HARPER'S
Pictorial History
OF THE

By Alfred H. Guernsey
and
Henry M. Alden.

CIVIL WAR

THE FAIRFAX PRESS

PREFACE.

WE have undertaken to write the History of the Great Conspiracy which finally culminated in the Great Rebellion in the United States. Our task was commenced during the agony of the great struggle, when no man could foretell its issue. We purposed at the outset to narrate events just as they occurred; to speak of living men as impartially as though they were dead; to praise no man unduly because he strove for the right, to malign no man because he strove for the wrong; to anticipate, as far as we might, the sure verdict of after ages upon events in which we felt the keenest personal interest.

We have based this History throughout upon authentic documents. We have made no statement which we have not believed to be true, and also substantiated by unquestioned evidence. We have drawn no deductions which we did not think warranted by the facts adduced. If our work has advanced slowly, it has been because at each step new materials came to light which demanded careful examination. The close of the war gave us access to documents before unattainable, which we yet judged essential to the proper understanding of our subject. We knew before how the war had been waged against the Confederacy, but we knew only in part how it had been waged by the Confederacy.

This was to be a "PICTORIAL HISTORY," in which the Illustrations were to form an integral part of the text. These are confined wholly to Maps and Plans illustrating military movements; representations of actual Scenes and Incidents; and Portraits of those who have borne an important part in the events described. The form of the work was chosen in order to enable us to introduce maps and illustrations upon a large scale.

We have wrought in common, each having access to all the materials, and consulting throughout upon the use to be made of them. We can now see clearly before us the labor which remains to be accomplished. We trust that within a few months, and within the compass of another volume similar to this, we shall be able to bring to a close this "History of the Great Rebellion in the United States."

A. H. G.
H. M. A.

NEW YORK, *May*, 1866.

CONTENTS.

[AT THE COMMENCEMENT OF EACH CHAPTER WILL BE FOUND A DETAILED SYLLABUS OF THE MATTERS THEREIN CONTAINED.]

ILLUSTRATIONS.

SCENES AND INCIDENTS.

MAPS AND PLANS.

PORTRAITS.

Harper's Pictorial History of the CIVIL WAR

INTRODUCTION.

COLONIZATION OF THE COUNTRY which became the United States of America.—The Colonists of one Race, and almost of one Condition.—Difference in Occupation, Religious Character, and Education.—Slavery.—British Arrogance and Oppression.—First Colonial Congress.—Continental Congress.—Revolutionary War.—Independence won, not by any Colony, but by the United Colonies.—A Nation in Fact, but not in Form.—Lack and Need of a Sovereign Power.—Constitutional Convention.—A "National" Government formed, and not a Confederation.—Sovereignty in the Central Government: States never Independent Sovereignties.—Constitution adopted by the People, and not by the State Governments.—Prosperity.—The one Element of Discord and Misfortune.—Necessary Compromise of Opinions and Interests.—Great political Advantages gained by the Slave Interest.—Consequent Tendencies in the Slave States to Oligarchy.—Addition of new States to the Union.—Slavery retains its political Advantage.—Great Increase of the Free States in Wealth and Population.—Formation of a Slavery Party.—Reprobation of Slavery throughout Christendom.—The Colonization Society.—The Missouri Compromise.—The Abolitionists.—Effect of the Abolition Agitation.—Aggressive and proscriptive Policy of the Fire-eating Slaveholders.—Endeavors to extend and to limit the Area of Slavery.—John C. Calhoun's Position.—The Fugitive-slave Law.—Obeyed to the Letter by the People of Massachusetts.—The Kansas-Nebraska Bill.—The Territorial Issue.—The Struggle in Kansas.—Assault on Senator Sumner.—The Dred Scott Decision.—Resistance by Free States.—Personal-liberty Laws.—Breaking up of the Democratic Party.—John Brown's Raid.—Presidential Nominating Conventions of 1860.—The Democratic Convention broken up on the Slavery Issue.—This Result brought about by the Politicians of the Cotton States.—Nomination of Bell and Everett, of Lincoln and Hamlin, of Douglas and Johnson, of Breckinridge and Lane.—Treason in President Buchanan's Cabinet.—Election of Abraham Lincoln.—No sectional Division of the Country.—Homogeneousness of the People of the United States.—The Difference produced by Slavery and Ignorance, and Freedom and Education.—Excitement

upon the Election of Mr. Lincoln.—Preparations for Secession in South Carolina.—The People of the other Slave States not ready or willing to Secede.—Agitation throughout the South.—Forced Inaction of the Government.—Gloom at the North.—Opposition to the Course of South Carolina throughout the Slave States.—Meeting of Congress.—President Buchanan's vacillating Message.—An empty Treasury.—Efforts to Preserve the Union.—Obstinacy of South Carolina.—Passage of her Ordinance of Secession.—President Buchanan found wanting.—Financial Disturbance and Ruin in Northern Cities. — Confidence at the South. — Fraud and Treason in the Cabinet.—Gloom and Despondency at the North.

THE people of the North American colonies lying between New Brunswick on the north and Florida on the south took a place among the nations in the year 1789. They were English people. For the Dutch colony of New Netherlands was so small and so inert that, even in its Dutch day, it made little impression upon the country, and none at all of an enduring kind upon the character of the new nation; while the Swedes, who settled near the mouth of the Delaware, were such a mere handful of men that, in this respect, they are not even to be taken into consideration.[1] The new nation was singularly homogeneous, whether in regard to the race or the condition of the people who composed it. The nation from which it

[1] In 1647 the population of Virginia and Maryland was 20,000; that of New England as many more; while in New Netherlands, including the Swedes on the Delaware, there were only between two and three thousand; and of these so large a proportion were Englishmen that, some years before, it had been found necessary to appoint an English secretary to the Dutch governor, and to promulgate ordinances in English. To New England, Virginia, and Maryland were afterward added the English colonies of Pennsylvania, the Carolinas, and Georgia.

had severed itself, being composed of English, Welsh, Scotch, and Irish elements—four distinct peoples, of widely different origin, traits, and habits, having been gathered by accident and the sword into the kingdom of Great Britain—was upon this point notably its opposite. But even in England proper there was not a greater predominance of sheer English blood; while the absence of any distinction of rank, and the comparative rarity of any wide difference of condition among its citizens, was almost peculiar to it among the states of Christendom. The sameness of its component parts was therefore so great that, compared in its substance with any other nation, it consisted of but a single element. Its marked and almost unprecedented homogeneousness was its distinctive character.

Such difference as there was between the people of the several commonwealths which formed this nation was caused almost entirely by variety of occupation, of religious conviction, and of consequent social habits; and thus the difference was, both in kind and in degree, merely such as always exists among people not only of the same nation, but of the same city and the same neighborhood. The settlements at the North were made by men who sought chiefly that liberty in religious affairs which they, in their turn, austerely denied to others: those at the South were planted, not settled, by men of wealth and rank in England, who sent over such adventurers as they could induce to embark in their enterprise, while they themselves remained at home to receive the lion's share of the profit. To those who went out as adventurers to the Plantations, as the American settlements were called,[2] there were added quite a large number of convicts, many of whom doubtless secured there the opportunity of reformation, and the means of reputable life. At the North the settlers clustered in farm-houses round their churches, and wrung a frugal living from a reluctant soil, seeking to lead a thrifty, independent, "godly" life, according to their stern notions of godliness. At the South men sought great profit by the rude culture of large tracts of rich land, upon which labor soon began to be performed chiefly by negro slaves; and dwelling-houses were consequently scattered widely through the Plantations, until at last each farm came to be called a plantation. At the North, religion, as distinguished from the practice of the Christian virtues, was mingled with all public and private affairs; the tone of society was ascetic; and there was no hierarchal church government. At the South religion was not regarded, except in so far as it was a proper and a reputable thing to be attended to; no artificial restraint was placed upon social intercourse; convivial habits prevailed; and in religious affairs, except among a few Scotch devotees of Presbyterianism, the Church of England had full control. To these traits of unlikeness must be added one other, which, in the event, proved to be of greater importance than either, or, indeed, than all of those which have been named. In New England, hardly were the comforts of life moderately secured, when provision began to be made for the intellectual education of the people; and this not only by the establishment of a college for the cultivation of the higher branches of learning, but by the instruction, in grammar-schools and by clergymen, of all the children in the colony. But at the South, only persons of some wealth and social position, and not all of those, sought the advantages of intellectual culture for their sons.[3] From the beginning to the present day this education of the mass of the people has been the grand distinctive feature between the country lying north of the Potomac and the Ohio, and that upon the south, with some exception as to Maryland and Kentucky. Consequently, the education of the country at large, and its position in literature, science, and the arts, are almost entirely due to the northern part of it. The men of the South who were educated received their education mostly at New England colleges, or in those of states which were settled by New England men, or had been brought under New England influence; or they were taught at home by tutors who were themselves educated in those colleges; and the comparatively little knowledge diffused through the mass of poor and untaught people around them has been due to intercourse with men who, born and bred in the northern, have sought homes in the southern part of the country. But, although the mental instruction of the whole country has thus come mainly from the North, the original difference in moral training and social organization between the northern and southern colonies has been mainly preserved.[4]

In one point society in these colonies was somewhat peculiar: the people of all of them, north and south, held negro slaves, and dealt in them. But neither the presence of the negroes nor their enslaved condition was due to the direct agency of the colonists; nor were they, in this respect, absolutely distinguished from their fellow-subjects of the mother country. Slaves were transported to the colonies at first against the wishes of the colonists; and whoever chooses to examine the London papers of the last century may find, even as late as 1776, advertisements of "black boys," and even of "black girls," who "have lived in England several years," and who are to be "sold at a bargain." There was, then, no essential difference between the Englishmen of America and the Englishmen of Great Britain. The former, taken as a whole, corresponded to the middle class of Englishmen in the mother country, exhibiting about the same moral, intellectual, and social variety of character, modified, and perhaps not for the worse, by the enterprise and self-reliance taught them by their comparative isolation, by privation, and adversity.

[2] Plantation was merely another English word for colony, colonizing.

[3] In 1671, more than sixty years after the settlement of Virginia, Governor Berkeley, of that colony, said, in a report to the Privy Council, "I thank God there are no free-schools nor printing, and I hope we shall not have these hundred years; for learning has brought disobedience, and heresy, and sects into the world, and printing has divulged them, and libels against the best government: God keep us from both."

[4] John Adams, writing to Joseph Hawley, Nov. 25th, 1775, says: "The characters of gentlemen in the four New England colonies differ as much from those in the others as that of the common people differs; that is, as much as several distinct nations almost. Gentlemen, men of sense, or any kind of education, in the other colonies, are much fewer in proportion than in New England. Gentlemen in the colonies have large plantations of slaves, and the common people among them are very ignorant and very poor. These gentlemen are accustomed, habituated to higher notions of themselves, and the distinction between them and the common people than we are."—*John Adams's Works*, vol. ix., p. 367.

Such was the people which the British government began to alienate, about 1750, by denying them their rights of birth as Englishmen; by treating them as mere creatures of convenience, to be worked for the benefit of British commerce and the aggrandizement of the mother country; by imposing burdensome taxes and irritating laws upon them without their consent; by rejoining to their plea in behalf of the establishment of a college in Virginia, that they had souls to be saved, "Souls! damn your souls! plant tobacco!"[5] Of this arrogance of purpose and insolence of manner, and of this notion that Anglo-Americans should exist chiefly for the benefit of British commerce and British manufactures, we shall see that two wars and the lapse of more than a hundred years have not quite rid the governing classes of Great Britain. This unnatural and selfish policy had its natural antagonizing effect. The outside pressure bound together the people upon whom it was brought to bear. Though scattered over a wide extent of country, and having separate local governments, they had free intercourse; and their common trial made them feel that they were not only one in blood, but one in interest. They began to act in concert, not for independent political existence, but for self-defense within the British Constitution.

In 1765 the first Colonial Congress for redress of grievances assembled at New York. But it was in no sense an authoritative body. It was composed of delegates from the several Colonial Assemblies, with three exceptions, who acted under special instructions. They set forth a Declaration of Rights and Grievances; they petitioned the King, and sent memorials to Parliament. But they only claimed all the privileges of Englishmen as their birthright, and therefore protested against being taxed by a body in which they were not represented. Their doings were warmly approved by the Assemblies and the people of all the colonies, and the first step was unconsciously taken toward the political union, the separate national existence, of the English race in America. The lapse of nine years, passed in the endurance of a common oppression from their common mother, and in continuous consultation as to their means of resistance, developed rapidly a unity of feeling in the colonies, which took form in the Continental Congress, composed of leading men from twelve provinces, which assembled in Philadelphia. Under the guidance of this body the power of the British government was in the course of events defied, and the independence of the colonies declared and maintained; but at first it merely imitated its predecessor in adopting a Declaration of Rights, in which the privileges of Englishmen and British subjects were claimed—most important of all, the right of being bound by no law to which they had not consented by their representatives. It took no active measure of resistance, and merely recommended one which may be called passive—a voluntary association, pledging the associators to entire commercial non-intercourse with Great Britain. It is desirable to bring to mind these well-known facts in view of the character and the pretensions of the rebellion the course of which we are about to trace, and also of the grounds on which the government of the United States took up arms for its suppression.

The Continental Congress, assembling first as a mere deliberative body, assumed, in the rapid course of events, the sole and absolute direction of the common interests of the colonies; and this assumption received the hearty, though informal, assent of a majority of the people so large that to all intents and purposes it was unanimous. As the War of Independence went on, as the people of the several provinces shared each other's anxieties and bore each other's burdens, as they stood shoulder to shoulder in defense of their common birthright, their common liberty, and their common interests, and saw each other in great masses face to face, as the leading men of one province were placed in authority over the people of another—the Virginia planter, Horatio Gates, commanding the northern army, and the Rhode Island iron-master, Nathaniel Greene, the southern—as social intercourse became at once more diffused and more intimate, they felt with unanimity that since they had declared themselves no longer part of the British nation, they were one nation of themselves. Their identity of blood was a patent fact, like the presence of the sun in the heavens, neither to be denied nor to be asserted; and sentiment, interest, and future security led them to regard their union as of paramount importance.

HORATIO GATES.

NATHANIEL GREENE.

These people were at last solemnly

[5] Reply of Seymour, Attorney General under William and Mary. See Franklin's Correspondence, vol. i., p. 155.

absolved from the bond which bound them politically to the mother country—a bond which, instead of being a tie of kindred, love, and mutual respect, as they at first assumed it was and then hoped it might be, had been made, against the protests of the best and brightest intellects in the British Parliament—chief among them Pitt (Lord Chatham) and Edmund Burke—

WILLIAM PITT.

EDMUND BURKE.

a galling fetter. They were independent, they were united, they were one people. In the fierce heat of their fiery trial and under the blows which had fallen so thickly and heavily upon them, they had been welded together as iron is welded into iron. But, although a nation in fact, they were not a nation in form. Distinguished as we have seen that this people was among the nations by its essential homogeneousness, it yet lacked that formal political unity which was necessary alike to its government as one nation at home and its recognition as one nation abroad. This great defect was felt the more from the exhaustion, the confusion, and the partial disorganization of society which followed the long War of Independence. But it was chiefly brought to the attention of the thinking men of the country by the jealousy with which the states began to watch and defend their interests, and by the inability of the Continental Congress, which was the representative power of the Confederation, to fulfill treaties, raise revenue, and maintain an army. There was no sovereign authority. The colonies or provinces had never possessed sovereignty. They had their Assemblies, by which their local laws were made, which, in most of them, required the assent of a governor appointed by the British crown; but the sovereignty over all of them was in the government of Great Britain. In 1776 they declared, not their individual sovereignty, but their independence as "united colonies;" as united colonies they won that independence, under the almost absolute exercise of power by the Continental Congress. Not only did no colony assert its sovereignty, but no colony won its independence. Yet it is not strange that a people who had just cast off the restraint of one sovereignty should have been slow, in their first days of relief, to assume that of another, especially when they were provided with local governments of ample powers to administer their local affairs. And beside all this, local interests, local ambitions, local jealousies, such as exist in the oldest and most compact nations, could be used by designing men to prevent consolidation, and might have an influence that way even with the candid and the patriotic. So the very Articles of Confederation themselves were adopted only after long hesitation.[6] Proposed by the Continental Congress in 1777, they were not ratified by all the states until 1781. By these articles the states entered into "a firm league of friendship" with each other for their common defense and general welfare; each state renounced the right to send embassies, make treaties, and declare war; and the union was to be perpetual. But aside from the fact that a league implies sovereign "high contracting" parties, by the second of these Articles of Confederation it was expressly set forth that each state retained its sovereignty, freedom, and independence, and all rights and powers not explicitly granted by that instrument to the Congress. The vote in the Congress was by states; each state had but one vote; and each paid its own delegates. There was no supreme executive, legislative, or judicial power for the whole country. The ministers and commissioners of the Congress, and the people themselves, proudly claimed the position due to "an independent nation;" and yet the nation was, politically, not one, but many. In a very few years the consequence was discord and confusion within, impending anarchy and threatening danger without. The Continental Congress, once omnipotent, was every day more and more disregarded. The new nation found that, in spite of its colonial Assemblies, which had been renamed State Legislatures, if it would continue its existence, something was needed in place of the sovereignty which had been cast off. That needed, but perhaps not altogether desired, supremacy, it found at last in the Constitution of the United States.

---

[6] *Articles of Confederation and perpetual Union between the States of New Hampshire, Massachusetts Bay, Rhode Island and Providence Plantations, Connecticut, New York, New Jersey, Pennsylvania, Delaware, Maryland, Virginia, North Carolina, South Carolina, and Georgia.*

ARTICLE 1. The style of this confederacy shall be, "The United States of America."

ART. 2. Each state retains its sovereignty, freedom, and independence, and every power, jurisdiction, and right, which is not by this confederation expressly delegated to the United States in Congress assembled.

ART. 3. The said states hereby severally enter into a firm league of friendship with each other for their common defense, the security of their liberties, and their mutual and general welfare; binding themselves to assist each other against all force offered to, or attacks made upon them, on account of religion, sovereignty, trade, or any other pretext whatever.

ART. 4. The better to secure and perpetuate mutual friendship and intercourse among the people of the different states in this Union, the free inhabitants of each of these states (paupers, vagabonds, and fugitives from justice excepted) shall be entitled to all privileges and immunities of free citizens in the several states; and the people of each state shall have free ingress and regress to and from any other state, and shall enjoy therein all the privileges of trade and commerce, subject to the same duties, impositions, and restrictions, as the inhabitants thereof respectively, provided that such restrictions shall not extend so far as to prevent the removal of property imported into any state to any other state, of which the owner is an inhabitant; provided, also, that no imposition, duties, or restriction shall be laid by any state on the property of the United States, or either of them.

If any person guilty of or charged with treason, felony, or other high misdemeanor, in any state, shall flee from justice, and be found in any of the United States, he shall upon demand of the governor, or executive power of the state from which he fled, be delivered up, and removed to the state having jurisdiction of his offense.

Full faith and credit shall be given in each of these states to the records, acts, and judicial proceedings of the courts and magistrates of every other state.

ART. 5. For the more convenient management of the general interests of the United States, delegates shall be annually appointed in such manner as the Legislature of each state shall direct, to meet in Congress on the first Monday in November in every year, with a power reserved to each state to recall its delegates or any of them, at any time within the year, and to send others in their stead for the remainder of the year.

No state shall be represented in Congress by less than two nor by more than seven members; and no person shall be capable of being a delegate for more than three years in any term of six years; nor shall any person, being a delegate, be capable of holding any office under the United States, for which he, or any other for his benefit, receives any salary, fees, or emolument of any kind.

Each state shall maintain its own delegates in any meeting of the states, and while they act as members of the committee of the states.

In determining questions in the United States in Congress assembled, each state shall have one vote.

Freedom of speech and debate in Congress shall not be impeached or questioned in any court or place out of Congress; and the members of Congress shall be protected in their persons from arrests and imprisonments, during the time of their going to and from and attendance on Congress, except for treason, felony, or breach of the peace.

ART. 6. No state, without the consent of the United States in Congress assembled, shall send an embassy to, or receive any embassy from, or enter into any conference, agreement, alliance, or treaty, with any king, prince, or state; nor shall any person holding any office of profit or trust under the United States, or any of them, accept of any present, emolument, office, or title of any kind whatever, from any king, prince, or foreign state; nor shall the United States in Congress assembled, or any of them, grant any title of nobility.

No two or more states shall enter into any treaty, confederation, or alliance whatever between them, without the consent of the United States in Congress assembled, specifying accurately the purposes for which the same is to be entered into, and how long it shall continue.

No state shall lay any imposts or duties, which may interfere with any stipulations in treaties entered into by the United States in Congress assembled, with any king, prince, or state, in pursuance of any treaties already proposed by Congress to the courts of France and Spain.

No vessels of war shall be kept up in time of peace, by any state, except such number only as shall be deemed necessary by the United States in Congress assembled for the defense of such state or its trade; nor shall any body of forces be kept up by any state in time of peace, except such number only as, in the judgment of the United States in Congress assembled, shall be deemed requisite to garrison the forts necessary for the defense of such state; but every state shall always keep up a well-regulated and disciplined militia, sufficiently armed and accoutred, and shall provide and have constantly ready for use, in public stores, a due number of field-pieces and tents, and a proper quantity of arms, ammunition, and camp equipage.

No state shall engage in any war without the consent of the United States in Congress assembled, unless such state be actually invaded by enemies, or shall have certain advice of a resolution being formed by some nation of Indians to invade such state, and the danger is so imminent as not to admit of a delay till the United States in Congress assembled can be consulted; nor shall any state grant commissions to any ships or vessels of war, nor letters of marque or reprisal, except it be after a declaration of war by the United States in Congress assembled, and then only against the kingdom or state, and the subjects thereof, against which war has been so declared, and under such regulations as shall be established by the United States in Congress assembled, unless such state be infested by pirates, in which case vessels of war may be fitted out for that occasion, and kept so long as the danger shall continue, or until the United States in Congress assembled shall determine otherwise.

ART. 7. When land forces are raised by any state for the common defense, all officers of or under the rank of colonel shall be appointed by the Legislature of each state respectively by whom such forces shall be raised, or in such manner as such state shall direct; and all vacancies shall be filled up by the state which first made the appointment.

ART. 8. All charges of war, and all other expenses that shall be incurred for the common defense or general welfare, and allowed by the United States in Congress assembled, shall be defrayed out of a common treasury, which shall be supplied by the several states in proportion to the value of all land within each state granted to or surveyed for any person, as such land and the buildings and improvements thereon shall be estimated, according to such mode as the United States in Congress assembled shall from time to time direct and appoint.

The taxes for paying that proportion shall be laid and levied by the authority and direction of the Legislatures of the several states, within the time agreed upon by the United States in Congress assembled.

ART. 9. The United States in Congress assembled shall have the sole and exclusive right and power of determining on peace and war, except in the cases mentioned in the sixth Article: of sending and receiving embassadors: entering into treaties and alliances; provided that no treaty of commerce shall be made whereby the legislative power of the respective states shall be restrained from imposing such imposts and duties on foreigners as their own people are subjected to, or from prohibiting the exportation or importation of any species of goods or commodities whatsoever: of establishing rules for deciding in all cases what captures on land or water shall be legal, and in what manner prizes taken by land or naval forces in the service of the United States shall be divided or appropriated: of granting letters of marque and reprisal in time of peace: appointing courts for the trial of piracies and felonies committed on the high seas, and establishing courts for receiving and determining finally appeals in all cases of captures; provided, that no member of Congress shall be appointed judge of any of the said courts.

The United States in Congress assembled shall also be the last resort on appeal in all disputes and differences now subsisting, or that hereafter may arise between two or more states concerning boundary, jurisdiction, or any other cause whatever; which authority shall always be exercised in the manner following: whenever the legislative or executive authority or lawful agent of any state in controversy with another shall present a petition to Congress, stating the matter in question, and praying for a hearing, notice thereof shall be given by order of Congress to the legislative or executive authority of the other state in controversy, and a day assigned for the appearance of the parties, by their lawful agents, who shall then be directed to appoint by joint consent commissioners or judges to constitute a court for hearing and determining the matter in question; but if they can not agree, Congress shall name three persons out of each of the United States, and from the list of such persons each party shall alternately strike out one, the petitioners beginning, until the number shall be reduced to thirteen; and from that number not less than seven nor more than nine names, as Congress shall direct, shall, in the presence of Congress, be drawn out by lot; and the persons whose names shall be so drawn, or any five of them, shall be commissioners or judges, to hear and finally determine the controversy, so always as a major part of the judges, who shall hear the cause, shall agree in the determination; and if either party shall neglect to attend at the day appointed, without showing reasons which Congress shall judge sufficient, or being present shall refuse to strike, the Congress shall proceed to nominate three persons out of each state, and the Secretary of Congress shall strike in behalf of such party absent or refusing; and the judgment and sentence of the court to be appointed in the manner before prescribed, shall be final and conclusive; and if any of the parties shall refuse to submit to the authority of such court, or to appear, or defend their claim or cause, the court shall nevertheless proceed to pronounce sentence or judgment, which shall in like manner be final and decisive, the

PORTRAITS OF THE SIGNERS OF THE DECLARATION OF INDEPENDENCE.

through half a century—brief period though that seems to the student of history—as their very independence was declared and won by a body appointed originally for no such purpose, so the constitution under which they assumed political form and unity was but the perfected fruit, the bud and blossom of which were the old Colonial and Continental Congresses; and it was elaborated by a convention at first designed for a minor, incidental purpose connected with commerce and navigation, and which finally assembled with nothing more than the bettering of the Articles of Confederation as its avowed and immediate object. Among that assembly of fifty-five men were George Washington, Benjamin Franklin, Alexander Hamilton,

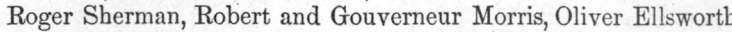

Roger Sherman, Robert and Gouverneur Morris, Oliver Ellsworth, Rufus King, Edmund Randolph, Charles Cotesworth Pinckney, John Rutledge, William Livingston, and James Wilson, a man whose reputation is beneath his merits, of whom Washington said that he was "as honest, candid, able a member as the Convention contained." It is not surprising that a convention composed of such men, and of those who were worthy to be their associates, soon found that the Articles of Confederation were past all mending, except such as

JOHN RUTLEDGE.

consists in remaking. In fact, the nation had far outgrown them. In spite of some jealous, short-sighted anxiety about state "sovereignty," and some doubts whether the Convention was empowered to do more than amend and work over the old confederation, the very first resolution adopted in Committee of the Whole, after twenty-one days' debate, was, "That a National government ought to be established, consisting of a supreme Legislature, Executive, and Judiciary." The national and supreme character of the government which they were about to frame being thus deliberately decided upon, and explicitly declared, they addressed themselves to their labors. These were based in the main upon two plans by Edmund Randolph, of Virginia, and Charles Pinckney, of South Carolina. Mr. Randolph's plan proposed a national Legislature of two branches, the most numerous to be chosen by the people, the right of suffrage being in proportion to the rate of free population, or taxes paid; a national ex-

As the formation of the people of the colonies into one independent state, or nation, had been brought about not suddenly, but by events extending

judgment or sentence, and other proceedings, being in either case transmitted to Congress, and lodged among the acts of Congress for the security of the parties concerned: provided, that every commissioner, before he sits in judgment, shall take an oath, to be administered by one of the judges of the supreme or superior court of the state where the cause shall be tried, "well and truly to hear and determine the matter in question, according to the best of his judgment, without favor, affection, or hope of reward;" provided also, that no state shall be deprived of territory for the benefit of the United States.

All controversies concerning the private right of soil, claimed under different grants of two or more states, whose jurisdictions as they may respect such lands and the states which passed such grants are adjusted, the said grants or either of them being at the same time claimed to have originated antecedent to such settlement of jurisdiction, shall, on the petition of either party to the Congress of the United States, be finally determined, as near as may be, in the same manner as is before prescribed for deciding disputes respecting territorial jurisdiction between different states.

The United States in Congress assembled shall also have the sole and exclusive right and power of regulating the alloy and value of coin struck by their own authority, or by that of the respective states; fixing the standard of weights and measures throughout the United States: regulating the trade and managing all affairs with the Indians not members of any of the states; provided, that the legislative right of any state within its own limits be not infringed or violated: establishing and regulating post-offices from one state to another, throughout all the United States, and exacting such postage on the papers passing through the same as may be requisite to defray the expenses of the said office: appointing all officers of the land forces in the service of the United States, excepting regimental officers: appointing all the officers of the naval forces, and commissioning all officers whatever in the service of the United States: making rules for the government and regulation of the said land and naval forces, and directing their operations.

The United States in Congress assembled shall have authority to appoint a committee to sit in the recess of Congress, to be denominated "a Committee of the States;" and to consist of one delegate from each state, and to appoint such other committees and civil officers as may be necessary for managing the general affairs of the United States, under their direction: to appoint one of their number to preside, provided that no person be allowed to serve in the office of President more than one year in any term of three years: to ascertain the necessary sums of money to be raised for the service of the United States, and to appropriate and apply the same for defraying the public expenses: to borrow money or emit bills on the credit of the United States, transmitting every half year to the respective states an account of the sums of money so borrowed or emitted: to build and equip a navy: to agree upon the number of land forces, and to make requisitions from each state for its quota, in proportion to the number of white inhabitants in such state; which requisition shall be binding, and thereupon the Legislature of each state shall appoint the regimental officers, raise the men, and clothe, arm, and equip them in a soldier-like manner, at the expense of the United States; and the officers and men to be clothed, armed, and equipped, shall march to the place appointed, and within the time agreed on by the United States in Congress assembled; but if the United States in Congress assembled shall, on consideration of circumstances, judge proper that any state should not raise men, or should raise a smaller number than its quota, and that any other state should raise a greater number of men than the quota thereof, such extra number shall be raised, officered, clothed, armed, and equipped in the

same manner as the quota of such state, unless the Legislature of such state shall judge that such extra number can not be safely spared out of the same; in which case they shall raise, officer, clothe, arm, and equip as many of such extra number as they judge can be safely spared. And the officers and men so clothed, armed, and equipped, shall march to the place appointed, and within the time agreed on by the United States in Congress assembled.

The United States in Congress assembled shall never engage in a war, nor grant letters of marque and reprisal in time of peace, nor enter into any treaties or alliances, nor coin money, nor regulate the value thereof, nor ascertain the sums and expenses necessary for the defense and welfare of the United States or any of them, nor emit bills, nor borrow money on the credit of the United States, nor appropriate money, nor agree upon the number of vessels of war to be built or purchased, or the number of land or sea forces to be raised, nor appoint a commander in chief of the army or navy, unless nine states assent to the same; nor shall a question on any other point, except for adjourning from day to day, be determined, unless by the votes of a majority of the United States in Congress assembled.

The Congress of the United States shall have power to adjourn to any time within the year, and to any place within the United States, so that no period of adjournment be for a longer duration than the space of six months; and shall publish the journal of their proceedings monthly, except such parts thereof relating to treaties, alliances, or military operations, as in their judgment require secrecy; and the yeas and nays of the delegates of each state on any question shall be entered on the journal when it is desired by any delegate; and the delegates of a state, or any of them, at his or their request, shall be furnished with a transcript of the said journal, except such parts as are above excepted, to lay before the Legislatures of the several states.

ART. 10. The Committee of the States, or any nine of them, shall be authorized to execute in the recess of Congress such of the powers of Congress as the United States in Congress assembled, by the consent of nine states, shall, from time to time, think expedient to vest them with; provided that no power be delegated to the said Committee, for the exercise of which, by the Articles of Confederation, the voice of nine states in the Congress of the United States assembled is requisite.

ART. 11. Canada, acceding to this Confederation, and joining in the measures of the United States, shall be admitted into, and entitled to, all the advantages of this Union; but no other colony shall be admitted into the same unless such admission be agreed to by nine states.

ART. 12. All bills of credit emitted, moneys borrowed, and debts contracted by or under the authority of Congress, before the assembling of the United States, in pursuance of the present Confederation, shall be deemed and considered as a charge against the United States, for payment and satisfaction whereof the said United States and the public faith are hereby solemnly pledged.

ART. 13. Every state shall abide by the determination of the United States in Congress assembled, on all questions which, by this Confederation, are submitted to them. And the Articles of this Confederation shall be inviolably observed by every state, and the Union shall be perpetual; nor shall any alteration at any time hereafter be made in any of them, unless such alteration be agreed to in a Congress of the United States, and be afterward confirmed by the Legislatures of every state.

These Articles shall be proposed to the Legislatures of all the United States, to be considered, and if approved of by them, they are advised to authorize their delegates to ratify the same in the Congress of the United States; which being done, the same shall become conclusive.

ecutive and a national judiciary, both to be chosen by the national Legislature; the national Legislature to have a negative on all state laws inconsistent with the Articles of Union, and the national executive and judiciary to have, as a Council of Revision, a qualified negative upon all laws, state as well as national. These were its most important and characteristic points. Mr. Pinckney's plan proposed essentially the same system, but attained its ends by simpler means; and this seems to have been the actual groundwork of the present Constitution of the United States.

Another plan was proposed by the delegates from New Jersey, Delaware, and New York. This plan was the result of an avowed attempt to perpetuate the old confederation. It proposed to empower the Congress to appoint an executive of federal laws, officers for the federal army, and to establish a federal judiciary. It was but a make-shift; but even this plan proposed that the acts of Congress in accordance with the Articles of Confederation, and the treaties ratified by it, should be the supreme law of the land—a proposition which showed the necessity of that which the plan sought to avoid; for, without the establishment of a supreme government, it would have been impossible to enforce this provision against any powerful state which chose to set it at naught. The vital difference between the government proposed by this plan and that proposed by Virginia and South Carolina was, that the former dealt with states as the individuals responsible to it, and the latter with the whole people individually, as citizens of the United States, into which union, for all national purposes, the individuality and so-called "sovereignty" of the states was entirely merged. There was no misapprehension of the issue. It was clearly stated. "The true question is," said Mr. Randolph, "whether we shall adhere to the federal plan, or introduce the national plan. . . . A national government alone, properly constituted, will answer the purpose." After a debate of four days, the national plan was adopted, Massachusetts, Connecticut, Pennsylvania, Virginia, the two Carolinas, and Georgia voting for it, New York, New Jersey, and Delaware against it, the vote of Maryland being divided.[7] It is worthy of special note that Virginia, North Carolina, South Carolina, and Georgia, which then included Kentucky, Tennessee, Alabama, and Mississippi, were all supporters, in express terms, of the "national" government, and that the plan which was the foundation of the system adopted was proposed by a delegate from South Carolina, while that which was its counterpart came from Virginia.

After four months of patient, thoughtful labor, free discussion, consideration, reconsideration, commitment, and recommitment, and of mutual concession to interest and to feeling, the Convention perfected the Constitution as it now exists, without the amendments made immediately upon its adoption. Probably not one of the delegates was entirely satisfied with it. Franklin avowed his dissatisfaction with several parts of it; Hamilton had proposed a

ALEXANDER HAMILTON.

JOHN JAY.

system essentially different from that which it established; yet they both devoted themselves earnestly to the task of securing its adoption by the people, the latter (aided by Madison and Jay) in a series of papers which enjoy the rare distinction of having moulded popular opinion in their day, and of becoming authority in statesmanship and classics in political literature. But, whatever the merits of the system of government established by this Constitution, there was no misapprehension of its character in any quarter. Of two men in Virginia who opposed its adoption, Patrick Henry said in the Convention of that state, June, 1788, "Who authorized them to speak the language of 'We, the people,' instead of 'We, the states?' States are the characteristic and the soul of a confederation. If the states be not the agents of this compact, it must be one great consolidated national government of the people of all the states." And George Mason in the same body also said, "Whether the Constitution

PATRICK HENRY.

be good or bad, the present clause clearly discovers that it is a national government, and no longer a confederation." The reply was not a denial of the nationality of the government, or an attempt to soften or gloze over its

consolidated character, but the avowal of these features, and the showing, by James Madison, that they were necessary. The same eminent patriot and statesman replied also to an inquiry by Hamilton, on the part of New York, whether the Constitution could be adopted with a reserved right to secede, in case certain amendments were not made, by a decided negative; the Constitution "required an unconditional adoption *in toto*, and forever." By June, 1788, nine states had adopted the Constitution, and thus merged their independent political existence in that of a new nation; but it was not until May, 1790, that Rhode Island, the last of the thirteen, consented to be absorbed into the Union, and the many became one.

As by the Constitution the powers not delegated by it to the United States, or prohibited to the states, are reserved to the states respectively, or to the people, let us see what rights and powers they were which the people of each state gave up. They were the right and power to levy taxes and impose duties, to regulate commerce, to make naturalization laws, to coin money, to regulate post-offices and post-roads, to define and punish piracies, to declare war, to provide an army and navy, to enter into any treaty, alliance, or confederation, to issue letters of marque and reprisal, to emit bills of credit, to keep troops, ships of war in time of peace, and to enter into any agreement or compact, either with each other, or with a foreign power. They placed the decision in any controversy between either one of them and another, or the citizen of another, or the United States, in the hands of the national judiciary; and, most important and significant concession of all, they gave up the right to change their very form of state government. This Constitution, according to one of the most eminent of its framers, was adopted by all the states " unconditionally, in toto, and forever;" this Union, by the terms of that Constitution, was to be " perpetual." Had the revolted colonies secured an individual sovereignty when they won their collective independence, this instrument would have left them none of it, according to the manifest intention of its framers. After its adoption there would have remained no semblance of sovereignty, but simply the right of independent self-government in local matters—that wise reservation which has secured the strength of centralization with the protection of local interests and the development of local resources by the people who are most concerned in them and best understand them; which insures the vast fabric based upon this Constitution from falling to pieces by its own weight, like the great empires of the past, by giving it stable support throughout its wide extent, instead of making it rest solely upon its central point; which frees us from an exhibition of that political incongruity seen in the mother country, where all interests, small or great, are controlled by the Imperial Parliament, and where we see the attention of that most important body given, day after day, to one petty county or parish matter or other, about which its members know little and care less. But this sovereignty the revolted states did not achieve. Sovereignty is the attribute of that power alone which has no superior; and of that sovereignty the colonies had none before their declaration of independence; and by that declaration which they made as united colonies, and which they won only as united colonies or states, they can not be said to have gained an individual sovereignty which they had not before. Upon this very point Charles Cotesworth Pinckney, of South Carolina, one of the delegates for the formation of the Constitution, in course of the debates in the Legislature of South Carolina herself on the adoption of the Constitution (January, 1788), said of the Declaration of Independence, "This admirable manifesto sufficiently refutes the doctrine of the individual sovereignty and independence of the several states. * * * * The several states are not even mentioned by name in any

CHARLES COTESWORTH PINCKNEY.

part, as if it was intended to impress the maxim on America that our freedom and independence arose from our union, and that without it we never could be free and independent. Let us, then, consider all attempts to weaken this union by maintaining that each state is separately and individually independent, as a species of political heresy which can never benefit us, but may bring on us the most serious distresses." If this be the bearing of the Declaration of Independence upon state sovereignty, what is that of the Constitution—an instrument which vests all the attributes of sovereignty in the national government, and which does this not by the act of the individual states, but by that of "the people of the United States?" It is also of importance to note that the Constitution was submitted, not to the Legislatures and corporate representatives of the states, but to the people; and for the very reason that it was supposed that the pride of state sovereignty would prevent the former from adopting it. James Wilson said, "I know that they [the Legislatures and state officers] will oppose it. I am for carrying it to the people of each state." It was unavoidable that the people should act by states, not only because that was the only mode of combined action in their power, but because the very question to be decided touched the resignation of power by the state as an individual. It seems impossible to avoid the conclusion that, after the adoption of that Constitution, there was no avoidance of its obligations or withdrawal from its pale, except in virtue of that inalienable right of revolution, which, to be

[7] New Hampshire and Rhode Island were not represented in this Convention.

B

DECLARATION O

A Declaration by the Representatives of the UNITED STATES
OF AMERICA, in General Congress assembled.

When in the course of human events it becomes necessary for one people to
dissolve the political bands which have connected them with another, and to
~~assume among the powers of the earth the~~ separate and equal station to
which the laws of nature & of nature's god entitle them, a decent respect
to the opinions of mankind requires that they should declare the causes
which impel them to the ~~change~~ separation.

We hold these truths to be self-evident: that all men are
created equal, ~~& independent~~: that ~~from that equal creation they derive~~
~~rights~~ inherent & inalienable, rights: that these among ~~which~~ these are
life & liberty, & the pursuit of happiness; that to secure these rights, go-
-vernments are instituted among men, deriving their just powers from
the consent of the governed; that whenever any form of government.
~~shall~~ becomes destructive of these ends, it is the right of the people to alter
or to abolish it, & to institute new government, laying it's foundation on
such principles & organising it's powers in such form, as to them shall
seem most likely to effect their safety & happiness. prudence indeed
will dictate that governments long established should not be changed for
light & transient causes: and accordingly all experience hath shewn that
mankind are more disposed to suffer while evils are sufferable, than to
right themselves by abolishing the forms to which they are accustomed but
when a long train of abuses & usurpations [begun at a distinguished period
&] pursuing invariably the same object, evinces a design to ~~reduce~~
them under absolute Despotism, it is their right, it is their duty, to throw off such
government & to provide new guards for their future security. such has
been the patient sufferance of these colonies & such is now the necessity
which constrains them to [expunge] their former systems of government.
the history of the present king of Great Britain is a history of [unremitting] injuries and
usurpations. [among which appears no solitary fact to contra-
-dict the uniform tenor of the rest, all of which have] in direct object the
establishment of an absolute tyranny over these states. to prove this, let facts be
submitted to a candid world, [for the truth of which we pledge a faith
yet unsullied by falsehood]
he has refused his assent to laws the most wholesome and necessary for the pub-
-lic good:
he has forbidden his governors to pass laws of immediate & pressing importance,
unless suspended in their operation till his assent should be obtained,
and when so suspended, he has utterly neglected to attend to them.
he has refused to pass other laws for the accomodation of large districts of people
unless those people would relinquish the right of representation in the legislature, a right
inestimable to them & formidable to tyrants only:
he has called together legislative bodies at places unusual, uncomfortable & distant from
the depository of their public records, for the sole purpose of fatiguing them into compliance
with his measures.
he has dissolved Representative houses repeatedly & continually for opposing with
manly firmness his invasions on the rights of the people.
~~~~, he has refused for a long time after such dissolutions, to cause others to be elected.

whereby the legislative powers, in
the people at large for their exer
exposed to all the dangers of in
he has endeavored to prevent the po
obstructing the laws for naturali
to encourage their migrations h
-propriations of lands:
he has obstructed the administratio
refusing his assent t
he has made our judges dependant
and amount of their salaries:
he has erected a multitude of nee
-ther swarms of officers to harrass
he has kept among us in times of pe
he has affected to render the military
he has combined with others to subje
tions and unacknoleged by our la
of legislation, for quartering la
for protecting them by a mock
they should commit on th
for cutting off our trade with all p
for imposing taxes on us without c
for depriving us in many cases of the benefits of t
for transporting us beyond seas to be
for abolishing the free system of English laws in
and enlarging it's boundaries so as to render it
rule into these colonies:
for taking away our charters, & al
for suspending our own legislatures
legislate for us in all case
he has abdicated government here,
of his allegiance & protection:
he has plundered our seas, ravag
lives of our people:
he is at this time transporting la
the works of death, desolation & t
scarcely paralleled in the most barb
of cruelty & perfidy unworthy th
he has endeavored to bring on the in
savages, whose known rule of wa
all ages, sexes, & conditions of e
he has incited treasonable insur
allurements of forfeiture & con
he has waged cruel war against
-ered rights of life & liberty in th
fended him, captivating & carr
-sphere, or to incur miserable
piratical warfare the opprobri
Christian king of Great Brita
where MEN should be boug

John Hancock Fran⁵ Lewis Rich⁴ Stockton Francis
Carter
Rob⁴ Morris John Penn W™ Whipple Casa
Benjamin Rush W™ Paca Samuel Chase John Hart
Benj. Franklin Tho⁵ Stone Geo Taylor Geo Ross Abra Clark
Jn⁵ Witherspoon Button Gwinnett
Joseph Hewes W™ Floyd Phil. Livingston Lyman Hall Thos
W™ Hooper
John Morton James Wilson Fras Hopkinson Geo Walton

UGHT BY JEFFERSON OF THE

INDEPENDENCE

July, 1776.

e of annihilation, have returned to
e state remaining in the mean time
rom without, & convulsions within:
tion of these states; for that purpose
of foreigners; refusing to pass others
& raising the conditions of new ap-

stice [totally to cease in some of these
for establishing judiciary powers:
will alone, for the tenure of their offices,

[by a self-assumed power] & sent hi-
ple & eat out their substance:
without the consent of our legislatures
nding armies [& ships of war]
ndent of & superior to the civil power:
a jurisdiction foreign to our constitu-
ng his assent to their acts of pretended ~~acts~~
lies of armed troops among us;
from punishment for any murders
bitants of these states;
the world;
sent;
jury;
for pretended offences:
ing province, establishing therein an arbitrary government
example & fit instrument for introducing the same absolute
aws:
ndamentally the forms of our governments,
ring themselves invested with power to
tsoever:
ing us out of his protection & waging war against us.
during his governors & declaring us out
coasts, burnt our towns & destroyed the
Scotch and other
nies of foreign mercenaries to compleat
; already begun with circumstances
is and totally
of a civilized nation.
nts of our frontiers the merciless Indian
s an undistinguished destruction of
s:]
s of our fellow-citizens with the
n of our property
to bear arms against their country & to become the executioners of their friends & brethren
nature itself, violating it's most sa
s of a distant people who never of
em into slavery in another hemis-
their transportation thither. this
fidel powers, is the warfare of the
termined to keep open a market
and
d he has prostituted his negative

for suppressing every legislative attempt to prohibit or to restrain this
~~determining to keep open a market where MEN should be bought & sold:~~
execrable commerce: and that this assemblage of horrors might want no fact
of distinguished die, he is now exciting those very people to rise in arms
among us, and to purchase that liberty of which he has deprived them
by murdering the people upon whom he also obtruded them: thus paying
off former crimes committed against the liberties of one people, with crimes
which he urges them to commit against the lives of another.]
in every stage of these oppressions we have petitioned for redress in the most humble
terms: our repeated petitions have been answered only by repeated injuries. a prince
whose character is thus marked by every act which may define a tyrant, is unfit
to be the ruler of a free people [who mean to be free. future ages will scarce believe
that the hardiness of one man, adventured within the short compass of twelve years
only to lay a foundation so broad & undisguised for tyranny over a people fostered & fixed in principles
of ~~liberty~~ freedom.]

Nor have we been wanting in attentions to our British brethren. we have
warned them from time to time of attempts by their legislature to extend an unwarrantable juris-
-diction over [these our states]. we have reminded them of the circumstances of
our emigration & settlement here, [no one of which could warrant so strange a
pretension: that these were effected at the expence of our own blood & treasure
unassisted by the wealth or the strength of Great Britain: that in constituting
indeed our several forms of government, we had adopted one common king, thereby
laying a foundation for perpetual league & amity with them: but that submission to their
parliament was no part of our constitution, nor ever in idea, if history may be
credited: and] we have appealed to their native justice & magnanimity [as well as to] the ties
of our common kindred to disavow these usurpations which [were likely to] interrupt
our connection & correspondence ~~& connection~~. they too have been deaf to the voice of justice &
of consanguinity, [& when occasions have been given them by the regular course of
their laws, of removing from their councils the disturbers of our harmony, they
have by their free election re-established them in power. at this very time too they
are permitting their chief magistrate to send over not only soldiers of our common
blood, but Scotch & foreign mercenaries to invade & destroy us. ~~deluge us in blood~~ these facts
have given the last stab to agonizing affection and manly spirit bids us to re-
-nounce for ever these unfeeling brethren. we must endeavor to forget our former
love for them, and to hold them as we hold the rest of mankind enemies in war,
in peace friends. we might have been a free & a great people together; but a commu-
-nication of grandeur & of freedom it seems is below their dignity. be it so, since they
will have it: the road to happiness & to glory is open to us too; we will tread it in
apart from them, and acquiesce in the necessity which denounces our eternal separation!]
we must therefore and hold them as we hold the rest of mankind enemies in war, in peace friends.

We therefore the representatives of the United States of America in General Con-
-gress assembled, appealing to the supreme judge of the world for the rectitude of our intentions, do in the name & by authority of the good people of these [states] colonies
[reject and renounce all allegiance & subjection to the kings of Great Britain
& all others who may hereafter claim by, through, or under them; we utterly
dissolve ~~& break off~~ all political connection which may have heretofore sub-
-sisted between us & the people or parliament of Great Britain; and finally
we do assert and declare these colonies to be free and independant states,
and that as free & independant states they have full power to levy
war, conclude peace, contract alliances, establish commerce, & to do all other
acts and things which independant states may of right do. And for the
support of this declaration] we mutually pledge to each other our lives, our
fortunes, & our sacred honour.

foot Lee
gston Arthur Middleton Step. Hopkins Th. Jefferson
dney George Wythe Benj. Harrison Thos. Nelson jr.
d Richard Henry Lee John Adams
. Read Josiah Bartlett Matthew Thornton
Roger Sherman
Rutledge Sam. Huntington William Ellery Charles Carroll of Carrollton
y ward jun. Geo Clymer
ynch Junr. Wm Whipple William Robt Treat Paine
ewis Morris Jas. Smith Elbridge Gerry
Saml. Adams Oliver Wolcott

complete, must have good cause, and power to maintain that cause. And this right belongs not to the people by virtue of state organization, or of residence within state limits, but to the inhabitants of any country or locality who are like-minded, and can make their rebellious determination good. As if to put this question, as far as he could, beyond a peradventure, the leader of the armies in the War of Independence, the president of the Convention who formed the Constitution, the first president of the United States under that Constitution, said of it in his Farewell Address to his Countrymen, "Until changed by an explicit and deliberate act of the whole people, it is sacredly obligatory upon all."[8]

---

[8] CONSTITUTION OF THE UNITED STATES.

PREAMBLE.

WE, the people of the United States, in order to form a more perfect union, establish justice, insure domestic tranquillity, provide for the common defense, promote the general welfare, and secure the blessings of liberty to ourselves and our posterity, do ordain and establish this Constitution for the United States of America.

ARTICLE I.

SECTION I.

All legislative powers herein granted shall be vested in a Congress of the United States, which shall consist of a Senate and House of Representatives.

SECTION II.

1. The House of Representatives shall be composed of members chosen every second year by the people of the several states: and the electors in each state shall have the qualifications requisite for electors of the most numerous branch of the State Legislature.

2. No person shall be a representative who shall not have attained to the age of twenty-five years, and been seven years a citizen of the United States, and who shall not, when elected, be an inhabitant of that state in which he shall be chosen.

3. Representatives and direct taxes shall be apportioned among the several states which may be included within this Union, according to their respective numbers, which shall be determined by adding to the whole number of free persons, including those bound to service for a term of years, and excluding Indians not taxed, three fifths of all other persons. The actual enumeration shall be made within three years after the first meeting of the Congress of the United States, and within every subsequent term of ten years, in such manner as they shall by law direct. The number of representatives shall not exceed one for every thirty thousand, but each state shall have at least one representative; and until such enumeration shall be made, the state of New Hampshire shall be entitled to choose three, Massachusetts eight, Rhode Island and Providence Plantations one, Connecticut five, New York six, New Jersey four, Pennsylvania eight, Delaware one, Maryland six, Virginia ten, North Carolina five, South Carolina five, and Georgia three.

4. When vacancies happen in the representation from any state, the executive authority thereof shall issue writs of election to fill such vacancies.

5. The House of Representatives shall choose their speaker and other officers, and shall have the sole power of impeachment.

SECTION III.

1. The Senate of the United States shall be composed of two senators from each state, chosen by the Legislature thereof, for six years, and each senator shall have one vote.

2. Immediately after they shall be assembled in consequence of the first election, they shall be divided as equally as may be, into three classes. The seats of the senators of the first class shall be vacated at the expiration of the second year, of the second class at the expiration of the fourth year, and of the third class at the expiration of the sixth year, so that one third may be chosen every second year; and if vacancies happen, by resignation or otherwise, during the recess of the Legislature of any state, the executive thereof may make temporary appointments until the next meeting of the Legislature, which shall then fill such vacancies.

3. No person shall be a senator who shall not have attained to the age of thirty years, and been nine years a citizen of the United States, and who shall not, when elected, be an inhabitant of that state for which he shall be chosen.

4. The Vice-President of the United States shall be President of the Senate, but shall have no vote, unless they be equally divided.

5. The Senate shall choose their other officers, and also a president pro tempore, in the absence of the Vice-President, or when he shall exercise the office of President of the United States.

6. The Senate shall have the sole power to try all impeachments. When sitting for that purpose, they shall be on oath or affirmation. When the President of the United States is tried, the chief justice shall preside: and no person shall be convicted without the concurrence of two thirds of the members present.

7. Judgment in case of impeachment shall not extend farther than to removal from office, and disqualification to hold and enjoy any office of honor, trust, or profit, under the United States, but the party convicted shall, nevertheless, be liable and subject to indictment, trial, judgment, and punishment according to law.

SECTION IV.

1. The times, places, and manner of holding elections for senators and representatives, shall be prescribed in each state by the Legislature thereof; but the Congress may at any time, by law, make or alter such regulations, except as to the place of choosing senators.

2. The Congress shall assemble at least once in every year, and such meeting shall be on the first Monday in December, unless they shall by law appoint a different day.

SECTION V.

1. Each house shall be the judge of the elections, returns, and qualifications of its own members, and a majority of each shall constitute a quorum to do business; but a smaller number may adjourn from day to day, and may be authorized to compel the attendance of absent members, in such manner and under such penalties as each house may provide.

2. Each house may determine the rules of its proceedings, punish its members for disorderly behavior, and, with the concurrence of two thirds, expel a member.

3. Each house shall keep a journal of its proceedings, and from time to time publish the same, excepting such parts as may in their judgment require secrecy; and the yeas and nays of the members of either house, on any question, shall, at the desire of one fifth of those present, be entered on the journal.

4. Neither house during the session of Congress shall, without the consent of the other, adjourn for more than three days, nor to any other place than that in which the two houses shall be sitting.

SECTION VI.

1. The senators and representatives shall receive a compensation for their services, to be ascertained by law, and paid out of the treasury of the United States. They shall in all cases, except treason, felony, and breach of the peace, be privileged from arrest during their attendance at the session of their respective houses, and in going to or returning from the same; and for any speech or debate in either house, they shall not be questioned in any other place.

2. No senator or representative shall, during the time for which he was elected, be appointed to any civil office under the authority of the United States, which shall have been created, or the emoluments whereof shall have been increased, during such time; and no person holding any office under the United States shall be a member of either house during his continuance in office.

SECTION VII.

1. All bills for raising revenue shall originate in the House of Representatives; but the Senate may propose or concur with amendments, as on other bills.

2. Every bill which shall have passed the House of Representatives and the Senate shall, before it become a law, be presented to the President of the United States; if he approve, he shall sign it; but if not, he shall return it, with his objections, to that house in which it shall have originated, who shall enter the objections at large on their journal, and proceed to reconsider it. If, after such reconsideration, two thirds of that house shall agree to pass the bill, it shall be sent, together with the objections, to the other house, by which it shall likewise be reconsidered, and if approved by two thirds of that house, it shall become a law. But in all such cases the votes of both houses shall be determined by yeas and nays, and the names of the persons voting for and against the bill shall be entered on the journal of each house respectively. If any bill shall not be returned by the President within ten days (Sundays excepted) after it shall have been presented to him, the same shall be a law in like manner as if he had signed it, unless the Congress by their adjournment prevent its return, in which case it shall not be a law.

3. Every order, resolution, or vote to which the concurrence of the Senate and House of Representatives may be necessary (except on a question of adjournment), shall be presented to the President of the United States; and before the same shall take effect, shall be approved by him, or being disapproved by him, shall be repassed by two thirds of the Senate and House of Representatives, according to the rules and limitations prescribed in the case of a bill.

SECTION VIII.

The Congress shall have power—

1. To lay and collect taxes, duties, imposts, and excises, to pay the debts and provide for the common defense and general welfare of the United States; but all duties, imposts, and excises shall be uniform throughout the United States;

2. To borrow money on the credit of the United States;

3. To regulate commerce with foreign nations, and among the several states, and with the Indian tribes;

4. To establish a uniform rule of naturalization, and uniform laws on the subject of bankruptcies, throughout the United States;

5. To coin money, regulate the value thereof, and of foreign coin, and fix the standard of weights and measures;

6. To provide for the punishment of counterfeiting the securities and current coin of the United States;

7. To establish post-offices and post-roads;

8. To promote the progress of science and useful arts, by securing for limited times to authors and inventors the exclusive right to their respective writings and discoveries;

9. To constitute tribunals inferior to the Supreme Court;

10. To define and punish piracies and felonies committed on the high seas, and offenses against the law of nations;

11. To declare war, grant letters of marque and reprisal, and make rules concerning captures on land and water;

12. To raise and support armies; but no appropriation of money to that use shall be for a longer term than two years;

13. To provide and maintain a navy;

14. To make rules for the government and regulation of the land and naval forces;

15. To provide for calling forth the militia to execute the laws of the Union, suppress insurrections, and repel invasions;

16. To provide for organizing, arming, and disciplining the militia, and for governing such part of them as may be employed in the service of the United States, reserving to the states respectively the appointment of the officers and the authority of training the militia according to the discipline prescribed by Congress;

17. To exercise exclusive legislation, in all cases whatsoever, over such district (not exceeding ten miles square) as may, by cession of particular states and the acceptance of Congress, become the seat of government of the United States, and to exercise like authority over all places purchased, by the consent of the Legislature of the state in which the same shall be, for the erection of forts, magazines, arsenals, dock-yards, and other needful buildings; and,

18. To make all laws which shall be necessary and proper for carrying into execution the foregoing powers, and all other powers vested by this Constitution in the government of the United States, or in any department or officer thereof.

SECTION IX.

1. The migration or importation of such persons as any of the states now existing shall think proper to admit, shall not be prohibited by the Congress prior to the year one thousand eight hundred and eight, but a tax or duty may be imposed on such importation, not exceeding ten dollars for each person.

2. The privilege of the writ of *habeas corpus* shall not be suspended unless when, in case of rebellion or invasion, the public safety may require it.

3. No bill of attainder, or ex-post-facto law, shall be passed.

4. No capitation, or other direct, tax shall be laid, unless in proportion to the census or enumeration herein before directed to be taken.

5. No tax or duty shall be laid on articles exported from any state.

6. No preference shall be given by any regulation of commerce or revenue to the ports of one state over those of another; nor shall vessels bound to or from one state be obliged to enter, clear, or pay duties in another.

7. No money shall be drawn from the treasury but in consequence of appropriations made by law; and a regular statement and account of the receipts and expenditures of all public money shall be published from time to time.

8. No title of nobility shall be granted by the United States; and no person holding any office of profit or trust under them shall, without the consent of the Congress, accept of any present, emolument, office, or title of any kind whatever, from any king, prince, or foreign state.

SECTION X.

1. No State shall enter into any treaty, alliance, or confederation; grant letters of marque and reprisal; coin money; emit bills of credit; make any thing but gold and silver coin a tender in payment of debts; pass any bill of attainder, ex-post-facto law, or law impairing the obligation of contracts; or grant any title of nobility.

2. No state shall, without the consent of the Congress, lay any imposts or duties on imports or exports, except what may be absolutely necessary for executing its inspection laws: and the net produce of all duties and imposts laid by any state on imports or exports shall be for the use of the treasury of the United States; and all such laws shall be subject to the revision and control of the Congress.

3. No state shall, without the consent of Congress, lay any duty of tonnage, keep troops or ships of war in time of peace, enter into any agreement or compact with another state, or with a foreign power, or engage in war, unless actually invaded, or in such imminent danger as will not admit of delay.

ARTICLE II.

SECTION I.

1. The executive power shall be vested in a President of the United States of America. He shall hold his office during the term of four years, and, together with the Vice-President, chosen for the same term, be elected as follows:

2. Each state shall appoint, in such manner as the Legislature thereof may direct, a number of electors, equal to the whole number of senators and representatives to which the state may be entitled in the Congress: but no senator or representative, or person holding an office of trust or profit under the United States, shall be appointed an elector.

The electors shall meet in their respective states, and vote by ballot for two persons, of whom one at least shall not be an inhabitant of the same state with themselves. And they shall make a list of all the persons voted for, and of the number of votes for each; which list they shall sign and certify, and transmit sealed to the seat of the government of the United States, directed to the President of the Senate. The President of the Senate shall, in the presence of the Senate and House of Representatives, open all the certificates, and the votes shall then be counted. The person having the greatest number of votes shall be the President, if such number be a majority of the whole number of electors appointed; and if there be more than one who have such majority, and have an equal number of votes, then the House of Representatives shall immediately choose by ballot one of them for President; and if no person have a majority, then, from the five highest on the list, the said House shall in like manner choose the President. But in choosing the President, the votes shall be taken by states; the representation from each state having one vote; a quorum for this purpose shall consist of a member or members from two thirds of the states, and a majority of all the states shall be necessary to a choice. In every case, after the choice of the President, the person having the greatest number of votes of the electors shall be the Vice-President. But if there should remain two or more who have equal votes, the Senate shall choose from them by ballot the Vice-President.*

3. The Congress may determine the time of choosing the electors and the day on which they shall give their votes, which day shall be the same throughout the United States.

4. No person except a natural-born citizen, or a citizen of the United States at the time of the adoption of this Constitution, shall be eligible to the office of President; neither shall any person be eligible to that office who shall not have attained to the age of thirty-five years, and been fourteen years a resident within the United States.

5. In case of the removal of the President from office, or of his death, resignation, or inability to discharge the powers and duties of the said office, the same shall devolve on the Vice-President; and the Congress may by law provide for the case of removal, death, resignation, or inability, both of the President and Vice-President, declaring what officer shall then act as President; and such officer shall act accordingly, until the disability be removed or a President shall be elected.

6. The President shall, at stated times, receive for his services a compensation, which shall neither be increased nor diminished during the period for which he shall have been elected, and he shall not receive within that period any other emolument from the United States, or any of them.

7. Before he enter on the execution of his office, he shall take the following oath or affirmation:

"I do solemnly swear (or affirm) that I will faithfully execute the office of President of the United States, and will, to the best of my ability, preserve, protect, and defend the Constitution of the United States."

SECTION II.

1. The President shall be commander-in-chief of the army and navy of the United States and

* Altered by the 12th amendment.

Thus one in blood and like in condition, blessed with an unexampled diffusion of intelligence and Christian morality, possessor of a vast expanse of rich and varied soil yielding wealth and inviting immigration, freed from the political burdens which oppressed and the social bonds which cramped the people of older states, presenting to the world outside a single, compact government, but secured from centralization within by absolute local independence, this nation rapidly rose to the first rank; and so solidly based were its power and prosperity, that, but for one element of internal discord, it would have remained forever, as nearly as man can judge, a happy example of the working of republican institutions. Nor, in fact, are republican principles at all affected by the events which shook that power and disturbed that prosperity.

At the time of the formation of the Constitution all the states but two admitted negro slavery. But in all except two this institution was regarded as an exotic, inherited evil, to be borne as well as might be until it should pass away with time. All the statesmen and leaders of the Revolutionary period, including those from Virginia, so regarded it. Jefferson himself did not hesitate to denounce it openly as "a violation of human rights," and to say that not only the honor, but "the best interests of the country" demanded its extinction. In the original draft of the Declaration of Independence, which is in Jefferson's own hand, one of the grievances most strongly insisted on as a justification for the Revolution is the infliction of slavery upon the colonists, and the perpetuation of the infamous traffic in human beings.[9] But in the Convention for the formation of the Constitution, the delegates from South Carolina and Georgia announced, upon the proposal to suppress the slave-trade immediately, that if this were done those states would not become part of the Union, for they must have slaves. Rutledge said, "Religion and humanity had nothing to do with this question. Interest alone is the governing principle with nations. The true question at present is whether the Southern states shall or shall not be parties to the Union." Charles Pinckney said, "South Carolina can never receive the plan if it prohibit the slave-trade. In every proposed extension of the powers of Congress, that state has expressly and watchfully excepted the power of meddling with the importation of negroes. If the states be all left at liberty on this subject, South Carolina may perhaps, by degrees, do of herself what is wished, as Maryland and Virginia already have done."

---

of the militia of the several states, when called into the actual service of the United States; he may require the opinion in writing of the principal officer in each of the executive departments, upon any subject relating to the duties of their respective offices; and he shall have power to grant reprieves and pardons for offenses against the United States, except in cases of impeachment.

2. He shall have power, by and with the advice and consent of the Senate, to make treaties, provided two thirds of the senators present concur; and he shall nominate, and by and with the advice and consent of the Senate, shall appoint embassadors, other public ministers and consuls, judges of the Supreme Court, and all other officers of the United States, whose appointments are not herein otherwise provided for, and which shall be established by law; but the Congress may by law vest the appointment of such inferior officers as they think proper in the President alone, in the courts of law, or in the heads of departments.

3. The President shall have power to fill up all vacancies that may happen during the recess of the Senate, by granting commissions, which shall expire at the end of their next session.

SECTION III.

He shall, from time to time, give to the Congress information of the state of the Union, and recommend to their consideration such measures as he shall judge necessary and expedient; he may, on extraordinary occasions, convene both houses, or either of them; and in case of disagreement between them, with respect to the time of adjournment, he may adjourn them to such time as he shall think proper; he shall receive embassadors and other public ministers; he shall take care that the laws be faithfully executed, and shall commission all the officers of the United States.

SECTION IV.

The President, Vice-President, and all civil officers of the United States, shall be removed from office on impeachment for and conviction of treason, bribery, or other high crimes and misdemeanors.

ARTICLE III.

SECTION I.

The judicial power of the United States shall be vested in one Supreme Court, and in such inferior courts as Congress may, from time to time, ordain and establish. The judges, both of the supreme and inferior courts, shall hold their offices during good behavior; and shall, at stated times, receive for their services a compensation, which shall not be diminished during their continuance in office.

SECTION II.

1. The judicial power shall extend to all cases in law and equity arising under this Constitution, the laws of the United States, and treaties made, or which shall be made, under their authority; to all cases affecting embassadors, other public ministers, and consuls; to all cases of admiralty and maritime jurisdiction; to controversies to which the United States shall be a party; to controversies between two or more states; between a state and citizens of another state; between citizens of different states; between citizens of the same state claiming lands under grants of different States; and between a state, or the citizens thereof and foreign states, citizens or subjects.

2. In all cases affecting embassadors, other public ministers, and consuls, and those in which a state shall be party, the Supreme Court shall have original jurisdiction. In all the other cases before mentioned, the Supreme Court shall have appellate jurisdiction, both as to law and fact, with such exceptions, and under such regulations as the Congress shall make.

3. The trial of all crimes, except in cases of impeachment, shall be by jury; and such trial shall be held in the state where the said crimes shall have been committed; but when not committed within any State, the trial shall be at such place or places as the Congress may by law have directed.

SECTION III.

1. Treason against the United States shall consist only in levying war against them, or in adhering to their enemies, giving them aid and comfort. No person shall be convicted of treason, unless on the testimony of two witnesses to the same overt act, or on confession in open court.

2. The Congress shall have power to declare the punishment of treason; but no attainder of treason shall work corruption of blood, or forfeiture, except during the life of the person attainted.

ARTICLE IV.

SECTION I.

Full faith and credit shall be given in each state to the public acts, records, and judicial proceedings of every other state. And the Congress may, by general laws, prescribe the manner in which such acts, records, and proceedings shall be proved, and the effect thereof.

SECTION II.

1. The citizens of each state shall be entitled to all privileges and immunities of citizens in the several states.

2. A person charged in any state with treason, felony, or other crime, who shall flee from justice and be found in another state, shall, on demand of the executive authority of the state from which he fled, be delivered up, to be removed to the state having jurisdiction of the crime.

3. No person held to service or labor in one state, under the laws thereof, escaping into another, shall, in consequence of any law or regulation therein, be discharged from such service or labor, but shall be delivered up on claim of the party to whom such service or labor may be due.

SECTION III.

1. New states may be admitted by the Congress into this Union; but no new state shall be formed or erected within the jurisdiction of any other state; nor any state be formed by the junction of two or more states, or parts of states, without the consent of the Legislatures of the states concerned, as well as of the Congress.

2. The Congress shall have power to dispose of, and make all needful rules and regulations respecting the territory or other property belonging to the United States; and nothing in this Constitution shall be so construed as to prejudice any claims of the United States or of any particular state.

SECTION IV.

The United States shall guarantee to every State in this Union a republican form of government, and shall protect each of them against invasion; and, on application of the Legislature, or of the executive (when the Legislature cannot be convened), against domestic violence.

ARTICLE V.

The Congress, whenever two thirds of both houses shall deem it necessary, shall propose amendments to this Constitution, or, on the application of the Legislatures of two thirds of the several states, shall call a convention for proposing amendments, which, in either case, shall be valid to all intents and purposes, as part of this Constitution, when ratified by the Legislatures of three fourths of the several states, or by conventions in three fourths thereof, as the one or the other mode of ratification may be proposed by the Congress; provided, that no amendment which may be made prior to the year one thousand eight hundred and eight shall in any manner affect the first and fourth clauses in the ninth section of the first Article; and that no state, without its consent, shall be deprived of its equal suffrage in the Senate.

ARTICLE VI.

1. All debts contracted and engagements entered into, before the adoption of this Constitution, shall be as valid against the United States under this Constitution, as under the Confederation.

2. This Constitution, and the laws of the United States which shall be made in pursuance thereof; and all treaties made, or which shall be made, under the authority of the United States, shall be the supreme law of the land; and the judges in every state shall be bound thereby, any thing in the constitution or laws of any state to the contrary notwithstanding.

3. The senators and representatives before mentioned, and the members of the several state Legislatures, and all executive and judicial officers, both of the United States, and of the several states, shall be bound by oath or affirmation to support this Constitution; but no religious test shall ever be required as a qualification to any office, or public trust, under the United States.

ARTICLE VII.

The ratification of the conventions of nine states shall be sufficient for the establishment of this Constitution between the states so ratifying the same.

Done in Convention, by the unanimous consent of the states present, the seventeenth day of September, in the year of our Lord one thousand seven hundred and eighty-seven, and of the Independence of the United States of America the twelfth. In witness whereof, we have hereunto subscribed our names.

GEORGE WASHINGTON; *President and Deputy from Virginia.*

New Hampshire.—JOHN LANGDON, NICHOLAS GILMAN.
Massachusetts.—NATHANIEL GORHAM, RUFUS KING.
Connecticut.—WILLIAM SAMUEL JOHNSON, ROGER SHERMAN.
New York.—ALEXANDER HAMILTON.
New Jersey.—WILLIAM LIVINGSTON, WILLIAM PATERSON, DAVID BREARLEY, JONATHAN DAYTON.
Pennsylvania.—BENJAMIN FRANKLIN, ROBERT MORRIS, THOMAS FITZSIMONS, JAMES WILSON, THOMAS MIFFLIN, GEORGE CLYMER, JARED INGERSOLL, GOUVERNEUR MORRIS.
Delaware.—GEORGE READ, JOHN DICKINSON, JACOB BROOM, GUNNING BEDFORD, jun., RICHARD BASSETT.
Maryland.—JAMES M'HENRY, DANIEL CARROLL, DANIEL OF ST. THO. JENIFER.
Virginia.—JOHN BLAIR, JAMES MADISON, jr.
North Carolina.—WILLIAM BLOUNT, HUGH WILLIAMSON, RICHARD DOBBS SPAIGHT.
South Carolina.—JOHN RUTLEDGE, CHARLES PINCKNEY, CHARLES COTESWORTH PINCKNEY, PIERCE BUTLER.
Georgia.—WILLIAM FEW, ABRAHAM BALDWIN.

Attest, WILLIAM JACKSON, *Secretary.*

ARTICLES IN ADDITION TO AND AMENDMENTS OF THE CONSTITUTION.

ART. 1. Congress shall make no law respecting an establishment of religion, or prohibiting the free exercise thereof; or abridging the freedom of speech, or of the press; or the right of the people peaceably to assemble, and to petition the government for a redress of grievances.

ART. 2. A well-regulated militia being necessary to the security of a free state, the right of the people to keep and bear arms shall not be infringed.

ART. 3. No soldier shall, in time of peace, be quartered in any house without the consent of the owner; nor in time of war, but in a manner to be prescribed by law.

ART. 4. The right of the people to be secure in their persons, houses, papers, and effects, against unreasonable searches and seizures, shall not be violated; and no warrants shall issue but upon probable cause, supported by oath or affirmation, and particularly describing the place to be searched, and the persons or things to be seized.

ART. 5. No person shall be held to answer for a capital or otherwise infamous crime, unless on a presentment or indictment of a grand jury, except in cases arising in the land or naval forces, or in the militia when in actual service in time of war, or public danger; nor shall any person be subject for the same offense, to be twice put in jeopardy of life or limb; nor shall be compelled, in any criminal case, to be a witness against himself; nor be deprived of life, liberty, or property, without due process of law; nor shall private property be taken for public use without just compensation.

ART. 6. In all criminal prosecutions, the accused shall enjoy the right to a speedy and public trial, by an impartial jury of the state and district wherein the crime shall have been committed, which district shall have been previously ascertained by law, and to be informed of the nature and cause of the accusation; to be confronted with the witnesses against him; to have compulsory process for obtaining witnesses in his favor; and to have the assistance of counsel for his defense.

ART. 7. In suits at common law, where the value in controversy shall exceed twenty dollars, the right of trial by jury shall be preserved; and no fact tried by a jury shall be otherwise re-examined in any court of the United States than according to the rules of the common law.

ART. 8. Excessive bail shall not be required, nor excessive fines imposed, nor cruel and unusual punishments inflicted.

ART. 9. The enumeration in the Constitution of certain rights, shall not be construed to deny or disparage others retained by the people.

ART. 10. The powers not delegated to the United States by the Constitution, nor prohibited by it to the States, are reserved to the States respectively, or to the people.

ART. 11. The judicial power of the United States shall not be construed to extend to any suit in law or equity commenced or prosecuted against one of the United States by citizens of another state, or by citizens or subjects of any foreign state.

ART. 12. The electors shall meet in their respective states, and vote by ballot for President and Vice-President, one of whom, at least, shall not be an inhabitant of the same state with themselves; they shall name in their ballots the person voted for as President, and in distinct ballots the person voted for as Vice-President; and they shall make distinct lists of all persons voted for as President, and of all persons voted for as Vice-President, and of the number of votes for each, which list they shall sign and certify, and transmit sealed to the seat of government of the United States, directed to the President of the Senate; the President of the Senate shall, in the presence of the Senate and House of Representatives, open all the certificates, and the votes shall then be counted; the person having the greatest number of votes for President shall be the President, if such number be a majority of the whole number of electors appointed; and if no person have such majority, then from the persons having the highest numbers, not exceeding three, on the list of those voted for as President, the House of Representatives shall choose immediately by ballot the President. But in choosing the President, the votes shall be taken by states, the representation from each state having one vote; a quorum for this purpose shall consist of a member or members from two thirds of the states, and a majority of all the states shall be necessary to a choice. And if the House of Representatives shall not choose a President whenever the right of choice shall devolve upon them, before the fourth day of March next following, then the Vice-President shall act as President, as in the case of the death or other constitutional disability of the President.

The person having the greatest number of votes as Vice-President shall be the Vice-President, if such number be a majority of the whole number of electors appointed, and if no person have a majority, then from the two highest numbers on the list the Senate shall choose the Vice-President: a quorum for the purpose shall consist of two thirds of the whole number of senators, and a majority of the whole number shall be necessary to a choice.

But no person constitutionally ineligible to the office of President shall be eligible to that of Vice-President of the United States.

[9] See this complaint in the fac simile of the original draft given on pages 6–7. It was stricken out before the adoption of the instrument in deference to the feelings of South Carolina.

Baldwin, of Georgia, also declared that that state "would not confederate if not allowed to import slaves." The existence of the nation as one and indivisible seemed of more importance at that period to the men to whom this announcement was made than the immediate suppression of a traffic which was then looked upon without the horror which it now excites; and so, to satisfy South Carolina and Georgia, in the dainty phraseology of the Constitution, "the migration or importation of such persons as any of the states existing shall think proper to admit" was allowed until the year 1808. Men who held negroes as property naturally expected, and reasonably claimed, that if they united themselves under a national government with other men who would soon pass laws for the extinction of such a right of property under their own local governments, these laws should not operate to the injury of those who did not adopt them; and so that other dainty but stringent clause was added, providing that any person "held to service and labor in one state under the laws thereof," escaping into another, "shall be delivered up on claim of the party to whom such service or labor may be due." It had been proposed in the Continental Congress that in the apportionment of taxation (which was to be according to population) slaves should be reckoned at three fifths of their actual numbers, because, as it was argued, the labor of five negroes was not more than equal to that of three white men. This principle of tax apportionment was adopted in the Constitution; and, consequently, as taxation and representation were to go hand in hand, representatives were apportioned in the same manner. Slaves were not to be represented as property; but three fifths of their actual number in each state went to swell the aggregate, according to which the representation of each state was more or less numerous in the popular branch of Congress and in the College of Electors for President and Vice-President.

The two former provisions of the Constitution in regard to slaves were, at the time of their making, the more highly prized by the slaveholders, but the last was of far the greatest importance in regard to the strength and perpetuation of slavery. For it gave to every citizen of a slave state, whether a slaveholder himself or not, a preponderance in the national government greater than that of a citizen of a free state, by three fifths of the number of slaves in his state; so that while thirty thousand citizens of a free state would send but one representative to Congress, twelve thousand citizens of a slave state would also send one representative if they collectively owned thirty thousand slaves. This provision also made it desirable, as far as regarded political preponderance, for slaveholders to discourage the presence in their state of citizens who were not also slaveholders, and to increase the aggregate number of slaves; for it is clear that, the greater the number of slaves and the fewer the number of their owners, the greater the concentration of political power in the hands of the latter. Thus a provision of the Constitution, made for the purpose of insuring the proper relation between representation and taxation, actually destroyed the political equality of citizens of the United States, in theory the very corner-stone of the republican government which it was framed to establish, while, at the same time, in the states which got the advantage in this inequality, two fifths of what was really productive property was exempted from direct taxation. Thus special privilege was added to the disproportionate political preponderance of the slaveholder. It was the power conferred by this inequality and this privilege on the one side, co-operating with the growth of the feeling against slavery throughout civilized Christendom on the other, which brought about the great rebellion against the government of the United States.

At the time when the Constitution of the United States was adopted, seven of the thirteen states which formed the Union, New Hampshire, Massachusetts, Rhode Island, Connecticut, New York, New Jersey, and Pennsylvania, either had abolished slavery or were sure to do so; but the six which retained it, Delaware, Maryland, Virginia, North and South Carolina, and Georgia, were in the aggregate the more populous and the wealthier, while, as we have just seen, their citizens had by the terms of the Union acquired peculiar privileges and advantages of representation. Consequently, at the beginning, the interests of the slave states, as a body, outweighed those of the free states, as a body. This advantage was assiduously preserved, until it was swept away by the irresistible onflow of events. On the 11th of March, 1784, Thomas Jefferson, Virginia's most eminent representative, proposed, in the Continental Congress, that after the year 1802 there should be "neither slavery nor involuntary servitude" in any state to be thereafter formed from the territory of the United States. This proposition failed to become an ordinance only by the lack of the vote of New Jersey, which was lost by the absence of one of her delegates. But in 1787 the important ordinance was passed by which slavery was prohibited in all territory of the Union northwest of the Ohio River. It was more than thirty years, however, before this ordinance had a direct influence upon the great question which was to shake the Union. Meantime Kentucky and Vermont, offshoots of Virginia and New Hampshire severally, were admitted to the Union in 1792, the former slave, the latter free. The slave state of Tennessee came in in 1799, and in 1802 the free state of Ohio. In 1803, the Territory of Louisiana, then a French colony, and including (after the indefinite fashion of colonial boundary claims) all the vast tract of land lying around the mouth of the Mississippi, and stretching westward and northwest thence from the banks of the Mississippi to the Pacific Ocean. Slavery was already established in this territory, from which, in 1812, a slave state was admitted into the Union. Free Indiana followed in 1816. Mississippi and Illinois, Alabama and Maine, alternately slave and free, were formed and recognized between 1817 and 1820.

Ten states had now been added to the original thirteen. Five admitted

slavery, and five excluded it; so that in the Senate, where the states, large and small, were equally represented, the original distribution of power between the free and the slave states had not been disturbed. But in the House of Representatives and in the College of Presidential Electors the aspect of affairs was much changed. At the time of the first census, 1790, the aggregate population of the states which had abolished slavery, or were about to abolish it, and of those which had not and since have not done so, was about equal; while the advantage of wealth and the anticipated increase in numbers were altogether on the side of the latter. But the census of 1820 showed authoritatively what all observing men well knew in a general way, that the states which had abolished slavery were increasing in population and in wealth much more rapidly than those which had retained it. In that year the population of the free states was found to be nearly three quarters of a million greater than that of the slave states, and the tide of immigration from Europe, which had then begun to set strongly in, bore its wealth of labor to the free states almost entirely. In itself there was nothing either surprising or alarming in this revelation. Had the country been in its normal condition, with its political power equally distributed, and all its citizens counting each a unit, and no more, in the choice of its executive and legislative officers, it would have been a matter of no political moment to any particular number of states where the increase of wealth and population was, so long as they were individually prosperous. For, as to their local affairs, the absolute control of those was secured to them by the Constitution, which also pledged to the preservation of their equal voice in the Senate. But in the thirty years which had passed since the formation of the national government a great and important change had taken place in the relations of slavery to the country at large. We have seen that it was regarded at that period, except by two of the states, as a legacy from the mother country, which conferred no benefit sufficient to compensate for its reproach and its disadvantages, and as an institution which must gradually disappear. The two states which were not of this mind were South Carolina and Georgia, who, it will be remembered, had refused to enter the Union if the slave-trade were immediately made illegal. In these states a small and active school of politicians soon arose, which devoted itself not only to the protection of slavery where it already existed, but to its extension and the increase of its power. This school rapidly attained a potent influence throughout the slave states, where it soon included nearly all the wealthy planters. This class of men saw the advantage which, in virtue of their slaves, they enjoyed by reason of their more numerous representation in Congress and the choice of President. They saw, too, that the tendency of affairs under their local government was to make them richer, and the poor men round them, who owned few or no slaves, poorer, and thus their mere dependents and creatures; and so, misled by mistaken self-interest, their power was gradually massed and marshaled under the direction of what may be conveniently and correctly called the South Carolina school of politicians, and slavery became a compact interest, to be protected and advanced in the councils of the nation. The only single and sectional interest to be so cared for, in fact; for in the free states men asked for nothing else than that freedom of action which was already secured to every citizen of the republic; nothing else was needful to their prosperity. Agriculture, manufactures, commerce, were interests, indeed, in which different parts of the country had different stakes; but they existed in a greater or less degree in all parts of the country; they were natural and universal manifestations of activity and civilization; and they existed in virtue of no special law, and required none for their undisturbed security. But with slavery it was not so; and the politicians who had chosen it, both as the interest which they were to defend and the weapon which they were to wield, saw with apprehension the rapidly increasing voice of the free states in the House of Representatives and in the Electoral College. The privilege which they feared to lose had become more precious in the very lapse of time which had also brought about the events which threatened them with its loss. By the invention of the cotton-gin the means of producing that staple in a marketable condition had been increased a hundred-fold, and the introduction of the steam-engine into the sugar-mill had more than doubled the value of the plantations in Louisiana. Not only so. These new processes, requiring capital and inviting capital, tended not more to the increase of the aggregate wealth of the states which profited by them than to the concentration of wealth of all kinds, and particularly of land and slaves, in the hands of the few. Consequently, the rich planters saw themselves, year by year, with more political power in their hands; and society in the slave states came to consist in the main of a small governing class of planters, with the bankers, merchants, and professional men whose functions were required by the business of the plantations, and a large class of poor people, becoming every day poorer, more wretched, more dependent, and, at the same time, prouder of their political advantages over the poor men of the free states, by which they were raised to a sort of equality with the wealthy slaveholders upon whose sufferance they existed. This anti-republican, oligarchal system of society the South Carolina school of politicians sought to protect, perpetuate, and propagate.

Meantime the anti-slavery sentiment had spread widely over the civilized world, which in this respect followed the humane lead of the government and the mass of the people of the United States. In the year 1794 Congress passed an act against fitting out vessels for the slave-trade, and in 1800 another, forbidding citizens of the United States from holding property in foreign slave-ships, and also authorizing United States ships to seize slavers. In 1807, as the bringing of slaves into the United States was to become unlawful by constitutional provision in 1808, an act was passed prescribing heavy penalties for this crime. During all this time the slave-trade was lawfully carried on in British ships; and it was not until March 25, of this very year 1807, that the carrying off of negroes from Africa into slavery under the British flag was forbidden by act of Parliament. The returns of the Charleston Custom-house, quoted in Congress, show that, of 39,075 negroes imported into South Carolina from Africa between the years 1804 and 1808, 19,649, or more than one half, were imported by British subjects. 25,834, or nearly two thirds of the whole number, were imported by foreigners, while traders of the maritime free states imported only 8838. In 1820 Congress passed an act declaring the slave-trade piracy, punishable with death. In 1833 slavery was abolished throughout the British Possessions after the 1st of August, 1834, as it had been a generation back in the most enlightened and Christianized states of the American Union, and as it would have been in all were it not for the absolute protection secured by the Constitution to every state in regard to its local government. The special advocates of universal freedom may think ill of a provision which resulted in the perpetuation of bondage in a part of the republic. But we must never forget that the men who framed our national government found slavery in the land, or that this provision has but incidentally kept in bonds a race which takes easily to compelled servitude, which under kind treatment can be happy in bondage, which continues servile after generations of freedom, taking pleasure in serving the superior race, pleased when it pleases that race, and proud when noticed by it, or, finally, that this provision was absolutely necessary to secure the political unity, and therefore the independence and peaceful progress of the race, which has made the American Republic the hope and the lode-star of the advocates of popular government throughout the world.

But the rights of states, however guarded, could not stay the advance of opinion; and the year 1816 saw a new attempt to do away with slavery—the Colonization Society was formed at Washington, having for its object the removal of free negroes from a country where they were in contact with a superior race having instinctive repugnance to equal association with them, to one where, being surrounded only by people of their own blood, they could attain such elevation as they were capable of, and even become the nucleus of a negro civilization. The benevolent hope was also expressed by the founders of this society, that slavery might be gradually abolished in the states which then permitted it, and that this so much desired end might be furthered by the means afforded of ridding the country of the freed negro, and enabling him to set out in his new life with some comfort and prospect of success. The leading members of this association were slaveholders, James Madison, John Randolph, and Judge Bushrod Washington, of Virginia, Henry Clay, of Kentucky, Charles Carroll, and Wright, of Maryland, being among them. The feeling of which this society was the fruit was akin to that which, according to Professor St. George Tucker, of William and Mary College, Virginia, produced ten thousand manumissions in that state between 1782 and 1797. But the leading men of the cotton-growing states looked askance upon this project, although it was directed neither directly nor indirectly against any of their rights as slaveholders.

Such was the position of affairs when the question of the organization and admission of Missouri as a state came before Congress. Missouri, as part of the ceded French territory, Louisiana, was already slave soil; as lying northwest of the Ohio River, it was debarred from slavery by the ordinance of 1787. The residents asked to be admitted to the Union with a state Constitution allowing slavery. The delegates from the slave states said "Yes; for slavery is already attached to the soil:" those from the free states said "No; for slavery is excluded forever northwest of the Ohio." Upon this question suddenly great warmth of feeling was manifested on both sides, and all party distinctions at once faded away. The occasion is of particular interest to us, not only as the beginning of that strife which, after a lapse of forty years, came to bloody arbitration, but from the fact that, in the course of the fierce altercations to which it gave rise, the determination of the extreme slavery party to carry their point, at all hazards to the country, was even then distinctly avowed. It having been proposed by James Talmadge, of New York, to restrain the further introduction of slavery into Arkansas, and by John Taylor, of the same state, to impose a similar restriction as to Missouri, the debate thereon was long and violent; and Mr. Cobb, of Georgia—ominous name!—in the course of a furious speech said, directing himself particularly to Talmadge, that "a fire had been kindled which all the waters of the ocean could not put out, and which only seas of blood could extinguish;" adding that if the Northern members persisted "the Union would be dissolved." To this fierce onslaught Talmadge replied by firmly and calmly reasserting his position and that of his constituents, maintaining it with arguments which even those who do not allow them to be conclusive must admit are clear and cogent, and saying, " If the civil war which gentlemen so much threaten must come, I can only say, let it come!" Thus early did the two parties to this question show the style in which they would act upon it: the one in passion and with ferocity, the other in calmness and with fortitude.

Few readers need be told how this dispute was then settled. Missouri was admitted with her slave-bearing Constitution, with the proviso that forever after there should be neither slavery nor involuntary servitude in any territory of the United States north of the parallel of 36° 30′ (the southern boundary of Missouri), but that south of that line states might be admitted either with slavery or without it. With this " Missouri Compromise," although it was first proposed by a Northern member, John Taylor, of New York, the whole country, and particularly the South, appeared to be well content; and it was believed that the firebrand of disunion was extinguished. But, alas! it smouldered.

From this period the political power of the slaveholding states became

practically a unit upon the subject of slavery, and all questions which bore upon it; and this being the only subject upon which there was a compact organization, and a united and vigorous policy conducted by men born and bred to conduct it, the slave interest soon came to be the controlling power in the government. The leaders of its extreme, or South Carolina school, generally assumed an arrogant, insolent tone to the members from the free states, and attempted, too often with success, to browbeat them openly upon the floor of Congress. Seeing how much destructive power the dogma of "state sovereignty" placed in their hands, they assumed it as the cardinal point of their political creed, in the very teeth of the assertions, the teachings, and the counsels of their own statesmen of the Revolutionary and post-Revolutionary generations. At what she thought a convenient occasion, South Carolina undertook to act upon this principle; but what short and sufficient measures for the maintenance of the power of the national government her attempted nullification of the Tariff Act of 1832 met at the hands of General Jackson, need not be told here. Her conduct in this affair, and her headlong rush into the rebellion of 1861, impatient to be the leader in the attempt to destroy the republic, form her chief claims to distinction in American annals.

In her nullification outbreak, South Carolina had not the support of even her sister slave states. Yet after her subjection the slave power continued to maintain its united front, and through an alliance, rarely broken, with the great Democratic party, North and South—each using the other for its own ends, after the universal practice of politicians—it always had a potent, and generally a controlling voice in the national government. For a few years there was no occasion for political controversy as to slavery. But soon a small, virulent, and fanatical body of men did yeoman's service to the cause of the extreme school of slaveholders by commencing an agitation upon the subject, which had, under the circumstances, no possible good end in view. But this mattered little to the Abolitionists. They were in their very nature impracticable men. Either not knowing, or not caring for the fact that government has to deal with existing powers and obligations, and not with abstract principles, they reduced statesmanship in America to one simple syllogism: It is wrong to hold man in bondage; the negro is a man; therefore negro slavery is wrong; therefore it ought at once to be abolished utterly. Regardless of all the circumstances by virtue of which the master found himself in possession of the slave; regardless of all traits of race in the slave and considerations of treatment by the master which modified the nature of the relation between them; and equally regardless whether the government of the United States, or even the people, had either the right or the power to abolish slavery, they clamored and agitated for its abolition. The people of the slave states, solemnly guaranteed in the undisturbed possession of their slaves by the organic compact of the nation, were naturally indignant at this movement toward a violation of their vested constitutional rights. Nor were they alone in this feeling. The mass, practically the whole of the people of the free states, wrongful as they felt slavery to be, yet knew that as citizens of the United States, or members of free commonwealths, they were in no way responsible for it, and had no power over it, and they regarded this agitation as dangerous to society and subversive of government. The Chancellor (Walworth) of the State of New York, and David B. Ogden, one of its most eminent and upright jurists, declared that "the doctrine of immediate emancipation" was "a direct and palpable nullification of the Constitution." This it undoubtedly was, and an attempt to carry it into effect would have been revolution, rebellion.

But the multitudinous opponents of the Abolitionists, North and South, not content with discountenancing, persecuted them, and, as a natural consequence, abolitionism took firm root and began to spread. Placed under a ban, it became bitter, vehement, denunciatory, void alike of common decency and of Christian charity. It denounced slavery, an institution which prevailed over one half the country, and among some of the purest and most eminent citizens of the republic, as "the sum of all villainies,"[10] and it did not hesitate to brand the Constitution itself as " a covenant with death and a compact with hell." It is not in the nature of man that an agitation should be carried on in such a spirit without provoking violent antagonism. Every man who held slaves—every man who, although he owned no slaves, did not believe that George Washington, and Thomas Jefferson, and Charles Carroll, to say nothing of perhaps his own grandfather or father, had passed their lives in villainy—every man who did not believe that the Constitution was a bargain with death and hell, was an opponent of abolitionism; and in the South the new movement did more than any other possible agency could have done to produce a unity of Southern feeling, to imbitter that feeling toward the North, and to mass more compactly the vast political power of slavery. The leaders of the extreme school were not slow to avail themselves of the weapons which their opponents had placed in their hands. Working remorselessly toward their end, and having already almost entirely the political leadership in their several states, they boldly assumed the whole control of Southern social and political affairs. They brought the press of their own states into entire subserviency to their purposes; they made it social damnation to subscribe for any newspaper or periodical in the free states which was not itself also subservient to their faction; they managed to exclude from political preferment all rising men who were not heart and soul devoted to that faction. By all manner of misrepresentation and craft they exasperated their numerous poor slave-less dependents against the Abolitionists; and taking ground that whoever was not for them was against them, they fixed the stigma of abolitionism upon all who did not look upon negro slavery as a just, wise, and beneficent institution—a test which, it need hard-

---

[10] John Wesley furnished the first of these stock phrases, and William Lloyd Garrison the second

ly be said, ranged nearly all the people of the free states among the Abolitionists, where, indeed, it would have placed the best, if not the most of those of the slave states a generation before. Thus these adroit and unscrupulous managers were enabled to excite among the residents of the slave states what they most desired—a wide-spread prejudice, deepening into enmity, against their fellow-citizens north of the Potomac and the Ohio. They represented the latter as a body of fanatics, ready to set the Constitution recklessly at naught in their disregard of the rights of those who differed with them in opinion. The loose and reckless lives of a large proportion of the Southern and Southwestern population, and their readiness to quarrel and to use arms, especially the knife, upon slight provocation; the rigid conformity to the "code of honor" among the better born and bred; and, on the other hand, the devotion of the people at the North to the pursuits of peace, their absolute subservience to law, their disuse of the duel, and the contempt and odium into which it rapidly fell among them, made it easy to implant a belief among the former that the latter were poor, mean-spirited, cowardly creatures, bound up in fanaticism and love of money. This was done; and no means were left untried by the Southern leaders to produce a conviction among their blinded followers that the inhabitants of the free states and the slave states were a different and an antagonistic people, the former being the superiors of the latter in all the heroic virtues, as the latter were their superiors in mechanical arts and the tricks of trade.

The feeling thus excited was, however, factitious and artificial; and it was possible only because the mass of those in whom it was implanted were ignorant—so uneducated, in fact, as generally to be unable to write, and, in a large proportion of cases, even to read; because, also, the great mass of them were never in a free state, or out of their own neighborhood, and never saw a "Yankee," except a peddler, who, perhaps, cheated them, and who certainly had to worry them for payment if they bought of him; and chiefly because their leaders, or "big men," as they called them, were able to shut out from them all knowledge of the free states through newspapers, except by extracts either from those which lauded or palliated slavery, or from those which denounced it and slaveholders in rancorous and unmeasured terms. But their influence in this regard stopped at the boundaries of slavery. The animosity which they excited was not reciprocal. Throughout the free states there was a disposition to soothe and to conciliate, and to make all sacrifices of feeling and of interest which could reasonably be asked, and even more, to what was regarded as the waywardness, the morbid sensitiveness, and the exasperated feeling of the people of the slave states. The interests of trade, too, interposed their influence; and merchants and manufacturers brooked without resentment many a provocation upon the subject of slavery from alarmed and apprehensive men, who, if deprived of their slaves, would be both without the occasion to buy and the means of paying for that which they had bought already. Of these feelings, as well as of the political importance which their compact organization and positive policy gave them, the extreme, or, as they began now to be called, the "fire-eating" Southern men took advantage. There were no bounds to their assumption of superiority in Congress, and little to their insolence and arrogance of manner. To any stand against the aggression of slavery they replied by threats of disunion; to any protest against insult, by such retort as brought the issue to the alternative of submission or a bloody encounter. All this the free states endured for peace' sake and for the Union.

But the South was not content. Encouraged by the deprecatory attitude of their opponents, and impelled by economical considerations, the leaders of the slavery interest undertook to make the whole power of the government subservient to their will; to break down the landmarks which, with their own consent, had been set up; and to change the political standing of slavery from that of a local institution, existing in virtue of municipal law, and having certain specified and sharply-limited guarantees in the Constitution, to that of a national institution, existing in virtue of the Constitution, and protected every where by the national flag.

Exhausted in its agriculture, and constantly needing new soil to make the labor of the wasteful, shiftless negro profitable, seeking also to preserve its superiority in the national government, slavery was unsatisfied with the acquisition of Florida and Louisiana, especially after the establishment of the Missouri Compromise line. For below the parallel of 36° 30′ the advance of slavery westward was stopped by the territory of Mexico, which bounded Louisiana and Arkansas on the west, and stretched along the Arkansas River and the 42d parallel of latitude to the Pacific Ocean. Hence the discussion in the Southern and Southwestern states of the annexation of Texas, as early as 1829, on the express ground that it would strengthen and extend the influence of slavery, and raise the price of slaves. Hence the indecorously-hasty recognition of the independence of that vast country and its admission to the Union, the consequent Mexican war, and the acquisition of California, New Mexico, and Utah. Hence the attempts, by browbeating and bowie-knife, to drive the free state settlers from the golden shores of California—an attempt which, after a little promise of success, failed utterly; and California, rapidly becoming populous and rich, and stretching far below the Missouri Compromise line, chose to exclude slavery, and was admitted to the Union as a free state, with Oregon soon to follow her. The manifest intention of the leading Southern politicians to use the national flag and the national forces, not only for the protection of slavery where it existed in virtue of local law, but for its diffusion throughout the national domain, led to the counter attempt in the bill brought in by David Wilmot, of Pennsylvania, and known as the Wilmot Proviso, which provided that slavery should be excluded from all territory which had been or should be acquired from Mexico. In spite of the union, for better for worse, between the Democrats of the slave and the free

states, this bill passed the House of Representatives, and only failed to become an act by a majority of ten against it in the Senate. The feeling against the propagation of slavery was now becoming stronger and stronger in the free states; petitions for the abolition of the internal slave-trade and of slavery in the District of Columbia were presented to Congress; and the Free Soil party came into existence, with the motto, "Free soil, free speech, free men." The counter move was one, not of conciliation or of compromise, but of extreme audacity. Mr. Calhoun, who had been a member of

JOHN C. CALHOUN.

President Monroe's cabinet when the Missouri Compromise was adopted, but who had led the nullification movement in South Carolina, who had nursed the doctrine of state sovereignty, and developed it from a querulous crotchet into a dangerous dogma, and who was the unblushing advocate and fearless champion of negro slavery, brought a series of resolutions into the Senate which denied the right of Congress to legislate upon the subject of slavery in the Territories, and declared any law which prevented the citizens of any state from going with their "property" into any of the Territories of the United States unconstitutional and void. This he did in face of the action of Congress in first establishing the Missouri Compromise line, and afterward extending that line to Texas. The effect and the intent of these resolutions was to throw the whole territory of the United States, from the southern boundary of New Mexico to the line of the British Possessions on the north, open to slavery. Mr. Calhoun also wrote and published a letter, in which he said to his fellow-citizens of the slaveholding states, "It is our duty to ourselves, to the Union, and our political institutions, to force the issue on the North," for the reason, as he sagaciously saw, that "we are now stronger relatively than we shall be hereafter, politically and morally." He also proposed, in direct violation of the Constitution, if the free states did not allow slaveholders to bring their slaves when they visited or traveled through them, and did not refrain from putting any hinderance in the way of returning fugitive slaves, to exclude their ships from the ports of the slaveholding states; and he recommended a convention of the cotton-growing states to take these matters into consideration. His resolutions did not pass, and his proposed convention was not then held; but his movement was only a few years too early.

From this time events tending toward the rebellion of the slaveholders succeeded each other rapidly. The passage of the Fugitive Slave Act in 1850 was another attempt to allay the excitement in which the "fire-eaters" at the South, with the aid of the reckless Abolitionists of the North, managed to keep the country. As this act imposed no new duties upon the residents of the non-slaveholding states, but, on the contrary, relieved their local officers of any responsibility in the matter of returning fugitives by the appointment of special commissioners for that purpose, and as its only operation was to give efficiency to a provision of the Constitution, delegates from the free states, not admirers of slavery, gave it their votes, and justified their course by the state of feeling in the slaveholding states. There had been a convention of delegates from the slave states at Nashville; the Legislatures of South Carolina and Mississippi had proposed the assembling of a Southern Congress; in the former body secession from the Union was openly advocated; and on the 4th of July, 1850, the memories of the day were not allowed to abate, for even a few hours, the feverous folly of the slave-monomaniacs, whose festivities were deformed by toasts defamatory of the Union. But the great excitement which was produced at the North by the passage of this law for the mere enforcement of a compact as old as the nation, and yet not so old as to have become antiquated and obsolete, showed the great change of feeling which the aggressive policy of the slavery propaganda had produced in a single generation. The Abolitionists, of course, were frenzied; and even those who were not of that faction regarded the law in form and spirit as intentionally aggravating and humiliating. The feeling upon the subject was deepened by the sudden flight to Canada, from the most northern free states, of large numbers of negroes, some of whom had lived there many years. The people of these states, although not very anxious to retain the negroes for their own sakes, yet saw with sorrow, and sad foreboding, what a multitude of their humble fellow-creatures they might have been, and still might be, called upon to send back into bondage. Yet they did not, as a body, flinch from their loyalty to the Constitution. Slaves claimed were delivered to claimants who established their cases, repulsive though the duty of rendition was. The slaveholders pressed their claims with a pertinacity which would have been very unwise if they had desired unity and good feeling; but which, as their object was to either provoke discord, hatred, and disunion, or to bring about the absolute subjection of the free states to their dominion, was shrewdly politic.

At last a negro named Anthony Burns was claimed in Boston, and put in detention during the investigation of the claim. Some of the more reckless of the Abolitionists, assisted by free negroes, attacked the building in which he was detained pending the examination, and a deputy marshal was shot. There was popular commotion, and a riotous disposition among a small part of the townspeople. But order was preserved and the law sustained by the state and city, as well as by the national authorities. The ablest counsel in the state appeared for the negro, and the investigation was protracted. The excitement increased and quickly spread throughout the state and the whole country. The claimant established his ownership, the negro was remanded; and on that day was seen in Boston one of the most imposing sights the world ever looked upon. Popular feeling was at its height, and the streets swarmed with people, not only from the city itself, but the adjacent country. It was feared that there would be an attempt to take the slave from the marshal as he was on his way to the vessel which was to carry him southward. The marshal had special aids well armed, and there was a company of marines at his command; but, in addition to these, and to prevent any contact between the excited people and the United States officers, the whole militia force of the vicinity was placed under arms, and acted as an escort to the marshal and the slave. Considerably more than ten thousand men thus voluntarily took up arms in support of a law which they loathed, and throughout that swarming, excited city there was not an act of violence committed on that day. Such deference to law merely as the law, in a populous city where feeling upon the subject of the law was all-pervading, and excitement had been rising for days, is unprecedented. But the slavery party were not satisfied with such sacrifices. They declaimed against the necessity of calling out ten or fifteen thousand troops to insure the return of one slave, as an evidence of a desire on the part of the community in which it occurred to violate their constitutional obligations; they did not see, or, seeing, chose to disregard the fact that those troops were volunteers, residents of Boston and the surrounding villages, and that, had not the people of Massachusetts been determined to fulfill their constitutional duty to the very letter, the United States would have been obliged to send an army, and a large one, to take that one negro away from Boston. The slaveholders claimed, in effect, a hearty and cheerful performance of this duty; but that they could not have, and had no right to exact.

The last test of the willingness of the free states to submit to aggression for peace' sake was applied in 1854 by the passage of the bill for the territorial organization of Kansas and Nebraska. Senator Douglas, of Illinois, a

STEPHEN A. DOUGLAS.

bold, adroit, persistent man, having in some excess the politician's failing of regarding the end rather than the means, and almost openly ambitious of the presidency, brought the bill for the organization of these territories into the Senate, and made one enormous, and, as he thought, overwhelming bid for the support of the whole South by introducing a clause which (in accordance with Mr. Calhoun's resolutions before mentioned) set aside the Mis-

souri Compromise as unconstitutional, and opened the whole western territory up to the British line to slavery. The proposition fell upon the country like a thunder-clap. The Missouri Compromise was looked upon as a solemn settlement of the question to which it referred for all time, and was held in the free states and in the border slave states in veneration second only to that felt for the Constitution itself. Yet such was the condition of parties, such the ability of those who undertook to bring about the passage of this important and portentous measure, such, too, the effect of the suddenness with which it was sprung upon the country, that it received a majority of both houses of Congress, and became the law of the land. But the event created a deep-seated and wide-spread alarm throughout the whole population of the free states. Large numbers of Northern Democrats, who dreaded the advance of slavery more than the breaking up of their party, clove away from it; and of these, and the Free Soil party, and a large remnant of the old Whig party, whose leader was slaveholding but not slavery-propagating Henry Clay, was formed the Republican party, which waxed

HENRY CLAY.

strong apace, and soon found that it must fight its way with weapons physical as well as moral.

The issue before the country was now sharply defined. The Democratic slavery party said, "You shall not exclude the Southerner from the territory of the republic, purchased with the common blood and treasure of its citizens. You can go there with your property, and shall he not go there with his?" To this the Republican replied, "There is no such exclusion. The Southerner can go into the Territories and take with him all that the Northerner can. There is, as there should be, no difference in this respect between them. But no; the Southerner demands that he shall not only take with him such property as the Northerner takes, but something else—property of a very extraordinary character, which is property only in his state by local law or custom, and which is not secured to him by the Constitution any where else except for its return to him there—property, the presence of which excludes the Northern *citizen*, whereas the exclusion of that property does not exclude the Southern *citizen*. This can not be." And then began the open, final struggle.

The first battle-ground of the new party was Kansas itself, whither the free soil men flocked to secure that fair land for free labor. Some went only of their own motion and with their own means; but many were sent out by emigrant-aid societies formed in the East. They went, however, as settlers in good faith. But how they were harried by ruffians from the border of Missouri; how they were outvoted at the polls by armed men, who swarmed into the Territory just before the elections, to return to Missouri immediately after they were over; how they were shot in cold blood and in hot blood; how they had to stand guard over their log cabins, their wives and children, and their cattle, as our forefathers stood guard over theirs against the savages; how there were two capitals and two constitutions, and governor after governor was sent out at the bidding of the South to support the false and crush the true; and how not one had either the ability, or the conscience, or the heart to do it; and how, finally, after a Congressional investigation, the shameful story was all rightly told, and truth triumphed—this we all know. But in all these sad commotions the country took great strides toward revolution, though at the time we did not see it. Then came an outrage which shocked the world—the assault upon Senator Sumner. He was not entirely blameless. A member of the highest legislative body of one of the foremost civilized nations might have done a wiser and a better thing in a set speech upon a momentous subject than call one senator, who was tall, "the Don Quixote," and another, who was short, "the Sancho Panza of slavery;" for this designation of Mr. Butler, of South Carolina, and Mr. Douglas, of Illinois, may be called the point of a studiously irritating speech by which Mr. Sumner provoked the wrath of the slaveholders, without any hope of either curbing their party or strengthening his own. What he said might have been wiser and better, indeed, but not more cutting, because it was severe, personal, and true. But for all that, when Preston Brooks attacked Mr. Sumner as he sat bending over his desk in the deserted Senate-chamber, and beat him senseless, he played not only the part of a ruffian, but of a traitor to the liberties of his country. He brought shame upon it throughout all Christendom; shame which the free states cast from them without soil by their indignant denunciation of the act at the voice of men of all parties among them; shame which the South Carolina politicians and their followers took with effrontery to themselves by making a hero of the assailant, and by assuming in Washington an air of greater defiance and insolence than ever. This act of violence provoked the resistance it was meant to intimidate, and added many thousands to the large vote cast in 1856 for Colonel Fremont, the first candidate of the new Republican party. Bearing the Sumner outrage in mind, men voted for Colonel Fremont who had never gone to the polls before since they became of age. Indeed, so strong had the conviction become in the free states that the safety of the republic demanded a firm check upon the aggressions of slavery, that it seemed at one time as if the Republican party would carry the day at its first struggle; and then went up the usual threats of disunion from the "fire-eaters;" and Governor Wise, of Virginia, declared that, if Colonel Fremont were elected, he would march with the militia of his state upon Washington and seize the Capitol and the national archives. But Fremont was not elected, and the country had another breathing-spell, and the rule or ruin party of the South another four years' period of preparation—preparation for their attempt to destroy the republic; for as to aggression they had no more to make; the Supreme Court having decided, in the case of Dred Scott, a negro who claimed to be free on the ground that his owner had taken him into a free state, and afterward into a part of the old Louisiana territory north of 36° 30', that the Missouri Compromise Act, in prohibiting slavery north of that parallel, was unconstitutional, and also that slave-owners might take their slaves into any state of the Union without detriment to their right to the service and labor of those slaves. This decision virtually converted the whole Union to the purposes of slavery, regardless of any local law; and in the Union there was nothing left for slavery to gain.

The position taken by the Supreme Court in this case was regarded throughout the free states as a direct attack, under cover of law, upon that independence in local legislation so carefully secured by the Constitution, and consequently as an open attempt upon their liberties. Nearly all of them at once took measures of the same kind as the resolution passed in the Legislature of New York, which body declared, by large majorities in both houses, "that this state will not allow slavery within its borders, in any form, or under any pretense, for any time, however short, let the consequences be what they may." This, however justifiable, was revolution—indirect, and it might have been bloodless, but still revolution; for either the State of New York must fail to make good its solemn asseveration, or else maintain a position in the teeth of the Constitution, as it was declared by the authority appointed to interpret it. So also were the Personal Liberty Laws passed in some of the free states revolutionary. That of Vermont, for instance, which provided that every person who might have been held as a slave who should in any manner go into that state should be free; and that any person who should attempt to hold any free person as a slave in that state for any time, however short, on the pretense that that person was or had been a slave, should be subject to imprisonment for five years or a fine of not less than $1000 and not more than $10,000. Upon this point, however, no occasion offered of open rupture. The free states continued to return fugitive

JAMES BUCHANAN.

slaves, though sometimes rescues were attempted; and no slaveholder ventured to test the willingness of New York or any other free state to allow slavery within its jurisdiction at the bidding of the Supreme Court. President Buchanan, Colonel Fremont's successful competitor, acted on the assumption that the only way to preserve the Union was to yield every thing to the de-

mands of the South Carolina faction, whose infamous policy in Kansas he sustained so unscrupulously that he disgusted even those who used him as their tool, and gave Mr. Douglas an opportunity to win support in the North by opposing him upon the very question which Mr. Douglas himself had thrown like a fire-brand into the country. The support even of the border slave states fell away from President Buchanan. Mr. Douglas gained some of it, the Republican party the rest.

While these events were taking place, the aggressive slaveholders were lashing themselves and the humble non-slaveholders around them into hatred and fury against their fellow-citizens of the free states. Of the manner of doing this and the result, there is one notable and melancholy instance. In the summer of the year 1855 the towns of Norfolk and Portsmouth were desolated by the yellow fever. The pestilence was so fearful that many of the native physicians fled before it, and of those in the neighboring country few could be induced to visit the scene of its ravages. Under these circumstances, a large number of medical men from Northern states hastened to the aid of their suffering countrymen, and remained with them, serving them night and day until the scourge had passed. Unacclimated as they were, weary and worn with watching in the pest-houses, many of them were attacked by the fever, and fourteen died and were buried in the land whither they had gone as ministers of mercy. It might be reasonably supposed that where their bodies lay would be hallowed ground; that it would be marked by some enduring token of the gratitude of the people for whom these men laid down their lives; that fathers would take their children there to teach them the noblest lesson of Christianity, self-sacrifice. But the truth is sadly, shamefully otherwise. The simple stones that marked their graves were made the targets of opprobrium. They stood there silent witnesses of what Northern men could dare to do for their countrymen, their brethren, who had reviled them for years without mitigation or remorse; they testified without ceasing that opposition to the spread of slavery did not spring from hatred of slaveholders; and to those who hardened their hearts they became an unendurable reproach. At last a leading newspaper in one of these towns[1] openly declared (it can hardly be believed of men in civilized Christendom) that the state of feeling toward the North "required the removal" of the bodies of these martyrs to benevolence. Such was part of the machinery, the infernal machinery, which was contrived for the destruction of the republic!

This was the condition of affairs when an event occurred which, although without immediate consequences of moment, except to the actors in it, seems as if it had been foreordained to precipitate the impending revolution. John Brown, an anti-slavery fanatic of the blindest and most furious sort,

JOHN BROWN.

but with determination in his nature and method in his madness, who had been harried and hunted by border ruffians in Kansas, and had in turn harried and hunted them as they deserved, made in October, 1859, that raid upon Harper's Ferry which is so fresh in all memories. How we all wondered when the telegraph told us that the national arsenal at that place had been seized by a band of men who proved to be only twenty-two in number! How we wondered still more when it proved that this treason against the United States was committed merely for the purpose of running off as many slaves northward as could be excited to fly! How, in the midst of our condemnation of the act, we felt a certain admiration of the calm self-devotion of the old man and his followers, whom it took a company of marines to dislodge, and whom the State of Virginia hanged with great pomp and formality, and with a display of military force which the pretense of an apprehended rescue by the Abolitionists did not prevent from being ridiculous. Virginia should not have been allowed to punish an offense committed, not against her local law, but against the sovereignty of the United States. But she boldly assumed the control of the affair. The occasion was too valuable

---

[1] The Norfolk *Argus*.

to the conspirators against the republic (for such we must now call them) to be lost. It must not be slobbered over, but made the most of, as a means of stirring up the masses of the people in the slave states into the proper state of turbulence for revolt. And, indeed, like all of the radical abolitionist movements, its only effect, its only possible effect, was, to carry the excitement, the antagonism, and the genuine fears of the slave states to a higher pitch than before. Had the disunionists of the South deliberately contrived to bring about some event which would give a new and resistless impulse to their cause, they could not have planned one which would have served their purpose half as well as this reckless raid of a poor old fanatic frontiersman. And so, although the closest and most jealous investigation of "the John Brown affair" had failed to connect any party or any leader at the North with it, the militia of Virginia were kept under arms until the middle of November, and South Carolina was placed under martial law, not for defense, but to beget an opinion that defense was necessary.

Opportunely for the disunion party, this strange event—unique of its kind in the annals of the country—happened but a short time before the canvass for the presidential election of 1860 was about to begin. John Brown was hanged in December, 1859, and the Democratic Nominating Convention assembled in Charleston in April, 1860. In that body the delegates from the slave states demanded an adoption of the doctrine that slavery existed by virtue of the Constitution in all of the Territories, as one of the principles of the Democratic party. They made this demand knowing that it would not be acceded to; and they were not disappointed. The Democrats from the free states had yielded year after year, for the sake of the party and the Union, until they felt that it would be ruinous to both to yield any farther. The platform of the slavery propaganda was rejected by a decided, immovable majority, and that of the free state delegates, which on the great question conformed to the decision of the Supreme Court as to the territories, but asserted the right of the people of the territories to admit or exclude slavery, was adopted. Upon this the delegates from Alabama, South Carolina, Mississippi, Louisiana, Arkansas, Florida, and Texas withdrew from the Convention, which, thus diminished to a bare majority of its members, adjourned to meet at Baltimore on the 18th of June. It should be observed that, of the fifteen slave states, eight, Georgia, North Carolina, Virginia, Maryland, Delaware, Kentucky, Tennessee, and Missouri, including, as will be seen, four of the most important, did not join in this attempt to disorganize the Democratic party for the purpose of making the election of the Republican candidate sure. This purpose was clearly seen at once by all the people of the free states, and equally by all the members of the Democratic party in the great and important slave states whose delegates had not taken part in the movement; and Mr. Douglas, the acknowledged leader and presidential candidate of the Democratic party in the free states and this part of the slave states, exposed in his speeches thoroughly and mercilessly the underhand measures by which the South Carolina faction had sought to use the Democrats of the North for the furtherance of their designs. The feeling occasioned by these events was profound; and it was seen that the old alliance between the slavery party and the Democratic party was at an end, that the power of the latter was destroyed, and, as regarded the immediate issue, that Mr. Douglas's chances of an election had vanished.

Foreseeing and dreading evil consequences from the election of a President by the Republican party, a large and influential body of citizens in both slave and free states sent delegates to a convention at Baltimore, in which John Bell, a Tennessee slaveholder of moderate views and unsuspected patriotism, was nominated for the presidency, and Edward Everett, of Massachusetts—a man who had been United States Senator, Governor of Massachusetts, President of Harvard College, and American minister to Great Britain, and who, with the knowledge, as it afterward appeared, of the great need of his exertions, had devoted himself for a few years to the preservation of the bond of union between the free and the slave states, and who had thereby incurred the sneers of the extreme Republicans as a "Union-saver," which was with them a term of reproach—was nominated as vice-president. The representatives of no party, and having no political organization or electioneering machinery at their command, the gentlemen who nominated these eminent citizens had no hope of electing them at the ballot-box. But it was thought probable that they would receive votes enough to prevent any choice by the people, and that thus the election would be thrown into the House of Representatives; in which case the election of Messrs. Bell and Everett or Messrs. Douglas and Lane was looked for.

Third in order, but first in importance, was the Convention of the Republican party, which took place at Chicago on the 16th of May. The nomination of Senator Seward, the congressional leader of this party, was regarded as a foregone conclusion. But, to the surprise of the country, Mr. Seward failed of a unanimous nomination at the first ballot; and one Abraham Lincoln, of Illinois, was his chief competitor. Of Mr. Lincoln little was known out of his own state. Only those who devoted more than a common attention to politics remembered that he had been a member of the House of Representatives for Illinois; that he had "stumped the state" with some effect in opposition to Mr. Douglas as candidate for the Senate in 1859; and that he had made a clever speech upon the great issue before the country at the Cooper Institute, in New York, in February, 1860. Yet the plea that he could be elected, and that Mr. Seward certainly could not, was urged with such effect that after a sharp contest he received a large majority of the votes. The nomination of Mr. Polk, or of Mr. Pierce, was not a greater surprise to the country; and as the captain of the homeward-bound China ship, when he approached Sandy Hook, hailed an outward-bound vessel and inquired, "Who's President of the United States?" and being answered "James K. Polk," hallooed back, "Who in —— is James K. Polk?" so the

people of the United States with one accord asked, "Who is Abraham Lincoln?" The answer had some significance. He was the grandson of a Kentucky pioneer, a fellow-emigrant and friend of Daniel Boone. Left an orphan at six years of age, the eldest of a family of four, he could be spared to go to school but six months, and began to earn his living ere he was well out of his childhood—first as a shepherd-boy, then as an apprentice in a saw-mill, then as a Mississippi boatman, then as a farm-hand on new clearings, in which employment he performed great feats in splitting rails. All this before he was legally a man; and when he came of age he went to Illinois, where he became general helper in a country store, then salesman, giving all his spare time to self-education. In the Black Hawk war he volunteered; and his capacity and popularity were soon acknowledged by his election to the captaincy of his company. His military service over, he was chosen member of the State Assembly of Illinois, to which position he was re-elected thrice. He now was admitted to the bar of his state, and practiced with no little success. He mingled much in politics, and in 1846 was elected member of Congress, but soon found it necessary to give his attention exclusively to his profession and his family. But the crisis of 1859 was too momentous for him to stand quietly aside, taking no part in it; and he entered the field again as candidate for the Senate in opposition to Mr. Douglas, his controversy with whom showed him a match for that daring, dexterous debater and practiced politician. He had early gained, and through all these vicissitudes of fortune had kept, with the consent of co-workers and opponents, the name of "Honest Abe." Such was the man who was suddenly placed before the American people as a candidate for the most important office in their gift. Of all those who had been placed in a like position, Mr. Lincoln was the most perfect example of the working of that republican principle which puts the highest honors of the state within the reach of the humblest born and bred among its citizens. Not one of the men who had preceded him as a candidate for the presidency had started in life upon so low a level, or had passed so many years without any advantages of intellectual and social culture. Born in a slave state, and having chosen his wife from the same community, he was, although a Republican, a conservative—not tinged in the least with the revolutionary mania of abolitionism. The Republican Convention selected him because of his availability; he accepted its nomination modestly.

The adjourned Democratic Convention, which assembled at Baltimore in June, excluded the delegates which had withdrawn from its Charleston session, but admitted new delegates from Alabama and Louisiana who were known to be supporters of Mr. Douglas. Upon this the delegates from Virginia withdrew, accompanied by most of those from the other slave states, and some of those from the free states—all, in fact, who were determined, in Mr. Calhoun's words, to "force the issue" upon the country of slavery throughout the Union or disunion. This faction organized itself, and nominated as president John C. Breckinridge, of Kentucky, a man who had hard-

JOHN C. BRECKINRIDGE.

ly attained middle age, and who, without remarkable ability, had been made a pet by the extreme slavery party and by the politicians of the South generally, and as vice-president General Lane, of Oregon. The original body nominated Senator Douglas for the presidency, and Herschel V. Johnson, of Georgia, for the vice-presidency.

Of the four parties now in the field, only one—that of Breckinridge and Lane—represented the rule or ruin, slavery or disunion, principles. Indeed, this party was obliged to nominate its candidates only because of the distinct avowal of all the other three that slavery in the Territories of the United States was not placed by the Constitution out of the control of the people of the United States, and that in any case the perpetuity of the republic was before the propagation of slavery. The party at the other extreme, whose candidates were Lincoln and Hamlin, were the advocates of free soil in the Territories, but absolute non-interference with slavery in the States. This party the Abolitionists not only refused to vote with, but constantly denounced; so that the latter were not represented in the contest. It is important to remember these facts in measuring the significance of the vote cast at this strange and momentous election.

The influence of the President, the Cabinet, and the holders of office throughout the country was openly and shamelessly exerted for the rule or ruin party. Mr. Howell Cobb, Secretary of the Treasury, while on a visit to

HOWELL COBB.

New York pending the canvass, avowed himself a disunionist; said that, in case of Mr. Lincoln's election, secession would have the sympathy and co-operation of the administration; and even declared that he did not believe another Congress of the United States would meet. The threats of disunion in case the Republican candidate were elected increased in violence; but, such was the temper of the people, they were no longer regarded as of old. "Gentlemen," said a Virginia planter, trembling with passion, in a conversation between half a dozen persons in the parlor of a New York insurance office, before the Republican nomination had been made, "gentlemen, if you elect Mr. Seward President, we shall break up this Union." "I think not, sir," calmly replied the man to whom he seemed more particularly to address himself. "You'll see, sir—you'll see; we will surely do it." "Then, sir," said the other, as quietly as before, but looking him steadily in the face, "we shall nominate Mr. Seward. Mr. Seward is not my man; for I am a free trader and an old Democrat. But if Virginia, or any other state or states shall declare that, upon the constitutional election of any citizen of the United States to any office, the Union shall be broken up, then I nominate that man and vote for him on principle;" and all present, with a single exception, uttered a hearty Ay. Such was the feeling of the canvass: a canvass conducted, nevertheless, with a notable moderation of language and bearing, except in a few isolated places in the Gulf states; a canvass remarkable, too, for the fact that, while in the free states the advocates of the extreme slavery or disunion party spoke freely and worked vigorously, without hinderance and almost without rebuke, in the slave states, with one or two exceptions, no word was uttered—none would have been allowed to be uttered—in behalf of the Republican party. Had any man ventured to declare publicly in South Carolina, or south of that state, that Mr. Lincoln was a proper person for President of the United States, he would have done so at imminent peril of his life. Not, as we shall see, because there were not many persons there who were willing, though not desirous, that he should assume that office, if constitutionally elected to it, but because the fierce faction which had seized the control of affairs in those states were determined, right or wrong, to brook no interference, and would either have made way with their presumptuous fellow-citizen by the knife, or driven him with violence out of their states into others where the freedom of speech guaranteed by the Constitution really existed, and where respect for law was enforced by an enlightened public opinion. In those states the Repub-

JOHN B. FLOYD.   ISAAC TOUCEY.

licans, the better to marshal and manage their forces, organized "Wide Awake Clubs," the chief, in fact the only function of which seemed to be to parade the streets at night in oilskin caps and capes, each man carrying a

swinging lamp. But, as if even this harmless way of wasting time and oil could not be contrived without helping the disunionists, these torch-light processions were made, not in the customary order of civic processions, but by platoons in companies, with captains and lieutenants, each club having a sort of military organization. It was at once pretended that the real object of all this nightly drill and parade was a preparation to invade the South, and a new impulse was given to the formation of volunteer companies and bodies of minute-men in the slave states. Secession, in case of the election of Mr. Lincoln, was openly proposed in the Legislatures of South Carolina and Alabama; the governor of the former recommending the reorganization of the militia of the state, and the immediate enlistment of one thousand volunteers.

Meantime a species of treason was going on in the very cabinet at Washington. Mr. Floyd, Secretary of War, and Mr. Toucey, Secretary of the Navy, used their official authority to place the government for a time at the mercy of the conspirators. The former sent to arsenals and forts in slave states all the arms and ammunition of the United States which he could move without attracting too much attention, and dispersed the little army to widely distant quarters, where it was not needed, placing at the same time officers born in slave states, as far as possible, in command at the most important points. Mr. Toucey, a Connecticut tool of the South Carolina faction, dismantled many vessels of the navy, and scattered the remainder to the four winds of heaven.

Under these foreboding circumstances the presidential election of 1860 took place on the 6th of November; and so complete were the arrangements for counting the votes and transmitting the returns to the telegraph stations, that on the morning of the 7th it was known from Maine to Texas, from Florida to Iowa, that Mr. Lincoln was elected. Thirty millions of people, scattered over an area of more than three millions of square miles, learned within a few hours of its occurrence an event more momentous to their country than any other which had taken place since its Declaration of Independence. Mr. Lincoln's majority over all his opponents in the electoral college proved to be sixty-four; but of the popular vote Mr. Douglas received nearly as many as Mr. Breckinridge and Mr. Bell did together, and

JOHN BELL.

within less than five hundred thousand of as many as were given for Mr. Lincoln himself.[2] Indeed, of the popular vote, Mr. Douglas and Mr. Bell together had nearly one hundred thousand more than Mr. Lincoln; and the majority of Douglas, Breckinridge, and Bell over Lincoln was nearly a million, and the entire electoral votes of Virginia, Kentucky, and Tennessee were given for Bell. Let us analyze this vote more carefully; for the South Carolina politicians at once began to take measures to bring about an immediate disruption of the Union, on the ground that the election had drawn a geographical line across the country, dividing it into two hostile sections of radically different people; and it is necessary to our purpose that we should see the audacity (for when impudence and outrage attain large proportions they have that name) both of the pretense and of the undertaking founded upon it. We must remember that Mr. Breckinridge represented the people whose purpose was that slavery should rule or the republic be destroyed; the other three candidates, however divergent their principles upon other

[2] The electoral vote was: for Lincoln, 180; for Breckinridge, 72; for Bell, 39; for Douglas, 12. The popular vote, for Lincoln, 1,857,610; for Douglas, 1,365,976; for Breckinridge, 847,953 (exclusive of South Carolina, where there is no popular vote); for Bell, 590,631. It must be remembered, in estimating the popular vote, that every ballot in the free states represents a citizen of the United States, while the ballots in the slave states represent three fifths of the slaves.

subjects, having been nominated in express opposition to the disunion faction. Now, the entire popular vote for Breckinridge in the slave states was 571,135, while in those very states the vote for Bell and Everett was

EDWARD EVERETT.

515,953, and that for Douglas 163,525, so that by adding the 26,430 votes which Mr. Lincoln himself received in the five slave states of Virginia, Kentucky, Missouri, Maryland, and Delaware, there were 705,908 voters who declared themselves distinctly opposed even to bringing the Calhoun issue before the country, while of the 571,135 who in effect declared for it, many, it is known, and multitudes, there is reason to believe, gave their votes for Mr. Breckinridge without regarding the mere election of Mr. Lincoln, in case it should take place, as sufficient cause for an attempt to break up the Union. So far, in fact, was the result of this election from showing an absolute division of the free and the slave states upon the question at issue, or, in truth, upon any other, that of Mr. Douglas's 1,365,976 votes, 1,202,451 came from the free states and 163,525 from the slave; and of Mr. Bell's 590,631 votes, 515,953 came from the slave states and 74,678 from the free; while in the free states Mr. Breckinridge himself received 276,818, or nearly one third of his entire number—California giving him 34,334; Connecticut, 14,641; Indiana, 12,295; Ohio, 11,405; Pennsylvania, 178,871; and even Massachusetts 5939.

These facts make it plain that, whatever division of feeling or interest there was between the mass of the people of the free states on the one side, and those of the slave states on the other, Mr. Lincoln's election was in itself no proof or sign of it. Still less was there at the time of his election any radical or material unlikeness between the masses of the people of those two divisions of the country. They were not different nations or peoples, united by a mere political bond, as those of England, Wales, Scotland, and Ireland are in the kingdom of Great Britain, but one nation, composed to all intents and purposes of but a single element. We have seen that in the beginning the people of the United States were English people, and that, as a nation, they were distinguished above all others for their homogeneousness. An English people they continued to be, with their homogeneousness not materially impaired in the course of two generations; while of such bonds as bind the inhabitants of one country together, not only did those which first existed between them still endure, but they had been greatly strengthened and multiplied by the passage of events, and the development of the national character and resources, during more than half a century. The most mobile people in the world, and favored in this respect by the natural formation of the country, intercourse among them had been more constant and intimate than among the people of any other nation. Having equal, or rather identical, political rights in all parts of the country, vast numbers of them continually exercised those rights, sometimes in one state, at others in another,

E

as business, inclination, or necessity caused them to change their places of residence. Men born and bred in the free states went into the slave states, became slaveholders as merchants or planters, and rose to distinction in the professions, in society, and in politics. An enormous and entirely unrestricted internal trade caused a constant and assimilating attrition among the whole people. As a consequence of this daily intermingling, intermarriage was constantly going on, if, indeed, that can be properly called intermarriage which is the union of individuals of the same race and the same nation. There was no town or considerable neighborhood, no society or corporation, no social circle in one of these divisions which was not bound by interest, or blood, or close association to some town, or neighborhood, or society, or social circle in the other. The language and the literature of the several parts of the country could not properly be called like: for likeness implies some difference; they were identical; the variations in speech and idiom being of such a trifling nature that, unlike the people of Switzerland, for instance, where the people of one canton, or those of England, where those of one county, can not understand those of another, the people of this country, even in its rudest and remotest districts, had not two dialects of their vernacular tongue. The ties of a common religion stretched over the land from north to south and from east to west. Not only so, but the chief religious and benevolent organizations of the various slightly divergent sects included the whole country in their scope, and derived their support from its people at large. Since the adoption of the Constitution a Spanish and a French province had been added to the country at the South; and of the large immigration, coming chiefly from Ireland and Germany, the greater part, but by no means all, had settled in the Northern states. But in the case of Louisiana and Florida, the number of citizens of a different race which were added to the republic was too insignificant to effect any change in the character of the population, except in two or three towns; and the same remark is even more true with regard to the influx of immigrants into the free states, which, having mainly taken place since 1816, there had not yet been time for it to effect any material change in the native blood of the country, even had that been possible. But such an event seems impossible; for, owing to intermarriage, and still more to the dominant influence of that English race which peopled this country, the immediate descendants of Germans and Irishmen, born therein, pass at once indistinguishably into the mass of its inhabitants; and, as in the mother country under like circumstances they become Anglo-Britons, so here they become Anglo-Americans. It was such a nation, thus homogeneous, thus bound together, and the individuals of which were ceaselessly commingling, as the very soils of the various parts of their country were commingled by a system of navigable rivers, unlike that which exists in any other country on the globe, and the various commonwealths of which were separated, not by natural boundaries, but by imaginary lines studiously drawn so as not to make visible separation, establish lines of defense, or secure exclusive privileges—a nation more marked by unity than any other in the world—a nation, those individuals of which who had enjoyed a like and moderate advantage of social and intellectual culture, could not, in familiar intercourse, be distinguished one from another in manners or in speech by a stranger, although they were born and bred a thousand miles apart—it was such a nation that the political leaders whom the election of Mr. Lincoln had unseated undertook to break into hostile fragments, and partly on the ground that the people of the states whose electoral votes had been cast for him were a different people from those of the states whose electoral votes had been cast against him.[3]

But with all the likeness, the real identity between the people of the whole country, there was a line which divided universal freedom and the elevation and intelligence of the mass of the citizens on the one side from the enslavement of an inferior race and the degradation and ignorance of the mass of the citizens on the other. In these points of difference and their consequences consisted the entire difference between the people whom the defeated Southern leaders sought to array against each other. To perpetuate the enslavement of that race, and to carry slavery into the territory of the Union, and with it the degradation of labor and of all citizens not slaveholders, was the object of the leaders of the rebellion. And that which made rebellion desirable made it also possible; for the ignorance, the poverty, the dependent position, and the blunted sensibilities of the millions of non-slaveholding citizens in the slave states, enabled the few thousand slaveholders to deceive them as to the issues involved, to excite in them groundless animosity against the people of the free states, to cause them to underrate the courage

[3] See, for instance, the following extract from the Louisville (Ky.) *Courier*, published at Nashville, whither its editor had fled before the advance of the national forces in March, 1862:

"This has been called a fratricidal war by some, by others an irrepressible conflict between freedom and slavery. We respectfully take issue with the authors of both these ideas. We are not the brothers of the Yankees, and the slavery question is merely the pretext, not the cause of the war. The true irrepressible conflict lies fundamentally in the hereditary hostility, the sacred animosity, the eternal antagonism between the two races engaged.

"The Norman cavalier can not brook the vulgar familiarity of the Saxon Yankee, while the latter is continually devising some plan to bring down his aristocratic neighbor to his own detested level. Thus was the contest waged in the old United States. So long as Dickinson doughfaces were to be bought, and Cochrane cowards to be frightened, so long was the Union tolerable to Southern men; but when, owing to divisions in our ranks, the Yankee hirelings placed one of their own spawn over us, political connection became unendurable, and separation necessary to preserve our self-respect.

"As our Norman kinsmen in England, always a minority, have ruled their Saxon countrymen in political vassalage up to the present day, so have we, the 'slave oligarchs,' governed the Yankees till within a twelvemonth. We framed the Constitution, for seventy years moulded the policy of the government, and placed our own men, or 'Northern men with Southern principles,' in power.

"On the 6th of November, 1860, the Puritans emancipated themselves, and are now in violent insurrection against their former owners. This insane holiday freak will not last long, however, for, dastards in fight, and incapable of self-government, they will inevitably again fall under the control of the superior race. A few more Bull Run thrashings will bring them once more under the yoke as docile as the most loyal of our Ethiopian 'chattels.'"

and the determination of those whom they taught them to hate, and generally to mislead these poor hoodwinked people and mould them to their own selfish purposes. For a whole generation the disunionists had devoted themselves to undermining the loyalty of their fellow-citizens to the republic and its flag, and inflating them with the petty pride of state sovereignty, to the representation of the people of the free states as mean-spirited cowards, who were scheming to cheat them of their birthright, and to the exaltation of that sort of chivalry which consists in the use of the bowie-knife and the revolver. Now the time had arrived when or never all this wicked work was to bear its natural fruit.

The Republican party was somewhat surprised and very exultant over its decided victory; but, although the country at large had become used to violent threats from the political leaders and writers of the slave states, the election of a Republican to the presidency was felt on every side to be no ordinary political event. Over the whole land there was a pause of expectation; the stock-market was troubled, and all eyes were turned southward. And first upon South Carolina, whose governor, William H. Gist, only the day before the election, had formally recommended secession to the Legislature of that state "in event of Abraham Lincoln's election to the presidency." Men were not left long in doubt as to the purposes of the leaders of opinion in that fractious and presuming commonwealth. They were bent upon the destruction of the Union, and that immediately. The Legislature of the state, which was in session, proceeded at once to consider the propriety of calling a convention of the people; and, in spite of some attempts to induce delay until there could be a consultation leading to combined action among the slave states, took ground in favor of instant and separate state action. The United States senators for South Carolina resigned their seats. The Grand Jury of the United States District Court at Charleston declined making its usual presentment, on the ground that the election of Mr. Lincoln had "swept away the last hope for the permanence of the federal government of these sovereign states;" and Judge Magrath, the United States judge

JUDGE MAGRATH.

for the district of South Carolina, formally laid off his robes and resigned his office, saying that he felt assured of what would be the action of the state, and considered it his duty to prepare to obey its wishes by ceasing to administer the laws of the United States within the State of South Carolina. His example was promptly followed by all the United States officers in Charleston, except the postmaster, the officers of the army, and those in the revenue service. The inhabitants of the town began to enroll themselves as minute-men, and the palmetto flag was hoisted on some of the vessels in the harbor.[4]

Georgia, which, in the Convention for the formation of the Constitution, had united with South Carolina in insisting that the slave-trade should be left open for a term of years, now quickly joined her former colleague in the attempt to destroy the government which was then established on their own conditions, and which had since been administered in their own interests, and chiefly by men of their own choice. The Governor of Georgia also recommended separate state action. He did not deem a general convention of the slave states practicable. He proposed that Georgia and each other slave-state should protect itself by imposing, in defiance of the Constitution, heavy duties upon the manufactures of Massachusetts, Vermont, Maine, and other "offending" states. He urged the appropriation of a million of dollars for putting the state in a condition of defense, and said that to all propositions for conference and compromise the answer should be, "Argument is exhausted; we stand to our arms." A public meeting was held in Savannah, at which it was resolved that "the election of Lincoln and Hamlin ought not to be, and will not be submitted to;" and it was recommended to the gov-

ernor to call a convention of the people. Blue cockades, the old sign of South Carolina nullification, began to appear in the streets.

In the other slave states, although there was no little excitement, there was not such ardor and precipitancy in the cause of disunion. In North Carolina, in Maryland, Virginia, Kentucky, Tennessee, Louisiana, and Missouri, the general feeling, in spite of isolated outbursts of wrath and denunciation, was decidedly in favor of waiting, at least, until the President elect had assumed office, and made some attack upon the peculiar interest of the slave states. Mississippi alone of the other slave states seemed ready to emulate the headlong course of South Carolina and Georgia. The extreme men of the South Carolina school in all quarters broke out in denunciation, in incitements to resistance, and in frothy declamation; but, in all the slave states except these three, there were various opinions expressed; the situation was discussed with a greater or less degree of calmness; and the weight of public opinion, as shown both by public meetings and the press, was largely and decidedly against any violent and unprovoked opposition to the proper results of a constitutionally conducted election. Thus, although Governor Wise, the previous governor of the State of Virginia, had declared before the election that, if Mr. Lincoln were chosen, he "would not remain in the Union one hour," and although some Virginia minute-men at once offered their services to South Carolina, a large meeting was held in Rockbridge County, in the centre of the state—a county containing a large number of slaves, and where is the Virginia Military School, and a college endowed by Washington—at which resolutions were unanimously adopted denying that "Virginia is so hitched to the Southern states that they can drag her into a common destiny;" asserting that "nine tenths of the people are opposed to resisting the general government so long as it is administered in conformity with the Constitution;" and also that "Virginia owes no duty to the South." These declarations are of value as indications of the state of feeling in central and eastern slaveholding Virginia. The vast division of the state which lay west of the Shenandoah Valley, containing one quarter of its inhabitants, one third of its agricultural wealth, and its chief commercial town, was unconditionally and heartily devoted to the Union. Like demonstrations were made in Maryland, in North Carolina, in Tennessee, Kentucky, and in Alabama. Thus divided were the people of the slave states upon the issue, as it was at first presented; the great majority being directly opposed to an attempt to break up the government because of the constitutional election of a president who not only had made no war upon their interests, but who, for four months, would have no more power to do so than the humblest of his fellow-citizens. It seemed for a day or two—for then days were counted—as if South Carolina would be left to herself, or perhaps to the company of Georgia. Nevertheless, she and those whom she had infected with her poison kept up their rebellious agitation, availing themselves of the pettiest means to foment an anti-Union feeling where none existed, and to magnify that which did exist. So, some foolish, loose-tongued, if not loose-lived, medical students in New York, having met and resolved to "withdraw their patronage from Northern institutions" and to leave the city for their homes, much was made of this silly proceeding. All this and much more like it had happened within a week of the election, and on the 12th of November, only six days after that event, Lawrence M. Keitt, member of the House for South Carolina—he who had stood by pistol in hand while his colleague beat Senator Sumner senseless in the Senate-chamber—openly declared in a public speech at Washington, that President Buchanan "was pledged to secession, and would be held to it," and that "South Carolina would shatter the accursed Union;" adding, in that blind, bombastic language, which political speakers and writers of his stamp so much affect, that, "if she could not accomplish it otherwise, she would throw her arms round the pillars of the Constitution, and involve all the states in a common ruin." This declaration of the complicity of President Buchanan in the schemes of the disunionists, which, it will be remembered, had also been made by his own Secretary of the Treasury, furnishes a clew to their precipitate action, which subsequent events will enable us to follow out to a conclusion shameful to the nation, and deeply dishonorable to all who were involved in it.

The effect of this single week upon the country was itself a disaster. Trade was seriously disturbed; stocks fell rapidly; foreign and domestic exchanges were embarrassed. The payment of debts to creditors in the free states was very generally refused in South Carolina and in Georgia, on the ground that they were due to men who might prove enemies. Nevertheless, the banks of those states drew on New York and Boston, and had their drafts honored in specie, although their own suspension of payment was daily expected. The government was powerless for the time. Congress was not in session; and therefore the President could not declare the policy of his administration during the remainder of its existence, which, brief though it was, was big with woe to the nation—to the world. Nothing had been done, even in South Carolina, which required executive interference, or even furnished occasion for a proclamation. The agitation of any subject, however dangerous, he had neither the right nor the power to restrain, and thus far only agitation had been attempted. Had he desired to strengthen the garrisons of the military posts in the most disturbed districts, he could not have done so; for the army was so small, and had been so scattered, that he could not have concentrated a sufficient force in time to be of any service. The navy was equally out of his reach. He was embarrassed, also, by the fact that not only had no overt act been committed, but no authoritative revolutionary declaration had been made; there was only much excitement every where, and fierce agitation in some quarters. But the determination of the agitators was clearly seen; and it was seen, too, that, instead of attempting to attain their end by a convention of the people of the United States, which, by amending the Constitution or abrogating it, could

_____
[4] The arms of South Carolina are a palmetto-tree.

have permitted the peaceable withdrawal of certain states, or have resolved the republic again into its elements, they were determined to set the Constitution at naught by the mere exercise of their own will, and thus force the alternative of resistance to their action, or the humiliation, and, in fact, the extinction of the national government. Gloomy forebodings filled the public mind, and a financial panic fell upon the whole country.

Yet it can not be too clearly or too constantly borne in mind by those who would justly appreciate the manner in which the rebellion was brought about, that thus far South Carolina was the only state in which the movement for secession was so general as to seem virtually unanimous. Even in Georgia many meetings were held to denounce the leaders of the movement for secession, although in the Legislature resolutions were introduced and ordered to be printed, which demanded that, as the States of Massachusetts, Vermont, Maine, Rhode Island, Connecticut, New York, Michigan, Wisconsin, and Pennsylvania had "nullified the Constitution," they should be regarded as no longer constituent parts of the United States of America, and that their votes in the electoral college should be thrown out; and instructing the members of Congress for Georgia, if this were not done, to resign their seats. This those members were ready and anxious enough to do; for at the head of the agitators of disunion were Alfred Iverson and Robert Toombs, United States Senators from Georgia, the former of whom had not hesitated to suggest, under his own signature, the outlawing and killing of any man who should accept office under Mr. Lincoln. Yet on the 4th of November, Alexander H. Stephens, a man whose integrity and ability had justly won him the first place among the political leaders of Georgia, which he had long represented in the Congress of the United States, addressed, by formal invitation, a large concourse in the State Hall of Representatives at Milledgeville on the condition of the country, and took ground, without hesitation or qualification, not only against secession, but against the right to secede under the circumstances. Upon this, the cardinal, in fact, the only point of the issue then presented, he said: "The first question that presents itself is, Shall the people of the South secede from the Union in consequence of the election of Mr. Lincoln to the presidency of the United States? My countrymen, I tell you frankly, candidly, and earnestly that I do not think that they ought. In my judgment, the election of no man, constitutionally chosen to that high office, is sufficient cause for any state to separate from the Union. It ought to stand by and aid still in maintaining the Constitution of the country. To make a point of resistance to the government, to withdraw from it because a man has been constitutionally elected, puts us in the wrong."[5] A slaveholder, an unqualifying advocate of slavery, a politician of long experience and continued success, his estimate of the causes of the secession movement are of the highest significance and of the greatest weight;

ROBERT TOOMBS.

[5] *Speech of A. H. Stephens, delivered in the Hall of the House of Representatives of Georgia, Nov.* 14, 1860.

FELLOW-CITIZENS,—I appear before you to-night at the request of members of the Legislature and others to speak of matters of the deepest interest that can possibly concern us all of an earthly character. There is nothing—no question or subject connected with this life—that concerns a free people so intimately as that of the government under which they live. We are now, indeed, surrounded by evils. Never, since I entered upon the public stage, has the country been so environed with difficulties and dangers that threatened the public peace and the very existence of society as now. I do not now appear before you at my own instance. It is not to gratify desire of my own that I am here. Had I consulted my own ease and pleasure, I should not be before you; but, believing that it is the duty of every good citizen to give his counsels and views whenever the country is in danger, as to the best policy to be pursued, I am here. For these reasons, and these only, do I bespeak a calm, patient, and attentive hearing.

My object is not to stir up strife, but to allay it; not to appeal to your passions, but to your reason. Good governments can never be built up or sustained by the impulse of passion. I wish to address myself to your good sense, to your good judgment; and if, after hearing, you disagree, let us agree to disagree, and part as we met, friends. We all have the same object, the same interest. That people should disagree in republican governments upon questions of public policy is natural. That men should disagree upon all matters connected with human investigation, whether relating to science or human conduct, is natural. Hence, in free governments, parties will arise. But a free people should express their different opinions with liberality and charity, with no acrimony toward those of their fellows, when honestly and sincerely given. These are my feelings to-night.

Let us, therefore, reason together. It is not my purpose to say aught to wound the feelings of any individual who may be present; and if, in the ardency with which I shall express my opinions, I shall say any thing which may be deemed too strong, let it be set down to the zeal with which I advocate my own convictions. There is with me no intention to irritate or offend.

The first question that presents itself is, Shall the people of the South secede from the Union in consequence of the election of Mr. Lincoln to the presidency of the United States? My countrymen, *I tell you frankly, candidly, and earnestly that I do not think that they ought.* In my judgment, the election of no man, constitutionally chosen to that high office, is sufficient cause for any state to separate from the Union. It ought to stand by and aid still in maintaining the Constitution of the country. To make a point of resistance to the government, to withdraw from it because a man has been constitutionally elected, puts us in the wrong. We are pledged to maintain the Constitution. Many of us have sworn to support it. Can we, therefore, for the mere election of a man to the presidency, and that, too, in accordance with the prescribed forms of the Constitution, make a point of resistance to the government without becoming the breakers of that sacred instrument ourselves, withdraw ourselves from it? Would we not be in the wrong? Whatever fate is to befall this country, let it never be laid to the charge of the people of the South, and especially to the people of Georgia, that we were untrue to our national engagements. Let the fault and the wrong rest upon others. If all our hopes are to be blasted, if the republic is to go down, let us be found to the last moment standing on the deck, with the Constitution of the United States waving over our heads. (Applause.) Let the fanatics of the North break the Constitution, if such is their fell purpose. Let the responsibility be upon them. I shall speak presently more of their acts; but let not the South, let us not be the ones to commit the aggression. We went into the election with this people. The result was different from what we wished; but the election has been constitutionally held. Were we to make a point of resistance to the government, and go out of the Union on that account, the record would be made up hereafter against us.

But it is said Mr. Lincoln's policy and principles are against the Constitution, and that, if he carries them out, it will be destructive of our rights. Let us not anticipate a threatened evil. If he violates the Constitution, then will come our time to act. Do not let us break it because, forsooth, he may. If he does, that is the time for us to strike. (Applause.) I think it would be injudicious and unwise to do this sooner. I do not anticipate that Mr. Lincoln will do any thing to jeopard our safety or security, whatever may be his spirit to do it; for he is bound by the constitutional checks which are thrown around him, which at this time renders him powerless to do any great mischief. This shows the wisdom of our system. The President of the United States is no emperor, no dictator; he is clothed with no absolute power. He can do nothing unless he is backed by power in Congress. The House of Representatives is largely in the majority against him.

In the Senate he will also be powerless. There will be a majority of four against him. This, after the loss of Bigler, Fitch, and others, by the unfortunate dissensions of the National Democratic party in their states. Mr. Lincoln can not appoint an officer without the consent of the Senate; he can not form a cabinet without the same consent. He will be in the condition of George III. (the embodiment of Toryism), who had to ask the Whigs to appoint his ministers, and was compelled to receive a cabinet utterly opposed to his views; and so Mr. Lincoln will be compelled to ask of the Senate to choose for him a cabinet, if the democracy of that body choose to put him on such terms. He will be compelled to do this or let the government stop, if the National Democratic men—for that is their name at the North—the conservative men in the Senate, should so determine. Then, how can Mr. Lincoln obtain a cabinet which would aid him, or allow him to violate the Constitution?

Why then, I say, should we disrupt the ties of this Union when his hands are tied, when he can do nothing against us? I have heard it mooted that no man in the State of Georgia, who is true to her interests, could hold office under Mr. Lincoln. But, I ask, who appoints to office? Not the President alone; the Senate has to concur. No man can be appointed without the consent of the Senate. Should any man then refuse to hold office that was given to him by a Democratic Senate? [Mr. Toombs interrupted, and said, if the Senate was Democratic, it was for Mr. Breckinridge.] Well, then, continued Mr. S., I apprehend no man could be justly considered untrue to the interests of Georgia, or incur any disgrace, if the interests of Georgia required it, to hold an office which a Breckinridge Senate had given him, even though Mr. Lincoln should be President. (Prolonged applause, mingled with interruptions.)

I trust, my countrymen, you will be still and silent. I am addressing your good sense. I am giving you my views in a calm and dispassionate manner, and if any of you differ with me, you can, on any other occasion, give your views as I am doing now, and let reason and true patriotism decide between us. In my judgment, I say, under such circumstances, there would be no possible disgrace for a Southern man to hold office. No man will be suffered to be appointed, I have no doubt, who is not true to the Constitution, if Southern senators are true to their trusts, as I can not permit myself to doubt that they will be.

My honorable friend who addressed you last night (Mr. Toombs), and to whom I listened with the profoundest attention, asks if we would submit to Black Republican rule. I say to you and to him, as a Georgian, I never would submit to any Black Republican *aggression* upon our constitutional rights. I will never consent myself, as much as I admire this Union for the glories of the past, or the blessings of the present, as much as it has done for the people of all these states, as much as it has done for civilization, as much as the hopes of the world hang upon it, I would never submit to aggression upon my rights to maintain it longer; and if they can not be maintained in the Union, standing on the Georgia Platform, where I have stood from the time of its adoption, I would be in favor of disrupting every tie which binds the states together.

I will have equality for Georgia and for the citizens of Georgia in this Union, or I will look for new safeguards elsewhere. This is my position. The only question now is, Can they be secured in the Union? That is what I am counseling with you to-night about. Can it be secured? In my judgment, it may be, but it may not be; but let us do all we can, so that in the future, if the worst come, it may never be said we were negligent in doing our duty to the last.

My countrymen, I am not of those who believe this Union has been a curse up to this time. True men, men of integrity, entertain different views from me on this subject. I do not question their right to do so; I would not impugn their motives in so doing. Nor will I undertake to say that this government of our fathers is perfect. There is nothing perfect in this world of a human origin—nothing connected with human nature, from man himself to any of his works. You may select the wisest and best men for your judges, and yet how many defects are there in the administration of justice? You may select the wisest and best men for your legislators, and yet how many defects are apparent in your laws? And it is so in our government.

But that this government of our fathers, with all its defects, comes nearer the objects of all good governments than any other on the face of the earth, is my settled conviction. Contrast it now with any on the face of the earth. [England, said Mr. Toombs.] England, my friend says. Well, that is the next best, I grant; but I think we have improved upon England. Statesmen tried their apprentice hand on the government of England, and then ours was made. Ours sprung from that, avoiding many of its defects, taking most of the good and leaving out many of its errors, and from the whole constructing and building up this model republic, the best which the history of the world gives any account of.

Compare, my friends, this government with that of Spain, Mexico, the South American republics, Germany, Ireland—are there any sons of that down-trodden nation here to-night?—Prussia, or, if you travel farther East, to Turkey or China. Where will you go, following the sun in its circuit round our globe, to find a government that better protects the liberties of its people, and secures to them the blessings we enjoy? (Applause.) I think that one of the evils that beset us is a surfeit of liberty, an exuberance of the priceless blessings for which we are ungrateful. We listened to my honorable friend who addressed you last night (Mr. Toombs) as he recounted the evils of this government.

The first was the fishing bounties, paid mostly to the sailors of New England. Our friend stated that forty-eight years of our government was under the administration of Southern presidents. Well, these fishing bounties began under the rule of a Southern president, I believe. No one of them, during the whole forty-eight years, ever set his administration against the principle or policy of them. It is not for me to say whether it was a wise policy in the beginning; it probably was not, and I have nothing to say in its defense. But the reason given for it was to encourage our young men to go to sea and learn to manage ships. We had at the time but a small navy. It was thought best to encourage a class of our people to become acquainted with seafaring life, to become sailors to man our naval ships. It requires practice to walk the deck of a ship, to pull the ropes, to furl the sails, to go aloft, to climb the mast; and it was thought, by offering this bounty, a nursery might be formed in which young men would become perfected in these arts, and it applied to one section of the country as well as to any other.

and upon this subject he said: "Some of our public men have failed in their aspirations; that is true, and from that comes a great part of our troubles." The feeling of his audience may be gathered from the fact that this statement was received with prolonged applause. Yet in less than three months from that night a Georgia Convention had passed an ordinance of secession, and Mr. Stephens himself was vice-president of the provisional government set up by the insurgents. Some notion of the sort of influence which was brought to bear during that interval upon him and others like minded may be formed from the fact that, during this long, carefully considered, and solemnly uttered speech, he was constantly interrupted by Mr. Toombs, in a tone of sneering menace, on one occasion for the purpose of objecting to Mr. Stephens's suggestion that nothing should be done by Georgia without submitting the great question of the day to a convention of the people!

The persistency and precipitancy of South Carolina offended the border states. They even resented it as a wrong done to the common cause. They claimed a right to be consulted upon a question of such stupendous importance as the severance of the republic for the cause of slavery. The Virginians proposed to South Carolina a convention of the slave states; but this South Carolina, with flippant haughtiness, refused to entertain, on the ground that Virginia was "completely demoralized" because she had "placed the Union above the rights and institutions of the South." The truth was, that the Virginia leaders knew that it was the purpose of South Carolina and Georgia to open the slave-trade; and to this they were opposed, because the chief wealth of the Virginia planters was in the slaves which they bred. This the South Carolina leaders, wise in their generation, saw at once, and used now and afterward to their advantage. On the 26th of November the Legislature of South Carolina met at Columbia. The governor (Gist), in his message, took ground in favor of immediate state action, declared his belief that Georgia, Alabama, Mississippi, Florida, Texas, and Arkansas would not hesitate to follow South Carolina, which, he said, would be "wanting in self-respect to entertain propositions looking to a continuance of the Union." It was determined that the delegates to the House of Representatives should go to Washington and resign, but remain there for consultation with other Southern members of Congress; and it was confidently announced that the

---

The result of this was, that in the war of 1812, our sailors, many of whom came from this nursery, were equal to any that England brought against us. At any rate, no small part of the glories of that war were gained by the veteran tars of America, and the object of these bounties was to foster that branch of the national defense. My opinion is that, whatever may have been the reason at first, this bounty ought to be discontinued—the reason for it at first no longer exists. A bill for this object did pass the Senate the last Congress I was in, to which my honorable friend contributed greatly, but it was not reached in the House of Representatives. I trust that he will yet see that he may with honor continue his connection with the government, and that his eloquence, unrivaled in the Senate, may hereafter, as heretofore, be displayed in having this bounty, so obnoxious to him, repealed and wiped off from the statute-book.

The next evil that my friend complained of was the tariff. Well, let us look at that for a moment. About the time I commenced noticing public matters, this question was agitating the country almost as fearfully as the slave question now is. In 1832, when I was in college, South Carolina was ready to nullify or secede from the Union on this account. And what have we seen? The tariff no longer distracts the public councils. Reason has triumphed! The present tariff was voted for by Massachusetts and South Carolina. The lion and the lamb lay down together—every man in the Senate and House from Massachusetts and South Carolina, I think, voted for it, as did my honorable friend himself. And if it be true, to use the figure of speech of my honorable friend, that every man in the North that works in iron, and brass, and wood has his muscle strengthened by the protection of the government, that stimulant was given by his vote, and, I believe, every other Southern man. So we ought not to complain of that.

Mr. Toombs. The tariff assessed the duties.

Mr. Stephens. Yes, and Massachusetts with unanimity voted with the South to lessen them, and they were made just as low as Southern men asked them to be, and that is the rates they are now at. If reason and argument, with experience, produced such changes in the sentiments of Massachusetts from 1832 to 1857, on the subject of the tariff, may not like changes be effected there by the same means—reason and argument, and appeals to patriotism on the present vexed question? and who can say that by 1875 or 1890 Massachusetts may not vote with South Carolina and Georgia upon all those questions that now distract the country, and threaten its peace and existence? I believe in the power and efficiency of truth, in the omnipotence of truth, and its ultimate triumph when properly wielded. (Applause.)

Another matter of grievance alluded to by my honorable friend was the navigation laws. This policy was also commenced under the administration of one of these Southern presidents who ruled so well, and has been continued through all of them since. The gentleman's views of the policy of these laws and my own do not disagree. We occupied the same ground in relation to them in Congress. It is not my purpose to defend them now; but it is proper to state some matters connected with their origin.

One of the objects was to build up a commercial American marine by giving American bottoms the exclusive carrying trade between our own ports. This is a great arm of national power. This object was accomplished. We have now an amount of shipping, not only coastwise, but to foreign countries, which puts us in the front rank of the nations of the world. England can no longer be styled the Mistress of the Seas. What American is not proud of the result? Whether those laws should be continued is another question. But one thing is certain: no president, Northern or Southern, has ever yet recommended their repeal. And my friend's efforts to get them repealed were met with but little favor, North or South.

These, then, were the true main grievances or grounds of complaint against the general system of our government and its workings—I mean the administration of the federal government. As to the acts of the federal states, I shall speak presently; but these three were the main ones used against the common head. Now, suppose it be admitted that all of these are evils in the system, do they overbalance and outweigh the advantages and great good which this same government affords in a thousand innumerable ways that can not be estimated? Have we not at the South, as well as the North, grown great, prosperous, and happy under its operation? Has any part of the world ever shown such rapid progress in the development of wealth, and all the material resources of national power and greatness, as the Southern states have under the general government, notwithstanding all its defects?

Mr. Toombs. In spite of it.

Mr. Stephens. My honorable friend says we have, in spite of the general government; that without it I suppose he thinks we might have done as well, or perhaps better, than we have done this in spite of it. That may be, and it may not be; but the great fact that we have grown great and powerful under the government as it exists, there is no conjecture or speculation about that; it stands out bold, high, and prominent, like your Stone Mountain, to which the gentleman alluded in illustrating home facts in his record—this great fact of our unrivaled prosperity in the Union as it is admitted; whether all this is in spite of the government—whether we of the South would have been better off without the government—is, to say the least, problematical. On the one side we can only put the fact against speculation and conjecture on the other. But even as a question of speculation I differ with my distinguished friend.

What we would have lost in border wars without the Union, or what we have gained simply by the peace it has secured, no estimate can be made of. Our foreign trade, which is the foundation of all our prosperity, has the protection of the navy, which drove the pirates from the waters near our coast, where they had been buccaneering for centuries before, and might have been still had it not been for the American navy, under the command of such spirits as Commodore Porter. Now that the coast is clear, that our commerce flows freely outwardly, we can not well estimate how it would have been under other circumstances. The influence of the government on us is like that of the atmosphere around us. Its benefits are so silent and unseen that they are seldom thought of or appreciated.

We seldom think of the single element of oxygen in the air we breathe, and yet let this simple, unseen, and unfelt agent be withdrawn—this life-giving element be taken away from this all-pervading fluid around us, and what instant and appalling changes would take place in all organic creation!

It may be that we are all that we are in "spite of the general government," but it may be that without it we should have been far different from what we are now. It is true there is no equal part of the earth with natural resources superior perhaps to ours. That portion of this country known as the Southern states, stretching from the Chesapeake to the Rio Grande, is fully equal to the picture drawn by the honorable and eloquent senator last night, in all natural capacities. But how many ages and centuries passed before these capacities were developed to reach this advanced age of civilization? There these same hills, rich in ore, same rivers, same valleys and plains, are as they have been since they came from the hand of the Creator; uneducated and uncivilized man roamed over them, for how long no history informs us.

It was only under our institutions that they could be developed. Their development is the result of the enterprise of our people under operations of the government and institutions under which we have lived. Even our people without these never would have done it. The organization of society has much to do with the development of the natural resources of any country or any land. The institutions of a people, political and moral, are the matrix in which the germ of their organic structure quickens into life—takes root and develops in form, nature, and character. Our institutions constitute the basis, the matrix, from which spring all our characteristics of development and greatness. Look at Greece. There is the same fertile soil, the same blue sky, the same inlets and harbors, the same Ægean, the same Olympus; there is the same land where Homer sung, where Pericles spoke; it is in nature the same old Greece, but it is living Greece no more. (Applause.)

Descendants of the same people inhabit the country; yet what is the reason of this mighty difference? In the midst of present degradation we see the glorious fragments of ancient works of art—temples with ornaments and inscriptions that excite wonder and admiration—the remains of a once high order of civilization which have outlived the language they spoke—upon them all Ichabod is written—their glory has departed. Why is this so? I answer, their institutions have been destroyed. These were but the fruits of their forms of government, the matrix from which their grand development sprung; and when once the institutions of a people have been destroyed, there is no earthly power that can bring back the Promethean spark to kindle them here again any more than in that ancient land of eloquence, poetry, and song. (Applause.)

The same may be said of Italy. Where is Rome, once the mistress of the world? There are the same seven hills now, the same soil, the same natural resources; nature is the same, but what a ruin of human greatness meets the eye of the traveler throughout the length and breadth of that most downtrodden land! Why have not the people of that Heaven-favored clime the spirit that animated their fathers? Why this sad difference?

It is the destruction of her institutions that has caused it; and, my countrymen, if we shall in an evil hour rashly pull down and destroy those institutions which the patriotic band of our fathers labored so long and so hard to build up, and which have done so much for us and the world, who can venture the prediction that similar results will not ensue? Let us avoid it if we can. I trust the spirit is among us that will enable us to do it. Let us not rashly try the experiment; for if it fails, as it did in Greece and Italy, and in the South American republics, and in every other place, wherever liberty is once destroyed, it may never be restored to us again. (Applause.)

There are defects in our government, errors in administration, and shortcomings of many kinds, but, in spite of these defects and errors, Georgia has grown to be a great state. Let us pause here a moment. In 1850 there was a great crisis, but not so fearful as this, for of all I have ever passed through, this is the most perilous, and requires to be met with the greatest calmness and deliberation.

There were many among us in 1850 zealous to go at once out of the Union, to disrupt every tie that binds us together. Now do you believe, had that policy been carried out at that time. we would have been the same great people that we are to-day? It may be that we would, but have you any assurance of that fact? Would you have made the same advancement, improvement, and progress in all that constitutes material wealth and prosperity that we have?

I notice in the Comptroller General's report that the taxable property of Georgia is $670,000,000 and upward, an amount not far from double that it was in 1850. I think I may venture to say that for the last ten years the material wealth of the people of Georgia has been nearly, if not quite doubled. The same may be said of our advance in education, and every thing that marks our civilization. Have we any assurance that, had we regarded the earnest but misguided patriotic advice, as I think, of some of that day, and disrupted the ties which bind us to the Union, we would have advanced as we have? I think not. Well, then, let us be careful now before we attempt any rash experiment of this sort. I know that there are friends, whose patriotism I do not intend to question, who think this Union a curse, and that we would be better off without it. I do not so think; if we can bring about a correction of these evils which threaten—and I am not without hope that this may yet be done—this appeal to go out, with all the provisions for good that accompany it, I look upon as a great, and, I fear, a fatal temptation.

When I look around and see our prosperity in every thing, agriculture, commerce, art, science, and every department of education, physical and mental, as well as moral advancement, and our colleges, I think, in the face of such an exhibition, if we can, without the loss of power, or any essential right or interest, remain in the Union, it is our duty to ourselves and to posterity to—let us not too readily yield to this temptation—do so. Our first parents, the great progenitors of the human race, were not without a like temptation when in the garden of Eden. They were led to believe that their condition would be bettered—that their eyes would be opened—and that they would become as gods. They in an evil hour yielded; instead of becoming gods they only saw their own nakedness.

I look upon this country, with our institutions, as the Eden of the world, the paradise of the universe. It may be that out of it we may become greater and more prosperous, but I am candid and sincere in telling you that I fear, if we rashly evince passion, and, without sufficient cause, shall take that step, that instead of becoming greater or more peaceful, prosperous, and happy—instead of becoming gods, we will become demons, and at no distant day commence cutting one another's throats. This is my apprehension. Let us, therefore, whatever we do, meet these difficulties, great as they are, like wise and sensible men, and consider them in the light of all the consequences which may attend our action. Let us see first clearly where the path of duty leads, and then we may not fear to tread therein.

I come now to the main question put to me, and on which my counsel has been asked. That is, What the present Legislature should do in view of the dangers that threaten us, and the wrongs that have been done us by several of our confederate states in the Union, by the acts of their Legislatures nullifying the Fugitive Slave Law, and in direct disregard of their constitutional obligations? What I shall say will not be in the spirit of dictation. It will be simply my own judgment, for what it is worth. It proceeds from a strong conviction that, according to it, our rights, interests, and honor—our present safety and future security, can be maintained without yet looking to the last resort, the "*ultima ratio regum.*" That should not be looked to until all else fails. That may come. On this point I am hopeful, but not sanguine. But let us use every patriotic effort to prevent it while there is ground for hope.

If any view that I may present, in your judgment, be inconsistent with the best interests of Georgia, I ask you, as patriots, not to regard it. After hearing me and others whom you have advised with, act in the premises according to your own conviction of duty as patriots. I speak now particularly to the members of the Legislature present. There are, as I have said, great dangers ahead. Great dangers may come from the election I have spoken of. If the policy of Mr. Lincoln and his Republican associates shall be carried out, or attempted to be carried out, no man in Georgia will be more willing or ready than myself to defend our rights, interest, and honor at every hazard, and to the last extremity. (Applause.)

What is this policy? It is, in the first place, to exclude us by an act of Congress from the Territories with our slave property. He is for using the power of the general government against the extension of our institutions. Our position on this point is, and ought to be, at all hazards, for perfect equality between all the states, and the citizens of all the states, in the Territories, under the Constitution of the United States. If Congress should exercise its power against this, then I am for standing where Georgia planted herself in 1850. These were plain propositions which were then laid down in her celebrated platform as sufficient for the disruption of the Union if the occasion should ever come; on these Georgia has declared that she will go out of the Union; and for these she would be justified by the nations of the earth in so doing.

I say the same: I said it then; I say it now, if Mr. Lincoln's policy should be carried out. I have told you that I do not think his bare election sufficient cause; but if his policy should be carried out in violation of any of the principles set forth in the Georgia Platform, that would be such an act of aggression which ought to be met as therein provided for. If his policy shall be carried out in repealing or modifying the Fugitive Slave Law so as to weaken its efficacy, Georgia has declared that she will in the last resort disrupt the ties of the Union, and I say so too. I stand upon the Georgia Platform, and upon every plank; and say, if those aggressions therein provided for take place, I say to you and to the people of Georgia, keep your powder dry, and let your assailants then have lead, if need be. (Applause.) I would wait for an act of aggression. This is my position.

Now upon another point, and that the most difficult, and deserving your most serious consideration, I will speak. That is the course which this state should pursue toward these Northern states, which by their legislative acts have attempted to nullify the Fugitive Slave Law. I know that in some of these states their acts pretend to be based upon the principles set forth in the case of PRIGG against Pennsylvania; that decision did proclaim the doctrine that the state officers are not bound to carry out the provisions of a law of Congress—that the federal government can not impose duties upon state officials; that they must execute their own laws by their own officers.

state would be "out of the Union" by the 18th of December. In all this time there not only had not been a single overt act of treason, but the laws of the United States had been scrupulously obeyed.

The temper and the purposes of the radical Abolitionists were now most significantly shown by their choice of this time, of all others, for a public apotheosis of John Brown. The 3d of December, the day on which Congress was to assemble, was also the anniversary of his death by execution of the law; and this occasion was to have been celebrated at the Tremont Temple, in Boston, by various exercises, which were to continue morning, afternoon, and evening. But the organizers of so flagrant an affront to public decency were doomed to disappointment. At the opening of the doors there was a small assemblage of negroes and white men, to the latter class of which there were soon large additions, among them the Chief of Police, with part of his force. Upon an attempt to organize the meeting for the purpose for which it was called, groans and hisses broke out all over the house, followed by cheers for the Constitution. Mr. Richard S. Fay, an eminent merchant and a strong anti-Abolitionist, was then nominated from the floor as chairman, and elected by acclamation, to the utter astonishment of the John Brown people. Resolutions were adopted strongly denouncing John Brown, his aiders, abettors, and admirers, and the meeting adjourned. The defeated party attempted forcible resistance, but they were ejected by the police and the house was closed—proceedings somewhat irregular, it must be confessed, but under the circumstances not quite unjustifiable. They gathered together again in the evening in the Negro Baptist Church, and were protected by the police during their meeting against a large concourse of exasperated citizens who surrounded the building.

On the 3d of December Congress assembled at Washington. The attendance of members was unusually large in both houses. In the lower the representatives of South Carolina appeared in their places; but in the Senate-chamber stood two empty chairs, silent witnesses of her refusal to be any longer numbered as one of the states of the Union. On the 4th of December President Buchanan sent his message to Congress. Never was an important state paper more eagerly looked for; never did one more entirely disappoint all expectations. The President attributed the attitude of the

---

And this may be true. But still it is the duty of the states to deliver fugitive slaves, as well as the duty of the general government to see that it is done.

Northern states, on entering into the federal compact, pledged themselves to surrender such fugitives; and it is in disregard of their obligations that they have passed laws which even tend to hinder or obstruct the fulfillment of that obligation. They have violated their plighted faith; what ought we to do in view of this? That is the question. What is to be done? By the law of nations you would have a right to demand the carrying out of this article of agreement, and I do not see that it should be otherwise with respect to the states of this Union; and in case it be not done, we would, by these principles, have the right to commit acts of reprisal on these faithless governments, and seize upon their property, or that of their citizens wherever found. The states of this Union stand upon the same footing with foreign nations in this respect. But by the law of nations we are equally bound, before proceeding to violent measures, to set forth our grievances before the offending government, to give them an opportunity to redress the wrong. Has our state yet done this? I think not.

Suppose it were Great Britain that had violated some compact of agreement with the general government, what would be first done? In that case our minister would be directed, in the first instance, to bring the matter to the attention of that government, or a commissioner be sent to that country to open negotiations with her, ask for redress, and it would only be when argument and reason had been exhausted that we should take the last resort of nations. That would be the course toward a foreign government, and toward a member of this confederacy I would recommend the same course.

Let us, therefore, not act hastily in this matter. Let your Committee on the State of the Republic make out a bill of grievances; let it be sent by the governor to those faithless states, and if reason and argument shall be tried in vain—all shall fail to induce them to return to their constitutional obligations, I would be for retaliatory measures, such as the governor has suggested to you. This mode of resistance in the Union is in our power. It might be effectual, and if in the last resort, we would be justified in the eyes of nations not only in separating from them, but by using force.

[Some one said the argument was already exhausted.]

Mr. Stephens continued: Some friend says that the argument is already exhausted. No, my friend, it is not. You have never called the attention of the Legislatures of those states to this subject, that I am aware of. Nothing has ever been done before this year. The attention of our own people has been called to this subject lately.

Now, then, my recommendation to you would be this: In view of all these questions of difficulty, let a convention of the people of Georgia be called, to which they may be all referred. Let the sovereignty of the people speak. Some think that the election of Mr. Lincoln is cause sufficient to dissolve the Union. Some think those other grievances are sufficient to dissolve the same, and that the Legislature has the power thus to act, and ought thus to act. I have no hesitancy in saying that the Legislature is not the proper body to sever our federal relations, if that necessity should arise. An honorable and distinguished gentleman the other night (Mr. T. R. R. Cobb) advised you to take this course—not to wait to hear from the cross-roads and groceries. I say to you, you have no power so to act. You must refer this question to the people, and you must wait to hear from the men at the cross-roads and even the groceries; for the people in this country, whether at the cross-roads or the groceries, whether in cottages or palaces, are all equal, and they are the sovereigns in this country. Sovereignty is not in the Legislature. We, the people, are the sovereigns. I am one of them, and have a right to be heard, and so has any other citizen of the state. You legislators, I speak it respectfully, are but our servants. You are the servants of the people, and not their masters. Power resides with the people in this country.

The great difference between our country and all others, such as France, and England, and Ireland, is, that here there is popular sovereignty, while there sovereignty is exercised by kings and favored classes. This principle of popular sovereignty, however much derided lately, is the foundation of our institutions. Constitutions are but the channels through which the popular will may be expressed. Our Constitution came from the people. They made it, and they alone can rightfully unmake it.

Mr. Toombs. I am afraid of conventions.

Mr. Stephens. I am not afraid of any convention legally chosen by the people. I know no way to decide great questions affecting fundamental laws except by representatives of the people. The Constitution of the United States was made by the representatives of the people. The Constitution of the State of Georgia was made by representatives of the people chosen at the ballot-box. But do not let the question which comes before the people be put to them in the language of my honorable friend who addressed you last night. Will you submit to abolition rule or resist?

Mr. Toombs. I do not wish the people to be cheated.

Mr. Stephens. Now, my friends, how are we going to cheat the people by calling on them to elect delegates to a convention to decide all these questions without any dictation or direction? Who proposes to cheat the people by letting them speak their own untrammeled views in the choice of their ablest and best men, to determine upon all these matters, involving their peace?

I think the proposition of my honorable friend had a considerable smack of unfairness, not to say cheat. He wished to have no convention, but for the Legislature to submit their vote to the people—submission to abolition rule or resistance? Now, who in Georgia would vote "submission to abolition rule?" (Laughter.)

Is putting such a question to the people to vote on a fair way of getting an expression of the popular will on all these questions? I think not. Now, who in Georgia is going to submit to abolition rule?

Mr. Toombs. The Convention will.

Mr. Stephens. No, my friend, Georgia will never do it. The Convention will never secede from the Georgia Platform. Under that there can be no abolition rule in the general government. I am not afraid to trust the people in convention upon this and all questions. Besides, the Legislature were not elected for such a purpose. They came here to do their duty as legislators. They have sworn to support the Constitution of the United States. They did not come here to disrupt this government. I am, therefore, for submitting all these questions to a convention of the people. Submit the question to the people whether they would submit to abolition rule or resist, and then let the Legislature act upon that vote? Such a course would be an insult to the people. They would have to eat their platform, ignore their past history, blot out their records, and take steps backward, if they should do this. I have never eaten my record or words, and never will.

But how will it be under this arrangement if they should vote to resist, and the Legislature should reassemble with this vote as their instruction? Can any man tell what sort of resistance will be meant? One man would say secede; another pass retaliatory measures; these are measures of resistance against wrong—legitimate and right—and there would be as many different ideas as there are members on this floor. Resistance don't mean secession—that, in no proper sense of the term, is resistance. Believing that the times require action, I am for presenting the question fairly to the people; for calling together an untrammeled convention, and presenting all the questions to them whether they will go out of the Union, or what course of resistance in the Union they may think best, and then let the Legislature act when the people in their majesty are heard; and I tell you now, whatever that convention does, I hope and trust our people will abide by. I advise the calling of a convention with the earnest desire to preserve the peace and harmony of the state. I should dislike, above all things, to see violent measures adopted, or a disposition to take the sword in hand, by individuals, without the authority of law.

My honorable friend said last night, "I ask you to give me the sword; for, if you do not give it to me, as God lives, I will take it myself."

Mr. Toombs. I will. (Applause on the other side.)

Mr. Stephens. I have no doubt that my honorable friend feels as he says. It is only his excessive ardor that makes him use such an expression; but this will pass off with the excitement of the hour. When the people in their majesty shall speak, I have no doubt that he will bow to their will, whatever it may be, upon the "sober second thought." (Applause.)

Should Georgia determine to go out of the Union, I speak for one, though my views might not agree with them, whatever the result may be, I shall bow to the will of her people. Their cause is my cause, and their destiny is my destiny; and I trust this will be the ultimate course of all. The greatest curse that can befall a free people is civil war.

But, as I said, let us call a convention of the people; let all these matters be submitted to it; and when the will of a majority of the people has thus been expressed, the whole state will present one unanimous voice in favor of whatever may be demanded; for I believe in the power of the people to govern themselves when wisdom prevails and passion is silent.

Look at what has already been done by them for their advancement in all that ennobles man. There is nothing like it in the history of the world. Look abroad from one extent of the country to the other; contemplate our greatness. We are now among the first nations of the earth. Shall it be said, then, that our institutions, founded upon principles of self-government, are a failure?

Thus far it is a noble example, worthy of imitation. The gentleman, Mr. Cobb, the other night, said it had proven a failure. A failure in what? In growth? Look at our expanse in national power. Look at our population and increase in all that makes a people great. A failure? Why, we are the admiration of the civilized world, and present the brightest hopes of mankind.

Some of our public men have failed in their aspirations; that is true, and from that comes a great part of our troubles. (Prolonged applause.)

No, there is no failure of this government yet. We have made great advancement under the Constitution, and I can not but hope that we shall advance higher still. Let us be true to our cause.

Now, when this convention assembles, if it shall be called, as I hope it may, I would say, in my judgment, without dictation, for I am conferring with you freely and frankly, and it is thus that I give my views, I should take into consideration all those questions which distract the public mind; should view all the grounds of secession so far as the election of Mr. Lincoln is concerned, and I have no doubt they would say that the constitutional election of no man is a sufficient cause to break up the Union, but that the state should wait until he at least does some unconstitutional act.

Mr. Toombs. Commit some overt act.

Mr. Stephens. No, I did not say that. The word overt is a sort of technical term connected with treason, which has come to us from the mother country, and it means an open act of rebellion. I do not see how Mr. Lincoln can do this unless he should levy war upon us. I do not, therefore, use the word overt. I do not intend to wait for that. But I use the word unconstitutional act, which our people understand much better, and which expresses just what I mean. But as long as he conforms to the Constitution he should be left to exercise the duties of his office.

In giving this advice I am but sustaining the Constitution of my country, and I do not thereby become a Lincoln aid man either (applause), but a Constitutional aid man. But this matter the Convention can determine.

As to the other matter, I think we have a right to pass retaliatory measures, provided they be in accordance with the Constitution of the United States, and I think they can be made such. But whether it would be wise for this Legislature to do this now is the question. To the Convention, in my judgment, this matter ought to be referred. Before we commit reprisals on New England, we should exhaust every means of bringing about a peaceful solution of the question.

Thus did General Jackson in the case of the French. He did not recommend reprisals until he had treated with France, and got her to promise to make indemnification, and it was only on her refusal to pay the money which she had promised that he recommended reprisals. It was after negotiation had failed. I do think, therefore, that it would be best, before going to extreme measures with our confederate states, to make presentation of our demands, to appeal to their reason and judgment to give us our rights. Then, if reason should not triumph, it will be time enough to commit reprisals, and we should be justified in the eyes of a civilized world. At least let the states know what your grievances are, and if they refuse, as I said, to give us our rights under the Constitution of our country, I should be willing, as a last resort, to sever the ties of this Union. (Applause.)

My own opinion is, that if this course be pursued, and they are informed of the consequences of refusal, these states will secede; but if they should not, then let the consequences be with them, and let the responsibility of the consequences rest upon them. Another thing I would have that convention to do—reaffirm the Georgia Platform, with an additional plank in it. Let that plank be the fulfillment of the obligation on the part of those states to repeal these obnoxious laws as a condition of our remaining in the Union. Give them time to consider it, and I would ask all states south to do the same thing.

I am for exhausting all that patriotism can demand before taking the last step. I would invite, therefore, South Carolina to a conference. I would ask the same of all the other Southern states, so that if the evil has got beyond our control, which God, in his mercy, grant may not be the case, let us not be divided among ourselves—(cheers)—but, if possible, secure the united cooperation of all the Southern states; and then, in the face of the civilized world, we may justify our action; and, with the wrong all on the other side, we can appeal to the God of battles to aid us in our cause. (Loud applause.) But let us not do any thing in which any portion of our people may charge us with rash or hasty action. It is certainly a matter of great importance to tear this government asunder. You were not sent here for that purpose. I would wish the whole South to be united if this is to be done; and I believe, if we pursue the policy which I have indicated, this can be effected.

In this way our sister Southern states can be induced to act with us, and I have but little doubt that the states of New York, and Pennsylvania, and Ohio, and the other Western states, will compel their Legislatures to recede from their hostile attitudes, if the others do not. Then, with these, we would go on without New England, if she chose to stay out.

A voice in the assembly. We will kick them out.

Mr. Stephens. I would not kick them out; but if they chose to stay out they might. I think, moreover, that these Northern states, being principally engaged in manufactures, would find that they had as much interest in the Union under the Constitution as we, and that they would return to their constitutional duty; this would be my hope. If they should not, and if the Middle states and Western states do not join us, we should at least have an undivided South. I am, as you clearly perceive, for maintaining the Union as it is, if possible. I will exhaust every means thus to maintain it with an equality in it. My principles are these:

First, the maintenance of the honor, the rights, the equality, the security, and the glory of my native state in the Union; but if these can not be maintained in the Union, then I am for their maintenance, at all hazards, out of it. Next to the honor and glory of Georgia, the land of my birth, I hold the honor and glory of our common country. In Savannah I was made to say by the reporters, who very often make me say things which I never did, that I was first for the glory of the whole country, and next for that of Georgia.

I said the exact reverse of this. I am proud of her history, of her present standing. I am proud even of her motto, which I would have duly respected at the present time by all her sons—Wisdom, Justice, and Moderation. I would have her rights and that of the Southern states maintained now upon these principles. Her position now is just what it was in 1850 with respect to the Southern states. Her platform, then, has been adopted by most, if not all the other Southern states. Now I would add but one additional plank to that platform, which I have stated, and one which time has shown to be necessary.

If all this fails, we shall at least have the satisfaction of knowing that we have done our duty, and all that patriotism could require.

Mr. Stephens continued for some time on other matters, which are omitted, and then took his seat amid great applause.

slave states to the fear of servile insurrections; when the planters, on the contrary, said, and, as it proved, with reason, they had no fears whatever on this score. He placed the responsibility for the disturbed state of the country entirely upon the shoulders of the anti-slavery party in the free states, utterly ignoring the aggressions of the slavery propagandists and the radical difference between the principles of the slaveholding founders of the republic and those of which John C. Calhoun was the great exponent; he declared that, in his opinion, unless the personal liberty laws of some of the free states were repealed the Union could not be preserved; but he passed no censure upon the studiously harsh and insulting provisions of the fugitive slave law which provoked their passage, but, on the contrary, he recommended the incorporation of that law into the Constitution; he denied the right of a state to break up the government merely of its own motion, and he admitted that he was bound to execute the laws of the United States throughout all the territory of the United States; but he added that neither the President nor Congress had the power to coerce a state, thus passing by the vital point that, according to the Constitution, the executive officers of the United States had to do, not with states, but with individual citizens of the United States. The message, in fact, said to the country, "First, in this quarrel the free states are all wrong and the slave states all right; next, no state has a right to secede; but, finally, if any state choose to do so, no one has any right to stop her." The effect of this pitiably shuffling manifesto was to encourage the seceders, to irritate the Republicans, and to dishearten the public at large. With the message came another document which deepened the despondency now fallen upon the country. The report of the Secretary of the Treasury showed the public coffers empty, large and pressing liabilities to be met, the national credit failing, and the revenue rapidly diminishing. All this in the face of a real wealth and prosperity during the previous year, indicated by an export trade of $400,000,000, an import of $362,000,000, and the more than sufficiency of the customs duties, $60,000,000, for the ordinary expenses of government. For the change the political condition of the country was entirely answerable. Wealth was vanishing, prosperity was at an end, for national dissolution seemed impending. The events of one month had cast over the future an impenetrable gloom.

The nation fell into a pitiable condition of uncertain opinion and vacillating action. A similar crisis in the affairs of a country dependent for the direction of affairs upon one central government would have brought on the inevitable alternative of anarchy or despotism. But this nation was saved by the complete sufficiency of its local governments, sustained as these were by the intelligence and the integrity of the mass of the people, whom they directly represented. Within the limits of each state, the relations between man and man, and between the individual and society, were undisturbed.

On the 10th of December the House of Representatives appointed a committee of thirty-three, one from each commonwealth, on the State of the Union. What was the state of the Union thus far we have already seen; and a mere recital of the principal events of the few days which intervened between the appointment of this committee and the nominal severance of the Union will give a better idea than can be conveyed by any other means of the confusion which prevailed in political affairs and the distracted condition of the public mind. A report had been circulated at the South that the Secretary of War, Mr. Floyd, had said that he would employ the United States troops to resist any attempt to seize the United States forts in the slave states. This rumor that he would perform his sworn duty he hastened to deny by telegraph, on the very day of the appointment of the committee on the State of the Union. At this time it was suggested among some of the corrupter politicians of the city of New York, that that city, with Brooklyn, Long Island, and Staten Island, should secede from the state, and form themselves into an independent commonwealth. But as Brooklyn was jealous of New York, and deemed that the two places had conflicting interests, it was feared that, if secession once began, Brooklyn might secede from New York; the inconvenience of which, as most of the inhabitants of the former were engaged in business in the latter, was so apparent, that the suggestion, after a little newspaper ventilation, vanished into silence. The excitement in Charleston rose apace, and, on the 8th of December, a guard was placed over the United States Arsenal at Charleston to prevent the transfer of supplies of ammunition to Fort Moultrie, the United States military post in that harbor, which was about four miles from the city. On the 10th, the Secretary of the Treasury, Mr. Cobb, resigned his portfolio, giving as his reasons that the honor and safety of his state, Georgia, were involved in the consequences of the presidential election; that his duty to her was paramount; and that his views made it improper for him to remain any longer a member of the cabinet: decorous scruples, the mere assumption of which was not common among those who, having like responsibilities, had like designs. On the 12th, Senator Wigfall, of Texas, a man whose extravagance and bombast made him laughed at, and whom we shall meet again under circumstances both rueful and ludicrous, made a set speech in the Senate-chamber, in which he announced that the Union would be dissolved; that "the eight cotton states" would secede; that they would be followed by Virginia, Tennessee, Maryland, and Kentucky; and that then Washington would be the seat of government of the new confederation. He also declared that he owed allegiance, not to the United States, but to his own state; a declaration afterward repeated in the same body by Senator Mason, of Virginia, with regard to his relations to his own state. On the 15th it was announced that General Lewis Cass, Secretary of State, had resigned, because of the President's determination not to re-enforce Fort Moultrie, and of his consequent conviction that the republic was approaching its dissolution. General Cass was one of the oldest and most experienced among the promi-

LEWIS CASS.

nent politicians of the past generation who kept the field, and he had thus far been a strong supporter of what was called "the Southern Rights Party." The resignation of such a man, for such a cause, however honorable to himself, was a most depressing occurrence. It made that painfully clear concerning which before there had been little doubt, that the President was about to shrink meanly from the responsibility of his office upon a great occasion. Preparations now were heard of from Louisiana to bring about the secession of that state. At the North efforts at conciliation began to be made, and a repeal of the Personal Liberty bills was freely talked of. On the 15th a private meeting was held of the most influential bankers, merchants, manufacturers, lawyers, and other professional men of conservative politics, for the purpose of appointing a committee of conference to urge delay upon the states about to secede, and to give assurances that any reasonable concessions for the sake of the preservation of the Union would be made. Such a position, taken by such men, seems, as we look back upon it, almost abject; but, in the excitement and under the feverous apprehension of the time, it appeared to most men the mere putting forth of a brotherly hand of deprecation. It failed utterly. An announcement that a committee of conference would shortly visit Charleston, met with a rebuff, in which cold-blooded arrogance was thinly concealed beneath the forms of courtesy. Judge Magrath, who spoke for his state, wrote, that nothing could swerve South Carolina from the course she had resolved on; adding, "The presence of any persons among us, however respectable, charged with the task of urging upon us a change of purpose, would be unprofitable and unpleasant." On the 17th, the South Carolina Convention assembled at Columbia, but, in consequence of the epidemic prevalence of the small-pox there, it adjourned the next day to Charleston, where it became immediately apparent that its members were bent upon ringleading the disunion movement. Throughout the state military drill was constantly kept up by all men capable of bearing arms. On the 18th, a bill for arming the State of North Carolina passed the Senate by a vote of forty-one to three. On the other hand, the repeal of the Massachusetts Personal Liberty Law was urged upon the state in an earnest manifesto, signed by numbers of its most respected citizens, headed by ex-Chief-justice Shaw, Judge Curtis, of the United States Supreme Court, and four ex-governors. On the 18th, Senator Crittenden, of Kentucky, one of the oldest, ablest, and most esteemed of the slaveholding members of Congress, brought forward a series of resolutions in that body which he and many others hoped would be adopted by both parties as a final settlement of the controversy. These resolutions, which were known as the Crittenden Compromise, after a preamble which stated their object to be that the sectional differences then distracting the country might be permanently quieted and settled by constitutional provisions, proposed certain amendments to the Constitution. These prohibited slavery north of the line of 36° 30′ north latitude, and admitted it south of that line; they deprived Congress of the power either to abolish slavery in places under its jurisdiction in slave states, and (except under certain specified conditions) in the District of Columbia, or to interdict the transportation of slaves from one slave state to another; they provided that, in case of resistance to the Fugitive Slave Law, and the rescue of a slave, the United States should pay the owner the value of the slave, and have a claim upon the county in which the rescue took place, which, in its turn, should recover from individuals. These articles, and others upon the same subject in the Constitution, were to be declared unalterable. Mr. Crittenden's compromise was not received with favor by the extreme members of the party whose prospective advent to power had occasioned its proposal. But, on the 19th, the General Assembly of Virginia passed resolutions inviting the various states to send commissioners to Washington to adjust the sectional differences of the nation, and recommending the Crittenden Compromise as the basis of action. This assembly, thus called together, obtained the name of "The Peace Congress." But this effort toward the preservation of the Union met with a sudden and severe rebuff; for, on the very next day, the South Carolina Convention formally passed an ordinance of secession by a unanimous vote.[6] That 20th of December, 1860, was a sad day in the annals of America and of the world—a day full of woes and bitter memories—a day on which disappointed politicians, the representatives of an arrogant and selfish oligarchy, essayed the destruction of the most beneficent government ever established, and vainly strove to stem the tide of human progress, which was about to sweep their petty personal interests and parish politics into oblivion. But the event itself produced at the moment a comparatively slight impression. Some guns were fired and some meetings held in a few towns in the country lying on the Gulf of Mexico; but in the slave states north of Charleston, the taking of the final plunge by South Carolina created no more excitement than many of the minor incidents which had previously occurred in the sad tragedy then beginning to be acted. One reason of the apparent apathy with which this secession was regarded was, because it was South Carolina, factious, querulous, headstrong, and loud-mouthed, which had passed with words a verbal Rubicon; another was, that, after what the political leaders of the state had said and done, the passage of an ordinance of secession was inevitable, unless they wished to stand confessed the merest braggarts and boasters. But the chief cause was, that the country had been stunned by the suddenness with which its national politics had fallen into disorder, and its national government had been brought to a dead lock without violence or even the threat of violence from any quarter. Its capacity for excitement seemed to be exhausted; and when that came which had been apprehended from the first, it was taken as a thing of course. South Carolina, however, did not treat the matter as one of course, but exhibited to the full that sense of the importance of her own acts which had always made her the subject of remark among her sister states, especially by those who were as much her superiors in power, and wealth, and general culture, as they were her inferiors in pre-

tension. Immediately upon the passage of the Ordinance of Secession, a declaration of the causes which led to it was issued to the world;[7] an oath of supreme allegiance to the state was prescribed for all officials, the first form of which having contained the words "exercise my office," these were altered, after grave consideration and debate, to "exercise my *high* office;" and commissioners were appointed to proceed to Washington to treat with the United States. Immediately, too—most characteristic fact—the newspapers of Charleston headed their letters and the extracts from journals which they received from the other parts of the country, "Foreign News," bringing derision upon themselves far and near by this childishness. On the 24th the South Carolina delegates withdrew from the House of Representatives, not resigning, but sending a letter to the Speaker, in which they informed the House that their state had dissolved their connection with the House; and, putting their destructive and debasing doctrine in its most offensive form, spoke of their fellow-members as those with whom they had been "associated in a common agency."[8] Thus far had South Carolina politicians been led to pervert the truth to gain their little ends. Thus did the state which was the first, as we have seen, to propose the formation of a national government, and whose leading man in the convention which framed the government solemnly pronounced the doctrine that each state was separately and individually independent a "political heresy," did not hesitate to declare before the world that George Washington, Benjamin Franklin, Alexander Hamilton, and their peers had thought and toiled, not to bring about a real union of the people of the country into one nation, but only to make a bargain or contract between different corporations, in which, for certain considerations, and upon certain conditions, those corporations agreed to submit to a general administration of affairs for certain distinctly specified purposes of

---

[6] SECESSION ORDINANCE OF SOUTH CAROLINA.

An Ordinance to Dissolve the Union between the State of South Carolina and other States united with her under the compact entitled the Constitution of the United States of America.

We, the people of the State of South Carolina, in Convention assembled, do declare and ordain, and it is hereby declared and ordained, that the ordinance adopted by us in Convention, on the 23d day of May, in the year of our Lord 1788, whereby the Constitution of the United States of America was ratified, and also all acts and parts of acts of the General Assembly of this state ratifying the amendments of the said Constitution, are hereby repealed, and that the union now subsisting between South Carolina and other states under the name of the United States of America is hereby dissolved.

[7] *South Carolina's Declaration of Causes.*

The people of the State of South Carolina in Convention assembled, on the 2d day of April, A.D. 1852, declared that the frequent violations of the Constitution of the United States by the federal government, and its encroachments upon the reserved rights of the states, fully justified this state in their withdrawal from the federal Union; but, in deference to the opinions and wishes of the other slaveholding states, she forbore at that time to exercise this right. Since that time these encroachments have continued to increase, and farther forbearance ceases to be a virtue.

And now the State of South Carolina, having resumed her separate and equal place among nations, deems it due to herself, to the remaining United States of America, and to the nations of the world, that she should declare the immediate causes which have led to this act.

In the year 1765, that portion of the British Empire embracing Great Britain undertook to make laws for the government of that portion composed of the thirteen American colonies. A struggle for the right of self-government ensued, which resulted, on the 4th of July, 1776, in a declaration, by the colonies, "that they are, and of right ought to be, FREE AND INDEPENDENT STATES; and that, as free and independent states, they have full power to levy war, conclude peace, contract alliances, establish commerce, and to do all other acts and things which independent states may of right do."

They farther solemnly declared that whenever any "form of government becomes destructive of the ends for which it was established, it is the right of the people to alter or abolish it, and to institute a new government." Deeming the government of Great Britain to have become destructive of these ends, they declared that the colonies "are absolved from all allegiance to the British crown, and that all political connection between them and the state of Great Britain is, and ought to be, totally dissolved."

In pursuance of this Declaration of Independence, each of the thirteen states proceeded to exercise its separate sovereignty; adopted for itself a Constitution, and appointed officers for the administration of government in all its departments—legislative, executive, and judicial. For purposes of defense they united their arms and their counsels; and in 1778 they entered into a league known as the Articles of Confederation, whereby they agreed to intrust the administration of their external relations to a common agent, known as the Congress of the United States, expressly declaring, in the first article, "that each state retains its sovereignty, freedom, and independence, and every power, jurisdiction, and right which is not, by this Confederation, expressly delegated to the United States in Congress assembled."

Under this confederation the War of the Revolution was carried on; and on the 3d of September, 1783, the contest ended, and a definite treaty was signed by Great Britain, in which she acknowledged the independence of the colonies in the following terms:

"ARTICLE 1. His Britannic majesty acknowledges the said United States, viz.: New Hampshire, Massachusetts Bay, Rhode Island and Providence Plantations, Connecticut, New York, New Jersey, Pennsylvania, Delaware, Maryland, Virginia, North Carolina, South Carolina, and Georgia, to be FREE, SOVEREIGN, AND INDEPENDENT STATES; that he treats with them as such; and, for himself, his heirs and successors, relinquishes all claims to the government, propriety, and territorial rights of the same, and every part thereof."

Thus were established the two great principles asserted by the colonies, namely, the right of a state to govern itself, and the right of a people to abolish a government when it becomes destructive of the ends for which it was instituted. And concurrent with the establishment of these principles was the fact that each colony became and was recognized by the mother country as a FREE, SOVEREIGN, AND INDEPENDENT STATE.

In 1787, deputies were appointed by the states to revise the Articles of Confederation; and on the 17th of September, 1787, these deputies recommended, for the adoption of the states, the Articles of Union known as the Constitution of the United States.

The parties to whom this Constitution was submitted were the several sovereign states; they were to agree or disagree; and when nine of them agreed, the compact was to take effect among those concurring; and the general government, as the common agent, was then to be invested with their authority.

If only nine of the thirteen states had concurred, the other four would have remained as they then were—separate sovereign states, independent of any of the provisions of the Constitution. In fact, two of the states did not accede to the Constitution until long after it had gone into operation among the other eleven, and during that interval they each exercised the functions of an independent nation.

By this Constitution certain duties were imposed upon the several states, and the exercise of certain of their powers was restrained, which necessarily impelled their continued existence as sovereign states. But, to remove all doubt, an amendment was added, which declared that the powers not delegated to the United States by the Constitution, nor prohibited by it to the states, are reserved to the states respectively, or to the people. On the 23d of May, 1788, South Carolina, by a Convention of her people, passed an ordinance assenting to this Constitution, and afterward altered her own Constitution to conform herself to the obligations she had undertaken.

Thus was established, by compact between the states, a government with defined objects and powers, limited to the express words of the grant. This limitation left the whole remaining mass of power subject to the clause reserving it to the states or the people, and rendered unnecessary any specification of reserved rights. We hold that the government thus established is subject to the two great principles asserted in the Declaration of Independence; and we hold farther, that the mode of its formation subjects it to a third fundamental principle, namely, the law of compact. We maintain that in every compact between two or more parties the obligation is mutual; that the failure of one of the contracting parties to perform a material part of the agreement entirely releases the obligation of the other; and that, where no arbiter is provided, each party is remitted to his own judgment to determine the fact of failure, with all its consequences.

In the present case that fact is established with certainty. We assert that fourteen of the states have deliberately refused for years past to fulfill their constitutional obligations, and we refer to their own statutes for the proof.

The Constitution of the United States, in its fourth article, provides as follows:

"No person held to service or labor in one state under the laws thereof, escaping into another, shall, in consequence of any law or regulation therein, be discharged from such service or labor, but shall be delivered up on claim of the party to whom such service or labor may be due."

This stipulation was so material to the compact that without it that compact would not have been made. The greater number of the contracting parties held slaves, and they had previously evinced their estimate of the value of such a stipulation by making it a condition in the ordinance for the government of the territory ceded by Virginia, which obligations, and the laws of the general government, have ceased to effect the objects of the Constitution. The states of Maine, New Hampshire, Vermont, Massachusetts, Connecticut, Rhode Island, New York, Pennsylvania, Illinois, Indiana, Michigan, Wisconsin, and Iowa have enacted laws which either nullify the acts of Congress, or render useless any attempt to execute them. In many of these states the fugitive is discharged from the service of labor claimed, and in none of them has the state government complied with the stipulation made in the Constitution. The State of New Jersey at an early day passed a law in conformity with her constitutional obligation; but the current of anti-slavery feeling has led her more recently to enact laws which render inoperative the remedies provided by her own laws and by the laws of Congress. In the State of New York even the right of transit for a slave has been denied by her tribunals; and the states of Ohio and Iowa have refused to surrender to justice fugitives charged with murder, and with inciting servile insurrection in the State of Virginia. Thus the constitutional compact has been deliberately broken and disregarded by the non-slaveholding states, and the consequence follows that South Carolina is released from her obligation.

The ends for which this Constitution was framed are declared by itself to be "to form a more perfect union, to establish justice, insure domestic tranquillity, provide for the common defense, promote the general welfare, and secure the blessings of liberty to ourselves and our posterity."

These ends it endeavored to accomplish by a federal government, in which each state was recognized as an equal, and had separate control over its own institutions. The right of property in slaves was recognized by giving to free persons distinct political rights; by giving them the right to represent, and burdening them with direct taxes for three fifths of their slaves; by authorizing the importation of slaves for twenty years; and by stipulating for the rendition of fugitives from labor.

We affirm that these ends for which this government was instituted have been defeated, and the government itself has been destructive of them by the action of the non-slaveholding states. Those states have assumed the right of deciding upon the propriety of our domestic institutions, and have denied the rights of property established in fifteen of the states and recognized by the Constitution; they have denounced as sinful the institution of slavery; they have permitted the open establishment among them of societies whose avowed object is to disturb the peace of and eloin the property of the citizens of other states. They have encouraged and assisted thousands of our slaves to leave their homes; and those who remain have been incited by emissaries, books, and pictures to servile insurrection.

For twenty-five years this agitation has been steadily increasing, until it has now secured to its aid the power of the common government. Observing the *forms* of the Constitution, a sectional party has found within that article establishing the Executive Department the means of subverting the Constitution itself. A geographical line has been drawn across the Union, and all the states north of that line have united in the election of a man to the high office of President of the United States whose opinions and purposes are hostile to slavery. He is to be intrusted with the administration of the common government because he has declared that that "government cannot endure permanently half slave, half free," and that the public mind must rest in the belief that slavery is in the course of ultimate extinction.

This sectional combination for the subversion of the Constitution has been aided in some of the states by elevating to citizenship persons who, by the supreme law of the land, are incapable of becoming citizens; and their votes have been used to inaugurate a new policy, hostile to the South, and destructive of its peace and safety.

On the 4th of March next this party will take possession of the government. It has announced that the South shall be excluded from the common territory, that the judicial tribunal shall be made sectional, and that a war must be waged against slavery until it shall cease throughout the United States.

The guarantees of the Constitution will then no longer exist, the equal rights of the states will be lost. The slaveholding states will no longer have the power of self-government or self-protection, and the federal government will have become their enemy.

Sectional interest and animosity will deepen the irritation; and all hope of remedy is rendered vain by the fact that the public opinion at the North has invested a great political error with the sanctions of a more erroneous religious belief.

We, therefore, the people of South Carolina, by our delegates in Convention assembled, appealing to the Supreme Judge of the world for the rectitude of our intentions, have solemnly declared that the union heretofore existing between this state and the other states of North America is dissolved, and that the State of South Carolina has resumed her position among the nations of the world as a separate and independent state, with full power to levy war, conclude peace, contract alliances, establish commerce, and to do all other acts and things which independent states may of right do.

[8] *Letter of South Carolina Members of the House of Representatives.*

SIR,—We avail ourselves of the earliest opportunity since the official communication of the intelligence, of making known to your honorable body that the people of the State of South Carolina, in their sovereign capacity, have resumed the powers heretofore delegated by them to the federal government of the United States, and have thereby dissolved our connection with the House of Representatives. In taking leave of those with whom we have been associated in a common agency, we, as well as the people of our commonwealth, desire to do so with a feeling of mutual regard and respect for each other, cherishing the hope that in our future relations we may better enjoy that peace and harmony essential to the happiness of a free and enlightened people.

JOHN M'QUEEN,
M. L. BONHAM,
W. W. BOYCE,
J. D. ASHMORE.

Dec. 24.
To the Speaker of the House of Representatives.

mere material interest—"a common agency," in fact, which was to be regarded only as the result of a bargain, and be administered as a bargain, with this difference, that any party to it might withdraw from it at pleasure, without liability to restraint or punishment. They proclaimed that the national flag had been only a shop-sign, and the American eagle a mere trade-mark; the sign and the mark, too, of a firm which was unworthy of credit, because any member of it might abscond whenever he pleased, and take with him whatever of the assets he could lay his hands upon. Having withdrawn from this "common agency," and set up on her own account as a nation, South Carolina set about preparations to establish foreign relations and create a navy. These, however, did not go very far; for, although it seems as if the self-assertion of this little commonwealth would have led her so far as to assume at once all the style of an independent nation, it began to be but too plain that she would not long be left alone.

At this very time the people of the free states were shocked by the announcement of the intended removal of seventy-eight guns of the largest calibre (10-inch columbiads) from the Alleghany Arsenal, opposite Pittsburg, in Pennsylvania, to Newport, near Galveston Island, Texas, and to Ship Island, in the Gulf of Mexico. At those places there were fortifications which had never yet been mounted; and the placing of these guns in them at this time, when they were not, and could not be garrisoned, seemed plainly to indicate a purpose that both the guns and the forts should fall into the hands of the men who were rapidly driving the whole South into open revolt. The officer in command at the arsenal and he who was to superintend the transportation of the guns were from slave states. There was an instant determination manifested in Pittsburg and the country round that the guns should not be removed; and the exhibition of feeling was so strong and so wide-spread that the order for their removal was countermanded.

This incident was a fair exponent of the course of the administration and the condition of the country. The former was vacillating and faithless, the latter distracted and torn by faction. Mr. Buchanan's weak policy encouraged the seceding faction without satisfying them, while it exasperated and humiliated all who were faithful to the republic. The seceders of South Carolina came to believe, or at least to the bold declaration of a belief, that there would be no attempt to defend the government by force of arms against destruction. Coercion of "a sovereign body" was pronounced absurd on general principles, and in the present case impossible; and, at the same time, the right of any state to break up the Union for any reason, or without any reason, and at any time, was asserted in another dogma, that "sovereign" parties to a contract are themselves the only judges whether the contract is violated and they absolved from it; a declaration which set utterly at naught the prescribed authority of the Supreme Court to decide upon the constitutionality of any state or national law, and which thus showed the radically destructive purposes of those who avowed it. The seceders also looked to the accomplishment of their purposes with impunity, by reason of the support, or at least the protection, of a powerful party—the well-disciplined rank and file of the pure Democratic party—in the free states. And these expectations were not entirely without reason. Many men still looked upon secession as a mere political movement, the last, most desperate effort of the slavery propaganda to retain its control of the national government, the culmination of the great game of bluff and brag which that party had so successfully played for so many years. This, indeed, was doubtless the original purpose of the greater number of those who took part in the secession movement. Indeed, they openly avowed among themselves that they proposed to secede, not for the purpose of destroying the Union, but to force the free states to amend the Constitution in favor of slavery.[9] Seeing this, and seeing, too, that without the Southern states the Democratic party would practically cease to exist, there were quasi-assurances held out privately, and even publicly in newspapers, by those who were blindly or corruptly committed to the fortunes of that party, that all in the free states who voted for other candidates than Mr. Lincoln (a large proportion, as we have seen) would support the slave states in a contest with the national government. On the other hand, the Abolitionists rejoiced at the prospective destruction of the government and extinction of the republic, which they had openly labored for fifteen years to bring about;[10] and the leading organ of the advanced section of the Republican party—the *New York Tribune*—admitted in terms the absolute right of secession claimed by the insurgents.[1] And, finally, the Southern leaders believed, or professed to their followers to believe, that any attempt of the government to maintain its authority would be followed by such an utter derangement of trade, manufactures, and all the public relations of life in the free states, as to bring on starvation and anarchy, and thus render the government powerless for offense, if not even to defend itself against the insurgent forces. These views were in a measure justified by the deplorable condition into which, in a few weeks, commercial affairs at the North fell from a state of remarkable and soundly-based prosperity. The South owed the North a sum estimated by competent persons at three hundred millions of dollars; and, even supposing that this was one third too large, the consequences of a refusal to pay, or even a temporary withholding so vast a sum, must needs be hopeless derangement and sudden ruin. The secessionists from the beginning looked only to success, regardless of the nature of the means they used and the consequences of their conduct to others; and this sum was in a great measure withheld, for the double purpose of crippling those to whom it was due, and using it to pay the expense of war with them. Collections of debts in slave states by creditors in free states became impossible in most cases, and the consequence was wide-spread bankruptcy and ruin at the North. The banks of the South had been allowed by law to suspend specie payments, and had availed themselves of the privilege; and consequently they had been followed in this respect by most of the banks at the North. The New England mills were either closed or running on half time; and throughout the North merchants and retail dealers reduced their force of salesmen, and manufacturers their force of workmen, or the time for which they employed and paid them. Winter and want were coming rapidly upon hundreds of thousands of Northern people who had hitherto lived in comfort if not in plenty. This was sad enough, but rumor exaggerated it, and designing politicians and corrupt journalists magnified and multiplied the exaggerations of rumor. For these reasons the seceders rested in confidence that no attempt would be made at coercion (which was the name they gave to the use of the power of the government for the maintenance of the integrity of the republic), and that they would be able first to defy the authority of the national government, and then, if they chose, to usurp it.[2] But in the free states there was a steadily growing conviction that there would be a determined attempt to detach all the Gulf and cotton-growing states from the Union permanently, and with this conviction another, that such a severance could not be accomplished, or even attempted, peaceably. Why the North believed thus few could have told; but the belief pervaded the community as latent electricity the air. The explosion seemed impending, and men began to look the awful probability of civil war in the face. In the President no one placed any trust, and Congress seemed incapable to cope with the emergency—capable of nothing except vain babbling of compromise. Committees on the State of the Union and peace conferences of all grades, public and private, came together and poured out a flood of talk upon each other and the country, and then rose and separated, no nearer union or wisdom than they were before. Men began to doubt, and to have reason to doubt, whether there were patriotism, and virtue, and vigor enough in the land to make even a respectable attempt to save the republic from disintegration. In the midst of all this trouble, a great cabinet scandal broke forth. It was found that $870,000 had been fraudulently abstracted from the Indian Trust Fund and acceptances substituted, to which the name of the Secretary of War (Mr. Floyd, of Virginia) were attached, and for the benefit of parties with whom he had intimate relations. The effect of this shameful discovery—made more shameful by the fact that the custodian of the bonds, the Secretary of the Interior, Jacob Thompson, of Mississippi, was at this very time in North Carolina as a commissioner from his state, working for secession—was to sap still farther the confidence of the nation in its own integrity. What could be hoped of the people or the government when the President's very cabinet was thus rotten and honeycombed with corruption? The only gleam of hope was in the fact that the falsehood, the treachery, and the peculation were without exception on the part of the enemies of the republic. And so loyal men here and there began to take heart, and gird themselves up for conflict.

[9] The commissioners sent by Mississippi to Maryland, and whom Governor Hicks, of the latter state, declined receiving, in the course of an address to the citizens of Baltimore, on the evening of December 9th, 1860, said:

"Secession is not intended to break up the present government, but to perpetuate it. We do not propose to go out by way of breaking up or destroying the Union as our fathers gave it to us, but we go out for the purpose of getting farther guarantees and security for our rights, not by a convention of all the Southern states, nor by Congressional tricks, which have failed in times past, and will fail again. But our plan is for the Southern states to withdraw from the Union for the present, to allow amendments to the Constitution to be made guaranteeing our just rights; and if the Northern states will not make those amendments, by which these rights shall be secured to us, then we must secure them the best way we can. This question of slavery must be settled now or never. The country has been agitated seriously by it for the past twenty or thirty years. It has been a festering sore upon the body politic; and many remedies having failed, we must try amputation, to bring it to a healthy state. We must have amendments to the Constitution, and if we can not get them we must set up for ourselves."

[10] "The abolition enterprise was started in 1831. Until 1846 we thought it was possible to kill slavery and save the Union. We then said, over the ruins of the American Church and the Union is the only way to freedom. From '46 to '61 we preached that doctrine."—*Wendell Phillips's Speech at Music Hall, Boston, July 6, 1862.*

[1] "Whenever any considerable section of our Union shall deliberately resolve to go out, we shall resist all coercive measures designed to keep it in."—*N. Y. Tribune, Nov. 9, 1860.*

[2] Senator Iverson, of Georgia, speaking in his seat on the 5th of December, 1860, said: "We intend, Mr. President, to go out peaceably if we can, forcibly if we must; but I do not believe, with the senator from New Hampshire (Mr. Hale), that there is going to be any war. If five or eight states go out, they will necessarily draw all the other Southern states after them. That is a consequence that nothing can prevent. If five or eight states go out of this Union, I should like to see the man who would propose a declaration of war against them, or attempt to force them into obedience to the federal government at the point of the bayonet or the sword. If one state alone was to go out, unsustained by her sister states, possibly war might ensue, and there might be an attempt made to coerce her, and that would give rise to civil war; but, sir, South Carolina is not to go out alone. In my opinion, she will be sustained by all her Southern sisters. They may not all go out immediately, but they will, in the end, join South Carolina in this important movement; and we shall, in the next twelve months, have a confederacy of the Southern states, and a government inaugurated and in successful operation, which, in my opinion, will be a government of the greatest prosperity and power the world has ever seen."

The cool defiance which was thus freely given in the halls of the national capital was supported by such declarations as the following in the leading journals of the slave states:

"The Northern people have an enemy at their own doors who will do our work for us, if we are not insane enough to take their myrmidons off their hands. 'The winter of their discontent' is but beginning to dawn. They have a long, dark winter, of cold and hunger, impending over their heads; before it is over they will have millions of operatives without work and without bread.

"In all human probability, before another summer melts their ice-bound hills, blood—human blood—will have flowed in their streets. When cold and hunger begin their work, this deluded rabble will ask alms at the doors of the rich with pike and firebrand in their hands. Our Northern enemies will then find that they have business enough to attend to at their own doors, without troubling themselves about keeping forts on Southern soil. 'They have got the wolf by the ears,' and they have a fair prospect of being bit, unless we are charitable enough to take the beast off their hands. If the North can furnish bread for its paupers for the next five months, well; if not, their rulers will answer for it in blood. It was simply the want of bread that brought Louis XVI. to the guillotine; and New York, as well as Paris, can furnish her Theroign de Maricourt, who may sing her *carmagnole* up Broadway with Seward's head upon a pike.

"Our Northern enemies are locked up with their million of operatives for the winter, and how they are to be kept quiet no man can tell."—*Charleston Courier.*

FORT SUMTER.

Major Anderson at Fort Moultrie.—His Character.—Weakness of his Position.—His Instructions.—He occupies Fort Sumter.—Effect of the Movement throughout the Country.—Authorities of Charleston seize the Arsenal, Custom-house, and Revenue Cutter.—Insulting Letter of the South Carolina Commissioners to President Buchanan.—Defiant Avowal of Secession Principles and Purposes in Congress.—The Government begins to assert itself.—Sagacity and Patriotism of Lieutenant General Scott and of General Wool.—Investment of Fort Sumter.—Underhand Attempt to supply and re-enforce it.—The "Star of the West" fired upon by the Rebel Batteries.—Major Anderson calls Governor Pickens to Account.—The first Flag of Truce.—Efforts of the Insurgent Leaders.—Seizure of Forts and Arsenals throughout the Gulf States.—Events in the Border States.—Formal successive Secession of the Gulf States.—Audacity of the Insurgents, mild Measures of the Government, and placid Patriotism of the People.—Seizure of Arms on their way to Georgia, and Retaliation of the Governor of Georgia.—Resignation of Secretary Thompson.—South Carolina demands the Evacuation of Fort Sumter.—Withdrawal of Senators of the seceded States from Congress.—General Dix's spirited Action and Order.—Formation of the "Confederate" Provisional Government.—Adoption of a Provisional Constitution, and Election of Officers.—Jefferson Davis, his Character and Career.—Alexander H. Stephens.—Opposition to Secession in Slave States.—Treachery of General Twiggs in Texas.—Jefferson Davis's Threat to expel the National Troops in Texas. — Mr. Lincoln declared President elect.—Plots against his Life.—Measures taken to discover and defeat them.—Mr. Lincoln's sudden Appearance at Washington.—Effect upon the Public.—Proposed Compromise Constitutional Amendments.—Inauguration of Mr. Lincoln.—His Inaugural Address.—Its Effect upon the Country.—General Beauregard takes Command at Charleston.—Numerous Army and Navy Officers resign their Commissions and take Service with the Insurgents.—State Sovereignty their alleged Justification.—Pierre Toutant, who and what.—The "Confederate" Commissioners in Washington.—Can Fort Sumter be re-enforced?—Fort Pickens can.—The Expedition of Relief.—Batteries around Fort Sumter.—Notice: "peaceably if we can, forcibly if we must."—Beauregard ordered to demand an Evacuation. — Major Anderson refuses.—Bombardment and Evacuation of the Fort.

WHILE all hearts were thus filled with anxiety and sad foreboding; while loyal men saw only that the great, long-dreaded calamity was about to fall upon the country—that the struggle for the nation's life must soon begin, and yet did not confess to themselves in what exact form that calamity must come, or conjecture where the first throes of that struggle would be felt; while even the men who were bent on the destruction of the republic, unless they could usurp the control of it in the interests of their class, were certain only of their purpose, uncertain as to the way in which they should accomplish it; while doubt and undefined dread thus brooded over the land, an almost unknown man was about to take a step in the mere exercise of ordinary prudence and the faithful performance of a soldier's duty, which decided in an hour the question whether the seceders were to accomplish their purpose without resistance, placed at once the relations of

FORT SUMTER, SEEN FROM THE REAR, AT LOW WATER.

the government and those who defied it upon a war footing, and fixed the spot where one party or the other must assert itself by force or be humiliated before the world. Robert Anderson, a major of artillery, was in garrison at Fort Moultrie as commander of the United States military post of Charleston Harbor. He had graduated with honor at West Point in 1825; he had served not only with gallantry, but with distinction, in Florida, and afterward in the Mexican war, having been severely wounded in the attack on El Molino del Rey; he was the author of the text-book of the United States army upon artillery service; and yet, so absorbed had Americans of this and the last generation been in the arts and employments of peace, so regardless of mere military merit, except in a very few eminent cases, that out of the professional circle of the army and that of his own friends and acquaintances, Major Anderson's name was rarely heard. But, wherever known, it was spoken as that of a man of bravery, sagacity, determined purpose, and umblemished honor. Upon all these points Major Anderson was now about to be tested, with the eyes of all nations upon him and the verdict of posterity before him. A native of one slave state, and connected by marriage with the people of another, it was hoped on the one side that he might betray his trust, and feared on the other that he might at least resign it. But hopes and fears alike proved vain. Thoughtless of the world and of posterity, regardless of the ties of family and friendship, he kept a single eye upon present duty, sought only to absolve himself of the responsibility which had been laid upon him, and so won the undying honors which ever fall to faith and firmness shown on great occasions.

When the secession excitement in South Carolina, and particularly in Charleston, had reached its height, but ten days before the State Convention had taken a final step, he busied himself in strengthening the defenses of Fort Moultrie and Fort Sumter to the best of his ability with the small force under his command. That force, all told, consisted of nine officers, fifty-five men (artillerists), fifteen musicians, and thirty laborers—one hundred and nine men, of whom only sixty-three were combatants, one of the officers being an assistant surgeon. With this little band, among whom all proved true, he determined to defend his flag and maintain his post to the last moment. He began to be watchful of the approaches to Fort Moultrie, which is about four miles from Charleston, upon Sullivan's Island, where, during a generation and a half of peace, a village had sprung up around it. After the 11th of December no one was admitted within the works unless he was known to some officer of the garrison. Events justified this precaution; for within a few days military organizations were set on foot in Charleston, the almost avowed object of which was the occupation of Forts Moultrie, Sumter, and Pinckney. On the 19th of this month Mr. Porcher Miles, in the South Carolina State Convention, said that members might allay any fears which they might have had on account of the forts in Charleston Harbor, because a conversation with the President had convinced him that the post would not be re-enforced, and the garrison of Fort Moultrie was "but seventy or eighty men," while Sumter was an "empty fortress which they might seize and control in a single night." The next day the Ordinance of Secession was passed; and on the 21st, as we have already seen, the Charleston newspapers, with childish precipitancy and petulance about trifles, announced occurrences in the Northern states under the heading "foreign news." Childish and petulant although this was, it showed Major Anderson very clearly the light in which the community which was equipping and drilling troops within sight of his ramparts were determined to regard him—as the officer of a power which they defied, and who held a military position upon their soil which might be made the base of operations against them. He felt the danger and the delicacy of his position. On the 24th of December he wrote a private letter in which he set forth the precarious circumstances in which he was placed: with a garrison of only sixty effective men, in an indifferent work, the walls of which were only fourteen feet high, within one hundred yards of sand-hills which commanded the position and afforded covers for sharp-shooters, and with numerous houses within pistol-shot, he confessed that, "if attacked in force by any one but a simpleton, there is scarce a possibility of our being able to hold out long enough for our friends to come to our succor." General Scott, too, saw and declared that the fort could be taken from Major Anderson by five hundred men in twenty-four hours. Meanwhile volunteer troops began to pour into Charleston, and there was much discussion in regard to the policy and possibility of seizing all the national forts in the harbor; and, in fact, under the circumstances, the opportunity was too tempting to warrant a belief that it would be long resisted. As to all this Major Anderson was well informed, for intercourse between the garrison and the city was kept up as usual. Nevertheless, his duty was clear, not only from the general nature of his responsibility to the government, but from special instructions sent to him by the Secretary of War—instructions so manifestly required in the emergency, that even John B. Floyd, false to his country and false to his honor, could not refrain from giving them. They were sent to Major Anderson verbally through Assistant Adjutant General Butler, whose written memorandum was afterward made public. According to this memorandum, Major Anderson was instructed "carefully to avoid any act which would needlessly provoke aggression," and on that reason "not, without necessity, to take up any position which could be construed into the assumption of a hostile attitude; but," the order continues, "you are to hold possession of the forts in the harbor, and if attacked, you are to defend yourself to the last extremity. The smallness of your force will not permit you, perhaps, to occupy more than one of the three forts, but an attack on, or attempt to take possession of either of them, will be regarded as an act of hostility, and you may then put your command into either of them which you may deem most proper to increase its power of resistance. You are also authorized to take similar steps whenever you have tangible evidence of a design to proceed to a hostile act."

Christmas day dawned upon Major Anderson under these circumstances and bound by these instructions. It may be supposed that he was not in a festive mood; but, whatever his apprehensions or his purposes, he kept them to himself, and accepted an invitation to dinner in Charleston. Had his entertainers known the already settled determination of their gentle, placid guest, he would probably never have been allowed to leave the city, certainly he would have been prevented from returning to his post. They parted for the last time as friends that night, which, indeed, was the last occasion on which he set foot in that nest of traitors. Lulled into confidence by a belief that under no circumstances would the President take any steps whatever to assert the authority of the government or protect the national honor in South Carolina, and confirmed in this belief by the manner of Major Anderson, the Charlestonians went on with their preparations, and awaited their own time for effecting their purposes. Meantime Mr. Robert W. Barnwell, Mr. J. H. Adams, and Mr. James L. Orr were sent as commissioners from the "sovereign state" of South Carolina, to "treat with the government of the United States for the delivery of the forts, magazines, light-houses, and other real estate, with their appurtenances, in South Carolina, and also for an apportionment of the public debt, and for a division of all other property held by the government of the United States as agent of the Confederated States, of which South Carolina was recently a member," etc., etc. It may be that this commission was appointed with the notion that it could be received by the President; it may be that some of those whom it represented could not perceive the effrontery of sending such a commission to the President of the United States, and actually believed that it would be able to open some kind of negotiation with the national government. Mayhap some citizen of this newly-hatched "sovereignty" saw in his excited imagination the commissioners returning with the deeds of Forts Sumter and Moultrie, Castle Pinckney, the arsenal and the light-houses, in their pockets, given in return for the promises to pay of the treasury of South Carolina. But fancies and visions like these, as well as those of a more modest and reasonable character, were very suddenly dispelled without the aid of the report of the commissioners; for the good people of Charleston, looking seaward on the morning of the 27th of December, saw, instead of the United States flag flying from the flag-staff of Fort Moultrie, only a cloud of smoke rolling upward; and soon the look-outs brought the news that Major Anderson had evacuated and dismantled that fortification, and had retired with his little command to Fort Sumter.

KEY OF THE FORT MOULTRIE MAGAZINE.   MAJOR ANDERSON'S CANDLESTICK.

The news caused great excitement in Charleston. The rebels saw themselves at once defied and baffled. They were thousands, and could soon make themselves tens of thousands; yet here a band of one hundred men had been placed in a position where they could assert, and, for a time at least, maintain the authority of the government, and uphold its flag in the very harbor of the chief city of the seceding state. Fort Sumter commanded the entrance to the port, and, being a very strong work, stood, as it were, sentinel over Charleston, and controlled its commercial exits and entrances. But this was not the chief reason of the turmoil in the town. The rebels were exasperated at finding that they had been outwitted, and that not only was the little garrison which they had calculated upon turning out of Fort Moultrie, civilly if they could, but forcibly if they must, placed safely beyond their reach, but that the empty fortress which they had taken for granted that they could seize and control in a single night, was effectually secured against all attempts except those of siege, bombardment, or storm by overwhelming force.

Major Anderson had kept his secret well, and done his work thoroughly. During the day, the wives and children of the troops were sent away from the fort, on the plea that, as an attack might be made upon it, their removal was necessary. Three small schooners were hired, and the few inhabitants of Sullivan's Island saw them loaded, as they thought, with beds, furniture, trunks, and other luggage of that kind. About nine o'clock in the evening, the men were ordered to hold themselves in marching order, with knapsacks packed, ready to move at a moment's notice. No one seemed to know the reason of the movement, and probably no one but Major Anderson himself and his next in command knew their destination. The little garrison was paraded, inspected, and then embarked on boats which headed for Fort Sumter. The schooners had taken, or then took, all the provisions, garrison fur-

ENTRY OF MAJOR ANDERSON'S COMMAND INTO FORT SUMTER ON CHRISTMAS NIGHT, 1860.

niture, and munitions of war which could be carried away on such short notice, and with such slender means of transportation—enough to enable fourscore men to sustain and defend themselves in a strong, sea-girt fortress for a long time. What could not be carried away was destroyed. Not a keg of powder or a cartridge was left in the magazine; the small-arms and military supplies of all kinds were removed; the guns were spiked, the gun-carriages burned, and the guns thus dismounted; partly-finished additions and alterations of the work were destroyed; the flag-staff was cut down; and nothing, in fact, was left unharmed but the round shot which were too heavy to carry off, and which the spiking and dismounting of the guns had made useless. The dawn saw Major Anderson safely established with his com-

MAJOR ANDERSON'S QUARTERS AT FORT SUMTER.

mand in Fort Sumter, secure from immediate attack, though Fort Moultrie was occupied only by a corporal's guard, left there to complete the work of destruction. He saw what a responsibility he had assumed, and fully appreciated the delicacy and the importance of the trust committed to him. Perhaps, if he could have looked forward for three months, and foreseen all the consequences of his act during that period, he would have remained at Fort Moultrie until he was summoned to yield by a force too great for him

to resist, or until he received orders to yield his post. It is well for the country, as well as for his own reputation, that he was tempted into no such speculations, but did to the best of his ability the duty which lay before him. The step which he took proved of more importance to the permanent safety of the republic than any other which he could have determined upon, had he spent months in deliberation, with the astutest politicians of the country as his counselors. A devout man, and impressed with the importance of his position, he was desirous of awakening in his officers and men the same profound sensations which filled his breast. He marked the occupation of their new position with a little religious ceremony. The flag which they were there to defend as a symbol of their nationality and their government was to be raised, and Major Anderson determined that he would raise it himself, and ask the blessing of Heaven upon their endeavor. So at noon of the 27th of December, all under his command, non-combatants as well as combatants, were assembled round the flag-staff. Major Anderson, with the halyards in his hand, knelt at its foot, and the officers and men, impressed with the solemnity of the occasion, needed no orders to assume a reverential position as the chaplain stepped forth in the midst and offered up an earnest prayer—a prayer, says one who was present, which was "such an appeal for support, encouragement, and mercy as one would make who felt that 'man's extremity is God's opportunity.'" After he had ceased, and the earnest Amen from manly lips had died away in the hollow casemates, the commander hauled up the flag, the band saluted it with "Hail Columbia!" the accents of supplication gave way to those of enthusiasm, and cheers broke forth from the lips of all present—cheers which proved to be not only cheers of exultation and confidence, but of defiance; for just then it happened that a boat sent down from Charleston to bring up exact reports of the condition of affairs at Moultrie and Sumter approached the latter fortress, and saw the national standard rise amid the shouts of those who then vowed in their hearts that, while in their hands, it should suffer no dishonor, and who through four weary watchful months and two dreadful days kept well their vow.

In their rage the Charlestonians denounced the President as false to his word and Major Anderson as a wanton provoker of civil war. The accusation against the President was based on his avowed determination not to re-enforce the forts, and on a declaration of four of the representatives of South Carolina—Messrs. John M'Queen, M. L. Bonham, W. W. Boyce, and Lawrence M. Keitt—that it was their "strong conviction that the people of the State of South Carolina would not either attack or molest the forts in Charleston Harbor before negotiating for them, provided no re-enforcements were sent to them, and their relative military status was not disturbed. This declaration was made, and, at the President's suggestion, put in writing on the 9th of December. This mere announcement of intention on the one part and declaration of opinion on the other, the seceders in South Carolina and in Washington, both in and out of the cabinet, chose to regard as a pledge—an obligation binding upon both parties to it. Mr. War Secretary Floyd immediately, on the 27th of December, formally asserted in the cabinet that "the solemn pledges of the government had been violated by Major Anderson," and as formally demanded permission to withdraw the garrison from the harbor of Charleston, as the only alternative by which to vindicate the honor of the government and prevent civil war. Yet this very Secretary of War had, on the 11th of December, two days after the declaration by the four South Carolina delegates, instructed Major Anderson to put his command into either of the forts which he deemed would make it most effective in case he should have tangible evidence of a design on the part of the South Carolinians to proceed to a hostile act, an attempt to take possession of either of the forts being especially indicated.

The effect of Major Anderson's change of position was even greater throughout the country at large than at Charleston. It flashed the gleam of arms upon the eager eyes of the people, and men saw suddenly what before they had only imagined. Those who had felt strongly, and talked earnestly of maintaining the national honor and integrity by the sword, had thought vaguely, and perhaps doubtfully, upon the mode in which this dreadful issue should be brought about. But here it was done without violence, without proclamation, at a word, and in the simplest manner. Major Anderson's movement placed the Charlestonians in the attitude of open enemies of the national government, with whom intercourse was thereafter to be upon a war footing. Unless what he had done was disavowed by the President, and he was ordered to retire from Charleston Harbor, or at least to return to Fort Moultrie, his occupation of Fort Sumter was an official declaration to the seceders that they could accomplish even the first of their purposes only by proving too strong in arms for the military force of the United States. His movement, but not himself, accomplished this. The rebels themselves were alone responsible for the grave significance of the fact; for, as commandant of the harbor, he might house his garrison in whichever of the forts he thought best, and no one, save the head of the War Department, have the right to ask a question. If the transfer of fourscore men from one fort to another meant war, it acquired that meaning only by reason of what had been done and planned in Charleston. So the cry of wrath which went up from the rebel city was answered by a voice of admiration, encouragement, and, above all, of confidence, from almost the entire country outside of South Carolina. Among the very people at the North upon whose sympathy the seceders had most surely counted —even in some of the very states at the South whose fortunes South Carolina believed with reason to be indissolubly linked with hers—the occupation of Fort Sumter was regarded as the most prudent and dignified course which could have been taken under the circumstances. It touched the national honor and awoke the national pride wherever patriotism was superior to local prejudices and class interest. It brought the conviction home to every citizen that he had a country and a government to which, although he himself was part of that government, he owed allegiance and support. The man who thus impressed a nation became the hero of the hour. Major Anderson's name and his praises were upon all lips which did not mutter treason. The most influential journals among those which had opposed the party whose success was made the occasion of the rebellion—even those in the states south of the Potomac and the Ohio—the political leaders of which were not already committed to the conspiracy against the republic, vied with their late political

THE PRAYER AT SUMTER, DEC. 26, 1860.

opponents in approbation of the position which Major Anderson had taken, and in showing how important it was to the self-respect of the nation, to its position before the world, and to its very existence, that he should be sustained by the government at Washington. The sensitive test of the money-market indicated the general feeling, and the price of stocks went up.

The pace of treason, rapid before, was quickened by this movement. On the 27th troops were ordered out in Charleston; military aid was proffered to South Carolina by Georgia and Alabama; and Governor Magoffin, of Kentucky, bent upon secession, called an extra session of the Legislature of that state. On this day, too, the rebels obtained through treachery the first vessel of their navy. The revenue cutter William Aiken was lying in Charleston Harbor, under command of Captain N. L. Coste, of the revenue service. Two weeks before he had told his second in command, Lieutenant Underwood, that he would not serve under Mr. Lincoln as President; and that, in case the expected secession of South Carolina took place, he should resign and place the cutter in command of Lieutenant Underwood. But, in spite of the passage of the Ordinance of Secession, he remained in command, and on the afternoon of the 27th he hauled down the United States revenue flag, raised the Palmetto standard of revolt, and placed his vessel as well as himself at the disposal of the insurgent authorities. His subordinate officers, true to their oaths, reported themselves for duty at Washington. This trifling incident is worthy of notice at the beginning of our sad story, as indicative of the violation of individual trust which marked this stage of the insurrection.

On the 28th the authorities of Charleston determined to assert their newly-assumed powers to the extent of their ability. They seized the custom-house, the post-office, and on the 30th the arsenal, and raised the state flag upon them, and sent an armed force to occupy Fort Moultrie and Castle Pinckney. The few soldiers at each of those fortifications yielded, of course, without any resistance, and on those walls also the palmetto-tree replaced the stars and stripes.

The President having refused to withdraw the garrison from Charleston Harbor, on the 29th the Secretary of War, Mr. Floyd, resigned his office, closing his resignation with these words: "I deeply regret that I feel myself under the necessity of tendering to you my resignation as Secretary of War, because I can no longer hold it under my convictions of patriotism, nor with honor, subjected as I am to a violation of solemn pledges and plighted faith." These fair phrases sounded well at the end of such a letter; but the truth was that, in consequence of Mr. Floyd's connection with the Indian Trust Fund fraud, for which he was afterward indicted, the President had intimated to him, through a distinguished statesman, that he deemed it improper that he should longer remain a member of the cabinet. On the twenty-ninth of December, also, the commissioners from South Carolina formally addressed the President, laid their authority before him, sent him an official copy of the Ordinance of Secession, and expressed a desire for such negotiation as would secure mutual respect, general advantage, and a future good-will and harmony; but added that, as Major Anderson, by dismantling one fort and occupying another, had made important changes in the affairs in relation to which they had come

H

to Washington, they were obliged to suspend all discussion until the movement which they referred to had been satisfactorily explained. They styled the retention of the government troops in Charleston Harbor a standing menace which rendered negotiation impossible, and urged their immediate withdrawal. Mr. Buchanan refused to receive them in an official capacity, but on the 30th replied to their letter. He denied that he, or his Secretary of War by his order, had given any pledge in regard to the garrison of Fort Moultrie, referred the commissioners to a memorandum of the instructions sent by Mr. Floyd to Major Anderson, and positively refused to withdraw the troops from Charleston Harbor; adding, "Such an idea was never thought of by me in any possible contingency." To the President's letter the commissioners the next day sent a rejoinder, polite in terms but so insulting in its implications, and so arrogant and insolent in its tone, that it was returned to them with the indorsement, "This paper, just presented to the President, is of such a character that he declines to receive it," and on the 5th of January they went home, having accomplished nothing.[1]

[1] *Correspondence between the South Carolina Commissioners and the President of the United States.*

Washington, December 29, 1860.

SIR,—We have the honor to transmit to you a copy of the full powers from the Convention of the people of South Carolina, under which we are "authorized and empowered to treat with the government of the United States for the delivery of the forts, magazines, light-houses, and other real estate, with their appurtenances, in the limits of South Carolina; and also for an apportionment of the public debt, and for a division of all other property held by the government of the United States, as agent of the Confederated States, of which South Carolina was recently a member, and generally to negotiate as to all other measures and arrangements proper to be made and adopted in the existing relation of the parties, and for the continuance of peace and amity between this commonwealth and the government at Washington."

In the execution of this trust, it is our duty to furnish you, as we now do, with an official copy of the Ordinance of Secession, by which the State of South Carolina has resumed the powers she delegated to the government of the United States, and has declared her perfect sovereignty and independence.

It would also have been our duty to have informed you that we were ready to negotiate with you upon all such questions as are necessarily raised by the adoption of this ordinance, and that we were prepared to enter upon this negotiation, with the earnest desire to avoid all unnecessary and hostile collision, and so to inaugurate our new relations as to secure mutual respect, general advantage, and a future of good-will and harmony, beneficial to all the parties concerned.

But the events of the last twenty-four hours render such an assurance impossible. We came here the representatives of an authority which could, at any time within the past sixty days, have taken possession of the forts in Charleston Harbor, but which, upon pledges given in a manner that we can not doubt, determined to trust to your honor rather than to its own power. Since our arrival here an officer of the United States, acting, as we are assured, not only without, but against your orders, has dismantled one fort and occupied another, thus altering to a most important extent the condition of affairs under which we came.

Until these circumstances are explained in a manner which relieves us of all doubt as to the spirit in which these negotiations shall be conducted, we are forced to suspend all discussion as to any arrangement by which our mutual interests may be amicably adjusted.

And, in conclusion, we would urge upon you the immediate withdrawal of the troops from the harbor of Charleston. Under present circumstances, they are a standing menace which renders negotiation impossible, and, as our recent experience shows, threatens speedily to bring to a bloody issue questions which ought to be settled with temperance and judgment. We have the honor to be, very respectfully, your obedient servants,

R. W. BARNWELL,
J. H. ADAMS, Commissioners.
JAS. L. ORR,

To the President of the United States.

The President's Reply.

Washington City, Dec. 30, 1860.

GENTLEMEN,—I have had the honor to receive your communication of 28th inst., together with a copy of "your full powers from the Convention of the people of South Carolina," authorizing you to treat with the government of the United States on various important subjects therein mentioned, and also a copy of the ordinance, bearing date on the 20th inst., declaring that "the union now subsisting between South Carolina and other states, under the name of the United States of America, is hereby dissolved."

In answer to this communication, I have to say that my position as President of the United States was clearly defined in the message to Congress on the 3d inst. In that I stated that, "apart from the execution of the laws, so far as this may be practicable, the executive has no authority to decide what shall be the relations between the federal government and South Carolina. He has been invested with no such discretion. He possesses no power to change the relations hitherto existing between them, much less to acknowledge the independence of that state. This would be to invest a mere executive officer with the power of recognizing the dissolution of the confederacy among our thirty-three sovereign states. It bears no resemblance to the recognition of a foreign *de facto* government, involving no such responsibility. Any attempt to do this would, on his part, be a naked act of usurpation. It is, therefore, my duty to submit to Congress the whole question in all its bearings."

Such is my opinion still. I could, therefore, meet you only as private gentlemen of the highest character, and was entirely willing to communicate to Congress any proposition you might have to make to that body upon the subject. Of this you were well aware. It was my earnest desire that such a disposition might be made of the whole subject by Congress, who alone possess the power, as to prevent the inauguration of a civil war between the parties in regard to the possession of the federal forts in the harbor of Charleston; and I, therefore, deeply regret that, in your opinion, "the events of the last twenty-four hours render this impossible." In conclusion, you urge upon me "the immediate withdrawal of the troops from the harbor of Charleston," stating that "under present circumstances, they are a standing menace, which renders negotiation impossible, and, as our recent experience shows, threatens speedily to bring to a bloody issue questions which ought to be settled with temperance and judgment."

The reason for this change in your position is, that since your arrival in Washington, "an officer of the United States, acting, as we (you) are assured, not only without, but against your (my) orders, has dismantled one fort and occupied another, thus altering to a most important extent the condition of affairs under which we (you) came." You also allege that you came here "the representatives of an authority which could, at any time within the past sixty days, have taken possession of the forts in Charleston Harbor, but which, upon pledges given in a manner that we (you) can not doubt, determined to trust to your (my) honor rather than to its power."

This brings me to a consideration of the nature of those alleged pledges, and in what manner they have been observed. In my message of the 3d of December last, I stated, in regard to the property of the United States in South Carolina, that it "has been purchased for a fair equivalent, by the consent of the Legislature of the state, for the erection of forts, magazines, arsenals, etc., and over these the authority 'to exercise exclusive legislation' has been expressly granted by the Constitution to Congress. It is not believed that any attempt will be made to expel the United States from this property by force; but if in this I should prove to be mistaken, the officer in command of the forts has received orders to act strictly on the defensive. In such a contingency the responsibility for consequences would rightfully rest upon the heads of the assailants." This being the condition of the parties, on Saturday, 8th December, four of the representatives from South Carolina called upon me and requested an interview. We had an earnest conversation on the subject of these forts, and the best means of preventing a collision between the parties, for the purpose of sparing the effusion of blood. I suggested, for prudential reasons, that it would be best to put in writing what they said to me verbally. They did so accordingly, and on Monday morning, the 10th instant, three of them presented to me a paper signed by all the representatives from South Carolina, with a single exception, of which the following is a copy:

To his Excellency James Buchanan, President of the United States:

In compliance with our statement to you yesterday, we now express to you our strong convictions that neither the constituted authorities, nor any body of the people of the State of South Carolina, will either attack or molest the United States forts in the harbor of Charleston previously to the act of the Convention, and we hope and believe not until an offer has been made, through an accredited representative, to negotiate for an amicable arrangement of all matters between the state and the federal government, provided that no re-enforcements shall be sent into these forts, and their relative military status shall remain as at present.

JOHN M'QUEEN,
M. L. BONHAM,
W. W. BOYCE,
LAWRENCE M. KEITT.

Washington, Dec. 9, 1860.

And here I must, in justice to myself, remark, that at the time the paper was presented to me, I objected to the word "provided," as it might be construed into an agreement on my part, which I never would make. They said that nothing was farther from their intention—they did not so understand it, and I should not so consider it. It is evident they could enter into no reciprocal agreement with me on the subject. They did not profess to have authority to do this, and were acting in their individual character. I considered it as nothing more, in effect, than the promise of highly honorable gentlemen to exert their influence for the purpose expressed. The event has proven that they have faithfully kept this promise, although I have never since received a line from any one of them, or from any member of the Convention on the subject. It is well known that it was my determination, and this I freely expressed, not to re-enforce the forts in the harbor, and thus produce a collision, until they had been actually attacked, or until I had certain evidence that they were about to be attacked. This paper I received most cordially, and considered it as a happy omen that peace might be still preserved, and that time might be thus given for reflection. This is the whole foundation for the alleged pledge.

But I acted in the same manner as I would have done had I entered into a positive and formal agreement with parties capable of contracting, although such an agreement would have been on my part, from the nature of my official duties, impossible. The world knows that I have never sent any re-enforcements to the forts in Charleston Harbor, and I have certainly never authorized any change to be made "in their relative military status." Bearing upon this subject, I refer you to an order issued by the Secretary of War, on the 11th instant, to Major Anderson, but not brought to my notice until the 21st instant. It is as follows:

Memorandum of Verbal Instructions to Major Anderson, First Artillery, commanding Fort Moultrie, South Carolina.

You are aware of the great anxiety of the Secretary of War that a collision of the troops with the people of this state shall be avoided, and of his studied determination to pursue a course with reference to the military force and forts in this harbor which shall guard against such a collision. He has, therefore, carefully abstained from increasing the force at this point, or taking any measures which might add to the present excited state of the public mind, or which would throw any doubt on the confidence he feels that South Carolina will not attempt by violence to obtain possession of the public works, or interfere with their occupancy.

But as the counsel and acts of rash and impulsive persons may possibly disappoint these expectations of the government, he deems it proper that you should be prepared with instructions to meet so unhappy a contingency. He has therefore directed me, verbally, to give you such instructions.

You are carefully to avoid every act which would needlessly tend to provoke aggression, and for that reason you are not, without necessity, to take up any position which could be construed into the assumption of a hostile attitude; but *you are to hold possession of the forts in the harbor, and if attacked, you are to defend yourself to the last extremity.* The smallness of your force will not permit you, perhaps, to occupy more than one of the three forts; but an attack on, or attempt to take possession of either of them, will be regarded as an act of hostility, and you may then put your command into either of them which you may deem most proper to increase its power of resistance. *You are also authorized to take similar steps whenever you have tangible evidence of a design to proceed to a hostile act.* D. P. BUTLER, Assistant Adjutant General.

Fort Moultrie, S. C., Dec. 11, 1860.

This is in conformity to my instructions to Major Buell.

JOHN B. FLOYD, Secretary of War.

These were the last instructions transmitted to Major Anderson before his removal to Fort Sumter, with a single exception, in regard to a particular which does not in any degree affect the present question. Under these circumstances, it is clear that Major Anderson acted upon his own responsibility, and without authority, unless, indeed, he had "tangible evidence of a design to proceed to a hostile act" on the part of South Carolina, which has not yet been alleged. Still he is a brave and honorable officer, and justice requires that he should not be condemned without a fair hearing.

Be this as it may, when I learned that Major Anderson had left Fort Moultrie and proceeded to Fort Sumter, my first promptings were to command him to return to his former position, and there to await the contingencies presented in his instructions. This would only have been done with any degree of safety to the command by the concurrence of the South Carolina authorities. But before any step could possibly have been taken in this direction, we received information that the "Palmetto flag floated out to the breeze at Castle Pinckney, and a large military force went over last night (the 27th) to Fort Moultrie." Thus the authorities of South Carolina, without waiting or asking for any explanations, and doubtless believing, as you have expressed it, that the officer had acted not only without, but against my orders, on the very next day after the night when the removal was made, seized by a military force two of the federal forts in the harbor of Charleston, and have covered them under their own flag instead of that of the United States.

At this gloomy period of our history, startling events succeed each other rapidly. On the very day, the 27th instant, that possession of these two forts was taken, the Palmetto flag was raised over the federal custom-house and post-office in Charleston, and on the same day every officer of the customs—collector, naval officer, surveyor, and appraiser—resigned their offices; and this, although it was well known from the language of my message that, as an executive officer, I felt myself bound to collect the revenue at the port of Charleston under the existing laws. In the harbor of Charleston we now find three forts confronting each other, over all of which the federal flag floated only four days ago; but now, over two of them, this flag has been supplanted, and the Palmetto flag has been substituted in its stead. It is under all these circumstances that I am urged immediately to withdraw the troops from the harbor of Charleston, and am informed that without this negotiation is impossible. This I can not do; this I will not do. Such an idea was never thought of by me in any possible contingency. No such allusion had been made in any communication between myself and any human being. But the inference is that I am bound to withdraw the troops from the only fort remaining in the possession of the United States in the harbor of Charleston, because the officer there in command of all of the forts thought proper, without instructions, to change his position from one of them to another.

At this point of writing, I have received information by telegraph from Captain Humphreys, in command of the arsenal at Charleston, that "it has to-day (Sunday, the 30th) been taken by force of arms." It is estimated that the munitions of war belonging to this arsenal are worth half a million of dollars.

Comment is needless. After this information, I have only to add, that while it is my duty to defend Fort Sumter, as a portion of the public property of the United States, against hostile attacks, from whatever quarter they may come, by such means as I possess for this purpose, I do not perceive how such a defense can be construed into a menace against the city of Charleston. With great personal regard, I remain yours very respectfully, JAMES BUCHANAN.

To Hon. Robert W. Barnwell, James H. Adams, James L. Orr.

Second Letter of the Commissioners to the President.

Washington, D. C., Jan. 1, 1861.

SIR,—We have the honor to acknowledge the receipt of your letter of the 30th December, in reply to a note addressed by us to you, on the 28th of the same month, as commissioners from South Carolina.

In reference to the declaration with which your reply commences, that your "position as President of the United States was already defined in the message to Congress of the 3d instant;" that you possess "no power to change the relations heretofore existing between South Carolina and the United States," "much less to acknowledge the independence of that state," and that consequently you could meet us only as private gentlemen of the highest character, with an entire willingness to communicate to Congress any proposition we might have to make, we deem it only necessary to say that the State of South Carolina having, in the exercise of that great right of self-government which underlies all our political organizations, declared herself sovereign and independent, we, as her representatives, felt no special solicitude as to the character in which you might recognize us. Satisfied that the state had simply exercised her unquestionable right, we were prepared, in order to reach substantial good, to waive the formal considerations which your constitutional scruples might have prevented you from extending. We came here, therefore, expecting to be received as you did receive us, and perfectly content with that entire willingness of which you assured us, to submit any proposition to Congress which we might have to make upon the subject of the independence of the state. The willingness was ample recognition of the condition of public affairs which rendered our presence necessary. In this position, however, it is our duty, both to the state which we represent and to ourselves, to correct several important misconceptions of our letter into which you have fallen.

You say, "It was my earnest desire that such a disposition might be made of the whole subject by Congress, who alone possess the power, as to prevent the inauguration of a civil war between the parties in regard to the possession of the federal forts in the harbor of Charleston; and I therefore deeply regret that in your opinion the events of the last twenty-four hours render this impossible." We expressed no such opinion; and the language which you quote as ours is altered in its sense by the omission of a most important part of the sentence. What we did say was, "But the events of the last twenty-four hours render such an assurance impossible." Place that "assurance," as contained in our letter, in the sentence, and we are prepared to repeat it.

Again, professing to quote our language, you say, "Thus the authorities of South Carolina, without waiting or asking for any explanation, and doubtless believing, as you have expressed it, that the officer had acted not only without, but against my orders," etc. We expressed no such

From the time of Major Anderson's transfer of his command, Washington had been in a state of deplorable and even disgraceful excitement. The delegates from the states which were ripe for revolt, but which had not seceded, retained their seats in Congress, and by their open threats and secret intrigues increased the alarm of the country, and crippled the feeble and already bewildered administration. They sat in the chairs to which they were sent for the support of the Constitution of the United States and contrived its overthrow; they lived in Washington upon the pay of the republic while they plotted its destruction; they held their positions only for the purpose of insuring the success of their conspiracy—only that they might counterbalance the votes of loyal men, and keep at dead-lock all the essential functions of the government. These are no general phrases, no vague deductions. The records of treacherous conspiracy show no page more infamous than that written by Senator Yulee, of Florida, in a letter to one of his constituents, in which he revealed the counsels of his fellow-conspirators, the senators of six states, and said that they had all determined to retain their places in the councils of the nation with the deliberate purpose of keeping Mr. Buchanan's hands tied, and depriving Mr. Lincoln, on his accession to office, of the legitimate powers of government. That not the smallest item might be lacking to the sum of its shame and the perfection of its perfidy, this letter was secured a swift and free passage to its destination under the Honorable writer's senatorial frank.[2] While such was the direct course of secret machination, open counsel went darkly groping. In both houses the debates were vague, wordy, colloquial, and from the

purpose. Abstract points were discussed sometimes with acrimony, at others jocosely; but no decisive action was proposed for the maintenance of the authority of the government and the integrity of the republic. The small minority who were already rebels at heart and in purpose, if not in act, were defiant and overbearing; their opponents sought only to pacify and restrain them by proffered concessions; and between these two was a considerable number who waited and watched to trim their course according to the current. On the 27th, in the House Committee of Thirty-three upon the State of the Union, Mr. Adams, of Massachusetts, proposed a resolution, " That it is expedient to propose an amendment to the Constitution to the effect that no future amendments of it in regard to slavery shall be made, unless proposed by a slave state and ratified by all the states." This resolution was passed with only three dissenting voices. Coming from a representative of Massachusetts, and proposing terms which would put the question of slavery in the states absolutely and forever out of the reach of the free states, no matter how greatly in the majority, and thus removing the ground of that apprehension for the future which was made the excuse of secession, this resolution might have been the first step toward the much-sought compromise. It was regarded with favor by many delegates from slave states; and after a free conference between all the members of the committee, even Mr. Cobb, of Alabama, declared that the question at issue might now be settled. It might, indeed, had not the politicians of South Carolina, and those of other states, but of their school, been bent upon attaining their purpose, in or out of the Union, by defiance

opinion in reference to the belief of the people of South Carolina. The language which you have quoted was applied solely and entirely to our assurances obtained here, and based, as you well know, upon your own declaration—a declaration which, at that time, it was impossible for the authorities of South Carolina to have known. But, without following this letter into all its details, we propose only to meet the chief points of the argument.

Some weeks ago the State of South Carolina declared her intention, in the existing condition of public affairs, to secede from the United States. She called a convention of her people to put her declaration in force. The Convention met and passed the Ordinance of Secession. All this you anticipated, and your course of action was thoroughly considered in your Annual Message. You declared you had no right, and would not attempt, to coerce a seceding state, but that you were bound by your constitutional oath, and would defend the property of the United States within the borders of South Carolina if an attempt was made to take it by force. Seeing very early that this question of property was a difficult and delicate one, you manifested a desire to settle it without collision. You did not re-enforce the garrison in the harbor of Charleston. You removed a distinguished and veteran officer from the command of Fort Moultrie because he attempted to increase his supply of ammunition. You refused to send additional troops to the same garrison when applied for by the officer appointed to succeed him. You accepted the resignation of the oldest and most eminent member of your cabinet rather than allow the garrison to be strengthened. You compelled an officer stationed at Fort Sumter to return immediately to the arsenal forty muskets which he had taken to arm his men. You expressed not to one, but to many, of the most distinguished of our public characters, whose testimony will be placed upon the record whenever it is necessary, your anxiety for a peaceful termination of this controversy, and your willingness not to disturb the military status of the forts, if commissioners should be sent to the government, whose communications you promised to submit to Congress. You received and acted on assurances from the highest official authorities of South Carolina, that no attempt would be made to disturb your possession of the forts and property of the United States, if you would not disturb their existing condition until the commissioners had been sent, and the attempt to negotiate had failed. You took from the members of the House of Representatives a written memorandum that no such attempt should be made, " provided that no re-enforcements should be sent into those forts, and their relative military status shall remain as at present." And although you attach no force to the acceptance of such a paper—although you " considered it as nothing more in effect than the promise of highly honorable gentlemen"—as an obligation on one side, without corresponding obligation on the other—it must be remembered (if we were rightly informed) that you were pledged, if you ever did send re-enforcements, to return it to those from whom you had received it, before you executed your resolution. You sent orders to your officers, commanding them strictly to follow a line of conduct in conformity with such an understanding. Besides all this, you had received formal and official notice from the Governor of South Carolina that we had been appointed commissioners, and were on our way to Washington. You knew the implied condition under which we came; our arrival was notified to you, and an hour appointed for an interview. We arrived in Washington on Wednesday, at 3 o'clock, and you appointed an interview with us at 1 the next day. Early on that day (Thursday) the news was received here of the movement of Major Anderson. That news was communicated to you immediately, and you postponed our meeting until 2½ o'clock on Friday, in order that you might consult your cabinet. On Friday we saw you, and we called upon you then to redeem your pledge. You could not deny it. With the facts we have stated, and in the face of the crowning and conclusive fact that your Secretary of War had resigned his seat in the cabinet, upon the publicly avowed ground that the action of Major Anderson had violated the pledged faith of the government, and that, unless the pledge was instantly redeemed, he was dishonored, denial was impossible; you did not deny it. You do not deny it now, but you seek to escape from its obligation on the grounds, first, that we terminated all negotiation by demanding, as a preliminary, the withdrawal of the United States troops from the harbor of Charleston; and, second, that the authorities of South Carolina, instead of asking explanation, and giving you the opportunity to vindicate yourself, took possession of other property of the United States. We will examine both.

In the first place, we deny positively that we have ever in any way made any such demand. Our letter is in your possession; it will stand by this on record. In it we informed you of the objects of our mission. We say that it would have been our duty to have assured you of our readiness to commence negotiations with the most earnest and anxious desire to settle all questions between us amicably and to our mutual advantage, but that events had rendered that assurance impossible. We stated the events, and we said that until some satisfactory explanation of these events was given us, we could not proceed; and then, having made this request for explanation, we added, " And in conclusion we would urge upon you the immediate withdrawal of the troops from the harbor of Charleston. Under present circumstances they are a standing menace, which renders negotiation impossible," etc. " Under present circumstances!" What circumstances? Why, clearly the occupation of Fort Sumter and the dismantling of Fort Moultrie by Major Anderson, in the face of your pledges, and without explanation or practical disavowal. And there is nothing in the letter which would, or could, have prevented you from declining to withdraw the troops, and offering the restoration of the status to which you were pledged, if such had been your desire. It would have been wiser and better, in our opinion, to have withdrawn the troops, and this opinion we urged upon you; but we demanded nothing but such an explanation of the events of the last twenty-four hours as would restore our confidence in the spirit with which the negotiations should be conducted. In relation to this withdrawal of the troops from the harbor, we are compelled, however, to notice one passage of your letter. Referring to it, you say, " This I can not do; this I will not do. Such an idea was never thought of by me in any possible contingency. No allusion to it had ever been made in any communication between myself and any human being."

In reply to this statement, we are compelled to say, that your conversation with us left upon our minds the distinct impression that you did seriously contemplate the withdrawal of the troops from Charleston Harbor. And in support of this impression, we would add, that we have the positive assurance of gentlemen of the highest possible public reputation and the most unsullied integrity—men whose name and fame, secured by long service and patriotic achievements, place their testimony beyond cavil—that such suggestions had been made to and urged upon you by them, and had formed the subject of more than one earnest discussion with you. And it was this knowledge that induced us to urge upon you a policy which had to recommend it its own wisdom and the might of such authority. As to the second point, that the authorities of South Carolina, instead of asking explanations, and giving you the opportunity to vindicate yourself, took possession of other property of the United States, we would observe: 1. That even if this were so, it does not avail you for defense, for the opportunity for decision was afforded you before these facts occurred. We arrived in Washington on Wednesday; the news from Major Anderson reached here early on Thursday, and was immediately communicated to you. All that day men of the highest consideration—men who had striven successfully to lift you to your great office—who had been your tried and true friends through the troubles of your administration, sought you and entreated you to act—to act at once. They told you that every hour complicated your position. They only asked you to give the assurance that if the facts were so—that if the commander

had acted without and against your orders—and in violation of your pledges—that you would restore the status you had pledged your honor to maintain. You refused to decide. Your Secretary at War, your immediate and proper adviser in this whole matter, waited anxiously for your decision, until he felt that delay was becoming dishonor. More than twelve hours passed, and two cabinet meetings had adjourned, before you knew what the authorities of South Carolina had done; and your prompt decision at any moment of that time would have avoided the subsequent complications. But, if you had known the acts of the authorities of South Carolina, should that have prevented your keeping your faith? What was the condition of things? For the last sixty days you have had in Charleston Harbor not force enough to hold the forts against an equal enemy. Two of them were empty—one of those two the most important in the harbor. It could have been taken at any time. You ought to know better than any man that it would have been taken but for the efforts of those who put their trust in your honor. Believing that they were threatened by Fort Sumter especially, the people were with difficulty restrained from securing, without blood, the possession of this important fortress. After many and reiterated assurances, given on your behalf, which we can not believe unauthorized, they determined to forbear, and in good faith sent on their commissioners to negotiate with you. They meant you no harm—wished you no ill. They thought of you kindly, believed you true, and were willing, as far as was consistent with duty, to spare you unnecessary and hostile collision. Scarcely had these commissioners left than Major Anderson waged war. No other words will describe his action. It was not a peaceful change from one fort to another; it was a hostile act in the highest sense, and only justified in the presence of a superior enemy, and in imminent peril. He abandoned his position, spiked his guns, burned his gun-carriages, made preparations for the destruction of his post, and withdrew, under cover of the night, to a safer position. This was war. No man could have believed (without your assurance) that any officer could have taken such a step, " not only without orders, but against orders." What the state did was in simple self-defense; for this act, with all its attending circumstances, was as much war as firing a volley; and war being thus begun, until those commencing it explained their action and disavowed their intention, there was no room for delay; and even at this moment while we are writing, it is more than probable, from the tenor of your letter, that re-enforcements are hurrying on to the conflict, so that when the first gun shall be fired, there will have been on your part one continuous, consistent series of actions, commencing in a demonstration essentially warlike, supported by regular re-enforcements, and terminating in defeat or victory. And all this without the slightest provocation; for, among the many things which you have said, there is one thing you can not say—you have waited anxiously for news from the seat of war, in hopes that delay would furnish some excuse for this precipitation. But this " tangible evidence of a design to proceed to a hostile act, on the part of the authorities of South Carolina," which is the only justification of Major Anderson you are forced to admit, " has not yet been alleged." But you have decided, you have resolved to hold, by force, what you have obtained through our misplaced confidence; and by refusing to disavow the action of Major Anderson, have converted his violation of orders into a legitimate act of your executive authority. Be the issue what it may, of this we are assured, that, if Fort Moultrie has been recorded in history as a memorial of Carolina gallantry, Fort Sumter will live upon the succeeding page as an imperishable testimony of Carolina faith.

By your course you have probably rendered civil war inevitable. Be it so. If you choose to force this issue upon us, the State of South Carolina will accept it, and, relying upon Him who is the God of Justice as well as the God of Hosts, will endeavor to perform the great duty which lies before her hopefully, bravely, and thoroughly.

Our mission being one for negotiation and peace, and your note leaving us without hope of a withdrawal of the troops from Fort Sumter, or of the restoration of the status quo existing at the time of our arrival, and intimating, as we think, your determination to re-enforce the garrison in the harbor of Charleston, we respectfully inform you that we purpose returning to Charleston to-morrow afternoon.

We have the honor to be, sir, very respectfully, your obedient servants,

R. W. BARNWELL, ⎫
J. H. ADAMS, ⎬ Commissioners.
JAMES L. ORR, ⎭

To his Excellency the President of the United States.

The following is the indorsement upon the document:

Executive Mansion, 3½ o'clock, Wednesday.

This paper, just presented to the President, is of such a character that he declines to receive it.

[2] The original of this letter was found by the correspondent of the New York Times among some papers which fell into the hands of the United States forces upon their sudden occupation of Fernandina, Florida. It is here (p. 32) reproduced in fac-simile. The resolutions to which it refers were not distinguished in any way from the rest of the rebellious resolves of the period.

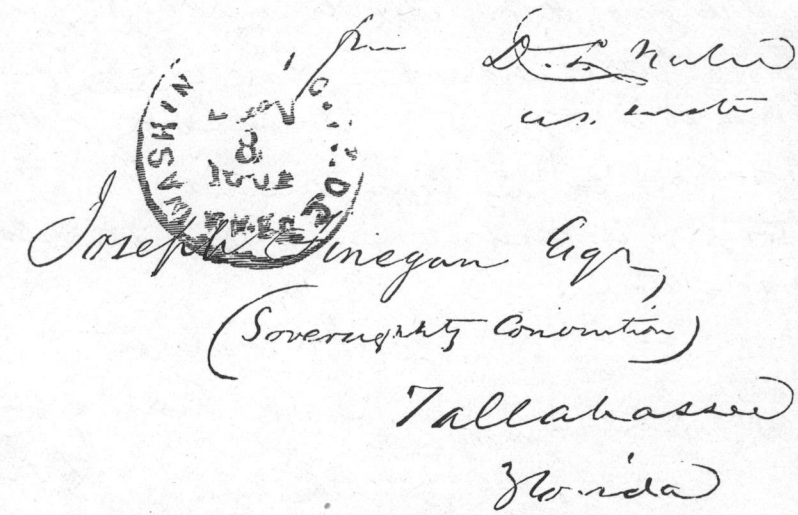

FAC-SIMILE OF THE SUPERSCRIPTION AND FRANK OF THE LETTER.

of the government and disruption of the republic. With these men secession was a foregone conclusion, and delay and vacillation on the part of the supporters of the government only aided the accomplishment of their designs. This was made plain on the 31st by Senator Benjamin, of Louisiana, a state which had not yet taken even the preliminary steps to secession. In a speech meant both as a threat and a valedictory, he announced to the Senate that during the next week Mississippi, Alabama, and Florida would separate from the Union; that a week after Georgia would follow them, to be followed shortly by Louisiana and Arkansas. He declared that the day of adjustment was past, and that when the members of that body parted, they would part to meet again as senators in one common council-chamber of the nation no more forever; and, announcing it as his belief that there could not be peaceable secession, he defied the attempt to subdue the revolted people to the authority of the Constitution. Couching this defiance in the phraseology adopted by the conspirators, he closed his speech with these words: "What may be the fate of this horrible contest none can foretell; but this much I will say—the fortunes of war may be adverse to our arms; you may carry desolation into our peaceful land, and with torch and firebrand may set our cities in flames; you may even emulate the atrocities of those who in the days of our Revolution hounded on the bloodthirsty savage; you may give the protection of your advancing armies to the furious fanatics who desire nothing more than to add the horrors of servile insurrection to civil war; you may do this and more, but you never can subjugate us; you never can subjugate the free sons of the soil into vassals paying tribute to your power; you can never degrade them into a servile and inferior race—never, never, never!"

This burst of bombastic prophesying, in which, with equal reason, vindictiveness was assumed as the motive, ruthlessness as the means, and servile subjection as the end in view of those who insisted that all should submit to the Constitution which all had adopted, and all obey the laws which all had had a voice in framing, was received with an uproar of applause in the galleries, which were filled with the sympathizers with disunion, who swarmed then in Washington and for a long time afterward. The outcries and confusion were so disgraceful, that even Mr. Benjamin's friends on the floor of the chamber were ashamed, and Mr. Mason, of Virginia, moved the clearing of the galleries, and the Senate immediately adjourned. Thus the people of the United States saw the year close upon them in turmoil, gloom, distress, and weakness, which had opened upon them united, happy, prosperous, and powerful.

With the beginning of a new year a new attitude was assumed at Washington. President Buchanan, no longer daring to stand before the country as an accomplice by default in the conspiracy against the republic, at last made some show of an attempt to preserve the existence and exert the power of the government of which he was the head. It was high time for him to do so. The purposes of the conspirators developed themselves rapidly; and it became clear that they aimed not only at secession, but at usurpation, by the occupation of the national capital, the possession of the archives, and the consequent recognition of their faction as the government of the United States, to the exclusion of the free states, except such as it should suit them to admit to a share of their stolen privileges.[3] And it should be always remembered that they labored constantly under the supposition, at first not entirely unfounded, that there was a large, if not a controlling party in the free states who looked with favor upon their movement, and who would give to them a moral, and perhaps a material, support. They threatened that the President elect should never be inaugurated; and some of them even went so far as to avow a belief that they would be able to reconstruct the Union in their interest, with the omission of the New England states. That they were grievously in error, all their fellow-citizens, except their Northern accomplices, knew in their inmost hearts; but few then knew how deeply that feeling was rooted, and how strongly nourished, which they supposed would wither away in the first heat of adversity; and in forming the plan of a new republic, from which New England should be excluded, they must have left out of their calculation the significant fact that New England had mostly peopled the Northern states, and had entirely given them their moral tone and intellectual character. Such, however, were their plans; and Mr. Buchanan found that it was no longer safe for him to fail to interpose such checks upon their execution as a decent regard for the duties of his high office demanded. Lieutenant General Scott was called into consultation with the cabinet, in which General John A. Dix had replaced Mr. Cobb, and Postmaster General Holt, an able, patriotic, and honorable Democrat, had been charged with the functions of the War office. Measures were taken for the military protection of the capital by the organization of the militia of the District, and the concentration of a few regular companies of artillery; and means were sought of increasing the garrisons of the principal forts in the slave states, and particularly those in the harbor of Charleston. But for the latter object the time had long passed, and even for the former it proved to be almost too late. The steam frigate Brooklyn, just arrived at Norfolk navy yard after a three years' cruise, was almost the only national ship of any consequence manned and equipped, and within reach of the government. She was ordered not to discharge her crew, and to remain in readiness to sail with a smaller vessel at an hour's notice. The purposes of the government got wind immediately, and reached the ears of the secessionists. At Norfolk they prepared to seize the ships should they attempt to sail; at Charleston they removed the buoys, obstructed the channel, and left the light-house darkling. The enterprise was abandoned. But the defense of Washington, and the measures necessary to insure the inauguration of Mr. Lincoln, went on as rapidly as possible, under the eye of Captain Charles Stone, of the Ordnance corps, to whom, at General Scott's recommendation, was committed the organization of the District militia, which, though not numerous, was thought sufficient for the emergency. A company of marines was sent to Fort Washington, fourteen miles below the capital, on the Potomac, and the

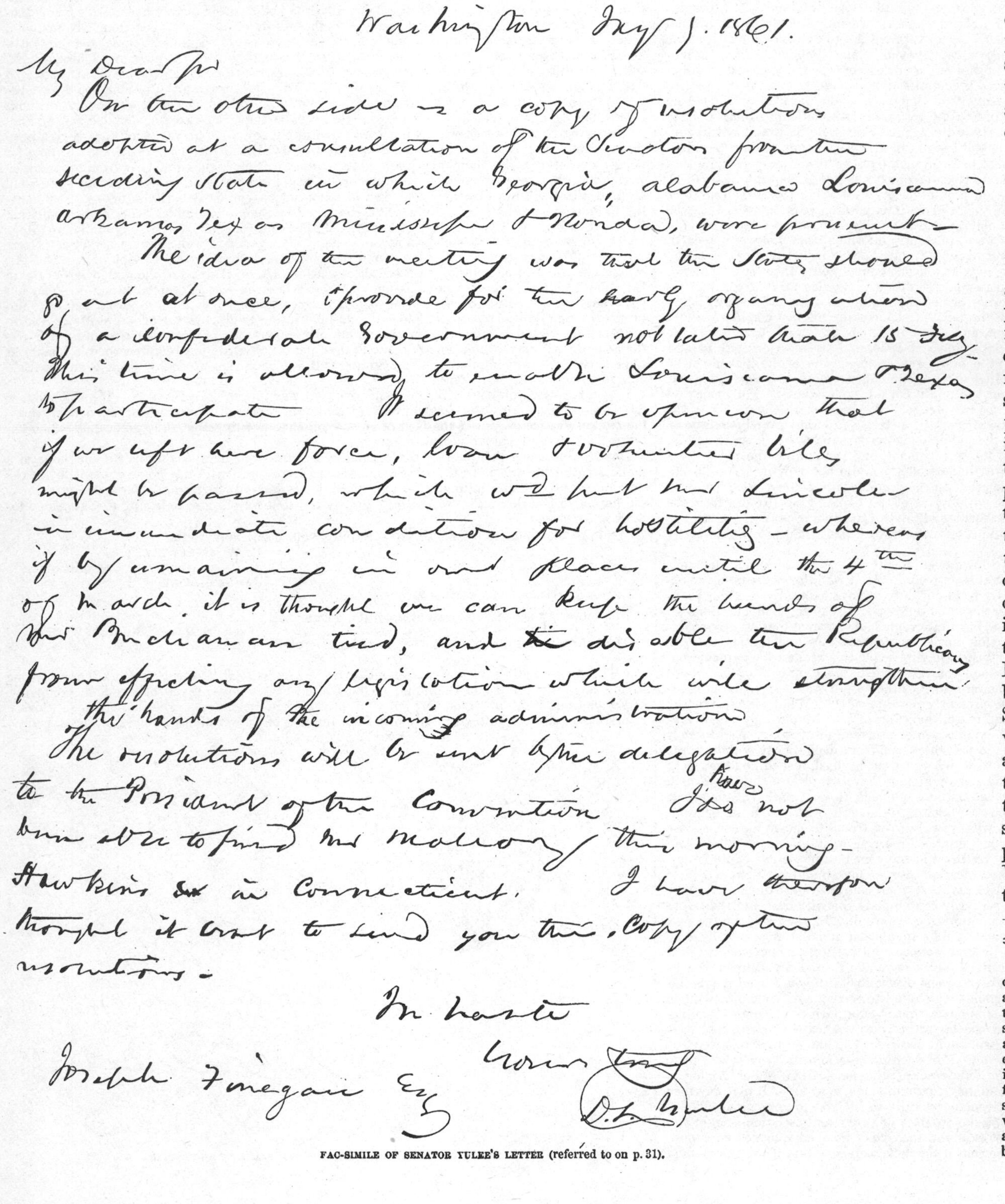

Washington Jany 1. 1861.

My Dear Sir

On the other side is a copy of resolutions adopted at a consultation of the Senators from the seceding States in which Georgia, Alabama, Louisiana, Arkansas, Texas, Mississippi & Florida, were present.

The idea of the meeting was that the States should go out at once, & provide for the early organization of a Confederate Government not later than 15 Feby. This time is allowed to enable Louisiana & Texas to participate. It seemed to be & will of force, loan & volunteer bills might be passed, which would put Mr Lincoln in immediate condition for hostilities—whereas if by remaining in our places until the 4th of March, it is thought we can keep the hands of Mr Buchanan tied, and disable the Republicans from effecting any legislation which will strengthen the hands of the incoming administration.

The resolutions will be sent by the delegation to the President of the Convention. I have not been able to find Mr Mallory this morning—Hawkins is in Connecticut. I have therefore thought it best to send you this copy of the resolutions—

In haste

Yours truly
D. L. Yulee

Joseph Finegan Esq

FAC-SIMILE OF SENATOR YULEE'S LETTER (referred to on p. 31).

[3] From the *Charleston Courier*, *Feb. 12th*, 1861.

"The South *might*, after uniting, under a new confederacy, treat the disorganized and demoralized Northern states as *insurgents*, and deny them recognition. But if peaceful division ensues, the South, after taking the federal capital and archives, and being recognized by all foreign powers as the government *de facto*, can, if they see proper, recognize the Northern confederacy or confederacies, and enter into treaty stipulations with them. Were this not done, it would be difficult for the Northern states to take a place among nations, and their flag would not be respected or recognized."

THE UNITED STATES SLOOP OF WAR "BROOKLYN."

volunteer military companies of Washington were paraded, inspected, and furnished with ball cartridges.

General Scott, to whom, for services in peace and war, his country owed more than to any other living man, devoted himself to meeting the military demands of a crisis which he had foreseen, and for which, if his counsels had been regarded, the government would have been fully prepared. There is no doubt of this, sad as it is to believe that all the woes which fell upon the republic might have been warded off if he had been listened to, who, at such a time, had the best right to be heard. The political sagacity and foresight which had made General Scott the great peace-maker, as well as the great captain of the republic, had not deserted him in his advancing years; and he had, as early as October 29th, 1860, addressed a memorandum to the President and the Secretary of War, in which he set forth the almost certain endeavor to destroy the Union upon the election of Mr. Lincoln; among whose supporters he was not, but whose election he could not believe would be followed by "any unconstitutional violence or breach of law." Such violence or breach he, in his integrity and love of country, regarded as the only justification of armed insurrection; but he knew the men of whom he wrote, and he did not believe that they would wait until they had either law or right on their side. In this remarkable paper he pointed out, with singular sagacity, as the event proved, that the Southern people, or those who spoke and acted for them, would seize the United States forts within their reach even before they had seceded. He recommended the immediate garrisoning of all these forts, and particularly of Forts Moultrie, Monroe, Pickens, and M'Rea, with such a force as to make any attempt to seize them by coup-de-main impossible; and he suggested that, in case of secession, commerce should remain unrestricted, but duties be collected on imports by forces stationed in forts or ships of war. But, alas! he was obliged to admit, in this very memorandum, that for the defense of the nine great forts which he mentioned, the government had, except the small garrisons of Moultrie and Monroe, but five companies of troops within reach, and those scattered at five posts separated hundreds of miles from each other; and, sadder still, he was obliged to send his patriotic warning and his wise counsels to a President who was supinely faithless to his trust, and to a Secretary of War who was one of the most active conspirators against the very government of which he was a member.[4] General Wool, too, one of the ablest and most honorable soldiers of the Union, had, as early as the 6th of December, addressed General Cass, Secretary of State, a letter, in which he set forth the imminent peril of the country, the frightful proportions which a civil war, inevitable upon secession, would assume, and pointed out the way in which to avoid it, by firm, decided, prompt, and energetic measures. Among these he particularly named the immediate increase of the garrison of Fort Moultrie.[5] But General Wool's letter was as little heeded as the

[4] GENERAL SCOTT'S VIEWS.

Views suggested by the imminent Danger (October 29, 1860) of a Disruption of the Union by the Secession of one or more of the Southern States.

To save time, the right of secession may be conceded, and instantly balanced by the correlative right, on the part of the federal government, against an *interior* state or states, to re-establish by force, if necessary, its former continuity of territory.—[Paley's Moral and Political Philosophy, last chapter.]

But break this glorious Union by whatever line or lines that political madness may contrive, and there would be no hope of reuniting the fragments except by the laceration and despotism of the sword. To effect such result, the intestine wars of our Mexican neighbors would, in comparison with ours, sink into mere child's play.

A smaller evil would be to allow the fragments of the great republic to form themselves into new confederacies, probably four.

All the lines of demarkation between the new Unions can not be accurately drawn in advance, but many of them approximately may. Thus, looking to natural boundaries and commercial affinities, some of the following frontiers, after many waverings and conflicts, might perhaps become acknowledged and fixed:

1. The Potomac River and the Chesapeake Bay to the Atlantic. 2. From Maryland, along the crest of the Alleghany (perhaps the Blue Ridge) range of mountains, to some point in the coast of Florida. 3. The line from say the head of the Potomac to the west or northwest, which it will be most difficult to settle. 4. The crest of the Rocky Mountains.

The southeast confederacy would, in all human probability, in less than five years after the rupture, find itself bounded by the first and second lines indicated above, the Atlantic and the Gulf of Mexico, with its capital at say Columbia, South Carolina. The country between the second, third, and fourth of those lines would, beyond a doubt, in about the same time, constitute another confederacy, with its capital at probably Alton or Quincy, Illinois. The boundaries of the Pacific Union are the most definite of all, and the remaining states would constitute the northeast confederacy, with its capital at Albany.

It, at the first thought, will be considered strange that seven slaveholding states and parts of Virginia and Florida should be placed (above) in a new confederacy with Ohio, Indiana, Illinois, etc.; but when the overwhelming weight of the great Northwest is taken in connection with the laws of trade, contiguity of territory, and the comparative indifference to free-soil doctrines on the part of Western Virginia, Kentucky, Tennessee, and Missouri, it is evident that but little, if any coercion, beyond moral force, would be needed to embrace them; and I have omitted the temptation of the unwasted public lands which would fall entire to this confederacy—an appanage (well husbanded) sufficient for many generations. As to Missouri, Arkansas, and Mississippi, they would not stand out a month. Louisiana would coalesce without much solicitation, and Alabama, with West Florida, would be conquered the first winter, from the absolute need of Pensacola for a naval dépôt.

If I might presume to address the South, and particularly dear Virginia—being "native here and to the manor born"—I would affectionately ask, Will not your slaves be less secure, and their labor less profitable, under the new order of things than under the old? Could you employ profitably two hundred slaves in all Nebraska, or five hundred in all New Mexico? The right, then, to take them thither would be a barren right. And is it not wise to

"Rather bear the ills we have,
Than fly to others that we know not of?"

The Declaration of Independence proclaims and consecrates the same maxim: "Prudence, indeed, will dictate that governments long established should not be changed for light and transient causes." And Paley, too, lays down as a fundamental maxim of statesmanship, "Never to pursue national *honor* as distinct from national *interest;*" but adds: "This rule acknowledges that it is often necessary to assert the honor of a nation for the sake of its interests."

The excitement that threatens secession is caused by the near prospect of a Republican's election to the presidency. From a sense of propriety as a soldier, I have taken no part in the pending canvass, and, as always heretofore, mean to stay away from the polls. My sympathies, however, are with the Bell and Everett ticket. With Mr. Lincoln I have had no communication whatever, direct or indirect, and have no recollection of ever having seen his person; but can not believe any unconstitutional violence, or breach of law, is to be apprehended from his administration of the federal government.

From a knowledge of our Southern population, it is my solemn conviction that there is some danger of an early act of rashness preliminary to secession, viz., the seizure of some or all of the following posts: Forts Jackson and St. Philip, in the Mississippi, below New Orleans, both without garrisons; Fort Morgan, below Mobile, without a garrison; Forts Pickens and M'Rea, Pensacola Harbor, with an insufficient garrison for one; Fort Pulaski, below Savannah, without a garrison; Forts Moultrie and Sumter, Charleston Harbor, the former with an insufficient garrison, and the latter without any; and Fort Monroe, Hampton Roads, without a sufficient garrison. In my opinion, all these works should be immediately so garrisoned as to make any attempt to take any one of them, by surprise or *coup-de-main*, ridiculous.

With the army faithful to its allegiance, and the navy probably equally so, and with a federal executive, for the next twelve months, of firmness and moderation, which the country has a right to expect—*moderation* being an element of power not less than *firmness*—there is good reason to hope that the danger of secession may be made to pass away without one conflict of arms, one execution, or one arrest for treason.

In the mean time, it is suggested that exports should remain as free as at present; all duties, however, on imports, collected (outside of the cities*), as such receipts would be needed for the national debt, invalid pensions, etc., and only articles contraband of war be refused admittance. But even this refusal would be unnecessary, as the foregoing views eschew the idea of invading a seceded state. WINFIELD SCOTT.

New York, October 29, 1860.

Lieutenant General Scott's respects to the Secretary of War to say,

That a copy of his "Views," etc., was dispatched to the President yesterday in great haste; but the copy intended for the Secretary, better transcribed (herewith), was not in time for the mail. General Scott would be happy if the latter could be substituted for the former.

It will be seen that the "Views" only apply to a case of secession that makes a *gap* in the present Union. The falling off say of Texas, or of all the Atlantic states, from the Potomac south, was not within the scope of General Scott's provisional remedies.

It is his opinion that instructions should be given at once to the commanders of the Barrancas, Forts Moultrie and Monroe, to be on their guard against surprises and *coups-de-main*. As to *regular approaches*, nothing can be said or done, at this time, without volunteers.

There is one (regular) company at Boston, one here (at the Narrows), one at Pittsburg, one at Augusta, Georgia, and one at Baton Rouge—in all five companies only, within reach, to garrison or re-enforce the forts mentioned in the "Views."

General Scott is all solicitude for the safety of the Union. He is, however, not without hope that all dangers and difficulties will pass away without leaving a scar or painful recollection behind. The Secretary's most obedient servant, W. S.

October 30, 1860.

* In forts or on board ships of war. The great aim and object of this plan was to gain time—say eight or ten months—to await expected measures of conciliation on the part of the North, and the subsidence of angry feelings in the opposite quarter.

[5] *General Wool's Letters.*

Troy, December 31, 1860.

MY DEAR SIR,—South Carolina, after twenty-seven years—Mr. Rhett says thirty years—of constant and increasing efforts by her leaders to induce her to secede, has declared herself out of the Union; and this, too, without the slightest wrong or injustice done her people on the part of the government of the United States. Although she may have seized the revenue cutter, raised her treasonable Palmetto flag over the United States Arsenal, the Custom-house, Post-office, Castle Pinckney, and Fort Moultrie, she is not out of the Union, nor beyond the pale of the United States. Before she can get out of their jurisdiction or control, a reconstruction of the Constitution must be had, *or civil war ensue.* In the latter case, it would require no prophet to foretell the result.

It is reported that Mr. Buchanan has received informally the commissioners appointed by the rebels of South Carolina to negotiate for the public property in the harbor of Charleston, and for other purposes. It is also reported that the President disapproved of the conduct of Major Anderson, who, being satisfied that he would not be able to defend Fort Moultrie with the few men under his command, wisely took possession of Fort Sumter, where he could protect himself and the country from the disgrace which might have occurred if he had remained in Fort Moultrie. Being the commander in the harbor, he had the right to occupy Fort Sumter, an act which the safety of the Union as well as his own honor demanded. It is likewise stated that apprehensions are entertained that Major Anderson will be required to abandon Fort Sumter and reoccupy Fort Moultrie. There can be no foundation for such apprehensions; for surely the President would not surrender the citadel of the harbor of Charleston to rebels. Fort Sumter commands the entrance, and in a few hours could demolish Fort Moultrie. So long as the United States keeps possession of this fort, the independence of South Carolina will only be in name, and not in fact. If, however, it should be surrendered to South Carolina, which I do not apprehend, *the smothered indignation of the free states would be roused beyond control.* It would not be in the power of any one to restrain it. *In twenty days two hundred thousand men would be in readiness to take vengeance on all who would betray the Union into the hands of its enemies.* Be assured that I do not exaggerate the feelings of the people. They are already sufficiently excited at the attempt to dissolve the Union for no other reason than that they constitutionally exercised the most precious right conferred on them, of voting for the person whom they considered the most worthy and best qualified to fill the office of President. Fort Sumter, therefore, ought not, and, I presume, will not be delivered over to South Carolina.

I am not, however, pleading for the free states, for they are not in danger, but for the Union and the preservation of the cotton states. Those who sow the wind may expect to reap the whirlwind. The leaders of South Carolina could not have noticed that we live in an age of progress, and that all Christendom is making rapid strides in the march of civilization and freedom. If they had, they would have discovered that the announcement of every victory obtained by the hero of the nineteenth century, Garibaldi, in favor of the oppressed of Italy, did not fail to electrify every American heart with joy and gladness. "Where liberty dwells there is my country," was the declaration of the illustrious Franklin. This principle is too strongly implanted in the heart and mind of every man in the free states to be surrendered because South Carolina desires it in order to extend the area of slavery. With all christianized Europe and nearly all the civilized world opposed to slavery, are the Southern states prepared to set aside the barriers which shield and protect their institutions under the United States government? Would the separation of the South from the North give greater security to slavery than it has now under the Constitution of the Union? What security would they have for the return of runaway slaves? I apprehend none; while the number of runaways would be greatly augmented, and the difficulties of which slaveholders complain would be increased tenfold. However much individuals might condemn slavery, the free states are prepared to sustain and defend it as guaranteed by the Constitution.

In conclusion, I would avoid the bloody and desolating example of the Mexican states. I am now, and forever, in favor of the Union, its preservation, and the rigid maintenance of the rights and interests of the states, individually as well as collectively. Yours, etc., JOHN E. WOOL.

General Wool to General Cass, before the resignation of the latter.

[Private.] Troy, Dec. 6, 1860.

MY DEAR GENERAL,—Old associations and former friendship induce me to venture to address to you a few words on the state of the country. My letter is headed "private" because I am not authorized to address you officially.

I have read with pleasure the President's Message. South Carolina says she intends to leave the Union. Her representatives in Congress say she has already left the Union. It would seem that she is neither to be conciliated nor comforted. *I command the Eastern Department,* which includes South Carolina, Georgia, Florida, Alabama, and Mississippi. You know me well. I have ever been a firm, decided, faithful, and devoted friend of my country. *If I can aid the President to preserve the Union, I hope he will command my services. It will never do for him or you to leave Washington without every star in this Union is in its place.* Therefore, no time should be lost in adopting measures to defeat those who are conspiring against the Union. Hesitancy or delay may be no less fatal to the Union than to the President or your own high standing as a statesman.

It seems to me that troops should be sent to Charleston to man the forts in that harbor. You have eight companies at Fort Monroe, Va. *Three or four of these companies should be sent, without a moment's delay, to Fort Moultrie.* It will save the Union and the President much trouble. It is said that to send at this time troops to that harbor would produce great excitement among the people. That is nonsense, when the people are as much excited as they can be, and the leaders are determined to execute their long-meditated purpose of separating the state from the Union. So long as you command the entrance to the city of Charleston, South Carolina can not separate herself from the Union. Do not leave the forts in the harbor in a condition to induce an attempt to take possession of them. It might easily be done at this time. If South Carolina should take them, it might, as she anticipates, induce other states to join her.

Permit me to entreat you to urge the President to send at once three or four companies of artillery to Fort Moultrie. The Union can be preserved, but it requires firm, decided, prompt, and energetic measures on the part of the President. He has only to exert the power conferred on him by the Constitution and laws of Congress, and all will be safe, and he will prevent a civil war, which never fails to call forth all the baser passions of the human heart. If a separation should take place, you may rest assured blood would flow in torrents, followed by pestilence, famine, and desolation, *and Senator Seward's irrepressible conflict will be brought to a conclusion much sooner than he could possibly have anticipated.* Let me conjure you to save the Union, and thereby avoid the bloody and desolating example of the states of Mexico. A separation of the states will bring with it the desolation of the cotton states, which are unprepared for war. Their weakness will be found in the number of their slaves, with but few of the essentials to carry on war, while the free states will have all the elements and materials for war, and to a greater extent than any other people on the face of the globe.

Think of these things, my dear general, and save the country, and save the prosperous South from pestilence, famine, and desolation. Peaceable secession is not to be thought of. Even if it should take place, in three months we would have a bloody war on our hands. Very truly your friend, JOHN E. WOOL.

Hon. Lewis Cass, Secretary of State, Washington, D. C.

LIEUTENANT GENERAL WINFIELD SCOTT.

THE STEAM-SHIP "STAR OF THE WEST."

Lieutenant General's had been, and the consequences were just what both the military patriots had foreseen and foretold. The government would now have gladly followed their counsels, but it was too late.

At Charleston, on the contrary, alacrity as well as audacity characterized all that was done. The return of the South Carolina commissioners from Washington with the announcement that the President had refused to hold any farther communication with them, gave a new stimulus to the pride and the pugnacity of the secessionists. They affected to regard this refusal as an insult, and began to lash themselves into fury, but also to take most vigorous measures against the government by which they chose to regard themselves as insulted. They hastened the repairs and the armament of Fort Moultrie, commenced the erection of batteries upon Sullivan's Island and Morris's Island, two points which commanded both the entrance to the harbor and Fort Sumter; the commander of Castle Pinckney ordered that no boat should approach the wharf-head without permission; the city was put under the protection of a military patrol, look-out boats were stationed in the outer harbor at night, and the telegraph was placed under censorship. All the citizens of Charleston liable to military duty were, without exception, called to arms. The collector of the port, appointed to his office by the United States government, announced that all vessels from and for ports outside of South Carolina must enter and clear at Charleston. The Convention passed an ordinance defining treason against the state, and declaring its punishment, which, with a misunderstanding of an old criminal law-phrase, ludicrous in itself, but horrible in the vengeful purpose indicated by it, was to be "death without benefit of *the* clergy."[6] Delegates were appointed to attend a convention of seceding states. An appeal was made by the leading newspaper of Charleston to the people of Florida, to seize the national forts at Pensacola and Key West, and the capture of the California treasure-ships bound northward through the Gulf of Mexico was recommended. This appeal was addressed to the people of a commonwealth which had not yet even gone through the form of seceding from the government which had bought and paid for the very soil on which they lived! With a similar disregard of the proprietary rights of that government, the South Carolina authorities forbade the United States sub-treasurer of Charleston to cash any more drafts from Washington. But in this respect their dishonest move received one honest counter-check, which provoked some merriment; for Governor Pickens, writing to the Secretary of the Treasury for a balance of $3000 due upon his salary as United States minister to Russia, received in reply a draft upon the sub-treasury the payments of which he had assumed to stop.

These bold steps were met only by timidity and hesitation on the part of the government. If Fort Sumter were to be retained, it must needs be re-enforced. An attempt was therefore made to send supplies and men to Major

Anderson, but in such a shuffling way, and with such a pitiful result, that it is a shame to tell the story. A large steam-ship, the Star of the West, was chartered, and with a supply of commissary stores and ammunition, and two hundred and fifty artillerists and marines, she sailed from New York on the 5th of January. But, although her destination was Charleston Harbor, she cleared for New Orleans and Havana, and she did not take the troops on board until she was far down the Bay. The attempted deceit entirely failed. The Charleston people were fully informed as to the project by some of their innumerable spies, who swarmed over the country. The vessel arrived off Charleston Bar in the middle of the night of the 9th. She there lay to of necessity; for the lights in the light-houses were all out, and the buoys removed. She put out her own lights, and awaited the dawning. As the day began to break she discovered a small steamer just inshore of her, which, on making the reciprocal discovery, steamed away for the ship channel, burning blue and red signals, and sending up rockets as she went. The Star of the West followed, with the national flag at her peak, until she was within about two miles of both Fort Sumter and Fort Moultrie, when a battery on Morris's Island, about half a mile off, not noticed until then, opened fire upon her. Another large United States flag was immediately run up at the fore, but still the battery continued its fire. Perhaps this surprised the officers of the vessel, for before she was headed for the harbor the troops were all sent below, so that they could not be seen, no one but the crew being allowed on deck; and it really did seem as if the government of the United States might be allowed to smuggle two hundred and fifty men into one of its own fortresses. But the well-informed seceders thought otherwise; and as to the flag of their country, they were but too glad of an opportunity for insulting it. So the fire was kept up upon the advancing steamer, which soon found herself in a very awkward position. The shot were flying over her deck and through her rigging; she had been hit once. To reach Fort Sumter, she would be obliged to pass within three quarters of a mile of Fort Moultrie, from which already an armed schooner had put off, towed by two steam-tugs. Thus cut off, hemmed in, and fired upon, without the means of returning fire, the commander of the Star of the West concluded that, if he persisted, there was no chance of any other event than the loss of his vessel and of many lives; and after remaining under fire for ten minutes, during which seventeen shots were fired at him from the battery, and some from Fort Moultrie, he turned his ship about and headed for New York, where he arrived on the 12th, to the great disappointment and humiliation of all true men, who were hardly less disgusted at this skulking attempt than chagrined at its failure.[7]

---

[6] The old penalty of death without benefit of clergy is now, and, from the changed condition of things, has been, of necessity, long obsolete. It had no reference to the attendance of a clergyman or minister of the Gospel upon the condemned criminal, but was a barbarous sign of the peculiar privileges of the clergy of the Roman Church, which asserted and maintained a right to try its clergy at its own tribunals. When, therefore, a man was condemned and about to be sentenced, he claimed, if he could, that he was a clergyman; and, as proof, offered to show that *he could read*, then an accomplishment confined to clergymen. But, as learning advanced, it became necessary to do away with this "benefit of clergy."

[7]   *Report of the Captain of the Star of the West.*

Steam-ship Star of the West, New York, Saturday, Jan. 12, 1861.
M. O. ROBERTS, ESQ. : SIR.—After leaving the wharf on the 5th inst., at 5 o'clock P.M., we proceeded down the Bay, where we hove to, and took on board four officers and two hundred soldiers, with their arms, ammunition, etc., and then proceeded to sea, crossing the bar at Sandy Hook at 9 P.M. Nothing unusual took place during the passage, which was a pleasant one for this season of the year.

We arrived at Charleston Bar at 1 30 A.M. on the 9th inst., but could find no guiding marks for the Bar, as the lights were all out. We proceeded with caution, running very slow and sounding, until about 4 A.M., being then in four and a half fathoms water, when we discovered a light through the haze which at that time covered the horizon. Concluding that the lights were on Fort Sumter, after getting the bearings of it we steered to the S.W. for the main ship channel,

FIRING ON THE "STAR OF THE WEST" FROM THE SOUTH CAROLINA BATTERY ON MORRIS'S ISLAND, JANUARY 10, 1861.

K

THE FIRST FLAG OF TRUCE.

Anderson, therefore, immediately addressed a note to the governor of South Carolina, asking whether this firing upon an unarmed vessel bearing the flag of his government was authorized, and informing him that if it were not disavowed he should regard it as an act of war, and not permit any vessel to pass within range of the guns of Fort Sumter. This letter he sent with a flag of truce to Charleston. Under the circumstances, a flag of truce was perhaps proper, and even necessary, and doubtless, to a military man, the proceeding was a mere formality; but to the people there were gloomy shadows in the folds of that white, peaceful token. To send a flag of truce confessed a state of war —of civil war; it recognized the existence of a second power in the land; and then what humiliation to see an officer of the United States army obtaining audience of the governor of one of the states, and one of the least important of them too, only by virtue of a protection, a safeguard! Governor Pickens, in reply, assumed the responsibility of the firing, informed Major Anderson that attempts to re-enforce him would be regarded as hostile acts, and resisted accordingly, and left him to decide whether he would fulfill his threat as to firing upon vessels coming within range of his guns. The situation proved to be graver, and the case more complicated, than Major Anderson was prepared to meet without superior orders. Of this he informed Governor Pickens, asking permission for the passage of a messenger to Washington, which was granted.[8] This incident added greatly to the excitement throughout the North, where, however, no violence or even vivacity of feeling was yet displayed; but a gloomy, gnawing, fierce unrest pervaded the whole land. It was felt that the government had acted pitifully, and had been publicly caught in the act; but that Major Anderson had borne himself only as became a brave and prudent soldier. In the first sentence of his demand upon the insurgent governor, the words " the flag of my government" touched the sensitive public heart. He had been the first to assert the existence of that government among the insurgents and to support its flag, and he rose higher than before in public favor.

While the South Carolina insurgents were conducting their affairs with such promptitude, such boldness, and such success, and the government was moving with such hesitation into such miserable failure, what was the course of events in the country at large? In the slave states the self-constituted leaders of the insurrection were doing their best, by acts of usurpation without even the shadow or pretense of authority, to bring about a bloody issue.

But what did Major Anderson under these circumstances? He behaved with the judgment and firmness which marked his conduct throughout his severe trial. It must be remembered that communication had been cut off between Fort Sumter and the main land, and that Major Anderson knew nothing of the intention of sending him supplies and re-enforcements. When, therefore, the Star of the West hove in sight of his battlements, she was to him merely a merchant steamer entering Charleston Harbor, and having no special claim on his protection. His orders were strictly to act upon the defensive; but all the little garrison of the fort were on the alert, and he himself stood, glass in hand, upon the ramparts. To his grief, but perhaps not to his surprise, he sees the first shot fired from Morris's Island, and he orders his shotted guns which bear upon that battery to be run out. A second shot, and up goes another flag at the fore. Is this a signal to him? He can not tell. Shall he fire upon the assailants? He longs to give the word; but he is not attacked; his orders justify him only in self-defense, and to fire begins the horrors of civil war. Still the steamer keeps her course, and shot after shot is fired upon her. The men at the guns begin to fret, and the captain of one begs, " Do let us give them one, sir." " Patient—be patient," was the calm reply. But the battery keeps up its fire; the steamer is hit; Fort Moultrie also opens its guns upon her. It is becoming too much even for that firm and prudent man to bear, and he is about to give the word, when, all at once, the steamer puts about, and makes way out to sea as rapidly as possible, and the puzzled commander's doubt is settled for him. But, although he was relieved from the necessity of opening fire upon the insurgents at that time, the occurrence was of so grave a nature that it could not be permitted to pass unquestioned, or repeated with impunity. Major

<hr>

where we hove to, to await daylight, our lights having all been put out since 12 o'clock, to avoid being seen.

As the day began to break, we discovered a steamer just inshore of us, which, as soon as she saw us, burned one blue light and two red lights as signals, and shortly after steamed over the Bar and into the ship channel. The soldiers were now all put below, and no one allowed on deck except our own crew. As soon as there was light enough to see, we crossed the Bar and proceeded on up the channel (the outer-bar buoy having been taken away), the steamer ahead of us sending off rockets, and burning lights until after broad daylight, continuing on her course up nearly two miles ahead of us. When we arrived about two miles from Fort Moultrie, Fort Sumter being about the same distance, a masked battery on Morris's Island, where there was a red Palmetto flag flying, opened fire upon us—distance about five eighths of a mile. *We had the American flag flying at our flag-staff at the time, and soon after the first shot hoisted a large American ensign at the fore.* We continued on under the fire of the battery for over ten minutes, several of the shots going clear over us. One shot just passed clear of the pilot-house, another passed between the smoke-stack and walking-beams of the engine, another struck the ship just abaft the fore-rigging and stove in the planking, while another came within an ace of carrying away the rudder. At the same time there was a movement of two steamers from near Fort Moultrie, one of them towing a schooner (I presume an armed schooner), with the intention of cutting us off. Our position now became rather critical, as we had to approach Fort Moultrie to within three quarters of a mile before we could keep away for Fort Sumter. A steamer approaching us with an armed schooner in tow, and the battery on the island firing at us all the time, and having no cannon to defend ourselves from the attack of the vessels, we concluded that, to avoid certain capture or destruction, we would endeavor to get to sea. Consequently we wore round and steered down the channel, the battery firing upon us until the shot fell short. As it was now strong ebb tide, and the water having fallen some three feet, we proceeded with caution, and crossed the Bar safely at 8 50 A.M., and continued on our course for this port, where we arrived this morning, after a boisterous passage. A steamer from Charleston followed us for about three hours, watching our movements.

In justice to the officers and crews of each department of the ship, I must add that their behavior while under the fire of the battery reflected great credit on them.

Mr. Brewer, the New York pilot, was of very great assistance to me in helping to pilot the ship over Charleston Bar, and up and down the channel. Very respectfully, your obedient servant, JOHN M'GOWAN, Captain.

<hr>

[8]   *Correspondence between Major Anderson and Governor Pickens.*

To his Excellency the Governor of South Carolina:

Sir,—Two of your batteries fired this morning on an unarmed vessel bearing the flag of my government. As I have not been notified that war has been declared by South Carolina against the United States, I can not but think this a hostile act committed without your sanction or authority. Under that hope I refrain from opening a fire on your batteries. I have the honor, therefore, respectfully to ask whether the above-mentioned act—one which I believe without parallel in the history of our country or any other civilized government—was committed in obedience to your instructions, and notify you, if it is not disclaimed, that I regard it as an act of war, and I shall not, after reasonable time for the return of my messenger, permit any vessel to pass within the range of the guns of my fort. In order to save, as far as it is in my power, the shedding of blood, I beg you will take due notification of my decision for the good of all concerned, hoping, however, your answer may justify a farther continuance of forbearance on my part. I remain, respectfully,   ROBERT ANDERSON.

Governor Pickens's Reply.

Governor Pickens, after stating the position of South Carolina toward the United States, says that any attempt to send United States troops into Charleston Harbor, to re-enforce the forts, would be regarded as an act of hostility; and, in conclusion, adds that any attempt to re-enforce the troops at Fort Sumter, or to retake and resume possession of the forts within the waters of South Carolina, which Major Anderson abandoned, after spiking the cannon and doing other damage, can not but be regarded by the authorities of the state as indicative of any other purpose than the coercion of the state by the armed force of the government; special agents, therefore, have been off the Bar to warn approaching vessels, armed and unarmed, having troops to re-enforce Fort Sumter aboard, not to enter the harbor. Special orders have been given the commanders at the forts not to fire on such vessels until a shot across their bows should warn them of the prohibition of the state. Under these circumstances, the Star of the West, it is understood, this morning attempted to enter the harbor with troops, after having been notified she could not enter, and consequently she was fired into. This act is perfectly justified by me.

In regard to your threat about vessels in the harbor, it is only necessary for me to say, you must be the judge of your responsibility. Your position in the harbor has been tolerated by the authorities of the state; and while the act of which you complain is in perfect consistency with the rights and duties of the state, it is not perceived how far the conduct you propose to adopt can find a parallel in the history of any country, or be reconciled with any other purpose than that of your government imposing on the state the condition of a conquered province.   F. W. PICKENS.

Second Communication from Major Anderson.

To his Excellency Governor Pickens:

Sir,—I have the honor to acknowledge the receipt of your communication, and say that, under the circumstances, I have deemed it proper to refer the whole matter to my government, and intend deferring the course I indicated in my note this morning until the arrival from Washington of such instructions as I may receive.

I have the honor also to express the hope that no obstructions will be placed in the way, and that you will do me the favor of giving every facility for the departure of the bearer, Lieut. T. Talbot, who is directed to make the journey.   ROBERT ANDERSON.

On the 2d of January, Governor Ellis, of North Carolina, took possession of Fort Macon, at Beaufort, the forts at Wilmington, and the United States Arsenal at Fayetteville; and on the same day Fort Pulaski, near Savannah, was seized by the order of Governor Brown, of Georgia. At Mobile, the Alabama secessionists demanded and received possession of the United States Arsenal, thereby securing 1500 barrels of powder, 300,000 cartridges, besides arms and other munitions of war. They also seized upon Fort Morgan, at the entrance of Mobile Bay, and garrisoned it with two hundred Alabama militia. All these forts and arsenals fell into their hands without resistance; for so benign and peaceful was the government against which they revolted, that its very military posts were left entirely without military protection, in the mere keeping of a corporal and his guard. Of this absence of protective force, the secessionists of North Carolina, Georgia, and Alabama availed themselves; this trust of the whole nation in the honor of all its constituent parts, they abused before they had even nominally dissolved the bonds which bound them to the government of the United States. Of the border states Virginia alone showed a readiness to swell the ranks of the insurgents. At Norfolk, almost within the very precincts of a great government naval station, a meeting was held on the 5th of January, at which speeches were made and resolutions passed urging resistance to "coercion and invasion"—the favorite phrases by which thoroughly disloyal men designated the maintenance of its power by the government. But this disposition was not yet general even in the eastern part of the state; and the governor, in a message to the Legislature in special session, condemned South Carolina, although he defied the United States.

GOVERNOR PICKENS.

The people of the northern tier of slave states, forming the border line between freedom and slavery, spoke out strongly for the Union, or remained in a state of quiet but anxious expectation. In Baltimore five thousand substantial citizens addressed a letter to Governor Hicks, approving his refusal to convene the Legislature of Maryland, which measure was advocated in the interests of the secessionists; and the governor replied to the commissioner from the State of Alabama, who had solicited the co-operation of Maryland, that he regarded co-operation between the slave states as an infraction of the Constitution, which he, as Governor of Maryland, swore to support. He declared that the people of that state were firm in their friendship for the Union, and would never swerve from it; that they had seen, with mortification and regret, the course taken by South Carolina; because, in their opinion, it was better to use the Union for the enforcement of their rights, than to break it up because of apprehensions that the provisions of the Constitution would be disregarded, and they would cling to it until it should actually become the instrument of destruction to their rights, and peace, and safety. There were then a few secessionists in Maryland at both extremes of the social scale; but the great bulk of the thrifty and intelligent people of the state found their feelings and their opinions expressed for them in this letter of their governor, who also spoke the convictions, at that time, of a large body of conservative men throughout the slave states. A like reply was given by the Legislature of Delaware to the commissioner from Mississippi, who approached them with like proposals. The condemnation of the course of the seceding states by the people of Delaware was prompt and unqualified. But around the Gulf seceders were more numerous, and had obtained absolute control of public affairs. In Georgia, in Florida, in Alabama, and in Mississippi, the Legislatures, or the Conventions which they had called, moved rapidly and steadily on to the business of the disruption of the republic; and in the Senate of Missouri, the Committee on Federal Relations was instructed to report a bill calling a state convention. A series of outrages upon the national military posts and property accompanied these more deliberative movements, and illustrated their spirit. In North Carolina, Forts Caswell and Johnson were taken possession of by the militia and other persons living near them. On the 11th of January a party of Louisiana militia seized upon the United States Marine Hospital, about two miles below New Orleans, which contained over two hundred patients, all of whom who could leave their beds were turned out immediately. At Pensacola, a body of Florida and Alabama militia appeared before the gate of the navy yard, and demanded possession. The officer in command, having no force to resist the demand, yielded his post of necessity. Fort Barrancas was also taken possession of in like manner. The navy yard contained over one hundred thousand dollars worth of ordnance stores. The perpetrators of this outrage had the assurance to send word to the government, through their senators, that it was the consequence of the re-enforcement of Fort Pickens, and to propose a restoration on both sides of the *status quo ante bellum!* The claims of science, beneficently devoted to the interests of all mankind, were not recognized as a safeguard, and the United States Coast Survey schooner Dana was seized on the 15th, by order of the state authorities of Florida. The freedom of commercial intercourse was equally disregarded by the Governor of Mississippi, who planted artillery at Vicksburg, on the banks of the river, to stop, for examination, all steamers passing southward. This arbitrary interruption of the traffic of that great water highway of the continent did much to open the eyes of the people of the Western and Northwestern country to the consequences of the disruption of the Union. At Augusta, the United States Arsenal was surrendered to the militia of the place upon the demand of the Governor of Georgia.

In most of these cases the forcible seizure of the nation's property on the part of states took place before those states had gone through the formality of passing an Ordinance of Secession. But it was not long lacking, this home-made salve for wounded honor. The Mississippi Convention passed the ordinance on the 9th of January, Alabama on the 11th, Florida on the 12th, Georgia on the 19th, and, to look forward a few days, Louisiana on the 28th, and Texas on the 1st of February. In Mississippi there were fifteen dissenting voices; in Florida, only seven against sixty-two; but in Alabama there were thirty-nine nays to sixty-one yeas; and in Georgia itself, secession was openly denounced and voted against by eighty-nine of the delegates, among whom were Alexander H. Stevens and Herschel V. Johnson, the Democratic candidate for the vice-presidency at the last election, and Judge Linton Stevens, of the Supreme Court. It is important to observe how large a proportion of the people, and what eminent and influential citizens, in some of these states, were so earnestly opposed to secession that, in spite of the attempts by social exclusion, browbeating, deceit, and even actual violence, to bring about unanimity, they boldly declared themselves against it. Of the evidence that the leaders and active instigators of the insurrection would not permit that free expression of public opinion through the ballot-box which alone could have excused, though it would not have justified their acts, some should be placed directly upon the pages in which the story of this woeful time will be told with candor, and with as much good feeling as comports with justice. There is no lack of it. "It is a notable fact" (the "Southern Confederacy," of Atalanta, Georgia, says this), "that, wherever the 'Minute-men,' as they are called, have had an organization" (they were armed vigilance committees), "those counties have voted, by large majorities, for immediate secession. Those that they could not control by persuasion and coaxing, they dragooned and bullied by threats, jeers, and sneers. By this means thousands of good citizens were induced to vote the immediate secession ticket through timidity. Besides, the towns and cities have been flooded with sensation dispatches and inflammatory rumors, manufactured in Washington City for the especial occasion. To be candid, there never has been as much lying and bullying practiced, in the same length of time, since the destruction of Sodom and Gomorrah, as has been in the recent state campaign." The doctrine of state sovereignty, which, in the face of the solemn teachings of the Southern fathers of the republic, the Calhoun school had so long and so ceaselessly poured into the ears of Southern people, now served the purpose for which it was intended, and men submitted to a state ordinance which set at naught the Constitution, and sought to destroy the Union, as they would have obeyed a law with regard to any minor matter of daily life. Only in this manner was this insurrection made possible. But even under these circumstances the leaders of the movement did not dare to submit the Ordinance of Secession to the people for confirmation, except in one state, Texas, which, it is worth while to observe, was the only one of the states which had a sovereign independent political existence before it became merged in the Union. It is needless to notice farther the forcible appropriation of national forts, arsenals, and ships by state authority. But in one instance the exertion of "sovereign" state authority was accompanied by incidents which were marked with the character of the time. To understand this, we must turn our eyes northward, and observe what was passing this while in the loyal free and slave states.

The promptitude and vigor of the insurgents was not imitated more by the people of the loyal states than by the government with which they kept their faith. From the nature of man and man's institutions, this was to have been expected. Revolutionary and destructive forces, unless they fail miserably at the very outset, must always act more quickly and more vigorously than those which protect that which they would overturn and destroy. For an essential element of established power is a *vis inertiæ*, the very disturbance of which, even for the purpose of resistance, is not only the first task, but, if accomplished, the first triumph of revolution. Established government rests upon the basis of a strong tranquillity; and revolution, which seeks to displace established government, can accomplish its purpose, even if it controls an equal body, only by adding movement to its weight, thus attaining momentum. The loyal people and the government of the United States wished to allay disturbance and to prevent a struggle; therefore, when they did any thing, they confined themselves to mild, but, as they then thought, firm repressive measures. They did not yet see that the business before them was not one of restraint, but of extinction; that they must destroy the power they feared, or be destroyed by it. So it is even in minor matters of police. Half a dozen riotous, reckless, liquor-maddened men will give employment to twice their number of policemen, acting under the authority of law and under a sense of responsibility, and, if not put down at once by the strong hand, may peril the peace of a neighborhood. The insurgents having openly defied the government, seized its forts, its arsenals, and its armed vessels, and established themselves in force, the people of the loyal states began to think that it was almost time for them to begin to think about beginning to do something. So meetings, decorously enthusiastic, were held in New York, in Boston, Philadelphia, Cincinnati, Chicago, Portland, Trenton in New Jersey, Wilmington in Delaware, and elsewhere, at which many laudable patriotic sentiments were uttered, and a sense of "the value of the Union" was strongly expressed (as if the existence of the nation and the government was a thing or an interest by itself, which was to be priced like goods or railway shares), and the administration was assured of the willingness of the people to support it against the insurgents. On the other hand, that the purposes of the loyal people might not be misapprehended, abolition demonstrations were interfered with; as at Rochester, in New York, where a meeting of abolitionists was broken up, amid cheers for the Union, General Scott, and Major Anderson; and where a banner, with the inscription "No compromise with slavery," had to be taken down. In Boston, Mr. Wendell Phillips, the apostle of abolitionism, having avowed himself, as he had often done before, "a disunion man," expressed joy at the secession of the Gulf states, and denounced the compromise spirit of Mr. Seward and Mr. Charles Francis Adams, was hissed and hooted, and followed home by a great crowd of excited people, from whom he was protected by policemen. The Legislature of New York, by resolutions, denounced secession, avowed a determination to support the national government, and offered men and money to the President. In the Massachusetts Legislature like resolutions were passed, and with them a bill increasing the militia of the state. On the 15th of January Major General Sanford offered the services of the whole first division of the militia of New York, which was under his command, for the support of the authority of the government. But it is worthy of note that there was some, though very trifling, objection to this offer, and to the general's right to make it.

Thus far, however, though much had been said at the North, nothing had been done as a set-off to the activity and audacity of the insurgents at the South. When, at last, something was attempted, it was not by the government, or even by state authority. The seceders had, from the beginning of their movement, busied themselves in buying arms and munitions of war in Northern cities as well as in Europe. Muskets, sabres, powder, percussion caps, and even cannon, were shipped to them from Northern ports, where the traffic in arms was the only branch of trade not paralyzed by the political disturbances. With this traffic an officer of police, John A. Kennedy, Chief of the Metropolitan District of New York, took the responsibility of interfering. He seized and detained several cases of muskets about to be shipped to Georgia. Information of the seizure was telegraphed to the consignees, and immediately there came back a dispatch from Mr. Toombs to Fernando Wood, Mayor of New York, containing a query as to the act and a threat as to its consequences. The reply of the mayor was one of exculpation and abject submission to the insurgent demagogue, to whom he said that if he had the power he would punish Kennedy.[9] Georgia at once retaliated, and in a most effective manner. The governor seized and held by military possession two barks, two brigs, and a schooner, lying in the harbor of Savannah, and belonging to residents of New York, and sent on word that they would be held until the arms were released. The Governor of New York replied that the seizure had been unauthorized, and that the arms should be given up. The vessels were then released, and made sail quickly from Savannah. But there being some difficulty and delay in releasing the arms, the Governor of Georgia seized three other vessels, a ship, a bark, and a brig, all owned in New York, and detained them until the arms were placed again at the disposal of their Georgia consignees. In these relative attitudes we shall always find the parties to this struggle: on the side of the insurgents, a determination to gain their point by any means, right or wrong, at any cost, and without hesitation; and on the part of the government, a reluctance to violent measures unless driven to them by sheer necessity.

At Washington, the House of Representatives, not until ten days had gone by, passed a resolution approving of Major Anderson's change of position, and assuring the President of support in the enforcement of the laws and the preservation of the Union, but nothing more momentous was attempted. In the cabinet, Secretary Thompson, of the Interior, on learning the attempt to supply and garrison Fort Sumter, resigned his portfolio; and on the 15th of January, Colonel Hayne, a commissioner from South Carolina, and attorney general of the state, demanded the withdrawal of the troops which were in the fort. On being requested to submit the demand in writing, he sent in a proposal to buy the fort, with the declaration that "if not permitted to purchase it, South Carolina would take it by force of arms," a safe threat against a work already engirdled by batteries, and containing not quite fourscore fighting men. On the 20th of January, the senators from Alabama, Florida, and Mississippi, among whom was Jefferson Davis, withdrew from the Senate. The latter made a parting speech, not resigning, but taking leave of the senators, on the ground that, as his state had passed an Ordinance of Secession, he had no longer a right to sit in his seat. Looked upon as one of the ablest men of his party, and as a politician of determined purpose, and little scruple as to the means of attaining a political end, his retirement attracted more attention than that of any other seceding member of Congress. His speech was listened to with profound attention, and at the close of it, all the Democratic senators crowded round him and the other seceding senators, and shook hands warmly with them.[10] Just a week after the withdrawal of the man who was to assume so prominent a part in the rebellion, another, also to be heard of again in the annals of the period, ex-Secretary of War Floyd, was presented for indictment by the grand jury of the District of Columbia on three findings: malversation in office, complicity in the abstraction of the Indian Trust Fund Bonds, and conspiracy against the government. But he had taken himself well out of reach of grand juries and marshals, and he wisely kept so thereafter. The original members of Mr. Buchanan's cabinet, with the exception of General Cass, who retired early, and Mr. Attorney General Black, who was honorable and loyal, brought disgrace upon themselves, upon his administration, and the country; but one of its new ministers, General Dix, Secretary of the Treasury, was the first member of the government to assert its authority, in a manner which met the expectations and called forth the sympathies of the people. The revenue cutters of the United States are, of course, in the keeping of the Secretary of the Treasury, and under his orders. Among those which were exposed to the peculiar practices of the insurgents, with regard to the property of the "common agency," were the Lewis Cass, at Mobile, and the Robert M'Clelland, at New Orleans. General Dix had not been at the head of the Treasury Department four days when he sent a special agent to those ports to save those vessels by ordering them to New York. Having reached New Orleans, the agent delivered the secretary's order to Captain Breshwood, of the M'Clelland, who, after consultation with the collector of the port, flatly refused to obey it. Upon this the agent telegraphed for instructions to the secretary, who telegraphed back orders for the arrest of the captain by the lieutenant of the cutter, and his treatment as a mutineer if he offered any resistance, closing the order with the memorable words, "If any one attempts to haul down the American flag, shoot him on the spot." This dispatch was intercepted both at Mobile and New Orleans, where the insurgent leaders had already placed the telegraph under supervision, and so did not reach the agent of the Treasury Department. The

Correspondence between Senator Toombs and Mayor Wood.

Milledgeville, Jan. 24, 1861.

To his Honor Mayor Wood:

Is it true that any arms intended for and consigned to the State of Georgia have been seized by public authorities in New York? Your answer is important to us and to New York. Answer at once.

R. Toombs.

To this the Mayor returned the following answer:

Hon. Robert Toombs, Milledgeville, Ga.:

In reply to your dispatch, I regret to say that arms intended for and consigned to the State of Georgia have been seized by the Police of this state, but that the city of New York should in no way be made responsible for the outrage.

As mayor, I have no authority over the Police. If I had the power, I should summarily punish the authors of this illegal and unjustifiable seizure of private property.

Fernando Wood.

10 *Speech of Jefferson Davis on leaving the Senate.*

I rise for the purpose of announcing to the Senate that I have satisfactory evidence that the State of Mississippi, by solemn ordinance in convention assembled, has declared her separation from the United States. Under these circumstances, of course, my functions terminate here. It has seemed to be proper that I should appear in the Senate and announce that fact, and to say something, though very little, upon it. The occasion does not invite me to go into the argument, and my physical condition will not permit it, yet something would seem to be necessary on the part of the state I here represent, on an occasion like this. It is known to senators who have served here that I have for many years advocated, as an essential attribute of state sovereignty, the right of a state to secede from the Union. If, therefore, I had not believed there was justifiable cause—if I had thought the state was acting without sufficient provocation—still, under my theory of government, I should have felt bound by her action. I, however, may say I think she had justifiable cause, and I approve of her acts. I conferred with the people before that act was taken, and counseled them that, if they could not remain, they should take the act. I hope none will confound this expression of opinion with the advocacy of the right of a state to remain in the Union, and disregard its constitutional obligations by nullification. Nullification and secession are indeed antagonistic principles. Nullification is the remedy which is to be sought and applied within the Union against an agent of the United States when the agent has violated constitutional obligations, and the state assumes to act for itself, and appeals to other states to support it. But when the states themselves, and the people of the states, have so acted as to convince us that they will not regard our constitutional rights, then, and then for the first time, arises the question of secession in its practical application. That great man who now reposes with his fathers, who has been so often arraigned for want of fealty to the Union, advocated the doctrine of nullification because it preserved the Union. It was because of his deep-seated attachment to the Union that Mr. Calhoun advocated the doctrine of nullification, which he claimed would give peace within the limits of the Union, and not disturb it, and only be the means of bringing the agent before the proper tribunal of the states for judgment. Secession belongs to a different class of rights, and is to be justified upon the basis that the states are sovereign. The time has been, and I hope the time will come again, when a better appreciation of our Union will prevent any one denying that each state is a sovereign in its own right. Therefore I say I concur in the act of my state, and feel bound by it. It is by this confounding of nullification and secession that the name of another great man has been invoked to justify the coercion of a seceding state. The phrase "to execute the law," as used by General Jackson, was applied to a state refusing to obey the laws and still remaining in the Union. I remember well when Massachusetts was arraigned before the Senate. The record of that occasion will show that I said, if Massachusetts, in pursuing the line of steps, takes the last step which separates her from the Union, the right is hers, and I will neither vote one dollar nor one man to coerce her, but I will say to her, "God speed!" Mr. Davis then proceeded to argue that the equality spoken of in the Declaration of Independence was the equality of a class in political rights, referring to the charge against George III. for inciting insurrection as proof that it had no reference to the slaves. But we have proclaimed our independence. This is done with no hostility or any desire to injure any section of the country, nor even for our pecuniary benefit, but from the high and solid foundation of defending and protecting the rights we inherited, and transmitting them unshorn to our posterity. I know I feel no hostility to you senators here, and am sure there is not one of you, whatever may have been the sharp discussion between us, to whom I can not now say, in the presence of my God, I wish you well. And such is the feeling, I am sure, the people I represent feel toward those whom you represent. I therefore feel I but express their desire when I say I hope and they hope for those peaceful relations with you, though we must part, that may be mutually beneficial to us in the future. There will be peace if you so will it, and you may bring disaster on every part of the country if you thus will have it. And if you will have it thus, we will invoke the God of our fathers, who delivered them from the paw of the lion, to protect us from the ravages of the bear; and thus putting our trust in God, and our own firm hearts and strong arms, we will vindicate and defend the rights we claim. In the course of my long career, I have met with a great variety of men here, and there have been points of collision between us. Whatever of offense there has been to me, I leave here. I carry no hostile feelings away. Whatever of offense I have given, which has not been redressed, I am willing to say to senators in this hour of parting, I offer you my apology for any thing I may have done in the Senate; and I go thus released from obligation, remembering no injury I have received, and having discharged what I deem the duty of man, to offer the only reparation at this hour for every injury I have ever inflicted.

JEFFERSON DAVIS.

cutters were thus lost to the government; but the publication of the intercepted order, a few days afterward, sent an awakening thrill through the public heart in the loyal states, which, after the dull oppression caused by the course of affairs at Washington thus far, was worth ten times the value of the vessels. Dear as his country's flag is to every true-hearted man, it is dearest of all to the citizen of the United States; for it is not only the symbol of his nationality, but the standard under which that nationality was achieved, beneath whose folds the fathers of the Revolution fought, and suffered, and died; and besides, it is the only outward and visible sign with which he, having no hereditary master, can connect his idea of patriotism, to which he can be loyal; it is the representative to him of the government of which he forms a part, of the eternal principles of liberty, and justice, and Divine benevolence upon which that government is founded, and of the noble land of which he ever thinks with love and pride. What the crown, the king, and the flag together are to another man, the flag alone is to the citizen of the republic. It is the rainbow of hope and promise in his sky, and his heart leaps up when he beholds it.[1] So, when Secretary Dix's order was made public, there was an outcry of joy all over the land; it was felt that the honor of the flag had at last found a defender in the government. A second impulse was given to the popular feeling which first broke forth when Major Anderson entered Fort Sumter, and which was to receive its highest exaltation when he was forced to leave it. The shameful fact must needs be recorded here, that both these revenue cutters were purposely brought within the power of the authorities of Alabama and Louisiana, before their secession, by the collectors of Mobile and New Orleans, who were the sworn officers and business agents of the government of the United States.[2] About the same time the Mint and the Sub-treasury of New Orleans, with all the public money they contained, together with private deposits, were seized by the secessionists of that city.

The six Gulf states and South Carolina having now passed Ordinances of Secession, and seized all the national forts, arsenals, mints, custom-houses, and ships within their reach, a convention of their representatives was held at Montgomery, the capital of Alabama, for the purpose of forming a joint provisional government, or "common agency," to take the place of that from which they had withdrawn themselves and whatever was within their reach. Texas passed its Ordinance of Secession on the 1st of February, and on the 4th the Convention of the seceding states organized itself, with Howell Cobb, only a few months before Secretary of the Treasury of the United States, as president. In four days they had named themselves "The Confederate States of America," adopted a Constitution, and formed a provisional government, of which Jefferson Davis, of Mississippi, was president, and Alexander H. Stephens, of Georgia, vice-president.

---

[1] Slavery, secession, and state sovereignty could not eradicate this love. An officer of the United States, taken prisoner after the war had lasted a year, received from a rebel officer, whose quarters he visited, the confession that he had no attachment to the confederate colors which floated above them, and that "the hardest thing about this war was to fire upon the old flag." This incident is known to the writer on private information.

[2] Mr. W. Hemphill Jones, the special agent of the Treasury Department, made a report to Secretary Dix, from which the following passages are taken:

New Orleans, Jan. 29, 1861.

SIR,—You are hereby directed to get the United States revenue cutter M'Clelland, now lying here, under way immediately, and proceed with her to New York, where you will await the further instructions of the Secretary of the Treasury. For my authority to make this order you are referred to the letter of the Secretary, dated the 19th inst., and handed you personally by me. Very respectfully,   WM. HEMPHILL JONES, *Special Agent.*

To Capt. J. G. Breshwood, commanding U. S. Revenue Cutter Robert M'Clelland.

Breshwood conferred with Collector Hatch, of New Orleans, and then returned the following answer, flatly refusing to obey the order:

U. S. Revenue Cutter M'Clelland, New Orleans, January 29, 1861.

SIR,—Your letter, with one of the 19th of January from the Hon. Secretary of the Treasury, I have duly received, and in reply refuse to obey the order. I am, sir, your obedient servant,
JOHN G. BRESHWOOD, *Captain.*

To Wm. Hemphill Jones, Esq., Special Agent.

Believing that Captain Breshwood would not have ventured upon this most positive act of insubordination and disobedience of his own volition, I waited upon the collector at the custom-house, and had with him a full and free conversation upon the whole subject. In the course of it, Mr. Hatch admitted to me that he had caused the cutter to be brought to the city of New Orleans by an order of his own, dated January 15, so that she might be secured to the State of Louisiana, although at that time the state had not only not seceded, but the Convention had not met, and, in fact, did not meet until eight days afterward. This, I must confess, seemed to me a singular confession for one who at that very time had sworn to do his duty faithfully as an officer of the United States; and, on intimating as much to Mr. Hatch, he excused himself on the ground that in these revolutions all other things must give way to the force of circumstances. Mr. Hatch likewise informed me that the officers of the cutter had long since determined to abandon their allegiance to the United States, and cast their fortunes with the independent State of Louisiana. In order to test the correctness of this statement, I addressed another communication to Captain Breshwood, of the following tenor:

New Orleans, January 29, 1861.

SIR,—By your note of this date I am informed that you refuse to obey the orders of the Honorable Secretary of the Treasury. As, on accepting your commission, you took and subscribed an oath faithfully to discharge your duties to the government, and, as you well know, the law has placed the revenue cutters and their officers under the entire control of the Secretary of the Treasury, I request you to advise me whether you consider yourself at this time an officer in the service of the United States. Very respectfully,   WM. HEMPHILL JONES, *Special Agent.*

To Captain Breshwood.

To this letter I never received any reply. I then repaired again on board the cutter, and asked for the order of the collector bringing her to New Orleans. The original was placed in my possession, of which the following is a copy. And here it may be proper to observe that the order is written and signed by the collector himself:

Custom-house, New Orleans, Collector's Office, Jan. 15, 1861.

SIR,—You are hereby directed to proceed forthwith under sail to this city, and anchor the vessel under your command opposite the United States Marine Hospital, above Algiers. Very respectfully, your obedient servant,   F. H. HATCH, *Collector.*

To Captain J. G. Breshwood, United States Revenue Cutter M'Clelland, Southwest Pass, La.

Defeated at New Orleans, Mr. Jones then took his way to Mobile, to look after the Lewis Cass. Her captain (Morrison) could not be found, but Mr. Jones discovered in the cabin the following letter, which explains the surrender of that vessel:

State of Alabama, Collector's Office, Mobile, January 30, 1861.

SIR,—In obedience to an ordinance recently adopted by a convention of the people of Alabama, I have to require you to surrender into my hands, for the use of the state, the revenue cutter Lewis Cass, now under your command, together with her armaments, properties, and provisions on board the same. I am instructed also to notify you that you have the option to continue in command of the said revenue cutter, under the authority of the State of Alabama, in the exercise of the same duties that you have hitherto rendered to the United States, and at the same compensation, reporting to this office and to the governor of the state. In surrendering the vessel to the state, you will furnish me with a detailed inventory of its armaments, provisions, and properties of every description. You will receive special instructions from this office in regard to the duties you will be required to perform. I await your immediate reply. Very respectfully, your obedient servant,
T. SANFORD, *Collector.*

To J. J. Morrison, Esq., Captain Revenue Cutter Lewis Cass, Mobile, Ala.

Upon Captain Breshwood's refusal to obey the order of the Secretary of the Treasury, the following telegraphic correspondence ensued:

New Orleans, Jan. 29, 1861.

Hon. J. A. Dix, Secretary of the Treasury:

Capt. Breshwood has refused positively, in writing, to obey any instructions of the department. In this I am sure he is sustained by the collector, and believe acts by his advice. What must I do?   W. H. JONES, *Special Agent.*

To this dispatch Secretary Dix immediately returned the following answer, before published:

Treasury Department, Jan. 29, 1861.

W. Hemphill Jones, New Orleans:

Tell Lieut. Caldwell to arrest Capt. Breshwood, assume command of the cutter, and obey the order through you. If Capt. Breshwood, after arrest, undertakes to interfere with the command of the cutter, tell Lieut. Caldwell to consider him as a mutineer, and treat him accordingly. If any one attempts to haul down the American flag, shoot him on the spot.
JOHN A. DIX, *Secretary of the Treasury.*

Probably no better choice of men for president and vice-president of the rebellious confederacy could have been made if as many months as there were days had been spent in the selection. Jefferson Davis was not a statesman, not even a high-toned politician; but he was a cool, astute, adroit political manager. He was not a man of either great military capacity or acquirement; but he was a good soldier, and a daring, determined commander. His temperament fitted him for such a bad eminence as that to which he had been raised, and it seemed as if his whole life had been but a training to fit him for its functions. Born in Kentucky in 1808, he had been brought up in Mississippi, of which state his father, a planter and a Revolutionary officer, became a resident while it was yet mere territory of the United States. He was thus familiar from his earliest youth with the men of the Southwest, where were gathered the most desperate, lawless, loose-lived of the citizens of the republic. During his youth, and long after he had entered vigorous manhood, New Orleans was the social sink of the Union, and Vicksburg but a by-way to the bottomless pit. Toward that corner of the Union, swept down by the resistless current of commerce, emigration, and adventure flowing between the banks of three mighty rivers, tended all the scum and sediment of an ever-moving population, to seethe and fret, in a vitiated tropical atmosphere, into moral pestilence. Parents in the well-ordered, well-instructed, God-fearing commonwealths of the North and East, whose sons went thither upon commercial ventures, saw not even in rapidly-accumulated wealth a recompense for the contamination of the very few years that sufficed to acquire it; and, parting with them, almost gave them up as lost. There both life and fortune were held by precarious tenure. There gambling was the general occupation, and bloody assault the social distinction of a "gentleman." There drunkenness, in a greater or less degree, was regarded as the normal condition of any creature who had intelligence above the brute; though a lapse into sobriety, when palliated by the temptations of great gain, was looked upon as venial. There a dialect of ingenious and elaborate blasphemy, half-savage slang, and abominable filth was made tolerably intelligible to strangers, who were accustomed only to the ordinary phraseology of the English race, by the occasional introduction of words of which necessity and the idioms of our language compelled the use. There statute law and common law were rarely enforced, except against an oppressed and degraded race; but the judgments of Lynch courts were pronounced with incorruptible austerity, and executed with inexorable certainty and swiftness. Such was the general tone of society in Mississippi and the surrounding country during the first thirty or forty years of this century; but above this general level, yet descending occasionally to it and resting upon it, was a small class of planters, who, with a very few professional men, and merchants of the more honorable sort, possessed all the little moral worth and intellectual culture of the region; and to this Mr. Davis belonged. But in such a community — a community whose moral sense was blunted by the presence of a class whom every member of every other class might oppress with impunity—even the men whose motives were just and whose tastes more or less refined, were obliged to maintain their position by a certain conformity to the social habits, and a certain assumption of the defiant bearing, of the men around them. Few men can live from early youth to mature manhood among desperadoes without acquiring something of their desperation—at least a familiarity with desperate issues. Among such a people Jefferson Davis passed his life until he went in 1824 as a cadet to West Point. Thence he graduated with honor in 1828, and was, at his own request, assigned immediately to active service with Colonel Zachary Taylor, afterward general and president, but then engaged in frontier warfare at the West. On the rough and adventurous battle-field of the borders, the future insurgent leader so quickly distinguished himself that upon the formation of a new regiment of cavalry he obtained in it his commission as first lieutenant, in which position he did good service against the Indians, and, it is said, made a warm friend of the well-known chief Black Hawk while he was held a prisoner of war. After seven years of active frontier service Mr. Davis resigned his commission, and in 1835 became a cotton-planter in Mississippi, diversifying the dull routine of Southern agricultural life with political studies. When the Democratic party nominated Mr. Polk for president, Mr. Davis canvassed, or "stumped" the state on his behalf, was made presidential elector to vote for him, and in 1845 was elected a member of the House of Representatives, where he soon proved himself in debate an active and energetic supporter of the measures of his party. He took his place in the front rank of the extreme advocates of slavery and state sovereignty. Upon the breaking out of the Mexican war he was elected colonel of a Mississippi rifle regiment, and resigned his seat in Congress for a post of honor in the field. Here he again distinguished himself by his coolness and determination, and at the battle of Buena Vista rendered such efficient service at the head of his regiment, where he remained throughout the day, though badly wounded, that General Taylor praised his conduct highly in his dispatches. His term of service having expired, he returned home, but was met on his way by a commission as brigadier general of volunteers, sent to him by President Polk. Almost any other man would have at once accepted such an honor. But here was an opportunity for an exhibition of a sort of perverse, pertinacious consistency in pushing the doctrine of state sovereignty to the last extreme, and of giving a civil rebuff to the government at Washington. Colonel Davis had been commissioned as a Mississippi volunteer; and, although he was in the service of the United States, under command of a general in the regular army of the United States, and paid by the United States, he was yet not to be insulted as a Mississippian by being made a general of brigade by the President of the United States; and so he declined the commission, on the ground that its bestowal was an infraction—well meant and pardonable, perhaps, but still an infraction—of the sovereignty of the "republic" of Mississippi!—a poor, struggling, debt-repudiating commonwealth, created by an act of Congress of the United States, and sparsely peopled by such emigrants as could best be spared from the older commonwealths of the same great nation. But still, ridiculous as it was, Mr. Davis made his point.

One of Mississippi's senatorial chairs at Washington being casually vacant in 1847, Mr. Davis was appointed by the governor of the state to fill it; and this he did so much to the satisfaction of his constituents that he was twice re-elected to the same position. In the Senate-chamber he attained the reputation of a ready, dexterous, and fearless debater, and a clear-headed, energetic man of business. His views of the superiority of state authority to that of the central government grew stronger as he grew older. It was in the nature of the man that they should. His notions of state responsibility for pecuniary obligation were brought into unpleasant notoriety during his senatorship by the position which he took in regard to the repudiation of her bonds by Mississippi. This he defended, and his sneer at "the crocodile tears which had been shed over ruined creditors" excited sorrow at home and indignation abroad.[3] In 1851 he resigned his seat in the Senate to be nominated Governor of Mississippi as the representative of the party in that state which held his principles; but, having been defeated by Henry S. Foote, the candidate of the Union party, he retired into private life for a year. In 1852 he electioneered for Mr. Pierce, the successful presidential candidate of the Democratic party, who acknowledged his services and his capacity by calling him into his cabinet as Secretary of War. In his new position he showed great activity and energy. He added to the coast defenses, improved the manufacture of arms and ammunition, and introduced the French light infantry tactics—wrongly styled Hardee's—into the army. Leaving the cabinet when Mr. Buchanan entered the White House, he returned to the Senate-chamber, where he remained until the Ordinance of Secession was passed by Mississippi, when, his doctrines of state sovereignty having accomplished the purpose for which they were devised, in compliance with them, he withdrew.

Mr. Davis owes his position purely to intellectual ability and to tenacity of purpose. He is not, like Toombs, a boaster and a bully of the fire-eating school; but he has a cool and almost serene audacity, which accomplishes his ends at least as effectually as noisier methods, and in a manner much better suited to his taste and his temperament. His nature is not rich, his soul not magnanimous, or his mind either strong or subtle. He influences men neither by convincing nor by winning them. His talent is that of clear perception; his power, that of nervous energy; and these are directed by an inflexible will. While other men pause over their scruples, and endeavor to reconcile their purpose and their conscience, he strikes directly at success. Devoid alike of enthusiasm and of sentiment, he yet knows the exaltation of entire commitment to a great purpose. His body is spare; his brain large; his face attenuated and purely intellectual in expression; his manner placid and precise, but decided. He could not have aroused the storm of insurrection, but he is just the man to guide its destructive energies.

In his character and his career, the man who was elected to the second place in the insurgent provisional government is very unlike him who holds the first. Alexander H. Stephens was born in Georgia in 1812, of parents in very humble life. Deprived, alike by the poverty of his family and the polity of his state, of the means of obtaining that grammar-school education which no child in the free states need ever be without, his career might have been obscure (it could not have been dishonorable or mean) had not the quickness of his parts attracted the attention of observant friends, who kindly supported him at school and at college, and during the first struggles of a professional career. He was admitted to the bar, and soon fully justified the judgment of his benefactors. It was not many years before he was able to gratify that love of home which distinguishes the English race no less in America than in Great Britain, and repurchased the small plantation of two hundred and fifty acres on which he was born, and which had necessarily been sold on his father's death. The possessor of such a freehold as Mr. Stephens's father had owned, in almost any other country than the slave states of America, would not have been without the means of sending his boy to school; but there, the children of men who, without capital either in money or in slaves, till so comparatively small a tract, wander about barefooted and bareheaded, and are given up to low associations. From 1837 to 1842 Mr. Stephens was a member of the Georgia Legislature, and in 1848 he was elected to the House of Representatives as a candidate of the old Whig party; but when that party, shaken to its already undermined foundation by the early throes of the convulsion which was to upheave the nation, fell into ruin, he took refuge in the Union wing of Southern Democracy. Of feeble frame, wasted by disease, and with a voice like the shrill pipe of an adolescent lad, which, indeed, he almost seemed to be, he yet soon attained distinction in Congress as a sound thinker, a skillful and eloquent debater, and a clear-headed, hard-working committee-man. His character, both as a politician and a man, is above reproach: the purity of his motives has never been impeached by friend or foe. It was as a lawyer, a legislator, and an orator that he won his reputation. He has no executive ability, or power to lead men into action. The cast of his mind is deliberative and argumentative. As we have already seen, he resisted secession to the very last; but when his state, or the majority of its residents, passed an Ordinance of Secession, he submitted; and, bound hand and foot by the doctrine of state sovereignty, was delivered over into the hands of the very faction whom he had so ably and so courageously opposed. They

[3] See his letter to the Washington *Union*, and the just animadversions upon it in the London *Times* of July 13th, 1849.

ALEXANDER H. STEPHENS.

made him vice-president, and he did not feel at liberty to resist their will. By the election of these two men, the insurgent leaders appealed directly to both classes of the people whose fortunes they had taken into their hands. The election of Jefferson Davis satisfied entirely the fire-eaters and uncompromising secessionists; and that of Mr. Stephens attracted to the new government the men of moderate views, who were still attached to the Union. Each man, too, was put into his proper place: the former where his varied experience of life, his military knowledge, and his executive ability would be called into play; the latter into a nominally executive office of all but the highest rank, but where his duties were really to preside over the deliberations of a legislative body. Soon after his elevation to this office he delivered a speech which was even more remarkable than that in which he endeavored to stay the movement toward secession, and to which there will be occasion to refer hereafter. Could reason, sanctioned by the character and upborne by the influence of a blameless and beloved man, have checked the madness of secession, Mr. Stephens's first effort would have checked it; but that proving impossible, he lent the same mental gifts and the same personal beauty of character to the support and adornment of a cause which he had not at heart.

With regard to a Constitution, the labors of the Convention were light and short: they adopted the Constitution of the United States with a very few variations. Of these, two only—the admission of absolute state sovereignty, involving the formation of the new government by states and not by the whole people, and the recognition of slavery as normal throughout the confederation—were the only radical differences between the new Constitution and that from which its framers had revolted.[4] And as to the last, it worked no practical change, because the absolute inviolability of slavery, as of every other local institution not inconsistent with the Constitution of the United States, was secured by that instrument itself. Thus their very organic law became a witness forever against those men who had undertaken the destruction of that which the vice-president of their confederation himself called "the most beneficent government the world ever saw." It showed that the reason of their rebellion was, not that they were in danger of losing any political right or personal privilege, not that they were in danger of becoming slaves, or even that their slaves were in danger of becoming free men, but merely that the interest of slavery had ceased to be dominant in the republic. Unanimity of feeling and unity of action marked the proceedings of this Convention, and of the government which was formed by it, though not of the people of whose destinies it had assumed control. But the government none the less exhibited immediately that promptness and decision which had marked the movements of the insurgent leaders from the very first. On the 18th of February Jefferson Davis was inaugurated provisional president;[5]

[4]   *Constitution of the Confederated States.*

The Preamble reads as follows:

"We, the deputies of the sovereign and independent states of South Carolina, Georgia, Florida, Alabama, Mississippi, and Louisiana, invoking the favor of Almighty God, do hereby, in behalf of these states, ordain and establish this Constitution for the provisional government of the same, to continue one year from the inauguration of the President, or until a permanent constitution or confederation between the said states shall be put in operation, whichsoever shall first occur."

The seventh section, first article, is as follows:

"The importation of African negroes from any foreign country other than the slaveholding states of the United States is hereby forbidden, and Congress is required to pass such laws as shall effectually prevent the same."

Article second: "Congress shall also have power to prohibit the introduction of slaves from any state not a member of this confederacy."

Article fourth of the third clause of the second section says:

"A slave in one state escaping to another shall be delivered up, on the claim of the party to whom said slave may belong, by the executive authority of the state in which such slave may be found; and in case of any abduction or forcible rescue, full compensation, including the value of the slave, and all costs and expenses, shall be made to the party by the state in which such abduction or rescue shall take place."

[5]   INAUGURAL ADDRESS OF JEFFERSON DAVIS.

Gentlemen of the Congress of the Confederate States of America, Friends and Fellow-Citizens:

Called to the difficult and responsible station of chief executive of the provisional government which you have instituted, I approach the discharge of the duties assigned me with an humble distrust of my abilities, but with a sustaining confidence in the wisdom of those who are to guide and aid me in the administration of public affairs, and an abiding faith in the virtue and patriotism of the people. Looking forward to the speedy establishment of a permanent government to take the place of this, and which, by its greater moral and physical power, will be better able to combat with the many difficulties which arise from the conflicting interests of separate nations, I enter upon the duties of the office to which I have been chosen with the hope that the beginning of our career as a confederacy may not be obstructed by hostile opposition to our enjoyment of the separate existence and independence which we have asserted, and which, with the blessing of Providence, we intend to maintain.

Our present condition, achieved in a manner unprecedented in the history of nations, illustrates the American idea that governments rest upon the consent of the governed, and that it is the right of the people to alter and abolish governments whenever they become destructive to the ends for which they were established. The declared compact of the Union, from which we have withdrawn, was to establish justice, insure domestic tranquillity, provide for the common defense, promote the general welfare, and secure the blessings of liberty to ourselves and our posterity; and when, in the judgment of the sovereign states now composing this confederacy, it has been perverted from the purposes for which it was ordained, and ceased to answer the ends for which it was established, a peaceful appeal to the ballot-box declared that, so far as they were concerned, the

government created by that compact should cease to exist. In this they merely asserted the right which the Declaration of Independence of 1776 defined to be inalienable. Of the time and occasion of its exercise they, as sovereigns, were the final judges, each for itself. The impartial, enlightened verdict of mankind will vindicate the rectitude of our conduct, and He who knows the hearts of men will judge of the sincerity with which we labored to preserve the government of our fathers in its spirit.

The right solemnly proclaimed at the birth of the states, and which has been affirmed and reaffirmed in the Bills of Rights of the states subsequently admitted into the Union of 1789, undeniably recognizes in the people the power to resume the authority delegated for the purposes of government. Thus the sovereign states here represented proceeded to form this confederacy; and it is by the abuse of language that their act has been denominated revolution. They formed a new alliance, but within each state its government has remained. The rights of person and property have not been disturbed. The agent through whom they communicated with foreign nations is changed, but this does not necessarily interrupt their international relations. Sustained by the consciousness that the transition from the former Union to the present confederacy has not proceeded from a disregard, on our part, of our just obligations, or any failure to perform every constitutional duty, moved by no interest or passion to invade the rights of others, anxious to cultivate peace and commerce with all nations, if we may not hope to avoid war, we may at least expect that posterity will acquit us of having needlessly engaged in it. Doubly justified by the absence of wrong on our part, and by wanton aggression on the part of others, there can be no cause to doubt that the courage and patriotism of the people of the Confederate States will be found equal to any measures of defense which soon their security may require.

An agricultural people, whose chief interest is the export of a commodity required in every manufacturing country, our true policy is peace, and the freest trade which our necessities will permit. It is alike our interest, and that of all those to whom we would sell and from whom we would buy, that there should be the fewest practicable restrictions upon the interchange of commodities. There can be but little rivalry between ours and any manufacturing or navigating community, such as the Northeastern states of the American Union. It must follow, therefore, that mutual interest would invite good-will and kind offices. If, however, passion or lust of dominion should cloud the judgment or inflame the ambition of those states, we must prepare to meet the emergency, and maintain by the final arbitrament of the sword the position which we have assumed among the nations of the earth.

We have entered upon a career of independence, and it must be inflexibly pursued through many years of controversy with our late associates of the Northern states. We have vainly endeavored to secure tranquillity and obtain respect for the rights to which we were entitled. As a necessity, not a choice, we have resorted to the remedy of separation, and henceforth our energies must be directed to the conduct of our own affairs, and the perpetuity of the confederacy which we have formed. If a just perception of mutual interest shall permit us peaceably to pursue our separate political career, my most earnest desire will have been fulfilled. But if this be denied

and by the 20th he had formed his cabinet, in which Mr. Toombs had the Department of State, Mr. Memminger that of the Treasury, and Mr. Pope Walker that of War. Thus, in three months and two weeks from the election in which the people of these seven states had taken part, they had been hurried into secession, had been provided, by the summary process of seizure, with fifteen forts, an immense amount of arms and ammunition, large sums of money and several armed vessels, had drilled thousands of troops, had a Constitution and a provisional government bestowed upon them, which government had put its administrative machinery in working order. In fact, nearly all these things were ready at their hand; they had only, as individuals, as states, or through a "common agency," to take them. An insurrection under like favorable circumstances the world never saw before.

The insurgent government found itself, however, not only jealously regarded by some of the most important slave states, but with a large and outspoken opposition in some of the very states by which it had been formed. From the small state of Delaware little aid could have been expected, and hope of that little was entirely given up on account of that state's unqualified devotion to the republic. Maryland and Kentucky were loyal by very large majorities. The former was under loyal rule; and, although the governor of the latter (Magoffin) was a secessionist, his hands were so tied by his constituents that he could not yet give any aid to the insurgent cause. Attempts to force Tennessee into rebellion had failed; and in the eastern part of the state the whole population was devoted to the Union. Of the people of Missouri a large majority also were unwavering in their allegiance to the Constitution and the flag. Virginia was busying herself to bring about a compromise and a restoration of the power of the government by amendments to the Constitution, and to that end she made propositions to South Carolina, who spurned them in a series of resolutions, one of which was, "That the separation of South Carolina from the federal Union was final, and she has no farther interest in the Constitution of the United States." In South Carolina there appeared to be almost an entire unanimity of feeling. There were many who were still loyal, but they comparatively were so few in number that they were quite overborne and practically extinguished. Only one man of them felt that his position warranted him in speaking out his loyalty. The name of John S. Pettigru, a venerable and much-esteemed resident of Charleston, where he gracefully occupied the highest social position, will always be held in honor as the one faithful among the many faithless to the republic in that city. The rector of the Episcopal church at which he was an attendant having, after the act of secession, omitted the President of the United States from the Collect for rulers and all in authority, Mr. Pettigru rose and left the church, thus silently protesting in the face of the congregation against the omission. It is said that only the veneration in which he was held secured him impunity in this opposition to the seceding party; but it is much to be deplored that all who were like-minded with him throughout the slave states were not, like him, bold and constant in their assertion of their loyalty and their love for the republic. The course of events would thereby have been greatly changed. But in other states of the new confederacy there was not only devotion to the Union, but speech and action in its support. When, after the Louisiana Convention had passed the Ordinance of Secession, her senators, John Slidell and Judah P. Benjamin, withdrew from Congress with insult and defiance on their lips, one of her delegates to the House of Representatives, John E. Bouligny, declared in his place that he would not withdraw, and that he would live by and die for the flag under which he was born. In Frankfort, Alabama, the state in which was the capital of the rebel confederacy, a meeting was held at which not only was a resolution passed sustaining the delegates of that district in their refusal to sign the Ordinance of Secession, but it was declared that secession was "inexpedient and unnecessary," that those present were "opposed to it in any form," and that "the refusal to submit the so-called Secession Ordinance to the decision of the people was an outrage upon their rights and liberty, and manifested a spirit of assumption, unfairness, and dictatorship." And, finally, it was resolved, that if the congressional nominee of those who took part in these proceedings were elected, he should represent them "in the United States Congress, and not in the Congress of this so-called 'Southern Confederacy.'"[6] In Georgia itself, and in the very capital of the state, a leading journal, assuming, of course, to speak strongly in the Southern interest, openly opposed the union of the fortunes of the state to "a confederacy of disorganizing charlatans" and "chimerical schemers;" admitted that the greatest danger to the new confederacy was threatened, not from the North, but from its own people; and warned its readers that indications were daily growing stronger that "organized, if not armed opposition to the new order of things might arise in states or parts of Southern states not vitally interested in the slavery question."[7] Other manifestations of the same kind appeared in various quarters of the confederacy; and on the floor of Congress, in both houses, many members, chiefly from Virginia, Maryland, and Kentucky, uttered boldly their devotion to the fortunes of the republic. But in the Legislature of North Carolina, where no Ordinance of Secession had yet been passed, and not even a convention called, a most significant resolution was unanimously adopted. It was declared that if reconciliation failed, North Carolina would go with the other slave states. This was a hardly needed indication of the line of policy to be pursued by the insurgent leaders, if they would strengthen their confederation by the accession of all the slave states. So, while within their own states intimidation, intrigue, social exclusion, and all possible moral and physical forces were brought to bear with increased urgency upon those who opposed secession, a belligerent attitude was at once assumed toward the government of the United States, in order, as we shall see, to make reconciliation speedily appear impossible, that thus the movement of the halting Northern slave states toward secession might be quickened. Enticements of a peculiar kind were also spread before the people of those states. The importation of negro slaves, except from the slaveholding states in the Union, was forbidden in the Constitution, which also, in the next section, gave the Confederate Congress power to prohibit the introduction of slaves from any state not a member of the confederacy. Thus foreign prejudices were conciliated by the forbidding of the African slave-trade, and the old market was still offered to Maryland, Virginia, Kentucky, and Tennessee, for the slaves they bred; while, at the same time, the power to exclude any one of them from that market, unless they joined the confederacy, was held up in terror over them. The rebel Congress also immediately passed an act declaring the navigation of the Mississippi free. This was addressed to Kentucky, Tennessee, and Missouri, and to the free states upon the great river and the Ohio, in the hope of detaching their interest from that of the Eastern and Middle states, and thus weakening the power of the government at Washington.

Meantime, arming, and the seizing of arms, and the betrayal of forts and armed vessels, went on almost as matters of course in the seceded states, and in some of those which had not seceded. On the 8th of February the United States Arsenal at Little Rock, containing 9000 muskets, 40 cannon, and a large supply of ammunition, was seized in the name of the people of Arkansas, who had not yet declared their separation from the Union. In Texas a more important surrender was accompanied by circumstances much more disgraceful to all concerned in it, and to the cause in the interest of which it was made. The troops in that state were under the command of Brigadier General David E. Twiggs, to whose custody were also committed the forts and all the military property of the United States in that department. General Twiggs had served creditably in Mexico, but with no particular distinction, and had attained his rank in the regular course of promotion. He was supposed to be at least a man of personal honor and integrity; but, availing himself of his position, and the trust which had been placed in him, he, not being threatened by an overwhelming force, delivered all the army posts under his command, together with all the other property in his keeping, into the hands of the rebellious authorities of Texas. Property worth over a million and a half of dollars, exclusive of the forts and public buildings, for which he was responsible as a man, aside from his military oath, was by his treachery lost to the United States. He, of course, expected his connection with the army of the United States to cease; but he was not permitted to resign, as many officers had been before him: an order for his ignominious expulsion from the army was issued immediately upon the receipt of proper information by the government at Washington. But he did not find all his subordinates ready to obey the orders by which he betrayed his trust. Captain Hill, who was in command of Fort Brown, refused to surrender that post, and made preparations to defend it; but, finally, as it appeared that it could not be held by the force under his com-

---

us, and the integrity of our territory and jurisdiction be assailed, it will but remain for us with firm resolve to appeal to arms, and invoke the blessing of Providence on a just cause.

As a consequence of our new condition, and with a view to meet anticipated wants, it will be necessary to provide a speedy and efficient organization of the branches of the executive department having special charge of foreign intercourse, finance, military affairs, and postal service. For purposes of defense the Confederate States may, under ordinary circumstances, rely mainly upon their militia; but it is deemed advisable, in the present condition of affairs, that there should be a well-instructed, disciplined army, more numerous than would usually be required on a peace establishment. I also suggest that, for the protection of our harbors and commerce on the high seas, a navy adapted to those objects will be required. These necessities have, doubtless, engaged the attention of Congress.

With a Constitution differing only from that of our fathers in so far as it is explanatory of their well known intent, freed from sectional conflicts, which have interfered with the pursuit of the general welfare, it is not unreasonable to expect that the states from which we have recently parted may seek to unite their fortunes to ours, under the government which we have instituted. For this your Constitution makes adequate provision, but beyond this, if I mistake not, the judgment and will of the people are, that union with the states from which they have separated is neither practicable nor desirable. To increase the power, develop the resources, and promote the happiness of the confederacy, it is requisite there should be so much homogeneity that the welfare of every portion would be the aim of the whole. Where this does not exist, antagonisms are engendered which must and should result in separation.

Actuated solely by a desire to preserve our own rights and to promote our own welfare, the separation of the Confederate States has been marked by no aggression upon others, and followed by no domestic convulsion. Our industrial pursuits have received no check, the cultivation of our fields progresses as heretofore, and even should we be involved in war there would be no considerable diminution in the production of the staples which have constituted our exports, in which the commercial world has an interest scarcely less than our own. This common interest of producer and consumer can only be intercepted by an exterior force which should obstruct its transmission to foreign markets, a course of conduct which would be detrimental to manufacturing and commercial interests abroad.

Should reason guide the action of the government from which we have separated, a policy so detrimental to the civilized world, the Northern states included, could not be dictated by even a stronger desire to inflict injury upon us; but if it be otherwise, a terrible responsibility will rest upon it, and the suffering of millions will bear testimony to the folly and wickedness of our aggressors. In the mean time there will remain to us, besides the ordinary remedies before suggested, the well-known resources for retaliation upon the commerce of an enemy.

Experience in public stations of a subordinate grade to this which your kindness has conferred has taught me that care, and toil, and disappointments are the price of official elevation. You will see many errors to forgive, many deficiencies to tolerate; but you shall not find in me either want of zeal or fidelity to the cause that is to me the highest in hope and of most enduring affection. Your generosity has bestowed upon me an undeserved distinction, one which I neither sought nor desired. Upon the continuance of that sentiment, and upon your wisdom and patriotism, I rely to direct and support me in the performance of the duties required at my hands.

We have changed the constituent parts, but not the system of our government. The Constitution formed by our fathers is that of these Confederate States. In their exposition of it, and in the judicial construction it has received, we have a light which reveals its true meaning. Thus instructed as to the just interpretation of that instrument, and ever remembering that all offices are but trusts held for the people, and that delegated powers are to be strictly construed, I will hope, by due diligence in the performance of my duties, though I may disappoint your expectation, yet to retain, when retiring, something of the good-will and confidence which will welcome my entrance into office.

It is joyous in the midst of perilous times to look around upon a people united in heart, when one purpose of high resolve animates and actuates the whole, where the sacrifices to be made are not weighed in the balance against honor, right, liberty, and equality. Obstacles may retard, but they can not long prevent the progress of a movement sanctioned by its justice and sustained by a virtuous people. Reverently let us invoke the God of our fathers to guide and protect us in our efforts to perpetuate the principles which by His blessing they were able to vindicate, establish, and transmit to their posterity; and with a continuance of His favor ever gratefully acknowledged, we may hopefully look forward to success, to peace, to prosperity.

[6] Report in the *North Alabamian*, Tuscumbia.

[7] Augusta *Sentinel*.

DAVID E. TWIGGS.

March 4th, 1861. Probably no political event ever occurred more significant and peculiar in all its circumstances. The unpracticed politician, and, till then, almost unknown man, who was thus declared the constitutionally elected chief magistrate of the republic, had been raised to that high office by a party which owed its very existence to the opposition awakened by a measure which had been brought forward by his principal opponent as his own stepping-stone to the highest position in the country. By his Kansas Bill Mr. Douglas made Mr. Lincoln President of the United States. The man also who, in the performance of his duty, declared him constitutionally elected, was his next most powerful opponent, as the candidate and representative of a faction who had predetermined to make that election the occasion of breaking in pieces the government of which they had so long had almost absolute control. If Mr. Douglas and Mr. Breckinridge met that day, it must have been as difficult for them as for two Roman augurs to look each other in the face without a smile —a smile no less rueful than subdued.

At this time Mr. Lincoln was in Springfield, Illinois, where his modest and almost humble home had become the shrine of political pilgrimage. He was beset by cabinet-makers, would-be ministers, office-seekers of a lower rank, political meddlers of all kinds, and newsmongers of all grades. Unasked advice was poured out upon him without stint; and from some quarters came importunate calls for a declaration of the policy of his coming administration. It was thought by many that if he announced a determination not to interfere with slavery, to respect the rights of local law and local custom, and to abide by the Constitution as interpreted by the Supreme Court, the progress of the rebellion would be crippled, if not entirely checked. But these expectations were not well founded. For, as it afterward appeared, such a declaration would have been without effect upon the leaders of secession in the seven states which had declared themselves no longer part of the republic; and the subsequent accession to their force from the remaining slave states was brought about, as we shall see, not by any apprehensions that the new administration would seek to disturb the relations between the negro slaves and their masters, but by a determination to insist upon the extension of slavery, and to defend the preposterous principle of state sovereignty.

Mr. Lincoln issued no declaration, but preferred that his future should be conjectured from his past. He busied himself in preparation for the momentous duties which would be laid upon him in the first hour after he had sworn as President to "defend the Constitution of the United States." Meanwhile steps were taken with the desperate intention of excluding him from the presidential chair, at the cost, if necessary, of his life and the lives of many others. As the 4th of March approached, some of the most violent of the secessionists (who swarmed in all the principal cities of the North) said, menacingly, that he would never be inaugurated; and bets were offered and accepted that he would never be in power at Washington:—accepted freely; for these threats were looked upon as empty bluster, the spiteful words of men accustomed to talk without restraint, and who were now smarting under a political defeat, and irritated by a prospective loss of power and patronage. They were, in fact, entirely disregarded, because it was not supposed for a moment that people who had declared that they had no connection with the government at Washington, and no interest in it, would think of attacking a place in which they were deprived of no rights, and from which they were not threatened. As to any other mode of preventing the inauguration, none could be thought of in the free states; and the slaveholders sojourning at the North, when asked how Mr. Lincoln could be deterred from assuming the office to which he had been elected, made no definite answer. They knew more than their querists dreamed they did; and the rebellion, still regarded as a passing political turmoil by the larger part of the people at the North, had already assumed a desperate phase and a bloody purpose, almost beyond the comprehension of the peace-loving, law-abiding people against whose constitutional rights and political interests it was directed. From the beginning, the leaders and principal actors in the rebellion added to the great advantages gained by base and wide-spread treachery, that of an entire readiness, if not a foregone determination, to do, with an utter recklessness of all consequences, except their own success, that which the government and the loyal people did not suppose that they would venture to do, or even think of doing. No one save themselves suspected how remorselessly they were in earnest.

But, although such was the general misapprehension of the spirit and the purposes of the rebellion, some men were sufficiently alarmed to take measures of precaution. The chairman of a railway company, over whose road the President elect was sure to pass, was waited upon by a lady who had

mand, he yielded it in a manner entirely honorable to himself both as a man and a soldier. The promptness and direct movement toward success which marked the rebel administration of affairs was shown in regard to the United States soldiers thus left without orders and without barracks in Texas. Mr. Davis, hardly well seated in a presidential chair hardly set up, wrote through his Secretary of War to the Texas Convention that these soldiers should be allowed a reasonable time to leave the territory of the confederacy (of which, it should be observed, Texas was not yet a member, as her Ordinance of Secession was only to go into effect on the 2d of March, after confirmation by the people); but that, should the United States government refuse to withdraw them, "all the powers of the Southern confederacy should be used to expel them."

But it was in another quarter, and under the administration of another president of the United States that Mr. Davis was first to use the powers of his confederacy to expel the troops and the flag of the United States from the borders of a seceded state. The beleaguered, but not yet completely invested fort in Charleston Harbor was still the cynosure of all eyes. Mr. Buchanan did nothing, and was plainly determined to do nothing for its relief; deeming, apparently, the nation's honor and his own abundantly satisfied if he could slink away from Washington while Major Anderson's flag was flying. Major Anderson took care that he should have that satisfaction. But a man was on his way to the capital, all unconscious that his way was sore beset, who could not be so easily contented.

On the 13th of February, in presence of the Senate and the House of Representatives, assembled in the chamber of the latter body, John C. Breckinridge, Vice-president of the United States, after opening and reading before them the certificates of election from all the states of the Union, declared that Abraham Lincoln had been duly elected President, and Hannibal Hamlin Vice-president of the United States for the term beginning

M

traveled through much of the South on a mission of mercy, and who told him that in the course of her journeys she had seen at least twenty thousand men under arms, and that she had become convinced that there was a conspiracy to seize upon Washington and prevent Mr. Lincoln's inauguration. Listened to with incredulity at first, in spite of the respect which her character and experience demanded, her anxiety finally produced such an impression upon the gentleman that he sent a proper messenger to Lieutenant General Scott to put him upon his guard, yet was inclined to apologize for calling his attention to such vague and extravagant apprehensions. What was his surprise to learn in reply from General Scott that he had for some time been quite sure of the existence of some such conspiracy; that he had made the proper representations to President Buchanan and to others, but that he was listened to with incredulity, and was absolutely powerless. Upon this, measures were at once taken to ferret out the truth. Detectives were employed, and placed upon the line of the railway in question near Baltimore and Washington. They soon discovered that the soldier's fears, no less than the lady's, were more than justified. They found volunteer military companies drilling at various points along the road, which they soon saw were composed entirely of men of the extreme slavery-secession faction, although they professed to be strong Union men. To these companies they joined themselves in the assumed character of Southern and Southwestern men of like principles and purposes, and then learned that the object of their formation was the proffer of their services to the directors of the railway as an escort to Mr. Lincoln at some convenient point of the road, where, having secured entire control of it for a sufficient time, they would kill Mr. Lincoln, and, if necessary, the whole party which accompanied him; they being determined and prepared to destroy, at some bridge or other fit place, the whole train in which he was a passenger, should that be needful to the attainment of their object. Similar investigations set on foot in Baltimore, by other persons whose suspicions had been excited, revealed a similar conspiracy in that city. The detectives were engaged three weeks in obtaining a full revelation of the designs of the plotters there. But they discovered, and themselves became seemingly a part of, a body of men well organized with the fell purpose that if the President elect survived to enter Baltimore, he should not leave it alive. They were to mingle with the shouting crowd which would be sure to surround his carriage on his arrival, to prolong and increase the excitement, and, in the confusion, to thrust themselves forward as overeager friends, and thus get near enough to put him surely to death with pistols and hand-grenades. In the first moments of surprise and alarm they could easily escape, and a vessel was to be ready to transport them immediately to safety within the limits of the confederacy in whose interests, if not by whose procurement, the diabolical scheme was concocted. Of course, the immediate actors in this intended slaughter were of the baser sort; but it was discovered that men of wealth, and social position, and political influence countenanced and supported it. The plot was a good one, and, owing to the informal, democratic, and overconfident habits of the country, easy of execution, had it not been detected.

Mr. Lincoln, as unsuspecting as every one of his constituents who was not fully informed, left Springfield on the 11th of February for Washington; and, after the inevitable series of congratulations and speech-makings on the route, arrived at Philadelphia on the 21st of the month. There he first learned the designs upon his life from the detective who had been principally instrumental in discovering them in Baltimore. Late in the evening of the same day a special messenger from General Scott and Mr. Seward—Mr. Seward's son—roused him from his bed with an earnest warning. Deeply impressed as Mr. Lincoln was by such monitions, received through such channels, he yet refused to abandon an engagement to be present at Independence Hall in Philadelphia on the morning of the next day—Washington's birthday—and one to meet the Legislature of Pennsylvania at Harrisburg in the afternoon; but, these fulfilled, he consented to abandon his original plan, and go immediately and privately to Washington. The day passed off without any incident worthy of remark, except that some attention was attracted by Mr. Lincoln's declaration in his speech at Independence Hall that, rather than abandon the principles of the Declaration of Independence, he would be "assassinated upon that spot." But this was regarded merely as a strong and not very happily phrased asseveration. The interview at Harrisburg with the Legislature of Pennsylvania being over, Mr. Lincoln placed himself in the hands of his friends, and retired to his hotel, assuming, by advice, an air of extreme fatigue, which his constant traveling and speaking made very natural. At about 6 o'clock in the evening he was conveyed in a close carriage to a special train, which started instantly for Philadelphia, and at the same time all the telegraph wires leading from the city were cut. With him the president of the road sent a trusty and intelligent confidential agent known as "George," whose authority was recognized by all the servants of the company, and who bore with him a large package of "dispatches," about which he seemed very anxious, and which was the alleged reason of sending the special train. At Philadelphia the party took the regular train, which they found waiting, and into which they quietly stepped just as it was starting. The detective was on the train, but "George" still considered himself in charge, and was astounded and alarmed soon after the train was under way by being accosted reproachfully by the engine-driver for not telling him that "Lincoln was on board." George instantly saw that his only way was to trust his friend, and replied, "Yes, he is on board." "Well," said the other, with a look of serious apprehension and determination, "now we have him, we must put him through." His own observation had led him to suspect the designs of the people along the road, and he felt that he carried Cæsar and his fortunes. Oddly enough, however, the man whom he supposed to

be the President elect was not he, but quite another person. The train passed swiftly through the perils prepared for the morrow, and Mr. Lincoln arrived at Washington about daybreak on the 23d of February. The telegraph wires had been united again, and George sent back the message, "The dispatches have arrived, and are safely delivered."[8]

Although the knowledge of this conspiracy had been confined to those who were concerned in it and those who had detected it, the fact that Maryland was the only slave state through which Mr. Lincoln was obliged to pass on his way to Washington, and the well-known riotous character of the baser part of the people of Baltimore, had made his reception in that city a subject of special interest. The Republicans of the place were counseled by the authorities to abandon their intention of receiving Mr. Lincoln with the honors due to a President elect, which they were told "would certainly produce a disturbance of the most violent and dangerous character to the President and all who were with him." They prudently followed the advice. On the evening of the 22d a Baltimore newspaper published an article calculated to produce an attack on Mr. Lincoln, who was to arrive there on the 23d, and the marshal of the city placed an unusually large body of the police under orders, to be used both as an escort and a general force of observation and restraint. When, therefore, on the day of his expected arrival at that city, it was announced that he was already in the national capital, which he had reached in privacy, in darkness, almost by flight, there was throughout the country a sensation of the liveliest surprise; surprise which was changed to shame and profound humiliation when the cause of this surreptitious entry of the seat of government was revealed. Except on the part of those who felt it their duty to sustain the successful candidate of the Republican party at all hazards, there was a universal and indignant expression of unbelief, and the affair became immediately the subject of a rueful kind of ridicule. The story was widely regarded, and especially in Baltimore and at the South, as trumped up for political effect, and the event for a time degraded Mr. Lincoln in the people's eyes. They refused to accept the alleged conspiracy against his life as any excuse for the ignominious secrecy with which he, the future chief magistrate of the country, made his way through one of its principal cities. They scouted the notion that any of their countrymen could seek to repair a political defeat by assassination. They resented the accusation brought against these Baltimore desperadoes as a national insult. The Anglo-Saxon race, they said, are not assassins; least of all are they so in the United States of America. The affair elicited on almost all sides mingled expressions of incredulity, bitterness, and ridicule. From the point of view of the people of the free states, this judgment was justified, and this feeling was correct. It may be safely said that among their native-born population the formation of such a conspiracy would have been morally impossible. But they forgot to take into account, as elements of their judgment, the debasing and brutalizing influences of slavery as an institution; they did not stop to think of the pitiless infliction of torture and death upon rebellious slaves throughout the South, and of the bloody duels and street-brawls between "gentlemen" so constantly occurring there; they forgot for the moment that the bowie-knife was strictly a slave-state weapon, and that of the bloody assaults and murders committed within their own borders by natives of the United States, the large majority were committed by men born and bred under the malign influence of the worst form of slavery.[9] And last, and perhaps most important omission, they had not yet even begun to conceive that the leaders of this insurrection, set on foot among a people so accustomed to scenes of blood, and in whom a spirit of arrogant domination was bred by the very constitution of their society, were determined, with the determination of the desperate, to carry their point at every hazard. It was long, indeed, before this conviction came effectually home to them.

The excitement caused by this disgraceful occurrence, however, soon gave place to profounder, if less vivid, emotions. On the 28th, the Plan of Adjustment adopted by the Peace Congress was sent to the Senate and the House, where they were followed, on the next day, by the report of the Committee of Thirty-three. It at once became apparent that they would not command the support either of Congress or the mass of the non-slaveholding people, and that, consequently, all hopes of harmony and peace which had been based upon them must be abandoned. Looking back upon these propositions, made after such long consultation among men who were practiced politicians, if not sagacious statesmen, we can but wonder at the failure which they exhibit to comprehend the revolutionary nature of the crisis. That of the Committee of Thirty-three was in the form of a brief amendment to the Constitution, which provided that no amendment should be made to that instrument which would give Congress power over the domestic institutions of any state. But as this was a mere solemn confirmation of a political right which no man denied, or ever had denied, to any or to all the states, it was therefore of no more consequence than the paper on which it was written.[10] The proposals of the Peace Congress were embodied in seven sections, of

[8] Statement of Mr. Thurlow Weed in the Albany Evening Journal, and private account of Mr. S. M. Felton, president of the Philadelphia and Baltimore Railway Company.

[9] Of the hundreds of cases which I might cite in support of this position, one in which there was no bloodshed seems to me very characteristic. A gentleman well known to me, being in the principal city of a slave state in 1861, was sitting upon the piazza of the best hotel in the place. Near him sat a man, in a dreamy, contemplative mood, having his back turned to the window of a barber's shop which opened with vertical sashes to the floor of the piazza. A light passing gust blew one of these sashes to, when instantly this man sprang up, and, drawing a revolver, fired five shots directly through the window into the barber's shop. Fortunately there were few persons in the shop, and he hit neither of them. But it is significant that he thought, of course, that the noise he heard was a pistol-shot; and, of course, that some person had attempted to shoot him "on sight;" and that, of course, he had a revolver in his pocket, which he drew, of course, and fired recklessly in the direction of the sound which startled him.

[10] "No amendment shall be made to the Constitution which will authorize or give Congress power to abolish or interfere, within any state, with the domestic institutions thereof, including that of persons held to labor or servitude by the laws of said state."

er to regulate, abolish, or control slavery in any state or territory of the United States, or in the District of Columbia, or any other place belonging to the United States; to prohibit the bringing of slaves into the District, or the transfer of them from one part of the country to another. The remaining sections forever prohibited the slave-trade, secured a more stringent enforcement of the Fugitive Slave Law, and declared that the foregoing sections should never be amended or abolished without the consent of all the states.[1] Except in the restoration of the line of the Missouri Compromise, this plan placed the republic, bound hand and foot, in the power of slavery. It could not but fail miserably, as it did. The Republicans were against it in a body; and, indeed, they opposed any adjustment other than that which should be effected by a Constitutional Convention of the people of the United States, which Congress had no power to convoke. It was plain that compromise was at an end, and that the government must sustain itself under existing conditions, or else be utterly destroyed.

Meantime the 4th of March came on apace; and in spite of their betting and their threatening, the secessionists on that day saw Mr. Lincoln duly invested with the office to which their own candidate in the contest had declared him constitutionally elected. The provision which General Scott had been able to make for the preservation of order within the District of Columbia, in spite of the small force at his disposal for that purpose, was sufficient to deter any attempt which evil-disposed persons, without as well as within its boundaries, were then prepared for. On the appointed day Mr. Lincoln went in procession to the Capitol, in company with President Buchanan, and, after visiting the Senate-chamber, proceeded to the east front of the

ABRAHAM LINCOLN.

which the first virtually re-established the Missouri Compromise; the second prohibited the acquirement of any territory by the United States "without the concurrence of a majority of all the senators from the states which allow involuntary servitude, and a majority of all the senators from the states which prohibit that relation;" and the third denied forever to Congress the pow-

building, where, in the open air, in presence of both houses of Congress, the foreign ministers, and a vast concourse of people, he delivered his inaugural address,[2] and took the oath of office at the hands of Chief Justice Taney.

President Lincoln's inaugural address was scanned with even more anx-

---

[1]   *Plan of Adjustment adopted by the Peace Congress.*

SEC. 1. In all the present territory of the United States north of the parallel of thirty-six degrees thirty minutes of north latitude, involuntary servitude, except in punishment of crime, is prohibited. In all the present territory south of that line, the status of persons held to service or labor, as it now exists, shall not be changed. Nor shall any law be passed by Congress or the Territorial Legislature to hinder or prevent the taking of such persons from any of the states of this Union to said territory, nor to impair the rights arising from said relation. But the same shall be subject to judicial cognizance in the federal courts, according to the course of the common law. When any Territory, north or south of said line, with such boundary as Congress may prescribe, shall contain a population equal to that required for a member of Congress, it shall, if its form of government be republican, be admitted into the Union on an equal footing with the original states, with or without involuntary servitude, as the Constitution of such state may provide.

SEC. 2. No territory shall be acquired by the United States, except by discovery, and for naval and commercial stations, dépôts, and transit routes, without the concurrence of a majority of all the senators from the states which allow involuntary servitude, and a majority of all the senators from the states which prohibit that relation; nor shall territory be acquired by treaty, unless the votes of a majority of the senators from each class of states hereinbefore mentioned be cast as a part of the two-third majority necessary to the ratification of such treaty.

SEC. 3. Neither the Constitution nor any amendment thereto shall be construed to give Congress power to regulate, abolish, or control, within any state or territory of the United States, the relation established or recognized by the laws thereof touching persons bound to labor or involuntary service in the District of Columbia, without the consent of Maryland, and without the consent of the owners, or making the owners who do not consent just compensation; nor the power to interfere with or prohibit representatives and others from bringing with them to the city of Washington, retaining, and taking away persons so bound to labor or service; nor the power to interfere with or abolish involuntary service in places under the exclusive jurisdiction of the United States within those states and territories where the same is established or recognized; nor the power to prohibit the removal or transportation of persons held to labor or involuntary service in any state or territory of the United States to any other state or territory thereof where it is established or recognized by law or usage; and the right, during transportation by sea or river, of touching at ports, shores, and landings, and of landing in case of distress, but not for sale or traffic, shall exist; nor shall Congress have power to authorize any higher rate of taxation on persons held to labor or service than on land. The bringing into the District of Columbia of persons held to labor or service for sale, or placing them in dépôts to be afterward transferred to other places for sale as merchandise, is prohibited, and the right of transit through any state or territory against its dissent is prohibited.

SEC. 4. The third paragraph of the second section of the fourth Article of the Constitution shall not be construed to prevent any of the states, by appropriate legislation, and through the action of their judicial and ministerial officers, from enforcing the delivery of fugitives from labor to the person to whom such service or labor is due.

SEC. 5. The foreign slave-trade is hereby forever prohibited; and it shall be the duty of Congress to pass laws to prevent the importation of slaves, coolies, or persons held to service or labor, into the United States and the Territories from places beyond the limits thereof.

SEC. 6. The first, third, and fifth sections, together with this section and the third paragraph of the second section of the first Article of the Constitution, and the third paragraph of the second section of the fourth Article thereof, shall not be amended or abolished without the consent of all the states.

SEC. 7. Congress shall provide by law that the United States shall pay to the owner the full value of his fugitives from labor, in all cases where the marshal, or other officer whose duty it was to arrest such fugitive, was prevented from so doing by violence or intimidation from mobs or riotous assemblages, or when, after labor, such fugitive was rescued by like violence or intimidation, and the owner thereby prevented and obstructed in the pursuit of his remedy for the recovery of such fugitive. Congress shall provide by law for securing to the citizens of each state the privileges and immunities of the several states.

[2]   *Inaugural Address of President Lincoln.*

Fellow-citizens of the United States:

In compliance with a custom as old as the government itself, I appear before you to address you briefly, and to take, in your presence, the oath prescribed by the Constitution of the United States to be taken by the President before he enters on the execution of his office.

I do not consider it necessary, at present, for me to discuss those matters of administration about which there is no special anxiety or excitement. Apprehension seems to exist among the people of the Southern states that, by the accession of a Republican administration, their property, and their peace and personal security, are to be endangered. There has never been any reasonable cause for such apprehension. Indeed, the most ample evidence to the contrary has all the while existed, and been open to their inspection. It is found in nearly all the public speeches of him who now addresses you. I do but quote from one of those speeches when I declare that "I have no purpose, directly or indirectly, to interfere with the institution of slavery in the states where it exists." I believe I have no lawful right to do so, and I have no inclination to do so. Those who nominated and elected me did so with the full knowledge that I had made this, and made many similar declarations, and had never recanted them. And, more than this, they placed in the platform, for my acceptance, and as a law to themselves and to me, the clear and emphatic resolution which I now read:

"*Resolved,* That the maintenance inviolate of the rights of the states, and especially the right of each state to order and control its own domestic institutions according to its own judgment exclusively, is essential to that balance of power on which the perfection and endurance of our political fabric depend; and we denounce the lawless invasion by armed force of the soil of any state or territory, no matter under what pretext, as among the gravest of crimes."

I now reiterate these sentiments; and, in doing so, I only press upon the public attention the most conclusive evidence of which the case is susceptible, that the property, peace, and security of no section are to be in any wise endangered by the now incoming administration. I add, too,

iety than the message with which Mr. Buchanan, months before, had so astonished and dissatisfied all men, except the seceders at home and abroad. Mr. Lincoln, on the contrary, satisfied all but the same unconditional secessionists, whom no duly qualified President of the United States could content, except at the cost of treachery. That he expressly disavowed the intention of interfering with slavery, or any other local institution, in the states where it then existed, and denied his right of such interference; that he declared that the Fugitive Slave Law, like all other constitutional laws, should be enforced; that he avowed respect for the constitutional rights of all parts of the Union, and the intention to pursue a peaceful course in his administration—this was really of no moment; for he also declared that no state, upon its own mere motion, could lawfully go out of the Union; that Ordinances of Secession were void; that resistance to the authority of the United States was insurrection; and that his official power should be used to "hold, occupy, and possess the property and places belonging to the government." To the leaders of the secession party, and their active, determined supporters, this message was a summons to submission, with the alternative of war. It was susceptible of no other construction. And yet so strangely did a large part, it would seem the greater part, of the loyal people throughout the country mistake the temper and the deliberate purpose of those who were directing the secession movement, that they regarded the address as significant of a peaceful restoration of the Union. This was especially the case with those members of the Democratic party in whom party considerations had not entirely extinguished love of country, and a reverence for the Constitution and the laws. Those who spoke for these men cast aside party considerations at once, and sustained the President in the position which he had taken. They fondly supposed that the members of their party at the South would do the same. How much they overrated the influence of patriotism and a devotion to the republic among the leading slaveholders, how incorrectly they estimated the relative value of slavery and the existence of the republic in the eyes of those men, the sequel sadly showed.

President Lincoln's address made little change in the course of events

that all the protection which, consistently with the Constitution and the laws, can be given, will be cheerfully given to all the states when lawfully demanded, for whatever cause, as cheerfully to one section as to another.

There is much controversy about the delivering up of fugitives from service or labor. The clause I now read is as plainly written in the Constitution as any other of its provisions:

"No person held to service or labor in one state under the laws thereof, escaping into another, shall, in consequence of any law or regulation therein, be discharged from such service or labor, but shall be delivered up on claim of the party to whom such service or labor may be due."

It is scarcely questioned that this provision was intended by those who made it for the reclaiming of what we call fugitive slaves; and the intention of the lawgiver is the law.

All members of Congress swear their support to the whole Constitution—to this provision as well as any other. To the proposition, then, that slaves whose cases come within the terms of this clause "shall be delivered up," their oaths are unanimous. Now, if they would make the effort in good temper, could they not, with nearly equal unanimity, frame and pass a law by means of which to keep good that unanimous oath?

There is some difference of opinion whether this clause should be enforced by national or by state authority; but surely that difference is not a very material one. If the slave is to be surrendered, it can be of but little consequence to him or to others by which authority it is done; and should any one, in any case, be content that this oath shall go unkept on a merely unsubstantial controversy as to how it shall be kept?

Again, in any law upon this subject, ought not all the safeguards of liberty known in the civilized and humane jurisprudence to be introduced, so that a free man be not, in any case, surrendered as a slave? And might it not be well, at the same time, to provide by law for the enforcement of that clause in the Constitution which guarantees that "the citizens of each state shall be entitled to all the privileges and immunities of citizens in the several states?"

I take the official oath to-day with no mental reservations, and with no purpose to construe the Constitution or laws by any hypercritical rules; and while I do not choose now to specify particular acts of Congress as proper to be enforced, I do suggest that it will be much safer for all, both in official and private stations, to conform to and abide by all those acts which stand unrepealed, than to violate any of them, trusting to find impunity in having them held to be unconstitutional.

It is seventy-two years since the first inauguration of a president under our national Constitution. During that period fifteen different and very distinguished citizens have in succession administered the executive branch of the government. They have conducted it through many perils, and generally with great success. Yet, with all this scope for precedent, I now enter upon the same task, for the brief constitutional term of four years, under great and peculiar difficulties.

A disruption of the federal Union, heretofore only menaced, is now formidably attempted. I hold that in the contemplation of universal law and of the Constitution, the union of these states is perpetual. Perpetuity is implied, if not expressed, in the fundamental law of all national governments. It is safe to assert that no government proper ever had a provision in its organic law for its own termination. Continue to execute all the express provisions of our national Constitution, and the Union will endure forever, it being impossible to destroy it except by some action not provided for in the instrument itself.

Again, if the United States be not a government proper, but an association of states in the nature of a contract merely, can it, as a contract, be peaceably unmade by less than all the parties who made it? One party to a contract may violate it—break it, so to speak; but does it not require all to lawfully rescind it? Descending from these general principles, we find the proposition that in legal contemplation the Union is perpetual, confirmed by the history of the Union itself.

The Union is much older than the Constitution. It was formed, in fact, by the Articles of Association in 1774. It was matured and continued in the Declaration of Independence in 1776. It was farther matured, and the faith of all the then thirteen states expressly plighted and engaged that it should be perpetual, by the Articles of Confederation in 1778; and, finally, in 1787, one of the declared objects for ordaining and establishing the Constitution was to form a more perfect Union. But if the destruction of the Union by one, or by a part only of the states, be lawfully possible, the Union is less than before, the Constitution having lost the vital element of perpetuity.

It follows from these views that no state, upon its own mere motion, can lawfully get out of the Union; that resolves and ordinances to that effect are legally void; and that acts of violence within any state or states against the authority of the United States are insurrectionary or revolutionary, according to circumstances.

I therefore consider that, in view of the Constitution and the laws, the Union is unbroken, and, to the extent of my ability, I shall take care, as the Constitution itself expressly enjoins upon me, that the laws of the Union shall be faithfully executed in all the states. Doing this, which I deem to be only a simple duty on my part, I shall perfectly perform it, so far as is practicable, unless my rightful masters, the American people, shall withhold the requisition, or in some authoritative manner direct the contrary.

I trust this will not be regarded as a menace, but only as the declared purpose of the Union that it will constitutionally defend and maintain itself. In doing this, there need be no bloodshed or violence, and there shall be none unless it is forced upon the national authority. The power confided to me *will be used to hold, occupy, and possess the property and places belonging to the government, and collect the duties and imposts;* but beyond what may be necessary for these objects, there will be no invasion, no using of force against or among the people any where. Where hostility to the United States shall be so great and so universal as to prevent competent resident citizens from holding the federal offices, there will be no attempt to force obnoxious strangers among the people that object. While the strict legal right may exist of the government to enforce the exercise of these offices, the attempt to do so would be so irritating, and so nearly impracticable withal, that I deem it better to forego for the time the uses of such offices. The mails, unless repelled, will continue to be furnished in all parts of the Union. So far as possible, the people every where shall have that sense of perfect security which is most favorable to calm thought and reflection.

The course here indicated will be followed, unless current events and experience shall show a modification or change to be proper; and in every case and exigency my best discretion will be exercised according to the circumstances actually existing, and with a view and hope of a peaceful solution of the national troubles, and the restoration of fraternal sympathies and affections.

That there are persons, in one section or another, who seek to destroy the Union at all events, and are glad of any pretext to do it, I will neither affirm nor deny. But if there be such, I need address no word to them.

To those, however, who really love the Union, may I not speak, before entering upon so grave a matter as the destruction of our national fabric, with all its benefits, its memories, and its hopes? Would it not be well to ascertain why we do it? Will you hazard so desperate a step, while any portion of the ills you fly from have no real existence? Will you, while the certain ills you fly to are greater than all the real ones you fly from? Will you risk the commission of so fearful a mistake? All profess to be content in the Union if all constitutional rights can be maintained. Is it true, then, that any right, plainly written in the Constitution, has been denied? I think not. Happily the human mind is so constituted that no party can reach to the audacity of doing this.

Think, if you can, of a single instance in which a plainly-written provision of the Constitution has ever been denied. If, by the mere force of numbers, a majority should deprive a minority of any clearly-written constitutional right, it might, in a moral point of view, justify revolution: it certainly would, if such right were a vital one. But such is not our case.

All the vital rights of minorities and of individuals are so plainly assured to them by affirmations and negations, guarantees and prohibitions, in the Constitution, that controversies never arise concerning them. But no organic law can ever be framed with a provision specifically applicable to every question which may occur in practical administration. No foresight can anticipate, nor any document of reasonable length contain, express provisions for all possible questions. Shall fugitives from labor be surrendered by national or by state authorities? The Constitution does not expressly say. Must Congress protect slavery in the Territories? The Constitution does not expressly say. From questions of this class spring all our constitutional controversies, and we divide upon them into majorities and minorities.

If the minority will not acquiesce, the majority must, or the government must cease. There is no alternative for continuing the government but acquiescence on the one side or the other. If a minority in such a case will secede rather than acquiesce, they make a precedent which in turn will ruin and divide them, for a minority of their own will secede from them whenever a majority refuses to be controlled by such a minority. For instance, why not any portion of a new confederacy, a year or two hence, arbitrarily secede again, precisely as portions of the present Union now claim to secede from it? All who cherish disunion sentiments are now being educated to the exact temper of doing this. Is there such perfect identity of interests among the states to compose a new Union as to produce harmony only, and prevent renewed secession? Plainly, the central idea of secession is the essence of anarchy.

A majority held in restraint by constitutional check and limitation, and always changing easily with deliberate changes of popular opinions and sentiments, is the only true sovereign of a free people. Whoever rejects it, does, of necessity, fly to anarchy or to despotism. Unanimity is impossible; the rule of a majority, as a permanent arrangement, is wholly inadmissible. So that, rejecting the majority principle, anarchy or despotism in some form is all that is left.

I do not forget the position assumed by some that constitutional questions are to be decided by the Supreme Court, nor do I deny that such decisions must be binding in any case upon the parties to a suit, as to the object of that suit, while they are also entitled to very high respect and consideration in all parallel cases by all other departments of the government; and while it is obviously possible that such decision may be erroneous in any given case, still the evil effect following it, being limited to that particular case, with the chance that it may be overruled and never become a precedent for other cases, can better be borne than could the evils of a different practice.

At the same time, the candid citizen must confess that if the policy of the government upon the vital questions affecting the whole people is to be irrevocably fixed by the decisions of the Supreme Court, the instant they are made, as in ordinary litigation between parties in personal actions, the people will have ceased to be their own masters, unless having to that extent practically resigned their government into the hands of that eminent tribunal.

Nor is there in this view any assault upon the court or the judges. It is a duty from which they may not shrink, to decide cases properly brought before them; and it is no fault of theirs if others seek to turn their decisions to political purposes. One section of our country believes slavery is right, and ought to be extended, while the other believes it is wrong, and ought not to be extended; and this is the only substantial dispute; and the fugitive slave clause of the Constitution, and the law for the suppression of the foreign slave-trade, are each as well enforced, perhaps, as any law can ever be in a community where the moral sense of the people imperfectly supports the law itself. The great body of the people abide by the dry legal obligation in both cases, and a few break over in each. This, I think, can not be perfectly cured, and it would be worse in both cases after the separation of the sections than before. The foreign slave-trade, now imperfectly suppressed, would be ultimately revived, without restriction, in one section, while fugitive slaves, now only partially surrendered, would not be surrendered at all by the other.

Physically speaking, we can not separate—we can not remove our respective sections from each other, nor build an impassable wall between them. A husband and wife may be divorced, and go out of the presence and beyond the reach of each other, but the different parts of our country can not do this. They can not but remain face to face; and intercourse, either amicable or hostile, must continue between them. Is it possible, then, to make that intercourse more advantageous or more satisfactory after separation than before? Can aliens make treaties easier than friends can make laws? Can treaties be more faithfully enforced between aliens than laws can among friends? Suppose you go to war, you can not fight always; and when, after much loss on both sides, and no gain on either, you cease fighting, the identical questions as to terms of intercourse are again upon you.

This country, with its institutions, belongs to the people who inhabit it. Whenever they shall grow weary of the existing government, they can exercise their constitutional right of amending, or their revolutionary right to dismember or overthrow it. I can not be ignorant of the fact that many worthy and patriotic citizens are desirous of having the national Constitution amended. While I make no recommendation of amendment, I fully recognize the full authority of the people over the whole subject, to be exercised in either of the modes prescribed in the instrument itself, and I should, under existing circumstances, favor, rather than oppose, a fair opportunity being afforded the people to act upon it.

I will venture to add that to me the convention mode seems preferable, in that it allows amendments to originate with the people themselves, instead of only permitting them to take or reject propositions originated by others not especially chosen for the purpose, and which might not be precisely such as they would wish either to accept or refuse. I understand that a proposed amendment to the Constitution (which amendment, however, I have not seen) has passed Congress, to the effect that the federal government shall never interfere with the domestic institutions of states, including that of persons held to service. To avoid misconstruction of what I have said, I depart from my purpose not to speak of particular amendments, so far as to say that, holding such a provision to now be implied constitutional law, I have no objection to its being made express and irrevocable.

The chief magistrate derives all his authority from the people, and they have conferred none upon him to fix the terms for the separation of the states. The people themselves, also, can do this if they choose, but the executive, as such, has nothing to do with it. His duty is to administer the present government as it came to his hands, and to transmit it unimpaired by him to his successor. Why should there not be a patient confidence in the ultimate justice of the people? Is there any better or equal hope in the world? In our present differences, is either party without faith of being in the right? If the Almighty Ruler of nations, with his eternal truth and justice, be on your side of the North, or on yours of the South, that truth and that justice will surely prevail by the judgment of this great tribunal, the American people. By the frame of the government under which we live, this same people have wisely given their public servants but little power for mischief, and have, with equal wisdom, provided for the return of that little to their own hands at very short intervals. While the people retain their virtue and vigilance, no administration, by any extreme wickedness or folly, can very seriously injure the government in the short space of four years.

My countrymen, one and all, think calmly and well upon this whole subject. Nothing valuable can be lost by taking time. If there be an object to hurry any of you, in hot haste, to a step which you would never take deliberately, that object will be frustrated by taking time; but no good object can be frustrated by it. Such of you as are now dissatisfied still have the old Constitution unimpaired, and on the sensitive point, the laws of your own framing under it; while the new administration will have no immediate power, if it would, to change either. If it were admitted that you who are dissatisfied hold the right side in the dispute, there is still no single reason for precipitate action. Intelligence, patriotism, Christianity, and a firm reliance on Him who has never yet forsaken this favored land, are still competent to adjust, in the best way, all our present difficulties. In your hands, my dissatisfied fellow-countrymen, and not in mine, is the momentous issue of civil war. The government will not assail you. You can have no conflict without being yourselves the aggressors. You have no oath registered in heaven to destroy the government, while I shall have the most solemn one to "preserve, protect, and defend" it. I am loth to close. We are not enemies, but friends. We must not be enemies. Though passion may have strained, it must not break our bonds of affection. The mystic cords of memory, stretching from every battle-field and patriot grave to every living heart and hearthstone all over this broad land, will yet swell the chorus of the Union, when again touched, as surely they will be, by the better angels of our nature.

toward the point to which they were now surely tending, but that little was a quickening of their progress and an increase of their force. Its plump denial of the right of secession, and its avowal of a determination to possess the national mints, arsenals, and military posts, put those in authority in the states which had passed Ordinances of Secession, and appropriated the property of the republic to their own use, upon their mettle; while its peaceful professions did nothing to mitigate to the advocates of state sovereignty, in the slave states which had not seceded, its assertion of the supreme and absolute authority of the central government in all national affairs. In the free states, and in the slave states still under loyal control, it made the idea of an armed struggle for the support of the government more familiar; and, by awakening the generous glow of patriotism, it softened and sundered the rigid bonds by which the Democratic party, the only well-organized and well-disciplined body in the country, had been for more than a generation so strongly bound together.

At the South the leaders allowed the people little time for such superfluous business as the consideration of a speech which merely showed that there was no ground of apprehension that their interests would suffer under the new administration of the United States government. They drove them sharply up to the work of rebellion. Military preparation and hostile action against the government had gone on vigorously under state authority during the three months preceding Mr. Lincoln's inauguration; and hardly had that event taken place when the confederate president ordered General Beauregard to Charleston to take command of the forces which had been assembled, and the works which had been erected there, for the investment of Fort Sumter. On the 9th of March the confederate Congress passed an act for the establishment and organization of an army. On the 14th the Legislature of Florida passed an act defining treason, and declaring that, in the event of a collision between the troops of the United States and those of Florida, the holding office under the government of the former by any resident of the latter should be punished with death! Supplies were cut off from the Gulf fleet and from Fort Pickens—an important post, the preservation of which to the government will form an interesting episode in the early part of our narrative. The various states under control of the confederate government ratified the Constitution adopted at Montgomery, and were called upon to furnish their quota of troops for the defense of the insurgent cause. The whole number called for was less than twenty thousand, and these, from a population of five millions, an unusually large proportion of whom were shifting adventurers or local desperadoes, and accustomed to the use of arms upon each other, were soon forthcoming. In certain places the young men of the more respectable and cultivated classes also formed themselves into military companies, and volunteered their services in the insurgent army. The South seemed to be animated with a lively and widespread enthusiasm for the confederate cause. For those whose hearts were in it were outspoken, active, and self-asserting; while those who preserved their allegiance to the old Constitution, their loyalty to the old flag, and their love for the republic, were, with comparatively few exceptions, silent and reserved. To officer the troops mustered under this levy there were more than enough of men well qualified. From the beginning of the commotion it was manifest that many officers of the United States army, professionally educated, and supported during their education by the republic, would, at the bidding of state politicians, disown the flag which they had sworn to defend, and turn their swords against the mother who had cherished them. The event surpassed anticipation. As state after state passed the Ordinance of Secession, officers of the army and navy, West Point cadets, and midshipmen, resigned in rapid succession, under the convenient plea that they were bound to follow the fortunes of their "sovereign" state. So overwhelmed were their minds by this shallow doctrine, or by the deep purpose which it was used to veil, that they did not see that under it their allegiance shifted with their residence, and could be moved about the country from one "sovereignty" to another as easily as a peddler moves his pack. Not one in five of them was born and bred in the state to whose fortunes he chose to regard himself as bound; and some of them, as we shall see, were (like thousands, if not tens of thousands, of the men they were to lead to battle against the flag of the republic) natives of free states. So mildly did the government of the United States use its powers, even in this extremity, that the resignations of these, its sworn defenders, who deserted it in the hour of its peril, were accepted, and they were allowed to retire with nominal honor. In this manner more than one hundred of the officers of the army and navy threw up their commissions, and offered their swords to the insurgent cause before the 4th of March. Let us, however, though we can not justify or even excuse this sad and shameful defection, consider fairly all the circumstances which palliated it. With few exceptions, all these officers had been imbued from their boyhood with the doctrine of state sovereignty. They had heard it insisted upon by the politicians of their part of the country, in the one-sided domestic discussions of the public assembly and the social circle—the very politicians upon whose recommendation they were appointed to their cadetships and their midshipmen's berths. For John C. Calhoun and the men of his school, who had obtained, partly by intrigue and partly by arrogation, the almost absolute control of the politics of the slave states, astutely seeing that the power of those states as units was a far more formidable weapon to wield against the advance of freedom than the power of the people of those states in mass, made the adoption of this dogma a sine-qua-non to political preferment. That the interest of slavery must either control the republic or destroy it was

N

for thirty years as a religion and an aggressive policy to them, and this monster of state sovereignty was both the fetich of their worship and the bugbear of their threats. When men brought up under such teaching saw the government at Washington pass into the hands of a party which they styled "Abolitionist"—when they saw their own states secede from the Union—when the voice of their elders, the spur of ambition, the hopes of social distinction, and the blandishments of women, all incited them to espouse the cause of the insurgents—and when to all this was added the consciousness that, if they fought under the flag of the republic, they must meet their brothers and their friends in battle, what wonder that so many of them, yielding to all these influences, resigned their commissions, often soothing their consciences, at first, with the self-assurance that they would not take up arms either under the old flag or the new one! Nay, considering how men are influenced by interest, by association, and by antagonism, is it not somewhat surprising that so many of them remained faithful to the flag which, if the doctrines taught by modern politicians of their part of the country were true, was the mere sign of "a common agency?" The greater part of the guilt of their defection must be laid upon the shoulders of the men who for so many years had labored to debauch the patriotism and pervert the judgment of the people of the South. To the men of the free states, on the contrary, loyalty to the republic, one and indivisible, was a sentiment, almost an instinct. They were not taught it any more than they were taught to breathe or to see; they debated it no more than they questioned the certain action of the great laws of nature. They imbibed it with their mother's milk, and it became a part of their very being. They had no peculiar abnormal institution to bias their judgments and debase their sentiments, and both their reason and their feelings united in their patriotism. They knew that their states had local rights which they prized; and they loved those states as a man loves his home, and his neighborhood, and his native town, and whatever is nearest to him; but they looked upon all these only as parts of one great whole. They gloried in the great republic; in its wise and humane principles of government, in its power, its wealth, its beneficent institutions, and its marvelous progress; they rejoiced in the prosperity of all parts of it; and their desire to wipe out the blot of slavery, which was one of the causes of the great rebellion, was due to a generous assumption of responsibility in regard to its existence which in no wise belonged to them. As to their country, they looked upon themselves only as citizens of the great American republic; and they inwardly smiled with pity upon men who went about introducing each other as "of South Carolina" and "of Virginia." It was easier for most of these men to stand by their colors than it was for some of those to abandon them.

Prominent among those who resigned their commissions before the breaking out of hostilities was Major Pierre Gustave Toutant, called Beauregard,

GENERAL BEAUREGARD.

Cummings's Point.

Iron-clad Battery.

Battery from which the "Star of the West" was fired upon.

MORRIS'S ISLAND, AS SEEN FROM FORT SUMTER.

Sand Battery, connected by covered gallery with

whom the confederate president placed in command at Charleston, with the rank of brigadier general in the provisional confederate army. This officer, the son of a Louisiana planter, was born near New Orleans in 1819. As his name indicates, he is of French descent, his grandfather having been a French Royalist refugee. The present writer bought at a book-stall, and has now in his possession, a copy of a History of the Life of Louis XVI. of France, with its terrible events and tragic ending, by a French writer, which was printed in Hamburg in 1802, nine years after that weak, but thoroughly good-hearted monarch died by the guillotine. Upon the portrait frontispiece of this volume is written, in a French hand of the last century, "Pierre Toutant à été heureux jusque a '93"[3]—touching evidence of a mistaken fidelity to the cause of aristocratic oppression, which events have shown has descended with the blood and the name of the exiled Royalist. In 1834, Pierre Toutant, the grandson, whose mother was an Italian woman, left his father's plantation for the Military Academy at West Point. That plantation, it is said, was called Beauregard, and the young cadet, introduced as Pierre Toutant de Beauregard, was mistakenly called by the latter name, which, being a territorial designation, gratified his vanity, and he retained it. He passed through his cadetship with much credit, graduated in 1838, and received his second lieutenant's commission in the First Artillery. Soon transferred to the Engineers, in which corps he was made first lieutenant before the expiration of his second year of service, he accompanied the small column of troops at the head of which General Scott, with a daring as much greater than of Cortez as the superiority of his enemy in arts and arms to that of the half savage and nearly overawed foe encountered by the Spanish conqueror, undertook to penetrate Mexico from its shores to its capital.[4] In this expedition he distinguished himself by gallantry and professional skill. At Contreras and Cherubusco he won a captain's brevet, and a major's at Chepultepec. In the final assault upon the city of Mexico he was wounded at the Belen Gate, and, with Lieutenants Gustavus W. Smith and George B. M'Clellan—of whom, also, we are to hear anon—received the honor of a special mention in General Scott's dispatches. Camp stories are told of his quick penetration and excellent judgment, and also of his somewhat notable self-reliance; and, although these are probably highly colored, if not exaggerated, there can be no doubt of the more than ordinary capacity and acquirements of Beauregard. At the close of the Mexican war his services were rewarded by the appointment of chief engineer for the building of the Mint and the Custom-house at New Orleans, and also of the important fortifications on the Mississippi below that city. Just before the outbreak of the insurrection, Major Beauregard was appointed by President Buchanan to the important and honorable post of superintendent of the Military Academy at which he received his education. He went to West Point, and nominally entered upon the duties of his new position. But he had been in authority less than a week when an order arrived superseding him. The traditions of West Point are that he spoke and acted as became a loyal citizen and soldier, and especially that he dissuaded the Louisiana cadets from resigning their commissions. But the Secretary of War *ad interim*, Mr. Postmaster Holt, distrusted him because of his Louisiana birth, and unwisely, it would seem, put him in disgrace. At all events, the temptation to a States Rights man to soothe his wounded vanity by yielding to the demands of his "sovereignty" to enter its service proved too tempting for him to resist, and he resigned his commission in the United States army. But it is more than probable that, sooner or later, in any case, he would have taken this step, influenced thereto by the associations of all his life, and by the prominent part taken in the conspiracy for the destruction of the republic by his brother-in-law, ex-Senator John Slidell, of New Orleans. Having arrived at Charleston within a few days of the inauguration of President Lincoln, General Beauregard found much already done toward the investment of Fort Sumter by the active zeal of the insurgents of South Carolina. Not only had Fort Moultrie, Castle Pinckney, and Fort Johnson been strengthened, but batteries had been erected at various points which either commanded the water-girdled ramparts from which the flag of the republic still floated, or the approaches by which succor could be carried to its defenders. To the completion and increase of these works, which were already so large as to require six hundred men for their garrisons, General Beauregard immediately devoted all his energy and engineering skill. But we must turn our eyes from Charleston to Washington, where maimed negotiations were halting toward the inevitable issue of civil war.

The provisional government at Montgomery had been in power but a few days when it appointed Mr. John Forsyth, former minister of the United States to Mexico; Mr. Martin J. Crawford, late United States senator from Georgia; and Mr. A. B. Rodman, an ex-Governor of Louisiana, as its commissioners to the government at Washington, for the purpose of opening negotiations upon all questions growing out of the revolutionary movement, which their appointment assumed to have been complete. The cabinet which President Lincoln had formed for the administration of the government to which these commissioners were accredited consisted, first, of William H. Seward, whom all the world, including himself, had expected to be president, if the Republican party were victorious, and who magnanimously accepted from his successful rival the appointment of Secretary of State, and thus gave his country, to the extent of his power, the advantage of his statesmanship and his experience. Next in importance at that time was the Department of War, which had been placed in the hands of Simon Cameron, late United States senator from Pennsylvania, who began life as a printer, and who had accumulated a large fortune. His reputation for integrity, however unjustly, was not without blemish; and Mr. Lincoln, when pressed, before his inauguration, to give him a cabinet office, had made objections on this ground, which his friends would seem to have satisfactorily set aside, without the ability, however, of preventing their recurrence. Mr. Gideon Welles, of Connecticut, was made Secretary of the Navy; an appointment which he owed rather to the influence of powerful friends than to any prominence as a politician or a publicist, or to any reputation as a man of affairs. He had been editor of a Hartford paper, and was a Democrat in the administrations of Van Buren and Polk. The Treasury was placed under the direction of Salmon P. Chase, a nephew of the venerated Bishop Chase, of Ohio and Illinois. A lawyer of eminence in Cincinnati, he had distinguished himself in suits which involved constitutional questions in regard to slavery, in which he always appeared against the slaveholding interest. As candidate of the Free-soil party, he had been elected to the Senate of the United States, and afterward was made Governor of Ohio, in which position his sound and wise views of finance at a critical period had done the commonwealth much service. For his Attorney General Mr. Lincoln had selected Edward Bates, a leading lawyer and politician of Missouri, who had done much service to the Re-

---

[3] " Pierre Toutant was happy until '93"—the year of Louis XVI.'s death.

[4] Cortez had five hundred Spanish troops, but his Tlascalan allies were numbered by thousands, and treachery served him better than either his own or the native forces. General Scott entered the country at the head of only fifteen thousand men, and the whole force under General Taylor was less than six thousand. The Mexicans fought with skill and desperate valor. Treachery was enlisted only in the councils of their leader, Santa Anna. And General Scott and his little army bore themselves so magnanimously and so wisely, that the Mexicans invited him to remain with them at the head of affairs. Happy would it have been for them had he done so.

publican party, and not a little during the canvass which resulted in Mr. Lincoln's own election. The Department of the Interior was committed to the hands of Caleb Smith, of Indiana; and the Post-office to Montgomery Blair, of Maryland, a graduate of West Point, whose whole life had been passed in the observation, if not in the conduct of public affairs, and who was expected to take, and did take, a much more prominent part in the cabinet counsels than the office which he accepted would have made necessary. To this cabinet the confederate commissioners made their approach almost ere it was well formed. They arrived in Washington on the 5th of March; but it was not until the 12th that Messrs. Crawford and Forsyth, representing the commission, addressed a note to the Secretary of State, Mr. Seward, informing him of the character in which they presented themselves at the capital, and asking him to appoint an early day on which they might present their credentials and proceed to negotiations. Their note was couched in those smooth and formal phrases of conventional courtesy with which men of social culture and diplomatic experience can cover even the most offensive assertions and the most injurious assumptions. They claimed that the seven states which they represented had withdrawn from the Union, and formed a confederation, "in the exercise of the inherent right of every free people to change or reform their political institutions," when they knew that the inhabitants of only one of those states—Texas—ever were, in the political sense of the word, a distinct people, and that four other states of the seven—Alabama, Mississippi, Louisiana, and Florida—were the mere creatures of the government and people of the United States, the very soil of two of them—Florida and Louisiana —having been bought and paid for out of the United States Treasury. They claimed recognition and consideration for their government on the ground that it was "endowed with all the means of self-support," when those means consisted largely of the arms, the money, the forts, public buildings, and vessels which it had seized from the very government from whom they demanded recognition. They professed that "amity and good-will" which diplomatic agents always profess until there is an open rupture; and they declared that the people whom they claimed to represent did not wish to do any act to injure their late confederates, when they knew that their very presence in that capital, as commissioners of part of the Union to a government administered by men constitutionally elected to govern the whole, was an evidence that their "late confederates" had already received at their hands the greatest injury in their power. Mr. Seward replied to this note on the 15th by a memorandum in which he informed them, with the utmost courtesy, that he had no authority to recognize them as diplomatic agents, or enter into correspondence with them. The events which had caused their mission to Washington he regarded, not as a rightful and accomplished revolution, but as a perversion of a temporary and partisan excitement to an unjustifiable and unconstitutional aggression upon the rights and authority vested in the federal government. The remedy for the deplorable condition of affairs then existing he expected to find, not in such irregular negotiations as those upon which they desired to enter, but in the regular and considerate action of the people whom they professed to represent, and in a constitutional convention for the amendment of the organic law of the land. In brief, plain phrase, the Secretary of State, speaking for his government, refused to not only recognize the government under which the commissioners acted, but to admit the right to establish it, and told them that they and all their constituents were then, as they had been before, citizens of the United States.

The reply of the insurgent commissioners to this memorandum is one of the curiosities of diplomatic literature. Still studiously preserving the hollow form of diplomatic courtesy, and making almost evangelical declarations of peace and good-will to men, the commissioners, in fact, took a high tone of defiance; read the Secretary and the President a presumptuous lecture upon the first principles of free government; held the innocence of the insurgent government up to the admiration of posterity; and styled the determination of the President to keep his solemn oath of office a determination "to appeal to the sword to reduce the people of the Confederate States to the will of the section or party whose president he is"—a most impudent remark, whether we consider Mr. Lincoln's constitutional position, or the distribution of the popular vote in the election which made him President, or the majorities in that by which secession was carried in any state of the confederation except South Carolina. They denied, too, that they had asked the government of the United States to recognize the independence of their confederation, but merely to adjust with them the relations springing from a manifest and accomplished revolution. In other words, they asked the government, by receiving them, to admit the very point in dispute, and they declared that the innocence, the peacefulness, and the good-will of the confederate government was to endure just so long as it was allowed to have its own way, regardless of the interests, the honor, and, in fact, the very existence of the government in defiance of which it had been set up.[5]

⁵   *Correspondence between Mr. Seward and the Confederate Commissioners.*

The following is the correspondence between the Secretary of State and the Commissioners from the Confederate States:

Messrs. Forsyth and Crawford, to Mr. Seward, opening Negotiation and stating the Case.

Washington City, March 12, 1861.

Hon. Wm. H. Seward, Secretary of State of the United States:

SIR,—The undersigned have been duly accredited by the government of the Confederate States of America as commissioners to the government of the United States, and in pursuance of their instructions have now the honor to acquaint you with that fact, and to make known, through you, to the President of the United States, the objects of their presence in this capital.

Seven states of the late federal Union having, in the exercise of the inherent right of every free people to change or reform their political institutions, and through conventions of their people, withdrawn from the United States and reassumed the attributes of sovereign power delegated to it, have formed a government of their own. The Confederate States constitute an independent nation *de facto* and *de jure*, and possess a government perfect in all its parts, and endowed with all the means of self-support.

With a view to a speedy adjustment of all questions growing out of this political separation, upon such terms of amity and good-will as the respective interests, geographical contiguity, and future welfare of the two nations may render necessary, the undersigned are instructed to make to the government of the United States overtures for the opening of negotiations, assuring the government of the United States that the President, Congress, and people of the Confederate States earnestly desire a peaceful solution of these great questions; that it is neither their interest nor their wish to make any demand which is not founded in strictest justice, nor do any act to injure their late confederates.

The undersigned have now the honor, in obedience to the instructions of their government, to request you to appoint as early a day as possible, in order that they may present to the President of the United States the credentials which they bear and the objects of the mission with which they are charged. We are, very respectfully, your obedient servants,   JOHN FORSYTH,
MARTIN J. CRAWFORD.

The Reply of Mr. Seward.

[Memorandum.]

Department of State, Washington, March 15, 1861.

Mr. John Forsyth, of the State of Alabama, and Mr. Martin J. Crawford, of the State of Georgia, on the 11th inst., through the kind offices of a distinguished senator, submitted to the Secretary of State their desire for an unofficial interview. This request was, on the 12th inst., upon exclusively public consideration, respectfully declined.

On the 13th inst., while the secretary was preoccupied, Mr. A. D. Banks, of Virginia, called at this department, and was received by the assistant secretary, to whom he delivered a sealed communication, which he had been charged by Messrs. Forsyth and Crawford to present the secretary in person.

In that communication Messrs. Forsyth and Crawford inform the Secretary of State that they have been duly accredited by the government of the Confederate States of America as commissioners to the government of the United States, and they set forth the objects of their attendance at Washington. They observe that seven states of the American Union, in the exercise of a right inherent in every free people, have withdrawn, through conventions of their people, from the United States, reassumed the attributes of sovereign power, and formed a government of their own, and that those Confederate States now constitute an independent nation *de facto* and *de jure*, and possess a government perfect in all its parts, and fully endowed with all the means of self-support.

Messrs. Forsyth and Crawford, in their aforesaid communication, thereupon proceeded to inform the secretary that, with a view to a speedy adjustment of all questions growing out of the political separation thus assumed, upon such terms of amity and good-will as the respective interests, geographical contiguity, and the future welfare of the supposed two nations might render necessary, they are instructed to make to the government of the United States overtures for the opening of negotiations, assuring this government that the President, Congress, and people of the Confederate States earnestly desire a peaceful solution of these great questions, and that it is neither their interest nor their wish to make any demand which is not founded in strictest justice, nor do any act to injure their late confederates.

After making these statements, Messrs. Forsyth and Crawford close their communication, as they say, in obedience to the instructions of their government, by requesting the Secretary of State to appoint as early a day as possible, in order that they may present to the President of the United States the credentials which they bear and the objects of the mission with which they are charged.

The Secretary of State frankly confesses that he understands the events which have recently occurred, and the condition of political affairs which actually exists in the heart of the Union to which his attention has thus been directed, very differently from the aspect in which they are presented by Messrs. Forsyth and Crawford. He sees in them, not a rightful and accomplished revolution and an independent nation, with an established government, but rather a perversion of a temporary and partisan excitement to the inconsiderate purposes of an unjustifiable and unconstitutional aggression upon the rights and the authority vested in the federal government, and hitherto benignly exercised, as from their very nature they always must so be exercised, for the maintenance of the Union, the preservation of liberty, and the security, peace, welfare, happiness, and aggrandizement of the American people. The Secretary of State, therefore, avows to Messrs.

Forsyth and Crawford that he looks patiently but confidently for the cure of evils which have resulted from proceedings so unnecessary, so unwise, so unusual, and so unnatural, not to irregular negotiations, having in view new and untried relations, with agencies unknown to and acting in derogation of the Constitution and laws, but to regular and considerate action of the people at those states, in co-operation with their brethren in the other states, through the Congress of the United States, and such extraordinary conventions, if there shall be need thereof, as the federal Constitution contemplates and authorizes to be assembled.

It is, however, the purpose of the Secretary of State, on this occasion, not to invite or engage in any discussion of these subjects, but simply to set forth his reasons for declining to comply with the request of Messrs. Forsyth and Crawford.

On the 4th of March inst., the newly-elected President of the United States, in view of all the facts bearing on the present question, assumed the executive administration of the government, first delivering, in accordance with an early, honored custom, an inaugural address to the people of the United States. The Secretary of State respectfully submits a copy of this address to Messrs. Forsyth and Crawford.

A simple reference to it will be sufficient to satisfy those gentlemen that the Secretary of State, guided by the principles therein announced, is prevented altogether from admitting or assuming that the states referred to by them have, in law or in fact, withdrawn from the federal Union, or that they could do so in the manner described by Messrs. Forsyth and Crawford, or in any other manner than with the consent and concert of the people of the United States, to be given through a national convention, to be assembled in conformity with the provisions of the Constitution of the United States. Of course the Secretary of State can not act upon the assumption, or in any way admit that the so-called Confederate States constitute a foreign power, with whom diplomatic relations ought to be established.

Under these circumstances, the Secretary of State, whose official duties are confined, subject to the direction of the President, to the conducting of the foreign relations of the country, and do not at all embrace domestic questions, or questions arising between the several states and the federal government, is unable to comply with the request of Messrs. Forsyth and Crawford to appoint a day on which they may present the evidences of their authority and the objects of their visit to the President of the United States. On the contrary, he is obliged to state to Messrs. Forsyth and Crawford that he has no authority, nor is he at liberty to recognize them as diplomatic agents, or hold correspondence or other communication with them.

Finally, the Secretary of State would observe that, although he has supposed that he might safely and with propriety have adopted these conclusions without making any reference of the subject to the executive, yet, so strong has been his desire to practice entire directness, and to act in a spirit of perfect respect and candor toward Messrs. Forsyth and Crawford, and that portion of the Union in whose name they present themselves before him, that he has cheerfully submitted this paper to the President, who coincides generally in the views it expresses, and sanctions the secretary's decision declining official intercourse with Messrs. Forsyth and Crawford.

Confederate Commissioners' final Letter to Secretary Seward.

Washington, April 9, 1861.

Hon. Wm. H. Seward, Secretary of State of the United States, Washington:

The "memorandum" dated Department of State, Washington, March 15, 1861, has been received through the hands of Mr. J. T. Pickett, secretary to this commission, who, by the instructions of the undersigned, called for it on yesterday at the department.

In that memorandum you correctly state the purport of the official note addressed to you by the undersigned on the 12th ult. Without repeating the contents of that note in full, it is enough to say here that its object was to invite the government of the United States to a friendly consideration of the relation between the United States and the seven states lately of the federal Union, but now separated from it by the sovereign will of their people, growing out of the pregnant and undeniable fact that those people have rejected the authority of the United States, and established a government of their own. Those relations had to be friendly or hostile. The people of the old and new governments, occupying contiguous territories, had to stand to each other in the relation of good neighbors, each seeking their happiness and pursuing their national destinies in their own way, without interference with the other, or they had to be rival and hostile nations. The government of the Confederate States had no hesitation in electing its choice in this alternative. Frankly and unreserved, seeking the good of the people who had intrusted them with power, in the spirit of humanity, of the Christian civilization of the age, and of that Americanism which regards the true welfare and happiness of the people, the government of the Confederate States, among its first acts, commissioned the undersigned to approach the government of the United States with the olive-branch of peace, and to offer to adjust the great questions pending between them in the only way to be justified by the consciences and common sense of good men who had nothing but the welfare of the people of the two confederacies at heart.

Your government has not chosen to meet the undersigned in the conciliatory and peaceful spirit in which they are commissioned. Persistently wedded to those fatal theories of construction of the federal Constitution always rejected by the statesmen of the South, and adhered to by those of the administration school until they have produced their natural and often-predicted result of the destruction of the Union, under which we might have continued to live happily and gloriously together had the spirit of the ancestry who framed the common Constitution animated the hearts of all their sons, you now, with a persistence untaught and uncured by the ruin which has been wrought, refuse to recognize the great fact presented to you of a complete and successful revolution; you close your eyes to the existence of the government founded upon it, and ignore the

Although Secretary Seward's memorandum was dated March 15th, this reply was not written until the 9th of April, the memorandum itself not having been sent to the commissioners until the 8th, with their own consent, they having been willing to await the result of negotiations still more irregular than those which they themselves had undertaken. These negotiations had reference entirely to the condition of Fort Sumter, and the course which the government meant to pursue in regard to it. This, indeed, was the material question of the day, the first great problem which the government was called upon to solve after the coming in of the new administration. On the 5th of March, President Lincoln's first full day in office, and the day on which the confederate commissioners arrived in Washington, he received through the War Department a letter from Major Anderson, giving his opinion, and that of all the officers in his command, that reenforcements could not be thrown into the fort in time to prevent its capitulation, from want of food, with less than a body of 20,000 good and well-disciplined men. After a full examination of the case thus submitted, General Scott and the army officers at Washington coincided with Major Anderson's judgment. But no such body of men was at the disposal of the government, or could be raised before the garrison at Sumter would be starved out. All that could be done, therefore, under the circumstances, was either to send provisions to the fort, if that would be allowed, or, if not, to evacuate it. But as a peaceful evacuation, unsupported and unexplained by any concurrent act of authority, would justly be regarded by the world as an admission of the incompetency of the government even to resist its own destruction, it was wisely determined to accomplish the re-enforcement of the important post of Fort Pickens, that thus it might be seen that, while the government was obliged to yield to military necessity on the one hand, it none the less asserted its power and maintained its dignity on the other. Orders were dispatched (necessarily by sea) for the transfer of troops from the frigate Sabine, then lying off Pensacola Harbor, to Fort Pickens; but the officer in command, conceiving himself bound by some such sort of armistice or agreement on the part of Mr. Buchanan's administration as was claimed to exist with regard to Major Anderson's force at Fort Moultrie, refused to disembark the troops. The news of this strange and untoward complication reached Washington at such a late period of the time allotted by circumstances for action, that Fort Pickens could not be re-enforced before the garrison at Fort Sumter would be famished. With regard to that garrison, therefore, the problem for the government was either to furnish it with supplies, or to get it out of the fort, as soon as possible, without loss of honor or virtual abdication of authority.

It was during this perplexity of the government that the confederate commissioners awaited a reply to their note to Secretary Seward. Meantime they received assurances from persons of high position, who, to use the mildest phrase, availed themselves of their advantages to act as observers and go-betweens in the interest of the rebellion (and, sad to relate, an associate judge of the Supreme Court was the chief of those who performed these ambiguous functions)—first, that Fort Sumter would be evacuated, and, next, that it would not be supplied or re-enforced without notice to the Governor of South Carolina. Seeing that thus the government would be as nearly as possible tied hand and foot by its own acts, and placed at the mercy of the

insurgents, the commissioners were quite willing to leave the Secretary of State's memorandum at the State Department, subject to such modifications as this anticipated military course of the government might compel. But when they learned on the 7th that Fort Sumter was to be provisioned and Fort Pickens re-enforced, if the government had power to do so, they sent their reply to the memorandum, and, solemnly shaking the dust from their feet, turned their backs on Washington.

The expedition for the relief of Fort Sumter was got under way with all possible dispatch; and notice was sent to Governor Pickens, of South Carolina, that a peaceable attempt would be made to provision the fort, and that if this were resisted, force would be used. The fleet was not a very imposing one, considering the important occasion of its dispatch. It consisted of but three armed vessels, three transport ships, and two steam-tugs. The last of these, the Yankee and the Uncle Ben, carried only their ordinary crews; the transports (the mail steamers Atlantic, Baltic, and Illinois) bore eight hundred men, with provisions; and of the armed ships, the steam sloop-of-war Pawnee carried ten guns and a crew of two hundred men; the Powhatan, of like grade, eleven guns and two hundred and seventy-five men; while the third was but a steam revenue cutter, the Harriet Lane, which had hastily assumed the naval colors, and which carried but five small guns and ninety-six men—the military and naval force, all told, consisting of but 1380 men and twenty-six cannon. Yet even this meagre armament was raised with difficulty under pressure of the great emergency. But not even all of these vessels left port with Charleston as their ultimate destination. The Atlantic and the Illinois, with eight hundred and fifty of the troops, were ordered to Fort Pickens; the armed steamers, the Baltic, with one hundred and sixty troops, and the steam-tugs, were instructed to rendezvous off Charleston Harbor, the commander having put to sea with sealed orders as to his farther operations. Those orders were that unarmed boats should be first sent in with provisions to Fort Sumter, and that, if these met with resistance, all means should be used to re-enforce as well as to supply it.

Nearly four months had now elapsed since Major Anderson had hastily sought the protection of this isolated strong-hold for his little band of fifty-five artillerists, nine officers, fifteen musicians, and thirty laborers. When he took up that position, it seemed to people generally as if he was absolutely unassailable, except by a fleet and by hunger. The former, it was well known, the insurgents were without; and it was supposed that the possession of it by the government would deprive them of the assistance of the latter. Fort Sumter was regarded as one of the strongest works within the limits of the republic. Built upon an artificial island in Charleston Harbor, at the cost to the nation of a million of dollars, it had all the advantages of inaccessible position, and the highest resources of engineering skill. Its pentagonal walls of brick and compact concrete were twelve feet thick at the base and eight at the parapet, which rose sixty feet from the foundation. On four of its five sides it was pierced for two tiers of guns, to which were added a third (called en barbette), fired from the parapet; but the fifth side, looking southward upon Charleston, was almost without defense, and weakened by the sally-ports and the docks; for the strong-holds of the republic, like its Constitution, were constructed upon the reasonable supposition that

high duties of moderation and humanity which attach to you in dealing with this great fact. Had you met these issues with the frankness and manliness with which the undersigned were instructed to present them to you and treat them, the undersigned had not now the melancholy duty to return home and tell their government and their countrymen that their earnest and ceaseless efforts in behalf of peace had been futile, and that the government of the United States meant to subjugate them by force of arms. Whatever may be the result, impartial history will record the innocence of the government of the Confederate States, and place the responsibility of the blood and mourning that may ensue upon those who have denied the great fundamental doctrine of American liberty, that "governments derive their just powers from the consent of the governed," and who have set naval and land armaments in motion to subject the people of one portion of the land to the will of another portion. That that can never be done while a freeman survives in the Confederate States to wield a weapon, the undersigned appeal to past history to prove. These military demonstrations against the people of the seceded states are certainly far from being in keeping and consistency with the theory of the Secretary of State, maintained in his memorandum, that these states are still component parts of the late American Union, as the undersigned are not aware of any constitutional power in the President of the United States to levy war without the consent of Congress upon a foreign people, much less upon any portion of the people of the United States.

The undersigned, like the Secretary of State, have no purpose to "invite or engage in discussion" of the subject on which their two governments are so irreconcilably at variance. It is this variance that has broken up the old Union, the disintegration of which has only begun. It is proper, however, to advise you that it were well to dismiss the hopes you seem to entertain that, by any of the modes indicated, the people of the Confederate States will ever be brought to submit to the authority of the government of the United States. You are dealing with delusions, too, when you seek to separate our people from our government, and to characterize the deliberate, sovereign act of the people as a "perversion of a temporary and partisan excitement." If you cherish these dreams you will be awakened from them, and find them as unreal and unsubstantial as others in which you have recently indulged. The undersigned would omit the performance of an obvious duty were they to fail to make known to the government of the United States that the people of the Confederate States have declared their independence with a full knowledge of all the responsibilities of that act, and with as firm a determination to maintain it by all the means with which Nature has endowed them as that which sustained their fathers when they threw off the authority of the British crown.

The undersigned clearly understand that you have declined to appoint a day to enable them to lay the objects of the mission with which they are charged before the President of the United States, because so to do would be to recognize the independence and separate nationality of the Confederate States. This is the vein of thought that pervades the memorandum before us. The truth of history requires that it should distinctly appear upon the record that the undersigned did not ask the government of the United States to recognize the independence of the Confederate States. They only asked audience to adjust, in a spirit of amity and peace, the new relations springing from a manifest and accomplished revolution in the government of the late federal Union. Your refusal to entertain these overtures for a peaceful solution, the active naval and military preparation of this government, and a formal notice to the commanding general of the confederate forces in the harbor of Charleston, that the President intends to provision Fort Sumter by forcible means, if necessary, are viewed by the undersigned, and can only be received by the world, as a declaration of war against the Confederate States; for the President of the United States knows that Fort Sumter can not be provisioned without the effusion of blood. The undersigned, in behalf of their government and people, accept the gage of battle thus thrown down to them; and appealing to God and the judgment of mankind for the righteousness of their cause, the people of the Confederate States will defend their liberties to the last against this flagrant and open attempt at their subjugation to sectional power.

This communication can not be properly closed without adverting to the date of your memorandum. The official note of the undersigned, of the 12th of March, was delivered to the Assistant Secretary of State on the 13th of that month, the gentleman who delivered it informing him

that the secretary of this commission would call at 12 o'clock, noon, on the next day, for an answer. At the appointed hour Mr. Pickett did call, and was informed by the Assistant Secretary of State that the engagements of the Secretary of State had prevented him from giving the note his attention. The Assistant Secretary of State then asked for the address of Messrs. Crawford and Forsyth, the members of the commission then present in this city, took note of the address on a card, and engaged to send whatever reply might be made to their lodgings. Why this was not done it is proper should be here explained. The memorandum is dated March 15, and was not delivered until April 8. Why was it withheld during the intervening twenty-three days? In the postscript to your memorandum you say it "was delayed, as was understood, with their (Messrs. Forsyth and Crawford's) consent." This is true; but it is also true that on the 15th of March Messrs. Forsyth and Crawford were assured by a person occupying a high official position in the government, and who, as they believed, was speaking by authority, that Fort Sumter would be evacuated within a very few days, and that no measure changing the existing status prejudicially to the Confederate States, as respects Fort Pickens, was then contemplated, and these assurances were subsequently repeated, with the addition that any contemplated change as respects Pickens would be notified to us. On the 1st of April we were again informed that there might be an attempt to supply Fort Sumter with provisions, but that Governor Pickens should have previous notice of this attempt. There was no suggestion of any re-enforcements. The undersigned did not hesitate to believe that these assurances expressed the intentions of the administration at the time, or, at all events, of prominent members of that administration. This delay was assented to for the express purpose of attaining the great end of the mission of the undersigned, to wit: a pacific solution of existing complications. The inference deducible from the date of your memorandum, that the undersigned had, of their own volition, and without cause, consented to this long hiatus in the grave duties with which they were charged, is, therefore, not consistent with a just exposition of the facts of the case. The intervening twenty-three days were employed in active unofficial efforts, the object of which was to smooth the path to a pacific solution, the distinguished personage alluded to co-operating with the undersigned; and every step of that effort is recorded in writing, and now in possession of the undersigned and of their government. It was only when all these anxious efforts for peace had been exhausted, and it became clear that Mr. Lincoln had determined to appeal to the sword to reduce the people of the Confederate States to the will of the section or party whose president he is, that the undersigned resumed the official negotiation temporarily suspended, and sent their secretary for a reply to their official note of March 12.

It is proper to add that, during these twenty-three days, two gentlemen of official distinction as high as that of the personage hitherto alluded to, aided the undersigned as intermediaries in these unofficial negotiations for peace.

The undersigned, commissioners of the Confederate States of America, having thus made answer to all they deemed material in the memorandum filed in the department on the 15th of March last, have the honor to be,   JOHN FORSYTH,
                                                                              MARTIN J. CRAWFORD,
                                                                              A. B. ROMAN.

A true copy of the original by me delivered to Mr. F. W. Seward, Assistant Secretary of State of the United States, at 8 o'clock in the evening of April 9, 1861.
      Attest,   J. T. PICKETT, Secretary, etc., etc.

Mr. Seward, in Reply to the Commissioners, acknowledges the Receipt of their Letter, but declines to Answer it.

                                        Department of State, Washington, April 10, 1861.
Messrs. Forsyth, Crawford, and Roman, having been apprised by a memorandum which has been delivered to them that the Secretary of State is not at liberty to hold official intercourse with them, will, it is presumed, expect no notice from him of the new communication which they have addressed to him under date of the 9th inst., beyond the simple acknowledgment of the receipt thereof, which he hereby very cheerfully gives.

A true copy of the original received by the commissioners of the Confederate States, this 10th day of April, 1861.   Attest,   J. T. PICKETT, Secretary, etc., etc.

INTERIOR OF THE SALLY-PORT AT SUMTER.

singular battery had been built. It was constructed of heavy yellow pine logs, and was protected from shell by a slanting roof of the same material. But over the logs was laid a mail armor of railway iron, strongly clamped and dovetailed. The port-holes were provided with doors like those of a man-of-war, and these also were covered with iron armor, and fell at the recoil of the guns, thus affording complete protection to the men who served the guns, except at the moment of aiming and firing. This battery mounted three heavy columbiads. Another battery, even more novel and curious, had been built at Charleston itself with an enterprise and mechanical ingenuity altogether unexpected. This was a floating battery, made, like that on Cummings's Point, of pine logs, and covered with a double layer of railway iron. It was a nondescript structure, not at all like either a vessel or a fort. It looked like a large shed, some hundred feet in length and twenty-five in width, and had been much laughed at while it was building. It presented no perpendicular face at the point of attack, only sloping surfaces of heavy iron. The magazine stretched along in the rear below the water-line, and was protected with layers of sand-bags, which helped to balance the weight of the four enormous siege-guns which it mounted. A floating hospital was attached to the stern of this grotesque, but, as it proved, really formidable structure. Other batteries of inferior power spotted the sandy shore within cannon or mortar range of Sumter; and all this preparation for the destruction of his post and the humiliation of his flag Major Anderson had been obliged to see going on unchecked within range of his batteries for four weary months. Strange, unprecedented, absurd, anomalous position! Sorely-tried major of artillery, found faithful in all things —faithful even to what seemed sure-coming death, and what was sure-coming surrender—while life and military honor were both to be saved by one word from your lips, Fire! which would have been answered by cheers over half a continent! Standing, not supine, not with hands tied, but vigilant, with hands free and full of arms, while your enemy dug his pits and set up his engines before your face and within your reach, affronting you each morning with some new device, which you, each morning, could have blown straight into the limbo where all such works deserve to go—will go forever where the cause of truth, and right, and universal good-will, for which you and your worthy comrades, with patient heroism, endured so much, prevails. Your foes did not quite trust your forbearance; for yonder upon Sullivan's Island, behind that brushwood and those slopes of sand, which, even to your penetrating glass, seem but the common fringing of a barren beach, is a tremendous battery of siege-guns and mortars, of which you will see nothing and hear nothing until you see their fire and hear their roar.

Such preparation had been made in Charleston Harbor for the reduction of Fort Sumter when the news arrived that the mission of the insurgent commissioners to Washington had entirely failed, and also that an expedition for the relief of the fort was about to sail. Immediately there was bustle and excitement of a military sort—the going to and fro of aids-de-camp and orderlies, and marching. Not a little of it superfluous, we may honestly believe; but somewhat may be pardoned to the ardor of such very inexperienced aids, and orderlies, and soldiers, in virtue of their earnestness; for they were in earnest, and actually meant to fight the government of the United States, and, what was worse, believed, and not without some reason, that they could fight it and live. To man the batteries of the insurgents in

there would be little occasion for defense against domestic violence. Charleston, indeed, being three miles and a half from Fort Sumter, was out of reach of any ordnance in use at the time when it was built, and, in fact, of any among its armament at the time when it was first threatened—threatened by the people whom it was built chiefly to protect. Around it, uniting haste, determination, and ingenuity, they had drawn a nearly complete circle of heavy batteries. The guns which Major Anderson had left maimed in Fort Moultrie had been unspiked; others had been added; the repairs which he had begun were nearly completed; and, strengthened with some traverses, the old fort, though not so large or so strong as Sumter, was yet a very formidable work. It mounted eleven heavy siege-pieces and several mortars, and was a little more than a mile from Sumter. At Fort Johnson—the name retained by the site of an old and long-abandoned and ruined fortification—two large sand batteries had been erected, and armed with heavy guns and mortars. These batteries were distant one mile and a quarter from Fort Sumter, and were the nearest to the city of all the guns which bore upon Major Anderson. Upon Cummings's Point, the part of Sullivan's Island nearest to Fort Sumter, and only three quarters of a mile distant, a

THE IRON-CLAD BATTERY ON CUMMINGS'S POINT, AS SEEN FROM FORT SUMTER.

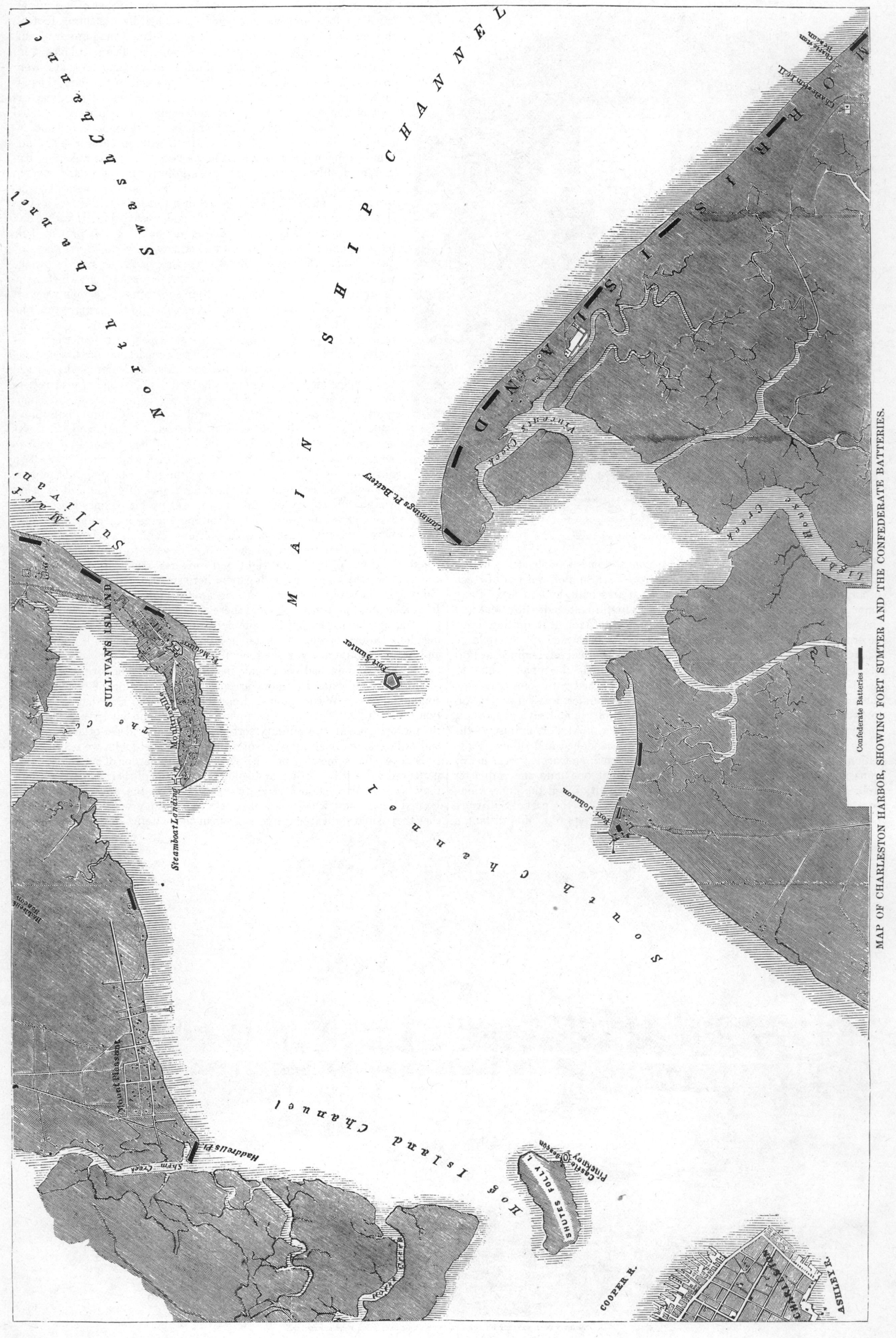

MAP OF CHARLESTON HARBOR, SHOWING FORT SUMTER AND THE CONFEDERATE BATTERIES.

Charleston Harbor a force of one thousand men would have been more than enough; but about seven thousand men were assembled there under the command of General Beauregard, and of these, four thousand were sent to the works, the remaining three thousand being held in reserve at the city.

It was on the 8th of April, 1862, that the issue was presented to the insurgents that they must allow the government to retain peaceful possession of its own fortress or expel its garrison by force. No communication was held with the insurgent administration at Montgomery; but on that day a messenger arrived from Washington to the Governor of South Carolina, informing him that provisions would be sent to Fort Sumter, and that, if they were not permitted to reach it peaceably, force would be used. Such had been the nature of the abnormal negotiations, understandings, or what not, between the representatives, authorized and unauthorized, open and secret, of the insurgents at Washington and the government, that honor, as well as policy, was thought to require the giving of this information. Upon receiving it, General Beauregard immediately communicated it by telegraph to Montgomery, where the question which it presented was considered for twenty-four hours; and on the 10th the confederate commander received an order to demand the evacuation of the fort, and, if this was refused, to commence the attack. He made the demand the next day at noon, in courteous phrase, of course, with the usual expressions of a desire to avoid the effusion of blood, and with a compliment to the constancy of Major Anderson, which came gracefully from a late companion in arms. The terms were the most honorable that could be offered. The abandonment of his post, which they were intended to grace, was promptly refused by Major Anderson as inconsistent with his sense of honor and his obligations to his government. As he bade General Beauregard's messengers farewell, he said to them that he should be starved out in a few days, unless the fort was previously brought about his ears by their fire. This casual remark, natural enough to a military man under all the circumstances, was reported at once all over the country, and seemed as strangely peaceful and superfluous, to say the least, to the multitude, as the good-natured mutual admissions of opposing counsel do to their incensed and mutually glowering clients; and it was even made the occasion of the impeachment of Major Anderson's loyalty. General Beauregard, however, although he did not so misunderstand it, yet immediately telegraphed it, with the refusal, to the confederate government, from whom he as promptly received authority to accept from Major Anderson, as an alternative of an attack, an agreement to evacuate the fort within a few days, and not to use his guns against the insurgent batteries unless they first opened fire on him. Two of General Beauregard's aids arrived at Fort Sumter about midnight of that day, the 11th, with a proposal of this alternative, and the authority to enter at once into the agreement in question. The negotiation was thus hastily pressed through that sleepless night because the relieving flotilla was known to the insurgents to be already in the offing, though he for whose relief it came was ignorant of their presence, and even of the purpose of the government; for communication with him had been cut off for four days, and the last messenger from Washington—Lieutenant Talbot, one of his own garrison—had not been allowed to return to him. In his final summons General Beauregard requested Major Anderson to communicate to his aids an open answer, which they awaited. This he did at half past two, offering to evacuate the fort on the 15th if he did not previously receive controlling instructions or supplies, and agreeing, meantime, not to open fire unless in case of hostile demonstration against the fort, or against the flag of his government. This offer, which was to go out unless he was ordered to remain, and was able to do so, and which secured him the right of defending any vessel which entered the harbor under the United States flag, was not at all what General Beauregard required; and so, at twenty minutes past three o'clock on the morning of the 12th, the aids-de-camp informed Major Anderson that fire would be opened upon him in one hour, and thereupon took final leave.[6]

---

[6] The following is the correspondence immediately preceding the hostilities:

Charleston, April 8.

L. P. Walker, Secretary of War:
An authorized messenger from President Lincoln just informed Governor Pickens and myself that provisions will be sent to Fort Sumter peaceably, or otherwise by force.
G. T. Beauregard.

Montgomery, 10th.

Gen. G. T. Beauregard, Charleston:
If you have no doubt of the authorized character of the agent who communicated to you the intention of the Washington government to supply Fort Sumter by force, you will at once demand its evacuation, and, if this is refused, proceed in such a manner as you may determine to reduce it. Answer.
L. P. Walker, Secretary of War.

Charleston, April 10.

L. P. Walker, Secretary of War:
The demand will be made to-morrow at 12 o'clock.
G. T. Beauregard.

Montgomery, April 10.

Gen. Beauregard, Charleston:
Unless there are especial reasons connected with your own condition, it is considered proper that you should make the demand at an early hour.
L. P. Walker, Secretary of War.

Charleston, April 10.

L. P. Walker, Secretary of War, Montgomery:
The reasons are special for 12 o'clock.
G. T. Beauregard.

Head-quarters, Provisional Army, C. S. A., Charleston, S. C., April 11, 1861—2 P.M.

Sir,—The government of the Confederate States has hitherto forborne from any hostile demonstration against Fort Sumter in the hope that the government of the United States, with a view to the amicable adjustment of all questions between the two governments, and to avert the calamities of war, would voluntarily evacuate it. There was reason at one time to believe that such would be the course pursued by the government of the United States, and under that impression my government has refrained from making any demand for the surrender of the fort.

But the Confederate States can no longer delay assuming actual possession of a fortification commanding the entrance of one of their harbors, and necessary to its defense and security.

I am ordered by the government of the Confederate States to demand the evacuation of Fort Sumter. My aids, Colonel Chesnut and Captain Lee, are authorized to make such demand of you. All proper facilities will be afforded for the removal of yourself and command, together with company arms and property, and all private property, to any post in the United States which you may elect. The flag which you have upheld so long and with so much fortitude, under the most trying circumstances, may be saluted by you on taking it down.

Colonel Chesnut and Captain Lee will, for a reasonable time, await your answer. I am, sir, very respectfully, your obedient servant,
G. T. Beauregard, Brigadier General Commanding.
Major Robert Anderson, Commanding at Fort Sumter, Charleston Harbor, S. C.

Head-quarters, Fort Sumter, S. C., April 11th, 1861.

General,—I have the honor to acknowledge the receipt of your communication demanding the evacuation of this fort; and to say in reply thereto that it is a demand with which I regret that my sense of honor and of my obligations to my government prevent my compliance.

Thanking you for the fair, manly, and courteous terms proposed, and for the high compliment paid me, I am, general, very respectfully, your obedient servant,
Robert Anderson, Major U. S. Army, Commanding.
To Brigadier General G. T. Beauregard, commanding Provisional Army, C. S. A.

Montgomery, April 11.

Gen. Beauregard, Charleston:
We do not desire needlessly to bombard Fort Sumter, if Major Anderson will state the time at which, as indicated by him, he will evacuate, and agree that, in the mean time, he will not use his guns against us, unless ours should be employed against Fort Sumter. You are thus to avoid the effusion of blood. If this or its equivalent be refused, reduce the fort as your judgment decides to be most practicable.
L. P. Walker, Secretary of War.

Head-quarters, Provisional Army, C. S. A., Charleston, April 11, 1861, 11 P.M.

Major,—In consequence of the verbal observations made by you to my aids, Messrs. Chesnut and Lee, in relation to the condition of your supplies, and that you would in a few days be starved out if our guns did not batter you to pieces, or words to that effect, and desiring no useless effusion of blood, I communicated both the verbal observation and your written answer to my communication to my government.

If you will state the time at which you will evacuate Fort Sumter, and agree that, in the mean time, you will not use your guns against us unless ours shall be employed against Fort Sumter, we will abstain from opening fire upon you. Colonel

FORT JOHNSON, AS SEEN FROM FORT SUMTER.

Without a doubt this issue was expected. It at least found General Beauregard prepared to keep the appointment of his representatives with sufficient punctuality. The hour went slowly by, and the batteries were silent. Five anxious minutes more were counted, and the dark quiet of the night was yet unbroken; but hardly were another five completed when the flash and the dull roar of a mortar came from the battery on Sullivan's Island. The conscious shell went up shrieking and wailing along its fiery curve, and, lingering reluctantly before its downward plunge, burst as it fell directly over the doomed fortress. No meteor of more direful portent ever lit the sky; for this told surely of the beginning of a civil war, compared to which all civil wars before it were as squabbles in a corner—a war in which millions of men were to be engaged, and which was to scatter ruin and want, not only through the country in which it raged, but across the sea, among two of the most powerful nations of the world; which was to convert half a continent into one great battle-ground, and strew it from east to west with the graves of its citizens slaughtered to gratify the base ambition and the disappointed pride of a small factious oligarchy, who justified to themselves their attempt to destroy a government upon the monstrous assumption of the right of one man to own and use another as his property. But to the eager neophytes in war who manned the Charleston batteries, this shell was merely the signal for the beginning of a bombardment in which they expected to run some risk and to gain much glory; for they knew well their overwhelming superiority both in numbers and in weight of artillery, and they knew how wasted, worn, and weary their handful of opponents were with want of food, anxiety, and watching. They expected, too, that after a few such contests—enough to show the government and the people of the free states that they really meant rebellion, they would attain their purposes, and be in a position so to remodel the map of North America as to secure the perpetuation of negro slavery throughout the larger part of its temperate climes, and (what was the real object sought by their insurrection) the political and social predominance of the slaveholding oligarchy. So miserably had politicians been able to cause the citizens of the republic to misunderstand each other! so miserably had some of them deceived themselves! After the firing of this signal mortar, the discharge of which was fitly committed to the hands of Edmund Ruffin, a Virginian, who had grown gray during his untiring efforts to bring about the struggle which he then began, there was a short pause of preparation, and then fire was opened from the whole crescent of batteries which more than half encircled the fort; for the water battery had been towed down two days before, and anchored on the undefended side which looked toward Charleston. From this time the discharge of shot and shell against the fort was kept up without ceasing; but the fort did not reply. The insurgent artillerists could see their balls strike against its sides, splintering the parapet and the embrasures, and their bombs fall within its inclosure, and hear them explode. An hour of this firing passed, and not a shot came back. Time wore on, and the bombardment was kept up until those to whom had been committed the doubtful honor of opening it grew tired with their unaccustomed task, and yielded their places to others, and still the fort was silent. More than two hours had thus passed in this one-sided contest. What could it mean? Did Major Anderson intend to preserve the inoffensive attitude which he had maintained for months, bear without resistance the fierce attacks of the batteries which he had allowed to be constructed around him, and, trusting solely to the endurance of his walls and his men, leave to his assailants, already committed to an inglorious contest, only the contemptible business of a fierce onslaught upon men who refused to fight them? Perhaps it would have been as well had he added that shame to the meed of their two days' labor; but his duty, of course, prevented his thought of such a purpose. He was not politic, he was only prudent.

Upon the departure of General Beauregard's aids from the fort the flag was raised, the posterns closed, the sentinels withdrawn from the parapet, and orders given that the men should not leave the bomb-proofs without special orders. At half past six o'clock the shrill notes of "Peas upon a trencher," piercing the uproar of the bombardment, called the garrison, as usual, to breakfast, which they ate leisurely and calmly. Major Anderson knew that if eighty men (only enough to work nine guns properly) were to do any thing against such a fire as had been opened upon him, it could only be with the careful husbanding of their strength and nervous energy; and therefore he had reserved his fire until he could use his guns in broad daylight, and send his men to their work with the support of the best breakfast his meagre stores could furnish. He then divided his command into three reliefs, assigning officers and men as equally as possible to each. The great inequality of the contest did not exist only in the numbers of men and the weight of metal which were opposed. The fort, though its magazines were well stored with powder, had a very small supply of cartridges; there were no scales with which to weigh powder, and only six needles with which to sew cartridge-bags; and there were neither tangent scales, nor breech sides, nor any other instrument for pointing a gun. Bread there was none; only salt pork. Under these privations, accurate firing and a long defense were equally impossible. The fire which had now been kept up for two hours and a half was much severer and more extended even than Major Anderson had looked for; for the masked battery of heavy columbiads on Sullivan's Island, the existence of which he had not suspected, enfiladed the fort, and was served with great energy and precision. It proved, too, that there was only one face of the work which was not seen in reverse (that is, open to a fire in the rear) from mortars. It was to such an attack that Major Anderson gave the order to reply soon after seven o'clock on the morning of Friday, the 12th of April. Captain Doubleday, his second in command, fired the first gun, and immediately the fort opened upon all the principal assailing batteries.

How unequal the fight was to be was not discovered in Sumter until after it had well begun; for it had been decided to use but two of the three tiers of guns with which the fort was mounted—those in the lower casemates and those upon the parapet; and the embrasures of the second tier were built up with earth, and brick, and stone. The parapet, or barbette guns, being of the heaviest calibre, capable of crushing even the armor of the iron-plated batteries, and also being, on account of their position, those only from which shells could be thrown, were most relied upon, and, for the protection of the artillerists at these, much labor had been expended since the time when an attack seemed imminent. But the vertical fire of shells from the insurgent batteries was so copious and well directed that this tier of guns had to be abandoned in the very beginning of the contest, and only two or three of them were fired surreptitiously by some of the men, whom neither danger nor command could deter from yielding to the temptation of using these formidable weapons against the enemy. But these stolen delights were merely imaginary; the hasty and careless firing of these great guns proving more dangerous to the fort and its defenders than to its assailants. One of them was not only thrown from its carriage by its own recoil, but dismounted another near it. Thus, in the very beginning, Major Anderson found himself deprived of what he relied upon as his main stay, and confined to the use of his lower tier of casemates. The rebel artillerists thus attained comparative security during almost the entire bombardment; for while they deprived the fort of the service of the only guns which could breach their walls, and, what was of more consequence, of the mortars which could have made havoc in their crowded open batteries, they themselves were able to pour a continuous shower of bursting shells upon every part of the fort which was exposed. This they did with notable skill and regularity of fire; but their direct fire was not nearly so effective. A large proportion of the solid shot missed the fort in the first hours of the bombardment, and those which were better aimed scattered themselves all over its sides, and thus did little injury of immediate importance. Two of the guns upon the parapet were hit, however—one being dismounted, and the other broken; and three of the iron cisterns over the hallways were penetrated by shot, the water pouring in floods upon the quarters below. The parade, where five large columbiads had been arranged for the purpose of throwing shells, was made absolutely untenable by the constant explosion of those dreadful missiles. It was in the midst of such a fire as this that the first relief in the fort went to their work. But they were allowed to fight alone only a very short time. No duty of the soldier is so trying as that of bearing an attack without resistance. Under such circumstances, raw troops in the field almost invariably waver, and, if the trial be continued too long, break and fly: only well disciplined veterans can bear the moral strain which such circumstances put upon them. In the present case, the whole garrison had been wrought up to a high pitch of excitement by a nearly three hours' bombardment without a shot in reply; and soon after the fort first opened fire they broke through the order of the day, and were all engaged heart and soul in the fight, with the tacit consent of their commander. Thus for the first four hours they kept up such a fire that the assailants were astonished, and believed that their watchfulness had been outwitted, and that the fort had been largely re-enforced. Soon the musicians and the workmen, functionally noncombatant, caught the infection. They joined the artillerists in working the guns, and, after a little practice as assistants, went off by themselves and brought new pieces into action. But, although every man of that small band thus did even more than his duty, and did it like a hero, it was soon apparent that they could work little harm to their multitudinous and well-protected assailants. A gun was silenced for a while in Fort Moultrie, the embrasures of which were somewhat injured, and the barracks riddled. One shot penetrated the floating battery, and wounded one man; but from the mailed side of this battery all the other shot which struck it glanced off harmlessly. The much more formidable iron-clad battery on Cummings's Point proved invulnerable to the shot of any piece which could be used against it; and, although the embrasures were hit two or three times, no serious injury was done to the guns or those who manned them. The other batteries seemed to be almost entirely unharmed. Lack of skill was not the cause of this ineffectiveness any more than lack of courage. But it proved that the calibre of the guns in the lower tier of casemates, to the use of which Major Anderson was confined, was too small to make their fire effective on iron-clad batteries, or even on such a strong piece of masonry as Fort Moultrie, at the distances at which they stood.

Four hours had passed since the besieged had opened fire, making, in

---

Chesnut and Captain Lee are authorized by me to enter into such an agreement with you. You are therefore requested to communicate to them an open answer. I remain, major, very respectfully, your obedient servant, G. T. Beauregard, Brigadier General Commanding.

Major Robert Anderson, commanding at Fort Sumter, Charleston Harbor, S. C.

Head-quarters, Fort Sumter, S. C., 2 30 A.M., April 12, 1861.

General,—I have the honor to acknowledge the receipt of your second communication of the 11th inst., by Col. Chesnut, and to state, in reply, that, cordially uniting with you in the desire to avoid the useless effusion of blood, I will, if provided with the proper and necessary means of transportation, evacuate Fort Sumter by noon on the 15th inst., should I not receive, prior to that time, controlling instructions from my government, or additional supplies; and that I will not, in the mean time, open my fire upon your forces unless compelled to do so by some hostile act against this fort, or the flag of my government, by the forces under your command, or by some portion of them, or by the perpetration of some act showing a hostile intention on your part against this fort, or the flag it bears. I have the honor to be, general, your obedient servant,

Robert Anderson, Major U. S. A., Commanding.

To Brigadier General G. T. Beauregard, commanding Provisional Army, C. S. A.

Fort Sumter, S. C., April 12, 1861, 3 20 A.M.

Sir,—By authority of Brigadier General Beauregard, commanding the provisional forces of the Confederate States, we have the honor to notify you that he will open the fire of his batteries on Fort Sumter in one hour from this time. We have the honor to be, very respectfully, your obedient servants,

James Chesnut, Aid-de-camp.
Stephen D. Lee, Captain C. S. Army and Aid-de-camp.

Major Robert Anderson, United States Army, commanding Fort Sumter.

A 10-INCH COLUMBIAD MOUNTED AS A MORTAR AT FORT SUMTER.

FORT MOULTRIE, AS SEEN FROM FORT SUMTER.

vain, a better fight than they could hope to make again; and now the tremendous converging fire of the assailants was beginning to tell upon the walls and parapet, and their shells made the ramparts and the parade untenable. Still the garrison were all unharmed, for they kept within the casemates as much as possible, and look-outs were stationed at commanding points, who gave warning when a shot was about to strike or a shell to burst. About twelve o'clock, through the port-holes was seen the welcome sight of armed vessels under the old flag. The fleet had arrived off the Bar. They dipped their flags in token of salutation and encouragement, and, although bombs were pouring ceaselessly into the parade of the fort, where the flag-staff stood, Sumter's flag was dipped in answer. In fact, men could not have behaved with more intrepid gallantry than was displayed by the few defenders of this fort. During the first day of the bombardment, the quarters were set on fire three times by the enemy's shells, and put out amid a storm of missiles which made the escape of any of those who thus exposed themselves to it seem almost miraculous. The fire upon one gun was so constant and so close that it was abandoned; but, ere long, fire was renewed from it, and an officer, going to the spot, found a party of laborers engaged in serving it. They had turned it upon the floating battery, and one of them was still watching the effect of the last shot, forgetting his danger in his delight, as he saw the ball take effect in the very middle of the battery.

In the afternoon the fire of the rifled guns in the iron-clad Cummings's Point battery became very accurate and severe. It was aimed at the embrasures, the masonry of which was cut out and scattered among the artillerists at almost every shot, bruising and stunning them often, but, fortunately, killing none. They all kept at their work without respite, and had their meals served to them at their guns. Soon after midday, the number of cartridges, of which it had been possible to prepare only seven hundred, had been so much reduced, and the ability to supply them was so small, that it became necessary to abandon all the guns but six. With these, a regular but not very formidable fire was kept up until darkness fell upon the scene, when the port-holes were closed for the night, and the besieged garrison withdrew to pass the anxious hours in brief alternations of rest, work, and watching.

Thus began one of the strangest contests known to the annals of war—a contest strange not only in the circumstances under which it was brought about, but in those under which it was carried on. For, thus far, no war had been declared, directly or by implication, between the government of the United States and the confederate insurgents at Montgomery, although an act of insurrectionary violence had been committed by the residents of Charleston in firing upon the Star of the West. Intercourse between all parts of the country was still nominally free, and to all the people of the seceding states actually so. The telegraph—that marvelous invention which, more than realizing the fairy gifts that dazzle and delight our wondering childhood, makes every man an enchanted prince, by bestowing upon him eyes that see and ears that hear what is passing at the farthest corners of the earth—still kept, though under supervision, all points of the country in communication. Little restraint was placed upon it in Charleston on this day; and the inhabitants of that decaying, stiff-necked sea-port, who, women as well as men, assembled on its battery-promenade to look at the bombardment, much as similar mixed companies looked in classic days upon bloodier contests in the arena, were hardly more immediate spectators of the fight than the millions of those throughout the land who, whether loyal or disloyal to the old flag which was then assailed, found their dearest interests involved in the issue of that contest. Every stage, every vicissitude of the struggle, was reported all over the land with the speed of lightning. The daily tasks and pleasures of a great nation were thrown aside, and the whole country became one vast amphitheatre, in which the combatants fought out their unequal fight with the eyes of thirty millions full upon them. Night fell upon the thrilling spectacle with the contest undecided, and sent home the spectators of both inclinings, quivering with excitement—the partisans of the rebels, however, full of hope and of defiance, those of the soldiers of the republic doubtful, depressed, and bitter; yet with their hearts full of an inspiring trouble and a noble wrath, born of a love which they had often talked about, but the sweet pangs of which few of them had ever felt before. Throughout the country on that night there was proportionately almost as little sleep as there was within Fort Sumter. The night in Charleston Harbor was dark, wet, and stormy. All through it the insurgents kept up a fire of mortars upon the fort, which provoked no reply, but accomplished the purpose of depriving the weary garrison of any except the most fitful slumber. Expecting both an attack by boats and re-enforcements from the fleet, Major Anderson posted guards at the most exposed points of the fort; but his watchfulness proved to have been unneeded. The insurgent commander saw that the reduction of the fort by bombardment was sure and speedy, and therefore wisely refrained from an assault which must needs be very bloody; and the naval forces found themselves entirely unable to move to the support of Major Anderson. Only the Pawnee, 10 guns, the Harriet Lane, 5 guns, and the transport Baltic, had arrived off the Bar on the 12th, the tug-boats having been detained by rough weather. Without these, the orders under which the expedition sailed could not be carried out. These were, as we have already seen, that unarmed boats should be first sent in with stores, and that, if these were fired upon, an attempt should then be made to send in both re-enforcements and supplies by force. But the Baltic, the only unarmed vessel, was too deep to pass the Bar; and, besides, the fort was already under fire. The naval commanders, however, upon consultation, formed a plan for the relief of Major Anderson, which was to hoist out all the boats and launches in the night, load them with the men and stores on board the Baltic, tow them in as far as possible, and, in the gray of the dawning, let them pull in to the fort, under cover of the guns of the Pawnee and the Harriet Lane. A good plan, though a perilous and a daring; but it was entirely frustrated by the nature of the harbor, which did the insurgents in this place such good service throughout the whole war. The Baltic got aground in the night, during the preparations for the disembarking of her troops and stores, and the project was necessarily abandoned. Others were formed; but, before they could be put into effect, they proved to be unavailing.

The storm subsided, and the sun rose brightly to usher in the final contest of Saturday. The bombardment was resumed by the insurgents with more vigor than they had shown before; and about nine o'clock the quarters and barracks were for the fourth time on fire. The men who were not actually engaged in serving the few guns in use tried to extinguish the flames. For a short time they worked like heroes, fighting one fire, and enduring another against which they could not fight. Here two non-combatants distinguished themselves in this their maiden battle—Mr. Hall, a musician, who, throughout the whole bombardment, won the admiration of all by his coolness, intrepidity, and energy; and Mr. Peter Hart, a sergeant in the New York Metropolitan Police Force, who visited the fort in company with Mrs. Anderson, and, on her departure, volunteered to remain there. On this occasion the orders of the commander could hardly restrain him from fruitless exposure of his life, and he afterward performed an act of signal daring. The efforts to put out the fire proved to be equally vain and perilous, for the enemy now poured in a steady fire of red-hot shot; and as fast as the flames were extinguished in one place, they broke out in another. The task was necessarily abandoned for another, yet more important and more dangerous—the protection of the magazine, and the securing enough powder to keep up the fight. Nearly a hundred barrels were taken out amid the roar of flames, the crash of falling beams, the flying of red-hot shot, and the explosion of shells, and were thrown into the sea. Meantime men were making cartridges as rapidly as possible in the magazine itself, using for that purpose blankets, sheets, and shirts, and all similar material that the fort could furnish. The supply obtainable in this manner was, however, soon exhausted; and the heat became so great from the blazing quarters and barracks that the magazine could no longer be left open with safety. The

REMOVING POWDER FROM THE MAGAZINE OF FORT SUMTER DURING THE BOMBARDMENT.

doors were, therefore, finally closed and locked, and the fight kept up only in name, by the occasional irregular discharge of a gun. The situation of the garrison, actually desperate from the beginning, was now rapidly approaching the last extremity. The main gates took fire, and were soon destroyed, leaving the fort open to assault from this quarter by overwhelming force. The chassis of the barbette guns were burned upon the gorge. The heat became so intense, and diffused itself so widely, that the shells and fixed ammunition in the upper service magazines exploded, scattering ruin and threatening death. The fire from all the insurgent batteries increased in fury; and the continued thunder of their heavy guns, the roar of the flames inside the fort, the crash of falling masonry and timber, the bursting of the enemy's shells, and the explosion of the ammunition in the service magazines, combined to make a scene in which grandeur rivaled peril. The great extent of the fort, the small number of men within it, and the care with which they were kept inside the casemates, thus far prevented any serious casualties. But it seemed as if the garrison were to escape death by shot and shell only to meet it by suffocation. The day was warm and

sultry, the smoke did not rise freely, and the fort became so filled with it that the men could hardly see or breathe. The heat itself grew stifling, and increased to such a point that it became necessary to protect all the powder left of that which had been taken out of the great magazine—only four barrels—with wet blankets and other bedding. The men themselves were able to get breath only by lying down upon the floors of the casemates, and spreading wet cloths over their faces to exclude the smoke. An eddying gust of wind occasionally dispersed the stifling clouds, and relieved their distress for lack of air, while it revealed to their sight the terrors of their situation. About this time the flag-staff, which, though hit nine times · had thus far escaped with slight injury, was shot away near the top. The look-out cried, "The flag is down," and instantly Mr. Hall sprung out into the flaming, shot-raked parade, and brought the flag away. But the halliards were so entangled that it could not be righted and raised again. What should be done? The flag must float, for, terrible as the situation was, no one had yet spoken of surrender. A temporary staff was rigged upon the ramparts, and Police-sergeant Hart volunteered to climb it and

POLICE-SERGEANT HART NAILING THE FLAG TO THE TEMPORARY FLAG-STAFF.

nail the flag fast. This he did while the enemy's batteries kept up their furious fire of shot and shell, in the face of which he accomplished his perilous undertaking, and descended the staff in safety. The enemy, determined rebels though they were, could not see unmoved this heroic defense of a fortress and a flag for which they felt that only a little while before they would have fought with no less gallantry; and at each of the now rare and irregular discharges of a single gun, they leaped upon their own ramparts and cheered Major Anderson and his men.

Under these circumstances, when the only four barrels of powder out of the magazine were practically inaccessible, when only three more cartridges remained, and they were in the guns, when the tragic interest of the day was at its height, the comic actor of the occasion entered upon the scene, and affairs took a ludicrous turn toward peace. The fall of the flag had, of course, been noticed, and it had been mistaken in one quarter at least for a sign of surrender. Soon after Mr. Hart had nailed it in its new position upon the outer wall, a man appeared at an embrasure with a handkerchief tied upon a sword, symbolic of the semi-military condition of his mind and person in

other respects, and demanded admission. It was allowed, and he scrambled in. He proved to be the Hon. Mr. Wigfall, of Texas, who had been the occasion of much laughter in the Senate-chamber, and who was now volunteer aid to General Beauregard. In a fuss and flurry, which provoked the smiles of the smoke-grimed soldiers whom he addressed, he said that he came from that officer, and asked for Major Anderson. He had gone to the main gate to meet the flag of truce, the approach of which had been observed; and before he could be summoned, Colonel Wigfall (for such was his new title) said, "Your flag is down; you are on fire; let us quit this;" and asked to have his extemporized flag of truce displayed from the ramparts. He was shown the national flag still flying, and told that if he wished his friends to stop firing *he* must display the flag of truce. This he at once did, waving it out of an embrasure, which, nevertheless, was nearly hit by two or three shots. As it was his flag, and not that of the fort, a corporal was then ordered to relieve him; but the firing being still kept up, because of the national flag again floating above the fort, the corporal declined to continue his useless exposure, and leaped back into the casemate, where the excited aid-de-camp soundly rated him for his cowardice. At this point Major Anderson came up, and the subsequent colloquy is thus reported by an eye-witness to the interview:

"Wigfall said, 'I am Colonel Wigfall, and come from General Beauregard, who wishes to stop this.' Major Anderson, rising on his toes, and coming down firmly upon his heels, replied, 'Well, sir.' 'Major Anderson,' said Wigfall, 'you have defended your flag nobly, sir. You have done all that is possible for men to do, and General Beauregard wishes to stop the fight. On what terms, Major Anderson, will you evacuate this fort?' Major Anderson's reply was, 'General Beauregard is already acquainted with my only terms.' 'Do I understand that you will evacuate upon the terms proposed the other day?' 'Yes, sir, and on those conditions only,' was the reply of the major. 'Then, sir,' said Wigfall, 'I understand, Major Anderson, that the fort is to be ours?' 'On those conditions only, I repeat.' 'Very well,' said Wigfall; 'then it is understood that you will evacuate. That is all I have to do. You military men will arrange every thing else on your own terms.' He then departed, the white flag still waving where he had placed it, and the stars and stripes waving from the flag-staff, which had become the target of the rebels."

But hardly was he half way to the shore when a more formal and numerous deputation from the staff of General Beauregard—Major Lee, Mr. Porcher Miles, ex-Senator Chesnut, and Mr. Roger A. Pryor—appeared with a flag of truce and asked admission, which, of course, was given. They also said that they came from General Beauregard. He had noticed that the flag had been down; that the fort was on fire; and he desired to know if he could render any assistance. As Major Anderson's position was the consequence of General Beauregard's own acts, this was, of course, but a delicate way of asking a surrender. The beleaguered commander was surprised, as well he might be, at this deputation from a man with whom he had already agreed upon general terms of evacuation, and he replied accordingly, to the great discomfiture of the members of the new deputation. These, however, after a few minutes' conference, informed Major Anderson that the extempore Texan colonel had not seen the rebel commander-in-chief for two days. They requested, however, a suspension of hostilities while they bore a written memorandum of Major Anderson's terms to General Beauregard; but, in the midst of this embarrassment, yet a third flag of truce arrived, borne by Major D. R. Jones, the insurgent general's chief of staff, offering the same terms of evacuation, with a single exception, which had been proposed before the bombardment—to wit, the departure of the whole command, with company arms and property, and all private property, and the privilege of saluting and keeping the flag—the exception being the salute to the flag. These terms Major Anderson positively refused then to accept without the salute, but consented that that point should remain open for consideration.

The salute was finally admitted by General Beauregard, who also (with equal courtesy, and regard for the condition of a fort which was about to pass into his possession) proffered assistance for the extinction of the fire, which was declined. The intrepid national commander had no alternative as to the course which he should pursue. He had not lost a man; but the fort had become untenable, and his means of defense were exhausted. Had there been time to let the walls cool so that the magazine might be opened, to blow down the parapet and build up the great gates with stones and rubbish, the defense might have been prolonged, as far as the fort itself was concerned, until the men were exhausted by a diet of sheer salt pork. But, even had these circumstances existed, the lack of cartridges and the means of making them would have made effective offensive operations impossible.[7]

It is said that yet another and still more ludicrous incident lightened the closing scenes of this eventful day within the fort. Mr. Roger A. Pryor, of Virginia, one of the first deputation from General Beauregard (and who seems to have been one of that high (but not highest) style of Southern man who vaunts his good-breeding and his chivalry, but has not yet attained to quiet self-respect and unassuming confidence in himself, united to scrupulous regard for the feelings of others, but maintains his superiority by offensive self-assertion), appeared on this occasion loaded down with arms incisive and explosive, and bore himself in keeping with his personal appearance. Seeing upon a table what appeared to be a glass of brandy, he swallowed it, without pause or ceremony. Surgeon Crawford having caught sight of him as he was turning down the dose, approached quickly, and informed him that what he had drank as brandy was iodide of potassium, a deadly poison. Instant collapse on the part of the patient followed this announcement; but whether it was due to the poison, or only to the announcement, the Muse of History has not been informed. She records with pleasure, however, that the valiant Virginian, having been seized upon by the benevolent surgeon, was put instantly through such a course of pumping and purgation that his life was saved, to be again, in like manner, devoted to the cause which he had espoused. It may be cruel, but it is human, to suggest that the surgeon, having failed of a single loyal patient through a two days' bombardment, was determined to have one at least from the rebel side, and seized the occasion of an equally thoughtless and harmless drinking to gratify at once his professional craving and his excited patriotism.

Agitating as this day had been in Charleston Harbor, it was none the less so outside the bounds of the insurgent confederacy. Throughout the free states, and the slave states still under loyal rule, the people rose on that Saturday morning with their souls filled with the one anxiety which had prevented or disturbed their rest. The bombardment and the defense would, of course, be renewed; but would Major Anderson be able to hold out until he received the re-enforcements and supplies which lay within sight of his ramparts? What of good or ill to the republic would this day bring forth? What of honor or dishonor to the flag? The excitement was not turbulent; it hardly ruffled the surface of society. It was a strong, deep-seated trouble; a sad and almost awful apprehension. It sank deeper and spread wider as the hourly dispatches told how the stirring fight went on. In the great centres of population and business the streets were filled by eager, anxious people, who spoke nervously upon the one great theme; and around the many bulletin-boards the crowds were so great as to impede the public passage. The announcements successively made of the feebleness of Major Anderson's resistance, of the inactivity of the fleet, of the fire, the throwing powder into the water, the explosions, the silencing of the fort, the incomprehensible display of the flag of truce at the same time with the national standard, were received with amazement, indignation, and incredulity. The southern end of the telegraph was, of course, in the hands of the insurgents; and soon these astonishing, and, as it was thought, absurd reports began to be attributed to the malicious perversion of those who sent them. The inactivity of the fleet seemed inexplicable; the story that the fort was on fire was scouted as quite incredible. Fort Sumter was believed to be an almost impregnable mass of solid masonry, as incombustible as the Rock of Gibraltar; and here it was, if the truth were told, burning like a tinder-box. Men turned away in scorn; they could not and would not believe it. And when, in the afternoon, the final dispatch came from Charleston, by way of Augusta, that the fort had surrendered; that the confederate flag floated over its walls, and that none of the garrison or confederate troops were hurt, it was thought that this was the cap-sheaf of malicious invention, and that it was only sure that the fight had gone on during the day with varying fortunes. The effect of the news, however, was to work the public mind up to a terrible pitch of excitement; and the most widely-circulated daily paper in the city of New York, having been thus far the apologist and the advocate of the secessionists, the indignation of the people was so roused against it that an attack upon its office was expected, and would

SCENE AROUND A BULLETIN-BOARD.

Q

[7] See the "Engineer Journal of the Bombardment of Fort Sumter," by Capt. J. G. Foster, Corps of Engineers, U. S. A., New York, 1861.

BOMBARDMENT OF FORT SUMTER BY THE BAT[

doubtless have been made, except for the prompt and vigorous preventive measures taken by the chief of police.

Little of the next day was given wholly to religious duties, for patriotism is an element of piety, not of religion; and the two days' attack upon the national flag was the only subject which really occupied men's minds—the only topic of their conversation. To satisfy the anxiety of the public, the principal newspapers, the publication of which, with one exception, was intermitted, of course, on Sunday, issued a number on this morning; and thus commenced a custom which was continued far into the period of the ensuing war. The dispatches of the previous day proved to be substantially true, and the people found themselves forced to bear the national humiliation with such resignation as they could summon. Here and there a voice was heard denouncing Major Anderson, or at least questioning his patriotism or his determination. But these were the views only of the most headstrong and least considerate folk; the mass of the people felt that he had a right to their entire confidence. At this very time he was evacuating the fort upon terms, and in a manner, creditable alike to himself and to his opponents in the recent contest. Having packed up all company and personal property, and made preparations for saluting his flag, Major Anderson was waited upon by several officers of General Beauregard's staff, Commander Hartstein, formerly of the United States Navy, but who had preferred his state to his country, and Captain Gillis, commander of the Pocahontas. The steamer Isabel, which the confederate authorities had provided as a transport to the vessels outside the Bar, lay at the wharf behind the gorge. The old battle-torn flag, which had been displayed four months before, amid prayers apparently unheard and hopes doomed to bitter disappointment, was raised to receive the honors which showed that it had fallen without disgrace. Fifty guns were fired, and it was lowered before solemn faces and tearful eyes. But, it would seem, the outraged genius of the republic demanded that some sacrifice of blood, even innocent, should atone for this humiliation, and at the seventeenth gun an accidental explosion of fixed ammunition instantly killed one of the artillerists, and severely wounded several others, one of them mortally. This casualty proved more fatal than the two days' bombardment to either party; for, in spite of reports long circulated to the contrary in regard to the insurgent force, there is no reasonable room for doubting the assertion that neither side lost a single man, while the wounds received were few and trifling. The salute finished, the victim to the honor of his country's flag, Private David Hough, was buried with military honors in the parade of the fort where he had done so gallantly a soldier's duty; and the garrison, in full uniform, were formed in line, and marched out to the air of "Yankee Doodle." The confederate officers present vied with each other in demonstrations of courtesy to their vanquished foes. The flag of Fort Sumter, which Major Anderson took away with him, was raised on board the Isabel as she put off, so that he and his command were under no flag but that of their government from the beginning to the end of the memorable series of events in which they bore so prominent a part.

Of the insurgent force in this affair little has been, and little need be said. They were in overwhelming numbers, and the fire of the fort—restricted as Major Anderson proved to be to his guns of smallest calibre—was so ineffective that their performance was little more than artillery practice. Their numbers, and their guns, and the work they did, have been thus precisely stated in an elaborate article written upon the best authority.[8] They had fourteen batteries in action, mounting forty-two heavy guns and mortars. From these there were thrown, during the two days, two thousand three

[8] Published in the Charleston Mercury of May 2d and 3d, 1861.

hundred and sixty shot and nine hundred and eighty shells. The number of men engaged in the confederate works was certainly over three thousand, and between four and five thousand were held in reserve. Of the officers who distinguished themselves—with such distinction as was possible where the officers on one side were three times as many as the men on the other, and no one was hurt—General Beauregard's report mentions Lieutenant Colonel R. S. Ripley, commanding the batteries on Sullivan's Island; Lieutenant Colonel W. G. De Saussure, commanding those on Morris Island; Major P. F. Stevens, in command of the iron-clad battery at Cummings's Point; Captain Thomas, who commanded the British rifled cannon at this point; and Majors Whiting and Gwin, and Captain Hartstein. Colonel Wigfall comes in for a share of commendation; and let us not forget that, with all his fluster and flurry, and the absurdity of his false position in regard to the capitulation, his motive was a good one, and he showed real fortitude in passing from the shore to the fort in an open boat during a heavy fire of shot and shell. Captain Hartstein, having but to superintend the patrolling of the harbor and carrying of messages in tug-boats, gained more distinction by his courtesy and fraternal kindness after the surrender than by the duties which he had performed before.

It was not to be expected that the official representative of the vaunting and insolent politicians and planters of South Carolina would emulate the honorable consideration shown by Captain Hartstein and the officers who accompanied him to those who had so gallantly defended the flag of the republic—the flag which, not long before, they had all been sworn to uphold at peril of their lives. Governor Pickens, in a speech which he made to the people of Charleston on the evening of the evacuation, exposed without reserve the spiteful, domineering, braggart spirit in which he, and those of his constituents who had really any voice in the direction of affairs, had gone into their rebellion. Alluding to the vast majority of their fellow-citizens, whom they had been told they would find arrayed on the side of the Constitution and the laws, he said: "We have defeated their twenty millions, and we have made the proud flag of the stars and stripes, that never was lowered before to any nation on this earth, we have lowered it in humility before the palmetto and the confederate flags." The humiliation of the national flag, though under circumstances which could bring no honor of any kind to its assailants, was too pleasant a theme to be passed over with one exulting outburst; and thus again the rebellious demagogue rolled the sweet morsel under his tongue: "We have humbled the flag of the United States. I can here say to you, it is the first time in the history of this country that the stars and stripes have been humbled. It has triumphed for seventy years; but to-day, on the thirteenth day of April, it has been humbled, and humbled before the glorious little state of South Carolina." On the same occasion, and in the same bombastic strain, he spoke of the independence of his constituents as already achieved, and as having been "baptized in blood." Now the twenty millions defeated by the insurgent forces (numbering seven thousand, and having in action forty-two heavy guns and mortars) were one hundred and nine half-famished men, including musicians, laborers, and the surgeon; and the blood in which the Charlestonian independence was baptized was that of four men, slightly wounded. Governor Pickens's speech was received with vociferous applause; and so was one of more significance, made in Montgomery, the confederate capital, the day before, by Mr. Pope Walker, the insurgent Secretary of War: "No man," he said, "can tell where the war this day commenced will end; but I will prophesy that the flag which now flaunts the breeze here will float over the dome of the old Capitol at Washington before the first of May. Let

THE GORGE OF FORT SUMTER.

them try Southern chivalry and test the extent of Southern resources, and it may float eventually over Faneuil Hall itself."

It was upon a people thus miserably mistaking their countrymen and themselves, thus blind with fury, thus bloated with insolence and besotted with pride, thus bent upon the humiliation and final destruction of the republic in which at last they had ceased to rule, that the heroes of Fort Sumter, defeated but not dishonored, turned their backs, on Sunday, the 14th of April, 1861, and sailed northward, under the very flag which they had so nobly defended, to tell in simple, modest words the story of their struggle.[9]

THE UPRISING AT THE NORTH.

Effect of the Bombardment of Fort Sumter.—War Proclamation of President Lincoln.—Response of the Free States; of the Governors of the Border Slave States.—Measures of the Rebel Government.—Seizure of the Navy Yard and Forts Barrancas and M'Rea at Pensacola.—Occupation of Fort Pickens by Lieutenant Slemmer.—Insolent Propositions for Truce, and degrading Compliance.—Re-enforcement of Fort Pickens.—Washington in danger.—The Convention of Virginia secretly passes a Provisional Ordinance of Secession, and an Ordinance uniting the State to the insurgent Confederacy.—Destruction of the Arsenal and Armory at Harper's Ferry, and its Occupation by the Insurgents.—Incomplete Destruction of the Portsmouth Navy Yard, and its Seizure.—Massachusetts leads the Van.—Reasons for her Promptness.—Attack upon a Massachusetts and a Pennsylvania Regiment in Baltimore.—March of the New York Seventh.—Communication between Washington and the North cut off.—Union Meetings.—The Flag.—Badges.—Show your Colors.—Gifts and Appropriations for the War.—A Blockade.—Rebel Privateers.—Neutral Treason.—Condition of Washington Society.—Spies.—Seizure of Telegraphic Dispatches.—Habeas Corpus practically suspended.—Commotion in Missouri.—Kentucky for the Union.—New Proclamation calling for 48,000 Men for three Years.—Military Preparations at the South.—Seat of the Rebel Government transferred to Richmond.—Nature and Purposes of the impending Conflict.

THE depression which followed the bombardment of Fort Sumter was but momentary. It did not last a single day. The rebound was instantaneous and tremendous. In spite of four months' warning, the event actually came with all the suddenness of surprise. In fact, it was absolutely necessary to the arousing of the loyal men of the republic from a state of mingled confidence and bewilderment, which had almost the seeming, and all the effect, of stupor. A keen and practiced observer, who had visited many parts of the world and many scenes of strife in the service of the most influential journal of Europe, and who had been sent to the United States to observe and report the course of events during the civil troubles, after remaining in New York two weeks, wrote, on the 20th of March, that to his eyes that city was "full of divine calm and human phlegm;" that the commercial queen of the West, in his opinion, "would do any thing rather than fight; her desire is to eat her bread and honey and count her dollars in peace." To him, judging from what he heard as well as what he saw, the disruption of the republic was then already accomplished; for, on the one side, a representative secessionist said to him, "No concession, no compromise; nothing that can be done or suggested shall induce us to join any confederation of which the New England states are members;" and, on the other, an equally eminent Republican, of the extreme school, declared to him on the same day, "If I could bring back the Southern states by holding up my little finger, I should think it criminal to do so."[10] The swift agency of steam could not take the letter containing these statements to London, print it, and send it back again, before the conclusion based upon them was entirely falsified. The secessionist doubtless stood firm in his rebellious determination; but the Abolitionist had found that, whatever might be his feeling upon the subject, the people of the free states did not regard the question of negro slavery in any of its bearings as worthy to be weighed one moment in the scale with that of the maintenance of constitutional government and the perpetuity of the republic; and the divine calm of the city that would do any thing rather than fight had been swept away by an intensely human excitement which strangely united all the heat of fury to all the coolness of resolution. In all this there was no sudden gyration of opinion or change of feeling. The national sentiment of loyal men was not touched to the quick until the bombardment of Fort Sumter. The secessionists might have held conventions and passed resolutions until the crack of doom, and it would have been regarded as of but little moment. Southern conventions had become a laughing-stock at the North on account of their wordy folly. They had been held for various ostensible objects, but chiefly for that of turning, by preamble and resolutions, the tide of commerce from New York, Boston, and Philadelphia to Norfolk and Charleston. In this they had not been successful; and the discredit which attached to them affected greatly all the preliminary steps taken in the more dangerous designs to which they were in part a cloak. In fact, much as the country had been disturbed by the outbreak at the South upon the election of Mr. Lincoln, it seemed but a continuation or expected consequence of the preceding presidential canvass. It was no new thing. It did not have a beginning; it was merely a going on. It seemed, nay, it was, the last move in the stupendous game of intimidation and braggadocio which had been played for twenty years and more. Much the same turmoil had been heard before, when the slavery propaganda had only feared defeat. What was to be expected upon its actual discomfiture? These men had talked so much about secession if a Republican were elected, that, unless they were willing to be looked upon as the merest braggarts, they must do something to back their words. Their conventions and their ordinances were mere brute thunder, harmful in effect upon the country, but harmless against its government. Their refusal to pay their Northern debts was regarded as far more injurious, and more indicative of hostile determination.

Thus thought and felt too many men throughout the country through the gloomy winter of 1860 and 1861; for even the seizure of forts and arms, and the very establishment of the insurgent government, were looked upon rather as extreme measures of intimidation than as the first steps of a desperate rebellion. The firing upon the Star of the West, strange to say, did not quite open the eyes of all of those who should have seen that it meant absolute defiance. But when, upon the announcement that Fort Sumter was to be provisioned, the insurgents bombarded the garrison out of it, then, with a sudden shock, the loyal citizens of the republic felt what secession really was. Indignation flashed through the astonished land. The whole country quivered with a new emotion. Men lived in the open air, that they might read in each other's faces, eye to eye, the noble wrath, the fixed determination, the lofty purpose that ruled the hour. Two could hardly speak together in the street above their ordinary tone without being surrounded with eager listeners. Every public place was thronged with unbidden crowds, intent upon discourse of the momentous situation. A nation of freemen, each of whom felt, at last, his own responsibility for his country's safety and honor, was pierced through brain and heart with the barbed conviction that that safety was in peril and that honor at stake. The strong barriers of party vanished as by magic, and men became so intensely absorbed in the present that, forgetful of the past, they saw each other for the first time only as fellow-citizens, with one feeling and one purpose. It was a moment of supreme grandeur in the life of the nation. Patriotism, which had been trodden under foot of politicians, which had withered in the arid soil of selfishness under the blazing sun of prosperity, which had been choked with the thorns of care, and wealth, and pleasure, struck at once its roots to the very centre of the nation's being, and in a single night blossomed into fruitfulness. That fruit was a stern resolve to sacrifice life and fortune in defense of the republic.

It was to a people who had passed through this mental experience that President Lincoln addressed a proclamation dated upon the day of the evacuation of Fort Sumter.[1] That was Sunday; and on Monday morning the President's appeal, distributed by telegraph, was read throughout the country. It was remarkably cool and dispassionate. It set forth that the laws of the United States had been for some time defied in the seven seceded states by combinations too powerful to be dealt with by the officers of the law; it called out 75,000 of the militia of the several states for the purpose of suppressing those combinations, and first, if not chiefly, of repossessing the forts which had been seized; it especially, and with great care in the use of words, disavowed any intention of "devastation, destruction, or interference with property in any part of the country." It commanded the insurgents to dis-

[9] *Major Anderson's Dispatch concerning the Bombardment and Evacuation of Fort Sumter.*

Steam-ship Baltic, off Sandy Hook, April 18, 1861.

Hon. S. Cameron, Secretary of War, Washington, D.C.:

SIR,—Having defended Fort Sumter for thirty-four hours, until the quarters were entirely burned, the main gates destroyed by fire, the gorge wall seriously injured, the magazine surrounded by flames, and its door closed from the effects of the heat, four barrels and three cartridges of powder only being available, and no provisions but pork remaining, I accepted terms of evacuation, offered by General Beauregard, being the same offered by him on the 11th instant, prior to the commencement of hostilities, and marched out of the fort Sunday afternoon, the 14th instant, with colors flying and drums beating, bringing away company and private property, and saluting my flag with fifty guns. ROBERT ANDERSON, Major First Artillery.

[10] Correspondence of the London *Times*, April 17th, 1861.

[1] *Proclamation of President Lincoln.*

Whereas the laws of the United States have been for some time past and now are opposed, and the execution thereof obstructed, in the states of South Carolina, Georgia, Alabama, Florida, Mississippi, Louisiana, and Texas, by combinations too powerful to be suppressed by the ordinary course of judicial proceedings or by the powers vested in the marshals by law: now, therefore, I, ABRAHAM LINCOLN, President of the United States, in virtue of the power in me vested by the Constitution and the laws, have thought fit to call forth, and hereby do call forth, the militia of the several states of the Union to the aggregate number of 75,000, in order to suppress said combinations and to cause the laws to be duly executed. The details for this object will be immediately communicated to the state authorities through the War Department. I appeal to all loyal citizens to favor, facilitate, and aid this effort to maintain the honor, the integrity, and existence of our national Union, and the perpetuity of popular government, and to redress wrongs already long enough endured. I deem it proper to say that the first service assigned to the forces hereby called forth will probably be to repossess the forts, places, and property which have been seized from the Union; and in every event the utmost care will be observed, consistently with the objects aforesaid, to avoid any devastation, any destruction of, or interference with property, or any disturbance of peaceful citizens of any part of the country; and I hereby command the persons composing the combinations aforesaid to disperse and retire peaceably to their respective abodes within twenty days from this date.

Deeming that the present condition of public affairs presents an extraordinary occasion, I do hereby, in virtue of the power in me vested by the Constitution, convene both houses of Congress. The senators and representatives are, therefore, summoned to assemble at their respective chambers at 12 o'clock, noon, on Thursday, the 4th day of July next, then and there to consider and determine such measures as, in their wisdom, the public safety and interest may seem to demand.

In witness whereof, I have hereunto set my hand, and caused the seal of the United States to be affixed.

Done at the City of Washington, this 15th day of April, in the year of our Lord one thousand eight hundred and sixty-one, and of the independence of the United States the eighty-fifth.

ABRAHAM LINCOLN.

By the President.
WILLIAM H. SEWARD, Secretary of State.

The following call on the respective state governors for troops was simultaneously issued through the War Department:

SIR,—Under the act of Congress for calling out the militia to execute the laws of the Union, to suppress insurrection, to repel invasion, etc., approved February 28, 1795, I have the honor to request your excellency to cause to be immediately detailed from the militia of your state the quota designated in the table below, to serve as infantry or riflemen for a period of three months, unless sooner discharged. Your excellency will please communicate to me the time at about which your quota will be expected at its rendezvous, as it will be met as soon as practicable by an officer or officers to muster it into service and pay of the United States. At the same time the oath of fidelity to the United States will be administered to every officer and man. The mustering officers will be instructed to receive no man under the rank of commissioned officer who is in years apparently over 45 or under 18, or who is not in physical strength and vigor. The quota for each state is as follows:

Maine	1	Pennsylvania	16	Missouri	4
New Hampshire	1	Delaware	1	Ohio	13
Vermont	1	Tennessee	2	Indiana	6
Massachusetts	2	Maryland	4	Illinois	6
Rhode Island	1	Virginia	3	Michigan	1
Connecticut	1	North Carolina	2	Iowa	1
New York	17	Kentucky	4	Minnesota	1
New Jersey	4	Arkansas	1	Wisconsin	1

It is ordered that each regiment shall consist, on an aggregate of officers and men, of 780. The total thus to be called out is 73,391. The remainder to constitute the 75,000 men under the President's proclamation will be composed of troops in the District of Columbia.

LIBERTY UN

UPRISING

perse within twenty days, and summoned a special session of Congress on the 4th of July. The command was a matter of form, prescribed by act of Congress; the summons, a matter of necessity. On that Monday morning, too, the flag of the republic—how dear to those who were true to it, they never knew till then—was raised by spontaneous impulse upon every staff which stood on loyal ground; and from the Lakes to the Potomac, from the shores of the Atlantic to the banks of the Mississippi, the eye could hardly turn without meeting the bright banner which symbolized in its stripes the union and the initial struggle, and in its stars the consequent growth and glory of the nation and the government which the insurgents had banded themselves together to destroy.[2]

The response of the free states to the proclamation was so unanimous and so instantaneous that it seemed to be by acclamation. The official responses of the several governors became almost matters of course and of form. They were dignified, calm, and resolute messages. The people in Delaware were equally prompt and hearty in their devotion to the republic; and over the vast extent of country lying north of the Potomac and the Ohio, its intelligent millions, throughout all grades of the social scale, were at once busied in preparing for the coming war, or, at least, in cheering those who were thus engaged. President Lincoln doubtless asked for 75,000 men with some fear and trembling; for, since the nation came into political existence, it had never had half that number of men under arms together. But before a day had passed it was manifest that more than twice as many were ready at his call. The proclamation, however, was not addressed to the free states only; and all those who were not under the control of the insurgent government (except California, Oregon, and Kansas, on account of their remoteness) were called upon to furnish their several quotas. From the governors of all the slave states except Delaware and Maryland there came a flat, and, in some cases, a defiant and an insolent refusal. Governor Letcher, of Virginia, was content with being decided. Governors Ellis, of North Carolina, and Magoffin, of Kentucky, added to their refusal a denunciation of the course of the government as "wicked." Governor Rector, of Arkansas, stigmatized the demand as "adding insult to injury," and talked of defense against "Northern mendacity and usurpation." Governor Harris, of Tennessee, said he had not a man for coërcion, but fifty thousand for the defense of the rights of his Southern, *i. e.*, his slaveholding brothers; while Governor Jackson, of Missouri, poured out his wrath in the words "illegal, unconstitutional, revolutionary, inhuman, diabolical."[3] The governors of Delaware and Maryland (Burton and Hicks) answered with bated breath, in the form of proclamation. The former announced that he found himself without power to comply with the requisition from the Secretary of War, but he recommended the raising of a regiment, which he announced would be at liberty to offer its services to the general government. The regiment was immediately raised and mustered into service; and before the year was out, this small state had furnished two thousand more men to the armies of the Union. Governor Hicks's proclamation was little else than a public wringing of the hands and bemoaning himself over the perplexities of his situation, which indeed were great and trying; for, although Maryland was loyal by a large majority, the disloyal men were actually numerous, and made up by their activity and defiant bearing for their inferiority of numbers. Among them, too, were the greater part of the wealthy slaveholders in the state, and the people of high social position. Governor Hicks endeavored to placate his constituents by assuring them that no troops should be sent from Maryland unless for the protection of the national capital, and reminding them that a special election would soon give them an opportunity of expressing their devotion to the Union, or their desire to see it broken up.[4]

The first step of the confederate government to meet this condition of affairs beyond their borders was to issue a call for 32,000 more troops. The governors of the seceded states thereupon issued flaming proclamations, denouncing, exhorting, commanding, and recommending; and in one instance, that of Governor Brown, of Georgia, the command took the needless, but, therefore, none the less dishonorable form of an interdiction of payment of any debt due to a resident of an anti-slavery state, while the recommendation shrewdly suggested that these confiscated funds should be paid into the treasury of Georgia.

These were preparations for future movements. But already the government of the United States had brought an important military operation to the verge of a successful issue. This was the re-enforcement of Fort Pickens—much the strongest fortification at the very important post of Pensacola Harbor in Florida, which it in a great measure commanded. At this post was a navy yard, which was used as a naval station for Gulf cruisers, and which was therefore rich in ammunition and supplies. The bay or harbor was defended first by Fort Pickens, a large and formidable stone casemated work, which stands on the point of Santa Rosa Island, a long and narrow strip of sand which almost closes the bay, and between which and the opposite shore there is a distance of but a mile and a half. Directly opposite Fort Pickens is a water-battery known as Fort M'Rea; and about two miles farther along the shore, and within less than the same distance of Fort Pickens, is a larger work than the former, which is called the Barrancas, or Fort San Carlos. The greedy eyes of the insurgents were early turned upon these important strong-holds and store-houses; and on the 12th of January a band of about five hundred men, led by Captain V. M. Randolph, of the United States Navy, and, it is said, by one Colonel Lomax, whose commission was in the Florida militia, appeared at the gates of the navy yard, and demanded its surrender to the State of Florida, which had that day passed its Ordinance of Secession. It was on this day that the Star of the West returned to New York, with the marks of two rebel cannon upon her hull, after her miserable attempt to re-enforce Fort Sumter. The scene at Pensacola Navy Yard was more shameful, and incomparably more calamitous. There was no attempt at decency on the part of Lieutenants E. Farrand and F. B. Renshaw, who were there in authority; and in their presence, and, it is asserted, by the command of the latter, the flag of the republic was hauled down amid the jeers of a drunken rabble, and the yard, with all its guns, stores, and ammunition, passed at a word into the hands of the insurgents.[5] On the same day, Commander Armstrong, of the Navy, caused the Barrancas to be abandoned; but he had the grace to spike the guns, and remove some, at least, of the munitions. Farrand and Renshaw were treacherously false to their colors; but Armstrong's plea was inability to cope with the forces which could be brought against him. At little Fort M'Rea, however, was a man of another mould. Lieutenant Adam J. Slemmer, a young officer of artillery, distinguished thus far only by his proficiency in the scientific branches of his profession, was stationed there; and he determined at once to do all that a brave and able soldier could to save the key to the position. The garrison under his command at Fort M'Rea was very small, but he did not despair. Hastily gathering from the Barrancas and the navy

---

[2] The feeling of the time when this spontaneous display of the stars and stripes lit up the face of all the North, found a truthful and spirited expression in this fine lyric, which appeared in the Boston *Transcript:*

THE FLAG. BY HORATIO WOODMAN.

Why flashed that flag on Monday morn
  Across the startled sky?
Why leaped the blood to every cheek,
  The tears to every eye?
The hero in our four months' woe,
  The symbol of our might,
Together sunk for one brief hour,
  To rise forever bright.

The mind of Cromwell claimed his own,
  The blood of Naseby streamed
Through hearts unconscious of the fire,
  Till that torn banner gleamed.
The seeds of Milton's lofty thoughts,
  All hopeless of the spring,
Broke forth in joy, as through them glowed
  The life great poets sing.

Old Greece was young, and Homer true,
  And Dante's burning page
Flamed in the red along our flag,
  And kindled holy rage.
God's Gospel cheered the sacred cause
  In stern, prophetic strain,
Which makes His rite our covenant,
  His Psalms our deep refrain.

Oh, sad for him whose light went out
  Before this glory came,
Who could not live to feel his kin
  To every noble name!
And sadder still to miss the joy
  That twenty millions know
In Human Nature's holiday
  From all that makes life low.

[3] REPLIES FROM THE DISLOYAL GOVERNORS TO THE REQUISITION FOR TROOPS UNDER THE PRESIDENT'S PROCLAMATION.

From Governor Letcher, of Virginia.

"I have only to say, that the militia of Virginia will not be furnished to the powers at Washington for any such use or purpose as they have in view. Your object is to subjugate the Southern states, and a requisition made upon me for such an object—an object, in my judgment, not within the purview of the Constitution or the act of 1795—will not be complied with. You have chosen to inaugurate civil war, and having done so, we will meet it in a spirit as determined as the administration has exhibited toward the South."

From Governor Ellis, of North Carolina.

"Your dispatch is received; and, if genuine, which its extraordinary character leads me to doubt, I have to say in reply, that I regard the levy of troops made by the administration for the purpose of subjugating the states of the South as in violation of the Constitution, and a usurpation of power. I can be no party to this wicked violation of the laws of the country, and to this war upon the liberties of a free people. You can get no troops from North Carolina."

From Governor Magoffin, of Kentucky.

"Your dispatch is received. I say emphatically that Kentucky will furnish no troops for the wicked purpose of subduing her sister Southern states."

From Governor Harris, of Tennessee.

"Tennessee will not furnish a single man for coercion, but fifty thousand, if necessary, for the defense of our rights, or those of our Southern brethren."

From Governor Rector, of Arkansas.

"In answer to your requisition for troops from Arkansas, to subjugate the Southern states, I have to say that none will be furnished. The demand is only adding insult to injury. The people of this commonwealth are freemen, not slaves, and will defend to the last extremity their honor, lives, and property against Northern mendacity and usurpation."

From Governor Jackson, of Missouri.

"There can be, I apprehend, no doubt that these men are intended to make war upon the seceded states. Your requisition, in my judgment, is illegal, unconstitutional, and revolutionary in its objects, inhuman and diabolical, and can not be complied with. Not one man will the State of Missouri furnish to carry on such an unholy crusade."

[4] *Proclamation of Governor Hicks, of Maryland.*

To the People of Maryland:

The unfortunate state of affairs now existing in the country has greatly excited the people of Maryland.

In consequence of our peculiar position, it is not to be expected that the people of the state can unanimously agree upon the best mode of preserving the honor and integrity of the state, and of maintaining within her limits that peace so earnestly desired by all good citizens.

The emergency is great. The consequences of a rash step will be fearful. It is the imperative duty of every true son of Maryland to do all that can tend to arrest the threatened evil. I therefore counsel the people, in all earnestness, to withhold their hands from whatever may tend to precipitate us into the gulf of discord and ruin gaping to receive us.

I counsel the people to abstain from all heated controversy upon the subject; to avoid all things that tend to crimination and recrimination, in order that the origin of our evil day may be forgotten now by every patriot in the earnest desire to avert from us its fruit.

All powers vested in the governor of the state will be strenuously exerted to preserve the peace and maintain inviolate the honor and integrity of Maryland.

I call upon the people to obey the laws, and to aid the constituted authorities in their endeavors to preserve the fair fame of our state untarnished.

I assure the people that no troops will be sent from Maryland, unless it may be for the defense of the national capital.

It is my intention in the future, as it has been my endeavor in the past, to preserve the people of Maryland from civil war; and I invoke the assistance of every true and loyal citizen to aid me in this emergency.

The people of this state will, in a short time, have the opportunity afforded them, in a special election of members of Congress of the United States, to express their devotion to the Union, or their desire to have it broken up. T. H. HICKS.

Baltimore, April 18, 1861.

[5] Report of a Select Committee to Congress, Feb. 21, 1861.

LIEUTENANT A. J. SLEMMER.

LIEUTENANT J. H. GILMAN.

yard a few troops who had proved faithful among the faithless, and joining to these some marines from the war steamer Wyandotte, then at that station, he threw himself with his little force, numbering in all but about eighty men, into Fort Pickens, where he hoped, and it proved not without reason, that he could hold out until re-enforcements should arrive. He secured himself against immediate attack from Fort M'Rea by destroying all the ammunition not locked up in the magazine, and by spiking the guns and ramming the tompions so firmly into the muzzles that they had to be bored out. All the other works were unimportant compared to Fort Pickens, which commanded every gun upon them; and although the insurgents addressed themselves vigorously to the task of strengthening the old forts, Lieutenant Slemmer, by his bold and spirited move (in which he was ably supported by Lieutenant Gilman), had foiled their main purpose utterly.

The news of these transactions flew quickly to Washington, for as yet there was no attempt at secrecy of movement, and steps were taken which resulted in a strategic defeat for the rebels. Their attention and the interest of the whole country was mainly concentrated upon Fort Sumter. As a strategical point, this fort was absolutely worthless, owing to the unimportance of the city which it defended, either as a commercial port, a centre of population, or a base of operations. The honor of the flag and humanity to the garrison were the chief, if not the only questions to be considered in regard to the situation at Charleston Harbor. But Fort Pickens was one of the keys of the Gulf of Mexico, and Washington was the capital of the republic. While, therefore, the flag of the Union was flying defiantly from Fort Sumter, the concentration round it of all the available force of the confederated insurgents was enabling the government to secure more easily the

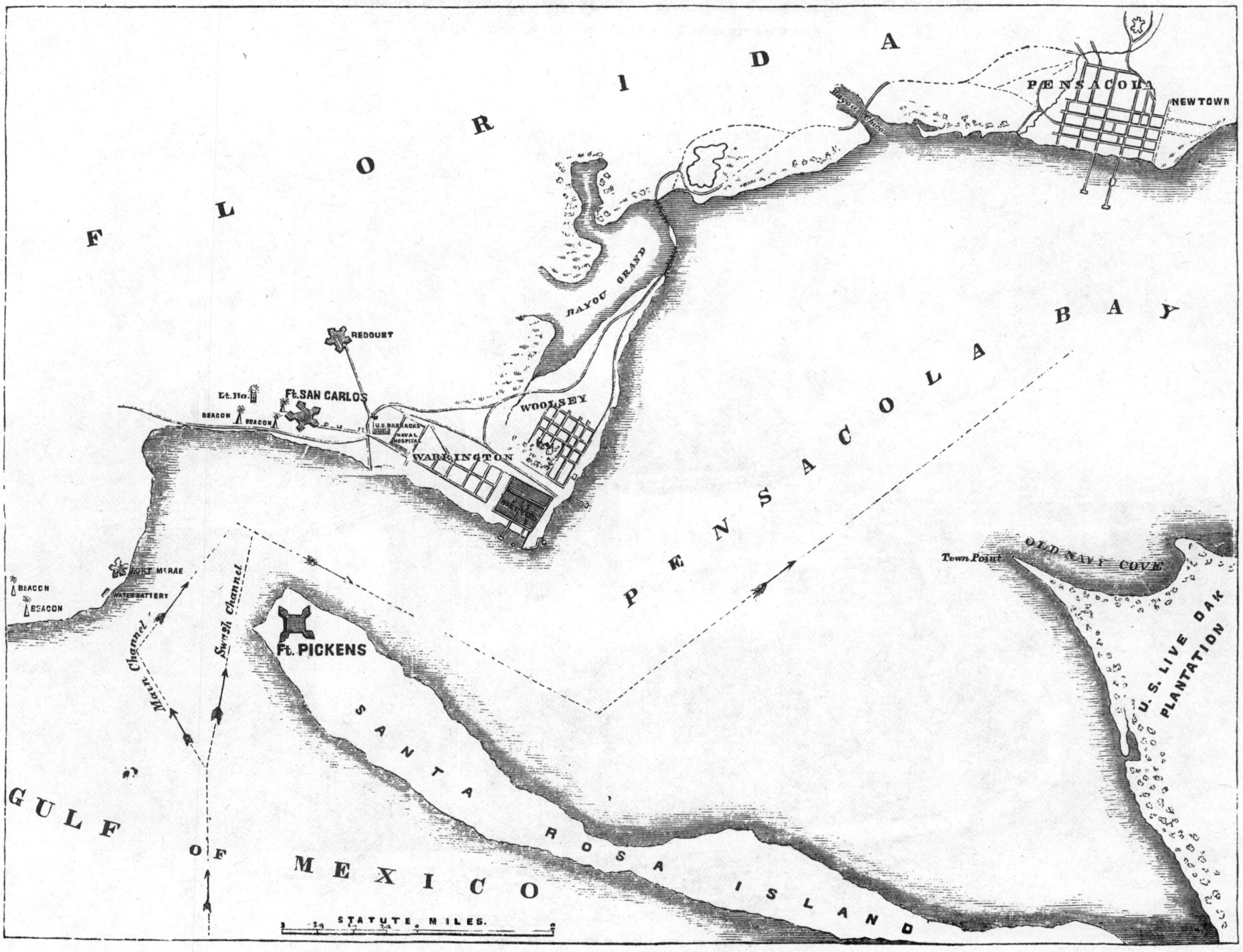

THE HARBOR OF PENSACOLA, FLORIDA, SHOWING THE FORTS, NAVY YARD, ETC.

ONE OF THE TEN FLANK CASEMATE BATTERIES AT FORT PICKENS, FLORIDA.

THE FLAG-STAFF BASTION AT FORT PICKENS, FLORIDA.

FRONT VIEW OF FORT PICKENS, PENSACOLA, SHOWING THE SALLY-PORT AND GLACIS.

immediate safety of the two most important points. On the 24th of January the war steamer Brooklyn was dispatched from Fortress Monroe with provisions, military stores, and a company of regular artillery under the command of Captain Vodges. The frigate Macedonian, and one or two other smaller vessels, were ordered to rendezvous at Santa Rosa Island; and these, upon an emergency, could have spared some hundreds of men for the defense of the fort. It was feared that this aid would not reach Lieutenant Slemmer in time; but, pending this movement, on the 28th of January a telegraphic dispatch was received at Washington from ex-Senator Mallory, of Florida, not addressed to President Buchanan, but intended for his eye, expressing the usual formal desire for peace, and proffering assurances that no attack would be made upon the fort if the *status quo* was not disturbed. The proposition was sufficiently insolent; but it suited the expectant, temporizing policy of President Buchanan to accept it, in order that the Peace Convention, then, as we have seen, in session, might carry on, without interruption, deliberations of which it was supposed that nothing could be hoped if they were disturbed by the clash of an armed collision.[6] For more than two months this little re-enforcement was kept back by the singular course of events which we have heretofore followed at Washington. The Brooklyn and her attendant vessels lay wearily off and on the coast at the mouth of Pensacola Harbor. Lieutenant Slemmer kept up good heart and strict discipline; and, on their side, the insurgents undertook to obtain possession of the fort by treachery. A letter was smuggled within the walls addressed to a sergeant, offering him two thousand dollars and a commission in the rebel army to betray the fort, and to every private who would aid him five hundred dollars. The men proved incorruptible, and the sergeant was placed under arrest. This attempt was in itself a treacherous violation of the truce (but treachery, personal bad faith, had marked the insurrection from the very beginning), and would have justified the commander of the Brooklyn in throwing his men into Fort Pickens. But he was relieved of the consideration of the question by the immediate receipt of orders from Washington to effect the landing.[7] This was on the 12th of April; and it

---

[6] *Extract from Instructions addressed to the Commanders of the Macedonian, Brooklyn, and other Naval Officers in command, and to Lieutenant Slemmer, commanding at Fort Pickens, Florida.*

"In consequence of the assurances received from Mr. Mallory, in a telegram of yesterday to Messrs. Slidell, Hunter, and Bigler, with a request it should be laid before the President, that Fort Pickens would not be assaulted, and an offer of such an assurance to the same effect from Colonel Chase, for the purpose of avoiding a hostile collision, upon receiving satisfactory assurances from Mr. Mallory and Colonel Chase that Fort Pickens will not be attacked, you are instructed not to land the company on board the *Brooklyn* unless said fort shall be attacked, or preparations shall be made for its attack. The provisions necessary for the supply of the fort you will land. The *Brooklyn* and the other vessels of war on the station will remain, and you will exercise the utmost vigilance, and be prepared at a moment's warning to land the company at Fort Pickens, and you and they will instantly repel any attack on the fort. The President yesterday sent a special message to Congress commending the Virginia resolutions of compromise. The commissioners of different states are to meet here on Monday, the 4th of February, and it is important that during their session a collision of arms should be avoided, unless an attack should be made, or there should be preparations made for such an attack. In either event, the *Brooklyn* and the other vessels will act promptly.

"Your right, and that of the other officers in command at Pensacola, freely to communicate with the government by special messenger, and its right, in the same manner, to communicate with yourself and them, will remain intact as the basis on which the present instruction is given."

[7] *Letter from General Scott.*

The following letter from Lieutenant General Scott was published in the Washington *National Intelligencer* of October 21, 1862:

October 30, 1860, I emphatically called the attention of the President to the necessity of strong garrisons in all the forts below the principal commercial cities of the Southern states, including, by name, the forts in Pensacola Harbor. October 31, I suggested to the Secretary of War that a circular should be sent at once to such of those forts as had garrisons, to be on the alert against surprises and sudden assaults. [*See my "Views," since printed.*]

After a long confinement to my bed in New York, I came to this city (Washington) December 12. Next day I personally urged upon the Secretary of War the same views, viz., strong garrisons in Southern forts—those of Charleston and Pensacola Harbor at once; those on Mobile Bay and the Mississippi, below New Orleans, next, etc., etc. I again pointed out the organized companies and the recruits at the principal dépôts available for the purpose. The Secretary did not concur in any of my views, when I begged him to procure for me an early interview with the President, that I might make one effort more to save the forts and the Union.

By appointment, the Secretary accompanied me to the President December 15, when the same topics, secessionism, etc., were again pretty fully discussed. There being at the moment (in the opinion of the President) no danger of an early secession beyond South Carolina, the President, in reply to my arguments for immediately re-enforcing Fort Moultrie, and sending a garrison to Fort Sumter, said:

"The time has not arrived for doing so; that he should wait the action of the Convention of South Carolina, in the expectation that a commission would be appointed and sent to negotiate with him and Congress respecting the secession of the state and the property of the United States held within its limits; and that if Congress should decide against the secession, then he would send a re-enforcement, and telegraph the commanding officer (Major Anderson) of Fort Moultrie to hold the forts (Moultrie and Sumter) against attack."

And the Secretary, with animation, added:

"We have a vessel of war (the *Brooklyn*) held in readiness at Norfolk, and he would then send three hundred men in her from Fort Monroe to Charleston."

To which I replied, first, that so many men could not be withdrawn from that garrison, but could be taken from New York. Next, that it would then be too late, as the South Carolina commissioners would have the game in their own hands by first using and then cutting the wires; that as there was not a soldier in Fort Sumter, any handful of armed secessionists might seize and occupy it, etc., etc.

Here the remark may be permitted, that if the Secretary's three hundred men had then, or some time later, been sent to Forts Moultrie and Sumter, *both* would now have been in the possession of the United States, and not a battery below them could have been erected by the secessionists; consequently, the access to these forts from the sea would now (the end of March) be unobstructed and free.

The same day, December 15, I wrote the following note:

"Lieutenant General Scott begs the President to pardon him for supplying in this note what he omitted to say this morning at the interview with which he was honored by the President.

"Long *prior* to the *Force Bill* (March 2, 1833), *prior* to the issue of his proclamation, and in part *prior* to the passage of the Ordinance of Nullification, President Jackson, under the act of March 3, 1807, 'authorizing the employment of the land and naval forces,' caused re-enforcements to be sent to Fort Moultrie, and a sloop of war (the *Natchez*), with two revenue cutters, to be sent to Charleston Harbor, in order, 1, to prevent the seizure of that fort by the nullifiers; and, 2, to enforce the execution of the revenue laws. General Scott himself arrived at Charleston the day after the passage of the Ordinance of Nullification, and many of the additional companies were then *en route* for the same destination.

"President Jackson familiarly said at the time, 'that by the assemblage of those forces for lawful purposes *he* was not making war upon South Carolina; but that, if South Carolina attacked them, it would be South Carolina that made war upon the United States.'

"General Scott, who received his first instructions (oral) from the President, in the temporary absence of the Secretary of War (General Cass), remembers those expressions well.

"Saturday night, December 15, 1860."

December 28. Again, after Major Anderson had gallantly and wisely thrown his handful of men from Fort Moultrie into Fort Sumter—learning that, on demand of South Carolina, there was great danger he might be ordered by the Secretary back to the less tenable work, or *out* of the harbor—I wrote this note:

"Lieutenant General Scott (who has had a bad night, and can scarcely hold up his head this morning) begs to express the hope to the Secretary of War—1. That orders may not be given for the evacuation of Fort Sumter. 2. That one hundred and fifty recruits may instantly be sent from Governor's Island to re-enforce that garrison, with ample supplies of ammunition and subsistence, including fresh vegetables, as potatoes, onions, turnips; and, 3. That one or two armed vessels be sent to support the said fort.

"Lieutenant General Scott avails himself of this opportunity also to express the hope that the recommendations heretofore made by him to the Secretary of War respecting Forts Jackson, St. Philip, Morgan, and Pulaski, and particularly in respect to Forts Pickens and M'Rea, and the Pensacola Navy Yard, in connection with the last two named works, may be reconsidered by the Secretary.

"Lieutenant General Scott will farther ask the attention of the Secretary to Forts Jefferson and Taylor, which are wholly *national*, being of far greater value even to the most distant points of the Atlantic coast and the people on the upper waters of the Missouri, Mississippi, and Ohio Rivers than to the State of Florida. There is only a feeble company at Key West for the defense of Fort Taylor, and not a soldier in Fort Jefferson to resist a handful of filibusters or a row-boat of pirates; and the Gulf, soon after the beginning of secession or revolutionary troubles in the adjacent states, will swarm with such nuisances."*

December 30, I addressed the President again as follows:

"Lieutenant General Scott begs the President of the United States to pardon the irregularity of this communication. It is Sunday, the weather is bad, and General Scott is not well enough to go to church.

"But matters of the highest national importance seem to forbid a moment's delay, and, if misled by zeal, he hopes for the President's forgiveness.

"Will the President permit General Scott, without reference to the War Department, and otherwise as secretly as possible, to send two hundred and fifty recruits from New York Harbor to re-enforce Fort Sumter, together with some extra muskets or rifles, ammunition, and subsistence?

"It is hoped that a sloop of war and cutter may be ordered for the same purpose as early as to-morrow.

"General Scott will wait upon the President at any moment he may be called for."

The South Carolina commissioners had already been many days in Washington, and no movement of defense (on the part of the United States) was permitted.

I will here close my notice of Fort Sumter by quoting from some of my previous reports.

It would have been easy to re-enforce this fort down to about the 12th of February. In this long delay Fort Moultrie had been rearmed and greatly strengthened in every way by the rebels. Many powerful new land-batteries (besides a formidable raft) have been constructed. Hulks, too, have been sunk in the principal channel, so as to render access to Fort Sumter from the sea impracticable without first carrying all the lower batteries of the secessionists. The difficulty of re-enforcing has thus been increased ten or twelve fold. First, the late President refused to allow any attempt to be made, because he was holding negotiations with the South Carolina commissioners.

Afterward Secretary Holt and myself endeavored in vain to obtain a ship of war for the purpose, and were finally obliged to employ the passenger steamer *Star of the West*. That vessel, but for the hesitation of the master, might, as is generally believed, have delivered at the fort the

* It was not till January 4 that, by the aid of Secretary Holt (a strong and loyal man), I obtained permission to send succor to the feeble garrison of Fort Taylor, Key West, and at the same time a company—Major Arnold's, from Boston—to occupy Fort Jefferson, Tortugas Island. If this company had been three days later, the fort would have been preoccupied by Floridians. It is known that the rebels had their eyes upon these powerful forts, which govern the commerce of the Mexican Gulf, as Gibraltar and Malta govern that of the Mediterranean. With Forts Jefferson and Taylor, the rebels might have purchased an early European recognition.

was decided to make the attempt that very night. Early in the evening the boats were hoisted out, volunteers selected (for, volunteers being called for, the whole ship's crew came forward), the men well armed, and boats also brought up from the Sabine and the St. Louis. The enemy was expected to resist the landing, and was known to have stationed strong coast-guards for that purpose. After the moon had set, between ten and eleven o'clock,

men and subsistence on board. This attempt at succor failing, I next verbally submitted to the late cabinet either that succor be sent by ships of war, fighting their way by the batteries (increasing in strength daily), or that Major Anderson should be left to ameliorate his condition by the muzzles of his guns—that is, enforcing supplies by bombardment and by *bringing to* merchant vessels, helping himself (giving orders for payment), or, finally, be allowed to evacuate the fort, which, in that case, would be inevitable.

But, before any resolution was taken, the late Secretary of the Navy making difficulties about the want of suitable war vessels, another commissioner from South Carolina arrived, causing farther delay. When this had passed away, Secretaries Holt and Toucey, Captain Ward, of the Navy, and myself, with the knowledge of the President (Buchanan), settled upon the employment, under the captain (who was eager for the expedition), of three or four small steamers belonging to the Coast Survey. At that time (late in January), I have but little doubt Captain Ward would have reached Fort Sumter with all his vessels. But he was kept back by something like a *truce* or armistice (made here), embracing Charleston and Pensacola Harbors, agreed upon between the late President and certain principal seceders of South Carolina, Florida, Louisiana, etc., and this truce lasted to the end of that administration.

That plan and all others, without a squadron of war ships and a considerable army, competent to take and hold the many formidable batteries below Fort Sumter, and before the exhaustion of its subsistence, having been pronounced, from the change of circumstances, impracticable by Major Anderson, Captain Foster (chief engineer), and all the other officers of the fort, as well as by Brigadier General Totten, Chief of the Corps of Engineers; and, concurring in that opinion, I did not hesitate to advise (March 12) that Major Anderson be instructed to evacuate the fort, so long gallantly held by him and his companions, immediately on procuring suitable transportation to take them to New York. His relative weakness had steadily increased in the last eighteen days.

It was not till January 3 (when the *first* commissioners from South Carolina withdrew) that the permission I had solicited October 31 was obtained to admonish commanders of the few Southern forts with garrisons to be on the alert against surprises and sudden assaults. (Major Anderson was not among the admonished, being already straitly beleaguered.)

January 3. To Lieutenant Slemmer, commanding in Pensacola Harbor:

"The general-in-chief directs that you take measures to do the utmost in your power to prevent the seizure of either of the forts in Pensacola Harbor by surprise or assault, consulting first with the commander of the navy yard, who will probably have received instructions to co-operate with you." (This order was signed by Aid-de-camp Lay.)

It was just before the surrender of the Pensacola Navy Yard (January 12) that Lieutenant Slemmer, calling upon Commodore Armstrong, obtained the aid of some thirty common seamen or laborers (but no marines), which, added to his 46 soldiers, made up his numbers to 76 men, with whom this meritorious officer has since held Fort Pickens, and performed, working night and day, an immense amount of labor in mounting guns, keeping up a strong guard, etc.

Early in January I renewed, as has been seen, my solicitations to be allowed to re-enforce Fort Pickens, but a good deal of time was lost in vacillations. First, the President "thought, if no movement is made by the United States, Fort M'Rea will probably not be occupied nor Fort Pickens attacked. In case of movements by the United States, which will doubtless be made known by the wires, there will be corresponding local movements, and the attempt to re-enforce will be useless."—(*Quotation from a note made by my Aid-de-camp Lay, about January* 12, *of the President's reply to a message from me.*) Next, it was doubted whether it would be safe to send re-enforcements in an unarmed steamer, and the want, *as usual*, of a suitable naval vessel—the Brooklyn being long held in reserve at Norfolk for some purpose unknown to me. Finally, after I had kept a body of three hundred recruits in New York Harbor for some time—and they would have been sufficient to re-enforce temporarily Fort Pickens and to occupy Fort M'Rea also—the President, about January 18, permitted that the sloop-of-war *Brooklyn* should take a single company, ninety men, from Fort Monroe, Hampton Roads, and re-enforce Lieutenant Slemmer in Fort Pickens, but without a surplus man for the neighboring fort, M'Rea.

The *Brooklyn*, with Captain Vodges's company alone, left the Chesapeake for Fort Pickens about January 22, and on the 29th, President Buchanan, having entered into a *quasi* armistice with certain leading seceders at Pensacola and elsewhere, caused Secretaries Holt and Toucey to instruct, in a joint note, the commanders of the war vessels off Pensacola, and Lieutenant Slemmer, commanding Fort Pickens, to commit no act of hostility, and not to land Captain Vodges's company unless that fort should be attacked.*

[That joint note I never saw until March 25, but supposed the armistice was consequent upon the meeting of the Peace Convention at Washington, and was understood to terminate with it.]

Hearing, however, of the most active preparations for hostilities on the part of the seceders at Pensacola, by the erection of new batteries and arming Fort M'Rea—that had not a gun mounted when it was seized—during the Peace Convention and since, I brought the subject to the notice of the new administration, when this note, dated March 12, to Captain Vodges, was agreed upon, viz.: "At the first favorable moment you will land with your company, re-enforce Fort Pickens, and hold the same till farther orders." This order, in duplicate, left New York by two naval vessels about the middle of March, as the mail and the wires could not be trusted, and detached officers could not be substituted, for two had already been arrested and paroled by the authorities of Pensacola, dispatches taken from one of them, and a third, to escape like treatment, forced to turn back when near that city. Thus those authorities have not ceased to make war upon the United States since the capture by them of the navy yard, January 12.

Respectfully submitted. WINFIELD SCOTT.

Head-quarters of the Army, Washington, March 30, 1861.

Letter from ex-President Buchanan in Reply to General Scott.

To the Editors of the National Intelligencer:

On Wednesday last I received the *National Intelligencer* containing General Scott's address to the public. This is throughout an undisguised censure of my conduct during the last months of the administration in regard to the seven cotton states now in rebellion. From our past relations I was greatly surprised at the appearance of such a paper. In one aspect, however, it was highly gratifying. It has justified me, nay, it has rendered it absolutely necessary, that I should no longer remain silent in respect to charges which have been long vaguely circulating, but are now indorsed by the responsible name of General Scott.

I. The first and most prominent among these charges is my refusal immediately to garrison nine enumerated fortifications, scattered over six of the Southern states, according to the recommendation of General Scott in his "views" addressed to the War Department on the 29th and 30th of October, 1860; and it has even been alleged that if this had been done it might have prevented the civil war.

This refusal is attributed, without the least cause, to the influence of Governor Floyd. All my cabinet must bear me witness that I was the President myself, responsible for all the acts of the administration; and certain it is that during the last six months previous to the 29th of December, 1860, the day on which he resigned his office, after my request, he exercised less influence on the administration than any other member of the cabinet. Mr. Holt was immediately thereafter transferred from the Post-office Department to that of War; so that, from this time until the 4th of March, 1861, which was by far the most important period of the administration, he performed the duties of Secretary of War to my entire satisfaction.

But why did I not immediately garrison these nine fortifications in such a manner, to use the language of General Scott, "as to make any attempt to take any one of them by surprise or *coup-de-main* ridiculous?" There is one answer, both easy and conclusive, even if other valid reasons did not exist. There were no available troops within reach which could be sent to these fortifications. To have attempted a military operation on a scale so extensive by any means within the President's power would have been simply absurd. Of this General Scott himself seems to have been convinced, for on the day after the date of his first "views" he addressed (on the 30th of October) supplemental views to the War Department, in which he states, "*There is one (regular) company in Boston, one here (at the Narrows), one at Pittsburgh, one at Augusta, Ga., one at Baton Rouge*"—*in all, five companies only within reach to garrison or re-enforce the forts mentioned in the* "*views*."

Five companies—four hundred men—to occupy and re-enforce nine fortifications in six highly-excited Southern states! The force "within reach" was so entirely inadequate that nothing more need be said on the subject. To have attempted such a military operation with so feeble a force, and the presidential election impending, would have been an invitation to collision and secession. Indeed, if the whole American army, consisting then of only 16,000 men, had been "within reach," they would have been scarcely sufficient for this purpose. Such was our want of troops that General Scott, believing, in opposition to the opinion of the committee raised in the House of Representatives, that the inauguration of Mr. Lincoln might be interrupted by military force, was only able to assemble at Washington, so late as the 4th of March, 653 men, rank and file of the army; and, to make up this number, even the sappers and miners were brought from West Point.

But why was there no greater force within reach? This question could be better answered by General Scott himself than any other person. Our small regular army, with the exception of a few hundred men, were out of reach, on our remote frontiers, where it had been continuously stationed for years to protect the inhabitants and the emigrants on their way thither against the attacks of hostile Indians. All were insufficient, and both General Scott and myself had endeavored in vain to prevail upon Congress to raise several additional regiments for this purpose. In recommending this augmentation of the army, the general states, in his report to the War Department of November, 1857, that "it would not more than furnish the re-enforcements now greatly needed in Florida, Texas, New Mexico, California, Oregon, Washington (T.), Kansas, Nebraska, Minnesota, leaving not a company for Utah." And again, in his report of November, 1858, he says:

"This want of troops to give reasonable security to our citizens in distant settlements, including emigrants on the plains, can scarcely be too strongly stated; but I will only add, that as often as we have been obliged to withdraw troops from one frontier in order to re-enforce another, the weakened points have been instantly attacked or threatened with formidable invasion."

These "views" of General Scott exhibit the crude notions then prevailing, even among intelligent and patriotic men, on this subject of secession. In the first sentence, the general, while stating that, "to save time, the right of secession may be conceded," yet immediately says, "this is instantly balanced by the correlative right on the part of the federal government against an *interior* state or states to re-establish, by force if necessary, its former continuity of territory." (For this he cites *Paley's Moral and Political Philosophy*, last chapter. It may be there, but I have been unable to find it.) While it is difficult to ascertain his precise meaning in this passage, he renders what he did *not* mean quite clear in his supplementary "views." In these he says, "It will be seen that the 'views' only apply to a case of secession that makes *a gap* in the present Union." The falling off say of Texas, or of all the Atlantic states from the Potomac south (the very case which has occurred), was not within the scope of General Scott's "provisional remedies;" that is to say, to establish by force, if necessary, the continuity of our territory. In his "views" he also states as follows: "But break this glorious Union by whatever line or lines that political madness may contrive, and there would be no hope of reuniting the fragments except by the laceration and despotism of the sword. To effect such result, the intestine wars of our Mexican neighbors would, in comparison with ours, sink into mere child's play." In the general's opinion, "a smaller evil (than these intestine wars) would be to allow the fragments of the great republic to form themselves into new confederacies, probably four." He then points out what ought to be the boundaries between the new unions, and at the end of each goes so far as even to indicate the cities which ought to be the capitals of the three first on this side of the Rocky Mountains, to wit, "Columbia, South Carolina;" "Alton or Quincy, Illinois;" and "Albany, New York," excluding Washington City altogether. This indication of capitals contained in the original now in my possession is curiously omitted in the version published in the *National Intelligencer*. He designates no capital for the fourth union on the Pacific. The reader will judge what encouragement these views, proceeding from so distinguished a source, must have afforded to the secessionists of the cotton states.

I trust I have said enough, and more than enough, to convince every mind why I did not, with a force of five companies, attempt to re-enforce Forts Jackson and St. Philip, on the Mississippi; Fort Morgan, below Mobile; Forts Pickens and M'Rea, in Pensacola Harbor; Fort Pulaski, below Savannah; Forts Moultrie and Sumter, Charleston Harbor; and Fort Monroe, in Virginia.

These "views," both original and supplementary, were published by General Scott in the *National Intelligencer* of January 18, 1861, at the most important and critical period of the administration. Their publication at that time could do no possible good, and might do much harm. To have published them without the President's knowledge or consent was as much in violation of the sacred confidence which ought to prevail between the commanding general of the army and the commander-in-chief as it would have been for the Secretary of War to publish the same documents without his authority. What is of more importance, their publication was calculated injuriously to affect the compromise measures then pending before Congress and the country, and to encourage the secessionists in their mad and wicked attempt to shatter the Union into fragments. From the great respect which I then entertained for the general I passed it over in silence.

It is worthy of remark that, soon after the presidential election, representations of what these "views" contained, of more or less correctness, were unfortunately circulated, especially throughout the South. The editors of the *National Intelligencer*, in assigning a reason for their publication, state that both in public prints and in public speeches allusions had been made to them, and some misapprehensions of their character had got abroad.

II. and III. General Scott states that he arrived in Washington on the 12th, and, accompanied by the Secretary of War, held a conversation with the President on the 15th of December. While I have no recollection whatever of this conversation, he doubtless states correctly that I did refuse to send three hundred men to re-enforce Major Anderson at Fort Moultrie, who had not then removed to Fort Sumter. The reason for this refusal is manifest to all who recollect the history of the time. But twelve days before, in the annual message of the 3d of December, I had urged upon Congress the adoption of amendments to the Constitution of the same character with those subsequently proposed by Mr. Crittenden, called the "Crittenden Compromise." At that time high hopes were entertained throughout the country that these would be adopted. Besides, I believed, and this correctly, as the event proved, that Major Anderson was then in no danger of attack. Indeed, he and his command were then treated with marked kindness by the authorities and people of Charleston. Under these circumstances, to have sent such a force there would have been only to impair the hope of compromise, to provoke collision, and disappoint the country.

There are some details of this conversation in regard to which the general's memory must be defective. At present I shall specify only one. I could not have stated that on a future contingent occasion I would telegraph "Major Anderson, of Fort Moultrie, to hold the forts (Moultrie and Sumter) against attack," because, with prudent precaution, this had already been done several days before, through a special messenger sent to Major Anderson for this very purpose. I refer to Major Buell, of the army.

The general's supplementary note of the same day, presenting to me General Jackson's conduct in 1833, during the period of nullification, as an example, requires no special notice. Even if the cases were not entirely different, I had previously determined upon a policy of my own, as will appear from my annual message. This was, at every hazard, to collect the customs at Charleston, and outside of the port, if need be, in a vessel of war. Mr. Colcock, the existing collector, as I had anticipated, resigned his office about the end of December, and immediately thereafter I nominated to the Senate, as his successor, a suitable person, prepared at any personal risk to do his duty. That body, however, throughout the entire session, declined to act on this nomination. Thus, without a collector, it was rendered impossible to collect the revenue.

IV. General Scott's statement alleges that "the *Brooklyn*, with Captain Vodges's company alone, left the Chesapeake for Fort Pickens about January 22, and on the 29th President Buchanan, having entered into a *quasi* armistice with certain leading seceders at Pensacola and elsewhere, caused Secretaries Holt and Toucey to instruct, in a joint note, the commander of the war-vessels off Pensacola, and Lieutenant Slemmer, commanding Fort Pickens, to commit no act of hostility, and not to land Captain Vodges's command unless the fort should be attacked." He afterward states, within brackets, "That joint note I never saw, but supposed the armistice was consequent upon the meeting of the Peace Convention at Washington, and was understood to terminate with it."

These statements betray a singular want of memory on the part of General Scott. It is scarcely credible that this very joint note, presented in such odious colors, was submitted to General Scott on the day it was prepared (January 29), and met his entire approbation. I would not venture to make this assertion if I did not possess conclusive evidence to prove it. On that day Secretary Holt addressed me a note, from which the following is an extract: "*I have the satisfaction of saying that on submitting the paper to General Scott, he expressed himself satisfied with it, saying that there could be no objection to the arrangement in a military point of view or otherwise.*" This requires no comment. That the general had every reason to be satisfied with the arrangement will appear from the following statement:

A revolutionary outbreak had occurred in Florida; the troops of the United States had been expelled from Pensacola and the adjacent navy yard; and Lieutenant Slemmer, of the artillery, with his brave little command, had been forced to take refuge in Fort Pickens, where he was in imminent danger every moment of being captured by a vastly superior force. Owing to the interruption of regular communications, Secretary Holt did not receive information of these events until several days after their occurrence, and then through a letter addressed to a third person. He instantly informed the President of the fact, and re-enforcements, provisions, and military stores were dispatched by the *Brooklyn* to Fort Pickens without a moment's unnecessary delay. She left Fortress Monroe on the 24th of January.

Well-founded apprehensions were, however, entertained at the time of her departure that the re-enforcements, with the vessels of war at no great distance from Fort Pickens, could not arrive in time to defend it against the impending attack. In this state of suspense, and while Lieutenant Slemmer was in extreme peril, Senators Slidell, Hunter, and Bigler received a telegraphic dispatch from Senator Mallory, of Florida, dated at Pensacola on the 28th of January, with the urgent request that they should lay it before the President. This dispatch expressed an earnest desire to maintain the peace, as well as the most positive assurance that no attack would be made on Fort Pickens if the present *status* should be preserved.

This proposal was carefully considered, both with a view to the safety of the fort and to the unhappy effect which an actual collision, either at that or any other point, might produce on the

* It was known at the Navy Department that the *Brooklyn*, with Captain Vodges on board, would be obliged, in open sea, to stand off and on Fort Pickens, and in rough weather might sometimes be fifty miles off. Indeed, if ten miles at sea, the fort might have been attacked and easily carried before the re-enforcements could have reached the beach, in open sea, where alone it could land.

the Brooklyn got under way, and moved toward the shore as slowly and as silently as possible. When the soundings showed but seven fathoms of water, she hove to, and the troops were disembarked. Under command of

Lieutenant Albert N. Smith, they pulled off with swift and steady strokes, and made for a point three miles from the fort, from which it was the intention that they should march to their destination. But the surf was found to

---

Peace Convention then about to assemble at Washington. The result was, that a joint dispatch was carefully prepared by the Secretaries of War and Navy accepting the proposal, with important modifications, which was transmitted by telegraph on the 29th of January to Lieutenant Slemmer and to the naval commanders near the station. It is too long for transcription; suffice it to say, it was carefully guarded at every point for the security of the fort and its free communication with Washington.

The result was highly fortunate. The *Brooklyn* had a long passage. Although she left Fortress Monroe on the 24th of January, she did not arrive at Pensacola until the 6th of February. In the mean time, Fort Pickens, with Lieutenant Slemmer (whose conduct deserves high commendation) and his brave little band, were placed, by virtue of this arrangement, in perfect security until an adequate force had arrived to defend it against any attack. The fort is still in our possession. Well might General Scott have expressed his satisfaction with this arrangement. The general was correct in the supposition that this arrangement was to expire on the termination of the Peace Convention.

V. But we now come to an important period, when dates will be essentially necessary to disentangle the statements of General Scott. The South Carolina commissioners were appointed on the 22d, and arrived in Washington on the 27th of December. The day after their arrival it was announced that Major Anderson had removed from Fort Moultrie to Fort Sumter. This rendered them furious. On the same day they addressed an angry letter to the President, demanding the surrender of Fort Sumter. The President answered this letter on the 30th of December with a peremptory refusal. This brought forth a reply from the commissioners on the 2d of January, 1861, of such an insulting character that the President instantly returned it to them with the following indorsement: "This paper, just presented to the President, is of such a character that he declines to receive it." From that time forward all friendly, political, and personal intercourse finally ceased between the revolutionary senators and the President, and he was severely attacked by them in the Senate, and especially by Mr. Jefferson Davis. Indeed, their intercourse had previously been of the coldest character ever since the President's anti-secession message at the commencement of the session of Congress.

Under these changed circumstances, General Scott, by note on Sunday, the 30th of December, addressed the following inquiry to the President:

"Will the President permit General Scott, without reference to the War Department, and otherwise as secretly as possible, to send two hundred and fifty recruits from New York Harbor to reenforce Fort Sumter, together with some extra muskets or rifles, ammunition, and subsistence? It is hoped that a sloop-of-war and cutter may be ordered for the same purpose 'to-morrow.'"

The general seems not to have then known that Mr. Floyd was out of office.

Never did a request meet a more prompt compliance. It was received on Sunday evening, December 30. On Monday morning I gave instructions to the War and Navy Departments, and on Monday evening General Scott came to congratulate me that the secretaries had issued the necessary orders to the army and navy officers, and that they were in his possession. The *Brooklyn*, with troops, military stores, and provisions, was to sail forthwith from Fortress Monroe for Fort Sumter. I am, therefore, utterly at a loss to imagine why the general, in his statement, should have asserted that "the South Carolina commissioners had already been many days in Washington, and no movement of defense (on the part of the United States) was permitted." These commissioners arrived in Washington on the 27th of December; General Scott's request was made to the President on the 30th; it was complied with on the 31st, and a single day is all that represents the "many days" of the general.

Again: General Scott asserts, in the face of these facts, that the President refused to allow any attempt to be made—to re-enforce Fort Sumter—because he was holding negotiations with the South Carolina commissioners. And still again, that "afterward Secretary Holt and myself endeavored in vain to obtain a ship-of-war for the purpose, and were finally obliged to employ the passenger steamer *Star of the West*." Will it be believed that the substitution of the *Star of the West* for the powerful war steamer *Brooklyn*, of which he now complains, was by advice of General Scott himself? I have never heard that doubted until I read the statement.

At the interview already referred to between the general and myself, on the evening of Monday, the 31st of December, I suggested to him that, although I had not received the South Carolina commissioners in their official capacity, but merely as private gentlemen, yet it might be considered an improper act to send the *Brooklyn* with re-enforcements to Fort Sumter until I had received an answer from them to my letter of the preceding day; that the delay could not continue more than forty-eight hours. He promptly concurred in this suggestion as gentlemanly and proper, and the orders were not transmitted to the *Brooklyn* on that evening. My anticipations were correct, for on the morning of the 2d of January I received their insolent note, and sent it back to them. In the mean time, however, the general had become convinced, by the representations of a gentleman whom I forbear to name, that the better plan, as the Secretaries of War and the Navy informed me, to secure secrecy and success, and reach the fort, would be to send a fast side-wheel mercantile steamer from New York with the re-enforcement. Accordingly, the *Star of the West* was selected for this duty. The substitution of this mercantile steamer for the *Brooklyn*, which would have been able to defend herself in case of attack, was reluctantly yielded by me to the high military judgment of General Scott.

The change of programme required a brief space of time; but the *Star of the West* left New York for Charleston on the evening of the 5th of January. On the very day, however, when this ill-fated steamer left New York, a telegram was dispatched by General Scott to Colonel Scott to countermand her departure; but it did not reach her destination until after she had gone to sea. The reason for this countermand shall be stated in the language of Secretary Holt, to be found in a letter addressed by him to Mr. Thompson, the late Secretary of the Interior, on the 5th of March, 1861, and published in the *National Intelligencer*. Mr. Holt says:

"The countermand spoken of (by Mr. Thompson) was not more cordially sanctioned by the President than it was by General Scott and myself; not because of any dissent from the orders on the part of the President, but because of a letter received that day from Major Anderson, stating, in effect, that he regarded himself secure in his position; and yet more from intelligence which late on Saturday evening (January 5, 1861) reached the department, that a heavy battery had been erected among the sand-hills at the entrance to Charleston Harbor, which would probably destroy any unarmed vessel (and such was the *Star of the West*) which might attempt to make its way to Fort Sumter. This important information satisfied the government that there was no present necessity for sending re-enforcements, and that, when sent, they should go, not in a vessel of commerce, but of war. Hence the countermand was dispatched by telegraph to New York; but the vessel had sailed a short time before it reached the officer (Colonel Scott) to whom it was addressed."

A statement of these facts, established by dates, proves conclusively that the President was not only willing, but anxious, in the briefest period, to re-enforce Fort Sumter.

On the 4th of January, the day before the departure of the *Star of the West* from New York, as General Scott in his statement admits, succor was sent to Fort Taylor, Key West, and to Fort Jefferson, Tortugas Island, which reached those points in time for their security. He nevertheless speculates on the consequences which might have followed had the re-enforcements not reached their destination in due time; and even expresses the extraordinary opinion that, with the possession of these forts, "the rebels might have purchased an early recognition."

I shall next advert to the statement that the expedition, under Captain Ward, "of three or four small steamers belonging to the Coast Survey," was kept back by something like a truce or armistice [made here], embracing Charleston and Pensacola Harbors, agreed upon between the late President and certain principal seceders of South Carolina, Florida, Louisiana, etc. And this truce lasted to "the end of the administration." Things altogether distinct in their nature are often so blended in this statement that it is difficult to separate them. Such is eminently the case in connecting the facts relative to Charleston with Pensacola.

Having already treated of the charge of having kept back re-enforcements from Pensacola, I have now to say something of the charge of having also kept them back from Charleston. Neither a truce, nor quasi truce, nor any thing like it, was ever concluded between the President and any human authority concerning Charleston. On the contrary, the South Carolina commissioners, first and last, and all the time, were informed that the President could never surrender Fort Sumter, nor deprive himself of the most entire liberty to send re-enforcements to it whenever it was believed to be in danger, or requested by Major Anderson. It is strange that General Scott was not apprised of this well-known fact. It was, then, with some astonishment that I learned from the statement of the general that he had, on the 12th of March, 1861, advised that Major Anderson should be instructed to evacuate the fort as soon as suitable transportation could be procured to carry himself and his command to New York. A military necessity for a capitulation may have existed in case there should be an attack upon the fort, or a demand for its surrender, but surely none such could have existed for its voluntary surrender and abandonment.

Probably that to which the general means to refer was not the *quasi*, but the actual truce of arms concluded at Charleston on the 11th of January, 1861, between Governor Pickens and Major Anderson, without the knowledge of the President. It was on the 9th of January that the *Star of the West*, under the American flag, was fired upon in the harbor of Charleston, by order of Governor Pickens. Immediately after this outrage, Major Anderson sent a flag to the governor, stating that he presumed the act had been unauthorized, and for that reason he had not opened fire from Fort Sumter on the adjacent batteries; but demanding its disavowal, and, if this were not sent in a reasonable time, he would consider it war, and fire on any vessel that attempted to leave the har-

bor. Two days after this occurrence, on the 11th of January, Governor Pickens had the audacity to demand of Major Anderson the surrender of the fort. In his answer of the same date the major made the following proposition: "Should your excellency deem fit, previous to a resort to arms, to refer this matter to Washington, it would afford me the sincere pleasure to depute one of my officers to accompany any messenger you may deem proper to be the bearer of your demand." This proposition was promptly accepted by the governor, and, in pursuance thereof, he sent, on his part, Hon. J. W. Wayne, the attorney general of South Carolina, to Washington, while Major Anderson deputed Lieutenant Hall, of the United States Army, to accompany him. These gentlemen arrived together in Washington on the evening of the 13th of January, when the President obtained the first knowledge of the transaction. But it will be recollected that no time intervened between the return of the *Star of the West* to New York and the arrival of the messenger bearing a copy of the truce at Washington within which it would have been possible to send re-enforcements to Fort Sumter. Both events occurred about the same time.

Thus a truce, or suspension of arms, was concluded between the parties, to continue until the question of the surrender of the fort should be decided by the President. Until this decision, Major Anderson had placed it out of his own power to ask for re-enforcements, and equally out of the power of the government to send them without a violation of public faith. This was what writers on public law denominate "a partial truce, under which hostilities are suspended only in certain places, as between a town and the army besieging it." It is possible that the President, under the laws of war, might have annulled this truce upon due notice to the opposite party; but neither General Scott nor any other person ever suggested this expedient. This would have been to cast a reflection on Major Anderson, who, beyond question, acted from the highest and purest motives. Did General Scott ever propose to violate this truce during its existence? If he did, I am not now, and never was, aware of the fact. Indeed, I think he would have been one of the last men in the world to propose such a measure.

Colonel Hayne did not deliver the letter which he bore from Governor Pickens, demanding the surrender of the fort, to the President until the 31st of January. The documents containing the reasons for this worrying delay were communicated to Congress in a special message of the 8th of February, to which I refer the reader. On the 5th of February, the Secretary of War, under the instructions of the President, gave a peremptory refusal to this demand, in an able and comprehensive letter, reviewing the whole subject, explaining and justifying the conduct of the President throughout. Its concluding sentence is both eloquent and emphatic:

"If," says Mr. Holt, "with all the multiplied proofs which exist of the President's anxiety for peace, and of the earnestness with which he has pursued it, the authorities of that state shall assault Fort Sumter, and imperil the lives of the handful of brave and loyal men shut up within its walls, and thus plunge our country into the horrors of civil war, then upon them and those they represent must rest the responsibility."

The truce was then ended, and General Scott is incorrect in stating "that it lasted to the end of that administration."

An expedition was quietly fitted out at New York, under the supervision of General Scott, to be ready for any contingency. He arranged its details, and regarded the re-enforcements thus provided for as sufficient. This was ready to sail for Fort Sumter on five hours' notice. It is of this expedition that General Scott thus speaks:

"At that time, when this (the truce) had passed away, Secretaries Holt and Toucey, Captain Ward, of the Navy, and myself, with the knowledge of the President, settled upon the employment, under the captain, of three or four steamers belonging to the Coast Survey, but he was kept back by the truce."

A strange inconsistency. The truce had expired with Mr. Holt's letter to Colonel Hayne on the 5th of February, and General Scott, in his statement, says, "it would have been easy to re-enforce this fort down to about the 12th of February." Why, then, did not the re-enforcements proceed? This was simply because of communications from Major Anderson. It was most fortunate that they did not proceed, because the three or four small steamers which were to bear them would never have reached the fort, and in the attempt must have been captured or destroyed. The vast inadequacy of the force provided to accomplish the object was demonstrated by information received from Major Anderson at the War Department on the last day of the administration.

I purposely forbear at present to say more on this subject, lest I might, however unintentionally, do injustice to one or more of the parties concerned, in consequence of the brevity required by the nature of this communication. The facts relating to it, with the appropriate accompaniments, have been fully presented in a historical review, prepared a year ago, which will ere long be published. This review contains a sketch of the four last months of my administration. It is impartial; at least such is my honest conviction. That it has not yet been published has arisen solely from an apprehension, no longer entertained, that something therein might be unjustly perverted into an interference with the government in a vigorous prosecution of the war for the maintenance of the Constitution and the restoration of the Union, which was far, very far, from my intention.

After a careful retrospect, I can solemnly declare before God and my country that I can not reproach myself with any act of commission or omission since the existing troubles commenced. I have never doubted that my countrymen would yet do me justice. In my special message of the 8th of January, 1861, I presented a full and fair exposition of the alarming condition of the country, and urged Congress either to adopt measures of compromise, or, failing in this, to prepare for the last alternative. In both aspects my recommendation was disregarded. I shall close this document with a quotation of the last sentences of that message, as follows:

"In conclusion, it may be permitted me to remark that I have often warned my countrymen of the dangers which now surround us. This may be the last time I shall refer to the subject officially. I feel that my duty has been faithfully, though it may be imperfectly, performed; and, whatever the result may be, I shall carry to my grave the consciousness that I at least meant well for my country.   Your obedient servant,   JAMES BUCHANAN.
Wheatland, near Lancaster, October 28, 1862.

Rejoinder of Lieutenant General Scott.

To the Editors of the National Intelligencer:

I regret to find myself in a controversy with the venerable ex-President Buchanan.

Recently (Oct. 21) you published my official *report* to President Lincoln, dated March 30, 1861, giving a summary of my then recent connection with our principal Southern forts, which, I am sorry to perceive, has given offense to the ex-President. That result, purely incidental, did not enter into my purpose in drawing up the paper, but, on reflection, I suppose that, under the circumstances, offense was unavoidable.

Let it be remembered that the new president had a right to demand of me—the immediate commander of the army—how it had happened that the incipient rebels had been allowed to seize several of those forts, and from the bad condition of others were likely to gain possession of them also. Primarily, the blame rested exclusively on me. Hence, to vindicate my sworn allegiance to the Union and professional conduct, the report was submitted to President Lincoln at an early day (in his administration), and recently to the world.

To that short paper ex-President Buchanan publishes a reply, of double the length, in *The Intelligencer* of the 1st instant. My rejoinder, from necessity, if not taste, will be short, for I hold the pen in a rheumatic hand, and am without aid-de-camp or amanuensis, and without a printed document and my own official papers.

Unable, in my present condition, to make an analysis of the ex-President's long reply, I avail myself of a substitute furnished by an accidental visitor, who has kindly marked the few points which he thinks may require some slight notice at my hands.

1. To account for not having garrisoned sufficiently the Southern forts named against anticipated treason and rebellion, according to my many recommendations, beginning Oct. 29, 1860, repeated the next day, and again, more earnestly, Dec. 13, 15, 28, and 30, the ex-President says, "There were no available troops within reach."

Now, although it is true that, with or without the ex-President's approbation, the Secretary of War had nearly denuded our whole eastern sea-board of troops in order to augment our forces in Texas and Utah, I nevertheless pointed out, at several of the above dates, the 600 recruits (about) which we had in the harbor of New York and at Carlisle Barracks, Pennsylvania, nearly all organized into temporary companies, and tolerably drilled and disciplined—quite equal to the purpose in question—besides the five companies of regulars near at hand, making about 1000 men.

These disposable troops would have given (say) two hundred men to the twin forts Jackson and St. Philip, below New Orleans; an equal number to Fort Morgan, below Mobile; a re-enforcement of one hundred men to Fort Pickens, Pensacola Harbor; and a garrison of the like number to the twin fort M'Rea; a garrison of one hundred men to Fort Jefferson, Tortugas Island, and the same to Fort Pulaski, below Savannah, which, like Forts Jackson, St. Philip, Morgan, and M'Rea, had not at the time a soldier—leaving about two hundred men for the twin forts Moultrie and Sumter, Charleston Harbor, where there were two weak companies, making less than ninety men. Fortress Monroe had already a garrison of some eight companies, one or two of which might, in the earlier period of danger, have been spared till volunteers could have been obtained, notwithstanding printed handbills were every where posted in Eastern Virginia by an eccentric character, inviting recruits to take that most important work.

Now I have nowhere said that either of those forts, even with the re-enforcement indicated, would have had a *war* garrison. Certainly not. My proposition was to put each in a condition,

Gun-boat "Wyandotte."   Store-ship "Supply."   Frigate "Sabine."

THE UNITED STATES FL

United States Steam-sloop "Brooklyn."   Gun-boat "Crusader."   "St. Louis."

FORT PICKENS, FLORIDA.

be so heavy that Lieutenant Smith regarded the danger from the elements as more to be feared than that from the enemy; and he therefore instantly formed the resolution of passing directly up and landing in front of the fort. It was accomplished without attack; and he had the satisfaction of seeing the gates of the fort close upon the full re-enforcement. The boats returned to the ships, and, taking off the marines from the Brooklyn, placed them safely too in Fort Pickens, and pulled back past Fort M'Rea and the Barrancas in broad daylight unharmed. It will be remembered, however, that this re-enforcement was only the result of a hasty attempt to meet the great emergency of the period immediately succeeding the seizure of the forts, the navy yard, and the arsenal by the insurgents, in the early stages of the movement for secession. The disgraceful truce had intervened. A few days after the Brooklyn had landed her artillerists, two large transports, the Atlantic and the Illinois, arrived off Santa Rosa, bringing seven hundred and fifty men, under the command of Colonel Brown, horses for a company of flying artillery, muskets, other munitions of war, and provisions. Under protection of the Sabine, of 50 guns, the Brooklyn, 14 guns, the St. Louis, 22 guns, the Water-Witch, the Wyandotte, the Crusader, and the Mohawk, of 10 guns each, to which was added afterward the Powhatan, a powerful steamer carrying 12 heavy guns, this important re-enforcement was landed—the troops in a single night; the horses, munitions of war, and provisions in the course of three days; and the 20th of April saw Fort Pickens, the most important post upon the Gulf, amply garrisoned and provisioned, and under the command of an officer, Colonel Brown, to whom the firm and gallant Lieutenant Slemmer might cheerfully, both as a soldier and a patriot, yield the precedence due to his superior rank. The batteries upon the hostile shores were under the command of Colonel Bragg, who had won laurels as an officer of artillery under the command of General Taylor in Mexico.

Important as the possession of Fort Pickens was, the position of Washington awakened a far livelier and more immediate interest throughout the country. To attack and gain possession of the national capital was the first impulse which found expression among the insurgents, excited almost to frenzy by the successful bombardment of Fort Sumter and the war-proclamation of the President. To secure its safety was the first care of every patriot. The cry, Washington is in danger, flew from lip to lip over the whole land; and men went about their necessary business with the ever-present apprehension of hearing at any moment of a bloody struggle upon the very steps of the yet unfinished Capitol for its possession. These were no vague fears, excited by the sudden peril of the country; for one of the first effects of the proclamation had been to cause the passage of an Ordinance of Secession in Virginia, and thus virtually to open the way for the march of the insurgent forces directly upon Washington. In January, a resolution had been passed unanimously in the Senate of Virginia declaring that, if the sectional differences of the country could not be reconciled, honor and interest demanded that she should unite her fortunes with those of her sister slaveholding states. At the same time, however, a resolution, bringing up the question of the policy of secession, was refused to be entertained by a vote of nine-

as I expressly said, to guard against a surprise or *coup-de-main* (an off-hand attack, one without full preparation).

That these movements of small detachments might easily have been made in November and December, 1860, and some of them as late as the following month, can not be doubted. But the ex-President sneers at my "weak device" for saving the forts.

He forgets what the gallant Anderson did with a handful of men in Fort Sumter, and leaves out of the account what he might have done with a like handful in Fort Moultrie, even without farther augmentation of men to divide between the garrisons. Twin forts, on the opposite sides of a channel, not only give a cross-fire on the head of an attack, but the strength of each is more than doubled by the flanking fire of the other. The same remarks apply to the gallant Lieutenant Slemmer, with his handful of brave men, in Fort Pickens. With what contempt might he not have looked upon Chase or Bragg in front of him, with varying masses of from 2000 to 6000 men, if Fort Pickens and its twin fort, M'Rea, had had between them only 200 men!

I have thus shown that small garrisons would, at first, have sufficed for the other twins, Forts Jackson and St. Philip also. My object was to save to the Union, by any means at hand, all those works, until Congress could have time to organize a call for volunteers—a call which the President, for such a purpose, might no doubt have made, without any special legislation, with the full approbation of every loyal man in the Union.

2. The ex-President almost loses his amiability in having his neglect of the forts "attributed," as he says, "without the least cause, to the influence of Governor Floyd;" and he adds, "All my cabinet must bear me witness that I was the President myself, responsible for all the acts of the administration."

Now, notwithstanding this broad assumption of responsibility, I should be sorry to believe that Mr. Buchanan specially consented to the removal by Secretary Floyd of 115,000 extra muskets and rifles, with all their implements and ammunition, from Northern repositories to Southern arsenals, so that, on the breaking out of the maturing rebellion, they might be found without cost, except to the United States, in the most convenient positions for distribution among the insurgents. So, too, of the 120 or 140 pieces of heavy artillery which the same secretary ordered from Pittsburgh to Ship Island, in Lake Borgne, and Galveston, Texas, for forts not yet erected! Accidently learning, early in March, that, under this posthumous order, the shipment of these guns had commenced, I communicated the fact to Secretary Holt (acting for Secretary Cameron) just in time to defeat the robbery.

But on this point we may hear ex-Secretary Floyd himself. At Richmond he expressly claimed the honor of defeating all my plans and solicitations respecting the forts, and received his reward —it being there universally admitted that, but for that victory over me, there could have been no rebellion!

3. Mr. Buchanan complains that I published, without permission, January 18, 1861, my views, addressed to him and the Secretary of War, October 29 and 30, 1860. But that act was caused, as I explained to him at the time, by the misrepresentations of the views in one of the earlier speeches of the same ex-secretary after his return to Virginia.

4. One of my statements, complaining of the joint countermand sent through the Secretaries of War and Navy to prevent the landing at Fort Pickens of Captain Vodges's company *unless the fort should be attacked*, is cited by the ex-President to prove a "singular want of memory" on my part; and a note from Secretary Holt is adduced to show that I had entirely approved of the joint countermand the day (Jan. 20) that it was prepared. Few persons are as little liable to make a misstatement by accident as Mr. Holt, and no one more incapable of making one by design; yet I have not the slightest recollection of any interview with him on this subject.

I do remember, however, that Mr. Holt, on some matter of business, approached my bedside about that time, when I was suffering greatly from an access of pain. Mr. Buchanan, Mr. Holt, and myself were all landsmen, and could know but little of the impossibility of landing troops on an open sea-beach, with a high wind and surf. Mr. Toucey, Secretary of the Navy, with officers about him of intelligence and nautical experience, ought to have said plumply that if Vodges was not to land except in the case of attack on Fort Pickens, he might as well have remained at Fortress Monroe, as the prohibition placed the fort, so far as he was concerned, at the mercy, or (as the event showed) on the want of enterprise on the part of the rebel commander at Pensacola.

Possibly there are other parts of the reply which a superficial reader may think require comment or elucidation; and, indeed, here is another marked for me by my kind visitor.

5. The ex-President has brought together a labyrinth of dates respecting the arrival and departure of rebel commissioners, armistices, etc., with which, as I had no official connection, I may have made an unimportant mistake or two; but, as I have not by me the means of recovering the clew to those windings, I shall not attempt to follow him. WINFIELD SCOTT.

New York, Fifth Avenue Hotel, November 8, 1862.

Ex-President Buchanan's Rejoinder to General Scott.

To the Editor of the National Intelligencer:

With a few remarks I shall close the controversy with General Scott, into which I have been most reluctantly forced by his voluntary and unexpected attack. This has, nevertheless, afforded me an opportunity of correcting many unfounded reports which I had long borne in patience and in silence. In my answer, I have already furnished clear and distinct responses to all the allegations of General Scott; and in his rejoinder he has not called in question any of my statements with a single exception. Which of us is correct in this particular depends upon the question whether his recollection of an event which occurred more than eighteen months ago, or the statement of Mr. Holt, reduced to writing on the very day, is entitled to the greater credit.

The general, in the introduction of his rejoinder, assigns as an excuse for the criticism on my public conduct, that this was merely incidental to his alleged official report to President Lincoln on the condition of our fortifications, and was not primarily intended for myself. From this statement, one would conclude that he had made such a report. But where is this to be found? For it he refers to the *Intelligencer* of the 21st of October; but there I discover nothing but his letter of four points to Mr. Seward, dated on the 3d of March, 1861, advising the incoming President how to guide his administration in the face of the threatened dangers to the country. In the single introductory sentence to this letter he barely refers to his "printed views" (dated in October, 1860), which had been long before the public; but it contains nothing like an official report on the condition of the fortifications.

Whether the introduction of this letter to the public, without the consent of President Lincoln, by one of the general's friends, in a political speech during a highly excited gubernatorial canvass, had influenced him to prepare his criticism on my conduct, it is not for me to determine.

At what period did General Scott obtain the six hundred recruits to which he refers in his rejoinder? This was certainly after the date of his "views," on the 30th of October, 1860; because in these he states emphatically that the forces then at his command were, "in all, five companies only within reach to garrison or re-enforce the (nine) forts mentioned in the 'views.'"

Did he obtain these recruits in November? If so, had he visited Washington, or written and explained to me in what manner the military operation could be accomplished by the four hundred men in the five companies and the six hundred recruits, I should have given his representations all the consideration eminently due to his high military reputation.

But he informs us he did not arrive in Washington until the 12th of December. His second recommendation to garrison these forts must consequently have been made, according to his own statement, on the 13th, 15th, 28th, or 30th of December, or on more than one of these days. At this period the aspect of public affairs had greatly changed from what it was in October. Congress was now in session, and our relations with the seceding cotton states had been placed before them by the President's Message. Proceedings had been instituted by that body with a view to a compromise of the dangerous questions between the North and the South, and the highest hopes and warmest aspirations were then entertained for their success. Under these circumstances, it was the President's duty to take a broad view of the condition of the whole country, in all its relations, civil, industrial, and commercial, as well as military, giving to each its appropriate influence. It was only from such a combination that he could frame a policy calculated to preserve the peace and to consolidate the strength of the Union. Isolated recommendations proceeding from one department, without weighing well their effect upon the general policy, ought to be adopted with extreme caution.

But it seems from the rejoinder that Secretary Floyd, at Richmond, had claimed the honor of defeating General Scott's "plans and solicitations respecting the forts;" "it being there," says the general, "universally admitted that, but for that victory over me, there could have been no rebellion." This is, in plain English, that the seceessionists of the cotton states, who have since brought into the field hundreds of thousands of undoubtedly brave soldiers, would have abandoned in terror their unlawful and rebellious designs, had General Scott distributed among their numerous forts 480 men in October or 1000 men in December! This requires no comment. I have never been able to obtain a copy of the speech of Mr. Floyd at Richmond to which I presume General Scott refers; but I learned, both at the time and since, from gentlemen of high respectability, that in this same speech he denounced me most bitterly for my determination to stand by and sustain the Union with all the power I possessed under the Constitution and the laws.

And here permit me to remark that it is due to General Scott, as well as myself, to deny that there is any portion of my answer which justifies the allegation that "the ex-President sneers at my 'weak device' (the words 'weak device' being marked as a quotation) for saving the forts." This mistake I must attribute to his "accidental visitor."

And in this connection I emphatically declare that the general, neither before nor after the publication of his "views" in the *National Intelligencer* of the 18th of January, 1861, without my consent, assigned any reason to me for making this publication, or ever even alluded to the subject. In this I can not be mistaken from the deep impression which the occurrence made upon my memory, for the reasons already mentioned in my answer.

I should have nothing more to add had General Scott, in his rejoinder, confined himself to the topics embraced in his original letter. He has extended them, and now for the first time, and in a sarcastic and no kindly spirit, refers to the alleged stealing of public arms by Secretary Floyd, and their transportation to the South in anticipation of the rebellion. The most conclusive answer to this allegation is that, notwithstanding the boasting of Mr. Floyd at Richmond, evidently with the view of conciliating his new allies, cited by the general as his authority, no public arms were ever stolen. This fact is established by the report of the Committee on Military Affairs of the House of Representatives, now before me, made by Mr. Stanton, of Ohio, their chairman, on the 18th of February, 1861, and to be found in the second volume of the Reports of Committees of the House for the session of 1860–61. This report, and the testimony before the committee, establish,

1. That the Southern states received in 1860 less instead of more than the quota of arms to which they were entitled by law; and that three of them—North Carolina, Mississippi, and Kentucky—received no arms whatever, and this simply because they did not ask for them. Well may Mr. Stanton have said in the House "that there are a good deal of rumors, and speculations, and misapprehension as to the true state of facts in regard to this matter."

2. Secretary Floyd, under suspicious circumstances, on the 22d of December, 1860, and but a few days before he left the Department, had, without the knowledge of the President, ordered 113 columbiads and 11 32-pounders to be transported from Pittsburgh to Ship Island and Galveston, in Mississippi and Texas. The fact was brought to the knowledge of the President by a communication from Pittsburgh; and Secretary Holt immediately thereafter countermanded the order of his predecessor, and the cannon were never sent. The promptitude with which we acted elicited a vote of thanks, dated the 4th of January, 1861, from the Select and Common Councils of that city "to the President, the Attorney General, and the acting Secretary of War" (Mr. Holt).

After this statement, how shall we account for the explicit declaration of General Scott that, "accidentally hearing early in March that under this posthumous order (that of Mr. Floyd of the 22d of December) the shipment of these guns had commenced, I communicated the fact to Secretary Holt (acting for Secretary Cameron) just in time to defeat the robbery?" And this is the same Secretary Holt who had countermanded "the posthumous order" in the previous December. And, strange to say, these guns, but for the alleged interposition of General Scott, were about to be sent so late as March from the loyal states into those over which Jefferson Davis had then for some time presided!

Had General Scott reflected for a moment, he could not have fallen into this blunder. It is quite manifest he was "without a printed document and my (his) own official papers."

3. The government had on hand in the year 1859 about 500,000 old muskets, which had been condemned "as unsuitable for public service," under the act of the 3d of March, 1825. They were of such a character that, although offered both at public and private sale for $2 50 each, purchasers could not be obtained at that rate, except for a comparatively small number. On the 30th of November, 1859, Secretary Floyd ordered about one fifth of the whole number (105,000) to be sent from the Springfield Armory, where they had accumulated, to five Southern arsenals, "in proportion to their respective means of proper storage." This order was carried into effect by the Ordnance Bureau in the usual course of administration and without reference to the President. It is but justice to say that, from the testimony before the committee, there is no reason to suspect that Secretary Floyd issued this order from any sinister motive. Its date was months before Mr. Lincoln's nomination for the presidency, and nearly a year before his election, and while the secretary was still an avowed opponent of secession. Indeed, the testimony of Colonel Craig and Captain Maynadier, of the Ordnance, before the committee, is wholly inconsistent with any evil intention on his part.

And yet these "condemned muskets," with a few thousand ancient rifles of a calibre then no longer used, are transformed by General Scott into "115,000 extra muskets and rifles, with all their implements and ammunition." This is the first time I have heard—certainly there was nothing of the kind before the committee—that ammunition was sent with these condemned and inferior arms to their places of storage—just as though they had been intended, not for sale, but for immediate use in the field. The truth is, that it is impossible to steal arms and transport them from one depository to another without the knowledge and active participation of the officers of the Ordnance Bureau, both in Washington and at these depositories. It may be observed that Colonel Craig, the head of the Bureau at this period, was as correct an officer, and as loyal and as honest a man as exists in the country. Yours very respectfully, JAMES BUCHANAN.

Wheatland, near Lancaster, Nov. 17, 1862.

RE-ENFORCEMENT OF FORT PICKENS BY COMPANY A, FIRST ARTILLERY, ON SATURDAY MORNING, APRIL 13, 1861.

THE SECOND RE-ENFORCEMENT OF FORT PICKENS, ON APRIL 16, 1861.

ty-six to thirty-six. A state convention had assembled at Richmond on the 13th of February, and its deliberations had continued up to the time of the bombardment of Fort Sumter. A very decided majority of this body was opposed to any movement toward secession; and, except with a very small minority, there was a purpose and a hope that Virginia should yet act as a mediator between the revolted states and the government. But the members of the extreme slavery party were indefatigably active. They plied the Convention day after day with resolutions and speeches upon the "injury and oppression" which the sisterhood of slavery had suffered from the "federal government," the duty of resisting "coercion," the "sovereignty of the states," and the consequent "right of secession." They procured the appointment of a commission to catechise the President upon "the course he intended to pursue toward the seceded states."[8] In this body the dogma of state sovereignty again worked out those logical results so fatal to the Union; for coercion, or, in other words, the assertion and maintenance of a supreme government for the execution of the supreme law of the land, was the bugbear that disturbed all concert of action against the seceding faction; and therefore, when, even after the attack upon Fort Sumter, the President called for troops to retake it and the other military posts which had been seized, most of the very Union men in this Virginia Convention felt compelled to declare that, "if the President meant the subjugation of the South," Virginia had but one course to pursue—to make common cause with her sister slave states, and resist. And so Governor Letcher having, on the 16th of April, as we have already seen, refused to furnish Virginia's quota of the troops called for by the President, and threatened resistance,[9] on the 17th an Ordinance of Secession was secretly hurried through the Convention, receiving, in the excitement of the moment, a vote of eighty-eight against fifty-five. Even this, however, was but a provisional ordinance, which was to take effect only when ratified by the votes of a majority of the people of the state at a poll to be taken on the fourth Thursday of May following.[10] This was the first instance in which the insurgent leaders had ventured to submit an Ordinance of Secession to the votes of the people. But in this very case they pursued their policy of precipitation and usurpation of power with a more guilty recklessness than ever before; for, in spite of this special provision in the ordinance itself, requiring a vote of the people for its establishment, another ordinance was immediately passed, adopting the Constitution of the Confederate States, and a solemn convention was entered into with commissioners from the government at Montgomery, by which Virginia became a member of the confederacy, submitted her entire military force and military operations to the control of the President of the confederacy, and made over to the insurgent government all the public property, naval stores, and munitions of war, which, in delicate phrase, she might have "acquired" from the United States.[1] This ordinance was passed with indecent haste on the 17th day of April, and the convention was entered into upon the 25th. True, the former was in terms dependent upon the vote to be taken in May upon the Ordinance of Secession. But as the state was meantime placed entirely in the military power of the insurgents, this provision was but the hollowest form of external decency. The effect of this action in Virginia was of inestimable advantage to the insurgents. It transferred their frontier from the obscure and remote line of the northern boundary of the Gulf states to the Potomac River, and placed one end of the Long Bridge, which is the southern outlet of Washington, upon hostile soil.

The temper and purposes of the people who had thus usurped control of the most important of the slave states was instantly manifested by hostile movements of the most alarming character. Hardly was the conditional Ordinance of Secession passed, when the custom-house and the post-office at Richmond were seized, and on the evening of the same day, the 18th of April, an attack was made upon Harper's Ferry. At this place, famous for the bold beauty of the scene, where the Potomac receives the waters of the Shenandoah, and pushes its way through a sharply-cut gap in the Blue Ridge, was one of the largest arsenals of the United States, to which was attached a factory of arms of corresponding magnitude. The former usually contained ninety-five thousand stand of arms; and the latter, when in full operation, turned out twenty-five thousand yearly. Here, too, at the outlet of the Shenandoah Valley, which pierces the centre of Virginia, was one of the principal stations of the Baltimore and Ohio Railway, by which the great river commerce of the West passed eastward to the sea-coast; and a great and well-stored flour-mill, one of the largest in the country. Around these

---

[8] *The President's Speech to the Virginia Commissioners, Messrs. Preston, Stuart, and Randolph.*

GENTLEMEN,—As a committee of the Virginia Convention, now in session, you present me a preamble and resolution in these words:

"Whereas, in the opinion of this Convention, the uncertainty which prevails in the public mind as to the policy which the federal executive intends to pursue toward the seceded states is extremely injurious to the industrial and commercial interests of the country, tends to keep up an excitement which is unfavorable to the adjustment of the pending difficulties, and threatens a disturbance of the public peace; therefore,

"*Resolved*, That a committee of three delegates be appointed to wait on the President of the United States, present to him this preamble, and respectfully ask him to communicate to this Convention the policy which the federal executive intends to pursue in regard to the Confederate States."

In answer I have to say, that having, at the beginning of my official term, expressed my intended policy as plainly as I was able, it is with deep regret and mortification I now learn there is great and injurious uncertainty in the public mind as to what that policy is, and what course I intend to pursue. Not having as yet seen occasion to change, it is now my purpose to pursue the course marked out in the inaugural address. I commend a careful consideration of the whole document as the best expression I can give to my purposes. As I then and therein said, I now repeat, "The power confided in me will be used to hold, occupy, and possess property and places belonging to the government, and to collect the duties and imposts; but beyond what is necessary for these objects there will be no invasion, no using of force against or among the people any where." By the words "property and places belonging to the government," I chiefly allude to the military posts and property which were in possession of the government when it came into my hands. But if, as now appears to be true, in pursuit of a purpose to drive the United States authority from these places, an unprovoked assault has been made upon Fort Sumter, I shall hold myself at liberty to repossess it, if I can, like places which had been seized before the government was devolved upon me; and in any event I shall, to the best of my ability, repel force by force. In case it proves true that Fort Sumter has been assaulted, as is reported, I shall, perhaps, cause the United States mails to be withdrawn from all the states which claim to have seceded, believing that the commencement of actual war against the government justifies and possibly demands it. I scarcely need to say that I consider the military posts and property situated within the states which claim to have seceded as yet belonging to the government of the United States as much as they did before the supposed secession. Whatever else I may do for the purpose, I shall not attempt to collect the duties and imposts by any armed invasion of any part of the country; not meaning by this, however, that I may not land a force deemed necessary to relieve a fort upon the border of the country. From the fact that I have quoted a part of the inaugural address, it must not be inferred that I repudiate any other part, the whole of which I reaffirm, except so far as what I now say of the mails may be regarded as a modification.

[9] *Proclamation of the Governor of Virginia.*

Whereas seven of the states formerly composing a part of the United States have, by authority of their people, solemnly resumed the powers granted by them to the United States, and have framed a constitution and organized a government for themselves, to which the people of those states are yielding willing obedience, and have so notified the President of the United States by all the formalities incident to such action, and thereby become to the United States a separate, independent, and foreign power; and whereas the Constitution of the United States has invested Congress with the sole power "to declare war," and until such declaration is made the President has no authority to call for an extraordinary force to wage offensive war against any foreign power; and whereas, on the 15th instant, the President of the United States, in plain violation of the Constitution, issued a proclamation calling for a force of seventy-five thousand men to cause the laws of the United States to be duly executed over a people who are no longer a part of the Union, and in said proclamation threatens to exert this unusual force to compel obedience to his mandates; and whereas the General Assembly of Virginia, by a majority approaching to entire unanimity, declared at its last session that the State of Virginia would consider such an exertion of force as a virtual declaration of war, to be resisted by all the power at the command of Virginia; and subsequently, the Convention now in session, representing the sovereignty of this state, has reaffirmed in substance the same policy, with almost equal unanimity; and whereas the State of Virginia deeply sympathizes with the Southern states in the wrongs they have suffered and in the position they have assumed, and having made earnest efforts peaceably to compose the differences which have severed the Union, and having failed in that attempt, through this unwarranted act on the part of the President; and it is believed that the influences which operate to produce this proclamation against the seceded states will be brought to bear upon this commonwealth if she should exercise her undoubted right to resume the powers granted by her people, and it is due to the honor of Virginia that an improper exercise of force against her people should be repelled; therefore I, John Letcher, Governor of the Commonwealth of Virginia, have thought proper to order all armed volunteer regiments or companies within the state forthwith to hold themselves in readiness for immediate orders; and upon the reception of this proclamation to report to the adjutant general of the state their organization and numbers, and prepare themselves for efficient service. Such companies as are not armed and equipped will report that fact, that they may be properly supplied.

In witness whereof, I have hereunto set my hand, and caused the seal of the Commonwealth to be affixed, this 17th day of April, 1861, and in the eighty-fifth year of the Commonwealth.

JOHN LETCHER.

[10] *Ordinance of Secession passed by the Virginia Convention, April 17th,* 1861.

An Ordinance to repeal the Ratification of the Constitution of the United States of America by the State of Virginia, and to resume all the Rights and Powers granted under said Constitution:

The people of Virginia, in the ratification of the Constitution of the United States of America, adopted by them in convention, on the 25th day of June, in the year of our Lord one thousand seven hundred and eighty-eight, having declared that the powers granted under the said Constitution were derived from the people of the United States, and might be resumed whensoever the same should be perverted to their injury and oppression, and the federal government having perverted said powers, not only to the injury of the people of Virginia, but to the oppression of the Southern slaveholding states;

Now, therefore, we, the people of Virginia, do declare and ordain, that the ordinance adopted by the people of this state in convention, on the twenty-fifth day of June, in the year of our Lord one thousand seven hundred and eighty-eight, whereby the Constitution of the United States of America was ratified, and all acts of the General Assembly of this state ratifying or adopting amendments to said Constitution, are hereby repealed and abrogated; that the union between the State of Virginia and the other states under the Constitution aforesaid is hereby dissolved, and that the State of Virginia is in the full possession and exercise of all the rights of sovereignty which belong and appertain to a free and independent state. And they do farther declare that said Constitution of the United States of America is no longer binding on any of the citizens of this state.

This ordinance shall take effect and be an act of this day, when ratified by a majority of the votes of the people of this state, cast at a poll to be taken thereon, on the fourth Thursday in May next, in pursuance of a schedule hereafter to be enacted.

Done in convention, in the city of Richmond, on the seventeenth day of April, in the year of our Lord one thousand eight hundred and sixty-one, and in the eighty-fifth year of the Commonwealth of Virginia.

A true copy. JNO. L. EUBANK, Secretary of Convention.

[1] *An Ordinance passed by the Virginia Convention for the adoption of the Constitution of the Provisional Government of the Confederate States of America.*

We, the delegates of the people of Virginia, in convention assembled, solemnly impressed by the perils which surround the commonwealth, and appealing to the Searcher of hearts for the rectitude of our intentions in assuming the grave responsibility of this act, do by this ordinance *adopt and ratify* the Constitution of the provisional government of the Confederate States of America, ordained and established at Montgomery, Alabama, on the eighth day of February, eighteen hundred and sixty-one; provided that this ordinance shall cease to have any legal operation or effect if the people of this commonwealth, upon the vote directed to be taken on the Ordinance of Secession passed by this Convention on the seventeenth day of April, eighteen hundred and sixty-one, shall reject the same.

A true copy. JNO. L. EUBANK, Secretary.

Convention between the Commonwealth of Virginia and the Confederate States of America.

The Commonwealth of Virginia, looking to a speedy union of said commonwealth and the other slave states with the Confederate States of America, according to the provisions of the Constitution for the provisional government of said states, enters into the following temporary convention and agreement with said states, for the purpose of meeting pressing exigencies affecting the common rights, interests, and safety of said commonwealth and said confederacy.

1. Until the union of said commonwealth with said confederacy shall be perfected, and said commonwealth shall become a member of said confederacy, according to the constitutions of both powers, the whole military force and military operations, offensive and defensive, of said commonwealth, in the impending conflict with the United States, shall be under the chief control and direction of the President of said Confederate States, upon the same principles, basis, and footing as if said commonwealth were now, and during the interval, a member of said confederacy.

2. The commonwealth of Virginia will, after the consummation of the union contemplated in this convention, and her adoption of the Constitution for a permanent government of the said Confederate States, and she shall become a member of said confederacy under said permanent Constitution, if the same occur, turn over to the said Confederate States all the public property, naval stores, and munitions of war, etc., she may then be in possession of, acquired from the United States, on the same terms and in like manner as the other states of said confederacy have done in like cases.

3. Whatever expenditures of money, if any, said Commonwealth of Virginia shall make before the union, under the provisional government as above contemplated, shall be consummated, shall be met and provided for by said Confederate States.

This convention entered into and agreed to, in the city of Richmond, Virginia, on the twenty-fourth day of April, 1861, by Alexander H. Stephens, the duly authorized commissioner to act in the matter for the said Confederate States, and John Tyler, Wm. Ballard Preston, Samuel M'D. Moore, James P. Holcombe, James C. Bruce, and Lewis B. Harvie, parties duly authorized to act in like manner for said Commonwealth of Virginia, the whole subject to the approval and ratification of the proper authorities of both governments respectively.

In testimony whereof the parties aforesaid have hereto set their hands and seals, the day and year aforesaid, and at the place aforesaid, in duplicate originals.

ALEXANDER H. STEPHENS, Commissioner for Confederate States.

JOHN TYLER,
WM. BALLARD PRESTON,
S. M'D. MOORE,
JAMES P. HOLCOMBE,
JAMES C. BRUCE,
LEWIS B. HARVIE.
} Commissioners for Virginia.

Approved and ratified by the Convention of Virginia, on the 25th of April, 1861.

JOHN JANNEY, President.

JNO. L. EUBANK, Secretary.

GENERAL VIEW OF HARPER'S FERRY AND THE MARYLAND HEIGHTS.

HARPER'S FERRY, VIRGINIA.

points of attraction there had grown up a manufacturing town of between nine and ten thousand inhabitants, which was connected with the Maryland shore by a bridge nine hundred feet in length, the alternate possession and abandonment, destruction and rebuilding of which played a prominent part in the approaching war. The commanding position of the place, and the great value of the arms and the founderies there, made it one of the most important internal military posts of the United States. It was at this time held by Lieutenant Roger Jones, who had under his immediate command only a small company of about forty men. That the post was in danger the government well knew, but there were no means of re-enforcing it sufficiently; and Lieutenant Jones had received orders that, in case of an attack which could not be successfully resisted, it should be destroyed. The peril came sooner than it was expected. But the commander was watchful, and he received information, on the 17th, the very day on which the Ordinance of Secession was passed within closed doors, that preparations were making at Winchester and in the surrounding country for an attack upon him in overwhelming force. He immediately prepared the work of destruction by piling the arms in heaps and surrounding them with combustible matter, and by mining the work-shops and laying trains. He was not an hour too soon. Orders were sent down from Richmond on the morning of the 18th for the seizure of the place, and three thousand men were expected to move upon it. Owing to the suddenness

of the call, however, only two hundred and fifty infantry assembled at the rendezvous, Halltown, a small village about four miles from Harper's Ferry. To these, however, were added a squad of Fauquier County cavalry and a piece of artillery; and thus the force was more than amply strong for the purpose, even without the help of the inhabitants of the town, which it was sure to receive. About nine o'clock in the evening this force moved swiftly and silently upon the Ferry; but they were not able to surprise its little garrison. They were challenged by sentry after sentry, until they began to apprehend that more formidable preparations for resistance had been made than they were able to encounter, and concluded to send in a flag of truce to obtain information from the townspeople. But, while the flag was on its way, and the officers were in consultation during the halt, a sudden flash broke forth in the direction of the armory; it was followed by others in quick succession, accompanied by explosions like the firing of heavy artillery. The cause was instantly suspected, and the cavalry, dashing into the village, soon returned with the information that the arsenal and the work-shops were blown up and on fire, and that the government troops had retreated across the Potomac toward Hagerstown in Pennsylvania. Lieutenant Jones had been prompt, and as thorough as circumstances permitted. Within three minutes from the time of firing the trains, the arsenal and the arms which it contained were destroyed, and the work-shops were all ablaze. But of the arms in the latter many were saved by the insurgents after they had put out the fire. Their way lit by the conflagration which they had kindled, Lieutenant Jones and his little band fled across the Potomac bridge, pursued by a threatening mob, which, however, they easily kept at bay, and, pushing on through the night, arrived, weary and footsore, at Carlisle Barracks, in Pennsylvania, the next afternoon, with the loss of only four men by desertion and straggling. Mr. Jones's faithfulness and his success won him commendation and a captaincy. But in what a situation was that country which esteemed itself fortunate in the escape of its soldiers with their lives from an important post, and the destruction of one of its most considerable arsenals and armories, filled with arms and implements which never could have been more needed!

To the loss of Harper's Ferry there was immediately added another of far more consequence, that of the great naval station at Portsmouth, which lies upon the Elizabeth River, eight miles from the noble harbor of Hampton Roads. The great capacity of this harbor, its safety, and its easy access to ships of the deepest draught, had early pointed it out as the most desirable place south of New York for the naval purposes to which it was appropriated. It was filled with the maritime and military wealth of the nation, and within its limits were the most extensive and complete array of shops, founderies, ship-yards, mills, and docks in the country; among them a dry dock of granite, built at an enormous cost, and capable of the largest vessels. Lying at the navy yard, which was at Gosport, a little suburb of the little

MARCH OF THE VIRGINIANS ON HARPER'S FERRY, 9 00 P.M., APRIL 18, 1861.

DESTRUCTION OF THE UNITED STATES NAVY YARD AT NORFOL

United States.   Tug Yankee.   Cumberland.   Merrimac.

DESTRUCTION OF THE UNITED STATES SHIPS AT T

INIA, BY FIRE, BY THE UNITED STATES TROOPS, ON APRIL 20, 1861.

Pennsylvania.

FOLK NAVY YARD, BY ORDER OF THE GOVERNMENT.

BURNING OF THE UNITED STATES ARSENAL AT HARPER'S FERRY, 10 P.M., APRIL 18, 1861.

town of Portsmouth, which, with the neighboring city of Norfolk, containing only about fourteen thousand inhabitants, were literally kept from decay and death by the business thrown into their hands by the government, were twelve vessels of war of various sizes, from the Pennsylvania, four-decker, of 120 guns, to the brig Dolphin of 4. Most of them were of large size; and although all were more or less in need of repairs, or were not quite completed, only one was unfit for service. Among them was the sloop-of-war Cumberland, Captain Pendergrast, which was in commission as the flag-ship of the home squadron, and the Merrimac, a noble steam frigate of 40 guns, which was launched at Charlestown, Massachusetts, in 1855, and which, in a voyage over the world, had won universal admiration by her union of speed, power, and weight of metal. Both the Cumberland and the Merrimac were destined to play, as antagonists, a striking part in the coming war; the latter by affording the first example of a new system of naval warfare; the former by a devotion to the flag and a stubborn resistance which threw the brightest halo of heroism over her destruction. In addition to these vessels there were in the yard nearly two thousand five hundred pieces of heavy ordnance, three hundred of which were Dahlgren guns. The quantity of small arms, ammunition, and other munitions of war in store here was immense; and at old Fort Norfolk, which was used as a magazine, were three hundred thousand pounds of powder, with shot and loaded shell in vast amount. The ships, docks, shops, naval stores, arms, and ammunition at Gosport Navy Yard and its immediate dependencies were worth, at a moderate valuation, thirty-five millions of dollars. This great prize was taken without the sacrifice of a drop of blood by the promptness and audacity of the insurgents, and lost by the cautious, good-natured scruples of the government. The place was entirely without protection. On the land-side, its space of many acres was inclosed only by a low wall, easily scaled or battered down at any point; and as to the ships, there were not on the spot seamen enough to man a single one of them. Though the station and its invaluable contents were thus exposed to attack, of which, from the very accession of President Lincoln to power there had been constant apprehension, no measures, even of prevention, were taken for its preservation. The ever-present fear of exciting animosity and provoking attack, the never-dying hope that some way, which no one could point out, would be found of maintaining the national authority, without asserting it by force, and of restoring the Union to its normal condition with the consent of all its parts, prevented any attempt to retain Portsmouth and the navy yard securely in the hands of the government. This was openly avowed by a member of President Lincoln's administration, of whose loyalty, and of the faithfulness of whose intentions, there can not be the slightest doubt. Secretary Welles, in his report to the President, submitted to Congress in the following July, says: "Any attempt to withdraw the ships, or either of them, without a crew, would, in the then sensitive and disturbed condition of the public mind, have betrayed alarm and distrust, and been likely to cause difficulty."

In this timid and hesitating policy thirty-seven priceless days were passed; and when, at last, in the words of the same officer, he became "apprehensive that action might be necessary," the action taken was of little more

effect than the inaction which it followed. Commodore M'Cauley, who was in command of the yard, was directed to use "extreme vigilance and circumspection;" but this vigilance and circumspection seem, by the terms of the order, which was dated April 10th, to have been quite as much addressed to the avoidance of offense to the disloyal as to the preservation of the nation's property and the maintenance of the authority of the government. He was directed "to put the shipping and public property in condition to be moved and placed beyond danger, but in doing this he was warned to take no steps that could give needless alarm." What a warning, to be solemnly addressed by the representative of the government of a great nation to one of its most important officers in such a crisis of its affairs! As at Charleston, so here at Portsmouth. Could the Star of the West, with her re-enforcements and supplies for Fort Sumter, have been promptly sent to Major Anderson, convoyed by the steam frigate Brooklyn, or some other sufficient naval force, with orders to demolish any battery that fired a gun upon the national flag, the revolt would almost surely have been crushed in its very birth. Strange, incomprehensible, that after the lesson in that quarter, and after the insurrection had made headway by audacity on the one side and hesitation on the other, it was not seen that the way to save Portsmouth and its dependencies was not to deal tenderly with disaffection, and avoid giving needless alarm, but to lay a frigate or two opposite the place, with orders to open fire with shot and shell upon the first attempt at violence! But matters went on in the same old timid way. At last the engines of the Merrimac were reported ready for use, and Commodore M'Cauley received orders from Washington to lose no time in getting her armament on board, in loading her, the Plymouth, the Dolphin, and the Germantown with the more valuable ordnance and other public property, and in putting these vessels in a position to be moved at any moment out of danger. The Cumberland, well manned and fully equipped, was placed in a position to command Portsmouth, the navy yard, and Norfolk; and orders were issued to repel by force all attempts to seize vessels or any other property, by whomsoever made, or under whatever pretense of authority. Thus, at the very last moment, the government took the measures it should have taken thirty days before. At the last—at the very last; for this was not done until the 17th of April, the day on which the Ordinance of Secession was passed in secret conclave at Richmond. Yet it might not have been quite too late but for another exhibition of that blind confidence on the one side, and that personal faithlessness on the other, which, in the beginning of this rebellion, brought defeat to the government and dishonorable success to the insurgents.

A large number of the officers under Commodore M'Cauley's command were from slave states—many of them from Virginia. He was betrayed into trusting the loyalty, and, what is more, the personal good faith of these men. They were good officers, and he could not believe that they would at once prove false to the country and the flag of which they were the sworn defenders; he could not insult them and degrade his own profession by acting upon the supposition that a whole body of men would remain in a service in which they had grown up only just so long as they could use their positions for the purpose of deceiving him and betraying their trust; he felt bound to believe that if they meant to abandon the old flag they would do so at once, and openly like men, and that, like men of honor, they would sedulously avoid an ambiguous position, which made them masters of the secrets, and gave them measurable control over the affairs of a government against which, while wearing its uniform and receiving its pay, they intended to fight when the time arrived. But they were not content with leaving him to these conclusions, so natural to an officer and a gentleman. They went to him with frequent professions of loyalty upon their lips, saying at one time, "You have no Pensacola officers here, commodore; we'll never desert you; we will stand by you to the last, even to the death."[2] Yet these words were only uttered to lure him into fatal security, as we shall see in the sequel.

The people of Norfolk, true to the feeling which, according to their own journal, required the removal of the bodies of the Northern physicians who died while ministering to them in the time of pestilence,[3] were among the earliest and bitterest of the secessionists in Eastern Virginia. Their streets were filled with murmuring and threatening. They paraded their militia companies, and openly declared that if the government attempted to remove any of the ships or the munitions of war, or the commander of the yard made any preparations to defend it, they would attack it instantly. The unreasonableness of such a threat might be a just subject of remark, were it not that the men who made it were thinking and acting far outside the pale of reason. On the night of the 16th of April a band of these people seized two light-ships and sunk them in the shallowest part of the entrance to the harbor. On the next day, it will be remembered, the very day on which the secret but discreetly disseminated Ordinance of Secession was passed, the Merrimac was ready to go to sea; but Mr. Isherwood, the engineer-in-chief, who had been sent expressly from Washington to expedite her preparations, was surprised at receiving the order from Commodore M'Cauley not to get up steam until the day after. On that day the fires were lighted, and again the commodore spoke doubtfully about sending the vessel out, and ordered a delay of a few hours. A remonstrance from the engineer-in-chief, who directed the commodore's attention to the urgent orders of the Navy Department, and the probability that the obstructions in the channel would be increased during the night, elicited only a tardy announcement that the Merrimac would not go to sea that day, and an order to draw the fires; whereupon the engineer started post-haste for Washington. Commodore M'Cauley appears, by his own admission, to have allowed his junior officers to persuade him that still farther delay would be most prudent. On the very morning, the 18th, when he issued the fatal order of procrastination, all of those officers who were from slave states, with one or two honorable exceptions, resigned their commissions; the greater part of the workmen of the yard absented themselves from duty; General Taliaferro, of Virginia, arrived at Norfolk to take command of the military forces there, and Commodore M'Cauley's eyes at last were opened. But they were opened only to see his imminent peril and his utter helplessness; to see that he could not save, but only destroy; and to the work of destruction he at once addressed himself. He ordered all the guns to be spiked—an enormous task. It was but partly performed; and of the pieces which were spiked, only a few were permanently injured. The 19th passed in this and like futile efforts to destroy the property which the commodore had concluded to abandon. On the 20th the tumult outside the yard rose yet higher, and at twelve o'clock an officer was sent out bearing a flag of truce. He was taken to General Taliaferro's quarters, where a consultation was held, the result of which was renewed humiliation and disgrace to the national government. Commodore M'Cauley promised that none of the vessels should be taken from the yard, or a shot fired except in self-defense. But again he decided to destroy what he could not remove, and he gave orders—the last which he issued as commander of the yard—to scuttle all the vessels except the Cumberland.

Meanwhile measures were taken at Washington to supersede him in his command; but they proved to be too late. When the engineer-in-chief reported at the Navy Department the detention of the Merrimac, the secretary saw that the error promised to be well-nigh fatal. Captain Paulding was immediately dispatched to Portsmouth with the powerful steam frigate Pawnee, on which were placed one hundred marines in addition to her regular crew, and three hundred and fifty Massachusetts volunteers, under command of Colonel Wardrop, who were taken on board at Fortress Monroe. With this force Captain Paulding arrived at Portsmouth on the evening of the 20th, under instructions to take command of all the vessels at that station, to repel force by force, and prevent the ships and other property, at all hazards, from falling into the hands of the insurgents—most fitting orders, but, like all others issued by the government since the breaking out of the insurrection (except those in reference to Washington and Fort Pickens), withheld until they were of no avail; for Captain Paulding arrived at Portsmouth only in time to see the scuttled ships settling down into the water, and to witness Commodore M'Cauley's helpless condition before the now overwhelming and partly organized force of the insurgents. What might have been accomplished with the Cumberland, the Pawnee, and the troops in the latter, under such circumstances, we can not, perhaps, rightly judge. It seems, indeed, as if such a force, promptly and vigorously used against a body of men, however large, who were unprotected by works of any kind, and who had little artillery, and that not in position, would have held them completely at bay, and, if necessary, dispersed them with great slaughter, and with the destruction of the towns of Norfolk and Portsmouth. But such an exertion of the strength of the government, it seems, was not to be

put forth; and Captain Paulding used the large discretionary powers with which he was clothed only to make as thorough as possible the destruction which Commodore M'Cauley had begun. He detailed one hundred men to render the heavy ordnance unserviceable by knocking off the trunnions; but they worked for an hour with the heaviest sledges, and produced no effect. The dry dock, the pride of the station, was mined; combustibles were scattered through the scuttled ships, the ship-houses, and barracks, and trains were laid through them, so that they might all be fired at once. It was two o'clock at night before all was reported ready, when all the force, except the few who were to light the trains, took ship on the Pawnee and the Cumberland. At four o'clock the former took the latter in tow and stood down the harbor; and at half past four, a rocket from the Pawnee gave the signal, and in a few minutes Gosport Navy Yard was all ablaze. The conflagration was an awful one, as may be easily imagined. By its terrible splendor the country was lit up for miles around; and the roar of the flames, as they devoured the work of years and the wealth of a nation, was heard with horror far and wide. The burning of the great four-decker Pennsylvania, the largest ship afloat, was in itself a spectacle of destructive grandeur worthy of mention in the naval annals of the republic, of whose fate her disastrous end might, to superstitious minds, have seemed an omen, enhanced as its effect was by the solemn booming of her heavy guns, as the fire reached them, at brief intervals.

While this ruin was going on, its huge proportions and its appalling means made it seem far more destructive than it really was; for when the flames had subsided, and the excited people, to baffle whom they were lighted, rushed into the yard, and began to save what could be saved, it was found that little harm was done except to the ship-houses and to the ships, all of which that were sea-worthy might have been removed from the harbor within the forty-eight hours previous; and even of these, two, the Plymouth and the Merrimac, were afterward raised and made serviceable. But the dry dock, all the various founderies and shops, the ordnance buildings, the tools, provisions, and officers' quarters, were but little injured, and were almost immediately put in use for the manufacture of arms, shot, and shell, and all the other military and naval purposes to which such a large establishment was adapted. Fort Norfolk, with its immense stores of powder, was taken without resistance. From the whole North there went up a cry of mingled grief and wrath at this great loss. The importance of the station for the naval purposes of the government in the coming struggle, and, no less, of the James River, the control of which was by this event virtually lost as an avenue of approach to the interior, and the immense value of the ships and stores which had been destroyed or given up, were instantly appreciated by the country. But the real significance of the capture was in the enormous quantity of heavy ordnance, which was not only lost by the government, but gained by the rebels. A capture of any thing like its importance in this respect is not recorded in history. As far as regarded heavy artillery, it virtually amounted to the disarming of one side and the arming of the other; and, combined with the various seizures which have already been enumerated, it chiefly contributed to produce the result, as we shall see, of an incomparable superiority in arms, on the part of the insurgents, upon the beginning of actual hostilities. We are not left without their own testimony upon this point. Mr. Peters, a commissioner of the State of Virginia, appointed to take an inventory of the property thus abandoned by the United States and seized by the insurgents, says, in a report published in the *Richmond Enquirer* of February 4th, 1862: "I had purposed some remarks upon the vast importance to Virginia, and to the entire South, of the timely acquisition of this extensive naval dépôt, with its immense supplies of munitions of war, and to notice briefly the damaging effects of its loss to the government at Washington; but I deem it unnecessary, since the presence at almost every exposed point on the whole Southern coast, and at numerous inland intrenched camps in the several states, of heavy pieces of ordnance, with their equipments and fixed ammunition, all supplied from this establishment, fully attests the one, while the unwillingness of the enemy to attempt demonstrations at any point, from which he is obviously deterred by the knowledge of its well-fortified condition, abundantly proves the other, especially when it is considered that both he and we are wholly indebted for our means of resistance to his loss and our acquisition of the Gosport Navy Yard."[4]

Within forty-eight hours after Commodore M'Cauley's agreement with General Taliaferro, troops from Virginia and from Georgia, to the number of a thousand men, with fourteen pieces of rifled cannon, had been added to the force already at Portsmouth and Norfolk, and the hull of the old frigate United States had been sunk in the narrowest part of the entrance to the harbor, within easy range of Forts Calhoun and Monroe, which guard the approach; and thus the insurgents were placed in complete possession of this important station, where they remained unmolested many months, while they successfully planned and executed enterprises which had an important influence upon the progress of the war.

Leaving the rebels now virtually masters of the Gulf states and the eastern slopes of the Alleghanies south of the Potomac, we must look northward upon scenes not less exciting and far more encouraging to those whose interest was bound up in the fortunes of the great republic. We have seen

---

[2] See the Reply of Commodore M'Cauley to the censure of the Congressional Committee, published in the *National Intelligencer*, May 5, 1862.　　　[3] See Introduction, page 14.

[4] The authority for this account of the destruction of Harper's Ferry and the Portsmouth Navy Yard will be found in the Richmond and New York newspapers of the day, in the Virginia correspondence of *Harpers' Weekly* of May 11th, 1861, in the Report of the Select Committee of the Senate for investigating the Facts relative to the Loss of the Navy Yard, etc., submitted by Mr. Hale, of New Hampshire, April 18, 1862, and the Reply of Commodore M'Cauley to the censure of the Congressional Committee, published in the Washington *National Intelligencer*, May 5, 1862.

that among the troops vainly brought by Commodore Paulding to the defense of Portsmouth Navy Yard was part of a Massachusetts regiment, which he took on board at Fortress Monroe. This was on the 19th of April. The President's proclamation was issued only on the 15th. The presence of a regiment of citizen soldiers at a point five hundred miles from their homes in less than four days from the time when the government called for their services, is an event characteristic of the temper of the people of the North at this turning point of the existence of the Union. The President's war proclamation, and the event which called it forth, had stirred the whole North not only to the liveliest exhibition of feeling, but to prompt and vigorous action. From the Atlantic shore to the banks of the Mississippi there was a generous rivalry of effort for the triumph of the republic over those who sought its destruction. The state authorities, the town councils, the public moneyed institutions, all addressed themselves to the task of providing men and money for the great emergency. Citizens formed themselves into Union, relief, and vigilance committees. Money was subscribed on all sides with a free hand, and volunteers came forward in eager throngs. Within a fortnight of the bombardment of Fort Sumter over thirty millions of dollars had been given at the North as a free gift in aid of the war from various quarters, public and private. New York was asked for 17,000 men for three months; the Legislature authorized 30,000 for two years, and a war loan of $3,000,000. Pennsylvania and Ohio each appropriated an equal sum. The city of New York alone voted $1,000,000 for the same purpose, and the sum was instantly advanced by the banks. The spirit of New York was but the spirit of the country. The West was not behind the East. The state of Indiana voted a million dollars; and Maine, Vermont, and New Jersey did the same. Foremost among the vast multitude which thus sprang forward to the support of the national cause and the principles of constitutional liberty were the people of the Commonwealth of Massachusetts. The proclamation had found her citizens and her authorities not unprepared. The inevitable conflict had been more clearly foreseen there than in any other part of the country north of the Potomac; and it was looked for with the inflexible determination to meet it without swerving or hesitation. Aside from the patriotism, the diffused intelligence, and the hatred of slavery for which the people of Massachusetts had been distinguished from the earliest days of colonial history, there were particular reasons for their ardor and alacrity at this crisis; for the insurrection had broken out and was for a long time openly sustained only in South Carolina; and from South Carolina Massachusetts had twice received insult and outrage: first, when, on sending, in 1844, by vote of her Legislature, Judge Hoar, of her Supreme Court, as a commissioner to Charleston, to make respectful inquiry as to the reasons for imprisoning certain of her negro residents on their arrival at that port in ships, for the purpose of testing the constitutional right of such action before the Supreme Court of the United States, her representative was not even allowed to state the object of his mission, and, though accompanied by his daughter, was driven out of the city with threats of violence if he ventured to remain; next, when, in 1855, Preston Brooks, member of the House of Representatives from South Carolina, aided and abetted by his colleague, Lawrence Keitt, attacked in the Senate Chamber, and beat senseless Charles Sumner, senator from Massachusetts. These injuries had ever rankled deeply in the breasts of Massachusetts men; and now, upon this great and fit occasion, the long-smothered flames of a righteous vengeance—if righteous other than almighty vengeance can ever be—burst forth on all sides with a fury which had been for years accumulating. To confound for a moment the feeling which thus exhibited itself with personal hatred and vindictiveness would be to degrade that which was high and almost holy. It was wrath, but wrath the spring of which was not self, but country: it was no petty personal resentment of an affront offered to the citizen in his representative, but a vindication of the dignity of an ancient and honorable commonwealth; not even the mere execution of retributive justice, but the burning desire of the most intelligent and right-minded body of freemen in the world to crush forever a power which they had had peculiar reason to feel was animated by a deadly and an undying hatred to liberty and the vital principles of Christianity, and bent on waging savage and remorseless war upon them and their advocates and supporters when they opposed its perpetuation and aggrandizement. And this sentiment, hard-tempered in the flow of thoughtful years, was whetted to a keen-edged purpose by the stern spirit of the old Puritanism, the intolerance of which had not yet been quite weeded from the soil to which it had been so early transplanted, where it had taken such firm root and grown with such a hardy growth. Always earnest, always devoted to the cause of freedom, and the prosperity and glory of the republic, and thus goaded by the memory of wrongs received at the hands of the men who were now in arms for the dismemberment of the Union and the destruction of its government, Massachusetts moved more promptly to the rescue than any other state. Within eighteen hours after the receipt of orders, the sixth regiment of her militia, Colonel Edward F. Jones, was on its way, 700 strong, from its head-quarters at Lowell, to Boston. Early on the morning of the 18th of April, only three days after the President's call for troops, it passed through New York on its way to Washington, and its march along the streets of the great commercial capital was one continued scene of enthusiastic welcome, congratulation, and encouragement. Thus, on the very first occasion, the confident predictions of the partisans of slavery that the people of the Middle States, and particularly those of the city of New York, would never permit the passage over their soil of troops going southward to crush a revolt in the slave states, were falsified, and in a manner which must have added to the surprise of the prophets a now clearer and surer foresight of the nature of the revolt which they had set on foot. The Sixth Massachusetts has the honor of being the

first regiment which mustered and marched to the defense of the capital; but its promptness was so successfully emulated throughout that old commonwealth that, in less than one week from the day on which the requisition of the Secretary of War, which accompanied the proclamation, was received by telegraph, the full quota of troops assigned to the state was either in Fortress Monroe or on the way to Washington.[5] Thus it happened that within five days of the bombardment of Fort Sumter, Commodore Paulding could steam into Portsmouth Harbor with a regiment of Massachusetts men ready to defend the navy yard.

All the Massachusetts troops, however, were not to reach their destination so quickly or so safely. The regiment first to report for duty, and which we have seen marching through the city of New York amid the cheers of its inhabitants, was destined to meet a bloody check in Baltimore. Passing through Philadelphia, where it was received with welcome, and quickly dispatched, by railway, with God-speed, it crossed, in the night, to stormier fortune, the boundary which separated slavery from freedom, and arrived at the Baltimore station on the morning of the 19th. As, upon the expected arrival of Mr. Lincoln himself upon his way to the capital, riotous conduct was apprehended by the authorities of Baltimore, so, for like reasons, upon this occasion it was feared that the presence of Northern troops, and particularly of a part of the militia of that state which was justly regarded as the leader in the anti-slavery movement, would excite feelings of antagonism, which would break forth in violence. I have before observed that the majority of the people in Maryland, and particularly of those in Baltimore, were unswerving in their loyalty to the Constitution and the government of the republic—a condition of public feeling in a slave state, which is to be attributed less to the geographical position of this one than to the system of popular education, which, as the reader of the Introduction to this history will remember, distinguished Maryland from the other states of like social and political organization. But still the large number of slaves held there, and the close relations of the people with those of the farther South, produced a division of sentiment so strong that the governor was obliged to recognize it in the proclamation which he issued upon the President's call for troops, and the mayor of Baltimore, also, in one which he issued, earnestly invoking all the inhabitants of that city to refrain from every act leading to outbreak or violence, and to render prompt assistance to the public authorities in their efforts to preserve the peace.[6] And here again, as always, the partisans of aggressive slavery were active, loud-mouthed, violent, while those who owned a supreme devotion to the republic were almost without exception quiet, orderly, unassuming people, who concerned themselves about their own affairs, and gave to social intercourse and intellectual culture the time which the others devoted to political intrigue and agitation, or to the coarser diversions of low life in a great city notorious throughout the country for the almost exceptional license and lawlessness of a certain part of its inhabitants, who might almost be classed with the dangerous element in the populations of London and Paris.

Upon the arrival of the long train containing the Massachusetts regiment and some other troops, which was at about ten o'clock in the morning, a threatening crowd quickly gathered around the station. It grew apace, and was plainly bent on mischief. The troops remained in the cars; and, could an engine have been at once attached to the train, they might have passed on unmolested; but a city ordinance required that, within certain limits, the cars should be drawn through the streets by horses, which of course separated them from each other; and of this separation and slow movement the mob were quick to take advantage. Threats and curses had been heaped upon the militia from their first appearance; but words were soon accompanied by deeds. The horses were seized, impediments were thrown upon the track, and at last the cars were pelted with paving-stones. The police, though in considerable force, were either in such insufficient numbers or so lukewarm in their duty (perhaps both conditions may be assumed) that the riot met no check; but the drivers whipped up their horses—the momentum of the cars was too great for the crowd to withstand—and in this manner nine of the eleven cars occupied by the Massachusetts regiment pushed through, and escaped with their freight of quiet, unresisting soldiers. But the mob increased in activity and daring as well as in numbers; some heavy anchors near by were dragged up and thrown across the track; and the movement of the last two cars, which contained four companies, became so difficult, and their situation so dangerous, that it was determined that the men should alight and march to the Washington station. They filed out of the cars and formed amid howls of defiance and derision, mingled with cheers for the South, for Jefferson Davis, for South Carolina and Secession, and groans for Massachusetts and the President of the United States, under the name of Abe Lincoln. The colonel of the regiment was with the companies in the advance; and the officers of those thus left behind, holding a hurried consultation, devolved the command of their detachment upon Captain Albert S. Follansbee, of Lowell. He wheeled his men into column, and began the march in close order. Stones, bricks, and every missile at hand soon flew thick and fast, and men armed with pistols and muskets began to appear in the ever-increasing mob. To that which had gathered immediately around the station another now was added. A large and tumultuous crowd, headed by the insurgent flag, rushed down the street in face of the troops, shouting to them to turn back, and threatening death to every "white nigger" of them who should attempt to reach the other station. But Captain Follansbee, calling upon the police to lead the way, he and his little band kept on their march, steady and unresisting. They had

<hr />

[5] Message of Governor Andrew to the Legislature of Massachusetts.
[6] Proclamation of George William Brown, mayor of Baltimore, April 17th, 1861.

FIRST BLOOD.—THE SIXTH MASSACHUSETTS REGIMENT FIGHTING THEIR WAY THROUGH BALTIMORE, APRIL 19, 1861.

gone but a short distance when their progress was retarded and their lines broken by a small bridge, from which the mob had torn up the planks; but the soldiers jumped from timber to timber, and got over, though in confusion. Many of them had by this time been severely hurt, and now two were struck down and effectually put *hors de combat* by missiles, which came thicker and faster than ever. A shot was at last fired into their ranks, and Captain Follansbee, thinking that the assault had been borne long enough, ordered his men to cap their pieces and defend themselves. The order was instantly obeyed, and with deadly effect; but the fire was returned from guns and pistols as well as with paving-stones. The Mayor of Baltimore now placed himself at the head of the little column, and endeavored to restrain the rioters by a bold exertion of his authority; but the protection which the municipal power of Baltimore had often before failed to afford to its own citizens it could not extend to strangers under these strange circumstances. The mayor's efforts proved futile, his position became dangerous, and he retired baffled, though not dismayed. The mob had now become a vast surging mass of infuriated men. Its numbers were estimated at from eight to ten thousand; but it has been found that in such conjectures numbers are usually exaggerated to three times the truth, and this case was not at all likely to be an exception to the rule. Yet it may be safely assumed that the Massachusetts men, who were little more than one hundred strong (the entire body consisted of eight hundred and sixty, rank and file), were now making their way through three thousand rioters. They kept together, however, in close ranks, opposing obedience and endurance to lawlessness and fury, wheeling upon their assailants and firing only when the attack became too severe to be borne without resistance; and in this manner they fought their way, with patient valor, one mile through the raging throng to the Washington station. But they had not yet escaped the perils of Baltimore. They and the rest of the regiment which had preceded them were enabled, indeed, by the exertions of the police and by their own large and well-armed numbers, to take the Washington cars, and the train was detained for some time, in hopes that the mob would now disperse; but it still increased, and, as it dared not face the muskets of a whole regiment, it turned its energies to the destruction of the train. The crowd dashed off upon the track in such numbers that, in the words of an eyewitness, for a mile it was black with an excited, rushing mass. Great logs and telegraph-poles, which required a dozen men to move them, were now thrown upon the rails, and rocks were rolled down upon the track from the embankment. Attempts were made to tear up the rails, and a cry was raised for pickaxes and crowbars; but only one or two could be found so suddenly. The police, now in large force, went forward and removed the obstructions, and the train, under a discharge of revolvers and stones, steamed slowly after; but the mob kept ahead of the police, continuing its destructive efforts. This dreadful scene covered a space of a mile and more; and the exertions, though not the fury of the rioters, ceased only from physical exhaustion. At last the track was clear; and the citizen soldiers, who had so promptly obeyed the orders of the elected chief magistrate of the nation, were borne swiftly beyond reach of their infuriated countrymen to the defense of their common capital.

At the same time with the Massachusetts regiment, upon the same road, and with the same destination, arrived ten companies of Pennsylvania militia. They were unarmed as well as ununiformed. But their helpless condition and their civil garb failed alike to protect them against the excited passions of the mob. Incapable of any effectual defense, they remained quietly in their cars, and were there stoned unmercifully for two hours. The sides of the cars afforded them protection; but many missiles went through the windows and inflicted serious bruises. Some attempted to escape; but they were attacked furiously, and obliged either to return to the cars or seek refuge in neighboring houses. After a time, the police, aided, it is said, by George P. Kane, United States marshal of that district, and some bold and loyal citizens, succeeded in partly quieting the tumult, and the Philadelphia troops were protected from farther injury, but were obliged to abandon their journey, and return as they came to Philadelphia. Two cars of baggage and munitions, which had been seized by the mob, were also rescued by the police.

GEORGE P. KANE.

In this deplorable and disgraceful affair, by which the pro-slavery faction of Baltimore gained the bad distinction of spilling the first blood shed in the great rebellion, at least thirty-nine men, according to the most trustworthy reports, were killed and wounded, in addition to the larger number who received unreckoned injuries more or less serious. Of the thirty-nine, eight rioters, one unoffending citizen, and two soldiers were killed outright, and three rioters and twenty-five soldiers were wounded, one of the last mortally. The three men who thus first gave up their lives in the cause of liberty and the republic were Sumner H. Needham, of Lawrence, and Addison O. Whitney and Luther C. Ladd, of Lowell. Their names will ever live in the memory of their countrymen.[7] In Massachusetts their fate and that of their wounded comrades excited a profound emotion, in which grief and indignation were tempered, though not abated, by a certain pride that this noble old commonwealth had been the first to offer the blood of her citizens in the defense of the liberties of the country, as she had also been the first to make the same sacrifice in the struggle by which those liberties were won. By a strange, and, it was fondly thought, a significant coincidence, it happened that the same day of the same month saw the sacrifice on both occasions. The skirmish at Lexington in 1775 and the street-fight at Baltimore, eighty-six years afterward, both occurred on the 19th of April. A correspondence by telegraph immediately took place between the Governor of Massachusetts and the Mayor of Baltimore as to the disposition of the bodies of the dead Massachusetts soldiers and the care for the wounded. On both sides it was touching and earnest; on both it showed state pride; but only on one, the Southern, that pernicious feeling of state independence, as if the state were something outside of rather than within the republic, which not even the solemnity of the occasion could repress, and which, no less than the fear for the life of slavery, was the cause of the struggle the first blood in which had been thus ominously shed. The one put forward the passage of armed troops of another state over the soil of his own as a palliation of the onslaught, if not an excuse for it; the other, though at the head of one of the oldest and most honorable commonwealths of the Union, and the one which had originally possessed and exercised the nearest approach to sovereignty, saw in the troops which he had sent and in any state over which they passed only the citizen soldiers and the common soil of the republic.[8]

Not in Massachusetts alone, however, did this attack upon the Massachusetts militia incense the people. The whole North burned with fierce resentment. Had the spirit which then animated the inhabitants of the free states, and even those of Kentucky and Missouri, who did not place the interests of slavery above those of the country, continued through the war, that lack of vindictiveness in them, which was publicly noticed by more than one observer and on more than one occasion, would not have softened the asperities and prolonged the continuance of the struggle.[9] The very advocates of slavery and apologists of the South, who were so numerous in the North, were profoundly moved at this flagitious attempt to stay the peaceful march of citizen soldiers through one of the United States at the command of the chief magistrate of them all. The demand that Baltimore should be humbled, and, if necessary to the opening of a safe highway to Washington, destroyed, was on every lip. Men whose interests and whose family connections were not only at the South, but in South Carolina, declared that, in this respect at least, the majesty of the nation should be asserted, and old black Federal cockades, exhumed from recesses where they had long been left in oblivion, began to appear on the breasts and hats of men whose blood boiled at the outrage upon the republic, but who were the very Gallios of slavery. Those who before sneered at the story of the attempt to assassinate Mr. Lincoln now believed it; the city which was the scene of the intended crime and of that actually committed was looked upon as an offense to the nation, and the cry, Through Baltimore or over it, went up over the whole Northern country. There was reason in the demand, and honor and justice, though not charity, in the feeling. The road to Washington lay through Baltimore; the people of Maryland had not even attempted to throw off the authority of the government at the former place; and that there was any aggression in the mere passage of their fellow-citizens through their chief town upon the order of their common government could not be for a moment pretended. No semblance of a defense was set up for them, except that strong municipal pride which causes the inhabitants of one place to resent the assertion of authority over them by the armed forces of another—an excellent plea in extenuation, if it were pertinent; but in this case it was entirely from the purpose. The Massachusetts men were in Baltimore, not to assert any authority there, not for the purpose of establishing relations of any kind with its people; they were merely travelers; and it was so plain as to need no demonstration that the passions of

---

[7] This account of the Baltimore riot is based upon a published letter of Captain Follansbee, and the reports of the affair in the Baltimore newspapers, and in the correspondence of those of New York.

[8] CORRESPONDENCE BETWEEN THE GOVERNOR OF MASSACHUSETTS AND THE MAYOR OF BALTIMORE.

Governor Andrew to Mayor Brown.

I pray you cause the bodies of our Massachusetts soldiers, dead in battle, to be immediately laid out, preserved in ice, and tenderly sent forward by express to me. All expenses will be paid by this commonwealth. JOHN A. ANDREW, Governor of Massachusetts.

Mayor Brown to Governor Andrew.

Baltimore, April 20, 1861.

The Hon. John A. Andrew, Governor of Massachusetts:

SIR,—No one deplores the sad events of yesterday in this city more deeply than myself, but they were inevitable. Our people viewed the passage of armed troops to another state through the streets as an invasion of our soil, and could not be restrained. The authorities exerted themselves to the best of their ability, but with only partial success. Governor Hicks was present, and concurs in all my views as to the proceedings now necessary for our protection. When are these scenes to cease? Are we to have a war of sections? God forbid. The bodies of the Massachusetts soldiers could not be sent out to Boston, as you requested, all communication between this city and Philadelphia by railroad, and with Boston by steamers, having ceased; but they have been placed in cemented coffins, and will be placed with proper funeral ceremonies in the mausoleum of Greenmount Cemetery, where they shall be retained until farther directions are received from you. The wounded are tenderly cared for. I appreciate your offer, but Baltimore will claim it as her right to pay all expenses incurred.

Very respectfully, your obedient servant, GEO. W. BROWN, Mayor of Baltimore.

Governor Andrew to Mayor Brown.

To his Honor George W. Brown, Mayor of Baltimore:

DEAR SIR,—I appreciate your kind attention to our wounded and our dead, and trust that at the earliest moment the remains of our fallen will return to us. I am overwhelmed with surprise that a peaceful march of American citizens over the highway to the defense of our common capital should be deemed aggressive to Baltimoreans. Through New York the march was triumphal.

JOHN A. ANDREW, Governor of Massachusetts.

[9] See particularly a speech delivered by the Hon. Joseph Holt, in New York, September 3d, 1861, and the letters of the special correspondent of the London *Times*.

the mob which attacked them were excited, not by any feeling of municipal pride, but by sympathy with the cause the suppression of which was the object of their journey. The New England men were going to sustain a government which the rioters hated because it had fallen under New England influence. Their object clearly was the obstruction of the Northern road to the capital until it could be seized and held by the insurgent army.[10] In this they were foiled by circumstances and the steadiness of the Northern troops.

The Massachusetts militia had escaped to Washington, the Pennsylvanians to Philadelphia; but the rioters did not abandon their designs. They were practically masters of Baltimore. Gun-shops and other stores of arms were broken open and pillaged. Places of business were generally closed. A public meeting was called for the afternoon, and the militia of the city were placed under arms. The preservation of public order was the professed, and, indeed, the actual object of these latter measures; but so strong, and so apparently pervading was the animosity excited by the events of the day, that the municipal and state officers were obliged to seek peace and quiet, not by the assertion and maintenance of the local law and the rights of the national government, but by placing themselves at the head of the insurgents, and giving to their purposes the sanction of constituted authority. This may have been a wise policy. It is by no means certain that if they had directly opposed the turbulent stream of excited popular feeling they would not have been swept away by it, or that, by yielding to and going with it for a while, they did not acquire an influence which enabled them to divert its current. And although events took place in the disturbed city within a few weeks, and in the state within a few months, which justify the belief that the excitement in Baltimore was produced by the efforts of a comparatively small, though energetic and desperate faction, the conclusion is not therefore warranted that the course of the mayor and the governor was not the wisest (it seems certainly to have been the most politic) that could have been pursued. On the afternoon of the collision the Mayor of Baltimore sent a telegraphic dispatch, and on the next morning, by special train, a deputation of three eminent citizens, to the President, imploring him neither to order nor to permit more troops to pass through the city, and assuring him that no more could go through without fighting their way at every step. Governor Hicks, whose sincere loyalty to the Constitution and supreme devotion to the republic there is no reason to doubt, united with him in this request. The President replied instantly, and with tender consideration for the distracting position of his petitioners; and, on the suggestion of General Scott, he assured them that, although troops must continue to come from the North to Washington, they should thenceforward march round Baltimore instead of through it, that thus the people of that city might not find rebellion lying in their way, but be compelled to seek it.[1] But it is sad to relate, and it is a most significant evidence of the condition of excitement into which the men of the pro-slavery faction were able to throw a city which, within a fortnight, exhibited an entire and spontaneous reaction of sentiment, that the authorities themselves took steps, before the receipt of the President's reply, to prevent the passage of troops from the North to the defense of Washington. The avenues of approach to the capital from the north and

GOVERNOR HICKS.

east available for the transportation of troops were the Northern and Central Pennsylvania and the Philadelphia and Baltimore Railways. These crossed several deep streams within the boundaries of Maryland, and, on the night of the 19th, the bridges over them were destroyed by order of the authorities of Baltimore![2] They also suspended the transmission of the mails and the removal of provisions from the city, and detained military stores and equipments belonging to the government sufficient for a thousand men.[3]

[10] *Extract from a Message of Mayor Brown to the City Council of Baltimore, July 10th*, 1861.

After recapitulating the occurrences of the 19th of April last, in which he agrees with Marshal Kane's account of the affair published on May 4, he says:

It is doing bare justice to say that the Board of Police, the Marshal of Police, and the men under his command, exerted themselves bravely, efficiently, skillfully, and in good faith, to preserve the peace and protect life. If proper notice had been given of the arrival of the troops, and of the number expected, the outbreak might have been prevented entirely; and but for the timely arrival of Marshal Kane with his force, as I have described, the bloodshed would have been great. The wounded among the troops received the best care and medical attention at the expense of the city, and the bodies of the killed were carefully and respectfully returned to their friends. The facts which I witnessed myself, and all that I have since heard, satisfied me that the attack was the result of a sudden impulse, and not of a premeditated scheme. But the effect on our citizens was for a time uncontrollable. In the intense excitement which ensued, which lasted for many days, and which was shared by men of all parties, and by our volunteer soldiers as well as citizens, it would have been impossible to convey more troops from the North through the city without a severe fight and bloodshed. Such an occurrence would have been fatal to the city; and, accordingly, to prevent it, the bridges on the Northern Central Railroad, and on the Philadelphia, Wilmington, and Baltimore Railroad, were, with the consent of the governor, and by my order, with the co-operation of the Board of Police—except Mr. Charles D. Hinks, who was absent from the city—partially disabled and burned, so as to prevent the immediate approach of troops to the city, but with no purpose of hostility to the federal government. This act, with the motive which prompted it, has been reported by the Board of Police to the Legislature of the state, and approved by that body, and was also immediately communicated by me in person to the President of the United States and his cabinet.

Dispatch of Secretary Cameron to Governor Hicks.

War Department, Washington, April 18, 1861.

To his Excellency Thomas H. Hicks, Governor of Maryland:

SIR,—The President is informed that threats are made and measures taken, by unlawful combinations of misguided citizens of Maryland, to prevent by force the transit of United States troops across Maryland, on their way, pursuant to orders, for the defense of this capital. The information is from such sources, and in such shapes, that the President thinks it his duty to make it known to you, so that all loyal and patriotic citizens of our state may be warned in time, and that you may be prepared to take immediate and effective measures against it.

Such an attempt could have only the most deplorable consequences; and it would be agreeable to the President, as it would be to yourself, that it should be prevented or overcome by the loyal authorities and citizens of Maryland, rather than averted by any other means.

I am very respectfully yours, etc., SIMON CAMERON, Secretary of War.

[1] CORRESPONDENCE BETWEEN THE GOVERNOR OF MARYLAND AND THE MAYOR OF BALTIMORE AND THE PRESIDENT OF THE UNITED STATES.

Governor Hicks and Mayor Brown to President Lincoln.

Mayor's Office, Baltimore, April 19, 1861.

To his Excellency the President of the United States:

SIR,—A collision between the citizens and the Northern troops has taken place in Baltimore, and the excitement is fearful. Send no more troops here. We will endeavor to prevent all bloodshed.

A public meeting of citizens has been called, and the troops of the state and the city have been ordered out to preserve the peace. They will be enough. Respectfully,

THOS. H. HICKS, Governor.
GEO. WM. BROWN, Mayor.

Mayor's Office, Baltimore, April 19, 1861.

To his Excellency the President of the United States:

SIR,—This will be presented to you by the Hon. H. Lenox Bond, Geo. W. Dobbin, and John C. Brune, Esqrs., who will proceed to Washington by an express train, at my request, in order to explain fully the fearful condition of our affairs in this city. The people are exasperated to the highest degree by the passage of troops, and the citizens are universally decided in the opinion that no more troops should be ordered to come.

The authorities of the city did their best to-day to protect both strangers and citizens, and to prevent a collision, but in vain; and but for their great efforts a fearful slaughter would have occurred.

Under these circumstances, it is my solemn duty to inform you that it is not possible for more soldiers to pass through Baltimore unless they fight their way at every step.

Z

I therefore hope and trust, and most earnestly request, that no more troops be permitted or ordered by the government to pass through the city. If they should attempt it, the responsibility for the bloodshed will not rest upon me.

With great respect, your obedient servant, GEO. WM. BROWN, Mayor.

I have been in Baltimore since Tuesday evening, and co-operated with Mayor Brown in his untiring efforts to allay and prevent the excitement and suppress the fearful outbreak as indicated above, and I fully concur in all that is said by him in the above communication.

Very respectfully, your obedient servant, THOS. H. HICKS, Governor of Maryland.

President Lincoln to Governor Hicks and Mayor Brown.

Washington, April 20, 1861.

Governor Hicks and Mayor Brown:

GENTLEMEN,—Your letter, by Messrs. Bond, Dobbin, and Brune, is received. I tender you both my sincere thanks for your efforts to keep the peace in the trying situation in which you are placed. For the future, troops *must* be brought here, but I make no point of bringing them *through* Baltimore.

Without any military knowledge myself, of course I must leave details to General Scott. He hastily said this morning, in the presence of these gentlemen, "March them *around* Baltimore, and not through it."

I sincerely hope the general, on fuller reflection, will consider this practical and proper, and that you will not object to it.

By this a collision of the people of Baltimore with the troops will be avoided, unless they go out of their way to seek it. I hope you will exert your influence to prevent this.

Now and ever I shall do all in my power for peace, consistently with the maintenance of the government. Your obedient servant, ABRAHAM LINCOLN.

The governor's agitation was not calmed, however, by the good-natured sympathy of President Lincoln and his readiness of concession. On the contrary, each day the disaffected people of Maryland became more threatening and their governor more alarmed. He now begged that no more troops should be sent not only through Baltimore, but through Maryland, while he proposed, with a strange disregard of the dignity of the government to which he claimed to be loyal, that the English embassador at Washington should be invited to mediate between the United States and its rebellious citizens!

Executive Chamber, Annapolis, April 22, 1861.

To his Excellency A. Lincoln, President of the United States:

SIR,—I feel it my duty most respectfully to advise you that no more troops be ordered or allowed to pass through Maryland, and that the troops now off Annapolis be sent elsewhere; and I most respectfully urge that a truce be offered by you, so that the effusion of blood may be prevented. I respectfully suggest that Lord Lyons be requested to act as mediator between the contending parties of our country.

I have the honor to be, very respectfully, your obedient servant, THOS. H. HICKS.

[2] *Proclamation of the Governor of Maryland.*

Frederick, May 11, 1861.

To the People of Maryland:

A communication from the Mayor of Baltimore to the House of Delegates, published by that body yesterday, is designed to implicate me in the destruction of the railroad bridges near Baltimore on the 19th ultimo; this, too, in face of the fact that I had, in a recent official communication to the Senate, positively denied any complicity in the matter. If the mayor's communication and accompanying certificates have induced any person to doubt my true position in the premises, I respectfully ask a suspension of judgment until a sufficient time be afforded me to collect the necessary proof, and show, as I shall be able to do most conclusively, that the destruction of the bridges was a part of the conspiracy of those acting against the government, and was known and proclaimed in other parts of the state before the destruction was consummated. Whether Mayor Brown did or did not know of this part of the programme, I am unable to say. I am charitable enough to believe that he did not know it. His peculiar surroundings, and agitated condition of mind at the time referred to, may reasonably enough account for his assent to the transaction. But any person who knows my opinion of George P. Kane and Enoch L. Lowe will at once admit that I would be very slow to assent to any proposition emanating from or endorsed by them. Their introduction into my chamber at the late hour of the night to urge my consent to the perpetration of an unlawful act was not calculated to convince me of the propriety or necessity of that act. Men do not readily take counsel of their enemies. So soon as the heavy pressure upon my time shall have somewhat subsided, I will lay before the public a full refutation of this nefarious attempt to involve an innocent person in an unwarranted proceeding. Until that time I request a suspension of public opinion. THOMAS H. HICKS.

[3] *Embargo at Baltimore.*

Baltimore, April 22, 1861.

It is ordered by the Mayor and the Board of Police that no provisions of any kind be transferred

Not only were the militia of the city and the neighborhood kept under arms, but volunteers were enlisted to the number of many thousand men, and an attack upon Fort M'Henry, a national work three miles from the city, was openly threatened. Governor Hicks was swept along with the popular torrent, and on the 22d of April he sent an official advice to the President that no more troops should be allowed to pass, not only through Baltimore, but over the boundaries of Maryland; and to this unreasonable request he added the humiliating recommendation that the President should propose a truce to the insurgents, and ask the British minister at Washington to act as a mediator between them and the government. This communication was of such an extraordinary nature that the President placed it in the hands of the Secretary of State for formal treatment. Mr. Seward, not lowering the government which he represented by a refusal in terms, administered a dignified and considerate rebuke to Governor Hicks for both his proposals, which it was unmistakably, though courteously, intimated could not even be taken into consideration. But the secretary gave just ground of complaint both to the supporters of the government and to the insurgents by telling Governor Hicks that the troops which were coming through Maryland were intended for no other service than the defense of Washington.[4] The men themselves, and those who sent and contributed to equip and provision them, expected that they were to be used to crush the insurrection; and when, not three months after, some of those very troops crossed into Virginia to give battle to the rebel army, the pledge of the United States cabinet minister to the Maryland governor appeared to have been either unauthorized or violated. But the commotion and turbulence of the distracted times confused so many sober minds, and deranged so many carefully-laid plans, that there was excuse for far graver discrepancies than this. The last violent demonstrations on the part of the Baltimoreans against the government were the seizure on the 24th of Relay House, a station on the Baltimore and Ohio Railway, which was held by six hundred picked men and four field-pieces, the object being to cut off the communication of Pennsylvania with Washington by that route; and, after the removal of about twenty-five hundred men, chiefly Pennsylvania militia, from Cockeysville, a village on the Baltimore and Susquehanna Railway, seventeen miles from the former place, the destruction of all the bridges except one upon that line

BURNING OF THE BRIDGE AT CANTON, MARYLAND, BY THE MOB.

within the limits of the state. Meanwhile the carriage-roads leading from Baltimore were thronged with vehicles filled with households and household goods, seeking safety in more peaceful places.

But although Massachusetts, by her promptitude, obtained the post of honor and of danger in these early days of the insurrection, the people of the other loyal states were no laggards, and those of New York strove with their brethren of the East in noble emulation. The annals of these days can not be silent upon the march of the New York Seventh Regiment, "National Guard," to Washington, without passing over some of their most interesting incidents. This regiment, which for two generations had represented, more than any other body of militia, the higher social and intellectual culture of the great commercial metropolis, had early attained and steadily preserved an equal distinction in drill and in discipline. And, unlike the other regiments of the same city, its service had not been entirely confined to encountering the perils of Broadway upon parade-days, between the Battery and Union Square. It had been called into service at the time of the Astor Place Riot, on which occasion, after having distinguished itself for hours in the face of the mob by the preservation of discipline, and the patient and even good-natured endurance of injuries from showers of paving-stones, it had obeyed promptly the command to fire, and by three compact and well-delivered volleys had put an end forever to riots in New York. The imbecility of the city government, which needlessly allowed this disturbance to grow to such a terrible issue, could bring no reproach upon the body of citizen soldiers who bore the brunt of it so manfully, and ended it so effectually. At another time, when Fernando Wood, the same mayor of New York whom we have seen so ready to meet the demands of the insurgents of Georgia for their arms, and to follow their example by proposing a secession of the city from the state, forcibly resisted the execution of the Metropolitan Police Law, which secured peace and order to the city and the surrounding district by removing its police from the influence of party politics, this regiment exhibited its *esprit de corps* and its discipline by twice instantly facing about to meet the requirements of the Police Commissioners, though at the apparent loss of formal and long-prepared festivities in honor of the regiment by the citizens of Boston, to join in which it was on its march at the receipt of the order; and such was the reliance upon this body of men, that although, at the time of the second order, it was in Boston, and there were several other regiments in New York, it was summoned by telegraph from the former city. Its reputation, like its name, was national, and, in fact, had extended across the ocean. The whole division, of which this regiment formed a part, had been placed at the service of the government by its major general at a time when there was yet hope that an appeal to arms might be avoided; and now, when the seat of the national government was in hourly peril, the Seventh at once stepped forward to assume a three months' service, and to go immediately on to Washington. The announcement that it was going begat a sort of confidence in those days, when, dark and gloomy though they were, the nature, the extent, and the duration of the coming conflict was entirely unforeseen. It was felt that the presence of the regiment in Washington, in support of the handful of regular troops assembled there, would deter any attack not more formidable and thoroughly organized than the insurgents were supposed to have prepared. The excited patriotic feeling of the city concentrated for the moment upon the movements of this regiment; during the two or three days of preparation an eager throng surrounded its head-quarters, where recently-recruited members, young men of fortune and fashion, and the highest education, were drilling day and night to attain such proficiency as would admit them as privates to the ranks upon the projected expedition. It was on the 19th of April that the Seventh set out for Washington. Its departure from the armory had been delayed for some hours, and meantime the news had come on by telegraph of the attack upon the Massachusetts men in Baltimore. It flew through the city, quickening general apprehension, deepening the general gloom, and stimulating the military ardor of the departing soldiers by the spur of emulation and the hope of distinction. The whole city seemed to pour out its population upon the line of march and the point of embarkation of this specially favored corps. The ranks were full, and more than full; never upon a gala-day had they shown more muskets. The moment of departure at last arrived. Pale with suppressed excitement, the peace-bred soldiers heard the command which ordered them to begin their march toward the enemy; a thousand feet with steady tread at once responded, and the regiment moved swiftly onward. Decked in no holiday garb, but grimly panoplied in gray and steel, with its colonel marching at its head, its serried files wheeled into the great thoroughfare in which its fine discipline and soldierly bearing had so often been objects of admiring comment; and there a spectacle met the eye never seen before in this country, without a doubt never to be seen again. For the occasion gave it its peculiar character. Broadway had been before as crowded (for what is full can not be fuller), but never with a throng so animated, so admiring, so solicitous, so self-sacrificing. The great artery of New York life throbbed and palpitated throughout its length with the big emotions of the public heart. As the head of the column appeared, a shout burst forth that flashed like the fire of a *feu-de-joie* from lip to lip along the line of march, advancing before the regiment and following after, and never ceasing or dying away while a musket remained in sight. Not a cheer, or a succession of cheers, but a great cry that went up continuously to heaven, and bore up with it the unspeakable aspirations of the vast multitude. The sound fell strangely and never to be forgotten upon the ears of all within its reach, for in its tone there was a wild and plaintive yearning which they had never heard before. The Seventh began its service by a march through two miles of such a crowd, uttering ceaseless encouragement and benediction. Thus the great city gave up the flower of its young men freely to the country's cause; though, as their bayonets passed out of sight, they flashed the rays of the setting sun on manly eyes all dim with unaccustomed moisture. New York saw in after times hundreds of thousands of brave men march through her streets on like errands and to bloodier business, and gave them all a hearty

from the city of Baltimore to any point or place, from this time until farther orders, without special permission.

The execution of this order is intrusted to Colonel I. R. Trimble.

The following order has been issued:

It being deemed necessary for the safety and protection of the city that no steam-boat be permitted to leave our harbor without the sanction of the city authorities, I hereby, by authority of the Mayor and Board of Police, direct that no steam-boat shall leave the harbor without my permit.

I. R. TRIMBLE, Commanding.

[4] *Secretary Seward to Governor Hicks.*

Department of State, April 22, 1861.

To his Excellency Thomas H. Hicks, Governor of Maryland:

SIR,—I have had the honor to receive your communication of this morning, in which you inform me that you have felt it to be your duty to advise the President of the United States to order elsewhere the troops then off Annapolis, and also that no more may be sent through Maryland, and that you have farther suggested that Lord Lyons be requested to act as mediator between the contending parties in our country, to prevent the effusion of blood.

The President directs me to acknowledge the receipt of that communication, and to assure you that he has weighed the counsels which it contains with the respect which he habitually cherishes for the chief magistrates of the several states, and especially for yourself. He regrets, as deeply as any magistrate or citizen of the country can, that demonstrations against the safety of the United States, with very extensive preparations for the effusion of blood, have made it his duty to call out the force to which you allude.

The force now sought to be brought through Maryland is intended for nothing but the defense of this capital. The President has necessarily confided the choice of the national highway which that force shall take in coming to this city to the lieutenant general commanding the army of the United States, who, like his only predecessor, is not less distinguished for his humanity than for his loyalty, patriotism, and distinguished public service.

The President instructs me to add that the national highway thus selected by the lieutenant general has been chosen by him, upon consultation with prominent magistrates and citizens of Maryland, as the one which, while a route is absolutely necessary, is farthest removed from the populous cities of the state, and with the expectation that it would, therefore, be the least objectionable one.

The President can not but remember that there has been a time in the history of our country when a general of the American Union, with forces designed for the defense of its capital, was not unwelcome any where in the State of Maryland, and certainly not at Annapolis, then, as now, the capital of that patriotic state, and then, also, one of the capitals of the Union.

If eighty years could have obliterated all the other nobler sentiments of that age in Maryland, the President would be hopeful, nevertheless, that there is one that would forever remain there and every where. That sentiment is that no domestic contention whatever that may arise among the parties of this republic ought in any case to be referred to any foreign arbitrament, least of all to the arbitrament of a European monarchy.

I have the honor to be, with distinguished consideration, your excellency's most obedient servant,

WILLIAM H. SEWARD.

THE SEVENTH REGIMENT MARCHING DOWN BROADWAY TO EMBARK FOR THE WAR.

welcome and God-speed; the Seventh itself was cheered and petted by the whole country through which it passed on its way to Washington; but this was the first, and they were felt (though perhaps partially) to be the best; and neither the men who went nor the people who sent them ever knew again the chivalrous enthusiasm of that day, the tender, solemn rapture of that parting.

It was not until six days afterward that the Guard reached Washington; but it will be well to follow them directly to their destination, for their progress thither was immediately involved with some of the many significant occurrences which throng so thickly along this eventful period. They passed swiftly upon the railway through New Jersey, a state which has the reputation of being somewhat sluggish in its sympathies, and yet its people poured out along the track in such numbers, that one member of the regiment, who gave an account of its march, said that he "did not see a rod of ground without its man from dusk till dawn, from the Hudson to the Delaware."[5] Philadelphia welcomed their coming, but could not speed their parting. All communication by railway between that city and Baltimore was effectually cut off before they reached it on the 20th; and for many hours they trod with fretful steps the formal streets of the hospitable town, which was but to them a station on the road to Baltimore. At last, all other modes of transportation proving hopeless, a steam-boat was chartered, and they started for Washington by way, not of Baltimore, but of Annapolis, the old and drowsy capital of Maryland. In taking this step their colonel (Marshall Lefferts) followed the lead of a man whose position and peculiar talents obtained for him a singular prominence in the drama to which the events which have been thus far recounted were but a prelude.

General Butler, an eminent member of the bar, and an officer of the militia of Massachusetts, had been placed by Governor Andrew in command of the Massachusetts regiments which were sent as part of the contingent of that state, under the President's proclamation, to the relief of Washington. He was a Democrat of the straitest sect, an active and life-long supporter of the party which for years had ruled the country by its alliance with the slaveholders of the South. He had been a member of the presidential nominating convention which met at Charleston; and he had given his hearty support, during the subsequent canvass, to Mr. Breckinridge, the candidate of the extreme slavery faction. But secession had opened his never very closely shut eyes to the policy of the men who ruled that convention, and he had declared at once and with the earnestness of a whole-hearted nature for the nation against his late political associates. In this he was a representative man, and his appearance in the service of the republic against the insurgents had for them and for the country at large a very great significance. It told more unmistakably, perhaps, than any other single event which had taken place, the supreme devotion of the people of the free states to the Union. The presence of such a man at the head of a brigade of Massachusetts troops on the march to put down the slaveholders' insurrection

was made yet the more striking by the fact that he was placed in command by Governor Andrew, who was prominent among the extreme, or, so-called, radical Republicans.

The news of the attack upon one detachment of his command flying northward, passed General Butler at Philadelphia, where he had arrived with the Eighth Massachusetts regiment. With a sagacious perception and prompt decision, which showed at the very first step that he was a leader, he saw that the consequence of the attack would be the destruction of the bridges between Philadelphia and Baltimore, and he determined to move instantly upon the latter place by way of Annapolis, occupying and holding the capital of Maryland; thus, in the words of his dispatch upon the occasion, calling the state to account for the death of Massachusetts men, his friends and neighbors. On the evening of the 20th he transported his command to Havre de Grace, upon the Susquehanna, and, seizing upon the large and powerful ferry-boat Maryland, steamed down the Chesapeake. He arrived at Annapolis on the morning of the 21st, and found there the Governor of Maryland and a body of insurgents—the one powerless in the hands of the other. The disaffected controlled the city, held the grounds of the United States Naval Academy there, and were about to seize upon the school-ship "Old Ironsides," as the superannuated frigate Constitution, the war-worn victor of many fights, had, for more than a generation, been fondly named. General Butler at once called for mariners from his command, and enough stepped forward to man the old ship for the nonce. They were placed on board, and by their aid and that of the Maryland she was towed out into the stream, where her guns were shotted and trained upon the shore; but the Maryland herself, with the troops still on board, ran aground, and remained fast until the next day. Meantime the New York Seventh Regiment, which had left Philadelphia in the steamer Boston, arrived, and was placed by its colonel under the command of General Butler; the Maryland was hauled off, and both regiments landed and took possession of the grounds of the Naval Academy. Against this landing of "Northern troops" upon the soil of Maryland Governor Hicks sent General Butler a formal protest; but the latter persisted—first showing, in reply, that the necessities of his position, the health of the men under his command, and the instructions of his government, made it imperative that he should land and march quickly through Maryland to Washington, respecting private property, outraging the rights of none, but, on the contrary, using his force, if necessary, to preserve the peace of Maryland as well as the authority of the national government, and having issued strict orders as to the drill and discipline of his soldiers, and congratulations upon their saving the Constitution—and the governor could not do otherwise than submit. It is worthy of notice that the Massachusetts general administered a respectful rebuke to the Maryland governor for his "ill-advised designation" of the troops under the general's command. "They are," said he, "not Northern troops; they are a part of the whole militia of the United States, obeying the call of the President."[6] Thus

---

[5] Major Theodore Winthrop, in the *Atlantic Monthly* for June, 1861.

[6] *General Butler to Governor Hicks.*

Off Annapolis, April 22, 1861.

To his Excellency Thomas H. Hicks, Governor of Maryland:

In reply to the communication from you on the 21st, I had the honor to inform you of the necessities of my command, which drew me into the harbor of Annapolis. My circumstances have not changed. To that communication I have received no reply. I can not return, if I desire so to do, without being furnished with some necessary supplies, for all which the money will be paid. I desire of your excellency an immediate reply whether I have the permission of the state authorities of Maryland to land the men under my command, and of passing quickly through the state on my way to Washington, respecting private property and paying for what I receive, and outraging the rights of none—a duty which I am bound to do in obedience to the requisitions of the President of the United States.

I have received some copies of an informal correspondence between the Mayor of Baltimore and the President of the Baltimore and Ohio Railroad, and a copy of a note from your excellency, inclosing the same to Captain Blake, commandant of the Naval School. These purport to show that instructions have been issued by the War Department as to the disposition of the United States militia, differing from what I had supposed to be my duty. If these instructions have been in fact issued, it would give me great pleasure to obey them. Have I your excellency's permission, in consideration of these exigencies of the case, to land my men, to supply their wants, and to relieve them from the extreme and unhealthy confinement of a transport vessel not fitted to receive them? To convince your excellency of the good faith toward the authorities of the State of Maryland with which I am acting, and I am armed only against the disturbers of her peace and of the United States, I inclose a copy of an order issued to my command before I had the

honor of receiving the copy of your communication through Captain Blake. I trust your excellency will appreciate the necessities of my position and give me an immediate reply, which I await with anxiety.

I would do myself the honor to have a personal interview with your excellency, if you so desire. I beg leave to call your excellency's attention to what I hope I may be pardoned for deeming an ill-advised designation of the men under my command. *They are not Northern troops; they are a part of the whole militia of the United States, obeying the call of the President.*

I have the honor of being your excellency's obedient servant,

BENJ. F. BUTLER, Brigadier General in the Militia of the United States.

P.S.—It occurs to me that our landing on the grounds at the Naval Academy would be entirely proper, and in accordance with your excellency's wishes. B. F. B.

Special Brigade Order, No. 37.

Head-quarters Second Division Massachusetts Volunteer Militia, on board Steamer Maryland, off Annapolis, April 22, 1861.

Colonel Munroe is charged with the execution of the following order: At 5 o'clock A.M. the troops will be paraded by company, and be drilled in the manual of arms, especially in loading at will, firing by file, and in the use of the bayonet; and these specialties will be observed in all subsequent drills in the manual. Such drill to continue until 7 o'clock, when all the arms will be stacked on the upper deck, great care being taken to instruct the men as to the mode of stacking their arms, so that a firm stack, not easily overturned, shall be made. Being obliged to drill at times with the weapons loaded, great damage may be done by the overturning of the stack and the discharge of the pieces. This is important. Indeed, an accident has already occurred in the regiment from this cause, and, although slight in its consequences, yet it warns us to increased diligence in this regard. The purpose which could only be hinted at in the orders of yesterday

REFERENCES.—1. Catholic College.—2. City Hotel.—3. Battery.—4. Capitol.—5. Midshipmen's Quarters.—6. *Constitution.*—7. Recitation Hall.—8. Chapel.—9. Observatory.—10. Officers' Quarters.—11. St. John's (Episcopal) College.—12. Hospital.—13. Monument—the same that was in front of the Capitol at Washington.—14. Naval Monument.

GENERAL VIEW OF ANNAPOLIS, WITH THE "CONSTITUTION" IN THE FOREGROUND.

THE MEN OF THE EIGHTH MASSACHUSETTS REGIMENT REPAIRING THE BRIDGES ON THE RAILROAD FROM ANNAPOLIS TO WASHINGTON.

sharply did this question define, and thus continuously present itself in the earlier stages of the conflict of which it was the great issue, though not the exciting cause. That cause I shall consider more particularly hereafter. But accident furnished General Butler with opportunity of showing how far from his intention was the attempt to change, or even the acquiescence in any violent attempt to change, the relation between master and slave. An insurrection of the slaves around Annapolis was at the time feared, and General Butler offered the governor the services of his troops for its suppression, or that of any other resistance to the laws of Maryland. For this offer he met with a mild though firm rebuke from his Abolitionist govern-

or; but in turn he defended himself with entire success, on the grounds both of humanity and policy.[7]

The difficulties in the apparently simple and easy task of landing two thousand loyal citizens of the United States, in obedience to the command of the President, upon the soil of one of those states which still acknowledged its old allegiance, having been thus overcome, there remained the not less serious task of moving across its territory. The insurgents had torn up the rails of the Annapolis and Elk Ridge Railway, of which General Butler took possession, and to the repairing of which the men of the Eighth Massachusetts at once addressed themselves. Indeed, the various capacity of this

has been accomplished. The frigate *Constitution* has lain for a long time at this port substantially at the mercy of the armed mob, which sometimes paralyzes the otherwise loyal State of Maryland. Deeds of daring, successful contests, and glorious victories had rendered "Old Ironsides" so conspicuous in the naval history of the country, that she was fitly chosen as the school-ship in which to train the future officers of the navy to like heroic acts.

It was given to Massachusetts, and Essex County, first to man her; it was reserved for Massachusetts to have the honor to retain her for the service of the Union and the laws.

This is a sufficient triumph of right, and a sufficient triumph for us. By this the blood of our friends shed by the Baltimore mob is in so far avenged. The Eighth Regiment may hereafter cheer lustily on all proper occasions, but never without orders. The old *Constitution*, by their efforts, aided untiringly by the United States officers having her in charge, is now safely "possessed, occupied, and enjoyed" by the government of the United States, and is safe from all her foes.

We have been joined by the Seventh Regiment of New York, and together we propose peaceably, quickly, and civilly, unless opposed by some mob or other disorderly persons, to march to Washington, in obedience to the requisition of the President of the United States. If opposed, we shall march steadily forward.

My next order I hardly know how to express. I can not assume that any of the citizen soldiery of Massachusetts or New York could, under any circumstances whatever, commit any outrages upon private property in a loyal and friendly state. But, fearing that some improper person may have by stealth introduced himself among us, I deem it proper to state that any unauthorized interference with private property will be most signally punished, and full reparation therefore made to the injured party to the full extent of my power and ability. In so doing I but carry out the orders of the War Department. I should have done so without those orders.

Colonel Munroe will cause these orders to be read at the head of each company before we march.

Colonel Lefferts's command not having been originally included in this order, he will be furnished with a copy for his instruction. By order of

[Signed],   B. F. BUTLER, Brigadier General.
                             WM. H. CLEMENS, Brigade Major.

State of Maryland, Executive Chamber, Annapolis, April 22, 1861.

To Brigadier General B. F. Butler:

SIR,—I am in receipt of your two communications of this date, informing me of your intention to land the men under your command at Annapolis, for the purpose of marching thence to the city of Washington. I content myself with protesting against this movement, which, in view of the excited condition of the people of this state, I can not but consider an unwise step on the part of the government. But I most earnestly urge upon you that there shall be no halt made by the troops in this city. Very respectfully, your obedient servant,   TH. H. HICKS.

[7]   *General Butler to Governor Hicks.*

Head-quarters Third Brigade Massachusetts Volunteer Militia, Annapolis, Maryland, April 23, 1861.

To his Excellency Thomas H. Hicks, Governor of the State of Maryland:

I did myself the honor in my communication of yesterday, wherein I asked permission to land the portion of the militia of the United States under my command, to state that they were armed only against the disturbers of the peace of the State of Maryland and of the United States.

I have understood within the last hour that some apprehensions were entertained of an insurrection of the negro population of this neighborhood. I am anxious to convince all classes of persons that the forces under my command are not here in any way to interfere with or countenance any interference with the laws of the state. I am, therefore, ready to co-operate with your excellency in suppressing most promptly and effectively any insurrection against the laws of Maryland.

I beg, therefore, that you announce publicly that any portion of the forces under my command

is at your excellency's disposal, to act immediately for the preservation and quietness of the peace of this community.

And I have the honor to be your excellency's obedient servant,
                             B. F. BUTLER, General of the Third Brigade.

Correspondence between Governor Andrew and General Butler.

Commonwealth of Massachusetts, Executive Department, Council Chamber, Boston, April 25, 1861.

GENERAL,—I have received through Major Ames a dispatch transmitted from Perryville, detailing the proceedings at Annapolis from the time of your arrival off that port until the hour when Major Ames left you to return to Philadelphia. I wish to repeat the assurance of my entire satisfaction with the action you have taken, with a single exception. If I rightly understood the telegraphic dispatch, I think that your action in tendering to Governor Hicks the assistance of our Massachusetts troops to suppress a threatened servile insurrection among the hostile people of Maryland was unnecessary. I hope that the fuller dispatches, which are on their way from you, may show reasons why I should modify my opinion concerning that particular instance; but, in general, I think that the matter of servile insurrection among a community in arms against the federal Union is no longer to be regarded by our troops in a political, but solely in a military point of view, and is to be contemplated as one of the inherent weaknesses of the enemy, from the disastrous operations of which we are under no obligation of a military character to guard them, in order that they may be enabled to improve the security which our arms would afford so as to prosecute with more energy their traitorous attacks upon the federal government and capital. The mode in which such outbreaks are to be considered should depend entirely upon the loyalty or disloyalty of the community in which they occur; and in the vicinity of Annapolis, I can, on this occasion, perceive no reason of military policy why a force summoned to the defense of the federal government, at this moment of all others, should be offered to be diverted from its immediate duty to help rebels who stand with arms in their hands, obstructing its progress toward the city of Washington. I entertain no doubt that whenever we shall have an opportunity to interchange our views personally on this subject, we shall arrive at entire concordance of opinion.

Yours faithfully,   JOHN A. ANDREW.

To Brigadier General Butler.

Department of Annapolis, Head-quarters, Annapolis, May 9, 1861.

To his Excellency John A. Andrew, Governor and Commander-in-Chief:

SIR,—I have delayed replying to your excellency's dispatch of the 25th of April in my other dispatches, because, as it involved disapprobation of an act done, couched in the kindest language, I supposed the interest of the country could not suffer in the delay; and incessant labor up to the present moment has prevented me giving full consideration to the topic. Temporary illness, which forbids bodily activity, gives me now a moment's pause.

The telegraph, with more than usual accuracy, had rightly informed your excellency that I had offered the services of the Massachusetts troops under my command to aid the authorities of Maryland in suppressing a threatened slave insurrection. Fortunately for us all, the rumor of such an outbreak was without substantial foundation. Assuming, as your excellency does in your dispatch, that I was carrying on military operations in an enemy's country, when a way *à l'outrance* was to be waged, my act might be a matter of discussion. And in that view, acting in the light of the Baltimore murderers, and the apparent hostile position of Maryland, your excellency might, without mature reflection, have come to the conclusion of disapprobation expressed in your dispatch. But the facts, especially as now aided by their results, will entirely justify my act, and reinstate me in your excellency's good opinion.

True, I landed on the soil of Maryland against the formal protest of its governor and of the corporate authorities of Annapolis, but without any armed opposition on their part, and expecting opposition only from insurgents assembled in riotous contempt of the laws of the state. Before,

A A

fine body of men, which seemed to be largely composed of skilled artisans, was one of the noteworthy features of their march to Washington. As they had furnished mariners to work the Constitution, so now, upon call, machinits, engineers, and iron-workers stepped forward in great numbers. The rails had not only been torn up, but carried off and hid; but they were unearthed, and even traced to and taken from the bottom of the river as if by instinct. The only engine to be found had been taken to pieces and partly destroyed, and, upon inquiry for a man who could put it in running order, one of the Beverly Light Guard, recognizing in a piece of the machine his own handiwork, promptly and successfully undertook to mend what he had made, some of his companions erecting, and others working, the temporary forges which were required. Cheerfully and thoroughly they did these tasks while they were starving; for, owing to some blunder or accident, few had eaten any thing for twenty-four, and some not for thirty hours. The Seventh found this out, and in a moment their own haversacks were opened, and the hungry men were filled, and furnished for the morrow. Governor Hicks continued to protest—this time against the occupation of the railway, on the ground that by this act the members of the Legislature, which was about to meet at Annapolis, would be prevented from reaching the seat of government. But this plea General Butler extinguished by reminding the governor that he himself had objected to the landing of the troops on the ground that, as the railway was hopelessly destroyed, they could not leave the city by it, and demurely pointing out that, if the troops could not pass one way, the Legislature could not pass the other; adding, with an irony all the keener because its edge was fact, that he only sought means of transportation that he might vacate the capital, and not encumber that "beautiful city" during the session of the Legislature.[8]

The railway repaired, and the engines and cars sufficient for the sick, the small howitzer battery of the Seventh, and the baggage, put in running order, the march to Washington began on the morning of the 24th, and, leaving the good people of Annapolis astonished at the strictly correct behavior, the universal courtesy, and even the open-handed generosity of a body of men whom the disorganizers had led them to believe were but a well-drilled band of ruffians, the Seventh led the column toward the capital. The picture of their patriotic journey would be incomplete were the gallantry which animated them left unillustrated by a declaration made on their behalf as to some of the foes whom they had reason to believe they would encounter. As individuals they had visited residents of Maryland and Virginia, and as a body they had enjoyed the hospitality of some of the military companies of those commonwealths, where they had friends whom they in turn had welcomed and entertained at New York. *These* men were furious in their denunciations of the Seventh in particular, and in their threats of bloody vengeance on it; but the members of that regiment, expressing their wonder at the hostility thus manifested on occasion of their mere march to the defense of Washington, said, "If, in the performance of duty, we shall be compelled to meet our friends of the Baltimore City Guard and the Richmond Grays in hostile array, we shall receive their first fire with presented arms, but on the second we shall be compelled to defend ourselves." Thus implacably malevolent were the self-styled chivalry of the labor-loathing slave section; and with such high-toned and truly chivalrous bearing, reminding us of the elaborate courtesy of the French Guard at Fontenoy, were they met by the simple and unpretending citizen soldiers of a commonwealth whose greatness was based on industry, and whose chief glory was in freedom. The march to Washington tried the endurance of the Seventh sorely. Begun in the morning, it was continued through the day under a blazing sun, over ground on which long stretches of hot and shifting sand were varied only by the wooden sleepers of the railway, progress over which was extraordinarily fatiguing. The railway was chosen instead of the turnpike road because it had been discovered that parties of cavalry had been posted along the latter route for the purpose of cutting off the regiment. Needful caution and the difficulties of the way made the march a very slow one; but the men kept steadily on, with an occasional halt at a station for brief rest and refreshment. All suffered greatly from fatigue and heat; and a few broke down and increased the sick-list. Night fell upon the slowly advancing column: it was the fourth which most of them had been obliged to give to service instead of to slumber, and they staggered wearily through the monotonous obstacles of their march, startled at intervals to life and braced to action by the distant dropping shot of an outlying rebel, watching vainly for their blood. In this way, scouting the country round and feeling every rod of the road, they advanced little more than one mile an hour; and, although the last stages of their progress were easy, it was not until the 25th, six days after their departure from New York, that they arrived at the capital. Before them there were only five hundred raw, undrilled men from Pennsylvania, and the Sixth Massachusetts regiment, fresh from its bloody initiation into military life at Baltimore. As they marched up the broad avenue to the White House, the roll of their drums made loyal hearts leap for joy, and sounded like the doom of treachery. But, to look forward, and to dismiss this regiment honorably from our sight, the fortunes of the war decreed that the New York Seventh should see no active service. They remained the full time for which the President's proclamation summoned them, and longer; these New York dandies worked in trenches and lay down to rest in mud; they again returned to the defense of Washington, but they never were under fire as a body. So high, however, was the reputation of the regiment for drill and discipline, that its members, even non-commissioned officers and privates, were eagerly sought as company and field-officers for newly-formed volunteer regiments, and a very large number thus entered the army and served through the war, in many cases with distinction. The composition of the corps, its reputation, the fact that it was regarded as representing the peculiarly conservative classes of the commercial metropolis of the country, and the promptness with which it volunteered to lead what was believed at the time to be the forlorn hope of the republic, have entitled it to a more prominent place in the earlier pages of this history than can be given hereafter to some bodies of men which displayed all its spirit and its patriotism, and which had ten times its numbers.

While these events were taking place near the capital, which had been so suddenly isolated from the loyal millions of the North, they were every where assembling to express, in a formal and solemn manner, their determination to support the government with their lives and their fortunes.

---

by letter, and at the time of landing, by personal interview, I had informed Governor Hicks that soldiers of the Union, under my command, were armed only against the insurgents and disturbers of the peace of Maryland and of the United States. I received from Governor Hicks assurances of the loyalty of the state to the Union—assurances which subsequent events have fully justified. The Mayor of Annapolis also informed me that the city authorities would in nowise oppose me, but that I was in great danger from the excited and riotous mobs of Baltimore pouring down upon me, and in numbers beyond the control of the police. I assured both the governor and the mayor that I had no fear of a Baltimore or other mob, and that, supported by the authorities of the state and city, I should repress all hostile demonstrations against the laws of Maryland and the United States, and that I would protect both myself and the city of Annapolis from any disorderly persons whatsoever. On the morning following my landing I was informed that the city of Annapolis and environs were in danger from an insurrection of the slave population, in defiance of the laws of the state. What was I to do? I had promised to put down a white mob, and to preserve and enforce the laws against that. Ought I to allow a black one any preference in a breach of the laws? I understood that I was armed against all infractions of the laws, whether by white or black, and upon that understanding I acted, certainly with promptness and efficiency. And your excellency's shadow of disapprobation, arising from a misunderstanding of the facts, has caused all the regret I have for that action. The question seemed to me to be neither military nor political, and was not to be so treated. It was simply a question of good faith and honesty of purpose. The benign effect of my course was instantly seen. The good but timid people of Annapolis, who had fled from their houses at our approach, immediately returned; business resumed its accustomed channels; quiet and order prevailed in the city; confidence took the place of distrust, friendship of enmity, brotherly kindness of sectional hate, and I believe to-day there is no city in the Union more loyal than the city of Annapolis. I think, therefore, I may safely point to the results for my justification. The vote of the neighboring county of Washington, a few days since, for its delegate to the Legislature, wherein 4000 out of 5000 votes were thrown for a delegate favorable to the Union, is among the many happy fruits of firmness of purpose, efficiency of action, and integrity of mission. I believe, indeed, that it will not require a personal interchange of views, as suggested in your dispatch, to bring our minds in accordance; a simple statement of the facts will suffice.

But I am to act hereafter, it may be, in an enemy's country, among a servile population, when the question may arise, as it has not yet arisen, as well in a moral and Christian, as in a political and military point of view, What shall I do? Will your excellency bear with me a moment while this question is discussed?

I appreciate fully your excellency's suggestion as to the inherent weakness of the rebels, arising from the preponderance of their servile population. The question, then, is, In what manner shall we take advantage of that weakness? By allowing, and of course arming, that population to rise upon the defenseless women and children of the country, carrying rapine, arson, and murder—all the horrors of San Domingo, a million times magnified, among those whom we hope to reunite with us as brethren, many of whom are already so, and all who are worth preserving will be, when this horrible madness shall have passed away or be thrashed out of them? Would your excellency advise the troops under my command to make war in person upon the defenseless women and children of any part of the Union, accompanied with brutalities too horrible to be named? You will say, "God forbid!" If we may not do so in person, shall we arm others so to do over whom we can have no restraint, exercise no control, and who, when once they have tasted blood, may turn the very arms we put in their hands against ourselves, as a part of the oppressing white race? The reading of history, so familiar to your excellency, will tell you the bitterest cause of complaint which our fathers had against Great Britain in the war of the Revolution was the arming by the British ministry of the red man with the tomahawk and the scalping-knife against the women and children of the colonies, so that the phrase, "May we not use all the means which God and Nature have put in our power to subjugate the colonies?" has passed into a legend of infamy against the leader of that ministry who used it in Parliament. Shall history teach us in vain? Could we justify ourselves to ourselves? Although, with arms in our hands, amid the savage wildness of camp and field, we may have blunted many of the finer moral sensibilities in letting loose four millions of worse than savages upon the homes and hearths of the South, can we be justified to the Christian community of Massachusetts? Would such a course be consonant with the teachings of our holy religion? I have a very decided opinion upon the subject, and if any one desires, as I know your excellency does not, this unhappy contest to be prosecuted in that manner, some instrument other than myself must be found to carry it on. I may not discuss the political bearings of this topic. When I went from under the shadow of my roof-tree, I left all politics behind me, to be resumed only when every part of the Union is loyal to the flag, and the potency of the government through the ballot-box is established.

Passing the moral and Christian view, let us examine the subject as a military question. Is not that state already subjugated which requires the bayonets of those armed in opposition to its rulers to preserve it from the horrors of a servile war? As the least experienced of military men, I would have no doubt of the entire subjugation of a state brought to that condition. When, therefore—unless I am better advised—any community in the United States, who have met me in honorable warfare, or even in the prosecution of a rebellious war in an honorable manner, shall call upon me for protection against the nameless horrors of a servile insurrection, they shall have it, and from the moment that call is obeyed, I have no doubt we shall be friends, and not enemies.

The possibilities that dishonorable means of defense are to be taken by the rebels against the government I do not now contemplate. If, as has been done in a single instance, my men are to be attacked by poison, or, as in another, stricken down by the assassin's knife, and thus murdered, the community using such weapons may be required to be taught that it holds within its own border a more potent means for deadly purposes and indiscriminate slaughter than any which it can administer to us.

Trusting that these views may meet your excellency's approval, I have the honor to be, very respectfully, your obedient servant,
BENJ. F. BUTLER.

8 *Correspondence between Governor Hicks and General Butler.*

Executive Chamber, Annapolis, Friday, April 23, 1861.

To Brigadier General B. F. Butler:

SIR,—Having, by virtue of the powers vested in me by the Constitution of Maryland, summoned the Legislature of the state to assemble on Friday, the 26th instant, and Annapolis being the place in which, according to law, it must assemble; and having been credibly informed that you have taken military possession of the Annapolis and Elk Ridge Railroad, I deem it my duty to protest against this step, because, without at present assigning any other reason, I am informed that such occupation of said road will prevent the members of the Legislature from reaching this city. Very respectfully yours, THOMAS H. HICKS.

To which General Butler replied as follows:

Head-quarters United States Militia, Annapolis, Maryland, April 23, 1861.

To his Excellency Thomas H. Hicks, Governor of Maryland:

You are credibly informed that I have taken possession of the Annapolis and Elk Ridge Railroad. It might have escaped your notice, but at the official meeting which was held between your excellency and the Mayor of Annapolis, and the committee of the government and myself, as to the landing of my troops, it was expressly stated as the reason why I should not land that my troops could not pass the railroad because the company had taken up the rails, and they were private property. It is difficult to see how it can be, that if my troops could not pass over the railroad one way, the members of the Legislature could pass the other way. I have taken possession for the purpose of preventing the execution of the threats of the mob, as officially represented to me by the Master of Transportation of the railroad in this city, "that if my troops passed over the railroad, the railroad should be destroyed."

If the government of the state had taken possession of the road in any emergency, I should have long hesitated before entering upon it; but as I had the honor to inform your excellency in regard to another insurrection against the laws of Maryland, I am here armed to maintain those laws, if your excellency desires, and the peace of the United States, against all disorderly persons whatsoever. I am endeavoring to save and not to destroy; to obtain means of transportation, so that I can vacate the capital prior to the sitting of the Legislature, and not be under the necessity of encumbering your beautiful city while the Legislature is in session.

I have the honor to be, very respectfully, your excellency's obedient servant,
B. F. BUTLER, Brigadier General.

THE SEVENTH REGIMENT NEW YORK STATE MILITIA HALTING FOR A REST ON THE MARCH TO ANNAPOLIS JUNCTION.

"Union Meetings," as they were called, were held at all the cities and principal towns of the free states; and at all of them there was an expression of the same fervid devotion to the cause of constitutional liberty and the republic, varied only, and not too much, in the form of words in which it was uttered. Of these meetings, that held at New York on the 20th of April deserves notice as of national consequence. The pre-eminence of the place in which it was held made it the most important, the distinction and the various political views and relations of its managers and speakers the most characteristic, and its numbers the most imposing. The city of New York was, of all places in the free states, the one in which there was the least disposition to resist any demands made in the interests of slavery. No insignificant proportion of her inhabitants was directly bound by ties of blood and intermarriage to the people of the slave states; a still larger number were closely connected with them by business relations; and within her walls, chiefly by its command of the votes of naturalized Irish emigrants, the Democratic party, the ever-faithful ally of the slave power, ruled supreme. And in an age and in a country in which commerce, trade, and labor have a social and political consideration which they never before enjoyed, the city, which was at once the great mart, treasure-house, and labor exchange of the land, had acquired an influence whose extent was limited only by the bounds of civilization, and whose power was diminished little by the effect of distance. There was no part of the country the prosperity of which was not more or less involved in her stability and welfare. The vast crops of the West moved to the sea-board upon railways and canals, and those of both West and South were borne to Europe in ships, built chiefly by her capital, which seemed to have no limit except the demands for its employment. Every trader in the country, from the merchant who sold cargoes in the quiet of a luxurious office, to the peddler who painfully bore his little stock upon his bending back, was directly or indirectly her tributary debtor. To her the agriculturist and the manufacturer looked to find at home or make abroad a market for the fruits of his labor. The harbors of the Atlantic and the Pacific Ocean filled with her ships, and the expanse of the great interior seas of the North plowed by keels floated from her harbor through canals, showed her the great carrier as well as the great factor and the great negotiator of a continent. Her capital insured the goods and even the lives that her commercial enterprise sent out upon these waters. With this position of command came a corresponding responsibility. Agriculture may flourish upon any field not trodden under foot of hostile armies; but trade thrives only amid general stability, and the sails of commerce must be wafted by the gales of peace. Therefore from the first mutterings of sectional discord the efforts of New York had been to set aside the issue and still the trouble; for she knew that she must provide the bulk of the means for carrying on a war which would at once drain her coffers and cripple her clients. En-

thusiasts, men of extreme views, men of reckless purposes, stigmatized her endeavors as the fruits of a base disposition to compromise with crime and to barter the principles of humanity for the good things of this life; and during the fierce debate of years, many were the sneers at the commercial patriotism of the so-called Union-savers, whose voices were heard only in deprecation. Honest in some cases, in many others this clamor was but a manifestation of that subtle hypocrisy by which the human heart seeks even to deceive itself. Self-sacrifice, conscious, seems heroic. Nothing higher toned, more unselfish, benevolent, patriotic, than to insist on carrying out one's principles without care for consequences. Being jocosely scornful of the meanness of looking after gold and silver in preference to the misty glories of abstract philanthropy is a grand sort of humor, a pipe the music of which costs little to those among whom it finds the readiest, most untiring dancers. For there is this difference between the position of most merchants and that of most enthusiasts in philanthropy—that profound political agitation threatens the former with present pecuniary loss and prospective ruin, while to the latter it generally brings little personal inconvenience, and often increase, if not of gain, at least of influence. Therefore, under such circumstances, the one is always called upon to sacrifice a tangible personal good in possession to the possible establishment of an abstract principle in which he has no direct interest; while the other has his triumph, gains his glory, sacrifices nothing, and, especially if he is a journalist or a man of letters, perhaps gets money by the very curiosity which he has provoked, the very solicitude which he has awakened. To the former, therefore, any grave disturbance of society is a very serious matter; it touches with inexorable finger that sensitive spot of almost every civilized man's organization, the pocket—a region in which the philanthropic agitator is often equally callous and flaccid. The penniless traveler knows that he can sing before the robber. Nor is the mercantile view of politics, whatever the motives and ends of individuals, narrow or selfish in its actual horizon. For to the great majority of any people serious political disturbance ushers in a troubled present and a cloudy future. It brings anxious days and sleepless nights; it darkens the father's brow with care, and wrings the mother's heart with sorrow; and it may pinch the whole household with the pangs of actual poverty. Without claiming, then, that the commercial scope of politics is taken from the sublimest moral plane, and, on the other hand, recognizing the existence of times when considerations of present material good must be given to the winds, it must be admitted that the merchant may justly claim that the philanthropist should respect his scruples and deal tenderly with his fears, and that the statesman should remember that there may be too great a sacrifice made for an abstraction, or even for a principle, unless national safety or honor is at stake. For such reasons New York could afford to bear the reproach of selfishness and timidity so long as the struggle could with any honor be avoided; but when that period was past she took her position instantly and without reserve upon the side of constitutional government, and her prompt movement now was all the more imposing from her foregone caution and reserve.

To the meeting at Union Square, where centred the main avenues of the city, it seemed as if nearly all the male adult population poured in steady streams from an early hour after noon. The vast expanse was packed close with people, and the outskirts of the crowd stretched into the tributary streets. Five platforms were set up for officers and speakers, and, these proving insufficient, the people most remote from them were addressed from the balconies and steps of houses, the windows and even the roofs of which were occupied by ladies drawn thither by the unwonted scene. Major Anderson and the other officers of Fort Sumter had arrived, bringing with them the tattered flag which they had maintained so long and defended so well, and their presence added needless fuel to the patriotic fire which fused into one glowing mass the incongruous political elements of this great gathering. For the men who took prominent parts on this occasion were the leaders of all parties; Democrats and Republicans, Old Whigs and Native Americans, the living and the dead organizations, were all represented; and as the speakers came not only from the city and the State of New York, but from the East and the West, and from the very South, the demonstration assumed a national as well as a municipal importance. The resolutions at this meeting, unlike those passed at meetings in the slave states, were neither defiant nor denunciatory. They calmly set forth the occasion of the coming war, and declared it the duty of all good citizens to uphold with their fortunes and their lives the authority of the government against acts of lawless violence, which, if longer unresisted, would inevitably end in the destruction of the institutions established by the fathers of the republic for the protection of life, liberty, and property, and involve the country in universal anarchy and confusion.[9] Of the many speeches made in support of these resolutions, nearly all may be passed by as of no permanent interest, though well adapted to the time and the occasion. But three of them were so characteristic of the spirit of the people, and so significant, not only in their terms, but in the sources whence they came, that without them the record of that day would be tame and incomplete.

Six months before, Robert J. Walker, of Mississippi, was perhaps one of the very last men in the country, outside the ranks of the raving "fire-eaters," who would have been expected to raise his voice against any movement of the slave states, and in support of any act of a Republican president. He had been through all his manhood an active, and through much of it a leading, member of the Democratic party. For six years he had represented Mississippi as her senator in Congress. As Secretary of the Treasury, he had been one of the most influential of President Polk's cabinet ministers, and had acquired, even among his political opponents, a reputation for sagacity, knowledge of affairs, and administrative ability—three of the chiefest qualifications of a statesman. Bound up not only with the Democratic party, but in the most intimate political and personal relations with the leading men of the Gulf states, the defender of their utmost rights, the apologist of their very excesses, he was selected by President Buchanan as the fourth governor of Kansas Territory; and it is to his enduring honor that he resigned that responsible position as soon as he saw that the course marked out for him by the administration which he served was flagrantly in violation of the principles of liberty and justice. Cautious by nature, schooled by long experience, and prejudiced only in favor of the men whose insurrection was the occasion of his presence, after a brief peroration, he thus coolly exposed their pretenses and condemned their action: "The question is, Shall this Union be maintained and perpetuated, or shall it be broken and dissolved? No question so important has ever occurred in the history of our race. It involves not only the fate of this great country, but the question of free institutions throughout the world. The case of self-government is now on trial before the forum of our country and of the world. If we succeed and maintain the Union, free institutions, under the moral force of our example, will ultimately be established throughout the world; but if we fail, and our government is overthrown, popular liberty will have made its last experiment, and despotism will reign triumphant throughout the globe. Our responsibilities are fearful. We have a solemn duty to perform—we are this day making history. We are writing a book whose pages can never be erased—it is the destiny of our country and of mankind. For

more than seventy years this Union has been maintained, and it has advanced our country to a prosperity unparalleled in the history of the world. The past was great, but the future opened upon prospects beyond the power of language to describe. But where are we now? The world looks on with scorn and derision. We have, it is said, no government—a mere voluntary association of independent states—a debating society, or a moot court, without any real power to uphold the laws or maintain the Constitution. We have no country, no flag, no Union; but each state at its pleasure, upon its own mere whim or caprice, with or without cause, may secede and dissolve the Union. Secession, we are told, is a constitutional right of each state, and the Constitution has inscribed its own death-warrant upon its face. If this be so, we have indeed no government, and Europe may well speak of us with contempt and derision. This is the very question we are now to solve—have we a government, and has it power to maintain its existence? This question is not for the first time presented to the consideration of the American people. It arose in 1832, when South Carolina nullified the revenue laws of the Union, and passed her secession ordinance. In that contest I took a very active part against the doctrines of nullification and secession, and upon that question, after a struggle of three years, I was elected by Mississippi as a senator of the United States. A contest so prolonged and violent had never before been witnessed in this country. It was fought by me in every county of the state under the banner of the Union. The sentiments contained in the many speeches then made by me, and then published, are the opinions I now entertain. They are all for the Union and against secession, and they are now the opinions of thousands of Union men of the South and of Mississippi. These opinions are unchanged; and deeply as I deplore our present situation, it is my profound conviction that the welfare, security, and prosperity of the South can only be restored by the re-establishment of the Union. I see, in the permanent overthrow of the Union, the utter ruin of the South and the complete prostration of all their interests. I have devoted my life to the maintenance of all their constitutional rights, and the promotion of their happiness and welfare; but secession involves them and us in one common ruin. The recognition of such a doctrine is fatal to the existence of any government—of the Union: it is death—it is national suicide. This is the question now to be decided: Have we a Union—have we a flag—are the stars and stripes a reality or a fiction—have we a government, and can we enforce its laws, or must the whole vanish whenever any one state thinks proper to issue the despotic mandate? Is the Union indissoluble, or is it written on the sand, to be swept away by the first angry surge of state or sectional passion which may sweep over it? It was the declared object of our ancestors to found a perpetual Union. The original Articles of Confederation, by all the states, in 1778, declared the Union to be 'perpetual,' and South Carolina (with all the states) then plighted her solemn faith that 'the union of the states shall be perpetual.' And in modifying these articles by the formation of the Constitution in 1787, the declared object of that change was to make 'the Union more perfect.' But how more perfect, if the Union is indissoluble in 1787, but might at any moment be destroyed by any one state after the adoption of the Constitution? No, my countrymen, secession is not a constitutional right of any one state. It is war—it is revolution—and can only be established on the ruins of the Constitution and of the Union. We must resist and subdue it, or our government will be but an organized anarchy, to be surely succeeded, as anarchy ever has been, by military despotism. This, then, my fellow-citizens, is the last great contest for the liberties of our country and of the world. If we are defeated, the last experiment of self-government will have failed, and we will have written with our own hands the epitaph of human liberty. We will have no flag, we will have no government, no country, and no Union; we will cease to be American citizens, and the despots of Europe will rejoice in the failure of the great experiment of republican institutions. The liberties of our country and of the world will have been intrusted to our care, and we shall have dishonored the great trust and proved ourselves traitors to the freedom of our country and of mankind. This is not a sectional question; it is not a Northern or a Southern question; it is not a question which concerns our country only, but all mankind. It is this: Shall we, by a noble and united effort, sustain here republican institutions, or shall we have secession and anarchy, to be succeeded by despotism, and extinguish forever the hopes of freedom throughout the world? God grant you, my dear countrymen, courage, and energy, and perseverance to maintain successfully the great contest. You are fighting the last great decisive

---

[9]   *Resolutions at the Union Meeting, New York, April 20th, 1861.*

Whereas the union of the states, under the guidance of Divine Providence, has been the fruitful source of prosperity and domestic peace to the country for nearly three quarters of a century; and

Whereas the Constitution, framed by our Revolutionary fathers, contains within itself all needful provisions for the exigencies of the government, and, in the progress of events, for such amendments as are necessary to meet new exigencies; and

Whereas an armed combination has been formed to break up the Union, by throwing off the obligations of the Constitution, and has, in several of the states, carried on its criminal purpose, and, finally, by assaulting Fort Sumter, a fortress of the United States occupied by a slender but heroic garrison, and capturing it by an overwhelming force after a gallant defense, thus setting the authority of the government at defiance, and insulting the national flag; and

Whereas the government of the United States, with an earnest desire to avert the evils of civil war, has silently submitted to these aggressions and insults with a patient forbearance unparalleled in the annals of history, but has at last deemed it due to the public honor and safety to appeal to the people of the Union for the means of maintaining its authority, of enforcing the execution of the laws, and of saving our country from dismemberment and our political institutions from destruction; therefore,

Resolved, That the Declaration of Independence, the war of the Revolution, and the Constitution of the United States have given origin to this government, the most equal and beneficent hitherto known among men; that under its protection the wide expansion of our territory, the vast development of our wealth, our population, and our power, have built up a nation able to maintain and defend before the world the principles of liberty and justice upon which it was founded; that by every sentiment of interest, of honor, of affection and of duty, we are engaged to preserve unbroken for our generation, and to transmit to our posterity, the great heritage we have received from heroic ancestors; that to the maintenance of this sacred trust we devote whatever we possess, and whatever we can do, and in support of that government under which we are happy and proud to live, we are prepared to shed our blood and lay down our lives.

Resolved, That the founders of the government of the United States have provided, by the institution of the Supreme Court, a tribunal for the peaceful settlement of all questions arising under the Constitution and the laws; that it is the duty of the states to appeal to it for relief from measures which they believe unauthorized; and that attempts to throw off the obligations of the Constitution, and to obtain redress by an appeal to arms, can be considered in no other light than as levying war against the United States.

Resolved, That the Constitution of the United States, the basis and the safeguard of the federal Union, having been framed and ratified by the original states, and accepted by those which subsequently became parties to it, is binding upon all; and that any resumption by any one of them of the rights delegated to the federal government, without first seeking a release from its obligations through the concurrence of the common sovereignty, is unauthorized, unjust to all the others, and destructive of all social and political order.

Resolved, That when the authority of the federal government shall have been re-established, and peaceful obedience to the Constitution and laws prevail, we shall be ready to confer and co-operate with all loyal citizens throughout the Union, in Congress or in Convention, for the consideration of all supposed grievances, the redress of all wrongs, and the protection of every right, yielding ourselves, and expecting all others to yield, to the will of the whole people as constitutionally and lawfully expressed.

Resolved, That it is the duty of all good citizens, overlooking past differences of opinion, to contribute by all the means in their power to maintain the union of the states, to defend the Constitution, to preserve the national flag from insult, and uphold the authority of the government against acts of lawless violence, which, if longer unresisted, would inevitably end in breaking down all the barriers erected by our fathers for the protection of life, liberty, and property, and involve the country in universal anarchy and confusion.

Resolved, That a committee of twenty-five, to be nominated by the president, be appointed by this meeting to represent the citizens in the collection of funds and the transaction of such other business in aid of the movements of the government as the public interests may require.

battle for the liberties of our country and of mankind; faint not, falter not, but move onward in one great column for the maintenance of the Constitution and the Union. Remember it was a Southern man, a noble son of Kentucky, who so gloriously sustained the flag of our country at Fort Sumter, and never surrendered that flag. He brought it with him to New York, and there it is, held in the hands of Washington, in that marble column now before us representing the Father of his Country, and whose lips now open and urge us, as in his Farewell Address, to maintain the Constitution and the Union. And now, while I address you, the news comes that the city of Washington, founded by the Father of his Country and bearing his sacred name, is to be seized by the legions of disunion. Never, never must or shall this disgrace befall us. That capital must and shall be defended, if it requires every Union man in America to march to its defense. And now, then, fellow-citizens, a desperate effort is made to make this a party question —a question between Democrats and Republicans. Well, fellow-citizens, I have been a Democrat all my life, and never scratched a Democratic ticket, from Constable up to President, but say to you this is no party question. It is a question of a maintenance of the government and the perpetuation of the Union. The vessel of state is rushing upon the breakers, and, without asking who may be the commander, we must all aid in her rescue from impending disaster. When the safety of my country is involved, I will never ask who is President, nor inquire what may be the effect on parties of any particular measure. Much as I love my party, I love my country infinitely more, and must and will sustain it at all hazards. Indeed, it is due to the great occasion here frankly to declare that, notwithstanding my earnest opposition to the election of Mr. Lincoln, and my disposition most closely to scrutinize all his acts, I see thus far nothing to condemn in his efforts to maintain the Union. And now, then, my countrymen, one word more before I close. I was trained in devotion to the Union by a patriot sire, who fought the battles of liberty during the war of the Revolution. My life has been given to the support of the Union. I never conceived a thought, or wrote or uttered a word, except in its defense. And now let me say that this Union must, will, and shall be perpetuated; that not a star shall be dimmed or a stripe erased from our banner; that the integrity of the government shall be preserved, and that, from the Atlantic to the Pacific, from the Lakes of the North to the Gulf of Mexico, never shall be surrendered a single acre of our soil or a drop of its waters."

Conclusive, comprehensive, and untemporizing as this speech was, it lacked the fervor which animated the great body of the loyal men in those days, and which found expression in the words of others who spoke for and to that immense multitude. Among these were two who afterward gave their lives in the defense of the republic. Edward Dickinson Baker was born a British subject. A native of London, he came to the United States in his boyhood, and, going to Illinois nearly forty years before these troublous times, he grew to man's estate in and with the rising West. His mind was active and powerful; to his professional reading of the law he added an unusual cultivation of letters; and a remarkable energy of character raised him steadily to distinction. Attracted to political life, he adhered from the beginning to those principles of freedom which it is the glory of the English race on both sides of the Atlantic to have asserted and maintained consistently with the stability of society and the best conditions of human progress; the notable and unmistakable exception being those places in which the perpetuation of slavery produced its inevitable results—oligarchical rule, and a society at once controlled and disturbed by violence. Senator Baker had followed General Scott as colonel of a volunteer regiment in the Mexican war, in which he served with distinction. He lived for some years in the chaotic but rapidly self-organizing society of California, and finally settled in Oregon, from which state he took his seat as senator in 1859. Believing that, although in the states where slavery was already established it was immovable except by the action of the people of those states, the future additions to the great republic should be consecrated to free soil, free speech, and free men, he attached himself to the Republican party, and gave it the zealous and untiring support which sprung from his earnest convictions and energetic character. With this creed and this experience, and with his ardent temperament fired by the outrages at Fort Sumter, Harper's Ferry, Portsmouth Navy Yard, and Baltimore, and his sympathetic nature roused by the excitement of the community in which he found himself, he thus broke forth in burning words, thus pledged the honor which he well maintained, and the life which, ere long, all vainly he gave up:

"The majesty of the people is here to-day to sustain the majesty of the Constitution, and I come, a wanderer from the far Pacific, to record my oath along with yours of the great Empire State. The hour for conciliation has passed, the gathering for battle is at hand, and the country requires that every man shall do his duty. Fellow-citizens, what is that country? Is it the soil on which we tread? Is it the gathering of familiar faces? Is it our luxury, and pomp, and pride? Nay, more than these, is it power, and might, and majesty alone? No, our country is more, far more than all these. The country which demands our love, our courage, our devotion, our heart's blood, is more than all these. Our country is the history of our fathers—our country is the tradition of our mothers—our country is past renown—our country is present pride and power—our country is future hope and destiny —our country is greatness, glory, truth, constitutional liberty—above all, freedom forever! These are the watchwords under which we fight; and we will shout them out till the stars appear in the sky, in the stormiest hour of battle. I have said that the hour for conciliation is past. It may return; but not to-morrow, nor next week. It will return when that tattered flag is avenged. It will return when rebel traitors are taught obedience and submission. It will return when the rebellious confederates are taught that the North, though peaceable, are not cowardly—though forbearing, are not fearful. That hour of conciliation will come back when again the ensign of the republic will stream over every rebellious fort of every confederate state. Then, as of old, the ensign of the pride and power, and dignity and majesty, and the peace of the republic will return. Young men of New York—young men of the United States—you are told this is not to be a war of aggression. In one sense that is true; in another, not. We have committed aggression upon no man. In all the broad land, in their rebel nest, in their traitors' camp, no truthful man can rise and say that he has ever been disturbed, though it be but for a single moment, in life, liberty, estate, character, or honor. The day they began this unnatural, false, wicked, rebellious warfare, their lives were more secure, their property more secure, by us—not by themselves, but by us—guarded far more securely than any people ever have had their lives and property secured from the beginning of the world. We have committed no oppression, have broken no compact, have exercised no unholy power; have been loyal, moderate, constitutional, and just. We are a majority of the Union, and we will govern our own Union, within our own Constitution, in our own way. We are all Democrats. We are all Republicans. We acknowledge the sovereignty of the people within the rule of the Constitution, and under that Constitution and beneath that flag let traitors beware. In this sense, then, young men of New York, we are not for a war of aggression. But in another sense, speaking for myself as a man who has been a soldier, and as one who is a senator, I say, in the same sense, I am for a war of aggression. I propose to do now as we did in Mexico—conquer peace. I propose to go to Washington and beyond. I do not design to remain silent, supine, inactive, nay, fearful, until they gather their battalions and advance their host upon our borders or in our midst. I would meet them upon the threshold, and there, in the very state of their power, in the very atmosphere of their treason, I propose that the people of this Union dictate to these rebels the terms of peace. It may take thirty millions; it may take three hundred millions. What then? We have it. Loyally, nobly, grandly do the merchants of New York respond to the appeals of the government. It may cost us seven thousand men. It may cost us seventy-five thousand men in battle; it may cost us seven hundred and fifty thousand men. What then? We have them. The blood of every loyal citizen of this government is dear to me. My sons, my kinsmen, the young men who have grown up beneath my eye and beneath my care, they are all dear to me; but if the country's destiny, glory, tradition, greatness, freedom, government, written constitutional government—the only hope of a free people—demand it, let them all go. I am not here now to speak timorous words of peace, but to kindle the spirit of manly, determined war. I speak in the midst of the Empire State, amid scenes of past suffering and past glory: the defenses of the Hudson above me, the battle-field of Long Island before me, and the statue of Washington in my very face—the battered and unconquered flag of Sumter waving in his hands, which I can almost now imagine trembles with the excitement of battle. And as I speak, I say my mission here to-day is to kindle the heart of New York for war—short, sudden, bold, determined, forward war. The Seventh Regiment has gone; let seventy and seven more follow. Of old, said a great historian, beneath the banner of the Cross, Europe precipitated itself upon Asia. Beneath the banner of the Constitution let the men of the Union precipitate themselves upon disloyal, rebellious confederate states. A few more words, and I have done. Let no man underrate the dangers of this controversy. Civil war, for the best of reasons upon the one side and the worst upon the other, is always dangerous to liberty, always fearful, always bloody; but, fellow-citizens, there are yet worse things than fear, than doubt and dread, and danger and blood. Dishonor is worse. Perpetual anarchy is worse. States forever commingling and forever severing are worse. Traitors and secessionists are worse. To have star after star blotted out—to have stripe after stripe obscured—to have glory after glory dimmed—to have our women weep and our men blush for shame throughout generations yet to come—that and these are infinitely worse than blood. People of New York, on the eve of battle allow me to speak as a soldier. Few of you know, as my career has been distant and obscure, but I may mention it here to-day with a generous pride, that it was once my fortune to lead your gallant New York regiment in the very shock of battle. I was their leader, and upon the bloody heights of Cerro Gordo I know well what New York can do when her blood is up. Again, once more, when we march, let us not march for revenge. As yet we have nothing to revenge. It is not much that where that tattered flag waved, guarded by seventy men against ten thousand—it is not much that starvation effected what an enemy could not compel. We have as yet something to punish, but nothing, or very little, to revenge. The President himself, a hero without knowing it—and I speak from knowledge, having known him from boyhood—the President says, 'There are wrongs to be redressed, already long enough endured;' and we march to battle and to victory because we do not choose to endure this wrong any longer. They are wrongs not merely against us; not against you, Mr. President, not against me, but against our sons and against our grandsons that surround us. They are wrongs against our ensign; they are wrongs against our Union; they are wrongs against our Constitution; they are wrongs against human hope and human freedom; and thus, if it be avenged, still, as Burke says, 'it is a wild justice at last,' and we will revenge them. While I speak, following in the wake of men so eloquent, so conservative, so eminent, so loyal, so well known —even while I speak, the object of your meeting is accomplished; upon the wings of the lightning it goes out throughout the world that New York, the very heart of a great city, with her crowded thoroughfares, her merchants, her manufacturers, her artists—that New York, by one hundred thousand of her people, declares to the country and to the world that she will sustain the government to the last dollar in her treasury—to the last drop of your blood. The national banners leaning from ten thousand windows in your city to-day proclaim your affection and reverence for the Union. You will gather in battalions,

"'Patient of toil, serene amid alarms,
Inflexible in faith, invincible in arms;'

and as you gather, every omen of present concord and ultimate peace will surround you. The ministers of religion, the priests of literature, the historians of the past, the illustrators of the present, capital, science, art, invention, discoveries, the works of genius—all these will attend us in our march, and we will conquer. And if, from the far Pacific, a voice feebler than the feeblest murmur upon its shore may be heard to give you courage and hope in the contest, that voice is yours to-day; and if a man whose hair is gray, who is well-nigh worn out in the battle and toil of life, may pledge himself on such an occasion and in such an audience, let me say, as my last word, that when, amid sheeted fire and flame, I saw and led the hosts of New York as they charged in contest upon a foreign soil for the honor of your flag, so again, if Providence shall will it, this feeble hand shall draw a sword, never yet dishonored, not to fight for distant honor in a foreign land, but to fight for country, for home, for law, for government, for Constitution, for right, for freedom, for humanity, and in the hope that the banner of my country may advance, and wheresoever that banner waves, there glory may pursue and freedom be established."

Few among the more intelligent and cultivated of the throng that he addressed did not respect the reputation of Ormsby M'Knight Mitchell; but probably no one of them expected from the eminent mathematician and astronomer, the superintendent of the Dudley Observatory, such an impassioned and stirring appeal as he made to them, such an earnest warning, and such a demand for instant, energetic action. What he was he told himself. A native of one slave state, born of parents who were natives of another, a resident of a free state (like many of his military fellow-students and quondam brother officers who had disowned and deserted the flag of the government which had bred and fed them), loving kindred and neighbors, and honoring the commonwealth of which he was a member, he yet disavowed any allegiance except to the republic, and thus, in his speech and in himself, he was a typical man for the times and the occasion. The hearts of all that great congregation went with him as he spoke these words: "I am infinitely indebted to you for this evidence of your kindness. I know I am a stranger among you. I have been in your state but a little while; but I am with you, heart and soul, and mind and strength, and all that I have and am belongs to you and our common country, and to nothing else. I have been announced to you as a citizen of Kentucky. Once I was, because I was born there. I love my native state as you love your native state. I love my adopted state of Ohio as you love your adopted state, if such you have; but, my friends, I am not a citizen now of any state. I owe allegiance to no state, and never did, and, God helping me, I never will. I owe allegiance to the government of the United States. A poor boy, working my way with my own hands, at the age of twelve turned out to take care of myself as best I could, and beginning by earning but $4 per month, I worked my way onward until this glorious government gave me a chance at the Military Academy at West Point. There I landed with a knapsack on my back, and, I tell you God's truth, just a quarter of a dollar in my pocket. There I swore allegiance to the government of the United States. I did not abjure the love of my own state, nor of my adopted state, but all over that rose proudly triumphant and predominant my love for our common country. And now to-day that common country is assailed, and, alas! alas! that I am compelled to say it, it is assailed in some sense by my own countrymen. My father and my mother were from Old Virginia, and my brothers and sisters from Old Kentucky. I love them all; I love them dearly. I have my brothers and friends down in the South now, united to me by the fondest ties of love and affection. I would take them in my arms to-day with all the love that God has put into this heart; but if I found them in arms, I would be compelled to smite them down. You have found officers of the army who have been educated by the government—who have drawn their support from the government for long years—who, when called upon by their country to stand for the Constitution and for the right, have basely, ignominiously, and traitorously either resigned their commissions, or deserted to traitors, rebels, and enemies. What means all this? How can it be possible that men should act in this way? There is no question but one. If we ever had a government and Constitution, or if we ever lived under such, have we ever recognized the supremacy of right? I say, in God's name, why not recognize it now? Why not to-day? Why not forever? Suppose those friends of ours from old Ireland—suppose he who has made himself one of us, when a war should break out against his own country, should say, 'I can not fight against my own countrymen,' is he a citizen of the United States? They are no countrymen longer when war breaks out. The rebels and the traitors in the South we must set aside; they are not our friends. When they come to their senses, we will receive them with open arms; but till that time, while they are trailing our glorious banner in the dust, when they scorn it, condemn it, curse it, and trample it under foot, then I must smite. In God's name I will smite, and as long as I have strength I will do it. Oh, listen to me, listen to me! I know these men; I know their courage; I have been among them; I have been with them; I have been reared with them; they have courage; and do not you pretend to think they have not. I tell you what it is, it is no child's play you are entering upon. They will fight, and with a determination and a power which is irresistible. Make up your mind to it. Let every man put his life in his hand, and say, 'There is the altar of my country; there I will sacrifice my life.' I, for one, will lay my life down. It is not mine any longer. Lead me to the conflict. Place me where I can do my duty. There I am ready to go, I care not where it leads me. * * * * I am ready to fight in the ranks or out of the ranks. Having been educated in the Academy; having been in the army seven years; having served as commander of a volunteer company for ten years, and having served as an adjutant general, I feel I am ready for something. I only ask to be permitted to act; and, in God's name, give me something to do." The burden which Mitchell solicited was laid upon his shoulders; the sacrifice which he offered was accepted. He died in the service of the republic during the coming struggle, but, as we shall hereafter see, not before he had led its armies to victory in the very heart of the country over which, while he spoke, the rebels, whom he denounced, but whose courage and determination he so justly acknowledged, held undisputed sway. If that be eloquence which, as has been said, produces the effect desired upon those to whom it is addressed, the simple directness of this short speech was eloquence itself. It raised all who heard it to such a pitch of enthusiasm that they gave vent to their feelings in demonstrations rarely seen in public among people of the English race. Tears, sobs, outcries half suppressed, and movements showing the deepest agitation, broke forth all around. Such moments do not last; our nature could not support them; and the emotion, though not the attention, of the assembly subsided under the discourse of speakers less fervid, but perhaps equally patriotic. The presence of certain of the men who took an active part on the occasion was justly regarded as worthy of special note, for they were known to all as the industrious advocates and apologists of secession hardly more than a week before. One of these stands out from among his fellows. The reader has, perhaps, divined his name. As Saul was among the prophets, so Fernando Wood appeared among the patriots. He not only appeared, but spoke. What he said was in itself of little interest or consequence; but it is noteworthy as indicative of the influence of the times upon a man of great sagacity, and boldness, and few scruples, who sought to efface by a successful political career the published records of a criminal tribunal. He declared it to be his official duty to support the Union, the government, the laws, and the flag; as a man, he professed that he threw himself into the coming contest with all his power and all his might, that the authority of the government and the integrity of the republic might be maintained, peaceably if possible, but, if not, forcibly; he spontaneously assumed the responsibility of pledging the corporation of the city for the sum necessary to fit out a brigade of troops; and, alluding to the threats of successful invasion made by the insurgents, he proclaimed that before the confederate flag could fly over Faneuil Hall in Boston, it must be carried over the dead bodies of the citizens of New York.[10] Into such a well-voiced semblance of patriotism was this man startled by the sight of the

[10] *Mayor Wood's Speech.*

FELLOW-CITIZENS,—The President has announced that Colonel Baker, the gentleman who has so eloquently addressed you to-day, proposes to raise a New York brigade, if the state will bear the expense of outfit; and here, as mayor of this city, so far as I have the power to speak, I pledge for the corporation that sum. When I assumed the duties of the office I have now the honor to hold, my official oath was that I would support the Constitution of the United States and the Constitution of the State of New York; and I imply from that that it is not only my duty, as it is consistent with my principles and sense of right, to support the Constitution, but the Union, the government, the laws, and the flag. And, in the discharge of that duty, I care not what past political associations may be severed. I am willing to give up all past prejudices and sympathies if in conflict with the honor and interest of my country in this great crisis. I am willing to say here that I throw myself entirely into this contest with all my power and with all my might. My friends, the greatest man next to Washington that this country has ever produced—Andrew Jackson—has said that "the Union must and shall be preserved," and in that connection he has said, and it is directly pertinent to the present contest, "the Union must and shall be preserved—peaceably if we can, but forcibly if we must." There are those of us who have heretofore held antagonist positions to what is supposed to be the policy and the principles of this administration, who are willing to accept that noble declaration of the sacred Jackson as a resort to force upon this occasion. Why, gentlemen, what is the nature of your government? Ours is a government of opinion expressed through the laws. The laws, being made by the people through their representatives, are simply the expressions of popular sentiment; and the administrators of the laws should be maintained in the exercise of all legal authority. I have always advocated a strong executive power; because, to be efficient, it requires ample authority, and under our form of government, the agent being merely the exponent of the popular will, he should be provided with every means to maintain that will. Thus, in maintaining the government, we maintain ourselves, our inalienable rights, and the basis of free institutions. It is true that individuals retain the right of independent criticism, and at the ballot-box have an opportunity to exercise this right; yet we are all bound to abide by the result. These views are pertinent to the occasion, so far as the people of the city and state of New York are concerned. This city is a portion of the state, and this state retains its position as one of the United States of America; therefore we must stand by the government, we must obey the laws, we must respect official authority, we must respond with alacrity to the calls of patriotism, and, so long as we may have the strength, support the Constitution and the Union. In accordance, then, with these views, I have no hesitation in throwing whatever power I may possess in behalf of the pending struggle. If a military conflict is necessary, and that military authority can be exercised under the Constitution and consistently with the laws, dreadful as the alternative may be, we have no recourse except to take up arms. In times of great peril great sacrifices are required. When the human frame is upon the verge of death, every effort of skill and the most desperate experiments are resorted to to preserve life and prevent dissolution. This may be said to be an apt illustration of the present condition of the body politic. In the expression of these views, which I design to be understood as a public proclamation in favor of maintaining the authority of government as such, "peaceably if we can, but forcibly if we must," I desire also to be understood as taking back no sentiment I have ever uttered on the political issues of the day. If the Presidential election was to be held over again to-morrow, my vote and my sentiments would be unchanged; nor am I to be regarded as countenancing or justifying mob law or violence. The people themselves have elected or established tribunals for the adjudication of offenses against the laws, and all of us are restrained and must conform thereto. Every man's opinion is to be respected; and he who denies to a fellow-citizen the right of independent thought, violates the first principles of republicanism, and strikes a blow at the theory of our government. My friends, it has been said here to-day that your flag has been insulted. Ay! not only has your flag been insulted, but the late Secretary of War, assuming to represent the Confederate States, has said that the confederate flag shall wave over your Capitol before the first of May. And, more than that, that the confederate flag shall wave over Faneuil Hall in Boston. My friends, before that banner can fly over Faneuil Hall in Boston, it must be carried over the dead body of every citizen of New York. In behalf of you I am prepared to say here, and, through the press, to our friends of the South, that before that flag shall float over the national Capitol, every man, woman, and child would enlist for the war. Gentlemen, I have no voice, although the heart, to address you longer. Abler and more eloquent men than myself are here. I can only say, therefore, that I am with you in this contest. We know no party now. We are for maintaining the integrity of the national Union intact. We are for exhausting every power at our command in this great, high, and patriotic struggle; and I call upon every man, whatever may have been his position heretofore, whatever may be his individual sympathy now, to make one great phalanx in this struggle, that we may, in the language of the eloquent senator who preceded me, proceed to "conquer peace." My friends, it has been already announced by the chairman that the Baltic and other vessels at the foot of Canal Street are ready to take five thousand men to-morrow to the capital of Washington. I urge a hearty response to that call, that New York may speak trumpet-tongued to the people of the South.

HON. FERNANDO WOOD.

their beauty, and fresh stimulus to the patriotism of their admirers. In this fancy they were at once followed, if indeed they had not been preceded, by their sisters at the South, who adopted with equal spirit and with almost equal unanimity the emblem of rebellion into their costume; so that from the great Lakes to the Gulf the entire population were decked in the same red, white, and blue, but arranged at the North as to signify devotion to, and at the South alienation from, and, in fact, hatred for, the government, which, with so much blood and toil, Washington and his compeers had so painfully established. Yet throughout the free states, and in the very midst of this outburst of patriotic feeling, the well-wishing friends, the active partisans, the very paid supporters, spies, and emissaries of the insurgents thronged unmolested, and, even when known, almost unheeded. The persecutions by which the insurgent party at the South brought about an appearance of unanimity in the insurrection will hereafter engage our attention; but it may here be appropriately said, once for all, that at the North, Southern birth and connection, and even well-known active sympathy with the revolted slaveholders, brought no man harm or even discomfort. Men from the states under control of the insurgents remained at the North in the absolute enjoyment of all their rights as citizens of the republic. The government at Washington and the people of the North regarded the resident of South Carolina and Massachusetts alike as individual members of the nation; and they remained alike undisturbed by government or people, unless there appeared good reason for believing that they were actually engaged in treasonable service against the United States. The few acts of violence by the people at the North (and they were so few and so trifling as to be almost unworthy of notice) were directed entirely against Northern men who affronted the aroused patriotism of their neighbors by an unblushing support of the cause of the insurgents. Two or three presses in New England and in Pennsylvania were attacked or threatened, and one man was tarred and feathered and ridden on a rail. To this extent only, in a time of war and most intense excitement, did the people of the free states emulate the outrages of their fellow-citizens of the slave states upon those whose political views were offensive to them—outrages committed during a period of thirty years, at intervals of a few days, in some part of the extended territory south of Mason and Dixon's line, sometimes perpetrated upon women, and often ending in the maiming and even the death of their victims. With this great difference, however, between the teacher and the taught, that these few and comparatively unimportant deviations from the respect for law and the rights of the citizen, though the fruits of such an exceptional public disturbance, were checked by the magistrates, and, in one case at least, followed by the trial, condemnation, and punishment of the offenders, and in all by reparation on the part of the county authorities; while the actors in the lynchings and mobbings in the slave states, during the peaceful period of thirty years, went about their outrageous business, as all the world well knows, with absolute impunity. But, with all this restraint in the midst of great agitation, there was a strong, and, under the circumstances, a not unreasonable determination that people in public positions, and particularly the conductors of public journals, should exhibit at least an outward loyalty to the government. Most of the newspaper offices were surmounted with flag-staffs, and upon these, with few exceptions, as upon all others similarly situated, the national colors were raised on the Monday after the bombardment of Fort Sumter. The offices at which this sign of nationality was not displayed were those of papers in New York and Philadelphia, which, during the few months preceding that event, had supported the cause of aggressive slavery. Before these offices crowds assembled, and demanded, with no threats of violence, but with good-natured determination, that they should show their colors. A few at first refused to comply with the demand, but not for many hours. Policy surely counseled them to yield so trivial a point at such a period; and perhaps fear of immediate consequences might have had some effect, though the demand was made by laughing and inoffensive throngs, which, in New York at least, were surrounded by a police force instructed to preserve order and competent to restrain violence.[1] A few private persons in the rural districts audaciously raised the standard of insurrection, more from a mischievous or a party spirit than with any really rebellious purpose. These flags were immediately torn down by the people of the neighborhood when they were not taken down by those who raised them; but no injury was done to the offenders. Had disaffection been more common it might have provoked a warmer resentment; but it was so insignificant that, although the people were determined that it should not be openly flaunted, its few displays were passed by as of little moment.

uprising North. Ere many months had passed events took place which tested his sincerity. The excitement of the day on which he appeared in such a new character was rendered more profound by the arrival during the meeting of news by telegraph that the Seventh Regiment had been attacked and cut to pieces in Baltimore. The incident and its effect are noteworthy, as showing the disturbed and sensitive state of the public mind, consequent chiefly upon the cutting off of the capital and of Baltimore from communication with the North. The state of apprehension and suspense throughout all the region north of the Chesapeake was such that the wildest rumor obtained belief and awoke alarm. The monster meeting did not dissolve, nor did the excitement immediately subside upon the adjournment. The people clung for a time around the great centre of the day's impression; and as the shades of evening fell, and they separated toward their homes, the waves of popular emotion slowly expanded in widening circles to the remotest bounds of the great city, till in the hush of night they gradually subsided.

But it was not only upon special occasion that awakened patriotism displayed itself. The cause of the republic was ever present to men's minds, and they loved to have some symbol of it ever present to their eyes: they found that symbol in the flag. The spontaneous raising of the national standard immediately after the bombardment of Fort Sumter grandly ushered in the exhibition of the loved emblem in every possible form and upon every possible place. Flag-staffs shot up by magic from public and private buildings, places of business, and dwelling-houses, and even from the towers and spires of churches, upon some of which the advance standard of freedom, justice, human progress, and Christian civilization appeared supported by the cross that glistened on their highest pinnacles. The demand for flags was so great that in one fortnight the price of bunting rose one hundred and fifty per cent. The enthusiasm did not stop here. Tiny flags were made for badges, and worn as a decoration upon the left breast. For a long time hardly a man was seen north of the Potomac and the Ohio without one. The brilliant token of loyalty was easily adapted to the flowing lines and varying hues of woman's costume, and the fairer part of the loyal North, with the accustomed tact of the sex, moulded the humor of the hour into fashions which gave new piquancy to

The leaders of the powerful faction which had obtained control of the seceded states having long preceded the government and the people of the loyal states in the work of preparation, had given at once the challenge and the first blow at Sumter. While these slept, those had worked; and now, with the people and the resources of eleven states practically under its control, and with the larger part of the military material of the republic in its possession, the government at Montgomery, upon the appearance of President Lincoln's war proclamation, had only to maintain the advantage of the initiative and proceed at once to active hostilities. To that proclamation Mr. Jefferson Davis's reply was the issuing of proposals to grant letters of marque and reprisal against the commerce of the United States.[2] This step

As to the behavior of these crowds in the city of New York I speak from personal observation.
2   *Proclamation by Jefferson Davis.*
Whereas Abraham Lincoln, the President of the United States, has, by proclamation, announced

did more to provoke the Northern people to wrath than any other which the insurgents had yet taken. In the progress of the world toward a more perfect humanity, privateering, or the subjecting of private property on the sea to capture by any person who for his own advantage chooses to undertake the business upon certain conditions, had come to be regarded as little better than legalized piracy, a relic of barbarism which should be cast aside with the license of pillaging private property upon land, than which it was regarded as even less tolerable, because the object of an army is the destruction of the military power of the enemy, and pillage, even when permitted, is but an accidental concomitant of military movements, while it is the sole purpose of the privateer. The great powers of Europe had agreed by the treaty of Paris to abolish privateering as a means of war, and to this article of that treaty the United States had offered to become a party, if those powers would agree to except all peaceful commerce from the ravages of war. But the government of Great Britain was not yet willing to sacrifice to humanity the advantages accruing from the large naval force which it kept up in the time of peace; and the government of the United States, having a small navy to protect a very large commerce and an extended sea-board, was therefore compelled, in self-preservation, to refuse its adherence to this article of the treaty. Such being the position of civilized Christendom upon this subject, and the people of the United States at the North (where only the people could truly be said to exercise a controlling influence upon the government) being thus, as ever, in advance of all others upon a question of enlarged philanthropy, the assumption by the chief of a junto of rebels of the right to license whoever would to rove the seas for the robbery and destruction of merchant vessels was looked upon as a monstrous outrage, a shameless affront to the intelligence and humanity of the age quite worthy of those who, to secure the perpetuity and the extension of slavery, had attempted the destruction of the republic on which rested the hopes of freedom for all mankind. The rebel privateers of the future were at once stigmatized by the universal voice of the free states as pirates; and, sailing under no recognized flag, such, according to the law of nations, they would have been, had they put to sea only under circumstances then existing. But events were soon to take place, both in America and Europe, which made a change in their prospective position.

Of these events the first was a proclamation, issued on the 19th of April by President Lincoln, declaring a blockade of the ports of the seceded states: the same act pronounced all privateers in the service of the rebels amenable to the laws for the prevention and punishment of piracy. The establishment of a blockade is always a matter of extended international importance, as it involves the interests of commerce, and abridges the rights of neutrals. In the present case the proclamation proved to be unusually momentous, because, according to the code established for themselves by the maritime powers of Europe, the right of blockade pertains only to belligerents, belligerent rights on one side implying the same rights on the other; and therefore, according to European dogmas, by this proclamation of blockade the government of the United States had at one word raised the insurgents to the rank of a belligerent power. It was, indeed, a matter of prime necessity to deprive the rebels of the means of replenishing their coffers by the sale of their cotton and tobacco to Europe, and to cut off their supplies of arms and munitions of war, which end might have been attained, and the international complications consequent upon an extended blockade avoided, by closing the ports of the seceded states to commerce. But the great naval and commercial power of Great Britain, acting as ever, even in foreign affairs, with a single eye to its own interests, and limiting its action only by its strength, had taken the position that, although in times of tranquillity a government may close its ports at pleasure, in time of insurrection it can only close ports in the hands of insurgents by effective blockade;[3] or, in other words, that while the people of a certain part of any country are obe-

dient to their laws and loyal to their government, that government may shut them off from commerce, but if those people should defy the law and resist the government, it can only exercise this function by a proceeding which raises them to the rank of belligerents. By this decision Great Britain, presuming on its naval strength, assumes not only to dictate, in the interests of its manufacturers and shipowners, the means by which alone other governments shall reduce their rebellious citizens to submission, but, in fact, to deprive entirely of one means those nations which do not constantly maintain a sufficient number of vessels of war to establish an effective blockade of all the ports in a rebellious quarter. In such an assumption the government of the United States could not acquiesce: the toleration of it in practice by any government would be a confession of inability to resist an intrusion upon its own sovereign functions; and, to look forward a little, at the extra session of Congress which met in July, an act was passed authorizing the President to close the ports in the seceded states at his discretion. Ports of entry are created in the United States by act of Congress; and the power of closing them, like the power of making war, belongs to Congress. But President Lincoln, in the emergency of the republic, had assumed the power of calling out the militia and commencing hostilities against the rebels; and, as far as the internal relations of government were concerned, he might, with equal certainty of indemnity, have closed the Southern ports. Had the ports been closed, although it was certainly possible that Great Britain might refuse to respect an assumption of power, or even to regard an act of Congress, which interfered with the trade of her citizens, yet it may be reasonably doubted whether, if the government of the United States had boldly asserted its sovereignty in its own affairs, and made active preparation to maintain it, the British government would have defied and insulted that sovereignty with the certain prospect of immediate war. But it was thought better to avoid this complication of difficulty; a temporizing policy again prevailed; and instead of a closing of the ports, a blockade was established. The privateering and the blockade gave to Great Britain welcome opportunity of throwing all her moral influence against the preservation of the republic, as we shall see hereafter.

Active hostilities did not immediately commence, and the attention of both parties was chiefly turned to the attitude of the border states. With a population of five and a half millions, rich, fertile, and extending in a broad belt, nearly two hundred miles wide at its narrowest part, between the insurgent slave states and the free, they held in their hands the immediate fate of the country. Had they all remained heartily and firmly faithful to the cause of the republic, the preponderance of power would have been so overwhelming, the advantage of position so great, that the rebellion would have had but a short life, and would have been strangled upon the soil which gave it birth. They did not take this position; and by their various policies (various in form, but little divergent in purpose) they swelled the proportions and prolonged the duration of the war, and brought its blood and its devastation home to their own fields and firesides. Maryland, Virginia, North Carolina, Tennessee, Kentucky, and Missouri were the debatable ground of the first days, and so of the whole war, of the rebellion. Both parties appreciated their importance, and both sought to secure them; the one, as usual, by a cautious, the other by a daring policy. We have already seen how Virginia, if not the most powerful, from her situation the most important of them all, was, on the first assertion of national authority, and in spite of all her previous denunciations of the course of South Carolina, at once thrown into the hands of the insurgents. North Carolina and Tennessee soon followed her. Kentucky and Missouri, distracted between the loyalty of the large majority of their people and the strong disaffection of their leading politicians, nearly all of whom were heartily in the interests of the rebel faction, wavered and temporized, and fell into civil commotion within their own borders; and Maryland was saved to the Union and from the fate of war only by the patriotism of her governor, and the sagacity and decision of his sometimes seeming opponent, but always actual co-worker, General Butler. Abandoning Virginia hopelessly to the insurgents, and passing her by until the beginning of active hostilities, I follow the immediate fortunes of the insurrection through the other five states upon the border.

The New England general who had so promptly settled the question of communication between the North and the national capital by moving directly upon Annapolis was immediately honored by being placed in command of a new military department, called the Department of Annapolis, which included the country twenty miles on each side of the railway as far as Bladensburgh. He established his head-quarters temporarily upon the heights commanding the seat of the state government. Whether it was a point of honor for the state Legislature not to meet in a town virtually in possession of the national authorities, or whether the members were in fear that General Butler, who had shown himself to be a man of his word, would carry out a threat which he was said to have made, that if they passed an Ordinance of Secession he would arrest the whole body, the meeting took place on the 27th of April at Frederick City, far westward of the Yankee muskets. In his message the governor opposed secession as unprovoked and unjustifiable, and advised that the state should array itself on the side of Union and peace, that thus it might act as a mediator between the insurgents and the government, and transfer the field of battle to other soil. In spite of the efforts of an active and disaffected minority, the Legislature decided, by the overwhelming vote of fifty-three to thirteen, that that body had not the right to pass an Ordinance of Secession; all efforts to bring about a convention of the people, and to place the military affairs of the state in the

the intention of invading this confederacy with an armed force, for the purpose of capturing its fortresses, and thereby subverting its independence and subjecting the free people thereof to the dominion of a foreign power; and whereas it has thus become the duty of this government to repel the threatened invasion, and to defend the rights and liberties of the people by all the means which the laws of nations and usages of civilized warfare place at its disposal;

Now, therefore, I, Jefferson Davis, President of the Confederate States of America, do issue this my proclamation, inviting all those who may desire, by service in private armed vessels on the high seas, to aid this government in resisting so wanton and wicked an aggression, to make application for commissions or letters of marque and reprisal, to be issued under the seal of these Confederate States.

And I do further notify all persons applying for letters of marque to make a statement in writing, giving the name and a suitable description of the character, tonnage, and force of the vessel, and the name and place of residence of each owner concerned therein, and the intended number of the crew, and to sign said statement, and deliver the same to the Secretary of State or to the Collector of any port of entry of these Confederate States, to be by him transmitted to the Secretary of State.

And I do further notify all applicants aforesaid, that before any commission or letter of marque is issued to any vessel, the owner or owners thereof, and the commander for the time being, will be required to give bond to the Confederate States, with at least two responsible sureties not interested in such vessel, in the penal sum of five thousand dollars; or if such vessel be provided with more than one hundred and fifty men, then in the penal sum of ten thousand dollars, with condition that the owners, officers, and crew who shall be employed on board such commissioned vessel shall observe the laws of these Confederate States, and the instructions given to them for the regulation of their conduct, that shall satisfy all damages done contrary to the tenor thereof by such vessel during her commission, and deliver up the same when revoked by the President of the Confederate States.

And I do further specially enjoin on all persons holding offices, civil and military, under the authority of the Confederate States, that they be vigilant and zealous in discharging the duties incident thereto; and I do, moreover, solemnly exhort the good people of these Confederate States, as they love their country, as they prize the blessings of free government, as they feel the wrongs of the past, and these now threatened in an aggravated form by those whose enmity is more implacable, because unprovoked, that they exert themselves in preserving order, in promoting concord, in maintaining the authority and the efficacy of the laws, and in supporting and invigorating all the measures which may be adopted for the common defense, and by which, under the blessings of Divine Providence, we may hope for a speedy, just, and honorable peace.

In testimony whereof I have hereunto set my hand, and caused the seal of the Confederate States to be affixed, this seventeenth day of April, 1861.
By the President, (Signed), JEFFERSON DAVIS.
R. TOOMBS, Secretary of State.

[3] Letter of Hon. Charles Francis Adams, United States Minister to Great Britain, to Secretary Seward, June 28, 1861.

hands of a Board of Safety (both of which measures were pressed by the sympathizers with the insurrection), failed; and no more disloyal measure was extorted than a strong condemnation of a war of subjugation, and a protest against the military occupation of the state.[4] On the 14th of May the Legislature adjourned. In the mean time troops rapidly concentrated under the command of General Butler, and on the 5th of May he advanced a force within a few miles of Baltimore, and took possession of Relay House, an im-

RELAY HOUSE.

portant railway station, which commanded both the passage southward toward Washington, and that westward toward Harper's Ferry. While here he met constant manifestations not only of a rebellious, but of a bloodthirsty and vindictive spirit. Two of his officers arrested a man who openly justified the murderous onset upon the Massachusetts regiment in Baltimore, and, according to his official statement, he found well-authenticated evidence of an attempt to poison his soldiers by persons who obtained admission to his camp in the disguise of pie-peddlers. Upon this discovery, he threatened the rebels with the swiftest and most condign punishment for such barbarity; and he who had, on the score of humanity, withstood the remonstrance of his own governor against his offer to put down a threatened insurrection of the slaves, reminded his rebellious enemies in a general order that they were teaching him a dangerous lesson, and that with a word he could mingle death in the food of their every household.[5] His movement toward Baltimore was the signal for a rapid departure of the rebellious Marylanders of that neighborhood westward. They went with such arms as they could command; and, at the same time, an attempt was made to send to Harper's Ferry, then in the possession of the insurgents, a steam gun, invented by a Mr. Winans, of Baltimore, who expected to effect by it an entire change in artillery warfare. But on the 10th General Butler seized this much-talked-of weapon on its passage, arrested those who accompanied it, and placed it among the less pretending, but, as it proved, more efficient batteries with which he commanded the important railway viaduct at what was known as

VIADUCT AT WASHINGTON JUNCTION.

the Washington Junction. On the 14th he entered the city of Baltimore itself with the Eighth New York Regiment, a detachment of the very Sixth Massachusetts which had been attacked three weeks before, and a battery, and, marching through the city, undisturbed by the rebellicus and cheered by the loyal, encamped upon Federal Hill, a high point of ground which commanded both Baltimore and Fort M'Henry, where he fixed his head-quarters. Having thus obtained quiet and absolute possession of this important city, he issued, on the same day, a proclamation, setting forth to the Baltimoreans that he was among them to sustain the laws, local as well as national; that, preferring to trust to their good faith and loyalty, he had come with little more than the guard suited to his rank; that no attempts to incite sedition or give aid and comfort to the insurgents would be permitted; and that the formation and drill of bodies of men not part of the enrolled militia of the state were forbidden. He invited the citizens to furnish rations for his command at fair prices, and promised that any outrage whatever upon person or property by those under his command should be visited with rigorous punishment. His tone was forbearing, courteous, and kind, but unmistakably firm and earnest.[6] At this proclamation the small minority of bitter and desperate secessionists muttered threats and treason between their teeth; but there was general acquiescence, and in some quarters outspoken approbation. The course which it marked out was followed with comparative ease; for a great change had taken place in Baltimore and its neighborhood since the attack upon the Massachusetts men. In spite of the activity, the virulence, and the audacity of the secessionists, the loyal citizens found that they were largely in the majority, and that, although the greater part of the wealthy and cultivated people, being all slaveholders and closely connected with the corresponding class in Eastern Virginia, were

---

4 *Resolution passed in the Maryland Legislature, May 10.*

Whereas the war against the Confederate States is unconstitutional and repugnant to civilization, and will result in a bloody and shameful overthrow of our institutions; and while recognizing the obligations of Maryland to the Union, we sympathize with the South in the struggle for their rights—for the sake of humanity, we are for peace and reconciliation, and solemnly protest against this war, and will take no part in it;

Resolved, That Maryland implores the President, in the name of God, to cease this unholy war, at least until Congress assembles; that Maryland desires and consents to the recognition of the independence of the Confederate States. The military occupation of Maryland is unconstitutional, and she protests against it, though the violent interference with the transit of federal troops is discountenanced; that the vindication of her rights be left to time and reason, and that a Convention, under existing circumstances, is inexpedient.

5 General Orders, Relay House, May 8, 1861.

6 *General Butler's Proclamation.*

Department of Annapolis, Federal Hill, Baltimore, May 14, 1861.

A detachment of the forces of the federal government under my command have occupied the city of Baltimore for the purpose, among other things, of enforcing respect and obedience to the laws, as well of the state—if requested thereto by the civil authorities—as of the United States laws, which are being violated within its limits by some malignant and traitorous men, and in order to testify the acceptance by the federal government of the fact that the city and all the well-intentioned portion of its inhabitants are loyal to the Union and the Constitution, and are to be so regarded and treated by all. To the end, therefore, that all misunderstanding of the purpose of the government may be prevented, and to set at rest all unfounded, false, and seditious rumors; to relieve all apprehensions, if any are felt, by the well-disposed portion of the community, and to make it thoroughly understood by all traitors, their aiders and abettors, that rebellious acts must cease, I hereby, by the authority vested in me as commander of the Department of Annapolis, of which Baltimore forms a part, do now command and make known that no loyal and well-disposed citizen will be disturbed in his lawful occupation or business, that private property will not be interfered with by the men under my command, or allowed to be interfered with by others, except in so far as it may be used to afford aid and comfort to those in rebellion against the government, whether here or elsewhere; all of which property, munitions of war, and that fitted to aid and support the rebellion, will be seized and held subject to confiscation, and, therefore, all manufacturers of arms and munitions of war are hereby requested to report to me forthwith, so that the lawfulness of their occupation may be known and understood, and all misconstruction of their doings be avoided. No transportation from the city to the rebels of articles fitted to aid and support troops in the field will be permitted, and the fact of such transportation, after the publication of this proclamation, will be taken and received as proof of illegal intention on the part of the consignors, and will render the goods liable to seizure and confiscation.

The government being ready to receive all such stores and supplies, arrangements will be made to contract for them immediately, and the owners and manufacturers of such articles of equipment and clothing, and munitions of war and provisions, are desired to keep themselves in communication with the Commissary General, in order that their workshops may be employed for loyal purposes, and the artisans of the city resume and carry on their profitable occupations.

The acting Assistant Quartermaster and Commissary of Subsistence of the United States here stationed has been instructed to proceed and furnish, at fair prices, 40,000 rations for the use of the army of the United States, and farther supplies will be drawn from the city to the full extent of its capacity, if the patriotic and loyal men choose so to furnish supplies.

All assemblages, except the ordinary police, of armed bodies of men, other than those regularly organized and commissioned by the State of Maryland, and acting under the orders of the governor thereof, for drill and other purposes, are forbidden within the department.

All officers of the militia of Maryland, having command within the limits of the department, are requested to report through their officers forthwith to the general in command, so that he may be able to know and distinguish the regularly commissioned and loyal troops of Maryland from armed bodies who may claim to be such.

The ordinary operations of the corporate government of the city of Baltimore and of the civil authorities will not be interfered with, but, on the contrary, will be aided by all the power at the command of the general, upon proper call being made, and all such authorities are cordially invited to co-operate with the general in command to carry out the purposes set forth in the proclamation, so that the city of Baltimore may be shown to the country to be, what she is in fact, patriotic and loyal to the Union, the Constitution, and the laws.

No flag, banner, ensign, or device of the so-called Confederate States, or any of them, will be permitted to be raised or shown in this department, and the exhibition of either of them by evil-disposed persons will be deemed, and taken to be evidence of, a design to afford aid and comfort to the enemies of the country. To make it more apparent that the government of the United States by far more relies upon the loyalty, patriotism, and zeal of the good citizens of Baltimore and vicinity than upon any exhibition of force calculated to intimidate them into that obedience to the laws which the government doubts not will be paid from inherent respect and love of order, the commanding general has brought to the city with him, of the many thousand troops in the immediate neighborhood, which might be at once concentrated here, scarcely more than an ordinary guard, and, until it fails him, he will continue to rely upon that loyalty and patriotism of the citizens of Maryland which have never yet been found wanting to the government in time of need. The general in command desires to greet and treat in this part of his department all the citizens thereof as friends and brothers, having a common purpose, a common loyalty, and a common country. Any infractions of the laws by the troops under his command, or any disorderly, unsoldierlike conduct, or any interference with private property, he desires to have immediately reported to him, and pledges himself that if any soldier so far forgets himself as to break those laws that he has sworn to defend and enforce, he shall be most rigorously punished.

The general believes that if the suggestions and requests contained in this proclamation are faithfully carried out by the co-operation of all good and Union-loving citizens, and peace and quiet, and certainty of future peace and quiet are thus restored, business will resume its accustomed channels, trade take the place of dullness and inactivity, efficient labor displace idleness, and Baltimore will be in fact, what she is entitled to be, in the front rank of the commercial cities of the nation.

Given at Baltimore, the day and year herein first above written.

Benj. F. Butler, Brig. General Com. Department of Annapolis.

E. G. Parker, Lieutenant Colonel, Aid-de-Camp.

SAND-BAG BATTERY.

disaffected, a very large and influential minority even of these, including men eminent for their talents no less than from their social position, were strenuous upholders of the Constitution and the Union. In Western Maryland the national flag was raised at Frederick City, at Hagerstown, and else-where, with due honors, and loyal defenders thronged around it. On the 13th of May a train from Philadelphia passed through Baltimore with the flag displayed; and the same token of devotion to the undivided republic was raised upon many public and private buildings. On the morning of the 14th, the day of General Butler's arrival, a Pennsylvania regiment, in complete array, passed unmolested, and even with some tokens of welcome, over the very route which three weeks before had been the scene of bloody conflict. On this day, too, Governor Hicks issued his proclamation calling for four regiments in compliance with the requirement of the President, to serve for three months; admitting that requirement to be "in the spirit and in pursuance of the law," though setting forth, as a salve to wounded state pride, the assurance of the Secretary of War that these troops should serve "within the limits of the State of Maryland, or for the defense of the capital of the United States." From this day sedition and treason gradually, though slowly, subsided in Baltimore, and lurked in secret places. Violence was suppressed by law, not made for the occasion, though supported by a force required by circumstances. General Butler, who, by his wisdom, his tact, and his activity, had so completely foiled the plans of the violent secessionists, and sustained a loyal state which was in imminent peril of being dragooned into secession, was made a major general, and placed in command of a new military district, including Virginia and the two Carolinas, his head-quarters being at Fortress Monroe; and the Winans steam gun, from which so much had been hoped on the one side and feared on the other, being found

RAISING THE STARS AND STRIPES OVER THE CUSTOM-HOUSE AT BALTIMORE.

THE WINANS GUN.

sent of *all* the slave states. Beyond these there was only one other demand to be made—that the free states should adopt slavery and make it perpetual. But all the governor's constituents did not think with him. The Legislature proved to be strongly conservative, and averse to disunion. A Convention was called, but with sufficient safeguards against the juggling or precipitation of the state into secession. At Nashville a meeting was held in January, at which it was declared by the agitators for secession that the "Constitutional Union party," whose candidate Mr. Bell was, had held the doctrine that the election of Mr. Lincoln would justify the dissolution of the Union. Mr. Bell himself, being present, rose and denied the charge, and his denial called forth cheers from all parts of the hall. At the election, on the 9th of February, of delegates to the Convention, the Union candidates were chosen by a majority of more than sixty-four thousand; and by a majority of nearly twelve thousand it was decided that there should not even be a Convention. This decision was more significant than the very majority of four hundred by which the Union delegates were elected in

a harmless monster after all, was fitly sent to Boston—that city so much threatened with the visitation of rebellious arms—a trophy.

At the beginning of the secession movement, hardly less loyal than Maryland, amid the commotion which followed the issuing of the President's proclamation, Tennessee and North Carolina were swiftly swept into the vortex of secession. This was partly because of the larger proportion of their slave property,[7] but chiefly because to them were not granted a governor like Hicks and a general like Butler. For, at the election which resulted in the choice of President Lincoln, the vote of Tennessee had been given for the conservative nominees, John Bell and Edward Everett; and although not a ballot had been cast for Lincoln, the people acquiesced in his election as the legitimate result of the canvass. But the governor, Isham G. Harris, being of the South Carolina school of politicians, at once began endeavors to carry the state into the hands of the secessionists. He called a special session of the General Assembly, avowedly upon the ground of the election of the Republican candidate, and the triumph of a party whose bond of union he declared to be uncompromising hostility to the rights and institutions of the fifteen Southern States. And here it is well to notice that of the fifteen states thus styled Southern, two, Delaware and Maryland, being north of the Potomac, belong to the Middle, and one, Missouri, to the Western geographical division of the Union. But they were slave states; and, in the mouth of slaveholders like Governor Harris, Southern thus used meant slave, even when applied to persons. To them a man born upon the iciest verge of Maine, if he came to a slave state and sustained slavery, was a Southern man; one born upon the point where Florida pushes itself almost within the tropics, if he had doubts as to the wisdom of perpetuating and diffusing negro bondage, was no Southerner, but a Yankee abolitionist. Governor Harris declared in his message to the Assembly which he had called together that these imperiled Southern rights could only be secured by the extension of a line to the Pacific, all territory south of which should be *forever* slave territory; by allowing slaveholders to travel and sojourn in the free states with their slaves; by the prohibition of the abolition of slavery in the District of Columbia, and all places in slave states under national jurisdiction; and by making these provisions unchangeable, except by con-

Memphis, the strong-hold of the aggressive slavery party, because it showed an unwillingness on the part of the people even to entertain the question of breaking up the Union, or to expose the political fortunes of the state to the chances which they must encounter in an assemblage meeting under circumstances of great excitement, and liable to be hurried into extreme measures, and even diverted from its purpose, by reckless and designing men—a disposition which, in the consideration of after-events, it will become us to remember. The President's proclamation was received with general disfavor, and caused such a change in the current of popular feeling that the secessionists, quick to see and to use their advantage, were enabled to turn the western tide almost entirely in their favor. We have already seen Governor Harris's defiant refusal to the call for troops. He immediately summoned another special session of the Assembly on April 25th; and an address was at the same time issued to the people of the state by some of its most eminent citizens, in which secession was disapproved of and the policy of the administration condemned, a refusal of aid to the government in its attempt to suppress the rebellion justified, assistance to the enemies of the government equally deprecated, and a course of neutrality recommended which should not offend "either party," but leave to the state the grand function of peace-maker between the states of the South and the general government. Strange to say, this policy was advocated on the ground that any other would transfer the war to the soil of Tennessee, and defeat all hopes of reconciliation.[8] The notion that they could assume a neutral position, and play the part of mediators between the government and the rebellion, took entire possession of such of the leading men of the border states as were not at heart with the rebels at the outset. They trusted that such a course would lead them safely through the difficulties of their position, which, it must be confessed, considering the division of their love and interest between slavery and the Union, were great and perplexing. It led them only into the very disaster which they sought to avoid; and while it brought upon their soil and their people the calamities which they seemed most to dread, it prolonged for the government that attitude of timid hesitation which from the beginning had paralyzed its en-

---

[7] According to the census of 1860, Maryland had a white population of 516,128, and 87,188 slaves; Tennessee a white population of 826,828, and 275,784 slaves; and North Carolina a white population of 631,489, and 331,081 slaves.

[8] *Address to the People of Tennessee.*

In the perilous times upon which our country is thrown, we trust it will not be deemed presumptuous or improper in us to express to our fellow-citizens our united opinion as to the duty of the state in this dire emergency.

We are threatened with a civil war, the dreadful consequences of which, if once fully inaugurated, no language can depict. In view of such consequences, we deem it the duty of every good citizen to exert his utmost powers to avert the calamities of such a war. The agitation of the slavery question, combined with party spirit and sectional animosity, has at length produced the legitimate fruit. The present is no time to discuss the events of the past. The awful presence is upon us, and the portentous future is hanging over us. There has been a collision, as is known to you, at Fort Sumter, between the forces of the seceded states and those of the national government, which resulted in the capture of the fort by the army of the Confederate States. In view of this event, and of other acts growing out of the secession of seven of the Southern States, the President has issued his proclamation calling out the militia of the states of the Union to suppress what the proclamation designates a "combination too powerful to be suppressed by the ordinary course of judicial proceedings, or by the powers vested in the marshals by law."

Tennessee is called upon by the President to furnish two regiments, and the state has, through her executive, refused to comply with the call. This refusal of our state we fully approve. We commend the wisdom, the justice, and the humanity of the refusal. We unqualifiedly disapprove of secession, both as a constitutional right and as a remedy for existing evils; we equally condemn the policy of the administration in reference to the seceded states. But while we, without qualification, condemn the policy of coercion as calculated to dissolve the Union forever, and to dissolve it in the blood of our fellow-citizens, and regard it as sufficient to justify the state in refusing her aid to the government in its attempts to suppress the revolution in the seceded states, we do not think it her duty, considering her position in the Union, and in view of the great question of the peace of our distracted country, to take sides against the government. Tennessee has wronged no state of this Union. She has violated the rights of no state, north or south. She has been loyal

to all where loyalty was due. She has not brought on this war by any act of hers. She has tried every means in her power to prevent it. She now stands ready to do any thing within her reach to stop it; and she ought, as we think, to decline joining either party; for, in so doing, they would at once terminate her grand mission of peace-maker between the states of the South and the general government. Nay, more; the almost inevitable result would be the transfer of the war within her own borders—the defeat of all hopes of reconciliation, and the deluging of the state with the blood of her own people.

The present duty of Tennessee is to maintain a position of independence—taking sides with the Union and the peace of the country against all assailants, whether from the North or South. Her position should be to maintain the sanctity of her soil from the hostile tread of any party.

We do not pretend to foretell the future of Tennessee in connection with the other states or in reference to the federal government; we do not pretend to be able to tell the future purposes of the President and cabinet in reference to the impending war; but, should a purpose be developed by the government of overrunning and subjugating our brethren of the seceded states, we say unequivocally that it will be the duty of the state to resist at all hazards, at any cost, *and by arms,* any such purpose or attempt. And, to meet any and all emergencies, she ought to *be fully armed,* and we would respectfully call upon the authorities of the state to proceed at once to the accomplishment of this object.

Let Tennessee, then, prepare thoroughly and efficiently for coming events. In the mean time, let her, as speedily as she can, hold a conference with her sister slaveholding states yet in the Union for the purpose of devising plans for the preservation of the peace of the land. Fellow-citizens of Tennessee, we entreat you to bring yourselves up to the magnitude of the crisis. Look in the face impending calamities. Civil war—what is it? The bloodiest and darkest pages of history answer this question. To avert this, who would not give his time, his talents, his untiring energy—his all? There may be yet time to accomplish every thing. Let us not despair. The border slave states may prevent this civil war; and why shall they not do it?

NEIL S. BROWN,　　　　S. D. MORGAN,
RUSSELL HOUSTON,　　JOHN S. BRIEN,
E. H. EWING,　　　　　ANDREW EWING,
C. JOHNSON,　　　　　JOHN H. CALLENDER,
JOHN BELL,　　　　　　BAILLIE PEYTON.
R. J. MEIGS,

Nashville, April 18, 1861.

ergies and developed those of the insurgents. Such neutrality was both treason and folly. It was treason, because it sought to disqualify the constitutional government of the republic, the paramount authority in all of its affairs, and practically asserted that a commonwealth into which its citizens had formed themselves by its consent upon its soil was not an integral part of it, but an independent and a sovereign power. For a mediator must be independent; a party to a cause can not decide it as a judge; and a declaration of neutrality and the interdiction of the passage of troops are alike the attributes only of absolute sovereignty, the admission of the right to which would have enabled any state of the Union, at any time and upon any issue, to defy with impunity the central authority behind the barrier of a soil declared neutral and impassable by a component part of that very authority. Such pretended neutrality, if not making war upon the United States, would amply fulfill the constitutional conditions of treason by giving aid and comfort to their enemies in the most effective manner, and would make the suppression of insurrection quite impossible. Such neutrality was folly, because it brought upon the states which adopted it the very calamities which they sought to shun. Had the border states, the people of which before the fall of Sumter professed, and even showed, a devotion to the Union, declared boldly for it, for good or ill, the war, which the vacillation of some and the assumed neutrality of others drew inevitably upon their own soil, would instantly have been transferred to that of the Gulf States, to be waged by such an overwhelming superiority of force that it would have briefly ended. An ambiguous course is always perilous; between two great destructive powers it is inevitably fatal; and the neutrality of the border states ended in such mediation as the neutral grain offers between the upper and the nether millstone. In other respects the position assumed by those who first pretended to the direction of these states was no less unreasonable and destructive. They declared secession to be unjustifiable; and yet, in the same breath, denounced the exercise of authority which sought to restrain this unjustifiable act as a coercion which they would not endure themselves or permit to be applied to others. They demanded that the government should wait, and the fate of the nation tremble in the balance, while they debated the question in a Border State Convention. They expected that, in any case, their terms should be accepted, and in this case they would remain in the Union as long as it suited their interests or their inclinations.

Governor Harris, however, advocated no half-way measures. He recommended to the Assembly the passage of an ordinance declaring Tennessee independent of the federal government, and the "reaffirming" each and every function belonging to a separate sovereignty. Thus the governor of a commonwealth, whose imperfect political individuality was the mere creature of the government and the citizens of the republic, and whose very local Constitution declared that its people had their sovereignty and their right of soil only "so far as is consistent with the Constitution of the United States," could with bare face recommend his constituents to reassume a sovereignty which they not only had never possessed, but had never pretended to possess. Such, however, was the resentment provoked by the forcible assertion of its authority by the central government that Governor Harris's recommendation was followed, and the 8th of June was appointed by the Assembly for the vote of the people upon a declaration of independence; but long before that time arrived the state had passed out of the control of the government at Washington and even of its own people. For, as in Virginia,

there was a league formed with the insurgents through a commissioner from them; and the whole military force of the state, and all the property and munitions of war which it had "acquired" from the United States, were turned over to the government at Montgomery. Simultaneously with the ratification of this league, an act was passed authorizing the governor to raise a force of fifty-five thousand men. This he proceeded at once to do; and, to look forward a few weeks to the consummation of this scheme, the 8th of June saw the whole state filled with the armed emissaries of the insurgent government; and, except in East Tennessee, denunciation and intimidation had done their work so thoroughly that the very people who had given a majority of more than sixty-four thousand against secession, now gave a majority of more than fifty-seven thousand for it—or seemed to give; for it was openly charged that this result had been brought about not without fraud, and the open acts of those who had obtained control of the state were such as to justify this accusation against their secret practices.

It is needless to follow closely the steps by which North Carolina trod the road of treason to the Constitution. Let the names be changed, and the story of Tennessee's defection is substantially hers also. She pursued with somewhat more celerity the same course with her sister slave state upon her western border, and by the 20th of May she had thrown herself without reserve, for better for worse, into the arms of the insurgent government. Nor would the fate of Kentucky and Missouri, in which the emissaries and the well-wishers of the rebels played the same part which they had assumed with such success in Virginia, North Carolina, and Tennessee, be worthy of particular attention, were it not that in those states their machinations were unsuccessful. Kentucky, though of her eleven hundred thousand inhabitants more than two hundred and fifty thousand were negro slaves, and although she was bound by strong ties to Virginia, numbered among her people a large proportion of noble men who were ready to give themselves and all that they then had for the imperiled existence of the republic. It is true that the majority of her political leaders, and perhaps even of her citizens, were so far infected with the poison of state sovereignty that they condemned a policy of coercion, and declared that her duty was to maintain an independent and neutral position between the contending parties, declaring, as they did declare, "her soil to be sacred from the hostile tread of either, and, if necessary, to maintain this neutrality by arms."[9] But while they were thus distracted by the conflicting claims of divided duty, even the warmest partisans of state sovereignty and slavery deplored the precipitation, while the majority denounced the contumacy, and all resented the arrogance of the South Carolina politicians, by whom this distressing dilemma had been prepared. At the election on the 4th of May for delegates to the Border State Convention, the Union nominees were chosen by a majority of two to one. At the Convention itself, which was held on the 27th of the same month, only Kentucky and Missouri were represented, and an address was issued to the people of Kentucky by her delegates, headed by the venerable Mr. Crittenden, declaring that the crisis presented the grand commanding question, Union or no Union, Government or no Government, Nationality or no Nationality; that the coming war was unnecessary, and resulted from the ambition of a few rather than the wrongs done to the people; and that Kentucky would continue loyal to the Constitution, the government, and the flag of the United States, and refuse alliance with any who would destroy the Union.[10] On the 30th of June the election for representatives to Con-

[9] *Resolutions of a Meeting at Louisville, Kentucky, April 20th, at which the Hon. James Guthrie presided.*

Resolved, 1. That, as the Confederate States have, by overt acts, commenced war against the United States, without consultation with Kentucky and their sister Southern States, Kentucky reserves to herself the right to choose her own position, and that while her natural sympathies are with those who have a common interest in the protection of slavery, she still acknowledges her loyalty and fealty to the government of the United States, which she will cheerfully render until that government becomes aggressive, tyrannical, and regardless of our rights in slave property.

2. That the national government should be tried by its acts, and that the several states, as its peers in their appropriate spheres, will hold it to a rigid accountability, and require that its acts should be fraternal in their efforts to bring back the seceding states, and not sanguinary or coercive.

3. That, as we oppose the call of the President for volunteers for the purpose of coercing the seceding states, so we oppose the raising of troops in this state to co-operate with the Southern Confederacy when the acknowledged intention of the latter is to march upon the City of Washington and capture the Capitol, and when, in its march thither, it must pass through states which have not yet renounced their allegiance to the Union.

4. That secession is a remedy for no evil, real or imaginary, but an aggravation and complication of existing difficulties.

5. That the memories of the past, the interests of the present, and the solemn convictions of future duty and usefulness in the hope of mediation, prevent Kentucky from taking part with the seceding states against the general government.

6. That "the present duty of Kentucky is to maintain her present independent position, taking sides not with the administration, nor with the seceding states, but with the Union against them both, declaring her soil to be sacred from the hostile tread of either, and, if necessary, to make the declaration good with her strong right arm."

7. That, to the end Kentucky may be prepared for any contingency, "we would have her arm herself thoroughly at the earliest practicable moment," by regular legal action.

8. That we look to the young men of the Kentucky State Guard as the bulwarks of the safety of our commonwealth, and that we conjure them to remember that they are pledged equally to fidelity to the United States and Kentucky.

9. That the Union and the Constitution, being mainly the work of Southern soldiers and statesmen, in our opinion furnish a surer guaranty for "Southern Rights" than can be found under any other system of government yet devised by men.

[10]   *To the People of Kentucky.*

Having been elected by you as your delegates to "a Convention of the border slave states and such other slave states as have not passed Ordinances of Secession," with power to meet with delegates from other states in convention, "to consult on the critical condition of the country, and agree upon some plan of adjustment;" and having met at Frankfort, on the 27th of May, in pursuance of the act, we deem it proper to inform you, briefly, of what was done by us in the Convention.

It was a matter of regret to us that, while the call for this Convention originated in Virginia, and had, apparently, the concurrence of all the border slave states, yet there were delegates in attendance from Kentucky and Missouri only. One representative chosen by the counties of M'Minn and Sevier, in Tennessee, appeared, and, although not coming with such credentials as were necessary to constitute him a delegate, he was invited to participate in our deliberations.

After a continuous session from day to day, during which the condition of the country, and the various causes that led to it, were maturely considered, it was resolved that the Convention should address an appeal to the people of the United States, and the delegates from Kentucky determined to present to you a separate address, in which views of your members should be embodied. In the discharge of this duty we now attempt to address you.

Your state, on a deliberate consideration of her responsibilities—moral, political, and social—has determined that the proper course for her to pursue is to take no part in the controversy between the government and the seceded states but that of *mediator* and *intercessor.* She is unwilling to take up arms against her brethren residing either north or south of the geographical line by which they are unhappily divided into warring sections. This course was commended to her by every consideration of patriotism, and by a proper regard for her own security. It does not result from timidity; on the contrary, it could only have been adopted by a brave people—so brave that the least imputation on their courage would be branded as false by their written and traditional history.

Kentucky was right in taking this position, because, from the commencement of this deplorable controversy, her voice was for reconciliation, compromise, and peace. She had no cause of complaint against the general government, and made none. The injuries she sustained in her property from a failure to execute laws passed for its protection, in consequence of illegal interference by wicked and deluded citizens in the free states, she considered as wholly insufficient to justify a dismemberment of the Union. That she regarded as no remedy for existing evils, but an aggravation of them all. She witnessed, it is true, with deep concern, the growth of a wild and frenzied fanaticism in one section, and a reckless and defiant spirit in another, both equally threatening destruction to the country, and tried earnestly to arrest them, but in vain. We will not stop to trace the causes of the unhappy condition in which we are now placed, or to criminate either of the sections to the dishonor of the other, but can say that we believed both to have been wrong, and, in their madness and folly, to have inaugurated a war that the Christian world looks upon with amazement and sorrow, and that Liberty, Christianity, and Civilization stand appalled at the horrors to which it will give rise.

It is a proud and grand thing for Kentucky to stand up and say, as she can, truthfully, in the face of the world, "We had no hand in this thing; our skirts are clear." And, in looking at the *terrorism* that prevails elsewhere—beholding freedom of speech denied to American citizens, their homesteads subjected to lawless visitation, their property confiscated, and their persons liable to incarceration and search—how grandly does she not loom up, as she proclaims to the oppressed and miserable, We offer you a refuge! Here, constitutional law, and respect for individual rights, still exist! Here is an asylum where loyalty to the name, nation, and flag of the Union predominates; and here is the only place, in this lately great republic, where true freedom remains—that freedom for which our fathers fought—the citizen being free to speak, write, or publish any thing he may wish, responsible only to the laws, and not controlled by the violence of the mob.

Is not this an attitude worthy of a great people, and do not her position and safety require her to maintain it? If she deviates from it; if she suffers herself, in a moment of excitement, to be led off by sympathy with one side or the other—to ally herself with either section—inevitable and speedy ruin must fall upon her. What reason can be urged to incline her to such a fatal step? She is still, thank God, a member of the Union, owing constitutional allegiance to it—an allegiance voluntarily given, long maintained, and from which she has derived countless benefits. Can she, by her own act, forfeit this allegiance, and by the exercise of any constitutional power sever herself from that government? In our opinion the statement of the proposition insures its rejection. It is of no more rational force than the argument of the suicide to commit self-slaughter. Secession is not a right. That the right of revolution exists is as true in states as the right of self-defense is true of individuals. It does not exist by virtue of legal enactment or constitutional provision, but is founded in the nature of things—is inalienable and indestructible, and ought to be resorted to only when all peaceable remedies fail. Revolution is an extreme remedy, finds its justification alone in an escape from intolerable oppression, and, hazarding the consequences of failure, as success or defeat makes the movement one of rightful resistance or rebellion, it becomes the stern duty of Kentucky to look not only to the motives that might impel her to revolt, but to the probable results. She must contemplate her condition in a complex character—national and state—and see what must be her fate in the event of a separation.

gress took place, the issue presented being between Union on the one side, and States Rights on the other; when the Union delegates were elected by an overwhelming majority, the State Rights men having polled but a few more than one quarter of the ballots.

Leaving Kentucky thus firmly bound to the fortunes of the republic, though with her patriotism chilled by the affectation of a cold neutrality, we turn our eyes upon Missouri, the state whose political birth forty years before had been ushered in by the inauspicious omens of the tremendous conflict in which she was now summoned to take a part. Were it not that fanaticism, whether in a good cause or a bad, always forgets or disregards the obligations and even the teachings of the past, the people of Missouri could not for a moment have been led by the delusions of state sovereignty into the denial of a paramount allegiance to the constitutional government of the republic; for there were men still living within her borders who could remember that at the time of her admission as one of the commonwealths entitled to a voice in that government, it was at Washington, and not at St. Louis or at Jackson City, that it was decided whether her Constitution should protect the institution of negro slavery. But a population which furnished the border ruffians who undertook to decide, and who, in a struggle of four years, so nearly decided, by the bowie-knife and the revolver, the political and social future of a neighboring community, could not but include a large number of men who would hasten to serve the cause they had most at heart, in the company of the great body of its devotees, and to dignify their former violence by making it appear the first step in a great revolution. These men were not wanting to their faction or to themselves. They took the field at once with the spirit and the audacity which had marked the movements of the insurgents from the beginning; and Claiborne Jackson, governor of the state, was at their head. Governor Jackson came into office on the 4th of January; and in his inaugural message he did not hesitate at taking the extreme ground that Missouri must stand by the other slave states, whatever course they might pursue. A Convention was called; but Union delegates were elected by large majorities; and the usual commissioner from the insurgents having pleaded the cause of the rebellion before it, he was informed by resolution that Missouri refused to join her fortunes with the states represented at Montgomery. In the resolutions, which were the result of the deliberations for which the Convention was called together, it was declared unanimously that the state had no cause for dissolving her connection with the Union; but another was passed by the large majority of eighty-nine to six, recommending, as a means of avoiding civil war, the withdrawal of the federal forces from the forts where collision with the insurgents might be apprehended.[1] Thus, indeed, might civil war have

been avoided; and so might a certain man who went down from Jerusalem to Jericho have avoided an unpleasant collision by presenting his purse to certain other men among whom he fell upon the road. To yield what is demanded, irrespective of the justice of the demand, may be at times the part of discretion; it can never be that of honor, of dignity, or of sovereign power. There was another resolution, recommending a National Convention for the amendment of the Constitution; but on the 27th of the month (it was March) the state Legislature passed a resolution that it was inexpedient to take any steps toward the National Convention, or toward the amendment of the Constitution of the Union which had been recommended by the state Convention. The stirring events of the latter half of April failed to produce in Missouri the effect which followed them in the other border states, and the excitement which they created soon passed away.

But, although the people of Missouri pronounced thus unhesitatingly, thus so decidedly, and by such large majorities for the Union, the restless and reckless men, who loved slavery more than the republic, did not cease their machinations. A secret association had already been formed for the purpose of forcing the state into the ranks of the insurrection; it numbered among its members many influential politicians; and its object, at least, if not its means, were approved by the governor himself. He began at once the organization of a State Guard, ostensibly for the purpose of keeping the peace and protecting the soil of the state against invasion—that term meaning, when so used, the presence of national troops. But the government at Washington had favored the formation of a military organization called Home Guards, composed of loyal Missourians, which, under spirited and determined leadership, soon checked the development of Governor Jackson's plans and those of his co-workers, who began their movement by seizing the United States Arsenal at Liberty, a small town in the extreme western part of the state, and distributing the arms to the malcontents in that neighborhood. The same fate threatened the more important arsenal at St. Louis; but in command there was Captain Nathaniel Lyon, of the United States Army, who had served with honor in Florida and in Mexico, and with discretion and loyalty in Kansas during her early trial. His force was very small, and the Police Commissioners of St. Louis, undertaking to make a little war upon the government, required him to confine the exercise of his authority to the grounds belonging to the United States. The city swarmed with the partisans of the rebels; the governor himself had ordered two thousand men down from Jefferson City, whose purpose could only be to seize the arms in the arsenal. This a Captain Stokes, also of the army, prevented by a daring and energetic movement. Provided by Governor

---

Under the national government, she has a right to the protection of thirty-three great states, and with them, thus protected, can defy the world in arms. Under it, she becomes prosperous and happy. Deprived of it, she finds herself exposed to imminent danger. She has a border front on the Ohio River of near seven hundred miles, with three powerful states on that border. She has four hundred miles on the south, by which she is separated from Tennessee by a merely conventional line. Her eastern front is on Virginia, and part of her western on Missouri, thus making her antagonistic, in the event of collision, to Virginia, which is our mother, and to Missouri, which is our daughter. Hemmed in thus on every side by powers, each one of which is equal to her own, her situation, and her sense of loyalty to the Union, imperatively demand of her to insist on the integrity of the Union, its Constitution, and government. Peace is of vital consequence to her, and can only be secured to her by preserving the Union inviolate. Kentucky has no cause of quarrel with the Constitution, and no wish to quarrel with her neighbors, but abundant reason to love both. Of the great West she was the pioneer, and became the starting-point of emigration to all around her. There is not a Western or a Southwestern state in which Kentucky families are not settled, and she is bound to all by ties of interest and brotherhood. She has ever been loyal to the government, answering to its requisitions and sharing its burdens. At the command of that government, when war was declared to protect the rights of sailors, although she had no vessels to float on the ocean, yet she offered up her blood freely in the common defense from the Lakes to the Gulf of Mexico. Again, when war, growing out of a territorial controversy, far from her own borders, was proclaimed, she was among the foremost in the fight, and Monterey and Buena Vista were made famous in history by the valor of Kentuckians. Never has she faltered in her duty to the Union.

In declining to respond to a call made by the present administration of the government, and one that we have reason to believe would not have been made if the administration had been fully advised of the circumstances by which we were surrounded, Kentucky did not put herself in factious opposition to her legitimate obligations; she did not choose to throw herself in hostile collision with the slave states of Missouri, Maryland, and Delaware, which have not seceded on the one hand, nor the slave states which have and are in process of secession on the other, and shed the blood of brethren and kindred at the very moment when she was striving to be an apostle of peace. Nature herself revolted at the thought, and her conduct in this matter had so much of love to God, and love to man in it, that it will meet the sanction of an approving world. So far from being denounced for this action, it is every where looked upon as an act of purest patriotism, resulting from imperious necessity, and the highest instincts of self-preservation—respected by the very administration that alone could have complained of it, and will, we doubt not, be ratified by it, if not in terms, at least by its future action. That act did not take her out of the Union.

Kentucky, in so grave a matter as this, passes by mere legal technicalities and a discussion of theoretical difficulties of government, poises herself upon her right to do what the necessities of her condition imperatively demanded of her, and relies upon the good sense and magnanimity of her sister states, seeing that there is no parallel in her condition and theirs to do her justice.

In all things she is as loyal as ever to the constitutional administration of the government. She will follow the Stars and Stripes to the utmost regions of the earth, and defend them from foreign insult. She refuses allegiance with any who would destroy the Union. All she asks is permission to keep out of this unnatural strife. When called to take part in it, she believes there is more honor in the breach than in the observance of any supposed duty to perform it.

Feeling that she is clearly right in this, and has announced her intention to refrain from aggression upon others, she must protest against her soil being made the theatre of military operations by any belligerent. The war must not be transferred by the warring sections from their own to her borders. Such unfriendly action can not be viewed with indifference by Kentucky.

Having thus referred to this subject in its general aspects, we would invite your individual attention to its direct bearings upon yourselves.

It is not now a question of party politics, although it may be the interest of some to make it so. The day of mere party platforms has, we trust, gone forever. It has passed from being a mere struggle for place that may gratify personal ambition, to one for the present and future welfare of a whole people, for the safety of homes and firesides. Whatever divisions have heretofore existed should now cease. In times past, in our elections, the questions which divided men related to mere party differences, and the members of all the parties rivaled each other in their expression of devotion to the Union, and were equally clamorous for their rights, in the Union and not out of it. Now these party differences are passed away and forgotten. The direct question is Union or no Union—Government or no Government—Nationality or no Nationality. Before this grand and commanding question every thing else gives way.

All can see that such a state of things can not continue without war, and that such a war was unnecessary. It resulted from the ambition of men rather than from the wrongs done the people. There was a remedy for every thing already provided by the Constitution, which, with wise foresight, provided against the trials to which it might be subjected. There were countervailing powers to check encroachments, whether by a President or by Congress; and it so happened that at this dangerous crisis, when a sectional president had been elected, there was a majority in opposition to him in both houses of Congress, by which he could have been controlled and the people

protected. It was the duty of the opposition to have stood to their posts till the danger of encroachment had passed away. But senators and representatives, following the example of their states, vacated their seats, and placed a president who would have been in a minority at the head of a triumphant majority. It was a great wrong, for which they must answer to posterity. Kentucky remained true to herself, contending with all her might for what were considered to be the rights of the people; and although one after another of the states that should have been by her side ungenerously deserted her, leaving her almost alone in the field, yet she did not surrender her rights under the Constitution, and never will surrender them. She will appear again in the Congress of the United States, not having conceded the least item of power to the government that had not heretofore been granted, and retaining every power she had reserved. She will insist upon her constitutional rights in the Union, and not out of it.

Kentucky is grieved to think that any thing should have been done by her sister states that has made it necessary for her to assume the position she now occupies. It is not one of submission, as it has been insultingly called—it is one of the most exalted patriotism; but, if she had no higher or holier motive—if she were not earnestly for peace among her brethren, the great law of self-protection points out her course, and she has no alternative. Already one section declares that there will be no war at home, but that it shall be in Kentucky and Virginia. Already the cannon and bayonets of another section are visible on our most exposed border. Let these hostile armies meet on our soil, and it will matter but little to us which may succeed, for destruction to us will be the inevitable result. Our fields will be laid waste, our houses and cities will be burned, our people will be slain, and this goodly land be rebaptized "the land of blood;" and even the institution, to preserve or control which this wretched war was undertaken, will be exterminated in the general ruin. Such is the evil that others will bring upon us, no matter which side we take, if this is to be the battle-field. But there is danger at home more appalling than any that comes from beyond. People of Kentucky, look well to it that you do not get to fighting among yourselves, for then, indeed, you will find that it is an ill fight where he that wins has the worst of it. Endeavor to be of one mind, and strive to keep the state steady in her present position. Hold fast to that sheet-anchor of republican liberty, that the will of the majority constitutionally and legally expressed must govern. You have, in the election by which this Convention was chosen, displayed a unanimity unparalleled in your history. May you be as unanimous in the future; may your majorities be so decided that a refusal to obey may be justly called factious. Trust and love one another. Avoid angry strife. Frown upon the petty ambition of demagogues who would stir up bad passions among you. Consider, as wise men, what is necessary for your own best interest, and, in humble submission, trust and look to that Almighty Being who has heretofore so signally blessed us as a nation for His guidance through the gloom and darkness of this hour.

J. J. CRITTENDEN, President.   C. A. WICKLIFFE,
JAMES GUTHRIE,   G. W. DUNLAP,
R. K. WILLIAMS,   C. S. MOREHEAD,
ARCH'D DIXON,   J. F. ROBINSON,
F. M. BRISTOW,   JOHN B. HUSTON,
JOSHUA F. BELL,   ROBT. RICHARDSON.

[1] *Resolutions reported in the Missouri Convention.*

Resolved, That at present there is no adequate cause to impel Missouri to dissolve her connection with the federal Union, but, on the contrary, she will labor for such an adjustment of the existing troubles as will secure peace, rights, and equality to all the states.

Resolved, That the people of this state are devotedly attached to the institutions of our country, and earnestly desire that by a fair and amicable adjustment the present causes of disagreement may be removed, the Union perpetuated, and peace and harmony be restored between the South and North.

Resolved, That the people of this state deem the amendments to the Constitution of the United States, proposed by Mr. Crittenden, with the extending of the same to Territories hereafter to be acquired, a basis of adjustment which will successfully remove the causes of difference forever from the arena of national politics.

Resolved, That the people of Missouri believe that the peace and quiet of the country will be promoted by a Convention to propose amendments to the Constitution of the United States; and that this Convention urges the Legislature of this state to take steps for calling such Convention.

Resolved, That, in the opinion of this Convention, the employment of military force by the federal government to coerce the seceding states, or the employment of force by the seceding states to assail the government of the United States, will inevitably plunge the country into civil war, and thereby extinguish all hope of an amicable settlement of the issues now pending.

We therefore earnestly entreat the federal government, as well as the seceding states, to stay the arm of military power, and on no pretense whatever bring upon the nation the horrors of civil war.

Resolved, That, when the Convention adjourns, it adjourn to meet at Jefferson City on the third Monday in December.

Resolved, That a committee be elected, a majority of which shall have power to convene the Convention at such time and place prior to the third Monday in December as the exigencies may require.

FORTIFICATIONS THROWN UP TO PROTECT THE UNITED STATES ARSENAL AT ST. LOUIS, MISSOURI.

A CORNER SCENE IN ST. LOUIS.

Yates, of Illinois, with a requisition from the Secretary of War for ten thousand muskets, he went to St. Louis. With the assistance of Captain Lyon, he managed to deceive a tumultuous mob which surrounded the arsenal by sending off a large quantity of worthless arms in such a manner as to attract attention. They were seized by the watchful multitude; and while these were triumphing in their success, Captain Stokes got on board a steamer not only the ten thousand muskets for which he came, but eleven thousand more, with five hundred rifle carbines, as many revolvers, one hundred and ten thousand cartridges, and some cannon and accoutrements, leaving only seven thousand muskets to arm the St. Louis volunteers. He steamed safely past a battery which the secessionists had erected near St. Louis, and, arriving at Alton, Illinois, sent his valuable prize to Springfield, in that state, thus executing the first successful and important enterprise for the preservation to the government of the material of war of which it was so much in need. Success generally begets success. The organization of the Home Guard went rapidly on, and soon there were five thousand armed and equipped in the vicinity of St. Louis, under the command of Colonels Francis P. Blair and Franz Sigel, the former a brother of President Lincoln's Postmaster General, the latter a German officer who had served with great distinction in the European troubles which had succeeded the French revolution of 1848. On the outskirts of St. Louis a camp of Governor Jackson's State Guards had been established, under the command of General Frost. Captain Lyon, knowing the object with which this encampment was formed, determined to break it up; and, in spite of a specious protest of loyalty on the part of General Frost, on the 10th of May he marched upon him at the head of the full commands of Colonels Blair and Sigel, with some pieces of artillery. The secessionists took the alarm and poured out after the troops, armed with whatever weapons they could seize; and even the townsfolk went in crowds to witness the fight. The former were foiled by the military dispositions of Captain Lyon; they could not approach the camp which they would so gladly have re-enforced; and General Frost, finding himself surrounded by a force four or five times as great as his own, surrendered at discretion upon Captain Lyon's summons.[2] By this prompt movement a dangerous nucleus of rebellion was broken up, about seven hundred prisoners, inclusive of fifty officers, were taken, and a large quantity of small arms, artillery, and ammunition captured. In this camp, which its commanding officer, with the effrontery and duplicity which the partisans of the rebellion so constantly, and often so successfully, practised, had voluntarily declared by letter to Captain Lyon not hostile to the United States, it was found that the two main streets were named Davis and Beauregard; that a part of its occupants were in the rebel uniform; and that the command was in great

measure armed with muskets seized by the Louisiana insurgents at Baton Rouge, and sent surreptitiously up the Mississippi![3] The prisoners having refused to take the oath of allegiance, the only condition proposed for their release, on the ground that they had already taken it, and that to take it again would be to admit that they had been in rebellion, were marched under guard to the arsenal. While they were on the way, preceded and followed by detachments of the Union troops, and shut in on either side by a single file, the front ranks of the guard were pressed upon by a tumultuous crowd, which, after insulting them with the most opprobrious epithets, proceeded to blows, and at last attacked them with stones and pistols. Several of the soldiers, without orders, fired into the crowd. Fortunately, or, as the issue proved, perhaps unfortunately, no person was injured, and the soldiers who had fired were immediately placed under arrest. Quiet and order were hardly restored when the tumult broke out afresh. Encouraged by their impunity, the mob renewed their attack, now in the rear, with stones and pistols. A captain ordered his company to fire, and twenty-five persons were killed or wounded. In a popular tumult, the innocent and the imprudent are always sure to suffer with the guilty, through no fault of those in authority. On this occasion a miscellaneous crowd, including even some women and children, had followed the troops, and it is sad to relate that those who fell were mostly citizens, who, however they might have sympathized with the purposes of the rioters, had not joined them in their attack. The rage of the secessionists, and the excitement of all the people, was tremendous; throughout the night St. Louis was heaving with suppressed tumult. On the following day a large body of the Home Guard, chiefly Germans, marched into the city from the arsenal, where they had been armed and equipped. The streets were thronged with people, through which they passed for a time unmolested. But at length hooting and hissing began, and finally a revolver was fired from the crowd. A soldier fell dead in the ranks. Firing now began from the windows of the houses, when the leading company of the Germans—not exhibiting the steadiness and self-possession of the Massachusetts militia-men under like circumstances in Baltimore—wheeled and fired down the street with fatal effect. The consternation which ensued was overwhelming; but the fury with which it was accompanied was mitigated by the discovery that of the six persons who were killed four were soldiers. The Germans, in their bewilderment, had fired into their own ranks. The excitement caused by these bloody occurrences was not confined to St. Louis. The news flew rapidly to Jackson City, and stimulated the instant passage of a Military Bill, which before was languishing through the debates. By this bill a military fund was created for the purpose of arming and equipping the militia; and all the money in the treasury, or to be received during the current year, however it had been previously appropriated, was devoted to this purpose. Every able-bodied man in the state was made subject to military duty; and, most important provision of all, this large force was placed under the orders of the governor, and required to take an oath to obey him alone.

Meantime General Harney, an army officer of more experience and vigor than discretion, had been appointed to the command of the Department of the West. He arrived at St. Louis on the 11th, in the midst of the turmoil caused by the bloody scenes of the two previous days. He issued first a curt soldier's proclamation, informing the people that he should discharge his delicate duties with decision; that he had not the power of disbanding the Home Guards, but that he would gratify the prejudices of the Missourians by putting down riotous demonstrations with the soldiers of the regular army.[4] On the 14th he issued another proclamation, in which he declared the Military Bill an indirect Secession Ordinance, which indeed it was, and pronounced it null and void. He pointed out to the Missourians that, whatever became of the people around the Gulf, their commonwealth must share the destiny of the republic, and that, if necessary, the whole power of the government would be used to enforce obedience to the "supreme law of the land," and to retain Missouri in the Union.[5] General Harney soon found

[2]   *Captain Lyon, U. S. A., to General Frost, Missouri State Guard.*
                                    Head-quarters United States Troops, St. Louis, May 10, 1861.
   To General D. M. Frost:
   SIR,—Your command is regarded as evidently hostile toward the government of the United States. It is, for the most part, made up of those secessionists who have openly avowed their hostility to the general government, and have been plotting at the seizure of its property and the overthrow of its authority. You are openly in communication with the so-called Southern confederacy, which is now at war with the United States, and you are receiving at your camp from the said confederacy, under its flag, large supplies of material of war, most of which is known to be the property of the United States. These extraordinary preparations plainly indicate none other than the well known purpose of the governor of this state, under whose orders you are acting, and whose purpose, recently communicated to the Legislature, has just been responded to by that body in the most unparalleled legislation, having in direct view hostilities to the general government, and co-operating with the enemy. In view of these considerations, and your failure to disperse in obedience to the proclamation of the President, and of the eminent necessity of state policy, and the welfare and obligations imposed upon me by instructions from Washington, it is my duty to demand, and I do hereby demand of you, an immediate surrender of your command, with no other conditions than that all persons surrendering under this demand shall be humanely and kindly treated. Believing myself prepared to enforce the demand, one half hour's time before doing so will be allowed for your compliance therewith.
                    N. LYON, Captain Second Infantry, commanding Troops.

[3] General Harney's proclamation to the people of Missouri, May 14, 1861.

[4] *General Harney's Proclamation to the People of the State of Missouri and the City of St. Louis.*
                                    Military Department of the West, St. Louis, May 11, 1861.
   I have just returned to this post, and have assumed the military command of this department. No one can more deeply regret the deplorable state of things existing here than myself. The past can not be recalled. I can only deal with the present and the future.
   I most anxiously desire to discharge the delicate and onerous duties devolved upon me so as to preserve the public peace. I shall carefully abstain from the exercise of any unnecessary powers, and from all interference with the proper functions of the public officers of the state and city. I therefore call upon the public authorities and the people to aid me in preserving the public peace.
   The military force stationed in this department by the authority of the government, and now under my command, will only be used in the last resort to preserve the peace. I trust I may be spared the necessity of resorting to martial law, but the public peace *must be preserved*, and the lives and property of the people protected. Upon a careful review of my instructions, I find I have no authority to change the location of the "Home Guards."
   To avoid all cause of irritation and excitement, if called upon to aid the local authorities in preserving the public peace, I shall, in preference, make use of the regular army.
   I ask the people to pursue their peaceful avocations, and to observe the laws and orders of their local authorities, and to abstain from the excitements of public meetings and heated discussions. My appeal, I trust, may not be in vain, and I pledge the faith of a soldier to the earnest discharge of my duty.   WILLIAM S. HARNEY, Brigadier General U. S. A., commanding Dep't.

[5]   *General Harney's Second Proclamation.*
                                    Military Department of the West, St. Louis, May 14, 1861.
   To the People of the State of Missouri:
   On my return to the duties of the command of this department, I find, greatly to my astonishment and mortification, a most extraordinary state of things existing in this state, deeply affect-

VOLUNTEERS ATTACKED IN ST. LOUIS.

himself involved in negotiations with Sterling Price, a wary and persistent man, under whose command, as major general, Governor Jackson had placed the forces enlisted under the Military Bill. On the 20th of May General Price brought General Harney to an agreement, by which the former pledged the whole of the force under his command and the whole power of the state to the preservation of order, and the latter consented to make no farther military movement in the state. This specious compromise, which tied the hands of the government and left those of the secessionists free, and, what was of more importance, recognized in effect the right of the state to make terms with the nation as to the treatment of rebellious citizens resident in Missouri, met with no favor outside the pale of the rebellion and the boundaries of Missouri, and with much opposition within the latter. Whether it was thought at Washington that General Harney had been for the first time in his life too cautious in the discharge of his duty, or that he had been overreached, did not appear in the order which, ten days after this concession, relieved him from the command of the Department of the West, and placed it in the hands of Captain, now Brigadier General Lyon. Of Arkansas, hardly a border state, it is only necessary to say that, after once refusing by her Convention to secede, she at last was carried over, on the 6th of May, to her Southern neighbors.

From the spectacle of shaken or subverted loyalty in the border states,

I turn to one yet more unpropitious to the fortunes of the republic—the condition of Washington itself. That which should have been the moral strong-hold and citadel of the nation, was, by its position, the weakest, and, by its political affinities and its social condition, the most disaffected city outside of the seceded states—a place which the government had not only to protect, but to protect itself against. Among the many advantages gained by the slave states in the early days of the republic, not the least was the establishment of the seat of government on the banks of the Potomac. The Eastern and Middle States wished it to be placed on the Susquehanna; but they also much desired the passage of a bill by which the government should assume the debts of the several states contracted during and because of the War of Independence, and thus pay from the common fund an expense incurred for the common benefit. This the Southern States, the people of which owned very few of those debts, opposed. Two causes, of what proved to be a sharp contention, were removed by a compromise of these two interests. The Southern States agreed to the assumption of the debts; the Eastern and Middle States consented to the final establishment of the seat of government upon the Potomac. The price which the Southern States paid for this advantage was small in comparison with its value; for it contributed largely to the preservation of the preponderance which they soon obtained and always kept in the general government; and now that they sought to destroy the republic, and build up a great slaveholding oligarchy upon its ruins, they expected and they found in Washington a multitude of co-workers, none the less valuable because they were always secret and generally treacherous. Washington—being without commerce, without manufactures, not even the chief city of a commonwealth or the county town of an agricultural district, not dignified by institutions of science and literature, or graced by galleries of art or places of elegant amusement—was the mere political capital of the country, the place for the transaction of the business of the nation. Thus barren of the chief interests which fill the daily life of men in the highest civilization, surrounded by slave territory and being itself slave ground, it had small attractions and many discomforts for the residents of free states. Few of them sought it except at the call of political duty, or for some advantage to be obtained only through political influence; and those few only in search of recreation or to gratify curiosity during the sessions of Congress. The duty performed, the end attained of profit or of pleasure, the visitor from the North, weary of politics in public, politics in society, and slavery in both politics and society, gladly turned his face homeward toward tranquillity and freedom. But while the residents of the most populous, the wealthiest, and the most cultivated part of the republic were thus strangers, or at most sojourners in its capital, the slave states naturally furnished it nearly the whole of its permanent population. In the appointment of clerks and subordinate officers of the government, it came gradually to pass that places at Washington were mostly given to men from the slave states, and the departments there were filled by incumbents who had received their situations at the hands of the leaders in the insurrection. The Northern and Western States furnished comparatively few men who sought subordinate public employment, except as a temporary resort, or as a step to higher position; but the lack of incentive to honorable exertion in commerce or in manufactures, in arts or in letters, in the slave states, and the concentration of land and slaves in the hands of a few, had for inevitable consequence the production of a numerous class of needy, shiftless, but well-connected men, of a certain degree and kind of social culture, who were glad to settle down at the capital as the recipients of comfortable salaries, which, by the influence of the slave power, they were able to retain through the brief and rare periods during which that power was not absolutely in the ascendant. In Washington the tone of society was given entirely by men and women who had been born and bred under the shadow of slavery; and the bankers, the lawyers, and men of minor occupations, who, for the sake of business, made it their home, soon adopted, if they did not bring with them, a creed and a conduct without which gain was difficult and social enjoyment impossible. Thus even the annual influx of members of Congress from the North came to be regarded much as the Saracens looked upon the stream of unbelieving pilgrims to

Jerusalem—something to be endured while the visitors paid tribute and suffered indignity, but which was resented and resisted when made in force and with a claim to possession. The presence of a president, a vice-president, and a cabinet, neither of whom was a slaveholder or even a Democrat, and who owed their elevation to the avowed opponents of the slave interest, was regarded by the Washingtonians, and particularly by the placemen, with mingled disgust and apprehension. They had come to think that the capital of the nation belonged to them. They trembled alike for their social ascendency and their salaries. They scorned the new men; they hated those who would replace them; they raged at the sight of abolitionists, and, worst of all, abolitionists in power. Many of the new-comers were rustic in appearance and in manners, and the city placemen felt, or affected to themselves to feel, as the Faubourg St. Germain really felt when the *bourgeoisie* entered *salons* without buckles in their shoes, and began to ask, By what right do you misgovern France? In only one direction was there hope for them, and they looked southward for deliverance. Their feelings were shared by the whole of the ruling faction of the slave states, of which, in fact, they were but representatives. The insurgents shrieked in type (a figure less violent would not express the truth) over what they pretended to regard as the desecration of Washington. In their copious but somewhat monotonous vocabulary of abuse—a vocabulary which hardly supported their continually asserted claims to superior refinement—they compared it, since the 4th of March, to a filthy cage of unclean birds, a wallow of swine, a festering sink of iniquity. They called the members of the new administration dogs and caitiffs, harpies who had come down to defile and brutalize the place; and they clamored frantically for the expulsion of the beast and the Illinois ape (these were the names which they gave to the President) from the desecrated city of Washington. Such was the cry that went up from the press in all quarters of what now in the North had received no worse name than "Secessia."[6] The purpose of attacking Washington, and asserting the power of the insurgent government over all the country south of Pennsylvania and the Ohio River, was undoubtedly entertained by the rebel leaders, but was necessarily abandoned on account of the dispositions of General Scott, the course of events in Maryland, Kentucky, and Missouri, and especially the tremendous and most unexpected uprising at the North. But still the government lived in constant apprehension. From the 19th (the day of the attack on the Massachusetts men in Baltimore) to the 25th of April, no communication from North or South was received at Washington, and the loyal and the disaffected alike suffered the torture of suspense. The public buildings were guarded, barricaded, and fortified. So lively was the apprehension of a sudden raid upon Washington by a force which, though not large enough to hold, might yet sack it, and carry off the archives

---

[6]　　*The Capture of Washington.*—*From the Richmond Examiner of April* 23, 1861.

The capture of Washington City is perfectly within the power of Virginia and Maryland, if Virginia will only make the effort by her constituted authorities; nor is there a single moment to lose. The entire population pant for the onset; there never was half the unanimity among the people before, nor a tithe of the zeal, upon any subject, that is now manifested to take Washington, and drive from it every Black Republican who is a dweller there.

From the mountain tops and valleys to the shores of the sea, there is one wild shout of fierce resolve to capture Washington City at all and every human hazard. The filthy cage of unclean birds must and will assuredly be purified by fire. The people are determined upon it, and are clamorous for a leader to conduct them to the onslaught. That leader will assuredly arise, ay, and that right speedily.

It is not to be endured that this flight of abolition harpies shall come down from the black North for their roosts in the heart of the South, to defile and brutalize the land. They come as our enemies—they act as our most deadly foes—they promise us bloodshed and fire, and this is the only promise they have ever redeemed. The fanatical yell for the immediate subjugation of the whole South is going up hourly from the united voices of all the North; and for the purpose of making their work sure, they have determined to hold Washington City as the point from whence to carry on their brutal warfare.

Our people can take it—if they will take it—and Scott the arch-traitor, and Lincoln the beast, combined, can not prevent it. The just indignation of an outraged and deeply injured people will teach the Illinois ape to repeat his race and retrace his journey across the borders of the free negro

states still more rapidly than he came; and Scott, the traitor, will be given an opportunity at the same time to try the difference between "Scott's tactics" and the Shanghae drill for quick movements.

Great cleansing and purification are needed and will be given to that festering sink of iniquity, that wallow of Lincoln and Scott—the desecrated City of Washington, and many indeed will be the carcasses of dogs and caitiffs that will blacken the air upon the gallows before the great work is accomplished. So let it be.

From the Richmond Whig of May 22, 1861.

We are not enough in the secrets of our authorities to specify the day on which Jeff. Davis will dine at the White House, and Ben. M'Cullough take his siesta in General Sickles's gilded tent. We should dislike to produce any disappointment by naming too soon or too early a day; but it will save trouble if the gentlemen will keep themselves in readiness to dislodge at a moment's notice! If they are not smitten, however, with more than judicial blindness, they do not need this warning at our hands. They must know that the measure of their iniquities is full, and the patience of outraged freedom is exhausted. Among all the brave men from the Rio Grande to the Potomac, and stretching over into insulted, indignant, and infuriated Maryland, there is but one word on every lip—"Washington;" and one sentiment on every heart—vengeance on the tyrants who pollute the capital of the republic!

See, also, the *Richmond Enquirer*, the *New Orleans Picayune*, the *Enfaula* (Ala.) *Express*, the *Goldsborough Tribune*, and the *Raleigh Standard*, and various other slave-state newspapers of the same period.

GALLERIES UNDER THE SENATE-CHAMBER.

E E

BREAD-OVENS UNDER THE CAPITOL.

BARRICADE IN THE TREASURY BUILDING.

THE EIGHTH MASSACHUSETTS VOLUNTEERS IN THE ROTUNDA OF THE CAPITOL.

and the treasure of the nation, that the principal passage-ways of the Treasury and the Capitol were defended by howitzers, which raked their length, and by heavy planks, which, stretched across them at short intervals about the height of a man's knee from the floor, made a charge upon the gun impossible. The iron plates cast for the dome of the Capitol were set up as breast-works between its columns, where they were supported by barrels of cement and heaped-up stone and timber. The statuary and the pictures were protected by heavy planking; and the basement of the building was used as a kitchen. But, when the communication was established, and regiments began to pour in, the public buildings were given as quarters to the troops which came to defend them; the basement of the Capitol became first a store-house and then a bakery, and the very chambers of the Senate and the House were turned into barracks. As the hopes of the loyal rose, those of the rebellious fell; and the Washington secessionists, seeing their chances of open attack upon the government diminish, turned their thoughts and their endeavors to treachery. More disheartening and perplexing circumstances than those under which President Lincoln assumed the control of government can not well be imagined. Entirely without administrative experience himself, and arriving at Washington with a cabinet, no member of which had any practical knowledge of the routine of his department, or any official acquaintance with his subordinates, pursued by an army of office-seekers, whose claims demanded at least consideration, and whose pretensions were generally great in proportion as their capacities were small, he and his ministers were obliged to make themselves familiar with the practical condition of the machine of administration, and prepare it instantly for a kind of service to which, even under the most favorable conditions, it was not too well adapted. The new administration was dependent both for information and assistance upon the subordinate officers of the old, in which the very members of the cabinet itself had proved not only politically traitorous, but personally perfidious. Nor, had the case been otherwise, would it have been prudent to chill the ardor and alienate the interests of the Democratic party by a general removal of officers appointed under its auspices. Necessity and policy therefore dictated the retention of a large proportion of the force which had been left in possession of the public offices by the retiring president. Of these, the greater number had declared that they never would hold office under a "Black Republican" administration. But with placemen the claims of personal interest are rarely waived in favor of abstract principles; and in this case, interest was seconded by the hope of serving the faction which sought the establishment of a new government in the old capital. The result was that spies swarmed not only in the city, but in the very departments. True, these men professed to be loyal, and had taken the oath of allegiance to the United States; but so had Secretaries Floyd, and Cobb, and Thompson, who betrayed the country while they formed a part of its government; so had Senator Yulee, who sat in the Senate-chamber, and wrote traitorous counsels to a brother-conspirator, while he and his yoke-fellows held their positions, that they might cast down the very power which they had sworn to support; so had the naval officers, whose voluntary assurances of patriotism and allegiance beguiled Commodore M'Cauley into the security which cost the country the Portsmouth Navy Yard; so had General Frost, who, from a camp flaunting the names and penetrated with the spirit of Davis and Beauregard, and defended by arms torn by the insurgents from a national arsenal, sent like, though not like trusted, assurances to Captain Lyon at St. Louis. To most of the men who had undertaken the destruction of the republic in the interests of slavery, no oath seemed binding, no obligation sacred; and so the new administration was surrounded with spies and traitors in the very capital. It knew not whom to trust. It could

not ask a question without fearing the revelation of its needs; it could not give an order or send a dispatch without risking the betrayal of its intentions. These apprehensions were fully justified; not only in these early days of the rebellion, but throughout the war, the enemies of the government received early information of its purposes. And the emissaries of the insurgents not only thus filled Washington: as I have before remarked, they pervaded the whole country. While from the states subject to the confederated government, men from the loyal states, and even Union men born on the soil, were mercilessly expelled by those in authority, when they were not hanged or shot by whomever chose to hang or shoot, at the North citizens of all parts of the republic lived as usual, undisturbed and unquestioned, and some time had passed before men who were known to be actively engaged in treasonable practices were arrested. Thus surrounded, thus mainly filled with a hostile population, with the very offices of the government swarming with spies, Washington, which its position upon the very southernmost border of doubtful loyalty would, in any case, have subjected to great and peculiar danger, became a city at once beleaguered and betrayed; and in fact, though not in name, the nation's capital was in the enemy's country. If it could have been immediately abandoned without loss of moral power and position before the world, the benefit to the country would have been great and instant; could its archives have been safely deposited elsewhere, its destruction would have saved enough treasure to rebuild it thrice in marble.

To the knowledge that agents and active sympathizers of the rebellion were spread over the land, that their communication was constant with their fellow-laborers in Washington, and to the rapidly developed fact that the rebellion was no sudden outbreak, but the result of a long-concerted scheme, is to be attributed an arbitrary order, by virtue of which officers of the government seized copies of telegraphic dispatches kept on file at the principal offices. The seizure was made simultaneously throughout the country, at 3 P.M. on the 20th of April; and it included all the dispatches which had been sent for a year. Those which betrayed purposes hostile to the government, or which related to supplies of arms purchased for the Southern rebels, were selected and sent to the capital. This measure, unwarranted by written law, was justified in the eyes of the people by the necessities of the situation. It furnished the government much valuable information; it limited somewhat the freedom of action of the rebel emissaries; and the only excitement which it caused was manifested among those who showed their loyalty by the earnestness with which they insisted that the rebels should have the full benefit of the Constitution which they had set at naught. About the same date citizens in various parts of the country were arrested simply in virtue of a Secretary of State's warrant, without process of law, and confined in Fort M'Henry at Baltimore, Fort Lafayette at New York, or Fort Warren at Boston. On the issuing of writs of *habeas corpus* on behalf of the persons thus imprisoned, the officers in command of those posts refused to produce their prisoners, by the order of the President; but a spirited officer, Major Morris, of the Artillery, in command at Fort M'Henry, had first assumed the responsibility of refusing obedience to the writ.[7] That the Constitution warranted the suspension of the writ of *habeas*

---

[7]   *Major Morris's Letter to Judge Giles, at Baltimore.*

At the date of issuing your writ, and for two weeks previous, the city in which you live and where your court has been held was entirely under the control of revolutionary authorities. Within that period United States soldiers, while committing no offense, had been perfidiously attacked and inhumanly murdered in your streets; no punishment had been awarded, and I believe no arrests had been made for these atrocious crimes; supplies of provisions intended for this garrison had been stopped; the intention to capture this fort had been boldly proclaimed; your most public thoroughfares were daily patrolled by large numbers of troops armed and clothed, at least in part, with articles stolen from the United States; and the federal flag, while waving over the federal offices, was cut down by some person wearing the uniform of a Maryland soldier. To add to the fore-

FORT M'HENRY.

corpus in time of rebellion the people well knew; and as there was doubt only whether the power to do so was vested in the President or in Congress, this important step also was taken with general acquiescence. But Chief Justice Taney, of the Supreme Court, in a case brought before him, denied the right of the President to suspend the privilege of *habeas corpus*, or to authorize its suspension by any military officer.[8] Against bayonets and cannon, however, supported by public opinion, the mandates even of a chief justice of the Supreme Court were powerless. The arrests went on; and the writ, having been several times disregarded, soon ceased to be issued.

Although neither the government nor the loyal people of the Union yet suspected how well matured were the plans and how fixed were the purposes of the insurgent leaders, the President now saw—what, indeed, no man of sense could fail to see—that, to cope successfully with the forces which the power at Montgomery had brought or was about to bring into the field, a larger levy was necessary than he had made, and that a longer and severer contest was impending than he had anticipated at the date of his first proclamation. He therefore, on the 3d of May, issued another, by which he called into service forty-two thousand volunteers for three years, directed the increase of the regular army by twenty-two thousand seven hundred men, and added eighteen thousand seamen to the navy.[9] The first proclamation called the state militia into service, and for only three months—the limit of the period for which their services could be so required; but the volunteers were to take service for three years. Such was the enthusiasm of the loyal people, and such their readiness to do battle for the republic, that volunteers poured in more rapidly than they could be organized, and it was at once apparent that within a few weeks the government would have at its disposal a body of one hundred and forty thousand men. The unanimity of the people of the free states seemed absolute; their patriotism, boundless in its self-sacrifice. Of money as well as men, more was offered than could at first be used, and more than in the raw judgment of a peace-bred people seemed to be required. The men who staid at home thought it their duty to provide in every way for the comfort of those who went into the army. Bounties were large; and the families of the volunteers were placed beyond the reach of suffering. Before the 7th of May, more than twenty-three millions of dollars had been contributed for these patriotic purposes.[10]

This devotion to the national cause was not manifested only by the men who would be obliged to do the fighting, or to pay the expenses as well as to bear the losses of a war. The clergy and the women threw themselves with all their souls into the enthusiasm of the hour. The former preached patriotism, and taught their people, in the pulpit as well as out of it, the lesson of self-devotion which they were so ready to learn, and showed them support in the Scriptures for the cause which they were so anxious to sustain. The latter began to make lint and bandages, and garments needful for the sick; they offered themselves as nurses, each one seeing herself the consoler and the savior of at least one defender of his country, the recipient of his gallantry and his gratitude; and they demanded, with sweet clamor, the immediate defeat of General Beauregard and the speedy arrest of Mr. Jefferson Davis. Their simple enthusiasm and their unreasonable expectations, in which they were not very far in advance of the cooler and more calculating patriots of the sterner sex, should not diminish one jot the credit which is due to their devotion. No demonstration could have been more whole-hearted, more encouraging, or more serviceable. In the seceded states, however, exactly the same devotion was exhibited; but its spirit was intensified and all its features heightened. There rebellion raved both in church and parlor: it inspired the prayer at the altar; it was heard in the song by the cradle. The very consecrated cup of the communion-table seemed to be drunk by men as a pledge of undying hostility; and if the sweet nourishment of infants was not curdled by the gall of bitter hatred, it was because the fair and kindred sources whence it should have flowed were closed by the dictates of an unnatural fashion, and that to servile arms and swarthy breasts was committed the tenderest office of maternity. There women not only sighed for the defeat of the armies and the destruction of the government of the republic; they longed for Mr. Lincoln's teeth, and ears, and limbs.[1] The inferior clergy, not content with preaching sedition at home or in the camp, exchanged the sword of the Spirit for the bowie-knife of the flesh; and bishops, rivaling the mail-clad abbots of the Dark Ages, put off the mitre and the lawn for the cocked hat and the epaulettes, and, casting aside the crosier, went out in arms as God's ministers charged with seeing that the curse was well visited upon Canaan. Although these demonstrations did much to heighten the enthusiasm of both sides, they were of little real significance on either. It can not be reasonably denied that if the clergy and the women had with like unanimity and earnestness opposed the action of

going, an assemblage elected in defiance of law, but claiming to be the legislative body of your state, and so recognized by the executive of Maryland, was debating the federal compact. If all this be not rebellion, I know not what to call it. I certainly regard it as sufficient legal cause for suspending the writ of *habeas corpus*. Besides, there were certain grounds of expediency on which I declined obeying your mandate.

1st. The writ of *habeas corpus* in the hands of an unfriendly power might depopulate this fortification, and place it at the mercy of "a Baltimore mob" in much less time than it could be done by all the appliances of modern warfare.

2d. The ferocious spirit exhibited by your community toward the United States Army would render me very averse from appearing publicly and unprotected in the city of Baltimore to defend the interests of the body to which I belong. A few days since a soldier of this command, while outside the walls, was attacked by a fiend or fiends in human shape, almost deprived of life, and left unprotected about half a mile from garrison. He was found in this situation and brought in, covered with blood. One of your evening prints was quite jocose over this laughable occurrence.

And now, sir, permit me to say, in conclusion, that no one can regret more than I this conflict between the civil and military authorities. If, in an experience of thirty-three years, you have never before known the writ of *habeas corpus* to be disobeyed, it is only because such a contingency in political affairs as the present has never before arisen. I claim to be a loyal citizen, and I hope my former conduct, both official and private, will justify this pretension.

In any condition of affairs except that of civil war I would cheerfully obey your order, and as soon as the present excitement shall pass away I will hold myself ready not only to produce the soldier, but also to appear in person to answer for my conduct; but, in the existing state of sentiment in the city of Baltimore, I think it your duty to sustain the federal military and to strengthen their hands, instead of endeavoring to strike them down. I have the honor to be, very respectfully, your obedient servant,

W. W. MORRIS,
Major Fourth United States Artillery, commanding Fort M'Henry.

May 14.

8 *The Merryman Habeas Corpus.*

In the case of John Merryman, a secessionist arrested in Baltimore and detained a prisoner in Fort M'Henry, a writ of *habeas corpus* was issued by Judge Taney, made returnable in the United States District Court. General Cadwallader declined surrendering the prisoner till he heard from Washington, and an attachment was issued for General Cadwallader.

General Cadwallader having declined acceding to the demand for the body of Merryman until he could hear from Washington, a writ of attachment was issued against him for contempt of court. The marshal reported that, on going to Fort M'Henry to serve the writ, he was refused admittance.

Chief Justice Taney then read the following statement:

"I ordered the attachment yesterday, because upon the face of the return the detention of the prisoner was unlawful, upon two grounds:

"*First.* The President, under the Constitution and laws of the United States, can not suspend the privilege of the writ of *habeas corpus*, nor authorize any military officer to do so.

"*Second.* A military officer has no right to arrest and detain a person, nor subject him to the Rules and Articles of War for an offense against the laws of the United States, except in aid of the judicial authority, and subject to its control; and if the party is arrested by the military, it is the duty of the officer to deliver him over immediately to the civil authority, to be dealt with according to law.

"I forbore yesterday to state orally the provisions of the Constitution of the United States which make these principles the fundamental law of the Union, because an oral statement might be misunderstood in some portions of it, and I shall therefore put my opinion in writing, and file it in the office of the Clerk of the Circuit Court in the course of this week."

The judge added that the military authority was always subordinate to civil; that, under ordinary circumstances, it would be the duty of the marshal to proceed with *posse comitatus* and bring the party named in the writ into court; but, from the notoriously superior force that he would encounter, this would be impossible. He said the marshal had done all in his power to discharge his duty.

During the week he should prepare his opinion in the premises, and forward it to the President, calling upon him to perform his constitutional duty, and see that the laws be faithfully executed, and enforce the decrees of this court.

9 *A Proclamation by the President of the United States.*

Washington, Friday, May 3, 1861.

Whereas, existing exigencies demand immediate and adequate measures for the protection of the national Constitution and the preservation of the national Union by the suppression of the insurrectionary combinations now existing in several states for opposing the laws of the Union and obstructing the execution thereof, to which end a military force, in addition to that called forth by my proclamation of the fifteenth day of April in the present year, appears to be indispensably necessary; now, therefore, I, Abraham Lincoln, President of the United States, and Commander-in-Chief of the Army and Navy thereof, and of the militia of the several states when called into actual service, do hereby call into the service of the United States forty-two thousand and thirty-four volunteers, to serve for a period of three years, unless sooner discharged, and to be mustered into service as infantry and cavalry. The proportions of each arm, and the details of enrollment and organization, will be made known through the Department of War; and I also direct that the regular army of the United States be increased by the addition of eight regiments of infantry, one regiment of cavalry, and one regiment of artillery, making altogether a maximum aggregate increase of 22,714 officers and enlisted men, the details of which increase will also be made known through the Department of War; and I farther direct the enlistment, for not less than one nor more than three years, of 18,000 seamen, in addition to the present force, for the naval service of the United States. The details of the enlistment and organization will be made known through the Department of the Navy. The call for volunteers hereby made, and the direction of the increase of the regular army, and for the enlistment of seamen hereby given, together with the plan of organization adopted for the volunteers and for the regular forces hereby authorized, will be submitted to Congress as soon as assembled.

In the mean time, I earnestly invoke the co-operation of all good citizens in the measures hereby adopted for the effectual suppression of unlawful violence, for the impartial enforcement of constitutional laws, and for the speediest possible restoration of peace and order, and with those of happiness and prosperity throughout our country.

In testimony whereof, I have hereunto set my hand, and caused the seal of the United States to be affixed.

Done at the City of Washington this third day of May, in the year of our Lord one thousand eight hundred and sixty-one, and of the Independence of the United States the eighty-fifth.

By the President. ABRAHAM LINCOLN.

WILLIAM H. SEWARD, Secretary of State.

10 *Patriotic Contributions to May 7, 1861.*

Abington, Mass......	$5,000	Great Falls, N. H....	$10,000	Ottowa, Ill.............	$18,000
Acton, Mass.	5,000	Greensburg, Ind.	2,000	Palmyra, N. J.........	6,000
Albany, N. Y.	46,000	Hamilton, Ohio......	1,000	Paterson, N. J.........	10,000
Amesbury, Mass.....	5,000	Harrisburg, Pa.......	5,000	Pennsylvania, State..	3,500,000
Auburn, N. Y.........	4,000	Hartford, Conn.......	64,000	Philadelphia...........	330,000
Barre, Mass...........	2,000	Hoboken, N. J.	2,000	Piqua, Ohio............	20,000
Batavia, N. Y.........	4,000	Hornellsville, N. Y..	1,000	Plymouth, Mass.......	2,000
Bath, Me.	10,000	Hudson, N. Y.........	4,000	Portland, Me.	31,000
Bedford, Mass........	2,000	Illinois, State.........	2,000,000	Poughkeepsie, N. Y..	10,000
Bedford, N. Y.	1,000	Indianapolis, Ind. ...	5,000	Princeton, N. J.	2,000
Bennington, Ver.....	10,000	Indiana, State........	1,000,000	Quincy, Mass..........	10,000
Binghampton, N. Y.	10,000	Iowa, State............	100,000	Rhode Island, State..	500,000
Bordentown, N. J....	3,000	Ipswich, Mass.........	4,000	Rochester	69,000
Boston, Mass.	186,000	Ithaca, N. Y.	10,000	Rockland, Me.	10,000
Bradford, Ver.	2,000	Janesville, Wis.	6,000	Sag Harbor, N. Y. ...	3,000
Braintree, Mass......	2,000	Jersey City, N. J. ...	32,000	Salem, Mass.	15,000
Bridgeport, Conn....	31,000	Keene, N. H..........	10,000	Salisbury, Mass.......	5,000
Bridgetown, N. J....	1,000	Kenton, Ohio	2,000	Sar. Springs, N. Y. ...	2,000
Brooklyn, N. Y.......	75,000	Lancaster, Pa.	5,000	Schenectady, N. Y....	2,000
Brunswick, Me.......	1,000	Lawrence, Mass......	5,000	Schuylkill Co., Pa....	30,000
Buffalo, N. Y.	110,000	Lebanon County, Pa.	10,000	Seneca Falls, N. Y...	3,000
Burlington, N. J.....	4,000	Lockport, N. Y.......	2,000	Shelburne, Ver........	1,000
Burlington, Ver......	3,000	London, Ohio	1,000	Southborough, Mass.	2,000
Camden and Amboy R.R. Company	10,000	Lowell, Mass..........	8,000	Stockbridge, Mass....	3,000
		Lynn, Mass.	10,000	Stowe, Mass.	2,000
Canandaigua, N. Y..	7,000	Madison, Ind.........	6,000	St. Albans, Ver........	10,000
Canton, Mass.........	5,000	Madison, Wis.........	9,000	Sutton, Mass..........	6,000
Cass County, Ind....	6,000	Maine, State..........	1,300,000	Sycamore, Ill..........	4,000
Charlestown, Mass...	10,000	Malden, Mass.	2,000	Syracuse, N. Y........	34,000
Chicago, Ill...........	20,000	Marblehead, Mass...	5,000	Taunton, Mass........	40,000
Cincinnati	280,000	Marlborough, Mass..	10,000	Toledo, Ohio...........	5,000
Circleville, Ohio	2,000	Marshfield, Mass.....	5,000	Troy, N. Y.............	48,000
Clinton, Ill.	5,000	Michigan, various pl's.	50,000	Upper Sandusky, O..	5,000
Clinton, N. Y.........	1,000	Milwaukee, Wis......	31,000	Utica, N. Y.............	20,000
Cohasset, Mass.	1,000	Morristown, N. J. ...	3,000	Vermont, State........	1,000,000
Concord, Mass........	4,000	Mount Holly, N. J...	3,000	Waltham, Mass.......	5,000
Concord, N. Y........	10,000	Mystic, Conn.	7,000	Warsaw, N. Y.........	3,000
Connecticut, State...	2,000,000	Needham, Mass......	3,000	Waterford, N. Y......	8,000
Damariscotta, Me....	3,000	Newark, N. J.........	136,000	Watertown, Mass.....	2,000
Detroit, Mich.........	50,000	New Brunswick, N.J.	2,000	Watertown, N. Y.....	3,000
Dover, N. H.	10,000	Newbury, Mass.......	3,000	Waynesville, Ohio....	2,000
Dunkirk, N. Y.	20,000	Newburyport, Mass..	4,000	Webster, Mass.........	4,000
Elizabeth, N. J.......	11,000	New Haven, Conn...	30,000	Westborough, Mass..	8,000
Elkhart, Ind.	8,000	New Jersey, State...	1,000,000	W. Cambridge, Mass.	10,000
Erie, Pa.	25,000	New London, Conn.	10,000	West Troy, N. Y.	7,000
Evansville, Ind.......	15,000	Newtown, Mass.	3,000	Weymouth, Mass.....	5,000
Fall River, Mass.....	10,000	New York, City	2,173,000	Wilmington, Ohio....	3,000
Flemington, N. J....	5,000	New York, State.....	3,000,000	Wisconsin, State......	225,000
Fond du Lac, Wis...	4,000	N. Andover, Mass....	3,000	Woburn, Mass.........	5,000
Galena, Ill............	1,000	Noblesville, Ind......	10,000	Woodbury, Conn.....	5,000
Georgetown, Mass...	5,000	Norwich, Conn.......	13,000	Woodstock, Ver.......	1,000
Glen Falls, N. Y.....	10,000	Ohio, State	3,000,000	Xenia, Ohio............	14,000
Gloucester, Mass.....	10,000	Oswego, N. Y.........	13,000	Zanesville, Ohio	3,000
				Total..........	$23,277,000

[1] Mr. William H. Russell's *Diary North and South*.

the North or of the South, much would have been effected toward the triumph of the opposing party; but so monstrous a condition of society as such a course would have revealed is unheard of in the annals of any nation. The occasions are of extremest rarity, if not altogether wanting, on which the clergy have withheld their blessings and their prayers from the cause of the people who honored their office and furnished their living, or women refused to bestow their cares and their smiles upon the men who were, or might hope to be, their husbands. This is right; it is inevitable. Especially is it woman's function to give to those she loves her sympathy and her support in time of trial. She will not, she can not question of the cause. Did she do so, mankind, divided against itself, would cease to be. Regardless of the nature of the issue, she fights, with weak, resistless weapons, her child's, her husband's, lover's battle. It is theirs, and that makes it hers. The wife of an Italian bandit or a Highland robber acts in this respect upon the same heaven-implanted impulse that filled the bosom of a Roman matron. It was not patriotism alone that fired the heart of the bereaved Maid of Saragossa, and nerved the arm of Charlotte Corday; nor was it *against* the cause of the men of France that the world saw lifted the bloodless sword of the fanatic of Orleans, that noble monster of a heroism female though not womanly. And thus throughout the land women, as ever, proved true women, and loyal men and rebels both found cheer and comfort.

The attitude of the government, and the spirit and unanimity of the people of the free states, astonished and alarmed, though it did not intimidate, the insurgent slaveholders. Mr. Davis hastily summoned a congress of the confederated states, and the delegates met at Montgomery on the 29th of April. His message upon the occasion is one of the most important and significant documents of the time, and one which, perhaps, more than any other, exercised a forming influence upon public opinion abroad.[2] To this lat-

[2] *Message of Jefferson Davis, April* 29, 1861.

Gentlemen of Congress:—It is my pleasing duty to announce to you that the Constitution framed for the establishment of a permanent government of the Confederate States of America has been ratified by the several conventions of each of those states which were referred to to inaugurate the said government in its full proportions and upon its own substantial basis of the popular will. It only remains that elections should be held for the designation of the officers to administer it. There is every reason to believe that at no distant day other states, identical in political principles and community of interests with those which you represent, will join this confederacy, giving to its typical constellation increased splendor; to its government of free, equal, and sovereign states a wider sphere of usefulness; and to the friends of constitutional liberty a greater security for its harmonious and perpetual existence.

It was not, however, for the purpose of making this announcement that I have deemed it my duty to convoke you at an earlier day than that fixed by yourselves for your meeting. The declaration of war made against this confederacy by Abraham Lincoln, President of the United States, in his proclamation, issued on the 15th day of the present month, renders it necessary, in my judgment, that you should convene at the earliest practicable moment to devise the measures necessary for the defense of the country. The occasion is, indeed, an extraordinary one. It justifies me in giving a brief review of the relations heretofore existing between us and the states which now unite in warfare against us, and a succinct statement of the events which have resulted, to the end that mankind may pass intelligent and impartial judgment on our motives and objects.

During the war waged against Great Britain by her colonies on this continent, a common danger impelled them to a close alliance, and to the formation of a confederation by the terms of which the colonies, styling themselves states, entered severally into a firm league of friendship with each other for their common defense, the security of their liberties, and their mutual and general welfare, binding themselves to assist each other against all force offered to, or attacks made upon them, or any of them, on account of religion, sovereignty, trade, or any other pretense whatever. In order to guard against any misconstruction of their compact, the several states made an explicit declaration in a distinct article, that each state retain its sovereignty, freedom, and independence, and every power of jurisdiction and right which is not by this said confederation expressly delegated to the United States in Congress assembled under this contract of alliance.

The war of the Revolution was successfully waged, and resulted in the treaty of peace with Great Britain in 1783, by the terms of which the several states were each by name recognized to be independent. The Articles of Confederation contained a clause whereby all alterations were prohibited, unless confirmed by the Legislatures of every state after being agreed to by the Congress; and in obedience to this provision, under the resolution of Congress of the 21st of February, 1787, the several states appointed delegates for the purpose of revising the Articles of Confederation, and reporting to Congress and the several Legislatures such alterations and provisions therein as shall, when agreed to in Congress, and confirmed by the states, render the federal Constitution adequate to the exigencies of the government and the preservation of the Union.

It was by the delegates chosen by the several states under the resolution just quoted that the Constitution of the United States was formed in 1787, and submitted to the several states for ratification, as shown by the seventh article, which is in these words: "The ratification of the conventions of nine states shall be sufficient for the establishment of this Constitution between the states so ratifying the same."

I have italicized certain words in the resolutions just made for the purpose of attracting attention to the singular and marked caution with which the states endeavored in every possible form to exclude the idea that the separate and independent sovereignty of each state was merged into one common government or nation; and the earnest desire they evinced to impress on the Constitution its true character—that of a compact between independent states—the Constitution of 1787, however, admitting the clause already recited from the Articles of Confederation, which provided in explicit terms that each state reclaimed its sovereignty and independence.

Some alarm was felt in the states, when invited to ratify the Constitution, lest this omission should be construed into an abandonment of their cherished principles, and they refused to be satisfied until amendments were added to the Constitution placing beyond any pretense of doubt the reservation by the states of their sovereign rights and powers not expressly delegated to the United States by the Constitution.

Strange, indeed, must it appear to the impartial observer, but it is none the less true, that all these carefully worded clauses proved unavailing to prevent the rise and growth in the Northern States of a political school which has persistently claimed that the government is set above and over the states; an organization created by the states, to secure the blessings of liberty and independence against foreign aggression, has been gradually perverted into a machine for their control in their domestic affairs. The creature has been exalted above its creator—the principals have been made subordinate to the agent appointed by themselves.

The people of the Southern States, whose almost exclusive occupation was agriculture, early perceived a tendency in the Northern States to render a common government subservient to their own purposes by imposing burdens on commerce as protection to their manufacturing and shipping interests. Long and angry controversies grew out of these attempts, often successful, to benefit one section of the country at the expense of the other, and the danger of disruption arising from this cause was enhanced by the fact that the Northern population was increasing, by emigration and other causes, more than the population of the South. By degrees, as the Northern States gained preponderance in the national Congress, self-interest taught their people to yield ready assent to any plausible advocacy of their right as majority to govern the minority. Without control, they learn to listen with impatience to the suggestion of any constitutional impediment to the exercise of their will; and so utterly have the principles of the Constitution been corrupted in the Northern mind, that, in the inaugural address delivered by President Lincoln in March last, he asserts a maxim which he plainly deems to be undeniable, that the theory of the Constitution requires, in all cases, that the majority shall govern. And in another memorable instance the same chief magistrate did not hesitate to liken the relations between states and the United States to those which exist between the county and the state in which it is situated, and by which it was created. This is the lamentable and fundamental error in which rests the policy that has culminated in his declaration of war against these Confederate States.

In addition to the long-continued and deep-seated resentment felt by the Southern States at the persistent abuse of the powers they had delegated to the Congress for the purpose of enriching the manufacturing and shipping classes of the North at the expense of the South, there has existed for nearly half a century another subject of discord, involving interests of such transcendent magnitude as at all times to create the apprehension in the minds of many devoted lovers of the Union that its permanence was impossible.

When the several states delegated certain powers to the United States Congress, a large portion of the laboring population were imported into the colonies by the mother country. In twelve out of the fifteen states, negro slavery existed, and the right of property existing in slaves was protected by law; this property was recognized in the Constitution, and provision was made against its loss by the escape of the slave. The increase in the number of slaves by foreign importation from Africa was also secured by a clause forbidding Congress to prohibit the slave-trade anterior to a certain date, and in no clause can there be found any delegation of power to the Congress to authorize it in any manner to legislate to the prejudice, detriment, or discouragement of the owners of that species of property, or excluding it from the protection of the government.

The climate and soil of the Northern States soon proved unpropitious to the continuance of slave labor, while the reverse being the case at the South, made unrestricted free intercourse between the two sections unfriendly. The Northern States consulted their own interests by selling their slaves to the South and prohibiting slavery between their limits. The South were willing purchasers of property suitable to their wants, and paid the price of the acquisition, without harboring a suspicion that their quiet possession was to be disturbed by those who were not only in want of constitutional authority, but by good faith as vendors, from disquieting a title emanating from themselves.

As soon, however, as the Northern States, that prohibited African slavery within their limits, had reached a number sufficient to give their representation a controlling vote in the Congress, a persistent and organized system of hostile measures against the rights of the owners of slaves in the Southern States was inaugurated and gradually extended. A series of measures was devised and prosecuted for the purpose of rendering insecure the tenure of property in slaves. Fanatical organizations, supplied with money by voluntary subscriptions, were assiduously engaged in exciting among the slaves a spirit of discontent and revolt. Means were furnished for their escape from their owners, and agents secretly employed to entice them to abscond. The constitutional provision for their rendition to their owners was first evaded, then openly denounced as a violation of conscientious obligation and religious duty. Men were taught that it was a merit to elude, disobey, and violently oppose the execution of the laws enacted to secure the performance of the promise contained in the constitutional compact. Often owners of slaves were mobbed and even murdered in open day solely for applying to a magistrate for the arrest of a fugitive slave.

The dogmas of the voluntary organization soon obtained control of the Legislatures of many of the Northern States, and laws were passed for the punishment, by ruinous fines, and long-continued imprisonment in jails and penitentiaries, of citizens of the Southern States who should dare ask of the officers of the law for the recovery of their property. Emboldened by success, on the theatre of agitation and aggression, against the clearly expressed constitutional rights of the Congress, senators and representatives were sent to the common councils of the nation, whose chief title to this distinction consisted in the display of a spirit of ultra fanaticism, and whose business was not to promote the general welfare or insure domestic tranquillity, but to awaken the bitterest hatred against the citizens of sister states by violent denunciations of their institutions.

The transaction of public affairs was impeded by repeated efforts to usurp powers not delegated by the Constitution, for the purpose of impairing the security of property in slaves, and reducing those states which held slaves to a condition of inferiority.

Finally, a great party was organized for the purpose of obtaining the administration of the government, with the avowed object of using its power for the total exclusion of the slave states from all participation in the benefits of the public domain acquired by all the states in common, whether by conquest or purchase, surrounded them entirely by states in which slavery should be prohibited, thus rendering the property in slaves so insecure as to be comparatively worthless, and thereby annihilating in effect property worth thousands of millions of dollars. This party, thus organized, succeeded in the month of November last in the election of its candidate for the presidency of the United States.

In the mean time, under the mild and genial climate of the Southern States, and the increasing care for the well-being and comfort of the laboring classes, dictated alike by interest and humanity, the African slaves had augmented in number from about six hundred thousand, at the date of the adoption of the constitutional compact, to upward of four millions. In a moral and social condition they had been elevated from brutal savages into docile, intelligent, and civilized agricultural laborers, and supplied not only with bodily comforts, but with careful religious instruction, under the supervision of a superior race. Their labor had been so directed as not only to allow a gradual and marked amelioration of their own condition, but to convert hundreds of thousands of square miles of the wilderness into cultivated lands covered with a prosperous people. Towns and cities had sprung into existence, and it rapidly increased in wealth and population under the social system of the South. The white population of the Southern slaveholding states had augmented from about 1,250,000, at the date of the adoption of the Constitution, to more than 8,500,000 in 1860, and the productions of the South in cotton, rice, sugar, and tobacco, for the full development and continuance of which the labor of African slaves was and is indispensable, had swollen to an amount which formed nearly three fourths of the export of the whole United States, and had become absolutely necessary to the wants of civilized man.

With interests of such overwhelming magnitude imperiled, the people of the Southern States were driven by the conduct of the North to the adoption of some course of action to avoid the dangers with which they were openly menaced. With this view, the Legislatures of the several states invited the people to select delegates to conventions to be held for the purpose of determining for themselves what measures were best to be adopted to meet so alarming a crisis in their history.

Here it may be proper to observe that, from a period as early as 1798, there had existed in all of the states of the Union a party almost uninterruptedly in the majority, based upon the creed that each state was, in the last resort, the sole judge as well of its wrongs as of the mode and measures of redress. Indeed, it is obvious that under the law of nations this principle is an axiom as applied to the relations of independent sovereign states, such as those which had united themselves under the constitutional compact.

The Democratic party of the United States repeated, in its successful canvass in 1836, the deduction made in numerous previous political contests, that it would faithfully abide by, and uphold the principles laid down in the Kentucky and Virginia Legislatures of 1799, and that it adopts those principles as constituting one of the main foundations of its political creed.

The principles thus emphatically announced embrace that to which I have already adverted—the right of each state to judge of and redress the wrongs of which it complains. Their principles were maintained by overwhelming majorities of the people of all the states of the Union at different elections, especially in the election of Mr. Jefferson in 1805, Mr. Madison in 1809, and Mr. Pierce in 1852. In the exercise of a right so ancient, so well established, and so necessary for self-preservation, the people of the Confederate States in their conventions determined that the wrongs which they had suffered, and the evils with which they were menaced, required that they should revoke the delegation of powers to the federal government which they had ratified in their several conventions. They consequently passed ordinances resuming all their rights as sovereign and independent states, and dissolved their connection with the other states of the Union. Having done this, they proceeded to form a new compact among themselves by new Articles of Confederation, which have been also ratified by conventions of the several states, with an approach to unanimity far exceeding that of the conventions which adopted the Constitutions of 1787. They have organized their new government in all its departments. The functions of the executive, legislative, and judicial magistrates are performed in accordance with the will of the people, as displayed not merely in a cheerful acquiescence, but in the enthusiastic support of the government thus established by themselves; and but for the interference of the government of the United States, this legitimate exercise of a people to self-government has been manifested in every possible form.

Scarce had you assembled in February last, when, prior even to the inauguration of the chief magistrate you had elected, you expressed your desire for the appointment of commissioners, and for the settlement of all questions of disagreement between the two governments upon principles of right, justice, equity, and good faith.

It was my pleasure as well as my duty to co-operate with you in this work of peace. Indeed, in my address to you on taking the oath of office, and before receiving from you the communication of this resolution, I had said that "as a necessity, not as a choice, we have resorted to the remedy of separating, and henceforth our energies must be directed to the conduct of our own affairs, and the perpetuity of the confederacy which we have formed. If a just perception of mutual interest shall permit us to peaceably pursue our separate political career, my most earnest desire will then have been fulfilled."

It was in furtherance of these accordant views of the Congress and the executive that I made choice of three discreet, able, and distinguished citizens, who repaired to Washington. Aided by their cordial co-operation and that of the Secretary of State, every effort compatible with self-respect and the dignity of the confederacy was exhausted before I allowed myself to yield to the conviction that the government of the United States was determined to attempt the conquest of this people, and that our cherished hopes of peace were unobtainable.

On the arrival of our commissioners in Washington on the 5th of March, they postponed, at the suggestion of a friendly intermediator, doing more than giving informal notice of their arrival. This was done with a view to afford time to the President of the United States, who had just been inaugurated, for the discharge of other pressing official duties in the organization of his administration, before engaging his attention in the object of their mission. It was not until the 12th of the month that they officially addressed the Secretary of State, informing him of the purpose of

HENRICO COUNTY JAIL, RICHMOND

THE CAP[

THE CITY OF R

RICHMOND.

REBEL PRISONS ON MAIN, NEAR TWENTY-FIFTH STREET, RICHMOND.

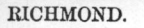

OND, VIRGINIA.

ter end, indeed, it was, like all the more important state papers of the insurgent leader, in a great measure directed, for he had no little skill in the lower arts of state-craft. He could mask an utterly selfish purpose behind a seeming magnanimity; pervert the truth with an air of frank simplicity; throw a veil of courtesy over the most arrogant assumption; and with a certain dignity of manner (sometimes too consciously assumed), and a pretense of wide philanthropy, appeal without a blush to those baser motives which influence nations as well as individuals. What he must and could conceal, he concealed adroitly; what he would have concealed, yet must maintain, he did not excuse or even vindicate; he boldly proclaimed it good, and put his adversaries on their defense. Yet, with all this, he was not personally corrupt or false. He was but a cunning politician, thrusting aside scruples in his public which he might cherish in his private life, and directing his course by that immoral law which has too generally been the guide of ruling men in all ages and of all nations. He now told Europe—Great Britain and

---

their arrival, and stating, in the language of their instructions, their wish to make to the government of the United States overtures for the opening of negotiations, assuring the government of the United States that the President, Congress, and people of the Confederate States desired a peaceful solution of these great questions; that it was neither their interest nor their wish to make any demand which is not founded on the strictest principles of justice, nor to do any act to injure their late confederates.

To this communication no formal reply was received until the 8th of April. During the interval, the commissioners had consented to waive all questions of form, with the firm resolve to avoid war if possible. They went so far even as to hold, during that long period, unofficial intercourse through an intermediary, whose high position and character inspired the hope of success, and through whom constant assurances were received from the government of the United States of its peaceful intentions—of its determination to evacuate Fort Sumter; and farther, that no measure would be introduced changing the existing status prejudicial to the Confederate States; that in the event of any change in regard to Fort Pickens, notice would be given to the commissioners. The crooked path of diplomacy can scarcely furnish an example so wanting in courtesy, in candor, and directness, as was the course of the United States government toward our commissioners in Washington. For proof of this, I refer to the annexed documents, taken in connection with farther facts which I now proceed to relate.

Early in April the attention of the whole country was attracted to extraordinary preparations for an extensive military and naval expedition in New York and other Northern ports. These preparations commenced in secrecy, for an expedition whose destination was concealed, and only became known when nearly completed; and on the 5th, 6th, and 7th of April, transports and vessels of war, with troops, munitions, and military supplies, sailed from Northern ports bound southward.

Alarmed by so extraordinary a demonstration, the commissioners requested the delivery of an answer to their official communication of the 12th of March, and the reply dated on the 15th of the previous month, from which it appears that during the whole interval, while the commissioners were receiving assurances calculated to inspire hope of the success of their mission, the Secretary of State and the President of the United States had already determined to hold no intercourse with them whatever—to refuse even to listen to any proposals they had to make, and had profited by the delay created by their own assurances in order to prepare secretly the means for effective hostile operations. That these assurances were given has been virtually confessed by the government of the United States, by its act of sending a messenger to Charleston to give notice of its purpose to use force if opposed in its intention of supplying Fort Sumter. No more striking proof of the absence of good faith in the confidence of the government of the United States toward the confederacy can be required than is contained in the circumstances which accompanied this notice.

According to the usual course of navigation, the vessels composing the expedition, and designed for the relief of Fort Sumter, might be looked for in Charleston Harbor on the 9th of April. Yet our commissioners in Washington were detained under assurances that notice should be given of any military movement. The notice was not addressed to them, but a messenger was sent to Charleston to give notice to the Governor of South Carolina, and the notice was so given at a late hour on the 8th of April, the eve of the very day on which the fleet might be expected to arrive. That this manœuvre failed in its purpose was not the fault of those who controlled it. A heavy tempest delayed the arrival of the expedition, and gave time to the commander of our forces at Charleston to ask and receive instructions of the government. Even then, under all the provocation incident to the contemptuous refusal to listen to our commissioners, and the treacherous course of the government of the United States, I was sincerely anxious to avoid the effusion of blood, and directed a proposal to be made to the commander of Fort Sumter, who had avowed himself to be nearly out of provisions, that we would abstain from directing our fire on Fort Sumter if he would promise to not open fire on our forces unless first attacked. This proposal was refused. The conclusion was, that the design of the United States was to place the besieging force at Charleston between the simultaneous fire of the fort and the fleet. The fort should, of course, be at once reduced. This order was executed by General Beauregard with skill and success, which were naturally to be expected from the well-known character of that gallant officer; and, although the bombardment lasted some thirty-three hours, our flag did not wave over the battered walls until after the appearance of the hostile fleet off Charleston. Fortunately, not a life was lost on our side, and we were gratified in being prepared. The necessity of a useless effusion of blood by the prudent caution of the officers who commanded the fleet, in abstaining from the evidently futile effort to enter the harbor for the relief of Major Anderson, was spared. I refer to the report of the Secretary of War, and the papers accompanying it, for farther particulars of this brilliant affair.

In this connection I can not refrain from a well-deserved tribute to the noble state, the eminently soldierly qualities of whose people were conspicuously displayed. The people of Charleston for months had been irritated by the spectacle of a fortress held within their principal harbor as a standing menace against their peace and independence—built in part with their own money—its custody confided with their long consent to an agent who held no power over them other than such as they had themselves delegated for their own benefit, intended to be used by that agent for their own protection against foreign attack. How it was held out with persistent tenacity as a means of offense against them by the very government which they had established for their own protection, is well known. They had beleaguered it for months, and felt entire confidence in their power to capture it, yet yielded to the requirements of discipline, curbed their impatience, submitted without complaint to the unaccustomed hardships, labors, and privations of a protracted siege, and when at length their patience was relieved by the signal for attack, and success had crowned their steady and gallant conduct, even in the very moment of triumph they evinced a chivalrous regard for the feelings of the brave but unfortunate officer who had been compelled to lower his flag. All manifestations or exultations were checked in his presence. Their commanding general, with their cordial approval and the consent of his government, refrained from imposing any terms that would wound the sensibility of the commander of the fort. He was permitted to retire with the honors of war, to salute his flag, to depart freely with all his command, and was escorted to the vessel on which he embarked with the highest marks of respect from those against whom his guns had so recently been directed. Not only does every event connected with the siege reflect the highest honor on South Carolina, but the forbearance of her people and of this government from making any harangue of a victory obtained under circumstances of such peculiar provocation attest to the fullest extent the absence of any purpose beyond securing their own tranquillity, and the sincere desire to avoid the calamities of war.

Scarcely had the President of the United States received intelligence of the failure of the scheme which he had devised for the re-enforcement of Fort Sumter, when he issued the declaration of war against this confederacy which has prompted me to convoke you. In this extraordinary production, that high functionary affects total ignorance of the existence of an independent government, which, possessing the entire and enthusiastic devotion of its people, is exercising its functions without question over seven sovereign states—over more than five millions of people—and over a territory whose area exceeds five hundred thousand square miles. He terms sovereign states "combinations too powerful to be suppressed in the ordinary course of judicial proceedings, or by the powers vested in the marshals by law." He calls for an army of seventy-five thousand men to act as the posse comitatus in aid of the process of the courts of justice in states where no courts exist, whose mandates and decrees are not cheerfully obeyed and respected by a willing people. He avows that the first service to be assigned to the forces which have been called out will not be to execute the processes of courts, but to capture forts and strong-holds situated within the admitted limits of this confederacy, and garrisoned by its troops, and declares that this effort is intended to maintain the perpetuity of popular government. He concludes by commanding the persons composing the "combinations" aforesaid, to wit, the five millions of inhabitants of these states, to retire peaceably to their respective abodes within twenty days.

Apparently contradictory as are the terms of this singular document, one point was unmistakably evident. The President of the United States calls for an army of 75,000 men, whose first service was to be to capture our forts. It was a plain declaration of war which I was not at liberty to disregard, because of my knowledge that under the Constitution of the United States the President was usurping a power granted exclusively to the Congress.

He is the sole organ of communication between that country and foreign powers. The law of nations did not permit me to question the authority of the executive of a foreign nation to declare war against this confederacy. Although I might have refrained from taking active measures for our defense if the states of the Union had all imitated the action of Virginia, North Carolina, Arkansas, Kentucky, Tennessee, and Missouri, by denouncing it as an unconstitutional usurpation of power to which they refuse to respond, I was not at liberty to disregard the fact that many of the states seemed quite content to submit to the exercise of the powers assumed by the President of the United States, and were actively engaged in levying troops for the purpose indicated in the proclamation. Deprived of the aid of Congress, at the moment I was under the necessity of confining my action to a call on the states for volunteers for the common defense, in accordance with the authority you had confided to me before your adjournment.

I deemed it proper farther to issue a proclamation, inviting applications from persons disposed to aid in our defense in private armed vessels on the high seas, to the end that preparations might be made for the immediate issue of letters of marque and reprisal, which you alone, under the Constitution, have the power to grant. I entertain no doubt that you will concur with me in the opinion that, in the absence of an organized navy, it will be eminently expedient to supply their place with private armed vessels, so happily styled by the publicists of the United States the militia of the sea, and so often and justly relied on by them as an efficient and admirable instrument of defensive warfare. I earnestly recommend the immediate passage of a law authorizing me to accept the numerous proposals already received.

I can not close this review of the acts of the government of the United States without referring to a proclamation issued by their president under date of the 19th inst., in which, after declaring that an insurrection has broken out in this confederacy against the government of the United States, he announces a blockade of all the ports of these states, and threatens to punish as pirates all persons who shall molest any vessel of the United States under letters of marque issued by this government. Notwithstanding the authenticity of this proclamation, you will concur with me that it is hard to believe that it could have emanated from a President of the United States. Its announcement of a mere paper blockade is so manifestly a violation of the law of nations, that it would seem incredible that it could have been issued by authority; but, conceding this to be the case, so far as the executive is concerned, it will be difficult to satisfy the people of these states that their late confederates will sanction its declarations—will determine to ignore the usages of civilized nations, and will inaugurate a war of extermination on both sides, by treating as pirates open enemies acting under the authority of commissions issued by an organized government. If such proclamation was issued, it could only have been published under the sudden influence of passion, and we may rest assured that mankind will be spared the horrors of the conflict it seems to invite.

For the details of the administration of the different departments, I refer to the reports of the secretaries of each, which accompany this message.

The State Department has furnished the necessary instructions for those commissioners who have been sent to England, France, Russia, and Belgium, since your adjournment, to ask our recognition as a member of the family of nations, and to make with each of these powers treaties of amity and commerce. Farther steps will be taken to enter into like negotiations with the other European powers, in pursuance to resolutions passed at your last session. Sufficient time has not yet elapsed since the departure of these commissioners for the receipt of any intelligence from them.

As I deem it desirable that commissioners or other diplomatic agents should also be sent at an early period to the independent American powers south of our confederacy, with all of whom it is our interest and earnest wish to maintain the most cordial and friendly relations, I suggest the expediency of making the necessary appropriations for that purpose. Having been officially notified by the public authorities of the State of Virginia that she had withdrawn from the Union, and desired to maintain the closest political relations with us which it was possible at this time to establish, I commissioned the Honorable Alexander H. Stephens, Vice-president of the Confederate States, to represent this government at Richmond. I am happy to inform you that he has concluded a convention with the State of Virginia, by which that honored commonwealth, so long and justly distinguished among her sister states, and so dear to the hearts of thousands of her children in the Confederate States, has united her power and her fortunes with ours, and become one of us. This convention, together with the ordinance of Virginia adopting the Provisional Constitution of the confederacy, will be laid before you for your constitutional action.

I have satisfactory assurances from other of our late confederates that they are on the point of adopting similar measures; and I can not doubt that, ere you shall have been many weeks in session, the whole of the slaveholding states of the late Union will respond to the call of honor and affection, and, by uniting their fortune with ours, promote our common interests and secure our common safety. * * * *

The Secretary of War, in his report and accompanying documents, conveys full information concerning the forces, regular, volunteer, and provisional, raised and called for under the several acts of Congress—their organization and distribution; also an account of the expenditures already made, and the farther estimates for the fiscal year ending on the 18th of February, 1862, rendered necessary by recent events.

I refer to the report, also, for a full history of the occurrences in Charleston Harbor prior to, and including the bombardment and reduction of Fort Sumter, and of the measures subsequently taken for common defense on receiving the intelligence of the declaration of war against us made by the President of the United States.

There are now in the field at Charleston, Pensacola, Forts Morgan, Jackson, St. Philip, and Pulaski, 19,000 men, and 16.000 are now en route for Virginia. It is proposed to organize and hold in readiness for instant action, in view of the present exigencies of the country, an army of 100,000 men. If farther force be needed, the wisdom and patriotism of the Congress will be confidently appealed to for authority to call into the field additional numbers of our noble-spirited volunteers, who are constantly tendering their services far in excess of our wants.

The operations of the Navy Department have been necessarily restricted by the fact that sufficient time has not yet elapsed for the purchase or construction of more than a limited number of vessels adapted to the public service. Two vessels have been purchased and manned, the Sumter and M'Rea, and are now being prepared for sea, at New Orleans, with all possible dispatch. Contracts have also been made at that city with two different establishments for the casting of ordnance—cannon, shot, and shell—with the view to encourage the manufacture of these articles, so indispensable for our defense, at as many points within our territory as possible. I call your attention to the recommendation of the secretary for the establishment of a magazine and laboratory for the preparation of ordnance stores, and the necessary appropriation required for that purpose. Hitherto such stores have been prepared at the navy yards and no appropriation was made at your last session for this object. * * * *

In conclusion, I congratulate you on the fact that in every portion of our country there has been exhibited the most patriotic devotion to our common cause. Transportation companies have freely tendered the use of their lines for troops and supplies. The presidents of the railroads of the confederacy, in company with others who control lines of communication with states that we hope soon to greet as sisters assembled in convention in this city, have not only reduced largely the rates heretofore demanded for mail service and conveyance of troops and munitions, but have voluntarily proffered to receive their compensation at their reduced rates in the bonds of the confederacy, for the purpose of leaving all the resources of the government at its own disposal for the common defense.

Requisitions for troops have been met with such alacrity that the numbers tendering their services have in every instance greatly exceeded the demand. Men of the highest official and social position are serving as volunteers in the ranks. The gravity of age, the zeal of youth, rival each other in the desire to be foremost in the public defense; and though at no other point than the one heretofore noticed have they been stimulated by the excitement incident to actual engagement and the hope of distinction for individual deportment, they have borne, what for new troops is the most severe ordeal, patient toil, constant vigil, and all the exposure and discomfort of active service with a resolution and fortitude such as to command the approbation and justify the highest expectation of their conduct when active valor shall be required in place of steady endurance.

A people thus united and resolute can not shrink from any sacrifice which they may be called on to make, nor can there be a reasonable doubt of their final success, however long and severe may be the test of their determination to maintain their birthright of freedom and equality as a trust which it is their first duty to transmit unblemished to their posterity. A bounteous Providence cheers us with the promise of abundant crops. The fields of grain, which will, within a few weeks, be ready for the sickle, give assurance of the amplest supply of food, while the corn, cotton, and other staple productions of our soil afford abundant proof that up to this period the season has been propitious.

We feel that our cause is just and holy. We protest solemnly, in the face of mankind, that we desire peace at any sacrifice save that of honor. In independence we seek no conquest, no aggrandizement, no cession of any kind from the states with which we have lately confederated. All we ask is to be let alone—that those who never held power over us shall not now attempt our subjugation by arms. This we will, we must resist, to the direst extremity. The moment that this pretension is abandoned, the sword will drop from our grasp, and we shall be ready to enter into treaties of amity and commerce that can not but be mutually beneficial. So long as this pretension is maintained, with a firm reliance on that Divine Power which covers with its protection the just cause, we will continue to struggle for our inherent right to freedom, independence, and self-government.

JEFFERSON DAVIS.

Montgomery, April 29, 1861.

MONTGOMERY, ALABAMA: FIRST SEAT OF THE REBEL GOVERNMENT.

France especially—that the confederate government had been established upon the substantial basis of the popular will; but he was silent as to the violent and insidious means by which that seeming popular unanimity had been brought about. He claimed for his confederacy the sympathy of the friends of constitutional liberty; when he knew that according to no meaning attached to those words was the course of his confederates other than an outrage on that liberty. He asserted that the free states had endeavored to reduce the slave states to a condition of inferiority; when he knew that, from the very construction of the republic, no state could possibly suffer from any other inferiority than that which might be the inevitable consequence of its natural resources, the number and character of its inhabitants, and the nature of its local institutions. He did not hesitate to say that the party whose candidate Mr. Lincoln was had been organized with the avowed object of excluding the slave states from all participation in the benefits of the public domain; when he knew that no man had ever proposed that the people of the slave states should have a single right of possession or enjoyment less than those of the free states in the common territory of the republic, but that the former had claimed to have a privilege there in effect peculiar to themselves. He could not conceal the fact that the insurgents were slaveholders, and the loyal men free laborers; but he covered up with cloudy words and euphemisms the other fact, that the sole grievance of the former was that the latter had refused to allow the farther propagation of slavery under the flag and the protection of the republic. He did not hesitate to say that the African slaves had been elevated from brutal savages into docile, intelligent, and civilized agricultural laborers, supplied with bodily comforts and careful religious instruction; when he knew that not one in a thousand of them had ever been in a country more savage than that into which they, and their ancestors for two generations, and sometimes for six, had been born as slaves; that their docility was a sad and sullen cowering under the lash and the revolver; their intelligence—except among those whose veins flowed mostly with white blood—not one whit above that of their race in Africa; their civilization, with like exceptions, only a compelled and stolid submission to the police of a superior people; their bodily comforts no more than such bare necessaries, not including wholesome food, as enabled them to live and labor for their owners;[3] and their religious instruction only such a use of the allurements of heaven and the terrors of hell as could be made auxiliary to the whip of the overseer—a religious instruction from which the reading of Christ's Word, and the teaching of the one great doctrine upon which Christianity is founded, "Whatsoever ye would that men should do to you, do ye even so to them," were solicitously and of necessity excluded. The wily leader told his fellow-confederates that the pro-

ductions of the South in cotton, rice, sugar, and tobacco had become necessary to the wants of civilized man, and that to the continuance of the supply the labor of African slaves was necessary; a statement utterly superfluous when made to them at any time, and entirely foreign to the emergency upon which he had called them together, but which he put forth as a threat to Europe of impending famine and misery, by which the commercial and the manufacturing classes might be driven to encourage a rebellion against a constitutional government in support of African slavery and their own interests. For already, and before a blow had been struck on the side either of the insurgents or the government, the former, as Mr. Davis told the world in this message, had sent commissioners to the British, French, Russian, and Belgian governments, to ask recognition and to make treaties. Assumption and self-assertion, pushed to the verge of absurdity, were weapons upon which the insurgent slaveholders much relied for the triumph of their cause, and in which their armory, not supplied, in this particular, by "acquirements" from the North, was inexhaustible. But men are too often taken at their own valuation; an arrogant, active, and unscrupulous pretender will for a time overbear and sweep away the claims of him who rests quietly in his consciousness of right; and so, as it appeared ere long, the presuming policy of the insurgents accomplished more than they could have expected, if not all that they desired. But it was in the closing sentences of this message that Mr. Davis assumed the position which most won for the rebels the sympathy of which they were so much in need. "In independence," he said, "we seek no conquest, no aggrandizement, no cession of any kind from the states with which we have lately confederated. All we ask is to be let alone—that those who never held power over us shall not now attempt our subjugation by force of arms. This we will, this we must resist to the direst extremity. The moment that this pretension is abandoned, the sword will drop from our grasp, and we shall be ready to enter into treaties of amity and commerce that can not but be mutually beneficial. So long as this pretension is maintained, with a firm reliance on that Divine Power which covers with its protection the just cause, we will continue to struggle for our inherent right to freedom, independence, and self-government." The picture which these words presented of an inoffensive, peaceful people seeking but to enjoy their own without detriment to others, and driven to resistance only by an attempt to deprive them of freedom and self-government, and bring them under foreign subjugation, produced a strong impression in Europe, and furnished the ill-wishers of the great republic a welcome text from which to preach against the tyrannical aggressiveness of democracy. That men who only asked to be let alone should not be awarded that small boon did indeed seem wrongful. But at the North, where this change from the insolent bravado which claimed Washington and threatened Boston was attributed to the right cause—the uprising which had so astounded the insurgents—

[3] In Cincinnati, the refuse of the immense lard factories is compressed into huge cakes, and this loathsome, indigestible mass is sent southward as food for slaves.

G G

where it was known that no other subjugation was purposed than the obedience of all to the supreme law enacted by all, and that freedom, independence, and self-government were insured by the Constitution which the insurgents had defied as completely, and by the very same safeguards and provisions, as by that which they had adopted—where it was also known that a cession of territory would be an absolute demand, and the conquest of Mexico an ultimate and speedy undertaking on the part of the insurgents if they were successful—and where it was felt in men's inmost hearts that the unresisted and accomplished secession of a single state was national ruin, Mr. Davis's peaceful professions, and his airs of injured innocence, were met with merited derision, and the phrase, "All we ask is to be let alone," became the satirical by-word of the day.

Other parts of this document were of even more importance than those to which the above remarks apply, but I postpone their consideration while I recount briefly the events which took place at the South between the meeting and the adjournment of this Congress, and until I attempt to show the nature and the purposes of the impending conflict. The Congress itself devoted its attention solely to the business of resistance. Letters of marque and reprisal were authorized. Authority was also given to Mr. Davis to accept the services of volunteers without regard to the place of their enlistment. The export of cotton during the blockade, except from the sea-ports of the Confederate States and through Mexico, was forbidden under both heavy penalty and imprisonment. A bill was passed authorizing the issue of fifty millions of dollars in bonds payable in twenty years, with interest at eight per cent., or, in lieu of bonds, treasury notes for small sums, without interest, to the amount of twenty millions of dollars. These bonds were offered to planters for their cotton—a politic measure, which sought at once to recruit the treasury, and to bind the planters to the new government by the ties of interest. The payment of debts to any persons or corporations in the loyal states was prohibited, and the loan of the money to the confederate treasury was recommended; but from this scandalous enactment the slave states of Delaware, Maryland, Kentucky, and Missouri, and the District of Columbia, were shrewdly excepted, in the vain hope that the proffered bribe might buy a lukewarm patriotism.

RESIDENCE OF MR. JEFFERSON DAVIS AT MONTGOMERY, CALLED "THE WHITE HOUSE."

Meantime the people of the seceded states were inflamed with an unquenchable military ardor. Having been taught to believe that one Southern man was a match for five Northerners, and that the Yankees (as they called the inhabitants of all the free states) would be slow to battle, even for a cause which they had at heart, the slaveholders, and the mean whites who did their bidding, looked for a sudden and an easy victory, and they thronged into the insurgent ranks to share its cheap-bought glory. The bulk of the newly-levied army was poured into Virginia, which was threatened by the forces rapidly accumulating around Washington. General Robert Lee, of Virginia, who had been one of Lieutenant General Scott's military family, and who had grieved the heart of his old chief by deserting for his state the cause of the republic, had been placed in command of the Virginia militia. To prevent confusion of state and confederate authority, on the 10th of May he was directed by the government at Montgomery to take command of all the troops in Virginia. Other officers soon superseded him; but this is the first appearance upon our scene of a man who was destined to exercise a controlling influence upon the fortunes of the war now about to open. On the 22d of May the Congress at Montgomery adjourned to meet on the 20th of July at Richmond. The former parted finally with its short-lived distinction, and the latter became in fact, if not in name, the confederate capital.

Fort Sumter had been attacked before the government had taken any steps for the suppression of the insurrection, and even before the President had issued a formal proclamation commanding the obedience of the insurgents to the constitutional authorities of the republic. In the bombardment of that strong-hold not a life had been lost or a serious wound received on the part either of the assailants or the garrison; and its evacuation was the consequence of a lack of food and a conflagration, both brought about by the means of batteries, the erection of which under his guns its commander, by orders from Washington, had made no effort to prevent. The collisions in Baltimore and St. Louis were produced by mere outbreaks of mob violence; and thus far, therefore, the war ushered in by the attack upon Fort Sumter may be regarded as not having begun. Before entering upon the details of a struggle of which the civil and the moral are far more interesting and significant than the military and the material aspects, it will be well to examine into the causes and the purposes of the conflict, and the means for its prosecution in the hands of each party at its commencement.

War, whether civil or between opposing nations, is always the fruit of aggression. It is resistance to aggression which produces collision of arms, although arms may be first taken up by the aggrieved. Civil wars, when they are not wars of races or religions, or between the partisans of rival claimants to supreme authority, or the results of two or all of these causes, are brought about by the attempts of the party in power to assert or to perpetuate the right of using that power for its own interests, regardless of the principles of justice and of the general good. Thus our ancestors fought King Charles at Naseby, at Worcester, and at Marston Moor, because he attempted to perpetuate the absolute royal prerogative which he blindly thought had come down to him unimpaired from the Tudors, and to rule English men as a father rules a family of children. He did not see that the nation had come to its majority. Thus, again, they fought King George at Bunker Hill, at Saratoga, and at Yorktown, because he and his ministers undertook to deny them—they being born on the western side of the Atlantic—their rights as Englishmen, and to tax them by the votes of a body in which they were not represented. And thus the French people swept away, in a storm of blood, the men who were banded together to rule France in the interests of an aristocratic class, and in utter disregard of the well-being of their social inferiors. In the United States there were no distinctions of race, of religion, or, properly, of rank or birth, in which might breed the germs of internal enmity. The homogeneousness of the nation at the time when it came into political existence had been indeed somewhat modified during the lapse of seventy years, but so slightly that this circumstance is not to be taken into consideration in an examination of the causes of the rebellion. For not only were the Irish and German immigrants who poured into the country after the year 1816 rapidly absorbed and assimilated by the Anglo-American people, among whom in the second generation they were lost, but by those of their number who went southward and were subjected to the influences of slavery, the sentiments and prejudices which led to the rebellion were adopted with the greatest facility; and among the recently arrived Irish immigrants in the free states the slaveholders' party found its constant supporters and allies. In the first armies which moved northward to meet the forces of the republic Irishmen and Germans bore a proportion to the whole number about equal to that of their countrymen in the opposing ranks; and amid the planters whom they left behind them there were no more strenuous advocates of progressive slavery and secession than those who were of British birth.[4] And it was to the Northwestern states, whither had thronged most of the German immigrants, that the insurgent planters, ere many months had passed, looked to find aid in forming a great confederacy, from which the purely English blooded Eastern states were to be excluded. Indeed, from the very beginning, this alliance, and that of the Irish-ruled city of New York, had been counted upon as main elements of strength in the attempted revolution. When to these facts there is added another, greatly significant, that among the strongest supporters and most active agents of the insurrection were a host of men born and bred in the free states, but who had political and personal interests involved in the success of the party of progressive slavery, and who served as officers in the insurgent army, in the civil affairs of the confederacy, or, still more effectively, as its emissaries at the North or in Europe, demoralizing public opinion at home and perverting it abroad; when of the regular army we find thirty officers born and bred in the free states who, in November and December of 1861, resigned their commissions and soon afterward entered the rebel service, and, on the other hand, one hundred and thirty-three officers of that army born and bred in slave states remaining true to their colors, and under sorely trying circumstances fighting the battles of the republic,[5] it will be seen how shallow was the pretense of the mouthpieces of the insurgent leaders that secession was the consequence of a difference between the people of the slave and free states. Some slight difference there was, but no such difference.

Still less were there opportunities for the development of that hatred which through so many centuries has shown religion and impiety walking hand in hand, inciting Mohammedan to slay Christian, Roman Catholic to burn Protestant, Church of England man to persecute Puritan, and Puritan to hang Quaker. On the contrary, a Christian faith essentially uniform pervaded the land, throughout which nearly all the known sects were harmoniously diffused. Even the slight difference in this regard between the two

[4] Mr. William Henry Russell's *Diary North and South* gives foreign, unbiased, and partly unwilling support to this statement, which is known to be true by every observant and thoughtful man in the United States.

[5] See the extracts from the Army Register in "Are the West Point Graduates Loyal?" by E. C. Marshall.

sides of the Potomac which had existed in the early years of the country had passed away. A great increase of the Baptists and Methodists in the slave states had deprived the Church of England of its predominance in that quarter; while in the free states, and in New England itself, that sect had grown rapidly, and with a constantly increasing growth, from a period which dated before the War of Independence. Nor were hostile and clashing interests of a normal kind the springs of this rebellion. Various interests, truly, had various preponderance in different parts of the country; but there must be variety of interest in every nation the people of which are not so rude as to have neither commerce, manufactures, arts, nor literature, or the territory not so small as to be monotonous. But such varieties of interest and occupation, so far from producing discord and division, compensate each other, harmonize with each other, and bind together the people among whom they obtain, making of them one complex, highly-developed, self-sustaining individual, while the nation of a single interest is, like an animal of simple organization, a feeble creature of low grade. The isolation and narrowness of view consequent upon exclusive devotion to one employment causes a nation surely to remain in or relapse into a state little above a semi-barbarism. The variety of normal interests in the United States was no greater and no other than comported with the well-being and the progress of a great and powerful nation, either as a whole or in regard to its component parts. Agriculture prevailed in the South, but not more than at the Northwest; and it was a powerful interest in the Northeast, where manufactures and commerce prevailed, and where the spirit of trade, though predominant, was not more active than at New Orleans or at Chicago. The mariners and the shipwrights of the North, who lived by carrying the cotton, the sugar, and the tobacco of the Southern planter, and the grain and pork of the Western farmer, and bringing the produce of other lands within their reach, furnished also the naval force which secured them the quiet possession of their fields, and the safe transhipment of their produce. The Northern forges and furnaces, which chiefly supplied the mills, the engines, and the railways of both South and West, earned whatever the tariff brought them in excess of the cost of like manufacture from Europe by furnishing also the arms which defended them; and, in case of foreign war, the mills of Massachusetts and Rhode Island were able to provide at once a market for the raw cotton of the South, and a full and certain supply of the fabrics into which it had been converted. So that, in fact, at the time of the attempted disruption of the republic, as at that of its formation (I have before remarked the fact, but it can not too constantly be kept in mind), it exhibited a homogeneousness in every respect far more nearly absolute than that of the kingdom of Great Britain—like itself a union, but a union of three distinct peoples, ancient, radically diverse, and for centuries inimical—or that of France, not to speak of the small republic of Switzerland, the larger empire of Austria, or the vast domain ruled by the autocrat of Russia. Save for one single point of difference, there was no nation in the world so homogeneous as the great republic; save for one single element of discord, not one so stably built, so strongly buttressed into unity. That point of difference, that element of discord, it is almost superfluous to say, was slavery. Yet slavery was not the cause of the rebellion.

In the introductory part of this history, it has been shown that at the adoption of the Constitution the slaveholders obtained political advantages, seen to be incidental and supposed to be temporary, to the preservation of which as slaveholders they soon began solicitously to devote themselves. It has been remarked but a few sentences above that civil wars, when not of race, religion, or dynasty, are the fruit of an attempt of men in power to keep that power in their own hands for their own selfish interests; and we shall now see that the civil war in the United States was not caused by any attack upon slavery, or by the denial of equal rights to slaveholders and free laborers either in the government or in the territory of the republic. We shall see, on the contrary, that it was due to the determination of the former not to yield the power conferred upon them by the abnormal social institution which they had preserved; and to their unwillingness to lapse into the condition of simple citizens, having the same rights as their fellow-citizens, and no more. This equality the fathers of the republic supposed that they would, and intended that they should, assume; but they resolved to perpetuate their predominance in the councils of the nation and their oligarchical supremacy in their own commonwealths, and to use this predominance for the purpose of administering public affairs entirely in the interests of their order. Foiled in this by the attitude and the numerical strength of the people of the free states, they determined to destroy the republic, with the hope, at first, of reconstructing it in such a manner as would inevitably and forever secure their object.

The election of Mr. Lincoln put slavery in no peril. Before he became a candidate for the presidency, or had the thought of becoming one, and in the course of an address to the people of a free state, he had avowed, in clear, decided terms, that, whatever might be his feelings and opinions in regard to slavery, he did not believe that the national government had the constitutional power to disturb it where it was established, or to control the local action of the people in its regard, or to deny the slaveholders the benefit of an effective Fugitive Slave Law.[6] His election found the party of the slaveholders in power. The presidential chair was filled by a man who was their creature, if he was not their tool; and from it he could not be removed for four months. They commanded a majority in the Senate and in the House of Representatives. The bench of the Supreme Court was filled by judges of their appointment, and who had always ruled in their interest; and throughout the country all the executive offices were under their control. Nor, as I have shown by an examination of the votes cast at the presidential election, did the success of Mr. Lincoln indicate any sectional division of the country upon the question of the administration of the national government;[7] while, on the contrary, the divided vote of the slave states, in consequence of which he was elected, though a plurality of one million of the entire popular vote of the country was given for his opponents collectively, did show that in those very states there was at that time a majority of two hundred thousand voters ready to maintain the paramount importance of the Union. There was, therefore, at the time of the secession of South Carolina, not only no impending danger to the interests of the slave states, but, in the view of the great body of their people (except in South Carolina itself), no such danger threatened in the future as induced them to give their votes in favor of a candidate who represented the party of progressive slavery or disunion. But the five hundred and seventy thousand slaveholders who did so vote,[8] and the leaders of whom immediately set on foot secession, knew well that the social institution peculiar to their states was in no peril; they were but putting into effect a long-cherished purpose to dissolve the Union when they had ceased to rule it. We are not left to infer this purpose from the furious and frothy outpourings of their provincial presses;[9] it had been distinctly avowed, though in private, by their representative man, John C. Calhoun. Forty-eight years before the election of Mr. Lincoln, and eight years previous to the agitation which resulted in the Missouri Compromise, he had confessed to Commodore Charles Stewart, an honored and successful commander in the United States Navy, that the leading slaveholders united themselves with the Democratic party in the North in defiance of their tastes and preferences, and only as a means of obtaining political power; adding this memorable declaration: "When we [the slaveholders] thus cease to control this nation through a disjointed democracy, or any material obstacle in that party which shall tend to throw us out of that rule and control, we

---

[6] *Remarks of Mr. Lincoln upon a Series of Questions addressed to him by Mr. Douglas during their canvass for the Senatorship of Illinois.*

Question 1. I desire to know whether Lincoln to-day stands pledged, as he did in 1854, in favor of the unconditional repeal of the Fugitive Slave Law?

Answer. I do not now, nor ever did, stand pledged in favor of the unconditional repeal of the Fugitive Slave Law.

Q. 2. I desire him to answer whether he stands pledged to-day, as he did in 1854, against the admission of any more slave states into the Union, even if the people want them?

A. I do not now, nor ever did, stand pledged against the admission of any more slave states into the Union.

Q. 3. I want to know whether he stands pledged against the admission of a new state into the Union with such a Constitution as the people of that state may see fit to make?

A. I do not stand pledged against the admission of a new state into the Union with such a Constitution as the people of that state may see fit to make.

Q. 4. I want to know whether he stands to-day pledged to the abolition of slavery in the District of Columbia?

A. I do not stand to-day pledged to the abolition of slavery in the District of Columbia.

Q. 5. I desire him to answer whether he stands pledged to the prohibition of the slave-trade between the different states?

A. I do not stand pledged to the prohibition of the slave-trade between the different states.

Q. 6. I desire to know whether he stands pledged to prohibit slavery in all the Territories of the United States north as well as south of the Missouri Compromise line?

A. I am impliedly, if not expressly, pledged to a belief in the *right* and *duty* of Congress to prohibit slavery in all the United States' Territories.

Q. 7. I desire him to answer whether he is opposed to the acquisition of any new territory unless slavery is first prohibited therein?

A. I am not generally opposed to honest acquisition of territory; and, in any given case, I would or would not oppose such acquisition, according as I might think such acquisition would or would not aggravate the slavery question among ourselves.

Now, my friends, it will be perceived, upon an examination of these questions and answers, that so far I have only answered that I was not *pledged* to this, that, or the other. The Judge has not framed his interrogatories to ask me any thing more than this, and I have answered in strict accordance with the interrogatories, and have answered truly, that I am not *pledged* at all upon any of the points to which I have answered. But I am not disposed to hang upon the exact form of his interrogatory. I am rather disposed to take up at least some of these questions, and state what I really think upon them.

As to the first one, in regard to the Fugitive Slave Law, I have never hesitated to say, and I do not now hesitate to say, that I think, under the Constitution of the United States, the people of the Southern States are entitled to a Congressional Fugitive Slave Law. Having said that, I have had nothing to say in regard to the existing Fugitive Slave Law farther than that I think it should have been framed so as to be free from some of the objections that pertain to it, without lessening its efficiency. And inasmuch as we are not now in an agitation in regard to an altera-

tion or modification of that law, I would not be the man to introduce it as a new subject of agitation upon the general question of slavery.

In regard to the other question, of whether I am pledged to the admission of any more slave states into the Union, I state to you very frankly that I would be exceedingly sorry ever to be put in a position of having to pass upon that question. I should be exceedingly glad to know that there would never be another slave state admitted into the Union; but I must add that, if slavery shall be kept out of the Territories during the territorial existence of any one given Territory, and then the people shall, having a fair chance and a clear field, when they come to adopt the Constitution, do such an extraordinary thing as to adopt a slave Constitution, uninfluenced by the actual presence of the institution among them, I see no alternative, if we own the country, but to admit them into the Union.

The third interrogatory is answered by the answer to the second, it being, as I conceive, the same as the second.

The fourth one is in regard to the abolition of slavery in the District of Columbia. In relation to that, I have my mind very distinctly made up. I should be exceedingly glad to see slavery abolished in the District of Columbia. I believe that Congress possesses the constitutional power to abolish it. Yet, as a member of Congress, I should not, with my present views, be in favor of *endeavoring* to abolish slavery in the District of Columbia, unless it would be upon these conditions: *first,* that the abolition should be gradual; *second,* that it should be on a vote of the majority of qualified voters in the District; and, *third,* that compensation should be made to unwilling owners. With these three conditions, I confess I would be exceedingly glad to see Congress abolish slavery in the District of Columbia, and, in the language of Henry Clay, "sweep from our capital that foul blot upon our nation."

In regard to the fifth interrogatory, I must say here, that as to the question of the abolition of the slave-trade between the different states, I can truly answer, as I have, that I am *pledged* to nothing about it. It is a subject to which I have not given that mature consideration that would make me feel authorized to state a position so as to hold myself entirely bound by it. In other words, that question has never been prominently enough before me to induce me to investigate whether we really have the constitutional power to do it. I could investigate it if I had sufficient time to bring myself to a conclusion upon that subject; but I have not done so, and I say so frankly to you here and to Judge Douglas. I must say, however, that if I should be of opinion that Congress does possess the constitutional power to abolish the slave-trade among the different states, I should still not be in favor of the exercise of that power unless upon some conservative principle, as I conceive it akin to what I have said in relation to the abolition of slavery in the District of Columbia.

My answer as to whether I desire that slavery should be prohibited in all the Territories of the United States is full and explicit within itself, and can not be made clearer by any comments of mine. So I suppose, in regard to the question whether I am opposed to the acquisition of any more territory unless slavery is first prohibited therein, my answer is such that I could add nothing by way of illustration, or making myself better understood than the answer which I have placed in writing.   [7] See the Introduction, p. 17.

[8] Deducting from the 874,953 votes cast for Mr. Breckinridge the 276,818 which he received in the free states, we have 571,135 as his party in the slave states.

[9] See the extract from the Louisville (Ky.) *Courier,* Introduction, p. 17.

shall then resort to the dissolution of the Union."[10] The time and the occasion supposed by Calhoun had come. Slavery was in no peril; but a disjointed democracy had thrown the slaveholders out of control of the nation, and, true to their purpose, that which they ceased to rule they began to ruin. It was by the agitation of the question of slavery that the democracy had become disjointed. But slavery in itself was no bar to the perpetuity of the Union; for, at its formation, slaves were held in every commonwealth but one of those which, under the Constitution, passed from a confederacy into a nation. It is true that in six of the remaining twelve slavery was felt to be wrongful, and was doomed to speedy extinction by irresistible forces both moral and material; but it is no less true that among the majority of the people of the other six which retained it there was at that time a similar estimate both of its justice and its economy, and that their leading statesmen, including those who spoke for them in the formation of the Constitution, expected and desired its abolition by legislative enactment. Washington wrote of slavery, "I can only say that there is not a man living who wishes more sincerely than I do to see some plan adopted for the abolition of it; but there is only one proper and effectual mode by which this can be accomplished, and that is by legislative authority; and this, so far as my suffrage will go, shall never be wanting."[1] Thomas Jefferson predicted, "Nothing is more certainly written in the book of fate than that these people [the negroes] are to be free."[2] In the debate in the Constitutional Convention on the apportionment of taxes to population, Hugh Williamson, of North Carolina, thought that "slaves should be excluded altogether [from the enumeration of taxable inhabitants], as being an encumbrance instead of increasing the ability to pay taxes."[3] Such being throughout the country the feeling of the people as to slavery at the time of the formation of the Constitution, it was not difficult to effect a compromise upon that subject which safely provided for the existing condition of affairs in regard to it, and which seemed to provide equally well for the future. But, as we have seen, slavery not only brought then unimagined wealth to the slaveholder; it conferred upon him political power and peculiar privileges. In virtue of his slaves, his vote was of more weight than that of his fellow-citizen of the free states; and his superiority in this regard became greater as the number of bondsmen owned by him and his neighbors increased. Slave states became oligarchies, and slaveholders a bastard kind of aristocracy. It was this power, and not his slaves, which the slaveholder saw slipping from his hands, and therefore he rebelled. For power is sweet; and when held by an intelligent and determined body of men, whether rightfully or wrongfully, whether for good or for evil, for selfish ends or for the benefit of mankind, it will not be yielded without a struggle. Most especially is this true of men whose notions of right and wrong have been perverted by the seeking after pleas in justification of the holding of an inferior race in chattel bondage. There had been compromise before, but now the slaveholders saw that no compromise which was not absolute concession would restore and preserve their lost supremacy. On the other hand, the question of slavery was just the one on which the men of the free states could no longer compromise. There the feeling that slavery was moral wrong and political ruin, though not universal, had taken such firm hold of the public mind, that any arrangement which looked toward a spread of the evil would not have endured for half a generation. The leading slaveholders were wise enough to see this; and, therefore, they refused all compromise which was not full concession of their claims in perpetuity, accompanied by the power for their enforcement. These, then, were the causes of the rebellion. First, the determination of the slaveholders to maintain their political supremacy, and not to subside into the condition of simple citizens of the republic; second, a radical change during the two generations which had passed since the adoption of the Constitution in the attitude of the people, both of the free and the slave states, toward slavery. Among the former this change had been effected by the progress of humanity and Christian civilization, which was unchecked within their borders; among the latter, by the rank-grown lust of riches and of power, and by the perverted moral sense of the people. Slavery was thus not the cause of the rebellion, but it was its indispensable condition. There was one other: the ignorance, the social degradation, and the sordid poverty and pride of the mass of the inhabitants of the slave states, which made the development among them of jealousy, suspicion, unfounded hate, and arrogant defiance of the people of the free states, by the machinations of the leading slaveholders, not only possible, but easy.

Having seen why the faction of progressive slavery, though in the minority in every slave state except South Carolina and perhaps Georgia, brought about the secession of eleven of the thirty-three divisions of the republic, let us now examine the grounds on which the government, supported by the whole people of the free states and a large majority of those in the border slave states, resisted the movement for the dissolution of the Union. Such an inquiry would seem superfluous were it not for the peculiar circumstances which distinguish the origin of this civil war from that of any other known to history. A nation, though ranking among the four great powers of the world, might, indeed, contain the seeds of its own dissolution; the statesmen who planned its Constitution might have been, from their lack of wisdom, of foresight, or of honesty, the architects of its ruin; but that a nation which attained its political independence and its unity by a noble sacrifice of blood, and treasure, and of local interest, and the organic law of whose existence was not extorted from power by peril, but evolved from circumstance and precedent through the cautious and protracted consultation of its own best representatives, should have been deliberately constituted so that it should die at the caprice of any one or two commonwealths formed out of its people and its territory; that its Constitution was purposely so framed that it would crumble to dust at the withdrawal of one of the parties to it, and that the right so to destroy it was carefully protected by its framers, the men who had given their lives to objects which it was intended to secure and perpetuate; that this should be, is morally so monstrous, so inconsistent with all the laws and the motives of human action, that it is difficult to believe that men in their senses could base upon such an assumption a great political and social revolution. And yet it was upon this ground that their action was defended by the insurgent slaveholders. They denied that they were rebels. They claimed that they were not resisting a government and setting at naught a Constitution to which they owed allegiance. They admitted that, until they passed their Ordinances of Secession, they were bound to obey the laws of the republic, and to respect the government at Washington; but they asserted that the right of secession belonged to every state; that its just exercise depended solely upon the will of the people of the state, who alone were to be consulted in the matter; and that by the mere passage of an Ordinance of Secession they were actually and rightfully absolved from all connection with, and responsibility to the government of the Union, and themselves became a sovereign, independent nation. The government at Washington and the people who were loyal to it looked in vain for the foundation of a theory so destructive, of a claim so extraordinary. It was not to be found in the Constitution, the organic law by virtue of which the nation existed. That instrument contained no clause which could be distorted into a justification of this preposterous plea; but, on the contrary, a positive declaration that the Union, even when confined to the states which originally entered into it, should be perpetual, and a provision for the punishment of treason and the putting down of rebellion. Equally vain was the search among the records of the debates and consultations which accompanied the formation of the Constitution, and in which all the differing views of its framers were brought forward, and all the various interests of the people whom they represented were urged, and either maintained, or yielded in a spirit of compromise. Throughout those protracted discussions there was no hint from any quarter of a reserved right of secession; but, on the other hand, from all quarters, and particularly from Virginia and South Carolina, the manifestation of an anxious desire to provide for the ample maintenance of the power of the national government against that of any state which might be tempted to deny or to resist it. Mr. Randolph, of Virginia, in his plan, especially provided that Congress should "call forth the force of the Union against any member of the Union failing to fulfill its duty under the articles thereof." Mr. Pinckney, of South Carolina, moved "that the national Legislature should have authority to negative all laws of state Legislatures which they should judge to be improper;" and Mr. Madison, of Virginia, "could not but regard an indefinite power to negative legislative acts of the states as absolutely necessary to a perfect system." And in the final discussion of the Constitution itself, treason having been defined in the third Article as "levying war against the United States or any of them," Mr. Morris, of Pennsylvania, objected that "in case of a contest between the United States and a particular state, the people of the latter must, according to the disjunctive terms of the clause, be traitor to one or the other authority," this view prevailed at once, and the words "or any of them" were stricken out. Thus clearly was it seen by the fathers of the republic that national government might be resisted by one or more of the states; thus unmistakably intended that in such case the authority of that government should be maintained; thus explicitly set forth that such resistance was treason and rebellion, to be put down by the whole force of the Union. The pretense of the insurgents that their secession was not resistance was too shallow to deceive the loyal people for a day. The distinction

[10] *Extract from a Letter from Commodore Stewart to Mr. G. W. Childs, of Philadelphia.*

Bordentown, May 4, 1861.

My dear Sir,—Agreeably to your request, I now furnish you with the reminiscences of a conversation which passed betwen Mr. John C. Calhoun and myself in the latter part of December, 1812, after the declaration of war by the Congress of the United States against Great Britain on the 18th of June previous. * * * *

Mr. Calhoun's age, I thought, approximated my own, which was thirty-four; and being a man of the highest order of talent, and representing a state in our Union which scarce ever permitted themselves to be represented by inferior ability in the national councils, I could not have commenced my object with one more fitted for the purpose I had in view. He was also a high-minded and honorable man, kind and friendly, as well as open and confiding to those he deemed worthy. We soon formed an intimacy, and I frequently had long conversations with him on the war, the subjects relating thereto, and matters growing out of its existence—the navy being the most prominent—the gunboats, the merchants' bonds then on the tapis in Congress, and other matters of political or minor interest. One evening I struck on the divided views of our sectional interests of the war—stated to him that the opposite feelings on this subject had puzzled me exceedingly, and asked him how it was that the planting states were so strongly and so decidedly in favor of the war, while the commercial states were so much opposed to it. With this latter section of our country it seemed to me that the punishment of England, through the medium of war, ought to meet their highest approbation and call for their greatest efforts, as they were the greatest sufferers, through her instrumentality and power over our commercial affairs, since 1792, which were so arrogantly urged by plunder and impressment on the highway of nations, while the southern portion of the Union had felt but little in comparison. I observed, with great simplicity, "You in the South and Southwest are decidedly the aristocratic portion of this Union; you are so in holding persons in perpetuity in slavery; you are so in every domestic quality; so in every habit in your lives, living, and actions; so in habits, customs, intercourse, and manners; you neither work with your hands, heads, nor any machinery, but live and have your living, not in accordance with the will of your Creator, but by the sweat of slavery, and yet you assume all the attributes, professions, and advantages of democracy."

Mr. Calhoun replied: "I see you speak through the head of a young statesman, and from the heart of a patriot, but you lose sight of the politician and the sectional policy of the people. I admit your conclusions in respect to us Southrons. That we are essentially aristocratic I can not deny, but we can and do yield much to democracy. This is our sectional policy; we are from necessity thrown upon and solemnly wedded to that party, however it may occasionally clash with our feelings for the conservation of our interests. It is through our affiliation with that party in the Middle and Western States that we hold power; but when we cease thus to control this nation through a disjointed democracy, or any material obstacle in that party which shall tend to throw us out of that rule and control, we shall then resort to the dissolution of the Union. The compromises in the Constitution, under the circumstances, were sufficient for our fathers; but, under the altered condition of our country from that period, leave to the South no resource but dissolution; for no amendments to the Constitution could be reached through a convention of the people under their three-fourths rule." I laughed incredulously, and said, "Well, Mr. Calhoun, ere such can take place, you and I will have been so long *non est* that we can now laugh at its possibility, and leave it with complacency to our children's children, who will then have the watch on deck." * * * *

[1] Washington's letter to Robert Morris, April 12th, 1786. *Sparks' Washington*, vol. ix., p. 159.

[2] *Jefferson's Writings*, vol. i., p. 48.

[3] *Madison Papers.*

between South Carolina's nullification of a law constitutionally passed which displeased her, and her secession upon the constitutional election of a President whom she did not like, was based upon a difference too slight and formal to receive even a respectful consideration from the straightforward, practical common sense of the intelligent and patriotic masses of the free states. Both proceedings had one end and aim—to make void the constitutional sovereignty of the republic, the will of the majority of the people lawfully expressed.

Peaceful national dismemberment, however, though difficult, is possible, and sometimes justifiable. Circumstances might arise under which justice, prudence, and humanity would all demand the severance of one part of a nation from the other. Did, then, justice, prudence, and humanity, or either of them, counsel the dismemberment of the Great Republic at the bidding of the controlling faction in eleven of the thirty-four commonwealths of which it was composed?

To determine the justice of their claim, we have only to consider the nature of the government from which they proposed to absolve themselves by their own action, and the organization of the nation which they proposed to destroy. Had the power or the nation known as the United States been a confederation, there might or might not have been reason in their claim to withdraw from it merely of their own motion. But we have seen that this was not the nature of the government which was formed in 1789. The government which preceded that was a confederacy; but that confederacy proving entirely inadequate to the absolute needs of the country, it was deliberately superseded by a government or national organization which was, and was asserted and recognized to be, not a confederacy, but a Union—a Making One—of the elements of the former confederacy—a fusion of them into one republic, which, admitting, and in fact preserving, the local independence of its various commonwealths in their local affairs, had one supreme government in its national affairs—one sovereign ruler, that sovereign being the will of the majority of its united people. This union was also (as in its very nature a Union—a Making One—must be) not a transient connection for profit or pleasure, but a merging of separate individuals into one, and was, for better for worse, perpetual.

The dictates of justice are absolute, and should be obeyed whatever ruin may ensue; but prudence looks to consequences. What, then, were the inevitable results of the division sought by the secessionists? For our purpose it is necessary to consider but one of them, the partition of a territory which, from its vastness, its fertility, its means of internal communication, its geographical position, and the character of the people by which it was inhabited, was, and must have remained, the dominant power of a continent, and which was united under one benign government, a government hardly felt by those who lived under it, or who rather were the government—the division of this territory among at least three rival powers, whose clashing interests and mutual jealousy must surely produce constant war, or that hardly less ruinous and demoralizing evil, a position of armed watchfulness

against aggression, or even aggrandizement by neighboring powers. If the slave states of the Union were separated from the free states, as the secessionists claimed, and which would have been the sure results of their success, the Ohio and the Potomac would have been the southern boundary of the free republic, which would thus have been almost bisected by the northernmost county of Virginia, called the "pan-handle;" and even if this strip had been ceded to the Northern republic, the bulk of the free states of the East and West would have been connected with each other only by the comparatively narrow isthmus of the State of Ohio.

But justice refusing, and prudence failing to sustain the plea first set up at Charleston for a dissolution of the Union, perhaps humanity claimed what justice did not dictate or prudence counsel. For what reason, then, did the insurgents seek to dissolve their connection with the old government, and to set up a new one for themselves? For an answer to this question the historian is not left to inference, or even to the unauthorized though unmistakable statements of private persons, or the indications of a general current of events. On the 21st of March, 1861, Alexander H. Stephens, then recently elected vice-president of the insurgent confederacy, delivered at Savannah, Georgia, a formal and elaborate exposition of the character and purposes of the new government which he and his associates were attempting to set up. In that speech he avowed, in very explicit terms, not only that slavery was the cause of the revolt, but that the insurgents had taken their position of armed hostility to the government in direct opposition to the opinions and the purposes of the founders of the republic, the framers of the Constitution, including those from the slave states. He admitted that those statesmen whose wisdom, whose force, and whose dignity had compelled a reluctant admiration from the Old World, held that the enslavement of the negro was in violation of the laws of Nature, and that it was therefore a social, moral, and political wrong. This part of the political ethics of the framers of the government, however, he, with the approbation of his audience, pronounced fundamentally fallacious. "Our government," he declared, "is formed upon exactly opposite ideas." "Slavery," he continued, "which was rejected by the first builders, is become the chief stone of the corner in our new edifice."[4]

His words found their ready echo in every insurgent's breast throughout the whole disaffected region, where more than two years afterward a leading organ of public opinion still avowed the rebellion "a protest against the mistaken civilization of the age." Is it to be wondered at that, such being the declared purpose of the insurgents, and so clear being their departure from the spirit and purpose of the founders of the republic in this regard, they were forced to admit this antagonism? Every citizen of the United States, in whose breast the love of gain or the love of ease, the lust of power or the canker of party spirit had not eaten out all patriotism and all humanity, should have decided, without a second thought, that they were to be resisted to the death. Such was the decision announced by the spontaneous and almost instantaneous UPRISING AT THE NORTH.

---

[4] After referring to a few points in which he argued that the Constitution of the Confederate States was an improvement upon that of the United States, Mr. Stephens continued:

"But, not to be tedious in enumerating the numerous changes for the better, allow me to allude to one other—though last, not least: the new Constitution has put at rest *forever* all the agitating questions relating to our peculiar institutions—African slavery as it exists among us—the proper *status* of the negro in our form of civilization. *This was the immediate cause of the late rupture and present revolution.* Jefferson, in his forecast, had anticipated this, as the 'rock upon which the old Union would split.' He was right. What was conjecture with him is now a realized fact; but whether he fully comprehended the great truth upon which that rock *stood* and *stands* may be doubted. *The prevailing ideas entertained by him and most of the leading statesmen at the time of the formation of the old Constitution were, that the enslavement of the African was in violation of the laws of nature; that it was wrong in principle, socially, morally, and politically.* It was an evil they knew not well how to deal with; but the general opinion of the men of that day was, that, somehow or other, in the order of Providence, the institution would be evanescent and pass away. This idea, though not incorporated in the Constitution, was the prevailing idea at the time. The Constitution, it is true, secured every essential guarantee to the institution while it should last, and hence no argument can be justly used against the constitutional guarantees thus secured, because of the common sentiment of the day. *Those ideas, however, were fundamentally wrong. They rested upon the assumption of the equality of races. This was an error.* It was a sandy foundation, and the idea of a government built upon it—when the 'storm came and the wind blew, it *fell*.'

"*Our new government is founded upon exactly the opposite ideas; its foundations are laid, its corner-stone rests, upon the great truth that the negro is not equal to the white man; that slavery, subordination to the superior race, is his natural and moral condition. This, our new government, is the first in the history of the world based upon this great physical, philosophical, and moral truth.* This truth has been slow in the process of its development, like all other truths in the various departments of science. . . .

"As I have stated, the truth of this principle may be slow in development, as all truths are, and ever have been, in the various branches of science. It was so with the principles announced by Galileo. It was so with Adam Smith, and his principles of political economy. It was so with Harvey, and his theory of the circulation of the blood. It is stated that not a single one of the medical profession, living at the time of the announcement of the truths made by him, admitted them. Now, they are universally acknowledged. May we not, therefore, look with confidence to the ultimate universal acknowledgment of the truths upon which our system rests? It is the first government ever instituted upon principles in strict conformity to Nature and the ordination of Providence in furnishing the materials of human society. Many governments have been founded upon the principles of certain classes; but the classes thus enslaved were of the same race, and in violation of the laws of Nature. Our system commits no such violation of Nature's laws. The negro by nature, or by the curse against Canaan, is fitted for that condition which he occupies in our system. The architect, in the construction of buildings, lays the foundation with the proper material—the granite—then comes the brick or the marble. The substratum of our society is made of the material fitted by Nature for it, and by experience we know that it is the best, not only for the superior, but for the inferior race, that it should be so. It is, indeed, in conformity with the Creator. *It is not for us to inquire into the wisdom of His ordinances or to question them.* For His own purposes He has made one race to differ from another, as He has made 'one star to differ from another in glory.' The great objects of humanity are best attained, when conformed to his laws and decrees, in the formation of governments as well as in all things else. Our confederacy is founded upon principles in strict conformity with these laws. This stone which was rejected by the first builders '*is become the chief stone of the corner*' in our new edifice."

How unwillingly Mr. Stephens embarked in the cause of secession is shown by his speeches in the Georgia Convention. We have given (*ante*, p. 19–21) a full report of a speech delivered on the 14th of November. We repeat a few of the leading points. He said:

"That this government of our fathers, with all its defects, comes nearer the objects of all good governments than any other on the face of the earth, is my settled conviction. . . . Where will you go, following the sun in his circuit round the globe, to find a government that better protects the liberties of its people, and secures to them the blessings that we enjoy? I think that one of the evils that beset us is a surfeit of liberty, an exuberance of the priceless blessings for which we are ungrateful. . . . Have not we at the South as well as the North grown great and happy under its operation? Has any part of the world ever shown such rapid progress in the

development of wealth, and all the material resources of power and greatness, as the Southern states have under the general government? . . . These [the civilization and institutions of Greece and Rome] were but the fruits of their forms of government, the matrix from which their grand development sprang; and when once the institutions of a people have been destroyed, there is no earthly power that can bring back the Promethean spark to kindle them here again any more than in that ancient land of eloquence, poetry, and song. And if we shall in an evil hour rashly pull down and destroy those institutions which the patriotic band of our fathers labored so long and so hard to build up, and which have done so much for us and the world, who can venture the prediction that similar results will not ensue? Let us avoid it if we can." . . .

The same opinions were reiterated by Mr. Stephens on the 18th of January, less than a month before he accepted the vice-presidency of the confederacy whose formation he had so persistently opposed. In this speech he says:

"I am frank to say, that if we are to secede for existing causes, without any farther effort to secure our rights under the Constitution in the Union—if a majority of this Convention has lost all hope, and look upon secession as the only remedy left—in my opinion, the sooner we secede the better. Delay can effect no good. How this Convention stands upon that question I do not know. Some claim a large majority for immediate and unconditional secession, while others think there is a majority still looking with hope to redress and conciliation. I, for one, am very desirous of having this point settled and put to rest in good feeling and harmony among ourselves by a test vote. My action hereafter shall be influenced by that vote. . . . . My judgment is against secession for existing causes. *I have not lost hope of securing our rights in the Union and under the Constitution;* that judgment on this point is as unshaken as it was when this Convention was called. . . . *I have ever believed, and do now believe, that it is to the interest of all the states to be and remain united under the Constitution of the United States, with a faithful performance by each of all its constitutional obligations; if the Union could be maintained on this basis, and on these principles, I think it would be the best for the security, the liberty, happiness, and common prosperity of all.* I do farther feel confident, if Georgia would now stand firm, and unite with the border states, as they are called, in an effort to obtain a redress of those grievances on the part of some of their Northern confederates whereof they have such just cause to complain, that complete success would attend the effort, our just and reasonable demands would be granted. In this opinion I may be mistaken, but I feel almost as confident of it as I do of my existence. . . . If, however," he concludes, "on the test vote, a majority shall be against the line of policy I indicate, then, sir, upon the point of immediate secession, or a postponement to some future day between this and the 4th of March, *I am clearly of the opinion that no good can come from any such delay or postponement.* . . . This is my view on that point. My judgment, as is well known, is against the policy. It can not receive the sanction of my vote; but if the judgment of a majority of this Convention, embodying as it does the sovereignty of Georgia, be against mine—if a majority of her delegates in this Convention shall, by their votes, dissolve the compact of union which has connected her so long with her confederate states, and to which I have been so ardently attached, and have made such efforts to continue and perpetuate upon the principles on which it was founded, I shall bow in submission to that decision. *I have looked, and do look, upon our present government as the best in the world.* This, with me, is a strong conviction. I have acted upon it as a great truth. But another great truth also presents itself to my mind, and that is, that *no government is a good one for any people who do not so consider it. The wisdom of all governments consists mainly in their adaptation to the habits, the tastes, the feelings, wants, and affection of the people.* The best system of government for our people might be the worse for another. If, therefore, the deliberate judgment of the sovereignty of Georgia shall be pronounced that our present government is a bad one, and shall be changed to some other better suited to our people, more promotive of our peace, security, happiness, and prosperity, while my individual judgment shall be recorded against it, yet my action shall conform to the decision made. Nay, more, sir, the cause of the state shall be my cause, her destiny shall be my destiny. To her support, defense, and maintenance all that I have and am shall be pledged. And however widely we of this Convention, as well as the people of the state, may have differed, or may now differ, as to the proper line of policy to be pursued at this juncture, I trust there will be but one feeling and one sentiment here and throughout our limits after the policy shall be adopted, let that be what it may. The cause of Georgia, whether for weal or woe, must and will be the cause of us all. Her safety, rights, interests, and honor, whatever fortunes await her, must and will be cherished in all our hearts, and defended, if need be, by all our hands."

MONTGOMERY, ALABAMA, FEBRUARY 8, 1861.

THE WAR FOR THE UNION.

CHAPTER I.

THE UNION AND THE CONFEDERACY.

Design of this History.—Materials.—Secession of seven States.—Formation of the Confederacy. —Accession of Virginia, Arkansas, Tennessee, and North Carolina.—The Ordinances of Secession.—The free Population of the Union and the Confederacy.—The slave Population.—Its military Bearing. — Characteristics of the North and the South. — Towns and Cities. — The South better armed at the Outset.—Its Advantages in Position.—King Cotton.—Unanimity of the People at the South.—State Sovereignty and the Union.—The public and private Property seized by the Confederacy. — Railroad Communication at the South. — The two weak Points of the Confederacy.—Opening of Hostilities.

WE have now traced the origin and described the development of the Great Conspiracy against the Union, fortifying our statements by a copious array of documents. We have shown how, after forty years, it culminated in the Great Rebellion. We have depicted the great Uprising of the North to oppose that rebellion. Henceforth it remains for us to tell the story of the War for the Union. We are to show how a peaceful people, whose armies had for generations numbered only a few thousand men, found itself suddenly transformed into two great military nations, equipping and bringing into the field the greatest armies of modern times. We shall have to tell of many errors and not a few crimes—to speak of living men as freely as though they were dead—to narrate deeds of heroism and self-sacrifice on both sides. We shall have to tell of great victories and of great defeats —of opportunities thrown away and of disasters overcome. We shall unduly praise no man because he strove for the Right; we shall malign no man because he fought for the Wrong. We shall endeavor to anticipate the sure verdict of after ages upon events in which we have the deepest personal interest. Whether we shall in the end have to speak of a nation made stronger by the sharp trial through which it passed, or of that nation broken and shattered, the future must unfold.

The materials for our history are abundant. No war was ever before so waged in the world's eye. Many of the commanders have prepared, or propose to prepare, Commentaries upon their campaigns as minute as those of Cæsar. There is not a regiment, and hardly a company, which does not contain a man capable of describing the events which he saw and a part of which he was; and, above all, the Newspaper—the Fourth Estate in our modern civilization—has sent its ablest representatives into the field to watch and describe events as they occur. The files of any one of our great newspapers will contain more and better materials for the historian of the American War than were comprised in the libraries from which Gibbon elaborated the story of the Decline and Fall of the Roman Empire, or the dusty archives from which Motley wrought out the History of the Rise and Growth of the Dutch Republic. From these constantly accumulating materials we propose to write the history of the War for the Union.

We may consider this war to have fairly begun on the 8th of February, 1861, when the Southern Confederacy was formally inaugurated. All that had before been done was the isolated action of disaffected individuals and local communities. From that moment these individuals and communities became formidable by the league into which they had entered, and by the farther accessions upon which they might reasonably count. The die was cast when that Confederacy was formed. All previous steps might have been retraced; now, nothing was left but to submit the question to the arbitrament of strength, and to abide the consequences. We propose to pass in rapid review over the events which resulted in the formation of the Confederacy.

South Carolina formally seceded from the Union on the 20th of December, 1860. In the Convention which gave utterance to the feeling of the state there was no dissentient voice. If in the Convention or among the people there were any who opposed the measure, they kept discreet silence. Charleston, which is to South Carolina more than Paris is to France or London to England, was jubilant upon the passage of the ordinance of secession. Every man, young or old, exulted that the Palmetto State had overthrown a great government. A few wiser men looked farther into the future. "We have," said a delegate in the Convention, "pulled down the temple that has been built for three quarters of a century. We must now clear the rubbish away and reconstruct another. We are houseless and homeless. We must shelter ourselves from storms."

A month had hardly elapsed before five other states ranged themselves by the side of South Carolina. Three of these did so almost simultaneously during the second week of January. In Mississippi an effort was made to postpone action; but this proving unavailing, all the delegates in Convention voted for the ordinance of secession on the 9th of the month. In Alabama the opposition was more decided. The ordinance of secession was passed in secret session by a vote of 61 to 39. The minority had vainly striven to have it referred to the people. One delegate affirmed that, unless this was done, the northern section of the state would not submit to the action of the Convention. The impetuous Yancey denounced the people of this section as traitors and rebels who should be forced to submit. The opposition was overawed; some of the delegates pledged their constituents to the support of the ordinance; the others held their peace. In Florida the opposition was merely nominal. A resolution affirming the right of the state to secede passed by a vote of 62 to 5. Upon the question of the adoption of the ordinance, only 7 out of 69 voted against it. In these three states the ordinances for secession were hurried through within two or three days after the assembling of the Conventions. In Georgia the contest was sharp, and for a while the result seemed doubtful. A fortnight before the secession of South Carolina the Legislature had, by a large majority, passed resolutions declaring that the interests of the slaveholding states were identical, and that they must remain one; affirming the right of any state to secede; denying the right of the federal government to attempt to coerce a state; and pledging Georgia, in case such attempt were made, to support the seceding state. These resolutions were afterward rescinded by a close vote, but were subsequently re-enacted in substance. The Convention met on the 16th of January. A resolution declaring it to be the duty of the state to secede, and appointing a committee to frame an ordinance for that purpose, was passed only by a vote of 165 to 130. But the victory was won. The ordinance, as drawn up, was passed by 208 to 89, and was subsequently signed by all the members. How strenuously those who opposed the measure struggled against it under the able lead of Mr. Stephens, and how unwillingly he, though voting against it, finally gave it his support as a matter of necessity, has been already shown in these pages. The Convention of Louisiana met on the 24th of January, and two days afterward passed an ordinance of secession by a vote of 113 to 17.

Delegates from these six states — Alabama, Florida, Georgia, Louisiana, Mississippi, and South Carolina—met at Montgomery, Alabama, on the 4th of February. The hall in which they assembled was adorned with portraits of Washington, Marion, Jackson, and Clay. There was little occasion for debate. The states which they represented had decided upon the formation of a Southern Confederacy. In four days all preliminary arrangements were completed, a Provisional Constitution, almost identical with that of the United States, framed, and Jefferson Davis elected president, and Alexander H. Stephens vice-president of the new nation. To the original six states Texas should properly be added, as her representatives appeared within a week, were admitted to seats, sanctioned all the previous proceedings of the Congress, and took part in those that followed. We have already narrated the early measures of this government. We now propose to glance briefly at the strength which was absolutely at its disposal, and that upon which it might reasonably count from accessions of states which had not yet seceded from the Union.

By the census of 1860 the entire population of the United States was thirty-one and a half millions, of whom twenty-seven and a half millions were free and four millions slaves.[1] The seven seceding states had a little more than two and a half millions of free persons, and a little less than that number of slaves. Leaving the slaves for the present out of view as an element of either strength or weakness, two and a half millions had thrown down the gage of battle to twenty-five millions. But the contest was not be waged against such odds. Arkansas was, in any case, sure to join the Confederacy. If war ensued, the accession of Virginia, North Carolina, and Tennessee might safely be reckoned upon. The result justified these anticipations.

Virginia was the first to join the Confederacy. We have already narrated the successive steps by which this was accomplished. The ordinance of secession and the ratification of the Provisional Constitution were passed on the 17th of April, subject to the decision of the people at an election to be held six weeks later; but, in the mean while, a compact had been entered into by which the state virtually became at once a member of the Confederacy. The result of the popular vote was a majority of more than a hundred thousand in favor of secession. There were, however, no returns sent in from thirty-four counties. These, with some others, finally organized themselves into the new state of Western Virginia. Virginia became virtually a member of the Confederacy on the 24th of April. In Arkansas a Conven-

tion met on the 4th of March. A small majority of the members were thought to be opposed to immediate secession. The Convention adjourned until the 6th of May without taking any decided action. During this interval an entire change had come over the popular mind, and an ordinance of secession was passed almost as soon as the Convention reassembled, with only a single dissenting vote, and within a week Arkansas became a member of the Confederacy. Tennessee was at first wholly opposed to the precipitate action of South Carolina. At the presidential election she had voted for Mr. Bell, the candidate of a party whose platform was "the Constitution, the Union, and the enforcement of the laws." But from the moment when it was apparent that the extreme Southern states would secede, the governor, Isham G. Harris, undertook to urge Tennessee to follow their example. He kept up an active correspondence with the leaders of the secession, and called the Legislature together to deliberate upon the state and the federal governments. The South, he said, should demand concessions which would never be granted. The Legislature were loth to follow the lead of the governor. It indeed passed a bill authorizing the election of delegates to a Convention, but at the same time submitting to the people the question whether they should meet. Out of 106,000 votes, the disunion candidates received only 25,000, and at the same time it was voted by a majority of 12,000 that the Convention should not be held. It seemed that the question of secession was put at rest; but the call of President Lincoln for troops produced intense excitement throughout the state. The Legislature had before declared that if any troops were sent to the South, Tennessee would resist at all hazards and to the last extremity. To the President's call the governor replied that the state would not furnish a man for the purpose of coercion, but would, if necessary, furnish fifty thousand to aid the South. The Legislature was convened, and the governor recommended the passage of an ordinance declaring Tennessee independent of the federal Union, and another adopting the Montgomery Constitution. These ordinances were passed on the 6th of May by a vote of 66 to 25, to be subject to a vote of the people on the 8th of June. On the 7th of May, a compact, entered into by commissioners, was sanctioned, by which the military power of the state was placed under the control of the President of the Confederate States. In Eastern Tennessee, out of 48,000 votes, 33,000 were against separation; but this majority was largely overbalanced by the other parts of the state, 104,913 votes in all being given for separation, and only 47,700 against it. Tennessee became formally a member of the Confederacy on the 8th of June; but her real adhesion must be dated from the 7th of May, when the Legislature sanctioned the compact placing the whole military force of the state under the control of the President of the Confederate States. North Carolina drifted more slowly, but not less surely, into the confederate vortex. Early in January the forts upon her coast had been seized by mere local authority. The governor disavowed the action, and offered to restore them to the possession of the United States upon condition that they should remain ungarrisoned. This condition was accepted by the feeble Buchanan and his treacherous cabinet. The consequence was that they were soon repossessed by the enemy, now acting under the authority of the governor. After many delays the State Convention assembled, and on the 20th of May passed ordinances for withdrawing from the Union and joining the Confederacy. On that same day, eighty-six years before, had been put forth the Mecklenberg Declaration of Independence, in virtue of which the State of North Carolina has always plumed herself upon being the real founder of the United States.

The eleven states which now composed the Confederacy had a free population of five and a half millions, leaving twenty-one and a half millions in the Union. But it was confidently believed at the South, and for a time feared at the North, that Kentucky, Maryland, and Missouri would go with the other slaveholding states. This would bring the population of the Confederacy up to eight millions, leaving nineteen millions to the Union. These anticipations and fears have not been realized, although the confederates have received much support from individuals of these states, and Kentucky and Missouri have been nominally admitted as members of the Confederacy, and are represented in the Congress.

But, besides the free population, the Confederate States contain three and a half millions of slaves. There was room for great difference of opinion as to the influence of this class of the population upon the military resources of the nation. The North believed that instead of adding strength it was an element of positive weakness. Not only was society so constituted that from more than three eighths of the able-bodied population not a soldier could be raised for the army or a dollar for the revenue, but they were from their very condition so hostile to their masters that a large part of the whites must remain at home to keep the blacks in subjection. In the war of 1812, it was said, a British force of less than 5000 men, so weary with long confinement on shipboard that they hardly deserved the name of an army, had marched many miles through a populous country, burned our national Capitol, and retired without meeting any serious opposition. Imagine, it was said, 5000 weary and footsore men landing somewhere on the New England coast, marching under a fierce August sun to Albany, doing what damage they pleased, and retiring unmolested. The very women, with their shovels and brooms, would have made prisoners of the whole invading force. The only explanation was that the masters were afraid of their slaves, and thought only of saving their own throats from the knives of their servants. In the slaves the British had good friends and sure means of information. Like causes would always produce like effects. The march of a Union army into the South would be the signal of a general servile uprising.

The South denied all this. They affirmed that their domestic institution gave them power as a military nation altogether beyond their mere population. In every state, they said, there must be men who govern, and if need

[1] In the following paragraphs the estimates have been expressed approximately in round numbers. The succeeding table presents the exact figures, according to the Census of 1860:

THE UNION.	Whites.	Free Colored.	Slaves.	Total.
California	376,200	3,816		380,016
Connecticut	451,609	8,542		460,151
Delaware	90,697	19,723	1,798	112,218
Illinois	1,704,684	7,069		1,711,753
Indiana	1,340,072	10,869		1,350,941
Iowa	673,925	1,023		674,948
Kansas	106,487	623		107,110
Kentucky	920,077	10,146	225.490	1,155,713
Maine	627,081	1,195		628,276
Maryland	516,128	83,718	87,188	687,034
Massachusetts	1,221,611	9,454		1,231,065
Michigan	742,289	6,823		749,112
Minnesota	171,793	229		172,022
Missouri	1,064,369	2,983	114,965	1,182,317
New Hampshire	325,622	450		326,072
New Jersey	647,084	24,947		672,031
New York	3,831,730	49,005		3,880,735
Ohio	2,303,374	36,225		2,339,599
Oregon	52,343	121		52,464
Pennsylvania	2,849,997	56,373		2,906,370
Rhode Island	170,703	3,918		174,621
Vermont	314,534	582		315,116
Wisconsin	774,392	1,481		775,873
District of Columbia	60,788	11,107	3,181	75,076
Territories	219,781	299	63	220,143
Total Union	21,557,370	350,721	432,685	22,340,776
THE CONFEDERACY.				
Alabama	526,534	2,630	435,132	964,296
Arkansas	324,186	137	111,104	435,427
Florida	77,778	908	61,753	140,439
Georgia	591,638	3,439	462,232	1,057,329
Louisiana	357,642	18,638	333,010	709,290
Mississippi	353,969	731	436,696	791,396
North Carolina	631,489	30,097	331,081	992,667
South Carolina	291,623	9,648	402,541	703,812
Tennessee	826,828	7,235	275,784	1,109,847
Texas	421,411	339	180,682	602,432
Virginia	1,047,613	57,579	490,887	1,596,079
Total Confederacy	5,450,711	131,401	3,520,902	9,103,014

be fight, and others who hold the place of rulers and legislators. Every where else in the civilized world these two classes merge into each other so gradually that no one can draw the line between them. With us the line is clear and palpable. Every black man knows that he is a laborer, and can be nothing more. Every white man feels that he is a ruler to-day, and may be called upon to be a soldier to-morrow. So completely under our institutions are the ordinary labors of the day performed by the slaves, that every able-bodied white man could take the field at a week's notice, and every thing would go on almost as before. Try this at the North: take three fifths of your men of military age from their farms and their workshops, and every thing would come to a stand in a month. There is no danger of an uprising of the slaves. If they were disposed to rise, they have no means of arming themselves or of acting in concert. Besides, they have no disposition to rise. They have been for generations so trained to obedience, that the women, the old men, and the boys, who can not take the field, will be amply able to keep them in subjection.

There was something of truth in both of these representations. For a short war, waged abroad, or even upon the frontiers of the country, slavery, as the event proved, undoubtedly gave great facilities for raising and equipping an army. There is probably no other nation of eight millions who could raise from nothing the armies which the Confederacy has brought into and maintained in the field. The habits of the people furnished a basis for a military organization. The population was almost entirely rural. New Orleans was indeed a great city, with 170,000 inhabitants; next, but at a wide interval, came Charleston, Richmond, Montgomery, and Mobile, each with 30,000 or 40,000; then came half a dozen cities with from 15,000 to 25,000; beyond these there was hardly a town with more than 5000. Of the rural population every man owned a gun, most of them a horse, and there were few who were not to a good degree expert in their use and management. Men living far apart, with abundant leisure, naturally seek occasions of coming together. These, in the South, were mainly afforded by the regular sessions of the courts and by militia musters. The court-houses are usually placed as nearly as possible in the centre of the county. The militia musters were held at the same place. From all the region the people thronged to court and muster. The parade of the militia was the least attraction at these gatherings; but every man was enrolled in some company, and had learned something of discipline. Rude as this militia organization was, it formed a basis for something better, and did good service when the people were summoned to actual warfare. The South, in a few months, was enabled to transform itself into a great military camp, with no serious breaking in upon the routine of its daily life.

At the North, and especially in the East, the case was different. Every man was engaged in some regular occupation. A large proportion were gathered into cities and towns. Besides New York and Philadelphia, whose population exceeded 600,000 each, there were six cities with more than 100,000, averaging 150,000; nearly a score with from 40,000 to 80,000, and fully fifty more with 10,000 each, besides towns almost without number with more than 5000, which were so closely connected with the cities that they might be considered suburban. Nearly one half of the people of the North lived in cities and large villages; nine tenths of the South lived in the country. The tendency of the free states was toward an aggregation of population; that of the South toward segregation. With few exceptions, the urban population of the North increased more rapidly than the rural; with few exceptions, the rural population of the South increased more rapidly than the urban. The consequence of this is inevitable. The man in the country may need to protect himself and his household, and so provides himself with arms; the man in a town is protected by the police, and requires no arms. The rule was, therefore, that the Southern man was armed and the Northern man was not. Our farmers, mechanics, and laborers undoubtedly furnished better materials for an army than the Southern planters and idlers, but it required more time to transform them into soldiers.

For the purpose which they had in view, the South had also the advantage in position. They contemplated only a defensive war; for their meditated capture of Washington was considered merely taking possession of what geographically and politically belonged to them. If the Union would consent to be broken up without a contest, there would be no fighting. The Union must carry the war, if there was to be war, into the confederate territory, and could reach no vital point except by long marches. The difficulties in the way of an invading army increase with every mile. The great master of war was conquered rather by the space and climate of Russia than by her arms. We had equal space to traverse, and a not less unfavorable climate to encounter before we could reach any vital point. Indeed, with the exception of the three or four ports from which her cotton was shipped, the South had no points of such vital importance that a blow reaching any one of them would have been of serious consequence. To the blockade of her ports and the consequent destruction of her commerce she could for a while submit; the more so, as she had plausible reason to believe that the great powers of the world could not suffer this to last long. Favored by climate, soil, and circumstances, the South had gained the monopoly of an article which had come to be a necessity for the world. Europe must have cotton, and she could get it only from the South. A quarter of the people of England, and a considerable part of those of every other civilized country, lived by the manufacture of cotton; without a supply of the raw material they must starve. If, therefore, in consequence of the war, this supply was cut off, the nations must somehow find a pretext for putting an end to the war. Nay, the North itself could not live without cotton. Cotton fed the manufactories of Massachusetts, and freighted the ships of New York. The woolens from England, the wines from Germany, the silks from France, and the teas from China, were paid for by cotton. Without cotton the industry and commerce of all nations must languish. The world would suffer more from the want of cotton than the South could from the want of an open market for it. For every negro prevented by the war and blockade from raising cotton, five white men would be doomed to idleness and consequent privation from the want of it to manufacture. "Cotton is King" passed into a proverb at the South.

The Confederacy was strong, also, in the entire unanimity of its people. Some of the states hesitated whether they should secede; but, that step once taken, there was no perceptible opposition except in Western Virginia and Eastern Tennessee. Every man felt bound to go with his state, right or wrong. The dogma of the supremacy of the states, inculcated for forty years, had become an absolute article of political faith. The federal government was only an agent created by the states, to be used or discarded at pleasure. A Southerner hardly styled himself an American; he was a Virginian or a Carolinian, a Georgian or a Mississippian. When his state seceded he must follow her fortunes. He might have sworn a thousand civil oaths to be faithful to the Constitution; he might even have taken the military oath—the *sacramentum*, the most sacred obligation known among men—so sacred, that when the founders of our faith needed a term for the obligation which bound a Christian to his Lord, they could only borrow this, and designate the supreme rites of the Church as "sacraments;" he might, like Lee and Davis, like Beauregard and Johnston, have taken this sacramental oath a hundred times, and yet it had no binding force when his state chose to absolve him from it. Many of these men sacrificed much in following their states. Lee had to abandon Arlington House, the spot next after Mount Vernon most closely associated with the memory of the Father of his Country; the two Johnstons gave up posts of honor and profit which it had cost them years to win. There were knaves like Floyd and Thompson, visionaries like Stephens and Jackson, schemers like Davis and Wise, adventurers like Maffit and Semmes; but we can not deny, what future ages will affirm, that not a few of the men who acted prominent parts upon the wrong side in this great war were moved by the sternest sense of what they deemed to be right. In violating their obligations to the Union they acted in obedience to what they deemed the higher law of state sovereignty. If men who had taken upon themselves such obligations thus violated them, it is no wonder that the mass of the people were led away. It was as much as a man's social standing was worth to refrain from joining the army. The women were even in advance of the men. No man who cared to be received in society dared be other than a secessionist. Thus the entire available force of the South was from the outset at the disposal of the confederate leaders.

The North, though vastly superior in numbers and accumulated wealth, showed at first no such unanimity. The ties between the great Democratic party of the North and the South had been so close that many believed the members of this party would yield every thing to their old associates rather than engage in a war to be waged on the platform of their political opponents. The President was not the first choice of a majority even at the North. Many hoped and more feared that he would not be sustained even at home. He was new in public affairs—was unacquainted with most of the men upon whose support he must rely. He could not know whom to trust and whom to suspect. No man ever assumed responsibilities under more trying circumstances than Abraham Lincoln. How he has discharged these responsibilities, the events which we are to relate will show.

The Confederacy, completed by the accession of the Border States, showed a united front. There was every prospect of a Union divided against itself to be opposed to it. It was apparently justified in its first arrogant measures. It could not anticipate the results shown by the great uprising at the North, which proved that love for the Union and a determination to uphold it were paramount to all party considerations. It could not foresee that Democrats would not be behind their old Republican opponents in supporting the war. The Confederacy held firm possession of almost every rood of territory which it claimed. Fortress Monroe in Virginia, Forts Pickens in Florida, Taylor on Key West, and Jefferson on the Tortugas, were all that remained to the Union within the bounds of the Confederate States. With the exception of the few hundred acres within the walls of these fortresses, a narrow strip on the Potomac, and the northwestern corner of Virginia, not a rood remained to the Union of the nearly eight hundred thousand square miles within the eleven seceding states. These four fortresses were, indeed, of inestimable value. Monroe commanded Hampton Roads, the only good harbor on the Atlantic coast south of the Delaware; had that fallen into the hands of the enemy, we should have had no place on the Southern coast for a rendezvous for our naval expeditions. Pickens commanded Pensacola, the only good harbor and naval dépôt on the Gulf of Mexico. Taylor and Jefferson commanded the throat of the Gulf; every vessel entering or leaving it must pass within sight of both. The other forts, a score in number, which had been built by the United States at a cost of ten millions of dollars, and were mounted with more than 1500 guns, had been seized by the states in which they were situated and turned over to the Confederacy. Besides these was the great arsenal at Norfolk, with 2500 great guns in store, and various other arsenals containing some hundreds of cannon, and small-arms sufficient for 150,000 men. There were also mints, hospitals, and custom-houses which had cost fully six millions; stores and supplies worth many millions, and nearly 150 light-houses along the coast from the capes of Virginia to the farther extreme of Texas. Apart from the public lands, it is safe to estimate that national property worth a hundred million dollars was seized by the Confederacy. The South, moreover, had always been a large debtor to the North. Southern merchants and planters made their purchases upon the credit of the cotton crop to be brought to market. The

BALLOON VIEW OF THE SEAT OF WAR.

Pictorial Map
of
Portions of Delaware, Maryland,
Virginia and North Carolina
and
Map of the Southern States

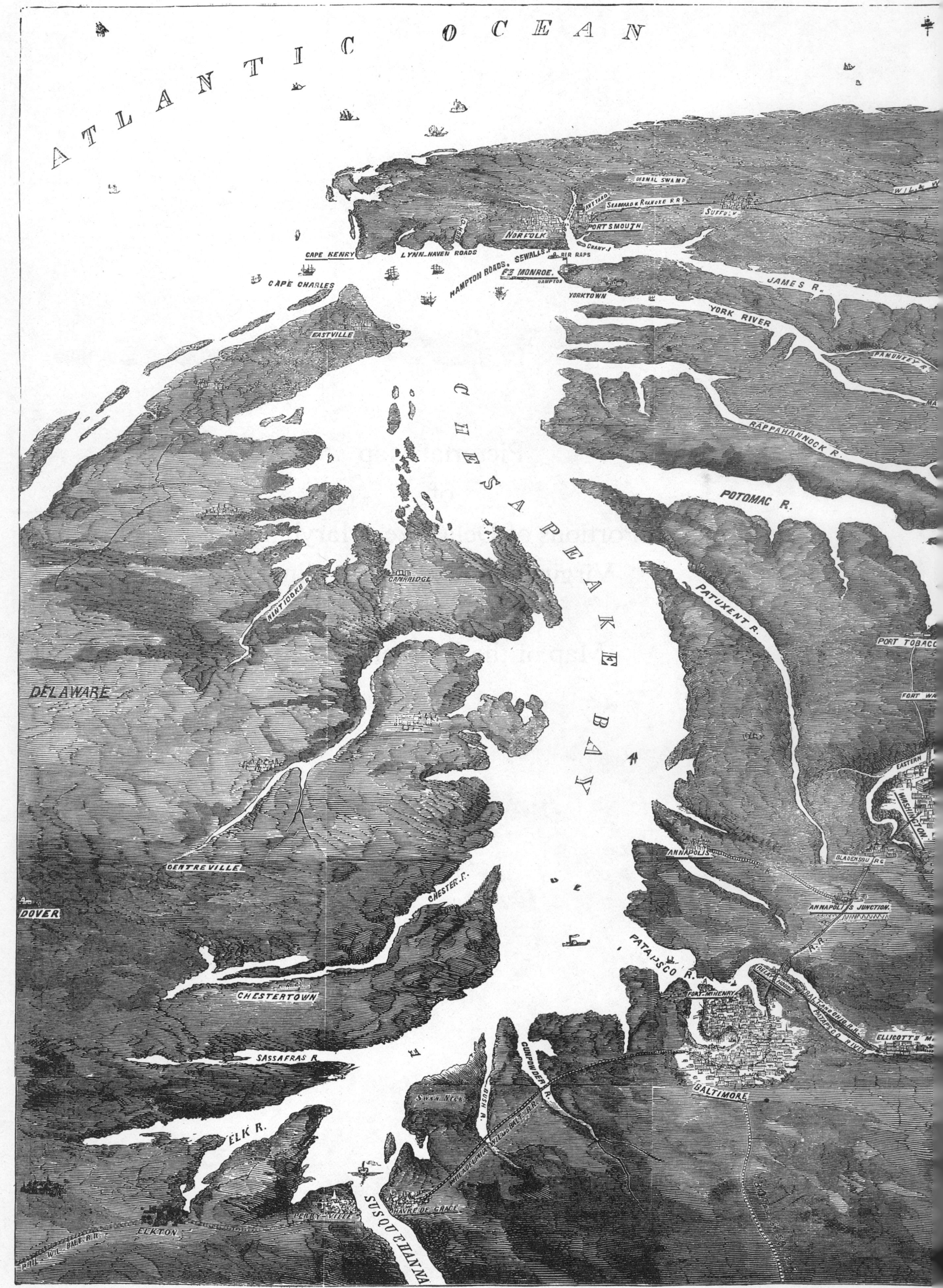

PICTORIAL MAP OF PORTIONS OF DELAWARE, MARYLAND, VIRGINIA, AND

CAROLINA, WITH THE COAST LINE FROM CAPE HENRY TO FORT PICKENS.

MAP OF THE SOUTHER[N]

RAIL ROADS, COUNTY TOWNS, STATE CAPITALS, COUNTY ROADS, THE SOUTHERN COAST FROM

LINCOLN

SCOTT

GULF OF MEXI[CO]

EXPLANATION

Rail Roads	Blockading Ships
Common	County Towns
Bounding States	State Capitals

SCALE OF MILES.

PREPARED FOR HARPER'S HISTORY

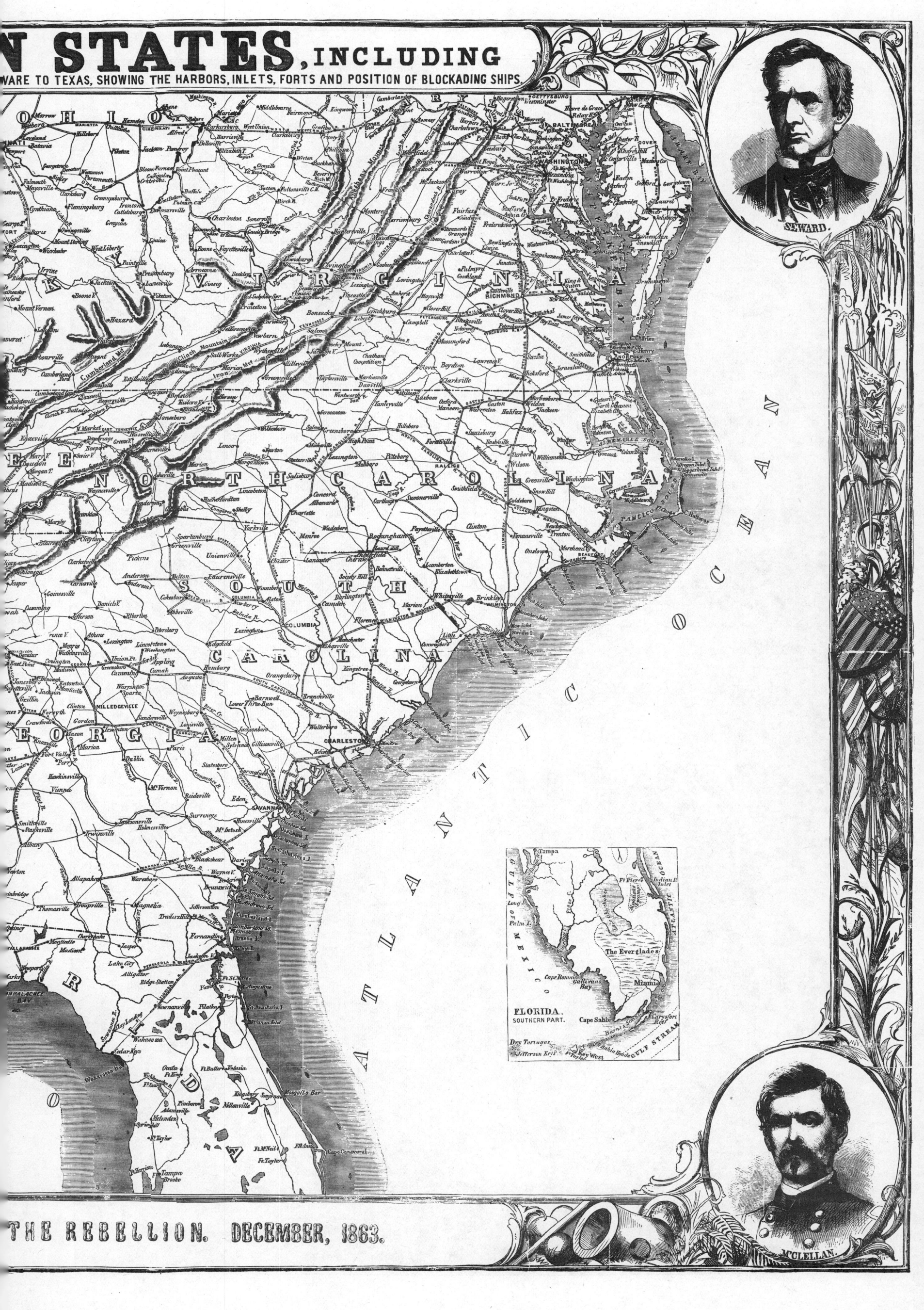

N STATES, INCLUDING

WARE TO TEXAS, SHOWING THE HARBORS, INLETS, FORTS AND POSITION OF BLOCKADING SHIPS.

SEWARD.

FLORIDA.
SOUTHERN PART.

THE REBELLION. DECEMBER, 1863.

McCLELLAN.

BALLOON VIEW OF FORTRESS MONROE AND HAMPTON ROADS.

amount of the debt thus due at the time of secession has been variously estimated at from one hundred to three hundred millions of dollars. The most reliable estimate is framed on the supposition that the cotton crop was in effect mortgaged for half its value. This crop was worth three hundred millions. Southern merchants and planters, therefore, owed one hundred and fifty millions to the North. This was at once confiscated, and the debtors were ordered to pay the amount into the Confederate treasury.

If war was to be waged, it was clearly for the interest of the cotton states that it should be waged on the border. Accordingly, Virginia had hardly joined the Confederacy before the seat of government was removed from Montgomery to Richmond, which then became for a time the centre from which military operations were directed. It was admirably adapted for this purpose. It was so far inland that it could be assailed only by a force vastly superior to its defenders. It had large manufactures of arms and provisions. It was connected by a system of railways with the extreme south and southwest, which would enable the whole force of the Confederacy to be speedily concentrated for its defense. If the system of Southern railways had been constructed especially for military purposes, it could hardly have been better contrived. One line, commencing in Central Georgia, follows the general run of the coast, touches at Savannah and Charleston, then, striking into the interior, reaches Richmond. Another line, starting at New Orleans, runs northward, parallel with the Mississippi, to the neighborhood of Memphis; then, turning almost due east, traverses the very heart of the South, through Tennessee and Virginia, to Richmond. These two great trunk lines are connected by branches reaching into every portion of the Southern States, and from Richmond sending offshoots to the Potomac. Thus, if Richmond were threatened, troops and supplies could be hurried by rail from the far south and southwest. If Charleston or Mobile were threatened, forces from Virginia, Mississippi, and Tennessee could be concentrated there. If Tennessee or Georgia were menaced from Ohio or Kentucky, all the available force of the Confederacy could be dispatched by short routes to the point assailed. A careful study of the general map of the Southern states which we furnish will show that the South had a great advantage in position for carrying on a war of defense. It occupied the centre of a circle, around the circumference of which the North must move. The advantage was hardly less for an offensive movement. If our armies on the Potomac were weakened to support those in the Valley of the Mississippi, the Confederacy could speedily concentrate its armies in Virginia, and hurl them in a mass upon Maryland and Pennsylvania. The Union had to maintain two great armies, one upon the Potomac, the other upon the Mississippi and its great affluents, which must act in a measure independently of each other, on account of the long distances which separated them, while the Confederacy could at pleasure throw its whole force upon either. Thus it happened that while the armies of the Union in the aggregate far outnumbered those of the Confederacy, the latter might be able, as they did, to confront their opponents at almost any given point with equal or superior strength.

The Confederacy thus entered into the contest with a strength altogether beyond that indicated by its population. It had, indeed, two weak points closely connected with each other. The accumulated capital of the South was mainly invested in slaves. If a Southron gained money, he invested it in negroes. The value of an ordinary field-hand had trebled in a few years in consequence of the regular demand for and high price of cotton. If the production of cotton were permanently suspended, slaves would lose their value. A long war of necessity involved this result, and the finances of the South would become embarrassed. Moreover, the character of property which attached to slaves depended upon positive law. If the federal government should pass an act of emancipation, with the power to enforce its execution, the wealth of the slaveholders would be swept away at a blow. That the government had a right to do this, if it were necessary as a war measure, was undisputed; but the public sentiment of the North was, at the outset, wholly opposed to the exercise of this right, and it was long kept in abeyance.

Thus, during the spring of 1861, the Union and the Confederacy stood fairly opposed to each other; all attempts at conciliation had failed, and the forces of each party were confronting each other. The confederate government had established itself at Richmond, and had pushed its outposts so far northward that they could see the dome of the federal Capitol across the Potomac. The national capital had been secured from the immediate danger which threatened it, but the determination to capture it was the prevailing sentiment of the Confederacy. It was commanded by the heights on the Virginia side of the Potomac, and the occupation of these by the federal forces was absolutely essential to the safety of Washington. Forces were also gathering in Western Virginia and Missouri, and were on the point of coming into collision. We turn to these three regions, so widely separated in space, where the first actual military operations commenced almost simultaneously near the close of May, 1861.[1]

[1] THE ORDINANCES OF SECESSION.

The following are the Ordinances of Secession of the several states, arranged in the order in which they were passed. Mere formal expressions and supplementary provisions are omitted or abridged; but the essential portions, which are embraced within quotations, are copied textually. To her brief Ordinance of Secession South Carolina added an elaborate "Declaration of Causes," which will be found at length on page 23 of this History:

SOUTH CAROLINA.—"We, the people of the State of South Carolina, in Convention assembled, do declare and ordain, and it is hereby declared and ordained, that the ordinance adopted by us in Convention on the 23d day of May, in the year of our Lord 1798, whereby the Constitution of the United States was ratified, and also all acts and parts of acts of the General Assembly of the state ratifying amendments of the said Constitution, are hereby repealed, and the union now subsisting between South Carolina and other states, under the name of 'The United States of America,' is hereby dissolved."—Passed December 20, 1861.

FLORIDA.—"*Whereas* all hope of preserving the Union, upon terms consistent with the safety and honor of the slaveholding states, has been fully dissipated by the recent indications of the strength of the anti-slavery sentiment of the free states, *therefore be it enacted*," that it is the undoubted right of any state to withdraw from the Union when it pleases, and that Florida should now exercise this right; and "the State of Florida hereby withdraws herself from the confederacy of states existing under the name of the United States of America, and from the existing government of the said states; and that all political connection between her and the government of the said states ought to be, and the same is hereby totally annulled, and said union of states dissolved, and the State of Florida is hereby declared a sovereign and independent nation; and that all ordinances heretofore adopted, in so far as they create or recognize said union, are rescinded; and all laws or parts of laws in force in this state, in so far as they recognize or assent to said union, be, and they are hereby repealed."—Passed January 7, 1861.

MISSISSIPPI.—"The people of Mississippi, in Convention assembled, ordain," etc., "That all the laws and ordinances by which the said State of Mississippi became a member of the federal Union of the United States of America be, and the same are hereby repealed; and that all obligations on the part of the said state, or the people thereof, be withdrawn; and that the said state does hereby resume all the rights, functions, and powers which by any of the said laws and ordinances were conveyed to the government of the said United States, and is absolved from all the obligations, restraints, and duties incurred to the said federal Union, and shall henceforth be a free, sovereign, and independent state." The provision of the state Constitution requiring officers to swear to support the Constitution of the United States is annulled; and the state consents to form a union with other seceding states "upon the basis of the present Constitution of the United States, except such parts thereof as embrace other portions than such seceding states."—Passed January 9, 1861.

ALABAMA.—"*Whereas* the election of Abraham Lincoln and Hannibal Hamlin to the offices of President and Vice-President of the United States by a sectional party, avowedly hostile to the domestic institutions and to the peace and security of the people of the State of Alabama, preceded by many and dangerous infractions of the Constitution of the United States by many of the states and people of the northern section, is a political wrong of so insulting and menacing a character as to justify the people of the State of Alabama in the adoption of prompt and decided measures for their future peace and security: *Therefore be it declared*," etc., that the State of Alabama now withdraws "from the Union known as 'The United States of America,' and henceforth ceases to be one of the said United States, and is, and of right ought to be, a sovereign and independent state;" and all powers heretofore delegated to the United States are "resumed and vested in the people of the State of Alabama." And as it is the wish of the State of Alabama to meet the slaveholding states of the South to form a provisional as well as permanent government, the people of these states are requested to meet by delegates at Montgomery on the 4th of February, 1861, for the purpose of securing "concerted and harmonious action in whatever measures may be deemed most desirable for our common peace and safety."—Passed January 11, 1861.

GEORGIA.—"We, the people of the State of Georgia, ordain," etc., "That the ordinance adopted by the people of Georgia in Convention, in the year 1788, whereby the Constitution of the United States was assented to, ratified, and adopted, and also all acts and parts of acts of the General Assembly ratifying and adopting the amendments to the said Constitution, are hereby repealed, rescinded, and abrogated; and we do farther declare and ordain that the union now subsisting between the State of Georgia and other states, under the name of 'The United States of America,' is hereby dissolved; and that the State of Georgia is in full possession and exercise of all those rights of sovereignty which belong and appertain to a free and independent state."—Passed January 19, 1861.

TEXAS.—"*Whereas* the federal government has failed to accomplish the purposes of the compact of union between these states, in giving protection either to the persons of our people upon an exposed frontier or to the property of our citizens; and *whereas* the action of the Northern states is violative of the compact between the states and the guarantees of the Constitution; and *whereas* the recent developments in the federal affairs make it evident that the power of the federal government is sought to be made a weapon with which to strike down the interests and property of the people of Texas and her sister slaveholding states, instead of permitting it to be, as it was intended, our shield against outrage and oppression; *therefore* we the people ordain," etc., "That the ordinance adopted by our convention of delegates on the 4th day of July, A.D. 1845, and afterward ratified by us, under which the republic of Texas was admitted into the Union with other states, and became a party to the compact styled 'The United States of America,' be, and is hereby repealed and annulled; that all the powers which by the said compact were delegated by Texas to the federal government are resumed; that Texas is of right absolved from all restraints and obligations incurred by said compact, and is a sovereign and independent state, and that her citizens and people are absolved from all allegiance to the United States and the government thereof."—Passed February 7, 1861.

LOUISIANA.—"We, the people of the State of Louisiana, ordain," etc., "That the ordinance passed by us in Convention on the 22d day of November, in the year 1811, whereby the Constitution of the United States, and the amendments of said Constitution, were adopted, and all laws and ordinances by which the State of Louisiana became a member of the federal Union, be, and the same are hereby repealed and abrogated; and that the union now subsisting between Louisiana and other states, under the name of 'The United States of America,' is hereby dissolved. That the State of Louisiana hereby resumes all rights and powers heretofore delegated to the government of the United States of America, and that her citizens are absolved from all allegiance to said government, and that she is in full possession and exercise of all those rights of sovereignty which appertain to a free and independent state."—Passed January 26, 1861.

VIRGINIA.—"The people of Virginia, in the ratification of the Constitution of the United States of America, adopted by them in Convention on the 25th day of June, in the year of our Lord 1788, having declared that the powers granted under the said Constitution were derived from the people of the United States, and might be resumed whenever the same should be perverted to their injury and oppression; and the federal government having perverted said powers, not only to the injury of the people of Virginia, but to the oppression of the Southern slaveholding states," the people of Virginia ordain that "the ordinance adopted by the people of this state in Convention in the year of our Lord 1788, whereby the Constitution of the United States of America was ratified, and all acts of the General Assembly of this state ratifying or adopting amendments to said Constitution, are hereby repealed and abrogated; that the union between the State of Virginia and the other states, under the Constitution aforesaid, is hereby dissolved; and that the State of Virginia is in the full possession and exercise of all rights of sovereignty which belong and appertain to a free and independent state. And they do further declare that said Constitution of the United States of America is no longer binding on any of the citizens of this state."—Passed April 17, 1861.

ARKANSAS.—"*Whereas*, in addition to the well-founded causes of complaint set forth by this Convention in resolutions adopted on the 11th of March, A.D. 1861, against the sectional party now in power in Washington City, headed by Abraham Lincoln, he has, in the face of resolutions passed by this Convention, pledging the State of Arkansas to resist to the last extremity any attempt on the part of such power to coerce any state that seceded from the old Union, proclaimed to the world that war should be waged against such states until they should be compelled to submit to their rule, and large forces to accomplish this have by this same power been called out, and are now being marshaled to carry out this inhuman design; and to longer submit to such rule, or remain in the old Union of the United States, would be disgraceful and ruinous to the State of Arkansas: Therefore we, the people of Arkansas, ordain," etc., "That the 'Ordinance and Acceptance of Compact,' passed by the General Assembly of the State of Arkansas on the 18th day of October, A.D. 1836 [here follows a minute description of this Compact and other acts], and all other laws, and every other law and ordinance, whereby the State of Arkansas became a member of the federal Union, be, and the same are hereby in all respects and for every other purpose herewith consistent repealed, abrogated, and fully set aside; and that the union now subsisting between the State of Arkansas and the other states, under the name of 'The United States of America,' is hereby forever dissolved." Then follows the usual declaration resuming all rights delegated to the federal government, absolving the citizens from allegiance to that government, and pronouncing Arkansas a "free and independent state."—Passed May 6, 1861.

TENNESSEE.—"We, the people of the State of Tennessee, waiving an expression of opinion as to the abstract doctrine of secession, but asserting the right as a free and independent people to alter, reform, or abolish our form of government in such manner as we think proper, do ordain and declare that all the laws and ordinances by which the State of Tennessee became a member of the federal Union of the United States of America are hereby abrogated and annulled, and that all obligations on our part be withdrawn therefrom, and we do hereby resume all the rights, functions, and powers which by any of the said laws and ordinances were conveyed to the government of the United States, and absolve ourselves from all the obligations, restraints, and duties incurred thereto, and do hereby become henceforth a free, sovereign, and independent state." The provisions of the Constitution of the state requiring civil and military officers to swear to support the Constitution of the United States, making citizenship of the United States a qualification for office, and recognizing the Constitution of the United States as the supreme law of the state, are abrogated and annulled.—Passed May 6, 1861.

NORTH CAROLINA.—"We, the people of North Carolina, ordain," etc., "That the ordinance adopted by the State of North Carolina, in the Convention of 1789, whereby the Constitution of the United States was ratified and adopted, and also all acts and parts of acts of the General Assembly ratifying and adopting amendments to the said Constitution, are hereby repealed, rescinded, and abrogated. We do further declare and ordain, that the union now subsisting between the State of North Carolina and the other states, under the title of 'The United States of America,' is hereby dissolved, and that the State of North Carolina is in the full possession and exercise of all those rights of sovereignty which belong and appertain to a free and independent state." Another ordinance was passed, ratifying the Montgomery Constitution, and declaring that "North Carolina will enter into the federal association of states upon the terms therein proposed when admitted by the Congress or any competent authority of the Confederate States."—Passed May 20, 1863.

BALLOON VIEW OF WASHINGTON, MAY, 1861.

MOAT AND SEAWARD FACE OF FORTRESS MONROE.

CHAPTER II.

EASTERN VIRGINIA, MISSOURI, AND WESTERN VIRGINIA.

Occupation of Alexandria.—Death of Ellsworth.—Fortress Monroe.—Battle of Big Bethel.—Condition of Missouri.—General Lyon's Measures.—Battle of Booneville.—Action at Carthage.—Governor Jackson deposed, and Gamble appointed.—Battle of Wilson's Creek.—Death of Lyon.—Western Virginia.—The Mayor of Wheeling.—M'Clellan appointed to the Command of the Department of the Ohio.—Skirmish at Clarksburg.—M'Clellan's Instructions.—Grafton.—Battle of Philippi.—Union Convention at Wheeling.—Letcher's Proclamation.—Rich Mountain.—Battle of Carrick's Ford.—Wise's and Floyd's Campaigns in Western Virginia.—Battle of Carnifex Ferry.—M'Clellan's congratulatory Address.

THE month of April saw the insurrection extravagant in hope, prodigal in the promise of success. The success of its first move had made secession rampant. State after state had wheeled into the line. Even Virginia, that had for a time hesitated, now stood in the van of that insurgent column which looked defiance at the general government which it had paralyzed. The attitude of the Confederacy was not that of resistance, but that of aggression. It hoped to possess itself, almost without opposition, of such commanding positions as would at the outset give it a decided advantage over the federal government both in prestige and power. The capture of Washington, secretly planned by the cautious, was talked of by the indiscreet leaders of the confederates. It is possible that all which prevented the realization of this scheme was the inertness of Virginia in regard to her final decision of the question of secession. The very time of the attack was fixed upon, which was to be between the 17th and 21st of April. It was doubtless with this view that the raid had been made upon Harper's Ferry, and that to embarrass the government still farther, a very large number of officers in the army and navy had suddenly handed in their resignations. It must be remarked, however, that Governor Letcher—whatever may have been his feeling in the matter, declined to sanction the raid upon Harper's Ferry, as also that upon the government property in and near Norfolk. These events occurred or were planned before the state had fully committed itself to secession, and therefore Letcher was undecided whether to give them his official sanction. Thus the hesitancy of Virginia became the salvation of Washington, for without the hearty co-operation of that state it was impossible that Washington, already forewarned and partially forearmed, could be taken.

When it is considered that Washington was the seat of the federal government, and that no hint of aggression had as yet issued from the administration, and when, indeed, no act of war had taken place, excepting that which the insurgents had inaugurated and consummated, it is not difficult to see that the revolutionary programme, in its very earliest movements, contemplated no less than the destruction of the entire fabric of the republic. When Mr. Walker, the rebel Secretary of War, said, on the 12th of April, that before the 1st of May the confederate flag would float over the dome of the old Capitol, President Lincoln had not yet called for his first quota of troops; and when, three days afterward, he did call for seventy-five thousand men, it was for the purpose mainly of protecting the capital against the threats of its enemies—threats that were even then on the verge of execu-

tion. Such was the position of the secession leaders in this month of April, when the sun shone for their hay-making.

But the month of May reversed the picture. The hope which had well-nigh led secession to triumph, and to justify that triumph which it sought, was crushed. The North had uprisen, and rushed to the defense of the capital; and in the middle of May it was seen that the time for taking the old seat of government without a desperate struggle had gone by. Yet it was declared that "the fixed and unalterable determination to capture this city is the prevailing sentiment of our people, and satisfaction gleams from the eye of every soldier whose destination is Washington."

The occupation of the "sacred soil" of Virginia soon became necessary to the safety of the national capital. It was undertaken in the latter part of May. The enthusiasm with which the loyal states had met the crisis of danger encouraged the government to push on and punish the aggression which had precipitated that crisis.

With a view of attacking, if possible, but, at any rate, of strenuously defending its position, the Confederacy held, in considerable force, the whole line from the Chesapeake to Edwards's Ferry, 25 or 30 miles above the capital. With a vigor which would have been afterward repeated with good effect, the government decided to take the offensive and to occupy Alexandria, about six miles below Washington, and on the opposite side of the Potomac. General Mansfield, with about thirteen thousand men, led this important movement. It was an impressive scene which the night preceding the attack ushered in. Vague hints had been given out of a storm about to burst forth at a moment's warning; and, in profound stillness, under a full moon, a busy preparation was being made; scouts were sent out in every direction; the men were suddenly summoned to the novel business of war, their bayonets glittering in the cold light; upon the river, steamers were being laden with troops and the machinery of strife: then the movement was made; and when the citizens of Washington awoke on the morning of the 24th of May, the ripe result was announced of operations that had been begun and consummated while they were asleep. At about daybreak the New York Seventh touched the Virginia soil, landing at the Alexandria bridge, near which they encamped. A detachment of soldiers, with some cavalry and artillery, crossed the Potomac below Georgetown, and took possession of the Loudon and Hampshire Railroad. The Manassas Gap Railroad also, running out of Alexandria, was held by the New York Sixty-ninth, and seven hundred passengers were captured and held as hostages. Meanwhile Colonel Ellsworth, early in the morning, entered the town with his Zouaves, severed its communication with the South both by railroad and telegraph, and so completely surprised the rebel troops that a large number of them, unable to effect an escape, were captured. Thus was an important entrance into Virginia opened to the federal army without a battle. One single life was lost, that of the brave but imprudent Colonel Ellsworth, who was shot by Jackson, the landlord of a hotel, to the roof of which he had incautiously ascended to pull down a confederate flag. "Behold my trophy," said the ardent Ellsworth, as he descended from the trap-door down the stairs. "And behold mine," replied Jackson, as, springing from his hiding-place, he lodged the contents of his gun in Ellsworth's breast. But the se-

ELMER E. ELLSWORTH.

cessionist quickly paid life for life at the hands of private Brownell. Ellsworth was looked upon as a noble martyr in the North, and so was Jackson in the South.

Simultaneously with the occupation of Alexandria, the heights commanding Washington were taken possession of by the national troops preparatory to a defensive fortification of the city. A few skirmishes and accidental collisions with the enemy were the only occurrences upon which the intense popular excitement of the people fed itself until the reverse at Big Bethel. This takes us from the Potomac to the Peninsula between the James and York Rivers.

Fortress Monroe is, strictly speaking, the only fortress or fortified inclosure in the United States. It was at first constructed for the protection of Gosport Navy Yard, and at the beginning of the war it had cost the government two and a half millions of money. Its area embraces about seventy acres, and in the centre it has a magnificent parade-ground of twenty-five acres, finely shaded with live-oaks. It is a bastioned work, heptagonal in form; its walls, which are of granite, rise to the height of thirty-five feet; and about the entire work a moat extends, from seventy-five to a hundred and fifty feet wide, and faced with dressed granite. On the side facing the sea there is a water-battery of forty-two embrasures, the slope of which, covered with a green turf, affords a favorite promenade. Fortress Monroe has been the final head-quarters of all the military and naval expeditions that have been sent to the Southern coasts. So completely does its possession control the commerce of Virginia, that it almost supersedes the necessity for a blockade along the coast of that state. Governor Letcher was, at an early period, fully aware of the importance of its capture, but this was an undertaking which, like the seizure of Washington, required a stronger force than could be marshaled together previous to the secession of Virginia. The Confederacy had no navy, and the land approach to the fortress was exceedingly difficult, the only access being by means of a strip of beach not over forty rods in width. After Virginia had finally seceded, this strong-hold stood in great peril, but was promptly re-enforced.

On the 22d of May, General Butler, whose decided policy in Maryland had saved that state to the Union, arrived at Fortress Monroe, and there assumed the command of a new department, the main object of which was a military occupation of the Atlantic coast.

On precisely the same day that Mansfield occupied Alexandria, Butler made a reconnoissance in force toward Hampton, a little village just north of Fortress Monroe. The confederate troops stationed there retreated as soon as they were aware of his approach, and, having made their escape across Hampton Creek into the town, attempted to burn the bridge in their rear, which they partially succeeded in doing. General Butler immediately established a camp near Hampton, and another eight miles farther west, at Newport News: in these two encampments, together with the troops inside

the fortress, Butler had in the early part of June about 12,000 men.

On the 10th of June the battle of Big Bethel was fought. The enemy had a strong position at Yorktown, about twenty-five miles from Fortress Monroe, and on the opposite side of the Peninsula. From this point southward they established outposts, which became centres whence cavalry squads were sent all over the country to compel tribute from the inhabitants, and frequent detachments were sent forth under cover of the night to harass the federal encampments and render their position untenable. The nearest of these outposts was situated at Little Bethel, a church which stood at the vertex of an equilateral triangle, each side measuring eight miles, and whose base is the line connecting Hampton and Newport News. Five miles farther, on the road to Yorktown, was the Great Bethel Church, near which the confederate Colonel Magruder was strongly intrenched, with a command of about 2000 men.

Butler determined to break up these two posts. On the 9th of June, he had his naval brigade busily engaged all day in learning the management of the flat-boats, in which a portion of his troops were to be ferried across Hampton Creek that night, to co-operate with another column moving from Newport News against Little Bethel. The expedition started secretly, under cover of the darkness, about midnight, as it was intended to reach its destination at daybreak. The force at Little Bethel was to be attacked simultaneously in front and rear by the two separate columns, and, having been routed, was to be driven toward Big Bethel and into Magruder's intrenchments. Fast upon their heels, and taking advantage of the entrance that would be opened to the fugitives, the federal forces were to rush in and take possession. In case of any failure in effecting this surprise, it was left to General Pierce's discretion whether or not he should attempt an assault upon Big Bethel.

A single miscarriage spoiled the intended surprise. Colonel Duryea's regiment was ferried across at one o'clock in the morning, and proceeded on the road to Bethel as far as to Newmarket Bridge, having crossed which it passed to the rear of the enemy, having captured his picket guard. So far all was well; but Colonel Townsend's regiment was yet to arrive from Hampton to act as support to Duryea. The roads from Hampton and from Newport News join just before Little Bethel is reached, and no sooner had Duryea's regiment passed this point of junction than the column from Newport News came up under Colonel Phelps, who left Colonel Bendix behind with a small force and a field-piece, to act as rear guard in case of an attempt being made by the enemy to cut off the retreat. But the Third New York (Colonel Townsend) was yet due. The arrival of this regiment and its junction with Bendix were a part of the programme, therefore it was expected, and its arrival promptly followed that of Bendix, who had taken position at the crossing of the roads; but, before it could emerge into plain sight, it had to ascend a slight elevation in the road. Phelps and Pierce were just in advance, and as they appeared above the rising crest alone and mounted, Bendix, in the dim light, conjectured that a cavalry force was approaching; but no cavalry were in the federal force, so that this body was assumed to belong to the enemy. They were fired upon, and ten of Townsend's men were wounded.

Pierce now ordered a retreat of the regiment. Meanwhile the firing alarmed the federal forces in advance, who also fell back. It was now broad daylight, and the mistake of the last hour was painfully evident, but it was too late to retrieve it, for already the enemy at Little Bethel had taken the alarm, and had added their strength to the already formidable position of Magruder. Pierce determined to try an assault, and sent to the fortress for re-enforcements. At first there was some promise of success; the outer line of the enemy's intrenchments was taken; but it was immediately retaken, and the bravest advances of the national troops were unavailing against the well-sheltered foe, and were repulsed with a loss of about forty men. Two of these, Major Winthrop and Lieutenant Greble, fell under circumstances worthy of distinct commemoration. Winthrop was shot by a North Caro-

ONLY ENTRANCE TO FORTRESS MONROE.

THE ADVANCE GUARD OF THE ARMY OF THE UNITED STATES CROSSING THE LONG BRIDGE OVER THE POTOMAC, MAY 24, 1861.

JOHN T. GREBLE.

lina drummer-boy while standing upon a log and brandishing his sword. He was in the act of rallying his men for a fresh encounter. Greble was working his gun within two hundred yards of a masked battery; a position which he retained until he had lost six out of eleven of his artillerists, during which time he had with his single piece repelled a sortie on the part of the enemy with great slaughter. He was falling back himself, when his head was taken off his shoulders by a cannon ball.

This reverse, though not without its value to the federal army, aroused a storm of popular indignation in the North. But Butler held his position on the Peninsula, which was so strong that Magruder, in spite of his success at Big Bethel, soon deemed it prudent to withdraw to Yorktown.

Leaving Eastern Virginia, penetrated from the north and east by the national forces, whose advance was as nearly as possible in the form of an arc reaching from Washington to Fortress Monroe, while at Richmond, the centre of this arc, the confederates were marshaling in strength, and from thence radiating forth and seizing upon the strongest natural positions, we turn to contemporaneous events in the West.

By a vote of one hundred and thirty-five thousand against thirty thousand, Missouri had, in the presidential election of 1860, decided against the extremists of the South. In this state, as in Maryland, there were men determined that Missouri should share the fate and fortunes of the Southern confederacy, but they were few. The events which have previously been narrated in this history: the President's call for troops to aid in suppressing insurrection, and Jackson's refusal; the conflict of the Home with the State Guards; the raid of the Illinois troops upon the St. Louis Arsenal, and the capture of Camp Jackson, near that city, by Lyon; the conflict of United States troops with the mob of St. Louis; Lyon's reversal of the policy adopted by Harney—a policy which, while it crippled the general government, yet allowed Jackson and Price, whom Harney knew to be secessionists at heart, to mature the military organizations of the state for purposes of their own—all these events had been gradually establishing a line of division on the question of state sovereignty as opposed to the sovereignty of the general government. That the very idea of state sovereignty, conceived thus absolutely, was the root of secession, was not popularly understood. It was so regarded by the secession leaders, and by Lyon also, who was persistently counteracting their movements. But a large portion of the people blindly believed that a state had the right to assume at option and to maintain an attitude of independence of the general government. Some states had already done this. In the opinion of the Missourians that was an unwise proceeding, but thoroughly legitimate; that is, they justified secession as to the principle involved, though they by no means favored its adoption. Missouri, at any rate, did not want it; if South Carolina wanted it, however, she had a perfect right to it. It was this position which, seemingly so innocent, still wrought all the mischief in the border states; for it was impossible that a state could hold that position and not advance beyond it. Clearly, any opposition by force of arms to secession, on the part of the general government, must of necessity array Missouri, and all other states in a similar situation, upon the one side or the other; for, judged from the stand-point of these states, such opposition was unjust and despotic. This judgment, which was entertained by a large portion of the people of Missouri, taken in connection with the prevailing sympathy of the state for Southern institutions, was sufficient, if not to throw the state over into the confederacy, at least to array it against the national government.

Accordingly, on the 11th of June, Jackson and Price held an interview with Lyon and Blair at St. Louis, and demanded of the latter that no more United States troops should be quartered in or should pass through the state. This was an attempt on the governor's part to renew with Lyon the

compact previously made between Price and Harney. In case his requisition was complied with, he offered, on his part, to disband the State Guards; to nullify the organization of the state militia, which had been going on under the provisions of the Military Bill; to protect the rights of all the citizens of Missouri, and to repel any invasion from without. That these offers were not made in good faith is evident from the fact that it was the governor himself who had in secret organized the State Guards before the Home Guards had any existence; indeed, these latter were rendered necessary by the violence of the former directed against loyal citizens. Moreover, the governor knew that what he had offered to do it was utterly impossible for him to accomplish.

But, whether made in good faith or not, these offers could not be met by Lyon; for, even assuming Jackson to have been desirous that Missouri should be neutral—and certainly that was all which the great body of his supporters desired—yet, in the assumption by any state of a neutral attitude, there was involved the right of separation. For Missouri to demand the abandonment of the state by the United States troops was no more than for South Carolina to demand the national government to evacuate the forts in Charleston Harbor; and the same principle which led to the refusal of the one demand compelled the rejection of the other. Lyon accordingly refused compliance with the terms proposed. The very next day Governor Jackson issued from Jefferson City a proclamation to the people of Missouri, making the most of his unsuccessful attempts at compromise; representing that he himself, desirous only of peace, had proposed terms of agreement most humiliating to the state, and that even these were rejected; and, finally, calling for fifty thousand of the state militia to repel the invaders. The majority of these "invaders," it will be remembered, were loyal Missourians.

The war was now fairly inaugurated, and the next day, the 13th of June, saw Jackson, with all the available troops under his command, retreating from the capital, and Lyon on his way to the capital, having started from St. Louis with about fifteen hundred men. On the day before, Sigel, with the Second Missouri, had been dispatched toward Springfield by the South Pacific Railroad for a purpose which will hereafter become evident.

Jackson, in his retreat, had given orders for the destruction of the Moreau bridge, four miles below Jefferson City, on the Missouri, while General Price attended to the severing of telegraphic communications. The flight was executed by means of the railroad, and all the bridges, as soon as passed, were burned. As General Lyon proceeded by water, this destruction was of course utterly useless. Even the destination of the fugitive executive was concealed, though conjecture pointed to Booneville, a strong-hold of secession some fifty miles up the river. Meanwhile, in the absence of the recreant governor, General Lyon instituted a provisional government, and called upon all loyal men to rally to the support of order and legitimate authority.

Thus far there had been no hostile collision between those representing the authority of the United States and Jackson's forces. But, now that war had been unmistakably declared, Lyon did not wait for the enemy to perfect his organizations; and, although General Harney had so illy appreciated the importance of a decided policy, yet it can not be denied that the federal troops at this crisis held their opponents in the State of Missouri at a great disadvantage. A firm course from the first would have held Missouri as strongly to her allegiance as Maryland was held. That had not been done. Still, so energetic and prompt were the measures of the national government, that they elicited praise even from the lips of the enemy. "Energy and promptitude," says the Charleston Mercury of May 31, "have characterized their movements both in Maryland and St. Louis, and their success along the border has so far been complete. They have, in the West, obtained and secured the great repository of arms for that section, equipped our enemies of St. Louis, Illinois, Indiana, and Ohio, leaving the resistance-men of Missouri poorly provided, Kentucky unarmed and overawed, and Tennessee also, with a meagre provision for fighting, dependent on the cotton states for weapons of defense. In all this, the military proceedings of the North since the fall of Sumter have been eminently wise."

Missouri was favorably situated for the influx, on a large scale, of confederate troops from Kentucky and Tennessee on the east, and from Arkansas on the south; and, curiously enough, at the very moment when Jackson was so confidently offering to repel all invaders, Ben M'Culloch, a noted Texan Ranger, had already crossed the southern border of the state with a force of 800 men, which rapidly increased as he moved upon Springfield. In view of this movement, General Sigel had been sent, on the 12th, in that direction, with the Second Missouri. Price was sending on other confederate forces as speedily as possible to Booneville and Lexington, and on the western border of the state Rains was mustering together still another army.

While these forces in the various parts of Missouri had not as yet been able to concentrate in any one place, it was evidently Lyon's opportunity to dispose of them in detail. For accomplishing this purpose he had inconsiderable means at his disposal. Leaving a force at Jefferson City sufficiently large to preserve order, he set out in three steamers and with about 2000 men for Booneville. This was on the 17th of June.

A few miles below the town the confederates had posted a battery on a bluff commanding the river. Instead, however, of passing this battery—which, indeed, he could hardly have effected with safety—Lyon landed his troops lower down, and marched along the road running through the bottom-land and parallel to the river. A mile and a half brought them upon the enemy's pickets, and another half mile brought them upon the enemy himself, in full force, under Colonel Marmaduke, who was posted in a lane running at right angles with the road upon which Lyon was approaching, and terminating at the river. A heavy cannonade was opened, driving the confederates to an adjacent wood. In order to draw them from this covert,

LYON'S MARCH FROM BOONEVILLE.

from which they kept up a brisk fire upon the federals, Lyon ordered a feigned retreat. The ruse was successful, and the whole force of the artillery was opened on the enemy, who turned and fled in confusion. The enemy seem to have been deficient in artillery; at least not a single cannon was fired by them during the engagement. Marmaduke's men had insisted upon fighting contrary to their colonel's judgment, who wished to retreat to some more tenable position. Jackson is said to have watched the battle from a distant hill, and, seeing the disastrous result, to have fled. Price was at home. The force of the enemy was inferior to that of the federal army making the attack, and was, besides, so indiscreetly managed, that in twenty minutes from the firing of the first shot it was in full retreat.

Every effort was now made by the state forces in Missouri to concentrate. There was no hope of their being able to effect this in the northern part of the state, but there was a chance in favor of a concentration of the forces retreating southward with those of M'Culloch in the southwest. Jackson fled from Booneville with only about five hundred men, and Captain Totten followed close upon him with a thousand. Rains was hurrying forward in order to join Jackson, pursued by Major Sturgis of the United States regular army. Rains, however, by the destruction of the bridge over the Osage at Papinsville, put a check upon the pursuit, and Sturgis was obliged to go into camp and wait for the high water to subside. Lyon, who had remained behind to get together an additional force, was soon able to join Sturgis on the Osage.

Meantime, on the 23d of June, Sigel arrived at Springfield. Price was then encamped at Neosho, a town in the southwest corner of the state, and Jackson was speedily moving southward to join him. To prevent this junction, Sigel advanced rapidly upon Neosho, which he entered without opposition on the 1st of July, and the next day learned that Price, Jackson, and Rains had already united their forces at a point just north of Carthage. Informing General Sweeny, who was at Springfield, of this fact, he received orders immediately to attack the confederate position. On the 4th of July he set out, and on the 6th came upon the enemy, posted in the open prairie. His force was greatly inferior, but he unlimbered his artillery and opened fire, to which the confederates briskly replied. A sharp artillery duel was kept up across the level prairie until two o'clock in the afternoon, when the enemy's guns had all been dismounted and his ranks broken. The confederate cavalry now attempted to outflank Sigel; but the latter, sending two six-pounders to the rear, and changing front, fell steadily back to his baggage-wagons, which were laboring forward, and, having secured these, he fell slowly back to the bridge over Dry Fork Creek, where the road ran between two high bluffs. Here, at the opening, were stationed the enemy's cavalry, which, baffled in its attack on the baggage train, sought at this point to cut off the retreat. Sigel, dispatching two cannon to the right and two to the left, supported by a small portion of his force, drew the enemy out of his solid and impregnable position against these his feigned movements, and waiting patiently their approach on either side, he opened upon them a terrific cross-fire, and, at the same time, by a sudden movement in front, cleared the bridge. The cavalry were routed, and Sigel moved rapidly to Carthage, which, to his surprise, he found occupied by the enemy. The only course left was to effect a junction as quickly as possible with a Union force stationed at Mount Vernon, midway between him and Springfield. But his immediate route, which led through a forest, was disputed by a large force

of the enemy. Here there was no opportunity for the enemy's cavalry, and, though he was largely outnumbered, Sigel, by the superiority of his Minié rifles over the old-fashioned arms of his antagonists, was able to contest the ground. Here the battle lasted for over two hours, until after sunset, and, indeed, was prolonged even into the darkness, when finally the enemy retreated, and Sigel, not daring even to rest his tired army, kept up his march all night, and the next day reached Mount Vernon.

Sigel had seen service in Europe, and in this battle proved both the temper of his courage and his able strategy. His entire loss was reported at forty-four, while that of the confederates was much greater, owing to the superiority of Sigel's artillery, that of the enemy being very poor and poorly managed.

At this time all the state, except the southwest quarter, was under the control of the Union forces. North of the Missouri River hostile collisions were frequent between the state troops and the small bodies of Illinois volunteers that had been stationed at various points. Skirmishes followed one another in rapid succession, and a vast amount of property was destroyed. On the 19th of July General Pope assumed the command of Northern Missouri, having under him a force of 7000 men. Meanwhile, on the 16th, Lyon and Sturgis had reached Springfield. An expedition under Sweeny was immediately dispatched to break up a secession camp at Forsyth, fifty miles south of Springfield, just above the Arkansas border. This was accomplished without opposition.

The situation in Missouri at the latter end of July assumed a very critical aspect. General Fremont, who a month previously had returned from Europe with a large amount of arms for the government, had just been appointed to the command of the Western Department. This was no enviable position. Every thing was in disorder. Forces which ought already to be matured were only preparing to be organized; they lacked arms, and even the harnesses for the baggage trains were unprovided. The enemy, on the other hand, had already prepared himself, and was ready to strike boldly. The successes of the confederates in Virginia had wrought up to the highest pitch their hopes of a speedy and victorious close to the war. The Southern journals of this date exulted in the anticipation of the most splendid success in Missouri, and with good reason. Price, and Rains, and Jackson had united their forces, and had forced Sigel to retreat. These forces were now joined to those of M'Culloch, making an army four times as large as that under Lyon. In the southeast, General Pillow had an army at New Madrid ready to march against St. Louis.

In the face of all these unfavorable circumstances, the political movements going on in the state were of an encouraging nature. On the 22d the State Convention met, and, after a few days' earnest consultation, declared the seats of the governor and his associates in office vacant, and appointed as provisional governor Hamilton R. Gamble. An address was also prepared for the people, justifying the measures which had been taken. This address reprimands in the most scathing terms the efforts which Governor Jackson and his lieutenant had made to carry Missouri out of the Union even previously to any interference on the part of the general government in the affairs of the state. On the same day that this document was issued, Lieutenant Governor Reynolds put forth a proclamation from New Madrid, which was meant as a preface to General Pillow's advance northward; and in two or three more days Governor Gamble issued a proclamation offering protec-

NATHANIEL LYON.

tion to all loyal citizens, and notifying the officers and troops of the Confederate States that their continuance in the state would be considered as an act of war. Certainly, so far as proclamations were concerned, the provisional government had the best of it, for, besides holding the capital, the proper and accustomed seat of the state sovereignty, they were also backed by the popular convention. But proclamations could neither disarm or discourage a confident confederate army like that which now threatened to overrun the state from the southwest.

On the 1st of August, the federal army at Springfield, under Lyon, whose principal commands were intrusted to Sweeny, Sigel, and Sturgis, encamped at Crane's Creek, two miles south of Springfield. The next day they resumed their march, and about five o'clock in the afternoon there was a slight skirmish with a small force of the enemy at Dug Springs. Having marched to Curran, twenty-six miles from Springfield, Lyon fell back again upon the latter place. His position was one of great peril. His force was inadequate to meet the enemy, and Fremont could spare no re-enforcements from St. Louis without weakening his own position, which was of greater importance; but, if he retreated, he would leave the inhabitants of Springfield unprotected, and could not, after all, save himself from a conflict, which must yet take place at some point sooner or later. Therefore he determined to make one effort to stay the progress of the enemy northward and to maintain his own position. Upon this determination followed the battle of Wilson's Creek, which, next to Bull Run, was the severest engagement of the year.

There is something sublime in the bold march of Lyon, on the night of the 9th of August, with a force of 5000 men, to Wilson's Creek, to encounter in the morning a force of more than 20,000. The enemy, meanwhile, was making elaborate arrangements for attacking him. For some time there had been considerable delay in the movements of the confederates toward Springfield, owing to a disagreement between the two leading generals, Price and M'Culloch, the former advocating, and the latter opposing an immediate attack upon the federal army. This question had been settled, however, by a peremptory order from General Polk to M'Culloch, commanding an immediate advance upon Springfield. Then M'Culloch, seemingly determined upon a quarrel, insisted upon having the chief command, which Price conceded without dispute.

On the 9th of August the confederate army had reached a point on Wilson's Creek about nine miles south of Springfield. They had determined to attack the national forces on four sides at once, when suddenly they were aware that they themselves were assailed by two columns—one, under Lyon, in front, and another, under Sigel, on their right flank. It was the expectation of Lyon to fall upon an enemy unprepared, but in this he was disappointed, and all that he had hoped from a surprise was lost. At first the powerful batteries of Totten and Dubois told fearfully upon the enemy, and it was even doubtful whether the inferiority in numbers, and particularly in cavalry, might not be compensated for by the superiority in artillery. Against Totten's battery the enemy directed an overwhelming force, and for half an hour the contending lines surged to and fro over the disputed ground, neither force giving way to the other. On the left of the battery the enemy had gained an advantage; but, in a moment, Lyon led his horse along the line to rally the troops. The horse was killed at his side, when, mounting another, he led on his men into the thickest of the fight. On our left, the enemy, meanwhile, was pressing hard, but there Dubois's battery held him in check. On the right, the First Missouri was being forced back by an overwhelming force, when Lyon promptly ordered two regiments to its sup-

port. Patiently at the brow of the hill they waited the approach of the enemy, until only a few yards separated the combatants, when the simultaneous discharge of their Minié rifles poured forth its volume of death against the astonished and panic-stricken foe. Lyon now ordered a bayonet charge, and himself took the lead of an Iowa regiment which had lost its colonel. He fell dead, pierced in that shower of hail; but the regiments stood firm and unwavering until the enemy, again baffled, withdrew.

Major Sturgis, upon whom the command now devolved, stood doubtful whether to advance or retreat. The former seemed impossible, and, if the latter was concluded upon, there was a dreary march of twelve miles before men who since yesterday morning had not tasted water. Sigel was to have attacked the rear, but there was no token that he had entered upon the work. Once, while this suspense lasted, the federal troops were deceived by the approach of a confederate column under the Union flag, and, hoping to receive their friends, they were mowed down by the fire of the cunning enemy. But against every movement, open or treacherous, our troops stood firm, and with their artillery drove the enemy back to his own ground. After six hours of this unavailing slaughter, Major Sturgis ordered a retreat, and having done so, received tidings of Sigel's rout and withdrawal from the rear. The enemy was too severely cut up to molest the leisurely retreat of either column. In this battle, as in that at Carthage, the artillery alone saved the Union army from utter annihilation.

No sooner had Virginia, on the 17th of April, passed the Ordinance of Secession, than Governor Letcher addressed a letter to Andrew Sweeny, Mayor of Wheeling, informing him of the fact, and ordering him to seize at once upon the Custom-house of that city, the Post-office, and all public buildings and documents, in the name of the sovereign State of Virginia. The mayor promptly replied: "I *have* seized upon the Custom-house, the Post-office, and all public buildings and documents, in the name of Abraham Lincoln, President of the United States, whose property they are." In this reply, Andrew Sweeny represented the whole northwestern portion of the state, and the attitude which it assumed toward secession.

By every natural association, Western Virginia was allied to Ohio and Pennsylvania, and therefore to Northern sentiments and institutions. Between the eastern and western portions of the Old Dominion there was little affinity; the low-lying lands of the former invited slavery, while the mountainous tracts of the latter absolutely excluded it. All along, therefore, there had been a natural disaffection between the two sections, and this had certainly not been weakened by the extraordinary exemption from taxation which, under the existing state of affairs, the East had always enjoyed. But the treason of Richmond furnished abundant occasion to the West to assert its dignity and independence. The triumph of secession upon the James naturally led to the triumph of loyalty among the mountains; and while Governor Letcher was training the state militia for service against the general government, Union meetings were held all over the western counties for the support of that government. The series of measures which resulted in the formation of the State of Western Virginia will hereafter be narrated. We have here only to do with the military events in that portion of the state. The topographical features of the region precluded it from becoming a permanent arena of warfare. M'Clellan's short campaign, lasting from the middle of May to the middle of July, 1861, comprises the history of secession in Western Virginia.[1]

On the 11th of May, the Department of the Ohio, including Ohio, Indiana, and the western portions of Pennsylvania and Virginia, was organized; and General M'Clellan, who had been invited by Governor Dennison, of Ohio, to abandon the presidency of the Ohio and Mississippi Railroad for a brigadier generalship, was put at its head. M'Clellan's career as military engineer in Mexico had brought him great distinction; but the office which he was now to undertake was novel, and accompanied by many difficult trials. An army had actually to be created out of undisciplined volunteer forces. To this task he proved himself fully competent. One of the prominent objects of the department thus instituted was to guard the line of the Ohio River, but, as the policy of the general government became more aggressive and determined, this object was lost sight of in view of a bolder purpose. The campaign in Western Virginia was in no sense an invasion, and this feature distinguished it from the operations that were going on for the occupation of the eastern part of the state. Indeed, it was some time before the federal army entered Western Virginia even for the purposes of protection. Thus, for a long period, this portion of the state had to take care of itself against the secessionists. Union companies were formed every where.

[1] As the terms were formerly used, the Blue Ridge was the boundary between Eastern and Western Virginia. In 1850, the former contained 401,540 whites, 45,783 free colored persons, and 409,793 slaves; the latter, 492,609 whites, 8123 free colored, and 62,233 slaves. The long-standing dispute between these sections, growing mainly out of the questions of taxation and representation, were temporarily compromised by amendments to the Constitution made in 1850, by which a mixed basis for representation was adopted, giving to the West a majority in the House, and to the East a majority in the Senate. By this compromise, slaves under twelve years of age were not subjects of taxation, while upon those above that age $1 20 was levied. The West complained that a large proportion of the property of the Eastern planters, which consisted of slaves, was either wholly or in effect free from taxation, while all of theirs was taxed; and moreover affirmed that they derived no benefit from the sums expended for internal improvements. From this time many leading men began to plan for a separation between the two sections. Mr. John S. Carlisle, in a speech at the Wheeling Convention, said: "There is no difference in opinion between the advocates of a separation of this state. If I may be allowed, I can claim some credit for my sincerity when I say that it has been an object for which I have labored at least since the year 1850. The Convention which met at Richmond in that year, and adopted our present State Constitution, clearly disclosed to my mind the utter incompatibility consistent with the interests of the people of Northwestern Virginia of remaining in connection with the eastern portion of the state." Governor Letcher, in his proclamation to the people of Northwestern Virginia, June 14, 1861, admits that these complaints were well founded. He says: "There has been a complaint among you that the eastern portion of the state has enjoyed an exemption from taxation to your prejudice. By a display of magnanimity in the vote just given, the East has, by a large majority, consented to relinquish this exemption, and is ready to share with you all the burdens of government."

THE MOUNTAIN REGION OF WESTERN VIRGINIA.

The first collision between these companies and Governor Letcher's forces occurred at Clarksburg on the 23d of May. Immediately measures were taken to organize regiments at Wheeling for the protection of loyal citizens; for no sooner had the result of the election in Western Virginia and its unanimous declaration of loyalty been made known, than the signal was given for the secessionists, whom Governor Letcher had sent in their midst, to inaugurate a reign of terror. Union men were treated with violence; bridges were burned, and valuable property destroyed. It was now high time that the general government should come to the rescue.

Before the advent of his troops into Western Virginia, M'Clellan issued two proclamations, one to his soldiers, and the other to the people whom they were sent to protect. The former were commanded to preserve the strictest discipline, and to remember that their duty was confined to the protection of loyal men against traitors; and the latter were assured of the honest intentions with which the movement was undertaken, and reminded of the fact that, while the secessionists had sent their armed forces beforehand to terrify and intimidate, the United States had patiently awaited the result of their election. They were moreover assured that there would be no interference with their slaves, but, on the contrary, that they should be protected even against any insurrection of the latter.

The instructions given to M'Clellan were to cross the Ohio, join Colonel Kelly, who was in command of the regiment at Wheeling, and, having driven out the confederate force, to advance on Harper's Ferry. His movements were hastened by the rapidity with which the secessionists were destroying bridges that would be necessary to his line of communication. The first point of approach was Grafton, which was the centre of all the railroad lines in Northwestern Virginia. Toward this point, on the morning of the 27th, Kelly moved with the First Virginia; and immediately afterward Colonel Irvine, with the Sixteenth Ohio, crossed the Ohio and followed Kelly's command. Another column, consisting of the Fourteenth Ohio, crossed at Marietta, and moved on Parkersburg. The confederates, having been informed of this advance, hastily retreated from Grafton at midnight, falling back to Philippi, where Colonel Porterfield was stationed with a small force of infantry and cavalry. Porterfield had been sent on by General Lee to recruit an army for the rebellion in Western Virginia, but his attempts proving entirely unsuccessful in that loyal section, he was obliged to write a very despondent letter to Lee, asking for re-enforcements in order to enable him even to maintain his position.

The occupation of Grafton had thus been effected without the firing of a single gun, and, on the afternoon of June 2d, there were assembled on the parade-ground of that place 3000 Union troops, under the command of Colonel Crittenden, of Indiana, to receive orders for a forced march that very night against the enemy at Philippi. At 8 o'clock they marched southward. It commenced early to rain, and rained all night; but through the wet and the mud the federal forces pushed on to their destination, which the most of them believed to be Harper's Ferry. They moved in two separate columns. One column, under Colonel Dumont, proceeded on the Northwestern Virginia Railroad to Webster, twelve miles from Philippi, and thence marched against the enemy's front. Kelly, accompanied by Colonel Lander, moved another column eastward to Thornton, from which point they marched twenty-two miles, and got in the rear of Porterfield's force. As soon as the column attacking in front was in position, the enemy's pickets commenced firing, and our artillery opened upon the surprised camp and threw it immediately into utter confusion. Had not the darkness and the storm impeded the movements of the flanking column, the entire confederate force at Philippi must have been captured; but Kelly only arrived in time to aid in the pursuit, and himself to meet with a severe wound from a stray shot after the enemy had mainly been put to flight.

But the military opposition to secession was no more decided than was the political. On the 11th of June the Union Convention met at Wheeling. Forty counties were represented, and each county delegation came forward and took the following oath: "We solemnly declare that we will support the Constitution of the United States, and the laws made in pursuance thereof, as the supreme law of the land, any thing in the ordinance of the Convention which lately met at Richmond to the contrary notwithstanding." The next day a committee of thirteen reported a Bill of Rights, repudiating all allegiance to the Southern Confederacy; resolutions were offered to maintain the rights of Western Virginia *in* the Union, and commanding all forces in arms against the United States to disband and return to their allegiance; and an ordinance was reported providing for the establishment of a provisional government. Frank H. Pierpont was appointed governor; and the principle set forth in his inaugural, that to the loyal people belong the government and governmental authority, was the principle that controlled the entire proceedings of the Convention.

On the 14th of June, Governor Letcher, having posted troops at Hattonsville, issued a proclamation, insisting that the majority of the state should rule the state, and calling upon Western Virginians, in the name of past friendship and historic memories, to co-operate with secession and join the Southern army. But this proclamation was as ineffectual as Porterfield's recruiting had been, although the governor offered to redress the wrongs which the western part of the state had so long suffered.

Returning to the military situation, as we find it in the latter part of June, we have M'Clellan personally at the head of the Union army in Western Virginia, and General Garnett commanding the confederate forces. The former had about 20,000 men, and his communications open and easy; while the confederate general had an inferior force, and, although posted in a position highly advantageous so far as fighting was concerned, was yet completely isolated from any possible basis of military operations. To have held

this position for a single day after the battle at Philippi, unless it were with a force so overwhelming as to make defeat impossible, was simply a military blunder. Yet Garnett held it even when he knew that M'Clellan was moving steadily on, and rapidly increasing in the number of his command. This position of the confederates was some twenty or thirty miles southward from Philippi, at Rich Mountain, a gap in the Laurel Hill Range, where the Staunton and Weston turnpike crosses it, about four or five miles from Beverly. The road which runs along its western slope was the only possible line of communication between this position and Garnett's base. This road ran through Beverly, and to hold the latter place was effectually to intercept the possibility of the enemy's retreat. Here, at Rich Mountain, Garnett had posted Colonel Pegram with 3000 men, while he himself, with about 8000, occupied Laurel Hill, fifteen or sixteen miles farther westward. The fortified position at this latter point was very strong. Having ordered General Morris to occupy Garnett's forces by a direct attack, M'Clellan himself, with the main body of his army, passed around by Buckhannon to the rear, that is, to the western slope of Rich Mountain. Here he divided his force into two columns, and giving one of these to Colonel Rosecrans, he sent the latter to the rear of Pegram, while he remained in front, ready to attack simultaneously. Rosecrans obtained the rear, sent a courier back to M'Clellan to give the signal, and went to work. The messenger missed his way, and passed into the encampment of the enemy, thus giving them full information of the movement. Meanwhile M'Clellan awaited the signal, and the enemy, acquainted with the peril of his position, made his way toward Laurel Hill. Garnett, also, had been warned of the danger, and, hastily leaving his intrenchments, proceeded southward, hoping to reach Beverly before M'Clellan; but, on his way thither, he met the fugitives of Pegram's army, and learned that Beverly was already in the possession of the Union forces. Thus all retreat to the southward was cut off. The only way of escape left him was to follow the course of the Cheat River toward the northeast until he should find some outlet into the valley of Virginia. Then followed M'Clellan's, or, rather, Morris's forces, in swift and unrelenting pursuit, Captain Benham leading the advance. At a bend of the Cheat River, where it winds about a bluff of fifty or sixty feet high, the enemy made a stand, and, planting a cannon on the top of the bluff, disputed the advance. It was an admirable position; but Benham led his men directly under the bluff and around to its left, where they could gain the road, and as they appeared upon his flank the enemy fled, leaving one of his guns and a number of killed and wounded. About a quarter of a mile farther on, where the stream made another turn, Garnett, with a few skirmishers, attempted to make another stand, and, while rallying his men, received a Minié ball which caused his death. This was called the battle of Carrick's Ford. In the mean time, Pegram's force, finding escape impossible, had surrendered to M'Clellan.

The federal success was complete. Only a small portion of the enemy escaped, and all their material fell into our hands. The immediate and natural result of this battle was the evacuation of Harper's Ferry, and the abandonment by the enemy of all Western Virginia.

In the mean time, while General M'Clellan was moving southward from the Ohio, along the Alleghany Ridge, and driving the enemy before him, General Wise, near the western and southern borders of the state, was gathering together another confederate army. He had just been appointed a brigadier general, with orders, first, to clear Western Virginia of federal troops and keep it clear, and, secondly, to occupy Wheeling, and disorganize the Union Legislature. In order to accomplish this in the face of M'Clellan's rapidly advancing army, he demanded of his government an adequate force, and was told that he must raise it himself. With the meagre nucleus of an army he advanced to Louisburg, about fifty miles south of Cheat Mountain Gap, and from this point moved in a northwesterly direction down the Kanawha Valley, his force gradually increasing, until, by the accession of Colonel Tompkins's detachment, already in the valley, it numbered full 4000 men, with a considerable cavalry force, and three or four battalions of artillery; but he was poorly supplied with ammunition, his recruits were undisciplined, and he was by a long distance removed from his base of supplies, which, besides that it might easily be cut off by the enemy, could only be reached through a portion of the state which was bitterly hostile to secession. Plainly, therefore, he must fall back to Charleston. Every conceivable advantage was in favor of the Union arms; every conceivable disadvantage frowned upon the confederates. The movements of the federal army were controlled by a single mind; its appointments were complete: the confederates had two armies, distinct in their organization and operations, and, if the most elaborate arrangements had been made to secure the possibility of their being conquered in detail, these two armies could not possibly have been more conveniently posted for that purpose than they were. The federal army had at its disposal every desirable means of communication both by land and water; the confederates had to communicate across the mountains. It is true that nowhere on the continent could be found positions of greater natural strength than those in which Garnett and Wise might fortify themselves at their leisure; but it is also true that, with equal leisure, M'Clellan could cut them off, and compel engagement or flight. This was pointedly illustrated in the battle at Rich Mountain, the news of which, coming like a thunderbolt upon Wise, precipitated his retreat, which stopped not short of Gauley Bridge, and in the course of which a great number of troops deserted him.

Thus ended the month of July, which in the eastern portion of the state had proved so disastrous to our arms. It was at this point that M'Clellan assumed command of the army of the Potomac, leaving Rosecrans to take his place in Western Virginia. Wise had handed in his resignation to the authorities at Richmond. General Floyd was ordered to re-enforce him, which

BATTLE OF RICH MOUNTAIN, JULY 13, 1861.

he did at his own convenience; and after the two generals had come together in Greenbrier County, there was a continual hostility between them, arising, no doubt, from the supercilious airs which Floyd indulged in toward Wise; to say the least, we may be sure that no love was lost between them. Floyd hesitated to support Wise; and Wise, though more honest in the discharge of his duty, could not help laughing at the blunders of Floyd. The latter started from Whiteville with over 3000 men, which force, before it was joined to Wise's legion, dwindled down to less than half that number. Floyd appointed as chief of his staff the editor of the *Lynchburg Republican*, for his first aid-de-camp a sub-editor—intending, probably, to have his conquests duly set forth in print—and for the leader of his cavalry a farmer, whom he seriously promised that horses and men should come out of the campaign as safe and sound as they went in; and this gentle general bragged that he would in a single fortnight drive Rosecrans across the Ohio. While he planned these large results, he forgot all about his transportation, and his baggage trains passed out from Whiteville no less than three times before they were fairly on the way for White Sulphur Springs, the place of junction.

From this position, which was more secure than any other, being near to the great central route to the eastward, the confederate army, largely re-enforced, and having the means at its disposal for carrying on the campaign considerably increased, ventured to advance to Sewell Mountain, a short distance to the west, and thence to Dogwood Gap, where the road from Summersville strikes the main turnpike from Louisburg to Charleston. Thus far there had been no important engagement in the valley of the Kanawha; but on the 10th of September a battle was fought at Carnifex Ferry.

General Rosecrans, on the last day of August, had proceeded to gather up his scattered army for a brisk autumn campaign against Floyd. Leaving Reynolds to keep General Lee in check at Cheat Mountain, he had advanced southward over Kreitz and Powell Mountains to Summersville, driven back the enemy's advanced posts, and pushed on by a forced march of seventeen miles and a half toward the Gauley River. It was not until he had nearly come up with the enemy that he learned the exact position of the latter, which was on the heights overlooking Carnifex Ferry.

Here Floyd had posted himself, having left Wise at a point farther southward to guard against a rear attack from the federal force at Hawk's Nest. He had expected to find a detachment of General Cox's division here, but the latter had retreated, and, unfortunately for Floyd, had sunk the ferry-boats. Floyd pushed his men across, and then, for the first time, discovered his ludicrously awkward position, with his infantry on one side of the river and his artillery on the other; so he posted off on horseback to General Henningsen for an engineer to build boats. While he was in this position, Colonel Tyler, with a small Union force, attacked him, but was repulsed. No sooner had Floyd extricated himself from his difficulty, than Rosecrans suddenly came upon him from Summersville. Floyd's position was naturally one of great strength, protected in the rear both by the river and the mountain ridge, and having but one avenue of approach, which was commanded by two powerful batteries. Rosecrans's troops were exhausted by a long and weary march; it was nearly night, too, and nothing could be accomplished but a reconnoissance, yet this came as near as possible to being a battle. An attempt was made to outflank the enemy on the left, where he was driven from his breastworks to the centre, but it was too late to bring up a supporting force; and, at the same time, two unsuccessful attempts were made in front to take the enemy's batteries by assault, in which Colonel Lytle was wounded and Colonel Lowe killed. Thus the day closed, and in the morning it was discovered that the enemy had retreated, and by the destruction of the bridge over the Gauley had cut off all pursuit. The retreat was continued to Meadow Bridge, whither General Wise was invited to follow; but the latter, having secured himself in a strong position in Fayette County, declined to fall back.

General Lee, who had assumed the command of Garnett's scattered forces in the northwest, and who had a considerable force at his disposal, proceeded to take up a position between the two principal positions of Reynolds—at Elkwater and at Cheat Mountain summit—and to carry them by a simultaneous attack, advancing against Elkwater himself, and giving to General Jackson the other column. Meeting with a repulse, however, he joined Floyd at Meadow Bridge, and after having personally examined Wise's position at Camp Defiance, brought to that point the entire confederate force (which amounted to about 30,000 men), with the exception of General Jackson, who remained in the vicinity of Cheat Mountain. Here, at Sewell's Mountain, the two main armies confronted one another; but no sooner was this the case, than Rosecrans, by a sudden movement, advanced against Jackson, surprising and totally routing his forces, and then returned back as far as to Gauley River.

At this crisis, Lee, Henningsen, and Wise were ordered to report at Richmond, and Floyd, who was left in the chief command, went into winter quarters at Cotton Hill, opposite the mouth of the Gauley, where the latter empties into the Kanawha. From this position, about the middle of November, being attacked suddenly and unexpectedly by a division of Rosecrans's forces under General Benham, he was driven in great confusion to Raleigh, through Fayetteville, a distance of thirty miles. Benham's men were worn out by the long march through mud and rain, and were obliged to rest for the night. The next morning, when about to continue the pursuit with almost a certainty of capturing Raleigh, and with it the entire train, if not the whole force of the enemy, he was recalled by an order from General Schenck, and Floyd continued his flight without farther molestation.

A writer in the *Lynchburg Virginian* gives a full account of the flight of Floyd, which he pronounces to be "another dark shadow in the campaign of Western Virginia." He says, "On the evening of November 11 the enemy made strong demonstrations, near Cotton Hill, of an attack on the next day, and General Floyd ordered the army to fall back three miles. Next morning it was reported that the enemy were advancing to Fayetteville, to cut off our retreat and surround our brigade. This news caused General Floyd to order a retreat, which took place about eight o'clock at night, when the brigade retreated back to Fayetteville, two and a half miles, and halted to guard the road which the enemy were expected to come in to attempt to cut off our retreat. Here the brigade remained until just daylight, without shelter, victuals, or repose, when they were ordered to continue their retreat. The brigade continued its retreat ten miles on the 13th, and halted for the night. During the whole of the retreat thus far there was a great deal of excitement, fear, and especially loss of baggage, property, and provisions; and on the night of the 11th they burned about three hundred tents, several bales of new blankets and overcoats, and a number of mess chests, camp equipages of all kinds; and flour barrels were burst, contents scattered on the ground, and all kinds of provisions wasted and scattered, all to prevent the enemy from getting them. Wagoners were compelled to take the horses from the wagons, mount them, and fly for safety, leaving about fifteen wagons in the hands of the enemy. On the morning of the 14th the brigade took up their march, and had gone but two miles, when it was reported that the enemy were near and rushing on the brigade. At this the cavalry, under command of Colonel Croghan, were ordered back to scout the country and ascertain the enemy's distance. When they had gone back two miles they met the enemy's pickets advancing, when Colonel Croghan ordered his men all to dismount, though he did not, when the pickets of the enemy fired on him, and he fell mortally wounded. His men took him up and carried him some two hundred yards to a house, when they discovered that the enemy were closing in, and the colonel told them to fly and save themselves, for he was dying. At the moment those who were with the colonel discovered that their horses had been taken by the Yankee pickets, who had rushed upon them, they turned and fled, and the whole cavalry came within five minutes of being all cut off and captured. The cavalry then all swept on in abreast until they came up with the rear of our infantry, and proclaimed that the enemy were pursuing in double-quick time. Then appeared a scene in our army indescribable, and of terrific confusion. At the word 'the enemy are pursuing,' all broke off in a wild run, some so frightened that they threw away their knapsacks and all they had, but gun and knife to defend themselves with. It required great effort upon the part of the officers, who were somewhat cool, to prevent a perfect rout. After this day the brigade continued its retreat, but with a great deal of toil and difficulty, and finally encamped here on the 24th of November. This encampment is near Peterstown, in the south edge of Monroe County, and it is expected that the brigade will winter near here."

Colonel Croghan fell into our hands mortally wounded, and died in a few hours. His body was sent by General Benham to the confederate commander, with a note hoping that he would appreciate the desire thus expressed of mitigating the horrors of war. He was a Kentuckian, the son of that George Croghan who, in 1813, with only 160 men, defended Fort Stephenson in Ohio against 1000 British regulars and Indians, and who, a quarter of a century later, received the thanks of Congress and a medal for his gallantry on that occasion, and died as inspector general of the United States army.

This pursuit of Floyd brought to an end the campaign in Western Virginia. After this there was no engagement—nothing but an unimportant though severe skirmish between a confederate force at Camp Alleghany, about twenty-five miles from Cheat Mountain summit, and a portion of Reynolds's division. Floyd was ordered with his brigade to Tennessee, and Wise's legion went to Richmond, from which place it was sent to Roanoke Island, where at the proper moment we shall find it, under the general's son, doing battle against the federal troops under General Burnside.

On the 19th of July M'Clellan had issued an address to his soldiers summing up the results of his campaign. He said: "You have annihilated two armies, commanded by educated and experienced soldiers, intrenched in mountain fastnesses, and fortified at their leisure. You have taken five guns, twelve colors, fifteen hundred stand of arms, one thousand prisoners, including more than forty officers. One of the second commanders of the rebels is a prisoner; the other lost his life on the field of battle. You have killed more than two hundred and fifty of the enemy, who has lost all his baggage and camp equipage. All this has been accomplished with the loss of twenty brave men killed and sixty wounded on your part. You have proved that Union men, fighting for the preservation of our government, are more than a match for our misguided and erring brothers. You have made long and arduous marches, with insufficient food, frequently exposed to the inclemency of the weather. I have not hesitated to demand this of you, feeling that I could rely upon your endurance, patriotism, and courage. In the future I may have still greater demands to make upon you, still greater sacrifices for you to offer. I have confidence in you, and I trust you have learned to confide in me. Remember that discipline and subordination are qualities of equal value with courage."

This address of M'Clellan seems almost prophetic. Two days before it was issued our army of the Potomac came in sight of the enemy before Manassas; two days after it was issued we met with the disaster of Bull Run. The greater demands of which M'Clellan spoke were to be made, the greater sacrifices offered; and we had to learn by bitter experience that "discipline and subordination are qualities of equal value with courage."

From our triumph in Western Virginia we now turn to our great defeat at Bull Run.

BULL RUN, NEAR UNION MILLS, CROSSED BY THE ORANGE AND ALEXANDRIA RAILROAD.

CHAPTER III.

THE BATTLE OF BULL RUN.

The Proclamation and Volunteers.—The opposing Armies.—Popular Impatience.—Forward to Richmond.—Determination to Advance.—McDowell's Appointment.—Forces at his Command. —Beauregard and Johnston.—The Situation at Manassas.—Beauregard's Proclamation.—Topography of the Region.—Movements of the Confederates.—The Ambush at Vienna.—Johnston and Patterson.—Treachery in the Departments.—Patterson out-generaled.—Johnston sets out to join Beauregard.—McDowell's Advance.—The Halt at Fairfax.—Outrages by the Soldiers.—McDowell's Order.—The March to Centreville.—Skirmish at Blackburn's Ford.— McDowell's First Plan of Operations.—Why abandoned.—His Second Plan.—Johnston and Beauregard at Manassas.—Their Plan of Attack.—War and Chess.—Strength of the two Armies.—The Advance upon Bull Run.—Time lost.—Tyler in Position.—Topography of the Battle-field.—General Position of the Confederates.—The Battle of the Morning.—The Confederates repulsed.—They fall back to the Plateau.—Jackson's Stand.—Johnston and Beauregard on the Field.—Reorganization of the Confederates.—Estimate of Forces.—The Battle of the Afternoon.—The Confederate Position.—Rout of the New York Zouaves.—The Zouaves and the Black Horse Cavalry.—Keyes's Movement.—The Fight on the Hill.—The Federal Batteries disabled.—The Fight on the Ridge.—Federal Anticipations of Victory.—Confederate Re-enforcements.—The Rout.—Arrival of Jefferson Davis.—Stand of Sykes with the Regulars.—The Flight of the Federals.—The Pursuit by the Confederates.—Civilians on the Field. —At Cub Run Bridge.—Miles's Division.—Miles and Richardson.—The Halt at Centreville. —The Flight to Washington.—Reports of the Battle.—General Resumé.—Object and Means of the Expedition.—Causes of its Failure.—Burnside and Schenck.—General Note.—Authorities for the History.—Name of the Battle.—Patterson's Explanation.—List of Regiments.—The New York Zouaves.—Losses on both Sides.

THE President's proclamation of April 15, calling for 75,000 militia for three months, also summoned Congress to meet in extra session on the 4th of July. Notwithstanding the contemptuous refusal of the governors of six states, whose quotas amounted to 12,000 men, more than 80,000 promptly responded to the call. They saved the national capital from seizure; but it soon became evident that this force was wholly inadequate to the task of "suppressing the combinations and causing the laws to be duly executed." On the 3d of May another proclamation was put forth by the President calling for 42,000 volunteers for three years, and ordering an increase of 23,000 men to the regular army, and 18,000 to the navy. The nation uprose to the greatness of the occasion rather than to the smallness of the demand. In a month five men volunteered for one who had been asked. When Congress met, just two months from the date of the call, it was formally announced by the Secretary of War that there were in active service 260,000 men, of whom 153 regiments, with 165,000 men, were volunteers for three years, 25,000 regulars, and 80,000 volunteers for three months; besides these, fifty-five regiments, 50,000 strong, had been accepted, and would be in the field in twenty days; so that after the three months' men had withdrawn there would remain an army 230,000 strong. Government seemed to doubt whether this was a sufficient force. The Secretary of War said, "It will remain for Congress to determine whether the army shall at this time be in-

creased by the addition of a still larger volunteer force." The President, with a deeper but yet inadequate insight into the magnitude of the rebellion, asked that Congress, "in order to make the contest a short and decisive one, should place at the control of the government for this work at least 400,000 men."

While the administration was thus in doubt as to the adequacy of the force at its disposal for the work to be done, there was now no doubt on the part of the people. When men saw regiment after regiment hurrying to camp or parading the streets, when they heard of them pouring forward in a continuous stream which seemed to block up every approach to the capital, they were confident that the Confederacy had no power to withstand the forces arraying themselves on its borders. Great as were these forces, they were exaggerated in popular estimation. A regiment proposed to be raised was set down as accepted; one accepted was considered to be in the field; one in the field to be ready for immediate service. The people did not know, and the government dared not tell them, that there was a fearful lack of arms, munitions, and equipments—of every thing necessary to transform a crowd of men into an army. Through the villainy of Floyd, the complicity of Toucey, and the imbecility of Buchanan, the loyal states had been stripped of arms. Of the three great armories, two had fallen without opposition into the hands of the Confederates. Norfolk, with its accumulation of 2000 great guns, was theirs. Harper's Ferry, with its machinery almost uninjured, was theirs, needing only to be transported to a safe place. The Union had merely the armory at Springfield, which was then capable of turning out only 25,000 muskets a year. The private armories then in existence could furnish only a few thousand more. As far as men were concerned, government could create an army by a word; to supply the arms, without which in modern warfare there can be no army, was a work of time. A few could be furnished by importation from abroad; for the rest, not only the arms themselves, but the means of creating them, must be created. The enemy was for the time abundantly supplied. The sudden seizure of the forts and arsenals from the Chesapeake to the Rio Grande, from Virginia to Alabama, had put into his hands more weapons than he could use. Men were not wanting on either side; but while the Federal regiments stood idle in camp for want of arms, the Confederates had weapons ready for every company that could be raised. The Confederates availed themselves of this initial advantage. The ink with which the Virginia Ordinance of Secession was written was hardly dry before Richmond was chosen as the capital, where their Congress was to meet on the 20th of July, and troops from the farthest South were pushed to the northern frontiers of the Confederacy, within sight of the dome of the Federal Capitol.

The people of the North could see no sign of a corresponding activity. Their forces never moved southward far enough to lose sight of the Potomac. Day by day they grew more impatient of this delay, for which they could see no good reason. Buchanan's administration had been feeble and treacherous; was not that of Lincoln treacherous and feeble? Twenty thousand men had twelve years before marched from Vera Cruz to Mexico; why could not ten times as many, under the same commander, march from Washington to Richmond or Montgomery? That commander, it was hinted rather than said, was a Southerner by birth. It was acknowledged that for more than half a century he had been true and loyal, but were not Davis and Stephens loyal, Twiggs, Lee, and Johnston faithful, and even Floyd, Cobb, and Thompson honest, until the time came when they must choose between their country and their section? Had the old treason gone out when the new administration came in?

Such were the questions which all men were asking themselves during the months of May and June, and it needed but a word, fitly or unfitly spoken, to rouse a storm of indignation against the government. That word was supplied by the New York *Tribune*, a newspaper which, from various causes, was at the moment the exponent of popular feeling. For a score of years it had, through evil report and through good report, maintained the principles of the Republican party, always earnestly, if not always wisely. That party had now, after a long and weary contest, triumphed in every free state but one. The circulation of the paper was large. It reached every hamlet in the North and West; it passed from house to house, from hand to hand, and had every week a million of readers, by a large portion of whom it was accepted as authority. At length, on the 26th of June, it contained an article headed "the Nation's War-cry," which in just thirty words gave expression to the common feeling, and form to the general demand. "Forward to Richmond!" it said. "The Rebel Congress must not be allowed to meet there on the 20th of July. By that date the place must be held by the national army." Day after day these thirty electric words were repeated without change, like the Roman senator's "Carthage must be destroyed." Day after day this brief text was followed up by an elaborate discourse. Government was charged with indifference, if not treachery. The rebels were ready to fly at our approach. If the right men were in the right places, the war could be virtually ended in three months. If this was not done, it would be the fault of incompetent or treacherous leaders; politicians in or out of uniform, who did not wish the rebels routed, and in whose official statements no reliance was to be placed. If the rebellion was not thoroughly put down by spring, it would be because the nation had been betrayed by the government; it must acknowledge itself beaten, and recognize the independence of the Confederacy. And so on through every form of direct or insinuated accusation.[1]

The force of these appeals lay in that they were echoes of the popular feeling to which they gave form and expression. It pressed upon government with a force which could not be withstood. Members of Congress crowded upon the President and General Scott complaining of the inactivity of the army, and urging them to heed the cry, "Forward to Richmond!" The administration was in a sore strait. If the movement was attempted, there was a more than equal chance of its failure; if it was not attempted, government would lose the confidence of the country. A lost battle might be retrieved; public confidence lost could never be regained. The President, looking mainly at the political aspect of the case, was in favor of the movement. The commanding general, looking mainly at the military aspect, was opposed to it; but at last, against his judgment, gave a reluctant consent.

The movement having been determined upon, it only remained to make the best preparations possible. General Scott could not take the command in person. Age and infirmity had come upon him. For three years he had been unable to mount a horse; it was with difficulty that he could walk a few steps; he was tormented with dropsy and harassed by vertigo. Four months later he was compelled to ask to be suffered to retire from active service. The request was granted, and, full of age and honors, he was released from the command which he had so long and honorably held. Meanwhile the actual conduct of the enterprise must be intrusted to other hands. The choice fell upon General Irvin McDowell. He was in the prime of manhood; had graduated twenty-seven years before at the Military Academy with high honor; had served through the Mexican war, and was breveted as captain for gallant and meritorious conduct in the hard-fought battle of Buena Vista. When peace came he relinquished his rank in the line, and entered the adjutant general's department. At the outbreak of the rebellion he returned to duty in the field, and was appointed brigadier general in the regular army, his commission dating from May 14, 1861. To consid-

IRVIN McDOWELL.

erable military experience he joined a personal character beyond reproach, and loyalty above suspicion. In selecting him for the command, government made the wisest choice then possible. It had yet to learn who were the generals endowed with great military genius. On the 27th of May McDowell was appointed to the command of a new military department, comprising all Virginia east of the Alleghany Mountains and west of the James River, with the exception of Fortress Monroe and its immediate vicinity. He set himself at once to the task of organizing into an army the regiments placed under his command. He took up his head-quarters at Arlington House, once the residence of the adopted son of the Father of our Country, from whom it had passed by marriage into the hands of General Lee, who had forsworn his military oath, thrown up his commission in the national army to head the insurgent forces in Virginia, and was soon to be appointed to the chief command of the entire Confederate army.

The force at the disposal of government for the execution of this enterprise was far less than was supposed. On the morning of the 27th of June, when the nation's war cry—"Forward to Richmond"—reached Washington, there were in and around Washington 38,600 Federal troops. Of these, 15,700 were across the Potomac in Virginia, the remainder being in the District. Patterson, with about 18,000 men, was fifty miles away, near Harper's Ferry, watching an equal Confederate force in the Valley of the Shenandoah. All that was expected of him was to prevent that army from interfering with the march into Virginia. Butler at Fortress Monroe, Banks in Maryland, and McClellan in West Virginia, with some 40,000 men in all, could not directly co-operate. Of the 310,000 men whom the Secretary of War a week after announced to be at the disposal of the government, about 100,000 were in actual service. Of these, something more than 50,000 could be concentrated near the capital, from which, after leaving behind a force to garrison Washington and its defenses, McDowell must draw the army which was to advance. The 8th of July was fixed upon as the day for the commencement of the movement. But the regiments came up slowly, many of them eight or nine days after the time fixed upon, and were sent forward without ever having been formed into brigades or having been seen by their commanders. Time passed on until the 15th, and yet the arrangements were far from complete; but the pressure from without was so strong, that orders were given for the advance on the following day. The force had been organized into five divisions. The First Division, under Tyler, consisted of eleven volunteer regiments, and three companies of cavalry and artillery. The Second Division, under Hunter, seven volunteer regiments, a battalion of regulars, a corps of marines, and six companies of cavalry and artillery. The Third Division, under Heintzelman, had ten volunteer regiments, and three companies of cavalry and artillery. The Fourth Division, under Runyon, had seven regiments of New Jersey volunteers. The Fifth Division, under Miles, had nine volunteer regiments, with two companies of artillery. The entire army numbered 35,000, of whom about 33,000 were volunteers. Of these one third were for three months, whose term of service was about to expire. About 1000 were regulars from a number of regiments, 500 were marines, and the remainder were cavalry and artillery. Of cavalry there were but four companies. Though falling fully 20,000 short of the number generally attributed to it, this was the largest army ever brought together under one command on this continent.

The Confederates, meanwhile, having resolved to make Virginia the seat of war, and having transferred their seat of government from Montgomery to Richmond, had pushed forward two considerable armies toward the Potomac. Beauregard's bloodless capture of Fort Sumter had made him the hero of the South, and to him was intrusted the command of the most important of these armies, that of the Potomac; while to Johnston, his superior in rank, was confided the command of the Army of the Shenandoah. The

---

[1] "THE NATION'S WAR-CRY. — *Forward to Richmond! Forward to Richmond! The Rebel Congress must not be allowed to meet there on the 20th of July!* By that date the place must be held by the national army!"—*Tribune*, June 26 to July 3.

" . . . . If the rebels are not virtually whipped when the next spring opens, and if they shall meanwhile have steadily confronted our troops without losing ground, we may consider that the republic has been betrayed by the folly or incompetence of its trusted leaders, and that disunion is a fixed fact."—*The Same*, June 27.

" . . . . The war can not much longer be conducted and held in check by politicians, whether in uniform or out. . . . If the men in Washington wish to convince the public that they have really repented, and are ready to do their duty, let them see to it that the national flag floats over Richmond before the 20th of July."—*The Same*, June 27.

"The real question is this: *Does General Scott* (or whoever it may be) *contemplate the same end, and is he animated by like impulses with the great body of the loyal, liberty-loving people of the country?* . . . . Does he want the rebels routed, or would he have them conciliated? If the national forces shall be beaten in a fair stand-up fight — which we do not believe possible — the patriot millions will acknowledge the corn and the independence of Secessia. If our side beats, the rebel leaders must abscond . . . . and we may just as well determine who is who in three months as in thirty."—*The Same*, July 1.

" . . . . Forward, then, and anticipate the rebel force, which only awaits our approach to flee. Forward to Richmond, and place the national foot on the neck of the traitor who already sues for peace."—*The Same*, July 1.

" . . . . Unfortunately, the credit to be given to declarations from the State Department is much impaired."—*The Same*, July 2.

Army of the Potomac took up a position judiciously chosen, either to threaten Washington or to defend Richmond. From Alexandria on the Potomac, just below Washington, starts the Orange and Alexandria Railroad, running southwestwardly, and forming the northern link in the great southern chain of railways. After traversing the flat Potomac region, it begins to climb the gradual slope of the outlying ranges of the great Alleghany chain. Twenty-seven miles from Alexandria it meets the Manassas Gap Railway, which, running almost due west for fifty miles, pierces the valley of the Shenandoah at Strasburg, thence turning south for a score of miles down the valley. These two roads meet on an elevated plateau. The point of union is known as Manassas Junction. From this point the railway runs southwardly, past Warrenton and Culpepper, fifty miles, to Gordonsville, where it connects with the great network of railway which, reaching every point in the South, has its focus at Richmond. From Manassas to Washington is about thirty miles; to Richmond about eighty in a direct line, but almost twice as far by the circuitous railway routes. Practically, however, it is nearer to Richmond for defensive purposes than to Washington for offensive. Before its military occupation the Junction was an insignificant place. It consisted of a low wooden dépôt, a dingy house for refreshments, and half a dozen small cottages scattered about over the bleak plain.

Beauregard, who had been ordered to the Mississippi, and was actually on his way thither when he was recalled, and ordered to take the command of the Army of the Potomac, reached Manassas early in June, and on the 5th issued a violent and mendacious proclamation addressed to the people of the region. "A reckless and unprincipled tyrant," he said, "has invaded your soil. Abraham Lincoln, regardless of all moral, legal, and constitutional restraints, has thrown his abolition hosts among you, who are murdering and imprisoning your citizens, confiscating and destroying your property, and committing other acts of violence and outrage too shocking and revolting to be enumerated. All rules of civilized warfare are abandoned, and they proclaim by their acts, if not on their banners, that their war-cry is 'Beauty and Booty.' All that is dear to man—your honor and that of your wives and daughters—your fortunes and your lives, are involved in this momentous contest." The people were summoned to rally to his camp. The neighboring planters responded to his call, partly in person, and more freely by sending their slaves, by whom, in a short time, a strong earthwork was thrown up, which was named Camp Pickens, in honor of the governor of South Carolina. The troops, thus freed from all other labor, could devote their time to military drill, and were soon brought into a state of tolerable efficiency.

The position, apart from its fortifications, was by nature a strong one. From the foot of the Blue Ridge a plain of about twenty miles in width slopes eastward down to the lowland region of the Potomac. This whole plain is broken and intricate, sparsely dotted with hamlets, plantations, and solitary houses, with patches of woodland, partly forests of considerable size, and partly of the scrubby growth of pine and oak which springs up spontaneously in the exhausted and abandoned fields of Virginia. It is intersected in every direction by streams, elsewhere denominated creeks, but in the local dialect known by the more picturesque name of "runs." Roads, which are hardly more than by-paths, traverse the plain in every direction, leading through the fields and woods to the solitary dwellings. The principal of these streams, which almost claims the rank of a river, is Bull Run. Pursuing a winding course, with a general direction from northwest to southeast, it drains a considerable tract of country, and falls into the Occoquan about twelve miles from its junction with the Potomac. It has worn a deep channel through the limestone strata, and the banks are generally steep and rocky. At intervals of a mile or two these banks are broken down so as to form fords, which are the only places where the stream can be crossed, with the exception of two bridges—one a substantial stone structure over which passes the Warrenton turnpike, the other a mere wooden bridge at Blackburn's Ford, seven miles below, on the direct road from Centreville to Manassas. A mile or so below this is the bridge by which the Orange and Alexandria Railway is carried over the Run. Three miles beyond the Run is Manassas Junction, where the Army of the Potomac had intrenched itself. The Run itself formed an admirable defensive line, eight miles long, from the Stone Bridge to the railroad. It could only be crossed by an army at the fords, and such was the nature of the approaches to these that they could be maintained against a greatly superior force. There was no necessity for fortifications, and with the exception of a strong abattis across the road at the Stone Bridge, there were no artificial defenses on the whole line. The wooded slopes of the hills furnished masks for batteries better than could be provided by art.

Beauregard, having securely intrenched himself at Manassas, pushed forward detachments toward Washington. An outpost was established at Fairfax Court House, ten miles on the road to Washington, where intrenchments were thrown up. The cavalry and light artillery made dashes to within sight of the Federal works at Arlington Heights, and could catch glimpses of the dome of the national Capitol, of which they hoped soon to have possession. One of the boldest of these dashes was made by Colonel Gregg to the north of Washington. He penetrated forty-five miles to the Potomac, and returning, on the 17th of June, when at Vienna, on the Loudon railway, he learned that a train of cars loaded with Federal soldiers was at hand. Placing two guns in ambush at a curve of the road, he awaited their approach, and as they rounded the curve poured in a well-aimed fire, which raked the cars from front to rear, killing a number of the soldiers, and scattering the rest. They then hastily pushed back without suffering any loss. With this exception, and a few unimportant rencounters between small squads of scouts, there had been no active hostilities between the two

MANASSAS JUNCTION AFTER ITS EVACUATION BY THE CONFEDERATES, FEBRUARY, 1862.

armies of the Potomac. Nor had there been any serious encounters between the forces to the north of Washington.

JOSEPH E. JOHNSTON.

General Joseph E. Johnston, who had been assigned to the Army of the Shenandoah, arrived at Harper's Ferry on the 23d of May, and assumed the command. He found there nine regiments and two battalions of infantry, four companies of artillery, with sixteen guns, and about three hundred cavalry. He saw at once that the place was untenable against even an equal force. It was so completely overlooked that it was more favorable to an attacking than a defending force. Patterson, across the Potomac, was watching him, ready to cross and advance up the valley from the east, while McClellan, after his successes in West Virginia, was expected to come into the valley from the west; with these forces in his rear, he would be cut off from giving any aid in case of need to the Army of the Potomac. He therefore wished to abandon Harper's Ferry, and fall back twenty-five miles to Winchester, where all the practicable roads from the west and northwest, as well as from Manassas, meet the main route from Pennsylvania and Maryland. But the military authorities at Richmond overruled him, and directed him still to occupy Harper's Ferry. On the 13th information came that Romney, fifty miles to the northwest, had been seized by a strong body of Federal troops, who were supposed to be the vanguard of McClellan's army coming down to form a junction with Patterson, and three days later information came that Patterson had crossed the Potomac at Williamsport, and was apparently advancing up the valley upon Winchester. Johnston then took the responsibility of abandoning Harper's Ferry, and threw his army by a flank movement across Patterson's presumed line of march. Patterson at once recrossed the Potomac, and Johnston, having received a dispatch from Richmond sanctioning the movement which he had already made on his own responsibility, resumed his original plan, and fell back to Winchester, where he intrenched himself strongly. Here he could oppose McClellan from the west, Patterson from the northeast, or form a junction with Beauregard at Manassas if necessary. On the 23d of Ju , Patterson again crossed the Potomac and marched toward Winchester. Johnston slowly retired, and some skirmishing took place, with no decisive results.

McDowell's advance had now been determined upon. In making his estimates of the force necessary to accomplish the work before him, he had stipulated that Johnston should be so "taken care of" as not to be able to come to the assistance of Beauregard. This work was intrusted to General Patterson. Johnston's army had been increased by eight regiments from the far South, and about 2500 militia called out from the neighboring counties in Virginia. As it lay strongly intrenched at Winchester at the middle of July, it numbered about 18,000 of all arms. Patterson's army was of about the same strength. They were almost all volunteer regiments whose term of service was about to expire; they were dissatisfied with the treatment they had received, and would not stay one hour beyond their time. Patterson vastly overrated the strength of the enemy, and dared not attack them; he would rather lose the chance of accomplishing something brilliant, than, by hazarding his column, endanger the success of the campaign by defeat. So he was satisfied with merely watching Johnston, and endeavoring to hold him at Winchester. On the 17th of July he received a telegram from Washington that McDowell had advanced, and that on the next day Manassas Junction would probably be carried. He believed that Johnston's forces were still before him, and that he had detained them until it was too late for them to assist Beauregard. He lay all the 18th awaiting an attack, not dreaming that his skillful opponent was then, with all his available force, on the way to join the Army of the Potomac; and it was only on the 20th, at the very hour when Johnston was joining Beauregard, that Patterson learned that he had been thoroughly out-generaled. It was too late to retrieve the error, even had he been capable of making a bold movement; and so, on the 21st, while the fight at Bull Run was going on, Patterson fell

quietly back to Harper's Ferry. While the smart of the great defeat at Bull Run was yet fresh, Patterson was charged with gross negligence, if not with absolute treachery. A calmer view showed nothing to sustain these charges. A task had been imposed upon him beyond his powers, and he failed in accomplishing it. He was simply incompetent, not wantonly negligent, still less treacherous. The decision of the government, by which he was honorably discharged from service, was just and proper.

Treason, however, was rife in every department of the government at Washington. For years a system had been growing up under which the clerkships in the various departments had been mainly bestowed upon Southerners. When cabinet ministers and naval and military officers were false, it could hardly be expected that civil clerks should be true. By their means the Confederate government was fully informed of every movement made or contemplated at Washington. The most secret dispatches, and the most private documents of the government at Washington, were copied and sent to the authorities at Richmond. A military map of Eastern Virginia had been prepared by government officials. It was thought to be of such importance that it was furnished only to Federal officers of the highest rank; yet a copy of it was found on the table of a Confederate captain at Fairfax.

McDowell's advance was commenced on the morning of the 17th of July. Beauregard was notified of it from "a trusty source" in time to give orders in the evening of that day that his advanced brigades should fall back from Fairfax. He also sent an aid-de-camp to Johnston at Winchester, calling for assistance, and indicating the point to which his march should be directed. By the time that this message reached Johnston, he had received direct communications from Richmond ordering him to go to the support of Beauregard. This order was received by Johnston at Winchester at one o'clock on the morning of the 18th. To comply with this order, Johnston must either defeat or elude Patterson. He chose the latter course. Leaving his sick, nearly 1700 in number, at Winchester, with the Virginia militia, and posting a strong rear-guard to induce Patterson to believe that his whole army was still in front, he pushed his whole available force up the Valley of the Shenandoah, and thence, through Ashby's Gap in the Blue Ridge, to the line of the Manassas Railway, which brought him by noon of the 20th to Manassas Junction, where, in virtue of his superior rank, he assumed the command of the entire army. He was at Manassas before Patterson dreamed that he had left Winchester, two days' march away. All that he dared hope was that he had gained a day and a half upon Patterson, who, he presumed, would join McDowell during the 22d.

McDowell's advance set out from the camps near Washington on the afternoon of July 16, but the main body did not commence its march until daybreak on the following morning, moving in four columns by roads nearly parallel. The advance was slow, for the men were unaccustomed to marching, and were incommoded by carrying the loads to be borne in light marching order. The roads also had been obstructed, and ambuscades were to be expected. Fairfax Court House was reached at about noon. The works thrown up here had been deserted, and the place was seized without opposition, only a few straggling shots being fired, by which three or four men were wounded. The greater part of the men had marched only six miles, and McDowell wished to push on at once to Centreville, six miles farther, but he was told that the men were worn out, not so much by the distance marched as by the more wearying work of waiting on foot. So a halt was ordered for the day. The troops were in high spirits. They looked upon the falling back of the Confederate forces as the first step in the retreat which would not cease until Richmond was reached. "It is ardently hoped,"

ROBERT PATTERSON.

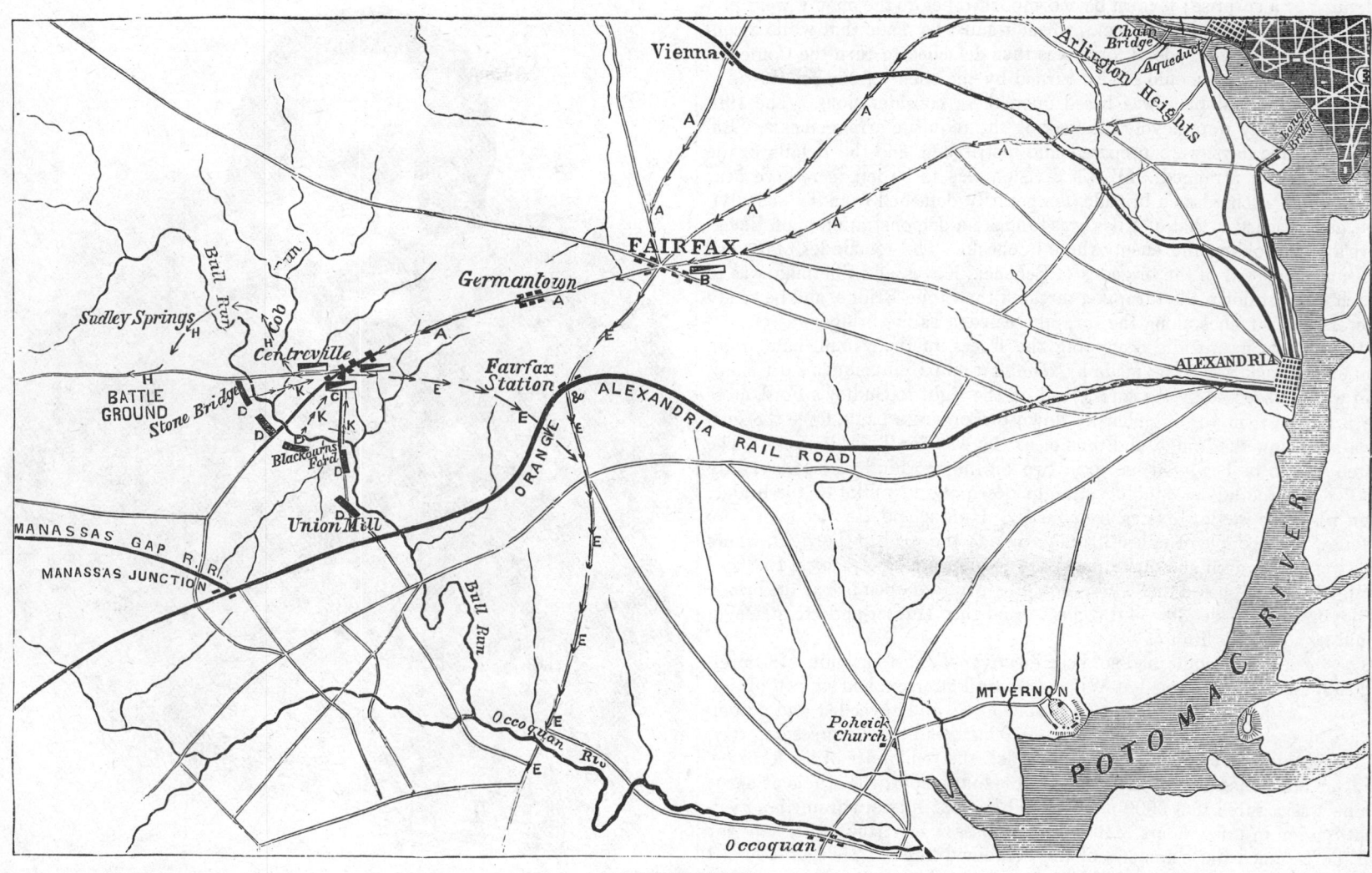

PLANS OF OPERATIONS.

This map indicates, in a general way, the operations, actual or proposed, on both sides, previous to the battle of Bull Run.—A A shows McDowell's advance to Centreville.—B Runyon's division, left in reserve near Fairfax Court House.—C C McDowell at Centreville.—D D Confederate brigades across Bull Run.—E E McDowell's first plan to turn the Confederate right.—H H McDowell's second plan to turn the Confederate left, which brought on the battle.—K K Beauregard's original plan of attacking with his right the Federals at Centreville.

wrote one newspaper correspondent, "that the rascals will make a stand at Manassas. But it is greatly feared that they will run again. If Beauregard does not give us battle at Manassas, his army will be thus thoroughly demoralized, and he is beaten past a ray of hope." The march was looked upon as a picnic excursion; the men gave themselves up to the humors of camp life. Some dressed themselves in women's clothes, and paraded the town; one fellow donned an imitation of a clerical gown and band, and with an open book in his hands stalked through the street, reading the funeral service of the President of the Southern Confederacy. Some—only a few—did not content themselves with these unmilitary displays. They set out on predatory excursions to the neighboring houses, and came back swinging their plunder upon their bayonets. Several houses were sacked and burned, though no personal injury was inflicted. McDowell repressed these outrages by a sorrowful and stern order. "It is with the deepest mortification," he said, "that the commanding general finds it necessary to reiterate his orders for the preservation of the property of the inhabitants of the district occupied by the troops under his command. It is again ordered that no one shall arrest or attempt to arrest any citizen not in arms at the time, or search, or attempt to search any house, or even to enter the same, without permission. The troops must behave themselves with as much forbearance and propriety as if they were at their own homes. They are here to fight the enemies of the country, not to judge and punish the unarmed and defenseless, however guilty they may be." The severest military penalty was threatened for any violation of this order. No more outrages were committed. The troops bivouacked under the open sky, the general and his staff, like the men, sleeping on the ground. Next morning the army resumed its march, and the whole force, with the exception of Runyon's division, which was left at Fairfax, was soon concentrated near Centreville.

Centreville is a village of a score or two of houses, straggling along a ridge at the confluence of several roads, about four miles from Bull Run. One of these roads—the Warrenton turnpike—goes almost due west, crossing the Run at the Stone Bridge. Another, going southwestward, and crossing the Run at Blackburn's Ford, goes directly to Manassas Junction, three miles beyond the stream, connecting by cross-roads with the different fords above and below. Tyler, whose division now led the advance, reached the village early on the 18th, and finding that the enemy had fallen back, pushed forward to make a reconnoissance in the direction of Blackburn's Ford, taking with him four regiments of Richardson's brigade. They found the enemy in considerable force hidden in the woods which bordered the Run. Some sharp though random firing from artillery was interchanged for several hours. The New York Twelfth was thrown into confusion; Richardson wished to charge with the other regiments, and carry the hostile position; but Tyler, who knew that it was no part of the commanding general's plan to bring on an action here, refused his consent. A reconnoissance only had been intended, and this had been made in stronger force than was desirable. The troops were accordingly withdrawn. In this skirmish the loss on each side was about equal. The Confederates lost 15 killed and 53 wounded,

several of them mortally—68 in all; the Federals lost 19 killed, 38 wounded, and 26 missing—83 in all.

McDowell could never have contemplated a march upon Richmond, with the army under his command, in face of the force directly opposed to him and of the re-enforcements which could be hurried up from Richmond and beyond. He did not even intend to assail them directly in the strong position at Manassas. His purpose was to gain their rear, and break their railway communication both with the forces at Richmond and in the Valley of the Shenandoah. The two armies of the enemy, cut off from communication with each other and with Richmond, would be forced to fall back from their position threatening the capital, leaving Manassas, the key of the direct route to the south, in his hands. To accomplish this, he proposed to make a sudden movement to the left, cross the Occoquan just below its junction with Bull Run, and strike a blow at the enemy's railroad communication in this direction. He had not, therefore, accompanied his army in its advance from Fairfax to Centreville. He had indeed expected to encounter the army at Fairfax, and was disappointed at their abandonment of that place without a struggle. The march to Centreville was intended merely as a demonstration. On the morning of the 18th he set out on a reconnoissance of the country to his left, through which he proposed to advance. He was soon convinced that the country in that direction was impracticable for the advance of his army, and was forced to abandon his first plan and form another. Coming to Centreville, he learned the results of Tyler's and Richardson's reconnoissance to Blackburn's Ford. This showed that the enemy had done wisely in falling back to the line of Bull Run, and that they were in too great force there to allow an attempt to force the passage with any reasonable hope of success; and even if the passage were forced, he would find himself in front of the strong position at Manassas, which was not to be desired. Still, something must be done, or the whole expedition would be an absolute failure; a failure without even an attempt to strike a blow. What was to be done must be done speedily. A large and the best part of his force consisted of three months' men, whose term of service was about to expire. They, at least, had had a few weeks of discipline. The three years' men were all new to military life. In a few days he would have lost ten thousand of his best troops. Every day's delay, while it would probably add to the strength of the enemy, would diminish his. The march to the left having been found impracticable, and a direct advance in front being too dangerous to be risked, the only alternative was to attempt to turn the enemy's position on the right.

From reconnoissances made and information received on the 19th, he learned that the enemy's extreme left was at the Stone Bridge, directly in his front, where the Warrenton turnpike crosses Bull Run; and that some two or three miles above was Sudley's Ford, which was unguarded, and could be reached by an almost unused forest road. The enemy apparently expected an attack some miles below; if his feeble left could be turned by surprise before he could bring up his force to sustain it, it could be forced back, the turnpike seized, and a detachment sent forward by it to cut the railroad in the rear of Manassas Junction. This movement, to be successful, must be a surprise; it must be accomplished before the enemy were prepared to resist it; and, moreover, provision must be made that while a considerable part of the Federal force was thus detached to turn the Confederate left, his own left should not be turned by the enemy from below.

McDowell's final plan was based upon these considerations. The 19th and 20th of July were devoted to making the requisite arrangements. Rations for three days were prepared and distributed, and the details of the enterprise were arranged. Miles's division was to be left in reserve near Centreville; Richardson's brigade, temporarily detached from Tyler's division, and attached to that of Miles, was to make a demonstration upon Blackburn's Ford, holding the enemy there in check. The remainder of Tyler's division, composed of the brigades of Schenck, Keyes, and Sherman, was to march straight down the turnpike, threaten the Stone Bridge, and be ready to cross and advance along the turnpike as soon as the bridge was cleared of the enemy, meanwhile occupying the forces in their immediate front. The main attack was to be made by Hunter's and Heintzelman's divisions, who were to proceed by the forest road on the right to Sudley's Ford, cross the Run, and then, turning sharply down the opposite bank, force the enemy's left below the bridge, and thus clear the way for Tyler to cross. The march was to be begun at half past two on the morning of Sunday, July 21, Tyler in the advance, going straight down the turnpike to the bridge, upon which he was to open a cannonade. Hunter and Heintzelman were to follow for a couple of miles till they came to the road to the right, where they were to turn off and make their way to their crossing-place at Sudley's Ford. It was supposed that Tyler would be ready to open fire at the bridge by daybreak—a little after four o'clock—and that Hunter and Heintzelman would be across the Run at six.

The enemy, meanwhile, had not been inactive. Johnston, whom McDowell had supposed to be detained at Winchester by Patterson, had slipped off unperceived with the whole of his available force, and, preceded and accompanied by eight regiments, numbering 6000 men, had, on the preceding day, joined Beauregard at Manassas. He had left the remainder of his force behind, for the Manassas Railway was not able to transport the whole at once; but he was assured that 5000 more would be sent forward from the Piedmont Station in a few hours. Reaching Manassas, in virtue of his superior rank he assumed the command of the combined forces. He had assumed that Patterson would discover his departure from Winchester, and, hastening to join McDowell, would reach him on the 22d, giving him a decided superiority in force; but, in the mean while, if his own expected 5000 came up on the evening of the 20th, he would, for a night and a day, have the greater numbers. Beauregard, being thoroughly acquainted with the ground, and apprised of the approach of the Army of the Shenandoah, had prepared a plan of battle, to which Johnston at once gave his assent. He proposed to cross Bull Run below the Stone Bridge with the whole force of the two armies, and attack McDowell, whom he expected to find lying at Centreville, before the expected re-enforcements from Patterson should join him. The Confederate troops were posted with this view, and orders were given for carrying the movement into effect; but the 5000 from Piedmont did not come up; the order was countermanded just at daybreak; the Confederates remained at their posts on their side of Bull Run without attempting their proposed offensive movement on the Federal left. At that same moment the Federal army—two hours behind its appointed time—had fairly commenced its offensive advance upon the Confederate left. If either commander had fathomed the plans of the other, the battle would have been fought on different ground, and probably with a different result.

War has been compared to the game of chess. The parallel fails in many important particulars. In chess each piece has a fixed and absolute value, and each player may know exactly his own force and that of his opponent. He who plays most skillfully must win. In war neither commander knows the exact value of his own force, and can only conjecture that of his adversary. Above all, there is the great disturbing element of time. A movement which would insure success if made at the right instant, may be useless or fatal an hour later. This element of time modified the whole course of the battle of Bull Run, and in the end decided its result. The Confederate re-enforcements did not come up as was expected, and the order for attack was countermanded. The Federal forces made their attack some hours later than was designed, and lost the expected advantage of surprise; and, finally, when the battle hung in even balance, a Confederate re-enforcement, of which neither side could know, turned the scale.

The two armies opposed to each other at the dawn of July 21 were almost equal. McDowell had set out with 35,000, of these, Runyon's division of 5000 had been left behind to hold the communications with Washington. At Centreville, on the evening of the 20th, he had 30,000; but among these were the Pennsylvania Fourth regiment and the battery attached to the New York Eighth: their term expired on the 20th, and they insisted upon their discharge. McDowell vainly tried to induce them to stay a few days longer. They refused. They had fulfilled the letter of their enlistment; and, on the morning of the 21st, while their comrades were marching forward to battle, this recreant Pennsylvania Fourth regiment, with the battery of the New York Eighth, slunk back to the rear to the sound of the enemy's cannon. Deducting these dastards, the killed and disabled of the 18th, and the sick of the various divisions, the Federal army, on the morning of the 21st, numbered, within a few hundreds more or less, 28,000 available men. At that same time the Confederate Army of the Potomac numbered about 22,000 (by the official statement, exactly 21,833) effective men. Of the Army of the Shenandoah 6000 had already arrived, making 28,000 in all. During the battle other re-enforcements to the Confederates came up, raising the Army of the Shenandoah from 6000 to 8334, besides Hill's Virginia regi-

DAVID HUNTER.

ment of 550. The entire force at the command of the Confederate general was a little less than 31,000.[1] What portion of either army were brought into action at each stage of the battle will appear hereafter. McDowell, after the discharge of the battery of the New York Eighth, had forty-nine guns. The Confederates had at the commencement of the action precisely the same number; another battery of four pieces was brought up by the re-enforcements, making fifty-three in all. The Confederate artillery was generally inferior in calibre and range, but as the firing was at close distance, this disadvantage was more than made up by the greater ease and rapidity with which they could be handled and discharged. The organization of the Confederate troops was decidedly superior. They had been brought together into brigades, under commanders whom they knew, while the greater portion of the Federals had been thus organized only since the march began, and were to a great extent unacquainted with their commanding officers. In cavalry the Confederates were much the stronger. They had at least twelve companies, while the Federals had but four.

The Federal divisions were set in motion by moonlight, at that stillest hour which just precedes the dawn. The time for each movement was carefully designated. Tyler, who lay in front of Centreville, was to lead the way, and go straight down the turnpike to the Stone Bridge, which he was to threaten. Hunter, who was encamped a mile or two in the rear, was to follow for two or three miles along the turnpike till he came to the forest road branching off to the right toward Sudley's Ford, where he was to cross the Run, and then turn sharply down the west bank. Heintzelman was to follow Hunter for about two miles on the forest road, then turn and cross the Run below him. All were to move at half past two. It was thought that Tyler would be in position to open fire at daybreak, a little after four; that Hunter, entering the forest road as soon as daylight enabled him to thread its tortuous course, would cross the Run at six, followed closely by Heintzelman, so that the whole force would be on the expected battle-ground in the cool of the morning. But a night movement is always liable to interruptions. These occurred at every step. Tyler occupied the turnpike two hours longer than was expected, keeping Hunter and Heintzelman so much behind their time. Then the road through the Big Forest was longer and more difficult than had been supposed, and the passage of the Run was made at nine instead of six. Three hours were thus lost when minutes were of priceless worth.

McDowell had anticipated the probability of delay, and wished to move his columns a few miles forward the preceding night; but he yielded to the wishes of some of his officers, who thought it would be more pleasant to make but a single march. For the second time within three days he threw away a victory which a more enterprising commander would have grasped. If, instead of halting at Fairfax on the 17th, after a march of only six miles, he had pushed on at once to Centreville, the battle of Bull Run would have been fought two days earlier. The Federals would have gone into action two thousand stronger and the Confederates ten thousand weaker on the

[1] Exactly 30,715, according to the lowest rendering of General Beauregard's official report. He may have intended to state the total number at from 600 to 2000 greater, his report being somewhat obscure on this point. See, on this subject, the note at the end of this chapter.

SAMUEL P. HEINTZELMAN.

19th than on the 21st. With 28,000 against 31,000, the battle was hardly lost on Sunday; with 30,000 against 21,000, it might have been won on Friday. So, if but one of the three hours lost on the morning of the 21st had been saved by a march on the evening of the 20th, the victory, almost within the grasp of McDowell, would not have been wrested from him by the unexpected arrival of the Confederate re-enforcements brought on by Smith. But we turn from what might have been to what was.

At six o'clock, two hours behind time, Tyler's three brigades were in front of the Stone Bridge; Hunter's two brigades were threading their way, Burnside leading, along the forest road; Heintzelman's two brigades were just turning into the forest. They had all crossed Cub Run, a narrow stream whose steep banks were spanned by a wooden bridge. They hardly noticed it in the morning twilight, but had occasion to remember it before evening. McDowell and his staff now rode up. Still apprehensive of a strong attack upon his left and rear, he ordered Howard's brigade, of Heintzelman's division, to remain in reserve, in case it should be necessary to re-enforce Miles at Centreville.

At half past six a shot from Tyler's 30-pounder announced to the other divisions that he was in position. Stationing a scout among the branches of a tall tree, which commanded a view of the opposite side of the Run, he waited for two hours until Hunter and Heintzelman, coming down on the other side, should drive back the enemy, and render it possible for him to cross to their direct support. In the mean while, to carry out his feigned attack, he sent one brigade a mile down the Run toward the next ford guarded by the enemy, upon whom he opened fire, which was vigorously returned, with little damage on either side. All this time he kept up a slow cannonade without eliciting any reply from the enemy in his front. They had beforehand ascertained that he was beyond the range of their guns, and did not care to waste ammunition and disclose their position by useless firing. At half past nine Burnside had reached the Run, crossed without opposition, followed by Porter's brigade and Heintzelman's division, and, after a brief halt for rest, pushed down the Run, and found himself confronted by the enemy on the northern slope of what was to be the battle-field of the day.

The course of Bull Run for half a mile above and below the bridge is nearly north and south. The turnpike crossing it goes almost due west from Centreville. Beyond the bridge it traverses a low wooded bottom half a mile broad, mounts a slight ascent, then sinks again down to a little hollow, by which a small brook, called Young's Branch, comes from the west, and then, making a short turn to the south, finds its way into Bull Run. The road following the valley of Young's Branch ascends for a mile by an easy slope until it gains the level of the plain about two miles from the Run. Here it is crossed by another road winding southward from Sudley's Springs. This road formed the western boundary of the battle-field. The valley of Young's Branch is shaped somewhat like a sickle, lying with its edge to the south and west. Upon that side the ground rises by a sharp ascent about a hundred feet to a plateau of an irregular oval form, containing about one hundred and fifty acres of cleared land, cut up into small fields, with here and there patches of young oaks and pines. Along the eastern and southern sides of the plateau was a dense thicket of second-growth pines, and across the upper edge of the fields a broad belt of oaks upon both sides of the Sudley road. Near the upper edge of the plateau was a house occupied by Mrs. Henry, and half a mile below another owned by a free negro named Robinson. Both were small wooden buildings densely embowered in trees, and surrounded by fences. This plateau, a mile long from east to west, and half a mile broad from north to south, was the bat-

tle-field of the afternoon, the sharpest fighting being in the oak woods, at the two houses, and in front of the pine thicket. The other side of the valley of Young's Branch slopes gently up to the north in a succession of open, undulating fields, covered with grass, and dotted over with groves and thickets. This slope was the scene of the battle in the morning.

While the Federal army was advancing to the attack, the Confederates were in the same position which they had occupied for some days along the southwestern side of Bull Run. Ewell's brigade was at Union Mills Ford, on the extreme right. The brigades of Jones, Longstreet, Bonham, and Cocke were successively posted close to the Run, in front of the principal fords, up to the Stone Bridge, a distance of eight miles. Between these, but slightly in their rear, so as to be able to support either of the front brigades that might be assailed, were the brigades of Holmes, Early, Jackson, and Bee. Beauregard, sanctioned by Johnston, assuming all along that the battle would be fought on his right, had concentrated his main strength upon that wing, leaving his left at the Stone Bridge comparatively weak. The front line of brigades consisted wholly of the troops of the Army of the Potomac; those of the Army of the Shenandoah, who were wearied by their rapid march from Winchester, being placed in reserve in the rear. But the battle being fought upon the left, the main brunt fell upon the Army of the Shenandoah.

Colonel Evans, who held the extreme Confederate left at Stone Bridge, deceived by Tyler's demonstrations, notified Beauregard that a strong attack had been commenced on that flank. The Confederate commander, directing that position to be held at all hazards, sent orders that a rapid and determined attack should be made upon the Federal flank and rear at Centreville. By this movement they expected to achieve a complete victory by noon. Johnston and Beauregard then took a position on a commanding hill in the rear of the centre of the Confederate lines, where for two long hours they awaited tidings of the battle. They came at last in an unwelcome shape. The order for an advance by their right had miscarried, and it was too late to renew it. Three hours would be required to effect the movement, and minutes were beyond price, for the action opened by the Federals on the left had gone sorely against the Confederates. After giving hasty orders countermanding that for an advance of the right, dispatching aids to Manassas to hurry up the re-enforcements momentarily expected by railway, and directing the reserve regiments to hasten to the scene of action, Beauregard and Johnston galloped to their left, where the roll of musketry and the din of artillery announced that a severe conflict was going on. An hour's sharp riding brought them at noon to the plateau in the rear of the Henry and Robinson houses. They looked upon a battle to all appearance lost. We now turn to that point where the battle had been fought.

Before nine o'clock, while Hunter and Heintzelman were winding their way unseen along the forest road, Evans became convinced that the attack on his front was a feint, and suspected that an attempt was making to turn his left. He had but fifteen companies at the Bridge. Leaving four in position there, with the other eleven and two guns he marched across the fields and took up a position to check the advance of the enemy, sending word to Bee, who commanded the nearest brigade in reserve, to hurry up to the scene of action. At half past ten the head of Burnside's column came in sight of Evans, and the action was opened. Bee, a gallant South Carolinian, who had been trained at West Point, had fought under Scott in Mexico, had been twice breveted for meritorious conduct at Cerro Gordo and Chapultepec, and who in this his last action gave proof of great military capacity, brought on his brigade of four regiments and two companies, with Imboden's battery, and drew them up on the edge of the plateau; but, seeing Evans sorely pressed by Burnside, he advanced down the slope, across the turnpike, over Young's Branch, and threw himself into the action. Burnside was now overmatched, and called for aid. Sykes's eight companies of regulars hurried down from Porter's column on the right, and restored the balance. At this moment, Hunter, whose division comprised the two brigades of Porter and Burnside, was wounded, and borne from the field. The command nominally devolved upon Porter, the senior officer; but, as he was throughout the action with his own brigade, Burnside was actually in command on his part of the field. Porter's column, coming down the Sudley road, were now in striking distance, and poured in a heavy fire from the right. The Confederate line began to waver, then fell back slowly and sullenly toward the turnpike. Just then, when the fight had continued for more than an hour, a fresh column appeared over the low ridge which separated Bull Run from the Federal left. This was Sherman's brigade of Tyler's division, which had been all the morning on the opposite side waiting for an opportunity to cross and take part in the conflict.

Tyler, warned from his observatory in the tree-top of the progress of the real attack, had withdrawn his feigned assault, and had brought up his three brigades in front of the Stone Bridge. Assured that the enemy were in no condition to molest him, he had ordered Sherman's brigade to cross the Run above the bridge, and support the forces hotly engaged on the opposite side. The crossing was effected without opposition, and just before noon Sherman came upon the field. The Confederates, now attacked by Sherman on the right, pressed by Burnside and Sykes on their centre, and galled by Porter on their left, rushed broken and shattered up the slope of the plateau, and half way across it, beyond the Robinson and Henry houses. Here they met support. Jackson, who had been in reserve next behind Bee, had brought forward his five regiments, and gained the eastern edge of the plateau across which Bee's broken, though not routed force was flying. "They are beating us back," said Bee to Jackson, as they met. "Sir, we will give them the bayonet," replied Jackson. Bee, encouraged by Jackson's firm front, tried to rally his men. "Here is Jackson," he cried, "standing like a stone wall!" The word fitted the mood of the moment. "Stonewall! Stonewall!" was passed from man to man; from that moment this became a part of the name by which the favorite Confederate leader was known. We shall have need, in describing the events of the next two years, to speak often of "Stonewall Jackson."

It was now past noon. Jackson's firm stand had gained a breathing-space for the Confederates upon the lower, or southeastern brow of the plateau. Sherman had joined the rear of Hunter and Heintzelman, who, coming down upon the upper margin of the plateau, had fairly outflanked the Confederate left. Tyler had brought over Keyes's brigade directly after Sherman's, and was menacing the lower edge of the plateau, where the Confederates were making what seemed their last stand in and in front of the pine thicket. Howard's brigade, detached in the morning from Heintzelman's division, had been ordered forward, and had secured the Run. Burnside's brigade, which had first entered into action, had exhausted its ammunition, and been withdrawn a little to the rear to replenish it, but could almost immediately be brought into action. Eighteen thousand men had now passed the Run, and as the Confederates had been driven clear away from the Stone Bridge, there was nothing but an undefended abbatis of felled trees to hinder Schenck, with Tyler's remaining brigade, from crossing and adding two thousand more to the force actually engaged.

Johnston and Beauregard now came upon the plateau. The Confederate forces there consisted at this moment of Jackson's five regiments which had not yet been engaged, and the shattered remains of Bee's and Evans's commands. These in the morning had numbered about 7500 men, but fully five hundred had been killed and wounded, so that the Confederate forces on the field at that moment were about 7000. Their position was strong. The pine thicket and the clumps of trees afforded admirable shelter. Their artillery, consisting of thirteen guns, was posted so as to play upon the coming enemy, and yet so sheltered as to be itself hardly exposed. The first task of the Confederate commanders was to reorganize the broken regiments. Johnston placed himself by the colors of the Fourth Alabama, which had lost all its field-officers, and Bee's shattered companies rallied around him on the right. Beauregard, as he posted the lines on the left, where the first onset of the enemy would fall, addressed the men in sharp and decisive words. That position was of the last importance; re-enforcements were close at hand, but until these came they must hold their posts at all hazards and against any odds. Order having been restored, and the forces posted, Johnston took his station at a point from which he could overlook the whole scene in every direction, and send forward the re-enforcements to the precise point where they could be most effective, while Beauregard remained in command of the field. Just beyond a ravine which forms the southern boundary of the plateau is a commanding elevation, upon which stands a house known as the "Portico," or "the Lewis House," overlooking the course of the Run above and below, and the field of battle. Here Johnston took up his head-quarters. Re-enforcements had begun to come up, and by the time that the Federal right was fairly in position for attack, the Confederates had on the field twelve full regiments of infantry, two hundred and sixty cavalry, and twenty-two guns, in all about 9500 men, with other re-enforcements approaching. Against these, upon their left, were advancing four brigades of the Federal army, with Ricketts's, Griffin's, and Arnold's batteries, sixteen guns. The brigades were those of Porter, of Hunter's division; Franklin and Wilcox, of Heintzelman's; and Sherman's, of Tyler's. Keyes's brigade, of Tyler's division, was engaged far to the left. In all,

THOMAS J. JACKSON.

13,000 men and sixteen guns were fairly in movement against the Confederates on the plateau.

The Federal right now moved confidently down along the Sudley road upon the Confederate left, sorely galled by the fire from the artillery, which was admirably served. But they pressed on up the slope, outflanked the enemy's line, and seized upon the upper edge of the plateau. Ricketts's and Griffin's artillery led, and took up position after position. The enemy's strongest position was on a swell west of the Henry house; a little to the south was another hill which commanded this. If that could be gained and held, the whole plateau would be commanded. The two batteries were ordered here, with the New York Eleventh as their support. Of this regiment, commonly designated as Ellsworth's Zouaves, high anticipations had been formed. Men had heard fabulous stories of the achievements of the French Zouaves in Algeria and the Crimea. Ellsworth had come from the West to New York at the head of a company whom he had trained to marvelous perfection in the Zouave drill. He had speedily recruited a regiment in New York, in a great measure of the class from which the French Zouaves were supposed to have been drawn. That they were not, when in camp, very pleasant neighbors, even to their friends, was admitted; but that they would be still less so to the enemy was sure. No one doubted that in action they would stand fire; and, above all, it was thought that every man of them was sworn to avenge the slaying of Ellsworth. The Zouaves went forward with bravado enough. Some of them had thrown off their gay jackets, that they might "fight freer." But when they came in sight of a Confederate regiment half hidden by a clump of pines, and at the same moment saw two mounted companies coming down upon them by a road through the woods, their courage vanished. They broke in utter confusion, and the cavalry rode straight through them, harming scarcely a man. A few of the Zouaves kept presence of mind enough to fire random shots at the horsemen, killing four, wounding one, and dispersing the whole body. But the regiment of Zouaves was scattered. Farnham, their colonel, and some of the officers, tried gallantly to stem the rout; many of the men fell in with other regiments, and did good service as skirmishers; but as a regiment it was wholly dispersed, not a few of the members heading the flight, and being among the first to bring to Washington and New York tidings of the rout, with wild stories of their own prowess on the fatal field, where they had shown themselves such arrant cowards.[1]

At about the same time, a little past two, Keyes's brigade of Tyler's divi-

ERASMUS D. KEYES.

[1] This is the whole story of the famous charge of the "Black Horse Cavalry" upon the Zouaves, with accounts of which the newspapers of the day were filled. By way of sample, we quote, with abridgments, some paragraphs of these reports. One of the lieutenants of the regiment writes:

"The Zouaves rushed out of the woods only to find themselves the target for another body of infantry beyond, while the Black Horse Cavalry were seen charging full upon them. They formed hastily in line, kneeling, semi-kneeling, and standing, that, Ellsworth fashion, they might receive their enemies with successive volleys. On came the Horse, splendidly mounted. To an early discharge from the cavalry the Zouaves made no response, although several of the men were killed, but waited patiently until the enemy were almost upon them, when, in quick succession, the three ranks fired. The shock to the rebels was great; but they rallied, and attempted a renewal of the charge, for which they paid dearly. They were completely shattered, broken up, and swept away. Not more than a hundred of them rode off, and as they went their ears were saluted with 'One, two, three, four, five, six, seven, tigah, Zouave!'"...... Another Zouave says: "The Black Horse Guard came upon the Zouave regiment at a gallop, and were received by the brave firemen upon their poised bayonets, followed instantly by a volley, from which they broke and fled. They quickly returned, with their forces doubled—perhaps six or seven hundred—and again dashed, with fearful yells, upon the excited Zouaves, and the slaughter commenced. No quarter, no halting, no flinching now, marked the rapid and death-dealing blows of our men as they closed in upon the foe in their madness and desperation. Our brave fellows fell; the ranks filled up; the sabres, bowie-knives, and bayonets glistened in the sunlight; horse after horse went down; platoon after platoon disappeared—the rattle of musketry, the screams of the rebels, the shout of 'Remember Ellsworth!' from the lungs of the Zouaves, and the yells of the wounded and crushed belligerents, filled the air, and a terrible carnage succeeded. The gallant Zouaves fought to the death, and were sadly cut up; but of those hundreds of Black Horse Guards, not many left that bloody rencounter."

A ZOUAVE AT WASHINGTON RELATING HIS EXPLOITS AT BULL RUN.

sion, which had come upon the field just at the close of the Confederate repulse in the morning, was ordered forward. Crossing the turnpike, he marched straight up the northern slope of the plateau in front of the Robinson house. The Third Connecticut and Second Maine regiments charged up the hill, crowned its summit, brushed away the enemy, and for a moment held the house and field. Their position was, however, commanded by a battery in the rear, which poured in so hot a fire that a few moments' exposure to it would have annihilated the whole line; as it was, the Maine regiment lost fifteen killed and forty wounded. Keyes withdrew below the brow of the hill, around which he skirted in search of an opportunity to charge; but the light battery of the enemy, shifting front as he changed ground, was always in his front, ready to pour in its shot whenever the head of a column should appear above the crest. This movement, lasting for more than an hour, took Keyes clear around the eastern edge of the plateau, out of sight of the battle which was raging two miles to the west.

The great struggle of the day was going on at the western end of the plateau. A Confederate battery of thirteen guns, supported by Jackson's and Bee's brigades, had been posted in a small open field five hundred yards southeast of the Henry house, just below the crest of a low elevation. From this shelter it poured in a fierce fire upon the Federal column coming down southwardly along the Sudley road. But the column pressed on until its head, now the extreme Federal right, had outflanked the batteries, which, with their supports, formed the extreme Confederate left. Five hundred yards southeast of these—a thousand from the Henry house—a hill rises fifty feet above the general level, and half as much above the ridge behind which the Confederates were posted. From this hill the Confederate left could be completely enfiladed. It was the key of the position. Whoever held that hill with artillery, held the plateau. The hill had just been seized by the batteries of Griffin and Ricketts, and the Zouaves had been ordered up as supports, while the Federal column coming from the north had passed the Henry house, and was bearing down upon the Confederate position. It was now almost three o'clock. Beauregard, informed that re-enforcements were close at hand, pushed forward his whole line to recover the plateau. Jackson advanced his "stone wall" against Ricketts and Griffin. The Zouaves, catching sight of his line and the two companies of cavalry, broke and fled ignominiously. Heintzelman ordered up the First Minnesota, the nearest regiment, to take their place. As they emerged from the wooded road down which they had come, and passed the crest of the hill, they found themselves face to face within fifty yards of a body of troops. The two lines had now become so intermingled that from position alone neither could tell friend from foe. Gorman, the colonel of the Minnesota regiment, was at a loss; Griffin was equally uncertain; some one had told them that this was another of Heintzelman's regiments. Heintzelman, apparently also in doubt, dashed between the two regiments, within pistol-shot of either. The enemy hesitated in like manner for a few moments. But the pause was brief. Each caught sight at the same moment of the colors of the other, and poured in a deadly fire. The two Federal batteries offered a conspicuous mark. A third of the cannoneers and half of the horses were shot down at the first volley, and the batteries were disabled. They had played a conspicuous part in the action of the day, and now, when they were to be most wanted,

they were useless. The only question was who should have them. Jackson dashed forward and seized the guns, trying to drag them from the field. Fresh regiments on each side were brought up; the line wavered to and fro for an hour; the guns were taken and retaken three times, but at the last remained in the hands of the Federals, who were dragging them away.

All this time a fierce battle had been going on a little to the left of this hill, along the ridge held by the Confederate forces. Griffin's and Ricketts's batteries, which would have swept the position, were thrown out of service, and, though not taken, were rendered useless. A strong Federal column was directed upon this ridge. Regiment after regiment was brought up; each, one after the other, was hurled back, some in tolerable order, some in sheer disorder. In the confused melée of the next hour it is impossible to trace clearly the action of each regiment along that short line of barely half a mile from the Henry house to the hill. The First Minnesota fell back; the First Michigan was brought forward and driven off. The Fourteenth New York came on in gallant style, but, coming in sight of the enemy's line, broke and ran. "I considered it," says Heintzelman, "useless to attempt to rally them. The most of the men would run from fifty to several hundred yards to the rear, and continue to fire high in the air, compelling those in the front to retreat." The New York Thirty-eighth tried hard to save the battery; forced back, they dragged off three of Ricketts's guns, leaving them, as they thought, out of the enemy's reach. Rallying, they advanced, and for a few moments thought themselves in possession of the field; then, without knowing how, they found themselves opposed to a superior force, swept by musketry and pierced by artillery, from which they fell back in sudden panic. "This," says their colonel, "was the last rally made by my regiment." Close by, but a little to the left, the New York Seventy-ninth charged up the ridge upon the Confederate batteries. Receiving a severe fire, they broke; rallied, and finally broke again, and fell back, leaving their colonel, Cameron, brother of the Secretary of War, dead upon the field. The New York Sixty-ninth took their place. "Now, boys, is your time," shouted Corcoran, their colonel, as they rushed into action. They held the crest for barely a quarter of an hour, and then fell back in disorder.

The advantages gained by the Confederates had been dearly won. Bee and Bartow, who had been all day long in the thickest of the fight, fell almost side by side near the Henry house; Jackson was wounded, but still kept the field; many other of the best officers had been killed or wounded in the desperate struggle. In spite of these checks, the Federal generals were still confident of victory. "The enemy was evidently disheartened and broken," says McDowell. "Every thing was in favor of our troops, and promising decisive victory," says Burnside, at four o'clock. "The prestige of success had thus far attended the efforts of our gallant but inexperienced troops," says Porter. Single regiments had been sent forward to the ridge who had been driven back overmatched; but now a determined assault was to be made by a strong column. The flags of eight regiments, though borne somewhat wearily, were pointed to the hill from which the disordered masses of the Confederates were seen, or thought to be seen, hastily retiring. But before this final and decisive charge was made upon the crest near the Henry house, which had now become the centre of the field, the whole Federal right came rushing down in utter rout, men, horses,

Q Q

and caissons mingled together in the wildest confusion. The instant that this hot torrent of fugitives touched a regiment which had before seemed solid, it melted away like a snow-bank before a jet of steam. The panic spread from regiment to regiment, and in a quarter of an hour the whole Federal force was transformed from an army into a frightened crowd.

To understand whence came the blow which so suddenly shattered the Federal right, we must go back to the Lewis house, where Johnston, with the whole field before him, was watching the progress of the fight in his front and the arrival of re-enforcements from his rear. All day long he had been harassed by groundless apprehensions that Patterson was close at hand. At ten o'clock he saw a column of dust rising up in the northwest, such as might be raised by an army on the march. This may have been a cloud blown up by a gust of wind, or have been raised by McDowell's columns near Sudley's Ford; but Johnston suspected that it indicated the approach of Patterson. Again, at two o'clock, an officer galloped up from Manassas with the report that a Federal force had reached the railway, and were now close upon the position which Beauregard was so stoutly defending. Upon the heels of this unwelcome messenger came another with tidings that this force was Kirby Smith's brigade of the Army of the Shenandoah. Johnston's course was now clear. An hour or two before he had ordered Cocke to bring up his brigade from the edge of Bull Run; but, learning that this position was threatened from across the stream, he had countermanded the order. It was now repeated, and Cocke's brigade, four regiments strong, came upon the field. In half an hour Fisher's North Carolina, and Cash's and Kershaw's South Carolina regiments, from Bonham's brigade, came up from below, followed almost at the same moment by Kirby Smith from Manassas with half of the long-awaited re-enforcements from Piedmont. Smith had started at daylight by rail, reaching the Junction at noon with four regiments and a battery. Leaving a weak regiment at the Junction, with the other three he had hurried across the fields to the Lewis house. Early's three regiments came up from their position down the Run just after Smith.

To the twelve regiments with which Beauregard had for two hours held the field, thirteen were now added. The re-enforcements were skillfully directed. A part were sent to strengthen Beauregard's line, which had just begun to advance. Among these were Smith's division. He himself was wounded, and the command devolved upon Elzey. A part made a circuit south and west to and beyond the Sudley road, outflanking the Federal right, fell upon its flank and rear, and hurled it in wild confusion upon the column just ready to assail the Confederate line near the Henry house. In fifteen minutes all was lost. The whole Federal force was swept clear off the plateau and up the slopes beyond the Sudley road, which swarmed with crowds of flying, disorganized troops, through whom dashed riderless horses and artillery teams driven at utmost speed. Regiments which a few minutes before stood firm, melted away at a touch. Some of the officers strove by entreaties and threats to rally their commands; but they would not stand even when beyond the reach of the Confederate fire. It was not a retreat; it was a flight; a rout as complete as any battle-field ever saw. Yet three regiments standing firm for half an hour, and presenting a "stone wall" behind which their broken comrades should rally, might even then have changed the issue of the day. A decisive victory could hardly have been won, but the Confederates could have been repulsed, and the result would have been a drawn battle. The odds were indeed at the moment against the Federals, but they were less than those against which the Confederates had held their ground for hours. McDowell had upon the immediate field 13,000 men. In half an hour he could have brought up Burnside's troops, who had been out of action since noon; Keyes's regiments, which were wholly intact; and Schenck's brigade, which had not been in action, but, having cleared away the abattis, were on the point of crossing the Stone Bridge—in all 7000 men, which would have given him 20,000. To oppose these the Confederates had 19,000. They had brought up every man who would be within reach for two hours. But no orders were given to bring up the Federal re-enforcements, and scarcely an attempt to present a front to the enemy. The New York Sixty-ninth, indeed, formed for a short time into an irregular square against a body of cavalry, and repelled their charge, but it soon broke and joined in the flight. Its colonel, Corcoran, became separated from his men, and was made prisoner. He was, by special order of the Confederate government, "confined in a cell appropriated to convicted felons," as hostage for certain privateers who had been captured by the Federals and put on trial for piracy. After a year's captivity he was exchanged, and was made brigadier general, his commission dating from the day of the battle of Bull Run.

The only real opposition to the pursuit of the Confederates was made by Sykes, with his eight companies of regulars, who marched to the right straight through the crowds of flying troops, vainly attempting to rally them, threw themselves in the way of the advancing enemy, whom they held in check until the broken regiments had gained a fair start. They then slowly retired, always showing a firm front, and covering the escape of those who were fleeing toward Sudley's and the fords below. They were the last to leave the field, and the only force opposed to the enemy in this quarter.

Jefferson Davis came upon the field just after the victory had been won. The Confederate Congress had been "allowed to meet at Richmond on the 20th." On that day the President had delivered his message, and in the evening had received tidings of the impending battle. He set out by railway for Manassas next morning, at the very moment when Tyler's first gun was fired, reached the Junction at four, mounted, and rode to Johnston's head-quarters at the Lewis house, and thence to the battle-field in time to

MICHAEL CORCORAN.

see the broken regiments of the Federals flying in the distance. He sent a glowing dispatch to Richmond. "Night," he said, "has closed upon a hard-fought field. Our forces were victorious. The battle was fought mainly on our left. Our force was 15,000; that of the enemy estimated at 35,000." Writing before the smoke of battle had cleared away, it is not strange that he doubled the strength of the Federals, and diminished by one third that of the Confederates.

The victors were in no condition to make a vigorous pursuit. One half of their infantry had been for hours under fire; the other half were exhausted by their rapid march and strenuous assault. A few of the freshest regiments started in pursuit, but were soon recalled; none of them went a mile. The artillery, which all day long had played an important part, were, with the exception of a few light guns, equally unavailable. The rest, from their positions, played upon the fugitives with little effect. The pursuit devolved wholly upon the cavalry. Of the dozen companies nearly all were now at hand. Stuart, whose charge had scattered the Zouaves, went upon the heels of those who were flying toward the upper fords, but the firm line of Sykes's regulars in the rear forbade any serious attack. They picked up many stragglers who had fallen out of the line of flight, but accomplished no more. Radford, with six companies—barely five hundred men—crossed the Run below the Stone Bridge, came upon the turnpike, and pressed upon the rear of the Federals. Schenck had just cleared away the abattis at the bridge, when he received intelligence of the rout, and that the army was retreating. He fell back toward Centreville, leaving the road open for the light battery of the Confederates to come on behind.

By various routes the Federal troops had now crossed the Run and gained the turnpike, along which they pressed in one confused mass. Here and there a regiment presented something like a military form, but intermingled with these was a crowd of officers, soldiers, and civilians, on foot, mounted, and in carriages. When the tidings of an impending battle reached Washington, all the idlers in the capital rushed forward to see the sight. Congressmen, newspaper correspondents, and loungers of every grade besieged the livery-stables. The man who had a horse or carriage for hire was lucky; he could let it at a war risk. All that long July day a constant stream poured out from Washington. Encouraged by the reports of the morning's success, many had ventured beyond Centreville; some had even crossed the Run. There was no one to hinder, and they went where they listed. This advancing current met the receding one. The opposing streams made a whirlpool, the vortex of which was where the road crossed the narrow bridge over Cub Run. Just below another human stream had poured in down the forest road up which Hunter and Heintzelman had marched in the morning. Behind were the Confederate cavalry, their hundreds multiplied in apprehension to thousands. An occasional sharp report, and a shot dropping here and there, showed that the pursuers had artillery—how many guns no man could know. All struggled and fought to pass the narrow bridge, beyond which lay safety. The light guns of the pursuers came within long range and opened fire. A shot struck a caisson on the bridge, over-

BLENKER'S BRIGADE COVERING THE RETREAT NEAR CENTREVILLE.

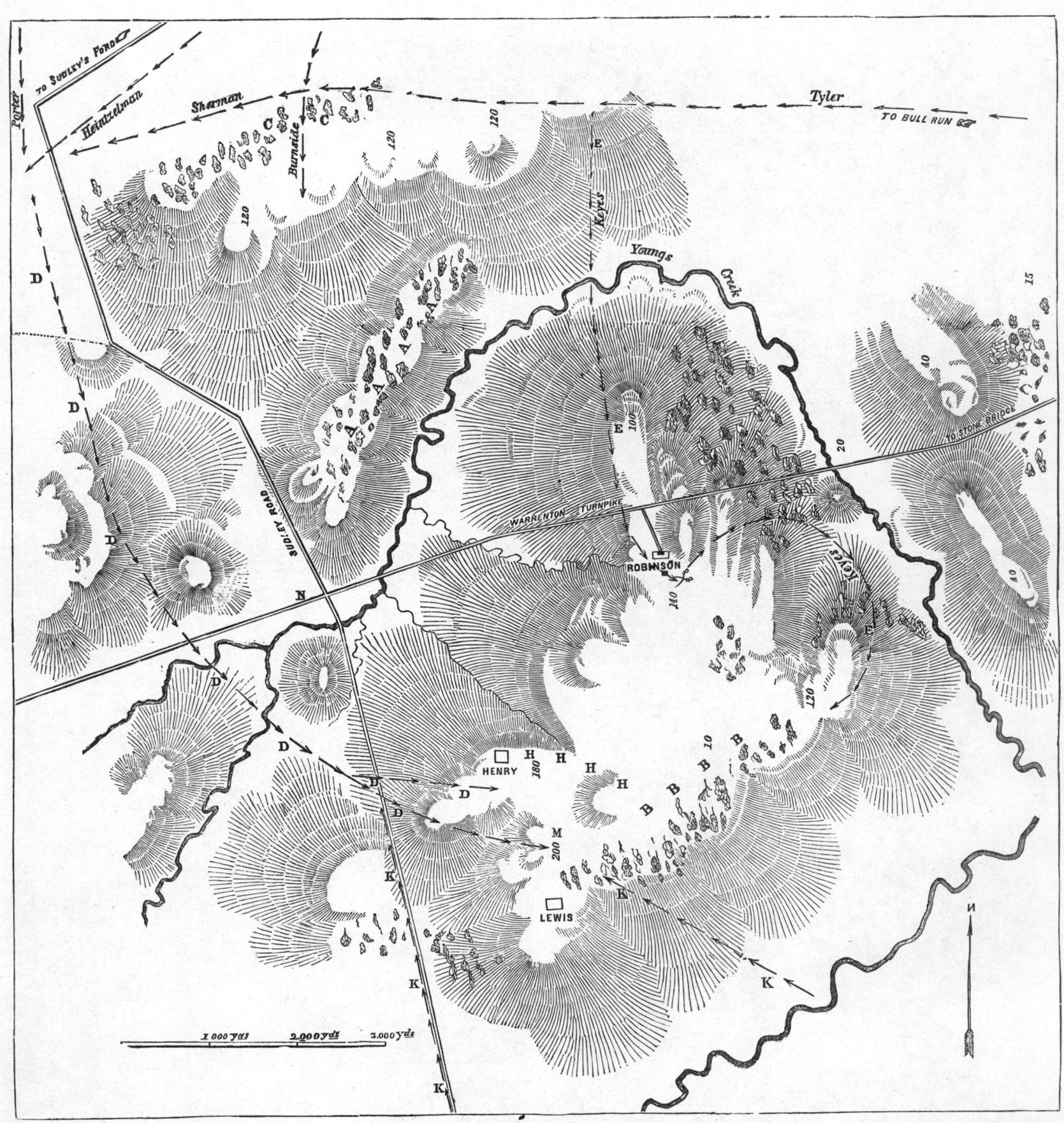

THE BATTLE-FIELD OF BULL RUN.

This map shows the topography of the field, and the principal positions during the battle, Bull Run being about half a mile to the east. **A A** scene of the Confederate repulse in the morning. **B B** Confederate stand on the southern edge of the plateau. **C C** Burnside withdrawn from the action after the fight of the morning. **D D** general line of advance of the united columns of Porter, Heintzelman, and Sherman upon the Confederate right. **E E** Keyes's movement after the separation of his brigade from that of Sherman, of Tyler's division. **H H** final advance of the Confederates. **K K** advance of the last Confederate re-enforcements. **M** hill where Griffin's and Ricketts's batteries were disabled. **N** Sykes's stand with the regulars after the rout. The figures denote the elevation above the level of Bull Run.

turned it, and blocked up the passage. The artillery horses were cut from their traces, and mounted by their drivers. Wagons loaded with ammunition, ambulances freighted with wounded, guns which had been dragged so far, were abandoned. A full third of the lost artillery was left here. The Confederate guns poured their shot into the writhing mass. Somehow the throng cleared itself; some got over the bridge; some crossed the stream above, some below. Once fairly beyond Cub Run, the fugitives found themselves in presence of Blenker's regiment, hastily drawn up in a firm line. Through this they were suffered to pass, and were beyond reach of harm. Almost twenty thousand men had been driven for miles by scarcely five hundred, and had left behind every thing but their lives. Evening had now closed in upon the rout. In the gathering darkness some squadrons of Confederate cavalry came up to Blenker's outposts. They were met by a fire, and wheeled back. For an hour or two they hovered around, and then retired across Bull Run.

Miles's division, 7000 strong, which had been left in reserve, had not been wholly inactive. Blenker's brigade was left in guard at Centreville. The brigades of Davis and Richardson marched down to Blackburn's Ford, near where the skirmish of three days before had been fought. A slow fire was opened upon the opposite bank, to which no reply was made, and no enemy was visible except at long distances until about eleven o'clock; then suddenly the opposite bank seemed full of them. They moved back and forth in a puzzling way. Now they seemed to be massing themselves as if to cross the Run in force; a small body was sent across who drove in the Fed-

eral skirmishers, but were in turn driven back by artillery. Then they appeared to be retreating—before the attack on their left, as Richardson supposed. Again the tide turned, and still larger masses were concentrated. These troops were the brigades of Jones and Longstreet, who had received the order to fall upon the Federal left, and were preparing to execute it, when it was countermanded because a similar order sent to Ewell had miscarried. The Federal commanders little knew the peril from which they had escaped. It was owing to sheer accident that they were not assailed by a threefold force, while the rest of the army was miles away, utterly beyond reach of giving them support.

So the day went on till past five o'clock, when an order came to retreat upon Centreville and endeavor to hold that position, for the attack upon the right had failed, and McDowell was retreating in utter rout. Richardson and Davis fell back, and took up a position to protect the retreating regiments from below, while Blenker guarded them in front.

The conduct of Miles, the commander of the division, had been singular all day. Several times he rode over to the posts of Davis and Richardson, changed the dispositions which they had made, countermanded the orders which they had given, and then hurried back to his quarters at Centreville. Toward evening Richardson had established his defensive line, when, returning to one of the regiments, he found that it had been entirely altered. He inquired by whose orders it had been done, and was told by Stevens, the colonel, that it was by express order of Miles. "Why the change was made," he added, "I do not know; but I have no confidence in Colonel

Miles, for he is drunk." Richardson replaced the regiment as before, and then reported to McDowell's aid that he had been interfered with all day in the disposition of his troops, and could not carry out the orders of the commanding general so long as he was under orders of a drunken man. He was directed to take the command. He began placing another regiment, when Miles met him and ordered him to form it in a different manner. Richardson replied that he should obey no more orders from him. Miles ordered him in arrest. Richardson paid no attention, and rode off. McDowell soon came up. Miles said the dispositions made were faulty, and asked to be allowed to remain in command of his division. The request was refused.

By nine o'clock the last of the fugitives from the battle-field were safely beyond the lines at Centreville. Beyond the cavalry chase, no attempt was made at pursuit from that quarter. Johnston ordered Longstreet's and Bonham's brigades to cross the Run below the bridge, and fall upon the Federals. They advanced some distance, but night coming on they were recalled, without coming near enough to be perceived by the Federal rearguard. A brief and informal council was held, and it was resolved that Centreville should be abandoned, and the army fall back to Washington. But the routed regiments had waited for no orders. They were already far in the rear, hurrying forward in the same panic with which they had come in. They reached their camps at Vienna and Arlington before daylight the next morning. In less than six hours of darkness they had accomplished in their flight a distance which it had taken them more than forty hours to traverse in their advance. Scarcely a regiment which had been driven from the battle-field presented the slightest trace of military order. The regiments of the reserve followed on more leisurely, but long before night they were all back in front of Washington.

The Confederate loss in this battle was 378 killed, 1489 wounded, and 30 missing—1887 in all. Of these, 1262 were of the Army of the Shenandoah. As the re-enforcements brought up last were in action but a short time, the greater part of this loss—probably about 1100—fell upon Bee's and Jackson's brigades, which went into battle 6000 strong. The whole loss in the Army of the Potomac was 630. Not quite half of this army, 22,000 strong, was in action at all, and of these only Evans's half brigade of barely 1500 men, until afternoon; fully half the loss of the Army of the Potomac must have fallen upon them. Bee's brigade, 3000 strong, was the only part of the Army of the Shenandoah which took part in the bloody repulse of the morning; it was also engaged through the afternoon, and thus suffered more than Jackson's; it must have lost 700 men. Of the 4300 men which composed the commands of Bee and Evans, one man in four must have been killed or wounded.

The Federal loss is officially stated at 481 killed, 1011 wounded, and 1460 missing—3051 in all. This is probably a close approximation to the entire loss. But as all the dead were left on the field, and the greater part of those who were severely wounded fell into the hands of the enemy, their number can be given only by estimate. The estimates are certainly below the truth. The Confederate official report states that 1421 prisoners were sent to Richmond, of whom 871 were unwounded. Deducting these from the total loss, there remain 2180 killed and wounded. According to the usual ratio of casualties in battle, the Federal loss must have been about 550 killed and 1630 wounded. They lost 27 cannon, of which 10 were captured on the field, and the remainder abandoned in various stages of the pursuit—a large part of them at the crossing of Cub Run—besides 4000 muskets, 4500 sets of accoutrements, and a considerable quantity of ammunition.

We have described the battle of Bull Run in detail because it presents an epitome of the errors which marked the conduct of the Federals during the first months of the war. The conception was unwise; the plan faulty; the execution imperfect. The conception was unwise, because defeat was more than probable, and little real advantage could be gained by entire success. All that could be gained was a temporary interruption of railroad communications. When the second plan of operations was decided upon, which it was supposed would bring on a battle with an enemy presumed to be of not inferior force, strongly posted, McDowell still left one fifth of his army behind at Fairfax, more than ten miles from the battle-field, where they could be of no use. He could not expect to rout the Confederates, and either destroy their army or drive them from their strong post at Manassas. That point was to be carefully avoided in any case. If repulsed by surprise at Stone Bridge, the Confederates could at worst fall back behind the guns of Camp Pickens. The only real object sought to be gained by the battle of the 21st was to cut the railroad connection near Gainesville, ten miles in a straight line from Centreville, and thus break up the communication between the enemy's forces at Manassas and those in the Valley of Virginia. That he was not aware that this communication had already been made, and that Jackson, with half of his army, had already joined Beauregard, and that he would be followed by the other half before his detachment could by any possibility reach the road, is not to be laid to the charge of McDowell. He had every reason to suppose that Patterson was still holding Johnston in check at Winchester. But the tearing up of a few rods of railway by a force which must in any case be withdrawn at once, could only hinder, not prevent the junction of the two armies of the enemy. In the endeavor to accomplish even this McDowell divided his army, leaving one third around Centreville, hardly five miles from where he knew the centre of the main force of the enemy to be, and stretching the other over ten miles of road, with an interval between the wings so wide that either might have been crushed without the least possibility of aid from the other. Had the Confederate commanders understood the design of McDowell, their wisest course would have been to have allowed him to pass the Stone Bridge without opposition, and so separate Tyler, Hunter, and Heintzelman as widely as he pleased from Miles. Two courses would then have been open: to fall upon Miles and annihilate him; or to march up Bull Run on the precise route by which their re-enforcements actually were brought up, throw themselves between Miles and Tyler, and assail the rear of the latter. The advancing columns of the Federals would have been thus cut off by superior force from their base of supplies at Centreville. They had set out with rations for three days, and only ammunition for a single battle, with no provision for a renewal. The Federal army having been thus effectually divided by its commander, either part might have been attacked and destroyed. The Confederate generals, not dreaming that the great movement had so small a purpose, assumed that its design was to interpose between Manassas and their army lying along Bull Run. They therefore ordered the position at the Stone Bridge to be held at all hazards, and brought up their forces to repel what they presumed to be the movement upon Manassas. At the same time, as the most effective method of relieving their threatened left flank, they ordered a determined attack by their right and centre upon the rear and left flank of the Federals at Centreville. Had a successful attack been made here, as McDowell says, "our whole force would have been irretrievably cut off and destroyed." The accidental miscarriage of the order sent to Ewell was all that prevented this result.

The long withdrawal from action of Burnside's brigade is wholly inexplicable. The battle of the morning was over by noon. It had lasted less than two hours. Burnside had not suffered severely, and his men were in perfect order, and confident of victory. Their ammunition had indeed become well-nigh exhausted, and they were very properly withdrawn a little to the rear to replenish it. This was only partially accomplished at half past four, when Burnside received orders to protect the retreat. More than four hours were thrown away, while a fierce action was going on in plain sight at the distance of scarcely a mile.

Hardly less unaccountable is the long delay of Schenck's brigade at the Stone Bridge. From eight in the morning the passage was only obstructed by an abattis, and defended by four companies of infantry with two guns. This weakness could not, indeed, be known at once; but before eleven Tyler was assured that the enemy had no force in that quarter, and crossed the Run with Sherman's and Keyes's brigades. The weak guard at the bridge was swept away by noon, when Bee and Evans fell back, and very soon after Keyes marched clear above and beyond the vacant position which it had occupied. There was nothing in the way but the abattis, which could have been avoided by a slight detour on either side, or removed in a few minutes. No attempt to remove it was made for almost four hours, and then the removal was made just in time to open the road for a few Confederate guns to come down upon the rear of the flying army.

Keyes's movement also, though gallantly made, was without significance in the general result. Every step after the assault at the Robinson house took him farther and farther from the spot where he was wanted, clear out of sight of the battle, of the result of which he was ignorant until the order reached him to join in the retreat. As it was, he was almost cut off. The forces of Burnside, Schenck, and Keyes, or any one of them, at the hill, might probably have secured a victory, or, at all events, could have prevented the utter rout.

The Confederate commanders, who had held their position against great odds, threw a superior force at the decisive moment upon the decisive point, and so won a victory as decisive and complete as is recorded in the annals of war.

NOTE ON THE BATTLE OF BULL RUN.

Sources and Authorities.—The main sources for the history of the battle of Bull Run are the reports of the commanders on both sides. The newspaper accounts, Northern and Southern, are of little value. The system of "War Correspondence," which furnishes abundant and valuable information respecting the later periods of the war, had not yet been fairly organized. The current accounts of the day abound in misapprehensions and exaggerations. In the Southern papers the number of the Federals is stated any where from 50,000 to 135,000, with from 75 to 150 guns, and regular cavalry by the thousand. The Northern papers were filled with accounts of heights stormed, intrenchments carried, and masked batteries encountered. But the battle was fought upon ground which neither side had anticipated. Until after ten o'clock in the morning there had not been a single soldier upon the plateau, and not a yard of intrenchment was thrown up, and, with the exception of the abattis at the Stone Bridge, there were no artificial defenses nearer than Camp Pickens, almost ten miles distant. Neither were there any masked batteries. The Confederate artillery was, indeed, very judiciously posted, every advantage being taken of the natural formation of the ground. Thus Imboden's battery of four guns was placed by Bee early in the day in a ravine running down the slope of the plateau in front of the Henry house, opening directly upon the road by which Porter's brigade and Heintzelman's division were advancing. Across the mouth of this ravine was a slight swell, behind the crest of which the guns were sheltered, and over which they played upon the Federal columns. When Bee and Evans were driven back, their line of retreat took them to the east of this battery, which was left wholly unsupported. For more than three hours Imboden never saw a Confederate except those belonging to his own battery. All this time he kept up a fire upon the Federal columns until his guns became so heated that it was dangerous to load them. During all this time he was fired upon by Griffin's and Ricketts's batteries, but so well was he covered by the slight swell before him that only three men were harmed by fragments of exploding shells; and at last, when the Federal column was close upon him, by going up the ravine he carried away all his guns except one, which was disabled by the accidental breaking of the axle. This was the only semblance of a masked battery upon the field. Neither was there any hand-to-hand fighting. The battle was wholly an affair of artillery and musketry. It is doubtful whether, until the rout, there was a bayonet-thrust or a sword-cut given on either side. The misstatements of the newspapers have been reproduced and multiplied in most of the formal accounts of the battle. Thus a Colonel Estvàn, who professes to have been with the Confederate army, says that Beauregard had 65,000 infantry and 4000 cavalry, including "Kirby Smith's corps of 30,000 men, which came up at the close of the action." He also a little more than doubles the Confederate loss. He brings General Scott on the battle-field, when he was never nearer it than Washington; describes the conduct of Ewell's, Holmes's, Longstreet's, and Jones's brigades, none of which were in the action; and narrates an interview on the field between Davis, Johnston, and Beauregard, at a moment when the first was half way between Richmond and Manassas, the second at the Lewis house, and only the third on the field. Estvàn's book was first published in England. It is false in every possible particular. Some American writers have given accounts hardly less incorrect.—McDowell's report of the battle itself is vague and indefinite. The reports of the division, brigade, and regimental commanders are mainly devoted to the special operations of their several commands; but by comparing and collating the whole, a fair idea may be gained of the phases of the action on the Federal side.—Johnston's report is, as far as it goes, clear and intelligible. It is chiefly valuable as affording means of correcting some important misstatements in that of Beauregard.—Beauregard's report, made out more than a month after the battle, is elaborate and minute. He, however, studiously exaggerates the force of the Federals at each important moment, and as studiously understates his own. But in most cases he unintentionally furnishes the means of correcting his misstatements; and where these are wanting, Johnston's less elaborate report supplies the deficiency.

NAME OF THE BATTLE.—The Confederate writers usually call the action of the 21st "the battle of Manassas," styling the skirmish of the 18th "the battle of Bull Run." But as the battle of the 21st was fought some miles from Manassas, and close by the bank of the Run, the Northern designation seems the most appropriate.—The title of the battle of "Blackburn's Ford," applied to the action of the 18th, is really incorrect. The ford near which the action took place is Mitchell's, Blackburn's being a mile or more lower down the stream. But as the reports all give the name of the ford as Blackburn's, it is hardly worth while to correct the error. It is precisely like that which has given the name of the "Battle of Bunker's Hill" to the fight on Breed's Hill. This skirmish was wholly unimportant, though at the time much was made of it. The losses on both sides are given from official sources. Beauregard says that upon "a cursory examination" of one part of the field, "sixty-four corpses" of the Federals "were found and buried." But this statement is clearly erroneous.

PATTERSON AND JOHNSTON.—"About one o'clock on the morning of the 18th I received from the government a telegraphic dispatch, informing me that the Northern army was advancing upon Manassas. . . . The best service which the Army of the Potomac could render was to prevent the defeat of that of the Potomac. To be able to do this, it was necessary, in the first instance, to defeat General Patterson or to elude him. The latter course was most speedy and certain, and was therefore adopted. Our sick, nearly 1700 in number, were provided for in Winchester. For the defense of that place the militia of Generals Carson and Meem seemed ample; for I thought it certain that General Patterson would follow my movement as soon as he discerned it. Evading him by the disposition made of the advance guard under Colonel Stuart, the army moved through Ashby's Gap to Piedmont, a station on the Manassas Gap Railroad. Hence the infantry were to be transported by the railway, while the cavalry and artillery were ordered to continue their march. I reached Manassas about noon on the 20th." [Here follows a list of the troops with him, amounting to a little more than nine regiments, 6000 men, as stated by Beauregard.] "The president of the railroad company had assured me that the remaining troops" [elsewhere stated at 5000 men] "should arrive during the day. . . . I regarded the arrival of the remainder during the night as certain, and Patterson's, with the Grand Army, on the 22d as probable."—*Johnston's Report*.

Patterson, at a public dinner on the 16th of November, made a speech, explaining and vindicating his conduct. The following are the essential points, as given in the newspapers of the day. On the 12th of July he wrote to General Scott, proposing to go to Harper's Ferry and Charleston, and asking when Manassas would be attacked; he was informed that the attack would be on the 16th. On the 13th he was directed, "If not strong enough to beat the enemy early next week, make demonstrations to detain him in the valley of Winchester." He made the demonstrations, and, on the 16th, drove the enemy's pickets into the intrenchments at Winchester. Three days before he had written to General Scott, informing him that Johnston was in a position to have his strength doubled, and asked for instructions; but none came. On the 17th Scott telegraphed, "To-morrow the Junction will probably be carried." He supposed that he had detained Johnston the appointed time, and that the work of his column was done. On the 18th, at half past one in the morning, he telegraphed and asked, "Shall I attack?" but received no reply. He expected to be attacked where he was [Johnston was then on the point of setting out to join Beauregard]; and if Manassas was not to be attacked on that day, "he ought to have been ordered down forthwith to join in the battle, and the attack delayed until he came. He could have been there on the day the battle was fought, and his assistance might have produced a different result." On the 20th he heard that Johnston had marched with 35,000 Confederates and a large artillery force in a southeasterly direction. [This must have been at about the hour when Johnston reached Manassas, whither he had marched with a little more than 11,000 men.] He telegraphed the information to General Scott, and knew that the message was received the same day. In accordance with instructions, he came to Harper's Ferry on the 21st.—In a letter written on that day from Harper's Ferry, General Patterson states, "I could have turned Johnston's position, and have attacked him in the rear; but he had received large re-enforcements from Mississippi, Alabama, and Georgia, a total force of over 35,000 Confederate troops and 5000 Virginia militia. My force is less than 20,000—nineteen regiments, whose term of service was up, or will be within a week. All refused to stay one hour over their time but four. Five regiments have gone home; two more go to-day; and three more to-morrow. To avoid being cut off, I fell back and occupied this place." At the time when Patterson with his 20,000 men was expecting to be attacked and cut off, the Confederates had near him only the Virginia militia, about 6000, and the 1700 sick at Winchester. All the others were then either at or near Manassas. Johnston had thus completely deceived Patterson both as to the number and position of his army.

THE FORCES.—"McDowell's army at Centreville numbered within a fraction of 30,000, with 55 pieces of artillery" [of these, six pieces, belonging to the New York Eighth, were thrown out of service, leaving 49 pieces.—*Report of Major Barry, Chief of Artillery*]. "A Pennsylvania regiment and a New York artillery company were discharged on the evening of the 20th, which, with the sick, reduced the effectives to about 28,000."—*Report of Major Barnard, Chief of Engineers.*

Beauregard, having mentioned that General Holmes had been directed to push forward his brigade from Fredericksburg, and that Hampton's legion of six companies of infantry, having arrived that morning by the cars from Richmond, was subsequently, as soon as it arrived, ordered forward," proceeds to give the following summary of his force: "The effective force of all arms of the Army of the Potomac on that eventful morning, including the garrison at Camp Pickens, did not exceed 21,833, and 29 guns. The Army of the Shenandoah ready for action on the field may be set down at 6000 men and 20 guns—that is, when the battle began; Smith's brigade and Fisher's North Carolina came up later, and made the total of the Army of the Shenandoah engaged, of all arms, 8334. Hill's Virginia regiment, 550, also arrived, but was posted as a reserve to the right flank. The brigades of General Holmes mustered 1265 bayonets, 6 guns, and a company of cavalry about 90 strong." It is not quite clear, from the foregoing statement, whether Beauregard includes Holmes's and Hampton's forces in the Army of the Potomac. We have assumed that they were included, making the entire Confederate force 31,000 effective men. If they are not included, the Confederate force would be raised to about 33,000.

A considerable part of the force on either side was not brought into actual service at any stage of the action. The battle presented three distinct periods, the precise time of which can not be given with absolute precision. As a general rule, the Confederate reports place them about half an hour earlier than those of the Federals. The exact moment is of little consequence. We give the time only by approximation. These periods are, *First*, The fight in the morning, from 10½ to 12, when the Confederates were repulsed. *Second*, The Confederate stand on the plateau from 12 to 3. *Third*, The advance of the Confederates and the rout of the Federals, from 3 to 4. The following is a statement of the forces actually engaged at each of these periods, gathered from the official reports on both sides. In all cases where actual numbers are furnished in the reports, these are given. In other cases, a "regiment" is assumed to have consisted of 750 effective men, and a "company," whether of artillery, cavalry, or infantry, of 75. Some were stronger and some weaker; but this is the average. The numbers given are those with which the regiments went into action; the losses at the several periods were so nearly equal as not materially to vary the general result.

1. *The Fight in the Morning.*

The Confederate force actually engaged consisted of Bee's brigade ["2732 bayonets," *Beauregard*, besides officers and artillery], 3000 men, and 11 companies of Evans's, with artillery, 900 men —in all, about 3900. The Federals actually engaged consisted of Burnside's brigade, four regiments, with two companies of artillery—3200 men in all, and Sykes's eight companies of regulars, 600 strong, together making 3800 men. Porter's artillery had begun to play upon the Confederates; his infantry regiments were also coming upon the field, when the Confederates broke. Sherman's brigade just then appeared, and aided in the repulse, when the Confederates, wholly outnumbered, fell back in confusion upon the plateau.

2. *The Confederate Stand on the Plateau.*

The Confederates, consisting of Bee's brigade, 3000 strong, and Evans's whole half brigade, 1300, fell back in confusion upon the plateau, where they met Hampton's legion, six companies, and Jackson's brigade ["2611 strong," *Beauregard*, besides artillery], about 2800—in all, about 7500 men were the forces on the plateau at the moment when Johnston and Beauregard came up. They were almost immediately followed by Smith's battalion of the Virginia Forty-ninth, and seven companies from Hunter's Virginia Eighth, ordered up from Cocke, and two additional regiments of the Army of the Shenandoah—Falkner's Second Mississippi and Fisher's North Carolina—which had just come up, 2500 men in all. The entire force which held the plateau was thus about 10,000, from which the losses must be deducted. Beauregard indeed says, after having enumerated all these regiments, "Confronting the enemy at this time my force numbered at most not more than 6500 infantry and artillerists, with but thirteen pieces of artillery and two companies of cavalry. . . . . The enemy's force, now bearing confidently down on our position, consisted of over 20,000 infantry, seven companies of regular cavalry, and 24 pieces of improved artillery." This is but a part of Beauregard's studious system of understating his own force, and overstating that of his opponents. The entire Federal force which crossed the Run was but 18,000; of these, at that moment, Burnside's brigade, with the exception of one regiment, was withdrawn, and Howard's brigade had not crossed the Run. These brigades numbered fully 5000, so that there remain but 13,000 Federals then "bearing down" upon the Confederate position; and these, according to Barnard, "were in a single column, strung along over several miles of road."—Johnston's report here furnishes additional means for correcting the error of Beauregard. Speaking of the time before the arrival of Fisher and Falkner, he says: "We had now 16 guns and 260 cavalry, and a little above nine regiments of the Army of the Shenandoah, and six guns and less than the strength of three regiments of that of the Potomac, engaged with about 35,000 United States troops, among whom were full 3000 men of the old regular army." Johnston here gives the Confederate force accurately, 12 regiments, equal to 9000 men, and 22 guns. He, however, more than doubles the Federal force.

3. *The Confederate Advance and the Federal Rout.*

Beauregard says: "By this time, between half past two and three o'clock P.M., our re-enforcements, pushed forward and directed by General Johnston to the required quarter, were at hand, just as I had ordered forward to a second effort for the recovery of the disputed plateau the whole line, including my reserves, which at this crisis of the battle I felt called upon to lead in person. The attack was general, and was shared in by every regiment then in the field." After enumerating the new re-enforcements, with less particularity than is done by Johnston, whose report we follow, he says: "About the same time, at three o'clock P.M., Brigadier General E. K. Smith, with some 1700 infantry of Elzey's brigade of the Army of the Shenandoah, and Beckham's battery, came upon the field from Camp Pickens, Manassas, where they had arrived by railroad at noon." This was the last re-enforcement; and the two reports enable us to give the number of the Confederates on the field, all of whom were in action at the time of the rout. These consisted of the 6000 men of the Army of the Shenandoah originally engaged; Evans's half brigade, 1300; Hampton's legion, 400; Kirby Smith's, 1700—9400 specially enumerated; with the following regiments of infantry, of which the numbers are not stated: Fisher's North Carolina, Falkner's Mississippi, of the Army of the Shenandoah; Cash's and Kershaw's, from Bonham's brigade; Cocke's whole brigade of five regiments; and Early's brigade of three regiments—in all, twelve regiments, equal to 9000 men, making 18,400 infantry. There is some obscurity in the enumeration of the cavalry and artillery; but at least ten companies are specially mentioned as engaged, which brings the entire Confederate force actually on the plateau at the time of the rout to a little more than 19,000 men. The remaining 11,000 (or perhaps 13,000) men not actually engaged consisted of Holmes's, Ewell's, Jones's, Longstreet's, and a part of Bonham's brigades.

The Federal forces engaged, or in a position to be brought into action at the time of the rout, consisted, as stated in the text, of the 18,000 who crossed the Run, deducting Keyes's brigade of 2500, and an equal number of Burnside's brigade—5000 in all, leaving 13,000 at that moment on the field.

THE ZOUAVES.—"The evanescent courage of the Zouaves prompted them to fire perhaps a hundred shots, when they broke and fled, leaving the batteries open to a charge of the enemy's cavalry, which took place immediately."—*Porter's Report*. "As soon as the Zouaves came up, I led them forward against an Alabama regiment partly concealed in a clump of small pines in an old field. At the first fire they broke and fled to the rear, keeping up a desultory firing over the heads of their comrades in front; at the same moment they were charged by a company of secession cavalry on their rear, who came by a road through two strips of wood on our extreme right. The fire of the Zouaves killed four and wounded one, dispersing them. The discomfiture of this cavalry was completed by a fire from Captain Collum's company of United States cavalry, which killed and wounded several men. Colonel Farnham, with some of his officers and men, behaved gallantly, but the regiment of Zouaves, as a regiment, did not appear again on the field. Many of the men joined other regiments, and did good service as skirmishers. . . . Since the retreat more than three fourths of the Zouaves have disappeared."—*Heintzelman's Report*. "The new position [of Griffin's and Ricketts's batteries] had scarcely been occupied when a troop of the enemy's cavalry, debouching from a piece of wood close upon our right flank, charged down upon the New York Eleventh. The Zouaves, catching sight of the cavalry a few minutes before they were upon them, broke ranks to such a degree that the cavalry dashed through them without doing them much harm. The Zouaves gave them a scattering fire as they passed, which emptied five saddles and killed three horses. A few minutes afterward a regiment of the enemy's infantry presented itself in line at not more than 60 or 70 yards' distance, and delivered a volley full upon the batteries and their supports. The Eleventh and Fourteenth regiments instantly broke and fled in confusion to the rear, and refused to rally and return to the support of the batteries."—*Barry's Report.*

THE ROUT.—The completeness of the rout is testified to in almost all the reports of the Federal commanders. *McDowell* says: "This soon degenerated into disorder, for which there was no remedy. Every effort was made to rally them, even beyond the reach of the enemy's fire, but in vain. The battalion of regular infantry alone moved up the hill, and there maintained itself until our men could get down to and across the Warrenton turnpike. The plain was covered with the retreating troops, and they seemed to infect those with whom they came in contact. The retreat soon became a rout, and this soon degenerated still farther into a panic. . . . . I gave the necessary orders to protect their withdrawal, begging the men to form in line, and offer at least the appearance of organization. . . . . Once on the road, and the different corps coming together in small parties, many without officers, they became intermingled, and all organization was lost. . . . . In the panic [at the crossing of Cub Run] the horses hauling the caissons and ammunition were cut from their traces by persons to escape with, and in this way much confusion was caused, the panic aggravated, and the road encumbered. . . . . By sundown most of our men had got beyond Centreville ridge, and it became a question whether we should or not endeavor to make a stand there. . . . . The utter disorganization and demoralization of the mass of the army seemed, to all who were near enough to be consulted, to admit no alternative but to fall back. . . . . On sending the officers of the staff to the different camps, they found that our decision had been anticipated by the troops, most of those who had come in from the front being already on the road to the rear, the panic with which they came in still continuing, and hurrying them along."

Porter says: "The slopes behind us were swarming with our retreating and disorganized forces, while riderless horses and artillery teams ran furiously through the flying crowd. All farther efforts were futile. The words, gestures, and threats of our officers were thrown away upon men who had lost all presence of mind, and only longed for absence of body. . . . . The rear-guard [mainly Sykes's regulars] followed our panic-stricken troops to Centreville, resisting the attacks of the rebel cavalry and artillery, and saving them from the inevitable destruction which awaited them had not this body been interposed."

Heintzelman says: "Soon after the firing commenced, the Brooklyn Fourteenth broke and ran. I considered it useless to attempt to rally them. The want of discipline in these regiments was so great that the most of the men would run from fifty to several hundred yards in the rear, and continue to fire—fortunately for the braver ones—very high in the air, and compelling those in front to retreat. . . . Finding it impossible to rally any of the regiments, we commenced our retreat at about half past four P.M. There was a fine position a short distance in the rear, where I hoped to make a stand with a section of Arnold's battery and the United States cavalry, if I could rally a few regiments of infantry. In this I utterly failed, and we continued our retreat on the road we had advanced on in the morning. I sent forward my staff officers to rally some troops beyond the Run, but not a company would form. . . . Such a rout I never witnessed before. No efforts could induce a single regiment to form after the retreat had commenced."

McClellan says: "I assumed command of the troops in the vicinity of Washington on Saturday, July 27th, 1861, six days after the battle of Bull Run. I found no army to command; a mere collection of regiments, cowering on the banks of the Potomac, some perfectly raw, others dispirited by the recent defeat. . . . The city was almost in a condition to have been taken by a dash of cavalry."

THE PURSUIT.—"Early's brigade, etc., pursued the now panic-stricken, fugitive enemy. Stuart, with his cavalry, and Beckham, had also taken up the pursuit along the road by which the enemy had come upon the field in the morning; but, soon encumbered by prisoners who thronged the way, the former was unable to attack the mass of fast-fleeing, fugitive Federalists. Withers's, Preston's, Cash's, and Kershaw's regiments, Hampton's legion, and Kemper's battery, also pursued along the Warrenton road by the Stone Bridge, the enemy having opportunely opened a way for them through the heavy abattis which my troops had made on the west side of the bridge several days before; but this pursuit was soon recalled. . . . Colonel Radford, with six companies of Virginia cavalry, was ordered to cross Bull Run, and attack the enemy from the direction of the Lewis house. In the immediate vicinity of the Suspension Bridge [over Cub Run] he charged a battery with great gallantry, took Colonel Corcoran, of the 69th New York, prisoner, and captured the colors of that regiment. . . . Lieutenant Munford also led some companies of cavalry in hot pursuit, and captured prisoners, cannon, etc., abandoned in the flight."—*Beauregard's Report*. "Stuart pressed the pursuit of the enemy's principal line of retreat, the Sudley road. Four companies of cavalry, under Radford and Munford, were ordered to cross the stream to reach the turnpike, the line of retreat of the enemy's left. Our cavalry found the roads encumbered with dead and wounded (many of whom seemed to have been thrown from wagons), arms, accoutrements, and clothing. . . . Instructions were sent to Bonham to march by the quickest route to intercept the fugitives; and to Longstreet to follow as closely as possible upon the right. Their progress was checked by the enemy's reserve, and by night at Centreville."—*Johnston's Report*.

"The order [to take up a position in front of Centreville] was executed with great difficulty, as the road was nearly choked up by retreating baggage-wagons of several divisions, and by the vast number of flying soldiers belonging to various regiments. . . . Nevertheless, I was enabled to take a position which would prevent the advance of the enemy, and protect the retreat of the army. . . . The retreat of great numbers of flying soldiers continued until nine o'clock in the evening, the great majority in wild confusion, and but few in collected bodies. Soon afterward several squadrons of the enemy's cavalry advanced along the road, and appeared before the outposts. . . . . The skirmishers fired, when the enemy turned around, leaving several killed and wounded on the spot. Afterward we were several times molested from various sides by the enemy's cavalry. At about midnight, the command to leave the position and march to Washington was given by General McDowell."—*Blenker's Report*.

GEORGE B. McCLELLAN.

CHAPTER IV.

THE ARMY OF THE POTOMAC.—BALL'S BLUFF.

The new Army.—Its Organization.—General McClellan.—Difficulties in his Way.—The *Materiel* of War.—Fortifications about Washington.—Popular impression as to the early close of the War.—McClellan's Memorandum addressed to the President.—His Estimate of the Force requisite for an aggressive Campaign.—Operations during the Summer and Autumn.—Reconnoissance toward Lewinsville.—Evacuation of Munson's Hill by the Confederates.—Confederate Batteries at Matthias Point.—Blockade of the Lower Potomac.—Operations on the Upper Potomac.—Position of Forces.—Confederate Occupation of Leesburg.—McCall's Advance to Drainesville.—Ashby's Raid on Harper's Ferry.—Devens's Reconnoissance toward Leesburg.—The Battle of Ball's Bluff.—Death of Baker.—The Defeat and Slaughter of the Federals.—Cause of the Disaster.—The Confederate Army in Virginia.—Ord's Advance to Drainesville.—Object of the Movement.—McCall's Division.—The March.—The Enemy flanked.—His Retreat.—Losses.

THE battle of Bull Run had been lost. The enemy had not improved his opportunity against our panic-stricken capital; no victory gained in the war was more fruitless of benefit to the victors, and to the vanquished there could have been no success more fortunate, on the whole, than was their defeat. The battle had been a test-battle for a continent that for three generations had been nursed in peace—a test-battle both for the North and South, it is true, but, as usually happens in such a case, the former, whose strength had been broken, learned the lesson, while the latter, blinded by temporary and easily-won success, became over-confident, and saw in the Federal rout of July only a magnificent illustration of the martial superiority of Southern chivalry. Thus it happened that while the South relaxed its strength, the muscular North contracted and prepared to strike blows. The great uprising in April had brought to the capital a vast assemblage of *militia;* and these, not waiting for the mature results of discipline, but pushed on by the incessant clamor of people and press, had shouldered arms, to which the majority of them were unused, and marched forth of a hot summer's day to meet the defiant foe beyond Centreville, very much as the same number of men would have gone to a picnic or a fancy tournament, and with not half the regularity that would have marked an ordinary training day; and this mock army had been swept from the field, disorganized and useless. Following upon this disaster came a second uprising, which gave us, at length, an army of *soldiers.*

But this was the work of time, and it was also a work of great difficulty. Perhaps the chief obstacle in the way of such a military organization as was required was the habitual predisposition of the people to peaceful occupations. Among the many shrewd sayings of Lord Bacon was this: that a nation devoted to the minute operations of mechanism and to lucrative commerce is the least likely, of all others, to be martially disposed. In addition to this we were a republic, and there was no distinction of classes, as between the ruling and the ruled, and thus none of that subserviency of one class to another which leads naturally to military subordination and discipline. It was an easy matter for Congress to vote and to raise half a million of men. But the manner in which recruiting was carried on introduced into this body an absolutely worthless element. Officers were appointed at the head of regiments as the reward for filling up their ranks, and the motives to deception were too powerful to be resisted; sometimes one third of a regiment which had been mustered into the army was found, upon inspection, to be unfit for active service. Here was one difficulty. But if there was a large class of "incapables" among the privates, there was a still larger class in proportion among the officers, who, for the most part, had no military knowledge whatever. This was the kind of army which displaced the armed

crowd of the summer campaign; this was the army which, at a week's notice, rushed to the protection of the capital; but it was not the kind of army that could carry on a campaign—that could stand reverses or bear success. There was not a sufficiently large force of the regular army to form a respectable nucleus about which this crude mass might be gathered and organized. The army that was needed had to be *made*, and it must be made out of unpromising material.

But who was to transform this half million of men into good and trustworthy soldiers? We had one general—Winfield Scott—who had been tried, and in whom the country had great confidence. But he was infirm, and had arrived at that period of life when it was beyond his power to endure the fatiguing duties that must inevitably fall upon the commander of so large an army. He himself, aware of this, although unwilling wholly to disengage himself from the struggle, suggested that another be placed at the helm, he himself retaining a general oversight of operations. For this important office he proposed General George B. McClellan.

The campaigns in West Virginia in the summer of 1861 contrasted most favorably with the operations carried on at the same time in the eastern part of the state. The topography of West Virginia presented a very great obstacle to military operations; but these difficulties existed in a greater degree for the Confederates than for ourselves, inasmuch as we had the advantage—in this case a decisive one—of having the surrounding people on our side. The attempts, therefore, which were made by Garnett and his fellow-officers to occupy this mountainous region were thwarted, without any great sacrifice except the labor involved in arduous marches, and somewhat more than the ordinary exposure that belongs of necessity to a soldier's life. However strongly the enemy might be fortified, he had always a long line of communication to protect, and, by simply cutting this line, he would always be compelled to risk the chances of battle, in which the advantages were mostly in our favor. The campaign was wisely planned in every part, and McClellan was unusually fortunate in the vigorous support given him by Rosecrans. Nor does the fact that the commander himself was not always personally present on the field of conflict at all diminish the credit due to the military skill which planned and controlled the battle. The good degree of military sagacity developed in these battles, and the rapidity with which one victory followed upon the heels of another, at a time when the whole country was impatient for activity, brought McClellan into a prominence which he enjoyed without a rival. Another quality, more characteristic of McClellan than of any other general, and one which was more than all others calculated to make him the centre of popular attraction, was his extraordinary capability of creating enthusiasm in his army. This enthusiasm was of no ordinary character, but rather a sort of inspiration, by which the troops became identified with their leader, a part and parcel of his personal ambition and destiny as well as of his military operations. It was not a simple, frank outburst of admiration, but it was personal sympathy, fervent devotion. Fortunate beyond the usual estimate put upon them were all these characteristics, and they doubtless had great weight with General Scott; but with the lieutenant general there was another consideration of at least equal importance—McClellan, having been from the first scrupulously jealous of what the Southern states deemed to be their rights, would be likely to conciliate the South, if conciliation were yet possible, and his appointment would unite the country by bringing even the pro-slavery party of the North over to the support of the war, whereas the appointment of a member of the Republican party, as it seemed to Scott, would provoke the enemy to a more determined resistance and distract our counsels at home. But there was a greater danger which was not foreseen, viz., the possibility, nay, the almost inevitable certainty of disagreement between a general and an administration representing sentiments radically opposite to his own; and the jealousies growing out of this opposition in sentiment lost us many a battle and many an opportunity of bringing the war to a speedy termination. These troubles were, however, in the background, and it will not be necessary to consider their origin and development until we come to treat of the Peninsular Campaign of 1862.

In the mean time, the difficulties which McClellan had to encounter and overcome at the outset, and before any active operations could be attempted, were very great and numerous. Some of these we have indicated in connection with the raw material which was given him to make into an army. This particular class of difficulties McClellan looked directly in the face, and it is probable that so great a number of men were never in so short a space of time organized into an efficient army. In this organization the regiment was the unit. Four regiments constituted a brigade, and three brigades a division. Each division had four batteries, three served by volunteers and one by regulars, the captain of the latter commanding the entire artillery of the division. The regulars were not distributed, but were kept together in divisions by themselves. In the constitution of this army, McClellan's intimate acquaintance with European tactics became of very great value and assistance. The result was perhaps not an equivalent to the Southern army in some important respects, for the latter entered more naturally into military organization; the officers were men accustomed to rule, the men to be ruled, and the existence of slavery in the South had always necessitated a very near approach to martial law as the ordinary status of society.

But soldiers are only the muscular basis of an army; it is the mechanical appliances of war that give an army availability and multiply its power. These appliances are of two sorts, offensive and defensive. And here again the difficulty did not consist in obtaining the raw material or a sufficient supply of money, but in elaborate construction, requiring the tedious labor of months. As Congress could vote half a million of men, so it could vote

INTERIOR OF THE UPPER BATTERY AT CHAIN BRIDGE, WASHINGTON.

half a thousand millions of dollars; but it could no more easily metamorphose money into muskets, cannon, and pontoon bridges than raw militia into soldiers. If we consider merely the amount of food necessary to five hundred thousand men, it sums up in the short space of one week to nearly three million pounds of meat and four millions of flour, besides three hundred and fifty thousand pounds of coffee and five hundred and twenty-five thousand pounds of sugar. The systematic regulation of this enormous supply presupposes arrangements the most complicate in advertisement of proposals, in shipment and transportation, and finally in distribution. Then the arrangements for equipments and munitions required still more time for their completion. The number of small arms at the disposal of the government was fearfully inadequate. These had either to be manufactured in this country or imported. The Springfield armory and that at Harper's Ferry were the principal sources of the home supply at the beginning of the war, and the latter of these had been destroyed in April. There were not enough muskets in the North to supply the 75,000 men of the President's first call. Even the Springfield armory could furnish no more than 25,000 per year. Evidently, then, new armories had to be set in operation, and those already existing enlarged, while in the mean time the most strenuous efforts were made to secure a foreign supply. Not only was the quantity of small arms necessary to carry on an extensive campaign slowly produced, but there was an equal impediment in the way of promptly furnishing heavy artillery.

The very tents of the soldiers taxed all the sail-makers of the country to the utmost extent of their working powers. Wagons, and harness, and cavalry equipments of every sort existed only in the raw material, and slowly advanced out of this primitive form under the manufacturer's busy hand. The industrial activity of the North was thoroughly aroused to meet the

sudden and pressing demand; all that could be done quickly was done. But skill is the result of experience; it does not spring up at any momentary emergency; and, therefore, all work requiring a great degree of mechanical elaboration was of slow completion; and the number of laborers fitted for such work being insufficient, others must be trained before they could be of any efficiency.

Not only must there be a vast increase of *materiel* for offensive warfare, but the disorganization of the army after its defeat at Bull Run made it necessary to surround Washington with defensive works of great strength. This was partially begun on the occasion of our first advance into Virginia and the occupation of Alexandria, when Forts Runyon and Corcoran were constructed as *têtes-de-pont* to the Long Bridge and the Aqueduct. A fortnight afterward Fort Albany was laid out, commanding the Columbia and the Aqueduct and Alexandria roads. After McClellan assumed command of the Army of the Potomac, the interval between Fort Corcoran and Fort Albany was filled by a series of works within supporting distance of each other; and strong works were built controlling the principal routes leading to Washington from the north. Thus was established the basis of an adequate fortification for the defense of the capital; but to complete the works so far as to justify any great depletion of the army in front of Washington for the purposes of an offensive campaign was the work of months.[1]

---

[1] "The theory of these defenses is that upon which the works of Torres Vedras were based—the only one admitted at the present day for defending extensive lines. It is to occupy the commanding points within range of each other by field-forts, the fire of which shall sweep all the approaches. These forts furnish the secure emplacements of artillery. They also afford cover to bodies of infantry. The works may be connected by lines of light parapets, or the ground (where practicable) may be so obstructed that the enemy's troops can not penetrate the interval without being exposed, for a considerable time, to the destructive effects of the artillery or musketry fire of the forts.

"With such a system established, the defense against a powerful attack requires that all the

INTERIOR OF FORT RUNYON.

FORT CORCORAN, ARLINGTON HEIGHTS.

In the face of all these impediments, it was the popular impression that the war would be, by great victories gained on the field, brought to completion in two or three months. Besides, there were a few who supposed that our immense and formidable preparations would intimidate the South, and obviate the very necessity of fighting. But the South was not intimidated. She herself voted 500,000 men, and brought a large proportion of that number into the field, partly by volunteering, and in great measure by conscription. Then it was apparent to every military eye that the whole strength of the two sections must meet, and that the side to yield would be that which was more rapidly exhausted. It was also evident that the preliminary preparations in the matter of organization must be thoroughly completed before a campaign could be ventured against an enemy whose force, though not equal to our own in point of numbers, had a great advantage in position, being situated at the centre of an arc along whose circumference it would be necessary for us to operate in any aggressive movement. The popular impression, however, as to the early termination of the war still remained; indeed, a shorter time elapsed before the date which had been set for a final settlement than would have sufficed for our army to learn how to build a pontoon bridge.

The season suitable for active operations previous to the winter of 1861 passed by without any important movement. In a memorandum addressed to the President early in August of that year, McClellan expressed his convictions in regard to the nature of the coming campaign in the most explicit terms. Having stated that the war differed from all others in this respect, viz., that in ordinary wars the purpose was simply to conquer a peace and make a treaty on advantageous terms, while in this it was necessary to crush a population sufficiently numerous, intelligent, and warlike to constitute a nation, he proceeded to urge the necessity for an overwhelming display of physical force. Our foreign relations and financial credit, he said, demanded that the military action of the government should be prompt and irresistible. The plan of operations which he advised was the following:

The rebels having made Virginia their main field of operations, it was therefore necessary that the great conflict should take place in that state. But, to weaken the resistance at this point, movements should be made both by land and water in other directions, and especially in the West, upon the Mississippi, and, as soon as Kentucky was sufficiently cordial in her loyalty, through that state into Eastern Tennessee. These separate and co-operative movements would not require a very large force; but for the main

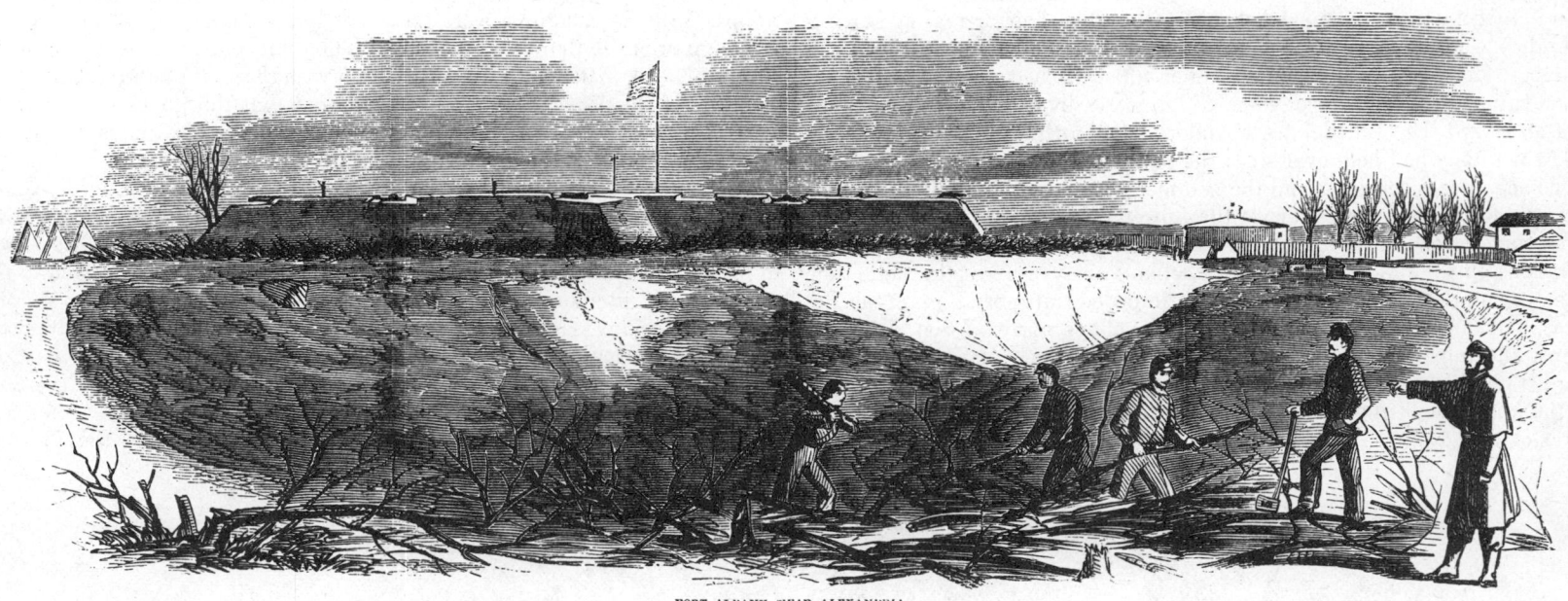

FORT ALBANY, NEAR ALEXANDRIA.

army—that of the Potomac—he urged a force of 273,000 men, to be supplied with the necessary engineer and pontoon trains and transportation. In direct co-operation with this force, a strong naval armament should be prepared to move against important points along the enemy's sea-coast. As an argument in favor of so large an army in the East, he suggested that the capture of Richmond was only the first step into the enemy's country; and as every successful advance lengthened our line of communications, large detachments of force would be necessary to protect that line, while the enemy, at every withdrawal, would be able to make a greater concentration of his own forces.

Undoubtedly, in his proposed distribution of forces, McClellan underrated the difficulties of the Western campaign. At least, it soon became evident

that to subdue the Confederates in Kentucky and Missouri alone required a force much larger than McClellan considered necessary for an advance into East Tennessee.

This memorandum was addressed to the President, at his own request, within two weeks after the battle of Bull Run. Three months afterward, in the latter part of October, there being a strong desire on the part of the country and the President for an immediate advance of the Army of the Potomac, McClellan made another statement to the President, representing the force available for an advance movement as only about 76,000 men, while that of the enemy behind intrenched fortifications was fully 150,000. It is true there was present for duty a force of 147,000 men, but over 13,000 of these were either unarmed or unequipped. Out of the 134,000 left, 58,000 must remain to protect Washington, to guard the Potomac, and to garrison Baltimore and Annapolis, leaving only 76,000 for the aggressive movement against Richmond.

In order to an advance, McClellan thought that 35,000 men should be left to protect Washington, 13,000 to guard the Potomac, 10,000 to garrison Baltimore and Annapolis, while there should be a column of 150,000 for active operations. This would require an aggregate, present and absent, of 240,000 men. As to the force of the enemy at Manassas, McClellan was no

forts shall be garrisoned; that a certain amount of infantry, cavalry, and movable artillery be distributed along the lines sufficient to hold them until reserves can be brought to support; and, finally, it requires a movable force held as a reserve, which may be shifted from point to point, to meet the enemy's effort wherever it may be made, and where, aided by the works, they can repel superior numbers.

"It is evident that *without* fortifications a place can not be considered secure unless held by considerably *greater* numbers than the enemy can bring to assail it. No less an authority than Napoleon says that, aided by fortifications, 50,000 men and 3000 artillerymen can defend a capital against 300,000 men, and he asserts the necessity of fortifying all national capitals."—*General Barnard's Report*, p. 12.

MUNSON'S HILL.

doubt egregiously mistaken. His information was gathered from unreliable sources, and any reports that militated against his preconceived opinions he summarily rejected. There is no good reason to believe that the enemy at Manassas numbered over 50,000 men; for even at a later period, when their ranks had been re-enforced by conscription, they were estimated at only about 80,000.

Thus so far as the main operations against Richmond were concerned. But the army was not idle during the summer. Reconnoitring parties were continually scouring the country to within a short distance of the enemy's lines. Frequently these reconnoissances resulted in skirmishes, which accustomed the soldiers to being under fire. One of the most important of those which occurred during the summer was that made by General Smith, on the 25th of September, toward Lewinsville. The general had several thousand troops in his command, and, shortly after their arrival at Lewinsville, they were attacked by a large force of the Confederates from Falls Church. The result of the sharp conflict which ensued was the retreat of the enemy and the capture of some of his stores by General Smith. Two days afterward the Confederates abandoned the fortifications on Munson's Hill, which they had held ever since the battle of Bull Run.

The enemy was active during the summer and autumn chiefly in two directions—to prevent navigation on the Lower Potomac, and to find his way across some of the fords of the Upper Potomac into Maryland; and these operations on the right and left of McClellan's army were at the same time offensive and defensive, as they not only impeded transportation on the Potomac, and threatened raids into the fertile valleys north of that river and against the important line of the Baltimore and Ohio Railroad, but also guarded either flank of the Confederate army at Manassas. Preparations for the blockade of the Lower Potomac were commenced previous to the battle of Bull Run. The Secretary of the Navy was not uninformed of

these movements, and as early as June suggested to the War Department the necessity of occupying Matthias Point, the possession of which in force would secure the navigation of the river from the threatened interruption, and at the same time furnish a foothold on the Virginia shore for operations against the enemy's right flank. The extreme left of the Federal army, in the neighborhood of Alexandria, was not more than five or six miles above a line run directly east from Manassas Junction, which was distant twenty-five miles. From Alexandria the Potomac runs almost directly south to the mouth of Acquia Creek, a distance of thirty miles; then it runs directly east for fifteen miles, where it rounds Matthias Point—a very prominent projection northward into the stream, and almost entirely separated from the main land by Gamble's Creek. It was a point which, at that early period of the war, might easily have been held by a small detachment of troops. But no measures were taken for its occupation by General Scott. His suggestions to the War Department being unheeded, the Secretary of the Navy took the matter into his own hands with the best material at his command. At this time, it must be remembered that the government had no gun-boats or iron-clad monitors, and the engagement of batteries by wooden ships of war were serious undertakings, in which the batteries had clearly the advantage. The United States steamers the Pawnee and the Pocahontas, and a naval flotilla under Commander Ward, with several steam-boats under naval officers, constituted the Potomac squadron, whose office it was to prevent communication with that part of Virginia which belonged to the Confederacy, intercepting supplies, and protecting transports and supply-vessels in their passage up and down the river. Commander Ward having discovered, by means of a reconnoissance off Matthias Point, that the Confederate troops encamped there were about to erect a battery, on the 26th of June sent up to the Pawnee, at Acquia Creek, for two boats armed and equipped. Two small cutters' crews were dispatched from the Pawnee,

CONFEDERATE BATTERIES AT EVANSPORT.

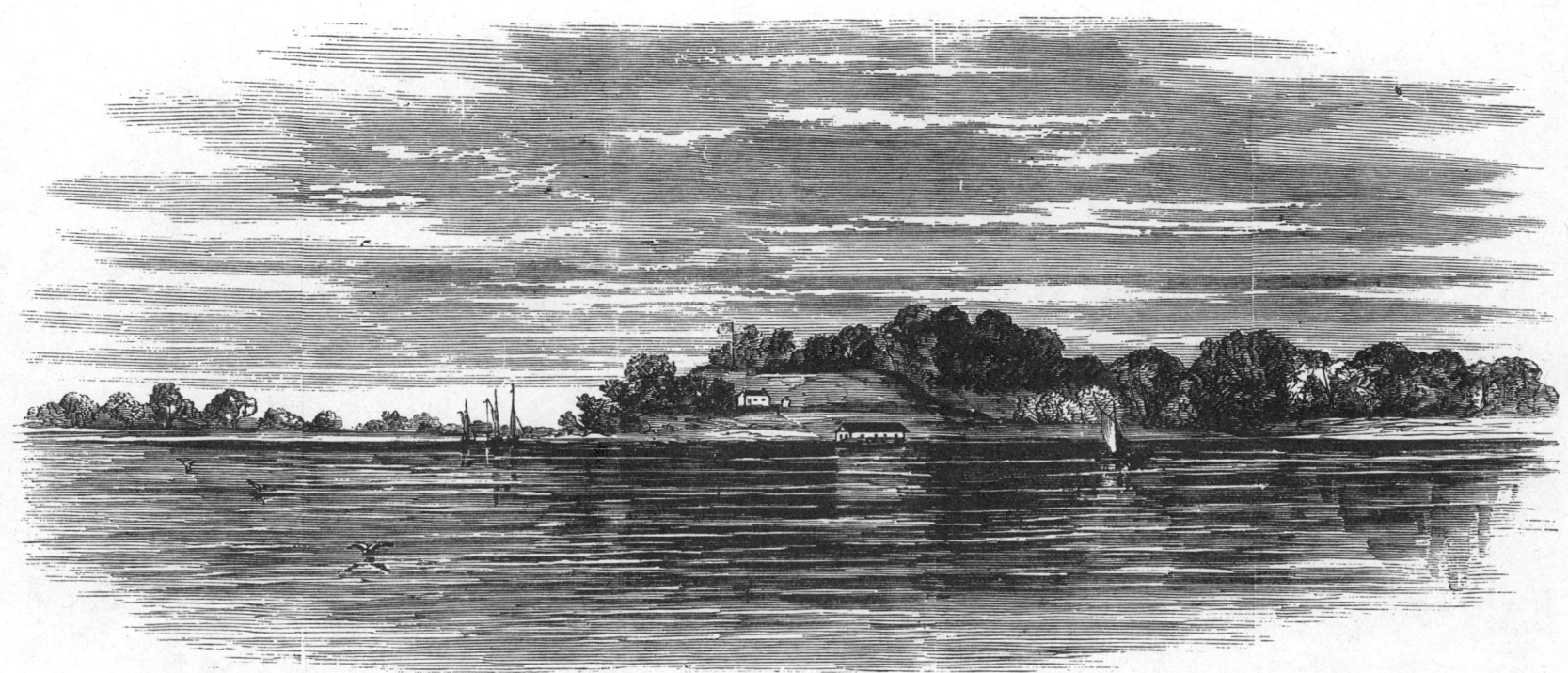

CONFEDERATE BATTERIES AT BUDD'S FERRY, ON THE POTOMAC.

which, with a boat's crew from Ward's vessel—the Freeborn—made between thirty and forty men. This party effected a landing at the Point the next morning, driving in the rebel pickets. They found preparations for erecting a battery, and, under cover of the Freeborn's guns, they proceeded immediately to throw up a sand-bag breast-work, which they completed before night, when, leaving their work in order to bring guns from the vessel to mount them, they were surprised by a party of the enemy concealed in the bushes on the shore; a few of them were taken prisoners, and the rest escaped to the steamer. Commander Ward was killed in the engagement. No Confederate battery, however, was maintained on Matthias Point, it being beyond supporting distance of the main army. In a few weeks the right bank of the Potomac was lined with batteries from High Point to Matthias Point, a distance of from thirty to forty miles. After McClellan assumed the command of the Army of the Potomac, the subject was again brought to the attention of the War Department by Secretary Welles. The President was anxious that something should be done, and in this anxiety he represented the feelings of the Northern people, who deemed it a humiliation that the Confederates should be able to maintain an efficient blockade of one of our principal channels of transportation. The Navy Department threw the responsibility upon the military, and, in return, the military shifted it off upon the naval. In a letter addressed to the Secretary of the Navy on the 12th of August, General McClellan says:

"I have to-day received additional information which convinces me that it is more than probable that the enemy will, within a very short time, attempt to throw a respectable force from the mouth of Acquia Creek into Maryland. This attempt will probably be preceded by the erection of batteries at Matthias and White House Points. Such a movement on the part of the enemy, in connection with others probably designed, would place Washington in great jeopardy. I most earnestly urge that the strongest possible naval force be at once concentrated near the mouth of Acquia Creek, and that the most vigilant watch be maintained day and night, so as to render such passage of the river absolutely impossible. I recommend that the Minnesota, and any other vessels available from Hampton Roads, be at once ordered up there, and that a great quantity of coal be sent to that vicinity sufficient for several weeks' supply. At least one strong war vessel should be kept at Alexandria; and I again urge the concentration of a strong naval force in the Potomac without delay. If the Navy Department will render it absolutely impossible for the enemy to cross the river below Washington, the security of the capital will be greatly increased. I can not too earnestly urge an immediate compliance with these requests." But the measures urged in this letter only looked to the defensive, and seemed quite unsatisfactory. If there was occasion to fear that the enemy's audacious operations on the south bank of the Potomac really threatened an advance into Maryland, which might place Washington in jeopardy, this only seemed to furnish an additional argument in favor of an attempt to dislodge the enemy from his positions. From this view of the case, it was only natural that a great pressure should be brought to bear on McClellan to induce him to co-operate in such an attempt, with as strong a force as might be necessary to secure its success. Really there was no occasion to fear an advance of the enemy from the mouth of Acquia Creek into Maryland; no movement could have been more unwise on the part of the Confederates; and, if it had been made, it is far more probable that the invading column of the enemy would be put in jeopardy than the Federal capital. But there was real occasion to fear that the Potomac might be rendered impassable to Federal vessels; and yet, while McClellan recommended "the strongest possible naval force" to be stationed in the Potomac to guard against a fancied danger, no means were taken to guard against that which was really threatened. The attitude of McClellan in respect to this matter was characteristic of his general policy. So formidable did the force of the enemy seem to him, that he even feared the event of a battle in which he himself should take the defensive, thinking it a matter of doubt, in case General Johnston should advance against him in front, flanking him at the same time by a movement across the Lower Potomac into Maryland, whether he might not be overwhelmed by such superior numbers in his front as to be unable to take care of the flanking column of the enemy, which would march triumphantly into Washington. If he was apprehensive as to the results of an attack, he was naturally far more apprehensive of the result of any movement on his own part which might bring on a general engagement. It was this latter motive which was really the ground of his disinclination to co-operate in any undertaking involving a direct assault upon the enemy's works. His idea of a campaign was that complete preparation ought to be made before any thing should be accomplished, and then to dispose of the enemy by a single decisive victory. It was now scarcely a month since the battle of Bull Run. Hardly any thing had been done as yet toward the re-organization of the army. From their previous impatience of inactivity, the people had gone over to the opposite extreme, and a rash movement now would incur a double measure of condemnation. Without any doubt, therefore, McClellan was both consistent and prudent in his determination not to tempt a general engagement at this time by a movement against the position of the enemy on the right bank of the Potomac. He should also have been firm. But so strong was the feeling of the President and the Secretary of the Navy in favor of the movement, that he vacillated, and made preparations for throwing Hooker's division across the river to carry the Confederate batteries by assault. On one occasion he promised that this force should be ready at an appointed time, and the Navy Department provided the necessary transports, and Captain Craven collected his flotilla together; but when the time came McClellan had changed his mind, and the troops were not on hand. The disappointment was aggravated by the fact that no notification was given that the troops would not be sent. The reason given for this alteration of purpose was, that the troops, according to the opinion of McClellan's engineers, could not be landed with safety. It was replied that the Navy Department would be responsible on that score, and the troops were again promised, and the disappointment was repeated. This led to some ill feeling; and Captain Craven gave up his command very unwisely, on the ground that he would be held responsible for the blockade of the Potomac. McClellan's fault was in his vacillation. He should have been steadfast in his refusal so long as the matter was left to his discretion. His position was thoroughly supported by his corps of engineers. On the 27th of September, General Barnard, chief engineer, in company with Captain Wyman, of the flotilla, made a reconnoissance of the enemy's batteries as far as to Matthias Point. In his report he says: "Batteries at High Point and Cockpit Point, and thence down to Chopawamsic, can not be prevented. We may, indeed, prevent their construction on certain points, but along here, somewhere, the enemy can establish, in spite of us, as many batteries as he chooses. What is the remedy? Favorable circumstances, not to be anticipated, nor made the basis of any calculations, might justify and render successful the attack of a particular battery. To suppose that we can capture all, and by mere attacks of this kind prevent the navigation being molested, is very much the same as to suppose that the hostile army in our own front can prevent us building and maintaining field-works to protect Arlington and Alexandria, by capturing them, one and all, as fast as they are built." In another communication on the subject of crossing troops for the purpose of destroying these batteries, he says: "The operation involves the forcing of a very strong line of defense of the enemy, and all that we would have to do if we were really opening a campaign against them there. It is true, we hope to force this line by turning it at Freestone Point" [a few miles below the mouth of the Occoquan]. "With reason to believe that this may be successful, it can not be denied that it involves a risk of failure. Should we, then, considering all the consequences which may be involved, enter into the operation merely to capture the Potomac batteries? I think not. Will not the Ericsson, assisted by one other gun-boat, capable of keeping alongside these batteries, so far control their fire as to keep the navigation suffi-

THE SEMINOLE AND POCAHONTAS ENGAGING THE CONFEDERATE BATTERIES AT EVANSPORT.

ciently free as long as we require it? Captain Wyman says yes." In the mean time conflicts were every day occurring with the batteries along the bank, but never with any decisive results, and not unfrequently resulting in serious injury to the vessels engaged. We need only refer to a single instance of these conflicts—that in which the Seminole and Pocahontas figured, early in the month of October. These two vessels on this occasion engaged the three batteries at Evansport. The action was commenced by the Seminole, but her fire was not returned until she came within full range of the batteries, which then opened upon her in earnest, striking her in several places. A heavy shell exploded close under the bows, throwing the water over the forecastle deck. A ball passed through the rails over the engine hatch, another through the hammock nettings, and one struck the mizzen-mast a few feet above the deck, badly injuring it. It was evident that only iron-clad vessels could reduce fortifications of this nature; and in this case, as in all others, the attempt had to be given up. No disastrous results followed from the erection of the Confederate batteries, nor was either the War or the Navy Department responsible for their existence, they having been erected at a time when neither of these departments were in a condition to prevent it. After the Potomac flotilla left to co-operate with the Port Royal Expedition, the river was effectually closed. Whatever embarrassment this may have been to the government, a careful consideration of the subject must lead to the conclusion that the difficulty was inevitably incident to the peculiar situation of the opposing armies. But, if the responsibility must rest any where, it should be with the Navy Department, which might have sent vessels of sufficient strength to reduce the enemy's works. This, however, was not done, for the very good reason that new batteries could be built as rapidly as the old ones were destroyed. Nothing could have effectually protected the navigation of the Potomac except the military occupation of its entire right bank by our army, and this occupation, clearly unadvisable at an early period, did not, at a later epoch, harmonize with General McClellan's plan of operations. What that plan was we shall consider in its appropriate place.

We now turn to the movements of the enemy on the Upper Potomac, which led to the battle of Ball's Bluff.

While, in October, the two main armies of Virginia were facing each other at Manassas, or rather, through their advanced pickets, at Fairfax Court House, each watching the movements of the other and expecting attack, considerable activity prevailed on the upper Potomac. General Banks, who had superseded Patterson after the battle of Bull Run, had been pushing his outposts several miles up the valley from his position at Harper's Ferry. This was in great measure occasioned by the movements of the enemy, who, having consumed every thing in the vicinity of Manassas and Centreville, found it necessary to make expeditions up the river for provisions, and especially into Loudon county, in the vicinity of Leesburg, where, through the numerous fords of the Potomac, raids could be easily made into Maryland. Leesburg was about forty miles from Harper's Ferry. Between twenty and thirty miles to the north the Federal troops held a favorable position on Sugar-loaf Mountain for observing the movements of the enemy in this direction. General Stone also had an important command

at Poolesville, in the vicinity of Edwards's Ferry. Our pickets lined the river from Harper's Ferry to Washington; and to avoid this uninterrupted series of police, the enemy resorted to the most elaborate manœuvring. His force, which had been detailed to Leesburg, consisted of the brigade of General Evans, or four regiments of soldiers; but this number was supposed by the Federal commanders to be much greater, they being misled by the *ruse* to which the enemy resorted, of showing himself at various places at short intervals of time, so as to multiply the apparent number in his command. The Federal position was in every way favorable for cutting off and surrounding Evans's brigade. To the north was General Banks at Harper's Ferry, and Geary at the Sugar-loaf; directly east was Stone at Edwards's Ferry, and sixteen miles farther to the eastward was McCall, with a large force at Drainesville. A little to the eastward of Leesburg, Goose Creek empties its waters into the Potomac, and across this small stream lies the Gum Spring road leading to Manassas. McCall's position at Drainesville bore upon this line of communication. The town of Leesburg itself, in a military point of view, was of great value to either army, lying on the railroad line from Washington to Winchester, and its possession securing the crops both of the Loudon and Shenandoah valleys. It was also a good position from which to carry on an irregular aggressive campaign against Maryland. But McClellan was on his guard; every ford was strongly defended, every movement of the enemy subjected to the strictest examination, and fortifications were erected at every available point. The Confederates, not being in sufficient force to man a great number of works if they had had them, relied not upon intrenchments or fortifications, but upon making a sudden attack in some unexpected quarter. They had, therefore, but a single battery, which was situated between Leesburg and Edwards's Ferry.

At this time the Confederate General Ashby, with his cavalry, was stationed at Charlestown, in the Shenandoah Valley, whence he continued, by a series of raids, to harass our forces at Harper's Ferry, a few miles to the northwest. The Confederates having now undisputed control of the lower Potomac, through their batteries at Acquia Creek, were seeking, by the co-operation of Evans with Ashby, to obtain a similar advantage on the upper part of the river. On the 13th of October, Ashby's troops, with four companies of Evans's brigade, and two pieces of his artillery, made an unusually daring expedition to Harper's Ferry. Taking up his position on the Loudon Heights, a severe skirmish occurred between the opposing forces, and some of the store-houses and mills in the village of Harper's Ferry were fired by the shells of the enemy. Otherwise no important result was gained, and it was with great difficulty that Ashby was able to withdraw from the position which he had so boldly taken.

Evans, in the mean time, in danger of being cut off by McCall, fell back to a position on Goose Creek, still holding Leesburg. Besides the danger of an attack from the direction of Drainesville, it will be remembered that General Stone threatened Evans's force from two points on the river, viz., from Edwards's Ferry and Harrison's Island, both being about five miles from Leesburg, and the same distance from each other. At Harrison's Island Colonel Devens was stationed, with a few companies of the 15th Massachusetts. Pickets were sent out by Evans in each of these directions. This

CHARLES DEVENS.

was the situation on Saturday night, the 19th of October. The next day General Stone, having evidently the impression that the main force of the enemy was in some other quarter, and that Leesburg was defended by only two or three companies, made his arrangements to cross the river and bring on an engagement. This determination led to the battle of Ball's Bluff, which has also been called the battle of Leesburg. Considering merely the disposition of the Federal forces, and the number of men available for an attack, it seems almost impossible that the combination formed should result in a disaster so complete as that which followed, and which we must now consider.

Ball's Bluff rises to the height of thirty feet from the river's edge, directly opposite and about a hundred yards from Harrison's Island. A reconnoissance had been made a few days previously from this point by Federal scouts, accompanied by engineers, and it was found that only a few companies held Leesburg. All the arrangements for attack seem to have proceeded on the basis of this reconnoissance. On Sunday at sunset, after furiously attacking the enemy's position from Edwards's Ferry, and devoting especial attention to a battery called Fort Evans, known to be at the right, General Stone landed a few of his troops on the Virginia side, but at dusk returned them to camp. At evening Colonel Lee, with a battalion of the 20th Massachusetts, and the 20th New York, or Tammany regiment, and a section of artillery, was in position at Conrad's Ferry, between Edwards's Ferry and Harrison's Island, ready to act in support of Devens, who had been ordered to cross the river to Ball's Bluff, and, proceeding toward Leesburg, to disperse an encampment which scouts had reported as existing a mile north of the town.

Devens had not completed his crossing before sunrise Monday morning, so inadequate were the means of transportation. Not long after he had crossed, Colonel Edward Baker came upon the island with his 1st California regiment, and commenced crossing. Early in the day he reported in person to General Stone, who directed him to cross at the island and take command of all the forces on the Virginia side. In this interview, according to Stone's report, made a week after the fight, the latter had distinctly intimated to Baker the nature of the situation; he had informed him what means of transportation he might have at his disposal; he had distinctly warned him that it was impossible to support him directly by a column crossed at Edwards's Ferry on account of the battery (Fort Evans) which interposed; he advised him to make no advance except against an inferior force, and to take no more artillery across than he had infantry to protect; and distinctly, in his written orders, he left it to the brave colonel's discretion whether to advance or retire, after that he had crossed and reconnoitred. With these instructions, Colonel Baker hurried to the field.

Devens, in the mean time, had accomplished his reconnoissance. He found that the scouts had been deceived, mistaking certain openings in the woods for white tents; but he encountered a Mississippi regiment on picket duty, and had retired fighting all the way to his landing-place, where his retreat was covered by Colonel Lee. The position to which he retired was a semicircular opening in the forest, stretching out from the bluff; and thither the enemy boldly followed him, taking a position under cover of the woods in his flank, and pouring upon his men a merciless fire. Random firing was thus continually heard by Baker's regiment as it was crossing the river. Gorman's brigade had crossed in the morning at Edwards's Ferry, on a reconnoissance toward Goose Creek, for the purpose of drawing Evans's attention from the right; still there was a sufficient force retained at the latter point to outnumber Colonel Devens, leaving out of sight the advantage of the enemy in the matter of position.

The California regiment was from seven o'clock in the morning until four in the afternoon crossing the river, and in the mean time numbers of them fell victims to the concealed fire of the enemy. At first there was no means of conveying the men across except an old water-logged scow, carrying about

T T

forty men; but another scow, capable of holding sixty, was afterward dragged up from the canal. This leisurely proceeding plainly indicates that the Federal commanders had no conception of the number of the enemy on the other side. The reconnoissances which had been made were notably deficient; in each case a picket guard of the Confederates had been encountered, when the reconnoitring force had retired, and, beyond the number of the combatants directly met, no information had been gathered. A small cavalry force, though it would not have mended the deficiency in boats, would at least have obtained the position and numbers of the foe to be encountered, and thus have awakened the Federal officers to the peril of making an attack in the careless manner in which it was made, both in regard to transportation and the number of men detailed. General Stone reports that he sent such a force, but his order was disobeyed.

After having crossed, the men climbed up the steep banks with their artillery, consisting of five pieces; skirmishers were sent out and the line of battle formed, with the California regiment on the left, the 15th Massachusetts and the Tammany regiment on the right, and the 20th Massachusetts in the centre, making, all told, a force of 1720 men. But in the woods was a much superior force. Gorman had retired from Goose Creek without accomplishing any thing more than a temporary diversion, and thus the force of the enemy at Ball's Bluff was continually re-enforced from the main body opposite Edwards's Ferry.

Our forces were received with a volley from the enemy; then followed random firing, and then again the volley, every fire being preceded by a hideous yell. This continued for half an hour, our men being leisurely picked off, as in an ambuscade, while the enemy was securely covered by the woods both from our musketry and artillery. In the severity of this onslaught the Rhode Island artillerists deserted their pieces, which were immediately manned by Colonels Wistar and Coggswell, the former of whom was killed and the latter wounded. Every moment the enemy grew bolder and more desperate, our men suffering terribly from the incessant fire, and having no possible protection except that furnished by a slight elevation of the ground. But there was no wavering. For two hours the brave men stood their ground thus, every minute telling its quota of murders. Then a council of war was held. What was to be done? Evidently three courses lay before Colonel Baker, and with him was left the decision between them. One was to retreat. But that involved recrossing the river, and, with the terrible advantage now held by the enemy, this would necessitate incalculable loss. Another course which might be taken was for Baker to cut his way through the woods to Edwards's Ferry. But in that case there was a considerable force of the enemy to be encountered in front, and a powerful battery, besides the overwhelming force which would pursue them from behind; the way, moreover, led through the woods. The only other course left was to remain and await re-enforcements. But how were these to come? Even the scanty supply of boats at hand were scattered, under no command or management; indeed, re-enforcements which *had been sent* could not, on this very account, find their way to the field. There seems to have been no possible escape from the net in which our forces had been carelessly immeshed. But in this extremity Baker dreams not of surrender. It is reported (and the report is accredited by General Stone) that at this point, and just as our officers had decided to hold the field, a mounted Confederate officer came out from the covert and beckoned our forces to advance, and that Colonel Baker, seizing upon this suggestion, led his men in a charge upon the enemy's position in the woods. However it may be as regards the suggestion, it is true that the colonel did lead his men in an impetuous charge, riding himself far in the front; that, with his hand placed in his breast after his usual manner, he coolly gave orders to his men, advising them to **fire** lower, and encouraging them with the hope of final success; and that in a moment a sheet of flame surrounded him as with the illumination of lightning, and he fell at the head of his column, the victim of an ill-advised battle. His body was with difficulty recovered. The command devolving upon Coggswell, he resolved to cut his way out to Edwards's Ferry; but this was now impossible, as our men in broken ranks were already hastening to cross the river. Colonel Devens had deserted his command and crossed the river on horseback. The scow was soon filled with men, when it was swamped, and many of the men lost. In utter confusion, the troops rolled over each other down the bank; some, attempting to swim across, were drowned, and a greater number were shot by the enemy, who never for one moment slackened fire. There was a sufficient force on the island to prevent pursuit, and with the retreat of our forces the engagement terminated. The Federal loss was 350 killed and wounded, and 500 taken prisoners. Among the wounded was a son of Oliver Wendell Holmes.

It seems almost a miracle of negligence that, with several thousand men available for this very field, and with abundant facilities for procuring suitable transportation, so small a force of men should have been placed at the mercy of an enemy whose numbers were unknown, and that, too, without adequate means of safe retreat in case of disaster. Nor was this the whole sum of the error. Why did Gorman retire from Goose Creek? His command was not very much inferior in numbers to that of the enemy, all told, and yet he simply exchanges shots with a Mississippi regiment and withdraws. If he had held his ground, and hung upon the flanks of Evans, his co-operation with Baker might have been efficient, and the day have ended with victory instead of defeat. Whoever may have been responsible for this reverse, no blame in connection with it is to be attributed to General McClellan, who only ordered Stone to make a feint at crossing, so as to co-operate with McCall at Drainesville.

The success of the enemy led to no important results. Our most serious loss was the death of Colonel Baker. His career had been one of unusual

GENERAL STONE'S DIVISION AT EDWARDS'S FERRY, OCTOBER 20, 1861.

EDWARD D. BAKER.

brilliance. He was born in London, but his father, soon after the birth of his son, emigrated to Philadelphia, and in a few years went to the West. Edward studied law, and rose to a high degree of eminence in that profession. From his fine address, the impressiveness of his presence, and his irresistible eloquence, he became a general favorite in the West. In Illinois, California, and Oregon, he, as resident of those states successively, carried on a successful political career. In Oregon he was elected United States senator in 1859. He was one of the ablest debaters in the Senate. The most striking characteristic of the man was that a great occasion inevitably inspired him and swayed his course. In the incipiency of any important movement he seemed to interpret its full meaning, and clearly to see the end from the beginning. This made him both ready and transparent in utterance; and these elements, added to the fire of eloquence that was in him, made him one of the best orators of the country. Thousands will remember, till they cease to remember any thing, his speech at the great Union Meeting in New York City when the war first broke out. Every sentence was like the full wave of a powerful sea, and carried the whole multitude on before it, swaying them and thrilling them like music. Yet there was no sentiment nor extravagant verbiage in his rhetoric. No sooner had he made that speech than he immediately began the work of recruiting a regiment for the war. He was afterward offered a higher position, even that of a major general, but he preferred to serve as colonel of his original regiment. Previous to the battle of Ball's Bluff he seems to have had a presentiment of his fate; he hurried to Washington, disposed of all his affairs, even to his own burial-place, and then returned to the field to die there doing his duty. This battle, in which one half of the men in the field were killed, wounded, or taken prisoners, and the loss of Colonel Baker, awakened throughout the country a determination that the officers concerned in the management of the affair should be held responsible.

In the mean time, directly after the engagement, orders were received from McClellan to hold the island and the Virginia shore at Edwards's Ferry

at all hazards. Re-enforcements were sent, but it was finally deemed best to withdraw entirely to the Maryland side of the river.

The Confederate army in Virginia at this time consisted of three separate armies, styled respectively the Army of the Potomac, the Army of the Valley, and the Army of the Acquia. The first of these, comprising four divisions, under Doren, Longstreet, and the two Smiths (G. W. and Kirby), was under the command of Beauregard; Jackson commanded the Army of the Valley, and Holmes that of the Acquia. The entire army, with its left threatening the upper, and its right the lower Potomac, while its centre rested on Manassas, covering the direct route to Richmond, was under the command of General Johnston. This was the position during the winter. On the 20th of December an engagement of some importance occurred near Drainesville. General Ord, following instructions from McCall, proceeded with five regiments, including Lieutenant Colonel Kane's regiment, a battery, and two squadrons of cavalry, on the Leesburg pike in the direction of Drainesville. The purpose of this movement was to drive back the enemy's pickets, which had advanced to within four or five miles of the Federal lines, with a reserve force at Drainesville, and to procure forage from the farms of disloyal citizens in the vicinity. A few miles to the east of Drainesville Difficult Creek crosses the pike. Here General J. F. Reynolds was posted with the first brigade ready to support the main column. Brigadier General Meade was also called up with the second brigade for a similar purpose. Thus McCall's entire division was involved in the general movement, though General Ord's brigade was the only one directly engaged. General McCall's division, immediately after the occupation by our forces of Munson's Hill and Falls Church, had been stationed at the right of these positions, with its encampments stretching away over a beautiful tract of country toward Lewinsville, thus forming the right wing of the great Potomac division, securing the Chain Bridge, guarding against a flank movement from Leesburg, and, in connection with Banks's division on the upper Potomac, against an invasion of Maryland, or a raid upon the Baltimore and Ohio Railroad. The Leesburg pike, starting from Chain Bridge, passes through Lewinsville, and, ten miles farther on, through Drainesville, running nearly parallel with the railroad from Alexandria to Leesburg. This railroad beyond Falls Church was occupied by a portion of the Confederate force holding possession of Leesburg, and at Hunter's Mill, a little to the southeast of Lewinsville, intrenchments had been thrown up, with rifle-pits and batteries. Drainesville also was threatened, and this being an important position on McCall's right, it was no small part of his duty to keep it clear of the enemy. At the present time, as we have already indicated, there was a strong reserve picket of the enemy in the neighborhood of Drainesville; there was also a full brigade at Herndon's Station, about four miles south of the town, and a force of five hundred infantry and cavalry at Hunter's Mill, besides a small infantry detachment, numbering two hundred, between Drainesville and the Potomac. The position of these forces, taken in consideration with the facility with which Confederate re-enforcements might be brought up by the road from Centreville, made it necessary that General Ord's movement should be supported by the entire strength of the division. The troops of this division were from Pennsylvania. Those selected for the main column of the expedition were the third brigade, consisting of the Sixth, Ninth, Tenth, and Twelfth regiments, to which was added a regiment of riflemen —the "Bucktails"—under the command of Lieutenant Colonel Kane. The Easton Battery, consisting of two 24-pounders and two 12-pounders, and a detachment of Colonel Bayard's cavalry, made up the entire column which started out of camp on Friday morning at six o'clock, with the cavalry and the "Bucktails" in the advance. It was a clear, frosty morning; the road was rugged, stretching through the woods, whose wintry foliage somewhat solemnized the picture. At half past ten a dispatch was sent to General McCall, acquainting him with the position of the enemy, which we have already indicated. The general mounted his horse, and, with his staff and a cavalry escort, followed in the road which Ord's brigade had taken in the

THE VILLAGE OF LEWINSVILLE, VIRGINIA.

BUILDING HUTS FOR THE ARMY OF THE POTOMAC.

morning, arriving on the field shortly after the battle commenced. General Ord, having dispatched a foraging party to the farms of prominent secessionists between the pike and the river, moved on to Drainesville, where he waited for the Tenth, Sixth, and Twelfth to come up. Upon his arrival the Confederate cavalry picket was dispersed, and two companies of the "Bucktails," together with the Ninth regiment, Colonel Jackson, were so disposed, in connection with the battery, as to cover the approaches to Drainesville from the south. The enemy in the mean time, with four regiments under command of General Stuart, advanced along the Centreville road, which was skirted by a dense wood on either side. Where the road debouches into an open clearing the Sumter battery was stationed, mounting six guns, and skirmishers were deployed to the left and right. In front of the enemy's battery, and five hundred yards distant, was the Easton battery; and between these two an artillery duel was kept up for half an hour. Then an attempt was made by the enemy, who advanced from the cover of the woods, to turn our left, which was repulsed by Colonel McCalmont and two or three shells from the battery, when it was given up. The Confederates were strongly flanked on the right by the Ninth and Twelfth, the former of whom met the enemy in close quarters. The front was held by the Sixth and by the Kane Rifles on opposite sides of the road, which, in its entire length, was commanded by our battery. Discovering that the enemy's guns were in a position open to an attack from their right and in the rear, General Ord detached two or three guns from the battery for this purpose, which soon poured in their enfilading fire with brilliant effect. It was this feature of the attack which most annoyed the Confederates, and finally compelled their retreat. So accurate was the fire from our battery, that every shot seemed to tell upon the enemy; one of his caissons was blown up; another was left behind; gun-carriages were broken, while the road was strewn with other evidences of destruction. The retreating columns of Stuart were pursued for a short distance, after which the entire command, having won the day, returned to camp. The Confederate loss was estimated at over two hundred and thirty, while that of the Union troops, all told, was no more than sixty-nine. This victory had no important result, but, as being the first important success achieved by the Army of the Potomac, received more attention than would otherwise have been given it, and called forth a special congratulatory letter from Secretary Cameron.

The situation in the West differed very materially from that in Virginia. In the latter, preparations were necessarily made on a gigantic scale. Here was gathered the concentrated strength of both armies—the Federal and the Confederate; and upon these, as it seemed, the final issue of the war depended. But this issue was not to be developed through impetuous and rashly-undertaken onsets, as was supposed, but very much through that stationary attitude which, by shallow critics on both sides, was sneered at as "masterly inactivity"—through the careful measuring of strength against strength in quiet, and the patient waiting for opportunity. This attitude followed as a necessity from a situation in which the advantage could rest with the assailant only on the condition of his having an available force vastly superior to that assailed. Whichever side assumed the offensive must be able to face two disadvantages—one, that of marching against a fortified position, and the other, that involved in a distant source of supplies. These disadvantages

could only be overcome by overwhelming odds. And how was this counterbalancing advantage to be gained by either side over an enemy forever watchful, and able, at least for a long time to come, to encounter re-enforcement with re-enforcement? So long as this situation remained, it was inevitable that whichever of these two armies should advance beyond a certain point, and risk an engagement with the other, must, unless there be some fatal mistake in the conduct of the defense, be beaten and driven back. If our naval force could have been made available in a direct attack upon the enemy's strong-hold, we should have needed no other advantage. But the situation did not allow any calculation of our naval resources as a direct element. It was impossible, therefore, that the conflict in Virginia should come to a decisive crisis until operations elsewhere should have brought one of the combatants to the verge of exhaustion, or at least to such an extremity as would give the other a decided advantage in the matter of available strength. Since it was morally certain that a vigorous series of campaigns in the West and along the sea-board must in the end bring the South to that point, our Army of the Potomac could afford to wait. The magnitude of that army was, in this connection, a fortunate circumstance for us; for, although it could not at first materially affect the general situation, yet, when the South should begin to be exhausted, it would enable our Western armies to aim rapid and effective blows against points disproportionately weak, or compel such a concentration of the Confederate forces as would necessitate the abandonment of important positions. The "quiet on the Potomac," therefore, did not diminish the importance of our Virginia army.

But in the West the situation, as we have said, was very different. Here what was to be done invited dispatch. We started on good vantage ground, moreover, inasmuch as we had superior facilities for the transportation of troops and supplies, and a more adequate supply of excellent arms; and the promptness of our military movements forestalled the enemy both in Missouri and Kentucky. While the Confederate generals in all their offensive operations put themselves at a distance from their supplies both of food or ammunition, we had the rivers on our side, answering both as avenues of communication and as a means of moving into the heart of the enemy's country. This made our naval resources more available in the Western campaign than they could be in Virginia. The operations of the enemy in the West always partook of the nature of an extensive raid rather than of a regular combination of forces for a sustained effort; and whenever they erected fortifications, they were soon compelled to abandon them, on account of the ease with which they were flanked and cut off from their distant base.

Our operations in the West were of course, from the first, mainly flank movements in relation to the position in Virginia. The objective point was East Tennessee. This was involved in McClellan's plan, as developed in his memorandum addressed on the 4th of August to the President. There were, as we shall see hereafter, two plans or routes by which this point might be reached But, gained by whatever plan, East Tennessee was even then seen to be the very keystone of the Confederate arch.

The critical situation, as regards popular sentiment, in the border states of Missouri and Kentucky, demanded a prompt and adequate display of force in those states, in order to secure the passive loyalty of Southern sympathizers and the active co-operation of Unionists. The progress of events in these two states will be the subject of our next chapter.

WATER BATTERIES AT COLUMBUS.

CHAPTER V.

KENTUCKY AND MISSOURI.

Neutrality of Kentucky.—Her Devotion to the Union.—Governor Magoffin's Position.—Confederate Occupation of Columbus.—Grant at Paducah.—Proceedings of the Legislature.—Its Address to the People of Kentucky.—Zollicoffer's Invasion.—Buckner's Operations.—Importance of Columbus.—Jeff. Thompson.—Battle near Fredericktown.—Battle of Belmont.—Object of the Battle.—The Retreat.—Losses.—McClernand's Address.—The Situation in Central Kentucky.—Skirmish at Munfordsville.—Nelson's Operations in Eastern Kentucky.—Battle at Pikeville.—Missouri.—General Fremont's Department.—Confederate Plans.—McCulloch, Pillow, Hardee, and Thompson.—Fremont's Proclamation.—Skirmishes.—Advance of Price.—Siege of Lexington.—Mulligan's Surrender.—Price's Retreat and Fremont's Advance.—Price's Proclamation.—Zagonyi's Charge.—Fremont's Removal.—Hunter's Retreat.—Advance of Price to the Osage.—Battle of Milford.—The Confederate Retreat.—The Situation at the close of 1861.—McClellan appointed General-in-chief.—Reorganization of the Western Armies.—The new Commanders.—McClellan's Instructions.—His Plans in the West.

UNTIL the autumn of 1861, Kentucky had quite successfully maintained a perfectly neutral position as regards any active participation in the war on either side. Her governor, Beriah Magoffin, had curtly replied to the President's call for troops in April, that Kentucky would "furnish no men for the wicked purpose of subduing her sister Southern states;" and he had also given the President to understand that no Federal troops were desired within the limits of that state. And, as no direct assistance was given to the Confederacy, and a like restriction was laid upon the Confederate forces, the general government had, as a matter of policy, respected this neutral position. Whatever may have been the secret inclination of the governor toward the Confederacy, the people of the state and its Legislature were, in the main, loyal to the Union. In the election of members of Congress, called to meet in special session on the 4th of July, 1861, every district but one elected strong Union men; and the election for members of the Legislature in August had a similar result. This disposition of the state, as soon as it became apparent to the Confederates, aroused their indignation, and it was openly proposed in the South to cut off all commercial intercourse with the Kentuckians. The New Orleans Delta of August 20th declared: "We will not pay the 'Blue Grass' country of Kentucky for its loyalty to Lincoln by opening our markets to its hemp fabrics. We must discriminate in favor of our gallant ally, Missouri, and give her the benefit of our marts in preference to either open foes or insidious neutrals. It is the clear duty of our government to declare Kentucky under blockade." This was certainly a very impolitic suggestion; for, at this very moment, the government at Washington was considering in what way it might completely cut off the Confederacy from the one sole communication now open to it from the North, viz., by the Louisville and Nashville Railroad; and it was only by reason of its reluctance to irritate the people of Kentucky that the Federal government hesitated to lay its positive embargo upon this road, by which the South was every day gaining every thing and

U u

losing nothing. It seems strange, therefore, that at this juncture Tennessee herself should have put out her hand and shut to the door of her prison-house. This stopped the passage of cotton, rice, and turpentine to Louisville; but it also shut out from Tennessee a rich supply of grain and pork, which at this time were of the greatest value to the South.

It became immediately evident that Kentucky must take an active part in the war on one side or the other. The prevailing sentiment of the people was in favor of the Union. But the southern portion of the state was in great part secessionist, and it was the cherished plan of the Confederacy to take advantage of this by throwing a large force into the counties just across the border. Measures were taken to carry out this plan, and early in August the Confederate Congress had passed an act authorizing enlistments in Kentucky. A Federal force also was being collected together at "Camp Dick Robinson," under General Nelson, for the purpose of insuring protection to loyal citizens. This led to a correspondence between the governor and the President, the former demanding the removal of this force, and the latter refusing to comply with the demand.

When the Legislature met, on September 5th, the governor, in his message, insisted on neutrality, and recommended that a force be raised by the state for its own defense, and that all other military bodies should be disbanded. But on this same day the Legislature was notified that Confederate troops had invaded the state, occupying and fortifying strong positions at Hickman and Chalk Bluffs. The invading force, which was commanded by Leonidas Polk, also occupied Columbus, that commander giving as a reason for so doing that he was only anticipating the occupation of the place by a Federal force, which intended, if not to take direct possession of Columbus, at least to plant batteries on the Missouri side of the river so as to command the town. Thus the neutrality of Kentucky was ended forever. It is a matter of little consequence whether it was a Federal or a Confederate force which first entered the state, since the purpose of either must have regarded, not Kentucky, but the main issue of the war, which had already assumed such proportions that it overleaped all ordinary boundaries, and the geographical position of Kentucky made it absolutely necessary that the state should become the most important arena of the coming campaign. Two days after the occupation of Columbus, General Grant, accompanied by two gun-boats, took possession of Paducah, at the mouth of the Tennessee, and a few miles above Cairo; and extensive preparations were made by the Federal government to resist the advance northward of the Confederates.

Polk had insisted upon it as a condition of his own withdrawal that the Federal forces in the state should likewise be removed. The Legislature, however, decided that the very mention of any condition of this nature was an insult to Kentucky, and passed a resolution demanding the unconditional withdrawal of the Confederate forces. The proceedings of the Legislature

LEONIDAS POLK.

during the rest of the month were honorable both to itself and to the state. The State Guard was disarmed; a series of resolutions was passed, requesting Major Anderson to take command of the military forces in the state, and indicating the stern resolution of the people to repel the invasion upon which the Confederates had so daringly entered; and, upon the veto of these resolutions by Governor Magoffin, they were passed by the requisite vote over his veto. A bill also was passed authorizing the Military Board to borrow three million of dollars, in addition to the million authorized May 24th. Another bill was passed calling out forty thousand volunteers, and one tendering the thanks of the Legislature to Ohio, Illinois, and Indiana, for prompt and needed assistance in forwarding troops for the defense of the state. A resolution was voted demanding the resignation of Senators Breckenridge and Powell; and at the close of the session, an address, memorable for its patriotism, was issued to the people of the state. In this latter, the condition of the state is briefly summed up in the following terms:

"Every effort was made for compromise and settlement. The Federal government did not insist upon our active aid in furnishing troops, seeming content if we obeyed the laws. Those engaged in the rebellion, however, planted camps of soldiers all along our southern border, seized by military power the stock of our railroad, impudently enlisted soldiers upon our soil, made constant raids into this state, robbed us of our property, insulted our people, and seized and carried off our citizens. Thus exposed to wrongs, with no power to prevent them, some of our citizens formed camps under the Federal government for the defense and protection of the state. In this condition we found Kentucky when the Legislature met on the first Monday in September. We were assured by the President of the Confederate States that our position should be respected; but the ink was scarcely dry with which the promise was written when we were startled by the news that our soil was invaded, and towns in the southwest of our state occupied by Confederate armies. Our warnings to leave were only answered by another invasion in the southeastern portion of the state. These sudden irruptions of such magnitude, skillfully directed, show that the assault on Kentucky was preconcerted, prepared, and intended long before. Thrice have the revolutionists appealed to the ballot-box in this state, and thrice have the people expressed by overwhelming majorities their determination to stand by the Union and its government. The attempt to destroy the union of these States we believe to be a crime not only against Kentucky, but against all mankind; but up to this time we have left to others to vindicate by arms the integrity of the government. The Union is not only assailed now, but Kentucky is herself threatened with subjugation. We have no choice but action, prompt and decided. Let us show to insolent invaders that Kentucky belongs to Kentuckians, and that Kentucky's valor will vindicate her honor."

This position was fully supported by the people. In the mean time, while General Polk was invading the western portion of the state, Zollicoffer was operating in the southeast. A slight skirmish took place on the 17th of September at Barboursville; and, to give notice of his hostile approach, Zollicoffer, on the same day, telegraphed to the state authorities that the safety of Tennessee necessitated his occupation of Cumberland and the long mountains of Kentucky, and that he had accordingly taken possession.

A month afterward he met with a severe repulse at Camp Wild-cat, in Laurel County. He had nearly eight thousand men, including two regiments of cavalry, which he had determined to bring against Colonel Garrard's Kentucky regiment; but the latter was speedily re-enforced, and the entire command given to General Schoepf, who maintained his position, which was one of great natural strength, against the repeated assaults of a foe numerically superior to his own. At about the same time, General Buckner was operating on the line of the railroad between Louisville and Nashville, in the central portion of Kentucky. On the 21st of September General Anderson assumed command both of the state and national forces.

The Confederate force at Columbus—more formidable than any other in the state—was soon increased to thirteen regiments, with six field and one siege battery, and three battalions of cavalry. It had also three steamers on the river. This force was concentrated at Columbus, which was strongly fortified, as also was Hickman, twenty-five miles farther south. The strength which was massed at Columbus was not only to be feared for its bearings on the campaign in Kentucky, but from the ease with which it might exert a decisive influence upon military operations in Missouri. One of the strongest motives which led to the Confederate occupation of Kentucky was the desperate state of affairs in Missouri. Arkansas had failed to support General Price. The battle of Wilson's Creek, which had been won with so great sacrifice and against terrible odds by the Federal forces under Lyon and Sigel, had interposed a check against the advance of the combined armies of the Confederacy from which they could not readily recover. McCulloch had withdrawn to Arkansas with his forces, leaving Price to continue the campaign as best he might. All eyes were turned to Columbus for a retrieval of the fortunes of the Confederacy in the West. In the early part of November it would have been very practicable for General Polk to disturb our military operations on the west of the Mississippi. It was to prevent a disturbance of this nature that the battle of Belmont was fought early in November. For three weeks Jeff. Thompson had been pushing his way up the river into Missouri. In the middle of October, from his camp in St. François County, he had issued one of his characteristic proclamations.

"Patriots of Washington, Jefferson, Ste. Genevieve, St. François, and Iron Counties!" exclaims he, "I have thrown myself into your midst to offer you an opportunity to cast off the yoke you have unwillingly worn so long. Come to me and I will assist you, and drive the invaders from your soil or die with you among your native hills. Soldiers from Iowa, Nebraska, and Illinois, go home! we want you not here, and we thirst not for your blood. We have not invaded your states; we have not polluted your hearthstones; therefore leave us, and, after we have wiped out the Hessians and Tories, we will be your friendly neighbors if we can not be your brothers!"

A few days later found him at Fredericktown, a little farther in the interior of Missouri, with a force of thirty-five hundred men. At Pilot Knob, a short distance north of this point, were three or four Federal regiments. General Grant immediately formed a combination which in two days completely routed Thompson, sending him southward at a somewhat brisker rate of speed than had marked his advance. This is the proper place to speak of this engagement, although it occurred in Missouri, because Thompson's movements so entirely depended upon co-operation from Columbus. A force of fifteen hundred men, under Colonel Plummer, of the 11th Missouri, was dispatched along the road from Jackson to Dallas, to move upon Fredericktown in such a manner as to cut off Thompson's retreat, and, co-operating with Colonel Carlin at Pilot Knob, to compel an engagement, greatly to the disadvantage of the enemy. Upon his approach, Plummer sent to Pilot Knob a messenger, with a letter, informing Carlin of his intention to attack the enemy on Monday, October 21st, and requesting co-oper-

STERLING PRICE.

PILOT KNOB, MISSOURI.

ation in front. This letter was intercepted by the enemy, and Thompson fell back about a mile from Fredericktown on the Greenville road, and there awaited attack. Through the information thus gained by the enemy an important advantage had been lost; yet by the re-enforcement which Plummer might have from Pilot Knob, and the superior artillery force which was at his disposal, the chances of success were yet all on his side. Accordingly, on Monday, he advanced against the enemy, who were commanded by Thompson and Lowe, attacked them, and, after a spirited fight, in which he received very important aid from Major Schofield, of the 1st Missouri Light Artillery, he drove the enemy routed from the field. The Confederate Colonel Lowe was killed in the engagement; and of the Federal officers, Major Gavitt and Captain Hingham were killed. The pursuit was kept up with considerable vigor. To prevent any interference from Columbus with columns sent to continue this pursuit was one of the chief objects of the movement against Belmont.

Belmont is just opposite Columbus, on the western or Missouri side of the river, and at this time was held by a small Confederate force under Colonel Tappan. Columbus itself was so strongly garrisoned that it would have been useless for General Grant, with the force at his disposal, to have attempted either a siege or an assault upon that strong-hold; and Belmont, being entirely commanded by the guns of Columbus, was worth nothing as a military position without the latter. The movement, then, as is also evident from written statements of General Grant previous to the battle, was of the nature of a reconnoissance, with the objects already indicated.

As soon as General Polk had any notice of our approach, he anticipated that Columbus would be directly attacked, and General Grant had taken special pains to make him think so, by sending General Smith (commanding at Paducah) with a considerable force, which marched in two columns, the one on Mayfield, and the other to within a few miles of Columbus; and, to help on the effect of this demonstration, a small detachment was ordered to Ellicott's Mills, twelve miles from Columbus, on the Kentucky side. These movements were made simply for the purpose of misleading the Confederate commander. Grant's forces, in the mean time, started from Cairo on the evening of November 6th, a great part of them being under the immediate command of General McClernand, and also landed on the Kentucky side of the river, nine miles below Cairo. In this way the enemy was entirely put off his guard as to Belmont, the point of direct approach. When, at daylight the next morning, Grant and McClernand's forces landed on the Missouri side, a short distance from Belmont, then it was that Polk's attention was for the first time turned in this direction, and he sent Pillow across from Columbus to support Tappan, still supposing, however, that Columbus was the main object of attack.

Pillow had crossed not a moment too soon; for the Federal army had promptly formed their line of battle, and driven in the Confederate outposts and sentries, and, having left a battalion in reserve near the transports, companies were thrown out as skirmishers, and in a few minutes the general engagement ensued. Grant's whole force, with the exception of his reserve, was thrown out in skirmishing columns, which led to a useless waste of his strength; whereas, if he had known the weakness of the enemy on the field at his first arrival, he might have literally crushed him by a sudden onset with his full force, and before the arrival of re-enforcements. The Confederates were driven back to their encampment—a strong position, lumber having been felled for several hundred yards about it, and an abattis formed. General McClernand, at the onset, attempted to outflank the enemy's right wing, and cut off re-enforcements from Columbus. Here the struggle was continued with great severity for half an hour; but Betzhoven's battery kept him back, and the attempt failed. Not so, however, in the centre. Here the attack was so vigorous that the enemy's line was almost immediately broken and the men thrown into confusion. Pillow was obliged to bring up his reserve of artillery, consisting of two batteries and a half, with which he kept the Federal army in check until he had restored communication between the two wings of his army. But his efforts to recover himself proved unavailing; for he had no sooner made his arrangements for a spirited resistance, than it was reported to him that three of his regiments and his most important battery were out of ammunition. Only one course was left him in this extremity, and that was to keep the battery in position, and to make a bayonet charge with the three otherwise defeated regiments, trusting to Polk to send him speedily the help which every moment he needed. But the commander at Columbus, still believing that his own position was in jeopardy, hesitated and held back assistance until Pillow had sent message after message, and was completely exhausted. Grant, seeing how matters stood, pushed his advantage to the utmost, and by furious and repeated onsets carried the abattis, and drove the enemy, foot by foot, and from tree to tree, pell-mell down the banks of the river, and within protection of the guns of Columbus. Pillow's division was so severely cut up that not a single company remained intact, and the whole body were crowded together in confusion.

But here the defeated enemy was re-enforced by several thousand fresh troops, and Grant was attacked in front, flank, and rear, and was in danger of being cut off from his transports. To prevent this, he retreated, the Confederates all the time charging upon his ranks, until he came up with his reserve, when he collected his forces together, and, ordering up fresh regiments and artillery from his reserve, recommenced the contest. Throwing his forces with great fury against General Cheatham's division, which was leisurely approaching, he broke the ranks of the latter, and, advancing his batteries close to the banks of the river, opened a murderous fire upon Pil-

WILLIAM NELSON.

low's flank and upon some steamers, which, with re-enforcements, were crossing the river from Columbus. Then the heavy guns of Columbus poured in their cannonade upon the battle-field, and were answered by Federal cannon from Belmont. It soon became evident, however, that so many re-enforcements had been sent across that it would be impossible for General Grant's men, who had been engaged from half past ten in the morning until five in the afternoon, to successfully hold their ground, and a retreat was again ordered. The enemy had been re-enforced to about thirteen thousand men, a force nearly three times as large as our own, and closely followed the retiring, but really victorious army of General Grant. The latter retreated in good order, embarked upon his transports, and left a battle-field which he had certainly won, but could not hope to keep. Our loss in killed, wounded, and missing was, according to General Grant's report, one hundred and eighty-four; that of the enemy was, by their own admission, over two thousand. Yet the battle was claimed by the Confederates on the ground that Grant was unable to hold the field.

After the battle, McClernand issued the following address to his soldiers:

"Few of you had ever seen a battle. You were imperfectly disciplined, and had inferior arms; yet you marched upon a concealed enemy superior in numbers, and on ground of their own choosing. You drove them steadily for two miles of continued fighting, and forced them to seek shelter under the heavy batteries at Columbus. You drove them from their position and destroyed their camp, bringing with you, on retiring, two hundred prisoners, two field-pieces, and a large amount of other property. Re-enforced from Columbus, they formed in large numbers in your rear to cut you off, while the heavy guns of Columbus were playing upon your ranks. Fighting the same ground over again, you drove them a second time. A portion of the command, becoming separated from the rest, made a successful and well-ordered movement by another route, and returned to the river. After a day of fatiguing marches, fighting as you marched, having been nearly six hours actually engaged, you re-embarked and returned to your camp."

Turning from the western to the central portion of the state, we find military movements in progress on a very extensive scale, Louisville, on the Ohio, being the head-quarters of the Union Department. When General Anderson assumed the command of this department, September 21, General Buckner was at Bowling Green, on the railroad between Louisville and Nashville, about seventy-one miles from the latter. This was an important military position, being at the junction of two roads leading into Tennessee. Buckner had been led to believe that, if he should come to Louisville, or even to Bowling Green, with a competent force, he would receive re-enforcements by thousands; but he hardly got a regiment, and kept very close to Bowling Green, in the southern part of Kentucky, though he had made a boast that he would winter in Louisville.

In the month of November great accumulations of Federal troops were collecting together from the states north of the Ohio River; and by the 1st of December there was in Kentucky alone an army of seventy thousand men, of which twenty thousand were citizens of the state. About four thousand of these were located at "Camp Dick Robinson," in Garrard County. This vast force had nothing between it and Nashville, and therefore noth-

ing between it and the virtual occupation of the State of Tennessee, except the army of Buckner, numbering thirty thousand men. No hostile collision between these two opposing forces occurred with the exception of an unimportant, though uncommonly severe skirmish at Munfördsville, on the Green River, and a few miles north of Bowling Green, on the road to Louisville. This action took place on the 17th of December, on the south bank of the river; but only a few companies were engaged, and the result had no bearings upon the general issue.

In the southeast, Zollicoffer, whom we left at Barboursville after his repulse at Camp Wild-cat, advanced, on the 10th of December, with strong force toward Somerset, compelling Schoepf, who occupied that town with a Federal division, to retire. The Confederate commander then encamped at Mill Spring, where he fortified his position, and remained until his overwhelming defeat at that place early in 1862.

General Nelson was in command of a small Federal force which he had been organizing in the eastern portion of the state, on the Virginia border. On the 2d of November he occupied Prestonburg, on the west fork of the Big Sandy. From Prestonburg he moved upon Pikeville in two columns, one of which, under Colonel Sill, was sent by a circuitous route to attack Colonel Williams in the rear, while Nelson, with the other, took the direct river route. Williams, who occupied Pikeville with about a thousand troops, made every preparation to offer a vigorous resistance. Two hundred of his men waited in ambush for General Nelson's advance (under Colonel Marshall) about twelve miles down the river from Pikeville. The Federal troops had had a very difficult march through the mud and rain, and, besides this, were living on half rations; but their resistance was successful, and the next day the Confederate force made an unconditional surrender. This short campaign of General Nelson, lasting only twenty days, drove the rebels from the eastern part of Kentucky.

Thus closed the year's campaign in Kentucky. General Anderson, on account of ill health, had resigned his command; and Sherman, his successor, for the same reason, gave way to Buell, who, with his head-quarters at Louisville, took command of the new army that was accumulating at the close of the year.

After the death of Lyon, who had given his life to wrest Missouri from the tightening grasp of the Confederacy, the burden, not only of responsibility, but of active duty in the field, rested upon Fremont, who assumed the command of the West a short time before the battle of Wilson's Creek. General John C. Fremont, a native of Georgia, of French descent, reared and educated in South Carolina, and afterward distinguished as an engineer and explorer, was appointed colonel of the United States Army in 1846, and commanded a battalion in the Mexican War. He was the first candidate of the Republican party for the presidency, but failed of being elected. At the breaking out of the war in 1861, Fremont was in Paris; but, receiving information of the events of April, he immediately purchased a large quantity of arms for the government, and returned to his native country in June. In July he received his commission as major general with the following order: "The State of Illinois, and the states and territories west of the Mississippi and on this side of the Rocky Mountains, including New Mexico, will in future constitute a separate command, to be known as the Western Department, under the command of Major General Fremont, of the United States Army, head-quarters at St. Louis." We have previously stated the

JOHN C. FREMONT.

BEN McCULLOCH.

difficulties incident to this command, which were very much heightened by the necessities of the Eastern Department. It was under these difficulties that the hard-contested battle of Wilson's Creek had been fought. This battle, however, so severely punished the Confederate army that it did not venture any farther advance; and as forces were rapidly accumulating under the President's new call, every month's delay was favorable to our army in the West.

In the mean time, large bodies of Confederate troops were collecting in the southeastern part of the state, threatening Cairo. The western portion of Missouri had furnished a great number of recruits, which were accumulated together at points most available for a contemplated advance against Cairo and St. Louis. McCulloch, after the battle of Wilson's Creek, had returned to Arkansas, and was recruiting his wasted strength from the border counties. Pillow was at New Madrid, on the Mississippi, with an army of about thirty thousand men; while Hardee occupied Greenville, east from Cairo, on the St. Francis River, with five thousand men; and Thompson, still nearer Cairo, was collecting a large force of disloyal Missourians. With this combination of forces, the Confederate generals were confident of their ability to drive our forces north of the Missouri River before the end of August.

It was under these circumstances that Fremont issued a proclamation declaring Missouri under martial law, and ordering that all persons taken with arms in their hands within the lines of his army—lines extending from Leavenworth, by way of the posts of Jefferson City, Rolla, and Ironton, to Cape Girardeau on the Mississippi—should be tried by court-martial, and, if found guilty, should be shot; also that the property, real and personal, of all persons in the state, who should take up arms against the United States, or who should be directly proven to have taken active part with their enemies in the field, should be confiscated to the public use, and their slaves, if they had any, should be declared free. This proclamation, so far as it related to slavery, was afterward modified by President Lincoln to suit the provisions of the Confiscation Act, passed by Congress August 6th, 1861.

This proclamation of Fremont called forth a counter-proclamation from Jeff. Thompson at Camp Hunter, wherein the latter most solemnly promised that for every member of the Missouri State Guard, or soldier in alliance with them, who should be put to death in pursuance of Fremont's order, he would *hang, draw,* and *quarter* a Union man in retaliation. Fremont's measure, in its main features, seemed to be necessary to restore quiet in the state. Neither life nor property were secure from violence; murders were committed by the wholesale; bridges were ruthlessly destroyed; and every where indiscriminate plunder and outrage attempted to shelter itself under the Confederate flag, and to claim privileges not even accorded to regularly organized combatants.

The month of September was for the most part a month of preparation on the Federal side. There was considerable skirmishing. Thus, during the first week of the month, Colonel Williams, with about eleven hundred national troops—Kansas and Iowa Third—was compelled to retreat from Shelbina, in Northern Missouri, before a superior force commanded by Martin Green, a self-appointed Confederate officer. This force of Green's, however, after having been increased to about three thousand men, was in a very few days effectually dispersed by Pope, who captured his baggage and provisions. Another skirmish, in which the Third Iowa also figured, on the 12th of the month, was one of uncommon severity, five hundred Union troops having been attacked by about four thousand rebels. After the struggle had lasted for an hour, and a hundred and twenty of our men had been disabled, their commander, Lieutenant Colonel Scott, ordered a retreat. A short time afterward, Colonel Smith's command, with four pieces of can-

non, met the enemy by another road, and, engaging them as they were about to cross the Missouri River, severely punished and routed them.

As a precaution, and in order that he might be able to use the greater portion of his army for a movement which he was planning against Price in the southwestern part of the state, Fremont, at some expense, fortified St. Louis.

In the mean time, Price, who had found an able ally in General Harris, marched northward, and joined his forces with those of the latter. As they were about to encamp, at the beginning of September, they received information that some moneys, amounting to a hundred thousand dollars, were at that very time on the point of being conveyed by a detachment of Federal troops to Lexington from Warrensburg. Although the Confederate troops were wearied with long marches when this communication was made to them, the prospect of securing so valuable a prize was an incentive not to be withstood. They marched at double-quick upon Warrensburg, but, upon their arrival there, found that they had been anticipated by the Federal troops. Their indignation was not at all mollified by certain caricatures which the German soldiers of our army had sketched on the walls in charcoal drawings, representing in a rude but vivid manner the disappointment of the Confederates in finding the money-boxes empty. After halting at Warrensburg for two days, Price moved upon Lexington, on the south bank of the Missouri River, whither the money had been conveyed. The Federal force at Lexington, consisting of about half a regiment of Home Guards, was strongly intrenched, and gave the enemy a severe repulse. Colonel Mulligan, with his Irish brigade, was sent to re-enforce Lexington. Price, too, found no difficulty in obtaining a vast number of recruits; for it was generally known that victory would bring with it the coveted gold. The Federal force had been increased to 2500 men, and the fortifications greatly extended and strengthened. On the 12th of September, scouts and advanced pickets, driven in, reported the approach of the enemy. The attack was at first concentrated upon the college, which had been strongly fortified; but the fire was so briskly answered by our troops that a retreat was ordered to Fair Ground until Price's supplies of ammunition should come up. In six days the attack was renewed. General Rains took up a position on the east and northeast of the town, while General Parsons attacked from the southwest, all the guns in front firing upon Colonel Mulligan's works at the same time. Affairs with the garrison soon began to assume a critical position, for sharpshooters had been detached which had cut them off from their supplies of water. Messengers had been sent by Mulligan to Jefferson City urging on re-enforcements, but they were captured by the enemy. So, too, small detachments of force dispatched to his assistance were cut off in detail, and defeated or captured. While matters were at this pass, a steamer came down the river bringing clothes, provisions, and ammunition; but these also fell into the hands of the enemy, who, indeed, stood in immediate need of the last two articles. At the same time, the hills north of the town were taken by Harris's and McBride's troops. Against these Colonel Mulligan made a *sortie* to drive them from the position, but his force was insufficient. This important point was protected by the Confederates by means of extensive movable breast-works constructed from hempen bales. About two o'clock of the 20th, after fifty-two hours of uninterrupted fighting, his troops and the means of defense having been entirely exhausted, Mulligan displayed the white flag, and surrendered his brave garrison as prisoners of war. Besides a great number of stands of arms, a considerable quantity of ammunition, and a vast amount of commissary stores, nine hundred thousand dollars in hard cash was also captured.

Fortunately for us, Price, for want of sufficient ammunition, was unable to follow up his victory with that decisive movement for which his success opened the way. Fremont, in alarm, hastened to Jefferson City, and hurried up his preparations to attack Price, who, upon the concentration of the

JAMES A. MULLIGAN.

THE DEFENSE OF LEXINGTON.

Union troops at Jefferson City, retired to Springfield, thus bringing himself into easy communication with Arkansas, and tempting Fremont to a distance from his source of supplies.

The Federal advance into Southwestern Missouri was made in five divisions, under Hunter, Pope, Sigel, Asboth, and McKinstry. This advance followed closely upon Price's retreat. The latter arrived at Neosho, in the southwest corner of the state, just in time to be present at the meeting of the State Legislature, and to celebrate the secession of Missouri with a salvo of one hundred guns. Here he joined McCulloch, but the meeting between the two was far from cordial.

Price's proclamation, issued at Neosho shortly afterward, indicates very forcibly the critical situation of the Confederate affairs in Missouri. "In the month of June last," he says, "I was called to the command of a handful of Missourians. . . . When peace and protection could no longer be enjoyed but at the price of honor and liberty, your chief magistrate called for fifty thousand men to drive the ruthless invaders from a soil made fruitful by your labors and consecrated by your homes; and to that call less than five thousand responded out of a male population exceeding two hundred thousand men. Some allowances are to be made on the face of the want of military organization, a supposed want of arms, the necessary retreat of the army southward, the blockade of the river, and the presence of an armed and organized foe. But nearly six months have now elapsed. The army of Missouri, organized and equipped, fought its way to the river. And where now are the fifty thousand? Had fifty thousand men flocked to our standard, with their shot-guns in their hands, there would now be no Federal hirelings in the state to pollute our soil. Where are those fifty thousand men? A few men have fought your battles. A few have dared the dangers of the field. Come to us, brave sons of the Missouri Valley. I must have fifty thousand men. I call upon you, in the name of your country, for fifty thousand men. Where are our Southern Rights friends? We must drive the oppressors from the land. I must have fifty thousand men. Numbers give strength. Numbers intimidate the foe. Numbers make our arms irresistible. Numbers command universal respect and insure confidence. We must have fifty thousand men! Come with your guns of any description that can be made to bring down a foe. If you have no arms, come without them. We must have fifty thousand men. Give me these men, and, by the help of God, I will drive the hireling thieves and marauders from the state. Be yours the office to choose between a free country and a just government and the bondage of your children. I, at least, will never see the chains fastened upon my country. I will ask for six and a half feet of Missouri soil on which to repose, for I will not see my people enslaved. Come on, my brave fifty thousand heroes—gallant, unconquerable Southern men! We await your coming."

Fremont arrived in Springfield on the 27th of October. He had sent Sigel forward to the south of Springfield, toward Wilson's Creek, who, coming up with the rear of the enemy just as the latter was about to retreat, made a spirited attack upon him. And here it was that Major Zagonyi, commander of Fremont's body-guard, made his brilliant and ever-memorable charge, leading his men up a steep hill in the face of the most murderous fire, and driving the enemy through the town.

Just at this crisis the order came from Washington for the removal of Fremont, who was succeeded by Hunter. The latter in a few days abandoned Springfield and moved toward Rolla, thus allowing Price to recover the ground from which he had just been driven by Fremont. General Fremont had created a great degree of enthusiasm in the West, and, without any doubt, every secessionist was delighted at his removal. As he had just begun his campaign when he was superseded, it is impossible to criticise his generalship, whether favorable or unfavorable.

As soon as Hunter began to recede, Price again advanced, moving in three divisions toward Kansas, with the intention of making that his field of operations. He had under his command about 20,000 men; and on the last day of November he was at Monticello with his centre, his right wing resting on Stockton, and his left on Nevada. His plan was to reach Kansas, and then, having supplied his troops with arms, to destroy the track of the Northern Railroad, and cut off communication with St. Louis. But General Halleck, who had superseded Hunter on the 18th of November, had, ere a month was passed, completely upset Price's project by more deeply-laid strategy of his own. Instead of succeeding in cutting off St. Louis, Price found himself, at Christmas, compelled to look out for his own communications, which, so far as Northern Missouri was concerned, were entirely cut

FREMONT'S BRIDGE ACROSS THE OSAGE.

SPRINGFIELD, MISSOURI.

off by Halleck's operations between the Missouri and the Osage Rivers. This was accomplished by a movement of General Pope from Sedalia on the 15th of December, which cut off Price's army on the Osage from a large body of recruits then on their way to its support from the counties north of the river, and at the same time from its northern base of supplies. Price was deceived by a feint movement against Warsaw on the Osage, while Pope, after moving about eleven miles in that direction, turned suddenly into Henry County toward a point farther west, placing his force, numbering four thousand, between the main body of the enemy and the squads of recruits scattered about at different points on the north side of the river. Most of these bodies—one of which was 2200 strong, encamped six miles north of Chillhouse—were dispersed by Pope's pursuing cavalry, and returned to their homes; and at the mouth of Clear Creek, near Milford, a force of the enemy numbering over 1500 were surrounded and captured on the 18th, together with a large amount of ammunition and subsistence, and a thousand stand of arms. In these movements Pope had guarded against an attack on his flank by stationing a considerable force at Clinton to intercept any columns which Price might dispatch from Osceola. Thus cut off from supplies of men and food, the position of the enemy, at any moment open to attack, was no longer tenable, and he was forced to retreat from his camp on Sac River, in St. Clair County, to Springfield, where General Price received considerable supplies of clothing and camp equipage, and prepared to go into winter quarters. Here also he gained three or four thousand recruits. But these were of no avail against the force which Halleck was preparing to hurl against him. Therefore, in the latter part of January, when this force was concentrating at Rolla, he fell back from Springfield to Arkansas, where, from his camp on Cove Creek, he reported to self-exiled ex-Governor Jackson. He had failed to get his fifty thousand men.

The fall and winter campaign of Price in Missouri was of critical importance, yet it seems not to have been appreciated by the Confederate authorities. General Price held throughout the year, from the commencement of his operations in Missouri, an independent position, acting quite entirely on his own responsibility. He was neither supplied with men nor with the material of war. Even in the fight at Wilson's Creek, where he had so vast a superiority in point of numbers, his old rifles and his miserable artillery put him at a decided disadvantage. At that time he had McCulloch with him; but the two officers were always at variance, and after that battle he was left entirely alone. Meantime our forces were daily increasing in numbers, and threatened, in a short time, merely by numerical superiority, to drive the entire Confederate force from the state. If, after the capture of Mulligan, Price had been abundantly supplied with ammunition, he would, without any doubt, have attacked General Fremont before the latter could have had time to concentrate his army; but, when Lexington surrendered, it is said that he had only two thousand percussion-caps in his whole command. Had his situation been otherwise, it is difficult to say what might have been the result, but it is certain that he would have held important advantages over Fremont, which might have entirely reversed the actual events of the year. By reason of the deficiencies in Price's commissary and ammunition, Fremont was allowed sufficient time to concentrate his own forces and to compel the retreat of the enemy. When the indefatigable Confederate leader again advanced, he was driven back, as we have seen, before Halleck's superior strategy and an overwhelming superiority of numbers. And here, in connection with the difficulties which all along followed Price in his operations during the year, the reader will allow us again to allude to the importance of the battle fought by General Grant at Belmont, which,

although it availed nothing toward the reduction of the strong-hold of Columbus, yet entirely cut off General Polk from any possible opportunity of co-operating with the Confederate forces in Missouri. It was upon this co-operation that the prospects of Confederate success in Missouri chiefly depended. When Polk and Pillow occupied Columbus, Jeff. Thompson, at the same time, established himself on the opposite side of the river; but when the latter attempted to operate in the interior and keep up his connection with Columbus, Grant came promptly upon the field between him and his base, thus, by the engagement at Belmont, cutting off both him and Price from their most important centre of support. In this way the vast combination of forces which the Confederates had prepared in the southeastern portion of Missouri, along the line of the Mississippi, with the view of an advance against Cairo and St. Louis, was baffled. This combination had been in preparation since July. At first it assumed the most threatening aspect. Fremont, however, had kept the enemy in check by a display of naval force on the Mississippi which deceived the enemy as to his ability to defend Cairo. Then the battle of Wilson's Creek was fought, and the force of the enemy very much weakened. In a month or two they again begun to hold up their heads; Columbus was occupied by Polk and Pillow; then followed the defeat of Thompson and the battle of Belmont. And thus the year closed, but not without hope to the Federal army in Missouri; for the enemy had been defeated in the western part of the state; Pope held the north securely by his small but active force; the Confederates in the southeast had lost more than they had gained, and were powerless to advance; and, finally, re-enforcements were daily bringing the Union army nearer to a position favorable for aggressive movements in the coming spring, that should forever clear the state of the Confederate armies.

The retirement of General Scott in October immediately affected the situation in the West. On the 31st of October he addressed a letter to the Secretary of War, requesting that his name might be placed on the list of army officers retired from service. For three years, he said, he had been unable to mount a horse, or even to walk without difficulty. On the afternoon of the day in which the letter was received by the secretary, the President, accompanied by his cabinet, visited the lieutenant general at his residence, and read him the official order carrying out his request, and placing him upon the list of retired officers, without any reduction of his current pay, subsistence, or allowances—this latter provision having been specially made in his behalf by Congress on the 5th of August, in anticipation of his early withdrawal from active service. The interview was an affecting one. The last great officer of the old school of military tactics thus disappeared from the stage, retaining his well-earned laurels as the veteran hero of two important wars.

An order was immediately issued by which George B. McClellan became commander-in-chief, under the President, of all the armies of the United States. Two days after assuming this command, McClellan, in a brief speech made at Philadelphia, said, "It is for the future to determine whether I shall realize the expectations and hopes that have been centred in me. The war can not last long. It may be desperate. I ask in the future forbearance, patience, and confidence. With these we can accomplish all." McClellan's mind, largely speculative, had looked inevitably upon the whole field, even when he was in command of only the Army of the Potomac. The command of all the armies in the field gave full scope for the execution of his comprehensive plans. The Department of the West had now to be entirely reorganized. The next day after McClellan was made general-in-chief, Fremont was relieved of his command,[1] and about the middle of November his

<hr />

[1] It is not meant to be indicated here that Fremont was removed solely at the instigation of McClellan; nor, if that were the case, is any fault meant to be found with the order, which, under the circumstances, was perfectly justifiable. The difficulties and jealousies growing out of political differences between the prominent actors engaged in the suppression of the Southern insurrection were already becoming only too painfully evident. The three of these actors who were most prominently representative were the President and Generals McClellan and Fremont. The latter two had each of them a preconceived bias of opinion, which controlled their respective policies in regard to the conduct of the war. McClellan's sympathies determined in favor of the South and its institutions; Fremont's in exactly the opposite direction. And as in each case the bias of opinion ruled the practical policy of these men, it is fair to call the disposition in each a partisan one. The President had also his bias of opinion, which was in favor of Northern institutions; but he was no partisan, inasmuch as his conduct was regulated solely by the Constitution, his interpretation and administration of which was affected only by imperative circumstance. No domestic institution of the South was touched by his hand until it became evident that the in-

terference became either an absolute necessity, or at least an important means in order to preserve the integrity of the national government. Apart from the peculiar attitude of the border states, there was no doubt as to the expediency of striking directly at slavery as the chief support of the insurrection. In order to secure Maryland, Kentucky, and Missouri, the blow was postponed. It was the necessary policy of government, during the period when these states were trembling in the balance between loyalty and treason, to desist from any interference with slavery unless some greater gain could come to the nation from the opposite policy. It was during this period that Fremont had command in Missouri. Without authority, he adopted a political policy which excited the opposition of those who, though desirous that the military authority of the nation should prevail in the state, were yet determined that the constitutional rights of the state should remain inviolate. This exercise of authority was at the time both arbitrary and unwise, and could easily have been avoided. The opposition to Fremont in the border states was a sufficient reason for his removal; and when McClellan was placed at the head of the entire field, that step became necessary to prevent political jealousy and rivalry from impeding the onward movement of the war.

DON CARLOS BUELL.

department was subdivided into three: first, New Mexico, which was assigned to Colonel Canby; second, the Kansas Department, the command of which was given to General Hunter, including Kansas, part of the Indian Territory, Nebraska, Colorado, and Dacotah; and, third, the Department of Missouri, under Halleck, including, besides that state, Iowa, Minnesota, Wisconsin, Illinois, Arkansas, and all of Kentucky west of the Cumberland River. The Department of the Ohio, including the portion of Kentucky not under Halleck's command, Ohio, Michigan, Indiana, and Tennessee, was given to General Buell. The Department of West Virginia, under Rosecrans, and that of the Potomac, continued the northern lines of occupation to the Atlantic. There could hardly have been a greater change than McClellan's new position produced in the military prospect of the Western armies. New commanders took the place of the old in every important field. General Hunter, a graduate of West Point, had commanded the second division at the battle of Bull Run, and on the removal of Fremont had assumed the command in Missouri until Halleck's arrival. The latter, from California, was also a graduate of West Point, was at one time a professor in the institution, and was the author of several well-known military works. He had served with distinction in Mexico, and entered the civil war with the rank of major general. Don Carlos Buell, commander of the Ohio Department, had served in the Mexican war, where he had twice been promoted by brevet. At the beginning of the war he had received a command on the Potomac, with the rank of brigadier general.

These new commanders in the West were appointed at McClellan's suggestion, with the approval of the President. They were to act under McClellan's instructions; and what the tenor of these instructions were we gather from the letters addressed to them at this time by the general-in-chief. In regard to the Department of Missouri, the general had evidently the impression that every thing had gone wrong under Fremont's administration. In his letter to Halleck, dated November 11th, he expressed his dissatisfaction in the strongest terms. He said that Halleck would have extraordinary duties, apart from those devolving upon him as a military commander, to perform. Chaos must be reduced to order; the personnel of the staff of the department would have to be changed, and a system of reckless expenditure, and fraud perhaps unheard of before in the history of the world, would have to be reduced to the limits of an economy consistent with the interests and necessities of the state. Contracts would have to be overhauled; and it was to be very carefully considered whether the existing organization of the troops were perfectly legal. In regard to military operations, he advised that Rolla, Sedalia, and other interior points should be held in considerable strength, while the main army should be concentrated on the Mississippi. His instructions to General Buell intimated that he considered the Department of Ohio second only to his own in importance. "It is possible," he said, "that the conduct of our political affairs in Kentucky is more important than that of our military operations. The military problem would be a simple one could it be entirely separated from political influences; such

is not the case. Were the population among which you are to operate wholly or generally hostile, it is probable that Nashville should be your first and principal objective point. It so happens that a large majority of the inhabitants of Eastern Tennessee are in favor of the Union; it therefore seems proper that you should remain on the defensive on the line from Louisville to Nashville, while you throw the mass of your forces, by rapid marches, by Cumberland Gap, or Walker's Gap, on Knoxville, in order to occupy the railroad at that point, and thus enable the citizens of Eastern Tennessee to use, while you at the same time cut off, the railway communication between Eastern Virginia and the Mississippi." This letter was addressed to Buell on the 7th. Five days afterward he wrote again, urging an advance into Eastern Tennessee as soon as it could be made with a reasonable prospect of success. In the mean time, all the avenues by which Kentucky lay open to invasion were to be carefully guarded. Previous to McClellan's appointment there had been no carefully elaborated plan comprehending the entire field of military operations in the East and West. In the East, McClellan, upon whose army the safety of the capital so entirely depended, had been able to gather together a large army—not so large as he desired, but still large enough to secure him against successful attack—thus giving him ample opportunities for fortification and extensive organization and discipline. In the West, the Federal generals had been compelled to fight at the very outset; to fight battles, moreover, in which they had terrible odds to encounter, without hope of support or re-enforcement from the government. There was no time for preparation, nor was there an opportunity for extensive organization. There was a force barely sufficient to meet the enemy in the field, and there could be found no reserve to prepare and to organize in camps and by means of camp drills. What troops there were in the West had an organization by which they managed somehow to hold the enemy in check, whether it was a legal organization or not; but they had been reduced to a minimum, in order to supply the Army of the Potomac. But, now that the Western field had come under his own command, McClellan began to appreciate its importance and its necessities. In August he advised the smallest possible force in this field, estimating that, if Kentucky took the right position—and she did—there would be no more than 20,000 needed, together with those which could be raised in that state and Eastern Tennessee, "to secure the latter region and its railroads, as well as ultimately to occupy Nashville." In October he had said that it was a matter of regret to him that it had not been deemed expedient by the national government to concentrate the forces of the nation in his then special field on the Potomac, but that some amends for this oversight might still be made by transferring from all the other armies their superfluous strength, thus re-enforcing his "main army." With this same end in view he recommended that all the cavalry and infantry arms, as fast as procured, be sent to this army; that the Western armies should be put entirely on the defensive, in order to allow his to assume the offensive; and that no more outside expeditions be attempted until he had fought the great battle in front. It was less than four days after he made these important suggestions that he was made general-in-chief. Thus placed at the head of the entire field, his estimate of the necessities of the West was materially different from what it had been when that section had been under Fremont's administration. For the first time it was discovered that a new order of things must be inaugurated in the West. "I soon found," says McClellan, "that the labor of preparation and organization had to be performed there; transportation, arms, clothing, artillery, discipline, all were wanting." Now, instead of giving the Army of the Potomac the initiative, he purposed to make the advance into East Tennessee a preliminary movement, after which his Virginia army would come in with a coup de main, and end the struggle. Nashville and Richmond would be captured by a simultaneous attack, and the Confederate line of defense would be thrown southward within the limits of the cotton states. From Richmond the Potomac army would advance to Charleston, where it would be met by a naval expedition; Buell would be pushed forward to Montgomery, or meet the Potomac army in Georgia; while Halleck would meet another naval expedition in New Orleans, and the occupation of the Southern sea-ports would render all farther resistance to the national government as useless as it would be desperate. The plan was brilliant and comprehensive, and showed that the general-in-chief had great powers of speculative combination. But we allude to it in this connection merely to show the importance which McClellan attached to the Western armies the moment they passed out of other hands into his own. It was a matter, therefore, for national congratulation that the West and the East had been thus included within a single command, since, within the short space of a single week, so remarkable a change had been effected, by which armies hitherto reduced in force, crippled in every appliance of war, and undervalued as to their comparative importance, were now to be made as efficient as they were worthy, and to be allotted their full share of the glories as well as the hardships of future campaigns. In the last week of October, McClellan expresses to the Secretary of War his regret that there has not been such a concentration of forces in Virginia as to allow the Army of the Potomac to enter upon an aggressive campaign before the season for such a campaign should be past. The very next week, all the armies of the West as well as of the East are placed at his disposal; but we find no longer an inclination on his part to withdraw any portion of the Western armies into Virginia. Indeed, his reason for delaying the campaign is now no longer the one given a week ago, viz., the inferiority of the Potomac army in respect of numbers, but the neglect from which the Western army has itself been suffering all along—its lack of preparation and organization. Henceforth he waits, not to fill up the ranks of the Virginia army, but to make preparations in the West.

In regard to the other charges made against Fremont—those made by Frank Blair, and partially reiterated in McClellan's instructions to Halleck—they were simply puerile. The expenses incident to Fremont's administration were no greater in proportion than those of any other department. His fortification of St. Louis was imperatively demanded by the condition of his own command, and the threatened advance of an enemy superior in numbers; and as to Western contracts, it is yet to be discovered that they were any more fraudulent or unsatisfactory than those made nearer Washington. The charge that Fremont was inaccessible to those seeking his presence for the purposes of business is wholly without foundation.

THE DESTRUCTION OF THE NASHVILLE BY THE IRON-CLAD MONITOR MONTAUK.

CHAPTER VI.

NAVAL OPERATIONS.

The Blockade of Southern Ports.—Naval Superiority of the North.—The New England Fisheries.—Condition of the United States Navy at the beginning of the War.—The Proclamation of the Blockade by President Lincoln.—Vessels recalled from Service in Foreign Waters.—Blockading Squadrons.—Jefferson Davis grants Letters of Marque.—Confederate Privateers.—Fortress Monroe.—The Hatteras and Port Royal Expeditions.—Confederate Attack on Santa Rosa.—Bombardment of Fort McRea.—Hollins's Confederate Fleet on the Mississippi.

IN a war whose successful termination depended upon the exhaustion of the South, the blockade of the Southern ports constituted of necessity an important feature. Herein it was that the naval superiority of the North was chiefly available. There were undoubtedly certain disadvantages arising out of the commercial character of the Northern people. Nor were these slight in a war like that waged between the North and the South, where it was precisely the case of an elaborate network of civilization, as vulnerable as it was complex and extensive, liable to be deranged by the minutest fluctuations even of a peaceful time, and much more by the violent changes incident to a period of civil strife, pitted against a feudal status of social life, the very atmosphere of which is martial aspiration. Yet these disadvantages were more than compensated for by our power to cut the Southern States almost entirely off from all foreign supply and re-enforcement. At the first outbreak of hostilities, however, the successful blockade of a coast measuring more than three thousand miles in length seemed utterly out of the reach of the national government, and was, doubtless, not even calculated upon by the Southern leaders as a possible event, since the cotton states, dependent upon their exports for their very wealth, were financially ruined the moment the gates of the sea were closed against them. Knowing this, they would never have ventured the chances of a war on such unfavorable conditions; and, indeed, it seemed a task, requiring some miracle to be performed in order to its accomplishment, for a nation which on the 1st of January, 1861, had but a single war-steamer available for the defense of its entire Atlantic coast, to proclaim a blockade whose regulations extended over the coast of half a continent. But this aspect of the case was essentially a delusive view. The inlets and harbors of our coast were not crowded with fleets, it is true; but the essential basis of a navy consists not in ships, but in trained seamen. The basis of a substantial navy had been firmly established for the North, not only through the ordinary channels of commerce, but more especially through the extensive New England fisheries.

The first commercial link connecting America with the Old World was established by means of the fisheries off Newfoundland. Not long afterward the Cape Cod fisheries came into prominence, and formed the basis of New England commerce. As in the case of ancient Attica, New England, on account of the sterility of her soil, impelled her sons, by the pressure of necessity, to devote a great measure of their activity to fisheries and commerce. About the middle of the seventeenth century it was the habit of Virginia planters to speak of the sterility of New England and of her fisheries with ridicule; it was sometimes even hinted that the Puritans would have shown a larger wisdom in settling the Bahamas than in sticking so closely to Plymouth Rock. Strangely enough, just two centuries later we find New England, in spite of her sterility, in advance of her more fruitful

sisters of the South in all material as well as moral prosperity, and able, through her naval power, to blockade the entire Southern coast; and this naval power, which, though chiefly resident in New England, is, through her steadfast loyalty, a national possession, is due mainly to her fisheries. The only season of the year in which the fisheries can be carried on with success is that which of all others is the most tempestuous, and only the most courageous and hardy men could face its dangers and endure its hardships. It is from men trained in this school that the navies of great nations are nourished. The naval service, while it demands and exhausts hardy seamen, is incapable of producing them; and both France and England have always looked to their fisheries to supply the demand for fresh material. The great Italian cities, at the height of their commercial prosperity, acknowledged their obligation to fishermen, and at Venice there was a yearly festival established to commemorate this obligation. In view of the national importance of our fisheries, the measures relating to them, and which formed a part of the Reciprocity Treaty between the United States and Great Britain, were held to be of momentous interest. These articles of the treaty allowed the citizens of either nation, under certain specified restrictions, to carry on fisheries in the waters of the other, thus extending for each nation its field for the training of seamen.

But, notwithstanding that there were about 20,000 men directly engaged in our fisheries, besides the great number of seamen engaged in commerce available for naval use, there were still great impediments to be removed before an actual navy could grow out of the resources at hand. The naval establishment of the United States at the beginning of the war, in regard to the number of vessels and the quantity of ordnance at its disposal, was exceedingly weak. This nation had always pursued a policy in regard to foreign powers which, while securing herself against attack from abroad, made it unnecessary to maintain an army and navy establishment proportioned to her comparative power. In March, 1861, the number of vessels of all classes belonging to the navy was only ninety, of which not more than forty-two were in commission, these latter mounting between five and six hundred guns. Nearly all of those in commission were on foreign stations, the Home Squadron consisting only of twelve vessels, mounting one hundred and eighty-seven guns; and only four of these were in Northern ports, the remainder being for the most part in the Gulf of Mexico. The complement of these vessels was about 2000 men. The number of naval officers disaffected to the government was very large. In the four months from March 4th to July 4th there were on this account two hundred and fifty-nine resignations. The destruction of the Norfolk Navy Yard had been chiefly injurious on account of the large amount of ordnance sacrificed, a large quantity of which fell into the hands of the enemy. The Cumberland, which was the only vessel of the yard in commission, fortunately escaped.

Such was the inadequate force at the disposal of the government when the war began. But the President promptly issued his proclamation, laying an embargo on the ports of the seven states then belonging to the Confederacy. This was on the 19th of April. On the 27th he included within the limits of his proclamation the ports of Virginia and North Carolina. To carry into effect these two proclamations, Flag-officer Pendergrast, in command of the Home Squadron, was sent, with all the ships available for the purpose, to establish non-intercourse, and to notify foreigners of the embargo, giving them fifteen days in which to complete their preparations for departure. Seventeen more vessels were put in commission, and the commandants of the navy yards in Boston, New York, and Philadelphia were directed to purchase and equip suitable steamers, in order to render the blockade as effective as possible. In the mean while vessels were continually arriving from foreign waters. The *Niagara* reached Boston from Japan on the 24th, and was immediately dispatched to Charleston Harbor. Shortly afterward she was removed to the Gulf, to intercept shipments of arms and munitions of war said to be on their way to Mobile and New Orleans. The East India, Mediterranean, Brazil, and African Squadrons were recalled, adding to the navy a force of 200 guns and 2500 men. Twelve steamers were purchased by the government, and nine more were chartered; and several small vessels which had been captured were taken into the service.

Thus, before July 4th, the blockade had been rendered so effective that foreign nations could not evade it, and were obliged to recognize its legality. The duties of the blockade were divided between two squadrons—the Atlantic Squadron, under the command of Flag-officer S. H. Stringham, and the Squadron of the Gulf, under Flag-officer Mervine: the former consisted of 22 vessels, 296 guns, and 3300 men; the latter of 21 vessels, 282 guns, and 3500 men. There were, in addition to these, the Potomac Squadron, under Commander Ward, the squadron in the Pacific, under Flag-officer John B. Montgomery, consisting of 6 vessels, 82 guns, and 1000 men, and the West India Squadron, which was assigned to Pendergrast.

THE SAVANNAH.

It was understood that transports secured on the spur of the moment could be of only temporary use, and accordingly, to secure vessels available in all weathers and for all sorts of service, the Navy Department contracted for the building of twenty-three gun-boats of about five hundred tons burden. The eight sloops-of-war which had been ordered by Congress in its previous session were being built as rapidly as the demand for vessels immediately needed would allow. Arrangements were also being made for the construction of larger and fleeter vessels, to be used not only on blockade, but also for the pursuit and destruction of privateers.

It was only through privateering that the Confederacy had the means of carrying on the war upon the seas. As soon as the President's proclamation calling out the militia was made known at the Confederate capital, Davis issued a proclamation inviting applications for letters of marque and reprisal, those applying to make a written statement, being required to give a suitable description of the character, force, and tonnage of the vessel to be employed, and the number of its proposed crew. Before receiving their commissions, all applicants were compelled to give bonds to the amount of $5000 or $10,000 that the laws of the Confederate States should be observed, that all damages done contrary to those laws should be satisfied, and that the commission should be surrendered when revoked by the President. Early in May this measure of President Davis was sanctioned by the Confederate Congress, and it was farther provided that prizes should be distributed among the owners, officers, and crews of the capturing vessels; but that these must first be carried into some port of the Confederacy, or of some friendly state, to be condemned by a competent tribunal. A bounty of $20 was offered for each person on board any armed ship belonging to the United States which should be burnt, sunk, or destroyed, and one of $25 for each person captured and brought into port.

There were two difficulties in the way of successfully carrying out this scheme. One was the blockade, which, in the first instance, impeded the egress of privateers, and after their escape prevented their return with captured vessels to Confederate ports; the other was the refusal of neutral powers to allow these armed vessels to bring prizes into any of their ports. Unless, therefore, privateers should be able to elude the blockade, both in their egress from Confederate ports and in their return to the same, the entire value of the prizes captured would be lost to the captors. It was inevitable, however, that some of these cruisers would get out to sea; and this once accomplished, it became absolutely impossible for the Federal government to maintain so effective a police as to secure our commerce against the threatened danger. There was an advantage gained by that government

even in this, inasmuch as the partial annihilation of our commerce diverted the activity and capital hitherto directed into that channel to the development of our naval resources against the Confederacy.

At the beginning of May, 1861, the Confederacy had purchased two vessels—*Sumter* and *McRae*—which were then being rapidly prepared for sea at New Orleans. The first privateer which eluded the blockade was the *Savannah*, which was also the first to be captured. This vessel was by no means a formidable one, her burden being only fifty tons, and at a little distance could not have been distinguished from an ordinary pilot-boat. She was fitted out at Charleston, where she took in a crew of twenty men, and carried an 18-pounder, mounted on a swivel amidships. She escaped on Sunday, the 2d of June, while the United States frigate *Minnesota*, on duty off Charleston, was in pursuit of a suspicious craft cruising to the southward. The next day she captured the brig *Joseph*, with a cargo of sugar, from Cuba. The same day, about 5 P.M., the brig *Perry* came in sight, and the *Savannah* gave chase, expecting to take another prize. Unfortunately for the privateer, the brig *Perry* was a United States man-of-war, and she caught a Tartar! The tables were turned; the chase was reversed, and at 11 o'clock the next morning the *Savannah*, with her officers and crew, were captured and brought to the port of New York.

A month later, the *Sumter*, mounting five guns, escaped from New Orleans, with a crew of sixty-five men and twenty marines, under the command of Raphael Semmes. This vessel was the old *Marques de la Habana*, which had been captured by the United States fleet off Vera Cruz in 1860, and taken as a prize to New Orleans. After her escape, which she effected while the *Brooklyn* was pursuing an English vessel attempting to run the blockade, the *Sumter* captured several brigs, which she carried as prizes to Cienfuegos, Cuba, where they were released by the Spanish government and sent to New York. On the 26th of July the *Sumter* was at Venezuela, having captured on her way from Cuba the *Abby Bradford*, which was sent to New Orleans with Semmes's first dispatch. After having captured and burned several valuable vessels, the *Sumter* reached Cadiz early in February, 1862. Here her career was virtually ended, as the *Tuscarora*, lying off Gibraltar, kept her under embargo, until Semmes finally, after waiting two months to effect an escape, discharged his crew and sold the ship. The career of the *Jeff. Davis*, which escaped from Charleston about the same time that the *Sumter* ran out from New Orleans, was far less fortunate than that of the latter vessel. She captured and burned a number of American vessels, but about the middle of August was wrecked near St. Augustine, Florida. In October, 1861, the *Nashville*, commanded by Lieutenant Pegram, escaped from Charleston. The next January she was at Southampton, England, which port she was ordered to quit on the 4th of February. At this time she was closely blockaded by the *Tuscarora;* but the latter was not permitted to pursue until after the expiration of twenty-four hours, which gave the privateer every chance of escape. The *Nashville* ran the blockade at Beaufort, and anchored safely in a Confederate port on the 1st of March, bringing with her $3,000,000 worth of stores, but no arms. Just one year from her arrival at Beaufort she was destroyed by the Federal iron-clads in the Great Ogeechee River, and under the guns of Fort McAllister. The *Montauk* (Captain Worden) led in the attack. She had grounded in that part of the river known as the Seven Miles' Reach, when the fleet approached to within twelve hundred yards, and opened fire both on the ship and the battery. The *Nashville* soon caught fire, and her magazine exploded. The attempts made by the Confederacy to build up its navy in foreign ship-yards will be considered in some future chapter.

THE SUMTER.

Apart from the measures taken to secure an effective blockade, the naval arm of the service, like the military, during the year 1861 was engaged only

THE BURNING OF HAMPTON BY MAGRUDER.

in detached operations. Two important expeditions were planned and carried out, having for their object the seizure of points on the Southern coast, and a diversion of the enemy's forces from Virginia, in view of a possible advance by McClellan's army in the autumn. Besides the Hatteras and Port Royal Expeditions, our occupation of Ship Island in September, and the attack made by the rebels on Santa Rosa Island in October, were the only events of interest worthy of note in the record of naval operations for the year.

Nothing of any importance occurred in General Butler's department during the month of July; but the Confederate General Magruder still had a large force on the Peninsula, which, shortly after the battle of Bull Run, signalized itself by burning the little village of Hampton. On the 7th of August Magruder had posted a force of seven thousand men, with eight pieces of artillery, on Black River, three miles from the village, with the intention of forcing an engagement upon our soldiers at Newport News or at Hampton, or at least of destroying the latter place, and thus preventing its being used by Butler's men for winter quarters. But these men already, as will presently appear, had their eye upon a sunnier clime, and would, therefore, hardly realize the injury which had been intended. The circumstances incident to the conflagration were every way disgraceful to the Confederate commander. No warning was given, and helpless non-combatants were aroused from their beds at midnight to look upon the destruction of their homes. Nothing, however, was accomplished by the enemy beyond this conflagration, as our forces were prepared to meet him, and with the chances of victory on their side.

On the 18th of August General Butler turned over his command at Fortress Monroe to General Wool, having been at the head of the department of Virginia for nearly three months. Assigned to no other post, he reported to General Wool for orders, and received quietly the command of the volunteer forces outside the fortress, viz., at Camps Butler and Hamilton, serving as a subordinate where he had, almost from the beginning of the war, been accustomed to the supreme command. But it was not long before work of great moment was intrusted to him for execution. The resources of the fortress had up to this time been used chiefly with a view to secure it from the possibility of capture; that security had now been fully gained, and henceforth Fortress Monroe was to become the centre from which the naval strength of the nation might be hurled against the trembling and almost defenseless coasts of the Southern Atlantic. In a single day the full importance of the possession of the fortress to our government flashed like an illumination upon the popular mind; it was the day when the expedition to Hatteras Inlet was brought to light as an accomplished result.

The Confederacy had not been without its serious apprehensions as to the vulnerability of its coast defenses; indeed, it was the sorest of anticipated evils; and the more the boasting in relation to heroic defenses against these daily-expected raids upon their coast, the greater their apprehension of ruin which must inevitably result from them. Within but a day or two of the

landing of our forces at Hatteras, the Augusta *Chronicle and Sentinel* gave the following reasons for immediately organizing a coast defense:

"1. Because there are many places where the enemy might commit raids and do us damage before we could organize and drive them off. Beaufort District, opposite to Savannah, has several fine ports and inlets, navigable for large vessels, wholly unprotected. This district has five black to one white inhabitant. Several inlets on our coast, which our enemies know like a book, from surveys in their possession, are equally unprotected.

"2. In two months more they will not fear our climate. By that time they might be ready to make a sudden descent and find us unprepared.

"3. A small force might eject them if ready to go at once; when, if we have to wait, a much larger one will be necessary.

"4. By organizing and drilling infantry and guerrillas at home, there will be no need to call upon the President for troops, and a feint from the enemy would not injure our Virginia operations."

Hardly had this note of alarm been sounded before the blow was struck and the danger illustrated. The point of attack was not that which would have been conjectured by the enemy; apparently no position along the coast, with the exception of cities, was better protected than Hatteras Inlet. This point was chosen by Butler himself, who both originated and planned the expedition, aided, however, in the execution of his scheme by Commodore S. H. Stringham, of the Navy. The first suggestion leading to this undertaking was furnished by a Union man who had been wrecked and detained as a prisoner at the Inlet, and who brought home the important information that through that opening in the sand-reef which lines the North Carolina coast, blockade runners were continually gaining access to the main land. This was before Butler had been relieved of his command; and when General Wool arrived at the fortress, he found that preparations were already being made, by order of General Scott, for an expedition whose object should be to block up the Inlet and reduce the forts in the vicinity. There were two of these fortifications—Forts Hatteras and Clark—which the Confederates had for the last three months been erecting upon the point north of the Inlet, one of them mounting ten and the other seven guns. These earthworks were constructed of sand, turfed over; were twenty-five feet in thickness, and contained bomb-proofs. The position of Fort Hatteras was one of great strength, being nearly surrounded by water, and accessible only by a circuitous march of five hundred yards over a neck of sand, and then over a narrow causeway commanded by two 32-pounders. Its bomb-proof sheltered four hundred men. Fort Clark, seven hundred yards farther north, was smaller, and less formidable in its armament.

General Butler volunteered to command the expedition, which started out from Hampton Roads a little after noon on Monday, August 26th, and which consisted of two frigates—the Minnesota and Wabash, the sloop-of-war Pawnee, and three war steamers—the Monticello, Harriet Lane, and Quaker City, together with two transport steamers—the George Peabody and the Adelaide, and the steam-tug Fanny, besides some surf-boats, and an

S. H. STRINGHAM.

old schooner which it was proposed to sink in the bulk-head. The Cumberland and the Susquehanna were expected to be on hand in time to join in the attack. Nine hundred troops made up the small military detachment of the expedition.

By two o'clock on Tuesday the fleet arrived off Hatteras, and the Monticello was dispatched to reconnoitre the position and to look out a suitable landing-place. The next morning the troops were landed two and a half miles north of the forts, under cover of the gun-boats. Upon the voyage, every thing had gone on pleasantly; but just now there was a heavy sea, and it was with great difficulty that a small portion of the force was landed, and all farther attempts at disembarkation were given up. In the mean time the fleet opened fire upon the forts, particularly upon Fort Clark. The return fire fell short, amid the contemptuous laughter of our blue-jackets. This was the first instance in the war of an assault by gun-boats, and the excitement was intense. Every soldier was promptly at his post. One of the spongers, dropping his sponge overboard, jumped over after it and recovered his place before there was time even to reprimand him for his offense. After a heavy bombardment, lasting from nine o'clock in the morning until night, Fort Clark was evacuated; the flag on Fort Hatteras also was hauled down, and our victory seemed secure. The Monticello steamed into the Inlet to within six hundred yards of the fort, when suddenly the heavy guns of the latter opened upon her with such terrible effect that she was in danger of sinking. But she escaped, though considerably injured; and the other boats reopened the attack, which was continued until dark, apparently with little effect. Things began to look despondently, and there was among the men a dim conjecture of failure; and, to complete the discouragement, the weather threatened serious work ahead. The vessels stationed near the shore to protect our troops were compelled during the night, for their own safety, to retire. The number of men landed were insufficient to resist attack, and, fortunately, no attack was made by the enemy.

On Thursday morning the assault upon Fort Hatteras was renewed, and, after a few hours of rapid firing, the white flag was displayed above the fort, and the Confederate flag-officer, Commodore Barron, offered to surrender the position to General Butler if the garrison might be permitted to retire with all the honors of war, stating, moreover, that he had in the fort seven hundred men, and fifteen hundred within call. Butler returned his compliments, and assured the Confederate commander that no terms were admissible save those of an unconditional surrender—terms which Barron was compelled to accept; and, giving himself up as prisoner, he had the additional humiliation of having to pass directly under the guns of the Wabash, which, six months before, he had himself commanded with honor.

At the very moment when the terms of capitulation were under consideration by the enemy, the Adelaide and the Harriet Lane were grounded in attempting to pass the bar, and both of them were under the guns of the fort. What if Barron, seeing his advantage, should renew the attack? It was a critical moment; but the terms were accepted, and the object of the expedition was accomplished. Instead, however, of destroying the port, as originally proposed, Butler thought it of great importance that it should be retained, and, in order to present this view of the case to General Scott, returned to Washington. The government, convinced of the wisdom of his proposition, determined to hold the place, and immediately provisioned the garrison for that purpose. The importance of this particular victory, considered alone and by itself, was no doubt extravagantly overrated by the people; but it must be remembered that it was preceded by a summer of disaster, and furnished the first glimpse of the possibilities for victory that

Z z

were involved in our naval resources; and it lifted from Butler's shoulders the heavy burden of the reverse at Great Bethel.

These events were soon followed by the occupation of Ship Island in the Mississippi Sound. The Confederates evacuated the island September 16th, and our forces, under Commander Smith, immediately took possession.

The importance of Hatteras Inlet to the government was in a very short time fully illustrated: first, by the great number of prizes taken—five schooners having been captured in a single day—and, secondly, by the opportunities offered for aggressive action in the immediate vicinity, an instance of which occurred within three weeks of the capture of Fort Hatteras, in the expedition against Fort Ocracoke, situated off an inlet of the same name, on the seaward face of Beacon Island. The expedition proceeded under the leadership of Lieutenants Maxwell and Eastman, and was a complete success, resulting in the destruction of the fort, which was deserted, and the capture of twenty-two guns. At Portsmouth, on the opposite side, there had been a camp, which the Confederate troops abandoned at the approach of the Fanny, to whom was intrusted the execution of the enterprise.

The success which attended General Butler in his descent upon the coast of North Carolina, gaining for our government not merely the key to the entire coast of that state, but also such a foothold on the main land as to furnish a nucleus for future movements in the interior as time should prepare the way for them, encouraged the Naval Department to fit out a second expedition, on a larger scale, to operate in waters farther south. The expedition, under the joint command of General Sherman and Commodore Dupont, and consisting of fifty vessels including transports, sailed from Fortress Monroe on Tuesday, the 29th of October, under sealed orders, the specific object of attack being left, in great measure, to the discretion of the officers commanding. The time that transpired between the sailing of the expedition and its arrival at its destination was a period of great suspense to the whole country—to the curiosity of the North and to the apprehension of the South. The entire uncertainty as to where the uplifted arm of the national power was to fall completely bewildered the states along the sea-board; every probable point of attack was fortified; Charleston, in particular, waited anxiously, expecting daily to see the menacing fleet across the bar of her harbor. The tenor of General Sherman's orders, of which some report in a Northern newspaper fell into the hands of the Confederates, indicating that considerable resistance might be expected on the part of the enemy, led the South to suppose that some strong point was to be assailed —Charleston, for instance, or Savannah, or New Orleans. But this was not the case. The leaders of the expedition, after careful deliberation, determined to take possession of Port Royal Harbor, on the coast of South Carolina. It was supposed that in five days the voyage would be completed; but on Friday, the 1st of November, rough weather set in, with a high southeaster, so that the fleet was dispersed and placed in a perilous situation. One of the ships had to throw a powerful battery overboard in order to save her crew, and some transports were lost. On the fourth of November the fleet arrived at Port Royal bar.

It was originally intended that the military forces should co-operate with the naval; but this, upon a consideration of the distance—which was five or six miles—over which the troops would have to be conveyed to the nearest point of landing, and by reason of a considerable loss, in the recent storm, of a greater portion of the means of disembarkment, was found to be a plan quite impossible of execution, and therefore the navy alone was involved in the engagement. The bar of Port Royal is ten miles seaward. After crossing this, the channel leads between St. Philip's Island and Hilton Head into the harbor. Upon each side of the channel, or Broad River, were situated batteries of considerable strength, viz., on Hilton Head, Fort Walker, mounting twenty-three guns; and on St. Philip's Island, Fort Beauregard, mounting fifteen guns; and at the left of the latter, a battery of four guns behind earthworks. Fort Walker was a formidable strong-hold, but those on the opposite side were less elaborate. There was no protection afforded by either of the forts from shells or bombs, as they had been hastily erected to meet a possible emergency of this nature. The Confederate forces on Hilton Head were under the command of General Drayton.

The attack, on account of unfavorable weather, was postponed until the 7th of November. The day was clear and beautiful, without a cloud, and in every way favorable to the operations of the fleet. A reconnoissance had been made three or four days previously, in which the strength and position of the batteries was ascertained. The attack was made at an early hour of the day. The transports being left in the rear, the most formidable steamers of the fleet, to the number of thirteen, with the Wabash, the flag-ship of Commodore Dupont, in the van, swept in with open ports; and all was silence until the Minnesota came directly opposite Fort Walker, when every gun of the fort fired simultaneously upon the frigate. There was no reply from the fleet. The batteries of Fort Beauregard poured in their fire, but still there was no answer. Then the second steamer in the line came within range, was fired upon from both sides at once, when, from the first three vessels, seventy-five guns delivered their terrible broadsides upon Fort Walker. From this moment the bombardment ceased not for four hours. In single file, as they had commenced, the steamers moved on until nine of them had passed out of range up toward the harbor; then they returned, describing an ellipse, and saluted Fort Beauregard. After sailing around this circle several times, another and far more successful plan was adopted— that of enfilading the batteries in either direction with our fire, while an attack was at the same time made from the front. Very soon nearly every gun was dismounted. A little after eleven the batteries on St. Philip's Island were silenced, Fort Walker maintaining its fire only for two hours longer. The battering of the fort was terrible; the guns were scattered in every direction, surrounded by the dead and the dying. In this extremity it was determined to abandon the fort. Back of this work there was an open space of a mile, over which the defeated troops ran in a panic, subject every moment to the fire of the fleet. They found shelter in the woods, through which they made their way across the peninsula to the main land. The ground over which they fled was covered with their muskets and knapsacks.

Upon the arrival of the fleet the harbor was guarded, in addition to the fortifications, by a squadron of Confederate steamers under Commodore Tatnall; but this miniature navy was of no avail, and at the first onset was driven away. Forty-three guns were captured, and possession was taken of Hilton Head, which has since been an important centre of naval operations. Situated midway between Charleston and Savannah, and commanding easily the railroad connecting those two cities, this military position was of very great value.

Previous to the sailing of the Port Royal expedition occurred the attack on Santa Rosa Island.

The Atlantic and Gulf coasts are almost entirely walled in from the open violence of the sea by long, narrow islands or reefs of sand, between which and the main land are inclosures of water, sometimes large enough to be called bays, that find or make an outlet through the before-mentioned reefs. Santa Rosa Island is a sand-reef of this character opposite Florida, on the Gulf coast, inclosing the Pensacola Harbor, which was the finest in the Gulf. On the Gulf side there are three or four sand-ridges parallel to the coast, running along the island, and on the opposite or harbor side the ground is low and swampy, covered with a few bushes and trees. On the lower or western extremity of the island Fort Pickens is situated, directly opposite Fort McRea. The Confederate authorities were keenly alive to the importance of Fort Pickens. As early as March, 1861, a month previous to the actual commencement of hostilities, Major General Bragg, commanding the Confederate forces at Pensacola, had issued an order prohibiting all traffic or communication with the fort, which was shortly afterward strongly re-enforced, and assumed a threatening attitude, whereupon formidable preparations for its assault began to be made at Pensacola. The coast fronting Fort Pickens takes the form of a semicircle, stretching from the navy yard to Fort McRea, a distance of two and one half miles, along which was constructed an uninterrupted line of redoubts and batteries, together with a water-battery beyond Fort McRea. Bragg had over six thousand men in his command, who, inflamed by the success at Sumter, were eager to repeat it against Pickens, at that time under the command of Lieutenant Slemmer, whose conduct during these eventful days this history has recorded in the proper place. He was succeeded in command by Colonel Harvey Brown. On the 13th of June the celebrated Sixth New York Regiment, Zouaves, commanded by Colonel William Wilson, who was one of the very first to offer his services to the government on the breaking out of the war, took its departure for Santa Rosa Island, where it encamped about a mile eastward from the fort. The island at this point is three fourths of a mile in width.

As a matter of course, there was the usual jealousy and bickering between the regulars in the fort and the volunteer Zouaves. But, so far as the enemy was concerned, "Billy Wilson" was the foremost man on the island; and although the prospect of taking the fort had long been despaired of, yet it

BILLY WILSON.

seemed to them to be no unworthy object to break up the Zouave encampment. It was to accomplish this object that on the evening of the 8th of October a force of between twelve hundred and two thousand Confederates, transported by two steamers and a few launches, under the command of Brigadier General Anderson, effected a landing on the island four miles above the camp. Except for a short distance beyond the camp in that direction there was no guard posted, although there was every reason to apprehend an early attack, on account of the strength of Bragg's army on the other side. The camp could hardly have been less favorably situated to repel an assault. Colonel Wilson's regiment had been depleted of quite four fifths of its number, having hardly two hundred men able to take the field.

The enemy, having landed without opposition, marched down the island in three columns, one down the centre of the island, and the other two along either coast. In this order they came upon the picket-guard, which altogether consisted of seventy men variously disposed. Here the attack commenced just as the Confederates came over the back hill of the beach; but the close ranks of the attacking columns received a destructive fire from the squads of men opposed to them, and were even thrown into considerable disorder. So persistently did the pickets hold their ground, retreating only step by step, delivering all the time a continuous fire into the enemy's ranks, that all the results calculated upon through a surprise of the camp were lost, the uninterrupted firing having completely alarmed the Zouaves and brought them promptly into line. There was even time given to send a dispatch to the fort, notifying Colonel Brown of the attack. So many false alarms had been given that this was received incredulously; but the heavy volley-firing, as the engagement became more general, aroused the regulars to an appreciation of the situation. In the mean time, Colonel Wilson and Lieutenant Colonel Creighton encountered the centre column of the enemy; but only a small force was left to receive the attack of this column, the greater number of men having been detached for the purpose of preventing the flank movement which was being effected by the enemy's left column. The main portion of the Confederate force was already in the very midst of the camp, to which they were setting fire, having completely plundered it of clothing, money, and baggage. From the fort a company of about thirty men, under Major Vogdes, marched toward the left of the field, and the major, being in advance of his men, was surrounded and taken prisoner. His men, however, made objections to surrendering, and bravely stood their ground. If the enemy had not become very much dispersed for the purposes of plunder and destruction, and had not thus also given time to the federal troops to gather themselves together for an attack, matters would have assumed a much more serious aspect. Supposing, from the severity of the fire, that the force upon the island was very much larger than they had counted upon, and fearing lest they might be cut off from their transports, the Confederates soon commenced a retreat, and were closely followed by the Zouaves and the force from the fort. This force attacked them as they were re-embarking, and fired upon them with terrible effect. The Confederate loss at this point was great, particularly as the swampy ground very much impeded their operations.

The expedition, though in some measure successful, was far from being thoroughly fortunate. In the first place, it did not accomplish what with so great a force might have been reasonably expected. The darkness of the night, and the dissipation among the men consequent upon their indiscriminate plunder, led to a great deal of confusion, and many of the troops were killed by men in their own ranks. And, again, whatever punishment they inflicted upon our men in the destruction of their camp and in robbing them of their personal effects, certainly in the more serious matter of the fight, namely, the loss of life, they were much the greater sufferers.

As to the conduct of Wilson's Zouaves, it must be remembered that it was their first battle, and that very little precaution had been taken against an attack. The disparity in numbers was terribly against them, and, to complete their embarrassment, Lieutenant Colonel Creighton had, through a mistaken order at an early period in the fight, retired with his men to the fort. The bravery of the guard was almost marvelous, and it was this that saved the regiment from destruction.

Fort Pickens, surrounded by a cordon of Confederate batteries, was threatened with the fate of Sumter, beleaguered as it was by a force ten times as large as its own. Partly in retaliation for the night attack on Santa Rosa Island, and partly because some active measures must be adopted to reduce the enemy's fortifications, Colonel Brown, on the morning of the 22d of November, assisted by Flag-officer McKean, with the Niagara, Richmond, and Montgomery, commenced the bombardment of the enemy's batteries, which, as we have said, stretched in a continuous line from Fort McRea on the left to the navy yard on the right. On this line, at the right of Fort McRea, was Fort Barrancas. These forts were mounted with some of the heaviest guns in the country. There were, besides, fourteen batteries, mounting from one to four guns. Conjointly with the attack from Fort Pickens, the fire from three batteries on the island was also directed against the enemy's works. The fire was returned with great accuracy and vigor. It was hardly noon, however, when the guns of Fort McRea were all silenced but one. Pickens was originally intended to resist an attack from the sea, and not from the coast; but sand-bag traverses and similar precautions prevented any serious injury of the works. The fire of Barrancas, and that from the navy yard, was perceptibly reduced during the afternoon. The next day Colonel Brown reopened the bombardment, but, owing to the shallowness of the water, the frigates were obliged to withdraw from the contest. They could, however, have availed nothing against the rifled guns of the enemy. Fort McRea was silent all day, and in the afternoon the village of Warring-

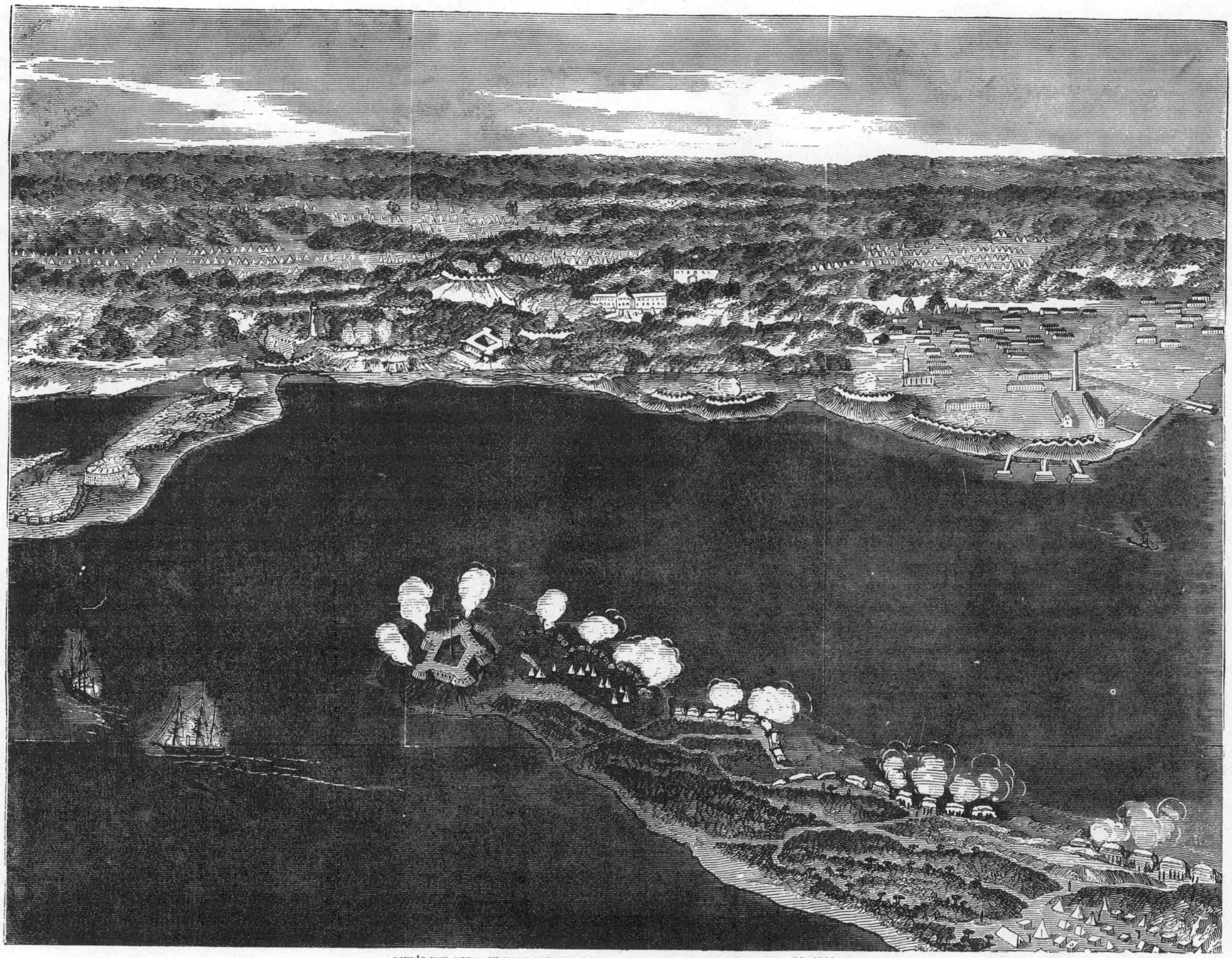

BIRD'S-EYE VIEW OF FORT PICKENS DURING THE BOMBARDMENT, NOVEMBER 22, 1861.

ton, in the rear of the Confederate batteries, was set on fire from our shells and almost entirely destroyed. On the 1st of January, 1862, the bombardment was again opened. The firing was continued into the night, and the splendor of the illumination was visible for forty miles out at sea. At midnight the bombardment ceased. No important results were gained on either side, the casualties to either force not exceeding a dozen men killed and wounded. But it was proved that the batteries in the vicinity of Pensacola were harmless against Fort Pickens, and Bragg's mission a useless one.

The next week after the fight on Santa Rosa, our fleet lying at anchor inside the Southwest Pass of the Mississippi, and consisting of the steamers Richmond, Huntsville, Water-witch, and the two sloops-of-war Preble and Vincennes, was suddenly attacked by the Manassas, a Confederate battering-ram, under the command of Captain Hollins. The onset was made on the night of the 12th by a charge of the ram against the sides of the Richmond, knocking a hole in her timbers below water-mark, but doing only a trifling damage, though the steamer was struck with such violence as to be torn from her fastenings. The crew, however, were on their guard, and deliver-

ed a broadside into the Manassas, one of whose engines would no longer work, and by the severity of their fire compelled Hollins to haul off his ram, and to signal for support. At the given signal a new danger became imminent to our vessels, for a row of fire-ships at that moment appeared moving down the river, and threatening complete destruction to the fleet. To avoid this calamity, the fear of which was enhanced by the approach of gun-boats down the river, the Federal ships of war fell down the Pass one after another; but, unfortunately, both the Richmond and the Vincennes got aground in attempting to pass the bar. The former, however, was in a favorable position to give full effect to her heavy guns, having her broadside up the stream, and thus the entire fleet was enabled to escape.

The motive which incited the Confederates to this attack was to break up the blockade, which had ruined the prospects of the Crescent City. For this purpose several gun-boats had been constructed during the summer, and the more formidable Manassas had been built at Algiers, just opposite New Orleans, and armed with a 64-pound Dahlgren. But the long-contemplated assault resulted in little immediate damage, and accomplished absolutely nothing in its attempt to break up the blockade.

HOLLINS'S ATTACK ON THE FEDERAL FLEET IN THE SOUTHWEST PASS.

WILLIAM H. SEWARD.

CHAPTER VII.

THE POLICY OF THE FEDERAL GOVERNMENT.

Opening of the Extra Session.—The Fourth of July.—Changes in the House.—Election of Speaker.—Galusha A. Grow.—Changes in the Senate.—Former Preponderance of the South.—Want of a Leader.—William H. Seward.—Salmon P. Chase.—Stephen A. Douglas.—Henry Wilson.—John C. Breckinridge.—Jesse D. Bright.—Expulsion of Breckinridge, Bright, Polk, and Johnson.—The President's Message.—The Army and the Navy.—War Bills proposed in the Senate.—Resolution to approve the President's Acts.—The Debates.—Expulsion of Senators.—The Army Bill.—The Crittenden and Johnson Resolution.—McClernand's Resolution.—Military Laws of the Session.—Financial Measures.—The Confiscation Bill.—Receipts and Expenditures.—Foreign Relations.—Instructions to Ministers.—Privateering.—Confederate Commissioners.—British, French, and Spanish Decrees of Neutrality.—The Affair of the Trent.—Views of the British and American Governments.—First regular Session of Congress.—President's Message.—Number and Constitution of the Army.—Mr. Stanton appointed Secretary of War.—The Navy.—Receipts and Expenditures.—Plan of the Secretary of the Treasury.—Change of Views in Congress.—Peace Propositions laid aside.—War Measures.—Appropriations.—Financial Measures adopted.—Paper Money a Legal Tender.—The Argument for and against it.

IT is proposed in this and the following chapter to describe the domestic and foreign policy of the Federal government from the opening of the extra session of Congress, July 4, 1861, to the close of the first regular session, July 17, 1862.

Congress met in extra session at the call of the President on the 4th of July. That day is memorable in American history. On that day, eighty-five years before, the delegates of the thirteen United States had formally put forth the declaration claiming a place among the sovereign and independent nations of the earth. Now delegates from thirteen states (for Kentucky and Missouri were nominally represented in the Confederate Congress) were preparing to convene at Richmond to complete the destruction of the Union. Three of the five successive presidents who had borne a part in the struggle for national existence had died on the 4th of July. On that day, thirty-five years before, just half a century after the signing of the Declaration, Jefferson, its author, and Adams, its most eloquent advocate, had died. On that day, thirty years before, Monroe, the last of the Revolutionary presidents, had died. On that day, ten years before, just fifty-eight

years after the corner-stone of the original capital had been laid by the hands of Washington, the corner-stone of the edifice in which Congress was now assembled had been laid by the President. Daniel Webster delivered an oration, in which he declared that the distinctive nature of American liberty, as distinguished from that of Greece, Rome, and modern Europe, was the capacity for self-government, giving to the will of the majority, fairly expressed through its representatives, the binding force of law, and the formation of a written constitution, founded upon the will of the people. Under that corner-stone he deposited a document, written by his own hand, setting forth, in his own massive diction, that on this day the Union of the United States stood firm; the Constitution was unimpaired, and growing every day stronger in the affections of the American people, and attracting more and more the admiration of the world.[1]

The Thirty-seventh Congress, thus convened in extra session five months before its regular time of meeting, would hardly have been recognized by one who had known the capital in former days. In the House of Representatives 159 members answered to their names at roll-call. When all the seats claimed were filled there were 178 members of the House. In the preceding Congress, whose term had closed four months before, there were 237 representatives. Of the 66 members to which the eleven seceding states were entitled, only six appeared. Five of these were from Virginia, chosen at an election of somewhat doubtful validity, and one from Tennessee. The nineteen free states sent 149 representatives; the four border states, which still adhered to the Union, sent 23. In no preceding Congress within the memory of living men had there been so large a proportion of new members. Barely one third of the representatives had been members of the preceding Congress. Some states changed their delegation entirely; some changed a majority. From Maine every representative was a new man; of the thirty-three members from New York, only eight had held seats in the last Congress; of the five representatives from New Jersey, three were new men. Two thirds of the entire delegation in the House consisted of men who had never before held seats in Congress. This great change of persons did not, however, involve a corresponding change in parties. The elections had been held before the plans of the Secessionists had been fully developed, and so before the great uprising of the North, which for a time swept away all the old party distinctions. In the previous Congress, out of 237 representatives, 109 were Republicans, 101 Democrats, while 27, mainly from the border states, who held the balance of power, maintained a position independent of either party. It had only been after a violent contest of two months that a Republican speaker was elected by a bare majority. In the present Congress the Republicans had 106 members, having actually lost three members; but the defection of the South gave the Republicans a majority of three to two, and there were, besides, about 30 members who, without belonging to the party, sustained the administration in its leading measures for the prosecution of the war.

Three members, Grow, of Pennsylvania, Blair, of Missouri, and Colfax, of Indiana, were prominently named as the Republican candidates for speaker. Colfax, whose chances of success stood high, and who was chosen speaker of the next Congress, peremptorily declined. He would not, by being a candidate, delay the organization of the House. The first ballot stood 71 for Grow and 40 for Blair; but, before the result was announced, Blair withdrew, asking his friends to change their votes. Most of them voted for Grow, giving him 99 votes out of 159. The remaining votes were scattered; of these, 12 were cast for Mr. Crittenden, who, having been superseded as senator from Kentucky by Mr. Breckinridge, had been chosen a member of the House. Several more were cast for other Union men, leaving the actual strength of the Opposition about 40.

Galusha A. Grow, the new speaker, though barely thirty-eight years of age, had been a member of the House for ten years. He had first taken his seat in 1850, being the youngest member. He soon gave evidence of decided ability, and was at successive sessions appointed chairman of several important committees. He ranked originally among the Democrats, but when the great disruption of parties began, he took his place in the new organization among the Republicans. In 1857 he was the candidate of that

---

[1] "If, therefore, it shall hereafter be the will of God that this structure shall fall from its base, that its foundations shall be upturned, and the deposit beneath this stone brought to the eyes of men, be it then known that on this day the Union of the United States of America stands firm, and that their Constitution still exists unimpaired, and with all its original usefulness and glory, growing every day stronger and stronger in the affections of the great body of the American people, and attracting more and more the admiration of the world. And all here assembled, whether belonging to public or to private life, with hearts devoutly thankful to Almighty God for the preservation of the liberty and happiness of the country, unite in sincere and fervent prayers that this deposit, and the walls and arches, the domes and towers, the columns and entablatures, now to be erected over it, may endure forever. God save the United States of America!"

party for speaker, but was defeated by Mr. Orr, of South Carolina, the candidate of the Democratic party, who had then a majority of fully three to two.

Before the speaker had been chosen several members of the Opposition party gave significant indications of the course which they were to pursue. When the names of the members from Virginia were called, Cox, of Ohio, and Burnett, of Kentucky, objected to their reception. Some members had been sworn into the military service of the United States; Vallandigham, of Ohio, moved that they were thereby disqualified from holding seats in Congress. Of Cox and Vallandigham we shall have occasion to speak hereafter. Burnett, after strenuously opposing every measure of the government, went over to the Confederacy, was formally expelled from his seat in Congress, and was subsequently appointed, by the body claiming to be the Council of State of Kentucky, a representative in the Confederate Congress at Richmond.

The change in the Senate was as notable as that in the House. The South had long since abandoned the hope of maintaining an equality in the popular branch of Congress. The population of the North increased more rapidly than that of the South. Its majority in the House was augmented with each successive apportionment. A united North was consolidating to oppose a united South, already consolidated. In the House, also, the members from the South had long been, as a whole, inferior in character and ability to those from the North. The lawless voters of Arkansas and Mississippi, the ignorant denizens of the sand-hills of Georgia and North Carolina, had sent members of their own class. "Fire-eaters," bullies, and demagogues had found constituents in various districts of other states. That there were many men in the House of ability, culture, and education from the Southern states is true; but, as a body, they were types of a low class of Southern society.

With the Senate it was different. There the South was nearly equal in numbers to the North; and as it was united on all sectional questions, and was always in close affiliation with a large party in the North, it had always a practical majority in the Senate. The South had always sedulously cared for its representation in this body of the national Legislature. The selection of senators was not determined by mere local or personal influences. Any rude district might send an incapable representative to the House, but a whole state would rarely agree upon any one incapable man. In the choice of senators, therefore, the combined intellect and culture of each state had the predominance. Now and then, indeed, in the complication of partisan politics, an incompetent man found his way to the Senate from a Southern state. But these cases were exceptional; as a general rule, the South sent its strongest men to the Senate, and kept them there. This long service added to their prominence. Of late years, also, Southern senators had gained an influence beyond that growing out of their individual talents and services. They were a compact body. When one acted or spoke he spoke and acted as a representative of all, and practically as the representative of all the Northern men of Southern principles. So long as the South controlled the Senate it controlled the government. Without its consent no law could be passed; without its sanction no officer could be appointed to execute a law.

The domination of the South in the Senate was never more absolute than during the session which closed with the termination of Buchanan's administration. The Democratic party, Southern and Northern, had a clear majority of three to two.[1] This gave them the control of all the standing committees; for, according to established usage, the dominant party in the Senate assembled in caucus and settled the constitution of all the committees. They apportioned among themselves the chairmanship and the majority of every important committee. The list was formally presented to the Senate for acceptance. It had been previously agreed upon by the majority in a private caucus from which the minority were excluded. The adoption of the list thus made out was certain. The minority had only to accept it, which they usually did without opposition, for opposition would have been unavailing.

The construction of the standing committees was a matter of great importance. Except in cases where a special committee was ordered—when the senator who proposed the committee was usually appointed its chairman by courtesy—these standing committees gave shape and form to the action of the Senate. Of the twenty-two regular committees, the control of sixteen was given to the slave states. These embraced every important committee. Mason, of Virginia, was chairman of the Committee on Foreign Relations;

GALUSHA A. GROW.

Hunter, of the same state, had that on Finance; Clay, of Alabama, had Commerce; Jefferson Davis had Military Affairs; Mallory, of Florida, had Naval Affairs; Bayard, of Delaware, had the Judiciary; Yulee, of Florida, the Post-office; Johnson, of Arkansas, had Public Lands; Benjamin, of Louisiana, had Public Land Claims; Brown, of Mississippi, had the District of Columbia; and to Green, of Missouri, was assigned the lead in the Committee on Territories, so long accorded to Douglas, whose recently promulgated doctrine of popular sovereignty had rendered him obnoxious to the oligarchy of the South. The six committees confided to senators from the free states had to do only with mere routine business. They were the Committees on Pensions, Patents, Public Buildings, Printing, Engrossed Bills, and Enrolled Bills. Even Bright, of Indiana, the facile tool of the South, and its mouthpiece when any communication was to be intrusted to a Northern man, was put off with the chairmanship of the Committee on Public Buildings.

The conspiracy against the Union was organized and directed in the Senate of the United States, if it did not originate there. Early in 1861, when South Carolina only had seceded, a meeting of Southern senators was convened, in which Georgia, Alabama, Louisiana, Arkansas, Mississippi, Florida, and Texas were represented. Resolutions were passed in favor of the simultaneous secession of all the Southern states, and the establishment of a Southern Confederacy. The conspiring senators, however, resolved still to retain their seats until the inauguration of the new administration; for, if they left, "force, loan, and volunteer bills might be passed, which would put Mr. Lincoln in immediate condition for hostility;" whereas, if they remained in their places until the 4th of March, they "could keep the hands of Mr. Buchanan tied, and disable the Republicans from effecting any legislation which would strengthen the hands of the incoming administration." A committee was appointed to carry out the objects of this meeting. Its members were Jefferson Davis, then United States senator from Mississippi, chairman of the Committee on Military Affairs, soon to be President of the

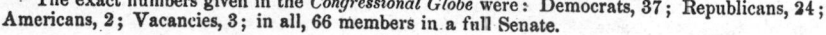

[1] The exact numbers given in the *Congressional Globe* were: Democrats, 37; Republicans, 24; Americans, 2; Vacancies, 3; in all, 66 members in a full Senate.

Southern Confederacy; Stephen R. Mallory, then United States senator from Florida, chairman of the Committee on Naval Affairs, soon to be Secretary of the Navy for the Confederacy; and John Slidell, a native of New York, then United States senator from Louisiana, soon to be the Confederate Envoy to the court of France.[1] Some of these conspirators abandoned their seats before the specified day, others retained them beyond that time; but enough remained to prevent the passage of any bills for strengthening the military or naval power of the government. Scarcely a regiment of soldiers, scarcely a vessel of war, scarcely a dollar in the treasury was at the disposal of the new administration when it came into office on the 4th of March.

The Senate which convened on the 4th of July consisted of but 47 members.[2] Andrew Johnson, of Tennessee, was the only one who appeared from the seceding states, and he had made his way to the national capital with a price upon his head. The seceding senators embodied their full proportion of the ability, and more than their proportion of the notability, of the Senate. Half of them were in their second and third terms. Their average service had already been eight years; the remaining senators averaged but four. To gain position in the Senate is usually a work of time. The new members had yet to acquire a national reputation. Of the senators now assembled thirty-one were Republicans; five others, though not belonging to that party, now supported the administration; two held an indeterminate position, but generally acted with the Opposition; the remaining nine persistently opposed every military or financial measure which implied the exercise of force for the maintenance of the Union. Of these nine four were within a few months formally expelled from the Senate for open complicity with the insurgents, and another subsequently resigned because the Senate demanded of its members an oath of fealty to the Constitution and government.

Although there were many able men in Congress, there was no one who could be considered a leader of the dominant party. That position had long been conceded to Mr. Seward. Even while in a meagre minority, he had for years exercised a personal influence greater than that of any other senator. He possessed many of the highest attributes of a statesman. He was ambitious, but in a noble way, for he was always ready to sacrifice present popularity to future renown. He never frittered away his influence or wasted his strength upon trifles. He took no part in mere Congressional skirmishing, and never condescended to reply to personal attacks. He spoke much, but only upon important subjects, and after full preparation. In every separate attribute of an orator he was excelled by some other senator. Hale could deliver a keener retort, Sumner pronounce a more scathing philippic; Douglas was a more skillful debater, Davis a more persuasive pleader. The two famous phrases, "the higher law" and "the irrepressible conflict," seem to have fallen from his lips by accident, without his imagining that they would be caught up and denounced on the one hand, and accepted on the other as symbols of a political faith.[3] He lacked that personal magnetism by which a leader sometimes binds the members of his party to himself. Strong men wept like children when the last chances of the election of Clay and Webster to the presidency were lost; the hold of Calhoun and Douglas upon their parties was quite as much personal as political. When Mr. Seward failed to receive the nomination, his supporters evinced no bitter regret. He was, in their view, the best exponent of the principles of the party; but if another man could secure a larger vote, they were content that he should be nominated. Mr. Seward was, however, conceded to be the foremost statesman of his time and country, the nearest representative of the great men of the last generation. That he was the representative man of his party was acknowledged, and it was a foregone conclusion with friends and foes that he would receive the nomination for the presidency. His vote on the first ballot, though not a majority, far exceeded that given for any other; but the second ballot showed that influences were at work which would prevent a majority from being concentrated upon him, and upon the third trial Mr. Lincoln was nominated. Mr. Seward then resolved to retire from public life; but, at the earnest request of his successful competitor, he consented to accept the position of Secretary of State. It was honorable to both men that such an offer should be made and accepted; but it would probably have been more for the interest of the country had he remained in his former position as leader of his party in the national Legislature.

Salmon P. Chase had risen rapidly into a leading position in the party. He had entered into public life as a Democrat, and as such had served for

one term as senator. When the great disruption took place in that party, he joined the Republicans, was twice chosen Governor of Ohio, and was a prominent candidate for the presidential nomination. He was chosen as senator for the Congress which had now convened; and had he taken his place as such, the position of leader must have fallen to him. But he had previously resigned his seat and accepted the office of Secretary of the Treasury. In this position he was to undertake heavier responsibilities than had ever before fallen to the lot of a financial minister. It is worthy of note that the four leading competitors of Mr. Lincoln for the presidential nomination accepted seats in his cabinet.[1]

There was one senator to whom, until within a month, men's eyes had been turned as likely to be the Congressional leader of the great Union party. Stephen A. Douglas, of Illinois, had for fifteen years been a determined opponent of the Whig or Republican party. He early foresaw the danger which threatened the Union from the controversy growing out of the agitation of the question of slavery. He perceived that there was but one principle upon which a union between free and slave states could be maintained, and that was the denial of the right of the general government to act in any way upon the permission or prohibition of slavery. It was admitted on all hands that this was true so far as the states were concerned: that South Carolina might any day abolish slavery, or Vermont establish it, within their limits, without question from any other state or from the Federal government. This principle was affirmed by the Compromise Act of 1850. The question was thus narrowed down to the Territories. Mr. Douglas maintained that the same principle should apply there also. In his view this involved the repeal of the Missouri Compromise. The emigrants to Kansas and Nebraska he considered to have the same rights in this matter which had been conceded to inhabitants of Utah and New Mexico. His doctrine on this point was finally wrought out and elaborated in his famous paper on the "Dividing Line between State and Federal Authority." This he regarded as the crowning act of his political life. "I believe it to be my mission," he said to the writer of these pages, "to settle forever the question of slavery; and I believe that it will be settled on the principles which I have here laid down." The essential points of this elaborate paper may be stated in a few words: Every distinct political community, loyal to the Constitution and the Union, is entitled to all the rights, privileges, and immunities of self-government in respect to their local concerns and internal polity, subject only to the Constitution of the United States; every Territory of the United States, when duly organized under a legal Territorial government, is a distinct political community; and slavery is a matter of local concern and internal polity; therefore the Territories, each for itself, have the sole right, under the Constitution, to legislate upon the subject of slavery. The Southern leaders would not assent to this doctrine. The nominating Convention of the Democratic party met at Charleston, April 23, 1860. The dividing line between the Northern and Southern branches of the party was then sharply run. The South demanded that the party should affirm not only that Congress should have no power to abolish slavery in the Territories, but that the Territorial Legislatures had no power to abolish slavery, or to prohibit the introduction of slaves, or to exclude slavery, or in any way to impair the right of property in slaves; and that it was the duty of the Federal government to protect slave property in the Territories. The North was willing to submit the question to the decision of the Supreme Court. More than half of the votes for President were cast for Mr. Douglas, but he lacked 50 of the 202 votes which, under the two thirds rule, were required for a nomination. The Convention broke up without making any nomination, and reassembled at Baltimore on the 18th of June. Here a schism took place, resulting in two Conventions. Mr. Douglas was nominated by one, and Mr. Breckinridge by the other. Had Douglas been nominated unanimously either at Charleston or Baltimore, his election was certain; but the disruption of these Conventions, making it sure that the vote of the South would be against him, drove hundreds of thousands of Northern Democrats over to Mr. Lincoln. An attempt to stay this popular current was made by nominating Mr. Bell as a "Union" candidate; but the nomination came too late. Mr. Lincoln received 180 electoral votes, being all from the free states except three from New Jersey. Mr. Breckinridge received 72 votes, being the whole from the strictly Southern states, together with those of Maryland and Delaware. The votes of Virginia, Kentucky, and Tennessee, 39 in all, were cast for Mr. Bell; while Mr. Douglas received only 9 votes from Missouri and 3 from New Jersey. The popular vote, indeed, showed a very different result. For Lincoln were cast, in round numbers, 1,850,000 votes; for Douglas, 1,360,000; for Breckinridge, 840,000; and for Bell, 590,000. Douglas, therefore, retained his place in the Senate as the representative of nearly one third of the people of the United States, who, while opposed to the Republican party, were still more opposed to every scheme of secession. His first effort was to secure the passage of the Crittenden Proposition. It was not, indeed, in accordance with his own cherished views, but he was eager to accept it in order to save the Union. This last hope failing, and the line having been clearly drawn, he saw that there was no way remaining by which a loyal citizen could show his devotion to his country except by ignoring all party politics, and sustaining the flag, the Constitution, and the Union under any administration, against all assailants at home and abroad. It was noted that, when Mr. Lincoln pronounced his inaugural address on the 4th of March, Douglas was by the side of his old personal opponent, holding his hat while he spoke; and that during the festivities which followed in the evening he was assiduous in his courtesies to the wife of the President. These acts,

---

[1] For a fac-simile of the letter describing this conspiracy, written and franked by David L. Yulee, then United States senator from Florida, and chairman of the Committee on the Post-office, see this History, page 32.

[2] Shortly afterward two senators were admitted representing the State of Virginia, and subsequently two others representing the newly-formed state of West Virginia.

[3] The phrase "the higher law" occurs in a speech delivered in the Senate, March 11, 1850, upon the admission of California into the Union. The following is the context:

"It is true, indeed, that the national domain is ours. It is true it was acquired by the valor and with the wealth of the whole nation. But we hold, nevertheless, no arbitrary power over it. We hold no arbitrary authority over any thing, whether acquired lawfully or seized by usurpation. The Constitution regulates our stewardship; the Constitution devotes the domain to union, to justice, to defense, to welfare, and to liberty. But there is a higher law than the Constitution, which regulates our authority over the domain, and devotes it to the same noble purposes. The Territory is a part, and no. inconsiderable part, of the common heritage of mankind, bestowed upon them by the Creator of the universe. We are his stewards, and must so discharge our trust as to secure in the highest attainable degree their happiness."

The phrase "irrepressible conflict" is found in a speech delivered at Rochester, October 25, 1858, in the following connection:

"It is an irrepressible conflict between opposing and enduring forces. It means that the United States must and will, sooner or later, become entirely a slaveholding nation or entirely a free-labor nation. Either the cotton and rice fields of South Carolina and the sugar plantations of Louisiana will be ultimately tilled by free labor, and Charleston and New Orleans become marts for legitimate merchandise alone, or else the rye-fields and wheat-fields of Massachusetts and New York must again be surrendered by their farmers to slave culture and to the production of slaves, and Boston and New York become once more markets for trade in the bodies and souls of men."

[1] The votes in the Convention on the first ballot were: for Seward, 173; Lincoln, 102; Cameron, 50; Chase, 49; Bates, 48. The remaining 48 votes were scattered among seven candidates.

which under ordinary circumstances would have been mere personal courtesies shown to a distinguished citizen of his own state, were accepted on all sides as significant indications of his political course. During the brief executive session of the Senate which followed, he took decided ground in favor of the line of policy indicated in the inaugural, accepting it, as it was intended, as a pledge that the aim of the administration was a peaceful solution of our national difficulties. But when the hostile measures of the Confederates rendered such a solution impossible, he remained firm in his resolution to uphold the Union by supporting the administration. His last public act was to dictate a letter to the chairman of the Democratic Committee of his own state, explaining and defending the course upon which he had resolved. This letter was dictated from a bed of sickness from which he was never to rise. Shortly after it was written, just one month before the meeting of the extra session of Congress, he was a corpse. He died at the age of forty-eight years, in the prime of manhood, at a moment when a career was opening before him nobler than has been presented to any American since the Father of his Country. He was more or less delirious during the closing days of his life. But his own impending death gave him no concern. The salvation of the republic was foremost in his thoughts; his last coherent words, before his farewell to his wife and his parting message to his absent children, breathed an ardent wish that the honor and safety of his country might be secured by the overthrow of her enemies.[1]

In the Senate the most important committee was now that on Military Affairs. Mr. Wilson, of Massachusetts, was appointed chairman of this committee, and was thus recognized as the leader of the dominant party in the Senate. His early life was spent on a farm. At twenty-two he learned the trade of a shoemaker, and soon after commenced business as a manufacturer of shoes. He entered warmly into politics and military affairs. At the age of forty he had already served eight years in the Legislature of Massachusetts, having twice been chosen President of the state Senate, and risen to the rank of brigadier general in the militia. In 1855 he was elected to the Senate of the United States, where he soon assumed a leading place. Earnest, fearless, and fluent, thoroughly appreciating the magnitude of the crisis, he was undoubtedly the best man for the position assigned to him. As all financial bills must originate in the House, the Committee of Ways and Means is the most important in that body. Thaddeus Stevens, of Pennsylvania, was appointed chairman of that committee, involving the lead of the House.

The lead of the Opposition in the Senate was accorded to Mr. Breckinridge. He had served for four years as Vice-president of the United States, and consequently as President of the Senate. He had been nominated for the presidency, with a fair chance of success if the election could be thrown into the House of Representatives. When this scheme failed, he had been chosen senator from Kentucky in place of Mr. Crittenden, who had labored

HENRY WILSON.

so earnestly to bring about a compromise. In presenting the credentials of his successor, Mr. Crittenden had said, "He succeeds to a place of great difficulty and high duties. I have no doubt that he will, and I hope that he may, occupy his seat more successfully than I have done for the good of our common country." Mr. Breckinridge had presided over the Senate with marked acceptance. His fine person, commanding address, courteous manners, and quick perception fitted him for that position. Just four months before the meeting of the extra session he had been thanked by the Senate for his conduct as its presiding officer. He had warmly supported the Crittenden Proposition. He had taken no part in the conspiracy against the Union. It cost him much to take the first steps against that Union over which he had hoped to preside. While the struggle was going on men marked his worn and haggard aspect; but, the steps once taken, he had neither the wish nor the power to retrace them. He took his seat as senator on the 4th of March in the executive session which followed the regular close of Congress. He then made a formal speech, urging the Senate to advise the President to withdraw all troops from the Confederate States, and to collect no large forces in any of the other Southern states. "The seven states which have gone out," he said, "are a protest against force in any form. From the eight Southern states which remain, making fifteen in all, there is also a protest against force." If force was used against any state which had seceded, or which might hereafter secede, he affirmed that his own state of Kentucky would "turn to her Southern sisters, with whom she was identified by geographical position, and by the ties of friendship, of intercourse, of commerce, and by common wrongs. She will unite with them to found a noble republic, and invite beneath its stainless banner such other states as know how to keep the faith of compacts, and to respect the constitutional obligations and the comity of the Confederacy." Thus, while under the sanction of his oath as senator of the United States, he avowed himself the advocate of those who had endeavored, or who should thereafter endeavor, to destroy the Union. Thus pledged to treason, he took his place as senator at the extra session. Henceforth his course was consistent. He

---

[1] The following are extracts from the last letter of Douglas:

"It seems that some of my friends are unable to comprehend the difference between arguments used in favor of an equitable compromise, with the hope of averting the horrors of war, and those urged in support of the government and flag of our country when war is being waged against the United States with the avowed purpose of producing a permanent disruption of the Union and a total destruction of its government. All hope of a compromise with the cotton states was abandoned when they assumed the position that the separation of the Union was complete and final, and that they would never consent to a reconstruction on any contingency, not even if we would present them with a blank sheet of paper, and permit them to inscribe their own terms. Still the hope was cherished that reasonable and satisfactory terms of adjustment could be agreed upon with Tennessee, North Carolina, and the border states, and that whatever terms would prove satisfactory to these loyal states would create a Union party in the cotton states which would be powerful enough at the ballot-box to destroy the revolutionary government, and bring those states back into the Union by the voice of their own people. This hope was cherished by Union men North and South, and was never abandoned until actual war was levied at Charleston, and the authoritative announcement made by the revolutionary government at Montgomery that the secession flag should be planted upon the walls of the Capitol at Washington, and a proclamation issued inviting the pirates of the world to prey upon the commerce of the United States. . . . . . In view of this state of facts, there was but one path of duty left to patriotic men. It was not a party question, nor a question involving partisan policy; it was a question of government or no government, country or no country; and hence it became the imperative duty of every Union man, every friend of constitutional liberty, to rally to the support of our common country, its government and flag, as the only means of checking the progress of revolution, and of preserving the union of the states. . . . . . I am neither the supporter of the partisan policy nor the apologist for the errors of the administration. My previous relations to them remain unchanged. But I trust the time will never come when I shall not be willing to make any needful sacrifice of personal feeling and party policy for the honor and integrity of my country. I know of no mode by which a loyal citizen may so well demonstrate his devotion to his country as by sustaining the flag, the Constitution, and the Union, under all circumstances, and under every administration, regardless of party politics, against all assailants at home and abroad. The course of Clay and Webster toward the administration of General Jackson in the days of nullification presents a noble and worthy example for all true patriots. . . . . . The gulf which separated party leaders in those days was quite as broad and deep as that which now separates the Democracy from the Republicans. But the moment an enemy rose in our midst, plotting the destruction of the government, the voice of party strife was hushed in patriotic silence. One of the brightest chapters in the history of our country will record the fact that, during this eventful period, the great leaders of the Opposition, sinking the partisan in the patriot, rushed to the support of the government, and became its ablest and bravest defenders against all assailants, until the conspiracy was crushed and abandoned, when they resumed their former positions as party leaders upon political issues."

opposed every measure looking to the strengthening of the Union or the weakening of the Confederacy. At the close of the session he returned to his home, threw up his office as senator, and joined the Confederates who were then invading Kentucky. They received him with open arms, and gave him a commission as brigadier general in their service. On the 4th of December, just nine months from the day when he had received the thanks of the Senate, he was formally expelled from that body without a single opposing vote.

Jesse D. Bright, of Indiana, was the only senator from a free state who took his place among the thorough opponents of the administration. He had been elected for three successive terms, and had now held his seat longer than any other member. He had always been a strict partisan. Though born in one free state and elected from another, there was no Southern man more entirely Southron than he. Other Northern members of his party sometimes hesitated to yield to the demands of their Southern colleagues—Bright never. He could be counted upon as surely as Davis or Mason. Though an indifferent speaker, he was a shrewd and dexterous party manager. He was placed on important committees, and had frequently been chosen temporary president of the Senate. He had taken no part in the great conspiracy. Facile tool as he was, that secret was not to be trusted to him. He urged his Southern colleagues to retain their places after the election of Lincoln. They did so as long as it suited their plan of preventing the passage of any bills which might strengthen the hands of the new administration. In these efforts they found a ready coadjutor in Mr. Bright. When the war finally broke out, he deliberately took the position of hostility to "the entire coercive policy of the administration." He was willing to furnish means to defend the capital then threatened by the Confederates, but would not give men or money to carry on the war against the states which had declared themselves out of the Union. During the extra session he spoke but little, for oratory was not his forte; but in his votes he followed Breckinridge like his shadow. In every division, important or unimportant, the name of Bright was sure to follow that of Breckinridge. That he misrepresented his constituents, opposed his country, and gave practical aid and comfort to the enemy was true; yet in his official capacity he only exercised his constitutional right of opposition, and furnished no grounds for parliamentary censure. But in a careless moment he had forged a weapon that could fairly be used against him.

A quarter of a century before he had a client, named Thomas Lincoln, who at length failed in business and emigrated to Texas. The connection had been a profitable one for Bright. After the annexation of Texas, Lincoln made his appearance at Washington in the character of schemer and speculator. Now he had a railroad scheme to urge upon Congress; then it was a machine for raising heavy weights which he wished to have employed in the erection of the public buildings at Washington. His last project was an alleged improvement in fire-arms. Bright was always ready to serve his old friend and client. He gave him letters of recommendation wherever they could be of use. He commended his fire-arms to Mr. Floyd, then Secretary of War, who seems to have been too busy in his treasonable projects to take any notice of it. At length, on the first of March, three weeks after the organization of the Confederate government, three weeks after Texas had formally seceded, and while the Confederate States were individually and collectively waging war against the Union, Mr. Bright wrote a letter introducing this Texan, with his improvement in fire-arms, to the President of the Confederacy.[1] What became of Lincoln for the next few months is unknown; but in August he was arrested in Ohio on charge of treason, and this letter was found upon him. Shortly after the meeting of Congress in December, a resolution was offered for the expulsion of Mr. Bright. He did not deny the genuineness of the letter; he had no recollection of having written it, but if Lincoln said that he wrote it he undoubtedly did so. The resolution was referred to the Committee on the Judiciary, who reported that the facts were not sufficient to warrant the expulsion of Mr. Bright from the Senate. This report was not accepted, and a long debate ensued. It was contended by Mr. Bright and his friends that it was a mere note of introduction; that in addressing Jefferson Davis as "His Excellency, the President of the Confederacy of States," the writer used only the usual form of courtesy, designating the person addressed by the title which he claimed; that at the time when the letter was written there was no war, and no probability of one until after the fall of Sumter. On the other side it was urged that the letter recommending an inventor of improved fire-arms to the notice of the leader in the insurrection was an evidence of the thorough disloyalty of the writer, for such a weapon could be wanted only for hostilities against the United States; and, moreover, some months later, while the country was actually engaged in a gigantic war, he had written another letter avowing that he "had opposed, and should continue to oppose, the entire coercive policy of the government." The resolution of expulsion passed by a vote of 32 to 14. Among those who voted against it were, besides the whole remaining body of Opposition senators, several Democrats who supported the administration, and two Republicans. These last took the ground that, however objectionable might be the general course of Mr. Bright, this letter, considering the circumstances in which it was written, did not necessarily imply a treasonable intent, which was necessary to warrant his expulsion. If treason, in its strict sense, were the only ground for expulsion, they were correct in their view, for upon this letter no jury could ever have convicted the writer of that crime. But there may be disloyalty which, falling short of actual treason, still disqualifies a man from acting as a legislator. In this sense the senator from Indiana was disloyal; but, to warrant expulsion, this disloyalty must be evinced by overt act. He had a right to the protection of law; but if there was any act of his which brought him fairly in opposition to the strictest law, that law should have been brought to bear with all its force against him. This letter would clearly have warranted his arrest and detention in a military prison; and surely no man who might rightly have been consigned to Fort Lafayette should have been allowed to retain a seat in the Senate of the United States.

Two other senators, Polk and Johnson, from Missouri, who sat in this extra session, were likewise expelled at the subsequent one. Both had gone to their homes and taken open ground in favor of the secession of their state; both had failed to claim their seats; and both were credibly reported to have made their way to the Confederate States. The case was so clear against them that there was no voice against the resolution for their expulsion. Even Bright, Powell, and Bayard voted for it.

The organization of Congress was completed on the first day of the session. The President's Message was transmitted on the following day. It opened with a summary of the events of the four months of his administration, and a statement and defense of the policy which he had adopted. In six states the functions of the government were suspended; forts and arsenals had been seized; the Confederacy had been organized, and was invoking recognition and aid from foreign powers. The administration had to prevent, if possible, the dissolution of the Federal Union. The policy decided upon was announced in the inaugural address. It looked to the exhaustion of all peaceful measures before proceeding to stronger ones. It sought only to hold the public places not already wrested from the government, and to collect the revenue. Every thing was forborne without which it was possible to keep the government on foot. Fort Sumter was to be provisioned, in order that the authority of the nation might be visibly maintained. It was assailed and reduced in order to destroy the visible authority of the Union. The assailants began the conflict while no force, immediate or in expectancy, menaced them, and thus forced upon the country the distinct issue of immediate dissolution or blood. No choice was then left but to call out the war power of the government, and so to resist the force employed for its destruction by force for its preservation. The Message closed with an argument against the constitutional right of any state or number of states to secede. This argument, though conclusive, was useless; the time for argument had passed; the question must be decided by arms.

But the essential points of the Message were contained in four brief paragraphs.[1] The first touched upon the position of "armed neutrality" which a

---

[1] *Jesse D. Bright to Jefferson Davis.*

"Washington, March 1, 1861.

"MY DEAR SIR,—Allow me to introduce to your acquaintance my friend Thomas B. Lincoln, of Texas. He visits your capital mainly to dispose of what he regards as a great improvement in fire-arms. I recommend him to your favorable consideration as a gentleman of the first respectability, and reliable in every respect.

"Very truly yours, JESSE D. BRIGHT.

"To His Excellency JEFFERSON DAVIS, *President of the Confederacy of States.*"

[1] The following is the text of the most important portions of the Message:

THE ISSUE.

"The assault upon and reduction of Fort Sumter was in no sense a matter of self-defense upon the part of the assailants. They well knew that the garrison in the fort could by no possibility commit aggression upon them. They knew—they were expressly notified—that the giving of bread to the few brave and hungry men of the garrison was all which would on that occasion be attempted, unless themselves, by resisting so much, should provoke more. They knew that this government desired to keep the garrison in the fort, not to assail them, but to maintain visible possession, and thus to preserve the Union from actual and immediate dissolution; and they assailed and reduced the fort for precisely the reverse object—to drive out the visible authority of the Federal Union, and thus force it to immediate dissolution. . . . . . Then and thereby the assailants of the government began the conflict of arms, without a gun in sight or in expectancy to return their fire, save only the few in the fort, sent to that harbor years before for their own protection, and still ready to give that protection in whatever was lawful. In this act, discarding all else, they have forced upon the country the distinct issue, 'immediate dissolution or blood.' And this issue embraces more than the fate of these United States. It presents to the whole family of man the question whether a constitutional republic or democracy—a government of the people by the same people—can or can not maintain its territorial integrity against its own domestic foes. It presents the question whether discontented individuals, too few in numbers to control administration, according to organic law, in any case, can always, upon the pretenses made in this case, or on any other pretenses, or arbitrarily, without any pretense, break up their government, and thus practically put an end to free government upon the earth. It forces us to ask, 'Is there, in all republics, this inherent and fatal weakness?' 'Must a government, of necessity, be too strong for the liberties of its own people, or too weak to maintain its own existence?'"

THE BORDER STATES.

"In the border states, so-called—in fact, the Middle States—there are those who favor a policy which they call 'armed neutrality'—that is, an arming of those states to prevent the Union forces passing one way, or the Disunion the other, over their soil. This would be disunion completed. Figuratively speaking, it would be the building of an impassable wall along the line of separation; and yet not quite an impassable one, for, under the guise of neutrality, it would tie the hands of Union men, and freely pass supplies from among them to the insurrectionists, which it could not do as an open enemy. At a stroke it would take all the trouble off the hands of secession, except only what proceeds from the external blockade. It would do for the Disunionists that which of all things they most desire—feed them well, and give them disunion without a struggle of their own. It recognizes no fidelity to the Constitution, no obligation to maintain the Union; and while very many who have favored it are doubtless loyal citizens, it is, nevertheless, very injurious in effect."

CALLING OUT TROOPS.

"Recurring to the action of the government, it may be stated that at first a call was made for 75,000 militia; and, rapidly following this, a proclamation was issued for closing the ports of the insurrectionary districts by proceedings in the nature of a blockade. So far all was believed to be strictly legal. At this point the insurrectionists announced their purpose to enter upon the practice of privateering. Other calls were made for volunteers to serve for three years, unless sooner discharged, and also for large additions to the regular army and navy. These measures, whether strictly legal or not, were ventured upon under what appeared to be a popular demand and a public necessity, trusting then, as now, that Congress would ratify them. It is believed that nothing has been done beyond the constitutional competency of Congress."

SUSPENSION OF THE WRIT OF HABEAS CORPUS.

"Soon after the first call for militia, it was considered a duty to authorize the commanding general, in proper cases, according to his discretion, to suspend the privilege of the writ of habeas corpus, or, in other words, to arrest and detain, without resort to the ordinary processes and forms of law, such individuals as he might deem dangerous to the public safety. This authority has purposely been exercised but very sparingly. Nevertheless, the legality and propriety of what has been done under it are questioned, and the attention of the country has been called to the proposition that one who has sworn to 'take care that the laws be faithfully executed' should not himself violate them. Of course, some consideration was given to the question of power and propriety before this matter was acted upon. The whole of the laws which were required to be faithfully executed were being resisted, and failing of execution in nearly one third of the states. Must they be allowed to finally fail of execution, even had it been perfectly clear that by the use of the

considerable part of the people of Kentucky and Missouri wished to assume. They wished their states to arm in order to prevent the Union troops from passing one way, or the Disunion troops the other way, over their soil. This project was condemned in a few brief and emphatic words.

The second important paragraph recited briefly the war measures adopted by the administration. A call had been made for 75,000 militia; the ports in the insurrectionary districts had been blockaded; farther calls had been made for volunteers for three years; and large additions had been made to the regular army and navy. It was assumed that in some or all of these measures the executive had exceeded the strict legal bounds of its authority; but they had been ventured upon under what appeared to be a popular demand and a public necessity, believing that they would be ratified by Congress.

The third paragraph related to the suspension of the writ of habeas corpus in certain cases. The facts were succinctly stated, and the opinion was expressed that in this case the executive had not gone beyond the power conferred upon it by the Constitution. But it was maintained by some that the authority to suspend this writ was vested in Congress; and to the judgment of the national Legislature the President submitted the question whether there should be any legislation upon this subject.

The fourth paragraph recommended that, in order to make the contest a short and decisive one, Congress should place at the disposal of government 400,000 men and $400,000,000, affirming that the country could sustain the burden; that the people were ready to bear it; and that the end to be attained was worth the sacrifice.

HANNIBAL HAMLIN.

The report of the Secretary of War presented only a general abstract of the operations of that department. The President's call of April 15 for 75,000 volunteers for three months had been responded to by more than 80,000 men. The proclamation of May 3 called for 42,000 volunteers for three years. Under this call 208 regiments had been accepted, of whom 153 were in actual service, and the remainder would be in the field within twenty days. These regiments, including the three months volunteers, numbered 285,000 men; besides these, the new regiments of the regular army numbered 25,000 men, making 310,000 in all. Deducting from these the 80,000 three months volunteers whose term of service was about to expire, there would remain an available force of 230,000 men, volunteers and regulars. The secretary submitted to Congress the question whether this force should be farther increased.

The report of the Secretary of the Navy showed that under the administration of Mr. Buchanan this department had not only been neglected, but such disposition had been made of the vessels as to render the navy powerless for immediate operations against the Confederacy. Nominally our navy, on the 4th of March, consisted of 90 vessels, carrying 2415 guns. But 21 vessels, with 1069 guns, were unfinished or unseaworthy, leaving 69 vessels, with 1346 guns, at all available. Of these, 21 vessels, with 791 guns, were dismantled or laid up in ordinary, so that we had actually in commission only 42 vessels, with 555 guns. Two of these vessels were 50-gun frigates, the remainder were sloops and steamers. The steam navy comprised only 26 vessels of all classes, with 216 guns. The fleet seems to have been posted with the express design of rendering it useless in the present emergency. Nearly all of the vessels were on foreign stations. The home squadron consisted of but 12 vessels, with 187 guns, and about 2000 men; and of these only 4 small vessels, carrying 25 guns and 280 men, were in Northern ports. Of the 69 serviceable vessels, which on the 4th of March were supposed to be available, one was lost in the Pacific, another was soon seized at Pensacola, and four were burned at Norfolk; there were four more which could not be put into commission for a considerable time. Thus, when all the vessels should be recalled from foreign service, there would remain 58 vessels of the former navy, with 1021 guns. Treachery was rife among the officers of the navy. Many of those occupying the most responsible positions were faithless. Among these was Matthew F. Maury, to whom had been for years intrusted the charge of the National Observatory. Only a few months before he had protested vehemently against the action of the examining board, which had retired him from the line of promotion, continuing him in his honorable and responsible scientific position. Without note or warning, he abandoned his post and went over to the enemy. In all, between the 4th of March and the 1st of July, 259 naval officers had resigned their commissions or been dismissed. Hardly a seaman followed their example of treachery. Thus, while the United States claimed to be and was considered one of the great maritime powers, their actual naval

---

means necessary to their execution some single law, made in such extreme tenderness of the citizen's liberty that practically it relieves more of the guilty than of the innocent, should to a very limited extent be violated? To state the question more directly: Are all the laws but one to go unexecuted, and the government itself to go to pieces, lest that one be violated? Even in such a case, would not the official oath be broken if the government should be overthrown, when it was believed that disregarding the single law would tend to preserve it? But it was not believed that this question was presented. It was not believed that any law was violated. The provision of the Constitution that 'the privilege of the writ of habeas corpus shall not be suspended unless when, in cases of rebellion or invasion, the public safety may require it,' is equivalent to a provision—is a provision—that such privilege may be suspended when, in case of rebellion or invasion, the public safety does require it. It was decided that we have a case of rebellion, and that the public safety does require the qualified suspension of the privilege of the writ which was authorized to be made. Now it is insisted that Congress, and not the executive, is vested with this power. But the Constitution itself is silent as to which or who is to exercise the power; and as the provision was plainly made for a dangerous emergency, it can not be believed the framers of the instrument intended that in every case the danger should run its course until Congress could be called together, the very assembling of which might be prevented, as was intended in this case, by the rebellion. No more extended argument is now offered, as an opinion, at some length, will probably be presented by the attorney general. Whether there shall be any legislation on the subject, and, if any, what, is submitted entirely to the better judgment of Congress."

MEASURES RECOMMENDED.

"It is now recommended that you give the legal means for making this contest a short and decisive one; that you place at the control of the government, for the work, at least 400,000 men and $400,000,000. That number of men is about one tenth of those of proper ages within the regions where, apparently, all are willing to engage; and the sum is less than a twenty-third part of the money value owned by the men who seem ready to devote the whole. A debt of $600,000,000 now is a less sum per head than was the debt of our Revolution when we came out of that struggle, and the money value in the country now bears even a greater proportion to what it was then than does the population. Surely each man has as strong a motive now to preserve our liberties as each had then to establish them. A right result, at this time, will be worth more to the world than ten times the men and ten times the money. The evidence reaching us from the country leaves no doubt that the material for the work is abundant, and that it needs only the hand of legislation to give it legal sanction, and the hand of the executive to give it practical shape and efficiency. One of the greatest perplexities of the government is to avoid receiving troops faster than it can provide for them. In a word, the people will save their government, if the government itself will do its part only indifferently well."

THE RIGHT OF SECESSION.

"This sophism derives much, perhaps the whole, of its currency from the assumption that there is some omnipotent and sacred supremacy pertaining to a state—to each state of our Federal Union. Our states have neither more nor less power than that reserved to them in the Union by the Constitution—no one of them ever having been a state out of the Union. The original ones passed into the Union even before they cast off their British colonial dependence; and the new ones each came into the Union directly from a condition of dependence, excepting Texas. And even Texas, in its temporary independence, was never designated a state. The new ones only took the designation of states on coming into the Union, while that name was first adopted by the old ones in and by the Declaration of Independence. Therein the 'United colonies' were declared to be 'free and independent states;' but even then, the object plainly was not to declare their independence of one another or of the Union, but directly the contrary, as their mutual pledge and their mutual action before, at the time, and afterward, abundantly show. . . . . . No one of our states, except Texas, ever was a sovereignty; and even Texas gave up the character on coming into the Union, by which act she acknowledged the Constitution of the United States, and the laws and treaties of the United States made in pursuance of the Constitution, to be for her the supreme law of the land. The states have their *status* in the Union, and they have no other legal *status*. If they break from this, they can only do so against law and by revolution. The Union, and not themselves separately, procured their independence and their liberty. By conquest or purchase the Union gave each of them whatever of independence or liberty it has. The Union is older than any of the states, and, in fact, it created them as states."

"Again: if one state may secede, so may another; and when all shall have seceded, none is left to pay the debts. Is this quite just to creditors? Did we notify them of this sage view of ours when we borrowed their money? If we now recognize this doctrine by allowing the seceders to go in peace, it is difficult to see what we can do if others choose to go, or to extort terms upon which they will promise to remain."

"If all the states save one should assert the power to drive that one out of the Union, it is presumed the whole class of seceder politicians would at once deny the power, and denounce the act as the greatest outrage upon state rights. But suppose that precisely the same act, instead of being called 'driving the one out,' should be called 'the seceding of the others from that one,' it would be exactly what the seceders claim to do; unless, indeed, they make the point that the one, because it is a minority, may rightfully do what the others, because they are a majority, may not rightfully do."

FUTURE POLICY.

"Lest there be some uneasiness in the minds of candid men as to what is to be the course of the government toward the Southern states after the rebellion shall have been suppressed, the executive deems it proper to say it will be his purpose then, as ever, to be guided by the Constitution and the laws; and that he probably will have no different understanding of the powers and duties of the Federal Government relatively to the rights of the states and the people under the Constitution than that expressed in the inaugural address. He desires to preserve the government, that it may be administered for all as it was administered by the men who made it. Loyal citizens every where have the right to claim this of their government, and the government has no right to withhold or neglect it. It is not perceived that in giving it there is any coercion, any conquest, or any subjugation, in any just sense of those terms."

"As a private citizen the executive could not have consented that these institutions shall perish; much less could he, in betrayal of so vast and so sacred a trust as these free people have confided to him. He felt that he had no moral right to shrink, or even to count the chances of his own life, in what might follow. In full view of his great responsibility he has so far done what he has deemed his duty. You will now, according to your own judgment, perform yours. He sincerely hopes that your views and your action may so accord with his as to assure all faithful citizens who have been disturbed in their rights of a certain and speedy restoration to them, under the Constitution and the laws. And having thus chosen our course, without guile and with pure purpose, let us renew our trust in God, and go forward without fear and with manly hearts."

force was less than that of any second-rate power. So patent was the insufficiency of the navy that the late administration had recommended the building of seven steam sloops-of-war, of light draught and heavy armament. The last Congress had authorized the construction of these vessels in spite of the vehement opposition of the Southern members who still retained their seats. "If these steamers are built," said Mr. Mason, "they will be part of the naval armament of the Confederation, to be used for any military purposes that the public exigencies may require. Until we know whether the arm of the government is to be raised against the states which have seceded, by no vote of mine shall there be any addition to the naval or military service of the country." These vessels were now in course of construction at the public navy yards, and the present administration had also contracted for twenty-three gun-boats, and had made preliminary arrangements for several larger and fleeter vessels. But the building of these was a work of time, and the demands of the service were pressing. A number of steamers had been purchased or chartered, so that on the 1st of July the government had in commission 82 vessels of war, carrying 1100 guns, with 13,000 men, besides officers and marines.

Congress determined from the outset to devote itself to the work for which it had been called together. The House voted to consider only bills and resolutions concerning military and naval operations, and financial and judicial matters therewith connected. In the Senate Mr. Wilson gave notice of a series of bills: First, To confirm certain acts of the President for the suppression of insurrection and rebellion. Second, To authorize the employment of volunteers to aid in enforcing the laws and protecting public property. Third, To increase the present military establishment of the United States. Fourth, For the better organization of the military establishment. Fifth, For the organization of a volunteer militia force to be called the National Guard of the United States. Sixth, To promote the efficiency of the army. Mr. Chandler gave notice of a bill to confiscate the property of civil and military officers who should be guilty of treason or of aiding and abetting it, and disqualifying them from holding any office of trust and emolument. These bills, more or less modified, together with the financial measures originating in the House, gave shape to the proceedings of the session.

The proposition to confirm the acts of the President was presented as a joint resolution. It recited that under extraordinary exigencies the President had exercised certain powers and adopted certain measures for the preservation of the government. He had (1.) called for 75,000 volunteers. He had (2.) set on foot a blockade of the ports of South Carolina, Georgia, Alabama, Florida, Mississippi, Louisiana, and Texas. He had (3.) blockaded the ports of Virginia and North Carolina. He had (4.) authorized the commanding general to suspend the writ of habeas corpus on the military line between Philadelphia and Washington. He had (5.) issued a proclamation calling into the service of the United States 42,000 volunteers, increasing the regular army by 22,700 men, and the navy by 18,000 seamen. He had (6.) authorized the commander of the forces in Florida to suspend the writ of habeas corpus if necessary. The resolution provided that all of these extraordinary acts should be approved, and declared as legal and valid as if they had been performed under the express authority and sanction of Congress.

After some preliminary discussion, which showed that there was among the Republicans a strong disinclination to sanction any permanent increase of the regular army, the debate was opened by Mr. Polk in opposition to the resolution. He said that Congress only has the right to make war, yet the President had, of his own motion and by his own wrong, brought on war. Secession was an accomplished fact before the close of the last Congress, yet that body had refused to pass any bills for the purpose of coercion. Provision was made by the Constitution for the enforcement of the laws when resisted by an individual or any number of individuals; but when a state or a number of states withdrew from the Union and denied the binding force of its laws, there was no provision for compelling their obedience. So the calling out of the militia was unconstitutional. Then, after seven states had seceded, the President, assuming them to be still in the Union, had ordered a blockade of their ports; and subsequently, when North Carolina and Virginia had resolved not to submit to the coercion of their sister states, he had ordered a blockade of their ports, in defiance of the provision of the Constitution that no preference should be given to the ports of one state over those of another. The Constitution provides that Congress shall have the power of regulating commerce with foreign nations and between the states. The President had undertaken to regulate commerce with the seceding states. The fact of their secession does not affect the case. If this secession was legal, they are foreign states; if illegal, they are still members of the Union. In either case the Constitution had been violated. The President had also, in acknowledged violation of the law, increased the force of the army and of the navy. He had also, in suspending the writ of habeas corpus, assumed a power which the sovereign of Great Britain dared not arrogate, and, in consequence, John Merryman had, in Maryland, been seized by the mere warrant of a military officer, and been shut up in Fort McHenry.[1] Thus the President had usurped the military

power of the government by making war and raising armies; he had usurped the commercial power by regulating trade and commerce; he had usurped the judicial power by setting aside the writ of habeas corpus. From these general charges Mr. Polk proceeded to specific allegations of abuses committed in his own state, the general purport of which was to justify all the acts of Governor Jackson, and to condemn all those of the Federal government. He closed by declaring that no measure which had for its object the prosecution of the war should ever command his vote.

Mr. Powell, of Kentucky, followed upon the same side, recapitulating in substance the points made by Mr. Polk. "If," he added, "the people justly appreciated the liberties given them by their fathers, and intended to be secured to them by the Constitution, the officer who had committed these usurpations would be arraigned at the bar of the Senate, and be upon trial under impeachment." In reply to a definite question, he declared that he approved of the action of the governor of his state in refusing to send volunteers for the defense of the national capital.

Mr. Breckinridge followed. His speech was made on the 16th of July, at the moment when the army was setting out on its disastrous expedition to Bull Run. He recapitulated in better form the arguments of Polk and Powell; denied that one branch of the government could indemnify another for a violation of the Constitution or laws, and declared that, so far from his acts being approved, the President should be rebuked by a vote of both houses of Congress.

Mr. Bayard, of Delaware, continued the discussion. His speech was delivered on the 19th of July, while the two armies were confronting each other at Bull Run. He thought the only alternative was an assent to secession or civil war. The secession of a state was indeed a revolutionary act. If a single state should secede, restriction and coercion, not to the extent of arms, might be employed, and this, coupled with conciliation, might bring the state back. But the power to coerce a state by arms had not been given to the general government. We could only make war upon the seceding states for a breach of compact, or make peace with them, and recognize the government which they had founded. He preferred peaceful separation to civil war. Congress had indeed the power to make war; but revolutions must be treated according to their magnitude, and a revolution by eleven states could not be met by war if its object was the restoration of the Union, and its preservation as a representative republic. He was therefore in favor of an armistice and negotiations. If compromise could restore these states to the Union, he would compromise; if not, he would part with them in peace on a just and equitable settlement. If their terms were unjust they should be rejected. Passing over the war measures of the President, which he conceded had been substantially endorsed by the subsequent action of Congress in passing war bills, Mr. Bayard went on to argue at length against sanctioning the suspension of the writ of habeas corpus. If that was done, the liberties of the country would be prostrated, and the rights of free citizens destroyed.

Among the supporters of the administration there was at first a wide difference of opinion in respect to this resolution. Some approved of every one of the specified acts; others objected to a part, and approved of the remainder. Mr. Trumbull would sustain or excuse all that had been done, but would not pronounce all the acts to have been legal. Mr. Sherman approved of all the acts as a matter of necessity, but would not as a senator vote that, in increasing the army and navy, and in suspending the writ of habeas corpus, the President had acted according to law. Mr. Howe would approve and sanction all these acts for the very reason that they had been done without direct sanction of law. Had there been law for them, the President would simply have done his duty and nothing more. As it was, he had taken upon himself the responsibility of saving the country without the sanction of express law, and in so doing he had acted more than well; he had acted bravely.

The debates on this resolution commenced near the beginning of the session, and were continued at intervals till the close. At first the opposition to the increase of the regular army and of the navy had been general, and amendments had been proposed providing that this increase should be only temporary. But the result of the battle of Bull Run, and the position of the Confederate forces almost in sight of the capital, convinced all Union men that a permanent addition to the army was a matter of necessity, and laws were accordingly passed sanctioning it. The theoretical objection to the suspension of the writ of habeas corpus still existed in many minds, but just now this was of no practical importance, and was tacitly dropped. The proposition to approve all the other specified acts of the President was at the last moment appended as an additional section to the act which passed both houses increasing the pay of privates in the army.[1]

The measures proposed from time to time furnished occasion for debating every aspect of the insurrection and of the policy of the government. A resolution was offered to expel the senators from the seceding states who had not withdrawn at the last session, and whose names still appeared on

---

[1] This case, which was most frequently dwelt upon in the debates, derives its special importance from the action of Chief Justice Taney in relation to it. Merryman, who resided near Baltimore, was arrested on the 25th of May, by order of the military commander, on charge of holding a commission as lieutenant in a company having in their possession arms belonging to the United States, and avowing his purpose of armed hostility against the government. He was taken to Fort McHenry, then commanded by General Cadwalader. He applied to Mr. Taney, Chief Justice of the United States, for a writ of habeas corpus. This was duly issued. General Cadwalader, through one of his officers, declined to produce Mr. Merryman, and asked the court to postpone farther action until instructions could be received from the President. Judge Taney issued an order of attachment against General Cadwalader for contempt of court. The marshal

to whom this order was given reported that he was not permitted to enter the fort, and so could not serve the order. The judge said that if the general could be brought before him he should punish him by fine and imprisonment; but as it was beyond the power of the posse comitatus to enforce the order, all that he could do was to place upon record a formal report of his proceedings, and to call upon the President to perform his constitutional duty by enforcing the process of the court.

[1] Public Acts of the 37th Congress, chap. lxiii.—"An Act to increase the pay of the privates in the regular army and of the volunteers in the service of the United States, and for other purposes:" Section 1 fixes the pay at $13 a month. Section 2 provides that the pay shall commence from the day when they were organized and accepted by the governors of their respective states. Section 3, "All the acts, proclamations, and orders of the President of the United States, after the 4th of March, respecting the army and navy of the United States, and calling out or relating to the militia or volunteers from the states, are in all respects legalized and made valid to the same intent, and with the same effect, as if they had been issued and done under the previous express authority and direction of the Congress of the United States."

the roll of the Senate, on the ground that they had engaged in a conspiracy against the Union. Mr. Bayard opposed this. He knew of no conspiracy on the part of these senators. They claimed that states had a right to secede, and acted openly with their states. Supposing them to be wrong in their view, should senators be expelled for an error in point of law? Should they be condemned individually for the action of their states? It was sufficient to declare their seats vacant. Mr. Latham would vote for striking their names from the roll, but not for expulsion, for that implied a stain upon the personal character of the individual. He knew that at least two of these senators did not endorse the right of secession, but they did not think they should remain in the Senate of the United States after their state had seceded. The senators, ten in number, were expelled by a vote of 32 to 10. Mr. Bayard also opposed the admission of Willey and Carlisle, who claimed the seats from Virginia vacated by Mason and Hunter. By admitting them, he said, a government would be recognized for that state which was not the regular government. The term of Mr. Letcher as governor had not expired. If he was in rebellion, that did not authorize a portion of the people of Virginia to form a Legislature and to elect senators. There was no authority to create a new state out of a part of an existing one. To do so would be to abandon the whole form of our government, and recognize insurrection in a state for the purpose of overthrowing the government of that state by a very small minority of its people. The members were admitted, only five senators voting in the negative.

In advocating the approval of the acts of the President, the impetuous Baker, who was soon to seal his faith with his blood, had said, "I propose to lend the whole power of the country, arms, men, money, and place them in the hands of the President. He has asked for $400,000,000; we propose to give him $500,000,000. He has asked for 400,000 men; we propose to give him 500,000. If the emergency be still greater, I will cheerfully add a cipher to either of these figures. I do that as a measure of war; but I look forward to returning peace. Bayonets are sharp remedies, but they are very powerful. I believe that the Union sentiment will yet prevail in the Southern states. But it may be that, instead of finding within a year loyal states sending members to Congress and replacing their senators on this floor, we may have to reduce them to the condition of Territories, and send from Massachusetts or Illinois governors to control them. If need come, I would be willing to do it. I would risk even the stigma of being despotic and oppressive rather than risk the perpetuity of the union of these states. Fight the war through; accomplish a peace; make it so permanent that a boy may preserve it; and when you have done that, you have no more need of a standing army."

Senator Powell moved as an amendment to the Army Bill that no part of the army or navy should be used to subject or hold as a conquered province any state now or lately one of the United States, or in abolishing or interfering with slavery in any of the states. Sherman opposed the amendment as out of place, but he declared that there was no purpose in conducting the war to subjugate a state or to free a slave. Its purpose was to preserve the Union, to maintain the Constitution in all its clauses and guarantees, without change or limitation. Dixon said that if, in the progress of the war, it should turn out that either the government or slavery should be destroyed, then let slavery perish. Lane, of Kansas, affirmed that we would have stood by the compromises of the Constitution, and permitted slavery to exist where it was planted; but the struggle has been forced upon us, and he was willing that it should be followed to its logical conclusion, believing that the institution of slavery would not in any state survive the march of the Union armies. Browning, the successor of Douglas, avowed that the war was one of subjugation. Where all the authorities of a state were disloyal, and banded in treasonable confederation against the government, he was for subjugation, it mattered not whether it was called subjugation of a state or of its people. If the issue was forced upon us, he was for the government against slavery, and would vote for sweeping that last vestige of barbarism from the face of the earth.

In the House, on the 22d of July, the day after the battle of Bull Run, Mr. Crittenden offered a resolution declaring that the war had been forced upon the country by Southern Disunionists; that it was not waged by the Union for the purpose of conquest or subjugation, or for interfering with the institutions of the states, but to maintain the supremacy of the Constitution and to preserve the Union, without impairing the equality and rights of the states; and that when these objects were attained, the war ought to cease. It passed with scarcely a show of opposition, only two votes being cast against it.[1] This resolution, in precisely the same words, was presented to the Senate by Andrew Johnson, of Tennessee. Mr. Polk proposed to amend it so as to read that "the war had been forced upon the country by the Disunionists of the Southern and Northern states." This was rejected by a vote of 33 to 4. This again brought up the question of subjugation. Mr. Trumbull disliked the use of that word in this connection. It had never been the purpose of the United States to subjugate or coerce states, but it was proposed to subjugate citizens who are standing out in defiance of the laws of the Union, and to coerce them into obedience to the laws of the Union. If the resolution meant that the war was not for this purpose, he was opposed to it. Mr. Fessenden said that the war was not carried on for

---

[1] "*Resolved*, That the present deplorable civil war has been forced upon the country by the Disunionists of the Southern states, now in revolt against the constitutional government and in arms around the capital; that in this national emergency Congress, banishing all feeling of mere passion or resentment, will recollect only its duty to the whole country; that this war is not prosecuted upon our part in any spirit of oppression, nor for the purpose of overthrowing or interfering with the rights or established institutions of those states, but to defend and maintain the supremacy of the Constitution and all laws made in pursuance thereof, and to preserve the Union, with all the dignity, equality, and rights of the several states unimpaired; and that as soon as these objects are accomplished the war ought to cease."

JOHN J. CRITTENDEN.

the purpose of subjugating the people of any state; but we had the definite purpose of defending the Constitution and the laws, and of putting down the revolt at any hazard, and it was for the South to say whether it was necessary to subjugate them in order to do it. If it were done, he would keep them subjugated no longer than was necessary for that purpose. Thus far it must go, and no farther.

Mr. Willey, of Virginia, said that there was a fear in his state that the design of the war was subjugation, to reduce the Old Dominion into a province. He did not believe that such was the object, and he was instructed and prepared to vote for every necessary measure and for every necessary man to carry on the war until the Constitution was vindicated and restored to its legitimate supremacy, and the Union re-established on a basis never to be overthrown. But if it was avowed that this was to be a war upon the domestic institutions of the South, and upon the rights of private property, every loyal arm on the soil of the Old Dominion would be instantly paralyzed. Pass the resolution, and vigor would be given to every loyal arm in the Old Dominion, and the friends of the Union would be multiplied by thousands.

Mr. Breckinridge would not vote for the resolution because he did not agree with the statement of facts contained in it. He believed there were errors on both sides. The present condition of affairs was owing to the refusal of the Senate to agree to any proposition of adjustment. The war was now prosecuted for objects of subjugation; and unless those states which had seceded would lay down their arms and surrender at discretion, the majority in Congress would listen to no terms of settlement.

The resolution was adopted by a vote of 30 to 5, Mr. Trumbull being the only Republican voting against it. On this question he found himself for once, though from very different reasons, voting with Breckinridge and Waldo Johnson; with Polk and Powell. This joint resolution, passing both houses of Congress almost unanimously, was accepted as an authoritative definition of the objects and limits of the war. Members on both sides had, in the heat of debate, loosely used the word subjugation; but, when it was fairly explained, it was found that by it those who supported the government meant merely bringing the revolted states under subjection to the recognized laws of the land. A small band in the Senate, most of whom were soon to take their proper place among the Confederates, refused to assent to this. In the popular branch of Congress, the Opposition members either voted for the proposition, or declined to vote at all. The two votes cast against it were from the Republican side.

In the House the debates took the same general turn as in the Senate. The same positions were taken, and enforced by similar arguments usually less elaborately presented. The attention of the House was mainly devoted to bills and resolutions pertaining to military and naval appropriations. The key-note to the predominant feeling in that body was struck by Mr. McClernand, a Democrat from Illinois, who offered a resolution that "this House hereby pledges itself to vote for any amount of money and any number of men which may be necessary to insure a speedy and effectual suppression of the rebellion, and the permanent restoration of the Federal authority every where within the limits and jurisdiction of the United States." This was adopted by a vote of 121 to 5. Taken in connection with the Crittenden resolution and the declarations embodied in the President's Message, it clearly defined the policy which all branches of the government, with rare unanimity, had at this time marked out in respect to the conduct of the war.

SALMON P. CHASE.

cent to 2 cents; that on silks, wines, and liquors was increased from 10 to 25 per cent.; upon most other articles the increase was about 10 per cent. A direct tax of $20,000,000 was levied upon the states, besides a tax of 3 per cent. upon all incomes in excess of $800 a year.[1] The Secretary of the Treasury was authorized to borrow $250,000,000, issuing therefor, at discretion, bonds at 7 per cent. interest, payable in twenty years; or treasury notes of not less than $50, at $7\frac{3}{10}$ per cent., payable in three years; or treasury notes of $5 and upward, payable on demand without interest; or similar notes at $3\frac{65}{100}$ per cent., payable in one year.[2]

The President was also authorized, in cases where the revenue laws could not be executed at a port of entry, to remove the custom-house to any secure place in the district, on land or on shipboard; or, if necessary, to close the ports of entry in any district. He might also, by proclamation, declare any state or part of a state in insurrection, and prohibit commercial intercourse with it, or license it upon such terms as might be prescribed by the Secretary of the Treasury.[3] A confiscation act was passed, providing that during the present or any future insurrection, after due proclamation by the President, all property used or intended to be used by the owner for aiding the insurrection should be lawful subject of capture and prize, and that it should be seized, confiscated, and condemned. This law specially provided that any owner of a slave, or any person having a legal claim to his services, who should require or permit such slave to take up arms against, or be in any way employed in military or naval service against the United States, should thereby forfeit all claim to him, any law of a state or of the United States to the contrary notwithstanding.[4]

This last provision, which met with strenuous opposition, and finally passed in the House only by a vote of 60 to 48, embodied the only direct action taken by Congress during the extra session upon the subject of slavery. The question, indeed, frequently came up incidentally in the course of debate, and members of both houses expressed their individual opinions upon it; but there was a manifest determination on the part of the administration and its supporters to take at this time no definite ground in relation to it. It will be the object of the next chapter to show how the government was subsequently forced from this position, and to set forth its whole course of action upon the question of slavery, which finally resulted in the proclamation for universal emancipation throughout the revolting states.

Congress thus placed the whole power of the nation at the disposal of the President for the suppression of the rebellion. The events of the last few months had proved that men would not be wanting; but the financial prospect gave occasion for the gravest apprehensions. The administration of Buchanan had left the treasury almost empty, and the credit of the government dubious. In December $5,000,000 of government notes were put into market at the lowest rates of interest offered. There were offers at 24 and 36 per cent.; only half a million was bid for it as low as 12 per cent.; all above that were rejected. But the money was needed to pay the interest on public stocks, and banks and bankers took a million and a half more at that rate on condition that it should be used only for this purpose. In January $5,000,000 more was borrowed at a little less than 11 per cent. In February $8,000,000 of six per cent. stock was sold, averaging 90 per cent. The tariff bill of March, and the hopes of peace inspired by the President's inaugural, raised the credit of government somewhat, and Mr. Chase, now Secretary of the Treasury, was able to dispose of $3,000,000 at 94 per cent. The attack upon Sumter brought down stocks again, and United States sixes sold at 83, while money could with difficulty be placed at 4 per cent.; $5,000,000 in treasury notes, made receivable for customs, was at length, by great exertions, sold to banks and bankers at par, which enabled the administration to go on a few weeks. Then, at the close of May, a new loan was offered, and $9,000,000 was secured at from 85 to 93 per cent. Just before the meeting of Congress $5,000,000 more was borrowed for 60 days on pledge of government notes. When Congress met, Mr. Chase estimated the probable expenditures of the year at about $320,000,000. To meet this he proposed to raise $80,000,000 by imposts and direct taxation, and the remaining $240,000,000 by loan. Congress passed the necessary bills, and the loan was thrown into the market. The banks of the three great commercial cities agreed to take, between August and December, $150,000,000. This would enable the treasury to meet the demands upon it until Congress should again assemble.

Our foreign relations meanwhile were a subject of uneasiness. The Con-

The extra session of Congress closed on the 6th of August, having lasted only thirty-three days. In it were passed many laws of the highest importance. All the military acts and orders of the President were approved and legalized.[1] The President was authorized to accept the services of 500,000 volunteers for a term of not less than six months or more than three years, but to be disbanded at the close of the war.[2] A farther increase of eleven regiments was made to the regular army during the rebellion; the whole army to be reduced at its close to 25,000 men, unless otherwise ordered.[3] The pay of private soldiers, regulars and volunteers, was raised to thirteen dollars a month.[4] Provision was made for the increase of the navy. The secretary was authorized to hire, purchase, or contract for, and to furnish and arm, as many vessels as were necessary.[5] The construction of iron-clad ships and floating batteries was directed, and a committee appointed to investigate plans for such structures. From the report of this committee in favor of the "Monitor" grew up the whole class of turreted vessels which constitute the distinctive feature of our iron-clad navy.[6] The duties were remitted upon all arms imported by states.[7] Ten millions of dollars were appropriated for the purchase of arms;[8] and two millions for transporting arms and munitions to loyal citizens in insurgent states.[9] The states were indemnified for all expenses incurred by them in raising, transporting, paying, and subsisting troops.[10]

The entire appropriations made amounted to $313,260,000, of which $227,938,000 were for the army, and $42,938,000 for the navy. To meet these expenditures recourse was had to an increase of the tariff, to direct taxes, to loans, and to the issue of treasury notes and bonds. An impost of 15 cents a pound was levied upon tea, and 4 cents upon coffee; these had hitherto been free. The duty on sugar was raised from three fourths of a

[1] Laws of the 37th Congress, Extra Session, chap. lxiii.   [2] Ibid., chap. viii.
[3] Ibid., chap. xxiv.   [4] Ibid., chap. lxiii.   [5] Ibid., chaps. xiii., liii.   [6] Ibid., chap. xxxviii.
[7] Ibid., chap. i.   [8] Ibid., chap. xl.   [9] Ibid., chap. xxviii.   [10] Ibid., chap. xxi.

[1] Laws of the 37th Congress, Extra Session, chap. xlv.   [2] Ibid., chaps. v., xlvi.
[3] Ibid., chaps. iii., xxxi.   [4] Ibid., chap. lx.

federates had confidently relied upon a prompt recognition of their independence by the great powers of Europe, and upon their armed intervention, if necessary, to put an end to the blockade. They believed that in their monopoly of the production of cotton they possessed the means compelling this action. The Federal government, on the other hand, directed its ministers to urge upon the governments to which they were accredited that the present disturbances had their origin only in popular passions excited under novel circumstances, and of a transient character; that it was for the interest of the world that our political system should remain unaltered; that any advantage which any foreign nation might derive from a connection with any discontented portion of our people would be ephemeral, overbalanced by the evils which it would suffer from a disseverance of the Union, whose policy had always been, and must hereafter be, to maintain peace, liberal commerce, and cordial amity with all other nations, and to favor the establishment of well-ordered government over the whole American continent; and that any thing which should induce discord or anarchy among us would tend to disturb the existing systems of government in other parts of the world, and arrest the progress of improvement and civilization. Our ministers were especially instructed to assure the governments to which they were sent that no foreign interference would be admitted in this or in any other controversy in which the government of the United States might be engaged with any portion of the American people; that foreign intervention would oblige us to treat as enemies those who should undertake it as allies of the insurrectionary party, and all the more so if such intervention should be undertaken by a combination of several European states; that the people of the United States deemed the Union, which would then be at stake, worth all the sacrifices of a contest with the world in arms, should such a contest prove inevitable.

Our ministers were also instructed to agree to the declaration of the Paris Conference of 1856, and enter into treaties in accordance with it. This declaration set forth, on the part of all the powers entering into it, that "Privateering is and remains abolished. The neutral flag covers enemy's goods, with the exception of contraband of war. Neutral goods, with the exception of contraband of war, are not liable to capture under enemy's flag. Blockades, in order to be binding, must be effective; that is to say, maintained by a force sufficient really to prevent access to the coast of the enemy." The non-maritime powers deferred their action to that of Great Britain and France. The preliminary negotiations opened in May. On the 18th of July Lord John Russell wrote to our minister, Mr. Adams, that her majesty's ministers would advise the queen to conclude such a treaty with the United States as soon as a similar one had been agreed upon by them with the Emperor of the French, so that the two might be signed simultaneously. Ten days later, upon learning that negotiations with the French government were completed, Russell renewed his declaration, adding parenthetically that the agreement must be wholly prospective. This proviso was subsequently explained to mean that the British government would undertake nothing which "should have any bearing, direct or indirect, upon the internal differences prevailing in the United States." The reasons given for this reservation were that the Confederates had been recognized as belligerents, and so that, by the general law of nations, they might arm privateers; the Federal government had designated such privateers as pirates, and any nation which had signed a convention with the United States declaring that privateering was abolished, might be called upon to treat Confederate privateers as pirates. To accept this condition would be to sacrifice the very object for which we had consented to recede from our former refusal to agree to the declaration of the Paris Congress. We had refused to accede to the abolition of privateering on the ground that it was not our policy to maintain large armies and navies. When we went to war, it was urged, we depended on our people for defense on land, and on our shipowners for defense on the water. England and France maintained vast fleets of public vessels to destroy the property of their enemies, which was precisely the work done by the vessels which we licensed as privateers. Why ask us to abandon our system of offense and defense while they maintained theirs? If they would make private property exempt from capture at sea by national vessels, we would consent to give up privateering. France, Russia, and the other powers of Europe were in favor of this modification of maritime law, but Great Britain would not accede to it, and the United States refused to become a party in the convention abolishing privateering. Now, in order to protect our commerce from Confederate privateers, we were disposed to accede to the treaty; but the British government insisted upon a proviso which expressly legalized Confederate privateers. To assent to this would also be to permit a foreign power to take cognizance of and adjust its relations upon internal and domestic differences assumed to exist among us. The proviso would, moreover, be unequal in its operation. Great Britain could modify her obligations to us on account of our internal difficulties, while our obligations to her would not be affected by any internal difficulties which might arise in any part of the British empire. Ireland might rise, India revolt, Canada or Australia secede from England, and our obligations to Britain would remain unchanged. The proviso was clearly inadmissible, and the negotiations were abandoned.

The Confederates had sent to Europe three commissioners, Yancey, Mann, and Rost, to endeavor to effect the recognition of their government. P. A. Rost was a judge in Louisiana, and had taken no prominent part in general politics. Dudley Mann had formerly been employed as diplomatic agent in Europe of the Federal government, and had of late years been engaged in unsuccessful efforts to open a direct trade between Virginia and Europe. William L. Yancey, of Alabama, was one of the earliest advocates of disunion. Earnest and eloquent, thoroughly sincere in his attachment to

WILLIAM L. YANCEY.

what he conceived the interests and rights of his section, and with a private character beyond reproach, no man out of the Senate of the United States had done so much to prepare the Southern mind for secession. In the presidential election of 1860 he took the lead in his state of the supporters of Mr. Breckinridge, who carried Alabama by a majority of 8000 over both Bell and Douglas. When a portion of the delegates in the Convention which passed the Ordinance of Secession declared that their constituents would not yield to it unless it was submitted to the popular vote, he denounced them as traitors and rebels who should be coerced into submission. On the 4th of May these commissioners waited upon Lord John Russell, the British Minister for Foreign Affairs, to lay before him a statement of the causes which had led to secession, and to urge the recognition of the Confederacy by Great Britain. The minister refused to communicate with them in his official capacity, but received them unofficially. Mr. Dallas, at that time our minister to Great Britain, was instructed, in case this unofficial intercourse was continued, to desist from any intercourse, official or unofficial, with the British government. The commissioners, at intervals, sent letters to the British government, but received only the briefest replies, and a final notice that no official communications would be entered into with them.

The British and French governments agreed to act together in regard to our affairs, with the expectation that all the other nations of Europe would concur in whatever measures they should adopt on the subject of recognition. They decided to recognize the Confederate States as a belligerent entitled to all the rights of war, and to maintain a strict neutrality between the contending parties. The queen's proclamation of neutrality was issued on the 13th of May. It commenced by reciting that, "Whereas hostilities have unhappily commenced between the government of the United States of America and certain states styling themselves 'the Confederate States of America;' and whereas we, being at peace with the government of the United States, have declared our royal determination to maintain a strict and impartial neutrality in the contest between the said contending parties," therefore all British subjects are warned "to abstain from violating or contravening either the laws and statutes of the realm in this behalf, or the laws of nations in relation thereto, as they will answer to the contrary at their peril." The laws of the realm in this respect are embodied in the Foreign Enlistment Act of 1819. This was quoted at length. In verbose and clumsy legal phraseology,[1] it provides, in substance, that any British subject who,

[1] As an illustration of the verbosity of this act, take the following sentence, which is repeated in substance seven times: "If any natural born subject of his majesty, his heirs and successors, without the leave or license of his majesty, his heirs or successors, for that purpose first had and obtained under the sign manual of his majesty, his heirs or successors, or signified by Order in Council or by proclamation of his majesty, his heirs or successors, shall take or accept, or shall agree to take or accept any military commission, or shall otherwise enter into the military service as a commissioned or non-commissioned officer, or shall enlist or enter himself to enlist, or shall agree to enlist or to enter himself to serve as a soldier, or to be employed, or shall serve in any warlike or military operation in the service of, or for, or under, or in aid of any foreign prince, state, potentate, colony, province or part of any province or people, or of any person or persons exercising or assuming to exercise the powers of government in or over any foreign country, colony, province, or part of any province or people, either as an officer or soldier or in any other military capacity," etc., "he shall be deemed guilty of a misdemeanor, and upon being convicted thereof, upon any information or indictment, shall be punishable by fine and imprisonment, or either of them, at the discretion of the court before which such offender shall be convicted."

without royal license, shall enter or engage to enter the military service of any foreign ruler or nation, shall be guilty of a misdemeanor, and shall be punished by fine and imprisonment. That no person within the British dominions shall, without royal license, equip, fit out, or arm any vessel to be employed for hostile purposes by any foreign ruler or nation; the offender to be punishable by fine and imprisonment, and the vessel, with all its appurtenances, to be seized and forfeited. That no person within the British dominions shall, without royal license, in any way augment the warlike force of any vessel of war belonging to any foreign ruler or people, under like penalty. Any person committing any of these offenses, or endeavoring to break any lawful blockade, or conveying articles contraband of war to either belligerent, is liable to the penalties prescribed in this statute, and also to those imposed by the law of nations. Any persons who commit these offenses are warned that they "do so at their peril and of their own wrong, and that they will in no wise obtain any protection from us against any liability or penal consequences, but will, on the contrary, incur our high displeasure by such misconduct." How this enactment and the proclamation based upon it was evaded will appear hereafter. This proclamation was followed by a circular to the governors of the different colonies, stating that, in order to give full effect to this principle of neutrality, her majesty had been pleased to interdict the armed ships, and also the privateers of both parties, from carrying prizes made by them into the ports or waters of the kingdom or its colonies.

The French proclamation was sharp and decisive. The Emperor, it said, "taking into consideration the state of peace which exists between France and the United States, has resolved to observe a strict neutrality in the struggle between the government of the Union and the states which propose to form a separate confederation." No vessel of war or privateer of either belligerent would be permitted to enter or stay with prizes in any French port for more than twenty-four hours, except in case of absolute necessity; no sale of prize goods would be allowed in French ports or roadsteads; every Frenchman was prohibited from accepting a commission from either party to arm vessels of war, to accept letters of marque, or to assist in any way in equipping or arming any vessel of war or privateer for either party; every Frenchman, whether residing at home or abroad, was prohibited from entering into the naval or military service of either belligerent; every Frenchman must abstain from any act in violation of French or international law which might be considered hostile to either party, and contrary to the neutrality which the Emperor had resolved to maintain. No Frenchman contravening the present enactment would have any claim to protection from his government against any acts or measures, whatever they might be, which the belligerents might exercise or decree.

The decree of the Spanish government was to the same effect, with the additional provisos that "transportation under the Spanish flag of all articles of commerce is guaranteed, except when they are directed to blockaded ports," and "the transportation of effects of war is forbidden, as well as the carrying of papers or communications for belligerents." The Portuguese decree was of the same tenor.

With the exception of the recognition of the Confederates as belligerents, the position of the European powers toward the United States during the first months of the war was not unfriendly. Some minor questions sprung up with Great Britain growing out of the blockade, but they were adjusted without much difficulty. But in November an affair occurred which threatened to involve us in actual war with Great Britain. The defeat at Bull Run, the inactivity of the Federal forces which ensued, and the increasing stringency of the blockade, which began to cause great uneasiness in Europe in relation to the supply of cotton, led the Confederate government to hope that there was a prospect of securing its recognition by Great Britain and

France, and thereby, in the end, to obtain foreign interposition in their favor. For this purpose it was determined to send commissioners of higher rank and wider reputation than those already on the ground. The choice fell upon James M. Mason, of Virginia, who was accredited to Great Britain, and John Slidell, of Louisiana, to France. Mason had been a member of the Senate of the United States since 1847, and had been for some years chairman of the Committee on Foreign Relations. This position gave him a kind of superintendence over the proceedings of the State Department. In 1857 he visited the East, where he was received with high honor. Upon occasion of the inauguration of the statue of Warren upon Bunker Hill, he was introduced by Mr. Winthrop as "a senator from the Old Dominion whose name is associated in more than one generation with eminent service in his native state and in the national councils." In reply he said, "I shall tell it in Old Virginia, when I return to her hallowed land, that I found the spirit of Massachusetts as buoyant, as patriotic, as completely filled with the emotions that should govern patriotism, when I visited Bunker Hill, as it was when that battle was fought." Thoroughly devoted to the dogma of state supremacy, he was yet among the last finally to resolve to abandon the Union. He retained his seat in the Senate to the close of Buchanan's administration, and during the executive session which followed Lincoln's accession; but during these months he strenuously opposed every measure looking toward strengthening the national government for the impending struggle. When his state at last seceded he went with her, and, failing to appear at the extra session, he was among the senators who were formally expelled. Slidell, though born in New York, had early taken up his residence in Louisiana. He represented that state in Congress in 1843, and was subsequently appointed minister to Mexico. He was elected to the Senate in 1853, and was a member when Louisiana seceded. His long residence in New Orleans, and the acquaintance thereby gained with the French language and character, fitted him for the position to which he was now appointed as commissioner to France.

Mason and Slidell, with their secretaries McFarland and Eustis, with several women of their families, embarked at Charleston late in October. Eluding the blockade, they reached Cardenas, in Cuba, and thence proceeded to Havana, where they were received with great consideration. Here they awaited the arrival of the British merchant-steamer Trent, plying between Southampton and the West India Islands, and carrying the British mails. They embarked on the morning of the 7th of November. The next day the Trent was intercepted by the American steamer San Jacinto, commanded by Captain Wilkes, and brought to by a shot across her bow. Boats were sent from the San Jacinto to the Trent, demanding the surrender of the commissioners and their secretaries. The commander of the Trent and the British mail agent protested against this. Mason and Slidell declared that they would not leave the Trent unless compelled to do so by force. A scene of confusion ensued. A daughter of Slidell struck one of the American officers in the face. They persisted in carrying out their orders. The commander of the Trent would not give up the men, nor would they give themselves up except to force. The force required was merely technical. It consisted in the display of strength, and the determination to use it, which would render resistance unavailing. This was at hand; and after a stormy scene of two hours' duration, the commissioners and secretaries, with their baggage, were transferred to the San Jacinto. Their families, declining to accompany them, were left on board the Trent, which pursued her voyage to England. The San Jacinto proceeded to the United States with the prisoners, who were placed in Fort Warren, near Boston.

The intelligence of the capture of these men was received with great rejoicing in the United States. The Secretary of the Navy wrote to the captain of the San Jacinto approving of his course, and in his report reiterated

JAMES M. MASON.

JOHN SLIDELL.

CHARLES WILKES.

the approval, saying that "the prompt and decisive action of Captain Wilkes on this occasion merited and received the emphatic approval of the Department," and that if he exhibited a too generous forbearance in not also capturing the Trent, it might be excused, but must not constitute a precedent for similar cases in the future. In the House of Representatives a resolution was adopted at the opening of the session, tendering the thanks of Congress to Captain Wilkes "for his brave, adroit, and patriotic conduct," and resolutions were adopted requesting the President of the United States to order Mason and Slidell to be confined in cells as convicted felons, in return for the similar treatment inflicted on Colonels Corcoran and Wood, captured at Bull Run, who had been so confined by the Confederate government as hostages for the crew of a privateer who had been thus shut up on charge of piracy. In the Senate the vote of thanks was referred to the Naval Committee, and received no farther action. A fortnight afterward, in the House, Mr. Vallandigham, who before and after was among the foremost opponents of the administration, offered a resolution declaring that it was the duty of the President to maintain the stand taken by the House; but circumstances had in the mean while arisen which changed the aspect of the case, and this resolution was referred to a committee, by whom it was never called up.

In Europe the seizure of these men was looked upon in a very different light. It was considered as alike an affront to the British flag and a violation of the law of nations. Our government foresaw from the beginning that the British government would not acquiesce in this proceeding. On the 30th of November the Secretary of State wrote to Mr. Adams, our minister at London, instructing him that Captain Wilkes had acted without instructions from the government, and that therefore the subject was free from the embarrassment which would have resulted had the act been specially directed. On the same day the British foreign minister, now become Earl Russell, forwarded a dispatch to Lord Lyons, minister at Washington, expressing the belief that the officer who committed the aggression had either misconceived his instructions or had acted wholly upon his own responsibility; but, in either case, the British government could not allow such an affront to pass without full reparation, and that the only satisfactory redress would be the liberation of the four prisoners, their delivery into the hands of Lord Lyons, that they might again be placed under British protection, and a suitable apology for the aggression which had been committed. This dispatch was to be communicated to the American government; but accompanying it was a private note to Lord Lyons, instructing him, in case a delay should be asked by the American government in order that the matter might be deliberately considered, to consent to wait ten days; but if, at the end of that time, the demands of the British government were not complied with, the minister was directed to leave Washington and repair to London with all the members and archives of the legation. This private instruction was not probably communicated to our government; but the official demand, though cautiously worded, was clearly an ultimatum of the British government, who meanwhile, by dispatching troops to Canada, and strengthening its naval force in the West Indies, made preparations looking to war. The French government agreed with the British, and M. Mercier, the French minister at Washington, was instructed to lay its opinion before the government of the United States, as one in which all neutrals were deeply concerned. The President and Secretary of State saw clearly that the demand must be complied with, or we must become involved in a war with Great Britain, and probably also with France; for, in case of war, the Confederate government would be recognized at once by Great Britain, and the two powers had agreed to act in concert.

Fortunately, the government of the United States had not committed itself in the matter, and was thus free to act in any manner without derogation from its honor and dignity. The question turned upon the provision of international law that vessels of neutrals conveying any thing contraband

of war belonging to a belligerent forfeit their character of neutrality and render themselves liable to seizure and condemnation. It has never been definitely settled what things are contraband of war. Arms, munitions of war, and soldiers are acknowledged to be so in all cases; provisions and articles which are used both in war and peace, such as materials for ship-building and coal, are considered contraband only when directly designed for the naval or military service of a belligerent. The question as to persons other than soldiers, and dispatches of the belligerent governments, has never been authoritatively settled. The decree of the Spanish government expressly forbade the carrying of papers or communications from belligerents. The orders of the Confederate government to the privateers which it authorized say that "neutral vessels conveying enemies' dispatches forfeit their neutral character, and are liable to capture and condemnation; but this rule does not apply to neutral vessels bearing dispatches from the public ministers of the enemy residing in neutral countries." The decision of our government was given in a long and elaborate dispatch from Mr. Seward, in which he maintained that ministers and their dispatches, as well as soldiers, were contraband; that Captain Wilkes had a right to search the Trent and capture these persons and their dispatches; but that all these proceedings must be conducted in a manner allowed and recognized by the law of nations. This law does not permit the captor to judge of the rights of the case; he must send the vessel which he charges to have forfeited its neutrality before a prize court for judicial examination. Captain Wilkes failed to do this, and permitted the Trent to proceed on her voyage, and by so doing effectually prevented the judicial examination which might have resulted in her release, including that of his prisoners. By this omission he vitiated the whole transaction, and for this error the British government had a right to expect the same reparation which we should have expected in a similar case. In coming to this conclusion, Mr. Seward said that he was really maintaining, not an exclusively British interest, but an old, honored, and cherished American cause. The principles were laid down in 1804 by James Madison, then Secretary of State, in instructions given to James Monroe, our minister to England. If he decided this case in favor of the American government, he must reverse its essential policy; if he maintained the principles and adhered to the policy, he must surrender the case itself. The American government could not deny the justice of the claim presented to it. The four persons held in custody would be cheerfully liberated, and Lord Lyons was requested to indicate a place and time for receiving them. It had previously been stated that Captain Wilkes had acted without the orders or knowledge of the government, which had neither meditated, nor practiced, nor approved any deliberate wrong.

The British minister accordingly dispatched a steamer to the neighborhood of Boston; Mason and Slidell, with their secretaries, were placed on board and formally delivered to the British government, and the steamer conveyed them to England.

But, while accepting the unconditional liberation of the prisoners and the accompanying explanation of the American government as the reparation which the British government had a right to demand, Earl Russell differed from Mr. Seward in his exposition of many points of international law, and in a paper equally elaborate with that of Mr. Seward proceeded to state

CHARLES FRANCIS ADAMS.

LORD LYONS.　　　　　　　　　　　　　　　　M. MERCIER.

wherein those differences consisted. It must be admitted that in view of positive law, so far as it is definitely settled, of the deductions fairly to be drawn in respect to other cases not specifically provided for, and of the general welfare of nations, to subserve which is the aim of international law, the general interpretation of Earl Russell must be accepted in preference to that of Mr. Seward.[1]

The affair of the Trent having been thus adjusted, the relations between the United States and Great Britain continued on a friendly footing. The British government, having occasion shortly after to send troops to Canada, asked permission to land them at Portland, and thence transport them by railway across the State of Maine. This was granted, and the British troops were saved from the risk and suffering of a wintry voyage up the St. Lawrence. Some few minor questions arose, but none of sufficient importance

to interrupt the harmony between the two nations. The American government tacitly withdrew its demand that the British minister should hold no intercourse, even unofficial, with the Confederate commissioners; and the British government endeavored in good faith to maintain its position of neutrality between those whom it had recognized as belligerents. It, however, declined to pass any new laws bearing upon the case, and the existing laws were so clumsily framed that the Confederates were subsequently able, by evading them, to fit out several cruisers in British ports to prey upon American commerce.

Congress convened in regular session on the 2d of December. The President's Message was devoted to a review of the condition of the country and the progress of the war. Our foreign relations had occasioned deep solici-

---

[1] The following, in a greatly abridged form, gives the essential points of these two elaborate papers:

Mr. Seward argues: Persons as well as property may become contraband, since the word means "contrary to proclamation, illegal, unlawful." It is agreed on all hands that persons in the naval or military service of the enemy are contrabands. Vattel says, "War allows us to cut off from the enemy all his resources, and to hinder him from sending ministers to solicit assistance;" and Sir William Scott says, "You may stop the embassador of your enemy on his passage;" and, "Dispatches are not less clearly contraband, and the bearers or couriers who undertake to carry them fall under the same condemnation."

Earl Russell rejoins: The neutral country has a right to preserve its relations with the enemy, and you are not at liberty to conclude that any communication between them can partake in any degree of the nature of hostility against you. The interests of the neutral state may require that the intercourse of correspondence should not be altogether interdicted. That might amount to a declaration that an embassador from an enemy shall not reside in a neutral state; for to what useful purpose could he reside there if he had no opportunities of communicating with his own government? Hence the practice of nations has allowed neutral states to receive ministers from belligerents and the means of immediate negotiations with them. Thus Sir William Scott, when England and France were at war, decided in the case of an American vessel—the Caroline—that the carrying of dispatches from the French minister in America to the French government was not a violation of neutrality, and that such dispatches were not contraband of war; and these principles must extend to embassadors and agents as well as to dispatches. Mr. Seward, he says, misapprehends the quotations which he makes from Sir William Scott, whose sole object was to explain the extent and limits of the doctrine of the inviolability of embassadors in virtue of that character. You may stop the embassador of the enemy when on his passage, but when he has reached his destination and taken upon him the functions of his office he is entitled to peculiar privileges. He indeed says that civil functionaries, if sent for a purpose intimately connected with hostile operations, may fall under the same rule with persons whose employment is directly military. The dictum of Vattel is in these words: "You may, moreover, attack and arrest the people of the enemy wherever you have the right to exercise acts of hostility. Not merely may you lawfully refuse passage to the ministers whom the enemy sends to other sovereigns, but you may even arrest them if they undertake to pass secretly and without permission into the places of which you are master," citing, by way of example, the seizure of the French embassador to Prussia when, France being at war with England, he attempted to pass through Hanover, which was then ruled by the King of England. The rule, as laid down by Earl Russell, is that "you may stop an enemy's embassador in any place of which you yourself are the master, or in any other place where you have a right to exercise acts of hostility. Your own territory or ships of your country are places of which you are yourself the master. The enemy's territory or the enemy's ships are places in which you have a right to exercise acts of hostility. Neutral vessels guilty of no violation of the laws of neutrality are places where you have no right to exercise acts of hostility." The doctrine that embassadors are contraband being denied, the conclusion is "that an embassador sent to a neutral power is inviolable on the high seas and in neutral waters while under the protection of the neutral flag."

Mr. Seward, proceeding from the point that dispatches and embassadors are contraband, assumes that "the circumstance that the Trent was proceeding from one neutral port to another

neutral port does not modify the right of the belligerent captor," and that consequently Captain Wilkes had the right, by the law of nations, to detain and search the Trent.

Earl Russell controverts this absolutely. He says, "It is of the very essence of the definition of contraband that the goods [or persons] should have a hostile and not a neutral destination. The articles must be taken in the actual prosecution of the voyage to an enemy's port." If indeed the real destination of the vessel be to an enemy's port, the pretense that it is to a neutral one will not protect her in conveying contraband articles; but in this case the Trent was bonâ fide on a voyage from one neutral port to another, and, therefore, had she on board articles in themselves contraband of war, she was not liable to capture. He points out at some length the injurious consequences which would result from the doctrines advocated by Mr. Seward. Thus: If, during the late war with Russia, a Russian minister to America was in an American ship bound from Hamburg to New York, the vessel might have been captured, taken to Portsmouth, and condemned; or a neutral packet, plying between Dover and Calais, with a Confederate agent on board, might be captured by a Federal cruiser and sent to New York; or a Cunard steamer, on its way from Halifax to Liverpool, with dispatches on board from Mr. Seward to Mr. Adams, might be arrested by a Confederate privateer.[a]

The essential point of Mr. Seward's dispatch is that the seizure of Mason and Slidell was vitiated only by the failure of Captain Wilkes to seize the vessel also and send her before a prize court, and that if this had been done the transaction would have been strictly legal.

Earl Russell replies to this, that, "in view of the erroneous principles asserted by Mr. Seward, and the consequences they involve, her majesty's government think it necessary to declare that they would not acquiesce in the capture of any British merchant-ship under circumstances similar to those of the Trent; and that the fact of its being brought before a prize court, though it would alter the character, would not diminish the gravity of the offense against the law of nations which would thereby be committed."

Mr. Seward closed his argument by adding: "In coming to my conclusion [to liberate the four prisoners], I have not forgotten that if the safety of this Union required the detention of the captured persons, it would be the right and duty of this government to detain them; but the effectual check and waning proportions of the existing insurrection, as well as the comparative unimportance of the captured persons themselves, when dispassionately weighed, happily forbid me from resorting to that defense."

Earl Russell replies to this: "Mr. Seward does not here assert any right founded on international law, however inconvenient or irritating to neutral nations; he entirely loses sight of the vast difference which exists between the exercise of an extreme right and the commission of an unquestionable wrong. His frankness compels me to be equally open, and to inform him that Great Britain could not have submitted to the perpetration of that wrong, however flourishing might have been the insurrection at the South, and however important the persons captured might have been. Happily, all danger of hostile collision on this subject has been avoided. It is the earnest hope of her majesty's government that similar dangers, if they should arise, may be averted by peaceful negotiations conducted in the spirit which befits the organs of two great nations."

[a] Such a capture would have been in accordance with the rule quoted above in the text, laid down by the Confederate government for its privateers. According to this, a neutral vessel renders herself liable to capture and condemnation if she carries dispatches from an enemy, except in the case of those from a minister residing in a neutral state—those sent to him by his government being contraband.

tude. A nation divided at home is exposed to disrespect from abroad; one party or the other was sure to invoke foreign intervention, and other nations were likely to accept the invitation. But the disloyal citizens of the United States had met with less encouragement than they expected. Even had foreign nations been disposed to act solely for the restoration of commerce, and especially for the acquisition of cotton, they had not been convinced that this end would be attained by the destruction of the Union; they perceived that a strong nation promised more durable peace and more reliable commerce than it would when broken into fragments. But as the integrity of our country depends upon ourselves and not upon foreign nations, we should make ample provision for the maintenance of our national defenses, especially those of our sea-coast, lakes, and great rivers. A military railroad should be constructed, connecting the loyal portions of Tennessee, North Carolina, and Kentucky with the other faithful parts of the Union. To protect our commerce, the commanders of sailing vessels, especially in the Eastern seas, should be authorized to recapture prizes which had been taken by pirates, and consular courts should be empowered to adjudicate respecting such prizes. There was no reason why the independence of Hayti and Liberia should not be acknowledged. Civil justice had been suppressed in the seceding states, in which there were two hundred millions of dollars due from insurgent to loyal citizens; but there were no courts to enforce these claims. He had been urged to establish military courts to administer summary justice in such cases, wherever our armies took possession of revolted districts; but he had declined to do so because he was unwilling to go beyond the most evident necessity in the unusual exercise of his power. He urged Congress to establish temporary tribunals for this purpose. The message embodied a brief dissertation upon the subject of capital and labor. It had been assumed on one side that labor is available only in connection with capital; that nobody would work unless some capitalist induced him do so; and the question had been mooted whether it was better that capital should hire laborers, inducing them to work of their own consent, or should buy them, forcing them to work without their consent, it being assumed in either case that the position of the laborer was one fixed for life. The President combated this whole theory. Labor, he said, was prior to and the source of capital, and there was no fixed position of laborer and capitalist. A large majority neither work for others nor have others working for them; many both work themselves and hire others to work for them, and the laborer of to-day is often the employer of to-morrow. The message contained two pregnant paragraphs bearing upon the question of slavery. These will be considered in the following chapter, in which the course of the government upon this subject will be narrated.

The army, according to the report of the Secretary of War, consisted, exclusive of 77,875 volunteers for three months, of 660,971 men. Of these, 640,637 were volunteers for three years or for the war, and 20,334 regulars.[1] The several arms of the service, volunteers and regulars, were distributed as follows: Infantry, 568,383; Cavalry, 59,398; Artillery, 24,688; Rifles and Sharpshooters, 8395; Engineers, 107. For the ensuing year appropriations were asked for a force of 500,000 men. The cavalry force was said to be larger than was necessary, and measures would be taken for its reduction. The secretary believed that "the army now assembled on the banks of the Potomac would, under its able leader, soon make such a demonstration as would soon re-establish the authority of the government throughout all the rebellious states."

A few weeks after the meeting of Congress Mr. Cameron resigned his post as Secretary of War, and was succeeded by Edwin M. Stanton, who had been for a short time attorney general under Mr. Buchanan. Much dissatisfaction had been expressed with the administration of Mr. Cameron. It was evident, from a report of a committee of Congress, that gross frauds had been perpetrated, but it should be borne in mind that the whole department had to be created almost anew, and that its operations had to be intrusted in a great measure to untried men. The retiring secretary retained the personal confidence of the President, who nominated him minister to Russia. Subsequently the House of Representatives passed a vote censuring the late secretary for having intrusted to a Mr. Cummings the control of large sums of money, and authority to purchase military supplies without restriction, and requiring from him no guarantee for the faithful performance of his duties, and for having involved the government in a vast number of contracts with persons not legitimately engaged in business pertaining to the subject-matter of such contracts. The President at once assumed the entire responsibility of the transaction for himself and for his cabinet.

The Secretary of the Navy furnished a comprehensive statement of the strength of the navy and of its operations since July. It had blockaded the insurgent ports along a coast of nearly 3000 miles, had captured 153 vessels which had attempted to run the blockade, and had achieved signal success at Hatteras and Port Royal. The number of seamen in the service had been raised since March from 7600 to 22,000. When all the vessels pur-

EDWIN M. STANTON.

chased and building were armed and equipped, we should have 264 vessels of all classes, mounting 2557 guns. Of these, 76 vessels, with 1783 guns, belonged to the old navy; 136 vessels, with 518 guns, had been purchased, and 52 vessels, with 256 guns, had been constructed. There were in all 163 steamers of all classes, with something more than 1000 guns.

The report of the Secretary of the Treasury was anxiously looked for, as indicating the financial condition of the government and the policy to be adopted. The estimated receipts for the fiscal year ending June 30, 1862, were in round numbers $329,000,000, of which only $37,000,000 were from customs and other usual sources, $20,000,000 from direct taxes, and the remaining $272,000,000 from loans already authorized. The entire expenditures of the year were estimated at $543,000,000, leaving $214,000,000 to be provided for by new loans. The secretary hoped the war would be brought to a close before midsummer, in which case the amount asked for would be amply sufficient; but if it should be protracted another year on the present scale, the expenditures would be $475,000,000, and the receipts $96,000,000. To raise this sum it would be necessary to increase the duty on tea, sugar, and coffee; to impose a direct tax of $20,000,000 on the loyal states, besides an income tax of $10,000,000, and a tax of $20,000,000 on liquors, tobacco, carriages, bank-notes, and other evidences of debt, making a direct tax in all of $50,000,000. There would then remain $379,000,000 to be procured by loans in some shape. The loans for the two years would then be $655,000,000. The whole amount of the public debt on the 1st of July, 1863, would, upon this estimate, be $900,000,000, a sum which the country could pay in twenty years as easily as it did the debt of $127,000,000 which existed in 1816, at the close of the war with Great Britain. It was proposed to raise a part of this loan indirectly by means of a national currency. There are, said the secretary, in circulation in the loyal states $150,000,000 of bank-notes, which is actually a loan without interest from the people to the banks. This may be transferred to the government in either of two ways. The notes may, by means of taxation upon them, be gradually withdrawn from circulation, and their place supplied by United States notes, payable on demand. This was partially attained by the Demand Notes of the treasury; but this mode was, in his opinion, liable to some grave objections. That which he suggested was to issue to individuals and associations notes redeemable by the proposed institutions themselves, secured by a deposit of United States stocks and an adequate provision of specie, the notes to be receivable for all government dues except customs. These notes, he thought, would form the safest currency which the nation had ever enjoyed, for they would be of equal and uniform value in every part of the Union. In a short time the whole circulating medium of the country, whether notes or coin, would bear the national impress, and its amount, being easily ascertainable, would not be likely to be increased beyond the wants of business. As the wants of the government increased with the protraction of the war, both these measures and several others were substantially adopted. The Demand Notes of the treasury, or "Greenbacks," as they were usually denominated, were first issued in large quantities, and became at first the common circulating medium. The establishment of national banks, based upon deposits of United States stocks, followed later.

[1] The volunteers for the war were furnished from the several states and territories in the following proportions:

California	4,688	New Jersey	9,342
Connecticut	12,400	New York	100,200
Delaware	2,000	Ohio	81,205
Illinois	80,000	Pennsylvania	94,760
Indiana	57,332	Rhode Island	5,898
Iowa	19,800	Vermont	8,000
Kentucky	15,000	Virginia	12,000
Maine	14,239	Wisconsin	14,153
Maryland	7,000	Kansas	5,000
Massachusetts	26,760	Colorado	1,000
Michigan	28,550	Nebraska	2,500
Minnesota	4,160	Nevada	1,000
Missouri	22,130	New Mexico	1,000
New Hampshire	9,600	District of Columbia	1,000

It was evident from the opening of the session that a great change had taken place in the views of Congress during the four months since the close of the extra session. The strength of the insurrection had proved far greater than had been anticipated, and it was perceived that the nation was engaged in a struggle for existence which would call for its utmost energies, and demand the use of every means within its power. Hitherto the government had proceeded on the assumption that the institution of slavery, and the sovereignty of the states as recognized in the written text of the Constitution, were not to be interfered with, though individual members of Congress had declared that in case of necessity either or both of these must yield to the paramount object of maintaining the Union. This change was clearly indicated when a resolution was offered in the House reaffirming the Crittenden resolution of the previous session, which declared that the war was not waged for the purpose of overthrowing or interfering with the established institutions of the states, and ought to cease as soon as the supremacy of the Constitution had been vindicated. This resolution had passed by an almost unanimous vote four months previously. It was now laid on the table by a vote of 71 to 65. Fifty-three of the members who had then voted for it now voted to lay it on the table, thus in effect saying that it might, and probably would, be necessary to interfere with the civil and domestic institutions of the insurgent states. In the Senate, Mr. Saulsbury, of Delaware, one of the few "peace" members who remained, offered a resolution appointing ex-Presidents Fillmore and Pierce, Chief Justice Taney, Edward Everett, John J. Crittenden, and six others, commissioners to meet a like number of commissioners to be appointed by the Confederacy, to confer together for the preservation of the Union and the maintenance of the Constitution; and that upon the meeting of this joint commission active hostilities should cease, and not be renewed unless the joint commission should be unable to agree, or their agreement be rejected either by Congress or the Confederacy. This resolution was laid upon the table and never called up.

The general character of the debates, and the arguments adduced, were similar to those of the last session, except that the supporters of the administration expressed themselves more firmly and decidedly upon every point. The opposition in the Senate, weakened by the expulsion of Breckinridge, Bright, Polk, and Johnson, made up in pertinacity what they lacked in numbers. In the House they were strengthened by the support of some members who had hitherto maintained a neutral position; still the administration had a large majority in both houses, and the most ample powers were conferred upon it for carrying on the war.

Until near the close of the session it was supposed that the army in service, numbering fully 700,000 men, was as large and even larger than was required. "There are," said Senator Fessenden, of Maine, at the end of March, "regiments in my own state to-day, raised and staying there, waiting to be called into the field, doing nothing, not armed, yet anxious to be in service. There are more men here on the Potomac than government knows what to do with. Half a million of men are all that we can possibly use." This opinion was general, and the enlistment of volunteers was virtually suspended. The estimates were based on an army of 500,000 volunteers for the war. Toward the close of the session, after the disastrous result of the campaign before Richmond, a law was passed authorizing the President to call out the militia of the states for not more than nine months; to cause an enrollment to be made of all citizens from eighteen to forty-five years of age; to accept the services of 100,000 volunteers to fill up existing regiments; and to receive into service, naval or military, persons of African descent; and in case such persons should be slaves of rebels, they, their wives, children, and mothers should be free.[1] Previous to this, the control of the army and navy was really vested in the President. He could select any naval officer of the grades of captain and commander, and appoint him to the command of a squadron, with the rank and title of "flag officer."[2] He was authorized and requested to dismiss from service any naval or military officer for any cause which he deemed advisable.[3] He might, when he deemed the public service to require it, take possession of any railroad or telegraph line, with all its appurtenances, and place all the agents and employés under military control, so that they should be considered a part of the military establishment of the United States.[4] It was made his duty to cause the seizure of all property of persons who should hold civil or military office under the Confederate government, and also of all other persons engaged in aiding the rebellion who should not within sixty days after public proclamation having been made return to their allegiance; personal property to be absolutely forfeited, and real estate during the lifetime of the offender. This proclamation was issued on the 25th of July, 1862. The penalty for treason was made death or imprisonment for not less than five years, with a fine of not less than $10,000, with disqualification to hold any office under the United States. The President was also authorized to grant pardon and amnesty upon such conditions as he deemed expedient.[5]

Appropriations were made on what then seemed to be the most liberal scale. To meet deficiencies in the army estimates for the year ending June 30, 1862, $209,000,000 were appropriated, besides $30,000,000 for the deficiency of pay to volunteers in the Western Department. For the ensuing year $538,000,000 were given.[6] The naval appropriation was $43,000,000, besides special sums amounting to $30,000,000 for building iron-clad steamers and gun-boats.[7] These are only the prominent items. There were, besides, large amounts appropriated for other objects directly connected with the war.

Vigorous financial measures were required to meet this great expenditure. Early in the session a joint resolution was passed declaring that, in order to pay the ordinary expenses of government, including the interest on the national loans, and to provide a sinking fund, taxes should be imposed which, together with the tariff, should yield an annual revenue of not less than $150,000,000.[1] In accordance with the demands of the treasury, duties of from 2 to 5 cents a pound were levied upon sugar, 5 cents on coffee, and 20 cents on tea, and an increase upon most other importations; a heavy excise was imposed upon the manufacture of distilled and fermented liquors; a tax of about three per cent. upon most articles of manufacture; licenses varying from $5 to $200 upon trades and professions, stamps were required upon legal and commercial documents; and a tax of three per cent. levied upon the excess over $600 of all incomes up to $10,000, and five per cent. upon all greater.[2] These, it was hoped, would produce sufficient to pay the ordinary expenses of government, including the interest on the public debt incurred and to be incurred. To meet the war expenses, recourse was had to the issue of paper money in the form of United States notes payable on demand, without interest. These were of various amounts, from one dollar upward. They were made receivable for all debts due to the United States except duties on imports, and payable for all debts due from the United States except the interest on the public debt, both of which must be paid in specie; for all other purposes they were made a legal tender. The entire amount of "greenbacks" authorized by different acts during this session and the last was $250,000,000. These notes might, at the option of the holder, be exchanged for treasury bonds, bearing interest at the rate of six per cent., redeemable at the pleasure of the government after five years, and to be paid in twenty years. Of these the Secretary of the Treasury was authorized at his discretion to issue $500,000.000 at par, in exchange for coin or demand notes.[3]

The provision making these notes payable for all government dues except interest of the public debt was, in effect, to make them payable at the pleasure of government. The proposition to make them a legal tender occasioned protracted debates, and met with strong opposition from some friends of the administration. It was urged in opposition that it was without precedent in our history; that it was unconstitutional by impairing the validity of contracts, since every contract for the payment of money was legally a contract for the payment of gold and silver coin, and that was the measure of the right of the one party and the obligation of the other. This provision divested one party of his right and released the other from his obligation. It said to one party, "Although you agreed to pay gold and silver, you shall be discharged by the payment of these notes;" and to the other, "Although you are entitled to demand gold and silver, you must be content to receive instead this paper." This would, moreover, be only the precursor of a brood of promises to pay, not one of which would be redeemed in the constitutional currency of the country. In support of the proposition it was urged that, while the states were by the Constitution prohibited from making any thing but gold and silver a legal tender, there was no such prohibition as to Congress. Congress had the power to coin money and to fix the value of it. Gold and silver had indeed been accepted as the usual measure of value, and governments, by affixing their stamps to them, gave them an extrinsic value; any other thing which governments might choose to thus stamp would answer equally as well for currency. If all governments agreed upon one thing, it would be equally valuable every where. If one fixed upon a thing, it would be valuable within the jurisdiction of that government. Congress had at different times, without question, changed the weight and alloy of gold and silver coin; that is, it had said that the man who had agreed to pay a certain number of dollars could now discharge the debt by the payment of a less quantity of gold or silver. And if it should happen that gold should become as plentiful as iron, no one doubted that government would have the power of substituting for it some other metal. If, when the public good so required, Congress had power to change the weight or alloy of gold or silver coin, or to substitute some other metal, and declare it legal tender, it had equally the power to issue paper money, and make that a legal tender. The prevailing argument for the measure, however, was the necessity of the case. Government had contracted large debts, and must contract still larger. The army must be paid and maintained. Gold and silver could not be had for this purpose, and something must be substituted. The abstract question of constitutionality must yield to the paramount law of necessity. Whether such necessity existed Congress must judge, and its judgment would be conclusive.

The first bill for this purpose, which authorized the issue of $150,000,000 of these notes, making them a legal tender, became a law on the 25th of February. It passed in the House by a vote of 93 to 59. In the Senate a motion to strike out the legal-tender clause was rejected by a vote of 22 to 17; and the bill, with the clause, passed by 30 to 7. Of the seventeen senators who wished to strike out the provision, five voted for the bill with the provision. This bill, in effect, decided the financial policy of the government. It sanctioned the view of the Secretary of the Treasury that "government can resort to borrowing only when the issue of notes has become sufficiently large to warrant a just expectation that loans of the notes can be had from those who hold or can obtain them at rates not less advantageous than those of coin loans before the suspension of specie payments." In other words, before government could hope to borrow the large amounts which it needed, it must supply the people with the money to lend.

Of deeper interest, and of more enduring consequence than even the military and financial measures of the Federal government, was its action in respect to slavery. To set this forth will be the purpose of the following chapter.

[1] Laws of the 37th Congress, First Session, chap. cci. [2] Ibid., chap. i. [3] Ibid., chap. cc.
[4] Ibid., chap. xv. [5] Ibid., chap. cxcv.; and Joint Resolution, No. 63.
[6] Ibid., chaps. xxxii., lxix., cxxxiii. [7] Ibid., chaps. xxiii., lvii., clxiv.

[1] Laws of the 37th Congress, First Session, Joint Resolution, No. 6.
[2] Ibid., chaps. ii., cxix. [3] Ibid., chaps. xxiii., cxlii.

THE WIGWAM AT CHICAGO, BUILT FOR THE MEETING OF THE REPUBLICAN CONVENTION OF 1860.

CHAPTER VIII.

THE FEDERAL GOVERNMENT AND SLAVERY.

Slavery in National Politics.—Whig and Democratic Conventions, 1840, 1844, 1848, 1852.—The Republican, American, and Democratic Conventions of 1856.—The Republican Convention of 1860.—Its Platform.—The Democratic Conventions of 1860.—Disruption of the Democratic Party.—The Union Party.—Formation of Sectional Parties.—Analysis of the Electoral and Popular Votes for President. — Principles of the Parties. — Position of Mr. Lincoln on the Question of Slavery.—His Inaugural and Messages.—Contrabands.—General Butler's Decision.—Action of the Government.—Fremont's and Hunter's Orders.—Modified by the President.—Mr. Lincoln's Letter to Horace Greeley.—His Policy defined.—The Border States.—Analysis of the Slave and Free Population.—Their Relations to Slavery.—The President's Proposition for Compensated Emancipation.—Meeting of Congress, December 2, 1861.—Antislavery Measures proposed.—The Debates.—Laws passed.—Abolition of Slavery in the District of Columbia.—Resolution in favor of Compensated Emancipation.—Colonization Schemes.—Prohibiting Slavery in the Territories.—Freeing the Families of colored Soldiers.—The Insurrection and Confiscation Act.—The President's proposed Veto.—Hesitation of the President.—Conference with Border State Representatives.—Premonitory Proclamation of Emancipation.—The new Policy of Government.

AFTER the adoption of the Missouri Compromise in 1820, the subject of slavery was first introduced into national politics as a party question during the presidential canvass of 1840, when the Democratic National Convention adopted as one of the cardinal principles of the party a resolution that the government had no power to interfere with the domestic institutions of the states, and that all efforts to induce Congress to interfere with questions of slavery, or to take incipient steps thereto, were calculated to endanger the stability and permanence of the Union. The convention of the opposition party, which had just assumed the name of Whig, put forth no formal declaration of principles, but confined itself to assailing the administration of Mr. Van Buren on the grounds of general mismanagement and corruption. Mr. Harrison was elected President, receiving the 234 electoral votes of eleven free and eight slave states; Mr. Van Buren having the 70 votes of two free and seven slave states. Of the popular vote Harrison received 1,275,000, Van Buren 1,153,000, and barely 7000 were cast for Birney, Abolition.[1]

In 1844, no allusion was made to slavery in the "platform" or declaration of principles of the Whig party. The Democratic National Convention merely reaffirmed the principle of the previous campaign. Mr. Polk received the 170 electoral votes of seven free and eight slave states; Mr. Clay having the 105 votes of seven free and four slave states. Of the popular vote, 1,368,000 were cast for Polk, 1,299,000 for Clay, and 62,000 for Birney, Abolition.

In the Whig Convention of 1848 a resolution was proposed affirming that, while Congress had no power to interfere with the institution of slavery within the states, it had the power, which it was its duty to exercise, to prohibit the existence or introduction of slavery into any territory possessed or to be acquired by the United States. This resolution was laid on the table without action. The Democratic Convention again affirmed the declaration in respect to slavery; and in consequence, a convention of a portion of the party assembled and adopted a series of resolutions affirming that slavery in the states depended upon state laws which the Federal government had no power to repeal or modify; but that it was the settled policy of the nation to localize and discourage slavery, and that it was the duty of Congress to prohibit its introduction into any territory now free. This convention nominated Mr. Van Buren for President. At the election General Taylor received the 163 votes of seven free and eight slave states, Mr. Cass that of eight free and seven slave states, 127 in all. The popular vote was 1,360,000 for Taylor, 1,250,000 for Cass, and 291,000 for Van Buren.

In the Whig Convention of 1852 it was resolved that the party acquiesced in the compromise measures of 1850, including the Fugitive Slave Law, as a settlement of all the questions which they embrace, and that it would discourage all efforts to renew the agitation of these questions. The Democratic Convention again affirmed the principle set forth in former platforms, with the addition that it covered the whole subject of slavery agitation in Congress; that the party would adhere to the compromise measures, including the Fugitive Slave Law, and would resist all attempts to renew, in or out of Congress, the agitation of the question of slavery, in whatever shape, or under whatever color the attempt might be made. A "Free Democratic Convention" then assembled. It put forth a declaration explicitly affirming that Congress had no power to make a slave or establish slavery; that it was the duty of the Federal government to relieve itself from all responsibility for the existence of slavery wherever it had the constitutional power to legislate for its extinction; that there ought to be no more slave states, no slave territories, no nationalized slavery, no national legislation for the extradition of slaves; that slavery was a sin against God and a crime against man which no human enactment or usage could make right; that the Fugitive Slave Law had no binding force upon the American people, and should be repealed; that the compromise measures were inconsistent with the principles of democracy, and inadequate for the settlement of the questions of which they were claimed to be an adjustment; and that there could be no permanent settlement of the slavery question except by the separation of the general government from slavery, the exercise of all its constitutional power and influence on the side of freedom, and by leaving to the several states the whole subject of slavery, including the delivery of fugitives from service or labor. Mr. Hale was nominated for President by this convention. At the election, Mr. Pierce received the 254 electoral votes of fourteen free and thirteen slave states, General Scott the 42 votes of two free and two slave states. The Democratic majority was much smaller in the electoral college than in the popular vote. Many large states were carried by small majorities. Of the popular vote, Pierce received 1,631,000, Scott 1,386,000, Hale 155,000.

After this decisive defeat the Whig party virtually disappeared from national politics. Many of its former members, especially at the South, went over to the Democrats; more, both North and South, formed themselves into a new organization, which assumed the name of Americans; while the great majority in the free states organized themselves into a new party, under the

---

[1] In this and the following paragraphs the popular vote is given in round numbers. In South Carolina no popular vote is cast even indirectly for President, the electors being appointed by the Legislature. The vote of this state is not included in the usual statements. She voted uniformly for the Democratic candidate. We have assumed the vote of the state to be 50,000, and that 40,000 would have been cast for the Democratic candidates, and 10,000 for the opposition. In making our statements, we have added this majority of 30,000 to the numbers usually assigned to the Democratic vote. In the election of 1860 we have put this down as cast for Mr. Breckinridge.

name of Republican, which received large accessions from Democrats who were dissatisfied with the position of their party in respect to slavery.

The first Republican National Convention assembled at Philadelphia June 17, 1856, in accordance with a call addressed to the people of the United States, without distinction of party, who were opposed to the policy of the administration of Mr. Pierce, opposed to the repeal of the Missouri Compromise, to the admission of slavery into a free territory, and in favor of the admission of Kansas as a free state. The platform declared that the Federal Constitution, the rights of the states, and the union of the states should be preserved; that the existence of slavery in the territories should be prohibited by express enactments; that neither Congress nor a territorial Legislature had authority to give slavery a legal existence in any territory; and that it was "the right and duty of Congress to prohibit in the territories those twin relics of barbarism, polygamy and slavery." Mr. Fremont, who had been a Democrat, though he had taken no prominent part in politics, was nominated for President, and Mr. Dayton, a former Whig, for Vice-president. The American party was ingrafted upon a half secret association, whose main object was to confine all offices of trust and emolument to citizens of native birth. Its first national convention, styling itself the American National Council, met at Philadelphia on the 19th of February. Its proceedings took a wider range than was originally contemplated. The main points in the declaration which it put forth were that Americans only should rule America; that Congress should not interfere in questions appertaining to the individual states, nor any state with the affairs of another; that a continuous residence of twenty-one years should be a requisite for the naturalization of an alien; that foreign paupers and criminals should not be suffered to land on our shores; and that all laws should be enforced until repealed, or pronounced null and void by competent judicial authority. A resolution was proposed that no person should be nominated for President who was not in favor of the prohibition by Congress of slavery in any territory north of the latitude of 36° 30': this was rejected by a large majority. Mr. Fillmore, formerly a Northern Whig, and Mr. Donelson, a Southern Democrat, were nominated for President and Vice-president. A Whig Convention met, and went through the form of indorsing these nominations. Its platform deprecated the formation of sectional parties, and affirmed that public safety required the election of a President pledged to neither geographical section. The Democratic Convention met at Cincinnati on the 2d of June. It reaffirmed the doctrines respecting slavery put forth by previous conventions, adding a resolution that Congress should not interfere with slavery in the District of Columbia or in the territories, and that every territory, whenever it had the requisite population, was entitled to enter the Union as a state, with a constitution admitting or prohibiting slavery, as its people might choose. Mr. Buchanan was nominated for President, and Mr. Breckinridge for Vice-president. Mr. Buchanan received the 172 electoral votes of fourteen slave and five free states, Mr. Fremont the 114 votes of eleven free states, and Mr. Fillmore the seven votes of Maryland. Of the popular vote, Buchanan received 1,868,000, Fremont 1,341,000, Fillmore 874,000.

In 1860, the Republican Convention met at Chicago on the 16th of May. Its platform declared that each state had the exclusive right to regulate its domestic institutions according to its own judgment; that the dogma that the Constitution carried slavery into the territories was a dangerous heresy; that the normal condition of all the territory of the United States was that of freedom; reaffirming the principle advanced by the previous convention that neither Congress nor a territorial Legislature had authority to give slavery a legal existence in any territory.[1] Mr. Lincoln, formerly a Whig, and Mr. Hamlin, formerly a Democrat, were nominated for President and Vice-president.

The Democratic Convention met at Charleston on the 23d of April. It was resolved that no nominations should be made until a platform had been adopted. The committee appointed to prepare this document could not agree, and two platforms were presented. That framed by the majority of the committee reaffirmed the Cincinnati platform, adding, "The democracy of the United States hold these cardinal principles on the subject of slavery in the territories: first, that Congress has no power to abolish slavery in the territories; second, that the territorial Legislature has no power to abolish slavery in the territories, nor to prohibit the introduction of slaves therein, nor any power to destroy or impair the right of property in slaves by any legislation whatever." Several reports were presented from the minority of the committee. After various amendments, these at last were embodied in a series of resolutions reaffirming the Cincinnati platform, with the addition that, as differences of opinion existed in the Democratic party as to the nature and extent of the powers of a territorial Legislature over the institution of slavery in the territories, the party would abide by the decision of the Supreme Court of the United States on the questions of constitutional law. This minority report was accepted in place of that of the majority. When the question of the final adoption of this report came up, the resolution submitting the decision of questions of constitutional law to the Supreme Court was rejected. The platform, as adopted, simply reaffirmed that of Cincinnati. About fifty of the Southern delegates then withdrew, and the remaining members, after voting that two thirds of a full convention should be required for a nomination, proceeded to vote for a candidate for President. A full convention consisting of 303 votes, 202 were requisite for a nomination. Fifty-seven ballots were taken. The votes for Mr. Douglas varied from 145 to 152. The remaining votes were scattered; Mr. Guthrie, of Kentucky, and Hunter, of Virginia, leading. A few votes were cast for Dickinson, of New York, Johnson, of Tennessee, and Lane, of Oregon. One delegate voted persistently from first to last for Jefferson Davis. At the 43d ballot Douglas received 151½, Guthrie 65½, Hunter (who had before had 42 votes) 16, Dickinson 5, Lane 13, Davis 1. After that there was no essential change in the vote. It was evident that no man could secure the 202 votes required for a nomination, and the Convention, after a fruitless session of ten days, adjourned to meet at Baltimore on the 18th of June. The members of the party in the several states were urged to appoint new delegates to fill the places of those who had withdrawn. The members who had seceded from the Convention had in the mean while held a convention of their own, lasting four days. After adopting the principles of the platform which had been voted down by the majority of the delegates, they adjourned to meet at Richmond on the 11th of June. They came together merely to adjourn till the 21st, awaiting the action of the Convention at Baltimore. When that Convention assembled, an angry discussion arose upon the admission of delegates. The disputed seats were mostly awarded to claimants who were in favor of the nomination of Mr. Douglas. Many members thereupon withdrew from the Convention; among them was Caleb Cushing, the chairman. The remaining delegates then proceeded to vote for a candidate for the presidency. There were left 194 votes; of these, 181 were given to Douglas, 7½ to Breckinridge, and 5½ to Guthrie. The nomination of Douglas was then made unanimous. Mr. Fitzpatrick, of Alabama, was nominated for Vice-president. He declined the nomination, and Mr. Johnson, of Georgia, was named in his place. The members who had seceded from this Convention assembled and nominated Mr. Breckinridge for President, and Mr. Lane, of Oregon, for Vice-president. These nominations were confirmed by the delegates who had seceded at Charleston, who were now in session at Richmond.

Thus the great Democratic party, which had, with three brief intervals, administered the affairs of the nation for more than half a century, was broken up. Neither portion could hope to succeed against the vigorous and united Republican party which had sprung to life. There was but one hope left for those who deprecated the success of this party. It was certain that Douglas could not gain the vote of the South, which was essential to his election. It was equally certain that, if the bare choice lay between Lincoln and Breckinridge, the slave states would vote for the latter and the free states for the former, giving him the election. But if a third candidate were brought into the field, obnoxious to neither section, he might draw from both sides votes enough to prevent either of the others from receiving a majority in the electoral college. Then the election would devolve upon the states represented by the popular House of Congress, all the members from each state casting a single vote, and their choice being restricted to one of the three persons who had received the highest number of electoral votes. A convention of the former "American" party, now styling itself the "Constitutional Union" party, had come together at Baltimore on the 10th of May, during the interval between the breaking up of the Democratic Convention at Charleston and its reassembling at Baltimore. Four years before this party had signally failed in its attempt to thrust itself between the Republicans and the Democrats. Now there seemed a fair chance for it to mediate between the free and the slave states. Its Convention laid down a platform "recognizing no principle other than the Constitution of the country, the union of the states, and the enforcement of the laws." To the text of this declaration all parties would assent; the only question would be as to its interpretation. In order to conciliate the South without offending the North, the nomination for President was given to John Bell, a respectable Tennessee lawyer, who had served in Congress with fair credit. To give some weight to the ticket, Edward Everett was nominated for Vice-president. The Conservatives at the North saw in this nomination a possible means of preventing the election of Mr. Lincoln. If the electoral vote of New York or Pennsylvania, and one other free state, could be taken from him, the choice would devolve upon the House of Representatives, where it was certain that he could not secure a majority of the states. Accordingly, in New York and several other states, "Fusion" tickets for electors were made up, containing the names of men who favored Douglas, Bell, or Breckinridge. The understanding was that all of these electors, if chosen, should cast their votes so as to prevent the election of Lincoln. This subtle scheme was too intricate to work. Its practical result was merely to give to Lincoln one half of the electoral vote of New Jersey, which would otherwise have been cast against him. In that state the vote was very close. The "Fusion" electoral ticket was made up of one half Douglas men, and one half who favored Breckinridge or Bell. Many of the Douglas voters struck off from their ballots the names of the Breckinridge or Bell electors, so that in their place three Republicans were chosen by a small majority.

The result of the presidential election of 1860 was that Mr. Lincoln received 169 electoral votes, being the whole of those of the sixteen free states except three votes from New Jersey; Mr. Bell the 39 votes of Virginia, Kentucky, and Tennessee; Mr. Douglas the 9 votes of Missouri, and 3 from New Jersey—12 in all; and Mr. Breckinridge the 72 votes of the remaining eleven slave states. The popular vote, apportioning that cast on Fusion

---

[1] The following is the text of the articles in the platform relating directly to slavery:

"The maintenance inviolate of the rights of the states, and especially the right of each state to order and control its own domestic institutions according to its own judgment exclusively, is essential to that balance of power on which the perfection and endurance of our political fabric depend; and we denounce the lawless invasion by armed force of the soil of any state or territory, no matter under what pretext, as among the gravest of crimes."

"The new dogma that the Constitution, of its own force, carries slavery into any or all of the territories of the United States, is a dangerous political heresy, at variance with the explicit provisions of that instrument itself, with contemporaneous exposition, and with legislative and judicial precedent; is revolutionary in its tendency, and subversive of the peace and harmony of the country."

"The normal condition of all the territory of the United States is that of freedom. As our republican fathers, when they had abolished slavery in all our national territory, ordained that 'no person should be deprived of life, liberty, or property without due process of law,' it becomes our duty, by legislation, whenever such legislation is necessary, to maintain this provision of the Constitution against all attempts to violate it; and we deny the authority of Congress, or of a territorial Legislature, or of any individuals, to give legal existence to slavery in any territory of the United States."

tickets according to the best estimates of the strength of the several parties, and giving to Breckinridge a clear majority of 30,000 in South Carolina, was, for Lincoln 1,855,000, for Douglas 1,360,000, for Breckinridge 870,000, for Bell 590,000.

Thus, previous to 1856, the question of slavery did not enter fairly into the presidential election, and there was no geographical line separating the great political parties. In 1840, Harrison was elected by the votes of eleven free and eight slave states; the votes of two free and seven slave states being cast against him. In 1844, Polk was elected by seven free and eight slave states; against him were seven free and four slave states. In 1848, Taylor was elected by seven free and eight slave states; opposed to him were eight free and seven slave states. In 1852, Pierce was elected by fourteen free and thirteen slave states; against him were two free and two slave states. But in 1856, Buchanan was elected by the votes of the whole fourteen slave states and five free states, while eleven free states voted against him. And in 1860 Lincoln received the entire vote of the sixteen free states, with the exception of the half vote of New Jersey, while the whole vote of the fifteen slave states was cast against him. It is worthy of note that the first Republican candidate for the presidency was a native of a slave state, and his opponent of a free state; while the second Republican candidate was born in a slave state, and his principal opponent in a free state.

The Republican party came into power pledged by their formal declaration of principles against any interference by the general government with slavery in the states where it existed. This doctrine was avowed by all parties and sections; but the Republicans were also pledged to prevent, by the action of the general government, the introduction of slavery into the territories. The Northern Democrats, in nominating Mr. Douglas, endorsed his doctrine of popular sovereignty, that the general government had no authority to decide the question of slavery in the territories, but that it belonged exclusively to the people of each territory, acting each for itself through its lawfully appointed Legislature. The Southern Democrats affirmed that by the Constitution slavery had a legal existence in the territories; denied that Congress or a territorial Legislature had any power to annul or impair that right; and demanded that the general government should, if necessary, protect slavery in the territories. The Union party took no definite position upon the disputed question, though a majority of its members would have been content with the non-intervention doctrine of Mr. Douglas. If they had nominated him, it is probable that he would have been elected.

Mr. Lincoln, in his inaugural address, explicitly avowed his adherence to the principle that the general government could not interfere with slavery in the states. "Apprehension seems to exist," he said, "among the people of the Southern states that, by the accession of a Republican administration, their property, and their peace and personal security, are to be endangered. There never has been any reasonable cause for such an apprehension. Indeed, the most ample evidence to the contrary has all the while existed and been open to their inspection. It is found in nearly all the published speeches of him who now addresses you. I do but quote from one of those speeches when I declare that 'I have no purpose, directly or indirectly, to interfere with the institution of slavery in the states where it exists. I believe I have no lawful right to do so, and I have no inclination to do so.' Those who nominated and elected me did so with the full knowledge that I had made this and many similar declarations, and that I had never recanted them. And more than this, they placed in the platform for my acceptance, and as a law to themselves and to me, this clear and emphatic resolution, 'That the maintenance inviolate of the rights of the states, and especially the right of each state to order and control its own domestic institutions according to its own judgment exclusively, is essential to the balance of power on which the perfection and endurance of our political fabric depend.' I now reiterate these sentiments." He also, in effect, pledged himself to enforce the execution of the Fugitive Slave Law. There was no question that the provision of the Constitution requiring the delivery of persons held to service or labor was intended to secure the surrender of fugitive slaves. The intention of the lawgiver was the law. There was some difference of opinion as to whether this constitutional provision should be enforced by national or state authority; but, if the slave was to be delivered up, it was of little consequence to him or others by what authority it was done. Every member of Congress had sworn to maintain this provision of the Constitution, and there could be no difficulty in framing a law by means of which to keep that oath. Such a law ought to embody adequate safeguards that no free person should be surrendered as a slave.

This emphatic declaration in favor of the maintenance of the constitutional right of each state to regulate and control slavery within its limits, presupposed, of course, that the states recognized the authority of the Constitution. If they attempted to set it aside by force and violence, they could not claim its protection. But, even after the war broke out, the President was anxious that the question of slavery should not be involved. But it soon became apparent that this was impossible. Slavery became involved from the moment when the national forces began to act in a slave state. On the 26th of May General McClellan issued an address to the people of Western Virginia assuring them that not only would the Federal troops abstain from all interference with their slaves, but that they would crush any attempt at servile insurrection. General Butler had hardly taken command at Fortress Monroe when three slaves came in, saying that they belonged to a Colonel Mallory, who had gone off to the enemy, and was about to send them to North Carolina to work on the fortifications. Butler needed laborers, and set them at work. Colonel Carey, of the Virginia Volunteers, soon presented himself, claiming to be the agent of Mallory, and demanded that the slaves should be given up. Butler refused. "Do you mean to set aside

BENJAMIN F. BUTLER.

your constitutional obligations?" asked Carey. "Virginia passed an ordinance of secession two days ago," was the reply, "and claims to be a foreign country. I am under no constitutional obligations to a foreign country." "You say we can not secede, and so you can not consistently detain them." "But you say you have seceded, and so you can not consistently claim them," rejoined Butler, one of the shrewdest of Massachusetts lawyers, never at a loss for finding law to sustain any position. "You are using negroes upon your batteries. I shall detain these as contraband of war."

It would be hard to find in Puffendorf or Vattell warrant for this extension of the definition of the term "contraband." It was an epigram, but an epigram which, in the end, pledged the United States to the abolition of slavery. This was on Friday, the 24th of May. From that day "contraband" became a synonym for slave. On Sunday eight more slaves came in, on Monday sixty, and so on from day to day, in families and by squads, until in a few weeks there were nine hundred, men, women, and children, in camp. Butler informed the War Department of his proceedings. They were sanctioned, and he was directed not to seize upon any slaves, and not to surrender any who came into his lines of their own accord. Two months later he again asked for instructions. There were in his camps three hundred able-bodied slaves, liable to be used in aid of the insurrection, who might fairly be detained as contraband; but what should he do with the six hundred old or infirm men, and women, and children, the fathers and mothers, wives and children of the contrabands? They were legally property, but property which had been abandoned by its owners, like a vessel adrift upon the ocean. The United States were the salvors, but salvors who would not hold such property. It seemed to him that all ownership of them had virtually ceased, and that they had resumed their natural condition of human beings. But General McDowell had issued an order forbidding fugitive slaves from coming into or being harbored within his lines. Was this order to be enforced in all the departments? If so, who were to be considered fugitives? Was a slave a fugitive whose master had run away from him? Must the army refuse food and shelter to slaves whose masters had run away or been driven off? Moreover, it was understood that slaves who had actually labored upon rebel intrenchments should be harbored and fed; but why should this favor be shown to those who had thus wrought against us and be denied to those who had, by escaping, avoided such hostility? "In a loyal state," said Butler, in conclusion, "I would put down a servile insurrection. In a state in rebellion, I would confiscate that which was used to oppose my arms, and take all the property which constituted the wealth of that state, and furnished the means by which the war is prosecuted, besides being the cause of the war; and if it should be objected that, in so doing, human beings were brought to the free enjoyment of life, liberty, and the pursuit of happiness, such objection might not require much consideration."

To a case thus keenly put there could be but one substantial reply. The question as to fugitives in the states which adhered to the Union was not involved. There the ordinary forms of judicial procedure could be observed. But these could not be enforced in the insurrectionary states; and the rights dependent on the laws of these states must be subordinated to military exigencies, if not wholly forfeited by treason on the part of those claiming them. Meanwhile the Confiscation Act of August 6, 1861, had provided for the case of slaves actually employed by their masters in aid of the rebellion. They were to be treated like other property; the rights of their owners

STAMPEDE OF SLAVES TO FORTRESS MONROE.

FEEDING NEGRO CHILDREN AT HILTON HEAD, SOUTH CAROLINA.

were forfeited; and forfeiture of the claim of their owners was equivalent to enfranchisement. The laws under which all slaves in these states were held had been superseded by the rebellion, and the enforcement of these claims, in the case of loyal owners, would be inconvenient and injurious. The rights of these men would be best secured by receiving the fugitives and giving them employment, leaving the question of indemnifying the masters to be settled after tranquillity had been restored. Butler was therefore directed to receive all fugitives who came to him, but he must not interfere with the servants of peaceful citizens, nor encourage any to leave their masters, nor prevent the voluntary return of any.

The Confiscation Act of August 6 was the only measure of the extra session bearing directly upon the question of slavery. This related solely to the case of slaves employed by their masters in the naval or military service of the enemy. Until, subsequently, other laws were enacted, the administration was careful not to transcend the provisions of that act. On the 31st of August, General Fremont, then commanding the Western Department, issued an order extending martial law throughout the State of Missouri, confiscating the property of all persons who should take up arms against the United States, or be proved to have taken an active part with their enemies in the field, and declaring their slaves to be free men. The President directed this order to be so modified as to conform to and not to transcend the provisions of the act of Congress. In May, 1862, General Hunter, commanding the Department of the South, issued an order putting the states of Georgia, South Carolina, and Florida under martial law, declaring that, as slavery and martial law were incompatible, the slaves in those states were forever free. The President set aside this declaration. He said that it belonged to him to decide whether, as commander-in-chief, he had the right to declare the slaves in any state to be free; and if he had the right, whether and when it should be exercised. This question was wholly distinct from that of police regulations in armies or camps. These were left to the discretion of the different commanders. Thus, while Butler, at Fortress Monroe, received fugitive slaves, Dix, in another part of Virginia, and Halleck, who had succeeded Fremont in Missouri, prohibited them from entering their lines. The same general principle was involved in instructions given in October, 1861, by the Secretary of War to General Sherman, who commanded the expedition to Port Royal. He was directed to avail himself of the services of any persons, whether fugitives from labor or not, who should offer themselves, organizing them into squads or companies, as he should find advisable, but not, as a general thing, to arm them for military service. Loyal masters were to be assured that compensation would be made to them for the loss of the services of persons so employed. These measures brought into the lines a large number of women and children, who were fed by the government, and earnest attempts were made to instruct the fugitives, and to employ their labor

usefully in the cultivation of abandoned plantations. It was many months before the plan of arming the slaves was adopted.

Mr. Lincoln's cardinal idea was that he was in law and right the chief magistrate of an undivided and indivisible nation, and that it was his duty to restore the Union by bringing back the disaffected portions to the dominion of the Constitution and the laws. Every military and political measure should be directed to this end. Eighteen months after his inauguration, when ample authority had been conferred upon him by Congress, he thus defined his policy: "As to my policy I have not meant to leave any one in doubt. I would save the Union. I would save it in the shortest way under the Constitution. The sooner the national authority can be restored, the nearer the Union will be—the Union as it was. If there be any who would not save the Union unless they could, at the same time, save slavery, I do not agree with them. If there be those who would not save the Union unless they could, at the same time, destroy slavery, I do not agree with them. My paramount object is to save the Union, and not either to save or destroy slavery. If I could save the Union without freeing any slave, I would do it; if I could save it by freeing all the slaves, I would do it; and if I could do it by freeing some and leaving others alone, I would also do that. What I do about slavery and the colored race I do because I believe it helps to save this Union; and what I forbear, I forbear because I do not believe it would help to save the Union. I shall do less whenever I shall believe that what I am doing hurts the cause; and I shall do more whenever I believe that doing more will help the cause. I shall try to correct errors when shown to be errors, and shall adopt new views as fast as they shall appear to be true views."[1] In his message of December 2, 1862, he reiterated all that he had said upon this subject in his inaugural address and in his message at the special session. "Nothing now occurs," he said, "to add to or to subtract from the principles or general purposes expressed in those documents." The reference to the Confiscation Act of the special session was cautious and guarded. He had strictly adhered to its provisions. If a new law on the same subject should be proposed, its propriety would be duly considered. But he threw out a hint against hasty and inconsiderate measures. "The Union," he said, "must be preserved, and hence all indispensable means must be employed; but we should not be in haste to determine that radical and extreme measures, which may reach the loyal as well as the disloyal, are indispensable."

Of hardly less importance than the vigorous prosecution of the war against the armed insurgents was the retention of the border slaveholding states. These states held peculiar relations to the two sections of the country. Slavery existed in them in law and in fact, but it was not their one great in-

[1] Letter to Horace Greeley, August 22, 1862.

stitution entwined with every fibre of their political, social, and domestic life. Slaveholders formed a small, and, in many parts, a numerically insignificant portion of the people. In Delaware there was but one slave to sixty free persons, and more than three fourths of these were in the least populous of the three counties, with but one fourth of the free inhabitants; in the other two counties there was only one slave to 180 free. It was fast becoming a free state. In ten years the free population had increased twenty-three per cent., and the slaves had decreased twenty-one per cent. In Maryland there was one slave to seven free. Half of the slaves were in counties with but one sixth of the free population. In Baltimore, with a population of 212,000, there were but 2500 slaves, a little more than one in a hundred. In ten years the free whites had increased twenty-four per cent., the free colored twenty, and the slaves only three and a half per cent. In Kentucky there was one slave to four whites; but half of the slaves were in counties with only a fourth of the population. The whites had in ten years increased twenty-one per cent., the slaves seven. In Missouri there was one slave to ten whites. There were a score of counties having each less than a hundred slaves. In St. Louis there were but 1500 slaves in a population of 160,000; less than one to a hundred. In ten years the whites had increased eighty per cent., the slaves thirty-two per cent. In that part of Virginia soon to be known as the State of West Virginia there was one slave to eighteen free persons. Three fourths of the slaves were in counties having only one fourth of the whites. There were whole counties with only three or four slaves. Of the fifty-one counties there were twenty each having less than a hundred slaves. In half the counties the ratio of slaves to whites was less than one to a hundred; in the most populous county it was one to 220. These Union slave states contained, in 1860, three fifths as many whites as the Confederacy, and a little less than one eighth as many slaves. Taken collectively, the population of whites to slaves was then about seven to one. But, during the first year of the war, a considerable portion of the slaves in Missouri and Kentucky had been taken South, so that now the ratio of slave to free was not more than one to ten, and of these the majority were owned by men notoriously disloyal.

There are no reliable statistics showing the number of slaveholders; but, considering that most men who owned slaves owned several, and many of them a large number, while there were considerable portions in which slavery had only a nominal existence, it may be assumed that in the border states not one citizen in fifty, and not one loyal man in a hundred, had any direct pecuniary interest in the perpetuation of slavery. It was almost universally acknowledged that the institution was injurious to the non-slaveholding citizens, and, consequently, to the general welfare of the state. It seemed, therefore, entirely feasible to detach these states from any complicity with the strictly slaveholding Confederacy. If they remained loyal, the Union would have 22,000,000 whites, and the Confederacy but 5,000,000. If they joined the secession, the Union would have 18,000,000 whites and the Confederacy 8,000,000, besides four and a quarter millions of slaves and free persons of color.[1]

Geographically and commercially the border states were connected as intimately with one section as with the other. The great highway of the Mississippi bound Kentucky and Missouri to New Orleans; the great lakes, and railways, and canals bound them equally to New York. If the Union was broken up, no matter to which fragment they adhered, they would be border states, and exposed to all the evils of that position. In either case they would hold one of their great avenues of communication at the mercy of a foreign power. If they went with the Confederacy they would lose the lakes; if they adhered to the Union they would lose the Mississippi. Their interest, more than that of any other section, lay in the maintenance of the Union, and few of the people had any interest in the maintenance of slavery. But the slaveholders exercised a power altogether disproportionate to their numbers. Public officers and leaders of opinion belonged almost exclusively to this class. Slavery was, moreover, a state institution, and attachment to the state took precedence over attachment to the nation, though less decidedly than in the Far South. The sentiment of the civilized world had gradually arrayed itself against slavery. This, by the law of antagonism, forced all slaveholding states into closer sympathy with each other, and so the institution of slavery formed a strong bond of union between all the states which maintained it. If the border states could be induced voluntarily to abandon slavery, this tie between them and the South would be destroyed.

To bring about the voluntary abandonment of slavery in the border states was a leading object in the policy of the President. To this end, in his message of December 2, 1862, he recommended that measures should be taken to compensate states which should undertake the gradual emancipation of their slaves. Three months later he sent in a special message recommending that Congress should pass a joint resolution declaring that "the United States, in order to co-operate with any state which may adopt gradual abolition of slavery, will give to such state pecuniary aid, to be used by such state in its discretion, to compensate it for the inconvenience, public and private, produced by such change of system." This proposition, he said, set up no claim of right on the part of the general government to interfere with slavery within the states. Whether they should accept it was left to their choice; but, he argued, the leaders of the rebellion hoped that the independence of some part of the disaffected region must be acknowledged, and then that the remaining part of the slaveholding section, finding the Union destroyed, would go with the South. To deprive them of this hope would substantially end the rebellion; and any state, by initiating emancipation, would in effect declare that in no case would it ever join the Confederacy.

[1] The statements in the preceding paragraphs are expressed approximately in round numbers. The following table exhibits the numerical relations of the Border States to the Union and the Confederacy, according to the census of 1860, West Virginia being included among the Border States:

BORDER STATES.	Whites.	Free Colored.	Slaves.	Total.
Delaware	90,697	19,723	1,798	112,218
Maryland	516,128	83,718	87,188	687,034
West Virginia	368,623	3,981	20,630	393,234
Kentucky	920,077	10,146	225,490	1,155,713
Missouri	1,064,369	2,983	114,965	1,182,317
	2,958,594	120,551	450,071	3,530,216
THE UNION.				
With Border States	21,925,370	354,702	453,315	22,634,010
Without Border States	18,966,776	234,151	3,244	18,104,794
THE CONFEDERACY.				
Without Border States	5,082,088	127,420	3,070,831	8,709,780
With Border States	8,040,682	247,971	3,520,902	12,239,996

Congress had hardly met in December when it became evident that the legislation upon the subject of slavery would assume a new aspect. The dominant party had come to the conclusion that slavery had not only furnished the occasion for the war, but supplied the means of carrying it on, and that, in order to put it down, it would be necessary to interfere directly with the institution in the insurrectionary states. A wide difference of opinion soon developed itself as to the extent and manner of this interference. Notices of bills and resolutions upon this subject were offered, and the debates upon these served to elicit the views of the members. The prevailing feeling was embodied in a series of acts, the debates upon which occupied a considerable part of the session. We shall describe these, keeping as nearly as possible to the order of time at which they became laws by receiving the approval of the President.

Naval and military officers were prohibited, by an additional article of war, under penalty of dismissal from the service, from employing the forces under their command for the purpose of returning fugitive slaves.[1]

In accordance with the recommendation of the President, a joint resolution was passed, declaring that the United States ought to co-operate with any state which may adopt the gradual abolition of slavery, by giving pecuniary aid to such state.[2] This resolution was denounced by the extreme opposition as an unconstitutional interference with the subject of slavery in the states. In the House, Mr. Wickliffe, of Kentucky, denied that the Constitution gave Congress any power to appropriate money to carry out the purposes of the resolution. In the Senate, Mr. Saulsbury, of Delaware, said that the resolution was extraordinary in its origin, source, and object; it was mischievous in tendency and unpatriotic in design; it was an attempt to induce some states to commence the work of abolition by holding out a pecuniary bribe to them. The states had never asked Congress for aid for any such purpose, and the offer was ill-timed and indelicate. In the House, Mr. Fisher, from the same state, said that he saw in the resolution a promise of a final settlement of the question of slavery. It was an olive-branch held out by the Northern states to the border states and to the whole South. In the Senate, Mr. Davis, of Kentucky, the successor of Mr. Breckinridge, who had been expelled, wished to amend the resolution so that it should affirm that although the whole subject of slavery within the states lay beyond the jurisdiction of the general government, yet when any state should determine to emancipate its slaves, the United States would pay a reasonable price for those emancipated, and the cost of their colonization in some other country. This amendment was rejected, receiving but four votes. The resolution received a lukewarm support from a large portion of the Republican members. That Congress had a right to pass the resolution, and to make the appropriations required by it, in case any state should avail itself of its provisions, was assumed, but it appeared to most of them to have no practical value. However, if it produced no good it could do no harm, and the resolution passed in the Senate by 32 to 10, and in the House by 89 to 31. It was looked upon as a means of testing the feeling of the border states, the only ones which would, in any case, accept the offer of compensation.

A far more important act was that by which slavery was abolished in the District of Columbia.[3] By this act all persons held to service or labor within the district, by reason of African descent, were freed from all claim for such service or labor; and no involuntary servitude, except for crime, and after due conviction, should hereafter exist in the district. A board of commissioners was appointed, to which all loyal persons might present claims against slaves discharged by this act. These commissioners might award a sum not exceeding $300 for each person thus discharged. These claims must be presented within ninety days from the passage of the act. No claims should be allowed for any slave brought into the district after the passage of the act, and none in any case from persons who had in any way aided or sustained the rebellion. The number of slaves in the district was about 3000. A million of dollars was appropriated for the indemnification of the owners of slaves thus freed, and $100,000 for the colonization of such as wished to emigrate to Hayti, Liberia, or any other country beyond the limits of the United States. Other acts, closely connected with this, provided that colored persons in the district should be amenable to the same laws, and liable to the same punishments as whites;[4] that any slave employed by the consent of his owner in the district after the passage of the Emancipation Act should be free, and that in judicial proceedings there should be no exclusion of any witness on account of color;[5] that ten per cent. of the taxes received from persons of color should be set apart to maintain schools for educating their children; and a special board of trustees was appointed for these schools.[6]

[1] Laws of 37th Congress, 2d Sess., chap. xl., March 13, 1862. [2] Ibid., Joint Resolution, No. 26, April 10, 1862. [3] Ibid., chap. liv., April 16, 1862. [4] Ibid., chap. lxxxiii., May 21, 1862. [5] Ibid., chap. cl., July 12, 1862. [6] Ibid., chaps. lxxxiii., cli., May 21, July 11, 1862.

The main bill for emancipating the slaves in the district passed in the Senate by 29 to 14; in the House by 92 to 13. The debate in the Senate was long and earnest. Mr. Davis, of Kentucky, said that the liberation of slaves where they were numerous would cause a conflict of races which would result in the exile or extermination of one or the other. If slavery were abolished by the general government in any of the states, the moment the white inhabitants were again reorganized they would either reduce the freedmen again to slavery or expel them, or would hunt them down like beasts and exterminate them. He affirmed that slavery and the slave-trade existed by public national law, based upon the usage of the civilized world, and not by positive enactment. This general national law existed in every country wherein it was not repealed by positive enactment, so that slavery was general, and the abolition of it local. He and the entire body of senators from the border states denied the right of Congress to emancipate the slaves in the district. Government might, if public necessity required it, take and use slaves like any other property, by making due compensation to the owners; but it could take property only for the purpose of employing it in the public use; and setting slaves free was not thus employing them. In the House, Mr. Crittenden said that this was a most unwise time to adopt such a measure. It would be looked upon only as the commencement of a series of measures for the entire abolition of slavery. It would give to the rebels the strength of desperation, by inspiring them with the belief that peace would bring the spoliation of their property of all descriptions.

The President, in signing the bill, merely suggested that the time for the presentation of claims should be extended in certain cases, and expressed his gratification that the two principles of compensation and colonization were recognized and applied in the act. The scheme of colonization was for a while a favorite one with the government. An act for the collection of taxes in the insurrectionary districts provided that lands, the taxes upon which should not be paid, might be sold or leased, one quarter of the proceeds to constitute a fund to aid in the colonization of persons of African descent in Hayti, Liberia, or any other tropical country.[1] A provision for the "transportation, colonization, and settlement in some tropical country, beyond the limits of the United States, of persons of African descent," made free by the Confiscation Act, who should be willing to emigrate, was appended to that important law.[2] The President was also authorized to make an arrangement with governments having possessions in the West India Islands to receive, employ, clothe, feed, and instruct, for a period of five years, all Africans taken from slavers captured by United States vessels.[3] In all these schemes of colonization it was assumed that arrangements would be made with the governments of the countries by which the rights of freemen should be secured to the colonists. Negotiations were informally attempted for this purpose with Hayti and the states of Central America. A small colony was dispatched to Hayti, but the experiment proved a failure. The Central American states were wholly averse to any such colonization, and the scheme was finally abandoned.

The distinctive principle of the Republican party, as formally enunciated in its conventions of 1856 and 1860, was that slavery should be prohibited in every part of the country over which the Federal government had the right of exclusive jurisdiction. This had been partially put into effect by the law emancipating the slaves in the District of Columbia. It was carried out to completion by the passage of an act "to secure freedom to all persons within the territories of the United States." This law enacted, in brief but expressive terms, that "from and after the passage of this act there shall be neither slavery nor involuntary servitude in any of the territories of the United States now existing, or which may be hereafter formed or acquired by the United States, otherwise than in punishment of crimes whereof the party shall have been duly convicted."[4] The bill passed with little debate. There was an important distinction between these two measures. It was tacitly admitted that slavery had a legal existence in the district, and therefore loyal owners were compensated for the loss of their slaves; it was assumed that slavery had no legal existence in the territories, and there it was merely prohibited. Except as a question of principle, this act was of little importance, for there were but sixty-three slaves in all the territories out of a population of 220,000; and the climate, physical nature of the country, and the character of the emigration, rendered it certain that no large number of slaves would ever be taken thither, and that when the territories came to be admitted into the Union as states, their Constitutions would prohibit slavery.

The government was slow to accept as soldiers persons of African descent, whether free by birth or enfranchised. The organization of negro regiments was discouraged until after the failure of the campaign before Richmond. It then became evident that all the force which the Union could by any means bring into the field would be required. The last important act of the session, which defined the power of the President in calling out the militia, empowered him to "receive into the service of the United States, for any military or naval service for which they may be found competent, persons of African descent, who shall be enrolled and organized under such regulations, not inconsistent with the Constitution and the laws, as he may prescribe." It was farther enacted that "any slave of a person in rebellion, rendering any such service, shall forever thereafter be free, together with his wife, mother, and children, if they also belong to persons in rebellion. The pay of these colored troops was fixed at ten dollars a month and one ration, being only a little more than half that given to white soldiers."[5]

But by far the most important act relating to slavery passed during the session was that known as the Confiscation Act. The various phases which this bill went through, and the debates which ensued in relation to it, evinced that there was a wide difference of opinion among the members of the Republican party as to the manner in which slavery should be dealt with. Those who took the most extreme ground, prominent among whom were senators Hale, Sumner, Wilson, and Trumbull, wished to legalize the absolute and perpetual forfeiture of the property, including slaves, of all persons engaged in the rebellion. The Constitution expressly declares that "no attainder of treason shall work corruption of blood or forfeiture except during the life of the person attainted;" but, as treason was punishable by death, the forfeiture of the life interest in the property of a condemned traitor would amount to very little. And as the persons of the rebels in the insurrectionary states could not be reached by judicial process, even this interest in their property could not be touched by attaint of treason. To reach this property absolutely was the design of a bill presented by Mr. Trumbull during the first week of the session. The bill came up for discussion on the 25th of February, when it was explained and defended by its author in a long and elaborate speech. The object of the bill, he said, was to operate upon property, and not to affect the person of the traitor, and applied only to cases where he was beyond the reach of judicial process. We had the right to take the property of our enemy and destroy it, if necessary. Again, the bill forfeited the claim of any person engaged in the rebellion to the service of any other person owing him service or labor, and declared the person free from any such claim. Congress had clearly the right to pass such a law. Government had the right to go to the farm or the work-shop, and take away and place in the army a man who by his own voluntary contract owed service to his employer. A parent had a right to the service of his son until he was twenty-one years of age; yet the government could take the son of eighteen and place him in the army. The claim of a master to the service of his slave was certainly not more sacred than that of an employer to the service of his workman, or of a parent to that of his son.

This sweeping measure for the universal confiscation of property and the general emancipation of slaves met with strenuous hostility not only from the opposition, including the members from the border states, but from some of the most earnest supporters of the administration. What would become of the loyal population of the South, asked Ten Eyck, of New Jersey, should all the slaves owned by rebels be set at liberty and allowed to roam the country at large? The policy involved in this measure, said McDougall, of California, would never secure peace, and would lead to a remorseless, relentless war, which would involve subjugation, if not extirpation. The bill, said Cowan, of Pennsylvania, proposed to strip fully 4,000,000 of whites of all their property, real, personal, and mixed, of every kind whatsoever, and reduce them to absolute poverty, and that at a time when they had in the field 400,000 men opposing us desperately. Should we, he asked, go back to the doctrine of forfeitures of the Middle Ages, and introduce feuds which centuries had not sufficed to quiet? The forfeitures of William the Conqueror sink into insignificance compared with those proposed by this bill. The act, said Browning, of Illinois, the successor of Douglas, sweeps away every thing, even the most ordinary comforts and necessaries of domestic life, and reduces all to absolute poverty and nakedness. It leaves them the ownership of nothing. They may repent of their past rebellion, and return to their allegiance, but they return bankrupts and beggars, with nothing on earth to render government desirable. The effect of the bill would be to make peace and reunion an impossible thing; it would fill the hearts of the entire Southern people with despair, and nerve their arms with the energy and desperation which despair inspires.

A special feature of the bill, which excited the strongest opposition of some of the most earnest Republicans, was that it freed the slaves of all persons who had been engaged in the rebellion, by the direct action of Congress, without the intervention of any judicial process. This, it was argued, was in direct violation of the most solemn pledges of the administration, and the repeated declarations of the Republican party. Mr. Collamer, of Vermont, perhaps the most thoroughly anti-slavery state in the Union, spoke at length upon these points, quoting from speeches by senators Sumner, Fessenden, and Sherman, expressly denying the right of Congress to interfere with slavery in a state, and maintaining that the pledges made to the country when Mr. Lincoln was elected should be religiously observed. He pointed out the distinction between this bill and the Confiscation Act of the last session forfeiting the property in slaves who had been actually employed in supporting the rebellion. The bill, he said, was, in his judgment, in direct violation of plighted faith, and of the provisions, prohibitions, and enactments of the Constitution. He did not think the people of his state wished him to aid in breaking any provision of the Constitution, and he would not do so if they wished it.

It was clear that Mr. Trumbull's bill could not pass the Senate. Several amendments were offered, and these were referred to a committee of nine, of which Mr. Clark, of New Hampshire, was chairman. They reported a bill designed to harmonize the various opinions, and thus to secure the adoption of some measure which should meet the pressing emergencies of the times. This bill differed from that of Mr. Trumbull in making the confiscation of property and the forfeiture of the right to slaves a punishment for treason, to be inflicted only after the trial and conviction of the offender. It also authorized the President to grant pardon and amnesty to all persons who had been engaged in the rebellion, at such time and upon such conditions as he should deem expedient for the public welfare.

This bill met with vehement opposition from the extremes on both sides. On the one hand it was said to be too lenient, and on the other hand too se-

[1] Laws of the Thirty-seventh Congress, Second Session, chap. xcviii., June 7, 1862. [2] Ibid., chap. cxcv., July 17, 1862. [3] Ibid., chap. cxcvii., July 17 1862. [4] Ibid., chap. cxi., June 18, 1862. [5] Ibid., chap. cci., July 17, 1862.

JOHN P. HALE.

God sometimes offered to nations as well as to individuals opportunity, which was of all things most to be desired. Never before had such an opportunity been presented. The blow which would smite the rebellion would scatter prosperity and happiness throughout the land. It would mark an epoch from barbarism to civilization. Congress, and not the President, had the supreme control over the operations of the war. By the old rights of war, freemen were made slaves; by those which he proposed, slaves were made freemen. The substitute was rejected. Mr. Trumbull opposed the bill because it made treason easy. On the other hand, amendments were proposed, striking out, one after another, every important section. These were all voted down; and the bill, as reported by the committee, passed the Senate by a vote of twenty-eight to thirteen; senators Trumbull and Sumner, notwithstanding their objections, voting for it, and several Republicans against it.

Meanwhile a bill similar to the one proposed by Mr. Sumner had passed the House. The Senate refused to accept it, adhering to its own. A committee of conference was appointed, and the House acceded to the Senate bill, with slight amendments, by a vote of eighty-two to forty-two.[1]

But the bill had hardly passed before it was known that the President would refuse to sanction it. He had prepared a message vetoing it. His main objections were against those parts of the first, second, seventh, and eighth sections which forfeited property beyond the life of the person attainted of treason. To obviate these objections and some others, a joint resolution was proposed limiting the class of state officers whose property was to be confiscated, and providing that real estate should be forfeited only during the life of the offender.[2] The President, considering this resolution to constitute a part of the bill, signed it, and it became a law.

The President was loth to change the avowed policy of the administration by exercising the great power thus placed in his hands. He clung to his favorite scheme of compensated emancipation. A week before the close of the session he sent a special message to Congress embodying the draft of an act providing that, in case any state should abolish slavery, bonds of the United States should be delivered to it of a certain sum for every slave, the whole to be paid at once if the emancipation was immediate, or in installments if it were gradual. The proposed bill was referred to committees, but no farther action was taken upon it. No border state, for whom it was especially intended, responded to the invitation.

On the same day, July 12, he requested all the members of Congress from the border states to meet him in conference. He laid before them his scheme, and urged them to favor it. If the war continued long, he said, slavery would be extinguished in those states. Much of its value had already gone, and all would soon be lost, with nothing to show for it. It would be better to take a step which would shorten the war, and secure substantial compensation for what would otherwise be wholly lost. How much better for these states as seller, and for the nation as buyer, to sell out and buy out that without which the war never could have been, than to sink both the thing to be sold and the price of it in cutting each other's throats. He hint-ed at the strong pressure exerted upon him to take stringent measures in regard to slavery.

A majority of those to whom this appeal was made presented a reply, dis-

vere. Mr. Sumner offered a substitute, which he advocated in several elaborate orations. He denied that the slaves of rebels could be regarded as property, real or personal. Though claimed as property and recognized as chattels by local law, the Constitution knew them only as persons. Being men, they were bound to allegiance and entitled to protection. No claim on the part of their masters could supersede the right inherent in the general government to demand the services of all. By declaring the slaves free, we should take from the rebellion its main spring of activity and strength.

[1] Laws of the Thirty-seventh Congress, Second Session, chap. cxcv., June 17, 1862.—The following is an abstract of the different sections of the bill, the title of which is, "An Act to suppress Insurrection, to punish Treason and Rebellion, to seize and confiscate the Property of Rebels, and for other Purposes."

Section 1. Every person who shall hereafter be convicted of the crime of treason against the United States shall suffer death, or be imprisoned for not less than five years, and fined not less than $10,000, and his slaves, if any, shall be declared free; the fine to be levied and collected on any or all of the property, real and personal, except slaves, of which the person so convicted was the owner at the time of committing said crime, any sale or conveyance to the contrary notwithstanding.

Section 2. If any person shall hereafter incite, assist, or engage in any rebellion against the authority of the United States, or give aid and comfort thereto, and be convicted thereof, he shall be punished by imprisonment for a period of not more than ten years, or by a fine of not more than $10,000, or both, and his slaves, if any, be set free.

Section 3 disqualifies all persons who shall commit these crimes from holding office under the United States.

Section 4 provides that this act shall not affect the case of any person guilty of treason before its passage, unless convicted under it.

Section 5 makes it the duty of the President to cause to be seized and applied to the support of the army of the United States all the property of the following classes of persons: (1) Officers of the rebel army and navy; (2) High officers, executive, legislative, judicial, and diplomatic, of the Confederacy; (3) Similar officers of any one of the Confederate states; (4) Those who, having held offices under the United States, shall hereafter hold offices under the Confederacy; (5) Those who shall hereafter hold any office under the Confederacy or any one of the Confederate states; provided, however, that those described in the third, fourth, and fifth classes shall have accepted their appointment since the secession of their respective states, or have taken the oath of allegiance to the Confederacy; (6) Those owning property in the loyal states who shall aid the rebellion; all sales or transfers of such property to be null and void; and it shall be a valid bar to any suit for the possession of such property that the owner belonged to any one of these six classes.

Section 6 provides that if any person, other than those described, aiding or abetting the armed rebellion, shall not, within sixty days after public warning and proclamation by the President, cease from rebellion and return to his allegiance, his property shall be in like manner seized.

Sections 7 and 8 prescribe the manner of proceedings by the courts in these cases.

Section 9 enacts that all slaves of persons who shall hereafter be engaged in rebellion, escaping and taking refuge within the lines of the army, all slaves captured from or deserted by such persons, or coming in any way under control of the government, shall be considered prisoners of war, shall be forever free from servitude, and not be again held as slaves.

Section 10 enacts that no slave, escaping from one state into another, shall be delivered up, except on oath of the claimant that the owner or master of the slave has not borne arms against the United States, or given aid and comfort to the rebellion; and prohibits all persons in the military service of the United States, under pain of dismissal, from deciding on the validity of any claim to the services of any escaped slave.

Section 11 authorizes the President to employ as many persons of African descent as he may deem necessary and proper for the suppression of the rebellion, and to organize and use them as he may deem best for the public welfare.

Section 12 authorizes the President to provide for the colonization, with their own consent, beyond the limits of the United States, of persons freed by this act; the consent of the governments of the countries having been first obtained, with a guarantee of the rights of freemen to the colonists.

Section 13 authorizes the President, by proclamation, to extend pardon and amnesty to all persons who may have participated in the rebellion, at such time, on such conditions, and with such exceptions as he may deem expedient for the public welfare.

Section 14 gives the courts of the United States authority to institute such proceedings, and to issue such orders, as may be necessary to carry this act into effect.

The joint explanatory resolution passed by both houses, which is essentially a part of this act, provides that the clause relating to state officers in section 6 "shall be so construed as not to apply to any act or acts done prior to the passage thereof, nor to include any member of a state Legislature, or judge of any state court, who has not, in accepting or entering upon his office, taken an oath to support the Constitution of the so-called Confederate states; nor shall the real estate of any offender under said act be forfeited beyond his natural life."

[2] Laws of the Thirty-seventh Congress, Second Session, Joint Resolution, No. 63.

senting from his opinion that the adoption of this policy would terminate the war or serve the cause of the Union. Their states were loyal, and had manifested beyond a doubt that in no case would they join the rebellion or go with the Confederacy, even if its independence was recognized. But the right of holding slaves belonged to the states. They could not see that they were called upon to make the sacrifice which was required by the proposition. They were asked to give up a valuable right, with no security for even the small compensation proposed. If, however, Congress would make the necessary appropriation of funds, and place them at the disposal of the President, to pay for the emancipated slaves and for their colonization, their states would consider the project. This reply was signed by twenty senators and representatives, most of them from Maryland, Kentucky, and Missouri. Another answer, signed by seven members, three of whom were from Western Virginia, was a little more favorable. They would ask their states to take the subject into consideration, adding, "We are the more emboldened to assume this position from the fact, now become history, that the leaders of the Southern rebellion have offered to abolish slavery among them as a condition to foreign intervention in favor of their independence as a nation. If they can give up slavery to destroy the Union, we can surely ask our people to consider the question of emancipation to save the Union."

The Confiscation Act was an attempt to harmonize different shades of opinion. It contained some apparent inconsistencies. The punishment for treason or rebellion, whether by death, imprisonment, fine, or the liberation of slaves, could be inflicted only after formal trial and conviction. But the property of all persons engaged in rebellion was to be seized and confiscated to public use, and their slaves, coming in any way under the control of the Federal power, were to be set free without the intervention of any judicial process. But these discrepancies were apparent rather than real. Trial, conviction, and punishment for treason were judicial acts, to be performed according to legal forms. The seizure of the property of an enemy was a military measure authorized by the laws of war. Slaves were considered in their twofold character of property and persons. As property they could be seized, but the United States could not hold them as slaves; and, consequently, when the title of their former owners was annulled, there was no other to take its place, and they reverted to their natural condition of freemen.

But, beyond this right of seizure of enemies' property, it was held that, in time of war, government had the right to employ any means not contrary to the laws and usages of civilized warfare to weaken the enemy. This power was affirmed to be inherent in the very nature of our government, even though it were not expressly granted by the Constitution. Among these rights was that of emancipating the slaves of the enemy. Some conceived that this right pertained to Congress, and should be carried into effect by express enactment; others held it to be a military right pertaining to the President in virtue of his function as commander-in-chief of the army and navy. But those who were in favor of the measure cared little by whom it was effected, so that it was effected at all. The President assumed that the power, and the responsibility for its exercise, devolved upon him.

Congress had hardly adjourned when the President was strongly urged to issue a proclamation for the universal emancipation of the slaves. He hesitated, upon grounds of expediency, to take this decisive and irrevocable step. On the 13th of September he was waited upon by a committee from various religious denominations in Chicago. They urged him to issue a proclamation of emancipation for the reasons that it would enlist the sympathy of the civilized world, would promote harmony at the North, would give new soldiers to the Union, and would be in accordance with the will of God.

Mr. Lincoln set aside the last argument by saying that very good men, claiming to represent the divine will, urged him to adopt very different measures. He thought that, if a direct revelation was to be made upon a subject so intimately connected with his own duty, it would be vouchsafed to him. But he expected no direct revelation, and could only study the physical facts of the case, and learn what was right, wise, and possible. A proclamation of emancipation might produce a good effect in Europe; it might help somewhat at the North; it might weaken the enemy by drawing off some of his laborers. But he did not think it would add available soldiers to our army. If the blacks should be armed, he feared that in a few weeks the arms would be in the hands of the enemy; besides, we had not arms enough to equip our white troops. Moreover, there were 50,000 soldiers in the Union army from the border slaveholding states, and it would be a serious matter should such a proclamation drive them over to the enemy. But

JACOB COLLAMER.

the main objection to issuing such a proclamation at that time was that it would be useless. "What good," he asked, "would a proclamation of emancipation from me do, especially as we are now situated? I do not want to issue a document that the whole world will see must necessarily be inoperative, like the Pope's Bull against the comet. Would my word free the slaves, when I can not even enforce the Constitution in the rebel states?"

The state of affairs at that time afforded no reason to hope that such a proclamation would produce any good effect. The campaign on the Peninsula had disastrously failed; the Army of the Potomac had been defeated and driven back upon the capital; the Confederates, flushed with victory, had crossed the Potomac and were threatening Baltimore, and, not impossibly, Philadelphia. On the very day when this interview took place, the general-in-chief telegraphed to General McClellan that he believed the Confederates were about to march in force upon the capital. On that day they seemed more likely to be able to dictate terms than to be forced to receive them. A proclamation from the President of the United States decreeing the emancipation of the slaves in the Confederacy would then have appeared as idle as a papal Bull against the comet.

A single week wrought an entire change in the aspect of affairs. The battle of Antietam, fought on the 17th of September, had put an end to the triumphal march of the enemy. The Confederates were in full retreat. They had, indeed, got safely back across the Potomac; but it was believed that the army which had foiled McClellan at Richmond, and defeated Pope at Manassas, would be captured or annihilated. Men passed at a bound from the depths of depression to the heights of exultation. The speedy overthrow of the Confederacy was confidently anticipated. It seemed that this might be hastened by a warning proclamation, giving the insurgents the choice between prompt submission, and subjugation with the liberation of their slaves.

So judged the President of the United States; and accordingly, on the

22d of September, he issued a proclamation declaring that hereafter, as heretofore, the object of the war would be to restore the Union; that at the next meeting of Congress he should again propose a measure to compensate any slaveholding state, not then in rebellion, which should voluntarily undertake the abolition of slavery within its limits; that on the first day of January, 1863, all persons held as slaves in any state then in rebellion should be free; and that the executive government of the United States, including its military and naval force, would recognize the freedom of these slaves, and would do nothing to hinder them from acquiring the actual possession of it; that on this day he would designate the states, and parts of states, which should then be considered to be in rebellion, and to which this provision of the forthcoming proclamation should apply.

This warning proved entirely ineffectual, and, at the appointed time, the proclamation of emancipation was issued. It marked a new phase in the conduct of the war. The object was indeed unchanged, but entirely new measures were called into requisition to effect that object. Heretofore the claims of rebel masters to their slaves had been put upon the same footing as their claims to any other property. This claim might be annulled precisely like the claim to a horse. The slave coming into possession of the government became free simply because the claim of the master having lapsed, there was no other to take its place, for the United States could not assume property in slaves. Henceforth slavery in all the insurrectionary states was declared to be abolished, and all the military and naval power of the government was solemnly pledged to maintain the freedom of all slaves in these portions of the United States.[1]

Delaware, Maryland, Kentucky, and Missouri, having remained loyal, were not included in this proclamation. A portion of Virginia, including the forty-eight counties soon to be known as the State of West Virginia, and seven others, subsequently recognized as the loyal state of Virginia, were also ex-

empt. Tennessee had all along been represented in the Federal Congress, and being in great part occupied by the national forces, was not held to be in insurrection. Thirteen parishes in Louisiana were held by our forces, and were not included in the insurrectionary districts. The number of slaves in these states and parts of states was 832,259. These remained, as before, slaves under the state laws. In the remaining slave states, Alabama, Arkansas, Florida, Georgia, Mississippi, North Carolina, South Carolina, and Texas, thirty-five parishes in Louisiana, and ninety-three counties in Virginia, were 3,108,197 slaves. These were all declared to be free.

During the interval between the issue of these two proclamations, and at various subsequent periods, the President and members of the cabinet expressed their views in respect to this measure and its probable influence upon the war. Mr. Seward wrote to the American minister to France[1] that the great problem of domestic slavery in the United States presented itself for solution when the war began. The people were intensely engaged in the difficult task of its solution. The President's message would carry the public mind still more directly and earnestly on its great work. Mr. Chase said that slavery, having come out of its shelter under state Constitutions and laws to assail the national life, must surely die. Who cared how its end came? In the rebel slave states it would come "by military order, decree, or proclamation, not to be disregarded or set aside in any event as a nullity, but maintained and executed with perfect good faith to all the enfranchised." In the loyal slave states it would come by the voluntary action of the people, aided by the free states. Meanwhile the American blacks must be called into this conflict as men, no longer as mere contrabands. We must follow the example of Andrew Jackson, who did not hesitate to oppose colored regiments to British invasion. We needed the good will of these men, and must make them our friends by showing ourselves their friends.[2] He had at first been averse to any interference with slavery in the states; but, as the war went on, "we put greater and greater armies into the field; but the slave population of the South was the real prop of the rebellion, raising provisions for the army while it was fighting in the field, so that they could have nearly all their laboring population in the battle-field, and they had another laboring population behind them to feed and support them. It seemed perfectly clear that we had to strike at this under-prop of the rebellion. The proclamation was the right thing in the right place."[3]

That the proclamation was irrevocable was firmly maintained. The President had been urged to retract it by some who considered it unconstitutional. He replied: "I think the Constitution invests the commander-in-chief with the laws of war in time of war. But, as law, the proclamation is either valid or invalid. If it is not valid it needs no retraction; if it is valid it can not be retracted any more than the dead can be brought to life."[4] Mr. Blair, the Postmaster General, said, "That measure, which involves both life and freedom in its results, when proclaimed was beyond revocation by either the civil or military authority of the nation. The people once slaves in the rebel states can never again be recognized as such by the United States. No judicial decision, no legislative action, state or national, can be admitted to re-enslave a people who are associated in our destinies in this war of defense to save the government, and whose manumission was deemed essential to the restoration and preservation of the Union and to its permanent peace."[5] Mr. Chase said, "Either the proclamation was a sham and an imposition in the face of the whole world, or else it was an effectual thing, and there are no slaves to-day in the rebel states. They are all enfranchised by the proclamation; for what says it? All the slaves are declared now and forever free, and the executive power of the nation is pledged to the maintenance of this freedom."[6]

It had been anticipated that this proclamation of emancipation would enlist the sympathy of the European governments upon the side of the Union. All our ministers abroad had urged the adoption of such a measure. The result failed to justify this anticipation. Mr. Dayton warned the government that it might look for efforts from portions of the foreign press to misstate the motives of the proclamation and the consequences which would follow it. Another effort in favor of recognition would be made, ostensibly on the ground of humanity, but really because emancipation would weaken the South and interfere with the production of cotton. On the other hand it was urged, especially in Great Britain, that the measure did not go far enough. Earl Russell, in a dispatch to Lord Lyons,[7] said that the proclamation was of a very strange nature. It professed to emancipate all slaves in places where the United States could not make emancipation a reality, but emancipate no one where the decree could be carried into effect. In some places a master could still recover his fugitive slave by process of law; in the other places, a slave, if arrested, was authorized to resist, and his resistance would be sustained by the military force of the United States. Slavery was therefore legal or illegal according to locality. There was no declaration of a principle adverse to slavery in the proclamation. It was merely a measure of war, and of a very questionable kind. The dispatch concluded by saying, "As President Lincoln has twice appealed to the judgment of mankind in his proclamation, I venture to say that I do not think it can or ought to satisfy the friends of abolition, who look for total and impartial freedom for the slave, and not for vengeance on the slave owner."

---

[1] The following is the text of the preamble and closing paragraph of the proclamation of September 22, 1862:

"I, ABRAHAM LINCOLN, President of the United States of America, and commander-in-chief of the army and navy thereof, do hereby proclaim and declare, that hereafter, as heretofore, the war will be prosecuted for the object of practically restoring the constitutional relation between the United States and each of the states, and the people thereof, in which states that relation is or may be suspended or disturbed.

"That it is my purpose, upon the next meeting of Congress, to again recommend the adoption of a practical measure tendering pecuniary aid to the free acceptance or rejection of all slave states so-called, the people whereof may not then be in rebellion against the United States, and which states may then have voluntarily adopted, or thereafter may voluntarily adopt, immediate or gradual abolishment of slavery within their respective limits; and that the effort to colonize persons of African descent, with their consent, upon this continent or elsewhere, with the previously obtained consent of the governments existing there, will be continued."

"And the Executive will in due time recommend that all citizens of the United States who shall have remained loyal thereto throughout the rebellion, shall (upon the restoration of the constitutional relation between the United States and their respective states and people, if that relation shall have been suspended or disturbed) be compensated for all losses by acts of the United States, including the loss of slaves."

Attention was also called to the provisions of the acts of Congress which forbid the naval and military force from returning fugitives; which declare all slaves of persons engaged in the rebellion, who in any way come into the control of the government, to be free; and which forbid the return of fugitive slaves unless the claimant makes oath that he has not been engaged in the rebellion. The most important paragraphs of this proclamation were textually repeated in that of January 1, 1863, which we give in full:

"PROCLAMATION.

"Whereas, on the 22d day of September, in the year of our Lord one thousand eight hundred and sixty-two, a proclamation was issued by the President of the United States containing, among other things, the following, to wit:

"That on the first day of January, in the year of our Lord one thousand eight hundred and sixty-three, all persons held as slaves within any states or designated part of a state, the people whereof shall then be in rebellion against the United States, shall be then, thenceforward, and forever free; and the executive government of the United States, including the military and naval authority thereof, will recognize and maintain the freedom of such persons, and will do no act or acts to repress such persons, or any of them, in any efforts they may make for their actual freedom.

"That the Executive will, on the first day of January aforesaid, by proclamation, designate the states and parts of states, if any, in which the people thereof respectively shall then be in rebellion against the United States; and the fact that any state, or the people thereof, shall on that day be in good faith represented in the Congress of the United States by members chosen thereto at elections wherein a majority of the qualified voters of such state shall have participated, shall, in the absence of strong countervailing testimony, be deemed conclusive evidence that such state, and the people thereof, are not then in rebellion against the United States.

"Now, therefore, I, ABRAHAM LINCOLN, President of the United States, by virtue of the power in me vested as commander-in-chief of the army and navy of the United States in time of actual armed rebellion against the authority and government of the United States, and as a fit and necessary war measure for suppressing said rebellion, do, on this first day of January, in the year of our Lord one thousand eight hundred and sixty-three, and in accordance with my purpose so to do, publicly proclaimed for the full period of one hundred days from the day first above-mentioned, order and designate as the states and parts of states wherein the people thereof respectively are this day in rebellion against the United States, the following, to wit:

"Arkansas, Texas, Louisiana (except the parishes of St. Bernard, Plaquemines, Jefferson, St. John, St. Charles, St. James, Ascension, Assumption, Terre Bonne, Lafourche, Ste. Marie, St. Martin, and New Orleans, including the city of New Orleans), Mississippi, Alabama, Florida, Georgia, South Carolina, North Carolina, and Virginia (except the forty-eight counties designated as West Virginia, and also the counties of Berkeley, Accomac, Northampton, Elizabeth City, York, Princess Anne, and Norfolk, including the cities of Norfolk and Portsmouth), and which excepted parts are for the present left precisely as if this proclamation were not issued.

"And by virtue of the power and for the purpose aforesaid, I do order and declare that all persons held as slaves within said designated states and parts of states are and henceforward shall be free; and that the executive government of the United States, including the military and naval authorities thereof, will recognize and maintain the freedom of said persons.

"And I hereby enjoin upon the people so declared to be free to abstain from all violence, unless in necessary self-defense; and I recommend to them that, in all cases when allowed, they labor faithfully for reasonable wages.

"And I farther declare and make known that such persons, of suitable condition, will be received into the armed service of the United States to garrison forts, positions, stations, and other places, and to man vessels of all sorts in said service.

"And upon this act, sincerely believed to be an act of justice, warranted by the Constitution upon military necessity, I invoke the considerate judgment of mankind, and the gracious favor of Almighty God.

"In testimony whereof, I have hereunto set my name, and caused the seal of the United States to be affixed.

"Done at the City of Washington this first day of January, in the year of our Lord one thousand eight hundred and sixty-three, and of the independence of the United States the eighty-seventh.

"By the President: ABRAHAM LINCOLN.
"WILLIAM H. SEWARD, Secretary of State."

[1] December 1, 1862.   [2] Letter to Loyal League, April 9, 1863.   [3] Speech at Cincinnati, October 15, 1863.   [4] Letter to the Springfield Convention, August 26, 1863.   [5] Speech at Cleveland, May, 1863.   [6] Speech at Cincinnati, October 15, 1863.   [7] January 17, 1863.

CHAPTER IX.

POLICY OF THE CONFEDERATE GOVERNMENT.

The Confederate Provisional Government.—Ultimate Object of the Secession Leaders.—First Session of Congress.—Military and Financial Bills.—The Slave Trade.—Second Session.—War accepted.—Privateering.—Debts to the North.—Adjournment to Richmond.—Third Session.—The President's Message.—Uprising of the South.—Wealthy Volunteers.—Hunter Secretary of State.—Judah P. Benjamin.—Men and Money voted.—Telegraph seized.—Alien and Confiscation Laws.—Number of alien Residents.—Result of the Confiscation.—Missouri received.—Last Session of the Provisional Congress.—President's Message.—The Danville Railroad.—The Permanent Government.—Constitution of the Congress.—Davis's first Message as permanent President.—Gloomy Prospects.—Too much attempted.—Conscription proposed.—Confederate Finances.—Cotton Loan.—Planters ask for Relief.—Reply of the Secretary of the Treasury.—Depreciation of the Currency.—Foreign Relations.—Lord John Russell and the Confederate Commissioners.—Yancey's Statement.—Weakened Condition of the Confederate Army.—Furloughs revoked.—The President's Conscription Message.—The first Conscription Act.—Its Provisions.—Exempts.—Opposition in Georgia and Alabama.—The Situation in the Spring of 1862.—Delays of the Federal Armies in Virginia.—The Movement upon the Peninsula.—Panic at Richmond.—Increase of the Confederate Forces.—Lee as Commander-in-chief.—Failure of the Federal Campaign.—The Confederate Triumph and its Cost.—New Conscription Laws.—Davis and Butler.—Policy with respect to colored Soldiers.

IT is proposed in this chapter to describe the foreign and domestic policy of the Confederate government from its organization in February, 1861, down to the close of the year 1862, dwelling especially upon the conscription laws, which enabled it to bring into the field a greater proportion of its population than had ever before been done by any civilized people.

The government established at Montgomery on the 8th, and formally inaugurated on the 18th of February, 1861, was simply a compact entered into between six states claiming to be independent and equal. Florida, with 77,000 whites, had an equal vote with Georgia, having more than ten times as many. This government was only provisional, to expire, by its own limitation, in a year, unless sooner superseded. Though the compact was formed by only six states, it was certain that some, and believed that all, of the nine remaining slave states would enter into it in less than a year. Provision was made in the Constitution for the admission of new states by the vote of two thirds of each house of Congress. If all the slaveholding states joined the Confederacy, it would have possession of the mouths of the Mississippi, of both banks of its lower course for more than a thousand miles, and of one bank of each of its great affluents, the Missouri and Ohio, for three hundred miles more. This would practically give it the control of the whole valley drained by the Mississippi and its main affluents, and it was confidently expected that, as soon as the Confederacy was firmly established, the northwestern free states would unite with it, either formally by becoming members, or actually by withdrawing from the Union and forming a separate government in close affiliation with that of the South. Some even went farther in their views, and believed that, the Union being dissolved, the Middle States would follow the presumed example of those of the Northwest, and form still another government. Thus the Southern slaveholding Confederacy, even if it were joined by none of the free states, would become the preponderating power of the continent.

Provision was moreover made in the Constitution for the acquisition of new territory. This was only desired upon the southern border. The leaders of secession had for years favored the filibustering expeditions against Mexico and Central America; they had secured the annexation of Texas, and had introduced into the Democratic platforms of 1856 and 1860 resolutions directly or indirectly advocating the acquisition of Cuba. A saving clause was indeed added, that this acquisition should be made "upon terms honorable to ourselves and just to Spain;" but it was perfectly understood that Spain would give up Cuba only upon compulsion, and had formally declared that any proposition for its purchase would be considered as an insult. Although it now suited the policy of the Confederate government to deny any purpose of aggression, it is certain that ultimate accessions of territory were expected to be made from its southern neighbors. In all territory, howsoever or whencesoever acquired, slavery was to be recognized and protected. The idea of a great slaveholding confederacy, ultimately to embrace the whole tropical and semi-tropical regions of the North American continent, was predominant in the minds of many, if not all of the leaders of the secession.

So firmly was the idea of the speedy accession of the remaining slaveholding states implanted in the Southern mind, that, although the Constitution forbade the "importation of negroes of the African race from any foreign country," an exception was made in the case of "slaveholding states or territories of the United States of America;" and when the Confederacy, on the 6th of May, declared war, or, as it was phrased, recognized the existence of war with the United States, these slaveholding states were formally excepted from the declaration. And when, subsequently, laws were passed forbidding the payment of debts to citizens of the United States, ordering the expulsion or imprisonment of all alien enemies and the confiscation of their property, citizens of these states who had not actually engaged in hostilities against the Confederacy were expressly excluded from the operation of these laws. And when, still later, the illegal Sovereignty Convention in Kentucky, and the regularly deposed Governor Jackson, of Missouri, undertook to bring these states into the Confederacy, their action was promptly recognized, these states were formally received, their delegates admitted to seats in Congress, and the states were claimed as members of the Confederacy.

The action of the Confederate Congress was mainly held in secret session, and there are few means of tracing the actual course of sentiment. This, however, is of little consequence, for almost from the outset the government assumed the form of a strict military despotism, all essential functions being centred in the President, Congress doing little more than act upon his suggestions and register his decrees. The idea was sedulously inculcated that there would be no real war; that the North dared not and could not fight, and, after a faint show of resistance, would recognize the independence of the Confederacy. But the leaders knew better. They were assured from the outset that their position must be maintained by arms if maintained at all. While talking of peace, they set at once about vigorous preparations for war. The President was directed to take charge of all military operations between the Confederacy and other powers; and on the 7th of March he was authorized to accept the services of 100,000 volunteers, to serve for twelve months unless sooner discharged, in order to "repel invasion, maintain the rightful possession of the Confederate States of America in every portion of territory belonging to each state, and to secure the public tranquillity against threatened assault." This warlike measure was adopted a full month before any attempt had been made to furnish supplies to Fort Sumter, and more than five weeks before the President of the United States had issued the call for 75,000 militia to suppress unlawful combinations and cause the laws to be duly executed.

The Congress adjourned after passing acts, none of which, with the exception of that calling for 100,000 volunteers, were of great importance. The principal ones provided for the issue of a million dollars in treasury notes to meet current expenses; authorized the appointment of commissioners to the European governments; regulated the transit of merchandise, and requested the various states to cede to the Confederacy the forts, arsenals, navy yards, and other public establishments which they had seized. The article in the Constitution prohibiting the foreign slave-trade had been adopted by the vote of four states against two, South Carolina and Florida opposing it. A bill was passed to carry this provision into effect. This was vetoed by the President on the ground that in one section of the bill provision was made to transfer slaves who had been illegally imported to the custody of foreign states or societies, upon condition of deportation and future freedom, and, in case this proposition was not accepted, the President was required to cause the negroes to be sold at auction to the highest bidder. This provision was held by Mr. Davis to be "in opposition to the policy declared in the Constitution, the prohibition of the importation of African negroes, and in derogation of its mandate to legislate for the effectuation of that object." The veto was sustained by Congress.

The government of the United States, having refused to receive Forsyth and Crawford, who announced themselves to be commissioners authorized by the Confederacy to enter upon negotiations upon all subjects growing out of the secession, gave formal notice, on the 8th of April, that provisions would be sent to Fort Sumter, peaceably if possible, otherwise by force. Thereupon ensued the bombardment and capture of that fort, the secession of other states, and other hostile measures which have already been fully detailed.

On the 12th of April the Confederate Congress was summoned to meet on the 29th, in consequence of the "declaration of hostile purposes contained in the message sent by President Lincoln to the government of South Carolina." In the mean time, the proclamation of President Lincoln of April 15, calling for 75,000 militia, and that of April 19, announcing the blockade of the Confederate ports, had been issued. The message of Mr. Davis, delivered at the opening of this session, has been cited at length in these pages.[1] On the 7th of May an act was passed recognizing war as existing between the Confederacy and the non-slaveholding states of the Union, and authorizing the issue of letters of marque and reprisal.[2] All captures and prizes made by these privateers were to be the property of the captors, and a bounty of twenty-five dollars was to be paid for every prisoner made by them and delivered into the hands of agents appointed for that purpose in Confederate ports, and a bounty of twenty dollars for each person on board of any armed vessel which should be destroyed by any privateer of equal or inferior force. But three weeks before the passage of this act the President had issued a proclamation inviting all persons to apply for letters of marque and reprisal. The military force then on foot was stated at 35,000 men, of whom 19,000 were at Charleston, Pensacola, Forts Morgan, Jackson, St. Philip, and Pulaski, and 16,000 on the way to Virginia. It was estimated that the government had control of arms and munitions to supply an army of 150,000 men. A law was passed forbidding the payment of any debt to any citizen of the non-slaveholding states, and all persons owing such debts were authorized to pay the amount in specie or its equivalent, or in treasury notes, into the public treasury, to be refunded with interest at the close of the war.

Virginia having in the mean while joined the Confederacy, it was evident that the immediate seat of hostilities would be transferred to that state,

[1] Ante, p. 113.

[2] The preamble to this act stated that, whereas the government of the United States had refused to treat with that of the Confederacy; the President of the United States had called for 75,000 men to capture forts and strong-holds belonging to the Confederate States; had announced his purpose to blockade their ports; "and whereas the State of Virginia has seceded from the Federal Union, and entered into a convention of alliance, offensive and defensive, with the Confederate States, and has adopted the provisional Constitution of the said states, and the states of Maryland, North Carolina, Tennessee, Kentucky, Arkansas, and Missouri have refused, and it is believed that the State of Delaware, and the inhabitants of the territories of Arizona and New Mexico, and the Indian Territory south of Kansas, will refuse to co-operate with the government of the United States in these acts of hostility and wanton aggression which are plainly intended to overawe, oppress, and finally subjugate the people of the Confederate States; and whereas, by the acts and means aforesaid, war exists between the Confederate States and the government of the United States and territories thereof, excepting" the states and territories before mentioned; therefore it is enacted "that the President of the Confederate States is hereby authorized to use the whole land and naval force of the Confederate States to meet the war thus commenced, and to issue to private armed vessels commissions, or letters of marque and general reprisal, in such form as he shall think proper, under the seal of the Confederate States, against the vessels, goods, and effects of the government of the United States, and of the citizens or inhabitants of the states and territories thereof, except the states and territories hereinbefore named."

THE FIRST CONFEDERATE CABINET.

JUDAH P. BENJAMIN, *Attorney General.* CHARLES G. MEMMINGER, *Treasury.* LEROY P. WALKER, *War.* JOHN H. REAGAN, *Postmaster General.*

STEPHEN M. MALLORY, *Navy.* ALEXANDER H. STEPHENS, *Vice-President.* JEFFERSON DAVIS, *President.* ROBERT TOOMBS, *Secretary of State.*

ROBERT M. T. HUNTER.

the states which originally organized the Confederacy; for, with the exception of three fortified islands, which were maintained by the preponderating naval power of the Union, its forces had been driven from every point, and now, at the expiration of five months from the organization of the government, not a single hostile foot pressed the soil of the original Confederacy. But the forces which had been sufficient to effect this would prove inadequate to repel invasion by half a million of troops now proposed by the enemy, and a large addition to the Confederate army would be necessary. The idea of any compromise or treaty which should involve the reconstruction of the Union was emphatically disavowed.

The South had, in the mean time, rushed to arms with an alacrity not less than that shown in the uprising of the North. Only 100,000 volunteers had been authorized by the law of the last session of Congress. More than this number offered themselves at once. In the Far South the question was not who should go, but who must stay. Companies were organized in every neighborhood and village, who urged their claims to acceptance. In answer to one such application, the Governor of Mississippi replied that he had but three regiments to fill, and had 150 companies to pick from. Large bounties were paid for the privilege of taking the place of an accepted volunteer. There were companies in which every private was wealthy, or the son of a wealthy man, every one having his negro servants in camp.[1] The report of the Secretary of War showed that early in July 194 regiments and 32 battalions had been accepted, numbering in all 210,000 men. At about the same time the Federal government had nominally in the field 230,000 men, exclusive of three months' volunteers, whose term was about to expire. The Federal Secretary of War hesitated to ask for more soldiers; the Confederate secretary recommended that Congress should call for and accept 300 regiments.

Robert Toombs resigned his post of Secretary of State, and was succeeded by Robert M. T. Hunter. It has long been a peculiarity of Virginia politics that the state is always supposed to have at least one man who is the embodiment of all political wisdom. In default of a better, the place has been at times assigned to a half-lunatic like Randolph, or an interminable declaimer like Wise. This position had somehow been accorded to Hunter, perhaps on the ground of long service; for, with a brief interval, he had been a representative or senator in Congress for nearly a quarter of a century. From 1849 onward he was chairman of the Committee of Finance in the Senate. He was chiefly noted for ponderous political platitudes to which constant repetition gave an air of profundity. In the Democratic Convention of 1860 he was named as a candidate for the presidency; in the first dozen ballots he received, though with a wide interval, the highest vote after that cast for Douglas. In the scheme of secession as at first drawn up by Southern senators, Hunter was to have been President, and Davis commander-in-chief of the army; but the rapid march of events which followed the first movements for secession demanded a leader of a different stamp from the sluggish Virginian. In a purely military government, the post of Secretary of State, though nominally the one of first dignity in the cabinet, was of no practical importance, and the vanity of Virginia might be safely flattered by bestowing it upon her stolid favorite,[2] for whom it was claimed by his admirers that "he possessed in a more eminent degree the philosophical characteristics of Jefferson than any other statesman now living." The ponderous, pragmatical Virginian soon found himself out of place in the fiery revolutionary government. His fine-spun theories were brushed away like cobwebs by the fierce exigencies of the times. In a few months he was succeeded as Secretary of State by Judah P. Benjamin, of Louisiana.

Mr. Benjamin, as is indicated by his name, and still more evidently by his face, belongs to that keen and aspiring Hebrew race which for the last

and from no point could they be so successfully conducted by the Confederates as from its capital. Accordingly, on the 22d of May the Congress adjourned to meet at Richmond on the 20th of July, and in the mean while the executive departments and the archives of the government were transferred to that city, which thus became the capital of the Confederacy.

The Congress met there at the appointed time, two days after the skirmish at Blackburn's Ford, and the day before the battle of Bull Run.

The message of President Davis announced that Alabama, Arkansas, North Carolina, Tennessee, and Virginia had become members of the Confederacy. The enormous military preparations made by the United States, he said, was a distinct avowal that they were engaged, not with mere rioters and insurgents, but in a conflict with a great and powerful nation. They were driven to the practical acknowledgment that the ancient Union had been dissolved; they recognized the separate existence of the Confederate States by a blockade of Southern ports, and a prohibition of all intercourse with the inhabitants of the Confederacy, whom they no longer recognized as citizens of the United States, and upon whom they were waging an indiscriminate and ferocious war. In this war rapine was the rule; private houses were burnt; the crops in the fields, and every article of use or luxury remaining in the dwellings from which the owners had fled, were destroyed; even the acquisition of medicines for the sick and wounded was interdicted. These sweeping accusations were put forth, not for the information of Congress, but in order to inflame the Southern mind. They were made before a single Federal soldier had advanced a score of miles into any portion of the territory to which the Confederates, upon their own principles, had the shadow of a claim. A large portion of the inhabitants of the border slave states, he said, were opposed to the prosecution of the war, and many of them, if unrestrained by the presence of large armies, would joyfully unite with the South; hence they had been excepted in the enactments which authorized hostilities against the United States. The policy which had been secretly entertained, and was now openly avowed and acted upon by the Confederate government, would greatly extend the operations in the field. The forces hitherto raised had amply provided for the defense of

[1] An Englishman, who thought himself fortunate in belonging to an accepted company, says that the hundred men of his company represented not less than $20,000,000. "All of us," he writes, "wished to go forth and fight the Yankees; not that the Northerners were deemed worthy of such an honor, but there was a strong desire to get to close quarters with the enemy, and settle the question without farther delay. There was not a youth but fancied himself a match for any half dozen New Englanders. Captains of other companies begged us to give up our call, and offered munificent compensation if we would let their companies report instead. Give up the chance of fighting the Yankees? No, indeed; we were the favored individuals, and not all the wealth of California could have bought us off in favor of others! Poor fellows! how soon the tune changed. Glad would some of these hot heads have been to return home months subsequently."—Battle-fields of the South, by an English Combatant.

[2] The Richmond Dispatch of July 26, 1861, announces this cabinet change in terms which, while meant to be congratulatory, would have been exquisitely ironical if irony had been intended. It says: "Mr. Toombs was of a temper to prefer the active duties of a soldier, in such a crisis as the present, to the monotony of an office which, for the present, is little more than nominal. . . . Virginia's position in the Confederacy has been acknowledged by assigning to one of her statesmen the highest post in the Confederate cabinet. Mr. Hunter is so well known to the country that it would be supererogatory to dwell upon the qualities of mind and character which fit him so eminently for the post to which he has been called. It would be difficult to define an instance in which the trite phrase of speech so justly applies, 'The right man in the right place.'"

half century has wielded an influence in Christendom altogether dispropor-tionate to its numbers. He was one of the most unscrupulous and by far the ablest member of the Louisiana bar. In 1853 he was elected to the Senate of the United States. He was soon recognized as one of the keenest debaters and the most finished orator in that assembly. As a lawyer, his main object was the acquisition of wealth; as a politician, to effect the dis-memberment of the Union. When Jefferson Davis organized his first cab-inet, Benjamin was appointed attorney general, a post for which he was expressly qualified by adroitness and unscrupulousness. After a while Le-roy Walker, the incompetent Secretary of War, was displaced, and Ben-jamin was named as his successor. In this department his career was far from brilliant. The Congressional committee of inquiry attributed to his incompetency the disaster which befell the Confederate cause at Roanoke Island. But if he was out of place as head of the War Department, the as-tute Southern dictator had discovered that he possessed faculties too valua-ble to be lost; so, in face of Congressional censure, Judah P. Benjamin was appointed Secretary of State in March, 1862.

The session of the Confederate Congress which commenced on the 20th of July was short. The triumph at Bull Run, exaggerated by public re-port, had inspired the South with an overweening confidence of immediate success, and Congress was ready to grant more than the executive asked. The Secretary of War had asked for 300,000 men; Congress authorized the acceptance of 400,000. The issue of $100,000,000 in treasury notes, payable in six months after the ratification of peace, and of a like amount in bonds, bearing eight per cent. interest, and payable in twenty years, was authorized, the notes to be receivable for all public dues except the export duty on cotton. A war-tax of fifty cents on the hundred dollars was im-posed upon all real and personal property, including slaves; heads of fam-ilies whose property amounted to less than $500 being exempt. The Pres-ident was authorized to take the control of all telegraphic lines and offices; to appoint agents wherever he chose to supervise all communications pass-ing over the lines; no communication in cipher, or any of enigmatical or doubtful character, could be transmitted until its real purport was explained to the agent, and not then unless the person sending it was known to be trustworthy. Any person sending any dispatch relating to military oper-ations without first submitting it to the inspection of the agent, or in any case sending a message calculated to aid the enemy, was to be punished by fine and imprisonment.

The Federal Congress had passed an act confiscating all property in the insurrectionary states which should be used in aid of the insurrection, in-cluding the enfranchisement of all slaves employed in the military or naval service of the insurgents. The Confederate Congress retaliated by passing sweeping acts ordering the banishment of all alien enemies, and the abso-lute confiscation of all their property of whatever kind, with the single ex-ception of debts due them from the Confederacy, or from a state belonging to it. This confiscation act was to be retrospective, its operation applying to every right or claim of any citizen of the Union subsequent to the 21st day of May. By these acts, and the proclamations issued in accordance with them, all citizens of the non-slaveholding states of the Union, who should not at once declare their intention of becoming citizens of the Con-federacy, and all subjects of neutral governments having a domicil within or carrying on business in the Union, were declared to be alien enemies. Ev-ery male of these classes above the age of fourteen years was required to leave the Confederacy within forty days. At the expiration of this period district attorneys and marshals were to make complaint against any such persons then remaining, the marshal arresting and keeping them in close cus-tody. If the court so ordered, they were to be removed in such a way as to prevent them from acquiring any information that could be prejudicial to the Confederacy. Any alien who should return after being removed should be delivered over to the military authority, to be dealt with as a spy or pris-oner of war, as the case might require. Receivers were appointed in the several districts, who were to summon before them all attorneys and coun-selors at law, all presidents and cashiers of banks, all administrative officers of railroads and other corporations, all agents of foreign merchants and cor-porations, all dealers in mercantile paper, all assignees and trustees of estates —all persons, in fine, "who were known to do business for others." To these persons a series of stringent questions was to be put, to which they were re-quired to answer upon oath. They were required to testify whether then, or at any time after the 21st of May, they had in their possession or under their control any property in which an alien enemy had any right, title, or interest, direct or indirect. If such was the case, they were to give minute and specific information respecting it. If they had disposed of any such property or interest, they were to state when, to whom, and for what the sale had been made, and by whom the property was then held. The same pro-vision applied to all debts due to any alien enemy. Every citizen was made a spy upon every other. Every person was to tell if he knew of any prop-erty held by or for, or any debts due to an alien enemy, describing them particularly, and giving the name and residence of the holder, debtor, trus-tee, or agent. The responsibility of the citizen was not limited to answer-ing the questions actually propounded, but he was especially directed, in ad-dition, to state every thing else that he knew "which may aid in carrying into full effect the sequestration act, and state the same as fully and particu-larly as if thereunto specially interrogated." If any attorney, agent, former partner, or trustee holding or controlling any property or interest in proper-ty belonging to an alien enemy failed to give information to the receiver, he was held to be guilty of a high misdemeanor, for which he was to be fined not more than $5000, be imprisoned not more than six months, besides be-ing liable to pay double the value of the property in question.

The number of persons directly affected by these laws was less than the framers supposed. There were residing in the Confederacy 233,000 persons born in neutral countries, of both sexes and of all ages. Of these a third were in Louisiana, another third in Texas and Virginia, leaving only a third in the eight remaining states. Of these only a few hundred came within the class of alien enemies by reason of having a residence or doing business in the Union. There were in the whole United States 4,136,000 residents of foreign birth, and of these 3,900,000 were in the Union states. There were resident in the Confederacy 98,000 natives of the border slave states. These were expressly excepted from the category of alien enemies, in ac-cordance with the fixed policy of the government to consider these states as quasi members of the Confederacy. By the census of 1860 there were 120,000 natives of the free states, men, women, and children, resident in the eleven states which ultimately seceded. A large portion of these went to the North before the passage of these acts. Of those who remained, many gave in their adhesion to the Confederate government, leaving only a few thousands to be dealt with as alien enemies. These were unmercifully har-ried, but rather by self-constituted vigilance committees than by the slower legal process prescribed by the law. It is doubtful if a thousand persons were arrested and banished in the manner and by the forms prescribed in this alien act.[1]

Apart from its retaliatory intent, this law had a double purpose. Besides compelling the support of all the residents of the Confederacy, or at least preventing any open opposition to the government, and thus enabling it to present an apparently united front before the world, it was expected that it would bring a large amount of money into the treasury, which was now in sore need. The private debts due from the South to the North were esti-mated at $200,000,000; the interest of Northern citizens in real estate, rail-road and other stocks, and similar investments, could not be estimated at less than $100,000,000 more. The whole $300,000,000 was to be nominally swept into the Confederate treasury. But the anticipations of the framers of the law were disappointed. Private debtors saw no advantage in paying their debts into the treasury, and securing a discharge, when they could as well leave them wholly unpaid. In spite of the searching inquisition order-ed, little actual property could be discovered in which alien enemies had an interest. The report of the Secretary of the Treasury nearly a year after the passage of the Confiscation Act set down the receipts, independent of loans, at $14,000,000. A million and a half was derived from customs, ten and a half millions from the war-tax, and two millions from miscellaneous sources. The proceeds of the confiscation must be included under, and form only a part of this last head. There is no reason to believe that the nett amount from confiscations exceeded half a million of dollars during the first year of the operation of the law.

An act was passed at this session to aid the disaffected citizens of Missou-ri in their opposition to the Federal government. This state was to be ad-mitted to the Confederacy when the provisional Constitution had been duly ratified by the old state government under Claiborne Jackson, and, in the mean while, the President of the Confederacy was authorized to send Con-federate troops to Missouri. An agreement for the accession of this state to the Confederacy was made at Richmond on the 31st of October, and ratified by an irregular meeting of the Legislature, where a quorum was obtained only by the admission of numerous proxies, on the 2d of November. Sen-ators and representatives appointed by this body, not by the people, were sent to Richmond, where they were admitted to seats in the Confederate Con-gress at the next session.

Congress adjourned in September to meet on the 18th of November. At the opening only twelve members were present; but they represented six states, and the provisional Congress represented states in their collective ca-pacity, and six states being a majority of the eleven, it was decided that these twelve members formed a quorum. The President's Message was delivered on the 19th. It gave a glowing account of the military operations in Vir-ginia and Missouri, and defended the invasion of Kentucky; spoke in hope-ful terms of the condition of the treasury; repeated the former charges against the Federal government for its manner of carrying on the war, and denounced the seizure of Mason and Slidell as a breach of international law and an insult to the British flag. The President made one suggestion, which was acted upon, and in the end became of great practical importance. For the successful prosecution of the war, it was indispensable that means should be supplied for transporting troops and military supplies. The war was to be waged mainly on the northern borders of the Confederacy, while men and supplies must be to a great extent drawn from the interior and the Far South. There were already two main systems of uninterrupted railroad communication between the northern and the southern portions. One was from Richmond along the sea-board, the other through Western Virginia to New Orleans. Besides these there was a third, complete with the exception

[1] The following table shows, as given in the census of 1860, the number of free persons residing in the seceding states who were born respectively in the free states, in the Union slave states, and in foreign countries:

States of the Confederacy.	Residents born in the Free States.	Residents born in the Union Slave States.	Residents born in Foreign Countries.
Alabama	5,930	2,955	12,352
Arkansas	11,049	20,298	3,741
Florida	2,010	375	3,309
Georgia	6,335	1,318	11,671
Louisiana	14,193	5,849	81,029
Mississippi	5,157	4,369	8,558
North Carolina	2,397	778	3,299
South Carolina	2,284	402	9,986
Tennessee	12,478	15,891	21,226
Texas	21,687	28,149	43,422
Virginia	36,757	17,744	35,058
	120,277	98,128	233,651

REUBEN DAVIS.   JEFFERSON DAVIS, *Senator.*   OTHO R. SINGLETON.
LUCIUS Q. C. LAMAR.   ALBERT G. BROWN, *Senator.*   JOHN J. McRAE.
                       WILLIAM BARKSDALE.

THE LAST DELEGATION FROM MISSISSIPPI IN THE CONGRESS OF THE UNITED STATES.

of an interval of forty miles between Danville, in Virginia, and Greensborough, in North Carolina. The construction of this short link would furnish a route through the interior of the Confederacy, and give access to a population and to military resources from which the government was then debarred, besides greatly increasing the safety and capacity of the transportation of troops and supplies from the farthest points. It was true that the Constitution prohibited Congress from appropriating money for internal improvements intended to facilitate commerce, but this prohibition might be obviated by considering this a military work. The mode suggested by the President was that Congress should give aid to a company organized to construct and carry on the work. The road was finally constructed directly by government, and in the end proved the salvation of the Confederacy by enabling it to transport troops rapidly between the East and the West. At more than one critical moment it practically increased by one half the offensive and defensive power of the Confederacy.

The provisional government of the Confederacy came to an end, by its own limitation, on the 15th of February, 1862. Electors had in the mean while been appointed to choose a President and Vice-president for the permanent government. The choice had been declared early in November. It was a mere matter of form. No candidates were named in opposition to Davis and Stephens, who received the unanimous vote of the electors. The provisional Congress had been a mere temporary junta, appointed by the Conventions and Legislatures of the several states. It was succeeded by a permanent Congress chosen by the people. This body convened on the 18th of February. Missouri and Kentucky having been recognized as members of the Confederacy, and sent delegates to both houses, all the slaveholding states were represented except Delaware and Maryland. The Senate, when full, consisted of 26 members. Nineteen were present at the opening. The House, if full, would have consisted of 112 members.

About twenty-five of these men had been members of the Congress of the United States in 1860. Of these, Alabama sent Clay to the Confederate Senate; Curry, Pugh, and Clopton to the House. Arkansas sent Johnson to

JOHN W. H. UNDERWOOD.
MARTIN J. CRAWFORD.
THOMAS HARDEMAN.
ROBERT TOOMBS, *Senator.*
PETER E. LOVE.
JOHN J. JONES.
ALFRED IVERSON, *Senator.*
JOSHUA HILL.
LUCIUS J. GARTRELL.
JAMES JACKSON.

THE LAST DELEGATION FROM GEORGIA IN THE CONGRESS OF THE UNITED STATES.

the Senate. Georgia sent Hill to the Senate, and Gartrell to the House. Mississippi sent Brown to the Senate; Reuben Davis, McRae, Singleton, and Barksdale to the House. North Carolina sent Smith to the House, all her other members being new men. South Carolina sent to the House Boyce, Miles, Bonham, and McQueen, four of her seven last representatives in the Federal Congress; she also sent to the Senate Orr and Barnwell, who had formerly represented her at Washington. Besides these former members of the Federal Congress, there were about half a score of men in this Confederate Congress who had acquired some political reputation. The other members were new men, thrown up from the masses by the fierce fires of secession.

The inauguration of Jefferson Davis as permanent President of the Confederacy took place on the 22d of February, the 130th anniversary of the birthday of Washington. Three days after he sent in his message, setting forth the condition of the Confederacy. The new government began under gloomy auspices. At the East, Burnside had captured Roanoke Island, and effected a firm lodgment in North Carolina. In the West, Grant had taken Fort Donelson; the Confederate forces, driven from Bowling Green, were evacuating Kentucky, and were in a few days to abandon Nashville, which had a few months before been named in Congress as the future capital of the Confederacy; Zollicoffer had been defeated and killed at Mill Spring; Price, driven from Missouri into Arkansas, had been defeated at Pea Ridge. Savannah was threatened by the Federal gun-boats. New Orleans, although no one then knew it, was in a few weeks to be captured by Farragut, inflicting what then seemed the one great blow to which the Confederacy was exposed. The great Federal force on the Potomac, which had been transformed from a crowd into an army, hung threatening over Virginia, and was almost ready to strike at Richmond, the heart of the Confederacy. The hope of foreign interference, upon which, in spite of protestations to the contrary, great reliance had been placed, was at an end. The maritime powers of Europe had recognized the efficiency of the blockade, and in shutting their ports to prizes had rendered useless the law for sending out privateers.

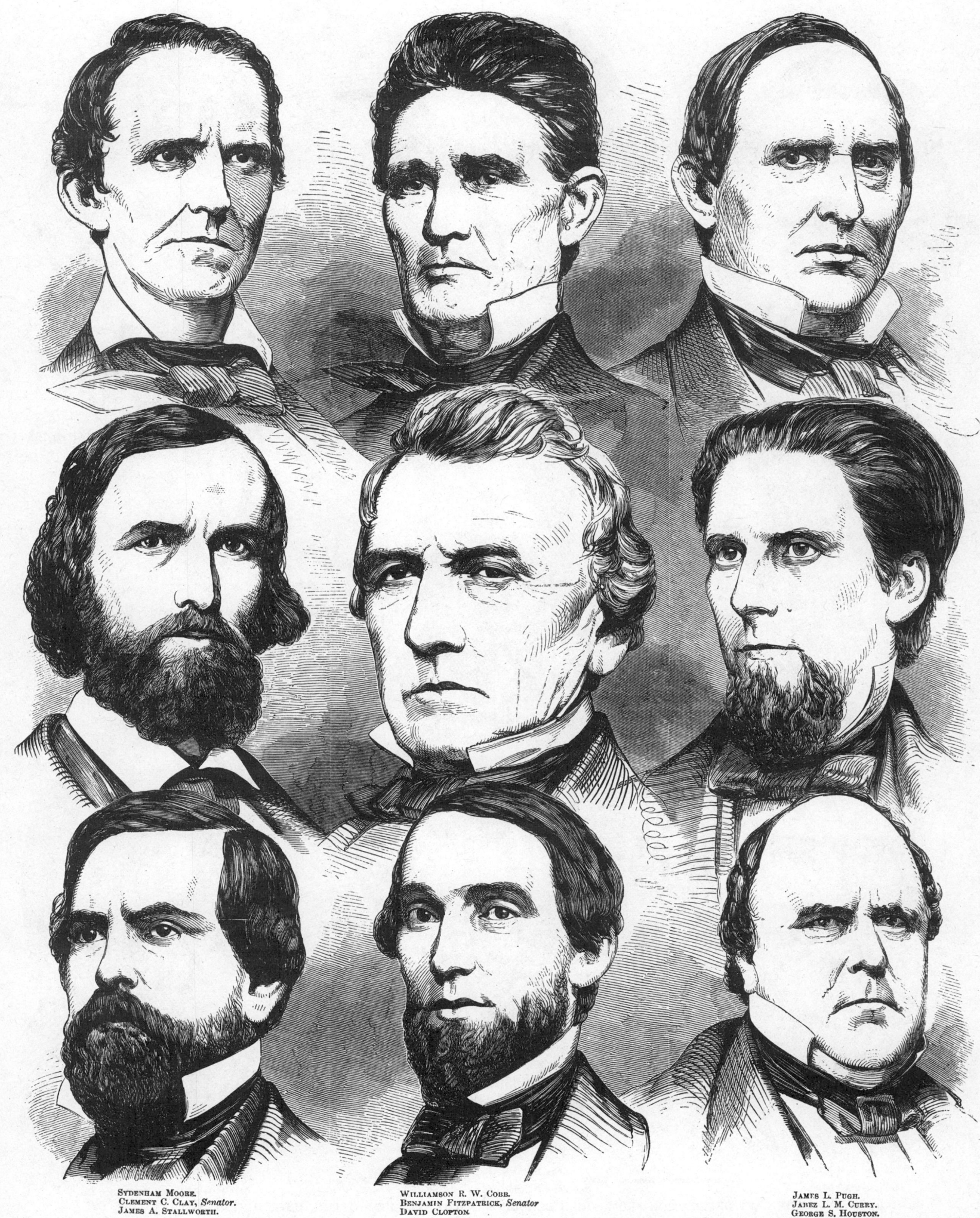

SYDENHAM MOORE.
CLEMENT C. CLAY, *Senator.*
JAMES A. STALLWORTH.

WILLIAMSON R. W. COBB.
BENJAMIN FITZPATRICK, *Senator*
DAVID CLOPTON.

JAMES L. PUGH.
JABEZ L. M. CURRY.
GEORGE S. HOUSTON.

THE LAST DELEGATION FROM ALABAMA IN THE CONGRESS OF THE UNITED STATES.

There was no way of turning a prize to profit. The Confederate ports were shut by the Federal blockade; neutral ports by the orders of the governments of Europe.

In face of these facts and many others of like nature, Davis frankly acknowledged what he could not deny. "Events," he said, "have demonstrated that the government had attempted more than it had the power successfully to achieve. Hence, in the effort to protect by our arms the whole territory of the Confederate States, sea-board and inland, we have been so exposed as recently to suffer great disasters." In this message the President intimated rather than declared what was necessary to enable the Confederate States to wage a successful war with their more numerous enemy. Troops must be enlisted for long terms, instead of the short ones for which they had hitherto taken the field. He hesitated even then to announce that the whole population of the South capable of bearing arms must be conscripted, and every man be made liable at any moment to be forced into the active army.

The one bright point which the President found in the general gloomy aspect of affairs was the condition of the finances of the Confederacy. "The financial system," he said, "devised by the wisdom of your predecessors, has proved adequate to supplying all the wants of the government. We have no floating debt; the credit of the government is unimpaired; the total expenditure for the year has been $170,000,000—less than the value of the cotton crop of the year." He could hardly have foreboded, or, if he foresaw, did not care to say, that in a few months the financial question would become quite as important as the military one; that the deficit in the Confederate funds would involve as much peril and suffering as any possible disaster in the field.

At the outset the Confederate government had no lack of money for immediate purposes. The treachery of Floyd, and the seizure of forts and arsenals, had furnished arms and munitions for the first volunteers. Regiments fitted out at their own cost, or by the states, were offered to the government. The first 100,000 men were put into the field costing the Confed-

LAWRENCE M. KEITT.
WILLIAM W. BOYCE.
JAMES CHESTNUT, *Senator.*
JOHN McQUEEN.
JOHN D. ASHMORE.
JAMES H. HAMMOND, *Senator.*
MILLEDGE L. BONHAM.
WILLIAM PORCHER MILES.

THE LAST DELEGATION FROM SOUTH CAROLINA IN THE CONGRESS OF THE UNITED STATES.

eracy hardly a dollar. A brief war, if any, was anticipated, requiring no great outlay. Wanting, and, to superficial view, likely to want very little money, the credit of the Confederacy at home was good; so, when a loan of $8,000,000 was asked, nearly double the amount was offered at or above par. The government wisely accepted the whole. At that time the Federal government could hardly borrow a less sum upon any terms. This loan was soon exhausted, and much larger amounts were required. The capital at the South seeking investment was small. For years, whenever any man had accumulated money, he invested it in lands and slaves, which were devoted to the production of cotton, which gave larger and surer returns than any other investment. The annual cotton crop of the South had been for some years worth not less than $200,000,000 a year, almost double the value of the gold product of California and Australia. Nearly all of this was exported. As a medium of exchange, cotton was equivalent to gold; but, unless as an article of export, it was worthless. If detained in the region where produced, it was a burden and nuisance. When the government found that it must contract large loans, it endeavored to make cotton a basis for secur-

ing them. The plan was that every cotton-grower should pledge himself by formal contract to lend to the government a certain portion of the proceeds of his cotton, receiving therefor bonds payable at a long day, with heavy interest. The government was not to buy the cotton directly. The planter was to sell it, as formerly, through his agents; but the money for the portion agreed upon, instead of being paid to him, was to be sent to the government, the planter receiving in lieu treasury bonds. It was estimated that one half of the product of his cotton might thus be spared by the planter. This, if the whole year's crop were sold as usual, would give the government $100,000,000. Agents were sent every where to urge the planters to make this conditional loan, and in a few weeks it was announced that $50,000,000 had been pledged; but, before any considerable part of the cotton could be sold, the blockade of the Southern ports shut it out from a market. The cotton was worthless. The government would have only the agreement of the planter to loan it half the proceeds when sold; the planter merely the agreement of government to give its bonds for it when sold and the proceeds paid over to it.

Meanwhile the planters were thrown into great distress. The usual practice at the South had been to sell the crop and receive the pay a year in advance. They had received the money for this crop from Northern merchants, and had spent it. As the market was cut off, they had no means of carrying on their estates the coming year. They asked government to come to their relief. Many modes were suggested, all of which resolved into two. Some proposed that the government should purchase the whole cotton crop; others that it should advance one half of its value, payment or advance to be made, not in bonds, but in treasury notes, which had become the general circulating medium of the country. Mr. Memminger, the Secretary of the Treasury, replied to these propositions on the 17th of October. Government, he said, wanted to raise money. These suggestions proposed that it should spend money. That which was the least objectionable, because it involved the smallest outlay, proposed that government should loan $100,000,000 on pledge of the forthcoming cotton crop, receiving only the notes of the planters. The other plan, that government should buy the whole existing crop, involved the issue of $150,000,000, being the whole value of the cotton, less the $50,000,000 of cotton loan pledged. But cotton, unless brought to market, was of no use to the government. In either case it would have to pay out the money which was essential to its very existence, and receive in exchange notes or produce which it did not need and could not use. To carry on the war, treasury notes to the amount of $100,000,000 had been issued, and these had become the measure of value; if another like amount were issued no new value would be created; the effect would be that two dollars must be paid for that which could now be purchased for one. Government, being the largest buyer, would thus pay double price for its purchases, and would actually sink the whole hundred millions which it had advanced. The planters were told that they could expect no special aid from government, and they must look out for themselves, like all the rest of the community. They were advised, in the first place, to produce little cotton, but to devote themselves to the cultivation of provisions, and to make their own clothing, looking for money to loans from the banks, to be secured by factors' acceptances based on pledges of produce. Banks could manage such loans much better than government, and, besides, much less advances would be looked for from them than from government. These suggestions were accepted to a great extent. The cotton crop of 1862 was estimated at less than a quarter of that of the preceding year, and the production of food was largely increased. The cotton already gathered was left on the hands of the planters, and, some months later, a law was passed ordering it to be destroyed whenever it was about to fall into the hands of the enemy, who were advancing into the Confederate States by the coast and in the West.

At a later period, when the value of cotton had been advanced fourfold in the European markets, the policy of the Confederate government in respect to it was changed. Swift steamers were built in the British ship-yards on the Clyde and Mersey to run the blockade, taking in arms and munitions, and carrying out cotton. The Confederate government purchased cotton and shipped it, receiving returns in gold and arms. The gold was employed in Europe for the purchase of arms and munitions; the arms and munitions partly by running the blockade and partly through Mexico. Every blockade-runner was compelled to take a certain part of its cargo on government account; the remainder was at the risk and for the profit of the owners. If one trip out of three was successful, the whole adventure was profitable.

The exigencies of the treasury in the mean time compelled the issue of paper money to an amount far exceeding the utmost estimates of the secretary. In January, 1861, the whole amount of currency in circulation at the South was $80,000,000. In January, 1863, it was $300,000,000. The decrease in value, when once it set in, was more rapid than the increase in amount. The old story of the Sibylline books was reversed. Every fresh issue of paper made the whole amount of less value than before. In September, 1861, when the issue of Confederate notes was $100,000,000, they were nominally equivalent to specie. Then the depreciation began. In November, specie commanded 20 per cent. premium; in April, 1862, 50 per cent.; in September, 100; at the opening of 1863, fully 300. That is, government, the largest purchaser, had to pay for its supplies four times as much in notes at the close of 1862 as it paid fifteen months before. Subsequently the depreciation became still greater. As we shall hereafter see, by the middle of 1864, in spite of stringent measures to reduce the amount of currency by imposing a tax which practically amounted to the repudiation of a large part of its old issues, Confederate notes were worth barely five cents upon a dollar.

The foreign relations of the Confederacy, when the permanent government was organized, were wholly unsatisfactory. The South had from the outset looked to the speedy recognition of the Confederacy by the European powers. Even if this were not followed by actual war between Great Britain and the United States, it was believed that it must result in measures which would greatly benefit the South. Great Britain, it was argued, must in any case have American cotton; the blockade prevented her from getting it except in small quantities and at enormous prices. She would therefore be driven, right or wrong, to refuse to regard the blockade. Her merchantmen, protected, if need were, by her fleet, would throng to Confederate ports, bringing in arms, supplies, and gold, and taking away cotton, tobacco, and rice. To effect such a recognition was the first object of Confederate diplomacy. To do this, it was necessary, in the first place, to neutralize the strong anti-slavery feeling in Great Britain, and then to convince her of the commercial advantages which would result from recognition and free trade with the South.

Yancey, Mann, and Rost, the first Confederate commissioners to Europe, sought an early interview with Lord John Russell, the British Foreign Secretary. He refused to receive them in their official capacity, but gave them an unofficial reception. They assured him that the real cause of the secession was not slavery, but the high price which the South was obliged to pay for manufactured goods, in order to protect Northern manufacturers. This, indeed, was in direct contradiction to the emphatic and really official declaration of Alexander H. Stephens, that "African slavery as it exists among us was the immediate cause of the late rupture and present revolution." It was in direct contradiction to every speech and declaration of Southern politicians and statesmen from first to last, before and after the secession. One of the first acts of the Southern Congress, the commissioners went on to say, was to reduce the duties upon imports, while the new tariff of the United States would nearly exclude British manufactures from the North. Of the $350,000,000 annually exported from the United States, $270,000,000 were the products of the Southern states. They had this amount to sell, and for it they wanted the manufactures of Europe, especially those of Great Britain. Russell intimated that the Confederacy would reopen the slave-trade. The commissioners denied this. The Confederate Constitution directly prohibited this trade, and there was no purpose to revive it. This interview took place on the 4th of March, 1861, and, although it was far from satisfactory to the Southern commissioners, they decided to remain in London for a while, hoping that the recognition of the Southern Confederacy would not long be delayed.

In August they addressed a formal note to the Foreign Secretary urging the recognition of the Confederacy upon the same general grounds, and complaining of the British proclamation of neutrality. The rule prohibiting prizes of either belligerent from entering British ports they declared to be a protection to the commerce and ships of the United States; for Southern ports being shut up by the blockade, and neutral ones closed by proclamation to Confederate prizes, they could only destroy any captures they might make. They then addressed themselves to the work of neutralizing the "anti-slavery sentiment so universally prevalent in England, which shrunk from the idea of forming friendly public relations with a government recognizing the slavery of a part of the human race." They declined discussing with a foreign power the question of the morality of slavery, but asserted that the Federal government was no more hostile to slavery than was the Confederate. The party in power in the Union, they said, had proposed to guarantee slavery forever in the states if the South would remain in the Union. "The object of the war, as officially announced, was not to free the slave, but to keep him in subjection to his owner, and to control his labor through the legislative channels which the Lincoln government designed to force upon the master." They therefore confidently believed "that, as far as the anti-slavery sentiment of England was concerned, it could have no sympathy with the North, and would probably become disgusted with a canting hypocrisy which would enlist those sympathies under false pretenses." The reply to this communication was that her majesty's government would not pretend to pronounce judgment upon the questions in debate between the United States and their adversaries; that it would not depart from its strictly neutral position; would not acknowledge the independence of the seceding states until the fortune of arms or the more peaceful mode of negotiation should have more clearly determined the respective positions of the two belligerents. Late in November the commissioners made one more attempt upon the British government. Under express instructions from Mr. Davis, they endeavored to show that the blockade was ineffective, and pointed out the commercial interests affected by it. The reply was sharp and decisive: "Lord Russell presents his compliments to Mr. Yancey, Mr. Rost, and Mr. Mann. He had the honor to receive their letters and inclosures of the 27th and 30th of November, but, in the present state of affairs, he must decline to enter into any official communication with them."

Mr. Yancey, having been elected to the Confederate Senate, returned to the South after the absence of a year. In giving an account of the results of his mission, he said that the Confederacy had no friends in Europe. The sentiment there was anti-slavery, and that portion of public opinion represented by the government of England was abolition. But the North, also, had no friends in Europe. The independence of the South would be recognized only when the North was forced to acknowledge it. The nations of Europe would never raise the blockade until it suited their interest, but he believed they would find it necessary to do so at an early day. Mason and Slidell had in the mean time been busy in London and Paris. Rost was sent to Spain, and Mann to Belgium; but they were unable to induce the European powers, all of whom had expressly or tacitly agreed to act in common, to recognize the Confederacy, or to depart from their position of absolute neutrality.

But the immediate difficulty which confronted the Confederacy at the organization of its permanent government was the condition of the army. The Confederate army of 1861 was composed mainly of men who had enlisted for a year, and their term of enlistment was about to expire. The time of 148 regiments would close in thirty days. Few of the men composing these regiments had re-enlisted. The rush of volunteers had ceased. Gay young men no longer contended for the honor of going to fight the Yankees. The long interval of inaction which had followed the battle of Bull Run, during which the Federal government was busy in gathering and training its recruits, had fearfully impaired the efficiency of the Confederate armies. The force which for months lay defiantly almost in sight of Washington was far less strong than was imagined. Had the Federal leaders known its real strength, they might have ventured a movement early in 1862 which would have swept it away. Beyond this army the Confederacy had at the moment no formidable force in the field. Richmond was almost destitute of defense.

The disasters which the Confederacy experienced in the early months of 1862 awoke the government to its danger, and pointed out its sole means of salvation. Their extended line of offense and defense must be contracted, and their forces concentrated upon vital points. Above all, the army must be largely increased. Furloughs had been so freely granted that the regiments in the field had been greatly weakened. By a general order of March 24, every furlough and leave of absence was summarily revoked; every officer and man absent from duty, except on a surgeon's certificate of disability, was ordered to return at once to his command. The President, in a special message to Congress, said that the laws for raising armies should be reformed. They had been so frequently changed that it was often impossible to determine what the law actually was. There was, moreover, a conflict between state and Confederate legislation. There must be some general system for raising armies, the power for which was by the Constitution vested in Congress. This necessity was now rendered imminent by the vast preparations made by the enemy for a combined assault at numerous points. The state had a right to demand military service of every citizen, but it was not wise to place in active service the very young or the very old. Those under eighteen required instruction; those of mature age were needed to maintain order at home. These two classes constituted the reserve, to be called out and kept in the field only in an emergency. To retain this reserve intact it was necessary, in a great war like this, that all capable persons of intermediate age should pay their debt of military service to the country. He therefore recommended that a law should be passed declaring that all persons residing in the Confederate States between the ages of eighteen and thirty-five, not legally exempt, should be held in the military service; that a prompt system should be adopted for their enrollment and organization, and that all laws conflicting with this system should be repealed.

The first general conscription law of the Confederacy, framed in accordance with this recommendation, was passed on the 16th of April, 1862. It withdrew every non-exempt citizen of the prescribed age from state control, and placed him absolutely at the disposal of the President during the war. It annulled all contracts made with volunteers for short terms, holding them in service for two years additional, should the war continue so long. All twelve months' recruits below eighteen and over thirty-five years, who would otherwise have been exempted by this law, were to be retained in service for ninety days after their term expired. The President might, with the consent of the several governors, employ state officers to make the enrollment, but, if this consent was not given, the President should appoint Confederate officers for that purpose. When all the companies and regiments from any state should have been filled, the remainder of enrolled men should be held as a reserve, from whom should be drawn by lot, at intervals of not less than three months, details to keep the companies always full. This reserve, while at home, was not to receive pay or be subject to the articles of war, except that, if they refused to obey the President's call, they should be treated as deserters. Whenever the exigencies of the service required it, the President was authorized to call out the entire reserve. This law was silent as to exemptions from service. The omission was remedied by subsequent orders; and as the course of events required still larger demands upon the people, these exemptions were more and more restricted, until they finally included only members of Congress and the state Legislatures, and such officials as were absolutely essential to administer the state and national governments; certain clergymen, teachers, and physicians; a few editors and printers; and a certain number of persons absolutely required to conduct agricultural operations and oversee slaves.[1]

Provision was made for carrying this sweeping conscription bill into prompt execution. Camps of instruction were established, where the enrolled men were collected and drilled, and in each state there was a commander of conscripts charged with the supervision of the new levies. These were sent off in squads and companies, to be formed into regiments as government pleased. State pride was, however, fostered by putting the recruits from each state together under officers from their own states.

There were some murmurs against this law, which virtually made every white male between the ages of eighteen and thirty-five a soldier, liable to be brought into active service at a moment's notice by the mere call of the President. These murmurs were promptly suppressed every where except in Georgia and Arkansas, where it seemed that a conflict might arise between state and Confederate authorities. Officers of the state militia had been arrested by the enrolling officers. The governor demanded their release, threatening to arrest any Confederate officer who should arrest any state officer. The Confederate authorities yielded the point; but adding, through the Secretary of War, "If you arrest any of our enrolling officers in their attempts to get men to fill up the Georgia regiments now in the face of the enemy, you will cause great mischief. I think we might as well drive out our common enemy before we make war upon each other." Brown, the irascible and pragmatic governor, was mollified by this concession to his dignity as chief magistrate of a sovereign state. He said that he was happy that the Confederate government had decided to respect the constitutional rights of the state so far as not to force her to the alternative of permitting any department of her government to be destroyed, or to defend herself by force. A local judge in Georgia pronounced the conscription law to be unconstitutional, but his decision was set aside by the Supreme Court of the state.

The disasters which compelled the Confederate government to adopt the policy of concentrating its forces in Virginia caused great excitement in the states beyond the Mississippi. Governor Rector, of Arkansas, issued an appeal to the people of that state calling them to arms, and more than insinuating that the Confederate government had deserted the state, and that the call of the President for troops from Arkansas should be disregarded, and even hinting at the formation of a new confederacy of the Southwest.[1] The Confederate government wisely forbore here, as in Georgia, to enter upon a controversy with one of the states. The wisdom of concentrating its force in Virginia was soon apparent, and at the next election Rector was defeated.

The conscription law was at once put into execution. Sweeping as it was, and rapidly as it was enforced, it was not an atom too sweeping, and barely in time to save the Confederacy from destruction. The Federal government, with the start in preparation of fully four months, delayed the advance of its troops upon Richmond, hesitating which line to adopt, when an advance upon either of the proposed lines could hardly have failed of success. A full month of precious time was lost before the advance was begun. Another month was wasted in the siege of Yorktown, where an army of fully 100,000 men was held in check by barely a tenth of their number. Three weeks more were taken up in the cautious advance across the Peninsula. Thus three full months, every day of which was of vital moment to the Confederacy, were lost by the Federal army before it was fairly in the neighborhood of Richmond.

For the greater part of this time the Confederate authorities well-nigh despaired of being able to defend their capital. On the 21st of April, while the Federal army was in check before Yorktown, the Confederate Congress adjourned in such haste as to show that the members were anxious to provide for their own personal safety. The newspapers were bitter in their invectives against the fugitives. One invented the euphonious word "skedaddle" to designate their flight. Another said that the stampeding members, afraid of railroad accidents, had gone off by canal, a regiment of ladies being sent to clear the tow-path. They would escort the members to the mountains, and, leaving them under the protection of the children until McClellan would suffer them to come forth, would return to the defense of the country. But the alarm was by no means confined to Congress. The railway trains were blocked up by fugitives; the President sent his family to Raleigh; the government archives were packed up ready to be sent to Columbia, South Carolina. The state Legislature, however, passed resolutions calling upon the Confederate authorities to defend Richmond to the last extremity, and this demand was seconded by the local authorities of the capital. Fortifications were thrown up around the city, and the approaches by the James River were blocked up. Above all, time had been gained. Early in June the conscription law began to produce its effects in filling up the ranks, and by the time the Federal army was prepared to open its direct attack it found itself confronted by fully equal forces, and in a few weeks was greatly outnumbered.

The President of the Confederacy had in the mean while given a great commander to its armies. Congress had not long before passed a bill creating the office of commanding general, who should take charge of the mili-

[1] The various conscription laws of the Confederacy were passed in secret session, and do not appear to have been published in full. The *Richmond Examiner*, an opposition journal, of January 30, 1864, published an abstract of the Military Bill which had not long before passed the Senate, and was then under consideration in the House. In this abstract, officers of the general and state departments are placed among the exempts. The *Richmond Sentinel*, the organ of the government, of February 17, gives an abstract of the bill as finally passed, the injunction of secrecy having been removed. The following is its abstract of exemptions:

"The tenth section provides that no person shall be exempt except the following: ministers, superintendents of deaf, dumb, and blind or insane asylums; one editor to each newspaper, and such employés as he may swear to be indispensable; the Confederate and state public printers, and the journeymen printers necessary to perform the public printing; one apothecary to each drug store, who was and has been continuously doing business as such since October 10, 1862; physicians over thirty years of age of seven years' practice, not including dentists; presidents and teachers of colleges, academies, and schools, who have not less than thirty pupils; superintendents of public hospitals established by law, and such physicians and nurses as may be indispensable for their efficient management. One agriculturist on each farm where there is no white male adult not liable to duty, employing fifteen able-bodied slaves between ten and fifty years of age, upon the following conditions: the party exempted shall give bond to deliver to the government in the next twelve months 100 pounds of bacon, or its equivalent in salt pork, at government selection, and 100 pounds of beef for each such able-bodied slave employed on said farm, at commissioners' rates. In certain cases this may be commuted in grain or other provisions. The officers and employés of railroad companies engaged in military transportation, not beyond one for each mile used in such transportation, and under certain restrictions. Also exempts mail contractors and carriers."

This abstract makes no mention of the officials of the general or state governments; but it is probable that they were exempted by other sections, for it is provided that the President may detail artisans, mechanics, or persons of scientific skill to perform indispensable services in various departments.

[1] "By the authority and sanction of the Military Board, whose duty it is to protect the state from invasion, whose right it is to call an army into the field when the Confederate States refuse or neglect to protect the people, I call upon each and every man capable of bearing arms to prepare at once to meet the enemy. The law is that every able-bodied free white male inhabitant between the ages of eighteen and forty-five shall constitute the militia of the state. . . . All men between these ages, if physically able, may be called to the field now, the state being invaded. The state, always sovereign, is sovereign yet in her reserved rights, one of which is to defend her own soil, her own government, her own people." Arkansas, he said, had severed her connection with the United States upon the doctrine of state sovereignty, and formed an alliance with the other Confederate states. She had lavished her blood in support of the Confederacy. "She had done this because of her generous confidence that, when the evil hour came upon her, the Confederate flag would be found floating from her battlements, defying the invader, and giving succor to her people. But untoward events had placed her beyond the pale of protection. Much impaired, though still capable of resistance, she will strike a blow for liberty, and continue to be free. If left to her fate, she will carve a new destiny rather than be subjugated. It was for liberty she struck, and not for subordination to any created secondary power North or South. Her best friends are her natural allies nearest at home, who will pulsate when she bleeds, whose utmost hope is not beyond her existence. If the arteries of the Confederate heart do not permeate beyond the east bank of the Mississippi, let Southern Missourians, Arkansians, Texans, and the great West know it, and prepare for the future. Arkansas lost, abandoned, subjugated, is not Arkansas as she entered the Confederate government; nor will she remain Arkansas, a Confederate state, desolated as a wilderness. Her children, fleeing from the wrath to come, will build them a new ark, and launch it on new waters, seeking a new haven somewhere of equality, safety, and rest." This address closed with a call for 4500 volunteers from the militia of the state. If sufficient volunteers were not forthcoming, the deficiency would be supplied by draft. "Troops raised under this call," it was significantly added, "will not be transferred to Confederate service, under any circumstances, without their consent, and on no account unless a Confederate force sufficient to prevent invasion is sent into the state. These are raised exclusively for home protection. Horses, horse equipments, and arms lost by the casualties of war will be paid for by the state."—*Address of Governor Rector*, May 5, 1862.

tary movements of the war. The design of the bill was to place Joseph E. Johnston at the head of the forces of the Confederacy. The President, with whom Johnston had never been a favorite, vetoed the bill; but Johnston, in virtue of his rank as senior general, commanded in the field before Richmond. A wound received on the 2d of June disabled him for a time; and on the following day Davis appointed Lee to the nominal office of commanding general, the order providing that he should "act under the direction of the President." There had been nothing in Lee's previous career indicating that he possessed qualities beyond those of a brave and energetic subordinate. As commander of the state forces he had not been successful in Western Virginia. His sudden appointment to the chief command of the Confederate forces was considered by the opponents of the administration as a part of Mr. Davis's plan of holding every thing under his own control, by studiously keeping down every man who might by possibility become his rival. It is hardly possible that in such a crisis this could have been the motive for the promotion of Lee. It is far more probable that in him the President saw the great general. But, be this as it may, in the appointment of Lee to the chief command the Confederate forces gained as their leader one of the great masters of the art of war.

The Federal campaign in the Valley and on the Peninsula was a failure. In the early days of June Richmond was in the utmost peril. In the early days of July the Federal forces had been forced to the James River. In the early days of August the Federals were driven back from Cedar Mountain. At the close of the month, after losing the battles near the old field of Bull Run, the Army of the Potomac was driven back upon Washington. In the early days of September the Confederates were crossing the Potomac, invading Maryland, and threatening Washington.

When the Confederate Congress reassembled at Richmond on the 15th of August, the President might well offer his congratulations upon the issue of the events of the last four months. "The vast army," he said, "which threatened the capital of the Confederacy has been defeated and driven from the lines of investment." The conscription law had saved the Confederacy; but this had been done at a fearful cost. The levy embracing all between eighteen and thirty-five had been exhausted. It was necessary to extend the conscription law so as to enable the President to call into active service all persons between thirty-five and forty-five. A law was passed to this effect on the 27th of September, but the power thus conferred was not exercised until the expiration of almost a year. In July, 1863, the President called into active service all between eighteen and forty-five. Seven months later, in February, 1864, a new law was passed still farther extending the conscription, by including in it all between the ages of seventeen and fifty. The full consideration of these two last conscription laws belongs to a subsequent period of this history.

The Confederates had from the very outset employed slaves and free colored persons in a military capacity. The works before Charleston, commenced late in 1860, were mainly thrown up "by large gangs of negroes from the plantations,"[1] and by free negroes of Charleston, of whom 150 in a single day offered their services to the Governor of South Carolina.[2] In April the Lynchburg Republican proposed "three cheers for the patriotic free negroes of Lynchburg," of whom seventy had "tendered their services to the governor to act in whatever capacity may be assigned them in defense of the state." It was triumphantly announced that all the fortifications required for the harbor of Norfolk could be erected by the voluntary labor of negroes.[3] In June the Legislature of Tennessee passed an act authorizing the governor to "receive into the military service of the state all male free persons of color between the ages of fifteen and fifty;" and if a sufficient number did not volunteer they were to be impressed. The Southern newspapers of 1861 were full of accounts of colored volunteers. One told of a grand display, held November 23, at New Orleans, where 28,000 troops were reviewed, among whom was a "regiment composed of 1400 free colored men." The works at Manassas Junction were mainly thrown up by the slaves of the neighboring planters.[4] In February, 1862, the Virginia House of Delegates passed a bill ordering the enlistment of free colored persons for six months. On the 10th of March Mr. Foote declared in the Confederate Congress that, when Nashville was surrendered, 1000 or 1500 slaves had been called out and employed on the fortifications. In November, Governor Brown, of Georgia, called for slaves to complete the fortifications of Savannah; if these were not voluntarily tendered, a levy would be made upon every planter in the state of one slave out of five, which would give a working force of 15,000. Subsequent to this time still more stringent measures were taken to bring negroes into the Confederate service.

Up to the beginning of 1863 the only law passed by the Federal Congress for the employment of colored soldiers was the act of July 17, 1862, authorizing the President to employ in the naval and military service of the United States persons of African descent, and freeing the families of such persons, provided they belonged to masters in rebellion. The passage of this law aroused an intense feeling throughout the South, of which the Confederate government promptly took advantage. In his message of August 15, President Davis complains that "two at least of the generals of the United States are engaged, unchecked by their government, in exciting servile insurrection, and in arming and training slaves for warfare against their masters, citizens of the Confederacy." Threats of vengeance were then made. These took form in a proclamation issued on the 23d of December, in which it was ordered that "all negro slaves captured in arms be at once delivered over to the executive authorities of the respective states to which they belong, to be dealt with according to the laws of said states," and that "like

orders be executed in all cases with respect to all commissioned officers of the United States when found serving in company with said slaves in insurrection against the authorities of the different states of the Confederacy." As the laws of the Southern States inflicted the punishment of death upon all insurgent slaves, and upon all who should aid them, the intent of this proclamation was to deny to all such persons who should be captured, and also to all white officers commanding them, the character of prisoners of war, directing them to be handed over for summary execution to the civil authorities of the several states. This proclamation was subsequently modified by an act passed in May, 1863. It declared that the commissioned officers of the enemy who might be captured should not be delivered to the state authorities, but should be dealt with by the Confederate government; that every white Federal officer commanding negro or mulatto troops should be deemed guilty of inciting servile insurrection, and if captured, be put to death or otherwise punished at the discretion of the military court; that every such person should be tried by the military corps or army capturing him, but the President might commute the punishment ordered by this court; but "all negroes and mulattoes who shall be engaged in war, or taken in arms against the Confederate States, or shall give aid and comfort to the enemies of the Confederate States, shall, when captured in the Confederate States, be delivered to the authorities of the state or states in which they shall be captured, to be dealt with according to the present or future laws of such state or states." The general principle thus attempted to be established was that no person of color should be recognized as a soldier of the Federal army, and as such be entitled, when captured, to the rights of a prisoner of war, but should be held to be a malefactor, liable to the severe penalties prescribed by local law against offenders of other than pure white descent. Out of this general provision grew in the sequel many questions relating to the exchange of prisoners.

The capture of New Orleans, at the close of April, 1862, had inflicted a severe wound upon Southern feeling. This was aggravated by the rigid government instituted over the conquered city by General Butler. Two special acts of his afforded a pretext for violent measures. Upon the informal surrender of the city the Union flag had been hoisted upon the Mint. There were then no Federal troops actually occupying the city, which was, however, commanded by the Union gun-boats, and virtually in their possession. The flag was cut down by a gang of desperadoes, prominent among whom was one Mumford, a notorious character of the city. He was arrested by General Butler, tried, and executed. Many women of New Orleans, after the complete occupation of the city, made it a point studiously to insult the Federal soldiers in the public streets. Butler determined to put down these insulting demonstrations, and issued his famous "General Order No. 28," declaring that "when any female shall, by word, gesture, or movement, insult or show contempt for any officer or soldier of the United States, she shall be regarded and held liable to be treated as a woman of the town plying her avocation." By the municipal law of New Orleans, any woman of this class "plying her avocation" in the street was liable to be arrested, detained over night in the calaboose, brought before a magistrate, and fined five dollars. This was the extent of the penalty threatened by the order. It assumed that only women of that class would endeavor to attract the attention of strangers. Still, the order was most unfortunately worded. It gave occasion to the charge that the women of the captured city were abandoned to the insults, if not to the passions, of lawless and excited soldiers. The Confederate authorities were not slow to take advantage of this. The charge was rung through the length and breadth of the land, where it aroused the fiercest frenzy. It was reiterated in Europe, where the recollection of atrocities committed in captured cities by ungoverned soldiers was fresh in men's memories. They had read of the outrages of the French under Suchet, at Tarragona; of the British, under Wellington, at Badajos; and of the thousand similar cases which marked the great war of the last generation. They were reading the accounts which began slowly to transpire of the outrages committed within a few months by the British troops in India, and were prepared to believe that similar scenes were enacting in New Orleans. Every instance of punishment which circumstances rendered necessary was repeated, exaggerated, and perverted, until the public mind in the South and in Europe was prepared not merely to justify, but to demand the most severe measures of retaliation. At length, on the 23d of December, President Davis issued a proclamation declaring that General Butler should no longer be considered a public enemy, but a felon deserving capital punishment, an outlaw and common enemy of mankind; ordering that, in case he was captured, he should be hung on the spot; that the commissioned officers serving under him should also, in case of capture, be reserved for execution; and that, until the execution of Butler, no commissioned officer of the United States should be released on parole.[1] The actual course of General Butler, while in command of New Orleans, will be narrated in full in a subsequent chapter.

From this survey of the foreign and domestic policy of the Federal and Confederate governments down to the beginning of the year 1863, we return to the series of great military operations of the year 1862.

---

[1] Dispatch from R. R. Riordan to Perry Walker, Mobile.   [2] Charleston Mercury, January 3, 1861.   [3] Petersburg Express, April 23.   [4] Beauregard's Report of the Battle of Bull Run.

[1] "I, Jefferson Davis, President of the Confederate States of America, and in their name, do pronounce and declare the said Benjamin F. Butler a felon deserving of capital punishment. I do order that he be no longer considered or treated simply as a public enemy of the Confederate States of America, but as an outlaw and common enemy of mankind, and that, in the event of his capture, the officer in command of the capturing force do cause him to be immediately executed by hanging; and I do farther order that no commissioned officer of the United States taken captive shall be released on parole before exchange until the said Butler shall have met with due punishment for his crimes. . . . All commissioned officers in the command of the said Benjamin F. Butler are declared not entitled to be considered as soldiers engaged in honorable warfare, but as robbers and criminals deserving death, and that they and each of them be, whenever captured, reserved for execution."—Proclamation of Jefferson Davis, December 23, 1862.

CUMBERLAND GAP.

CHAPTER X.

EASTERN KENTUCKY. MIDDLE CREEK AND MILL SPRING.

The General Situation at the beginning of 1862.—The Necessity for immediate Action.—The President's Order of January 27th.—The Situation in Eastern Kentucky.—Humphrey Marshall in the Big Sandy.—Garfield's Brigade.—The March on Paintville.—Retreat of Marshall.—Middle Creek.—The Battle.—Marshall retreats to Abingdon, Va.—The Course of the Cumberland.—Cumberland Gap.—Zollicoffer's Camp at Mill Spring.—General Crittenden joins Zollicoffer.—Thomas moves against the Confederate Encampment.—The Battle of Mill Spring.—Death of Zollicoffer.—Crittenden's Retreat to Gainesborough.

A NERVOUS disquiet pervaded the Southern mind at the commencement of a new year, the result, in a great measure, of the highly-wrought anticipations which had grown out of the Trent affair. It was presumed that the Federal government would decide blindly, and without regard to the claims of justice, upon the question which had been forced upon it by the unauthorized seizure of Mason and Slidell, and it was a painful surprise to the Confederates to learn that the two commissioners had been quietly and dispassionately rendered up to the British government. The extraordinary unanimity with which the people of the North supported the administration in its efforts to subdue a rebellious section of the country was a disappointment hardly less keen or more easily admitting of consolation. The South, along with its hope of foreign interference, had insanely nourished the fond expectation of what it called "a popular revulsion in the Northern people against the folly and pusillanimity of their rulers."[1] It also very much galled the Confederates to look back upon the closing events of the past year—the repulse at Drainesville and the reverse in Missouri. Nor was the immediate future any more hopeful. The Confederacy was prepared neither in the East nor the West to assume the offensive: in the West this policy was impossible; in the East it was perilous. There was no good reason to expect that the national army would rashly set out upon an ill-advised campaign, directly assailing the formidable strong-holds and fortifications of the Confederacy; there was no necessity compelling that army to rush desperately into any campaign of whatsoever sort and favored by whatsoever advantages; it could wait until its preparations had become so formidable as to be all but irresistible. The naval expeditions of the preceding year had inculcated a wholesome fear all along the Atlantic and Gulf coasts, and this apprehension was only matched by that which the threatened movements of the national forces in the West naturally occasioned. Price was in full retreat southward, with three Union armies in his rear. McCulloch, with his daring band of Arkansas recruits, had withdrawn from the field. Kentucky was overawed. The blockade interposed an almost insuperable barrier between the Southern cities and all foreign ports. The national finances had been efficiently sustained by the entire wealth of the North, while those of the South were already betraying their fundamental weakness. Very soon, too, the twelve months' soldiers of the Confederacy would have to be discharged. It was beginning to be seen, and already it was declared by the Southern press, that it is an old and ever-proven truism, that when two sections are at war, the one which has the least means must find success in early and rapid action, for it can gain little by time, while the other finds in time the power to bring into efficient use its more varied means. The clearest policy of the weaker section in such a conflict was to find in the rapid use of its revolutionary enthusiasm an overmatch for the slower, less spirited, but more enduring North.[1] The Southern people were impatient for an advance of the Confederate army of the Potomac. "We have gazed," they said, "imploringly on the lion while the fox has been weaving his toils. Are we to continue hemmed in for another six months, and lack all things, or shall our armies *on to Washington*, and lack nothing?"

There was somewhat of a restless spirit at the North also, but based upon entirely different grounds, and far more reasonable in its nature and its conclusions. It was not peevishness, nor the outgrowth of a desperate spirit that would venture all at a single throw; it was rather the expression of confident hope mingled with an element of considerable anxiety—hope so far as we ourselves were concerned, anxiety in regard to the attitude of European Powers. The aristocracy of the Old World was plainly committed to the interests of the Southern slaveholder, and it needed but a single stroke of policy or a change of ministry to give the sanction of authority to the opinions held by the Second Estate both in England and France. Nine months had passed since the declaration of war, and these nine months were especially signalized by reverses to the Federal armies. Every week's delay in moving against the enemy's works enfeebled that respect for our strength as a nation which foreign nations had always entertained, and made the policy of interference, already backed by motives of selfish interest, apparently justifiable as well as natural. If it should come to the worst—if Europe should despair of an early termination of the war on account of the vacillation of our military commanders—then nothing short of national ruin, as complete and irretrievable as any upon historic record, stared us in the face. And for vacillation and hesitancy, moreover, there seemed little occasion. Hitherto the case had been different; we had, in spite of the vast resources of the nation held in reserve, been compelled to create the very means and organization through which these resources should become available and effective. But now, through unparalleled activity and determination, the great want had been measurably supplied; and although it was impossible to calculate with certainty upon success in every movement which we were prepared to make, yet it is to be remembered, and was then earnestly insisted upon, that in no war of any magnitude was it ever possible to obviate the chances of failure, whatever may have been the previous preparation. The pressing exigencies urging on an immediate movement of our

[1] In addition to other disparagements, the Confederate army suffered very much from disease in camp, far more than the Federal army—not only by reason of less favorable location, but also, and chiefly, through negligence. Says E. A. Pollard, in his *Southern History of the War:* "The most distressing abuses were visible in the ill-regulated hygiene of our camps. The ravages of disease among the army in Virginia were terrible. The accounts of its extent were suppressed in the newspapers of the day; and there is no doubt that thousands of our brave troops disappeared from notice without a record of their end, in the nameless graves that yet mark the camping-grounds on the lines of the Potomac and among the wild mountains of Virginia. Our camps were scourged with pneumonia and diarrhœa. The armies on the Potomac and in Western Virginia suffered greatly—those troops in Cheat Mountain and in the vicinity of the Kanawha Valley most intensely. The wet and changeable climate; the difficulty of transportation; exposure to cold and rain without tents, the necessary consequence of the frequent forward and retrograde movements, as well as the want of suitable food for either sick or well men, produced most of the sickness, and greatly aggravated it after its accession." The Southern people, when made aware of these facts, with great generosity contributed immense sums in clothing and stores for the relief of their troops. During the latter quarter of 1861, the eleven states of the Confederacy contributed in this way a million and a half in money, besides the voluntary contributions which came from Missouri and Kentucky.

armies were those belonging naturally to the situation, and not the effect of popular clamor. Never was there more patience manifested by any people where so much—nothing less, indeed, than the life of the nation—was at stake, and manifested in connection with such stirring enthusiasm and ardent patriotism as was shown by the people of the loyal states in those quiet autumn and winter months, during which they waited without a murmur or the slightest breath of suspicion against the national authority. When, therefore, General McClellan states in his report that, about the middle of January, upon recovering from a severe illness, he found that "excessive anxiety for an immediate movement of the Army of the Potomac had taken possession of the minds of the administration," it is not to be understood that this anxiety was the result of any growing dissatisfaction among the people. There were currents from across the Atlantic drifting inevitably into a policy hostile to the United States, the bearings of which were more patent to the Department of State than to the nation at large. The altered policy which then became necessary was not, as has sometimes been alleged, and as General McClellan seems in this connection to indicate, the result of the change in the secretaryship of the War Department, by which Edwin M. Stanton took the place of Mr. Cameron. But for the complications rapidly being developed in the Department of State, the War Department could have prosecuted its operations according to a more leisurely policy. Whether, even under these circumstances, that would have been a wise policy, is an independent question; a necessity from without, urging an immediate movement, disposed summarily of the whole matter.

It is from this stand-point that we are to consider the important military order which his excellency the President issued from the executive mansion on the 27th of January, 1862, the substance of which was the following:

"That the 22d day of February, 1862, be the day for a general movement of the land and naval forces of the United States against the insurgent forces.

"That, especially,

"The army at and about Fortress Monroe,

"The Army of the Potomac,

"The Army of Western Virginia,

"The army near Munfordsville, Kentucky,

"The army and flotilla at Cairo,

"And a naval force in the Gulf of Mexico, be ready to move on that day.

"That all other forces, both land and naval, with their respective commanders, obey existing orders for the time, and be ready to obey additional orders when duly given.

"That the heads of departments, and especially the Secretaries of War and of the Navy, with all their subordinates, and the general-in-chief, with all other commanders and subordinates of land and naval forces, will severally be held to their strict and full responsibilities for prompt execution of this order."

This was followed on the 31st by a special war order, "That all the disposable force of the Army of the Potomac, after providing safely for the defense of Washington, be formed into an expedition for the immediate object of seizing upon the railroad southwestward of what is known as Manassas Junction, all details to be in the discretion of the commander-in-chief, and the expedition to move before or on the 22d day of February next."

The subsequent modification of this special order by the President, and the events of the Peninsular campaign, will form the leading subjects of a subsequent chapter. In the mean time we turn to the Western field, and to the events which there followed each other, in execution of the President's order, from Garfield's victories in the valley of the Big Sandy to the evacuation by the enemy of all the important strong-holds in Kentucky.

During the month of January, Eastern Kentucky was the one sole field of active military operations. The Confederate force in Kentucky at this time was distributed among the three important military positions commanding the southern part of the state and the main avenues into Tennessee, viz., Columbus, Bowling Green, and the region about Cumberland Gap. A small portion of this force, however, was located in the eastern part of the state, consisting of a few regiments of Kentucky troops under Colonel Humphrey Marshall, occupying an intrenched position at Paintville. We have previously given an account of the retreat of the Confederate force, not quite 1500 strong, under Colonel Williams, in November, from Prestonburg and Piketon into Virginia. This was the result of an attack by General Nelson, who, if he had pursued the retreating enemy, might, perhaps, have reaped important fruits from his victory by the destruction or occupation of the Virginia and East Tennessee Railroad. But this would have been a hazardous undertaking, considering the distance over which supplies would have to be transported, and the mountainous nature of the country to be traversed, added to the embarrassments which would have grown out of the hostile disposition of the inhabitants. General Nelson did not even continue the pursuit of Colonel Williams through Pound Gap, but withdrew to the central portion of the state with his forces. Immediately afterward Humphrey Marshall gathered together a brigade of Confederates at Paintville, with a battery of artillery and a few companies of cavalry.

The colonel—a man of aldermanic dimensions—had occupied a somewhat prominent position in politics, and had served in the Mexican war, having led the famous charge of the Kentucky volunteers at Buena Vista. He had been elected to Congress in 1849; was appointed commissioner to China by President Fillmore, and afterward became a leading member of the American party. He was not, however, destined to distinguish himself as a military hero in the valley of the Big Sandy, although great hopes were entertained at the South that he would make his way triumphantly to Frankfort, and establish the authority of the provisional governor Johnson in the place of the regular state government.

K K K

JAMES A. GARFIELD.

The Big Sandy, having its head waters in Virginia, forms the northwestern boundary between that state and Kentucky, emptying its waters into the Ohio. At Louisa, a small village situated some twenty-five miles southward from its mouth, West Fork joins the main stream. Following the road up this fork for twenty-five miles farther, we reach Paintville. At high water the river is navigable as far as Piketon, twenty-five miles beyond, and in November General Nelson had no difficulty in transporting his supplies to that point. On the 7th of January, however, when Colonel James A. Garfield broke up his camp on Muddy Creek and advanced against the enemy, the river was low, and occasioned great difficulty in the transportation of supplies. His force at starting was about 1500, consisting of the Forty-second Ohio and the Fourteenth Kentucky, accompanied by a squadron of cavalry. On the route he was re-enforced by a battalion of Virginia cavalry, under Colonel Bolles, and 300 of the Twenty-second Kentucky, making the entire force with which he marched on Paintville about 2200 men. Another battalion of cavalry, under Colonel Wolford, together with the Fortieth Ohio, was also moving toward the same point from the west along Paint Creek. Hearing of this threatened attack, Humphrey Marshall had left his intrenchments two days before, and retired to a position among the heights at Middle Creek, a little below Prestonburg, leaving only a small force of cavalry at the mouth of Jennie's Creek, three miles west of Paintville, to act as a corps of observation and to protect his trains. Before reaching Paintville, Garfield was made aware of the situation of this cavalry force, though he had no certain knowledge of the whereabouts of the other and main portion of the enemy. Dispatching Colonel Bolles's cavalry and a company of infantry to attack the former from the north side, he himself, with a thousand men, crossed the Paint at four o'clock in the afternoon, to make an armed reconnoissance, which resulted in the discovery that the main body of the enemy had withdrawn. It was over two hours since he had sent Bolles up the creek, and now, seeing that he had a fair opportunity of securing the Confederate cavalry force, he promptly sent a messenger with orders to the colonel not to attack until he should have time himself to get in the rear and cut off the retreat. The orders, however, came too late, as the attack had already been made, and the colonel was then engaged in pursuing the enemy up the Jennie; so that when Garfield, a little later, had gained, as he supposed, the rear of the enemy, he soon discovered their cavalry equipments, which they had left in the confusion of flight, strewing the road, and indicating with certainty that the Confederates had escaped. Bolles, in the mean while, after pursuing until he came up with Marshall's infantry rear-guard, returned to Paintville, where the Federal forces encamped for the night.

The next morning the arrival of the Fortieth Ohio and Wolford's cavalry brought the number of the Federal forces up to 2400 men. On the 9th, Garfield, detailing 1100 men from his four regiments, and detaching two cavalry squadrons to move along his right up Jennie's Creek, followed the river road south to Prestonburg, the distance to this town from Paintville being twelve miles. He had been delayed a whole day at the latter place, awaiting supplies from George's Creek, a few miles below on the river, which arrived in such scanty amounts as to render it impossible to give three days rations of hard bread—and it was useless to set out with less

MAP OF KENTUCKY AND NORTHERN TENNESSEE.

than that—to more than 1500 men. It was necessary, therefore, that fully 1000 men should remain behind until the arrival of farther supplies.

Humphrey Marshall, with over 3000 men, had taken up a position among the heights on the forks of Middle Creek, two miles below Prestonburg. His force consisted of two Virginia and two Kentucky regiments, one of the latter under the command of Colonel John S. Williams, being the same which Nelson had two months ago driven out of the state through Pound Gap. Two small detachments of cavalry and a battery of four pieces guarded the approaches to a position naturally very good for defense. On the evening of the 9th Garfield's advanced column drove in the Confederate pickets, and a messenger was dispatched to Paintville with orders to move forward all the available force to participate in the morrow's conflict. As another boat-load of supplies had arrived that day from below, Lieutenant Colonel Sheldon was enabled to take about 700 men, at the head of which force he started early the next morning. The main body of Garfield's force, having slept on their arms in the rain until four o'clock A.M., moved up Abbot's Creek one mile, and crossed over to the mouth of Middle Creek, a little north of Prestonburg, arriving there at eight o'clock. Supposing the enemy to be encamped on Abbot's Creek, it was Garfield's plan to gain his rear by moving up Middle Creek, thus cutting off the retreat, while an attack was made at the same time by the cavalry upon the front. Small bodies of Marshall's cavalry were met all along the march up Middle Creek for two miles and a half, when the Federal troops were drawn up on the slope of a semicircular hill. A thousand yards farther up the stream divided into two forks, which were held by the enemy. It was now noon, and with the small force available for an attack the approach was of necessity a cautious one, the re-enforcements not having arrived. It was not wise, through an armed reconnoissance, to seek information as to the numbers and disposition of the Confederate force, as this reconnoissance would inevitably bring on a general engagement, in which the Federal troops would not only be overwhelmed by a superior force, but would labor under the additional disadvantage of being precipitated into a battle without any previous plan of operation. Besides, the enemy was so posted in his concealed position as to command the road at the head of the gorge, and also to flank it from the left-hand side. His artillery, together with

Colonel Williams's regiment, was on the right-hand side of the road at the head of the gorge, and a crescent-shaped hill on the opposite side concealed another column just behind its crest. It was Marshall's design to draw the Federal forces up the road, and then to open upon them from the front and left. Anticipating a manœuvre of this nature, Garfield, having taken up his position on the slope of a semicircular hill on the right-hand side of the creek, dispatched twenty mounted men, who made a headlong charge up the valley, and, drawing the enemy's fire, disclosed the position above indicated. Two columns, consisting each of two companies, were sent, one along the crest to the right, behind which Colonel Trigg's Virginia regiment was stationed, and the other across the creek, to ascend the rugged crest farthest up the gorge on the left. The right column became immediately the target of the enemy's artillery, but the latter was so badly served that its shells did not explode, while the small force dispatched to the left, after climbing up the rocky ridge on their hands and knees, engaged the enemy on that side. Both columns were re-enforced. Trigg's regiment was withdrawn across the creek, and the battle raged chiefly on the left, which Garfield still farther re-enforced with one hundred and fifty men. The Confederates in the mean time had gained a commanding position on the top of the ridge, and directly in front of the Federal reserve force, on which they opened a heavy fire, that was returned with good effect. To guard against a flank movement, which was now threatened by the enemy's right, another column of one hundred and twenty men was ordered to cross at a point lower down and drive the enemy from his new position, a movement which was successfully accomplished. After some pretty severe fighting, a similar success attended the Federal column on the crest nearer the creek, the enemy being also driven from his position at that point. On account of the great disparity of the two opposing forces, the Federals were obliged to resort in many cases to an irregular mode of fighting, sheltering themselves whenever opportunity offered behind trees and rocks. They had no heavy artillery, and the cavalry, having gone in a mistaken direction, did not participate in the engagement. The battle had now continued in this desultory style for over three hours, and it was four o'clock P.M. when Sheldon came up with re-enforcements from Paintville. These had started early in the morning, and had marched fifteen miles without breakfast; but their courage, not daunted by these unfavorable circumstances, demanded to be tested in the fight with the already checked, if not baffled foe. The enthusiasm occasioned by their arrival was unbounded, and Garfield promptly dispatched his entire reserve to the right for an attack upon the enemy's main position and the capture of his guns. Appreciating the new phase which the battle was taking, Humphrey Marshall ordered a retreat, which was continued to Abingdon, in Virginia. It was a short winter's day, and was now too dark to admit of pursuit. The sky was illuminated with the burning of the enemy's stores preparatory to his disorderly flight. The next morning, on the arrival of the cavalry, a pursuit was sustained for several miles, and some prisoners were taken. Two or three days afterward the entire command returned to Paintville.

This success, disposing of the Confederate force in Northeastern Kentucky, had an additional brilliancy imparted to it from the fact that it inaugurated a long series of victories. Humphrey Marshall's political antecedents, and the reminiscences which haunted many citizens of the North of his plump presence in Congress and in the famous American Convention, gave somewhat of piquancy to the dramatic features of this episode of his defeat. The victor, the young colonel from Ohio, was soon promoted to a brigadier, and afterward a major generalship, and in 1863 was elected to Congress from Ohio, his native state. Although not a graduate of West Point, he proved a most efficient officer in the early Western campaigns.

If we now cross the mountains crowding the southeastern portion of Kentucky, we shall find ourselves in the valley of the Cumberland River, which has its rise among these mountains, and, taking a westward direction in its zigzag course, after its two head tributaries, coming down along either side of Pine Mountain, have formed a junction at Cumberland Ford, just north of Cumberland Gap, runs through Barboursville and Williamsburg, thence northwestwardly, just leaving Somerset to the north, while it sweeps down into Tennessee, and, after a long and very winding course to the east, passes through Nashville, and then returns through a more regular channel into Western Kentucky, and empties into the Ohio at Smithland, about fifty miles above Cairo, having described a course twice the length of the Hudson. That portion of Kentucky which this river cuts off before it first enters Tennessee was held by the Confederacy, and was a very important tract of country, guarding the entrance into Tennessee from Eastern Kentucky.

FELIX ZOLLICOFFER.

The Confederate government early in the summer guarded against a Federal advance into East Tennessee by way of Cumberland Gap by sending General Felix Zollicoffer, with a force of several thousand men, to the threatened point. Occupying the mountain ranges of Southeastern Kentucky, he had made advances into the interior as far as Manchester, his operations generally taking the form of raids, having for their purpose the destruction of railroads, the dispersion of Federal encampments, and, still more frequently, the obtaining of provisions. In September a slight skirmish had occurred at Barboursville between a portion of his troops and a body of Home Guards. In October he had met with a repulse at Camp Wild-cat, near Loudon. An expedition had been planned against him by General Schœpf in November; but a Confederate brigade having been sent to his

relief from Bowling Green, the scheme was abandoned. General Alvin Schœpf, a European officer of considerable experience, now took up a position at Somerset with about 5000 available men, a few cavalry, and a single battery of artillery. Fifteen miles to the southeast of this position was that occupied by Zollicoffer, at Mill Springs, on the south bank of the Cumberland. In itself considered, the Confederate position was one of great strength. The banks of the river, rising to the height of three or four hundred feet, afford sites favorable for fortification; and Zollicoffer had not only an intrenched camp at Mill Springs, but another on the opposite bank at Beech Grove. The northern encampment was occupied by five regiments, and fortified with twelve pieces of artillery; on the southern bank there were stationed two regiments and a considerable cavalry force. Apparently of great strength, the position was really a very weak one. The surface of the ground surrounding the encampment afforded no good range for artillery against an attacking infantry force; but a still greater disadvantage was the scarcity of provisions. Wayne County was the only fruitful portion of the state from which the Confederates could draw supplies. Over a hundred and thirty miles intervened between them and Knoxville, and the Cumberland, commanded by Federal troops, afforded a precarious channel of communication. The unfavorable situation was heightened by impassable roads; and as the immediate vicinity was rapidly exhausted, the Confederate soldiers were sometimes reduced to one third rations, while their mules and horses were often without any supply whatever. About the first of January General Crittenden arrived from Knoxville and assumed command of the army, which had been already re-enforced by Carroll's brigade.

GEORGE H. THOMAS.

Nearly at the same time that Crittenden arrived at Mill Springs, General Buell detached a force from his main army, and sent it against the Confederate strong-hold in Eastern Kentucky. The force thus dispatched consisted of seven regiments and a portion of Wolford's cavalry, under the command of General George H. Thomas, who had distinguished himself both in Florida and Mexico, and had, from 1850 up to the beginning of the war, been instructor of artillery and cavalry at West Point. A native of Virginia, General Thomas was still true to his country, and had already, in August, 1861, been appointed a brigadier general of volunteers. Thomas left Lebanon on the 31st of December, and, after a march of nearly two weeks, reached Columbia, and, after a rest of four or five days, pushed on eastward to Fishing Creek, a few miles west of Somerset. It was now the 17th; the march had been over roads almost impassable, and four regiments and one of the batteries—more than one half of Thomas's column—were yet struggling along on the road from Columbia. To await these, and also to communicate with Schœpf, Thomas halted at this point, ten miles north of the enemy's camp. The Tenth Indiana, of Colonel Manson's brigade, held the advance; and from this regiment two companies were sent out as picket guard on the road to Mill Springs, taking up their position beyond the junction of that road with the one leading from Somerset to Mill Springs. In advance of these was stationed a battalion of Wolford's cavalry. The camp of the Tenth was not far in the rear. Colonel R. L. McCook, with two regiments of his brigade, the Second Minnesota and the Ninth Ohio, were encamped a mile to the right, on the Robertsport and Danville road. This disposition of Thomas's forces guarded all the approaches to his encampment, and also to Somerset. This was the situation on Friday night. During the day Schœpf had visited Thomas, and arrangements were made for a co-operation of the two columns in the attack on Zollicoffer's camp, which was to take place on the succeeding Monday. Recent rains had swollen Fishing Creek to such an extent as to render it impossible for either of the divisions to support the other in case of an attack being made by the enemy; therefore, to supply the place of the regiments which were yet detained on the road, it was arranged that Carter's brigade should be sent from Somerset to General Thomas. This brigade consisted of the Twelfth Kentucky and two regiments of East Tennesseeans. On Saturday the Fourth Kentucky arrived on the field with Wetmore's battery, which, with the regiments and Standart's battery sent from Somerset, raised Thomas's force to a complement of six regiments and three batteries, besides the small detachment of Wolford's cavalry.

In the mean time, the peculiar situation of the Confederate army on the Cumberland led to a movement which anticipated the Federal attack, and resulted in the battle of Mill Spring, otherwise known as the battle of Somerset, though it was fought at neither of these places, but midway between them, at Cross Roads. By extraordinary efforts, Crittenden, having been informed of Thomas's advance, had collected together sufficient provisions for two or three days ahead, and on Friday night had sent out a reconnoitring party, which had met and exchanged shots with the picket guard of the Tenth Indiana and then retired. Saturday night the Confederate officers met in council and determined to advance against Thomas, surprise his camp, and give him battle at early dawn on Sunday morning. There were two considerations which led to this determination. The first related to the enemy, whose two columns would be united in an attack on the Confederate camp, but might be met separately in case Crittenden should take the initiative. The second regarded the position of the Confederate army, which could easily be turned, and which therefore made it necessary that Crittenden should either make the proposed advance, or retreat, leaving the way open into East Tennessee. The Federal force, moreover, was estimated, on the basis of the reconnoissance made the previous night, at considerably less than its real value. Although there was a great deal ventured in this advance, made thus upon a mistaken estimate of the enemy's strength, it had a reasonable hope of success if the surprise could have been calculated upon as certain. This was not the case; for Thomas, fully aware of the probability of an attack, had disposed of his forces accordingly.

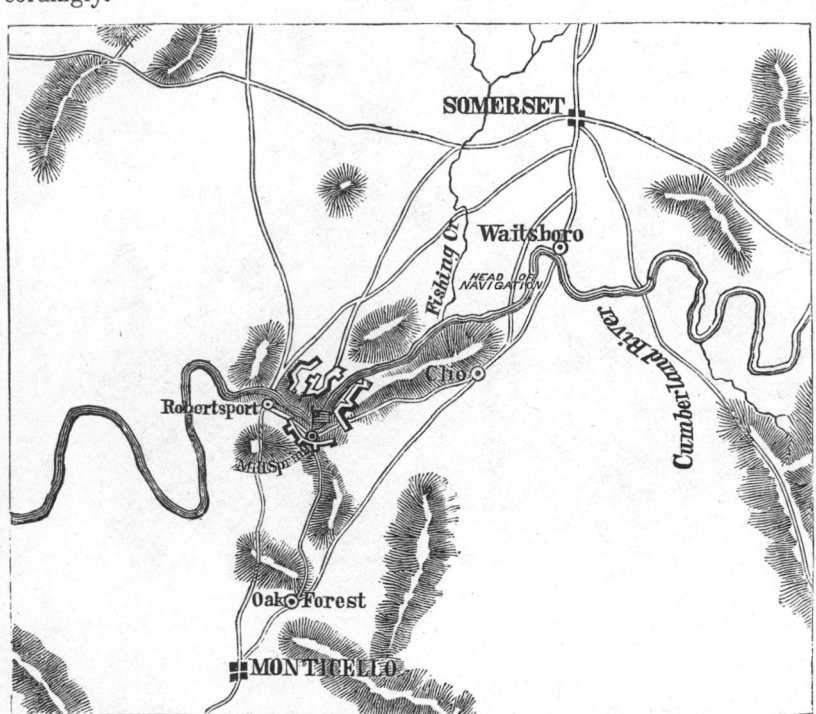

MAP OF MILL SPRING AND THE VICINITY.

The Confederates marched out of camp at midnight in perfect silence, with Zollicoffer's brigade in the van, followed by Carroll's, making altogether a force of eight regiments, with six pieces of artillery. After a march of six hours, through drizzling rain and over muddy roads, the skirmishers of the Fifteenth Mississippi encountered the Federal pickets at daybreak. The captain of one of the companies on picket guard had just reported to Colonel Manson that all was quiet, when a courier arrived with tidings of the attack. The long roll was instantly beat, and a company was promptly dispatched to the support of the pickets, followed immediately by the entire regiment, which had just formed in line of battle about seventy-five yards from the picket-firing, when Zollicoffer was seen close in front with the Mississippi regiment, supported by Battle's and Stanton's. For an hour the Indiana soldiers stood against these three regiments, when half of their number were obliged to retire from their position on the right of the road. At this moment the Fourth Kentucky came up on the left, and a part of McCook's brigade on the right, making the numbers engaged at this point, on each side, nearly equal. The position now held by the Federal troops was about a thousand yards in the rear of that originally taken by the Tenth, which, by the superior numbers opposed to it, had been driven over one hill and up the slope of another. Here the battle raged more hotly, and for a time without any sensible advantage on one side or the other, until at length the Fourth Kentucky and Tenth Indiana, their ammunition being nearly exhausted, took shelter in the woods along the crest of the second hill, when the Confederates rushed forward from their cover in the woods across the field intervening between the two positions. The crest once

ROBERT L. McCOOK.

gained, the field was theirs. Every nerve was strained to the utmost. Carroll's brigade was ordered up to support Zollicoffer, and on the Federal side McCook's two regiments were called into action. One of these, the Second Minnesota, rapidly made its way among the logs and brushwood to the left, taking the place of the Fourth Kentucky and the Tenth Indiana, and at the same time the Ninth Ohio got into position on the right of the road in the woods, where it was separated from the enemy by a corn-field. Only the road separated the two regiments. In the rapid movement of the Confederates under Zollicoffer, the latter was killed by S. S. Fry, colonel of the Fourth Kentucky; but the regiments under his command, maddened by the event, rushed furiously on till they came into an almost hand to hand encounter with McCook's brigade, the Second Minnesota and the Confederates opposed to them pushing their muskets through the same fence. For half an hour the desperate conflict continued, and still remained doubtful. The Confederates had clearly an advantage in the numbers engaged, while the Federals had a compensating advantage in position, and also in the management of artillery, for the Confederate batteries overshot McCook's brigade, while his told with fearful effect against the enemy. Suddenly the battle turned; the Confederates were driven back to their first position. In the mean while, Carter's brigade having gained the enemy's right flank, a bayonet charge was ordered along the whole line, and the retreat of the Confederates was turned into a rout. They had lost their favorite leader, and Crittenden in vain endeavored to rally them against the pursuing Federals. One or two feeble stands were made, but without effect, and before night they had been driven within their intrenchments at Beech Grove, having lost in killed and wounded 300 men, besides fifty taken prisoners. The Federal batteries were brought up, and from commanding positions on the neighboring hills opened a cannonade on the enemy's camp. Schœpf had joined Thomas, and it was intended to carry the fortifications the next morning by storm, but in the night the Confederates effected a retreat across the river. This movement was attended with great distress and a complete demoralization of the Confederate army, the scattered fragments of which were afterward collected together at Gainsborough, on the Cumberland, about thirty miles below the point at which that river enters Tennessee.

The part which Colonel McCook's brigade played in the battle of Mill Spring was prominent. The colonel, a native of Ohio, was thirty-five years of age, and was destined, in a few months, to lose his life, not on the fair field of battle, but by the hand of the assassin. He was murdered, August 6, 1862, by a company of guerrillas, in ambush near Salem, Alabama. Colonel McCook, at the beginning of the war, was placed in command of the Ninth Ohio regiment, which had reached so high a degree of discipline that McClellan pronounced it the first in the army. With this regiment he had passed through the West Virginia campaign; under Rosecrans he was given the command of the second brigade. At Philippi, Rich Mountain, and Carnifex Ferry his command was always foremost in the fight. The battle of Mill Spring was the last in which he participated. He was wounded here, but it was not long before he was again at the post of duty. For his energy and bravery in this battle he was appointed a brigadier general, but his attachment to his old regiment led him to decline the commission.[1]

---

[1] A large number of the McCook family were engaged in the civil war on the Federal side. Among them are the following: General Alexander McCook, the brother to whom Robert sent his last message: "Tell Aleck and the rest that I have tried to live like a man and do my duty;" Daniel McCook, jun., adjutant general in General McCook's staff, and who was to suffer death from wounds received at Kenesaw Mountain in 1864; Edwin McCook, then a captain in Colonel Logan's Illinois regiment; Lieutenant Edward S. McCook, of the regular army; Major Anson McCook, Second Ohio; Henry McCook, captain of an Illinois regiment; Sheldon McCook, a lieutenant in the navy.

ANDREW HULL FOOTE.

CHAPTER XI.

FORTS HENRY AND DONELSON.

The original Plan for the Advance of the Western Armies.—The Resistance to be overcome.—Estimate of Forces in the West.—The new Plan of Operations.—The Cumberland and Tennessee Rivers.—Their military Importance.—The Mississippi Flotilla.—Commodore Foote.—McClernand's Reconnoissance toward Columbus.—The Capture of Fort Henry, February 6, 1862.—Expedition up the Tennessee to Florence, Alabama.—Preparations for an Attack on Donelson.—Position of the Fort.—Disposition of the Confederate Army.—Buckner, Floyd, Johnson, and Pillow.—Floyd's Suggestion in regard to the Defense of the Fort.—Operations on Thursday, February 13; Investment of the Fort by General Grant; Assaults on the Confederate Lines.—Arrival of the Gun-boats.—Naval Attack on Friday; its ill Success.—Confederate Council of War Friday Night.—The Battle of Saturday; early Success of the Confederates; their final Repulse.—Floyd's second Council; its Deliberations.—Escape of Floyd and Pillow.—Surrender of Fort Donelson by Buckner, Sunday Morning, the 16th.—Evacuation of Bowling Green, Nashville, and Columbus.—Polk's Withdrawal to Island No. 10.

THREE times now within a period of three months had the way been laid open for an attack upon the Virginia and Tennessee Railroad; twice through Pound Gap and Virginia, and again, after the victory of Mill Spring, by way of Cumberland Gap. In neither case was the opportunity improved, because the Federal force at hand was not sufficiently large to secure a permanent possession, and because the plan of invading Tennessee through Eastern Kentucky had been given up for another, more feasible, and involving larger and more satisfactory results. It was deeply regretted by the government, and was the subject of complaint among many loyal people of the North, that the deliverance which had been promised through the original plan to the Unionists of East Tennessee had to be postponed; but any merely temporary relief would evidently have only aggravated their sufferings. The new plan of operations transferred the burden of the spring campaign in the West from the department of General Buell to that of General Halleck, and the field of activity from Eastern to Central and Western Tennessee. Originally it was proposed that Buell should advance through Cumberland Gap, and take possession of the line of communications connecting Tennessee with Richmond—a line which could be reached by a march of little more than thirty miles from the Gap—while Halleck should co-operate by the movement of a joint naval and land expedition down the Mississippi. The resistance to be overcome in this plan was very great in each department. Buell had two impediments; one was Buckner's army, now strongly fortified at Bowling Green, and the other the geography of Eastern Kentucky. Bowling Green was, in relation to Tennessee, a most important military position, situated a little to the south of the centre of Kentucky, at the head of navigation, on the Big Barren, a branch of Green River, and commanding the only two lines of railroad communication between the two states, namely, the Louisville and Nashville Road, and the branch of that route which, taking its departure five miles below Bowling Green, has its western *terminus* at Memphis. The Confederate army at this point must either be met in its intrenched position, or left in the rear. Though not impregnably fortified, Bowling Green was easily protected from an attack on the north, the approach in that direction being across the river; and, in order to cut off its communications with the South, it would be necessary to occupy in force each of the two railroad lines above mentioned. Whatever might have been the success of an attempt to capture it, it could not have been accomplished without great exhaustion of force; and to push

a large army into Tennessee, leaving Buckner in its rear, would have been absolutely ruinous. In Halleck's way, on the Mississippi, was Columbus—the Gibraltar of the West—thirteen miles below Cairo, and connected by railroad with Bowling Green and the South. From this point, at the beginning of the year, the Confederate line of occupation stretched westward through Bowling Green and into Virginia, where the Great Kanawha continued it on toward the eastern strong-hold of Manassas. Fort Columbus was originally a position of great natural strength. The eastern bank, on which it lay, was lined above and below by bluffs 150 feet in height; and north of the town, one of these bluffs, facing up the river, was fortified with three tiers of batteries, and mounting altogether upward of fifty guns; the other sides open to attack were also well fortified. The works on the summit of the hill cover an area of nearly four miles. To prevent the passage by the fort of gun-boats, a strong iron chain stretched across to the opposite bank. The entire armament of Columbus consisted of 140 pieces of artillery.

Still proceeding on the supposition that the plan which we have indicated, and which was the one originally proposed, was to be carried into execution, what was the amount of force on each side available for the campaign?

On the 1st of December, 1861, there were in Kentucky 70,000 Union troops, of which about 23,000 were raised in the state. These troops were under the command of General Buell, whose head-quarters were at Louisville. At that time upward of 18,000 of these troops had not yet been sworn in, and the greater portion were recently armed and undisciplined. But the work of recruiting and organization was rapidly going on, and it was to continue until Buell's command should number 100,000 men. In Missouri, at St. Louis and Cairo, Halleck was gathering another army, fully as large as that of Buell. Regiments from Illinois, under the command of General Grant, constituted the great proportion of this army. Nothing is easier than to overestimate the effective force of an army freshly recruited. Take, for instance, the combined force of Halleck and Buell at the beginning of 1862. It is set down in round numbers at 200,000 men. But from this flattering estimate made on paper we have, in the first place, to deduct between twenty to thirty per cent. for forces not yet fairly in the field. This would leave say 150,000 men in camp. Of this 150,000 a considerable proportion would be without arms and unorganized; a great number of regiments would be detached as garrisons at important points; and a still farther deduction would have to be made for those disabled by sickness, so that not more than 100,000 men could be counted upon as available for active operations in an offensive campaign. Neither Halleck nor Buell, therefore, could count upon a column of over 50,000 men each. That this estimate is not founded on conjecture will appear when we come to consider the forces engaged at the siege of Donelson. What was the force which was opposed to this by the Confederates? The two great centres about which this force gathered were, as we have already indicated, Columbus and Bowling Green, each of which was held by an army ranging from 20,000 to 30,000 strong. There were various detachments of force in Tennessee, the most important of which was Crittenden's little army, which Thomas had driven to Gainesborough. Bowling Green was the direct objective of Buell's attack, as Columbus of Halleck's. The scattered detachments in Tennessee might easily be gathered together to harass the right flank of Buell's army if he should pass across the mountains through Cumberland Gap. The forces at Columbus and Bowling Green, in their fortifications, were able to resist more than three times their own number in case of an attack made directly against them; they were so connected with each other and with their base of supplies that they would be able to stand a siege of any duration, as the Federal force would be clearly inadequate to their perfect investment; they occupied a central position, while the attack must move along the radii of an extended arc; the probabilities, therefore, in case of a direct attack, were decidedly in their favor. In the plan of operations originally proposed, such an attack was necessarily involved. This was clearly the case as regards Columbus; and no good general would ever dream of leaving so large a force as that at Bowling Green in his rear, unless his line of communication was secure against interruption. There could be no security like this in an advance through Eastern Kentucky. This advance, therefore, taken in connection with the co-operative movement of a naval and land force down the Mississippi, involved of necessity the capture both of Bowling Green and Columbus. Nothing would have better suited Albert Sidney Johnston, the Confederate general commanding in the West, than an attempt on the part of the Federal generals to reduce these two strong-holds. The attempt would certainly have resulted, if not in defeat, at least in such an exhaustion of force as would have made the Confederates masters of the situation in the entire West.

If, in relation to the above plan of operations, the Confederate position appeared to be one of extraordinary strength, it was yet, in relation to another plan, especially vulnerable; and every formidable difficulty incident to the one plan suggested some remarkable facility connected with the other. While East Tennessee was protected from invasion by Buckner's army and three ranges of mountains, West Tennessee was only protected by two small forts weakly garrisoned, one on the Cumberland River, and the other on the Tennessee. While, on the one hand, there was access only by mountain passes and over miserable roads, on the other there were two unobstructed rivers; while an advance, in the one case, left the only possible channel of communication with any source of supplies in the hands of the enemy, in the other it was not only secure against any interruption of this nature, but, on the other hand, threatened the communications of the enemy himself. The Confederate armies at Bowling Green and Columbus, which, in relation

COMMODORE FOOTE'S GUN-BOAT FLOTILLA ON THE MISSISSIPPI.

to the one plan, were impregnable towers of strength, were, in relation to the other, not simply deficient in force, but most unfortunately situated. They held advanced positions suitable as centres of offensive operations, but without a supporting force sufficient for an aggressive campaign; and while they could not be turned by a flank movement either on their right or left, they could yet be left in the rear by the movement of Halleck's entire naval and land force between them along the courses of two rivers, which, above Forts Henry and Donelson, were entirely in possession of the Federal armies. These two rivers were the Tennessee and the Cumberland.

The course of the Cumberland, from its rise among the mountains of Eastern Kentucky, and through its extensive curvature into Tennessee on its way eastward through Nashville, and then northward through Western Kentucky until it empties into the Ohio, we have already described. The head waters of the Tennessee are separated from those of the Cumberland by the Cumberland Mountains. After the Clinch and the Holston, which are the head tributaries of the Tennessee, have united just east of Knoxville, that river takes a southwesterly course, passing a little north of Chattanooga and down into Alabama, through the northwest corner of which it again returns into Tennessee, and, after traversing the entire breadth of the latter state, runs in a course nearly parallel to that of the Cumberland through Western Kentucky, and empties into the Ohio at Paducah, ten miles below the mouth of the Cumberland, having described a course of 700 miles in length. It was the existence of these two rivers which, leading into the very heart of the Confederacy, and constituting at the same time the most rapid, convenient, and secure channel of communication with the North, transformed the plan of the spring campaign in every important particular, and exchanged a very doubtful prospect for the glorious certainty of victory; and yet their importance was ignored both by the Federals and the Confederates—by the former until Buckner's increasing army at Bowling Green had made an advance into Tennessee by way of Cumberland Gap a perilous undertaking, by the latter until a Federal advance by way of the Tennessee and Cumberland was a danger imminent and no longer to be averted. The peril to the Confederate armies which was involved in this advance was not wholly unforeseen, but it was not contemplated as one likely to be realized, or, if it should be realized, one which was likely to be of great magnitude. At an early period, General Polk, commanding at Columbus, had intended to occupy Paducah at the mouth of the Tennessee; but he was anticipated in this movement by General Grant, who took possession of the place with a small force, which, by accessions from Cape Girardeau, was increased to about 5000 men. Not gaining any foothold in this quarter, the Confederates had built two forts—Henry and Donelson—the former on the Tennessee, and the latter on the Cumberland, near the Tennessee border, and just north of the railroad from Bowling Green to Memphis, hoping that these strong-holds could be sufficiently strengthened before the Federal armies would be prepared to advance. Here, at this time, was the great weakness of the western half of the Confederacy, and both Commodore Foote and General Grant strongly favored an advance in this direction. The plan involving this movement was formed suddenly by General Halleck, and, as has been shown already, entirely transformed the main features of the campaign as originally proposed. Fortunately, all the preparations which had been made with the view of proceeding directly against Columbus were just as available for an advance down the Tennessee.

The most important element in this preparation was the naval fleet which had been constructing on the Mississippi. It had been begun by General Fremont, who had found it necessary in this way to supplement his insufficient force. This fleet consisted of a flotilla of twelve gun-boats at Cairo, carrying in all 126 guns, and of thirty-eight mortar-boats, which had been built at St. Louis, and then towed down to Cairo to receive their armament. Some of the gun-boats had been iron-clad, and cost $89,000 each. The Benton, which was the most formidable, carried sixteen guns; the Mound City, Cincinnati, Louisville, Carondelet, St. Louis, Cairo, and Pittsburg, carried thirteen guns each; and the Lexington, Essex, Tyler, and Conestoga only nine. The mortar-boats were sixty feet long by twenty wide, surrounded by iron-plated bulwarks; and the mortars, weighing nearly a ton, with a charge of fifteen pounds of powder threw a shell three and a half miles. A portion of these boats were not yet ready for action. The entire fleet was under the command of Commodore A. H. Foote. This naval officer was a native of Connecticut. He had entered the navy as midshipman at the age of fifteen; and his memorable services against the pirates in the East Indies and against the slave-trade on the African coast had gained him an honorable fame. He was now fifty-five years of age. His strength of purpose, his unflinching energy in execution, and his Christian character placed his name among the noblest of American naval heroes.

Up to the very latest moment the Confederates were led in every possible way to expect an attack on Columbus by Halleck, and an advance by Buell into East Tennessee. This expectation on their part was doubtless heightened by quite extensive demonstrations against Columbus both on the river and by land, which were made by Grant and Foote in the middle of January. On the 7th of that month, Commodore Foote, with three gun-boats—the Essex, Lexington, and Tyler, made a reconnoissance down the Mississippi to within two miles of Columbus. At the same time, an expedition was organized by General Grant to operate by land in the same direction. This expedition was under McClernand's immediate command, and consisted of somewhat more than 5000 men, of which 4000 were infantry, 1000 cavalry, besides two batteries of light artillery. The men belonging to Schwartz's battery were the only soldiers in the entire command who were not from Illinois. On the 9th of January the cavalry crossed the river from Cairo to Fort Hall, on the eastern side, and guarded the approaches from Columbus,

JOHN A. McCLERNAND.

the infantry and artillery following the next day. Reconnoissances were made in all directions, and especially toward Columbus, not discovering the enemy, though coming within a mile and a half of his defenses. On the 14th, McClernand, with his whole force, took up a position north of Blandville, and commanding the road between Columbus and Paducah by the occupation of O'Neill's and the Blandville bridge across Mayfield Creek. The next day he crossed Mayfield Creek, and at Weston's General Grant came up with him. Proceeding to Milburn, ten miles east from Columbus, the expedition, at this point, might have been looked upon by General Polk either in the light of a demonstration against Columbus, or of a movement against the railroad running southward from Columbus to Union City. In the mean time General Smith had marched several columns from Paducah to Mayfield, whence communication was established with McClernand. After making this formidable demonstration in the vicinity of Columbus, the Federal troops were suddenly, on the 21st, returned to Cairo.

Movements were also made by General Buell, after the victory at Mill Spring, which indicated an advance in force into East Tennessee. The Cumberland River was crossed at Waitsborough, and a column pushed toward Cumberland Gap, while General Buell seemed to be massing his forces mainly on his left. That these operations had the designed effect on General Johnston is apparent from his sending a considerable force to Knoxville.

Just on the eve of conflict the Confederacy began to suspect that Forts Henry and Donelson were after all to be the objective points of attack. The sudden withdrawal of Grant's forces from the vicinity of Columbus, and Buell's change of front—General Thomas, instead of going to Tennessee, having turned back to Danville, forming a junction with Nelson, and thus flanked Bowling Green on the left—these movements revealed the secret of the whole campaign. The situation, from this point of view, became a critical one. Beauregard was immediately sent from Manassas to consult with Johnston in the West. It was too late, however, to readjust the elements involved in the impending conflict. The President's order for a general advance all along the line from Manassas to Columbus had gone forth, and the blow must soon fall. No forces could be spared from the eastern half of the Confederacy to Johnston's assistance; nothing but the delay of the Federal armies could relieve him. Perhaps he depended somewhat on this delay. The Federal fleet was not yet fully prepared; only a portion of the gun-boats had been iron-plated; several of the mortar-boats were yet only partly built; the Western army, also, was only partially organized. But this hope was vain. President Lincoln was determined to strike immediately with so many of the boats as *were* ready, and with so much of the army as could be made available for action, thinking that the Confederates would by delay gain more in the strength of their defensive positions than the Federal army would in its power to attack. And certainly, if the Confederates had been given time to re-enforce their weak positions on the Tennessee and the Cumberland, the whole prospect of the spring campaign would have been materially altered to their advantage.

The battles of Middle Creek and Mill Spring were not directly involved in the plan of the campaign, which really commenced with the operations against Fort Henry. All the preparations having been completed, General Grant, commanding at Cairo, proceeded up the Tennessee under convoy of Foote's flotilla of gun-boats. Ten regiments, with artillery and cavalry, and with three days' rations in their haversacks, embarked at Cairo, and, preceded by the gun-boats, reached Paducah on Monday, February 3d. The

next morning the fleet moored on the east bank of the Tennessee, nine miles below Fort Henry. A reconnoissance was then made to detect the presence of batteries, if there were any, along the bank, and to draw the fire of the fort for the purpose of ascertaining its range. While engaged on this reconnoissance, the Essex was pierced by a 32-pound shot. No serious injury was done, but a warning was received in regard to the inefficiency of this boat, which, originally employed as a ferry-boat at St. Louis, had been remodeled and fitted up as a gun-boat. That night the troops, having landed from the transports, were encamped at Bailey's Ferry, between three and four miles north of the fort, having their encampment on an elevated ridge running parallel with the river. Wednesday was spent on both sides in making preparations. When the Federal troops landed at Bailey's Ferry, General Tilghman, commanding the fort, was absent at Fort Donelson, but, having received information of the Federal approach, he immediately returned. Colonel Heiman, in the mean time, had guarded the approach to Fort Henry, on the Dover road, with two pieces of artillery. The garrison of Fort Henry at this time—Tuesday night—consisted of little more than 2500 men. These, together with the force on the Dover road, made an army of 3200 men. It was palpably impossible to hold the position against a formidable attack. The situation of the fort itself was very unfavorable. Occupying a position not high enough above the river to be secure against the violence of the spring freshets, it was surrounded on all sides by elevated positions, which, once gained by the enemy, enfiladed its own defenses. One of these, on the opposite bank, Fort Heiman, was thought so important that it had been occupied by a small force, and had been partially fortified. On Wednesday morning two Tennessee regiments were added to the garrison, and the force at Fort Heiman was recalled. A sudden rise of the river made the situation still more unfavorable for the Confederates. It not being possible to hold the commanding positions to which we have alluded, the Confederate force was concentrated within its intrenched camp, abandoning the outer series of rifle-pits.

The day passed by without an attack. General Grant was waiting for his re-enforcements to come up from Cairo. Reconnoissances, however, were made by the Federals on the road to Dover, which led Tilghman to believe that the main portion of Grant's land forces was to be sent against Fort Donelson. It was this supposition alone which determined him to remain and abide the issues of a battle. But on Thursday morning he was undeceived. Grant had, the previous night, issued his order for Commodore Foote to attack the fort on Thursday at eleven o'clock. His plan of co-operation was to march one column, consisting of eleven regiments of McClernand's division, to a point between Forts Henry and Donelson, on the Dover road, and another, consisting of ten regiments, under General C. F. Smith, to Fort Heiman, on the west bank; both columns to advance simultaneously with the gun-boats.

Seven gun-boats—the Essex, Carondelet, Cincinnati, St. Louis, Conestoga, Tyler, and Lexington, participated in the engagement. Four of these were partially iron-clad, the Essex being less perfectly inclosed in plates than the rest. These four formed the first line of the advance on Thursday. At half past ten the boats got under way, and the prompt and gallant commodore repeated his instructions to his men. The other three iron-clads were to keep in line with the flag-ship Cincinnati. It was urged upon the officers and men that it was of the greatest importance that they should keep cool during the engagement, and fire with slowness and deliberation, both to prevent heating the guns and random firing, and also to avoid unnecessary waste of ammunition. Somewhat more than a mile north of the fort Panther Island is situated. Thus there were two channels of approach; the one on the east side being commanded by the guns of the fort, while the other, more shallow, was covered by the island. Obstructions which had been placed in the latter had been partially removed, and the high water enabled the boats to pass over those which remained without injury. Steaming up this passage slowly, so as to allow the troops on the two banks time to get into position, the four iron-clads finally appeared at the head of the island, with the three other boats closely following in their rear. Under cover of the island, they had entirely escaped the long-range fire from the fort. They now took up a position and opened upon the fort, the three boats in the rear firing over those in front. Neither the fort nor the gun-boats were able to use their entire armament, the former, out of seventeen guns, only manning eleven, while only the same number were used by the latter out of seventy-five. The Confederates had twelve guns commanding the river: one ten-inch columbiad, one rifled 24-pounder, two 42-pounders, and eight 32-pounders.

Before the bombardment had fairly commenced, Tilghman, becoming aware of Grant's movements on his right and left flanks—for such, in fact, were the movements of McClernand and Smith—disappointed and alarmed, immediately determined upon the retreat of the main body of his small army, before these operations, which would render escape impossible, should have been completed. There was no time to lose, and there was but a single avenue of retreat. In a few minutes the attack of the gun-boats would render the intrenched camp untenable, as fully two thirds of it was exposed to their fire. There was no chance of holding the fort against the preparations which Tilghman saw being made against it, and the only object of an engagement on his part would be to give time to his retreating columns. Accordingly, the order for their withdrawal to Fort Donelson was given, only the heavy artillery, with about seventy men, being left in Fort Henry. While this movement was being executed under Colonel Heiman, and the gun-boats were commencing their attack on the fort, McClernand's division was slowly making its way through the woods, and through the mud which was the result of a storm on the previous night. But for this impediment

FOOTE'S GUN-BOATS ASCENDING TO ATTACK FORT HENRY.

W. D. PORTER.

the retreat of the Confederates would have been cut off and the investiture of the fort rendered complete.

The bombardment, however, proceeded successfully, the first shot being fired at half past twelve o'clock. There was no cessation in the firing, and every shot from the boats made its impression on the fort, upon which Foote concentrated his entire fire, leaving the movements going on in the rear to General Grant, who, as we have seen, was unavoidably behindhand. The action on both sides was carried on with great spirit. A single 80-pound shell disabled every one of the Confederates at one gun, and the bursting of another produced a similar catastrophe. Neither were the gun-boats unharmed. The Essex received a shot which penetrated her starboard boiler, and, filling the boat with steam, scalded her captain, W. D. Porter, and several of the crew, and she was compelled, disabled, to drift down the stream. The remaining gun-boats continued their fire, and steadily approached to within a thousand yards of the fort, and, after a hot engagement, lasting a little over an hour, achieved the victory. Tilghman had held out until all but four of his guns were disabled and the walls of the fort were giving way, when he pulled down his flag and surrendered the fort. This stubborn resistance had been prolonged to allow the main body under Heiman time to effect its retreat. Sixty-two prisoners were surrendered with the fort, among whom were twelve commissioned and six non-commissioned officers. Tilghman, who had been induced to remain to keep up the courage of his men, and who surrendered with them, was a stout man, and courteous in his manners, though of a somewhat haughty air. He was a graduate of West Point. On the occasion of his capitulation he expressed to the commodore his willingness to surrender to so brave a man. Foote replied, "You do perfectly right in surrendering; but you should have blown me out of the water before I would have surrendered to you."

From the extent of the outworks of Fort Henry, it was evidently the intention of the Confederates to re-enforce it very strongly. The rapidity, however, with which the Federal commanders proceeded to attack, prevented this re-enforcement; and it was only the failure of General Grant to move his land forces with the requisite promptness that allowed the Confederates to escape. A pursuit was ordered, and the rear of the enemy overtaken, but nothing was gained except a few prisoners who had lagged behind on account of exhaustion, and several pieces of light artillery.

The capture of Fort Henry opened the Tennessee River to the Federal gun-boats up to the head of navigation at Florence, in Northern Alabama. Immediately after the surrender, Lieutenant S. L. Phelps, commanding the Conestoga, proceeded up the river, accompanied by the Tyler and Lexington. About twelve miles south of the fort the Memphis and Ohio Railroad from Bowling Green crosses the river, after which it continues southeast to McKenzie, and from this point communication is established with Columbus by a branch road running northwest through Union City. The main road is continued from McKenzie on to Memphis. The connection, therefore, between Bowling Green and both Columbus and Memphis depended on the railroad bridge across the Tennessee. This point was reached by Phelps a little after dark, and not only was the draw closed, but the machinery for turning it had been disabled. At the same moment, several Confederate transports were half a mile above the bridge, trying to escape up stream. A party was landed, and it took an hour to open the draw; then, the Tyler being left behind to destroy the railroad, the other two boats gave chase to the transports. Some of the latter were laden with military stores, and these had to be abandoned and fired; the concussion produced by the explosion of considerable quantities of gunpowder on board broke the skylights of the Conestoga, and raised the light upper deck from its fastenings. The house of a Union man living on the river bank was blown to pieces by the force of the explosion. Proceeding up the river to Cerro Gordo, in Hardin County, a Confederate steamer, which was being converted into a gun-boat,

ALABAMA LOYALISTS GREETING THE FEDERAL GUN-BOATS.

was captured the next day, and the day after two more at Eastport. Florence, at the foot of the Muscle Shoal, was the natural terminus of the expedition. Here a deputation of citizens waited on the lieutenant deprecating violence, and especially praying that their railroad bridge might not be destroyed. As there was no military motive to the destruction of the bridge, the request was granted. The expedition then returned. The most important feature connected with it was the exhibition, all along the route, of the Union sentiment of the people. Lieutenant Phelps, in his report, says: "We have met with the most gratifying proofs of loyalty every where across Tennessee, and in the portions of Mississippi and Alabama which we visited. Most affecting instances greeted us almost hourly. Men, women, and children, several times gathered in crowds of hundreds, shouted their welcome, and hailed their national flag with an enthusiasm there was no mistaking; it was genuine and heartfelt."

Forts Henry and Donelson, although miles in the rear of Columbus and Bowling Green, were the front and centre of the Confederate line. Henry had been captured. It only remained to carry the works at Donelson, and the centre was broken. Johnston held, and now knew that he held, a wretched line of defense. It stretched from Bowling Green to Columbus, 120 miles; was protected by less than 50,000 men; at its central position, which was as weak as it was accessible, there could not be brought up in time to be of use one third of that number. Time had from the first been a master element in this campaign. The President's Military Order had contemplated the value of moments. It was not an order to move simply, or to prepare to move, but to move at once, even with an uncompleted armament. And after the movement had begun, time still controlled the chances and results. When Tilghman saw what was the disposition of the Federal forces on the forenoon of the 6th, he knew that he could not hold Fort Henry; yet, only to gain two hours and ten minutes, he risked an engagement, and lost twenty-one men killed and wounded, besides sixty prisoners. Those two hours' fighting netted him a profit of full 3000 men. The mud, which hindered Grant's troops moving on his flank, helped him to this result. And, now that Henry was captured, very much depended on the rapidity with which a blow could be struck at Donelson. Every day wasted amplified the defensive works of that fort, and brought behind them thousands more of defenders.

The gun-boats, however, had to be consulted in this matter of speed. It was thought impossible to do without them; they had taken Henry, and it was intended that they should play the most important part in taking Donelson. But Commodore Foote wanted time, the very thing which could not be spared. The Essex and the Cincinnati had been worsted on the 6th, and were in no condition to fight again. Of the iron-clads only the St. Louis and the Carondelet remained intact. It is true, the places of the two injured boats could be filled by others, but Fort Donelson was incomparably superior to Fort Henry in the resistance it would offer. More boats were needed; at least the two disabled ones ought to be repaired. While Foote protested on these grounds against an immediate attack on Donelson, Halleck and Grant insisted upon it as a military necessity. With the most rapid movement possible, much precious time would be consumed. The troops for Fort Henry had started with only three days' rations; the army must

FORT DONELSON, TENNESSEE.

be newly supplied. The prisoners, the sick, and the wounded must be attended to; new boats must be brought round from Cairo, also transports with re-enforcements; and, before the army at Fort Henry could move over from the Tennessee to the Cumberland, provision must be made for a change of base.

Tilghman had surrendered Fort Henry on Thursday; it was not until the next Wednesday, the 12th, that Grant had his entire column in motion toward Donelson, though a great portion of McClernand's division had moved the previous day. Here was a delay of six days, which, though necessary, was very costly. The distance between the two forts was twelve miles, over thickly wooded hills, broken by deep ravines, which, near the rivers, were choked with back-water. The roads were good, the weather pleasant and mild. The two main divisions of the army, McClernand's and Smith's, moved in separate columns; the strength of both, in round numbers, amounting to 20,000 men, including seventeen batteries, and from 1200 to 1500 horsemen. In the march, as in subsequent operations, McClernand kept to Smith's right. The two commands were in communication with each other early in the afternoon, within two miles of the fort. The rest of the day was occupied in manœuvring the troops into position, which was attended with slight skirmishing here and there, to test the enemy's strength and to find his line of works, a matter of great difficulty from the nature of the ground. The Confederate pickets and outstanding forces were pushed back to their defenses, and the Federal forces rested for the night on a line in general parallelism with that of the enemy. During the night batteries were posted in the most favorable position then accessible. It was General Grant's design to make an assault the next day simultaneously with the gun-boats.

Donelson was stronger, both by nature and art, than Henry. The position was a more commanding one, and it was more strongly fortified. The course of the Cumberland from Dover, where Fort Donelson was situated, toward its mouth, was almost due north; but just before reaching the town, and in passing it, westward. Upon a bluff, rising by a gentle slope from the river, just at the bend, to the height of a hundred feet, the State of Tennessee had built Fort Donelson. The fort was on the south, or left bank, its water batteries, from an elevation of thirty feet, commanding the river as far as their guns could reach. Back of the fort extended a *plateau* of a hundred acres; a deep gorge broke the bluff toward the south. The town of Dover, lying just above on the river, was also on an elevation, separated from the plateau on which the fort was situated by a long valley, filled to a considerable depth with back-water from the Cumberland. The country for miles around is uneven; not mountainous, but hilly and heavily timbered. The numerous elevations that diversify the surface terminate in bluffs, whose abrupt and precipitous sides, difficult of access even to the nimble goat, lead down into rough-looking ravines. The timber on the hills immediately skirting the lines of defense had been cut down by the Confederates to secure a full sweep for artillery, and to form an extensive abattis-work obstructing the approach. To return to the fort. The table-land on which it lay was the work of art, the ground having been leveled to afford room for the fortifications and rifle-pits, which covered the entire space. By ravines along its

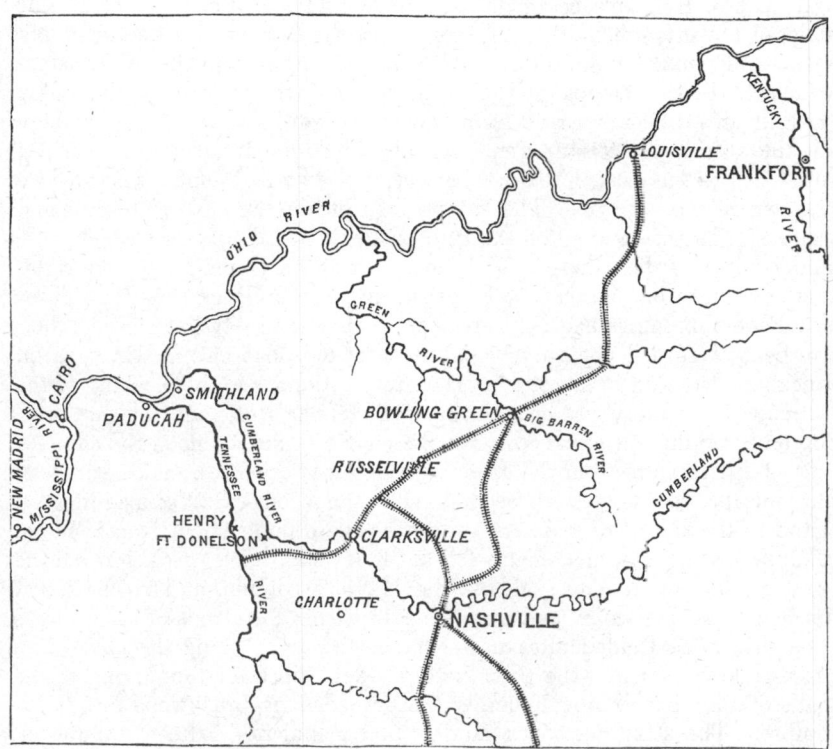

MAP ILLUSTRATING THE WESTERN CAMPAIGN IN FEBRUARY, 1862.

boundary the *tableau* was separated from a series of wooded hills, whose distance from the fortified line was about 800 yards.

The unfavorable feature of the defense was that the fort was so easily commanded by these neighboring ridges.

It was not until the middle of December that prominent attention was directed to the works at Henry and Donelson. "On reaching Donelson," says Tilghman, who was sent there at that time, "I found at my disposal six undisciplined companies of infantry, with an unorganized light battery, while a small water battery of two light guns constituted the available river defense. Four 32-pounders had been rightly placed, but were not available." With two forts on his hands, Tilghman found his time for preparation short. By the 25th of January, when re-enforcements were being brought up in anticipation of attack, the batteries had been completed, and a field-work, with a trace of 1000 yards, had been built in the rear of the fort, and the work of protecting the approaches by rifle-pits had been commenced. Two weeks later Fort Henry was surrendered, and the vital importance of Donelson, covering the approach to Nashville, seemed for the first time to be thoroughly understood. Beauregard and Johnston were in anxious consultation, and it was concluded between them that Nashville must be defended at Donelson—that the best engineers and the ablest generals should be sent to the fort, and all the re-enforcements which could be spared should be hurried up with all possible dispatch.

On the evening of the 6th, Heiman's command, 3000 strong, entered Donelson, with the not highly encouraging reminiscence of Foote's gun-boat fleet still clinging to them. This was the main force then occupying the defenses. Three Tennessee regiments were placed in the fort, constituting a garrison of about 1600 men. The re-enforcements which, during the next week, arrived at Donelson, came mostly from Bowling Green by railroad. General Bushrod R. Johnson came up on the 8th, and took the command until the arrival of Pillow on the 10th.

Pillow found the works incomplete. Two heavy guns for the water battery were yet unmounted; the works in the rear were deficient both in extent and strength, and competent artillerists were lacking. It was late to make these discoveries; but prompt measures were taken to supply all deficiencies, the soldiers working in their trenches day and night. Even the tools necessary for this kind of work were so scarce that they had to be passed from one regiment to another. In the mean time artillery companies were being exercised in the use of their guns. For three days the soldiers were at work constructing rifle-pits along the first line of heights, including within its crescent the fort and water batteries, with the field-work in their rear, and also the town of Dover, which it became now an imperative necessity to defend, since it had been made a dépôt for supplies.

On the night of the 11th Buckner came to hand, and was placed in command of the right, near the fort. Bushrod Johnson held the left, near Dover. Between the two, prominently advanced on a strong position on the left centre, was Heiman's command. The space to be defended was a quadrangle, lined by the Cumberland on the north, by two pretty large creeks on the east and west, and on the south by the outer line of rifle-pits. The quadrangle was intersected by the wide stream of back-water running between the fort and Dover, which divided the right from the left, making it difficult to manœuvre one division in support of another; a great disadvantage, considering the length of the line—nearly three miles. This line, distant from the river from 400 to 1200 yards, was only one third completed on Wednesday morning, when Grant started from Fort Henry.

The re-enforcements came to Donelson came in by detachments, some of them so tardily that they came near being left out altogether. Buckner's division, with the exception of one regiment, was all in before the 12th of February. The Second Kentucky came in with B. R. Johnson on the 8th; Brown's brigade on the 8th and 10th. Floyd's division, which, after its reverses in West Virginia, had been sent to Tennessee, was the last to arrive. His force

consisted of four Virginia and one Mississippi regiment, and was distributed into two brigades—Wharton's and McCausland's, to which a portion of Baldwin's brigade of Buckner's division was temporarily attached. Floyd had received the order to re-enforce Donelson on the 12th. He had already, on the 7th and 8th, sent on Wharton, but was hesitating about the policy of dispatching the rest of his division. From Clarksville, on the 12th, he wrote to Johnston, urging that the main portion of the defensive force should be concentrated at Cumberland City, "leaving at Fort Donelson enough to make all possible resistance to any attack which might be made upon the fort, but no more." He thought that the character of the country made it dangerous to concentrate the entire army in the fort, and that a large body at Cumberland City should flank the Federal army attacking the fort. He also advocated the obstruction of the river to make it impassable for gun-boats.

Whatever wisdom there may have been in these suggestions, they were too late to be applicable to the occasion. Grant was already within two miles of the fort, and Floyd had hardly dispatched his letter to Johnston before peremptory orders came from the latter to advance his force immediately. Floyd had been anxious to secure the adoption of his plan; and on the 11th, when Buckner left him to join Pillow, he carried to the latter an order from Floyd for the concentration of Buckner's and his own divisions at Cumberland City. Upon a consultation between Pillow and Floyd the plan was changed, and the morning of the 13th found Floyd's whole force inside of the Confederate intrenchments. The same morning also the Forty-first and Forty-second Tennessee arrived. On this Thursday morning the defensive army probably numbered at least 15,000 men.[1]

On Thursday, the day set for the attack, there was but little disparity between the opposing forces; what there was favored the Federals, but it did not amount at most to more than 3000 or 4000 men. The gun-boats and transports not arriving according to appointment, another twenty-four hours' grace was given the Confederates, of which they sedulously took advantage. Federal artillery was placed on the spurs opposing the lines of defense; McClernand's division was brought up as nearly as possible to the south of Dover, so as to command the river road to Charlotte, the main outlet for escape in that direction. Oglesby's brigade held the extreme right, supported on the left by W. H. L. Wallace; Smith's division was drawn up on the left. Skirmishers had the day almost entirely to themselves. Among those on the Federal side the most famous were Birge's regiment of sharpshooters, each one of whom, in gray uniform and gray felt cap, watched from behind his stump for the appearance of Confederate heads above their defenses. The distance between these keen-eyed watchers on one side and on the other was only about 300 yards. The fire was so incessant and so fatal that the Confederates were allowed no rest except in their uncomfortable rifle-ditches, it being impossible for them to reach their tents over the ridge without exposure. These ditches, with the earth-work in front, had been, as Floyd plaintively intimates in his report, carelessly, because hastily, constructed so far from the ridge as to compel this exposure.

The great event of the day was the gallant but useless assault made by three Illinois regiments—the Seventeenth, Forty-eighth, and Forty-ninth—supported by two others, on an advanced position of Heiman's. The Forty-eighth belonged to W. H. L. Wallace's brigade, the others to Payne's. When Wallace moved in the morning to the support of Oglesby, Colonel Hayne, with the Forty-eighth, had been left near the centre in support of a battery; 500 yards to his right were posted the Seventeenth and Forty-ninth, under Colonel Morrison. Hayne moved his regiment up to these, and, assuming the command of all three at Morrison's request, prepared to storm the redoubt in their front. This redoubt, separated from them by a wooded valley, formed Heiman's right centre. Heiman's position was an elevation shaped like a V in contour. On either side a valley separated his brigade from Buckner on the right, and on the left from Drake's brigade, which occupied another elevation, and which we have hitherto considered

---

[1] In the estimate of the number of men defending Donelson the Confederate accounts are various. Lieutenant F. H. Duquecron, one of the officers engaged, reports the number as 18,000. This also was the estimate given in an account of the battle by the *Richmond Dispatch.* He ought to have had some opportunity of knowing; he belonged to the Fourteenth Mississippi, which reached Dover from Bowling Green on the 9th, and was present until Saturday noon, when he received a wound in the leg. Contrary to this is Pillow's report, which puts the number at only 13,000. The *Nashville Patriot,* in the corrected copy of its list of casualties at Donelson, gives the following estimate of the numbers engaged:

48th Tenn.	230	3d Tenn.	650 (750)	3d Miss.	500
42d "	498	51st "	80	4th "	535
53d "	280	50th "	650	14th "	475
49th "	300	2d Ky.	618	20th "	562
30th "	654	8th "	300	26th "	434 (443)
18th "	615 (685)	7th Tex.	300	50th Va.	400
10th "	750	15th Ark.	270	51st "	275
26th "	400	27th Ala.	216	56th "	350
41st "	450 (575)	1st Miss.	280	36th "	250
32d "	558 (555)				
					11,480 (11,781)

Battalions of infantry: Colin's and Gowan's.......................... 330
Battalions of cavalry: Gantt's... 227 (800)
Milton's.. 15
Forrest's..................................... 600 (1200)
Artillerists... 677
————— 1,849 (2,922)

Total.............................. 13,329 (14,703)

The numbers in the parentheses are corrections made from the reports of Confederate officers. Wherever these reports give numbers at all, they, save in one instance, exceed the corresponding ones in the list. It is fair, then, to presume that where no number is given there would also be an increase. It is certainly evident that Pillow understated his force; and it is possible that Duquecron's would, if all the data were known, prove much nearer the truth. Two things should be remembered in this connection. One is, that, on account of hurry of preparation, so urgent as to forbid the ordinary roll-call in the morning, and also by reason of the irregularity with which re-enforcements came in, as well as the confusion consequent upon the surrender, no actual estimate was made. Floyd, when questioned by the Confederate Secretary of War, was entirely ignorant of the strength of his command. It is also to be remembered that, as a rule, Confederate reports studiously underestimate the forces engaged on that side. The estimate which we have given in the text is the one given by the Confederate Lieutenant Colonel Gilmer, chief engineer of the Western Department.

INTERIOR OF WATER BATTERY AT FORT DONELSON.

as a part of Heiman's command. Heiman's advanced salient was, at this stage of the investment, the only portion of the Confederate line distinctly visible. From this point the enemy's cannon had sweep of the valley across which the Federal troops filed in approaching Dover. Through the valley on Heiman's right ran a road from Dover westward to the Tennessee; here the line of rifle-pits was broken. On this side Heiman had two regiments; in the centre was posted Maney's battery, with two regiments, supported by another on the left side. The battery was on the summit of the hill and exposed. It was opposed on the 12th by two Federal batteries, which were under cover of the woods, one of them bearing on Heiman from the right, and the other from the left, the latter bearing also on Buckner's left. These two Federal batteries had kept up a bombardment all day Wednesday, their fire being returned not only by Maney's battery, but also by Graves's on Buckner's left, and by another at Drake's position. On the morning of the 13th another battery was brought against Heiman's left, and the one bearing on his right was advanced. In the course of the forenoon the advance line of skirmishers from the Illinois troops was observed making its way through the woods. Maney began to shell the woods; Graves also kept up a fire to the right, the gunners suffering severe punishment from Federal sharpshooters. Two lieutenants fell at Maney's in quick succession, but the guns were kept in play. Meanwhile Hayne's column, at 11 o'clock, had pushed across the valley and up the hill to within forty rods of the enemy's rifle-pits. The Confederates now commenced firing along the entire line from 2000 rifles, while the three batteries kept up their thundering. The path of the approaching Federals was impeded by brushwood and fallen timber. The slaughter was abundant and merciless. Fifteen minutes of this deadly work seemed enough for endurance that in the end only promised to be bootless. The brave Illinoisans began to give way. Then they rallied again, and were repulsed; and still again, when they finally withdrew, having been under fire for nearly an hour. Colonel Morrison was severely wounded in the action, and carried from the field.

Somewhat farther to the left, and at about the same time, a less formidable though equally gallant assault was made by a portion of Lauman's brigade, the fourth of General Smith's division. This brigade consisted of four regiments, together with which Birge's Sharpshooters were associated. On Lauman's right front Cavender's 20-pound rifled Parrots had been placed in a position commanding a portion of the enemy's works, the Seventh Iowa and Birge's regiment acting as support. This had been the position on the evening of Wednesday. Thursday morning two regiments—the Fourteenth Iowa and the Twenty-fifth Indiana—were ordered to assault the Confederate line one mile from their front. The movement was over rugged ground. In the wooded ravine just beneath the position to be assailed the line was formed. The Twenty-fifth Indiana then moved up the hill, "under a most galling fire of musketry and grape," says Lauman, "until their onward progress was obstructed by the fallen timber and brushwood." A position was gained and held at a severe cost in life for two hours, when the regiment was ordered back out of range. In the mean time the Fourteenth Iowa had crossed a ravine and gained a position away to the right, which it held to some purpose, while Lieutenant Parrott, who, with the Seventh, was supporting the Cavender Parrotts, came up between the two assailing columns, holding the centre. This position was held by Lauman's brigade till night. In addition to these assaults, a heavy cannonade was kept up all day, and nearly all night firing was continued, keeping the Confederates under arms in their trenches.

Thursday night, the weather, which had previously been genial for February, began to be cold and disagreeable; a storm of snow, mingled with sleet, caused great suffering among the troops. The change was so sudden that evidently no preparation had been made for it.

There was yet no sign of any of the gun-boats except the Carondelet, which reached Donelson on the 12th, and the next day gave the enemy a foretaste of good things to come by sending upward of one hundred and fifty shells into the fort. This was on the morning of the 13th, and was intended to aid the assaults made at that time on portions of the Confederate line. The enemy returned the fire with spirit, but most of their guns shot over the gun-boat, only two striking; one of these, a 128-pound shot, passed through the port casemate of the Carondelet, burst her steam-heater, and fell into the engine-room. No one, however, was seriously injured. During this engagement, which lasted about an hour, the Confederate Captain Dixon, of the Engineer Corps, was killed at the battery. As to the other boats besides the Carondelet, thus: Tuesday night, before Grant had left Fort Henry, the steamer Minnehaha, with Colonel Baldwin and his regiment, the Fifty-seventh Illinois, on board, came up to the fort, and transports with reenforcements were following after. These transports Grant ordered, through Baldwin, to be turned back to Paducah, whence they were to start under convoy of the gun-boat fleet for Smithland, and thence up the Cumberland to a point a few miles below Donelson, where they were to land the re-enforcements the next afternoon. The Minnehaha started down the Tennessee at midnight, and reached Paducah early the next morning, having met on the way eight or ten transports loaded with troops. But it was found that only a part of the fleet were at Paducah; the remainder straggled slowly up; and it was ten o'clock on Wednesday night when the whole armament arrived at the mouth of the Cumberland.

"The scene," writes the *Times* correspondent, "was magnificent beyond description. The night was as warm as an evening in August in our more northern latitudes; a full moon looked down from an unclouded sky, and glanced off from bayonets, plumes, and sword-hilts without number. At intervals long jets of fleecy smoke burst out along the parapets of the two forts on the heights overlooking the town, and the boom of the welcome went reverberating over the hills, till from the long distances in Kentucky it came back like a whisper. In turns the bands on the boats charmed the ear with most eloquent music, which, added to the effect of scores of gayly-dressed ladies promenading the upper decks, gave the scene more the character of some vast drawing-room gathering; so much like was it, that no one would have been surprised had the whole crowd suddenly resolved into eddies of whirling waltzes, or the swift, changeful currents of quadrille or gallopade."

The progress of the fleet, slow enough hitherto, now began to be impeded by the downward current of the Cumberland. Forty-five miles only were made in nine hours. This brought the fleet to Eddyville, where it was greeted with vociferous demonstrations of loyalty; one gray-haired man was so affected at hearing "Yankee Doodle," that he took off his hat and gave three cheers for the Union. At midnight, Thursday, the armament reached its destination. It consisted of six gun-boats and fourteen transports. From the latter a column of 10,000 men were landed, bringing Grant's army up to 30,000 strong. These fresh troops were General Lew. Wallace's division, consisting of regiments from Ohio, Indiana, Kentucky, and Nebraska. The landing was about three miles below the fort. The distance to be traversed by these troops before they could reach McClernand's left was very great, and the march could only be accomplished by means of a circuitous route, which, avoiding the back-water west of the fort, ran around by Smith's rear along the ridges held by the Federal army. In this way it happened that Lew. Wallace's men were all day Friday getting into position.

This delay led to a new disappointment. It had been intended that, as early as possible in the day, a combined attack should be made by the gun-boats on the water batteries and by the land forces on the rear. In the latter part of the programme the new troops were given an important part, but their necessarily tardy movements prevented any operations on Friday by Grant's army except the usual skirmishing and cannonade.

The gun-boats, however, steamed up the river, and at three o'clock P.M. commenced the attack. They were six in number. Four—the St. Louis, Carondelet, Louisville, and Pittsburg—were iron-clad, each mounting thirteen guns; the other two, the Tyler and Conestoga, were wooden, mounting each nine guns. There was one boat less than the number at Fort Henry, and the conditions of the conflict were materially altered. The armament of Fort Donelson was greater than that at Fort Henry. Besides eight pieces in the main fort, there were the two batteries, mounting thirteen guns. Then, again, the water batteries at Fort Henry were of no use on account of their inferior position; those at Donelson, on the other hand, were elevated thirty or forty feet above the river. Remembering, therefore, that at Fort Henry two of his iron-clads had been disabled, it is hardly possible that Commodore Foote entered upon this engagement without serious apprehensions regarding the result. He had discovered the vulnerable points of his gun-boats, but, before he had leisure to fortify them, he was called upon to expose them again to danger.

As at Fort Henry, the wooden boats kept well to the rear of the iron-clads, which steamed up to the fort in the form of a crescent, opening fire at a distance of a mile and a half. The Confederate batteries did not reply until the boats were within point-blank range of their guns. Only twelve bow-guns could be brought to bear from the fleet; the enemy, from the fort and the batteries, worked nearly twice that number. The fleet moved slowly up into closer and closer combat, until it reached a point only about 300 yards (Pillow says 150) from the Confederate guns. Foote probably hoped that close range would make his fire more effective. From where he stood he could have reached with his shot and shell nearly every spot within the Confederate lines. But he had no time to regard the opportunity, tempting as it was. These heavy guns, belching out ruin against the sides of his vessels, must be attended to first of all. Already the shot from a ten-inch columbiad and a rifled 32-pounder were beginning to tell on his boats, and Pillow was carefully watching their effect. But the fire from the fleet also was beginning to drive the gunners from their post; only give the gun-boats fifteen minutes more, and the victory would be theirs. But just at this critical moment "two unlucky shots"[1] turned the tide. One, penetrating the pilot-house and mortally wounding the pilot, carried away the wheel of the St. Louis; the other disabled the tiller-ropes of the Louisville, and both vessels drifted helplessly down the stream. The frightened gunners returned to their batteries and redoubled their efforts, and soon the Pittsburg and the Carondelet followed their retiring comrades. After a fight of an hour and a half the gun-boats had been defeated with a loss of fifty-four killed and wounded; among the latter was the commodore himself, whose foot was seriously injured. A portion of the casualties was due to the bursting of a rifled gun on board the Carondelet. The Confederate batteries, well protected and well served, were essentially uninjured; according to the report of Gilmer, the Confederate chief engineer, not a man in them was killed. The wooden gun-boats, as has been said, participated in the battle only at long range, and threw curveting shell, which, passing over the Confederate works, exploded in the air above them; on board these boats there were no casualties. It may have somewhat contributed to the defeat of the gun-boats that, in the excitement natural to a situation of more imminent peril, their guns were not worked with the deliberation which more than any thing else secured success for them at Fort Henry.[2]

---

[1] General Grant's Report.
[2] Foote's great difficulty for some weeks had been that he was unable to get enough men to man his gun-boats. Thus, when he was about to move against Fort Henry, he says in a letter to Secretary Welles,

"I have been obliged, for want of men, to take from the five boats remaining at Cairo all the men, except a sufficient number to man one gun-boat for the protection of that important post. . . . . . It is peculiarly unfortunate that we have not been able to obtain men for the flotilla, as

GUN-BOAT ATTACK ON FORT DONELSON.

After the attack, the cessation of which was like the clearing up of a thunder-storm, a consultation was held between Foote and Grant, in which it was decided that the former should return to Cairo to prepare a more formidable fleet, while General Grant should complete his investiture of Donelson. To prevent Columbus from re-enforcing Donelson, the Tyler was sent around to complete the destruction of the railroad bridge just above Fort Henry. Phelps's expedition of the previous week had failed, it seems, of doing its work thoroughly at this important point. The St. Louis and the Louisville were yet in a condition to remain, and it being thought necessary to keep up a show of force, or, at the least, to protect the transports, they did remain. The next day they steamed up the river and threw a few shells into the fort; but the only serious attack made by the gun-boats was that of the 14th.

Floyd, who as senior officer assumed the chief command on his arrival, had inferred, from the close pressure of the Federal troops up to his lines, and from the pertinacity of their assaults on Thursday, that he would certainly be attacked by Grant's whole army Friday morning. We have seen already how he came to be disappointed. All the forenoon he waited in vain; there was nothing but the usual skirmishing. Doubt made the Confederate commander restless, for something on one side or the other must be done quickly. If Grant would not fight him, then he must fight Grant. Of the two alternatives he very much preferred the former, remembering the assaults of yesterday; every repetition of these assaults exhausted the assailant. At last, after waiting nearly all day, the matter was decided for him; at three o'clock the gun-boats attacked in front, but the accompaniment of assault in the rear was not forthcoming. The gun-boats were driven away disabled, beaten. But, in spite of the shouts of victory arising from the two water batteries, Floyd had been disappointed. "I was satisfied," he says, "from the incidents of the last two days, that the enemy did not intend again to give us battle in our trenches. They had been fairly repulsed, with very heavy slaughter, upon every effort to storm our position, and it was but fair to infer that they would not again renew the unavailing attempt at our dislodgment, when certain means to effect the same end without loss were perfectly at their command. We were aware of the fact that extremely heavy re-enforcements had been continually arriving, day and night, for three days and nights,[1] and I had no doubt whatever that their whole available force on the Western waters could and would be concentrated here, if it was deemed necessary, to reduce our position. There was no place within our intrenchments but could be reached by the enemy's artillery from their boats or their batteries. It was but fair to infer that, while they kept up a sufficient fire upon our intrenchments to keep our men from sleep and prevent repose, their object was merely to give time to pass a column above us on the river, both on the right and left banks, and thus to cut off all our communication, and to prevent the possibility of egress."

It was Floyd's policy, therefore, to fight the enemy at the earliest possible moment. But it was too late to accomplish any thing that day. A little after dark, at Floyd's summons, all the division and brigade commanders of the Confederate army were gathered together for consultation at General Pillow's head-quarters. It was then and there unanimously agreed that an attack should be made, in accordance with Floyd's proposition, the next morning, for the purpose of cutting their way out into the open country southward. It fell upon Pillow and Buckner to plan the attack. The situation to be considered was this: there were three roads leading southward from Dover. One of these closely skirted the river for a distance of twelve or fifteen miles, then branched off toward Charlotte. Another ran farther to the west, connecting with the former road and also with Charlotte. The third, still farther west, is mentioned in the Confederate reports as the Wynn's Ferry road. Across these roads stood Oglesby's and W. H. L. Wallace's brigades—in fact, the great body of McClernand's division. Lew. Wallace's division held the ridge on the left of the Wynn's Ferry road. Every one of these roads was strongly fortified by Grant with 24-pound siege guns. In order to secure a retreat, Grant's right must be defeated and rolled up on his centre. But how dispose the forces for this attack? This was the great difficulty. Pillow's force alone, estimated by himself at 7000, including Floyd's, was incompetent for such a task; it was necessary that the great bulk of the three corps under Floyd, Pillow, and Buckner should be massed against the Federal right. Yet the proposition submitted by Pillow was that Buckner should lend him Hanson's Second Kentucky regiment, and that, with this and the troops already intrenched on the left, he (Pillow) would roll up Grant's right to a point opposite Buckner, where the latter should attack in flank and rear, and the enemy be driven to his gun-boats. A very satisfactory operation, if it could be accomplished. But one thing the over-sanguine Pillow had lost sight of in his calculations: if he should fail in his part, as most probably he must, then the battle would have been ventured in vain. Buckner, demurring to this impossible plan, had one of his own to suggest, which certainly was wiser, though it was doubtful if any more good would come out of it than from Pillow's. His plan was, that, leaving a regiment or two in his intrenchments on the right, he would move his command up near to Pillow's, and, while the latter attacked Grant's right, he would attack the right centre, "and, if successful, take up a position in advance of the works on the Wynn's Ferry road, to cover the retreat of the whole army." Buckner also lost sight of the fact that, in leaving his lines on the left, he left them open to the enemy. But this circumstance was of no serious moment except in the event of a failure in the main assault; but in that very possible event all would be lost! General Buckner's plan prevailed.

The night which followed—that of Friday—was as bitterly cold as the preceding. The next morning opened with a cold and cheerless sky. Pillow had ordered his men under arms at half past four, to march out of their works at five, more than an hour before light, but a halting brigade made the time of march fifteen minutes past five.

Baldwin's brigade, consisting of a Mississippi and a Tennessee regiment, had the advance, moving along the road west of the river road. A third of a mile on the march, and the enemy was found in some force. Baldwin found great difficulty in manœuvring. The Twenty-sixth Mississippi, in front, was three times broken up in disorder while deploying. On the left of the road was an open field of 400 or 500 acres, open to the enemy's fire. The Twenty-sixth Mississippi having been formed on the right, and the Twenty-sixth Tennessee filling up a gap still left between that regiment and the road, and also holding the road itself, Pillow sent the Twentieth Mississippi around to the left in the open field just mentioned, where it was only food for powder, and was soon afterward withdrawn. By this time Baldwin's right was re-enforced by the arrival of McCausland's Virginians and other regiments, while his left was strengthened by Wharton's brigade. Pillow's entire force operating against the Federal right was, at his own estimate, not less than 7000 strong.

The attack was wholly unexpected by the Federals, who were taken at considerable disadvantage. The several brigades of McClernand's division were very much detached from each other, and the difficulty of support was heightened by the masses of tangled brushwood, black-jack, and dense undergrowth of trees, which made the manœuvre troublesome. Opposed to the advancing column of attack was a portion of Oglesby's brigade, a few Illinois regiments, who held the road, inadequately supported by artillery.

At first the advanced Federal regiments occupied the crest of the hill at the foot of which Baldwin, McCausland, and Wharton were deploying their forces. The troops on both sides were mostly under cover of the woods—a circumstance which concealed the immense volume of the Confederate assault. Part way up the slope the Confederate column advanced and watched its opportunity, skirmishing and sharp-shooting, in the mean while, actively going on. Wharton tried to gain way in the open field on the left, but a storm of Minié balls kept him back. After an hour's skirmishing, the left of the column, under General Johnson, pushed up a ravine around to the left, flanking the Illinoisans, a dozen Confederate batteries in the mean while crashing the woods with their missiles. Hitherto Oglesby's favorable position had baffled the enemy's advance. The Confederate troops, many of them raw recruits, required "extraordinary exertions on the part of their field and company officers to prevent their being thrown back in confusion to their trenches."[1] But the movement to the left drove Oglesby's right back to another position. Here a determined attack was made, met by an equally determined resistance.

The battle extended along the lines, involving, at seven A.M., two regiments of W. H. L. Wallace's brigade, supporting Oglesby on the left. These were the Eleventh and Twentieth Illinois, under Ransom and Marsh. A Confederate column charged up the hill in their front, and gained the road—the one west of the river road—but were repulsed, giving way to a fresh line, which advanced boldly to repeat the assault. Wallace brought nearly his entire brigade, consisting of 3400 men, upon the hill, and, with the assistance of Taylor's and McAllister's batteries, again and again drove back the defiant foe.

It was now half past eight o'clock, and re-enforcements from the centre of the line, held by Lew. Wallace, were moving past to the extreme right, which, bent out of its original line, was yet obstinately disputing every step of ground. Lew. Wallace's division had been awakened in the morning by the noise of battle far away to their right, and had supposed that Oglesby was attacking the enemy. At eight o'clock a message came from McClernand asking for assistance. Wallace had been ordered to hold the centre at all risks, to prevent the enemy's escape in that direction. A messenger was dispatched to Grant's head-quarters, but the latter was on one of the gun-boats, consulting with Foote in regard to the possibilities of another naval attack. Lew. Wallace, receiving a second and more urgent message from McClernand, stating that his flank had already been turned, sent forthwith Colonel Cruft's brigade. This brigade, consisting of two Indiana and two Kentucky regiments, moved on to the woods beyond Taylor's battery, and nearly to the extreme right of the line. Here it became engaged with a column of the enemy emerging from a ravine in Oglesby's rear.

Oglesby's brigade, which had held on till the last, was now getting out of ammunition. Graves's battery, from the Confederate intrenchments, had now more effective range than it had had all the morning, and thinned the ranks at every discharge. In good order the brigade gave way, breaking through Cruft's line in its retreat, and leaving the latter fearfully exposed to the sweeping fire of the enemy's infantry and artillery. Cruft had been misled by his guide, and had taken a position too far to the right, which he was

---

they only are wanting to enable me to have at this moment eleven full-manned, instead of seven partially-manned, gun-boats ready for efficient operations at any point. The volunteers from the army to go in the gun-boats exceed the number of men required, but the derangement of companies and regiments, in permitting them to leave, is the reason assigned for not more than fifty of the number having been thus far transferred to the flotilla."

Again, starting for Donelson:

"I leave again to-night with the Louisville, Pittsburg, and St. Louis for the Cumberland River, to co-operate with the army in the attack on Fort Donelson. I go reluctantly, as we are very short of men, and transferring men from vessel to vessel, as we have to do, is having a very demoralizing effect upon them. Twenty-eight men ran off to-day (Feb. 11), hearing that they were again to be sent out of their vessels. I do hope that 600 men will be sent immediately. I shall do all in my power to render the gun-boats effective in the fight, although they are not properly manned; but I must go, as General Halleck wishes it. If we could wait ten days, *and I had men*, I could go with eight mortar boats and six armored boats."

[1] This was not true. The only considerable body of re-enforcements which had reached Grant by Friday night were Lew. Wallace's division. It was true, however, that Grant intended to complete the investment of Floyd's position, if it took 50,000 men to accomplish it.

[1] See Baldwin's Report.

soon compelled to abandon. Every thing now seemed to depend upon the steadfastness of W. H. L. Wallace's brigade. Upon his batteries, from three separate and commanding situations, the Confederate artillery was pouring its vials of wrath. Looking out upon his right hand, he could see Pillow's columns already pressing upon his rear. Between his brigade and them only a single regiment of Oglesby's command remained on the field. That regiment was the Thirty-first Illinois, commanded by Colonel John A. Logan, late a Congressman from Illinois, but who, at the beginning of the war, had resigned his seat for the colonelcy of this regiment. Colonel Logan had been wounded in the thigh, but he still kept his post. Having ordered the surgeon to dress his wound, he again went to the front, remarking that he had fired twenty-two rounds since his hurt, and he could fire at least as many more now that the wound was dressed. His regiment partook of his dauntless spirit, and remained on the field till the last cartridge was gone.

Matters were now, indeed, getting on rather badly in McClernand's division, and they got on worse and worse until nearly noon, when the Confederates had gained their first point, having pushed him off of the two roads to Charlotte. They had also captured a portion of his artillery. Swartz's battery they had taken and lost, and taken again. A part of McAllister's battery was also captured. McClernand's whole line was retreating, but in good order. "He did not retreat," says Pillow, "but fell back, fighting us and contesting every inch of ground." It had taken Pillow from six o'clock till noon to perform his part of the day's work, viz., to roll McClernand back upon Lew. Wallace, upon the Wynn's Ferry road. But where was Buckner?

LEWIS WALLACE.

Going back, then, to trace Buckner's progress during the day, we find it in the morning considerably behind time in its operations. In the first place, it had to wait for Head's regiment to come up from Heiman's left to take possession of the abandoned lines. In the second place, the roads were slippery with ice, and in the darkness this was a great inconvenience. The fight was already in progress with McClernand when Buckner reached the rifle-pits on the right of Pillow's previous line. Here, as the tardy regiments came up, the line was formed near the point where the Wynn's Ferry road crossed Pillow's intrenchments. Colonel John C. Brown's brigade, consisting of three Tennessee regiments, partly held the rifle-pits, and was partly held in reserve. Graves's battery was placed at the left of the road, bearing on two Federal batteries in its front, one on the road, the other opposite Buckner's left. This battery also gave a good share of its attention, as has been already seen, to McClernand's brigades on the Federal right, who were contesting the field with Pillow, and who were already gradually giving way.

Buckner's attack proceeded from a point on Heiman's left. The latter, however, kept his original position, and Drake, who had the day before held the hill on his left, was now with Pillow. Buckner's command amounted to over 4000 men. Not wishing to waste his force by assaults, he intended simply to hold his position and await the issue of the battle, which was now culminating on his left. But Pillow needed a more active co-operation than this; Buckner must relieve him by an advance. At nine Buckner was made to understand this, and sent the Fourteenth Mississippi, supported by two of his Tennessee regiments, against the batteries in his front, while Graves sent his compliments entirely to the Federal right, his fire in front being masked by Buckner's advance. Yesterday these compliments were lightly

thought of—"Valentines" the soldiers called them facetiously—it was the middle of February—but to-day it was more serious. Graves's artillery made more impression than even Buckner's advance. While McClernand's right was retiring, exhausted of ammunition, his left was pushing the Confederates back to their defenses. Here Buckner, thwarted, crouched till noonday, when Pillow, who had almost forgotten him in the excitement of his partial victory, began to bethink himself of his military partner—of operations then due on the Wynn's Ferry road.

Accompanied by Gilmer, he rode across the field, and found Buckner where we have just left him, resting behind his intrenchments, and contemplating the strength of the two Federal batteries yonder in his front. But that would not take the batteries. A movement was quickly made, at Pillow's order, flanking them on their left and rear, while Pillow himself, with Forrest, his right-hand cavalry-man, who had been harassing Oglesby's and W. H. L. Wallace's rear, made a charge from the right. The batteries were driven back, leaving four pieces in the hands of the enemy. Buckner had gone around by way of the valley just off Heiman's left, and now his forces joined those of Pillow, who had come round from the other side.

Now, if ever, was the time for this Confederate army, or "our people"— as Floyd, in his peculiar but unmilitary style, expresses himself—to escape southward toward Nashville. The route to Charlotte was open, and now the Wynn's Ferry road also was clear. This evidently was the design from the beginning. With a view to this, all the regiments had taken with them blankets and knapsacks, with three days' rations. But the excitement of successful pursuit made a mere escape appear a tame and unworthy consummation of so costly a victory. Why not continue the movement against Lew. Wallace, and then against Smith himself, and sweep Grant's army entirely away from the front of Donelson? This question was not modestly nor wisely answered by Pillow and his associates in command. It was forgotten that, although a portion of Grant's army, unprepared for assault, had been met and beaten in detail, the attack could no longer have this advantage. The fight had already lasted six hours; the regiments which had been driven had retired slowly, and were by no means demoralized. Many of these regiments had already had time to recover themselves, and with the troops yet untouched in their rear, presented a firm and irresistible front to their now well-nigh exhausted enemy. Nor this alone; but it was probable that in two hours more Floyd's army would itself be driven, and the avenue of escape which was now open be again closed against it. All this was forgotten in the excitement of victorious advance.

Instead of the whole army escaping by the river route to Charlotte, only Baldwin's two regiments remained on this route, B. R. Johnson having hurried off the others to the right for a new battle.

Lew. Wallace had not been idle all this time. After sending Cruft's brigade to McClernand's assistance, it was not long before fugitives from the right crowded in confusion upon his rear, and a mounted officer came galloping down the road, shouting, "We are cut to pieces!" To remain stationary longer would invite panic. Thayer's brigade was moved forward, with Wallace himself in advance. The junior Wallace, Oglesby, and McArthur, with portions of their brigades, were almost immediately met retiring in good order, and calling for more ammunition. The enemy was following close upon these. Between Pillow's advance and the retiring troops Thayer's brigade was interposed, being advanced to the tip of the ridge, and there formed in a line at right angles with the old one. This was the nucleus for a new front. Wood's battery, a portion of the Chicago light artillery, was posted in the road along which the enemy must advance—at its right an Illinois and Nebraska, and at its left an Illinois and Ohio regiment. Two Illinois and an Ohio regiment were held in reserve. In the mean time, McClernand's men were refilling their cartridge-boxes. Cruft's brigade had joined Thayer's on the right, and Taylor's battery was brought to bear on the enemy, whose advance was now completely checked. Now the waves of battle began to flow backward against the Confederates.

At three o'clock General Grant rode up the hill and ordered an advance against the retiring ranks of the enemy. At McClernand's request, Lew. Wallace, whose troops were comparatively fresh, undertook the assault. Cruft's brigade, headed by the Eighth Missouri and the Eleventh Indiana, from Smith's division, with two Ohio regiments in reserve, formed the assailing column. The ground to be gained was in great part the same which had been given up in the forenoon. Across the valley or extended ravine in Wallace's front was the ridge which had been last yielded. Here the Confederates were re-forming their line. Up this ridge a charge was made by two Missouri and Indiana regiments, led by Colonel M. L. Smith, while Cruft moved around the base of the hill to the right. Before Smith lay an ascent of one hundred and fifty yards, "broken by outcropping ledges of rock, and, for the most part, impeded by dense underbrush." Cruft had to make his way around upon the enemy's flank through brushwood. At intervals up the hill Smith's skirmishers were rapidly advanced, and a lively bushwhacking followed between them and the Confederate pickets, each side taking shelter, as opportunity offered, behind rock and tree. Slowly the two regiments followed, and, when less than fifty yards had been gained, received a volley from the hill-top. It now fared hard with the skirmishers. Smith ordered his men to lay down, and when the violence of the fire was exhausted, they rose again and pushed on up the hill. Thus falling when the fire was hottest, and then rising again, they at last reached the top, and Cruft at the same time attacking the enemy on the hill-side, the ridge was cleared. The fight and pursuit lasted for two hours, and by five o'clock the enemy had entirely disappeared from the field, taking refuge in his intrenchments.

While this was going on along the Wynn's Ferry road, an assault was also being made by Smith's division on Buckner's intrenchments. While Buckner was yet on his way back to his lines the storm fell upon Head's almost solitary regiment, which had been distributed along the rifle-pits for a distance of three quarters of a mile. The regiment altogether only numbered a little over 400 men fit for duty. These had been sharp-shooting all the forenoon. At two o'clock Buckner's men began to return to their rifle-pits, but in great disorder. An attack was made by Smith before Hanson's regiment, which was the first to return, had got into position.

General Smith's troops were fresh, and impatient to take part in the action. His division consisted of four Iowa, three Indiana, two Illinois, and one Missouri regiment. Three of these, the Second and Seventh Iowa, and the Twenty-fifth Indiana, supported by others, were selected for the assault, the main column of the division making a feint farther to the right. The ground to be gained was more precipitous and difficult than elsewhere along the lines.

The assault was undertaken under cover of Stone's Missouri battery. The regiments engaged in it were not surpassed by any in the service. It was at the head of the Second Iowa that General Lyon charged and fell at the battle of Wilson's Creek. After the fight had lasted an hour at the right of the entire Confederate line, this regiment made an onset and gained a portion of the rifle-pits. Stone's battery was brought forward, and although two regiments were ordered up from the fort, and others of Buckner's were now at hand, it was impossible for the enemy to regain what he had lost. This position enfiladed the entire right of the defenses of Donelson, and, if darkness had not intervened, Buckner's force would have been immediately routed.

The day had come to a close—a day of uninterrupted battle. For the first time during the war had it occurred that all day long an engagement had been continued between the two opposing armies. The troops engaged on either side must be credited with distinguished bravery. It was on this occasion, for the first time, that Southerners admitted that Northern troops would fight as well as their own, and even then it was given out that this was true of the Western troops alone. Those engaged on the Confederate side were mostly from Tennessee and Mississippi; those on the Federal mostly from Illinois. From the latter state were at least twenty-nine regiments, four of which were of artillery; from Iowa there were six regiments; from Indiana the same number; from Kentucky there were two, and from Missouri three. If these troops—and many of them were raw recruits—had not been pretty richly endowed with Western "grit," there is no doubt but that Pillow would have effected his design and delivered his army. But although, for nearly four hours, Oglesby almost entirely alone bore the brunt of the tremendous blow aimed at the Federal right, there was no flinching, and, until the ammunition gave out, there was no retreat. They so severely punished the Confederates that even after the latter had, by an obstinate contest of six hours, gained possession of the roads leading southward from Dover, they were no longer in a condition for the escape which they had fought to secure.

In a battle so severe, the casualties were on both sides remarkably small. Grant gives no definite estimate of losses in his report, but sets them in the rough at not less than 1200, which is far beneath the true figure.[1] Pillow estimates his losses at 2000. The list of Federal losses are especially remarkable for the number of field-officers killed and wounded. The two regiments which lost more than any others were the Eleventh and Thirty-first Illinois, these two being the last to give way when McClernand was driven. The loss of the Eleventh Indiana was almost half that of Wallace's entire brigade. It was the resolution with which both officers and men resisted the overwhelming attack of Pillow and Johnson that gained the day for the Federals. "We came to take that fort," said Oglesby, "*and we will take it!*" This was the sentiment of Grant's entire army.

That night the Confederate generals held a second council of war about midnight. It had taken till 12 o'clock to bury the Confederate dead. As on the previous night, the place of meeting was at General Pillow's head-quarters in Dover. Floyd was there, and Pillow, attended by his aids, and Buckner, and in the course of the consultation Colonel Forrest made his appearance. The council was held under circumstances of ill omen. "Our people" had made a desperate fight, but the gateways of escape which it had forced open were now shut against it. This had been clearly ascertained by scouts, who had returned with the gloomy intelligence that the Federal camp-fires were in the same positions as on Friday night. Forrest did not believe this testimony, but ocular evidence satisfied him of its truth. At one o'clock orders had been given for the entire command to be under arms at four o'clock in the morning, to march out on the road to Charlotte. Now these orders would have to be rescinded. And there was no other way of escape. Floyd had at night sent up the river to Nashville all the boats, with the wounded, and three hundred Federal prisoners which had been captured during the day, so that even this outlet was closed. The scene at Pillow's head-quarters at about three o'clock on Sunday morning had all the interest of a drama. The following dialogue will represent in substance the consultation which followed after the report of the investment of Dover had been made by the scouts.

FLOYD. "Well, gentlemen, what is now best to be done?"

Profound silence.

FLOYD (again). "General Pillow, what do you think it is best to do?"

PILLOW. "I think that we had better adhere to our previous resolution to cut our way out, sir."

FLOYD. "Well, General Buckner, what do *you* think it is best to do?"

BUCKNER. "We can try to cut our way out, as we did yesterday, but we should lose three fourths of our command, sir. I can not hold my position for half an hour after daylight. If I attempt to take my force out I shall be seen by these fellows that have ensconced themselves in part of my intrenchments. They will surely cut me to pieces!"

COLONEL FORREST. "But I will cover you with my cavalry."

BUCKNER. "That will make no difference. We can not cut our way out without its costing us three fourths of our men."

FLOYD. "I concur with General Buckner."

PILLOW. "If we can fight them another day in the trenches, by to-morrow we can have boats enough here to transport our troops across the river, and let them make their escape to Clarksville."

BUCKNER. "It will be impossible for me to hold my position for half an hour, as I have already informed you."

PILLOW. "But why can't you hold your position? I think you can hold your position; I think you can, sir."

BUCKNER (a little touched). "I know my position better, perhaps, than you do, sir. I can only bring four thousand men to bear against the enemy, while he can oppose me with any given number. You, gentlemen, know that yesterday morning I considered the Second Kentucky, Colonel Hanson's regiment, as good a regiment as any in the service; yet such was their condition yesterday afternoon, that, when I learned the enemy was in their trenches (which were to our extreme right, and detached from the others), before I could rally and form them, I had to take at least twenty men by the shoulders, and put them into line as a nucleus for formation."

FLOYD. "It is evident, as General Buckner says, that we can no longer hold out in the trenches. What shall we do?"

BUCKNER. "The other alternative, it appears to me, is a plain one. We can surrender. It is an alternative which we can accept without dishonor, considering our determined resistance of yesterday. To repeat that resistance to-morrow would cost three fourths of the command—a sacrifice which no commander has a right to make."

FLOYD. "We will have to capitulate; but, gentlemen, I can not surrender; you know my position with the Federals; it wouldn't do—it wouldn't do!"

PILLOW (still bent on "cutting out"). "I will neither surrender myself nor my command; I will die first!"

BUCKNER. "Then I suppose, gentlemen, the surrender will devolve upon me?"

FLOYD (looking out for the main chance). "General, if you are put in the command, will you allow me to take my brigade out by the river?"

BUCKNER. "Yes, sir, if you move your command before the enemy act upon my communication offering to capitulate."

FLOYD. "Then, sir, I surrender my command."

PILLOW (angrily). "I will not accept it; I will never surrender!"

BUCKNER (calling for pen, ink, and paper, and not forgetting the bugler). "I will accept, and share the fate of my command."

Floyd, Pillow, and Forrest then began to busy themselves about getting out of the way. The former escaped with about fifteen hundred men, one half of his command, on board the steamer General Anderson and another smaller boat. These had come down at about daybreak from Nashville. Curiously, considering the state of affairs at Donelson, one of these boats brought down four hundred raw troops. The manner of proceeding with the escape was to cross the river with a boat-load of troops, and then to return for more. Pillow and his staff got across in a small flat-boat, four feet by twelve, procured for him by an aid-de-camp, making their way to Clarksville by land. Forrest in the mean time, with a portion of his command, "cut out" by crossing the back-water on the left, and appear to have had an unpleasant time of it. To say nothing of the water, which was "saddle-skirt deep," the weather was so intensely cold that "a great many of the men were frostbitten, and it was the opinion of the generals that the infantry could not have passed through the water and have survived it." The two hundred were brave fellows, but Gantt, and Wilcox, and Henry — Forrest's subordinates — preferred to remain with Buckner, and were surrendered.

The scene at the river, where Floyd was embarking his "people," became exciting as the morning light grew more distinct. All Floyd's brigade, with the exception of the Twentieth Mississippi, consisted of Virginians under Wharton and McCausland. For these latter he showed the preference; they were embarked first; and, "to prevent stragglers from going aboard," Colonel Brown, commanding the Mississippi regiment, was directed to place a strong guard around the steam-boat landing. The boats had only come down a short time before daylight, and the rumor that the position was to be surrendered spreading through the camps, a multitude of soldiers flocked to the river "almost panic-stricken and frantic," hoping to escape. But the Twentieth Misssissippi "stood like a *stone wall*." After several trips

[1] The following is the list of casualties as given in the officers' reports immediately after the battle:

Twenty-fifth Kentucky	84	Second Iowa	198
Thirty-first Indiana	69	Twenty-fifth Indiana	115
Seventeenth Kentucky	40	Seventh Iowa	39
Forty-fourth Indiana	43	Birge's Sharpshooters	4
Eleventh Illinois	330	Eighth Missouri	45
Twentieth Illinois	133	Eleventh Indiana	34
Forty-eighth Illinois	42	Twelfth Iowa	30
Forty-fifth Illinois	22	Taylor's Battery	9
Seventeenth Illinois	81	McAllister's Battery	2
Forty-ninth Illinois	68	Total	1388

Less than half the regiments are here represented. The greatest number of casualties of course befell McClernand's division, Smith's suffering hardly any. Not a regiment of Oglesby's or Thayer's brigade is represented in this list; yet Oglesby must have suffered more in proportion than any other brigade engaged. W. H. Wallace's brigade lost 687. If we put Oglesby's loss at only 700, we have, together with the numbers given in the list, a little over 2000, without including Thayer's losses.

had been made, and nearly all of the Virginia regiments taken across, Buckner, who had already capitulated, began to grow uneasy, and ordered the boat to leave the landing, threatening, in case of delay, to send a shell in that direction.

Thus the night and morning with the Confederate army. Outside of their intrenchments, meanwhile, was a painful and heart-sickening scene. Thousands of dead and wounded were lying on the bloody field. On such a night, to be helpless from severe wounds was a suffering less dreadful than death itself, for it was bitter cold. Where Lew. Wallace's division held the battle-field, the terrible sufferings of these helpless soldiers were, so far as possible, relieved. The ground, according to Wallace's report, "was thickly strewn with the dead of McClernand's regiments. The number of Illinoisans there found mournfully attested the desperation of the battle, and how firmly they had fought it. All night, and till far in the morning, my soldiers, generous as they were gallant, were engaged in ministering to and removing their own wounded and the wounded of the first division, not forgetting those of the enemy."

As morning broke upon the Federal ranks, it found them on all sides drawn up ready for an assault on Donelson, in conjunction with an attack by the two gun-boats which Foote had left behind. Before the action was commenced a white flag was seen above Fort Donelson, the sound of Buckner's bugle was heard, and the following note came directed to General Grant from General Buckner:

"SIR,—In consideration of all the circumstances governing the present situation of affairs at this station, I propose to the commanding officer of the Federal forces the appointment of commissioners to agree upon terms of capitulation of the forces and post under my command, and in that view suggest an armistice until twelve o'clock to-day. I am, sir, very respectfully, your obedient servant, S. B. BUCKNER."

To which General Grant replied:

"Yours of this date, proposing an armistice and appointment of commissioners to settle terms of capitulation, is just received. No terms other than an unconditional and immediate surrender can be accepted.

"I propose to move immediately upon your works. I am, sir, very respectfully, your obedient servant, U. S. GRANT."

This elicited from General Buckner the following remarkable answer:

"SIR,—The distribution of the forces under my command, incident to an unexpected change of commanders, and the overwhelming force under your command, compel me, notwithstanding the brilliant success of the Confederate arms yesterday, to accept the ungenerous and unchivalrous terms which you propose. I am, sir, your very obedient servant, S. B. BUCKNER."

The Fifty-eighth Ohio Volunteers was the first regiment on the enemy's battery, and, immediately upon possession, its band opened with the "Star Spangled Banner."[1]

At the lowest estimate, 10,000 men were surrendered with the fort, besides forty pieces of artillery. Grant estimated the number of prisoners at from 12,000 to 15,000. The prisoners were, for the most part, dressed in citizens' clothes, having no military mark except black stripes on the pants. The officers had on gray uniforms, and were distinguished from Federals holding similar rank by the great profusion of gold lace. Most of the Tennessee regiments had enlisted only for twelve months, and had received no pay since they had entered the service.[2]

The results of the victory at Donelson distinguished it above any victory which had hitherto been gained in American history. The prisoners taken would have made a larger army than Scott led in Mexico. It was not merely a siege, but a great battle. In his congratulatory order to his troops General Grant said:

"The victory achieved is not only great in the effect it will have in breaking down rebellion, but has secured the greatest number of prisoners of war ever taken in any battle on this continent." And surely he did not overstep the limits of a becoming modesty in adding, "Fort Donelson will hereafter be marked in capitals on the map of our united country, and the men who fought the battle will live in the memory of a grateful people."

Very soon after the surrender of Donelson both General Floyd and General Pillow were relieved of their commands.[3]

---

[1] The German colonel, Bausenwein, commanding the Fifty-eighth, was full of innocent rapture over the Confederate booty. In his report to the adjutant general he breaks out in this wise: "I have some 4000 muskets, revolvers, Bowie-knives, etc., now under guard, and thousands of tents, provisions of enormous bulk (!)—in fact, every thing of war implements. Hundreds of horses and mules! Our company officers walk no more; they are supplied with Secesh saddles, horses, and mules, and happiness beams from their eyes and lips!"

[2] As regards the disposition made of the prisoners the following order will inform the reader:

"SPECIAL ORDER.
"Head-quarters, Army in the Field, Fort Donelson, February 16, 1862.
"All prisoners taken at the surrender of Fort Donelson will be collected as rapidly as practicable, near the village of Dover, under their respective company and regimental commanders, or in such manner as may be deemed best by Brigadier General S. B. Buckner, and will receive two days' rations preparatory to embarking for Cairo. Prisoners are to be allowed their clothing, blankets, and such private property as may be carried about the person, and commissioned officers will be allowed their side-arms. By order U. S. GRANT, Brig. Gen."

[3] The Confederate Congress commenced its session two days after the capture of Donelson. Just one week after the capture, Jefferson Davis was inaugurated as President of the Confederate States under the auspices of a permanent government. It is hardly any wonder that Mr. Davis should have resented the echoes of disaster coming to his ears at such a time. It was an ill omen for the so-styled permanent government. His resentment was certainly not diminished by the consciousness that he himself was responsible for the defeat. Anxious to divert popular vengeance from his own freshly-crowned head, he, on the 11th of March, sent to Congress, together with the official reports of the battle, the following special message:

"Executive Department.
"I transmit herewith copies of such official reports as have been received at the War Department of the defense and fall of Fort Donelson. They will be found incomplete and unsatisfactory. Instructions have been given to furnish farther information upon the several points not made intel-

BOWLING GREEN, KENTUCKY.

The more immediate results of the Federal victory were the evacuation of Bowling Green and Columbus by the Confederates. While the battle was being fought on Saturday, General A. S. Johnston was already at Nashville, awaiting the arrival of his command from Bowling Green.

The column dispatched by Buell against Bowling Green consisted of General Ormsby M. Mitchell's (third) division. General Mitchell was a na-

ORMSBY McKNIGHT MITCHELL.

ligible by the reports. It is not stated that re-enforcements were at any time asked for; nor is it demonstrated to have been impossible to have saved the army by evacuating the position; nor is it known by what means it was found practicable to withdraw a part of the garrison, leaving the remainder to surrender; nor upon what authority or principles of action the senior general aban-

tive of Kentucky, and a graduate of West Point, belonging to the same class as General Lee and General Joseph E. Johnston. For some time he held the professorship of mathematics at West Point; he afterward held a similar position in the Cincinnati college, where, in 1845, he founded an observatory. At one time he had been adjutant general of Ohio. When the war broke out he saw what would be its magnitude, and immediately offered his services. At this time fifty-seven years of age, he promised to become one of the most energetic and thorough of the Federal officers.

His division broke camp at Bacon Creek, a few miles north of Munfordsville, on Tuesday, February 11, marched across Green River to Camp Madison, and on Thursday and Friday completed the march from that point to

doned responsibility by transferring the command to a junior officer. In a former communication to Congress I presented the propriety of a suspension of judgment in relation to the disaster at Fort Donelson until official reports could be received. I regret that the information now furnished is so defective. In the mean time, hopeful that satisfactory explanation may be made, I have directed, upon the exhibition of the case as presented by the two senior generals, that they should be relieved from command, to await farther orders whenever a reliable judgment can be rendered on the merits of the case.   JEFFERSON DAVIS."

The charges intimated in the above were more specifically stated by H. B. Brewster, the Confederate A. A. General, in the following communication, addressed to Generals Floyd and Pillow, March 16:

"Under date of March 4 the Secretary of War says: 'The reports of Generals Floyd and Pillow are unsatisfactory, and the President directs that both these generals be relieved from command till farther orders.' He farther requests General Johnston 'in the mean time to request them to add to their reports such statements as they may deem proper on the following points:

"'1st. The failure to give timely notice of the insufficiency of the garrison of Fort Donelson to repel attack.

"'2d. The failure of any attempt to save the army by evacuating the post when found untenable.

"'3d. Why they abandoned the command to their inferior officer, instead of executing themselves whatever measure was deemed proper for the entire army.

"'4th. What was the precise mode by which each effected his escape from the post, and what dangers were encountered in the retreat.

"'5th. Upon what principle a selection was made of particular troops, being certain regiments of the senior general's brigade, etc.'"

The different answers made by the two generals to these charges were characteristic. Pillow's was manly but independent; and inasmuch as he had himself advised an effort to escape with the entire army, he could hardly have felt the burden of blame resting very heavily on his shoulders; still he answered as if the charges applied to himself as much as to any body. In regard to the failure to give timely notice of the need of re-enforcements, he said that up to Friday, the 14th, there was no such need; but if there had been, General Johnston had no men to spare. In this case it was clearly, as it appeared to him, the best policy to fight their way out. He seemed inclined to blame Buckner, as indeed he had reason to, for having failed to do his part of the work on Saturday, and thus enabling the enemy to recover himself. It was his own opinion that the assault might have been again tried with success on Sunday; but this was only his private opinion; and when the command was delivered over to him, he could not act upon it in the face of Buckner's and Floyd's assertion that it would cost three fourths of the army.

Poor Floyd, on the other hand, feeling that the onus of complaint unavoidably rested on himself, was disposed to resent the charges and to kick them back in the President's face.

In the first place, he had planned the whole defense to suit himself, but stupid Johnston did not agree to his plans. He knew that Johnston's whole army could not repel the Federal advance up the Cumberland.(!) He considered the fort illy chosen, to begin with. Then, again, it had only thirteen guns, and only three of these were available against iron-clads. [Pretty well available, we should say, considering the results of the gun-boat fight on Friday!] He did not call for re-enforcements because he thought there were already troops enough in the miserable fort, considering that it was only a trap after all. He thought the main object of the defense at Donelson was to gain time for Johnston to evacuate Bowling Green with all his supplies and munitions of war.

Hold Donelson, indeed! Why, it could not be held except with a force of 95,000 men; 50,000 at the fort, 20,000 at Clarksville, and 25,000 more at Nashville. What use, then, of making

GENERAL MITCHELL'S DIVISION CROSSING GREEN RIVER, FEBRUARY, 1862.

NASHVILLE, TENNESSEE.

RAILROAD BRIDGE ACROSS THE CUMBERLAND AT NASHVILLE.

Bowling Green, a distance of forty-two miles. The town was occupied on the 15th without resistance, only three regiments of the enemy remaining behind. Both of the bridges across the Big Barren River were destroyed, and the Confederates had succeeded in shipping all their artillery to Nashville. In the mean time, Johnston, as we have said, was at Nashville directing operations, and awaiting the event of the battle at Donelson. Up to the latest moment Pillow promised him success. So late as Saturday night that sanguine officer telegraphed to him, "On the honor of a soldier, the day is ours!" The telegram was received at midnight, and Nashville rang with the jubilations of an excited people. At dawn the news came of the surrender of the fort. Then cheers were exchanged for a tumult of fear. It was Sabbath morning, and the good people of the town were at church thanking God for a great victory, when Governor Harris galloped through the streets of the capital proclaiming that Donelson had fallen, and their army had been captured, and that at any moment the enemy might come down upon them. In an excited, hurried manner he summoned the state Legislature, and adjourned it to Memphis, leaving by a special train in the afternoon himself with the state archives. A scene of the utmost confusion followed. If the city had become the victim of a universal conflagration, the panic could scarcely have been greater. The churches were broken up, the streets were crowded with weeping women, and the side-walks were filled with trunks and baggage thrown hastily out of the houses, and sometimes from the third story windows. The more reckless of the citizens abandoned themselves to plunder. In the midst of this general and confused exodus, General Johnston's army might have been seen moving across

the Cumberland, with a long train following, which did not get over all night. Floyd had got up with his small detachment, and now remained as a rear guard until the retreat should be accomplished. On the following Thursday he too took his departure.

There was sufficient reason why Nashville should have been abandoned, but there was hardly any occasion for the panic which crazed its citizens, who expected to see the gun-boats coming up before sundown. General Johnston had received the tidings of defeat as early as four o'clock Sunday morning. If he had issued a simple proclamation to quiet the natural alarm of the citizens, the tumult which followed would have been avoided. He left all this in the governor's hands, who only made matters worse. It was true that Nashville was no longer tenable. The city had no natural situation which could be made available for defense. Good turnpike roads led to it from all sides, and through it ran the Cumberland, navigable for the Federal fleet. Johnston's engineer reported that the city could not be held by a force less than 50,000 strong. This, however, was only ground for the removal of the army, and need only have disturbed such of the citizens as were particularly desirous of leaving their homes and property for the sake of sharing the fortunes of the Confederacy. But that which moved the citizens of Nashville was not so much disinterested patriotism as mortal terror. The Southern leaders had studiously endeavored, and in a great measure had succeeded in producing a popular impression among the people that within the lines of the Federal armies they were secure from no violence. This had been the impression ever since Beauregard had said that "Beauty and booty" was the motto of the Union soldiers.[1]

The day after the surrender of Donelson, Commodore Foote, though still suffering from his wound, left Cairo with eight mortar-boats, two iron-clads, and the Conestoga, for another advance up the Cumberland — this time against Clarksville, a fortified position on the river, about fifty miles below Nashville, and on the Virginia Railroad. On the 20th, Clarksville, abandoned by its garrison, fell into Foote's hands. The railroad bridge across the river had been destroyed. The commodore, at the request of the mayor and other prominent citizens, issued a proclamation, guaranteeing safety to such citizens as chose to remain in the city. General Smith was left in command, while Foote returned to Donelson to prepare an expedition against Nashville. Buell had already sent large re-enforcements to Grant. A portion of these, under General Nelson, accompanied Foote on transports. These

an ado about a re-enforcement of a dozen or so thousands of men, which would be but a drop in the bucket.

As to the "failure of any attempt to save the army by evacuating the post when found untenable," this seemed to Floyd a biting sarcasm on Jeff. Davis's part. Pray, what had the bloody fight of the 15th meant, if it was not an "attempt to save the army by evacuating the fort." But perhaps the President was not satisfied because the attempt, unsuccessful on Saturday, was not repeated on Sunday. He would remind the President that "there is such a thing as human exhaustion—an end of physical ability in men to march and fight—however little such a contingency may seem possible to those who quietly sleep upon soft beds, who fare sumptuously every day, and have never tried the exposure of protracted battles and hard campaigns." Floyd then begins to grow somewhat extravagant in his details of what his army had suffered; he speaks pathetically of "the conflict, toil, and excitement of unsuspended battle running through eighty-four hours."(!) His excited imagination sees three Federal soldiers where there was but one. How was this force, six times his own, to be thrust aside? Then, besides, if his soldiers should cut their way out, "they would have to march over a battle-field strewn with corpses."(!)

The remaining charges related chiefly to Floyd's escape with a good part of his own division after a surrender had been determined upon. This was easily explained. There were two boats, and these came so late that it was impossible for only a small part of the army to escape. The senior general preferred, of course, to save his own troops to any others.

However ludicrous some parts of Floyd's report may appear, his arguments, on the whole, were perfectly just and reasonable. Like Tilghman at Fort Henry, Floyd could, by the defense of Donelson, effect nothing, except to gain time for Johnston to form a new line more defensible farther south. Donelson was, indeed, nothing else but a "trap," as Floyd called it; and if any one was culpable for setting this trap, it was Jefferson Davis himself. He had placed the Confederate army of the West in a situation adapted neither to offensive nor defensive operations, being too feeble for the former, and disposed in the worst possible manner for the latter.

[1] The following, from the Nashville *Banner of Peace* of about this date, indicates the manner in which this impression had been produced:

"We have felt too secure, we have been too blind to the consequence of Federal success. If they succeed, we shall see plunder; insult to old and young, male and female; murder of innocents; release of slaves, and causing them to drive and insult their masters and mistresses in the most menial services; the land laid waste; houses burned; banks and private coffers robbed; cotton and every valuable taken away before our eyes, and a brutal and drunken soldiery turned loose upon us."

COLUMBUS, KENTUCKY.

troops occupied the capital without opposition. General Buell himself arrived on the 26th, and issued a proclamation, the object of which was to secure the citizens of Nashville from spoliation or injury. By this order, soldiers were "forbidden to enter the residences or grounds of any citizens on any plea, without authority."

The next day, General Grant, accompanied by his staff, came up from Clarksville. Among other of the citizens, they called on Mrs. James K. Polk, the wife of a late President of the United States. This lady, then about fifty years of age, had all her life been associated with the South, and her sympathies were clearly with the Confederate rather than with the United States government. But these sympathies she did not express, from a courteous regard for her visitors. "She hoped that the tomb of her husband" (which was in a corner of the beautiful garden, surrounded by cedars and magnolias) "would protect her household from insult and her property from pillage; farther than this, she expected nothing from the United States, and desired nothing."

The Confederate government, by their too hasty abandonment of Nashville, lost a large amount of stores. These consisted especially of clothing and commissary supplies. The mob had, for the most part, taken care of this property. Floyd had great difficulty in driving off the greedy crowd. The Confederate quarter-master left the city eight days before the arrival of the Federal army; if he had remained, he could doubtless have saved property amounting in value to hundreds of thousands.

With remarkable rapidity, it was now proposed to move on Columbus with Foote's fleet. This was needless, as already General Beauregard had ordered Polk to evacuate that strongly fortified place, and to adopt a position on the river farther south. The position selected by Polk was Island No. 10, the main land in Madrid Bend, on the Tennessee shore, and New

Madrid, on the opposite bank. Island No. 10 was about ten miles below Columbus. Defensive works had been thrown up at these points the previous autumn, and heavy batteries were being constructed. On the 25th orders were issued for the removal of the sick, preparatory to the evacuation of Columbus. Two days afterward General McGown was assigned to the command of the new position, his division being ordered thither February 27. The commissary, quarter-master's, and ordnance stores had all been removed, and afterward the heavy guns. March 1, Polk's entire army, except the cavalry, evacuated Columbus—General Stuart's brigade moving, by way of the river, to New Madrid, the remainder by land to Union City. On the 3d, two days after Polk and his staff left the works, a scouting party, consisting of a portion of the Second Illinois cavalry, sent from Paducah by General Sherman, took possession of the town. The next day the fleet came down, and three regiments, under Generals Cullum and Sherman, took permanent possession.

The campaign commenced on the 1st of February had now terminated. It had been brief, but decisive. It had lasted but one month, but it was a continued series of victories. It renewed the enthusiasm of a people which had grown tired of waiting for results. Grant and Foote—the two heroes of this campaign—came before the people bearing splendid trophies in their hands. Henry, Donelson, Bowling Green, Nashville, and Columbus—all reduced within a period of thirty days—appeared to Unionists to speak prophetically of the fate awaiting all Confederate strong-holds. A month ago, and one half of Kentucky was firmly held in the grasp of the Confederate armies; now, not only that state, but the greater part of Tennessee also, was restored to Federal allegiance. Hopes were entertained that another year of vigorous work would bring back all the seceded states.

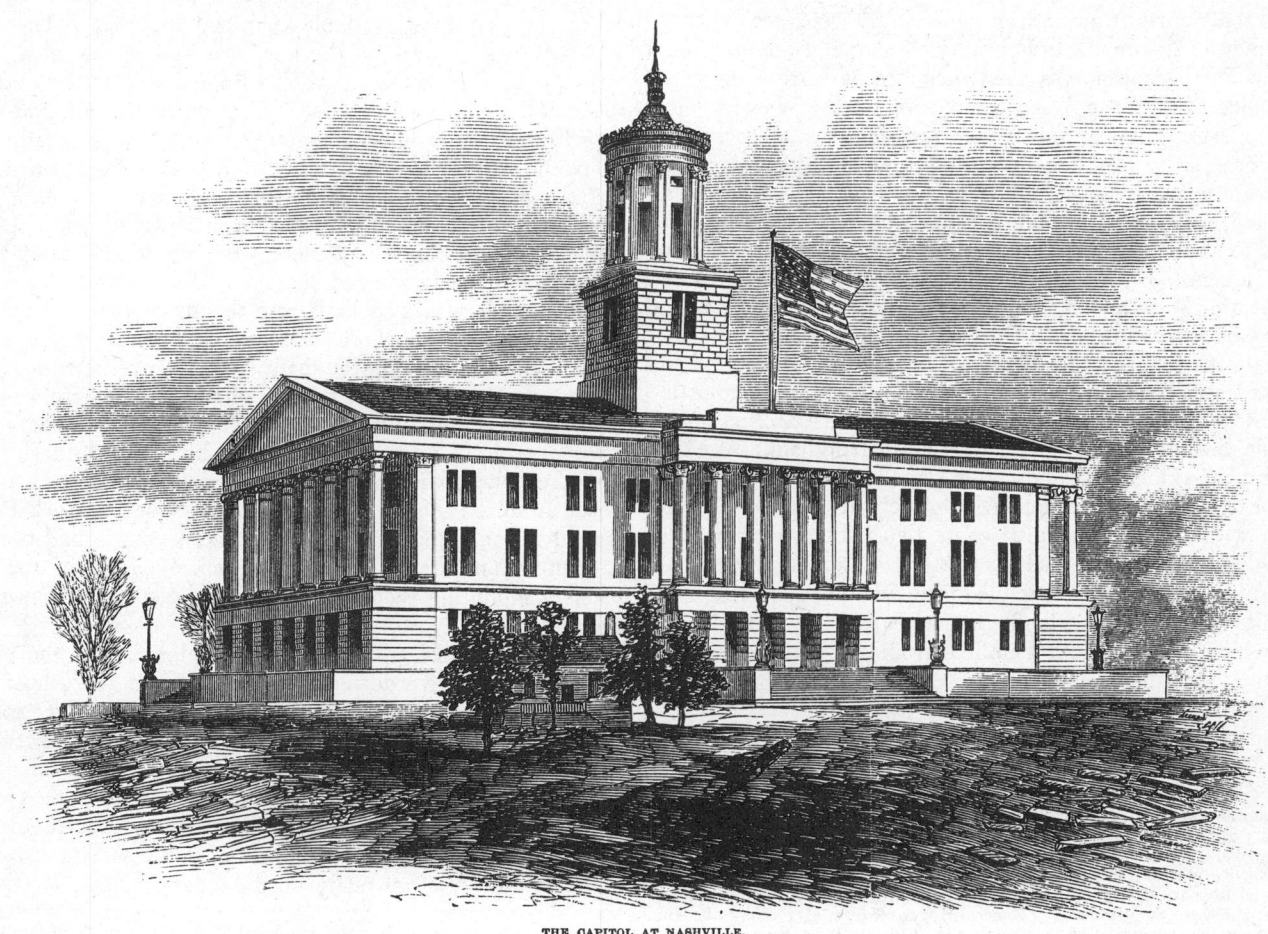

THE CAPITOL AT NASHVILLE.

P P P

BURNSIDE'S EXPEDITION OFF FORTRESS MONROE. NIGHT SCENE.

CHAPTER XII.

ROANOKE AND NEWBERN.

Hatteras Inlet at the beginning of 1862.—Situation and Importance of Roanoke Island; its defensive Works.—General Wise's Command.—The New England Coast Division; its original Destination.—McClellan's Instructions to Burnside.—The Burnside Expedition.—Commodore Goldsborough.—Arrival of the Fleet off Hatteras.—The Battle of Roanoke Island.—Destruction of the Confederate Fleet and Capture of Elizabeth City.—Capture of Edenton, Plymouth, and Winton.—The Battle of Newbern.—Capture of Washington.—Bombardment and Capture of Fort Macon.—Beaufort.

THE old proverb that "misfortunes never come singly" was proved true to the Confederacy in the month of February, 1862. Between the loss of Fort Henry and of Fort Donelson was sandwiched in, as it were, the capture of Roanoke Island. Floyd and Wise, compatriots in the Western Virginia campaign of the last autumn, but always at loggerheads with each other, were now fitly disposed by Mr. Benjamin, the Confederate Secretary of War, at points as wide apart as possible. Wise, with his legion, had been sent to Roanoke Island, the eastern terminus of the Confederate line. Floyd had been dispatched to Tennessee, the western limit. Just one week before Floyd surrendered Donelson, or, rather, left Buckner to transact the disagreeable business for him, Wise had surrendered Roanoke Island.

When North Carolina seceded from the United States, the Confederate authorities fortified Hatteras Inlet by the construction of Forts Hatteras and Clark. Other works were erected commanding Oregon Inlet, farther north. It was not long, however, before these works on the North Carolina coast were reduced by the Federal fleet under Butler and Stringham. Within the long, narrow sand-bar extending almost from Cape Henry to Cape Lookout, lie the waters of two extensive sounds, Albemarle and Pamlico. Pamlico Sound, together with the embouchures of its two tributary rivers, the Neuse and the Pamlico, had been gained by Butler's victories. The Confederate force defending these waters, compelled to resign the inlets, had concentrated on Roanoke Island. This island commands the only entrance to Albemarle Sound, which connects with Pamlico by means of Croatan and Roanoke Sounds on either side of the island.

Roanoke Island is the key not only to a large portion of Northeastern North Carolina, but also to an important slice of Virginia—an especially important slice, as including Portsmouth and Norfolk.[1] The island was de-

fended by a few regiments, mostly from North Carolina. General Wise was assigned to the command during the latter part of December, 1861. Benjamin desired him to bring his legion up to 10,000 strong by recruiting in North Carolina. It does not indicate any great enthusiasm in the Confederate cause on the part of that state that Wise was obliged to fall back upon the military authorities at Richmond for support. But no troops could be spared from the Virginia army. It appeared very likely that Roanoke Island would prove to be another of Secretary Benjamin's traps. The fortifications were on the western coast, commanding the Croatan Sound, which was the only channel available for naval approach. There were three sand forts built at intervals on the northern half of this coast: Fort Bartow, at Pork Point; Fort Huger, at Weir's Point; and midway between these, Fort Blanchard, mounting four guns. The works at Pork and Weir's Point were quite formidable, mounting together twenty-two guns, three of which were 100-pound rifles. Opposite Pork, at Redstone Point on the main land, was Fort Forest. On the east side of the island there was a battery, covering the passage of troops to or from Nag's Head, on the bar outside. On the southern end of the island there were no works whatever. Even if the marshy and densely-wooded character seemed to preclude the possibility of any formidable attack by land from this direction, it was still important that there should be some work commanding the entrance to Croatan Sound, either on the island or on the main land. To resist the approach of Federal troops toward the northern portion of the island, there was in the middle of it, nearly on a line with Fort Bartow, a strong redoubt, constructed with a pond covering it in front and flanking both extremities. This battery was thirty-five yards wide, and commanded a cart-road, the only available approach from the south. Across from Redstone to Pork Point a line of obstructions, consisting of piles and sunken vessels, had been formed, leaving an open channel under the guns of each of the two forts. A fleet of eight steamers, mounting each two guns, completed the defenses of Roanoke Island.

In the mean time an expedition was planning on the Federal side which would soon set these defenses at naught. On the 6th of September, 1861, General McClellan had requested the Secretary of War "to organize two brigades, of five regiments each, of New England men, for the general service, but particularly adapted to coast service." At the time this request was made, it was McClellan's intention to use this force in the inlets of Chesapeake Bay and on the Potomac. But so great was the difficulty of obtaining suitable vessels, and adapting them to the service required of them, that the expedition was not ready until January, 1862. McClellan, in the mean

---

[1] "Roanoke Island was the key to all the rear defenses of Norfolk. It unlocked two sounds, Albemarle and Currituck; eight rivers, the North, West, Pasquotank, the Perquimans, the Little, the Chowan, the Roanoke, and the Alligator; four canals, the Albemarle and Chesapeake, the Dismal Swamp, the Northwest Canal, and the Suffolk; two railroads, the Betersburg and Norfolk, and the Sea-board and Roanoke. It guarded more than four fifths of all Norfolk's supplies of corn, pork, and forage, and it cut the command of General Huger off from all its most efficient transportation. It endangers the subsistence of his whole army, threatens the navy yard at Gosport, and to cut off Norfolk from Richmond, and both from railroad communication with the South. It lodges the enemy in a safe harbor from the storms of Hatteras, gives them a rendezvous, and

large, rich range of supplies, and the command of the sea-board from Oregon Inlet to Cape Henry. It should have been defended at the expense of 20,000 men and of many millions of dollars."—*Report of General Wise.*

MAP OF THE NORTH CAROLINA COAST.

LOUIS M. GOLDSBOROUGH.

while, had been appointed general-in-chief. In his larger combinations he changed his original intention in regard to this expedition, and determined to give it a wider range, sending it to the North Carolina coast; partly because Butler's operations had opened the way, partly because permanent possession of Albemarle Sound would greatly facilitate the task of the blockading fleet, but chiefly because he hoped to be able to strike a blow at the Weldon Railroad after the capture of Newbern. In his letter of instructions, January 7, to General Ambrose E. Burnside, who was to command the expedition, he indicated the following series of operations: Burnside was first to unite with Flag-officer Goldsborough, in command of the fleet, at Fort Monroe; the first point of attack was to be Roanoke Island; then Newbern was to be attended to, and, if possible, the Weldon road also. Raleigh itself might perchance come within reach, but there must be caution about that. Having taken Newbern, Burnside was to push down to Beaufort, reduce Fort Macon, and open the port. Wilmington was brought up in prospect as the "next point of interest," but with a hint that its capture might require an additional force. The instructions concluded with the following caution regarding proclamations: "In no case would I go beyond a moderate joint proclamation with the naval commander, which should say as little as possible about politics or the negro; merely state that the true issue for which we are fighting is the preservation of the Union and upholding the laws of the general government, and stating that all who conduct themselves properly will, as far as possible, be protected in their persons and property."

The expedition, when completed, constituted a formidable armada. The naval force consisted of twenty light-draught vessels, having altogether an armament of over fifty guns, of which more than one fourth were 9-inch

guns; there were two 100-pound rifles, and only twelve of the guns were of less calibre than 30-pounders.[1] This part of the expedition was under the command of Flag-officer Louis M. Goldsborough, a native of the District of Columbia, and a citizen of Maryland. He had been fifty years in the naval service of the United States, and over eighteen years he had passed at sea. He was flag-officer of the North Atlantic blockading squadron. A late act of Congress had placed him on the retired list, but of the opportunity thus offered he had not availed himself.

The military division consisted, in the first place, of an army nearly fifteen thousand strong. There were seven gun-boats connected with this division: the Picket, which was Burnside's flag-ship; the Pioneer, the Hussar, the Chasseur, the Ranger, the Lancer, and the Vidette; the latter mounting three guns and the others four. The flotilla of transports numbered nearly forty vessels, each capable of conveying between four and five hundred men; in addition, there was a large amount of small craft, fifty or more additional vessels, for the transportation of supplies sufficient for sixty days' rations. General Ambrose E. Burnside, commanding the military division, was born in Indiana, May 23, 1824. He graduated at West Point in 1847, and was attached to the Confederate General (then Captain) Bragg's command in the Mexican war and the subsequent Indian campaigns. Retiring from military service in 1853, he did not enter it again until the civil war. He assumed command of the First Rhode Island Volunteers, but in the battle of Bull Run commanded a brigade. Soon after that battle he was made a brigadier general, and when the Coast Division was raised he was appointed its commander. Decisive in character, and at the same time a keen analyst of character in others, courteous in manner and of a commanding presence, he was more than any other man fitted for the important position assigned to him.

General John G. Foster, commanding the first brigade of Burnside's army, was a native of New Hampshire, and at the time of our history now reached was nearly forty years of age. He was second lieutenant of engineers in the regular army, belonging to the company of which McClellan was first lieutenant. He took part in the Mexican campaign, and at the battles of Contreras and Cherubusco earned the first lieutenancy. At El Morino del Rey he was severely wounded, and promoted to a captaincy. In 1854 he became Assistant Professor of Engineering at West Point. General Foster was one of the garrison of Fort Sumter when that work was assailed at the beginning of the insurrection.

The expedition sailed out of Hampton Roads January 11, at half past nine o'clock at night, and arrived off Hatteras on the 13th, just as a northeast gale began to blow up, threatening danger in any attempt to pass over the bulkhead. Even in the most quiet sea there were several vessels which must re-

STORM OFF HATTERAS.

main outside on account of their too great draught of water. The City of New York, drawing sixteen feet of water, attempted to pass the shoals on the 14th and got aground. The next day the vessel went to wreck in sight of thirty vessels that could render her no assistance. All day on the 14th and that night her crew were lashed to the rigging to prevent the waves from sweeping them overboard. Four of her boats were gone. In the remaining one, two brothers, William A. and Charles H. Beach, two mechanics from Newark, New Jersey, accompanied by the fireman, the second engineer, and the colored steward, managed to gain the fleet, and surf-boats were sent out to rescue their comrades. The next morning the gun-boat Zouave sunk at her anchorage, running foul of some obstruction. The Louisiana grounded the same day with the City of New York. A few days afterward the Pocahontas was wrecked. It was with great difficulty, and in connection with such dispiriting incidents as have been related, that the fleet was conveyed into the waters of the sound through "the shallow, narrow, and tortuous" channel of the bulk-head. Says Goldsborough, alluding to this channel, "Under the most favorable circumstances, scarcely an inch more than seven and a half feet of water can be found in it. It was only by the greatest exertions and perseverance on the part of my officers and men, and by turning every possible expedient to prompt account, that our vessels of the heaviest draught (some of them drawing quite eight feet) were worried through this perplexing gut." It was not until the 28th that this feat had been successfully accomplished.

[1] The following is a list of the naval vessels, with the names of their commanders and the character of their armament:

1. Stars and Stripes...	Lieut. Com'g Worden	4 8-in., 55 cwt.; 1 20-lb. Parrott.
2. Louisiana............	Lieut. Com'g Murray	1 8-in., 63 cwt.; 1 32-lb., 57 cwt.; 2 32-lb., 3 cwt.; 1 12-lb. rifled.
3. Hetzel..............	Lieut. Com'g Davenport......	1 9-in.; 1 80-lb. rifled.
4. Underwriter........	Lieut. Com'g Leffers	1 8-in., 63 cwt.; 1 80-lb. rifled; 1 12-lb. rifled; 1 12-lb. smooth bore.
5. Delaware...........	Lieut. Com'g Quackenbush ..	1 9-in.; 1 32-lb., 57 cwt.; 1 12-lb. rifled.
6. Valley City.........	Lieut. Com'g Chaplin........	4 32-lb., 42 cwt.; 1 12-lb. rifled.
7. Southfield...........	A. V. Lieut. Com'g Behm...	3 9-in.; 1 100-lb. rifled.
8. Hunchback..........	A. V. Lieut. Com'g Colhoun.	3 9-in.; 1 100-lb. rifled.
9. Morse...............	Acting Master Hayes	2 9-in.
10. Whitehead..........	Acting Master Trench	1 9-in.
11. Seymour............	Acting Master Wells	1 30-lb. rifled; 1 12-lb. rifled.
12. Shawsheen.........	Acting Master Woodward	2 20-lb. rifled.
13. Lockwood..........	Acting Master Graves	1 80-lb. rifled; 1 12-lb. rifled; 1 12-lb. smooth bore.
14. Ceres...............	Acting Master McDiarmid ..	1 30-lb. rifled; 1 32-lb., 33 cwt.
15. Putnam............	Acting Master Hotchkiss.....	1 20-lb. rifled.
16. Brinker............	Acting Master Giddings.....	1 32-lb. rifled,
17. Granite............	Act'g Master's Mate Boomer..	1 32-lb., 57 cwt.
18. Perry..............		— 9 in.
19. Birney.............		— 9 in.
20. Whitehall..........		

JOHN G. FOSTER.

On the 5th of February, the fleet, with fifteen days' rations, was in motion for Roanoke Island, which is distant thirty-eight miles from Hatteras Inlet. Williams's brigade, consisting of four regiments, was left at the Inlet. The naval division led, advancing in three columns, commanded respectively by Worden, Murray, and Davenport. It was a fine day, but the fleet moved slowly, and it was not until evening that the low, swampy shores of North Carolina were visible. Curiously, the enemy had forgotten to remove the buoy on the eastern extremity of Long Point Shoal, twenty miles from the Inlet, and thus probably the loss of several vessels was prevented. That night a force was dispatched to the main land to secure the services of a certain individual, peaceably or by force, as a pilot. The errand was successfully accomplished. The next day was unpromising. A thick fog obscured all distant objects. Once during the forenoon it cleared away, disclosing Roanoke Island and the vessels of the Confederate fleet; but the fog returned again when the channel of Croatan Sound was nearly reached, and it began to rain. The next day, Friday, February 7, was clear, and at nine o'clock the fleet weighed anchor for the third time, at the sign of the Union jack, and the Ceres and Putnam led the way, as on the previous day, in search of obstructions. Arriving soon at the entrance of Croatan Sound, there were then the marshes to be threaded. Through these the passage is so narrow that not more than two ships can pass abreast. At half past ten these had been cleared, and a signal gun was fired from one of the forts on the island announcing the impending attack. The Underwriter, which had been sent to discover the presence of a battery, if there was one, at Sandy Point, near Ashby's Harbor, where Burnside intended to land his troops, gave signal a little after eleven o'clock that the coast was clear at that point. A few minutes later the naval division, accompanied by the seven gun-boats of the coast division, approached Pork Point, beyond which the Confederate fleet was drawn up behind a double row of piles. Before the bombardment commenced, Goldsborough signaled from the Philadelphia, "This day our country expects every man to do his duty." All the forts and vessels opened fire upon the attacking fleet, but the latter, in return, gave especial attention to Fort Bartow. At one o'clock the flag-staff of this fort was carried away by a shot, and in less than half an hour afterward the barracks in the rear were in flames.

In the course of the afternoon the troops began to disembark at Ashby's Harbor, under cover of the gun-boats. The landing was not entirely unguarded by the enemy, who had posted a small force there with a field battery. But the Delaware, with Rowan on board, took up a position just south of Pork Point, and cleared the way with a few shots from her guns. In the mean time the bombardment went on. It had been hottest between two and three o'clock. Two hours later Fort Bartow ceased firing, and the Confederate fleet withdrew around Weir's Point.

Q q q

While this was going on, General Wise was lying sick at Nag's Head, four miles east of the island, on the sand-bar. The Confederate force upon the island on the morning of the 7th consisted of the Eighth North Carolina regiment, under Colonel H. M. Shaw, who, in the absence of Wise, was the senior officer; the Thirty-first, under Jordan, and three companies of the Seventeenth, under Major G. H. Hill. These, allowing for an absence of four or five hundred men, made up a garrison of nearly 1600 men. Early on the morning of the 7th this garrison was re-enforced by ten companies of the Wise Legion, under the command of Colonel Anderson and Captain Wise, the general's son. General Wise, notwithstanding his illness, issued all the necessary orders from his sick-bed, and attended to the wants of his army.

By midnight on the night of the 7th nearly 10,000 Federal troops had been landed at Ashby's Harbor. It was a dismal night for the soldiers, who, before emerging upon the firm sandy plain in the interior, had to wade through mud knee deep, and then to content themselves with such sleep as they could get with only their overcoats to protect them from the cold rain.

The next day, Saturday, the 8th, was Burnside's. The gun-boats, indeed, kept up their fire during the day, and a little after noon passed the obstructions in the Sound, but the burden of the day's labor fell on the military division. At seven o'clock in the morning the line of battle was formed. The advance up the island was in three columns: Foster's brigade in the centre, Parke's on the right, and Reno's on the left. Foster was to move along the cart-road in front, while Reno and Parke flanked the enemy's position by advancing through the woods on either side. The marshes and lagoons with which the island is covered rendered the approach difficult. A battery of six 12-pound boat howitzers headed the central column.

The field work, which constituted the enemy's sole defense against this land attack, was about a mile distant from Ashby's Harbor, on the cart-road. In its front the timber had been cut away to afford range for the artillery. It was garrisoned by 300 men, the remaining portion of the defensive force being held in reserve. Besides the clearing in front, the position was covered, front and flank, by an extensive lagoon.

The Confederate skirmishers were soon met and driven in, and at a curve in the road the battery of howitzers was placed to bear upon the enemy's battery a short distance ahead. The howitzers were exposed to a severe fire from three heavy guns in the Confederate work. An advance was made by the enemy with a view to flank Foster's brigade, the others not having yet come into action or even attracted the notice of the Confederate officers. A

JESSIE L. RENO.

pretty sharp action followed between the Twenty-third and Twenty-seventh Massachusetts regiments and a portion of the Wise Legion under Anderson and Captain Wise, in which the Confederates were repulsed. Here it was that Captain Wise received a wound which soon afterward proved mortal. The heroism of the Federal soldiers, who in many cases were obliged to stand waist-deep in water, was admirable. The wounded, as they were carried to the rear, smiled cheerfully and encouraged their companions. Nowhere did a single soldier flinch from the work in hand. Soon Parke passed Foster on the right and came into action. A charge was then ordered to be made by Hawkins's regiment of Zouaves, the Ninth New York, and simultaneously with this movement the flanking column under Reno was disclosed on the left. The Confederate battery was now enfiladed from both sides by a raking fire which the bravest soldier could not stand and live, and the only hope left was in flight. The stars and stripes were hoisted above the hostile battery, and the Federal columns hastened on in pursuit of the Confederates, who were retreating toward Nag's Head. The Twenty-first Massachusetts and the Fifty-first New York were in the advance, and just reached the shore in time to prevent the escape of a small number of prisoners, among whom was Captain Wise. The Confederate encampments were still farther north; from these the enemy's reserve force was driven toward the upper end of the island. But there was no chance for Shaw to make another stand. He therefore surrendered his entire command, which had that morning been re-enforced by four companies of the First North Carolina and a battalion under Colonel Green, bringing it up to a strength of at least 2500 men. Three thousand stand of small arms were also captured. Among the prisoners we have mentioned Captain Jennings Wise. He was wounded in the battle, and only survived it a few hours. Captain Wise had been previously editor of the Richmond Enquirer. The casualties in the Federal fleet amounted to twenty-five, of whom six were killed; in the military division Burnside reported a loss of 235, of whom thirty-five were killed.

The Confederate fleet endeavored to escape by running up the Pasquotank River to Elizabeth City. The day after the capture of Roanoke Island, thirteen steamers, under Commander Rowan, were sent in pursuit. It was also a part of Rowan's mission to proceed up the river and destroy a link of the Albemarle and Chesapeake Canal. At nine o'clock on the morning of the 10th, Rowan met the enemy's vessels off Elizabeth City, and captured or destroyed the entire fleet.[1] The Ellis, one of the Confederate steamers, was transferred to the Federal fleet. Between forty and fifty prisoners were taken.

LANDING OF THE TROOPS BELOW NEWBERN.

session of the town. Eight cannon, and a schooner on the stocks, were destroyed. Two schooners were captured, one of them having on board 4000 bushels of corn. On the 18th of February, Flag-officer Goldsborough and General Burnside issued a joint proclamation to the people of North Carolina.[1]

Albemarle Sound, at its western extremity, opens northward into the Chowan River, and eastward into the Roanoke. Leaving Croatan Sound on the afternoon of the 18th, Commander Rowan, with the Delaware, proceeded on a reconnoissance up this river. Two steamers were to follow him with Hawkins's Zouaves from Roanoke, and, stopping at Elizabeth City, he took away with him the force at that point, consisting of five steamers. Having ordered a reconnoissance to Plymouth, and anchored his fleet at the mouth of Roanoke River, with orders to follow him when the reconnoissance should be completed, he proceeded, with the Delaware and Perry, to Winton. At this place Union men were said to be in arms in expectation of the arrival of Burnside's men. His vessels were fired upon by a North Carolina battery. Early on the 20th, the entire command having arrived, after a short conflict the town was captured.

General Burnside, after the capture of Roanoke Island, directed his force, in conjunction with the naval division, now left under Rowan's command, against Newbern. This city was situated up the Neuse River, which empties into Pamlico Sound on the western side. The two commands embarked from Hatteras Inlet March 12, and that night anchored off the mouth of Slocum's Creek, eighteen miles below Newbern. Here, the next morning, the military division landed under cover of the fleet. The troops were disembarked in the midst of great enthusiasm, some of them, too impatient to wait for the boats, leaping into the water and wading waist-deep to the shore. It was twelve miles from the place of landing to the enemy's camp, and the roads were rivers of mire, through which the soldiers were obliged to march, dragging their heavy artillery with them. This toilsome march consumed the day, and the boat howitzers did not come up till three o'clock on the morning of the 14th. The vessels of the fleet, in the mean while, had moved up the river, shelling the woods in advance of the troops. At daylight on the 14th General Burnside ordered an advance, throwing General Foster with a column against the Confederate left. A second column, under Reno, was to attack the right; while a third, under Parke, was to attack in front. General Reno advanced along the railroad, and the other two columns by the turnpike. The soldiers had suffered much from tedious marches and exposure to rain, but they advanced to the attack with eager-

SINKING OF THE CONFEDERATE FLEET.

The next morning, after the conflict between the two fleets, the Federal steamers passed into the harbor off Edenton, at the west end of Albemarle Sound. A portion of a flying artillery regiment stationed in the town fled, and many of the citizens, excited by apprehension on account of some unfounded reports, left their homes. The Federal troops took undisturbed pos-

[1] "The names of the men-of-war vessels captured and destroyed by our vessels since we reached this island are as follows: Flag-steamer Sea-bird, destroyed; steamer Forest, destroyed; steamer Curlew, destroyed; steamer Fanny, destroyed; steamer Ellis, captured; steamer Black Warrior, destroyed, and a new gun-boat on the stocks at Elizabeth City, also destroyed—making seven vessels in all; and each of the first six, I may add, was remarkably well armed as a gun-boat. All of them, except the Curlew, were destroyed or captured in the attack at Elizabeth City; and it may be proper to mention that the whole of them, saving, of course, the one on the stocks, were struck by our projectiles of one kind or another in the course of the engagement they had with us off here on the 7th instant. The Curlew, during the engagement of the 7th, was so badly injured by one of our 100-pounder shells that she was compelled to seek shelter close under Fort Forest, where, as soon as our vessels burst through the double row of extensive obstructions (formed by piles and sunken vessels, and at, as we are credibly informed, a cost of $400,000) in order to get at her and also attack the fort, she was set on fire by her own crew, and, almost simultaneously, the fort, too, shared the same fate from the hands of those who were in it. In about an hour afterward, in the dark of the evening, both blew up."—Flag-officer Goldsborough's Report, February 20, 1862.

[1] "Roanoke Island, N. C., February 18, 1862.

"The mission of our joint expedition is not to invade any of your rights, but to assert the authority of the United States, and to close with you the desolating war brought upon your state by comparatively few bad men in your midst. Influenced infinitely more by the worst passions of human nature than by any show of human reason, they are still urging you astray to gratify their unholy purposes. They impose upon your credulity by telling you of wicked and even diabolical intentions on our part; of our desire to destroy your freedom, demolish your property, liberate your slaves, injure your women, and such like enormities, all of which, we assure you, is not only ridiculous, but utterly and willfully false.

"We are Christians as well as yourselves, and we profess to know full well and to feel profoundly the sacred obligations of that character. No apprehensions need be entertained that the demands of humanity or justice will be disregarded. We shall inflict no injury unless forced to do so by your own acts, and upon this you may confidently rely.

"These men are your worst enemies. They, in truth, have drawn you into your present condition, and are the real disturbers of your peace and the happiness of your firesides. We invite you, in the name of the Constitution, and in that of virtuous loyalty and civilization, to separate yourselves at once from their malign influence, to return to your allegiance, and not compel us to resort farther to the force under our control. The government asks only that its authority may be recognized, and, we repeat, in no manner or way does it desire to interfere with your laws constitutionally established, your institutions of any kind whatever, your property of any sort, or your usages in any respect.

"L. M. Goldsborough, Flag-officer commanding North Atlantic Blockading Squadron.

"A. E. Burnside, Brigadier General commanding Department of North Carolina."

ELIZABETH CITY, NORTH CAROLINA.

ness. They had the day before learned of the evacuation of Manassas by the Confederate army of the Potomac. Reno, on the railroad, had the advance. The enemy's works were five miles below Newbern, and were a mile in extent, protected on the river bank by a battery of thirteen guns, and on the opposite side by a line of redoubts over half a mile in length. This line of works was defended by eight regiments of infantry, five hundred cavalry, and three batteries of field artillery of six guns each. The Confederate forces were under the command of General Branch.

General Reno's column was moving upon the enemy's right flank. As it moved up the railroad, a train was observed which had just arrived, bringing re-enforcements to the enemy. This train was attacked, and the enemy driven behind his intrenchments. The engagement then commenced, the Twenty-first Massachusetts regiment coming within short range of the enemy's redoubts and drawing their fire. General Foster's brigade had come up on the main road at the right and had formed his line, the Twenty-fourth Massachusetts on the extreme right and the Tenth Connecticut on the left. Between the Tenth and Reno's position General Parke held the centre. The Federal line thus formed extended more than a mile. The action, which was already begun, was quite severe. In some parts of the Federal line, particularly on the right centre, the swampy ground, broken by ravines opening toward the enemy, exposed the soldiers to the enemy's fire. The Twenty-third Massachusetts, on the left of the Tenth Connecticut, had hardly got into position before its colonel, Henry Merritt, fell, a cannon shot having passed through his body. The naval battery was placed in the centre, and the officers in charge of the guns stood by them persistently, although in some cases but a single gunner remained. Hammond, in charge of the Hetzel, lost all his men. On Reno's right, also, the fire was very hot. Adjutant Frazer A. Stearns, son of President Stearns, of Amherst College, and attached to the Twenty-first Massachusetts, was shot early in the battle.

Thus far the Confederate troops had the advantage, for, although inferior in numbers, they fought behind breast-works. A charge was now made by four companies of the Twenty-first, who marched from the railroad at double-quick and drove the enemy from one of their breast-works, hoisted the Union colors, and were advancing against a second work, when a larger force attacked them, and they were obliged to withdraw. An assault made by the Fourth Rhode Island on Parke's right was more permanently successful, resulting in the capture of a battery and two flags. From this work, in the centre of the Confederate line, Colonel Rodman, pursuing his advantage, charged upon the enemy's works farther to the left, which Reno was also assailing with his entire command. Their centre being now broken, the enemy fell back under the combined attack on his right. While this was going on, the Twenty-fourth Massachusetts, holding the extreme right of the entire line of attack, pushed forward by a rapid movement and gained a position within the enemy's intrenchments, which were then occupied by Foster's whole brigade. The Confederates were now, after four hours' fighting, in full retreat to Newbern. All three of Burnsides brigades were soon engaged in pursuit, and reached the river bank opposite Newbern about the middle of the afternoon. In the mean time the gun-boats had come up, and, by means of a steamer which they had captured, the army was conveyed across the river. The Confederates had escaped, by means of the railroad, to Goldsborough, after having burned the bridge across the river.

The gun-boats had safely passed the obstructions below the city, and three or four forts which commanded the river, the most formidable of which was Fort Thompson, mounting thirteen guns, two of them rifled 32-pounders. This fort protected the left flank of the land force resisting Burnside's approach, and its reduction by the gun-boats formed an important part of the battle. Not a man was lost in the naval division. Several of the vessels were slightly injured in passing the obstructions.

WATER BATTERY AT NEWBERN.

LANDING OF TROOPS AT SLOCUM'S CREEK.

BOMBARDMENT OF NEWBERN.

As the results of this victory, besides the city, General Burnside took eight batteries, numbering forty-six heavy guns, and three batteries of light artillery of six guns each, two steam-boats, and a large amount of commissary and quarter-master's stores, and two hundred prisoners. The Federal loss, as estimated in Burnside's report, was ninety-one killed and 466 wounded; the loss in officers was very severe. The Confederates admitted a loss of 500, including the prisoners.

A week after the fall of Newbern, Washington, at the mouth of Pamlico River, was surrendered to a portion of the Federal fleet under Lieutenant Commander A. Murray. On the 19th of April, General Reno, with five regiments, took possession of Camden, the capital of Camden county, and situated on the Pasquotank River, opposite Elizabeth City. Three of the regiments were landed at midnight of the 18th–19th three miles below Camden, but, by an incompetent guide, were led nearly a dozen miles out of their way. The Confederates were intrenched at South Mills, across the road by which Reno the next morning approached the town. Their rear was protected by a thick wood. From this position they were driven after a sharp engagement, in which the Federal loss was fourteen killed and ninety-six wounded. Most of Reno's men were so much wearied with their long march and the heat that pursuit was impossible.

The work of the expedition, according to the plan laid down by General McClellan, was now almost accomplished. It is true nothing had been done to seriously threaten the Weldon Railroad, but the Confederate position at Norfolk had been effectually flanked, and complete possession had been gained of Albemarle and Pamlico Sound. The reduction of Fort Macon would give the national government the entire coast of North Carolina. This fort commanded the entrance of Beaufort Harbor, one of the best on the Southern coast. It was situated on the eastern extremity of Bogue Banks, opposite Morehead City, and was considered more formidable than either of the forts yet attacked by the Federal fleet. This fort was bombarded on the 25th of April by three steamers and by three siege batteries on shore. One of the latter was mounted with three 32-pounder Parrotts. These shore batteries were constructed behind sand-hills, and, besides the Parrott guns, mounted eight mortars. The naval squadron carried about thirty guns, and was under Commander Samuel Lockwood, of the Daylight. The military division consisted of two regiments, the Eighth Connecticut and Fourth Rhode Island, with five companies of the Fifth Rhode Island. The action commenced early in the morning from the batteries on shore. At half past eight the squadron began to fire on the fort, the three gun-boats moving in an ellipse, and delivering their fire by turns. It was evident, however, in a very short time, that these boats, in the unsteady waters where they were situated, would have little effect on the fort, while they were themselves suffering severe injury, and at ten o'clock they withdrew. The batteries on shore, also, during the early part of the day, fired too high, and most of their heavy shells exploded too far beyond the fort. About half an hour, however, after the withdrawal of the boats, this mistake was corrected. The bombardment from shore was continued nearly all day. There was not a strong garrison in the fort, not more than five companies, all told, under Colonel White, and they held out with great tenacity until their guns were all silenced. At four o'clock P.M. the flag of truce was displayed and the firing ceased. Four hundred prisoners were captured. The reduction of Fort Macon gave the Federal navy a port of entry and a harbor fitted for vessels of heavy draught. One of the most favorable results of the occupation of the North Carolina coast was the accession of a large number of negroes, who would otherwise have contributed greatly to the military strength of the Confederacy, as every slave on the plantation was equivalent to a white in arms. The slave population of the counties occupied was estimated in 1850 as over 30,000.

R R R

Bombardment of Fort Macon.

JOHN ERICSSON.

CHAPTER XIII.
THE VIRGINIA AND THE MONITOR.

Confederate Privateers. — Treatment of captured Privateersmen. — Necessity of Iron-clads. — Transformation of the Merrimac into the Virginia. — The Stevens Battery. — Iron-clads proposed to the Federal Government. — Approval of the Plan of the Monitor. — Its Inventor and Builder. — The Revolving Turret, and its Inventor. — Launch of the Monitor. — Hampton Roads. — Appearance of the Virginia. — Sinking of the Cumberland. — Destruction of the Congress. — The Minnesota, Roanoke, and St. Lawrence. — Wooden Vessels and Iron-clads. — Close of the first Day's Fight. — Appearance of the Monitor. — First Encounter of Iron-clads. — The Result. — The Monitor and Virginia watching each other. — Destruction of the Virginia. — Action at Drewry's Bluff. — Loss of the Monitor. — Perilous Voyage of the Passaic. — New Monitors built. — Obstacles to their Construction. — Forging Armor-plates. — Capacity of Turreted Vessels. — The Turrets as proposed by Timby. — Automatic Aiming and Discharge. — Advantages of the Turret System.

AT the commencement of the war the Confederates were without any naval force. Of the fifty vessels which they had seized in their ports and rivers only a few were capable of service on the ocean. They had neither time nor means to construct vessels of war; but the Federal merchantmen offered a tempting prize which it was hoped might be secured by private armed vessels sailing under letters of marque. During the spring and early summer of 1861 several privateers were fitted out. Most of them came to grief; none were successful. The revenue schooner Aikin was seized at Charleston, and fitted out as a privateer under the name of the Petrel. She had hardly got to sea when she came in sight of the frigate St. Lawrence, to which she gave chase, supposing her to be an unarmed merchantman. Coming within range, the frigate discharged a single broadside, which sank the privateer. The Echo, a condemned slaver, was seized at Charleston, and equipped as a privateer under the name of the Jeff. Davis. She made several prizes. Among these was the S. J. Waring, captured within less than two hundred miles from New York. The colored steward, William Tillman, and two seamen, were left on board, with a prize crew of five men, to take the vessel to Charleston. One night Tillman killed three of the captors, and, aided by one of the crew, compelled the others to take the Waring to New York, where salvage was awarded to him as the re-captor. The Jeff. Davis was soon after wrecked on the Florida coast. The Savannah, a pilot schooner of only 54 tons, was fitted out as a privateer. After making a single prize, she was captured by the frigate Perry, and her captain and crew were put in irons as pirates. They were brought to trial as pirates, but the jury failing to agree, they were remanded. The Confederate government thereupon selected an equal number of Federal officers, among whom was Colonel Corcoran, captured at Bull Run, and placed them in close confinement, to be treated in the same manner as the crew of the Savannah. In consequence of this action, and of the prevailing sentiment at home and abroad, the Federal government receded from its position, and the rights of prisoners of war were tacitly conceded to captured privateersmen.

The blockade of the Southern coast soon became so strict that privateers had no chance of sending their prizes into their own ports, and those of foreign nations were closed by proclamations of neutrality. Privateers could only destroy their prizes without gaining any profit for themselves. The only practical advantage which the Confederates derived from the issue of letters of marque was the tacit acknowledgment by the Federal government that they were actual belligerents, and that prisoners made from them on the sea as well as on the land were to be considered as prisoners of war.

Though Confederate citizens could not wage war upon the ocean with profit to themselves, government might greatly injure the enemy by preying upon its commerce. Armed vessels might be fitted out under the Confederate flag, bearing regular commissions as men-of-war. They had no ships built for this purpose, and no means for constructing them at home. Until they could buy or build them abroad, they could only arm and equip some of the merchant-steamers which had fallen into their hands. The Nashville, formerly plying as a packet between New York and Charleston, and the Marques de la Habana, a New Orleans and Havana trader, her name having been changed to the Sumter, were armed and sent to sea. The fate of these two vessels, which has already been described in this History, showed that steamers built for commerce were not adapted for cruisers. Steamers possessing great speed and sufficiently stanch to carry a heavy armament were demanded. In course of time several of these were procured in Great Britain. The career of two of these, the Florida and the Alabama, will be narrated hereafter. We now turn to a subject of greater importance, which comes up earlier in order of time.

The Confederate authorities early saw the necessity of floating batteries to defend their coasts, harbors, and inland waters. They could not hope to rival their enemy in the number of vessels. They must rely upon the superior offensive and defensive force of a few. The maritime powers of Europe had instituted experiments to test the practicability of rendering ships invulnerable by clothing them with iron. France had built La Gloire, and Great Britain the Warrior. These were ordinary men-of-war, covered wholly or in part with solid iron plates four or five inches thick, which was thought sufficient to withstand the heaviest shot possible in naval warfare. But to construct a vessel of this class, with all the appliances of European navy yards and founderies, required months. The Confederates needed such vessels in weeks. They had no means of building a hull or of making an engine. They had no iron which a European naval constructor would have thought fit for armor. But imbecility, treachery, and accident gave them a hull and engine ready for immediate use.

In 1855 the United States built at different navy yards three powerful steam frigates, the Merrimac, the Roanoke, and the Minnesota. They were all nearly alike, of about 3500 tons burden, carrying from forty to fifty heavy guns. In April, 1861, the Merrimac was at the Norfolk Navy Yard, undergoing repairs. When that place was abandoned, she was set on fire, scuttled, and sunk. She was soon after raised by the Confederates, and John M. Brooke, formerly a lieutenant in the United States Navy, John L. Porter, Confederate naval constructor, and William P. Williamson, chief engineer, were ordered to examine into her condition and the use to which she might be put. They reported that her upper works were so much damaged that she could not be rebuilt without great expense and delay; but the bottom part of the hull, the boilers, and heavy parts of the engine, were almost without injury, and that these could be adapted for a shot-proof steam battery more quickly and for one third of the sum which it would cost to construct such a vessel anew. The plan was furnished by Brooke and Porter. The central part of the hull, for something more than half of its length, was cut down to within three or four feet of the water-line to form the gun-deck, and the hull was plated with iron to a depth of about six feet below the water-line. A casemate of entirely novel construction was built upon the gun-deck. Pine beams, a foot square and fifteen feet long, were placed side by side, like rafters, at an inclination of about 45 degrees. These projected over the sides of the vessel like the eaves of a house, their ends dipping two feet below the water. Upon these beams were placed two layers of oak planks four inches thick, one layer horizontal, the other vertical. This was first overlaid with ordinary flat bars of iron four and a half inches thick. Experiments which were made under the care of Lieutenant Brooke showed that this thickness of iron was inadequate, and a layer of railroad iron was added. This casemate did not come to a point, like the roof of a house, but there was a flat space on the top, rendered bomb-proof by plates of wrought iron. From this roof projected a short smoke-stack. The armament consisted of eight 11-inch guns, four on each side, and a 100-pound rifled Armstrong gun at each end. The ends of the vessel were cut down still lower, so as to be two feet below water. A light bulwark, or false bow, of wood was built. This served the twofold purpose of preventing the water from banking up against the casemate when the vessel was in motion, and of a tank to diminish the draft. The inclined roof and submerged eaves and ends constituted the novel and distinctive features of this battery, to which was given the name of the Virginia. The draft of the Merrimac had been about twenty-three feet, and her speed was fourteen or fifteen miles an hour. The iron heaped upon her when she was converted into the Virginia brought her down about two feet more, and her speed was reduced quite one half.[1]

The construction of the Virginia was commenced in June, 1861, and pushed forward as rapidly as possible. The fact that this battery was being built could not long be concealed from the Federal authorities, and every effort was made to mislead them by false information. Now it was reported that the Virginia was ready for action, and would soon come out; then some Southern paper would contain a paragraph affirming that she was a failure;

---

[1] The description of the Virginia is necessarily imperfect. The plans were carefully concealed in the archives of the Confederate naval department, which has never divulged them. No one except her builders and crew appears ever to have been on board of her. When she was blown up, so complete was the destruction that no fragment of her armor has been discovered. There is some doubt as to the character and thickness of the iron which covered the casemate. We have accepted, with some doubt, the statement of the double thickness, flat bars and railroad iron, making from seven to nine inches in all. This is confirmed by the effect of the shot which she withstood, which would certainly have penetrated four inches if struck perpendicularly. The accompanying picture is the best ever taken. The submerged stern is not shown, as it was below water and invisible. The bow, which appears projecting before the casemate, was simply the light, false bow, built upon the real bow, which was below water. The sloping sides should have been represented as dipping below the water, instead of stopping at the edge of the hull, above the water-line.

THE VIRGINIA.

her armor had been found too thin to be of service; more had been piled upon her, until accurate calculation showed that she would never float. Again it was said that her back had been broken in attempting to launch her, and that she was abandoned. Several persons made their appearance in the Federal lines claiming to have been employed upon her, and furnished rude drawings of her construction. Whether they were treacherous or ignorant can not be known; but their descriptions were certainly far from accurate.

The Federal government was slow to perceive the necessity of iron-clad vessels. Before the rebellion it had made no direct experiments in this direction. Robert and Edwin Stevens, wealthy citizens of New Jersey, had indeed, for some years, been engaged in constructing an iron battery upon a plan of their own, and Congress had at different times made appropriations to the amount of half a million; the builders had also expended more than a quarter of a million dollars. In December, 1861, a commission was appointed to examine this vessel. They reported unfavorably. To complete her would cost more than $550,000, making the whole expense nearly $1,300,000, and it would be months before she could be made available. Meanwhile, when Congress met in extra session in July, 1861, the Naval Department asked for an appropriation of $50,000 for the purpose of testing iron plates. This was refused; but the President ordered that plate should be prepared, without waiting for an appropriation. At length, on the 3d of August, just before the close of the session, an appropriation of $1,500,000 was made for building one or more iron-clads. The next day an advertisement was issued for proposals, and a commission appointed to examine the plans suggested. Seventeen proposals were presented for vessels ranging from 83 to 400 feet in length, to cost from $32,000 to $1,500,000 each. The commission reported in favor of three different vessels. The Ironsides, by Merrick & Sons, of Philadelphia, was to be a regular man-of-war, covered with four and a half inch solid plates. She was to be 240 feet long, about 3500 tons burden, to carry 20 heavy guns in broadside. She would be completed in a year, at a cost of $780,000. The Galena, by C. S. Bushnell, of New Haven, was to be a steamer of 700 tons, brigantine rigged, pierced for 18 guns. Her frame to be of solid timber 18 inches thick, covered from 2 to 4 inches with plates of thin rolled iron. Her armor was found in the end to be wholly inadequate to resist heavy guns. Her cost was $235,000. Both these vessels were built upon general models which had been long in use.

Of an altogether different class was the Monitor proposed by John Ericsson, of New York.[1] Her design was so wholly new in every respect that the approval of the commission was cautiously guarded. They said: "This is novel, but seems to be based upon a plan which will render the battery shot and shell proof. We are somewhat apprehensive that her properties for sea are not such as a sea-going vessel should possess; but she may be moved from place to place on our coast in smooth water. We recommend that an experiment be made with one battery of this description on the terms proposed, with a guaranty and forfeiture in case of a failure in any of the points and properties of the vessel as proposed."

Novel as the plan was to others, it was no sudden conception of the inventor. It had been thought out to the minutest detail, and been constructed in drawings and models for years. So confident was Ericsson of the perfect success of his invention, that he proposed for it the name of the "Monitor," in order "to admonish the South of the fate of the rebellion, Great Britain of her fading naval supremacy, and the English government of the folly of spending millions in fixed fortifications for defense." These terms were accepted. The price was to be $275,000. The contract was signed on the 5th of October. The construction of the vessel was undertaken by Thomas F. Rowland, who, starting in life as the driver of a railway engine, then becoming an engineer and ship-builder, had, at the age of twen-

ty-eight, become proprietor of the "Continental Works" at Greenpoint, in the city of Brooklyn. Ericsson superintended the whole work in person. In spite of his threescore years, he was every where skipping up and down ladders, and over planks and gangways, as though he were a boy of sixteen. It seemed as though a plate could not be fitted or a bolt driven without his being at the workman's side. So rapidly was the work pressed forward that the vessel was launched, with her engines on board, on the 30th of January, just a hundred days after the keel was laid.

The hull of the Monitor was constructed of a double thickness of iron, three eighths of an inch thick, strengthened by iron ribs and knees. It was 140 feet long, 30 feet wide at the broadest part, and 12 feet deep. The shape and proportions were like those of the half of an egg-shell slightly flattened at the bottom. An Indian canoe is an almost perfect miniature of this hull, and is apparently hardly less frail, for a cannon ball would pierce the thin iron as easily as a pistol shot would the bark sides of the canoe. But this frail hull was so protected that when afloat no shot could reach it. Five feet below the top, an iron shelf, strongly braced, projected nearly four feet from the sides. This shelf was filled up with oaken blocks three and a half feet thick, over which were bolted five series of iron plates, each an inch thick. This armor-shelf or platform projected sixteen feet at the stern, in order to cover the rudder and propeller, and ten feet at the bow, to protect the anchor. The entire length on deck was 166 feet, the breadth 42. When afloat, the entire hull and three feet of the armor-platform were submerged. To the eye the vessel was merely a low raft, rising only two feet above water. No shot from a hostile vessel could reach the vulnerable hull without passing through the invulnerable armor. This defensive structure of the Monitor was solely the invention of Ericsson.

But a vessel of war must possess offensive as well as defensive power.

THOMAS F. ROWLAND.

---

[1] John Ericsson was born in Sweden in 1803. From boyhood he manifested decided aptitude for mechanical invention. In 1823 he went to England, where he acquired the highest reputation as a constructive engineer. He came to America in 1839, assuming at once and maintaining a foremost place in his profession.

ENGINE-ROOM

TURRET MACHINERY

WARD-ROOM

STIMERS NEWTON CAMPBELL SUNST...ANDS
THE MONITOR
JEFFERS GA...ER STODDER

INTERIOR OF THE TOWER.

WHEEL HOUSE

CAPTAIN'S CABIN.

BERTH DECK.

READY FOR ACTION.

LAUNCH OF THE MONITOR.

This in the Monitor was embodied in two 11-inch guns, a heavier ordnance than had ever before been placed on any vessel. Ericsson had struck upon a principle which all European engineers had strangely missed. In the field, the primary object in warfare is to slaughter the enemy's men; in naval warfare, to destroy his vessels. A rifle bullet will disable a man as effectually as a cannon ball; heavy shot only will destroy a ship. In the field, the combatant will succeed who can strike the more blows; on the water, the one who can strike the heavier. The guns of the Monitor could be placed only upon the deck; these, as well as the gunners, must be protected. For the means of doing this the Monitor was indebted to the revolving turret, the invention of another than Ericsson, though he displayed rare genius in first adapting it to practical use. Ten years before Ericsson had dreamed of the Monitor, a lad residing in an inland American village had thought of revolving turrets.

Theodore R. Timby was born in Duchess County, New York, in 1822. He received the education usual among the sons of American farmers. Before he was twenty years old he was engaged in active business; but the bent of his mind was toward mechanical invention. At sixteen he constructed a model of a floating dry-dock, but it was pronounced to be practically useless by those to whom it was proposed, and he abandoned it. Years after it was re-invented by others; but these docks now in use contain nothing essential which was not embodied in the model of this young resident of a country town. Several other inventions were more profitable. His first model for a revolving turret was made in 1841. It was hardly six inches in height, but contains the germ of the whole invention. On the 18th of January, 1843, he filed his first caveat for this in the Patent Office. The specifications are for a "revolving metallic tower, and for a revolving tower for a floating battery, to be propelled by steam." In the mean while he was constructing a large iron model, which was finished in the spring of 1843, and was during that year publicly exhibited throughout the country. He urged his invention upon the attention of the American government, besides constructing several models, one of which was sent to the French government, and another to the Emperor of China. Our military authorities admitted the practicability of the invention, but assumed it to be wholly superfluous. The defenses of the country, it was said, were already more than could ever be required. A favorable report was indeed made, in 1848, to the Senate, one of the committee being Jefferson Davis. No farther action was taken on this report, although it was endorsed by the chief of the Ordnance Bureau. Timby, however, took out patents covering the broad claim "for a revolving tower for offensive and defensive warfare, whether used on land or water." The advantages of the revolving turret for naval warfare are apparent at a glance. It furnishes a shield for guns and gunners which can be made invulnerable without using a weight of iron greater than can be floated; and it enables the vessel, without altering its own position, to bring its whole ordnance to bear upon any point in the circle. When Ericsson bent himself to the invention of a floating battery, he found the one essential thing necessary to give it practical offensive power ready to his hands, though it is not probable that he then knew to whom he was indebted for it.

The turret of the Monitor was constructed of plates of iron an inch thick, about three feet wide,

Sss

and nine feet long. Eight of these plates constituted its thickness. It was thus nine feet high and eight inches thick, with a diameter of about twenty feet. The two port-holes, side by side, were oval, just large enough horizontally to allow the gun to be run out, with sufficient vertical height to give room for the elevation of the guns to secure the range for different distances. It was made to revolve upon a central shaft by means of a separate engine. When not in action, by driving back a wedge it rested firmly upon a metallic ring upon the deck. The guns were loaded within the turret, and only run out to be discharged. The deck was perfectly flat, without even a permanent railing. The smoke-pipe and draft-pipe for admitting air to the hull could be lowered below the deck. When the vessel was prepared for action the deck presented a smooth surface, broken only by the huge round turret, and a low square pilot-house near the bow. The vessel drew ten feet of water, and was rated at 776 tons.

The work of the constructors was completed early in January. Two full months were spent in fitting the armament and testing the apparatus. On the 5th of March, in obedience to a sudden order, she set out for Fortress Monroe. She reached her destination on the night of the 8th, just in time to avert an overwhelming catastrophe, but just too late to prevent a great disaster; for the Virginia had come out ten hours before, and won the first battle in Hampton Roads.

Hampton Roads is an indentation setting in westward from Chesapeake Bay. The narrow entrance is guarded by Fortress Monroe, built on a peninsula jutting out from the southern shore. It then spreads out into an oval harbor some five miles in diameter. Here and there is a shallow place; but almost every part is deep enough to float the largest vessel. The estuaries of two rivers enter the top of the harbor from opposite directions: the James from the northwest, and the Elizabeth from the southeast. At the head of the estuary of the Elizabeth, eight miles from its opening, are Norfolk on the east side, and Portsmouth, with Gosport, its suburb, on the west. The navy yard is at Gosport, which is about twenty miles from the entrance to the Roads. The harbor formed by the bay and estuary is one of the best on the continent. Hampton Roads was made the great naval rendezvous for the Federal fleet. The north shore was occupied by the Federals, who had a camp at Newport News, at the mouth of the James. The Confederates had intrenched camps at Sewall's Point and Craney Island, on each side of the mouth of the Elizabeth, covering the approach to Norfolk. During the spring and early summer of 1861, Norfolk had been so feebly held that it might have been taken. Butler, who had 11,000 men at Fortress Monroe, projected an expedition for this purpose; but the battle of Bull Run put a stop, for a time, to all active operations by the Federal armies. Every possible man was withdrawn to Washington. Only 5000 were left at Fortress Monroe, and for six months the enemy were left to construct the Virginia without hinderance.

Meantime Federal fleets had assembled in the Roads and had been dispatched upon various expeditions. In the first days of March the only vessels of war at that point were the steam frigates Minnesota and Roanoke, twins of the Merrimac, and the sailing frigates Cumberland, 24 guns, saved from the seizure at Norfolk, and Congress, 50 guns. The St. Lawrence, 50-gun ship, mounting 12 guns, came in on the 6th from a cruise. Besides these was a fleet of transports and tugs. The Minnesota and Roanoke lay down the Roads, near Fortress Monroe. The Roanoke, always unlucky, was disabled, having broken her shaft five months before. She bore the flag of Captain Marston, then the senior officer of the post, for Goldsborough, the flag-officer in command, was absent with the Albemarle expedition. The Cumberland and Congress lay off the mouth of the Elizabeth River. Goldsborough had given strict orders that no sailing vessel should be left without a tug at hand to manage it. This provision was neglected. The apprehensions excited by reports of the near completion of the Merrimac or Virginia had died away. Men had come to look upon her as a bugbear, or,

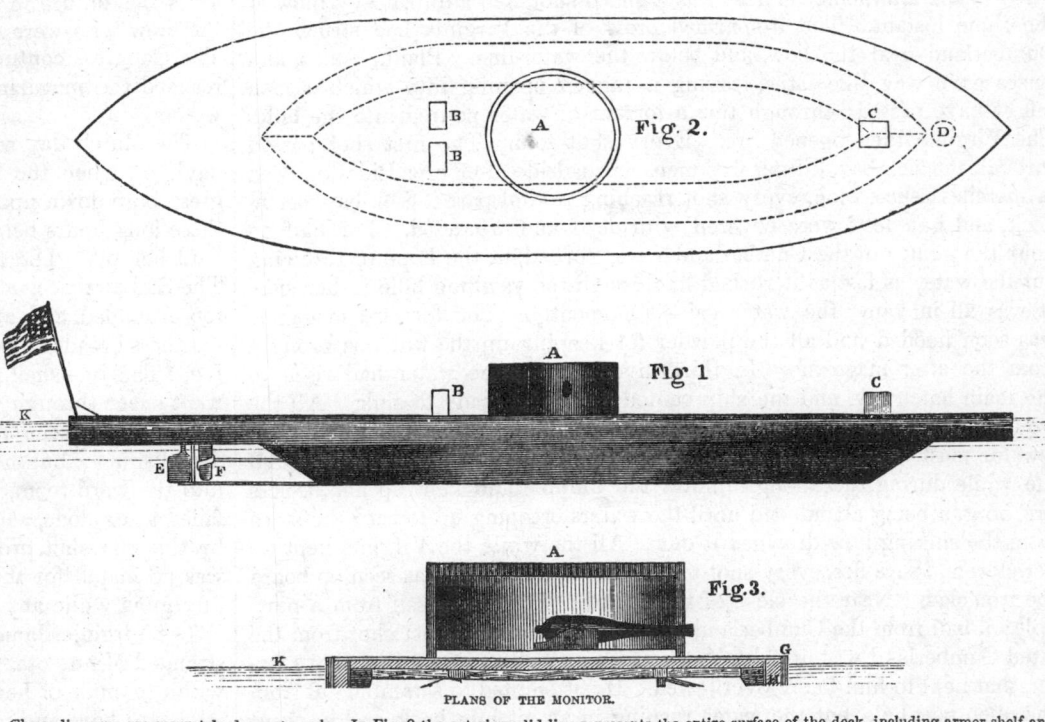

PLANS OF THE MONITOR.

These diagrams are accurately drawn to scale.—In Fig. 2 the exterior solid line represents the entire surface of the deck, including armor-shelf and overhang at bow and stern. The exterior dotted line represents the top of the proper hull; the interior line shows the dimensions of the flat bottom.—Fig. 1 is a profile of the vessel; the portion visible when the vessel is afloat is shown by the place of the water-line.—Fig. 3 is a vertical section of the turret.—The reference letters are the same throughout: A, Revolving Turret.—B, B, Smoke-pipe.—C, Pilot-house.—D, Anchor-well.—E, Rudder.—F, Propeller.—G, Iron Armor.—H, Braces for Deck Beams.—K, K, Water-line.—L, Gun.—M, Gun-carriage.

at worst, an enemy that could easily be managed by the Minnesota. "We are tired of waiting for the Merrimac," wrote Captain Van Brunt, of the Minnesota, "and wish she would come out."

At noon on Saturday, the 8th of March, what appeared to be three small steamers were seen coming down the Elizabeth. One of these, merely from the large size of her smoke-pipe, was conjectured to be the Virginia. Cut down as she was, she looked in the distance no larger than a tug. Her appearance at that time was a surprise. The two frigates lay at anchor, with the wash-clothes of the crew hanging from the rigging. Radford, the commander of the Cumberland, was on the Roanoke, miles away, acting as a member of a court of inquiry. He took horse and rode for Newport News, where he arrived just in time to see his vessel go down. Marston ordered the Minnesota to get under way at once, and summoned two tugs to tow the broken-shafted Roanoke to the scene of action. The Minnesota was soon under full headway. Her speed being twice that of the enemy, she could choose her own ground. Van Brunt meant to run her into the iron-clad, whose armor would be no protection against such a blow, and the shock would have broken her in two. Passing near Sewall's Point, fire was opened upon the Minnesota from the rifle battery, one shot crippling her mainmast. She returned a broadside, and steamed on till she came within a couple of miles of the enemy. The tide was running ebb; the Minnesota drew twenty-three feet, and there was now less depth of water at a shoal part of the channel; but the bottom was soft, and it was vainly hoped she might be forced over. She stuck fast, out of range of the Virginia, and lay an idle spectator of the destruction of the Cumberland and Congress. The Roanoke was dragged slowly on by two tugs. She too ran aground at the stern, in twenty-one feet of water, and could go no farther. Her head was dragged around, and the helpless hulk was pointed down the bay. Going and returning, she was fired upon from the batteries at Sewall's Point. They aimed wildly; some shot passed through the rigging and fell far beyond. The fire was returned, but the balls fell short of the mark.

The Virginia left the navy yard at Gosport at 11 o'clock in the morning. Her commander, Franklin Buchanan, had entered the United States Navy thirty-five years before. He had attained the rank of captain, and stood high on the roll. When the war broke out he was commander of the navy yard at Washington. He then threw up his commission and entered the Confederate service. Born in Maryland, he had not even the pretext of following his state in taking up arms against his country. As the Virginia left her dock, the wharves on both sides of the river were crowded with spectators. Two barricades which closed the river were opened, and the iron-clad, accompanied by the Beaufort and the Raleigh, tugs, each mounting a single gun, steamed down the stream. It was the trial trip of the Virginia, and she was found to move slowly. At one o'clock she cleared the Elizabeth River, and stood straight across the Roads toward Newport News. The Congress lay at anchor in the channel, three hundred yards from the shore; the Cumberland was two hundred yards beyond. As the Virginia came within range, she opened upon the Congress from her 100-pound bow gun. Passing the Congress at three hundred yards, she received a harmless broadside. She returned it with effect, a single shot disabling every man but one at a gun, and kept straight on for the Cumberland, which had been swung across the channel, to bring her full broadside to bear upon the approaching enemy. The Cumberland opened fire from her two pivot guns, and soon after with her whole broadside of eleven 9-inch Dahlgrens. Broadside after broadside followed in rapid succession, but the balls glanced harmlessly from the iron armor of the Virginia, which kept straight on, without returning a shot or showing a single man. She seemed to wish to give her defensive power a fair test. Nothing could be more satisfactory. Six full broadsides had been received at nearer and nearer range, with no essential damage. The Virginia kept straight on for minutes, which seemed hours, her bow pointed square at the side of the Cumberland. It was now three in the afternoon. There was a sharp shot, and a dull, heavy blow at the same instant. The iron-armed prow of the Virginia had struck the Cumberland near the bow, and below the water-line. Plank, beams, and knees gave way like laths, leaving a ragged opening into which a man might have passed; through this a torrent of water poured into the hold. The Virginia then opened fire. Every shot told. The first shot passed through the sick-bay, killing five men. Broadside after broadside followed in merciless succession, every shot reaching a vital part. Sick-bay, berth-deck, and gun-deck were covered with dead and wounded. For half an hour the pumps of the Cumberland were worked, in the hope of throwing out the water as fast as it rushed in through the yawning hole in her side. It was all in vain; the water gained momently. The forward magazine was soon flooded, and all the powder for keeping up the fire was brought from the after magazine. In thirty-five minutes the water had risen to the main hatchway, and the ship canted over, just ready to sink. All the wounded who could walk were ordered out of the cockpit. These were few, for most were unable to help themselves or be helped by others. All the while during these long minutes the Cumberland kept up her useless fire, no gun being abandoned until the waters creeping up toward the stern from the sinking bow drowned it out. All the while the Virginia kept up her slow and sure fire, every shot telling. Only one man was seen on board the iron-clad. Near the close of the fight he showed himself from a port-hole; a ball from the Cumberland cut him in two. The last shot from the fated Cumberland was fired by Matthew Tenney, from a gun just above water, that next to him being overflowed. He attempted to scramble out from the open port-hole, but the water rushing in swept him back, and he went down in the sinking vessel. In three quarters of an hour after the Virginia had given the fatal blow, the Cumberland went down in fifty-four foot wa-

ter, her pennant still flying from the mast-head above the waves. Not a man was captured. A few swam to land, and more were picked up by small boats from the shore. The Virginia ceased her fire when the frigate went down, and turned toward the Congress.

As soon as it was perceived that the Virginia had opened the fight, a number of Confederate steamers came out from the James River and joined in the action. These were the Teazer, of one gun, the Jamestown, of two guns, and the Patrick Henry, formerly known as the Yorktown, of six guns. The last two had formerly been packets, owned by New York merchants, and plying between New York and Richmond. They had been seized by the Confederates, and converted into armed vessels. Seeing the fate of the Cumberland, Lieutenant Smith, who commanded the Congress, hoisted sail, and, with the help of a tug-boat, ran the frigate ashore in water too shoal to permit the Virginia to run her down. All the small Confederate steamers assailed her with a sharp fire, which made terrible havoc among her crew. The Virginia, having finished the Cumberland, then turned upon the Congress. Taking up a position 150 yards astern, the iron-clad raked the frigate fore and aft with shell, every one, at that close range, telling with fatal precision. The fuses were cut short, and every shell burst inside the frigate. The first killed seventeen men at a single gun. During all the fire hardly a man was merely wounded; most who were hurt were killed outright, the head or shoulder being shorn off, or the body cut in twain. Surgical aid was useless. After the first fifteen or twenty minutes the surgeon of the Congress did not even pretend to amputate a limb. The most that he could do was to apply a tourniquet to stop the bleeding, and administer stimulants to prevent prostration. "The only insignificant wound which I dressed," he says, "was that of one of the crew who had his hand taken off."

The Congress was fast aground, and could meet the terrible broadsides of the Virginia only from her two stern guns. These were soon disabled; one was dismounted, the other had its muzzle shot off. Lieutenant Smith, the commander, was killed, and the command devolved upon Lieutenant Pendergrast. The frigate was disabled, and on fire in several places; not a gun could be brought to bear upon the enemy. If every gun had been brought to bear it would have been useless. A chance shot might enter a port-hole, but the armor of the Virginia was impenetrable. There was no hope of succor from the Minnesota, which lay three miles off fast aground. At four o'clock the colors of the Congress were hauled down. An officer of the Virginia took formal possession. The Congress prize was given in charge to Lieutenant Parker, who had brought the little gun-boat Beaufort alongside. He ordered that the frigate should be abandoned in a quarter of an hour, as he meant to burn her at once. The surgeon remonstrated. He said that it was impossible to remove the wounded in that time. A score or more of the crew of the Congress got on board the Beaufort. In the confusion it is said that they supposed her to be a Federal tug from the shore. The Congress lay within rifle-shot from the shore. A regiment or two had been hurried to the nearest point. They opened a sharp rifle and artillery fire upon the Beaufort. Several were wounded, among whom were Lieutenant Miner, of the Virginia. The gun-boat hauled off, and the Virginia again opened fire upon the ill-fated Congress, although she had a white flag flying to show that she was out of action. The Confederates reported, and doubtless believed, that they were fired upon from the Congress, after her colors had been hauled down and while the white flag was flying. They were certainly in error; but in the hurry and confusion they might well suppose that the shot which were fired from the shore came from the ship. They must stand fairly acquitted from the charge of having wantonly fired upon a defenseless enemy who had surrendered. The firing by the Federal forces from the shore can only be justified by presuming that the troops there did not see that the colors of the Congress had been hauled down, and were replaced by the white flag of truce. After firing a few shells the Virginia and her allies left the Congress and turned toward the Minnesota. The Congress was on fire in several places. Her boats were manned, and those of the crew who were unhurt, and a few of the wounded, were taken ashore. The Congress continued to burn for eight hours. At midnight the flames reached the magazine, and the frigate, blown up, disappeared beneath the waters.

The March day was wearing to a close, but there was still two hours of daylight, when the Virginia, having destroyed the Cumberland and Congress, bore down upon the Minnesota. This great steam frigate had lain all these long hours helplessly aground. Steam tugs had been vainly trying to haul her off. The Roanoke, after grounding, had gone down the Roads. The St. Lawrence, in tow of a steamer, had approached the Minnesota. She too grounded, and, after receiving a single shell, and throwing in return a harmless broadside, was dragged off, and steered down toward Fortress Monroe. This one shell, a chance shot, thrown from the distance of half a mile, went sheer through the side of the St. Lawrence just above the water-line, passed through the ward-room, the surgeon's state-room on the opposite side, demolishing a bulkhead; it then struck a heavy iron bar, and glanced back into the ward-room, where it rested, its force being expended. This shell failed to explode, and no person was injured; but the actual damage done by this one shot proved to the captain of the St. Lawrence that his vessel was no match for the Virginia. She was impervious to any shot from his fifty guns, while any shell from her might destroy the St. Lawrence.

The Virginia, Jamestown, and Patrick Henry had borne down upon the stranded Minnesota. The draft of the iron-clad prevented her from coming within a mile of her enemy. She took a position at this distance on the starboard bow, and opened fire. Only one shot hit its mark. The Minnesota returned from her 10-inch pivot, with no result. The Jamestown and Patrick Henry were more effective. They took a closer position on port-bow and stern, firing from rifled guns, and killing and wounding several men. The return from the Minnesota was quite as effective. The Patrick Henry received a shot which passed through her boiler, killing and wounding seven men, and disabling her for the moment. She was towed off by her consorts. Two full hours had been spent in this indecisive combat. Night was closing in. The Virginia, essentially unharmed by the fiery ordeal through which she had passed, dared not lie out the night in the Roads. At seven o'clock, an hour after sunset, she hauled off, and with her consorts steamed to the sheltering batteries at the mouth of the Elizabeth. She might well do so. No vessel that ever floated had done so great a work in a single half day. She had destroyed two powerful vessels, carrying three times her number of men, and fully six times her weight of armament. She, with two feeble consorts, had engaged two other great vessels, greatly her superiors measured by any standard before known, inflicting far more damage than she received, and only prevented from destroying them because she could not come to close quarters with them. Her first day's work might fairly be claimed as the greatest ever achieved in naval warfare. Great victories had before been won upon the ocean, but never had there been such a disproportion between the losses of victors and vanquished.

The Cumberland went into action with 376 men. When the survivors were mustered there were only 255. She lost 121 in killed and drowned. The crew of the Congress were 434 officers and men; of these, 298 got to shore, 26 of them being wounded, 10 mortally; there were in all 120 killed and missing; about 20 of these were made prisoners, leaving a roll of killed and drowned of 100 men. Besides these, 3 were killed on the Minnesota, and 16 wounded; an absolute loss of fully 250 officers and men. On the Virginia there were but 2 killed and 8 wounded. On the other Confederate vessels 4 were killed and a few more wounded; an absolute loss of not more than 10 officers and men—fully twenty-five to one in favor of the Confederates. The disproportion in the loss of vessels and material was still greater. The Roanoke and St. Lawrence were driven away, glad of the accident of low water, which kept off the Virginia and enabled them to escape. The Minnesota had inflicted as much damage as she had received. The Cumberland and the Congress were utterly destroyed. They had expended their utmost fire upon the iron-clad. The result was that they had riddled her smoke-stack and steam-pipe, shot away her flag-staffs and anchor, knocked off the muzzles of two guns, which were easily replaced, and had started an armor-plate here and there. The Virginia herself, in dashing upon the Cumberland, had twisted her iron prow. All the harm which she had received was immaterial, and could be wholly remedied in a few hours. She withdrew from action only because the coming darkness intervened. On the morning of the next day she was as efficient as before.

The Virginia steamed off in the gathering darkness, leaving the Minnesota fast upon the mud-bank where she had lain for so many eventful hours. The recoil from her own heavy broadsides had forced her farther on, and she seemed to have made for herself a cradle. At ten o'clock the tide commenced to run flood, and for six hours all hands were at work, steam-tugs assisting, to haul her off the bank. Every effort was unavailing. She lay fast, and at four o'clock, the tide having fallen, the work was suspended, and the Minnesota lay immovable, awaiting a new onset from the Virginia.

Not wholly helpless, however, for a new actor had come upon the scene whose powers were yet to be tested. The Monitor had left New York three days before for Hampton Roads. The first part of the passage was stormy. The waves swept clear over her low deck, the turret often being the only thing above water. The draft-pipe for conveying air to the crew quartered in the hold was too low, and the water poured down it. It was lowered, and its opening in the deck tightly closed. Farther provision had been made for drawing air down the turret. The machinery became disarranged. The crew were almost suffocated. Water also leaked down at the junction of the turret and the deck. These deficiencies were remedied, and the battery outrode the storm, proving to be in the main an excellent sea-boat. On the evening of the 8th she came to Hampton Roads. She had for hours heard the heavy sound of the cannonading which announced that an action had been going on. At nine in the evening she reached the fortress and learned what had happened. Lieutenant Worden was ready to test his untried craft

FIRST VOYAGE OF THE MONITOR.

JOHN L. WORDEN.

against the Virginia. In sixty minutes he was on his way to the Minnesota, by whose side the Monitor was anchored at an hour past midnight. The night passed, the morning broke, and the slow hours passed away until, at eight o'clock, the Virginia was seen bearing down upon the Minnesota.

The Christian day of rest has come to be the battle-day of Christendom. At sunrise the Virginia appeared coming down toward the Minnesota. All hands were beat to quarters; but the iron-clad ran directly past, almost within reach of the guns of Fortress Monroe, and then turning, stood straight up the channel through which the Minnesota had come the day before. Signal was made for the Monitor to engage. She ran down directly in the wake of the Minnesota, covering her as far as possible with her diminutive bulk, and laid herself directly alongside the Virginia. Never were antagonists apparently so unequally matched. The Monitor was only one fifth of the size of her antagonist, and appeared much smaller, for she presented to sight nothing but her flat deck just above the water, her low, square pilot-house, and round turret. The Virginia opened upon her with all her guns. Most of the shot flew over the low deck; a few struck the turret; but all except one glanced off, leaving hardly a mark. One rifled bolt, from the 100-pound Armstrong, struck fair and square, penetrating half through the nine inches of iron. The bolt broke off, leaving the head sticking in the wound. Soon the antagonists began to manœuvre for position, keeping up a fire all the while. The speed of the two vessels was about equal, but the light draught of the Monitor gave her an advantage. Once the Virginia got aground, and the Monitor steamed round and round her, trying bow, stern, and sides in search of a vulnerable point. She fired cast-iron shot of 168 pounds, and so short was the distance and so fair the mark that hardly one missed; but they struck the sloping sides of the Virginia at so great an angle that they glanced harmlessly off; had they struck a perpendicular wall they would have either gone through or been shattered.

The Virginia soon got afloat again, and finding that she could make nothing of the invulnerable Monitor, turned her attention once more to the Minnesota, which had already received an 11-inch shot just above the water-line. The iron-clad came head on, and received the full broadside of the Minnesota. Fifty solid shot struck square. Any wooden vessel that ever floated would have gone down under such a fire. The Virginia was apparently unharmed. She fired shell in return from her rifled bow-gun. The first shell passed sheer through four rooms, tearing them all into one, and in exploding set the ship on fire. The second shell went through the boiler of the steam-tug Dragon, which lay alongside, blowing her up, killing and wounding seven men. But the third shell was hardly fired when the Monitor interposed, compelling the Virginia to shift her position. She grounded again, and lay exposed once more to the full broadside of the Minnesota. Afloat again, she steamed down the bay, closely followed by the Monitor. Reaching more open water, she turned sharp around, and ran at full speed square against the Monitor. Her iron prow, which had pierced the ribs of the Cumberland as though they had been of wicker-work, left hardly a mark upon the armed side of the Monitor, upon whose turret and pilot-house she now concentrated her whole fire. Soon after the anxious spectators on the Minnesota saw the Monitor standing down the bay, while the Virginia, with the Patrick Henry and Jamestown, which had been hovering around, headed apparently straight for the Minnesota, still fast aground, badly crippled, most of her shot expended, and her crew worn out with fatigue. Why the Monitor had withdrawn could not be known. Perhaps she had expended her ammunition; perhaps she had sustained some vital injury. All that Van Brunt could know was that the Virginia and her consorts were coming down upon him, and could take up a position to rake his stern with no possibility

SCENE OF THE FIGHT OF THE IRON-CLADS.

1, Sewall's Point.—2, Craney Island.—3, The Patrick Henry.—4, The Jamestown.—5, The Monitor.—6, The Merrimac.—7, Confederate Camp.—8, The Minnesota.—9, 10, Batteries.—11, The Congress.—12, The Cumberland.—13, Newport News.—14, Steam Tug.—15, The Roanoke.—16, Rip-Raps.—17, French Man-of-War.

of an effective reply. He gave orders that preparations should be made for destroying his ship as soon as it was clear that all hope of saving her was gone; but, upon ascending to the deck, he saw that the Confederate vessels had no intention of continuing the fight. They had changed their course, and were heading with all speed for their refuge at Craney Island.

Such was the fight of the Monitor and the Virginia, as seen through the smoke from the deck of the Minnesota. From the Monitor itself it presented some different phases. At eight o'clock the Virginia was seen close at hand. Worden took his station in the pilot-house to direct the fight; Stimers controlled the movement of the turret; Greene had charge of the guns. The action began at a quarter before nine. At half past eleven a shot from the Virginia struck square against the pilot-house. One of the wrought-iron logs, 9 inches by 12, of which it was built, was shattered. Worden was looking from a narrow loop-hole just opposite the point where the shot struck. Fragments of cement were driven into his face, blinding him, and forcing him to give the command to Greene. The fight was kept up for three quarters of an hour longer, when the Virginia drew off, sagging down at the stern as though she was aleak; but her movements showed that her machinery was unharmed. The Monitor, which Van Brunt, in the excitement of the moment, thought to be heading for Fortress Monroe, soon came up to the Minnesota, but the Confederate vessels were close up to their refuge under the batteries at Craney Island. The Monitor did not pursue them. In the heat of the action it could not be ascertained how much damage had been sustained. It was certain that her pilot-house was seriously injured; another shot striking it fairly would have disabled her. Her heavy guns were an almost untried experiment; the explosion of one would probably have rendered her useless. In driving off the Virginia she had done her work. In attempting more all might have been lost. Even after the Virginia disappeared from view the safety of the Minnesota seemed by no means assured. She still lay fast, exposed to a new assault. Van Brunt determined to get her off at all hazards. Guns and provisions were thrown overboard, and water-tanks opened to lighten the steamer; more tugs were brought into use, and the great steamer was dragged half a mile from her mud bed; then the tide fell, and she was again fast. When the tide rose the next morning she was again afloat, and was brought back to Fortress Monroe.

If the importance of a battle were to be estimated solely by the actual loss inflicted or suffered, the first fight of iron-clads would be only a harmless duel. No man on the Virginia, it is affirmed, was harmed by the heavy shot of the Monitor or the great broadsides of the Minnesota. The firing had been going on for an hour and a half when a shot struck the Monitor turret fairly. One man happened to be standing so that his knee touched the wall just opposite; he was stunned, but soon recovered. Another man was partially stunned, but soon recovered. Besides Worden, no man was seriously harmed. On board the Minnesota three were killed and sixteen wounded, half of them only slightly. During the actions of the two days the Minnesota expended 247 solid shot, 282 shells, and more than two tons of powder, without any essential harm to her opponent. She was seriously damaged in hull and armament. At the close of the fight, what with guns disabled and thrown overboard, she had but eleven that could be equipped for service. During the three and a half hours of the engagement the Monitor fired 41 shot, few of which missed, but all except two or three were really harmless. She was fairly struck twenty-two times: nine times on the turret, eight times on the side armor, three times on the deck, and twice on the pilot-house. Of all these shot, delivered at close range from heavy guns, only one, which struck the pilot-house, did any perceptible damage.

The Monitor and the Virginia, exposed to such a terrible ordeal, both proved themselves invulnerable against any fire which had ever before been brought to bear by one ship against another. The conclusion seemed inevitable that wooden ships were to be of no farther use in naval warfare, and that the great navies which France and Great Britain had built at such an immense cost were practically annihilated. When the tidings of this fight crossed the Atlantic, the London Times affirmed that England had on the day before 149 first class war-ships; now there were only two; beyond these there was not one that could, without madness, be pitted against the Monitor. Even these were not invulnerable; for, being iron-plated only amidships, they would be set in a blaze at either extremity in a few minutes by shells from their unassailable antagonists. The Illustrated London News, echoing the expressions of statesmen in Parliament, urged that Great Britain should cease to erect sea-board fortifications, but should spend the money wasted upon them in cutting down the useless line-of-battle ships, plating their hulls with iron, and fitting them with cupolas armed with guns at least as heavy as those of the Monitor. Like most hasty conclusions, this was too sweeping. In a few weeks Farragut showed at New Orleans, and again in a few months at Mobile, that wooden ships, boldly and skillfully handled, could yet play an important part even against iron-clads.

The Monitor and the Virginia never again tried their strength against each other. For a month they lay watching each other, the one in the lower Roads, the other at the mouth of the Elizabeth. On the 11th of April, the Virginia, with her old consorts, steamed out, as if bent on an action. By a rapid dash the fleet captured three Federal transports lying unguarded, and then returned. Twice after she showed herself in the Roads, as if to provoke a fight, and then steamed back. The Monitor now and then went up toward the mouth of the Elizabeth, but always drew back when her enemy appeared. It was clear that neither side wished to risk losing their main defense. If the Virginia was lost, the water approach to Richmond would be in the hands of the Federals; if the Monitor was disabled, Hampton Roads would be in the power of the Confederates. All the movements of the rival iron-clads were mere feints, with no definite object. Meanwhile the Peninsular campaign had been inaugurated. McClellan had laid siege to Yorktown. The post was evacuated by the Confederates on the 3d of May. They resolved to withdraw all their force to the front of Richmond. Norfolk was abandoned, the work-shops and store-houses at the navy yard having been burned, and the great dry dock partially blown up. The troops by which this place had been garrisoned were ordered to Richmond. Norfolk was formally occupied by the Federal forces on the 10th of May. The withdrawal from Norfolk compelled the abandonment of the strong Confederate positions at Sewall's Point and Craney Island.

The Virginia had in the mean while been placed under the command of Josiah Tatnall, a veteran officer, who had spent a whole life in the naval service of the United States. Less than two years before he had commanded the fleet of the Union in the Chinese waters. In June, 1859, he rendered important aid to the French and English in their disastrous assault upon the Pei-ho forts. When recalled from the East by the approaching troubles at home, he threw up his commission, and joined the enemies of the nation which he had so long served. The Confederate government was then eagerly courting the support of foreign powers. Tatnall's opportune service had made his name popular in France and England. To this, rather than any ability which he had ever manifested, was owing his appointment to the command of the Virginia, the most important position in the Confederate navy. The abandonment of Norfolk shut the Virginia out from her refuge up the Elizabeth. She was liable at any moment to be assailed by a superior force. The James River was still open to her. If she could be taken up that stream she might be safe, and also aid in defending Richmond; but she drew quite twenty-five feet, and forty miles below Richmond was a shoal where there was only eighteen feet of water. If she could be brought to that draft the pilots said they could take her over. The work of lightening was begun. The commander went to bed; but he was awakened by an officer who told him that the vessel had been lifted just enough to render her unfit for action, yet more than two feet less than the pilots had declared necessary to take her over the shoal. Moreover, the westerly winds which had prevailed had driven the waters down the stream, so that there was less than the required eighteen feet. The poor old commander, awoke by these tidings, saw nothing to be done but to destroy his vessel; so he ran her ashore, landed her crew, and set her on fire fore and aft. She burned fiercely for an hour, and then, just before dawn on the 11th of May, blew up. So entire was the destruction, that no fragment was ever discovered of sufficient size to enable any one to describe the details of her construction. "The Virginia," reported Commander Tatnall, "no longer exists. I presume that a court of inquiry will be ordered to examine into all the circumstances, and I earnestly solicit it. Public opinion will never be put right without it." The court was ordered, and reported that the destruction of the Virginia was not necessary. She might have been taken up the James to a point of safety, where she could still have barred the ascent of the river. Then and there, if worst came to worst, was the time to decide upon the disposition to be made of the Virginia.

Four days after the destruction of the Virginia, the Monitor engaged in her second and last action. The James River was now open for operations, and Commander John Rogers was sent up the river with five vessels, among which were the Monitor and Galena. It was hoped that they could reach Richmond and compel the surrender of the city. The expedition met with no serious obstacles until it reached within eight miles of Richmond. The river here makes a sharp turn, with high banks on either side. On the western side is Drewry's Bluff, about 200 feet high, upon which the construction of a fort, since known as Fort Darling, had been hastily commenced. The river, here about 500 feet broad, was also obstructed by a double line of barriers, piles, and sunken vessels, and the banks were lined with sharpshooters. The three wooden vessels anchored 1300 yards below the fort. The Galena ran up to within 600 yards, swung across the river, and was at once exposed to the full fire from the fort. The Monitor went still nearer, but found that her guns could not be elevated sufficiently to reach the battery, and fell farther down to a point from which her guns could be brought to bear. The action was kept up for three hours. The Galena suffered se-

THE MONITOR IN THE STORM.

verely. Thirteen shot and shell penetrated her side; bulwarks were shattered and knees started; the deck was pierced by the plunging fire, the wheel injured, and armor started in several places. It was clearly shown that the light armor of this vessel was of no practical use when opposed to heavy guns. The Monitor was hit squarely three times, once on the turret and twice on the side armor, but received no damage beyond a slight bending of the armor-plates. The Naugatuck, which lay beyond the range of the fort, was disabled by the bursting of her 100-pound Parrott gun. Having expended nearly all her ammunition, the Galena withdrew, followed by the Monitor. The Galena lost thirteen killed and eleven wounded; three others, on the other vessels, were wounded by musketry from the shore. The Confederate loss was five killed and seven wounded. This action was at the time of far greater importance than is indicated by the loss suffered or inflicted. It was considered by both sides as proving that earth-works could not be reduced by gun-boats. "The action," said Lieutenant Jeffers, who now commanded the Monitor, "was most gallantly fought against great odds, and with the usual effect against earth-works. So long as our vessels kept up a rapid fire, the enemy rarely fired in return; but the moment our fire slackened, they remanned their guns. It was impossible to reduce such works except with the aid of a land force."

The Peninsular campaign had now been fairly commenced, and it was necessary to maintain a considerable fleet at Hampton Roads in order to convoy transports and protect the right flank of the army on its march along the York and Pamunkey Rivers. The Monitor remained here until nearly the close of the year. Then operations were contemplated against Charleston, and the Monitor, with the Passaic and Montauk, two vessels of the same general construction which had just been completed, was ordered to Beaufort, South Carolina. The Monitor set out on the 29th of December, in tow of the steamer Rhode Island. The second day out they approached the stormy point of Cape Hatteras. A gale sprung up, and the sea began to rise in heavy swells, breaking over the deck and pilot-house, and dashing against the base of the turret. The packing became loosened by the working of the turret, and the water began to leak in here and through the sight-holes in the pilot-house; but the pumps threw it out as fast as it entered until after dark. Then the gale increased, and the water began to dash into

THE PASSAIC AT SEA.

PUMPING AND BAILING.

LOSS OF THE MONITOR.

the turret and down the blower-pipes. A great wave would lift the vessel, and, when she descended to meet another, the flat under surface of her armor-shelf came down square with a heavy blow, which still farther loosened the packing of the turret, and caused other leaks. All the pumps were set to work; but the water gained, slowly at first, then rapidly. At half past ten it was above the ash-pits. A signal of distress was made, and the Rhode Island was requested to send boats to take off the crew. Two boats put off, which were filled to their utmost capacity. The sea dashed clear over the deck, sweeping off several men. By half past eleven the fires were all out, and the deck was on a level with the water. The men remaining on board were crowded into the turret. The boats from the Rhode Island had at length succeeded in getting alongside again. The men were ordered to try to get on board them. Some, stupefied by fear, would not make the attempt. Bankhead, the commander, was the last man to leave the sinking boat. The last that was seen of the Monitor was at midnight, when she drifted away, the red light gleaming from her turret. She must have gone down a few minutes after, carrying with her twelve of the sixty-five men on board. The Monitor was lost just eleven months from the day when she was launched.

The Passaic, in tow of the steamer Georgia, was a few miles behind the Monitor, and was nearly lost in the same gale. She began to leak first at the junction of the turret with the deck, and then toward the bows, and soon after near the stern. Ballast was thrown over, and then shot, in order to lighten the vessel. One after another the pumps gave out, and the men were set to bailing. Huge masses of water rolled over the deck, sometimes dashing clear over the top of the turret. There was no hope of relief, for not a boat could live. For three long hours the officers and men worked in the darkness. Then came a cry that the water was within three inches

of the fires, and the last pump had given out. Then there was a fierce swash, and the water hissed over the glowing grates, for even the firemen and engineers had worked knee-deep in water. The men now gave up all hope. Some sat down and gazed silently at the rising water; some wept; some prayed; others rushed to the turret to be the last to go down. The officers urged the men to the pumps again. They were found to work, and hope again dawned. The head of the ship was turned straight toward the shore, forty miles away. This change of position saved her. The waves no longer lifted the vessel, but pitched her from side to side. As morning dawned the wind subsided. By bailing and pumping the crew gained upon the leak. The men flung themselves down upon the cold wet deck, and in a few moments were fast asleep. The next night the gale sprung up anew, and the leak began to gain a little; it was feared that new ones would be sprung. A brief account of what had happened was written, sealed up in a bottle, to which was attached a red flag, and thrown overboard. But the pumps worked well, and the storm was outrode. On the evening of the 2d of January the Passaic made Beaufort Harbor.

The battle in Hampton Roads gave each side unbounded confidence in the soundness of the principle upon which its iron-clads had been constructed. The Virginia and the Monitor furnished the models upon which other vessels were constructed. None of the Confederate iron-clads equaled the first. They had no more hulls and engines ready furnished to their hands, and had not the facilities for constructing them. The Federal government immediately commenced the construction of nearly a score of the monitor class, but larger, and embodying many improvements. At a later period other turreted iron-clads were built, of far greater size, and with such changes in construction as were thought necessary to fit them for sea-going vessels. Some of these carried also a few heavy stationary guns; but their essential offensive feature was the revolving turret. The construction of these vessels was attended with no small difficulty. The French and English iron-clads had been clothed only with solid armor-plates. Four and a half inches —just the width of this printed column—had been fixed upon as the standard thickness. In Europe there were founderies provided with the means of rolling such plates. Nothing of the kind existed in America. These plates could be produced here only by the slow process of forging.

To produce a forged plate, a quantity of fragments of all sorts of iron is bound up into a fagot about two feet square. This is thrust into a furnace, heated to a bright red, when the mass becomes almost as plastic as wax. It is then placed under a heavy steam-hammer, a few blows from which reduce the fagot to a "bloom"—a homogeneous mass of iron, looking like a fragment of a wooden joist, about six inches square, and four feet long. To forge these blooms into plates, four or five layers are piled up upon the end

ASLEEP ON DECK.

FORGING A BLOOM.   FORGING A PLATE.

of an iron bar, and thrust into a furnace. This bar answers the purpose of a handle to move the mass, and is suspended by chains so as to balance. The blooms, piled up on the flattened end of the bar, are thrust into a furnace, and heated for hours until they become plastic. They are then withdrawn from the furnace, swung around, and placed under a hammer still heavier than that which has reduced them from fagots, and beaten out flat, forming the commencement of a plate. Upon the end of this other blooms are piled, heated, and hammered out in like manner. This process is repeated until the plate has acquired the required length, when it is chiseled off from the bar. It is then simply a plank of solid iron, twelve or fifteen feet long, three broad, and four or five inches thick. This process is necessarily slow. There were no national founderies, and only two or three private ones capable of executing it. These could furnish only the plates for the Ironsides, and for the Roanoke; for this unlucky vessel being useless in its original shape, it had been resolved to cut her down, and convert her into an armored ship. The Ironsides proved in the end to be an effective vessel; the Roanoke was as useless as before. The turrets of the new monitors and their side armor must in the mean while be composed of layers of inch iron. The thickness of the turrets was increased from eight to eleven and even thirteen inches. This was found at Charleston in 1863, and at Wilmington in 1865, to be sufficient to resist the most powerful shot that could be brought to bear upon them. With some exceptions, which arose from causes nowise affecting the principle upon which they were constructed, no monitors have been seriously injured by the fire to which they have been subjected, even when put to service for which they were never designed—that of assailing fortifications.

Still, the revolving turrets hitherto constructed embody only a portion of the possible offensive power involved in the design of their inventor. Those built afford perfect protection to ordnance and gunners. They also give the vessel the power of throwing its whole offensive power upon any required point of the circle within the range of its guns. But the fire is given from a gun moving around the circumference of a circle, and the slightest interval between the aim and the discharge sends the ball in a line different from that intended. In the turret as designed by Timby provision was made against this grave defect. His turret was to revolve, not upon a central shaft, but upon rollers around its periphery. From its centre rose a plat-

form resting upon a central shaft, moving independent of the revolution of the turret itself. This platform was to be the post of the commander during action. A telescope is firmly fixed upon this platform; by his side is a wheel, by which he turns the shaft in any direction, so as to keep the telescope pointed directly at the object of attack. If it moves he follows it with the telescope, just as a rifleman moves his piece when taking aim at a bird in flight. As the turret revolves, each gun is for an instant brought in a line exactly parallel with the commander's telescope, always pointed upon the object of attack. If the gun be discharged at that instant, the ball must go straight to its mark. Provision is made to effect this with an instantaneousness unattainable by the motion of human nerves and muscles. A galvanic battery is provided, with a separate conducting wire running to each gun; this is so arranged that the connection is formed at the instant when the gun is brought by the revolution of the turret in a vertical line below the telescope. If the fuse attached to the conducting wire is placed in the vent of the piece, the discharge is instantaneous, and the telescope, and consequently the gun, being pointed directly at the object, the aim is perfect, and the ball must go straight to its mark. The accompanying diagram represents a vertical section of a large turret, designed for a stationary battery, mounting sixty guns in two tiers. It shows the interior of such a turret, with the automatic sighting and discharging apparatus. The principle and arrangement is the same whatever may be the number of the guns. The commander within the turret aims every gun of the battery with as much precision as a sharpshooter aims his telescopic rifle, discharging it by an electric current at the instant when the aim is secured. The gunners have nothing to do but to load the guns, run them to the port-hole, and insert the fuse.

The correctness of the principle on which the monitor turrets is based has been proved to be sound by the severest practical tests. Great improvements may doubtless be made in the actual construction of the turrets and hulls. Thus, instead of having the turret entirely above deck, it may be sunk for fully a third of its height below deck. Its liability to be struck would thus be diminished in that proportion, while its chief vulnerable point, the base upon which it revolves, would be effectually shielded by the side armor of the vessel. The seaworthiness of the vessel would be increased by bringing the centre of gravity nearer the keel. The protected part of the

VERTICAL SECTION OF STATIONARY REVOLVING TURRET.

A, A, Exterior and interior Walls of the Turret, with dome-shaped Roof K, revolving by the Gearing F, upon friction Rollers G, G.—C, C, Artillery Platforms, the Gun-carriages radiating from the common Centre.—B, The Commander's Platform, revolving, independently of the Turret, upon the Shaft b, b, by means of the Rod and Gearing D.—On the left of the Shaft is the "Circuit Closer," forming the connection between the Galvanic Battery and Conductors passing to each Gun.—E, E, E, Ventilators.—H, H, Casemates, mounted with Guns, independent of Revolving Turrets.—I, I, Wall of subterraneous foundation for Turret, inclosing Chambers for Stores and Munitions.

turret would require a much less thickness of armor, and its diameter might be increased without adding to its weight. With a diameter of thirty feet instead of twenty there would be space for an armament of four or six instead of two guns. A vessel with such a turret, and with hull and engines capable of a high rate of speed, could not fail to be superior in offensive and defensive power to any iron-clad that can be built upon the European plan of vessels little differing from the old men-of-war, with lofty sides and presenting a great extent of perpendicular surface to attack, or even the Confederate plan of a long casemate with sloping sides. No vessel can be constructed upon either of these plans capable of floating the thirteen inches of iron which constitute the best monitor turrets. A man-of-war with its guns mounted in broadside can use only half its armament upon any one point at a time, and that only by exposing its whole side to the enemy. A monitor can bring its whole armament to bear upon any point at each revolution of the turret, which occupies about a minute; and if the turret should be furnished with the automatic sighting apparatus, every shot is under the absolute control of one governing mind. A monitor, moreover, fights with equal force in any position. Its whole fire can be delivered at will from bow, stern, or either side. If it have speed to enable it to choose its own position, it never needs to present any portion of its hull except its sharp bow to the enemy. This offers a mark so small that it could be hit only by the merest chance. Practically, its low turret is the only assailable point, and this, as already constructed, is capable of resisting any shot to which, in the present state of naval artillery, it can ever be exposed. It is safe to say that the defensive power of the turret can be increased more rapidly than the offensive power of artillery.

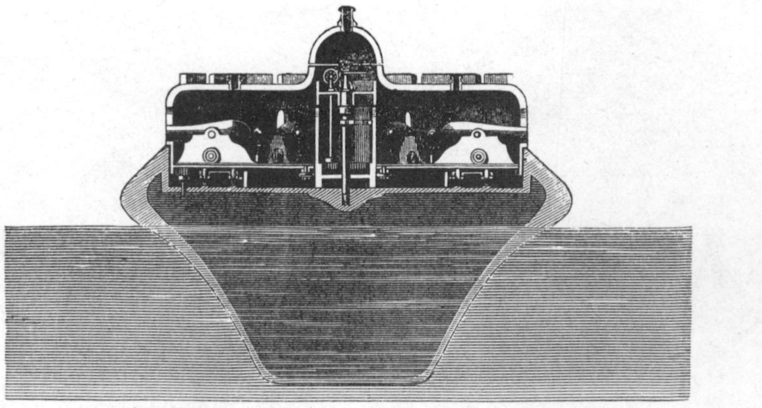

VERTICAL SECTION OF PROPOSED NAVAL TURRET AND HULL.

It was a part of the design of the inventor of the revolving turret to adapt it to fortifications of large size for harbor defense. The following diagram represents a cordon of turrets for the protection of the Harbor of New York, the approach to which is through the "Narrows," about one third of a mile wide. This would be reduced to a quarter of a mile by docks built out from each shore. Upon the extremity of each dock would be erected a turret, and another upon an artificial foundation midway between them. Each of these turrets would be one hundred feet in diameter, mounting sixty guns in two tiers. The turrets are to revolve once a minute, equal to about three and a half miles an hour. As every gun may be discharged at every revolution, the possible effective fire from each turret would be sixty shot a minute. The three turrets could thus, in case of need, concentrate a fire of 180 guns upon any point in the circle. A series of chains is stretched from turret to turret. When no attack is threatened these chains rest upon the bottom, leaving the passage unobstructed. They can be drawn up by a windlass, moved by the steam engine in the foundation of each turret. They are not to be drawn up "taut," but hang swaying in the water, at such a depth as to prevent the passage of a hostile fleet. They are furnished with buoys nearly sufficient to float the chains, so that only a small part of their tensile strength is expended in supporting them, leaving almost the whole strength to resist the passage of a hostile fleet. While detained here, any vessel would be exposed at point-blank distance to the whole fire of two turrets, which no ship ever built could sustain for a quarter of an hour. If thought necessary, movable torpedoes can be attached to chains in such a way as to be drawn directly below any vessel detained by the chains, and there exploded by a galvanic battery.

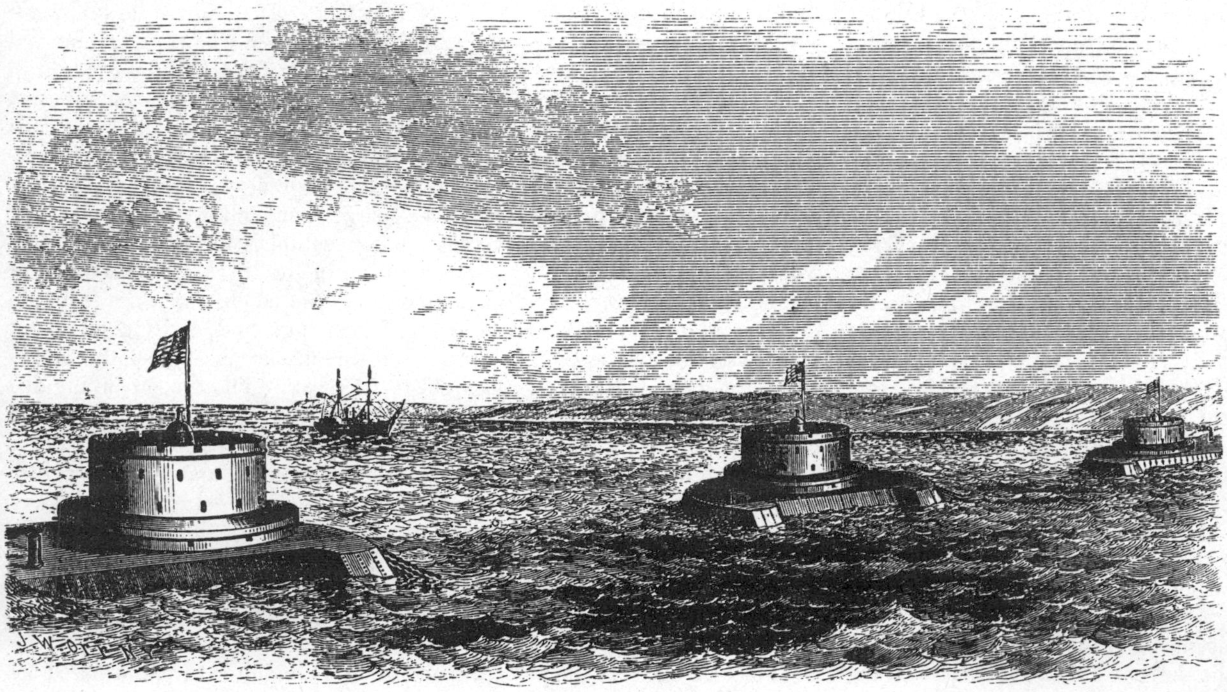

PROPOSED CORDON OF TURRETS FOR HARBOR DEFENSE.

NOTE ON THE MONITOR SYSTEM.

THE invention of the Revolving Turret has been attributed to Mr. Ericsson, and to Captain Cowper Coles, of the British Navy. The latter expressly claims it for himself upon the following grounds: He says[1] that in 1855 he sent to the British Admiralty drawings for an armored vessel of light draft, the guns protected by a *stationary* "hemispherical tower." This suggestion was not acted upon. In March, 1859, he sent in drawings in which this tower, or shield, was placed upon a "turntable," thus constituting it a revolving turret. In Blackwood's Magazine for December, 1860, is an article on this subject, containing a drawing of such a turret, with the mechanism for turning it by hand. Now, in September, 1854, Ericsson had forwarded to the Emperor of France plans for a vessel provided with "a semi-globular turret of plate iron six inches thick, revolving on a column and pivot, by means of steam power and appropriate gear-work."[2] Coles says that his plans were "so exactly similar" to that of the Monitor "that I think it will be apparent that this invention is of English origin, and I claim it for this country"—that is, for himself. But the date of Ericsson's proposition to the French Emperor for a revolving turret antedates by almost four years that of Coles to the British Admiralty. But Timby, as has been shown, exhibited his invention publicly, and secured a right to a patent for it in 1843, eleven years before Ericsson proposed it to the French Emperor, and sixteen years before Coles claims to have thought of it. During all this time it was in many ways a matter of public record, and his claim was so clearly undeniable that the contractors for the monitors purchased his patent for a large sum.

Much discussion arose as to the capabilities of the monitors, of which Ericsson says "the revolving cupola forms so important a feature."[3] In April, 1864, the Secretary of the Navy presented to Congress an elaborate "Report in Relation to Armored Vessels," detailing all the facts which had at that time transpired, and giving the opinions of prominent naval officers upon the subject. These opinions differed greatly. Lieutenant Jeffers, who commanded the Monitor at Drewry's Bluff, says, "I am of opinion that protecting the guns and gunners does not, except in special cases, compensate for the greatly diminished quantity of artillery, slow speed, and inferior accuracy of fire; and that, for general purposes, wooden ships, shell guns, and forts, whether for offense or defense, have not yet been superseded."[4] In the attack upon Fort Sumter, April 7, 1863, six monitors took part. The reports of Admiral Dupont and the commanders of these vessels was decidedly adverse to them. They were certainly considerably injured, but close examination shows that these injuries to the turrets in no wise affected the principle of their construction. Bolts were driven in, and some of the turrets were jammed at the base so as to prevent their revolution; but, although exposed to a heavier fire than any ships had ever endured, no turret was pierced. The Secretary of the Navy sums up the case thus: "Brief as was the conflict, the fire brought to bear upon the monitor vessels was such as could have been sustained by no *ordinary* boats, and demonstrates their power of resistance and their adaptation for harbor purposes. That the vessels in that engagement should have returned from the encounter with so few casualties, and the loss of but one life, is certainly remarkable."[5] In the second attack upon the Charleston forts, July 11, three monitors participated. Admiral Dahlgren "was favorably impressed with the endurance of these iron-clads. The Cattskill was struck 60 times, a large percentage of the hits being very severe. The pilot-house, turret, side-armor, and decks were all more or less damaged. Some of the shots were large; one, found on deck, where it fell after striking the turret, proved to be a 10-inch. . . . . . The test was very severe; yet, after firing 128 rounds, the vessel came out of action in good working order, as was proved by her going into action next day."[6] For two months during the siege of Fort Wagner the monitors were in action almost every day. Lieutenant Simpson, of the Passaic, reports: "The strength of the turret has been most severely tried. At one place two round shot of very large calibre (estimated by some as 11-inch, by others as 15-inch) have struck close together on the same plate, the impression of the second shot overlapping a portion of that made by the first. The mass of iron has been pressed in so as to form an extensive bulging on the inside, and the outer plate is broken, but no serious effect was produced. . . . . . The turrets are as near impregnable as any thing can be made, and eleven inches of iron seems to be enough for all purposes of defense. The only objection to them is the 'through bolts,' which allow the nut inside to fly when the head is struck. The new system of making turrets, now adopted by the Navy Department, obviates this difficulty. . . . . . I recommend that a system of turret should be devised by which it will have no connection with the spindle, but have a bearing all around its base, running on friction-rollers. I would also recommend that the base of the turret should be carried below the spar deck."[7] This officer was probably not aware that these two features formed a part of the design of the inventor of the turret. Inspector Hughes reports: "The shot make an indentation on the iron, and break the bolts that fasten the plating together. The greatest indentations that have come to my knowledge were to the depth of $2\frac{1}{2}$ and $2\frac{3}{4}$ inches. In my opinion, these indentations were made from 11-inch and 13-inch solid shot. A shot of this kind will generally break from one to five or six bolts. When the bolts break they can soon be replaced. I do not see that the turrets are injured practically."[8] Admiral Goldsborough says: "A difference of opinion exists among naval minds, at home and abroad, as to whether the better expedient is to use the guns of an iron-clad *turret-wise* or in broadside ports. The turret I regard as decidedly preferable. It renders one gun of a class equivalent to at least two of the same disposed in opposite broadside ports, and this with a great reduction of crew. It admits also of much heavier guns. It does not necessarily involve a breadth of beam antagonistic to velocity. It affords a better protection to guns and men, and, withal, it secures the fighting of guns longer in a sea-way."[9] Admiral Dahlgren, speaking of the whole of this two months' fighting, says: "The battering received by the monitors was without precedent. The Montauk had been struck 214 times, the Weehawken 187 times, and almost entirely by 10-inch shot. What vessels have ever been subject to such a test? It is not surprising that they should need considerable repair after sustaining such a severe pounding for so long a time, but only that they could be restored at all to serviceable condition. All the little defects of detail were marked by a searching process. Decks were cut through, cannon were worn out, side-armor shaken, tops of pilot-houses crushed, etc.; but all these were reparable, and no vital principle was seriously touched."[10] Commodore Rodgers, after comparing at length the relative advantages and disadvantages of the Ironsides and Monitor class of vessels, says: "To sum up my conclusions, I think that the Monitor class and the Ironsides class are different weapons, each having its peculiar advantages, and both needed to an iron-clad navy; but that when the Monitor class measures its strength against the Ironside class, then, with vessels of an equal size, the Monitor class will overpower the Ironside class; and as vessels find their natural antagonists in vessels, and only their exceptional antagonists in forts, it must be considered, upon the whole, that the Monitor principle contains the most successful elements for plating vessels for war purposes."[11] Admiral Porter says: "Any professional man who will lay aside his prejudices caused by the discomforts incident to monitors, must admit that as a harbor defense they are the best and only vessels to be built. If they have not been able to penetrate the harbor of Charleston, they have there done what no other vessels ever built could have accomplished. They held their own as no other vessels could have done, and under their shelter the army was enabled to perform its work successfully."[12] This favorable opinion, based upon the performances of the monitors at Charleston, was confirmed after Porter had occasion to test them at Fort Fisher, January, 1865, with the addition that the new ones which he had under his command proved themselves excellent sea-vessels, even upon the stormy coast of North Carolina. Captain Blakely, the celebrated English gun-maker, writing of the endurance of the monitors at the capture of Fort Fisher, says: "The fort contained not one gun powerful enough to sink an iron-clad ship. Most of these guns were more powerful than any gun mounted on any fort in England, or on any English ship except one, yet they failed to injure the Federal fleet. It follows that the fleet could attack Portsmouth or Plymouth with more impunity than Fort Fisher, so far as artillery fire is concerned."

1 Letter to the *London Times*, April 1, 1862. 2 Report on Armored Vessels, p. 13. 3 Ibid., p. 13. 4 Ibid., p. 29. 5 Ibid., p. 99. 6 Ibid., p. 217. 7 Ibid., p. 256–259. 8 Ibid., p. 289. 9 Ibid., p. 574. 10 Ibid., p. 585. 11 Ibid., p. 594. 12 Ibid., p. 592.

DAVID G. FARRAGUT.

CHAPTER XIV.

THE CAPTURE OF NEW ORLEANS.

Gulf Expeditions proposed.—The Lower Mississippi.—Ship Island.—General Phelps's Proclamation.—Reported Defenses of New Orleans.—Butler's Instructions.—His Voyage to Ship Island.—The Naval Expedition.—Porter and Farragut.—Farragut's Instructions.—Meeting at Ship Island.—Surveys of the River.—Forts Jackson and St. Philip.—Bombardment of the Forts.—Cutting the Barricade.—Preparations for Passing.—List of Vessels.—The Passage of the Barricade.—The Fight with the Forts.—The Naval Combat.—Destruction of the Varuna.—The Hartford on Fire.—The Brooklyn, Richmond, and Pensacola.—Destruction of the Manassas.—The missing Gun-boats.—The Losses.—The Passage up the River.—Capture of the Chalmette Regiment.—Panic in New Orleans.—Destruction of Property.—The Chalmette Batteries.—Arrival before the City.—The Summons to Surrender.—Bailey and Lovell.—Farragut and the Mayor.—The Union Flag hauled from the Mint.—Farragut's Warning.—The Mayor's Reply.—Waiting for Butler.—Surrender of Forts Jackson and St. Philip.—Treachery of Mitchell.—Destruction of the Louisiana.—Condition of the Forts.—Surrender of the Vessels.—Arrival of Butler at New Orleans.—Landing of Troops.—The March through the Streets.—Military Occupation of New Orleans.

THE Federal government had no sooner recovered from the panic of Bull Run than it resolved to attempt the recapture of some of the places on the Gulf of Mexico which had been seized by the Confederates. New Orleans was the most important of these. Not only was it the only large city in the Confederacy, but it was its chief commercial emporium. More than half the cotton sent abroad was shipped from its wharves; it was the entrepôt of the great valley of the Mississippi; its possession would open the whole course of the great river. But it was supposed to be so strongly defended that no force could be spared sufficient to take it. McClellan declared that it would require 50,000 men. Mobile was next in importance, and an expedition was planned against it, to be placed under the command of General Butler. Texas was then suggested as of more immediate importance. Galveston in our possession, the German cotton-planters would, it was thought, bring the state back to the Union.

Whether New Orleans, Mobile, or Galveston were finally fixed upon as the object of attack, Ship Island was the best place of rendezvous for the expedition, being within striking distance of every point on the Gulf of Mexico. The Mississippi, reaching its long arm downward, has built up a narrow mud causeway for a hundred miles into the centre of the Gulf. The country on each side, lying below the level of the river, is a strange compound of swamps, bayous, and lagoons. Between this causeway and Cape St. Blas, on the east, is a deep indentation of the Gulf, with several smaller bays penetrating still farther inland. Midway in this indentation, known as Mississippi Sound, Mobile Bay sets up into the Alabama coast. The shallow lagoons known as Lakes Borgne and Pontchartrain, opening from the sound, pierce far into the State of Mississippi, furnishing a water route for vessels of light draught from New Orleans to the Gulf, independent of that

by the river. Almost in the centre of the sound, ninety-five miles from the mouths of the Mississippi, sixty-five from New Orleans, and fifty from Mobile, is Ship Island, a low bank of shifting white sand, seven miles long and three quarters of a mile wide, almost the counterpart of Fire Island in Long Island Sound. On the eastern end, a few groves of stunted oaks and pine find sustenance; at the western end is an excellent harbor, capable of sheltering a fleet of the largest vessels. The island possesses, also, the prime advantage of an abundant supply of water. Sink a barrel any where, and it is filled with pure water filtered through the clean white sand. The island had been for some months in possession of a small detachment from the Federal blockading navy, when in December, 1861, General Phelps was sent there with a considerable body of troops, the advance part of Butler's expedition. He signalized his advent by a strange proclamation addressed to the people of the Southwest, in which he affirmed that the admission of any new slave state into the Union was a violation of the Constitution, and that the states in which slavery existed at the adoption of the Constitution were bound, by becoming parties to that compact, to abolish it. Monopolies, he said, were destructive to national prosperity, and slavery was the greatest of all monopolies. Labor was inherently noble, and the motto of the country should be, "Free labor and workingman's rights." This proclamation was never fairly published, and so it was quietly ignored by the government.

Butler was just about to embark for Ship Island from Fortress Monroe, when the order was countermanded. The affair of the Trent had occurred; England had demanded the surrender of Mason and Slidell, and there was a prospect of war with Great Britain. This question was adjusted, and government again took up the expedition to the Gulf. New Orleans was fixed upon as its object. If the accounts of its defenses, ostentatiously put forth by the Southern papers, were true, the city was unassailable by any force that could be brought against it. Forts Jackson and St. Philip, seventy-five miles below New Orleans, on opposite sides of the river, it was said, mounted 173 rifled 63-pounders of the best English manufacture. Just below them was a dam, which no fleet could force in less than two hours, during which it would be under the direct fire of the forts, many of whose guns were furnished with red-hot shot. The forts were manned by 3000 men, many of them experienced artillerists. Then there were almost ready two floating steam batteries, covered with four and a half inches of solid English and French iron plates, each carrying twenty 68-pounders, so arranged that their balls would "skim the water, striking the enemy between wind and water." Besides these, there were fire-ships, incendiary shells, Congreve rockets, and the like. Then there was a constant succession of redoubts all the way from the forts to the city; those at Chalmette, Jackson's old battlefield, had rifled cannon, with a proved effective range of five miles. All the

GODFREY WEITZEL.

navies in the world could not force their way up the rapid current of the Mississippi in the face of such obstacles. Moreover, in New Orleans itself were 32,000 infantry, and as many more quartered close by, all in "discipline and drill far superior to the Yankees." For generals they had Mansfield Lovell and Ruggles, "who possess our entire confidence;" and "for commodore old Hollins, a Nelson in his way."

But the Federal government had learned that the strength of the defenses of New Orleans had been greatly exaggerated, and was convinced that the city might be taken by a strong naval force, aided by a moderate army. Butler asked for only 15,000 men. These were given to him, with a conditional promise of 3000 more from Key West and Pensacola. The troops were sent by detachments to Ship Island, the commanding general accompanying the last, leaving Hampton Roads on the 25th of February. His instructions, dated two days before, directed him to keep the object of the expedition a profound secret. No one was to know the destination except Major Strong, his chief of staff, and Godfrey Weitzel, soon to be a general, but then only a lieutenant of the engineers, in which capacity he had aided in the construction of the forts on the Mississippi. "The object of your expedition," said McClellan in his order, "is one of vital importance—the capture of New Orleans. The route selected is up the Mississippi River, and the first obstacle to be encountered, perhaps the only one, is in the resistance offered by forts St. Philip and Jackson. It is expected that the navy can reduce the works. Should the navy fail to reduce the works, you will land your forces and siege train, and endeavor to breach the works, silence their fire, and carry them by assault. The next resistance will be near the English Bend, where there are some earthen batteries; here it may be necessary for you to land your troops, to co-operate with the naval attack, although it is more than probable that the navy unassisted can accomplish the result. If these works are taken the city of New Orleans necessarily falls." Then followed a plan for operations against Mobile, Pensacola, and Galveston. "It is probable," wrote McClellan, "that by the time New Orleans is reduced, it will be in the power of the government to re-enforce the land-forces sufficiently to accomplish all these objects;" but, in the mean time, Butler was "never to lose sight of the fact that the great object to be achieved is the capture and firm retention of New Orleans." This object was gained, but not in any respect in the manner proposed by McClellan. The forts were run, not reduced by the navy or carried by assault by the army; and when tidings came of the capture of the city, McClellan was calling for more men to enable him to hold his own before Richmond, instead of being able to send re-enforcements to New Orleans.

Butler took leave of the President and cabinet on the 24th of February. "Good-by, Mr. President," he said; "we shall take New Orleans, or you will never see me again." "The man that takes New Orleans," said the Secretary of War, "is made lieutenant general." The prophecy was fulfilled in spirit, if not in letter. New Orleans was taken by the navy, not by the army. The commander of the naval expedition was in time created vice-admiral, a rank in the navy corresponding to that of lieutenant general in the army. Of the man who was to be made lieutenant general, almost nothing was known, only that just a week and a day before he had "proposed to move immediately upon the works" at Fort Donelson, unless the "terms of an immediate and unconditional surrender" were accepted.

Butler, with the last of his command, left Hampton Roads for Ship Island

on the 25th of February, in the steamer Mississippi. The voyage, which should have been accomplished in a week, occupied a month. The steamer almost grounded near Hatteras Inlet; fairly grounded, and came near sinking, on the Frying-pan Shoals, off Cape Fear; put into Port Royal for repairs; started out, and ran aground again. The captain was clearly incompetent. If the vessel was to get to Ship Island by water she must have a new commander. Butler deposed the captain, put him under arrest, and appointed a new commander in his place. At length, on the 25th of March, the Mississippi reached Ship Island. The commanders of the naval expedition were already there, awaiting Butler's arrival.

The naval force had been laboriously organized. Besides the blockading squadron in the Gulf, a fleet of armed steamers, gun-boats, and a bomb flotilla consisting of twenty-one schooners, each carrying a mortar capable of throwing a bomb of 215 pounds, was provided. The mortar vessels were placed under the command of David D. Porter, then commander in the navy, since admiral. He was the son of that Commodore Porter whose exploits in the Essex form one of the most stirring chapters in the naval history of our war of 1812, and a younger brother of William D. Porter, of whom we have written, and shall have to write. The outbreak of the rebellion found him, after thirty years of service, a lieutenant in the navy, his name standing high on the list.

The government hesitated long in selecting the man who should have the chief command of the naval expedition. The choice was not made until the preparations were almost completed. It fell upon David G. Farragut, then a captain in the navy, to whom was assigned the rank of Flag-officer of the Western Gulf Squadron. The father of Farragut, a native of the island of Minorca, came to America in 1776. He entered the army, where he rose to the rank of major. After the war, having married in North Carolina, he migrated to Tennessee, taking up his residence near Knoxville, where his son was born in the first year of the present century. Like many another boy inland born, he would be a sailor. Porter, an intimate friend of the father, procured a midshipman's warrant for the child, then only ten years old, and took him upon his own vessel. Young Farragut, then fourteen years old, was with Porter in the famous Essex fight in Valparaiso Bay, and received the special commendation of his commander for his conduct, though he was too young to be recommended for promotion. In times of peace naval promotion comes slowly. Farragut, who had become lieutenant in 1825, was appointed commander in 1841, and captain in 1855. Meanwhile he had served at home and abroad, afloat and ashore, noted always for his diligence in mastering the duties of his profession, and for his facility in acquiring languages. He learned French at home, Spanish and Portuguese in South America, Italian and Arabic in the Mediterranean. The outbreak of the rebellion found him on shore duty at Norfolk, where he possessed a small estate. Of his sixty years, all but ten had been passed in the service of his country. He was proof against the temptations which assailed every officer of Southern birth or connections—temptations to which Buchanan and Tatnall, Maury and Page, Semmes and Maffit yielded. He managed to make his escape from Norfolk, leaving every thing behind him. He bore his three-score years lightly. No one who saw him would suppose that he was past middle age. A modest, quiet man, doing the duty which came to his hands without show or parade, he was now to have the opportunity of showing that he possessed the highest qualities of a commander.

Farragut received his first instructions on the 20th of January. They were followed by others three weeks later. As soon as his flag-ship, the

DAVID D. PORTER.

SHIP ISLAND AND THE APPROACHES TO NEW ORLEANS.

BIG GUN
Commanding Channel.

CHART
SHOWING THE POSITION OF
SHIP ISLAND

FORT MASSACHUSETTS
SHIP ISLAND

FIRE-RAFTS.

Hartford, was ready, he was to proceed to sea, and take the command of the Western Gulf blockading squadron. The mortar boats were to rendezvous at Key West. When all was ready, he was to collect such vessels as could be spared from the blockade, proceed up the Mississippi, and reduce the defenses which guarded the approaches to New Orleans. When he appeared off that city, he was to take possession of it under the guns of his squadron, hoist the American flag, and keep possession until the troops came up. Then, if the squadron from above had not descended, he was to push a strong force up the river, and take the defenses in the rear. "As you have expressed yourself perfectly satisfied with the force given to you," wrote the Secretary of the Navy, "and as many more powerful vessels will be added before you can commence operations, the Department and the country will require of you success. There are other operations of minor importance, but nothing must be allowed to interfere with the great object in view, the certain capture of the city of New Orleans. The Department relies upon your skill to give direction to the powerful force placed at your disposal, and upon your personal character to infuse a hearty co-operation among your officers free from unworthy jealousies." This confidence was fully justified. The great object in view was gained; and if the secretary's anticipations that "if successful, you open the way to the sea for the great West, never to be closed; the rebellion will be riven to its centre, and the flag to which you have been so faithful will recover its supremacy in every state," were not at once attained, it was through no fault of Farragut and his associates. Never before, save when Nelson, supported by Collingwood, and Hardy, and Harvey, won the great fight at Trafalgar, was a commander so truly and loyally supported by his subordinates as was Farragut by Porter, Bailey, Bell, and the officers and men of every vessel in the fleet. No trace of any unworthy jealousy appeared. In the fight every officer did his best; and in the reports, while each told what his own vessel had done, every one was eager to praise his associates. These reports, fully forty in number, leave nothing to be desired by the historian who has to describe the capture of New Orleans.

Farragut reached Ship Island on the 20th of February, more than a month before the arrival of Butler, who was daily expected. He ran down with his fleet to the mouths of the Mississippi, and for a full month was busy in getting his vessels over the bar. It was supposed that there was nineteen feet of water. If so, all the vessels could be got over, except, perhaps, the Colorado, which drew twenty-two when loaded, but lightened an inch for twenty-four tons. The Wabash drew eighteen feet on an even keel, and could be got over without difficulty. All the other vessels, it was thought, could easily pass. But fifteen feet was found to be the utmost depth. Neither the Colorado or the Wabash could cross. The Mississippi, lightened almost to the bare hull, was got over, tugs pulling her through a foot of mud. The fleet which entered the Mississippi consisted of forty-five vessels of all classes. Five were powerful steam sloops, the largest vessels which had ever crossed the bar; there were seventeen gun-boats, twenty-one mortar schooners, and two large sailing vessels. All told, they carried something more than 200 mortars and guns, many of them of heavy calibre.

The last of the large steamers were not fairly over the bar until the 8th of April. But meanwhile Farragut and Butler had met at Ship Island and concerted their plan of operations. Porter's bomb vessels were to assail the forts. If he reduced them, well; if not, Farragut would try to run past them. If he succeeded, Butler should bring up his forces through the bayous to the rear of the forts, cutting them off from New Orleans, which Farragut would have held with his fleet.

Three weary weeks passed before active operations were begun. But much work was done in this interval. The whole course of the river up to the forts was accurately surveyed. No more desolate region exists than that near the mouths of the Mississippi. On the right is swamp and lagoon; on the left lagoon and swamp. A stunted tree, a dilapidated house, only breaks the dull mud level. One hardly knows whether land or water predominates. Land first fairly gets the victory after a contest of thirty miles, when a thick belt of wood finds soil from which to grow on the west bank. Just here the river makes a bend, scarcely perceptible in a general map. At this bend, on the first patch of firm ground, were placed the first and the only seaward defenses of New Orleans. On the west, or convex side of the bend, was Fort Jackson; a little above, on the east, or concave side, was Fort St. Philip. Fort Jackson itself mounted seventy-four guns, with a supplementary battery of six. Fort St. Philip had forty guns. Both forts had been constructed by the best engineers that West Point could furnish, among whom were Beauregard and Weitzel. They were not quite completed when the rebellion broke out, but the deficiencies were thought to have been supplied by the zeal of the Confederates. They were thought to be impregnable, though the voyager up the Mississippi would hardly notice them, unless it were as the first two objects which broke the monotony of the dull mud level. All that he could see was two neatly sodded green slopes, surmounted by low brick walls, with a few black openings for guns. The river here is half a mile wide, with a current of four miles an hour, its course commanded by the guns of the two forts. But these guns were only a part of the defenses. Straight across the river from Fort Jackson a strong barrier had

been stretched. Upon this the Confederates had twice lavished their labor. First, they had placed a row of heavy logs, bound together by an iron chain, across the stream. The drift-wood from above lodged against this, forming a huge raft, the pressure of which in time became too great for the strength of the chain; one night it parted, and the whole structure was swept down to the Gulf. Taught by experience, the Confederates built a new barricade upon wiser principles. Eight hulks, partially dismasted and filled with logs, were strongly anchored in the stream, with intervals through which the drift-wood could pass. A chain passing from one to another bound all together. Near the left bank the barricade could be opened at will to permit a vessel to pass. One end of the barricade was covered by the guns of Fort Jackson; the other was protected by a battery, both sweeping its entire length, while Fort St. Philip, from above, could pour its whole fire upon any assailant. Above lay a fleet of rams, gun-boats, and fire vessels, whose number and strength were unknown. The whole was in charge of a recreant Pennsylvanian, J. K. Duncan, brigadier general commanding coast defenses. The two forts were especially commanded by Edward Higgins, once an officer in the army of the United States.

The western bank of the river, for eight miles below Fort Jackson, was lined by a belt of dense woods fifty yards wide, completely hiding the fort from the view except at one point, where the trees had been cleared away in order to afford unobstructed range upon ascending vessels. Porter had resolved to place his bomb schooners close to the bank and screened by these woods, over which they were to fling their shells into the invisible fort. The exact bearing and distance of the fort from the station assigned to each vessel must be ascertained. This work was performed with no little risk by members of the coast survey detailed for that purpose. They had to resort to all kinds of observations from all possible positions, hardly one of which was upon firm ground. Some stations consisted of flags among the overhanging branches, the angles between them being measured from boats in the stream below; other stations were the chimney-tops of deserted houses, to which the observers worked their way through the roofs. All the while they were exposed to a random fire from the guns of the fort, and to shots from riflemen lurking in the woods. But, in spite of all difficulties, the work was accomplished, and an accurate map was prepared, showing the bearing and distance of almost every point in the river from the flag-staffs of the forts.

On the morning of the 17th of April all the vessels of the expedition were drawn up closely together four miles below the forts. The enemy opened the fight by sending down a fire-raft, piled up with wood saturated with tar and turpentine. A boat which put off from the Iroquois dragged the raft ashore, where it burned itself harmlessly out. All that day and the following night fire-rafts came down, but it was soon found that they were harmless. The final preparations for the bombardment were now made. The mast-heads of the bomb vessels would rise just above the woods on shore. From them the walls of the fort could be seen, though the vessels were undistinguishable from the forts; for Porter had ordered the masts to be dressed off with branches and vines. Of the dense mass of green, no one in the fort could tell what was forest and what was mast and rigging. On the

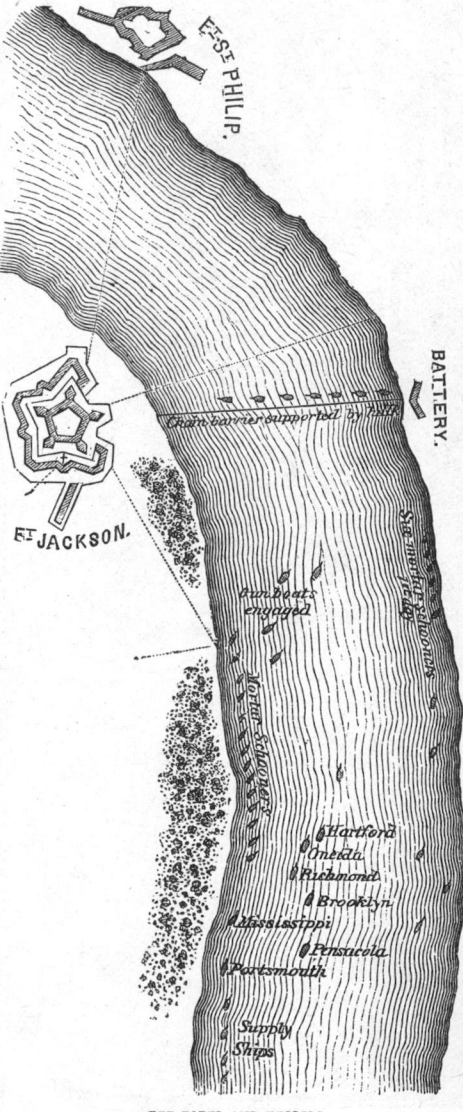

THE FORTS AND VESSELS.

morning of the 18th all the bomb vessels had taken their positions, the fore-most a little more than a mile and a half (2850 yards) from Fort Jackson. Behind this, in close order, were anchored twelve other vessels; across the river were six other mortar vessels, the foremost a little more than two miles (3680 yards) from Fort Jackson, upon which the whole fire was to be con-centrated. At nine o'clock the action commenced, the mortar vessels firing in order, each one every ten minutes. The forts replied. All day long the mortar boats kept up their constant fire, while gun-boats were dashing here and there, up and down the river, firing upon and receiving fire from the forts. Fire-rafts also came down, but they were easily disposed of. No one of the vessels lying under the lee of the woods was struck this day; two of those across the river were hit, killing one man and wounding three. The day was wearing to its close when a dense column of smoke and flame was seen rising from the fort. The citadel had been fired by the bombs; all the clothing and commissary stores were destroyed, and the magazine was in imminent danger. Porter could not know this. He supposed that it was another fire-raft ready to be launched against him. Night-firing was uncer-tain; the wind had set in fresh; no one could know how long the bombard-ment would last; the men were worn with labor and fasting, and so at dusk Porter ordered the firing to cease. If he had known all, he would have kept up the bombardment through the night. As it was, he thought it best to be prudent. This, he says, was the only mistake that occurred during the bombardment. Next day the bombardment was resumed, the fort respond-ing as briskly as before. One mortar vessel was struck by a shell and sunk, two men being wounded; another was hit by a shot which killed one man, and disabled the mortar for two or three hours. On the third day no harm was done to the fleet, and nothing showed that Fort Jackson was seriously injured by the 4000 bombs discharged at it. Porter began to lose confi-dence in mortars; but a deserter came in, telling a fearful story, only partly true, of the havoc made in the fort. Hundreds of shell, he said, had fallen within the works, casemates were broken in, citadel and outbuildings burnt, magazine endangered, levee cut, and men demoralized and dispirited. So the mortar fleet went to work with renewed vigor.

Farragut, meanwhile, had come to the conclusion that the mortar fleet would never reduce the forts. He must try what could be done by steam-ers and gun-boats. Whatever was to be done must be done quickly, or the great fleet would be again reduced to a mere blockading squadron, for shells, fuses, and cartridges were nearly expended. He would try to run the forts, or, if that could not be done, would engage them at close action, "and abide the result; conquer or be conquered; drop anchor or keep under way, as in his opinion was best," when the decisive moment should arrive.

Before the forts could be passed the barricade must be cut. This work was assigned to Bell, the fleet captain, commander of the flag-ship. Two gun-boats were given him for this work. One of these, the Pinola, was fur-nished with a petard, to be flung on board a hulk, and then ignited by a gal-vanic spark. The other, the Itasca, was to rely upon stout arms wielding hammer and chisel. The boats crept up on the night of the 20th, under cov-er of a fierce bombardment and of darkness. They reached the barricade. The Pinola, stopping her engine, threw her petard fairly upon one of the hulks; the strong current caught the vessel, whirling her down stream, and snapping the conducting wire before the spark could be transmitted. The Itasca was more fortunate. She steamed up to the middle hulk, and lashed herself to it. Her men leaped on board the hulk. In half an hour they cut the chain and loosed the hulk from its anchors. Gun-boat and hulk, lashed together, were swept by the current to the shore, the hulk luckily inside. The central hulk thus removed, the one on each side swung away, leaving an opening wide enough for three vessels to pass abreast. The Pinola, balked, through no fault of her own, in her own part of the enterprise, did good service in aiding her more fortunate consort. Getting again under way, she steamed up to the barricade, threw successively two five-inch haw-sers to the Itasca, broke both in trying to drag her off, started her at length with a larger one, and the two boats returned in triumph to the fleet. Their joint work was done. The way to New Orleans was open to Farragut, if he dared attempt it.

Farragut was ready to dare it. He made every preparation to fit his fleet for the venture which he saw must devolve upon it. The fleet would be ex-posed to hazards of every kind, and every precaution was taken against them. Foremost of all was one devised by Moore, the engineer of the Rich-mond. He proposed that the iron chain cables should be looped over the side of the vessels, so as to form a sort of armor protecting the line of the en-gines. This defense was adopted by the whole fleet. Months after, it was adopted by the Kearsarge in her memorable encounter with the Alabama. Each commander made, besides, his own special arrangements for preventing shot from reaching vital points in his vessel. Hammocks, coal, bags of ash-es, bags of sand, were piled up forward and abaft. Some rubbed their ves-sels with mud, to render them less perceptible; others whitewashed their decks, to make things more visible by night. Farragut's general order,[1] ad-dressed to the commander of each vessel, provided for almost every possible

BOMBARDMENT OF THE FORTS.

[1] The following are sentences from this order: Send down topgallantmasts. Rig in the flying jibboom, and land all the spars and rigging except what are necessary for the three topsails, fore-sail, jib, and spanker. Trice up the topmast stays, or land the whiskers, and bring all the rigging into the bowsprit, so that there shall be nothing in the range of the direct fire ahead. Mount one or two guns on the poop and topgallant forecastle, bearing in mind that you will always have to ride head to the current, and can only avail yourself of the sheer of the helm to point a broadside gun more than three points forward of the beam. Have a kedge in the mizzen chains; a hawser bent through the stern chock; also grapnels to tow off fire-ships. Have light Jacob ladders made to throw over the side for the use of carpenters in stopping shot-holes. See that pumps and hose are in good order for extinguishing fire. Have many tubs of water about the decks, for the pur-pose of extinguishing fire and for drinking. Have heavy kedge in the port main chains, and whip on the main yard, ready to run it up and let fall on the deck of any vessel you may run alongside of in order to secure her for boarding.

contingency. Much of it is hardly intelligible except to the nautical mind; but there are sentences which have the ring of Nelson or Napoleon: "I wish you to understand," he says, "that the day is at hand when you will be called upon to meet the enemy in the worst form for our profession. Hot and cold shot will, no doubt, be freely dealt to us, and there must be stout hearts and quick hands to extinguish the one and stop the holes of the other. I shall expect prompt attention to signals and verbal orders, either from myself or the captain of the fleet, who, it will be understood, in all cases acts by my authority."

Farragut had resolved to attempt to run past the forts. The time was fixed for the night of the 23d. The bombardment was to be kept up until then, mainly to occupy the enemy. So a rain of shells was kept up. Duncan, in the forts, reported cheerfully for the public in New Orleans. The enemy had fired 25,000 shells, of which a thousand had fallen in the fort, doing little real harm; "they must soon exhaust themselves; if not, we can stand it as long as they can." Confidentially, he writes less confidently. Mitchell, the naval commander, was urged to get the great ram Louisiana down at once, to draw off some part of the heavy fire from the mortar vessels. The position of the fort was critical; casemates were shattered and crumbling away, and the magazine was in peril. Duncan exaggerated his danger. Instead of 25,000 shells, barely 5000 had then been thrown against him; of these, not a third of a thousand had fallen within the fort. For all practical purposes, it was as strong when surrendered on the 28th as when first assailed ten days before.

Farragut's arrangements for passing the forts, like most great things when stripped of all accessories, were very simple. The mortar fleet, with its own steamers, and the sailing vessels, were to remain behind, yet covering the advance with their fire. Five steamers and twelve gun-boats were to run or fight the forts. All told, they carried 294 guns.[1] They were arranged in two columns. The barricade once passed through the opening made by the Itasca, Bailey, second in command, with the right column, was to deal with Fort St. Philip; Bell, captain of the fleet, with the left column, was to deal with Fort Jackson. Caldwell, of the Itasca, had in the mean while been sent up to ascertain if the gap which he had made in the barricade was still open. He found that the channel was clear, and that the whole fleet could pass.

Just after two o'clock on the morning of the 24th two small red lights were shown. This was the signal for advance. At half past three the whole fleet was fairly under way. The Hartford—Farragut, perched in the fore-rigging, peering anxiously through his glass into the thick darkness—led the left column of the blue; Bailey, in the Cayuga, led the right, all the other vessels following in close order. The forts were about two miles above. The vessels steamed slowly up against the strong current, making scarcely two miles an hour. As soon as they were fairly under way, the five small steamers belonging to the mortar flotilla threw a hot enfilading fire upon the water batteries, while the mortar schooners opened upon the forts a bombardment fiercer than had before been delivered. For an hour there was not an instant when five shells were not in the air; sometimes there were half a score. The ascending fleet was clearly in view from the flotilla below, every spar, man, and rope clearly visible through the flames, which seemed to be eating them up. When the last vessel disappeared in the smoke, Porter gave the signal to cease firing and drop down the river. He had done his share in the work. The rest must be left to Farragut.

Both columns passed the barricade without serious difficulty, only that three gun-boats missed the opening and were obliged to turn back. The real work was now to begin, for they were right under the guns of the forts, and open to the attack of the Confederate rams and gun-boats. Each man had now to fight at his own discretion; Farragut could only guess how each vessel was conducting itself; but he was able after the fight was over to report that "it has rarely been the lot of a commander to be supported by officers of more indomitable courage or higher professional merit."

Bailey, whose red flag was borne by the Cayuga, caught the first fire from Fort St. Philip. This fort had received no harm from the bombardment beyond the disabling of a single heavy gun. The flag-boat could bring no gun to bear at first, and steamed straight on, delivering a fire upon the fort in passing, and soon finding herself attacked by the whole fleet of Confederate gun-boats, with no supporting vessel in sight. "Hot but congenial work," says Bailey. Two large steamers, one on starboard bow, another astern, tried to board; off starboard beam was a third; but an 11-inch Dahlgren, at thirty yards' distance, quieted him; he shoved for shore, ran aground, and burned himself up. The Cayuga's forecastle Parrott drove off her enemy on the bow; by that time the Varuna and Oneida came dashing up, and took part in the fight.

The Varuna, Boggs in command, built for a merchant vessel, was the swiftest and weakest boat in the squadron. Giving Fort St. Philip a passing fire, she dashed up stream, and soon found herself in a nest of rebel steamers. She "worked both sides" upon these. Her first opponent, apparently crowded with troops, caught her starboard fire, and drifted ashore, with boiler exploded. Three more on either side soon shared the same fate. She then slacked steam, and was overhauled by two of the enemy, both iron-clad at the bows, and intent upon running her down. Hitherto not a man had been hurt on the Varuna. But now the Governor Moore, her foremost enemy, gave a raking fire, which killed three and wounded nine men, and almost simultaneously butted her twice. The Moore got more than she gave. Boggs managed to throw three shells into her abaft of her armor, besides a few favors from a stern rifled gun, when she dropped out of action partly disabled. Another boat, iron-clad at the bows, with an under-water beak, was at the same time assailing the Varuna. She struck her fairly, with damaging force, receiving shot which glanced harmlessly from her mailed bow; then she drew off, and came back, delivering another blow on the same spot, which crushed in the side of the Varuna. But in the melée her bows were dragged around, exposing her unarmored side. Five 8-inch shells, delivered from the now sinking Varuna, settled her, and she went ashore. Fifty of her crew were killed and wounded. She was set on fire by her own commander, who burned his wounded with his vessel. This fight was brief. In fifteen minutes after the Varuna was first butted she was on the bottom, her topgallant forecastle only being out of water. The Oneida had by this time come up. Boggs waved her on to finish the Moore. This accomplished, the Oneida returned and took off a part of the crew of the sinking Varuna; the rest were rescued by other vessels. The honors of the fight must be accorded to the Varuna, the only lost vessel. Before she went down she had helped to sink or disable six vessels of the enemy, any one of whom was fairly her match.

The large steamers were meanwhile having a rough time. The Hartford had hardly got under way when she received the fire of Fort Jackson. She replied from two forecastle guns, keeping straight on for the barricade. Passing this, Farragut sheered off at the distance of half a mile, and poured in full broadsides of grape and canister, which drove every man in the fort under cover; but the casemate guns kept up a hot fire. Fort St. Philip now opened upon the advancing fleet. The fire became general, but the smoke was so dense that it was difficult to distinguish friends from foes; the flash of the guns was the only object at which forts or fleet could aim. A huge fire-raft soon loomed up amid the blackness. Farragut, in trying to avoid it, ran his vessel on shore. The raft, pushed on by the ram Manassas, whose black hull was invisible, was shoved right upon the Hartford. In a moment the good ship was on fire half way up to her tops, the flames bursting through the ports and running up the rigging. "Fire quarters" were beaten, the flames extinguished, the steamer backed off from shore, extricating herself from the raft, and pointed up stream. This in a few minutes brought her opposite St. Philip, upon which she poured her fire from one broadside, while the other blazed at Jackson. A half hour more of this hot work carried the Hartford beyond the range of the forts, and brought her among the remains of the Confederate fleet, which had been pretty thoroughly dealt with by the gun-boats, which had gained the advance.

The Brooklyn, meanwhile, had had her share of hot work. Her place in the line was directly after the flag-ship. In the smoke and darkness she lost sight of the Hartford, and became entangled among the hulks of the barricade. She fell athwart the stream, her bow grazing the bank. Here she caught the fire of St. Philip. Regaining her position, she passed the opening, and met the Manassas, which delivered a shot at ten feet distance; this was stopped by the sand-bags which protected that vital point, the steam drum. The ram twice attempted to butt; but she was too close to get up full speed, and the blows were harmless. Morse's improvised chain armor proved a perfect protection to the sides of the Brooklyn. The Manassas slid off and disappeared in the darkness, to reappear only once more. A Confederate steamer then tried the Brooklyn, which was all the time raked from Fort Jackson. "Our port broadside," says Craven, the gallant captain of the Brooklyn, "at the short distance of fifty or sixty yards, completely finished him, setting him on fire almost instantaneously." The Brooklyn groped her way in darkness and smoke until she found herself abreast of St. Philip, so close that there was but thirteen feet of water. She was in a position to bring her full broadside to bear, and for a few minutes poured in a storm of grape and canister which drove the men from their guns and silenced the fire of the fort. Having passed the forts, the Brooklyn, still under way, engaged several of the enemy's gun-boats, pouring in a destructive fire at short range, generally from sixty to a hundred yards. "The effects of our broadsides," says Craven, "must have been terrific." The Brooklyn was under fire an hour and a half, and suffered severely both in men and in damage to the vessel.

The three other steam ships played worthy but less conspicuous parts. The Richmond, the slowest vessel, groped its way through the fiery channel after the way had been cleared, suffering little. The Pensacola took the full fire of St. Philip passing slowly up, frequently stopping to return it. Her men lay flat on deck to receive the first fire of the forts. The enemy overshot, and many lives were thus saved; but the loss on the Pensacola exceeded that of any other vessel. She did not come up with the enemy's gun-boats until the action with them was nearly over. The Mississippi, in a few months to go down at Port Hudson, felt the enemy's fire. She received ten shots, eight of which passed sheer through her, and got a severe wound from the Manassas, which she at last disabled.

The Manassas was the great reliance of the Confederate fleet. She was built somewhat after the model of the Virginia, and it was supposed that she could deal with the Federal fleet as the Virginia had dealt with the Cumberland. In the gray of the morning, when the Federal fleet had fairly passed the forts and had destroyed the Confederate flotilla, the Manassas appeared coming up after them, hoping even then to retrieve the fortunes of the fight.

[1] The following are the vessels, with the number of their guns, ordered to attempt to pass the forts: *Steam ships*—Hartford, 28; Brooklyn, 26; Richmond, 24; Pensacola, 24; Mississippi, 13. *Gun-boats*—Cayuga, 7; Oneida, 10; Varuna, 9; Katahdin, 7; Kineo, 6; Wissahickon, 6; Sciota, 5; Iroquois, 9; Kennebec, 5; Pinola, 5; Itasca, 4; Winona, 6: in all, 17 vessels, with 294 guns. The three gun-boats Itasca, Winona, and Kennebec failed to pass the barricade. No accurate list of the Confederate vessels encountered above the barricade has been preserved. There appear to have been in all 16 or 18 armed vessels, carrying about 50 guns. Many of them were designed for rams, so that the number of guns is no measure of their real offensive power. The iron-clad Manassas, which was supposed capable of clearing the whole river, carried but one gun. The following list, only partially accurate, is the most complete which can now be given of the Confederate flotilla: Louisiana, iron-clad, 16; Manassas, iron-clad, 1; McRae, 8; Governor Moore, 3; General Quitman, 2; Jackson, 2; Lovell, 1; Warrior, 2; Resolute, 2; Reliance, 2; Breckinridge, 1; Stonewall Jackson, 1; Galveston, 2; Anglo-Norman, 2; Star, 1.

THE HARTFORD ON FIRE.

Farragut ordered Smith of the Mississippi to turn and run her down. The head of the Mississippi was pointed down stream, and she dashed toward the ram with the full velocity of steam and stream. When only fifty yards apart, the ram put her helm aport and dodged the blow, but ran fast on the bank. Her crew got ashore as best they could. The Mississippi, balked of her blow, poured in two broadsides, thoroughly riddling the Manassas, and then boarded. But it was not worth while to save her. The hulk was dragged off from the bank, fire set to her, and she was sent drifting down the current without a man on board. Half an hour after, the Manassas came drifting down the river below the forts, seemingly ready to pounce upon the defenseless mortar vessels. Fire was opened upon the hulk, but it was soon discovered that she was harmless. Flame and smoke were pouring from every opening, and she was evidently sinking. Porter, wishing to save her as a curiosity, got a hawser on board and tied her to the bank. Hardly was this done when a faint explosion was heard, her only gun went off, and, emitting flames through her bow port, the Manassas gave a final plunge and disappeared under the turbid waters of the river.

The morning had hardly broken, and the fog was not lifted from the riv-

er, when Farragut, the battle won, looked round for his fleet. Three gunboats were missing, whether captured, sunk, or driven back he could not then know. He afterward learned that they were safe. The Winona and Kennebec had got fouled among the hulks of the barricade, and at daylight found themselves a mark for the whole fire of the two forts, against which it was madness to contend, and had turned their heads down stream. The Itasca, which had opened the barricade, had met with misfortune and disappointment. She tried bravely to pass, and only desisted when several shot from Fort Jackson passed through her. One pierced her boiler, making an opening through which the steam rushed in a dense cloud, filling fire-room and engine-room, driving every one from below. Others caused leaks which threatened to sink the boat. She was also forced to withdraw. Caldwell, her commander, gave pathetic utterance to his heartfelt sorrow and disappointment that his disabled condition prevented him from being a participant in the complete success of the enterprise to which he had contributed so much. The Varuna, victorious in death, was a total loss. The seven days' bombardment, and the three hours' fight with forts and fleet, had cost in all 37 killed and 171 wounded, more than half of which fell upon the five

THE CRESCENT CITY IN 1862.

steam ships.[1] The forts shot too high throughout, and the gun-boats, lying low, were overshot. Their injuries were mainly received in the combat with the enemy's flotilla.[2] The entire loss of the Confederates has never been ascertained. In the forts 14 were killed and 38 wounded. The loss on the boats must have been very severe, for at least twelve of them were sunk or burned.

Farragut found his fleet somewhat battered, but sufficient for the work which it had to do. Boggs, his own vessel being lost, volunteered to take a boat, make his way through the bayous bordering the Mississippi, and convey dispatches to Porter and Butler, still below the forts. Butler was told that the way was clear for him to send up his troops by the bayous in the rear of the forts, where their landing would be protected by gun-boats left for that purpose. For Porter there was a note from Farragut, telling in sharp sailor phrase of the rough time which he had had; how once he thought it was all up with him; how he fought his way through, destroyed the Confederate fleet, was starting for New Orleans; the city captured, he would come back and attend to the forts, which Porter should hold as they were, unless, indeed, they should surrender, as he thought they would, upon being summoned. Just now he was going ahead. "I wish," he concluded, "to get above the English Turn, where they say the enemy have not placed a battery yet, but have two above, nearer New Orleans. They will not be idle, and neither will I. You supported me nobly."

But after passing the forts there was no serious opposition. The batteries which had been reported to line the levee above had no existence. The Chalmette regiment was encamped at the quarantine station five miles above the forts. Bailey ran the Cayuga up to the bank, hailed the colonel, and ordered him to pile his arms and come on board. The regiment surrendered, and were released on parole, only they must remain where they were until next day. The fleet steamed up the river through a scene of almost pastoral quiet. The banks for a mile on each side were lined with sugar plantations, green with young cane, dotted over with gangs of negroes busy at work. Now and then a white flag, or the Union colors, was hung out from a villa, or waved from the levee. Sometimes a white man would appear, making gestures of hatred or defiance. Here and there the slaves swarmed up to the levee, hoe in hand, waving their battered hats, and shouting a welcome to those who, they had learned by the strange system of free-masonry peculiar to the negroes, had come to be their deliverers. On other plantations, where they were kept under more strict control, they dug doggedly on, not seeming to notice the unwonted spectacle of an armed fleet steaming up the river. As evening fell, the fleet came to anchor eighteen miles below New Orleans by the bends of the river, but only half that distance in a

straight line. Huge volumes of fiery smoke were seen rolling up. A great panic had suddenly fallen upon the Crescent City.

On the morning of the 24th no man in New Orleans dreamed that the city was in danger. Duncan had telegraphed the evening before, giving an account of affairs up to the morning. "Heavy and continuous bombardment all night, and still progressing. No farther casualties except two men slightly wounded. We are cheerful, and have an abiding faith in our ultimate success. Twenty-five thousand 13-inch shells have been fired by the enemy, one thousand of which fell into the fort. They must soon exhaust themselves; if not, we can stand it as long as they can." Duncan overcounted. Hardly 5000 shells had then been thrown. Eight or nine thousand was the utmost limit after two days' more.

This cheering report appeared in the New Orleans morning papers of the 24th. Every body thought every thing was well until half past nine, when the alarm-bell was heard. Twelve strokes, four times repeated, summoned all armed bodies to their head-quarters. A telegram from below, cut off at the fifteenth word, said, "It is reported that two of the enemy's gun-boats have succeeded in passing the forts." Not two, but seven times two, if the truth had been known. Five long hours passed without a farther word. Mansfield Lovell, commander at New Orleans, had the day before gone leisurely down toward the forts. He came back, dashing along the levee at racing speed, bringing tidings that the whole Union fleet—not merely two gun-boats—had passed the forts, destroyed the Confederate flotilla, and were approaching New Orleans. It was late in the afternoon. The panic set in. Officers rode about impressing carts to haul the cotton from the store-houses to the levee for burning. The foreign consulates were crowded with persons bringing their valuables to be deposited for safe-keeping under foreign flags. The banks sent off their four millions of gold, which soon found its way to the Confederate treasury, never to be reclaimed. The military bodies hurried to their armories; but instead of the 64,000 infantry in and about the city, "in discipline and drill far superior to the Yankees," there were less than 3000 troops and a few thousand militia. Lovell abandoned the city, taking off his soldiers, and followed by some thousands of the militia; the others doffed their uniforms and remained behind. The governor of the state fled up the river in the swiftest steamer he could find, scattering proclamations directing the burning of every bale of cotton and every barrel of sugar which the enemy could by any possibility reach. The whole city was mad with apprehension and rage, with bewilderment and fury. Some denounced Duncan, some upbraided Lovell, some demanded that the city should be made another Moscow, some clamored that every Union man should be brought to the lamp-post. Worse even than the coming of the Yankees, all the scoundrelism of the city, noted for the number of its scoundrels, broke loose. The municipal authorities, restored to administration by the cessation of martial law, were at their wits' end. The police was powerless. There was but one way to save the city from burning and plunder. The mayor called upon the European brigade, composed of foreigners, to take charge of the city. They accepted the charge, and suppressed the tumult. At evening the authorized work of destruction began. The torch was applied to 15,000 bales of cotton, piled up on the river bank; to nearly a score of cotton-ships, ready to elude the blockade through some of the fifty outlets; to as many steam-boats; the relics of that mighty fleet which once lined the levee, four deep, for miles; to a great iron-clad ram, almost completed, which was to sweep the river; to miles of steam-boat wood and acres of coal; to ship-timber, dry docks, board-yards—to every thing combustible which the Yankees could use. The heads of hundreds of barrels of sugar and hogsheads of molasses were stove in. Men, women, and children, white, black, and parti-colored, scooped up molasses and sugar from the ground, and carried it off in pails, baskets, tubs, and aprons. Few of the inhabitants of New Orleans, except the slaves, slept on the night of Thursday, the 24th of April.

At dawn the next day Farragut weighed anchor, and steamed cautiously up the river. Evidences of the panic in New Orleans were every where visible. Burning cotton-ships and ship-yard apparatus on fire came floating down. The destruction of property was awful. At half past ten they came in view of Jackson's old battle-field, three miles below the city. Earth-works were visible by the old lines on each shore. The fleet was drawn up in two lines as before, one to attend to each bank. Bailey, in the Cayuga, was far ahead, not having seen the signal to slacken speed and allow the slower vessels to come up. A raking fire was opened upon him for a mile from twenty guns—not the famous five-mile rifled cannon which the newspapers had placed there just twenty days before. He could reply with only two forecastle guns. In twenty minutes the fleet got up. Each vessel, in passing, bore away, and gave the forts a broadside of shells, shrapnel, and grape, silencing them effectually. This affair cost the fleet one man, Midshipman John Anderson, of the Brooklyn, knocked overboard by the wind of a ball and drowned. For the rest, it was, in Farragut's words, "one of the little elegancies of the profession—a dash and a victory."

At noon the fleet rounded the bend, came into full view of the Crescent City, and cast anchor. Fires were blazing all along the shore; the stream was full of burning vessels; the levee was aswarm with an angry mob, who

<hr>

[1] The following is the loss on each vessel belonging to the running fleet, as reported by the surgeon general:

BELL'S DIVISION.	Killed	Wounded		BAILEY'S DIVISION.	Killed	Wounded
Hartford	3	10		Mississippi	2	6
Brooklyn	9	26		Pensacola	4	33
Richmond	2	4		Cayuga	—	6
Sciota	—	2		Oneida	—	3
Iroquois	6	22		Varuna	3	9
Kennebec	—	—		Katahdin	—	—
Pinola	3	7		Kineo	1	8
Itasca	—	4		Wissahickon	—	—
Winona	3	5			10	65
	26	80				

Besides these, during the seven days' bombardment, 2 were killed (one by a fall from the masthead) and 26 wounded. One more was killed afterward. The entire cost of the capture of New Orleans was 39 men killed and 171 wounded; one mortar boat and one gun-boat sunk.

[2] According to the accounts of a deserter, the casemate guns which threw hot shot from Fort Jackson erred on the other side. The officer in command, fearing to fire too high, depressed his guns below the horizontal line; wishing to work his guns vigorously, they were run out with a jerk; the consequence was that the balls rolled out into the moat, while the guns blazed harmlessly away with powder and wadding. The officers on the rampart told him that his shot were falling short. He tried to remedy the defect, and, fixing a correct aim on one particular vessel, blazed away at it. Only when the Federal fleet had got out of range did he discover that he had been devoting himself to one of the Confederate chain hulks.

amused themselves with hunting down a few persons who raised a faint cheer for the Union. A fierce rain-shower came down and melted away a part of the crowd. In the midst of it a boat put off from the Hartford, with no white flag of truce flying. The crew were rigged in the freshest man-of-war style, as though they were on a pleasure-trip. In the stern sat three officers—Morton in command of the boat, Bailey and Perkins charged to see the authorities, whoever they might be, and demand the surrender of the city. These two stepped ashore, amid cheers for Jeff. Davis and the South, and groans for Lincoln and his fleet. Some of the crowd, wiser than the rest, conducted the two messengers to the City Hall, the mob yelling around. "No violence," said a newspaper next morning, "was offered to the officers, though certain persons who were suspected of favoring their flag and cause were set upon with great fury and roughly handled;" but it added, "on arriving at the City Hall it required the intervention of several citizens to prevent violence being offered to the rash embassadors of an execrated dynasty and government."

The story of the actual surrender of New Orleans reads like a farce, which might at any moment be turned into a tragedy; for the furious mob, and the city which sheltered it, lay at the mercy of the Union fleet.

The two officers entered the City Hall, and introduced themselves to his honor the mayor—a smug, pompous little gentleman, addicted to the use of flowery phrases. After formal salutations had been exchanged, Bailey announced that he had come to demand the surrender of the city and the hoisting of the Union flag on the public buildings. Mayor Monroe had no authority to surrender, and would not hoist the Union flag; General Lovell was the military commander; he should be sent for. Meanwhile conversation was kept up; courteous in form, but with an occasional sharp tang. The Union officers praised the valor of the Confederate forts and fleets, and regretted the destruction of so much property in the city. The mayor rejoined, tartly, that the property was their own; if they chose to destroy it, it was nobody's business. Bailey replied that, as things stood, it looked very much like biting off one's own nose to spite his face. Just then Lovell came in. After due hand-shakings, Bailey again announced his errand. Lovell could not think of surrendering the city. He had evacuated it with his troops; it was defenseless, and Farragut could shell it if he chose. He would retire and leave the city authorities to do as they thought proper. The mayor thereupon said that he would consult the City Council, and report the result next day.

Farragut was amused and puzzled; but, as his men were tired out, he concluded to wait till next day for the action of the city fathers, especially as there were several matters that could be attended to in the mean while. There were sundry rams, almost completed, meant to be the terror of the river; several forts; and, above all, a boom lying ready to swing across the river to prevent the descent of any fleet from above. It was a stupendous structure, three quarters of a mile long, composed of logs four feet in diameter and thirty feet long, lying three abreast, bound together with chains. There were ninety-six of these lengths. These were all rendered harmless.

An hour after daylight on Saturday a boat put off from the shore containing messengers from the mayor. The City Council would meet at ten, and the Federal commander should be apprized of the result of their deliberations. Farragut replied that it was not within the province of a naval officer to assume the duties of a military commander. He had come to reduce New Orleans to obedience to the laws of the United States. The city must be surrendered, all hostile flags must be hauled down, and that of the United States be hoisted on all public buildings by noon; there must be no more outrages upon loyal people; they should try to quell disturbances, restore order, and call upon the people of New Orleans to return to their usual avocations; the rights of person and property should be secure.

The city fathers met, and the mayor read to them the reply which he had prepared for Farragut. They approved it heartily. It was the most singular document ever offered to a conqueror by the authorities of a conquered town. The city had been evacuated by the troops, the administration of its government and the custody of its honor had been restored to the mayor, whose duty it became "to transmit the answer which the universal sentiments of his constituency, no less than the promptings of his own heart, dictated on that sad and solemn occasion. I am no military man," he continued; "it would be presumptuous in me to attempt to lead an army to the field, and I know still less how to surrender an undefended place. The city is yours by the power of brutal force. As to the hoisting of any other flag than the one of our own adoption, the man lives not in our midst whose hand and heart would not be palsied at the mere thought of such an act; nor could I find in my entire constituency so wretched and desperate a renegade as would dare to profane with his hand the sacred emblem of our aspirations." The mayor went on to compliment the commander upon the sentiments which he had manifested. "They sprung from a noble but deluded nature," were worthy of one "engaged in a better cause," and the mayor "knew how to appreciate the motives which inspired them." The Federal commander should remember that he had "a gallant people to administer; a people sensitive to all that can in the least affect its dignity and self-re-

THE LEVEE IN 1862.

spect. Do not allow them to be insulted by the interference of such as have rendered themselves odious and contemptible by their dastardly desertion of the mighty struggle in which we are engaged, nor of such as might remind them too painfully that they are the conquered and you the conquerors. Peace and order may be preserved without a resort to measures which could not fail to wound their sensibilities and fire up their passions." And more of the same sort, the purport of all being that the captors were modestly desired to withdraw the fleet which commanded the city, and leave the people to themselves, with full power to work their will upon any Union men in their midst. At all events, if they wanted the Federal flag raised, they must do it themselves. There was bravado, if not bravery, in this reply; but a man powerless to harm his opponent, who knows that he can be harmed only by being struck through the bodies of women and children, may safely venture upon bravado.

Next morning Farragut sent a small party ashore to hoist the Union flag on the Custom-house and Mint, with strict orders not to use their arms unless actually assailed. They were insulted, but not assaulted. The flags were left without a guard; but the guns of the Pensacola were trained upon the Mint, and the mob were warned that fire would be opened upon the building if any attempt was made to disturb the flag. At eleven o'clock the crews of all the ships were assembled on deck to "return thanks to Almighty God for his great goodness and mercy in permitting them to pass through the events of the last two days with so little loss of life and blood." An April shower seemed coming up, and the gunner of the Pensacola removed the wafers by which the guns are discharged. The report of a howitzer from the main-top turned all eyes toward the Mint. Four men were seen upon the roof; one cut the flag from the staff, and all dragged it off. Without orders, the strings to every gun of the Pensacola were pulled. No shot followed. The fortunate removal of the wafers alone prevented a full broadside from being poured into the city. The flag was carried into the street, paraded in a cart to the sound of fife and drum, trailed through the mire, and then torn into shreds, which were distributed among the screaming crowd.

Farragut hardly knew what to do. The insult had been committed; he could take ample vengeance, but only by opening fire, and punishing the innocent as well as the guilty. His kindly nature revolted at this. He took till next day to consider and to consult with Butler, who had come up the river, as yet without bringing any troops. The result was that Farragut wrote to the mayor, noticing the refusal to haul down the state flag, detailing the outrages which had been committed, and warning him that "the fire of this fleet might be drawn upon the city at any moment, and in such an event the levee would in all probability be cut by the shells, and an amount of distress ensue to the innocent population, which I have heretofore endeavored to assure you that I desired by all means to avoid. The election is therefore with you; but it becomes my duty to notify you to remove the women and children from the city within forty-eight hours, if I have rightly understood your determination."

The mayor returned an impudent reply. He could not conceive that the Federal flag had been hoisted by the orders of "Mr. Farragut;" the interference of any force while negotiations for surrender were pending was a flagrant violation of the courtesies, if not of the rights, recognized among belligerents. The city still contained a population of 140,000, and "Mr. Farragut" must be aware of the utter inanity of such a notification. "Our women and children," he continued, "can not escape from your shells, if it be your pleasure to murder them on a question of mere etiquette. You are not satisfied with the peaceable possession of an undefended city, opposing no resistance to your guns, because of its bearing its doom with something of manliness and dignity, and you wish to humble and disgrace us by the performance of an act against which our nature rebels. This satisfaction you can not expect to obtain at our hands. We will stand your bombardment, unarmed and undefended as we are. The civilized world will consign to indelible infamy the heart that will conceive the deed, and the hand that will dare to execute it."

This insolent message gave Farragut an opportunity to extricate himself from the dilemma of submitting to an insult to his flag or of avenging it by punishing the innocent with the guilty. He simply replied that the mayor had made his letter so offensive that it would terminate all intercourse between them. General Butler was close at hand with his forces. When he arrived the charge of the city would be turned over to him. But, in the mean time, the flag of the Union was to be raised on the Custom-house, and the mayor must see that it was respected. Every ensign and symbol of government, whether state or Confederate, except that of the United States, must be hauled down. This was done. Captain Bell, with a few marines, marched into the city, hauled down the Confederate flag, hoisted that of the Union, locked the Custom-house, put the key in his pocket, and returned, leaving the flag unguarded. It was not again molested.

By this time it was known that Forts Jackson and St. Philip had been surrendered, the remainder of the Confederate fleet destroyed or given up, and the river-road to New Orleans open to the unarmed transports which were to bring up Butler's troops. The forts had been passed—not reduced, or even seriously injured. The great iron-clad ram Louisiana was unharmed. She had taken no part in the action, though on the day before her work had been assigned. It is said that her crew were all drunk. Three armed steamers had moreover escaped. If they were no match for the Union armed vessels, they might yet make havoc of the mortar schooners and transports. As soon as the passage was achieved, Porter sent a flag demanding the surrender of the forts. Higgins had no official information that New Orleans had been occupied, and could not then entertain a proposition for surrender. The next day, the 28th of April, Colonel Higgins had occasion to change his mind. Weitzel, whose old duck-shooting experience came into use, had guided expeditions through the bayous; they had got above both forts, cutting them off from communication with New Orleans. A mutiny had broken out in Fort Jackson; 250 men had come out and surrendered to the Union pickets. Porter again demanded a surrender. "You have defended the forts gallantly," he said, "and no more can be asked of you. I know you can hold out some time longer, but in the end you must yield. You can gain nothing by farther resistance. You shall have terms sufficiently honorable to relieve you from any feeling of humiliation. Officers shall retire on parole, with their side-arms; soldiers shall be paroled, laying down their arms; public property shall be given up; private property shall be respected." Higgins replied that he would give up the forts on these terms, but he had no authority over the navy, and was not responsible for what it should do. There had been a quarrel between the military and naval commanders. Each accused the other of failure of duty. Four Union boats steamed up with white flags flying, answered by white flags on the forts. Duncan and Higgins came on board the Harriet Lane, where the articles of capitulation were to be formally drawn up. While this was being done, word was brought to Porter that the Louisiana, all ablaze, was coming straight down upon them. "This is not creditable to the naval commander," said Porter. "We are not responsible for the acts of these naval officers," responded Higgins. "Is there much powder aboard, and are the guns loaded?" "I presume so; but we know nothing of naval matters here." The heated guns now began to go off, with every probability of throwing shot and shell amid friends and foes. Porter coolly remarked to the Confederate officers, "If you do not mind the explosion which is soon to come, we can stand it." No one moved from his seat, and the conference proceeded as calmly as though nothing had happened. The current sheered the burning vessel across the river, and when it was just abreast of Fort St. Philip it blew up, scattering the fragments in every direction, and killing one man in the fort. The noise was heard for miles. When the smoke cleared away not a vestige of the Louisiana was visible; she had gone down in the deep waters of the Mississippi. Had the explosion occurred, as Mitchell, the treacherous naval commander, intended it should, in the midst of the Federal fleet, every vessel would have been destroyed.

Duncan and Higgins acted with perfect good faith. Not the slightest change was made in the forts while the articles of capitulation were being drawn up. Every thing was surrendered as it stood when the white flag was raised. Officers and men were released on parole. They came out from the fort looking more like school-boys going home than men who had just been made prisoners. Not a few were of Northern birth, who had enlisted to man the forts in the full belief that they would never be called upon to fight. New Orleans, it was thought, might be assailed from above; nobody dreamed that a fleet from below would seriously attempt to fight or pass the forts. Yet such is the marvelous power of discipline, that they stood to their work like men who were fighting for a cause dear to them, instead of one for which they had no sympathy. A part of them, indeed, took the first fair occasion to desert. Duncan appeared at New Orleans next day, and harangued the angry crowd on the levee. He declared, with tears in his eyes, that nothing but the mutiny of a part of his command could have induced him to surrender. But for that he could have held out for months.

Fort St. Philip was hardly scarred. Fort Jackson, to an unprofessional eye, had been severely handled. It had been plowed with shells, the citadel had been burnt, the magazine endangered, casemates crumbled and flooded, walls cracked, drawbridge broken down, causeways blown up, holes made by bombs every where visible. Naval officers, who knew that a shattered ship was defenseless, were justified in supposing that the fort was really reduced; that another day's bombardment would have finished it; that it could have stood but little more without coming down about its defenders' ears, and would need to be demolished and rebuilt if government ever intended to fortify the site again. Weitzel, who knew better the capabilities of a fort, told a very different story. The navy, he reported, passed the forts, but did not reduce them. St. Philip, with one or two exceptions, was without a scratch. To an unexperienced eye, Jackson seemed badly cut up; but to resist an assault, or even regular approaches, it was as strong as when the first shell was fired against it.

The forts having been surrendered, Porter turned his attention to Mitchell, who lay half a mile above with three steamers, one of which he had just scuttled. A shot fired over him from the Harriet Lane caused him to lower his flag. Twenty-one officers and 300 men surrendered at discretion. The men were dismissed on parole; the officers were retained as prisoners to answer for their perfidious conduct in continuing hostilities while they had a flag of truce flying.

The forts were surrendered on the 28th of April. Butler, hastening down to bring up troops some way, found the river-road open. The transports, among which was the Mississippi—not the war steamer of the same name—were soon under way, freighted with soldiers who had been wearily waiting at the Head of the Passes. At sunset on the 29th she reached the forts, now held by blue coats instead of gray. At midnight the general came on board, and the vessels passed up the river. The voyage occupied the whole of the last day of April. At noon on the 1st of May the Mississippi lay along the levee of New Orleans. A crowd had gathered, but not the angry mass which had been seen there for almost a week. They seemed to be disposed to make a joke of the circumstances. There was a popular song, set to a rollicking tune, telling how a mythical "Picayune Butler" had come to a mythical town. The coincidence of names struck the mob. "Picayune Butler" was asked to come ashore and show himself. The general grimly enjoyed the joke. He wished the tune of "Picayune Butler" played for the delectation of the mob. The band happened to be destitute of the score, and were obliged to give "Yankee Doodle" and the "Star Spangled Banner" instead.

But, apart from chaffing, there was work to be done. Butler determined to take military possession of the city at once. In four hours a company of the Thirty-first Massachusetts landed on the levee and quietly pressed the crowd back, making room for the remainder of the regiment and for the Fourth Wisconsin. Both regiments then formed, a file taking each side of the street, the general and his staff marching on foot. Strict orders had been given for the conduct of the troops. There was to be no plundering of public or private property. No officer or soldier should, upon any pretext, absent himself from his station without arms or alone. They were to march in silence, except that the bands were to play; no notice to be taken of offensive or insulting words. If a shot was fired from a house, they should halt, arrest the inmates, and destroy the house. If they were fired upon from the streets, the offender should, if possible, be arrested, but they should not fire into the crowd unless absolutely necessary for self-defense, and then not without orders. The troops moved steadily on, seemingly unconscious of the surging masses crowding the side-walks, hurrahing for Beauregard, Bull Run, and Shiloh, cursing Butler and the Yankees. They passed the St. Charles Hotel, now deserted; five days before it was the head-quarters of Lovell; to-morrow it was to be the head-quarters of Butler. They reached the unfinished, roofless Custom-house, which the government had been building, Beauregard being engineer, when the rebellion broke out. The Union flag floated, unguarded and unmolested, from its walls. The door was locked, and the key was on board the Hartford. Entrance was forced and, half an hour before sunset on the 1st of May, the Union troops were making preparations in an upper story for their first meal in New Orleans. Strong guards were posted at all needful points. The rage of the mob had exhausted itself; the city relapsed into perfect quiet. Butler returned to the vessel, to add the last words to the proclamation which was formally to announce on the morrow that New Orleans was again under the flag of the Union.

PASSING UP THE BAYOU.

THE CITY OF NEW ORLEANS.

CHAPTER XV.

BUTLER'S ADMINISTRATION AT NEW ORLEANS.

The Condition of New Orleans.—Character of its Population.—Butler at the St. Charles.—Interview with the Mayor.—Quelling the Mob.—Butler's Proclamation.—Soulé's Remonstrance.—Butler and the City Authorities.—Occupation of Baton Rouge.—Providing Food.—Charles Heidseck.—Feeding the Poor.—The City Authorities reproved.—The Women Order.—The General and the Mayor.—Deposition of the Municipal Government.—Regulating the Currency.—The Banks and their Issues.—Property sequestered by the Confederacy.—Cleaning the Streets.—The Quarantine.—Pardon of the Monroe Guard.—Execution of Mumford.—Execution of Plunderers.—Punishment of Outrages.—Mrs. Phillips.—The Oath of Allegiance or Neutrality required.—Protest of Consuls.—Modified Oath.—Butler and the Clergy.—Dr. Leacock.—Disarming the Population.—Consular Protest.—The Confiscation Act.—The Negro Question.—Colored Regiments.—Military Operations.—The Pass System.—Occupation of the Lafourche District.—Sequestration of Property.—Growth of Union Sentiment.—Butler's Plans.—Charges against him.—His Recall.—Butler and the Consuls.—His Farewell Address.

IN assuming the military government of New Orleans, General Butler undertook a difficult and delicate task. It will be the object of this chapter to show how he performed it. The people were heterogeneous. At the outbreak of the rebellion the resident population was 168,000; 155,000 were free and 13,000 slaves. Of the free population, 10,000 were colored; of the whites, 80,000 were born in the United States, 65,000 in foreign countries. Ireland sent 24,000, Germany 20,000, France 11,000, England 3000. Almost half of the free white population were born abroad; more than half out of the state. Of those of foreign birth, few became citizens by naturalization, as is shown by the small vote cast. In the presidential election of 1860 less than 11,000 votes were given; of these, Bell received one half, the remainder being almost equally divided between Douglass and Breckinridge; not a single vote was given to Lincoln. No city in the Union has so few citizens in proportion to its white population. The alien element was strong beyond its ratio of number. Two thirds of the business men were of foreign birth. They had come to New Orleans to make money. For the country which protected them they cared nothing. All that they cared for was the profits which they could gain by trading; so that these were safe, they cared not for king or emperor, for Union or Confederacy. Of citizens by birth, the majority belonged to the Creole race; that is, as the word is used in Louisiana, people born in the state, but of French or Spanish blood. They are fond of money, and yet not specially active in the pursuit of gain. In ordinary cases, they kept rather aloof from politics, preferring luxury to excitement. Under the impulse of passion or revenge they were ready for any desperate deed. Two or three assassinations, as many fights and "encounters" in street or bar-room, and as many more formal duels, were the average from day to day. Besides the resident population, there was a floating mass of renegadoes and desperadoes from all quarters of the globe, fiery Frenchmen, revengeful Spaniards, sneaking Cubans, and, worse than either, the refuse of all the gamblers, swindlers, and ruffians swarming down the Mississippi from every part of the Union. A desperado for whom Vicksburg or Natchez-under-the-Hill had become too hot, but who had no taste for roughing it in Texas, looked to New Orleans as a temporary refuge. This floating population, shifting from day to day, of which the census could take no account, numbered from 5000 to 10,000.

New Orleans was a purely commercial city. It owed its being to the fact that it stood on the first tolerably firm patch of land above the mouths of the Mississippi. The resident population were at first loth to imperil their interests by rushing into secession; but the controlling mass of aliens, who could lose nothing, and might hope to gain much by the overthrow of the Union, soon seduced or forced the indolent impetuous Creoles to their views. Secession became the fashion. No young man who cared to have a place in society dared to do other than volunteer for the Confederate army. The population of New Orleans was depleted by 30,000 of the flower of its youth. They were in every army of the Confederacy.

When New Orleans found itself powerless before the fleet of Farragut, its population numbered about 140,000. It was made up of the poor who could not leave, of the scoundrels who would not leave, and of people who cared not whether they staid or left, so that they could have either security or profit, going or staying. The scoundrels of the city, known by the Hindoo name of "Thugs," were those who thronged the streets, and with whom the Union commander had first to do.

The city of New Orleans had been built upon commerce. Most of its industrious population lived by trade. When the blockade from above and the blockade from below cut off all but the venturous trade of blockade-running, great distress ensued. The demand for labor was almost extinct. There was barely thirty days' provisions in the city. The ordinary sources of supply were cut off. No more flour came from Mobile, no more cattle from Texas, no more marketing from up the Mississippi and the fertile Red River country. The rich could hardly obtain food, for the markets were empty and provision-stores mostly closed. Prices rose enormously; a barrel of flour cost sixty dollars. Fifty thousand people were in danger of immediate starvation. The hot season was also at hand, and the appearance of yellow fever might reasonably be anticipated. Its last appearance as an epidemic was in 1853, when, out of the 30,000 unacclimated population, 29,020 were attacked and 8101 died in three months, 5269 dying in the single month of August.[1] There was every thing in the sanitary condition of the city to render its appearance as an epidemic probable, and in that case the utter annihilation of the unacclimated Northern army was almost inevitable. "You'll never see home again!" "Yellow Jack will have you before long!" yelled the mob, as the advance of Butler's force marched into the city.

[1] See Alexander Walker, editor of New Orleans Delta, in Harper's Magazine for November, 1853; and J. Snowdon Pigott, M.D., *ibid.*, June, 1857.

The whole actual force of the army now under the command of Butler was about 14,000 men. Ship Island, Forts Jackson and St. Philip, Baton Rouge, and many posts on the lagoons, must be occupied and garrisoned. To hold New Orleans, with its hostile population of more than 100,000, he had at the outset barely 7000 men. Should the yellow fever appear, he would in a month have not one. The enemy had a considerable force in the neighborhood, which might at any moment attempt to dislodge him. Farragut's fleet, indeed, commanded the city, but it could act only by destroying it. If the Confederates chose to make a Moscow of New Orleans, the army of occupation might be annihilated. Butler was not merely to hold the city, but to govern it. He could not deal with it as Davoust dealt with Hamburg, or as the British dealt with Delhi. It was to be treated as if it were in fact as well as in theory a city of the United States, with no severity or rigor which was not absolutely necessary to maintain the authority of the Union.[1]

Butler decided to make the St. Charles Hotel his temporary head-quarters. It was closed; but an entrance was effected, and a son of one of the proprietors discovered. He could not give up the hotel to General Butler; should he do so, he would be shot before he could reach the next corner; waiters, cooks, and porters would not serve, cook, or carry for him; besides, there were no provisions in the market. These difficulties were quietly set aside. Butler would take the hotel; the general and his attendants could, if need were, wait upon and cook for themselves; for food, they had become accustomed to army rations, and could live very well upon them. His head-quarters established, Butler sent to the mayor, informing him that he would be happy to meet him and the Common Council at two o'clock. The mayor, emboldened by the moderation displayed by Farragut, replied impudently that his place of business was in the City Hall, where he could be seen during office hours. He was courteously informed that such a reply would not be likely to satisfy the commanding general. Monroe finally concluded to accept the invitation to the St. Charles. At the appointed hour he made his appearance, accompanied by several friends, among whom, as counsel and mouthpiece, was Pierre Soulé, a shrewd lawyer, fluent speaker, and unscrupulous politician, of French birth, and a great favorite among the Creoles. Nine years before he had been appointed by Pierce, the most unprincipled, and, after Buchanan, the feeblest of our presidents, minister to Spain. He was a member of the noted Ostend Conference.

A cannon had been placed at each corner of the hotel, around which was drawn up a regiment, commanded by General Williams. The open space around was filled by a dense mob, who gathered courage from the quiet demeanor of the troops, and filled the air with hootings and execrations. Williams sent an aid to inform Butler that he feared he could not control the mob. "Then let him open upon them with artillery," replied Butler. "Don't do that!" shouted the mayor. "The mob must be controlled," replied Butler; "we can't have a disturbance in the streets." "Shall I go out and speak to the people?" asked Monroe. "As you please," answered Butler; "but order must be preserved in the public streets." The speeches of the mayor and his friends quieted the mob for a time; but their rage broke out anew at the sight of a half company of soldiers escorting the loyal Judge Summers, once Recorder of New Orleans, to a place of safety in the Custom-house. The orders given to Lieutenant Kinsman, who commanded the squad of fifty men, were brief and emphatic: "If any one molests or threatens you, arrest him. If a rescue is attempted, fire." The squad, drawn up in two lines, with a space between in which were the lieutenant and the judge, worked its way through the surging mob. Those nearest the soldiers kept quiet; those behind them, sheltered by the quiet ones, yelled and hooted. Half the way from the St. Charles to the Custom-house was accomplished without a collision. Then one of the noisiest of the crowd happened to be within reach. "Halt!" ordered the lieutenant; "bring out that man." In an instant he was dragged between the lines, still screaming and shouting. "Stop your noise," was the sharp order. "I won't," was the reply. "Sergeant, lower your bayonet. If another sound comes from that man's mouth, run him through." The man was as mute as a corpse. Once more on the way a similar scene was performed, with the same result. Their work accomplished, the squad marched back through a crowd as silent as a funeral. Nobody had been hurt; but the mob of New Orleans was cowed by the mere display of the force of the law embodied in one lieutenant and fifty men.

The afternoon had worn away, and the conference between the general and the mayor was adjourned, to be resumed in the evening. Butler opened it by reading his proclamation, printed copies of which were given to the other side. The printing of this proclamation had cost a little trouble. The printer, who was desired to print it, could not think of doing so, nor should it be done in his office with his consent. In two hours a file of soldiers were drawn up before the building. Half a dozen of them entered the office, laid down their muskets, and stepped quietly to the cases. The quick click of type was heard. In two hours more the proclamation was in type, proofs read, corrected, revised, and copies enough for present use worked off. Its purport was that the city of New Orleans was occupied by the forces of the United States, who had come to restore order under the laws and the Constitution. For the present—for the third time in its history—the city would be governed by martial law. No ensigns or flags except those of the United States and of foreign consulates could appear. All citizens who should renew their oath of allegiance to the United States would be fully protected. All who maintained their allegiance to the Confederate states would be considered rebels and enemies. Those who had been in the serv-

[1] Parton's "General Butler in New Orleans" furnishes full details of the administration of Butler in New Orleans.

ice of the Confederate States, who should give up their arms and return to peaceful avocations, would not be unnecessarily molested. Foreigners not naturalized would still enjoy the protection of the laws of the United States. The killing of any soldier would be considered as assassination; the owner of any house in which such act should be committed would be held responsible, and the house would be liable to be destroyed by military authority. All disorders, disturbances of the peace, and crimes of an aggravated character interfering with the forces or laws of the United States, would be tried and punished by a military court; other misdemeanors would be subject to the municipal authorities, if they desired to act; civil cases would be tried by the ordinary tribunals. The circulation of Confederate bonds and scrip was prohibited; but, as Confederate current notes were the only money in the hands of the poorer classes, they might circulate, if any one would take them. If a soldier of the United States should commit any outrage upon person or property, he would be promptly punished, and full redress be made. Martial law would be enforced, mildly if possible, rigorously if necessary, so long as the authorities of the United States deemed proper. In brief, Butler wished to govern only the military forces, and sustain the government of the United States against its enemies, leaving the authorities of the city in full exercise of their ordinary municipal and civil functions.

Soulé, still spokesman for the mayor, objected to the proclamation. It would give great offense, and the people would never submit to it. They were not conquered, and could not be expected to behave as a conquered people. The presence of the troops would irritate a high-spirited and sensitive people. The troops could have no peace while they remained. "Withdraw them," he said, "and leave the city government to manage its own affairs. If they remain, there will certainly be trouble." Butler flamed up at this. "I did not expect," he said, "to hear a threat from Mr. Soulé on this occasion. New Orleans is a conquered city. If not, why are we here? Have you welcomed us? Are we here by your consent? Would you not expel us if you could? New Orleans has been conquered by the forces of the United States, and by the laws of nations lies subject to the will of the conquerors. I have proposed to leave to the municipal government the free exercise of all its powers, and I am answered by a threat."

Soulé disclaimed any intention of threatening the troops, but had merely stated what he thought would be the consequence of their remaining. Butler replied that he would gladly take every one of his soldiers from the city, as soon as it could be shown that the city government had rendered it possible for him to ride alone, without insult or danger, from one end of the city to another. But the events of the afternoon had proved that the city authorities were unable to control the mob. Lovell himself had been forced to proclaim martial law to protect peaceable citizens against the rowdies. "I know," he concluded, "more about your city than you think. I know that this hour there is an organization established for the purpose of assassinating my men by detail. But I warn you that, if a shot is fired from any house, that house will never again cover a mortal's head; and if I can discover the perpetrator of the deed, the place that now knows him shall know him no more forever. I have the power to suppress this unruly element in your midst, and I mean so to use it that, in a very short period, I shall be able to ride through the entire city free from insult and danger, or else this metropolis of the South shall be a desert from the plains of Chalmette to the outskirts of Carrolton."[1]

The discussion was continued, but Butler was immovable. The mayor declared that the functions of the city government should be at once suspended, and the general could act his pleasure. This was objected to by others, and it was finally agreed that the City Council should deliberate upon the matter, and announce their decision the next day. They decided that the city government should continue to exercise its usual functions, but requested that the troops should be withdrawn from the vicinity of the Courthouse, so that there might be no appearance that the authorities were acting under military compulsion. The request was more than complied with. The camps within the city were one by one broken up. Some of the troops established a permanent camp at Carrolton, on the outskirts; others were posted across the river at Algiers; others garrisoned the abandoned forts on the lagoons. A full brigade was sent to occupy Baton Rouge, of which possession had been taken by Commander Palmer, of the Iroquois, belonging to Farragut's fleet.[2] When all these dispositions had been made there remained in New Orleans itself only 250 men, who were posted in the Custom-house, and served merely as a provost guard. Butler had resolved to try a conciliatory policy, confining himself solely to his strictly military functions, leaving the internal government of the city to the municipal authorities, aided, if necessary, by the European brigade, who had been requested to continue their organization. How ill this mild policy succeeded will soon appear; but under it the city for a few days enjoyed a tranquillity to which it had long been a stranger.

[1] Parton's "Butler in New Orleans," p. 296.

[2] The proceedings at Baton Rouge were, on a small scale, similar to those at New Orleans. The body of the fleet had passed up the river without stopping. On the 8th of May the Iroquois anchored off the town, and the commander sent a note to the mayor demanding that the town should be surrendered; the flag of the United States be hoisted on the Arsenal; the property of the Confederate states to remain intact, and be delivered over when demanded; the rights and property of citizens to be respected. The mayor and selectmen replied that the city of Baton Rouge would not be surrendered voluntarily to any power on earth; but it was without military force, and had no means of defense. Its occupation would be without the consent and against the wish of the peaceable inhabitants. The city had no control over the Arsenal, except for the purpose of preserving the buildings since its evacuation, and it could not be expected to surrender it, or exercise any act which would be offensive to the sensibilities of the people, by hoisting the flag of the United States. Palmer did not wait to bandy messages, but sent a few men ashore, took possession of the Arsenal and barracks, and hoisted the Union flag without opposition. He then sent a note to the mayor telling him what he had done, and warning him that, although he had left no force on shore to protect it, the flag must not be molested; adding, significantly, "The rash act of some individual may cause your city to pay a bitter penalty."

This quiet interval gave Butler an opportunity to provide against the famine and pestilence with which New Orleans was threatened. The question of food was the most pressing. There was at Mobile a quantity of flour purchased by the city for the subsistence of its citizens; a safe-conduct was to be given to steam-boats to come and return, conveying this flour. The Opelousas Railroad was authorized and required to run trains to bring provisions into the city. At the junction of the Mississippi and Red Rivers were large quantities of cattle, flour, and other provisions purchased for the subsistence of the city; a safe-conduct was granted to two steamers each day to bring these to New Orleans. The city authorities were to appoint an agent to superintend these transportations, the faith of the city being pledged that no aid or intelligence should be conveyed to the Confederates.[1] The orders which gave these privileges were drawn up on the suggestion of the city authorities. The faith of the city, solemnly pledged, was throughout deliberately and persistently abused. Under cover of it provisions were sent to Lovell's troops, and most important information was regularly furnished to the Confederate authorities. A small but scandalous case was that of Charles Heidseck. He was a Frenchman, a member of the firm whose Champagne bottles are known all over the world. He had come to America to look after the business of his house, and had for some time been a resident of Mobile. When the order appeared authorizing boats to convey flour from Mobile to New Orleans, he went on board as bar-tender. In this capacity he made several trips, conveying letters and information. He was finally detected, arrested, and sent to Fort Jackson. "I arrested him as a spy," wrote Butler; "I confined him as a spy; I should have tried him as a spy; and would have hanged him, upon conviction, as a spy, if I had not been interfered with by the government at Washington." After some months of confinement the Champagne dealer was released, and suffered to return unhung to France.

Food began to come in from all these sources. Butler contributed a thousand dollars to feed the poor. Much beef and sugar intended for the rebels in the field had been captured. A thousand barrels of this were distributed without charge. Supplies came from New York exceeding the wants of the army. The commissary was authorized to sell the surplus to families at cheap rates: flour, seven and a half cents a pound; salt meats, ten; "city bank-notes, gold, silver, or United States treasury notes to be taken in payment." All this brought down the market price of provisions. Flour fell in a few days from sixty to twenty-four dollars. Those who had or could get money other than Confederate paper need not starve. But more than a third of the population had no money or means of earning it. To find work for these, and the means of paying the laborers, came up in a short time.

The city was reeking with the filth accumulated for weeks, forming a train for the yellow fever whenever a chance spark from the tropics should be at hand to fire it. The authorities had undertaken to clean the streets. They neglected to do so. Butler, on the 9th of May, sharply reminded them of their neglect. "You have assumed this work," he said, "and it must be performed. The present suspension of labor furnishes ample supplies of hungry men who can be profitably employed to this end. Three days since I called the attention of the mayor to this subject, and nothing has been done." The mayor averred that he had set 300 men at work upon the streets; but not a man of them could be discovered. Butler put forth a general order inveighing sharply against the conduct of the city authorities, and of the wealthy leaders of the rebellion, who had gotten up the war, and were endeavoring to prosecute it, without regard to the starving poor. "They have betrayed their country; they have been false to every trust; they can not protect those whom they have ruined, but have left them to the mercies of a chronic mob; they will not feed those whom they are starving. The United States have sent forces here to fight and subdue rebellious armies in array against their authority. We find substantially only fugitive masses, runaway property-burners, a whisky-drinking mob, and starving citizens with their wives and children. It is our duty to call back the first, punish the second, root out the third, feed and protect the last."

The male mob of New Orleans had been cowed by the mere fear of artillery and bayonets; but there was a female mob, composed mainly of the wives and daughters of the upper classes, who could not thus be reached. Protected by the immunities of their sex, they embraced every opportunity of insulting the Union troops. They flaunted secession colors upon their dresses, they sung secession songs, and thrummed secession tunes upon their pianos. If a body of soldiers passed the balconies where they were standing, they would turn their backs contemptuously. If they met a Union officer on the pave, they would sweep aside their dresses as if to avoid defilement, and turn into the middle of the street with insulting words and gestures. If a Union officer entered a street car or a church pew, these women would leave in a body. These annoyances, petty in themselves, grew to be unendurable. The climax was reached when a woman deliberately spat in the faces of two officers who were quietly walking in the street. Butler resolved to put a stop to these insults, and to do it not by the exercise of military power, but simply by carrying into effect an old and well-known municipal law of the city. By this a prostitute plying her vocation in the street was liable to be arrested, confined over night in the calaboose, brought in the morning before a magistrate, and fined five dollars. What constituted plying this vocation in public? Simply that a woman openly and obtrusively endeavored to attract the attention of strange men. For this purpose opprobrious epithets and insulting gestures are used as often as smiles and blandishments. Thereupon, on the 15th of May, was issued the famous General Order No. 28. The result in New Orleans itself was precisely what

[1] General Orders, May 4, 1862.

was intended. Women who had grossly insulted soldiers and officers, knowing that their sex shielded them from personal resentment, and who would have courted military arrest and formal trial as a kind of martyrdom, shrank back from the prospect of the calaboose and the police court. Not a single arrest was made under the order. There was no occasion for one. The threat of the calaboose and the police court did for the women what the mere threat of cannon-shot and bayonet-thrust had done for the men.[1]

In New Orleans the import of the order was thoroughly understood. Beyond the city, where the municipal law upon which it was based was unknown, it was misunderstood and misrepresented. It was interpreted to give up the women of New Orleans to violence and outrage. Rewards were offered at the South for the assassination of Butler. In the British Parliament, Lord Palmerston denounced it as "infamous." Punch, the representative of British sentiment, compared Butler with Nena Sahib. The Secretary of State admitted to the English chargé that he "regretted that, in the haste of composition, a phraseology which could be mistaken or perverted had been used." This admission was correct in substance. Ten words explaining that each offending female was, "in strict accordance with the municipal law of New Orleans," to be regarded "as a woman of the town plying her avocation," would have obviated all chance of misconstruction or misrepresentation.

This order was the occasion, not the cause, of the deposition of the municipal government. Two weeks' trial had demonstrated that the government of New Orleans could not be administered conjointly by two authorities so utterly hostile in aim as the Union general and the Confederate mayor and council. The city authorities not only neglected to perform the duties which they had undertaken, but they undertook to perform offensive acts beyond their sphere. A French armed vessel, supposed to be the precursor of a large fleet, was in the river. The Common Council offered the hospitalities of the port to this fleet, the offer being couched in terms offensive to the Union. Butler rebuked them sharply. Your action, he said, is an insult both to the United States and to France. The tender of hospitalities by a government to which only police duties and sanitary regulations are intrusted, is simply an invitation to the calaboose and the hospital. The United States authorities are the only ones here capable of dealing with foreign nations. "The action of the city council in this behalf must be revised." This was on the day when Order No. 28 was published. When that order appeared, the mayor sent to Butler a letter written by his clerk, and signed by himself, protesting against the order. He could not suffer it to be promulgated without protest. Union officers and soldiers were by it allowed to place what construction they pleased upon the conduct of the women of New Orleans. He would not be responsible for the peace of the city while this order, which had "aroused the passions of the people, and must exasperate them to a degree beyond control," and was "a reproach to the civilization, not to say the Christianity of the age," was in force. Butler at once issued an order suspending the mayor, and ordering his committal to Fort Jackson. Before the order was executed, an interview was granted. Butler said the letter was insulting. The mayor protested that he had not meant to insult the general; he only wished to vindicate the virtuous ladies of New Orleans. The general expounded the order, showing that it could refer only to those whose conduct evinced that they were not virtuous. The mayor averred that he was perfectly satisfied, and asked to withdraw his offensive letter. Butler wrote an indorsement, which Monroe signed, and was relieved from arrest.[2] In a few hours the mayor sent a note asking to withdraw his withdrawal. This was on Saturday. The mayor reiterated his request on Sunday, but was told that this was not a business day; on Monday his affair would receive attention. He came on Monday, accompanied by a half score of friends and advisers. Butler, meanwhile, had received information which determined him to make short work. Each of the mayor's friends was asked whether he sanctioned the offensive letter. The mayor and three others who avowedly sanctioned it were sent to Fort Jackson; the others were discharged. Pierre Soulé, the mouthpiece of secession in the city, was also arrested, and sent to Fort Warren, in Boston Harbor. In a few weeks, however, he was released at the request of Butler, upon his parole not to return to New Orleans, nor to commit or advise any act hostile to the United States.

The city government was suppressed, and the work of governing New Orleans was intrusted to General Shepley. On the 20th of May he issued a notice saying that, "in the absence of the late mayor," he should "for the present, and until such time as the citizens of New Orleans shall elect a loyal citizen of the United States as mayor of the city, discharge the functions which have hitherto appertained to that office." Ample protection was assured to all peaceable citizens; any outrage committed by or upon soldiers would be punished; all city ordinances not inconsistent with the laws of the United States or with the general orders of the commanding general would be continued in force; all legal contracts made by or with the city authorities would be held inviolate. Captain Jonas H. French was appointed provost marshal, with the general functions of chief of police, and Major Joseph M. Bell provost judge, to try all charges of violation of municipal or national laws.

Four things claimed the immediate attention of the new government: to

GEORGE F. SHEPLEY.

supply food for the population; to furnish labor, so that the poor could procure food; to provide a safe currency; and to guard against the yellow fever.

Provisions soon began to appear in sufficient quantities to preclude the absolute necessity of famine. Dealers were at first disposed to close their stores, and it was necessary, for a few days, to order them to be kept open under penalty of a fine. The only currency in actual circulation consisted of "shinplasters," car and omnibus tickets, and Confederate notes, the latter depreciated seventy per cent. in value. The banks had sent off their specie, but it was supposed that it could be recovered, and in that case they would be perfectly solvent. The banks were anxious to regain their funds. They asked Butler to give protection to the specie, if it could be recovered and brought back, promising to hold it in good faith to protect their bill-holders and depositors. Butler agreed to this, with the proviso that banks as well as individuals should restore all the property belonging to the United States which had come into their hands. "I have come," he said, "to retake, repossess, and occupy all and singular the property of the United States, of whatever name and nature. Farther than that I shall not go, save upon the most urgent military necessity, under which right every citizen holds all his possessions. Therefore, as safe-conducts may be needed for agents of banks to go and return with the property, these will be granted for a limited but reasonable period of time."[1] No safe-conducts were required for this purpose. Memminger, the Confederate Secretary of the Treasury, wrote that "the coin of the banks of New Orleans was seized by the government to prevent its falling into the hands of the public enemy. It has been deposited in a place of security under the charge of the government; and it is not intended to interfere with the rights of property in the banks farther than to insure its safe custody. They may proceed to conduct their business in the Confederate States upon this deposit just as though it were in their own vaults."[2]

To produce any thing like a redeemable currency the Confederate notes must be driven out. These had been allowed to circulate provisionally. A general order was issued[3] directing that neither the city nor any bank should exchange its obligations for Confederate notes, nor put out any obligation payable in such notes; and that after the expiration of ten days[4] all circulation of and trade in such notes should cease; that all sales thereafter made in consideration of such notes should be void, and any property thus sold would be confiscated, a quarter of the proceeds to go to the informer. Banks and bankers at once issued notices requiring all persons having deposits with them of Confederate notes to withdraw them at once, those not withdrawn "to be at the risk of the owners;" that is, the banks, who had grown rich upon the traffic in these bills, now that they were worthless wished to throw the whole loss on the community. They had received them as money when they were supposed to be valuable, and wished to pay them out when they were mere waste paper. Butler promptly interposed. He ordered that no incorporated bank or private banker should pay out any thing but specie, United States treasury notes, or the current bills of city banks.[5]

REPAIRING THE LEVEE AT NEW ORLEANS.

The Bank of Louisiana alone protested against this order, and endeavored to avoid compliance; but Butler had might as well as right on his side. He was inflexible, and the bank, "having no alternative but compliance," yielded with the best grace in its power. Confederate notes and shinplasters disappeared, and were replaced by the currency of the United States, and by small notes issued by the city government.

Soon after[1] an order appeared with which the banks had to do. Any person who had in his possession or under his control any property belonging to the "so-called Confederate States," was required, under penalty of imprisonment and confiscation of property, to give information concerning it. This order signified, among other things, that money deposited in any bank to the credit of the Confederacy had become the property of the Union, and must be surrendered. The Citizens' Bank reported that the Treasurer of the Confederate States had upon its books a credit of $219,000. It proposed to pay over this sum in Confederate notes. Moreover, there were on deposit in the bank to the credit of various Confederate receivers $215,000; this, the bank thought, was to be considered a special deposit, which should be paid in the same currency in which it was received. Butler would not accede to this view of the case, and ordered that the latter sum should be paid at once in gold, silver, or United States currency. For various reasons, he would refer the former sum to the government for adjudication; but the bank must, in the mean time, hold the notes as a special deposit, and also keep a like amount of bullion to await the decision.[2] Nearly a quarter of a

million of dollars was thus recovered from the banks, and paid over to the treasury of the United States. "This," said Butler, "will make a fund upon which those whose property has been confiscated may have claim."

Soon[1] came another order which concerned individuals as well as corporations. It ordered that all sums due to any citizen of the United States which had been in any way sequestered by the ordinances of the Confederate States,[2] or by those of Louisiana, were to be paid over to the lawful owners. Not a few debts due to American citizens were thus recovered. Among those affected by this order was John G. Cocks, a judge at New Orleans. In 1860 he had bought a score and a half of slaves from Major Anderson, for which he had given his notes. A month after the fall of Fort Sumter, Cocks put forth in a New Orleans paper an insulting letter, addressed to "Major Robert Anderson, late of Fort Sumter," in which he said that these notes would never be paid. Butler took possession of the large estates of Cocks, who had fled from New Orleans, holding them as security for the liquidation of Anderson's claim.

In a few weeks provisions had poured into New Orleans in sufficient quantities to obviate a famine; but the laboring classes were without means to purchase, and the filthy condition of the streets invited pestilence. The poor must be fed, and the streets must be cleaned. It appeared to Butler that these two objects might be combined. He accordingly proposed[3] to the military commandant and city council that the city should employ 2000 men, to each of whom should be paid fifty cents a day by the city, the United States also issuing to each laborer a full soldier's ration, worth quite as much, and sufficient for the subsistence of a man and a woman. This suggestion was accepted; the force was placed under the charge of Colonel T. B. Thorpe, a native of New York, who had for many years resided in Louisiana. The work thus undertaken was well done. The accumulated filth of months was purged away, and the city placed in a better sanitary condition than it had known for years. Moreover, the changes of the river constantly create new lands within the city limits. This new land, known as

drafts in them as money, thus giving them currency and circulation. Now that the re-establishment of the authority of the United States rendered this paper worthless, the banks wished to throw the loss upon their creditors, depositors, and bill-holders. They refused to receive them, while they continued to pay them out; they required their depositors to take them; they changed the obligation of contracts by stamping their own bills "redeemable in Confederate notes;" they invested the savings of labor and the pittance of the widow in this paper, while they sent away their specie, so that the people could have nothing but these notes; while all other property had become nearly valueless, bank stocks were selling at great premiums, and stockholders were receiving large dividends. To equalize the loss, and have it fall, in part at least, where it ought, the order prescribing the medium by which payments were to be made was issued. Moreover, all persons who had issued "shinplasters" were required to redeem them in current funds, under penalty of confiscation and sale of property for the purpose of redemption, or, in lack of this, of imprisonment at hard labor.

[1] General Order No. 40; June 6.

[2] *Extracts from Butler's Reply to the Bank*, Jan. 13, 1862.—"The report finds that there is to the credit of the Confederate States $219,090 94. This is, of course, due *in presenti* from the bank. The bank claims that it holds an equal amount of Confederate treasury notes, and desires to set off these notes against the amount so due. This can not be permitted. Confederate treasury notes are not due till six months after the conclusion of a treaty of peace between the Confederate States and the United States. When that time comes it will be in season to set off such claims. The United States being entitled to the credits due the Confederate States in the bank, that amount must be paid in money or valuable property. I can not recognize the Confederate notes as either money or property. The bank having done so by receiving them, issuing their banking upon them, loaning upon them, thus giving them credit to the injury of the United States, is estopped to deny their value. But there are other considerations which may apply to this item: only the notes of the Confederate States were deposited by the treasurer in the bank, and by the order of the ruling authority then here the bank was obliged to receive them. In equity and good conscience the Confederate States could call for nothing more than they had compelled the bank to take. The United States succeed to the rights of the Confederate States, and should only take that which the Confederate States ought to take. But the United States, not taking or

recognizing Confederate notes, can only leave them with the bank, to be held by it hereafter in special deposit as so much worthless paper."

How far these considerations applied to the case of the sums deposited by the Confederate treasurer was left to the decision of the government; but the bank was required to give security for payment in case the decision should be against it. But the decision of Butler in case of the deposits made by Confederate receivers was clear and definite. He said:

"The several deposits of the officers of the supposed Confederate States were received in the usual course of business; were doubtless, some of them, perhaps largely, received in Confederate notes, but, for the reason above stated, can only be paid to the United States in its own constitutional currency. These are, in no sense of language, 'special deposits.' They were held in general account, went into the funds of the bank, were paid out in the discounts of the bank, and, if called upon to-day for the identical notes put into the bank, which is the only idea of a special deposit, the bank would be utterly unable to produce them. As well might my private banker, with whom I have deposited my neighbor's check or draft as money, which has been received as money, and paid out as money, months afterward, when my neighbor has become bankrupt, buy up other of his checks and drafts at a discount, and pay them to me, upon the ground that I had made a 'special deposit.'"

[1] July 9.　　　[2] For which, see *ante*, p. 212.　　　[3] June 4.

batture or "shoal," is at first a mere mud-bank, and requires to be protected from the water before it is available as property. By well-directed labor, batture worth a million of dollars was in a few months added to the city property.

The cleansing of the streets and canals was not alone an adequate safeguard against the yellow fever. Butler had adopted the theory that this pestilence is indigenous in no region where there is frost every winter. Wherever there is great summer heat acting upon decaying vegetable and animal matter, the fever may spread. This forms the train ready for explosion, but it must be fired from abroad. New Orleans furnishes every condition for the spread of the disease when once introduced.[1] To prevent the introduction of this spark, a vigorous and judicious quarantine was established. The duration of this was in each case left to the discretion of the health-officer. His instructions were to detain a vessel as long as he thought necessary to protect the city, whether the time were one day or a hundred. A vessel loaded with hides and wool, its hold reeking with dead and putrid matter, was not placed on an equality with a steamer carrying only passengers and merchandise not likely to absorb and generate contagion. The rule was simply that any vessel should be kept in quarantine just so long as the health-officer deemed necessary to secure the city from infection. For a few days there was an alarm. One man, who had come on a steamer which had touched at Nassau, was seized by the disease. The house was cleared of all persons except an acclimated attendant, and the whole block guarded by sentinels. The man died; every article in his room was burned or buried; his attendant was quarantined; the whole quarter of the city was cleaned and fumigated. This was the sole case of yellow fever in New Orleans during the summer of 1862.

Food sufficient to obviate the absolute peril of famine had been brought to New Orleans. Labor sufficient to feed 4000 persons was furnished; but there were ten times as many whose ordinary means of livelihood had been cut off. These must be cared for; and in a few weeks there were 35,000 persons, nearly a quarter of the population, fed from the public funds. Butler considered that this great burden ought to be made to fall, as far as possible, upon those who had been most active in bringing starvation upon the poor and helpless. A loan of a million and a quarter of dollars had been made by various corporations and individuals, and placed in the hands of a "Committee of Public Safety" for the defense of New Orleans. The subscriptions were in sums varying from a few thousand to more than two hundred thousand dollars. The subscribers to this loan showed that they had means to pay largely for the support of their starving neighbors. Butler[2] ordered a sum equal to one quarter of their subscriptions to be paid by each of these persons. This produced more than $300,000. Moreover, about a hundred cotton-brokers, the leading commercial men in New Orleans, had published a circular urging planters not to bring their produce to the city. Butler, by the same order, assessed a fine of from $100 to $500 upon each of these. Under this order nearly $350,000 was received, which was set apart as "a fund for the purpose of providing employment and food for the deserving poor." From this fund a thousand men were to be paid to work on the streets and canals. Each was to receive a dollar and a half a day, the wages which had been paid for labor on the fortifications; the rations heretofore issued by the United States to these laborers being discontinued. This fund was exhausted early in December, and one of the last acts of Butler[3] was to impose another assessment of a like amount upon the same parties.

Meanwhile William B. Mumford, the man who had hauled down the flag from the Mint, had remained in New Orleans. He appeared in public, boasting of his deed, and defying the authorities to molest him. He was apprehended, brought before a military commission, tried, and condemned to death. While this was going on, it was discovered that a number of men had organized themselves into a military company, under the name of the "Monroe Guard," with the purpose of breaking through the lines and joining the Confederate army. Among these were six soldiers who had been paroled at Fort Jackson. These were arrested and condemned to death, under the recognized laws of war. Strenuous efforts were made to procure their pardon. In these many of the Union men of the city joined. It was represented that they were ignorant men, who were totally unaware of the nature of their act. One of them, when brought before the commission, declared that he did not know any thing about paroling. "Paroling," he said, simply, "is for officers and gentlemen; we are not gentlemen." Butler yielded to the urgent petitions for mercy. To one of these he replied: "You, who have exerted your talents to save the lives of Union men in their hour of peril, ought to have a determining weight when your opinions have been deliberately formed. You ask for the lives of these men. You shall have them. You say that the clemency of the government is best for the cause we all have at heart. Be it so. You are likely to be better informed upon this than I am. But if this example of mercy is lost upon those in the same situation, swift justice can overtake others in like manner offending." The men were reprieved and sent to Ship Island. But the reprieve of these six rendered it impossible to spare Mumford. To pardon him would be judged by the mob as a confession of weakness. Butler firmly resisted all entreaties. One venerable man, one of the noblest in

the city, begged for mercy. "Give me this man's life," he prayed; "it is but a scratch of your pen." "True," replied Butler; "but a scratch of my pen could burn New Orleans. I could do the one act as soon as the other. I think one would be as wrong as the other." Mumford was hung on the 7th of July: a tall, black-bearded man, aged forty-two, rather prepossessing in appearance, a gambler by profession. He met his fate with composure. He said that the act for which he was condemned was committed under excitement, and he did not think that he was suffering justly. The Confederates endeavored to elevate Mumford to the rank of a martyr. His execution formed a leading part of the charge in virtue of which Jefferson Davis[1] declared Butler to be an outlaw, who was to be hung at once in case he was captured. The execution was justified by every law of war, and demanded by the exigencies of the times. It effectually subdued the mob, which otherwise would need to have been quelled by cannon and the bayonet.

No other military execution took place at New Orleans, except those of a gang of scoundrels who committed robbery and theft under the pretense of being Union officers. Early in June there were complaints that men wearing the Federal uniform, claiming authority to search for concealed arms, had repeatedly entered houses, and had gone off carrying with them valuable property. A flagrant case of this kind occurred on the 11th. The next day one of the perpetrators was detected. He betrayed his accomplices, two of whom were arrested on the 12th, and three more on the 13th. All were tried, convicted, and ordered to be executed on the 16th. They were William M. Clary, George William Crage, late officers on board Union vessels; Frank Newton, a private in a Connecticut regiment; and Stanislaus Roy and Theodore Leib, residents of New Orleans. Leib was a mere boy, and his punishment was commuted, as was that of the informer. The others were promptly hung just five days after the commission of their crime.

At the close of June reports reached New Orleans of disasters to the Federal armies in Virginia. These came by telegraph over Southern lines, and were greatly exaggerated. The spirits of the Confederate sympathizers rose. Fidel Keller, a bookseller, procured a skeleton from a medical student, and exposed it in his window, labeled "Chickahominy," intending that the bones should be taken by the populace to be those of a Union soldier slain before Richmond. John W. Andrews displayed in club-rooms and other public places a cross, which he declared to have been made from the bones of a Union soldier. These offenders were sent for two years to Ship Island. Lieutenant De Kay, a gallant young officer, had been fatally wounded by guerrillas while descending the Mississippi. After a month, he died on the 27th of June. His funeral took place the next day at an Episcopal church, where Leacock, the rector, an Englishman by birth, had promised to perform the rites of the Church. He failed to be present; but the sacred edifice was filled by a gang made up of the scum of the rabble, whose conduct was scandalous beyond description, and the solemn rites were hastily hurried over. The funeral procession was mocked and insulted as it passed along the streets. The most prominent among the insulters was a woman named Phillips, the wife of Philip Phillips, a native of Charleston, educated in Vermont and Connecticut, subsequently a member of the South Carolina Nullification Convention of 1832. He emigrated to Alabama, whence he was sent to Congress in 1853. At the close of his term he declined a re-election, and took up his residence in Washington. His wife was one of the leaders of fashion in the national capital during the administration of Buchanan. She was one of a clique of traitresses who, from their supposed influence in political matters, were popularly known as the "boudoir cabinet." She was exiled from the Union, and went to New Orleans, where she made herself notorious as an advocate of the Confederates. Her conduct at the funeral of De Kay exhausted the measure of Butler's forbearance. He ordered that she should be sent to Ship Island.[2] She was in a few weeks released and sent to Mobile.

The population of New Orleans, native and foreign, might be fairly divided into two main classes—Union men and rebels. Six weeks after the occupation of the city, Butler concluded that it was necessary, as a public exigency, "to distinguish between those who were well disposed to the government of the United States and those who still held allegiance to the Confederate States." He therefore directed[3] that every person claiming to exercise any official function, military or civil, should take the oath "to bear true faith and allegiance to the United States of America, and to support the Constitution thereof." Every official act performed by persons failing to take this oath within five days was to be null and void. All persons also, who had been citizens of the United States, who desired any right, favor, or privilege beyond mere protection from personal violence, must take the oath before their request could even be heard. Every person born in the United States, and every person of foreign birth who had resided therein for five years, and who had not claimed and received protection from the consul of his own government, was declared to be a citizen within the meaning of this order. Every alien was required to take an oath that "So long as my government remains at peace with the United States, I will do no act, or consent that any be done, or conceal any that has been or is about to be

---

[1] "Lying upon a low alluvial plain, below the level of the Mississippi River at high water, it is surrounded by extensive undrained swamps, and has itself been reclaimed from a marsh. Its rich alluvial soil contains great quantities of vegetable mould, and is so damp that water can be obtained any where at the depth of a few feet. There are a number of cemeteries within the city limits which greatly taint the air. The drainage is imperfect, and the scavenger duty very badly performed. The open lots are also sources of disease, being the receptacle of the offal of the surrounding houses."—DR. PIGOTT, in *Harper's Magazine*, June, 1857.

[2] General Order No. 55, August 4.   [3] December 9.

[1] Proclamation of Dec. 23, 1862; see *ante*, p. 219.

[2] "Mrs. Phillips, wife of Philip Phillips, having been once imprisoned for her traitorous proceedings and acts in Washington, and been released by the clemency of the government, and having been found training her children to spit upon officers of the United States at New Orleans, for which act of one of those children both her husband and herself apologized, and were again forgiven, is now found on the balcony of her house during the passage of the funeral procession of Lieutenant De Kay, laughing and mocking at his remains; and upon being inquired of by the commanding general if this fact were so, contemptuously replies, 'I was in good spirits that day:' It is therefore ordered that she be not regarded and treated as a common woman of whom no officer or soldier is bound to take notice, but as an uncommon, bad, and dangerous woman, stirring up strife and inciting to riot, and that therefore she be confined at Ship Island," etc.—*Butler's Order*, June 30, 1862.   [3] General Order No. 41, June 10.

FEEDING THE POOR AT NEW ORLEANS.

done, that shall aid or comfort any of the enemies or opposers of the United States." There were also in the city many thousands who had served in the Confederate army. To them the option was given either to take the oath, or to surrender themselves as prisoners of war, to be paroled until regularly exchanged, or to be put in confinement, as they might choose. The members of the Common Council, who had up to this time acted as the legislative power in the city, refused to take the oath, and their functions were suspended "until such time as there shall be a sufficient number of the citizens of New Orleans loyal to their country and their Constitution to entitle them to resume the right of self-government."[1] Nearly a half of the score of foreign consuls at New Orleans united in a protest against the oath required by this order. Their protest was sharply worded. Its substance was, that some persons of foreign birth, in order to receive protection, were required not merely to swear allegiance to the United States, but also not to "conceal" any acts done against the government. Butler rejoined with greater sharpness. If a foreigner wished to enjoy the privileges accorded to American citizens, let him take the oath of allegiance. If he did not choose to do this, but wished to remain a neutral, let him take the oath to do nothing to aid the enemies of the United States. If he wished to do neither, but was content to remain with mere protection from personal violence, let him "be quiet, and keep away from his consul." If he did not like any of these conditions, let him take himself away—the sooner the better for all parties. This reply concluded with an admonition that the foreign consuls, as a body, should present no more argumentative protests against his orders. This was no part of their duties or their rights. If any one of them had any suggestion to offer, he could easily learn the proper mode. Butler could not, however, refrain from one bit of grim humor. The French legion had been required to take an oath to "defend the Constitution of the State and the Confederate States," without any protest from the French consul. Butler modified the oath required of foreigners so as to correspond with this, merely inserting the words "Constitution of the United States" instead of "Constitution of the State and of the Confederate States;" the oath, for the benefit of foreigners, being given in French as well as English.[2]

The consuls had no farther protest to offer upon this topic. But some months after it was reopened by the Reverend Dr. Leacock, the clergyman who had promised and then neglected to perform the funeral rites of De Kay. Some 12,000 persons had taken the citizens' oath, 2500 the foreign neutrals' oath, and more than 5000 Confederate officers and soldiers had given the required parole. Leacock was moved "to speak affectionately and candidly" to the Union general. He had been "eating up God's people as it were bread," by inducing them to take oaths which they never intended to fulfill. The general was urged to "pause and consider his course," to take "a very different course from that which he was pursuing." The doctor had "great sympathy for the general," and prayed that "God would give him grace to see his error, and sustain him in the discharge of his arduous and manifold duties." Before the act of secession was performed Leacock had published a sermon, the concluding paragraph of which strongly urged secession. This was printed, and 30,000 copies had been sold. The doctor now said that this paragraph, printed from his own manuscript, was not actually delivered. In fact, he was, and always had been, a friend of the Union, in proof of which he adduced a paragraph of a sermon preached some weeks after the former one, in which the destruction of the Union was earnestly deprecated. If this sermon was actually delivered at the time stated, it was a strange sequel to the one already published.

A question had meanwhile come up which must be decided. The rubric of the Episcopal Church prescribed that prayers should be offered for the "President of the United States and all others in authority." For this had been substituted, by direction of the bishop, Major General Polk, a prayer for the President of the Confederate States. After the occupation of New Orleans by the Union forces this could not clearly be done. When that part of the service was reached, the priest was wont to invite the congregation to spend a few moments in silent prayer. This at length came to be so notorious as to demand attention. Butler invited the prominent Episcopal clergymen to a conference. The question was whether they should offer the prescribed prayer for the President of the United States. Leacock endeavored to make a side issue. "Your insisting upon the oath of allegiance is causing half of my flock to perjure themselves." "If that is the result of your preaching," rejoined Butler, "the sooner you leave the pulpit the better." "Are you going to shut up the churches?" "I am more likely to shut up the ministers." The result was that Butler gave them the choice either to read the prayer for the President, omit the silent act of devotion, or leave New Orleans as prisoners of state. Leacock, and Goodrich and Fulton, much better men, refused to comply, and were sent North. Their churches were, however, kept open, service being performed by army chaplains, as laid down in the rubric.

As a rule, every "gentleman" of New Orleans wore a pistol or a knife as

[1] Order, June 27.

[2] *Extract from General Order No.* 42, July 9.—"The commanding general has received information that certain of the foreign residents have scruples about taking the oath prescribed in General Order No. 41. Anxious to relieve the consciences of all who may honestly entertain doubts upon this matter, he hereby revises the order so as to permit any foreign subject, at his election, to take and subscribe the following oath, instead of the oath as set forth. He is sure that no foreign subject can object to this oath, as it is in the very words of the oath taken by every officer of the European brigade, prescribed more than a year ago, and claimed as an act of the strictest neutrality by the foreign officers taking it, and for more than a year passed by all the foreign consuls without protest:

"'I do solemnly swear that I will, to the best of my ability, support, protect, and defend the Constitution of the United States [the Constitution of the State and of the Confederate States]. So help me God.'

[TRADUCTION.]

"'Je jure solennement, autant qu'il sera en moi, de soutenir, de maintenir, et de défendre la Constitution des États Unis [de l'État et celle des États Confédérés]. Que Dieu me soit en aide.'"

certainly as he did a hat or a coat. For a time Butler refrained from interfering with this local practice. But when Breckinridge, on the 5th of August, made his determined but unsuccessful attack upon Baton Rouge, among the Confederate killed and wounded were found citizens wearing their usual arms, who only the day before had mingled with the Union officers, but who, on the approach of the Confederates, had hurried out to join them. Butler, on the representation of Weitzel, then resolved to disarm the population of New Orleans, and ordered that every private weapon, from a rifle to a dirk, should be given up, unless it were held by a written permit. The French consul remonstrated against the execution of this order, so far as it applied to French subjects. There were signs, he said, that the servile population meant to break the bonds which bound them to their masters, and they were only "partially kept in subjection by the conviction that their masters were armed, although their weapons were only such as could be used in self-defense." Butler replied by showing that the professed neutrality of many Frenchmen was not to be trusted. Few of them had taken the oath not to act against the United States. Bonnegras, the French consul at Baton Rouge, had been allowed to retain his arms, but his son was captured fighting against the Union. He could not see how arms which would serve for personal defense could not be used for offensive warfare. The fear that the blacks would wish to break the bonds which bound them to their masters was quite natural, since they, being an imitative race, would be quite likely to follow the example set them of rebellion against constituted authorities; "but surely the representative of the emperor, who did not tolerate slavery in France, could not desire that his countrymen should be armed for the purpose of preventing the negroes from breaking their bonds." But the United States could and would give better protection against outrage, whether from white men or negroes, than could be furnished by any improvised citizens' organization. Whenever the inhabitants of New Orleans should by a united act show their loyalty or neutrality, he would be glad of their aid to keep the peace, and would even restore the city to them. But, until that was done, he should require the arms of all the inhabitants, white and black, to be under his control.[1] This order was followed by another offering specific rewards for the discovery of hidden weapons. Concealment being an overt act of rebellion, any slave giving information of such hiding by his master was to be emancipated. Moreover, any offense which might be lawfully resisted by arms, whether committed by whites or blacks, would be capitally punished. Men known to be in favor of the Union were allowed to retain their arms by special permission. Some secessionists doubtless kept their weapons; but for the practical purpose of aiding in the recapture of New Orleans, they were disarmed.

The Confiscation Act[2] divided the rebels into two classes. The property of the first class, consisting mainly of high civil and military officials, was to be confiscated at once; that of the second class, comprising the great mass of the people, was liable to confiscation in case they did not return to their allegiance within sixty days after the issue of a proclamation to that effect. This proclamation was put forth on the 25th of July. One provision of this act made void all transfers of property made by rebels after the close of the sixty days of grace, which expired on the 23d of September. Disloyal citizens began to make nominal sales of their property to foreigners for the most paltry consideration. Before the passage of the Confiscation Act Butler had assumed the responsibility of sequestrating the property of Twiggs and Slidell, taking the house of the former for his own head-quarters. Twiggs, displaced from his command at New Orleans, had fled on the approach of the Union fleet, leaving behind him letters which showed that he had sought the command in Texas in order to betray his trust. He died, unregretted by friend or foe, soon after the capture of the city.

Ten days before the expiration of the time of grace every neutral foreigner was ordered to register himself, as it "might soon become necessary to distinguish the disloyal from the loyal citizens and honest neutral foreigners residing in the department." The day after the close of the period of grace, an order appeared pronouncing void every sale or contract, except for actual necessaries of life, made by any citizen who had not returned to allegiance to the Union, and ordering every one who had not renewed his allegiance to report himself, with a description of all his property, actual or contingent, to the nearest provost marshal, whereupon he would receive a certificate showing him to be a registered enemy of the United States. Every householder was ordered, under severe penalties, to furnish a list of all the denizens of his house, giving their names, age, sex, and occupation. These lists furnished a complete record of the *status* of every resident of New Orleans. It was added that every person who should within a week renew his allegiance to the United States, and remain truly loyal, would be recommended to the President for pardon for all previous offenses.[3]

The great slave question never came fairly before Butler for adjudication. His official instructions were silent on this point. His private verbal instructions were to the effect that the government had not been able to decide upon a comprehensive policy. The President, wisely resolved to take no step that must afterward be retraced, directed him, in his straightforward, homely phrase, to "run the machine as he found it;" in other words, to raise no issues, and to meet those which presented themselves in such a way as to avoid censure from radicals or conservatives. Hence Butler gave little encouragement for slaves to leave their masters. But flagrant abuses were redressed; the jails were no longer permitted to be used as whipping-places for slaves; and, more than all, blacks were made equal with whites in the eye of the law. The decision which established this point was rendered almost casually by Major Bell, the provost judge. A negro was called to the

[1] Butler to Count Mejan, August 14.

[2] See *ante*, p. 198, 206.

[3] General Order No. 76, September 24.

BATON ROUGE, THE CAPITAL OF LOUISIANA.

white man." "Has Louisiana gone out of the Union?" asked Bell. "Yes," responded the lawyer. "Then," rejoined Bell, "she took her laws with her; let the man be sworn."

The formation of regiments of free colored men had, however, an important though indirect bearing upon the question of slavery. The general government, sadly bestead in Virginia, could send no re-enforcements to Louisiana. Butler, who must have men, called upon the free persons of color to volunteer. The call was met; in a few weeks there were three colored regiments of infantry and two batteries of artillery ready for service. He was recalled before these troops had opportunity of showing their worth. His successor had occasion to prove it at Port Hudson. The conduct of these regiments demonstrated, what many, both North and South, had doubted, that the colored race are capable of becoming soldiers, and, consequently, of becoming freemen. How this fact came to be recognized on both sides, and how it influenced the policy of both parties in the war, must be narrated hereafter.

The capture of New Orleans had weakened the Confederacy, but had not given to the Union the additional strength which had been anticipated. It had not opened the Mississippi, whose navigation was interrupted by the fortifications at Vicksburg, impregnable against a naval attack. The attempts made by the fleet to reduce these works, and the failure of the plan devised by Butler to avoid them by changing the course of the river, so as to convert Vicksburg into an inland town, will be narrated hereafter. Toward the close of his administration he had the mortification of seeing the batteries at Port Hudson springing up almost under his eye. A re-enforcement of five thousand men and two monitors would have enabled him in October to have taken this place. But these could not be furnished to him. The disasters in Virginia, and the march of the enemy into Maryland, compelled the Federal government to concentrate all its strength for the defense of the heart of the nation.

Butler could undertake no important military operations, for, besides the occupation of Baton Rouge, he had a force barely sufficient to hold New Orleans and its approaches. It would have been cruel for him to have taken possession of any points which he could not permanently hold. The moment his troops abandoned any place, every person even suspected of Union feeling would have been exposed to the vengeance of the returning enemy. Moreover, under the strict orders of the Confederate authorities, all cotton and sugar would have been destroyed in advance of his march in any direction, entailing ruin upon innocent holders. Butler's wish was to have sent to him, or to be allowed to raise upon the spot, an army sufficient to hold every important point, with a supporting force that could not be overcome, the region being made to pay the expense. He believed that a few months under that régime would reduce the hostile population to subjection, and would convince Union men that they were not, by the withdrawal of the troops, to be given up to rapine and murder.

The pass-office at head-quarters presented the most striking illustrations of Butler's rigorous rule. Within the Union lines there were food, medicine, and clothing; beyond them were destitution and desolation. There were residents of New Orleans whose families were enduring the extremity of suffering; there were continuous applications for permission to convey food and medicine to them. These were at first freely granted; but it soon appeared that these permissions were systematically abused. Under cover of them supplies and munitions were conveyed to the hostile camps. A trunk of clothes would be found to have a false bottom concealing military supplies; thousands of percussion caps would be hidden in a barrel of flour; the persons of women were stuffed out with contraband articles. The restrictions upon the granting of passes were made more and more stringent, until at last they were almost invariably refused.

The most notable operation of Butler beyond New Orleans was the occupation of the Lafourche District, a fertile and wealthy region lying west of the Mississippi. This was accomplished by Weitzel late in October. A series of swift marches, one spirited action,[1] and some minor conflicts, accomplished the occupation of this district in four days. An immense amount of property liable to confiscation was found. The holders of it were glad to sell this at any price. Some of the officers of the invading force began to purchase sugar upon speculation. Butler, knowing that this practice would demoralize his army, put a stop to it by a sweeping general order. Believing, he said, that the district was largely occupied by persons disloyal to the United States, whose property was liable to confiscation, and that sales were made of it to the prejudice of the rights of the government, it was directed that all the property in the district should be sequestered, and all sales thereof be held invalid; that the movable property be brought to New Orleans, and sold at public auction, the proceeds to be held subject to the rightful claims of loyal citizens and neutral foreigners. A commission was appointed to take charge of this property, with authority to employ the negroes of any plantation in working the same; any person who had not been actually in arms against the United States since the occupation of New Orleans might, upon returning to his allegiance, work his own plantation, and retain possession of his property except such as was necessary for the military service of the United States. The commissioners were also empowered to decide upon all questions of loyalty and neutrality, and to report to the commanding general such persons as they should judge proper to be recommended to the President for amnesty, pardon, and the return of their property, "to the end that all persons that are loyal may

witness-stand to testify against a white man. The defendant's counsel objected that, "by the laws of Louisiana, a negro can not testify against a

---

[1] This action, fought at Labadieville October 27, is described at length by Captain J. W. De Forest as, "of all the combats which I have seen, the most scientific, orderly, comprehensible, and artistically satisfactory. Similar results would have followed the same tactics if a hundred thousand men had been opposed to each other instead of less than six thousand."—*Vide Harper's Magazine,* September, 1864.

suffer as little injury as possible, and that all persons who have been heretofore disloyal may have an opportunity now to prove their loyalty and return to their allegiance, and save their property from confiscation, if such shall be the determination of the government of the United States."[1] Major Bell, the provost judge, was president of this commission, but the chief labor devolved upon Colonel Kinsman. For six weeks he was employed in applying the provisions of the Confiscation Act to the District of Lafourche, setting the negroes at work upon abandoned plantations, and restoring to loyal men their estates which had been temporarily sequestered. The confiscated property was sold at auction to the highest bidder, and the proceeds paid over to the general treasury. No portion of Butler's administration, with the exception of the woman order, has been so sharply criticised as this. But if the claim be granted that secession is rebellion, and that those who had taken up arms against the government were rebels, this measure is fully justified by every provision of public law and policy.

Meanwhile a strong Union sentiment had been gradually growing up in New Orleans. This was shared only in a slight degree by the upper classes on the one hand, or by the lower classes on the other. But it was predominant among the middle classes. Large and enthusiastic Union meetings were convened, and an election was held on the 3d of October, by order of General Shepley, to choose two delegates to the Federal Congress. The canvass was eager, and no citizen who had taken the oath of allegiance was excluded from voting; 7500 votes were cast, of which nearly 5000 were given for Michael Hahn and Benjamin F. Flanders, both uncompromising Union men. The validity of this election was not, however, recognized, and the members-elect were not allowed their seats.

As winter approached, Butler urged the government to furnish him with a force sufficient to enable him to extend his operations, and especially to reduce the works at Port Hudson. Early in December Senator Wilson called upon the Secretary of War to urge the importance of the request. Mr. Stanton approved of Butler's vigor and ability, and promised to do what he could to aid him. Yet at this moment, not only was the recall of Butler determined upon, but his successor had been appointed more than three weeks before. On the 9th of November, the very day upon which Butler issued his Lafourche order, General Banks was assigned to the command of the "Department of the Gulf, including the State of Texas."

The reasons for the recall of Butler have never been made public.[2] There were, indeed, insinuations that he had prostituted his official position to serve his own private interests. Some color was supposed to be given to these charges from the fact that his brother, Andrew J. Butler, entered into large and profitable business transactions in New Orleans. When the port was opened in June, no man, with means and capacity, could fail to make money. Turpentine could be bought for $3 in New Orleans, and would sell for $38 in New York; flour was $24 in New Orleans, in New York $6; sugar was three cents in New Orleans, in New York more than twice as much. Andrew Butler, with large means and credit, entered into business, and, until prices at the two places were equalized, his profits were large. Later came large auction sales of confiscated property. Butler bought much of this; but there is not the slightest proof that he received any undue favor. He purchased in open market, and if he secured a larger share than most of his competitors, it was because he was able and willing to pay more than they. Even if it is true, as has been alleged, that the general advanced his own private funds to his brother, and shared the profits, this of itself forms no ground of accusation. It was for the interest of the government and the country that the trade of New Orleans should be revived. If the general could by his own means advance this object, he was so far a public benefactor. One transaction, indeed, had a suspicious look upon its face. A quantity of cotton had been seized; Butler sent this to his own agent, with directions to sell it. Government seized the cotton. Upon investigation, it appeared that the laborers upon Ship Island were without pay. Butler borrowed $4000 upon his own draft, paid the laborers with the proceeds, sent the cotton to his agent to be sold, the draft to be paid, and the balance held to his order, so that, when the account was stated, he might settle with the government. Government, having seized the cotton, suffered the draft to be protested, much to Butler's disadvantage; but when the affair was explained the money was refunded.

This, and one other transaction of a much larger amount, are averred[3] to have been the only operations of a mercantile nature in which Butler was engaged while in command of the Department of the Gulf. There was at the levee a large number of transports which, by the terms of their charters, were to be sent home in ballast. No ballast was to be had nearer than the sand of Ship Island, thirty hours' steam from the city. The steamer Mississippi, hired at $1500 a day, required 250 tons of ballast; to take this at Ship Island, and afterward discharge it, would require at least fourteen days, at a cost to the government of $21,000. There was on the levee sugar enough to ballast the whole fleet; sufficient to ballast the Mississippi could be taken on board and discharged in four days, at a cost of $6000, thus saving $15,000. Butler proposed to allow merchants to ship sugar at a moderate freight, say $5 a hogshead, amounting, in the case of the Mississippi, to $2000 more—$17,000 in all. The difficulty was to find money to buy sugar at the moment. Government had then no money at New Orleans; the general had none; but by pledging $150,000, his whole private fortune, he borrowed $100,000. This he placed in the hands of his brother, who with it bought and shipped sugar, receiving a commission on his shipments. Government took the sugar thus shipped, merely repaying the advance. Other merchants were also allowed to ship sugar upon payment of a moderate freight to the government. The transports went home ballasted with sugar instead of sand. How much was saved in all by this arrangement has not been stated. The saving to government on the Mississippi alone was $17,000. Some of the owners of the transports, who had contracted that their vessels should be sent back in ballast, conceived that they had a right to the payment of freight, now that the ballast was in the form of sugar instead of sand. Their unreasonable claim was not allowed; and whoever was dissatisfied, the Secretary of the Treasury was not.

The true reason for the recall of Butler is probably to be found in the determination of the government to avoid all difficulties with foreign nations, and more especially with France. For many reasons, the administration of Butler had become odious abroad. This was owing, in a great measure, to the relations in which he became involved with the foreign consuls. The active population of New Orleans being largely composed of foreigners, gave the consuls great influence. With, perhaps, a single exception, they were in favor of secession, and believed in the ultimate triumph of the Confederacy. Reichard, the Prussian consul, joined the Confederate army, raised a battalion, rose to the rank of brigadier general, and was now in Virginia, leaving as acting consul his partner, Krutschmidt, who had married a sister of his co-religionist Judah P. Benjamin, the Confederate Secretary of War. Mejan, the French consul, took such an open part against the Federal authority that the emperor was finally obliged to recall him. Others were more or less involved on the same side. For a while it seemed to be their main business to protest against Butler's acts. Half of them protested against the oath of neutrality required from foreigners. The British consul protested against an order directing the members of the British Guard to leave the city because they had sent their arms and uniforms to Beauregard's camp. The French consul protested against the order for disarming the population, and against that for imprisoning Heidseck, of Champagne and bar-tending notoriety, and against several other orders. The Spanish consul remonstrated against the quarantine regulations; and so on. Once the whole consular body, with the exception of the Mexican consul, joined in a formal protest. The occasion was this:

The Citizens' Bank, whose capital consisted mainly of bonds held by European owners, the interest upon which was payable semi-annually at Amsterdam, was in February alarmed at the probability of an attack upon New Orleans from above, and resolved to deposit $800,000 in silver with the agent of the bondholders, to meet the interest which would become due in the course of the year. The agent of the bondholders, apprehensive that in case the city was abandoned by the Confederate troops it would be plundered by the rabble, placed this money in charge of Mr. Conturié, the Dutch consul. Butler, thinking that this transaction was a fraudulent one, designed merely to get the specie under the control of the Confederate government, demanded that it should be given up to him until the matter could be investigated. Conturié refused. Butler had the key of the vault in which it was deposited taken by force from the consul, who was kept under formal arrest for a few hours. The consuls remonstrated, to Butler, to the Federal authorities, and to their own governments, against this violation of the person of a foreign representative. The Secretary of State, in reply to a communication from the Dutch minister at Washington, apologizing for the restraint put upon the consul at New Orleans, proposed to appoint a commissioner to investigate the matter; meanwhile government should hold the silver, to deliver it up to the claimants if it should prove to belong to them. The bank, just before the passage of the forts, moreover bought something more than $700,000 of foreign exchange, paying for it specie, which was deposited with the French consul, the bills not to be accepted until the coin had been shipped. Butler, believing this transaction to be a fraudulent pretense to get the coin out of the bank, requested Mejan to retain it under his charge.

Several other transactions, involving the same principles, occurred, the principal of which was the seizure of 3200 hogsheads of sugar which had been bought by Covas, a Greek, reputed to be the agent of an association of merchants in London and Havana. He had sold specie for Confederate notes, with which he had bought the sugar. Butler ordered the sugar to be retained until the transaction could be investigated. The English, French, and Greek consuls protested against this.

The Federal government appointed Reverdy Johnson, an eminent lawyer of Baltimore, as a commissioner to investigate these transactions. He reached New Orleans early in June, and, after spending six weeks in investigation, decided against Butler in every important case. The seizures, he said, "were evidently made under a misapprehension, to be referred to the patriotic zeal which governs him, to the circumstances encircling his command at the time so well calculated to awaken suspicion, and to an earnest desire to punish, to the extent of his supposed power, all who had contributed, or were contributing, to the aid of a rebellion the most unjustifiable and wicked that insane or bad men were ever engaged in."

Butler was deeply chagrined at this decision. He wrote to the Secretary of State[1] that another such commissioner as Mr. Johnson sent to New Orleans would render the city untenable; that the result of his mission had caused it to be understood that the general was not supported by his gov-

[1] General Order, November 9.

[2] He was received with great cordiality by the President and cabinet. He inquired the reason of his recall. The President referred him to the Secretary of War, who had recommended the measure. Mr. Stanton said that the reason was one which did not imply, on the part of the government, any want of confidence in his honor as a man or in his ability as a commander. "You have told me," answered Butler, "what I was *not* recalled for. I now ask you to tell me what I *was* recalled for." "You and I," replied the secretary, laughing, "are both lawyers, and it is of no use for you to file a bill of discovery upon *me*, for I sha'n't tell you."—PARTON's *Butler in New Orleans*, p. 613.

[3] By Mr. Parton, who claims to have fully investigated the subject, with full access to every document bearing upon it.—*Vide Butler in New Orleans*, p. 407–413.

[1] September 19.

ernment; that he was to be relieved, his acts overhauled; that a rebel might do any thing he pleased in the city, as the worst that could happen would be a few days' imprisonment until a new commander should arrive. If this state of things was to continue, he would prefer that the government should get some one else to govern New Orleans. This suggestion was acted upon. But three days[1] after his successor was appointed, and a month before the official notice was received, Butler had the pleasure of forwarding a report which showed so clearly the misdeeds of Mejan, the French consul, that he was recalled. Sanford, the American minister at Brussels, wrote home in September that the Confederate agents in Europe were seriously embarrassed by the non-arrival of a large quantity of coin which they expected from New Orleans, but that "assurances were now given that the money was in the hands of the French consul, and would be shortly received." The purveyors of cloth were specially mentioned as unable to get their pay from the Confederate agents. This letter was sent to Butler, with directions to investigate the matter. He had many reasons for doing this work thoroughly. It was discovered that a firm doing business in New Orleans, under the name of Ed. Gautherin and Co., with a branch house at Havre, had a year before contracted to furnish the Confederate government with a large quantity of cloths for uniforms. These were the unpaid cloths referred to by Sanford. Early in April these cloths reached Havana, whence they were shipped to Matamoras, in Mexico, were smuggled into Texas, and delivered to the Confederate agent. At this time, just before the Federal fleets passed the forts, De Bow, the Confederate produce-loan agent, borrowed of the People's Bank in New Orleans $400,000 in specie, without interest, upon a pledge of cotton. This specie, intended to pay for these cloths, was deposited for security with the French consul. It was far into June before the goods were delivered, and until this was done payment was not to be made. Mejan, in the mean while, had promised not to deliver up any specie held by him in trust without the consent of Butler. Reverdy Johnson's report induced the government to direct that Mejan should be released from this engagement. He delivered the specie to Gautherin, who got it conveyed to Havana on board a Spanish man-of-war. In consequence, a second installment of goods, which was not to be delivered until the first was paid for, was forwarded to the Confederate authorities. Mejan, indeed, averred that he knew nothing of Gautherin except that there was a French house of that name in New Orleans, and that there was no money in his hands to carry out their contract with the Confederates. But incontestable documents demonstrated his complicity. His wife had accepted a present "to close the affair well;" his clerk received a percentage for keeping the money in the consulate; besides which, there was good reason to believe that out of a sum of $19,000 charged to "expenses," the French consul received a fifth. "Count Mejan," wrote Butler in conclusion, "has connived at the delivery of clothing for the Confederate army since the occupation of New Orleans by the Federal forces; he has taken away nearly half a million of specie to aid the Confederates. His flag has been made to cover all manner of illegal and hostile transactions, and the booty arising therefrom. I am glad that my action here has been vindicated to the world, and that the government of the United States will be able to demand of the French government a recall of its hostile agent."

This vindication came too late. Before it was written the successor of Butler had been appointed; before it reached Washington that successor was on his way to New Orleans. Banks, bringing considerable re-enforcements, arrived at New Orleans on Sunday, the 14th of December, and proceeded to the residence of Butler. On Tuesday the two generals met at head-quarters, and Butler formally surrendered the command of the Department.

He took leave of his comrades in a touching general order addressed to "the Soldiers of the Army of the Gulf:" "I greet you, my brave comrades," he said, "and say farewell! You have deserved well of your country. Without a murmur, you sustained an encampment on a sand-bar so desolate that banishment to it, with every care and comfort possible, has been the most dreaded punishment inflicted upon your bitterest and most insulting enemies. You had so little transportation that but a handful could advance to compel submission by the Queen City of the rebellion, whilst others waded breast-deep in the marshes which surround St. Philip, and forced the surrender of a fort deemed impregnable to land attack by the most skillful engineers of your country and her enemy. At your occupation, order, law, quiet, and peace sprang to this city, filled with the bravoes of all nations, where for a score of years, during the profoundest peace, human life was scarcely safe at noonday. By your discipline you illustrated the best traits of the American soldier, and enchained the admiration of those that came to scoff. You have fed the starving poor, the wives and children of your enemies, so converting them into friends, that they have sent their representatives to your Congress by a vote greater than your entire numbers, from districts where you were tauntingly told that there was 'no one to raise your flag.' By your philanthropy you have won the confidence of the 'oppressed race' and the slave. Hailing you as deliverers, they are ready to aid you as willing servants, faithful laborers, or, using the tactics taught them by your enemies, to fight with you in the field. You have met double numbers of the enemy and defeated them in the open field. But I need not farther enlarge upon the topic. You were sent here to do that. I commend you to your commander. You are worthy of his love. Farewell, my comrades! Again farewell!" To the citizens of New Orleans he issued a farewell address, in which he declared the policy upon which he had acted, set forth and vindicated the measures he had employed, and urged upon the people to take the only measures compatible with duty or interest.[2] This done, he took leave of New Orleans, where he had for seven months exercised an authority as absolute as was ever committed to a single man.

VIEW IN THE FRENCH QUARTER OF NEW ORLEANS.

SAMUEL R. CURTIS.

CHAPTER XVI.

FROM DONELSON TO VICKSBURG.—THE TRANS-MISSISSIPPI CAMPAIGN OF 1862.

Price's Retreat from Springfield.—General Samuel R. Curtis.—Federal Occupation of Springfield and Advance into Arkansas.—The Indian Tribes West of the Mississippi ; the Sioux War ; Albert Pike's Intrigues.—Battle of Pea Ridge.—The Barbarities of War.—Operations in New Mexico.—Arizona ; its social Organization ; Hostility of the Apaches.—Resumé of the revolutionary Proceedings in Arkansas and Texas in 1861 ; Seizure of Arsenal at Little Rock ; Meeting in Austin, Texas, in 1860 ; Governor Houston's Career ; General Twiggs's Surrender ; Confederate Forces in Texas at the Beginning of the War.—Sibley's Invasion of New Mexico.—John R. Baylor.—Colonel Canby's Defense of Fort Craig ; Battle of Valverde.—Retreat of Sibley to Texas.—Curtis's Operations in Arkansas after the Battle of Pea Ridge ; Advance on Little Rock ; Governor Rector ; Expedition up White River ; Change of Base from Batesville to Helena.—Confederate Forces in Arkansas in the Autumn of 1862.—Guerrilla Operations.—Battles at Cane Hill and Prairie Grove.—The political Situation in Missouri ; General Halleck's Policy.—Capture of New Madrid and Island No. 10.

IN this and the subsequent chapter we purpose to follow the course of military events in the West from the capture of Fort Donelson down to the Vicksburg campaign. This will bring the history of the war in the West down to the close of 1862. The events narrated are naturally grouped under two separate departments. To the first belong the military operations west of the Mississippi ; to the second, the operations along the Mississippi and Tennessee Rivers — including the battle of Shiloh, the capture of Memphis, and the advance into Mississippi—and General Buell's and Rosecrans's campaigns in Kentucky and Tennessee.

These campaigns, even if we confine ourselves to the immediate field of active operations, disregarding the distant military centres from which instructions were issued and whence supplies were obtained, covered an area of nearly 100,000 square miles. The battle of Pea Ridge was fought on the very confines of civilization, at a point 500 miles distant from the line of General Bragg's march into Kentucky. From New Madrid to the mouth of the Arkansas was more than 200 miles in a straight line ; from the latter point to St. Louis was more than 300 ; and yet this field, so wide in extent, was but a part of the theatre of war. General Halleck's and Buell's forces were the right wing only of the Federal army, separated from the left, indeed, by nearly a thousand miles, and by the wild and tortuous ranges of the Alleghanies, but still co-operating with it as effectually as if there had been no such vast interval of space between.

At the close of 1861 General Price had fixed his head-quarters at Springfield, in the southwestern part of Missouri. At that time, of the four lines of railroad in the state starting from St. Louis, the two proceeding westward were entirely under Federal control. A portion of the lines to Springfield and to Ironton were in the hands of the Confederates. The situation of Price's army was not favorable for an offensive movement, but by retaining it during the winter he had gained a good supply of clothing for his troops and about 4000 fresh recruits from the state. He did not even regard his position as tenable. When, in the latter part of January, General Samuel R. Curtis advanced along the line of the railroad to Rolla and then to Lebanon, Price began to retreat toward Arkansas.

General Curtis, to whom General Halleck had given the command of the army in the field, was a native of Ohio, and at the time of which we are writing was fifty-five years of age. He had studied at West Point, and received an appointment in the army, but in 1832 had resigned his commission, and devoted himself to law and afterward to engineering. He fought under General Taylor in Mexico with the rank of colonel, was appointed military governor of Monterey and of other places occupied by the United States troops, and in these positions had developed a good degree of administrative ability. Subsequently he took a prominent part in the construction of railroads in the West. From Keokuk, in Iowa, he was elected to Congress in 1858 and again in 1860, but at the beginning of the war he resigned his seat in order to participate in the great struggle. He accompanied the New York Seventh from Philadelphia to Washington, and was made an honorary member of that regiment. He then went back to Iowa, superintended the earliest organization of troops in that state, and from the skirmish at Booneville was engaged in the war in Missouri under the conduct of General Lyon. He was at first colonel of the Second Iowa, but was soon made brigadier general of volunteers. He served under General Fremont, and afterward under General Halleck. The latter, upon the withdrawal of General Price to Springfield, gave General Curtis the command in the southwestern part of the state. The army committed to his hands was organized into four divisions, under Generals Sigel, Asboth, and Davis, and Colonel Carr. It was chiefly made up of troops from Missouri and Illinois. There were also some Indiana and Iowa regiments, and a battery from Ohio.

This army moved from Lebanon February 11th, and on the 14th General Halleck telegraphed to Washington that the Union flag then floated over the court-house in Springfield ; that, after a short engagement, Price had retreated, leaving behind a large amount of stores and equipments, and that Curtis's cavalry were in close pursuit. The fact that Price had abandoned his sick, amounting to about 600 men, proves that that general scarcely anticipated the Federal advance. He had waited, however, till the last moment, expecting re-enforcements from the Confederate army in Arkansas. This gave General Curtis a great advantage ; for, although Price was undisturbed in his retreat to Cassville, he was obliged from that point to keep up a running fight for four days, until he reached Cross Hollows in Arkansas. From this position he was soon driven fifty miles southward to the line of Boston Mountains, leaving behind him again his sick and most of his stores. Indeed, General Curtis's commissary had been mostly supplied by stores captured from the enemy during his march southward from Springfield. A large number of recruits were captured on their way from Missouri to join Price's army. Among these was Brigadier General Edward Price, son of the Confederate commander.

General Halleck kept up a series of dispatches to Washington of the most encouraging nature. Four days after he had announced that the Union flag floated over the Springfield court-house, he notified to General McClellan the fact that it was also floating in Arkansas. He added that Price had been driven several miles across the Arkansas line, that his rear was being cut up, and that stores and prisoners were being captured from him hourly. The country, wild with excitement over the capture of Donelson, accepted these dispatches as certain indications of victory already obtained by the Army

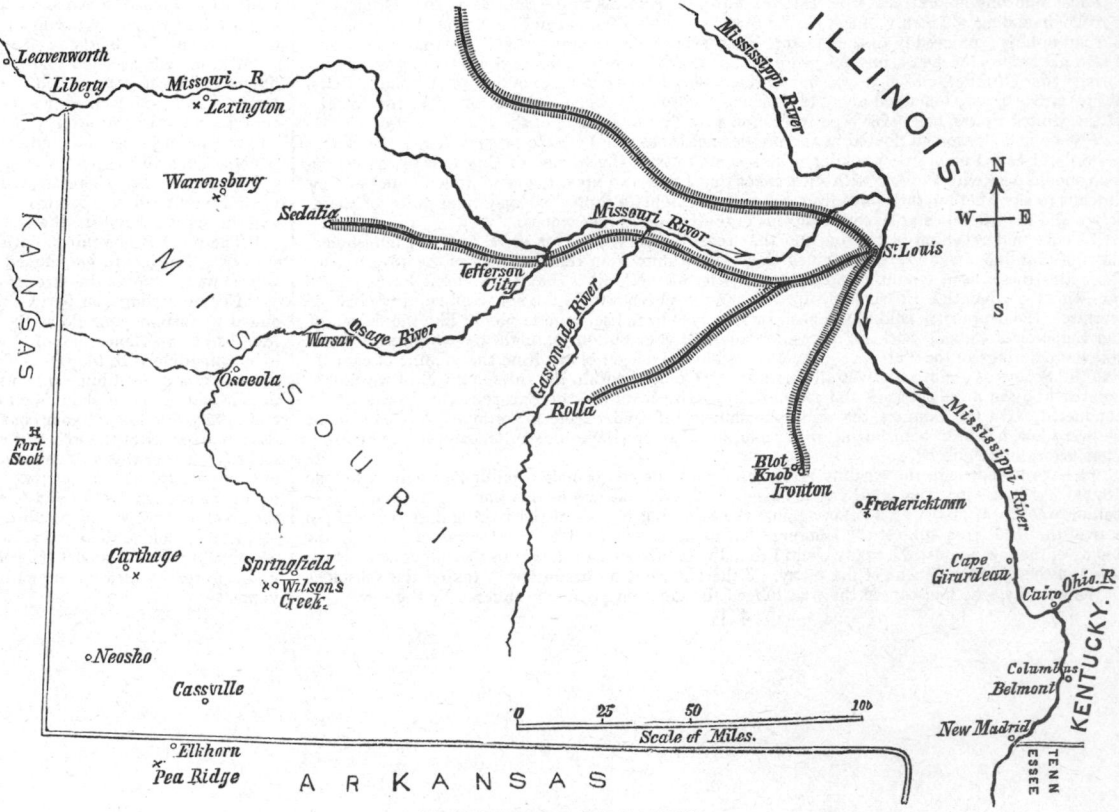

MAP OF THE SEAT OF WAR IN MISSOURI.

of the Southwest. In fact, not only had nothing decisive been accomplished by that army, but it was daily being drawn into a perilous situation. The danger was not chiefly in its distance from a military base, but in its inferiority in numbers to the force which was being gathered against it. All along his line of advance—at Rolla, at Lebanon, at Springfield, and at Cassville—Curtis had weakened his force by leaving detachments to guard his communications, and could not, therefore, bring into the field more than ten or twelve thousand men, while the available force of the enemy was nearly twice that number, without counting the Indian allies of the Confederates. Situated just south of the border line between Arkansas and Missouri, and flanked on the west by the Indian Territory, the field of the proposed contest was the one which would have been selected of all others as the most favorable for the concentration of Price's, McCulloch's, and the Indian forces. Yet General Halleck's confidence in the Army of the Southwest was not wholly without justification. A good portion of General Curtis's force had bravely met the enemy at Carthage, at Wilson's Creek, and in subsequent battles, and even when opposed to superior numbers had dealt very effective blows. The Confederate army, too, was badly armed and weak in artillery.

The attitude assumed by the Indian tribes toward the war should here be briefly noticed. In 1789 there were within the limits of the United States, including the Territories, less than 100,000 Indians. In 1853, by the extension of the territorial domain from the acquisition of Texas, New Mexico, Utah, and California, their number had increased to more than 400,000. In California alone, upon its accession, there were 100,000. In New Mexico the estimated number was upward of 50,000. In Texas there were nearly 30,000. In Utah there were 11,000. At the beginning of the war, the pressure of emigration westward for a score of years had driven all the great Indian tribes west of the Mississippi. What was known as the Indian Territory then covered only a small area comparatively upon the map, and was hedged in on all sides by territories which had either already become states of the Republic, or would soon become such. This limited space had been given by the United States to the Indian tribes which had been driven across the Mississippi. Elsewhere, in Minnesota, Iowa, Oregon, and in the Territories, the Indians existed in great numbers indeed, but they were limited to certain reservations. The relation of the government to all the Indian tribes in the West had been peculiar. The policy pursued regarded the permanent interest of the white man alone, while it bestowed temporary indulgences upon the red man. Every thing else was left in the hands of the missionaries, who exercised a favorable influence upon this rapidly declining

INDIAN SQUAWS WINNOWING WHEAT.

race. It was unfortunate, however, that the patronage which the government bestowed upon the Indians was frequently dispensed through agents who took many opportunities to defraud the beneficiaries. This, and the natural antipathy against the white man which it is almost impossible to eradicate from the Indian blood, led, finally, in the summer of 1862, to an outbreak of hostilities even among the tribes as far north as Minnesota. The Sioux Indians in that state, numbering about 1200 warriors, suddenly, in the month of August, attacked the settlements of the whites, and began a series of massacres, unrivaled in their horrible details except by the former outrages perpetrated by the same race upon the infant colonial settlements of the Eastern States. The only premonition of this terrible event had been a rumor which prevailed in the spring and early summer that the Indian tribes of Utah, Colorado, Dacotah, and Western Nebraska were making preparations to ravage the Territories and frontier states. It was given out that Confederate emissaries had been among them, instigating them to revolt. This rumor, taking so general a shape, and being, moreover, the natural product of an excited imagination, appears to have had no practical effect. It aroused no serious suspicions in the minds of the settlers, although it led the Commissioner of Indian Affairs to publish an advertisement warning the public of the dangers likely to be encountered by travelers on the overland route to the Pacific. Without attributing the outbreak in August directly to Confederate agencies, it is yet quite certain that the distraction of the country by civil war led the ignorant Sioux to hope for success in an undertaking upon which in more tranquil times they would scarcely have ventured. Apart from the first success of the marauders not much was effected by them. The loss of life was estimated in round numbers at 800, and that

of property at between two and three millions of dollars. A few companies of troops under Colonel H. H. Sibley, afterward promoted to a generalship,

INDIAN CAMP CAPTURED BY COLONEL SIBLEY.

soon quelled the insurrection. In giving these details of the Sioux War we have anticipated in regard to time, but this seemed the most fitting place in which to speak of them, as they were somewhat nearly related to events which had been going on during the few previous months among the tribes farther south upon the Confederate border. In the summer of 1861 Albert Pike had been among these tribes acting as "commissioner of the Confederate States to the Indian nations and tribes west of Arkansas." Here, on the 12th of August, he had entered into a treaty with the Camanches, according to the terms of which that nation agreed to settle upon reserves claimed to have been leased by the Confederates from the Choctaws and Chickasaws, in the southern portion of the Indian Territory, namely, that portion included between the Red and Canadian Rivers; in return for which agreement the Camanches were to be under Confederate protection, in token of which Albert Pike gave their chiefs letters of safeguard.[1] Other tribes than the Camanches were also decoyed from their allegiance to the Federal government. A few days before the above treaty was made, the Confederate government had been organized at Mesilla, in Arizona, under John R. Baylor as governor. This movement was undertaken in spite of, rather than by the assistance of, the Indians of that Territory. The evacuation of Fort Stanton by the Federal troops on the 8th of August left the enemy in possession of property equal to $300,000, including the fort, and there was not a single Federal soldier left within the limits of Arizona. The territory claimed to have been leased from the Choctaws and Chickasaws embraced an area of 23,437 square miles, or a little less than one fourth of the Indian Territory. If the Creeks, Seminoles, Osages, and Cherokees could also be alienated from the United States, the Confederacy would then have secured the entire Territory, having a population of nearly 72,000 souls. This country, with its 52,000,000 of acres, would add greatly to the resources of the Confederate government, and, if it could be retained, would become a valuable security for the payment of the vast debt which that government must incur in the course of the war. Its mountains were filled with iron and coal. The Red River ran along its southern border, and the Arkansas almost through its centre. Albert Pike spared no pains to secure this boon for the Confederacy. To some extent he succeeded in bringing over even the Cherokees to the side of his masters. On the 21st of August, a mass meeting, attended by about 4000 of that nation, at Tahlegue, declared their adherence to the Confederate cause. The proceedings of this Indian convention were transmitted by John Ross, the principal chief of the Cherokees, to General McCulloch.[2] The Rev. Mr. Robinson, a missionary to the Cherokees, also made a

[1] The following is a copy of the letters of safeguard:

"The Confederate States of America to all their officers, civil and military, and to all other persons to whom these presents shall come:

"The bearer of this is Bis-te-va-na, the principal chief of the Ya-pa-rih-ca band of the Ne-um, or Camanches of the Prairie, and those who accompany him are the head men of that band, all of whom have this day concluded and signed in behalf of the whole Ya-pa-rih-ca band articles of a convention of peace and friendship between that band and other bands of the Ne-um with us, and have thereby agreed to settle and live upon reserves in the country between the Red River and the Canadian, leased by us from the Choctaws and Chickasaws; and the said chief has also agreed to visit the other bands of the Ne-um, not parties to the same convention, and now on the Staked Plain or elsewhere, and persuade them also to settle upon reserves in the same country.

"We have accordingly taken the said chief and the said head men, and all other persons of both sexes and all ages, of the said Ya-pa-rih-ca band, from this day forward under our protection, until they shall for just cause forfeit the same, and that forfeiture be declared by us; and we have therefore granted, and do grant to them and to each of them, these our

"LETTERS OF SAFEGUARD

for their protection, and to avail each and all of them as far as our authority and jurisdiction extends.

"You are therefore hereby charged to respect these letters, and give all the said persons protection and safe-conduct; and any infraction by any of you of this safeguard will be visited by us with all the penalties due to those who violate the public faith and dishonor the Confederacy.

"In testimony whereof, Albert Pike, commissioner of the Confederate States to all the Indian nations and tribes west of those states, doth hereunto set his hand and affix the seal of [SEAL.] his arms.

"Done and granted at the agency of the Confederate States for the Camanches, Wichitas, and other bands of Indians near the False Wichita River, in the leased country aforesaid, this twelfth day of August, in the year of our Lord one thousand eight hundred and sixty-one.

"ALBERT PIKE,

"Commissioner of the Confederate States to the Indian nations and tribes west of Arkansas.

"Countersigned,   WM. QUEENSBURY,

"Secretary to the Commissioner."

[2] The following is a copy of John Ross's letter:

"Executive Department, Park Hill, Cherokee Nation, August 24, 1861.

"To MAJOR CLARK, ASS'T QUARTERMASTER, C. S. A.:

"SIR,—I herewith forward to your care dispatches for General McCulloch, C. S. Army, which I have the honor to request you will cause to be forwarded to him by the earliest express.

"At a mass meeting of about 4000 Cherokees at Tahlegue, on the 21st instant, the Cherokees, with marked unanimity, declared their adherence to the Confederate States, and have given their authorities power to negotiate an alliance with them.

"In view of this action, a regiment of mounted men will be immediately raised and placed under the command of Colonel John Drew, to meet any exigency that may arise.

"Having espoused the cause of the Confederate States, we hope to render efficient service in the protracted war which now threatens the country, and to be treated with a liberality and confidence becoming the Confederate States.

"I have the honor to be, sir, very respectfully, your humble servant,   JOHN ROSS,

"Principal chief of the Cherokee nation."

report of the affair to the Federal government. He stated that the Confederate commissioner had assumed the payment of the annuities hitherto received by the Cherokees from the national government. This was not a mere paper treaty. The Cherokees followed up the convention with active preparations to defend themselves and to assist their new ally. A home guard of 1200 men was formed. The Creeks, also, had raised a thousand men for service in the Confederate army. It is probable that in these movements the Cherokees, Creeks, and Camanches were led by the same motives which in that very month the next year led the Sioux Indians to revolt. There was the same natural antipathy to the white man, mingled with a sentiment of revenge for past wrongs, real or imagined, and the same ignorant belief that the fortunes of the republic were declining, while the star of the Confederacy was in the ascendant. There was this difference, however. The Indians farther south very naturally considered that their immediate, if not their future destiny must be linked with that of the Confederacy, which was now opposing a very bold front against the national armies. All the Indian tribes, moreover, were doubtless gratified by the spectacle that was being afforded them of millions of white men pitted, army against army, in fraternal strife, and were willing, so far as possible, to add fuel to the fire of rebellion. They never proved an ally of much consequence to the Confederates, who had an eye rather to their territory than to their services in the field. The Indian troops which were raised were placed under the command of Albert Pike, who received as the reward of his labors the rank of brigadier general in the Confederate army.

Although Mr. Davis, in his message to the Confederate Congress, had declared that the events of the previous year had demonstrated that the government had attempted more than it had power successfully to achieve, and that serious disasters had resulted from the effort to protect the whole territory of the Confederacy, sea-board and inland, yet there was no disposition manifested in the subsequent conduct of the war to attempt any thing less. Certainly no such disposition was shown west of the Mississippi. If Price had been retreating, it was only because of the military advantages to be gained by retreat. Indeed, he would have remained at Springfield if McCulloch had promptly come to his support. Besides, the Confederacy, at this time, was intent upon holding the power which it had gained over the Indian country on its border, and which would have to be given up if its Western army should fall back far from that border. Every effort was now made to secure victory in the impending battle. The command of the trans-Mississippi Department was given to General Earl Van Dorn, who reached the camp at Boston Mountains on the 2d of March. Price and McCulloch had been at loggerheads in previous campaigns, and this appointment of Van Dorn to the command of the entire army exercised a wholesome influence.

General Curtis selected Sugar Creek, on the confines of Missouri, Arkansas, and the Indian Territory, as a line of defense. Here he awaited the attack of the enemy, which was made on Thursday, the 6th of March. Colonel Jefferson C. Davis, acting as major general in command of the third division, held a position on Pea Ridge, north of the creek, commanding the Fayetteville road, one brigade on the right of the road, the other on the left. Two batteries, one of six and another of four guns, covered the approach, and one of them commanded the valley to the eastward and westward. Sigel's two divisions were seven miles south of the creek, at Bentonville. Carr's division held the eastern part of the ridge. This ridge, from which the battle receives its name, extends along the north bank of Sugar Creek, and is broken toward the north by gradual slopes, with an occasional ravine. From the position occupied by the army to the Missouri line was nearly eight miles. Two roads traverse the ridge, one from Bentonville, another from Fayetteville, and converge toward Keetsville. As the Missouri line is approached, these roads pass through a narrow valley, and are lined on either side by steep and continuous ranges of hills. Midway between the roads as they strike the ridge is Leetown, near the creek; on the road from Fayetteville, and northeast of Leetown, was Elk-horn Tavern. From this tavern the Confederates designated the action as the battle of Elk Horn. To the northwest of Leetown an extensive ravine, known as Cross-timber Hollow, crossed the Bentonville road. The camp was protected in the rear by a thick oak scrubbery, which extended to the road on the west. Beyond this was an open field, bounded on the right by a range of hills near Elk-horn Tavern.

On the 5th, General Sigel, at Bentonville, was apprised of the enemy's approach through a scout, and also by a message from General Curtis, which conveyed similar tidings, and ordered his return to Sugar Creek. He promptly dispatched his train of 200 wagons northward, protected by a rear-guard. This guard, consisting of the Thirty-sixth Illinois and part of the Second Missouri, was attacked the next day by greatly superior numbers, and surrounded. But Sigel had remained behind, and succeeded in bringing off his men with an inconsiderable loss. He joined Curtis on the afternoon of Thursday.

Van Dorn had begun to advance on Tuesday. With General Pike's Indian division, his numbers probably did not fall short of 20,000 men. In the newspaper reports of the time they were estimated at from twenty-five to thirty thousand.[1] His march was by way of Fayetteville and Bentonville. Sending only a small force to demonstrate in Curtis's front, his plan was to make a detour to the westward, turning the Federal right, and, if possible, to gain the defile in Curtis's rear. But for Sigel's admirable skill in his retreat from Bentonville, by which he availed himself of the advantages which the nature of the ground afforded for the use of artillery against the enemy, he must have been cut off, his trains captured, and the whole Federal army placed in a position of great peril. He, however, accomplished a junction with the main army near the western edge of Pea Ridge. Van Dorn had, on the night of the 6th, gained the rear of the Federal army, with Price on his left, fronting southward, and McCulloch on the right nearly opposite Sigel. The position taken by the Confederates compelled General Curtis to change front, after he had been all day engaged in obstructing the approaches on the south side. The new line thus formed was at right angles to the one previously occupied, and extended from Sugar Creek to Cross-timber Hollow. Davis held the centre, Sigel the left, and Carr the right.

The battle of Pea Ridge opened on Friday morning, Van Dorn, concentrated against the Federal right, bearing down heavily upon Carr's division. Curtis, also, had so distributed his force that, while he had three divisions on his right—Carr's, Davis's, and Asboth's—only Osterhaus's division had been left to Sigel. McCulloch endeavored early in the day to move eastward, so as to co-operate with Price and Van Dorn, and thus the action became general. Osterhaus's division, with two of Davis's regiments, moved out a mile beyond Leetown. Three pieces of flying artillery were sent in advance, supported by the Third Iowa Cavalry. This was to delay the movements of the enemy until Osterhaus could come up. But the cavalry and artillery were swept back from the field like chaff before the wind. Farther to the right, Carr was also being driven back toward Elk-horn Tavern. The low brushwood and numerous hollows and ravines afforded shelter to the Confederate troops as they advanced, and enabled them to engage the Federals at close quarters, where their shot-guns, loaded with buck-shot, were more than a match for the best long-range rifle.

The enemy was pressing closely up to the road, which was the only possible avenue of retreat to the Federal army. Once gained in force by Van Dorn, and the day would be lost to the Federals if only McCulloch should hold his own, and prevent Davis and Osterhaus from re-enforcing the right. The battle going on between Leetown and Elk-horn Tavern must decide the event. When the Third Iowa Cavalry had been driven back, and the forces of McCulloch had reached the cover of the brushwood beyond Leetown, Colonel Osterhaus came up and engaged the enemy in a large open field to the left. Then the second brigade of Davis's division was sent in on the right, but was soon driven back. The enemy had gathered in large force on this part of the field. Here were now several thousand of McCulloch's men, supported by a large body of Indians. Davis's First brigade was with Osterhaus in the open field to the west. This was ordered to change its front and attack in the rear that portion of the enemy which was pressing the Second brigade. This movement was accomplished with good effect, though not until the Second brigade had lost some of its guns, which were soon after recovered by the First. The success of the sortie made by Davis's First brigade allowed the Second an opportunity to recover itself, and the enemy was driven from this part of the field, leaving behind him his killed and wounded. Among the former were General McCulloch and General McIntosh, his second in command. Then two regiments of Sigel's command re-enforced Davis, and were sent in on the right to support Carr. The desperate fight on the left centre had saved the day. Price's men had by night reached the Fayetteville road in Curtis's rear, and Van Dorn made Elk-horn Tavern his head-quarters. But, though victorious on his left, the enemy had been badly defeated on his right, and it was doubtful whether he could sustain his position on the morrow. In regard to the ill success of the Confederate right, it can not be doubted that McCulloch's and McIntosh's death discouraged their troops, and contributed materially to their repulse.

The result of the day, though very unsatisfactory to either army, were especially discouraging to the Federals. The enemy held their line of communications. Their supplies were nearly exhausted. Their mules had been without food for forty-eight hours. There was no escape except by defeating Van Dorn, who had strongly posted himself on the hills commanding the defile northward.

Saturday morning opened from a sky overcast with clouds. The enemy's cannon looked menacingly down upon the Federal encampment from the bold eminences to the northward, 200 feet in height. Batteries and battalions were posted at the base of these hills on either side. The Federal line was again changed, so that Davis held the right, Carr the centre, and Sigel the left. To General Sigel was allotted the most important part of the day's operations. The battle commenced at eight A.M. Sigel opened a heavy cannonade on Van Dorn's position, and advanced around to the left under cover of the fire. The Confederate artillery replied, but without much effect. Davis pushed round on the right, turning the enemy's left. The advantage gained was that the Federal artillery enfiladed the Confederate lines. Some of the enemy's guns were captured, and, to save them all from capture, they had to be withdrawn. Before the battle had lasted two hours, it had terminated in the retreat of the enemy from the field. The Confederates had failed of their object; but, on the other hand, it can not be said that the Federals had gained a very decisive victory. On both sides men and guns had been captured. The loss in killed and wounded on both sides was nearly equal, amounting, in either case, to about 1000.[1] Van Dorn withdrew his forces from the field without molestation.

---

[1] Pollard says 16,000; but he evidently does not include the Indians.

[1] The Federal force engaged in the battle of Pea Ridge consisted of the following troops:
First division, Colonel Osterhaus: Thirty-sixth Illinois, Twelfth Missouri, Seventeenth Missouri, Twenty-fifth Illinois, Forty-fourth Illinois, battalion Third Missouri, two battalions Benton Hussars (cavalry), battalion Thirty-ninth Illinois Cavalry, two batteries of 6 guns each.
Second division, Brigadier General Asboth: Second Missouri, Fifteenth Missouri, Sixth Missouri Cavalry, battalion Fourth Missouri Cavalry, two batteries 6 guns each.
Third division, Colonel Jeff. C. Davis: Eighth Indiana, Twenty-second Indiana, Eighteenth Indiana, Thirty-seventh Illinois, Ninth Missouri, First Missouri Cavalry, two batteries, one of 4 guns another of 6.
Fourth division, Colonel Carr: Fourth Iowa, Ninth Iowa, Thirty-fifth Illinois, Twenty-fifth Missouri, Third Iowa Cavalry, Third Illinois Cavalry (two battalions), Bowen's battalion of cavalry, two batteries of 6 guns and one of 4.

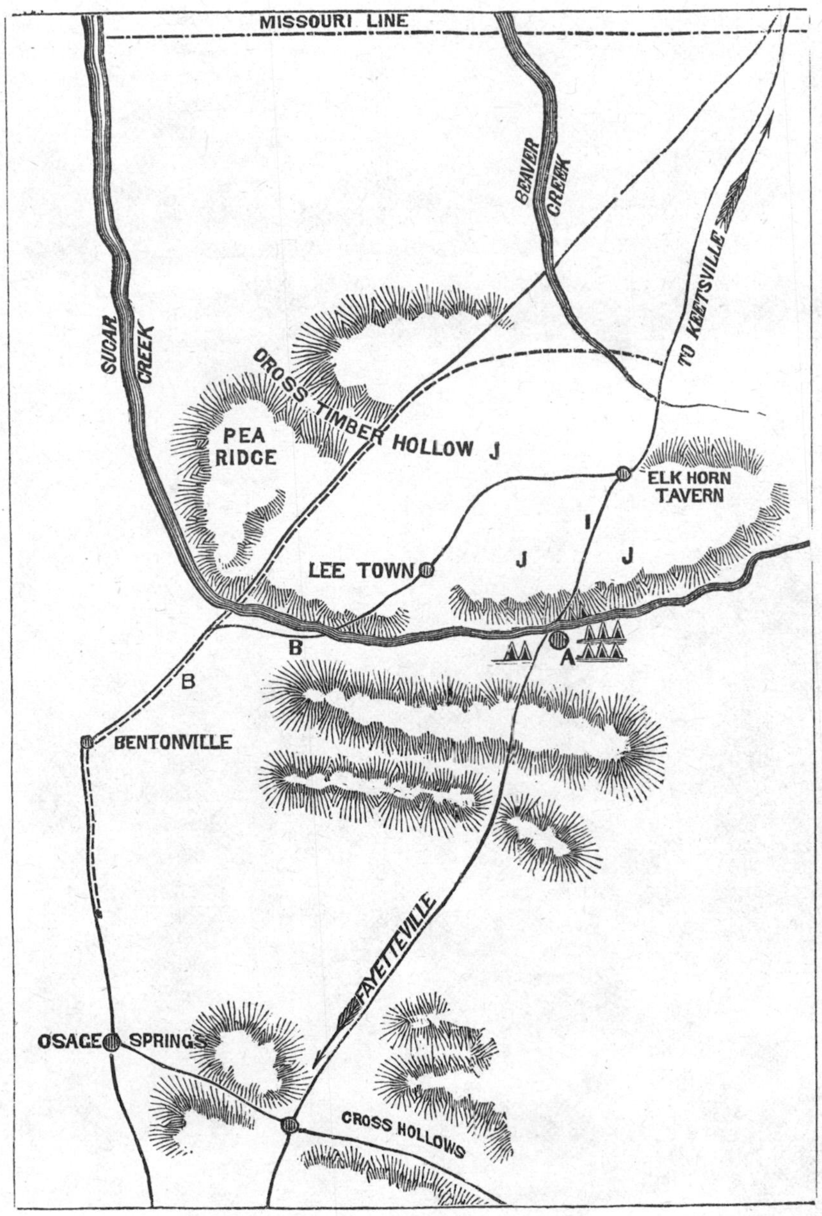

MAP OF THE BATTLE-FIELD OF PEA RIDGE.

A. Camp of General Curtis.—B B. Route of Sigel from Bentonville.—I. Spot where McCulloch fell.—J. Tableau of Pea Ridge.

The day after the battle, the Confederate commander sent a burial party to General Curtis, under a flag of truce, to ask for the dead left upon the field. The request was granted by the Federal commander, who took occasion to express his regret that he had found on the battle-field many of his dead who had been tomahawked, scalped, and otherwise shamefully mutilated. A few days afterward Van Dorn replied, making a counter-charge that some of his men who had surrendered themselves prisoners of war had been murdered in cold blood by Germans of Sigel's command. Sigel did not deny the charge, but stated, in a communication to General Curtis, that when Elbert's three pieces of artillery were taken, the men serving at the guns were surrounded and shot dead, although seeking refuge behind the horses. "When such acts are committed," said General Sigel in this letter, "it is very natural that our soldiers will seek revenge, if no satisfaction is given by the commander of the Confederate army."[1]

After the battle of Pea Ridge, Van Dorn retreated south of Boston Mountains. General Curtis fell back to Keetsville, where he received re-enforcements from Kansas and Missouri.

While General Curtis was on his march into Arkansas, events of considerable importance, though having no important bearing on the general campaign, were in progress farther westward, in that part of New Mexico which, since February, 1863, has been known as the Territory of Arizona.[1]

This country had a population of whites roughly estimated at 20,000. The Indian population was more than twice as numerous, about half of whom were friendly to the whites, while the other half were hostile. The Apaches, the most hostile of the tribes, had overrun the country several times, and were called "devils" by their own race on account of their fiendish outrages. Although rich in mineral treasure of every sort, the Territory had been but partially developed. This was due to three causes. The principal obstacle was the negligence of the government during the few previous years. The two other unfavorable elements in the way of rapid growth—the hostility of the Apaches and the sterility of the vast deserts—could have been either removed or counteracted if the authorities at Washington had properly appreciated the value of the Territory. The great motive to emigration which existed in the mineral wealth of the country lost its effect upon the people on account of the insecurity of life, which intimidated all except the adventurer, the speculator, and the reckless criminal from settling in a region known from time out of mind as the theâtre of Indian massacre. The essential defect was the absence of a military force adequate to protect settlers from pillage and murder.[2] This region of our Western territory has an additional importance from the fact that it furnishes the most convenient route for the proposed Pacific Railroad. While there were great objections to be brought against any of the projected routes, those against this were fewer and of a less formidable character. It was this route, running along the 32d parallel of latitude, that Jefferson Davis very ably advocated in the Senate. It was a much shorter route than any of the others which were under consideration, and it traversed a much milder region. The greatest obstacle was the scarcity of water along the route. Springs were, on an average, over twenty miles apart. In some cases as many as forty miles intervened between one supply of water and another. This scarcity of water was also a considerable obstacle to a continuous line of military posts. But this was a difficulty very easily obviated by a system of artesian wells. Such a system was, indeed, in 1858, in process of construction, in order to facilitate communication across the desert from Fort Fillmore to Albuquerque, and from Fort Union to Santa Fé. The events of 1861 not only interrupted the scheme of the Pacific Railroad route, but for more than a year threatened to deprive the United States of all military occupation of the Territory.

Upon the first outbreak of the Southern insurrection, and even before active hostilities were inaugurated, the revolutionists had their own way in the territory west of the Mississippi. In Arkansas, before that state had seceded from the Union, the United States Arsenal at Little Rock had been seized, with 9000 muskets, forty cannon, and a large supply of ammunition. Fort Smith was captured by the Confederates April 26, 1861. In Texas, General Twiggs, to whom had been committed all the forts and the military property of the United States in that department, had, before the secession of Texas, and without the slightest plea on the score of necessity, delivered up all the posts under his command, together with property which, not including forts and public buildings, was valued at a million and a half of dollars. The troops were allowed to leave the state. When the Ordinance of Secession had been passed, on March 2 of that year, there still remained in Texas a few detachments of Federal troops, and these were made prisoners and re-

Only a few of these regiments were full, a large number of sick having been left behind at Rolla and Lebanon.

The official report of losses was as follows: First division, 144; second division, 119; third division, 329; fourth division, 701: total, 1351, of which 203 were killed. General Van Dorn stated his loss at 600. This does not include the prisoners taken by General Curtis, which the latter claims to have amounted to 1000. Pollard says that Van Dorn took 300 prisoners.

[1] How far General Sigel's account is justified may be inferred from the following extract from a narrative of the battle which appeared a month afterward in the Richmond Whig. It was written by an officer of General Price's army. He gives a vivid description of the action on Friday in that part of the field near Leetown, where General McCulloch and McIntosh were killed, which we quote in full:

"After listening some moments to the terrible tumult in the distance" [the writer refers here to the conflict going on near Elk-horn Tavern between Price's column and the Federal right], "suddenly, and within 300 yards of me, two or three cannon opened their brazen throats, hurling their missiles of death through the undergrowth in almost every direction. As the sound of the cannon came the third or fourth time, like the noise in springtime on the marshy margin of a lake, only more shrill, loud, and apparently more numerous than even the frogs, came the war-whoop and hideous yell of the Indians. Here I was unconsciously in the midst almost of McCulloch's charging squadron, and in range of a battery of three guns that were hurling death and defiance at them." [These were the guns of Elbert's flying artillery, which had been sent in advance to arrest McCulloch's progress toward the Federal right centre.]

"The battery was speedily charged and captured, those supporting it being borne backward three quarters of a mile by the impetuous forward press of the Confederates. Their retreat, most of the way, was through a corn-field, down a road upon its borders, but continuing into woods adjacent, full of undergrowth, where the main force of the enemy's strongest wing was posted. Here began the rattling musketry, which soon increased to a Niagara in sound. For hours there was hardly an intermission, save that created by the stunning roar of the cannon, so close that the ears of both parties were deafened. Within this vortex of fire fell McCulloch and McIntosh. At one time, having concluded to make my way to the immediate command of General Price, after passing from the corn-field down to the edge of the woods, just as four of us entered the woods a shell was thrown at us, bursting in our midst. . . . . I then went leisurely over the corn-field, and rode back to the deserted guns.

"About forty-five men lay in the space of two or three hundred yards to the rear of the battery, all save one entirely dead, and all but three *Dutchmen*. . . . . Here was a sterner feature of war than any I had yet seen. *The Texans, with their large, heavy knives, had cloven skulls in twain, mingling blood, and brains, and hair. The sight was a sad one, but not devoid of satisfaction to our own exiles from home and wife. The character of the bloody victims, as denoted by their countenance, betoken victory for the South.* I looked upon the faces of many dead enemies that day, and among them all found no expression of that fixed, fierce determination which Yankees describe as belonging peculiarly to the heroic hirelings who enlist for pay to desolate our homes."

[1] The act establishing the Territory of Arizona was approved by the President February 24, 1863. The first section defines the Territory as "all that portion of the Territory of New Mexico situated west of a line running due south from the point where the southwest corner of the Territory of Colorado joins the northern boundary of the Territory of New Mexico, to the southern boundary-line of said Territory of New Mexico."

[2] In his report for 1858, the Secretary of War, John B. Floyd, afterward Confederate general, thus treats of the situation on the Western frontier at that time:

"The whole strength of the army, as posted, consists of 17,984 men, and the actual strength on the 1st of July last was 15,764. In addition to other movements, this force is called upon to garrison 68 forts of a large and permanent character . . . . and to occupy 70 posts less permanently established, where the presence of a force is absolutely required. The area over which these forts and posts are spread embraces a circuit of about 3,000,000 square miles, and requires a journey of many thousand miles to visit the principal ones of them.

"The external boundary of our country, requiring throughout a more or less vigilant military supervision, is 11,000 miles in length, presenting every variety of climate and temperature, from the inclement cold of our Canada frontier to the tropical regions of Southern Texas. But the occupation of this long line of frontier is a trifling difficulty in comparison with that of protecting the double line of Indian frontier, extending from the Lake of the Woods to the banks of the Rio Grande, on the east side of the Rocky Mountains, and from beyond the River Oregon on the British frontier, to the head of the Gulf of California on the western slope of those mountains. Superadded to these lines, requiring to be occupied, are the great lines of intercommunication between the Valley of the Mississippi and the Pacific Ocean, which imperatively demand that protection which only the United States troops can furnish. These lines are very long, and are now extremely important, while every year renders them more and more so. From our Western frontier of settlements to those of Northern Oregon the distance is about 1800 miles; from the same frontier to the settlements of California, *via* Salt Lake, is 1800 miles; from the frontier of Arkansas, at Fort Smith, by Albuquerque or Santa Fé, to Fort Tejon, is about 1700 miles; and from San Antonio, by El Paso, to San Diego, near the borders of the white settlements, is 1400 miles; constituting an aggregate line of 6700 miles, which ought to be occupied, and which we pretend in some sort to keep open. This simple statement of facts demonstrates, stronger than any arguments could do, the absolute necessity for an increase of the army. . . . If there is a higher duty than another devolving upon a well-regulated government, it is to afford perfect protection to its citizens against outrage and personal violence; yet this great obligation is not performed by the government of the United States. For a large portion of the year, scarcely a week elapses without bringing us intelligence of some Indian massacre or outrage more shocking than death itself; and it most frequently happens that these acts go unpunished altogether, either from the want of troops for pursuit, or from their remoteness from the scenes of slaughter, which renders pursuit useless. In former times, when the hardy pioneer was allured away from the line of white settlements by fertile lands alone, he scarcely ventured so far as to be beyond succor and protection from those he left behind. But far different is the state of things at present. Our Pacific settlements, with their great inducements of rich lands, salubrious climate, and fabulous mineral treasures, present to the inhabitants of the Atlantic states temptations to emigration which the privations of an intervening wilderness and desert, and continual danger from roving bands of savages, hanging upon their march for many hundred miles together, can not deter them from undertaking. This migration strengthens the natural ties between the Atlantic and Pacific states, and adds immensely to the defensive strength of that remote region. Justice and humanity alike demand protection for these emigrants at the hands of government."

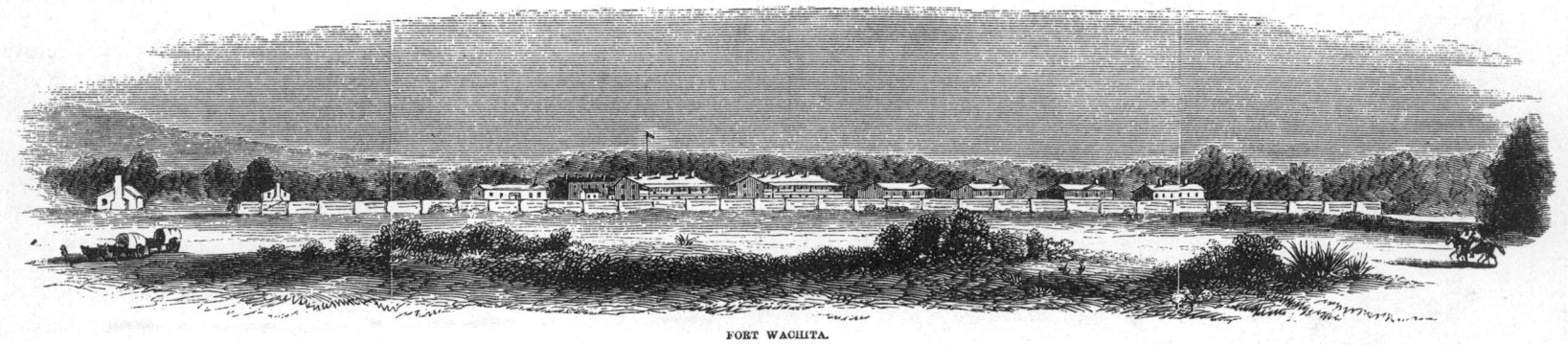

FORT WACHITA.

FORT ARBUCKLE

FORT DAVIS.

FORT BROWN.

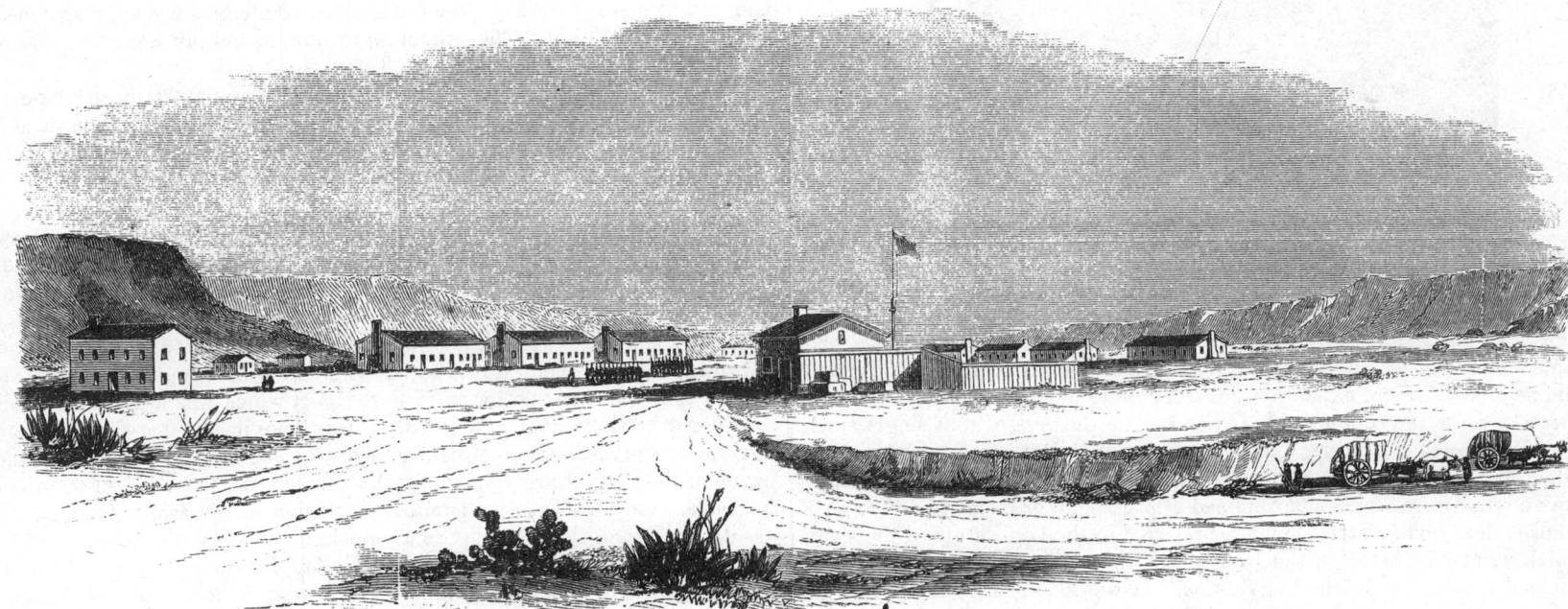

FORT LANCASTER

THE ALAMO, SAN ANTONIO, GENERAL TWIGGS'S HEAD-QUARTERS.

leased on parole. The secession sentiment in Texas had never been violent. In December, 1860, the largest meeting ever held in Austin passed enthusiastic resolutions in favor of the old Union, and the meeting was made the occasion for a gala-day. Governor Houston, in a letter to the commission-

SAM. HOUSTON.

er sent to Texas by the State Convention of Alabama, said that secession would involve civil war and the ruin of our institutions, if not liberty itself. The governor, it seems, from another portion of this correspondence, had some schemes of his own in connection with the future of Texas. "Texas," said he, "has views of expansion not common to her sister states." He proposed to make the conquest of Mexico by the prowess of that single state. He was opposed to holding a State Convention. But the Convention was called, and the sentiment of the people having undergone a rapid change, the vote in favor of secession obtained a large popular majority. The governor endeavored to have the matter referred to the Legislature of the state, which was to assemble on the 18th of March. His reluctant attitude provoked the members of the Convention. It was thought by many that he was opposed to the confederation of Texas with the other Southern states, and favored her setting up for herself. The Convention insisted upon its absolute authority, and declared the act of secession an accomplished fact. State troops were then dispatched to the Rio Grande to occupy the posts abandoned by the Federal troops. Subsequently an ordinance was passed in the Convention, requiring the state officers to appear before that body and take an oath of allegiance to the Confederacy. The governor and secretary of state refusing to comply with this demand, their chairs were declared vacant. Lieutenant Governor Clark then became acting governor of the state.[1] In June all intercourse with the people of the Northern states was forbidden, and all citizens of the latter states were warned to leave Texas within twenty days. During the year 1861 no offensive operations were undertaken by the national government against Texas, with the exception of a bombardment of the Confederate batteries at Galveston in the month of August.

Of the forts surrendered by General Twiggs, the principal ones were Forts Davis, Arbuckle, and Wachita. Fort Davis was situated on the Rio Grande, about 500 miles from San Antonio, in a cañon of the Lympia Mountains. It was in the midst of the most picturesque scenery. On either side, the immense rocks forming the sides of the cañon tower upward to a height of 500 or 600 feet. Fort Arbuckle was on the northern frontier of the state, and Fort Wachita was sixty miles northwest of Arbuckle. It was near Fort Wachita that General Van Dorn had, in 1858, routed the Camanches in a pitched battle. Fort Brown, on the Rio Grande, and Fort Lancaster, on the San Antonio and San Diego mail route, were also included in the terms of

the surrender. General Twiggs had served with great distinction in the Mexican War. He was breveted major general for his gallantry at Monterey, and received a sword from Congress. As a reward for his disgraceful surrender of the United States forts and property in Texas, he received from the Confederacy the command of a major general, and was for a short time in command of New Orleans. He died at Augusta, Georgia, September 15, 1862. The surrender was made to Colonel Ben. M'Culloch, who had been selected for this purpose by the revolutionary committee of the state, styling itself the "Committee of Public Safety." M'Culloch, also, had served in the Mexican War, and had earned especial commendation from General Taylor in the battle of Buena Vista. He had had a great deal of experience in partisan warfare on the Texan frontier, and had done much for the cavalry service of the United States. As soon as Lincoln's election was known, he had identified himself with the secessionists in Texas. He had 800 men under his command when he received the surrender of San Antonio. He was soon sent abroad to procure arms for the state; but, before he had succeeded in this mission, he was made a brigadier general. His part in the war in Missouri has already been shown in this history. He died, as we have seen, in the battle of Pea Ridge.

Texas, immediately after her accession to the Confederacy, sent forces into all parts of the field to sustain the cause which she had adopted. Three regiments, under Wigfall, Hood, and Archer, were sent to Virginia; two, under Terry and Gregg, to Kentucky; and two, under Green and Lock, to Missouri. By the 1st of November, 1861, there were nineteen regiments in the field, of which seven were disposed of as above stated. Six were dispatched to the coast of Texas. The others were sent to the northern frontier, or were organized for operations in the Territories.

Texas, from her geographical position, became the natural base for operations against New Mexico.[1] The troops designed for the campaign in that country consisted, in November, of three regiments, organized into a brigade under the command of Brigadier General W. U. Sibley. During the previous summer the Confederates had not been idle in New Mexico. In July, although they did not invade the Territory in any formidable force, they created such a panic that nearly all of the Federal military posts were abandoned without a struggle. Forts Breckinridge and Buchanan were abandoned upon the rumored approach of the Texan troops, without any attempt at defense, and even without an estimate of the amount of force likely to be brought against them. The garrisons, numbering about 450 men, started over the mountains eastward to Fort Craig, which was located near Valverde, on the Rio Grande. While they were moving in that direction, the garrison of Fort Fillmore, consisting of nearly 700 men, under Major Isaac Lynde of the regular army, disgracefully surrendered to a force of less than 200 Texans on the 27th of the month. Four months afterward Major Lynde was dropped from the army list as a punishment for his delinquency. The next week after the surrender of Fort Fillmore, Lieutenant Colonel John R. Baylor, commanding the Confederate forces in the southern portion (Arizona) of New Mexico, issued a proclamation taking possession of the Territory in the name of the Confederacy, assuming the title of military governor. Soon after Fort Stanton was abandoned, thus throwing into the hands of the revolutionists property valued at nearly half a million of dollars. Fort Craig was also abandoned. Messila became the military capital of Arizona. General Albert Sidney Johnston received from Governor Baylor the command of the Confederate forces in the Territory, which at this time numbered less than 1000 men. On the 8th of September, however, General Johnston became commander of the entire military department of the West, and the charge of the operations in New Mexico was committed to General Sibley, who was preparing a military expedition for the complete conquest of that Territory. Sibley's head-quarters were at Fort Bliss, in Texas.

In the mean time the small Federal force left in New Mexico was under the command of Colonel E. R. S. Canby, who, by a general order of the War Department, was soon after placed at the head of the Department of New Mexico, with his head-quarters at Santa Fé.

The Confederate General Sibley had proposed to reach the field of operations early in September, 1861, but failed to do so, as he explains in his report, "from misunderstandings, accidents, deficiency of arms, etc." He says: "I found myself at this point" [Fort Bliss] "as late as the middle of January, with only two regiments and a half, poorly armed, thinly clad, and almost destitute of blankets. The ranks were becoming daily thinned with those two terrible scourges to an army, small-pox and pneumonia. Not a dollar of quarter-master's funds was on hand, or had ever been, to supply the daily and pressing necessities of the service, and the small means of this sparse section had been long consumed by the force under the command of Lieutenant Colonel Baylor, so that the credit of the government was not as available a resource as it might otherwise have been." Having established a general hospital at Donna Anna, he prepared to move up the Rio Grande, and on the 7th of February reached a point seven miles below Fort Craig, which, together with Fort Stanton, had been retaken by Canby. The latter occupied Fort Craig, the immediate object of the Confederate attack, with a garrison of 2500 men, 1000 of which were regulars.

On the 16th of February Sibley reconnoitred, advancing to within a mile of the fort. Finding the latter too strong to be attacked, and the Federal commander declining a battle in the open field, he determined to cross the Rio Grande below the fort to the east bank, to turn the Federal position, and thus compel an engagement. It was supposed in the fort that Sibley was withdrawing his force, especially as Colonel Canby's scouts had declared it

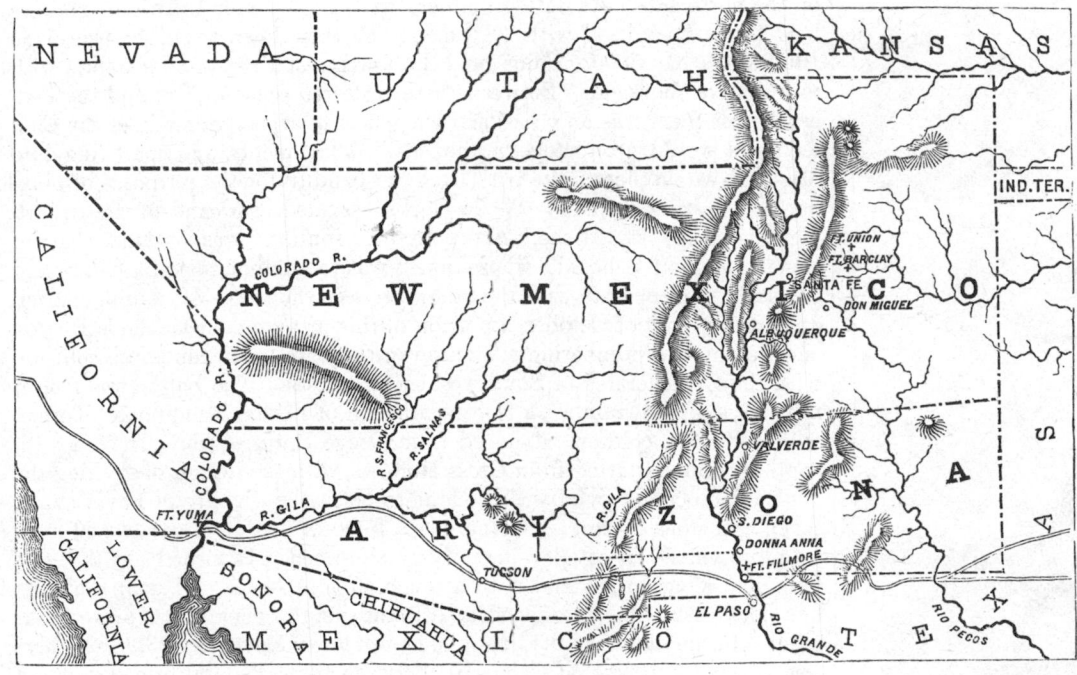

MAP OF NEW MEXICO.

impossible for the enemy to advance through the sand-hills on the east side of the river. In truth, General Sibley, by crossing, had placed his army in an unfavorable situation, as his camp was destitute of water, which could only be obtained by gaining a point above the fort. The Confederates crossed on the 20th. The day before, Canby had ordered his regulars—the Fifth, Seventh, and Tenth Infantry—together with Colonel Kit Carson's and Pino's regiments—also to cross the river and occupy an elevation opposite to and commanding Fort Craig. On the 20th he sent across some cavalry and artillery to cover the infantry. An engagement followed, which was confined to the artillery, but in the course of which Pino's regiment became demoralized, and the entire force had to be withdrawn to the fort.

The Confederates were without water all day, and their animals, suffering extremely from thirst, became exhausted, and so completely broken down that the wagons could not be moved. It was now of the utmost importance that a Federal force should cut off the approach of the enemy to the river at Valverde, where was the only supply of water in the vicinity. For this purpose, the regulars, with Carson's regiment, some cavalry, and two batteries, were moved up the west bank in that direction, but, upon arriving at their destination, it was found that the Confederates had already anticipated them. The batteries were opened upon the enemy, compelling his retreat with considerable loss. The Federals crossed to the east bank, and encountered the full strength of Sibley's command, which now made a desperate stand, and there followed the action known as the battle of Valverde.

Colonel Canby came upon the field at noon with Pino's regiment of New Mexicans, which had occasioned so much disorder on the previous day. The forces engaged on both sides were nearly equal, in either case amounting to a little over 1500 men. The earlier part of the battle was little more than an artillery duel. The two Federal batteries were situated, one of them, Lieutenant Hall's, on the right, and the other, Captain McRae's, on the left. The latter, about two P.M., was advanced toward a wood which covered the enemy's right. A furious charge was made by the Texans, under Captain Lang, against this battery. His regiment was thinned at every step by successive vollies; but it still pressed on, picking off the gunners, one by one, with shot-guns and pistols, until only two men remained to man the guns. The force detailed to support McRae could not be brought up. Captain McRae had fallen; and soon the impetuous advance of the enemy decided the contest in this part of the field. The battery was captured, and no attempt was made for its recovery. On the right a similar attempt was made against Hall's battery, but the latter was gallantly supported by Carson, and the enemy at this point was repulsed. But the confusion on the left, consequent upon the loss of McRae's battery, made it necessary that Canby should withdraw from the field. He retired upon the fort in good order. The Federal loss in this battle was estimated at about 200; that of the enemy somewhat less.

Not being in a condition to assault Fort Craig, General Sibley moved northward against Albuquerque and Santa Fé, which were evacuated by the Federals. About the same time, Tucson, near the southern border of the Territory, was occupied by a band of roving guerrillas under Captain Hunter. From this point Hunter advanced northward toward the Pimo villages, and even threatened Fort Yuma, on the California boundary. The hostile Indians united with the Confederates, and the whole Territory, with the exception of the strong forts held by the Federal troops, was devoted to rapine and murder.

General Canby, in March, was able to take the offensive. After successful skirmishes with the Confederates at Apache Pass and Pigeon's Ranch,

he threatened Albuquerque, the enemy's principal dépôt of supplies. This movement compelled Sibley to evacuate the Territory, leaving his sick and wounded behind in the hospitals at Santa Fé, Albuquerque, and Sorocco. The Confederates had, by their outrages upon peaceful citizens, exasperated the inhabitants and made them bitter enemies. This doubtless hastened their retreat into Texas, which, under the steady pressure of the Federal force in their rear, was a succession of disasters. As they withdrew, Fort Fillmore, Fort Bliss, and El Paso were immediately occupied by the Federals under the command of General Carleton, who, being now re-enforced by troops from California, was enabled to hold the Territory against the enemy, and turn his attention to the conquest of the hostile Apaches.[1]

After the battle of Pea Ridge, the military operations of either army in Arkansas were not especially significant. About a month after that battle, it was supposed that Price was moving toward Springfield. This led to a temporary withdrawal of the Federal army from Arkansas. But early in May General Curtis was again penetrating the state by a more easterly route. Moving southward from Salem, he occupied Batesville, on the White River. Between Batesville and Little Rock, on the Arkansas, was a distance of nearly eighty miles. This latter point, the capital of the state, was the object of the Federal advance. As Curtis moved in that direction, there was great excitement in the capital. Governor Rector, on the one hand, upbraided the Confederate government for having made no provision for the defense of the state, while, on the other, he frantically appealed to the Missourians and Texans to come to the rescue. He said: "It was for liberty that Arkansas struck, and not for subordination to any created secondary power, north or south. Her best friends are her natural allies, nearest at home, who will pulsate when she bleeds, whose utmost hope is not beyond her existence. If the arteries of the Confederate heart do not permeate beyond the east bank of the Mississippi, let Southern Missourians, Arkansians, Texans, and the great West know it and prepare for the future. Arkansas lost, abandoned, subjugated, is not Arkansas as she entered the Confederate government; nor will she remain Arkansas, a Confederate state, desolated as a wilderness. Her children, fleeing from the wrath to come, will build them a new ark, and launch it on new waters, seeking a haven somewhere of equality, safety, and rest."

But the governor does not appear to have rallied about him any formidable forces of resistance. He soon took a hasty departure from the capital, and the executive government passed over to the martial authorities. The pressing need of men in Tennessee had depleted the Confederate armies of the Southwest almost to the last extremity of weakness. But, on the other hand, the importance of the Tennessee campaign to the Federal cause also reduced Curtis's army to such an extent that he was forced to abandon the campaign against Little Rock. Thus there occurred a lull in the trans-Mississippi campaign, which was only partially disturbed by frequent military expeditions. The principal one of these was that undertaken in June, after the capture of Memphis, up the White River. The object of this expedition was to open communication with the army of General Curtis. Four gunboats—the St. Louis, Mound City, Lexington, and Conestoga—accompanied by a transport having on board Colonel Fitch's Indiana regiment, moved up the river toward St. Charles. The Mound City led, and, as it approached St. Charles, received the fire of two concealed batteries. The troops from

TUCSON, ARIZONA.

[1] At the close of the official report of his operations in New Mexico, General Sibley says:
"In concluding this report . . . it is proper that I should express the conviction . . . that, except for its political geographical position, the Territory of New Mexico is not worth one quarter of the blood and treasure expended in its conquest. As a field of military operations it possesses not a single element, except in the multiplicity of its defensive positions. The indispensable element, food, can not be relied on. During the last year, and pending the recent operations, hundreds of thousands of sheep have been driven off by the Navajoes. Indeed, such were the complaints of the people in this respect, that I had determined, as good policy, to encourage private enterprises against that tribe and the Apaches, and to legalize the enslaving of them."

JOHN M. SCHOFIELD.

the transport were landed with the purpose of taking the batteries in the rear, when a ball from the bluff penetrated the casement of the Mound City, and passed through her steam drum. The result was that only 23 out of a crew of 175 escaped scalding. A scene of great confusion followed. Frantic with pain, men leaped into the water, and some of them were drowned. Boats sent to their relief from the other vessels were fired upon with grape and canister with fearful effect. But Colonel Fitch, hearing of the accident, only pressed his regiment more rapidly forward, and carried the batteries at the point of the bayonet. But the expedition failed of its main object, and General Curtis, on the 24th of June, evacuated Batesville, and by the middle of the next month had securely established a new base at Helena, on the Mississippi, about fifty miles above the mouth of White River. The events of the year from this time resolve themselves into a bare chronicle. On the 19th of September General Curtis was called to the command of the Department of Missouri, which was so defined as to comprehend Missouri, Kansas, and Arkansas. General Steele, who had arrived at Helena with a division of troops, then assumed the command of that post.

About this time the Confederate forces in Arkansas numbered probably 25,000 men. General Hindman, with about 5000 men, covered Little Rock

on the north side. At Batesville there were 2000, under McBride. Holmes held Little Rock itself with 2000 men. Farther down the river, near Pine Bluff, Roan had 5000. Rains held the northwestern part of the state with four or five thousand. Between these scattered detachments and the Federal forces there was an occasional encounter of arms. Sometimes the Confederates would group together in small detachments, and, marching into Missouri, would there unite with irregular banditti for the purposes of plunder or guerrilla warfare. When Curtis assumed command of the department, an army, styled the "Army of the Frontier," was organized under General John M. Schofield, whose object was to subdue guerrilla bands, and generally to co-operate with the other forces in the trans-Mississippi district. Just at the close of October, a portion of this army, under Generals Herron and Totten, and numbering six or seven thousand men, came into collision with the Confederates in Southwestern Arkansas. The battle was fought near Fayetteville Hollows, a few miles north of Boston Mountains. Totten, with the main column, advanced from Osage Springs, while Herron, with another column, started from Cross Hollows, with the design of striking the flank of the enemy, who was thought to be in the vicinity of Fayetteville, seventeen miles distant. Herron had a force of less than a thousand men, made up chiefly of cavalry, imperfectly equipped. It turned out that this force had alone to contend with a much superior force of Texan Rangers; but, notwithstanding the disparity of numbers, the enemy was driven four miles. In the same vicinity, just one month later (November 28, 1862), there was a small skirmish at Cane Hill, between three Federal brigades, under General James G. Blunt, and a force of Confederates, made up of Marmaduke's men, considerably re-enforced by guerrillas. This also resulted favorably to the Federals.

A few days afterward there was a more stubbornly contested action at Prairie Grove, a short distance northwest of Cane Hill. After the battle of Cane Hill, General Blunt had held the country in the immediate vicinity of the battle-field, that being the great wheat and corn growing district of the state. The Confederate forces were strongly re-enforced by bringing up the several detachments scattered over the state, and were commanded by General Hindman. These forces may be roughly estimated at 15,000. Hindman, with great promptness, advanced northward to cut General Blunt off from his communications. Blunt, at the first notice of this movement, sent for General Herron, who was at Wilson's Creek with the second and third divisions of Schofield's army. Herron moved at the instant, and in three days had marched over a hundred miles. In the mean while Blunt remained at Cane Hill, and the enemy slipped by him on his flank, thus gaining a position which, while it was strong against either Blunt or Herron, also enabled him to prevent their conjunction. It was, however, a position favorable to the Federal generals, on the simple condition of the ability of both to participate in the critical battle.

On the morning of December 7 Herron had reached Fayetteville, and, resting for an hour, pressed on along the road from that place southward. Up to the previous night he had kept up communication with Blunt, but that was now broken off, for Hindman was planted between them, and hoped to fight them in succession. It was Sunday morning; "a more beautiful morning or a grander sunrise," says Herron, "I never beheld;" but it inaugurated a day of bloody, terrible battle. Herron had sent 3000 cavalry to Blunt's support, and now his own need of such a force was most urgent. Part of his infantry and artillery must be detailed to guard his train of 400 wagons, leaving him, at his own estimate, only 4000 available men. As he came out on the prairie by the mountain road seven miles south of Fayetteville, the Arkansas cavalry, which had the advance, came "dashing back in great disorder." His army and Hindman's had met, having, as a newspaper

BATTLE OF ST. CHARLES, ON WHITE RIVER, ARKANSAS.

JAMES G. BLUNT.

FRANCIS J. HERRON.

correspondent remarked, run together like two locomotives. Hindman's advance was pushed back on his main lines, which were found posted on a long ridge by a creek, and in Herron's immediate front. The Federal commander decided to attack, trusting that Blunt, who could not be more than ten miles away, would hear the booming of artillery, and attack in time to decide the contest in his favor. By ten o'clock the crossing began under cover of several batteries. Herron was fortunate in his artillery, as also in the superior discipline of his command. The contest went on fiercely on his left. A battery of the enemy, strongly posted on a hill, was captured, and then the position had to be abandoned. A counter-charge was ordered, but the Confederates could not stand up in the face of Herron's guns. Here, with varying fortune, the fighting was kept up till long after noon, and as yet nothing had been heard from Blunt.

General Blunt, when he first heard the sound of battle, a little after noon, was more than five miles from the scene of conflict. At two o'clock he was upon the field. He found the enemy on the ridge across the Fayetteville road. "On the north, and in front of the enemy's lines," says he, in his report of the battle, "was an open valley, divided into large fields, a portion of them cultivated in corn. At the east end of this valley, General Herron, with the second and third divisions, was engaged with the enemy." Blunt's column entered the valley at its western extremity, on the left wing of the enemy. Hindman was thus engaged in front and rear at the same time; but his force, though divided, was yet strong in each part. Between his and

Blunt's position there was a piece of woods, into which the greater part of Blunt's column was thrown. From three o'clock until nightfall there was no interruption of the battle. Both Herron's and Blunt's commands slept on their arms all night, prepared to renew the contest on Monday; but, under cover of the darkness, the enemy slipped away, and retreated across the Boston Mountains. The loss on both sides was severe; in Herron's command alone amounting to little less than a thousand. Blunt came upon the field later, and fought under less disadvantage, and suffered less severely. The Federal artillery had been worked with promptness and accuracy, and with terrible effect against the enemy, whose loss exceeded that of the Union army. The Confederates acknowledged that Hindman had been defeated. At the close of the month Blunt advanced south of Boston Mountains and took possession of Van Buren without any considerable resistance.

Early in 1863 a force of the enemy, under General Marmaduke, moved on Springfield, Missouri; but that place had been so carefully provided for against attack by General Browne that the Confederates were repulsed.

The military situation in Missouri was closely interwoven with the political. General Fremont's well-known political history, and his self-committal from the first to an anti-slavery policy, had excited against him the prejudices of the Missourians. His policy had been unwise, because it was both partisan and premature. When General Halleck was sent to take his place, in November, 1861, he was especially instructed to shape his political course in such a manner as to prove that President Lincoln's administration was committed, not to the abolition of slavery, but to the suppression of armed treason. To such a course Halleck steadfastly adhered so long as he was commander of the department. The necessity of severe military restrictions rendered political tolerance indispensable. Even after the Confederate armies were driven out of the state, there were thousands of citizens who still sympathized with the Confederate cause, and who were willing to sacrifice much for its success. Against these there could be only severity in so far as they gave actual aid to the enemy. But there were also thousands of citizens thoroughly loyal to the United States government. Severity against these, and in regard to points not involved in the main issue of the war, could not fail to alienate many of them from their adherence to the government, and drive them over to its opponents. In a state rent with intestine faction, it was wise to compose the strife so far as this could be done consistently with the simplest interpretation of loyalty.

With General Halleck the only test of loyalty was support of the government. Those who could not stand this test were singled out and treated as enemies. Any one was at liberty to think as he chose of slavery, but it fared hard with those who stumbled at the oath of allegiance. His measures against those found in arms against the government within the state, or contributing in any way to the comfort of the enemy, were justly severe. He ordered that all persons within his lines who, disguised as loyal citizens, were found giving information to the enemy, should be shot. Union families, crowding into St. Louis from all parts of the state, were quartered upon avowed secessionists. All the municipal officers of the city were required to take the oath of allegiance. His government, while it mulcted and punished the disloyal, yet protected them against all unauthorized violence. There could be no seizure of private property except on the plea of strict military necessity, and even in this case, if it was unauthorized, it was pun-

PLAN OF THE BATTLE OF PRAIRIE GROVE.

EXPLANATION
UNION TROOPS
REBEL TROOPS
ROADS
FENCES
DWELLINGS

ISSUING PASSES AT ST. LOUIS.

ished with death. No arrests were made except upon definite and substantial charges. No slaves were taken from their masters except in cases where the latter were disloyal, and had used their slaves, or permitted them to be used for disloyal purposes. No fugitive slaves were admitted into his camps. Martial law was strictly enforced. All civil authorities attempting to interfere with the execution of any order from the head-quarters of General Halleck were arrested and punished. An order was issued requiring all publishers of newspapers, those of St. Louis excepted, to furnish General Halleck a copy of each issue for inspection, under penalty of having their papers suppressed. The officers of mercantile associations were required to take the oath of allegiance to the Federal government. The president and faculty of the University of Missouri, and the officers of all the railroad companies in the state, were required to take the same oath. Lawyers were not allowed to practice before submitting to the oath. The oath of allegiance was made the test of the privilege of suffrage at elections. Citizens who, as such, engaged in acts of hostility, were treated with marked severity. The arrest and trial of some persons apprehended for destroying railroad bridges and other property became the occasion of a correspondence, in which General Price insisted that these men should be treated as prisoners of war. General Halleck replied that no orders of General Price could save from punishment spies, marauders, and incendiaries; that if armed forces in the garb of soldiers, and duly organized as legitimate belligerents, destroyed railroad bridges as a military act, they would be treated as prisoners of war; but that soldiers in the garb of citizens must suffer the usual penalties inflicted upon citizens for their crimes. In accordance with this response, eight persons, who were convicted of the crime of destroying the railroad bridges, were shot in the month of February, 1862. After the Federal victories in Tennessee, and the expulsion of Price from the southern border of the state, the military regulations hitherto in force were somewhat relaxed. During the remaining portion of General Halleck's career the disturbance from guerrillas was inconsiderable. General Schofield assumed the command of the department June 1, 1862, which position he resigned in September to General Curtis.

While Grant and Buell were preparing for an advance southward from Nashville, and Curtis was carrying on his campaign west of the Mississippi, General Pope and Commodore Foote moved upon the enemy's works at New Madrid and Island No. 10. The conflict on either side of the river was not more important than that for the possession of the river itself. Columbus had to be surrendered as the consequence of the capture of Donelson, but the new positions occupied by the Confederates at Island No. 10 and New Madrid were southward from Columbus only from twenty-five to thirty-five miles. The enemy determined to fall back step by step, in this way preventing the Federal gun-boats from establishing a connection with Farragut's fleet at the mouth of the river.

THE CARONDELET RUNNING THE CONFEDERATE BATTERIES AT ISLAND NO. 10.

Island No. 10 is situated in a bend of the Mississippi, on the Tennessee border, and although ten miles above New Madrid on the river, is southwest of that place. New Madrid is on the Missouri shore. It was upon this island that the Confederates had erected their principal fortifications, which consisted of eleven earth-works, mounting seventy heavy guns. At New Madrid there was a bastioned earth-work mounting fourteen guns, and in the upper part of the town a battery of seven pieces. The line of intrenchments between the upper and lower work constituted the defense of the

A MORTAR.

place. These works were occupied by five regiments of Confederate infantry, with several companies of artillery. In the river the enemy had also six gun-boats, carrying from four to eight guns. The Confederate General McCown commanded the troops holding New Madrid.

New Madrid, being below Island No. 10, and its possession cutting off that island from its natural communication southward, was the first to be attacked. General Pope appeared before the town on the 3d of March, but had no

heavy artillery, and no means of contending with the naval force in the river. While awaiting the arrival of his large guns, he posted a battery at Point Pleasant, twelve miles below, thus cutting off McCown from re-enforcements and supplies from the South. This battery had, of course, to be mounted with small guns, and, as a protection against the heavier artillery of the Confederate gun-boats, the guns were placed in sunk batteries, between the rifle-pits, which afforded protection to a thousand infantry. Thus invested on the south side, McCown drew re-enforcements from the island. The number of his command was nearly doubled, and three additional gun-boats increased the naval force, which was under the command of Commodore Hollins.

After waiting over a week, Pope received his siege guns from Cairo, which were, on the night of the 12th, placed within 800 yards of the enemy's main fortification, commanding the work and the river above it. At daylight the batteries were opened, and the fire of four heavy guns was concentrated upon the gun-boats with such effect as to disable some of them; also three guns in the enemy's land-works were dismounted. The only impression made by the Confederate batteries on Pope's lines was in the injury done to one gun, attended by the wounding of eight men, and in the loss of three men in an Ohio regiment. The result of the day's operations convinced the Confederate commander that it was useless to attempt farther resistance at that point, for General Pope was already about to cut off the line of retreat. McCown therefore abandoned New Madrid on the night of the 13th, leaving his dead unburied, and all his stores and ammunition, and even the knapsacks of his soldiers, and fell back upon the island. In regard to the military property abandoned by the enemy, the testimony of General Pope is that it included "all their artillery, field batteries, and siege guns, amounting to thirty-three pieces, magazines full of fixed ammunition of the best character, several thousand stand of inferior small-arms, with hundreds of boxes of musket cartridges, tents for an army of 10,000 men, etc." Untouched suppers, candles left burning in the tents, and the general appearance of the encampment, indicated that the retreat had been effected with unceremonious haste.

The Confederate force was now concentrated on the island. General Pope's occupation of New Madrid secured a perfect blockade of the river, and the defenders of Island No. 10 were too far removed from the main army under Johnston to receive any help from that source. The island, moreover, was not a good defensive position. It is flat, and commanded by the high ground on the left bank of the river. Its defenses had been constructed under the superintendence of General Beauregard, who, at the last moment, on the 5th of April, turned the command over to General McCall.

On the 14th of March, the day of the capture of New Madrid, Commodore Foote moved from Cairo with an armament consisting of eight gun-boats, all iron-clad except the Conestoga, and ten mortar boats, lashed to steamers.[1] Two regiments of infantry accompanied the expedition, which reached a point about four miles above Island No. 10 on the morning of the 15th. The next day a bombardment commenced, which continued until the 7th of April. The great point to be gained was the rear of the fortifications, which Beauregard had erected on the high ground commanding the island. To

[1] These mortar boats were constructed at St. Louis at the suggestion of General Fremont. They were about 60 feet long and 25 feet wide, surrounded on all sides by an iron plate bulwark six or seven feet high. The weight of the mortar itself was 17,210 pounds. Its bore admitted easily a 13-inch shell. From the edge of the bore to the outer rim was 17 inches. The weight of the mortar bed was 4500 pounds; that of the shell, filled with wet sand, was 230 pounds; filled with powder, 215 pounds.

MORTAR BOATS IN PROCESS OF CONSTRUCTION.

THE GUN-BOAT FLEET DROPPING DOWN STREAM TO RECONNOITRE.

STEAMERS TOWING MORTAR-BOATS INTO POSITION.

OPERATIONS AGAINST ISLAND NO. 10.—BOMBARDMENT FROM THE MORTAR BOATS.

ISLAND NO. 10 AFTER THE SURRENDER.

effect this, it was necessary that Pope should have transports to convey his troops from New Madrid to the Tennessee shore. Opposite Island No. 10, on the Missouri side, was a peninsula called Donaldson's Point, which widens inland. From New Madrid across the widest part of this peninsula Wilson's Bayou extends for about eight miles. Terminating in a large pond, it is only four miles distant from another pond which opens out into the river some distance above New Madrid. It occurred to General Hamilton, a subordinate of General Pope, that, by means of a canal, which should take advantage of the bayou and traverse the land between the two ponds, transports might be brought from Foote's fleet to New Madrid. This canal was undertaken, and cost the troops very much labor. It was twelve miles long, and for half of that distance it passed through heavy timber, which had to be sawed off by hand four feet under water. In this way the transports were brought through. But there was now another obstacle to the passage of the troops. From Tiptonville to the fortifications east of the island McCall had erected batteries commanding the river. It was necessary to have gun-boats to cover the passage. These fortunately succeeded in running the enemy's batteries on the island, the Carondelet on the 4th of April, and the Pittsburg on the 6th. These soon silenced the hostile works along shore, and by midnight on the night of the 7th the army was on the west bank of the Mississippi. "The passage of this wide, furious river by our large force," says General Pope, in his official report, "was one of the most magnificent spectacles I ever witnessed." Pope and Foote were now masters of the situation. The latter had been shelling the island for three weeks. During this bombardment the bursting of a rifled gun on board the St. Louis had killed and wounded fourteen men.

There was no battle. As soon as the crossing of Pope's command was ascertained, the Confederates withdrew from the island. Not a single life had been lost by Pope's army. There were captured three general officers, over 100 heavy siege guns, twenty-four pieces of field artillery, and several thousand stands of arms. A floating battery of sixteen guns was also taken, which had been brought from New Orleans to Memphis, and thence to Island No. 10. The prisoners, according to General Pope's estimate, including those taken on the main land, numbered 6700, including 273 field and company officers. Although the victory was bloodless, yet no battle-field had hitherto yielded so large results in captured material. The disaster to the Confederates was the more mortifying from the fact that, during the long siege, daily bulletins from the commanding general had assured them that the position was impregnable to the naval attack in front and unassailable in the rear. There appears to have been no knowledge on the part of the Confederate officers that the canal was being constructed on the west side of the river. The crossing of the Federals from New Madrid had all the effect of a surprise, which was followed by a panic, and those who escaped in the general confusion suffered very much from hunger and fatigue.

The same day that Island No. 10 was surrendered, the issue of the battle of Shiloh was being determined, more than 100 miles distant, on the banks of the Tennessee.

CHAPTER XVII.

FROM DONELSON TO VICKSBURG.—OPERATIONS IN KENTUCKY, TENNESSEE, AND NORTHERN MISSISSIPPI.

The Confederate Military Situation early in 1862; Lack of Munitions of War; Expiration of Terms of Enlistment.—Davis's War Policy an Offensive-defensive Policy.—Confederate Plans of Operation.—Beauregard and the Army of the Mississippi.—Battle of Shiloh, or Pittsburg Landing.—General Grant's Position; Lack of defensive Preparations.—Confederate Success of April 6th.—Arrival of Re-enforcements.—Defeat of the Confederates.—Halleck's Arrival at Pittsburg Landing; Reorganization of the Army.—Advance against Corinth.—Colonel Elliott's Expedition.—Capture of Memphis.—Naval Contest on the River.—Mitchell's Campaign in Northern Alabama.

Kirby Smith and Bragg North of the Tennessee.—Guerrilla Warfare.—John Morgan.—Invasion of Kentucky. — Battle at Richmond, Kentucky. — Excitement in Cincinnati and Louisville. — Kirby Smith's Proclamation.—Bragg's Movements; Capture of Munfordsville; the Race for Louisville.—Buell's Army at Louisville.—Tragic End of General Nelson.—Bragg's Proclamation to the People of the Northwest.—Junction of the two Confederate Armies.—Bragg's Retreat.—Battle of Perryville.—Evacuation of Cumberland Gap.

Grant's Army in Northern Mississippi.—Battles of Iuka and Corinth.—Grant's Advance along the Central Mississippi Railroad.—General Hovey's Expedition.—Confederate Occupation of Holly Springs.

Rosecrans in command of the Department of the Cumberland.—His Campaign for the Defense of Nashville.—Battle of Murfreesborough, or Stone River.—Retrospect of Political Events in Tennessee.—Governor Johnson's Administration.

AFTER the evacuation of Nashville, Albert Sidney Johnston's army had fallen back to Murfreesborough. This position covered the approach into East Tennessee. The Federal plan of the campaign clearly did not contemplate an advance in that direction, for, although such an advance would afford relief to many suffering Unionists, still, for that reason alone it was not worth while to forego certain obvious military advantages connected with a campaign pushed directly southward toward Corinth. The principal of these advantages was the celerity of movement which was possible in an advance up the Tennessee River, and there was added to this the greater facility of obtaining supplies. An attempt was made by the Confederates to anticipate this advance by the fortification of Pittsburg Landing, a few miles from the southern border of Tennessee. This attempt was frustrated by the prompt action of two of Foote's gun-boats securing that point as a base of operations for General Grant's column, which advanced about the middle of March. This column consisted of five divisions, under Smith, McClernand, Wallace, Sherman, and Hurlbut. The two latter, made up chiefly of Ohio troops, had been added since the capture of Donelson. It took eighty-two transports to convey this army with its material of war. Savannah, a few miles below Pittsburg, was made the grand dépôt for supplies, which were drawn from St. Louis and Cairo. General Buell's army had its head-quarters at Nashville, on the Cumberland, more than a hundred and twenty miles distant. Both armies were now under a single department, created by the President's order of March 11, and designated the Department of the Mississippi. To this department also belonged General Pope's command, and General Hunter's, in Kansas. The supervision of the Department of the Mississippi was given to General Halleck.

In the mean time the Confederate government had been making a great effort to reorganize its military forces in the field. In the first stage of the war troops had been enlisted only for the short period of twelve months, and during the early months of 1862 this term was expiring. Many of these re-enlisted. Calls were issued upon the states—upon Mississippi for seven regiments, upon Alabama for twelve, upon Georgia for 12,000 men, upon North Carolina for five regiments. These new levies, with the re-enlisted men, were all in the field by the 1st of April. All leaves of absence were revoked. Provision was also made for bringing into the army by conscription all able-bodied men between the ages of eighteen and thirty-five; those between these ages already in the army were compelled to remain.

Tennessee being the especial arena of the war in the West, her governor, Isham G. Harris, made extraordinary efforts to bring men into the field from that state. Before February 20 he had organized and put in the field fifty-nine regiments of infantry. He now proposed to "prepare for efficient service in the field the whole military strength of the state." As yet the war had done little toward exhausting the fighting material of the Confederacy. But few sanguinary battles had been fought. It has not been seldom that a single European battle has put out of combat a larger number of men than had been disabled or captured in the Confederate armies before April 1, 1862, and the number of captured had been considerably larger than that of the disabled. Even the most martial class of Southern fighting men, those who were readiest to volunteer, and who became fittest officers in the field, still remained almost intact. The streets of the larger towns and cities of the South were still thronged with able-bodied young men. The Confederate President urged as his plea for conscription not the fact that volunteer service was likely to prove inadequate, but that it confined the burden of the war to the most patriotic class of citizens; he proposed by conscription merely to regulate the supply of force, so that an effective reserve might be held back to await a future exigency.

copper, for a battery of six pieces. The bells furnished from Fredericksburg alone sufficed for two such batteries. Beauregard issued a similar notice to the people of the Southwest, which met with a prompt response. The public prints of the South were full of offers made by Southern women to give to the government all the bell-metal which could be gathered from their kitchen furniture. Lead for bullets was also scarce, and one lady sent the lead weight attached to the striking part of her clock to help supply this deficiency. Subsequently, munitions of war were brought in large quantities from abroad, some of which came through Atlantic ports, and a large quantity by way of Matamoras, on the Rio Grande; so that at the close of 1862 there was no longer any marked deficiency.

The general plan of military operations adopted by Davis, and which now began to be clearly developed, was an offensive-defensive policy; at any rate and always to check the Federal column of advance on a line as far northward as could be safely chosen, and to seize upon every opportunity for a counter-advance which should carry the war into the loyal states—this was the theory upon which the war was to be conducted by the Confederacy. Considering the main purpose of the revolution itself, and the circumstances under which it was undertaken, this policy was eminently wise. The war had been begun, on the part of the revolutionists, to secure the empire of slavery over a vast section of territory; for its support it rested upon the wealth of the slaveholding class, and the power which that wealth gave this class over the poor whites of the South. Undertaken in the interest of wealth and power, it was an unpopular war. The first principle controlling the conduct of the war was that every slave state must be retained within the bounds of the Confederacy, and as much of the Territories as could be held. The second principle was that the war must be removed as far as possible from the Southern states, partly because this would give the Confederacy a bold military front, but chiefly because the people, with the war at their thresholds, and levying upon them its utmost burden of want and horror, could not safely be trusted. With the presence of Federal armies on Southern soil the old Union sentiment would revive, the popular respect for the national flag would return, and the people, in conjunction with the Federal government, would turn the tables against the slaveholders. There would thus be a revolution within a revolution, in which event that class which was most directly interested in the war would suffer the entire burden of loss and shame. If the revolution had been a popular movement, then the problem involved would have been mainly a military one, unembarrassed by political entanglements. In that case, the more pressing the demand for sacrifice of property or life, the more firm and sacred would have been the purpose to resist invasion. Under the circumstances, therefore, Davis's plan was wise. Other plans there might have been displaying greater military sagacity, but there was none which promised so much as this one.

This plan was one which we have termed offensive-defensive. But in the early months of 1862 only the defensive features could have been developed, and even these were developed under great difficulties, such as have been already detailed. The armies of the Union immediately available for conflict considerably outnumbered the revolutionary armies. This relation was reversed in a few months by the action of the Confederate conscription law. But this law did not begin to affect the army until early in June. Now every thing must depend upon the new levies of volunteers.

THE WAR IN KENTUCKY AND TENNESSEE.

The principal difficulty now attending the military operations of the Confederates in the West, as in the East, was the lack of munitions. At the beginning of the war the seizure of all Federal forts along the coast had furnished material for a short period of war. But the Federal expeditions directed against important points on the sea-board soon called into requisition all the heavy guns thus captured. The Confederate factories were not yet adequate to supply the pressing demand either for small-arms or heavy artillery. Of the sixty regiments furnished by Tennessee, the government had only been able to arm but 15,000; the rest were armed with old rifles and shot-guns furnished by citizens. At Fort Henry, Donelson, New Madrid, and Island No. 10, hundreds of heavy guns and large numbers of small-arms had fallen into the hands of the Federals. The systematic evasion of the blockade, which, at a later period, contributed largely to the supply of the Confederate armies in war material, did not yet exist. Saltpetre for the manufacture of gunpowder was so scarce, and its possession so completely monopolized by speculators, that the Confederate Secretary of War, on the 4th of February, issued an order that all military commanders should impress the saltpetre in every district where it was found, paying therefor at the rate of 40 cents per pound. Then, again, in regard to the manufacture of light artillery, although there was an abundance of copper, there was not enough tin to convert the copper into bronze. The Ordnance Bureau, therefore, solicited from citizens the use of all bells which could be spared. The reason of this was that bells contained so large an amount of tin in their composition; a ton of bell-metal being sufficient, with the proper amount of

The defensive plan which, under these circumstances, was adopted by the Confederates, was a simple one. Two routes were open to the Federal advance, along two separate systems of railroad communication. One of these—the Georgia system—centred in Atlanta. The other, which drained the states of Alabama and Mississippi, and was connected with the Georgia system by means of the line eastward from Montgomery, had no one vital centre, and its destruction would therefore involve a more complex and extended campaign. The natural approach to the one system was through Chattanooga—to the other through Corinth and Memphis. Buell's army, at Nashville, threatened rather the one; Grant's, at Pittsburg, threatened rather the other. Johnston, so long as he remained at Murfreesborough, covered the approach to Chattanooga, and a large column was being gathered at Corinth to oppose Grant. The Federal armies united would outnumber the Confederate, and this fact favored a concentration either in East or West Tennessee. Almost every military consideration dictated an advance on Corinth from Pittsburg. Johnston, fully aware of these considerations, did not long remain at Murfreesborough.

On the 5th of March, General Beauregard, who had just left Island No. 10 to its fate, assumed command of the Confederate forces in the Department of the Mississippi. In an address to his soldiers issued that day from Jackson, he said that the Confederate losses since the commencement of the war were about the same as those sustained by the national arms, and that for the reverses lately experienced the enemy must be made to atone. He wish-

GENERAL BUELL CROSSING DUCK RIVER AT COLUMBIA, TO RE-ENFORCE GRANT.

SHILOH MEETING HOUSE.

PITTSBURGH LANDING.

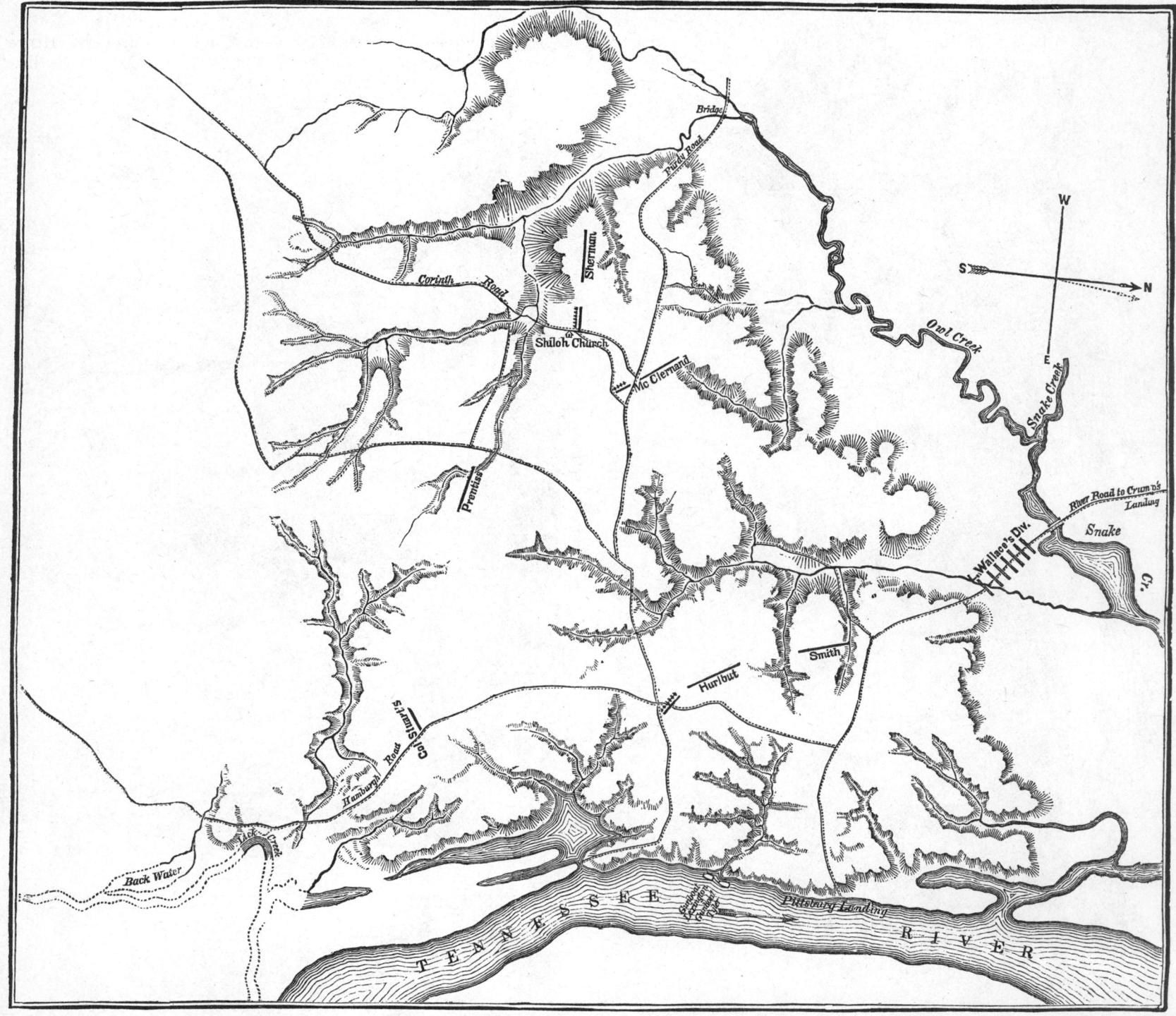

PLAN OF THE BATTLE OF SHILOH, OR PITTSBURG LANDING.

ed those who shrunk from the task to transfer their arms to braver and firmer hands, and to return home—a request which, at a later period, no Confederate officer would have dared to make lest it should be complied with. Beauregard's army consisted of troops which had been in service for a few months in Tennessee and the adjacent states, to which large additions were daily being made. He had for his associates in command Generals Bragg and Polk, both of whom brought re-enforcements to his commands. Bragg had evacuated Pensacola in January for the more perfect defense of Mobile, and had now brought up a "fine corps of troops" from that city to Beauregard's assistance. Polk brought his entire command, with the exception of the detachment left on the Mississippi. Johnston, too, was already on the march from Murfreesborough with an army of veterans. By the 1st of April the united army was well in hand in the vicinity of Corinth, holding the Mobile and Ohio and the Memphis and Charleston Railroads. Beauregard commanded the entire army, which was divided into three corps under Polk, Bragg, and Hardee.

Not until the 28th of March did Buell leave Nashville. Grant's army was located on the south side of the Tennessee River, only eighteen miles from the combined armies of Johnston and Beauregard, who had already perfected their arrangements for an attack. It was three days before Buell's army had crossed Duck River, and then they were ninety miles from Grant. The enemy had every advantage, if he could only bring up his three corps and compel a battle, which must terminate disastrously to the Federal column, so inferior in numbers, at Pittsburg. Why, with this overwhelming advantage, Beauregard did not precipitate a battle with greater promptness, will always be an enigma to the historian. It was known, Beauregard says, in his report of the battle, as early as the 2d of April, that Buell was on his way to join Grant. Orders were issued at one o'clock on the morning of the 3d for the movement, and there were only eighteen miles between Beauregard and Grant. Beauregard might have moved even sooner than this. The only reason he gives for not doing so is the "want of general officers needful for the proper organization of divisions and brigades of an army brought thus suddenly together." He had had nearly a month in which to supply this want, and it is to be supposed that Johnston's column was already properly organized and officered. At least it is certain that the army was no better off in this respect on the 2d than it was two or three days ear-

lier. There was considerable delay in the movement. The orders issued by General Beauregard on the morning of the 3d contemplated that, on the 4th, the three corps would have reached the vicinity of Shiloh Church, so that an attack might be made on the 5th; a not very difficult undertaking, considering the short distance to be traversed. But the delays on the first day were great, and a severe rain-storm on the 4th interposed a farther impediment, so that it was not until late on Saturday afternoon of the 5th that the army reached the intersection of the road from Pittsburg to Hamburg. It must be remembered, however, that the difficulties in the way of Beauregard were also impediments in an equal degree to Buell's march. Yet the latter had arrived at Savannah, seven miles from Pittsburg, with the advance of his army, on the evening of the 5th.

Turning now to General Grant's position, we find it most vulnerable to attack. Pittsburg Landing is a narrow ravine, with high bluffs on either side. Farther back from the river the country is broken and thickly wooded, with here and there an open field. On the very eve of battle we find Grant's army encamped without a single breast-work or a single protection for a battery. The time had not yet come when the armies on either side had learned the all-important lesson of the value of artificial defense; but it was inexcusable that a permanent encampment should have been so entirely destitute of intrenchments. There were two gun-boats on the river—the Tyler and Lexington. Grant's advance line, consisting of three divisions, under Sherman, Prentiss, and McClernand, extended, without any judicious arrangement, from Owl Creek, on the right, to Lick Creek, on the left. The arrangement on the left was extremely faulty. Here one brigade of Sherman's division, under Stuart, was posted beneath bluffs which commanded the position. The rest of Sherman's force was three or four miles distant, away off to the right of Shiloh Church. This gap was only filled by Prentiss's division, as McClernand's was massed close up to Sherman's left and rear. Behind, and nearer the Landing, were the divisions of Hurlbut and Smith. The latter was commanded by W. H. L. Wallace, in the absence of General Smith, who was suffering still from a wound received at the siege of Donelson. At Crump's Landing, some miles below on the river, lay Lew. Wallace's division.

Such was Grant's position when it was attacked by the enemy, Sunday morning, the 6th of April. The attack was made in three lines. The first was under Hardee, with one of Bragg's brigades; the second advanced in the rear of the first, under Bragg; while Polk's corps, with a reserve, under Breckinridge, in its rear, formed the third. The entire force attacking was estimated by Beauregard as a little over 40,000 men. The first blow, falling upon Prentiss and Sherman, amounted almost to a surprise. The pickets were driven in, and, close upon their heels, the enemy followed. There was the least possible preparation for an attack. Prominent officers were still in bed. Breakfasts were being prepared, as if no such an event as a battle were at hand; and there was an entire lack of readiness in all details. Sherman, although, like the rest, taken by surprise, not having his men under arms until his advance guard had been driven back upon the main body, yet acted with great promptness and coolness. He called immediately to McClernand to come to his support on the left; sent word to Prentiss that the enemy was in his (Sherman's) front in force, and called upon Hurlbut to come up to Prentiss's aid. Leaving out Stuart's brigade, which must, under the circumstances, be left to its separate commander, being on the extreme left near Lick Creek, Sherman's division was drawn up in the vicinity of Shiloh Church. McDowell's brigade held the extreme right, with a battery guarding the bridge on the Purdy road over Owl Creek. Next to the left, and just west of the Corinth road, on which stood Shiloh Church, was Buckland's brigade. Hildebrand's brigade was on the east side of the road, with the church between him and Buckland. In front of Sherman's position ran a creek along his entire line. The position was good for defense, and, if advantage had been taken of it, and an abatis been constructed, the approach of the enemy up the slope to his encampment might have been repelled with ease. As it was, however, there was not even a breast-work, while the woods in front afforded cover to the enemy. Along the road in rear of the church Sherman had eight companies of cavalry, used to service at Donelson. A little after seven o'clock the general rode along his line on the left and became directly exposed to the fire, the enemy having already gained the woods in front, where he was massing his forces for attack. Here his orderly was killed. Appler's regiment—the Fifty-third Ohio—held the extreme left, and was ordered to hold it at all hazards, being encouraged to do so by the presence of a battery on his right, which was supported by three of McClernand's regiments. Two other Ohio regiments were on Appler's left, also having a battery on their right, at the church.

The battle was fairly begun at about eight o'clock in the forenoon. In excellent order, Hardee's columns advanced out of the woods in Appler's front, a portion of them passing obliquely to the left to occupy the huge gap between Prentiss and McClernand, others advancing directly against Sherman, and all covered by a heavy artillery fire from the woods, to which the two batteries already mentioned, in Hildebrand's front, responded. Soon Sherman heard sounds of musketry and artillery away to the left, indicating that Prentiss was engaged. In less than an hour these sounds grew ominous, clearly announcing that Prentiss was falling back. Sherman's own left, too, was being broken. Appler had fired but two rounds when he fell back, and was heard from no more during the battle, the movements of his regiment from this point becoming what Hildebrand, in his report, styles "general." The regiment at his right followed soon, and the battery posted between them was thus compelled to retire, with a loss of three guns, McClernand's three regiments being unable to support it. Hildebrand's own regiment then breaking up completed the rout on the left of the church. This necessitated the retreat of the battery at the church, and the abandonment of Sherman's entire encampment. So complete was the demoralization of Hildebrand's brigade, that the officer commanding saw no more of it that day. A new line was formed by Buckland and McDowell on the Hamburg road, a short distance in rear of camp, but was no sooner formed than it was abandoned with the loss of a battery. The only thing now to be done was to fall back still nearer to the river and close up on McClernand's right. This movement was fortunate for McClernand, who was now being hard pressed. McDowell's brigade was thrown against the enemy's left flank. Here the struggle was maintained until three o'clock P.M., the men taking advantage of every cover which the nature of the ground afforded.

On the left the Confederates met even greater success than on the right. Prentiss, as we have seen, was attacked nearly at the same time as Sherman. At this point, also, the surprise had been more complete than on the right. Prentiss's command consisted of seven regiments, nearly one half of which were from Missouri. The line was formed on the open field, while the enemy were sheltered by woods. On both flanks the Confederate columns advanced. A portion of Bragg's corps came in on Hardee's right. Prentiss was soon driven from his position; his rear was gained by the enemy, and he himself, with nearly half of his division, were captured. Before ten o'clock Prentiss's encampment was in the enemy's possession. Stuart's isolated brigade was now placed in a perilous position. McArthur's brigade, of W. H. L. Wallace's command, started for his assistance, but, coming in too far on the right, became involved in the retrograde movement of Prentiss's division. Stuart was on the Hamburg road, and a column of the enemy which came in on the field by this route attacked him just after he had withdrawn so as to be out of Bragg's way. Unable to hold his position, which was commanded by high bluffs, he fell back from ridge to ridge, making gallant resistance at each point, until at noon he was completely disorganized, and withdrew from the field.

In the mean while the columns which had swept aside Prentiss's division bent their whole force upon McClernand's position. This division was the best and strongest in the advanced line. It numbered twelve regiments, all but one composed of Illinoisans. The other two divisions in front consisted of raw men; but McClernand's division had borne the brunt of the Confederate assault at Fort Donelson, and in some measure was used to the hor-

rors of the battle-field. But having no efficient support on either hand, and the enemy being able to bring forward fresh troops continually, McClernand fell back, though not until he had lost more than half his artillery. His retreat was in good order, bringing him out at length on a line with Hurlbut. Thus by noon the entire Federal advance was driven in, routed for the most part, leaving three large encampments in the hands of the enemy, and having sustained heavy loss in artillery.

Two divisions alone now remained intact, Hurlbut's and W. H. L. Wallace's. These alone barred the victorious foe in front from the dépôts of ammunition and the transports. Wallace was now on Hurlbut's left, partially filling up the gap caused by Prentiss's rout. Hurlbut, for the sake of a better position, abandoned his camp and fell to the dense wood in the rear, where from this cover he had an advantage in repelling the enemy's advance across the open fields in his front. Soon after Wallace also fell back, and at half past four o'clock the entire Federal army was crowded into a narrow semicircular area extending about half a mile from the Landing.

For eight hours the battle had lasted, and yet the Confederates, notwithstanding their success, still lacked a complete victory. They could see on every side many of the material fruits of victory, such, indeed, as rarely ever attends a decisive triumph; but the business still before them gave them no leisure to secure these fruits. The work of the day would not be done until the Federals were swept from the field—from the Landing itself—as they had been from their camps. Besides, notwithstanding they had inflicted heavy injuries on Grant's army, their plan of battle had failed. It had been Johnston's design to leave an outlet of escape toward the north down the river, and to drive Grant's army in this direction by massing overwhelming columns against his left. Instead of this, the Federals had fallen back on either side upon the centre, and still presented an obstinate front. One circumstance had especially daunted the Confederates. At half past two o'clock their commander in the field had been killed while leading a charge against Wallace's division. He had received a Minie ball in his leg which severed an artery, and soon died from loss of blood. This had led to some confusion and delay on the most critical part of the field. Beauregard, who was suffering from indisposition, was then obliged to take the field, and, in the mean while, the Federals had fallen back to their last line about the Landing, and organized their scattered commands.

General Albert Sidney Johnston, the deceased Confederate commander, had had a somewhat eventful military career. His military education was completed at West Point in 1820. He served in the Black Hawk War, after which he left the army until 1836, when he emigrated to Texas, arriving there shortly after the battle of San Jacinto. He then entered the Texan army as a private soldier. Soon he superseded General Felix Houston in the chief command. This led to a duel between the two officers, in which Johnston was wounded. In 1838 he was appointed Secretary of War in

ALBERT SIDNEY JOHNSTON.

HAMBURG LANDING.—COMMISSARY DÉPÔT ON THE TENNESSEE.

Texas, and the next year carried on a successful campaign against the Cherokees. He warmly advocated the annexation of Texas to the United States. In 1846 he commanded the volunteer Texan Rifles; was six months afterward an inspector general on General Butler's staff. President Taylor appointed him paymaster in 1849 with the rank of major, and upon the passage by Congress of the act authorizing the raising of additional regiments, he was made colonel of the Second Cavalry. In 1857 he was placed at the head of the forces sent to Utah, and was soon made the commander of that district. He resigned his position in the army at the beginning of the civil war, and upon his arrival at Richmond received a general's commission and the command of the Confederate Department of the Mississippi. He died upon the battle-field for lack of prompt surgical attendance. His death was at first carefully concealed from the army, and it was given out that it was not he, but George M. Johnston, provisional governor of Kentucky, who had been killed. The latter, who participated in the battle, was also mortally wounded.[1]

The Federal situation was discouraging, but far from hopeless. W. H. L. Wallace had been mortally wounded. Prentiss, with a good part of his division, had been captured. Half of the artillery of the army had been lost. The river, from Savannah to Pittsburg, was lined with stragglers, who were panic-stricken and unfit for fighting. Lew. Wallace's division of veteran troops, which had been expected all day from Crump's Landing, had mistaken its route, and had not yet reached the battle-field; and the whole army was now huddled together in the vicinity of the encampment which had been occupied by W. H. L. Wallace. The hospitals along the ridge near the Landing were full to overflowing with killed and wounded. All day the battle had been fought without any definite plan; at its opening Grant himself was miles away at Savannah, and when he came upon the field, at ten A.M., he saw nothing better to be done than to oppose the most stubborn resistance to the enemy. But the enemy had done his worst and spent his force. His loss in killed, wounded, and missing nearly equaled Grant's. Grant's dépôts of ammunition were still intact, and there was not the slightest doubt on his part that he would be able to hold with perfect ease the line which he had adopted. In this state of affairs General Grant visited Sherman's line. The two generals estimated their loss, and a plan was formed for future operations. The time was to come when these two officers were together to wield the united armies of the republic against the revolutionary forces which now, at the sunset of this 6th of April, were so defiant and confident of success. Grant naturally recurred to the battle of Donelson. He said to Sherman that, at a certain period of the battle, he saw that either side was ready to give way if the other showed a bold front. He

had taken the opportunity, and had ordered an advance all along the line, and the enemy had been beaten. It was just such a crisis now. The two instances were very nearly analogous. At Donelson, Pillow had succeeded in turning the Federal left upon its centre, driving one entire division from its camps. The reverse in the present instance was greater; but here, as before, the enemy had spent his force in exhausting charges, and a few fresh troops would be certain to turn the tide. These were now near at hand under Lew. Wallace. It was then decided that the army, thus re-enforced, should on the morrow assume the offensive.

In the mean time the defensive position at the Landing had been strengthened. All the artillery of the army had been placed by Colonel Webster, Grant's chief of staff, to cover every approach. For some time there had been a lull in the firing. The enemy was marshaling his columns for the final charge of the day. It was not long before these columns approached over the broken ground in front. But the fire from twenty guns checked their advance. They could make no headway against it. Suddenly, too, there burst forth against them a rapid and overwhelming fire from the two gun-boats, which had been waiting all day for an opportunity to share in the battle. This opportunity was now afforded by the position of General Grant's army. This new element in the conflict discomposed the Confederates, who were compelled to withdraw from the field.

That night Beauregard's head-quarters were at Shiloh Church. Just at dark Lew. Wallace came up. A portion of Buell's army had arrived. Buell came to Sherman at the close of the interview between the latter and General Grant, and assured him that he could bring 18,000 fresh men for to-morrow's battle. All night long these men were crossing in the transports. Nelson and Crittenden had been able to get on the field just at the close of the last repulse of the enemy. These divisions were formed near the Landing, in a line perpendicular to the river, stretching up to the Corinth road. This line was continued in the same direction west of the road, where Hurlbut, McClernand, and Sherman took up their position. Among these last three divisions were apportioned the fragments which were left of Prentiss's and W. H. L. Wallace's. Lew. Wallace came in on the extreme right, continuing the line to the neighborhood of Shiloh Church. During the night McCook's division of Buell's army took the position on Crittenden's right, close up to the Corinth road. At nine o'clock it began to rain—a fortunate circumstance for those of the wounded who had been left on the field of battle, and were suffering from thirst. The gun-boats kept up an annoying fire all night, thus depriving the enemy of that sleep which was so necessary in view of the duties to be met in the morning. It was owing to this cannonade that the enemy was found the next morning to have withdrawn from the camps which he had captured on Sunday.

The battle of Monday did not compare either in length or severity with that of the previous day. The advance was along either side of the Corinth road, Grant on the right and Buell on the left. It would have been better, doubtless, if this disposition had been exactly reversed, as in that event the hardest of the fighting would have fallen upon Buell's fresh men; for, while the enemy had yesterday massed against the Federal left, he now directed his heaviest column against the right, which was held in great part by the jaded troops of Grant's army.

Beauregard was now outnumbered, and, although he made a gallant resist-

<hr />

[1] The following extract from an article published in *Harper's Weekly*, January 30, 1858, shows in what esteem General Johnston was then held in the army:

"Colonel Johnston is now in the matured vigor of manhood. He is above six feet in height, strongly and powerfully formed, with a grave, dignified, and commanding presence. His features are strongly marked, showing his Scottish lineage, and denote great resolution and composure of character. His complexion, naturally fair, is, from exposure, a deep brown. His habits are abstemious and temperate, and no excess has impaired his powerful constitution. His mind is clear, strong, and well cultivated. His manner is courteous, but rather grave and silent. He has many devoted friends, but they have been won and secured rather by the native dignity and nobility of his character than by his powers of address. He is a man of strong will and ardent temper, but his whole bearing testifies the self-control he has acquired. As a soldier he stands very high in the opinion of the army. As an instance of this it may be mentioned that, in a large assembly of officers and gentlemen, the gallant and impetuous Worth, when asked who was the best soldier he had ever known, replied, 'I consider Sidney Johnston the best soldier I ever knew.'"

The General Hospital at Hamburg.

Commissary Store Boats.

The Interior of a Sanitary Steamer.

Landing Cannon.

Moving Siege Guns to our lines.

GENERAL HALLECK'S ARMY ON THE TENNESSEE.

FORT PILLOW.

Since the Confederates had taken the initiative of attack for the purpose of defeating one of two armies against which, combined, there was little hope of successful defense, and had failed in that purpose, the result of the battle, so far as they were concerned, was equivalent to a defeat. As a test of force it afforded encouragement to the Federal commanders. General Halleck determined to reorganize the armies under Grant and Buell, and to re-enforce them with every regiment that could be spared from other portions of the field. He started from St. Louis the very day after the battle. In less than two weeks after his arrival on the field, General Pope's division, 25,000 strong, had been brought up from New Madrid, and before the close of April the three columns, under their respective commanders, were ordered to hold themselves in readiness to move. The army thus gathered together under Halleck's command numbered more than a hundred thousand men. Beauregard, also, had increased his force by calling Price and Van Dorn from Arkansas, who

ance in the early part of the day, he had by noon brought into action his entire reserve force, and it was evident that he could neither hold his ground nor secure the fruits of yesterday's victory. He withdrew from the field in good order, falling back on Corinth.

We have called the attack on Sunday morning a surprise. General Grant claims that this was not the case, and that, if the enemy had sent him word when and where he would attack, he could not have been better informed. "Skirmishing," he says, "had been going on for two days between our reconnoitring parties and the enemy's advance." It is certain, however, that Johnston's attack had all the practical effect of a surprise. Grant himself admits: "I did not believe that they intended to make a determined attack, but simply to make a reconnoissance." It was just this determined attack, preceded by only a feeble and imperfect warning, which tended more than any thing to the Federal reverse on Sunday. A larger number of Grant's army were new troops as compared with the Confederate army. The enemy had the important advantage of attack also, while Grant's command had not even ordinary advantages in the way of defense. Thus the panic arose. With the exception of McClernand's division, there was not a regiment in the advance line, on the morning of the 6th, which had ever seen a battle, and Johnston gave these men their first impression of the fury of a charge, which came upon them so suddenly as immediately to produce demoralization. It was not the fault of field and company officers that this happened, for these officers did their best to rally their broken regiments, and themselves remained on the field after they had been totally abandoned by their commands.

The battle had no decisive effect on the campaign. The losses were not far from equal on both sides. The Confederate loss Beauregard estimates at nearly 11,000; that of the Federals was about 3000 more; and this difference may be explained by the number of prisoners lost in Prentiss's division. As to the forces engaged, there are no exact official estimates given on the Federal side. Grant had about forty regiments the first day, one fourth of which, at the lowest estimate, were of no use on the field. Buell and Lew. Wallace added to this force, on the second day, about 25,000 men.

added an army which, if we are to believe a statement made to his soldiers by General Bragg, almost equaled "the Army of Shiloh." Bragg's entire address to his soldiers on May 5 indicates that the Confederate army at Corinth was quite equal to Halleck's. He says: "You will encounter him" [the enemy] "in your chosen position, strong by nature and improved by art, away from his main support and reliance, gun-boats and heavy batteries, and, for the first time in this war, with nearly equal numbers." He continues: "The slight reverses we have met on the sea-board have worked us good as well as evil; the brave troops so long retained there have hastened to swell your numbers; while the gallant Van Dorn and invincible Price, with the ever-successful Army of the West, are now in your midst, with numbers almost equaling the Army of Shiloh. We have, then, but to strike and destroy, and, as the enemy's whole resources are concentrated here, we shall not only redeem Tennessee, Kentucky, and Missouri at one blow, but open the portals of the whole Northwest." It must be admitted that Halleck's army was much superior to Beauregard's in artillery and equipments.

The roads south from Pittsburg were at this season of the year peculiarly difficult. At all times low and marshy, the country was now almost impassable; bridges which the enemy had burned had to be rebuilt; but, on the 3d of May, over comparatively dry roads, the army had advanced to within eight miles of Corinth. This place is twenty miles west of the Tennessee River, and somewhat farther from Pittsburg Landing. It is situated at the intersection of the Charleston and Mobile railroads. Between the small village and the Tennessee the country was broken, the roads across the marshes had been torn up, and the bridges destroyed. In the advance General Pope commanded the left, Buell the centre, and Grant the right; afterward the right was given to Thomas, Grant being made second in command. Pope's division was re-enforced with a division drawn from Curtis's Army of the Southwest. In order to prevent the re-enforcement of Beauregard, and to cut off his retreat, an expedition was sent out under Colonel Elliott, consisting of two cavalry regiments, with orders to strike the Mobile and Ohio Railroad in the vicinity of Booneville, and destroy the track, so as to

COLONEL ELLET'S RAM FLEET.

CLOSING SCENE OF THE NAVAL FIGHT BEFORE MEMPHIS.

effectually prevent its use for the next few days. Elliott, it was intended, should then make his way through Northern Alabama, reporting there to General Mitchell at Huntsville. General Mitchell's division of Buell's army, instead of moving with the others to Pittsburg Landing, had, just before the battle of Shiloh, pushed directly south into Northern Alabama. Elliott was partially successful, destroying a large number of locomotives and cars at Booneville.

Notwithstanding the confident tone with which Beauregard and Bragg had both addressed the army, indicating that Corinth must not be abandoned without a desperate struggle, that place was evacuated at the close of May without any considerable conflict with the Federal forces marching against it. Not a piece of ordnance was left behind.

At the time of the evacuation the water was falling so low in the Tennessee River that Halleck could no longer rely upon his water-base, and was obliged to resort to railway communications. This caused great delay, and the enemy were able to withdraw no inconsiderable number of troops eastward for the defense of Richmond, then threatened by McClellan. But to give up Corinth was also to retire from Memphis.

Immediately after the surrender of Island No. 10, Commodore Foote, with his mortar boats and some transports, moved down the river against Fort Pillow. This and Forts Wright and Randolph were the fortifications guarding the approach to Memphis, which was seventy miles below Fort Pillow, and fifty-eight below Fort Randolph. Fort Pillow is situated on the First Chickasaw Bluffs on the Tennessee shore. These bluffs rise to the height of seventy-five or one hundred feet, and are broken by ravines. This point on the river is the first good position for defense below Island No. 10. The river here makes a wide bend around Plum Point, and immediately below, at the Bluffs, another bend, so that Fort Pillow commands several miles of the river both above and below. Upon the Second Chickasaw Bluffs stands Fort Randolph, with Fort Wright just above, so that these two works take up the line of defense where Fort Pillow leaves it off. Foote established his mortars at Craighead Point, opposite Fort Pillow, and three fourths of a mile distant. The bombardment commenced on the 17th of April by a fire from these mortars upon the fort and a small Confederate fleet in the vicinity of the latter. This attack was repeated daily, without any very sensible effect. In the mean time the Federal gun-boats lay at anchorage just out of range above the fort. There was no possibility of a co-operation of the land forces, at first on account of the height of the water in the river, and afterward because Pope's division was called upon to co-operate in the movement against Corinth. Pope's army of 20,000 men was withdrawn on the morning of the 17th to join Halleck's command at Pittsburg, which step, says Commodore Foote, "frustrated the best matured and most hopeful plans and expectations thus far formed in this expedition." Two regiments only, under the command of Colonel Fitch, were left to co-operate with the flotilla. The plan of attack proposed to be carried out, if Pope had remained, was, that a canal should be built on the Arkansas side, so as to enable the gun-boats and transports to get in the rear and thus cut off the Confederate batteries. Even with the small force left under Colonel Fitch, amounting

COLONEL ELLET'S RAM APPROACHING MEMPHIS.

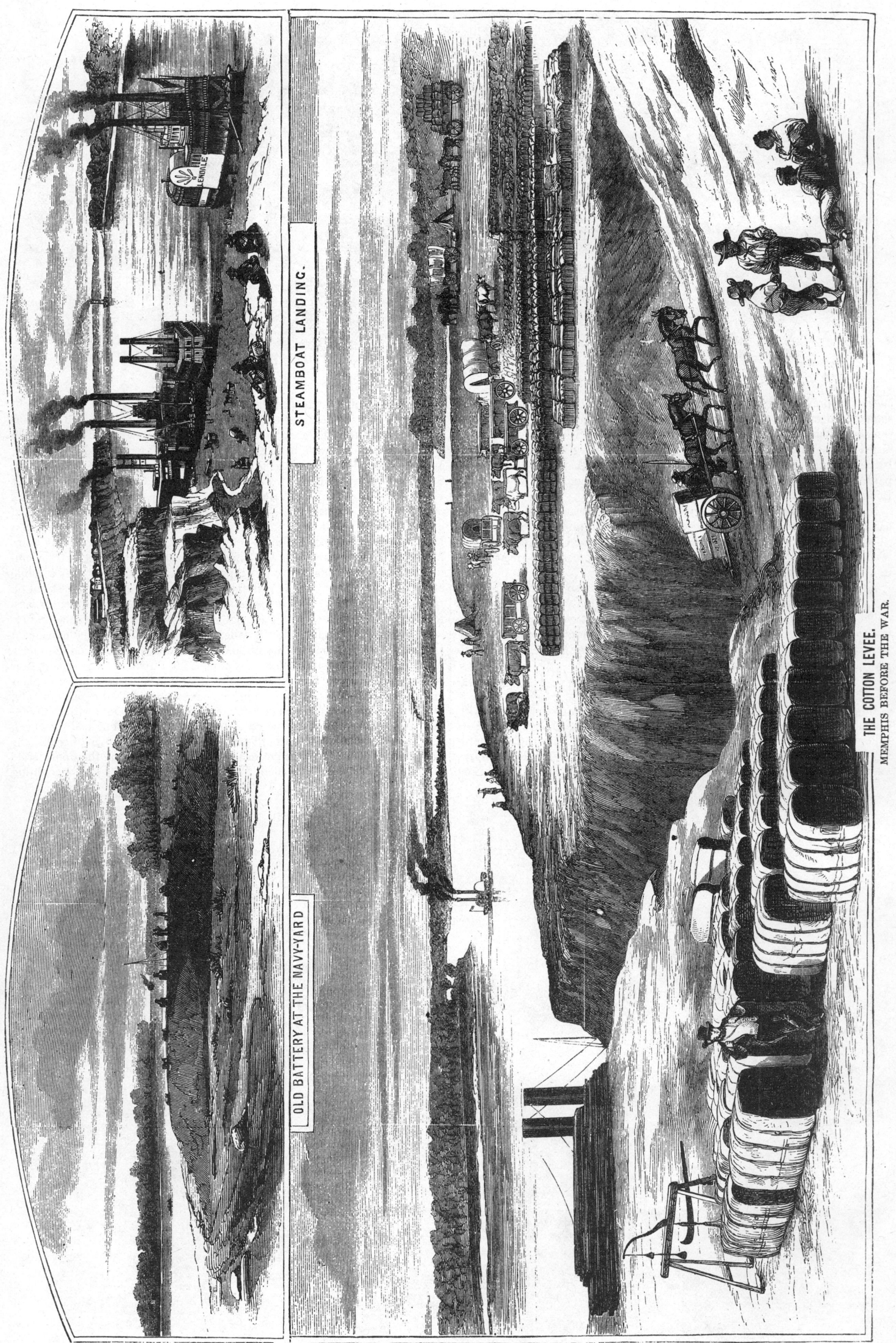

STEAMBOAT LANDING.

OLD BATTERY AT THE NAVY-YARD

THE COTTON LEVEE.
MEMPHIS BEFORE THE WAR.

JACKSON'S MONUMENT AT MEMPHIS.

to not more than 1200 men, an attempt was made to carry out this plan, but without success.

The circumstances in which Commodore Foote was placed greatly chafed his spirits. He expected, when he left New Madrid, to be able to capture Memphis within the space of one week, and the departure of Pope's army was, under these circumstances, a bitter disappointment. The wound which he had received at Fort Donelson added to his despondency. On the 14th of April he wrote to Secretary Welles:

"The effects of my wound have quite a dispiriting effect upon me from the increased inflammation and swelling of my foot and leg, which have induced a febrile action, depriving me of a good deal of sleep and energy. I can not give the wound that attention and rest it absolutely requires until this place is captured."

His position was one in which he could not make a formidable attack, and one even which occasioned him apprehension. His force consisted of seven iron-clad and one wooden gun-boat, sixteen mortar boats, "only available in throwing shells at a distance, and even worse than useless for defense," and the small land force under Colonel Fitch. Against him were nine Confederate gun-boats already at Fort Pillow, and ten others reported on their way to Memphis from the Lower Mississippi. He expected soon to hear of the arrival in his front of the heavy gun-boat Louisiana, just being completed at New Orleans. This boat occasioned him some alarm, though he had not much to fear from the others, most of which were wooden, though armed with heavy guns. Fort Pillow, according to his report, had not less than forty heavy guns. "Under these circumstances," he writes, "an attack on our part, unless we can first establish a battery below the fort under the protection of the gun-boats, would be extremely hazardous, al-

though its attempt might prove successful, and even be good policy under other circumstances; but it can hardly now be so regarded, as a disaster would place all that we have gained on this and other rivers at the mercy of the rebel fleet, unless the batteries designed to command the river from below are completed at No. 10, or at Columbus, which I very much doubt. I therefore hesitate about a direct attack upon this place now, more than I should were the river above properly protected." Commodore Foote doubtless retained a vivid recollection of his contest with the water-battery at Donelson. At New Madrid and Island No. 10 every thing had been made to depend upon a movement in the rear of the enemy's works. Such a movement was now scarcely possible. Even the tools necessary for cutting the proposed canal were not at hand, having been removed with Pope's army. Foote's indisposition, early in May, rendered it necessary for him to transfer the command of the Mississippi flotilla to Captain C. H. Davis. He returned to the East, and at Washington took the superintendence of the Bureau of Equipment until the summer of 1863, when he was appointed to supersede Admiral Dupont in the command of the South Atlantic squadron. While on his way to that destination he was taken ill, and died at New York on the 26th of June, 1863. His services in the West had been properly appreciated by the people and the government. He had been raised to the rank of rear-admiral, his commission dating from July 16, 1862.

On the 10th of May a naval action took place on the river between the Federal and Confederate fleets. The Confederate squadron consisted, according to Davis's report, of eight iron-clad steamers, four of which were fitted as rams from old New Orleans tow-boats, the upper works of which had been cut away, and their sides protected, in some instances, by railroad iron, and in others by bales of cotton, hooped and bound together by iron bands.

HOISTING THE NATIONAL FLAG OVER THE POST-OFFICE AT MEMPHIS.

HUNTSVILLE, ALABAMA.

These rams proceeded up the river and attacked the mortar boats. The gun-boat Cincinnati, under Commander Stembel, followed by the Mound City, under Commander Kilty, hurried up to the support of the mortar boats. The Cincinnati had hardly cut loose from the shore, and was in a position which prevented her from being easily handled, when the most formidable of the rams came up to close quarters. Twice the Cincinnati let fly her stern guns at the ram, but without effect, and the latter came against her with great force, although without effecting any serious damage. This blow enabled the Cincinnati to move out from shore, when she hurled broadside after broadside against the sides of her grim antagonist. The ram again trusted to her striking power, and the two vessels again struck with a violent blow, and, at the same moment, the ram received a full broadside from the gun-boat alongside, while on both sides there was a free discharge of musketry. At this crisis, and while all around him was in confusion, Commander Stembel shot the pilot on board the ram, and the next moment himself received a severe wound. But the ram was disabled and drifted down the stream. In the mean while the Mound City disabled two others of the enemy's vessels. The entire Confederate fleet had withdrawn before the action had lasted an hour. The Mound City and the Cincinnati were so badly crippled as to need repairing.

Fort Pillow was evacuated on the 4th of June, as a consequence of the evacuation of Corinth. Every thing of any value was either carried away or destroyed. All that now stood between the Federal force and Memphis was the Confederate fleet. Flag-officer Davis started immediately down the river, and, on the morning of the 6th, the enemy's fleet of eight vessels was discovered lying off the levee at Memphis. On both sides preparations were made for an immediate contest. Five gun-boats—the Benton, Cairo, Carondelet, Louisville, and St. Louis—with two vessels of the ram fleet, the Queen of the West and Monarch, under Colonel Ellet, moved down the river, the rams getting into action first. The Confederate fleet was ranged in two lines of battle. The contest was not long, lasting little more than an hour, and terminated in the destruction or capture of seven of the enemy's vessels. In the very beginning of the action the General Lovell was sunk by the Queen of the West, in the middle of the river, with most of her crew. The Beauregard and Little Rebel had their boilers blown up; the former went down, and the latter had to be abandoned by her crew. One boat, the Jeff. Thompson, took fire from the Federal shells, and burned to the water's edge. The General Price was run ashore and abandoned. The Sumter and Bragg were disabled and captured. A single boat—the Van Dorn—succeeded in effecting an escape. Only three men of the Federal flotilla were wounded in the engagement.

Memphis was immediately surrendered by the mayor, John Park; and Colonel Fitch, with his little command, took possession of the city. During the whole of the naval action the levee had been crowded with a throng of interested spectators. Not a few of these hoped that it might terminate in the triumph of the national arms. The capture of Memphis left the Confederates no large city in Tennessee. Indeed, with the exception of a small force in East Tennessee, about Chattanooga, Knoxville, and Cumberland Gap, there was not, at the time of the capture of Memphis, any Confederate army in the state. Beauregard's army had fallen back to Tupelo, about eighty miles south of Corinth, on the Mobile and Ohio Railroad, followed by the advance of the Federal army under General Pope. General Grant's army held the line of railroad skirting the southern boundary of Tennessee from Memphis to Corinth. Buell's column was already moving upon Chattanooga, which had been uncovered by Beauregard's retreat. In this direction, as we have already indicated, General Mitchell had been operating for the last two months, and had established himself at Huntsville, on the railroad connecting Memphis and Corinth with Chattanooga; but, for want of support, he had been obliged to withdraw from all territory occupied by him south of that point. On the 1st of May he wrote to the Secretary of War: "The campaign is ended, and I now occupy Huntsville in perfect security, while all of Alabama north of the Tennessee River floats no flag but that of the Union." When Buell moved against Chattanooga, Mitchell's command was given to General Rousseau, and General Mitchell received the command of Port Royal. Thus, about the middle of June, we find Southern Tennessee, from Memphis nearly to Chattanooga, held by three Federal armies, whose combined strength can not have been less than 125,000 men. Soon we shall see this line completely broken up by a formidable movement of the enemy in the rear.

Shortly after his retreat from Corinth, General Beauregard retired for a brief period from the army on account of ill health. His command was turned over to General Bragg, who forthwith prepared to assume the offensive. He began to move his army from Tupelo westward toward Chattanooga. One reason of this movement was to anticipate General Buell's march in the same direction; but Bragg had an ulterior purpose beyond that. He intended from Chattanooga to strike boldly into Kentucky. By this movement he expected not only to compel the abandonment by the Federals of their advanced positions, but also, by the aid of Kentuckians, to establish the Confederate government in Kentucky. He was certainly justified in assuming the offensive; for, although the Confederates had been steadily losing territory, they had, in the mean time, by this very contraction, been steadily gaining men. Detached forces had been drawn in from all parts of the Confederacy, and were available at the most critical points of conflict. The Conscription Act also had brought into the field large numbers of fighting men. The Federal armies, on the other hand, though, taken all together at this time, not far outnumbering the forces of the enemy, were scattered all along the rivers in the West, and all along the Atlantic coast. The advance southward of Halleck's army necessitated a series of detached garri-

JOHN MORGAN.

sons along the lines of railroad used for the transportation of supplies. These garrisons were made the more necessary on account of the guerrilla operations of the enemy, which in the summer of 1862 were especially troublesome in Kentucky.

Bragg's projected invasion was preceded by a series of guerrilla expeditions. The lower counties of Kentucky suffered chiefly from their ravages. Property was stolen, outrages of every sort were not unfrequently perpetrated upon Union citizens, bridges were burned, and even the friends of the Confederacy did not escape the lust of these desperadoes for plunder. The most successful of these expeditions was one undertaken by John Morgan, the most noted guerrilla leader of the war. Morgan was a native of Kentucky. When the war broke out he was a planter of considerable means, but he left his plantation and became attached to General Hardee's division of the Confederate army. He had protected Johnston's rear in the retreat from Nashville. Soon after that event he gathered about him a band of daring Kentuckians, whom he led in a series of predatory operations against railroads, supply-trains, and loyal citizens. His own regiment was joined on this occasion by some partisan rangers from Georgia, a Texas squadron, and two companies of Tennessee cavalry. He started from Knoxville July 4, and his expedition was accomplished in less than one month. During that time he penetrated two hundred and fifty miles within the Federal lines, captured a large number of defenseless towns, took a large number of small-arms, and destroyed a great amount of valuable military property. On the 11th of July Morgan had reached Lebanon, a short distance south of Frankfort. The place was protected by less than a hundred men, and fell easily into Morgan's possession. Here large government dépôts, filled with sugar, coffee, and other provisions, were destroyed. Morgan proceeded as far northward as Cynthiana, where the garrison was surrounded and captured, after a desperate conflict with superior numbers. This put an end to Morgan's successful career. He was soon overtaken at Paris, and defeated by a Federal force under the command of General Green C. Smith. At the same time Forrest was engaged in an expedition of a similar character. On the 13th of July, the day Morgan entered Cynthiana, Murfreesborough, in Tennessee, was surrendered to Forrest. The surrender was attended by the capture of an entire Michigan regiment. The impetuous onset of the Confederate cavalry appears to have at once nearly settled the fate of the town. The force defending the place no doubt exceeded Forrest's command. According to General Buell's report, the attack might have been effectually repelled. Encouraged by these successes, Colonel Morgan, who had retreated into Tennessee, even ventured to attack Clarksville, on the Cumberland River, below Nashville, and succeeded in capturing that place, with a large quantity of military stores.

The retreat of Beauregard's army from Corinth was without doubt a most judicious movement. It was, in great measure, a surprise to General Halleck, who was thus compelled to form new combinations. Bragg, who came into command on the 16th of June, had in this way gained time not only to re-enforce his army, but even to prepare for a formidable movement into Kentucky. Every day brought some new increment to his army through the operation of the Conscription Act. As we have said previously, the Confederacy had suffered very little from the exhaustion of its fighting population; and, in regard to the munitions of war, there soon ceased to be any

great uneasiness, for every week now brought into the several Confederate ports artillery of various calibre and small-arms without number; and, even apart from this foreign supply, there were already in operation, at Richmond and the great military centres in Georgia and the Carolinas, extensive manufactories devoted to the production of all the needed material for conducting the war. The situation since the early spring had wonderfully changed. The prospects of the Confederacy were every day growing brighter. The vast combinations which McClellan had formed for the capture of Richmond had miscarried, as will be shown in the subsequent chapter. The government established by the revolutionists had shown itself competent to meet emergencies which but a few months since had threatened its speedy overthrow. That government, although it had failed to obtain recognition from the great European powers, had elicited signal marks of respect by the energy with which it was conducting a war of so great magnitude; and by many eminent foreign statesmen, whose words carried with them great weight and authority, it was considered to be on the fair road to success. At home, that government had not yet betrayed its inherent weakness. Its hold upon the masses of the Southern people had not yet been relaxed. The bold front which it was now prepared to show in the field inspired the timid with respect and confidence, and silenced its strongest opponents. But this bold front must be maintained, and at much risk. Any very deliberate action was not within the scope of the policy which was forced upon the Confederate executive. Like all revolutionary governments, the Confederacy was in no position where it could exactly measure its resources and exercise a rigid economy in the exhaustion of its vital forces. Whatever else it might be, it *must* be audacious; when it ceased to be that, it gave up its prestige altogether. It was not permitted to stand upon the defensive, and await the developments of the national government against which it was arrayed. In a game of that sort it must inevitably be the loser. Depending for its very existence upon impulse rapidly awakened, it must be maintained also by popular impulse. To hesitate, even upon the most rational and carefully considered policy for effective defense, was to invite a popular reaction. Audacity was, therefore, the watchword of the revolutionists. The enemy must be stricken, blow upon blow, and paralyzed before he should have time given him to develop his more various resources for war. And with the splendid armies now in hand, both in the East and West, this seemed quite possible to the Confederates. It looked like an easy matter to push back the waves of war northward, and, by a contrary tempest, to sweep every battle-field, and in the heart of the great commercial cities of the North; and perchance in the national capital, to dictate the terms of peace. What these terms would be was significantly foreshadowed in the daily editorials of the Richmond journals. Among these were the acceptance by the Northern states of the Confederate Constitution, and the acknowledgment of the right of secession.

Evidently the Confederates were on the eve of important offensive movements, from which they expected the most extravagant measure of success. What these movements were in the West has already been indicated. To what issue they came, under the leadership of General Bragg, it will be our business to show in the remaining portion of this chapter.

The possession of Knoxville and East Tennessee gave General Bragg the

N. B. FORREST.

CINCINNATI, OHIO.

necessary foothold for the invasion of Kentucky. If General Mitchell's column had been sufficiently strengthened, it might have occupied such positions in Northern Alabama and Georgia as would have compelled the evacuation of East Tennessee. In the month of June the Confederates had abandoned Cumberland Gap. With a little exertion on General Buell's part, Chattanooga and Knoxville might have been captured. The summer months were occupied by Buell in straggling, impotent blows against the enemy. He sent an expedition where he ought to have marched with an army. Thus, on the 7th of June, General Negley appeared before Chattanooga with a handful of troops, and instituted what perhaps might be called the feint of a siege. A few more thousand men, who could easily have been spared for the purpose, would have captured the place, insured our possession of Knoxville, and have given the Federal army a strong position on the enemy's flank if he should advance into West Tennessee. By the want of energy displayed in the West, the Confederates were allowed two advantages. They were able to re-enforce their army in Virginia, and they were permitted in the West to take the initiative and to advance northward by the most auspicious route. It is true, doubtless, that the battle of Shiloh had been a heavy blow to the army. But this blow had fallen chiefly upon

General Grant's column. Buell's army was fresh and well organized. The great want in the West was of a military leader—a man with military intuitions—a man of sufficient nerve to hold in hand and effectively wield the columns of a large army. Such leaders there were. Grant, Sherman, and Thomas—afterward recognized as the great martial heroes of the continent —belonged to the Western army, and held prominent positions; but they were overshadowed by officers whose claims were more ostentatious. General Grant had shown great ability in the conduct of the operations against Fort Donelson. This the country had appreciated simply because it resulted in success; the coolness with which the general had formed new combinations when his first plan had been disturbed by the sudden attack on his lines, and the promptness with which he had done the right thing at just the right time—these qualities had passed unobserved. At Pittsburg Landing, on the 6th of April, he had exhibited the same coolness and nerve, and the result was a success; but, just at the point of success, Buell came on the field, and the sudden turn which eighteen thousand fresh men gave to the battle caused the latter to be regarded as the hero of the entire action. Both Grant and Sherman had made great mistakes—they had not yet learned all the lessons of the battle-field. We have seen how, at Fort Henry, Grant, by

VOLUNTEERS CROSSING THE OHIO FROM CINCINNATI TO COVINGTON.

waiting too long, had let the garrison slip by him on the road to Donelson. We have seen also what meagre preparation both he and Sherman had made against Beauregard's attack in the battle of Shiloh; but the time had not yet come when the armies on either side had learned to intrench themselves even in the most temporary encampment. General Thomas owed whatever elevation he had at this time to his victory over Zollicoffer at the battle of Mill Spring; but the time was to come yet when he should win most important victories—when, by a simple master-stroke, he should wipe out of existence the Confederate Army of the West. General Halleck, the commander of the department in which these generals were operating, was himself an officer of more than ordinary ability. He was a careful student of military science, and was capable of great strategic combinations. He lacked, however, those peculiar characteristics which insure success to the commander on the field. Early in July, just after McClellan's celebrated change of base, he was called to Washington to occupy the position of general-in-chief, a position for which he had eminent qualifications. His retirement from the West left Buell and Grant as the two great actors in that field, the former at that time being considered the greater general. Pope, who had won great distinction as the hero of New Madrid and Island No. 10, was also removed to the East, to take an important command in Virginia.

This latter general was fighting a desperate battle on the old field of Bull Run on the same day that an important engagement was going on between the Federal troops and the advance of General Kirby Smith at Richmond, Kentucky. Kirby Smith commanded the Confederate forces in East Tennessee. Early in August he had commenced to move northward in two divisions, commanded by Churchill and Claiborne. Though he met with little resistance in his march, he encountered many difficulties. For many days his men had nothing to eat but green corn. His ordnance train was brought through without loss. However troublesome the intermediate journey, Smith's army knew that it was marching to the fertile valley of the Kentucky. At Richmond the first formidable resistance was encountered. This place is situated about fifty miles southeast of Frankfort, the capital of the state. There was a force stationed here under the command of Brigadier General M. D. Manson, consisting of about eight regiments, mostly Indiana troops, a small squadron of cavalry, and nine pieces of artillery. Smith's army was met a short distance from Richmond by this force, and the action began early on the morning of August 30. The enemy executed a successful flank movement with a portion of Churchill's division, and broke the Federal lines. General Manson was captured. Just as the field was being abandoned to the enemy, General Nelson, coming from Lexington, tried to rally the flying troops, but without success; he was wounded in the effort. The superiority of the enemy in cavalry, as well as infantry, to a great degree decided the battle. The Federals left a large number of killed and wounded on the field, and lost largely in prisoners. Nearly all of their artillery, too, was captured.

This sudden movement of the enemy, who had already reached the banks of the Kentucky, created intense excitement both in Kentucky and Ohio. In Frankfort the Legislature was in session, but on receiving intelligence of the defeat at Richmond adjourned to Louisville, removing to that place the archives of the state, and about one million of money from the banks of Richmond, Lexington, and Frankfort. A proclamation was issued by Governor Robinson calling upon the citizens to take up arms in defense of the state. In two days time Lexington was taken. At this stage of his progress Kirby Smith proclaimed to the people the object of his invasion. He said: "We come, not as invaders, but liberators. We invoke the spirit of your resolutions of 1798. * * * We call upon you to join with us in hurling back from our fair and sunny plains the Northern hordes who would deprive us of our liberty that they may enjoy our substance." The Confederate cavalry entered Frankfort on the 6th of September. There was no efficient force, as it then seemed, to prevent Kirby Smith from reaching the Ohio River. It was even anticipated that he might capture Cincinnati.

The excitement in Cincinnati was so great that martial law was proclaimed, all places of business were closed, and the citizens were required to arm in defense of the city. Governor Tod issued a proclamation urging upon the citizens of Ohio the immediate requirements of the hour. General Lewis Wallace was placed in command of the force gathered together to cover the approach to Cincinnati.

In the mean time, while Kirby Smith was demonstrating against the line of the Ohio farther north, the great bulk of Bragg's army entered Kentucky, by way of Chattanooga, en route for Louisville. The season for this movement was well timed. If successful, the abundant harvests of the Kentucky and Ohio valleys, already ripening in the fields, would fall into the hands of the victors; for, while Kirby Smith was charging against the Federals that they were holding Kentucky in order to secure her substance, the Confederates were open to precisely the same charge.[1] Suddenly, as Bragg drew nearer to Frankfort, Kirby Smith left Cincinnati, and, by a forced march, succeeded in effecting a junction with him at the capital on the 4th of October. Here the two commanders amused themselves with the inauguration of Mr. Hawes as provisional governor of Kentucky.

General Bragg's own column when he entered the state on the 5th of September consisted of thirty-six infantry regiments, with five regiments of cavalry. In one week's time the advance of the column appeared in front of Munfordsville, at the crossing of the Louisville and Nashville Railroad over Green River, and demanded the surrender of the place. Up to this time Bragg had demonstrated against Nashville, in order to keep Buell at the latter place until he could strike the railroad between the Federal army and Louisville, which was its great base of supplies. He had, to a great degree, succeeded in deceiving Buell as to his real object, but his purpose was at length betrayed through intercepted dispatches. His movements had been well planned. Smith's column demonstrated against Cincinnati on the right, Bragg's against Nashville on the left; then suddenly, in both cases, the mask was laid aside, and both columns joined near Frankfort, a few miles from the real objective point of the campaign. The movement was as bold in conception as it was ingenious in design. But it failed in one important particular—it proceeded too leisurely. General Bragg was

[1] "The great and true source of meat supply is the State of Kentucky. If our armies could push directly forward over that state, and occupy it to the banks of the Ohio, the political advantages secured to the South would be of even small account compared with those she would derive in a sumptuary point of view. There are more hogs and cattle in Kentucky available for general consumption, two or three to one, than are now left in all the South besides; and steps ought to be taken by government to drive back these animals, as well as mules and horses, as our armies march forward, and place them within our lines. It is not only positively important to us that these animals should be promptly secured as they fall within our grasp, but it is negatively so, also, in depriving the enemy of the convenient supplies of meat for their armies which they have derived from Kentucky."—*Richmond Examiner*, September 12, 1862.

FEEDING TROOPS AT THE MARKET-PLACE IN CINCINNATI.

GENERAL BUELL'S ARMY ENTERING LOUISVILLE.

VETERAN TROOPS MOVING UP THE OHIO TO LOUISVILLE AND CINCINNATI.

too confident of the completeness of his disguise. It will be admitted that both columns of his army encountered great obstacles in the way of a rapid march. He was compelled, in a great measure, to depend upon the country for supplies; but the country was full of adherents to the Confederate cause. He had, in the earlier stage of his march, a difficult route; mountains were to be crossed, and here, where there must be the greatest delay, supplies were least abundant. Then, again, after a difficult march, his troops needed rest before they would be in a condition to fight decisive battles. All these difficulties must be admitted; but, in view of other marches made by great armies during the war—marches longer and far more difficult, but accomplished in one half the time—it is impossible not to lay the failure of Bragg's really splendid scheme for the occupation of the line of the Ohio to his slowness of movement. It was on the 21st of August that he had crossed the Tennessee River, just above Chattanooga. It was six weeks before his army was joined by Smith's at Frankfort. Yet he was delayed by no important battle. The battle of Richmond, in which Kirby Smith was engaged, was decided in one day. Bragg himself had fought a battle at Munfordsville on the 14th and 16th of September. The advance of his column, as previously stated, had demanded the surrender of this place on the 13th. The Federal force stationed there for the protection of the bridge, under Colonel Wilder, consisted of a little over three thousand men, with four guns. This force surrendered on the 17th, after having sustained two attacks, with a loss of eight men killed and twenty wounded. Re-enforcements had arrived, so that the number of prisoners taken by the enemy was four thousand five hundred men, with ten guns. Apart from these battles, which gave the enemy over seven thousand prisoners, there was no serious engagement on the line of march. There can scarcely be a reasonable doubt but that Bragg and Smith, if they had moved with greater rapidity, might have taken possession of Louisville without a struggle. What would have followed it is hard to say. Evidently General Bragg counted upon a more considerable demonstration in his favor from the citizens of Kentucky than he received. As had just been proved in Maryland, so too it was demonstrated in Kentucky, that the state was at heart loyal to the national government. Even the occupation of Louisville would not have, probably, added materially to the number of Bragg's army, while his advanced position would have been untenable against the combination of forces which must soon have gathered against him.

But in the race for Louisville Buell came out ahead. Having been made aware of Bragg's purpose, Buell kept in his front, covering Nashville at the same time. Although the enemy had destroyed the bridge across Green River, Buell's command forded that stream, driving the Confederates out of Munfordsville, and advanced rapidly toward Louisville. To this latter place had been transferred the intense excitement which a few days before had

prevailed in Cincinnati. Many veteran troops, chiefly from Grant's army, had been sent to both these places up the Mississippi and the Ohio, and, mingled with the new levies of troops, had done much to allay the popular apprehension. The command at Cincinnati was given to General Lewis Wallace, and General William Nelson commanded the troops at Louisville. Notwithstanding Buell's haste to reach Louisville, it is still quite certain that, but for one circumstance, Bragg would have beaten him in the race. The road which the latter was taking crossed Salt River near Bardstown, about thirty-five miles south of Louisville, and the bridge at this point he found destroyed. The delay thus occasioned gave Buell the start. Just before the Federal army entered Louisville, on the 25th of September, the panic there had reached its height. In twenty-four hours more Nelson would have abandoned the city. All non-combatants had been sent out, and every thing was in confusion. To confusion was added a want of confidence on the part of many in General Buell's generalship. Indeed, the latter had scarcely got his army into the panic-stricken city before he found that an order had been issued from the War Department placing General Thomas in command, and it was mainly on account of the persistent solicitation of the latter that Buell was retained.

The position which General Buell held was very similar to that of McClellan at the same period. Both generals were unfortunate from the political associations in which, whether by their own will or otherwise, they had become entangled. Americans do not easily forget the past histories of prominent public characters. This tenacity of memory is shown in the embarrassments which attended Fremont's administration in Missouri. It had not been forgotten that McClellan and Buell had in former times had political affiliations with men who were now leaders of the revolution. The great masses of the people, notwithstanding this knowledge, were willing to wait until the military competence or incompetence of these officers should have been proved, and to rest their judgment upon that basis alone, although there were many honest men who, from the well known sympathy of McClellan and Buell with a distinctively Southern sentiment, feared that they would conduct the war with less vigor than might else be expected. There are many circumstances which to the historian will show that this apprehension was well grounded, though, as regards patriotism, no impeachment will ever rest against the names of either of these generals. In the mean time, even if they had been so inclined, they were not allowed to pursue a purely military policy without disturbance. A few partisans were determined to meddle with their military policy. Those whose sympathies were allied to theirs pressed them to a lenient policy, which would soften the blows directed by their arms against the wealthy slaveholding classes of the South. These recommended the advance of those according with them in sentiment to the first commands. On the other hand, there were those equally partisan who pressed them in exactly the opposite direction. These were unwilling that the war should be conducted, no matter how successfully, upon a policy which should touch too lightly the institution of slavery. They did all in their power to incite popular opposition to McClellan and Buell, and they urged strongly upon the President the necessity of their removal from command. The latter, taking sides with the great masses of the people, waited the course of military events, determined that the war for the Union must succeed, and that, if success should seem to be more sure from leaving slavery intact, he would so leave it; if by its destruction, then it should be destroyed.

Buell's temporary removal had no other than military grounds, the justice of which was afterward fully proved. Thomas, as we have seen, though better fitted to command, protested against the decree from Washington, which was then retracted. He himself was made second in command, and thus occupied a position in which his military talent could not be made available.

General Buell's army, designated as the Army of the Ohio, numbered altogether, after its junction with Nelson, about a hundred thousand men, one half of whom were new recruits, who had been pouring into Louisville for the last few days. At Louisville he lost thousands by desertion. The army consisted of three corps. General Alexander McDowell McCook commanded the First Corps, and General Crittenden the Second. Both these corps had been engaged in the second day's fight at Shiloh. The Third Corps, commanded by General C. C. Gilbert, was Nelson's old command. The command had been assigned to Gilbert at first temporarily, when Nelson was sent to Louisville. Nelson's tragical end gave him the permanent command.

General Nelson was shot at Louisville on the 29th of September by General Jefferson C. Davis. The affair grew out of the insolence of General Nelson toward the latter, who immediately borrowed a pistol and shot him as he was ascending the stairs of the Galt House. General Nelson was a native of Kentucky. He had been, at the beginning of the war, over twenty years in the naval service, when he was suddenly transferred to a military department, relieving General Anderson of his command in Kentucky. When General Buell's army advanced to Nashville, Nelson had an important command. At the time of his death he had not yet recovered from the wound which he had received at the recent battle of Richmond. He was rough in his manner, but a good disciplinarian, and an excellent officer on the field. The difficulty between Generals Davis and Nelson appears to have sprung from some domestic dissension, and to have been aggravated by an exhibition of insolence on the part of Nelson, who had given Davis an insignificant command over the home guard defending the city. On the morning of the 29th Nelson met Davis at the Galt House, and asked him respecting the number of men in his command. Davis answered that he had about so many, giving the number approximately. Nelson replied angrily, mingling expressions of rage with those of insult, and upon Davis demanding an apology, struck the latter in the face. Davis then borrowed a pistol from a lawyer in the vicinity, followed Nelson up the stairs and shot him, inflicting a mortal wound. For this act he was subsequently tried by court-martial and acquitted. General Davis was not a graduate of the Military Academy, but had been, previous to the war, appointed from civil life to a command in the regular army. He was one of Major Anderson's sub-

ordinate officers in the defense of Fort Sumter. Immediately after the surrender of that fort he returned to Indiana, his native state, and took command of the Twenty-second Indiana Volunteers, joining General Fremont's army in Missouri, where he was promoted to the command of a brigade, and took a prominent part in the conflict with General Price, both under Fremont and subsequently under General Curtis. The spirit of General Davis was evinced in the affair at Milford in 1861, where, with a force of scarcely five hundred of the Iowa cavalry, he surprised a Confederate camp, capturing a force of the enemy nearly three times the number of his own command, with a thousand stand of arms, and a large quantity of military stores. It was not until this action that he received from the government a rank corresponding to his actual position. His commission as brigadier general dates from December 18, 1861.

General Bragg at Bardstown, September 26, issued a proclamation which is worthy of note, because it discloses the hopes at this time entertained by a large portion of the Confederacy in regard to the Northwestern states of the Union. Disclaiming any purpose of invasion, he said that his object was "to secure peace, and the abandonment by the United States of their pretensions to govern a people who never have been their subjects, and who prefer self-government to a union with them." He said that, at the inauguration of the Confederate government, commissioners were sent to Washington to adjust the difficulties growing out of a political separation, but that the national government refused them recognition. "Among the pretexts," said he, "urged for the continuance of the war is the assertion that the Confederate government desires to deprive the United States of the free navigation of the Western rivers." On the contrary, he stated that the Confederate Congress had, prior to the commencement of the war, publicly declared that the navigation of the Mississippi should be free to the states upon its borders. Having thus appealed to the interest of the people of the Northwest, he proceeded to make another appeal, namely, to their desire for peace. The Confederacy, he said, restricted itself to the moderate demand that the United States should cease to prosecute war against it; but, because the government at Washington was relentless in this particular, the Confederates were driven to protect their own country by transferring the seat of war to that of an enemy who pursued them "with an implacable and apparently aimless hostility." "So far," he said, "it is only *our* fields that have been laid waste, our people killed, our homes made desolate, and our frontiers ravaged by rapine and murder." It rested, therefore, with the people of the Northwest to put an end to the invasion of their homes, either by prevailing upon the general government to desist from war, or, if that should not prove possible, their own state governments, in the exercise of their sovereignty, should secure immunity from the desolations of war by making a separate treaty of peace, which the Confederate government would be "ready to conclude on the most just and liberal basis." "Nature," he said, "has set her seal upon these states" [i. e., the states of the South], "and marked them out to be your friends and allies. She has bound them to you by all the ties of geographical contiguity and conformation, and the great mutual interests of commerce and productions. When the passions of this unnatural war shall have subsided, and reason resumes her sway, a community of interest will force commercial and social coalition between the great grain and stock-growing states of the Northwest, and the cotton, tobacco, and sugar regions of the South. The Mississippi River is a grand artery of their mutual national lives, which men can not sever, and which never ought to have been suffered to be disturbed by the antagonisms, the cupidity, and the bigotry of New England and the East. It is from the East that have come the germs of this bloody and most unnatural strife. It is from the meddlesome, grasping, and fanatical disposition of the same people who have imposed upon you and us alike those tariffs, internal improvement, and fishing bounty laws, whereby we have been taxed for their aggrandizement. It is from the East that will come the tax-gatherer to collect from you the mighty debt which is being amassed mountain high for the purpose of ruining your best customers and natural friends. * * * You say you are fighting for the free navigation of the Mississippi. It is yours freely, and always has been, without striking a blow. You say you are fighting to maintain the Union. The Union is a thing of the past. A union of consent was the only union ever worth a drop of blood. When force came to be substituted for consent, the casket was broken, and the constitutional jewel of your patriotic adoration was forever gone."

General Bragg was not the only one who anticipated important results from the offer of peace to the Northwest based on a future alliance. The very same day that Bragg issued the above proclamation, the Committee on Foreign Affairs laid before the Confederate Congress a report in favor of recommending to the President the "issuance of a proclamation touching the free navigation of the Mississippi and its tributaries, and the opening of the markets of the South to the inhabitants of the Northwestern states upon certain terms and conditions." The time at which this report was made, and the likeness which in all respects it bears to Bragg's proclamation, indicates that the latter was a deliberately considered document, in which the military officer was the representative of a policy already approved by the great body of the Confederates. It is quite evident, also, that prominent men in the Northwest, in sympathy with the revolution, had given considerable encouragement as to the success of such a policy. As much as this is directly stated in one part of the report. "It is gratifying," the document reads, "to discover that high-spirited and intelligent public men in several of the Northwestern states have of late become exceedingly active in their endeavors to discourage and suppress the ferocious war spirit heretofore raging among their fellow-citizens, and that their honest and patriotic efforts have been already attended with the most marked success." At the same

JEFFERSON C. DAVIS.

time, a minority report was laid before Congress dissenting from the views expressed by the majority of the committee. This report was signed by E. Barksdale, J. R. McLean, and W. R. Smith. These individuals did not believe it advisable to offer exclusive commercial privileges to a portion of the people against whom the Confederacy was in arms. They did not see but that similar motives and arguments might be brought to bear upon the Eastern states as successfully as upon those of the Northwest. The manufacturers of the New England states, they thought, would be as likely to be conciliated by a discriminating tariff as the Northwestern farmers by the removal of all tariff, and their ship-owners by a monopoly of the carrying trade of the South as the people along the Mississippi by the free navigation of that river. Give the city of New York, said they, the conduct of our commercial affairs, and she would be as likely to desist from her wickedness toward the Confederates as Cincinnati would be if allowed to exchange her pork on profitable terms for Southern cotton and tobacco. The signs of returning reason, indicating a desire for the return of peace among the inhabitants of the Northwestern states, were not as apparent to them as to the majority of the committee.[1] But, notwithstanding this view of the case, as presented in the minority report, it is very evident that the prosperity of the South would have been enhanced to a far greater degree by an alliance with the Western than one with the Eastern states, if she should succeed in establishing her independence. The great obstacle in the way was the indisposition of the Western states to form such an alliance upon such a basis.

General Bragg's proclamation contained a formidable menace in the event of the refusal by the Northwest of the proposed adjustment. He said in effect: "Here I am with an army which, including Smith's off at my right, numbers not less than sixty thousand men. I bring also the olive-branch, which you refuse at your peril." But, unfortunately for him, the bridge across Salt River was down; and Buell, with his army, had already entered Louisville. At the same time that he menaced, it was likely that he must prove his ability to accomplish his threats. Indeed, it now was becoming quite clear that this Bardstown proclamation was to be the great feat of his boldly-planned campaign. He forthwith made arrangements for retreat. Instead of pushing on toward Louisville, he ordered his trains eastward toward Harrodsburg, leaving a strong force at Bardstown, with orders to keep Buell back until October 4th. In the mean time he went to Frankfort, where Kirby Smith arrived on the 4th, and the two officers on that day amused themselves with the inauguration of a Mr. Richard Hawes as provisional governor of the state.

Buell was slow to move against the enemy. His army was tired with long marching, and his men came to Louisville without shoes and poorly clad; but it can scarcely be doubted that the enemy were suffering even more inconvenience from precisely the same causes. He gave his army a full week's rest at Louisville, and it was only on the 1st of October that, forming a movable column out of his three corps, he marched out, with a train of nearly two thousand wagons, stretching over twenty-two miles, to

find the enemy. During the week he had been waiting the enemy's cavalry had swept the country in the vicinity of Louisville, destroying daily property estimated by hundreds of thousands. In this matter of cavalry Bragg had great advantages over Buell, whose army, on the other hand, was no doubt more perfectly equipped, and was certainly larger in point of numbers than Bragg could bring upon the field. Buell advanced at the rate of about ten miles per day, and reached Bardstown the very day Bragg had determined upon as that beyond which it was no longer necessary to hold the place. But, leisurely as were Buell's movements, they brought his army into such close proximity with Bragg's rear as to give the Confederate general some uneasiness. This brought on the battle of Perryville, which was fought on the 8th of October.

Buell, either from excessive caution, or because he was not aware of the enemy's situation, had already lost a precious opportunity. He ought to have been fighting the enemy at Bardstown on the 1st, instead of just then beginning his march. If he intended to fight at all, here he had every advantage in his favor. Let us see what he really did, and with what result.

Smith, after the mock inauguration of Governor Hawes was over, fell back toward Harrodsburg. Buell had dispatched one division—Sill's, of McCook's corps—to look after him. The other two divisions—Rousseau's and Jackson's—formed the left column of Buell's army, and took the road to Mackville. Gilbert, with the third corps, formed the centre column, moving by a road farther westward. Crittenden's corps, the right column, moved to Bardstown, and was delayed at that point by slight skirmishes. Gilbert reached the northern skirt of Perryville on the 7th, and began to annoy Bragg's rear with his artillery. McCook was within call; Crittenden would be in the course of twenty-four hours. Bragg had from fifteen to twenty thousand men within call. These were not all upon the field at Gilbert's first collision with Bragg's rear, for the reason that the latter had preferred to make a stand at Harrodsburg, where, on the 9th, he would be re-enforced by Kirby Smith's army. Buell's movements had altered this determination, and Bragg, with great promptness, brought up Hardee's two divisions, under Buckner and Anderson, and Cheatham's, which was commanded by General Polk. Buell, notwithstanding he could outnumber the enemy, still wished to avoid a battle at this point, and he ordered up McCook's corps from Mackville—a place equidistant from Harrodsburg and Perryville, and ten miles from either—only because he anticipated that he should meet with some resistance at this stage of his march.

McCook received this order at 2 o'clock on the morning of the 8th, and hurried up his column. His advance connected with Gilbert's left on the road to Perryville before eleven A.M. The march had been through a rugged country so destitute of water that the men suffered much, and even the hospitals were insufficiently supplied. Along the route Gilbert's artillery was heard all the morning, but there was no general engagement in the forenoon. McCook arrived upon the field not a moment too soon, as the enemy was already preparing to occupy the commanding position on Gilbert's flank, which Buell intended the First corps to hold. This position

---

[1] The following is the text of both reports:

MAJORITY REPORT.—The Committee on Foreign Affairs, to whom was referred certain resolutions relating to the true policy of the war, and recommending to the President the issuance of a proclamation touching the free navigation of the Mississippi and its tributaries, and the opening of the market of the South to the inhabitants of the Southwestern states upon certain terms and conditions, have had the same under consideration, and now report back said resolutions, with one or two slight amendments, and recommend that they be adopted.

The expediency of conducting the war in which we are engaged with all possible activity, and of carrying that war into the enemy's country, so soon as the same shall be found practicable, is believed to be now universally admitted by all enlightened men who have given their attention to the subject. It is evident that we must rely alone upon our own energies for success in the struggle of arms which is now in progress. In the present condition of affairs it is quite manifest that, in order to bring the sanguinary struggle in which we are engaged to an early termination, it will be necessary that every portion of our army should be kept in a state of constant readiness for active exertion, and that no opportunity should be neglected of striking the forces of the enemy, wherever to be found upon Southern soil, with that boldness and heroic energy which are so certain to secure to our arms the most signal success.

It is equally manifest that the enemy will never be willing to desist from the unjust and ferocious war which they are now waging until the evils and inconveniences thereof shall have been brought home fully to themselves. When our valiant and disciplined armies (enhanced in numbers and in strength, as it is hoped they will shortly be) shall have once found their way to the heart of the enemy's country, and have inflicted a just retaliation upon those who have so ruthlessly ravaged our territories, pillaged our towns, and desolated our homes, it is to be reasonably expected that even they will at last be able to discern the rank injustice and brutal cruelty which they have compelled us to experience, and for the perpetration of which they have not been heretofore subjected to any thing like adequate punishment.

Your committee are well satisfied that the issuing of some such proclamation by the President as that described in the resolutions referred to them, at such time as he shall deem expedient, could not but be attended with the most salutary effects. It is an undoubted fact that the government at Washington, aided by unscrupulous local demagogues in the Northwestern states, has succeeded to a considerable extent in deluding the people of that region into a general belief that, should we succeed in our struggle for independence, it is the intention of the government and people of the Confederate States to shut them out from the free navigation of the Mississippi River and its great tributaries; and though the Provisional Congress of these states long ago emphatically negatived this idea by well-known acts of formal legislation, yet your committee is assured that the delusion on this subject still continues to exist among the people of the Northwest, and that the gross misapprehension in regard to the intentions and policy of the Confederate States of America, thus engendered and kept in existence by wicked and designing men, has operated most effectively in prompting the people of the Northwestern states (so closely connected with the South heretofore, both by geographical and political ties) to contribute freely, both in men and money, to the prosecution of a war which, if successful on the part of those with whom it originated, would be, eventually, as disastrous in its effects to the people of the Northwestern states themselves as to those of the Confederate States of America. It is gratifying to discover that high-spirited and intelligent public men in several of the Northwestern states have of late become exceedingly active in their endeavors to discourage and suppress the ferocious war spirit heretofore raging among their fellow-citizens, and that their honest and patriotic efforts have been already attended with the most marked success.

Such a proclamation as that recommended in the resolutions referred to this committee, it is confidently believed, would have a tendency greatly to strengthen the efforts of the advocates of peace in the Northwestern states, be calculated to bring those states quickly into amicable relations with the states of the South, withdraw them ultimately altogether from their present injurious political connection with the states of the North and East, with which they have really so little in common, and thus enable us to dictate the terms of a just and honorable peace from the great commercial emporium of that region, through whose influence mainly has this wicked and unnatural war been thus far kept in progress.

MINORITY REPORT.—The undersigned, a minority of the Committee on Foreign Affairs, beg leave to dissent from the report of the majority upon certain resolutions referred to the committee, touching the issuing by the President of a proclamation to the inhabitants of the Northwestern

states, tendering to them the free navigation of the Mississippi River, and advantageous treaty stipulations at the close of the war.

It is submitted that subjects relating to the conduct of the war are not appropriate matters of investigation by the Committee on Foreign Affairs.

But, waiving this consideration, the undersigned totally dissent from the views of the majority touching the duties of this house. It is a work of supererogation for this body to undertake to decide and to declare the mode of conducting the war. It is a question involving consequences of vital moment, legitimately pertaining to the functions of the executive and those who have been chosen to lead our armies. But if such duty were, in fact, devolved upon this body, as is implied by the report of the majority, it would be in violation of all the rules of enlightened warfare to unfold the plan which it is designed to pursue in the prosecution of the war.

It is believed that thus far the executive has availed himself of the means placed at his disposal for conducting the war in the manner most judicious and effective; and that in the signal success which has attended our struggle for the maintenance of the independence of the Confederate States will be found sufficient reason for leaving him, without interference, to the exercise of the duties imposed by the Constitution.

The undersigned dissent from the recommendation that the government should tender to a portion of the citizens of the government with whom we are at war exclusive commercial privileges. It is not the part of wisdom to commit our government to any fixed policy in advance. Legislation should not be anticipated, but should be shaped by existing events. If a deviation from this plain suggestion of wisdom be advised in the present instance upon the idea of the influence of an appeal to the self-interest of the inhabitants of the Northwestern states, it should not be forgotten that the same argument might, with equal propriety, be addressed to the inhabitants of the New England states. The manufacturers of that section would be conciliated by pledges that a discriminating tariff would, at the close of hostilities, be put into speedy operation for building up their interests, and ship-owners would be propitiated by pledges that they would be permitted to perform the carrying trade of the South as under the old Union. And the city of New York would be induced to pause in her course of folly and wickedness toward the Confederate States if assured that they would confer upon her the privilege of conducting their commercial affairs and enriching herself upon the proceeds of her labor.

The Northern people derived, under the former government, an annual profit of not less than $100,000,000 upon Southern trade. Their implements of war will be laid aside when assured that their coffers shall be filled with the proceeds of Southern labor. But the undersigned do not hesitate to repel the suggestion that the people of the South are willing to purchase peace by such a sacrifice of their rights, and by so degrading a concession to Northern cupidity. To be respected, our course must be firm and our legislation rational and just.

At an early period after the organization of the government of the Confederate States, a law was passed declaring the free navigation of the Mississippi River, with certain salutary restrictions. The policy of the government has not been changed on this subject. It is presumed to have been known to the inhabitants of the Northwestern states before they embarked in a wicked and unjustifiable war against the people of the Confederate States. To proclaim this policy at the present time, coupled with offers of their lucrative trade, in the manner suggested by the majority, would be, in the highest degree, derogatory to the dignity of the government. It would bring upon it the imputation of pusillanimity. It would be accepted by the enemy as a confession of conscious weakness, and its inevitable tendency would be to prolong the war.

The undersigned are firm in the opinion that the most effective mode of conquering a peace is not to be found in extending to the enemy propositions of reconciliation, but in the vigorous prosecution of the war.

The signs of returning reason, indicating a desire for peace among the inhabitants of the Northwestern states, upon the discovery of which the majority have congratulated the House, are believed to be delusive. The undersigned regret to say that they have not been able to discern them. But, in the event of the actual existence of these alleged pacific indications, it is clear that they are the result, not of temporizing expedients on the part of the government of the Confederate States, but of its manifestations of purpose to prosecute the war with vigor and effect.

For these reasons the undersigned dissent from the views of the majority, and ask the concurrence of the house in the opinion that they should be rejected.

E. BARKSDALE,
J. R. MCLEAN,
W. R. SMITH.

on Gilbert's left was especially important, because it secured access to Chaplin's Creek. McCook formed his line on the range of hills known as Chaplin's Hills west of that stream, the road to Perryville being in the rear. Two of Rousseau's brigades held the right; Terrell's, of Jackson's division, held the left. This latter brigade not only guarded the left flank, but protected the trains in the rear. In order to still farther strengthen the left, Starkweather's brigade of Rousseau's division was placed in reserve behind Terrell. Another brigade of Jackson's division, under Colonel Webster, was in reserve farther to the right, near Russell's house.

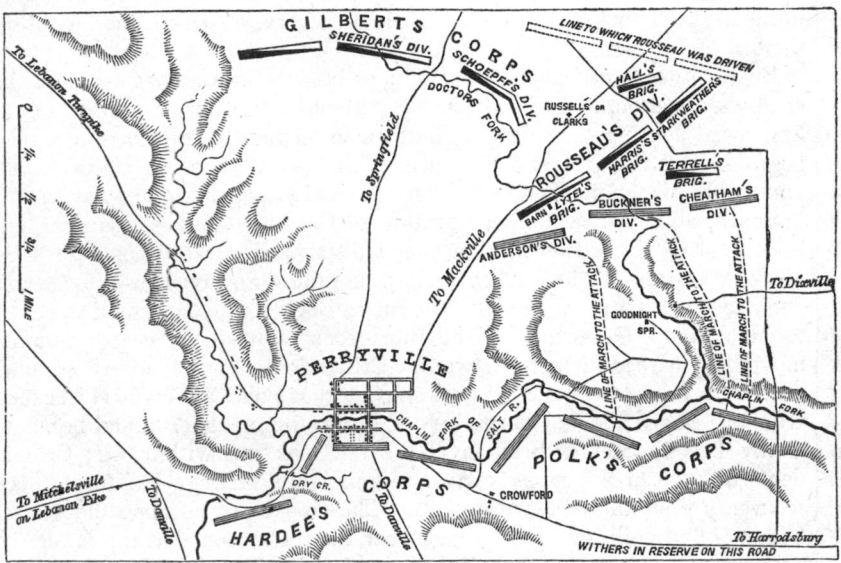

PLAN OF THE BATTLE OF PERRYVILLE.

Bragg attacked a little after noon. He was compelled by McCook's position to cross the stream more to the north, but his batteries played upon the national troops from favorable positions on both sides of the stream. Before long, Terrell's brigade was attacked with great impetuosity. This brigade consisted entirely of raw troops, and it was only through some mistake in manœuvre that it was not in reserve in the place of Starkweather's. Terrell's men wavered beneath the shock, and, although their division commander, General Jackson, advanced to rally them, they were swept from the field, leaving Parsons's battery in the hands of the enemy. Jackson was killed at the first fire. He was struck in the right breast by a piece of an exploded shell, and, with the exclamation "Oh God!" fell from his horse and died without a struggle. Even the enemy paid a tribute to his gallantry. Terrell also fell directly after, and McCook's left flank was uncovered, and would have been destroyed, with the loss of the trains, but for the pluck of Starkweather's men. These belonged to Rousseau's division, General O. M. Mitchell's old command.

As soon as McCook had become assured of the safety of his left, he rode over to the right only to find that Rousseau also had been driven back. He was even compelled to use Webster's brigade. His reserves were now all in the front, and he was obliged to call for re-enforcements. In his effort to support the right, Colonel Webster was killed; Lytle, who held the extreme flank, fell on the field. It was not until the position at Russell's house had been abandoned that McCook received any re-enforcements. Then Colonel Gooding's brigade, of R. B. Mitchell's division, came upon the field. This brigade consisted of three regiments, accompanied by a battery, and added fifteen hundred men to McCook's command, which in the morning had numbered thirteen thousand. Of these there were now not more than seven or eight thousand men capable of fighting.

It was nearly dark when Gooding had succeeded in wresting the position at Russell's house from the enemy and saving the line. But this had been accomplished at great sacrifice. At the close of the brief but desperate encounter, five hundred out of the fifteen hundred had been killed or wounded. Colonel Gooding himself had been taken prisoner. Then there came up another brigade from Gilbert, which went into position on Gooding's right. In fact, Buell was only just now aware that any battle was in progress. He had given orders that McCook should not fight; but as the enemy attacked, and so much depended upon McCook's position, it is hard to see what else could have saved the day but fighting. The battle was now over. McCook had with great difficulty held his own, and had saved his command, while Gilbert stood apart, with some twenty thousand men or more, giving scarcely more assistance or co-operation than if he had been fifty miles from the field. The enemy, with one third of the force which Buell had in his front, had, by making that force bear upon McCook's corps alone, overwhelmed the latter on both flanks, and almost swept it from the field.

The loss had been very heavy on the Federal side. In Rousseau's division alone the casualties amounted to over 2000; in Jackson's the loss was greater, but many of these were counted as missing. The Confederates must have lost nearly as many men, as they attacked formidable positions.

The next morning General Bragg withdrew his force to Harrodsburg, and, with Kirby Smith, moved southward toward Camp Dick Robinson, and thence out of the state altogether. The Confederates, although they failed in the military object of their invasion, succeeded in carrying out of Kentucky a great deal of plunder. According to a statement made by the Richmond Examiner, "the wagon train of supplies brought out of Kentucky by General Kirby Smith was forty miles long, and brought a million yards of jeans, with a large amount of clothing, boots, and shoes, and two hundred

wagon loads of bacon, six thousand barrels of pork, fifteen hundred mules and horses, eight thousand beeves, and a large lot of swine." Of the jeans nearly all were taken from a single establishment in Frankfort. A large amount of plunder was captured. The enemy staid there four weeks, and during all that time trains of cars were running southward laden with mess pork and other stores, and numerous wagon trains similarly laden were traversing all the roads in that direction. The fact that this was possible illustrates the need which then existed for an efficient Federal cavalry force. Indeed, the want of such a force shows an extraordinary degree of negligence on the part of the government at this stage of the war.

The invasion of Kentucky had made it necessary for the Federal troops under General Morgan to evacuate Cumberland Gap. This gap is nearly eighty miles in length, and is about one hundred and fifty miles southeast of Lexington. The mountain on either side rises to the height of twelve hundred feet; the gap itself is traversed by an excellent road. The position was important to the Confederates, chiefly because it guarded the approach to East Tennessee, and thus covered the line of railroad connecting Richmond with the valley of the Mississippi. It had remained in their hands until General Mitchell's campaign had compelled them to abandon it, about the middle of June, when it was occupied by a division of national troops under General George W. Morgan. A number of unsuccessful attempts were subsequently made by the Confederates to regain the Gap. It was only when Bragg's advance into Kentucky had cut off all supplies that General Morgan determined to withdraw. He held out bravely to the last moment. On the 11th of September he had no corn left, and only a meagre supply of beans and rice. On the 17th he withdrew from the Gap, blowing up the magazine, and burning the commissary building, with his tents, wagons, gun-carriages, and other martial appliances. His retreat of two hundred and fifty miles, through a mountainous and unproductive country, to the banks of the Ohio, forms an interesting episode of the war. Sometimes destitute of water, always dependent for its daily supply of food on foraging, harassed perpetually by Confederate cavalry, and sleeping at night under the open sky, his command reached the Ohio River on the 4th of October. The whole command numbered nearly twelve thousand men, and it succeeded, in spite of many embarrassments, in bringing off twenty-eight pieces of artillery and four hundred wagons. This success is the more remarkable when it is considered that Morgan was continually skirmishing with the enemy, and was obliged to build new roads, under very disadvantageous circumstances, for the conveyance of his trains. His sick he had been compelled to leave at the Gap.

Bragg's invasion had broken up the advanced line of the national forces in Eastern Tennessee. It had also, to a great extent, depleted General Grant's army in Mississippi, portions of which had been sent to Cincinnati and Louisville. But a sufficient force was left to retain the line already held, which extended from Corinth, in Mississippi, to Tuscumbia, in Alabama. Some important changes had occurred since the month of July. General Halleck had been called to Washington to assume the position of general-in-chief, and the command of that portion of the Western army not included in General Buell's department had been given to General Grant. Pope had been called away to take command of the Army of the Potomac, and his place was now taken by General Rosecrans.

ROBERT B. MITCHELL.

PERRYVILLE, KENTUCKY.

Though Bragg had taken the bulk of the Confederate army in the West into Kentucky, still a large Confederate force had been left in Northern Mississippi. This force, under the command of Generals Price and Van Dorn, confronted General Grant in September, holding a position which, from its uninterrupted railroad connection with Chattanooga, enabled it to co-operate with Bragg's movement. Van Dorn was the principal in command. If his force had been united to that of General Price, the whole would have constituted an effective army. Instead of this, the plan of operations agreed upon contemplated that Price should cross the Tennessee River to operate against the rear of General Buell, who was then advancing northward to intercept Bragg; and, in the mean time, while Grant's forces would thus be drawn eastward from Corinth, the latter place was to be captured by Van Dorn. Upon the first development of this plan, Grant began to concentrate his army by abandoning Tuscumbia and Iuka. A small force under Colonel Murphy was left at the latter place. Almost immediately afterward a body of Confederate cavalry dashed into the town, drove Murphy out, and captured the place, which contained a large quantity of medical and commissary stores. For neglecting to destroy the six hundred and eighty barrels of flour which were there stored, Colonel Murphy was arrested by General Buell. It was now determined by General Grant to attack General Price on the north, west, and south.

The left wing of Price's army rested near Iuka, a little village of about three hundred inhabitants. Against this position, Grant, accompanied by Ord's division, moved with about eighteen thousand men, taking the road to Burnsville, a little northwest of Iuka. Rosecrans, with two divisions, under

Generals Stanley and Hamilton, was ordered to Jacinto, to attack in the rear. Both columns started at the same time. Rosecrans reached Jacinto on the 18th of September, and the next day, after a march of twenty miles, advanced against the enemy. The enemy's skirmishers were met at Barnett's Corners, and were driven in. Grant in the mean time had arrived at Burnsville. By some misunderstanding, each column awaited for the attack to be commenced by the other. This occasioned considerable delay. At length a dispatch came from General Grant stating that he was waiting upon Rosecrans's attack. The latter promptly moved forward, and found the Confederates posted on a high ridge about two miles from Iuka. It was then four o'clock P.M. General Hamilton's division formed in line under a severe fire. The enemy had clearly an advantage in position. Hamilton could bring but a single battery, the Eleventh Ohio, to bear upon him. The ground was broken by ravines, and densely covered with undergrowth. It has been claimed for each side that it was outnumbered by the other. Rosecrans, in an order issued eight days after the battle, speaks of the unequal ground, which permitted the enemy to outnumber his men three to one. On the other hand, Pollard says that the Confederates were "overmatched by numbers."

It was almost night when the battle commenced, but in the two hours during which it lasted it raged with uncommon fierceness. Upon the Fifth Iowa and the Eleventh Missouri, supporting the battery, fell the most stunning blows from the enemy. The former lost seventy-six, the latter one hundred and sixteen, in killed and wounded. About the Eleventh Ohio battery there was the hottest work. The action had scarcely lasted half an

IUKA, MISSISSIPPI.

RICHARD F. OGLESBY.

hour before seventy-two of its men were put out of combat. The battery was charged and captured by the Confederates, and was again recaptured by the Fifth Iowa. Thrice again was it captured and recaptured. The fighting was in some instances hand to hand. It is said that in one spot, not over sixteen feet square, there were counted the next morning seventeen Confederate soldiers lying dead around one of their officers.

Grant did not attack, and during the night Price's army left the field. By casualties in the field and captures during the forced retreat, the loss sustained by that army amounted to upward of two thousand men. The Federal loss was nearly eight hundred. General Grant's combinations rendered it impossible for General Price to carry out his original plan of co-operation with Bragg. Van Dorn had also failed of his object, not having reached Corinth soon enough to insure its capture. The two armies, under Price and Van Dorn, were soon concentrated at Ripley, some distance west of Iuka, for an attack on Corinth. General Grant had abandoned Iuka and returned to Corinth. Four days afterward, Rosecrans, who had just been promoted to be a major general, assumed command of that place. In order to guard the line of railroad upon which the Federal army depended for supplies, General Grant proceeded to Jackson, fifty miles north of Corinth, having posted Ord's force on the same railroad farther south, at Bolivar. Thus Rosecrans was left at Corinth with an army numbering little more than twenty thousand men.

Van Dorn, in command of the Confederate army in Mississippi, moved against Corinth on the 2d of October, the day after Buell marched from Louisville against Bragg. The battle known as the Battle of Corinth was fought on the 3d. Van Dorn moved from Chewalla, on the line of the Memphis and Charleston Railroad, west of Corinth. It ought to have been evident to the Confederate commander that an attack on Corinth had scarcely a chance of success. He had a larger army than Rosecrans, it is true; but the latter held a position which, considering the situation of Grant's and Ord's columns, was defensible against an army more than twice as strong as that constituting its defense. The reason that Van Dorn moved from the west on Corinth was his knowledge of the fact that Beauregard, early in the year, had constructed fortifications on the north and east. These fortifications had been very much strengthened since the Federal occupation. Halleck had constructed a line of works inside of those constructed by Beauregard, and Grant had constructed still another inside of this latter. This interior line consisted of a chain of redoubts, arranged with a view to concentrate the fire of several heavy batteries upon an attacking force.

As soon as the enemy's approach assumed a definite shape, Rosecrans called in the outpost garrisons on the south side at Iuka, Burnsville, and Rienzi. The outpost on the Chewalla road was withdrawn a short distance and strengthened. It yet appeared doubtful to Rosecrans whether the main attack would be directed against himself, or against Bolivar, Bethel, or Jackson, at which places there were strong garrisons. But he would rather gain than lose on either supposition. If the attack was mainly against Corinth, then his position was eminently favorable for defense; if against any position farther north, then his position was equally favorable for offensive operations in the enemy's rear. Of the two cases offered, he would have much preferred the latter, as more fatal to Van Dorn. In an interview with his

division commanders on the morning of the 3d, Rosecrans instructed them "to hold the enemy at arm's-length" until the latter should assume a definite position, when they were to take a position where they could avail themselves of their batteries and the favorable ground in the vicinity of Corinth.

On the 3d, the Federal troops on the Chewalla road had been pushed back with severe loss. Brigadier General Hackleman was killed, and General Oglesby was severely wounded. It was Davies's division that had been principally engaged. The fight all day had been a general skirmish in the midst of dense timber, where heavy artillery could not be used to advantage. The plan of attack was, however, pretty fully developed. The main rebel column under Van Dorn rested its right upon the Chewalla road, and extended toward the north; its left, under Price, lay upon the Mobile and Ohio Railroad, almost directly north of Corinth, while Lovell held the extreme right. It was upon this side of the town—the northwest side—that Van Dorn expected to find the line of defense weakest. But during the past ten days other works had been built here, of which the Confederate commander was ignorant. The new line consisted of four redoubts. On the right, near Beauregard's old line, one of these was situated. On the night of the 3d, Fort Richardson, mounting five guns, was constructed, to cover the approach by the Bolivar road, which ran out from Corinth a little east of north. Fort Williams, which had been built to command the heights over which ran the road from Chewalla, was a very strong work, mounting several heavy Parrott guns; and Fort Robinette, built on a high, narrow ridge, enfiladed both the Bolivar and the Chewalla roads. Still another fort on the extreme left, near the Corinth Seminary, strengthened that flank, at the same time that it afforded additional protection to the centre. The ground along this line was unusually favorable to the use of artillery.

With admirable skill, Rosecrans had anticipated the probable approach of Van Dorn's army—had done his best, indeed, to tempt the latter in this very direction, and had made this part of his line as strong as any other. His line of battle on the morning of the 4th faced northward. Hamilton's division, which had just fought the battle of Iuka, held the right from Fort No. 1 to Fort Richardson. Then came Davies's division, joined on the left by six companies of Yates's sharpshooters. Stanley's division, consisting of two brigades, came next in order, its left resting on Fort Robinette, and McKean's division, with McArthur's brigade, held the extreme left. The cavalry, under Colonel Mizner, was posted on both wings and in the rear. The whole line was covered well in front by the undulations of ground, and the various batteries, under Lieutenant Colonel Lathrop, were either protected by fortifications or by an apron of hay or cotton-bales.

The near approach of the Confederates had placed the town of Corinth in an uncomfortable situation. There were a great number of non-combatants in the place, and the knowledge that the enemy was within a thousand yards of Rosecrans's line, and could easily shell the town, was a reasonable ground of uneasiness. Whatever apprehension there may have been on this point was realized before daylight. A battery had been planted by the enemy in Stanley's front, and not more than two hundred yards distant from Fort Robinette, from which, before daybreak, a fire was opened upon the town. The breakfast-fires of the Federal soldiers enabled the enemy to get the proper range, and a good number of shells were sent into the streets of Corinth. There was panic then among the non-combatants, who had been

DAVID S. STANLEY.

uneasy all night, and who now had recourse to hurried flight. At daylight a fire from Fort Williams in a very few minutes silenced the troublesome battery. The enemy meanwhile was forming at a little distance in the woods, while batteries on either side were already in action, and skirmishing was going on between sharpshooters in the marshy ground in front.

At about half past nine Price's column, in a dense mass, debouched on the Bolivar road. As it advanced it took the form of a wedge, and moved up with fierce velocity, as if it would pierce and overwhelm all opposition. Every Federal battery directed its full and unobstructed fire against this massive column, piercing it in front and on the flank, and making huge gaps in it—gaps which were no sooner made than filled. Musketry was then added to artillery; "but," says an eye-witness, "the enemy bent their necks downward and marched steadily to death, with their faces averted like men striving to protect themselves against a driving storm of hail." The Federal sharpshooters from behind their hastily-built breastworks poured in their fire, but still Price's column moved inflexibly onward. As it came nearer, the wedge had opened and developed into two columns, spreading out over the whole front of the field. Up the whole line pressed over every obstruction—up to the crest of the hill, flanking Fort Richardson on the right. Davies's division began to falter; but at the right moment Rosecrans was in its ranks, and they rallied, but not until the enemy had gained Fort Richardson. Even Rosecrans's head-quarters were captured, and from the shelter of the house a fire was opened on troops in the rear. In the yard of this house seven Confederate soldiers were found dead after the battle. Richardson, after a desperate and unequal contest for the possession of the fort, fell at last, and the enemy rushed into the captured work. Scarcely had the fort been taken before it was retaken by the Fifty-sixth Illinois.

Hamilton's division on the right had, in the mean time, swept the enemy's lines on the flank with a steady fire. Having fallen back a little when Stanley wavered, it now charged forward in the wake of the Fifty-sixth Illinois. There was an advance all along the line. A few minutes before, and it had appeared for a moment uncertain whether the enemy might not compensate for his terrible loss in approaching by an important success on Rosecrans's flank. But now all was changed. Price's entire column was broken and in swift retreat, flinging aside its arms, and scattering into the woods from which, but a little before, they had issued an immovable phalanx.

Van Dorn's column, which was to have attacked simultaneously with Price on the Chewalla road, was delayed by the nature of the ground. Ravines, and densely-wooded thickets, and artificial obstructions were in his way. The action with Price was over in a few minutes, and Van Dorn came on the field too late. Still the latter advanced. If the advance of Price's column had been gallant, yet it was surpassed by the almost incredible bravery of the Texan and Mississippian soldiers of Van Dorn's command. Besides the entanglements and topographical obstacles in their way, their line of advance was within point-blank range of the thirty-pound Parrott guns of Fort Williams and the guns of Fort Robinette. Supporting these works was a strong column of veterans as yet fresh for the battle. But Van Dorn's men overcame all obstacles with a courage that seemed irresistible. Colonel Rogers came on in advance at the head of his Texan brigade. But they paused at the ditch; Rogers fell just as he had leaped over. Then the Ohio brigade of Stanley's division, which Colonel Fuller had all this while kept lying with their faces to the ground behind the ridge on the right of the fort, rose and delivered six successive volleys, driving the Texans back. But the Confederate supports came up, and there was a severe hand-to-hand fight, which resulted at length in the success of the national troops. The victory had been gained at a fearful cost of life. The Sixty-third Ohio went into the fight with two hundred and fifty men, and left just one half that number of killed and wounded on the field. The rout of Van Dorn's column was as complete as had been that of Price's. Forts Williams and Robinette, the latter of which had borne the brunt of the assault, now poured their ruinous shower of shell into the midst of the flying enemy. Such had been the obstinacy of the assault on Fort Robinette that fifty-six dead Confederates were found heaped up in front of the redoubt.

The battle had lasted now for an hour and a half since Price's column came out on the Bolivar road. But the pursuit was an important part of the battle. Says the correspondent from whom we have already quoted: "The pursuit of the beaten foe was terrible. Sheets of flame blazed through the forest. Huge trunks were shattered by crashing shells. You may track the flying conflict for miles by scarified trees, broken branches, twisted gun-barrels and shattered stocks, bloodstained garments and mats of human hair, which lie on the ground where men died; hillocks which mark ditches where dead rebels were covered, and smoothly-rounded graves where slaughtered patriots were tenderly buried." The retreat was continued across the Hatchie River to within a short distance of Ripley. General Hurlbut, of Ord's command, joined in the pursuit. Hurlbut, while the battle was going on, had started from Bolivar, intending to strike the enemy's rear. On the 5th the enemy's retreat was intercepted. Eight guns were captured, many hundred small-arms, and several hundred prisoners.

As regards the generalship displayed in the battle of Corinth, there can be but one opinion. General Rosecrans planned and fought the battle with consummate skill. It must of course be admitted that he was exceedingly fortunate in having opposed to him two generals who were as rash in their attempt against Corinth as their attack was magnificent. Very few battles in the war were so obstinate and bloody as the battle of Corinth. General Rosecrans, in a congratulatory order issued October 25th, said to his troops: "Upon the issue of the fight depended the possession of West Tennessee,

E. O. C. ORD.

and perhaps even the fate of operations in Kentucky. The entire available force of the rebels in Mississippi, save a few garrisons and a small reserve, attacked you. They were commanded by Van Dorn, Price, Villipigue, Rust, Armstrong, Maury, and others, in person. They numbered, according to their own authorities, nearly forty thousand men—almost double your own numbers. You fought them into the position we desired on the third, punishing them terribly; and on the fourth, in three hours after the infantry entered into action, they were beaten. You killed and buried one thousand four hundred and twenty-four officers and men, some of their most distinguished officers falling, among whom was the gallant Colonel Rogers, of the Second Texas, who bore their colors at the head of his storming column to the edge of the ditch of Battery Robinette, where he fell. Their wounded, at the usual rate, must exceed five thousand. You took two thousand two hundred and sixty-eight prisoners, among whom are one hundred and thirty-seven field-officers, captains, and subalterns, representing fifty-three regiments of infantry, sixteen regiments of cavalry, thirteen batteries of artillery, and seven battalions, making sixty-nine regiments, thirteen batteries, seven battalions, besides several companies. You captured three thousand three hundred and fifty stands of small-arms, fourteen stands of colors, two pieces of artillery, and a large quantity of equipments. You pursued his retreating columns forty miles in force with infantry and sixty miles with cavalry, and were ready to follow him to Mobile, if necessary, had you received orders. * * * * * *

"But our victory has cost us the lives of three hundred and fifteen brave officers and soldiers, besides the wounded. * * * The memory of the brave Hackleman, the chivalrous Kirby Smith, the true and noble colonels Thrush, Baker, and Miles, and Captain Guy C. Ward, with many others, live with us and in the memory of a free people, while history will inscribe their names among its heroes."

The same day that this order was issued General Rosecrans was ordered from Corinth to Cincinnati to command the Department of the Cumberland, which was made to comprise that portion of Tennessee east of the Tennessee River, and such parts of Northern Georgia and Alabama as might be taken possession of by the national forces. The armies of the West were at this time reorganized, the troops under General Grant constituting the Thirteenth Army Corps, and those under Rosecrans the Fourteenth. On the 16th of October Grant had been assigned to the command of the Department of the Tennessee, which was defined to include Cairo, Forts Henry and Donelson, Northern Mississippi, and all of Kentucky and Tennessee west of the Tennessee River.

After the battle of Corinth, Van Dorn, collecting together the scattered fragments of his army, took a position in the vicinity of Holly Springs, on the Cairo and New Orleans Railroad. General Grant, having received a considerable re-enforcement from new levies, followed the line of this railroad, advancing southward from Bolivar and Jackson. He began this movement on the 4th of November. During the month of November it remained at Lagrange, three miles east of Grand Junction. The Federal occupation of New Orleans, and the advance which the national armies had made into Arkansas, seemed to render possible a successful campaign for the complete

GRAND JUNCTION, TENNESSEE.

Orleans Railroad. But there were great obstacles in the way of success in this direction, the most formidable of which was that the advance was far into the enemy's country. A long line of communications stretched back in the rear, which must be guarded against attack. No small portion of Grant's army must be detached for garrisons at Columbus, Humboldt, Trenton, Jackson, Bolivar, Corinth, and Grand Junction, and at every stage of the advance there must be a farther depletion. Much might have been effected by a large and effective force of cavalry; but this force was wanting. The distance over which supplies were to be transported, even to Grand Junction, was one hundred and forty miles. Memphis was far preferable to Columbus as a base of supplies, being only fifty miles distant from Grand Junction, but the road was not in running order.

On the 28th of November Grant moved from Lagrange. The next day Hamilton's advance entered Holly Springs, from which Van Dorn had retired, and was reported to be strongly fortified on the Tallahatchie River. By December 1 the main portion of Grant's army was in camp at Lampkin's Mills, south of Holly Springs, and seven miles north of the Tallahatchie. Simultaneously with Grant's advance General Curtis marched a column of seven thousand men, under General Alvin P. Hovey, from Helena, in Arkansas, on the Mississippi, intending to co-operate with Grant by striking Van Dorn's flank on the Tallahatchie. This caused Van Dorn to give up the position held by him on that river and to retire farther southward, through Oxford, closely followed by Grant.

Hovey's expedition was very successful. The cavalry which accompanied it, under Colonel Washburn, contributed greatly to this success. Hovey's column crossed the Tallahatchie on the 28th of November, and then destroyed the railroad line for some distance. At Oakland an engagement occurred with the Confederate cavalry, which resulted favorably to Colonel Washburn. The Confederate steam-boats on the Tallahatchie were destroyed, and some locomotives which had been left behind by the enemy. Having effected this much, and the enemy having fallen back nearly to Jackson, the expedition returned to Helena. A few days later, General Grant having made his head-quarters at Oxford, Van Dorn saw the way open for an attack on Grant's rear. He determined, therefore, to surprise and capture Holly Springs. About daylight on the morning of December 20, Van Dorn's cavalry, consisting of twenty-two regiments, appeared in the streets of Holly Springs. In the railroad dépôt, on the east side of the town, there were two trains of cars, one of them empty and the other loaded with cotton. These were fired. A hundred men were guarding the valuable government stores at the dépôt, but these were soon overwhelmed and captured. Other detachments of infantry in the suburbs of the town were surprised and captured in squads. Six companies of the Second Illinois Cavalry were surrounded, but, after a gallant fight, cut their way out, and the enemy began his work of destruction. All the Northern men in town were taken prisoners, and, after being plundered, were paroled. The passenger and freight dépôts were burned. The arsenal, full of arms and ammunition, suffered the same fate. Some twenty or thirty buildings on the public square and eighteen hundred bales of cotton were involved in the conflagration. It was estimated that the government property destroyed amounted to two millions of dollars, besides the cotton.

The attack on Holly Springs was not a surprise to General Grant, who had telegraphed to Colonel Murphy, commanding the town, that he would be attacked. He had sent on re-enforcements, which, however, arrived too late. The telegraphic dispatch to Colonel Murphy reached him on the evening of the 19th. He had under his command five or six hundred infantry, besides the Second Illinois Cavalry, and, with a proper disposition of this force, and making the necessary preparations for defense, he might have resisted the attack successfully until re-enforcements came to his assistance. General Grant, in his order four days afterward, properly stigmatized the surrender of the place as disgraceful. He said: "With all the cotton, public stores, and substantial buildings about the dépôt, it would have been perfectly practicable to have made, in a few hours, a defense sufficient to resist, with a small garrison, all the cavalry force brought against them, until the re-enforcements, which the commanding officer was notified were marching to his relief, could have reached him."[1]

Other stations along the line were captured, and it was the enemy's intention to destroy every bridge between Corinth and Columbus. The destruction of his dépôt of supplies at Holly Springs rendered it impossible for Grant to continue his advance southward. He returned to Holly Springs with his army, from which a detachment of ten thousand men was sent to General Sherman to assist in the operations against Vicksburg.

Returning from General Grant's department to that which was now under

conquest of the Northwest, or at least for the possession of the Cairo and New

[1] The Richmond Dispatch of January 15 contained the following estimate of the victory gained at Holly Springs:

"The surprised camp surrendered 1800 men and 150 commissioned officers, who were immediately paroled. And then commenced the work of destruction. The extensive buildings of the Mississippi Central dépôt—the station-house, the engine-house, and immense store-houses—were filled with supplies of clothing and commissary stores. Outside of the dépôt the barrels of flour were estimated to be half a mile in length, one hundred and fifty feet through, and fifteen feet high. Turpentine was thrown over this, and the whole amount destroyed. Up town, the court-house and public buildings, livery-stables, and all capacious establishments, were filled, ceiling-high, with medical and ordnance stores. These were all fired, and the explosion of one of the buildings, in which was stored one hundred barrels of powder, knocked down nearly all the houses on the south side of the square. Surely such a scene of devastation was never before presented to the eye of man. Glance at the gigantic estimates:

"1,809,000 fixed cartridges and other ordnance stores, valued at $1,500,000, including 5000 rifles and 2000 revolvers.

"100,000 suits of clothing and other quartermaster's stores, valued at $500,000; 5000 barrels of flour and other commissary stores, valued at $500,000.

"$1,000,000 worth of medical stores, for which invoices to that amount were exhibited, and 1000 bales of cotton, and $600,000 worth of sutlers' stores."

According to this account, General Grant's wife was among the captured.

HOLLY SPRINGS, MISSISSIPPI.

GROCERIES MITHELLS.

Railroad Depot.

Rebel Armory.

ALVIN P. HOVEY.

Rosecrans's command, we find the eastern, and a large portion of the central part of Tennessee occupied by the Confederate army which Bragg had withdrawn from Kentucky in October.

The army which Rosecrans received from Buell was now largely re-enforced by new levies. President Lincoln had, in July and August, called 600,000 new men into the field.[1] Buell's army had been greatly depleted by desertions. In June some 14,000 men were absent from his command. This demoralization increased to such an extent that, in September, special officers were appointed to arrest deserters and return them to service. Rosecrans had in his army so many raw recruits that he was compelled to devote considerable time to their discipline. In moving against Bragg, he had also to contend against another difficulty. Two large armies had ravaged the space intervening between the Ohio and the Tennessee Rivers since the middle of summer. It was now autumn; and, unless Rosecrans waited for the harvests of another year to ripen, he could enter upon an active campaign only after he should have accumulated a large store of provisions. Not only could he not supply his army from the country, but the very avenues of communication with a distant base of supplies must be provided. The Cumberland River was too low for his purpose. The Louisville and Nashville Railroad had been destroyed by Bragg. The bridges had been burned, and the tunnel at Gallatin, north of Nashville, had been destroyed. The railroad must be repaired, and even then it would be a poor substitute for the river. The enemy had a superior force of cavalry, under Forrest and Morgan, and it would be no difficult matter for Bragg to dispatch a force to his rear which would undo in an hour the work of days. It would not have been easy to interrupt the water communication except by elaborate fortifications. A river does not depend upon the safety of bridges, as does a railroad, for its continuous and perfect communication.

In the subordinate officers there was some change. We drop Gilbert, and have the good fortune of Thomas's company as an actual instead of a nominal commander. McCook and Crittenden are retained, and Rousseau is deservedly elevated to the command of a corps. In the exchange of Buell for Rosecrans we are also gainers, if we look for vigorous operations. There are many obstacles in the way, as we have pointed out; but Rosecrans meets these with a determined will. Little more than a month after his assumption of command he is on the move, and by the 1st of November has his advance at Bowling Green. A week later McCook's corps passed through Nashville. But the railroad had been completed only as far as to the northern border of Tennessee.

[1] The following table, prepared from official reports, shows the number of troops furnished by each of the loyal states up to December 1, 1862. This table does not include the 80,000 furnished just after the capture of Fort Sumter.

State		State	
Maine	30,240	Indiana	96,698
New Hampshire	16,000	Illinois	130,059
Vermont	19,006	Michigan	47,220
Massachusetts	72,107	Wisconsin	42,557
Rhode Island	10,000	Minnesota	10,957
Connecticut	28,551	Iowa	50,000
New York	219,059	Kansas	14,000
New Jersey	27,400	California	9,000
Pennsylvania	230,000	Oregon	1,500
Delaware	2,500	Colorado	3,300
Maryland	10,000	Nebraska	3,500
West Virginia	20,000	New Mexico	2,000
Kentucky	55,000	District of Columbia	2,000
Missouri	38,031	Total	1,355,087
Ohio	164,402		

This estimate includes nearly 100,000 volunteers furnished for special service and for a short period of time.

If the Confederates ever needed a commander bold, and at the same time wise, it was now. The opportunity offered to such a commander was even greater than it had been in the summer. Then the Confederate armies were being rapidly filled by the new Conscription Act, and numbers had made Bragg confident of great results to be gained by a march to the Ohio. His invasion had not gained the objects for which it was undertaken. He had failed to take Louisville and Cincinnati. He had not even gained any important victory in the field. The Northwestern states had not sued for peace, notwithstanding the magnanimous terms which he had offered. Even the citizens of Kentucky had not rallied around his standard. Those who joined him had been pressed into the service against their will. What might have been the attitude of Kentuckians if he had succeeded in the military objects of his invasion is only conjectural. Many had greeted his arrival when the way seemed open to a grand success. Many had been intimidated by the formidable appearance of his army when there was a panic in the great Northern cities on the line of the Ohio, and when as yet the Federal armies appeared incompetent to oppose an adequate resistance. But when his army began to halt, then to waver, and finally to retreat without the prestige of victory before Buell's army, the situation was reversed. Those who were intimidated lost their fears. Those whose expectations of Confederate success had been aroused now lost their hope, and began to fear for the consequences of their premature demonstrations in Bragg's favor. Bragg had been unable to accomplish what he had threatened against those who resisted him, and had disappointed those who had been too hasty and prodigal in their trust. When his troops left Lexington, women ran through the streets wringing their hands in terror and dismay, and his train was encumbered with the vehicles of panic-stricken refugees. When the more wealthy citizens looked upon the flaming piles in which their property was being consumed, because if left it would no longer enrich a Confederate army, the keen anguish of distress was mingled with a sentiment of disgust for the treachery of which they had become the unhappy victims. But an immense amount of stores which had been captured from the defenseless was carried away by the retreating army, and this was almost the solitary token of its poor success. When the train passed through Bryantsville, on the 13th of October, the few guns and ammunition wagons which had been captured had the precedence. Then came the long train of captured stores, which was followed by humiliated refugees, flying with their negroes in every imaginable sort of vehicle, from stately carriages and stage-coaches down to ambulances and Jersey wagons. The infantry, artillery, and cavalry of the army brought up the rear, and intermixed with the medley spectacle were vast herds of cattle, horses, and mules. "The effect of our retreat along the road every where," writes a Confederate historian,[1] "was sinking and depressing in the extreme. No miniature banners waved, no white kerchiefs greeted our troops with approving smiles from lovely women, and no wild cheer was heard responsive to the greetings which had attended their march into Kentucky. Trembling women stole to the doors to look upon the strange, mystified scene before them, and, as the truth gradually forced itself upon them, their eyes filled with tears, and they shrank back, fearing even to make the slightest demonstration of friendliness. All was sullen, downcast, and gloomy." The same writer farther on admits "that the South was bitterly disappointed in the manifestations of public sentiment in Kentucky." He says: "The exhibitions of sympathy in this state were meagre and sentimental, and amounted to but little practical aid to our cause. Indeed, no subject was at once more dispiriting and perplexing to the South than the cautious and unmanly reception given to our armies, both in Kentucky and Maryland. The reference we have made to the sentiment of each of these states leaves but little room to doubt the general conclusion that the dread of Yankee vengeance and love of property were too powerful to make them take risks against these in favor of a cause for which their people had a mere preference, without any attachment to it higher than those of selfish calculation."

In the summer, then, Bragg had been overconfident of his power to overwhelm the states of the Northwest by his newly-conscripted army. Now his force was less in number, but the opportunity offered was, even under this disparaging circumstance, more tempting to a vigorous military leader. It was possible now to make use of the solitary advantage gained by the summer campaign. The devastation of the country over which both armies had passed and repassed, while it hindered Rosecrans, in so far helped Bragg. The latter had shown a great degree of boldness in design in the summer campaign, but, at the same time, had betrayed his lack of great executive ability. So far as successful execution of a plan depended upon fearless firmness, he could be trusted; so far as it depended upon keen and comprehensive insight, he was almost certain to be foiled. It was just this latter element, which he so much wanted, that was most necessary in an encounter with Rosecrans, who was himself especially distinguished by this very characteristic of genius. The Confederate General Joseph E. Johnston was now in command of the department, but he was unable to take the field on account of a severe wound received in Virginia, in the battle of Seven Pines. That Johnston was a far abler general than Bragg can not well be questioned, but what would have been the prospect of success if he had been actually in command, it is scarcely possible to infer from the most careful scrutiny into his subsequent campaigns.

On the 26th of November the cars for the first time ran through to Nashville. A heavy force was posted at Gallatin to protect the road. From that time the preparations for the campaign were speedily pushed forward. At the close of December the army had been clothed, and sufficient ammuni-

[1] Pollard's Second Year of the War, p. 159.

WILLIAM S. ROSECRANS.

tion and supplies were brought to Nashville to secure the army against the needs which might at any time arise from the interruption of the railroad. Having made these preparations, Rosecrans awaited his opportunity, which was not long wanting. It was impossible for Bragg to make a false move which would not immediately lay him open to his wary antagonist. To all appearance Rosecrans was at his leisure. It was given out that he would no doubt go into winter quarters at Nashville. But, as soon as his army was provided for, he began to look with dissatisfaction upon the interval between Nashville and Murfreesborough. Which army should cross that intervening space to attack the other—his or Bragg's? Bragg's army numbered sixty thousand men, of which force nearly one third was cavalry. Rosecrans had 40,000 infantry and about 3000 cavalry. The question as between a movement from Nashville on Murfreesborough and one from Murfreesborough on Nashville was momentous. The army receiving the attack would avoid the waste of force attending an advance movement, and be able to avail itself of fortifications. But it was important that an action should not long be delayed. The enemy could well afford to wait, but every day materially diminished Rosecrans's stock of provisions. Happily for Rosecrans, Bragg solved the problem, and in a highly satisfactory manner, by sending off a large portion of his cavalry under Forrest and Morgan. Forrest was dispatched to General Grant's rear, while Morgan advanced into Kentucky to break Rosecrans's line of communication. This was a fortunate event for Rosecrans. One brigade of the enemy's cavalry, under the best horseman of the Confederacy, was thus out of the field. Morgan was not dangerous, acting in his rear, as provision had been made against that event. These "clouds of mounted men," as Rosecrans called them, had been his principal annoyance. They swept the country in every direction. Rosecrans's cavalry force was so small that it was kept within the infantry lines. Bragg had still a large cavalry command left under Generals Wheeler and Wharton. So settled was Bragg's opinion as to Rosecrans's indisposition to assume the offensive, that he had on neither of the roads leading in his direction any heavy force. Polk and Kirby Smith were at Murfreesborough, while Hardee held the left toward Franklin with an advanced guard at Nolensville. Rosecrans deemed that his opportunity had arrived, and moved December 26th. McCook's corps of three divisions advanced on the

Nolensville pike against Hardee. Thomas, with two divisions under Negley and Rousseau, advanced by the Franklin and Wilson pikes to threaten Hardee's flank, and then to fall in to Nolensville, ready, in the event of McCook's success, to support Crittenden against an attack at Stone River, south of Lavergne; for Crittenden had advanced along the Murfreesborough pike to the latter place with Wood's, Palmer's, and Van Cleve's divisions. Crittenden's corps at Lavergne was the pivot of the entire movement; McCook's was to strike hard upon Hardee; and Thomas's was to support either McCook or Crittenden, as circumstances should decide. The plan was admirably well conceived. There were two possible issues to the action: either Hardee would be re-enforced, and the main battle would be fought west of Murfreesborough; or he would fall back on Murfreesborough, uniting with Polk and Smith in the defense of that place.

On the 26th McCook was skirmishing all day, and at night occupied a strong position at Nolensville. The same night Crittenden was at Lavergne, having passed over a rough and difficult country, intersected by forests and cedar brakes. Thomas also had made good progress, meeting little resistance. All this day and the next the separate columns pushed on through a drenching rain. The Christmas holidays were now begun, but they were no holidays to the weary soldier. On the second day of his advance the movements of Hardee were clearly developed. He was retreating, but not southward. It was now certain that the battle would be fought at or a little north of Murfreesborough. On the night of that day Crittenden had reached Stewart's Creek. Thomas had brought his column to Nolensville. McCook was following Hardee closely and watchfully. On the 29th McCook's advance brought him within seven miles of Murfreesborough; Crittenden moved to within three miles of that place, at Stone River; and Thomas held the centre, Rousseau's division being nearer to Crittenden, and held in reserve; while Negley's was in the front. That night Rosecrans, having moved his head-quarters to Stewart's Creek, went to the front, where he remained. Although it was only about thirty miles from Nashville to Murfreesborough, Rosecrans's advance on the latter was greatly impeded by Wheeler's and Wharton's cavalry. The main cause of delay, however, was the necessity for Rosecrans to await the development of the affair between McCook and Hardee.

4 M

The situation of Bragg's army was a good one for defense. Upon Murfreesborough as a centre numerous important pikes converge. The railroad from Nashville, taking Lavergne upon its route, runs through the town in a southeasterly direction. As Rosecrans had little cavalry, it was not necessary for Bragg to detach from his army any considerable force to guard that portion of the railroad which was in his possession. He held a central position, while Rosecrans moved along the radii of a quadrant. One thing, however, was unfavorable. The topography of the country in the vicinity of Stone River rendered it difficult to operate successfully with cavalry. It was a broken and heavily-wooded country, with here and there an open field, and was well adapted to the use of infantry and artillery.

The battle known as the battle of Stone River lasted several days. But the main actions—those which decided its character and result—were fought on the 31st of December, 1862, and the 2d of January, 1863. The battle was fought on the banks of Stone River, a stream which, flowing eastward, crosses the pike a mile north of Murfreesborough, where it abruptly changes its course, flowing northward and parallel with the road. On the evening of December 30th, the left of Rosecrans's line lay along the river on its western bank. Two divisions of Crittenden's corps, Van Cleve's and Wood's, extended from the Murfreesborough pike to the river. The other division —Palmer's—held the cotton-field on the right of the pike. Thomas held the centre, with Negley on Palmer's right, and Rousseau in reserve. McCook lay off to the left, his line being extended to a great length toward the Franklin road, facing southeastward.

Stone River, which skirted the Federal left, ran through the enemy's line. The great mass of the Confederate army lay on the west bank opposite McCook. This portion of Bragg's lines was held by Hardee's corps. Breckinridge's division of this corps was detached from the rest, and held a position on the east bank. Polk held the ground between Hardee and Breckinridge.

Both Bragg and Rosecrans had determined to attack on the 31st, and the plan of attack formed by each exactly corresponded. On each side the bulk of the army was massed on the left wing. Bragg thought to whip McCook, and push Rosecrans off from the pike connecting him with Nashville. Rosecrans designed to crush Breckinridge, and, rapidly following up the blow, get in between the enemy and Murfreesborough. Neither had any positive expectation of being attacked by the other. As Rosecrans was obliged to bring his left wing across the river in order to carry out his plan, his movements were subject to greater delay. He was thus somewhat anticipated by Bragg. He had instructed McCook, in case of an attack being made upon his corps by Hardee, to hold out stubbornly, thus insuring the success of the attack on Breckinridge and Polk.

McCook's corps consisted of three divisions, which extended from left to right thus: Sheridan, Davis, Johnson. The latter division was surprised by Hardee at daybreak on the 31st, and while Rosecrans's movements on the left had hardly begun. The latter was not unwilling that McCook should be attacked, if only it did not disturb his prearranged plan. But in this respect he was destined to be disappointed. He was not aware of the advantage which Hardee was rapidly gaining on McCook. Perhaps he remembered the obstinacy with which this corps of McCook's had a few weeks before withstood the attacks of the same enemy at Perryville. Three or four hours of obstinate resistance on McCook's part would without doubt enable him to overwhelm Breckinridge; certainly such commanders as Davis and Sheridan could maintain the battle for that length of time. There was one thing, however, which disturbed Rosecrans's confidence. McCook's line, he feared, was not arranged in a proper manner. He had the night before spoken of this arrangement to McCook. Said Rosecrans: "I don't like the facing so much to the east, but must confide that to you, who know the ground." The battle had been going on about an hour, when one of McCook's staff officers announced that the right was heavily pressed, and needed assistance. The messenger was not sufficiently explicit. He certainly failed to impress upon Rosecrans's mind the impression that there was any danger. The fact was that two of Johnson's brigades—Kirk's and Willich's—had been routed, leaving their batteries in the enemy's hands. Davis, too, had been doubled up brigade by brigade, although gallantly resisting, and driven back. This was not reported to Rosecrans; and the latter, although he heard the battle swerving more and more to the left, supposed that McCook was refusing his right gradually, according to the instructions given him. He therefore directed the officer to return and direct General McCook to hold on obstinately.

It was not long before a second officer arrived, as Van Cleve was crossing Stone River, and stated that the right wing was being driven. This was now only too evident to Rosecrans, who could hear the sound of battle rapidly swaying northward. Sheridan had followed Davis, and the peril was now imminent. Van Cleve was recalled, and two of his brigades sent over to the centre. Rousseau's division was sent into the cedar brakes to support Sheridan, and become the nucleus of a new formation. The scene which met Rosecrans's eye as he went over to the right would have unnerved a man of less resource. The stragglers from McCook's routed command were swarming to the rear through the brakes in crowds. The enemy had succeeded in breaking up Rosecrans's plan of attack, and had carried his first position. Even Negley had given way in the centre, and Rousseau could scarcely bear up against the impetus of the attack. All the troops on Palmer's left had been sent to the right. The only division which retained its original position was Palmer's. Let us see how that division was situated, so much now depended upon it. Most of the division was now on the right of the pike. Cruft's brigade was a little in the rear, in the wood. Hazen stood across the pike, so that his front line extended eastward to the

railroad which runs between the pike and the river. It was of the first importance that this position of Hazen's should be held, in order to cover the formation of a new line, in which work Rosecrans was now engaged. The river on Palmer's left, being deep and having but a single ford, was a good flank defense. A rise of ground at the railroad afforded some protection against the enemy's artillery. Palmer's troops were well-disciplined veterans, and were fresher than the troops of the enemy, who had been fighting since morning. About ten o'clock Hazen and Cruft were attacked in great force; but, fortunately, the valor of the Federal troops and the strength of Parsons's artillery baffled every onset. The whole of Bragg's army, with the exception of Breckinridge, was now engaged. At one o'clock P.M. and at four o'clock fresh attempts were made to drive Hazen from his position, but without success.

In the mean time Rosecrans had been at work farther to the right. When McCook's routed battalions retreated out of the corn-fields and through the skirts of the woods on Rousseau's flank, the latter officer found it quite impossible, under the circumstances, to get his division into position in the cedar thicket. Galloping off to General Thomas, he described his situation. In the rear there was open ground, about three miles distant from Murfreesborough. Here the railroad and turnpike, about fifty rods apart, run through a slight cut, forming a natural rifle-pit. Farther back there is on either side of the road a swell of ground, which, once gained and held, constituted an impregnable position. To this favorable position Rousseau withdrew his division, with General Thomas's permission. Guenther's and Loomis's batteries were posted on the left, with Stokes's Chicago battery, and were strongly supported by a brigade of regulars. Scribner's brigade took position in the natural rifle-pit above mentioned, and Beatty's brigade held the crest on the right, which stretched away to the northern edge of a cedar wood. Scarcely had the line been formed, stretching from Hazen northwestwardly to Van Cleve's position on the right flank, when the gray uniforms of Hardee's troops were seen issuing from the edge of this wood. The hill on the left, where the batteries had been placed, commanded the entire space in front of the wood on the right, and as rapidly as the enemy came forth into the open ground his ranks were mown down without mercy. It was impossible for Bragg to move Rosecrans from his strong position, while every onset decimated the ranks of his own troops. The prompt formation of the Federal line in the strongest possible position had turned the fortune of the battle. But Rosecrans's loss in the early part of the day had been heavy. Over twenty-five pieces of artillery had fallen into the enemy's hands, and a large number of prisoners had been captured by Wharton's cavalry. Wheeler had the day before succeeded in gaining Rosecrans's rear, and captured a large number of wagons loaded with supplies and baggage, and so small was the Federal cavalry command that he made the entire circuit of the lines, and joined Wharton on the left. But these movements of the enemy's cavalry scarcely disturbed Rosecrans, who could not by any mere annoyance, or even partial reverse, be diverted from the end he had in view.

The battle on Wednesday ended with the complete repulse both of Hardee on the right and of Polk at the centre. Hazen at the close of the day withdrew from the advanced position which he had held with wonderful tenacity for ten hours. The next day opened the new year, 1863. Rosecrans's position was so strong that Bragg feared to make an assault, and contented himself with skirmishing and a few cavalry raids. Rosecrans had been re-enforced by Starkweather's and Walker's brigades; but he preferred to wait for fresh supplies of food and ammunition before resuming offensive operations.

On Friday, the 2d of January, the contest was renewed with some degree of vigor. Bragg early in the morning directed a heavy cannonade against the Federal centre from four strong batteries, and made demonstrations against the right. But this show of attack was not followed up, and, indeed, was intended merely to discover whether Rosecrans still kept his position in force; for the cavalry scouts had reported to Bragg indications of a retrograde movement on the part of the Federal commander.

While Bragg was speculating thus in regard to the movements of Rosecrans, the latter was quietly crossing Stone River with Van Cleve's division, and, before Bragg was fully aware of the movement, he had gained a position on and under cover of an eminence which commanded Polk's line, enfilading it. Either Polk must withdraw or Van Cleve. The whole of Breckinridge's division, therefore, was massed in front of the threatening position, and heavily supported by artillery, and by cavalry to the number of 2000. Before the formidable assault which was made by Breckinridge at about four o'clock P.M., Van Cleve retired in some confusion to the other side of the river. But it was not long before the situation at this point was exactly reversed, and the pursuers were the pursued.

Just on the other side of the river from the eminence carried by Breckinridge was the crest from which, on Wednesday, Loomis's, Guenther's, and Stokes's batteries had belched forth destruction against the enemy. Here General Crittenden, who commanded on this part of the field, directed his chief of artillery to dispose his batteries for a terrific cannonade, while three brigades—two of them from Negley's division—were ordered up to meet the enemy, who was endeavoring to push his advantages. At this point Rosecrans reports: "The firing was terrific and the havoc terrible. The enemy retreated more rapidly than they had advanced. In forty minutes they lost 2000 men." Bragg had timed his assault fortunately for himself. Had it occurred earlier, with the same disastrous result, there would have been no need of protracting the already sufficiently bloody battle of Stone River for another day. Rosecrans says: "It was now after dark and raining, or we should have pursued the enemy into Murfreesborough. As it was, Crittenden's corps passed over, and, with Davis, occupied the crests, which were in-

MURFREESBOROUGH, TENNESSEE.

THE APPEARENCE OF BRAGG'S DESERTED ENCAMPMENT.

trenched in a few hours." If Bragg had deemed Polk's line untenable with a single division in this commanding position, now that it was occupied by a whole corps it was absolutely necessary for the Confederate general to withdraw. In order to guard against an attack on his right, which might again, as on Wednesday, disturb his plans, Rosecrans resorted to a very ancient, but very effective species of strategy. By a heavy division of camp-fires, and by a feigned line of battle, whose only reality consisted in torches, he succeeded in impressing the Confederate commander with more respect for his forces in that direction than might have been entertained upon a closer inspection.

About noon on the 3d of January, Bragg determined to give up the contest. Up to that time there had been no fighting during the day. It had been raining since long before daybreak, and Rosecrans would have found great difficulty in pushing the enemy, dragging his artillery through the muddy fields. Besides, the troops of both armies were nearly exhausted by exposure and fatigue. That night Bragg retreated to Duck River with perfect security. It was an utter impossibility for Rosecrans, under the circumstances, to follow in pursuit. Even if the weather had been favorable, he had no cavalry, and his artillery horses were worn out.

Bragg and Rosecrans, in their official reports of the battle, both claim that they were opposed by superior numbers. Rosecrans estimates the force with which he left Nashville at nearly 47,000, and in the battle at 43,000. The enemy's force he estimates at over 62,000. Bragg, on the other hand, gives the number of his effective force, on the morning of December 31, as less than 35,000, and estimates the force opposed to him at nearly 70,000.

Considering the numbers engaged, the battle of Stone River was one of the bloodiest of the whole war. The entire Federal loss in killed was 1553, of whom 92 were officers. The wounded numbered a little over 7000, and the loss in prisoners was nearly 3000, making the Federal loss in the aggregate nearly 12,000, or more than one fourth of the entire army. The entire Confederate loss is stated by Bragg as 10,000. Both armies lost the services of important general officers by death or wounds. General Sill, of McCook's corps, was killed. On the Confederate side, Generals James E. Rains and Roger M. Hanson were killed, and Generals Chalmers and Adams were disabled.

THE STONE RIVER MONUMENT.

Turning now from the military operations in Tennessee, we will close this chapter with a review of the political situation in that state.

The manner in which Tennessee was first carried over to the side of the rebellion has been recorded in this history. The governor of that state, Isham G. Harris, had from the first identified himself with the Confederate leaders. With evident reluctance, Tennessee followed the policy urged upon it by its governor. The eastern portion of the state was intensely loyal, giving 33,000 out of 48,000 votes against secession. Among those who disapproved of secession was John Bell, who, as Presidential candidate, carried the largest vote in the state. But he equally disapproved of what was then styled the coercive policy of the administration in relation to the seceded states. He regarded this policy as a justification of the state in refusing aid to the general government, but, as a matter of expediency, advised the people to take the attitude of neutrals and mediators. It was impossible, however, after the President's proclamation of April 15, 1861, for the more conservative citizens to stem the tide which then set in in favor of the revolutionists. Those who had before counseled inaction now looked with favor upon that clause of Governor Harris's reply to Secretary Cameron, which, while it refused two regiments of militia to put down the insurrection, threatened to raise 50,000 troops, if necessary, for the defense of Southern rights. Even Neil S. Brown, formerly Governor of Tennessee, who had joined Bell in his efforts to sustain a neutral position, now recommended a vigorous war policy. He said: "I have hoped obstinately against such an alternative; but the conviction is forced upon my mind that it is the settled policy of the administration, and, so far as I can see, of the whole North, to urge a war of extermination against the South. The clouds are gathering in every direction, and the signs now are that the border states are to be the battle-ground. In this view, the first duty is to arm at once; and to talk of keeping out of such a contest, if it comes, is simply idle."

When the Legislature met in extra session on the 25th of April, Governor Harris, in his message, recommended the passage of an ordinance separating the state from the Union, with a view of joining the Confederacy as soon thereafter as possible. The members of the Legislature had not been elected upon any such issue as was now presented, and could not fairly be said to represent the views of the people. But the governor "could see no propriety for encumbering the people of the state with the election of delegates to do that which it was in the power of the Legislature to enable them to do for themselves." The Legislature had been in session about a week, when Henry W. Hilliard, commissioner from the Confederate States, appeared before it, and addressed the members. His object, he said, was to establish a temporary alliance between Tennessee and the Confederacy, as a movement preliminary to a permanent relationship. Something more was at issue than the right to hold slaves, namely, the right of self-government.

This address and the governor's message induced the Legislature, on the 1st of May, to instruct Governor Harris to enter into a military league with the Confederacy. The governor, in obedience to this instruction, appointed as commissioners for that purpose Gustavus A. Henry, Archibald O. W. Totten, and Washington Barrow. The league was established May 7th between these gentlemen and Mr. Hilliard. According to the terms of the Convention, the military operations, offensive and defensive, of Tennessee against the United States were, until the union of that state with the Confederacy, to be as completely under the control of President Davis as if the union had already been established. Upon becoming a permanent member of the Confederacy, the state would turn over to the Confederate government all the public property, naval stores, and munitions of war in her possession and acquired from the United States. The expenditures of the state in the interim were to be met and provided for by the Confederate government.

There was a great majority of the Legislature in favor of the ratification of this treaty. On the 6th of May an ordinance was passed submitting to the vote of the people a Declaration of Independence. At the same time with the Ordinance of Secession, another for the adoption of the Confederate Constitution was submitted to the people. The Legislature passed an act calling on the governor to raise 55,000 men for the defense of the state, 25,000 of whom were to be immediately fitted for the field. Before the day of election—June 8, 1861—Governor Harris had most of these 25,000 men in camp, equipped, for the most part, with munitions belonging to the United States. The presence of this army was intimidating to the people; it was an indication of the governor's determination to sustain the revolutionary party in any event; for these armed men had been put into the field before the people had expressed a desire to separate from the Union, and it was not likely that any expression of opinion which the people might now make would avail any thing. Apparently, the result of the election was a majority of 57,000 in favor of secession. What the vote really cast was it will never be possible to ascertain. The means already used by the governor to precipitate the secession of the state had not been so honorable as to preclude a reasonable suspicion that his agents would see to it that the revolutionary party should show an overwhelming majority.

In order to still farther strengthen the power which he had gained, Governor Harris, in May, ordered the disbandment of all organizations except his own, and that all arms belonging to such organizations be returned to the State Arsenal at Nashville. All debts due to the citizens of Northern states, he declared, must be repudiated.

So steadfast were the counties of East Tennessee to the Union, that the general government had not yet discontinued the mails in that section.[1] At Knoxville in May, and at Greenville in June, large Union Conventions were held. Several of the central and western counties joined in the protest against the revolution. The Convention at Greenville lasted three days. A declaration of grievances was adopted, in which it was stated that the right of free suffrage had been obstructed by Governor Harris's government; that the people had been insulted in their own homes, and that women and children had been shot down by brutal soldiery, and innocent citizens plundered and butchered. It was declared that the Ordinance of Secession was not binding upon loyal citizens. A memorial was prepared, petitioning the Legislature to afford the people of East Tennessee a separate government. But this portion of the state was unable to cope with Governor Harris and his army, and it was not yet possible for the United States to furnish any material assistance. In spite of weakness, the people held fast to their opinions, and were abundantly rewarded with persecution. Irregular squads of cavalry and infantry swept the country, conscripting the citizens, destroying the crops, and heaping every possible indignity upon defenseless women and children. Soon the thoroughfares into Kentucky were crowded with refugees, who made their way across the mountains with great difficulty. Able-bodied men also fled and entered the Union army. The first regiment of loyal Tennesseeans was composed of soldiers who had been exiled from their homes. Many of these were wealthy, and, for the Union cause, left all their possessions behind them to be ravaged by the secessionists, and many left behind them families. The number of men left, however, was sufficient to oppose an obstinate resistance, and the mountainous character of the country favored their efforts for self-defense. At length these men grew bolder, and, in an irregular manner, assumed a sort of offensive warfare, burning the bridges along the line of the railroads over which the Confederate forces received their supplies.

Tennessee was the first of the Confederate States occupied by the national

[1] The counties in which loyalty prevailed were the following: Anderson, Bledsoe, Blount, Bradley, Campbell, Carter, Claiborne, Cocke, Grainger, Green, Hamilton, Hancock, Hawkins, Johnson, Knox, Marion, McMuir, Meigs, Monroe, Morgan, Polk, Rhea, Sevier, Sullivan, and Washington.

UNIONISTS OF EAST TENNESSEE SWEARING BY THE FLAG.

armies. The fall of Donelson insured the fall of Nashville also. The Confederate government of the state then transferred its seat to Memphis. All the troops raised by Governor Harris had been ungrudgingly yielded up to the demands of General Albert Sidney Johnston, and at the time of the capture of Donelson the governor had not a single armed company subject to his command. General Buell occupied Nashville on the 25th of April, 1862. Three days before this, General Grant issued an order declaring West Tennessee under martial law. The capture of Memphis in the June following entirely disorganized Governor Harris's government. The governor himself took the field, and was present at some of the most important battles of the year.

The appointment of Andrew Johnson as military governor of Tennessee, with the rank of brigadier general, was confirmed by the United States Senate on the 5th of March, 1862. Andrew Johnson, who was to be the next Vice-President of the United States, and who was, through a melancholy occasion, to be also its President, was born at Raleigh, North Carolina, December 29, 1808. His parents occupied a humble station in life. The father died when the son was about four years of age, and the circumstances of the

family were still more straitened. When ten years old the boy became a tailor's apprentice, and in the shop, through an accidental acquaintance with a man of eccentric but studious habits, he learned to read, and acquired a rudimentary education. He went to Tennessee while still a young man, and there married. His choice of a partner proved quite fortunate to his future prospects, for his wife became his teacher. In 1829 Mr. Johnson held his first office, that of alderman of Greenville, of which city he was, in the subsequent year, elected mayor. In 1835 he was sent to the state Legislature, where he espoused the principles of the Democratic party. Under the auspices of this party he was elected a member of Congress in 1843, where, in regard to the important questions of the admission of Texas, the Mexican War, the Tariff of 1846, and the Homestead Bill, he strongly advocated the policy upon which his election was based. In 1857 he was elected to the United States Senate for the full term which would end in 1863.

Johnson was a Democrat after the school of Andrew Jackson. The Jacksonian element of his democracy was especially apparent in his career at the time of the first development of the secession theories in the Senate of the United States. Among the Southern senators he stood almost alone in his denunciation of secession as treason, and in his advocacy of the right of the general government to exact from the states submission to the Constitution and the laws. In his speech delivered December 19, 1860, his argument against disunion was very strong as affecting Southern interests. He predicted that disunion must destroy slavery; that a hostile or even alien government upon the border of a slaveholding state would be the natural haven of rest to the hunted slave. "If one division was allowed, others would follow; and," said he, "rather than see this Union divided into thirty-three petty governments, with a little prince in one, a potentate in another, a little aristocracy in a third, a little democracy in a fourth, and a republic somewhere else—a citizen not being permitted to pass from one state to another without a passport or a commission from his government—with quarreling and warring among the petty powers, which would result in anarchy—I would rather see this government to-day—I proclaim it here in my place—converted into a consolidated government." In view of the proposed aggression by the Southern states upon the Federal forts and Federal ships, his language was still stronger. In a speech delivered March 2, 1861, he said: "Show me those who make war on the government and fire on its vessels, and I will show you a traitor. If I were President of the United States I would have all such arrested, and, if convicted, by the Eternal God I would have them hung."

In assuming his position as Governor of Tennessee, Mr. Johnson was, of course, obliged to resign his seat in the Senate. Fortunately, he had been twice governor of the state in previous years, and knew well the temper of the people with whom he would have to deal. But even thus his course

was a difficult one to pursue. The state had not been wholly occupied by the national arms. Even those portions which had been brought again under Federal control were infested by the raids of Morgan and other daring partisan rangers. The Union sentiment among the citizens was not as fervent as had been anticipated, partly because sectional antipathies had been naturally intensified by the bloody strife, and partly because the chance of war might in a few weeks reverse the current of success in favor of the Confederates.

Governor Johnson reached Nashville on the 12th of March, accompanied by Emerson Etheridge, clerk of the House of Representatives, and Horace Maynard, member of Congress from Tennessee. The next evening after his arrival he was called upon by citizens, who desired to elicit an expression of opinion on the critical question of the day. The address which he delivered on the occasion he afterward published as an "Appeal to the People of Tennessee."[1] It was eminently conservative. Military rule was, for a time, a necessity. It did not arise from the desire of the Federal government to usurp powers belonging to the states, but from the constitutional obligation imposed upon the President to provide for every state a republican form of government. In the present instance, there was a state which had no government whatsoever. The government which had been had disappeared, and, in the confusion incidental to a period of strife, anarchy must ensue, unless, for a period, a provisional government could be established. His declaration of the policy which he intended to pursue was succinct, but very plain. Those who had been loyal would be honored; those who would become so would be welcomed on their return; but intelligent and conscious

---

[1] "The President has conducted this mighty contest, until, as commander-in-chief of the army, he has caused the national flag again to float undisputed over the Capitol of our state. Meanwhile the state government has disappeared. The executive has abdicated; the Legislature has dissolved; the judiciary is in abeyance. The great ship of state, freighted with its precious cargo of human interests and human hopes, its sails all set, and its glorious old flag unfurled, has been suddenly abandoned by its officers and mutinous crew, and left to float at the mercy of the winds, and to be plundered by every rover upon the deep. Indeed, the work of plunder has already commenced. The archives have been desecrated, the public property stolen and destroyed; the vaults of the State Bank violated, and its treasures robbed, including the funds carefully gathered and consecrated for all time to the instruction of our children.

"In such a lamentable crisis, the government of the United States could not be unmindful of its high constitutional obligation to guarantee to every state in this Union a republican form of government, an obligation which every state has a direct and immediate interest in having observed toward every other state; and from which, by no action on the part of the people in any state, can the Federal government be absolved. A republican form of government, in consonance with the Constitution of the United States, is one of the fundamental conditions of our political existence, by which every part of the country is alike bound, and from which no part can escape. This obligation the national government is now attempting to discharge. I have been appointed, in the absence of the regular and established state authorities, as military governor for the time being, to preserve the public property of the state, to give the protection of law actively enforced to her citizens, and, as speedily as may be, to restore her government to the same condition as before the existing rebellion.

"In this grateful but arduous undertaking, I shall avail myself of all the aid that may be afforded by my fellow-citizens. And for this purpose I respectfully but earnestly invite all the people of Tennessee, desirous or willing to see a restoration of her ancient government, without distinction of party affiliations or past political opinions or action, to unite with me, by counsel and co-

operative agency, to accomplish this great end. I find most, if not all of the offices, both State and Federal, vacated either by actual abandonment, or by the action of the incumbents in attempting to subordinate their functions to a power in hostility to the fundamental law of the state, and subversive of her national allegiance. These offices must be filled temporarily, until the state shall be restored so far to its accustomed quiet that the people can peaceably assemble at the ballot-box and select agents of their own choice. Otherwise anarchy would prevail, and no man's life or property would be safe from the desperate and unprincipled.

"I shall, therefore, as early as practicable, designate for various positions under the state and county governments, from among my fellow-citizens, persons of probity and intelligence, and bearing true allegiance to the Constitution and government of the United States, who will execute the functions of their respective offices until their places can be filled by the action of the people. Their authority, when their appointments shall have been made, will be accordingly respected and observed.

"To the people themselves the protection of the government is extended. All their rights will be duly respected, and their wrongs redressed when made known. Those who through the dark and weary night of the rebellion have maintained their allegiance to the Federal government will be honored. The erring and misguided will be welcomed on their return. And while it may become necessary, in vindicating the violated majesty of the law, and in reasserting its imperial sway, to punish intelligent and conscious treason in high places, no merely retaliatory or vindictive policy will be adopted. To those especially who in a private, unofficial capacity have assumed an attitude of hostility to the government, a full and complete amnesty for all past acts and declarations is offered, upon the one condition of their again yielding themselves peaceful citizens to the just supremacy of the laws. This I advise them to do for their own good, and for the peace and welfare of our beloved state, endeared to me by the associations of long and active years, and by the enjoyment of her highest honors."

A LOYAL SOUTHERN FAMILY FLYING NORTH.

FORT NEGLEY, NASHVILLE.

treason must be punished. A full amnesty was offered to all who in a private, unofficial capacity had been hostile to the government.

Upon the refusal of the Common Council of Nashville, and other officers, to take the oath of allegiance, Governor Johnson declared their places vacant, and appointed others to fill them. The mayor was arrested for "disloyal practices." The press was placed under military supervision. This firm policy elicited important results. The citizens began to express anxiety to take the oath, and even Confederate soldiers were desirous of availing themselves of the general amnesty. Trade began to revive; vacant houses were reoccupied; there was security of life and property.

That the majority of the citizens in Nashville was not any too loyal is apparent from the vote given May 22d for judge. A disunionist, Turner S. Foster, was chosen by a majority of 190. Governor Johnson gave Judge Foster his commission, and the same day had him arrested and sent to the Penitentiary. On the 12th of May a Union meeting was held at Nashville, and a fortnight afterward at Murfreesborough. Substantially the same resolutions were adopted on both occasions. The state to which the revolution had reduced Tennessee is touchingly depicted in the language of these resolutions. Schools, colleges, universities, churches, were closed; the common-school fund had been abstracted and carried away; the funds of the State Bank had been seized by Governor Harris and his adherents; the state debt had been increased by millions; commerce had been cut off and manufactures shut up; judicial proceedings were suspended—and all this was the result of the unfortunate alliance into which the state had entered with the Confederacy.

Governor Johnson's policy was such as the circumstances of his position compelled him to adopt. In all things he was firm. It would have pleased him better if he had not been so frequently forced to take arbitrary measures. But indulgence to the enemies of the government was certain to be abused. He was even obliged to force those who could not desist from the use of treasonable language to go south beyond the Union lines. He found loyal citizens who had been reduced to extremest poverty by the rebellion, and he deemed it not unjust to assess the wealthy sympathizers with the rebellion for the relief of these people.[1]

[1] The following was the form of the circulars sent by Governor Johnson to some of the richest secessionists of Nashville:

"State of Tennessee, Executive Department, Nashville, August 18, 1862.

"SIR,—There are many wives and helpless children in the city of Nashville and county of Davidson who have been reduced to poverty and wretchedness in consequence of their husbands and fathers having been forced into the armies of this unholy and nefarious rebellion. Their necessities have become so manifest, and their demands for the necessaries of life so urgent, that the laws of justice and humanity would be violated unless something was done to relieve their suffering and destitute condition.

"You are therefore requested to contribute the sum of ——— dollars, which you will pay over within the next five days to James Whitworth, Esq., Judge of the County Court, to be by him distributed among these destitute families in such manner as may be described.

"ANDREW JOHNSON, Military Governor."

Nashville, the military centre of the Federal armies in Tennessee, was four times isolated from the Northern states before the end of August. On the 28th of August General Rousseau was placed in command of the city. He was soon succeeded by General Thomas; but the presence of the latter with Buell's army being very much needed, Negley assumed the command. While Bragg was fighting Buell at Perryville, the Confederate Generals J. R. Anderson and Forrest, attended by Governor Harris, concentrated a large force east of Nashville for the purpose of making an attack upon the city. But the army which they had brought together was defeated at Lavergne on the 7th of October by a detachment of General Negley's troops, commanded by General Palmer. Other attempts were directed by the Confederates against Nashville, but these never succeeded. That which caused Negley the most annoyance was the busy persistence with which Morgan worried his line of communication with the North. At one time, soon after the battle at Lavergne, both Negley's army and the citizens were so far deprived of supplies that they were compelled to live off the country, and even the area allowed them to forage in was very much restricted by the Confederate cavalry. The troops had been for some days living on half rations when Rosecrans reached Nashville with his army in November.

The retreat of Bragg's army from Murfreesborough after the battle of Stone River brought the whole of Western and Middle Tennessee under Federal control. Afterward Burnside's operations in East Tennessee almost entirely defeated the forces of the Confederacy in that portion of the state. But for the power of Morgan and Forrest, it would have been possible to have reorganized the state under a permanent government. As it was, the provisional government continued throughout the year 1863, and it was not until January 26, 1864, that Governor Johnson issued his proclamation for a state election.[1]

[1] Governor Johnson would willingly have taken this step at an earlier stage if the people had been prepared for it. His views on the subject of reorganization are thus expressed in a public speech made in September, 1863:

"Tennessee is not out of the Union, never has been, and never will be out. The bonds of the Constitution and the Federal power will also prevent that. This government is perpetual; provision is made for reforming the government, and amending the Constitution, and admitting states into the Union, not for letting them out of it.

"Where are we now? There is a rebellion; this was anticipated, as I said. The rebel army is driven back. Here lies your state—a sick man in his bed, emaciated and exhausted, paralyzed in all his powers, and unable to walk alone. The physician comes. Don't quarrel about antecedents, but administer to his wants, and cure him as quickly as possible. The United States sends an agent or a military governor, whichever you please to call him, to aid you in restoring your government. Whenever you desire, in good faith, to restore civil authority, you can do so, and a proclamation for an election will be issued as speedily as it is practicable to hold one. One by one, all the agencies of your state government will be set in motion. A Legislature will be elected. Judges will be appointed temporarily, until you can elect them at the polls; and so of sheriffs, county court judges, justices, and other officers, until the way is fairly open for the people and all the parts of the civil government to resume their ordinary functions. This is no nice, intricate metaphysical question. It is a plain, common-sense matter, and there is nothing in the way but obstinacy."

CHAPTER XVIII.

THE PENINSULAR CAMPAIGN.

I. FROM THE POTOMAC TO THE CHICKAHOMINY.

Authorities for the Peninsular Campaign.—The Strength of the Army of the Potomac.—Impatience at its Inactivity.—Army Corps.—Lincoln's and McClellan's Plans for the Campaign.—McClellan's Argument.—Strength of the Confederate Army.—The Council of War adopts McClellan's Plan.—The President's Order for an Advance on the 22d of February.—Condition of Beauregard's Army.—Fortifications at Centreville and Manassas.—Beauregard replaced by Johnston.—New General Orders.—Centreville and Manassas abandoned.—McClellan's Promenade.—Condition of the Confederate Fortifications.—McClellan's Plan modified. The President orders it to be carried into Effect.—McClellan relieved from the general Command.—McClellan's Address to the Army.—His new Plan of Operations.—Topography of the Peninsula.—Yorktown.—The Defenses of the Peninsula.—Magruder's Force.—Landing of the Federal Troops at Fortress Monroe.—Conflicting Opinions as to the Strength of the Enemy.—Blenker, Wool, and McDowell withdrawn from McClellan's Command.—The Reasons for this. —Its Effect on future Operations.—Proposed Naval and Military Attack upon Yorktown abandoned.—Statements of McClellan and Goldsborough.—Unsuccessful Attempt to force the Lines at Lee's Mill.—Magruder's Account.—Siege Operations begun.—Smith's Attempt to force the Lines at Wynne's Mill.—The Force of the Parties.—McClellan and the President.—Progress of the Siege.—Arrival of Franklin's Division.—Strength of the Army, June 30.—Proposed Attack upon Gloucester abandoned.—The Sieges of Yorktown in 1781 and 1862.—Completion of the Federal Batteries.—Losses during the Work.—Effectiveness of the Army.—The Abandonment of Yorktown.—McClellan's Dispatch.—Weakness of the Warwick Line.—Johnston's Retreat.—The Battle of Williamsburg: Stoneman repulsed; Confusion as to Command; Hooker at first successful; he is hard pressed; is relieved by Kearney; Movements of Peck and Hancock; Hancock's decisive Charge; Losses; Movements of McClellan.—Franklin sent up the River.—He is attacked at West Point.—The White House taken as a Base.—Johnston's Plans.—Norfolk to be abandoned.—Its Surrender.—The Destruction of the Virginia.—Tatnall's Trial.—Note on the Virginia.—Drewry's Bluff.—Combined Attack on Fort Darling proposed by Goldsborough and declined by McClellan.—The Reason.—McClellan again demands Reenforcements.—McDowell's Corps promised.—The President's Order.—Johnston's Proceedings.—His probable Force.—Panic in Richmond.—Proceedings of the Authorities.—Jefferson Davis and his Family.—The Citizens and the Press.—McClellan's Advance from Williamsburg. —He reaches the Chickahominy.

FROM the survey of the operations in the West, we now turn to the more important and disastrous campaign on the Peninsula of Virginia.[1] McClellan, when, in July, 1861, placed in command of the Army of the Potomac, found in and about Washington hardly 50,000 men, with thirty imperfectly equipped field-pieces. The panic which followed the rout at Bull Run soon subsided. The nation had unbounded confidence in the new commander, to whom was ascribed the entire credit of the successful operations in Western Virginia. This confidence was not shaken by the disaster of Ball's Bluff. On the 1st of November he was appointed to the chief command of the armies of the United States. The whole nation applauded the action of the government.[2] Re-enforcements poured in, and by the middle of October there were in and about Washington 152,000 men, of whom 133,000 were present and fit for duty. On the 1st of November the Army of the Potomac numbered 168,000, of whom 147,000 were fit for duty; but there were 13,000 imperfectly equipped, leaving an effective force of 134,000. The artillery numbered nearly 300 guns. Its weakest arm was the cavalry. This numbered nominally about 15,000, of whom half were wholly or partially unarmed.[3] Yet, in the opinion of many generals, the cavalry force was

greater than was needed.[1] The importance of this arm of the service was yet to be learned. McClellan had from the first insisted that the war was to be mainly fought by the Army of the Potomac. The resources of the nation were lavished upon it; to it every other department was subordinated. Before the 1st of November it had nearly reached its utmost strength in numbers and discipline. Officers and men were eager to commence active operations. No one dreamed of going into winter quarters. The strength of this army was, indeed, much below that which McClellan thought requisite for an advance movement. He wished for a nominal force of 240,000, which would give about 208,000 effective men. Of these, 35,000 were to garrison Washington, 10,000 to garrison Baltimore and Annapolis, 13,000 to guard the Potomac above and below the capital, leaving 150,000 for the column of active operations. This force provided, he thought the Army of the Potomac might successfully assume active operations, the great object to be attained being "the crushing defeat of the rebel army at Manassas;" the advance "not to be postponed beyond the 25th of November, if possible to avoid it."[2]

The Confederate army of the "Department of Northern Virginia" lay mainly at Centreville and Manassas. Its outposts were pushed forward within a few miles of Washington; from their most advanced points the Capitol was visible. They had also a force in the Valley of the Shenandoah, threatening the capital from above; and had erected batteries at every commanding point along the lower Potomac, completely closing the approach by water. McClellan believed that at the close of October their "force on the Potomac was not less than 150,000 strong, well drilled and equipped, ably commanded, and strongly intrenched."[3]

The autumn months of 1861 had been unusually favorable for military operations; yet week after week passed, and no movement besides reconnoissances and consequent skirmishes was made by the Federal army. The impatience grew stronger as autumn lapsed into winter, and winter verged toward spring, with no indications of activity. The Confederate flag floated in plain view across the Potomac from the Capitol; the unmolested Confederate batteries barred the lower Potomac. Was the great national army, whose perfect organization had been so loudly vaunted, meant for work or for play? Were there not private plans, working against the public weal, which kept it motionless? Surmise grew into accusation. The administration was charged with wishing, for selfish purposes, to protract the war rather than to end it. A difference of opinion had arisen between the President and the general as to the organization of the army. Lincoln wished it to be divided at once into several corps. McClellan was opposed to this. It was a delicate matter, he said, to appoint major generals before they had been tried by actual service, and had shown their fitness to be selected to command 30,000 or 40,000 men. A major general could not be stowed away in a pigeon-hole, if he should prove incompetent, as easily as a brigadier general. He proposed to manage the entire army himself in some battle or campaign, and then select from the brigadier generals such as should prove themselves competent for higher commands;[4] yet he himself, wholly untried in military operations on a large scale, wished to have the sole command of an army of 150,000 men. The Secretary of War and most of the generals were in favor of the immediate organization of army corps; but the President, who was slowly feeling his way, deferred for a time to the opinion of McClellan, and the corps were not arranged until the very day when the Army of the Potomac was ordered to prepare for the expedition to the Peninsula.

Of far more importance was the difference of opinion as to the entire plan of the campaign. The bulk of the Confederate force lay at and near Centreville and Manassas, drawing its supplies mainly from Richmond by way of the Orange and Alexandria Railroad. The President wished the Army of the Potomac to advance directly upon this railroad, at a point between Manassas and Richmond, and, by assailing the enemy's base of supply, force him to come out of his intrenchments and give battle in the open field. McClellan wished to assume the lower Chesapeake Bay as his base of operations, transporting the army by water down the Potomac and up the Rappahannock, disembarking at Urbana, and thence marching upon Richmond, forty miles distant.

Two full months passed beyond the time which McClellan had fixed upon for the advance, and the direction in which it was to be made was not decided. The general laid his plan before the President, who disapproved it, and adhered to his own. To assure the country that this inaction was to come to an end, the President, on the 27th of January, issued a general order appointing the 22d of February as the day for a general advance of all the land and naval forces of the United States against the insurgent forces. This was followed, on the 31st of January, by a special order, directing that, after providing for the defense of Washington, the disposable force of the Army of the Potomac should be formed into an expedition for the immediate object of seizing and occupying a point upon the railroad southwestward of Manassas Junction, the details to be in the discretion of the commander-in-chief, and the expedition to move on or before the 22d of February. McClellan asked to submit in detail his objections to this plan,

---

[1] The conduct of the Peninsular Campaign has been assailed and defended upon purely partisan grounds. So differently has it been represented, that I have thought proper to give the authority upon which every important statement in the text has been made. The works which are only occasionally referred to are fully designated in the proper places. The following authorities, which are continually cited, are designated thus:

"*McC. Rep.*"—Report on the Organization and Campaigns of the Army of the Potomac, etc. By GEORGE B. McCLELLAN, Major General United States Army.—This report is a defense, as well as a statement, of the operations of the commander. The edition cited is that put forth by the author. Where the same document is found here and in other authorities, it is usually referred to this report.

"*Com. Rep.*"—Report of the Joint Committee on the Conduct of the War (1863).—This report is especially valuable for the official documents which it embodies, and for the sworn testimony of leading generals. Only Part I., which relates to the Army of the Potomac from its organization to the battle of Fredericksburg, is referred to in these chapters.

"*Sec. of War Rep.*"—Report of the Secretary of War, Dec. 1, 1862. This report embodies that of General Halleck, general-in-chief, after July 11, and several important documents from General McClellan, not embraced in his detailed report.

"*Reb. Rec.*"—The Rebellion Record, etc. Edited by FRANK MOORE.—My obligation to this valuable collection of documents is not to be measured by the frequency of direct citations. Usually, when documents are referred to without direct citation, they are to be found in this collection, where they are presented in a more accurate form than in the newspapers of the day. Not unfrequently they have been corrected by the authors themselves.

"*Art. Op.*"—Report of the Engineer and Artillery Operations of the Army of the Potomac, etc. By Brigadier General J. G. BARNARD, Chief Engineer, and Brigadier General W. F. BARRY, Chief of Artillery.

"*Pen. Camp.*"—The Peninsular Campaign and its Antecedents, as Developed by the Report of Major General George B. McClellan. By J. G. BARNARD, Brigadier General, etc.—This is a review of some points in McClellan's Report. It is strongly controversial in tone, but embodies some important semi-official statements.

"POLLARD."—Southern History of the War, etc. By EDWARD A. POLLARD, Editor of the Richmond Examiner.—This is chiefly valuable as the only formal attempt to present the history of the war from a Southern stand-point. It is thoroughly partisan. It is hard to tell whether hatred to the Union cause or hatred to the Richmond administration predominates in the author's mind. The work, however, embraces many citations from official reports not as yet accessible in any other form.

"MAGRUDER."—Report of Operations on the Peninsula. By Major General J. B. MAGRUDER, Commanding.—This report embraces only the first half of the period occupied by the siege of Yorktown, down to April 16, when Magruder was displaced by the arrival of Johnston. It is contained in "Official Reports of Battles" (p. 515-537, as republished in New York), published by order of the Confederate Congress.

"DE JOINVILLE."—The Army of the Potomac, etc.—This appeared in the *Revue des Deux Mondes* of Paris, over the signature of A. Trognon. It is attributed, without contradiction, to the Prince de Joinville, son of Louis Philippe, who accompanied his nephews, the Comte de Paris and the Duc de Chartres, with the Army of the Potomac, in which they served on the staff of General McClellan. It throws much light upon many points of the history.

"LEE."—Report of General ROBERT E. LEE of the Operations of the Confederate Army of Northern Virginia, from the Battle of Seven Pines to that of Fredericksburg.—This report, though printed by order of the Confederate authorities, has not as yet (July, 1865) been published. After the capture of Richmond a copy of it fell into the hands of the editor of the *New York Herald*, to whom I am indebted for it. Having it only in newspaper "slips," I am not able to cite the pages to which reference is made.

[2] "With the retirement of General Scott came the executive duty of appointing in his stead a general-in-chief of the army. It is a fortunate circumstance that neither in council nor country was there, so far as I know, any difference of opinion as to the proper person to be selected. The designation of General McClellan is, therefore, in a considerable degree, the selection of the country as well as of the executive, and hence there is better reason to hope that there will be given to him the confidence and cordial support thus by fair implication promised."—*President's Message*, Dec. 3, 1861.   [3] *McC. Rep.*, 47.

[1] "In my judgment, a large amount of cavalry is not useful, and can not be used south of the Potomac. I have always said that the regular cavalry would have been sufficient for the operations of this army—merely as advanced guards, and to carry reports and messages."—RICHARDSON, *Com. Rep.*, 113. "I think we have more cavalry than we want; I should suppose that one half of the cavalry that is across the river [less than 12,000] would be sufficient."—HEINTZELMAN, *Ibid.*, 119. "I have in my division one regiment of cavalry. I would be very glad to get rid of two thirds of it. I think, as things are situated now, that 2000 cavalry are as much as we want for the whole army."—FRANKLIN, *Ibid.*, 124. "There are twelve divisions. My division has one regiment of cavalry. I think we might do with less. I think I might have done with two thirds of the amount of cavalry I have. If we were organized by corps of three divisions each, two regiments of cavalry would be sufficient for the three divisions."—McDOWELL, *Ibid.*, 139.

[2] *McC. Rep.*, 46-49.   [3] *Ibid.*, 46.   [4] *Com. Rep.*, 6.

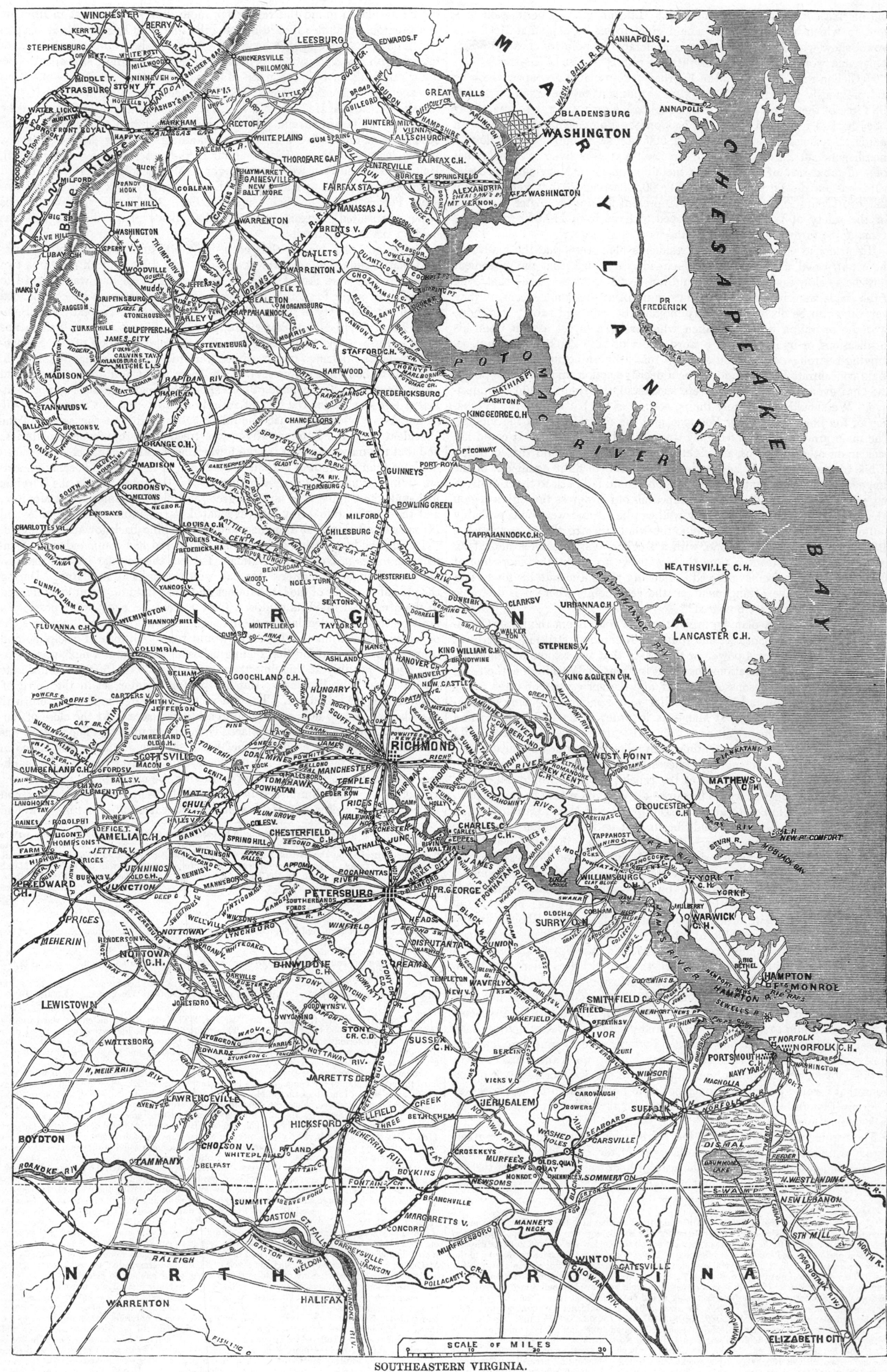

SOUTHEASTERN VIRGINIA.

and his reasons for preferring his own.[1] Lincoln granted permission in a note, in which he said that he would give up his own plan if McClellan would show wherein McClellan's was preferable in point of cheapness, certainty, and worth of victory, or facility for retreat in case of disaster.[2]

McClellan replied on the 3d of February, in an elaborate paper which he had previously prepared.[3] It proceeds throughout on the assumption that the force of the enemy was at least equal to his own. At the close of October he had estimated that they had on the Potomac 150,000 men. In March he reduced the estimate to 102,500, besides 13,000 in the Valley of the Shenandoah. In this paper no direct estimate was given. The nominal force of the Army of the Potomac, including those in Maryland and Delaware, was, on the 1st of February, 219,000, of whom 28,000 were sick, absent, or in confinement, leaving 191,000 present for duty.[4] After providing for the safety of Washington, he hoped to have from 110,000 to 140,000 troops to be thrown upon the new line.[5]

His principal objections to the President's plan were, that the nature of the country and the condition of the roads were such that the movement must be so slow that the enemy could not be taken by surprise; that, even if the roads were in a tolerably firm condition at the commencement, they were liable to be obstructed at any moment by rain and snow; that, however the operation was undertaken, whether by a direct assault upon his fortifications, or by an attempt to turn either or both flanks, the enemy, occupying a strong central position, with roads diverging in every direction, could concentrate his whole force for a decisive action upon any one point; and that, even if the operation were successful, the result would be indecisive. We should gain merely the possession of the battle-field, the evacuation of the line of the upper Potomac, and the moral effect of the victory. The main army of the Confederacy would not be destroyed. It could fall back upon other positions, and fight again and again, should the condition of his troops permit. If he was in no condition to fight again out of the range of his intrenchments at Richmond, he could fall back to them, destroying railroad bridges and otherwise impeding our progress through a region where the roads are as bad as they well can be; "and we would probably find ourselves forced at last to change the whole theatre of war, or to seek a shorter land-route to Richmond, with a smaller available force and at an expenditure of much more time than were we to adopt the short line at once. We would also have forced the enemy to concentrate his forces and perfect his defensive arrangements at the very points where it is desirable to strike him when least prepared."[6]

In favor of his own plan, he urged that the route from the lower Chesapeake Bay was the shortest land-route to Richmond, striking directly at the heart of the enemy's power in the East; that the region was more favorable for offensive operations than that in front of Washington, the roads being passable at all seasons of the year, and the spring two or three weeks earlier. A movement in force on that line would oblige the enemy to abandon his intrenched position at Manassas in order to cover Richmond and Norfolk; for, should he permit us to occupy Richmond, his destruction could be averted only by entirely defeating us in a battle, in which he must be the assailant. If the movement were successful, it would give us the capital, the communications, the supplies of the rebels; Norfolk would fall, all the waters of the Chesapeake would be ours—all Virginia would be in our power, and the enemy forced to abandon Tennessee and North Carolina. The alternative presented to him would be to beat us in a position selected by ourselves, disperse, or surrender. If we were beaten in battle, we should have a perfectly secure retreat down the Peninsula upon Fortress Monroe, with both flanks perfectly covered by the fleet. During the whole movement our left flank would be covered by the water; our right would be secure, for the enemy would be too distant to reach us in time; he could oppose us only in front, we bringing our fleet into full play. Should circumstances render it not advisable to land at Urbana, we could use Mob Jack Bay; or, "the worst coming to the worst, we can take Fortress Monroe as a base, and operate with complete security, though with less celerity and brilliancy of results, up the Peninsula." In conclusion, he said: "It is by no means certain that we can beat them at Manassas. On the other line I regard success as certain by all the chances of war. We demoralize the enemy by forcing him to abandon his prepared position for one which we have chosen, in which all is in our favor, and where success must produce immense results. Nothing is certain in war, but all the chances are in favor of this movement. So much am I in favor of the southern line of operations, that I would prefer the movement from Fortress Monroe as a base—as a certain though less brilliant movement than that from Urbana—to an attack upon Manassas."

The argument was ably stated; but, as the event proved, McClellan greatly overestimated the obstacles in the way of the President's plan, and as greatly underestimated those in the way of his own. The force of the enemy at Manassas was hardly half what he supposed.[7] When he reached the Peninsula he found the region far more difficult than that in front of Washington, even after he had adopted the line from Fortress Monroe, upon which he had supposed that he could "operate with complete security, although with less celerity and brilliancy of results, up the Peninsula." The order directing an advance upon Manassas was not formally revoked, but its execution was not required. The President, according to his wont, took time to consider. He was still in favor of his own plan, but he said he was not a military man, and would submit the question to a council of war consisting of the twelve generals commanding divisions, and be governed by the decision of the majority. Four of the generals, Sumner, McDowell, Heintzelman, and Barnard, were in favor of Mr. Lincoln's plan of an onward movement right on to Richmond. Eight generals, Fitz John Porter, Andrew Porter, Franklin, W. F. Smith, McCall, Blenker, Keyes, and Naglee (who represented Hooker), voted for McClellan's plan. This council was held on the 8th of March.[1]

McClellan's plan having thus been definitely sanctioned, Lincoln determined that it should be put into execution. On the same 8th of March two general orders were issued. By the first order McClellan was directed to organize his army for active operations into four corps, to be commanded according to seniority of rank: First Corps, McDowell; Second Corps, Sumner; Third Corps, Heintzelman; Fourth Corps, Keyes. Besides these was to be a Fifth Corps, under Banks, to operate in the Valley of the Shenandoah; and the defenses of the capital were to be placed under Wadsworth, who was to be military governor of the District of Columbia.[2] The second order directed that no change of base should be made without leaving a sufficient force to render the capital entirely secure; that not more than half of the Army of the Potomac should be moved, without the assent of the President, until the Potomac River was freed from the enemy's batteries; and that the movement toward the lower Chesapeake should be commenced not later than the 18th of March.[3] On the next day, March 9, came important tidings from two different quarters. In Hampton Roads the Virginia had sunk the Cumberland and Congress, and had encountered the Monitor; and the Confederate army had evacuated its position at Centreville and Manassas, and along the Potomac, and were falling back toward Richmond.

During the long period of inaction, Beauregard had commanded the Confederate forces in Northern Virginia. He was the popular hero of the day. He had taken Fort Sumter. He had won the fight at Bull Run. During the pleasant months of the late summer and early autumn, volunteers flocked to the army and filled its camps. They expected a short war; possibly a fight or two, to be decided by their terrible bowie-knives, at the very sight of which every Yankee who could would run. All idea of discipline and organization, every thing that distinguishes an army from a mob, was scouted. Quite possibly at this time there were 100,000 or 150,000 Confederate troops toward the Potomac. But by the time winter set in the spirit of volunteering had died out. The old volunteers were anxious to return to their homes, and no new ones came to fill their places. At the close of January, 1862, Beauregard was displaced from his command. The pretext was that his services were needed at the West. Joseph Johnston was placed in command. For the first, but not for the last time during the war, the thankless task was imposed upon him of retrieving the errors of his predecessors. He found an army diminished in numbers, ill disciplined, ill provided, and suffering from sickness.[4] He saw at once that it was beyond his power to

[1] *McC. Rep.*, 96, 97.

[2] *Lincoln to McClellan*, Feb. 3, 1862. "You and I have distinct and different plans for a movement of the Army of the Potomac. Yours to be done by the Chesapeake, up the Rappahannock to Urbana, and across and to the terminus of the railroad on the York River. Mine to move directly to a point on the railroad southwest of Manassas. If you will give me satisfactory answers to the following questions, I shall gladly yield my plan to yours: *First.* Does not your plan involve a greatly larger expenditure of time and money? *Second.* Wherein is victory more certain by your plan than mine? *Third.* Wherein is victory more valuable by your plan than mine? *Fourth.* In fact, would it not be less valuable in this, that it would break no great line of the enemy's communications, while mine would? *Fifth.* In case of disaster, would not a retreat be more difficult by your plan than mine?" [3] *McC. Rep.*, 98–107. [4] *Ib.*, 52. [5] *Ib.*, 106. [6] *Ib.*, 105.

[7] The Confederate government carefully abstained from making any public statement of the strength of its armies in the field. Their actual force in Northern Virginia at any period can be given only by approximation. At the close of October, when it was probably largest, McClellan had estimated it at 150,000. A few weeks later, Butler, collecting all accessible official evidence, calculated that there were 70,000. Three estimates of the number, near the beginning of March, have been preserved, all purporting to be based upon reports of McClellan's secret service corps. The first is stated by Colonel Lecompte, a Swiss officer serving on McClellan's staff, to have been furnished on the 21st of February by the Count of Paris, who was also on the staff (*Barnard, Pen. Camp.*, 13); the second was laid before a council of war on the 2d of March (*Ibid.*, 95); the third is given by McClellan (*Report*, 122), as furnished on the 8th of March by the chief of the secret service corps. These estimates, adapting the locations to those laid down in the last, are as follows:

McClellan, March 8.		*Council, March 2.*		*Count of Paris, Feb. 21.*	
At Manassas, Centreville, Bull Run, Upper Occoquan, and vicinity	80,000	Same region....	29,900	Same region............	47,000
At Brooks's Station, Dumfries, Lower Occoquan, and vicinity	18,000	Same region....	20,600	Same region............	18,000
At Leesburg and vicinity.......	4,500	Not given (say)	4,500	Leesburg................	6,000
In the Shenandoah Valley......	13,000	Not given (say)	13,000	Winchester...	12,000 to 18,000
	115,500		63,500		83,000 to 89,000

The Committee on the Conduct of the War say, "The strength of the enemy was variously estimated at from 70,000 to 210,000 men. Those who formed the highest estimates based their opinions upon information received at head-quarters. Subsequent events have proved that the force of the enemy was below even the lowest of these estimates; and the strength of their fortifications was very greatly overestimated."—*Com. Rep.*, 7.

[1] Sumner's and Barnard's testimony (*Com. Rep.*, 360, 387). This important council, whose vote fixed the general plan of the campaign, has been strangely unnoticed. The question before it was whether the plan of Lincoln or that of McClellan should be adopted. No one of the generals taking part in it who testified before the committee could even fix the date. It was, they thought, late in February or early in March. Mr. Raymond (*Administration of President Lincoln*, 225) says it was held "late in February." The true date is fixed incidentally by McClellan (*Report*, 116). But he speaks of it merely as a meeting of commanders of divisions, convened by his invitation "for the purpose of giving them their instructions, and receiving their advice and opinions respecting their commands." [2] *McC. Rep.*, 58. [3] *Ibid.*, 117.

[4] "It was really most surprising to observe the inertness which followed the battle of Manassas. Our War Department, our generals, our soldiers, were all reposing on their laurels, lost in the happiest dreams of their late success. Nothing was done toward insuring the fruits of this victory. The idea of having beaten the Northern army was so consoling that the Southerners began to think that the idea that the soldier should be taught was pure folly. 'We have now,' they said, 'beaten Scott, the greatest general of the age; we have destroyed his army, and, consequently, it would be a waste of time to drill, exercise, and do things of that kind. We need only to draw our dreaded bowie-knives, and every enemy who is able to run will do so.' These ideas predominated among the soldiers of the army, and the officers took no pains to counteract them. When McClellan was appointed to the chief command of the Federal army, and set to work to strengthen his position by the construction of field-works in order to be enabled to proceed the better with the organization of his forces, Beauregard at last began to bestir himself, and to rouse his officers and men from their lethargy. Fortified works on a grand scale were now undertaken, and, indeed, the preparations were so extensive that it appeared as if the whole state of Virginia was to be fortified. No steps were, however, taken for the erection of hospitals, the improvement of the roads, or the instruction of the soldiers. We were especially ill provided with medicines and clothes, and the troops suffered greatly in consequence. Added to this, sickness broke out in Beauregard's camp. It was the more serious, inasmuch as our authorities had never directed their attention to any sanitary precautions. Wounded men and horses were alike treated in the most negligent manner, and the consequences were indeed appalling. Dead horses lay about in hund-

RUINS OF BRIDGE AT BLACKBURN'S FORD.

withstand a serious attack, and resolved to fall back the moment any determined movement was made by the Federal forces. Beauregard had, indeed, laid out immense works at Centreville and Manassas. At Centreville were two lines. One faced east, a mile and three quarters long; the other faced north, two miles long. In both were thirteen distinct forts, connected by "infantry parapets," "double caponniers," and "redans." There were embrasures for seventy-one guns. On a high hill commanding the rear of both lines was a large redoubt with ten embrasures. Manassas was defended in all directions by a system of detached works, with platforms for heavy guns, arranged for marine carriages, and connected by infantry parapets; the system being rendered complete by a very large work with sixteen embrasures, commanding the highest of the other works by about fifty feet.[1] The works at Manassas had been mounted with guns. Those at Centreville had

been merely laid out, but no heavy artillery had been placed in them, and for weeks they were occupied only by a corps of observation, ready to fall back upon any alarm.

Beauregard's order upon giving up the command of the army, issued on the 30th of January, and Johnston's order upon assuming it, five days later, clearly indicate that both were aware of their perilous position. The main point of each was an urgent appeal to the troops not to disband.[1] Johnston, however, before giving the final orders for evacuation, waited for some definite movement on the part of the enemy. He had trusty friends who informed him at once of every thing that took place in Federal councils. So long as the Federal authorities were undecided where to strike, he might safely hold his position. But the moment he learned of the order to move by the way of the Peninsula he called back his corps from Centreville, destroyed the bridges over Bull Run, and fell back to Manassas. The next day, March 10, he evacuated this place, burning every thing which he could not carry away.[2]

Early on the 9th of March McClellan was apprised that the enemy was

reds as they had fallen, and nobody seemed to care any thing about it, or to take any steps to put an end to a state of things so detrimental to the health of the army. Before long the hospitals in Beauregard's camp became enormously overcrowded, and the scythe of death reaped a large harvest in the narrow lanes of the camp, mowing down the lately blooming youth of the South. Happily for the army, General Beauregard received orders to assume command of the army on the Mississippi. It was, indeed, high time for a change in the administration of the Army of the Potomac, as the demoralization, negligence, and the lax discipline which permitted the soldiers to assume a bearing which verged on actual insubordination were becoming quite unbearable. Pale, haggard faces peered out upon you from the tents, and forms worn to the bone by hunger and disease tottered about. Nobody seemed to exert any authority, and nobody was disposed to obey. Beauregard left his army in the most deplorable condition, hurrying straight to the scene of his future defeat."—ESTVAN, *War Pictures from the South*, 107–109.

"The Acts of Congress providing for re-enlistments had failed to effect the desired object. The spirit of volunteering had died out, and the resolution of our soldiers already in the field was not sufficient to resist the prospects, cherished for months amid the sufferings and monotony of the camps, of returning to their homes. The exigency was critical, and even vital. In a period of thirty days the term of one hundred and forty-eight regiments expired. There was good reason to believe that a large majority of the men had not re-enlisted, and of those who had re-enlisted a very large majority had entered companies which could never be assembled, or, if assembled, could not be prepared for the field in time to meet the invasion actually commenced."—POLLARD, ii., 23.   [1] *McC. Rep.*, 123.

[1] Beauregard said: "I can not quit you without deep emotion, without even deep anxiety in the moment of our country's trials and dangers. This is no time for the Army of the Potomac—the men of Manassas—to stack their arms and quit, even for a brief period, the standards they have made glorious by their manhood."—*Reb. Rec.*, iv., 66. Johnston said: "Accustomed to the comforts and luxuries of home, you have borne and met the privations of camp life, the exactions of military discipline, and the rigors of a winter campaign. Your country now summons you to a noble and a greater deed. The enemy has gathered up all his energies for a final conflict. He does not propose to attack this army so long as it holds its present position with undiminished numbers and unimpaired discipline; but, protected by his fortifications, he awaits the expiration of your term of service. Expecting a large portion of our army to be soon disbanded, he hopes that his immense numbers will easily overpower your gallant comrades who will be left here. The commanding general calls upon the twelve-months' men to stand by their brave comrades who have volunteered for the war. You can not, you will not draw back at this solemn crisis of our struggle, when all that is heroic in the land is engaged, and all that is precious hangs trembling in the balance."—*Reb. Rec.*, iv., 130.   [2] *Com. Rep.*, 250.

EVACUATION OF MANASSAS JUNCTION.

CONFEDERATE HUTS AT CENTREVILLE.

evacuating his positions at Centreville, Manassas, and on the upper and lower Potomac. This, he thought, presented a good opportunity for his troops to gain some experience on the march and bivouac preparatory to a campaign, and to get rid of the superfluous baggage and other impediments which accumulate around an army in camp. He hoped, though rather faintly, that by marching upon Manassas he might be able to harass the rear of the retreating enemy.[1] On the morning of the 10th the Army of the Potomac began its "promenade" toward Manassas. Centreville was reached at noon. For once the Virginia mud did not prevent a rapid march. The formidable works which had so long been an object of dread were found to be thoroughly dilapidated. They did not appear to have been touched for months. The banks and escarpments were washed down by the rains. The ditches were so filled up that a man might leap across them. There was not the slightest evidence that a single heavy gun had ever been mounted upon them. There were, indeed, huts sufficient to shelter an army of 50,000 or more men; but the utmost force collected here at any time was 12,000 or 15,000.[2] The army marched no farther than Centreville, but McClellan and a strong escort rode on to Manassas, wading Bull Run, for the rude bridge at Blackburn's Ford had been destroyed. The strong-hold at Manassas was a scene of ruin. Here the promenade ended. Stoneman, with a force of 2300 cavalry and infantry, pushed on fourteen miles in the track of the retreating Confederates. They found the roads strewed with abandoned small-arms, stores, and munitions, showing that the final retreat had been hasty. They were, however, far from disorganized. After ascertaining their position, and finding them too strong to be assailed, Stoneman returned. The whole army then marched back, and in less than a week after it had set out was again in its camps near Washington.

In the course of this week the plan of the campaign was modified. Instead of going up the Rappahannock to Urbana, and thence marching straight across the Peninsula, as McClellan had all along proposed, the "less brilliant" plan of landing at Fortress Monroe was adopted. This change was made at a council of the four newly-appointed corps commanders, McDowell, Sumner, Heintzelman, and Keyes, held at Fairfax Court-house on the 13th of March. According to the memorandum of the proceedings given by McClellan, it was unanimously voted "that, the enemy having retreated from Manassas to Gordonsville, behind the Rappahannock and Rapidan, it is the opinion of the generals commanding army corps that the operations to be carried on will be best undertaken from Old Point Comfort, between the York and James Rivers," provided that certain conditions were secured; but if this could not be done, "the army should then be moved against the enemy behind the Rappahannock at the earliest possible moment."[3] But Sumner testified that no such proposition was submitted to the council, and, had it been submitted, he should have voted against it.[4] McClellan assented to what he considered the decision of the council, and communicated it to the War Department. The Secretary of War replied that the President had considered the plan, made no objections to it, but ordered that in its execution sufficient force should be left at Manassas Junction to make it sure that the enemy would not repossess himself of that position and line of communication; that Washington should be left entirely secure, and then the general should "move the remainder of the force down the Potomac, choosing a new base at Fortress Monroe, or any where between here and there; or, at all events, move such remainder of the army at once in pursuit of the enemy by some route."[5]

The President had by this time become convinced that the direction of the active operations of the Army of the Potomac would fully occupy all of McClellan's powers, without the task of controlling the entire military operations of the nation. Accordingly, on the 11th of March, an order was issued stating that "General McClellan having personally taken the field at the head of the Army of the Potomac, until otherwise ordered, he is relieved from the command of the other military departments, he retaining the command of the Army of the Potomac." All the region west of Knoxville was formed into a new Department of the Mississippi, the command being given to Halleck; and a new Department of the Mountain, embracing all between those of the Mississippi and the Potomac, was created for Fremont. All commanders of departments were to report directly to the Secretary of War. McClellan, though chagrined that this order was published before it was officially communicated to him, yielded to it with a good grace. He wrote to the President, "I have said to you that no feeling of self-interest or ambition should ever prevent me from devoting myself to the service. I am glad to

---

[1] *McC. Rep.*, 118, 119. [2] *Com. Rep.*, 243–250. [3] *McC. Rep.*, 128.
[4] "When the army returned to Fairfax Court-house a council was convened there, consisting of the four corps commanders, McDowell, Heintzelman, Keyes, and myself, and the proposition was submitted to us in this form: Whether, as the enemy was then rapidly retreating through the country, and the roads were in a very bad condition, it would not be better to turn them by a movement by water—as my understanding was, to descend the Potomac and land at Urbana. With the understanding that the army was to land at Urbana, I yielded to the proposition; and I will add, that I was never more surprised in my life than, when I embarked at Alexandria, to learn that the whole army was going down to Fortress Monroe. I had not dreamed of any such movement, and would not have voted for it."—*Com. Rep.*, 360. The testimony of General Keyes, however, confirms the view of McClellan. He says: "About the 13th of March a council of corps commanders was held at Fairfax Court-house, at which were present Generals McDowell, Sumner, Heintzelman, and myself. General McClellan was not much present during the discussions. The subject of the campaign was talked of. I do not know that any minutes were made. It was finally agreed and understood that we were to take the army down to Old Point Comfort and move up the Peninsula. . . . The corps commanders were unanimous in their agreement. In consequence of the arrangements made there, the army was embarked for Old Point Comfort."—*Com. Rep.*, 598. He also wrote to Senator Harris, June 7: "The plan of campaign on this line was made with the distinct understanding that four army corps should be employed, and that the navy should co-operate in the taking of Yorktown, and also (as I understood it) support us on our left, by moving gun-boats up the James River. . . . The above plan was adopted unanimously by Generals McDowell, Sumner, Heintzelman, and Keyes, and was concurred in by General McClellan, who first proposed Urbana as our base. The army being reduced by 45,000 troops, some of them among the best in the service, and without the support of the navy, the plan to which we are reduced bears scarcely any resemblance to the one I voted for."—*McC. Rep.*, 165.
[5] *McC. Rep.*, 129.

have the opportunity to prove it; and you will find that, under present circumstances, I shall work just as cheerfully as before, and that no consideration of self will in any manner interfere with the discharge of my public duties."[1]

On the 14th McClellan issued a stirring address to his army. "For a long time," he said, "I have kept you inactive, but not without a purpose. You were to be disciplined, armed, and instructed. The formidable artillery you now have had to be created; other armies were to move and accomplish certain results. The patient labors of many months have produced their results. The Army of the Potomac is now a real army, magnificent in material, admirable in discipline and instruction, excellently equipped and armed. Your commanders are all that I could wish. The period of inaction has passed. I will bring you now face to face with the rebels, and only pray that God may defend the right. In whatever direction you may move, however strange my actions may appear to you, ever bear in mind that my fate is linked with yours, and all that I do is to bring you where I know you wish to be—on the decisive battle-field. I shall demand of you great, heroic exertions, rapid and long marches, privations perhaps. We will share all these together." And more in the same strain.[2]

McClellan then submitted to the War Department his proposed plan of operations. Fortress Monroe was to be the first base of operations, Richmond being the objective point, to be reached by the way of Yorktown and West Point. It was assumed that the enemy would concentrate his forces, and that a decisive battle would be fought between Richmond and West Point. The first object of the campaign was to capture Yorktown by a combined naval and military attack, which would be the work of only a few hours; then West Point would be established as the new base, about twenty-five miles from Richmond, "with every facility for developing and bringing into play the whole of our available force on either or both banks of the James." The co-operation of the navy was again and again insisted upon as an absolutely necessary part of this programme. "Without it the operations may be prolonged for many weeks, and we may be forced to carry in front several strong positions, which, by its aid, could be turned without serious loss of either time or men. . . . For the prompt success of this campaign, it is absolutely necessary that the navy should at once throw its whole available force, its most powerful vessels, upon Yorktown. There is the most important point—there the knot is to be cut."[3]

The Peninsula of Virginia lies between the James and York Rivers, which, running nearly parallel from the northwest, empty into Chesapeake Bay, their mouths forming wide estuaries. Fortress Monroe occupies the extremity of the Peninsula, and is connected with the main portion only by a narrow sand beach. The extreme length, from the fort to a line drawn between Richmond and West Point, is about sixty miles; the average breadth about twelve. At Yorktown, twenty miles up, it is narrowed to eight, which width it preserves ten miles, to Williamsburg; then the rivers begin to diverge. The shores of the lower portion of the Peninsula are deeply indented with creeks, some of which extend half way across. The land is flat and low,

THE NELSON HOUSE, YORKTOWN.

covered with swampy forests, through which sluggish streams flow lazily, expanding after every rain into miry ponds. Here and there is a small settlement, grouped around a rude church, a court-house, or a cross-road tavern. The roads, winding from one to another, hardly passable at any time, are, after a storm, impracticable for a wheel-carriage. The climate is unhealthy during the summer, but the soil is generally fertile, and the fisheries productive, the oysters of the York and James Rivers being among the finest in the world. The population is 45 to the square mile, about equal in density to that of Pennsylvania, the slaves slightly outnumbering the whites. Yorktown is a dilapidated village of some fifty houses, on the York River, twenty miles from Fortress Monroe. It is chiefly noted for the surrender of Cornwallis in 1781. In the colonial times it was much larger, and for a long time vied with Williamsburg, the capital of the colony. The principal building is the Nelson House, built by Thomas Nelson, one of the signers of the Declaration of Independence, and afterward governor of Virginia. For years it had been occupied as a tavern, the only one in the place. It stands upon a bluff, the highest point of land on the Peninsula below Richmond. Opposite is Gloucester Point, setting sharply in from the northern bank, reducing the width of the York River from two miles to one.

Strong fortifications had been thrown up at Yorktown under the direction of General Magruder, formerly an officer in the United States army. On one side they commanded the river, and on the other overlooked the narrow neck of land. He had also prepared an elaborate line of defense, stretching for miles down both rivers, and almost meeting in the centre of the Peninsula. Magruder was confident that, with 25,000 men to hold it, this line could not be broken by any force that could be brought against it. But 11,000 was the utmost force given him, and he had to adopt a shorter line, which could be held by his small force. This line, which was thirteen miles long, followed the course of the Warwick River, a muddy stream rising close by the Yorktown bluff, and flowing through swamps across the Peninsula into the James. At intervals of three or four miles were mill-dams, which set the water back, forming a series of shallow ponds. The only roads crossed these dams. Redoubts were thrown up at the heads of the bridges and at various points along the Warwick. Six thousand men were retained in garrison at Yorktown, Gloucester, and Mulberry Island, leaving five thousand to defend the line of the Warwick.[1]

The Federal army was hurried to the Peninsula as rapidly as transportation could be furnished. The advance, consisting of Heintzelman's corps, landed on the 23d of March. They were ordered to encamp close by Fortress Monroe, in order to leave the enemy in doubt whether Norfolk or Yorktown was to be the immediate object of attack. Four days afterward a reconnoissance was made as far as Big Bethel, but strict orders had been given by McClellan that no demonstration should be made. Heintzelman believed that, had he been permitted to advance, he could have forced the enemy's lines with a single brigade, have isolated the troops at Yorktown, and have compelled the surrender in a few days. Hooker was of the same opinion.[2] The

---

[1] *McC. Rep.*, 125.　　　[2] *Reb. Rec.*, iv., 306.　　　[3] *McC. Rep.*, 132-134.

[1] MAGRUDER, 516.

[2] Heintzelman testifies: "A few days after I got to Fortress Monroe, I got information, which I considered reliable, that General Magruder had about 7500 men on the Peninsula; at all events, not to exceed 10,000. . . . I think, if I had been per-

FORTIFICATIONS OF YORKTOWN, LOOKING TOWARD THE RIVER.

Confederates were fully aware of the weakness of their position, and of the disasters which would follow had it been forced.[1]

McClellan reached Fortress Monroe on the 2d of April, preceded or immediately followed by the bulk of his force. It was less than he had demanded. Blenker's division of 10,000 men had been withdrawn from his immediate command, to be held in a position to re-enforce Fremont. He had expected to be authorized to draw 10,000 men from Wool's force at Fortress Monroe. On the day following his arrival he received orders depriving him of all control over Wool's forces, and was forbidden to detach any of his troops without his consent. "This order," he says, "left me without any base of operations under my own control." The very next day he was informed that McDowell's whole corps was detached from his immediate command, and ordered to remain behind. It had been stipulated by the council which recommended the Peninsular movement that "the force to be left to cover Washington should be such as to give an entire feeling of security for its safety from menace." Sumner thought that 40,000 men in all for the defense of the city would be sufficient; the other corps commanders thought that, "with the forts on the right bank of the Potomac fully garrisoned, and those on the left bank occupied, a covering force in front of the Virginia line of 25,000 men would suffice." To man the forts, it was estimated, would require 25,000 first-rate troops—50,000 in all. McClellan proposed to leave for the defense of Washington and its approaches 73,000 men. Of these, 35,000 were in the Valley of the Shenandoah; 20,000 at Warrenton, Manassas, and on the lower Potomac; and 18,000 in and before the capital. But the military authorities at Washington "did not consider the force in the Valley of the Shenandoah as available for the immediate defense of the capital, being required for the defense of that valley;" and Wadsworth, who had been appointed military governor of the district, said that the force under his command was "nearly all new, imperfectly disciplined, several of the regiments in a very disorganized condition, and entirely inadequate to and unfit for the important duty to which it had been assigned." They reported that the stipulation and the order of the President "had not been complied with;" and, in consequence, Lincoln ordered McDowell's division to remain behind.[2]

The combined naval and military attack upon Yorktown, which McClellan had declared to be the essential feature of his plan of operations, was never made. It seems hardly to have been mentioned after his arrival at Fortress Monroe. It appears to have been set aside in consequence of the presence of the Virginia, which lay apparently ready for another raid upon the fleet. "Flag-officer Goldsborough," says McClellan, "then in command of the United States squadron in Hampton Roads, regarded it (and no doubt justly) as his highest and most imperative duty to watch and neutralize the Virginia, and as he designed using his most powerful vessels in a contest with her, he did not feel able to detach for the assistance of the army a suitable force to attack the water batteries at Yorktown and Gloucester. At no time during the operations against Yorktown was the navy prepared to lend us any material assistance in its reduction until after our land batteries had partially silenced the works."[1] Goldsborough, however, asserted that he had given to McClellan all the assistance for which he asked. "I was requested," he says, "to perform services in connection with the army, and every thing was done that was asked. General McClellan came on board my ship to consult me, and I pointed out to him what I thought the best plan, to which he assented. The plan of attack upon Yorktown was that I should furnish him with seven gun-boats, which I did. Every thing was furnished to General McClellan by the Navy Department that he desired in the way of gun-boats. He told me that he wanted no more than I had detailed for him." By the plan then agreed upon, the approach to Richmond was to be made by the York River, Goldsborough guaranteeing to prevent the Virginia from interfering with it, for which he said that he had ample means. The main body of the army was to advance direct upon Yorktown from Fortress Monroe; a strong force to be landed, under cover of the gun-boats, within four miles; while another column was to land on the northern side of the York, and attack Gloucester in the rear, where it was wholly unprotected. Gloucester, it was thought, would fall without any fighting, and its fall would involve that of Yorktown, whose river front could be attacked from the Point more effectually than by the fleet. No attempt was made to execute this plan—why, Goldsborough never knew.[2] The reason undoubtedly was that McClellan, who greatly overestimated the enemy's strength, dared not attempt it at once after the withholding of McDowell's corps, to whom he had assigned the attack upon Gloucester, nor even a fortnight later, when he was joined by Franklin, whose division formed a considerable part of that corps.

McClellan then undertook to carry out the plan, which Heintzelman had proposed, of piercing the Confederate line in the centre of the Peninsula, and interposing a force between Yorktown and Richmond. W. F. Smith's division of Keyes's corps was directed, on the morning of the 5th of March, to go straight up the Peninsula to the Half-way House, between Yorktown and Williamsburg, so as to prevent the escape of the garrison at Yorktown, and prevent re-enforcements from being thrown in. Heintzelman was to send Fitz John Porter's division by a road nearly parallel, but to halt at Powers's House, six miles below Yorktown, there to await farther orders. Heavy rains fell all the morning, which made the roads almost impassable for the infantry of Smith's column. He could bring forward only a few guns; ammunition, provision, and forage could not be brought up at all. Early in the afternoon he unexpectedly found himself brought to a stand by the Warwick River, and the works which guarded its passage at Lee's Mill. On all the maps of that region the river was laid down as running parallel with, and not crossing, the main road from Newport News to Williamsburg, re-entering a creek on the James, and making the so-called Mulberry Island a real island. Instead of this, the Warwick was now found to run directly

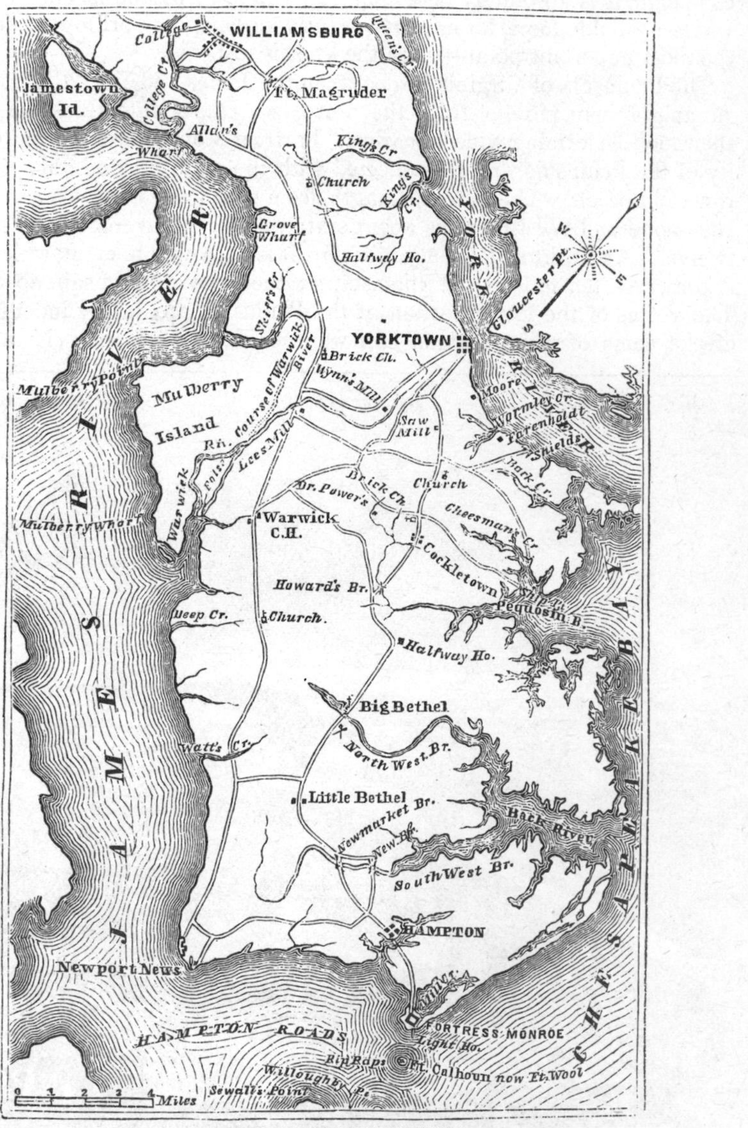

THE PENINSULA, BELOW WILLIAMSBURG.

mitted to advance when I first landed on the Peninsula, I could have isolated the troops at Yorktown, and the place would have fallen in a very few days. . . . I supposed that we could force the enemy's lines at about Wynne's Mill, so as to prevent the enemy from re-enforcing it. . . . I was always of opinion that we could have forced their lines; and, from information that we got at the Adams House, about two miles from Williamsburg, the day before the battle there [*i. e.*, May 4], I was satisfied we could have done so. We were willing to try it with a single brigade. General Hamilton made the application, and I forwarded it to the commanding general."—*Com. Rep.*, 346, 347.

Hooker testifies: "When General McClellan landed, there were somewhere between 8000 and 15,000 at Yorktown. . . . From my examination of the works at Yorktown, I felt that their lines could be pierced without any considerable loss by the corps with which I was on duty—Heintzelman's corps. We could have gone right through and gone to the rear of the enemy. They would have run the moment we got to their rear, and we could have picked up the prisoners. Right there at Yorktown they had expended a great deal of labor. But I would have marched right through the redoubts which were a part of the cordon they had, and got on the road between Yorktown and Richmond, and thus compelled the enemy to fight me on my ground, and not have fought them on theirs. If McClellan had thrown his army between Yorktown and Williamsburg, it would have resulted in the capture and destruction of the enemy's army. I know of no reason why that could not be done."—*Com. Rep.*, 575, 576.

McClellan estimated the enemy's force much higher. He says: "Information which I had collected during the winter placed General Magruder's command at from 15,000 to 20,000 men, independently of General Huger's force at Norfolk. Knowing that General Huger could easily spare some troops to re-enforce Yorktown, and that he had indeed done so, and that Johnston's army at Manassas could be brought rapidly by the James and York Rivers to the same point, I proceeded to invest the town without delay."—*Report*, 155. General Keyes wrote on the 7th of April: "Suppose we succeed in breaking through the line in front of us, what can we do next? The roads are very bad, and if the enemy retains the command of James River, and we do not first reduce Yorktown, it would be impossible for us to subsist this army three marches beyond where it is now. . . . The line in front of us is one of the strongest in the world, and the force of the enemy capable of being increased beyond the numbers we have to oppose to him. . . . If we break through and advance, both our flanks will be assailed from two great water-courses in the hands of the enemy; our supplies would give out, and the enemy, equal if not superior in numbers, would, with the other advantages, beat and destroy this army."—*McC. Rep.*, 167, 168. General Keyes appears subsequently to have modified his opinion. In testifying before the committee a year after, he said: "My impression now is that, if the whole army had been pushed forward, we should have found a point to break through. . . . I will not say that, if we had pressed on immediately on arriving in front of their lines, we might not have found a point where we could have broken the line, and then have invested Yorktown on two sides, when the fall of it would, of course, have been hastened. It is my opinion that if we had pressed on rapidly when we first arrived, we might have found a point through which we could have broken."—*Com. Rep.*, 600, 601.

[1] Colonel Cabell, the Confederate chief of artillery, reports: "From the topography of the ground, it was absolutely necessary to occupy the whole of this line in the then condition of our forces. Our forces were so few in number, that it was essential to the safety of the command that the whole should be defended, as the breaking of our lines at any point would necessarily have been attended by the most disastrous results; the centre broken or our flank turned, compelling a precipitate retreat to Yorktown or Mulberry Island, to stand a siege of the enemy's land force, assisted by the whole naval force, with but little prospect of relief or re-enforcements when the enemy occupied the intervening country. Three roads led up from the Peninsula and crossed our line of defenses. The first, on our right, was the Warwick Road, that crossed at Lee's Mill; the second crossed at Wynne's Mill; and the third was commanded by redoubts Numbers 4 and 5, near Yorktown. The crossing at Lee's Mill was naturally strong, and fortifications had been erected there and at Wynne's Mill. Below Lee's Mill, the Warwick River, affected by the tides, and assisted by swamps on each side, proved a tolerable protection; but the marshes could easily be made passable, and the river bridged."—MAGRUDER, 531.

[2] For full details of these withdrawals, see *McC. Rep.*, 134, 139–142; *Com. Rep.*, 251, 252, 303–305. McClellan, in reviewing his campaign, says this reduction of force "removed nearly 60,000 men from my command, and reduced my force by more than one third after its task had been assigned, its operations planned, its fighting begun. To me the blow was most discouraging. It frustrated all my plans for impending operations. It fell when I was too deeply committed to withdraw. It left me incapable of continuing operations which had been begun. It compelled the adoption of another, a different, and a less effective plan of campaign. It made rapid and brilliant operations impossible. It was a fatal error."—*Report*, 160.

[1] *McC. Rep.*, 156.

[2] Goldsborough's testimony, *Com. Rep.*, 631–633.

across the Peninsula. Heintzelman's division, after overcoming some slight resistance at Big Bethel and Howard's Bridge, found itself in like manner checked when almost in front of Yorktown.[1] Skirmishing, which Magruder magnifies into an attack of "furious cannonading and musketry," ensued at both points; but the result was that the Confederates held the line of the Warwick intact. If McClellan found the line "stronger than was expected, unapproachable by reason of the Warwick River, and incapable of being carried by assault,"[2] Magruder was still more astonished that the line was not forced. He believed that he had before him the whole army of the Potomac, "forming an aggregate of not less than 100,000, since ascertained to have been 120,000," and that he had held them in check with 5000. For several days he expected another attack; his men slept in the trenches under arms, but, to his surprise, day after day passed without an assault. In a few days the object of the delay became apparent. Long lines of earthworks began to appear in every direction through the intervening woods and along the open fields.[3] McClellan had become convinced that "instant assault upon Yorktown would have been simple folly," and that he must prepare for it by the preliminary employment of heavy guns and some siege operations."[4] The five thousand Confederates, who, without re-enforcements, held for at least six days the line of the Warwick, decided the whole course of the campaign. They delayed the entire Federal army for a month in the swamps of the Warwick.

Much was to be done before Yorktown could be formally invested. Miles of road were to be cut and corduroyed through swampy forests, and bridges to be built over sluggish streams. Direct hostile operations were suspended. McClellan ordered Keyes, whose corps was posted opposite the line of the Warwick, "not to move any of the troops from their positions unless the enemy actually lands or crosses the Warwick." Once only did he depart from this cautious policy. Smith, whose division was posted on the extreme right, chafed at this inactivity. Keyes, who had more than once "seen a disposition on his part to try to break through the enemy's lines with his division, or a part of it," ordered that no such attempt should be made. Smith had discovered that the weakest point was at Wynne's Mill, near the centre of the enemy's line. He was authorized by McClellan, without the knowledge of Keyes, to push a strong reconnoissance to this point, and sustain the reconnoitring party by a real attack, if found expedient.[5] At this point the enemy had only a single battery of three six-pounders. The fire of this was silenced, and four companies of the 3d Vermont, wading to the arm-pits, crossed the stream, and drove a North Carolina and Georgia regiment from their rifle-pits. These rallied, and, re-enforced by three regiments, forced the Vermonters out of the pits and back across the stream, with heavy loss. The other regiments who were preparing to support the advance were recalled. Later, an attempt was made by the 6th Vermont to cross by the dam; but a single gun of the enemy commanded this passage, and the attempt was abandoned. The four companies of the 3d which crossed the Warwick lost 25 killed and 50 wounded, most of them severely. The entire loss was 35 killed and 120 wounded. Magruder represents this affair as a decided victory; the Federal loss, he thought, could not be less than 600, his own being not more than 75; "but," he adds, "all the re-enforcements which were on their way to me had not yet joined me, so that I

[1] McC. Rep., 154, 159.   [2] Ibid., 160.   [3] Magruder, 517.
[4] McC. Rep., 162.   [5] McC. Rep., 177; Com. Rep., 599.

WILLIAM F. SMITH.

was unable to follow up the action by any decided step." He enumerates fourteen entire regiments of infantry, besides artillery and dragoons, as engaged or within supporting distance. These were the forces on the line of the Warwick. Adding to them the troops in the fortifications, the Confederate force in and about Yorktown probably numbered from 20,000 to 25,000 men. Additional re-enforcements soon arrived, and with them came officers who outranked Magruder, and he ceased to command.[1] This was the only serious engagement on the Peninsula previous to the evacuation of Yorktown, although an almost continuous artillery fire and picket shooting was kept up on various parts of the line.

Meantime for a fortnight an almost continuous dialogue was held by telegraph and mail between McClellan and the government at Washington, running thus:[2]

[1] Magruder, 517–535.   [2] Com. Rep., 319–323.

MAKING ROAD THROUGH THE SWAMP.

McCLELLAN, *April* 5. The enemy are in large force along our front. Deserters say they are daily re-enforced from Richmond and Norfolk. I beg you to reconsider the order detaching the first corps from my command. If you can not leave me the whole of that corps, let me not lose Franklin and his division. *April* 6. The order forming new departments, if enforced, deprives me of the power of ordering up wagons and troops absolutely necessary to enable me to advance to Richmond. I request that my orders for wagon-trains, etc., that I have left behind, as well as Woodbury's brigade, may be at once complied with. I repeat my request that Franklin may be restored to my command.

LINCOLN, *April* 6. Your orders for forwarding transportation and Woodbury's brigade under your command will not be interfered with. You have over 100,000 troops with you, independent of Wool's command. You had better break the enemy's line from Yorktown to Warwick River at once. They will probably use time as advantageously as you can.

McCLELLAN, *April* 7. Johnston arrived at Yorktown yesterday with strong re-enforcements. It seems clear that I shall have on my hands the whole force of the enemy—not less than 100,000 men, possibly more. When my present command all joins me, I shall have about 85,000 men. With this army I could assault the enemy's works, and perhaps carry them; but were I in possession of their intrenchments, and assaulted by double my numbers, I should not fear the result. I shall do all in my power to carry the works; but I should have the whole first corps to land upon York River, and attack Gloucester in the rear.

LINCOLN, *April* 9. My explicit directions that Washington should be left entirely secure have been neglected. Do you think I should permit the line from Richmond to this city to be entirely open except the resistance which could be offered by less than 20,000 unorganized troops? When I telegraphed that you had more than 100,000 men, I had just obtained a statement, taken from your own returns, making 108,000 with you or on the way. You say you have but 85,000. Where are the other 23,000? Wool's command is doing for you just what a like number of your own command would have to do if that command was away. I suppose your whole force is with you now. If so, it is the precise time for you to strike a blow. The enemy will gain faster by fortifications and re-enforcements than you can by re-enforcements alone. Let me tell you it is indispensable for you that you strike a blow. I am powerless to help this. I have always thought that going down the bay in search of a field, instead of fighting at or near Manassas, was only shifting, not surmounting a difficulty: we should find the same enemy, and the same or equal intrenchments at either place. The country is noting that the present hesitation to move upon an intrenched enemy is but the story of Manassas repeated. I will do all I can to sustain you; but you must act.

McCLELLAN, *April* 10. The reconnoissance of to-day proves that it is necessary to invest and attack Gloucester Point. Give me Franklin's and McCall's divisions, and I will at once undertake it. If you can not possibly send me the two divisions to carry out this final plan of the campaign, I will run the risk, and hold myself responsible for the result, if you will give me Franklin's. Grant me this request. The fate of our cause depends upon it. I wish the two divisions; Franklin's is indispensable. I have determined on the point of attack, and am engaged in fixing the positions of the batteries.

ADJUTANT GENERAL, *April* 11. Franklin's division has been ordered to embark immediately for Fort Monroe.

McCLELLAN, *April* 12. Thank you for the re-enforcements sent me. Franklin will attack on the other side. The moment I hear from him I will state point of rendezvous. I am confident. *April* 13. Arrangement proposed by Franklin would assist me much. Our work progressing well. We shall soon be at them, and I am sure of the result. *April* 14. Have seen Franklin. Thank you for your kindness and consideration. I now understand the matter, which I did not before. Our field-guns annoyed the enemy considerably to-day. Roads and bridges now progressing rapidly. Siege-guns and ammunition coming up very satisfactorily. Shall have nearly all up to-morrow. The tranquillity of Yorktown is nearly at an end.

SECRETARY OF WAR, *April* 20.[1] I am rejoiced to learn that your opera-

---

[1] In the Committee's Report this dispatch is dated the 27th. This is doubtless an error, as it clearly refers to the two preceding dispatches, and to McClellan's dispatches of the 18th (not given in the Report) relating to the affair of the 16th, in which he says, "The conduct of the Green Mountain Boys is spoken of in the highest terms. They drove a superior number of the enemy from their fortified position, but were forced to relinquish it on the rebels being re-enforced. The loss of the enemy must have been very heavy, as the well-directed fire of our artillery mowed them by acres."

REMAINS OF BRITISH WORKS AT YORKTOWN.

tions are progressing so rapidly, and with so much spirit and success, and congratulate you and the officers and soldiers engaged upon the brilliant affair mentioned in your telegrams. Every thing in the power of the department is at your service. I hope soon to congratulate you upon a splendid victory that shall be the finishing stroke of the war.

Here the colloquy appears to have closed for a while. The tranquillity of Yorktown was not disturbed for a fortnight; and it was many months before the splendid victory was achieved which was to be "the finishing stroke of the war." Franklin, with his division, 11,000 strong, reached Yorktown on the 14th, raising the effective force of the Army of the Potomac to more than 100,000 men,[1] besides the 10,000 of Wool, who at Fortress Monroe were doing just what, had they been removed, McClellan would have been obliged to do with the same number of his own command. McClellan's first plan, for the success of which he proposed to hold himself responsible, was to join Hooker's division to Franklin's, and, landing on the Severn, to make a diversion by attacking Gloucester in the rear. This plan was abandoned because "no more troops could be spared" to assist Franklin. He then determined to act on Gloucester by disembarking Franklin on the north bank of the York, under the protection of the gun-boats. A place for landing was selected, but nothing more was done. Franklin's division was kept for more than three weeks on board the transports, and was not disembarked until the 6th of May, after Yorktown had been abandoned and the battle of Williamsburg had been fought.[2]

By the middle of April the works at Yorktown had been reconnoitred, the locations for the batteries determined, and the roads and bridges to reach them well advanced. The topography of the place indicates the position of its defenses. The Confederate works occupied the precise lines of the British works of 1781, which were until recently in fair preservation. The level bluff upon which Yorktown stands forms an irregular parallelogram, the longer sides, running northwest and southeast, being 1200 yards, the shorter sides being 400 and 600 yards. It is inclosed by deep ravines, which almost meet in the rear. The American forces in 1781 advanced southwestwardly from Williamsburg. The Federal forces in 1862 advanced from the opposite direction; but the attack in both cases was directed against the southwestern face of the works. In 1781 the assailing batteries were advanced to within 200 and 300 yards from the defensive works; in 1862 they were from 1500 to 2500 yards; one battery, with two two-hundred pound and five one-hundred pound Parrotts, was 3810 yards from the nearest point of the defenses. All told, there were fifteen batteries, mounted with 111 guns and mortars. By the 3d of May these were essentially completed and armed. The work had been carried on under an incessant but inef-

---

[1] McClellan undesignedly gives the impression that Franklin joined him a week later. He says (*Report*, 176), "On the 22d of April, General Franklin, with his division from General McDowell's corps, had arrived and reported to me." The misdate here implied has been positively made by various writers; among others, by Hillard, who says (*Life and Campaigns of McClellan*, 180), "On the 22d of April, while the siege of Yorktown was going on, General Franklin's division of General McDowell's corps arrived, and reported to General McClellan. These troops were kept on board the transports, and not embarked for some days." The force of the Army of the Potomac at this precise date has not been given; but, on the 30th of April, no considerable re-enforcements having arrived in the interval, McClellan (*Report*, 53) says that there were, nominally, including Franklin, 126,387 men. Of these, however, 11,037 were absent by authority, and 6015 sick or under arrest, leaving an effective force of 109,335.

The Assistant Adjutant General furnished the following detailed statement, "accurately compiled from the morning Report of the Army of the Potomac on the 30th day of April, 1862, signed by Major General McClellan and his assistant adjutant general" (*Com. Rep.*, 323).

Number of Men composing the Army of the Potomac, April 30, 1862.

	Present for duty.	Sick and on special duty.	Aggregate absent.	Present and absent.
General Staff, Engineers, and Engineer Brigade, Cavalry Division, Escort to Head-quarters, and Provost Guard	13,787	798	2,072	16,657
Second Corps, General Sumner	19,054	887	2,061	22,002
Third Corps, General Heintzelman	34,633	2009	3,068	39,710
Fourth Corps, General Keyes	33,586	1886	4,089	39,561
Franklin's Division	11,332	270	846	12,448
	112,392	5850	12,136	130,378

The Assistant Secretary of War states (*McC. Rep.*, 109), "In thirty-seven days (and most of it was accomplished in thirty days) from the time I received the order [Feb. 28], there were transported to Fort Monroe 121,500 men." Franklin's division can not, from the dates, be included in this number.   [2] *McC. Rep.*, 176; *Com. Rep.*, 621, 632; *Art. Op.*, 71–82.

BATTERY NO. 1.

MORTAR BATTERY, NO. 4.

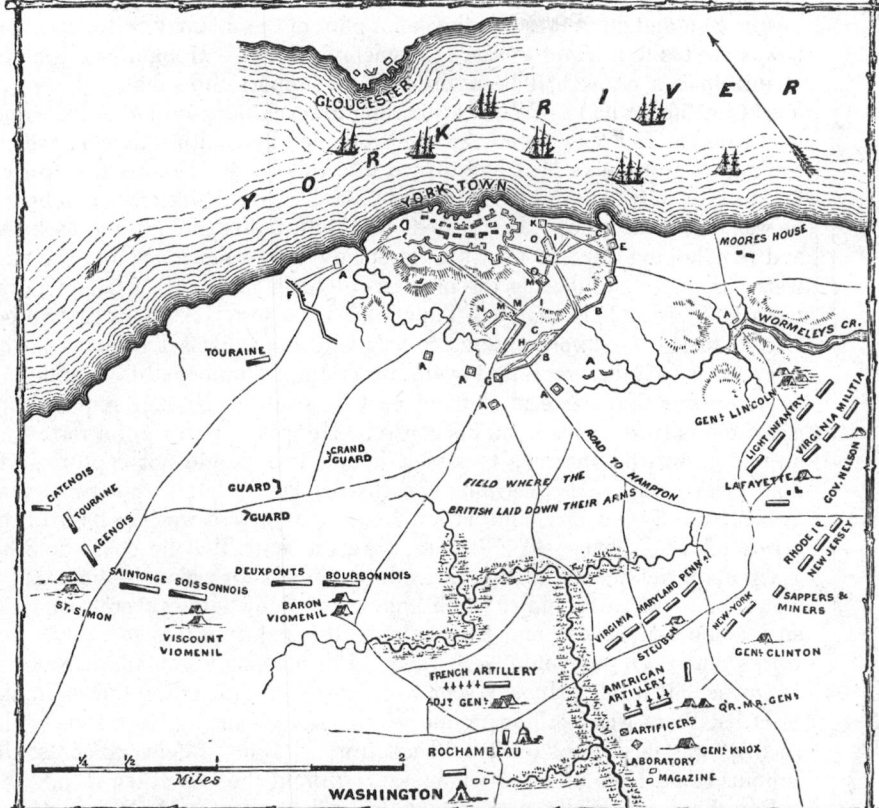

SIEGE OF YORKTOWN, OCTOBER, 1781.

A, British Outworks, taken possession of by the Americans on their arrival.—B, First Parallel.—C, D, American Batteries.—E, Bomb Battery.—G, French Battery.—H, French Bomb Battery.—I, Second Parallel.—K, Redoubt stormed by the Americans.—L, Redoubt stormed by the French.—M, M, M, French Batteries.—N, French Bomb Battery.—O, American Batteries.

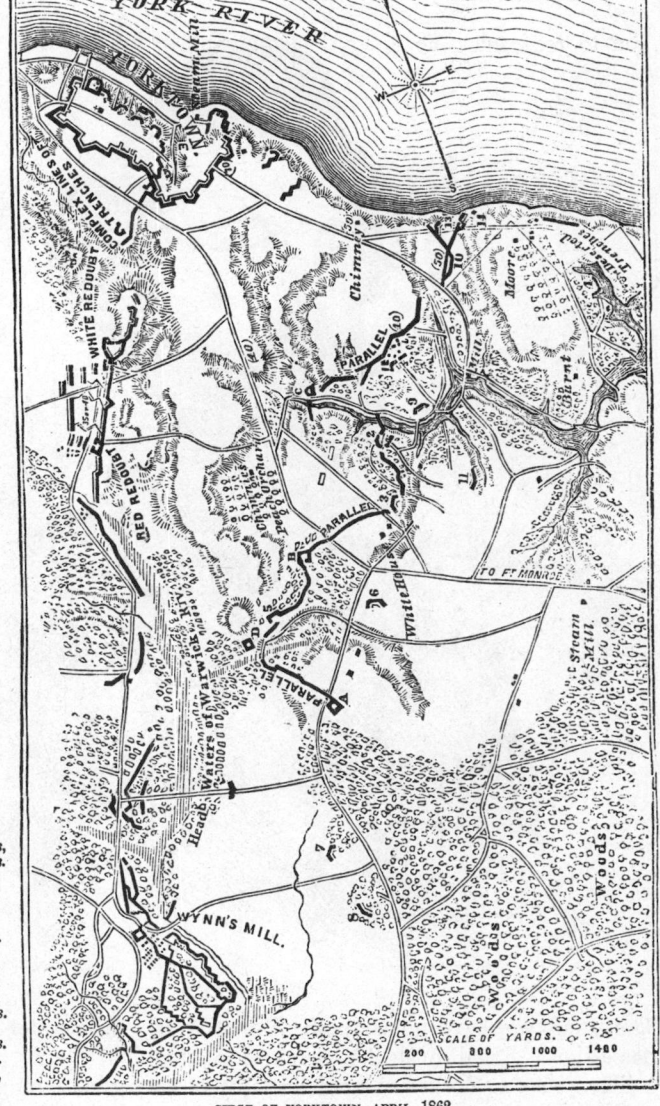

SIEGE OF YORKTOWN, APRIL, 1862.

The Figures (1—15) designate the Union Batteries.—The Letters (A, B, C, D) designate Redoubts.

NO.	ARMAMENT.
1,	2 200-pdr. Parrotts,
	5 100-pdr. Parrotts.
2,	3 4½-inch Rifled,
	6 30-pdr. Parrotts,
	6 20-pdr. Parrotts.
3,	7 20-pdr. Parrotts.
4,	10 13-inch Mortars.
5,	8 20-pdr. Parrotts.
6,	5 10-inch Mortars.
7,	6 20-pdr. Parrotts.
8,	6 20-pdr. Parrotts.
9,	10 10-inch Mortars.
10,	7 4½-inch Rifled,
	3 100-pdr. Parrotts.
11,	4 10-inch Mortars.
12,	5 10-inch Mortars,
	5 8-inch Mortars.
13,	7 30-pdr. Parrotts.
14,	3 10½-pdr. Parrotts,
	1 100-pdr. James.
15,	2 8-inch S. Howitzers.

fectual fire from the enemy. Not a score of lives were lost by this fire.[1] But the troops suffered severely from sickness during that month. Nearly an eighth of the army was disabled by disease. Its morale was also impaired; it was hard to bring officers and men to endure, day after day and week after week, the weary toil of digging in the Warwick swamps. The Army of the Potomac was less effective at the beginning of May than it had been a month before.[2]

McClellan, in opposition to the opinion of the chief of engineers, would not open fire from the batteries, one by one, as they were finished, but resolved to wait until all were ready, when he would have such an overwhelming force as would crush every thing before it. He departed from the plan only so far as to open with solid shot and shell from the 100 and 200 pounders of Battery No. 1, upon the wharf at Yorktown, 4800 yards distant, where the enemy were discharging several vessels. Most of the percussion shells failed to explode, and those filled with Greek fire produced no perceptible effect. The vessels were driven off, and took refuge across the river, behind Gloucester Point.[3] Daybreak on the 6th of May was the time fixed upon for the general fire to open. On the afternoon of the 3d the enemy began a vigorous fire of shells into Heintzelman's camp, which was nearest to Yorktown. A balloon, which was sent up to reconnoitre, seemed to be a special mark. They kept up a random fire, without any apparent object, until after midnight. Toward daylight, Heintzelman was awakened by a rattling fire of musketry. He telegraphed to the officer commanding the skirmishers in the trenches, and received answer that there was no fighting, but the light of a great fire in Yorktown was visible. At daylight it was reported that the enemy were evacuating their works. Heintzelman went up in the balloon, saw that the number of camp-fires about Yorktown was much dimin-

ished, and the guns had disappeared. Presently he saw the Federal skirmishers entering the works. He came down, and, presuming that he should be at once ordered in pursuit, gave direction for his troops to prepare three days' rations. But hour after hour passed, and no orders came. He rode over to head-quarters, and found that orders had been given for the pursuit; but it was past noon before they got off.[4] Magruder, who had constructed the works, and had so obstinately held them without re-enforcements, had ceased to command a fortnight before. A council of war had decided that the fortification was untenable, and must be abandoned; and the fire of the previous evening was merely to mask the evacuation. Of the ninety-four guns, fifty-six were left behind, only three of them disabled.[5] McClellan telegraphed to Washington, "We have the ramparts; have guns, ammunition, camp equipage, etc. We hold the entire line of his works, which the engineers report as being very strong. I have thrown all my cavalry and horse-infantry in pursuit, supported by infantry. No time shall be lost.

[1] "An incessant fire was kept up during the day with rifled projectiles and eight-inch shell and solid shot, and thirty-two and forty-two pounder shot, without retarding the work in the least. Since our first appearance before Yorktown (April 5), and particularly since the 15th, the ravines have been filled with men night and day, making roads, building batteries and parallels, and guarding the works. The loss of life has been most trifling. I have not the exact number, but I have reason to believe that it does not amount to a dozen."—Art. Op., 146.

[2] On the 30th of April the sick-list numbered 5618; there were also "absent by authority" 11,037 (McC. Rep., 53). It is fair to assume that two thirds of the leaves of absence must have been given by reason of disability. "April 19. Colonel Alexander states that the men worked well, but their officers do not attach sufficient importance to the work to be performed, many of them lying in the shade in place of superintending the work" (Art. Op., 159). "April 21. Of the 3000 men asked for, 2326 reported this morning for duty" (Ibid., 160). "April 26. Very little work was done last night; it was impossible to get the working parties to do any thing" (Ibid., 169). "April 27. A great deal of difficulty and delay is still experienced in regulating the working parties. Details, after waiting at the place where they have been directed to go, return to camp and report no engineer officer to be found; while the engineer officer waiting several hours without seeing them" (Ibid., 171). "April 28. To-day only 1000 men reported in place of 1500 to Lieutenant McAlester" (Ibid., 173). "We should probably have succeeded [in an immediate assault upon Yorktown], and if we failed, it may well be doubted whether the shock of an unsuccessful assault would have been more demoralizing than the labors of the siege. Our troops toiled for a month in the trenches, or lay in the swamps of the Warwick. We lost few men by the siege, but disease took a fearful hold upon the army, and toil and hardship, unredeemed by the excitement of combat, impaired the morale. We did not carry with us from Yorktown so good an army as we took there" (Ibid., 62).

[3] Art. Op., 63, 127; Com. Rep., 429.
[4] Com. Rep., 347.   [5] Art. Op., 189.

TAKING POSSESSION OF YORKTOWN.

GEORGE STONEMAN.

The gun-boats have gone up the York River. Gloucester is also in our possession. I shall push the enemy to the wall."[1]

The works at Yorktown were certainly of very great strength. Probably they could not have been carried by assault unless the assailants were fully twice as many as the defenders. There were also strong outworks, extending for a mile to the head waters of the Warwick. This stream, with its swampy borders, presented a very strong defensive line if held by an adequate force. But, extending for more than ten miles, a much larger force than the enemy had at his disposal would have been needed to hold them against a determined attack. They consisted of an infantry parapet and trenches along the bank, with three or four redoubts and batteries, mounting only two or three light field-pieces to sweep the main approaches. At no time before the 16th of April could Magruder have given more than 10,000 men to the defense of this whole line without stripping Yorktown of its garrison. A real attack by 20,000 men could have pierced the line. Once broken, there was nothing between the assailants and Williamsburg.[2]

Johnston, who had for a fortnight been in command on the Peninsula, conducted the retreat from Yorktown with rare ability. Besides the heavy guns, and ammunition belonging to them, he left little behind. His trains and the mass of his troops were well under way hours before their departure was perceived. The weather had favored him. Several clear days had put the roads in good condition, and before the pursuit was commenced he was past the defensive lines before Williamsburg, and well on his way to Richmond. A strong rear guard was left behind near Williamsburg, where works had been thrown up to check any pursuit. Two main roads run down the Peninsula from near Williamsburg; one, following the York River, goes to Yorktown; the other, following the course of the James, crosses the Warwick at Lee's Mill. These two roads, which are connected by numerous cross-roads, come together a mile east of Williamsburg. At this point was Fort Magruder, the centre of the Confederate works, which, to the number of thirteen, stretched clear across the narrow isthmus between the two rivers. All these works were hidden by heavy forests, concealing them from view until the observer was within a mile. The trees near the works had been felled, so that the occupants of the redoubts might have timely notice of the approach of an enemy and bring their artillery to bear.

McClellan, though he was convinced that the force of the enemy outnumbered his own, had no idea that they would make a stand before Williamsburg. He remained at Yorktown to direct the movements of Franklin's division by the York River to West Point, having ordered Stoneman, with all the available cavalry and four batteries of horse artillery, to pursue the enemy and harass his rear. A heavy and continuous rain-storm now set in, which soon rendered the roads difficult. But Stoneman pressed on, and, a little past noon of the 4th, debouched from the screen of woods, and found himself under a hot fire from Fort Magruder. He fell back, suffering some loss in men and guns, to await the coming up of the infantry, without whom it was useless to attempt to assail the enemy's works. Hooker's division of Heintzelman's corps had been ordered to support Stoneman. They left Yorktown about noon. While struggling to reach the position where Stoneman stood at bay, they found the road occupied by Smith's division, which, coming up from Lee's Mill, had turned into this road. Hooker had to stop for three or four hours until Smith had passed. Night was closing in before he was able to advance. He pressed on for four hours through the darkness and rain, hoping to come up with the enemy before morning; but the men were exhausted by laboring the previous night in the trenches before Yorktown and by the long march. They must have rest. An hour or two before midnight they were ordered to halt, and flung themselves down in the miry road. At daybreak they were aroused and summoned to march. In an hour after they came in sight of Fort Magruder. Hooker required but a few minutes to decide upon his course. He was in pursuit of a retreating army. It was his business to attack it, and, if he could not capture it, to hold it in check. His own force was hardly 9000; but within two hours' march were 30,000 men, and within four hours' march was the bulk of the Army of the Potomac, 60,000 more. He was sure that he could hold his grasp upon the enemy against thrice his numbers for twice the time that it would be required for aid to reach him. The Confederates were soon driven into Fort Magruder, and Hooker pushed his skirmishers so close to the works that not a gun could be worked. If a man showed his head or hand he got a ball in it. Hooker sent word to the commanding officer in the rear that there was nothing in the way of his advancing his troops. The enemy "was in a vice," and could not fire; the line of defenses across the isthmus could have been carried, he said, without the loss of ten men.[1]

But there was really no commanding officer there. McClellan was at Yorktown. Heintzelman had been ordered to take charge of operations in front; but Sumner had come up in person the night before without any troops of his own corps, and assumed command in virtue of seniority. "Sumner ranked me," says Heintzelman, "and I had nothing to do." That night nothing was done. Next morning a consultation was held. Sumner decided to assail the enemy's left, and troops were ordered up for that purpose. So hour after hour passed away. Hooker all the while had been hotly engaged upon the left. The sound of the firing was plainly heard at head-quarters. Heintzelman was sent in that direction to take charge of operations. He had scarcely gone when Hooker's letter came, telling Heintzelman that he had been hotly engaged all the morning; his men hard at work, but much exhausted; but communication was open; troops could come up, take post by his side, and whip the enemy. In twenty minutes the letter was returned from Sumner, with an endorsement that it had been opened and read by the senior officer on that field.[2] But no re-enforcements came up. For hours Sumner was apprehensive of an attack upon the centre, where he kept his post, though he repeatedly gave orders for the troops in the rear to move up on the same road which Hooker had taken.[3]

WINFIELD SCOTT HANCOCK.

[1] Reb. Rec., iv., 6.
[2] For the strength of the Confederate works on the Warwick, see especially Art. Op., 194–201. The most exaggerated reports were put forth respecting the strength of this line. Thus the New York Herald of April 22 furnishes an elaborate map showing three continuous lines of intrenchments running completely across the isthmus. The first line mounts 140 guns, the second, two miles in the rear, has 120 guns, both being provided with "hot shot furnaces." The third, two miles beyond, has 240 guns, and consists, besides the intrenchments, of six forts. Behind these appear the "encampments of the rebel army in four grand divisions," besides a "reserve at Williamsburg;" in all, 500 guns, besides those of Yorktown itself. The works on Gloucester Point were said to have "eighteen 100-pounder rifle guns." Instead of which, most of the pieces were light navy guns; "the others are believed to be as heavy as 32-pounders." Of the whole, only eight in all bore on the river and on our positions.—Art. Op., 193.

[1] Com. Rep., 577.   [2] Hooker's Report, Reb. Rec., iv., 15.
[3] Keyes, in his testimony (Com. Rep., 603), says that these orders were countermanded; but Sumner (Testimony, Ibid., 361) makes no reference to any such countermand; and Kearney's division, which relieved Hooker, and Peck's and Hancock's brigades, which performed important parts toward the close of the battle, came up under orders from Sumner. McClellan (Report, 183) merely mentions the countermanding by Sumner of orders to re-enforce Hancock.

Hooker had opened the battle at half past seven in the morning. At nine he had silenced the fire of Fort Magruder, and kept his advantage for two or three hours. But the enemy began to receive re-enforcements, and took the offensive. Longstreet, who commanded the rear, had retreated beyond Williamsburg; he turned back to strengthen the force which was engaged. Three times in succession the Confederates charged upon Hooker's centre, each time with fresh troops, and each time were thrown back with heavy loss. Hooker's ammunition began to give out. Longstreet made a furious charge upon a battery left for a moment without support, and captured four guns, but was again driven off. So the tide of battle ebbed and flowed until between four and five in the afternoon, when Kearney came upon the field. For six hours he had been struggling up along a single muddy road, encumbered with other troops and trains. He outranked Hooker, who gladly left the command to him, his wearied regiments resting from the fight. Kearney dashed impetuously forward, and, after a sharp contest, drove the enemy back, gained his rear, and won the fight on this part of the scene. Darkness now closed in, and the regiments bivouacked on the field which they had won.

Toward the close of the day the action had stretched to the right of Fort Magruder. Peck's brigade, which had come up, took position there, and held its ground against all attacks. Hancock had come up still farther to the right. He took possession of two redoubts, which were weakly held, and repeatedly asked for re-enforcements to enable him to advance and take another redoubt which commanded the plain between him and Fort Magruder. Sumner twice ordered this re-enforcement, and twice countermanded the order at the moment of execution. At length, the request being repeated, Sumner ordered him to fall back; but Hancock deferred the execution of this order to the last moment. He was unwilling to lose the advantage which he had gained. The enemy began to press hard upon him. Feigning to retreat slowly, he suddenly turned upon them, poured in some terrific volleys of musketry, and then giving the word, "Now, gentlemen, the bayonet!" charged with his whole brigade. The enemy broke into utter rout, leaving behind more than 500 killed, wounded, and prisoners. Hancock's loss was only 31. This brilliant charge, just in the dusk, closed the battle. The entire Federal loss was 2228; of these, 456 were killed, 1400 wounded, and 372 missing. More than two thirds of this was suffered by Hooker's division, which lost, in all, 1575, of whom 338 were killed, 992 wounded, and 335 missing. Nearly all of the prisoners were taken on the night preceding the battle. They were men who had straggled into the woods, and, not being able to extricate themselves in the darkness, were captured by the enemy's pickets. The loss of the Confederates must have been larger. During the greater part of the fight they attacked with superior numbers, and were flung back by cannon and musketry. Hooker believed that the killed of the enemy was double his own. The next day more than eight hundred of his wounded were found in the hospitals at Williamsburg; others were distributed among private houses, and all the available tenements in the vicinity of the battle-field were filled with them.

McClellan had remained at Yorktown to superintend the preparations for sending Franklin's troops up the river. He sent aids to observe operations in front. It was past noon before he heard any thing to lead him to suppose that there was any thing occurring beyond a simple affair of a rear guard. At one o'clock came a message importing that all was not going well in front. Soon Sprague, the governor of Rhode Island, who was acting as aid to the chief of artillery, dashed up, reported how matters stood in front, and urged him to go up there at once. "I thought they could take care of that little matter," replied McClellan; but promised to go up.[1] He reached Sumner's head-quarters between four and five, took the command in person, and, hearing heavy firing toward the right, ordered three brigades in that direction; but, before the orders could be executed, Hancock had decided the day on that part of the field.[2]

Night put an end to the contest, and the wearied troops slept upon the muddy field, many without food, and all without shelter. The enemy took advantage of the darkness to decamp, leaving their dead and wounded behind them. During the night McClellan sent word to Heintzelman not to renew the attack in the morning, as he was about to make other dispositions, and would send re-enforcements. The Confederates, making no delay at Williamsburg, pushed on up the Peninsula for Richmond. A few cavalry were sent after them, who succeeded in picking up some prisoners and four or five guns which had stuck fast in the mud.

The day after the battle four divisions were sent in transports up the York River. They landed at West Point. The landing had just been effected, when, at nine o'clock on the morning of the 7th, an unsuccessful attempt was made to drive them off by a body of Confederates who had got thus

THE WHITE HOUSE.

far on their retreat. A sharp musketry fire was kept up till afternoon, when the Confederates withdrew, and kept on their retreat. The Federal loss in this affair was 49 killed, and 154 wounded and missing. After two or three days' delay at Williamsburg, the army commenced its slow march up the Peninsula, and on the 16th of May the head-quarters were established at the White House, on the Pamunkey, one of the two streams which unite to form the York River. This place is thirty miles north of Williamsburg, and twenty-five east of Richmond, with which it is connected by the Richmond and York River Railroad.[3]

Johnston had determined to abandon Yorktown some days before the evacuation took place. On the 28th of April he wrote to Tattnall, the commander of the Virginia, "The enemy continues his cautious policy. The preparations for opening fire upon Yorktown seem to be nearly completed. His great superiority in artillery will probably enable him to dismount our guns very soon." He suggested to Tattnall that possibly he might make a dash past Fortress Monroe and destroy the Federal transports in the York River. On the 10th of May Johnston wrote: "Finding it necessary to abandon this position, and regarding the evacuation of Norfolk as a consequence of that measure, I have directed Major General Huger to withdraw his troops from that place and remove to Richmond. I have also desired Captain Lee to abandon the navy yard, and report to the Secretary of the Navy in Richmond, saving as much as possible of the public property, and destroying, if practicable, what he can not save." Norfolk had been held by Huger with 15,000 men. The greater part of these went toward Richmond almost simultaneously with the evacuation of Yorktown. A few thousand were left behind until the last moment. Intelligence of this reached Fortress Monroe on the 8th. Wool, with a few thousand men, set out to take possession. They approached Norfolk on the afternoon of the 10th. At the outskirts they were met by the mayor and a deputation of citizens with a white flag, and bearing a letter from Huger, stating that, being unable to hold the city, he had surrendered it into the hands of the civil authorities. The mayor said that he had come to surrender the city into the hands of the United States, and to ask protection for the persons and property of the citizens. This was assured by Wool. The general, Mr. Chase, the Secretary of the Treasury, who had accompanied the expedition, and the mayor, then entered a carriage and drove to the City Hall to inaugurate the new government. Wool issued a proclamation appointing General Viele military governor, who was to see that no peaceable citizen should be molested, and that no United States soldier entered the city without a written permit from the commanding officer of his regiment. Wool then left the city. A crowd of people assembled. The mayor made a speech. He said that if the question

[1] Sprague's testimony, Com. Rep., 570.
[2] De Joinville says (p. 55): "The success of Hancock had been decisive, and the reserves brought up by the general-in-chief, charging upon the field, settled the affair." McClellan (Report, 184) shows that the contest was over before these re-enforcements could come up. Estvan, who scarcely ever tells the truth even by accident, and whose work is only worthy of notice because others have repeated his statements, brings McClellan personally into the action. He says (War Pictures, 279): "Suddenly a shout of a thousand voices broke upon the ear like the rushing of a mighty wind from the wood. What did this portend? There was little time left for us to speculate. Charge after charge was made upon our men, and the news then spread that McClellan, with the main body of his army, had arrived on the field of battle. This explained the loud cheers from the wood. Our men could no longer stand their ground. McClellan in person led on his troops into the midst of the fire. Magruder, now finding that the battle was lost, ordered a retreat to be sounded."
[3] The place derived its name from a plain white wooden house, occupying the site of the residence of Mrs. Custis, afterward the wife of Washington. This, as well as Arlington House on the Potomac, had fallen to the daughter of George Washington Parke Custis, the son of Martha Washington by her former husband. She was now the wife of General Robert E. Lee. The family of Lee had been residing at the White House, but had, just before the arrival of the Federal troops, removed to the neighborhood of Richmond. Mrs. Lee left upon the wall the following note: "Northern soldiers, who profess to honor the memory of Washington, forbear to desecrate the home of his first married life, the property of his wife, now owned by her descendants.—A Granddaughter of Mrs. Washington." Under this one of the Union guards wrote: "A Northern officer has protected your property, in sight of the enemy, and at the request of your overseer." This residence was burned at the close of June, when the Federal forces abandoned West Point.

The Mayor & Councils of Norfolk meeting the Federal forces under a flag of truce

The Council tree

Hoisting the old flag on the Custom-house

Entering the City of Norfolk

Burning of the Gosport Navy-Yard

THE OCCUPATION OF NORFOLK.

had rested with him he would have defended the city to the last man, but the government had decided differently; the citizens of Norfolk had been deserted by their friends, and all that the city authorities could do was to make the best terms possible. The Union commander had granted all that had been asked, and now the citizens should yield, and abstain from acts of violence and disorder. The crowd dispersed, having given three cheers for Davis and three groans for Lincoln. No notice was taken of this impudent proceeding. The loss of Norfolk, as has already been related, involved the destruction of the iron-clad Virginia.[1] A court of inquiry decided that this was unnecessary. A naval court-martial was convened, before which Tattnall was arraigned. The court honorably acquitted him, affirming that, on the day before the evacuation of Norfolk, a council was held by order of the Secretary of the Navy to determine what should be done with the Virginia; that Tattnall was in favor of passing Fortress Monroe and taking the ship into York River, or of running to Savannah with her, but that he was overruled by the council, who directed that she should remain on this side of Fortress Monroe for the protection of Norfolk and Richmond; that she was

[1] Ante, page 257.

lightened in order to enable her to go up to a safe place on the James; that she could not be lightened sufficiently to enable her to reach that place, but was thereby rendered vulnerable;[1] that all which was necessary for the enemy to do was to keep a watch upon her until her provisions were exhaust-

[1] Note on the Virginia.—The report of the trial of Tattnall enables us to correct and supplement our account (ante, page 250) of the Virginia. It shows that she was far less formidable than was supposed. The iron plating of the roof or shield was only four inches thick. The "knuckle" formed by the projection of the eaves of the roof beyond the hull was twenty inches under water. Below this the hull was covered for a depth of two feet by three layers of iron, each an inch thick and eight inches broad, put on horizontally. She then drew between twenty and twenty-two feet of water. After her encounter with the Monitor she was put on the dock, with the purpose of putting additional plates two inches thick perpendicularly upon the hull; the iron, however, gave out before all her whole length could be covered. These additional plates reached about one hundred and eighty feet from the bows, leaving sixty feet at the stern with only three inches. Four shots from the Monitor struck within a space of eight feet. A rafter was cracked and the plates somewhat broken, but there was no serious injury. When the additional plating was put on she drew twenty-two feet forward and twenty-three feet aft. Her engines were very defective. They failed several times, and the engineer said they were liable to fail at any moment. It was often found difficult to start, to stop, or to reverse them. In the opinion of Buchanan, her first commander, she was not seaworthy, not being sufficiently buoyant, and would founder in a common sea; the moment a sea struck her it would wash into her ports; she was only fitted for harbor defense. Catesby Jones, her executive officer, thought her no match for the Monitor, if properly handled; the Monitor ought to have sunk her in fifteen minutes; one of the smallest tugs might have disabled her rudder and propeller.

ed, and then capture her; and that, under these circumstances, the only alternative of her commander was to abandon and destroy the ship, as he had done. The navy yard at Gosport was destroyed by fire, and an attempt, only partly successful, was made to blow up the great stone dry dock. All the batteries which guarded the James River were abandoned, and the water approach was open to within eight miles of Richmond.

Four days after the destruction of the Virginia, the Galena, Monitor, and two gun-boats were repulsed at Fort Darling on Drewry's Bluff. Among those who defended the fort were the crew of the Virginia.[1] The boats had been put to a work for which they were not adapted. Goldsborough urged McClellan to send a force to capture that fort, which was of no great strength.[2] He offered to lead the naval attack in person. If the fort should be captured, he said that the vessels could remove the obstructions above, go straight to the city, and shell it to surrender. McClellan considered the proposal, and concluded to defer a decision until he had got his army on the other side of the Chickahominy.[3] The truth was, that, in consequence of his urgent representations, an order had just been given to McDowell which rendered it necessary to move on the basis of the York River rather than on the far preferable line of the James.

Yorktown had scarcely been evacuated when McClellan again began to represent his force as wholly inferior to that of the enemy. On the evening of the battle of Williamsburg he telegraphed, "I find Joe Johnston in front of me in strong force, probably greater a good deal than my own, and very strongly intrenched." Five days later, Williamsburg having been abandoned, he writes from "three miles beyond Williamsburg," "I regard it as certain that the enemy will meet us with all his force on or near the Chickahominy. They can concentrate many more men than I have. Every effort should be made to re-enforce me with all the disposable forces in Eastern Virginia. If I am not re-enforced, it is probable that I will be obliged to fight nearly double my numbers strongly intrenched. I do not think it will be possible for me to bring more than 70,000 men upon the field of battle." Four days later he said, "I can not bring into actual battle more than 80,000 men at the utmost, and with them I must attack in position, probably intrenched, a much larger force, perhaps double my numbers. I beg that you will cause this army to be re-enforced without delay by all the disposable troops of the government. I ask for every man that the government can send me. Any commander of the re-enforcements whom your excellency may designate will be acceptable to me, whatever expression I may heretofore have addressed to you on the subject. I will fight the enemy, whatever their force may be, with whatever force I may have, and I firmly believe that we shall beat them; but our triumph should be made decisive and complete." He desired that these re-enforcements should be sent by water, because their arrival would be more safe and certain, and because he would then be free to rest his army on the James River whenever the navigation of that stream should be opened.

To these repeated and urgent requests, the President replied on the 18th that he was unwilling to uncover the capital entirely; that, even if this were prudent, the junction could be more speedily made by a land march than by water; but, in order to increase the strength of the attack upon Richmond, McDowell, whose forces had been augmented to 35,000 or 40,000 men, would march by the shortest route, and, keeping himself always in a position to save the capital from any possible attack, he should so operate as to put his left wing in communication with McClellan's right, which should be extended to the north of Richmond. The communication between the forces might be established either north or south of the Pamunkey River. After this had been effected, McDowell was to be under the orders of McClellan; but he must give no orders which could put McDowell out of position to cover Washington. This definitive order decided the plan of the operations against Richmond.[4]

The conduct of Johnston evinced that he was at no time in command of the powerful force attributed to him. He had made no attempt to interfere with the siege operations against Yorktown, but abandoned his strong works as soon as he found that they were likely to be assailed. He gave up his strong lines at Williamsburg after fighting just long enough to enable his trains to escape, abandoning his sick and wounded. He pursued his retreat to Richmond, making no attempt to impede or harass the enemy beyond the slight attack upon a single division which was for a moment isolated at West Point. Instead of 150,000 or 160,000 men, it is hardly possible that his strength could have exceeded 50,000 or 60,000.

The approach of the Federal army occasioned a fearful panic at Richmond. Congress adjourned in haste on the 21st of April. The Confederate officials sent off their wives and children, and packed up the government archives for transportation to Columbia. Packing-boxes and trunks became the staple wares, and encumbered all the sidewalks; the railway dépôts were crowded with baggage, the trains thronged with refugees. The panic increased as successive tidings came that Yorktown had been evacuated, Williamsburg abandoned, Norfolk surrendered, the Merrimac destroyed, and the Federal gun-boats were ascending the James River. The only obstruction to their ascent was the incomplete fort at Drewry's Bluff, and the unfinished barrier just above it. The Secretary of the Navy advertised for timber to construct new defenses; schooners loaded with plaster and guano were seized and sunk in the river; sharpshooters were called upon to organize into companies to line the banks. One enthusiastic individual

offered to be one of a hundred to board the whole fleet of gun-boats and take them at all hazards. The state Legislature resolved that the city should be defended to the last extremity, "if such defense is in accordance with the views of the President," and appointed a committee to wait upon him to learn his intentions. He said that it would be the effort of his life to defend Virginia and to cover the capital; he had never thought of abandoning the state; if Richmond should fall, which he did not anticipate, that would be no reason for withdrawing the army from Virginia; the war could be carried on in the state for twenty years. Notwithstanding his confident words, he was worn and haggard. His family feared for his life. He lost no time in putting his house in order. He was baptized at home one Tuesday morning, and was confirmed in church an hour later. His family should go to Raleigh; they only feared that they had delayed too long already. The 16th was appointed as a fast-day. On the day when the proclamation was issued, tidings had just come of the capture of New Orleans. The evacuation of Yorktown and the abandonment of Norfolk had been determined upon. Well might the proclamation declare that "recent disaster has spread gloom over the land, and sorrow sits at the hearth-stones of our countrymen." In the interim Norfolk had been seized, and the Virginia, "the iron diadem of the South, worth an army of 50,000 men," destroyed. On the day before the fast, Letcher, the governor, summoned all who were willing to unite in defending the capital of the state to assemble at the City Hall. He was there, in the vinous condition which was his wont, and made a speech. "I have been told," he said, "that the duty of surrendering the city would devolve upon the President, the mayor, or myself. I answered, if the demand is made upon me, with the alternative to surrender or be shelled, I shall reply, Bombard and be damned!" Mayo, the mayor, followed in the same vein. "When the citizens of Richmond," he said, "demand of me to surrender the capital of Virginia and of the Confederacy to the enemy, they must find some other man to fill my place. I will resign the mayoralty; and when that other man elected in my stead shall deliver up the city, I hope I have physical courage and strength enough left to shoulder a musket and go into the ranks."[1] The governor ordered all the stores and other places of business, except such manufacturing establishments as were engaged in fulfilling contracts for the government, to be closed at two o'clock in the afternoon, so that all persons should have time for drill and discipline, and directed the militia to assemble at three, every day excepting Sunday, to be drilled for the four hours until sunset. The city was thronged with refugees from the border states, the dregs of the Baltimore mob predominating. A few of these, with nothing to lose, held a public meeting and passed resolutions devoting Richmond to flames as soon as the Union troops should enter it. A portion of the city press clamored for this. "To lose Richmond," said the Dispatch, "is to lose Virginia, and to lose Virginia is to lose the key to the Southern Confederacy. Virginians, Marylanders! ye who have rallied to her defense, would it not be better to fall in her streets than to basely abandon them? The loss of Richmond in Europe would sound like the loss of Paris or London, and the moral effect will hardly be less. It is better that Richmond should fall as the capital of the Confederacy than that Richmond exist the dépôt of the hireling horde of the North. The next few days may decide the fate of Richmond. It is either to remain the capital of the Confederacy, or be turned over to the Federal government as a Yankee conquest. The capital is to be either secured or lost—it may be feared not temporarily—and with it Virginia. Life, death, and wounds are nothing if we only can be saved from the fate of a captured capital and a humiliated Confederacy. Let the government act—let the people act. There is time yet. If fate comes to its worst, let the ruins of Richmond be its most lasting monument."

McClellan's advance toward the panic-stricken city was slow. The distance from Williamsburg was a little more than forty miles. On the 8th the troops collected there began to move. In two days nineteen miles had been gained. On the 13th the army was concentrated near West Point. On the 14th and 15th rain fell. On the 15th and 16th two divisions set out for the White House, five miles farther. So bad were the roads, that the train of one division occupied thirty-six hours in passing this distance. About this time two provisional army corps were organized—the Fifth, consisting of the divisions of Porter and Sykes, and the reserved artillery, was placed under Fitz John Porter; the Sixth, consisting of Franklin's division and that of Smith, which was detached from Keyes's corps, was placed under Franklin. On the 16th head-quarters were at the White House; on the 19th five miles beyond. On the 20th more rain fell, but the advanced light troops reached the banks of the Chickahominy. On the 21st the main body of the army was near that stream, which was henceforth to be historic.[2]

---

[1] Tattnall's Trial, p. 89.   [2] POLLARD, i., 324; ii., 30, says that it mounted only four guns.
[3] Goldsborough's testimony, Com. Rep., 633.
[4] McC. Rep., 191–195; Com. Rep., 324–329. "Had McDowell joined me by water," says McClellan, "I could have approached Richmond from the James, and thus avoided the delays and losses incurred in bridging the Chickahominy, and would have had the army massed in one body instead of being necessarily divided by that stream."—Report, 195.

[1] For the panic in Richmond, see POLLARD, i., 322–325; ii., 28–34, 309–311. Reb. Rec., iv., 136, 424–426. An intercepted letter, written on the 7th of May by a niece of Jefferson Davis, resident in his family, furnishes some striking details. She writes: "I am ready to sink with despair. There is a probability of General Jackson's army falling back on Richmond; and, in view of this, no lady is allowed to go up on the railroad to Gordonsville, for fear, if allowed to one, that many others would wish to do it, which would incommode the army. General Johnston is falling back from the Peninsula or Yorktown, and Uncle Jeff. thinks we had better go to a safer place than Richmond. If Johnston falls back as far as Richmond, all our troops from Gordonsville and Swift Run Gap will also fall back to this place and make one desperate stand against McClellan. The Yankees are approaching Richmond from three different directions—from Fredericksburg, Harrisonburg, and Yorktown. Uncle Jeff. is miserable. He tries to be cheerful and bear up against such a continuation of troubles, but I fear he can not live long. Our reverses distressed him so much, and he is so weak and feeble, it makes my heart ache to look at him. What a blow the fall of New Orleans was! It liked to have set us all crazy here. Every body looks distressed, and the cause of the Confederacy looks drooping and sinking. We all leave here to-morrow morning for Raleigh. Three gun-boats are in the river on their way to the city, and may probably reach here in a few hours, so we have no longer any time to delay. I only hope we have not delayed too long already. I am afraid that Richmond will fall into the hands of the enemy, as there is no way to keep back the gun-boats. James River is so high that all obstructions are in danger of being washed away; so there is no help for the city. She will either submit, or else be shelled. Uncle Jeff. was confirmed last Tuesday, in St. Paul's Church, by Bishop Johns. He was baptized in the morning, before church."—POLLARD, ii., 31.   [2] McC. Rep., 187, 188.

THE MARCH FROM WILLIAMSBURG.

COLD HARBOR.—McCLELLAN'S HEAD-QUARTERS.

CHAPTER XIX.

THE PENINSULAR CAMPAIGN.

II. ON THE SHENANDOAH AND THE CHICKAHOMINY.[1]

The Chickahominy.—McClellan's Advance.—Correspondence between McClellan and the President.—McDowell ordered to move.—The Order suspended.—Jackson's Operations in the Valley of the Shenandoah.—Retreats from Winchester.—Joined by Ewell.—Battle of Kernstown.—The Order to McDowell.—Battle of Bull Pasture.—Position of the Union Forces.—Battle of Front Royal.—Retreat of Banks to the Potomac.—Crosses the River.—Panic at Washington.—Fremont's Movements.—Battle of Lewisburg.—McDowell ordered to follow Jackson.—He sends Shields reluctantly.—Jackson in Peril.—He Retreats up the Shenandoah.—Eludes Fremont and Shields.—The Pursuit by Fremont.—Battle of Cross Keys.—Battle of Port Republic.—End of the Pursuit.—Results of Jackson's Expedition.—The Union Army on the Chickahominy.—Battle of Hanover Court-house.—Elation of McClellan.—Condition of Johnston.—The Union Left across the Chickahominy.—*Battle of the Seven Pines:* Johnston's Plan.—His Statement of his Force.—The Storm at Richmond.—Casey driven back.—Conduct of his Division.—Keyes and Kearney forced beyond the Seven Pines.—New Line formed.—Close of the Action.—*Battle of Fair Oaks:* Sumner crosses the Chickahominy.—The first Action, May 31.—The second Action, June 1.—Repulses of the Confederates.—Hooker's Reconnoissance.—The Losses.—Results of the Battles of Seven Pines and Fair Oaks.—What might have been accomplished.—McClellan and McDowell.—Bridges and Intrenchments.—Lee takes Command.—His Antecedents and Character.—Resigns his Commission.—Enters the Southern Army.—Fortifies Richmond.—His Plan on assuming Command.—Stuart's Expedition.—McClellan ready.—Affair of King's School-house.—McClellan's Dispatches.—The Evening before the Seven Days.

THE Chickahominy, rising in swampy uplands northwest of Richmond, flows southeastwardly for about fifty miles, parallel with and midway between the James and the York rivers. It then turns sharply to the south, and, after a winding course of twenty miles, falls into the James forty miles below Richmond and ten west of Williamsburg. Toward its mouth it becomes a considerable stream, navigable by small steamers for twenty or thirty miles. The military operations of the Peninsular campaign embraced that part of the stream between Bottom's Bridge on the south, where it is crossed by the Williamsburg road, and Meadow Bridge, fifteen miles to the north, where it is crossed by the Fredericksburg Railroad. Richmond lies nearly opposite the centre of this line, about six miles from the Chickahominy at its nearest approach.

Between these points the river flows through a belt of wooded swamp three or four hundred yards wide. The swamp is bordered on both sides by low bottom lands sloping gently up to the level of the surrounding country. The entire breadth of the intervale is about a mile, in some places a little more, in others a little less. The tops of the trees rise to the level of the uplands, screening the view from one side to the other. In dry summer weather the stream is a mere rivulet, flowing sluggishly through the swamp, sometimes in a single channel, oftener in several. A moderate shower fills the channel, which is about a dozen yards wide and four feet deep. A heavy shower or a continuous rain-fall, causing a rise of two feet more, floods the swamp and overflows the bottom lands. These bottoms are intersected by deep ditches, and even when not overflowed are so soft as to be impassable for cavalry and artillery.

The swamp and stream had been crossed by several bridges. All of those in front of Richmond had been destroyed by Johnston when he fell back from Yorktown and Williamsburg, and the approaches to them were com-
manded by batteries on the southern side. Besides the bridges were a few fords, approached by side-roads, over which a pedestrian could in dry weather make his way over swamp and stream. But this season had been unusually rainy. The channel was always full to the brim, and every shower flooded swamp and bottoms. Infantry might possibly have picked their way across in loose order, but cavalry would have sunk to the horses' girths, and artillery and trains beyond their axles, in the spongy soil. For an army the Chickahominy was impassable except by bridges, and these, as experience soon proved, must be built above the level of the highest floods, and provided with long approaches across the swamp. The best places for the bridges were covered by the batteries of the enemy, and other points had to be chosen. Bridges of boats and pontoons were out of the question. The soil was too soft and spongy to afford a foundation for piles. It only remained to build the bridges upon trestles, the approaches being embanked or corduroyed. As a military obstacle, the narrow Chickahominy, with its bordering swamps and bottoms, liable to overflow at any moment, was more formidable than a broad river which could be crossed by boats, or over which a pontoon bridge could be thrown in a few hours.[1]

In moving from Williamsburg the right wing of the Federal army had kept to the north, striking the Chickahominy at New Bridge, directly in front of Richmond; the left wing, keeping to the south, had reached the river at Bottom's Bridge, thirteen miles below. On the 22d of May, Stoneman's advance guard of cavalry and Franklin's corps, on the right, were near New Bridge, with Porter at supporting distance in the rear; Keyes, on the left, was at Bottom's Bridge, with Heintzelman as a support; between Keyes and Porter was Sumner, connecting the right with the left. The head-quarters were established at Cold Harbor, just in the rear of the head of the right wing. The bulk of the enemy were across the Chickahominy, on the main road from New Bridge to Richmond; but a detachment had been left at Mechanicsville, on the north bank, four miles above.[2] This was brushed away on the 24th by the artillery, which forced it across the bridge, which was then destroyed.

The approaches to Richmond from below were only slightly held. Bottom's Bridge had been demolished, but close by was a practicable ford, which had been seized on the 20th, when a division crossed the river and occupied the opposite high ground. Naglee made a long reconnoissance in force down the right side of the Chickahominy, taking almost the same route by which, five weeks later, the Union army retreated to the James. He followed this by another reconnoissance directly toward Richmond, going beyond the Seven Pines, only six miles from the city. In neither reconnoissance was any serious resistance encountered, or the enemy found in force. Keyes's corps was then sent across the Chickahominy at Bottom's Bridge, with orders to take up a position near the Seven Pines. Heintzelman's corps was also sent across; and he, being the senior officer, was placed in command of all the forces then on the south side of the stream.[3] Johnston, in his retreat, had strangely neglected to obstruct the York River Railroad, running directly from Richmond to the White House on the Pamunkey. The bridge by which the railroad crossed the Chickahominy was indeed destroyed, but so little other damage was done that by the 26th the road was in operation up to the river, and the bridge nearly reconstructed.

---

[1] Since the date of note [1], p. 328, we have secured the Confederate "Reports of the Operations of the Army of Northern Virginia, from June, 1862, to and including the Battle of Fredericksburg, Dec. 13, 1862." They include the reports of Jackson and his subordinate officers of the operations in the Valley of the Shenandoah, and Lee's report of his operations from the Seven Days' Battles to the Battle of Fredericksburg. There are also about 350 reports of subordinate officers, the whole forming two large volumes. These will be cited as "*Lee's Rep.*;" the references being throughout to the pages of the edition printed by order of the Confederate Congress at Richmond in 1864.

[1] For the character of the Chickahominy as a military obstacle, see especially *Art. Op.*, 19, 20; *McC. Rep.*, 189; also both works *passim*.

[2] Strictly speaking, the banks of the Chickahominy are the northwest and the southeast. In reports and documents they are variously denoted as the *south* or *west*, and the *north* or *east*. The side toward Richmond, being the right looking down the stream, will be called by us the *right* or *south*; the opposite one, the *left* or *north*.   [3] *McC. Rep.*, 186–188; 213, 214.

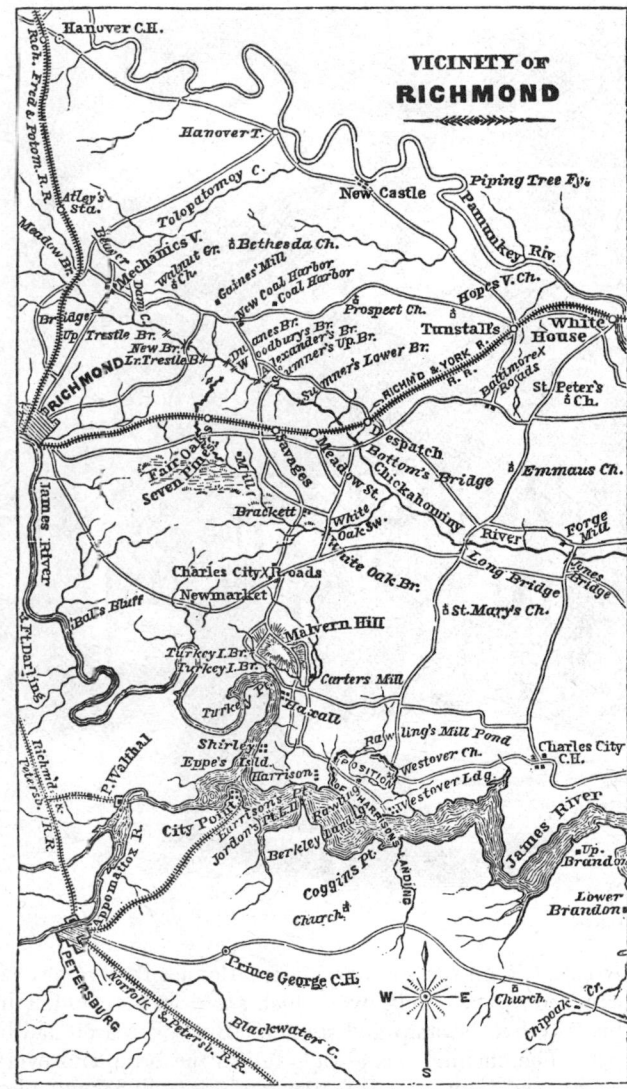

McClellan still continued to urge that his force should be re-enforced; especially that McDowell's whole corps should be sent to him at once by water. "My pickets," he writes,[1] "are within a mile of Bottom's Bridge, and scouts are within a quarter of a mile. I am advancing on the other roads. The indications are that the enemy intend fighting at Richmond. Our policy seems to be to concentrate every thing there. They hold central positions, and will seek to meet us while divided. I think we are committing a great military error in having so many independent columns. The great battle should be fought in mass; then divide if necessary." Sound advice: if he had himself acted upon it two weeks later at Fair Oaks, or six weeks later at Cold Harbor, his campaign would have had a different termination.

Three days later[2] he transmitted what the President calls his "long dispatch." It had been raining, and "rain on this soil soon makes the roads incredibly bad for army transportation;" yet this was the very region where he had insisted, not four months before, that "the roads are passable at all seasons of the year."[3] He had been a mile across the Chickahominy, the enemy being about half a mile in front. All the bridges were destroyed, and "the enemy were in force on every road leading to Richmond, within a mile or two west of the stream." Yet on the previous day they were not in great force opposite Bottom's Bridge,[4] upon the Williamsburg road; and on the same day Naglee had made his reconnoissance down the right bank for a dozen miles, crossing other roads, without serious resistance, or finding "the enemy in force;" and on the third, fourth, and fifth days after, "a very gallant reconnoissance was pushed by Naglee with his brigade beyond the Seven Pines," seven or eight miles beyond the river, meeting "considerable opposition," but none which his single brigade could not overcome.[5] Thus one of the main approaches to Richmond by way of the Williamsburg road and the York River Railroad for eight miles beyond the stream and within six of the city, was not, for a full week, "held by the enemy in force." All accounts, McClellan continued, represented the numbers of the enemy as greatly exceeding his own, and every thing gave positive assurance that the approach to Richmond involved a desperate battle between the opposing forces. All his divisions were moving toward the foe, and he should advance steadily and carefully, attacking in such a manner as to employ his greatest force. He regretted the state of things in McDowell's command; he had no means of knowing when he would start, what were his means of transportation, or when he would be in the vicinity of the Chickahominy; but there was little hope that he would come by land in time for the coming battle. He was, moreover, not sure that he comprehended the orders which had been given to McDowell; he wished that the extent of his own authority should be clearly defined, and hoped that McDowell would be placed under his orders, he himself being strictly responsible for the closest observance of the President's instructions; and, above all things, let McDowell be sent at once by water. "But, in any event," he concluded, "I shall fight with all the skill, caution, and determination that I possess, and I trust that the result may either obtain for me the permanent confidence of my government, or that it may close my career."

To this the President replied on the same day, "You will have just such

control of McDowell and of his forces as you indicate;" adding that McDowell could go by land quicker than by water; by land "he can reach you in five days after starting, whereas by water he will not reach you in two weeks, judging by past experience."[1]

On the morning of the 24th McClellan received a dispatch from the President announcing that McDowell would soon be with him. The President had left McDowell's camp the evening before. Shields's command was there, but so worn that he could not move till Monday, the 26th; but both he and McDowell said that they would positively move on the morning of that day. Meanwhile Anderson, the Confederate general who was opposing McDowell's advance, had as his line of supply and retreat the road to Richmond. Could not McClellan, almost as well as not, while he was building the Chickahominy bridges, send a force from his right to cut off the enemy's supplies from Richmond, preserve the railroad bridges across the two forks of the Pamunkey, and intercept the enemy's retreat? If he could do that, he would prevent the army now opposed to him from receiving an accession of nearly fifteen thousand men, and if he saved the bridges he would secure a line of railroad for supplies besides the one he then had. The President closed by reiterating, "You will have command of General McDowell after he joins you precisely as you indicated in your last dispatch to me of the 21st." There was in this dispatch one sentence ominous of evil: "We have so thinned our line to get troops for other places that it was broken yesterday at Front Royal, with a probable loss to us of a regiment of infantry and two companies of cavalry, and putting Banks in some peril."[2]

McClellan was greatly elated by this dispatch. McDowell's forty thousand would soon be added to his command, giving him a force "sufficiently strong to overpower the large army confronting him." His elation was brief. On the afternoon of the same day he received another dispatch from the President announcing that the order for McDowell to march toward Richmond had been suspended.[3]

The reason for this sudden change of order is to be found in the bold and skillful operations of "Stonewall Jackson," one hundred and fifty miles from McClellan, and half as far from McDowell. In the previous autumn Jackson had been assigned to the command of the Confederate forces in the Valley of the Shenandoah. During the winter and early spring his force was about ten thousand men, but his numbers were apparently doubled by the celerity of his movements. "The rapidity of his marches," says a Confederate writer, "is something portentous. He is heard of by the enemy at one point, and before they can make up their minds to follow him he is off at another. He keeps so constantly in motion that he never has a sick-list, and no need of hospitals. He will assuredly make his mark in this war, for his untiring industry and eternal watchfulness must tell upon a numerous enemy, unacquainted with the country, and incommoded by large baggage trains."[4] His operations were annoying rather than important, except as they compelled the Federal government to keep a considerable force to watch him; but by hard service his command was brought into a state of great efficiency.

Simultaneously with Johnston's abandonment of Manassas in March, Jackson fell back up the valley from Winchester toward Staunton, followed by Shields, with a division of Banks's Fifth Corps. This retreat, which was kept up as far as Newmarket, brought Jackson within fifty miles of Johnston, who lay near Gordonsville, awaiting the development of McClellan's plans. Shields undertook to decoy Jackson from joining Johnston. He made a feigned retreat back to Winchester, marching his whole force thirty miles in one day. The ruse was successful. Jackson turned to pursue. Banks, who thought it impossible that Jackson would venture to attack him, marched his whole corps, with the exception of Shields's division, toward Centreville. Shields, who still hoped that Jackson would venture an attack, secretly posted the bulk of his division in a secluded position two miles from Winchester. The people of that town, ignorant of this, reported to Jackson that the place was evacuated except by a small rear-guard. On the evening of March 22, Jackson's cavalry made a dash into Winchester, driving in Shields's pickets. The attack was repulsed after a sharp skirmish, in which Shields was severely wounded, his arm being broken by the fragment of a shell. Banks, confident that Jackson would not renew the engagement, set off next morning for Washington; but Shields, anticipating a strong attack, notwithstanding his wound, prepared to receive it. The assault began at noon with a sharp artillery fire, which met with a strong reply. At three o'clock Tyler's brigade charged upon the Confederate batteries on the left, and captured them. Then followed a general and successful assault upon the Confederate right and centre. The Confederates retreated, leaving their dead and wounded behind. Banks returned next morning, and pursued the retreating enemy thirty miles to Woodstock, ceasing the pursuit only when his men were thoroughly exhausted. The Federal loss in this engagement was 103 killed and 441 wounded. Of the Confederates, 270 were reported to have been buried on the battle-field, and many others by the inhabitants. Their entire loss was estimated at 500 killed and 1000 wounded.[5]

[1] May 18; Com. Rep., 327.   [2] May 21; McC. Rep., 196–198.   [3] Ibid., 104.
[4] Ibid., 190.   [5] Ibid., 213; Naglee's Report, Reb. Rec., v., 81.

[1] Com. Rep., 329.   [2] McC. Rep., 199.
[3] "In consequence of General Banks's critical position, I have been compelled to suspend General McDowell's movements to join you. The enemy are making a desperate push upon Harper's Ferry, and we are trying to throw General Fremont's force and a part of General McDowell's in their rear."—McC. Rep., 200.   [4] Southern Generals, 172.
[5] The Federals usually style this action, fought March 23, the Battle of Winchester. The Confederates more properly call it the Battle of Kernstown, from the hamlet near which it was fought. Shields states his own force to have been 6000 infantry, 750 cavalry, and 24 pieces of artillery. He estimates the force of the enemy at 9000 infantry, 1500 cavalry, and 36 guns.—(Reb. Rec., iv., 328–343.) Pollard says that the Confederate forces amounted to 6000 men, besides Ashby's cavalry, while Shields was 18,000 strong. "The enemy," he says, "was left in possession of the field of battle, two guns, four caissons, and about 300 prisoners. Our loss was about 100 killed,

JAMES SHIELDS.

This repulse was a severe check to Jackson. He fell back, faintly pursued by Banks, to Harrisonburg, where he remained for three weeks; and then, on the 19th of April, crossed the south fork of the Shenandoah, thus placing himself within supporting distance of Johnston, who, "shutting out his army from all intercourse with the public," held his position behind the Rappahannock and Rapidan, the main body being near Gordonsville. Toward the close of April, when the plans of McClellan had become developed, Johnston took the bulk of his forces to the Peninsula, but detached Ewell's division of about ten thousand to the support of Jackson. The junction took place on the last day of April.[1]

In the mean while great changes had been made, and were proposed to be made, in the disposition of the Federal forces in this region. A new Department, called that of the Rappahannock, including the District of Columbia, had been created, the command being assigned to McDowell. Shields's division was withdrawn from Banks and attached to McDowell, who, thus strengthened, was ordered on the 17th of May to join McClellan before Richmond, but still to keep himself in a position to cover Washington.[2] Banks, who had followed Jackson as far as Harrisonburg, was at the same time ordered to fall back fifty miles to Strasburg, and there fortify himself. Forces from Fremont's Mountain Department were approaching Jackson's

position from the direction of Romney. The advance, under Milroy, came along the western side of the Shenandoah Mountains as far as McDowell, a village forty miles southwest of Harrisonburg, which was still occupied by Banks. Here Milroy was attacked, on the 8th of May, by Jackson, and, although re-enforced by Schenck, who had come up just in time with a small re-enforcement, was compelled to retreat after a sharp engagement. In this action, sometimes called that of Bull Pasture, the Confederates sustained the heavier loss, but, having a strong supporting force at hand, though not actually engaged, they gained their point of driving Milroy from the field and capturing a considerable amount of stores.[1] Fremont, with his main body, had been coming down from the same direction. His advance having been thus driven back, he halted at Franklin for fully ten days.

The Federal forces in this region were now so widely scattered as to invite an attack upon some of their severed portions. Banks, stripped of Shields's division, was at Strasburg with barely 6000 men. Fremont was at Franklin, seventy miles away to the southwest, with the Shenandoah Mountains between him and Banks. McDowell was near Fredericksburg, as far to the southeast, just ready to march toward Richmond. A single regiment, and a few companies, 1400 men in all, were at Front Royal under Colonel Kenly; these, with a few at Rectortown, formed the only connection between Banks and McDowell. Jackson, who had concentrated his command at Harrisonburg, was practically nearer each of these bodies than any one of them was to any other. Banks was the nearer and weaker enemy, and Jackson resolved to strike at him. Concentrating his whole command at Newmarket, he marched down the South Fork of the Shenandoah, placing the three ranges of the Masanutten, the North, and the Shenandoah Mountains between himself and Fremont, and struck Kenly at Front Royal at noon on the 23d. The Union force was posted here merely as a protection against guerrilla raids, and was wholly too weak to resist an attack in force. It was swept away after a brave but brief resistance, four fifths being killed or captured.

The Confederates then pushed toward Winchester, hoping to gain the rear of Banks, who was still at Strasburg, and cut off his retreat down the Valley. Banks's position was perilous. To remain at Strasburg was to be surrounded, and either starved out or beaten. An attempt to retreat westward over the mountains would involve the abandonment of his trains at the outset, with the certainty of being attacked on his flanks by a superior force. All that remained for him was to retreat down the Valley, "entering the lists with the enemy in a race or a battle, as he should choose, for the possession of Winchester, the key of the Valley." The distance for each was about equal. At nine o'clock on the morning of the 24th the retreating column was on its march, the train in front. The rear had hardly gone three miles when reports came from the front that the enemy held the roads. The train was sent to the rear, and the troops moved to the front. After a short encounter, the head of the Confederate column was beaten back, and Banks succeeded in reaching Winchester. Before daybreak next morning he was assailed by Jackson with superior and constantly increasing force. After a desultory conflict of five hours, Banks began a hurried retreat toward Martinsburg. Here he halted a couple of hours, and then pushed on for the Potomac, which he reached at Williamsport by sunset. The river was still between him and the pursuing enemy. The ferry was barely sufficient to transport the ammunition train; the ford was occupied by the wagons; the cavalry could wade and swim the stream; but there was no apparent means

---

[1] Our casualties amounted to 28 killed, 80 severely wounded, 145 slightly wounded, and 3 missing, making a total of 256.—*Schenck's Report.* "The Confederate loss in this action was considerable. Of 350 killed and wounded, nearly two thirds were Georgians. We engaged the enemy with not more than one third of his own numbers, which were about 12,000."—POLLARD, ii., 35. But the official reports of Milroy and Schenck give their entire force at 2268, while they believed that the Confederates "brought into action not less than 5000, besides their reserved force of 8000 in the rear."

---

and probably twice as many wounded; that of the enemy was certainly more than double. The greater portion of our dead left on the field of battle were buried under the direction of the mayor of Winchester. Some fifty citizens collected the dead, dug a great pit on the battle-field, and gently laid the poor fellows in their last resting-place. Scarcely a family in the country but had a relative there."—*Southern History of the War,* i., 281–284.

Shields, in a published letter, congratulated himself that "Jackson and his stone-wall brigade, and all the other brigades accompanying him, will never meet this division again in battle." Yet he adds, somewhat inconsistently, "The enemy's sufferings have been terrible, and such as they have nowhere else endured during the war; and yet such were their gallantry and high state of discipline that at no time during the battle or pursuit did they give way to panic. They fled to Mount Jackson, and are by this time, no doubt, in communication with the main body of the rebel army." In his official report he says: "Jackson, with his supposed invincible stone-wall brigade, were compelled to fall back in disorder upon their reserve. Here they took up a new position for a final stand. A few minutes only did they stand, when they turned dismayed and fled in disorder."—*Reb. Rec.,* iv., 329–335.

[1] *Southern Generals,* 175, 263, 347.

[2] "Upon being joined by General Shields's division, you will move upon Richmond by the general route of the Richmond and Fredericksburg Railroad, co-operating with the forces under General McClellan, now threatening Richmond from the line of the Pamunkey and York Rivers. While seeking to establish, as soon as possible, a communication between your left wing and the right wing of General McClellan, you will hold yourself always in such a position as to cover the capital of the nation against a sudden dash of any large body of the rebel forces. General McClellan will be furnished with a copy of these instructions, and will be directed to hold himself in readiness to establish communication with your left wing, and to prevent the main body of the enemy's army from leaving Richmond and throwing itself upon your column before the junction of the two armies is effected."—*McC. Rep.,* 195.

FRONT ROYAL.

SCENE OF THE BATTLE NEAR FRONT ROYAL.

to get the infantry across. Fortunately, however, a pontoon train had been brought along all the way from Strasburg, and by its aid the infantry were all got across before noon of the next day. "Never," says Banks, "were more grateful hearts in the same number of men than when, at midday on the 26th, we stood on the opposite shore." In this retreat of fifty-three miles Banks lost six or eight hundred men, of whom the greater part were captured. Of his train of 500 wagons he lost 55, besides considerable stores destroyed at Strasburg and Winchester. Banks, some days after, estimated his entire loss at about 900, of whom 38 were known to be killed and 155 wounded, the rest missing.[1]

Jackson reached the river just in time to see his enemy safe on the Maryland side. He rested there for a single day, and had divine service performed in camp. He issued an address to his army congratulating them upon their success in driving the Federal army from the Valley of the Shenandoah, and capturing several thousand prisoners, and an immense quantity of stores and provisions.

This movement of Jackson caused a panic in Washington almost as great as that which the approach of McClellan had occasioned at Richmond. Rumor trebled his force. Geary, who was posted at Manassas Gap, reported that, besides those in pursuit of Banks, there were 10,000 at Front Royal, and as many more at Orleans, all pressing forward in the same direction. Washington was thought to be menaced. "I think," telegraphed the President to McClellan on the 25th, "that the time is near at hand when you must either attack Richmond or give up the job, and come back to the defense of Washington." The Secretary of War telegraphed to the governors of several states that "intelligence from various quarters left no doubt that the enemy in great force were marching toward Washington," and directed them to send all their militia and volunteers for the defense of the capital. Military possession was ordered to be taken of all railroads, and they were directed to hold themselves in readiness to transport troops and munitions to the exclusion of all other business.

Fremont was ordered to move southeastward from Franklin to Harrisonburg, thus throwing himself upon Jackson's rear. On the very day before this order was sent, and at the very hour when Kenly was annihilated at Front Royal, a brigade of Fremont's command, under Colonel Crook, had gained a decided advantage over a superior force of the enemy, under Heth, at Lewisburg, fifty miles to the southwest, across the Alleghany Mountains. Fremont issued a glowing order to his troops, announcing that "the results of this victory would be important," and that "the forces now under his immediate command lacked but the opportunity to emulate the gallantry and share the glory of their comrades of the Army of the Kanawha."[2] The opportunity was not wanting, for at that moment the order was on its way directing him to march against Jackson. Instead of going southeastward to Harrisonburg as ordered, he went northeastward toward Strasburg, making a much longer march, but, as he averred, by a more practicable route, to throw himself upon Jackson's rear.

McDowell was at the same time ordered to lay aside for the present the movement upon Richmond, and to put 20,000 men in motion at once for the Shenandoah, to operate either in conjunction with Fremont or alone against Jackson, and for the relief of Banks. He obeyed the order with a heavy heart. He wrote to the President, "Co-operation between General Fremont and myself to cut off Jackson is not to be counted upon, even if it is not a practical impossibility. I am beyond helping distance of General Banks, and no celerity or vigor will avail as far as he is concerned. The line of the retreat of

the enemy's forces up the Valley is shorter than mine to go against him. It will take a week or ten days for the force to get to the Valley by the route which will give it food and forage, and by that time the enemy will have retired. I shall gain nothing for you there, and shall lose much for you here. It is, therefore, not only on personal grounds that I have a heavy heart in the matter, but I feel that it throws us all back; and from Richmond north we shall have all our large masses paralyzed, and shall have to repeat what we have just accomplished." The President replied, in his simple, earnest way: "I am highly gratified at your alacrity in obeying my order. The change was as painful to me as it can possibly be to you or to any one. Every thing now depends upon the celerity and vigor of your movement."[1] McDowell seems not to have dreamed that Jackson would follow Banks up to the Potomac, placing himself, going and returning, almost twice as far from Strasburg as either Fremont or McDowell would have to go to reach that vital point. This remonstrance was dated on the 24th of May. Nine days after, Jackson, on his retreat, passed through Strasburg, just before the junction of Fremont and Shields, whose division of McDowell's corps was sent to the Valley, was to have been effected. Had either or both of these commands marched with only half the celerity of Jackson in his advance and retreat, the Confederate force would have been shut up in the lower portion of the Valley, with scarcely a possibility of escape.

Jackson perceived the full peril of his situation. Giving his wearied force but a single day's rest, he began his retreat on the 29th, masking the

---

[1] Com. Rep., 274, 275.

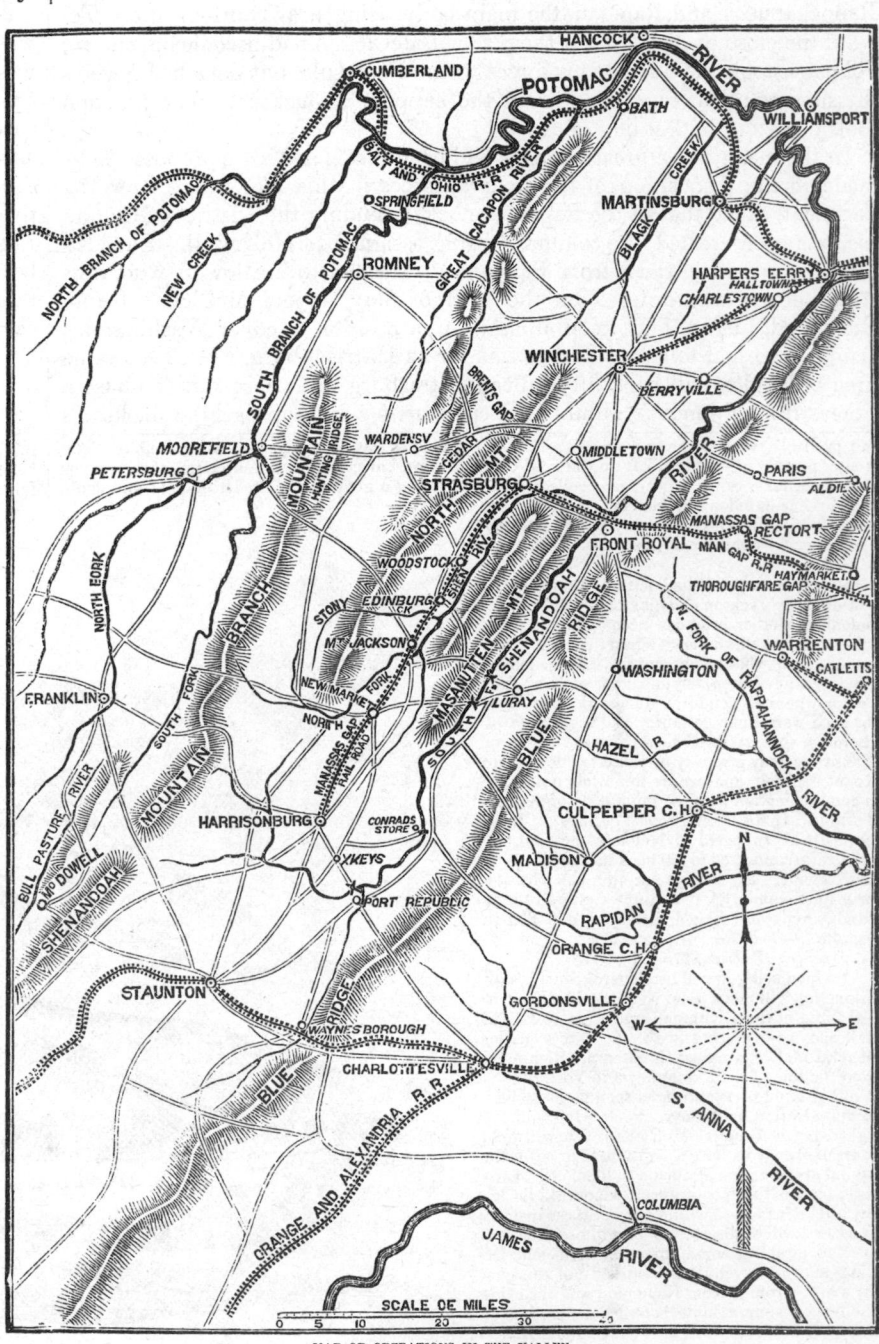

MAP OF OPERATIONS IN THE VALLEY.

---

[1] Banks's Report, etc., Reb. Rec., 52-67; 139-141.   [2] Reb Rec., 141.

movement by a feigned attack upon Harper's Ferry by Ewell's division. On the 30th his whole reunited force was at Winchester, but made no delay there, pushing straight on for Strasburg. On that same day, Fremont, after a hard march up the west side of the Shenandoah Mountains, had crossed this and its outlying range, Hunting Ridge, and was at Wardensville. Next day the advance was pushed forward to the road between Winchester and Strasburg. Jackson had passed that point only a few hours before on the way to Strasburg. Fremont followed, and on the morning of the 1st of June his advance came upon Jackson's rear. A skirmish ensued; but Fremont's advance was checked, and Jackson got clear to Strasburg. Here he was told that Shields had been for forty-eight hours in possession of Front Royal, but had not joined Fremont. He at once inferred that he was marching down the South Fork of the Shenandoah by way of Luray, meaning to cross and get first to Newmarket. Sending a detachment to burn the bridges over the South Fork, Jackson kept rapidly on up the turnpike, harassed by Fremont's pursuing force. So close were they upon him that his only means of escape seemed to be to put the North Fork of the Shenandoah between him and his pursuers. He crossed the stream at Mount Jackson on the 3d, destroying the bridge behind him. This was hardly accomplished when the Federal forces appeared on the opposite bank. It took a whole day to reconstruct the bridge. Jackson had thus secured so much the start, and on the 5th reached Harrisonburg, the point from which he had commenced his adventurous march a fortnight before. Here he made no delay, for Fremont was again close on his rear. He turned to the east toward Port Republic on the North Fork, hoping to cross that before Shields, who was marching more slowly down its east side, could come up. Ashby's cavalry, with some infantry, was left as a rear-guard at Harrisonburg. Colonel Wyndham, of the Union cavalry, making a reconnoissance on the 7th, fell into an ambuscade, and, with a considerable portion of his men, was captured; an infantry skirmish ensued, in which each side suffered some loss. In this skirmish Ashby was killed.

Thus far, owing to the happy accident which enabled him to slip between Fremont and Shields at Strasburg, and to the start gained by the destruction of the bridge at Mount Jackson, the Confederate army had retreated without serious loss. But the two commands of the Federals, each fully equal to his own, were marching in parallel lines about fifteen miles apart, but with the deep South Fork of the Shenandoah, over which all the bridges

THOMAS JONATHAN JACKSON.

below Port Republic had been destroyed, between them. If Shields reached this place first in force, Jackson would be hemmed in. There was now no alternative but to prevent this junction by checking Fremont, and then either out-fighting or out-marching Shields. Ewell, whose division had performed the main part of the fighting in this expedition, was posted at the Cross Keys, midway between Harrisonburg and Port Republic, while Jackson himself kept on four miles farther, to the neighborhood of the latter place.

Ewell's position was strong. In front was a valley and rivulet, with woods on either flank. He was attacked by Fremont on the 8th. The action lasted from eleven in the morning till four in the afternoon, skirmishing and artillery fire being kept up until dark. Ewell held his position during the night, but before dawn was ordered to join Jackson, who was seriously threatened at Port Republic by Shields. In this action Ewell had five brigades of 8000 men, but only 6000 were brought into close action. Fremont's whole force was about 18,000, less than half of whom were brought upon the field. Both Fremont and Ewell assert that they occupied the field of battle, and thus each claims the technical honors of victory. The real advantage was certainly with Ewell. He had checked Fremont's advance, and left Jackson's whole force for another day free to act against Shields.[1]

Port Republic is a forlorn village, situated in the angle formed by North and South Rivers, affluents of the South Fork of the Shenandoah. The South River is a shallow stream easily fordable, the North River crossed by a wooden bridge connecting the town with the Harrisonburg road. Shields's advance had reached this place on the morning of the 8th. A body of cavalry dashed across the South River into the town, and planted a gun opposite the entrance to the bridge. A Confederate brigade crossed, drove them back, and captured the gun, the cavalry falling back three miles to their infantry support. Night closed this skirmish, which was going on simultaneously with the battle at Cross Keys, seven miles distant. By dawn Ewell had joined Jackson, who resolved to throw his whole force across the river and attack Shields, burning the bridge in his rear, so as to prevent Fremont from joining Shields. His whole force was now upon the east side of the South Fork, which ran between him and Fremont. Tyler, who led the advance of Shields, had barely 3000 men. Posting these in a commanding position, covered by a battery of six guns, he awaited the attack. Several assaults of the enemy were repelled with heavy loss; but a Confederate brigade, marching through a dense forest, charged upon Tyler's left flank, and by a combined assault on front and flank forced him from his position, with the loss of all his guns except one; these were abandoned because the artillery horses had been killed. The retreat was orderly, the enemy pursuing for a number of miles.

Just at the close of the action the force of Fremont appeared on the opposite side of the river, but no attempt was made to cross. Jackson states his loss in this battle at 133 killed, 929 wounded, and 14 missing—1167 in all, of whom nearly two thirds belonged to Ewell's division, which had been also engaged the previous day. In these three days this division lost nearly 1000 men. The Union loss in killed and wounded must have been much smaller, but Jackson claims to have taken 450 prisoners.[2]

Here ended the pursuit of Jackson. Why the forces of Fremont and Shields were not united and brought against Jackson is one of the mysteries of this miserable campaign. On the 8th of June, the day of the battle of Cross Keys, orders were sent from the War Department that Fremont should "take post with his main force near Harrisonburg, to guard against operations of the enemy down the Valley of the Shenandoah;" and Banks, who had meanwhile recrossed the Potomac, should take position at or near Front Royal; and that McDowell, "having first provided adequately for the defense of the City of Washington, and for holding the position at Fredericksburg, should as speedily as possible execute his former instructions to march toward Richmond, whither, indeed, McCall's division of his army had in the mean while been ordered to go by water.[3] Fremont, instead of stopping at Harrisonburg, fell back in a few days as far as Mount Jackson, leaving his wounded behind; Shields took post at New Market; and Jackson, on the 12th, retired across the South River, where he remained near Weyer's Cave for three days, when he set out to join Lee at Richmond. The object which he had in view had been fully accomplished. With barely 20,000 men he had neutralized McDowell's 40,000, Fremont's 20,000, and driven Banks's 6000 beyond the bounds of the Confederacy, leaving McClellan to confront first Johnston and then Lee before Richmond.

The order of May 24th shut off McClellan from all hope of any immediate support from McDowell's corps, and he proceeded to shape his measures accordingly. The first thing to be done, in his estimation, was to throw a series of bridges across the Chickahominy, in order to enable his whole army to cross at different points. Of these there were eleven, "all long, difficult, and with extensive log-way approaches." The necessity of all these is not apparent, for nearly the whole army was finally passed over by two of them. "The entire army," McClellan affirms, "could probably

[1] Each commander, in his official reports, greatly exaggerates the loss of the other in this battle. Ewell says: "There are good reasons for estimating the loss of the enemy at 2000 in killed, wounded, and prisoners. On a part of the field they buried 101 at one spot, 15 at another, and a house containing some of their dead was said to have been burned by them; and this is only a part of their loss."—(Lee's Rep., i., 63.) Fremont, in his report, made next day, says: "The enemy's loss we can not clearly ascertain. He was engaged during the night in carrying off his dead and wounded in wagons. This morning, on our march, 200 of his dead were counted on one field, the greater part being badly mutilated by cannon-shot. Many of his dead were also scattered through the woods, and many have been already buried."—(Reb. Rec., v., 110.) Fremont estimated his own loss at 125 killed and 500 wounded, making no mention of prisoners, of whom, indeed, it is hardly possible there could have been many. Ewell's report states his loss specifically at 43 killed, 230 wounded, and 14 missing—287 in all.—(Lee's Rep., i., 120.)
[2] Lee's Rep., i., 55–60, 121; Tyler's Report, Reb. Rec., v., 110.　　　[3] Com. Rep., 275.

BRIDGE ACROSS THE CHICKAHOMINY SWAMP.

have been thrown across the Chickahominy immediately after our arrival, but this would have left no force on the left bank to guard our communications, or to protect our right and rear. If the communication with our supply dépôt had been cut by the enemy, with our army concentrated on the right bank of the Chickahominy, and the stage of water as it was many days after our arrival, the bridges carried away, and our means of transportation not furnishing a single day's supplies in advance, the troops must have gone without rations, and the animals without forage; the army would have been paralyzed."[1] But Bottom's Bridge and the railway bridge, only a mile apart, and on the direct line of his communications, were above the reach of the highest water, and, these protected, his communications across the river were safe. It was surely easier to protect these than a half score of points. He believed all the time that he was confronted across the river by a force greatly superior to his own; and yet, by some unexplained course of reasoning, he decided, "under the circumstances, to retain a portion of the army on the left bank of the river until our bridges were completed."[2] He divided his army into two parts, neither of them in a position to aid the other in case of a sudden attack in force. The troops that crossed the Chickahominy were directed in a General Order "to go prepared for battle at a moment's notice." They were to preserve discipline, obey orders, and especially to bear in mind "that the Army of the Potomac has never been checked; keep well together, throw away no shots, but aim carefully and low, and, above all things, rely upon the bayonet."[3]

By the 28th of May the two corps of Keyes and Heintzelman, forming the left wing, were on the south side of the Chickahominy, massed checker-wise along the Williamsburg road for a distance of about six miles. The right wing, comprising the corps of Sumner, Franklin, and Porter, was stretched for eighteen miles along the north bank of the Chickahominy. The two wings formed an acute-angled triangle of unequal sides, the apex being at Bottom's Bridge. The distance between the centre of the two wings was hardly five miles in a direct line, but between them flowed the Chickahominy, over which no practicable bridge had been thrown except at the apex of the triangle. If the left wing, which was thus thrown across the river toward Richmond, were attacked in force by the enemy massed in superior numbers on that side, the right wing could come to its aid only by a march of more than twenty miles; so if the right were assailed, it could be aided by the left only by an equal march.[4] For a hostile commander, with any thing like an equal force, there were two courses open. He could throw his entire strength upon the weaker left wing with a probability, as sure as any thing in war can be, of annihilating it; or he could fling his

whole army upon the Federal right, attacking its weak line of communication with its supplies. Johnston tried the former plan at the close of May. He failed only through accidents which neither party could anticipate. Lee tried the second plan at the close of June, under circumstances which should have insured its defeat. The result was that the Federal army, outgeneraled, but not outfought or outnumbered, was driven from the Chickahominy to the James, bringing the Peninsular campaign to a disastrous close.

For a few days McClellan's dispatches to the President were hopeful. On the 25th of May, the time was very near when he should attack Richmond. Next day, he was "quietly closing in upon the enemy preparatory to the last struggle." He had cut the Virginia Central Railroad in three places, and would try to cut the other railroad. He thought the Richmond intrenchments not very formidable, and hoped soon to be within shelling distance. His arrangements for the morrow were very important, and, if successful, would leave him free to strike on the return of the force detached.[1]

He had just learned that a considerable force of the enemy was near Hanover Court-house, to the right and rear of his army, threatening his communications, "and in a position either to re-enforce Jackson or to impede McDowell's junction, should he finally move to join us." This force, as it afterward appeared, was Branch's division of raw men from North Carolina. Fitz John Porter was ordered to dislodge them. Marching fourteen miles through a heavy rain, Porter's advance, under Emory, reached the neighborhood of Hanover Court-house at noon on the 27th, and found a portion of the enemy drawn up across the road to dispute their progress. Emory, re-enforced by a portion of Morell's brigade, routed this body after an hour's firing, and the main body of the Union force were ordered to pursue them northward, while Martindale, with three regiments, was sent westward toward Ashland to obstruct the railroad and cut the telegraph wires. He soon found himself opposed by a superior force, and sent to Porter for re-enforcements. For reply he received orders to march to the right, in which direction the enemy were, as Porter supposed, retreating north, pursued by the main part of the corps. Martindale rejoined that the enemy was on his left, but prepared to obey orders, when he was directed to march to a certain distance and halt. But so confident was he that Porter was misinformed of the position of the enemy that he obeyed the order only in part, keeping back a portion of his force to guard the van of the main column. Soon his force of 1000 men was attacked by the whole strength of the enemy, estimated at from 5000 to 7000 men. He stood his ground stoutly for two hours, but was sorely bestead. His centre was broken, and the enemy getting through the woods upon both his flanks. Porter at length found that he was mistaken in supposing the enemy was retiring to the north, and that he had been "pursuing a myth." He faced his whole column about, and fell upon the flanks of the enemy, who were held at bay by Martindale. The Confederates were routed, and fled in confusion.

¹ McC. Rep., 200.   ² Ibid., 201.   ³ Gen. Order, May 25th, Reb. Rec., v., 431.
⁴ McClellan, while attempting to explain why he failed to push his advantage at Fair Oaks, shows the complete isolation of his two wings. He says: "The only available means of uniting our forces at Fair Oaks for an advance upon Richmond, soon after the battle, was to march the troops from Mechanicsville and other points on the left bank of the Chickahominy down to Bottom's Bridge, and thence over the Williamsburg road to the position near Fair Oaks, a distance of about twenty-three miles. In the condition of the roads at that time this march could not have been made with artillery in less than two days."—Report, 223.

¹ McC. Rep., 204, 205.

SHELLING ACROSS THE CHICKAHOMINY SWAMP.

"The immediate results of these affairs," says McClellan, "were some 200 of the enemy's dead buried by our troops, 730 prisoners sent to the rear, one 12-pound howitzer, one caisson, a large number of small-arms, and two railroad trains captured. Our loss amounted to 53 killed, 344 wounded and missing."[1]

McClellan was jubilant at the result of this action, the first which had been fought by his direction. It was, he said, a glorious victory; the rout of the rebels was complete—not a defeat, but a complete rout. Porter had gained two complete victories over superior forces. The enemy were concentrating every thing on Richmond; he would do his best to cut off Jackson, but was doubtful whether he could. All the railroads had been cut but that from Richmond to Fredericksburg. The President replied that he was very glad of Porter's victory, but added, "If it was a total rout of the enemy, I am puzzled to know why the Richmond and Fredericksburg Railroad was not seized. Again: As you say you have all the railroads but the Richmond and Fredericksburg, I am puzzled to see how, lacking that, you can have any except the scrap from Richmond to West Point. The scrap of the Virginia Central from Richmond to Hanover Junction, without more, is simply nothing. That the whole of the enemy is concentrating upon Richmond I think can not be certainly known to you or me." McClellan was no wise satisfied with this guarded congratulation. "I do not think," he wrote, "that you at all appreciate the value and magnitude of Porter's victory. He has entirely relieved my right flank, which was seriously threatened; routed and demoralized a considerable portion of the rebel forces. It was one of the handsomest things of the war, both in itself and its results. Porter has returned, and my army is again well in hand. Another day will make the probable field of battle passable for artillery."[2] Martindale, whose firm stand against superior forces had secured the victory, was not so enthusiastic either as to the conduct of the affair or its value.[3]

Johnston was in no position to attack, or even seriously to threaten, McClellan's right on the eastern side of the Chickahominy. He had fallen back from Yorktown, from Williamsburg, and then across the Chickahominy, simply because he was opposed to a greatly superior force. Of course, plausible reasons must be given for these movements. Yorktown, it was said, was evacuated because "McClellan, by his arrangements, had made the place untenable;"[4] the strong lines at Williamsburg were abandoned because he wished to fight the enemy in the open field, out of the reach of gun-boats;[5] the Chickahominy was crossed because he did not wish to fight a great battle with so formidable an obstacle in the way of his retreat, in case he was worsted.[6] Branch's six regiments, so far from being sent from Richmond to threaten McClellan's right and his communications with his base of supplies, were moving down from Gordonsville to the defense of Richmond, whither Johnston was calling every man, with the exception of Jackson's command in the Valley of the Shenandoah. Two days before the

affair at Hanover Court-house, J. R. Anderson, who had been confronting McDowell near Fredericksburg, was on his way to Richmond, and the day after the battle his force passed Ashland, almost within sight of Porter's battle-field, and hurried on to the capital. There was now no enemy between McDowell and McClellan, and their advanced guards were only fifteen miles apart. Jackson was at this moment at Williamsport on the Potomac, 200 miles away. The terror excited at Washington by his bold movement alone prevented the junction of McDowell with McClellan.[1]

But if McClellan's right wing, stretched along the eastern branch of the Chickahominy, was unassailable by any force at Johnston's command, the weaker left, practically isolated on the other side of the stream, invited a sharp and sudden blow. About 30,000 men, belonging to Keyes's and Heintzelman's corps, had been sent across the Chickahominy.[2] Keyes, whose corps was in the advance, intrenched itself a mile behind a place on the Williamsburg road known as "The Seven Pines," nearly midway between the river and Richmond. The place was named from a clump of pine-trees which formerly stood at the crossing of several roads. Casey's division of this corps was pushed a thousand yards beyond the Pines to Fair Oaks Farm.[3] Here were two pleasant houses in a grove of fair oak-trees, with a long pile of wood cut for the railroad. Casey's pickets were advanced a thousand yards farther to the edge of a dense forest, through an opening in which the enemy were descried in force. The region was mostly wooded and intersected by marshes, with small clearings around the few houses. The trees were hastily cut down to form abatis, rifle-pits were dug, and one or two redoubts for artillery hastily constructed.

Heintzelman's corps lay behind that of Keyes, stretching also to the left, in order to cover the approaches to the White Oak Swamp, which came close up to the Williamsburg road. Although Keyes was in the advance, Heintzelman was told by McClellan that he was to command on that side of the Chickahominy, and if there was any fighting to do, he must do it. He thought the troops were too much scattered, but dared not change their position in face of the positive orders which he had received; but after a week he got authority to place his men as he saw fit, and sent half of them

[1] McC. Rep., 208. [2] Ibid., 208-212.

[3] "The whole line of our march and our left flank, by the order of the commander-in-chief, was left exposed and open to assault; following the directions which the general gave, instead of a victory, we should have been involved in an ugly catastrophe. . . . I went with a force of only about 1000 men to encounter the whole force of the enemy that day, from 5000 to 7000. The general results were these: A cross-fire opening upon us from the woods; I had my wings supported in columns—my centre was broken—and maintained my position there about two hours, while the rest of the army were pursuing a myth, when the return of the second brigade under Morell enabled us to take the rebels thus held at advantage, and repulse them, resulting in the rout of the enemy. . . . I never comprehended any object in the movement to Hanover Court-house except it was to intercept some of the enemy, if any should happen to be between Hanover Court-house and Fredericksburg."—Martindale's Testimony, Com. Rep., 635-637.

[4] Southern Generals, 265.   [5] Pollard, ii., 16.   [6] Memphis Appeal.

[1] McC. Rep., 211, De Joinville, 68.—As early as May 29th McClellan was apprized of the significance of the Confederate troops near Hanover Court-house. On that day he wrote to the Secretary of War: "General Anderson left his position in the vicinity of Fredericksburg at 4 A.M., Sunday [May 25th], with the following troops: 1st South Carolina; one battalion South Carolina Rifles; 12th, 13th, and 14th South Carolina; 3d Louisiana; two batteries of four guns each, namely, Letcher's Virginia, and McIntosh's South Carolina batteries. General Anderson and his command passed Ashland yesterday morning en route for Richmond, leaving men behind him to destroy the bridges over the telegraph road, which they traveled. This information is reliable. It is also positively certain that Branch's command was from Gordonsville, bound for Richmond, whither they have now gone. It may be regarded as positive. I think that there is no force between Fredericksburg and the Junction" [of the Virginia Central and Richmond and Fredericksburg Railroads, ten miles north of Ashland]. Yet the very next day he wrote that his right flank had been "seriously threatened" by Branch, the dispersal of whose division had effected "the clearing of our right flank and rear;" this "dispersal," apart from the loss of prisoners and killed, amounting only to hastening their march to Richmond. He repeats this statement in his Report prepared more than a year later, asserting that Branch's force "was in the vicinity of Hanover Court-house, to the right and rear of our army, thus threatening our communications."—(Report, 211, 212, 205.) They were certainly to the right, at a distance of fifteen miles, and endeavoring to get away; but they were not in his rear, and could only threaten his communications by almost reversing their line of march, and putting the Chickahominy and three fifths of the Union army directly between themselves and the Confederate force before Richmond. Lee, indeed, made this very movement a month later, but not until his strength was nearly double that of Johnston, and he had measured the capacity of his antagonist. He made it, also, with more than 60,000 men, instead of with six raw regiments.

[2] "There were four divisions on the right bank of the Chickahominy—one a very weak one. I should think the strength of the four divisions must have been 30,000 men, perhaps."—McClellan's Testimony, Com. Rep., 433.

[3] There are two Fair Oaks mentioned in the reports of the actions of May 31st and June 1st. The failure to discriminate these has given rise to much confusion. "Fair Oaks Farm" is on the Williamsburg road, something more than half a mile beyond the Seven Pines. "Fair Oaks Station" is a wooding point on the railroad, about a mile from the farm.

4 T

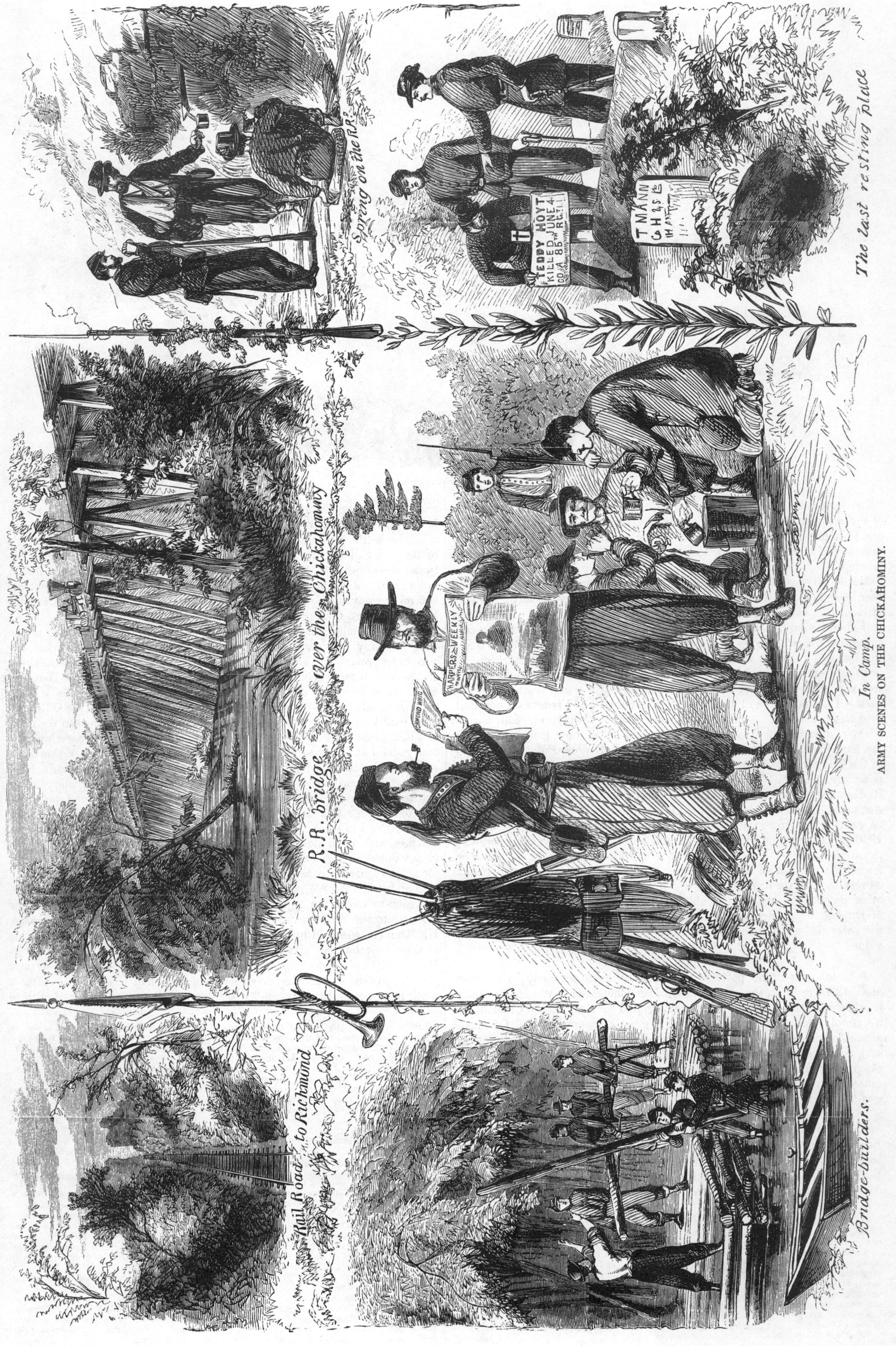

Spring on the R.R.?

The last resting place

R.R. bridge.

Over the Chickahominy

Rail Road to Richmond

In Camp.

ARMY SCENES ON THE CHICKAHOMINY.

Bridge-builders.

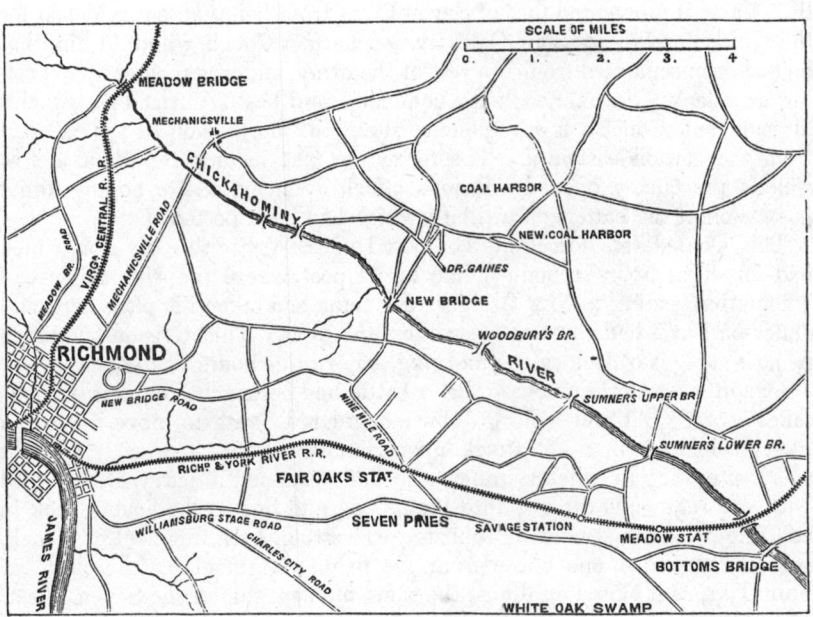

SEVEN PINES AND FAIR OAKS.

forward to the Seven Pines. This was only the day before the battle opened.[1]

Johnston, in the mean while, was informed, but only partially, of the movement across the Chickahominy. His "trusty scouts" could only tell him on the 30th of May that Keyes's corps had crossed, and were encamped on the Richmond side of the stream. He resolved to "attack them next morning, hoping to be able to defeat Keyes's corps completely in its advanced position before it could be re-enforced." The attack was to be made by the four full divisions of Huger, Longstreet, D. H. Hill, and G. W. Smith, comprising fully three fifths of Johnston's entire force.[2] The main assault was to be made in front by Longstreet, with his own division and that of Hill; Huger was to move down the Charles City road, and attack the left flank of the force engaged by Longstreet; and Smith was to march down to the junction of the New Bridge and Nine-mile roads, and be ready to assail the right flank of Keyes or to cover Longstreet's left.

During the afternoon and night of the 30th a storm more violent than had been known for a generation swept over Richmond. This seemed providential for the Confederates. The channel of the Chickahominy was already full to its brim. The stream, swollen by the storm, would overflow the swamp and bottom, preventing any aid to be sent to Keyes from the other side. The left wing of the Union army seemed doomed. Though it was twice as strong as Johnston supposed, it was still greatly overmatched, and its destruction would have been the greater success for the Confederates.[3]

The attack was to be made simultaneously at daybreak. The storm delayed the movements of the troops, but by eight o'clock Longstreet was in position, ready to begin. Hour after hour he waited for Huger, unwilling to make a partial attack instead of the combined movement which had been planned. Noon had passed before he decided to commence the assault, without waiting for the dilatory Huger.[4]

Casey's division of Keyes's corps was in the advance at Fair Oaks Farm, three quarters of a mile in front of the Seven Pines, its pickets being pushed a third of a mile farther, up to the very edge of the wood in and behind

which the enemy was posted, his strength being fully screened from view. There had been indications of an impending attack. The cars had been heard running all the night before from Richmond, indicating that troops were being brought to the front. Early in the morning an aid of Johnston was captured close to the Union lines. Keyes ordered his division to be under arms at 11 A.M. Soon tidings were brought that the enemy were coming in force down the Williamsburg road. Casey advanced several batteries toward his picket-lines to meet them, at the same time sending back for re-enforcements. He had scarcely done this when the enemy burst through the screen of woods. The pickets and supporting regiments were swept back in confusion. The artillery had been thrown forward; in order to save the guns, Naglee made a bayonet charge upon the advancing enemy, and pressed them back to the woods. Here he was met with a furious fire of musketry, and forced back; the guns were saved, with the exception of a single piece, and the whole division fell back to the line of defense at Fair Oaks Farm. Here this weak division, scarcely five thousand strong, held its ground for three hours against three times its number. But at length, pressed in front, almost enveloped on both flanks, and having lost one third of its number, it fell back to the second line of defense in front of the Seven Pines, then held by Couch's division. The retreat was made just in time. Had it been delayed a few minutes, the whole division would have been surrounded and captured. As it was, they lost a battery of five guns. Casey maintained that this stubborn resistance at this line really saved the day, and prevented this action from resulting "in a severe repulse, which might have resulted in a disastrous defeat."[1]

Couch's division at the Seven Pines had been weakened by sending regiments to the support of Casey. Their line of defense, protected by a slight abatis, lay across the road. Keyes, the corps commander, who was now on the ground, brought forward what re-enforcements he could from the rear, and made a stand. Thus far the weight of the fight on the Confederate side had been borne by Hill's division, which was in the advance. Longstreet's force now came up, and pressed the line in front, while its superior numbers enabled it to assail the right and left flanks at the same time. Couch, who was on the right with two regiments, was forced from his position. Instead of falling back, he withdrew along the Nine-mile road to Fair Oaks Station, where he took part in the action which soon began at that point. Longstreet, who was now on the field, leaving the Union right, pressed with all his force upon the centre and left, between Couch and the main body of the division. Heintzelman by this time had brought forward Kearney's division of his corps, Hooker's being then near White Oak

[1] Heintzelman's Testimony, *Com. Rep.*, 351.

[2] In the organization of the Confederate army, a "division" was the largest member, answering to a "corps" in the Union army. Each division comprised from four to six brigades. The strength of a division at this time was about 12,000, so that the attack, as planned, would have been made by 48,000 men; but, as Huger failed to execute his part, there were but 36,000 Confederates actually engaged. Including Branch and Anderson, who reached Richmond the day before with about 12,000, Johnston could have had barely 20,000 men beyond these four divisions; as Huger had only recently been brought from Petersburg, where he was posted for some time after his abandonment of Norfolk, Johnston could not have fallen back from Yorktown and Williamsburg with more than 45,000. For General Johnston's own statement of his force at different periods of the campaign, see note at the end of this chapter.

[3] "I determined to attack next morning [May 31st], hoping to be able to defeat Keyes's corps completely in its more advanced position before it could be re-enforced. . . . Heavy and protracted rains during the afternoon and night, by swelling the stream of the Chickahominy, increased the probability of our having to deal with no other troops than those of Keyes."—(*Johnston's Report.*) "The storm of May 30th was terrible. Never, even in the tropics, have I seen a more sudden and sweeping deluge. The creek which flowed at the bottom of the hill below the house in which I lived [in Richmond], and over which, in ordinary times, a boy might leap, filled the valley, on the morning of May 30th, with a shallow lake more than one hundred yards in width."—(Hurlbert, in *De Joinville*, 114.) "During the day and night of the 30th of May a very violent storm occurred. The rain, falling in torrents, rendered work on the rifle-pits and bridges impracticable, made the roads almost impassable, and threatened the destruction of the bridges across the Chickahominy. The enemy, perceiving the unfavorable position in which we were placed, and the possibility of destroying that part of our army which was apparently cut off by the rapidly-rising stream, threw an overwhelming force upon the position occupied by Casey's division."—(*McC. Rep.*, 215.) "General Keyes's corps and a part of General Heintzelman's were on the right bank of the Chickahominy. General Sumner's corps, with the rest of the army, were on the other bank of the river. The enemy took advantage of our position, and the small force that was on the right bank, and made their preparations to just gobble up Keyes's whole corps. They attacked me on the 31st of May. The preceding night was one of the worst I ever saw. I never before heard such a thunder-storm as there was on that night."—(Casey's Testimony, *Com. Rep.*, 443.) "On Friday night we had one of the worst rain-storms, thunder and lightning, that I ever saw. A man who had lived there twenty-nine years said that it was one of the worst storms they ever had in that country."—(Heintzelman's Testimony, *Com. Rep.*, 354.) "Through all the night of the 30th of May there was a raging storm, the like of which I can not remember. Torrents of rain drenched the earth. The thunderbolts rolled and fell without intermission, and the heavens flashed with a perpetual blaze of lightning. From their beds of mud and the peltings of this storm, the Fourth Corps rose to fight the battle of the 31st of May, 1862."—(*Keyes's Rep.*)

[4] Johnston says that the advance was made at 2 P.M., "the engagement being opened by artillery and skirmishers, and by 3 o'clock it had become close and heavy." But, according to the concurrent accounts of all the Union officers, the skirmishing began by noon, and within an hour the action became serious. Johnston's report was written nearly a month after the battle, and while he was still feeble from the effects of his wound. There can be no doubt that he is incorrect in his statements of time, placing the important periods of the action two hours later than they actually occurred. In giving the time, we adopt the general statements of the Union authorities.

[1] The conduct of Casey's division was at the time a matter of sharp discussion. Several officers, who saw only the disorganized regiments, reported that it had behaved disgracefully: McClellan, in his first dispatch, declared that "Casey's division, which was the first line, gave way unaccountably and discreditably." Upon more complete information, he officially withdrew the charge, saying, "I withdraw the expression contained in my first dispatch, and I cordially give my indorsement to the conclusion of the division commander, that 'those parts of his command which behaved discreditably were exceptional cases.'"—(*McC. Rep.*, 222.) Still it is certain that the division, as such, was broken by the overwhelming force to which it was opposed. A portion of it, with others, rushed back, a disorganized mass. Heintzelman, in his Report, states the case fairly. He says: "Some of the regiments fought gallantly till overwhelmed by superior numbers. After they were once broken, however, they could not be rallied" [as a body, that is, since, as he implies and as Keyes affirms, among the fragments of regiments which formed the line which finally checked the Confederate advance were portions of Casey's, as well as of Couch's and Kearney's divisions]. "The road was filled with fugitives (not all from this division) as far as Bottom's Bridge. Colonel Starr's regiment, of General Hooker's division, had to force its way through them with the bayonet, and a guard I placed at Bottom's Bridge stopped over a thousand men."

SILAS CASEY.

DARIUS N. COUCH.

Swamp, too far away to come up in time. The fight raged fiercely with varying success for an hour and a half, until five o'clock, when the Union force began slowly to give way, and fall back from the position at the Seven Pines. The right, with Couch, had moved northward toward Fair Oaks Station; the left, with Berry, of Kearney's division, held its ground, keeping the enemy before it in check until nightfall, when they fell back southward by way of the White Oak Swamp. The Union centre fell back fighting a few hundred yards to a narrow strip of woods crossing the Williamsburg road. Here Heintzelman in person succeeded in rallying about eighteen hundred men, the fragments of regiments, and checked the advance of the enemy, who never got beyond this belt of woods. It was almost by accident that this stand was successful. Keyes, who was on the left of the proposed line, saw that the key to the position was a spot where the wooded ground sloped abruptly to the rear. If the enemy gained this the day was lost. He called a single regiment to follow him across an open field of seven or eight hundred yards. They dashed on in the face of a scorching fire, and gained the spot just in time. "Had they been two minutes later," says Keyes, "they would have been too late to occupy that fine position, and it would have been impossible to have formed the next and last line of battle, which stemmed the tide of defeat, and turned it toward victory." The new line, formed of fragments from regiments from every division which had been engaged—Casey's, Couch's, and Kearney's—had hardly been formed, when a heavy mass of the enemy, which had been held in check, came down upon it. They were met by a fire so deadly that their advance was checked.

It was now past six o'clock, and, though it wanted an hour of sunset, the dense vapors rising from the swamp made all objects indistinct. The Confederates, who had pressed the Union forces for two miles from Fair Oaks Farm to beyond the Seven Pines, fell back a little toward Richmond, passing the night under arms on the battle-field and in the camps which they had won. The Union troops fell back a mile in the other direction to an intrenched camp.

The battle had hardly opened when the sound of musketry was heard at McClellan's head-quarters, six miles away in a direct line, on the other side of the Chickahominy. He was confined to his bed by illness, but sent an order to Sumner, whose corps lay nearest the battle-field, and who had just thrown two bridges over the Chickahominy, to hold himself in readiness to march to the scene of action. The storm which had on the previous evening burst so furiously over Richmond, had spent its force there and to the south; northward it was comparatively slight. The inundation which Johnston supposed would render the Chickahominy impassable by daybreak began to appear at noon. It was now two hours after noon. The bridges had become almost impassable, many of the timbers of the best one being already floating. Sumner more than obeyed the order which he had received. Instead of merely preparing to move, he advanced his two divisions—those of Sedgwick and Richardson—halting the leading company of each upon the bridge opposite it. He thus saved an hour, when, as events proved, minutes were priceless.

Tidings came to head-quarters that the day was going hardly, and Sumner, at half past two, was ordered to cross. Sedgwick's division in the advance pressed over the shaking bridge. The artillery was dragged with difficulty through the swamp on the other side. Sumner, with this division, guided by the sound of the firing, pushed on to Fair Oaks Station, where he arrived just in time to fight the battle of Fair Oaks, which, although no one

then knew it, prevented that of Seven Pines from being an entire defeat for the Union forces. At Fair Oaks Station he met Couch, who told him that he had been separated from the rest of the army, and was momently expecting an attack. Sumner took the command, and hastily formed Sedgwick's division and Couch's few regiments along the north side of the railroad from the station eastward. The formation was incomplete, when, at five o'clock, the enemy opened a furious attack upon his centre, hoping to get possession of the battery of artillery which had been posted there.

This Confederate force was composed of G. W. Smith's division, which had for eight hours remained idle at its post where the Nine-mile road joined that leading to New Bridge. Johnston had taken his place here, and Jefferson Davis had come out to witness the fight. This division had taken its post at eight o'clock in the morning. For three hours, from one till four, Johnston was utterly unaware that a battle had been going on scarcely four miles away.[1] At four o'clock Johnston ordered Smith to move, and in an hour he had begun a hot attack upon Sumner's line. The early twilight was just closing in, when Sumner, who had sustained a heavy fire, charged with six regiments directly into the woods, and hurled the enemy back in confusion. At this moment Johnston was struck by a fragment of a shell, severely wounded, and borne from the field. Night closed the battle of Fair Oaks, as it closed at almost the same moment that of the Seven Pines.

Just then Richardson's division of Sumner's corps came upon the field. He had begun to cross the Chickahominy by "Sumner's lower bridge," which was nearest to his own camp; but before his division was half over, the rising waters made this bridge impassable, and two brigades, with all the artillery, had to cross by the upper bridge, over which Sedgwick had crossed. When this division came up, it was posted along the railroad to the left of Sedgwick, connecting this with Birney's brigade of Heintzelman's corps, which had been sent in that direction, but had halted, without having taken part in the fight.[2] The two forces bivouacked in the field, their picket lines being within speaking distance.

The disabling of Johnston left the Confederates with an incompetent leader. Smith, who succeeded to the command, appears to have gone over to the Seven Pines, but found the forces there in no condition to renew their attack here on the next morning.[3] But the attack was fiercely renewed on

[1] We here follow Johnston's notation of time, as it relates to matters that came under his personal observation. He says: "I had placed myself on the left of the force employed in this attack, with the division of General Smith, that I might be on a part of the field where I could observe and be ready to meet any counter-movement which the enemy's general might make against our centre or left. Owing to some peculiar condition of the atmosphere, the sound of the musketry did not reach us. I consequently deferred giving the signal for General Smith's advance until four o'clock, at which time Major Jasper Whiting, of General Smith's staff, whom I had sent to learn the state of affairs with General Longstreet's column, returned, reporting that it was pressing on with vigor. . . . Smith's division moved forward at four o'clock, General Whiting's three brigades leading. Their progress was impeded by the enemy's skirmishers, which, with their supports, were driven back to the railroad. At this point Whiting's Own and Pettigrew's brigades engaged a superior force of the enemy. Hood's, by my orders, moved on to co-operate with Longstreet. General Smith was desired to hasten up with all the troops within reach. He brought up Hampton's and Hatton's brigades in a few minutes. The strength of the enemy's position, however, enabled him to hold it until dark. About sunset, being struck from my horse, severely wounded, by a fragment of a shell, I was carried from the field, and Major General G. W. Smith succeeded to the command."

[2] Birney was put under arrest by Heintzelman, and brought before a court-martial on charge of disobedience of orders in having halted his brigade. He was honorably acquitted, it being shown that he had obeyed orders received from Kearney, his immediate commander. His brigade, then commanded by Colonel Hobart Ward, did good service in the action of the following day.

[3] Thus only can we explain Johnston's statement that "General Smith, who succeeded to the command, was prevented from resuming his attack on the enemy's position next morning by the discovery of strong intrenchments not seen on the previous evening." He indeed adds: "Smith's division bivouacked on the night of the 31st within musket-shot of the intrenchments which they were attacking when darkness stayed the conflict." But there were no intrenchments near Fair Oaks Station, where Smith's attack upon Sumner was made. Johnston represents the sharp fighting on the railroad next day merely as a demonstration upon two of the Confederate brigades, which was repelled. But he was clearly misinformed as to the character of this action. The con-

EDWIN V. SUMNER.

SEARCHING FOR THE DEAD AND WOUNDED.

PICKETS IN THE WOODS.

the right, near Fair Oaks Station. The Confederates advanced down the railroad—avoiding Sedgwick's division, which had fought the previous day, and was still held to the right by Sumner in position at Fair Oaks—and fell upon Richardson's division, which formed the centre. The attack, repulsed at one point, was renewed at another, but without success, Richardson's line, supported by artillery, standing firm.

Meanwhile Hooker had come up from the left, making for the heaviest fire, for the ground was so densely wooded that the position of the combatants could not be seen. He found Birney's brigade, now commanded by Ward, drawn up in line of battle, and with this force fell upon the enemy's rear, and, after an hour's hard fighting, pushed them from the woods by which they were sheltered. He then ordered a bayonet charge. The enemy broke and fled toward Richmond. Almost at the same moment Richardson's whole line, farther to the right, advanced, pouring in its fire at close range, following up the advantage by a bayonet charge, which put the enemy to flight. The line of retreat followed by the Confederates took them from the railroad to the Williamsburg road, where the forces who had the day before gained the battle of Seven Pines still held the direct way to Richmond, and the whole force moved back, utterly foiled in the object for which the attack had been made. The Union force was too much scattered to venture a pursuit.[1]

The battle of Sunday, June 1st, began at seven in the morning, and was over at eleven. At noon McClellan came upon the field at Fair Oaks, but he had no orders to give; he was quite satisfied with what had been done.[2] On the next day the Union forces assumed the position at Fair Oaks Farm which Sumner had held before the battle. Sumner also retained his position at Fair Oaks Station, strengthening it by earthworks. The losses in killed and wounded in these two battles were nearly equal. That of the Confederates was 4233; that of the Union, 4517, of whom 890 were killed; there were also 1222 missing, three quarters of them from Keyes's corps.[3] The

current accounts of all the Union generals show that it was a serious attack by Smith's entire division, which was effectually repulsed.—See Richardson's *Letter, Reb. Rec.*, v., 87; Sumner's Testimony, *Com. Rep.*, 363; Hooker's Testimony, *ibid.*, 578; *McC. Rep.*, 220; *De Joinville*, 77.

[1] Heintzelman gave orders to pursue, but countermanded them at the urgent request of Kearney, who said it was better to let well enough alone, and that McClellan would order a general advance in a few days. Next day he learned that the Confederates had retreated in confusion, and sent Hooker forward, who penetrated to within less than four miles of Richmond. He was then stopped by order of McClellan, and directed to establish his command on the ground occupied before the battle by Casey's division at Fair Oaks Farm.—*Com. Rep.*, 352, 578.

[2] Sumner's Testimony, *Com. Rep.*, 363.

[3] These are the official statements. McClellan's report of his loss is:

Corps	*Killed.*	*Wounded.*	*Missing.*
General Sumner's	183	894	146
" Heintzelman's	259	980	155
" Keyes's	448	1753	921
	890	3627	1222

Johnston does not distinguish between killed and wounded. He says:

Longstreet reports the loss in his command at being about............. 3000
Smith reports his loss at....................................... 1233
                                                                  4233

Confederate attack was well conceived, and, had it been carried out according to Johnston's plan, would hardly have failed of success. If Huger had come down upon the left at any time, or if Smith had moved only an hour earlier from the right, Heintzelman and Keyes must have been utterly crushed. Or had the full flood of the Chickahominy come down, as was expected, four hours before instead of four hours after noon, Sumner could not have crossed, and the Union forces on the south side of the river would have been annihilated in plain sight of the whole army on the opposite bank, utterly powerless to give any aid.

As it was, the blow had utterly failed, and the Confederate force hurried back to Richmond broken and dispirited. Had McClellan known how utterly broken it was, he might have marched straight on to Richmond on the 1st of June.[1] The city itself and its approaches were then utterly unfortified. Even McClellan was convinced, only six days before, that the Richmond intrenchments were not formidable.[2] There was, indeed, nothing between him and Richmond except the six miles of space, a few rifle-pits and sand-works not mounted with artillery, and the disjointed fragments of a defeated army. The formidable works which in a few days crowned every hillock and swept every road were hardly begun. They were the work of Lee, constructed at a later date. Hooker saw nothing of them when he

McClellan indeed says (*Rep.*, 221), "General J. E. Johnston reports the loss of the enemy in Longstreet's and Smith's divisions at 4283; General D. H. Hill, who had taken the advance in the attack, estimates his loss at 2500, which would give the enemy's loss 6783." But Hill's division was included in Longstreet's "command," and his loss forms a part of Longstreet's. There is, indeed, reason to suspect that the Confederate loss is understated by Johnston. Hurlbert, the translator of De Joinville, who was at the time detained in Richmond under surveillance, says: "There were published in the Richmond papers detailed brigade and regimental reports of the losses in sixty out of seventy-two organizations, regiments, battalions, and companies mentioned as taking part in the engagements. I computed these losses as they were published. The sum total was 6733, killed, wounded, and missing." Correcting a probable misprint (6233 for 6283), this is within one of McClellan's statement of the Confederate loss, purporting to be taken from Johnston's Report. It is to be noted, however, that the 2500 loss ascribed to Hill's division make just the difference between the two statements (4233 and 6733). It might be supposed that some one, seeing these two statements, and finding in Johnston's Report no separate mention of Hill, whose loss must have been large, his division doing most of the fighting on the first day, assumed this number in order to make the accounts coincide, and that McClellan hastily adopted the statement without verifying it by Johnston's Report. From the nature of the actions, the Confederates charging intrenchments, and being exposed to artillery, while they brought none into the field, their loss might be presumed to be in excess. We, however, admit Johnston's statement into the text.

[1] Hurlbert (*Appendix to De Joinville*, 112) says: "They were in a perfect chaos of brigades and regiments. The roads to Richmond were literally crowded with stragglers, some throwing away their guns, some breaking them on the trees—all with the same story, that their regiment had been 'cut to pieces,' that the 'Yankees were swarming on the Chickahominy like bees, and fighting like devils.' In two days of the succeeding week the provost-marshal's guard collected between 4000 and 5000 stragglers, and sent them into camp. What had become of the command of the army no one knew. By some persons it was reported that Major General Gustavus W. Smith had succeeded Johnston; by others, that President Davis had taken the reins of the army. General Johnston himself was reported to be either actually dead or dying. . . . Had I been aware on that day of the actual state of things upon the field, I might easily have driven in a carriage through the Confederate lines directly into our own camps. It was not, indeed, till several days after the battle that any thing like military order was restored throughout the Confederate positions."

[2] *McC. Rep.*, 204.

FAIR OAKS FARM.—BURYING THE DEAD AND BURNING THE HORSES.

PICKET GUARD ON THE CHICKAHOMINY.

advanced within three and a half miles of Richmond. Had it been found inexpedient to endeavor to march into Richmond, there was nothing to prevent the Union lines from being advanced fully a mile and a half, clear beyond the woody belt which had sheltered the Confederates. Richmond would then have been within shelling distance. McClellan seems never to have imagined the possibility of an advance by his left wing, which then comprised three of his five corps. He simply said that he could not at once throw his whole army across the Chickahominy, and pronounced the idea of then marching upon Richmond as too absurd to be entertained by any one. But his ablest officers, who had met the enemy at Seven Pines and Fair Oaks, were of a different opinion.[1]

The Chickahominy continued to rise slowly but continuously all through Sunday, June 1st, though the rain had ceased. Many supposed that its upper waters had been dammed, and that the sluices had been opened. All the bridges, except the railroad bridge, were swept away or their approaches submerged. For several days the railroad bridge was the only communication between the two wings of the army, and that was made passable only by planks laid between the rails.[2] To build new bridges high above the water seemed to McClellan the work of the time. He kept up, however, a brisk correspondence with the government at Washington, the main topics being the weather, and what he was going to do when the weather should permit.[3] The weather was certainly unpropitious. Never, within the mem-

ory of the oldest inhabitant, had there been on the Peninsula such a rainy season as this.

McDowell was now, for the third time, ordered to join McClellan. He wrote from Manassas to McClellan joyfully announcing the fact. McCall's division was to go by water, the remainder of the corps by land. He himself, with the remainder, would be with him in ten days by way of Fredericksburg. This was on the 10th of June. Two days after, he wrote that McCall was on the way, but circumstances would prevent him from coming with the other troops at the time promised; but he asked that McCall's division should be so placed as to join the remainder of his corps when they arrived. McClellan had all along been jealous of McDowell. He wrote to the President intimating that McDowell was willing that the general interests should be sacrificed to increase his own command. He wished no troops not under his full control, but would prefer to fight the battle with what he had, and leave others responsible for the result.[1] McCall's division

[1] After having shown (see *ante*, p. 348, Note [4]) the utterly isolated position of the two wings of his army, he proceeds: "The idea of uniting the two wings of the army in time to make a vigorous pursuit of the enemy, with the prospect of overtaking him before he reached Richmond, only five miles distant from the field of battle, is simply absurd, and was, I presume, never for a moment seriously entertained by any one connected with the Army of the Potomac. An advance, involving the separation of the two wings by the impassable Chickahominy, would have exposed each to defeat in detail. Therefore I held the position already gained, and completed our crossings as soon as possible."—(*McC. Rep.*, 223.) But Keyes testified: "I think McClellan should have pushed right on after the battle of Fair Oaks. I do not know why he did not cross and attack, and win the battle. I think, if he had possessed the great quality of an energetic general, we should have taken Richmond."—(*Com. Rep.*, 445.) Sumner testified: "When the enemy had retreated after the battle of Fair Oaks, I know of no military reason for not immediately following them up to Richmond; and from information which we afterward received, I do believe that if the general had crossed the Chickahominy with the residue of the army, and made a general attack with his whole force, we could have carried Richmond. . . . If we had attacked with our whole force, we should have swept every thing before us; and I think the majority of the officers who were there think so now."—(*Ibid.*, 366.) Keyes testified: "I am not able to state why the enemy were not pursued; but it is my opinion that if they had been vigorously pursued by all the forces available for the pursuit, our army might have gone into Richmond."—(*Ibid.*, 609.) Hooker was asked, "Suppose that, the next day after the repulse of the enemy at Fair Oaks, General McClellan had brought his whole army across the Chickahominy, and made a vigorous movement upon Richmond, in your judgment, as a military man, what would have been the effect of that movement?" He replied, "In answer to that, I would say, that at no time during the whole campaign did I feel that we could not go to Richmond."—(*Ibid.*, 579.) Hooker had, the day after the battle, advanced his whole force toward Richmond beyond Fair Oaks Farm, meeting no resistance except a little picket-firing, when he was recalled by a telegram to the effect that he should "return from his brilliant reconnoissance: we can not afford to lose his division." "I had no expectation," he said, "of being lost."—(*Ibid.*, 578.) [2] *Art. Op.*, 26.

[3] June 2. "Our left is within four miles of Richmond. I only wait for the river to fall to cross with the rest of the force, and make a general attack. Should I find them holding firm in a

very strong position, I may wait for what troops I can bring up from Fortress Monroe" [he had just been officially informed that Wool's department had been merged into his own, General Dix there replacing Wool, who was sent to Fort McHenry, near Baltimore]. "But the *morale* of my troops is now such that I can venture much, and do not fear for odds against me. The victory is complete, and all credit is due to our officers and men."—(*Com. Rep.*, 333.) June 2. "Our left is every where advanced considerably beyond the positions it occupied before the battle." [This is erroneous. The left never occupied a position on the Williamsburg road in advance of Fair Oaks Farm; and Fair Oaks Station, where Sumner posted himself, was no nearer Richmond.] "I am in strong hopes that the Chickahominy will fall sufficiently to enable me to cross the right. We have had a terrible time with our communications, bridges and causeways, built with great care, having been washed away with the freshet. All that human labor can do is being done to accomplish our purpose." *June* 3. "The Chickahominy has been almost the only obstacle in my way for several days. Every effort has been made, and will continue to be, to protect the communications across it. Nothing of importance except that it is again raining." *June* 4. "Terrible rain-storm during the night and morning; not yet cleared off; bridges in bad condition, and still hard at work upon them. I have taken every possible step to insure the security of the corps on the right bank, but I can not re-enforce them from here until my bridges are all safe, as my force is too small to insure my right and rear, should the enemy attack in that direction, as they may probably attempt. I have to be very cautious now." *June* 5. "Rained most of the night—has now ceased, but it is not clear. The river is still high and troublesome. Enemy opened with several batteries on our bridges near here this morning; our batteries seem to have pretty much silenced them, though some firing is still kept up. The rain forces us to remain in *statu quo*." *June* 7. "The Chickahominy has risen so as to flood the entire bottom to the depth of three and four feet. I am pushing forward the bridges in spite of this; and the men are working night and day, up to their waists in water, to complete them. The whole face of the country is a perfect bog, entirely impassable for artillery or even cavalry, except directly in the narrow roads, which renders any movement either of this or the rebel army utterly out of the question until we have more favorable weather. I am glad you are pressing forward re-enforcements so vigorously. I shall be in perfect readiness to move forward and take Richmond the moment McCall reaches here, and the ground will admit the passage of artillery. I have advanced my pickets about a mile to-day, driving off the rebel pickets and securing a very advantageous position." [It is hard to see in what direction the pickets were advanced a mile: certainly not toward Richmond.] *June* 10 (much abridged). "I have information, not reliable, that Beauregard has arrived. I am completely checked by the weather; the Chickahominy is in a dreadful state; we have another rain-storm on our hands. I shall attack as soon as weather and ground will permit; but there will be a delay. I suggest that large detachments should be sent from Halleck's army to strengthen this. I will attack whenever the weather permits."—(*McC. Rep.*, 224–230.)

[1] McDOWELL TO McCLELLAN—*June* 10: "For the third time I am ordered to join you, and hope this time to get through. In view of the remarks made with reference to my leaving you and not joining you before by your friends, and something I have heard as coming from you on

WOODBURY AND ALEXANDER'S BRIDGE.

arrived on the 12th and 13th. They were posted on the extreme right, the point nearest to Fredericksburg. A few new regiments, seven in all, were sent from Baltimore and elsewhere to Fortress Monroe, and a like number of older ones were sent thence to the Chickahominy.[1] McClellan moved his head-quarters across the Chickahominy on the 13th. By the 20th the bridges over the Chickahominy were measurably finished—in all eleven, of which seven were practically of use: Bottom's Bridge; the Railroad Bridge, the means of bringing up most of the supplies to the left wing; the Foot Bridge, on the shortest line between the two wings, "available for infantry under certain circumstances;" Duane's Bridge, "practicable for all arms;" Woodbury's Infantry Bridge, "available for infantry;" Woodbury and Alexander's Bridge, "for all arms;" and Sumner's upper bridge, or the Grapevine Bridge, the one over which Sumner had crossed to win the battle of Fair Oaks, "in condition to be used in emergency by all arms."[2] Franklin's corps was now passed over, leaving only Porter's corps and McCall's division on the north side. Earth-works were in the mean while thrown up along the entire front on the south side, in an irregular semicircle, from the edge of White Oak Swamp up to Fair Oaks Farm and Station, then down to the Chickahominy at Woodbury's Bridge, five miles measured around the arc, and three along its chord formed by the river. The works were of no great strength, for the generals in command disapproved of them; they thought they made the men timid.[3] There were half a dozen redoubts, each mounting six or eight guns, connected by infantry parapets of timber and earth, with a ditch in front. The redoubts had parapets ten or twelve feet thick, and some were provided with magazines; the connecting lines were three or four feet thick at top.[4]

On the 3d of June, two days after the battle of Fair Oaks, Robert E. Lee was appointed to the command of the Confederate army in Virginia. For almost two centuries the Lees had been among the "First Families of Virginia." A century ago, Thomas Lee, grandson of the first American Lee, and grandfather of Robert E. Lee, was President of the Council and acting governor of the province. He kept almost royal state at his residence in Strafford.[5] Three of the sons of Thomas Lee bore prominent parts in our Revolutionary struggle. Two of them, Richard Henry and Francis Lightfoot Lee, were among the signers of the Declaration of Independence: the former, on the 7th of June, 1776, moved in the Continental Congress the famous resolution that "These United Colonies are, and of right ought to be, free and independent states; that they are absolved from all allegiance to the British crown, and that all political connection between them and the State of Great Britain is, and ought to be, totally dissolved." Another son, the father of the Confederate general, was Henry Lee—the famous cavalry commander "Legion Harry." He was chosen by Congress to deliver the funeral oration on the death of Washington, in which occurs the phrase, "First in war, first in peace, and first in the hearts of his countrymen." He fell into pecuniary embarrassments, and died in 1818, leaving among other children Robert Edmund Lee, a boy of twelve.[1]

It was not hard for the son of "Legion Harry" to gain admission to West Point. He entered this national institution in 1825, and, after four years, graduated with the highest honors of his class. It is recorded of him that "he never received a reprimand or had a mark of demerit against him." For more than thirty years his military record was not merely stainless, but most honorable. During the war with Mexico he was with Scott as Chief of Engineers. He was, indeed, the favorite officer of that veteran commander, and was mentioned with special honor in almost every one of his voluminous dispatches. This war over, he became Superintendent at West Point; but after two years he left, having received a commission in the cavalry. He served with honor in various quarters, fighting the Indians on the Texan frontier, and capturing John Brown at Harper's Ferry. The outbreak of secession in 1860 found him again in Texas, with the rank of colonel, but standing first on the list recommended for promotion to the rank of general. Thirty years before he had married the daughter and heiress of Mr. Custis, the step-child and adopted son of Washington. Through her he had become the proprietor of Arlington House, on the Potomac, and other large estates, all connecting him directly with the wife of Washington.

He was now fifty-five years old. For thirty-six years he had been in the military service of the United States. He had time and again sworn the military oath, binding him by the strongest obligation known among men to loyalty to the nation. He had risen high in his profession, and the highest rank in it was within his reach. To abandon the Union would peril every thing: professional rank, private fortune, and, if secession failed, his good name among men. But he was a Virginian, and, according to the theory of his section, his primary allegiance was due to his state. If she broke away from the nation, he must go with her. He came to Washington, and had a meeting with Scott, his old commander and friend. This was on the 18th of April, 1861, the day succeeding that upon which the Virginia Act of Secession was passed. He considered himself bound, he said, not to retain his commission in the army. Scott urged him not to resign. "I must," said Lee; "I can not consult my own feelings in the matter." Two days later he sent in his resignation, accompanying it with a pathetic letter, which breathed a hope that he might not yet be called to fight against the flag under which he had so long served.[2] The hope was

that subject, I wish to say I go with the greatest satisfaction, and hope to arrive with my main body in time to be of service. McCall goes in advance by water. I will be with you in ten days with the remainder, by Fredericksburg." June 12. "The delay of General Banks to relieve the division of my command now in the Valley beyond the time calculated upon will prevent my joining you with the remainder of the troops I am to take below at as early a day as I named. My third division (McCall's) is now on the way. Please to do me the favor so to place it that it may be in a position to join the others as they come down from Fredericksburg."—(Raymond's Administration of President Lincoln, 247.)

McCLELLAN TO THE SECRETARY OF WAR—June 14: ". . . It ought to be distinctly understood that McDowell and his troops are completely under my control. I received a telegram from him requesting that McCall's division might be placed so as to join him immediately on his arrival. That request does not breathe the proper spirit. Whatever troops come to me must be disposed of so as to do the most good. I do not feel that in such circumstances as those in which I am now placed, General McDowell should wish the general good to be sacrificed for the purpose of increasing his command. If I can not fully control all his troops, I want none of them, but would prefer to fight the battle with what I have, and let others be responsible for the result. . . ."—(McC. Rep., 232.)

[1] "On the 12th of June the 16th Massachusetts joined Hooker's division. Several regiments arrived about that time. I got about 5000 men for my corps about that time."—(Heintzelman, in Com. Rep., 355.)

[3] "I was never in favor of those field-works. I think they have a tendency to make the men timid, and do more harm than good; and I think the older officers of the army think so. Formerly it was a matter of army regulation not to throw up field-works, because it made the men timid."—(Sumner's Testimony, Com. Rep., 366. For the nature of these field-works, see Art. Op., 30, 31, with Plan No. 15.)

[5] "There is no structure in our country to compare with it. The walls of the first story are two and a half feet thick, and of the second story two feet, composed of brick imported from England. It originally contained about one hundred rooms. Besides the main building, there are four offices, one at each corner, containing fifteen rooms. The stables are capable of accommodating one hundred horses."—(Lossing's Field-Book of the Revolution, ii., 217.)

[2] Art. Op., 29, 30, 222.

[4] Art. Op., 29, 30, and Plate 15.

[1] General Charles Lee, dismissed from the Revolutionary army for his conduct at and after the battle of Monmouth, and thenceforth the bitter enemy of Washington, has been strangely confounded with "Legion Harry," one of his most trusted officers during the war, and his intimate friend thereafter. Charles Lee was born in Wales, and was in no way connected with the Lees of Virginia. For a sketch of the last days of Charles Lee, see John Esten Cooke, in Harper's Magazine for September, 1858, p. 502.

[2] LEE TO SCOTT, April 20, 1861: "Since my interview with you on the 18th instant, I have felt that I ought no longer to retain my commission in the army. I therefore tender my resignation, which I request you will recommend for acceptance. It would have been presented at once but for the struggle it has cost me to separate myself from a service in which I have devoted all the best years of my life, and all the ability I possessed. . . . Save in defense of my native state, I never desire again to draw my sword." To his sister he wrote on the same day: "The whole South is in a state of revolution, into which Virginia, after a long struggle, has been drawn; and though I recognize no necessity for this state of things, and would have forborne and pleaded to the end for redress of grievances, real or supposed, yet in my own person I had to meet the question whether I should take part against my native state. With all my devotion to the Union, and the feeling of loyalty and duty of an American citizen, I have not been able to make up my

ROBERT E. LEE.

futile. Lee soon found himself fighting with his state and against his na-tion, with what skill, and bravery, and ill-fortune is yet to be told. That very month, four years after, he surrendered the fragments of his great army to the successor of the man who had so vainly urged him against taking the fatal step.

Three days after his resignation, Lee formally accepted from the State Convention the position of command-er of all the forces of Virginia, not yet one of the Confederate states, though soon to become one. The President of the Convention, in formally an-nouncing the appointment, amplified the famous sentence which the father of the general had uttered respecting the Father of the Union. Lee re-joined, reiterating that he should only fight in behalf of Virginia.[1]

When the state forces of Virginia were merged into the army of the Confederacy Lee was appointed brig-adier general, but was still outranked by Cooper and A. S. Johnston, who

had held older commissions in the army of the United States.[1] His unsuc-cessful operations in Western Virginia have been already narrated.[2] He was then sent to superintend the coast defenses in Georgia and South Caro-lina. When the Union forces began to menace Richmond, he was recalled to superintend the defenses of the Confederate capital. Randolph was nominally Secretary of War, but the actual functions of the office were per-formed by Lee.

Little had been done to fortify Richmond before the battle of Fair Oaks. When Lee was appointed to the command he issued a stirring address to his troops. The army, he said, had made its last retreat, and henceforth its watchword must be "Victory or Death." He first set himself at work to surround the capital with defenses, while he awaited the arrival of new troops, and watched the developments of the plans of his opponent. By the time McClellan's bridges were complete Richmond had become a fortified camp, and Lee thought himself in a condition to assume the offensive at a favorable moment.[3] To ascertain the precise position of the Federal right,

SAMUEL COOPER.

mind to raise my hand against my relatives, my children, and my home. I have therefore re-signed my commission in the army, and, save in defense of my native state, with the sincere hope that my poor services may never be needed, I hope I may never be called on to draw my sword." —(Southern Generals, 36.)

[1] The President of the Convention said: "You are at this day among the living citizens of Virginia, 'First in War;' we pray to God most fervently that you may so conduct the operations committed to your charge that it will soon be said of you that you are 'First in Peace;' and when that time comes, you will have earned the still prouder distinction of being 'First in the hearts of your Countrymen.'" Lee replied: "I would have much preferred that your choice had fallen

upon an abler man. Trusting in Almighty God, an approving conscience, and the aid of my fel-low-citizens, I devote myself to the service of my native state, in whose behalf alone will I ever again draw my sword."—(Southern Generals, 44.)

[1] Of Albert Sidney Johnston, killed at Shiloh, we have had occasion to speak (ante, p. 299, 300). We shall not henceforth have to speak of Samuel Cooper, and will here dismiss him in a brief note. He was born in the State of New York in 1798; was educated at West Point; rose by slow seniority until 1852, when we find him colonel and adjutant general. He married into the Mason family of Virginia, and became a Virginian by adoption. When secession occurred he resigned his commission, offered himself to the Confederates, and was named adjutant general. Traitor to his state as well as to his nation, like Semmes of the Alabama, it is notable that his last official act as Adjutant General of the United States was to affix his signature to the order by which Twiggs was "dismissed from the army of the United States for his treachery to the flag of his country." Cooper sent in his resignation on the 7th of March, 1861. It was accepted, but was to take effect from the 1st, the day when he signed the order for the dismissal of Twiggs. On the 15th he was at Montgomery tendering his services to the Confederacy. He acted as Adjutant General of the Confederacy during the war.—(Southern Generals, 286-294.)   [2] Ante, p. 144.

[3] "After the battle of Seven Pines, the Federal army, preparatory to an advance upon Rich-mond, proceeded to fortify its position on the Chickahominy. . . . The intention of the en-

BIRD'S-EYE VIEW OF RICHMOND AND VICINITY.

JAMES E. B. STUART.

and the nature of its communications with its base of supplies on the York River, Stuart, with fifteen hundred cavalry, was sent to make a raid clear around the rear of the Union forces on the north bank of the Chickahominy. He set out on the 13th of June, veiling his purpose by going first northward, in order to give the impression that his object was to re-enforce Jackson. Then turning sharply southeastward to Hanover Court-house, he found himself unexpectedly clear to the right and rear of the Federal lines. Thence he dashed toward the White House, destroying some dépôts of provisions, which were protected by scarcely a corporal's guard, and turned southwestward to the Chickahominy, which he reached at midnight of the 14th, some miles below Bottom's Bridge. Here he found the ruins of an old bridge, from which a temporary foot-bridge was constructed, over which the men crossed, the horses swimming the stream. Only a single man was lost by Stuart in this daring expedition. He brought with him a hundred and sixty-five prisoners, and more than twice as many horses.[1] McClellan saw in this exploit only a raid productive of no important result.[2] But the real result was of immense moment. It showed that McClellan's communications were utterly unprotected, and that he was open to a blow on this vital point. Lee at once directed Jackson to move rapidly down from the upper valley of the Shenandoah, and join him upon the north side of the Chickahominy, where his main force would be at the appointed time. To mask this movement, Whiting's division was ostentatiously dispatched in the direction of Jackson, apparently with the design of strengthening him for a movement toward Washington.[3] The ruse succeeded. The movement was hardly made when it was known to McClellan and at Washington. The President saw in it a weakening of the Confederate force at Richmond equivalent to a corresponding strengthening of McClellan. The general saw in it an illustration of the strength and confidence of the enemy opposed to him. Lincoln wished to know when McClellan would attack; McClellan replied that the attack would be made "after to-morrow, as soon as Providence will permit."[4]

emy seemed to be to attack Richmond by regular approaches. The strength of his left wing rendered a direct assault injudicious, if not impracticable. It was therefore determined to construct defensive lines, so as to enable a part of the army to defend the city, and leave the other part free to cross the Chickahominy and operate on the north bank. By sweeping down the river on that side, and threatening his communications with York River, it was thought that the enemy would be compelled to retreat or give battle out of his intrenchments."—(*Lee's Rep.*, i., 5.) "The earthworks designed by Lee were of considerable magnitude, and were constructed in different shape, to suit the conformation of the ground. They swept all the roads, crowned every hillock, and mounds of red earth could be seen, in striking contrast with the rich green aspect of the landscape. Redoubts, rifle-pits, casemate-batteries, horn-works, and enfilading batteries were visible in great numbers in and out of the woods in all directions. Some were mounted with heavy siege-pieces of various calibre, but the majority were intended for field-guns."—(*Southern Generals*, 52.)

[1] Stuart's Report, *Reb. Rec.*, v., 192.

[2] "The burning of two schooners laden with forage, and fourteen government wagons, the destruction of some sutlers' stores, the killing of several of the guard and teamsters at Garlick's Landing, and some little damage done at Tunstall's Station, and a little *éclat*, were the precise results of this expedition."—*McC. Rep.*, 231.

[3] *Lee's Rep.*, i., 5, 6, 60.

[4] "Yours of to-day, making it probable that Jackson has been re-enforced by about ten thousand from Richmond, is confirmed. . . . If this be true, it is as good as a re-enforcement to you of equal force. I could better dispose of things if I could know about what day you can attack Richmond."—(Lincoln to McClellan, June 18.) "Our army is well over the Chickahominy . . . the rebel lines run within musket range of ours. Each has heavy supports at hand. A general engagement may take place any hour. An advance by us involves a battle more or less decisive. They have certainly great numbers and extensive works. If ten or fifteen thousand men have left Richmond to re-enforce Jackson, it illustrates their strength and confidence. After to-morrow we shall fight the rebel army as soon as Providence will permit. We shall await only a favorable condition of earth and sky, and the completion of some necessary preliminaries."—(McClellan to Lincoln, same day, *Com. Rep.*, 336, 337.)

Jackson commenced his march to join Lee on the 17th. It was expected that he would be at Ashland, fifteen miles from the extreme right of the Federal line, on the 24th. Up to this time McClellan believed him to be at Gordonsville, seventy miles away. Reports, industriously circulated so as to reach Washington, placed him every where: at Gordonsville, at Port Republic, at Harrisonburg, at Luray, and even at New Creek—a hundred or a hundred and fifty miles from his real position. Some informants said that he was moving toward Richmond; others that he was to march upon Washington and Baltimore as soon as McClellan should attack Richmond. The President believed that these reports were mere blinds, and suspected that the real movement was toward Richmond, as it proved to be.[1]

Picket-firing and desultory skirmishing with artillery had been going on all along at intervals. On the 25th, the "bridges and intrenchments being at last completed, an advance of our picket-line on the left was ordered, preparatory to a general forward movement." The object was to ascertain the nature of the ground beyond a belt of swampy woods half a mile in front of Fair Oaks Farm. The attempt was vigorously opposed, and a desultory fight occurred, lasting from eight in the morning to five in the afternoon: "not a battle, but merely an affair of Heintzelman's corps, supported by Keyes," with some aid from Sumner. According to McClellan, his point was fully gained. The Confederates give a different report of the "affair." As events happened, it matters little whether or not a few hundred yards were here won. The "forward movement" for which it was preparatory was made the next day, but by Lee, not by McClellan.[2]

At five o'clock McClellan telegraphed to Washington that the "affair is over, and we have gained our point fully . . . all is now quiet." An hour and a half later another dispatch from him went over the wires. It said that Jackson's advance was at Hanover Court-house; Beauregard was at Richmond; there were 200,000 men opposed to him; he should probably be attacked next day; he would do all he could, and, if his army was destroyed by overwhelming numbers, he could at least die with it, and share its fate; if the result of the coming action was disaster, he was not responsible; there was no use of again asking for re-enforcements.[3]

There were, indeed, some errors in this dispatch. None of Beauregard's army had come to Richmond. Instead of 200,000, the Confederates had barely half as many effective men; instead of "having to contend with vastly superior odds," McClellan's army was somewhat in excess of the enemy. Beauregard was at a quiet watering-place in Alabama, because his "physicians urgently recommended rest and recreation." These physicians were apparently none other than Jefferson Davis and his chief adviser Benjamin, who, to say nothing of old grudges dating as far back as Bull Run, were displeased with his abandonment of Corinth.[4] But the essential part was true. Jackson, for once a day behind his time, was near Hanover Court-house, with not merely his advance, but with his whole force. He himself had been that day at Richmond, where a general council of war was held, at which the plan of attack for the next day was settled;[5] and two hours before the dawn of the next morning six divisions of the Confederate army would be on their march beyond the Chickahominy, to fall upon the Union right, not half their number, isolated on the north side of the stream.[6]

[1] *McC. Rep.*, 235, 236.

[2] This "affair" is named by the Confederates the Battle of King's School-house. Its actual results appear to be that the Federals lost about 600 men—516, not including Palmer's brigade, as stated by McClellan; the Confederates, probably, not quite as many. McClellan says (*Rep.*, 236, 237): "Our object was fully accomplished; the enemy was driven from his camps." Wright, who commanded the Confederate centre, says (*Lee's Rep.*, i., 386): "When the fight ceased at dark, I occupied the very line my pickets had been driven from in the morning, and which I continued to hold until the total rout of the Federal army on the 29th." Lee says (*Rep.*, i., 6): "The enemy attacked on the Williamsburg road. The effort was successfully resisted, and our line maintained."

[3] "Several contrabands just in give information confirming supposition that Jackson's advance is at or near Hanover Court-house, and that Beauregard arrived with strong re-enforcements in Richmond yesterday.

"I incline to think that Jackson will attack my right and rear. The rebel force is stated at (200,000) two hundred thousand, including Jackson and Beauregard. I shall have to contend against vastly superior odds if these reports be true. But this army will do all in the power of men to hold their position and repulse any attack.

"I regret my great inferiority in numbers, but feel that I am in no way responsible for it, as I have not failed to represent, repeatedly, the necessity of re-enforcements; that this was the decisive point, and that all the available means of the government should be concentrated here. I will do all that a general can do with the splendid army I have the honor to command, and if it is destroyed by overwhelming numbers, can at least die with it, and share its fate.

"But if the result of the action, which will probably occur to-morrow, or within a short time, is a disaster, the responsibility can not be thrown on my shoulders; it must rest where it belongs. Since I commenced this, I have received additional intelligence confirming the supposition in regard to Jackson's movements and Beauregard's arrival. I shall probably be attacked to-morrow, and now go to the other side of the Chickahominy to arrange for the defense on that side. I feel that there is no use in my again asking for re-enforcements."—*McC. Rep.*, 238.

[4] *Southern Generals*, 237.—After the evacuation of Corinth, May 30th, "Mr. Davis telegraphed to General Bragg to assume permanent command. General Beauregard was thus laid on the shelf, not to be reinstated, as Mr. Davis passionately declared, though the whole world should urge him to that measure."—(General Jordan, Beauregard's Chief of Staff, in *Harper's Magazine* for *October*, 1865.) For some of the grounds of the old dispute between Davis and Beauregard, see *ibid.*; also *Southern Generals*, 223–225.

[5] POLLARD, ii., 311.

[6] *Lee's Rep.*, i., 122, 126, 173.

STRENGTH OF THE CONFEDERATE ARMY IN VIRGINIA FROM SEPTEMBER, 1861, TO JUNE, 1862.

General J. E. Johnston, at the request of the writer of this History, furnishes the following authentic statement of the force under his command during this period:

"January 3d, 1866.

"In September, 1861, the effective strength of the army under my command in Northern Virginia was about 37,000. It occupied Leesburg, Centreville and Manassas, and the Lower Occoquan.

"On the 31st of December it had been increased, by improved health and the addition of Loring's and Holmes's troops, to 54,000, including Jackson's command. Jackson's 8000 were near Winchester and Romney. There were 2600 at Leesburg; 31,800 at Centreville and Manassas; 7000 on the Lower Occoquan and near Dumfries; and 5000 about Fredericksburg. This army was much reduced during the winter by the effect of what we called the 'Bounty and Furlough Law,' but received some recruits from the South in the early spring. When, in April, it moved to Williamsburg, its strength (effective) was about 50,000, of which 6000 were left with Jackson in the Valley, and 6000 with Ewell, on the Rappahannock.

"The remaining 38,000 were sent to the position near Yorktown in two bodies. I accompanied the second, which arrived on the 17th of April. Magruder's own force was about 15,000, making our army at Yorktown near 53,000, exclusive of cavalry. Sickness and the fight at Williamsburg reduced this number by 6000. Our loss at Williamsburg was about 1800.

"According to the above numbers, the strength of this army, when it reached the neighborhood of Richmond, was about 47,000. To this were added, near the end of May, Anderson's and Branch's troops—about 13,000—and three brigades of Huger's division—not quite 7000. If the effect of sickness is not considered, this would make the army amount to 67,000 at the time of the fights at Fair Oaks and Seven Pines. On that occasion, four brigades of G. W. Smith's division were engaged at Fair Oaks; and at Seven Pines, D. H. Hill's four, and two of Longstreet's, were engaged on the 31st of May. On the morning of June 1st there were nine Confederate brigades at Fair Oaks, five of them fresh, and thirteen at Seven Pines, seven of them fresh—that is to say, which had not been engaged the day before."

CAMP LEE, HEAD-QUARTERS, NEAR RICHMOND.

CONSCRIPT OFFICE, CAMP LEE.

CHAPTER XX.
THE PENINSULAR CAMPAIGN.
III. FROM THE CHICKAHOMINY TO THE JAMES.

Plans of Operations.—The Strength of the Armies.—Lee's General Order.—*Battle of Mechanicsville*, or *Beaver Dam Creek*: The March from Richmond.—The Federal Position.—The Attack upon the Right.—The Attack upon the Left.—Repulse of the Confederates.—McClellan's Plans.—Change of Base resolved upon.—*Battle of Cold Harbor*, or *Gaines's Mill*: The Federals fall back.—The new Position.—Advance of the Confederates.—The Assault by A. P. Hill.—Its Repulse.—General Assault by Longstreet, D. H. Hill, and Jackson.—Porter hard pressed.—Slocum re-enforces him.—The Union Line broken.—Ineffectual Cavalry Charge.—Batteries captured.—Arrival of French and Meagher.—The Pursuit checked.—The Federals cross the Chickahominy.—Operations on the right Bank.—The Fight at Golding's Farm.—The Council of War.—McClellan's Letter to the Secretary of War.—Results of the Battle.—Peril of Richmond.—The Change of Base.—Topography of the Region.—The Federal Retreat.—Lee's Embarrassment.—Stuart at the White House.—The Confederate Pursuit.—Skirmish at Price's Farm.—*Battle of Savage's Station*: Heintzelman's unauthorized Retreat.—Destruction of Stores.—Magruder's Attack.—The Retreat continued.—*Battle of Frazier's Farm*, or *Charles City Cross Roads*: The Confederate Pursuit.—Lee's Plan of Operations.—Why it failed.—Holmes's and Wise's Movements.—The Federal Position.—Longstreet's Attack.—McCall's Defense.—The Fight in the Woods.—Hooker's and Kearney's Divisions.—A. P. Hill's Attack.—Gains Ground.—Is repulsed.—Close of the Action.—The Result.—McCall's Division.—*Battle of Malvern Hill*: The Federal Position.—Repulse of D. H. Hill in the Morning.—Lee's Order.—Magruder and D. H. Hill attack in the Afternoon.—The Battle as seen from both Sides.—The Confederates repulsed.—Condition of their Force.—McClellan retreats to Harrison's Landing.—Errors in this Campaign.—Lee's first Error should have been fatal.—McClellan's Error at Cold Harbor.—His Failure to attack Richmond.—His general Failure as a Commander.—Absent at all important Moments.—Lee's second strategical Error.—Position and Movements during the six Days.—Lee's Error at Malvern.—McClellan's last Error.—Jackson in the Battles.—General Review of the Subject.—The Losses in these Battles.

THURSDAY, June 26th, had been fixed upon by both McClellan and Lee as the day when each was to commence an offensive movement. Neither was aware of the intention, and each was deceived as to the object and position of the other. Lee presumed that McClellan intended to lay siege to Richmond by regular approaches. The city was in no condition to sustain a prolonged and close investment. It was not provisioned for a fortnight in advance, and its line of supply was liable to be interrupted at any moment. His object was simply to raise the siege. This he proposed to do by assailing McClellan at the point where he himself was most vulnerable: by threatening his line of communications with the York River, whence, as Stuart's raid had shown, his supplies were wholly drawn. McClellan's purpose was to attack Richmond by direct assault.[1]

The armies by which these two plans were to be carried out were almost equal in number, character of troops, and equipment. Each consisted of a little more than 100,000 effective men, present for duty. Making every allowance for defective reports on either side, the difference could not have been more than 5000. In a contest between forces so nearly balanced, the victory would rest with that which was most ably commanded. The general who made the fewest errors would win.[2]

---

[1] "The intention of the enemy seemed to be to attack Richmond by regular approaches. By sweeping down the Chickahominy on the north side, and threatening his communications with York River, it was thought that the enemy would be compelled to retreat or give battle out of his intrenchments."—(*Lee's Rep.*, i., 5.) "On the 25th, our bridges and intrenchments being at last completed, an advance of our picket line on the left was ordered, preparatory to a general forward movement." "On the 26th, the day upon which I had decided as the time for our final advance, the enemy attacked our right, and turned my attention to the protection of our communications and dépôts of supply."—(*McC. Rep.*, 236, 239.)

[2] The strength of McClellan's force at this time is fixed within a few hundreds by official evidence. McClellan (*Report*, 53) states its numbers (from which should properly be deducted 1101 men with Colonel Ingalls, Quartermaster, at the White House) on the 20th of June to have been, "Officers and men, present for duty, 105,825." This is exclusive of Dix's Corps of 10,000 at Fortress Monroe, which was too far removed to take any part in the operations. The Report of

Lee's plan of operations was carefully elaborated by himself and Jefferson Davis, and carried into execution under the eye and by the direction of both, who were on the field, and under fire at the most decisive points. A chance shot might at any moment, by killing either, have changed the whole course of the war.[1]

The whole scheme of operations was set forth on the 24th, in an elaborate General Order from Lee, in which the movements of each division were carefully prescribed. A. P. Hill, Longstreet, and D. H. Hill, with 34,000 men, were to march from before Richmond, cross the Chickahominy above the extreme right of the Union lines, and join Jackson, who, with 30,000, was coming down from the north. Half of the cavalry were also to cross the Chickahominy. On the south side of the river were left only Huger's and Magruder's divisions, numbering 24,000, and the reserve artillery and the remaining cavalry, about 3000 in all, making less than 30,000 men of all arms on that side.[2] This plan involved one error, which should have

---

McClellan's adjutant general of the same day (*Com. Rep.* 337) gives the apportionment of this force. From this number should be deducted the losses by casualty and sickness for the week between the 20th and the 26th. These, including the 600 killed and wounded in the "affair" of the 25th, could not vary greatly from 1500.

The Confederate force consisted of the divisions of Huger, Magruder, Longstreet, A. P. Hill, and D. H. Hill, the reserve artillery of Pendleton, and Stuart's cavalry, in front of Richmond; and Jackson's command, comprising the three divisions of himself, Ewell, and Whiting, coming down from the Valley of the Shenandoah. To these are to be added a portion of Holmes's division and Wise's brigade, brought over from the other side of the James River near the close of the operations. A. P. Hill (*Lee's Rep.*, i., 173), D. H. Hill (*Ibid.*, i., 187), and Holmes (*Ibid.*, i., 151) give the number of their force. Longstreet does not state his, but four of his six brigade commanders (*Ibid.*, i., 330, 331, 346, 353) give the number in their brigades, which enables us to fix very nearly the strength of the whole division. Magruder (*Ibid.*, i., 190) gives his, and (*Ibid.*, i., 191, 202) enables us, in connection with the statements of two of his four brigade commanders (*Ibid.*, i., 367, 371), to fix very nearly that of Huger. Pendleton (*Ibid.*, i., 224) enumerates fifteen batteries as constituting the reserve artillery; to each of these we assign 100 men. Stuart's cavalry (*Ibid.*, i., 398) consisted of six regiments and three legions: we give the strength wholly by estimate. The precise numbers are, however, of little consequence, as the cavalry was not actually employed on either side. The main possible source of error in estimating the Confederate force consists in fixing the strength of Jackson's command, of which we find no official statement. The lowest probable estimate is 27,000, the highest 35,000; we put it at 30,000, not merely as a medium between the two, but as the one which, upon careful examination, appears to be the closest approximation to the truth.

From the foregoing data we educe the following table, representing the effective force upon each side on the 26th of June.

UNION FORCES.		CONFEDERATE FORCES.	
Sumner's Corps	17,581	A. P. Hill's Division	14,000
Heintzelman's Corps	18,810	D. H. Hill's Division	10,000
Keyes's Corps	14,610	Longstreet's Division	10,000
Porter's Corps	19,960	Magruder's Division	13,000
Franklin's Corps	19,405	Huger's Division	11,000
McCall's Division	9,514	Holmes's Division	7,000
McClellan's Staff, Engineers, Cavalry Division, Provost Guard, etc.	4,844	Jackson's Command	30,000
		Pendleton's Artillery	1,500
	104,724	Stuart's Cavalry	4,000
Deduct losses, June 20 to 26 (say)	1,500		
Entire Force, June 26	103,224	Entire Force, June 26	100,500

Besides this effective force, "present for duty," each army contained many sick. Of these, on the 20th of June, there were in McClellan's army 12,225, probably increased on the 26th to 13,000; moreover, there were nearly 30,000 reported as "absent," a considerable portion of whom were undoubtedly away on sick-leave. We have no means of ascertaining the number of these in the Confederate army; but scattered incidentally through the reports are evidences that it was very considerable. It is clear, however, that Lee brought into the field every effective man at his disposal.

[1] "The plan was submitted to his Excellency the President, who was repeatedly on the field in the course of its execution."—(*Lee's Rep.*, i., 5.) The presence of Davis is repeatedly mentioned in the reports of different officers. We find him on the 26th giving direction for the battle at Mechanicsville; on the 27th and 28th we find him on the field; and on the 30th at Frazier's Farm, where "the fight was commenced by fire from the enemy's artillery, which swept down the road, and from which his Excellency the President narrowly escaped accident."—(*Ibid.*, i., 177.)

[2] The following are the most important portions of the General Orders of Lee, "No. 75; June 24th (*Lee's Rep.*, i., 44, 45):

"General Jackson's command will proceed to-morrow from Ashland toward the Slash Church, and will encamp at some convenient point west of the Central Railroad. Branch's brigade of A. P. Hill's division will also, to-morrow evening, take position on the Chickahominy, near Half Sink. At 3 o'clock Thursday morning, 26th instant, General Jackson will advance on the road

ASHLAND.

MECHANICSVILLE.

insured his destruction. It was made on the assumption that the bulk of the Union army was still on the north side of the Chickahominy, whereas, of the 100,000 men of which it was composed, only 30,000 were on that side; the remaining 70,000 had already crossed, and were strongly posted on the south side.[1] While thus assailing the Union army on that side with double its force, he left Richmond open to assault from more than twice the number by which it was defended. But the very magnitude of the error prevented its being suspected. Neither McClellan nor one of his generals ever imagined that Richmond was practically uncovered. It is curious to find that during the 27th—the decisive day—while on the north side of the river the Confederate force was two to one, and on the south side the Union force two to one, the commanders on both sides, and at all points, believed themselves to be fighting with or confronted against superior numbers.

TUESDAY, JUNE 26.—MECHANICSVILLE.[2]

During the evening of the 25th—at almost the hour when McClellan was awakened from the dream of rejoicing over what he thought the successful result of the advance of his picket line preparatory for the final advance of his whole army on the following day, by the unwelcome tidings that Jackson was close at hand, threatening his right and rear—A. P. Hill had marched northward and concentrated his whole division near Meadow Bridge. Branch's brigade had gone still farther in order to communicate with Jackson, who was to be at that point at early dawn; the whole movement being entirely hidden by the formation of the ground from the view of the Union pickets on the opposite side of the Chickahominy.[3] Two and three hours after midnight Longstreet and D. H. Hill commenced their still longer march through mud and darkness in the same direction, reaching their assigned positions in front of Mechanicsville at eight in the morning.[4] Branch waited for six hours for the approach of Jackson. At ten word was sent that he was close at hand. Branch then crossed the Chickahominy, and moved slowly down its north bank, driving the Union pickets before him. A. P. Hill, with the rest of his division, waited at their post for hours, also momently expecting the approach of Jackson. Three o'clock came, and yet no tidings.

JAMES LONGSTREET.

Jackson had been delayed by the Union skirmishers spread out along his line of march. Hill resolved to cross at once, rather than to hazard the failure of the whole plan by longer deferring the execution of his part of it. The crossing was effected without serious opposition, and the bulk of the division, Branch being yet far behind, pressed down toward Mechanicsville. Here, but on the south side of the stream, Longstreet and D. H. Hill were in waiting, and, after a little delay in repairing the bridge, also crossed the Chickahominy, the Union advance falling back from the village for a mile to a position beyond Beaver Dam Creek.

This was held by two brigades of McCall's Pennsylvania Reserves, who had joined McClellan a fortnight before. The position was a strong one—the creek curving around Mechanicsville for a mile; the water, waist-deep, was five or six yards wide, with steep banks. It was impassable for artillery except by bridges on two roads, one crossing at Ellison's Mill, near its mouth, the other a mile above. These roads and the open fields between them were commanded by artillery, and the whole line on the north bank was defended by rifle-pits and felled trees. The position could be carried in front only by a superior force, and with heavy loss. But it could be turned on the right; and A. P. Hill supposed that this had been already done by Jackson, who would then have interposed his force between McCall and Porter, cutting off both retreat and re-enforcements. Without waiting to ascertain whether this had been accomplished, Hill marched his whole division across the open fields, swept by the Union batteries. The main stress of his attack was at first directed upon the Union right at the upper road, which was held by Reynolds. The Confederates advanced gallantly under a murderous fire, and reached the edge of the creek. A few even succeeded in crossing above Reynolds's position, and gained a lodgment on the opposite side; but they effected nothing. Elsewhere the assault was repulsed, the assailants suffering fearfully.

Davis and Lee, who were watching the fight from different positions on the other side of the Chickahominy, ordered D. H. Hill to send forward a brigade to the support of the division which had been roughly handled. Ripley's was dispatched, and a little before dark aided A. P. Hill in a furious assault upon the Union left at Ellison's Mill, which was held by Seymour. The attack failed even more disastrously than that upon the right. At 9 o'clock, the Confederates, repulsed at all points, fell back beyond artillery range, and the firing gradually ceased.

This action was fought on the Union side wholly by Reynolds's and Seymour's brigades, numbering 6000, and five brigades of the Confederates, numbering about 12,000. The Confederate loss in killed and wounded was about 1500, of which two fifths fell upon Ripley's single brigade. The Union troops had every advantage in position, and their loss was not more than 300.[1]

---

leading to Pale Green [Walnut Green] Church, communicating his march to General Branch, who will immediately cross the Chickahominy, and take the road leading to Mechanicsville. As soon as the movements of these columns are discovered, General A. P. Hill, with the rest of his division, will cross the Chickahominy near Meadow Bridge, and move direct upon Mechanicsville. To aid his advance, the heavy batteries on the Chickahominy will at the proper time open upon the batteries at Mechanicsville. The enemy being driven from Mechanicsville, and the passage across the bridge opened, General Longstreet, with his division and that of General D. H. Hill, will cross the Chickahominy at or near that point—General D. H. Hill moving to the support of General Jackson, and General Longstreet supporting General A. P. Hill—the four divisions keeping in communication with each other, and moving *en echelon* on separate roads, if practicable. The left division in advance, with skirmishers and sharpshooters extending in their front, will sweep down the Chickahominy and endeavor to drive the enemy from his position above New Bridge; General Jackson, bearing well to his left, turning Beaver Dam Creek, and taking the direction toward Coal Harbor. They will then press forward toward the York River Railroad, closing upon the enemy's rear, and forcing him down the Chickahominy. Any advance of the enemy toward Richmond will be prevented by vigorously following his rear, and crippling and arresting his progress. The divisions of General Huger and Magruder will hold their positions in front of the enemy against attack, and make such demonstrations, Thursday, as to discover his operations. Should opportunity offer, the feint will be converted into a real attack; and should an abandonment of his intrenchments by the enemy be discovered, he will be closely pursued. . . . Commanders of divisions will cause their commands to be provided with three days' cooked rations. The necessary ambulances and ordnance trains will be ready to accompany the divisions, and receive orders from their respective commanders."

Magruder states (*Lee's Rep.*, i., 191) that when these orders had been executed "there were but 25,000 men between the enemy's army of 100,000 and Richmond." He underrates the actual force of all arms by some 3000.

[1] Lee seems never to have discovered this error, for in his Report, prepared eight months later, he says (p. 8): "The principal part of the enemy was now [June 27th] on the north side of the Chickahominy."

[2] The battle of Thursday, June 26th, is usually styled by Federal authorities that of Beaver Dam, from the small stream on whose banks it was fought; Lee, and all Confederate authorities, more properly call it that of Mechanicsville. Lee calls the battle of the 27th that of the Chickahominy; by the majority of Union authorities it is styled that of Gaines's Mill; but we follow all other Confederate Reports, and designate it as the battle of Cold Harbor. Various names have been given to the action of June 30th, such as Glendale, Charles City Cross Roads, and White Oak Swamp; we follow Lee and all other Confederate Reports, and call it the battle of Frazier's Farm, that being the place where the sharpest fighting occurred.

[3] *Lee's Rep.*, i., 173, 258.   [4] *Ibid.*, i., 122, 180.

ELLISON'S MILL.

[1] For the data upon which the losses in this and subsequent battles are estimated, see Note at

JOHN F. REYNOLDS.

From the moment when McClellan learned of the approach of the enemy on his right, he wisely gave up all idea of maintaining his position on the north bank of the Chickahominy. At noon of the 26th he telegraphed to the Secretary of War that his pickets were being driven in, he supposed by Jackson's advance-guard; that his communications would probably be cut off, and even Yorktown might be recaptured; the case was a desperate one, but he would do his best to outmanœuvre, outwit, and outfight the enemy.[1] The Quartermaster at West Point was directed to send supplies to the front to the last moment; to hurry the remaining stores up the James River, burning every thing which could not be got off—to prepare, in fact, for a change of base from the York to the James River—a change which should have been made weeks before.[2] More than a week before, McClellan had made some arrangements looking to this movement. Had it been undertaken in time, the whole course of the campaign must have been changed. Lee, instead of raising the siege of Richmond by threatening the line to the York River, must have assailed McClellan in his intrenchments, or subjected the ill-provisioned city, with its immense protecting army, to the hazard

of a siege or of direct assault. This change of base demanded that the whole army should be united on the south side of the Chickahominy. McClellan thought that Jackson—whose force was supposed to be the whole, instead of less than half, of that opposed to him on the right—was so close that the trains could be saved only by accepting battle on the north side. He did not expect to win a decisive victory. His utmost hope was to hold his own for a few hours.[1] The battle was to be fought by Porter, and McClellan wished to give him all the re-enforcements which could be spared from the other side of the river. He asked each commander of a corps on the south side how many men he could spare to re-enforce Porter, after retaining sufficient to hold his own position for twenty-four hours. The answers showed that not one of them imagined that the greater part of the force of the enemy which had confronted them had been withdrawn and was now on the other side. Keyes wanted to keep all the men he had, "if the enemy is as strong as ever in front;" Heintzelman would undertake to hold his intrenchments with four brigades, which would leave two disposable for service on the other side of the river. The afternoon of the next day, when the battle of Cold Harbor hung in even scale, Franklin, half of whose corps had already been sent over, did not think it prudent to take any more troops from him; and Sumner ventured only to say that he could send two of his eight brigades, and even that would be hazardous.[2] These two brigades were sent, but an hour too late to change the fortune of the day. They were too late to take part in the battle, but just in time to prevent a sore defeat from becoming a total rout.

FRIDAY, JUNE 27.—COLD HARBOR.

The position at Beaver Dam Creek was far in advance of the main force and easily turned. During the night the force which had held it was quietly withdrawn, leaving only enough to serve as a blind, and they were to retreat as the enemy advanced. A new line was taken up five miles below. The thirty heavy guns which had been placed in batteries between these two positions were removed across the Chickahominy, with nearly all the wagons of Porter's corps, and New Bridge, the upper one on the stream, was destroyed behind them. This was done during the night, and as the morning of the 27th broke, hot and sultry, Porter and McCall, freed from all impedimenta, stood ready for action.

The position was a strong one. A small unnamed stream, curving sickle-wise, empties into the Chickahominy. The banks are in most places fringed with a belt of swamp, but in places they rise steeply, and the bed of the stream forms a ravine. On the eastern side the land rises in a gradual slope crossed by gullies, about fifty feet above the swamp, and spreads into a flat table-land, with here and there a gentle swell. Patches of woodland dot the plain, which is mostly cleared and cultivated, the farm-houses standing alone each in the midst of its own fields. Two places find names on the map: New Cold Harbor, nearest the Chickahominy, and Cold Harbor a mile northward. Each consists of two or three dilapidated houses, a rifle-shot apart. Cold Harbor was the centre of Porter's line, which thence turned sharply eastward for a mile. The whole semicircular line covered the heads of the bridges crossing the Chickahominy. Hasty preparations had been made for defense. The trees in the swamp had been felled; rifle-

TRUMAN SEYMOUR.

the end of this chapter. The Reports of the various Confederate Commanders are very minute, and fully set forth the completeness of their defeat.

Lee says (*Report*, i., 6): "Jackson's march on the 26th was longer than had been anticipated, and his progress also being retarded by the enemy, A. P. Hill did not begin his movement until 3 P.M., when he crossed the river and advanced upon Mechanicsville. Longstreet and D. H. Hill crossed the Mechanicsville bridge as soon as it could be repaired, but it was late before they reached the north bank. D. H. Hill's leading brigade, under Ripley, advanced to the support of the troops engaged, and at a late hour united with Pender's brigade of A. P. Hill's division in an effort to turn the enemy's left; but the troops were unable, in the growing darkness, to overcome the obstructions, and after sustaining a destructive fire of musketry and artillery at short range were withdrawn."

D. H. Hill (*Ibid.*, i., 180) says: "I had received several messages from General Lee, and one from the President of the Confederate States, to send forward a brigade. In advancing this brigade I met General Pender, whose brigade had just been roughly handled, who told me that, with the assistance of two regiments of Ripley's brigade, he could turn the position at Ellison's Mill by the right, while two regiments should advance in front. General Ripley was ordered to co-operate with Pender, and the attack was made about dark. The enemy had intrenchments of great strength and development on the other side of Beaver Dam, and had the banks lined with his magnificent artillery. The approach was over an open plain, exposed to a murderous fire of all arms, and an almost impassable stream was to be crossed. The result was, as might have been anticipated, a disastrous and bloody repulse."

Ripley (*Ibid.*, i., 230) says: "I was informed by General A. P. Hill that the enemy had a strong and well-served battery and force in position near Ellison's Mill, to attack which he had sent Pender's brigade by the right, and other troops to the left; and it was arranged that my brigade should co-operate. While the troops were in motion I received orders to assault the enemy from General Lee, and also from General D. H. Hill. Night coming on, and it being deemed important to attack the position at once, the advance was ordered along the whole line. We drove back the enemy from his advanced positions, and closed in upon the batteries and their heavy infantry supports, all of which poured upon our troops a heavy and incessant fire of shell, canister, and musketry. The ground was rugged, and intersected by ditches, and covered with abatis a short distance in front of the position to be assaulted. A mill-race, with scarped banks, and in some places waist-deep in water, ran along the front of the enemy, at a distance ranging from fifty to one hundred yards. To this position our troops succeeded in advancing, notwithstanding the fire of the enemy was exceedingly severe. The loss was heavy in the extreme, amounting in the 44th Georgia to 335, and in the 3d North Carolina to 142. Some time after nightfall our troops were withdrawn. The fragments of the 3d North Carolina and the 44th Georgia were rallied some distance in the rear, under some difficulty, owing to the loss of all their field and many of their company officers." In this assault of hardly an hour's duration Ripley's single brigade of 2366 men lost 574 in killed and wounded—more than one fourth being killed outright.

A. P. Hill (*Ibid.*, i., 174), after describing the several assaults made by his division, and their "failure with heavy loss," adds: "It was never contemplated that my division alone should have sustained the shock of this battle; but such was the case, and the only assistance I received was from Ripley." Each of Hill's four brigade commanders who were engaged in this action speak of heavy losses in their command.   [1] McC. Rep., 240.

[2] *Ibid.*, 241, 243—"The superiority of the James River route, as a line of attack and supply, is too obvious to need exposition."—*Ibid.*, 242.

[1] "Our retreat was a contingency I thought of; but my impression is, that up to the time of the battle of Gaines's Mill, I still hoped that we should be able to hold our own."—(McClellan, in *Com. Rep.*, 435.) "By desperate fighting, our right wing inflicted so severe a loss upon the enemy as to check his movement on the left bank of the river, and give us time to get our materiel out of the way."—*Ibid.*, 434.   [2] McC. Rep., 250-253.

NEW COLD HARBOR.

pits and barricades had been flung up on the hill-side; and the crest was crowned by the artillery, which could thus play over the heads of the infantry upon an advancing enemy; but the elaborate earth-works which now seam the region were the work of Grant, almost two years later. The plain over which was the approach to the front of this line was also swept by the heavy guns two miles away on the other side of the Chickahominy.

Butterfield held the extreme left of this line, extending to the swamps of the Chickahominy; next came Martindale—both of Morell's division—then Griffin's brigade; then Sykes, with his division: all of these, of Fitz-John Porter's corps, formed the first line. Behind this was McCall's division: Meade, then commander of a brigade, who was a year and a week after to win the battle of Gettysburg, the true turning-point of the war, was on the left; next Reynolds, in a few hours to be a prisoner of war; then Seymour, who a few hours before had crushed Ripley and Pender at Beaver Dam, as reserve behind the second line. Stoneman's cavalry were miles away to the north; they could be of no use on this field, which must be contested by infantry and artillery. Porter, fearing that Stoneman would be cut off by the advance of Jackson, sent orders to him to retreat to the White House, and afterward rejoin the army as best he could—where, no one knew.

If a battle was to be fought here by these forces, no stronger position could have been chosen, and no better dispositions made. Porter expected to be hard pressed in front; he hoped to hold his position without aid long enough to cover the retreat of the army; but he asked that some division on the other side should be held ready to support him.[1]

At dawn of the 27th the Confederates at Mechanicsville were astir. They had been aroused by a sharp artillery fire, and expected a renewal of the fight at Beaver Dam. After an hour they discovered that the firing was a ruse to detain them, and that the Federal forces had retired. Another hour was spent in repairing the bridges so that the artillery could cross; and then the divisions took up the line of march, as prescribed in Lee's order. D. H. Hill bore to the left to unite with Jackson, who was still behind, having encamped for the night within sound of the cannonade. A. P. Hill and Longstreet—Hill in advance—kept to the right, following the road along the Chickahominy. The march was slow and cautious, for on rounding any swell of land they might come upon their enemy in force. Noon had passed before five miles had been accomplished. Passing Gaines's Mill, where a slight skirmish occurred, from which has been given one of the names to the whole battle, they came in sight of the Union force drawn up on the hill-side beyond the unnamed creek. Between them lay an open plain a quarter of a mile wide, swept by artillery from the crest in front and from the other side of the Chickahominy, and bounded by a wood tangled with undergrowth, and traversed by a sluggish stream which converted the soil into a dense morass. Here a slight delay occurred to form the line.

It was past two o'clock[2] when Hill was directed to begin the assault. Longstreet was held back, because it was thought by Lee that Jackson's approach on the left, which was every moment expected, would cause the extension of the Union line in that direction. Hill's brigades dashed across the plain, floundered through the swamp, and pressed up the opposite slope in the face of a fierce fire of artillery and musketry. Some brigades advanced close to the infantry lines; a

few regiments even pierced them. But they were soon forced back. For two hours the battle raged with equal obstinacy on either side. The Federal troops gained ground, and from being assailed became the assailants. Hill was defeated, crushed, and almost routed. Some of his regiments stood their ground; others threw themselves flat on the earth to escape the withering fire; others rushed from the field in disorder.

The completeness of the defeat at this point is fully shown in the Confederate reports. Lee[1] and Hill[2] affirm it in general terms. Archer[3] says: "My troops fell back before the irresistible fire of artillery and rifles. The obvious impossibility of carrying the position without support prevented me from attempting to check the retreat. Had they not fallen back I would myself have ordered it." Pender[4] says: "My men were rallied and pushed forward again, but did not advance far before they fell back; and I think I do but justice to my men when I say that they did not commence it. The enemy were continually bringing up fresh troops, and succeeded in driving us from the road." Whiting, of Jackson's command, who came to the relief of these troops, says:[5] "Men were leaving the field in every direction, and in great disorder; two regiments, one from South Carolina and one from Louisiana, were actually marching back from the fire. The 1st Texas were ordered to go over them, and through them, which they did. . . . Near the crest, in front of us and lying down, appeared the fragments of a brigade. Men were skulking from the front in a shameful manner; the woods on our left and rear were full of troops in a safe cover, from which they never stirred. . . . Still farther on our extreme right our troops appeared to be falling back. . . . The troops on our immediate left I do not know, and I am glad I don't. Those that did come up were much broken, and no entreaty or command could induce them to come forward, and I have great reason to believe that the greater part never left the cover of the wood on the west side of the ravine." Whiting does great injustice to the troops of Hill. They were, indeed, defeated and broken, but it was after two hours of desperate fighting, under every disadvantage of position, against a force quite equal to them, as the record of their losses shows. Thus the regiment from South Carolina, which "was actually marching back under fire," must have been the "1st Rifles, S. C. Volunteers." Of this regiment its colonel, Marshall, reports:[6] "In that charge we sustained a loss of 76 killed, 221 wounded, and 58 missing; and on the next morning I had only 149 officers, non-commissioned officers, and privates for duty. Early on the morning after the battle I made a detail from each company to bury their dead, and so severe was the work of death in some of the companies that it took the detail all day to bury their dead;" and of those "missing" in the morning all but four rejoined their regiment.[7] Hill states the case fairly. After acknowledging the repulse, he says:[8] "My division was engaged full two

[1] Lee's Rep., i., 8.　　　[2] Ibid., i., 176.　　　[3] Ibid., i., 256.　　　[4] Ibid., i., 253.
[5] Ibid., i., 154.　　　[6] Ibid., i., 502.　　　[7] Ibid., i., 505.　　　[8] Ibid., i., 176.

AMBROSE P. HILL.

FITZ-JOHN PORTER.

DANIEL BUTTERFIELD.

hours before assistance was received. We failed to carry the enemy's lines, but we paved the way for the successful attack afterward, and in which attacks it was necessary to employ the whole of our army that side of the Chickahominy. About four o'clock re-enforcements came up on my right from General Longstreet, and later Jackson's men on my left and centre, and my division was relieved of the weight of the contest."

Longstreet's division had been drawn up in the rear of Hill, covered from fire by a low ridge. Lee, finding Hill sorely worsted, ordered Longstreet to make a feigned attack upon the left, hoping to divert a part of the Union force to that direction, and thus relieve Hill. Longstreet soon found that the force here was too strong to be disturbed by a mere feint, and that to be of service he must make a real attack with his whole force. Jackson now came into view; D. H. Hill, who had joined him, in advance, on the extreme right, Ewell and Whiting on the left, and Lawton a little in the rear. The line was now complete, and a general advance along its whole extent was ordered.

Porter, in the mean while, seeing the immense force advancing upon him, had, two hours before, asked for re-enforcements. Slocum's division of Franklin's corps had been all day kept in readiness on the south side of the Chickahominy for this purpose. They had, indeed, been ordered over at daybreak, and had begun to cross; but when half way over the order was countermanded. They were now hurried over, and came upon the field at half past four, when the general Confederate attack had been fairly com-

menced. Porter's whole line was so severely pressed at every point that he was forced to divide Slocum's force, sending parts of it, even single regiments, to the points most threatened.[1]

The general Confederate assault was commenced by D. H. Hill upon the extreme Union right, held by Sykes with his regulars. He opened by a sharp artillery fire; but in half an hour the battery was withdrawn badly crippled. Meanwhile he could hear, by the direction of the fire on his right, that the Federals were forcing A. P. Hill and Longstreet back. The assault must be made hand to hand. In the face of a fierce fire, by which his force

[1] *McC. Rep.*, 243–251. McClellan says (*Rep.*, 248): "At 3 30 Slocum's division reached the field, and was immediately brought into action at the weak points of our line." It is clear that he places the arrival of Slocum a full hour too early; for at 3 25 he telegraphed to Porter (*Ibid.*, 251): "Slocum is *now* crossing Alexander's Bridge with his whole command." To finish the crossing, form, march up the bank, and reach the field of action, must have required an hour or more. There is some confusion as to the recall of Slocum's division in the morning. McClellan says (*Rep.*, 243): "General Franklin received instructions to hold General Slocum's division in readiness by daybreak of the 27th, and if heavy firing should at that time be heard in the direction of General Porter, to move it at once to his assistance without farther orders;" and (*Ibid.*, 251) "Slocum's division commenced crossing the river to support Porter soon after daybreak on the morning of the 27th; but as the firing in front of Porter ceased, the movement was suspended." Franklin testifies (*Com. Rep.*, 622): "At seven o'clock in the morning of that day I was ordered to send Slocum's division to assist Porter. This order was countermanded about nine o'clock, after a part of the division had crossed the Chickahominy. The order to send the division over was signed by Colonel Colburn, and I sent back some word, I do not remember what. General Marcy answered that he hardly supposed the general commanding could have intended to send the division over; that there must have been some mistake about it, he thought. Then about nine o'clock, perhaps nearly ten, the order was countermanded, the order countermanding coming from General McClellan, though I do not remember who signed it. What was the reason for ordering the division back I do not know."

HENRY W. SLOCUM.

GEORGE A. McCALL.

was sorely galled, and some of the regiments thrown into disorder, he succeeded in passing the swamp in his front, and pressed up the opposite slope, only to be forced back. Ewell had come up on Hill's left, and attempted to carry the position in front of him; but most of his command gave way under the fierce fire which they encountered. "We were attacked," he says, "in front and flank by superior numbers, and were for hours without re-enforcements." The "hours" were less than an hour, and the "superior numbers" existed only in the imagination of the assailants, justifiable, indeed, by the terrible fire to which they were exposed. Trimble, of this division, led his brigade toward the Confederate right; he met two regiments coming out of the field in confusion, who cried out, "You need not go in; we're whipped; you can't do any thing!" "Get out of our way!" his men replied; "we will show you how to do it!" and they charged at a run across the field against the Union lines.[1] Still Ewell was losing ground, when Lawton's brigade came upon the field. This brigade, 4000 strong, composed wholly of Georgian troops, was a

THE FINAL CHARGE AT COLD HARBOR.

part of the force sent from Richmond a fortnight before to join Jackson, and "mask his withdrawal from the Valley." Jackson had incorporated this brigade with his "own" division, and it held the rear of his entire command. It was ordered forward from the place where it had been halted, two miles from the battle-field. Lawton went as rapidly as possible over a road blocked up by artillery and ambulances. Coming upon the field, he learned that Ewell "was sorely pressed, and that re-enforcements were promptly needed." Here he met two regiments standing in the open field, who had just been driven from the open woods. "I moved," he says, "through the interval between these regiments, promptly formed line of battle, and accepted the position which they had abandoned. A continuous line of 3500 men moving forward in perfect order, and at once opening fire along its entire length, chiefly armed with Enfield rifles, promptly marked the preponderance of musketry on our side." This long line advanced toward the thickest of the fight. In the wood Ewell was seen. He shouted "Hurrah for Georgia!" as he saw Lawton's long line advancing.[2]

It was now half past six, an hour before sunset. The whole Confederate force on this side of the Chickahominy, with the exception of Kemper's single brigade of "1433 muskets," of Longstreet's division, which was held in reserve,[3] was brought into action. Opposed to them were only Porter's corps, McCall's division, and Slocum's sent over from the other side. Making allowance for losses on each side up to this time, the Confederate force on the field numbered about 56,000; the Union force, 33,000.[4] The Confederates, at a fearful sacrifice, had crossed the swamp at all points, and thus neutralized the former great advantage of position against them. The Union

line was pressed along its whole length by a force of almost two to one. The crowning attack was made half an hour before sunset, and the Union line gave way almost simultaneously on the right, centre, and left. Where it first broke no one can say. Each Confederate commander believed that his troops gave the decisive blow. In our judgment the most decisive blow was struck near the centre, where Hood's Texans, of Whiting's division, charged upon a battery which was so posted that it had done fearful execution all through the fight. "In this charge, in which upward of a thousand men fell, killed and wounded, before the fire of the enemy, and in which fourteen pieces of artillery were captured, the Fourth Texas, under the lead of General Hood, was the first to pierce these strong-holds and seize the guns."[1] About the same time, Longstreet, on the extreme left, had driven back the Union force opposed to him, and was pressing them toward the brink of the Chickahominy. Five companies of cavalry, who had been kept in reserve, charged upon the pursuers, but were scattered at the first fire.[2]

D. H. Hill, on the Confederate left, had been annoyed by an isolated battery which swept the road by which he proposed to attack in flank the Union right. A sudden charge by two of his regiments captured this battery; it was held only for a few minutes, then retaken, and the Confederates driven back, the regiment which had captured the guns losing half its number in the work. Brief as the time was, it was enough. The temporary

---

[1] Lee's Rep., i., 309.　　　[2] Ibid., i., 270.　　　[3] Ibid., i., 124, 353.

[4] Confederates: Jackson, Longstreet, A. P. Hill, D. H. Hill, 64,000; deduct losses, thus far, 8000=56,000. Union: Porter, 19,000; McCall, 9000; Slocum, 8000=36,000; deduct losses, thus far, 3000=33,000. These are given merely as a close approximation to the actual numbers at that moment.

[1] Jackson in Lee's Rep., i., 135.

[2] [McC. Rep., 248; Lee's Rep., i., 124.] This slight cavalry affair is the only one in which that arm was actively engaged on either side during the seven days, with the exception of a Confederate charge two days later, which McClellan (Rep., 258) calls "a sharp skirmish with the enemy's cavalry;" but Bowers, the commander of the Confederate cavalry regiment, tells the exact story. He says (Lee's Rep., i., 417) that he charged upon the Federal cavalry, but was driven back, carrying with him two officers and eleven privates wounded, but leaving behind two more officers and "forty-six non-commissioned officers [and privates?] missing, being wounded, killed, and thrown from their horses."

CAVALRY CHARGE AT COLD HARBOR.

SKIRMISHING IN THE WOODS.

silence of the terrible battery enabled the rest of Hill's division to advance. The extreme right of the Union line gave way; it rallied, and was again forced back, not without disorder, toward the river-bank. Hill asserts[1] that it was "this final charge upon their right flank which decided the fortunes of the day." The truth is, that the Union line, now pressed along its whole length by a twofold force, which had at a fearful sacrifice overcome the advantage of position, gave way on every point almost at once, and fell back toward the bluff which here bounded the Chickahominy. They were followed, though cautiously, by the enemy in the twilight which was fast closing in.

It was not a rout, though fast threatening to become one. The core of every division remained solid, but fragments were flying off, like sparks from an iron under the blacksmith's hammer. But all, soldiers and fugitives, pressed toward the bridges which stretched through swamp and over river, beyond which lay safety. All at once a great shout was heard, and French's and Meagher's brigades—Meagher, they say, leading in his shirt sleeves—dashed up the bluff, driving through the stragglers, who were thronging toward the bridge, and advanced to what was now the front. Their presence gave heart to the fugitives, who rallied behind them and marched up the hill. The Confederates paused in the pursuit, and, after delivering a few ineffectual volleys, withdrew as night set in, and the battle was over. An hour earlier, and these two brigades alone would have turned the wavering scale and won a victory. As it was, they were just in time to prevent a great defeat from becoming a disastrous rout. D. H. Hill, moralizing afterward, says: "A vigorous attack might have resulted in the total rout of the Yankee army and the capture of thousands of prisoners. But I was unwilling to leave the elevated plateau and advance in the dark along an unknown road, skirted by dense woods, in the possession of the Yankees."[2]

When morning broke the whole Union force was safely across the Chickahominy, and the bridges behind them were down. Three regiments, at different points, had been isolated by the Confederate rush, were surrounded and made prisoners. Many stragglers, scattered through the wood, were picked up next day by the cavalry who scoured the region. In all, the Federals lost about 2000 prisoners, among whom was General Reynolds, who, three days later, at Richmond, met his division commander, McCall, captured in a subsequent battle. The Union loss in this action was about 4000 in killed and wounded; that of the Confederates, 9500. The Federals also lost 22 guns, of which 20 were captured by the enemy; the others were run off the bridge while crossing.

During the whole of this action, while Lee was with his troops controlling their movements and directing the fight, McClellan was on the opposite side of the river.[3] He was kept in alarm by the messages sent to him hour by

hour from different positions on that side. At half past eight, Smith, on the extreme right, reported that six or eight regiments had moved down to the woods in front of Sumner. At eleven, Sumner telegraphed that the enemy threatened an attack on his right, near Smith; and an hour and a half later, that there was sharp shelling on both sides; and two hours after, that there was sharp musketry firing in front, to which he was replying with artillery and infantry, and the man on the look-out reported that there were some troops—how many could not be made out—drawn up in line of battle opposite his right. Then, at intervals, Franklin reported. In the morning the enemy were massing heavy columns on his right; then, an attack had been begun there on Smith, which proved to be an artillery fire;[1] but his own shells were bursting well, and Smith thought Sumner would soon have a cross-fire upon the enemy which would silence them. At a quarter past five, Franklin, half of whose corps, under Slocum, were across the river, thought it not prudent to take any more troops from him at present. Ten minutes after, McClellan replied that Porter was hard pressed, and it was not a question of prudence, but of possibilities; if Franklin could possibly hold his position until dark with two brigades, he should send one to support Porter. This last order seems not to have reached Franklin, for he says that during the whole day he did not know that a battle was going on across the river.[2]

All the movements by the Confederates on this side of the Chickahominy are detailed at length by the different commanders. The substance is, that with pickets, skirmishers, and artillery, they felt the Union line along its whole length, showing themselves at points here and there, and then the force vanished, to reappear at a different spot, thus trebling their apparent numbers. The nature of the ground afforded facilities for these operations. There was a series of swamps, forests, low ridges, and ravines, which shut out all sight of what was passing at a few hundred yards' distance. If a body of troops showed itself at any point, no one could say whether it was a single regiment or the head of a full division. So an artillery fire upon any point

[1] Lee's Rep., i., 183.   [2] Ibid., i., 181.
[3] "During the battle at Gaines's Mills I was on the right bank of the river, at Dr. Trent's house, as the most central position."—McClellan's testimony, in Com. Rep., 435.

[1] McClellan writes (Report, 252) "from 3 pieces." This is probably a simply clerical error, for Franklin testifies (Com. Rep., 622), "We had put up a work during the night of the 26th. The enemy opened upon that work, and such of our artillery as he could see, early on the morning of the 27th, and there was a very severe cannonading, with 30 guns on each side, I should judge, lasting about an hour. Their object appeared to be to drive us away from Golding's, but it was evidently a diversion to prevent our sending assistance to Porter. There was no infantry fighting till about dark."
[2] McC. Rep., 251–253. Franklin testifies (Com. Rep., 623): "At my position at Golding's, the woods were so dense between Fitz-John Porter and myself that we did not hear a musket or heavy gun of his all day. We did not know that there was any infantry fight going on. We saw some of the enemy's infantry going up to attack what we supposed to be his position, and we shelled them as well as we could from our side. I was about two miles distant from the field of battle at Gaines's Mills." General J. E. Johnston reports a similar occurrence at Fair Oaks. Though not more than three miles from the battle-field of May 31, he did not hear the cannonading, which was yet distinctly audible at the Federal head-quarters, ten miles or more distant, across the stream. Johnston supposed that this was occasioned by some peculiar condition of the atmosphere.

might be a mere feint, or the prelude to an attack in force. All the shows of force which had all day long disturbed McClellan were but feints. The only real attack on that day, south of the Chickahominy, was just at sunset, when Toombs, anxious to distinguish himself, sent two small infantry regiments, re-enforcing them afterward, to force the Union pickets. The attempt cost dearly. Half of the Georgia Second went into action 271 strong, and lost 120; the Fifteenth carried in 370, and lost 70 in killed and wounded. Toombs claims that after "two hours of fierce and determined conflict" the Federals were "driven back and repulsed." Franklin says: "There was no infantry fighting until about dark, when two brigades of the enemy attacked Hancock's brigade, which was in position as the advance of the picket line. He had a sharp engagement for about three quarters of an hour, when the enemy was driven back. It was then entirely dark, too late to make any pursuit."[1]

Toward midnight McClellan held a council of war —the only one, apparently, during the campaign. Even then he seems to have had some purpose of recrossing the Chickahominy and risking another battle on that side. If the purpose was a serious one it was soon abandoned, and orders were given for a retreat to the James River.[2] He then wrote a bitter letter to the Secretary of War: He knew the whole history of the day. On this side of the river, the right bank, we repulsed several strong attacks; on the left our men did all that men could do, but they were repulsed by vastly superior numbers soon after he had brought his last reserves into action. If he had 20,000, or even 10,000 fresh troops to use to-morrow, he could take Richmond; but he had not a man in reserve, and he should be glad to cover his retreat and save the material and personnel of the army. A few thousand more men would have changed this battle from a defeat to a victory; as it was, the government could not hold him responsible for the result. "If I save this army now," he concludes, "I tell you plainly that I owe no thanks to you or to any other persons in Washington. You have done your best to sacrifice this army."[3]

RICHARD S. EWELL.

SATURDAY, JUNE 28.—THE RETREAT.

Lee had indeed won a formal victory, but at a fearful cost. In the two actions he had suffered a loss in killed and wounded of almost 10,000 men, double that which he had inflicted. He had indeed driven the enemy from the field of battle, and across the river; but this crossing was just what his opponent was endeavoring to effect. He had cut McClellan's line of communication and supply with the York River; but that line had been already given up, and a far better one chosen. To accomplish this, he had placed his army in a position which, had his opponent known it, rendered its destruction inevitable. Two thirds of it, 54,000 strong after its losses, was on the north side of the Chickahominy. The other third, ten miles away in a straight line, was before Richmond. Between them, and more than equal to both, the Union army, at last united, lay like a solid wedge. The river, which McClellan had so long found to be an impassable barrier, lay right between Lee's two wings, which he could unite only by retracing his two days' march up the left bank to Mechanicsville, then down the other side to Richmond. Had McClellan on the 28th or 29th struck at Richmond with his whole available force, the city must have fallen in five hours. The bridges being down, 25,000 men could have held the whole line of the Chickahominy from Bottom's Bridge to New Bridge, leaving fully 70,000 for the assault of Richmond, which was defended by only 27,000, along a line of nearly ten miles. The fall of Richmond must have involved the destruction or dispersion of the force across the Chickahominy, for at Richmond were his only dépôts of supplies. His men had marched out with only three days' rations, and were followed by a very small train. The rapidity of Jackson's march, and the nature of the country traversed, show that he could have only a meagre train. There is not the slightest reason to suppose that, away from Richmond, the Confederates had within a hundred miles provisions sufficient to supply Lee's 54,000 men for five days; and without supplies, an army in that time becomes a disorganized and paralyzed mass, incapable of offense or defense. If McClellan had but known

his own position and strength, and that of his opponent, he could hardly have wished that Lee should have placed his troops in any other position than that occupied by them just after the battle of Cold Harbor. Magruder, who was in chief command on the left bank, appreciated the sore peril of the Confederate capital and cause. He saw that a vigorous attack upon him could not be other than successful.[1]

But McClellan had resolved, instead of giving battle to Lee on the left side of the Chickahominy, or of assaulting Richmond on the right, to abandon the whole position, and retreat with his entire force to the James River. The different commanders were ordered to load the wagons with ammunition and provisions, and the necessary baggage of officers and men, and to destroy every thing which could not be carried off. The sick and wounded, who could not march or be carried, were to be left behind. These were fewer than might have been expected. Of the 13,000 on the sick-list, and the 3000 wounded in the two previous days, about 2500 in all were thus abandoned.

The problem of the "Change of Base" was, after all, a very simple one. It was merely to march an army for ten or fifteen miles with no enemy in front, but with one, erroneously supposed to be superior, in its rear, and upon one flank. The main difficulty was to carry off the guns and trains of supplies and ammunition. The country over which the march was to be made favored the retreating army. The retreat must indeed be slow, for the roads were few and difficult, but the pursuit must be slower, for these roads could be obstructed at every step.

Some three or four miles from the extreme left of the Union position White Oak Creek empties into the Chickahominy. This creek is bordered by a swamp. For five miles the stream has some volume, and the swamp is narrow, three or four hundred yards wide; then it spreads out, for eight miles toward Richmond, to a breadth of three miles or more. From the Chickahominy to the head of the swamp it was crossed by only two roads. Southward, toward the James, the ground rises slowly, and becomes a dry flat instead of a wet flat, but with swamps along the sluggish streams, cov-

[1] Lee's Rep., i., 280; Com. Rep., 622. This skirmish at Golding's Farm is the only affair which in any way justifies McClellan's assertion (Report, 257): "On the right bank we repulsed several strong attacks."

[2] Of this council Heintzelman testifies (Com. Rep., 355): "At about eleven o'clock I got a telegram that General McClellan wished to see me immediately at his head-quarters, about a mile and a half off. I found them all packed up and ready to move. The general stated the situation of affairs and what he proposed to do. One thing was to move across to the James River. The other plan was to collect all the troops from my side of the Chickahominy and have a battle the next day, and throw every thing upon the result of that battle. I asked him what would be the result if we lost. He said that if we were defeated the army would be lost, but he was inclined to risk every thing upon that battle, but to fall back from there to the James River; that we could reach there with a loss, perhaps, of a few pieces of siege artillery and some wagons, and then we could receive re-enforcements. He said that was his opinion; still, he felt inclined to risk every thing on a battle. The next day we commenced to retreat. That was the first time I was consulted in that campaign, any thing more than by mere conversation."—See also McC. Rep., 254, 255.

[3] McC. Rep., 257, 258.

[1] Magruder, in Lee's Rep., i., 191: "From the time at which the enemy withdrew his forces to this side of the Chickahominy and destroyed the bridges to the moment of his evacuation—that is, from Friday night until Sunday morning—I considered the situation of our army as extremely critical and perilous. The larger portion of it was on the other side of the Chickahominy; the bridges had all been destroyed, and but one was rebuilt, the New Bridge, which was fully commanded by the enemy's guns from Golding's; and there were but 25,000 men between his army of 100,000 and Richmond. I received repeated instructions during Saturday night from General Lee's head-quarters, enjoining upon my command the utmost vigilance, directing the men to sleep on their arms, and to be prepared for whatever might occur. I passed the night without sleep, and in the superintendence of their execution. Had McClellan massed his whole force in column, and advanced it against any point of our line of battle, as was done at Austerlitz by the greatest captain of any age, though the head of his column would have suffered greatly, its momentum would have insured him success, and the occupation of our works about Richmond, and consequently the city, might have been his reward. Our relief was therefore great when information reached us that the enemy had evacuated his works, and was retreating."

COMMENCEMENT OF THE RETREAT.—JUNE 29.

5 A

MAP OF THE REGION NEAR RICHMOND.

ered with scrubby forests, with here and there a clearing. The maps show roads in abundance and intricate confusion, but they are mainly mere paths, over some of which no wheeled vehicle had passed for years. Three roads, however, starting from Richmond, spread out like the sticks of a fan, and then unite half way between the swamp and Malvern Hill, the point to which McClellan directed his retreat. Thence they branch out in every direction: toward the lower bridges of the Chickahominy, some miles below the railroad, and toward the rich plantations which border the James. Just skirting the swamp is the Charles City Road, then the Central or Darbytown, then the Newmarket. It was by these roads that Longstreet and A. P. Hill, who, having recrossed the Chickahominy and turned the head of White Oak Swamp, marched to make their attack on the 30th upon the retreating column; and Magruder, coming from near Richmond, reached Malvern, where he was so disastrously beaten back on the 1st of July.

McClellan's retreat was in the following order: At noon on the 28th, Keyes, who lay nearest, crossed White Oak Creek and took position on its opposite bank, to cover the passage of the other troops and trains. These, which would have stretched for a distance of forty miles if drawn up in

single line—accompanied by a herd of 2500 cattle—were got safely over, and proceeded on their way, Keyes's corps guarding the advance. They reached the James River without molestation on the morning of the 30th. Franklin and Porter followed from the rear by the same route, and were over on the morning of the 29th. At daybreak of this day Heintzelman and Sumner evacuated their works in front, falling back toward Savage's Station, which they were to hold until night, and then to cross the swamp by the upper road. A part of these several corps were to keep a line of battle fronting toward the creek to check pursuit from the rear, while others were to take position across the three roads, and so fronting toward Richmond, in order to protect the trains passing behind them from assault in flank. McClellan, having given general directions for the movements and positions of the troops, rode to the James to select the best position on that river, and to consult with the naval commanders there.[1]

On the morning of the 28th Lee was wholly at a loss what next to do. There was no force in front of him on his side of the Chickahominy; but

---

[1] McC. Rep., 255-265.

DESTRUCTION OF THE TRAIN.

still McClellan might propose to cross the river lower down, and give battle, in order to preserve his communications with the York River. The cavalry, with Ewell's division of Jackson's command, were sent down to the railroad to observe the state of things there. As they approached, the few troops guarding the railroad passed the river, burning the bridge behind them. Ewell remained until evening, and then rejoined his command. Stuart, with his cavalry, dashed down the railroad toward the White House, which they reached next morning. With him was the proprietor of that estate, Fitz-Hugh Lee, son of the Confederate commander. The house was in flames; nearly all the immense quantity of stores accumulated here had been removed, and were on their way to the James.[1] The abandonment of the railroad and the destruction of the bridge showed that no attempt would be made to hold that line; but still it might be McClellan's purpose either to move upon Richmond or to reach the lower bridges on the Chickahominy, cross the stream, and retreat down the Peninsula. Lee was therefore forced to wait until the intent of his opponent was developed. During the night it was evident that the Union army was in motion, and the Confederate pickets failing to detect any approach to the lower bridges, it became evident that the retreat was toward the James River. So, early on the morning of the 29th, Longstreet and A. P. Hill were ordered to cross the Chickahominy by the New Bridge, which had been rebuilt by Magruder during the night of the 27th, and, crossing in front of Richmond, to move down by the Central Road; Magruder and Huger were to move by the Charles City Road, thus taking the Federal army on the flank; while Jackson at a later hour was to cross by the Grapevine Bridge, and move down near the right bank of the river, thus threatening the rear.[2]

SUNDAY, JUNE 29.—SAVAGE'S STATION.

At dawn Magruder discovered that the Federal works at Fair Oaks were abandoned, and Sumner and Heintzelman were slowly falling back toward Savage's Station. The works on the extreme right were held a little longer. An attack was made upon them, but it was repulsed, with a loss of 150.[3] Magruder, in the mean time, followed cautiously down the railroad, opening a distant fire at intervals—Sumner's retiring troops turning occasionally, and then keeping on the retreat. Late in the afternoon they had fallen back nearly to Savage's Station from the front and the right. Sumner and Heintzelman had been ordered to hold this point until nightfall, the positions of each being assigned to them by McClellan. But Heintzelman abandoned his position before the time, and crossed the swamp by the upper road, giving orders for the destruction of the ammunition and stores remaining at Savage's Station which could not be carried off by the trains. The stores and provisions were piled up in a great pyramid and set on fire. The ammunition and shells were heaped upon a train, which, with steam up, was sent down the railroad to the Chickahominy. Fire was set to the train, and before it reached the site of the bridge it was ablaze, and the shells began to explode. So great was the momentum, that the engine and first car leaped clear across the chasm and landed on the opposite side.

[1] Stuart (Lee's Rep., i., 402) gives a glowing account of the quantity of munitions and stores destroyed here. He says: "The conflagration had raged fearfully at the White House during the night previous, while explosions of shells rent the air. I was informed that 5000 men held the place. . . . Provisions and delicacies of every description lay in heaps, and the men regaled themselves on the fruits of the tropics as well as the substantials of the land. Large quantities of forage were left also. Nine large barges loaded with stores were on fire as we approached. Immense numbers of tents, wagons, and cars in long trains, loaded, and five locomotives; a number of forges; quantities of every species of quartermaster's stores and property, making a total of many millions of dollars—all more or less destroyed." Ingalls, the quartermaster at the White House, however, testifies (Com. Rep., 448): "There were no stores of any importance destroyed. There was some pork destroyed, and some whisky, belonging to the Commissary Department. There were also the stores on one of the trains that I was going to send out at the time the rebels got possession of the road. Most of the stores on that train were abandoned. All the vessels, with the exception of two or three barges which had been got close to the shore, were got off."
[2] Lee's Rep., i., 10.　　[3] Ibid., i., 169. 285.

At the same instant the whole mass of powder exploded, and the remaining cars plunged, shattered, into the mud of the river.[1]

Magruder, in the mean time, had been delayed by various contradictory orders, but at length came in sight of Sumner's corps drawn up a little in front of Savage's Station, and about half past five o'clock opened a sharp attack with artillery, supporting it by infantry. He had one heavy gun mounted on a railroad car, protected from cannon-shot in front by a sloping iron roof, and from rifle-shot on the sides by thick walls of wood lined with iron. This contrivance, which the Confederates named "the land Merrimac," was used with considerable effect. The action continued hot for more than two hours, when, darkness coming on, the firing ceased as if by common consent, neither side gaining any perceptible ground from the other, though the action was so close that firing was sometimes suspended on account of the impossibility of distinguishing friends from foes. The numbers actually engaged on either side were small. Magruder brought fairly into action only McLaw's two small brigades, numbering together 2250 men; of these, 345 were killed and wounded. His entire loss was about 400. The loss on the Union side was considerably larger. Early next morning Magruder was ordered by Lee to cross over to the Newmarket Road in order to join in the flank attack of that day. Lee had counted in this action upon the co-operation of Jackson; but he was delayed by the necessity of rebuilding a bridge in order to cross the Chickahominy. Sumner's stand had effected its object of delaying the enemy, and before midnight his force was on its way to White Oak Swamp, leaving behind 2500 sick, wounded, and their attendants in the hospital at Savage's Station.[2]

MONDAY, JUNE 30.—FRAZIER'S FARM.

On the morning of the 29th Longstreet and A. P. Hill recrossed the Chickahominy at New Bridge, and after passing through the deserted Union lines, and going almost within sight of Richmond, headed the White Oak Swamp, went down the Darbytown Road, and encamped within striking distance of the centre of McClellan's retreating column. They had made a forced march under a fierce sun, and many of the men dropped from the ranks in utter exhaustion. Magruder and Huger were marching to the same point by parallel roads. Jackson and D. H. Hill crossed the Chickahominy on the 30th, and followed straight upon the line of McClellan's retreat to White Oak Swamp. In the mean while, Holmes, whose brigade was at Fort Darling, on the opposite side of the James River, was to cross with all his disposable force and join in the attack. McClellan's whole force was stretched in a line

[1] This retreat of Heintzelman has occasioned much censure. He himself (McC. Rep., 261; Com. Rep., 356) gives reasons for his movement which seem hardly reconcilable with each other. Sumner, he says, had taken a position in advance of that ordered, and "this movement of General Sumner uncovering my right flank, it became necessary for me to retreat." But immediately after he says that, after having been ordered to hold his position by Sumner, who was the commanding officer on the ground, he saw that Sumner and Franklin had "more troops than could be brought into action judiciously," and "the reason I left with my corps was that the ground was so constructed that there were absolutely more troops there than could find room. The roads in their rear were filled with artillery and wagons. . . . I knew that General Sumner had as many troops as were necessary, and my corps, in case of a forced retreat, would only have rendered it more disastrous. . . . Sumner and Franklin had a very sharp action that afternoon, and repulsed the enemy." Sumner (McC. Rep., 260) says: "When the enemy appeared on the Williamsburg road, I could not imagine why General Heintzelman did not attack him, and not till some time afterward did I learn, to my utter amazement, that General Heintzelman had retreated with his whole corps (about 15,000 men) before the action commenced. This defection might have been attended with the most serious consequences; and although we beat the enemy signally, and drove him from the field, we should certainly have given him a more crushing blow if General Heintzelman had been there with his corps." It is clear that not half of Sumner's force was engaged.
[2] McC. Rep., 259–262; Lee's Rep., i., 10, 160, 193, 290, 295, 298. No reliance can be placed upon the Confederate estimates of the Union loss in this action. Thus Magruder (Lee's Rep., 195) says: "I estimate the loss of the enemy to be not less than 3000 killed and wounded; Semmes [who lost 53] reporting not less than 400 dead in his front alone;" while Kershaw, who was more hotly engaged, "turns (Ibid., i., 299) with pride and satisfaction to 500 dead of the enemy left on the field" as evidence of the prowess of his troops.

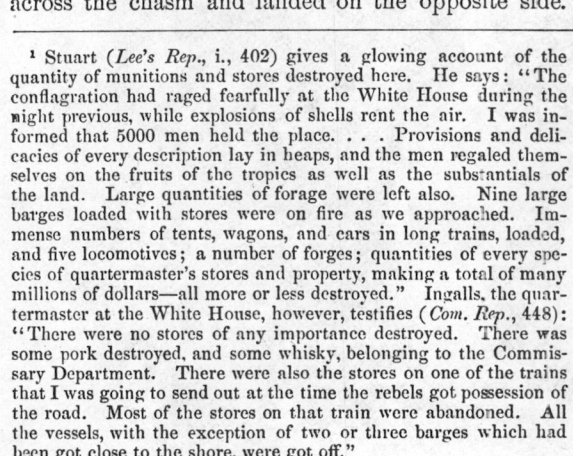

SAVAGE'S STATION ABANDONED.

eight miles long from the swamp to Malvern Hill, on the James; protected by this line, his artillery and trains were slowly floundering over difficult roads.

Lee's plan of battle for this day was an illustration of grand strategy—the only one deserving the name during the whole campaign. His purpose was to make an attack in column upon McClellan's long line, break through it at the centre, hurl the left back upon Jackson, and assault the right in the rear. To accomplish this plan, his whole strength—more than 80,000 men —were so situated that they might apparently be concentrated at the right moment upon the given point: Jackson upon the rear, all the rest upon the flank. The plan failed because the force could not be brought together in time; and instead of the attack being made by the whole, the action on his side was confined wholly to Longstreet and A. P. Hill, with 18,000 men; and in place of a grand and decisive battle, there were a series of combats, in which each brigade on both sides engaged almost without concert. From the accounts, more or less at variance, and all incomplete, we have to attempt to set forth the leading points in this fierce but desultory conflict.[1]

Holmes, joined by Wise, crossed the James with 7000 men, mostly fresh North Carolinians, and on the morning of the 30th came within sight of McClellan's retreating column, upon whom, in the afternoon, he opened fire from a distance. A few rounds of artillery and a few shells from the gunboats scattered his force, the cavalry and artillery breaking into a wild stampede, and riding over and through the infantry. Two were killed, forty-one wounded, and several others seriously hurt by being run over by the cavalry and artillery. Holmes and Wise made no farther appearance in this campaign, but the day after the battle of Malvern marched quietly back to their encampments across the James

Jackson reached the White Oak Creek at noon. He found the bridge destroyed and the approaches covered by artillery from the opposite side. In vain he attempted to repair it all through the afternoon. The men would not work under the heavy fire to which they were exposed. He was but two miles distant from the fierce battle in which Longstreet and Hill were engaged, and the noise of it could be distinctly heard; but he was powerless to aid the attack in which he had been expected to bear so prominent a part.

Longstreet and A. P. Hill resumed their march down the Darbytown Road in the morning, and about noon came in sight of a part of the Union line drawn up, its centre at Frazier's Farm, near a point where a road leading to the James River crosses the roads coming from Richmond, by which they were advancing. Huger was supposed to be coming down the Charles City Road, two miles on the right.

The whole Union line was so long that it was unoccupied in portions. At this point McCall was in the centre, with Kearney on the left, and Hooker, then Sumner, on the right. McCall was somewhat advanced, and upon his division, weakened by the two battles in which it had been engaged, the first onset fell.

After some skirmishing, at about four o'clock Longstreet made the onset with the fiery impetuosity which he ever manifested. The first attack was made by Kemper's brigade, which had not yet been engaged, it having been the only one held in reserve at Cold Harbor. The brigade was driven back, losing 250 killed and wounded, and nearly 200 prisoners—a quarter of its whole number. Its place was taken by others, who, in greater force, dashed upon the same point. They swept in the Union line for a space, but were checked by Hooker and forced back. This was on McCall's left. All the force of Longstreet and Hill now rushed in, each brigade commander apparently acting for himself. Foiled at one point, they dashed upon another, determined to break the line somewhere. At last, Wilcox's Alabama brigade leading, they poured over a swampy stream and through a dense wood, and across an open field upon McCall's right, straight in the teeth of his batteries.

Of this charge McCall says:[2] "On the right, Randall's battery was charged upon by the enemy in great force, and with a reckless impetuosity I never saw equaled. They advanced at a run over a space of six hundred yards of open ground. The guns of the battery mowed them down, yet they never paused. A volley of musketry was poured into them at a short distance by the 4th regiment, in support of the battery, but it did not check them for an instant; they dashed on, and pistoled and bayoneted the cannoniers at their guns. Part of the 4th regiment gave way; the remainder, however, with part of the 7th regiment in their rear, then coming forward, stood their ground like heroes. As I was with the battery at the time, it was my fortune to witness, in the bayonet fight that there took place, such a display of reckless daring on the part of the Alabamians, and of unflinching courage on the part of the Pennsylvanians, as is rarely beheld. My men were, however, overpowered and borne off the ground. The battery was taken, but immediately after abandoned by the enemy, who rapidly retired. Just before sunset, Cooper's battery in front of the centre was, after several charges had been repulsed, finally taken by the enemy, but only to be retaken by the 9th regiment in a most glorious charge."

Wilcox says:[3] "The enemy's battery had an open field of fire, the ground being perfectly level. The 11th Alabama advanced, and, entering upon the open field, came on the battery, which began a rapid fire of grape and canister. The regiment did not halt an instant, but continued to advance, steadily and rapidly, without firing, until it approached within two hundred yards of the battery, when it gave loud cheers and made a rush for the guns. Halting in front of it for an instant, they fire upon the battery and infantry

JACKSON IN CHECK AT WHITE OAK CREEK.

---

[1] Our authorities are: Lee (*Lee's Rep.*, i., 10), Longstreet (*Ibid.*, i., 125), A. P. Hill (*Ibid.*, i., 177), Jackson (*Ibid.*, i., 134), and Reports of the several Confederate brigade commanders engaged, all given in Lee's Report; McClellan's Report (p. 265–269); the testimony of Heintzelman, Sumner, and McCall (*Com. Rep.*, 357, 365, 586).

[2] *Com. Rep.*, 558.   [3] *Lee's Rep.*, i., 342.

immediately in rear of it, and then make a successful charge upon and take it. . . . . The enemy, at first repulsed and driven from the battery, retire to the woods, and deliver a terrible and destructive fire upon this regiment. With its ranks sadly thinned, it heroically stands its ground. The enemy, now seeing this regiment isolated and unsupported, advance from their cover against it. The sword and bayonet are freely used; many of the men received and gave in return bayonet wounds. There are no supports for them; no re-enforcements come, and they are at length forced to yield and retire to the woods in the rear, having left upon the field and around the battery in dead alone eight officers, of whom seven were captains or lieutenants commanding companies, and forty-nine privates."

The battle raged with almost equal fury along the whole line. Hill, on the Confederate left, pressed forward his brigades in a mass, and gained ground at first, capturing two full batteries, which he retained; but he was unable to gain any ground permanently, and at last it became apparent that Hooker and Kearney, on their right and left, were slowly gaining, while the earlier repulse of McCall's flanks had been retrieved, and his centre remained unbroken. Lee, indeed, says:[1] "The enemy had been driven with great slaughter from every position save one, which he maintained until he was enabled to withdraw under cover of darkness. At the close of the struggle nearly the entire field remained in our possession." Longstreet reports:[2] "The enemy was driven back slowly and steadily, contesting the ground inch by inch. He succeeded in getting some of his batteries off the field, and, by holding his last position till dark, in withdrawing his forces under cover of night." Sumner errs equally on the other side. He says:[3] "After a furious contest, lasting till dark, the enemy was routed at all points, and driven from the field." There was no rout; though, as most of the Confederate brigade commanders report, their brigades were greatly shattered. A. P. Hill[4] gives the true account of the condition when darkness closed the struggle: "On our extreme right matters seemed to be going badly. Two brigades of Longstreet's division had been roughly handled, and had fallen back. Archer was brought up and sent in, and in his shirt sleeves leading his gallant brigade, affairs were soon restored in that quarter. About dark the enemy were pressing us hard along our whole line, and my last reserve, General J. R. Anderson, was directed to advance cautiously. Heavy re-enforcements to the enemy were brought up at this time, and it seemed that a tremendous effort was being made to turn the fortunes of the battle. The volume of fire that, approaching, rolled along the line, was terrific. Seeing some troops of Wilcox's brigade who had rallied, they were rapidly re-formed, and, being directed to cheer long and loudly, moved again to the fight. This seemed to end the contest, for in less than five minutes all firing ceased, and the enemy retired."

The Confederates captured in the earlier part of the action about 20 guns, and lost about 300 prisoners. Their loss in killed and wounded exceeded that of their opponents. Their two divisions kept a part of the field after their enemy had retired, thus holding the honors of the battle; but they were so fearfully shattered, here and before, that not a man of them was brought into the greater fight fought next day at Malvern. A. P. Hill had crossed the Chickahominy four days before with 14,000 men, and at Mechanicsville, Cold Harbor, and Frazier's Farm had lost 4000 in killed and wounded. Longstreet had crossed with 10,000, and at Cold Harbor and here lost 4200. Some of his brigades had more than half their number killed and wounded. Wilcox carried 1850 into action at Cold Harbor; in the two battles he lost 1035. Pryor had 1400, and lost 850.

Accounts current at the time represent the division of McCall as having

BAYONET FIGHT AT FRAZIER'S FARM.

been thoroughly routed on this field. Parts of it were indeed shattered and broken; but, as a division, it fought bravely and held its ground firmly. Of the whole army it alone had fought in two battles—Mechanicsville and Cold Harbor. Here it was opposed to the first onset and the severest brunt of the fight. Meade, then leading one of its brigades, and a year after, lacking two days, to command the whole Army of the Potomac down to the close of the war, claimed for this division no more than its rightful due when he wrote: "It was only the stubborn resistance offered by our division, prolonging the contest till after dark, and checking till that time the advance of the enemy, that enabled the concentration during the night of the whole army on the James River, which saved it."[1] After the battle was over, McCall, riding out into the darkness, fell in with a regiment of the enemy and was captured. He had been almost the whole day under the hottest fire, escaping unharmed, though every one of his staff was killed or wounded.

TUESDAY, JULY 1.—MALVERN HILL.

The battle at Frazier's Farm was hardly over when the Union forces again took up their retreat toward Malvern Hill, the point selected for resisting the farther advance of the enemy. The rear of the wagons and reserve artillery had arrived there about four in the afternoon. Soon after daylight the last division was in, and the post of each was assigned.

The position was admirably chosen for a defensive battle. Malvern Hill is an elevated plateau, a mile and a half long and half as broad, the top nearly free from woods. It slopes gently toward the north and east down to the verge of a thick forest; westward it falls more abruptly into a ravine, which extends to the James River. All along the front are ravines, rendering the approach difficult except by the roads which cross them. On the crest of the hill seven heavy siege guns had been placed in position, and the reserve artillery was so posted that a concentrated fire of sixty guns could be brought to bear upon any point in front or on the left, the direction from which the enemy must advance to the attack. Here the main force was massed. The right, less strongly held, curved backward through a wooded region to the James. Both flanks thus rested upon the river, and were protected by the gun-boats. Porter's corps was on the left; then Heintzelman's, a part of Keyes's, Sumner's, Franklin's, and last, on the extreme right, the remainder of Keyes's.

Jackson crossed the White Oak Creek, and followed in the track of the retreating army. At Frazier's Farm he found Lee, who ordered him to press forward; at 9 o'clock, coming in sight of the Union line, he took up his position, Whiting on the left, then Ewell; D. H. Hill being on the right, who was thus brought in front of Hooker, near the Union centre. Hill was within range of the artillery on the plateau, and suffered severely. "Anderson's brigade was roughly handled, he being wounded and borne from the field." The division was then halted, and the Union position reconnoitred.[2] "The Yankees," says Hill,[3] "were found to be strongly posted on a commanding hill, all the approaches to which could be swept by his artillery, and were guarded by swarms of infantry, securely sheltered by fences, ditches, and ravines. Tier after tier of batteries were grimly visible on the plateau, rising in the form of an

[1] Lee's Rep., i., 11.   [2] Ibid., i., 126.   [3] McC. Rep., 268.   [4] Lee's Rep., i., 177.

ON THE FIELD.

[1] Com. Rep., 589.
[2] McClellan thus describes this part of the engagement: "About 3 P.M. a heavy fire of artillery opened upon Kearney's left and Couch's division, speedily followed up by a brisk attack of infantry on Couch's front. The artillery was replied to with good effect by our own, and the infantry of Couch's division remained lying on the ground until the advancing column was within short musketry range, when they sprang to their feet, and poured in a deadly volley, which entirely broke the attacking force, and drove them in disorder back over their own ground. This advantage was followed up until we had advanced the right of our lines some seven or eight hundred yards, and rested upon a thick clump of trees, giving us a stronger position and a better fire. Shortly after 4 o'clock the firing ceased along the whole front, but no disposition was evinced on the part of the enemy to withdraw from our front."—McC. Rep., 271.
[3] Lee's Rep., i., 185.

BATTERY D., FIFTH U. S. ARTILLERY, AT FRAZIER'S FARM.

FIRST MASSACHUSETTS BATTERY AT FRAZIER'S FARM.

amphitheatre. We could only reach the first line of batteries by traversing an open space of from three to four hundred yards, exposed to a murderous fire of grape and canister from the artillery and musketry from the infantry. If that was carried, another and another, still more difficult, remained in rear. I had expressed my disapprobation of a farther pursuit of the Yankees to the commanding general, and to Generals Jackson and Longstreet, even before I knew of the strength of their position. An examination satisfied me that an attack would be hazardous."

But Lee was resolved that his grand stroke of strategy should not fail. He sent a note to each of his division commanders ordering an assault. That brief note of forty words cost him more than 4000 men.[1]

Huger had been directed to march down the Charles City Road and join Longstreet and A. P. Hill in the battle of the 30th. He failed to reach the point in time. Next day he tried to move forward, but got entangled among the other divisions, and finally lost his way. He had had the same misfortune a month ago at Seven Pines; and now, when his divisions came up, they were one by one taken from him and given to Magruder, and formed a part of his command during the battle. At first he was inclined to ignore the arrangement, and even directed one of his brigade commanders not to place himself under Magruder;[2] but his order was disregarded, and he could only remonstrate afterward against the slight which had been put upon him, not for the first time. After the battle was over he was suffered to direct his division in removing the wounded and burying the dead.[3]

The afternoon was now wearing away when Lee ordered the artillery attack which he hoped would break the Union lines. "But, instead of one or two hundred pieces, only a single battery opened, and that was knocked to pieces in a few minutes; and one or two others shared the same fate of being beaten in detail." Hill knew not what to do. He "wrote to Jackson that the firing from the batteries was of the most farcical character;"[4] and received for reply that he must advance as ordered upon hearing the shout from Armistead. At length, an hour and a half before sunset, he heard shouting and firing on his right, and, supposing this to be the signal, urged his whole division forward. He shall tell the story of his charge in his own words, somewhat abridged:

"We advanced alone; neither Whiting on the left, nor Magruder or Huger on the right, moved forward an inch. The division fought heroically, but fought in vain. Garland, in my immediate front, showed all his wonted courage, but he needed and asked for re-enforcements. I found Toombs's brigade in our rear, and ordered it to support Garland, and accompanied it. The brigade advanced handsomely to the brow of the hill, but soon retreated in disorder. Gordon pushed gallantly forward and gained considerable ground, but was forced back. Ripley's brigade was streaming to the rear. Colquitt's and Anderson's brigades had also fallen back. Ransom's brigade had come up to my support from Huger; a portion of it had come, but without its brigadier. It moved too far to the left, and became mixed up with the mass of troops there, suffering heavily, and effecting little. Winder was sent up by Jackson, but he came too late, and also went to the same belt of woods already overcrowded with troops. Finally Ewell came up, but it was after dark, and nothing could be accomplished. I advised him to hold his ground, and not to attempt a forward movement."[5] Hill lost in this action,

THE GUN-BOATS AT MALVERN HILL.

lasting only an hour and a half, of his own division, 336 killed and 1373 wounded.[1]

McClellan thus describes this part of the engagement:

"At six o'clock the enemy suddenly opened upon Couch and Porter with the whole strength of his artillery, and at once began pushing forward his columns of attack to carry the hill. Brigade after brigade, formed under cover of the woods, started at a run to cross the open space and charge our batteries; but the heavy fire of our guns, with the cool and steady volleys of our infantry, in every case sent them back reeling to shelter, and covered the ground with their dead and wounded. In several instances our infantry withheld their fire until the attacking columns, which rushed through the storm of canister and shell from our artillery, had reached within a few yards of our lines. They then poured in a single volley and dashed forward with the bayonet, capturing prisoners and colors, and driving the routed columns in confusion from the field."[2]

Hill was mistaken in supposing that "neither Magruder nor Huger moved forward an inch," and in afterward reiterating, "So far as I can learn, none of our troops drew trigger excepting McLaw's, mine, and a portion of Huger's." McLaw's division was a part of Magruder's command; and all this time Magruder, with the whole of his own and Huger's force, was engaged in a fierce conflict on the right. From them came the shouting and firing which Hill supposed to be the signal for his own advance. To this attack by Magruder, as well as to that by Hill, belongs McClellan's account just quoted. So close were they in space and time that, viewed from the opposite lines, they appeared as parts of one movement.

Magruder, after a weary and harassing march from the battle-field at Savage's Station, was ordered by Lee to attack on the right of Hill, who was in position. He found Armistead, of Huger's division, awaiting the arrival of artillery. Magruder sent back to hurry it up, and pushed on some of his troops within range of a heavy fire. Just then he received a copy of Lee's note, ordering him, as soon as he heard the yell from Armistead, to "do the same," and charge. Armistead had driven in some skirmishers, and yelled. Lee, supposing that the Union line was broken, and that the troops were retreating, wrote to Magruder to advance and cut them off.[3] He attempted to carry out the order. His plan was "to hurl about 15,000 men upon the enemy's batteries and supporting infantry; to follow up any successes they might obtain; and, if unable to drive the enemy from his strong position, to continue the fight in front by pouring in fresh troops, and, in case they were repulsed, to hold strongly the line of battle where I stood, to prevent serious disaster to our arms."[4] But in a short time his whole force was engaged, breasting a terrific fire of artillery and musketry. "The battle-field," says Magruder, "was enveloped in smoke, relieved only by flashes from the lines of the contending troops. Round shot and grape crashed through the woods; and shells of enormous size, which reached far beyond the head-quarters of our gallant commander-in-chief, burst amidst the artillery parked in the rear. Belgian missiles and Minié balls lent their aid to this scene of surpassing grandeur and sublimity." This determined attack failed in making any impression upon the Union lines or in disturbing a single battery. The Federal troops had no occasion to leave their strong position. It was quite sufficient to mow down the enemy with artillery as they advanced. When darkness set in, Magruder "concluded to let the battle subside," and his wearied men sank down to sleep on the spot they had reached. Some of them were within a hundred yards of the Union batteries.

---

[1] Lee's note, given in *Report*, i., 212. See also p. 185, 199. "Batteries have been established to act upon the enemy's lines. If they are broken, as is probable, Armistead, who can witness the effect of the fire, has been ordered to charge with a yell. Do the same."
[2] *Lee's Rep.*, i., 200, 212, 368.
[3] "My brigades were, during the action, under the immediate command of General Magruder. As they were sent forward into the battle at Malvern Hill, I was directed to report them to another commander. As I was treated in the same manner at Seven Pines, I can only *hope* this course was accidental, and required by the necessities of the service. I therefore make no report, and refer to reports of others for details of the battle of Malvern Hill. After this battle, as required, the division was occupied, under my orders, in removing the wounded and burying the dead."—Huger, in *Lee's Rep.*, i., 149.   [4] D. H. Hill, in *Lee's Rep.*, i., 186.   [5] *Ibid.*

[1] *Ibid.*, i., 307.   [2] *McC. Rep.*, 271.
[3] Lee to Magruder, in *Lee's Rep.*, i., 210: "General Lee expects you to advance rapidly. It is reported that the enemy is getting off. Press forward your whole line and follow up Armistead's successes."   [4] Magruder, in *Lee's Rep.*, i., 200.

THE BATTLE OF MALVERN HILL.

Of these closing scenes, as viewed from the other side, McClellan writes: "About 7 o'clock, as fresh troops were accumulating in front of Porter and Couch, Meagher and Sickles were sent with their brigades to relieve such regiments of Porter's corps and Couch's division as had expended their ammunition, and batteries from the reserve were pushed forward to replace those whose boxes were empty. Until dark the enemy persisted in his efforts to take the position so tenaciously defended; but, despite his superior numbers, his repeated and desperate attacks were repulsed with fearful loss, and darkness ended the battle of Malvern Hill, though it was not until after 9 o'clock that the artillery ceased its fire."[1]

The Confederates were indeed repulsed fearfully—and, had McClellan only known it and followed up his advantage—disastrously.[2] But the superior forces of the enemy existed, as they had for months, only in the imagination of the Union commander. Neither Longstreet nor A. P. Hill had a man in this action. Jackson's own command was not engaged in the attack, though all of it was within the range of our guns, and suffered a loss of just 41 killed and 363 wounded by the distant fire.[3] D. H. Hill's division, reduced to less than 8000, and Magruder's and Huger's, then not exceeding 20,000, were all.[4]

General Trimble thus describes the condition of the Confederate army on the morning after the battle:[5] "The next morning, by dawn, I went off to ask for orders, when I found the whole army in the utmost disorder. Thousands of straggling men were asking every passer-by for their regiments; ambulances, wagons, and artillery obstructing every road, and altogether, in a drenching rain, presenting a scene of the most woeful and heart-rending confusion." The very show of an attack upon such an army by the unbroken Union force must have defeated it. But there was in the mind of its commander no thought of an attack. When, in the morning, the Confederates looked up the hill which they had so vainly attempted to scale, they saw not a trace of the grim batteries and serried lines which had confronted them the night before. In the storm and darkness the Union army had fled from a victory as though it had been a rout.

McClellan had "perceived that the position at Malvern Hill was the key to our operations in that quarter."[6] His whole army was concentrated here, having during the actions and retreat suffered far less loss than it had inflicted. Here he had wisely resolved to give battle; and yet before the battle was fought he had begun the retreat, and as soon as the "complete victory" was won, the troops were on the march, abandoning the key to the position.[7] Hitherto the retreat had been orderly, but for this last seven miles it presented the aspect of the flight of a routed army.[8] Keyes, who was to form the rear-guard, was instructed: "Bring along all the wagons you can; but they are to be sacrificed, of course, rather than imperil your safety. Celerity of movement is the sole security of this position." Next day, while the retreat was going on, the chief of staff wrote to Keyes: "It is of the utmost importance that we should save all our artillery and as many of our wagons as possible. If you bring in every thing you will accomplish a most signal and meritorious exploit, which the commanding general will not fail to represent in its proper light to the Department."[9] On the 3d, McClellan wrote to the Secretary of War that the army was thoroughly worn out, and required rest and very heavy re-enforcements; but he hoped that the enemy was equally worn out. He hoped the army would have breathing space before it was attacked again. It was impossible then to estimate the losses, but he doubted whether there were more than fifty thousand men with their colors. To "accomplish the task of capturing Richmond," re-enforcements should be sent to him "rather much over than less than one hundred thousand men."[10]

This hasty and disorderly retreat was performed with little molestation from the enemy. Stuart's cavalry, who had rejoined Lee after the battle, followed after, through the storm, making a few captures of straggling men and abandoned arms. Some of the Confederate infantry followed cautiously, and on the 3d came near enough to throw a few shells at the rear-guard,

THE RETREAT FROM MALVERN.

but were quickly dispersed by a fire from the batteries and gun-boats. But no serious attempt at annoyance was made; and after passing a few days near the battle-field of Malvern, burying the dead and gathering abandoned property, the Confederates, on the 8th, retired to Richmond. McClellan felt himself in a condition, on the 7th, to write to the President that his position was very strong, and daily becoming more so; if not attacked that day he should laugh at the enemy; his men were in splendid spirits, and anxious to try it again. Meanwhile the President was to alarm himself as little as possible, and, above all, must not lose confidence in the army.[1]

With the battle of Malvern Hill properly closed the campaign on the Peninsula. To the errors which marked its earlier period, as conducted by McClellan, we advert but briefly. They arose mainly from the exaggerated estimates which he made of the forces opposed to him. Thus, at the close of October, 1861, when the Confederates had at and around Centreville only 40,000 or 50,000, he believed that they numbered 150,000; when they abandoned this point, he put their numbers at 115,000 instead of 50,000. He was held in check at Yorktown for weeks by 11,000, 20,000, and finally 53,000, instead of 100,000, "and possibly more," as he believed. While lying idle in the Chickahominy swamps, confronted, as he thought, by a superior force, there was not a day up to the battle of Fair Oaks when his strength was not greater by half than that of the enemy. And when at length Lee had gathered all his re-enforcements, including Jackson, his utmost effective strength was barely 100,000, instead of the 180,000 or 200,000 which McClellan attributed to him, his own force being fully as great.

Into the six days—which have somehow passed into history as the Seven Days—from June 26 to July 1 in which this ill-starred campaign culminated, were concentrated on both sides more grave errors than can elsewhere be found in modern military history.

Of Lee's initial error in dividing his army, which should have lost him every thing, we have already spoken. The wild attack upon the strong Union position at Beaver Dam Creek can be justified only on the ground that it was made in utter ignorance of his own force at that point, and of that opposed to him. It finds its parallel upon a larger scale in our own attack upon Fredericksburg, six months later.

The battle of Cold Harbor was fought upon the Union side without any assignable object. McClellan indeed says:[2] "The objects sought for had been attained. The enemy was held at bay, our siege-guns and material were saved, and the right wing had now joined the main body of the army." But the material had all been saved hours before the action commenced. The very last of the siege-guns was carried off at sunrise, half past four, and it was not till "after noon that the enemy were discovered approaching in force, and it soon became evident that the entire position was to be attacked."[3] Here were fully eight hours of daylight during which Porter's and McCall's troops, unencumbered by trains, could have crossed wholly without molestation. Any two or three hours of that time would have been amply sufficient for the purpose. In the darkness, and after the fatigue and confusion of a lost battle, the crossing was effected in three or four hours by half more men. The crossing might indeed have been made during the night of the 26th, and the right wing, entirely fresh, with the exception of McCall's division, which had won the fight at Beaver Dam Creek, might have been with the main body of the army on the right bank of the Chickahominy, in the very position where McClellan had been for weeks trying to place them; with the wholly unexpected advantage that the force of the enemy was divided, with the whole Union army and the impassable Chickahominy between the portions. With the bridges destroyed, and the approaches covered by artillery, the whole Confederate force on the left bank of the Chickahominy, for at least two days, was wholly useless for the defense of Richmond.

This battle was not fought to preserve the communications with the White House, for on the day before orders had been given to abandon that base,[4]

[1] McC. Rep., 272.

[2] Some days after the retreat from Malvern Hill McClellan proposed to renew the movement upon Richmond, if he could have a re-enforcement of 20,000 men. In reply to the question, "In what do you consider your chances of success would have been greater, with the addition of 20,000 to the number which you had at Harrison's Landing, than they were when you were in front of Richmond, and before Jackson had formed a junction with the rest of the rebel forces?" he answered: "I should have counted upon the effect of the battles which had just taken place upon the enemy. We had then strong reason to believe that the enemy's losses had been heavier than our own, and that portions of his army were very much demoralized, especially after the battle of Malvern Hill."—Com. Rep., 438.   [3] Lee's Rep., i., 307.

[4] Magruder, indeed, says (Lee's Rep., i., 202) that "there was a force of 26,000 or 28,000 under my orders engaged and under fire." But he must have considered himself in command of the whole field, and so have included D. H. Hill's division. For he repeatedly states that his own division and that of Huger together numbered, on the 1st of July, 25,000; of these fully 800 had been killed and wounded at Golding's, Price's, and Savage's Station, and many of his men gave out in the march before reaching Malvern Hill. As one example out of many scattered through the minor Confederate reports, General Howell Cobb says (Lee's Rep., i., 279) that his brigade "commenced the march on the morning of the 29th of June with 2700 men, but fatigue and exhaustion had so reduced our ranks that less than 1500 were carried into the battle of the 1st of July." Of his own division and Huger's, Magruder could not have had more than 18,000 or 20,000 at Malvern Hill.   [5] Lee's Rep., i., 314.   [6] Ibid., 264.

[7] The greater portion of the transportation of the army having been started for Harrison's Landing during the night of the 30th of June and 1st of July, the order for the movement of the troops was at once issued upon the final repulse of the enemy at Malvern Hill.—Ibid., 273.

[8] "We were ordered to retreat, and it was like the retreat of a routed army. We retreated like a parcel of sheep; every one was on the road at the same time, and a few shots from the rebels would have panic-stricken the whole command."—Hooker's Testimony, Com. Rep., 580.

[9] Ibid., 611, 612.   [10] Ibid., 342.

[1] Lee's Rep., i., 13, 136, 404; McC. Rep., 279.   [2] McC. Rep., 249.

[3] Ibid., 247. According to all Confederate accounts, they were not in position to open the attack until nearly two o'clock.

[4] Ibid., 243. McClellan intimates that this was done in consequence of the operations of the 27th. He says (Ibid., 254): "The operations of this day [the 27th] proved the numerical superiority of the enemy, and made it evident that while he had a large army on the left bank of the

and unite the whole force on the right bank. The reasons which McClellan assigns for not effecting this junction on the left bank are valid, and it is only to be wondered at that, after having got his whole army together on the right bank during the night of the 27th, he should even have suggested the idea of recrossing with his whole force and giving battle on the other side. His whole army was now just where it should have been long before, whether for advance or for retreat. But the reasons which he assigns for failing to advance upon Richmond are wholly invalid, not only in view of what is now known, but in view of what was or should have been known at the time. "The enemy," he repeats, "was in our rear, and there was every reason to believe that he would sever our communications with our supply dépôt at the White House. We had on hand but a limited amount of rations; and if we had advanced directly to Richmond, it would have required considerable time to carry the strong works around that place, during which our men would have been destitute of food; and even if Richmond had fallen before our arms, the enemy could still have occupied our supply communications between that place and our gun-boats, and turned their disaster into victory." But, as we have seen, the communications had already been abandoned. The whole army was furnished with supplies on the right bank of the Chickahominy for at least a fortnight. After destroying an immense amount of stores, which the train, forty miles long, was unable to convey, the army was fed, until it reached Harrison's Landing, a period of seven days, from what it carried with it. Even then "some portions of the army had still some rations left."[1] The supplies could by no means have been exhausted; for, besides the amount remaining in the wagons when the army retreated from Malvern Hill to Harrison's Landing, "the large herd of 2500 beef cattle was transferred to the James River without loss."[2] A few hours' combat on the 28th or 29th of June must have resulted in the capture of Richmond. The victorious army, besides the supplies which it would have captured there, would have been in a condition to have drawn its supplies from its new and better base, while the Confederate army on the left bank of the Chickahominy would have been wholly destitute of supplies from any source.

There was not the slightest occasion for leaving Porter and McCall as a forlorn hope, merely to hold a superior force at bay for a few hours. The battle of Cold Harbor was one which might either have been accepted or avoided. But, if accepted, there was no reason why it should have been fought with forces so inadequate as to render defeat a foregone conclusion. Ten thousand out of three times the number of men unemployed within hearing, and almost within sight of the battle, would have changed the issue of the day. With these Cold Harbor would have been a victory instead of a defeat.

The Union army was united during the night of the 27th; the Confederate force was separated, the Chickahominy River and swamp lying between the two portions. The operations of the day showed that the main Confederate force was on the left bank. Whether the Union army was to endeavor to take Richmond, or was to retreat to the James River, and there to find a new and better base, the first thing was to keep the force of the enemy apart. This was all the more imperative now that it was determined to retreat. To do this long enough to secure that the retreat should be unmolested, it was only necessary to thoroughly destroy the bridges. This was done so imperfectly that it might as well not have been done at all. The bridges, which it had cost weeks to build, were so little damaged that they were repaired in hours. New Bridge was rebuilt by Magruder during the night of the 27th, without opposition, right under the guns of the Union batteries, and over this Longstreet and A. P. Hill crossed. The Grapevine Bridge, over which Sumner had so hardly passed a month before to repair the defeat at Seven Pines and win the victory at Fair Oaks, was left so little damaged that Jackson reconstructed it in a few hours of the night of the 29th. The thorough destruction of these two bridges would have kept the Confederate force, then across the Chickahominy, on that side long enough to have enabled the retreating army to have gained its new position without another battle.

But the Union army had no commander. From the moment when McClellan learned of the approach of Jackson, he seems to have lost head and heart. Having resolved to retreat instead of to advance, he posted his troops each morning, and his corps commanders saw no more of him for the day. He was busy selecting positions and expediting the passage of trains; doing the work of an engineer rather than that of a general. Each commander of a corps was left to himself to do the best he could. Except at Malvern Hill, the commanding general was not even constructively on the field at any important moment during the whole campaign. He was not present during the battles at Williamsburg or Hanover Court-house, at Seven Pines or Fair Oaks, at Cold Harbor, Savage's Station, or Frazier's Farm. Few of his generals even saw him at Malvern.[3]

Chickahominy, which had already turned our right, and was in position to intercept the communications with our dépôts at the White House, he was also in large force between our army and Richmond. I therefore effected a junction of our forces."

[1] Ingall's Testimony, Com. Rep., 449.　　　　　　[2] McC. Rep., 256.

[3] During the Seven Days' Battles "the corps commanders fought their troops entirely according to their own ideas. If any body asked for re-enforcements, I sent them. If I wanted re-enforcements, I sent to others. . . . General Sumner fought the battle of Savage's Station entirely himself. . . . The next day [Frazier's Farm] General McClellan again posted his troops, and then went off to the James River. That battle was fought entirely by the corps commanders; at least, I received no directions myself. At Malvern Hill I received no orders from General McClellan after the troops were posted. . . . During that fight he was down at his head-quarters on the James River. He came up some time late in the afternoon, and was with General Porter about half an hour. . . . He was the most extraordinary man I ever saw. I do not see how any man could leave so much to others, and be so confident that every thing would go right."—Heintzelman's Testimony, in Com. Rep., 358, 359. Sumner testifies (Ibid., 364, 365): "The action at Malvern commenced on the left at about ten o'clock in the morning. General McClellan had deemed it necessary to go down to Harrison's Landing to determine on the points to

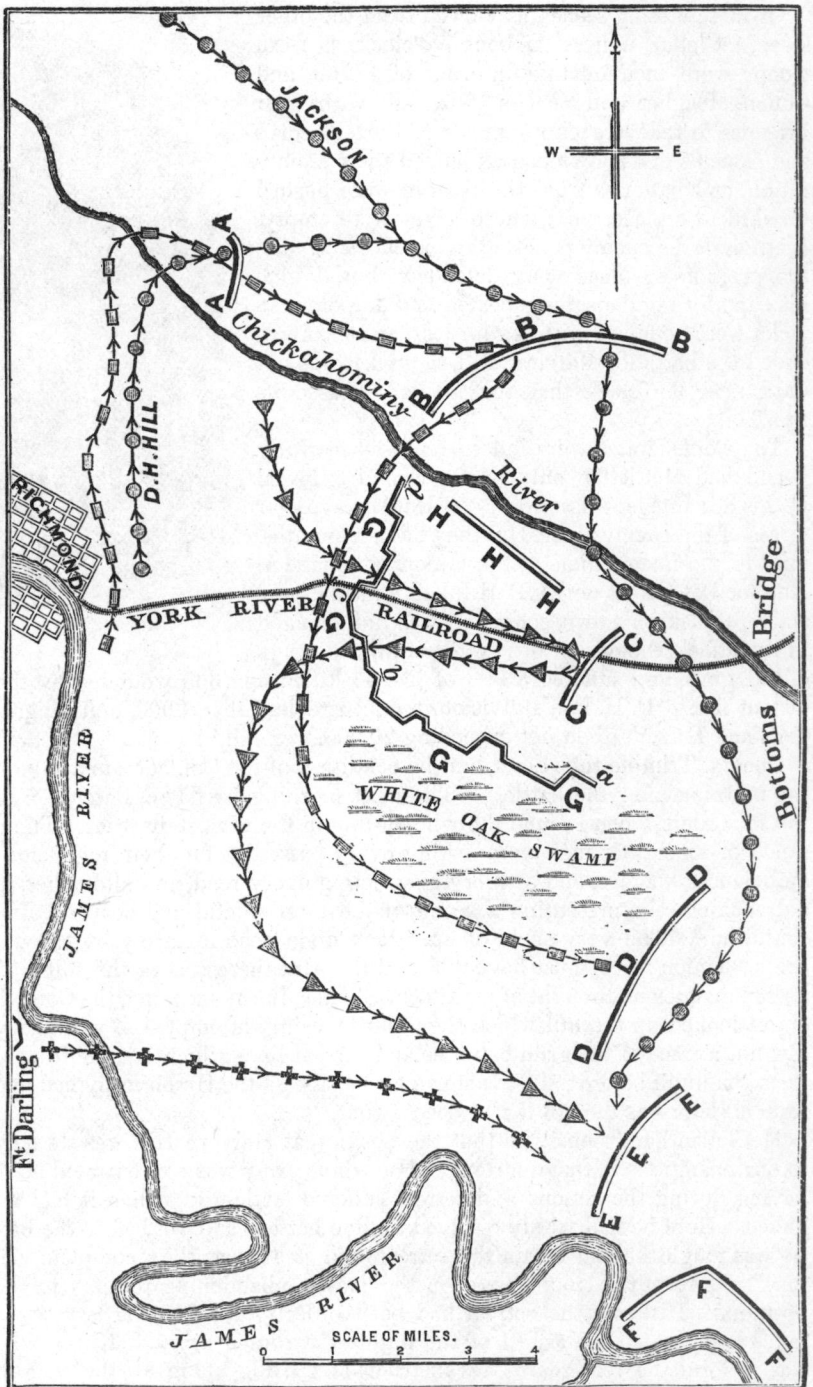

POSITIONS AND MOVEMENTS, JUNE 25 TO JULY 1.

This plan indicates, in a general way, the positions and movements of the armies from June 25 to July 1.

A. A. Union position at Mechanicsville, June 26.
B. B.   "   "   Cold Harbor, June 27.
C. C.   "   "   Savage's Station, June 29.
D. D.   "   "   Frazier's Farm, June 30.
E. E.   "   "   Malvern Hill, July 1.
F. F.   "   "   Harrison's Landing, July 4.

G. G. Union intrenchments before Richmond: a. Keyes: b. Heintzelman; c. Sumner; d. Franklin.
H. H. Porter and McCall, after crossing the Chickahominy.

Jackson's and D. H. Hill's march.
Longstreet's and A. P. Hill's march.
Magruder's and Huger's march.
Holmes's and Wise's march.

The retreat of the Union army was by the same line as Jackson's march, after crossing the Chickahominy.

Lee, unless he was greatly misinformed as to the strength of his opponent, or entertained the most profound contempt for his capacity, must have shared in Magruder's feeling of relief when he learned, on the morning of the 29th, that the Union army, instead of moving upon Richmond, was in full retreat for the James River. The siege of Richmond was indeed raised for the time, but if the retreating army safely reached its new base, the beleaguerment could be renewed under more favorable auspices. To secure any permanent advantage, this army must be signally defeated, or, at least, greatly crippled on its march. To effect this was the design of the movements of the 29th and 30th. If Lee had succeeded, as he proposed, in concentrating 70,000 men on the afternoon of the 30th, half upon the flank and half in the rear,[1] yet both so near as to constitute one body, his plan would have succeeded. The plan failed from contingencies which should have been taken into account. The attacking force had to march twice as far as the retreating one, and over a country of which they were ignorant. The

---

which the troops should retire. I therefore found myself, by virtue of my seniority of rank, in command of the army, without having been formally invested with that command, or having received any instructions in relation to it. I received a note from General McClellan's chief of staff to this effect, that any orders I gave on the field would be approved. About an hour or two afterward I received a verbal message from General McClellan. He was then down the river, two and a half miles from where the battle was going on. . . . Some time afterward General McClellan came on the field. I think he first went up on the left, and came down the line toward the right where I was. He stopped and conversed with me for some time, and then went down toward the right, in the direction of the river. I did not see him again that day. About four o'clock that afternoon a very furious attack was made on our left again. That was the time when Magruder made the assault. . . . I do not know where General McClellan was during this second fight. I presume he was at his quarters. I do not know of his being on the field." McClellan says (Rep., 269): "General Barnard then [the night of the 30th June] received full instructions for posting the troops as they arrived. I then returned to Haxall's, whence I went with Captain Rodgers to select the final location for the army and its dépôts. I returned to Malvern before the serious fighting commenced, and after riding along the lines, and seeing most cause to feel anxious about the right, remained in that vicinity." But he says, on the same page, "From the position of the enemy, his most obvious lines of attack would come from the directions of Richmond and White Oak Swamp, and would of necessity strike us upon our left wing." There was no fighting on the right, in the vicinity of which General McClellan remained.

[1] "When I was taken prisoner I was conducted at once to Lee's head-quarters. Here Longstreet told me that they had 70,000 men bearing on that point, all of whom would probably arrive during the night."—McCall, in Com. Rep., 588.

result was that the flank attack at Frazier's Farm was made by 18,000 men instead of 40,000, while Jackson, who was to have assailed the rear with 30,000, was held in check, utterly unable to cross the White Oak Creek.[1] The neglect of Lee to acquire minute information of the character of the country is inexplicable. The entire operations were carried on within a dozen miles of the capital of the Confederacy. One would suppose that every rood of ground, and every road and military point, would long before have been accurately surveyed and mapped. Moreover, even during the siege, this region, on the south side of the Swamp, had never been occupied by the enemy. It is doubtful whether, with the exception of a single cavalry reconnoisance in May, a single company of Union soldiers had crossed to the south side of the swamp until within a week. The first duty of a commander is to make himself acquainted with the country where he is to operate. If Napoleon owed to any one thing more than to another his marvelous triumphs, it was to the care with which he studied the topography of his campaigns. Thus alone was he enabled to manœuvre his forces so as to have them, however apparently separated, brought together at the right moment. "The great art of war," he said, "consists in knowing how to separate in order to subsist, and how to concentrate in order to fight." Lee had neglected this one essential thing, and, in consequence, his flank and rear assault failed utterly.

Had there been any real commander of the Union army on the field, the Confederate check at Frazier's Farm might have been rendered a severe defeat. Before the fight was fairly begun, the last of the Federal trains were safe at Malvern Hill. The army occupied a line from front to rear of barely eight miles. Jackson, in the rear, was held firmly in check across the Swamp, and could not advance a foot. Longstreet's and Hill's column struck this line near its centre. Keyes's corps, fully equal to Longstreet's and Hill's, had not been engaged at all. It had marched but eight miles in two days, and must have been fresher than the enemy, who had marched fully twice as far, after having fought at Cold Harbor. This corps, or half of it, brought back into the fight at Frazier's Farm, would have given such a preponderating strength to the Union force that Longstreet and Hill, instead of being merely checked, must have been overwhelmed. As it was, they suffered so severely that they could not be brought into the action of the next day. But the commanding general was miles away from the scene of action, and no one of the corps and division commanders could have any knowledge of the whole field and of the positions of the different troops. Each did the best he could under the circumstances, and no troops could have fought more bravely; "but no one knew who and where his next neighbor was; and, what is worse, there was no common head near at hand to direct, and give coherence and unity to the operations."[2] "It was very late at night," says McClellan,[3] "before my aids returned to give me the results of the day's fighting along the whole line, and the true position of affairs."

The battle of Malvern Hill was fought by the Confederates without plan or concert. Of more than 70,000 men, whom Lee had even then within two hours' march, less than 30,000 were brought into action.[4] Opposed to these was the whole Union force of fully 85,000 effective men, holding a position which they could have maintained against twice their number. With such odds, there could have been but one result. The mad Confederate assault failed utterly, and could not but have failed if it had been made with their whole force instead of less than half. D. H. Hill, who had opposed it, endeavors to show that, if properly supported by Jackson, he could have succeeded; but in the very attempt he is forced to point out the "blundering arrangements" of his superiors.[5]

In reviewing the operations of these six days one can not but be impressed by the slight part borne by Jackson. He failed to be at his designated place at Mechanicsville. He reached Cold Harbor only in time to turn the wavering scale. Had Porter been re-enforced, as he should have been, Jackson would have been too late. He was held at bay at White Oak Swamp, utterly unable to aid in the battle raging only two miles away. At Malvern Hill he did not even attempt to bring his own proper divisions into action, though he sent Hill upon his hopeless effort to storm the heights, which even that reckless fighter thought impregnable. Where, as in this case, all was accomplished by hard fighting, the losses sustained by each commander afford the best measure of his efficiency. Jackson had 30,000 men, and lost not quite 2300; Longstreet and D. H. Hill, out of 10,000 each, lost each 4000; A. P. Hill, out of 14,000, lost 3900; Magruder, out of 25,000 belonging to himself and Huger, lost nearly 4000, fully four fifths of them in the single battle at Malvern, in which, if it was to have been fought at all, Jackson should have borne the prominent part. The "blundering arrangements" in this battle, of which D. H. Hill complains, must be mainly charged to Jackson.

Never was there better fighting, and never worse generalship than during the six days on the Peninsula. "The Union army," says McClellan,[1] "fought an overwhelming enemy by day, and retreated from successive victories by night, through a week of battle, closing the terrible scenes of conflict with the ever-memorable victory at Malvern, where they drove back, beaten and shattered, the entire Eastern Army of the Confederacy." But at no point, as we have shown by an analysis of forces, was there an "overwhelming" or even a superior force of the enemy except at Cold Harbor, where such a supremacy should not have existed. "Richmond," as McClellan says, "was still within our grasp," as it had indeed been for a month; but the hand which should have grasped it was too feeble for the effort.

We have written, "In a contest between forces so nearly balanced, the victory would rest with that which was most ably commanded. The general who made the fewest errors would win." We might have said, where the whole campaign was a series of errors on both sides, the commander who made the last great error would lose. McClellan's retreat from Malvern was the last great error, and so Lee won. The fruits of victory remained with him; though at a heavy cost, he had won the object at which he aimed, and had good right to say, "The siege of Richmond was raised, and the object of a campaign which had been prosecuted, after months of preparation, at an enormous expenditure of men and money, completely frustrated."[2]

[1] *McC. Rep.*, 445. [2] *Lee's Rep.*, i., 14.

LOSSES FROM JUNE 26 TO JULY 1.

After the retreat to Harrison's Landing, the losses of each division of the Union army, in killed, wounded, and missing, were summed up, but no attempt was made to give the proportion in each engagement (*McC. Rep.*, 272). If any confirmation of the accuracy of the statement were needed, it would be found in a comparison of the official reports of June 20 and July 20 (*McC. Rep.*, 53; *Com. Rep.*, 337, 344). The entire loss, in killed, wounded, and missing, is undoubtedly accurately stated; but as the dead and many of the wounded were abandoned, probably some hundreds should be added to these and taken from the number put down as "missing." Lee, indeed, says (*Rep.*, i., 14) that more than 10,000 prisoners were taken; but this is clearly erroneous. Besides the 2000 at Cold Harbor, and the 2500 at Savage's Station, almost all of whom were sick or wounded, and perhaps 1000 (*Lee's Rep.*, i., 11, 134, 184) picked up by Jackson on his march to White Oak Bridge, very few prisoners were taken by the Confederates.

Of the Confederate commanders, Jackson, D. H. Hill, Longstreet, A. P. Hill, Holmes, and Pendleton, give their exact losses. The losses of Magruder and Huger can be made up very closely from the reports of their brigade commanders. Barksdale (*Lee's Rep.*, i., 296) says that "one third of his brigade fell upon the field: it numbered about 2400, which would make the loss 800. Cobb (*Ibid.*, i., 279) puts his loss in killed and wounded at "nearly 500." McLaw's (*Ibid.*, i., 161, 164), 97 killed, 456 wounded. D. R. Jones (*Ibid.*, i., 172), 103 killed, 708 wounded. Ransom (*Ibid.*, i., 370), 69 killed, 354 wounded. Mahone (*Ibid.*, i., 372, 378), 63 killed, 216 wounded. Armistead (*Ibid.*, i., 438, 439, 448, two regiments estimated), 320 killed and wounded. Wright (*Ibid.*, i., 397), 55 killed, 243 wounded. In all, 3984, of whom 656 were killed, and 3328 wounded. Of the cavalry and reserve artillery, we find mention of about 20 killed and 104 wounded.

The missing in A. P. Hill's division are not given; the number was evidently small, probably about 100. In Magruder's command we find about 400 missing in about two thirds of the brigades; we set down the whole at 600.

From the foregoing data we have compiled the following table of

KILLED, WOUNDED, AND MISSING.

Union.					Confederate.				
	Killed.	Wounded.	Missing.	Total.		Killed.	Wounded.	Missing.	Total.
McCall	253	1240	1581	3,074	Jackson	376	1,892	14	2,282
Sumner	187	1076	848	2,111	D. H. Hill	714	3,192	48	3,954
Heintzelman	189	1051	833	2,073	Longstreet	763	3,429	237	4,429
Keyes	69	507	201	777	A. P. Hill	619	3,251	100(?)	3,970
Porter	620	2460	1198	4,278	Magruder and Huger	656	3,328	600(?)	4,584
Franklin	245	1313	1179	2,737	Holmes	3	59	..	62
Engineers and Cavalry	19	62	118	199	Artillery and Cavalry	20	104	..	124
Total	1582	7709	5958	15,249	Total	3151	15,255	999	19,405

The losses in the separate battles can be given only approximately, by considering the troops engaged in each, and the nature of the fighting, aided by a few indicia scattered here and there through the various reports of Confederate commanders.

Keyes was engaged mainly at Malvern Hill; we put his entire loss in that battle. Sumner was engaged at Savage's Station, Frazier's Farm, and Malvern; we divide his loss between those three engagements. Heintzelman at Frazier's Farm and Malvern; we divide his loss between them. McCall was at Mechanicsville, where he lost about 300, and at Cold Harbor, and the Farm, losing about equally in each. Porter was chiefly engaged at Cold Harbor and Malvern; we put three fourths of his loss at the former. Of Franklin's corps, half with Slocum was at Cold Harbor, the other half with Smith at Garland's and Price's Farms, and elsewhere; we put two thirds of his loss at Cold Harbor, dividing the remainder among the other engagements.

Jackson was engaged at Cold Harbor and slightly at Malvern; D. H. Hill at Mechanicsville, Cold Harbor, and Malvern: both of these distinguish between their losses in each engagement. A. P. Hill was at Mechanicsville, Cold Harbor, and Frazier's Farm. We estimate his loss in the first at 750, in the last at 900, leaving the remainder for Cold Harbor. Longstreet was at Cold Harbor and Frazier's Farm; we put his loss in the latter battle at 1100, leaving the remainder for Cold Harbor.

From these data we construct the following approximate table of

KILLED AND WOUNDED IN THE SEVERAL ENGAGEMENTS.

	Union.			Confederate.		
	Killed.	Wounded.	Total.	Killed.	Wounded.	Total.
Mechanicsville	50	250	300	250	1,250	1,500
Cold Harbor	75	3250	3925	1500	8,000	9,500
Savage's Station	100	500	600	75	325	400
Frazier's Farm	300	1500	1800	325	1,700	2,025
Malvern Hill	375	1800	2175	900	3,500	4,400
Skirmishes (say)	82	509	591	101	480	581
Total	1582	7809	9391	3151	15,255	18,406

[1] "Huger not coming up, and Jackson being unable to force the passage of White Oak Swamp, Longstreet and Hill were without the expected support. The advantages in numbers and position were on the side of the enemy. Could the other commands have co-operated in the action, the result would have proved most disastrous to the enemy." . . . "Under ordinary circumstances the Federal army should have been destroyed. Prominent among the causes to which its escape is due is the want of timely information. This fact, attributable chiefly to the character of the country, enabled General McClellan skillfully to conceal his retreat, and to add much to the obstructions with which nature had beset the way of our pursuing columns."—*Lee's Rep.*, i., 11, 14.

[2] Barnard, *Pen. Camp.*, 44.

[3] *McC. Rep.*, 268.

[4] We estimate the effective Confederate force within five miles of Malvern Hill, on the 1st of July, thus: Jackson and D. H. Hill, 30,000; Longstreet and A. P. Hill, 15,000; Magruder and Huger, 20,000, Holmes, 7000: in all, 72,000. Longstreet, A. P. Hill, and Holmes were not under fire at all. Of Jackson's "command" only D. H. Hill's 8000 were brought fairly in; these, with Magruder's 20,000, were all that actually fought.

[5] "The battle of Malvern Hill might have been a complete and glorious success had not our artillery and infantry been fought in detail. My division batteries, having been three times engaged, had exhausted all their ammunition, and had been sent back for a fresh supply. If I had had them with me, with a good supply of ammunition, I feel confident that we could have beaten the force immediately in front of us. Again, the want of concert with the infantry divisions was most painful. Whiting's division did not engage at all, neither did Holmes's. My division fought an hour or more the whole Yankee force, without assistance from a single Confederate soldier. Some half hour after my division had ceased to struggle against odds of more than ten to one, I had to fall back. McLaw's division advanced but to share the same fate. Notwithstanding the tremendous odds against us, and the blundering arrangements of the battle, we inflicted heavy loss upon the Yankees. The actual loss in battle was, in my opinion (though most persons differ with me), greater on our side than on that of the Yankees."—D. H. Hill, in *Lee's Rep.*, i., 187.

CHAPTER XXI.
THE PENINSULAR CAMPAIGN.
IV. THE WITHDRAWAL FROM THE PENINSULA.

Position of the two Armies.—Petersburg fortified.—Pope placed in Command of the Army of Virginia.—Halleck appointed General-in-Chief.—McClellan asks for Re-enforcements.—His Plan of carrying on the War.—McClellan and Halleck.—Jackson and Hill sent to Gordonsville.—Night Attack from Coggin's Point.—Movement to Malvern Hill.—McClellan ordered to withdraw from the Peninsula.—His Remonstrance.—Hooker's Advice.—Halleck's Reasons for the Order.—The Withdrawal.—The Confederates march Northward.

SIX weeks of almost entire inactivity followed the battle of Malvern and the retreat of the Federal army to Harrison's Landing. The Confederate force remained for some days in the vicinity of the battle-field, and on the 8th of July returned to its positions near Richmond, the movement being so completely masked by the cavalry that no intelligence of it reached the Federal commander, who was still fearful of an attack.[1] Lee was apprehensive that an attempt might be made upon Richmond from the new Federal base by way of Petersburg. D. H. Hill was detached from his division, and placed in command of the Department of the South Side, extending from Drewry's Bluff to the South Carolina line. Petersburg was utterly defenseless, not a spadeful of earth having been thrown up around it. A system of fortifications was now begun, which were ultimately developed into the formidable works which afterward resisted for so long the approach of General Grant. All the troops that could be spared from before Richmond were set to work upon these intrenchments, besides a thousand negroes brought from North Carolina.[2]

On the 26th of June, General Pope had been called from the West, and placed in command of the Army of Virginia, comprising the forces of McDowell, Banks, and Fremont. Pope strenuously opposed the movement of McClellan to the James, urging instead that, if he found himself unable to maintain his position on the Chickahominy, he should mass all his force on the north bank, even at the risk of losing much material of war, and endeavor to make his way in the direction of Hanover Court-house, but in no case to retreat farther to the south than the White House on the Pamunkey. After the retreat to the James, it became apparent that the views of Pope and McClellan were wholly opposed to each other. Both commanders urged the appointment of a commander-in-chief over all the forces. General Halleck, who had successfully conducted operations in the West, was appointed to command the whole land forces of the United States as general-in-chief, and was directed to repair to the capital as soon as he could with safety to the operations within his Department of the Mississippi. This order was dated July 11, and Halleck assumed the command on the 23d.

McClellan had not fairly established himself in his new position when he began to urge that he should be largely re-enforced. On the 1st of July he asked for 50,000 men at once. Next day: "Re-enforcements should be sent to me rather much over than less than 100,000 men." In reply to the demand for 50,000, the President said that, according to McClellan's own plan, 75,000 were required for the defense of Washington; while, including Banks, Fremont, McDowell, and those about the capital, there were not more than 60,000; adding to these Wool at Baltimore, and Dix at Fortress Monroe, there were not, outside of the force then with McClellan, 75,000 men east of the Mountains. "Thus the idea of sending you 50,000, or any other considerable force promptly, is simply absurd." McClellan still continued to urge for re-enforcements from any and every quarter. The true defense of Washington, he said, was before Richmond; Burnside, with all his troops, should be brought thither from North Carolina; with a little more than half a chance he could take Richmond.

On the 25th of July General Halleck went to the James in order to consult with the commander of the Army of the Potomac. At that time McClellan's plan was to cross the James River, attack Petersburg, cut off the enemy's communications with the South, making no farther demonstrations against Richmond. Petersburg being then wholly unfortified, this attempt might probably have succeeded. Halleck was, however, utterly averse to the plan, and it was abandoned. McClellan then said that with 30,000 re-enforcements he could attack Richmond with a good chance of success, although he would then have but 120,000 effective men, while he estimated the force of the enemy at not less than 200,000. Halleck would promise only 20,000, and said that unless McClellan could attack Richmond with these, with a strong probability of success, it would be a military necessity to unite the forces of McClellan and Pope. McClellan, after consultation with his officers, decided that he would make the attempt with 20,000, although he would not say that the probabilities were in favor of success; still, there was a chance, and he would try it, and Halleck returned to Washington with the understanding that the attempt should be made. The next day McClellan wrote asking 15,000 or 20,000 more re-enforcements.[3]

The four weeks' quiet on the James was interrupted on the night of July 31. The Union fleet lay stretched along for two miles above and below Harrison's Landing. Just opposite, across the James, was Coggin's Point, a peninsular projection jutting out into the river, diminishing its breadth to 1000 yards. Hill ordered forty-three guns to be quietly placed on the point; this was done without being discovered from the opposite shore, and just after midnight fire was opened upon the Federal shipping and camp.

Innumerable lights from the vessels and camp served to show just where lay the objects of aim, and for half an hour there was a continuous bombardment. But, owing to the difficulty of the roads, and the necessity for concealing the operation, only a small quantity of ammunition had been brought forward. In all only 1000 shot were fired, by which ten men were killed and fifteen wounded. The attack failed of its main object, the injuring of the fleet. The fire was returned briskly from the gun-boats, but it was almost harmless, there being nothing to show the position of the enemy. Of the Confederates but one man was killed and two wounded. The ammunition being expended, the guns were withdrawn as silently as they had been advanced.[1] The south bank of the river opposite his position was then occupied by McClellan, who wrote cheerily to Halleck, who had urged him to press the enemy: "I will attend to your telegraph about pressing at once. I will send Hooker out. Give me Burnside, and I will stir these people up.[2]

On the 4th of August McClellan moved, as if to press the enemy. Hooker and Sedgwick advanced to Malvern Hill, drove back the enemy's pickets, took possession of the point, and pushed reconnoissances toward Richmond. McClellan reported: "This is a very advantageous position to cover an advance on Richmond, only 14¾ miles distant; and I feel confident that, with re-enforcements, I could march this army there in five days."[3] When intelligence of this advance reached Richmond, the greater part of the troops there were hurried down, and the night of the 6th closed upon the two armies occupying nearly the same positions as on the 1st of July. Next morning, when the Confederates looked to the hill, they found it abandoned by the Union force.[4] McClellan had, during the night, received peremptory orders from Halleck to withdraw his army from the Peninsula. He sent an earnest remonstrance against this order. His army, he said, was now in excellent condition; he held both sides of the James River, and could act in any direction. He was within 25 miles of Richmond, and was not likely to meet the enemy in sufficient force to fight a battle until he had reached 15 or 18 miles, thus practically bringing him within 10 miles of Richmond. His longest line of land transportation was 25 miles; but, by the aid of the gun-boats, his army could be supplied by water during its advance until within 12 miles of Richmond. The retreat would demoralize the army, would depress the people of the North, and would probably influence foreign powers to recognize the Confederacy. He therefore urged that the order should be rescinded; and that, so far from being recalled, his army should be promptly re-enforced to enable it to resume the offensive.[5] Hooker, indeed, wished to disobey the order of the general-in-chief. He said that they had then force enough to take Richmond; he himself was ready to take the advance. If the movement was unsuccessful, it would probably cost McClellan his head, but that "he might as well die for an old sheep as for a lamb." McClellan for a time seemed inclined to follow Hooker's counsel. On the 10th he gave Hooker a written order to supply himself with ammunition and three days' rations, and to be ready to march the next day. "This order," says Hooker, "was communicated to the whole army, and I firmly believed that order meant Richmond; but, before the time arrived for executing it, it was countermanded."[6]

To McClellan's remonstrance Halleck replied briefly by telegraph, "The order will not be rescinded, and you will be expected to execute it with all possible promptness;" and at length by letter, setting forth his reasons for giving and adhering to the order.[7]

After this definite and final order for the withdrawal from the Peninsula ten days passed before the army began to move. Sharp criminations and recriminations passed between Halleck and McClellan on account of this delay. But at length, on the 16th, the sick and stores had all been embarked, and the movement of the troops had begun. A long pontoon bridge had been thrown across the Chickahominy near its mouth, and by this and other bridges the troops recrossed that fatal stream. On the morning of the 18th the rear guard was over and the bridge was removed. McClellan, who had apprehended an attack upon his rear, did not feel secure until he had his whole army across the river.[8] But almost the entire Confederate force had been gradually withdrawn from Richmond. Jackson and Ewell had been sent to Gordonsville five weeks before; they had been followed a fortnight later by A. P. Hill. On the 13th of August, Longstreet's, Hood's, and the bulk of Magruder's and Huger's divisions marched northward; and while McClellan was congratulating himself that he had got safely across the Chickahominy, the whole Confederate force was a hundred miles away, confronting Pope on the Rappahannock.[9]

---

[1] "The rebel army is in our front, with the purpose of overwhelming us by attacking our positions, or reducing us by blocking our river communications. I can not but regard our position as critical."—*McClellan to the President*, July 7.

[2] D. H. Hill, in *Lee's Rep.*, ii., 110.   [3] *Com. Rep.*, 456.

[1] *Lee's Rep.*, ii., 232.   [2] *McC. Rep.*, 285.   [3] *Ibid.*, 289.
[4] *Lee's Rep.*, i., 16.   [5] *McC. Rep.*, 288–296.   [6] Hooker's Testimony, in *Com. Rep.*, 579.
[7] After replying to the strategical and political arguments advanced by McClellan, Halleck says: "If your estimate of the enemy's strength was correct, your requisition [for 35,000 re-enforcements] was perfectly reasonable; but it was perfectly impossible to fill it until new troops could be enlisted and organized, which would require several weeks. To keep your army in its present position until it could be so re-enforced would almost destroy it in that climate; and, even after you receive the re-enforcements asked for, you admitted that you must reduce Fort Darling and the river batteries before you could advance upon Richmond. It is by no means certain that the reduction of these fortifications would not require considerable time, perhaps as much as those at Yorktown. This delay might not only be fatal to the health of your army, but, in the mean time, General Pope's forces would be exposed to the heavy blows of the enemy without the slightest hope of assistance from you. . . . I have not inquired, and I do not wish to know by whose advice, or for what reasons, the Army of the Potomac was separated into two parts, with the enemy between them. I find the forces divided, and I wish to unite them. Only one feasible plan has been presented for doing this. If you or any one else had presented a better plan, I should have adopted it. But all of your plans require re-enforcements which it is impossible to give you. It is very easy to ask for re-enforcements, but it is not so easy to give them when you have no disposable troops at your command."—*McC. Rep.*, 299–301.

[8] *McC. Rep.*, 313–316.   [9] *Lee's Rep.*, i., 13, 18; ii., 3, 80.

Harper's Pictorial History of the CIVIL WAR

Part Second

HARPER'S

Pictorial History

OF THE

By Alfred H. Guernsey and Henry M. Alden

CIVIL WAR.

PREFACE.

THE writing of this History has extended over a period of five years. It began while the conflict of arms was at the hottest, and before it had passed its doubtful period; it is now concluded nearly three years after the surrender of the rebel armies, but before the final stage of Reconstruction can be fairly said to have been inaugurated. It has been a work of great magnitude, covering as it does the events of seven years—and those seven the most important in our national history.

The design of the Authors has been in no respect modified by the fact that this is an Illustrated History. We have written exactly as we should have done if the interest of our readers depended upon the unadorned recital of facts. No pains have been spared—no expense of time or of study—in order to make this the fullest and most complete history of the Civil War which at this time is possible. We have not compiled from other histories, but have depended entirely upon the original materials furnished by documents of every description, military and political, no small proportion of which have never been published, but have been obtained from prominent actors on both sides of the contest. If we had hastened to submit our work to the public, much of this material, both published and unpublished, would have been lost to us, and our work would to that extent have lacked completeness and maturity. By waiting we have also been enabled to bring the history down to the beginning of the present year, thus including the Reconstruction acts of the Thirty-ninth and Fortieth Congresses. In the whole scheme of the work no less prominence has been given to political than to military events.

The materials from which we have drawn consist of all the official reports, both National and Confederate, which have been published, and a large number of others which we have obtained in manuscript; the official returns of the several armies on both sides; the innumerable letters of war correspondents; conversations with prominent military officers, National and Confederate; miscellaneous documents, maps, memoranda, letters, and orders, furnished by such officers; the *Congressional Globe;* and numerous biographical sketches, more or less extended, of military and political characters. Wherever it has seemed sufficient, we have simply referred to these authorities by citation; and in numerous instances we have either quoted them in full or given a summary of their testimony.

The Introductory Chapters of the work were written early in the war by Mr. Richard Grant White. The remainder, commencing with the section headed "The War for the Union," is by us whose names appear on the title-page. Each of us has written independently of the other, except that we have had access to the same materials, and have consulted together at every stage of the work. As a rule, not however without exceptions, the chapters relating to military operations in the East, and the earlier ones upon political history, are by Alfred H. Guernsey. Those relating to military operations in the West, including the whole of Sherman's Campaigns, together with the later political chapters, are by Henry M. Alden.

While fully confident of the justice of the National cause in the Civil War, we have willingly conceded to those who opposed that cause the same sincerity of motive which we claim for ourselves, and the same conviction of justice in their appeal to arms. We have written of the living as if they were dead, and have endeavored to anticipate the impartial verdict of the future. If we have failed in this regard, it has been an error of judgment rather than of feeling. In the political chapters we have especially striven to avoid special pleading in behalf of any party, seeking to take the attitude of the spectator and judge rather than that of the advocate.

Such has been the scheme of our work, such the materials upon which it has been based, and such the spirit with which it has been conducted. The main outlines of the struggle which we have here portrayed we are confident will stand the test applied by time and by the judgment of posterity.

A. H. G.
H. M. A.

NEW YORK, *April,* 1868.

CONTENTS.

[AT THE COMMENCEMENT OF EACH CHAPTER WILL BE FOUND A DETAILED SYLLABUS OF THE MATTERS THEREIN CONTAINED.]

ILLUSTRATIONS.

SCENES AND INCIDENTS.

MAPS AND PLANS.

PORTRAITS.

HENRY W. HALLECK.

CHAPTER XXII.

POPE'S CAMPAIGN IN VIRGINIA.[1]

Pope placed in command of the Army of Virginia.—Fremont relieved.—Positions of Pope's Forces.—The Plan of Operations.—Pope's Address.—His General Orders.—Similar Confederate Orders.—Pope concentrates his Force.—Jackson ordered to Gordonsville.—Re-enforced by Hill.—Battle of Cedar Mountain.—Banks attacks and is repulsed.—The Losses.—Pope re-enforced.—Jackson retreats to Gordonsville.—Lee joins Jackson, and Pope withdraws beyond the Rappahannock.—Estimate of the Confederate Force.—The Design of Lee.—Manœuvring on the Rappahannock.—Speedy re-enforcements promised to Pope.—Stuart's Raid on Catlett's Station.—Capture of Pope's Dispatch-book, and its Consequences.—Lee's new Plan of Operations.—Jackson marches for Thoroughfare Gap.—Longstreet follows him.—Pope begins to fall back.—Jackson captures Stores at Manassas Junction.—Fight at Bristoe Station.—Fitz John Porter ordered to move.—Taylor's Brigade routed.—Jackson's Peril.—He falls back to Bull Run.—First Battle at Groveton, August 28.—Pope confident of destroying Jackson.—Jackson stands at Bay.—Pope's Plan.—Why it failed.—Affairs at Washington.—Halleck and McClellan.—Second Battle of Groveton, August 29.—Sigel's ineffectual Attack upon the Right.—Fighting upon the Centre and Left.—Longstreet reaches Thoroughfare Gap.—Skirmish at the Gap.—Longstreet's Advance unites with Jackson.—McDowell and Porter.—Pope orders Porter to

attack.—The Order not obeyed.—Hooker's and Reno's Attack upon the Left.—Hatch's Assault along the Turnpike.—Close of the Battle.—Pope claims a Victory.—Pope's new Order to Porter.—Third Battle at Groveton, August 30: Strength of the two Armies.—Pope's Forebodings.—Is convinced that the Enemy is retreating, and orders a Pursuit.—The Confederate Position.—The Union Line.—Porter attacks Jackson's Right.—Reno and Heintzelman attack the Centre.—Jackson demands Re-enforcements.—Longstreet's Movements.—Warren's Stand.—Retreat of the Union Forces.—Losses in the Battles of Groveton.—The Forces after the Battle.—Terror at Washington.—McClellan and his Friends.—The Battle of Chantilly, or Ox Hill.—Death of Kearney and Stevens.—The Retreat to Washington.—Pope relieved from the Command.—Estimate of Pope's Campaign.—The Difficulties in his Way.—His early Measures judicious.—His Error on the 29th.—The Time of Longstreet's arrival on the Field.—The greater Error of the 30th.—Estimate of Lee's Campaign.—Its different Phases.

ON the 26th of June, the day on which the closing operations before Richmond were commenced, General Pope was placed in command of the "Army of Virginia," made up of the corps of Fremont, Banks, and McDowell. Fremont took umbrage at being thus placed under an officer whom he outranked, and asked to be relieved from his command. The request was readily complied with, and he disappears from the history of the war, Sigel being placed in command of his corps. Pope found his army widely scattered. Of McDowell's corps of 18,500 men, one half, under King,

[1] In addition to the authorities heretofore mentioned, we use mainly in this chapter Pope's Report, citing from the official copy, published by order of Congress; and the Report of the Fitz John Porter Court-martial, cited as "Court-martial."

5 D

JOHN POPE.

was at Fredericksburg, on the Rappahannock, the other half, under Ricketts, at Manassas Junction, thirty miles to the north; Banks, with 8000, and Fremont, with 11,500, were at Middletown, fifty miles farther to the northwest, with the Blue Mountains between them and Manassas. Infantry and artillery numbered 34,000, and there were about 5000 cavalry. A considerable part of the force was in bad condition.

The Federal government was still nervously apprehensive for the safety of Washington, though there was not a single Confederate soldier within ten days' march; every man had been withdrawn from the Shenandoah and Rappahannock to the Chickahominy. Pope was ordered, as McDowell had been, to cover Washington from attack from the direction of Richmond, assure the safety of the Valley of the Shenandoah, and then, by menacing the Confederate lines of communication with the South by way of Gordonsville, to endeavor to draw off some of the force then opposed to McClellan before Richmond. The whole plan of the campaign was based upon the supposition that Jackson was still threatening the Valley, and thence Washington, Maryland, and even Pennsylvania. Pope's first object was to concentrate his scattered command upon the line of the Rappahannock, whence he could, by rapid marching, interpose between any body of the enemy moving up the Valley and their main force at Richmond. The retreat of the Army of the Potomac to the James changed the whole aspect of affairs. Pope soon found that his plan for operations was wholly at variance with that of McClellan; and at his suggestion Halleck was summoned[1] from the West, and, as general-in-chief, placed in command of both.

Pope, on taking the field, issued an address to his army[2] censuring, by implication, the course of McClellan, and breathing a spirit of confidence which belied the forebodings which he felt.[3] "I have come," he said, "from the

West, where we have always seen the backs of our enemies; from an army whose business has been to seek the adversary and beat him when found; whose policy has been attack and not defense. I presume that I have been called here to pursue the same system, and to lead you against the enemy. I desire you to dismiss from your minds certain phrases which I am sorry to find much in vogue among you. I hear constantly of taking strong positions and holding them; of lines of retreat and bases of supplies. Let us discard such ideas. The strongest position a soldier should desire is one from which he can most easily advance against the enemy. Let us study the probable lines of retreat of our opponent, and leave our own to take care of themselves."

This address was followed by a series of General Orders prescribing the mode in which the campaign was to be conducted. The troops were, as far as practicable, to subsist upon the country in which their operations were carried on; vouchers were to be given for all supplies taken, payable at the close of the war, upon proof that the holders had been loyal citizens.[1] The cavalry should take no trains for baggage or supplies, only two days' rations, to be carried on their persons; villages and neighborhoods through which they passed were to be laid under contribution for the subsistence of the men and horses.[2] People living along railroad and telegraph lines were to be held responsible for all damage done to them, and for guerrilla attacks. If roads or telegraphs were injured by guerrillas, the inhabitants living within five miles were to be turned out to repair them. If a soldier was fired upon from a house, it was to be razed to the ground, and the inhabitants sent as prisoners to head-quarters. If such an outrage occurred at a distance from any settlement, the people within five miles should be held accountable, and made to pay an indemnity. Any person detected in such outrages, either during the act or afterward, was to be shot, without awaiting civil process.[3] All disloyal male citizens near, within, or in the rear of the army lines were to be arrested; those who took the oath of allegiance, and gave security for its observance, were to be allowed to remain at home; those who refused were to be sent South, beyond the extreme pickets of the army, and if thereafter found behind, within, or near the lines, would be considered as spies, and subjected to the extreme rigor of military law. If any one violated the oath of allegiance, he should be shot, and his property confiscated. No communication should be held, except through the military authority, with any person residing within the lines of the enemy; and any person concerned in carrying letters or messages in any other way would be considered and treated as a spy.[4]

Stringent as these orders were, their severest provisions had been more than anticipated by the action of the Confederate government in Tennessee. Eight months before,[5] Judah Benjamin, then Secretary of War, issued official instructions "as to the prisoners taken among the traitors of East Tennessee." All, said the order, who can be "identified in having been engaged in bridge-burning, are to be tried summarily by drum-head court-martial, and, if found guilty, executed on the spot by hanging. It would be well to leave their bodies hanging in the vicinity of the burnt bridges." All who had not been so engaged were to be sent to Tuscaloosa, Alabama, and to be kept in confinement as prisoners of war. "In no case," continues the order, "is one of the men known to have been up in arms against the government to be released on any oath or pledge of allegiance. The time for such measures is past. They are to be held as prisoners of war, and kept in jail until the close of the war. Such as come in voluntarily, take the oath of allegiance, and surrender their arms, are alone to be treated with leniency." The Confederate government, however, denounced the orders of Pope as gross violation of the rules of war, and by a General Order[6] it was declared that General Pope, and the commissioned officers serving under him, were not entitled to the privileges of prisoners of war, and if any of them were captured they were to be kept in close confinement; and if any persons should be executed in pursuance of his General Orders, an equal number of these prisoners, selected by lot, should be hung.

Pope's first movement was to concentrate his scattered forces, so as to bring them within something like supporting distance of each other. Sigel, who now commanded Fremont's corps, and Banks, were withdrawn from the Valley of the Shenandoah, and posted near Sperryville, east of the Blue Mountains; Ricketts, with his division of McDowell's corps, was brought down from Manassas to Waterloo Bridge, twenty miles to the east; King's division of McDowell's corps was still left at Fredericksburg. The Army of Virginia was thus posted along a line of forty miles. The region having been abandoned by the Confederates, a rapid march of two days, either from his right or left, would have enabled Pope to seize Gordonsville, which commanded the main railroad communication between Richmond and the South. Banks, who had in the mean while pushed southward a score of miles to Culpepper, was ordered, on the 14th of July, to send Hatch, who commanded the cavalry, to seize Gordonsville, and destroy the railroads which centre there from both directions. Hatch failed to execute this order, and having again failed a few days after, he was superseded in the command of the cavalry by Buford.[7]

Tidings of the renewed activity of the Federal forces on the Rappahannock soon reached Richmond, and although the Confederate capital was still threatened by McClellan's great army on the James, so important was the possession of Gordonsville, the key of communication with the South, that Lee ventured to weaken his force at Richmond in order to counteract the menacing movements of Pope. On the 13th of July, Jackson, with his own division and that of Ewell, was ordered to proceed to Gordonsville, with the

carry out the plans of the government with all the energy and all the skill of which I was master."—*Pope's Report*, 6.

[1] July 11.   [2] July 14.
[3] I "took the field in Virginia with grave forebodings of the result, but with a determination to

[1] Order No. 5.   [2] Order No. 6.   [3] Order No. 7.
[4] Order No. 11.   [5] Nov. 25, 1861.   [6] No. 54, August 1, 1862.   [7] *Pope's Report*.

promise of re-enforcements in case there should be a chance to strike an effective blow without withdrawing troops too long from the defense of Richmond. Jackson found Pope too strong to warrant him in making any offensive movements, and for a fortnight contented himself with holding Gordonsville. But there being no indication that McClellan meditated moving upon Richmond, Lee, on the 27th of July, sent A. P. Hill to join Jackson.[1] The Confederate force at Richmond was thus reduced by 35,000 men, fully a third of its number.

On the 29th of July Pope left Washington to join his army in the field. On the 7th of August he advanced their position somewhat, concentrating his infantry within a space of ten miles along the road from Sperryville to Culpepper, the cavalry being thrown ten miles forward toward Gordonsville. On the same day, Jackson, having been informed that only a part of the enemy was at Culpepper, marched his command in that direction, hoping to strike a portion of Pope's army before it could be re-enforced. On the morning of the 9th, Banks was pushed six miles forward to a strong position near Cedar Mountain, and Ricketts was posted three miles in the rear. Sigel had been ordered to march to Culpepper, so as to be there in the morning; but, owing to misconception of orders, he did not arrive until late in the afternoon.

In the afternoon of the 9th, Ewell, whose division was in the advance, came in sight of Banks's position, near the northwestern flank of Cedar Mountain, a conical hill which rises sharply a few hundred feet from a plain intersected by creeks and low ridges. On the crest of one of these a body of Union cavalry was seen, the infantry and artillery being hidden by the opposite slope. Two brigades of Ewell's division, moving to the right, ascended Cedar Mountain, and planted their batteries two hundred feet up the side, so as to command the valley below. The remainder of Ewell's division, with a part of that of Jackson, keeping to the left, passed beyond the base of the mountain, and took up a position on a wooded ridge opposite the Union line. Hill's division had not yet come up. Lawton's brigade, the strongest of Jackson's division, was left behind to guard the trains, and took no part in the action. Between the wooded ridges occupied by the two armies lay an open plain a few hundred yards wide; here was a cornfield, and beyond this a wheat-field, upon which the yellow shooks of grain just reaped were still standing. At four o'clock a fierce fire of artillery had fairly opened. Some loss was sustained by the Federals from the batteries on the mountain side; more by the Confederates in the plain below. Winder, who now led the brigade which still bore the name of "Jackson's Own," was killed, and the command of it devolved upon Taliaferro. The cannonade was kept up for an hour, when Banks, believing that the enemy were in no great force,[2] threw his whole division in two columns across the grainfield. One column charged straight across the field upon the Confederate right. Early, who was posted there, being sorely pressed, called for re-enforcements. Hill had now come up, and one of his brigades was sent to Early's support. The main assault was upon the Confederate left. So sudden was the onset, that the extremity of the Confederate line was turned, and, before they were aware of it, they were charged directly in the rear, and forced back upon their centre, which also gave way. All seemed lost. The artillery, hurried to the rear, disappeared behind the crest of the ridge, while the greater part of the infantry broke away in confusion fast verging into rout. Jackson hurried in person to the front, and at length stopped the flight and re-formed his broken line. Two more brigades of Hill's division had now come up, and were pushed into action. The Confederates on the field now outnumbered the Federals by nearly two to one.[3] The Union advance was checked, and then forced back across the open field beyond the ridge from which they had come. In the mean while, Pope, who was with Ricketts's division, only three miles in the rear, became convinced, notwithstanding the assurances which he had just received from Banks, that the enemy was really in force, and that a serious action was going on. He hurried forward with Ricketts, and just at dusk met the retreating forces of Banks. A new line was formed, toward which Jackson advanced cautiously in the darkness, opening upon it a sharp artillery fire, which was returned so vigorously that a Confederate battery was disabled and withdrawn. Jackson then fell back, and passed the night on the battle-field.

In this accidental engagement, which might be denominated simply an "affair" were it not for the magnitude of the loss on both sides, the Confederates lost, in killed and wounded, about 1300; the Union loss was estimated at about 1400 killed and wounded, and 400 prisoners. Besides these there were a large number of stragglers, who never returned to their commands.[4]

[1] *Lee's Rep.*, i., 15; ii., 3.

[2] Banks's dispatches to Pope: "August 9, 2 25. The enemy shows his cavalry, which is strong, ostentatiously. No infantry seen, and not much artillery. Woods on the left, said to be full of troops. A visit to the front does not impress that the enemy intends immediate attack. He seems, however, to be taking positions."—"4 50. About four o'clock, shots were exchanged by the skirmishers. Artillery fire on both sides in a few minutes. One regiment of rebel infantry advancing. Now deployed in front as skirmishers. I have ordered a regiment on the right, Williams's, to meet them; and one on the left, Augur's, to advance on the left and in front."—"5 P.M. They are now approaching each other."—*Pope's Report*, 218.

[3] The Union force consisted only of Banks's corps, numbering at the outset only 8000. There were present, as is shown by the report of losses (*Lee's Rep.*, ii., 49), forty-two regiments of Confederate infantry, 21,000 men in all; but of these only about one half were seriously engaged in the actual fight. Two thirds of the loss, indeed, fell upon ten of the regiments of Jackson and Ewell.

[4] "No report of killed and wounded has been made to me by General Banks. I can, therefore, only form an approximation of our losses in that battle. Our killed, wounded, and prisoners amounted to about 1800 men, besides which, fully 1000 men straggled back to Culpepper Courthouse and beyond, and never entirely returned to their commands. . . . No material of war nor baggage-trains were lost on either side."—*Pope's Report*, 11. Jackson says: "We captured 400 prisoners, 5302 small-arms, one 12-pounder Napoleon and its caisson, with two other caissons and a limber, and three colors. The official reports of the casualties in my command show a loss of 223 killed, 1060 wounded, 31 missing—total loss, 1314. This was probably about one half that sustained by the enemy."—*Lee's Rep.*, ii., 7. There is reason to suppose that Pope's estimate of his loss was too low; for he puts down Banks's force before the battle at 8000, and afterward he counts it at 5000, a diminution of 3000. If half of the 1000 stragglers returned to their command, there remain 2500 for killed, wounded, and prisoners, or 2100 killed and wounded, which we think to be about the true number. If all of the stragglers returned, there would still be a loss of 400 prisoners, and 1600 killed and wounded.

During the next two days the armies lay watching each other, neither commander venturing upon any offensive movement. King had, on the day before the battle, been ordered from Fredericksburg to join Pope. He arrived on the evening of the 11th, raising Pope's force to about 33,000. With these, he proposed to fall at daylight upon Jackson, upon his line of communications, and compel him "to fight a battle which must have been entirely decisive for one army or the other."[1] Jackson, whose numbers were about the same, had learned of the re-enforcements of Pope, and, supposing them to be much greater than they were, fell back during the night of the 11th, in order to "avoid being attacked by the vastly superior force in front of me, and with the hope that General Pope would be induced to follow me until I should be re-enforced."[2]

The Union cavalry followed the retiring enemy to the Rapidan, and captured some stragglers. They then returned to their former position, and occupied the line of the Rapidan from Raccoon Ford to the base of the Blue Ridge. On the 14th, Reno joined Pope with 8000 men of Burnside's command, which had been brought from North Carolina to Fortress Monroe, and thence to Fredericksburg. Pope, with his infantry, now numbering 40,000 men, pushed forward a little beyond Cedar Mountain. A week had not passed, however, before Pope became assured that nearly the whole of the Confederate army had left Richmond, and were concentrated in his immediate front, designing to overwhelm him before he could be joined by any part of the Army of the Potomac. He thereupon fell back beyond the Rappahannock, and by the 19th his army, 45,000 strong, infantry and cavalry, was posted for eight miles along the north bank, from Rappahannock Station to Warrenton Springs. Across the river was Lee, with 85,000, being the whole of the Confederate army of Virginia, with the exception of D. H. Hill's division, which was left a few days longer at Richmond, and Holmes's, which was not moved at all.[3]

Burnside's corps had been brought from North Carolina to Fortress Monroe, and early in August it was known at Richmond that it was being embarked on transports. The direction in which it was sent would furnish a clear indication of the Federal designs. If it came up the James to McClel-

[1] *Pope's Report*, 11. [2] Jackson, in *Lee's Rep.*, ii., 7.

[3] The Confederate "Reports of the Army of Northern Virginia," while minute upon almost every other topic, are almost wholly silent as to the force engaged in the operations of August and September. We are forced to rely upon other sources for an approximative estimate of these forces. Four independent lines of investigation, taken in connection with a few hints scattered through the Reports, give results so nearly alike, that we consider our estimate as substantially correct.

I. It was shown (*ante*, pp. 361, 379) that the effective force at the commencement of the "Seven Days" was 100,000, and that the losses in battle were about 20,000; to which should be added probably 10,000 by sickness during the ensuing six weeks. The conscription law had been fairly in operation since the close of June, and had, as the writer was informed by General J. E. Johnston, during the five weeks after the battle of Fair Oaks, added about 40,000 to the army at Richmond. The operation of this law being very uniform, 40,000 were probably added during the six weeks preceding the middle of August. The recruits, instead of being sent on from the camps of instruction in regiments and brigades, were sent in squads to join the old regiments. This would make the entire force at the middle of August a little more than it was at the close of June—that is, 110,000. Every division and brigade, with the exception of that of Holmes, some 10,000 strong, was finally sent from Richmond and Petersburg in the following order: Jackson, July 13; A. P. Hill, July 27; Longstreet, August 13; D. H. Hill, August 21, joining Lee on the 23d of September, three days after the battle of Groveton. This makes the entire force at the outset 100,000 of all arms.

II. The reports of casualties, which will be cited in the appropriate places, give the loss by regiments in the whole series of battles; and as every regiment was apparently brought into action at one time or another, these lists contain the entire number of regiments. We find 177 different regiments of infantry from the different states, as follows: Virginia, 39; Georgia, 37; North Carolina, 26; South Carolina, 17; Alabama, 16; Mississippi, 12; Louisiana, 9; Texas, 3; Tennessee, 3; Florida, 2; Arkansas, 1. From indicia scattered here and there, we put the aggregate strength of the regiments at 500, which gives 88,500 infantry; the artillery and cavalry we put down at 5000 each, making a total of 98,500 of all arms.

III. There were, in all, 40 brigades; each of these comprised from three to six regiments. In many cases the numbers which were carried into the separate actions are noted in the reports. Comparing these, and taking into account the losses previously reported, we find the brigades to have averaged about 2250, making about 90,000 infantry, and 10,000 artillery and cavalry.

These data thus all indicate, without the probability of any material error, that the entire force of the Confederate army, previous to any losses on the march or in action, was about 100,000 of all arms. The regiments brought into each action, and the losses in every battle being given throughout, we shall be able to arrive at a very close approximation of the actual force at each important period of the campaign.

IV. After the foregoing estimate had been made, I obtained an abstract of the official returns of the various Confederate armies during almost the whole period of the war. These returns came into the hands of the government at the surrender of the army of Lee. An abstract of these was furnished by the War Department to Mr. William Swinton, author of the "Campaigns of the Army of the Potomac." For this, and many other documents as yet inaccessible to the general student, I am indebted to Mr. Swinton. These returns corroborate the accuracy with which my previous estimates had been framed. I here give the returns of the Confederate "Army of Northern Virginia" from Feb. 28, 1862, to Feb. 28, 1865. I shall have frequent occasion, in subsequent chapters, to refer to this table. The explanatory notes appended to it are my own. In referring to the strength of this army at different periods, I shall consider only those reported as "present for duty." It will be seen that the returns are wanting for some of the most important periods.

RETURNS OF THE CONFEDERATE ARMY OF NORTHERN VIRGINIA FROM FEB. 28, 1862, TO FEB. 28, 1865.

Date.	Present and Absent.	Absent.	Aggregate Present.	Present for Duty.
1862. Feb. 28[a]	84,225	27,829	56,396	47,617
" July 20[b]	137,030	42,344	94.686	69,559
" Sept. 30[c]	139,143	76,430	62,713	52,609
" Oct. 20	153,778	74,403	79,395	67,805
" Nov. 20	153,790	67,207	86,583	73,554
" Dec. 31	152,853	61,799	91,004	79,072
1863. Jan. 31	144,605	51,308	93,297	72,226
" Feb. 28[d]	114,175	39,740	74,435	58,559
" Mar. 31	109,839	36.460	73,379	60,298
" May 31	133,689	44,935	88,754	68,352
" July 31	117,602	63,991	53,611	41,135
" Aug. 31	133,264	61,300	71,964	56,327
" Sept. 30[e]	95,164	39,943	55,221	44,367
" Oct. 31	97,211	39,960	57,251	45,614
1863. Nov. 20	96,576	40,488	56,088	48,269
" Dec. 30	91,253	36,538	54,715	43,558
1864. Jan. 31	79,602	34,463	45,139	35,849
" Feb. 20	68,435	28,873	39,562	33,811
" Mar. 10	79,202	33,051	46,151	39,407
" April 10	97,576	36,358	61,218	52,626
" June 30	92,685	30,114	62,571	51,863
" July 10[f]	135,805	66,961	68,844	57,097
" May 31	146,838	87,854	58,984	44,247
" Oct. 31	177,103	94,468	82,635	62,875
" Nov. 30	181,826	93,966	87,860	69,290
" Dec. 20	155,772	76,454	79,318	66,533
1865. Jan. 31	141,627	71,954	69,673	53,445
" Feb. 28[g]	160,411	87,062	73,349	59,094

[a] It has been shown (*ante*, p. 360) that at the close of May this army numbered 67,000, and (*ante*, p. 361) that at the end of June it had fully 100,000 men present for duty.

[b] Three weeks after the close of the "Seven Days," its force present for duty, notwithstanding its losses, was nearly 70,000 on the 20th of July. The returns for the next six weeks are wanting; but it is certain that large additions were received, bringing its marching force in August fully up to 100,000.

[c] On the 30th of September, a fortnight after the battle of Antietam, there were but 72,000 "present," including sick and wounded. By this time all those who had fallen out in the march had rejoined their commands, so that the campaign from Cedar Run to Antietam cost 38,000, disabled and deserters. During the next two months the army was largely augmented by conscription.

[d] The diminution at this time was owing to a part of Longstreet's corps having been sent to North Carolina, where he remained until May.

[e] At this time Longstreet had been sent with re-enforcements to Bragg in Tennessee.

[f] From this time the effects of desertion and sickness became strikingly apparent. The number of the "absent" exceeds, sometimes very considerably, that of the "present;" while of those "present" only about two thirds were fit for "duty." The effective strength of the army was only about one third of its nominal force.

[g] The returns for the remainder of the period before the surrender are wanting.

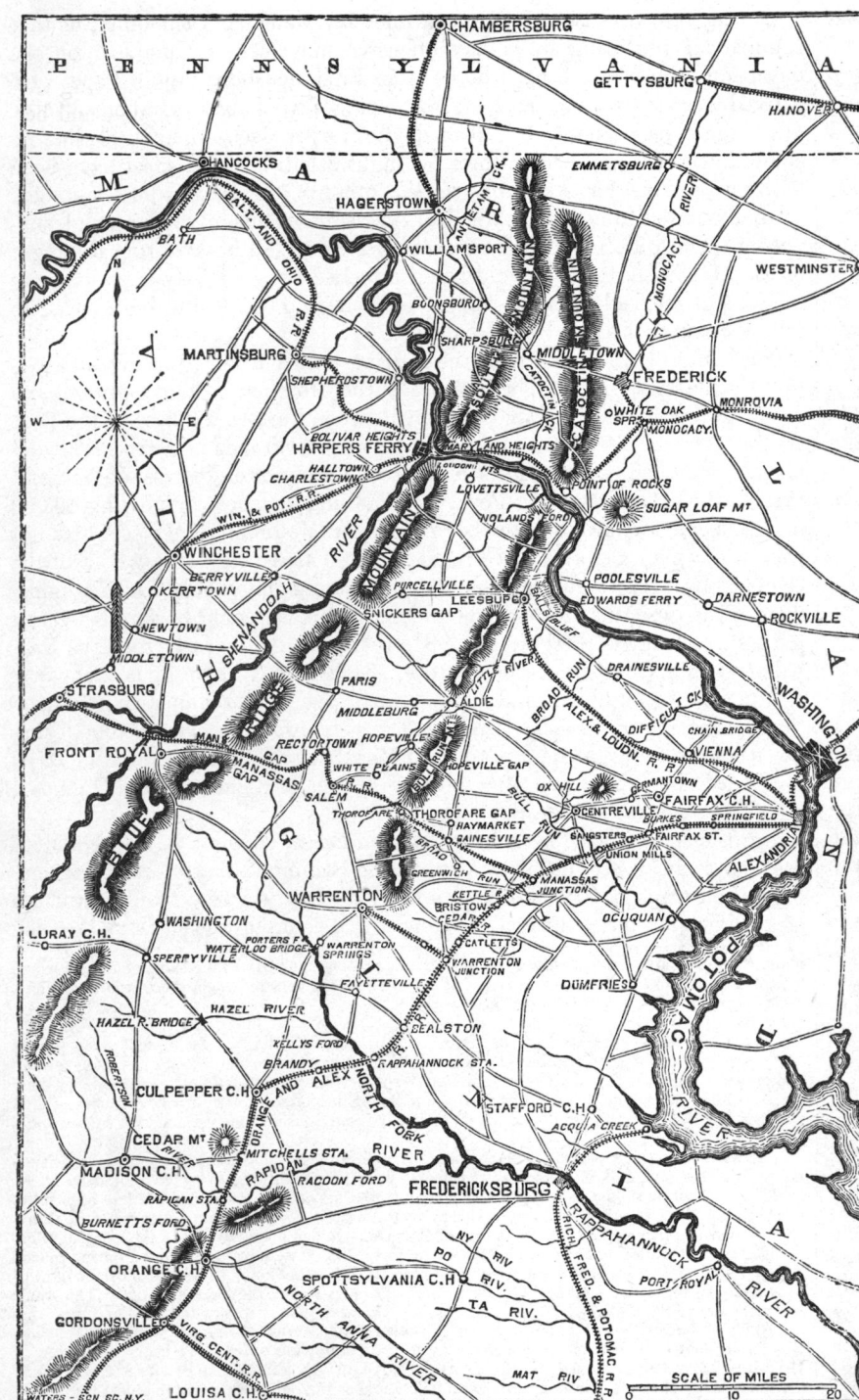

MAP OF THE CAMPAIGN IN VIRGINIA.

ed attempts to cross at various points, and an almost continuous artillery fire was kept up along the whole line of eight miles, with little loss on either side.[1] Lee then began to move slowly up the river, in order to turn the Union right. Pope had been directed to keep himself in communication with Fredericksburg, whither the Army of the Potomac was being brought, and could not extend his right to check the enemy. He was assured, however, that if he could hold his line until the close of the 23d, he would receive re-enforcements sufficient to enable him to assume the offensive.[2] On the 22d he resolved to cross the river the next morning, and fling his whole force upon the flank and rear of Lee's long column, which was passing toward his right. The manœuvre, except that it involved no long march of the attacking column, would have been almost a repetition of that by which Lee assailed McClellan's retreating column at Frazier's Farm; but such was the disparity of force that it could hardly have been other than a disastrous failure. But a fierce rain-storm during the night raised the waters of the shallow river six or eight feet, swept away the bridges and overflowed the fords, so as to render the movement impracticable, and also prevented Lee from any serious attempt to cross above, which he had begun to do.[3]

An episode occurred during that stormy night of the 22d which, though trifling in itself, changed the whole course of the campaign. Pope's head-quarters were at Catlett's Station, ten miles in the rear of the centre of his line. Here all the army trains were parked, guarded by 1500 infantry and five companies of cavalry. Stuart, with 1500 cavalry, had crossed the river above Pope's extreme right, and, gaining the rear of his line, pressed, without being discovered, down to Catlett's Station. Here, in the midst of the darkest night he ever knew, Stuart found himself in the very midst of the Union camp. By chance he encountered a negro whom he had known before, who offered to guide him to the spot occupied by Pope's staff. A few companies stole unperceived up to the tents "occupied by the convivial staff of Pope," charged upon them, captured one or two of the inmates, and seized some plunder. But of far more importance than all was Pope's dispatch-book, which revealed just the situation of his army, his imminent need of re-enforcements, and his expectation of the time when they would reach him.[4] This bold dash cost one man killed and one wounded. When that unnamed negro, accidentally encountered in the darkness, guided the Sixth Virginia cavalry to Pope's tent, he was potentially fighting the battles of Groveton and Antietam.

The disclosures made by this dispatch-book convinced Lee that, if he could at once throw his force directly upon the Union rear, cutting its communications with Washington, Pope's whole army could be destroyed or captured. To do this his force must be divided, a part marching rapidly around the enemy's right to his rear, the remainder occupying his attention in front until the departing column was well advanced, when it would follow by the same route.[5] The manœuvre was a delicate one, depending upon every movement being executed at the precise time. A sudden storm, or any other accident interfering for a single day, would thwart the whole plan. It was also hazardous, for the Union army might fall with equal or superior force upon either of the separated divisions. Still, the chance of great success was sufficient to warrant the attempt, and not a moment was lost in carrying it out.

The first part, upon the successful execution of which every thing depended, was confided to Jackson, whose capacity for conducting a rapid march had been abundantly tested. On the morning of the 25th he left his position, passed up the south bank of the Rappahannock, crossing the river beyond Pope's extreme right, and then pressed rapidly up the narrow valley between Blue and Bull Run Mountains. The column pressed on by strange country roads and by "nigh cuts" across open fields, and at midnight, after a march of twenty miles, reached Salem, a little town just opposite the Thoroughfare Gap, through which he hoped to pass the Bull Run Mountains, and emerge directly upon Pope's rear. If that pass should be defended the whole movement would be a failure. Stuart, with all the cavalry, accompanied the column on its right, scouring the region between it and the Union force. It was hoped that the movement would be unperceived and unsuspected by the enemy. "Don't shout, boys, the Yankees will hear us," said Jackson, as the long column passed by a point where he stood, proudly watching their rapid march. "Who could fail," he said, "to win victory with these men?"[6]

Pope, however, was not taken by surprise. Jackson's march had hardly been begun when he was informed that "a large detachment of the enemy, numbering 36 regiments of infantry, with the usual number of batteries of artillery and a large cavalry force, was marching rapidly up the North Branch, and was then pressing on toward White Plains and Salem, and from these points would be able to turn our right by the direction of Thoroughfare Gap, or even north of that place."[7] He was, however, compelled

lan, the siege of Richmond was to be pressed. If it went to the Rappahannock, McClellan would be withdrawn from the James. Mosby, soon to be known as a vigorous partisan leader, had been captured; being set free by exchange, he passed Fortress Monroe as Burnside was embarking. He learned from a sure source that the destination was the Rappahannock, and conveyed to Lee the long-wished-for information.[1] Reports, which, however, were premature, also affirmed that a part of McClellan's army had gone to the aid of Pope. It was clear, therefore, that active operations against Richmond were no longer contemplated; and Lee believed that he might venture to leave the Confederate capital, and advance with almost his whole army upon Pope, and overwhelm him before re-enforcements could reach him. Some changes had been made in the organization of his army. Huger, whose incompetency had been demonstrated, was displaced; Magruder was sent to Texas. Their divisions, and that of Whiting, which had been only temporarily attached to Jackson's force during the Seven Days, were united with that of Longstreet, and placed under his command. This body of 50,000 men left Richmond by the 13th of August, and moved with such rapidity that by the 16th it had passed Gordonsville, and was advancing toward the Rappahannock, whither Jackson had proceeded the day before.[2] Thus, two days before McClellan's advance corps and trains had fairly started from their camp on the James, Richmond and Petersburg were left defended only by about 20,000, the division of D. H. Hill and Holmes, with perhaps a few raw conscripts who had not been assigned to their places in the grand army. So secretly had this movement been made, that on this very day reports reached McClellan that the enemy were advancing against him from the Chickahominy; and on the 17th he wrote that he should not feel entirely secure until he had his whole army beyond the Chickahominy,[3] and a week later he thought it necessary to strengthen the defenses of Yorktown to resist an attack from the direction of Richmond. On that very day D. H. Hill left Petersburg with his division, the last to join in the movement toward Washington.[4]

Early on the morning of the 20th the pickets of Pope's right at Rappahannock Station were driven in, and before night the main body of the Confederate infantry, outnumbering him almost two to one, were in his front across the Rappahannock. During the two following days Lee made repeat-

[1] Cooke's *Stonewall Jackson*. [2] *Lee's Rep.*, i., 18; ii., 81, 90.
[3] *McC. Rep.*, 314, 317. [4] *McC. Rep.*, 320; *Lee's Rep.*, ii., 111.

[1] The Confederate loss, August 20-23, was 152 killed and wounded.—*Lee's Rep.*, i., 50.
[2] Halleck to Pope, August 21: "I have telegraphed to General Burnside to know at what hour he can re-enforce Reno. I am waiting his answer. Every effort must be made to hold the Rappahannock. Large forces will be in to-morrow."—Later, same day: "I have just sent [query received] General Burnside's reply. General Cox's forces are coming on from Parkersburg, and will be here to-morrow or next day. Dispute every inch of ground, and fight like the devil till we can re-enforce you. Forty-eight hours more, and we can make you strong enough. Don't yield an inch if you can help it."—*Pope's Report*, 221, 222.
General Haupt, Superintendent of Transportation at Alexandria, to Pope, received August 24: "Thirty thousand troops or more demand transport. We can manage 12,000 per day. The new troops might march, the veterans go in cars, horses driven; baggage, tents, etc., wait until they can be forwarded. Supplies take precedence."—Later, same day: "We expect to clean out all the troops now here, and all that are expected to-day."—*Ibid.*, 227. [3] *Pope's Report*, 13.
[4] Stuart, in *Lee's Rep.*, ii., 137. [5] *Lee's Rep.*, i., 21. [6] Cooke's *Stonewall Jackson*, 275.
[7] *Pope's Report*, 15. Colonel J. S. Clark, who at great risk watched Jackson's march, saw

by his orders to hold his force in such a position as to enable him to keep up his communication with Fredericksburg. Assurances of speedy re-enforcements were so precise and definite that he felt warranted in holding his position. He was assured that 30,000 would reach him by the 25th; but on the evening of that day only 8000 had come up.[1]

On the 26th, Longstreet, who had kept up a show of force in front of Pope, yet all the while creeping away to his right, commenced his march to unite with Jackson, who, having left Salem at daybreak, was pressing through Thoroughfare Gap. Pope then abandoned the line of the Rappahannock, and undertook to throw his whole force in the direction of Gainesville and Manassas Junction. On the morning of the 27th he had 54,000 infantry, made up of his own Army of Virginia, and the re-enforcements which had reached him from Burnside's corps and the Army of the Potomac. He had also nominally 4000 cavalry, but their horses were so broken down that hardly 500 were fit for service.[2]

Jackson, in the mean while, had passed Thoroughfare Gap on the morning of the 26th; pressed past Gainesville, which Pope supposed to be strongly occupied, but where there was not a single Union soldier, and by sunset was at Bristoe Station, on the railroad which formed Pope's chief means for supplies. At Manassas Junction, seven miles distant, was a large dépôt of supplies almost without guard.[3] A strong body of cavalry under Stuart, and about 500 infantry under Trimble, were dispatched to seize these stores. They pressed on through the darkness, though the infantry had made a march of more than twenty miles that day, and before dawn had effected their purpose, capturing the only considerable dépôt of stores between Pope's army and Washington.[4] These stores were destroyed by the Confederates, and so were of little advantage to Jackson beyond giving his hungry troops rations for a single day, but their loss proved a serious disadvantage to Pope.

On the morning of the 27th the greater part of Jackson's command moved to Manassas, leaving Ewell at Bristoe, upon which place Hooker was marching. A short action took place in the afternoon, in which Ewell was worsted, but he fell back in good order to Manassas.[5] Fitz John Porter, who, with 4500 men, was at Warrenton Junction, nine miles distant, was ordered by Pope to move during the night to Bristoe, to the support of Hooker, whose ammunition was entirely exhausted. He was to be there at daybreak, but did not reach the place until six hours later.[6] Meanwhile a considerable body of Union troops came down toward Manassas along the railroad. They found the Junction too strongly held to be recovered, and after a gallant fight, in which General Taylor was killed, they retreated with much loss.[7]

Pope's force was now concentrating in the neighborhood of Manassas. Had this concentration been effected one day earlier, Jackson would have marched into the jaws of destruction. As it was, he was in imminent peril. He had no alternative but to retreat, but whither it was hard to say. McDowell, marching to his right from Warrenton, was at Gainesville, with a force equal to his own, cutting him off to the west by the route by which he had advanced. To retreat northward toward Aldie would have removed him every step farther from the main army of Lee, which was yet beyond the Bull Run Mountains. He adopted the only course which could have saved him, and even in this the chances were fearfully against him. This was to fall back toward the point from which Longstreet was advancing, and at the same time deceive his opponent as to the direction of his retreat. His own division, now commanded by Taliaferro, moved from Manassas directly north, while Ewell and Hill, with the cavalry, marched northeastward, as if pushing straight for Washington. At Centreville they turned sharply west, and during the 28th rejoined Taliaferro a little west and north of the battle-field of Bull Run.[8] The ruse succeeded. Pope withdrew McDowell from Gainesville, marched him directly toward Centreville, and ordered Heintzelman in the same direction. Jackson had now secured a strong position a little north and west of the battle-field of Bull Run. McDowell's line of march led him close by the right of Jackson, and exposed him to a flank attack. This was made by Jackson just before sunset, and a sharp action, mostly of artillery, ensued, which was terminated by the darkness, neither side gaining any decided advantage,[9] and both suffering heavy loss. Ewell and Taliaferro were severely wounded.[10]

Pope, supposing that Jackson was in full retreat to Thoroughfare Gap, was confident that there was no escape for him. At half past nine he wrote to Kearney, "McDowell has intercepted the retreat of the enemy, and is now in his front. Unless he can escape by by-paths leading to the north to-night, he must be captured." McDowell must hold his ground at all hazards, prevent the retreat of Jackson, and by daylight the next morning the whole force would be up from Centreville and Manassas Junction, and between them the enemy must be crushed. Jackson had now, after his losses, exclusive of cavalry, not quite 30,000 men. Pope had, or rather supposed that he had, 50,000, who could be brought into action in the morning. Of these, 25,000, under McDowell, Sigel, and Reynolds, were supposed to be directly west of Jackson, between him and the Gap; 25,000 more, with Kearney, Hooker, and Reno, near Centreville, on the east. His only apprehension was that Jackson might retreat northward toward Leesburg, and to prevent this, Kearney was to keep close to him during the night of the 28th.[1]

This apparently well-conceived plan was based upon a misconception as to the purpose and position of the enemy. Jackson had no purpose of retreating, but had taken a position which he meant to hold until he should be joined by Longstreet, who was a full day's march nearer him than Pope supposed. The execution of his plan was prevented by a movement previously made by McDowell, who had sent Ricketts toward Thoroughfare Gap, and had before withdrawn King's division to Manassas Junction, near which place Porter now was. Pope's force, therefore, instead of being in the rear and on the front of Jackson, was on his right flank and front—Sigel's corps near Groveton, close on the flank; McDowell and Porter near Manassas; Reno and Heintzelman in front, toward Centreville. McDowell and Porter were ordered, on the morning of the 29th, toward Gainesville, and thus gain a position somewhat in Jackson's rear, while Sigel was to fall upon his flank, and Heintzelman and Reno, marching from Centreville, to attack him in front. These movements would bring the whole force together; and when communication was established, the whole command was to halt, and, above all things, to occupy a position from which they could reach Bull Run that night; for Pope presumed that it would be necessary to do this on account of supplies. "The indications," he said, "are, that the whole force of the enemy is moving in this direction at a pace which will bring them here by to-morrow night or next day."[2]

Pope's expectation upon the morning of the 29th was, with his whole force, two to one, to fall upon Jackson's front, right flank, and rear; and he hoped, with good reason, "to gain so decisive a victory over the army under Jackson, before he could have been joined by any of the forces under Longstreet, that the army of Lee would have been so crippled and checked by the destruction of this large force as to be no longer in condition to prosecute operations of an aggressive character."[3] This accomplished, he would have fallen back across Bull Run, and have awaited supplies and re-enforcements, which would in a day or two have given him a force superior to that of the enemy. This plan failed utterly through the determined resistance opposed by Jackson, and from the fact that Longstreet was nearer at hand than was supposed. At the very moment when this order was written, Longstreet was pressing through the narrow gorge of Thoroughfare Gap; and, instead of coming to Jackson's aid "to-morrow night or next day," he was able to give him essential support that afternoon, and by the next morning, the 30th, to bring his whole force upon the field.

In the mean while all was confusion, doubt, and ignorance at the Federal capital. McClellan left Fortress Monroe on the 23d for Acquia Creek, on the Rappahannock, whither a part of his army had preceded him, and the rest was to follow. Next day he telegraphed to Halleck for orders, and especially for information as to where Pope was, and what he was doing. "I do not know," replied the general-in-chief, "where Pope is, or where the enemy in force is. These are matters which I have been all day most anxious to ascertain." Two days later Halleck telegraphed, "There is reason to believe that the enemy is moving a large force into the Shenandoah Valley. Don't draw any troops down the Rappahannock at present; we shall probably want them all in the direction of the Shenandoah. Perhaps you had better leave Burnside in charge at Acquia Creek, and come to Alexandria, as very great irregularities are reported there." On the 27th still there was no sure information as to what was going on. Past midnight, McClellan had heard that heavy firing had been heard at Centreville; he had sent to ascertain the truth, and, meanwhile, asked anxiously whether the works in front of Washington were garrisoned and ready for defense. At 1 35 there is news that "Taylor's brigade, sent this morning to Bull Run Bridge, had been cut to pieces or captured;" and McClellan thinks the best policy will be to make the works at Washington "perfectly safe, and mobilize a couple of corps as soon as possible, but not to advance them until they can have their artillery and cavalry." At 2 30: "I still think that we should first provide for the immediate defense of Washington on both sides of the Potomac. I am not responsible for the past, and can not be for the future, unless I receive authority to dispose of the available force according to my judgment. Please inform me at once what my position is. I do not wish to act in the dark." At 6: "A dispatch from Pope, dated at 10 A.M., says, 'All forces now sent forward should be sent to my right, at Gainesville.' I have at my disposal here about 10,000 men of Franklin's corps, about 2500 of General Tyler's brigade, and Colonel Tyler's 1st Connecticut Artillery, which I recommend should be held for the defense of Washington. If you wish me to order any part of this force to march to the front, it is in readiness to march at a moment's notice to any point you may indicate."[4] At 4 10, on the 28th: "Franklin is with me here at Alexan-

only a part of his force. Instead of 36 regiments of infantry, Jackson had about 66, all of which were on the march. The entire cavalry force of the Confederate army was at this time with Jackson, for Longstreet (*Lee's Rep.*, ii., 81) says that on the 27th he had no cavalry.

[1] *Pope's Report*, 15. Also, considerably enlarged, *Reb. Rec.*, v., 348. Also Note [2], *ante*, p. 384.

[2] *Pope's Report*, 17.

[3] At half past ten on the evening of that day, McDowell, then at Warrenton, wrote to Pope, "Centreville and Manassas are fortified, the former sufficiently to offer a stout resistance, and the latter enough to aid materially raw troops."—*Pope's Report*, 200.

[4] Among the stores captured were 50,000 pounds of bacon, 1000 barrels of beef, 2000 of pork, 2000 of flour; two trains loaded with stores and clothing, large quantities of forage, 8 guns, 42 wagons and ambulances, 200 tents; 300 prisoners, 200 negroes, and 175 horses also fell into their hands.—*Lee's Rep.*, ii., 155. A sharp dispute arose between Stuart and Trimble as to the credit of this operation, each denying the claims of the other.—*Ibid.*, 143, 150–159. Jackson (*Ibid.*, 93) clearly gives it to Trimble.

[5] *Lee's Rep.*, 93.

[6] *Pope's Testimony on Porter's Trial.* The failure to execute this order formed one of the charges against Porter, who was subsequently tried by court-martial and cashiered.

[7] *Lee's Rep.*, ii., 93.

[8] Pope indeed says (*Report*, 18) that, if Jackson had massed his whole force and attacked the Union centre at Bristoe Station, the most serious consequences would have ensued; but the result fully justifies Jackson's course.

[9] Pope says, "Each party maintained its ground." Jackson says, "The Federals did not attempt to advance, but maintained their ground with obstinate determination. Both lines stood exposed to the discharge of musketry and artillery until about nine o'clock, when the enemy slowly fell back, yielding the field to our troops."

[10] The actions of this and the two following days are known as indifferently as the "Second Bull Run Battle," the "Battle of Manassas Plains," the "Second Manassas Battle," and the "Battle of Groveton." They were all one battle, fought on the same ground. We think Groveton the most appropriate, that being the name of a small hamlet near the centre of the battle-field.

[1] *Pope's Report*, 19.

[2] Pope's General Order, No. 5, August 29, to McDowell and Porter.—*Report*, 241.

[3] *Pope's Report*, 22.

[4] The dispatches are dated 1 35, 2 30, 6 P.M., August 27; but the context indicates that they

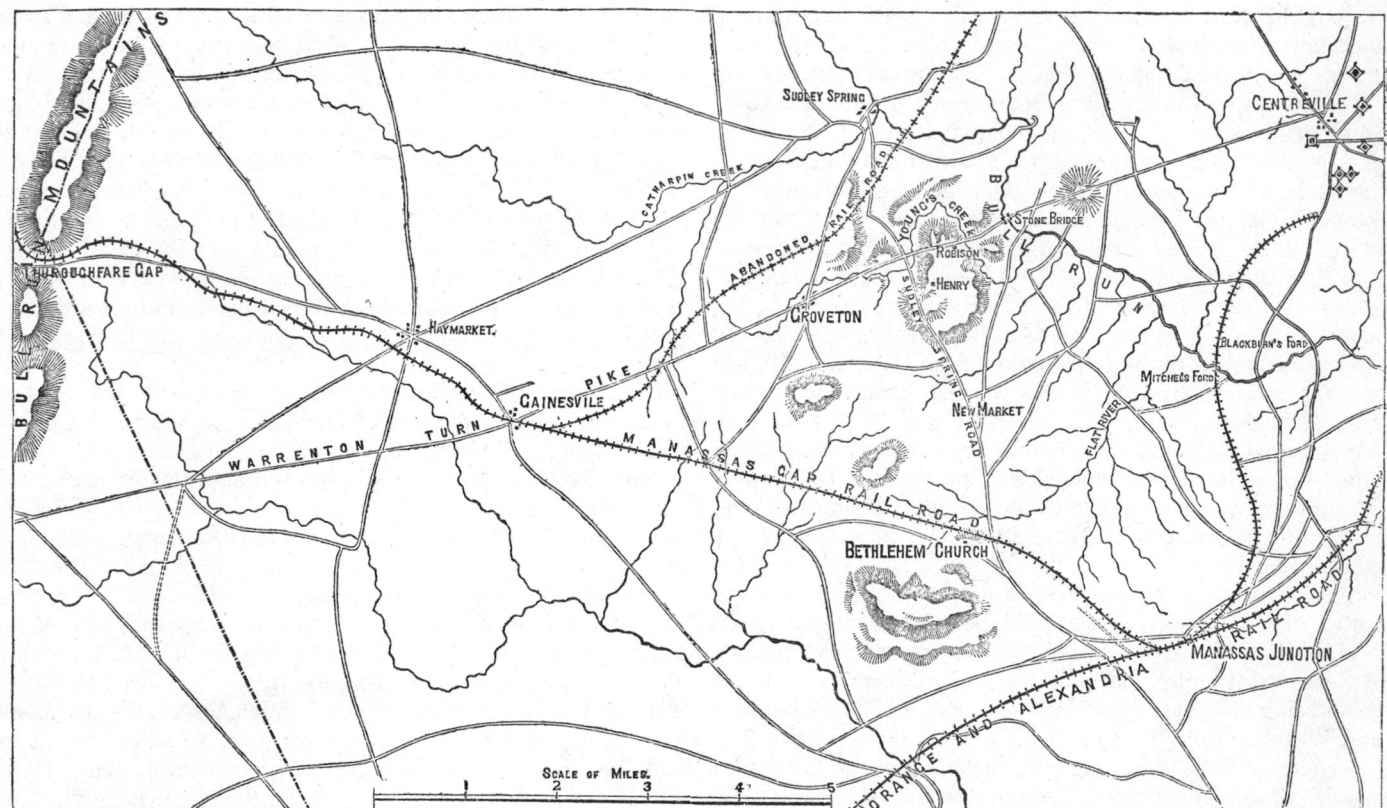

MAP OF OPERATIONS, AUGUST 28, 29, 30.

dria. I will know in a few minutes the condition of the artillery and cavalry. We are not yet in a condition to move; may be by to-morrow morning. I have ordered troops to garrison the works at Upton's Hill. They must be held at any cost. It is the key to Washington, which can not be seriously menaced as long as it is held." Halleck writes: "Place Sumner's corps, as it arrives, near the guns, and particularly at the Chain Bridge. The principal thing now to be feared is a cavalry raid into this city, especially in the night time." McClellan, on the 29th: "Franklin's corps is in motion; started about 6 P.M. He has but forty rounds of ammunition, and no wagons to move more. I do not think he is in condition to accomplish much if he meets with serious resistance. I should not have moved him but for your pressing order of last night." And in the afternoon, the battle then being fought, though no one at Washington knew it: "The last news I received from Manassas was from stragglers, to the effect that the enemy were evacuating Centreville and retiring toward Thoroughfare Gap. This is by no means reliable. I am clear that one of two courses should be adopted: (1st.) To concentrate all our available forces to open communication with Pope. (2d.) To leave Pope to get out of his scrape, and at once use all our means to make the capital perfectly sure. No middle ground will now answer. Tell me what you wish me to do, and I will do all in my power to accomplish it."[1]

Official reports from Washington notified McClellan that large bodies of the enemy were moving through Vienna, in the direction of the Chain Bridge; so McClellan halted Franklin at Annandale, only a few miles toward Pope.[2] Yet there was not a Confederate soldier within thirty miles, or between him and the forces at Washington. Jackson was sternly holding his ground beyond Bull Run, on almost the very spot where a year, a week, and a day before he had won the title of "Stonewall;" and Longstreet, having marched since early dawn, and for three successive days before, was within hearing of the noise of the battle which Jackson was so firmly waging.

Early on the morning of the 29th Sigel opened the attack on the Confederate right.[3] Jackson's left, under Hill, stretched northward toward Sudley Ford, on the Bull Run; then came Ewell's division, under Lawton, in the centre; then Jackson's own division, now commanded by Starke, on the right, resting near the little hamlet of Groveton. His force lay mainly behind an abandoned railroad, whose deep cuttings formed a strong intrenchment. The ground was thickly wooded. His artillery was mainly massed in on low ridges in the rear of his right. Jackson's front fell back about half a mile until they reached the abandoned railroad, where a fierce combat ensued.[4] Milroy and Schurz, of Sigel's corps, charged fiercely upon the enemy, sheltered by this embankment, but were driven back; the charge was repeated, and again repulsed. The Confederates then advanced, but were checked by a hot artillery fire, and fell back to their position.[5] Jackson was fighting a defensive battle, in order to hold his position until re-enforced by Longstreet, who was rapidly coming up. Pope came upon the field about noon, and, in reply to Sigel's request for aid, told him that he must hold his ground, but that he should not be again pushed into action, for McDowell and Porter were coming up from Manassas by the Gainesville

road, and would soon fall upon the enemy's flank and probably upon his rear.[1] Heintzelman's corps, comprising the divisions of Hooker and Kearney, had meanwhile come upon the field and taken position on the right, and Reno's corps between Sigel and Heintzelman. For four hours a series of sharp skirmishes ensued along the centre and left of the Confederate line.[2]

Longstreet's command, Lee accompanying, had been advancing in the track of Jackson. It reached White Plains, at the western entrance of the Thoroughfare Gap, on the evening of the 27th, where the night was passed, and at dawn of the 28th pressed forward to that narrow defile, which a thousand men could have held against five times their number. Presuming it to be held, Longstreet sent a part of his force by a rough mountain path to Hopewell Gap, three miles northward, to turn the Union rear. But Thoroughfare Gap, the key to every thing, was not held. After some skirmishing, the Confederates poured through and gained its eastern mouth. Ricketts, commanding a division of McDowell's corps, had been sent from Gainesville in that direction "to assist Colonel Wyndham, who, at 10 15 A.M., reported the enemy passing through Thoroughfare Gap." He pushed forward rapidly, but was too late. At three in the afternoon, before reaching the Gap, he met Wyndham's skirmishers retiring before the enemy, who were already in possession. After vainly attempting to check them, finding himself outflanked on both sides, he retreated to Gainesville, and thence to Manassas, and the way was open for Longstreet to come to the aid of Jackson, who stood at bay on his chosen ground.[3]

Early on the morning of the 29th Longstreet's columns were united, and the advance to join Jackson was resumed. Before they reached Gainesville, the noise of the battle, five miles distant, was heard. The wearied troops pressed on with renewed vigor. His advance passed through Gainesville about nine o'clock,[4] and in an hour began to come upon the field, and took positions on the rear and to the right of Jackson. The Confederate right now extended across the Warrenton Turnpike to the Manassas Railroad. The joint order to Porter and McDowell directing them to move toward Gainesville, found these commands near Bethlehem Church, two miles west of Manassas, and four or five miles from the field of battle. King's division had been detached from McDowell, and placed under Porter for a special purpose. McDowell, being senior officer, assumed command, and gave Porter an order for his movements,[5] and pushed his corps, including King's division, toward the battle-field, which he reached at about four o'clock. Pope, who was wholly unaware that Longstreet had united with Jackson,[6] now sent an order to Porter to come into action. "Your line of march," he wrote, "brings you in on the enemy's right flank. I desire you to push forward into action at once on the enemy's flank, and, if possible, on his

---

were sent during the night of the 27th, and should properly have been dated at these hours A.M. of the 28th.   [1] *McC. Rep.*, 321–330.   [2] *Ibid.*, 332.

[3] Pope says the attack began about daylight. Sigel says: "From half past six to half past ten our whole infantry and nearly all our batteries were engaged in a most vehement artillery and infantry contest." Jackson says: "In the morning, about ten o'clock, the Federal artillery opened with spirit and animation upon our right, which was soon replied to by our batteries."

[4] Pope says: "Jackson fell back several miles, but was so closely pressed that he was compelled to make a stand, and make the best defense possible." This is clearly an error, for Sigel says, "Milroy and Schurz advanced one mile, and Schenck two miles from their *original positions;*" and these were from three quarters of a mile to a mile and a half from a belt of woods occupied by the Confederate skirmishing-line. This simply fell back a few hundred yards to the railroad, Jackson's real line.   [5] Reports of Milroy and Schurz, in *Pope's Report*, 90, 109.

[1] *Pope's Report*, 21.

[2] After the attack in the morning, "the enemy moved around more to our left to another point of attack. This was vigorously repulsed by the batteries. About two o'clock P.M. the Federal infantry, in large force, advanced to the attack of our left."—Jackson, in *Lee's Rep.*, ii., 95. "From twelve until four o'clock very severe skirmishes occurred constantly at various parts of our line, and were brought on at every indication the enemy made of a disposition to retreat."—*Pope's Report*, 21.

[3] Longstreet, in *Lee's Rep.*, ii., 81; McDowell, in *Pope's Report*, 44; Ricketts, *Ibid.*, 169.

[4] General John Buford at this time counted 17 regiments of infantry, one battery of artillery, and about 500 cavalry. He estimates the regiments at 800 each; this is probably too high.—*Court-martial*, 188. He, however, saw only a part of Longstreet's force.

[5] There is an irreconcilable discrepancy as to the nature of this order. McDowell testifies that it was to this effect: "You put your force in here [pointing in the direction where a cloud of dust indicated that a body of the enemy were approaching], and I will take mine up at the Sudley Spring road, on the left of the troops engaged at that point with the enemy. . . . The question with me was how soonest, within the limits fixed by the order of General Pope, this force of ours could be applied against the enemy," the limitation being that "the troops must occupy a position from which they can reach Bull Run to-night or in the morning."—*Court-martial*, 85. Porter asserts that the order was that he should remain where he was. No other persons were within hearing when this order was given, or of the conversation which preceded and followed it.

[6] "I did not then believe, nor do I now believe, that at that time [4 30 P.M.] any considerable portion of Longstreet's corps had reached the vicinity of the battle-field."—Pope's Testimony, *Court-martial*, 35.

THOROUGHFARE GAP.

rear, keeping your right in communication with General Reynolds. The enemy is massed in the woods in front of us, but can be shelled out as soon as you engage their flank. Keep heavy reserves, and use your batteries, keeping well closed to your right all the time. In case you are obliged to fall back, do so to your right and rear, so as to keep you in close communication with the right wing." This order was dispatched at half past four, and received by Porter just two hours later. He attempted to get his leading division, Morell's, into position; but, thinking the enemy in front in too great force, and judging the country impassable for artillery, did not advance, and retained his former position during the remainder of the day, knowing nothing of the battle which was going on four miles away. The failure to execute this order forms the second and gravest charge against Porter.

Sharp fighting, something more than mere "skirmishing," had been going on all the afternoon, especially upon the Confederate left, somewhat weakly held by A. P. Hill, with considerable intervals between some of his regiments. By three o'clock the fighting here had assumed the proportions of a battle. Grover, with his brigade of Hooker's division, rushed in upon the enemy a little to the right of his extreme left. Of this charge Jackson says:[1] "The Federal infantry, in large force, advanced to the attack of our left, occupied by the division of General Hill. It pressed forward, in defiance of our fatal and destructive fire, with great determination, a portion of it crossing a deep cut in the railroad track, and penetrating, in heavy force, an interval of nearly 175 yards, which separated the right of Gregg's from the left of Thomas's brigade. For a short time Gregg's brigade, on the extreme left, was isolated from the main body of the command. But the 14th South Carolina Regiment, then in reserve, with the 45th Georgia, attacked the exultant enemy with vigor, and drove them back across the railroad track with great slaughter. The opposing forces at one time delivered their volleys into each other at the distance of ten paces." Grover says:[2] "After rising the hill under which my command lay, an open field was entered, and from one edge of it gradually fell off in a slope to a valley through which ran a railroad embankment. Beyond this embankment the forest continued, and the corresponding heights beyond were held by the enemy in force, supported by artillery. At three P.M. I received an order to advance in line of battle over this ground, pass the embankment, enter the woods beyond, and hold it. We rapidly and firmly pressed upon the embankment, and here occurred a short, sharp, and obstinate hand-to-hand conflict, with bayonets and clubbed muskets. Many of the enemy were bayoneted in their tracks; others struck down with the butts of pieces,[3] and onward pressed our line. In a few yards more it met a terrible fire from a second line, which in its turn broke. The enemy's third line now bore down upon our thinned ranks in close order, and swept back the right centre and a portion of the left. With the gallant 16th Massachusetts in our centre, I tried to turn his flank, but the breaking of our right and centre, and the weight of the enemy's lines, caused the necessity of falling back first to the embankment, and then to our first position, behind which we rallied to our colors." In this fierce conflict, lasting only twenty minutes, Grover, out of less than 2000 men, lost 484.

Kearney, on the extreme Union right, afterward advanced,[1] and swept "with a rush the first line of the enemy. This was most successful. The enemy rolled upon his own right. It presaged a victory for us all. Still, our force was too light. The enemy brought up rapidly heavy reserves, so that our farther progress was impeded."[2]

A. P. Hill[3] thus describes the fight toward evening: "The evident intention of the enemy was to turn our left, and overwhelm Jackson's corps before Longstreet came up; and to accomplish this, the most persistent and furious onsets were made by column after column of infantry, accompanied by numerous batteries of artillery. Soon my reserves were all in, and up to six o'clock my division, assisted by the Louisiana brigade of General Hayes, with a heroic courage and obstinacy almost beyond parallel, had met and repulsed six distinct and separate assaults, a portion of the time a majority of the men being without a cartridge. The enemy prepared for a last and determined attempt. Their serried masses, overwhelming superiority of numbers, and bold bearing made the chance of victory tremble in the balance. Casting about for help, fortunately it was here reported to me that the brigades of Generals Lawton and Early were near by, and, sending for them, they promptly moved to my front at the most opportune moment, and this last charge met the same fate as the preceding. Having received an order from General Jackson to endeavor to avoid a general engagement, my commanders of brigades contented themselves with repulsing the enemy and following them up but a few hundred yards." Both sides, as usual, claim to have fought against superior numbers; but a comparison of the divisions engaged, as shown in the respective reports, shows that the Confederates had at the close a considerable preponderance. That is, A. P. Hill, Ewell, and Lawton outnumbered Hooker, Kearney, and Reno, to whom they were opposed. The opportune arrival of Longstreet upon the right enabled Jackson to concentrate nearly his whole strength to resist this attack upon his left.

At half past five, McDowell having come up, Pope, supposing that Porter was advancing, in compliance with the order sent an hour before, but only received an hour later, ordered an attack upon Jackson's right, which, ignorant of Longstreet's arrival, he supposed to be the extreme right of the whole Confederate force on the field.[4] This attack was made along the Warrenton Turnpike by King's division, then commanded by Hatch, of McDowell's corps, who, "trusting to find the enemy in retreat, as he was told, and hoping to turn their retreat into a flight, took the men forward with an impetuosity akin to rashness."[5] Instead of finding a retreating enemy, he was confronted, after marching three quarters of a mile, by a strong force. A fierce struggle, lasting three quarters of an hour, took place, mainly between Doubleday's and Patrick's brigades on the Union side, and those

[1] In Lee's Rep., ii., 95.   [2] In Pope's Report, 76.
[3] John Esten Cooke says: "Without ammunition, the men of Jackson seized whatever they could lay their hands on to use against the enemy. The piles of stones in the vicinity of the railroad cut were used; and it is well established that many of the enemy were killed by having their skulls broken with fragments of rock."—Stonewall Jackson, 293.

[1] Heintzelman, in Pope's Report, 55, says not till several orders had been sent to him to do so, and after Hooker had been driven back.   [2] Kearney, in Pope's Report, 79.
[3] In Lee's Rep., ii., 125.
[4] Pope (Report, 17) strangely says: "About half past five I directed Generals Heintzelman and Reno to assault the left of the enemy," and then proceeds to describe Grover's assault on the railroad embankment; and adds: "The whole of the left of the enemy was doubled back toward its centre, and our forces, after a sharp conflict of an hour and a half, occupied the field of battle, with the dead and wounded of the enemy in our hands." And again (Report, 21): "While this attack [by McDowell] was going on, the forces under Heintzelman and Reno continued to push back the left of the enemy in the direction of the Warrenton Turnpike, so that at about eight o'clock in the evening the greater portion of the field of battle was occupied by our army." Whereas the truth is that Grover's attack began at three, and was soon repulsed, as was also the subsequent one by Kearney and Reno.   [5] McDowell, in Pope's Report, 46.

FRANZ SIGEL.

of Hood and Evans on the Confederate. The result, as told by Hatch, was: "Night had now come on. Our loss had been severe, and the enemy occupying a position in the woods on our left, I was forced to give the order for a retreat. The retreat was executed in good order, the attempt to follow being defeated by a few well-directed volleys from Patrick's brigade."[1] Longstreet says: "Hood, supported by Evans, made a gallant attack, driving the enemy back until nine o'clock at night. The enemy's entire force was found to be massed directly in my front, and in so strong a position that it was not deemed advisable to move on against his immediate front, so the troops were quietly withdrawn at one o'clock the following morning. After withdrawing from the original attack, my troops were placed in the line first occupied, and in the original order."[2]

The battle, as a mere conflict of force, was wholly undecisive. The Confederates had not been permanently driven a rod from any position which they wished to hold; at most, their extreme weak left, which was altogether "in the air," had been drawn in a little toward the centre. But Jackson had gained his object. He had held his ground until Longstreet's whole force had come up and taken position by his side and in his rear. Not so thought Pope. He believed that Jackson had suffered a defeat, which only the absence of Porter had prevented from being decisive.[3] Early next morning he sent to Washington the news of his success. "We fought," he wrote, "a terrific battle here yesterday with the combined forces of the enemy, which lasted with continuous fury from daylight until after dark, by which time the enemy was driven from the field, which we now occupy. Our troops are too much exhausted to push matters, but I shall do so in the course of the morning, as soon as Fitz John Porter's corps comes up from Manassas. The enemy is still on our front, but badly used up. We have lost not less than 8000 men killed and wounded, and from the appearance of the field, the enemy have lost at least two to our one. He stood strictly on the defensive, and every attack was made by ourselves. Our troops behaved splendidly. The battle was fought on the identical field of Bull Run, which greatly increased the enthusiasm of our men. The news just reaches us from the front that the enemy is retreating toward the mountains. I go forward to see. We have made great captures, but I am not able yet to form an idea of their extent." McDowell wrote a little more cautiously: "I have gone through a second battle of Bull Run, on the identical field of last year, and unhurt. The victory is decidedly ours."[4]

At half past eight on the evening of the 29th, Pope sent a peremptory order to Porter to march at once to the field of battle, where he was to appear at daylight.[5] Two of his brigades, that of Griffin, and Piatt's, temporarily attached to his corps, by some misconception of orders, marched

to Centreville, and took no part in the fighting of the day. The rest of his corps, 7000 strong, joined Pope near Groveton early in the morning. Pope's whole force, with the exception of these two brigades, 5000 strong, and Banks's corps of the same number, which was at Bristoe in charge of the railroad and wagon trains, was at last concentrated. Its effective strength was now reduced to 40,000. Opposed to them were the combined forces of Longstreet and Jackson, now under Lee, who was on the field and assumed command, numbering about 60,000.[1] Both armies were exhausted by their previous marching and fighting, and neither manifested a disposition for a while to assume the offensive. Pope was, indeed, greatly discouraged by a letter which he received at daybreak from Franklin, informing him that rations and forage would be sent from Alexandria if he would send a cavalry escort to bring out the trains. He had no cavalry to send, and if he had, they could not go and return in time to furnish his men with the supplies of which they were in sore need. "It was not till I received this letter," he says, "that I began to feel discouraged and nearly hopeless of any successful issue to the operations with which I was charged."[2] The natural course, under the circumstances, would seem to have been the one which he had contemplated the day before: to have fallen back to Centreville, or even beyond, and meet his supplies and the re-enforcements, which could not have been long delayed, from Alexandria. Meanwhile he became convinced that the enemy was actually retreating. Lee was drawing in Jackson's exposed left, and the movement of Longstreet's strong right was hidden from view by intervening hills and woods. A paroled prisoner came in and reported that the whole Confederate army was in rapid retreat. This soldier had come into Porter's lines, and was sent by him to Pope with an assurance that he did not believe a word of the story. Pope replied that he believed the soldier, and ordered Porter to advance.

At noon Pope gave a general order to pursue the enemy thus presumed to be retreating, and special orders to different commanders.[3] Lee had no occasion or intention of retreating, nor did he propose to attack, but chose to await the assault of the enemy. His position was the same as on the previous day, except that Jackson's extreme left was drawn in a little. His line stretched northward for a mile, in a somewhat irregular crescent form, the convex side facing the east, and following the course of thickly wooded heights; its centre was also protected by a deep cutting for an unfinished railroad, which formed an admirable earth-work. Longstreet's line ran southeastward behind the crest of another wooded ridge, which concealed him wholly from the view of the enemy, to whom his presence and position was entirely unknown. His reserves lay considerably beyond the rear of Jackson, so that at any moment, without disturbing his front, he could sustain Jackson. His force being larger and his line shorter than that of Jackson, his brigades were much more closely massed. The whole line resembled an irregular L,[4] Jackson forming the perpendicular, Longstreet the horizontal line. Between Jackson's right and Longstreet was a considerable interval; this was, however, swept by artillery massed behind the crest of a ridge in the rear, only the muzzles of the guns being visible. Pope, still believing that Jackson's right was the right of the entire Confederate force, instead of being in fact its centre, directed his main attack, or, as he fancied, his "pursuit," upon this point. His line of battle conformed closely to that of Lee. On the extreme right was Heintzelman, then Reno, then Sigel, forming the perpendicular, confronting Jackson; the other wing consisted of McDowell's command, which comprised his own corps, that of Porter, and the Pennsylvania Reserves under Reynolds—Porter being in the advance, and Reynolds to his right. During the action some changes took place. Of McDowell's corps, King's division, now, as on the previous day, under Hatch, were sent forward with Porter, and Ricketts was added to Heintzelman, while Reynolds was in effect left to act for himself.[5]

After some hours of sharp cannonading, Sykes's division of Porter's corps was pushed forward to support an advance to be made by Butterfield. Thus far they had seen none of the Confederate infantry or cavalry, and of his artillery only the muzzles of the cannon. Butterfield's advance must have been ordered upon the supposition that Jackson was in full retreat. It was gallantly made, and gallantly supported, but it failed utterly. Jackson, sheltered by the railway embankment, was as secure as earth-works could make him, and poured in a furious fire, which tore in pieces the assailants as they emerged from the woods, their own fire being almost harmless against a sheltered foe.[6] Reno and Heintzelman at the same time assailed Jackson farther to the right, aided by Reynolds, who had been moved thither from the rear, where they had been posted to support Porter's "pursuit."[7] Jackson found his centre and left sorely pressed. "The Federal infantry," he says, "about four o'clock moved from under the cover of the wood, and ad-

---

[1] *Pope's Report*, 179.　　　　　　　　　　[2] *Lee's Rep.*, ii., 82.
[3] *Pope's Report*, 22.　　　　　　　　　　[4] Newspapers, August 31.
[5] "Immediately upon receipt of this order, the precise hour of receiving which you will acknowledge, you will march your command to the field of battle of to-day, and report to me in person. You are to understand that you are to comply strictly with this order, and to be present on the field within three hours after its reception, or after daybreak to-morrow morning."

[1] These estimates include only infantry, the cavalry being of little avail on either side.
The Union force is stated by Pope (*Report*, 23) as follows: "McDowell, 12,000; Sigel, 7000; Heintzelman, 7000; Reno, 7000; Porter, 7000—40,000 in all.
We arrive at an approximation to the Confederate force from the following data: Longstreet's whole force was on the field, as well as that of Jackson. These comprised 35 brigades, and at the outset, according to our previous estimate, numbered 78,750. In the various engagements from Cedar Mountain to the battle of the 29th, they had lost about 8000. The march had been long and exhausting, and probably quite 5000 had fallen out of the ranks from fatigue or sickness, thus leaving 65,000 available. The entire force seems not to have been actually brought into action, for in the detailed list of casualties losses are mentioned in only 115 regiments, which probably at the time averaged 400 each—46,000 in all, leaving 19,000 not directly in action. Pope brought nearly his whole force into action, probably about 35,000.　　[2] *Report*, 23.
[2] EXTRACTS FROM ORDERS: "The following forces will be immediately thrown forward and in pursuit of the enemy, and press him vigorously the whole day. Major General McDowell is assigned to the command of the pursuit." McDowell to Porter: "Major General McDowell being charged with the advanced forces ordered to pursue the enemy, directs that your corps will be followed immediately by King's division, supported by Reynolds's. . . . . Organize a strong advance to precede your command, and push on rapidly in pursuit of the enemy until you come in contact with him."—*Pope's Report*, 47.
[4] Longstreet and Sykes describe the line as an irregular V reversed (<), but an L represents it more closely.　　[5] McDowell, in *Pope's Report*, 48.　　[6] Sykes, in *Pope's Report*, 147.
[7] *Pope's Report*, 24; Heintzelman, *Ibid.*, 56; Reynolds, *Ibid.*, 67; Hatch, *Ibid.*, 178.

vanced in several lines, first engaging the right, but soon extending the attack to the centre and left. In a few moments our entire line was engaged in a fierce and sanguinary struggle with the enemy. As one line was repulsed another took its place, and pressed forward as if determined, by force of numbers and fury of assault, to drive us from our positions. So impetuous and well sustained were these onsets as to induce me to send to the commanding general for re-enforcements."[1] Lee informed Longstreet of Jackson's peril; but, before any succor could be sent, Longstreet found that he could better aid Jackson by another movement. "From an eminence near by," he says, "one portion of the enemy's masses attacking General Jackson were immediately within my view, and within easy range of batteries in that position. It gave me an advantage that I did not expect to have, and I made haste to use it. Two batteries were ordered for the purpose, and one placed in position and immediately opened. As it was evident that the attack upon General Jackson could not be continued ten minutes under the fire of these batteries, I made no movement with my troops. Before the second battery could be placed in position the enemy began to retire, and in less than ten minutes the ranks were broken, and that portion of the army put to flight. A fair opportunity was offered me, and the intended diversion was changed into an attack. My whole line was rushed forward at a charge."[2]

Let us now look at the field on the Union left, as seen from its positions. Butterfield's brigade had marched up the hill upon the as yet invisible enemy. "As he advanced there was a great commotion among the rebel forces, and the whole side of the hill and edges of the wood swarmed with men before unseen. The effect was not unlike flushing a covey of quails."[3] Warren—then colonel, soon to be major general—commanding a weak brigade of two regiments, numbering together 1000 men, seized a commanding position which had been vacated by the withdrawal of Reynolds, and held it until he was fairly enveloped by the advancing enemy, and retreated only when the rest of Porter's corps had been driven back. Out of 480 men of the 5th New York, he lost, in killed, 79; wounded, 170; missing, 48. The 10th New York, out of 510 men, lost 23 killed, 65 wounded, 48 missing—412 out of 1000 in this one action.[4] Porter's corps was thus compelled to bear the whole onset of Longstreet's advance. Outnumbered fully three to one, outflanked on the left, and unsheltered on the right, where Reno and Heintzelman were falling back from the enfilading fire of Longstreet's batteries and the fierce onset of Jackson's advance, it retreated, first to the plateau of the Henry House—the scene of the final struggle at Bull Run a year before—and then, the enemy still outflanking, across Bull Run to Centreville. Warren's desperate stand had not, however, been unavailing. To all seeming, it saved the defeat from becoming a rout.[5] The retreat was made in good order. Porter's corps, though defeated, was not routed, and Sykes's regulars covered the retreat of a portion of the army. They had performed the same service on the same ground a year before. Out of scarcely 7000 men, Porter's corps lost, in the few hours during which this action lasted,

2164 men, of whom 323 are put down as killed, 1323 wounded, and 518 missing.[1]

The main stress of the battle had fallen upon the centre of both armies, from thence extending to the Confederate left and the Union right. Hooker, on the Union right, assailed Hill, and gained some advantage.[2] But when the main attack had failed, and the anticipated pursuit had become a retreat, the whole Union force was ordered to fall back toward Centreville. The order was given at eight o'clock. The army retreated in order. It had suffered a defeat; but there was no disgraceful panic like that which had marked the close of the battle fought a year before on almost the same ground.[3]

In this three days' battle the Confederate loss was about 8400: 1400 killed, 7000 wounded. The Union loss was much larger, probably about 11,000.[4] This, however, by no means measures the diminution which the army had undergone. Many had been made prisoners; Lee says "more than 7000, in addition to about 2000 wounded left in our hands." The straggling had been enormous. "Half of the great diminution of our

---

[1] Jackson, in *Lee's Rep.*, ii., 96.   [2] Longstreet, in *Lee's Rep.*, ii., 82.

[3] Warren, in *Pope's Report*, 150.   [4] Sykes, in *Pope's Report*, 147, 162.

[5] Longstreet says, "The commanding general soon joined me, and a few minutes after Major General Anderson arrived with his division." (This division, the largest in the force, numbering at least 24 regiments, formed the rear of Longstreet's command, and had been held in reserve a little to the rear.—*Lee's Rep.*, i., 25.) "The attack was led by Hood's brigade, closely supported by Evans. These were rapidly re-enforced by Anderson's division from the rear, Kemper's three brigades and D. R. Jones's division from the right, and Wilcox's brigade from the left. The attacking columns moved steadily forward from point to point, following the movements of the general line. These were, however, somewhat detained by an enfilade fire from a battery on my left." (This was Hazlitt's battery, attached to Warren's brigade. See Warren, in *Pope's Report*, 150.) "This threw more than its proper share of fighting upon the infantry, and enabled the enemy to escape with many of his batteries, which should have fallen into our hands."—Longstreet, in *Lee's Rep.*, ii., 83.

---

[1] General Pope says (*Report*, 24): "The attack of Porter was neither vigorous nor persistent, and his troops soon retired in considerable confusion. . . . As soon as they could be rallied, I pushed them forward to support our left, and they there rendered most conspicuous service, especially the brigade of regulars under Colonel Buchanan." Buchanan, however (*Ibid.*, 152), says: "About 5 P.M. the brigade was withdrawn in admirable order." Chapman, who commanded another brigade of Sykes's division, says (*Ibid.*, 172): "About 3 30 P.M., by General Porter's order, the brigade retired in admirable order to the point designated. . . . The movement was executed with surprising order, and elicited my warmest admiration." These, as well as Warren's brigade, belonged to Sykes's division. Of Morell's division of this corps we have no special reports; but Sykes incidentally mentions the gallantry with which Butterfield's brigade of this division made the attack upon Jackson. The losses in Morell's division of two brigades amounted to 1247, exceeding by a third those of Sykes, which certainly does not indicate any want of vigor in its attack. Among the specifications in the charges against Porter was, that on this day he "did so feebly fall upon the enemy's lines as to make little or no impression on the same, and did fall back and draw away his forces unnecessarily, and without making any of the great personal efforts to rally his troops or keep their lines, or to inspire his troops to meet the sacrifices and make the resistance demanded by the importance of his position," etc. This specification was, however, withdrawn by the judge advocate, without offering any proof to substantiate it.—*Court-martial*, 9.

[2] "Hooker's division now advanced into the woods near our right, and drove the enemy back some distance." — Heintzelman, in *Pope's Report*, 56. "The onset was so fierce, and in such force, that at first some headway was made; but their advance was again checked, and eventually repulsed with great loss."—A. P. Hill, in *Lee's Rep.*, ii., 126.

[3] The withdrawal was made slowly, quietly, and in good order, no pursuit whatever being attempted by the enemy."—*Pope's Report*, 24. "The obscurity of the night, and the uncertainty of the fords over Bull Run, rendered it necessary to suspend operations until morning, when the cavalry, being pushed forward, discovered that the enemy had escaped to the strong position at Centreville."—*Lee's Rep.*, i., 25.

[4] The Confederate loss can be fixed very closely upon official evidence. In *Lee's Rep.*, i., 50, is a detailed "List of Casualties at Manassas Plains in August, 1862," made out by regiments, giving the loss in each. The whole number there given is 1090 killed, 6154 wounded. This list is apparently not complete, the reports of Longstreet and Jackson adding considerably to the number.

	Killed.	Wounded.	Total.
Longstreet (*Ibid.*, ii., 89): "Total loss in the corps under my command between the 23d and 30th of August, embracing actions at Rappahannock, Freeman's Ford, Thoroughfare Gap, and Manassas	663	4016	4679
Jackson (*Ibid.*, ii., 98): "Losses in my command in its operations from the Rappahannock to the Potomac"	805	3547	4352
	1468	7563	9031

	Killed.	Wounded.	
Deduct from the above losses in minor engagements before the 27th (*Ibid.*, i., 50)	27	94	
And losses (estimated) at Chantilly, Sept. 1	100	400	127	494	621
Total in these actions	1341	7069	8410

This includes the losses at Bristoe on the 27th, which are also included in the Union losses.

The Union losses can be given to a considerable extent only by estimate. Porter's and Reynolds's loss is given in full, Heintzelman's with the exception of one brigade. Sigel puts his whole loss at 1983, but does not discriminate between killed, wounded, and missing. We put the last at 500, and apportion the others in the usual proportion. Of the losses of McDowell and Reno we find no lists.

	Killed.	Wounded.	Missing.
Porter	333	1323	518
Reynolds	67	397	189
Heintzelman (say)	200	1300	400
Sigel (say)	300	1200	400
Total in these divisions	900	4220	1507

The losses in McDowell's and Reno's corps were probably about equal to the above, and as the field remained in the hands of the enemy, many of those reported as missing were doubtless killed or wounded; these may be estimated at 600. Putting all these imperfect data together, we estimate the Union loss as in the text.

MONUMENT ON THE BATTLE-FIELD OF GROVETON.

PHILIP KEARNEY.

ISAAC I. STEVENS.

forces," says Pope, "was occasioned by skulking and straggling from the army. The troops which were brought into action fought with all gallantry and determination, but thousands of men straggled away from their commands, and were never in any action. I had posted several regiments in the rear of the field of battle on the 29th of August, and although many thousand stragglers and skulkers were arrested by them, many others passed around through the woods, and did not rejoin their commands during the remainder of the campaign."[1]

At Centreville, on the morning of September 1, Pope had remaining of McDowell's corps, 10,000; Sigel, 7000; Heintzelman, 6000; Reno, 6000; Porter, 9000, including the two brigades which had strayed thither on the morning of the 30th. Banks, with 5000, had rejoined the army, and Sumner, with 11,000, and Franklin, with 8000, had come up from Alexandria, raising the whole army to 62,000, exclusive of cavalry, which was so used up as to be unavailable.[2] Lee, after the battle, had, besides cavalry, about 60,000 present; but D. H. Hill, with his division, which had left Hanover Junction on the 26th, was close at hand, and on the 2d of September came up with his division of 10,000. The advantage of the situation was then really in favor of the Union army. The forces present were nearly equal; but Pope had strong intrenchments, and might certainly expect considerable re-enforcements at once.[3] His troops were, indeed, greatly exhausted by the fighting, and marching, and privations of the previous week; but Lee's could not have been in better plight. They had fought as much, marched as far, and fared quite as hard.[4]

But it was determined at Washington that Centreville should be abandoned, and the whole army once more retreat and take shelter within the defenses of Washington. The alarm for the safety of the capital rose again to its height. In their terror, the President and Halleck turned to McClellan. Pope had written to Halleck, charging "many brigade and some division commanders of the forces sent here from the Peninsula" with unsoldierly and dangerous conduct. "The constant talk, indulged in publicly and in promiscuous company, is, that the Army of the Potomac will not fight. You can have hardly an idea of the demoralization among officers of high rank in the Potomac Army, arising in all instances from personal feeling in relation to changes in commander-in-chief and others. I am endeavoring to do all I can, and will most assuredly put them where they shall fight or run away." He urged that Halleck "should draw back this army to the intrenchments in front of Washington, and set to work in that secure place to reorganize and rearrange it."[5] The President urged McClellan to telegraph to his friends in the old Army of the Potomac, adjuring them not to fail in their duty. He complied by writing to Porter: "I ask of you, for my sake and that of the country, that you and all my friends will lend the fullest and most cordial co-operation to General Pope in all the operations now going on. Say the same thing to my friends in the Army of the Potomac, and that the last request I have to make of them is that, for their country's sake, they will extend to General Pope the same support they ever

have to me." In writing thus, McClellan merely complied with the request of the President. "Neither then, nor at any other time," he says, "did I think for one moment that Porter had been, or would be, in any manner derelict in the performance of his duty." Porter replied, "You may rest assured that all your friends, as well as every lover of his country, will ever give, as they have given to General Pope, their cordial co-operation and constant support in the execution of all orders and plans. Our killed and wounded attest our devoted duty." Halleck wrote to McClellan, whom a hurried order had virtually stripped of all command, "You will retain the command of every thing in this vicinity not temporarily to be Pope's army in the field. I beg of you to assist me in this crisis with your ability and experience."[1]

On the 31st, the day after the battle, a heavy storm set in; but Jackson was pushed forward toward Fairfax to turn the Union right, and Pope sent McDowell, Heintzelman, and Reno in that direction, intending to attack on the morning of the 2d of September. But the heads of the two forces came in contact just before dark on the 1st, at Ox Hill, near Chantilly. A fearful thunder-storm was raging, in the midst of which the engagement began. A portion of the Confederates were thrown into some confusion; then re-enforced, they drove back Stevens's division of Reno's corps. Stevens was killed in the front of his troops. Kearney rushed in with his wonted dashing bravery, and, riding forward alone in advance of his men to reconnoitre the ground, fell in with a Confederate soldier, from whom he inquired the position of a regiment. Discovering his mistake, he turned to ride away, when the soldier fired, and Kearney fell from his saddle mortally wounded. Darkness closed the action, each army retaining a portion of the field, and both claiming a victory. But before morning the whole Union army was in retreat for Alexandria. Lee, with Longstreet's corps, came up during the day, and was joined on the battle-field by D. H. Hill, with his division fresh except for its rapid march.

With the battle of Chantilly, or Ox Hill, as the Confederates name it, closed Pope's campaign in Virginia. He requested at its close, as he had done at its beginning, to be relieved from the command of the Army of Virginia, and to be returned to his former post in the West. His request was granted, and on the 7th of September he departed from Washington. The Army of Virginia ceased to exist as such, and the whole force, resuming its old name of the Army of the Potomac, was again placed under the immediate command of McClellan.

It would be unjust to judge of the campaign of Pope by its unfortunate result, or by the censures to which it has been subjected, or even by the account of it as told by its commander. If we turn from what was said, and review what was actually done, in the light thrown upon it by the Confederate Reports, we shall find much to praise, and, until the last two decisive days, little to censure. The task imposed upon him was a difficult one. He found the army which he was to command disorganized and scattered. Some of the corps commanders were hostile to others.[2] His appointment was distasteful to many, and he had not acquired a reputation which would compel all to acquiesce in its wisdom, however much it might stand in the way of their advancement. Then his first address to his army alienated the feelings of the whole Army of the Potomac, a portion of whom were to serve under him. This feeling, though less strong than he supposed, stood

---

[1] Pope's Report, 26.   [2] Ibid., 25.
[3] Halleck to Pope: "August 31, 11 A.M. You have done nobly. All reserves are being sent forward. Conch's division goes to-day. Part of it went to Sangster's Station last night with Franklin and Sumner, who must be with you. Can't you renew the attack?"—Pope's Report, 246.
[4] "Many of the men were barefooted, and limped along weary unto death. They were faint from want of food, and broken down by absence of rest. The phenomenon was here presented of an army living for many days upon green corn and unripe apples only, and during this time making exhausting marches, engaging in incessant combats, and repulsing every assault. The flower of the Southern youth, raised in affluence and luxury, were toiling on over the dusty highways, or lying exhausted by the roadside, or fighting when so feeble that they could scarcely handle their muskets."—Cooke's Stonewall Jackson, 277.   [5] Pope's Report, 250.

[1] McC. Rep., 340, 344.
[2] We do not care to dwell upon this point. Abundant proofs of it may be found by any one who chooses to read the Reports of the commanders of corps and divisions.

in the way of that open and hearty co-operation which is essential to the highest efficiency of an army. While there was, we think, no purposed neglect in supporting him in act, still the fact that his plans and movements were openly censured by officers high in rank could not fail to demoralize those of lower grade, and through them the soldiers. Hence the fearful amount of straggling and skulking with which he had to contend from the outset. That he was opposed to a general who in this campaign, and ever after, manifested military capacity of a high order, and whose plans were carried out with unswerving fidelity, was a contingency always to be taken into account. That he was from the first called to meet greatly superior forces was owing to no fault on his part; it should be charged to those who failed to send to him the re-enforcements so absolutely essential and so positively promised. His first steps toward concentrating his forces were none the less commendable because so perfectly obvious. For the battle of Cedar Run he is nowise responsible. Had it proved a disastrous defeat instead of a bloody but indecisive passage of arms, no blame could have attached to him. Fettered by his instructions, and buoyed up by unfulfilled promises of aid, he could not afterward have done other than attempt to hold the line of the Rappahannock. The discovery of his weakness made by Stuart's dash upon Catlett's Station was an accident which might have happened to any one, and the like of which happened to Lee three weeks later. The destruction of the stores at Manassas could not have occurred had the assurances been true, as he had a right to believe, of the force by which that place was held. The marchings and countermarchings from Manassas to Gainesville, then back toward Centreville, and again toward Gainesville, were warranted, and in a measure compelled, by what he had at the moment good reason to believe to be the position and movements of the enemy.

The battle of the 29th was delivered, and all the orders given on the supposition that Jackson, with about 25,000 men, was the only enemy to be encountered, and that Longstreet was at a distance. In the morning he thought that "the indications are that the whole force of the enemy is moving in this direction at a pace that will bring them here by to-morrow night or the next day." He must have been of the same opinion at half past four in the afternoon, when the order was written informing Porter that "your line of march brings you in on the enemy's right flank," and directing him to "push forward into action at once on the enemy's flank." But before the order was received, and even before it was written, a considerable part of Longstreet's corps had come upon the field, and taken position upon Jackson's right, so that the line of march prescribed to Porter would have brought him far to the left of what was then the enemy's right flank, and directly in front of at least the advance of the enemy's "whole force." It is certainly strange that at this hour Pope should have been uninformed that Longstreet was on the field, instead of being thirty or forty hours' march away; for between nine and ten o'clock Buford reported to McDowell that before that time he had seen a large body of the enemy, estimated by him at more than 13,000 men, passing Gainesville and apparently marching directly to the battle-field.[1] Pope, indeed, on the morning of the 30th, when he supposed that he had won a victory and that the enemy were in retreat, declared that he had met and driven from the field "the combined force of the enemy," which can only be interpreted to mean the united commands of Jackson and Longstreet. Still, the battle of the day was indecisive, and if Pope had carried out his plan of the morning, and fallen back beyond Bull Run, the substantial fruits of victory would have been his.

[1] Buford, in *Court-martial*, 188. Whatever was then known or might have been known, nothing is now more certain than that a considerable part of Longstreet's force joined Jackson by noon, and bore a considerable part in the action of the 29th, and that before night his whole corps, with the exception of Anderson's division, had arrived, and this came up on the following morning. Lee says (*Report*, i., 23–25), "On the morning of the 29th the whole command resumed their march, the sound of cannon announcing that Jackson was already engaged. Longstreet entered the turnpike near Gainesville, and moving down toward Groveton, the head of his column came upon the field in the rear of the enemy's left." After some manœuvring, which is described, "Longstreet took position on the right of Jackson, Hood's two brigades, supported by Evans, being deployed across the turnpike, and at right angles to it. These troops were supported on the left by three brigades under Wilcox, and by a like force on the right under Kemper, D. R. Jones's division formed on the extreme right of the line, resting on the Manassas Gap Railroad." D. R. Jones (*Ibid.*, ii., 217) fixes the time of his arrival at "about noon." Longstreet says (*Ibid.*, 81) "that the noise of battle was heard before we reached Gainesville [which must have been about eight, for Buford saw his strong advance beyond that place by nine], and the head of my column soon after reached a position in rear of the enemy's flank, and within easy cannon shot." Hood, whose division was in the advance, says (*Ibid.*, 209), "Early in the day we came up with the main body of the enemy on the plains of Manassas, engaging General Jackson's forces."

The attack of the 30th was a grave military error, and wholly without excuse, if we regard General Pope's subsequent explanations as setting forth the knowledge which he then had of his condition and that of the enemy. Shortly after daylight he "began to feel discouraged and nearly hopeless of any successful issue to the operations with which he was charged." He was aware, by "twelve or one o'clock in the day, that we were confronted by forces greatly superior to our own, and that those forces were being every moment largely increased by fresh arrivals;" and he "therefore advanced to the attack," in order to "lay upon the enemy such blows as would cripple him as much as possible, and delay as long as practicable any farther advance toward the capital."[1] Yet at twelve o'clock he ordered the forces under McDowell to "be immediately thrown forward in pursuit of the enemy, and press him vigorously during the whole day."[2] That is, an inferior force was to pursue one already superior, which was every moment largely re-enforced, in the very direction from which those re-enforcements were advancing. Surely the thing then to be done was to fall back beyond Bull Run. If his force was sufficient to warrant him in attacking with any hope of escaping a complete defeat, it was more than sufficient to have enabled him to hold the line of Bull Run against the same enemy; and so long as this line was held, the enemy would be effectually prevented from making any farther direct advance toward the capital.

This campaign was conducted throughout by Lee and Jackson with rare ability. It grew in the end into something very different and far greater than was at first intended. Jackson was sent toward the Rappahannock merely to prevent the seizure of Gordonsville and the railroad. Lee's first object was to remove McClellan from his position on the James, and it seemed to him that "the most effectual way to relieve Richmond from any attack from that quarter would be to re-enforce Jackson, and advance upon Pope."[3] Halleck, at the same time, was equally desirous of relieving Richmond by withdrawing the Army of the Potomac, and McClellan, sorely against his wish, was carrying out this determination. As soon, therefore, as Lee was assured that Richmond was no longer threatened from the James, he pushed his main force toward the Rappahannock, hoping to overwhelm Pope before he could be joined by McClellan. To do this, he must cross the Rappahannock in front, or by the right or left of Pope, who confronted him on the opposite bank. While thus manœuvring, the seizure of Pope's dispatch-book informed him of the precise strength and position of the Union forces, and convinced him that it was possible by a rapid march to gain its rear, cut it off from retreat, supplies, and re-enforcements, and fall upon it with such a preponderance of force as to render its destruction almost inevitable. Rapidity of execution was essential to the success of this plan, and a slight failure in any point of detail might be fatal. We have seen how the plan was executed. Lee's operations from the 24th to the 30th of August must take a high place in the history of the war. To find its equal in boldness of conception, we must go forward nine months to the time when Grant passed the batteries at Vicksburg. To find its superior, we must go forward two years and three months to the time when Sherman began his great March to the Sea.

[1] *Report*, 23, 24.   [2] *Ibid.*, 47.   [3] *Lee's Rep.*, i., 19.

MONUMENT ON THE BATTLE-FIELD OF BULL RUN.

THE CONFEDERATES CROSSING THE POTOMAC.

CHAPTER XXIII.

THE INVASION OF MARYLAND.—ANTIETAM.

Result of the Campaign in Virginia.—The Invasion of the North.—Maryland! my Maryland!—Jackson's Scheme.—Lee's Design.—His Force.—Crossing the Potomac.—The Confederate Force.—Lee's Address to the People of Maryland.—His Reception.—The Command given to McClellan.—Reorganization of the Federal Army.—Movements of the Army.—Lee divides his Force.—Harper's Ferry.—The March upon the Ferry.—Lee's Order comes into the Hands of McClellan.—The Investment of Harper's Ferry.—Its Capture.—McClellan and Halleck.—McClellan advances.—Battle at Turner's Gap.—Battle at Crampton's Gap.—Lee's Position.—He falls back across the Antietam.—The Battle-field of Antietam.—Approach of the Union Force.—Confederate Troops come up from Harper's Ferry.—Movements of September 16.—McClellan's Plan of Battle for the next Day.—Hooker attacks the Confederate Left.—Is wounded.—His Corps repulsed.—Sumner attacks the Left and Centre.—Sedgwick repulsed on the Left.—The Fight in the Centre.—State of the Action at Noon.—Arrival of Franklin's Corps.—Its Part in the Engagement.—The Confederates worsted.—Their critical Position on the Left.—Over-caution of Sumner and McClellan.—Burnside's dilatory Movements.—He crosses the Antietam and drives back the Enemy.—A. P. Hill comes up from Harper's Ferry.—Burnside repulsed.—Close of the Battle.—Forces in and out of Action.—Estimate of Losses.—Results of the Battle.—The President's Proclamation freeing the Slaves.—After the Battle.—Lee recrosses the Potomac.—Affair at Shepherdstown.—McClellan and the Administration.—Stuart's Raid.—The President's Orders to Advance.—His Letter to McClellan.—McClellan's Plans.—He crosses the Potomac.—Advances toward Warrenton.—Lee moves to Culpepper.—Position of the Armies.—McClellan removed from Command, and Burnside appointed.

IN the brief campaign, lasting only twenty days from the time when the contending forces first encountered at Cedar Run, and only a week after the decisive movement for taking Pope's army in the rear was commenced, Lee had accomplished more than he had ventured to hope. Not only had the siege of Richmond been raised, but Virginia was virtually freed from the presence of the Federal armies; the main part of the force which had threatened North Carolina was withdrawn, and the whole plan of the Peninsular campaign thwarted; and, what was of still greater importance, the abundant harvests of the Valley of the Shenandoah would be reaped by Confederate sickles, and serve for the maintenance of Confederate armies. A bolder thought now came into the mind of the Confederate leader. There were yet some weeks, the most favorable in all the year for active military operations. During these, at least, the war might be carried on in the enemy's country. And so the noise of the battle of Groveton had scarcely ceased, when it was resolved to invade the State of Maryland.

Political considerations had much to do with this determination. It had come to be an article of faith that Maryland, from geographical position and community of institutions, belonged to the Confederacy. Richmond was thronged with refugees from Maryland who declared that the state was held within the Union by mere force, and that she wanted only an opportunity to break the hated bond. The song, "Maryland! my Maryland!" was thrummed on every piano, and sung by every voice. It was held to be the utterance of the people.[1] It needed only the presence of a powerful army to arouse the whole state, and bring her at once into the Confederacy. This accomplished, all the slave states—for Kentucky and Missouri were already claimed by the Confederacy and were represented in its Congress—would be detached from the Union. After the secession of Maryland, Washington could be no longer held as the Federal capital.

Jackson had long wished to lead or follow in an invasion of the North. Immediately after the battle of Bull Run he proposed to march directly into Western Virginia with 10,000 men, there recruit his army to 25,000, and then the Army of the Potomac, crossing at Leesburg, should unite with his own force; both should advance upon Harrisburg, and thence upon Philadelphia in the spring of 1862. With the heart of the North thus pierced by the Southern troops, the strategic points captured, and Washington evacuated, he believed that the Federal government would succumb and agree upon terms of peace.[2] How far Lee shared in these sanguine anticipations is doubtful. His Report, prepared seven months later, seems to imply that he proposed merely to occupy Maryland, and threaten Pennsylvania. He says: "To prolong a state of affairs every way desirable, and not to let the season for active operations pass without endeavoring to inflict farther injury upon the enemy, the best course appeared to be to transfer the army into Maryland. The condition of Maryland encouraged the belief that the presence of our army, however inferior to that of the enemy, would induce the Washington government to retain all its available force to provide against contingencies which its course toward the people of that state gave it reason to apprehend. At the same time, it was hoped that military success might afford us an opportunity to aid the citizens of Maryland in any efforts they might be disposed to make to recover their liberty." "It was proposed to move the army into Western Virginia, establish our communications with Richmond through the Valley of the Shenandoah, and, by threatening Pennsylvania, induce the enemy to follow, and thus draw him from his base of supplies."[3]

On the 2d of September Lee was joined at Chantilly by the division of D. H. Hill, consisting of five brigades. This gave him a force of about 70,000 men of all arms with which to undertake the invasion of the North; for by battle, disease, and straggling he had lost 30,000. The united army pushed rapidly on to the Potomac, Jackson in the advance. He crossed the river at a ford midway between Harper's Ferry and Washington, thirty miles from each, almost at the point where eight months before the Union

[1] Here are two stanzas of this song:

"The despot's heel is on thy shore,
Maryland! my Maryland!
His touch is on thy temple door,
Maryland! my Maryland!
Avenge the patriotic gore
That flecked the streets of Baltimore,
And be the Battle-queen of yore,
Maryland! my Maryland!

"I hear the distant thunder hum,
Maryland! my Maryland!
The Old Line's bugle, fife, and drum,
Maryland! my Maryland!
She is not dead, nor deaf, nor dumb,
Huzzah! she spurns the Northern scum,
She breathes, she burns, she'll come, she'll come,
Maryland! my Maryland!"

[2] Cooke's *Stonewall Jackson*, 86–88.

[3] *Lee's Rep.*, i., 27, 28.

forces had passed over into Virginia to meet the disaster of Ball's Bluff. There was nothing to oppose the passage. As the head of the column reached the middle of the river, Jackson, raised from his usual calm demeanor by what seemed the beginning of his cherished plan of an invasion of the North, paused, raised his hat, while bands and voices struck up the words and music of "My Maryland."[1] The entire Confederate force followed hard after, and on the 7th was concentrated near Frederick City, next after Baltimore the largest town in Maryland. All told they numbered barely 60,000, for without a battle thousands had fallen exhausted by the way, unable to keep up with the swift march.[2]

Lee issued an address to the people of Maryland. It was right, he said, that they should know, as far as concerned them, the purpose which had brought the Confederate army into the state. "The people of the Confederate States had long watched the wrongs and outrages which had been inflicted upon the citizens of a commonwealth allied to the states of the South by the strongest social, political, and commercial ties," and, "believing that the people of Maryland possessed a spirit too lofty to submit to such a government," the people of the South wished to aid them in "throwing off this foreign yoke." There would be no constraint or intimidation; "this army will respect your choice, whatever it may be; and while the Southern people will rejoice to welcome you to your natural position among them, they will only welcome you when you come of your own free will."

But if Lee had anticipated a general rising in Maryland, or even any considerable accession to his army, he was doomed to disappointment. Bradley Johnson, a Marylander who held a command in the Confederate army, was placed in charge of the provost-guard at Frederick. He put forth an address to the people calling upon them to join the delivering forces. "We have arms for you," he said; "I am authorized to muster in for the war companies and regiments. Let each man provide himself with a stout pair of shoes, a good blanket, and a tin cup. Jackson's men have no baggage." This prospect was not alluring to those to whom war had presented itself as a gay holiday show. When the theoretical secessionists of Maryland saw their liberators, officers as well as men, barefoot, ragged, and filthy,[3] they looked upon them with hardly concealed aversion. Yet that ragged and begrimed army was as brave a body of soldiers as the world ever saw. The enthusiasm of the Maryland secessionists exhausted itself in a few women secretly sewing clothing for the army, and in presenting to Jackson a magnificent horse, which threw him the first time he mounted it.[4]

The command of the Union army passed quietly and almost as a matter of course into the hands of McClellan even before Pope had asked to be relieved.[5] The President and General Halleck went to McClellan's house on the morning of the 2d. Lincoln said that things were going on badly in front; the army was in full retreat upon the defenses of Washington, and the roads were filled with stragglers. McClellan should go out and meet the army, take command of it as it approached the works, and put the troops in the best position for defense. Until this was said Halleck had no knowledge of the President's purpose.[6] Lincoln had resolved, in his quiet way, that he must exercise his authority as commander-in-chief of the army until he could find some man into whose hands this power could be intrusted. How often he tried to find such a man, and how fully he trusted him when found, this history will show. A formal order was forthwith issued: "Major General McClellan will have command of the fortifications of Washington, and of all the troops for the defense of the capital."

McClellan set vigorously to work to reorganize the shattered army. Some changes were made in the distribution of corps and commanders. Banks was placed in charge of the fortifications around Washington, the command of his corps in the field being given to Mansfield, a veteran officer who had never held any prominent command, but had shown at Norfolk high qualifications. Hooker was placed in command of the corps of McDowell, who disappeared from active duty. Burnside, Sumner, Franklin, and Porter retained the command of their corps. Thus, with the exception of Burnside, who was his personal friend, all the corps commanders had served under McClellan on the Peninsula. The core of the army consisted of the force brought from before Richmond. So admirably had this been organized by McClellan that, in spite of the shock which it had experienced in its retreat from the Chickahominy, its withdrawal from the James, and the disasters which a part of it had suffered under Pope, it took at once the form of a regular army, and formed a nucleus around which were rallied the troops gathered from every quarter. In a week, besides 72,000 men around Washington, and 13,000, mostly new recruits, left un-

[1] *Stonewall Jackson*, 308.

[2] The extent to which the army was reduced by fatigue and exhaustion is abundantly testified to by all Confederate accounts. Lee says (*Rep.*, i., 35): "The arduous services in which our troops had been engaged, their great privations of rest and food, and the long marches without shoes, had greatly reduced our ranks. These causes had compelled thousands of brave men to absent themselves, and many more had done so through unworthy motives." Cooke says (*Stonewall Jackson*, 341): "All the roads of Northern Virginia were lined with soldiers, comprehensively denominated 'stragglers;' but the great majority of these men had fallen out from the advancing column from physical impossibility to keep up with it; thousands were not with General Lee because they had no shoes, and their bleeding feet would carry them no farther, or the heavy march without rations had broken them down. This great crowd toiled on painfully on the wake of the army, dragging themselves five or six miles a day; and when they came to the Potomac, near Leesburg, it was only to find that General Lee had swept on, that General McClellan's column was between him and them, and that they could not rejoin their commands. The citizens of that whole region, who fed these unfortunate persons, will bear testimony that numbers sufficient to constitute an army in themselves passed the Blue Ridge to rendezvous, by General Lee's orders, at Winchester. These 20,000 or 30,000 men were not in the battle."

[3] "Never had the army been so dirty, ragged, and ill-provided as on this march."—D. R. Jones, in *Lee's Rep.*, ii., 221.

[4] *Stonewall Jackson*, 309, 312; *Lee's Rep.*, ii., 111.

[5] The government had, indeed, wished to remove him from the command, and had twice urged it upon Burnside. He declined to accept it, and declared that if matters could be so arranged as to remove the objections to him, McClellan could do more with the army than any other man.—*Com. Rep.*, 650.

[6] *McC. Rep.*, 345; Halleck, in *Com. Rep.*, 451.

MAP OF OPERATIONS IN MARYLAND.

accountably and against McClellan's wish at Harper's Ferry, there was a movable force of nearly 100,000 men to operate against Lee in Maryland. McClellan took the field at the head of this force.

McClellan took the field in Maryland in person on the 7th, when the march toward Lee was fairly begun. The army moved in three columns. The right wing, under Burnside, comprised his own corps and that of Hooker. The centre, under Sumner, comprised his own corps and that of Mansfield. Franklin, in command of his corps and Couch's division, had the left. Porter's corps, not fully organized, followed after. The movement was slow, for Lee's plan had not yet developed itself. In the six days, from the 7th to the 13th, the advance was barely thirty miles. McClellan was also deceived as to the strength of the enemy, estimating it at 120,000 men—twice the real number.

Lee's object in crossing the Potomac at a point so near Washington, instead of at Harper's Ferry or above, and thence advancing into the heart of Maryland, was to assume a position which should threaten both Washington and Baltimore. This he supposed would draw the enemy after him; and he proposed to give battle to the Union army as far as possible from its base of supplies. For the accomplishment of this purpose, he believed that the possession of Harper's Ferry was indispensable, in order to enable him to keep open his communications with Richmond through the Valley of the Shenandoah. He assumed that the march into Maryland would have caused the Union troops at Harper's Ferry to be withdrawn, as they should have been, and as McClellan wished. This not being done, Lee undertook to dislodge, and, if possible, capture the forces there. To effect this, he divided his army, sending the whole of Jackson's command and half of Longstreet's toward Harper's Ferry, retaining with himself D. H. Hill's division, half of Longstreet's corps, and the greater part of the cavalry.[1] McClellan's advance had been so slow that Lee trusted that

Harper's Ferry could be reduced and his army reunited before he would be called upon to meet the enemy.[1] In forming his plan of operations, Lee must have under-estimated the Federal force as greatly as McClellan over-estimated that of the Confederates. He could not have supposed that the enemy whom he had outnumbered and defeated at Groveton, and whom he had seen in full retreat to the fortifications at Washington, should within ten days have swelled to a force outnumbering his own almost three to one.[2] He must have supposed that his own effective force and that of the enemy were about equal.

Harper's Ferry is at the junction of the Potomac and the Shenandoah. The Potomac, coming from the north, meets the Shenandoah, ranging from the west, at the foot of a spur of the Blue Ridge, here known as Elk Mountain. The united streams have torn a narrow passage through the mountain, rending it from summit to base, leaving on either side steep cliffs a thousand feet high. The eastern cliff is Maryland Heights; the western, on the Virginia side, Loudon Heights. In the angle at the junction of the rivers is an elevated plateau, falling steeply toward the Potomac, and sloping gently toward the Shenandoah, and stretching backward at the level of the surrounding country. The ridge of this plateau is Bolivar Heights, at the foot of which nestles the village of Harper's Ferry. Some one had once

street's "command" properly comprised 21 brigades; but at this time 10 of these were detached for the Harper's Ferry operation, and did not act during the remainder of this campaign under Longstreet. In the remainder of this chapter "Longstreet's corps" will indicate only the 11 brigades which remained with him. The others will be designated by the name of the respective division commanders, McLaws, Anderson, and Walker. D. H. Hill's division consisted of 5 brigades. Thus 24 brigades were detached to Harper's Ferry, and 16 remained with Lee. The effective strength of a brigade at this time, previous to losses in battle, was 1500; some, however, were much stronger, some much weaker.   [1] Lee's Rep., i., 28.

[2] On the 20th of September, after the loss of 15,000 at South Mountain and Antietam, no considerable re-enforcements having been received in the interval, the Army of the Potomac numbered "present for duty" 164,359, of whom 71,210 were stationed within the defenses at Washington, leaving in the field directly under McClellan 93,169. The nominal force—present for duty, sick, and absent—was 293,798.—Com. Rep., 492.

[1] Jackson's "command," including A. P. Hill's division, comprised 14 brigades. Long-

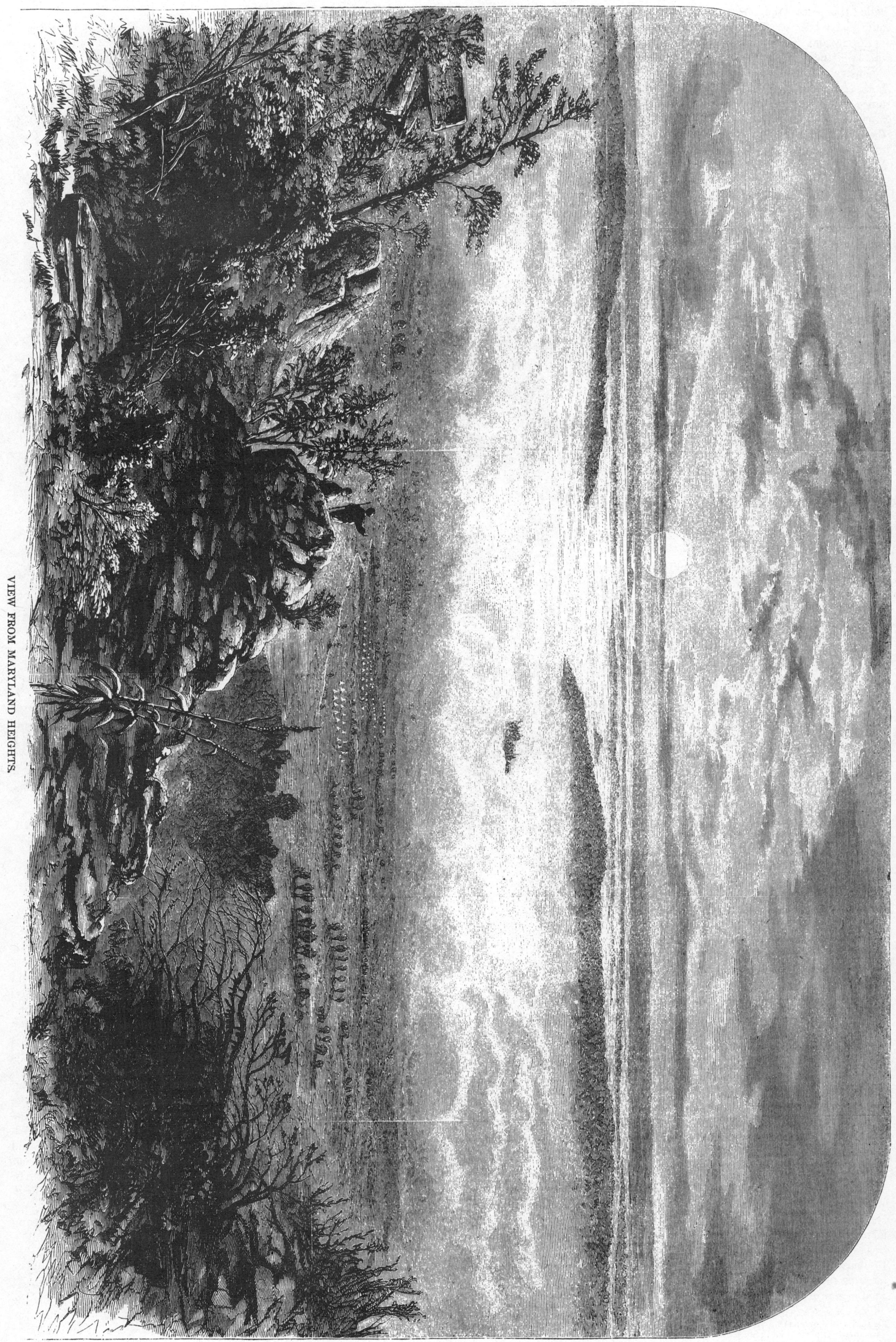

VIEW FROM MARYLAND HEIGHTS.

called this place "the Thermopylæ of America." It might have been so in the times when war was waged with bow and sword, with spear and sling, but with the appliances of modern warfare the place has no defensive value. It is completely overlooked by both Loudon and Maryland Heights at such a distance and height that a plunging fire of artillery or musketry can be poured into it from either without the possibility of reply. It is a mere military trap, unless the commanding heights are also held in force; and then it is worthless, as no enemy need go near it in order to cross the Potomac from either direction to invade Maryland or Virginia. Johnston had perceived this fifteen months before, and abandoned the place without resistance, and against positive orders, the moment it was menaced. Lee strangely considered its possession essential to his proposed operations, and, in order to seize it, divided his army. Had he done otherwise, the course of the campaign must have been wholly different. He would have fought the decisive battle far in the interior with the whole, instead of with a part of his force. Had he been defeated, his army must have been annihilated, for the victorious enemy would have been between him and Virginia, cutting off all possibility of succor or retreat. Had he been victorious, he might probably have anticipated Sherman's march to the sea, for beyond the Alleghanies there was no army to oppose him; and from Philadelphia he might have dictated terms of peace.

Harper's Ferry was held by a force of about 13,000, including an outpost at Martinsburg. They were raw troops, commanded by Colonel Miles. About 1500 men were posted on Maryland Heights, the remainder were intrenched on Bolivar Heights. Lee's plan was to surround this force, and thus capture it. His orders were issued on the 9th, and their execution commenced the next morning. Walker, whose two brigades had been sent to the mouth of the Monocacy to destroy the canal aqueduct, was to cross the Potomac, ascend its right bank, and seize Loudon Heights. McLaws, with eight brigades, was to march from Frederick, pass the South Mountain at Crampton's Gap, cross the narrow valley to the foot of Maryland Heights, which he was to ascend and occupy, disposing his forces in such a way as to hold the roads winding around its base, thus cutting off all retreat in that direction. Jackson, with fourteen brigades, was to cross the South Mountain at Turner's Gap, advance to the Potomac, cross it high above Harper's Ferry, sweep down its right bank, capturing or driving back the force at Martinsburg, and then march directly upon Harper's Ferry. The remainder of the army was to march toward Hagerstown, where, or at Boonesboro', it was to be rejoined by that portion which, it was assumed, would have succeeded in its designs upon Harper's Ferry.[1]

The directions of this order were executed with great precision. Walker took possession of Loudon Heights on the 13th, without encountering the slightest opposition. McLaws reached the foot of Maryland Heights on the 12th. He sent two brigades to scale the ascent and gain the summit. They encountered some resistance from the troops posted there, but this was overcome, the Federals abandoning their works, pitching the guns down the cliff, and making their way across the river to Harper's Ferry. Maryland Heights was in the possession of the infantry of McLaws on the evening of the 13th. The next morning was employed in cutting a road to the top of the Heights practicable for artillery, along which four guns were laboriously dragged, and from these fire was opened upon the town.

Jackson, in the mean while, was pressing upon his longer march with that speed which had gained for his command the name of the "foot cavalry." Leaving Frederick on the 10th, he reached the Potomac next day at Williamsport, 25 miles above Harper's Ferry, and on the 12th entered Martinsburg. The Federal troops abandoned this place at his approach, and fell back to Harper's Ferry. Jackson followed hard after, and on the following morning came in sight of the Union force, drawn up on Bolivar Heights. In three days he had marched 80 miles. The remainder of that day and the whole of the 14th were spent by Jackson in ascertaining, by courier and signal, the positions of Walker and McLaws upon Loudon and Maryland Heights. He found that they had gained the positions appointed for them, and commanded the only roads by which the Federals could retreat down the Potomac or up the Shenandoah, but that the enemy on Bolivar Heights were beyond the effective range of his light guns. Separated as they were from him by rivers, they could afford no direct assistance in capturing the Federal force as it then stood. Jackson undertook to

SIGNAL STATION, SUMMIT OF MARYLAND HEIGHTS.

dislodge the enemy from Bolivar Heights, and drive them down into the slaughter-pen of Harper's Ferry. The force with which he was to do this exceeded only slightly that opposed to him. Miles had 12,000 or 13,000. Jackson's "command" numbered at the outset about 32,000. It had fought at Cedar Run, Bristoe, the three battles near Groveton, and at Chantilly, losing in all 6000 men, killed and wounded. Not less than 10,000 had fallen out from sickness or exhaustion on the long march from the Rapidan to the Potomac. He could not have brought more than 15,000 to Harper's Ferry. For the rest, the affair reads almost like a farce, with a few tragic lines interpolated.

By the morning of the 15th Jackson had fairly surrounded Miles; batteries from one side opened upon the other on the Bolivar plateau; the guns from Loudon and Maryland Heights played at the heads of those below, and were duly answered; none doing harm, except that one Confederate shot struck a Federal caisson. Miles called a council of war, and said he had resolved to surrender; one or two of his officers wished to "cut their way out;" the cavalry, 1500 strong, rode up the Potomac, with or without orders, and got off, encountering no opposition, and destroying in their way 75 wagons of the Confederate train. If the infantry had gone the same way there was nothing to hinder; but they were raw troops, commanded by worse than raw officers. Miles raised the white flag in token of surrender. Before it was perceived, he was mortally wounded by a chance shot. White, his superior in rank, who, on coming in from Martinsburg, had waived the command in Miles's favor, went to Jackson to arrange terms of surrender. There was then nothing else to be done, for the troops had degenerated into a crowd of frightened men. He found the Confederate general fast asleep on the ground. Hill, whom White had first encountered, aroused Jackson. "General," said he, "this is General White,

[1] Lee's Rep., i, 28. For the full text of this order, see McC. Rep., 353. D. H. Hill had left his copy of the order in his room at Frederick, where it was found and given to McClellan three days after. It placed him in full possession of the plans of his enemy; too late, indeed, to enable him to thwart them entirely, but in time to enable him to strike an unexpected blow.

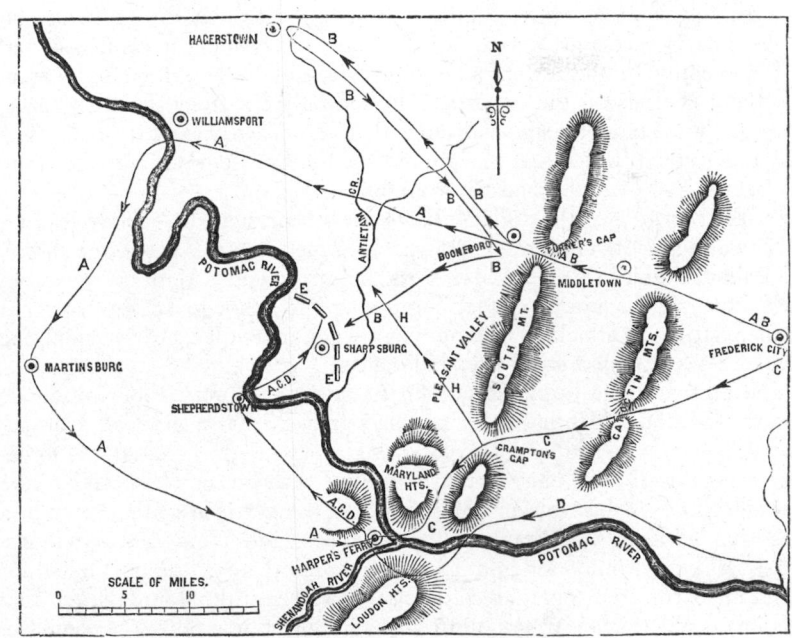

MOVEMENTS FROM SEPTEMBER 10 TO 17.

A, A. Jackson's March from Frederick to Sharpsburg.   D, D. Walker's March from the Monocacy to Sharpsburg.
B, B. Longstreet's   "   "   "   E, E. Confederate Position at Antietam.   [tietam.
C, C. McLaws and Anderson's   "   "   H. H. Franklin's March from Pleasant Valley to the An-

Franklin followed the same route as McLaws from Frederick to Pleasant Valley; the remainder of the Union army that of Longstreet from Frederick to Boonesboro', and thence to the Antietam. The arrows show the direction of the march. Where two or more letters come together, it indicates that the several bodies followed the same route.

of the United States army." Jackson made a gesture of recognition, and again closed his eyes. "He has come to arrange terms of surrender," continued Hill. Jackson made no reply; he was fast asleep. Again, half awakened, he said, drowsily, "The surrender must be unconditional; every indulgence can be granted afterward," then fell fast asleep once more, leaving Hill to decide upon the terms.[1] The terms granted were certainly liberal. All were to be paroled, retaining their personal effects, and officers their side-arms; transportation to be furnished to carry away the property. Upon these terms more than 11,000 men were surrendered. The Confederates gained 73 guns, with but little ammunition, 13,000 small-arms, and a considerable amount of stores. The capture cost the Confederates perhaps two score of lives, and the Federals about as many.[2]

Although the affair at Harper's Ferry proved of ultimate disadvantage to the Confederates, it was disgraceful alike to the military authorities at Washington, who left the force in a place where it was of no use, and to the officers who attempted no adequate defense. Miles died a few hours after the surrender, but his conduct was sharply censured by the Military Commission. Ford, who shamefully abandoned Maryland Heights, was dismissed from the service on the ground of "such lack of military capacity as to disqualify him from a command in the service." White was commended as having "acted with decided capability and courage."[3]

Slow as had been McClellan's advance, it yet carried him farther from Washington than was thought prudent by Halleck. With more than 70,000 men in garrison, the authorities at Washington were nervously apprehensive for the safety of the capital. When tidings were brought that a Confederate force had recrossed the Potomac, it was assumed that the whole army had crossed or was about to cross and assail Washington, either in front, or in the rear by recrossing into Maryland below McClellan. Even as late as the 16th, when the two armies were face to face on the Antietam, Halleck still believed that the bulk of the Confederate force was in Virginia.[4]

[1] Cooke's *Stonewall Jackson*, 325.
[2] McLaws speaks of a "sharp and spirited engagement" on Maryland Heights, but does not give his losses.—*Lee's Rep.*, ii., 163. Walker lost on Loudon Heights one killed and three wounded.—*Ibid.*, 204. A. P. Hill lost three killed and 66 wounded. There appear to have been no losses in the remainder of Jackson's command. [3] General Orders, 1862, No. 183.
[4] *The President to McClellan*, Sept. 12: "Governor Curtin telegraphs me, 'I have advices that

The Confederates left Frederick on the 10th, and the place was occupied by the Federals on the 12th, after a skirmish with the enemy's cavalry left behind as a rear-guard. On the evening of the next day, accident, which had three weeks before favored Lee by disclosing to him the situation of Pope, placed in McClellan's hands the order from Lee disclosing his designs, and the position and movements of every division of the Confederate army. Thus informed, McClellan's course was plain. He had 100,000 men within a few hours' march from Frederick. Lee had divided his army into two parts, neither of which, by McClellan's own exaggerated estimate, consisting of more than 60,000, and, in fact, of only half as many. By a rapid march, the whole Union army could be thrown right between these two portions. He proposed to "cut the enemy in two, and beat him in detail."[1] His arrangements were for once made with due promptness. That night orders were sent to every general. Franklin was to cross the South Mountain by Crampton's Gap, cut off McLaws, and relieve Harper's Ferry. The remainder of the army, Hooker and Reno in the advance, followed by Sumner with his own corps and that of Mansfield, with the division of Porter which had come up, was to march upon the heels of Lee toward Boonesboro', crossing the South Mountain at Turner's Gap, six miles above Crampton's, and fall upon that half of the Confederate army which had not been sent toward Harper's Ferry.

Lee had meanwhile moved leisurely past the South Mountain. On the 11th Longstreet had reached Hagerstown, D. H. Hill stopping at Boonesboro'. On the afternoon of the 13th the Confederate commander was startled by intelligence that the Federals, whom he had supposed to be quietly resting at Frederick, were pressing swiftly toward Turner's Gap. If they succeeded in passing the mountains they would be fairly between the portions of his divided army. Hill was hurried back to the Gap at once to keep the enemy in check until Longstreet could be recalled from Hagerstown. Lee felt the full peril of his position. He had with him barely 28,000 men, and these stretched along a distance of 25 miles. To provide for the worst, he sent his trains across the Potomac, escorted by only two regiments.[2]

Hill reached the summit of the Gap early in the morning of the 14th, just before the head of the Federal force came up. His division had left Hanover Junction, a few miles from Richmond, on the 26th of July, and joined Lee at Chantilly, fully 150 miles distant, on the 3d of September, and were then, without a day's rest, pushed forward to the Potomac and into Maryland. They had not been engaged in a single action. But "the straggling had been enormous, in consequence of heavy marches, deficient commissariat, want of shoes, and inefficient officers," so that he could bring less than 5000 men into action[3] out of more than twice that number with which he had set out.

The South Mountain rises to a height of about 1000 feet, the depression at Turner's Gap being about 400 feet. But the Gap is so narrow that a few hundred men with artillery could hold the summit against an army. But

Jackson is crossing the Potomac at Williamsport, and probably the whole rebel army will be drawn from Maryland.' Receiving nothing from Harper's Ferry or Martinsburg to-day, and positive information that the line is cut, corroborates the idea that the enemy is recrossing the Potomac." *Halleck to McClellan*, Sept. 13: "Until you know more certainly the enemy's force south of the Potomac, you are wrong in uncovering the capital. I am of the opinion that the enemy will send a small column toward Pennsylvania to draw your forces in that direction, then suddenly move on Washington with the forces south of the Potomac and those he may cross over." Sept. 14: "Scouts report a large force still on the Virginia side of the Potomac. If so, I fear you are exposing your left and rear." Sept. 16: "I think you will find that the whole force of the enemy in your front has crossed the river. I fear you more than ever that they will recross at Harper's Ferry or below, and turn your left, thus cutting you off from Washington."—*McC. Rep.*, 350.
General Halleck indeed testified (*Com. Rep.*, 453): "In respect to General McClellan's going too fast or too far from Washington, there can be found no such telegram from me to him. He has mistaken the meaning of the telegrams I sent to him. I telegraphed to him that he was going too far, not from Washington, but from the Potomac, leaving General Lee the opportunity to come down the Potomac and get between him and Washington." But, as McClellan's left actually hugged the Potomac, and his centre and right, moving by parallel roads, were more nearly within supporting distance than if they had followed in the rear, it is hard to see how, if he moved at all, he could have gone at a less distance from the river. [1] *McC. Rep.*, 360.
[2] This significant fact is mentioned only by D. H. Hill, and that merely incidentally, in his report of the battle of Antietam. "Our wagons had been sent off across the river on Sunday, the 14th, and for three days the men had been sustaining life on green corn and such cattle as they could kill in the fields. In charging through an apple orchard at the Yankees, with the immediate prospect of death before them, I noticed men eagerly devouring apples."—*Lee's Rep.*, ii., 118.
[3] D. H. Hill, in *Lee's Rep.*, ii., 114.

BOONESBORO' AND TURNER'S GAP, FROM THE WEST.

JESSE L. RENO.

a road, rough though passable, runs along the summits of each of the ridges which bound the Gap on either side; by these the main attack of the Federals was made, the object being to turn, either by the right or the left, or by both, the Confederate force holding the summit of the Gap. Reno's division took the road to the left, and, after sharp fighting, succeeded at noon in gaining the summit, or rather one of the summits, for the crest of the mountain is cloven by a deep ravine, and beyond this the enemy held a strong position. There was now a lull in the contest lasting for a couple of hours, while Hooker, who had reached the base of the mountain after Reno, was working his way up the road on the right of the pass. A solitary peak, which overlooked the country for miles, was the key to the whole position. Whoever held that held the pass. Both sides seemed to apprehend this at once, and each endeavored to gain it. Hooker's men were climbing the steep slope, too steep for artillery to be dragged up. Hill, from the valley below, trained his guns upon the peak, but with little effect. He sent three brigades of infantry up to hold the peak. The lines met, and engaged in a fierce but desultory combat, each availing itself of every natural defense.

Until late in the afternoon the battle on the Confederate side had been fought wholly by Hill. But about four o'clock Longstreet had come up with eight brigades, worn and exhausted by the long march from Hagerstown. Some of these were hotly engaged, but they came two hours too late to change the fortunes of the day. When night closed in the Federals had won every position and held the Gap, through which their whole force could pour on the following morning. Nothing was left for Lee but to retreat, leaving his dead and wounded behind. The action was fought with determined bravery on both sides. In all, the Federals had brought in about 30,000 men, the Confederates 17,000.[1] The Federal loss in this action was 312 killed, 1234 wounded. That of the Confederates was greater. Hill lost, in killed, wounded, and prisoners, nearly 2000; for at Antietam, three days later, he could bring into action only 3000.[2] Some of Longstreet's brigades also lost heavily. The Federals secured 1500 prisoners, most of them from the wounded. The entire loss of the Confederates, in killed and wounded, was probably something more than 2000. Reno was killed near the close of the battle. The Confederates lost Garland. Both were brave officers and accomplished gentlemen.[3]

Simultaneously with the battle at Turner's Gap, an action had been going on at Crampton's Gap, a few miles distant. Franklin, with his corps, lacking Couch's division, which had not come up, advanced toward this gap. The foot of the pass was slightly held, and the force pressed on up the slope. Tidings of the approach of Franklin reached McLaws, who had just established himself on Maryland Heights. He sent Cobb back with three brigades, directing him to hold the pass if it cost the last man. Cobb took post near the top of the mountain, behind a stone wall; Slocum's division

charged this in front, while Smith moved round to assail it in flank and rear. The Confederates broke and fled down the slope in confusion, and in the evening Franklin debouched into Pleasant Valley, three miles from Maryland Heights on the opposite side, and only six from Harper's Ferry, whence the sound of firing indicated that the place was still held. The Federals lost 115 killed and 416 wounded; the Confederates more, for they left behind 600 prisoners, mostly wounded.

On the morning of the 15th McLaws drew back his whole force, leaving only two regiments upon the heights, and formed it across the lower end of the Valley, Franklin forming his across the upper end. Both lay watching each other all the morning, each supposing the other to be superior, and neither daring to attack. The numbers were, in reality, nearly equal, the Confederates having a small preponderance.[1]

The passes of the South Mountain having been forced, the position of Lee was perilous. He had with him less than 25,000 men of all arms, infantry, cavalry, and artillery. So long as Harper's Ferry held out, the forces sent to capture it were cut off from reuniting with him. The position here was singular. If Jackson and McLaws held the garrison of the Ferry in a vice, that garrison and Franklin held McLaws and Walker in as close a grip. McLaws could not join Lee by marching up Pleasant Valley, for Franklin barred the way; he could not cross the Elk Mountain, for that was impassable for an army; until Harper's Ferry was taken, he could not cross the Potomac, and, by going up its south bank and recrossing, rejoin Lee. "There was," he says, "no outlet in any direction for any thing but the troops, and that very doubtful; in no contingency could I have saved the troops and artillery."[2] Walker, on Loudon Heights, was equally isolated, for between him and Lee was interposed both the Shenandoah and the Potomac. But when Turner's Gap was forced, Harper's Ferry was still uncaptured; but tidings had just come that the place must soon fall, when the troops beleaguering, and themselves beleaguered, would be set at liberty. If a battle could be postponed two days, Lee would be able to bring into action as many of these separated forces as would be able to endure the long march to join him. To shorten this march, he retreated during the night of the 14th toward the Potomac, and, placing the Antietam Creek between himself and McClellan, took up a strong defensive position near the village of Sharpsburg.

The Potomac makes a bend shaped somewhat like the two-horned antique bow, about six miles from tip to tip. The Antietam is like the loosened string of this bow. This stream in itself is no formidable military obstacle. It is passable for infantry at almost every point. Three stone bridges and several fords, within a distance of three or four miles, afford abundant passage for artillery, provided the approaches to them are not fully commanded by an enemy. The region beyond, that is, on the western side, is somewhat broken. There are low swells, with narrow intervening valleys, and patches of woodland and cultivated fields, cut up by roads, fences, and stone walls. The limestone rock every where crops up above the surface, affording tolerable shelter for troops. The position is such that, in case of need, a general with 20,000 men might fairly venture to hold it against 30,000; one with 30,000 might fairly venture to assail an enemy posted there with 20,000.

Lee reached this position on the morning of the 15th, the cavalry forming his rear-guard, somewhat closely pressed by the Union horse. The head of the foremost pursuing infantry column reached the east bank of the Antietam in the afternoon. McClellan had hoped to bring on an action that day. His orders were, that if the enemy were overtaken on the march, they should be attacked at once; if found in force and position, the advanced corps should halt and await his arrival. Coming to the front late in the afternoon, McClellan found the enemy drawn up beyond the Antietam, making an ostentatious display of infantry, artillery, and cavalry on the opposite crests. The Union corps, coming after in different columns, had become somewhat entangled, and McClellan decided, in view of what he saw and could then have known, that it was too late to attack that day. If he had been aware how weak was the force in his front, he might, perhaps, have determined otherwise.

Lee had scarcely crossed the Antietam before he learned that Harper's Ferry had been surrendered, and that all obstacles, except those of time and space, to the reunion of his army were removed. Orders were at once sent for the whole force near the Ferry to hasten to Sharpsburg. Jackson was the first to move.

At 3 in the afternoon his men were ordered to cook two days' rations, and be ready to march. The march was begun an hour past midnight. On the morning of the 16th the corps were within two miles of Sharpsburg. They had made a night-march of fifteen miles in less than six hours, fording the Potomac by the way. The addition which he brought to Lee was small in numbers. The two divisions, Jackson's, or the "Stonewall," and Ewell's, had set out from Richmond 20,000 strong. Within six weeks they had fought at Cedar Run, Bristoe, and during all the three days at Groveton. They had marched from the Rappahannock to Manassas, from Manassas to the Potomac, from the Potomac to Frederick, from Frederick to Harper's Ferry, from Harper's Ferry back to Sharpsburg, losing

---

[1] McClellan says: "We went into action with about 30,000 men." He supposed that he had encountered "D. H. Hill's corps, 15,500, and a part, if not the whole of Longstreet's, and perhaps a portion of Jackson's" (Rep., 372). But he had actually met eight brigades of Longstreet's, about 12,000, and D. H. Hill's, 5000. Such was, however, the strength of the position, that if the Confederates had been able in the morning to have brought 10,000 or 15,000 men to its defense, and so held the crests on the two sides of the Gap with artillery, they could not have been dislodged by five times their number.—See Longstreet and D. H. Hill, in Lee's Rep., ii., 84, 114.

[2] Lee's Rep., ii., 114.

[3] D. H. Hill thus brutally mentions the death of these two generals: "This brilliant service cost us the life of that pure, gallant, and accomplished Christian soldier, General Garland, who had no superior and few equals in the service. The Yankees, on their side, lost General Reno, a renegade Virginian, who was killed by a happy shot from the 23d North Carolina."

[1] Franklin's corps (Couch not having arrived) numbered not quite 13,000. McLaws's command was made up of troops which had suffered least in the previous actions, having been mostly in reserve, and only partially engaged at Groveton. His eight brigades would probably average at this time 1800 each. Deducting the losses of the day before, and the two regiments left on the Heights, there would be between 13,000 and 14,000. He himself says (Lee's Rep., ii., 167): "The force in Harper's Ferry was nearly, if not quite equal to my own, which was as far superior." He had just before estimated the "force above," that is, Franklin's, at "from 15,000 to 25,000 and upward." The force at Harper's Ferry he knew, at the time of making the report, to have been more than 11,000, for that number had surrendered, and the whole cavalry force had escaped. Our estimate of McLaws's strength is also confirmed by the numbers which he was able to bring upon the field at Antietam two days later.   [2] See McLaws, in Lee's Rep., ii., 167.

at each step of the long way. Of those 20,000 men, Jackson brought back to Lee on the Antietam only himself and 5000 others.[1] In the afternoon Walker came up. His two brigades had not as yet been engaged in any action. They had formed part of the rear-guard at Groveton. The two brigades numbered a little more than 3000 men when they rejoined Lee that evening. McLaws remained at Pleasant Valley until the morning of the 16th. He then crossed the Potomac by the railroad bridge, passed through Harper's Ferry, not giving his men time for rest and refreshment, and at dark encamped for a few hours on the south bank of the Potomac, close by the ford. At midnight the march was resumed, and by dawn of the 17th the command was halted close by Sharpsburg. Of the eight brigades comprised in this command, three had suffered severely at Crampton's Gap; the others had done hard duty on Maryland Heights, and in watching the outlets from Harper's Ferry. The march to Sharpsburg had been trying. Men dropped from the ranks in utter exhaustion. McLaws brought with him only 7000 men, barely half his force; of these about 3000 belonged to his own division, about 4000 to that of Anderson;[2] so that, on the morning of the 17th, Lee had, exclusive of cavalry, about 36,000 men, infantry and artillery.[3]

Meanwhile, on the afternoon of the 16th, McClellan began to move. Hooker was sent across the Antietam at a point above the extreme left of the Confederates. The passage was made without opposition. He then moved down the west bank, and came in contact with the Confederate left. Some sharp skirmishing ensued, the only result being that Hooker established himself in a position from which he could strike on the next morning; and Lee could infer from what quarter the first blow would come, and make his dispositions accordingly. Mansfield's corps followed Hooker across the Antietam during the night, and encamped a mile in the rear. McClellan's plan, if Hooker understood it rightly, was the true one. He had undertaken the offensive. The action at Turner's Gap had shown that he was in superior force. With half his strength he had forced the passage through the South Mountain, and his opponent had fallen back in full retreat. He had come up with Lee standing at bay at the farthest point to which retreat was possible. Every thing pointed to the one conclusion, that the whole Union force should be thrown at the earliest moment upon the Confederates. That this was to be done on the morning of the 17th was the decision, as understood by Hooker, to whom the initiative was assigned.[4]

Hooker opened the attack at dawn on the morning of the 17th. The onset fell upon a portion of Jackson's command, which, few in numbers, was strongly posted in a wood upon the Confederate left. This was soon swept back, with the loss of half its numbers, out of the wood, across an open field, and into another wood, where the outcropping rock gave shelter from the fierce fire poured in upon it. Lawton, who now commanded Ewell's division, called upon Hood for all the assistance which he could give. Hood threw his two strong brigades into action, and was soon followed by three brigades from Hill's division. Hooker still pressed on, meanwhile sending back for Mansfield's corps to come up to his support. This came upon the field at about 8 o'clock. While deploying his column, the veteran commander, who had joined his corps only the day before, was killed, and the command reverted to Williams. Hooker still pushed on upon the extreme left of the Confederates, and by 9 o'clock had gained an elevation which commanded the position of the enemy. He thought the battle won. The enemy, as far as he could see, were falling back in disorder, while his own troops, full of spirits, rent the sky with cheers. Just then, while looking for a point at which to post his batteries in order to sweep the retreating foe, he fell severely wounded. Having directed a telegram to his friends, announcing that he had won a great victory, and sending a message to Sumner, who was already close at hand, to hasten upon the field, he was borne half-conscious to the rear.[5]

But when Sumner came up the whole aspect of the battle had changed. Hill and Hood had sprung to the relief of Jackson. Their united force was far inferior in numbers to that of Hooker and Mansfield, but they were inordinately strong in artillery. Hill, with but 3000 infantry, had more than 80 guns at his command.[6] These, in front and upon the left, with the mounted artillery upon the right, under Stuart, were brought to bear upon Hooker's advancing corps. This was checked, then wavered, and when the enemy, with hardly half their numbers, charged from the sheltering woods, Hooker's corps broke and fled in utter rout, not to appear again upon the field. Their rout, moreover, threw into confusion a part of Mansfield's corps. The losses in Hooker's corps had been severe, but absolutely they had not been greater, and, relatively to the numbers engaged, had been less than they had inflicted. The killed and wounded had been about one sixth of the whole number, a ratio hardly one half of that of the forces which afterward bore the brunt of the fight on either side.[7]

JOSEPH K. MANSFIELD.

Sumner's large corps, more than 18,000 strong, was now thrown into action. It advanced in three columns. Sedgwick's division, on the extreme right, took the position from which Hooker had been driven so speedily that the Confederates were not aware of their signal success, but fell back to their former position before what they supposed to be merely re-enforcements brought up to support a force that had been driven back. Next on the left came the divisions of French's and Richardson's corps, pressing down toward the Confederate centre. Lee perceived that here was to be the main stress of the fight. To meet it, he ordered up every disposable man from his right. First came Walker's division, 3000 strong; then McLaws with 3000, and Anderson with 4000. So pressing seemed the emergency that Lee ventured still farther to weaken his right, detaching regiment after regiment, until D. R. Jones, who had been posted there with six brigades, had barely 2400 men with which to confront Burnside's corps of 14,000.[1] This withdrawal from the right was, however, screened from the view of the enemy by the wooded ridge along which the Confederate line was formed.

At ten it seemed that victory was secure for the Union forces. Sedgwick had gained a position a little beyond that from which Hooker had been driven an hour before, and Jackson's corps was streaming to the rear. Hood, having lost a third of his men and exhausted his ammunition, was withdrawn. Hill was sorely pressed by French and Richardson. Three of his five brigades were broken and retreating; the other two clung desperately to a sunken road which formed a natural rifle-pit. The Confederate left, worn by the fight in which it had been engaged for five hours, and pressed at every point by a superior force, was on the point of giving way. But the strong re-enforcements brought up not only restored the balance, but gave them a slight preponderance. All losses being deducted, Lee had here on his left about 24,000 men. Sumner had his own corps and half of that of Mansfield, now numbering together 22,000. The re-enforcements came up almost at the same moment. Jackson, strengthened by McLaws, advanced upon Sedgwick, who had gone considerably to the right, leaving a wide gap between himself and French. Into this gap Walker flung his division, assailing Sedgwick on the flank and threatening his rear. The combined attack was more than he could endure. The division was forced from the strip of woods which it held, and which Hooker had vainly attempted to win, across the open field, over which he had been driven for a full half mile, until they rallied behind a long line of post and rail fence. Here they re-formed, and poured in so fierce a fire that the Confederates were checked, and fell back again into the wood. Both sides now occupied here on the extreme right the positions which they had held in the morning, and the fighting in this quarter was closed. In this fierce encounter McLaws lost 1019 men and Walker 1103 out of the 6000 which they brought into the field. Jackson's loss during this final assault was nearly 1000. Sedgwick's loss was 1136, and Green's division of Mansfield's corps lost 650. Thus the Confederate loss in this final assault on the Union right was nearly double that of their opponents.[2]

---

[1] I accept this statement of the force brought by Jackson on the authority of the generals who commanded the divisions at Antietam: J. R. Jones, who commanded Jackson's division, says, "The old Stonewall division entered the action weary and worn, and reduced to the numbers of a small brigade . . . not numbering over 1600 men at the beginning of the fight."—*Lee's Rep.*, ii., 222. Early, who commanded Ewell's division, gives its losses at Antietam as 1352 "out of less than 3500, with which it went into that action."—*Ibid.*, ii., 196.

[2] *Lee's Rep.*, ii., 116, 172.

[3] From this point we take no account of the cavalry force on either side, as it was not engaged in the action of the day.

[4] "When I had left with my corps to make this attack, I had been assured that, simultaneous with my attack, there should be an attack upon the rebel army in the centre and on the left the next morning. I sent word to General McClellan when I proposed to attack, in order that he might direct the other attacks to be made at the same time. At dawn I made the attack."—Hooker, in *Com. Rep.*, 581.　[5] Hooker, in *Com. Rep.*, 581.　[6] *Lee's Rep.*, ii., 115.

[7] The completeness of the rout of Hooker's corps, after his wounding, is shown by evidence too conclusive to be questioned. Sumner says (*Com. Rep.*, 368): "On going upon the field, I found that General Hooker's corps had been dispersed and routed. I passed him some distance in the rear, where he had been carried wounded, but I saw nothing of it all, as I was advancing with my command upon the field. There were some troops lying down on the left, which I took to belong to Mansfield's command. General Mansfield had been killed, and a portion of his

corps also had been thrown into confusion. General Hooker's corps had been dispersed; there is no question about that. I sent one of my own staff officers to find where they were; and General Ricketts, the only officer we could find, said that he could not raise 300 men of the corps." General Meade, upon whom the command of General Hooker's men devolved, reported (*McC. Rep.*, 394): "There were but 6729 men present on the 18th; whereas, on the morning of the 22d, there were 13,093 men present for duty, showing that previous to and during the battle 6364 men were separated from their command."　[1] *Lee's Rep.*, ii., 219.

[2] The details of this action are given by McLaws and Walker in *Lee's Rep.*, 169, 205. Neither Lee nor Jackson make any separate mention of the defeat of Hooker in the morning. They

FRANCIS C. BARLOW.

French and Richardson were gaining slowly but steadily upon Hill. Colquitt's brigade had suffered severely, and fell back to the sunken road, where a vain attempt was made to rally them; they broke, and disappeared from the fight. Garland's brigade was pressing on, when an officer raised a shout, "They are flanking us!" "This cry," says Hill, "spread like an electric shock along the ranks, bringing up vivid recollections of the flank fire at South Mountain. In a moment they broke and fell to the rear." A part of it was rallied in the sunken road. Ripley's brigade had also fallen back to this road, and behind the crest of a hill which bordered it. Hill's numerous artillery had been withdrawn from his front. It had done good service in the conflict of the morning; but McClellan had posted his heavy guns near the Antietam in such a position as to command the position. "Our artillery," says Hill, "could not cope with the superior weight, caliber, range, and number of the Yankee guns. They were smashed up or withdrawn before they could be effectually turned against the massive columns of attack."[1]

Howard, who now commanded the division of Sedgwick, who, having been twice wounded, was borne from the field, was still engaged with Jackson, McLaws, and Walker, when French on the right, followed by Richardson on the left, pushed vigorously upon Hill, driving him back toward the right and rear, into and beyond the sunken road, which formed a right angle with his previous line. Kimball, of French's division, and Meagher, of Richardson's, gained the border of this natural rifle-pit at almost the same moment. Here ensued the fiercest fighting of the day. R. H. Anderson had now brought his division of 4000 men to the support of Hill, who had been farther strengthened by a number of regiments drawn from D. R. Jones, who held the extreme Confederate right, opposite Burnside, who had hardly made an attempt to cross the Antietam and take his assigned part in the action. The fight here was almost wholly with musketry, scarcely a battery being brought into action on either side. Meagher's Irish brigade suffered fearfully. Its commander was disabled by a fall from his horse. The brigade, having nearly exhausted its ammunition, was withdrawn to replenish, its place being taken by Caldwell's brigade. Both brigades moved, one to the front, the other to the rear, as steadily as though on drill. Barlow, then colonel, since major general, now dashed upon the flank of the sunken road, capturing the 300 men who still clung to it.

Anderson was wounded shortly after coming upon the field, and the command of his brigade devolved upon Pryor.[2] The ground upon which Richardson and French had been fighting was broken and irregular, intersected by numerous ravines, hills covered with corn, inclosed by stone walls, behind which the enemy could manœuvre and throw his strength, without being perceived, upon every part of the lines. More than half a score desperate attempts were made; all were repelled, and the conclusion of each found the Union troops in possession of some additional ground and

important position. Two of these repulses were given by Barlow, who, with his two regiments, the 61st and 64th New York, had won the sunken road. He fairly won his generalship upon this bloody field. Eighteen months before he had enlisted as a private. In one of the last of these, Richardson, whose services on this day were second to those of no other man, was mortally wounded, and the command of his division fell upon Hancock.

This action on the centre was fairly begun an hour before noon. By two hours after noon the Confederates here were worsted, and their force was so thoroughly shattered that it needed but a single heavy blow to shiver it to atoms, and, notwithstanding the reverse which Sedgwick had met, which was really only slight, to win a complete victory. McClellan had then at the very point where the blow should have been struck a force three-fold greater than was required to make it effectual. About noon, Franklin, with two divisions of his corps, 12,000 strong, had come up from Pleasant Valley.[1] The march had been an easy one, and these troops were perfectly fresh. McClellan had intended to keep this corps in reserve on the east side of the Antietam, to operate on either flank or on the centre, as circumstances might require. But when it came up the action was so critical that he properly abandoned this purpose, and sent the corps across the stream. The leading division, that of Smith, touched the edge of the fight somewhat sharply. It came upon the field between Sedgwick and French just at the moment when Sedgwick had been forced back. The third brigade met a force of the enemy coming out of the woods so often contested, drove them back, and attempted to enter the woods. Meeting a severe fire, it fell back, somewhat disordered, behind the crest of a hill, where it re-formed, the Confederates at the same time falling back into the shelter of the woods. Smith's second brigade was sent a little to the left to support French, and encountered a sharp fire from Hill's artillery.[2] Slocum's division of Franklin's corps followed directly after that of Smith, and the whole corps was ready for action. Franklin had given orders to advance. Had this been done, nothing in war can be more certain than that the absolute rout and capture of the Confederate army would have followed. This corps, 12,000 strong, perfectly fresh and eager for action, lay right in front of a great gap which had been left between the Confederate centre and left. On the left, Jackson, with McLaws and Walker, had left barely 8000 men; Hill, in the centre, with the remnants of his own division, of Anderson's, of the six brigades of Longstreet, including Hood's two, which returned to the field, had remaining not more than 13,000, and these were so utterly shattered and broken that, in the utmost emergency, not half that number could have been rallied for a fight. Confronting him were the divisions of Richardson, French, and Green, of Mansfield's corps, worn, exhausted, and reduced in numbers, it is true, but cheered with success, and still with quite 13,000 effective men.

Hill's condition, as told by himself and his brigade commanders, was indeed pitiable. Of his own five brigades four had been utterly routed. He had gone into action at South Mountain with 5000, and lost 2000; of the 3000 with which he entered the battle of Antietam, he could, the day after its close, muster less than 1700. In three days he had lost almost two thirds of his men. Thirty-four field-officers had gone into these two battles; when they were over, only nine were left; regiments, or the fragments of them, were commanded by lieutenants. His artillery, eighty guns and more, had been "smashed up," or withdrawn to avoid certain destruction. The Thersites of the Confederate army (saving only the point of cowardice; for, in spite of his foul pen and tongue, he was a skillful leader and desperate fighter), one can not wonder that Hill heaps invectives upon friend and foe. Reno is a "renegade Virginian," killed by "a happy shot;" the force opposed to him are always styled "Yankees," in which word he embodies the utmost of his detestation, save in one case, where, for deeper emphasis, they are denominated "the restorers of the Union." The Confederates failed of victory, he says, because McLaws and Anderson came up two hours too late; because the artillery was badly handled—"an artillery duel between the Washington artillery and the Yankee batteries was the most melancholy farce of the war;" and because "thousands of thievish poltroons had kept away from sheer cowardice; the straggler is generally a thief, and always a coward, lost to all sense of shame; he can only be kept in ranks by a strict and sanguinary discipline." Yet there is something almost sublime in the attitude of Hill at the close of the fight on his front. Two brigades had streamed to the rear in confusion, leaving a great gap, through which the enemy poured resistlessly. Rallying 150 men, Hill, musket in hand like a private, led them on.[3] He himself shall describe the closing moments of his part of the engagement: "There were no troops

---

were not at all aware that it was an utter rout. So closely had the advance of Sedgwick followed the retreat of Hooker that it was supposed to be a rally of the same troops with strong reinforcements. See also McClellan's Report, and Sumner, in Com. Rep., 368.

[1] D. H. Hill, in Lee's Rep., ii., 115.

[2] Lee's Report embodies no reports, either divisional or regimental, from Anderson's division, and its movements are barely alluded to by Hill. It was sharply engaged, losing more than 1000 men; but its efforts seem to have been desultory and ineffective.

[1] Franklin says (Com. Rep., 626): "The advance of my command arrived on the battle-field of Antietam about 10 o'clock." McClellan says (Report, 385): "Between 12 and 1 P.M. General Franklin's corps arrived on the field of battle." From a comparison of all the indicia of time, I conclude that Franklin gives the hour correctly, and that he was actually engaged before noon.

[2] This movement of Smith's division of Franklin's corps was of considerable importance. The Confederate reports respecting it are very full, and greatly exaggerated. Thus Hill says (Lee's Rep., ii., 115): "Franklin's corps advanced in three parallel lines, with all the precision of a parade-day, upon my two brigades. They met with a galling fire, however, recoiled, and fell back, and finally lay down behind the crest of a hill, and kept up an irregular fire. I got a battery in position, which partly enfiladed the Yankee line, and aided materially to check its advance." Walker (Ibid., ii., 206) describes at length the encounter between Smith's third brigade and two regiments of his division, which were ordered by Longstreet "to charge the enemy, who was threatening his front as if to pass through the opening between the point of timber. This order was promptly obeyed in the face of such a fire as troops have seldom encountered without running away, and with a steadiness and unfailing gallantry seldom equaled. Battery after battery, regiment after regiment, opened their fire upon them, hurling a torrent of missiles through their ranks; but nothing could arrest their progress, and three times the enemy broke and fled before their impetuous charge. Finally they reached the fatal picket fence. To climb over it in the face of such a force, and under such a fire, would have been sheer madness to attempt, and, their ammunition being now almost exhausted, Colonel Cooke very properly gave the order to fall back, which was done in the most perfect order; after which the troops took up their former position, which they held until night." [3] Lee's Report, ii., 346.

BURYING THE DEAD.[1]

SCENES ON THE FIELD AFTER THE BATTLE.[1]

AT THE FENCE.

near to hold the centre except a few hundred rallied from various brigades. The Yankees crossed the old road which we had occupied in the morning, and occupied a corn-field and orchard in advance of it. They had now got within a few hundred yards of the hill which commanded Sharpsburg and our rear. Affairs looked very critical. I found a battery concealed in a corn-field, and ordered it to move out and open upon the Yankee columns. It moved out most gallantly, though exposed to a terrible direct and reverse fire from the long-range Yankee artillery across the Antietam. A caisson exploded, but the battery was unlimbered, and, with grape and canister, drove the Yankees back. I was now satisfied that a single regiment of fresh men could drive the whole of them in our front across the Antietam. I got up about two hundred men, who said they were willing to advance to the attack if I would lead them. We met, however, with a warm reception, and the little command was broken and dispersed. About two hundred more were gathered, and I sent them to the right to attack the Yankees in flank. They drove them back a short distance, but were in turn repulsed. These two attacks, however, had a most happy effect. The Yankees were completely deceived by their boldness, and induced to believe that there was a large force in our centre. They made no farther attempt to pierce our centre, except on a small scale."[1]

McClellan thus relates the closing operations on this part of the field: "Hancock, seeing a body of the enemy advancing to the left of his position, obtained a battery from Franklin's corps, which assisted materially in frustrating this attack. The enemy seemed at one time to be about making an attack upon this part of the line, and advanced a long column of infantry toward this division" (this must have been Hill's last 200), "but on nearing the position, General Pleasanton opening on them with sixteen guns, they halted, gave a desultory fire, and retreated, closing the operations on this part of the field." Not dreaming that the enemy who had encountered them so stubbornly, and who still showed so bold a front, was so utterly broken that a single fresh regiment would have put them to utter rout, Hancock and French desisted from the attack, and rested in the positions they had won.

Jackson's plight, had Sumner known it, was no less critical than that of Hill. Of the 5000 men whom he had brought from Harper's Ferry, 2000 had been killed or wounded in the morning's fight with Hooker. Re-enforced, he had pressed Sedgwick back for half a mile, and then fallen back himself, having not more than 7000 effective men. Sumner, in front of him, had left wellnigh 5000 of Sedgwick's division; of Hooker's routed corps at least 6000 remained with their command, and might have been rallied; of Mansfield's first division, which had withdrawn in the morning, there must have been 3000. In all, Sumner had at his hand on the extreme right twice the force of Jackson at the time when Franklin, fairly on the field, was ready and anxious to attack. Had he then thrown his fresh 12,000 between Hill and Jackson, and upon the flank of both, striking either to the right or left, one or the other of these commands must have been annihilated, even without an effort on the part of the troops with which they had already been engaged.

That this was not done was no fault of Franklin. He had made every preparation, and given orders for an assault upon the woods which had been so hotly contested all day, when Sumner came up, and, in spite of Franklin's urgency, forbade the movement. Neither is it to be charged to McClellan except in so far that he approved of Sumner's action.[2] Sumner, indeed, showed on this day a want of vigor and resource utterly at variance with the whole tenor of his military career. For six hours he seems not to have made the slightest attempt to rally the corps of Hooker and Mansfield, which had retreated hardly a mile in his rear. Among these were some of the best soldiers in the army.

McClellan's plan on the evening of the 16th, as understood by Hooker,[3] was to make a simultaneous attack upon the Confederate right, centre, and left. By the morning of the 17th he had changed his scheme, and determined "to attack the enemy's left with the corps of Hooker and Mansfield, supported by Sumner's, and, if necessary, by Franklin's, and as soon as matters looked favorably there, to move the corps of Burnside against the enemy's extreme left; and whenever either of these flank movements should be successful, to advance our centre with all their forces then disposable.[4] Now Franklin's corps was fully four hours distant, and did not commence its march until an hour, and did not reach the ground until six hours after

---

[1] D. H. Hill, in *Lee's Rep.*, ii., 116, 117.—This closing attack "on a small scale" is quite differently described by others. McClellan says: "The 7th Maine, of Franklin's corps, without any other aid, made a gallant attack against the enemy's line, and drove in the skirmishers, who were annoying our artillery and troops on the right." Hill says that "Pryor had gathered quite a respectable force behind a hill, when a Maine regiment" (he gives the number erroneously as the 21st) "came down to this hill, wholly unconscious that there were any Confederate troops near it. A shout and a volley informed them of their dangerous neighborhood. The Yankee apprehension is acute; the idea was soon taken in, and was followed by the most rapid running I ever saw."

[2] Franklin's testimony, in *Com. Rep.*, 626: "The division of General Slocum arrived on the field. I formed two brigades of it in line of battle in front of the Dunker Church, with the intention of making an attack at once upon the enemy in that wood. I was waiting for the third brigade to be a reserve for the other two, when I was informed that General Sumner had detained the brigade at his head-quarters for the protection of his right. I sent for it, and it finally arrived, and General Sumner with it. The general advised me not to make the attack, for if it failed, the right would be entirely destroyed, as there were no troops there that could be depended upon. I informed him that I thought it a very necessary thing to do, and told him that I would prefer to make the attack, unless he assumed the responsibility of forbidding it. He assumed the responsibility, and ordered me not to make it. One of General McClellan's aids was there at the time. He informed General McClellan what had been done, and the general himself came up and stated that things had gone so well [ill?] on all the other parts of the field that he was afraid to risk the day by an attack there on the right at that time. Therefore no attack was made by that division that day." McClellan's account (*Report*, 387) is to the same effect: "General Franklin ordered two brigades of General Slocum's division, General Newton's and Colonel Torbert's, to form in column to attack the woods that had been so hotly contested by Generals Sumner and Hooker; General Bartlett's brigade was ordered to form the reserve. At this time General Sumner, having command on the right, directed farther offensive operations to be postponed, as the repulse of this, the only remaining corps available for attack, would peril the safety of the whole army." [3] *Ante*, p. 399. [4] *McC. Rep.*, 377.

[1] These views, and those on page 403, are reproduced from Photographs by M. B. Brady, taken a day or two after the action. They are introduced as presenting the real aspect of a great battlefield. My acknowledgments are due to Mr. Brady for access to, and free use of his immense collection of scenes and portraits.

THE STONE BRIDGE OVER THE ANTIETAM.

the opening of the attack which they were to support. The attack on the Confederate right was not opened until at least three hours after it should have been made. It is not easy to say how far the blame for this delay rests upon McClellan, and how far upon Burnside. McClellan affirms that the order to advance upon the bridge was sent at 8 o'clock, which was the proper time, unless the attack was to be simultaneous with that of Hooker; that the order was twice repeated, at considerable intervals, the second time most peremptorily. Burnside testifies that the order was not received until about ten o'clock.[1]

.The part assigned to Burnside was of the highest importance. His initial attempts to execute it were feebly made, and were repulsed one after another. At length two regiments dashed at the bridge, which had all along been commanded by Toombs with two small regiments, numbering together less than 500 men, hidden behind fences and in a narrow belt of woods. These had been withdrawn a little before, as well as the force which commanded the adjacent fords, so that the actual passage of the stream was made without opposition.[2] Burnside's whole corps, nearly 14,000 strong, was soon across the stream. Here an unaccountable delay

of two more hours took place, and it was only after McClellan had given repeated orders that Burnside advanced.[1] To appreciate the vital importance of these delays to the salvation of Lee's army, we must turn to the movements of the Confederates upon their extreme right.

Lee's right wing consisted of six of Longstreet's weakest brigades, under D. R. Jones. These had been reduced one half by various details of brigades and regiments, so that during the morning Jones had not quite 2500 men.[2] When Walker, McLaws, and Anderson came up from Harper's Ferry, they were at first posted on the right and in the rear of the centre; but when the heavy attack had fairly developed itself on the left, they were all withdrawn thither. This withdrawal took place at about ten. It could never have been made had Burnside's attack been begun at nine; and without it Jackson and Hill must have been crushed by Sumner, and driven in hopeless rout upon their right. Now, at almost four, two full hours after the action on the right and centre had ceased, Burnside fairly began his attack. It was at first successful. The heights which command Sharpsburg were won; the Confederates were driven back through the town. Had this been done two hours before, a position would have been secured from which the whole Confederate line would have been swept by an enfilading fire of artillery. But now A. P. Hill had come up from Harper's Ferry, having marched seventeen miles that day. He brought with him five brigades, or rather such portions of them as could endure the march. One

[1] McClellan (Report, 390) says: "At eight o'clock an order was sent to General Burnside to carry the bridge. After some time had elapsed, not hearing from him, I dispatched an aid to ascertain what had been done. The aid returned with information that but little progress had been made. I then sent him back with an order to General Burnside to assault the bridge at once, and carry it at all hazards. The aid returned to me a second time with the report that the bridge was still in possession of the enemy. Whereupon I directed Colonel Sackett, the Inspector General, to deliver to General Burnside my positive order to push forward his troops without a moment's delay, and, if necessary, to carry the bridge with the bayonet; and I ordered Colonel Sackett to remain with General Burnside and see that the order was executed promptly." Burnside testifies (Com. Rep., 640): "On the morning of the 17th I was ordered to place the command in position to enable us to attack the enemy at the bridge as soon as I was notified to commence the attack. About ten o'clock I received an order from General McClellan to make the attack on the bridge."

[2] This withdrawal of the troops before the final attempt at crossing is expressly affirmed by D. R. Jones and Toombs (Lee's Rep., ii., 219, 324). Burnside's Report, however, seems to imply, without positively affirming it, that there was a conflict here.

[1] McC. Rep., 390; Burnside, in Com. Rep., 641.

[2] This number is expressly given by both Lee and Jones. The words of the latter, indeed, seem to imply that this was the entire strength of his six brigades. He says (Lee's Rep., ii., 219): "My command had been farther reduced on the right, leaving me for the defense of the right with only Toombs's two regiments, and Kemper's, Drayton's, and Walker's brigades. When it is known that on that morning my entire command, of six brigades, comprised only 2430 men, the enormous disparity of force with which I contended may be seen." Now, although these brigades had suffered heavily at Groveton, where two of them lost nearly 1500 men, and considerably at South Mountain, it is hardly credible that their average strength should have been reduced to 600 each—not one third of their original strength. The whole six brigades took part in the fight with Burnside.

SITE OF A BATTERY.

SCENE OF A CHARGE.

brigade was reduced to 350 men;[1] all told there were not 4000, and of these only three brigades, including the weak one, numbering all together not more than 2000 men, were brought into the fight. It was over before the others could engage. With these and Toombs's brigade, then not 1000 strong, Burnside's whole corps was driven back, just as darkness was coming on, to the Antietam, which he recrossed the next morning. A. P. Hill hardly exaggerates when he says: "The three brigades of my division actively engaged did not number over 2000 men, and these, with the help of my splendid batteries, drove back Burnside's corps of 15,000 men."[2] Hill lost 346 killed and wounded; Jones lost about 700. Burnside's loss in killed and wounded was 2173.

Porter's corps had not been brought into action at all. It was posted in the centre, between the right and left wings, to guard the trains, for the safety of which McClellan was apprehensive. Portions of it were at times detached as supports to batteries. It lost only 130. Franklin's corps can hardly be considered as engaged, although in its brief encounter it lost 438; so that 25,000 men, wellnigh a third of McClellan's force, and as many as Lee had in action at any one moment, were practically unemployed. Lee had in all, and at all times, exclusive of cavalry, something more than 40,000, of whom all but about 2000 were engaged. McClellan had 83,000, of whom 58,000 were engaged; but they were sent in by "driblets," corps after corps, at intervals of hours. What the result was has been shown; what it would have been had the assault been made in full force can hardly be a matter of doubt.[3] Had the battle of Antietam been fought on the 16th, Lee

[1] Lee's Rep., ii., 263.
[2] A. P. Hill, in Lee's Rep., ii., 129.—It is indeed asserted by Burnside (Com. Rep., 641): "The enemy had brought away from opposite the extreme right of our army portions of their forces, and concentrated them against us." There was, indeed, time sufficient for such an operation in the interval between the cessation of the action on the right and the beginning of this on the left, had the Confederates been in a condition to make it; but I do not find in any of their reports, which fully detail the movements of every brigade, with the exception of those of Anderson's division, the least intimation of any such movement, and this division was apparently in no condition for offense.
[3] "I have always believed that, instead of sending these troops into action in driblets, as they

could have mustered barely 27,000 men, while McClellan had—Franklin's corps not being present—fully 70,000. The Union loss was 11,426 killed and wounded; that of the Confederates about 10,000. The disparity arises mainly from the great excess of Burnside's loss on the left. On the right and centre each side lost about equally. The entire Union loss in the series of actions in Maryland, not including missing, was 14,200; that of the Confederates about 12,500.[1]

were sent, if General McClellan had authorized me to march these 40,000 men on the left flank of the enemy, we could not have failed to throw them right back in front of the other divisions of our army on our left, Burnside's, Franklin's, and Porter's corps; and all escape for the enemy, I think, would have been impossible. Why that was not done I do not know."—Sumner, in Com. Rep., 368.
[1] The Union force at Antietam is given in detail in McClellan's Report. In summing up the Confederate force we have to estimate that under Longstreet. We put down the average strength of his brigades at 1500—some were less, some greater. He had eleven brigades, and had probably lost 500 at Turner's Gap; this would give him 16,000 at Antietam. The strength present in the other commands is stated with sufficient accuracy in the various reports, as previously cited. From these data, omitting cavalry on both sides, we construct the following table:

FORCES PRESENT AT ANTIETAM.

UNION.		CONFEDERATE.	
Hooker's corps	14,856	Longstreet's division	16,000
Sumner's "	18,813	Jackson's "	5,000
Porter's "	12,930	Walker's "	3,000
Franklin's "	12,300	McLaws's "	3,000
Burnside's "	13,819	Anderson's "	4,000
Mansfield's "	10,126	D. H. Hill's "	3,000
		A. P. Hill's "	4,000
		Reserve artillery	2,000
Total force	82,844	Total force	40,000
Not engaged: Porter and Franklin	25,230	Not engaged: Part of A. P. Hill	2,000
Total engaged	57,614	Total engaged	38,000

Probably, to make the comparison entirely just, some deduction should be made from McClellan's numbers, as the Confederate commanders report usually the numbers with which "they went into the action," while the Union report gives the number "present and fit for duty:" there will always be some discrepancy between these two modes of enumeration. Lee says (Report, i., 35): "This great battle was fought by less than 40,000 men on our side;" which we think a true statement. D. H. Hill, indeed, asserts (Lee's Rep., ii., 119): "The battle was fought with less than 30,000." Cooke (Stonewall Jackson, 340-342): "In General Lee's published official Report the exact numbers are given—33,000." I find in Lee's Report no such statement, but do find the one just cited. Again Cooke says: "Nor was the bulk of Jackson's corps present until four P.M., toward the end of the action. General Lee fought until late in the day with Longstreet, D. H. Hill, Ewell, and two other divisions, a force of about 25,000 men. The re-enforcements of McLaws, Anderson, and Hill increased this number to 33,000, with which force General Lee met the 87,164

BEHIND A BREASTWORK.

SHELTER FOR WOUNDED.

The action of Antietam was in all respects a drawn battle. The Confederates had inflicted a greater absolute loss than they had suffered; but they had suffered, in proportion to their strength, far more than they had inflicted. At the close of the fight the positions of the armies were nearly the same as at its commencement. On the extreme right and left, the Federals, after forcing back the Confederate lines, had been repelled in turn beyond the original Confederate lines; but the Confederates then fell back, so that neither side held the field of battle. In the centre the Confederate lines had been forced back a little, and here the Federals held some ground wrested from the enemy. During the night the Confederates changed ground a little, but in all essential respects their position was as advantageous as it had been in the morning. Nor did the battle decide the issue of the invasion of Maryland; that question had been decided three days before, when McClellan, forcing the passes of the South Mountain, interposed his army between Lee and his projected line of march into Pennsylvania. After the battle, Lee accomplished without hinderance just what he would have done had no action taken place. He gave up the invasion of the North, recrossed the Potomac, and awaited in Virginia the movements of his tardy opponent. But the moral effect of the battle was great. It aroused the confidence of the nation, who saw in it a sure presage of the speedy overthrow of the insurrection; and, what was more, it emboldened the President to issue his warning proclamation for the abolition of slavery. That proclamation had been written months before, though only his trusted advisers knew of it. If put forth at any time during the disastrous summer, it would have been a mockery. It would have sounded to the world like a despairing shriek for help. And so the proclamation, written and rewritten, touched and retouched, lay in his desk. How could he, without mockery, promise to "recognize and maintain" the freedom of all slaves in the insurgent states, when the victorious armies of those confederated states threatened the capital of the Union? And so, when urged to issue such a proclamation, he replied in one of the half-jesting phrases in which he was wont to couch his most serious thoughts, that it would be like "the pope's bull against the comet." But now it seemed that such a promise could be maintained. So five days after the battle of Antietam the proclamation was put forth, and the result of the contest was staked upon an issue from which a few months before the nation would have shrunk, and for which even now it was scarcely prepared. The principle upon which Mr. Lincoln acted then, before, and thereafter, was at the same time clearly expressed by himself: "My paramount object is to save the Union, and not either to save or destroy slavery. If I could save the Union without freeing any slave, I would do it; if I could save it by freeing all the slaves, I would do it; if I could save it by freeing some and leaving others alone, I would also do that. What I do about slavery and the colored race, I do because I believe it helps to save this Union; and what I forbear, I forbear because I do not believe it would help to save the Union. I shall do less whenever I believe that what I am doing hurts the cause; and I shall do more whenever I believe that doing more will help the cause."[1] The inexorable march of events had now brought things to such a state that the conflict between Slavery and the Union was irrepressible. One or the other must go down. In a few months more all men saw that, whether the Union was saved or lost, Slavery was inevitably destroyed.

The battle was over, except on the extreme right, while the sun was yet high in the heavens, and McClellan had to consider whether it should be renewed the next day. Burnside, in spite of his severe repulse, was in favor of renewing it in the morning if he could have 5000 fresh men. Franklin was of the same opinion; he was sure that he could take the hotly-contested wood, which would uncover the enemy's left. Sumner thought otherwise.[1] McClellan decided to postpone the attack. He reasoned that, "Virginia lost, Washington menaced, Maryland invaded, the national cause could afford no risks of defeat. One battle lost, and almost all would have been lost. Lee's army might then have marched as it pleased on Washington, Baltimore, Philadelphia, or New York, and nowhere east of the Alleghanies was there another organized force able to arrest its march."[2] Believing, as he and most of his generals did, that the enemy was equal or superior in numbers, he could not well have come to any other decision. But in truth his fresh troops were almost equal in number to Lee's entire remaining force, while those who were worst off were in better plight than the best of the enemy. During the morning Humphreys's and Couch's divisions, 14,000 strong, came up; Lee also received some accessions from those who had fallen out in the march from Harper's Ferry, and stood at bay all day awaiting an attack. McClellan ordered that this should be made on the morning of the 19th. But in the darkness of the night the Confederate forces slipped quietly away, and when McClellan looked for them in the morning they were safely across the Potomac, and as evening fell they encamped five miles from the river. Next morning a strong reconnoissance from Porter's corps was sent over at Shepherdstown to ascertain the position of the enemy. A. P. Hill, who brought up the Confederate rear, turned upon them and drove them back, with considerable loss.[3]

Gathering up the remnants of his army, and bringing on those who had been left behind at Harper's Ferry, and those who had fallen out on the march thence to the Antietam, numbering in all less than 40,000 effective men, Lee fell back to Martinsburg, and thence to Winchester, where he had ordered all his stragglers to rendezvous. On the 30th of September he had but 53,000 men present for duty. On that day, exclusive of 73,000 left behind for the defense of Washington, McClellan had with him 100,000 effective men.[4]

Six weeks of beautiful autumnal weather were passed in almost total inaction. McClellan, believing that his army was in no condition to provoke another battle, posted it along the eastern side of the Potomac, half near Harper's Ferry, and the remainder watching the fords above and below, for he still apprehended that Lee would attempt to recross the river. Meanwhile the old bickerings between the commander of the army in the field and the military authorities at Washington were renewed with increased pertinacity. McClellan wanted supplies, clothing, horses, and, above all, re-enforcements. The Washington authorities would not spare a man from the 73,000 lying idle in the defenses of the capital, and the clothing and horses forwarded were far less than McClellan demanded. On the 6th of October the President issued a peremptory order that the army should at once "cross the Potomac and give battle to the enemy, or drive him South." If the army crossed between the enemy and Washington, so as to cover the capital, it should receive 30,000 re-enforcements, otherwise not more than 15,000. McClellan paid no immediate attention to this order, but reiterated his demands and complaints. He assumed that he, being with the army in the field, was more competent to determine whether it was in a condition to move than was the general-in-chief in his office at Washington.[5] On the 10th, Stuart, with 1800 cavalry, crossed the Potomac above the Union positions, made a clear circuit around the Union army, and recrossed below, without having lost a man. On the 13th the President wrote to McClellan earnestly urging him to action, and indicating the true theory upon which operations should be conducted.

"You remember," he said, "my speaking to you of what I called your over-cautiousness. Are you not over-cautious when you assume that you can not do what the enemy is constantly doing? Should you not claim to be at least his equal in prowess, and act upon the claim? You say that you can not subsist your army at Winchester unless the railroad from Harper's Ferry to that point be put in working order.[6] But the enemy does now subsist his army at Winchester, at a distance nearly twice as great from railroad transportation as you would have to do. He now wagons from Culpepper Court-house, which is just about twice as far as you would have to do from Harper's Ferry. He is certainly not more than half as well provided with wagons as you are. I should certainly be pleased for you to have the advantage of the railroad from Harper's Ferry to Winchester, but it wastes all the remainder of the autumn to give it to you, and, in fact, ignores the question of time, which can not and must not be ignored. It is one of the standard maxims of war to operate upon the enemy's communications as much as possible, without exposing your own. You seem to act as if this applies against you, but can not apply in your favor. Change positions with the enemy, and think you not he would break your communications with Richmond in twenty-four hours? You dread his going into Pennsylvania. But if he does so in full force, he gives up his communications to you absolutely, and you have nothing to do but to follow and ruin him; if he does so with less than full force, fall upon and beat what is left behind all the easier. If he should move northward, I would follow him closely, holding his communications. If he should move toward Rich-

men reported by General McClellan as 'in action' on the Federal side." But McLaws and Anderson, instead of being absent until "late in the day," were hotly engaged before noon, the division of McLaws losing a larger proportion of its numbers than any other except that of D. H. Hill.

In giving their losses, the Confederate reports do not usually discriminate between the different engagements. The report by regiments (*Lee's Rep.*, ii., 107, 108) makes their entire loss 1567 killed, 8274 wounded, 10,291 in all; but this is clearly defective, as is shown by the separate reports of division commanders. Those of Longstreet, including his entire "command," are given in *Lee's Report*, p. 89; Jackson, excluding A. P. Hill's at Antietam and Shepherdstown, *Ibid.*, 105; A. P. Hill at Antietam, *Ibid.*, 131; D. H. Hill, *Ibid.*, 119. The Union loss in each engagement is given separately. The following table presents a summation:

LOSSES IN THE MARYLAND CAMPAIGN, SEPT. 14–17.

UNION.	Killed.	Wounded.	Missing.	Total.
Hooker	348	2,016	255	2,619
Sumner	860	3,801	548	5,209
Porter	21	107	2	130
Franklin	70	335	33	438
Burnside	432	1,741	120	2,293
Mansfield	274	1,384	85	1,743
Cavalry	5	32	—	37
At Antietam	2010	9,416	1043	12,469
Turner's Gap	312	1,234	22	1,568
Crampton's Gap	115	416	2	533
Total	2437	11,066	1067	14,970

CONFEDERATES.	Killed.	Wounded.	Missing.	Total.
Longstreet	964	5234	1310	7,508
Jackson	321	1809	57	2,187
A. P. Hill	63	283	—	346
D. H. Hill	464	1852	925	3,241
Reported losses	1812	9178	2292	13,282
Correcting the apportionment of killed, wounded, and missing, and adding prisoners as below, we give the following as a close approximation:	Killed.	Wounded.	Missing.	Total.
Total	2062	10,428	4792	17,282

A large proportion of those entered as "missing" in the Confederate Reports were undoubtedly killed or wounded. D. H. Hill says (*Lee's Rep.*, ii., 118): "Doubtless a large number of the 'missing' fell into the hands of the Yankees when wounded;" and Rodes (*Ibid.*, 347): "The 'missing' are either prisoners or killed." At South Mountain they were forced to abandon their killed and severely wounded, and could only enter as such upon the lists those whose fate was known. Nearly all the killed and many of the wounded were also left behind at Antietam. It is safe to estimate that of the 2292 reported as missing, 1500 were killed or wounded; apportioning these in the usual ratio adds 250 to the killed and 1250 to the wounded, as reported, diminishing the missing by the same numbers.

McClellan puts the Confederate loss much higher. He says (*Report*, 396): "About 2700 of the enemy's dead were, under the direction of Major Davis, Assistant Inspector General, counted and buried upon the battle-field of Antietam. A portion of their dead had been previously buried by the enemy. This is conclusive evidence that the enemy sustained much greater loss than we." Accepting this, and adding the dead at South Mountain, the Confederate killed must have numbered fully 3500, which would make their total loss more than 20,000, besides prisoners, of whom there were 6000, about two thirds of whom appear to have been stragglers. We do not undertake to reconcile these conflicting accounts as to the killed, and consequently of the wounded, but adopt the Confederate statement, with the exception above noted. To the "missing," however, we add 4000 unwounded prisoners.

The method of the Confederate generals in stating the number of the "missing" is wholly inexplicable. From the 23d of August to the 17th of September they put down in all only 2373, while it is certain that they lost nearly three times that number in prisoners during the three last days of this period, and all of their reports speak of thousands of stragglers.

[1] *Ante*, p. 202. For the proclamation, see *ante*, p. 208.

[1] *Com. Rep.*, 642, 627, 369.

[2] *McC. Rep.*, 394.

[3] Hill (*Lee's Rep.*, ii., 130) gives a most exaggerated account of this engagement: "A daring charge was made, and the enemy driven pell-mell into the river. Then commenced the most terrible slaughter that this war has yet witnessed. The broad surface of the Potomac was blue with the floating bodies of our foe. But few escaped to tell the tale. By their own account they lost 3000 men killed and drowned from one brigade alone. My own loss was 30 killed and 231 wounded."

[4] See *ante*, p. 383, for Lee's force. The strength of the Army of the Potomac on the 30th of September was, according to the official report, signed by McClellan, 173,745 present for duty, of whom 73,601 were around Washington.—*Com. Rep.*, 507.

[5] *McC. Rep.*, 426.

[6] This had been destroyed by the Confederates.

mond, I would press closely to him, fight him if a favorable opportunity should present, and at least try to beat him to Richmond on the inside track. If he made a stand at Winchester, moving neither north nor south, I would fight him there, on the idea that if we can not beat him when he bears the wastage of coming to us, we never can when we bear the wastage of going to him. In coming to us he tenders to us an advantage which we must not waive. We should not so operate as merely to drive him away. As we must beat him somewhere, or fail finally, we can do it, if at all, easier near to us than far away. If we can not beat the enemy where he now is, we never can, he again being within the intrenchments of Richmond."[1]

On the 21st McClellan was convinced that his army was nearly in a condition to move. The cavalry was indeed, he thought, in numbers much inferior to that of the enemy, but in efficiency was far superior. He now asked whether the President wished him "to march on the enemy at once, or to await the arrival of new horses." The reply was that no change was intended in the order of the 6th. The President did not expect impossibilities, but the season should not be wasted in inaction. McClellan's purpose had been to cross the Potomac above Harper's Ferry, on the western side of the Blue Ridge, and move directly upon the Confederate forces, expecting that they would either give battle near Winchester or retreat toward Richmond. He believed that if he crossed below, Lee would recross into Maryland. But now the season had come when the river might be expected to rise at any hour, rendering the apprehended Confederate movement too hazardous to be ventured. McClellan therefore decided to cross on the eastern side of the Blue Ridge, thus threatening Lee's communications. He thought it possible, though not probable, that he might throw his force through some pass in the mountains, and gain the Confederate rear in the Valley of the Shenandoah. Failing this, he still hoped to strike the flank of their long retreating column, separate their army, and beat it in detail, or, at all events, force them to concentrate as far back as Gordonsville, and thus leave his own army free to adopt the Fredericksburg line of advance upon Richmond, or to move by his old way of the Peninsula.[2]

The crossing of the Potomac began on the 26th of October, and continued until the 2d of November, when the whole army was over. Leaving 15,000 men at and near Harper's Ferry, the army marched more than 100,000 strong, besides 20,000 detached from the force at Washington[3] to co-operate with his movement. The weather was favorable, the roads good, and the great army moved rapidly. Keeping along the eastern foot of the Blue Ridge, Warrenton being the point of direction for the main body, its line of march for the greater part of the way being the same, but in a reverse direction, as that by which Lee had advanced upon Pope hardly three months before.

The Confederate army, during its two months' repose after Antietam, had been recruited to about 70,000.[1] As soon as Lee was aware of the threatening movement of McClellan, he hastened to counteract it by moving southward in the same direction. Jackson, with his own corps and Stuart's cavalry, was halted to observe, and, if occasion was given, assail the Union force upon its march, while the remainder of the army pressed up the Valley of the Shenandoah. For days the two hostile columns were moving parallel to each other, only a few miles apart, but with the Blue Mountains between them. Rapid as was the march of the Union army, that of the Confederates was still faster. Lee, in advance of his opponent, turned a spur of the Blue Ridge, passed from the Valley of the Shenandoah into that of the Rappahannock, and took position at Culpepper by the time that McClellan had massed his army near Warrenton, a half score of miles to the north. But in effecting this operation he had played into his opponent's hands, and given him an opportunity to strike more favorable than he had dared to anticipate. McClellan had hoped to separate the Confederate army. Lee had himself separated it. Jackson's corps was left fully three days' rapid march behind that of Longstreet. If an attack had then been made, it could hardly have failed to result otherwise than in a serious disaster to the Confederates. McClellan resolved upon an assault. For once he seemed satisfied that he had the preponderance of force.[2]

But this intent of vigorous action came too late. The breach between McClellan and the military authorities at Washington had become too wide to be closed. His removal from the command had been resolved upon, and had been delayed only from the difficulty of deciding upon his successor. The choice finally lay between Burnside and Hooker.[3] Why Sumner, who outranked each, and had seen more service than both, was passed over, it is hard to say. But the choice now fell upon Burnside. Upon the stormy evening of the 7th of November, when McClellan had given directions for the movements of the next two days, a messenger from Washington reached the head-quarters of the army. He bore an order, couched in briefest military phrase, bearing date two days before, removing McClellan from the command of the army, and directing Burnside to assume it; and another equally curt, from Halleck to McClellan, the writing of which one may imagine to have been a pleasant task.[4]

---

[1] Com. Rep., 524.

[2] McC. Rep., 428, 436. "I still considered the line of the Peninsula as the true approach to Richmond, but, for obvious reasons, did not make any proposal to return to it."—Ibid., 427.

[3] According to the official return (Com. Rep., 534) on the 20th of October, the Army of the Potomac numbered, "present for duty," 133,409, exclusive of 73,593 at Washington. McClellan (Report, 430) gives its strength at 116,000, besides some 5000 detached bodies. This discrepancy appears to be occasioned (see McC. Rep., 422) by about 12,000 teamsters, officers' servants, etc., being included in the regular returns.

[1] Present for duty, October 20, 67,805; November 20, 73,554.—Ante, p. 383.

[2] "The army was massed near Warrenton, ready to act in any required direction, perfectly in hand, and in admirable condition and spirits. I doubt whether, during the whole period that I had the honor to command the Army of the Potomac, it was in such excellent condition to fight a great battle. . . . The reports from the advance indicated the possibility of separating the two wings of the enemy's forces, and either beating Longstreet separately or forcing him to fall back at least upon Gordonsville to effect his junction with the rest of his army. . . . Had I remained in command I should have made the attempt to divide the enemy; and could he have been brought to a battle within reach of my supplies, I can not doubt that the result would have been a brilliant victory for our army."—McC. Rep., 438, 439.

[3] "General Hooker came very near receiving, instead of me, the command of the Army of the Potomac."—Burnside, in Com. Rep., 725.

[4] General Orders, No. 182.—"By direction of the President of the United States, it is ordered that Major General McClellan be relieved from the command of the Army of the Potomac, and that Major General Burnside take command of the army. By order of the Secretary of War."

Halleck to McClellan.—"GENERAL,—On the receipt of the order of the President, sent herewith, you will immediately turn over your command to Major General Burnside, and repair to Trenton, New Jersey, reporting on your arrival at that place, by telegraph, for farther orders."—Com. Rep., 565.

CAVALRY RECONNOISSANCE IN VIRGINIA.

AMBROSE E. BURNSIDE.

CHAPTER XXIV.
BURNSIDE'S CAMPAIGN.—FREDERICKSBURG.

Burnside in Command.—His Plan for the Campaign.—Its Merits and Demerits.—New Organization of the Army of the Potomac.—The Movement from Warrenton to Fredericksburg.—Delay in crossing the Rappahannock.—The Pontoons.—Fredericksburg threatened with Bombardment.—The Confederate Army reaches Fredericksburg.—The Position on the Rappahannock.—Burnside's Preparations for Crossing.—The Delay opposite Fredericksburg.—Lee's Plan of Operations.—Crossing the River, and Preparations for Attack.—Burnside's final Plan for two Assaults.—Franklin's Attack upon the Left.—Meade's Advance repulsed.—Gibbon advances, and is repulsed.—The Confederate Pursuit checked by Birney.—The Moments of the Action.—The Confederate Position on the Right at Marye's Hill.—Its Strength.—Assailed by Sumner.—French and Hancock repelled.—Hooker ordered to attack.—Humphreys assaults, and is driven back.—Close of the Battle.—The Numbers engaged.—Burnside proposes to renew the Battle the next Day.—Is dissuaded by his Generals.—He recrosses the Rappahannock.—Effects of the Battle of Fredericksburg.—Condition of the Union Army.—Burnside designs a new Movement.—The proposed Cavalry Expedition.—The President forbids the Movement.—The Reasons for the Prohibition.—Franklin and Smith criticise Burnside's Plan, and propose another.—Cochrane and Newton's Interview with the President.—Burnside and Halleck.—Burnside's third Plan.—The Mud Campaign.—Burnside's Order No. 8, dismissing Hooker and others.—The President refuses to sanction the Order.—Burnside resigns, and Hooker is placed in Command.—Sumner and Franklin relieved.—Death of Sumner.—Hooker takes Command.

THE command of the Army of the Potomac was thrust into the unwilling hands of Burnside. He had twice declined it, and would have done so now had it been left to his choice;[1] but the order was peremptory, and he had no alternative but to obey. Yet, as if foreseeing the issue, he repeated to the messenger who brought the order and to members of his own staff what he had before said to the President and the Secretary of War, that he did not consider himself competent to take the command of so large an army, and, moreover, that from the place which his command had held during the campaign, he knew less than any other general of the position,

tion, numbers, and character of the several corps.[1] Still, with the knowledge then possessed by the military authorities, the choice was the wisest that could have been made. No other general had held an important separate command. His expedition to North Carolina had been successful. He had become entangled in none of the jealousies which impeded, or were thought to impede, the efficiency of the army. His personal and military character was unreproached and irreproachable. Burnside's modesty, contrasted with Hooker's vehement self-assertion, decided the question of the generalship. He was taken at the high estimate which the administration placed upon him, rather than at the low one which he placed upon himself.

Burnside was required not only to take command of the army, but to state what he proposed to do with it.[2] He had been from the first opposed to the movement made by McClellan upon Warrenton. He argued that if the army was to go to Richmond by land, the only way was that by Fredericksburg. McClellan was half convinced of the truth of this, and on the day before he was superseded gave orders which looked toward the abandonment of his present line of operations.[3] Two days after he had been placed in command, Burnside presented his plan.

Its essential features were that McClellan's design of attacking Lee should be given up, the movement toward Gordonsville abandoned, and then there should be "a rapid move of the whole force to Fredericksburg, with a view to a movement upon Richmond from that point." In favor of his plan he urged that if the Union army should move upon Culpepper and Gordonsville, and even fight a successful battle, the enemy would still have many lines of retreat, and would be able to reach Richmond with enough of force to render necessary another battle there. Should the enemy fall back without giving battle, the pursuit would be simply following up a retreating army well supplied with provisions in dépôts in its rear, while the pursuing army would have to rely for supplies upon a single long line of communication, liable to be cut at any point. But in moving by the way which he proposed, the army would cover Washington until it reached Fredericksburg, where it would be on the shortest road to Richmond, the taking of which, he thought, "should be the great object of the campaign, as the fall of that place would tend more to cripple the rebel cause than almost any other military event, except the absolute breaking up of their army." The presence of a large army on the Fredericksburg line would render it impossible for the enemy to make any successful movement upon Washington. An invasion of Pennsylvania was not to be expected at that season of the year; and, even should a lodgment be made there by any force that could be spared, its destruction would be certain soon after winter set in. "Could the army before Richmond be beaten, and their capital taken," he added, "the loss of half a dozen of our towns and cities in the interior of Pennsylvania could well be afforded."[4]

This plan was undoubtedly a judicious one upon the assumption that the capture of Richmond was the main aim of the campaign. For an advance thither by way of Gordonsville, the main base of supplies must be Alexandria, involving transportation by land of fully 150 miles by the route which must be followed. For an advance by way of Fredericksburg, Acquia Creek, on the Potomac, would be the base to which supplies could be sent by water, leaving but 75 miles of land transportation, by a line much less exposed. The advantage of the Peninsular route are still greater. The base of supplies would be at West Point, only 30 miles from Richmond. The main objection to this, that the army here would not be in a position to cover Washington, would be obviated by concentrating there a force sufficient for its defense, which the great numerical preponderance of the Union troops rendered easy. In fact, there was at this moment in and around Washington, independent of Burnside's army in the field, a force very nearly equal to the whole Confederate Army of Northern Virginia.[5]

[1] Com. Rep., 650.   [2] Ibid., 650.   [3] Ibid., 649.
[4] For the entire text of this plan, see Com. Rep., 643; and for Burnside's own explanation of it, Ibid., 650.
[5] The advantages of the Peninsular route, or rather a modification of it, taking the James River instead of the York as the base, were set forth six weeks later by Franklin and Smith, in a letter to the President, first made public in Swinton's Campaigns of the Army of the Potomac, pp. 263–265. Mr. Swinton indeed affirms (Ibid., 233), upon the authority of "the corps commander then most intimate in his confidence," that "Burnside had not matured any definite plan of action, for the reason that he hoped to be able to postpone operations till the spring. He did not favor operating against Richmond by the overland route, but had his mind turned toward a repetition of McClellan's movement to the Peninsula; and in determining to march to Fredericksburg, he cherished the hope of being able to winter there upon an easy base of supplies, and in the spring embarking his army for the James River." Not only is there no trace of any such purpose to be found in Burnside's written plan, but every recommendation implies the design of moving by the overland route.

The fatal error in Burnside's plan was that it wholly misconceived the main object to be aimed at. The capture of Richmond would indeed have been in itself a great material and moral loss to the Confederacy, but it would have been of far less moment than the destruction, or even the signal defeat of the army. That army was the head and front of the offending, and at this the blow should have been aimed. The President, with a keener insight into the case than any other man had yet attained, had written, "We must beat the enemy somewhere, or fail finally. If we can not beat him where he now is, we never can, he being again within the intrenchments of Richmond." This was as true now as it was a month before. It so happened that the Confederate commander had placed his army in such a position as to invite an attack. A little more than half of it was massed at Culpepper, a little less than half was lying three days' march away in the Valley of the Shenandoah. The Union army was massed only a few hours' march from the enemy, outnumbering him more than two to one. An attack in force could hardly have resulted otherwise than in a decisive victory. Burnside proposed deliberately to throw away the advantage thus thrust into his hands, and march directly away from his inferior foe, in quest of an object which, even if attained, was of wholly secondary consequence. The President, however, though with some reluctance, acceded to Burnside's plan, but with the significant intimation, "I think it will succeed if you move rapidly, otherwise not."[1] While preparing for this movement, Burnside organized his force into three "Grand Divisions"—Sumner being placed in command of the "Right," Hooker of the "Centre," and Franklin of the "Left."[2]

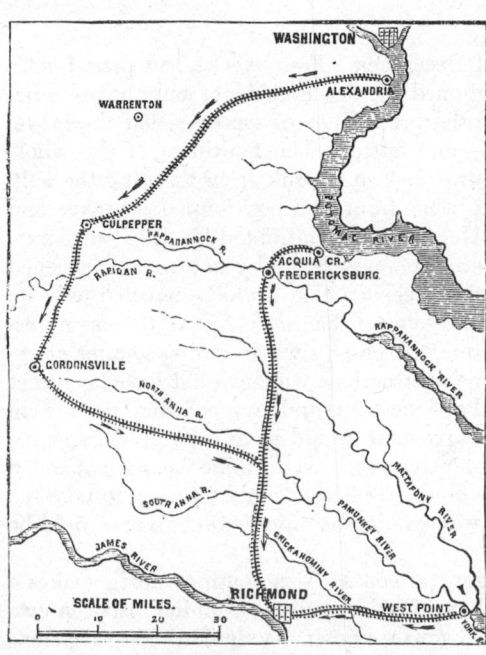

ROUTES TO RICHMOND.

This sketch illustrates the advantages, in point of distance, of the three proposed routes to Richmond. The first, abandoned by Burnside, assumes the basis of supply to be at Alexandria. The second, proposed by him, assumes it to be at Acquia Creek. The third, that adopted by McClellan, places it at West Point.

Burnside began his movement from Warrenton to Fredericksburg on the 15th of November. He had proposed to make it by concentrating his force at Warrenton, as though he intended to attack Culpepper or Gordonsville. But Lee was not deceived. On the 17th he learned that Sumner had marched from Catlett's Station toward Falmouth, and that Federal gun-boats had entered Acquia Creek. This, he thought, "looked as if Fredericksburg was to be reoccupied," and he dispatched two divisions of infantry, with cavalry and artillery, to augment the small force which had held the town. Next day a bold dash by Stuart's cavalry upon Warrenton disclosed that the Federal army were gone, whereupon Longstreet's whole command was sent toward Fredericksburg, while Jackson was ordered from the Valley to rejoin the main army.[3] Lee, having divined Burnside's movement, met it in just the manner in which one would suppose he would have done, but, as it would seem, just in the way his opponent did not anticipate. There were five conceivable things to be done: To repass down the Valley of the Shenandoah and again invade Maryland, and threaten Pennsylvania; to make a demonstration upon Washington, with the intent of recalling the march to Fredericksburg; to fall back at once toward Richmond; to remain where he was, and await the issue of events; or to throw himself directly across the new line of advance proposed by Burnside. The first two movements Burnside had ruled out as impracticable or ruinous. For the third there was no immediate necessity; it could be done, if need were, afterward as well as then. Burnside seems to have supposed that Lee would choose the fourth. As it happened, he chose the fifth course, which accident enabled him to carry out under auspices far more favorable than he could have dared to anticipate.

Sumner, with the advance of the Union army, reached Falmouth, opposite Fredericksburg, on the 17th. The design was that he should cross the Rappahannock at once, and seize the heights in the rear of Fredericksburg before Lee could re-enforce the small force stationed there. The river at that point could not be forded by an army in mass, and the railroad and turnpike bridges which had spanned it were destroyed. Burnside had, as he supposed, made arrangements by which pontoons sufficient to span the stream would have been sent to him from Washington so as to meet him on his arrival. But none came for a week, during which time nothing could be done to carry out the plan of operations.[4] Sumner, indeed, who

FREDERICKSBURG, FROM FALMOUTH.

son immediately concerned endeavored to shift from himself the burden of the responsibility. Burnside says (*Com. Rep.*, 651, 655): "My plan had been discussed by General Halleck and General Meigs at my head-quarters at Warrenton on the night of the 11th or 12th, and, after discussing it fully there, they sat down and sent telegrams to Washington, which, as I supposed, fully covered the case, and would secure the starting of the pontoons at once. I supposed, of course, that those portions of the plan which required to be attended to at Washington would have been carried out there. I understood that General Halleck was to give the necessary orders, and then the officers who should receive those orders were the ones responsible for the pontoons coming here. I could have carried out that part of the plan through officers of my own; but, having just taken the command of an army with which I was unacquainted, it was evident that it was as much as I could attend to, with the assistance of all my officers, to change its position from Warrenton to Fredericksburg."—Halleck says (*Ibid.*, 673): "On my visit to General Burnside at Warrenton on the 12th of November, in speaking about the boats and things which he required from Washington, I told him that they were all subject to his orders. To prevent the ne-

---

[1] *Com. Rep.*, 645.

[2] Sumner's Grand Division consisted of the 2d Corps, under Couch, lately Sumner's, and the 9th Corps, under Wilcox, formerly Burnside's. Hooker's Grand Division comprised the 3d Corps, under Stoneman, from the garrison of Washington, and the 5th Corps, formerly Fitz John Porter's, under Butterfield. Franklin's Grand Division consisted of the 1st Corps, formerly Hooker's, under Reynolds, and the 6th Corps, formerly Franklin's, under W. F. Smith. The 12th Corps, so briefly commanded by Mansfield, was left at Harper's Ferry, under Slocum. The 11th Corps, under Sigel, detached from the defenses of Washington, was near Manassas Junction, guarding the railway line. This corps did not strictly form a part of Burnside's movable army. Among the commanders of "divisions," as distinguished from the "Grand Divisions," were Birney, Doubleday, French, Gibbon, Hancock, Howard, Humphreys, Meade, Newton, Sykes.

[3] *Lee's Rep.*, i., 37.

[4] This delay, upon which so much hinged, was made the subject of strict scrutiny. Each per-

ACQUIA CREEK. BURNSIDE'S BASE OF SUPPLY.

had been fired upon by a battery from across the river, and had silenced it so easily as to show that the enemy were there in only trifling force, was disposed to send a detachment by a ford which was practicable for the purpose, and gave an order to that effect. But he had received explicit orders not to cross and occupy Fredericksburg; and, "upon reflection, he concluded that he was rather too old a soldier to disobey a direct order; besides, he had had a little too much experience on the Peninsula of the consequence of getting astride a river to risk it here." So, having revoked the order, he sent a note to Burnside, asking whether he should take Fredericksburg the next morning, provided he could find, what he had already found, a practicable ford. Burnside replied in the negative; he did not think it advisable to occupy Fredericksburg until his communications were established; and Sumner coincided in this decision.[1] Hooker, who brought up the rear of the army, requested permission, on the 20th, to send a division across the Rappahannock, which should march down the south side and seize the heights behind Fredericksburg. Burnside next day refused permission. He thought that although Hooker might "beat any force of the enemy he would meet on his way, yet it would be a very hazardous movement to throw a column like that beyond the reach of its proper support;" and, moreover, a rain-storm which had set in during the night rendered the movement impossible.[2] Sumner, on the 21st, sent over a message to the corporate authorities of Fredericksburg demanding the surrender of the town, under pain of bombardment in case of refusal. The civic authorities were told by the military commander that "while the town would not be occupied for military purposes, its occupation by the enemy would be resisted." Directions were given for the removal of the people, and almost the entire population left their homes.[3] No bombardment then took place; but a fortnight later, when the movement across the river was made, Fredericksburg, which was then used by the Confederates for "military purposes," and almost the entire population having been removed in consequence of the threat, was bombarded. This was fiercely denounced as a violation of the laws of war, but without the slightest ground. The town had been formally summoned to surrender; the unarmed population had abandoned it after abundant notice; and it was used for the direct "military purpose" of "resisting the occupation by the enemy."

A fortnight passed, during which time the Union army lay upon the north bank of the Rappahannock, waiting for means to cross the stream, and for the accumulation of supplies at the Acquia Creek, and the means of transporting them from the Potomac to the Rappahannock. The Confederate army was meanwhile concentrating on the southern side to resist any advance. About this time that army was formally organized into two corps, under the immediate command of Longstreet and Jackson, who had each been raised to the rank of lieutenant general. Longstreet's corps consisted of the troops formerly belonging to his command. To Jackson was assigned, besides those which he had heretofore commanded, the division of D. H. Hill. The two corps were now of nearly equal force, that of Longstreet being perhaps slightly in excess.[4]

It was almost the middle of December. Four weeks had passed since Burnside's plan had been sanctioned by the President; but the essential thing upon which he had based the probability of success—that the movement should be rapidly made—had failed. The faultiness of the whole scheme was now apparent. Burnside had shrunk from assailing the half of Lee's force which lay directly in his front, in a position hastily taken and of no great natural strength. He was now confronted by the Confederate army, drawn up in a position almost unassailable by nature, strengthened by the labor of three unobstructed weeks, which could be assailed only by crossing a formidable stream; and even if that were passed, the enemy assailed and driven from his position, the pursuit would still encounter at every step of the way just the same obstructions which would have been met on the line which had been abandoned. If military considerations were alone in question, no farther movement would have been made, and the army would have gone into winter quarters. But public feeling demanded a movement, and Burnside, sanctioned by his generals, resolved to take the offensive. The only question was where the intervening river should be crossed.[1]

The Rappahannock, with a general course from south to north, makes a sharp bend westward a mile above Fredericksburg, running between two lines of heights. Those on the north, known as Stafford Heights, slope steeply down to the river bank, with an elevation sufficient to command the valley across the river. On the south side, the hills just in the rear of Fredericksburg rise sharply something less than a mile from the river; then they trend away, in a semicircular form, until they sink down into the valley of the Massaponax, six miles below Fredericksburg, leaving an irregular broken valley, two miles broad at its widest point. This range of heights was mostly covered with dense woods, oaks with branches now leafless, skirted with sombre pines, rising southward by a succession of wooded ridges, each dominating the one below until lost in a wild wooded region soon to become famous under the name of the "Wilderness." Upon the crests and slopes of these wooded heights Longstreet's corps had been disposed, covering a front of about five miles. There was little need of artificial aid to the natural strength of the position; but artillery and rifle pits were dug and abatis constructed.[2] D. H. Hill's division was posted near Port Royal, twenty miles below, to prevent the Union gun-boats from ascending the river, and some skirmishing here took place.[3] The remainder of Jackson's corps was

and McLaws, comprising 21 brigades. Jackson's corps, the Second, consisted of the divisions of A. P. Hill, D. H. Hill, Ewell, and Taliaferro, comprising 19 brigades. The cavalry and horse artillery, under Stuart, acted somewhat independently with either corps; at the battle of Fredericksburg, mainly with Jackson.

[1] Sumner: "I was in favor of crossing the Rappahannock, because I knew that neither our government nor our people would be satisfied to have our army retire from this position or go into winter quarters until we knew the force that was on the other side of the river, and the only way of ascertaining that was by feeling them" (*Com. Rep.*, 658).

Franklin: "General Burnside called a council, in which it was the unanimous opinion, I think, of all the generals present, that if this river could be crossed, it ought to be crossed, no matter what might happen afterward. The point of crossing was not then definitely determined upon; but I thought at the time that we were to cross several miles farther down. Afterward General Burnside called us together again, and informed us that he had determined to cross at the two points at which we finally did cross. I had no objection to that, but thought they were as good as the point farther down" (*Ibid.*, 661).

Hooker: "After the pontoons arrived, it became a matter of importance to determine where and in what way we should cross the Rappahannock. The officers commanding the Grand Divisions were called together to discuss and determine that matter. General Burnside proposed that a portion of the command should cross at Fredericksburg, and a portion should cross about twelve miles below. I objected by my vote in the council to crossing two columns so far apart, and stated my preference that the whole army should cross at what is called the United States or Richards's Ford, about twelve miles above; but I was overruled" (*Ibid.*, 666).

[2] "Pits were made for the protection of the batteries; and, in addition to the natural strength of the position, ditches, stone fences, and road-cuts were found along different portions of the line, and parts were farther strengthened by rifle-trenches and abatis."—Longstreet, in *Lee's Rep.*, ii., 427.

[3] Hill always managed to say something quite out of harmony with the usual decorum of the Confederate official reports. Here, with abridgments, is his account of what took place at his extremity of the line: "Four Yankee gun-boats were then lying opposite the town of Port Royal. Rifle-pits were constructed to prevent the pirates from ascending. Hardaway opened upon the gun-boats. Finding the fire too hot for them, they fled back. Hardaway continued to pelt them, and, to stop his fire, the ruffians commenced shelling the town. A dog was killed and a negro wounded. The pirates fled down the river; but a worse fate awaited them than a distant cannonade—a section of artillery immediately on the bank gave them a parting salute. From Yankee sources we learned that the pirates lost six killed and twenty wounded. Whether they over-esti-

cessity of the commanding officer here reporting the order for the boats there, the order was drawn up on his table and signed by me directly to General Woodbury. I saw General Woodbury on my return, and he told me that he had received the order. I told him that in all these matters he was under General Burnside's direction; I had nothing farther to give him except to communicate that order to him. I gave no other order or direction in relation to the matter."—There seems to have been an unaccountable misapprehension as to the purport of the order which was addressed to General Woodbury, of the Engineer Brigade. It read: "Call upon the chief quarter-master to transport all your pontoons to Acquia Creek" (*Ibid.*, 663). Woodbury did not understand that this order demanded instant execution. "Had the emergency been made known to me in any manner," he says, "I could have disregarded the forms of service, seized teams, teamsters, and wagon-masters for instant service wherever I could find them. Then, with good roads and good weather, they might possibly have been in time. But I had no warrant for such a course, which, after all, could only have been carried out by the authority of the general-in-chief" (*Ibid.*, 665).—Quarter-master General Meigs said that the blame did not rest upon his department, "which was no more responsible for the march of a pontoon train than for the march of a battery of artillery or of a regiment of infantry. Its business was to provide material for the transportation of an army. If General Woodbury had orders from General Burnside, he was responsible for carrying them out" (*Ibid.*, 680).

[1] Sumner, in *Com. Rep.*, 657.   [2] *Com. Rep.*, 654, 666.   [3] *Lee's Rep.*, i., 38.

[4] Longstreet's corps, the First, consisted of the divisions of Anderson, Pickett, Ransom, Wood,

AN ARMY TRAIN.

BUILDING THE BRIDGE AT FREDERICKSBURG.

posted so as to be in a position to support either Hill or Longstreet. Two shots in immediate succession were to be the signal giving notice for the whole of the Confederate force to concentrate upon any point that should be menaced in force.

Burnside had resolved to cross at a point known by the euphoneous designation of Skinker's Neck, about twelve miles below Fredericksburg. The movements which were made for this purpose caused the enemy to concentrate much of his strength in that direction. The thought then occurred to him to detain this force there by ostentatious demonstrations, and to make the crossing at Fredericksburg. "I decided," he says, "to cross at Fredericksburg, because, in the first place, I felt satisfied that they did not expect us to cross here, but down below; and, in the next place, I felt satisfied that this was the place to fight the most decisive battle, because, if we could divide their forces by piercing their lines at one or two points, separating their left from their right, then a vigorous attack with the whole army would succeed in breaking their army in pieces."[1] No conclusion could, as matters stood, be more sound, provided that the premises upon which it was based were sure. If it was certain that Lee's left would be behind Fredericksburg, and his right a dozen miles or more away, then an adequate force flung into this great gap would divide the Confederate army, and a vigorous assault upon its left might be expected to crush it when cut off from aid from the right. To carry out this plan, it was necessary that the river should be crossed and battle be waged and won in a single day. Failing this, the rest must depend upon contingencies which no man could foresee.

The 11th of December was fixed upon as the day for crossing the river. During the previous night nearly one hundred and fifty heavy guns were placed in position upon the crest of Stafford Heights, commanding a great part of the opposite valley. The intention was to throw three bridges across at Fredericksburg, and as many more at a point two or three miles below. Sumner's Grand Division was to cross by the upper bridges, Franklin's by the lower, while Hooker's was to be held in reserve, ready, if the assault was successful, to spring upon the enemy in his retreat.[2] It was supposed that the bridges could be built in two or three hours.[3] Before dawn the pontoons were brought down to the river bank, and the work of laying the bridges was begun in the darkness. Two single shots broke the stillness which reigned through the Confederate lines. These were the signal for Longstreet's corps to concentrate upon the threatened point. Fredericksburg was held by only two regiments of sharp-shooters, who were sheltered in houses and rifle-pits, and behind walls on the river bank. In addition to the darkness of night, a dense fog filled the valley. The engineers had hardly begun to lay the bridges when they were assailed by rifle-shots at short range from the opposite shore, and driven off with severe loss. Again and again they returned, and again and again were driven off. The two or three hours had stretched to six, and the narrow stream was only half spanned, and not another length could be laid under the fierce fire. Burnside now ordered that fire should be opened upon the town from his artillery which crowned the opposite crests. Nearly one hundred and fifty heavy guns at once opened fire into the pall of mist which still shrouded the scene. After two hours a column of rising smoke indicated that a part of the town was in flames, and another attempt was made to complete the bridges. This was repelled as the former ones had been, showing that almost ten thousand shot had failed to dislodge the sharp-shooters from their coverts. When the fog lifted at noon, it was found that the elevation at which the guns were placed was so great that few of them could be sufficiently depressed to bear upon the river front of the town. The day was fast wearing away, and nothing had been accomplished. The officers reported that the bridges could not be built. Burnside said that it must be done, and some means must be found to dislodge the sharp-shooters. It was now decided that a detachment should cross in open pontoon boats and carry the town. Two regiments from Massachusetts and one from Michigan volunteered for the perilous work. They rushed down the bank and pushed the boats into the stream; a few strong strokes with the oars, and they were under shelter of the opposite bluffs, up which they dashed, and in a quarter of an hour carried the town.[4] In half an hour more the bridges were finished, and, as evening was falling, Couch's division was over and the first step in the enterprise fairly taken.[5] Franklin had indeed met with scarcely a show of opposition. His artillery covered the opposite shore, and his bridges were ready before noon; but Burnside had resolved that the attack should be made in two separate columns, and Franklin was not suffered to cross until the other bridges were completed.

It was no part of Lee's plan seriously to oppose the passage of the river by the Federal force, or even to assail it when over. He wisely chose to await its assault upon his strong position,[6] to which his opponent would

mated or under-estimated their losses I do not know; they sometimes lie on one side and sometimes on another. In a few days the pirates returned with some more of their thievish consorts. Guns were brought down to the river under cover of a dense fog, and when it lifted were opened upon them. We have learned from the same respectable Yankee source that three of the pirates were struck, one three times, and that a captain was killed, and four or five other thieves knocked on the head."—D. H. Hill, in *Lee's Rep.*, ii., 458.   [1] Burnside's Testimony, in *Com. Rep.*, 652.

[2] Hooker, in *Com. Rep.*, 667.   [3] Burnside, *Ibid.*, 655.

[4] McLaws says (*Lee's Rep.*, ii., 445) that the artillery fire was so severe that his "men could not use their rifles, and the different places occupied by them becoming untenable, the troops were withdrawn from the river bank at half past four, when the enemy crossed in boats, and, completing their bridges, passed over in force and advanced into the town."   [5] Burnside, in *Com. Rep.*, 656.

[6] Lee indeed believed that it was impossible to prevent the crossing. He says (*Rep.*, i., 39): "The plain of Fredericksburg is so completely commanded by the Stafford Heights, that no effectual opposition could be made to the construction of bridges or the passage of the river without exposing our troops to the destructive fire of the numerous batteries of the enemy. At the same time, the narrowness of the Rappahannock, its winding course and deep bed, presented opportunities for laying down bridges at points secure from the fire of our artillery. Our position was therefore selected with a view to resist the enemy's advance after crossing, and the river was guarded only by a force sufficient to impede his movements until the army could be concentrated."—Franklin, however, was confident that not only might his passage have been prevented, but that his division, when over, could have been crushed. He says (Testimony, in *Com. Rep.*, 661): "I always

SUMNER'S GRAND DIVISION CROSSING THE RAPPAHANNOCK.

FRANKLIN'S GRAND DIVISION CROSSING THE RAPPAHANNOCK.

have been pledged by crossing the river. He seems, indeed, to have been uncertain whether the movement in his front was a serious one, or merely a feint to cover an attempt upon one of his flanks; for it was not until from twenty-four to forty hours after the firing of the signal-guns that Jackson's corps was brought up from its positions nearly a score of miles down the river.[1] Could the bridges have been completed, as was expected, early on the morning of the 11th, and the attack made that day, Burnside would have encountered only half of the Confederate force, and the result of the action could hardly have failed to have been different.

The whole of the 12th was most unaccountably spent in crossing the river and deciding upon the order of the attack on the next day. It was found that the extreme Confederate right was protected by a canal, all the bridges crossing which had been destroyed; there was, besides, a sluiceway and mill-pond, so that this point was unassailable; and an attack upon the right could only be made against the steep front of Marye's Hill, rising in the rear of the town and presenting a front of a mile, then sloping off sharply to a ravine traversed by a small stream; thence the heights sweep away from the river, leaving a broken plain, its edges deeply indented by wooded spurs. This plain, about two miles broad, is traversed by the Richmond and Fredericksburg Railroad, which winds around the base of the heights, occasionally cutting through the extremities of the projecting spurs. Midway between the railway and the river runs the old Richmond or Port Royal Road, often embanked and fringed with trees, affording shelter behind which the Union force could be deployed. When the final arrangements had been made on both sides, the Confederate forces, 80,000 strong, were posted along the ridge of the range of hills, their advance line in places pushed forward to the wooded base, Jackson's corps holding the right and Longstreet's the left. The Union army, 100,000 strong, was posted along the Richmond Road, from Fredericksburg down; Couch's corps, of Sumner's division, in the town; then Wilcox's corps, forming the connection with Franklin's Grand Division on the left.

The character of the ground unmistakably indicated that the main attack should be made by Franklin; for not only was the Confederate position here manifestly weaker, but the plain in front of it was spacious enough to give room to deploy his whole force; while to the right, in front of Sumner, the plain was so narrow that only a fragment of his force could at any one moment be brought into action. If he assailed the strong position before him, it must be by successive blows, not by a single attack with his whole force. Franklin understood, on the afternoon of the 12th, that Burnside intended that he should make the attack with his Grand Division, to which had been added a part of Hooker's. Hooker understood that there was to be a twofold assault, at distinct points, the main one by Sumner, on the right.[2] Burnside clearly proposed a twofold attack in force, that on the left to be the first.[3] But when, on the morning of the 13th, Franklin received his order, it was so worded as to lead him and his generals to suppose that it meant he should make merely an armed reconnoissance of the enemy's lines with but one of his eight divisions, to be supported by another, keeping the remainder in position for a different movement.[4] Franklin was also informed that a column, consisting of a division or more, detached from Sumner's corps, was to move against the heights in the rear of Fredericksburg. Thus, as the plan was framed, not more than four divisions, one quarter of the force which had crossed or was ready to cross the river, were to assail the position held by the Confederates. We can only account for this plan by supposing that Burnside thought that the enemy in his front was really in inconsiderable force, its bulk being still a score of miles away, and that not only had he crossed the Rappahannock at a point where he was not expected, but that during the eight-and-forty hours which had passed since the attempt was begun the enemy had not concentrated his strength in his front. Thus only can we explain the part assigned to Hooker, to spring upon the enemy on his retreat, and the order to Franklin to be in readiness to march down the Richmond Road, that being the direction which the retreating Confederates would naturally take. If such was his belief, he must have been confirmed in it by the trifling opposition offered to his passage of the river. There was, indeed, nothing to show the neighborhood of a great hostile army. Hardly a reply had been made to his heavy bombardment; not

<hr />

doubted our power to cross, and I do not believe we could have crossed had the enemy chosen to prevent it; and I know, from what I have seen since and what I before suspected, that they could have prevented our crossing at those two points if they had chosen. However, the crossing was successfully made, under cover of a fog, and, as far as my wing was concerned, we got into position safely, with the loss of a very few men. Still, we were in such a position that, if the enemy had at any moment opened upon us with the guns they had bearing upon us, I think in the course of an hour our men would have been so scattered that it would have been impossible to rally them. For some unaccountable reason they did not open their batteries."

[1] "It having been definitely ascertained that the enemy had crossed the Rappahannock in large force, I was ordered to move my division at dawn on the 12th" (A. P. Hill, in Lee's Rep., ii., 461).—"Just before sundown on the 12th I received an order to march that night to Fredericksburg, as the Yankees were expected to attack General Lee that day. A portion of my command was twenty-two miles from that city, and the most of them from eighteen to twenty" (D. H. Hill, Ibid., 458).—"A. P. Hill moved his division at dawn on the morning of the 12th. At the same time, Taliaferro, then in command of Jackson's division, moved from his encampment. Early on the morning of the 13th, Ewell's division, under Early, and D. H. Hill, with his division, arrived, after a severe night's march, from their respective encampments, the troops of D. H. Hill being from fifteen to eighteen miles distant from the points to which they were ordered" (Jackson, Ibid., 434).

[2] "General Burnside said [in the council] that his favorite plan of attack was on the telegraph road."—Hooker, in Com. Rep., 667.

[3] "The enemy had cut a road along in the rear of the line of heights where we made our attack, by means of which they connected the two wings of their army, and avoided a long detour through a bad country. I wanted to obtain possession of that new road, and that was my reason for making an attack on the extreme left. I did not intend to make the attack on the right until that position had been taken, which I supposed would stagger the enemy, cutting their line in two; and then I proposed to make a direct attack on their front, and drive them out of their works."—Burnside, in Com. Rep., 653.

[4] Franklin, in Com. Rep., 708. The order is given in full in Com. Rep., 707. The essential portions are these: "The general commanding directs that you keep your whole command in position for a rapid movement down the old Richmond Road; and you will send out at once a division at least to pass below Smithfield, to seize, if possible, the heights near Captain Hamilton's, on this side of the Massaponax, taking care to keep it well supported and its line of retreat open. . . . . You will keep your whole command ready to move at once, as soon as the fog lifts."

an enemy showed himself during that day or the next besides the few regiments which had been driven from Fredericksburg, and the scanty line of sharp-shooters, hardly more than a picket-guard, scattered along the river bank. He had indeed been informed by a German prisoner, who represented that he had been impressed into the Confederate service, of the strength of the enemy, of their positions and batteries, and that they regarded it as an impossibility that the heights could be carried; but Burnside clearly placed no faith in his story.[1]

The morning of Saturday, December 13, broke with a dense fog resting in the valley, shutting the two armies from all sight of each other. So dense was it that the Confederates could hear the word of command given to the invisible lines before them.[2] The night had been bitterly cold. Some of the Confederate pickets were frozen at their posts.[3] About ten o'clock the fog lifted, and showed Franklin's command in motion. He had placed a liberal construction upon the order to assault with at least one division, and threw forward Reynolds's entire corps, Meade's division in advance in the centre, supported by Gibbon's on the right, and Doubleday's on the left, somewhat in the rear. The Confederate horse artillery, under Stuart, was so posted across the Richmond Road as to enfilade the Union line, and Doubleday was deflected still farther to the left to dislodge them. After an hour's sharp cannonading Stuart's guns were withdrawn, and Meade opened a fierce artillery fire upon the woods in his front. The Confederate batteries making no response, Meade pushed forward right against what proved to be the centre of Jackson's position.[4]

Jackson's front line was composed of three brigades of A. P. Hill's division, posted in the woods at Hamilton's Crossing, the point which Franklin had been ordered to assail with a single division; the other three brigades formed the second line along the military road, while the divisions of D. H. Hill, Ewell, and Taliaferro were in reserve beyond the crest of the heights. A wide gap had been left between two of Hill's front brigades, just behind a strip of boggy wood which was supposed to be inaccessible.[5] By one of those accidents which sometimes change the result of a battle, Meade advanced right upon this point, and his division thrust itself like a wedge through the unguarded opening, in the face of a fierce artillery fire now opened upon his column from the hitherto silent batteries. This wedge, by sheer force of impact, forced itself between and past the Confederate brigades of Lane and Archer, sweeping back the flanks of each, and gaining the second line along the military road. A part of Gregg's brigade was thrown into confusion, but the remainder of the line stood firm, and checked the rush of Meade's column. This had pushed in so rapidly that it was separated from Gibbon's division, which was to be its immediate support, and was enveloped, for it had pierced, not shattered, the first Confederate line, whose separated portions assailed each of its flanks, while its front was headed by the second line. It was now a mere question of force. Meade's three brigades were opposed to Hill's six, and they fell back in confusion over the ground which they had gained. Meanwhile Gibbon's supporting division, after a brief delay, which to Meade seemed long,[6] came up on his right, and for a moment stemmed the Confederate advance. But in the mean while a messenger from Hill had dashed up to Early, who was in the rear, bringing tidings that "an awful gap" had been left in the front line, through which the enemy were pouring, endangering not only the infantry of that line, but all the batteries. Early sent Lawton's brigade into the fight; they rushed in with the wild "cheer peculiar to the Confederate soldier, and which is never to be mistaken for the studied hurrahs of the Yankees,"[7] closely followed by the remainder of the division. At the same time Hood, whose division of Longstreet's corps was next to Jackson, and who had received orders to co-operate with him, sent a brigade to the scene of action. This united force swept back Gibbon's division, as well as the shattered remains of Meade's.[8]

The consequences of the wording of Burnside's order, and Franklin's understanding of it, were now apparent. Franklin held his Grand Division in a position for a "rapid advance down the Richmond Road," and so, with the exception of Meade and Gibbon, it was stretched along the road, the nearest part being a full mile from the scene of conflict, and most of it much farther, for Doubleday's division, which was to have directly supported the attack, had gone so far to the left as to be beyond reach. But, fortunately, Stoneman's corps of Hooker's Grand Division had begun to cross the river opposite the place of the fight. Birney's division of that corps, which led, had been ordered to follow Meade when he advanced; but the order was countermanded, and he was directed to retire his men from a hot artillery fire which was opening upon them. He had begun to do this when he was told to push forward to aid Meade, whose division was flying back in all direc-

tions. The fugitives rushed straight through Birney's lines, closely pursued by the enemy, who dashed within fifty yards of Birney's guns. Four batteries of these opened such a furious fire of canister that the Confederates were checked; they then recoiled, falling back to their original first line on the railroad.[1] The battle on the left was now over. It had lasted about two hours, counting from the time when Meade advanced down to the moment when the Confederates recoiled from the pursuit.[2] Burnside, indeed, sent an order to Franklin directing him to attack in front, but before this was received Franklin deemed it too late to make any change in his dispositions.[3] Jackson also planned an assault under cover of darkness upon the Federal position. He proposed to attack with his artillery in advance, followed by the infantry; but his first guns had hardly moved forward a hundred yards when the Federal artillery reopened its fire, and so completely swept his front as to satisfy him that the attempt must be abandoned.[4]

In this action upon the left the Federals lost, in killed and wounded, about 3700, of which nearly 2600 fell upon the two divisions of Meade and Gibbon, and 900 upon that of Birney. The Confederates lost about 3200, of which half fell upon the division of A. P. Hill, and a fourth upon that of Ewell. In their advance the Federals captured 500 prisoners, and lost about as many in the retreat.[5]

During this action on the left, a still more fiercely contested fight was raging three miles away on the right, at the foot of Marye's Hill, directly behind Fredericksburg. The Confederate position here was of great strength.[6] "Marye's Hill, covered with their batteries, falls off abruptly toward Fredericksburg, to a stone wall which forms a terrace on the side of the hill, and the outer margin of the Telegraph Road, which winds along the foot of the hill. The road is about twenty-five feet wide, and is faced by a stone wall, about four feet high, on the city side. The road having been cut out of the side of the hill in many places, this last wall is not visible above the surface of the ground. The ground falls off rapidly to almost a level surface, which extends about a hundred and fifty yards; then, with another abrupt fall of a few feet, to another plain, which extends some two hundred yards, and then falls off abruptly into a wide ravine, which extends along the whole front of the city." This road, invisible from the direction whence the attack was to come, was precisely like the ditch of a fortress, affording perfect protection to the men posted in it. Parts of two brigades, numbering in all not 2000 men, were stationed here, and yet so small was the space that they stood four deep.[7] The line of this sunken road was continued on each side by a stone wall raised above the ground, and by rifle-pits and trenches. The crest of the hill was covered with artillery, but so narrow was the space that there was here only room for eleven guns of the Washington Artillery; these were mostly 12-pounders. Other guns, about fifty in all, of heavier calibre, were posted so as to enfilade the approaches, while the bulk of the artillery was held in reserve beyond the crest of the hills, the ammunition trains being several miles in the rear.[8] Lee, indeed, seems to have assumed that the enemy would succeed in gaining the crest of the hills, and that the battle would be fought on the plateau beyond, where his whole system of defensive works had been constructed; while Burnside supposed that these crests once gained the victory would be won.

The attack upon Marye's Hill was committed to Sumner; but, as Wilcox's corps of his Grand Division had been stretched down the river to keep up the connection with Franklin, the burden of the assault was laid upon Couch's corps. French's division was to begin the attack, followed by that of Hancock, "two of the most gallant officers in the army, and two divisions that had never turned their backs to the enemy."[9] When the fog lifted at noon, these divisions were seen formed in two columns of attack, marching straight toward the base of the heights, along two roads which here run parallel, that on the right being the "Orange Plank Road," leading westward to the "Wilderness," four months hence to become historical in connection with

---

[1] Hooker, in *Com. Rep.*, 667.　　[2] *Lee's Rep.*, ii., 428.　　[3] *Ibid.*, ii., 487.
[4] Reynolds, in *Com. Rep.*, 698; A. P. Hill, in *Lee's Rep.*, ii., 452.　　[5] *Lee's Rep.*, ii., 466.
[6] "General Gibbon's division on my right, which I understood was to have advanced simultaneously with my own, did not advance till I was driven back. It advanced until it came within short range of the enemy, when it halted. The officers could not get the men forward to a charge, and the division was held at bay there some twenty or thirty minutes, during which time my division had gone forward. That delay enabled the enemy to concentrate their force and attack me on my front and both flanks. I had penetrated the enemy's lines so far that I had no support on either flank, and was therefore forced to fall back. As I came out, Gibbon's forces advanced, and got as far probably as the railroad, which was the enemy's outer line" (Meade, in *Com. Rep.*, 691).—Gibbon says: "I saw General Meade's troops moving forward into action, and I at once sent orders to my leading brigade to advance and engage the enemy. Shortly afterward I ordered up another brigade to the support of the first. The fire was very heavy from the enemy's infantry, and I ordered up the third brigade, and directed them to take the position with the bayonet, having previously given that order to the leading brigade. But the general commanding that brigade told me that the noise and confusion was so great that it was impossible to get the men to charge, or to get them to hear any order to charge. The third brigade went in, took the position with the bayonet, and captured a considerable number of prisoners. I had just received the report of the success of the third brigade, when shortly after I saw a regiment of infantry come out on the left of my line, between myself and General Meade. No troops came up in support of my division to enable me to hold the position which I had gained" (*Ibid.*, 715).
[7] Early, in *Lee's Rep.*, ii., 470.　　[8] *Lee's Rep.*, ii., 428, 457.

[1] Birney, in *Com. Rep.*, 705; Reynolds, *Ibid.*, 698; Jackson, in *Lee's Rep.*, ii., 436; A. P. Hill, *Ibid.*, 464; Early, *Ibid.*, 471.
[2] The moments of the fight are best given in the dispatches of General Hardie, of Burnside's staff, who was placed at Franklin's head-quarters to report upon the operations. We give the main points of his consecutive dispatches, as contained in *Com. Rep.*, 712–714: "*December* 13, 7 40 A.M. Meade's division is to make the movement from our left; but it is just reported that the enemy's skirmishers are advancing, indicating an attack upon our position on the left.—9 A.M. Meade just moved out; Doubleday supports him. Meade's skirmishers engaged with enemy's skirmishers.—9 40. Two batteries playing upon Reynolds. They must be silenced before he can advance.—11 A.M. Meade advanced half a mile, and holds on.—12 M. Birney's division now getting into position. That done, Reynolds will order Meade to advance.—12 5 P.M. Meade's line is advancing in the direction you prescribed this morning.—1 P.M. Enemy opened a battery enfilading Meade; Reynolds has opened all his batteries upon it. Reynolds hotly engaged.—1 15 P.M. Heavy engagement of infantry; Meade is assaulting the hill.—1 25 P.M. Meade is in the woods; seems to be able to hold on. Reynolds will push Gibbon in if necessary; the infantry firing is prolonged and quite heavy; things look well enough; men in fine spirits.—1 40 P.M. Meade having carried a portion of the enemy's position in the woods, we have 300 prisoners; tough work; men fight well; Gibbon has advanced to Meade's right; Meade has suffered severely; Doubleday, to Meade's left, not engaged.—2 15 P.M. Gibbon and Meade driven back from the woods; Newton gone forward; Jackson's corps of the enemy attacks on the left; Gibbon slightly wounded; Bayard mortally wounded by a shell. Things do not look so well on Reynolds's front; still we will have new troops in soon.—2 25 P.M. Franklin will do his best; new troops gone in.—3 P.M. Reynolds seems to be holding his own; things look better somewhat.—3 40 P.M. Gibbon's and Meade's divisions are badly used up, and I fear another attack can not be made this afternoon. Doubleday's division will replace Meade's as soon as it can be collected, and if it be done in time another attack will be made. The enemy is in force in the woods on our left, threatening the safety of that portion of our line. Just as soon as the left is safe, our forces here will be prepared for a front attack; but it may be too late this afternoon; indeed, we are engaged in front any how. Notwithstanding the unpleasant items I relate, the *morale* generally of the troops is good.—4 30 P.M. The enemy is still in force on our left and front. An attack on our batteries in front has been repulsed. A new attack has just opened on our left; but the left is safe, though it is too late to advance either to the left or front."
[3] *Com. Rep.*, 710.　　[4] Jackson, in *Lee's Rep.*, ii., 438.
[5] For detail of the losses in this action, and in that on the right, see *supra*, p. 416.
[6] This description is copied from Kershaw's Report (in *Lee's Rep.*, ii., 487). Of all the Reports on either side, this of Kershaw, who commanded here, is the only one which gives any adequate idea of the strength of the Confederate position. The existence of the sunken road, which, as it happened, was the key to the whole action here, seems never to have been known to any of the Union generals, even when they furnished their reports.
[7] *Ibid.*, 488.　　[8] *Ibid.*, 522, 533, 547.　　[9] Sumner, in *Com. Rep.*, 658.

THE ASSAULT UPON MARYE'S HILL.

the battle of Chancellorsville; the other, the "Telegraph Road," bending southwardly, and leading to Richmond, in which, hidden from view, lay the few regiments forming the advance line of the Confederate force, commanded by Cobb;[1] but he having been killed early in the day, the command was given to Kershaw, whose brigade was thrust forward into and near the sunken road.

No sooner had the Federal columns moved in dense masses out of the deep ravine, through which some suppose that the Rappahannock once flowed, and emerged upon the narrow plain at the foot of Marye's Hill, than they came within range of the Confederate artillery posted upon the crests. Every gun opened upon them with terrible effect, "making great gaps that could be seen at the distance of a mile."[2] The light guns of the Confederates, at this close range, were better than though they had been heavier, for they could be worked more rapidly. French's division, in the advance, pressed on in the face of the artillery fire, closing up the great gaps plowed through their ranks, and had crossed half of the narrow space toward the foot of the hill, when they were met by a sheet of fire full in their faces from an invisible foe. It came from the Confederate infantry hidden in the road "cut out of the side of the hill," not a man of whom was visible above the smooth slope. The heads of the advancing columns melted away before this solid wall of fire, delivered from ranks four deep,[3] like a snow-bank before a jet of steam.

French's division recoiled before this fierce fire, and streamed back over the narrow plain across which they had advanced, leaving almost half their number behind. Hancock's came close after; this, with French's remaining men, pushed straight on, disregarding the hot artillery fire from the heights; but no sooner did they come within musket-range of the sunken road than a solid sheet of lead poured upon them. The front which was to be carried was so narrow that scarcely more than a brigade could be brought upon it at once. Brigade dashed in after brigade, each taking the place of one which had been swept back so rapidly that it seemed, from the Union lines in the plain, but a single assault, lasting three hours; but, as seen from the Confederate positions on the hill, it seemed a succession of waves dashed against the rocky wall at its base. But it was not a question of numbers. Had twice as many men been brought up the result would have been the same, only the loss would have been twice as great. Nor was it a question of bravery; for never, not even when, seven months later, the Confederates in their turn dashed and were shattered against the steeps at Gettysburg, was an assault made with more desperate and unavailing valor.[4] The main stress of the assault had been borne by divisions of French and Hancock. They had pressed across the narrow plain, about 10,000 strong, and lost fully 4000 in killed and wounded.

Burnside had watched the action from the heights across the Rappahannock. Two full hours had passed, and nothing seemed gained. Assault after assault had been made by divisions which had "never turned their backs to the enemy." The regiments which he had expected to see crowning the crest had been repelled from the base. "That crest must be crossed to-night," he exclaimed, and directed Hooker to cross and attack upon the Telegraph Road—the very position against which French and Hancock had been "butting all day long." Of Hooker's six divisions, two, and these, he says, "were my favorite divisions, for the one was that which I had educated myself, and the other was that which Kearney had commanded, and of these I knew more than of any others in my command," had been sent to the left to support Franklin. Another division had been sent across to the upper end of Fredericksburg to support Howard, and still another lower down to support Sturgis, both of whom had been pushed forward to aid French and Howard. Hooker had then but two divisions left with which to act; they were that of Humphreys, composed of new men, and Sykes's regulars, who had fought at Bull Run and Cold Harbor, at Malvern and Groveton. Hooker rode forward across the river to consult with the generals who had been engaged in the attack. He saw Couch and Wilcox, French and Hancock. With a single exception, they were all of opinion that no attack could be successfully made there. Hooker examined the position himself, and sent to Burnside an aid with a message dissuading from a new assault. The messenger returned with orders that an attempt must be made. Hooker then rode back, and in person repeated his urgency

[1] T. R. R. Cobb, not to be confounded with Howell Cobb, once Buchanan's Secretary of the Treasury, but now also a general in the Confederate army.   [2] Lee's Rep., ii., 429.

[3] "I found, on my arrival, that Cobb's brigade occupied our entire front, and our troops could only get into position by doubling on them. This was accordingly done, and the formation along most of the line was consequently four deep. As an evidence of the coolness of the command, I may mention here that, notwithstanding that their fire was the most rapid and continuous that I have ever witnessed, not a man was injured by the fire of his comrades."—Kershaw, in Lee's Rep., ii., 488.

[4] The Confederate reports testify abundantly to the desperate bravery with which this assault was carried on. Lee says (Rep., i., 42): "Our batteries poured a rapid and destructive fire into the dense lines of the enemy as they advanced to the attack, frequently breaking their ranks, and forcing them to retreat to the shelter of the houses. Six times did the enemy, notwithstanding the havoc caused by our batteries, press on with great determination to within one hundred yards of the foot of the hill; but here, encountering the deadly fire of our infantry, his columns were broken, and fled in confusion to the town."—Ransom, whose division bore half the brunt of the fight, says (Ibid., 451): "Another line was formed by the enemy, he all the while keeping up a brisk fire with sharp-shooters. This line advanced with the utmost determination, and some few of them got within fifty yards of our line; but the whole were forced to retire in wild confusion before the telling fire of our small-arms at such short range. For some minutes there was a cessation; but we were not long kept in expectancy. The enemy now seemed determined to reach our position, and formed apparently a triple line, and, almost massed, moved to the charge heroically, and met the withering fire of our artillery and small-arms with wonderful stanchness. On they came to within less than one hundred and fifty paces of our line; but nothing could live before the sheet of lead that was hurled at them from this distance. They momentarily recovered, broke, and rushed headlong from the field. A few, however, more resolute than the rest, lingered under cover of some fences and houses, and annoyed us with a scattering but well-directed fire. Nothing daunted by the fearful punishment he had received, the enemy brought out fresh and increased numbers of troops. Our men held their fire until it would be fatally effective; meanwhile the artillery was spreading fearful havoc among the enemy's ranks. Still he advanced, and received the destructive fire of our line; even more resolute than before, he seemed determined madly to press on; but his efforts could avail nothing."

FRANKLIN'S DIVISION RECROSSING THE RAPPAHANNOCK.

against an attack. But Burnside was inflexible, and insisted that it should be made.[1]

The short December day was verging to a close before Hooker was prepared to attack. He thought that the assault had not been sufficiently concentrated, and proposed to breach "a hole sufficiently large for a forlorn hope to enter." He brought forward batteries, and poured in a fire from every gun at his command. It made no more impression than if it had been poured upon "the side of a mountain of rock;" indeed, the sunken wall, which formed the real Confederate defense, could not be touched by any fire from the plain. Just at sunset Hooker ordered Humphreys's division to form in column of assault. Knapsacks, overcoats, and haversacks were thrown aside, and the men were directed "to make the assault with empty muskets, for there was no time there to load and fire." At the word, they rushed forward with loud hurrahs, charging straight for the stone wall. As it happened, the Confederate artillery, which had been posted on the crest of Marye's Hill, had exhausted its ammunition, and was passing to the rear, while other guns were coming forward to supply their places.[2] Humphreys's men thus escaped the terrible artillery fire which had staggered French and Hancock, and the head of the column gained a few yards—possibly rods—beyond the point attained by those who had gone before, and had then been hurled back by the musketry fire from the sunken road.[3] Here they met, as those who had gone before had met, the solid sheet of lead, winged with flame, poured in their faces, and turned, as they had done, from that fierce fire. Of the 4000 men whom Humphreys led up to that hidden defense, almost a half were stricken down in a quarter of an hour, for so brief had been the time between their rush and their repulse. Had Humphreys succeeded in his assault, Hooker had proposed to support him by Sykes; but the assault had signally failed; and, says Hooker, grimly, "finding that I had lost as many men as my orders required me to lose, I suspended the attack, and directed that the men should hold, for the advance line between Fredericksburg and the enemy, a ditch that runs along about midway between the enemy's lines and the city, and which would afford a shelter for the men.[4]

The Confederate army lay on their arms that night, fully expecting that the battle would be renewed the next day. The attack had been made by so small a portion of the Union force, and had been repulsed, especially on the right, by so small a part of the Confederate force, that Lee could not believe it to be the final attempt, and he resolved to await its renewal in his strong position, rather than run the risk of attacking in turn.[5] Burnside had crossed the river with 100,000 men. About 55,000 of these were with Franklin on the left; of these, about 17,000 had been fairly put into action. Against these Jackson had brought in about 20,000, being half of his own corps, and a brigade of Hood's division of Longstreet's corps. Hooker and Sumner, on the Union left, had 45,000; of these, 15,000 had been thrown

against the stone wall. Actually opposed to them were not more than 5000 of Longstreet's corps, though the whole, 40,000 strong, exclusive of Hood, could have been brought in had it been necessary; so that, in this twofold action, less than one third on either side were actually engaged.[1]

Burnside passed the night in consultation with his officers and men. Notwithstanding their dissuasion, he resolved to renew the assault next morning. Sumner, with the corps which Burnside himself had originally commanded, and which had not been seriously engaged, was to assail the heights by a direct attack, conducted just as that had been which had been so disastrously repulsed. He thought that these regiments, "coming quickly after each other, would be able to carry the stone wall and the batteries in front, forcing the enemy into their next line, and, by going in with them, they would not be able to fire upon us to any great extent." And so the order was given. With Sumner, to receive an order was to set about its execution, and before the morning lifted the columns of attack were formed. Then, when all was ready for the desperate attempt, the veteran soldier felt at liberty to remonstrate. "General," he said, "I hope you will desist from this attack. I do not know of any general officer who approves of it, and I think it will prove disastrous to the army." Burnside could not but hesitate when such advice was given by one "who was always in favor of an advance when it was possible." He kept the column formed, but suspended the order for advance until he could consult with his generals. One and all —commanders of corps and divisions on the right—were against the attempt. He sent for Franklin from the left, and his opinion was the same. So, after hours of thought, Burnside resolved that he would not venture the attack, which he himself at the time believed would have been successful, though he soon became convinced to the contrary. Night had almost come when he informed his officers that he had determined to recross the river with the bulk of the army, but to leave enough to hold Fredericksburg itself, and to protect the bridges, which were to remain, in case he should want to cross again. But upon the representations of Hooker and Butterfield—two men into whose composition entered no feeble fibre—he was convinced that even Fredericksburg could not be held; that everything must be withdrawn across the river, and the whole enterprise abandoned as a failure.[2] Sumner alone, of all the council, was still in favor of holding on to Fredericksburg. He thought this might have been done by a single division, provided the batteries across the river were rightly posted, and so the upshot of the affair would have presented a better appearance:

<hr/>

[1] Hooker, in *Com. Rep.*, 667; Burnside, *Ibid.*, 723. Both generals agree precisely as to facts. Burnside, however, considered this delay on the part of Hooker as "loss of time, and a preparation on the part of an officer for a failure, inasmuch as it was his duty to attack when ordered."

[2] *Lee's Rep.*, ii., 532.

[3] Hooker says (*Com. Rep.*, 668): "The head of General Humphreys's column advanced to within perhaps fifteen or twenty yards of the stone wall, which was the advanced position which the rebels held, and then they were thrown back as quickly as they had advanced. Probably the whole of the advance and the retiring did not occupy fifteen minutes. They left behind, as was reported to me, 1760 of their number out of about 4000."—McLaws, describing the field as it appeared after the close of the action, says (*Lee's Rep.*, ii., 447): "The body of one man, supposed to be an officer, was found within about thirty yards of the stone wall, and other single bodies were scattered at increased distances, until the main mass of the dead lay thickly strewn over the ground at something over one hundred yards off, extending to the ravine, commencing at the point where our men would allow the enemy's column to approach before opening fire, and beyond which no organized body of men was able to pass."

[4] *Com. Rep.*, 668. This ditch is what is called in the Confederate Reports a "ravine."

[5] "The attack on the 13th had been so easily repulsed, and by so small a part of our army, that it was not supposed the enemy would limit his efforts to one attempt, which, in view of the magnitude of his preparations and the extent of his forces, seemed to be comparatively insignificant. Believing, therefore, that he would attack us, it was not deemed expedient to lose the advantages of our position, and expose the troops to the fire of his inaccessible batteries beyond the river by advancing against him. But we were necessarily ignorant of the extent to which he had suffered."—*Lee's Rep.*, i., 43.

[1] There is some discrepancy of statement as to the numbers of Union force which crossed the river, the forces constituting each wing, and the numbers actually engaged. Burnside, however, testifies (in *Com. Rep.*, 656): "We had about 100,000 men on the other side of the river. Every single man of them was under artillery fire, and about half of them were at different times formed into column of attack. Every man was put in column of attack that could be got in." But a careful perusal of all the testimony shows that of the divisions formed into "columns of attack," fully a third were not fairly thrown into action.—Franklin estimated (*Com. Rep.*, 709): "The force under my command was somewhat over 40,000 men. I do not think it was over 50,000, counting Stoneman's two divisions; but I can not tell without looking at the figures. There were six divisions engaged in supporting the attack—Meade's, Doubleday's, Gibbon's, Birney's, Sickles's, and Newton's; I think the number was about 40,000." But, as has been shown, only three of these six were seriously engaged—Meade's and Gibbon's, of Reynolds's corps, which together lost fully 2500 out of the 2800 in Franklin's Grand Division, leaving only 300 for the three divisions of Doubleday, Sickles, and Newton, and of these 200 were from Doubleday's. Birney's division of Hooker's command was also engaged, losing nearly 1000 (*Ibid.*, 706). Three days before the battle Meade's and Gibbon's divisions, according to the returns of the day, numbered not quite 12,000 "present for duty," of which Meade had 6800; but he says he brought into action only 4500. Birney's numbered 7000 (*Ibid.*, 691, 702, 706); so that the estimate of 17,000 brought into action by Franklin on the left is fully equal to the truth. On the right we have seen that the three divisions of French, Hancock, and Humphreys were the only ones brought directly into the fight: the utmost strength of these divisions was 5000 each.

In placing the Confederates at 80,000 I am guided mainly by the official returns (*Ante*, p. 406), which give the numbers "present for duty" on the 20th of November, a fortnight before the battle, at 73,554; and on the 31st of December, a fortnight after the battle, at 79,092. At each date there were about 12,000 reported as "present," besides those "present for duty;" while the nominal strength, "present and absent," exceeded 150,000, being greater at the first date than the last. Of the "absent" I suppose that none could in the interval have been brought back; of those "present," but not reported as "for duty," probably a few thousand might have been available in an emergency. The Confederate Reports give the movements and losses of every brigade and regiment, so that, assuming their whole force to have been 80,000 effective men, I am able to give, without the possibility of material error, the numbers actually engaged on any part of the field.

[2] Burnside, in *Com. Rep.*, 653.

it would have been merely "a change of tactics—a drawing back a little in order to try it again."[1]

During Sunday, the 14th, and the greater part of Monday, the 15th, the two great armies lay in their positions, each expecting when the morning fog lifted to be attacked by the other. There was some firing at different points along the extended lines, but nothing which approached to an engagement. On the afternoon of the 15th a formal truce for the purpose of removing the wounded was agreed upon between Jackson and Franklin on their part of the field—the Union left and the Confederate right.[2] Opposite Fredericksburg, on the Union right, while there was no formal truce, there was little actual hostility. Each force was waiting to see what the other would do. Burnside, after some hours of deliberation, ordered, on the afternoon of the 15th, that his whole force should recross the Rappahannock. A cold rain-storm had in the mean while set in during the night, under cover of which the passage was effected without its being suspected by the enemy. Next morning, the 16th, when the fog lifted from the valley, the whole Union force was seen across the Rappahannock; the pontoons were swung back, and the river once more separated the two armies. Burnside left nothing behind save a part of the dead in front of the stone wall, some ammunition, and 9000 muskets which had fallen from the hands of his slain and wounded.[3]

The Confederates lost about 4600 men, of whom 600 were killed and 4000 wounded. The Union loss was nearly twice and a half as great: about 1500 killed and 9000 wounded. The Confederates lost also 650 prisoners, the Federals 900,[4] besides 1200 stragglers who never rejoined their commands. In the action on the left the losses were not greatly disproportionate, that of the Federals being somewhat in excess. But on the right, in front of the stone wall, the disproportion was enormous. Of the 1800 losses in Longstreet's corps, 250 occurred in holding Fredericksburg on the 11th, and as many more in Hood's division which supported Jackson, leaving but 1300 who fell in the defense of Marye's Hill.[5] The Union loss here was fully 6500, of which probably 5000 fell before the fire of the 2000 infantry who held the stone wall. These lost not more than 500, and most of these fell while getting into position; when once behind that defense they were perfectly sheltered, except when a man exposed himself accidentally to a chance shot from a skirmisher. Two thirds of the Confederate loss at Marye's Hill was sustained by regiments posted on the surrounding slopes, and partially exposed to distant artillery fire. In the final charge, when Humphreys's division dashed with unloaded muskets toward the sunken road, and were flung back in a quarter of an hour with a loss of 1700 men, it is doubtful whether the Confederates suffered the loss of a single man killed or wounded.[6]

Severe as were the casualties of the battle, they formed a small part of the injury inflicted upon the Union army. Its morale was seriously impaired. It was clear to every man, the commanding general only excepted, that the whole plan of the campaign was thwarted. Whatever might have been the chances of its success had it been promptly executed, they were all destroyed by the fatal delay of a month. Officers in their tents, and soldiers by their bivouac fires, discussed the campaign, and declared that it was not possible even to cross the Rappahannock, much less to march to Richmond. The feeling of discouragement was universal from the private up to the commander of a grand division. Burnside alone appeared ignorant of the real condition of his army. "I do not," he said, "consider the troops demoralized, or the condition of the army impaired, except so far as it has been by the loss of so many men."[7] But his officers knew otherwise. Sumner, a week after the battle, thought the army far more demoralized than was warranted by its losses. "There is a great deal too much croaking; there is not sufficient confidence," he said; but he still thought that "within a few days, with sufficient exertion, the army will again be in excellent order."[1] But this revival of confidence never came. The tone of the army was indicated by resignations among officers and desertions among privates, which increased to an alarming extent.

Burnside meanwhile determined upon another attempt, which was in effect a repetition of the one which he had first proposed, of crossing the river some miles below Fredericksburg, and thus turning the Confederate right, wholly avoiding the strong position from which he had been so disastrously hurled. Meanwhile a cavalry force of 2500 was to cross the Rappahannock by the upper fords, and gain the rear of Lee's army; they were then to separate, a part returning by different routes, while a picked body of 1000 men, with four pieces of artillery, were to press on, passing to the south of Richmond, and joining General Peck at Suffolk, where steamers were to be in waiting to bring them back to Acquia Creek. The object of this cavalry expedition was twofold: To attract the attention of the enemy from his main movement, and to "blow up the locks on the James River Canal, the iron bridge over the Nottoway, on the Richmond and Weldon Railroad," thereby seriously interrupting the Confederate communications and sources of supply.

On the 26th of December, all the preparations for this movement were made. The place of crossing had been selected, the positions for artillery to protect the passage chosen, and orders given that three days' rations should be cooked for the whole army, while ten or twelve days' supply of food, forage, and ammunition should be provided, and the whole army be in readiness to move at twelve hours' notice. On the 30th the movement had been fairly commenced, when Burnside received a telegram from the President informing him that he had good reason to order that there should be no general movement until he had been informed of it. Burnside suspended the movement, and hastened to Washington to ascertain the reason for this order.[2]

A week before, Franklin and Smith had addressed a letter to the President, declaring that in their opinion the plan of the campaign already commenced could not be successful. It was, they said, sixty-one miles to Richmond, and for the whole distance it would be necessary to keep the communications open, and these communications were liable to be broken at many points. If the railroad was rebuilt as the army advanced, the enemy would destroy it at important points. If wagon transportation was depended upon, the trains must be so large that much of the strength of the army would be required to guard them, and the troops would be so separated by the trains blocking the road that the van and the rear could not be within supporting distance. The enemy would, moreover, be able to post himself defiantly in strong positions, whence probably the whole strength of the army would not be able to drive him; and even if he were driven away, the result would not be decisive. His losses in these strong positions would be slight, while ours would be enormous. To insure a successful campaign, it was in their judgment essential that all the troops in the East should be massed; that they should approach as near as possible to Richmond without an engagement; and that the line of communication should be absolutely free from danger of interruption. These requisites could only be secured by a campaign on the James River, and they accordingly drew up the outlines of such a campaign.[3]

While the President was deliberating upon this letter, Generals Newton and Cochrane went up to Washington, and laid before him what they considered the condition of the army. They told him that it was the general opinion of officers and men that it would be a dangerous and ruinous folly to attempt to cross the Rappahannock; that they knew they could not succeed, and would therefore be deprived of a great portion of their vigor.[4] The President thereupon gave the order prohibiting any movement of which he was not previously informed. Burnside urged that the movement should be made. The President refused his assent until he had consulted with his military advisers. The general returned to his camp, whence he wrote asking for distinct authority from Halleck to cross the river. He knew, he wrote, that there was hardly an officer holding any important command who would favor the movement, but he was confident that it should be made, and he would take the responsibility of making it upon himself; but he felt that the general-in-chief should at least sanction it. Halleck replied in general terms, laying down sundry general rules which ought to govern the management of an army, and saying that while he had always favored a forward movement, he could not take the responsibility of giving any directions as to how or when it should be made. The prohibitory order appears to have been withdrawn, for Burnside resolved to make another move upon his own responsibility, and without making any reply to this letter of Halleck.[5]

This movement was to be commenced by passing the Rappahannock

---

[1] Sumner, *Ibid.*, 659. [2] *Lee's Rep.*, ii., 438. [3] *Lee's Rep.*, i., 43.
[4] *Ibid.*, i., 43. [5] *Ibid.*, ii., 433.
[6] The Official Reports of Losses (Union, in *Com. Rep.*, 681; Confederate, in *Lee's Rep.*, ii., 433, 439) are as follows:

UNION.

	Killed.	Wounded.	Missing.	Total.
Sumner's Grand Div.	480	4159	855	5494
Hooker's " "	327	2469	748	3548
Franklin's " "	338	2430	1531	4679
Engineers' " "	7	43	100	50
	1152	9101	3234	13771

CONFEDERATE.

	Killed.	Wounded.	Missing.	Total.
Longstreet's Corps	251	1516	127	1894
Jackson's "	344	2545	526	3415
	595	4061	653	5409

This Union Report, furnished by the Medical Inspector General soon after the battle, requires some considerable emendations. Of those set down as "missing," about 1200 returned to their commands (*Halleck's Report of Operations*), reducing the missing to 2078. The Confederates claim about 900 prisoners (*Lee's Rep.*, i., 43), leaving nearly 1200 missing to be accounted for. I have no doubt that a third of these were slain outright on the field, in addition to those reported as killed. I attribute all these to the assault on the stone wall on the right, for on the left the dead and wounded were buried or removed by truce between Franklin and Jackson. It is only by making such an addition that I can explain the great disproportion between the killed and wounded on the right, as reported. The usual ratio in a close engagement is one killed to five or six wounded; here it is put down as a little more than one to ten, while all the circumstances of the fight indicate that the killed must have borne an unusual proportion to the wounded. Moreover, the Medical Inspector says, "The return of killed may be too small." I have therefore adopted these emendations into the text, increasing the killed by 450, and diminishing the missing by 1650.

As the Confederates remained in undisturbed possession of the entire field of battle, they were able to account for every man of their army. I adopt their Official Report as accurate. In *Lee's Report*, i., 33, there is a statement of the Confederate losses, making them 458 killed and 3743 wounded; and there seems to have been published a statement purporting to be Lee's Official Report, making his entire loss only 1800 killed and wounded. I find this reproduced in several histories, notably in Pollard's *Lost Cause*, p. 346, where it appears thus: "General Lee, in his official dispatch, writes, 'Our loss during the entire operations since the movements of the enemy began amounts to about 1800 killed and wounded.'" This was published fully two years after the real official report of Lee was printed by order of the Confederate Congress. I can account for this statement only by supposing that as Lee was with Longstreet's corps during the whole action, he only referred to the casualties in that corps, not including that in Jackson's corps, which were almost twice as many.

The estimate of losses at various movements, and on the different parts of the field, has been formed from a careful analysis of the reports on both sides. The absolute loss in each army was, however, much less than the reports indicate, the proportion of those wounded so slightly as not to be disabled having been unusually large on both sides. Several of the Confederate reports note this fact. The Union Medical Inspector General says (*Com. Rep.*, 681) that, of the 9101 reported as wounded, there were only 1630 whose cases required to be treated in hospitals; these, added to the 1152 reported as killed—which he thought probably too small—amounting in all to 2782, would, he was confident, "cover the whole amount of disabling casualties occurring at the battle of Fredericksburg."
[7] Testimony in *Com. Rep.*, 656.

[1] Burnside, in *Com. Rep.*, 716–718. [2] Sumner, *Ibid.*, 660.
[3] This letter is given entire in Swinton's *Army of the Potomac*, 263–265. The arguments in its favor were, that "on the James River our troops can be concentrated more rapidly than they can be at any other point; that they can be brought to points within twenty miles of Richmond without the risk of an engagement; that the communication by the James River can be kept, by the assistance of the navy, without the slightest danger of interruption." The principal features of the proposed plan were these: Concentrate 250,000 men; land 150,000 on the north, and 100,000 on the south side of the James, as near as possible to Richmond. Let both bodies advance in the lightest marching order, pontoons being ready to make a connection at any time. It was not probable that the enemy would have sufficient force to withstand the shock of two such bodies. If he declined to fight on the river, the army on the south bank should seize the railroads running from Richmond southward, while the remainder should either attack or invest the Confederate capital.
[4] Newton's Testimony, in *Com. Rep.*, 730–740; Cochrane's, *Ibid.*, 740–746. They must also have implied, if they did not express the opinion which Newton had formed (*Ibid.*, 731), "that the dissatisfaction of the troops arose from a want of confidence in General Burnside's military capacity."
[5] Burnside, in *Com. Rep.*, 718, 719.

at fords six miles above Fredericksburg, masked by a feint at crossing some miles below the town, the feint to be made in such force that it might be converted into the real attempt, if circumstances should warrant, for there were conflicting accounts of the positions of the enemy. This required that roads should be cut through forests in both directions, and corduroyed so as to be passable for artillery and trains; sites for batteries chosen and prepared, and other arrangements made. At last a trusty spy brought information which decided Burnside to make the real attempt above Fredericksburg.

It was now the 20th of January. After the friendly storm, under whose cover the Union army had safely recrossed the Rappahannock, there had ensued five weeks of serene weather. The roads were as good as the bad Virginia roads can be. Burnside gave the final order to move in a hopeful spirit. "The commanding general," he said, "announces to the Army of the Potomac that they are about to meet the enemy once more. The late brilliant actions in North Carolina, Tennessee, and Arkansas have weakened the enemy on the Rappahannock, and the auspicious moment seems to have arrived to strike a great and mortal blow to the rebellion, and to gain that decisive victory which is due to the country." The movement had been commenced the day before. The infantry of the grand divisions of Franklin and Hooker having marched up the river by parallel roads, screened from the observation of the enemy by the intervening heights, and encamped near the fords where the crossing was to be effected, while Couch's corps moved down the river to make the proposed feint, and Sigel's reserve corps, which had in the mean while been brought up, held the communications between the two wings. But the pleasant weather, upon the continuance of which every thing depended, had come to a close. Late in the afternoon a cold, fierce storm set in. The sleet, driven by a furious gale, penetrated the clothing, and cut the faces of the men as they staggered on in their weary march. In two hours every mud-hole became a little lake, and the clayey roads, unhardened by frost, were transformed into quagmires wherein the wagons sank beyond the axles, and the mules to their bellies. It seemed as though the bottom had dropped out. The storm raged all that night and the next day. There was but one man in the army who did not perceive that the movement must be a failure. That one man was Burnside. He still hoped against hope, and resolved to struggle against fate. So all day on the 21st the army staggered on in its march through the mud. Not a gun or a wagon could be moved except by doubling or trebling the teams, and often a hundred men and more pulling at a stout rope were required to drag a pontoon-wagon through the mire. By terrible exertions some were got forward, while the roads were strewed with a chaos of confusion—shipwrecked wagons, horses and mules dead and dying, pontoons and guns immovable in the mud. Still, a formidable force of all arms was got together upon the river bank at the points where the crossing was to be essayed. But before the artillery and pontoons could be put in position, the Confederates had divined every thing, and had posted their forces so as to render the possibility of even crossing the river a matter of doubt; while, had the passage been effected, any farther advance was impossible. So thought the general officers of the army; and the opinions of some of them were expressed in such a form, that Burnside perceived that either he or they must vacate their posts. He sought direction from Halleck, but vainly. Then he recalled the troops to their former positions, and the three days' mud campaign came to an end.[1]

Burnside had for weeks been aware that his entire plan of operations was denounced by some of his leading generals. While he would not charge them with any willful disobedience of orders, he thought that they manifested a want of alacrity which seriously affected the result of the operations. He now resolved to get rid of persons whom he regarded as of no use, and to make some strong examples to the army.[2] He drew up a general order dismissing from the service Hooker, the commander of a grand division, Brooks, Newton, and Cochrane, commanding army divisions, and relieving from duty Franklin, commander of a grand division, together with Smith, Sturgis, and Ferrero, commanding army divisions, and Colonel Taylor, the acting adjutant general of Sumner's grand division.[3] This sweeping order was drawn up with the knowledge of but two men besides the general, and was ordered to be issued. But one of these confidants, "a cool, sensible man, and a firm friend" of Burnside, intimated that while the order was just and should be issued, it transcended in some points the authority of the general. He could not dismiss an officer or hang a deserter without the express approval of the President; and, moreover, by publishing the order, he would force the President to take sides in the military dispute. If he sanctioned the order, his administration would incur the hostility of many influential men, friends of the dismissed officers; if he refused to sanction it after it was issued, he would appear to be the enemy of the commanding general. Still Burnside was firmly convinced he could not retain the command unless he issued the order, with the assurance that it should be sustained. He accordingly went to Washington with the order in one hand and his resignation in the other. He told the President, "If you will say to me, 'You may take the responsibility of issuing the order, and I will sustain it,' I will take that responsibility: this is the only way in which I can retain the command of the Army of the Potomac; otherwise here is my resignation; accept it, and here is the end of the matter as far as I am concerned." The President hesitated. He must consult his advisers. "If you consult any body," replied Burnside, "you will not sanction the order." And so it proved. After deliberating for a day, the President decided to relieve Burnside from the command of the Army of the Potomac, and place Hooker in command, making also some important changes in other respects, principal among which were that Sumner and Franklin should be relieved from their commands. Burnside was satisfied with this decision. "If Hooker can gain a victory," he said to the President, "neither you nor he will be a happier man than I shall be."

Burnside then supposed that his resignation would be accepted; but the President judged otherwise. "We need you," he said, "and can not accept your resignation." The truth was, that while Burnside's own opinion had proved true, that he was not fitted for the command of so large an army, he had yet shown so much capacity for a less onerous command, and had, above all, manifested such an entire absence of all selfish purposes, that the nation could not spare him. He still wished to resign; his private affairs required his attention; and, moreover, he said, if all general officers whom it was found necessary to relieve should resign, it would be better for the President, as it would relieve him from the applications of their friends. "True," replied the President; "but there is no reason for you to resign; you can have as much time as you please for your private business, but we can not accept your resignation." Several commands were proposed to him. He could have the department of South Carolina, or the departments of South and North Carolina would be combined and given to him. He declined both, because he thought these departments were then in good hands. He would remain in the army if his services were absolutely required; but, if he staid, he wished to be employed. Then came up the question as to the form in which his retirement from the command of the Army of the Potomac should be announced. An order had been drawn up at the War Department stating simply that Burnside had been relieved at his own request. To this he objected; he did not wish to appear as having voluntarily given up his command without good reason. This order did not express the real facts of the case, and he still wished to resign. The general-in-chief and the Secretary of War urged that by so doing he would injure himself and the cause. For himself, Burnside "did not care a snap," but he did not wish to injure the cause; the Department might issue just what order it chose; he would take thirty days' leave of absence, and would then come back and go wherever ordered, even if it were to command his old army corps under Hooker. So, when the official order appeared,[1] it announced that Burnside, "at his own request," had been relieved from the command of the Army of the Potomac, and Hooker assigned to the command; that Sumner, "at his own request," had been relieved from duty in this army, and that Franklin was also relieved, but without the significant addition of "at his own request."[2]

Sumner was soon after assigned to the command of the Department of Missouri; but while on his way to the West he died at Syracuse, in New York, on the 21st of March, leaving his name honorably identified with many of the severest struggles of the war. He entered the army in 1819, and had been in active service for forty-four years. He was twice breveted for gallant and meritorious conduct in the Mexican battles; then he was placed in command of the Department of New Mexico, where he directed important military operations against the turbulent tribes of savages. The opening of the civil war found him a colonel of cavalry, but with an appointment of brigadier general to command upon the Pacific coast. From this, at his own request, he was recalled to take part in the operations of the Army of the Potomac, where his services were rewarded by promotion to the rank of major general of volunteers, and, later, of major general by brevet in the regular army.

Burnside, his thirty days' leave of absence having expired, was assigned to the command of the Department of the Ohio, his own old army corps, the 9th, going with him. Subsequently, as we shall have occasion to see, he was recalled to the Army of the Potomac, acting an important part in the closing campaign of the war.

The formal transfer of the command of the Army of the Potomac from Burnside to Hooker was made on the 26th of January. Burnside, in his farewell order, said that the short time in which he had been in command "had not been fruitful in victory," but the army had shown qualities which, under more favorable circumstances, would have accomplished great results."

[1] "Before we could get the pontoons and artillery in position, the plan had been discovered by the enemy, which rendered the crossing very precarious, and the movement of artillery on the opposite bank, even if they had been got over, would have been rendered almost impossible from the state of the roads and the whole face of the country, in consequence of the storm. But a very serious objection to attempting the crossing after this occurred was the almost universal feeling among the general officers that the crossing could not be made there. Some of them gave vent to these opinions in a very public manner, even in the presence of my own staff officers, who informed me of the fact. I telegraphed to General Halleck that I would be very glad to meet him at Acquia Creek; or, if he wished it, I would run up for an hour to Washington. He sent me word that I must be my own judge about coming up. I at once telegraphed back, 'I shall not come up.' I then determined to order the commands back to their original encampments. After doing that, I went to my adjutant general's office, and issued an order which I termed General Order No. 8. That order dismissed some officers from service, subject to the approval of the President, and relieved others from duty with the Army of the Potomac."—Burnside's Testimony, in *Com. Rep.*, 719.

[2] Testimony in *Com. Rep.*, 723.

[3] GENERAL ORDER No. 8, *Jan.* 23, 1863 (Extracts): "General Joseph E. Hooker having been guilty of unjust and unnecessary criticisms of the actions of his superior officers, and of the authorities, and having, by the general tone of his conversation, endeavored to create distrust in the minds of officers who have associated with him, and having, by omissions and otherwise, made reports and statements which were calculated to create incorrect impressions, and of habitually speaking in disparaging terms of other officers, is hereby dismissed the service of the United States as a man unfit to hold an important commission during a crisis like the present." General W. T. H. Brooks was dismissed "for complaining of the policy of the government, and for using language tending to demoralize his command." Generals John Newton and John Cochrane were also dismissed "for going to the President of the United States with criticisms upon the plans of their commanding officer." These dismissals were made subject to the approval of the President. Then followed a list of officers who were "relieved from duty," it "being evident that they can be of no farther service in this army." The names on this list were Generals Franklin, commanding a grand division; Smith, commanding an army corps; Sturgis, Ferrero, and Cochrane, commanding army divisions; and Lieutenant Colonel Taylor, adjutant general of Sumner's Corps. Cochrane's name appears in both lists, as relieved absolutely by Burnside's authority, and dismissed subject to the approval of the President.

[1] Jan. 28, 1863.

[2] For the details of the transactions relating to the closing period of Burnside's command, see *Com. Rep.*, 57-60, and *Ibid.*, 716-722.

THE CAMPAIGN

IN THE MUD.

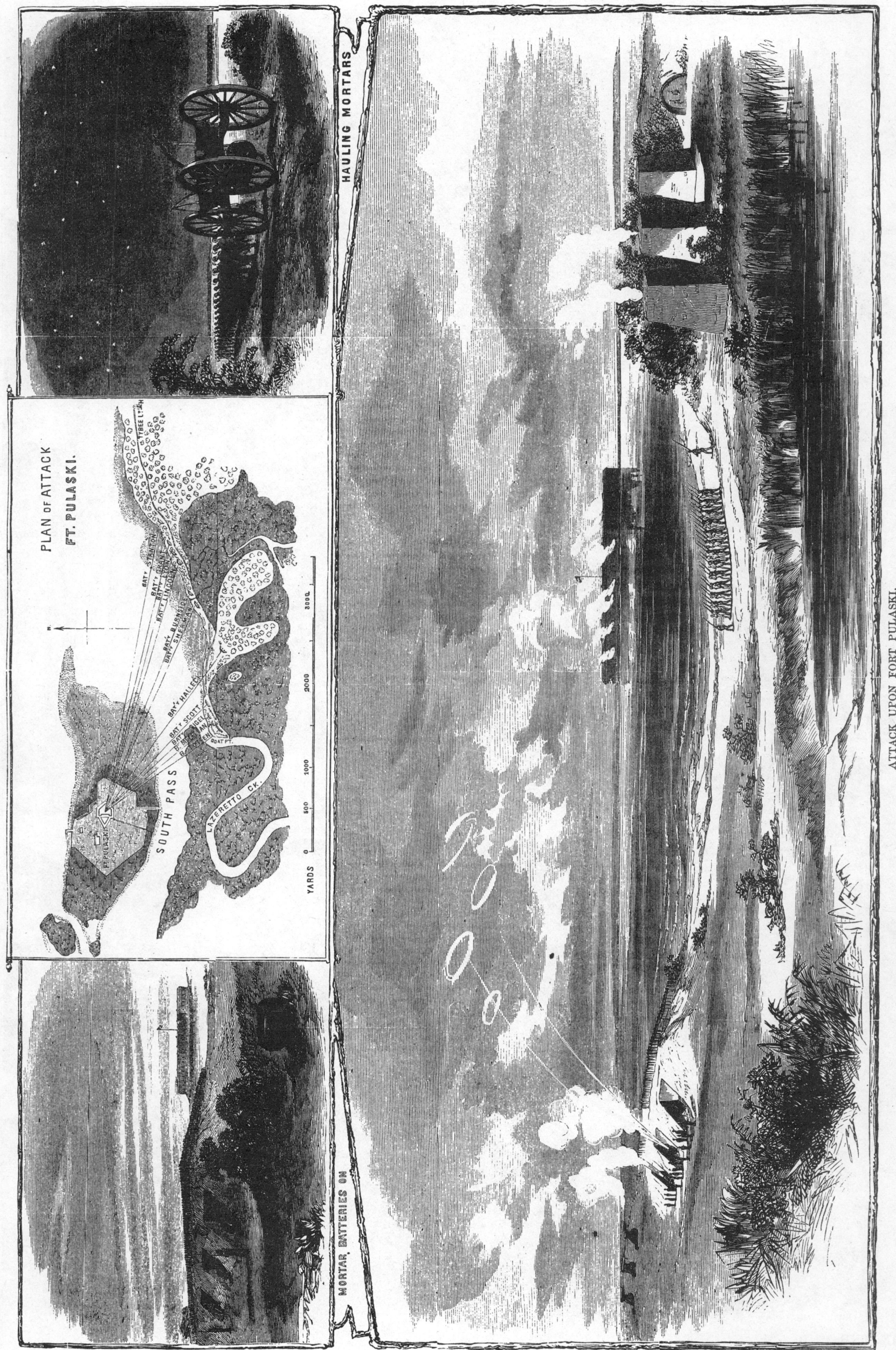

HAULING MORTARS.

MORTAR. BATTERIES ON

PLAN OF ATTACK FT. PULASKI.

ATTACK UPON FORT PULASKI.

CAPTURE OF THE HARRIET LANE.

CHAPTER XXV.

NAVAL AND COAST OPERATIONS.

The Blockade.—Capture of Fort Pulaski.—Capture of Galveston.—It is retaken by the Confederates.—Loss of the Harriet Lane and Westfield.—The Confederate Cruisers.—The Florida fitted out in England.—Runs the Blockade at Mobile.—Equipped and Escapes to Sea.—The Clarence, Tacony, and Archer.—Capture and Destruction of the Florida.—The Alabama built in England.—Escapes from Liverpool.—Takes on board Armament and Crew.—Semmes assumes Command.—His previous Career.—The Cruise of the Alabama in the North Atlantic.—Cruise in the Gulf of Mexico.—Captures the Ariel.—Destroys the Hatteras.—Cruise in the South Atlantic.—At the Cape of Good Hope.—Cruise in the Indian Ocean.—Returns to Europe.—Enters the Harbor of Cherbourg.—Destroyed by the Kearsarge.—The Results of her Depredations.—Operations in North Carolina.—Burnside recalled to the Potomac.—Foster's Expedition to Tarboro and Goldsboro.

WE have already narrated the brilliant naval exploit which insured the capture of New Orleans. The farther operations of the fleet upon the Mississippi and its tributaries will be described in their appropriate place, in connection with the military operations in the West. Vessels find their natural opponents in vessels, the cases in which they can be employed in the attack upon forts and towns being exceptional. The Confederacy being wholly destitute of a force upon the ocean, and its chief sea-ports being unassailable by a fleet, the operations of the Union fleet were mainly confined to a strict blockade of the coast, and to short expeditions up the rivers. These offensive operations were of necessity on a small scale, and though not unfrequently marked by great skill and boldness, had but little influence upon the general result of the campaign of 1862. One by one, however, the minor ports along the Atlantic and Gulf of Mexico were seized, leaving to the Confederates only Wilmington, Charleston, Savannah, and Mobile, which had been rendered unassailable by a direct naval attack. These ports came to be of great importance to the Confederates, and were not captured until their armies in the field had given up, or were about to give up, the contest.

The most important of these expeditions was that which resulted in the capture of Fort Pulaski, situated on a mud island at the mouth of the Savannah River, and commanding the approach to the city of Savannah. After a series of laborious approaches, conducted at first by General T. W. Sherman, and afterward by Hunter, who succeeded him in the command of this department, Gilmore succeeded in placing batteries bearing upon the fort, but at a distance greater than a serious bombardment of a fortification had ever been attempted. There were in all eleven batteries, mounting thirty-six mortars and heavy guns, the nearest battery being 1620 yards, almost a mile, from the fort. The batteries being placed, the surrender of Pulaski was demanded on the 10th of April. Olmstead, the Confederate commander, replied that he had been placed there to defend the fort, not to surrender it. Fire was then opened, and after a bombardment of eighteen hours the walls were thoroughly breached; and the fort, having been rendered untenable, was surrendered, with forty-seven guns, a large amount of ammunition and stores, and nearly four hundred prisoners. But Hunter had not sufficient force to warrant him in making any attempt upon the immediate defenses of the town. Savannah, therefore, remained in the possession of the Confederates until captured in December, 1864, by W. T. Sherman. But the possession of Fort Pulaski by the Federals barred all direct access to Savannah by sea, and the city became of no use to the Confederates as a port by which supplies from abroad could reach them.

Galveston, in Texas, was also a port of considerable importance to the Confederates, being the main entrepôt for the commerce of a great part of the state. In May a naval force appeared at the town and demanded its surrender, but for months no effective measures were taken to enforce the demand. At last, on the 8th of October, the town surrendered, with slight attempts at resistance, to a naval force of four steam vessels under Commodore Renshaw. Banks, who had succeeded Butler in command of this department, ordered a regiment to hold Galveston; a third of it was sent, the remainder being on its way, when the Confederate General Magruder, who had just been appointed to the chief command in Texas, formed a bold plan for the recapture of Galveston, which seems to have been most negligently guarded.

The plan was carried into effect before dawn on New Year's day, 1863. Galveston stood upon a long, narrow island in the bay, connected with the main land by a bridge two miles long, built upon piles. This bridge was not destroyed, and formed a ready means of approach. The town was occupied by less than three hundred men, without artillery, the naval force being supposed to be sufficient to hold it. This consisted of eight vessels, of which only two, the Westfield and the Harriet Lane, were in serviceable condition. The former, of 1000 tons, had been one of Porter's mortar fleet in the Mississippi; the latter, of 500 tons, had been built for the revenue service, of which it was the show vessel. The three infantry companies, numbering less than three hundred men, were encamped upon a wharf, a quarter of a mile from the market-place. The Westfield and the Harriet Lane were stationed in different channels down the bay, the other vessels being opposite the town. Magruder had collected a land force of five or six regiments, and several vessels. Two of these, the Neptune and the Bayou City, were protected by cotton bales piled twenty feet high upon the low decks, so that from a distance they looked like common cotton transports: they were manned by two or three hundred sharp-shooters. Coming down the bay, they were perceived in the moonlight from the Harriet Lane, which steamed up to meet them. Meanwhile the land force of Magruder had swarmed across the long bridge, and in overwhelming numbers assailed the three Federal companies on the wharf; aided by the fire from the weak vessels, these held their ground for a while. As day was dawning, the Harriet Lane, steaming up the bay, encountered the Neptune and the Bayou City, the Confederate steamers striking the Federal vessel almost simultaneously on each side. The Neptune was disabled by the shock, and grounded in shoal water; the Bayou City, turning, ran again into the Harriet Lane and grappled with her. A sharp fire was then poured from both vessels into the Harriet Lane from riflemen thoroughly protected by the barricades of cotton bales; the men were driven from their guns, and the Lane was carried by boarding, her commander, Wainwright, being killed in the mêlée. This fine vessel fell into the hands of the Confederates almost uninjured, all her crew being made prisoners.

Meanwhile the Westfield had got under way, and was steaming up to the scene of conflict, when she grounded fast upon the bar, within full range of

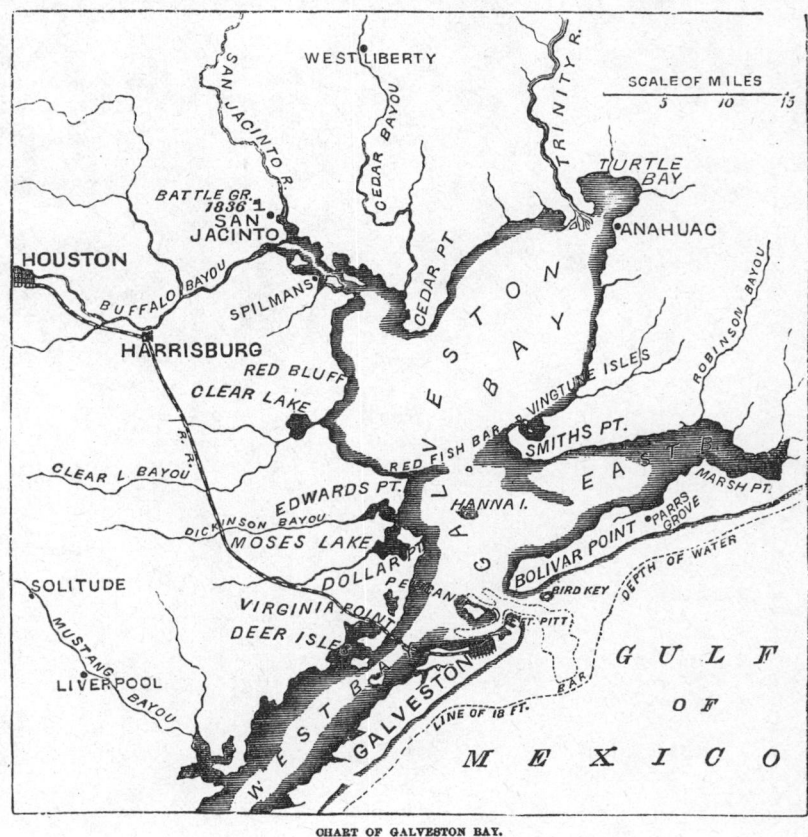

CHART OF GALVESTON BAY.

DESTRUCTION OF THE WESTFIELD.

batteries which the Confederates had established upon the shore. The other Federal gun-boats vainly endeavored to drag her off. Renshaw, perceiving that it was impossible to save his ship, resolved to destroy her, the crew to escape in boats to the transports lying hard by. A barrel of turpentine was unheaded, ready to be set ablaze as soon as the crew were free from the vessel. Nearly all had been taken to the other steamers near by, and Renshaw, who was the last to leave, was just stepping into his boat, in which were several persons, while another, loaded to the water's edge, was putting off. By some accident the turpentine was prematurely fired; the flames spread instantly to the forward magazine, and the vessel blew up, destroying the two boats and all on board.

Meanwhile an action had been going on upon the shore. The three companies of infantry, aided by the fire of the gun-boats, repelled the attack of the Confederate regiments. But the boats were at length withdrawn to attempt to aid the Westfield. The infantry, wholly destitute of artillery, and now commanded by Confederate batteries, had no alternative but to surrender at discretion.

The immediate results of this daring enterprise were that, with the loss of 26 killed and 117 wounded, the Confederates captured the Harriet Lane, wholly uninjured, two coal-barges which were lying at the wharf, destroyed the Westfield, and secured nearly 400 prisoners. But the indirect results were still more important. The whole State of Texas came into their almost undisturbed possession, and furnished many facilities for running the blockade. This was done principally by small schooners, which took out cotton and brought back munitions of war. The supplies thus acquired were of incalculable advantage to the Confederate government during the remainder of the war.

The successful career of the Sumter had demonstrated to the Confederate government the injury which might be inflicted upon the commerce of the Union by even a few vessels of a more efficient class. The resignation of more than two hundred officers of the Federal navy gave the Confederates an abundance of skillful officers; but, having no facilities at home for constructing vessels adapted for service upon the ocean, they were obliged to have recourse to foreign builders. The ship-yards of Great Britain were open to them. The first efficient cruiser which sailed under their flag was built at Birkenhead, near Liverpool, ostensibly for the Italian government.[1] In spite of the remonstrance of the American minister, she was suffered by the British government to put to sea under the British flag, bearing the name of the Oreto. After a brief detention at Nassau she was released, and, proceeding to a little island in the Bahama group, received on board her armament, which had been brought to the place of rendezvous in a British vessel, and in August, 1862, appeared off the harbor of Mobile, still carrying British colors. Commodore Preble, who commanded the blockading fleet, hesitated to fire upon her, supposing that she must be what she professed, a British man-of-war. When he discovered his mistake, it was too late; she had got beyond effective range, and steamed up the bay to Mobile. Here she remained until January, 1863, and then, her name having been changed to the Florida, she was placed under the command of John N. Maffitt, once an officer in the American navy; she escaped the blockading fleet under cover of night. The first day of her cruise she made her first prize, which was pillaged and burned. In three months the Florida captured fifteen merchantmen in the Gulf of Mexico, all of which were burned except two, which were armed, manned, and converted into Confederate privateers.

One of these, the brig Clarence, was placed under the command of Lieutenant C. W. Read, not long before a midshipman in the Federal navy, who steered northward, and made several prizes, among which was the bark Tacony, a swifter vessel than his own. Transferring his armament and crew to this, he passed up the coast as far as Massachusetts Bay, making a score of prizes. Learning that cruisers were on his track, he again shifted his guns and crew into his last prize, the Archer, burned the Tacony, and steered for Portland, Maine, where he learned that the steam revenue cutter Cushing was lying. Anchoring openly and unsuspected at the mouth of the harbor, when night fell on the 24th of June he sent two boats, fully armed, up to the city. They succeeded in capturing the Cushing and taking her out to sea. But two merchant steamers were hastily manned by volunteers, and overtook the Cushing. The captors abandoned the cutter, blew her up, and took to their boats and made for the Archer. But the pursuing steamers were too quick; they picked up the boats, overhauled the Archer, and brought her crew back to Portland as prisoners.

Meanwhile the Florida, after cruising among the West India Islands until August, steamed across the Atlantic, and on the 4th of September entered the French harbor of Brest, where she was detained a few days by the French authorities. Released from detention, she recrossed the Atlantic, cruising along the South American coast for months, but making few prizes, for the American flag had by this time been almost driven from the ocean. At length, in October, 1864, the Florida entered the Brazilian harbor of Bahia. Here she was found by the Federal steamer Wachusett, Captain Collins. Relying upon the safeguard of a neutral harbor, Morris, who now commanded the Florida, was quite at ease. Half his crew were allowed to go on shore. Collins determined to cut matters short by seizing the Florida; this was done with scarcely a show of resistance, and the Wachusett, with the prize, steamed homeward; but, coming into Hampton Roads, the Florida was run into by a United States vessel, probably designedly, and sunk. This capture was certainly made in violation of the neutral rights of Brazil. The Brazilian government put in a formal remonstrance; the

BAHIA, BRAZIL.

justice of this was conceded so far as the special act was concerned. The American government disavowed the capture, suspended Collins from command, and ordered the prisoners to be released, but at the same time took care to enter a counter complaint against the Brazilians for harboring Confederate "piratical ships." The Brazilian government protested, apparently, as a mere matter of form, and was satisfied with the course of our government; and the overthrow of the Confederate cause, which took place while negotiations were pending, removed all occasion for pressing farther the complaint against Brazil.

Of still greater importance to the Confederate cause was the Alabama, whose active career as a cruiser began some months earlier than that of the Florida. Among the great English shipbuilders was John Laird, a member of the British House of Commons. The war had just fairly commenced when he contracted with the Confederate government to build for it a steamer which should combine all the qualities of a formidable cruiser. She was to have sufficient strength, and be provided with an armament which would render her adequate to cope with any of the largest vessels in the American navy, while her speed should enable her to escape any superior enemy which she would be likely to encounter.

While this steamer, then known simply as the "290," lay upon the stocks, her destination was notorious; but the British officials would not, and the American minister could not, furnish evidence which the government judged sufficient to warrant its interference. At length, after she was launched and ready for sea, evidence was procured which eminent British counsel pronounced sufficient to require her detention.[1] For a week no action was taken by the British government. The Queen's Advocate had been seized with sudden illness, and could not attend to business, and other counsel had to be consulted. Their opinion was in favor of detention, and orders to that effect were sent by mail to Liverpool;[2] but the Confederate agents in London learned of this, and notified their friends in Liverpool by telegraph. No time was to be lost in forestalling the arrival of the order, and on the morning of the 29th of July the "290" dropped slowly down the Mersey, under pretense of a simple trial trip.[3] "To give color to this pretense, to which her even then unfinished condition lent a *primâ facie* sanction, a gay party was assembled on board." There were women, friends and acquaintances of the builder, and their accompanying gallants. Luncheon and all the appliances of naval hospitality were provided. But in the midst of the feasting, at a signal from the "290," a small steam-tug came alongside, and the astonished guests were requested to step on board. All that evening and the next day the bustle of preparation went on, and, two hours before dawn, the "290" started on her seaward voyage, bound for Nassau, in the Bahamas, as her crew supposed, but really for another port. She was away just in time, for the gold-laced custom-house officials were then coming down the river with the tardy order for her detention, and, moreover, the American steam frigate Tuscarora was hurrying—only two days too late—to the mouth of the Mersey to intercept the Confederate cruiser, as yet wholly unarmed.

The real destination of the "290" was the harbor of Porto Praya, in the Portuguese island of Terceira, where she was to meet another British vessel laden with the armament which was to form her equipment as a vessel of war. She had sailed under the command of Captain Bullock, who had superintended her construction; but when the farthermost British land was passed Bullock went ashore, and his place was taken by an Englishman,

[1] "Our collector at Liverpool states that he has every reason to believe that the vessel is for the Italian government."—Earl Russell to Mr. Adams, Feb. 22, 1862.

[1] "*Temple, July 23, 1862.*—I am of opinion that the Collector of Customs would be justified in detaining the vessel. Indeed, I should think it his duty to detain her; and that if, after the application which has been made to him, supported by the evidence which has been laid before me, he allows the vessel to leave Liverpool, he will incur a heavy responsibility—a responsibility in which the Board of Customs, under whose directions he appears to be acting, must take their share. It appears to be difficult to make out a stronger case of infringement of the Foreign Enlistment Act, which, if not enforced on this occasion, is little better than a dead letter. It well deserves consideration whether, if the vessel be allowed to escape, the Federal government would not have serious grounds of complaint."—R. P. COLLIER, Q. C.
[2] Diplomatic Correspondence, 1862-3, i., 163.
[3] "The Cruise of the Alabama, and the Sumter." This work is made up mainly from the journals of Semmes, and was evidently drawn up under his supervision. This has been followed almost exclusively in the following account, all quotations, unless otherwise expressly credited, being taken from it, although it has not been thought necessary, in all cases, to cite the pages. The work will be cited simply as "Semmes."

RAPHAEL SEMMES.

"Captain J. Butcher, late of the Cunard service. Of the other temporary officers, three out of five were Englishmen." The crew numbered about seventy men and boys, and were shipped for a feigned voyage, the Confederate captain "trusting to the English love of adventure to induce them to re-ship when the true destination of the vessel came to be declared."[1] In nine days the "290" reached Porto Praya. Soon after arrived a British vessel, the Agrippina, with coal, ammunition, and guns, and, not long after, still another British vessel from Liverpool, having on board "a number of seamen, shipped, like those on board the "290," for a feigned voyage, in the hope of inducing them to join when the ship was fairly in commission."[2] In this vessel also came Raphael Semmes, who had been appointed to command the "290" when, under a new name, she was to appear upon the ocean as a Confederate cruiser.

Semmes, now about fifty years of age, was a native of the State of Maryland. He had entered the American navy thirty years before. At the outbreak of the war he had attained the rank of commander in the navy, was a member of the Light-house Board, and resided at Washington. He wrote to Stephens, of Georgia, indicating his willingness to fight for the South, but did not wish to thrust himself upon the new government "until his State had moved." On the 14th of February, 1861, he received a telegraphic dispatch from the Chairman of the Naval Committee at Montgomery inviting him to repair to that place. Then, and not before, he sent in his resignation from the United States navy, and telegraphed back to Montgomery that he was "a free man to serve his struggling country." He had before this taken occasion to write to an Alabama Congressman, giving his views "of the situation of the Confederates, as regards their marine, for defense and means of inflicting damage on their opponents." Leaving his family at Washington, Semmes repaired to Montgomery, where he was soon dispatched to the Northern States to make "large purchases, and contracts for machinery and munitions, or for the manufacture of arms and munitions of war." The Confederate Secretary of the Navy had learned that there were for sale, "at or near New York, two or more steamers of speed, light draught, and strength sufficient for at least one heavy gun." In April Semmes was recalled to New Orleans, and placed in command of the Sumter,[3] whose career as a cruiser has already been narrated.

On the 24th of August, the "290," still under British colors, had received her armament, and was thus transformed into a man-of-war, and steamed out of the neutral port. When fairly a maritime league from land, and thus, according to international law, in the open sea, the common domain of all nations, Semmes, in full uniform, appeared on deck, and announced that the vessel was henceforth the Confederate States steam-ship Alabama. At the instant down came the British flag, and in its place appeared that of the Confederacy. The new commander made a speech to the men who had been entrapped on board under false pretenses, urging them to enlist with him, telling them that the main purpose of the cruise was to prey upon American commerce, which would give them abundance of prize money. The crew were a motley gang, all British, swept up "from the groggeries of Liverpool," in the belief that they were shipping in a sort of privateer, where they would have a jolly good time and a plenty of license.[4] "The

modern sailor," says Semmes, "has greatly changed in character. He now strikes for pay like a sharper." Semmes was glad to hire them upon their own terms. "I was afraid," he says, "that a large bounty in addition would be demanded of me."[1]

On the 29th of August the Alabama was fairly in trim to begin her cruise. The battle of Groveton was at that hour being fought, and the result hung in even scales. The Alabama had now assumed her true character. She was a wooden screw steam sloop, bark-rigged, of 1040 tons burden, provided with two engines of great power, pierced for twelve guns on deck, with two heavy guns amidships; her whole cost for building and equipment was a quarter of a million of dollars.[2] To man her fully required at least one hundred men; Semmes had only eighty, but he trusted that he could fill up the complement by volunteers from the prizes which he should make.[3]

The Alabama now steered straight for the great highway of commerce between Europe and America. This was reached in a week, and on the 5th of September she made her first capture. On that day the Confederate army crossed the Potomac into Maryland. "This vessel," notes Semmes in his journal, "was of course taken possession of, her crew brought on board the Alabama and placed in irons, and a quantity of rigging and small-stores transferred to the captor. Next morning the prize was fired, the Alabama having taken from her thirty-six prisoners."[4] The Alabama was now in the track of commerce, and within the next ten days captured half a score of vessels. The journal of Semmes describes the disposition made of some of them:

September 7. Captured the Starlight, from Fayal to Boston, with a number of passengers, among others some ladies. "Brought on board all the United States seamen, seven in number, including the captain, and confined them in irons." *September* 9. Several additional prizes having been made, "about 9 A.M. fired the Starlight; at 11, fired the Ocean Rover; and at 4 P.M., fired the Alert." *September* 14. "Captured a whaler, the Benjamin Tucker, from New Bedford, eight months out, with about 340 barrels of oil; crew thirty. Brought every body on board, received some soap and tobacco, and fired the ship." *September* 16. Captured another whaler; stood off to Flores; when within four or five miles, sent all the prisoners, sixty-eight in number, ashore in boats, and then, "having taken the prize some eight or ten miles distant from land, hove her to, called all hands to quarters, and made a target of her. The practice was pretty fair for green hands. At dark fired the prize." After this burst of good fortune there was a lull of a fortnight. The Alabama was crowded with prisoners taken within the last few days. "These," says Semmes, "were hard times for the prisoners, crowded together on deck, with no shelter but an extemporized tarpaulin tent between them and the pelting of the pitiless storm, which drenched the decks alternately with salt water and fresh."[5]

October passed, and at its close the Alabama, having in the mean time made twenty-seven captures, was off the American coast, hardly two hundred miles from New York. Semmes had hoped to lie off the harbor, and make some prizes at its very mouth; but his fuel was now running short, and he was obliged to run southeastward to the island where coal was to await him. On the 18th of November the Alabama made the French island of Martinique. Here she fell into sore peril, for the American steamer San Jacinto, of superior force, appeared off the harbor, and instituted a close blockade. But the Alabama managed to elude her antagonist under cover of darkness, and gained the coal rendezvous at the island of Blanquilla.

In the latter days of November the Alabama had got on board coal sufficient for nearly three weeks' steaming, and was ready for a fresh cruise. She made for the West India Islands, hoping to be able to intercept one of the treasure-ships conveying gold from the Isthmus to New York. A million of dollars in gold was a prize worth waiting for. On Sunday, December 7, a prize came within sight, though not the one which had been hoped for. A huge side-wheel steamer hove in view, pressing southward. It could be only a California steamer, bound southward, not northward; toward the Isthmus with passengers, not from it with gold. The Alabama shot from her lurking-place, and made way to cross the track of the stranger, who bore the Union flag. The Alabama, now carrying the same, was evidently taken for an American vessel. But as the steamers came within gun-shot, the stars and stripes fell from the Alabama, and the Confederate flag took their place, while a blank shot demanded a surrender. The warning was not heeded; the chase held on her way with full press of steam. But a shell from the Alabama, striking the foremast, showed that she was within the power of her enemy, and, abandoning all effort to escape, she rounded to and surrendered. The prize proved to be the Ariel, a California steamer bound from New York to the Isthmus, having on board 500 passengers, besides 140 Federal marines, on their way to join the Pacific squadron.

The Alabama was embarrassed by the magnitude of her prize. There was much which was of use: three boxes of specie, a 24-pound rifled gun, a few rifles and swords, and a thousand rounds of ammunition. The Ariel also would make a bonfire as brilliant as any of the twoscore with which Semmes had already illuminated the ocean. But this could not be lighted until the hundreds of prisoners were disposed of. The narrow deck of the Alabama could not give even standing-room for half of them. Semmes kept his prize by him for a couple of days, hoping to fall in with a homeward-bound California steamer, to which he would transfer his crowd of prisoners, and then burn the Ariel; but none appearing, he determined to take her toward Kingston, Jamaica, land the prisoners in boats, and then burn the ship. But, learning that the yellow fever was raging at Kingston, and unwilling to put a crowd of men, women, and children ashore in a

---

[1] Semmes, i., 277.   [2] Ibid., i., 283.   [3] Ibid., i., 1-8.   [4] Ibid., ii., 33.   [1] Semmes, i., 297.   [2] Ibid., i., 266.   [3] Ibid., i., 298.   [4] Ibid., i., 306.   [5] Ibid., i., 305, 320.

HOMER C. BLAKE.

plague-stricken port, he had no alternative but to release the Ariel upon bond, and "forego the pleasure of making a bonfire of the splendid steamer that had fallen into his hands."

The Alabama was still cruising among the West India Islands when intelligence came that Banks was about to dispatch a great naval and military expedition from New Orleans to the coast of Texas, Galveston being its immediate destination. Semmes was aware that this expedition "would be accompanied by one or more armed vessels, but the principal portion would be composed of troop-ships crowded with the enemy's soldiers; and should the Alabama but prove victorious in the fight, these transports would be of more practical importance than all the grain and oil ever carried in a merchantman's hold."[1] At noon on the 11th of January the Alabama was off Galveston, ignorant that the place had been recaptured by the Confederates, and the proposed Banks expedition delayed. Several vessels were seen lying off the bar. One of these, the gun-boat Hatteras, catching a glimpse of the Alabama on the distant horizon, stood out to reconnoitre. The Alabama edged slowly seaward, in order to draw this vessel away from her consorts, so that in case of a conflict the noise of the guns would not reach them. The rate at which the Hatteras had approached showed that she was in speed no match for the Alabama, which could thus escape if she perceived that she was overmatched in strength. Just after dark the Hatteras came within hailing distance, and from her deck came the inquiry, "What ship is that?" "Her majesty's ship Petrel. What ship is that?" was the reply from the Alabama. "I will send a boat aboard," was answered by Lieutenant Blake, the commander of the Hatteras, who gave orders accordingly, and the boat was lowered and put off. Up to this moment the commander of the Hatteras must have supposed that the Alabama was what she proclaimed herself, a British vessel, for he would have scarcely sent a boat on board what he believed to be an armed enemy. Hardly had the boat left the side of the Hatteras when a new hail, "We are the Confederate steamer Alabama," was heard, accompanied by the whizzing of a shell over the deck, followed by a full broadside. The Hatteras returned the fire, and endeavored to close, hoping to carry the enemy by boarding. But the greater speed of the Alabama enabled her to thwart the attempt, while her superior armament placed her opponent at her mercy. The only chance for the Hatteras was that a shot might strike some vulnerable point of the Alabama. In a few minutes a shell from the Alabama entered the hold of the Hatteras amidships; almost at the same instant another passed through the sick-bay, and exploded, both setting the vessel on fire, while another destroyed the steam cylinder, disabling the engine, and rendering the Hatteras wholly unmanageable. On fire in two places, utterly disabled, a mere wreck upon the water, there was nothing for Blake to do but to fire a lee gun in token of surrender, and to ask for assistance for his crew. The action had lasted only thirteen minutes, and the Hatteras was rapidly sinking. The boats from both vessels were employed in conveying the crew of the vanquished to the deck of the victor. Two minutes after the last man had left the Hatteras she went down, bow first, with her pennant at the masthead, carrying with her every thing but the living men. The Alabama suffered some injury, but not sufficient to cripple her, and had two men slightly wounded. On the Hatteras two were killed and five wounded; the boat's crew which had put off just before the action rowed back to the shore, only twenty miles distant; all the others, more than a hundred, were made prisoners, and carried to Kingston, where they were put ashore.

For two months the Alabama cruised among the West India Islands, and then, about the middle of March,[2] went southward along the coast, reaching Bahia, in Brazil, by the middle of May, making many prizes all the while. Here she found the Georgia, another Anglo-Confederate cruiser; took in coal, and, after being repeatedly warned by the Brazilian authorities that her stay was not desired, steamed away across the South Atlantic for the coast of Africa, making port near Cape Town on the 5th of August. She hovered in these waters for more than a month. Coming into the harbor of Simon's Town on the 16th of December, she found evil tidings: Vicksburg and Port Hudson had fallen; Lee, foiled at Gettysburg, had recrossed the Potomac into Virginia. "Our poor people," he writes, "seem to be terribly pressed by the Northern hordes; but we shall fight it out to the end, and the end will be what an all-wise Providence decrees." But, what was still worse for the Alabama, the Union steamer Vanderbilt, of superior force, which had been sent to look for the Alabama, was in the neighborhood. She had left the very harbor where the Alabama was, only five days before, and might return at any moment. The Confederate cruiser must go to another cruising ground. The Malay Archipelago was chosen, and, after a fortnight's run through heavy gales, the voyage of 3000 miles was accomplished early in November. But the American war-steamer Wyoming was in these waters, and the Alabama must be wary in encountering an adversary of superior force. The cruise among the intricate channels of the Indian Archipelago lasted three months. Few prizes were taken, for the American flag had almost disappeared from these waters. On the 13th of January[3] the Alabama set her head homeward, toward Great Britain, by

way of the Cape of Good Hope. The Cape was reached, after a rough voyage, on the 11th of March. Here Semmes got into a controversy with the governor for a breach of neutrality in bringing a prize into that port. The case was decided against him, and, entering a protest against the "unfriendly disposition of a government from which, if it represents truly the instincts of Englishmen, the Confederates had a right to expect at least sympathy and kindness in the place of rigor and harshness,"[1] he turned the head of the Alabama toward Europe on the 25th of March. For a month not a single vessel was encountered. On the 22d of April "the guano-laden ship Rockingham was boarded, taken possession of, employed as a target, and then set fire to." Five days after, the Tycoon shared the same fate. This was the last prize taken by the Alabama. Nineteen other vessels were overhauled before the cruiser, a fortnight after, entered the French harbor of Cherbourg, but not one of them sailed under the American flag.

The Alabama entered Cherbourg on the 11th of June,[2] and began to make some repairs, of which she stood in need after her long cruise. Three days after, the American steam-sloop Kearsarge, Captain Winslow, which had been cruising in the British Channel, looking out for several vessels apparently designed for the Confederate service, appeared off Cherbourg. The vessels were as nearly as possible equal in size and armament. Semmes, who wished to signalize himself by some exploit other than the burning of helpless merchantmen, requested Winslow to remain off the port for a day or two, when he would come out beyond neutral waters and give battle. Winslow, nowise loth to fight, complied with the request, and lay off the port. On the 19th the Alabama came out, escorted to the limit of the neutral waters by the French iron-clad Couronne. Following close after, fortunately as it happened for the Confederates, was an English steam yacht, the Deerhound, whose owner, Lancaster, wished to treat his family to the sight of a naval duel. When the neutral marine league was fairly passed, the Couronne turned back, leaving the expectant combatants to themselves. The Kearsarge edged slowly off as the Alabama advanced, wishing to make sure that the action should take place so far off shore that there should be no question about the line of national jurisdiction. The distance of seven miles from land having been gained, the Kearsarge turned, and steered straight for the enemy. The Alabama opened fire at the distance of a mile, repeating her broadsides three times. The shot passed harmlessly through the rigging of the Kearsarge, which kept head on toward the Alabama. At nine hundred yards the Kearsarge sheered round and delivered her broadside. This broadside told fearfully. Then, fearing that the Alabama would make for the shore, and take shelter in French waters, Winslow put his vessel to full speed, designing to run under the stern of the Alabama and deliver a raking fire. To counteract this, the Alabama also sheered, presenting her broadside instead of her stern. Both vessels being under full steam, the Alabama, in order to keep her broadside toward her enemy, and at the same time to avoid coming into close action, was forced to describe a series of circles around the Kearsarge, whose object was to come into close action. The Kearsarge, whose object was to gain a raking position, followed the course of the Alabama, and the combined result was that the two vessels

[1] Semmes, ii., 435.   [2] 1864.

JOHN A. WINSLOW.

[1] Semmes, ii., 42.   [2] 1863.   [3] 1864.

DESTRUCTION OF THE ALABAMA.

described a series of circles around each other; but the Kearsarge, having a slight advantage in speed, was able to diminish the orbit. The action lasted an hour. From the first the superiority of the aim of the Kearsarge had been apparent. At the seventh revolution around the shifting common axis, the Alabama perceived that victory was hopeless, and she headed for the shore, five miles distant. If she could accomplish but two of these, she would be within French waters.[1] But the attempt at retreat came too late.

The Alabama was disabled, and the Kearsarge, steaming ahead, took a raking position across her bows. The white flag of surrender was raised; a boat from the Alabama came alongside, bearing an officer, who said that the Alabama had surrendered, and was fast sinking. The boats of the Kearsarge were lowered to save the drowning enemy. The British Deerhound also approached, and was requested by Winslow to aid in the rescue of those who had now become his prisoners. The Alabama was going down; the officers and crew took to the water. Forty of them, among whom was the captain, were picked up by the Deerhound and carried to England; a dozen were saved by French pilot-boats and taken to Cherbourg; seventy

[1] It has been asserted that both commanders wished to fight the action at short range. The compiler of the Confederate account says (*Semmes*, ii., 290): "Captain Semmes had great confidence in the power of his Blakeley [7-inch] rifled gun. He wished to get within easy range of his enemy, that he might try this weapon effectively; but any attempt on his part to come to closer quarters was construed by the Kearsarge as a design to bring the engagement between the ships to a hand-to-hand conflict between the men. Having the speed, she chose her distance, and made all thoughts of boarding hopeless. It was part of the plan of Captain Semmes to board, if possible, at some period of the day, supposing that he could not quickly decide the question with artillery. It was evidently Captain Winslow's determination to avoid the old-fashioned form of a naval encounter, and to fight altogether in the new style; his superior steam power gave him the option."—Captain Winslow, on the other hand, says: "It was soon apparent that Captain Semmes did not seek close action. I became then fearful lest, after some fighting, that he would again make for the shore. To defeat this, I determined to keep full speed on, and with a port helm to run under the stern of the Alabama, and rake, if he did not prevent it by sheering and keeping his broadside to us. We adopted this mode as a preventive, and, as a consequence, the Alabama was forced, with a full head of steam, into a circular track during the engagement. The effect of this manœuvre was such that, at the last of the action, when the Alabama would have made off, she was near five miles from the shore; and had the action continued from the first in parallel lines, with her head in-shore, the line of jurisdiction would no doubt have been reached. . . . . I had endeavored to close in with the Alabama, but it was not until just before the close of the action that we were in a position to use grape; this was avoided, however, by her surrender. . . . . Nearly every shot told fearfully on the Alabama, and on the seventh rotation on the circular track she winded, setting fore-trysail and two jibs, with head in-shore."—Nothing can be more clear than that neither commander expected to decide the fight by the "old-fashioned form" of boarding. Such was the character of each vessel, and the armament of the other, that long before they could have come side by side, one or both must have been disabled. Each knew the armament of the other, and each considered his own to be superior.

A NIGHT ENCAMPMENT.

ocean. But Semmes wished to signalize himself by something more than the capture of defenseless merchantmen, and knowing that the ships were "equally matched,"[1] he challenged the Kearsarge to the contest. It was supposed that Semmes would soon be again at sea in command of a still more powerful vessel than the one which he had lost. This was iron-clad, and was almost completed by the builders of the Alabama; but the British government had now perceived the danger into which they were rushing by their interpretation of the neutrality laws, and took possession of the ship. Semmes, after a while, made his way to the Confederacy, and received the nominal rank of brigadier general in the army, and as such was, a year after, included in the surrender of Johnson's army.

The brilliant success which attended the early operations of Burnside at the commencement of the year has been already recorded.[2] The successive captures of Roanoke Island, Newbern, Elizabeth City, Fort Macon, and Beaufort, gave the Union forces command of the greater part of the coast of North Carolina, and of the Sound by which it is bordered. Wilmington, and the intricate approaches which lead to it, remained to the Confederates, and afforded facilities for running the blockade. It was supposed that these successes would be followed up by a march into the heart of the state, which would seize the lines of railroad connecting the far South with Richmond. But Burnside's force of 15,000 was insufficient for such an enterprise, and the exigencies of the campaign in Virginia left the Federal government no troops by which he could be re-enforced. The most that Burnside could do was to hold the points on and near the coasts which he had seized. When McClellan retreated from the Chickahominy to the James, Burnside was ordered to bring to Fortress Monroe all the troops which he could collect,[3] leaving Foster with just enough to garrison Newbern, Beaufort, and a few other points. The Confederates also brought all their available force from North Carolina to Virginia; so that, during the summer and early autumn, there was little fighting in North Carolina.

When Lee's invasion of Maryland had failed, and the Union and Confederate armies lay confronting each other on the Rappahannock, considerable re-enforcements were dispatched to Foster in North Carolina, so that he was able to assume the offensive. Early in November he pushed an expedition inland toward Tarboro, where he had learned that there were a few regiments of the enemy; but, finding that they had been largely re-enforced, he retreated. In December he planned a still more important enterprise, the main object being to reach Goldsboro, and destroy the railroads centering at that point. The Confederates meanwhile had strengthened their force in the Department of North Carolina. In November they had but 9000 men, of whom 6000 were reported as present for duty. By December these numbers were fully doubled, and Gustavus W. Smith was placed in command. After the wounding of Johnston at Fair Oaks, Smith had been placed in command of the army before Richmond. He had held it hardly for a day when he was struck down by an attack of paralysis, and Lee was appointed in his place. Foster left Newbern with his entire movable force,[4] about 10,000 strong, and encountered no serious opposition until he reached Kingston, half way between Newbern and Goldsboro. Here a sharp fight occurred,[5] the Confederates retreating. Foster pressed on toward Goldsboro,

were rescued by the Kearsarge. Of the crew of the Alabama seven were killed in the fight; nineteen, most of whom were wounded, went down with the vessel. On board the Kearsarge there were three wounded, one mortally.

The life of the Alabama had been two years lacking nine weeks, counting from Sunday, August 24, 1862, when she first hoisted the Confederate flag, down to Sunday, June 19, 1864, when she was sunk, leaving not a wrack behind. No one ship that ever floated ever inflicted such injury upon an enemy. In all, she had captured sixty-five vessels, burning all except the few required to save the lives of her prisoners. She had destroyed vessels and cargoes valued at ten millions of dollars, and, what was of more injury to the enemy, had well-nigh driven the American commercial flag from the ocean. She was to all intents a British vessel, built at a British dock, manned by a British crew, and sailing almost always under the British flag. Her keel was never wet in Confederate waters, and no man from her deck ever caught a glimpse of the shores claimed by the Confederates; and she rarely hoisted the Confederate flag, except when, having decoyed a prize by the show of false colors, she raised her own in the act of making a prize. Her long impunity from capture is not a matter for wonder. The whole wide ocean was her hiding-place. A hundred vessels might be in search of her, and it would be a matter of chance if one would encounter her. If heard from to-day at any point, to-morrow she would be hundreds of miles away, in what direction no man not on board of her could know. "Her stay in any neutral harbor was necessarily as short as the perching of a hawk on a bough. Like the hawk's in upper air, the Alabama's safety, as well as her business, was on the high seas."[1] At the very last, it was a mere matter of accident that the Kearsarge was at hand when the Alabama appeared at Cherbourg. No one supposed that she was then on this side of the globe. The last that had been heard of her she was in the Indian Ocean. Even at Cherbourg she might have declined to enter into combat with the Kearsarge. Safe while she remained in the neutral harbor, she might have waited her time, as she had done at Martinique, when watched by the San Jacinto, and again, fitted for sea, have crept out into the wide

[1] Semmes, ii., 280.

[1] Ibid., ii., 278. [2] Ante, pp. 242–249. [3] July 4, 1862. [4] Dec. 11. [5] Dec. 14.

BATTLE OF KINGSTON, DECEMBER 14.

ACTION AT WHITEHALL, DECEMBER 16.

hoping to strike the railroad. On the 16th he reached Whitehall, where a brisk skirmish ensued; the Confederates were driven back, and two gunboats which were there building were destroyed. Foster then pushed on toward Goldsboro, following the course of the Neuse, and sending detachments in various directions to destroy the railroad bridges. On the 17th another skirmish took place at a point near Goldsboro. In the mean while the Confederates had gradually concentrated a superior force at Goldsboro, and Foster found it unwise to attempt to reach this place, the point at which he had aimed. He therefore commenced a rapid retreat to Newbern, where his force arrived on the 24th, having been absent ten days, during which time it had marched nearly two hundred miles. Foster lost 90 killed and 478 wounded; the Confederates lost 71 killed, 268 wounded, besides 476 prisoners, most of whom were captured at Kingston, and immediately paroled. The expedition really accomplished nothing. The slight injury done to the railroad was soon repaired, and the communication between Richmond and the far South was hardly interrupted. With this attempt closed the active operations for 1862 in North Carolina. But in February of the ensuing year the Federal force was considerably strengthened, and Lee, perceiving that military operations on the Rappahannock would be suspended until spring, ventured to detach Longstreet, with a considerable part of his corps, from the army in Virginia, and send him to North Carolina. In March the Confederate force in this department nominally numbered 73,000 men, of whom 53,000 were reported as "present," and 45,000 "present for duty."

During the year various movements looking toward a siege of Charleston were attempted. The most important of these was an attempt on the 16th of June to take possession of James Island. The Federals were repulsed,

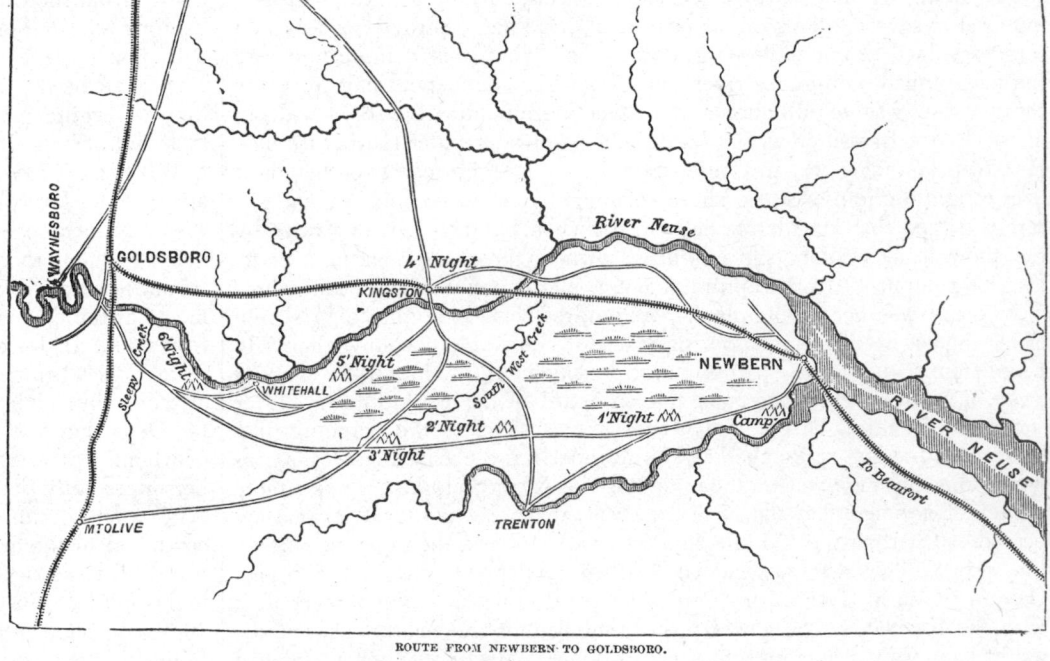

ROUTE FROM NEWBERN TO GOLDSBORO.

with a loss of 700. But the siege of Charleston forms an episode so complete in itself as to require a separate chapter.

SKIRMISH NEAR GOLDSBORO, DECEMBER 17.

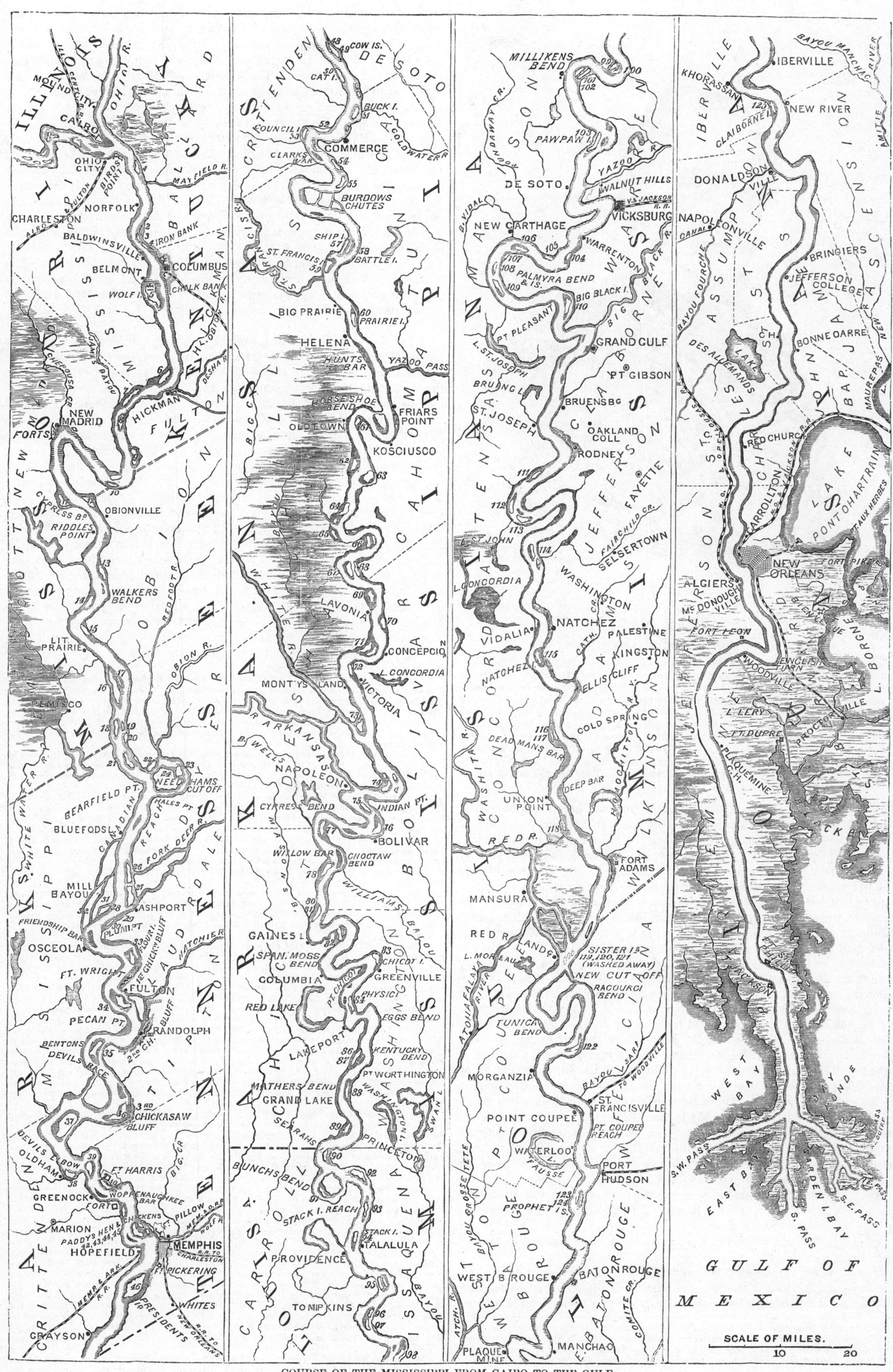

COURSE OF THE MISSISSIPPI FROM CAIRO TO THE GULF.

JOHN RODGERS.

CHAPTER XXVI.

THE WAR ON THE MISSISSIPPI.

The River.—Gun-boat and Mortar Fleet.—Farragut's Squadron.—A Succession of Victories.—Vicksburg becomes a Military Post.—Masked Batteries along the River Shore.—Shelling of Grand Gulf.—General Williams arrives before Vicksburg.—Farragut runs the Blockade.—Junction of the Fleets.—Bombardment of Vicksburg.—Escape of the Ram Arkansas.—Battle of Baton Rouge, and Destruction of the Arkansas.—Resumption of Operations against Vicksburg.—General Grant's Plan of the Winter Campaign.—An embarrassing Surrender.—Sherman's Defeat at Chickasaw Bayou.—McClernand in Command.—Capture of Arkansas Post.—General Grant's Army at Young's Point.—A Series of Naval Exploits.—The "pocket-full of Plans."—General Williams's Canal.—The Lake Providence Route.—The Yazoo Pass Expedition.—The "Deer-Creek Raid."—On to New Carthage.—The Transports run the Blockade.—Grierson's Raid.

"THE possession of the Mississippi," said General Sherman, in his speech at St. Louis just after the close of the war, "is the possession of America."[1] That this great river is not to the American what the Nile was to the Egyptian is owing to the greatness of America herself, who proudly refuses to be dependent upon even so important an ally; though, next to the two great oceans which skirt her continent, the river is the most important fact of her physical existence, and now (that is, in *anno Domini* 1866) has been proved to be the bond, sealed in blood, of her indissoluble union. Naturally, both in appearance and in fact, the river unites the North with the South, and, though seeming to divide between the Atlantic and the Pacific slopes, she in reality unites these also. The Algonquin Indians aptly named her *Missi Sepe*, "the Great River;" for, if the Missouri is to be considered—as it would have been but for a natural blunder on the part of the early American geographers—the parent, and not merely the tributary stream, the Mississippi is the longest river in the world. Even if we accept the more contracted limits which the geographers have given her, and date her origin from Itasca Lake, she drains a basin of more than a million of square miles—a basin which by possibility provides for a population of nearly four hundred millions, or almost one half of the present population of the entire globe. Even Aaron Burr, in his most splendid calculations respecting the destiny of this mighty garden—this granary of the world, under-estimated its gigantic possibilities. In the basin of the Mississippi the America of the future includes within its limits, as an *imperium in imperio*, a region, the population of which will outnumber the almost innumerable multitudes which have gathered about the Nile and the Ganges. For the present, however, the Englishman may well compare with the Mississippi his Thames, and the German his Rhine. Two centuries and a half go but a little way in the development of the resources of a nation, and far less than that period can be said to have been occupied in the real history of the Mississippi Valley.

The Mississippi is the most tortuous of rivers, and this circumstance, by the impediment which it offers to the current, doubtless favors navigation. Frequently the distance which has to be traversed is twelve, and sometimes even thirty times greater than it would be in a direct line. This circumstance also renders the river more capable of defensive fortification. Taken with its tributaries, the river affords nearly 17,000 miles of water which is navigable by steam. Its largest tributaries are the Missouri, Ohio, White, Arkansas, and Red Rivers. The Missouri is 3000 miles in length; it is a rapid and turbid stream, and asserts its lordship over the Mississippi by imparting to the latter a good measure of these characteristics. It enters the Mississippi a few miles above St. Louis. The Ohio, the largest eastern tributary of the Mississippi, enters the latter stream at Cairo, having previously received the waters of the Alleghany, the Kentucky, the Cumberland, and the Tennessee. From Pittsburg, where the Alleghany and Monongahela unite, to the mouth of the Ohio, is 948 miles; the river, with its tributaries, has 5000 miles of navigable waters. Within the limits of Arkansas, and not far apart, are the mouths of the White and Arkansas Rivers. The latter, much the more important tributary, is about 2000 miles long, and drains a basin of 178,000 square miles. The Red River enters the Mississippi from the west, about 200 miles above New Orleans. The greater part of its course is through fertile prairies of a reddish soil, which gives its color to the waters, and a name to the river. But for "The Raft" which obstructs its course, this river would be navigable for 400 miles from its mouth.

All of the western tributaries of the Mississippi drain the slopes of the Rocky Mountains, while its great eastern tributary, the Ohio, with *its* tributaries, drains the western slopes of the Appalachian range. Every one of these tributary and sub-tributary streams is swollen in the spring from the melting snows of the mountains. From the first of March, therefore, until the last of May—or for about ninety days—there is not simply a flood on the Mississippi, but literally an accumulation of floods. On the Missouri there is an average rise of fifteen feet, and this, added to the swollen Mississippi, makes a flood twenty-five feet in height. A second flood is heaped above this from the Ohio, below whose mouth the rise of the Mississippi is fifty feet. Above Natchez the flood begins to decline. At Baton Rouge it seldom exceeds thirty feet, and at New Orleans seldom twelve. At every flood the river overflows its banks for a distance of five hundred miles from its mouth, chiefly on the western side, inundating the country for the space of from ten to thirty miles. To guard against this, *levees* have been constructed, which confine the river within its original limits. Sometimes these levees are broken down by the violence of the current, and the consequent destruction of property is immense. To the yearly overflow of the Mississippi are to be attributed the large number of bayous in its vicinity. These vary in their extent, some of them scarcely exceeding a small river in size, while others spread out into lagoons and lakes.[1]

[1] When, at the beginning of this century, Monroe and Pinckney were negotiating with Napoleon I.—then First Consul of France—in regard to the purchase of Louisiana, Napoleon, anxious to transfer the province to the United States, lest it should fall into British possession, remarked that whatever nation held the Valley of the Mississippi would eventually be the most powerful on earth.

[1] "It is estimated that about 16,000,000 acres of the most fertile and productive lands of the states of Missouri, Arkansas, Mississippi, and Louisiana, are subject to overflow. To protect these lands from the annual devastation by the waters has been the object of incessant toil and immense outlays of capital by the inhabitants of the Valley of the Mississippi.

"So early as 1840, Congress made an appropriation for the construction of a chart of the "Hydrographical Basin of the Mississippi," which was executed by J. N. Nicollet, in the employ of the United States Topographical Bureau.

"In 1850, a corps of engineers was organized under Captain, now General A. A. Humphreys, which made a thorough survey of the Delta with special reference to the discovery of some system of works by which the country could be protected from overflow. These observations were made during and subsequent to the great flood of 1851.

"The constant increase of the volume of the flood revealed by each successive rise is ascribed by Captain Humphreys, in his Report, to the superior drainage produced by the cultivation of the country on the upper tributaries of the Mississippi, whereby the waters are thrown more rapidly into the main channel; the leveeing of the river and its tributaries in the states above Louisiana, so as to prevent the escape of the waters into the swamps and lowlands, whence it would be gradually drained to the river; the construction of cut-offs; the shortening of the channel, and more rapidly conveying the water to points below; and the lengthening of the Delta, thus extending the level mouth of the river, so that the current being retarded, the water is held back in the channel above.

"The remedies suggested are: Higher and stronger levees; prevention, by act of Congress, of the construction of additional cut-offs; formation of new outlets to the Lakes Borgne and Pontchartrain; opening of the closed bayous; enlargement of the Atchafalaya and Bayou Plaquemine, and the creation of artificial reservoirs in the swamps, to relieve the channel of the river in extreme cases.

"The early settlers, who selected the more elevated and fertile lands on the banks of the river, found little difficulty in protecting themselves from the floods. The whole country was then open to the waters, and a slight embankment, several inches high, would turn off the water, which was drained to the lowlands farther from the river. Other settlers, however, followed the pioneers; new plantations were established; and, by independent individual action, the slight embankments became linked together for many miles along both sides of the river. The waters, by reason of this confinement, rose higher every succeeding year, the embankments were enlarged, strengthened, and extended, until a line of levees, from fifteen to thirty feet wide at the base, and varying in height from five to twenty feet, stretched, with little interruption, from the lands on the coast, below New Orleans, along the channel of the river, to the boundaries of Tennessee and Missouri.

"The system, owing to its origin, was purely a selfish one. Each settler provided for his individual protection. If by a cut-off he could drain the water from his own place and throw it on the lands below, or by closing a bayou he could reclaim additional acres, the thing was done without reference to the effect it might have on the country lower down the stream. Much damage was thus done by shortening the channel of the river and by closing some of its natural outlets to the sea.

"The legislation of the states along the Mississippi has been little better than the individual action. The enactments depended more upon the comparative strength of the parties to be benefited and injured than upon any well-established plan for the control of the waters. Under authority of law, the channel of the river was shortened by the construction of cuts across the narrow necks formed by the great bends so frequent in the course of the stream. Bayous, which led from the main channel of the river to the gulf, forming independent outlets or mouths, were closed, and the water forced into one channel, which was unable to carry it to the sea.

"Before the war, therefore, the Father of Waters had become unmanageable in the hands of those who sought to control his floods. During the war, when labor that had been forced to the task day and night, and which at times was able to grapple successfully with the elements, was withdrawn, the waters swept away the levees at Morganzia, West Baton Rouge, at Chinn's and at Robertson's plantation, and at other points both above and below the mouth of the Red River, and inundated the country west of the Mississippi from Morganzia to Berwick's Bay.

"An attempt was made during last winter to rebuild these broken embankments. Under the combined efforts of the state authorities of Louisiana and the War Department at Washington, a large number of laborers were employed, and the work had been so far repaired that it was believed to be sufficiently strong to resist the pressure of the flood. Many planters and men from the North, believing that these levees would be rebuilt, engaged in the cultivation of the fertile lands in the parishes of Point Coupee, West Baton Rouge, Iberville, Lafourche, Terrebonne, and parts of others that were overflowed last year. Recent reports from Louisiana bring the sad intelligence that all these newly-constructed levees have been swept away, and that the water is rapidly filling up the swamps and spreading over the whole country, driving the homeless inhabitants before it.

"It is a grave question for the consideration of the country whether Congress should not undertake the protection of the whole Delta of the Mississippi against overflow. The present sys-

CREVASSE ON THE LOWER MISSISSIPPI.

The commercial development of the Mississippi Valley, although very rapid, has scarcely advanced beyond its first stage. It has been thus far a purely agricultural growth. The fertility of the valley is infinite, and along the banks of the river and its affluents large plantations have suddenly sprung up, and enjoyed an almost incredible prosperity. Oftentimes a single cotton or sugar crop has brought its planter a fortune. Necessity has given rise to towns, sparsely populated, and whose sole importance consists in their convenience as dépôts for the shipment of cotton or sugar. The necessity of securing the sites of these towns against the violence of perennial floods led to their situation upon the bluffs which rise here and there along the river banks. In the development of these towns—for they could scarcely be called cities—manufactures and the arts could have but little scope. In some cases, indeed, an easy communication by railroad with the Atlantic sea-board gave them some of the characteristics of our Eastern cities. The principal towns situated upon the banks of the Mississippi are St. Louis, Cairo, Columbus, Memphis, Vicksburg, Natchez, Baton Rouge, and, near the mouth of the river, New Orleans, which alone can be said to compare in commercial importance with the great cities of the East.

All of these were in our civil war points of great military importance. Their very situation, in nearly all cases, was such as to give them many facilities for defense against a naval attack. The city of New Orleans was, however, not in itself favorably located in this respect; it was not built upon bluffs like Memphis and Vicksburg, and had to be defended against inundation by artificial levees. But the approach to the city from the Gulf was well guarded by Forts Jackson and St. Philip. With the exception of these two forts, there were no military defenses worth considering on the Mississippi at the beginning of the war, and if the nation had possessed any considerable naval strength, the entire river from Cairo to New Orleans might have been secured at the outset. But, while a navy was being provided, there were constructed at favorable points fortifications which for some time secured the greater portion of the river to the Confederacy. The two points which were the last to surrender to the national arms were Vicksburg and Port Hudson. The campaigns—naval and military—which had for their object the reduction of these two strong-holds form the main subject of this and the succeeding chapter. But, before entering directly upon these campaigns, we shall briefly review the previous naval history of the war on the Mississippi.

The importance of a navy on our Western rivers was early appreciated. A month after the capture of Fort Sumter, Commander John Rodgers was summoned to Washington, and to him was assigned the duty of creating the Western navy. In the first stages of the undertaking, the War Department, under Secretary Cameron, assumed the expense and supervision; and it was not until the autumn of 1861 that the matter was transferred to the charge of the Navy Department, where it properly belonged.

Rodgers, an officer fitly chosen to organize the armed flotilla of the West, was son of the distinguished Commodore John Rodgers, one of the fathers of the American Navy. A native of Maryland, he had entered the naval service of the United States in 1828, at an early age. He had seen much service as midshipman and lieutenant; had been for two years engaged in boat service on the coast of Florida, in the war with the Seminoles and in the Coast Survey Expedition; in 1852 had been appointed second in command of the North Pacific and Behring Straits Exploring Expedition, and, succeeding to the chief command of that expedition on account of the severe illness of Captain Ringgold, had taken his vessel, the Vincennes, farther into the Arctic region than a ship-of-war had ever before penetrated; and when the rebellion broke out he had reported for active service, and had been sent to Norfolk to attempt the rescue of the vessels there, but, arriving too late to accomplish this, had been assigned to the difficult and dangerous duty of blowing up the dry-dock. It was from Norfolk that Rodgers was, on May 16, 1861, summoned to Washington to receive orders respecting his mission to the West. Entering immediately upon this mission, he went to work heartily. He purchased steamers, which, under his supervision, were fitted, armed, and armored as gun-boats. But it was a slow and difficult undertaking, demanding much skill, and more than ordinary perseverance. The question of the comparative power of even iron-clad gun-boats as against forts was still one about which a great deal might be said on both sides. Even as we look back now and consider what the war has taught us in regard to the solution of this vexed problem, we hesitate to pronounce definitely, satisfying ourselves with the somewhat vague conclusion that the result depends as much upon one member of the equation as the other. In the instances of successful reduction of forts by gun-boats, the case might have been reversed if the enemy had constructed better fortifications. Certain it is that Foote was severely repulsed at Donelson, though he had been so victorious at Henry; and that nearly all the captures of forts during the war were the immediate consequence of assaults with an overwhelming military force, the ships accomplishing little beyond the silencing of the enemy's guns.

Commander Rodgers never took any of his vessels into action. He became the victim of covetous contractors, and, at the suggestion of General Fremont, who afterward regretted the circumstance, was relieved by A. H. Foote, September 6, 1861. The new naval commander, on his arrival in the West, found three wooden vessels in commission, besides which there were, in process of construction, nine iron-clad gun-boats and thirty-eight mortar-boats. There was not a single navy yard or dépôt on any of the rivers. Much embarrassment was occasioned by the paucity of funds and the want of ordnance. Even after the boats were completed it was found difficult to man them. These obstacles were surmounted by Flag-officer[1] Foote, "whose perseverance and courage," says Secretary Welles, "were scarcely surpassed by the heroic qualities displayed in subsequent well-fought actions on the decks of the gun-boats he had under so many discouragements prepared."

In the month of February Foote was able to bring against Fort Henry seven gun-boats—the Essex, St. Louis, Carondelet, Cincinnati, Tyler, Lexington, and Conestoga, of which the last three were wooden. In that fight the Cincinnati and Essex were disabled, and could not be brought against Fort Donelson a week later. In the naval action at Donelson the Tyler also was absent on the Tennessee, but the two iron-clads were replaced by the Louisville and Pittsburg. Foote declared that if the battle could have been postponed one week, he could also have brought eight of his mortar-boats into action. Besides the nine gun-boats involved in the attacks on Henry and Donelson, three others—the Benton, Mound City, and Cairo—were ready for action in a few days. At Island No. 10, in March, sixteen mortar-boats were engaged. From a letter written about this time by General Strong to Foote, it appears that the Confederates then had "thirteen gun-boats independent of the five below New Madrid, and the Manassas, or ram, at Memphis." These vessels were, however, far inferior to Foote's gun-boats, as was shown shortly afterward; yet they excited considerable apprehension, for Farragut's fleet had not then entered the river from below. From this time additions to the gun-boat fleet of the Western navy were slowly made. By the close of 1862, the Tuscumbia, the Baron De Kalb, and the Osage had been added, and there were in process of construction the Neosho, Indianola, Choctaw, and Chillicothe. The Ozark was completed in 1863. Including these, the gun-boat fleet consisted of twenty vessels, with an armament of about 170 guns, and a tonnage of nearly 10,000 tons. Nine or ten more gun-boats were added before the close of the war.[2] Of the gun-boats added to the Western fleet during the year after the fight at Donelson, the Tuscumbia was among the largest.[3] The Mound City was blown up in July, 1862, on the White River, and subsequently the Cairo met a similar fate on the Yazoo.

Next to the vessels known as gun-boats, Ellet's steam-ram fleet held the most important place in the Mississippi squadron. Charles Ellet bore the same relation to steam rams as Ericsson to the monitors. He was a native of Pennsylvania. As a civil engineer he had gained a reputation which was well earned. His treatise on "The Laws of Trade in Reference to Works of Internal Improvement," published in Philadelphia in 1837, was an exhaustive work on the subject, and attracted considerable attention. A few years afterward he was chosen by the War Department to survey the Lower Mississippi. It was an important object of his life to carry out a scheme which he had conceived for improving the navigation of the Western rivers.[4] He was so impressed with this project that, in honor of it, he named his son Charles *Rivers* Ellet. It is not more remarkable that De Soto found

tem, or rather want of system, seems to be a failure; and, unless some such combination of works as is suggested by General Humphreys be adopted, planting on the fertile river lands must ever be a precarious undertaking, with the weight of the chances largely against success. The distinguished engineer who conducted the survey referred to estimated the total cost of works to protect the country from the Ohio to the Gulf at $26,000,000. The country thus reclaimed and protected would easily bear a tax of an amount sufficient to pay the interest on this sum, to keep the works in repair, and, finally, to liquidate the debt. This, like all other physical problems, must be capable of determination. The water brought down the Mississippi is not infinite; its quantity, its velocity, its pressure, are measurable; the height and strength of levees, and the capacity of outlet required to confine and discharge the annual floods brought down, are therefore determinable measurements. To solve the problem, it is only necessary that a competent superintendent, clothed with ample authority over every portion of the territory to be protected, be charged with the task, so that the whole work may be carried on and completed in accordance with some well-established system."—*N. Y. Tribune*, May 26th, 1866.

[1] This title remained in existence until the operation of an act of Congress of July 16, 1862. By this act the officers of the navy were distributed into nine grades, taking rank according to the date of commission in each grade, as follows:

GRADES IN THE NAVY.	CORRESPONDING GRADES IN THE ARMY.
1. Rear Admirals.	1. Major Generals.
2. Commodores.	2. Brigadier Generals.
3. Captains.	3. Colonels.
4. Commanders.	4. Lieutenant Colonels.
5. Lieutenant Commanders.	5. Majors.
6. Lieutenants.	6. Captains.
7. Masters.	7. First Lieutenants.
8. Ensigns.	8. Second Lieutenants.
9. Midshipmen.	

In regard to the change thus introduced, Secretary Welles, in his Report for 1862, says: "The act of July 16, 1862, 'to Establish and Equalize the Grade of Line Officers of the United States Navy,' does justice in conferring ranks and grades that had until that time been withheld from as meritorious and gallant a class of officers as ever devoted their days and periled their lives for their country. Though the justice to which they were entitled has been long delayed, it was gracefully and generously rendered by the present Congress, and has been and is appreciated by the brave men who are its recipients, and by all attached to the service, as a just recognition of the worth and ability of the officers of the American Navy. . . . The commanders of our squadrons now hold rank with those of other naval powers on the ocean, on distant service, and wherever they carry our flag, or appear as the representatives of their country."—Page 40.

Flag-officers Goldsborough, Dupont, Farragut, and Foote were nominated to the Senate for the grade of rear-admiral on the day subsequent to the approval of the act. Other officers—among whom were captains Stewart, Read, Gregory, Stringham, and Paulding—were the same day nominated for rear-admirals on the retired list.

Subsequently, in 1864, the rank of vice-admiral was created by Congress, to correspond with the revived grade of lieutenant general in the army. The bill creating this rank, originating in the Senate, passed the House December 20, and was approved on the 21st by the President, who the same day nominated Farragut to the new office. After the close of the war Congress created the rank of general in the army, and the corresponding rank of admiral in the navy, to which ranks U. S. Grant and David G. Farragut were respectively assigned.

[2] There were building in May, 1864, the following iron-clad vessels for the Mississippi squadron: The Catawba, 2 guns, 970 tons; the Chickasaw, 2 guns, 970 tons; the Etlah, 2 guns, 614 tons; the Kickapoo, 4 guns, 970 tons; the Klamath, 2 guns, 614 tons; the Koka, 2 guns, 614 tons; the Milwaukee, 4 guns, 970 tons; and the Oneota, 2 guns, 1034 tons.

[3] The Tuscumbia had an armament of five guns—three eleven-inch Dahlgrens forward, and two 100-lb. rifled guns in battery aft. Her sides were plated with three-inch, and her deck with one-inch wrought iron; the plates over the batteries, or gun-rooms, were six inches thick forward, and four aft. Her timbers were very strong, her build stanch, and her outfit complete. A bulwark of iron, loop-holed for musketry, was placed around her guards. She had also an apparatus for throwing a stream of water 200 feet.

[4] "Mr. Ellet found that the use of dikes, or levees, along the banks caused the water to rise higher between them, because the river was previously wont to fill the swamps adjacent. Either fresh outlets must be formed for the tremendous accumulation of water somewhere above the present Delta, or the levees must be raised indefinitely, at an enormous cost, and with a continual danger of breaking away. His remedy proposed for the navigation of the Ohio seemed to be the most natural, the most secure, and the cheapest, as well as the most beneficial to apply to the Mississippi. He advocated the building of dams on the Ohio or other tributaries, to improve their navigation and secure the lower valley from inundation, and urged Congress to adopt the work for the general benefit of the country."—*Harper's Magazine*, vol. xxxii., p. 297.

his grave in the waters of the Mississippi, which he discovered, than that both the Ellets, father and son, perished in the attempt to secure, by their warlike invention of rams, that very navigation which the father had sought to improve by peaceful measures for so many years.[1]

After the seizure of the Norfolk Navy Yard, and when uneasiness had been aroused by the report that the Confederates were converting frigates and steamers into iron-clad rams, Ellet appreciated the threatened danger, and in a printed memorial to Congress, dated Georgetown, February 6, 1862, a month before the appearance of the Merrimac, he gave the government a warning as to the consequences which might ensue upon the appearance of these Confederate rams.[2] The government listened to this final appeal, though it was not until the appearance of the Merrimac, and the events which followed had fully vindicated Ellet's judgment, that the latter was summoned to the aid of Secretary Stanton. Foote was at this time very anxious on account of Confederate rams on the Mississippi, and he knew he had no vessels which could meet these rams on equal terms. Here was an opportunity to test Ellet's favorite project. He was sent West by Secretary Stanton with authority to purchase and convert into rams such vessels as he should deem suited to his purposes. With a colonel's commission, he set out on the 26th of March. At Pittsburg he purchased five powerful tow-boats, the Lioness, Samson, Mingo, Fulton, and Homer. The hulls were strengthened, the bows filled with solid timber, the boilers protected by a double tier of oak twenty-four inches thick, and the pilot-house plated against musketry. At Cincinnati he purchased four side-wheel steamers of great power, as being more readily handled in the strong current of the Mississippi—the Queen of the West, Monarch, Switzerland, and Lancaster. But for Colonel Ellet's extraordinary personal influence he would never have been able to obtain men for his rams, although he had permission to recruit from the army. The project was deemed not only a visionary, but a perilous one. His brother, Alfred W. Ellet, then a captain in the Fifty-ninth Illinois, brought his own company, with another from the Sixty-third Illinois, and met the boats at Cairo. For firemen Ellet was mainly indebted to negroes.

CHARLES ELLET.

We turn now from the Mississippi squadron, which before the end of 1862 numbered about 80 vessels—gun-boats, rams, mortar-boats, and side-wheel steamers—to Farragut's fleet, which, after the fall of New Orleans, occupied the Lower Mississippi. This fleet consisted of two parts: vessels of the West Gulf squadron, and Admiral D. D. Porter's mortar flotilla.[3] At the close of 1861 the entire Gulf squadron numbered 21 vessels, with 282 guns and 1000 men. This squadron was divided into an Eastern and Western, February 21, 1862. The former was under the command of Flag-officer McKean, who was relieved June 4, 1862, by acting Rear-admiral Lardner, who was shortly succeeded by Commodore Theodorus Bailey. The limits of this eastern squadron comprised the southern and western portions of the Florida coast, commencing at Cape Canaveral and extending to Pensacola. Westward from and including Pensacola, the West Gulf squadron extended to the Rio Grande. This latter was a very important command, for two reasons: first, on account of the operations against New Orleans, which had been contemplated ever since the early autumn of 1861; and, secondly, on account of the importance of the blockade in this quarter, within the limits of which were included the ocean outlets of the Mississippi Valley. David G. Farragut, then captain, afterward admiral, vice-admiral, and finally Admiral of the United States Navy, was wisely chosen to command this de-

CHARLES RIVERS ELLET.

[1] In order that the reader may fully comprehend Mr. Ellet's connection with steam rams previous to the war, we transcribe a few paragraphs from the article in *Harper's Magazine*, already referred to:

"It was in the winter of 1854–5, at Lausanne, in Switzerland, that home of wandering savans, during the siege of Sebastopol, when the Russians spoke of sinking their splendid fleet, that Mr. Ellet first revolved in his mind the plan of protecting and strengthening war vessels, so that they might be used as rams; that thus, instead of sinking their fleet, the Russians might sink that of the allies, and raise the blockade of the harbor. In December, probably, he wrote to the Russian government, giving a detailed statement of his plan, which was thankfully received, but, in consequence of the death of the emperor soon after, was overlooked and never acted upon. In the following April (26th) he addressed a letter to the Secretary of War, through Mr. John Y. Mason, our minister at Paris, with the same propositions. These, with a reply and rejoinder from our Navy Department, were afterward published (Richmond, 1855) in pamphlet form, and circulated widely both in the South and in Europe. We were at that time slightly menaced with war with England on the Right of Search question.

"In his prefatory note, dated Richmond, December 1, 1855, Mr. Ellet says:

"'People are accustomed to regard the art of naval warfare as the art of manœuvring cannon, and throwing shot and shell. I wish them to reflect upon the power of a moving steam-boat driven against the enemy who has no means of resistance but his batteries, and to decide which is the more certain warfare. I wish, therefore, to compare the number of fighting steamers which may be sent to any port in the United States from the shores of Europe with the number of river steamers, coasting steamers, steam-tugs, and even ferry-boats, which might be found ready to meet them here.'

"This remarkable pamphlet, upon which must be based his claims to the paternity of the steam ram, is so forcible and explicit, that it should be given entire did space allow. Like all he ever wrote, it is clear, earnest, well reasoned, and nervous in style. He says:

"'My plan is simply to convert the steamer into a battering-ram, and to enable her to fight, not with her guns, but with her momentum. In short, I propose to strengthen the steamer throughout in the most substantial manner, so that she may run head on into the enemy, or burst in his ribs, or drive a hole into his hull below the water-line. A hole only two feet square, four feet under water, will sink an ordinary frigate in sixteen minutes.'

"He then minutely details the altering or building of ships for his purpose. And then he adds:

"'I have read accounts of five or six accidental collisions at sea in the last six months—sometimes by steamers running into sailing vessels, and sometimes by sailing vessels running into steamers—and in every case the vessel struck in the waist was sunk, and the vessel which ran into her was able to keep on her course. For harbor defense, however much we may continue to build and arm forts and batteries, I think we should not neglect also to build *floating batteries—rams*—great steamers, as near shot and shell proof as they can be made, with a strength of hull, speed, and power that will enable them to crush in the side of a man-of-war by simple collision.

"'To my understanding, the efficacy of the plan which I recommend is self-evident. *And I hold myself ready to carry it out in all its details whenever the day arrives that the United States is about to become engaged in a naval contest.*'

"To this letter the following remarkable answer was returned:

"'Navy Department, Washington, D. C., March 21, 1855.

"'SIR,—The receipt of your letter of the 25th ult. is acknowledged, and the Department tenders you its thanks for the views expressed therein. The suggestion to convert steamers into battering-rams, and, by the momentum, make them a means of sinking an enemy's ships, was proposed as long ago as 1832, and has been renewed many times since by various officers of the navy. No practical test has been undertaken; but with the necessary speed, strength, and weight, a large steamer on the plan proposed by you would introduce an entire change in naval warfare.

"'Very respectfully, your obedient servant,

"'CHARLES W. WELCH, Acting Secretary of the Navy.'

"In reply to this, Mr. Ellet, on the 16th of August, sent another letter to the Navy Department, through Mr. Buchanan, then our minister in London, in which letter he still more strenuously urges the adoption of his plan. The Secretary of the Navy, J. C. Dobbin, in a very courteous reply, dismissed the subject, stating that the Department had no power, but by special vote of Congress, 'to undertake the construction of proper vessels and machinery for experimenting.'

"In the letter which elicited this last reply Mr. Ellet discusses the objections which are likely to be raised against his plan, such as that his own vessel might be sunk or hopelessly damaged in engine or vital parts by the collision or by hostile shot. With our late remarkable experience we can see that these objections fall to the ground. But from the data before him he reasoned correctly that the danger from collision would be immensely against the vessel struck; and in the danger from shot, he entered into a nice calculation of the probabilities of a vessel being struck in a vital part, between the points of extreme range and that of close contact, by which he showed that the chances were reduced to an inappreciable fraction.

"When we consider how the allied fleet bombarded the fortress of Sweaborg, defended by about 800 guns, for the space of forty-five hours, without suffering the loss of a single man by the enemy's shot, 'in consequence of the continual movement of the ships,' as the Russian general alleged, and as we also recall some very remarkable engagements of our own in the late war, we may appreciate the prevision of our advocate. The bombardment of Port Royal and the experience of blockade-runners confirm the result of his calculations.

"Among the cases of accidental collisions cited are several remarkable ones, all tending to the support of his theory. The well-known sinking of the Arctic by the Vesta, with great loss of life; the Wellington, of 131 guns, damaged by a sailing ship; the Imperatrice, steamer, sunk almost immediately by the schooner Commerce; the Victoria, ship, sunk in two minutes by a small Sardinian steamer; the brigantine Henry, run into by a diminutive steamer and lost immediately.

"In 1842, the Hudson River steamer Empire, coming into New York with a new pilot on a misty morning, ran fairly into a new wharf with the full power of the engine, forcing the bow of the boat through the timber facing of logs eighteen inches square, then through a solid stone filling eight and a half feet thick, and then through earth and rubbish seventeen feet farther, making a chasm of twelve feet wide at the logs, twenty-seven feet long, and seventeen feet deep. The only injury sustained by the boat was the breaking of one of her oblique braces and a slight leak at the stem.

"Now, if such is the effect of a frail river steamer upon an object of this sort, what must be expected of a vessel built and armed for the very purpose of a ram? There is another example, memorable for the tragical, mysterious manner in which it occurred. It may be recollected that, a few years ago, an American vessel, with an English captain, was hired, it is supposed, to run down a Russian ship of war in the Baltic. He strengthened his bows with solid timber, and followed the war vessel out of St. Petersburg, and in the gray of dawn next morning, when near the Categat, while his crew were asleep or below decks, he took the helm himself and ran into the Russian ship with the power of sails merely, and instantaneously sunk her with her crew of three hundred souls.

"'The practical conclusion,' says Mr. Ellet, 'to be drawn from these facts is apparent. If vessels built for ordinary commercial purposes, and propelled either by steam or sail, invariably sink the vessel they strike with their bow when running with any considerable velocity, while themselves receiving but little injury from the collision, it follows, of necessity and *à fortiori*, that a steamer expressly designed for such conflict, well fortified at the bow, strongly built throughout, divided longitudinally and centrally by a solid partition reaching from kelson to deck and from stem to stern, and transversely by other partitions, separating the hull into six or eight water-tight compartments, and horizontally by one or more partitions or floors, of which one shall be below the water-line when light—I say it follows of necessity that such a vessel, skillfully framed and properly fastened, may be driven at high speed against any ship of ordinary construction in the certainty that the ship struck will go down and the battering ship float.'

"All this, which is familiar knowledge to us in 1865, was foreseen and reasoned out in 1855. At that time Mr. Ellet was living in Richmond. His views, as set forth by his pamphlet, addresses to Congress, and by conversation and newspaper communications, were all well known. Here, indeed, is the germ of the idea wrought out but partially by the rebels after their seizure of the navy yard at Norfolk. To the suggestion that the enemy could strengthen his ships, and meet them ram with ram, it is only necessary to add that this is a fundamental condition of all civilized warfare, and will occur under every species of construction, armament, or defense."

[2] We make the following extract from this memorial:

"STEAM RAMS.—It is not generally known that the rebels now have five steam rams nearly ready for use. Of these, two are on the Lower Mississippi, two are at Mobile, and one is at Norfolk. The last of the five is doubtless the most formidable, being the steam frigate Merrimac, which has been so strengthened that, in the opinion of the rebels, it may be used as a ram. But we have not yet a single vessel at sea, nor, so far as I know, in course of construction, able to cope with a well-built ram. If the Merrimac is permitted to escape from the Elizabeth River, she will be almost certain to commit great depredation on our armed or unarmed vessels in Hampton Roads, and may even be expected to pass out under the guns of Fortress Monroe and prey upon our commerce in Chesapeake Bay. Indeed, if the alterations have been skillfully made, and she succeed in getting to sea, she will not only be a terrible scourge to our commerce, but may prove also to be a most dangerous visitor to our blockading squadron off the harbors of our Southern coasts.

"I have attempted to call the attention of the Navy Department and of the country so often to this subject during the last seven years that I almost hesitate to allude to it again, and would not do so here but that I think the danger from these tremendous engines is very imminent, but not at all appreciated."

[3] Farragut's fleet was constituted thus:

Steam-sloops.		*Steam-sloop.*		*Mortar Fleet.*	
Hartford	24 guns.	Sciota	4 guns.	H. Beals.	
Richmond	26 "	*Sailing-sloop.*		J. Griffith.	
Pensacola	24 "	Portsmouth	17 "	Racer.	
Brooklyn	24 "	*Mortar Fleet.*		S. Bruen.	
Mississippi	12 "	Norfolk Packet.		H. Jones.	
Colorado	28 "	Arletta.		Dan. Smith.	
Gun-boats.		Sophronia.		*Vessels accompanying Mortars.*	
Iroquois	9 "	Para.		Harriet Lane	4 guns.
Oneida	9 "	C. P. Williams.		Miami	7 "
Varuna	12 "	O. H. Lee.		Westfield	6 "
Cayuga	6 "	W. Bacon.		Clifton	6 "
Winona	4 "	T. A. Ward.		Uncas	5 "
Katahdin	4 "	A. Dugel.		Owasco	5 "
Itaska	4 "	M. Vassar.		Octorara	10 "
Kineo	4 "	C. Mungham.		Sea Foam	5 "
Wissahickon	4 "	M. J. Carlton.		A. Houghton	2 "
Pinola	4 "	S. C. Jones.		*Coast Survey Vessel.*	
Kennebec	4 "	Orvetta.		Sachem	5 "

The Octorara did not arrive until after the capture of New Orleans. Each of the mortar-boats mounted a bomb and two guns. Some of the vessels accompanying the mortars were only armed tugs.

ADMIRAL PORTER'S MORTAR FLEET.

partment. After July 11 Pensacola became the great naval dépôt for the West Gulf squadron.

Farragut sailed from Hampton Roads to take the command on February 2, 1862, and, arriving at Ship Island on the 20th, began to organize his fleet. Two months were consumed in these preparations, the greatest difficulty being encountered in landing the vessels of heavy draught. After every effort had been made, the Colorado and the Wabash could not be got over the bar. The entire fleet sent against New Orleans, including the vessels withdrawn from the blockade, consisted of 48 vessels, with about 300 guns and 20 bombs. Porter's mortar flotilla had been organized at the Brooklyn Navy Yard in the winter of 1861–2, and performed a very important part in the opening of the Mississippi. In Farragut's entire fleet there was not a single iron-clad vessel.

The most brilliant naval period of the war — if the brilliancy of naval operations depend upon their success in actual engagement with the enemy's ships and forts — is comprised within the brief space of four months, beginning February 6, and ending June 6, 1862. Yet this was far from being the period of our greatest naval strength. Very much stronger expeditions were fitted out afterward, but they failed of success, except in one or two instances.[1]

Let us review the brief, but eventful and satisfactory record of these four months. The capture of Fort Henry, February 6, was the first of a series of victories on the Western rivers that aroused the nation from a situation, if not of doubt, at least of a negative sort of confidence, to one of positive hope and courage. The capture of Donelson ten days later, though it could scarcely be called a naval victory, still derived a large measure of its importance from its bearings upon the progress of naval operations. It gave us command of the Cumberland, as the victory at Fort Henry had given us command of the Tennessee. It was followed, within the space of a fortnight, by the evacuation of Columbus and Nashville. The Confederates held New Madrid until March 14, when their communications had been cut off by General Pope. In the capture of Island No. 10, April 7, the army under Pope, and the naval squadron under Foote, had an equal share. Here there was no battle, but there were captured nearly 7000 prisoners and a large amount of war material, including 100 siege-guns. The crossing of Pope's force to the rear of the enemy, on the west side of the Mississippi, by the aid of the gun-boats, had secured the victory without the loss of a single man.

Before the close of April, Farragut, with his fleet, had steamed past Forts Jackson and St. Philip, and, arriving before New Orleans, held the city under his guns. Lovell's fleet had been disposed of in a short but sharp conflict during the passage by the forts. This was purely a naval victory. New Orleans was conquered by Farragut, and the forts surrendered to Admiral Porter, commanding the mortar fleet. Butler's army, numbering about 14,000 men, became an army of occupation. The capture of New Orleans

---

[1] It would be unfair to infer that because our navy was not always successful in these gigantic expeditions, that it ceased, after the period we have indicated, to be an important element in the war. Our blockading squadrons were from the first indispensable to success. If the monitors accomplished little in actual service, they were none the less a security against foreign intervention. The extent of our iron-clad fleet made it useless for the Confederates to organize a fleet of any sort. Though the Confederates could construct forts which baffled our fleets, yet the latter, co-operating with the army, were of the greatest service, of which service one of the most memorable instances was the capture of Fort Fisher. And the instances are not a few in which our armies were saved from disaster by the presence of gun-boats. Two or three of the inferior gun-boats of the Mississippi squadron, in several important Western battles, were of greater value than an entire military division could have been. At Belmont, the Tyler and Lexington saved Grant's army from defeat. At Pittsburg Landing, the same gun-boats, if they did not save the first day's battle, at least, by the moral effect of their presence, rendered the defeat far less disastrous than it might otherwise have been. On February 4, 1863, the Lexington, assisted by the A. S. Robb and other boats, repulsed 4500 Confederates at Dover, Tennessee. At Helena, five months later, the Tyler enabled an inferior national force to hold the position against an attack which, under other circumstances, might possibly have succeeded. In the same month (July), at Bluffington Island, Indiana, John Morgan's force was terribly cut up by the Alleghany, Naumkeag, and three other boats. Although the navy, acting alone, was unable to capture Vicksburg, it not only rendered some of the most brilliant feats of General Grant's campaign against that post possible, but also, after the victory, secured the permanent possession of the river far more effectively than a reserve force of one hundred thousand men could have done. It was due to our great naval strength alone that, after the termination of the Vicksburg campaign, the Confederates were compelled to adopt the line of defense running eastward and southward from Chattanooga, keeping aloof from the great Western rivers.

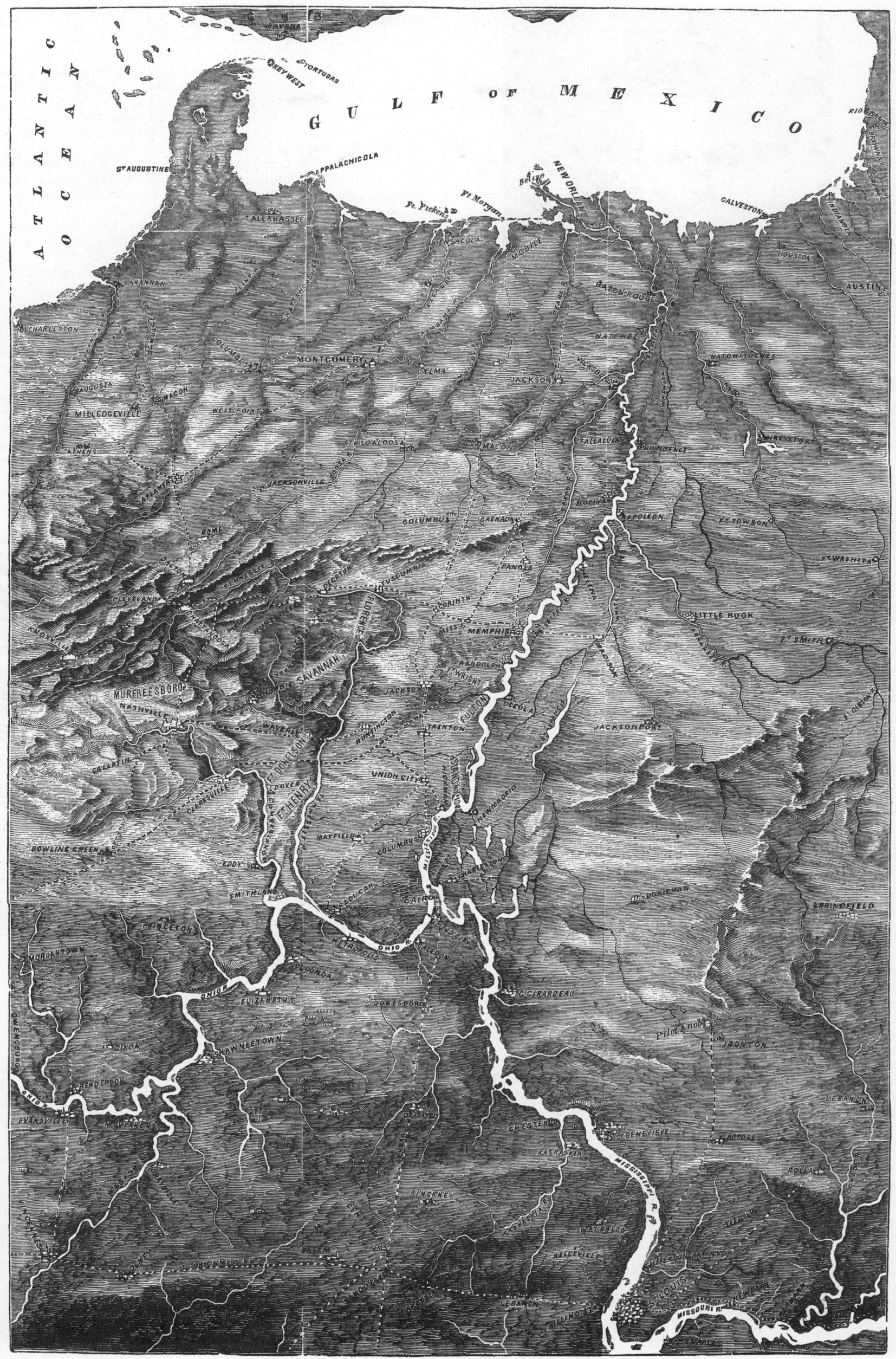

BIRD'S-EYE VIEW OF THE BASIN OF THE MISSISSIPPI.

CHARLES H. DAVIS.

was, thus far, the most substantial triumph of the war. It was to the South a greater disaster, comparatively, than the loss of New York City would have been to the North.

In the mean time, Foote was engaged in an expedition against Fort Pillow, which he had undertaken directly after the surrender of Island No. 10. But Pope's army abandoned him April 17th, to join the army moving upon Corinth, and left him helpless. Early in May, this gallant naval officer, still suffering from his wound, was, at his own request, relieved, and the command of the Mississippi squadron was assigned to Captain C. H. Davis. A little more than a year after his resignation of this command Admiral Foote died, while making preparations to depart for Charleston, to relieve Admiral Dupont. The day after Davis assumed the command—May 10—the Confederate fleet at Memphis came up the river and engaged the squadron, but withdrew, defeated, after an hour's fight, having, however, succeeded in badly crippling the Cincinnati and the Mound City. The evacuation of Corinth gave us Fort Pillow without a battle, June 4, and the next day the city of Memphis was surrendered.

But before the surrender of Memphis there was a spirited conflict with Montgomery's fleet. Davis left Fort Pillow, June 5, with a fleet of nine boats—five gun-boats, two tugs, and two of Colonel Ellet's rams, the Queen of the West and the Monarch. Montgomery, with his eight boats, had threatened to "send Lincoln's gun-boats to the bottom," and the inhabitants of Memphis gathered upon the hill-side to witness this expected catastrophe. The fight which followed has already been described in a previous chapter. It was here that Ellet redeemed all the promises which he had made for his rams. The two rams alone could have sunk the entire fleet.[1] Colonel

Ellet in person commanded the Queen of the West, which was his flag-ship. His brother, Alfred Ellet, commanded the Monarch. During the progress of the fight, Colonel Ellet, stepping out upon the forward part of the deck to observe the effect of a blow which he had given the Lovell, and which was sinking the latter, received a bullet in his knee. The wound proved to be a dangerous one, and amputation became necessary; but the colonel resisted stoutly, declaring that "the life should go first." Two weeks after the battle he was conveyed to Cairo on one of his rams—the Switzerland—and died on reaching the wharf on the morning of June 21. He left his brother Alfred in command of the ram fleet.

After the capture of Memphis, four of the gun-boats, with an Indiana regiment under Colonel Fitch, were dispatched to the White River to open communication with General Curtis, who had advanced to Batesville. Some batteries were carried at St. Charles, but the main object of the expedition was not accomplished, and General Curtis, in order to find a base of operations, was obliged to transfer his army from Batesville to Helena, on the Mississippi.

Meanwhile Farragut's fleet had been advancing up the river. The Iroquois, under Commander Palmer, arrived off Baton Rouge May 7. The authorities, ordered to surrender, indulged in the same mock-heroic nonsense which the mayor and council of New Orleans had been indulging in the week before. They were determined that the city of Baton Rouge should not "be surrendered voluntarily to any power on earth." There was no military force, the mayor added, in the city, and its possession by the Federals "must be without the consent and against the wish of the peaceable inhabitants." He declined to hoist the national flag because it was "offensive to the sensibilities of the people." Palmer, "determined to submit to no such nonsense," took possession of the arsenal, barracks, and other public property of the United States. No resistance was offered. In a note to Mayor Bryan, on the 9th, Palmer informed him that he had taken possession of the arsenal, and hoisted over it the United States flag, and added: "War is a sad calamity, and often inflicts severer wounds than those upon the sensibilities. I therefore trust I may be spared from resorting to any of its dire extremities; but I warn you, Mr. Mayor, that this flag must remain unmolested, though I have no force on shore to protect it. The rash act of some individual may cause your city to pay a bitter penalty." Farragut, having come up on May 10, continued the mayor in office, and encouraged the employment which the latter had already made of the foreign corps as a police guard for the maintenance of good order. Baton Rouge was the first place of importance above New Orleans, from which it was distant about 140 miles. It was situated on a plateau 40 or 50 feet above high water, on the east bank of the river; was the capital of Louisiana, and had a population, in 1860, of 5498.

Fifteen miles above Baton Rouge is Natchez, in Mississippi. This place Palmer, with the Iroquois and other gun-boats, reached on the 12th. He addressed a note to the mayor, which the citizens at the landing refused to receive. Palmer then seized a ferry-boat which was loading with coal, put aboard of it a force of seamen, a few marines, and two howitzers, and sent the expedition across the river, with orders to see that the mayor received the note. But there was no occasion to land this force, as two members of the Common Council were already in waiting with the mayor's apology. Mayor Hunter submitted to the necessities of the situation, if not with remarkable grace, at least without any heroic bluster. But Natchez was of

---

[1] "While the engagement," writes Captain Davis, "was going on in this manner, two vessels of the ram-fleet, under command of Colonel Ellet, steamed rapidly by us, and ran boldly into the enemy's line. Several conflicts had taken place between the rams before the flotilla (of gun-boats), led by the Benton, moving at a slower rate, could arrive at the closest quarters. In

the mean time, however, the firing from the gun-boats was continuous, and exceedingly well directed. The General Beauregard and the Little Rebel were struck in the boilers and blown up.

"The ram, Queen of the West, which Colonel Ellet commanded in person, encountered with full power the rebel steamer General Lovell, and sunk her, but in so doing sustained pretty serious damage. Up to this time the rebel fleet had maintained its position, and used its guns with great spirit. These disasters compelled the remaining vessels to resort to their superiority in speed as the only means of safety. A running fight took place, which lasted nearly an hour, and carried us ten miles below the city. The attack made by the two rams under Colonel Ellet, which took place before the flotilla closed in with the enemy, was bold and successful."

NATCHEZ UPON THE HILL.

NATCHEZ UNDER THE HILL.

little military importance, and had never been occupied by any military force; it was therefore abandoned.

Thus far no resistance had been encountered by the fleet since the capture of New Orleans. It was therefore somewhat of a surprise, doubtless, to S. P. Lee, commanding the advanced naval division of Farragut's squadron, when, on May 18, in reply to his demand for the surrender of Vicksburg, he received the defiant response, "Mississippians don't know, and refuse to learn, how to surrender to an enemy. If Commodore Farragut or General Butler can teach them, let them come and try!" Such, indeed, was the answer returned to the demand by James L. Antry, military governor and colonel commanding the post. M. L. Smith, a brigadier general in command of the military defenses of Vicksburg, replied, on his own account, that he had been ordered to hold the defenses, and that it was his intention to do so as long as it was in his power. L. Lindsay, mayor of the city, added his refusal to that of the military authorities. "As far as the municipal authorities are concerned," he said, "we have erected no defenses, and none are within the corporative limits of the city." Phillips, on the 21st, gave Mayor Lindsay notice to remove the women and children of Vicksburg beyond the reach of his guns, as any attack upon the defenses must injure or destroy the town. This notice was given by Phillips for the purpose of placing it at his own option whether he should fire or not immediately upon the expiration of the truce. And thus the matter rested. Phillips, however, did not make an attack.

Above and below Vicksburg the river was now entirely in the possession of the national forces. A co-operating military force only half as large as that which secured the victories at New Madrid and Island No. 10 could at this time have compelled the surrender of Vicksburg, and opened the Mississippi from Cairo to New Orleans. But the whole available military force in the West was then being collected together against Beauregard's army at Corinth. Even Curtis's force in Arkansas had been so far reduced for this purpose that it was unable to assume the offensive. From General Butler's department no troops could be spared, since, after garrisoning Forts Jackson and St. Philip, Ship Island and Baton Rouge, there was left a force barely sufficient to defend New Orleans against such an attack as might be expected.

But for Vicksburg—an obstacle which was not overcome for nearly fourteen months—the river, we have said, was completely possessed. But armed vessels and transports, passing up and down, were frequently annoyed by attacks from guerrillas and concealed batteries. Porter, on his way up the river with the mortars, was thus attacked at Ellis's Bluffs on June 3.

Whenever these attacks were made in the vicinity of towns, it was found necessary to retaliate by holding the inhabitants responsible; and if they were repeated, the villages or towns, as the case might be, were in some instances destroyed. Natchez, Grand Gulf, and Donaldsonville, in the course of the year, suffered severely from punishments inflicted upon them in this way. The most serious collision of this nature took place early in June, at Grand Gulf. The Confederates were just then beginning to fortify that place, and Commander Palmer, fearing that the passage down the river might be obstructed, sent down the Wissahickon and Itaska, under Commander De Camp, to reduce the newly-erected batteries. These vessels arrived off Grand Gulf on the morning of June 9, when they were attacked from the shore with rifled and other cannon. After an action of two hours, in which the gun-boats were quite roughly handled, one of them being hulled seventeen and the other twenty-five times, the batteries were silenced. On the vessels one man was killed and five wounded. Palmer then decided to bring down the rest of the squadron from below Vicksburg. His position was one of some difficulty. The batteries above him were manned by a force of 500 artillerists. Their position upon the hill seemed to protect them against serious injury, and the gun-boats had much to fear from their plunging fire. He did not dare to leave a few vessels only at Vicksburg. He expected that at any moment the iron-clad ram Arkansas might come down from the Yazoo. Fort Pillow, too, had just been evacuated; and, not aware of the destruction of the Confederate fleet at Memphis, he feared that the vessels of that fleet might, in conjunction with the Arkansas, attempt a raid against his little squadron. The fortifications of Vicksburg were daily being strengthened by the arrival of new guns and ammunition. His gun-boats were "all of them in a most crippled condition;" the sick-list had largely increased; the time of the men on the Colorado had expired; he was almost out of both coal and provisions, and had little oil left for his engines. "Unless supplies come up," he writes, June 10, "we can not stay here a week longer."

Palmer sent the Katahdin and Itaska down as far as to the mouth of Red River to discover if there were any more of those formidable obstacles in the shape of batteries in process of erection, and on the afternoon of the 10th dropped down and shelled the Grand Gulf batteries for an hour. This effected nothing, and he determined, in case of the repetition of an attack from the shore, to burn the town. The attack was repeated, and the town was burned.[1]

ELLIS'S BLUFFS.

---

[1] Captain Craven, of the Brooklyn, passing up the river a week afterward, reports that he was molested nowhere on his route from Baton Rouge to Vicksburg. Speaking of Grand Gulf, he says: "The town there was in ruins, having been first riddled by shot and then destroyed by fire. On a small hill just to the right of the town was a small earthwork, which had been but recently thrown up, and was capable of receiving three or four field-pieces. This work, as well as the town, was entirely deserted."

Grand Gulf had been fired upon previously, on which occasion Lieutenant Commander E. T. Nichols, of the Winona, had notified the Mayor of Rodney, a few miles below, that a similar punishment would be visited upon that place in the event of the batteries in that vicinity firing upon the national vessels. This notification led to the following correspondence:

[No. 1.]

"Jackson, Mississippi, June 12, 1862.

"SIR,—I have the honor to inclose a copy of a letter received by the Mayor of Rodney, notifying him, in substance, that if the vessels of the United States Navy are fired upon by our troops from or near the town, vengeance will be taken upon the women and children, or, as the writer is pleased to term it, 'punishment for the offense will be visited upon the town;' and this, too, that 'we are not here to war upon unarmed and peaceable citizens.'

"Where two nations are at war, it has been customary, among civilized people, 'to punish the offense' of an attack by the armed forces of one upon those of the other by a combat with the attacking party. If such attack be made from a town, the assaulting party is not entitled to, and, so far as our troops are concerned, does not claim, any immunity by reason of the presence of women and children. What we do claim, however, and insist upon, is, that when your vessels or transports are fired upon by our troops, they shall not hasten to the nearest collection of unarmed and peaceable women and children, and wreak their vengeance upon them, as was done lately at Grand Gulf by United States vessels in retaliation for an attack with which the town had nothing more to do than had the city of St. Louis.

"My batteries are located at such points upon the river as are deemed best suited for the desired purposes, and without reference to or connection with the people of the town. Should the site happen to fall within a village, you, of course, are at liberty to return the fire. Should it be

VIEW OF VICKSBURG FROM THE RIVER.

Vicksburg, which, as regards heroic and obstinate resistance to the national arms, held almost equal rank with Richmond and Charleston, lies in the State of Mississippi, on the east bank of the river, 400 miles above New Orleans, and about the same distance from Cairo. Its commercial importance is due to its location in the midst of the great cotton-growing country along the Yazoo. It is connected with Jackson, the state capital, by railroad; and from De Soto, on the opposite bank, a railroad, running to Monroe, drains the land commerce of Northern Louisiana. It is the most important, and, at the same time, the most defensible military position on the Mississippi. At the time of the capture of New Orleans, this fact was little appreciated on either side.[1] The population of Vicksburg, before the war, was, in round numbers, 5000. The town, situated on the shelving declivity of high hills, with its dwellings scattered in groups on the terraces, presents a very picturesque appearance.

On the 20th of June, a month after the first appearance of Farragut's fleet off Vicksburg, Brigadier General Thomas Williams left Baton Rouge with a large portion of the garrison which had been there posted, and in four days' time reached a position on the peninsula opposite Vicksburg. He had only four regiments and eight field-guns. The force defending Vicksburg at this time consisted of about 10,000 men.[2] General Williams immediately set about constructing a canal across the narrow neck of the peninsula, on the Louisiana side, which, if successful, would throw Vicksburg and its defenses six miles inland. Of this we shall have more to say hereafter in connection with the projects for getting a position to the rear of the city. Porter's mortar fleet of sixteen vessels had in the mean while moved up the river to Vicksburg. It was now proposed that a junction should be effected between Farragut's fleet and that under Davis's command, as preliminary to as formidable an attempt against the city as it was possible for this combined naval force to make.

In two or three instances already the national vessels had run the gauntlet of Confederate batteries on the Mississippi. The Carondelet on the 4th, and the Pittsburg on the 6th of April, had run past the enemy's fortifications on Island No. 10. In the latter part of the same month, Farragut, with nearly his entire fleet, passed Forts Jackson and St. Philip. He did not, therefore, reckon it an enterprise of very great magnitude or peril to run the Vicksburg blockade. It is not likely that he anticipated any very important results from this operation. He knew well enough that batteries could be passed with much greater ease than they could be taken. But he had been ordered by the Navy Department and the President to do something against Vicksburg, and was disposed to strike the heaviest blow possible with the force he had in hand; and on the night of the 27th of June he had every thing in readiness for the undertaking. The order was given for a movement the next morning. Porter, who had got his mortar fleet and his gun-boats in an advantageous position, and who had been for the past two days employed in ascertaining the range of the enemy's works, was to open fire upon the latter at four o'clock A.M. He was to perform a part similar to that which had been assigned him at New Orleans—that is, he was to stand still and engage the enemy's batteries, while Farragut should pass them with his fleet. This fleet of Farragut's consisted of the

in the vicinity of one, however, the usages of civilized warfare do not justify its destruction, unless demanded by the necessities of attack or defense.

"I can not bring myself to believe that the barbarous and cowardly policy indicated in the inclosed letter will meet with the approval of any officer of rank or standing in the United States Navy. I have, therefore, thought proper to transmit it to you under a flag of truce, with the confident expectation that you will direct those under your command to confine their offensive operations as far as possible to our troops, and forbid the wanton destruction of defenseless towns, filled with unoffending non-combatants, unless required by imperious military necessity.

"The practice of slaying women and children as an act of retaliation has happily fallen into disuse in this country with the disappearance of the Indian tribes, and I trust it will not be revived by the officers of the United States Navy, but that the demolition and pillage of the unoffending little village of Grand Gulf may be permitted to stand alone and without parallel upon record.   M. LOVELL, Major General Commanding.

"Commanding Officer United States Navy, Mississippi River, near Baton Rouge."

[No. 2.]

"Baton Rouge, June 17, 1862.

"SIR,—I have to acknowledge the receipt of your communication of the 12th instant, together with its inclosure, in which you are pleased to say that vengeance will be visited upon the women and children of Rodney if our vessels are fired upon from the town. Although I find no such language contained in the letter of Lieutenant Commanding Nichols, or even any from which such inference might be drawn, still I shall meet your general remark on your own terms. You say you locate your batteries 'at such points on the river as are deemed best suited,' etc., without reference to the people of the town, and claim no immunity for your troops. Now, therefore, the violation is with you. You choose your own time and place for an attack upon our defenseless people, and should therefore see that the innocent and defenseless of your own people are out of the way before you make the attack; for rest assured that the fire will be returned, and we will not hold ourselves answerable for the death of the innocent. If we have ever fired upon your 'women and children,' it was done here at Baton Rouge, when an attempt was made to kill one of our officers, landing in a small boat manned by four boys. They were, when in the act of landing, mostly wounded by the fire of some thirty or forty horsemen, who chivalrously galloped out of the town, leaving the women and children to bear the brunt of our vengeance. At Grand Gulf, also, our transports were fired upon in passing, which caused the place to be shelled, with what effect I know not; but I do know that the fate of a town is at all times in the hands of the military commandant, who may at pleasure draw the enemy's fire upon it, and the community is made to suffer for the act of its military.

"The only instance I have known where the language of your letter could possibly apply took place at New Orleans, on the day when we passed up in front of the city, while it was still in your possession, by your soldiers firing on the crowd. I trust, however, that the time is past when women and children will be subjected by their military men to the horrors of war; it is enough for them to be subjected to the incidental inconveniences, privations, and sufferings.

"If any such things have occurred as the slaying of women and children, or innocent people, I feel well assured that it was caused by the act of your military, and much against the will of our officers; for, as Lieutenant Commanding Nichols informs the mayor, we war not against defenseless persons, but against those in open rebellion against our country, and desire to limit our punishment to them, though it may not be always in our power to do so.

"Very respectfully, your obedient servant,   D. G. FARRAGUT.

"Major General MANSFIELD LOVELL."

[1] So little notion was there of any farther struggle for the possession of Vicksburg, that we find, in an intercepted letter from Mr. Davis's niece, dated May 7, 1862, and addressed to her mother in Mississippi, the following passage: "Uncle Jeff. thinks you are safe at home, as there will be no resistance at Vicksburg, and the Yankees will hardly occupy it, and, even if they did, the army would gain nothing by marching into the country, and a few soldiers would be afraid to go so far into the interior."

[2] This was Captain Craven's estimate (*Rep. Sec. Navy, Accompanying Documents*, p. 309). This estimate tallies with that given by A. S. Abrams, one of the Vicksburg garrison. (See *Abrams's Siege of Vicksburg*, pp. 6 and 7.)

three steam-sloops Brooklyn, Hartford, and Richmond, and the gun-boats Iroquois, Oneida, Wissahickon, Sciota, Winona, Pinola, and Kennebec. The fleet was to form a double line of sailing, so that the gun-boats, advancing in the order named, should form a second line, and fire between the ships. The Hartford, as occasion offered, was to fire her bow guns on the forts at the upper end of the town, while the broadside batteries of all the ships were to be particularly directed to the guns in the forts below and on the heights. "When close enough," ordered Farragut, "give them grape." Upon reaching the bend of the river, which was just above Vicksburg, the Wissahickon, Sciota, Winona, and Pinola were in any case to continue their course, but the other gun-boats were to drop down the river again if the enemy's batteries were not thoroughly silenced.

The signal to weigh anchor was given at 2 A.M. on the 28th. At four o'clock, as had been ordered, Porter opened fire from the mortars, and almost at the same moment the Confederates fired their first gun, which was returned by the leading vessels of the fleet as they came up. On Farragut's starboard quarter, Porter brought up the Octorara, Westfield, Clifton, Jackson, Harriet Lane, and Owasco, and united in the attack. By the united efforts of the fleet and the mortar flotilla the Confederate guns were soon silenced, sometimes not replying for several minutes, and then again with but a single gun. The Hartford, in its attack upon the summit batteries, succeeded better than had been expected. The passage up the river was slow, the flag-ship having but eight pounds of steam, and even stopping once in order that the vessels in its stern might close up. The Brooklyn, Kennebec, and Katahdin failed to follow the flag-ship past the batteries, and turned back. The commanders of these vessels gave various explanations of this failure, but they do not seem to have been satisfactory to the commander of the fleet. The vessels which succeeded in passing received some injury, not of a serious character, from the upper batteries, after the latter had been passed, and suffered a loss in men of fifteen killed and thirty wounded. On the vessels which failed to pass there were no casualties. General Williams, on the Louisiana side, had a battery in operation during the action, thus affording a slight support to the fleet.

The whole significance of this bold affair is summed up in a few words by Admiral Farragut, namely, "that the forts can be passed; and we have done it, and can do it again as often as may be required of us." And that was all. We can do no more, he added, than silence the batteries for a time, as long as the enemy has a large force behind the hills to prevent our landing and holding the place. He said that it was impossible to take Vicksburg without an army of from 12,000 to 15,000 men. Admiral Porter, in his official report of the action on the 28th, says: "It is to be regretted that a combined attack of army and navy had not been made, by which something more substantial might have been accomplished. Such an attack, I think, would have resulted in the capture of the city. Ships and mortar vessels can keep full possession of the river and places near the water's edge, but they can not crawl up hills 300 feet high, and it is that part of Vicksburg which must be taken by the army. If it was intended merely to pass the batteries at Vicksburg, and make a junction with the fleet of Flag-officer Davis, the navy did it most gallantly and fearlessly.[1] It was as

PORTER'S MORTAR FLEET IN TRIM.

handsome a thing as has been done during the war, for the batteries to be passed extended full three miles, with a three-knot current against ships that could not make eight knots under the most favorable circumstances."

By six o'clock the batteries were passed, and Farragut met Lieutenant Colonel Charles Rivers Ellet, of the ram fleet, who had made his way down the river bank during the night, and who now offered to forward communications to Flag-officer Davis, and to General Halleck, then at Memphis. After effecting a junction with Davis, Farragut applied to Halleck for a military force to co-operate in an immediate attack on Vicksburg. Halleck's reply on the 3d of July was an utter disappointment.

In the mean while Vicksburg was subjected to a bombardment from the mortar-boats above and below. When Farragut passed the batteries there were but few guns mounted.[1] During the progress of the bombardment which followed, General Earl Van Dorn[2] was sent to Vicksburg, and placed in command over Brigadier General M. L. Smith. Soon afterward the garrison was re-enforced by Breckinridge's brigade from Beauregard's army. Van Dorn's appointment to this post, for which he certainly had no peculiar fitness, was received by the Mississippians with enthusiastic pleasure. The hope of successful resistance at this point was every day growing brighter. It was with no little pride that the citizens of Vicksburg contrasted their own position, and the fate of their city thus far, with what they naturally regarded the too facile surrender of other posts on the river. In this pride the ladies of the heroic city had their full share. On the morning of June 28, when Farragut's fleet was on its way past the city, and shells were falling like hail in the streets, crowds of these enthusiastic ladies might have been seen on the Court-house, the "Sky Parlor," and other prominent places in the city, gazing upon "the magnificent scene."[3]

While Vicksburg was being bombarded by mortars, Farragut and Davis

---

[1] In regard to the conduct of his own men in the bombardment, Admiral Porter says: "They know no weariness, and they really seem to take a delight in mortar-firing, which is painful even to those accustomed to it. It requires more than ordinary zeal to stand the ordeal. Though I may have been at times exacting and fault-finding with them for not conforming to the rules of the service (which requires the education of a lifetime to learn), yet I can not withhold my applause when I see these men working with such earnest and untiring devotion to their duties while under fire."—Rep. Sec. Navy, 1862, Acc. Doc., p. 410.

[1] Abrams says only seven.—Siege Vicks., p. 6. This estimate is probably considerably below the mark.
[2] "This doughty Confederate cavalier, of Rosecrans's class at West Point, has greatly astonished his old associates. West Point men of his time remember him as a small, handsome, modest youth, literally at the foot of his class. In Mexico he was on the staff of General P. F. Smith, and was very popular, for to his other qualities he added dashing bravery. His conspicuous course in the rebel interests at the breaking out of the war deceived them into thinking him a general. A good soldier he certainly was—brave, dashing, a splendid horseman, but he lacked head, and was always taking his men into culs de sacs. He died by the hand of a man who believed he had seduced his wife."—Coppee's Grant and his Campaigns, p. 133.
[3] Abrams's Siege Vicks., p. 7.

PASSAGE OF THE VICKSBURG BATTERIES BY FARRAGUT'S FLEET.

organized an expedition to ascend the Yazoo River. General Williams offered to send up a few sharp-shooters from his army to co-operate with the gun-boats Tyler, Carondelet, and the ram Queen of the West, which formed the naval part of the expedition. The object of the movement was to procure correct information concerning the obstructions and defenses of the river. It was known that eighty miles from the mouth there was a raft obstructing the passage with a battery near it below, and above, the new Confederate ram Arkansas, "a vessel represented to be well protected by iron, and very formidable in her battery." To find and capture this ram was the most important part of the expedition. The gun-boats, early on the morning of July 15, had scarcely passed the mouth of the Yazoo when they encountered the Arkansas coming down. This vessel, in her construction, resembled the Louisiana and Mississippi, destroyed at New Orleans. She was built at Memphis, and at the time of the capture of this place she succeeded in escaping up the Yazoo, while a consort of hers, built in the same manner, was destroyed. She was a sea-going steamer of 1200 tons. Her cutwater was a sharp, cast-iron, solid beak. She was thoroughly covered with T rail iron, with heavy bulwarks of thick timber, with cotton-pressed casemating, impervious to shot. Her port-holes were small, with heavy iron shutters; all her machinery was below the water-line, and she had a battery of ten guns.[1] She was commanded by Isaac N. Brown, and had a picked crew. The gun-boats met the ram about six miles above the mouth of the Yazoo. They were commanded, the Carondelet by Captain H. Walke, the Tyler by Captain Gwin, and the ram Queen of the West by Colonel Alfred Ellet. When the ram was discovered, the gun-boats were proceeding at intervals of a mile apart, the Queen of the West ahead, the Tyler next, and the Carondelet behind. The result of a conflict with the Arkansas was, to say the least, uncertain, and all the national vessels reversed their course, and retreated down the river, keeping up a running fight with

MORTAR BOATS FIRING ON VICKSBURG AT NIGHT.

the Tyler was seen to proceed from the mouth of the Yazoo, with the Arkansas closely following. It was to Admiral Farragut a moment of surprise and of mortification. Had the event been anticipated, the fate of the Arkansas could have been decided in thirty minutes. As it was, the vessels of the fleet were lying with low fires, but none of them had steam, or could get it up in time for so instant an emergency, and the ram escaped without serious injury, though she received a broadside fire from all the national vessels. The Benton, it is true, got under way and pursued the ram for some distance, but at her snail's pace the pursuit seemed only less ludicrous than the situation which would have followed if she had been so unfortunate as to overtake and come into close quarters with her adversary.

Thus far the result of the ram's appearance had not been seriously disastrous. Indeed, though this was not known at the time to her opponents, she was incapable of inflicting a very severe blow. Her smoke-stack had been shivered in pieces early in the action, and for want of steam she could not be used as a ram with any effect. The Carondelet had run ashore, her wheel-ropes being shot away, and would probably have fallen a prey to the Arkansas if the latter had had leisure for improving her opportunity. The Tyler was partially injured. About thirty men on the Federal side were killed, wounded, or missing, and

DAVIS'S FLEET ON ITS WAY TO JOIN FARRAGUT'S.

the ram for about an hour. The firing was distinctly heard by both the squadrons in the Mississippi, and it was supposed that the gun-boats were engaging batteries. But the true cause of the firing became apparent when

many of these casualties occurred among Williams's sharp-shooters, who were especially exposed. The loss on the Arkansas was ten killed and fifteen wounded.

Partly to support the few vessels of his fleet on the Lower Mississippi,

[1] *Naval Scenes on the Western Waters*, p. 59.

THE ARKANSAS RUNNING THROUGH THE UNION FLEET OFF VICKSBURG.

and partly to make another attempt against the Arkansas, Admiral Farragut determined, on the night of the 15th, to repass the Vicksburg batteries. He was supported by Davis's squadron and the mortar flotilla; but the ram, lodged under the guns of Vicksburg, was so well concealed by her situation that she escaped the destruction intended for her.

On the 22d another attack was made upon the ram, which now lay between two forts at the upper bend of the river. Farragut's fleet was four miles below, and it was understood that he would receive the ram if she should attempt to escape down the river. The attack was made by the Queen of the West, commanded by Colonel Ellet, and the Essex, under Commander W. D. Porter; but it proved a failure. The Queen of the West and the Essex passed down under cover of a fire opened upon the upper batteries by the Benton, Cincinnati, and Louisville. The Essex boldly attacked the ram, but the bow-line of the latter being let go, the current drifted her stern on, and the gun-boat, missing the Arkansas, ran ashore. There was less than a rod's distance between the two vessels, and in these close quarters the three nine-inch guns of the Essex told with serious effect upon the ram. The Queen of the West also ran at the ram, but was so severely damaged by the fire from the shore that she with difficulty escaped. "This attempt on the part of Colonel Ellet," says Farragut, "was a daring act, and one from which both Flag-officer Davis and myself tried to deter him." The Sumter, which had come down with the other vessels, on account of some misunderstanding did not join in the attack. The Essex remained aground for ten minutes, under a heavy fire, and then, getting afloat, ran down to Farragut's fleet through a storm of shot and shell, but without receiving a single blow after she left the upper forts. From the latter and from the ram she was penetrated with three projectiles, one of which went through her casemates, and, exploding inside, killed one man and wounded three of her crew. The Queen of the West steamed back, exposed to the fire from the shore and struggling against the current of the river, to Davis's squadron. She had on board two officers, four soldiers, and three negro firemen, not one of whom were injured.

Farragut had on the 20th received an order to descend the river to New Orleans. Owing to the fall in the river, this was becoming an imperative necessity. Waiting only a day or two after the engagement with the ram, and until General Williams had completed his arrangements for departure with his small force, he proceeded to obey this order. It was arranged that the Essex and Sumter, under Commander W. D. Porter, should take charge of the lower part of the river. Left in this situation, the fleet on the Mississippi, so far from being competent to make any offensive movement, was likely to have difficulty in holding its ground against the enemy, who now had, besides the Arkansas, two gun-boats on the Red River and two on the Yazoo. "I presume," says Farragut, writing from New Orleans, July 29, "Flag-officer Davis will destroy those in the Yazoo; and my gunboats chased the Music and Webb up the Red River, but drew too much water to go far."

The situation before Vicksburg, therefore, at the beginning of August, was discouraging. There was no longer any co-operating army. Flag-officer Davis's fleet was reduced in power, both by the absence of a large number of gun-boats—undergoing repairs or engaged in special duty—and by sickness among the men.[1] The garrison of Vicksburg had been largely increased, nearly doubled, and a large number of additional guns had been mounted in the batteries. The canal, which had been finished for about ten days, had proved a failure. The bulkhead was knocked away on the 22d of July, but the Mississippi, which had so often been known to change its channel in a single night on the slightest occasion, refused by a singular caprice to take the course which General Williams had opened for it, and Vicksburg, instead of becoming an inland city, had joyful occasion for self-congratulation and for laughter at the foiled project of "the Yankees." But, although the canal failed to answer the purpose for which it had been constructed, it was of great service so long as Williams remained. It had been made a means of defense "by constructing a continued breastwork and rifle-pit on the lower border, and an angle on the upper border to enfilade the canal where it was crossed by the levee. This levee, distinguished as the *new* levee, formed in itself a convenient breastwork."[2] When Williams left, however, it was no longer safe for the ordnance, commissary, hospital, and mail boats to lie at the bank. It was also impossible to maintain communication with the vessels below Vicksburg across the neck, and the latter could no longer be used to co-operate in a bombardment from below. The Sumter and Essex must now depend upon Baton Rouge and New Orleans for their supplies. Davis found, moreover, that he would be compelled to exhaust a large measure of his force in maintaining his own connection with Cairo. He determined, therefore, to abandon his position before Vicksburg, and withdraw to the mouth of the Yazoo River. From this point there was a lull of five months in the operations against Vicksburg.

The Confederate line of defense in the West at this time ran from Vicks-

BATON ROUGE, LOUISIANA.

---

[1] Davis writes, July 23, just before Williams's departure, thus: "My force is also reduced by the absence of eight gun-boats, three of which are guarding important points on the river, and five of which are undergoing repairs. I have said that I am in want of 500 men to insure the efficiency of the flotilla. In this calculation I make allowance for the return to duty of many of the sick; but 600 men would not be too many to send to me. The most sickly part of the season is approaching, and the Department would be surprised to see how the most healthy men wilt and break down under the ceaseless and exhausting heat of this pernicious climate. Men who are apparently in health at the close of the day's work, sink away and die suddenly at night under the combined effects of heat and malarial poison. The enemy, however, suffers a great deal more than we do. He counts seventeen or twenty thousand men on his rolls, but can hardly muster five thousand in his ranks. To sickness are added, in his case, the want of hospital accommodations, the want of medicines, and the want of suitable food. I learn that General Williams is about to move down the river. Should it prove so, it will be very unfortunate in its results. This is one of the points at which the co-operation of the army is most essential."

[2] *Rep. Sec. Navy*, 1862, Acc. Doc., p. 517.

burg southward parallel with the river, and from the same point deflected northward to the northern boundary of the State of Mississippi, and thence turned eastward, following the Virginia and East Tennessee Railroad. Morgan and Forrest had just been raiding through Kentucky and Tennessee, preparatory to Bragg's invasion. General Grant, on the northern border of Mississippi, was confronted by large Confederate armies under Price, Lovell, and Van Dorn. As soon as General Williams left Vicksburg, Breckinridge withdrew his division in order to attack Baton Rouge, and, in co-operation with the ram Arkansas, to secure the Lower Mississippi. If the expedition could have been undertaken a few days sooner, it would have been a success so far as Baton Rouge was concerned. Breckinridge doubtless knew that a large proportion of Williams's troops were suffering from sickness. He could not have reckoned too strongly upon this element in his favor, for when Williams left Vicksburg he had scarcely well soldiers enough to take care of the sick ones.

Breckinridge's force received marching orders on the 26th of July. It was transported by railroad as far as Tangipahoa, in St. Helena Parish, Louisiana, which became the base of operations. Between forty and fifty miles from this place, at Camp Moore, on the Comite River, there was a body of Louisiana troops being fitted for active duty in the field. There were only one or two regiments here, with a battery, and a few cavalry, the whole under the command of General Ruggles. This became one of the two columns acting against Baton Rouge, and remained under Ruggles's immediate command, while the column from Vicksburg was assigned to General Charles Clarke. The latter consisted of two brigades, of four regiments, or parts of regiments, each. The troops of this column were all veterans. The design was to attack Baton Rouge from the rear, while the Arkansas, with the help of the Webb and Music from the Red River, engaged the Federal gun-boats. Several days were occupied in waiting until the ram should have recovered from the wounds inflicted upon her in her recent conflicts with the Mississippi squadron. At length Van Dorn telegraphed to Breckinridge that the ram was ready, and would be due at Baton Rouge on the morning of August 5th, which time, therefore, was fixed for the attack.

General Williams had not returned to Baton Rouge a moment too soon. He was well aware of the enemy's design, and industriously provided for the coming battle. On the river were the Essex, Cayuga, Sumter, Kineo, and Katahdin. On the land Williams had nearly 2500 men available for action. These were encamped in the rear of the city, and it was determined to meet the enemy just on the skirts of the town, and there dispute his nearer approach.

The march to Comite River from Tangipahoa, a distance of about fifty miles, was at this season very exhausting to the Confederates under Breckinridge. The heat was intense, and the men fell rapidly out of the ranks from sickness or fatigue. Almost every farm-house on the roadside was converted into a hospital. There was a brief halt at Camp Moore, and on the 4th, a little before midnight, the two columns were pushing on over a smooth sandy road that led through well-cultivated plantations to Baton Rouge. About dawn, when these columns were within three miles of the city, there occurred a strange misadventure. They were passing by a piece of woods when they were fired upon by a company of partisan rangers, who mistook them for Federal troops. Before the mistake was rectified several casualties had occurred, and the line had been thrown into confusion. General Helm, commanding one of the brigades, was disabled by the fall of his horse into a ditch, and was withdrawn from the field. It was here that Captain Alexander A. Todd, a brother-in-law of President Lincoln and an officer on General Helm's staff, met his end. He was instantly killed by a shot from the woods.[1] Order was soon restored, and the columns marched on, Clarke's to the right and Ruggles's to the left. They first appeared in the open fields bordering on the Greenwell Springs Road, toward the upper part of the city and southeast of the Arsenal. Here they attempted without success to draw out the national forces. Failing in this, they veered to the southward a little farther, and it was in the position thus taken that the battle of Baton Rouge was fought.

The streets of the city ran out to the verge of the Federal encampments. The battle-field was flat in surface, extending in the form of an arc about the city from the Arsenal grounds to those of the Capitol. Bayou Gross ran north and east of the Arsenal grounds. Within the latter were two guns, sweeping the field to the left of the Fourth Wisconsin and Ninth Connecticut, on the opposite or right bank of the bayou. In the rear of the centre of the Ninth were two guns, and on the other side of a knoll in the Government Cemetery two more. Farther to the right was the Fourteenth Maine, on the left of the Greenwell Springs Road and in rear of the Bayou Sara Road, which crosses at right angles the two main approaches to the city. In the road itself were four guns, afterward increased to six. On the right of the Greenwell Springs Road was the Twenty-first Indiana (which was under cover of a wood), with the Magnolia Cemetery in its front. To the right

of Magnolia Cemetery the Sixth Michigan continued the line across a country road and another known as the Clay Cut Road, supporting two guns in the country road. The Seventh Vermont was stationed in the rear of the two latter regiments, on the right of the Catholic cemetery. The extreme right was held by the Thirtieth Massachusetts, a short distance in the rear of the Capitol, and supporting Nims's Battery. Considering that the attack was expected on the Greenwell Springs Road, this disposition of force was an admirable one, the only fault consisting in the unfortunate position of the encampments of the Fourteenth Maine and Twenty-first Indiana, which were in front of those regiments, and liable to capture in case of their retreat, an event which really did occur.[1]

The Confederates at daylight drove back the Federal pickets. General Breckinridge in person led the right wing, his young son, Cabell, acting as aid-de-camp. The full force of the first determined attack fell upon the Indiana, Maine, and Michigan regiments. The resistance was obstinate. The Federal flanks were called in to support the centre; but the enemy succeeded, after a sharp conflict, in driving in the regiments in the advanced front and capturing their encampments. The Seventh Vermont failed to give efficient support at the critical moment, and Colonel Roberts, its commander, was killed while vainly attempting to urge forward his men. "He was worthy," said General Butler, "of a better disciplined regiment and a better fate." The Indiana regiment lost all its field-officers before retreating. General Williams had just given the order for the line to fall back, when, seeing the condition of this regiment, he advanced to its front, and told the Indianians that, in the absence of their officers, he would lead them himself. Scarcely had the responding cheers died away when he fell, mortally wounded.[2] The batteries had done good execution. The soldiers, though many of them had never seen a battle before, disputed bravely every advance of

DEATH OF GENERAL THOMAS WILLIAMS.

the enemy. It had come at length to a hand-to-hand conflict, the result of which seemed to be in favor of the Confederates. As the national forces withdrew from the vicinity of Magnolia Cemetery, where had been the deadliest conflict, the gun-boats in the river opened on both of the enemy's flanks, their fire over the city being directed by a system of signals from the Capitol, instituted by Lieutenant Ransom.

In the mean time Breckinridge was listening anxiously in the intervals of conflict for the guns of the Arkansas; but he heard them not. About six miles from the city the ram had stopped in her progress down the river, unable to proceed on account of her inefficient engine machinery. She had left Brown, her former commander, sick at Vicksburg, and was now commanded by Lieutenant Stevens. Her crew numbered 180 men, well chosen; she had ten heavy guns (six 8-inch and four 50-pounders), but could not be brought into action.

Disappointed at the non-appearance of this indispensable ally, and seeing

[1] A Confederate, alluding to this event, says: "Captain Todd was a young gentleman of fine accomplishments, great personal daring, exceeding amiability, and the warmest home affections. But the evening before he wrote to his mother, and just before the accident he was conversing with Lieutenant L. E. Payne, ordnance officer of the brigade, communicating the messages he wished conveyed home in case of his fall. . . . Brave boy! he met his end serenely, and his body was interred by gentle and loving hands."

[1] See Weitzel's Report in Reb. Rec., vol. v., p. 301, Doc. Fletcher, an English historian of the war, says: "The position does not appear to have been well selected, as in front of the centre of the line, between the two roads, was a large cemetery, overgrown with high grass, and affording both cover for an advancing enemy, and, when occupied, a strong offensive position." This is probably true so far as the position was related to the shape which the attack finally took.
[2] The following General Order (No. 56) was issued by General Butler after the battle:

"The commanding general announces to the Army of the Gulf the sad event of the death of Brigadier General Thomas Williams, commanding Second Brigade, in camp at Baton Rouge.

"The victorious achievement—the repulse of the division of Major General Breckinridge by the troops led by General Williams, and the destruction of the mail-clad Arkansas by Captain Porter, of the Navy—is made sorrowful by the fall of our brave, gallant, and successful fellow-soldier.

"General Williams graduated at West Point in 1837; at once joined the Fourth Artillery in Florida, where he served with distinction; was thrice breveted for gallant and meritorious services in Mexico as a member of General Scott's staff. His life was that of a soldier devoted to his country's service. His country mourns in sympathy with his wife and children, now that country's care and precious charge.

"We, his comrades in arms, who had learned to love him, weep the true friend, the gallant gentleman, the brave soldier, the accomplished officer, and the devoted Christian. All this and more went out when Williams died. By a singular felicity, the manner of his death illustrated each of these generous qualities.

"The chivalric American gentleman, he gave up the vantage of the cover of the houses of the city, forming his lines in the open field, lest the women and children of his enemies should be hurt in the fight.

"A good general, he made his dispositions and prepared for battle at break of day, when he met his foe.

"A brave soldier, he received the death-shot leading his men.

"A patriot hero, he was fighting the battle, and died as went up the cheer of victory.

"A Christian, he sleeps in the hope of the blessed Redeemer.

"His virtues we can not exceed; his example we may emulate; and, mourning his death, we pray, 'May our last end be like his.'"

DESTRUCTION OF THE ARKANSAS.

the impossibility of attempting to fight the national infantry, artillery, and gun-boats at the same time, Breckinridge ordered the captured camps to be burned as a preliminary to withdrawal from the field. His forces found some shelter from the shells of the fleet in the woods which skirted the battle-field all around. It was not noon yet when the battle was over, and the field was left in possession of the national forces, under Colonel Cahill, who had succeeded to the command after the death of General Williams.

The enemy had suffered severe loss, especially in officers, among whom General Clarke was left in our hands mortally wounded. His dead, to the number of seventy, were left upon the field, so hasty had been his retreat. The battle-field gave striking evidence of the nature of the conflict. In front of the Indiana and Michigan regiments some of the enemy were found who had been killed with rails, which the Union soldiers, having lost their arms, had used as weapons. "In one spot," says an eye-witness, "behind a beautiful tomb, with effigies of infant children kneeling, twelve dead rebels were found in one heap."

The forces engaged in the battle, though variously estimated, were probably not very far from equal.[1] The loss on the national side was 90 killed and 250 wounded.

The morning after the battle, the Essex, accompanied by the Cayuga and Sumter, advanced up the river to where the Arkansas was lying, abandoned by her companions, the Webb and Music. There was no serious conflict. Commander W. D. Porter engaged the ram for a short time, when the latter was fired, deserted, and then blown up. Very soon the vessels of the national fleet saw floating past them the shattered fragments of their most formidable antagonist on the Mississippi. In informing the Naval Secretary of this event, Admiral Farragut said: "It is one of the happiest moments of my life that I am able to inform the Department of the destruction of the ram Arkansas, not because I held the iron-clad in such terror, but because the community did."

A few days after the battle (August 16) Baton Rouge was evacuated by the national troops, and the place was afterward held by the naval force.

Sherman had been confirmed major general of volunteers on the 1st of May, 1862. In urging this appointment, Halleck, writing from the West shortly after the battle of Shiloh, said: "It is the unanimous opinion here that Brigadier General W. T. Sherman saved the fortunes of the day on the 6th, and contributed largely to the glorious victory of the 7th." At the time when Halleck wrote thus, Grant was under a cloud; his military qualities were scarcely appreciated; he was thrust somewhat into the background, and subjected to much mortification, enjoying little of that confidence which he afterward won from the government. But in this unfortunate period of his career his rightful claims were supported heartily and in full by General Sherman.[2] Afterward when, at the very close of the war, the latter was for one single act bitterly and unjustly calumniated, he received from General Grant a full return of sympathy and support. Grant had always believed in Sherman, even when the latter had

been called insane. He always gave him the most responsible position under his command. In recommending his promotion to the rank of brigadier general in the regular army in 1863, he says: "At the battle of Shiloh, on the first day, he held, with raw troops, the key-point of the landing. It is no disparagement to any other officer to say that I do not believe there was another division commander on the field who had the skill and experience to have done it. To his individual efforts I am indebted for the success of that battle."

When Halleck was called to Washington in July, 1862, to assume the duties of general-in-chief, the Department of the Mississippi was assigned to the hero of Fort Donelson.[1] There was at that time a lull in military operations, and Grant had leisure to give attention to the general administration of affairs in this department. One of the very first things which he did was to send Sherman, with his own and Hurlbut's divisions, to occupy Memphis as its military commander. Sherman assumed command of the district, superseding General Hovey, on the 21st of July, stationing his own division in Fort Pickering, Hurlbut's on the river below, and sending the other troops to Helena. He retained the mayor and other civil officers of the city in their offices, and confined the action of provost-marshal guards to persons in the military service, and to buildings and grounds used by the army. All citizens were required to yield obedience to the United States government or leave the district; if they staid, and gave aid to the enemy, they were to be treated as spies. He did not exact from all a formal oath of allegiance. He required no military passports for inland travel, but he restricted it to the five main roads leading from the city, and there was a minute inspection of all persons and property going in or out. The principal matter requiring stringent regulations was that of trade. The exportation of salt and of all war material was prohibited. All cotton bought beyond the lines and brought in had to be purchased on contracts for payment at the close of the war, because, if paid for in coin or in treasury notes, these were almost always sure to find their way into the coffers of the Confederate treasury.

As the army penetrated the southern districts along the Mississippi, the temptation to indulge in cotton speculation became a great obstruction to military discipline. But, notwithstanding this, it was found expedient to allow a partial trade in cotton, though every effort was made by General Grant to prevent this commerce from demoralizing his subordinate officers. It was manifestly the policy of the government to drain the South of its cotton. This important staple was an invaluable aid to the enemy; it was a part of his war material, since his foreign loans were based entirely upon a cotton basis. It seemed wise, therefore, to make it for the interest of Southern cotton-holders to retain the staple, instead of burning it or allowing it to pass into the hands of the Confederate government. This temptation was afforded by allowing a partial trade.[2]

[1] It was on October 16, 1862, that General Grant was made commander of the Department of the Tennessee, this department being made to include Cairo, Forts Henry and Donelson, Northern Mississippi, and portions of Kentucky and Tennessee west of the Tennessee River.
[2] The connection of the cotton question with the Confederate conduct of the war is so important that some of its details may be interesting to the reader.
The first auction sale of confiscated cotton from Port Royal took place in New York on the 10th of June, 1862. At this sale seventy-nine bales were sold, at an average of sixty cents per pound. From this time on to the close of the war such sales were quite frequent. Before a single bale of cotton had been confiscated, however, the Confederates had contemplated the possibility of such conquests on the part of the United States government as would bring into its possession a portion of their accumulated stores. As early as February 26, 1862, a meeting of cotton and tobacco planters was held at Richmond to consider the expediency of the purchase by the Confederacy, or of a voluntary destruction of the entire tobacco and cotton crop. The Richmond Examiner describes the audience as "one of the largest, wealthiest, and most intellectual meetings" ever

COTTON HOARDS IN SOUTHERN SWAMPS.

[1] Whatever odds there may have been were certainly in favor of the Confederates. The wide discrepancy in the estimates given is somewhat singular. Pollard says Breckinridge had less than 3000 men, and Williams nearly 6000. Abbott, on the other hand, makes Williams's force less than 2500, and Breckinridge's 8000. The only authority for this latter estimate of the enemy's numbers is a soldier's letter published in the Rebellion Record (vol. v., p. 307, Doc.). This letter is throughout wholly unreliable. In a later statement Abbott estimates the enemy's force at 5000. Cahill makes Williams's force 2500, and that of the enemy ten regiments, or 5000 men. Weitzel estimates Breckinridge's force at 6000. Fletcher makes the numbers on both sides about 4000. It is possible that the enemy may have numbered between 3000 and 4000; Williams certainly had not 3000 men.
[2] A staff-officer of General Grant thus writes of this period: "La Fontaine truthfully says, 'Aucun chemin de fleurs ne conduit à la gloire.' Detraction was busy with her poisonous tongue. Grant was more bitterly assailed now than at any previous time, as a 'butcher,' as 'incompetent,' and as being a 'drunkard.' Some one was disparaging Grant in Sherman's presence, when the latter broke out with, 'It won't do, sir, it won't do; Grant is a great general! He stood by me when I was crazy, and I stood by him when he was drunk, and now, sir, we stand by each other.'"

Toward the close of October Sherman was summoned to meet Grant at Columbus for military consultation. The Department of the Mississippi had been broken up, and General Grant was at the head of the Department of the Tennessee. About this time Rosecrans assumed command of the Department of the Cumberland. Corinth and Perryville had been fought, and both battles—that of Corinth especially—had resulted in important national victories. The objective point in the campaign now contemplated by General Grant was Vicksburg.

During the interval of some months in which Vicksburg had been left undisturbed, the enemy had strengthened its fortifications. Several additional batteries had been erected above the town, and a strong line of defenses had been thrown up from Chickasaw Bayou to Haines's Bluff on the Yazoo River. The bluff itself had been fortified, and opposed an insuperable obstacle to the ascent of the national fleet farther up the river. Port Hudson, in the mean time, had become a strong-hold second only to Vicksburg in importance, and between these two points the Mississippi (as also the Red River) was in full possession of the Confederates, who had thus an opportunity of availing themselves, to an almost unlimited extent, of the abundant supplies to be obtained from Louisiana and Texas. After Van Dorn's defeat at Corinth, he had been superseded by John C. Pemberton, a favorite of President Davis, who, that he might outrank Van Dorn and Lovell, had been made a lieutenant general. This officer has been very severely criticised by Southern writers on the ground of his general incompetency for the position assigned him, and, in particular, for his apathy during this important period, when the opportunities for provisioning Vicksburg and increasing its efficiency as a defensive point appear to have been neglected. He made his head-quarters, it is said, at this time rather at Jackson than at Vicksburg, only paying an occasional visit to Vicksburg. He thought, probably, and with good reason, that his presence was imperatively demanded to the rear and westward of Vicksburg, to guard against

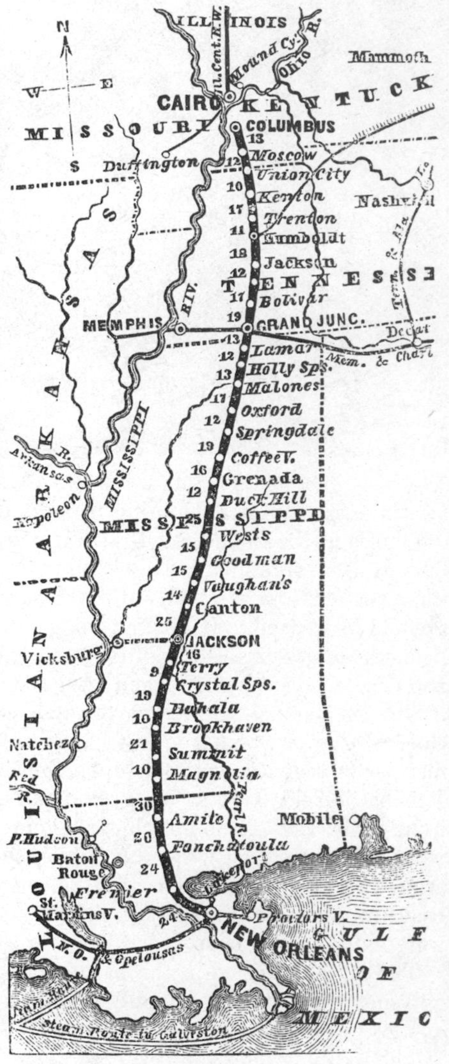

MAP OF THE MISSISSIPPI CENTRAL RAILROAD.

sembled in that city. The speeches made and the resolutions adopted were certainly characteristic. General T. J. Green, of North Carolina, having called the meeting to order, the Hon. C. K. Marshall arose to read the resolutions. "We have it in our power," he said, by way of preface, "to do what will have a serious influence not only within the city of Richmond, but may ameliorate the condition of the race of mankind at large."

The following is a copy of the resolutions:

"Whereas, the government of the United States have made an unprovoked, flagrant, and wicked war on the government and people of the Confederate States, and have conducted that war on principles hitherto unknown among civilized nations; and, whereas, we feel that our only safety against so ruthless and unrelenting a foe is to be found in the courage, patriotism, and self-sacrificing spirit of our people; and, whereas, no sacrifice, however enormous, is too great if it only brings us freedom from our oppressors; and, whereas, the tyrants and despots of the North have openly proclaimed their purpose to desolate our homes and appropriate our property to their own use, and have, in various instances, carried the infamous threat into practical execution by plundering our people of cotton, tobacco, rice, and other property; and, whereas, fire, when applied by heroic hands, is more formidable than the sword, therefore it is by this meeting

"*Resolved*, That as a means of national safety, dictated alike by military necessity and true patriotism, we deem it the imperative duty of this government to adopt measures for the purchase of the entire crops of cotton and tobacco now on hand, with the purpose of at once preventing the appropriation of them by the invaders of our soil and country, and making a fair and equitable compensation for the same to their owners, by such arrangements as shall enable the government to meet the debt incurred thereby without involving the public treasury in any serious liability on account of the said purchase. Certificate of government liability to be given for the entire property.

"*Resolved*, That, as the owners of these great staples, the government would hold in its hands the power of removing so great temptation from the path of the Federal army, now making its raids into our country, and robbing our citizens under the avowed pledges of supplying, by force, the markets of the world with these valuable articles of demand, which must necessarily be done, if those pledges are redeemed, by the total bankruptcy of our planting interests on the one hand, and the utter subjugation and enslavement of the people of the South on the other.

"*Resolved*, That, possessed of these products, it would become the solemn duty of the government to take immediate action through commissioners appointed for that purpose, or otherwise to take an account of such portions of said crops as are at exposed places, first furnishing the owners thereof with certificates of the amount and value of their crops as evidences of debt by the government therefor, and consign the property to the devouring flames.

"*Resolved*, That in case the owners of said staples decline to accept the terms offered by the government, a tax of —— cents per pound should be assessed and collected from such crops, and if finally lost or sacrificed, as a measure of public safety thereafter, such owners should not be allowed any compensation for the same.

"*Resolved*, That where other articles of produce or stock are exposed to the raids of the enemy, they should be removed if practicable, and if not practicable, an inventory of them should be taken, with an estimate of their value, by military authority, or a government agent, or, in the absence of either, by competent citizens, and certified to by them, and said property forthwith destroyed, and the parties thus deprived of their property should be indemnified by the government."

Mr. Marshall then made a speech on the resolutions. He alluded, in terms so extravagant as to appear ludicrous, to the expedients to which the Confederates had been driven by the blockade. "Men," he said, "have seized pikes and lances, for want of proper arms, to defend their wives, and daughters, and mothers." He thought the Richmond government did not fully appreciate the exigency of the times. If it had purchased the first cotton crop, the Southern navy might then have boasted of thirty such vessels as the Merrimac. The last crop was now actually rotting unbaled. They had been taught to believe that France and England wanted cotton so badly that they would come and get it. Why didn't they come? He had begun to doubt whether there were such countries as France and England. "The enemy found cotton at Ship Island; some, it is true, they found in flames, but not enough of it. At Florence they went up and took an inconsiderable quantity. No one seemed to think of setting fire to it. At Nashville they will perhaps get fifty thousand bales, and the owners, to save their property, will have to swear allegiance to that miserable tyrant, Abe Lincoln. And presently they will descend the Mississippi with perhaps fifty gun-boats, and compel the negroes to load them with cotton, and send it to Europe, and say, We have opened a cotton port—there is the evidence. I want us to do something manly—something grand. I want the Confederate government to buy all the cotton, and, if need be, destroy it. If one of those pillars which support this temple were cotton, and the other tobacco, and England, France, Russia, and the United States of America, *and ourselves* depended on them for existence, and it were necessary, I would, Samson-like, drag them down, *and let one universal ruin overwhelm civilization*. Suppose, as these resolutions propose, the government buys the cotton and tobacco crops, it is not to be expected that it will soon be able to pay for them. Hardships will be the consequence. Great numbers must suffer. A tax will have to be imposed. I will suppose that half of the cotton and tobacco crop has been burned. My cotton has been burned, and I have received seven cents a pound from the government, while my neighbor's, whose crop has not been burned, has been enhanced double in value. His small crop of cotton would be a fortune, yet who among us would hesitate to apply the torch to it sooner than it should fall into the hands of the enemy? But suppose the government were to buy the whole crop, and determine to burn it (as I want them to do), that the world may see that this little republic, as they may choose to consider us, can strike a blow that will send consternation through the world, while they are talking about conquering the republic and hanging the President. I want the government to come forward and say, Here is the money for four million bales of cotton, and give it to her commissioners, and say, Burn it. I want the government to go in search of the cotton, instead of leaving it to be captured by her [that is, the enemy's] iron-clad steamers. The government have two million of bales as a financial measure. There are some gentlemen present who raise as much as four thousand bales of cotton, and who say they will themselves burn it, indemnity or not, rather than the Yankees shall get possession of it. A lady of my acquaintance has said she will not only burn her crop, but her house itself, and take to the forest, rather than see the enemy possess it. We shall ruin our own interest by letting this crop lie here, and putting another crop upon it. Cotton, instead of being ten cents, will not command more than three cents. Suppose the blockade were opened now, we could not get it to market by August. The boats which used to transport our cotton are engaged in making war upon us, and some of them have got well peppered at Fort Donelson. They are to-day planting cotton in Texas, and next week they will begin to plant farther north. I needn't enlarge on this to planters. It is evident to them there will be two crops on the market before next January. Some will say we will force England to go to India for cotton. I will say to her, Go! England has spent three hundred and fifty million pounds, and gotten Louisiana planters to go to those distant countries, and has been obliged to give it up as a forlorn hope. But suppose England finds other cotton-fields, I'd like to know if we can't find other spinners for our crops, and be forever independent of her. To the west of us are two little countries, China and Japan. In China they desire to put all their lands in tea, but they fear to discontinue the raising of cotton. If they could get cotton elsewhere, they would put all the land in tea. Well, then, the best spinners and weavers in China can be hired for nine cents a day, and we can get them to spin and weave our cotton long before England can find other cotton-fields. China and Japan are not so distant from us as we were from England when Whitney put the first cotton-gin in operation in Savannah. I hope Congress will take up and pass these resolutions. I have great hope from this meeting. So much have these resolutions to recommend them to the people of the Southern Confederacy, that, were I addressing them to-night, I believe I could get an overwhelming vote for government buying the entire crops of cotton and tobacco, and consigning them to the flames."

Governor Moore, of Kentucky, then addressed the meeting, advocating the resolutions.

On motion of Edmund Ruffin, who fired the first gun of the war, and who blew his brains out after the defeat of the Confederacy, the resolutions were put to vote, and unanimously adopted. Henry S. Foote, the Tennessee senator in the Confederate Congress, was then called to the stand, and strongly approved of the resolutions.

About the same time, a bill was reported in the Confederate Senate to indemnify planters for property destroyed to prevent its capture. The bill, as passed, made no such provision, but made it the duty of all military commanders to destroy all cotton, tobacco, or other property that might be useful to the enemy, if the same could not be safely removed, whenever said property was, in their judgment, liable to capture. It was estimated that the amount of cotton and tobacco which would thus be destroyed would be about one twentieth of the entire crop. On the 3d of March a resolution was passed in the House advising planters to raise provisions and cattle in place of cotton and tobacco. This came before the Senate March 12, and Mr. Brown, of Mississippi, proposed a substitute, in the form of a bill to curtail the cotton crop for 1862, the amount being limited to three bales for each planter, and an additional bale per head for each hand employed in its culture, and inflicting a penalty of forty dollars for every bale raised above this quota. He thought the House measure would affect injuriously the patriotic planters, while it enriched the disloyal.

Mr. Orr, of South Carolina, thought the number of "patriotic planters" was very small. Wigfall, of Texas, was not so sure about the expediency of neglecting to raise cotton. Mr. Barnwell, of South Carolina, thought that on the cultivation of cotton, and the increase of supplies of that staple for the market, depended not only the sources of wealth, but the importance, consequence, and weight of the Confederacy with foreign nations. "We must," he said, "raise it, hold it, and fight for it." Besides, he thought the power assumed by Mr. Brown's substitute the grossest assumption of authority he had ever witnessed. Mr. Hunter, of Virginia, objected on the ground that the measure taxed the patriotism of the planters, and was an interference with state rights. Like Barnwell, he thought that reducing the supply would so advance the price that other sources of cotton would be sought. Mr. Brown urged that the main object of the United States in descending the river was to get cotton, and that there should be as little of it to be found as possible. The idea that cotton could be raised in India was "played out." He was in favor of burning all the cotton they had, and raising no more until the world was disposed to do them justice. Semmes, of Louisiana, said he had long since abandoned the idea that cotton was king. England would not interfere for it. "Rather than make war with the United States, she would convert her government into an eleemosynary for the maintenance of her hordes of starving operatives." He should vote for the resolution, to warn the people of a lengthy war, and that they must raise provisions. The resolution, being put to vote, was lost.

On the 6th of May, in answer to an inquiry made by a Southern firm whether cotton purchased on foreign account would be exempted from the order enjoining the destruction of all cotton about to fall into the enemy's hands, J. P. Benjamin, the Confederate Secretary of State, replied that if purchases of that sort were made, it must be at the risk of the purchasers.

The Charleston *Courier* of May 14 published a circular which it claimed to be "the deliberate expression of the wealthiest and most influential class of the citizens of New Orleans." For manifest reasons no signatures were attached. After a chivalric prelude, the circular goes on to urge the destruction of every bale of cotton liable to capture on the Western rivers, and the refusal to ship or sell a bale until the independence of the Confederacy was recognized. "Let the conquest of the United States," it said, "be a barren one. If we are true to ourselves there will be no trade, and the countless millions of foreign products will be without a purchaser. How long will they remain idle spectators of such a scene," etc. For copying this circular, the New Orleans *Bee* was on the 16th suppressed by General Butler. The same day, for publishing an article of similar purport, the general took possession of the New Orleans *Delta*.

The planters, for the most part, justified Mr. Orr's doubt of their patriotism. They were very reluctant to burn their cotton, and in most cases where the destruction was accomplished it was by Confederate guerrillas. Such, for instance, was the case near Memphis, where, toward the last of June, a large body of Confederate cavalry visited a number of plantations on the line of the Memphis and Charleston Railroad, burning great quantities of cotton, and arresting all persons found purchasing that staple. But, in spite of every effort made by the Confederate government, large quantities of cotton were seized by the United States at every step of the army's progress southward. A portion of the cotton found belonged to the Confederate government, and a portion to private citizens, who had in many instances secreted it against the very occasion of possible capture.

Mr. Pollard, the Southern historian, thinks it was a great mistake that the Confederate government did not, in 1861, purchase the entire cotton crop, and make it the basis of its credit. He estimates that there were at this time 3,500,000 bales of cotton in the South, which might have been secured at the rate of seven cents a pound. He enters into an indignant protest against the illicit trade in cotton indulged in by the planters: "The country had taken a solemn resolution to burn the cotton in advance of the enemy; but the conflagration of this staple soon became a rare event; instead of being committed to the flames it was spirited to Yankee markets. Nor were these operations always disguised. Some commercial houses in the Confederacy counted their gains by millions of dollars since the war, through the favor of the government in allowing them to export cotton at pleasure. . . . The cotton and sugar planters of the extreme South, who prior to the war were loudest for secession, were at the same time known to buy every article of their consumption in Yankee markets, and to cherish an ambition of shining in the society of Northern hotels. It is not surprising that many of these affected patriots have found congenial occupation in this war in planting in copartnership with the enemy, or in smuggling cotton into his lines. The North is said to have obtained in the progress of this war [Pollard is writing this in 1863], from the Southwest and Charleston, enough cotton at present prices to uphold its whole system of currency—a damning testimony to the avarice of the planter. Yet it is nothing more than a convincing proof, in general, that property, though very pretentious of patriotism, when identified with selfishness, is one of the most weak and cowardly things in revolutions, and the first to succumb under the horrors of war."—*Pollard's Second Year of the War*, p. 289.

the operations of General Grant, which were threatened in that quarter. It has been said that Pemberton was in favor of evacuating all points held by the Confederates on the water, and had even recommended the abandonment of Charleston and the destruction of its works.[1] He certainly did not act upon this theory in the Vicksburg campaign.

The first thing to be accomplished by General Grant was the expulsion of the enemy from the line of the Tallahatchie. Then, while Rosecrans occupied Bragg, Grant, with Sherman's help, proposed to take Vicksburg. The details of the campaign were admirably planned, and, so far as the principal movements were concerned, successfully carried out up to just the last point, when the whole scheme miscarried, not by reason of a great defeat, but by the disgraceful and unnecessary surrender of Holly Springs.

In the first stage of the campaign, as arranged by Grant and Sherman, three columns were to move—one, under Grant, from Jackson, in Tennessee; a second, under Sherman, from Memphis; and a third, consisting mainly of a cavalry force, under C. C. Washburne, from Helena—against Pemberton's army on the Tallahatchie, numbering 40,000 men.[2] The success of this first part of the campaign is thus concisely summed up by Sherman: "Grant moved direct on Pemberton, while I moved from Memphis, and a smaller force under General Washburne struck directly for Grenada; and the first thing Pemberton knew, the dépôt of his supplies was almost in the grasp of a small cavalry force, and he fell back in confusion, and gave us the Tallahatchie without a battle."[3]

From the vantage-ground thus gained Grant could almost see his way into Vicksburg. To him, then, Jackson seemed almost within his grasp, and thence it was but a step into the coveted strong-hold. The force sent from Helena, which had now been recalled (perhaps too soon), had swept a clear course for him to Grenada. Pemberton had fallen back to Canton, a few miles north of Jackson. On November 29th Grant reached Holly Springs; on December 3d his head-quarters were at Oxford, and his cavalry in the advance were driving Van Dorn out from Water Valley and Coffeeville. Not a score of miles from Coffeeville is Grenada; and if all holds well behind—at the dozen points in the rear where garrisons have been left to keep open communications—Jackson must fall before Christmas, and Vicksburg before New Year.

So sure was Grant of his goal, that, while at Oxford (December 8), he dispatched General Sherman, commanding the right wing of his army,[4] to undertake a co-operative expedition from Memphis against Vicksburg. Sherman was to take with him one division of his present command, and all the spare troops from Memphis and Helena. Scarcely a fortnight was allowed for the preparation of this important but ill-fated expedition. In the mean while Grant waited, or pushed on slowly, so as to give the appearance of a continuous movement. On the 14th of December he wrote to Sherman, saying that, for a week hence, his head-quarters would be at Coffeeville, and expressing particular anxiety to have the Helena cavalry back again with him—evidently not at ease about Van Dorn's movements in his rear. With one eye on Vicksburg, he was forced to cast the other suspiciously on Holly Springs, his principal dépôt of provisions and ammunition, garrisoned with little over a thousand men under Colonel R. C. Murphy. Van Dorn was leading his cavalry against this place, and Grant, knowing this, gave Murphy timely warning. The blow fell suddenly, on December 20, and found Murphy unprepared. The place was surrendered, and Grant, cut off from his base, was obliged to fall back to Grand Junction, and to give up a campaign which, but for this fatal surrender, promised a fortunate issue.

Sherman embarked from Memphis on the 20th of December,[5] the very day on which Holly Springs was surrendered. He had in his command Morgan's and the two Smiths' divisions—about 30,000 men. At Helena this army was re-enforced by over 12,000 men under General Frederick Steele, comprising the brigades of Hovey, Thayer, Blair, and Wyman.

From a letter written by Sherman to Porter (December 8), we gather a pretty definite idea of the objects which the expedition was intended to ac-

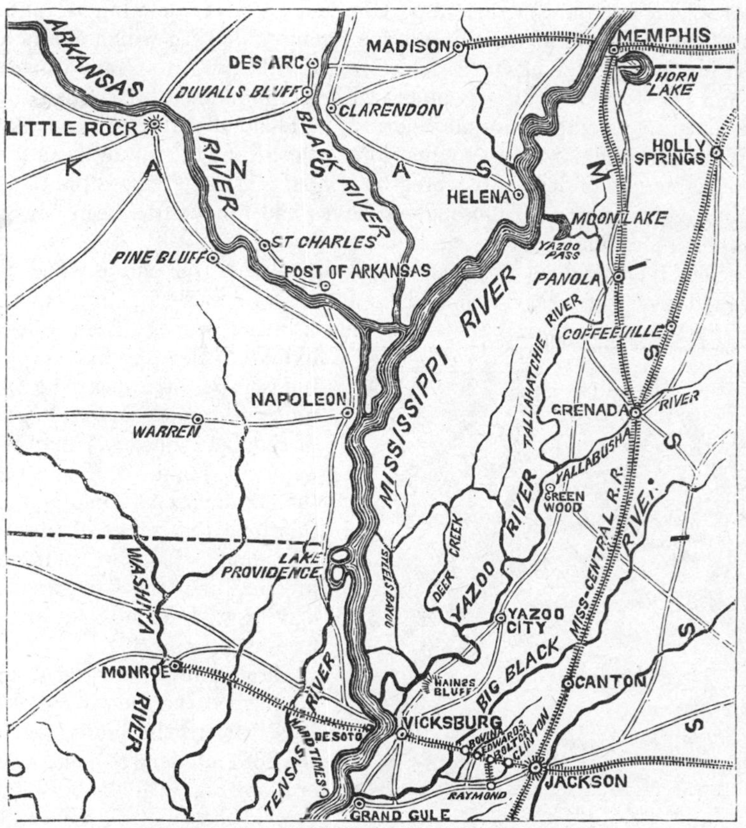

MAP ILLUSTRATING OPERATIONS ON THE YAZOO AND THE ARKANSAS.

complish. Sherman at this time, and, indeed, up to the time of his own defeat, confidently expected that Grant would succeed on the northeast of Vicksburg—a result which, so far as he was concerned, was chiefly valuable because it would keep Pemberton on the line of the Yalabusha, and thus insure his own success on the Yazoo. "We hope," he writes, "that they (the rebels) will halt and re-form behind the Yalabusha, with Grenada as their centre. If so, General Grant can press their front, while I am ordered to take all the spare troops from Memphis and Helena, and proceed with all dispatch to Vicksburg." He intended first to break the inland communications of Vicksburg, and then to make a combined attack upon the city by land and water, Porter co-operating with the fleet. He would "cut the road to Monroe, Louisiana, to Jackson, Mississippi, and then appear up the Yazoo, threatening the Mississippi Central Road where it crosses the Big Black," thus disconcerting the enemy and throwing him on to Meridian, leaving Vicksburg an easy capture.

The want of sufficient transportation for Sherman's large force was the cause of much embarrassment in fitting out the expedition, and of great confusion and inconvenience on its route to Friar's Point. The confusion was increased by the necessary haste of the embarkation. The transports, suddenly pressed into service, were crowded so closely as to afford scarcely more than standing-room, and, of course, there were no adequate accommodations for the comfort or cleanliness of the men. The discomforts of this situation were exaggerated by the embarkation of Steele's force at Helena. The negroes along the river were greatly impressed at sight of an expedition which they confidently believed had been sent down for the express purpose of their liberation. Many of them, indeed, came upon the boats, and were taken under the protection of the flag. The fleet arrived at Milliken's Bend on Christmas eve, and not a few of the enthusiastic soldiers expected to eat their Christmas dinner in Vicksburg.

The next day troops were landed, and destroyed the railroad leading from Vicksburg to Texas. The expedition was convoyed by Porter's gun-boats, on December 26th, to Johnston's Landing, twelve miles up the Yazoo River.[1] On the transport fleet Morgan's division led the advance, followed in order by Steele, Morgan L. Smith, and A. J. Smith.

Vicksburg itself is situated upon very high bluffs, which extend southward along the river to Warrenton, and northward till they touch the Yazoo, about fifteen miles from Haines's Bluff. Between these bluffs, upon which the Confederates were now strongly fortified, and the Yazoo is a low country, full of swamps, lagoons, sloughs, and bayous. The points of approach to the bluffs from the river are few and difficult—far more difficult than Sherman had anticipated. In this bed of mire and quicksand the national troops were landed, on the 27th, near Chickasaw Bayou, which runs from Vicksburg around the hills in the rear of the city and into the Yazoo, taking a sharp turn northward before it reaches the river.

Scarcely had Holly Springs fallen into Van Dorn's hands before Pemberton was warned of the attempt about to be made against the northern de-

[1] *Abrams*, p. 8. [2] This is Bowman's estimate.—*Sherman and his Campaigns*, p. 77.

[3] Speech at St. Louis after the war.

[4] General Grant's army constituted the Thirteenth Army Corps, of which the right wing was under command of General Sherman. This right wing consisted of three divisions:

The First, commanded by A. J. Smith, and consisting of two new brigades, Burbridge's and Landrum's.

The Second, commanded by Morgan L. Smith, consisting of G. A. Smith's and David Stuart's brigades.

The Third, commanded by G. W. Morgan, comprising the new brigades of Osterhaus, Lindsay, and De Courcey.

The other brigades remained at Memphis.

[5] Before embarkation General Sherman issued the following characteristic order:

"I. The expedition now fitting out is purely of a military character, and the interests involved are of too important a character to be mixed up with personal or private business. No citizen, male or female, will be allowed to accompany it, unless employed as a part of the crew, or as servants to the transports. Female chambermaids to the boats and nurses to the sick alone will be allowed, unless the wives of captains and pilots actually belonging to the boats. No laundress, officer's or soldier's wife, must pass below Helena.

"II. No person whatever, citizen, officer, or sutler, will, on any consideration, buy or deal in cotton, or other produce of the country. Should any cotton be brought on board of any transport, going or returning, the brigade quarter-master, of which the boat forms a part, will take possession of it, and invoice it to Captain A. R. Eddy, chief quarter-master at Memphis.

"III. Should any cotton or other produce be brought back to Memphis by any chartered boat, Captain Eddy will take possession of the same, and sell it for the benefit of the United States. If accompanied by its actual producer, the planter or factor, the quarter-master will furnish him with a receipt for the same, to be settled on proof of his loyalty at the close of the war.

"IV. Boats ascending the river may take cotton from the shore for bulkheads to protect their engines or crew, but on arrival at Memphis it must be turned over to the quarter-master, with a statement of the time, place, and name of its owner. The trade in cotton must await a more peaceful state of affairs.

"V. Should any citizen accompany the expedition below Helena in violation of these orders, any colonel of a regiment or captain of a battery will conscript him into the service of the United States for the unexpired term of his command. If he show a refractory spirit, unfitting him for a soldier, the commanding officer present will turn him over to the captain of the boat as a deck-hand, and compel him to work in that capacity, without wages, until the boat returns to Memphis.

"VI. Any person whatever, whether in the service of the United States or transports, found making reports for publication which might reach the enemy, giving them information, aid, or comfort, will be arrested and treated as spies."

[1] "On entering the Yazoo, the first object that attracted the attention was the ruins of a large brick house and several other buildings, which were still smoking. On inquiry, I learned that this was the celebrated plantation of the rebel General Albert Sidney Johnston, who was killed at Shiloh. It was an extensive establishment, working over three hundred negroes. It contained a large steam sugar refinery, an extensive steam saw-mill, cotton-gins, machine-shop, and a long line of negro quarters.

"The dwelling was palatial in its proportions and architecture, and the grounds around it were magnificently laid out in alcoves, with arbors, trellises, groves of evergreens, and extensive flower-beds. All was now a mass of smouldering ruins. Our gun-boats had gone up there the day before, and a small battery planted near the mansion announced itself by plugging away at one of the iron-clads, and the marines went ashore after the gun-boats had silenced the battery, and burned and destroyed every thing on the place. If any thing were wanting to complete the desolate aspect of the place, it was to be found in the sombre-hued pendent moss, peculiar to Southern forests, and which gives the trees a funereal aspect, as if they were all draped in mourning, as on almost every Southern plantation there were many deadened trees standing about in the fields, from the limbs of all of which long festoons of moss hung, swaying with a melancholy motion in every breeze."—*Missouri Democrat.*

fenses of Vicksburg. In this respect he had an overwhelming advantage over Sherman (who knew nothing of the unfavorable turn which affairs had taken in the rear of Vicksburg), and Grant's withdrawal to Grand Junction left him free to pursue his advantage without hinderance. He faced about with his army; and by the time Sherman had landed on the south bank of the Yazoo, he had not only an equal force to confront the latter, but also an impregnable line of defense, covered by abatis, constructed from the thicket in front of his works. Thousands of slaves had for months been engaged upon these fortifications.

The emergency which Sherman was about to meet was one in which neither the bravery of his Western soldiers nor his own fertile ingenuity availed him any thing. It is true, the enemy had a line of works fifteen miles in extent to defend; and, supposing that he was attacking a force much inferior to his own in point of numbers, Sherman may well be justified in the confident hope that he might, at some point in this long line, make an impression, and that, by persistent pressure, he must succeed in driving the enemy out of his fortifications.

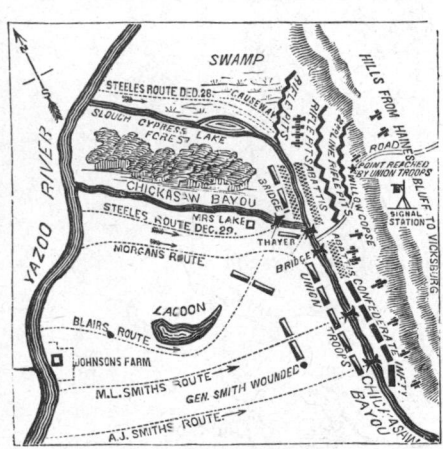

BATTLE OF CHICKASAW BAYOU.

Having debarked his troops, he pushed the enemy's pickets back toward the bluffs, and on the 28th intended to make a general assault. Chickasaw Bayou proved the chief obstacle to his plan of attack. Dividing the country in the enemy's front into nearly equal portions, it could be crossed only at two points, each completely covered by the enemy's fire. This necessitated either a division of the attacking force, or the restriction of the assault to the west side of the bayou; and, as the bayou turned westward along the base of the bluffs, it covered the enemy's entire left, and had in this section only four points at which a crossing could be effected, and even at these only in the face of rifle-pits on the table-land behind, of rifle-trenches on the hill-sides farther back, and of heavy batteries posted on the summits of the hills. Along the base of these hills, and back of the bayou, ran the road from Vicksburg to Yazoo City, serving the enemy as a covered way along which he could at leisure move his artillery and infantry, concentrating them upon any of the points which might be selected for crossing the Federal troops.

Steele advanced on the east side of the bayou, but, encountering a swamp over which there was no passage except by a long corduroy causeway, and

that, too, at the risk of losing one half of his division, wisely concluded to give up the attempt. Morgan, on the other side of the bayou, advanced up to the enemy's centre as far as to the bank of the bayou in front of the bluffs, where his progress was arrested, though he held his ground during the ensuing night. Morgan L. Smith advanced simultaneously farther to the right. While reconnoitring the ground he was disabled by a bullet lodged in his hip, and Brigadier General David Stuart succeeded to the active command. Where this division reached the bayou there was a crossing by means of a narrow sand-slip, but the attempt was deemed too perilous. On the extreme right General A. J. Smith advanced, and Burbridge's brigade—arriving on the field about noon, having just returned from a raid on the Vicksburg and Shreveport Railroad—was pushed forward by Smith to the bayou, with orders to cross on rafts under cover of a heavy cannonade. Landrum's brigade occupied a high position on the main road, within three fourths of a mile of the enemy's works, and with Vicksburg in plain view on his right.

On the morning of the 29th Steele had been recalled, and held the left, supporting Morgan. The entire army lay opposite the Confederate centre and left, with the inevitable bayou on its own left and front. Nothing had been heard from Grant, but his near presence was conjectured from a signal rocket which had been seen ascending in the east the first night after landing.

Sherman determined to assault the hills in Morgan's front, while A. J. Smith should cross at the sand-spit to the right. The assault was made, and a lodgment effected on the table-land across the bayou, the heads of the supporting columns being brought well up to the enemy's works. The audacity of the troops up to this point was never surpassed. Blair's brigade, originally holding a position between Morgan and M. L. Smith, in advancing, had crossed the track of Morgan's division till it reached the extreme front on the left, in Steele's van. Here it crossed the bayou at a point where both banks were covered by tangled abatis, and the quicksand bed of the bayou was covered by water three feet deep. Through this bed Blair led his brigade across, leaving his horse floundering in the quicksands behind, and carried two lines of rifle-pits beyond, under a fire which struck down one third of his command. But, despite such instances of valor, beyond the crossing of a few regiments, and the slight foothold gained on the southern bank of the bayou, no impression was made; and so scathing was the fire from the enemy's rifle-pits, and the cross-fire from his batteries, that the advanced columns faltered and fell back, leaving many dead, wounded, and prisoners.

Still Sherman urged A. J. Smith, on the right, to push his attack across the sand-bar. The latter had already crossed the Sixth Missouri, who lay on the other side, under the bank of the bayou, with the enemy's sharp-shooters directly over their heads. They were about to make a road by undermining the bank, when the utter failure of Morgan's assault on the left led to an order for their withdrawal, which was accomplished, as the advance

POSITION OF THE SIXTH MISSOURI AFTER CROSSING THE BAYOU.

ADMIRAL PORTER'S FLEET AT THE MOUTH OF THE YAZOO.

had been, with heavy loss. All this time Burbridge had been skirmishing across the bayou, and Landrum pushing ahead through the abatis toward Vicksburg.

The night of the 29th was spent by the troops in the position of the night before, lying, exposed to a heavy rain, upon the miry ground, with no shelter but their blankets, and with no consolation from victory for their past loss or present hardship.

Sherman now gave up all hope of success from his present position. His only resource left was an attempt to turn the enemy's line by carrying his extreme right, the batteries upon Drumgould's Bluff, some miles farther up the Yazoo. While his army was encamped in the swamp on the night of the 29th, Sherman visited Admiral Porter on board his flag-boat, where was concerted the following plan of operations: Porter was to move up the Yazoo and bombard the batteries, while about 10,000 picked troops should make a determined assault, the rest of the army making a strong demonstration on the enemy's left. If successful in carrying out this plan, the national forces would have complete possession of the Yazoo River, and would hold the key of Vicksburg.

Steele's division, and one of Morgan L. Smith's, were accordingly embarked on the night of the 31st. But a dense fog made it impossible for Porter to advance his gun-boats, and the expedition was deferred to another night. But the next night the clear moonlight, which would last till morning, proved as unfavorable as the fog of the night before, since there would be no cover of darkness for landing the troops, and the attempt to secure a lodgment on the ridge between Yazoo and Black Rivers was abandoned.

Porter had previously (on the 24th and 27th) assailed the position at Haines's Bluff without success. In the second attempt the gun-boat Benton had been disabled, and Captain Gwin, her gallant commander, received a wound of which he died January 3, 1863.

The entire expedition was now a pronounced failure. The loss suffered by the national forces was 191 killed, 982 wounded, and 756 missing. The Confederate loss was very slight. It was also evident to General Sherman that the army under Grant, due a week ago, must have failed to co-operate with him. On the morning of January 2d the expedition was re-embarked for Milliken's Bend, and before nightfall the last of the transports had passed out of the Yazoo. At the mouth of the river Sherman met General McClernand, who had come down on the steamer Tigress with orders to assume command of the expedition. To him General Sherman resigned his command.[1]

[1] On January 4 Sherman issued the following order:

"Pursuant to the terms of General Order No. 1, made this day by General McClernand, the title of our army ceases to exist, and constitutes in the future the Army of the Mississippi, composed of two 'army corps,' one to be commanded by General G. W. Morgan, and the other by myself. In relinquishing the command of the Army of the Tennessee, and restricting my authority to my own 'corps,' I desire to express to all commanders, to the soldiers and officers recently operating before Vicksburg, my hearty thanks for the zeal, alacrity, and courage mani-

The War Department had, on December 18, 1862, issued a general order dividing the Army of the Tennessee into four separate army corps, to be

fested by them on all occasions. We failed in accomplishing one great purpose of our movement, the capture of Vicksburg, but we were part of a whole. Ours was but part of a combined movement, in which others were to assist. We were on time. Unforeseen contingencies must have delayed the others.

"We have destroyed the Shreveport road, we have attacked the defenses of Vicksburg, and pushed the attack as far as prudence would justify, and, having found it too strong for our single column, we have drawn off in good order and good spirits, ready for any new move. A new commander is now here to lead you. He is chosen by the President of the United States, who is charged by the Constitution to maintain and defend it, and he has the undoubted right to select his own agents. I know that all good officers and soldiers will give him the same hearty support and cheerful obedience they have hitherto given me. There are honors enough in reserve for all, and work enough too. Let each do his appropriate part, and our nation must in the end emerge from this dire conflict purified and ennobled by the fires which now test its strength and purity. All officers of the general staff not attached to my person will hereafter report in person and by letter to Major General McClernand, commanding the Army of the Mississippi, on board the steamer Tigress, at our rendezvous at Gaines's Landing, and at Montgomery Point.

"By order of Major General W. T. SHERMAN.

"J. H. HAMMOND, A. A. G."

The connection of General McClernand with this expedition against Vicksburg is chiefly worthy of note as being so characteristic of the entire want of system—and, we might add, of judgment—in the general direction of the national armies at this time, and, indeed, until Grant became lieutenant general. It appears that, independently of any consultation with Grant, of whose winter campaign Vicksburg was the objective point, McClernand had in the autumn of 1862 been intrusted by the War Department with the organization of an expedition down the Mississippi. This, we understand, was done at McClernand's own instance. There was a long correspondence between him and the Department, the latter adopting his suggestions and urging him to hasten his preparations. The President and the Secretary of War united in drafting a document ordering him to organize the troops remaining in Indiana, Iowa, and Illinois, and to forward them with all dispatch to Memphis and Cairo, that, as soon as a sufficient force, not required elsewhere, should be got together, an expedition against Vicksburg might be organized under his command. The troops, however, were "subject to the designation of the general-in-chief," and were to be employed "according to such exigencies as the service in his judgment might require." The order was a confidential one, but the President, in his indorsement, allowed McClernand to show it to governors or others at his discretion, and expressed his "deep interest" in the proposed expedition.

McClernand was all in earnest. On the 16th of December he writes:

"Having substantially accomplished the purpose of the order sending me to the states of Indiana, Illinois, and Iowa, by forwarding upward of 40,000 troops, as was particularly explained in my letter of the 1st instant to the Secretary of War, and referred by him to you, I beg to be sent forward in accordance with the order of the Secretary of War on the 21st of October, giving me command of the Mississippi expedition."

Whether General Halleck looked with disfavor upon the arrangements made with McClernand by the President or Secretary of War, thinking it would be better to leave the disposition of the troops at Memphis to General Grant, does not appear. Certain it is, however, that when Grant, early in December, received the order to send an expedition down the river, no mention of McClernand was made. When Halleck received McClernand's letter of the 16th, the expedition was upon the point of starting under Sherman's command. Yet, two days after the receipt of this letter, the following telegram was transmitted to Grant from Halleck:

"The troops in your department, including those from General Curtis's command which join the down-river expedition, will be divided into four corps. It is the wish of the President that General McClernand's corps shall constitute a part of the river expedition, and that he shall have the immediate command under your directions."

McClernand was detained by his correspondence with the War Department until December 25th, when he left Springfield (Illinois), with his staff, for Cairo—nearly a week after Sherman's expedition had started from Memphis. Grant had dispatched an order the same day that he received Halleck's telegram, giving McClernand the command, but the dispatch was interrupted at Jackson, Tennessee, and could proceed no farther.

Finally, McClernand received the dispatch and was ready to leave Memphis December 30th, reaching the mouth of the Yazoo, as we have seen, just in time to meet the retreating expedition, with which he had been so curiously connected.

In regard to Sherman's conduct of the expedition, General Grant, writing after the capture of

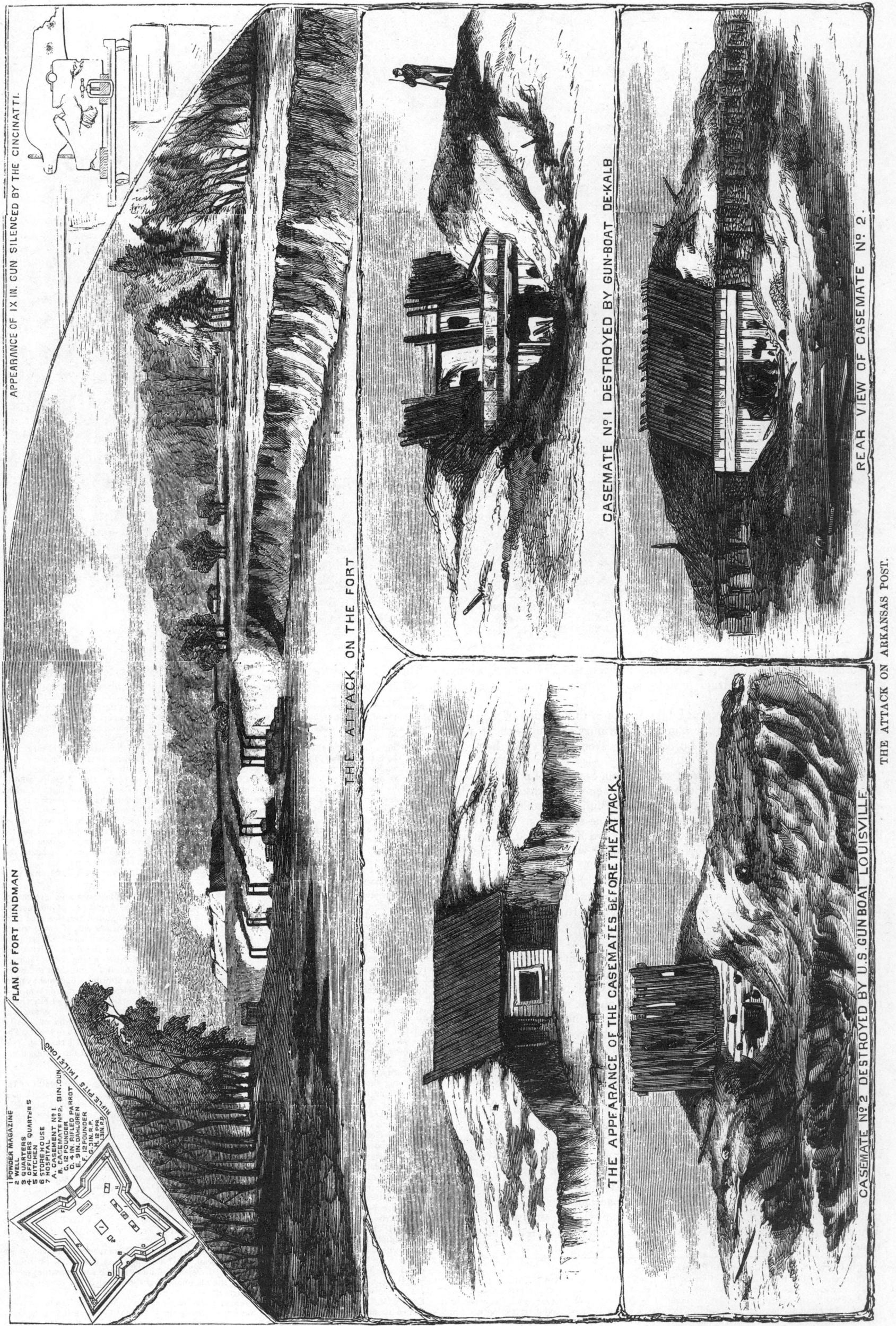

PLAN OF FORT HINDMAN

1 POWDER MAGAZINE
2 WELL
3 QUARTERS
4 OFFICERS QUARTERS
5 KITCHEN
6 STORE HOUSE
7 HOSPITAL
A. CASEMENT Nº 1
B. CASEMATE Nº 2,
C. 12 IN RIFLED PARROT
D. 4 IN RIFLED PARROT
E. 9 IN DAHLGREN
F. 10 POUNDER
G. 3 IN. N.P.
H. 12 PR.
RIFLE PITS 1 MILES LONG

APPEARANCE OF IX IN. GUN SILENCED BY THE CINCINATTI.

THE ATTACK ON THE FORT

CASEMATE Nº I DESTROYED BY GUN-BOAT DE-KALB

REAR VIEW OF CASEMATE Nº 2.

THE APPEARANCE OF THE CASEMATES BEFORE THE ATTACK.

CASEMATE Nº 2 DESTROYED BY U.S. GUNBOAT LOUISVILLE.

THE ATTACK ON ARKANSAS POST.

CONFEDERATE TRANSPORT BRINGING CATTLE TO VICKSBURG.

known as the Thirteenth, Fifteenth, Sixteenth, and Seventeenth, and to be commanded respectively by McClernand, Sherman, Hurlbut, and McPherson, while General Grant was to retain command of the whole. Upon assuming command of the expedition, now returned to Milliken's Bend, McClernand gave the command of his own corps to General Morgan, this command comprising the divisions of A. J. Smith and Morgan's own division, now commanded by General P. J. Osterhaus. Sherman's corps comprised also two divisions, Steele's and M. L. Smith's (now commanded by Stuart)..

These two corps, with McClernand in chief command, embarked upon the same transports which had brought them from Memphis, and, under convoy of Admiral Porter's gun-boats, proceeded up the river to attack Fort Hindman, commonly known as Arkansas Post, on the north bank of the Arkansas River, fifty miles from its mouth, and a little more than twice that distance below Little Rock. Here a settlement had been made by the French in 1685. The fort was situated on the first high ground to be found in ascending the Arkansas; it had a parapet eighteen feet across, with a ditch of twenty feet wide by eight deep, strong casemates, and a cordon of rifle-pits. Its commander was General T. J. Churchill, who had under him a garrison of about 5000 men. The fort was mounted with eight guns, and its capture was an affair of no great difficulty. But Churchill had orders from Lieutenant General Holmes, the Confederate commander in Arkansas, "to hold on till help arrived, or till all were dead."

The expedition entered White River, and, after ascending it for fifteen miles, through a cut-off, moved into Arkansas River January 9, and by noon of the next day the troops were all debarked three miles below the fort. The story of the capture is soon told. The gun-boats, even while the troops were landing, had shelled the sharp-shooters out of their rifle-pits along the levee, and, moving up to the fort, opened a bombardment. By land the army was pushed up around the fort, across bayous and swamps, and during the night of the 10th slept on their arms, in readiness for the assault of the next day. The gun-boats opened again a little after noon on the 11th, and in two or three hours the guns of the fort had been completely silenced. In the mean time several brigades had charged up to within musket-range of the enemy's works, where they found partial shelter in the ravines. In this advance General Hovey was wounded, and General Thayer had a horse shot under him. General A. J. Smith pressed back the Confederate right until, as he sent word to McClernand, he could "almost shake hands with the enemy." As soon as the guns of the fort were silenced, McClernand ordered a general assault, when a white flag appeared on the ramparts, just as the Eighty-third Ohio and Sixteenth Indiana, with General Burbridge at their head, were entering the intrenchments on the east side, while Sherman's and Steele's advanced regiments were on the point of entering on the north and west, and the fort was in McClernand's hands, with 5000 prisoners, 17 guns, and 3000 small-arms. Churchill professed, even after the capture, his intention to have held out till the last man was slain, and said he was only prevented from doing so by the unauthorized display of the white flag by some of his Texan soldiers. So much the better, it would seem, for the Texans! The Confederate loss in killed was 60, and in wounded from 75 to 80. McClernand reports his own loss 129 killed,

831 wounded, and 17 missing. A few days later, the fortifications at Arkansas Post, the command of which had been assigned to General Burbridge, were dismantled and blown up. The position was of no importance, and was therefore abandoned. Before the withdrawal from Arkansas, however, an expedition under General Gorman and Lieutenant Commanding Walker was sent up the White River, and Des Arc and Duval's Bluff were captured.

Grant, having attended to the reorganization of his forces into four army corps, proceeded to Memphis, and on the 18th of January he went down the river and met Sherman, McClernand, and Porter near the mouth of the White River, returning from their successful raid into Arkansas, and, accompanying them to Helena, he consulted them in regard to farther operations for the reduction of Vicksburg. Three days later, McClernand's force reached Young's Point, nine miles above Vicksburg, on the opposite bank of the river, facing the mouth of the Yazoo. For over two months—until the movement on New Carthage—Grant's army was engaged in several unsuccessful attempts at an approach to Vicksburg from above. Before entering upon a review of these experiments, let us for a moment turn our attention to the interesting exploits of some of our gun-boats during this interval.

On the 2d of February, Colonel Charles R. Ellet, with the Queen of the West, ran past the batteries, with orders to destroy the City of Vicksburg, a vessel which had, after Sherman's failure, been brought down by the enemy from the Yazoo to the front of Vicksburg. This movement had not escaped Porter's observation. It was also known to him that supplies were continually being obtained both at Vicksburg and Port Hudson by means of transports. To these transports, also, Colonel Ellet was expected to pay his regards. The Queen of the West was a wooden steamer, strengthened so as to carry an iron prow. Her armament consisted of an 80-pounder rifled Parrott gun on her main deck, one 20-pounder and three 12-pounder brass howitzers on her gun-deck. In order to protect her from the shot and shells of the batteries, she had had her steering apparatus removed and placed behind the bulwarks of her bows, and three hundred bales of cotton covered her machinery. The change in her steering apparatus proved a great inconvenience, and, after starting on her trip, it was found necessary to return it to its original position. This caused some delay, and she did not pass into full view of the batteries before sunrise, thus becoming a fair target for a hundred guns bearing upon her at once. Only three or four shots, however, struck her before she reached the City of Vicksburg, which was made fast to the river's bank at the centre of the bend. Colonel Ellet made for the steamer at once, and struck her, but the force of the blow was broken by wide guards, which overlapped the prow of the ram, and prevented the latter from reaching the hull of the Vicksburg. The current, which was very strong at this point, swung the Queen round side by side

5 X

THE QUEEN OF THE WEST AND THE VICKSBURG.

LOSS OF THE QUEEN OF THE WEST.

with the enemy. At this moment Colonel Ellet fired his starboard bow gun, loaded with incendiary shells, into the Vicksburg, his own cotton bales being at the same time set on fire by shells from the batteries. It was impossible to attempt any thing farther at this point, and the Queen, without material injury, passed the lower batteries. Below Natchez she captured and burned three small steamers laden with provisions. During the night a flat-boat, with a cargo of coal, was cast loose from the fleet above, and floated down to the ram.

A week later (February 10) the Queen started upon another expedition down the river, accompanied by the De Soto as tender. The next evening she reached the mouth of Old River, into which Red River runs. On the 12th, leaving the De Soto to guard the mouth of Old River, the Queen entered the Atchafalaya, and made some captures of army wagons and provisions, and, on the way back to her anchorage of the previous night, was fired upon from the shore and her master mortally wounded. On the 12th the two steamers passed up into Red River, and, moving up to the mouth of the Black River, where they anchored for the night, they the next morning captured the Era, No. 5, a steamer of 100 tons, with fourteen Texan soldiers, $28,000 in Confederate money, and 4500 bushels of corn destined for Little Rock. The pilot of the Era was taken on board the Queen, and, either by accident or design, he grounded the steamer directly under the guns of Fort Taylor, located at a bend in the river twenty miles above the spot where the Era was captured, and where she now lay under guard. The guns of the fort opened with frightful accuracy upon the unfortunate Queen, nearly every shell striking her, and one shot pierced her smoke-pipe, filling the boat with steam. It was impossible for the Queen to reply to the shots that were crashing through her machinery. There was the greatest confusion on board; cotton-bales were tumbled into the river, and men, jumping overboard, clung to them, hoping to float down to the De Soto, a mile below; negroes, frightened to death, were plunging into the water, where, with no means of preservation within their reach, they were drowned. The De Soto endeavored to come to the rescue, but the attempt proved too perilous, and she withdrew out of range. As she floated down she picked up several of the crew. Colonel Ellet escaped in this manner. By 11 o'clock P.M. the De Soto reached the Era, and, proving unmanageable, was blown up. Upon the Era, with the Confederate ram Webb sixty miles behind him and in swift pursuit, Colonel Ellet worried his way out of Red River and up the Mississippi, past Ellis's Cliffs, where he met the Indianola, one of the finest of the national gun-boats. Just as the Era came alongside of her unlooked-for deliverer the fog lifted, and revealed her pursuer, the Webb, not far in the rear. The tables were then turned, and the Webb was pursued by the two boats, but, being a swift vessel, she escaped.

The Era was now furnished with supplies, and sent back to Admiral Por-

ter. The Indianola[1] had set out from the mouth of the Yazoo on the night of February 13. She passed the batteries without steam, floating down with the current at the rate of about four miles an hour. Although her crew could hear the voices of the Confederate soldiers on the bank, yet she passed by unobserved until she drifted by a camp-fire on the levee, when she was discovered by a soldier, who discharged his musket at her. This was the signal for a general discharge of muskets and cannon. As the Indianola now put on steam to hasten her progress her position became known, and she was opened upon from every battery which she had now to pass; but she suffered no injury. She was commanded by Lieutenant Commander Brown. How she arrived in time to rescue the Era has been already shown.

The Queen of the West was being repaired by the enemy, and as it would be difficult to manœuvre so long a boat as the Indianola in the waters of the Red River, and no pilots could be obtained, Brown returned with his boat up the river. When he reached the mouth of the Big Black River, forty miles below Vicksburg, on the 24th, the Webb and the Queen of the West hove in sight behind him, accompanied by two cotton-clad steamers. Brown had expected another vessel to come down to assist him in meeting the emergency which now threatened, but he had been disappointed. It was now half past nine P.M., and the night was very dark. Clearing for action, Brown stood down the river to meet them. The Queen of the West led in the attack, striking through a coal-barge against the Indianola, but harmlessly; then came the Webb. "Both vessels came together, bows on," says Brown, "with a tremendous crash, which knocked nearly every one down on board both vessels, doing no damage to us, while the Webb's bow was cut in at least eight feet." Not minding the cotton-clads, which kept up an incessant fire with small-arms, Brown turned his attention to the rams, with whom he was now engaged at close quarters. From his forward guns

[1] "The Indianola was a new iron-clad gun-boat, one hundred and seventy-four feet long, fifty feet beam, ten feet from the top of her deck to the bottom of her keel, or eight feet four inches in the clear. Her sides (of wood) for five feet down were thirty-two inches thick, having beveled sticks laid outside the hull (proper), and all of oak. Outside of this was three-inch-thick plate iron. Her clamps and keelsons were as heavy as the largest ship's. Her deck was eight inches solid, with one-inch iron plate, all well bolted. Her casemate stood at an incline of twenty-six and a half degrees, and was covered with three-inch iron, as were also her ports. She had a heavy grating on top of the casemate that no shell could penetrate, and every scuttle and hatch was equally well covered. She was ironed all round, except some temporary rooms on deck, and, besides the amount of wood and iron already stated, had coal-bunkers seven feet thick alongside of her boilers, the entire machinery being in the hold. She had seven engines—two for working her side wheels, two for her propellers, two for her capstans, and one for supplying water and working the bilge and fire pumps. She had five large five-flued boilers, and made abundance of steam. Her forward casemate had two eleven-inch Dahlgren guns, and her after casemate two nine-inch. Her forward casemate was pierced for two guns in front, one on each side, and two aft, so that she could fire two guns forward, one on each side, and four at an angle sideways and astern. She had also hose for throwing scalding water from her boilers that would reach from stem to stern, and there was communication from the casemates to all parts of the vessel without the least exposure. The pilot-house was also thoroughly iron-clad, and instant communication could be had with the gunners and engineers, enabling the pilot to place the vessel in just such position as might be required for effective action."—*Appleton's Annual Cyclopædia*, 1863, p. 44.

he fired at his antagonists as opportunity offered. He received a third blow, which crushed the starboard coal-barge. Two more blows were struck without seriously damaging the Indianola. The sixth blow from the Webb crushed the starboard wheel and disabled the starboard rudder, starting a number of leaks back of the shaft. The Webb now struck a fair blow in the stern, starting the timbers of the Indianola, which let in the water in large volumes. Finally, the gun-boat, with two feet and a half of water over her floor, was run ashore. Unable longer to hold out against four vessels, mounting ten guns, and manned by over a thousand men, Brown surrendered, after a fight of an hour and a half. All his guns had been either thrown overboard or rendered useless.

The enemy intended immediately to repair the Indianola, which was an important accession to his fleet. Her destruction afterward was probably the most ludicrous incident of the war. It happened in this way. Porter observed the Queen of the West on the morning of February 25th at Warrenton, seven miles below Vicksburg. He had not heard of the capture of the

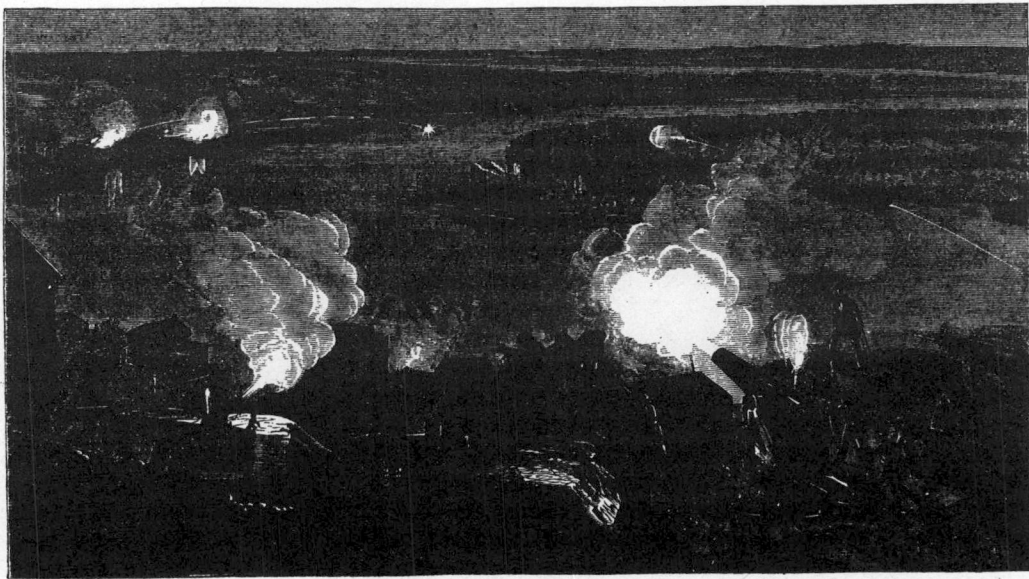

THE INDIANOLA RUNNING THE VICKSBURG BATTERIES.

Indianola, and the appearance of this boat excited alarm. He had no expectation that the Queen would so soon be repaired, and began to fear (too late) for the safety of the Indianola. In a letter written by him on the 26th, he expresses his anxiety on her account. It appears that he stood in becoming awe of the Queen (whose loss he considered more to be deplored than the disaster at Galveston), but had little fear of the Webb, which really gave the death-blow to the Indianola. The latter vessel (the Indianola) Porter characterizes as weak, the only good thing about her being her battery. But a trivial instrument of war at this crisis was destined to effect more than the Queen of the West or the Indianola had been able to accomplish. Admiral Porter had observed that while the Queen and the Indianola were running past the batteries, five of the enemy's guns were burst and dismounted. He therefore tried to provoke the fire of the batteries by placing a mortar so that its fire bore upon that portion of the town where there was nothing but army supplies. For a time the mortar accomplished its object, when the enemy gave up firing.

"Finding," says the admiral, "that they could not be provoked to fire without an object, I thought of getting up an imitation monitor. Ericsson saved the country with an iron one, why could I not save it with a wooden one? An old coal-barge, picked up in the river, was the foundation to build on. It was built of old boards in twelve hours, with pork-barrels on top of each other for smoke-stacks, and two old canoes for quarter-boats; her furnaces were built of mud, and only intended to make black smoke and not steam."

Porter considered his "dummy" a very much better-looking affair, after all, than the Indianola. Well, he let slip this formidable dog of war one night (that of the 24th), hardly expecting of it such good service as it really accomplished before the enemy discovered how he had been fooled. When the dark monster, without a soul on board, was disclosed by the first dim

morning light, the Confederates appear to have had no hesitation about firing. "Never," says Porter, "did the batteries of Vicksburg open with such a din; the earth fairly trembled, and the shot flew thick around the devoted monitor." Of course the "dummy" could not be sunk, for the shots went in one side and out at the other. The soldiers of Grant's army lined the banks, and "shouted and laughed like mad" to see the fun. In the very midst of this frolic the Queen of the West appeared off Warrenton, and a damper was thrown upon the jollity of the spectacle on which all eyes had been fixed, by apprehensions as to the fate of the Indianola.

In the panic occasioned by the appearance of the "dummy," the enemy had given warning to the Queen of the West, who, supposing that she was pursued by a monster gun-boat, and trembling for her life, turned and fled down the river. The sham monitor, though it deigned no reply to the Confederate guns, did pursue the Queen as rapidly as a five-knot current would allow. Dispatches had been already sent from Vicksburg ordering the Indianola to be blown up without delay, that she might be saved from the clutches of her novel antagonist. The Queen of the West took refuge in the Red River, but, having no support, was not long afterward blown up to avoid capture. The order to blow up the Indianola was obeyed, and the gun-boat was annihilated. This exploit of the "dummy,"[1] strange as it may

[1] In regard to the effects produced by Porter's "dummy," the Richmond Examiner of March 7, 1863, says:

"The telegraph brings us tidings of something which is tremblingly described as a 'turreted monster.' Gun-boats are deemed not more dangerous than dug-outs, but when the case is altered to an interview with a 'turreted monster,' then the brave defenders of the Father of Waters can do nothing better than make two-forty toward the mountains.

"The reported fate of the Indianola is even more disgraceful than farcical. Here was perhaps the finest iron-clad in the Western waters, captured after a heroic struggle, rapidly repaired, and destined to join the Queen of the West in a series of victories. Next we hear that she was of necessity blown up, in the true Merrimac-Mallory style, and why? Laugh and hold your sides, lest

ADMIRAL PORTER'S "DUMMY."

THE LANCASTER AND SWITZERLAND RUNNING THE VICKSBURG BATTERIES.

seem, broke up that naval supremacy of the river below Vicksburg which had been almost secured by the enemy. If a few more regular gun-boats had run the blockade with the same results as the Queen of the West and Indianola, the Confederates would have soon had a powerful and almost irresistible fleet. It was certainly ingenious in Admiral Porter to send the "dummy" down instead.

Precisely a week after the victory of the "dummy" the rams Lancaster and Switzerland attempted to pass the batteries, being wanted by Admiral Farragut in the Red River. By some delay, it was daylight when they came under fire. The Lancaster was sunk, and the Switzerland, though she succeeded in passing, was badly cut up. Colonel Charles Rivers Ellet[1] com-

manded the latter vessel; the Switzerland was commanded by Lieutenant Colonel John A. Ellet, brother of Alfred Ellet.

The aspect of military affairs at the close of 1862 was for the nation a discouraging one. The repulse at Fredericksburg in the East had its Western counterpart in Sherman's defeat on the Yazoo. Indeed, the whole year just closed had presented no grand results in favor of the national arms except the capture of New Orleans.

The Yazoo expedition had been an experiment, and a somewhat costly one; and, following upon its failure, for several weeks, so far as Vicksburg was concerned, every operation of Grant's army was an experiment, and proved a failure. The state of the river did not allow of those brilliant operations which in the end were successful. But Grant had a large army, consisting of McClernand's command, and of his own troops brought down from Memphis. It would almost seem that it was to keep this immense force out of idleness that he embarked upon the series of adventures which preceded the advance to New Carthage in April.

you die of a surfeit of derision, oh Yankeedom! Blown up because, forsooth, a flat-boat or mudscow, with a small house taken from the back garden of a plantation put on top of it, is floated down the river before the frightened eyes of the Partisan Rangers. A turreted monster!

"'A most unfortunate and unnecessary affair,' says the dispatch. Rather so! 'The turreted monster proved to be a flat-boat, with sundry fixtures to create deception!' Think of that! 'She passed Vicksburg on Tuesday night, and the officers (what officers?), believing her to be a turreted monster, blew up the Indianola, but her guns fell into the enemy's hands.' That is passing odd. Her guns fell into 'the enemy's hands after she was blown up!' Incredible! Mallory and Tatnall did better than that with the Merrimac.

"'The Queen of the West,' continues the facetious dispatch, 'left in such a hurry as to forget part of her crew, who were left on shore.' Well done for the Queen of the West and her brave officers! 'Taken altogether,' concludes the inimitable dispatch, 'it was a good joke on the Partisan Rangers, who are notoriously more cunning than brave.' Truly an excellent joke — so excellent that every man connected with this affair (if any resemblance of the truth is contained in the dispatch) should be branded with the capital letters 'T. M.,' and enrolled in a detached company, to be known by the name of 'The Turreted Monster' henceforth and forever."

[1] A few weeks afterward, at the close of the summer, Colonel Charles Rivers Ellet applied for leave of absence on account of illness, and in Au-

gust retired to the home of his uncle, Dr. Ellet, at Bunker Hill, Illinois. He had been troubled with a severe attack of neuralgia in the face, for which he was in the habit of taking some opiate. On the night of October 16th he died, either from an overdose of morphine or from prostration. He was little more than twenty years old, was a man of great literary culture and refinement, and had shouldered responsibilities such as few of much riper years were called upon to bear.

POSITION OF WILLIAMS'S CANAL.

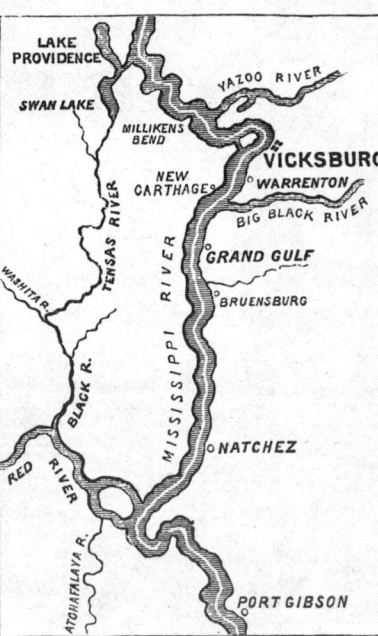

THE LAKE PROVIDENCE ROUTE.

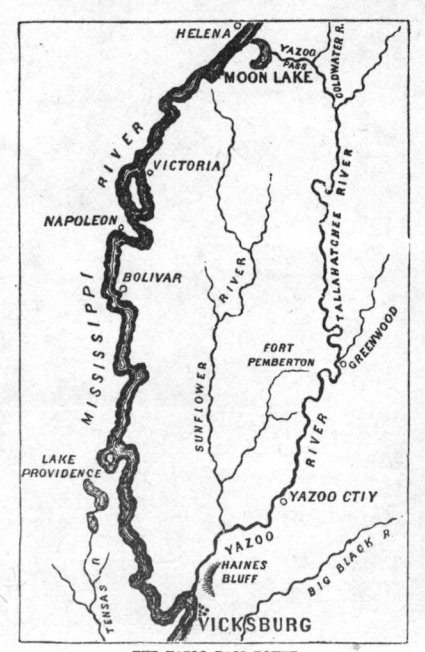

THE YAZOO PASS ROUTE.

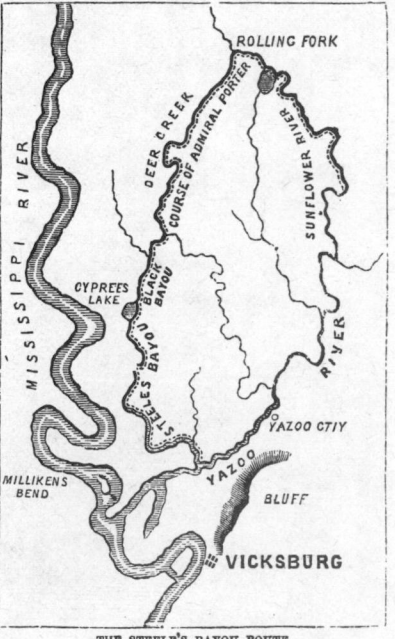

THE STEELE'S BAYOU ROUTE.

NEGROES AT WORK ON THE CANAL.

First among these was General Williams's Canal, to which allusion has already been made. Grant came down to Young's Point in person on the 2d of February, and under his superintendence the work on the canal was reopened and vigorously prosecuted. To secure the encampment from inundation, a levee was constructed on the eastern side. The river was rising rapidly, and it proved difficult to keep the gathering flood out of the canal and the camps. While the work was still going on, on the 8th of March the levee gave way suddenly just west of the canal, and the waters with great violence rushed in, carrying away the dikes which had been built and the implements of the workmen, and, entering the camps, drove the soldiers to the refuge of the levee. The entire peninsula south of the railroad was flooded.

Failing to find a route for his transports to a point below Vicksburg by means of the canal, Grant directed his attention more prominently toward another mode of effecting this object, by a route which his engineers had pronounced practicable. By cutting a channel into Lake Providence from the Mississippi, it was thought possible that transports might be conveyed through that lake, then through the Tensas, Black, and Red Rivers into the Mississippi below Natchez. Work had been begun on the channel shortly after the work on the canal had been reopened. This Lake Providence route would have brought the army down to a point far below Vicksburg, but it would have enabled Grant to co-operate with Banks at Port Hudson. The channel, about a mile in length, was completed March 16th. Before, however, any thing had been fairly done in making this plan available, the promise of success by means of a similar route on the east side of the river created a diversion. The flood, to which a path was opened by the Lake Providence Canal, inundated a large district of country in Louisiana, some portion of which was a fine cotton-growing region.

The plan of operations on the east of the Mississippi, by the Yazoo Pass route, had at first for its object only the destruction of the enemy's transports on the Yazoo, and the gun-boats which were being built on that stream. Eight miles below Helena (but on the opposite bank) a canal was cut into Moon Lake, from which, by Yazoo Pass and the Coldwater and Tallahatchie Rivers, there was a passage into the Yazoo. The navigation by this route proving better than was expected, Grant entertained a hope of gaining in this way a foothold on the high land above Haines's Bluff. Major General J. B. McPherson, commanding the Seventeenth Corps, was directed to hold his men in readiness to move by this route, and he was re-enforced by one

BREAK IN THE MISSISSIPPI LEVEE, NEAR THE CANAL.

division from McClernand's and another from Sherman's corps. "But," says General Grant, "while my forces were opening one end of the pass, the enemy was diligently closing the other end, and in this way succeeded in gaining time to strongly fortify Greenwood, below the junction of the Talla-hatchie and Yalabusha." The passage into the Coldwater River was an af-fair of great difficulty. The flood which had been occasioned by the cutting of the canal, the swift current of the stream, and the gigantic branches of the cypress and sycamore overhanging the boats and obstructing their passage, rendered the progress of the expedition very slow, the rate of speed being about one mile in four hours. The boats were greatly damaged, but the ex-pedition succeeded in reaching the junction at Greenwood, where Fort Pem-berton opposed such a resistance that it was compelled finally to withdraw. An unsuccessful attempt was made by the gun-boats to reduce the fort, which they bombarded for two days. The land about the fort was loose, and at this time flooded with water, a circumstance which debarred the army from co-operation in the attack. The Confederate force was estimated at over

IN THE SWAMPS.

BAYOU NAVIGATION.

AMONG THE BAYOUS.

McCLERNAND'S CORPS MARCHING THROUGH THE BOGS.

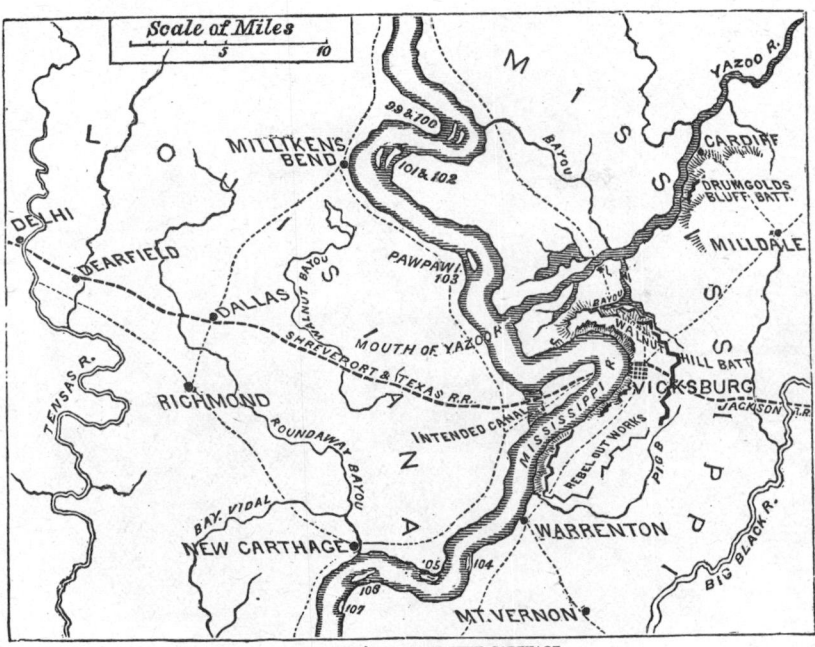

FROM MILLIKEN'S BEND TO NEW CARTHAGE.

5000 men, under the command of General Tilghman, who a year before had been captured at Fort Henry, in Kentucky.

Another plan was then attempted by which Fort Greenwood might be avoided and left in the rear. This was to be effected by a passage up the Yazoo River to Cypress Bayou (opposite the position occupied by Sherman in the attack on Chickasaw Bluffs the previous December), thence into Steele's Bayou, and through Little Black Fork into the Big Sunflower River, and turning at Rolling Fork southward into Deer Creek, which empties into the Yazoo above Haines's Bluff. The expedition, commanded by Admiral Porter, consisted of the gun-boats Pittsburg, Louisville, Mound City, Cincinnati, and Carondelet, with a number of small transports. Porter found a co-operating military force essential, and a column was sent under Sherman. "The expedition failed," says Grant, "probably more from want of knowledge as to what would be required to open this route than from any impracticability in the navigation of the streams and bayous through which it was proposed to pass. Want of this knowledge led the expedition on until difficulties were encountered, and then it would become necessary to send back to Young's Point for the means of removing them. This gave the enemy time to move forces to effectually checkmate farther progress, and the expedition was withdrawn when within a few hundred yards of free and open navigation to the Yazoo."

Grant then reverted to his original plan of moving his transports to the south of Vicksburg. His engineers had prospected a route through the bayous which ran from near Milliken's Bend on the north and New Carthage on the south, through Roundabout Bayou into Tensas River. The route was opened, and one small steamer and a number of barges were taken through the channel. But about the middle of April, the river beginning to fall rapidly, the roads became passable between Milliken's Bend and New Carthage, and communication by water was out of the question.

In the course of the Deer Creek raid a Federal soldier is reported to have been captured and taken before a Confederate officer, when the following colloquy took place: "What in the devil is Grant in here for? what does he expect to do?" "To take Vicksburg," was the reply. "Well, hasn't the old fool tried this ditching and flanking five times already?" "Yes," replied the soldier, "but he has got thirty-seven more plans in his pocket."[1] It is quite impossible to conceive what these other thirty-seven plans could have been; for, certainly, with the exception of that which was next put in operation, and which resulted in the capture of Vicksburg, it seems that every possible mode of approaching, turning, or avoiding the city had been tried.

Grant's idea, from his first arrival at Young's Point, was to get his army across the river at a point below Vicksburg, having effected which, he proposed to attack the city from the rear. He was now able to set about this work in earnest. It was with this view that he had sought to open a water communication between Milliken's Bend and New Carthage. At the same time, he had determined to occupy the latter place with his troops. New Carthage was the first point below Vicksburg that could be reached by land at the stage of water then existing. On the 29th of March, McClernand, with his corps, was ordered to advance and occupy this position, to be followed by Sherman's and McPherson's corps as soon as supplies and ammunition for them could be transported. The roads, though level, were intolerably bad, and as McClernand's advance reached Smith's Plantation, two miles from New Carthage, it was found that the levee of Bayou Vidal was broken in several places, and New Carthage had been insulated. The troops were therefore compelled to take a more circuitous route by marching twelve miles around the bayou to Perkins's Plantation. Supplies of provisions, ammunition, and ordnance for the troops had to be hauled

[1] *Iowa Colonels and Regiments*, p. 223.

over bad roads for a distance of thirty-five miles from Milliken's Bend. McClernand's advance was therefore one of extreme difficulty.

As the water fell it was found necessary to get the transports which were to convey the army across the Mississippi down the river by running the Vicksburg batteries. The gun-boats selected to convoy the transports were the Benton, Lafayette, Price, Louisville, Carondelet, Pittsburg, Tuscumbia, and Mound City—all iron-clad except the Price. Three transports were selected—the Forest Queen, Henry Clay, and Silver Wave—their machinery being protected by cotton bales. They were laden with supplies. On the night of April 16th the expedition set out. The iron-clads were to pass down in single file, and when abreast of the batteries were to engage the latter, covering the transports with the smoke of their cannonade. Fire was not opened upon the fleet until it was squarely in front of Vicksburg, and then the gun-boats responded, pouring their full broadside of twenty-five guns into the city. Into the cloud of smoke which now rolled heavily above the gun-boats the three transports entered. The Forest Queen, in the advance, received a shot in the hull and another through the steam-drum, which disabled her instantly. The Henry Clay, next in order, was stopped to prevent her running into the crippled vessel, and at the same moment received a shell which set fire to her cotton. Her demoralized crew launched the yawl and made for the shore, while the transport, in a blaze of flame, floated down the river, finally disappearing below Warrenton. The Forest Queen was towed down by a gun-boat, and the Silver Wave escaped uninjured.

Succeeding in getting these two transports down, Grant ordered six more to be sent in the same manner. Five of these, on the 22d, succeeded in passing the batteries with slight damage; the other was sunk just after passing the last battery.

Admiral Porter repaired the damaged transports, five of which were brought into running order, while the other two were in a fit condition to serve as barges. The limited number of transports in his possession led Grant to extend his line of movement to Hard Times, in Louisiana, seventy-five miles from Milliken's Bend. Here, before the end of April, the Thirteenth Corps (McClernand's) was in readiness for the campaign about to be undertaken across the river.

It was at this crisis that Colonel Grierson's raid was undertaken, under directions from General Grant. The entire Confederate force in the states bordering on the Mississippi was now being gathered together to meet the blows which Grant was preparing to strike. Thus the way was open for one of those bold cavalry incursions for which hitherto only the Confederates had distinguished themselves, but which, from this time, became a prominent feature in the national conduct of the war. Morgan, Forrest, and Van Dorn had set the example, which was to be followed now by Colonel Grierson in a bold movement from La Grange, in Tennessee, through the State of Mississippi to Baton Rouge, in Louisiana.

At the outbreak of the war, Colonel Grierson, a native of Illinois, entered the army as an aid to General Prentiss. Subsequently colonel of the Sixth Illinois, he soon rose to the command of a brigade in Grant's army. The force placed at his disposal for his celebrated raid consisted of a brigade 1700 strong, composed of the Sixth and Seventh Illinois and Second Iowa Cavalry.

La Grange, the starting-point of the expedition, is an inland town, about fifty miles east from Memphis, on the southern border of Tennessee. Grierson's command set out from this place on the morning of April 17th, the Sixth Illinois in the advance. At night the head of the column encamped within four miles of Ripley, the first town reached after crossing the Mississippi border. The route of the expedition through Mississippi, as will be seen from the following map, passed entirely around Pemberton's army, between the Ohio and Mobile and the New Orleans and Jackson Railroads, crossing the railroad leading east from Vicksburg a little south of Decatur, and the New Orleans Railroad just in the rear of Natchez. After three days of adventurous riding, and meeting only inconsiderable detachments of the enemy, which were easily scattered, the command on the night of the 19th reached Mr. Wetherall's plantation, eight miles south of Pontotoc, and

GRANT'S TRANSPORTS RUNNING THE BATTERIES.

BENJAMIN H. GRIERSON.

SAVING THE BRIDGE ACROSS PEARL RIVER.

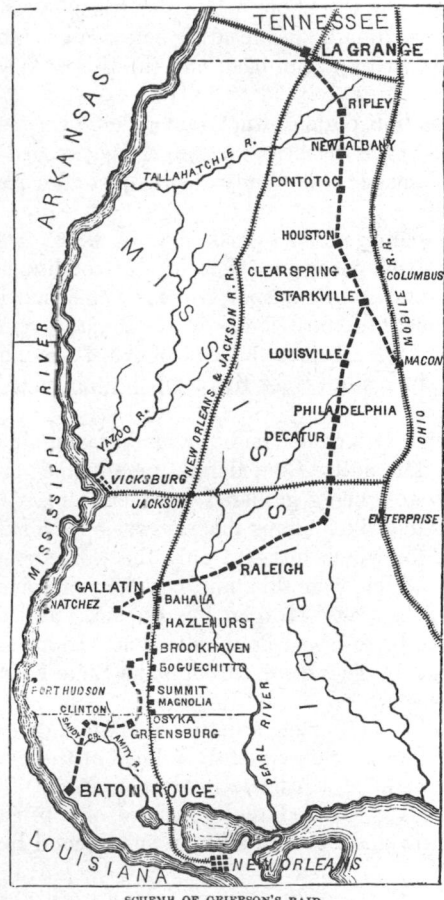

SCHEME OF GRIERSON'S RAID.

DESTROYING RAILROADS.

GRIERSON'S COMMAND ENTERING BATON ROUGE.

sixty miles from its first night's encampment. Forty miles were made the next day; and on the 21st, Colonel Hatch, with the Iowa regiment, in an excursion, the object of which was the destruction of the Mobile Railroad at Columbus, was confronted by a superior force of the enemy. In the fight which ensued Colonel Hatch was seriously wounded, and his command dispersed. On the 27th the expedition reached Pearl River, where it was joined by a detachment of thirty-five men who about a week before had been sent from the main column to cut the telegraph running northward from Macon. This little party had succeeded in marching to Macon and safely returning to the main column, under the leadership of Captain Forbes. It had been in great peril, for the whole state was now alarmed. Unable to capture Macon, it was misled by false information to Enterprise, where, but for the boldness of Captain Forbes, it would have fallen into the hands of three thousand Confederate soldiers. The captain, understanding his danger, tried to bluff the enemy, and succeeded. He rode boldly up to the town with a flag of truce, and demanded the instant surrender of the place to Colonel Grierson. Colonel Goodwin, commanding the Confederate force, asked an hour to consider the proposition, to which request Forbes was only too willing to accede. That hour, with rapid riding, delivered his little company from its embarrassing situation.

In the mean time, the main column, which, after Hatch's defeat, only numbered 1000 men, had been rescued from imminent peril by a deliverance still more remarkable, because it was providential rather than strategic. During the 22d and the following night, the expedition made the most difficult march of the raid. Waiting in the morning for the return of a battalion which had been detailed to destroy a large shoe factory near Starkville, it had been delayed, and toward night found itself entangled in the swamps of the Okanoxubee River, a few miles south of Louisville. The water in many

places on the roads was four or five feet deep, and the tired horses, after a march already accomplished of over fifty miles, and now confronted by a waste of water, without the light of day to guide their path, were many of them drowned. Fortunately not a man was lost, and the next morning (that of the 23d) found the entire column hurrying forward to reach the bridge across Pearl River. Confederate scouts had gone before them, and if the bridge should be destroyed there was no hope of escape. It was not till late in the afternoon that Colonel Prime, with the Seventh Illinois, neared the bridge. Upon a closer approach it was discovered that the enemy's scouts were already engaged in the destruction of the bridge, stripping up the planks and hurling them into the river. The scouts were driven from the bridge, which in a few minutes more would have been rendered useless. This was near Decatur, where, on the next day, Grierson destroyed two warehouses full of commissary stores, several carloads of ammunition, and burned the railroad bridges and trestle-work, besides capturing two trains of cars

THE ADVANCE ON PORT GIBSON.

It was Grierson's raid which first demonstrated that the Confederacy was but a shell, strong at the surface by reason of organized armies, but hollow within, and destitute of resources to sustain or of strength to recruit those armies.

The same day that Grierson entered Baton Rouge was fought and won the battle of Port Gibson, the first of a series of victorious battles in the rear of Vicksburg which in the course of two months had their crowning success in the capture of the "heroic city."

CHAPTER XXVII.

THE WAR ON THE MISSISSIPPI.—(Continued.)

Opening of the new Campaign against Vicksburg.—Getting into Position.—Battle of Port Gibson and Evacuation of Grand Gulf.—Feint Attack at Haines's Bluff.—General Banks's Progress in Louisiana.—Port Hudson.—Farragut runs the Blockade.—Battle at Raymond.—Capture of Jackson.—Battle of Champion Hill.—McClernand's Fight on the Black River.—Investment of Vicksburg.—First Assault, May 19th.—Second Assault, May 22d.—The Siege.—The Capitulation.—Results of the Campaign.—Capture of Port Hudson.

and two locomotives. On the morning of the 27th they reached the Pearl River at a point sixty miles nearer its mouth. Here again they were fortunate in obtaining ferriage across the river. At Gallatin, on the night of the 27th, they captured a 32-pounder rifled Parrott gun and 1400 pounds of powder. At Bahala, on the 28th, four companies, detailed for that purpose, destroyed the railroad dépôt and transportation. The next day, at Brook Haven, on the New Orleans and Jackson Railroad, the Seventh Illinois dashed through the streets, burned the railroad dépôt, cars, and bridges, and paroled over 200 prisoners. After farther destruction of railroads and stores at Bogue Chito and Summit, Grierson's command on the 1st of May, near Osyka, returned to the main road to avail itself of a bridge, its only means of crossing an important stream. Here it fell into an ambuscade, and Lieutenant Colonel Blackburn was severely wounded. That night it crossed Amite River, evading the sleeping pickets of the enemy. Finally, at noon on May 2, the raiders galloped into the streets of Baton Rouge, as dusty, ragged, and wayworn a band of heroes as ever was seen.

In this raid, Grierson's command, by a succession of forced marches, often through drenching rain and almost impassable swamps, sometimes without rest for forty-eight hours, had in sixteen days traversed 800 miles of hostile territory, destroying railroad bridges, transportation, and commissary stores, paroling a large number of prisoners, and destroying 3000 stand of arms, at a cost of only twenty-seven men.

As a result of his observations, Grierson writes:

"The strength of the rebels has been over-estimated. They have neither the arms nor the resources we have given them credit for. Passing through their country, I found thousands of good Union men, who were ready and anxious to return to their allegiance the moment they could do so with safety to themselves and families. They will rally around the old flag by scores whenever our army advances. I could have brought away a thousand with me, who were anxious to come—men whom I found fugitives from their homes, hid in the swamps and forests, where they were hunted like wild beasts by conscripting officers with blood-hounds."

Five hundred negroes followed the raiders into Baton Rouge on the captured horses.

AT length the campaign was opened which was to result in the capture of Vicksburg. The transports had been brought down, and three corps of troops were in motion. McClernand, who had the advance, had been waiting—"impatiently waiting," according to his report, for an opportunity, had with considerable difficulty crossed the peninsula from Milliken's Bend to New Carthage. "Old roads," says he, "were repaired, new ones made, boats constructed for the transportation of men and supplies, twenty miles of levee sleeplessly guarded day and night, and every possible precaution used to prevent the rising flood from breaking through and ingulfing us." He had also to contend with Harrison's cavalry, which finally retreated to Perkins's Plantation, six miles below New Carthage. Upon McClernand's approach, New Carthage was hastily abandoned by the enemy, who, taking refuge at James's Plantation, a mile and a half below, was dislodged also from that position. The arrival of the transports at this point accelerated the movement of the corps, which advanced from New Carthage to Perkins's Plantation, General Hovey constructing on this route nearly 2000 feet of bridging out of extemporized material, thus in the short space of three days completing the military road from the river above to a point on the river forty miles below Vicksburg.

On the 22d of April Porter notified McClernand that on the following morning he would attack Grand Gulf, requesting the latter to send an infantry force to occupy the place so soon as he should succeed in silencing the enemy's guns. Osterhaus's division was detached for this purpose; but, after farther consideration, the attack was postponed. The line being now extended southward on account of the limited number of transports, McClernand advanced to Hard Times, fifteen miles below Perkins's Plantation, and seventy miles from Milliken's Bend. This position was three miles above Grand Gulf. It being desirable to get below this strong-hold, the cavalry, followed by McClernand's, and afterward by McPherson's corps, crossed Coffee Point to D'Schron's Plantation, and on to a point opposite Bruinsburg. While the cavalry were reconnoitring this route, an attack was made (April 29th) on Grand Gulf by the gun-boats, a military force 15,000 strong having embarked on transports for the purpose of effecting a landing in case the attack succeeded. Seven gun-boats participated in the attack—the Louisville,

ATTACK ON GRAND GULF.

Carondelet, Mound City, Pittsburg, Tuscumbia, Benton, and Lafayette. The three last mentioned attacked the upper and more formidable batteries. The batteries below were soon silenced, and the entire force of the bombardment was directed against the upper one, which had been hotly engaged by the Benton and Tuscumbia. Both these vessels were now suffering severely. Many on board were numbered among the killed and wounded; and, just as the Pittsburg came up to their support, a large shell passed through the Benton's pilot-house, wounding her pilot and disabling her wheel, so that she was forced to drift down and repair her injuries. In a very short time the Pittsburg had lost eight killed and sixteen wounded. The Tuscumbia, too, was badly cut up. General Grant was watching the conflict from a tug-boat, and to him the prospect of success in this direct attack did not appear promising. The gun-boats had now fought at a disadvantage for nearly six hours in the strong currents and eddies of the stream, and were being very much crippled, while the guns of the enemy's batteries were apparently uninjured.

It was therefore determined to cross over to Bruinsburg—the landing for Port Gibson—and to turn the position at Grand Gulf. McClernand's corps was disembarked at Bruinsburg before noon on the 30th, and, after a distribution to the troops of three days' rations, which took up three or four hours, the army began its advance toward Port Gibson. McPherson's corps followed as rapidly as possible.

The march began at three o'clock P.M. Carr's division moved in the van, followed in order by Osterhaus's, Hovey's, and A. J. Smith's. There was no halting except for the preliminary packing of haversacks, and, in the case of Benton's brigade, even this had been dispensed with. This brigade, the first of Carr's division, had moved forward as soon as it was landed, and had left a detail behind to bring its supplies; not a light labor, when it is remembered that the brave fellows carried these provisions upon their backs under a broiling sun for a distance of four miles. Benton's command having gained the hills, four miles back from the river, and waited there for its rations, the whole corps was soon in motion. It marched on until midnight, when, about eight miles out from Bruinsburg, there was a smart encounter with the enemy. A fight of two or three hours ensued, in which the artillery took chief part, resulting in the withdrawal of the enemy. Farther advance was impossible, and the soldiers laid down and slept upon their arms until daylight. They had been awakened the morning before at three o'clock by the bombardment of Grand Gulf—covering the movement of the transports down the river—and for twenty-four hours had not had a moment's sleep. At dawn the march was resumed, and continued for four miles, when the enemy was encountered in his chosen position on Centre Creek, three miles west of Port Gibson.

Grant's movement had proved a complete surprise to Pemberton, who, until the last fortnight, had supposed Tullahoma, in Tennessee, to be the object of the impending campaign rather than Vicksburg. As late as April 13th, three days before the first passage of Grant's transports below Vicksburg, Pemberton telegraphed to Joe Johnston, then at Tullahoma, "I am satisfied Rosecrans will be re-enforced from Grant's army. Shall I order troops to Tullahoma?" But on the 17th the descent of the transports had apparently convinced him of his mistake, as he then telegraphed to Johnston the "return" of Grant, and the "resumption" of operations against Vicksburg. From this time he was scarcely allowed either the chance of a doubt as to Grant's real intentions, or time for preparation. And what time he had slipped leisurely away without any show of positive energy on his part. He must have known, when he saw the transports going down, that an at-tempt would be made by Grant to cross the river *somewhere* below Vicksburg, and that probably it would be made at Grand Gulf. Thus, on the 29th of April, he telegraphed to Johnston, "The enemy is at Hard Times in large force, with barges and transports, indicating a purpose to attack Grand Gulf, with a view to Vicksburg."

The only preparation which he had made against this contemplated attack was to send a few thousand troops, under command of General Bowen, to Grand Gulf. The attempt to occupy Grand Gulf was made, as we have seen, on the 29th; it was going on, indeed, while Pemberton was telegraphing the above dispatch to Johnston. But suddenly the attack was given up, and Bowen, leaving a small force at Grand Gulf, found it necessary, with an incompetent army, to move southward from the mouth of the Big Black, putting that river between himself and Vicksburg. Re-enforcements were on the way; but Grant was moving with precipitate rapidity, and nothing could now prevent his immediately landing two corps. On the morning of the 1st of May, Bowen found himself, with only two brigades, in a position which should have been taken ere this by the greater portion of Pemberton's army. His situation made victory for him impossible, for Grant almost inevitable. One thing, and but one, was in his favor; this was the character of the country in which he must venture battle—"a country," said Grant, "the most broken and difficult to operate in I ever saw." It is, of course, useless to speculate as to what might have happened had Pemberton appreciated the importance of the strongest possible resistance at this point; but it is none the less a damaging fact that he did *not* appreciate it. But it was too late now for Pemberton to speculate about the matter; the Vicksburg campaign was already virtually decided. Bowen, resist however bravely he might, must retreat; and Grant must advance, carrying with him the key of Vicksburg.

Bowen's resistance was as gallant and as obstinate as the circumstances of his situation allowed. His army, if it might be called an army, was posted on Centre Creek, where, out of the road leading from Bruinsburg, two others branched in opposite directions, but each conducting to Port Gibson. Upon the one rested his right, and his left upon the other. He had between five and six thousand men. Opposed to him were more than twice his own numbers, supported by a full corps, which was moving rapidly upon the field. But in such a position a small force easily opposes a very much larger one. The roads run along narrow ridges, with deep and almost impenetrable ravines on either side. Only a comparatively small army can be brought into action at one time in such a field, and it is only by long-continued fighting that the superiority in numbers is made to tell.

It was McClernand's corps which, on the national side, fought the battle of Port Gibson. Carr's division held the front, the first brigade on the right, and the second on the left. Hovey's division occupied the ridges on Carr's right. Osterhaus's confronted the enemy's left, and secured McClernand's rear. When A. J. Smith's division came up, it moved into the position first occupied by Hovey, while the latter advanced to the support of Benton's brigade (Carr's right), which had been fighting against odds for nearly two hours. Opposite the Eighteenth Indiana regiment, which was Benton's right, touching the road from Bruinsburg at Magnolia Church, was a Confederate battery, situated on an elevated position, and which was a source of great annoyance. A spirited charge was made by detachments from both Carr's and Hovey's divisions, resulting in the capture of this battery and 400 prisoners—an achievement which should be credited to both divisions. From this time the enemy was steadily though slowly driven back. Several attempts on his part, directed against McClernand's centre, had already

GENERAL LOGAN CROSSING THE BAYOU PIERRE.

failed; against Osterhaus's position on the left he still maintained his ground, until finally J. E. Smith's brigade, of McPherson's corps, came to the assistance of Osterhaus, when, by a flank movement, Bowen was driven from the field; yet, from the nature of the ground and the approach of darkness, he was able to retire in good order. The next morning Port Gibson was occupied by McPherson's corps, after bridging the Bayou Pierre, the enemy having burned the bridge in his retreat. The national loss in the battle had been 130 killed and 718 wounded; that of the enemy was in proportion probably much heavier.

On the 3d of May, as a consequence of his defeat at Port Gibson, the enemy evacuated Grand Gulf just as Admiral Porter was about to subject that position to another bombardment. As soon as the place was abandoned, Grant determined to make it his base of supplies. His forces had now advanced fifteen miles out, to Hankinson's Ferry, on the Big Black. Before any farther progress could be ventured, it was necessary to complete the arrangements occasioned by the change of base from Bruinsburg to Grand Gulf, and to wait for Sherman's corps.

This corps had been left behind until the last, as a blind to Pemberton, to prevent his sending heavy re-enforcements southward from Vicksburg to Bowen's army. Sherman, on April 28th, received an order from Grant to make a feint the next day against the Confederate batteries on the Yazoo simultaneously with the attack on Grand Gulf. The field in which this demonstration was to be made was the scene of his repulse four months before, and the associations revived were doubtless not of a pleasant character to General Sherman, who was now called upon—by a threatening advance, to be followed by a hasty retreat—to incur the popular suspicion of a second defeat. But Sherman could afford to look past disaster in the face, and to defy the popular impression which his present task must occasion, but which succeeding events would shortly dispel. So far as his own army was concerned, there would also exist, for a brief period, this unfavorable impression; but it could not last long enough to cause demoralization, or to impair the confidence of his soldiers in his military leadership. He embarked General Blair's division on ten steam-boats, and at 10 A.M. on April 29th entered the waters of the Yazoo, where he found the flag-boat Black Hawk, the iron-clads Choctaw and De Kalb, the gun-boat Tyler, and several smaller wooden boats, ready for co-operation. During that night this military and naval force lay off the mouth of Chickasaw Bayou, and early next morning got within range of the Confederate batteries. A vigorous bombardment of the latter was kept up for four hours, and, toward evening, Blair's division was disembarked in full view of the enemy, as if intending an assault. The ruse succeeded; for, although there was no road across the submerged field which lay between the river and the bluff, it seemed to the enemy, from his previous experience of Sherman's movements, more than probable that a real attack would be ventured. After the landing of the troops, the gun-boats and the batteries resumed their cannonade. The 1st of May, while the battle of Port Gibson was being fought, was occupied on the Yazoo in movements similar to those of the day before. In the midst of these movements, orders came from Grant hurrying Sherman's corps forward down the river to Grand Gulf. The force in front of the Yazoo batteries vanished as rapidly as it had appeared. Sherman, dispatching orders to Steele and Tuttle to march to Grand Gulf by way of Richmond, silently fell down to Young's Point on the night of May 1st.

At noon on May 6th Sherman's corps reached Hard Times. In the course of the next two days it had crossed the Mississippi and marched to Hankinson's Ferry, where it relieved Crocker's division, and enabled it to join McPherson's corps in the advance movement which had been ordered by Grant the day previous.

Grant's purpose had originally been to collect all his forces at Grand Gulf, accumulate a good supply of provisions and ordnance stores before moving, and, during the time thus occupied, detach one of his corps to co-operate with General Banks in the reduction of Port Hudson, after which, by a junction of the two armies, he would have an additional force of about 12,000 men to bring against Vicksburg. But, after the advantage he had gained at the outset in defeating Bowen, he wisely deemed it not worth his while to wait for Banks, who was now west of the Mississippi, and could not be at Port Hudson before May 10th, and determined, from the foothold already acquired, to push rapidly northward to the rear of Vicksburg. He knew that Johnston would, as quickly as possible, re-enforce Pemberton, and that if he waited for the capture of Port Hudson, while the delay might bring him a few thousand more men, it would bring Pemberton a much larger force. He therefore, on the 7th, had ordered a general movement of his army against the railroad conducting from Vicksburg westward to Jackson.

Before following the course of this campaign through the battles immediately preceding the investment of Vicksburg, let us glance at General Banks's progress in Louisiana up to the commencement of operations against Port Hudson.

General Banks arrived at New Orleans December 14th, 1862, when he assumed the command of the Department of the Gulf, relieving General Butler. He brought with him a military force of about 10,000 men, and the fleet with which he sailed consisted of twenty-six steam and twenty-five sailing vessels. The entire Army of the Gulf, thus re-enforced, numbered 30,000 men, and was designated the Nineteenth Army Corps. General Banks's object was threefold—to regulate the civil government of Louisiana; to direct the military movements against the rebellion in that state and in Texas; and to co-operate in the opening of the Mississippi by the reduction of Port Hudson. This latter post, lying within his department,

BANKS LANDING AT BATON ROUGE, LOUISIANA.

BURNING OF THE MISSISSIPPI.

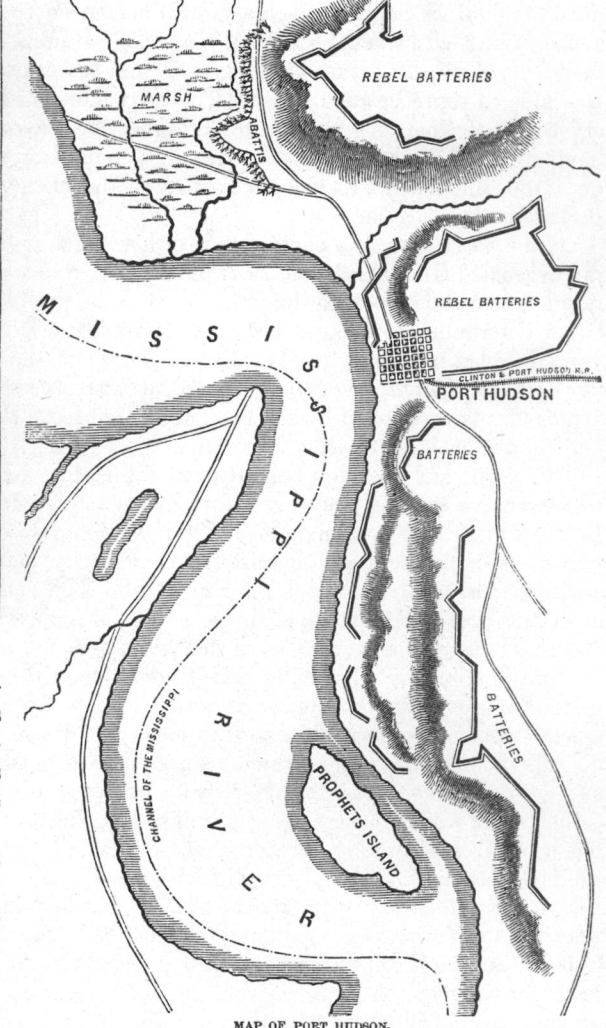

MAP OF PORT HUDSON.

was on the east bank of the Mississippi, at the terminus of the Clinton and Port Hudson Railroad, twenty-five miles above Baton Rouge.

The first notice taken of Port Hudson as a military post was in the latter part of August, 1862, when W. D. Porter, of the Essex, went up the river to reconnoitre the batteries reported to be in process of erection at this point. At that time no guns could be discovered, but earthworks were being constructed. About a week after this reconnoissance, the Anglo-American, in passing Port Hudson, was opened upon from three batteries, and received seventy-three shots.

In March, 1863, General Banks had concentrated at Baton Rouge, which he had reoccupied immediately after his arrival at New Orleans, an army of 25,000 men, and on the 13th made a strong demonstration against Port Hudson. All that was intended to be effected by this was a diversion in favor of Admiral Farragut, who, with a naval force (consisting of the Hartford, Mississippi, Richmond, and Monongahela, and the gun-boats Albatross, Genesee, Kineo, Essex, and Sachem, and six schooners), was about to run the Port Hudson batteries, which had been multiplied and strengthened during the last six months. Had Banks, instead of merely making a demonstration, invested Port Hudson, it might, according to Halleck's report, have been easily reduced; but as the garrison consisted at this time of about 18,000 men, this result would not probably have been reached.

Farragut had to pass a line of batteries commencing below the town and extending along the bluff about three and a half miles. Early on the 14th his fleet reached Prophet's Island, five miles below Port Hudson. In the afternoon the mortars and two of the gun-boats opened on the batteries, and at 9 30 P.M. the signal to advance was given. The Hartford, with the admiral on board, took the lead, with the gun-boat Albatross lashed to her side. The Richmond and the gun-boat Genesee followed; the Monongahela, with the Kineo, came next, and the Mississippi brought up the rear, the mortars still bombarding the batteries. The admiral's ship passed without difficulty, but the smoke from their fire obscured the river from the vessels following. The Richmond, receiving a shot through her steam-drum, dropped out of fire, with three of her crew killed and seven wounded. The captain of the Monongahela also dropped down the river and anchored. The gun-boat Kineo, her propeller fouled by a hawser, and with a shot through her rudder-post, followed their example. So accurate was the fire from the batteries that the destruction of the whole fleet was imminent. The Mississippi grounded, and, after destroying her engines, spiking her guns, and setting her on fire, Captain Smith, with the officers and crew, abandoned her, escaping to the shore opposite Port Hudson. The vessel soon drifted down the river, and finally exploded. Such is the story of the fleet. General Banks had a slight encounter with the enemy, and returned to Baton Rouge. Far-

ragut's object in passing up the river was to cut off Vicksburg from supplies brought from the Red River.

General Banks now turned his attention to the borders of the Bayou Teche. From Algiers, opposite New Orleans, starts the New Orleans and Opelousas Railroad, terminating at Brashear City, eighty miles distant, where Grand Lake forms a junction with the Atchafalaya. Opposite Brashear City is Berwick, near the entrance of the Bayou Teche into the Atchafalaya. Starting from a point near Opelousas, the Teche runs southeastwardly about two hundred miles. The principal towns on its banks are Franklin, Martinsville, and Opelousas. It was up this river that, only a few weeks previous, General Weitzel had attempted to advance, but, meeting so stubborn a resistance from the Confederate General Mouton, aided by the gun-boat Cotton, had been compelled to fall back. Apprehending a second advance, however, the enemy had burned the gun-boat. The obstructions put in Weitzel's way had also been swept away by the current of the bayou. But, a few miles above Pattersonville, on the river, Fort Bisland had been constructed, and was held by several thousand Confederates.

This region was the richest in the state, and Banks devoted himself to its reclamation from the enemy. Having concentrated his forces at Brashear City, Weitzel's brigade was crossed over to Berwick on the 10th of April, followed shortly by General Emory's division. As Banks advanced up the bayou, General Dick Taylor, commanding the Confederates, retired upon Fort Bisland. On the 12th, Grover's division, embarked on transports, and accompanied by the national gun-boats Clifton, Estrella, Arizona, and Calhoun, entered Grand Lake, the object of the expedition being to get in Taylor's rear, and either to cut off his retreat if he evacuated his works, or, if he remained, to attack him, co-operating with the forces in front. On the 13th this division landed about three miles west of Franklin. The enemy, on its approach, blew up the Queen of the West, which he had only recently captured. A fight occurred at Irish Bend, where Grover landed, and the enemy retreated, destroying, as he fell back, his gun-boat Diana, and some transports at Franklin. Banks meanwhile pushing him in front, Taylor was obliged to abandon his fortified position. He was vigorously pursued; at New Iberia, on his retreat, he destroyed five transports loaded with commissary stores and ammunition, and a gun-boat not yet finished. This place was reached by Banks's army on the 17th, and a cannon foundery was taken, and two regiments sent to destroy a celebrated salt mine in the town. Already 1500 prisoners had been captured, besides a large number of horses, mules, and beeves.

Taylor retreated on Opelousas after a brief stand against Grover at Bayou Vermilion. His destruction of bridges as he fell back occasioned some delay in Banks's advance, but the latter reached Opelousas on April 20th, Taylor continuing his retreat toward Alexandria, on the Red River. The gun-boats at the same time oc-

VIEW ON THE TECHE.

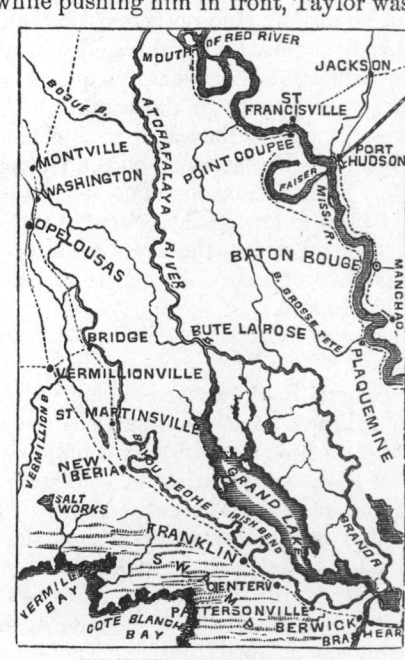

MAP OF THE BAYOU TECHE CAMPAIGN.

OCCUPATION OF ALEXANDRIA.

6 A

BANKS'S ARMY LEAVING SIMMSPORT.

JOHN A. LOGAN.

cupied Butte-à-la-Rose, opening the Atchafalaya to Red River, and thus establishing communication with Admiral Farragut, who held the mouth of that river. During the first week in May, while Grant was preparing for an advance from Grand Gulf, Taylor evacuated Fort De Russey and Alexandria, falling back to Shreveport, near the border of Texas, with orders from General Moore to withdraw into the latter state if pressed by General Banks. On the 6th of May Admiral Porter appeared before Alexandria with a fleet of gun-boats, and took possession of the town without opposition. Thus, after the capture of 2000 prisoners, two transports, and twenty guns, and compelling the destruction by the enemy of eight transports and three gun-boats, General Banks had conquered all of Louisiana west of New Orleans and south of the Red River, and had possession of the latter stream from its mouth to Shreveport.

He now put his army in motion against Port Hudson, sending as many as possible by water, and marching the remainder to Simmsport, where they were ferried across the Atchafalaya, and moved down the west bank of the Mississippi to a point opposite Bayou Sara, where they crossed on the night of May 23d, and the next day Port Hudson was besieged on the north, while General C. C. Augur, with 3500 men from Baton Rouge, invested it on the south. These two investing armies joined hands on the 25th, after a repulse of the enemy by Augur, and a steady advance of the right wing, under Generals Weitzel, Grover, and Dwight, resulting in the enemy's retiring within his outer line of intrenchments.

General Frank Gardner commanded the garrison at Port Hudson, which had now been very much reduced to meet the more pressing exigencies of the Vicksburg campaign. Leaving this position thus invested by an army of 12,000 men, we return to the battles around Vicksburg.

The movement ordered by General Grant on May 7th, and which had been scarcely begun before the arrival of Sherman's corps, consisted of an advance by two parallel roads up the southeast bank of the Big Black River, McPherson hugging the river closely, McClernand moving on the higher or ridge road, and Sherman following, with his corps divided on the two roads. The movements of these two corps after the battle of Port Gibson had indicated an immediate advance across Black River at Hankinson's or Hall's Ferries toward Warrenton. But their real objective was the Vicksburg and Jackson Railroad, which Grant wished to reach somewhere between Bolton and Edwards's Station. He knew what he had to apprehend from Joe Johnston's army, and that vigorous efforts would be made by the Confederate authorities of Mississippi to arouse the militia against him (Governor Pettus, indeed, had, on May 5th, called upon every man in the state to take up arms) to harass his movements. His eyes were turned now not directly upon Vicksburg—they looked eastward to Jackson. This was a point which

he must secure at once; the railroads centring there must be destroyed, as also the military stores there accumulated. This was the special duty assigned to McPherson, while McClernand and Sherman were to strike the railroad farther to the west.

General Grant moved with Sherman. On the evening of May 11th he telegraphed to General Halleck that his forces were across Fourteen-mile Creek, that he should communicate no longer with Grand Gulf, and therefore might not be heard from for several weeks. This telegram, in the general's own mind, meant "Success is certain, but no time is to be lost; I must look to the country for my soldiers' rations, and fight my way round Vicksburg to a new base of supplies on the Yazoo!"

The next day, McPherson, having nearly reached Raymond, a few miles west of Jackson and south of the railroad, met two brigades of the enemy, under Generals Gregg and Walker. A battle followed between General Logan's division, which was in the advance, and the Confederates, who held a strong position on a creek within three miles of Raymond, with two batteries posted on an eminence commanding the road on which McPherson was moving, and with his infantry lying on the hills to the right of this road, and in the timber and ravines in front. Although the fight was severe enough to inflict upon Logan a loss of 69 killed and 341 wounded, it was of short duration. After an unsuccessful attempt to execute a flank movement on Logan's left, and a furious charge for the purpose of capturing De Golyer's battery, which was repulsed with severe loss to the assailants, the enemy was driven from the field, and Logan entered Raymond. The Confederate loss in this battle was severe both in killed and wounded, and on account of desertion. The killed amounted to 103, the wounded and captured to 720. The forces engaged were nearly equal. Johnston reports Gregg's and Walker's force as 6000. Logan's division was inferior in numbers, but Crocker's arrived in time to accelerate the enemy's retreat.

At this stage of Grant's progress his army extended from Raymond westward toward Edwards's Station. As the enemy defeated by McPherson retreated toward Jackson, where re-enforcements were continually arriving, and where Johnston was hourly expected to take command in person, both Sherman and McClernand were ordered to move toward Raymond preparatory to an attack on Jackson. McPherson, on the 13th, advanced to Clinton, the first important position directly west from Jackson, where he destroyed the railroad and telegraph. Sherman approached Jackson from the southwest by the Mississippi Springs Road, while McClernand moved to Raymond, and on the 14th occupied with one division Clinton, with a second Mississippi Springs, a third remaining at Raymond.

McPherson and Sherman were the same day moving against Jackson. When, at about 10 A.M., the former was within three miles of Jackson, he was met by the bulk of the enemy's forces under General W. H. T. Walker, whose command, consisting of South Carolina and Georgia troops, had arrived the previous evening. At the same time, and about the same distance south of Jackson, Sherman encountered the enemy in a position apparently of great strength. After some delay, caused by a heavy shower, McPherson disposed his forces for an attack. Crocker's division was in the advance. The battle here was almost an exact repetition of that which took place two days before at Raymond, though shorter and less severe. A brief artillery duel was followed by an impetuous charge of Crocker's division across the ravine in front, up the hill held by the Confederates—a charge which swept the enemy up to and out of their breastworks. The national troops pursued until they came within range of the guns defending Jackson, when McMurray's and Dillon's batteries were brought up and shelled the flying Confederates.

The resistance offered to Sherman was feeble, the enemy soon retreating into his interior defenses. The town was then immediately abandoned by the Confederates, and at 4 P.M. the flag of the Fifty-ninth Indiana was waving over the Capitol, McPherson's and Sherman's commands entering the place almost simultaneously. McPherson's loss in this battle was 37 killed, and 228 wounded and missing. The Confederate loss in killed, wounded, and prisoners amounted to 845.

General Joe Johnston had reached Jackson on the night of May 13th.

CROCKER'S CHARGE AT JACKSON.

JOHN C. PEMBERTON.

He conducted the battle of the 14th, superintended the evacuation of Jackson, and then withdrew his army northward. This general—probably the most able officer in the Confederate service—after his wound at the battle of Seven Pines, in Virginia, in May, 1862, was incapable of military service until November following, when he was assigned to the command of the West.[1] He left Richmond with his staff November 29, and on December 4 reached Chattanooga. The next day he went to Murfreesborough, but was still, on account of his wound, prevented from any other than a general supervision of Bragg's army. At this time President Davis was on a tour of inspection in the West. He visited Murfreesborough with Johnston. The next notice we have of Johnston he was with Davis (December 26, 1862) at Jackson, before the Mississippi Legislature. On this occasion the Confederate President addressed a long and eloquent speech to the Legislature. The fact that Davis belonged to Mississippi imparted an unusual interest to this address, which was also very characteristic of the man. He had left his constituency two years before to assume his present position. He alluded in eloquent terms to his political connection with the state, and to his interest in her welfare; he glanced backward to the time when he had last addressed them, and admitted that, while he then had thought war inevitable as the result of secession, the conflict had assumed proportions more gigantic than he had anticipated; this was due to a want of moderation, sagacity, and morality in the Northern people; he wondered now how it had ever been possible for the people of the South "to live for so long a time in association with such miscreants," and loved so rotten a government. They of Mississippi knew as yet but little of the horrors of the war; but *he*, from his post at Richmond, had witnessed them in the captivity of old men, and the insults offered by "dirty Federal invaders" to delicate women, in the wanton destruction of property, and every imaginable outrage. There was a difference between the two peoples. "Our enemies," he said, "are a traditionless, homeless race;" they had, from the time of Cromwell, been disturbers of the world's peace, first in England, then in Holland, and again in England on their return; unable to let Papacy alone in the Old World, they could not let Quakers and witches alone in the New. Hence, knowing the savagery of the Yankees, it had been his chosen policy to carry on the war on the fields of the enemy—a policy which had been thwarted by the superior power of the North; and this disparity of power it was which had necessitated the rigors of conscription in the South. He appealed to the Mississippians to send every available man to the front, and alluded in complimentary terms to the bravery of the Mississippian soldiers—to the old men

among them, and the gentle boys of sixteen, of whom he had heard on Virginia battle-fields. He warned them that every effort would be made by the enemy to capture Vicksburg and Port Hudson, and told them about the brilliant commanders whom he had chosen to defend these positions; then again he invoked them, by the glorious dead of Mexico, and by the still more glorious dead of the battle-fields of the Confederacy, by the desolate widows and orphans left behind, and by their maimed and wounded heroes, to rush forward and place themselves at the disposal of the state. Against the capture of New Orleans he offset the repulse formerly sustained by the enemy's fleet before Vicksburg, and his recent repulse at Fredericksburg; he referred to the smiles of the Emperor Napoleon; prophesied the conversion of the Northwest to the Confederate cause; pointed to the bright hopes of the trans-Mississippi campaign; and, as the climax of hope, mentioned the interesting fact that the gallant State of Kentucky was "still the object of the ardent wishes of General Bragg," and that he had even heard that officer, in an address to his troops, speak longingly of Kentucky and the banks of the Ohio! Such was the address of President Davis. General Johnston was then called upon for a speech. "The scar-worn hero," says a report of the proceedings, "looked a little nervous, while the house rang with loud and prolonged applause. He rose and said: 'Fellow-citizens, my only regret is that I have done so little to merit such a greeting. I promise you, however, that hereafter I shall be watchful, energetic, and indefatigable in your defense.'"

As soon as Davis reached Richmond he was pressed to remove General Bragg and give Johnston command of the Army of Middle Tennessee. Davis referred the matter to Johnston, who (February 12, 1863) expressed his approbation of General Bragg, and his belief that the interests of the service required that the latter should not be removed. A month later, while at Mobile, on his way to Mississippi, Johnston received an order to assume command of the Army of Middle Tennessee, and to direct General Bragg to report to the War Department. When Johnston reached Tullahoma he informed the Secretary of War (March 19th) that the change could not be made, on account of the critical condition of Bragg's family. On the 10th of April he repeated this to President Davis, and added that he himself had been sick, and was not now able to serve in the field. On the 9th of May he was ordered to proceed at once to Mississippi and take chief command of the forces there. Up to this time Johnston had been physically unable to undertake any responsibility for the conduct of the war in Mississippi.

And he assumed the command too late for his assistance to be of any value. Grant's army was already within a short distance of Jackson, while Pemberton, completely deceived by the Federal demonstrations toward Warrenton, was holding the main body of his army on the west bank of the Big Black, in the vicinity of Edwards's Station, where he continued to hold it until after the capture of Jackson, making no attempt to find out the real movements of Grant, or to harass his exposed flank and rear.

This was the situation when Johnston reached Jackson, where his little army of about 6000 men was of course unable to save the place from capture. In retreating he took the Canton Road, by which alone he could preserve communication with Pemberton. Upon Grant's first landing, Johnston had urged Pemberton to attack him without delay, and with all his army. "Success," he said, "will give back what was abandoned to win it." He telegraphed on May 1st to Richmond that Pemberton was calling for re-enforcements, which could not be sent from Bragg's army without giving up Tennessee. "Could not one or two brigades be sent from the East?" A week later Johnston again begged for re-enforcements.

On the night of his arrival at Jackson, Johnston for the first time knew what had been the result of the battle at Port Gibson, and the progress of Grant's army. He urged Pemberton to immediately attack the Federal division at Clinton, and promised co-operation. But his own hands were tied the next day by Grant's advance on Jackson. After abandoning the town, he marched his army six miles the same day, and encamped for the night. He from this encampment sent a dispatch to Pemberton, informing the latter of his situation, and that re-enforcements—under General Gist from the East, and General Maxey from Port Hudson—had been ordered to assemble at some point forty or fifty miles from Jackson. The re-enforcements, he said, would, when gathered together, number from 12,000 to 13,000. As soon as these had joined the two commands under himself and Pemberton, the whole army ought to concentrate and fight a decisive battle.

This dispatch Pemberton says he did not receive until the evening of May 16th. In the mean time this general had ventured a battle on his own account. He had disobeyed Johnston's order to move toward Clinton, compliance with which would have secured the junction of the two commands on the 15th, and proceeded forthwith, against the advice of his subordinate generals, to make a movement which would render union impossible.[1] This

[1] The following is the order issued from the Adjutant and Inspector General's office at Richmond, November 24th, 1862:

"General J. E. Johnston, Confederate States Army, is hereby assigned to the following geographical command, to wit: Commencing with the Blue Ridge of mountains, running through the western part of North Carolina, and following the line of said mountains through the northern part of Georgia to the railroad south of Chattanooga; thence by that road to West Point, and down the west or right bank of the Chattahoochee River to the boundary of Alabama and Florida, following that boundary west to the Choctawhatchee River, and down that river to Choctawhatchee Bay—including the waters of that bay—to the Gulf of Mexico. All that portion of the country west of said line to the Mississippi River is included in the above command. General Johnston will, for the purpose of correspondence and reports, establish his head-quarters at Chattanooga, or such other place as in his judgment may best secure facilities for ready communication with the troops within the limits of his command, and will repair in person to any part of said command whenever his presence may for the time be necessary or desirable.

"By command of the Secretary of War. JOHN WITHERS, A. A. G.

"His Excellency the President, Richmond, Va."

[1] Pemberton, upon the receipt, on the morning of the 14th, of Johnston's order, or rather suggestion, to attack Sherman at Clinton, replied that he would at once move from Edwards's Station in compliance with the order, though he considered the movement a hazardous one. Pemberton thought he ought to remain behind the Big Black, and near Vicksburg. He called a council of war, and the majority decided in favor of the movement indicated by Johnston. The others—including Generals Loring and Stevenson—preferred a movement for the purpose of cutting off Grant from his supplies by the Mississippi. Little did Loring and Stevenson know about Grant's supplies, or the facility with which the latter could feed his army, even if there were no such river as the Mississippi. Pemberton was in favor of neither movement, fearing that either would "remove him from his base," but determined finally (i. e., on the afternoon of the 14th) to direct all his disposable force—about 18,000 men (probably a low estimate)—toward Raymond or Dillon's, in Grant's rear. This plan of the campaign completely ignored the existence of Johnston or his army. Johnston's plan was to attack Grant, and to attack him in such a manner as to secure, first, the co-operation of the two commands, and afterward their concentration. Johnston ignored Vicksburg; it seemed plain enough to him that if Grant could not be beaten in the field, it was not only useless to attempt the defense of Vicksburg against a siege, but involved, moreover, in the end, the capture of the besieged army. Pemberton, on the other hand, was willing to risk every thing for Vicksburg, and would risk nothing which might involve its abandonment. On

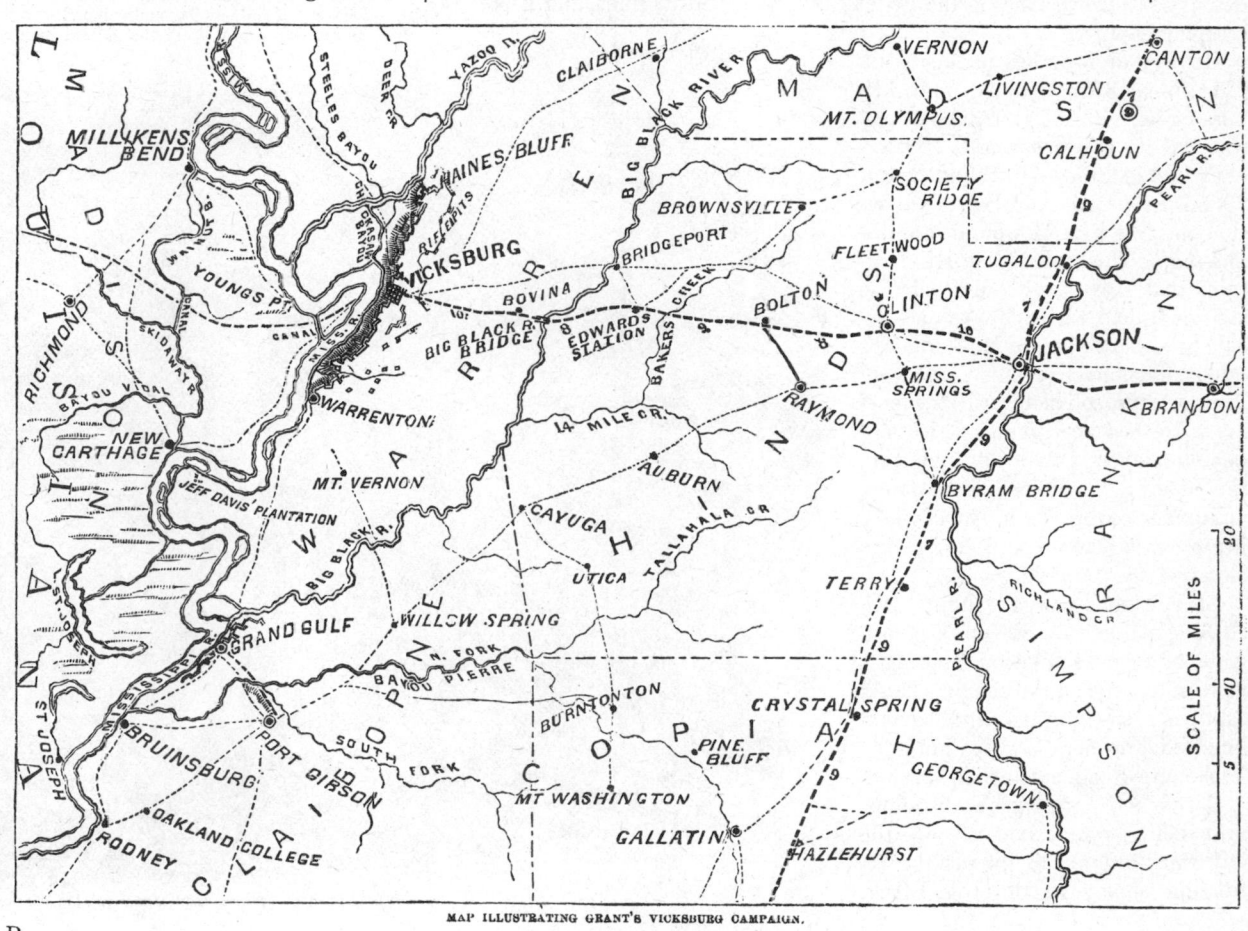

McPHERSON AND HIS CHIEF ENGINEERS.

movement led to the battle of Champion's Hill, or Baker's Creek. Johnston, in the mean while, was falling back on Canton, with his hands completely tied so far as any possible co-operation with Pemberton was concerned.

The capture of Jackson was followed by the destruction of the railway station, arsenals, workshops, etc., in the town. It would have been well if the work of destruction had here stopped; but some soldiers of Sherman's corps got possession of some bad rum, and burned private houses, the Roman Catholic church, the hotel, and the penitentiary.

In the mean time Pemberton was crossing the Big Black. Having remained idle while Johnston was at hand and fighting, as soon as the latter had retreated he advanced and offered battle. Grant became informed of these movements of the enemy, which were sufficiently convenient to his own purpose. He was now ready to face about toward Vicksburg with his three corps.

Early on the morning of the 16th, Sherman, who had been occupying Jackson, was ordered to join as rapidly as possible the main body of Grant's army, then in the vicinity of Bolton. Blair's division of Sherman's corps was hurried on to Edwards's Station. This division supported the left of McClernand's corps, which moved at the same time.

Three roads to the north of Raymond, leading out from the Raymond and Bolton Road, conducted to Edwards's Station, uniting two miles east of that place. The longer of these roads was a mile and a half north of Raymond, another was two miles farther north, and a third ran out from the Raymond and Bolton Road one mile south of Bolton, and was separated from the second or middle road by a distance of four miles. Upon these roads McClernand advanced on the morning of the 16th. Grant had ordered the advance on the night of the 15th to be made that morning, and McClernand,

his own plan he acted without consistency. It was plainly absurd for him to refuse a battle with Johnston's co-operation, and forthwith to bring on one in which only his own command could participate.

when he received the order, was ready to move. Hovey's division was at the entrance of the northern road; A. J. Smith's at that of the southern, with Blair in support; and Osterhaus's at that of the middle, supported by General Carr. Grant had already ordered on McPherson's corps, which was ready to support Hovey's division. As these columns advanced, the several divisions supporting each other, their position was one equally fitted for defense and attack.

The enemy, under General Pemberton, had taken a strong position along a ridge of hills east of Edwards's Station, and on the right bank of Baker's Creek, his front covered by cavalry skirmishers and artillery. Early on the morning of the 16th (6 30 A.M.) Pemberton received a dispatch from General Johnston instructing him to move northward in order to effect a junction of the two commands. It was Pemberton's intention to obey this or-

MAP ILLUSTRATING GRANT'S VICKSBURG CAMPAIGN.

der. His trains were ordered back to the Big Black, and the army would have followed had it not been already too late. He wrote to Johnston that he was coming in obedience to orders; but the most important part of his communication was the postscript, which told of heavy skirmishing already begun at the front. The skirmishing went on, and grew into a general engagement. The battle of Champion's Hill had to be fought, and General Pemberton could not help himself.

Five miles out from Edwards's Station the enemy's skirmishers were first met on A. J. Smith's front. Half a mile brought the division within range of the enemy's artillery, and the advance at this point was delayed till the opposing guns were silenced. Osterhaus, in the centre, heard the firing on his left, and soon after came himself into collision with the enemy on the skirt of a thick wood, "covering," to use McClernand's phrase, "a seeming chaos of abrupt hills and yawning ravines." Soon he came upon the enemy in full force. Two hours and a half after the first skirmishing on the left, McClernand learned from Hovey that the latter "had found the enemy strongly posted in front," and that McPherson was close on his rear. McClernand had been ordered to find the enemy, but to risk an engagement only upon the assurance of certain victory. Grant was on the right, with Hovey and McPherson. He had left Clinton for the front at an early hour. When he reached the junction of the Vicksburg Railroad with the Raymond and Bolton Road, he found McPherson's advance and his pioneer corps rebuilding a bridge which Osterhaus's cavalry had destroyed the night before. Passing on to the front, after seeing McPherson's two divisions well under way, Grant found Hovey's division ready at any moment to bring on a battle.

The top of the ridge on which the enemy rested was covered with dense forest and undergrowth. On the south side of the Vicksburg Road, which here makes a sharp turn to the left, was a precipitous height resembling in character the adjacent ridge. The country to the right of the road sloped gently through a short reach of timber, then opening into cultivated fields and into a valley of considerable extent. On the road, and into the wooded ravine on the left, lay Hovey's division disposed for attack. McPherson operated on the right of the road, threatening the enemy's rear.

McClernand, as we have seen, had been delayed, skirmishing and driving away the artillery in his front, while Grant, on the right, was waiting to hear from him. McClernand appears to have been extremely solicitous about McPherson's supporting Hovey. Grant, having already settled this matter to his own satisfaction, signified to McClernand a little after noon that he wished him to push forward with all rapidity, and that he would himself attend to Hovey and McPherson.

The Federal left had been made secure by McClernand's judicious disposition of his own and Blair's divisions. When the order came urging forward the left and centre, the right, under Hovey, had been contending for nearly two hours against superior numbers. Hovey's division bore the brunt of the whole conflict. Directly in his front was the Confederate General Stevenson's division, posted in a strong position on Champion Hill, from which the battle is named. One brigade, and then a second, of Crocker's division, was sent to re-enforce Hovey, who, after a difficult approach to the enemy's position under a galling fire, was contending against great odds, and had been borne back by the overwhelming forces of the enemy. Logan had in the mean time gained an important position on Pemberton's left flank, and Grant, appreciating the opportunity thus afforded him, again ordered Hovey's division forward, re-enforced as above stated, and this attack, with that upon the flank, finally drove the enemy from the field. Logan's movement had so far succeeded that the Confederate General Loring's division was cut off from Pemberton, and was compelled to retreat by a long detour southward, evading the Federal left, losing all its guns, and narrowly escaping capture.

Hovey's division lost in this battle 211 killed, 872 wounded, and 119 missing—a total of 1202, about one third of its entire strength. Osterhaus lost 14 killed, 76 wounded, and 20 missing. In A. J. Smith's division the loss was 24 wounded and 4 missing. This record clearly indicates that Hovey, with McPherson's assistance, had really fought and decided the battle before McClernand's other divisions had come into any very serious collision with the enemy. He had been repulsed, leaving behind eleven guns captured from the enemy; but his men, undaunted, and under cover of a heavy artillery fire, again advanced, and carried the closely-contested field.

McPherson's corps fought with equal gallantry — Stevenson's brigade, of Logan's division, making a brilliant charge on the enemy's flank, capturing seven guns and several hundred prisoners, and, gaining the Vicksburg Road, cutting off Loring.

Carr's and Osterhaus's divisions, now being well advanced on the left, were ordered to pursue the retreating enemy to the Big Black.

The pursuit was continued till after dark, resulting in the capture of a large amount of munitions and stores.

Sherman's corps had no part in the battle, not coming upon the field at all. McPherson fought only two of his divisions, Ransom's brigade not having yet arrived from Milliken's Bend. The entire Federal loss in the battle was 426 killed, 1842 wounded, and 189 missing—total, 2457. The Confederate loss was not probably less in killed and wounded, besides that of some 2000 prisoners, from fifteen to twenty guns, and thousands of small-arms. Among the killed was General Lloyd Tilghman, of Fort Henry renown, now commanding one of Loring's brigades, who was shot while attempting to check the Federal pursuit.[1]

The pursuit was continued on the 17th, McClernand's corps in the advance. Sherman, having reached Bolton, was turned northward toward Bridgeport, where Blair soon joined him.

The only stand made by Pemberton's retreating and demoralized army was on the banks of the Big Black River. Here it was found by McClernand on the 17th, strongly posted on both sides of the river. At this point, on the west bank—the main position of the enemy—bluffs extend to the water's edge. On the east bank there is an open bottom a mile wide, surrounded by a stagnant bayou two or three feet in depth and from ten to twenty in width, extending in the form of a segment from the river above to the river below; behind this bayou the enemy had thrown up rifle-pits. McClernand made the most elaborate disposition of his command for an attack. Carr's division held the right, and Lawler's brigade the extreme right. After Carr's division had been delayed by the enemy's artillery for two or three hours, Lawler discovered a way of approach by which the position could be successfully assaulted. A charge was made at this point by Lawler. His brigade, coming into close quarters with the enemy, received a volley in flank, bringing down 150 men; but the charge was sustained. No shot was fired by the gallant assailants until they had crossed the bayou. They then poured in their volley, and, without reloading, swept on with fixed bayonets, and the position was abandoned by the Confederates, leaving in their works eighteen guns, 1500 prisoners, and large quantities of small-arms and commissary stores. McClernand's loss was 29 killed and 242 wounded. Those of the enemy who were not captured escaped across the river by a bridge which had been constructed of three steam-boats. This temporary bridge and the railroad bridge were burned by the fugitives, and it was impossible for the Federals to cross the river in the face of the enemy, whose sharp-shooters lined the opposite bluffs.

That night Pemberton's disordered army straggled into the streets of Vicksburg, bringing panic with its approach.[2]

[1] As to the numbers engaged on the Confederate side in the battle of Champion's Hill, we have taken Pemberton's estimate (18,000 men). This is, no doubt, below the mark. Grant estimates the enemy's numbers at 25,000. Abrams, to whom we have formerly referred, and who was well acquainted with the defense of Vicksburg, gives Pemberton a command of from 23,000 to 26,000 men, positioned as follows:

"Major General Stevenson's division, composed of the brigades commanded by Brigadier Generals Lee, Barton, and Cummings, and Colonel, now Brigadier General Reynolds, in front; General Loring's division, composed of the brigades commanded by Brigadier Generals Tilghman, Featherstone, and others, in the centre; and Bowen's division, composed of two brigades under Brigadier General Green and Colonel Cockrell. There was also one brigade commanded by Brigadier General Baldwin, detached from Major General M. L. Smith's division, Wanl's legion of Texans, and Wirt Adams's cavalry regiment, the whole making an effective force of between 23,000 and 26,000 fighting men."

[2] Abrams thus describes the entrance of the Confederate army into Vicksburg:

"At about 10 o'clock on Sunday night the main body of the Confederate forces commenced entering Vicksburg, and then ensued a scene that almost beggars description. Many planters living near the city, with their families, abandoned their homes and entered our lines with the Confederate forces. We were among the troops when they entered, and never in our life beheld any thing to equal the scene. As if by magic, the stillness of the Sabbath night was broken in upon by an uproar, in which the blasphemous oath of the soldier and the cry of the child mingled, and formed a sight which the pen can not depict. It was a scene which, once beheld, can not be forgotten. There were many gentle women and tender children torn from their homes by the advance of a ruthless foe, and compelled to fly to our lines for protection; and mixed up with them, in one vast crowd, were the gallant men who had left Vicksburg three short weeks before,

COTTON BRIDGE BUILT BY McPHERSON ACROSS THE BIG BLACK.

Johnston, as soon as he learned the result of the fighting on Baker's Creek, dispatched to Pemberton: "If Haines's Bluff be untenable, Vicksburg is of no value, and can not be held. If, therefore, you are invested in Vicksburg, you must ultimately surrender. Under such circumstances, instead of losing both troops and place, you must, if possible, save the troops. If it is not too late, evacuate Vicksburg and its dependencies, and march to the northeast." But before the dispatch was received Pemberton had already shut himself up in Vicksburg, and Grant had locked him in.

Was Haines's Bluff untenable? Sherman had found it impregnable on the river side last December. But where was the Confederate army to defend this post now — this post now so absolutely necessary to General Grant?

While McClernand was crossing the Big Black on the morning of the 18th by floating bridges a short distance above the scene of the preceding day's battle, Sherman crossed the same river at Bridgeport. From that point he approached Vicksburg until within about three miles of the town, when he turned to the right and took possession of Walnut Hills and the adjacent banks of the Yazoo without resistance.

McPherson struck into and followed Sherman's course up to the point where the latter had turned eastward. McClernand advanced on the Jackson and Vicksburg Road, and thence, at St. Alban's, turned to the left into the Baldwin's Ferry Road, so as to cover the approaches to Vicksburg from the southeast.

That night Vicksburg was fairly invested. It was the night of May 18th, 1863. Precisely one year had elapsed since the first attempt had been made against Vicksburg, and since, in return to S. P. Lee's demand of surrender, the authorities of the town had replied that Mississippians did "not know, and refused to learn, how to surrender to an enemy."

Admiral Porter, in the mean time, having returned to the Yazoo, on May 16th was able to open communication with Grant's army and send it provisions; he also attacked Haines's Bluff, the evacuation of which had already begun. On the approach of the gun-boats the garrison made a precipitate retreat, leaving forts, guns, munitions, tents—every thing.[1]

The way was now open to Yazoo City and the whole valley of the Yazoo. Lieutenant Walker, with five gun-boats, was sent up the river by Admiral Porter, and, upon reaching Yazoo City (May 20th), found the Confederate navy yard there in flames and the city defenseless. There were also found two rams—the Red Republic, 310 feet long by 75 wide, and the Mobile, ready for plating—and some other vessels. In the hospital were 1500 Confederate sick and wounded.

Pemberton's army, as we have seen, began to enter Vicksburg on the night of the 17th. The eastward or land defenses of the town were not yet wholly completed, but no time was lost in repairing their defects. While Haines's Bluff was being evacuated, the Confederate troops were entering their defenses, distributed as follows: On the left was Major General M. L. Smith's division, composed of brigades under Shoup, Baldwin, Vaughan, and Buford; in the centre, Major General J. H. Forney's division, consisting of Moore's and Herbert's brigades; and on the left, Major General C. L. Stevenson's division, consisting of brigades under Barton, Cummings, Lee, and Reynolds. Bowen's division, consisting of two brigades under Green and Cockrell, was held in reserve. This army, now the garrison of Vicksburg, numbered about 25,000 effective men. Including the non-combatants, there was an accumulation of provisions sufficient to last nearly two months. The fortifications consisted of strong bastioned forts on the right, centre, and left, favorably located on high points, and without these ran an exterior line of intrenchments. The works had been admirably well planned by M. L. Smith, but the execution had been imperfect. They were neither high enough nor thick enough; the position of the guns was too much exposed, and the guns themselves, being *en barbette*, were easily dismounted. During the interval which elapsed, however, between the occupation of these intrenchments on Sunday night, and the first attempt made against them on Tuesday afternoon (the 19th), the axe and spade were diligently used, and a strong front was presented to the assailants.

McClernand's command—the left corps of the besieging army—advanced on the 19th to Two-mile Creek (so called on account of its distance from Vicksburg), after driving in the enemy's skirmishers. Overlooking this creek, a long hill ran north and south in general conformity with the Vicksburg defenses, which were in plain view on a similar range a mile westward. The intervening space between the two ranges consisted of a series of deep hollows, separated by long, narrow ridges, both the hollows and the ridges running from the enemy's works toward McClernand's position until they terminated in the valley of the creek, being covered near their termination with a thicket of trees and underbrush. McClernand had scarcely occupied the hills across Two-mile Creek, and posted his artillery, when he received an order from General Grant instructing all the corps commanders to gain as close a position to the enemy as possible, preliminary to a general assault, which was to be made at 2 o'clock P.M. A. J. Smith's division, on the right of the Vicksburg Road, and Osterhaus on the left, with Carr in reserve, by 2 o'clock had approached to within 500 yards of the enemy. General Os-

in all the pride and confidence of a just cause, and returning to it a demoralized mob and a defeated army, all caused through one man's incompetency."

[1] Admiral Porter, in his dispatch to the Secretary of War, May 20th, says:

"The works at Haines's Bluff were very formidable. There are fourteen of the heaviest kind of mounted 8- and 10-inch and 7½-inch rifled guns, with ammunition enough to last a long siege. As the gun-carriages might again fall into the hands of the enemy, I had them burned, blew up the magazine, and destroyed the works generally. I also burned up the encampments, which were permanently and remarkably well constructed, looking as though the rebels intended to stay some time. Their works and encampments covered many acres of ground; and the fortifications and rifle-pits proper of Haines's Bluff extend about a mile and a quarter. Such a network of forts I never saw."

VICKSBURG FROM THE HILLS IN ITS REAR.

terhaus, who had been wounded in the fight on the Big Black, was now able to resume the command of his division.

To the right of A. J. Smith, McPherson's corps, holding the centre, advanced in like manner. The right was held by Sherman, who had on the 18th pushed forward Tuttle's division, supported by Blair's, on the northernmost approach to Vicksburg, while Steele's division, taking a blind road still farther to the right, moved toward the Mississippi. On the morning of the 19th Sherman had his right resting on the Mississippi, in plain view of Porter's fleet at the mouth of the Yazoo and at Young's Point, while his front, in sight of Vicksburg, was separated from the enemy by only 400 yards of very difficult ground, cut up by almost impracticable ravines. The Fourth Iowa Cavalry had taken possession of Haines's Bluff, and communication had been opened with Admiral Porter.

This was the situation when Grant ordered the general assault on the 19th. Sherman alone was in a position to make a determined attack; and Grant, counting on the demoralization of the enemy, hoped, by a vigorous onset against the Confederate left, to win an immediate victory. At the hour designated Blair's division moved forward, with Ewing's and Giles Smith's brigades on the right of the road, and T. K. Smith's on the left, artillery being disposed in the rear to cover the point where the road entered the Confederate intrenchments. Tuttle's division held the road, Buckland's brigade, however, being deployed to Blair's rear. The assault was not successful, though it was a most gallant affair. The line advanced across the intervening chasms, filled with standing and fallen timber, up to the trenches, and the Thirteenth Regulars (Giles Smith's left), reaching the works first, succeeded in planting its colors upon the outer slope; but this was effected at a cost of 77 out of 250 men, the commander of the regiment, Captain Washington, being mortally wounded, and five other officers more or less severely. Almost simultaneously, two other regiments (the Eighty-third Indiana and the One Hundred and Twenty-seventh Illinois) reached the same position, but, though able to hold their ground by making it fatally hazardous for any head to appear above the parapet, they could not enter the works. Other regiments on either side obtained similar positions, but night came on finding them still outside of the works, which they could only threaten but not take. Under cover of the darkness Sherman withdrew his advanced columns to a safer position.

The next two days were occupied by the Federals in perfecting their system of supplies (twenty days of marching and fighting had now been passed with but about five days' rations drawn from the commissary), opening military roads, and posting artillery in positions more commanding. The enemy, inspirited by his own success in resisting Sherman's assault, was employed meanwhile in a similar task.

On the 22d Grant determined to venture a second assault, this time engaging his whole line. He gives, in his report, four reasons for this second attempt: 1st. He hoped the assault, from the position already gained, would be successful. 2d. His present force was inadequate to maintain a complete investment of Vicksburg and at the same time attend to Johnston's army, now at Canton, and daily increasing in numbers by re-enforcements from the East. His own effective army now numbered scarcely more than 30,000 men, being but little superior in this respect to that immediately in his front. 3d. Success would close the campaign, and not only save the government from sending him large re-enforcements, but also free his own army for farther operations. 4th. Even if the attempt should prove unsuccessful, the troops, impatient now to take Vicksburg, would not work so willingly in the trenches before as after such an assault. Accordingly, the assault was made. If it had succeeded, it would have been a victory almost unparalleled in the annals of war; for success involved the forcing of a strong line of intrenchments eight and a half miles in length, by operations carried on over the most difficult ground; it involved the capture of a strong-hold defended by a garrison of 25,000 men—one third of which was fresh, and not yet dispirited by defeat—by an army of about 30,000 men, already exhausted by twenty days of rapid marching and severe fighting. It was not an impossible achievement, but its only chance of accomplishment must rest upon the utter demoralization of the enemy. This demoralization might have been counted upon in the case of an impetuous attack immediately following upon the entrance into Vicksburg of Pemberton's defeated army; but, just as truly, it could not be counted upon after the repulse of Sherman on the 19th. But as Grant had tried every conceivable approach to Vicksburg before attempting the only one which really promised success, so now, with the alternative before him of an almost hopeless assault or of a siege which must result in his favor, he refused to depend upon certain but delayed victory until he had first risked a somewhat serious loss upon the precarious chance of instant triumph; he refused to believe any thing hopeless until Fortune had added her denial to that furnished by military casuistry.

The assault was ordered on the 21st to take place at 10 o'clock A.M. on the 22d; and so fastidiously was a simultaneous attack insisted upon, that Grant had the watch of each of his corps commanders timed exactly to his own. We will follow the fortunes of the battle—the last which was fought for the possession of Vicksburg—beginning with Sherman's attack on the right.

At the appointed hour, even at the appointed moment, Sherman's assailing column, consisting of Blair's division (G. A. Smith's and T. K. Smith's brigades), led by Hugh Ewing's brigade,[1] advanced along a road selected the night before. This road followed the crown of an interior ridge, being thus partially sheltered, and finally entered the parapet of the enemy's works

HUGH EWING.

at a shoulder of the bastion. Tuttle supported Blair, and Steele, from his position half a mile to the right, attacked simultaneously the enemy in his front. As Blair advanced, not a head could be seen above the enemy's works except now and then that of some sharp-shooter, who quickly discharged his piece and then disappeared. To keep these down a line of picked skirmishers was placed. The advancing column was led by a volunteer storming-party of 150 men, carrying boards and poles to bridge the ditch. Meanwhile five batteries concentrated their fire on the bastion commanding the approach; but no enemy appeared, although the assailing column, as it came upon the crown of the ridge, was fully exposed. Unassailed the storming-party had reached the salient of the bastion, and passed toward the sally-port, followed closely by Ewing's brigade, when from behind the parapet rose the enemy in double rank, and poured on the head of the column a terrific fire, staggering and sweeping it back to cover. The rear pressed on, but vainly attempted to brave this reserved storm of bullets. Still undaunted, Ewing's advance shifted to the left, crossed the ditch, climbed up the outer face of the bastion, and planted its colors near the top, burrowing in the earth from the fire upon its flank. Giles Smith's brigade meanwhile formed line in a ravine, and threatened the parapet 300 yards to the left of the bastion, while Kilby Smith, from the slope of a spur, assisted by Ewing's brigade, kept up a constant fire on any object appearing above the parapet.

It had been impossible for the two rear brigades to pass the point in the road where Ewing had been driven back; but Giles Smith had connected with Ransom's brigade—the right of McPherson's command—and held a position which Blair reported (at 2 P.M.) as favorable for an assault. Sherman, therefore, kept up the attack on his front. But Smith and Ransom, charging up to the parapet, were met, as Ewing had been, with a reserved fire, before which they recoiled to the cover of the hill-side. Steele all this while was fighting with equal desperation on the extreme right, and with as little profit.

All along the line the battle had been raging for more than three hours. McPherson's whole corps was engaged. On the left, McClernand had from dawn until 10 o'clock kept up a bombardment from thirty-nine guns (including four 30-, six 20-, and six 10-pounder Parrott's), breaching the enemy's works at several points, and temporarily silencing his guns. Carr's division had relieved A. J. Smith's, in advance on the right of the corps, and, at the time designated for the combined attack, Lawler's brigade of the former division, and Landrum's of the latter, charged the enemy's line, and in fifteen minutes had carried the ditch, slope, and bastion of a fort in their front, which was entered by Sergeant Griffith with eleven men of the Twenty-second Iowa regiment. All of these fell inside the fort except the sergeant, who captured and brought off thirteen Confederates. The colors of two Illinois regiments (the Forty-eighth and Seventy-seventh) were planted on the bastion, and those of the Thirteenth Ohio on the counterscarp of the ditch. Within the next quarter of an hour the ditch and slope of another earthwork were carried by Benton's and Burbridge's brigades (of Carr's and Smith's divisions), and their colors were planted on its bastion. Captain White, of the Chicago Mercantile Battery, vying with Sergeant Griffith,

---

[1] Blair commanded the second division of Sherman's corps, formerly Sherman's fifth division. Hugh Ewing's brigade had belonged to Rosecrans's army, but joined Sherman's command after the battle of Murfreesborough.

THE APPROACHES TO VICKSBURG.

THE INVESTMENT OF VICKSBURG—SHERMAN'S EXTREME RIGHT ON THE MISSISSIPPI.

carried forward one of his guns by hand to the ditch, and, double-shotting it, fired into an embrasure of the work, disabling a gun in it about to be discharged, and cutting down its gunners. The works thus partially occupied by these two divisions were separated from each other by a curtain. Hovey and Osterhaus, on the left, advanced on a more extended line of attack, but, encountering an enfilading fire, were repulsed.

Thus far, the battle on the left had not in any essential feature differed from that on the right and centre. Each corps had succeeded in planting colors on the outer slopes of the enemy's bastions. Thus much had been effected, and nothing more seemed possible. The works partially carried were of no value unless the works at their left and right were also carried. Grant, who had taken a commanding position in McPherson's front, saw all this, and was almost ready to withdraw his forces, when he received a dispatch from McClernand which excited his astonishment. The dispatch informed him that McClernand had gained two of the enemy's forts, and asked for re-enforcements. It found Grant in Sherman's front. Now Grant had held a better position during the attack for observation of what was going on in McClernand's corps than McClernand himself. He had not seen any possession of forts, nor any necessity for re-enforcements. In reply to a dispatch previously received from the same source, asking for aid, he had ordered the latter to re-enforce from his left. He knew that, from the nature of the ground, "each corps had many more men than could be used in the assault. More men could only avail in case of breaking through the enemy's line or in repelling a sortie." Moreover, McArthur's division was on its way from Warrenton, and this he ordered McClernand to bring up to his aid. He showed McClernand's dispatch to General Sherman, who ordered a renewal of the attack on his front. While going back to the centre Grant received from McClernand a third dispatch, stating that the latter had gained the enemy's intrenchments *at several points*, but was brought to a stand. Grant doubted the accuracy of this information, but he could not disregard these reiterated statements, which *might*, after all, be true, and, that no possible opportunity of success should be allowed to escape through any fault of his, he ordered Quinby's division to report to McClernand, leaving McPherson with only four brigades to hold the centre. The dispatches were shown to McPherson, to satisfy him of the necessity of making a diversion in his front. At half past three a fourth dispatch was received from McClernand, still expressing a hope of forcing the enemy's line, stating that he had taken several prisoners, and that his men were still in the forts. The prisoners alluded to were probably the baker's dozen brought in by Sergeant Griffith; and the "men still in the forts" were doubtless there, but in the same condition with the eleven unfortunate braves whom Griffith had left behind. But Quinby's division did McClernand no good, and McArthur's did not get up till the next day. The only result of McClernand's illusory dispatches was a mortality list longer by half than it would have been if the troops had been withdrawn at three instead of at eight o'clock P.M. Sherman had ordered Tuttle to detail for the assault one of his brigades. Mower's was selected for this duty, but, upon advancing against the bastion, encountered a more severe fire, if possible, than that which had repulsed Ewing in the forenoon. Steele, too, renewed his attack midway between the bastion and the river. He advanced over ground exposed to a flank fire, and deeply cut by gullies and washes up to the parapet, which was found too strongly defended to be carried, and, after holding the hill-side, to which he had retreated for cover until night, he withdrew his division.

Thus ended the assault of the 22d of May, which, though it made no impression upon the Vicksburg defenses, attested the valor of the national troops. For ten hours they had fought against fortune, but had not won the battle. Repeatedly they had charged the three strong bastioned forts on the right, centre, and rear of the enemy's line, only to be swept back each time with decimated ranks. Partial successes, indeed, they had had, standing upon the very edge of victory, with their colors flaunting in the faces of the foe; but these had only excited false hopes and led to greater carnage; death had been the sole reward of their enthusiasm. McClernand's loss alone amounted to 1487 killed, wounded, and missing, making three fourths of the entire loss of this corps during the whole campaign. Nearly one half (677) of the casualties occurred in Carr's division. A. J. Smith's loss was nearly as great, amounting to 499. Sherman's corps lost about 600 men. The casualties in the three corps counted up to almost 3000, of which, therefore, nearly one third must have been in McPherson's command, which confronted the most formidable redoubt in the whole line—that commanding the main approach (by the Jackson Road) to Vicksburg.

The Confederates—mostly drawn from the Cotton States—also fought with determined bravery. Opposed to Sherman were Baldwin's and Shoup's brigades (W. L. Smith's division); Herbert's brigade (J. H. Forney's division) met the persistent attack which was made on both sides of the Jackson Road, the Third, Twenty-first, and Twenty-third Louisiana regiments especially distinguishing themselves; while farther to the right, Moore and Lee (the latter of Stevenson's division) held their ground against McClernand. Bowen's two brigades re-enforced the other commands as occasion required. The Confederate loss was upward of 1000 men. If Pemberton had not prevented sharp-shooting and artillery duels from the time of the investment—which he was probably compelled to do in order to save ammunition—the national troops would have found much greater difficulty in approaching so near the Confederate line; as it was, however, the Federal sharp-shooters had got so close that it was dangerous for the enemy's gunners to rise from cover to load their pieces; and, besides this, many of the enemy's guns were dismounted. The charges, therefore, made by the Federals in this battle met with little or no resistance from artillery.

Admiral Porter co-operated in the assault. On the evening of the 21st he was notified of the proposed attack by General Grant, and ordered to shell the water batteries before and during the first stage of the engagement. All that night he kept up a bombardment on the works and the town from six mortars which he had stationed in the river, and sent up three gun-boats to shell at the same time the water batteries. In the morning another gun-boat was added, and the four vessels crossed the river and opened on the hill batteries, which they finally silenced. The water batteries were then engaged for two hours at a distance of 440 yards. Such was the noise and smoke on the river front that Admiral Porter neither saw nor heard any thing of the battle in the rear. At 11 o'clock A.M. the spectacle presented to an occupant of Vicksburg must have been one of terrible sublimity. An unceasing storm of fire enveloped the city on all sides. The gun-boats engaged the batteries; the mortars and the Parrott guns, mounted on rafts in the river, and guns posted on the opposite peninsula, shelled the town; and Grant's army was concentrating every available gun against the forts in the rear, while his columns were forming into line for the assault. Still, though environed by this circle of fire, stores in Vicksburg were opened as usual, the streets were promenaded by women and children, and only a very few persons were injured.[1]

On the 27th of May the gun-boat Cincinnati was sunk in the attempt to silence one of the land batteries. She was abreast of the mortars, and rounding to, when a well-directed shot from a fine piece of ordnance called "Whistling Dick" entered her magazine, and she began to sink rapidly; and other shots in quick succession crashed through her iron plating. The gun-boat managed to reach the right bank of the river, and her crew was landed before she sank. She was afterward (August, 1863) raised and towed to Cairo.

After the failure of his second assault, Grant was compelled to resort to a regular siege of Vicksburg. His army was largely re-enforced.[2] McArthur was already on hand; Lauman's division and four regiments had already been ordered from Memphis; these were soon joined by Smith's and Kimball's divisions of the Sixteenth (Hurlbut's) Army Corps, which were assigned to Major General C. C. Washburne. Herron's division, from the Department of Missouri, arrived June 11th, and was put on the extreme left, Lauman's connecting it with McClernand; and, three days later, two divi-

<hr />

[1] Says a citizen who occupied Vicksburg during the siege, "Such cannonading has, perhaps, scarcely ever been equaled; and the city was entirely untenable, though women and children were in the streets. It was not safe from behind or before, and every part of the city was alike within range of the Federal guns. The gun-boats withdrew after a short engagement, but the mortars kept up the shelling, and the armies continued fighting all day. . . . . It would require the pen of a poet to depict the awful sublimity of this day's work—the incessant booming of cannon and the banging of small arms, intermingled with the howling of shells and the whistling of Minié-balls, made the day most truly hideous."

[2] Grant's army, thus re-enforced, consisted of the following sixteen divisions:

1. F. Steele's,	9. J. A. Logan's, } McPherson's Corps.
2. F. Blair's, } Sherman's Corps.	10. M. M. Crocker's,
3. J. McArthur's,	11. J. G. Lauman's, } Washburne's Command.
4. J. M. Tuttle's,	12. W. S. Smith's,
5. P. T. Osterhaus's,	13. N. Kimball's,
6. A. J. Smith's } McClernand's Corps.	14. F. J. Herron's,
7. A. P. Hovey's,	15. J. Welsh's, } Parke's Corps.
8. E. A. Carr's,	16. R. B. Potter's,

There were also belonging to Washburne's command four regiments from Memphis. The whole army numbered nearly 70,000 men.

C. C. WASHBURNE.

WILLIAM H. EMORY.

sions of the Ninth Army Corps (now belonging to Burnside's Department of the Ohio), under command of J. G. Parke, reached the field, and with Washburne's command were sent to Haines's Bluff.

On the 28th of June General McClernand's connection with Grant's army ceased, Major General Ord superseding him in command of the Thirteenth Corps. His military career had for himself been an unfortunate one. As to his bravery or his fidelity, no doubt had ever been entertained. A great favorite in the southern portion of Illinois, he was yet unpopular among his peers and superiors in the army. He had been very successful in political life, and had always identified himself with the Democratic party. At twenty years of age he took an honorable position at the bar; he established (1835) the first Democratic press in Shawneetown, Illinois, his native town; in 1836 he was elected to the State Legislature from Gallatin, his native county; in 1838 the office of lieutenant governor was tendered him, which he declined, not being of the constitutional age (thirty years); he was again in the Legislature in 1840, and during the session accepted a challenge to personal combat from Judge J. W. Smith, who had been offended by some strictures made by McClernand on the conduct of the Supreme Court, but, the judge not appearing, the duel was not fought; he was again elected in 1842, and the next year was sent as representative to Congress, being reelected in 1844, 1846, and 1848; in 1850 he prepared and offered the first draft of the famous compromise measures of that year; the next year he retired to Jacksonville, Illinois, removing thence to Springfield in 1856, and in 1859 was elected representative in Congress from the capital district; twice he had been a presidential elector (for Van Buren and Pierce); in April, 1861, at the instance of Governor Yates, he accompanied a volunteer force to Cairo and occupied that place, and in July he resigned his seat in Congress. Such are the naked outlines of his political career. But when he entered the service of his country against the rebellion he was not without military experience, having at an early age served as a private in the Black-Hawk War until its close. It was rather to his disadvantage that he was urged forward in the first stages of the civil war by his political friends. If he could have done in his military as he had in his political life—taken his position where circumstance assigned him, and let his aspirations follow the appreciation of his military merits by his superior officers—he would then have found his true place, whether high or low. He fought well at Fort Donelson, and again at Shiloh; afterward he commanded the army corps of the reserve in Halleck's campaign against Corinth. We next hear of him in connection with the expedition against Vicksburg at the close of 1862. At that time Grant had command of the Army of the Mississippi. But Grant's time had not yet come. If the capacities for generalship which he afterward revealed had been then known, he would, at any rate, have been allowed to command his army without interference from Washington. Unhappily, this interference could not then be avoided. Grant assigned Sherman to command the Vicksburg expedition; the War Department relieved Sherman, and put McClernand in command. If any attribute was peculiarly characteristic of Grant, it was his knowledge of men. He had faith in Sherman, he had not in McClernand; but McClernand was forced upon him. It soon proved that Grant was right. McClernand, in com-

mand of a single corps, very soon assumed to be a *quasi* commander-in-chief. Military courtesy as well as military discipline requires absolute subordination; but McClernand's aspirations were disagreeably prominent; he was officious in advice and suggestions as to how the campaign ought to be conducted. The assault of May 22d, and the false hopes entertained on account of his dispatches to Grant, soon brought on a crisis. In addition to this, McClernand's congratulatory order to his command, on May 31st, amounted to an insinuation against his superior officer, and he was promptly relieved. Afterward we find McClernand engaged in the advocacy of McClellan for President in opposition to Lincoln. He resigned his place in the army in November, 1865.

Four days after the second assault on Vicksburg, General Banks had invested Port Hudson. Port Hudson is located on a bend in the Mississippi River, about twenty-two miles above Baton Rouge, and one hundred and forty-seven from New Orleans. Batteries had been erected along the river on high bluffs, extending from Thompson's Creek above the town southward for three and a half miles. The land defenses began from Thompson's Creek, and ran in a semicircular form for ten miles till they connected with the lower battery. The line of investment from right to left was held by Weitzel's brigade, and Grover's, Paine's, Augur's, and T. W. Sherman's divisions. The Confederate works had been skillfully planned, consisting, like those around Vicksburg, of strong redoubts commanding all the approaches to the town, and supporting each other, with rifle-pits between and in front; the garrison, however, had been reduced to about 6000 men. An attempt was made on May 27th to carry the works by assault. A heavy bombardment preceded the attack, which was begun by Weitzel, Grover, and Paine on the right at 10 A.M. The left, under Augur and Sherman, did not attack with any vigor until four hours later, and thus all the value of a simultaneous assault was lost. The river batteries in the mean time were engaged by Farragut's fleet —the Hartford and Albatross above, and the Richmond, Monongahela, Genesee, and Essex below. The naval attack was not entirely unsuccessful; the gun-boats compelled the enemy to abandon his southernmost battery, dismounted many of his heavy guns, and even reached the landward defenses with a fire in reverse.

But on the land side the assault was a complete failure. Not because of any want of gallantry in the troops; no men ever fought better. The enemy's rifle-pits were protected by impassable abatis swept by heavy guns. The battle on the right lasted till 4 o'clock in the afternoon. Weitzel, Grover, and Paine—neither of whose commands amounted to more than a brigade—with two regiments of colored troops, crossed Sandy Creek in the morning, and succeeded in driving the enemy through the woods to his fortifications. Augur and Sherman in the afternoon achieved a similar success on the left, moving up to the fortifications until they held the sides of the parapet opposite the enemy, but, toward night, being exposed to a flank fire, they withdrew. The position gained on the right was maintained. The negro troops were posted on the extreme right, a position well calculated to test their steadiness and bravery. They made during the day three charges

CUVIER GROVER.

THE ASSAULT ON PORT HUDSON, MAY 27, 1863.

FORT HUDSON FROM THE OPPOSITE BANK.

on the enemy's batteries, and, although losing heavily, they held their position with the other troops without flinching until nightfall. This was the first instance in which negro troops fought during the war. In this action General T. W. Sherman was severely wounded. The entire National loss was 1842, of whom 293 were killed. The Confederate loss was inconsiderable.

The troops now went to digging, mining, and sharp-shooting. They were mostly nine-months' men, whose time had nearly expired. In a hostile region, with a large body of Confederate cavalry in their rear, and all Louisiana left open to Dick Taylor by Banks's concentration against Port Hudson, their situation was not an enviable one, and would have been perilous if, at this time, the attention of the enemy had not been so wholly given to the more important post of Vicksburg.

After several days' bombardment a second assault was made on Port Hudson. The chief point of attack was the northeasterly corner of the enemy's line of intrenchments. The result of the assault was a nearer approach to the works, and on the left, while Grover and Weitzel made the more palpable attack on the right, General Dwight succeeded in carrying and holding an eminence which commanded a vital point in the defenses known as "the Citadel." But what had been thus gained had cost 700 more men, and no subsequent assaults were made. Among the wounded was General Paine.

On the west side of the Mississippi, Dick Taylor had had the field in Louisiana almost entirely to himself. Early in June he reoccupied Alexandria and Opelousas. Upon his advance down the Atchafalaya, apparently threatening New Orleans, the advanced federal posts were withdrawn to Brashear. To this latter point Lieutenant Colonel Stickney had been sent by General Emory from New Orleans, to take command. From mismanagement, and lack of preparation and discipline, the enemy succeeded in taking Thibodeaux, Terre Bonne, and Bayou Bœuf, capturing their garrisons, while another column, under Mouton and Green, threatened Brashear from Berwick. Brashear was surrounded and captured with 1000 prisoners, Fort Buchanan, 10 heavy guns, and thousands of liberated negroes were reduced to slavery. Ryder, who had a few weeks before needlessly burned Berwick, managed to escape with the only national gun-boat left in the bayou. The road was now open for Taylor to advance to Algiers, the western suburb of New Orleans, Lafourche having been evacuated by Stickney. But the enemy fortunately had too weak a force to attempt the recapture of New Orleans; therefore he moved northward and threatened Donaldsonville; but, even after his storming-party had entered the fort, he was repulsed by the aid of the gun-boats, with a loss of 200 killed and 124 prisoners.

In the mean time Grant's army held its ground before Vicksburg. Five days after the investment the garrison had been reduced to 14½ ounces of food per day to each man, and it is reported that Pemberton had expressed his determination never to surrender the town till the last dog had been eaten and the last man slain. The only hope of relief from the alternative of starvation or surrender was in Joe Johnston; but if Pemberton entertained any hope from this source he leaned upon a broken reed. Grant's re-enforcements enabled him to give Sherman a detached command, consisting of the forces at Haines's Bluff, a division from each of the Thirteenth, Fifteenth, and Seventeenth corps, and Lanman's division, for the especial purpose of looking after Johnston. The character of the country was also in his favor, enabling him by intrenchment to secure himself against an attack in his rear, while the Big Black formed a strong defensive line on the south, and his means of communication were beyond the enemy's reach. Johnston was also embarrassed by the frequency of straggling and desertion in his army. The evil was so great and of such extent as to cause Governor Brown, of Georgia, through which state the delinquents found their way to the East, to issue a proclamation, ordering their arrest by associations of citizens as well as by state troops.

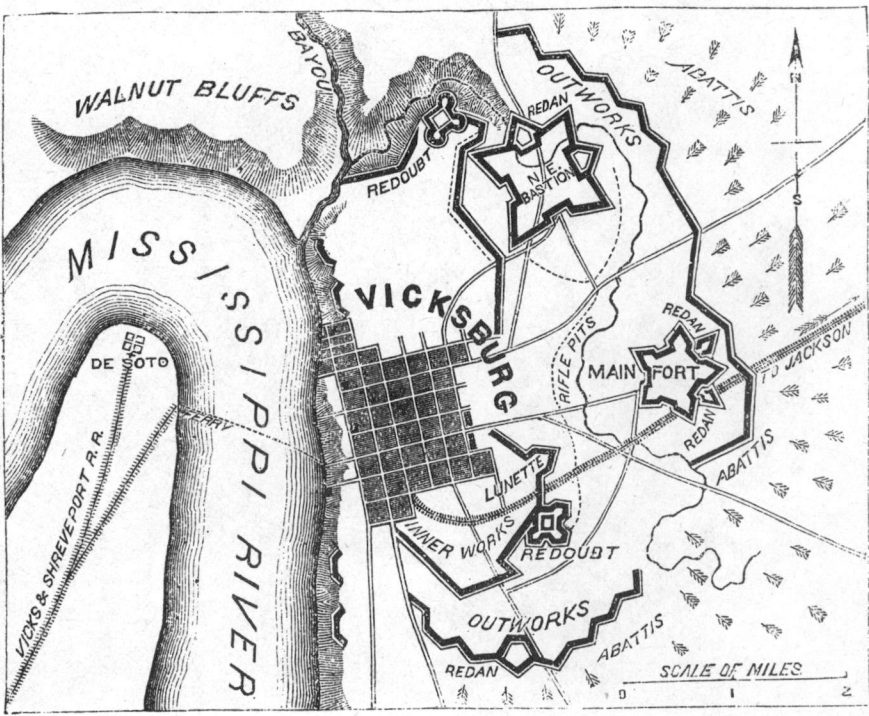

PLAN OF THE VICKSBURG DEFENSES.

ENTRANCE OF GALLERY LEADING TO THE MINE.

MINERS AT WORK UNDER THE FORT.

The irregularities of the ground between the two lines afforded opportunities for the construction of winding covered ways leading up to the outworks of the enemy. This circumstance facilitated the construction of mines. The excavations were well guarded from the observation of even the Federal troops. The first mine was sprung on June 25th, under a fort opposite the centre, in McPherson's front, and to the left of the Jackson Road, where Logan, early in the siege, had occupied and erected a fort upon a hill near the enemy, and overlooking his works. The explosion threw down a part of the face of the fort which had been undermined. An attempt was made to get possession, but without success. The Confederate General Herbert had built a second fort in the rear, so that the explosion of the first was of no great importance. A grandson of Henry Clay was killed in the struggle with the Federal troops on this occasion. In the same way other forts were undermined, the enemy countermining at a great disadvantage, and often the miners and counterminers approached so nearly that they could hear each other's picks. If it had been necessary, Grant's army would, no doubt, have dug itself into Vicksburg.

The garrison, exhausted from an insufficient supply of food, was wearied moreover by uninterrupted confinement in the rifle-pits, where many, escaping the accurate shots of Grant's sharp-shooters, fell victims to disease. The national troops, on the other hand, sheltered by the kindly covering of woods from the burning heat of the summer sun, well supplied with food —for they had the resources of the entire West at their backs and within their command—and finding innumerable springs of the best water in the deep ravines, improved daily in health; thousands of men became available who were numbered among the non-effectives just after the assault of May 22d.

Next to the hardships endured by the brave defenders of Vicksburg were those suffered daily by the non-combatants. Starvation confronted these latter in its worst forms. All the beef in the city was exhausted before the end of June, and mule-meat was resorted to as a last expedient.[1] The poor were without money, and, but for the charity of those possessed of better means, must have starved, with flour at $1000 per barrel, meal $140 per bushel, molasses $10 per gallon, and beef at $2 50 per pound. The city looked like a pile of half-ruined buildings, so searching were the Federal shells. For safety, the inhabitants went to caves dug into the sides of the hills, and here too the missiles of death reached them, not sparing even innocent children. The spirits both of the citizens and the troops were kept up, in a measure, by the rumors continually reaching them that Johnston was about to raise the siege. Couriers frequently found their

[1] Abrams says that he "partook of mule-meat for three or four days, and found the flesh tender and nutritious, and, *under the peculiar circumstances*, a most desirable description of food."

EXPLOSION OF FORT ON McPHERSON'S FRONT.

THE SIEGE OF VICKSBURG—BATTERY HICKENLOOPER.

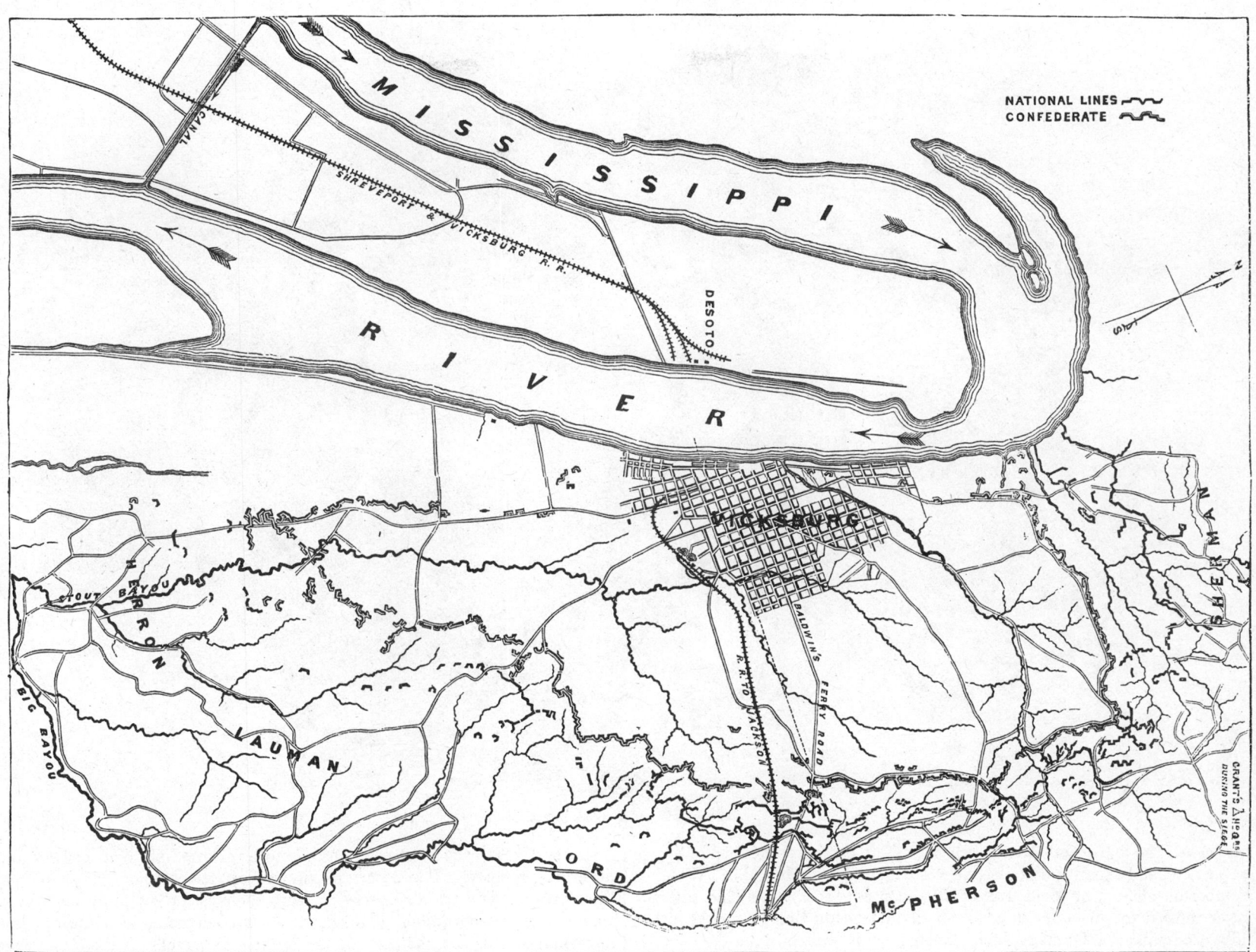

MAP ILLUSTRATING THE SIEGE OF VICKSBURG.

way through the swamps and thickets of the Yazoo to Grant's rear, and on their return gave out these vague hints, exciting the most extravagant expectations. Many believed that Johnston had gathered together an army of 50,000 men for the relief of Vicksburg. By the same route used by these couriers, Pemberton supplied himself with percussion caps during the siege.

Johnston himself, with an army of about 24,000 men, gathered together from all possible sources under the pressure of necessity, and poorly equipped, had no hope of raising the siege by an attack on the rear of Grant's army. He could obtain no assistance from Bragg, who was firmly held by Rosecrans, and the diminution of whose force would have compelled the abandonment of Tennessee, without securing the possession of Vicksburg. But it seemed not impossible that some help might come from the west side of the Mississippi if Kirby Smith and Taylor could re-establish their communications with the Vicksburg garrison. Even such help could only have protracted the campaign. But, whatever it promised, it was not to be had. An unsuccessful attempt was made, in April, by the Confederate General Marmaduke, to capture Cape Girardeau, above Cairo, which, if it had succeeded, would have somewhat seriously embarrassed General Grant's operations. General Kirby Smith's attempt to open communications with Vicksburg proved equally abortive. An attack was made early in June upon the Federal camp at Milliken's Bend. The first stage of the attack promised a favorable result to the Confederates, who succeeded in driving the small detachment of national troops from their outer line of intrenchments to the river's bank, but with the aid of a gun-boat the tide of battle was turned, and the Iowa regiments, assisted by negro troops, rallied and repulsed the assailants. After another fight at Richmond, nine miles from Milliken's Bend, in which it was defeated, Kirby Smith's army retired into the interior. His 8000 men, says Johnston, had been mismanaged, and had fallen back to Delhi. From the West no farther attempt was made for the relief of Vicksburg and Port Hudson.

A correspondence was kept up between Pemberton and Jackson during the siege. Again and again the latter professed his inability to raise the siege, or to do any thing more than co-operate with Pemberton in an attempt to extricate the garrison. To urgent appeals from the War Department at Richmond, Johnston repeatedly replied that he could effect nothing with so inadequate a command. "If I attack," he said, "there is the Big Black in my rear, cutting off my retreat." Finally, on June 21st, Pemberton wrote to Johnston recommending him to make a demonstration on the Federal right, and promised to himself move out his garrison, if possible, by the Warrenton Road and across Hankinson's Ferry. Upon mature consideration this plan was deemed impracticable. On the 22d of June, the day after he had made this bold proposition, Pemberton suggested that Johnston should make to Grant propositions to pass his army out, with all its arms and equipages. He could hold out, he said, fifteen days longer. In reply to this, Johnston

complimented Pemberton upon his determined spirit, and held out hopes of aid from Kirby Smith. He hoped that "something might yet be done to save Vicksburg" without resorting to any mode of merely extricating the garrison, but he declined to confess his own weakness by making the proposed terms to General Grant. Such terms, if necessary, must come from Pemberton, though they might be considered as made under his authority. Johnston, in the mean time, having obtained his field transportation and supplies, marched toward the Big Black, June 29th, hoping better results from an attack on the south than on the north of the railroad. On the night of July 3d he sent a messenger to notify Pemberton that he was ready to make a diversion to enable the garrison to cut its way out, but before the arrival of this messenger Vicksburg had been surrendered.

It may seem wonderful that Vicksburg should have been surrendered on the Fourth of July, a "Yankee anniversary," as the enemy was now pleased to call it. Pollard, the Southern historian, takes especial umbrage at this circumstance. Surrendered it must have been, doubtless; but why, of all days of the year, on *that* day? The explanation must rest with General Pemberton. He knew that Grant was preparing for an overwhelming attack. This attack, he thought, would certainly be made on the 4th. The chances in such an event were wholly in Grant's favor. Of the garrison not more than 15,000 men could probably be made available for the defense of a line eight miles long, and against a brave, well-fed, and confident enemy numbering over 60,000 men. It was bad enough to surrender on the 4th of July, but it was still worse to be ingloriously beaten on that day. Moreover, it was quite natural that Pemberton should be confident of securing better terms for his army by indulging the enemy a little in this particular.

At any rate, on the morning of July 3d an unusual quiet rested upon the defenses of Vicksburg, which was soon explained by the appearance of a flag of truce upon the works in front of A. J. Smith. This flag ushered into our lines two Confederate officers, Colonel Montgomery and General Bowen, with a sealed communication from Pemberton to Grant. The letter proposed the arrangement of terms of capitulation by the appointment of commissioners, three on each side. Of course Pemberton said that he was "fully able to maintain his position for an indefinite period." General Grant replied, refusing to submit to the terms of a commission, and demanding an unconditional surrender. He, however, consented to meet Pemberton at 3 o'clock P.M., and to arrange the terms of surrender by a personal interview.

The two generals met at the appointed hour under a gigantic oak in McPherson's front. Many and various have been the accounts published of this important interview. By some Pemberton is represented as having chatted in an indifferent manner, making arrangements for the surrender of a large army and of the Mississippi River while chewing straws with marvelous *sang froid*; others report that he was stormy, irascible, and even im-

INTERVIEW BETWEEN GRANT AND PEMBERTON.

pertinent. As to General Grant's behavior there can be no doubt; of course he smoked, and equally, of course, he was cool and imperturbable. Whether Pemberton chatted or scolded is of little consequence. It is said that the latter refused to surrender unconditionally, declaring that he would rather fight it out, and that Grant replied, "Then, sir, you can continue the defense. My army has never been in a better condition for the prosecution of the siege." However this may have been, the interview ended with the understanding that Pemberton would confer with his subordinate officers, and return an answer the following morning. The oak-tree has long since disappeared through the ravages of relic-hunters. Upon the spot where it stood a monument was erected. This also was soon so much defaced that in 1866 it was displaced by a sixty-four-pounder cannon placed in an erect position, with the muzzle pointing upward.[1]

Grant, after consultation with his generals, anticipated any communication which Pemberton might make by writing him a letter on the evening of the 3d. He proposed the following scheme: Pemberton's army should be allowed to march out of the city as soon as paroled, the officers taking with them their regimental clothing, while staff, field, and cavalry officers might

[1] The original monument was a pyramid twenty feet high, surmounted with a fifteen-inch globe. On one of its faces was an American eagle sustaining on its wings the Goddess of Liberty. On another face was the following inscription: "To the memory of the surrender of Vicksburg by Lieutenant General J. C. Pemberton to Major General U. S. Grant, on the 3d of July, 1863."

retain one horse each; the rank and file to be allowed all their clothing, but no other property. The necessary amount of rations could be taken from the stores in Pemberton's possession, with utensils for cooking; also thirty wagons for transportation. The sick and wounded would be subject to similar conditions as soon as they should be able to travel. If the terms were accepted, he would march in one division and take possession at 8 A.M. on the 4th.

Early the next morning Pemberton's reply was received, accepting the proposed terms in the main, but submitting that, in justice both to the honor and spirit of his army, manifested in the defense of Vicksburg, it ought to be allowed to march out with colors and arms, stacking them in front of the lines, after which Grant should take possession; that the officers should be allowed their side-arms and personal property, and that the rights and property of citizens should be respected.

Some of these requests were acceded by General Grant; others were refused. He had no objection to paying Pemberton's troops the compliment

THE OLD MONUMENT, MARKING THE SITE OF THE SURRENDER.

THE NEW VICKSBURG MONUMENT.

of allowing them to march to the front and stack their arms, provided they then marched back again, remaining as prisoners until they were paroled. The parole was insisted upon in its strictest form, to be signed in each case by the paroled soldiers individually. He refused to be bound by any stipulations as to the treatment of citizens, confining himself simply to the assurance that he did not propose to cause any of them any undue annoyance or loss. With these modifications the parley must close. If the terms were not accepted by 9 A.M. they would be regarded as refused, and hostilities would recommence. Acceptance would be indicated on Pemberton's part by the display of white flags along his lines.

These terms were promptly accepted by Pemberton. Three hours were occupied by the Confederate army in marching out and stacking their arms. In the afternoon the national troops marched in and took possession. This was the third recurrence of the national anniversary since the beginning of the war. The first saw Congress convoked to assist the executive in meeting, for the first time in our history, an aggressive enemy within our own borders. The second witnessed McClellan's return to Harrison's Landing after a most disastrous campaign. But on the third was celebrated the surrender of Vicksburg and the victory of Gettysburg, the two events which, taken together, mark the turning-point of the war against the Southern Confederacy.

By 3 o'clock P.M. the national fleet of rams, gun-boats, and transports lined the levee. Grant, with McPherson, Logan, and their several staffs, entered Vicksburg. After an active campaign of eighty days— counting from the first passage of the transports below Vicksburg—he had won the most important and stupendous victory of the war. His loss had been 8575,[1] of which 4236 fell before Vicksburg. Not more than half of the wounded had been permanently disabled. The enemy's loss before the surrender amounted to at least 10,000 killed and wounded, not counting stragglers. In addition to these, 27,000 men were captured with Vicksburg, including fifteen general officers, one hundred and twenty-eight pieces of artillery, and about eighty siege-guns, besides arms and munitions of war for an army of 60,000, together with a large amount of public property, consisting of railroads, locomotives, cars, steam-boats, cotton, etc. Much property had also been destroyed to prevent its capture.

Grant had acted at his own discretion in paroling so large a number of troops. It saved the government the expense of removing them North, which at this time would have been very difficult with the limited transportation on hand, and also of their subsistence, and it left the army free to operate against Johnston.

The enthusiasm of the national forces upon their entrance into Vicksburg surpasses description. To Pemberton's army, in addition to the distressing hardships of the siege, was added the humiliation of defeat. One of the most interesting features connected with the capture of Vicksburg was the exultation of the negroes. Crowds of them congregated upon the side-walks,

[1] Grant sums up his loss in the series of battles about and before Vicksburg as follows:

	Killed.	Wounded.	Missing.
Port Gibson	130	718	5
Fourteen-mile Creek	4	24	—
Raymond	69	341	32
Jackson	40	240	6
Champion's Hill	426	1842	189
Big Black Bridge	29	242	2
Before Vicksburg	245	3688	303
Total	943	7095	537
Sum total			8575

THE SURRENDER OF VICKSBURG, JULY 4, 1863.

FEDERAL TROOPS BEFORE JACKSON, MISSISSIPPI.

welcoming Grant's army with broad grins of satisfaction. On the next day, which was Sunday, they dressed themselves in the most extravagant style, and promenaded the streets with a more palpable expression of triumphant joy than the conquerors themselves.

When Johnston was apprised of the surrender of Vicksburg he withdrew from the Big Black to Jackson. Immediately after the capture, Grant sent the remainder of the Thirteenth and Fifteenth Corps to re-enforce the five divisions already assigned to Sherman for operations against Johnston. Sherman had constructed a line of defense in Grant's rear from Haines's Bluff to the Big Black. This line had kept Johnston from his proposed attack north of the railroad, and the surrender of Vicksburg had made a diversion on the Big Black as unnecessary as it was impracticable.

Johnston's four divisions covering Jackson on the morning of July 9th were commanded by Major Generals Loring, Walker, French, and Breckinridge, while a division of cavalry, under General Jackson, guarded the fords of Pearl River above and below the town. Sherman in the mean time had been marching his command over the intervening fifty miles in the heat and dust, and through a country almost destitute of water—so destitute, indeed, that Johnston considered a siege of Jackson impossible. His advance appeared before the enemy's intrenchments on the 9th, and on the 12th had invested the town, both flanks resting on Pearl River. While skirmishing was going on in front, the cavalry were operating on the north and south of Jackson, destroying railroads and other property.

Johnston's position was entirely untenable. Batteries posted upon the surrounding hills were within easy range, commanding the town. Sherman's army fell but little short of 50,000 men, and he had a hundred guns planted upon the hills. In this situation he only waited for his ammunition train, which arrived on the 16th. This delay gave Johnston time for retreat; to remain was certain disaster.

In a too close approach to the works on the 12th, Lauman's division suffered a severe loss—about 500 men, of whom two hundred were captured, with the colors of the Twenty-eighth, Forty-first, and Fifty-third Illinois. This unfortunate loss was the result of a misapprehension of orders. Lauman's division was under Ord's command, and held the extreme right, confronting Breckinridge. Ord, thinking the position of the division too much retired, ordered it forward, so as to connect with Hovey's. This advance was not designed to bring on an engagement, nor would it have done so but for a careless misapprehension on Lauman's part. Pugh's brigade, after crossing the New Orleans and Jackson Railroad at a point about two miles south of Jackson, and driving back the enemy's skirmishers, found itself, with less than 1000 men, confronted by a strong line of works held by two brigades of the enemy, with two full batteries, and protected by abatis in front. The intervening space was open, affording no cover to a charging column. Pugh reported this situation to Lauman; but the latter repeated the order to move forward. It was certain death to every other man in the brigade, but the order was obeyed. No other result was possible but that which followed, namely, the useless murder of half the column. Well may Lauman have wept when he looked upon the remnant of his old brigade. He was afterward relieved of his command by General Ord.[1]

Jackson was evacuated on the night of July 16th, Johnston retreating across Pearl River, burning the bridges behind him, and through Brandon toward Meridian, about 100 miles east of Jackson. The town, thus again left in possession of the national troops, was once more devoted to destruction. Sherman pursued the enemy as far as Brandon, and then returned with his army across the Big Black. The Confederate loss at Jackson, by Johnston's report, was 71 killed, 504 wounded, and about 25 missing. Desertions were frequent from his army both during the siege and in the retreat.

The navy had necessarily a less conspicuous share than the army in the capture of Vicksburg, but its co-operation had been absolutely essential to Grant's success. The gun-boats had been constantly engaged in shelling the town from below. For forty-two days the mortar-boats had also been at work without intermission, throwing shells into all parts of the city, and even reaching the works in the rear of Vicksburg, three miles distant, with a fire in reverse; thirteen guns had been transferred from the fleet to the army; the river had been patrolled from Cairo to Vicksburg, to clear out the guerrillas who had on several occasions built batteries on the shore, and attempted to sink or capture the transports conveying stores, re-enforcements, and ammunition to the besieging army; and the gun-boats, with General Ellet's marine brigade, had frustrated the schemes of Kirby Smith by their co-operation with the small force on the right bank of the Mississippi at Milliken's Bend.[2]

---

[1] Sherman, speaking of this affair, attributes the disaster to "misunderstanding or a misinterpretation of General Ord's minute instructions on the part of General Lauman."

[2] Immediately after the surrender Sherman penned the following impromptu, but characteristic letter to Admiral Porter:

"I can appreciate the intense satisfaction you must feel at lying before the monster that has defied us with such deep and malignant hate, and seeing your once disunited fleet again a unit; and, better still, the chain that made an inclosed sea of a link in the great river broken forever. In so magnificent a result I stop not to count who did it. It is done, and the day of the nation's birth is consecrated and baptized anew in a victory won by the united navy and army of our country. God grant that the harmony and mutual respect that exists between our respective commanders, and shared by all the true men of the joint service, may continue forever, and serve to elevate our national character, threatened with shipwreck. Thus I muse as I sit in my solitary camp out in the woods, far from the point for which we have justly striven so long and so well; and though personal curiosity would tempt me to go and see the frowning batteries and sunken pits that have defied us so long, and sent to their silent graves so many of our early comrades in the enterprise, I feel that other tasks lie before me, and time must not be lost. Without casting anchor, and despite the heat, and the dust, and the drought, I must again into the bowels of the land, to make the conquest of the land fulfill all the conditions it should in the progress of this war. Whether success attend my efforts or not, I know that Admiral Porter will ever accord to me the exhibition of a pure and unselfish zeal in the service of our country.

"Though farther apart, the navy and army will still act in concert, and I assure you I shall never reach the banks of the river or see a gun-boat but I will think of Admiral Porter, Captain

The 4th of July, 1863, also witnessed a conflict of some importance at Helena, Arkansas, on the right bank of the river, above Vicksburg. This place, since its occupation in the summer of 1862 by the advance of General Curtis's army, had rested undisturbed in the possession of the national forces, and had been of great use as a dépôt of recruits and supplies for operations farther south. It threatened also the most important points in those portions of the state occupied by the enemy.

Toward the close of the siege of Vicksburg, Lieutenant General Holmes, the Confederate commander in Arkansas, at the suggestion of Secretary Mallory, and with Kirby Smith's permission, prepared an expedition to attack Helena. He left Little Rock on the 25th of June, and made Clarendon, sixty miles east of the capital, on White River, the rendezvous for his forces. Fagan, Sterling Price, and Marmaduke were to command in the attacking army. It was Holmes's design to surprise the Federal force; but Price, owing to high water, was four days behindhand, and in the mean time General B. M. Prentiss, commanding at Helena, became acquainted with the enemy's intentions. The garrison numbered about 4000 men, and was intrenched behind strong earth-works, well mounted with artillery, and with their main approaches covered by abatis. Prentiss had also an important ally, upon whose presence the enemy had not calculated, in the gun-boat Tyler, commanded by J. M. Pritchett.

The town lies upon the river flat, but near it are high commanding ridges, with ravines opening toward the river. Upon a low ridge nearer the town Fort Curtis was located, while upon the higher ridges commanding it outworks had been constructed by Brigadier General F. Salomon, to whose charge also had been assigned their defense. These outworks consisted of four strong batteries, designated from right to left by the first four letters of the alphabet in their succession. The flanks, which, being between the ridges and the river, were open, were protected by rifle-pits and batteries.

Holmes reports his total force to have been 7646, or about twice the strength of the garrison. The Missourians were under Price, Parsons, and Marmaduke, while the brigades of Fagan, McRae, and Walker consisted of troops gathered together from Arkansas. The Confederate command was not lacking in bravery, and the attack was admirably conducted, but the assailing force was too weak by half for any chance of success against a determined garrison in so strong a position. The Confederate Governor of Arkansas, Harris Flanagan, with his adjutant general, Colonel Gordon Rear, were on the field, acting as volunteer aids to General Holmes.

On the morning of July 4th Holmes's army was within a mile of the outworks. Price led the brigades of Parsons and McRae (3095 men) against Battery C on Grave-yard Hill, and succeeded, after great loss, in carrying the

single regiment lost its colonel, lieutenant colonel, and over 100 men. The remainder withdrew to the rifle-pits already captured, where, exposed to the fire from the fort, they held their ground until 11 o'clock, when a general retreat was ordered.

Marmaduke, with 1750 men, had been ordered to take the fort on Righton Hill (Battery A) on the north, but he failed even to make a vigorous assault, not being supported by Walker's brigade.

Holmes reports his loss in this battle as 173 killed, 687 wounded, and 776 missing. Thus, by his own admission, he lost over one fifth of his command. Prentiss says he buried nearly 300 of the enemy's killed, and took 1100 prisoners. His own loss was less than 250, all told. The gun-boat Tyler had a large share in the havoc which was made among the charging columns of the enemy.

The capture of Port Hudson and its garrison followed as the immediate and necessary consequence of the surrender of Vicksburg. In any case, Gardner could not have held out much longer. His ammunition for small-arms was almost gone, only twenty rounds remaining to each man, and the garrison was on the verge of starvation. Its mill had been fired by a shell, 2000 bushels of corn being burned with it. No meat was left, and the mules were being killed to satisfy the demand; even rats, it is reported, were eaten by the famishing soldiers. Only fifteen serviceable guns remained on the land defenses, the others having been, one after the other, disabled by the accurate fire of the Federal guns. Banks's sappers and miners had dug their way up to the works, and General Dwight had a mine ready on the left, charged with thirty barrels of powder, in such a position that its explosion would have destroyed " the Citadel," already referred to as a vital point in the enemy's defenses. The hospitals were full of the sick, and the men in the trenches were so exhausted and enfeebled that they were unfit for action. The capture of Vicksburg, however, precipitated the capitulation of Port Hudson. Grant had embarked an expedition, under General Herron, to reenforce Banks, but scarcely were the men on board when the tidings was brought of the capture of Port Hudson, and Herron's expedition was ordered up the Yazoo.

It was on the 6th of July that the news of the victory at Vicksburg reached Port Hudson. Gardner could hardly by any possibility have misinterpreted the tremendous salute of the gun-boats, re-echoed from the land batteries, or the news shouted across his lines. He forthwith convened a council of war, and a surrender was determined upon. On the 7th he communicated with General Banks, asking the latter to give him official assurance of the news. If Vicksburg had really been surrendered, he asked for a cessation of hostilities, with a view to the consideration of terms for the capitulation of Port Hudson. Banks replied by sending Grant's own dispatch, but refusing a cessation of hostilities. Conferees were appointed on each side, and on July 8th terms of surrender were concluded upon, and the next morning formal possession was taken of the town.

Banks does not report his loss before Port Hudson, but it probably fell not far short of 3000. The enemy admitted a loss of only 610 men during the forty-five days' campaign, but this, Banks is confident, must have been too low an estimate, as he found 500 wounded in the hospitals. The number of prisoners taken was 6408, of whom 455 were officers. The captures of the whole campaign, including the trans-Mississippi operations, Banks estimates at 10,584 men, 73 guns, 6000 small-arms, three gunboats, eight other steam-boats, besides cotton and cattle of immense value.

The capture of Port Hudson scared Dick Taylor out of the country east of the Atchafalaya, compelling him to evacuate Brashear City just one month after its capture. Both Grant and Banks now urged an immediate combined movement against Mobile,

SALUTING THE FLAG AT PORT HUDSON.

work, capturing some of its guns, which were either spiked or devoid of friction-primers, and therefore useless to the captors. Price had great difficulty in bringing his own artillery over the broken country and up the hill. Meanwhile his infantry was falling under a fire from all the other works. Instead of retreating, hundreds of his command pushed forward in disorder and without support, and encountering a cross fire, until, unable to retreat, as many as had escaped death surrendered. Price reports a loss in this action of over one third of his command.

Fagan's small command of four regiments had attacked at the same time, attempting the still more difficult task of carrying Battery D on the left. The charge at this point was exceedingly gallant, but met with only partial success. The brave Arkansans rushed up the precipitous ravines, and drove the Federal sharp-shooters out of their rifle-pits; but every assault upon the fort itself only added to the useless slaughter of the assailants. A

but were overruled at Washington. It seems some Texan refugees were anxious that operations should be recommenced on the line of the Red River, and Banks was advised accordingly. The history of the campaign thus opened we reserve for a subsequent chapter.

Herron, in the mean time, having transferred his troops to vessels of lighter draft, moved up the Yazoo, his transports preceded by the iron-clad De Kalb and two tin-clad gun-boats under Captain Walker. The expedition had for its object the destruction of a large number of Confederate steam-boats which had run up the Yazoo to find refuge from Porter's fleet. When nearly opposite Yazoo City the De Kalb was sunk by a torpedo. The Confederate garrison abandoned the city upon the approach of the expedition. Only one of the steam-boats was captured, the others making their escape up the river. The fugitive vessels were, however, pursued by Herron's cavalry, and all of them, to the number of twenty-two, were burned or sunk. Three hundred prisoners were captured, six heavy guns, 250 small-arms, 800 horses, and 2000 bales of cotton.

Breese, and the many elegant and accomplished gentlemen it has been my good fortune to meet on armed or unarmed decks of the Mississippi squadron."

6 F

OPENING OF THE MISSISSIPPI—ARRIVAL OF THE "IMPERIAL" AT NEW ORLEANS.

Thus ended the campaign for the possession of the Mississippi River, which now, to use the happy expression of President Lincoln, "ran unvexed to the sea." On the 16th of July the steam-boat Imperial arrived at New Orleans from St. Louis, the first steamer which had made the trip for more than two years.

The foremost man in this campaign was General Grant, the taker of guns and armies. His name was on every tongue. The shout of joy which arose from a whole people on account of his victory was mingled with a pæan of praise to the victor. He was at once appointed to the vacant major generalship in the regular army, to date from July 4th, 1863. In the midst of these acclamations to his honor, President Lincoln addressed him a letter[1] acknowledging the inestimable service he had rendered his country,

and adding a personal acknowledgment of his own error of judgment as to the propriety of re-enforcing Banks after the battle of Port Gibson instead of moving directly against Vicksburg. In this Vicksburg campaign General Grant showed his capacity for the command of a large army, and for the conduct of movements the most extensive; a remarkable boldness of conception, almost unlimited resources, and a steady persistence of purpose not to be moved by any obstacle, and not to be conquered by a succession of partial defeats. As to total defeat with such a commander, *that* was clearly impossible.

"Executive Mansion, Washington, July 13th, 1863.

" To Major General Grant:
"My dear General,—I do not remember that you and I ever met personally. I write this now as a grateful acknowledgment for *the almost inestimable service you have done the country.* I

wish to say a word farther. When you first reached the vicinity of Vicksburg I thought you should do what you finally did—march the troops across the neck, run the batteries with the transports, and thus go below; and I never had any faith, except a general hope that you knew better than I, that the Yazoo Pass Expedition and the like could succeed. When you got below, and took Port Gibson, Grand Gulf, and vicinity, I thought you should go down the river and join General Banks; and when you turned northward east of the Big Black, I feared it was a mistake. I now wish to make a personal acknowledgment *that you were right and I was wrong.*
"Yours, very truly,   A. Lincoln."

JOSEPH HOOKER.

CHAPTER XXVIII.

HOOKER IN COMMAND.—CHANCELLORSVILLE.

FROM this survey of operations in the West we turn again to Virginia, where, at the opening of the year, the two great armies of the Union and the Confederacy lay confronting each other upon the banks of the Rappahannock.[1]

Hooker was invested with the command of the Army of the Potomac on the 26th of January. Just three days before, his predecessor had drawn up an order dismissing him from the service, and on the very day before it was doubtful whether that order should be put in force. But the transfer of command was executed with all due military courtesy. "Give," said Burnside, in his parting address to the army, "to the brave and skillful general

[1] The following are the leading authorities for Chancellorsville: Testimony before the Committee on the Conduct of the War, contained in volume i. of the second series (cited as *Com. Rep.*, ii.).—Lee's Report of Chancellorsville (cited as *Lee's Rep.*): it embraces his own report and those of nearly all of his principal commanders.—Hotchkiss and Allan, engineers in the late Confederate army, have put forth a monograph upon Chancellorsville. It is specially valuable for its elaborate maps, which clearly represent the topography of the region, and show every movement upon both sides.—Dabney's Life of Stonewall Jackson embraces some valuable information respecting the operations of that commander. The author had access to many materials which are now probably destroyed.

who has so long been identified with your organization, and who is now to command you, your full and cordial support and co-operation, and you will deserve success." Hooker, in assuming command, said that "he only gives expression to the feelings of this army when he conveys to our late commander, Major General Burnside, the most cordial good wishes for his future."

Hooker took command with a confidence in himself which contrasted strongly with the self-distrust which had been expressed by Burnside. The position had come to him unsought, but, as he believed, not undeserved. "No being lives," he averred, "who can say that I ever expressed a desire for the position. It was conferred on me for my sword, and not for any act or word of mine indicative of a desire for it."[1] He had, indeed, grave misgivings, not as to his own capacity, but as to the state of the force placed under his command.[2] Foremost among these causes of misgiving was the hostility of Halleck, who for six months had sat, and for thrice as long was to sit, under the title of general-in-chief, as an incubus upon the Union armies. Hooker knew, or at least believed, that Halleck had been hostile to him from the first, and the sole request that he made of the President was that he would stand between him and his superior in command.[3] The condition of the army was a still more grave matter for apprehension. Burnside had received it from McClellan strong in numbers, discipline, and spirit. In three months he transmitted it to Hooker reduced in numbers and impaired in efficiency. Much of this was owing to causes over which Burnside had no control. Lincoln's policy, as finally indicated by his emancipation proclamation, was looked upon with disfavor by a very considerable part of the army. Many of the officers in high command, especially those who had belonged to the regular army, were far from hostile to slavery. McClellan, just escaped from the Chickahominy swamps, had found time six months before to present his views of the principles upon which the war should be waged. "The rebellion," he said, "has assumed the character of a war; as such it should be regarded. It should not be a war looking to the subjugation of the people of any state in any event. It should not be at all a war upon population, but against armed forces and political organizations. Neither confiscation of property, political executions of persons, territorial organizations of states, or forcible abolition of slavery, should be contemplated for a moment. Unless the principles governing the future conduct of our struggle shall be made known and approved, the effort to obtain the requisite forces will be almost hopeless. A declaration of radical views, especially upon slavery, will rapidly disintegrate our present armies."[4] McClellan gave voice to the prevailing feeling among the leading officers of the army. No inconsiderable part of the private soldiers had been drawn from a class which looked with bitter aversion upon the negro. This was especially the case with the regiments raised in the large cities of the North. To them the very name of Abolitionist was a word of reproach. But now the proclamation issued on New Year's day of 1863 had solemnly pledged the nation to the abolition of slavery as an essential feature of the future conduct of the war.

For a time it seemed that McClellan's prophecy that a declaration of radical views upon the subject of slavery would be verified by the rapid disintegration of the Army of the Potomac. Officers high in rank openly declared that they would never have embarked in the war had they anticipated this action of the government.[5] When rest came to the army after the disaster of Fredericksburg and the failure of the mud campaign, the disaffected began to show themselves and to make their influence felt. The army fell into a course of rapid depletion. Express trains, and even the mails, were burdened with civilian clothing, sent to soldiers by their friends to facilitate their escape from camp. When Hooker took command desertions numbered 200 a day. In a week the army lost as many men as were killed in any pitched battle. What with deserters and absentees, 85,000 men, almost 4000 of whom were commissioned officers, wellnigh half the nominal strength of the army, were away from the field, scattered all over the country.[6] The great body of the disaffected, whether in or out of the army, believed that the government would soon be forced to restore McClellan to the command, and practically to abandon its declared policy of emancipation. By these men the appointment of Hooker was looked upon with no favor. They could not fail to remember the unsparing terms in which he had attributed the disaster of the Peninsular campaign to the utter want of capacity of their favorite commander.[7] They looked eagerly forward to the time when he should be placed at the head of the army, and thence, as political affairs seemed to be shaping themselves, raised to the Presidency of the United States. The feeling in the army and that in the country acted and reacted upon each other, and for a time it seemed that the policy of the government would be condemned alike by citizens and soldiers.

In spite of these untoward circumstances and the grave misgivings which he felt, Hooker grasped the command with a firm hand. It was midwinter, and operations in the field must be postponed until early spring

should render the roads passable. In that interval much could be done. Hooker set himself strenuously at work to improve the condition of the army. At the very outset he broke up the grand divisions, and restored its former organization into corps, each being placed under the command of a general in whom he had confidence. Then the great evil of desertions was to be encountered. The loose system of furloughs was thoroughly revised. Hitherto the corps commanders had granted leaves of absence at discretion. By the new regulations no leave of absence could be granted except from head-quarters to officers of high rank. In no regiment could more than one field officer or two line officers be absent at the same time. Not more than two privates out of a hundred in any regiment could be absent on furlough at the same time, and no man could receive a furlough unless he had a good record for attention to his duties. The leaves of absence being of short date, fifteen days being the utmost limit, even these strict rules enabled all deserving men who wished it to visit their homes. Disloyal officers were carefully weeded out. Express trains were examined, and all citizens' clothing found therein was burned. The police and commissariat of the army received special attention. Comfortable winter huts were built; vegetables and fresh bread were ordered to be issued twice a week. The good result of these measures was soon apparent. Desertions ceased; absentees returned to their commands; the ratio of sickness sank from more than ten per cent. to less than five. The cavalry, which had heretofore been scattered among the grand divisions, was organized into a separate corps, and soon grew into a powerful arm, wanting only a fitting man to wield it; but Hooker was not, as commander of this army, to find such a leader. He did the best he could by giving the cavalry corps to Stoneman, with Averill next in command. Sheridan was yet to be brought from a subordinate position in the West. The outpost duty had been grossly neglected; the Confederates knew what was passing within the Union lines almost as accurately as did its own commanders. Hooker changed all this. The picket lines were rendered impenetrable. One division lay encamped on Falmouth Heights, opposite Fredericksburg, in plain view of the enemy. The camps of the other divisions, a score or more in number, covering a circuit of a hundred miles, lay beyond the wooded crests of Stafford. What passed beyond this screen was hidden from the keenest view which the Confederate commander could gain, saving when some ostentatious demonstration, or a sharp, sudden dash of pickets was made, with the object, as Hooker explained, "to encourage and stimulate in the breasts of our men, by successes however small, a feeling of superiority over our adversaries." Knowing, moreover, that idleness was the bane of all armies, every effort was made to keep the troops employed, and whenever the weather permitted they were engaged in field exercises.

As winter wore away and spring opened, the commander felt assured that he had at length "a living army well worthy of the republic," or, as he was wont to express it in larger phrase, "the finest army upon the planet." All through those winter weeks he had pondered the problem how and where he should strike.[1] His instructions were of the most general character. Halleck wrote: "In regard to the operations of your own army, you can best judge when and where it can move to the greatest advantage, keeping in view always the importance of covering Washington and Harper's Ferry, either directly or by so operating as to punish any force of the enemy sent against them."[2] Hooker had, however, caught the true idea of the work to be done. It was not so much to capture Richmond as to destroy the Confederate Army of Northern Virginia which lay in his front. Lincoln had months before vainly sought to impress this idea upon McClellan.[3] Grant seized upon it months later. In seeking to solve the problem of attack, Hooker soon came to the decision that it was impossible to cross the Rappahannock and assail the enemy directly in front. The misadventure of Burnside had demonstrated this point; and, moreover, since that luckless attempt, the Confederate position had been greatly strengthened. The mere passage of the river in front of the Confederate lines presented, indeed, no very serious difficulty, for Lee adhered to his former plan, rather inviting than threatening such an operation.[4] But his long lines of intrenchment, stretching for a distance of twenty miles along the sides and crests of the heights, were in plain view. Interspersed with the infantry parapets were epaulements for artillery which would sweep the hill-sides and bottom-lands over which an

[1] Com. Rep., ii., 112.
[2] "I entered upon my duties with many misgivings and forebodings. When it was announced to me that I had been placed in command of the Army of the Potomac, I doubted, and so expressed myself, if it could be saved to the country."—Ibid., 112.
[3] "I was informed by a member of the cabinet that [when it was first proposed to remove McClellan] the President and five members of it were in favor of placing me at the head of the Army of the Potomac, and one or two members of the cabinet and General Halleck were opposed to it." (Hooker, in Com. Rep., ii., 175.)—"I had been reliably informed that I was again opposed by him on the removal of Major General Burnside." (Ibid., 112.)—"In my interview with the President, among other subjects relating to the new position I had been called to fill, I stated that I hoped to succeed, provided he would stand between me and the commanding general of the army. This was the only request I made of the President in assuming command."—Ibid., 111.
[4] McClellan to the President, July 7, 1862, McC. Rep., 280–282.
[5] Com. Rep., ii., 112.   [6] Ibid., 112.
[7] "I do not hesitate to say that the failure of the Peninsular campaign is to be attributed to the want of generalship on the part of our commander."—Hooker, in Com. Rep., i., 575.

[1] "The subject of the campaign was one to which General Hooker gave much thought and attention. But, while getting the views of every body else, he did not give his own, but kept his intentions in regard to the proposed campaign entirely secret from every one, fearing that what he intended to do might come to the knowledge of the enemy. When he assumed command of the army there was not a record or document of any kind at headquarters of the army that gave any information at all in regard to the enemy. There was no means, no organization, and no apparent effort to obtain such information. We were almost as ignorant of the enemy in our immediate front as if they had been in China. An efficient organization for that purpose was instituted, by which we were soon enabled to get correct and proper information of the enemy, their strength and movements." (Butterfield, in Com. Rep., ii., 74.)—"Knowing that the passage of the river would be resisted, and perhaps defeated, if brought to the knowledge of the enemy, I had taken every precaution to keep it a profound secret. I had not even communicated it to my corps commanders, or the officers of my staff." (Hooker, in Com. Rep., ii., 118.)—A close examination of Hooker's dispatches and orders, compared with what is now known, shows that he was almost as well aware of the strength and positions of the Confederate force as of his own.
[2] Com. Rep., ii., 115, 285.
[3] "I would press the enemy closely; fight him if a favorable opportunity should present. If he make a stand at Winchester, I would fight him there, on the idea that if we can not beat him when he bears the wastage of coming to us, we can never when we bear the wastage of coming to him. We should not so operate as merely to drive him away. As we must beat him somewhere or fail finally, we can do it, if at all, easier near to us than far away. If we can not beat the enemy where he now is, we never can, he again being within the intrenchments of Richmond. I think he should be engaged long before such point is reached." (Lincoln to McClellan, October 13, 1862, abridged, Com. Rep., i., 525.)—"General Hooker finally determined upon a plan of campaign, the intent and purpose of which was to destroy the army of General Lee where it then was; not merely to fight a battle and gain possession of the battle-ground, and have the enemy fall back to Richmond, but to destroy him there; for General Hooker believed that we could better afford to fight the enemy nearer Washington than Richmond."—Butterfield, in Com. Rep., ii., 75.
[4] "As in the battle of Fredericksburg, it was thought best to select positions with a view to resist the advance of the enemy than incur the heavy loss that would attend any attempt to prevent his crossing."—Lee's Rep., 6.

Blacksmiths' Department, Head-Quarters.

Stables and Negro Servants' Tent.

General Hooker's Tent.

HEADQUARTERS OF THE ARMY OF THE POTOMAC.

assailing force must march. Abatis of fallen timber guarded every point between the impassable swamps at the foot of the hills, while in the rear these outer lines were covered by rifle-pits, and every little rise of ground bristled with intrenchments like a miniature fortress. To attack these works in front seemed hopeless. "Previous exposure in attempting it under Burnside, when the enemy's preparations were far less complete, had made this a conviction in the mind of every private in the ranks."[1]

The enemy could then be assailed only by turning his position either below or above. Against the former operation was the fact that the river increases so rapidly in width that it would require a thousand feet of bridging, and the pontoon trains and artillery must march twenty miles over a broken and wooded country, by roads still axle-deep with clayey mud. This march could not be concealed from the enemy on the opposite bank, who could easily extend his intrenchments down the river faster than the assailants could construct practicable roads. This movement was, then, clearly impracticable.[2]

It only remained to turn the Confederate right far above Fredericksburg, and this was possible only upon condition that the movement should be a surprise. Three miles above Fredericksburg, in a straight line, but twice as far following the bend of the river, is Banks's Ford; seven miles farther is the United States Ford,[3] neither of them to be waded except in the dry season; now the water was so high that the passage could be made only by bridges. These points were defended by works so strong and strongly held as to preclude all possibility of carrying them. A little above the United States Ford the Rappahannock receives the Rapidan, an affluent almost equal to itself. Here was the extremity of the Confederate lines, although small detachments were posted up the Rapidan for some miles. If the Rappahannock should be crossed above the position, the Rapidan was still to be passed. Lee never imagined that his opponent would attempt to turn his flank by marching such a distance, over roads almost impassable, into a region where his army must subsist upon what it could carry with it, crossing, also, two rivers which a single shower would so swell as to cut him off from his ammunition and provision trains. Yet this was the bold operation which Hooker resolved to undertake.

The army of Hooker was divided into seven corps. Many changes had been made in the principal commands. The Ninth Corps, which Burnside had brought back from North Carolina, and which had fought under him at South Mountain and Antietam, was detached from the Army of the Potomac, and, under the immediate command of W. F. Smith,[4] sent with its old leader to the West. Its place was supplied by the Twelfth, under Slocum, which had been posted at Harper's Ferry. The Eleventh, under Sigel, which had guarded the approaches to Washington, was brought down to the main army. Sigel had applied for leave of absence, and, at the urgent request of Hooker, the command of this corps was given to Howard. Butterfield was made chief of staff, and the Fifth Corps was assigned to Meade. Stoneman was placed at the head of the cavalry, and the Third Corps was given to Sickles. Sedgwick replaced Smith in the command of the Sixth Corps. Reynolds retained the First Corps, and Couch the Second. The army which Hooker had in hand numbered in effective men, "present for duty," 120,000 infantry and artillery, besides 13,000 cavalry.[5] The cavalry, excepting a single brigade of perhaps 1000, under Pleasanton, as we shall have to show, were sent away on an expedition in which they accomplished nothing, and so must be placed out of the account in estimating the effective force with which the opposing generals encountered each other in that series of actions which we call the battle of Chancellorsville. The Confederate force was far inferior.[6] Three months before it had numbered 80,000; but, confident in the strength of his position, and somewhat embarrassed by the scarcity of forage, Lee had sent Longstreet with half of his corps southward toward North Carolina, where offensive operations were threatened. There remained on the Rappahannock the divisions of Anderson and McLaws, and Jackson's entire corps, consisting of the divisions of A. P. Hill, D. H. Hill, Trimble (formerly that of Jackson), and Early. But D. H. Hill had been put in command of the Department of North Carolina, and his division was now under Rodes; Trimble was at home on sick-leave, and his division was commanded by Colston. Besides these, there was Stuart's cavalry, reduced to two brigades, and a strong reserve artillery. The entire effective strength of all arms was something more than 60,000 men. Anderson's and McLaws's divisions guarded the line from the United States Ford downward beyond Fredericksburg, a distance of ten miles; Early held the intrenchments at the foot of the hills opposite Franklin's Crossing; the remainder of Jackson's corps lay near Port Royal, twenty miles below Fredericksburg. Both armies had built for themselves comfortable winter huts in the wooded region on either side of the Rappahannock, which formed for the time a barrier which neither could overpass.

Hooker, having matured his plan of campaign, wished to commence its execution as early as possible. The term of enlistment of 40,000 men, a third of his army, would soon expire, and he knew that there was little use of putting troops into action just before the close of their time of service. Before the middle of April, though the roads were still too heavy for artillery and wagon trains, he thought that mounted men might move. On the 12th he ordered Stoneman to take the whole cavalry force, with the exception of a single brigade, 12,000 sabres strong, turn the hostile position on the left, throw himself between the enemy and Richmond, isolate him from his supplies, and check his retreat. Every where and all told, Stoneman could not encounter a force half equal to his own. In sharp phrases, which rang like battle orders, Hooker gave his directions to Stoneman: "Harass the enemy day and night, on the march and in the camp unceasingly. If you can not cut off from his column large slices, do not fail to take small ones. Let your watchword be Fight! and let all your orders be Fight! Keep yourself informed of the enemy's whereabouts, and attack him wherever you find him. Take the initiative in the forward movement of this grand army; bear in mind that celerity, audacity, and resolution are every thing in war." The primary object of this cavalry expedition, to which every thing was to be subservient, was to cut the enemy's communication with Richmond by the Fredericksburg route.[1] The movement was premature. The cavalry rode two days up the Rappahannock, and threw a division across, but a sudden storm swelled the capricious stream, and this division, in order to avoid being isolated, was forced to recross by swimming. The storm continued, the river became wholly impassable, and the cavalry were ordered to remain where they were.

A fortnight of genial spring weather now intervened. It seemed that the rainy season was over, the swollen river was confined within its banks, the roads grew firmer. Hooker in the mean while had matured his grand enterprise. "I concluded," he says, "to change my plan, and strike for the whole rebel army instead of forcing it back upon its line of retreat, which was as much as I could hope to accomplish in executing my first design." This plan was the one which has been already indicated. It was to ascend the Rappahannock beyond the hostile lines, throw a strong force across, which should sweep down the opposite bank, "knock away the enemy's force holding the United States and Banks's Fords by attacking them in their rear, and, as soon as these fords were opened, to re-enforce the marching column sufficiently for them to continue the march upon the rebel army until his whole force was routed, and, if successful, his retreat intercepted. Simultaneous with this movement on the right, the left were to cross the Rappahannock below Fredericksburg, and threaten the enemy in that quarter, including his dépôt of supplies, to prevent his dispatching an overwhelming force to his left."[2] How near this plan came of success, and how utterly it failed, is now to be shown.

On the 26th of April Hooker issued the orders which gave the first inti-

---

[1] Warren, in *Com. Rep.*, ii., 52.

[2] *Ibid.*, 53.

[3] More properly, the United States Mine Ford; sometimes called the Bark Mill Ford.

[4] As it happened, however, Smith did not accompany the corps to the West. He remained at the East, and the command of the corps was given to Parke.

[5] There is no absolutely official report, to which I have been able to gain access, showing the exact strength of Hooker's army, but scattered through the testimony given in the Report of the Committee on the Conduct of the War are data which enable me to fix it without possibility of any material error. Hooker (*Com. Rep.*, ii., 120) gives the strength "for duty" of the Fifth, Eleventh, and Twelfth Corps at 44,661—say 45,000. The Eleventh was the weakest in the army, numbering (*Com. Rep.*, ii., 121) 11,000. There remain 34,000 for the Fifth and Twelfth. These were apparently of about equal strength, 17,000 each. The Sixth was the strongest corps; Sedgwick, its commander (*Ibid.*,95), places it at 22,000; Hooker (*Ibid.*, 128) says it numbered 26,233; but he adds, "not the whole of which, by a few thousands, it is reasonable to suppose, appeared in line of battle." This difference between 22,000 and 26,000 is about the normal discrepancy between those borne upon the muster-rolls as "present" and those actually at any moment "present for duty." Sedgwick, who had for a time the First and the Third, as well as his own corps, the Sixth, gives (*Ibid.*, 95) the numbers of the two former at 35,000. Sickles (*Ibid.*, 7) says that the strength of his corps, the Third, was 18,000, which would leave 17,000 for the First, that of Reynolds. There then remains only the Second Corps, that of Couch; of the strength of this I find no special mention. I assume it to have been 17,000, that being the average number of each of the other corps.

[6] Confederate writers usually place the numbers of Lee's army at 45,000. But the official returns (see *ante*, p. 381) show that on the 31st of March there were present in the Army of Northern Virginia 73,379 men, of whom 60,298 were present for duty. The force was certainly not diminished during the next month, for Longstreet was detached a month before. Lee says (*Rep.*, 5), "General Longstreet, with two corps, was detached for service south of the James River in February." I am inclined to suspect a clerical error here, and that for "two divisions" we should read "three;" for Longstreet's Corps consisted of five divisions, those of Anderson, McLaws, Hood, Ransom, and Pickett. Only the first two are in any way mentioned in the Reports of the Battle of Chancellorsville, and in the list of regiments I find none belonging to the last three divisions. Moreover, Dabney says (*Stonewall Jackson*, 664): "The three divisions of Hood, Pickett, and Ransom were absent in Southeastern Virginia, making a demonstration against Suffolk, whither they had been directed by the scarcity of forage and food in Spottsylvania." Dabney, who seems to have had access to authentic reports as to Jackson's force, says: "His four divisions now contained about 28,000 muskets, and an aggregate of more than 30,000 men and officers. They were supported by 28 field batteries, containing 115 guns; besides these batteries, the army was still accompanied by a reserve corps of artillery. Stuart's division of cavalry was also acting upon the left." Adding the artillery and cavalry to the 28,000 muskets and more than 2000 officers, will bring the strength of Jackson up to fully 35,000. This writer, indeed, adds: "Lee had, in all, an aggregate of about 45,000 men." But, even apart from the actual returns which have been cited, this is clearly an under estimate, for Longstreet's Corps was always much stronger than that of Jackson, and the divisions of Anderson and McLaws were much the largest in that corps, and had suffered less in the previous actions than the others. They probably numbered, including artillery and cavalry acting with them, fully 25,000 men; so that the most reliable indirect evidence attainable corroborates the accuracy of the official returns, which give Lee a little more than 60,000 men.

The foregoing was written before the appearance of Hotchkiss and Allan's work, previously noted. They give the force of each division as follows: Jackson's Corps—A. P. Hill, 11,100; D. H. Hill, 9000; Trimble, 6000; Early, 7400; in all, 33,500. Anderson and McLaws, 17,000; Artillery, 170 pieces, 5000 men; Cavalry, present, 2700—a total of 58,200. But it is expressly stated that these are the numbers of "muskets," that is, privates and non-commissioned officers. They add (page 24): "We have not the exact data on which to give the effective strength, but an addition of 4000 to the total above would be a liberal estimate." This addition to the "effective" must mean the officers, who are included in the Union returns. This statement differs only slightly from my estimate as to the total force, but makes that of Jackson larger, and those of Anderson and McLaws smaller. Anderson's division contained three more regiments than that of McLaws, and was probably the stronger by 1000. I adopt their statement, distributing the 3800 "additional," as nearly as may be, among the different organizations.

From these data is framed the following table:

FORCES AT CHANCELLORSVILLE.

UNION.	
REYNOLDS (1st Corps). *Divisions:* Doubleday, Robinson, Wadsworth..	17,000
COUCH (2d Corps). *Divisions:* French, Gibbon, Hancock	17,000
SICKLES (3d Corps). *Divisions:* Berry, Birney, Whipple	18,000
MEADE (5th Corps). *Divisions:* Griffin, Humphrey, Sykes	17,000
SEDGWICK (6th Corps). *Divisions:* Brooks, Howe, Newton...............	22,000
HOWARD (11th Corps). *Divisions:* Devens, Schurz, Steinwehr..........	11,000
SLOCUM (12th Corps). *Divisions:* Geary, Williams	17,000
PLEASONTON (Cavalry)..................	1,000
Total Force................	120,000

CONFEDERATE.		
JACKSON'S CORPS.	A. P. Hill.............	11,800
	Rodes	9,600
	Colston	6,400
	Early	7,800
LONGSTREET'S CORPS.	Anderson.............	9,500
	McLaws	8,500
	Artillery..............	5,400
	Cavalry	3,000
	Total Force.........	62,000

[1] Hooker's Instructions, in *Com. Rep.*, ii., 113

[2] Hooker, in *Com. Rep.*, ii., 116.

PICKET GUARD.

mation of his plan. The corps of Meade, Slocum, and Howard were to form the main turning column. They were to march at sunrise next day, ascend the Rappahannock to Kelly's Ford, twenty-seven miles above Fredericksburg, cross the river, and move for the Rapidan, cross, and sweep down its southern bank. They were to move as lightly as possible, the men to carry eight days' rations on their persons; each corps to have but a single battery and six ambulances, the small ammunition to be carried on mule-back. Most of the artillery, and several regiments whose term was about to close, being left behind, this column marched 36,000 strong. Couch, with two of his divisions—that of Gibbon being left opposite Fredericksburg—was to follow after as far as the United States Ford, there halt in readiness to cross the moment that the hostile force guarding it should be swept away. Sedgwick, with his own corps and those of Sickles and Reynolds, were to cross the Rappahannock below Fredericksburg, and make a vigorous demonstration to distract the attention of the enemy.

The main turning column pressed rapidly up the Rappahannock, and before night of Tuesday, the 28th, reached Kelly's Ford. The stream was unfordable, but a pontoon bridge was quickly thrown over, and early on the

morning of the 29th the crossing was effected. The force, separated into two columns, pressed rapidly on to the Rapidan. Slocum and Howard crossed at Germania Ford; Meade at Ely's Ford, ten miles below. The Rapidan was hardly fordable, the water reaching to the armpits of the men; but they waded through, bearing their knapsacks on their bayonets. So wholly unanticipated was this advance, that a small party of the Confederates were surprised at Germania Ford in the act of building a bridge; these were all captured. Meade swept eastward down the right bank of the Rapidan, directly toward Fredericksburg, until he came in view of the United States Ford over the Rappahannock. Two Confederate brigades which had been guarding this point fell back. As soon as Couch caught sight through the mist of the head of Meade's column, pontoon bridges were laid, his divisions passed over, and all the four corps headed straight for Chancellorsville, their appointed place of rendezvous, where they were concentrated late in the afternoon of the 30th.

Chancellorsville was a solitary brick house, with a few insignificant outbuildings, standing in a clearing on the eastern verge of a wild, wooded region known as the Wilderness. Looking eastward toward Fredericksburg,

CAVALRY CROSSING AT ELY'S FORD.

CROSSING AT UNITED STATES FORD.

eleven miles distant, are two roads; to the right the Orange plank road, to the left the turnpike. These diverge for a space, and then, converging, unite half way between Chancellorsville and Fredericksburg. Both are excellent roads; the one planked, the other macadamized. Westward from Chancellorsville they run together for a couple of miles, and then separate, the turnpike running to Culpepper, the plank road to Orange Court-house. This road is the essential feature of the military position. From the north comes in another road, which after a mile divides, sending branches to the different fords of the Rapidan and the Rappahannock. The cleared fields around Chancellorsville have a circuit of a mile; the belt of woods surrounding them eastward toward Fredericksburg, and southward toward Spottsylvania, is a mile or two in breadth. Beyond this, in both directions, lies an open cultivated country.

The Wilderness, henceforth to be historic, stretches westward from Chancellorsville. The region for a space of a dozen miles is seamed with veins of iron ore. These have been wrought for five generations. Here indeed were erected the first regular iron furnaces in North America. The forests had been cut down to furnish fuel for these furnaces. The soil being generally too poor to repay culture, the region was left to Nature, which soon covered it with a dense mass of dwarf pines, scrubby oaks, chinquapins, and the like. Every stump left by the woodman's axe sent up a cluster of sprouts in place of the parent trunk. Whortleberries and brambles of every kind, availing themselves of the temporary flood of sunshine, twined and matted themselves into thickets through which the solitary huntsman could make his way only by dragging his rifle after him. The surface was an elevated plateau, swelling every where into low hills and ridges, with swampy intervales between, along which sluggish brooks made their way toward the Rapidan on the north and the Mattapony on the south. Here and there is a little farm-house, or tavern, or church, with a small clearing around it, surrounded by the forests, like an island in the midst of waters. Four miles west of Chancellorsville, the Brock Road, leaving the turnpike, runs southeastward. Besides these, other roads, mostly mere wood-paths, penetrate the thickets. In this Wilderness, and upon its eastern and western verge, Lee, with the Confederate army of Northern Virginia, was within a year and a day thrice to encounter and foil the Union Army of the Potomac under the successive commands of Hooker, Meade, and Grant.

Hooker's turning movement, apparently the critical point of his whole plan, had been successfully performed. His wary opponent was taken by surprise. He knew nothing of it until it was practically accomplished. On the 28th, Sedgwick, with his own corps and those of Sickles and Reynolds, moved down the river, screened from the view of the enemy by the intervening heights. All that rainy night they lay upon their arms, with no camp-fires to betray their position. Before dawn, while the flanking column was crossing the river thirty miles above, the pontoons were borne silently to the river bank and swung across. When day broke, Jackson saw a great force of the enemy across the stream, holding the very ground from which they had dashed upon his lines four months and a half before. He sent the news to the commanding general. "I heard firing," said Lee to the messenger, "and was beginning to think it was time that some of you lazy young fellows were coming to tell me what it was all about. Say to General Jackson that he knows just as well what to do with the enemy as I do."[1] Noon came before Lee received tidings that Hooker had crossed the Rappahannock and was then pressing toward the Rapidan, the columns converging upon Chancellorsville. He sent a message to Anderson, who held the lines, sharply censuring him for his negligence.[2] During the night of the 29th Anderson's brigade retired from the ford to Chancellorsville, but, learning of the great force that was advancing against them, fell back the next morning six miles farther toward Fredericksburg, where they intrenched themselves. Saving some skirmishing between Pleasonton's cavalry and the retiring Confederates,[3] so slight that no Federal commander reports it, Hooker's columns reached Chancellorsville without opposition. To all human seeming, Hooker was justified in the congratulatory orders which he issued that evening. "It is with heartfelt satisfaction that the commanding general announces to the army that the operations of the last three days have determined that our enemy must either ingloriously fly, or come out from behind his intrenchments and give us battle on our own ground, where certain destruction awaits him."[4] To those around him he spoke in the same strain. "The rebel army," he said, "is now the legitimate property of the Army of the Potomac. They may as well pack up their haversacks and make for Richmond, and I shall be after them."[5] Sedgwick was ordered, should the enemy in his front show any symptoms of falling back, to pursue him with the utmost vigor along the road leading to Richmond; "pursue until you destroy or capture."[6] It was a foregone conclusion with Hooker that Lee must retreat the moment his flank was fairly turned. He hoped to force him to fall back toward Gordonsville rather than by the direct route to Richmond, for which place he would then strike, having fifty miles less to march. In anticipation of these results, he had a

[1] Dabney, 661.
[2] "During the forenoon of the 29th Stuart reported that the enemy had crossed the Rappahannock at Kelly's Ford on the preceding evening. Later in the day he announced that a heavy column was moving from Kelly's toward Germania Ford on the Rapidan, and another toward Ely's Ford on that river. The routes that they were pursuing, after crossing the Rapidan, converge near Chancellorsville, whence several roads lead to the rear of our position at Fredericksburg." (Lee's Rep., 6.)—"I captured a courier from General Lee, with a dispatch in Lee's own handwriting. It was dated at 12 o'clock that day, and I captured it at one o'clock, only one hour from Lee's hand. It was addressed to General Anderson, and read: 'I have just received reliable intelligence that the enemy have crossed the river in force. Why have you not kept me informed? I wish to see you at my head-quarters at once.'"—Pleasonton, in Com. Rep., ii., 27.
[3] "The enemy's cavalry skirmished with Anderson's rear-guard as he left Chancellorsville, but, being vigorously repulsed by Mahone's brigade, offered no farther opposition to his march."—Lee's Rep., 6.
[4] Hooker's General Order, No. 47, April 30.   [5] Swinton, 275.   [6] Com. Rep., ii., 103.

THE ADVANCE OF SEDGWICK'S CORPS CROSSING THE RAPPAHANNOCK.

million and a half of rations placed on board lighters, with gun-boats ready to tow them down the Potomac and up the Pamunkey, so that his advance would not be impeded by want of supplies.[1]

Hooker had done much, but he left undone the one thing which was needed to place his complete success beyond all reasonable doubt. On that Thursday night he halted his force in the Wilderness around Chancellorsville, where it was cooped up as effectually as though it had been on an island, instead of pushing forward another hour's march, which would have brought it into open country beyond. To oppose this march Lee had then at hand only the single division of Anderson. McLaws and Early were yet on the heights at Fredericksburg, the nearest troops fully ten miles away. The bulk of Jackson's corps were twice as far off. It was not until the night of the 30th was far spent that Lee was fully assured that the operations upon his front were a feint, and that the main danger was to come from his flank and rear. He was not minded to retreat without a struggle. The Union army was divided; if one half could be defeated, the whole would be neutralized, and if worst came to worst, he could retreat after a battle as well as before. Leaving Early's division and Barksdale's brigade—less than 10,000 men in all—to hold the line near Fredericksburg, Lee began at midnight of the 30th to concentrate the remainder of his force in front of Hooker. McLaws was hurried up from the extreme left, and Jackson, with the divisions of A. P. Hill, Rodes, and Colston, from the right. By eight o'clock on Friday morning, the first of May, the head of Jackson's column began to come up to Anderson, and three hours later all had arrived and formed line of battle at the very place upon which Hooker was now directing his advance.[2]

For now, as the morning was wearing away, Hooker began to prepare to move out of the skirts of the Wilderness into the open space beyond. He had ordered Sickles's corps to join him, and it had come up, raising his force to more than 60,000, a number greater by a quarter than Lee could bring against him after providing for the maintenance of the lines at Fredericksburg. There were three roads centring at Chancellorsville and running eastward. Upon each of these a column was to be pushed out. Meade's corps was to lead: the divisions of Griffin and Humphreys on the left, by the river road; Sykes, to be supported by Hancock, of Couch's corps, in the centre, along the turnpike; Slocum's corps on the right, by the plank road, while French's division of Meade's corps was to strike still farther south. Two o'clock in the afternoon was assigned for the completion of these movements. After that time the headquarters were to be at Tabernacle Church, close by the junction of the plank road and the turnpike, half way toward Fredericksburg.[3]

Hooker was destined never, during the war, to see the spot which he had assigned for his headquarters. The left column moved five miles down the river road, and came in sight of Banks's Ford without meeting an enemy. The right column marched unopposed half as far, when it was arrested by tidings from the central column. This column, Sykes leading, Hancock behind, had pressed down the plank road, and soon came upon the enemy's advance. Sykes drove them back for a space, and at noon gained the point assigned to him. After some sharp fighting he was forced back for a little, and took up a position which he desired to hold. But orders came that he, with all others, should fall back to the positions from which they had set out. Warren, who bore the order, had vainly urged that it should not be sent; Couch protested against it; Hancock thought they should advance instead of retreating.[4]

Thus, in opposition to the opinions of every general who had felt the enemy, Hooker withdrew his advancing columns, and instead of keeping up the offensive which he had assumed, threw himself upon the defensive. With

[1] *Com. Rep.*, ii., 145.

[2] "The enemy in our front, near Fredericksburg, continued inactive, and it was now apparent that the main attack would be made upon our flank and rear. It was therefore determined to leave sufficient troops to hold our lines, and with the main body of the army to give battle to the approaching column. Early's division of Jackson's corps, and Barksdale's brigade of McLaws's division, with part of the reserve artillery under General Pendleton, were intrusted with the defense of our position at Fredericksburg, and at midnight on the 30th General McLaws marched with the rest of his command toward Fredericksburg. General Jackson followed at dawn next morning with the remaining divisions of his corps. He reached the position occupied by General Anderson at eight A.M., and immediately began preparations to advance."—*Lee's Rep.*, 7.

[3] Hooker's Order, in *Com. Rep.*, ii., 124.

[4] "On gaining the ridge about one and a quarter mile from Chancellorsville, we found the enemy advancing and driving back our cavalry. This small force resisted handsomely, riding up and firing almost in the faces of the Eleventh Virginia infantry, which formed the enemy's advance. General Sykes moved forward in double-quick time, attacked the enemy vigorously, and drove him back with loss till he had gained the position assigned to him. This he attained at about 12 o'clock. No sound yet reached us indicating that any other of our columns had encountered the advance of the enemy. General Sykes bravely resolved to hold the position assigned him, which his command had so gallantly won from the enemy, and I set out with all possible speed to report the condition to the commanding general. From information received since the advance began, the general decided to countermand it, and receive the enemy on the line occupied the night before."—Warren, in *Com. Rep.*, ii., 56.

"I was in favor of advancing, and urged it with more zeal than convincing argument. I thought with our position and numbers to beat the enemy's right wing. This could be done by advancing in force upon the two main roads toward Fredericksburg, each being in good supporting distance, at the same time throwing a heavy force on the enemy's right flank by the river road." (Warren, in *Com. Rep.*, ii., 56.)—"The ground upon which I had posted Hancock in support of Sykes was about one and a half mile from Chancellorsville, and commanded it. Upon receiving orders from General Hooker to come in, I sent to him urging that on account of the great advantages of the position it should be held at all hazards. The reply was to return at once. General Warren also went in person and urged the necessity of holding on." (Couch, *Report of Chancellorsville*.)—"I have no doubt that we ought to have held our advanced positions, and still kept pushing on and attempt to make a junction with General Sedgwick."—Hancock, in *Com. Rep.*, ii., 66.

"At 11 o'clock the troops moved forward upon the plank and turnpike roads—Anderson, with the brigades of Wright and Posey, leading on the former; McLaws, with his three brigades, preceded by Mahone's, on the latter. Wilcox and Perry, of Anderson's division, co-operated with McLaws; Jackson's troops followed Anderson on the plank road. The enemy was soon encountered on both roads, and heavy skirmishing with infantry and artillery ensued, our troops pressing steadily forward. A strong attack upon McLaws was repulsed with spirit by Semmes's brigade; and Wright, by direction of Anderson, diverging to the left of the plank road, marched by way of the unfinished railroad from Fredericksburg to Gordonsville, and turned the enemy's right. His whole line thereupon retreated rapidly, vigorously pursued by our troops until they arrived within about one mile of Chancellorsville."—*Lee's Rep.*, 6.

LAYING THE PONTOONS FOR SEDGWICK'S CORPS.

a force largely superior, instead of attacking, he prepared to receive the attack of the enemy. His reasons, as stated by himself, were based wholly upon the character of the region. "The ground in our vicinity," he says, "was broken, and covered with dense forests, much of which was impenetrable to infantry. The ravines to the north of the road were deep, and their general direction was at right angles to the Rappahannock, affording the enemy a formidable position behind each of them. Here was the enemy's entire army, with the exception of about 8000 men which had been left to hold the line from below Hamilton's crossing to the heights above Fredericksburg, a distance of between five and six miles. The right and central corps had proceeded but a short distance when the head of the column emerged from the heavy forest, and discovered the enemy to be advancing in line of battle. Nearly all of the Twelfth Corps had emerged from the forest at that moment, but as the passage-way through the forest was narrow, I was satisfied that I could not throw troops through it fast enough to resist the advance of General Lee, and was apprehensive of being whipped in detail. Accordingly, instructions were given for the troops in advance to return and establish themselves on the line they had just left, and

to hold themselves in readiness to receive the enemy."[1] But Warren, who had scanned the ground with the eye of an engineer, thought the physical conditions favorable to the Union force. "If," he says, "the attack found the enemy in extended lines across our front, or in motion toward our right flank, it would have secured the defeat of his right wing, and consequently the retreat of the whole. The advantages of the initiative in a wooded country like this, obscuring all movements, are incalculable, and so far we had improved them."[2]

The defensive position which Hooker now assumed formed a line of nearly five miles from east to west, running mainly parallel and a little south of the united plank road and turnpike. The left, a short distance east of Chancellorsville, was bent back a little northward; the right presented a similar

[1] Hooker, in *Com. Rep.*, ii., 125.
[2] Warren, in *Com. Rep.*, ii., 56.—Hancock indeed states that Hooker too late countermanded the order for withdrawal: "General Warren, who brought the order, suggested to General Couch that he should not fall back, although the order was to that effect. But General Couch did not feel at liberty to follow that suggestion, having received peremptory orders to fall back. It appears, however, that General Warren rode off to General Hooker and explained the advantages of the position we held, and came back with an order that it should be held. But, in the mean time, the position had been abandoned, and the enemy had taken possession of it."—*Com. Rep.*, ii., 68.

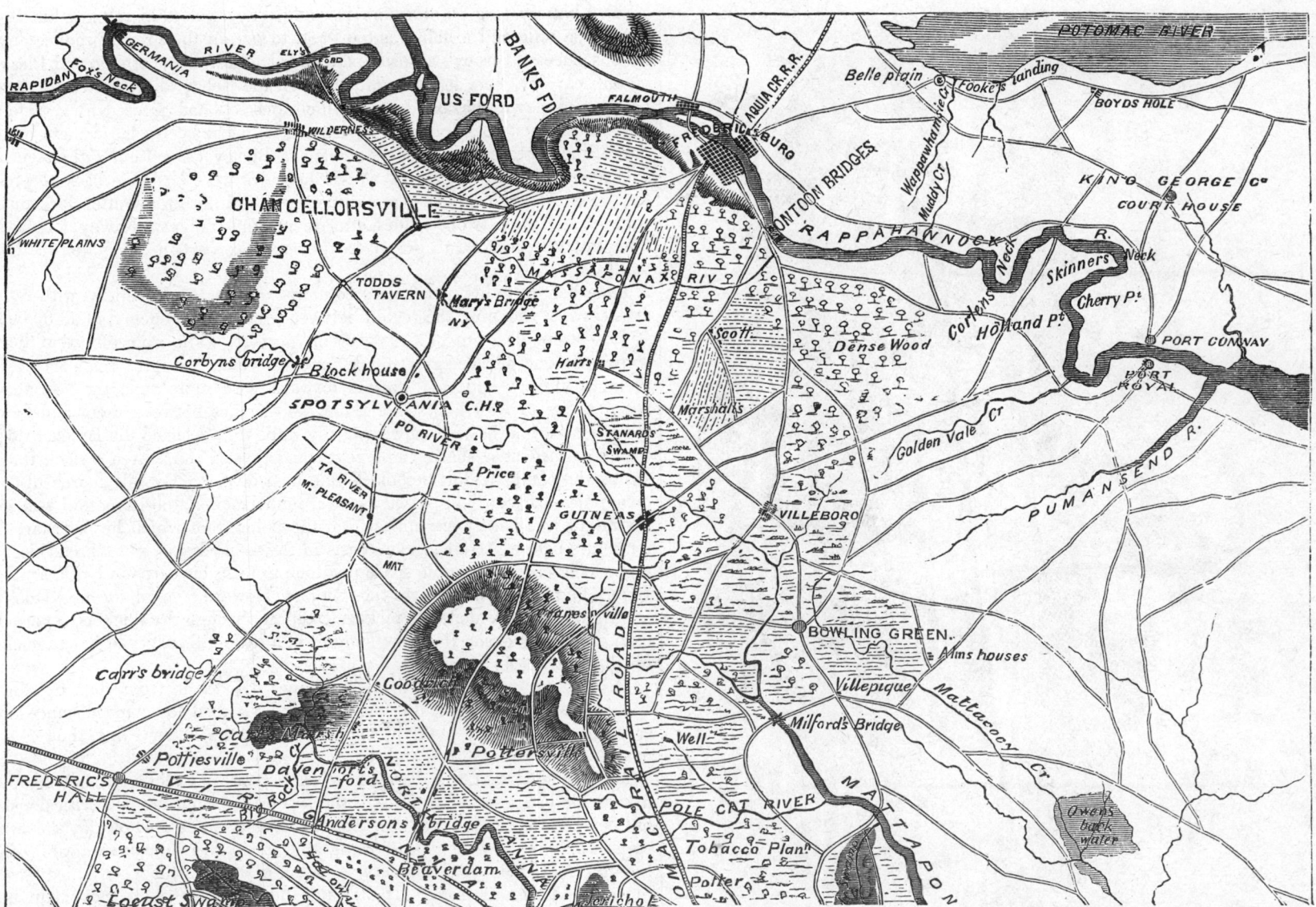

MAP OF THE REGION NEAR CHANCELLORSVILLE.

curve. The general shape was nearly that of the letter **C**, the main front facing southward, the upper and lower curves looking west and east. The corps and divisions were somewhat broken up. The general placing in front was, Meade on the extreme left, toward Fredericksburg; Slocum in the centre; Howard on the right. The corps of Couch and Sickles were mainly in reserve, though a division of each was thrust forward into the front line, which was strengthened by abatis and breast-works. The right was weakly posted, but it was, in military phrase, flung out into the air; but as the enemy were wholly on the left, hardly reaching to the centre, it was thought that an attack was not to be looked for in that direction, and Howard gave assurance that he could hold his position against any force that could be brought against it.[2]

At nightfall Lee and Jackson, who had been engaged on different parts of the field, met upon the brow of a little hill covered by a clump of pines which had escaped the woodman's axe, whose annual shedding of leaves formed a soft carpet upon the ground. They retired apart to consult upon the situation. This was critical. They must either win a battle or retreat. Hooker having assumed the defensive, they must attack. The Confederate skirmishers which had been pushed into the belt of wood had succeeded in ascertaining that the Union lines were unassailable in front of Chancellorsville.[3] But Stuart, whose cavalry had been reconnoitring westward and northward, reported that in these directions the Federal camps were open, and that almost all of his cavalry force was absent. Jackson proposed that while a part of the Confederate force should demonstrate upon Hooker's front, the remainder should march clear around his line, and assail it upon its right flank and rear. The measure was hazardous in the extreme. The Federals, now in position, outnumbered the whole Confederate force, and

this was to be divided. But it was certain that Hooker must soon learn how small was the force remaining near Fredericksburg, and would then bring up Sedgwick from the Rappahannock, increasing the disparity nearly two to one. And even if the flank attack should miscarry, the Confederate army, then separated into three portions, would still have lines of retreat as favorable as they now had. Jackson's three divisions would have the plank road westward, or the road southward through the open country; McLaws and Anderson had the latter route; Early could fall back toward the others, and the three bodies could reunite and make a stand upon new ground, or, if need were, press on to Richmond; so that, barring the risk, which must be run, of a total defeat, their position would be no worse than it now was.[1]

This plan was settled, and the two Confederate commanders lay down to rest without shelter upon the bare ground. Jackson had neither blanket nor overcoat. He declined an overcoat offered him by one of his staff. Thinking him asleep, the officer took off the cape, spread it over Jackson, and fell into slumber. Jackson rose and spread the cape over its owner, and laid down again uncovered. Before dawn he was seen sitting crouched over a scanty fire, almost hugging it, and shivering with cold, yet busy studying a rough map of the region, inquiring of his chaplain, who knew something of the country, if there were no roads by which the Federal flank might be turned. The chaplain only knew that a little beyond was a blind forest-path, which, by various windings and turnings, struck the plank road four miles west of Chancellorsville. The line was traced on the map. "That is too near," said Jackson; "it goes within the lines of the enemy's pickets. I wish to get well to his rear without being observed." An inhabitant of the region was now brought up, who said that the furnace road, upon which they were, ran southward for a few miles, and then was intersected by the Brock road from the northwest, which struck the plank road, so that by making a circuit of fifteen miles a point would be reached several miles above Hooker's extremest outposts. This was just what Jackson desired, and at sunrise he began the march with his three divisions.[2]

SATURDAY, MAY 2.

A mile of dense forest intervened between the road and Hooker's front, completely hiding the march from observation. But at one point the road crossed a bare hill just opposite Sickles's position. For two hours the long column, with its trains and ambulances, filed over the hill in plain view.[3] It was clearly a movement in force, but with what purpose was a matter of doubt. It might be for offense upon the right, and so Hooker directed Howard to be fully prepared, to keep heavy reserves in hand to meet it, and especially to throw out pickets in his front.[4] How utterly and criminally this order was disregarded remains to be shown. But the road on which the column was observed ran here due south, straight away from the Union lines; this indicated that the movement was a retreat. Sickles sent

---

[1] This map shows, in a general way, the topography of the region in which Hooker proposed to operate. Though not perfectly accurate, it is the best then accessible. Of the actual character of the Wilderness he was almost wholly ignorant, and had no means of becoming acquainted with it. The essential features of the map are the relative positions of Fredericksburg and Chancellorsville, the fords by which the Rappahannock and Rapidan were to be passed, and the roads leading away from Fredericksburg by which it was supposed that the Confederate army must retreat. The roads are: (1.) The railroad to Richmond, and the Telegraph Road, running southwardly nearly parallel with it; (2.) The plank road and turnpike. These are represented on the map as one road from Fredericksburg to the point marked as the "Wilderness," where they diverge. The road from "Todd's Tavern" to the "Wilderness" shows nearly the line of Jackson's flank movement. With these exceptions, the roads laid down are mere rude country roads, hardly passable for an army with artillery and trains. In moving from near Falmouth, Meade, Slocum, and Howard crossed the Rappahannock at Kelly's Ford, north of Germania Ford, on the Rapidan; Couch and subsequently Sickles and Reynolds, at United States Ford. Lee's chief dépôt was at Guinea's Station, on the railroad, near which Jackson's corps had its winter quarters; but they had been moved half way up to Fredericksburg, near which place McLaws and Anderson were posted. The distance between Fredericksburg and Chancellorsville is 11 miles, which will indicate the scale upon which the map is drawn.

[2] *Com. Rep.*, ii., 56.

[3] "The enemy had assumed a position of great natural strength, surrounded on all sides by a dense forest filled with a tangled undergrowth, in the midst of which breast-works of logs had been constructed, with trees felled in front so as to form an almost impenetrable abatis. His artillery swept the few narrow roads by which his position could be approached in front, and commanded the adjacent woods. Darkness was approaching before the strength and extent of his line could be ascertained; and as the nature of the country rendered it hazardous to attack by night, our troops were halted and formed in line of battle in front of Chancellorsville, at right angles with the plank road, extending on the right to the mine road, and to the left in the direction of Catharine Furnace."—*Lee's Rep.*, 8.

[1] *Dabney*, 672.   [2] *Ibid.*, 675.   [3] Birney, in *Com. Rep.*, ii., 34.
[4] Hooker's Order, 9.30 A.M., in *Com. Rep.*, ii., 126.

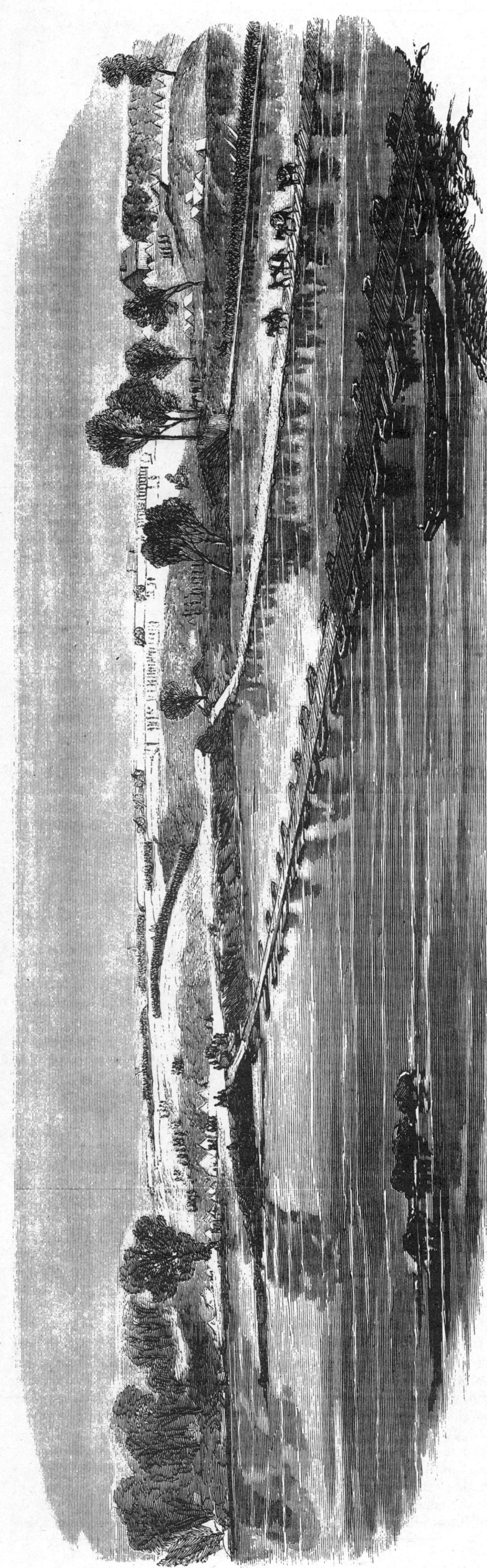

SEDGWICK'S BRIDGE LAID.

a rifled battery to a point where it could play upon this column, but the distance, a mile and a half, was too great to permit the fire to produce any serious effect. Birney's division, afterward followed by others, and Pleasonton's cavalry, were sent forward through the woods to reconnoitre. Birney passed down the blind road which Jackson had refused to take, fell upon a regiment of McLaws's division which had been placed there as a guard, and captured it. This movement of Birney's so seriously threatened Jackson's trains in the rear that two brigades were hastened back to protect them. As it happened, however, Birney did not follow after Jackson's column, and these two brigades, after seeing the trains well away, followed after, but were unable to get up in time to take part in the action of this day.[1]

Long before midday, Jackson's column—infantry and artillery, with Stuart's cavalry patroling the region between him and the enemy, in all 30,000 strong—were clear out of sight of friend and foe. The troops felt that they were upon one of those great flank marches which had more than once led them to victory, and they pressed forward with more than their wonted speed, every step for hours increasing the distance between them and Lee. Their march had been southwestwardly until they reached the Brock road; then it turned at a sharp angle to the northwest. At three o'clock they struck the plank road at the old Wilderness tavern. By this march of fifteen miles Jackson had passed clear around Hooker's position, and was in a straight line hardly six miles from the point from which he had started ten hours before. Here, like an oasis in the forest desert, was a broad clearing, which gave him ample space in which to form his corps in battle array. Barely two miles away, down the road, lay Howard's corps, forming Hooker's right. The Confederate pickets, creeping through the thickets, reported its position. Jackson from the summit of a little hill surveyed it, and made his dispositions for an assault.

His column was formed into three lines—Rodes in front, then Colston, and, last, A. P. Hill, stretching across the plank road for some distance on each side, completely overlapping the head of the Federal line, thus commanding it on front, flank, and rear.

Lee, with parts of the divisions of Anderson and McLaws,[2] not 20,000 men in all, had reserved to himself the less brilliant but not less critical task of keeping in check a force three times as strong. For a whole day the two corps would be isolated, neither being able to aid or even communicate with the other. If Hooker changed the position of his right, Jackson's meditated blow would miss its mark. If, divining the character of the movement, he should assail Anderson and McLaws either in front from Chancellorsville, or on the flank and rear by bringing Sedgwick up from Fredericksburg, their destruction was inevitable. Between Sedgwick's 30,000[3] and him lay only Early's 10,000, guarding a line of six miles. Lee confined himself during the morning to demonstrations all along Hooker's front. Early in the morning he got a few guns into a position which commanded the field in front of the Chancellorsville House, and drove all the wagons back into position. Then, at intervals, his infantry crept into the woods, delivered a yell and a volley, and disappeared, to reappear at a different point.[4] Sickles's advance was so threatening that Lee was obliged to resist it in force.[5] Sickles, with Birney's division, maintained his ground successfully, and sent back for re-enforcements; his other divisions were promised him, together with a brigade from Slocum, and one from Howard. Sickles was just about to open his attack with all this force, fully equal to the whole of Anderson's and McLaws's, when some officer came dashing up, breathless, with a report that Stuart's cavalry were moving in his rear, and might cut him off; that Jackson's infantry were very near; that the Union troops were retreating. Sickles disbelieved this story. Surely such a thing could not have happened without a serious engagement, and had there been a battle he would have heard the noise. But almost instantly an aid came up with tidings from Howard. The right flank had been turned; Howard's corps had given way, and Jackson was right on Sickles's rear. Hooker also sent word that he could not give the promised re-enforcements; he had to use them to check the enemy, who had broken through the Eleventh Corps. Sickles must withdraw his whole force, and save as many of them as he could.[6]

Jackson had struck his blow. A little after five o'clock he had formed his lines, and began to press through the dense thickets which skirted the plank road, down which, only three miles away, lay a part of Howard's corps, forming the extreme right of Hooker's army. No assault here had been dreamed of. Intrenchments had been thrown up, but they were left unguarded. The men had stacked their arms, and were scattered about cooking their suppers; ambulances, ammunition-wagons, pack-mules, and cattle were huddled together.[7] Not a picket was thrown out into the woods in front, nor even up the road, where for more than two hours Jackson had been deploying his divisions, hardly three miles away. The Union right was like a militia regiment at the close of a holiday muster rather than an army in presence of an enemy.[8]

[1] Thomas and Archer, in *Lee's Rep.*, 54–58.
[2] These divisions consisted of nine brigades; but Barksdale's, of McLaws's, had been left at Marye's Heights, and Wilcox's, of Anderson's, had been sent back to Banks's Ford.
[3] Reynolds's corps was withdrawn from Sedgwick that morning, and ordered to Chancellorsville, where it arrived during the night. Sedgwick had then his own corps and Gibbon's division of Couch's.   [4] Warren, in *Com. Rep.*, ii., 45; Pleasonton, *Ibid.*, 27; Hooker, *Ibid.*, 127.
[5] "At midday the enemy appeared in some force at the furnace. Posey's brigade was sent to dislodge him, and was soon engaged in a warm skirmish with him. The increasing numbers of the enemy made it necessary to move Wright's brigade over to the support of Posey's."—Anderson, in *Lee's Rep.*, 25.   [6] Sickles, in *Com. Rep.*, ii., 6.   [7] *Com. Rep.*, ii., 45, 127.
[8] Devens, whose division occupied the extreme right, testifies (*Com. Rep.*, ii., 173): "About two or three o'clock in the afternoon, two soldiers, who had been sent out to observe the enemy's lines as spies from one of the other commands, came in and reported that the enemy were massing heavily on our right," and that he sent them to Howard with the tidings. But that no pickets could have been pushed out upon the road is evident. The attack which came down that road, and on both sides of it, was an utter surprise.

With a yell and a volley the Confederates dashed out of the woods into the open space occupied by this unsuspecting division. The regiments upon whom the onset first fell scattered without firing a shot, and rushed in wild confusion upon those behind them; these in turn gave way before the wild rush of their own comrades. Some of the regiments made a stand to stem the torrent; but it was vain, and the whole corps was soon streaming down the road, and through the woods toward Chancellorsville. Rodes, who commanded the front line of the Confederates, thus describes the conflict: "At once the line of battle rushed forward with a yell, and Doles at the moment debouched from the woods, and encountered a force of the enemy and a battery of two guns intrenched. Detaching two regiments to flank the position, he charged without halting, sweeping every thing before him; and pressing on to Talley's, gallantly carried the works there, and captured five guns by a similar flank movement of his command. So complete was the success of the whole manœuvre, and such was the surprise of the enemy, that scarcely any organized resistance was met with after the first volley was fired. They fled in the wildest confusion, leaving the field strewn with arms, accoutrements, clothing, caissons, and field-pieces in every direction. The larger portion of his force, as well as intrenchments, were drawn up at right angles to our line; and being thus taken in the flank and rear, they did not wait for the attack. On the next side, which had an extended line of works facing in our direction, an effort was made to check the flying columns. For a few moments they held this position; but once more my gallant troops dashed at them with a wild shout, and, firing a hasty volley, they continued their hasty flight to Chancellorsville. It was at this moment that Trimble's division, which had followed closely in my rear, headed by Colston, went over the works with my men, and from this time the two divisions were mingled in inextricable confusion. Pushing forward as rapidly as possible, the troops soon entered a second piece of woods, thickly filled with undergrowth. The right, becoming entangled in an abatis near the enemy's first line of fortifications, caused the line to halt, and such was the confusion and darkness that it was not deemed advisable to make a farther advance. I at once sent word to Lieutenant General Jackson, urging him to push forward the fresh troops of the reserve line, in order that mine might be reformed. Riding forward on the plank road, I satisfied myself that the enemy had no line of battle between our troops and the heights of Chancellorsville, and on my return informed the chief of artillery of the fact, and he opened his batteries on that point. The enemy instantly responded by a most terrific fire, which silenced our guns, but did little execution on the infantry. When the fire ceased General Hill's troops were brought up, and, as soon as a portion were deployed in my front, I commenced withdrawing my troops by order of the lieutenant general."[1]

Rodes was right. Between him and Chancellorsville, hardly half a mile away, there was no line of battle, and nothing from which to form one. Jackson was almost justified in declaring that with half an hour more of daylight he could have carried that place.[2] The check to the Confederate rush came from an unexpected quarter. When the tidings came to Sickles of the flight of Howard, Pleasonton, with two regiments of cavalry, was riding leisurely back to the rear, for in the dense forest there was nothing for cavalry to do. He found the open space which he had left a few hours before filled with fugitives, ambulances, and guns. He had with him a battery of horse artillery. The moment was critical. The enemy must be checked then and there, and to do it there was but this battery and those few horsemen. Turning to Major Keenan, he said, "You must charge into those woods with your regiment, and hold the rebels in check until I can get some of these guns into position; you must do it at any cost." "I will do it," responded Keenan, with a smile, though both knew that the order was equivalent to a death-warrant. The charge was made; a quarter of the regiment fell, their leader at their head. But ten priceless minutes were gained. Pleasonton brought up his battery at a gallop, double-shotted the guns with canister, and pointed them at the ground line of the parapet, telling the gunners to aim low. Then getting a score of guns into position out of the confused mass around, he had all double-shotted, pointed at the woods in front, and bade the gunners to await his order to fire. Hardly was this done when the whole forest, whose verge was a quarter of a mile distant, seemed alive with men. Just as he was about to give the order to fire, a Federal flag appeared on the front. He sent an aid to learn whether these men were friends or foes. "Come on," they shouted; "we are friends!" The order to fire was suspended for a moment. During that moment the woods blazed with musketry, and the enemy, leaping over the parapet, dashed straight up toward the guns. Then came the order to fire, and the low-pointed guns swept the whole line away like chaff. They returned again and again to the charge. At one time they came within fifty yards of the guns. Had they known it they might have captured them, for the artillery were utterly without infantry support. Pleasonton had left but two squadrons of raw cavalry. These he disposed in a single line, with drawn sabres, in the rear of his batteries, with orders to charge should the enemy come up to the guns.[3]

Lee had all day kept up demonstrations against Hooker's front. Anderson and McLaws had been ordered, as soon as the sound of Jackson's guns was heard, to press strongly upon the Union left, to prevent re-enforcements from being sent to the right, but not to make any attack in force, and inclining all the while to their left, so as to connect with Jackson's right, as he closed in upon the centre.[4] A fierce artillery fire from several commanding positions was kept up, accompanied by ostentatious infantry demonstrations upon the line held by Slocum and Couch. Meade had been posted upon the extreme Union left, quite out of the reach of the battle, so

ALFRED PLEASONTON.

that Hooker had at hand only Berry's division of Sickles's corps, and a single brigade of Couch's, which had been held in reserve at Chancellorsville. Berry's division was the one which Hooker had commanded, and it had never failed him. He pushed this forward at double-quick to meet the enemy. It was vain to attempt to check the wild rout of the Eleventh Corps. Hooker ordered the few cavalry with him to charge the flying mass, sabre in hand. Some of the fugitives were shot down by his staff, but no human power could arrest their flight,[1] though they had already outstripped their pursuers. Berry's division, with fixed bayonets, pressed through the flying mass, hoping to regain the high ground which they had abandoned. They were too late; it was in possession of the enemy. The most that he could do was to take a stand upon a ridge, known as Fairview, upon the hither side of the forest which bounded the clearing at Chancellorsville, and thence to pour a fire of artillery and musketry up the road and into the woods.

Night was closing in. The full moon shone brightly, throwing into deep shade the forests, just bursting into leaf. The divisions of Rodes and Colston, which had chased Howard's corps two miles through the dense thickets, had fallen into inextricable confusion. Seeing no enemy before them, they had halted, and there was a lull in the contest. Jackson, who had been urging on the pursuit, ordered A. P. Hill's division to come to the front and take the place of Rodes and Colston, and, accompanied only by his staff, passed down the road to examine the position. Some of his companions remonstrated against his exposing himself. "There is no danger," he replied; "the enemy is routed. Go back and tell Hill to press on." A few minutes after a musketry fire from Berry's pickets pattered among the trees. Jackson turned back toward his own lines. Some of Hill's troops were coming down from the opposite direction. Seeing this little group of horsemen, they mistook them for Union cavalry, and fired upon them. Half of Jackson's escort fell dead or wounded. He himself received three balls at the same instant. One passed through his right hand, a second through his left, while a third struck the left arm near the shoulder, severing the main artery and shattering the bone. His frightened horse darted back into the woods toward the Union lines. Jackson was bruised and almost dismounted by striking his face against the overhanging bough of a tree. His left arm was useless, but, mastering the horse with his wounded right hand, he turned back to the road, and fell almost lifeless into the arms of an aid, one of the two who had kept up with him. One of these remained, while the other rode off in search of a surgeon. Just then Hill, with his staff, came to the spot. With his own hand Hill bandaged the broken arm of his commander, and then rode off toward where the battle was about to reopen.

A little group was soon gathered around, and the wounded general was placed upon a rude litter and borne back toward the rear. They had gone but a few rods when Berry's guns poured a fierce fire up the road. One of the litter-bearers was killed, the others fled, leaving Jackson with but two companions. These flung themselves flat upon the ground to escape the canister which hurtled over them. The fire slackening for a moment, Jackson rose, and, supported on each side by an aid, staggered into the

---

[1] *Lee's Rep.*, 111.   [2] *Dabney.*   [3] *Pleasonton, in Com. Rep.*, ii., 28.   [4] *Lee's Rep.*, 9.

[1] *Com. Rep.*, ii., 126.

THE STAMPEDE OF THE ELEVENTH CORPS.—BERRY'S CORPS CHECKING THE PURSUIT.

NEAR CHANCELLORSVILLE, MAY 1.

wood which bordered the road. He came upon Pender's brigade lying flat to avoid the shot pouring into the gloom. "I fear," said Pender, recognizing his wounded commander, "that we can not maintain our position here." "You must hold your ground," replied Jackson, for a moment blazing into his old battle-fire. This was the last order ever given by Jackson on the field. He was soon replaced in the litter and borne back through the tangled brushwood. One of the bearers stumbled and fell. Jackson was thrown to the ground, striking heavily upon his broken arm, and bruising his side. An ambulance was soon found, in which he was borne to the rear, where the broken arm was amputated. The operation promised well. Two days later he was borne to the hospital a score of miles away. But pneumonia set in, occasioned probably by the exposure of that Friday night before his great flank march, when he had slept unsheltered upon the bare ground, aggravated perhaps by the bruise which he had received when thrown from the litter. He died on Sunday, the 10th of May. When the supreme hour approached, his mind wandered. Visions of the battle-field and of Paradise mingled together. "Order Hill to prepare for battle—pass the infantry to the front rapidly—tell—" Then a change passed over his delirium; and murmuring gently, "Let us cross over the river and rest under the shade of the trees," he fell into the sleep which knows no earthly wakening.

The military career of Thomas Jonathan Jackson as a Confederate commander lasted just two years. On the 2d of May, 1861, he was placed in command at Harper's Ferry; on the 2d of May, 1863, he received his mortal wound in the Wilderness of Virginia. His great fame was won within the last year of his life, for in May, 1862, took place his operations in the Valley of the Shenandoah, wherein, by foiling Fremont and Shields, he showed that he possessed qualities higher than those of a stubborn fighter and a daring partisan. Born of a respectable family, fallen into decay, accident gave him an appointment as cadet at West Point. Passing in due course from the Military Academy into the army, he served with credit in the war with Mexico. Soon after he left the army, and became Professor of Natural and Experimental Philosophy and Artillery Tactics in the Virginia Military Academy at Lexington. Meanwhile a great change had occurred in his moral nature—that alteration which theologians denominate "a change of heart." He embraced that form of Christianity which finds its exponents in Calvin and Edwards. Major Jackson, Professor in the Military Academy, was also Deacon Jackson of the Presbyterian Church. His ten-years' career as professor was far from brilliant. He was rather a laughing-stock to the gay youths who thronged the Academy. That he was master of the management of guns was admitted; that he understood the science which he was set to teach was possible; but he had little faculty for imparting his knowledge. There were eccentricities in his mode of life, arising, materialists would say, rather from a disordered stomach than from

a disturbed brain, but still sufficiently marked to furnish occasion for men to consider him as "half-cracked." The few who knew him well, however, saw that these eccentricities were but superficial; that underlying them was a firmness and persistence of character which would enable him to run a great career if an opening to such should ever occur. Few even of these few knew the boundless ambition, and the unquestioning, almost fatalistic self-confidence which lay hidden below all the outward manifestations of his character.

When the great rebellion broke out, any one would have been justified in assuming that Jackson would have taken sides with the Union. He had been educated by the Union; he had fought with honor under the flag of the Union; all his interests, and, as might be supposed, all his feelings, were with the Union rather than with the Confederacy. His personal concern in slavery was of the slightest. The region in which he was born and where he resided was farming rather than planting. Most of the owners of slaves wrought in the fields as laboriously as their servants. Unless, as was not often the case, they reared slaves for the Southern market, they would have been richer without than with the ownership of these laborers. Society in the Valley was constructed like that of Massachusetts rather than like that of South Carolina. But somewhere and somehow Jackson, during his quiet ten years as Professor, had become imbued with the extremest Southern ideas; not merely the "State-right" doctrine that the primary allegiance of the citizen was due to his state—that to the nation being secondary and dependent—but with the extremest views of the extremest men of the extreme South. As early as 1856 he was a Disunionist.[1] He spent a part of the summer of 1860 in New England, and on his return said that he had "seen enough to justify the division that had just occurred in the Democratic party, which resulted in the defeat of Douglas and the election of Lincoln—a division which, he predicted, would render a dissolution of the Union inevitable.[2]

When the war broke out, it would have been hard to find a man so fully prepared for extremes as Jackson. The deacon who had gone round asking for subscriptions of a few dimes from negroes in aid of the Bible Society—who had, with infinite misgivings, consented, upon the representations of his pastor, to "lead in prayer" at "evening meetings"—calmly declared that no quarter should be given. It was, he said, "the true policy of the South to take no prisoners in this war."[3] He threw himself

[1] Dabney, 143.   [2] Ibid., 145.
[3] I venture this statement solely upon the assertion of Dabney, whose words I quote. This writer professes to give the substance of what was, months after, said by Jackson in justification of the ground which he had assumed. The war, he said, as reported by Dabney, "was different from all civilized wars, and therefore should not be brought under their rules. Its intention was a wholesale murder and piracy. It was the John Brown raid resumed and extended; and as Virginia had righteously put to death every one of those cut-throats upon the gallows, why were their comrades in the same crime to claim now a more honorable treatment? Such a war was an offense against humanity so monstrous that it outlawed those who shared its guilt beyond the

NEAR CHANCELLORSVILLE, MAY 1.

into the conflict with all the fervor of a firm but narrow mind, in which there was not room for doubt. In the long list of enthusiasts who have devoted themselves to a cause, there is not one whose faith was more undoubting than that of Jackson. From the moment that he took the field his hypochondria vanished. Heretofore he had timed his hours and measured his food; thenceforth the hardest lot of a soldier's life was endured without a thought. He left his home almost without warning, and never returned to it alive. He was never for a day absent from the field. The mooning professor was at once inspired with the genius of command.

In all the annals of war there can be found no general who held more absolute sway over his troops. Some have regarded him as the hand to execute what others conceived; but this certainly falls far below his military merit. Two great movements, each of which postponed for a year the issue of the war, were conceived as well as executed by him. The flank march whereby Pope was routed in the summer of 1862, and this of the spring of 1863, whereby alone, as it happened, Lee was saved from destruction at Chancellorsville, were Jackson's, both in conception and execution. The Confederates might better have lost a battle than this one man.

Hooker was greatly discouraged by the rout of Howard's corps. His first impulse was to withdraw from Chancellorsville and the road leading thence from the Wilderness; but he changed his plan during the night, and resolved to await the Confederate attack, meanwhile causing Couch to draw up an entirely new line, to which he might fall back in case of need,[1] and ordering Sedgwick up to his aid from Fredericksburg. The line of battle was necessarily somewhat contracted. What had before been the extreme Union right had been won, and was still held by the enemy. On the line now assumed, the right, instead of stretching westward parallel with

the plank road, was bent sharply northward, directly across it. The position on the centre and left remained unchanged. Howard's corps, now partly reorganized, was sent to the extreme left, where no assault was anticipated. Reynolds's corps, which had come up during the night, was halted some two miles away from the actual right; Meade's was partly in reserve, and partly guarding the road leading to the river. These two corps took no part in the action which ensued.

The real line of battle for Sunday, the 3d of May, formed three sides of an irregular square. The left, facing eastward toward Fredericksburg, was held by Hancock's division of Couch's corps; the centre, facing southward, by Slocum's corps; the right, facing westward, by Sickles's corps, with French's division of Couch's corps. Sickles's extreme left, on a small plateau known as Hazle Grove, projecting southward beyond the general line, was somewhat isolated and open to assault; but it commanded the centre of the Union position. If the enemy won that, he could hold it with artillery, and pour an enfilading fire along Slocum's line. Hazle Grove was the key to every thing, and should have been held at every hazard;[1] but Hooker, knowing only of its exposure, and unaware of its vital importance, ordered Sickles to abandon it, and fall back to the line on the heights at Fairview. The movement began at daybreak, but before it was completed the battle of Sunday—the main action at Chancellorsville—was opened.

Jackson had fallen before he had accomplished half his plan. He had intended, after having driven in Hooker's right, to move still farther northward, and intrench himself at the point where the roads unite which lead from Chancellorsville to the river. He believed that he could seize and hold that point, which was vital, inasmuch as it commanded Hooker's line for supplies. "My men," he said, "sometimes fail to drive the enemy from their positions, but the enemy are never able to drive my men from theirs."[2] But the execution of this design was impossible, even had Jackson been there to attempt it, for Reynolds's corps had come up and occupied this very point.

Leaving Jackson wounded upon the battle-field, Hill had on Saturday evening pressed through the woods to the right, where Pleasonton had got his guns into position, and renewed the assault. This was repulsed, and

pale of forbearance." The war, he averred, would soon assume an internecine character; the North would arm the slaves against their masters; the Confederate States could not, and should not, submit to this, and should retaliate, rather, however, "against the instigators than the ignorant tools. But," he continued, "by the time this stern necessity had manifested itself, the Federal government might have many of our soldiers and much of our territory in their clutches, so that retaliation would be encumbered with additional difficulties. It would be better, therefore, to begin upon a plan of warfare which would place none of our citizens in their power alive;" and if, he concluded, "quarter was neither given nor asked," the Confederate soldiers "would be only the more determined, vigilant, and unconquerable;" while the Union soldiers "would be intimidated, and enlistments would be prevented" (Dabney, 192–194). It must be added, however, that when the murderous principle upon which Jackson wished the war to be carried on failed to meet the approval of the Confederate government, there was no general in their service who more strictly observed the amenities of warfare. When he lay wounded almost within the Union lines, he objected to being removed in case it would do him any injury. "If the enemy comes," he said, "I am not afraid of them. I have always been kind to their wounded, and I am sure they will be kind to me."—Hotchkiss, 124.

[1] "About midnight, or after, I was awakened by General Couch, who told me that we were ordered to withdraw, I supposed to some new position, and that the Second Corps was to form the rear-guard; but at daylight, just as the movement was about to commence, as I understood, General Couch informed me that we were going to remain there and fight a battle."—Hancock, in Com. Rep., ii., 67.

[1] "I immediately"—that is, on Saturday night—"set to work, knowing the importance of this position, to fix it up for the fight of the next morning. I managed to get forty pieces in position, and I cleared out behind us the débris of the Eleventh Corps, that had gone off—the caissons, guns, ambulances, etc., all piled up in great confusion in a marsh that was there. I built three bridges across the marsh, and, with the support of Sickles's corps, we could have defeated the whole of the rebel army there that morning. At 3 o'clock I received an order to fall back in rear of the position at the Chancellorsville House. Before I left, General Sickles informed me that he also had orders to leave with his corps. I mentioned to him the importance of this position, and he agreed with me that we ought to make an effort to hold it. I feel perfectly satisfied that, had General Hooker been able to see the position that I occupied there, he would never have abandoned it; and I looked upon it as a great misfortune that he did not see that point. The rebels, having this position, could enfilade our whole line to the Chancellorsville House with their batteries at this point."—Pleasonton, in Com. Rep., ii., 29.   [2] Dabney, 700; Hotchkiss, 125.

CHANCELLORSVILLE, MAY 1.

Hill was wounded. Rodes was next in rank, but Hill sent for Stuart, who was five miles away, and desired him to take command of the whole corps. When he came, Rodes yielded, not with the best grace.[1] Stuart found every thing in confusion. This was increased by a midnight attack made by Birney, who forced the Confederates back for a space through the woods, and recovered some of the guns which had been abandoned by Howard's corps in its precipitate flight. In the darkness some of the Confederate brigades fired upon each other.[2]

All that night Stuart was busy in reorganizing the shattered corps which had so unexpectedly come under his command. He was separated from Lee by six miles of dense forest. Morning was approaching before he could inform his commanding general of his position, and receive instructions. The messenger said that Jackson had urged that "the enemy should be pressed in the morning." Lee's response was, "Those people shall be pressed."

The odds on that Sunday morning were greatly in favor of Hooker. At and about Chancellorsville he still had fully 78,000 effective men. Lee proposed to press this force in its intrenchments with 30,000 less.[3] Moreover Sedgwick, with his own strong corps, and Gibbon's division of Couch's corps, quite 27,000 men in all, were near Fredericksburg, not fifteen miles away. They were confronted by Early with not more than 11,000. It was

clearly possible that Sedgwick would force his way to Hooker, and, assuming that Early should escape destruction and join Lee, the Federal preponderance would be greatly increased. Taking no account of probable losses on either side, Hooker would have 95,000 men, Lee 59,000. Apart from numbers, Hooker's position was far the better. His 78,000 lay together, Lee's 48,000 were separated, and it depended upon the chances of battle whether they could be united. Hooker, moreover, was intrenched upon ground mainly of his own choosing; Lee, assuming the offensive, must assail these intrenched lines. The region was indeed a difficult one, but the physical obstacles were as great for the one side as for the other, and the one venturing the offensive must undertake to overcome them. Considering that each commander was well informed of the force of his opponent, one can not but wonder that Lee should have ventured an attack, and that Hooker should have awaited it.

SUNDAY, MAY 3.

The action was opened at dawn by Stuart, earlier than he had intended. He had ordered his right to be swung around through the woods, from the position to which his men had fallen back during the night. This brought two of his brigades right in front of Hazle Grove, from which Sickles had withdrawn every thing except Graham's brigade, which formed his rear-guard. Stuart's direction was mistaken for an order to attack. A sharp conflict ensued, with loss on both sides; but Graham got safely off to Fairview, and Stuart took possession of Hazle Grove. A glance showed him the value of the position which had been abandoned to him. In a few minutes he occupied it with thirty guns. His whole force was then ordered to advance upon the Union lines, which, as the fog lifted, were seen crowning the Fairview ridge, a third of a mile in front. Between lay the valley of a little creek covered with a tangled forest growth, through which the attacking columns must force their way, in the face of a fierce fire of artillery and musketry. Again and again they charged down the valley, through the woods, and up the slope, and as often were thrown back in confusion, only to advance again with fresh force and unabated resolution.

Sickles, upon whom all this onset fell, first sent word to Hooker that he could hold his position so long as his ammunition lasted, and then, a little later, that he needed prompt support. This last urgent demand came in an evil time. For two hours and more the Confederate guns at Hazle Grove had been playing upon Chancellorsville. The house was riddled by shot. A ball struck a pillar of the veranda against which Hooker was leaning. He fell senseless. Those around thought him dead or dying. There was no one at hand with authority to send the re-enforcements so urgently asked by Sickles, though the two corps of Reynolds and Meade were wholly disengaged. Half of either of these sent to Sickles would have been enough to

---

[1] "Captain Adams, of General A. P. Hill's staff, reached me post-haste, and informed me of the sad calamities which had for the time deprived the troops of the leadership of both Jackson and Hill, and of the urgent demand for me to come and take command as quickly as possible" (Stuart, in *Lee's Rep.*, 17).—Rodes says (*Ibid.*, 112): "I yielded the command to General Stuart, not because I thought him entitled to it, belonging as he did to a different arm of the service, nor because I was unwilling to assume the responsibility of carrying on the attack, as I had already made the necessary arrangements, and they remained unchanged, but because, from the manner in which I had been informed that he had been sent for, I inferred that General Jackson or General Hill had instructed Major Pendleton to place him in command; and for the still stronger reason that I feared that the information that the command had devolved upon me, unknown except to my own immediate troops, would, in their shaken condition, be likely to increase the demoralization of the corps."

[2] "The attack was made precisely at midnight by Ward's brigade, with the remaining part of Birney's division in support. It was admirably conducted under General Birney, and was in all points successful. It was made entirely with the bayonet. We drove Jackson back to our original line, and reoccupied General Howard's rifle-pits, and recovered several pieces of artillery and some caissons which had been abandoned during the day. Jackson's force was thrown into great confusion, and his own artillery opened upon his own men" (Sickles, in *Com. Rep.*, ii., 7).—"At about midnight on Saturday, General Sickles ordered me to attack Jackson's corps with my division, driving them from the plank road and the small earthworks. At one o'clock I reported that we held the road and works, and had recaptured the artillery and caissons taken from us during the stampede of the Eleventh Corps" (Birney, *Ibid.*, 35).—"There was much confusion on the right, owing to the fact that some troops mistook friends for the enemy, and fired upon them."—Stuart, in *Lee's Rep.*, 18.

[3] Hooker had with him the corps of Reynolds, Meade, Sickles, Howard, and two divisions of Couch, numbering at the outset 81,000. Howard's corps had lost 2500, the greater part prisoners; all other losses up to this time could not have exceeded 500, leaving an effective force of 78,000. Lee's entire force, exclusive of cavalry, was 60,000. Of these, Early's division, and two brigades from Anderson and McLaws, about 11,000, were left near Fredericksburg. The entire losses on Friday and Saturday could not have exceeded 1000, leaving with Lee, near Chancellorsville, about 48,000. We take no account of the cavalry, because the character of the region prevented them from being brought into active service, on either side, in this operation.

DANIEL E. SICKLES.

have secured the victory.[1] That attack repulsed, the remainder of Hooker's unengaged force, sweeping around, would have enveloped Stuart's broken corps, and crushed it to powder. Reynolds was indeed minded to bring his corps into the fight. This seems to have been the plan of Hooker, as understood by some of his officers.[2] But if such was the purpose of Hooker, its execution was prevented by the blow which disabled him. For two eventful hours the Union army was without a commander. Hooker lay insensible for a time, then, partly recovering, mounted his horse; but pain overmastered him, and he lay upon the ground as if in a doze, the Confederate shells bursting all around him. Now and then he was partially aroused when some important dispatch required a prompt answer.[3]

Sickles's ammunition was almost exhausted. Again he sent to headquarters asking for aid, but there was no one there even to reply to his urgent demand. He withdrew his now useless artillery, and fell back with his infantry to a second line, which he resolved to hold by the bayonet. He was not followed, and, looking to his front, it seemed that the enemy was routed. They had the aspect of a disorganized crowd rather than an army. Just then French, with his division, had advanced upon the Confederate left, and driven it back.[4] Stuart concentrated all his force upon this point, and succeeded in repelling the attack, the only offensive movement made by the Union forces at Chancellorsville on that day. Had it been supported by a half, or even a quarter of Reynolds's corps, which lay idle only a few furlongs off, Stuart could not have escaped destruction.

While Stuart was thus with varying fortune pressing the attack upon the Union right, Lee, with the divisions of Anderson and McLaws, assailed the centre held by Slocum, under an enfilading fire from the batteries posted at Hazel Grove. The left, held by Hancock's division of Couch's corps, was threatened, rather than attacked,[5] for Lee was all the time edging to his left in order to make a junction with Stuart. This was effected at ten o'clock, at the very moment when the battle hung in even scales. Both sides had lost terribly. Stuart's three divisions, numbering in the morning about 27,000, had lost fully 6000 in killed and wounded, and 1500 prisoners. Sickles and French had lost well-nigh 5000 out of 22,000. The united Confederate force, 40,000 strong after all its losses, pressed on converging toward Chancellorsville. In their way lay Sickles, French, and Slocum, with some 10,000 less. Barely two miles away on either hand were Reynolds, Meade, and Howard, with fully 42,000, not a regiment of whom were moved to the scene of conflict at the supreme moment. The stress of the Confederate assault now again fell upon Sickles. His ammunition exhausted, he could only hold his line with the bayonet. Five times the enemy dashed upon him; five times they were thrust back. Then the whole front melted away, Sickles's corps first yielding the position.[1] Then, in obedience to orders from Couch, who had in some sort assumed temporary command, the army retreated to the line which had been traced out the night before.

As a defensive position to be held against a superior force, a better could hardly have been desired. It formed a sharp curve, the apex three quarters of a mile back of Chancellorsville, the sides stretching back right and left to the Rappahannock and Rapidan, covering the fords. Each flank was covered by a little stream bordered by dense woods. An enemy could assail it only by its narrow front, and this was covered by the skirt of the forest, pierced with only a few rough roads. It was a position which any general might venture to hold against double his force. Hooker had here fully 70,000 men, half of whom had not been seriously engaged. Lee had left barely 40,000; yet, in the face of these odds, he was on the point of renewing the fight, when he was arrested by ominous tidings. While the fierce fight had been going on around Chancellorsville, Sedgwick had marched from below Fredericksburg, stormed the heights, and was advancing to unite with Hooker.[2] Sedgwick had now his own corps, 22,000 strong. These were across the river, two or three miles below Fredericksburg. Gibbon's division of Couch's corps, 5000 strong, which had been left behind at Falmouth, opposite Fredericksburg, was also under Sedgwick's command; thus, all told, he had 27,000. Confronting him along the heights was Early, who had been left from Jackson's corps, and Barksdale's brigade of McLaws's, and Wilcox's of Anderson's, in all 11,000 strong. Just after four o'clock on Saturday afternoon Hooker sent an order to Sedgwick directing him to march upon Fredericksburg, capture it, and vigorously pursue the enemy. "We know," he added, though he did not himself believe it,[3] "that the enemy is flying, trying to save his trains. Two of Sickles's divisions are among them." This order did not reach Sedgwick until dusk. Almost simultaneously came another, dated three hours later, directing the route which should be taken in pursuit. At this time Jackson had struck his blow and shattered Howard's corps. At an hour before midnight another order came to Sedgwick. Hooker, not aware that he had already crossed the river, and supposing him still to be on the north bank, directed him to "cross the Rappahannock on the receipt of this order, take up your line of march on the Chancellorsville road until you connect with the major general commanding, and attack and destroy any force you may fall in with on the road. You will leave all your trains behind except the pack trains of your ammunition, and march to be in vicinity of the general at daylight. You will probably fall upon the rear of the force commanded by General Lee, and between you and the major general commanding he expects to use him up. Be sure not to fail." This peremptory and special order was dispatched after Jackson's assault had been checked.[4] Sedgwick put his corps in motion at once. The moon shone almost as brightly as day upon the hills, but thick fogs were gathering in the valley. The Confederates were on the alert, and their skirmishers presented some annoyance. Still Sedgwick's march was unaccountably slow. It took the head of his column until daybreak—a space of fully six hours, to reach Fredericksburg, a distance of three miles.

Two or three attempts were made to carry the heights on the Confederate right, which were held by Early with the main strength of his division. These attempts were repulsed with little difficulty. Gibbon, who had now crossed the river, made a demonstration against their left, but a deep canal, the bridges over which had been removed, prevented any advance. It had the effect, however, of detaining there a Confederate brigade which was moving from that direction toward Marye's Hill in the centre. This hill was

[1] "If Hooker had been well enough to have answered my request for re-enforcements, it would have turned the whole tide of battle. I have no doubt it would have been won in thirty minutes; at least it would have been won in an hour. It would have been won just as soon as you could have got ten thousand men from the right or the left to have repulsed that attack."—Sickles, in *Com. Rep.*, ii., 10.

[2] "We expected that Jackson's forces would assault us in the morning at Chancellorsville, and the intention was that General Sickles, with all his force, was to meet him at once; and the First Corps, Reynolds's, was also to attack him and envelop him; and, if necessary, more forces were to be drawn from the left of our line, leaving only forces enough to hold Lee's forces in check" (Warren, in *Com. Rep.*, ii., 46).—"I can not tell why the First Corps was not brought into action. I thought that the simple advance of two corps would take the enemy in flank, and would be very beneficial in its result. General Reynolds once or twice contemplated making this advance upon his own responsibility. Colonel Stone made a reconnoissance, showing it to be practicable."—Doubleday, in *Com. Rep.*, ii., 17.

[3] Pleasonton, in *Com. Rep.*, ii., 31.

[4] Sickles (in *Com. Rep.*, ii., 8) thus describes the aspect at this moment: "The enemy seemed to be satisfied with having forced me to withdraw my infantry from their front line to this second position, and the battle paused for half an hour or more. The loss inflicted upon the enemy, especially by my artillery, was most severe. Their formation for the attack was entirely broken up, and from my head-quarters they presented to the eye the appearance of a mass—a crowd without definite formation."—Stuart (in *Lee's Rep.*, 16) thus describes the situation: "In the mean time the enemy was pressing our left with infantry, and all the re-enforcements I could obtain were sent there. Colquitt's brigade of Trimble's division, ordered first to the right, was directed to the left to support Pender. Johnson's brigade, of the second line, was also engaged there, and the three lines were more or less merged into one line of battle, and reported hard pressed. Urgent requests were sent for re-enforcements, and notices that the troops were out of ammunition. I ordered that the ground must be held at all hazards, if necessary with the bayonet."—Several of the Confederate brigade commanders report how hardly they were pressed by the advance of French. Thus Pender (in *Lee's Rep.*, 52) says: "My men were about out of ammunition, broken down, and badly cut up."—Ramseur (*Ibid.*, 74) tells how he was obliged to run over the Confederate troops in his front, and how his line was "subjected to a horrible enfilade fire, by which it suffered severely." Out of 1509 men he lost 788.

[5] The left, that is of the line as actually engaged, for the corps of Meade and Howard, forming the absolute left, were not engaged at all. Hancock says (*Com. Rep.*, ii., 68): "Although the enemy massed their infantry in the woods very near me, and attempted to advance, and always held a threatening attitude, I judge they had exhausted their troops so much that they dared not attack me. There was no forcible attack on me."

[1] "No supports coming up, and the enemy meanwhile having had time to restore order in his own lines and bring up fresh reserves, I was again attacked, and, having no means of resistance except the bayonet, after repelling five successive attacks I again fell back to General Hooker's headquarters, which were then within easy range of the enemy's cannon, and were rapidly becoming a pile of ruins, almost every shot telling upon the building" (Sickles, in *Com. Rep.*, ii., 9).—Hancock, who, from his position on the left, could see something of what was going on upon the right, says (*Com. Rep.*, ii., 67): "The first lines finally melted away, and the whole front appeared to pass out. First, the Third Corps (Sickles's) went out; then the Twelfth Corps (Slocum's), after fighting a long time, and there was nothing left on that part of the line except my own division. I was directed to hold that position until a change of line of battle could be made, and was to hold it until I was notified that all the other troops had gotten off."—The Confederate reports uniformly give 10 o'clock as the time when Chancellorsville was carried; the Federal reports place the time an hour later.

[2] "The troops, having become somewhat scattered by the difficulties of the ground and the ardor of the contest, were immediately reformed preparatory to renewing the attack. The enemy had withdrawn to a strong position nearer the Rappahannock, which he had previously fortified. His superiority of numbers, the unfavorable nature of the ground, which was densely wooded, and the condition of our troops after the arduous and sanguinary conflict in which they had been engaged, rendered great caution necessary. Our preparations were just completed, when farther operations were arrested by intelligence received from Fredericksburg."—*Lee's Rep.*, 10.

[3] "It was based on a report sent in from General Sickles that the enemy was flying at the time he was sent out to follow up Jackson's corps. I was of the impression that the general was mistaken, but nevertheless felt that no harm could follow from its transmission to General Sedgwick."—Hooker, in *Com. Rep.*, ii., 147.

[4] Sedgwick (*Com. Rep.*, ii., 95) says that this dispatch was dated at ten minutes past 10. He probably gave the hour from memory. Hooker (*Ibid.*, 129) gives its date at 9 o'clock. There is no doubt, however, as to the time when it was received, although Howe (*Ibid.*, 23) says it was "received just after dark, say 8 o'clock; but he evidently confounds it with a previous order. As to the character of the night, I have endeavored to reconcile statements which upon their face appear wholly inconsistent. Hooker and Butterfield say expressly and in almost the same words (*Ibid.*, 76, 129): "It was a bright moonlight night, and clear, sufficiently light for staff officers to write dispatches by moonlight." Howe says (*Ibid.*, 22): "It was bright starlight, so that I could see what was in the advance." Sedgwick, on the other hand, says (*Ibid.*, 100): "In consequence of the enemy and the darkness, it took us until daylight to make a little over three miles. It was a very foggy night."

held by only two brigades—that of Barksdale occupying the stone wall at its base, from which it had so disastrously repulsed Burnside a few weeks before. The morning was wearing away, and nothing had been effected. At length Sedgwick, urged by Warren, resolved to assail Marye's Hill in front. At 11 o'clock, just as the fight at Chancellorsville was closing, he formed two strong columns, which dashed at the wall. The enemy reserved their fire until the nearest column, led by Colonel Johns, was within a few score yards; they then poured in a solid sheet of musketry. The column faltered and fell back. In a couple of minutes it rallied, and pressed fifty yards nearer. Again it met the sheet of fire, and again broke. It seemed that the tragedy of December was to be re-enacted. But Johns, though wounded, rallied his men for a third charge. This time they did not stop; they rushed over and around the wall, and in fifteen minutes from their first advance carried it, killing or capturing its defenders. Johns was again wounded and borne from the field. Colonel Spear, who led the other column, was killed. Other regiments now swarmed up the height from both sides. The Confederates made a fierce fight, but it was vain. Early fell back southward along the telegraph road. Sedgwick's corps thus stood directly between Early and Lee, with only two brigades in his front. This little force retreated sullenly along the plank road, closely followed by Sedgwick.

Such were the tidings which reached Lee at Chancellorsville. His situation was full of peril. Sedgwick might overwhelm Early, and then the Confederate lines of communication would be cut, or he might press straight on to Chancellorsville, and fall upon Lee's rear. This corps must be defeated at every cost, or all was lost. Four brigades of McLaws and Anderson, which had suffered least in the fight of the morning, were sent back to check the Federal advance. They came up with the retreating regiments at Salem Church, midway between Chancellorsville and Fredericksburg. Here a brief stand had been made upon a low wooded ridge. This was carried by the divisions of Brooke and Newton, for Howe had been posted in the rear to keep Early in check, and Gibbon had been left behind to occupy Fredericksburg. The Confederate re-enforcements now pressed Brooke and Newton back through the wood with heavy loss, and were in turn checked by the artillery. Night coming on, both armies slept upon the field. All this afternoon, Hooker, with 70,000 men, lay supinely behind his intrenchments, in front of which were barely 30,000 of the enemy. He made no attempt to aid Sedgwick, who had at length, though tardily, accomplished two thirds of his march.

MONDAY, MAY 4.

No army ever found itself in a more dangerous position than that of Lee on Monday morning, the 4th of May. All counted, it now numbered less than 50,000 men. Stuart, with nearly all of Anderson, confronted Hooker at Chancellorsville. Six miles to the east was McLaws, with less than 10,000, holding Sedgwick in check. Three miles farther to the south was Early, with 8000. Sedgwick had lost heavily, but he still had quite as many as McLaws and Early together. It was hardly within the range of possibility that Hooker would not discover the situation, and either assail Stuart in front with twofold numbers, or, leaving enough to hold him fast, fall upon the rear of McLaws, who would thus be crushed between two fires. Lee's only hope lay in dislodging Sedgwick. To do this he must still farther weaken his force at Chancellorsville. Anderson's remaining three brigades were moved down, leaving only Stuart, with 20,000 men, in front of Hooker. These took position toward Sedgwick's left, threatening to cut him off from the river, while Early marched along the ridge and retook Marye's Hill, thus throwing himself in Sedgwick's rear and cutting him off from Fredericksburg, which was thereupon abandoned by Gibbon, who recrossed the river.[1] Sedgwick's position was now a defensive one, for Hooker directed him not to renew the attack upon Salem Heights. By noon Lee had about 27,000 men opposed to Sedgwick, who had about 18,000, having lost 3000 on the previous day. There was some skirmishing all through the day, but no serious attack was made until 6 o'clock, when, Anderson having united with Early, these two divisions fell upon Howe, who, with 6000 men, was on the Union left. Howe met the assault with great stubbornness, and then fell slowly back toward Banks's Ford, to a strong position which he had previously chosen. The enemy dashed furiously upon this, but were met by a galling fire and driven back, broken and apparently routed. Howe was confident that they would not venture another attack, as, indeed, they did not. Two hours after dark he was surprised to learn that Sedgwick was about to fall back to the ford. He refused to abandon his position without a positive order. The order came, and was obeyed.[2] The division marched to the ford without the slightest molestation, having occupied its strong position two hours after having repulsed the attack.

Hooker all this day lay wholly inactive with his great force of 70,000 men, within two hours' march. Between him and Sedgwick, by the road along which Meade had marched out on Thursday, there was at no time more than three brigades. Hooker's orders to Sedgwick indicate the uncertainty under which he labored all that day, even when he had resumed the command after his injury. Long before daybreak he directed Sedgwick not to resume his assault upon Salem Heights unless he himself attacked, for he hoped that the enemy would assail him; but he was too far away to give any directions; only, if Sedgwick thought best to cross the river, he could go either to Banks's Ford or Fredericksburg. At 11 o'clock in the morning he directed Sedgwick not to cross unless compelled to do so, but, if possible, to hold the position at the ford. Half an hour later, Hooker sent word that he proposed to advance upon the enemy the next day, and in that case Sedgwick's position would be as favorable as could be desired. Sedgwick had all day been doubtful whether he could maintain himself on the south side of the river; but after the repulse of the attack made upon him, he wrote that he could hold his position. But, just ten minutes before Hooker received this, he sent an order to Sedgwick to cross. He immediately countermanded the order, but, before this was received, which was just before daylight, nearly the whole corps were over, and the enemy had taken a position which commanded the bridge, and it was too late to return.[1] Sedgwick lost in all nearly 5000 in killed, wounded, and missing, the greater portion of them on Sunday, and captured nearly 1400 prisoners. The Confederates lost about 4000.[2]

But, during the night, Hooker had resolved to abandon his own position. He summoned his corps commanders to a consultation. Slocum was not present. Howard wished an advance. Sickles and Couch were in favor of withdrawing. Reynolds went to sleep, saying his opinion would be the same as that of Meade. Meade at first opposed the crossing of the river mainly on the ground that the movement could not be effected in the presence of an enemy flushed by success; he, however, ceased to press his objections upon Hooker's confident assurance that the army could be withdrawn without loss. Hooker had no doubt that he could hold his position, and perhaps force the enemy to retire; but he urged that, as he would fall back toward Richmond, he would become constantly stronger, while we were growing weaker; he could be better assailed near Washington than at Richmond. So the order to cross the river was issued, and a new line of intrenchments was thrown up close by the United States Ford to cover the passage. When Sedgwick announced that he could hold his ground, Hooker appears to have proposed to recross back again at Banks's Ford, unite with Sedgwick, and give battle. But this purpose was frustrated by Sedgwick's movement.[3]

Lee, leaving Early on the heights at Fredericksburg to prevent Sedgwick from recrossing, reunited his remaining force, now reduced to 40,000, before the position from which Hooker was preparing to retire. In the afternoon of Tuesday a fierce storm sprung up. The river rose rapidly, submerging the approaches to the bridges. One of these was taken down and used to piece out the others, over which the army retreated without being perceived by the enemy. The storm passed away during the night, and Lee had made preparations to attack the Federal works at daylight; but, upon advancing his skirmishers, he found that the great Union army was beyond the river.[4]

The cavalry movement, upon which Hooker had relied for destroying the enemy by cutting his communications, proved equally fruitless. Stoneman divided his corps. Averill, in command of one column, ascended the Rapidan some twenty miles. At Rapidan Station, on the Orange Railroad, he came up, on Friday, with W. F. Lee, with 900. He reported the next day that he had been engaged with the cavalry of the enemy, and destroying communications. His loss in this "engagement" was one man killed and two wounded. On Sunday he retraced his steps, whereupon Hooker displaced him from command, and appointed Pleasonton in his place. But meanwhile the battles had been fought and lost. Stoneman, with the main cavalry column, pushed on farther southward. Arriving at a point thirty miles northwest of Richmond, he divided his force into six bodies. "We dropped," he says, "like a shell in that region of country, intending to burst it in every direction, expecting each fragment would do as much harm and create nearly as much terror as would result from sending the whole shell. The result of this plan satisfied my most sanguine anticipations." One regiment struck the James River Canal, and attempted ineffectually to destroy the aqueduct which spans the Rivanna River. They then returned to the main body. Four others were sent in various directions to break up the railroad from Richmond to Fredericksburg, which was the primary object of the whole movement. Davis, with one regiment, reached to within seven

[1] Sedgwick appears to have supposed that Early's force were re-enforcements from Richmond. He says (*Com. Rep.*, ii., 106): "I was informed, at an early hour, that a column of the enemy, 15,000 strong, coming from the direction of Richmond, had occupied the heights of Fredericksburg, cutting off my communication with Fredericksburg."

[2] "The movement was commenced very late, and Hays's and Hoke's brigades were thrown into some confusion by coming in contact; and it becoming difficult to distinguish our troops from those of the enemy, on account of the growing darkness, they had therefore to fall back to reform" (Early, in Lee's *Rep.*, 35).—"The attack was delivered with a violence that I had never before encountered. We resisted the first attack better than I expected, and at a favorable time the left of my line was thrown back partially behind some woods. As I expected, the enemy seemed to be under the impression, from this movement, that we were giving way. They advanced until they reached a point that we should have desired above all others they should have advanced upon, and where a reserve force, which I had placed under cover, had an opportunity to get a flank fire upon them with full effect. When the fire from our new position struck them, it was but a short time before they were entirely broken, and fell back in a rout. After this repulse, the position of the Sixth Corps, in my judgment, was less liable to a serious attack than it had been at any time since it crossed the Rappahannock, and I saw no necessity for recrossing the river" (Howe, in *Com. Rep.*, 21).—"Some time after we had returned to our old camps, I met General Hooker, and spoke to him of the movements we had made and the position we held. I stated to him that after the fight of the 4th of May I could have gone with my division to the heights of Fredericksburg, and held them. He expressed his surprise that those heights could have been held on the night of the 4th, and said, 'If I had known that you could have gone on those heights and held them, I would have re-enforced you with the whole army.' I told him that if I had not received orders to go back to Banks's Ford, I could have marched uninterruptedly to Fredericksburg Heights after 9 o'clock that night; for, after the fight we had had, the rebels abandoned the Heights, and there was nothing to be seen of them. There was a bright moon that night, and we could see an object of the size of a man or a horse at a great distance" (*Ibid.*, 25).—"The attack on Brooks was easily repulsed, chiefly by the skirmish line and the battery of the First Massachusetts. That on Howe was of a more determined character. It was gallantly resisted by our infantry by a counter-charge, while the artillery of the division played with fearful effect upon their advance. At length our line was forced back upon the left, and Howe directed his right to retire to a less advanced position. The division reformed promptly, the batteries keeping up a most effective fire. The advance of the enemy was checked, his troops were scattered and driven back with fearful loss, and the new position was easily maintained until nightfall. Several hundred prisoners, including one general officer and many others of rank, and three battle-flags, were captured from the enemy in this engagement."—Sedgwick, in *Com. Rep.*, ii., 107.

[1] Sedgwick, in *Com. Rep.*, ii., 97; Hooker, *Ibid.*, 133.

[2] Early, who encountered only Sedgwick, reports his entire loss at 1474; McLaws, 1889, the greater portion being in the action with Sedgwick; Anderson, 1445, probably half here.

[3] Butterfield, in *Com. Rep.*, ii., 77; Hooker, *Ibid.*, 135.

[4] *Lee's Rep.*, 13.

miles of Richmond, tore up a few rails, and destroyed some stores; captured a train filled with wounded, who were paroled; then, finding himself likely to be cut off, he headed southeastwardly for Williamsburg, but, discovering Confederate cavalry in his way, turned northward, crossed the Mattapony, and, following down its bank, reached the Union outposts at Gloucester Point, opposite Yorktown. Kilpatrick, with another regiment, on Monday struck the railroad still nearer Richmond, destroyed the dépôts at Hungary Station, then rode to within two miles of the city, passing through the outer line of defenses. With his small force it was useless to attempt any thing farther; so he turned eastward, passing the Chickahominy at Meadow Bridge, which he destroyed, and crossed the Mattapony without having encountered any opposition. Here he fell in with Davis, and both proceeded to Gloucester Point. Stoneman himself remained near the point where his divisions had separated, with only 700 men, which he kept as a nucleus around which the different parties could rally in case of need, having sent out three regiments to destroy the bridges in his vicinity. These reunited on Tuesday, and Stoneman set out on a rapid retreat to the Rapidan and Rappahannock, crossing the latter river at Kelly's Ford on Thursday, the 8th. The alarm caused by the "explosion of the bomb" was great, but the injury inflicted was small. In three days the railroad to Fredericksburg was in running order. Had it been known that almost the whole transportation of the road was collected at Guinea's Station, eighteen miles from Chancellorsville, where also were the main dépôts of supply, and that these were left wholly unguarded, a rapid dash made by half of the cavalry upon this point at any time during this eventful week would have changed the whole course of the campaign.[1]

The Federal loss in these operations at Chancellorsville was something more than 17,000, of whom 5000 were unwounded prisoners. They also lost 13 guns, some 20,000 muskets, and a considerable quantity of ammunition and accoutrements. The Confederate loss was about 13,000, of whom 1581 were killed, 8700 wounded, and about 3000 prisoners.[2]

Hooker issued an order congratulating his army on its achievements. "If," said he, "it has not accomplished all that was expected, the reasons are well known to the army. It is sufficient to say that they were of a character not to be foreseen or prevented. . . . . . We have made long marches, crossed rivers, surprised the enemy in his intrenchments, and, wherever we have fought, have inflicted heavier blows than we have received . . . . . . have placed *hors de combat* 18,000 of his chosen troops, destroyed his stores and dépôts filled with vast amounts of stores, deranged his communications, captured prisoners within the fortifications of his capital, and filled his country with fear and consternation." But no dépôts were destroyed or communications deranged except by the cavalry; the stores destroyed were not sufficient to interfere with Lee's scanty accumulations, and the interruptions to communications were so slight that they were restored in two or three days. Far more truthful was Lee's statement to his army: "Under trying vicissitudes of heat and storm, you attacked the enemy, strongly intrenched in the depths of a tangled wilderness, and again on the hills of Fredericksburg, fifteen miles distant, and, by the valor that has triumphed on so many fields, forced him once more to seek safety beyond the Rappahannock."

Hooker declared that when he returned from Chancellorsville he "felt that he had fought no battle," for the reason that he could not get his men into position to do so, though he had more men than he could use;[3] that he failed in his enterprise from causes "of a character not to be foreseen or prevented by human sagacity or resources." A careful examination of all that was done, or left undone, evinces that every one of these circumstances was of a character which lay fairly within the limits of probability; and that there was not, in fact, any moment between Thursday afternoon and Tuesday morning when success was not wholly within the grasp of the Union army. The movement by which Chancellorsville was reached, and the Confederate position rendered worthless, was brilliantly conceived and admirably executed. The initial error, by which alone all else was rendered possible, was that halt at Chancellorsville. Had the march been continued for an hour longer, or even been resumed early in the following morning, the army would have got clear of the Wilderness without meeting any great opposing force, and then it would have been in a position where its great superiority of numbers would have told.[1] The rout of Howard's corps was possible only from the grossest neglect of all military precautions. Jackson, after a toilsome march of ten hours, halted for three hours in open ground not two miles from the Union lines. A single picket, sent for a mile up a broad road, would have discovered the whole movement in ample time for Hooker to have strengthened his position, or to have withdrawn from it without loss. The blame of this surprise can not, however, fairly be laid upon Hooker. He had a right to presume that whoever was in command there would have so picketed his lines as to prevent the possibility of being surprised in broad daylight. But even as it was, the disaster to the Eleventh Corps should have had no serious effect upon the general result. That was fully remedied when the pursuit was checked. On Sunday morning Hooker was in a better position than he had been on the evening before. He had lost 3000 men and had been strengthened by 17,000, and now had 78,000 to oppose to 47,000. The Confederate army was divided, and could reunite only by winning a battle or by a day's march. The only thing which could have lost the battle of that day was the abandonment of the position at Hazle Grove, for from this alone was it possible to enfilade Slocum's line. But surely it is within the limits of military forethought that a general who has occupied a position for two days and three nights should have discovered the very key to that position, when it lay within a mile of his own headquarters. The disabling of Hooker could not, indeed, have been foreseen; but such an accident might happen to any commander upon any field, and there should have been somewhere some man with authority to have, within the space of three hours, brought into action some of the more than 30,000 men within sound, and almost sight, of the battle then raging. Sedgwick's assault upon the heights of Fredericksburg was certainly dilatory. He could not, indeed, have safely executed to the letter his orders, which involved a night assault upon the heights; but they could have been more easily stormed at 5 o'clock than at 11, and this would have brought him upon Lee's rear by 9, when the action was going sorely against the Confederates. How the hours from Sunday noon till Monday night were wasted, has been shown. Hooker, indeed, reiterates that he could not assail the Confederate lines through the dense forests. But Lee broke through those very woods on Sunday, and was minded to attempt it again on Wednesday, when he found that the enemy had disappeared. The golden opportunity was lost never to be recovered, and the Confederate Army of Northern Virginia gained a new lease of life.

If final success were a certain test of the merits of a military plan, we must accord the highest success to that of Lee. But it succeeded only through a series of accidents, any one of which failing would have involved ruin; and a general, save in the direst emergency, has no right to reckon upon the favors of fortune. His first movement, that of marching with the bulk of his army to confront Hooker at Chancellorsville, was wise, for he had good reason to suppose that then and there the force of the enemy was inferior to his own. He had no means of knowing that Sickles's corps had come thither; and, at the worst, he could fall back if he found himself overmatched, and return to his former position, or retreat upon his communications, and make a stand at any favorable point. But when, on the next morning, he divided his army, sending three fifths of it a day's march away, he staked upon an unlikely chance every reasonable possibility of safety. He had no right to assume that the Union right would be surprised, or that Hooker would fail to fall with overwhelming force upon one part or the other of his divided army. So, on Sunday morning, he had no right to anticipate that an attack made by an inferior force upon lines strongly intrenched could succeed, or that his opponent would meet him with only half of his force. How hardly, and by what accidents only, the battle of Sunday morning was won, has already been shown. He tempted fortune still more desperately when, on that afternoon and the next morning, he still farther divided his force. How could he suppose that Stuart's 20,000 would for a long day hold in check Hooker's 70,000, while a great battle was being fought close by between forces so equally matched that a tenth of this idle force added to the enemy would assuredly turn the scale? To retreat promptly and rapidly upon and along the railroad was the only course which any man knowing what both commanders knew, and, still more, what we now know, would have pronounced safe for Lee, when he was startled by the tidings that Sedgwick had stormed the heights and was advancing upon his rear. Lee, reversing the words of Hooker, might have said, "We succeeded only through circumstances of a character not to be foreseen or brought about by human sagacity or resources."

[1] "General Lee had but two regiments of cavalry, under W. H. F. Lee, to oppose to the large force under Stoneman. The whole country in the rear of the Confederate army, up to the very fortifications of Richmond, was open to the invader. Nearly all the transportation of that army was collected at Guinea's Station, eighteen miles from Chancellorsville, with little or no guard, and might have been destroyed by one fourth of Stoneman's force. Such was the condition of the railroads and the scarcity of supplies in the country, that the Confederate commander could never accumulate more than a few days' rations ahead at Fredericksburg. To have interrupted his communications for any length of time would have imperiled his army or forced him to retreat."—*Hotchkiss*, 101–9. See also Hooker and Stoneman, in *Com. Rep.*, 137–40.

[2] The official report of Union losses is given by Hooker in *Com. Rep.*, ii., 143; the Confederate in *Lee's Rep.*, 131–133. In the Union report, the respective numbers of killed, wounded, and missing are not given; but Lee (*Rep.*, 15) states that he took "about 5000 prisoners, exclusive of wounded." This statement has been adopted, and an attempt has been made to apportion the missing among the several corps, but the estimate is almost wholly conjectural. The Confederate report, while giving separately the killed and wounded in every regiment, makes no mention of the missing. But in their separate reports (in *Lee's Rep.*, 27, 33, 36, 117), Anderson, McLaws, Early, and Rodes give the missing in their respective divisions. Hill and Colston do not report their missing; but, as they were in the hottest of the fight on Saturday and Sunday, it is presumed that their loss in missing was at least equal to the average of the others. From these data the following table has been constructed:

Losses at Chancellorsville.

Union.	Killed and Wounded.	Missing.	Total.
First Corps (Reynolds)	192	100	292
Second Corps (Couch)	1,525	500	2,025
Third Corps (Sickles)	3,439	600	4,039
Fifth Corps (Meade)	399	300	699
Sixth Corps (Sedgwick)	3,601	1000	4,601
Eleventh Corps (Howard)	508	2000	2,508
Twelfth Corps (Slocum)	2,383	500	2,883
Cavalry, etc.	150		150
Total	12,197	5000	17,197

Confederate.	Killed and Wounded.	Missing.	Total.
Early's Division	851	500	1,351
A. P. Hill's Division	2,583	500?	3,083
Colston's Division	1,868	450?	2,310
Rodes's Division	2,178	713	2,891
Anderson's Division	1,180	210	1,390
McLaws's Division	1,379	380	1,760
Artillery and Cavalry	227		
Total	10,277	2753	13,030

There is reason to suppose that the losses on each side were some hundreds greater than officially given. Thus Sedgwick reports his loss to have been 4925 (*Com. Rep.*, 107), and Sickles says (*Ibid.*, 10) that on Sunday he "lost 260 officers and about 4500 men in a couple of hours." Such of the Confederate generals as gave their losses state them considerably above those put down in the general report. In four divisions, the excess is about 400 in killed and wounded. Then, as to the missing, Sedgwick states that he made about 1400 prisoners, while in the division opposed to him the Confederate reports acknowledge only 1090, and some of these must have been captured before they encountered Sedgwick. Still we must consider the final official reports on both sides as the highest authority attainable in this case.

[3] *Com. Rep.*, ii., 142.

[1] "A mile or more in advance of the position I then had would have placed me beyond the forest, where, with my superior force, the enemy would probably have been beaten."—Hooker, in *Com. Rep.*, ii., 142.

GEORGE G. MEADE.

CHAPTER XXIX.

THE INVASION OF PENNSYLVANIA.—GETTYSBURG.

Hooker's Plans.—The President's Views.—Pleasonton's Cavalry Reconnoissance.—Lee's Plans.
—Reasons for invading the North.—Elections at the North.—State of public Feeling.—Opinion of the British Minister.—Strength of the Confederate Army.—Route of Milroy.—The Advance into Pennsylvania.—Cavalry Encounters.—Hooker's Policy.—Halleck and Hooker.—
Hooker resigns.—Meade appointed to the Command.—His Antecedents.—Lee's Movements.
—The Armies concentrate toward Gettysburg.—Meade selects
a Position on Pipe Creek.—Pleasonton marks Gettysburg as the Battle-field.—*Battle of July*
1: Topography of Gettysburg.— Reynolds and Hill approach.— Reynolds killed.— Howard
takes Command.—Meade sends Hancock to the Field.—The Federals driven back.—Hancock
decides to accept Battle.—The Position chosen.—Lee's Dilemma.—*Battle of July* 2: Meade's
Line of Battle.—Sickles goes too far in advance.—Hood's Attack upon Round Top.—The Attack repulsed by Vincent.—Sickles and Hood wounded.—Birney attacked and driven back.—
Crawford checks the Confederate Attack.—Humphreys assailed and falls back.—The Union
Line re-formed.—The Confederates fall back.—Confederate Advantage on the Right.—The
Situation at Night.—*Battle of July* 3: Lee's Plan of Attack.—Ewell forced back on the Right.
—The Cannonade on the Centre.—Pickett and Pettigrew advance.—Lieutenant Haskell.—
The Confederate Rout.—Cavalry Attack.—Close of the Fight.—Order for Pursuit given and
countermanded.—The third of July at Gettysburg and Vicksburg.—Meade holds a Council of
War.—Lee retreats to the Potomac.—Meade slowly advances.—Lee recrosses the Potomac.
—Losses at Gettysburg.—Criticism on the Battle.

6 L

FROM Chancellorsville and the Wilderness both armies returned to their
old positions on opposite banks of the Rappahannock.[1] Hooker meditated repeating, with some modifications, the attempt in which Burnside had
failed.[2] He proposed to pass the river at Franklin's Crossing, and assail the
enemy's intrenchments in front; for he could not anticipate that with their
inferior force they would come out of their strong works, and meet him on

[1] For this campaign and the ensuing ones in Virginia, the full reports of the Confederate Army
of Northern Virginia are wanting. If they were ever made, I have not been able to gain access
to them. I presume that they were among the lost archives of the Confederacy. General Lee,
a few days after the battles of Gettysburg, made a Preliminary Report, which will be found in the
Rebellion Record, vol. vii. Some months later he made a somewhat more detailed report. This,
I believe, has never been printed. For a MS. copy of it I am indebted to Mr. William Swinton.
It, however, adds little to the information contained in the earlier Report. I find no reports
from corps, division, and brigade commanders. The testimony given before the Congressional
Committee on the Conduct of the War is the best authority upon the Union side. This (cited as
Com. Rep., ii.) will be found in the first volume of the second series of this Report. Not a few of
the newspaper accounts of this battle, Northern and Southern, are very accurate. From these
sources the following account has been mainly drawn.

[2] "As soon as I heard that General Sedgwick had recrossed the river, seeing no object in maintaining my position where it was, and believing that it would be much more to my advantage to
hazard an engagement with the enemy at Franklin's Crossing, where I had elbow-room, than
where I was, the army on the right was directed to recross the river."—Hooker, in *Com. Rep.*, ii.,
134.

the open plain. This was an enterprise which he had before pronounced to be wholly impracticable. It is vain to inquire what had happened within the week to make the project more feasible. His army had been much reduced by the departure of the nine-months' and two-years' men. On the 13th of May he informed the President that his "marching force of infantry was cut down to 80,000 men;" he added, "I hope to commence my movement to-morrow; but this must not be spoken of to any one." Lincoln replied that he did not think any thing was to be gained by an early renewal of the attempt to cross the Rappahannock; still, if Hooker believed that he could renew the attack successfully, he would not restrain him.[1] Whatever the proposed movement was, it was not attempted.

The result at Chancellorsville had inspired the Confederates with the most unbounded confidence. There was a universal clamor that the invincible army of Virginia should assume the offensive, carry the war beyond the bounds of the Confederacy, and conquer a peace upon Federal soil. To do this, it was necessary that the entire force, except what was engaged upon the Mississippi, should be concentrated in Northern Virginia. Before the close of May it became evident to Hooker that some great operation was in contemplation. Longstreet's three divisions, which had been engaged south of Richmond, were brought up one by one toward the Rappahannock. During the month of April he had been besieging Peck at Suffolk. But on the 2d of May, the ominous tidings that Hooker had advanced upon Lee caused Longstreet to abandon the siege, and put his force upon the march northward. The issue at Chancellorsville caused the movement to be suspended, and the force moved slowly by separate divisions. During the first week of June the whole army was concentrated near Culpepper, with the exception of A. P. Hill's division, which was left at Fredericksburg to mask the contemplated movement. Hooker, discovering that something was in progress, sent over on the 5th of June a part of Sedgwick's corps for the purpose of observation. Hill made such a display of his troops as to convince Hooker that the force in his front was not seriously diminished. Prisoners reported that the movements were merely a change of camps. Hooker indeed suspected that the van of the Confederate column would be heading toward the Potomac, while its rear was still left at Fredericksburg. He asked permission in that case to cross the river and fall upon their rear: this was refused, Halleck deeming that it would be perilous to permit the main force of Lee to move upon the Potomac, while the Union army was attacking a part of it in an intrenched position. The President concurred in this view, couching his opinion in his own quaint language.[2] But if it was Hooker's purpose to cross at Banks's Ford or the United States Ford, instead of marching right upon the front of the Confederate intrenchments, one can hardly see how he could have failed to inflict serious damage upon their rear, which would be thus severed from the main body at Culpepper, sixty miles away. Hooker in the mean time had learned that the Confederate cavalry at least was concentrated at Culpepper, and, in order to break up their camps, sent Pleasonton with two brigades of cavalry and 3000 infantry in that direction. This force ascended the north bank of the Rappahannock on the 9th of June, and marched in two columns toward Culpepper. The columns soon found themselves in presence of the enemy in large force, both of cavalry and infantry. A succession of sharp skirmishes ensued, lasting from early morning until late in the afternoon. The loss was about equal, four or five hundred on each side; but Pleasonton, finding himself confronted by superior numbers of both arms, retreated. Lee claims to have taken 400 prisoners; Pleasonton claims to have taken 200. This movement, and subsequent reconnoissances, which showed that the enemy were moving into and down the Valley of the Shenandoah, clearly indicated that they were bent either upon interposing between Hooker's army and Washington, or crossing the Potomac and invading the North.

Lee's design was first to detach Hooker from his strong position at Fredericksburg, then to free the Valley of the Shenandoah from the Union force which had occupied it during the winter and spring, "and, if practicable, to transfer the scene of hostilities north of the Potomac." He also hoped that there would be an "opportunity to strike a blow at the army commanded by Hooker;" or, in any case, that "this army would be compelled to leave Virginia, and perhaps would draw with it troops from other quarters; and so their plans of the campaign would be disarranged, and a part of the season for active operations would be consumed in forming new combinations."[3]

Apart from these purely military reasons, there were grave political motives for an invasion of the North. A numerous party, and one active even beyond its numerical strength, had bitterly opposed the war. The Emancipation Proclamation had concentrated and intensified this opposition. During the hundred days which intervened between the announcement of Lincoln's purpose to put forth this proclamation and its actual issue, elections had been held in ten of the states of the Union. In these states Mr. Lincoln had, in 1860, a majority of more than 200,000; now the opposition majority was 35,000. In 1860 these states had sent 78 Republican and 37 Democratic representatives to Congress; now they elected 51 Administration and 67 Opposition members. This change was specially notable in the large states. New York, Pennsylvania, Ohio, Indiana, and Illinois, which had sent 65 Republicans and 34 Democrats, now returned 40 Administration and 59 Opposition members. In Ohio Clement C. Vallandigham had been arrested on account of a speech in bitter denunciation of the war; had been tried by a court-martial, and sentenced to imprisonment in a fortress until the close of the war. This sentence was commuted by the President to banishment into the Confederacy. A great Democratic meeting was held at Albany, in which the leaders of the party in the State of New York inveighed bitterly against this proceeding; and at home Vallandigham was nominated by acclamation as the Democratic candidate for Governor of Ohio. At the time no one doubted that he would be elected. No one could dream that a state which had just sent to Congress 14 Opposition and but 5 Administration representatives would in a few months give a majority of a hundred thousand for the administration; nor could any one presume that a very large portion of the members of Congress elected as opposition would range themselves on the side of the administration in upholding the war. The draft, moreover, which was soon to go into effect, was vehemently denounced, declared to be unconstitutional, and threats were openly made that its enforcement would be violently resisted. There was fair occasion for the South to be persuaded that any great success gained over the Union army would elicit such a feeling throughout the North that the government would be compelled to desist from the prosecution of the war. "It was hoped," says Lee, "that, in addition to military advantages, other results might be attained by the success of our army." Nor was this opinion that the people of the North were becoming weary of the war confined to those whose interests and feelings were so strongly enlisted. The British minister at Washington had six months before shared in this opinion, and so informed his government.[1] Since then an almost uninterrupted series of successes had been gained by the Confederates. They had defeated Burnside at Fredericksburg, and foiled Hooker at Chancellorsville; Vicksburg and Charleston still held out against all the Federal assaults; none of the operations on the Lower Mississippi and the Gulf had succeeded; the capture of Galveston had given all Texas into the hands of the Confederates; the Alabama and the Florida had swept American commerce from the high seas. Saving the few miles occupied by the main armies, the Union forces actually held no part of the Confederate territory of which they had taken possession. During the first six months of the year 1863 it seemed as though the tide of success had fully set in favor of the Confederacy, and it appeared that nothing but a successful invasion of the North was wanting to secure its final triumph, recognized by all the great powers of Europe.

The invasion once determined upon, the entire disposable strength of the Confederacy was placed at the disposal of Lee. Southern Virginia and North Carolina were almost stripped of troops, to augment the Army of Northern Virginia. By the middle of June, when the movement toward the North was fairly commenced, Lee found himself in command of a force of fully 100,000 men of all arms.[2] This was divided into three corps, commanded by Longstreet, A. P. Hill, and Ewell, the cavalry being under Stuart. The advance of this great army was made with a deliberation in strong contrast with the hurried invasion of Maryland the year before.

Hooker, having learned of the advancing movement on the 12th of June, withdrew his army from opposite Fredericksburg, and moved northward so

[1] *Com. Rep.*, ii., 105.

[2] "In case you find Lee coming to the north of the Rappahannock, I would by no means cross to the south of it. If he should leave a rear force at Fredericksburg, tempting you to fall upon it, he would fight in intrenchments, and have you at disadvantage; and so, man for man, worst you at that point, while his main force would in some way be getting an advantage of you northward. In one word, I would not take any risk of being entangled up on the river, like an ox jumped half way over a fence and liable to be torn by dogs, front and rear, without a fair chance to gore one way or kick the other."—*Com. Rep.*, ii., 155.

[3] *Lee's Rep.*

[1] "The success of the Democratic—or, as it now styles itself, the Conservative party—has been so great as to manifest a change in public feeling among the most rapid and the most complete that has ever been witnessed even in this country. . . . The Conservative leaders seemed to be persuaded that the result of the elections would be accepted by the President as the will of the people; that he would seek to terminate the war, not to push it to extremity; that he would endeavor to effect a reconciliation with the South, and renounce the idea of subjecting or exterminating them." (*Dispatch of Lord Lyons*, November 17, 1862.)—The minister indeed goes on to say that at that moment "the Conservative party were calling loudly for a more vigorous prosecution of the war;" but he adds, "I thought I perceived a desire to put an end to the war, even at the risk of losing the Southern States altogether." He goes on to affirm that while they "would, if possible, obtain an armistice without the aid of foreign governments, they would be disposed to accept an offer of mediation, if it appeared to be the only means of putting a stop to hostilities."

[2] Pollard (*Lost Cause*, 402) gives the numbers as 75,000 infantry and 15,000 cavalry. But as the Confederate government never published official returns of the strength of its armies, this statement must be conjectural. I think it fully 10,000 too low. The captured returns (*Ante*, p. 383) are wanting for Lee's army for the month of June, which would have given its strength when this movement commenced. At the close of May the numbers of this army were 88,754 "present," of whom 68,352 were "present for duty." But it is clear that during the ensuing weeks it was considerably augmented. The statement in the text is based upon the following data:

I. It has been shown that after the close of the actions at Chancellorsville, Lee had with him, exclusive of 9000 wounded, 47,000 infantry and artillery, and 3000 cavalry. It may be assumed that of the wounded 5000 would in the ensuing six weeks be able to return to duty. This would give him, apart from re-enforcements, 55,000 men. The re-enforcements consisted mainly of Longstreet's three corps, which had been sent south of Richmond, and rejoined the Army of Northern Virginia late in May and early in June. The captured returns show that in March there were under Longstreet "present for duty," in the Department of North Carolina and South Virginia, 45,103, and in the Department of Richmond, under Elzey, 5789. In June there were in these departments, that of North Carolina now being under D. H. Hill, 25,997, a diminution of almost 25,000. These were all sent to Lee, and, added to his 55,000, would give him 80,000 infantry, apart from new levies raised in the interim. The number of these new levies was certainly very considerable, for we find that the cavalry, which at the close of April numbered less than 3000, had by the middle of June swelled, according to Pollard, to 15,000. It is certain, also, that under the stringent conscription laws very considerable accessions were made to the infantry. For example, we find it specially noted that Pettigrew's entire division, which acted so important a part at Gettysburg, were "raw troops from North Carolina, who had never been under fire," and consequently formed no part of the former Army of Northern Virginia, which had fought on the Peninsula, at Groveton, Antietam, and Fredericksburg. If we allow only 10,000 for the absolute increase of infantry during May and early June, these, added to Lee's 80,000 and the 10,000 new cavalry, would give a sum of 100,000, the number set down.

II. Longstreet (Swinton's *Army of the Potomac*, 310) says that when the army was concentrated at Chambersburg, in Pennsylvania, it numbered 67,000 "bayonets," that is, privates; adding to these the officers, there would be a total of fully 75,000 infantry and artillery, besides about 5000 cavalry, the remaining 10,000 having been sent elsewhere. This would make the whole force which crossed the Potomac 90,000. As there was a long line, from the Rappahannock to the Potomac, to guard, a considerable number must have been left behind for that purpose. Estimating these at only 10,000, we have fully 100,000 as the original number.

III. As the army passed through Hagerstown it was carefully counted. Of the results of this count we have two reports. Hooker says (*Com. Rep.*, ii., 173): "With regard to the enemy's force I had reliable information. Two Union men counted them as they passed through Hagerstown. In round numbers Lee had 91,000 infantry and 280 pieces of artillery; marching with that column were about 6000 cavalry; a portion of the enemy's cavalry crossed the Potomac below Edwards's Ferry; this column numbered about 5000 men." Butterfield, now his chief of staff, as he had been of Hooker's, reported this to Meade (*Ibid.*, 420), who seems to have adopted it as the basis of his estimate (*Ibid.*, 337) of the force opposed to him, although on the day after he took command he had telegraphed to Washington (*Ibid.*, 479) that "Mr. Logan, Register of Wills, and Mr. Preston, very fine men in Hagerstown, have taken pains to count the rebels, and could not make them over 80,000; they counted the artillery, made it 275 guns; 2000 comprise the mounted artillery and cavalry." These two counts, apparently independent of each other, confirm our estimate that the Confederate force which entered Pennsylvania numbered of all arms fully 90,000 men.

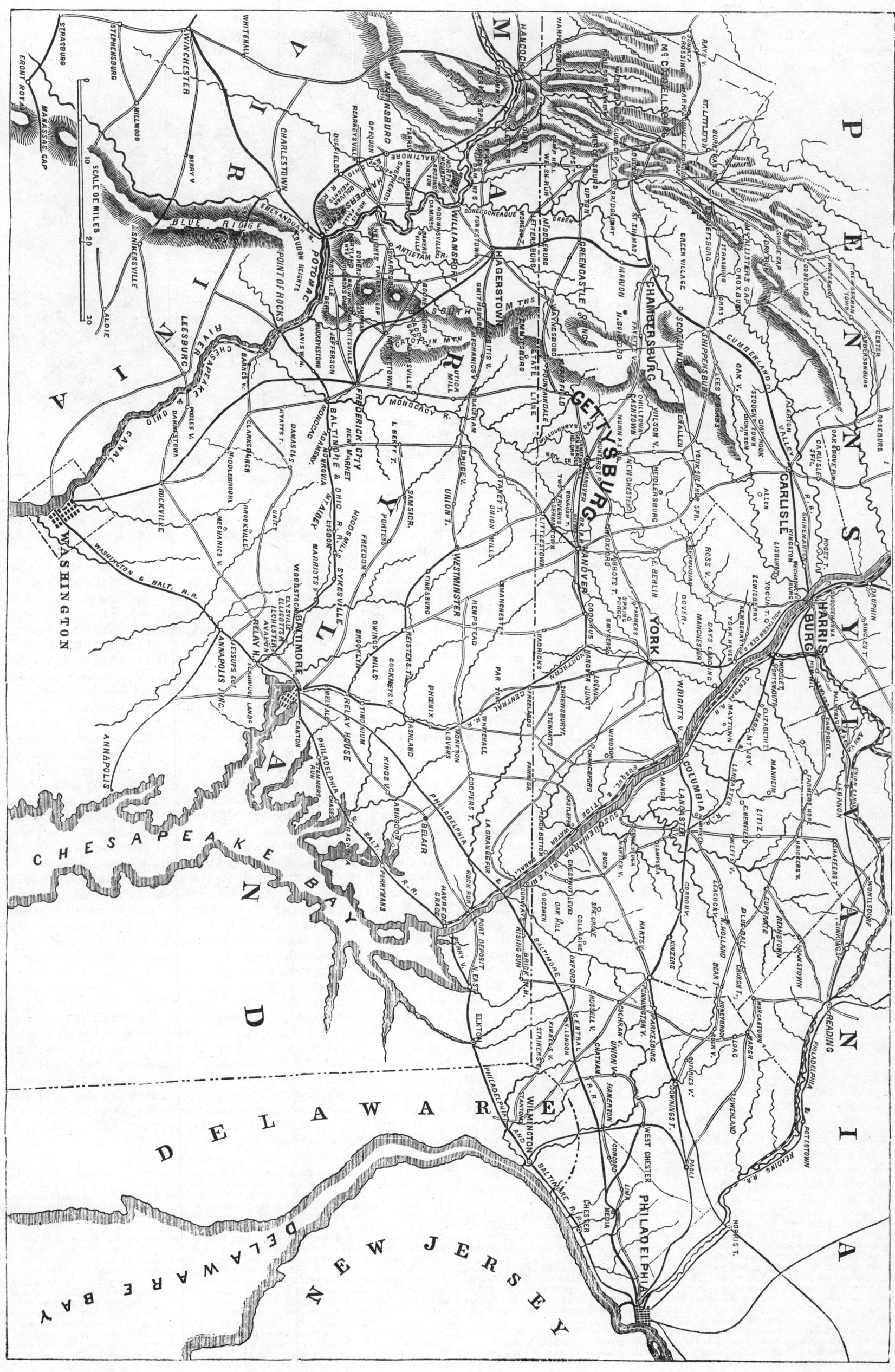

BURNING THE BRIDGE OVER THE SUSQUEHANNA, COLUMBIA, PENN.

as to cover Washington. A. P. Hill forthwith left Fredericksburg, and joined the main army at Culpepper. Lee then pushed forward his divisions one by one, and by different routes, all centring upon Winchester, the key of the lower valley of the Shenandoah. Milroy, with 7000 men, had been long lying at Winchester. On the 12th of June he began to get tidings that the enemy were pressing down upon him, in what force he could not learn; but on the next day his doubts were solved by authentic tidings that the Confederates were advancing in overwhelming force. Then was the time to retreat; but this was delayed until the 15th, when, before dawn, he destroyed what he could of his stores, spiked his guns, and started for Harper's Ferry; the Confederates having in the mean while sent a strong force, which gained his rear, while he was also attacked in front. Milroy's whole force was dispersed, and 2300 of them were captured.[1] The others made their way, utterly broken, to and across the Potomac; some of them never halted in their wild flight until they had reached Chambersburg, far into Pennsylvania. Ewell's corps, which had gone on in advance, followed on and entered Maryland, the cavalry pushing as far as Chambersburg.

Lee had supposed that this partial movement would cause Hooker to leave Virginia and cross the Potomac to defend the threatened North, rendering an attack upon Washington feasible. But Hooker was not entrapped by this manœuvre, and kept his army near the old battle-field of Manassas, effectually covering Washington. Lee now began to move the corps of Hill and Longstreet down the Valley of the Shenandoah, along the west side of the Blue Ridge, Hooker being on the east side. The cavalry of each army, sent out as feelers, came into frequent collision, sometimes in considerable force, the advantage, on the whole, being with the Federals.[2] Lee hoped by all these movements to draw Hooker farther from Washington, which had now become his base, and even to induce him to pass the Blue Ridge and venture an attack. The opportunity seemed, indeed, a favorable one. For some days the Confederate army was stretched from Culpepper a hundred miles to the Potomac. To strike that long line somewhere seemed feasible. So thought the President. "If," he wrote to Hooker, "the head of Lee's army is at Martinsburg, and the tail of it on the plank road between Fredericksburg and Chancellorsville, the animal must be very slim somewhere; could you not break him?"[3] But Hooker determined not to make the attempt. In his view, the wisest course was to move his army on a concentric but inner circle to that followed by the main body of the enemy, and thus be enabled to thwart his general design, whatever that should prove to be. Any slight advantages which he might hope to gain over portions of the hostile force would be more than counterbalanced by the necessity which would be involved of marching his army away from the point where it was most needed. Although the rear of the Confederate army was so far away from its front, it was moving to unite, and there was no probability that a Union force could strike it strongly any where without encountering a superior force. For the time

the true policy was that adopted by Hooker, and thereafter for a time by Meade, to be governed in his operations by those of the main body of the hostile army.[1]

Lee having failed in finding an opportunity to strike a blow at the Union army in Virginia, or inducing Hooker to assail him upon unfavorable terms, now resolved to transform the raiding operations in Pennsylvania into a serious invasion by his whole army. Longstreet's and Hill's corps pushed rapidly to the Potomac. On the 24th and 25th, the river, now so low as to be easily fordable, was passed at Williamsport and Shepherdstown, almost within sight of the battle-field of Antietam, and the columns, uniting at Hagerstown, pressed forward toward Chambersburg. Hooker's course was now clear. On the 26th his army crossed the Potomac at Edwards's Ferry, the point where Lee had crossed into Maryland nine months before, and headed toward Frederick City. Lee had advanced so far from the Potomac as to leave his base of communications and supply greatly exposed. Hooker's plan was in the first place to assail these rather than to precipitate a battle; for every day would weaken the invaders, while it would give him new strength. He now, more urgently than ever, urged that every soldier within reach should be added to his available army.

It so happened that there were 10,000 men at Harper's Ferry, under French, who had not long before been put in command there. The place, as we have before seen, was utterly worthless for either side. For all military purposes, these men might as well have been a thousand miles away as at Harper's Ferry. The strength of the two opposed armies was so nearly equal that 10,000 men might make the difference between victory and defeat. The force at Harper's Ferry had been in a manner placed under the command of Hooker; but, in reply to an inquiry whether there was any reason why the place should not be abandoned, and the troops there brought into use, Halleck rejoined that much expense and labor had been incurred in fortifying the works there and thereabout, and he could not approve of their abandonment except in case of absolute necessity. Hooker thereupon sent back to Halleck two dispatches at the same time. One, which was to be shown to the President and the Secretary of War, briefly reiterated his views as to the retention of Harper's Ferry; the other contained his resignation of the command of the Army of the Potomac,[2] evidently intended to be acted upon in case the former should be unavailing. Halleck replied forthwith that Hooker had been appointed to the command by the President, to whom the application for being relieved must be referred. Brief time was taken for consideration, for on that same day, already far advanced into the afternoon, Hooker's resignation had been accepted, and the command of the Army of the Potomac formally assigned to General Meade.

Viewed simply as an isolated act, this sudden resignation of Hooker at a moment when the two armies were inevitably approaching a decisive con-

---

[1] "In a short time the whole infantry force, amounting to more than 2300 men, with eleven stand of colors, surrendered, the cavalry alone escaping. These operations resulted in the expulsion of the enemy from the Valley, the capture of 4000 prisoners with a corresponding number of small-arms, 28 pieces of superior artillery, about 300 wagons, and as many horses. Our entire loss was 47 killed, 219 wounded, and 3 missing."—Lee's Rep., MS.

[2] "On the 17th the enemy's cavalry encountered two brigades of ours under General Stuart, near Aldie, and was driven back with loss. The next day the engagement was renewed, the Federal cavalry being strongly supported by infantry, and General Stuart was in turn compelled to retire."—Lee's Rep. "On the 21st the enemy attacked with infantry and cavalry, and obliged General Stuart to fall back to the gaps of the mountains. In these engagements the cavalry sustained a loss of 510 killed, wounded, and missing."—Ibid., MS.

[3] Lincoln to Hooker, June 14th (Com. Rep., ii., 260). Two days later (Ibid., 160) Lincoln recurs to the same topic: "Your idea may be right, probably is; still, it pains me to abandon the fair chance presented of breaking the enemy's lengthy and necessarily slow line, stretched now from the Rappahannock to Pennsylvania."

[1] When A. P. Hill's corps "took up its line of march, following those of Ewell and Longstreet, I was clearly of the opinion that it was my duty to be governed in my operations by those of the whole rebel army, and not a part of it, and accordingly I directed my marches with that view."—Hooker, in Com. Rep., ii., 161.

[2] These dispatches both bear date June 27, 1 P.M. They were received almost at the same moment, 2.55 and 3 P.M. (See Com. Rep., ii., 174, 292.)—No. 1. "I have received your telegram in regard to Harper's Ferry. I found 10,000 men here in condition to take the field. Here they are of no earthly account. They can not defend a ford of the river; and, as far as Harper's Ferry is concerned, there is nothing of it. As for the fortifications, the work of the troops, they remain when the troops are withdrawn. No enemy will ever take possession of them. This is my opinion. All the public property could have been secured to-night, and the troops marched to where they could have been of some service. Now they are but a bait for the rebels, should they return. I beg that this may be presented to the Secretary of War and his Excellency the President."—No. 2. "My original instructions require me to cover Harper's Ferry and Washington. I have now imposed upon me, in addition, an enemy in my front of more than my number. I beg to be understood that I am unable to comply with this condition with the means at my disposal, and earnestly request that I may at once be relieved from the position that I occupy."

flict would seem uncalled for and unjustifiable. The immediate occasion was not of sufficient consequence to warrant a step which involved such grave consequences. But the question now mooted as to the troops at Harper's Ferry was but the culminating point of a long course of discord. Hooker knew that Halleck had opposed and twice defeated his appointment to the command of the Army of the Potomac. He perceived, or thought he perceived, a fixed determination to thwart him in every way.[1] This ill feeling had by this time grown to such a height, and assumed a form so personal, that it was clearly out of the question for the two men to act together in the positions which they occupied. Halleck took early occasion to vent his spite. There was an order prohibiting officers from visiting Washington without permission. Hooker, four days after his supercedure, went to the capital. He had hardly left his carriage ten minutes when he was put under arrest by order of the general-in-chief. How many opportunities were lost, and how many lives sacrificed by the personal ill feeling and professional jealousy which had sprung up among officers high in rank in the army, it would be vain to inquire.

The country and the army were astounded on the 28th of June by the announcement that the command of the Army of the Potomac had been relinquished by Hooker and was conferred upon Meade. Despite the misadventure at Chancellorsville, Hooker still retained the confidence of the soldiers who served under him. There was a kind of self-assured confidence in the man which begat confidence in others. Of Meade, who was so suddenly called upon to replace him, less had been heard than of almost any other corps commander in the army. Just a year before he had commanded a brigade at Cold Harbor. Four days later his brigade made its mark at Frazier's Farm. Glimpses were caught of him at South Mountain and Antietam. At Fredericksburg he won a partial success, but this was lost sight of in the disasters which accompanied and followed. At Chancellorsville, his corps, through no fault of his, hardly touched the fight. He had little of that imposing personal presence to which McClellan owed all, and Hooker much of power. His aspect was that of a scholar rather than of a captain. Those who knew him best could only say that wherever tried he had never been found wanting, but that he had never been subjected to a great trial. If the question had been simply whether Meade should replace Hooker, it would have been difficult to find a man to favor the change. But things had suddenly come to such a condition that a great change must be made at a critical moment. Either Halleck must be displaced as general-in-chief, or Hooker must vacate the command of the Army of the Potomac. The smaller the change at the urgent crisis involved the less of apparent peril, and so Hooker's request to be released from command was promptly granted. What special reasons fixed the choice upon Meade as his successor can only be conjectured. There were no open cliques of generals in his favor, and consequently no ostensible ones against him. Herein, perhaps, lies the secret.[2]

No man in or out of the army could have been more surprised than was Meade when the tidings came that he was appointed to the command. He took upon himself his new duties in a quiet way, which strongly contrasted with the self-distrust of Burnside and the self-assertion of Hooker. The movements planned by his predecessor were carried out by the same staff. Only that the orders were issued over a new name, the army would scarcely have known that it had a new commander. The only important changes made were that Hancock was placed in command of the Second Corps, vacated by Couch's appointment to the Department of the Susquehanna, and Sykes took the Fifth, formerly led by Meade. Reynolds retained the First Corps, Sickles the Third, Sedgwick the Sixth, Howard the Eleventh, and Slocum the Twelfth.

Lee, having crossed the Potomac, pushed rapidly forward into Pennsylvania with his whole force. Cutting loose from its supplies, his army was to live upon the country. But Lee ordered that supplies should be extorted in an orderly manner, upon formal requisitions duly made, payment being tendered in Confederate notes; if these were declined, certificates were to be given showing the amount and value of the property thus taken. If the local authorities neglected to meet these requisitions, the required supplies were to be seized. These requisitions were frequently onerous. Thus the town of York, with but 7000 inhabitants, was called upon, among other things, for 165 barrels of flour, 3500 pounds of sugar, 32,000 pounds of beef, 2000 pairs of boots or shoes, and $100,000 in cash. Probably the whole borough did not contain this amount of stores and money. At all events, only a quarter of the money could be raised.

[1] "Almost every request I made of General Halleck was refused. It was often remarked that it was of no use for me to make a request, as that of itself would be sufficient cause for General Halleck to refuse it. . . . . . . I may add as my conviction that if the general-in-chief had been in the rebel interest, it would have been impossible for him, restrained as he was by the President and the Secretary of War, to have added to the embarrassment he caused me from the moment I took command of the Army of the Potomac to the time I surrendered it."—Hooker, in *Com. Rep.*, ii., 175.

[2] "I have said that there were no "open" cliques in favor of Meade as opposed to Hooker. That there was some secret opposition to Hooker's retention of the command soon after Chancellorsville is clear. On the 14th of May the President writes to Hooker (*Com. Rep.*, ii., 150): "I have some painful intimations that some of your corps and division commanders are not giving you their entire confidence. This would be ruinous if true."—General Couch was the ranking officer of the corps commanders. But early in June he was detached from the Army of the Potomac and placed in command of the "Department of the Susquehanna," that is, of Pennsylvania. This change seems to have been quite acceptable to Hooker: "I can give a command to General Couch," telegraphed the Secretary of War to Hooker on the 9th of June; "I can spare General Couch," returned Hooker at once (*Com. Rep.*, ii., 252). Just after the battle of Gettysburg, Halleck notified Couch that Meade had the command of all the troops in the Department of the Susquehanna, and that his orders must be obeyed. To which Couch rejoined: "General Meade's wishes, instructions, and recommendations have been carried out so far as practicable. As I prominently mentioned that officer for his present position, it may be inferred that I would show no lukewarmness in carrying out his orders" (*Com. Rep.*, ii., 501).—Now, as there seems to have been no time between the resignation of Hooker and the appointment of Meade in which Couch, then in Pennsylvania, could have been consulted, it must be presumed that this "prominent mention" by Couch was made at an earlier day.

This formidable invasion aroused the most intense apprehension. Directly after the rout of Milroy at Winchester, the President issued a proclamation calling for 100,000 militia from the nearest states. Of these, Pennsylvania was to furnish 50,000, Ohio 30,000, Maryland 10,000, West Virginia 10,000. These were called out for six months, unless sooner discharged. Besides these, the Governor of New York was asked to order out 20,000. Within a few days New York sent nearly 16,000, of whom 14,000 were from the Empire City. Their absence gave opportunity for the fearful riots which ensued in the city of New York about the middle of July. In Pennsylvania, which was immediately threatened, the President's call was slightly responded to. In that state the militia system was so imperfect that there was not a brigade or regimental organization in existence. The governor called for 60,000 volunteers, who would be "mustered into the service of the state for ninety days, but would be required to serve only so much of the period of the muster as the safety of the people and the honor of the state should require." About 25,000 in all responded to these calls from Pennsylvania, but so tardily that not a man of them ever came in sight of the enemy. The Pennsylvania militia did not fire a gun to relieve their state from invasion. Some of the New York regiments came up in time to touch the van of the enemy as they halted in their advance. In New Jersey a few thousand men were raised, and a few companies actually went as far as Harrisburg. About 2000 were furnished by Delaware to guard the railroads in Maryland. The other states which were called upon did absolutely nothing. Before, indeed, any of the militia could be brought up, the battle of Gettysburg had been fought, and the crisis was past; for events had been so shaping themselves as to render a great battle inevitable. The time and place of this was determined more by accident and the physical character of the region than by any purpose on the part of either commander.

The South Mountain, a continuation of the Blue Ridge of Virginia, runs northward through a corner of Maryland far into Pennsylvania. Lee had crossed the Potomac on the west of this ridge, Hooker on the east. The line of march of the two armies was nearly parallel, the mountains between them, and each commander for a few days knew little of the movements of the other. Meade in the mean time followed out the plans conceived by Hooker. Lee, having some days the start, was considerably northward of Meade; Ewell, in the advance, was as far as Carlisle, and preparing to move toward Harrisburg, the capital of Pennsylvania, while Longstreet and Hill halted at Chambersburg. Meade had gone about half as far from the Potomac, and was in such a position that, by a rapid march to the west through the unobstructed passes of the South Mountain, which his left column had almost reached, he could throw himself right in the rear of Lee, and effectually cut him off from his supplies, wholly isolating him in a hostile country. Tidings of this movement reached Lee on the night of the 28th of June. He saw at once that the great invasion could be carried no farther, at least until he had destroyed the army which thus hung menacingly upon his flank and rear. The whole Confederate army was thereupon ordered to concentrate toward the enemy. The point of concentration was Gettysburg, beyond South Mountain. Thither Longstreet and Hill were to march eastward from Chambersburg, and Ewell southward from Carlisle.[1] Now Meade's left column, consisting of the corps of Reynolds and Howard — Sickles's corps, though not so far in advance, forming part thereof, with Buford's cavalry, had advanced farther northward than the remainder of the army, and on the 30th were close by Gettysburg. On that morning Meade learned that the enemy were moving against him. He thereupon resolved to concentrate his forces, which were now spread over many miles of country. The natural mode was to withdraw his advance, and bring up his centre and rear. His leading purposes were to compel the enemy to withdraw from the Susquehanna, and then to give or receive battle at the first favorable opportunity. The position which he selected as most likely to be the scene of conflict was on Pipe Creek, a little stream fifteen miles southeast from Gettysburg.[2]

When Lee appointed Gettysburg as the place of rendezvous for his army, he knew nothing of its supreme strategical importance. Meade, also, knew

[1] "Preparations were made for the advance upon Harrisburg; but on the night of the 29th [so printed, but it should clearly be the night of the 28th; that is, the night before the 29th] information was received that the Federal army, having crossed the Potomac, was advancing northward, and that the head of the column had reached the South Mountain. As our communications with the Potomac were thus menaced, it was resolved to prevent his farther progress in that direction by concentrating our army on the east side of the mountains. Accordingly, Longstreet and Hill were directed to proceed from Chambersburg to Gettysburg, to which point Ewell was also instructed to march from Carlisle."—*Lee's Rep.*

[2] "I determined to move my army as promptly as possible on the main line from Frederick to Harrisburg, extending my wings on both sides of that line as far as I could consistently with the safety and rapid concentration of that army, and to continue my movement until I either encountered the enemy or had reason to believe that he was about to advance upon me; my object being, at all hazards, to force him to loose his hold on the Susquehanna, and meet me in battle at some point. It was my firm determination to give battle wherever and as soon as I could possibly find the enemy, modified, of course, by such considerations as must govern every general officer. On the night of the 30th I had become satisfied that the enemy was apprised of my movements; that he had relinquished his hold on the Susquehanna; that he was concentrating his forces, and that I might expect to come in contact with him in a very short time—when and where I could not at that moment tell. I instructed my engineers to select some general ground, having reference to the existing position of the army, by which, in case the enemy should advance upon me across the South Mountain, I might be able, by rapid movement of concentration, to occupy this position, and be prepared to give him battle upon my own terms. The general line of Pipe Creek was selected, and a preliminary order issued notifying the corps commanders that such line might possibly be adopted, and directing them how they might move their corps, and what their positions should be along this line. This order was issued on the night of the 30th of June, possibly on the morning of the 1st of July; certainly before any positive information had reached me that the enemy had crossed the mountain and were in conflict with any part of my force." (Meade, in *Com. Rep.*, ii., 330.)—This statement is given in full, as it sets at rest the assertion often made that Meade proposed to retreat before the enemy, and that he was forced to fight at Gettysburg by an unauthorized attack made by Reynolds. His purpose of assuming the line of Pipe Creek was contingent upon circumstances which might or might not arise. It was, as will be seen, accident, so far as any previous purpose on the part of either commander was concerned, that made Gettysburg the scene of the conflict—the speedy occurrence of which, somewhere hard by, had become inevitable, unless, indeed, Lee should consent to retreat without having fairly attempted any thing—and this he was by no means inclined to do.

GETTYSBURG.

quite as little thereof. "It was a place," as he told the Congressional Committee on the Conduct of the War, "which I had never seen in my life, and had no more knowledge of than you have now." Yet it would seem that a glance at a map should have revealed its importance. This little town occupies, as it were, the hub of a wheel, from which roads, or spokes, radiate in every direction: northwestward toward Chambersburg; northeastward toward Harrisburg and Philadelphia; southwestward toward the Potomac; southeastward toward Baltimore. Whosoever held Gettysburg, held, if he knew it, the key to a campaign. It so chanced that one soldier had happened to study the topographical features of this region, and he had made up his mind that Gettysburg was the one spot whereat, if so it could be, to have a fight. And it so happened, also, that this man was the only one, who, as things stood, could have so ordered events that the fight should have happened just then and there. That man was Alfred Pleasonton, now commanding the cavalry corps; the man to whom primarily it was owing that the fierce rush of Jackson had been stayed at Chancellorsville. In the distribution of his troopers, he had sent the strongest division, that of Buford, to cover the left flank of the army, that is, Reynolds's column, which was nearest the enemy. His order to Buford was to hold Gettysburg to the last extremity, until the army could be concentrated there.[1] Buford reached Gettysburg early on the morning of the last day of June, in advance of the infantry of Reynolds's column, whereof the First Corps, properly his own, but now under the immediate command of Doubleday, and the Eleventh, Howard's, encamped that night four miles from Gettysburg.

WEDNESDAY, JULY 1.

On the morning of the 1st of July Buford pushed his troopers northwestward. At the same time the advance of the Confederate army was approaching from that direction. Lee had moved his force slowly from Chambersburg and Carlisle, not imagining that any considerable Union force was in the neighborhood of Gettysburg, for, as it chanced, Stuart, with his vigilant cavalry, was far away. He had been left behind in Virginia to harass the Union rear, and was then to cross into Maryland. This crossing was made far to the south of the point where Hooker went over, so that Stuart found the whole Union army between him and Lee, and he could reach Carlisle, the place appointed for rendezvous, only by making a wide circuit. When he came there on the 1st of July, he found the place evacuated, and the army on the way to Gettysburg, whither he hastened, but not in time to take any part in the action of the first two days. Reynolds set his command in motion toward Gettysburg. He had evidently discerned the supreme necessity of preventing the enemy from seizing this point.[2] No one who looked upon the ground could fail to perceive this.

The quiet town of Gettysburg nestles in a little hollow ten miles east of the South Mountain range. The surrounding country is rough and broken, granite ridges cropping up all around. This granite had been, in the formative period of the earth's history, flung up through the soft shale, which, worn away by water-currents, left exposed the bare ridges of the harder stone. The general course of these ridges is north and south; they are not continuous for any great extent, and are not unfrequently cast into irregular forms. Looking westward from the town at a distance of half a mile, one sees a long, wooded height, its centre crowned by the buildings of a Theological Seminary, whence it receives the name of Seminary Ridge. Looking southward, at the distance of a mile, is the rounded extremity of another ridge, broken into several separate hills. Ascending the nearest of these, the ridge is seen falling away for a space, then, at the distance of three miles, rising again into a broken spur, closing in a rocky, wooded peak. This whole range bears the name of Cemetery Ridge, for upon it was the burying-ground where rest generations of the dwellers of the quiet town. But now, hard by is a great City of the Dead, made populous in three short days. This ridge, running first northward, then, with a sharp curve, eastward, then, again, bending to the south, is, in shape, not unlike a fish-hook. Each of the rugged hills which rise from the clearly-marked line of the crest bears its own name. That at the extremity of the stem of the hook is Round Top, with Little Round Top its prolongation. Cemetery Hill is at the bend; Culp's Hill forms the barb. These two ridges are now historic, for on Cemetery Ridge the Union Army took its position, the Confederate force being drawn up on Seminary Ridge. The valley between them, half a mile wide at its narrowest point, near the town, then gradually spreading southward to twice that breadth, consists of cultivated fields, interspersed with patches of woodland. In these fields and woodlands, and up the rough slopes of Cemetery Ridge, was waged for two days the mightiest conflict of the war.

On Wednesday morning, July 1, Hill, who, leading the Confederate advance, had encamped the previous night half a dozen miles west of Gettysburg, learned, to his surprise, that the town was occupied by the Union cavalry. What force of infantry lay behind he could not know. He put his divisions in motion, and sent back to urge forward Longstreet's corps, which was yet fifteen miles in the rear. Buford had meanwhile gone out two

[1] Pleasonton, in *Com. Rep.*, ii., 359.
[2] Otherwise we can not explain his conduct in acting in direct contradiction to the order which he had just received to fall back in the opposite direction to Pipe Creek. It was clearly one of those cases in which a subordinate commander was justified in disregarding a positive order, which he knew must have been given in ignorance of the real position of affairs. Sickles, later in the day, did precisely the same thing. He was some fourteen miles behind Reynolds, and had also been ordered to fall back; but, learning that an action was going on at Gettysburg, he marched directly thither. "I assumed," he says, "that this new fact [the action then going on] was not known to General Meade when the order to retreat was issued. The emergency did not admit of the delay that would have been required to communicate with General Meade, who was ten miles distant. I moved to Gettysburg on my own responsibility. As soon as I had determined to do that, I sent to General Meade informing him of what I had done, and expressed my anxiety to have his sanction of it. I received a communication from him informing me that he approved of my course."—*Com. Rep.*, ii., 296.

JOHN BUFORD.

THEOLOGICAL SEMINARY, GETTYSBURG.

ing their commander. Cutler's brigade of this division was now sorely pressed, and fell back; but two regiments of the Confederates, advancing along a deep cutting for an unfinished railway, were swept upon by a flank movement, and, shut up in this gorge, were forced to surrender. Thus far the contest had been waged between a single division on each side. The balance of success was against the Confederates. The two remaining divisions of Reynolds's corps now came up, closely followed by Howard's corps. Howard assumed command of the field.

But still heavier re-enforcements were coming up to the aid of Heth. First came Pender's division of Hill's corps, northwestward from toward Chambersburg; then from the north, Ewell from toward Carlisle, pressing down upon the Union right. They struck Robinson's division of Reynolds's corps. Their first blow was unsuccessful, and three North Carolina regiments were captured. Howard, leaving Steinwehr's division of his corps in reserve on the Cemetery Ridge behind Gettysburg, pushed Schurz and Barlow forward to meet the advance of Ewell. The roads by which the Federal troops had advanced diverge from Gettysburg like the spokes of a wheel, so that at each step the line grew thinner and thinner; while the Confederates, coming to the centre along these same spokes, were concentrating at every moment. As the afternoon wore away, Ewell's whole corps, and two thirds of that of Hill, fully 50,000 strong, were steadily pressing down upon the two corps of Reynolds and Howard, numbering at the outset not more than 21,000 men, including the division of 4000 left in reserve, which was not brought forward.[1] Howard now sent back to Sickles, a dozen miles away to the south, urging him to come up to his relief. Sickles

miles in that direction, crossing Seminary Ridge. At nine o'clock Hill's leading division, that of Heth, came upon Buford, who, knowing that Reynolds was on the march, resolved to contest the Confederate advance. Unlimbering the guns of his horse artillery, and deploying his troopers, he held the enemy briefly in check, but was soon forced back to the crest of the ridge. The sound of his guns quickened the march of Reynolds, whose leading division, under Wadsworth, 4000 strong, was now within a mile of Gettysburg. These were soon formed, under fire, in line of battle. The action had scarcely opened when Reynolds fell dead, shot through the head by a rifle-ball. There were but few men who could not have been better spared. There were not wanting those who had begun to look upon him as the most promising general in the Union army. Doubleday, who had come up, now took command; but he brought no re-enforcements to Wadsworth, for the other divisions of Reynolds's corps, and the whole of Howard's, were yet two hours' march behind. For two hours this one division maintained the fight, and then began slowly to give way. The enemy pressed on, a part of Archer's brigade so eagerly that they were isolated. Meredith swung round his "Iron Brigade," and captured 800 men, includ-

[1] "I do not believe that our force actually engaged, belonging to the two corps, amounted to over 14,000 men. There was a reserve of 3000 or 4000 of the Eleventh Corps, which did not join actively in the fight. It fired some shots from Cemetery Hill, but the most of them fell short into our own front line." (Doubleday, in Com. Rep., ii., 309.)—Doubleday adds: "According to the reports rendered to me, we [i. e., apparently Reynolds's corps] entered the fight with 8500 men, and came out with 2450." I suspect that there is here some error in the printing of these figures; for Wadsworth states that in his division "about 4000 men went into action," and that of these, on the next morning, he had but about 1600 men to answer to their names. It is hardly to be supposed that the two remaining divisions of this corps were so greatly inferior in numbers to any of the others. I think it safer, on many grounds, to estimate the six divisions of these two corps at 3500 each.

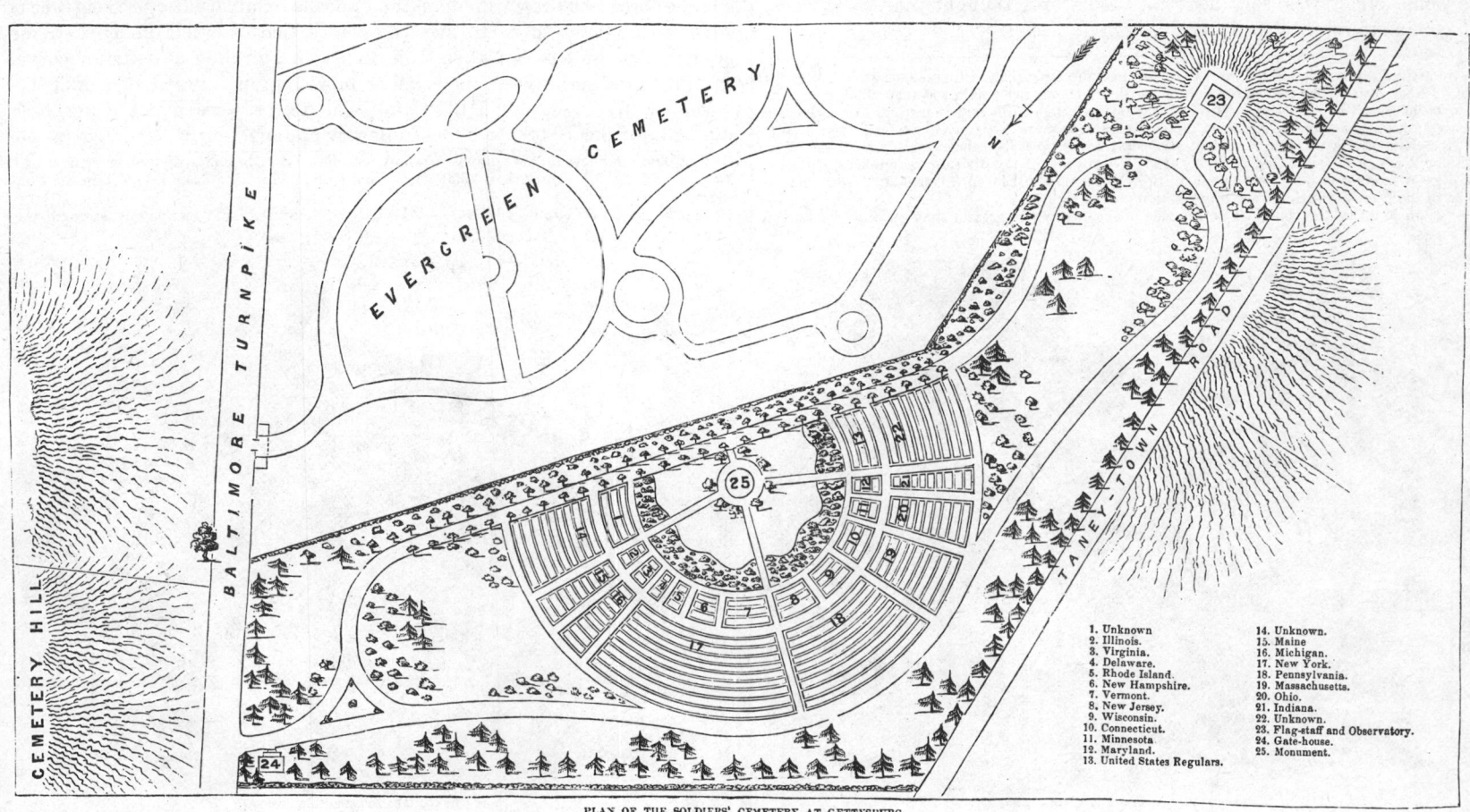

PLAN OF THE SOLDIERS' CEMETERY AT GETTYSBURG.

1. Unknown.
2. Illinois.
3. Virginia.
4. Delaware.
5. Rhode Island.
6. New Hampshire.
7. Vermont.
8. New Jersey.
9. Wisconsin.
10. Connecticut.
11. Minnesota.
12. Maryland.
13. United States Regulars.
14. Unknown.
15. Maine.
16. Michigan.
17. New York.
18. Pennsylvania.
19. Massachusetts.
20. Ohio.
21. Indiana.
22. Unknown.
23. Flag-staff and Observatory.
24. Gate-house.
25. Monument.

THE WHEAT-FIELD WHERE REYNOLDS FELL.

put his corps in motion, but a forced march only enabled him to reach Gettysburg after the action was over.

At an hour past noon, Meade, who, with his column of the centre, was at Taneytown, fourteen miles southeast of Gettysburg, learned that a fight was going on, and that Reynolds had fallen. He perceived "that the matter was being precipitated very heavily upon him." Of Gettysburg himself he knew nothing, and the first thing to be done was to ascertain whether it was a place whereat to give or receive battle. Calling to Hancock, the corps commander in whom he most confided, he ordered him to hurry to the field and take command there. Hancock was outranked by Howard, who was there, and by Sickles, who might be there; but it was no time to regard the niceties of military etiquette. Hancock sprang into an ambulance, that he might study the maps on his way, and in two hours was on the field, in time to see a lost battle, which, indeed, bore the aspect of a rout;[1] for Rodes's division of Ewell's corps had thrust itself right into a wide gap between the right of the First and the left of the Eleventh Union Corps, folding completely around the right of the First, pressing it back toward the Seminary. Here, behind a slight rail intrenchment, a stand was made long enough to permit the trains and ambulances to get off. Doubleday threw his personal guard of twoscore men into the Seminary building, whose quiet walls had never before witnessed any thing more stirring than debates upon points of theological controversy. But by this time the whole region was filled with the advancing lines of the enemy, double, sometimes triple. When the remnants of this gallant corps finally abandoned their position, they fell back to Gettysburg, right between two lines of the enemy. The Eleventh Corps at the same time was driven back to the same point, and the two retreating columns became entangled in the streets. The First Corps, being a little in advance, got well through. The Eleventh was struck heavily by Ewell's advance, and three fourths of the survivors of its two divisions engaged were made prisoners.[2] This battle cost the two Union corps not less than 10,000 men, of whom half were killed or wounded. Well-nigh half of the killed and wounded fell upon Wadsworth's division of 4000, which had for six hours withstood the enemy. The loss of the Confederates was very heavy. Wadsworth thought that his division inflicted more injury than it received.[3]

[1] "I arrived on the ground not later than half past three o'clock. I found that, practically, the fight was then over. The rear of our column, with the enemy in pursuit, was then coming through the town of Gettysburg. General Howard was on Cemetery Hill, and there had evidently been an attempt on his part to stop and form some of his troops there."—Hancock, in Com. Rep., ii., 405.

[2] Lee claims to have taken here 5000 prisoners; these must have been mainly from the Eleventh, for Wadsworth says (Com. Rep., ii., 413): "Very few of my division were taken prisoners; but a great many prisoners were taken on the right from the Eleventh Corps, and from one division of the First Corps that went into position on the right."

[3] "I am sure that the slaughter on the side of the enemy was greater than on our own side on

When Hancock rode up to Gettysburg, he bore with him the responsibility of all that was to follow; for he was charged not only to take the command of whatever force he should find there, but to decide whether that force should fall back, or whether the whole army should be brought forward and concentrated there. In a brief interval, what remained of the First and Eleventh Corps were assembled on the rocky ridge fronting Gettysburg, and presented so imposing an appearance as to cause Lee to hesitate to assail them. Looking back in the light of what is now known, the decision of the Confederate commander was most erroneous; but for one knowing only what he could then have known, it was the only safe one. Of his three corps only two had come up—Longstreet's, the strongest of all, was still behind. What part of the Union force lay upon and behind that rugged ridge he could not know. So the attack was suspended, and the Confederate army paused, waiting to see what the next day should bring forth. Hancock sent back to Meade such a report as to determine him to fight at Gettysburg, and during the night all the army was set in motion for that point. Sickles had already arrived two hours before night set in. Hancock's corps, and Slocum's, with that of Meade, now commanded by Sykes, came up in the morning. Sedgwick's did not reach the ground till afternoon, after a fatiguing march of thirty-five miles.

When the Federal army was finally posted, Slocum was on the extreme right, on Culp's Hill, the barb of the fish-hook; next was the remnant of Wadsworth's division, Howard's corps, on Cemetery Hill; then, along the stem of the hook, the corps of Hancock and Sickles, with Sykes's and Sedgwick's on the extreme left, behind the rocky rampart of the Round Tops. Reynolds's corps, to the command of which Newton had now been appointed, was in reserve behind the centre of the whole line, which was three miles in extent, measured along the ridge; but, owing to its curving form, no part of it was an hour's march from any other. As the line was intended by Meade, two thirds of the entire force could in half an hour have been concentrated upon any point; but by a misapprehension, arising from the nature of the ground, Sickles took a position considerably in advance, and upon this movement hinged the battle of the day. The bulk of the Confederate force was drawn up upon the opposite Seminary Ridge, Longstreet's corps on the right, then Hill's in the centre, that of Ewell on the extreme left, being at the foot of Culp's Hill. This line, forming an exterior curve, was fully five miles long, there being, however, an interval of a mile between Ewell's right and Hill's left. The forces were about equal, each numbering from 70,000 to 80,000 infantry and artillery.[1] The Federal po-

the first day. I know that we almost annihilated one or two brigades that came against us." (Com. Rep., ii., 415.)—More than 2000 prisoners are claimed to have been taken from the Confederates.

[1] Meade (in Com. Rep., ii., 337) says: "Including all arms of the service, my strength was

MEADE'S HEADQUARTERS, CEMETERY RIDGE.   LEE'S HEADQUARTERS, SEMINARY RIDGE.

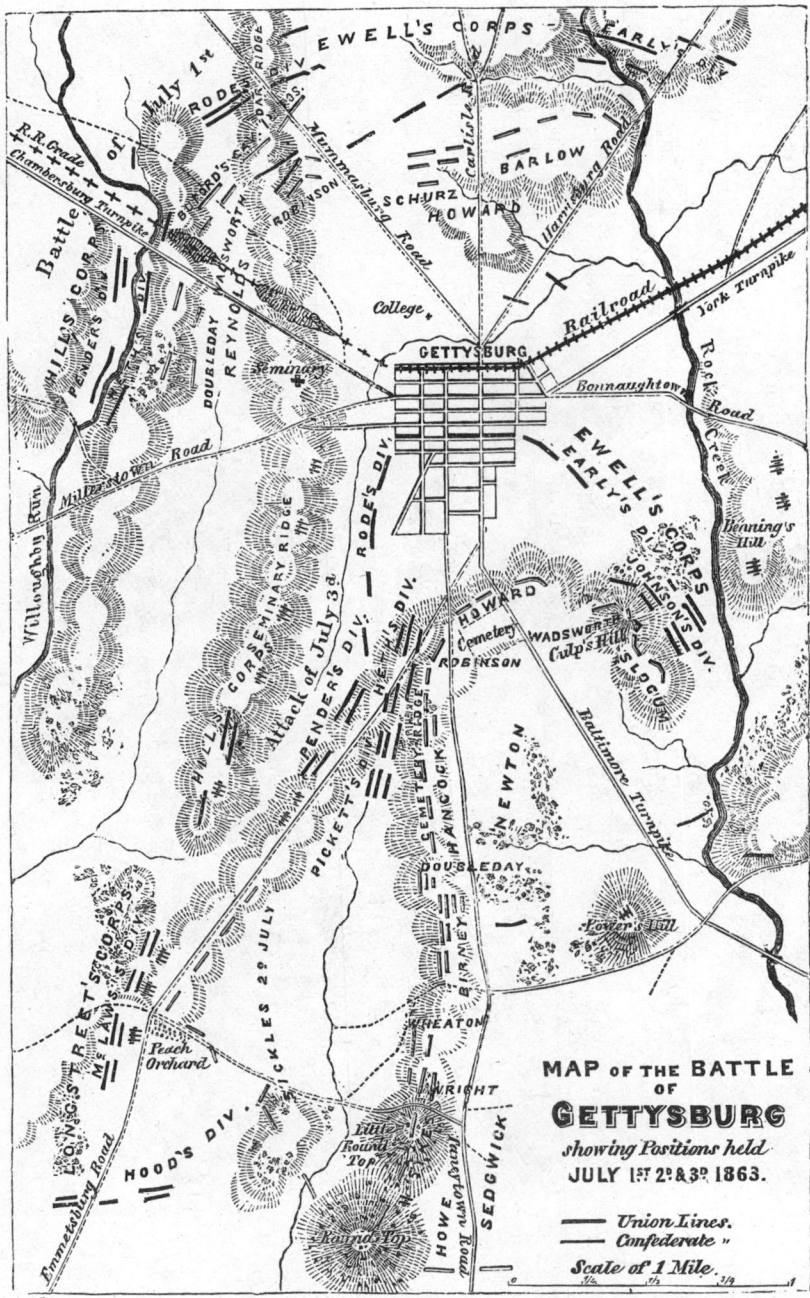

MAP OF THE BATTLE
OF
GETTYSBURG
showing Positions held
JULY 1ST 2D & 3D. 1863.

—— Union Lines.
—— Confederate "
Scale of 1 Mile.

a "demonstration on the right, to be converted into a real attack should opportunity offer."[1] The points of attack were fully five miles apart.

Meade had intended, and s > ordered, that his line should occupy the ridge directly between Cemetery Hill and Round Top; and from the point where he was, the course of this ridge was plain enough; but this crest, at its centre, where Sickles was to take position, is low, and, sinking down into a valley in front, rises at a few hundred yards into another wooded ridge, running diagonally to the one in its rear. To Sickles this seemed the position contemplated in the order, so he marched out upon it. This movement left a wide gap between him and Hancock, who was to have connected with his right. But he was also to rest his left upon Round Top. Now, as the course of this ridge is such that its extremity is a mile in advance of this hill, Sickles could only fulfill this condition by bending his left back, so that his line described two sides of a triangle. Birney's division formed the left, facing southwestward; Humphreys's division the right, facing northwestward. The Confederate right overlapped the Union left, and, swinging round to attack, completely enveloped it. At four o'clock, Meade, coming to the front, saw the perilous position in which Sickles had placed his corps, and commenced an order to withdraw, but before the sentence was completed the Confederates opened the attack, and it was thought that it was too late for any change of position. Meade determined to support Sickles, even at the hazard of disarranging all his carefully-formed plans. Troops were hurried up from every part of the field: from Slocum on the extreme right, Hancock in the centre, Sykes on the left; Sedgwick, whose corps, wearied by their long march of twenty hours, had been halted in the rear. Hood, in the mean time, had swung round his overlapping right, and penetrated the interval which separated Birney's extreme left from Little Round Top. This steep, rocky ridge, strangely enough, was not occupied. It was the key to the whole position; for, if the enemy could gain it, they could hold it, and a few guns planted there would enfilade the whole line[2] as far as Cemetery Hill. It was to Gettysburg what Hazle Grove was to Chancellorsville. They commenced scaling its rugged sides, for a time meeting no opposition except from its steep ascent. But it so happened that Warren, who, with no troops, had gone out as engineer to survey the field, reached the summit just in time to take in the peril of the situation. Hurrying back, he encountered Barnes's division of Sykes's corps marching out to the aid of Sickles. From this, Vincent's brigade and a single regiment of Ayres's were directed to scale the ridge on the side opposite to that up which the Confederates were climbing. The crest was reached from each side almost at once, the Federals a moment in advance. A fierce hand-to-hand fight ensued among the gray granite boulders piled up in wild confusion. The Confederates were flung back from the face of the hill, but, working around through the ravine at its base, some of them penetrated between the two Round Tops. Vincent's ammunition was exhausted, but the enemy were driven back by a bayonet charge, and, as darkness began to close in, this vital point was safe. Regiments from the Eastern, the Western, and the Central States were among the little band who, on this barren cliff, rendered possible the victory which was finally to crown the heights of Gettysburg.[3]

---

[1] Lee's Rep.

[2] "The enemy threw immense masses upon General Sickles's corps, which, advanced and isolated in this way, it was not in my power to support promptly. At the same time that they threw these immense masses upon General Sickles, a heavy column was thrown upon the Round Top Mountain, which was the key-point of my whole position. If they had succeeded in occupying that, it would have prevented me from holding any of the ground which I subsequently held to the last. Immediately upon the batteries opening I sent several staff officers to hurry up the column under General Sykes, of the Fifth Corps, then on its way, and which I had expected would have been there by that time. This column advanced, reached the ground in a short time, and fortunately General Sickles was enabled, by throwing a strong force upon Round Top Mountain, where a most desperate and bloody struggle ensued, to drive the enemy from it, and secure our foothold upon that important position." (Meade, in Com. Rep., 332.)—"I went to what is called Bald Top, and from that point I could see the enemy's line of battle. I sent word to General Meade that we would at once have to occupy that place very strongly. He sent, as quickly as possible, a division of General Sykes's corps; but, before they arrived, the enemy's line of battle, I should think a mile and a half long, began to advance. The troops under General Sykes arrived barely in time to save Round Top Hill, and they had a very desperate fight to hold it."—Warren, Ibid., 377.) See also Crawford, Ibid., 470.

[3] The regiments which repelled the attack here were the 16th Michigan, the 44th and 140th New York, the 33d Pennsylvania, and the 20th Maine. Vincent was mortally wounded. Early next morning Meade telegraphed to Halleck: "I would respectfully request that Colonel Strong Vincent, 33d Pennsylvania Regiment, be made a brigadier general of volunteers for his gallant conduct on the field yesterday. He is mortally wounded, and it would gratify his friends as well as myself. It was my intention to have recommended him with others, should he live." The Secretary of War replied: "According to your request, Colonel Vincent has been appointed brigadier general for gallant conduct on the field."—Com. Rep., ii., 492.

---

sition was very strong, its chief disadvantage being that a great portion of it was so broken and rocky as to allow not more than a third of the artillery to be brought into position. But this was counterbalanced by the advantage which it gave for infantry.

It was evident that Lee could not, for any time, retain his present position. He was far from his base of supply, and the country around would not long subsist his great army, even could he forage at will, as he had done in the fertile valley of the Cumberland; and, moreover, his foraging parties would be likely to be cut off in the mountain passes.[1] He was then shut up to a choice of one of three things. He must attack the enemy in their strong position, or he must draw them from it by continuing his march, and threatening Washington and Baltimore, or he must retreat to Virginia. The third course would be a complete abandonment of the enterprise which had been so deliberately undertaken; the second was strongly urged by Hood, but it would only be prolonging the suspense, for an action must soon take place somewhere, and the enemy would, beyond all doubt, become stronger every day.[2] He decided upon the first. The controlling reason is doubtless to be found in the temper of his army. They had won a series of great victories; among these they even counted Antietam. At Fredericksburg, with but a fraction of their available force, they had beaten Burnside, though here they had position in their favor. At Chancellorsville, with two thirds of their present numbers, they had foiled and driven off Hooker, whose force was known to be much larger than that now led by Meade. There they had successfully attacked the enemy in his intrenchments; why should they not do so now with equal success? Besides, it would seem that Lee, not without reason, greatly under-estimated the numbers in his front. The force which he had driven back the day before was certainly small, and there was nothing to indicate the great army which had been concentrated during the night, and now lay hidden behind that rocky crest.[3] So Longstreet was ordered to assail the extreme Federal left, while Ewell at the same time to make

---

about 95,000." This I understand to be the entire force at the commencement of operations; but the losses on the previous day reduced this number by 10,000; the cavalry numbered about 10,000, but these took no part in the action of this day. Longstreet (see ante, p. 502) states that when the three Confederate corps were concentrated at Chambersburg, "the morning reports showed 67,000 bayonets," equivalent to about 75,000 officers and men; they had lost on the previous day not far from 5000. The Confederate artillery formed a separate corps, probably 5000 strong. I am not certain whether these are to be included in the 67,000 "bayonets." If they are not, then Lee's infantry and artillery would number about 75,000. Some thousands on each side were left behind with the trains. Thus, of the Confederates, Pickett's division was in the rear, and was not brought upon the field until the next day.   [1] Lee's Rep.

[2] "The enemy are here," said Lee to Hood, "and if we do not whip him he will whip us." Longstreet was opposed to making an attack this day; he wished to wait until Pickett's division should come up. "He did not want to walk with one boot off."—These facts were narrated after the close of the war by General Hood to General Crawford, from whom I receive them.

[3] We infer that Lee under-estimated the force of Meade, not only from the fact that he nowhere speaks of the "superior numbers of the enemy," but also from the nature of the attacks which he made on this and the following day.

BREASTWORK IN THE WOODS.

BATTLE OF GETTYSBURG —

UNION POSITION NEAR THE CENTRE —

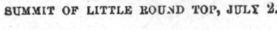

SUMMIT OF LITTLE ROUND TOP, JULY 2.

BATTLE OF GETTYSBURG, JULY 2.

Longstreet, with the remainder of Hood's division, soon joined by that of McLaws, was pressing fiercely upon Birney's division.[1] Sickles was borne from the field with his right leg shattered. Hood was also wounded, losing an arm. Birney's line was so thin that when the enemy attacked any point he was forced to draw regiments thither from other places. Caldwell and Ayres, of Sykes's corps, were sent to his support. They held the ground stubbornly, but were forced back, and their retreat soon became almost a rout.[2] Crawford, with the Pennsylvania Reserves, was now coming up. He ordered a charge with his whole division, himself leading. The color-bearer of his leading regiment had been shot down; Crawford leaned from his horse, snatched the flag, and, waving it over his head, shouting "Forward, Reserves!" dashed down the slope, and met the enemy's skirmishers advancing through the open wheat-field. They recoiled, and then fled back to their line of battle, posted behind a stone wall. Here they made a brief stand, but were driven back, with heavy loss, to a ridge in their rear. Crawford, having advanced without supports, halted, and took position behind the stone wall, the enemy holding the ridge in front and the woods on his left. It was now dusk, and the action closed upon the extreme left.

For a time Humphreys, whose division had formed Sickles's extreme right, had hardly been molested, but in front of him lay Hill's whole corps, ready to be launched upon him at any moment. When Birney found that he could no longer hold his ground, he ordered Humphreys to change front, so as to join with him upon a new line, or rather upon that from which the corps had originally advanced. Just then the enemy, who had opened a sharp artillery fire, pressed down upon his front and both flanks. Humphreys fell back deliberately, although suffering fearfully. In a few minutes he lost 2000 out of his 5000 men. By the time he reached the crest of the Cemetery Ridge the enemy were close upon him. Birney's broken force streamed beyond the crest. But the line had now been formed, patched up, indeed, by brigades from almost every corps. Some of these, as well as Birney's, had been fearfully cut up. The Confederates surged up against this line, but were encountered with a fire so fierce that they halted, then recoiled. Hancock now ordered a counter-charge. Humphreys's men, who had never broken, turned and joined in the charge. The enemy had exhausted the impulse of their onset, and were driven back to the position where they had fallen upon Sickles.

Ewell's demonstration on the right was delayed until the fight on the left was drawing to a close. Most of Slocum's corps had been brought away from Culp's Hill, and the Confederates succeeded in effecting a lodgment within the exterior intrenchments of the extreme Union right. Elsewhere the assault was repelled.

The Federal losses on this day were fully 10,000 men, of which three fifths fell upon Sickles's corps, which lost fully half its numbers.[3] The Confederate loss could not have been less, and was probably somewhat greater. The action of this day had decided nothing as to the ultimate issue. Lee indeed held the advanced line from which Sickles had been driven, but it was a line which Meade had never intended to occupy, and from which he would gladly have receded without a fight. Ewell's foothold upon the left had no significance unless it could be extended. Cemetery Ridge, from Round Top to Culp's Hill, remained intact. Still these "partial successes" encouraged Lee to hope that a stronger assault the next day might prove successful.[4]

FRIDAY, JULY 3.

Lee's general plan of attack was the same as that on the preceding day. Ewell was to press his advantage on the extreme right, while the main assault was to be upon the centre. But at daybreak Meade assumed the offensive against Ewell, and after a sharp contest, which lasted all the morning, drove him from the foothold which he had won within the Federal intrenchments on the extreme right. Now this point was fully two miles from the Seminary, where Lee had taken his post, and wholly hidden from it by the intervening heights. By some strange accident he received no tidings of the mishap which had befallen Ewell, and which, in the result, neutralized that third of the Confederate army on their left, leaving Meade at liberty to use almost his whole force, if need were, at any point. Supposing that Ewell would be able to aid by a strong demonstration, if not by a direct attack, upon the Union right, Lee resolved to assail the left centre, which held the low ridge between Cemetery Hill and Round Top.

All the morning was spent in preparation. The Confederate line along Seminary Ridge afforded an admirable position for artillery. Here, directly in front of the Union centre, at the distance of a mile, were concentrated a hundred and twenty guns. A great part of the Union line was so rugged that artillery could not be brought upon it, so that, although Meade had three hundred guns, he could reply with only about eighty at the same time. At an hour past noon the Confederates opened with all their batteries. For two hours, from a space of less than two miles, there was an incessant cannonade from two hundred guns. Upon no battle-field in the

world's history had such a bombardment been witnessed. The Confederate fire told fearfully upon the Federal guns; many were disabled, but their place, as well as that of those which had expended their ammunition, was supplied by others brought up from the rear. The infantry, sheltered behind the crests, suffered little. The contest was not to be decided by artillery. At length Hunt, the chief of artillery, ordered the fire to be slowly slackened, partly "to see what the enemy were going to do, and also to make sure that there should be a sufficient supply of ammunition to meet the attack,"[1] of which this cannonade was the sure prelude.

It was now three o'clock. Lee, supposing that the Federal batteries had been silenced and the infantry disordered, now slackened his fire, and at the instant his infantry columns emerged from the woods which crown Seminary Hill and advanced down its slope. Pickett's strong division of Longstreet's corps had early that morning come upon the field. They were veteran Virginians, and had not been engaged. To them, supported by Wilcox, was assigned the right of the attacking force; Heth's division, supported by two brigades, had the left.[2] Lee had proposed to advance his artillery to the support of his infantry, but found too late that it had expended its ammunition.[3] In all, the attacking columns numbered about 18,000 men. They marched down the slope and across the plain in compact order and swiftly, but not with the fierce rush and wild yells which were wont to mark the Confederate onset. Never upon any stricken field since when, at Wagram, Massena wedged his column between the Austrian lines, was a more imposing spectacle than that now presented to friend and foe, watching from opposite crests, as this great column pressed on. All the Federal batteries from Round Top to Cemetery Hill opened upon them. Great gaps were plowed in their lines only to be closed again. At first the column headed for the left of the Union centre. Here Doubleday was posted. His division, which had suffered fearfully on the first day, had been strengthened by Stannard's Vermont brigade, and now numbered 2500 men. They were in lines five deep, and well strengthened by hasty intrenchments of rails and stones. The Confederates turned a little to their left, where Hancock's corps lay only two lines deep. In making this movement, Pickett's right wing, bending to his left, exposed his centre to a flank fire from Stannard, which threw it into some confusion,[4] and was the first of the disasters crowded into the space of a few minutes. Still the column pressed on, galled by artillery in front, and obliquely from batteries on Round Top and Cemetery Hill. Hancock's infantry withheld their fire until the enemy were within three hundred yards, and then poured in volley after volley. Pettigrew's division, on the left, first meet this sheet of flame, melted away before it like a snow-bank, and in five minutes were streaming back in wild confusion, leaving, besides their dead, a third of their numbers prisoners. Wilcox, meanwhile, had not advanced, and, Pettigrew being routed, Pickett's division was left alone, but undaunted. Their fierce onset struck first upon Webb's brigade, which, posted behind a low stone wall, occupied Gibbon's front line.[5] They broke this, and charged right among the batteries, where a fierce hand-to-hand struggle took place. The officers on each side fought pistol to pistol, the men with clubbed muskets. Gibbon, as it chanced, was a little to the right, urging the regiments there to follow Pettigrew's routed troops, and was struck down. Webb's brigade fell back from the stone wall over which the assailants were surging, but only to the second line behind the crest. Gibbon had a little before sent Lieutenant Haskell to Meade with tidings that the enemy were upon him. He was returning, and had just reached the brow of the hill, when he met Webb's brigade falling back. Without waiting to find Gibbon, Haskell rode to the left, and ordered the whole division to the right to meet the advancing foe. At that critical moment the virtual command was exercised by this young lieutenant.[6] The troops "came up helter-skelter, every body for himself, their officers among them," the only thought being to throw themselves into the breach. All that mortal men could do to win victory was done by Pickett's veterans in the five or ten immortal minutes which followed the instant when their battle-flags flaunted above the stone wall. Of his three brigade commanders, Garnet lay dead and Armistead fatally wounded within the Union lines, and Kemper was borne off to die; of fifteen field officers but one was unhurt. But all was vain; they were checked in front, and a murderous fire was poured into their flank. To advance, stand, or retreat was impossible; they flung themselves upon the ground with hands uplifted in token of surrender. Of that gallant band not one in four escaped; the others were dead or prisoners.

The few shattered remains of Pickett's and Pettigrew's commands were flying wildly to the rear, pelted by the Federal artillery and by that of the Confederates, who opened fire from all their batteries.[7] Wilcox, who had

---

[1] It must be borne in mind that a "division" in the Confederate army corresponded nearly to a "corps" in the Federal army.

[2] "I heard the cheers of the enemy, and looking in front across a low ground, I saw our men retreating in confusion; fugitives were flying across in every direction; some of them rushed through my lines. The plain in front was covered with the flying men. A wheat-field lay between two masses of wood directly in my front. The enemy in masses were coming across this field, driving every thing before them."—Crawford, in *Com. Rep.*, ii., 470.

[3] On the 10th of June this corps numbered 11,898; on the 4th of July there were but 5766, a loss of 6132. It took no active part in the action of July 3.—*Com. Rep.*, ii., 428.

[4] "In front of General Longstreet the enemy held [that is, on Thursday] a position from which, if he could be driven, it was thought that our army could be used to advantage in assailing the more elevated ground beyond, and thus enable us to reach the crest of the ridge. After a severe struggle Longstreet succeeded in getting possession of and holding the desired ground. Ewell also carried some of the strong positions which he assailed, and the result was such as to lead to the belief that he would ultimately be able to dislodge the enemy. These partial successes determined me to continue the assault the next day."—*Lee's Rep.*

[1] Hunt, in *Com. Rep.*, ii., 451.   [2] Heth's division was now commanded by Pettigrew.

[3] "The enemy's fire slackening, Longstreet ordered forward the column of attack, consisting of Pickett's and Heth's divisions in two lines, Pickett's division on the right; Wilcox's brigade marched in rear of Pickett's right to guard that flank, and Heth's was supported by Lane's and Scale's brigades, under General Trimble. . . . Our batteries, having nearly exhausted their ammunition in the protracted cannonade that preceded the advance of the infantry, were unable to reply, or render the necessary support to the attacking party. This fact was unknown to me when the assault took place."—*Lee's Rep., MS.*

[4] "The prisoners state that what ruined them was Stannard's brigade on their flank, as they found it impossible to contend with them in that position, and they drew off all in a huddle to get away from it."—Doubleday, in *Com. Rep.*, ii., 310.

[5] Hancock in this action took charge of the whole line of battle, leaving Gibbon in command of the Second Corps.

[6] "There was one young man on my staff who has been in every battle with me, and who did more than any other one man to repulse that last assault at Gettysburg, and he did the part of a general there, yet he has been [April, 1864] only a first lieutenant until within a few weeks. I have now succeeded in getting the Governor of Wisconsin to appoint him to a colonelcy, and I have no doubt he will before long come before the Senate for a star."—Gibbon, in *Com. Rep.*, ii., 445.—He never came before the Senate for a star; among the killed at Cold Harbor not two months later we read the name of the gallant Colonel Franklin A. Haskell, 36th Wisconsin.

[7] "As soon as that attack was over, and the enemy saw that their men had given up, they opened their batteries at once, upon their own men and ours at the same time, and after that cannonade they formed another column of attack, which advanced, but more upon our left."—Hunt, in *Com. Rep.*, ii., 451.

not advanced, moved forward as if to renew the assault. But he was checked by a hot artillery fire, and never came within musket-shot of the Union line. To Stannard, who had struck the first sharp blow in this fight, it was reserved to strike the last. He launched two regiments upon the retreating force, and cut off some hundreds from its rear.

Meanwhile Ewell on the Confederate left, and Hood and McLaws upon the right, lay wholly inactive. Hood had been held in check by Kilpatrick's cavalry upon his rear, and by Crawford upon what was now his flank. The cavalry had indeed made a sharp attack upon Hood, which, though disastrous to them, had much to do with the fortune of the day. Farnsworth's brigade leaped a fence and charged up to the very muzzles of a Confederate battery, from which they were repulsed with heavy loss, their commander being among the killed.[1]

After the decisive repulse of the Confederate assault there were yet three hours of daylight. Meade rode to the left of his line and ordered Sykes to advance his corps. Crawford, who had held the position which he had won the night before, pushed a few regiments into the wood in his front. They struck Hood's foremost brigade, which broke and fled, running over another brigade which had thrown up strong intrenchments. These also fled without firing a shot, and Hood's whole division fell back a mile, leaving two or three hundred prisoners and 7000 stand of arms. Many of these had been flung away the previous day by Sickles's corps; these were piled up in heaps in order to be burnt.[2] But before the widely-scattered corps could be concentrated night was approaching, and the order for pursuit was countermanded.

Another scene in the great drama of the war was being enacted twelve hundred miles away. At the very moment when the Confederate column started upon its march to death two guns were fired from the confronting lines at Vicksburg. They were the signal that Grant and Pemberton were approaching to confer upon the terms of surrender for that strong-hold. During that hour in which two armies were struggling upon the heights of Gettysburg, those two men, seated apart in the shade of a great oak, were debating upon the conditions upon which the great Western prize should pass from the hands of those who had so long and stoutly held it into the hands of those who had so long and stoutly sought to win it. At the moment when the fragments of the Southern army streamed back in wild rout from the Northern cliffs, the great river of the West was permitted to run unvexed to the sea. The same shadow on the dial marked the time of the defeat at Gettysburg and the virtual surrender of Vicksburg.

When the Confederate army had, apparently, firmly established itself in Pennsylvania, it was thought that a favorable opportunity was presented to open negotiations with the Federal government. Alexander H. Stephens, the Vice-President, had offered to proceed to Washington as a military commissioner. On this 3d of July he set out, bearing a letter signed by Jefferson Davis as Commander-in-Chief of the Confederate forces, addressed to Abraham Lincoln as Commander-in-Chief of the army and navy of the United States. In case the President should refuse to receive a letter thus addressed, Mr. Stephens was to procure a duplicate of it, addressed to Lincoln as President of the United States, and signed by Davis as President of the Confederacy. Apparently there was no political purpose involved in this mission. Its ostensible object was to enter into stipulations by which the rigors of war might be mitigated; but it can not be doubted that it was undertaken just at this time in the confident persuasion that Lee had met with such success in the invasion of Pennsylvania as would dispose the Federal government to consent to negotiations of wider scope. But, while Stephens was awaiting permission to pass the Union lines, tidings came of the great victories at Gettysburg and Vicksburg, and the government refused to receive the commissioner, declaring that "the customary agents and channels are adequate for all needed communications and conference between the United States forces and the insurgents."

When Lee saw the remnants of Pickett and Pettigrew rushing back from their fruitless assault, he perceived that all hope of successful offensive operations had vanished. "We can not expect always to win great victories," he said. He could only hope to avoid a total rout. He contracted his lines from the right and left toward the centre, expecting and perhaps hoping to be attacked in turn.

When morning broke it became a matter of grave doubt with Meade what course to pursue. That the enemy had suffered severely was certain, but how severely could not be known. His own losses were great, and were supposed to be greater than they were. The corps commanders made hurried estimates of their remaining force. These summed up only 51,514 infantry.[3] A council of war was held, to which Meade propounded four questions: Shall the army remain at Gettysburg? If we remain, shall we resume the offensive? Shall we move upon him by way of Emmettsburg? If the enemy is retreating, shall we pursue on his direct line of retreat? The decision was to remain.[1] During the day a heavy rain set in, and at nightfall Lee, finding that an attack would not be ventured upon his position, began his retreat to the Potomac. This having been discovered on the morning of the 5th, Sedgwick's corps, which had not been engaged, was dispatched to follow him up and ascertain his whereabouts. After a march of eight miles he found their rear-guard strongly posted in the mountain passes, where a small force could hold him in check for a long time, and thought it unadvisable to pursue upon that road. Meade thereupon decided, on the 6th, to follow Lee by a flank movement, by way of Frederick and Boonesboro, involving a march of eighty miles, to Williamsport, on the Potomac, whither Lee was clearly heading. Lee, having but forty miles to march, reached the river on the 7th. But the stream which he had crossed almost dry-shod a fortnight before had been swollen by the heavy rain, and was unfordable. A bridge which he had flung across had been destroyed by a sudden cavalry dash made by French from Harper's Ferry, and Lee had no alternative but to intrench himself, with his back to the river, and await an attack.

Meade marched slowly, feeling the way with his cavalry, but on the 12th his army came in front of the Confederate lines. He had been strengthened by French with 8000 men from Harper's Ferry; Couch had sent 5000 militia, under W. F. Smith, from Carlisle, and, moreover, considerable numbers were close at hand from Baltimore and elsewhere; but these were nine months' men, just brought from North Carolina and the Peninsula, who had only one or two days more to serve. Meade judged that these would add nothing to the real strength of his army for attack, and left them behind. Still his actual numbers exceeded those of the enemy by quite a half. Meade, although he supposed the enemy to be nearly of his own strength, was disposed to attack at once, but submitted the question to his seven corps commanders. Wadsworth and Howard were in favor of attack, the other five were opposed to it until after farther examination of the position. Meade yielded his opinion, and the next day was spent in reconnoissances. The result was that in the evening an order was issued for an advance of the whole army at daylight. But when morning broke the enemy had disappeared. Lee had succeeded in patching up a bridge, and the river had fallen so that it was barely fordable at a single point. Ewell crossed by the ford, Hill and Longstreet by the bridge. The Confederate army stood once more in Virginia, and the invasion of Pennsylvania, upon which so much had been staked, was at an end.

The Federal loss at Gettysburg was 23,190, of whom 2834 were killed, 13,733 wounded, and 6643 missing. The Confederate loss was about 36,000, of whom 13,733, wounded and unwounded, remained as prisoners. The entire loss to this army during the six weeks from the middle of June, when it set forth from Culpepper to invade the North, to the close of July, when it returned to the starting-point, was about 60,000.[2]

The Confederates were slow to admit the great disaster at Gettysburg. Three weeks after the battle Alexander H. Stephens, in a speech at Charlotte, N. C., declared that "General Lee's army had whipped the enemy on their own soil, and obtained vast supplies for our own men, and was now ready to again meet the enemy on a new field. Whatever might be the movements and objects of General Lee, he had entire confidence in his ability to accomplish what he undertook. He would come out all right in the end. The loss of Vicksburg was not an occurrence to cause discouragement or gloom. It was not as severe a blow as the loss of Fort Pillow, Island No. 10, or New Orleans. The Confederacy had survived the loss of these points, and would survive the loss of Port Hudson and other places. If we were to lose Mobile, Charleston, and Richmond, it would not affect the heart of the Confederacy. After two years' war the enemy had utterly failed, and if the war continued two years longer they would fail. So far they had not broken the shell of the Confederacy."[3]

Meade, having determined "to act on the defensive, and receive the attack of the enemy, if practicable," his dispositions for the battle were to be mainly determined by the movements of the enemy. He must place his force so as to meet the assault, at whatever point it should be made, only, of course, holding the strong points of his position. It is incomprehensible, therefore, why, during all the day of July 2, the Round Tops were left wholly unguarded; for this, as Meade clearly states, was "the key-point of my whole position. If the enemy had succeeded in occupying that, it would

---

[1] "I have always been of the opinion," says Pleasonton (*Com. Rep.*, ii., 360), "that the demonstration of cavalry on our left materially checked the attack of the enemy on the 3d of July, for General Hood was attempting to turn our flank when he met Farnsworth's and Merritt's brigades of cavalry; and the officers reported to me that at least two divisions of infantry and a number of batteries were held back, expecting an attack from us on that flank.—Gregg, also on the right, engaged Stuart's troopers, who had now, after a wide detour, come upon the field in that quarter. In modern warfare, the great results of a campaign, when brought to an issue upon a stricken field, are decided by the shock of infantry and artillery,—the hands of an army; the services of cavalry—its eyes, being mainly preliminary. If, in narrating a great campaign, the historian could detail every striking episode, he would find in this campaign nearly a score of cavalry encounters, any one of which in the earlier stages of the war would have ranked as a battle.

[2] Crawford, in *Com. Rep.*, ii., 471, and private statement.

[3] First Corps, 5000; Second, 5000; Third, 5676; Fifth, 10,000; Sixth, 12,500; Eleventh, 5500; Twelfth, 7838. These corps had marched from the Rappahannock 78,245 strong (Butterfield, in *Com. Rep.*, ii., 428), and had been re-enforced by fully 6000. This would give a loss of fully 33,000, besides that of the cavalry, which had been considerable, Buford's division having been so severely cut up on the first day that it had been sent to Westminster, twenty miles to the rear, to protect the trains and to recruit. (Pleasonton, *Ibid.*, 359.)—This estimated loss was, however, half greater than it actually proved to be. "This," says Butterfield (*Ibid.*, 427), "is always the case after a battle. A great many commanders come in and say that half their force is gone; the colonel reports that half his regiment is gone; that is reported to the brigade commander, who reports that half his brigade is gone, and so on."

[1] Birney, Sedgwick, Sykes, Hays, and Warren were for remaining for a day, and await the development of the enemy's plans; Slocum and Pleasonton were for a direct pursuit of the enemy, if he were retreating; Newton would move by way of Emmettsburg; Howard was doubtful.—See Butterfield, in *Com. Rep.*, ii., 427; Birney, *Ibid.*, 368.

[2] The statement of the Union loss and of the number of Confederate prisoners is unquestionable, being given in Meade's official report. Of the Confederate losses no reports were published, and probably none were ever rendered; for Lee, in his report, says that he is not able to give them. Recourse must therefore be had to collateral evidence. The only point absolutely fixed is the report of numbers on July 31 (*ante*, p. 383), which shows that on July 31 there were "present for duty 41,000 men." If we accept Pollard's statement that this army set out 90,000 strong, the loss would be nearly 49,000. If our estimate of 100,000 as the original strength be accepted, the loss will be 60,000. This includes not only the losses at Gettysburg, but those incurred by casualty and wastage in the march from Culpepper to Gettysburg and back, which must have amounted to many thousands. Lee especially notes that the cavalry suffered severely from toil and privation. Farther, if we accept the estimate of the forces actually present at Gettysburg, based upon Longstreet's statement (*ante*, p. 502), at 80,000, the losses of all kinds from July 1 to 31 would be 39,000, including those incurred from wastage and skirmishes on the way back from the Potomac to the Rappahannock; allowing 3000 for these, there remain 36,000 for Gettysburg and the days immediately following. Of this 14,000 prisoners, we judge from various indicia that 8000 were unwounded—1500 captured on the field on the 1st of July, 5000 on the 2d, and 1500 in the pursuit. This leaves 28,000 for killed and wounded. Apportioning these in the same ratio as in the Union loss, there will be about 5000 killed and 23,000 wounded of the Confederate army.

[3] *Richmond Dispatch*, June 25.

GETTYSBURG.

JULY 3, 1863.

have prevented me from holding any of the ground which I subsequently held to the last;" and it was only "fortunately that General Sykes was enabled, by throwing a strong force upon Round Top Mountain, where a most desperate and bloody struggle ensued, to drive the enemy from it, and secure our foothold upon that important position."[1] It was, indeed, a fortunate accident that a division of Sykes's corps, who were marching in quite a different direction, happened to be near enough to reach the summit of Round Top as the enemy were on the point of gaining it. "They arrived barely in time to save it, and they had a very desperate fight to hold it."[2] Again, if the advanced position taken by Sickles was as disadvantageous as it seemed to Meade, one may wonder why he was not withdrawn. The enemy were indeed advancing to the attack, but there was as yet some space between, and it would seem to have been easier to withdraw from an untenable position than to be driven from it.[3] It is not easy to comprehend why Sedgwick's corps, stronger by half than any other one in the army, took no active part in the action of either day,[4] or, at least, was not held in such a position that, when the enemy broke and fled at the close of the action, it could have been launched in pursuit,[5] for there was yet three hours of daylight.

But, granting that it was not advisable to pursue and assail the enemy in the position of unknown strength which he occupied on the evening of the 3d, there can be little hesitancy in condemning Meade's failure to follow when it had been ascertained that Lee was in full retreat toward the Potomac. To make a wide detour with the expectation of striking him on the flank was equivalent to declining a battle; for Lee had so far the start that he reached the river at the same time that Meade began his flank march of eighty miles. He would have crossed at once, had he been able; but the stream, swollen by rains, was not fordable, and his only bridge had been destroyed. The Confederate army was in bad plight, and looked eagerly for the falling of the waters.[6] When, upon the 12th, Meade came up with the enemy, he had every chance in his favor. He was in superior force; his army was in excellent condition and in high spirits; the enemy could not be other than wearied and disheartened. If the attack was unsuccessful, it could amount to no more than a check, for he could fall back to the South Mountain, where he would be unassailable; but if the assault was successful, the Confederates would be ruined, for they had at their back a swollen river, which they had no means of crossing. Meade was minded to fight; he had come for that purpose; but, unfortunately, he submitted the question to a council of war. He had been hardly a fortnight in command, and would not assume the responsibility of acting in opposition to the views of his corps commanders, so he yielded his opinion to theirs;[7] unwisely as it seems to us, wisely as he was himself afterward convinced.[8] When, after spending a day or two in reconnoitring, he ordered the attack to be made at daybreak on the 14th, he was too late. The enemy had crossed, and the swollen Potomac lay between. "The fruit was so ripe, so ready for plucking," said Lincoln, "that it was very hard to lose it." The President, indeed, expressed himself in terms of censure so sharp that Meade asked to be relieved from the command of the army.[9] The request was refused.

[1] Meade, in *Com. Rep.*, ii., 332.

[2] Warren, in *Com. Rep.*, ii., 377. See also Crawford, *Ibid.*, 469

[3] Sickles indeed affirms that the position which he took was a good one. He says (*Com. Rep.*, ii., 298): "I took up that line, because it enabled me to hold commanding ground, which, if the enemy had been allowed to take—as they would have taken it if I had not occupied it in force—would have rendered our position on the left untenable, and, in my judgment, would have turned the fortunes of the day hopelessly against us." But the enemy did actually take the position held for a time by Sickles at the cost of half his corps, and were only repelled from the very line which Meade had proposed to hold.

[4] "My corps did not take any important part in the battle of Gettysburg. It was frequently sent to different parts of the field to re-enforce and support other troops that were more vigorously engaged."—Sedgwick, in *Com. Rep.*, ii., 460.

[5] "I think that our lines should have advanced immediately, and I believe that we should have won a great victory. I was very confident that the attack would be made. General Meade told me before the fight that, if the enemy attacked me, he intended to put the Fifth and Sixth Corps on the enemy's flank. I therefore, when I was wounded, and lying down in my ambulance, and about leaving the field, dictated a note to General Meade, and told him if he would put in the Fifth and Sixth Corps, I believed he would win a great victory. I asked him afterward, when I returned to the army, what he had done in the premises. He said he had ordered the movement, but the troops were slow in collecting, and moved so slowly that nothing was done before night, except that some of the Pennsylvania Reserves went out and met Hood's division, and actually overthrew it. There were only two divisions of the enemy on our extreme left, opposite Round Top, and there was a gap of one mile that their assault had left; and I believe that if our whole line had advanced with spirit, it is not unlikely that we should have taken all their artillery at that point. I think that we should have pushed the enemy there, for we do not often catch them in that position; and the rule is, and it is natural, that when you defeat and repulse an enemy, you should pursue him."—Hancock, in *Com. Rep.*, ii., 408.

[6] "The Potomac was found to be so much swollen by the recent rains as to be unfordable. Our communications with the south side were thus interrupted, and it was difficult to procure either ammunition or subsistence. The enemy had not yet made his appearance, but, as he was in condition to obtain large re-enforcements, and our situation, for the reasons above mentioned, was becoming daily more embarrassing, it was deemed advisable to recross the river. Part of the pontoon bridge was recovered, and new boats built. Our preparations being completed, and the river, though still deep, being pronounced fordable, the army commenced to withdraw to the south side on the night of the 13th."—*Lee's Rep.*

[7] The objections of the council were not to fighting, but to attacking them. "We all," says Pleasonton (*Com Rep.*, ii., 361), "wanted to fight There was one general, General French, I think, who remarked, after General Meade declared that he would not order an attack against the vote of the council, 'Why, it does not make any difference what our opinions are. If you give the order to attack, we will fight just as well under it as if our opinions were not against it.'"

[8] Testimony, in *Com. Rep.*, ii., 336.

[9] Halleck to Meade, July 14: "I need hardly say to you that the escape of Lee's army without another battle has created great dissatisfaction in the mind of the President, and it will require an active and energetic pursuit on your part to remove the impression that it has not been sufficiently active heretofore." Meade to Halleck: "Having performed my duty conscientiously and to the best of my ability, the censure of the President is in my judgment so undeserved that I feel compelled most respectfully to ask to be immediately relieved from the command of this army." Halleck to Meade: "My telegram stating the disappointment of the President at the escape of Lee's army was not intended as a censure, but as a stimulus to an active pursuit. It is not deemed a sufficient cause for your application to be relieved."

The operations of Lee at Gettysburg can be justified, or even explained, only upon the supposition that he was wholly deceived as to the strength of the enemy in his front. He had, indeed, very good reasons to suppose himself to be in greatly superior force. On Wednesday, when he had won a decided advantage, he had clearly two to one on the field. On Thursday morning he was, after his losses, stronger by more than half, and there was nothing in the operations of that day to evince that the Federals had been greatly strengthened. He had, indeed, gained important apparent advantages at two points. Ewell had effected a lodgment within the intrenchments on the Union right. On their left, the Federals had been driven back from what seemed to be a strong part of their chosen line; and though the attack had been finally repelled, still the ground contended for had been won, and was held. Owing to two accidents—the temporary withdrawal of Slocum's corps on the right, and the advance of Sickles on the left beyond the main lines—the Confederates had seen only a force inferior to their own, and it was reasonable to infer that this formed all which could have been brought into action by the enemy. On Friday, every thing, up to the moment of the final charge, confirmed this impression. Lee was ignorant that by noon Ewell had been driven out of the intrenchments which he had won the night before. The fierce cannonade, which was opened an hour after noon, was replied to by little more than half the number of guns, and of these the fire was slackened in such a way as to indicate that the Union batteries were effectually silenced. To suppose that Lee assailed the heights of Gettysburg knowing, or imagining that they were held by an army fully equal in numbers to his own, is to attribute to him a degree of rashness which is belied by his whole military career.

Lee's attack on the last day has been subjected to grave censure. If it was made with a knowledge of the numbers opposed to him, it was wholly indefensible. But it must be judged in the light of what he knew at the time. He was under no necessity of giving or even of receiving battle. The main object of the invasion had indeed failed. There was no chance that he could seize Baltimore or Philadelphia; none, indeed, that he could hold his position in Pennsylvania. But the way of return to Virginia was open to him. He was in a position where a battle which should be less than a victory so great as to involve the destruction of the army opposed to him would have been useless, while a defeat could hardly be other than ruinous. Having decided to attack, the assault should have been made with his whole force. After all his losses he had certainly 60,000 men; his plan of attack involved the use of hardly half of these, including Ewell's proposed demonstration. The main assault was committed to only 18,000.[1] What, asked Longstreet, would have been the result if the assault had been made by 30,000 men instead of 15,000? There can be no doubt that if this attack was to be made, it should have been made by twice the force. Yet, in the light of what we now know, it was well that this was not done. If twice as many men had been sent in they must have equally failed, and with twice the loss. The Confederates only just succeeded in touching the Union line of defense, and from this they were repelled in utter rout by less than a fifth of the force which could have been brought there in another twenty minutes. Only two divisions of Hancock's corps, with a single other brigade, were really engaged.[2] The other division of that corps, together with the corps of Howard, Reynolds, and Sickles, which had been badly cut up during the two previous days, were at hand; Slocum's corps had cleared itself from Ewell at Culp's Hill, on the right, and could have been brought into action on the left; moreover, there was Sedgwick's whole corps, which had not yet even touched the fight. Meade, while holding his right and left, could easily, if need were, have brought 50,000 men to the defense of his centre. What with his artillery, which swept the approach, it is safe to say that no 50,000 or 80,000 men, if they could have been hurled at once upon the Cemetery Ridge, could ever have carried it. "The conduct of the troops," says Lee, "was all that I could desire or expect, and they deserved success so far as it can be deserved by heroic valor and fortitude. More may have been required of them than they were able to perform, but my admiration of their noble qualities, and confidence in their ability to cope successfully with the enemy, has suffered no abatement from the issue of this protracted and sanguinary conflict." This task, "more than they were able to perform," was imposed upon his votaries by Lee. Upon him, therefore, must rest the blame for the failure to execute it.

[1] It is indeed said that McLaws and Hood, with some 15,000 more, were to have taken part, and that Lee was bitterly indignant at the "slow-footed McLaws" for not coming up. But there is in his report no indication that such was any part of his plan. The wording of it, indeed, seems to exclude any such purpose, and implies that the carrying of Cemetery Heights was intrusted to Pickett and Pettigrew.

[2] "The shock of the assault fell upon the second and third divisions of the Second Corps, and these were the troops, together with the artillery of our line, which fired from Round Top to Cemetery Hill at the enemy as they advanced, whenever they had the opportunity. Those were the troops that really met the assault. No doubt there were other troops that fired a little, but these were the troops that really withstood the shock of the assault and repulsed it. The attack of the enemy was met by about six small brigades of our troops, and was finally repulsed after a very terrific contest at very close quarters."—Hancock, in *Com. Rep.*, ii., 408.

IN CAMP.

CHAPTER XXX.

MEADE'S CAMPAIGN IN VIRGINIA.

The Armies.—Meade's Advance into Virginia.—Lee's Retreat.—The Armies on the Rappahannock.—Both Armies reduced.—Cessation of Operations.—Appeals of Davis and Lee.—Lee advances and Meade retreats.—Fight at Bristoe.—Meade falls back to Centreville.—Lee returns to the Rappahannock.—Meade slowly follows.—Stuart in Peril.—Imboden's Dash upon Charlestown.—Cavalry Fight near Warrenton.—Meade proposes to go to Fredericksburg.—Capture of Rappahannock Station.—The Mine Run Attempt.—Butler's Movement toward Richmond.—Kilpatrick and Dahlgren's Raid.—The Army in Winter-quarters.

IN a year and a week, from the beginning of the Seven Days before Richmond to the close of the battle at Gettysburg, the Union Army of the Potomac and the Confederate Army of Northern Virginia had encountered in six desperate struggles, each lasting for days. In four—on the Peninsula, at Groveton, Fredericksburg, and Chancellorsville—the Confederates won the honors and advantages of victory; in two—at Antietam and Gettysburg—they had been defeated. Besides these great conflicts, there had been many minor engagements. The losses upon each side had been singularly alike. In killed, wounded, and prisoners, each had lost about 110,000. If to these are added the scores of thousands who died from disease in pestilential camps, and upon the long and weary marches, each army lost more than its muster-rolls embraced when at the fullest.[1] During nine months they were to confront each other, neither striking or hardly attempting a blow; and then to enter upon that terrible campaign of eleven months, which resulted in the annihilation of the Confederate army, and the overthrow of the cause which it had so long and valiantly upheld. Of that nine months' indecisive campaign in Virginia I am now to write.

When Lee, after Gettysburg, had succeeded in making good his escape

[1] In the following table an attempt is made to give as nearly as possible in round numbers the losses in the two armies during the period of a year and a week, commencing with the battle of Mechanicsville, June 26, 1862, and ending with that of Gettysburg, July 3, 1863. The number of killed and wounded can be very closely ascertained. The errors in one case will be about balanced by contrary ones in another. The number of prisoners is much less certain. Very many prisoners claimed on both sides were also wounded, and entered on the lists as such. I have endeavored to distinguish between the wounded and unwounded prisoners, giving as "prisoners" only those not left wounded on the field. In the list of prisoners taken by the Confederates I have not included the 11,000 captured by Jackson at Harper's Ferry, for they were paroled at once, and were never actually in the hands of the enemy. I have, however, included the 2500 captured from Milroy at Winchester, for they were actually held. The "prisoners" column is therefore to be taken merely as a rough estimate. Only the losses in the great actions have been given. Some thousands besides these fell or were captured in minor engagements, bringing the numbers fully up to those given in the text. Of the losses from disease no even approximate estimate can be formed. Fifty thousand upon each side would certainly be a moderate estimate.

Battles.	UNION.		CONFEDERATE.	
	Killed and Wounded.	Prisoners.	Killed and Wounded.	Prisoners.
The Seven Days on the Peninsula..	10,000	5,000	18,000	1,000
Pope's Campaign	14,000	7,000	11,000	1,000
Antietam, etc.	14,000	1,000	12,000	5,000
Fredericksburg	10,000	1,000	4,500	500
Chancellorsville	12,000	5,000	10,000	2,500
Gettysburg	16,500	5,000	28,000	8,000
Total	76,500	25,000	83,500	18,000

across the Potomac, he took up the same position which he had, after Antietam, assumed ten months before.[1] To Meade was presented the same question which had been offered to McClellan after Antietam. In what manner should he, with his superior force, assail the enemy? The decision was promptly made. It was the same to which McClellan came after long hesitation and delay. Instead of following directly upon Lee's rear, on the west side of the Blue Ridge, he would threaten his flank and menace his communications by advancing along the east side of this mountain chain. This decision was based upon the admitted impossibility of supplying his great army by the single line of railroad which traversed the Valley of the Shenandoah. Lee would be compelled, as he had before been compelled, to retreat up the valley. Meade moreover hoped, having the shorter line, to be able to throw a heavy column through some gap of the Blue Ridge, and assail the flank of Lee's long line as it passed in its retreat.[2] On the 17th and 18th the Potomac was crossed, and the army commenced its march. Some slight changes were made in the commands. Butterfield had been hurt at Gettysburg, and Humphreys was appointed chief of staff, a position which Meade had urged upon him when he took command. Sickles and Hancock had been severely wounded. French's division, from Harper's Ferry, had been added to Sickles's corps, which had suffered so terribly, and French was put at its head. Warren, who had long been chief engineer of the army, was a little after placed in command of Hancock's corps.

As soon as he discovered the Federal advance, Lee broke up his camps near Winchester, and commenced a rapid retreat up the Valley of the Shenandoah, hoping to pass from it into the Valley of the Rappahannock, and so reach the railroad leading to Richmond in advance of Meade. Thus the two armies were moving rapidly in parallel lines, but with the Blue Ridge between, shutting each from all information as to the movements and positions of the other, except such as could be gained by scouts posted at some commanding point of observation.

On the 22d, when the Union army had reached Manassas Gap, Meade learned that the enemy were marching right opposite to him. This seemed the desired opportunity to throw a column through the gap, and fall upon the centre of his line. French pushed his corps through, meeting with slight opposition, and next morning saw the Confederates drawn up at

[1] Lee seems to have had in mind some offensive operation when he crossed the Potomac. In his report he says: "Owing to the swollen condition of the Shenandoah River, the plan of operations which had been contemplated when we recrossed the Potomac could not be put in execution, and before the waters had subsided the movements of the enemy induced me to cross the Blue Ridge, and take position south of the Rappahannock."—We can only conjecture that this contemplated plan was to march down the south side of the Potomac, and strike a blow at Washington. If this was the plan, it must have been based on the supposition that Meade would loiter upon the north bank of the Potomac, as McClellan had done after Antietam.

[2] "It was impracticable to pursue the enemy in the Valley of Virginia, because of the difficulty of supplying an army in that valley with a single-track railroad in very bad order. I therefore determined to adopt the same plan of movement as that adopted the preceding year, which was to move upon the enemy's flank through Loudon Valley."—Meade, in Com. Rep., ii., 339.

ANDREW A. HUMPHREYS.

Front Royal in what seemed to be a strong line of battle. Meade now made dispositions for a fight the next day, for he believed that he had interrupted Lee's retreat, and that he would be compelled to fight in order to secure his trains. But when morning dawned the enemy had vanished. The seeming strong line of battle was but a rear-guard; the main army had been all the time swiftly marching by roads farther to the west. Lee, having thus eluded the threatened attack, pressed on, passed through a lower gap out of the Valley of the Shenandoah into that of the Rappahannock, and at length halted at Culpepper, the goal of the retreat, the point where he had six weeks before reviewed the great army with which he had set out for the invasion of the North. Meade, having missed his blow, withdrew his forces from the Manassas Gap, and marched leisurely on toward the Rappahannock.[1]

On the last day of July the Confederate Army of Northern Virginia numbered only 41,000 men "present for duty." Besides these there were 12,500 "present," a few more than the wounded whom they had brought away from Gettysburg. Through all the week during which Lee had been detained by the swollen Potomac, he had been sending his wounded across in boats, so that he had gained a full fortnight in which to transport them to Culpepper and beyond without molestation. The Union army could not have numbered less than 75,000, probably more. Meade knew that he was greatly superior, how greatly he most likely did not suspect. He wisely resolved to advance upon Lee, but unwisely consulted the authorities at Washington. The movement was forbidden. He might only "take up a threatening attitude upon the Rappahannock."[2] What any attitude upon the Rappahannock which did not involve the passage of that stream could threaten, is hard to see. Certainly not the Confederate army which lay beyond; not its communications or sources of supply; not Richmond, or any one of its connections with any part of the Confederacy.

Lee's army was strengthened from day to day. On the 31st of August it numbered 56,000 present for duty. This increase was the first, and, indeed, the only fruit of Jefferson Davis's earnest appeal, issued on the 15th of July, to those "now absent from the army without leave," in which he promised amnesty and pardon to all who should "with the least possible delay return to their posts of duty;" but this period of grace was limited to twenty days.[3] Meade's army was in the mean while considerably dimin-

ished. A division was sent to South Carolina to aid in the siege of Charleston. The draft riots in New York, which broke out the very day upon which Lee recrossed the Potomac, had indeed been suppressed, but the opposition to the draft was still so strenuous that military aid was deemed necessary to enforce it, and a large body of troops were taken from the Army of the Potomac and sent to New York for that purpose. During the first days of September Lee's force was fully equal to that of Meade. But, in the mean time, Bragg, in Tennessee, was hardly pressed by Rosecrans, and Longstreet, with his corps, was sent to his aid. Meade was soon aware of this diminution of the force opposed to him, and this time, without waiting for instructions, moved his army across the Rappahannock, and established himself at Culpepper, while Lee fell back beyond the Rapidan, and took a position strong by nature and strongly fortified.

Meade was now in a region of which he knew nothing, and could learn nothing except by sending his cavalry in every direction to reconnoitre. This took time, and he had just decided upon a plan of operations when he was told that his army must be reduced. Things had gone badly at the West. Rosecrans had been defeated at Chickamauga, and Meade must spare a quarter of his army to restore the balance in Tennessee. The corps of Slocum and Howard were chosen. Thereafter these corps ceased to form a part of the Army of the Potomac, and belong to that of the West. The command of these two corps was given to Hooker, who had never lost the confidence of the President and the Secretary of War. He had, indeed,

soldiers to return to their respective regiments at once. To remain at home in this, the hour of our country's need, is unworthy of the manhood of a Southern soldier. . . . . The commanding general appeals to the people of the states to send forth every man able to bear arms to aid the brave soldiers who have so often beaten back our foes."—The following are passages from the address of Jefferson Davis: "You know too well what the enemy mean by success. Their malignant rage aims at nothing less than the extermination of yourselves, your wives, and children. They propose, as the spoils of success, that your homes shall be partitioned among the wretches whose atrocious cruelties have stamped infamy on their government. . . . . No alternative is left you but victory or subjugation, slavery, and the utter ruin of yourselves, your families, and your country. The victory is within your reach. The men now absent from their posts would, if present in the field, suffice to create numerical equality between our force and that of the invader. . . . . I call upon you, then, to hasten to your camps, in obedience to the dictates of honor and of duty, and summon those who have absented themselves without leave to repair without delay to their respective commands; and I do hereby declare that I grant a general pardon and amnesty to all officers and men within the Confederacy, now absent without leave, who shall, with the least possible delay, return to their posts of duty; but no excuse will be received for any delay beyond twenty days after the first publication of this proclamation in any state in which the absentee may be at the date of the publication. This amnesty shall extend to all who have been accused, or who are undergoing sentence for absence without leave or desertion, except only those who have been twice convicted of desertion."

MAP OF CAMPAIGN, JULY—NOVEMBER, 1863.

---

[1] Meade, in *Com. Rep.*, ii., 339.—Lee (*MS. Rep.*) thus describes these operations: "As the Federals continued to advance along the eastern slope of the mountains, apparently with the purpose of cutting us off from the railroad, Longstreet was ordered, on the 19th of July, to proceed to Culpepper Court-house by way of Front Royal. He succeeded in passing part of his command over the Shenandoah in time to prevent the occupation of Manassas and Chester Gaps by the enemy. As soon as a pontoon bridge could be laid down, the rest of his corps crossed, and marched through Chester Gap to Culpepper, where they arrived on the 24th. He was followed by Hill's corps. Ewell reached Front Royal the 23d, and encamped near Madison Court-house on the 29th."

[2] "Upon my arrival at the Rappahannock, which was toward the close of July, I communicated my views to the government, in which I expressed the opinion that the farther pursuit of General Lee should be continued at that time, inasmuch as I believed that our relative forces were more favorable at that time than they would be at any subsequent time, if we gave him time to recuperate. It was thought proper, however, by the general-in-chief to direct me to take up a threatening attitude upon the Rappahannock, but not to advance."—Meade, in *Com. Rep.*, ii., 340.

[3] *July* 26. Lee issued the following General Order to the Army of Northern Virginia: "All officers and soldiers now absent from this army, who are able to do duty, and are not detached on special service, are ordered to return immediately. The commanding general calls upon all

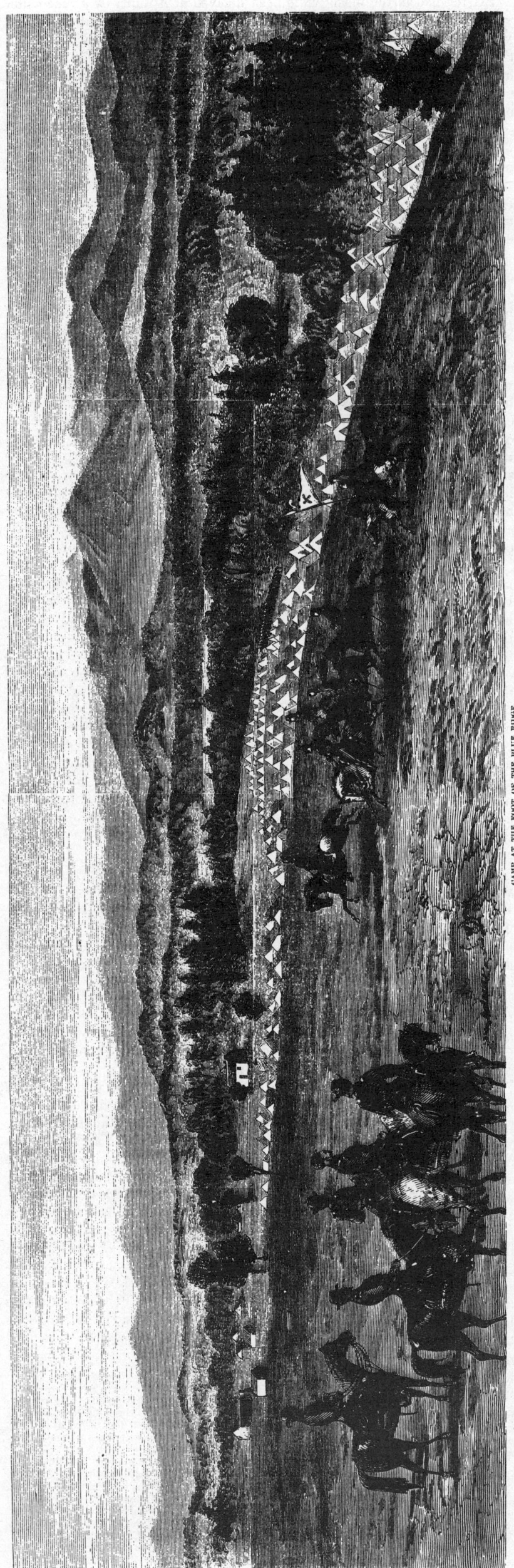

CAMP AT THE FOOT OF THE BLUE RIDGE.

wished to receive the command of a corps under Meade, but one can easily understand that this proposition could not be acceptable to that general.[1] Whatever honor Hooker lost at Chancellorsville was abundantly regained at Lookout Mountain.

The armies in Virginia, thus again brought to an equality, remained inactive until early in October. By that time the troops sent to New York had returned, diminished in number by a third; the draft also furnished some accessions, but of a character which added little real strength. Still, according to his own estimate, Meade had well-nigh 70,000 effective men. The force of the enemy he thought to be considerably less.[2] Now occurred Meade's retreat to Centreville, which, with McClellan's flight to Malvern Hill, Hooker's abandonment of Chancellorsville, and Butler's "bottling up" at Bermuda Hundreds, yet to take place, must stand as the inexplicable incidents of the war.

Early in October there appeared a very evident diminution of the Confederate forces along the Rapidan, while cavalry and some infantry were seen moving toward Meade's right flank. These operations were susceptible of two interpretations. Lee might be falling back still farther, in which case the movements observed on the Union right were simply a demonstration to throw the enemy off the track while the Confederate army was withdrawing; or it might be the purpose of Lee to gain the rear of the Union army, and fall upon its communications, which were kept up mainly by the single line of railroad from Alexandria southward. Meade, coming to the front, was satisfied that the former was the design of his opponent,[3] and made preparations to throw his cavalry and two of his five infantry corps across the Rapidan. But before this was done he became satisfied that the enemy, instead of retreating, was in full advance. He could not believe that with his inferior force Lee would venture to assail him at Culpepper, and therefore the movement must be to turn his right flank and assume a position in his rear which would compel him to attack at disadvantage. He thereupon, on the morning of the 11th, withdrew his whole army across the Rappahannock. Hardly had this been done, when he learned that the Confederate force had actually moved upon Culpepper, as if with the design of offering battle in the very position which he himself had chosen. Now Meade had no desire to avoid a battle, if he could fight upon his own terms, and so he directed three of his corps to recross the Rappahannock and move toward Culpepper. Hardly had this been done, when Gregg, whose cavalry had been thrown out to the right, came in with reports that he had been attacked and driven back by a heavy force of all arms, and that the whole Confederate army, after the delay of a day at Culpepper, was on the march to gain the Union rear.

The information proved true in the main. Lee, knowing how greatly the Union army had been depleted a few weeks before, but ignorant of the strong accessions which it had received within a few days, meditated a repetition of the movement by which he had a year before defeated Pope; only instead of, as Meade supposed, marching west of the Bull Run Mountains, and crossing them at Thoroughfare Gap, he designed to skirt the southern extremity of this range, and gain a position just in the Union rear, upon the railroad. Meade's communications being thus interrupted, he would be forced to attack upon the ground which the enemy should select. Lee reasoned that Meade, forced to withdraw from the Rappahannock, would not be able to resume offensive operations that season. Meade presumed that Lee's design was to occupy the strong position at Centreville, and saw nothing to be done but to retreat with all speed upon that point, hoping to reach it in advance of the enemy. But, as it happened, Lee, instead of aiming at Centreville, directed his march upon Bristoe. He moved also with much less than his wonted celerity, delaying, indeed, for a whole day, the 13th, at Warrenton, in order to supply his troops with provisions. Thus it happened that when the head of Lee's columns, moving eastward, came on the 14th near Bristoe, Meade's whole army, moving northward, had passed that point, with the exception of Warren's corps, which was bringing up the rear. Had Meade known that the army were behind instead of before him, he would, as he avers, have paused and given battle;[4] but, misinformed of the true position, he continued his retreat, crossed Bull Run, and took position at Centreville.

[1] "When I came to Washington, the Secretary of War informed me that he very much regretted the step that I had taken [in resigning the command of the Army of the Potomac]; that it was the intention of the President to give me the command of all the troops I had asked for; but that fact had never been communicated to me, nor had I any intimation of it before. I inquired of the President why he had not given me a corps in that army after he had relieved me, and he said it was for the reason that he thought it would not be agreeable to me or to General Meade. Subsequently he communicated his desire to this effect to General Meade, which was acceded to by the latter first, and afterward objected to by General Meade."—Hooker, in Com. Rep., ii., 178.

[2] Meade (Com. Rep., ii., 343) testified: "As near as I can judge, my army contained of efficient men, equipped and armed such as I could bring into battle, between 60,000 and 70,000 men. I think the enemy had about 60,000. I thought I was probably from 8000 to 10,000 his superior."—General Howe (Ibid., 318) relates a conversation which he had with Meade at this very time. He says: "General Meade remarked that our strength was 74,000 men, and of that number he said that 68,000 were armed and in a condition to fight. Then he spoke of the strength of Lee's army. He ran over the data that he had obtained from divers and sundry sources, and made out that Lee could not have over 45,000 men. He referred to the different corps and divisions of the rebel army; to the movements that had been made, with which he seemed to be familiar; and, as I remember, he stated that Lee's army could not be over 45,000 men, showing that we had such a preponderance of force that with any thing like a fair ordinary chance we could have our own way. That was on Friday" [October 9].—This estimate of 45,000 was singularly accurate, for on the last day of September Lee's muster-rolls showed 44,367, and on the last day of October 45,614, present for duty.

[3] "I said to General Meade, 'I do not see but one thing that Lee can do with advantage with his army, and that is to throw himself suddenly upon our rear.' General Meade replied, 'Oh, he can not do that; he would not think of doing such a thing as that.'"—Howe, in Com. Rep., ii., 318.—General Meade, in his testimony before the Committee on the Conduct of the War (Report, ii., 340–342), gives a very full account of his movements at this time, and of the reasons which governed them.

[4] "Notwithstanding my losing a day, I had moved with more celerity than the enemy, and was a little in his advance. If I had known this at the time, I would have given the enemy battle the next day in the position that I had occupied at Auburn and Greenwich."—Com. Rep., ii., 341.

IN CAMP AT WARRENTON SPRINGS.

Warren had in the mean while been delayed at Auburn by a rencounter with a portion of Ewell's corps. This, after some skirmishing, drew off, and Warren followed on after the rest of the army, between which and him there was now a considerable interval. When the head of Lee's army came in the afternoon to Bristoe, they saw Sykes's corps marching out. Hill made some dispositions to assail the rear of Sykes, when he became aware of the approach of Warren from the opposite direction. Hill turned to assail Warren, while Sykes, strangely enough, kept on his retreat for a space.[1] Warren's position was perilous. His single corps was isolated from the remainder of the army, while the whole force of the enemy was coming up right upon his flank. Only a part of it was actually up, and on the next few minutes every thing depended. With quick decision, Warren sent his two leading divisions, which were a mile in advance of the other, to seize upon a deep cutting in the railroad. They dashed forward at a run, and were just in time to gain the position when Hill's advancing line of battle came up. They were received with so hot a fire that they fell back with considerable loss. Heth's division—the same which, under Pettigrew, who had been mortally wounded at Williamsport, had suffered so severely at Gettysburg—made a feeble attack upon the right flank, when it encountered Webb's division, the same which it had met on Cemetery Ridge; they again retreated in confusion. In all, the Confederates lost 400 killed and wounded and 450 prisoners—the entire Union loss being about 200. Hill had been checked, but Warren was far from being free from peril, for Ewell's corps and the remainder of Hill's were rapidly approaching, while the other Union corps, apparently ignorant of what was going on, had kept up the retreat, and were now miles away. Warren could not hope, with his single corps, long to withstand the whole Confederate army, nor while daylight lasted could he safely abandon his strong position and pursue his march. But night was approaching, and before Lee could make the necessary dispositions for attack, darkness closed in, and under its thrice welcome cover Warren marched on, and rejoined the main army at Centreville.

Had Meade on that day known the position of the enemy, he would certainly never have crossed Bull Run. He would most likely have marched back to Bristoe, before it had been abandoned by Warren, where there can be little doubt that a battle would have taken place, under such advantages that victory would have been certain.[2] But so erroneous was Meade's information that even on the next day Birney's division was ordered to march on to Fairfax Station, half way between Centreville and Washington, to hold that point against an expected attack. Had Lee really purposed to throw his army through Thoroughfare Gap, Meade should have welcomed such a movement. The Confederate army, wholly cut off from its sources of supply, would have been hemmed in between Meade's superior forces and the defenses of Washington. It could have neither food nor ammunition except what it bore with it. It could neither hold its position, nor advance nor retreat without winning a battle, against greatly superior forces. The case was widely different from what existed a year before, when Lee, fully twice as strong, had made the same flank march against Pope's disjointed and dispirited army.

After a couple of days' repose at Centreville, Meade perceived that Lee was not minded to follow him any farther, and he resolved to retrace his steps. But now a storm set in and swelled the little stream of Bull Run into a foaming torrent, which could be crossed only by pontoons. These had been left ten miles behind, and so for two days the army could not move a mile. Lee pushed a few troops as far as Bull Run, and on the 18th commenced his retreat toward the Rappahannock, marching along the railroad, which he thoroughly destroyed behind him. The next day, the Run having fallen, Meade began his advance. He moved slowly, for there was nothing to be gained by haste. More than a week was occupied in the twenty miles' march back to Warrenton, and ten more days were lost in repairing the road so that supplies could be kept up.

Besides Warren's stand at Auburn and his fight at Bristoe, there had been no fighting except by the cavalry, who were flung out from either army. On the 13th Stuart was near coming to grief hard by Catlett's Station, where he had last year performed good though accidental service by the capture of Pope's dispatch-book. He had pushed forward quite in advance of the infantry, and, coming upon the head of the leading Federal column, had fallen back toward Catlett's, where he bivouacked in a low spot among a dense pine thicket. Meantime the other Federal column had moved by a parallel road, and Stuart was hemmed in between the two, not two miles from Meade's head-quarters, and within less than a quarter of a mile from a ridge whereon Warren had pitched his camp. Stuart was hidden from observation by the thicket and by the heavy night mist, while the enemy on the hill-tops was in plain view. His destruction was inevitable should he be discovered. Sending two or three soldiers disguised in Federal uniforms to creep through the hostile lines and notify Lee of his peril, he waited till morning was beginning to dawn, and then opened a sudden artillery fire upon Warren. So unexpected was the attack that the troops upon whom

[1] "When I began the fight, the last of General Sykes's corps was moving off. I do not suppose that he got more than three or four miles away, and a part of his corps did come back just before dark. I think the orders were to concentrate at Centreville that night; but when I was engaged in battle, it seemed to me plain enough that he ought to have helped me without solicitation or orders."—Warren, in *Com. Rep.*, ii., 384.

[2] "Under the conviction that the enemy was moving on, and had moved on, I that night [of the 13th] gave orders for a further retrograde movement, until I occupied the line of Centreville and Bull Run. In performing this movement the next day, I ascertained, when too late to take advantage of it, that the enemy had not moved on the pike [leading through Thoroughfare Gap to Centreville], but that he had moved across, with the expectation of falling upon my flank and rear, and that his advance had encountered my rear-guard, under the command of General Warren, and had been severely handled."—(Meade, in *Com. Rep.*, ii., 341.)—Warren says (*Ibid.*, 387): "We lost another opportunity when the enemy attacked me at Bristoe; perhaps not at that point exactly, but during that movement we missed an opportunity that we should be very glad to have again."

DÉPÔT OF SUPPLIES ON THE RAILROAD.

it fell were thrown into momentary confusion, and moved across the crest to escape the cannonade. Stuart sprang to horse, and passing safely with all his men, rode clear around the Union rear. The scouts whom he had sent out had in the mean time succeeded in reaching Ewell, who set his column in motion, and it was the head of this which encountered Warren at Auburn.

While Meade was resting at Centreville, Imboden, with a division of Confederate cavalry, was stationed in the Valley of the Shenandoah. From Winchester, on the 16th, he made a sudden dash down to Charlestown, close by Harper's Ferry, where he captured more than 400 prisoners, and secured a large quantity of supplies, and then, upon the approach of a superior force from the Ferry, he fell back, preserving all his spoils. On the 19th Kilpatrick, with his cavalry division, having crossed Bull Run, pressed on toward Warrenton. When within a few miles of that place he encountered Hampton's troopers, who were covering the Confederate rear. Hampton fell back for a space until joined by Stuart and Fitz Lee. Kilpatrick was in turn driven back, not without confusion, losing 200 prisoners. What with Imboden's captures at Charlestown, the Confederates had made, during these five days, about 2500 prisoners, and had lost not more than a quarter as many. In killed and wounded the losses were about equal, not far from 500 on each side. Lee had, however, succeeded in his chief purpose, that of securing himself against any probable attack during the few remaining weeks of the autumn.

While, however, Meade was waiting at Warrenton for the repair of the railroad, he meditated an indirect offensive movement, being nothing other than a repetition of Burnside's, entered upon just a year before. He proposed to march rapidly to Fredericksburg, cross there and seize the heights, and thus transfer his base of operations from the Orange and Alexandria to the Fredericksburg Railroad. He argued that this movement would be a complete surprise to the enemy; that the heights of Fredericksburg could be seized before Lee could get down there; and then, he says, "if Lee followed me down there, it would be just what I wanted; if he did not, then I could take up my position there, open my communications, and then advance upon him or threaten Richmond." But Halleck refused his consent to this plan; he was opposed to any change of base—a phrase which indeed had come to have an ominous sound. If Meade chose to make any movement against Lee, he was at liberty to do so, but there must be no change of base.[1] Why, in November, Halleck should sanction the very operation which he had positively forbidden in July, is inconceivable. Lee's army was somewhat stronger now than then;[2] Meade's was considerably weaker. Then there were four months of favorable weather; now there was no likelihood of as many weeks. Then the Union army was flushed by the great victory, and the Confederate dispirited by the great defeat of Gettysburg;

now the Confederates were inspirited, and the Federals dispirited by the result of the subsequent operations.

The Confederate army lay meanwhile behind the Rappahannock, widely scattered. Two brigades were on the north bank, occupying intrenchments at Rappahannock Station which had been thrown up by the Federals. On the 7th of November Meade put his army in motion. It was formed into two columns—the First, Second, and Third Corps under French; the Fifth and Sixth under Sedgwick. In the early morning Birney's division of French's corps waded across the river at Kelly's Ford, captured 500 prisoners, and prevented any supports from coming up to Rappahannock Station, where Sedgwick's corps was to cross. Sedgwick was delayed until afternoon before the works on the north bank. Russell, who led the first division, just at sunset reported that he would with his 3000 men undertake to storm the intrenchments. He charged upon them with fixed bayonets without firing a shot. He met a fire so fierce that in ten minutes his leading regiment, the Fifth Maine, lost 16 out of its 23 officers, and 123 out of 350 men; but the works were carried. At the same moment the One Hundred and Twenty-first New York and the Fifth Maine, firing but a single volley, swept through the rifle-pits and gained the pontoon bridge, cutting off the retreat of the garrison. A few escaped by swimming, but 1600 out of 2000 surrendered. This brilliant achievement redressed the balance of losses in this campaign.

It was now dark. Birney, in command of the Third Corps, sent word to French, across the river, that he would advance at daylight. He began to move, but was checked by an order from Meade. In the afternoon, having been joined by Sedgwick's corps, he advanced to Brandy Station, half way to Culpepper, whither Lee had fallen back, with some 30,000 men, being all that he could then concentrate from his widely-scattered cantonments. Birney was eager to follow, confident that he could strike a telling blow. But Meade, cautious every where except upon the actual battle-field, would not consent. He brought up his whole army to the Station, and Lee, availing himself of the hesitation, recrossed the Rapidan. Meade pushed his advance posts to Culpepper and beyond, and for nearly three weeks lay inactive.[1] It is difficult to understand why the signal advantage which had been gained was not followed up, and the whole day of the 8th wasted in uncertain movements. But the golden opportunity of falling with his whole force upon a portion of the Confederate army was lost; and when Lee had fallen back behind the Rapidan, it was hazardous to follow until the railroad could be put in thorough repair.[2]

[1] Com. Rep., ii., 342.
[2] Confederate returns: July 31, 41,135; October 31, 45,614; November 20, 48,269.

[1] Birney, in Com. Rep., ii., 372; Warren, Ibid., 385.
[2] "I succeeded in surprising the enemy, forcing a passage [across the Rappahannock], compelling him to retreat hurriedly and rapidly to the Rapidan. The army was then moved across the Rappahannock, and placed in position between the Rappahannock and the Rapidan, somewhere near its former position, but not quite so far to the front as before, because I had not my communications open. Here a farther delay was rendered necessary until the railroad could be completed from Warrenton Junction and the Rappahannock, and my communications opened."—Meade, in Com. Rep., ii., 342.

MINE RUN.—CENTRE OF CONFEDERATE POSITION.

MINE RUN.—RECROSSING AT GERMANIA FORD.

MINE RUN.—WARREN'S LAST POSITION.

As November drew near a close, Lee evidently supposed that active operations for the season were over. He therefore scattered his troops in winter quarters over a wide extent of country. Ewell's corps, on the right, rested upon Mine Run, a mere brook, with a depth of water of from a few inches to two feet, creeping through swamps and dense undergrowth. It runs along the western margin of the Wilderness, and empties into the Rapidan a dozen miles west of Chancellorsville. Along this stream intrenchments had been formed and abatis constructed. These were not very strongly held; and all the lower fords of the Rapidan were left wholly unguarded. The Confederate army was somewhat stronger than at any period since Longstreet's departure for the West. The returns of November 20 showed 56,000 men, of whom 48,000 were present for duty; but it was widely scattered. Ewell's corps was posted along Mine Run, thence stretching southward as far as Orange Court-house, a distance of fully fifteen miles. Still farther lay Hill's corps, its extremity being at Charlottesville, thirty miles farther. The distance from the extreme right to the extreme left was forty-five miles, and there was an interval of some miles between Ewell and Hill. Meade had in all about 70,000 men, closely concentrated within a few miles of Lee's right at Mine Run; of these, about 60,000 were brought forward in aid of the operation which was now to be undertaken.[1]

It seemed to Meade that by suddenly crossing the Rapidan at the fords where Hooker had before crossed, then striking the plank road and turnpike leading westward toward Orange Court-house, he would, by a rapid march of barely twenty miles, fall upon Ewell's corps, crush that before Hill could come up, and then turn upon that corps, drive it back, and thus gain an effective lodgment at Orange Court-house and Gordonsville. The movement was undoubtedly a feasible one, provided no mischance occurred, and every part of it was conducted precisely as planned; but its success depended upon the contingencies of time, space, and weather.

The 24th of November was the time set for the movement; but, as if by way of premonition, a furious storm arose, which delayed every thing for two days. On the 26th the march was begun. The several corps marched in two separate columns, by several different roads. It was supposed that all would reach their points of concentration beyond what had been ascertained to be the extremity of the Confederate intrenchments on Mine Run by noon of the 27th. Warren reached the Rapidan at Germania Ford at the time appointed; but French, who was to cross hard by, was three hours behind time, and thus the passage was delayed, for Meade would not send one corps over alone. Then, again, somebody had blundered in measuring the width of the stream; every pontoon bridge was just one boat too short, and the difficulty had to be supplied by bridging. Thus almost a day was lost in taking the first step, the passage of the Rapidan, which was not effected until the 27th. Warren then pushed on rapidly. He had, indeed, a good road from the Rapidan southward, and within an hour of the appointed time was at the point where he was to be joined by the Third Corps. But French got entangled in the labyrinth of paths, and halted four miles short of the place for junction, where he was held in check by a body of the enemy who had been pushed forward in advance of their line of intrenchments. These two corps, with the First, which was to follow, formed the left column; the right—the First and Fifth Corps—had not got within communicating distance, and till this was effected Meade would not venture an advance. Next morning this was made, but the enemy had fallen back to his intrenched position, and all that day and the next were spent in reconnoitring the position and fixing upon some point for attack. As Sunday, the 29th, drew to a close, Sedgwick, on the right, and Warren, on the left, reported that an attack was feasible on their fronts. Warren indeed, at 9 o'clock, assured Meade that he was confident that the enemy would not be found before him in the morning.[2] French was opposed to attacking on his own front, in the centre, so it was resolved to attack on the left and right, Warren being strengthened by two of French's divisions, giving him a force of 26,000. Sedgwick opened fire with his artillery, and was just about advancing to the assault, when an aid came from Warren with a dispatch stating that he had suspended his assault, finding that the enemy was in great force on his front. There had been ample time to bring up the bulk of the Confederate army, and Warren had the day before demonstrated so ostentatiously that Lee's attention was strongly directed to that part of his line, which he had strengthened by weakening the others.[3] Meade rode over to Warren's position, and was reluctantly obliged to acknowledge that he had done wisely in not making the attack. Sedgwick now reported that the enemy had strengthened himself also in his front; so the order to attack was reversed, and Birney, who had actually begun a strong demonstration upon the centre, was surprised by being ordered to fall back again. Meade was indeed half-minded to accede to Warren's suggestion—to keep on until he had passed beyond the extremity of the Confederate works, and assail them

in some position where they would not have time to intrench themselves before the attack could be made. But it was now winter, and favorable weather could not be anticipated from day to day; any sudden storm would prevent the bringing forward of supplies, and of those which had been brought half were exhausted.[1] So Meade concluded that, under the circumstances, nothing more—and nothing more was equivalent to nothing at all—could be done. He withdrew his army to its former position.

With the Mine Run attempt—an enterprise which could have been successful only in case that out of a score of untoward circumstances, all of which were probable, and some of which were almost certain—the closing campaign of 1863 in Virginia came to an end, and both armies retired to winter quarters to await the opening spring.

That during the autumn and winter Richmond had been left almost wholly without troops, was ascertained from sure sources. Between October, 1863, and March, 1864, there were there at no time more than 7000 effective troops, while fully 10,000 Union prisoners were known to be confined in the military prisons. Several plans were formed of making a sudden dash upon the Confederate capital, and at all events liberating these prisoners. Early in February, General Butler, now in command at Fortress Monroe, sent a considerable body of cavalry, supported by infantry, from Yorktown toward Richmond. The cavalry reached Bottom's Bridge, on the Chickahominy, on the 7th; but tidings of the expedition had somehow preceded them, and the roads were so thoroughly obstructed as to be impassable for cavalry, and the expedition returned, having effected nothing.

At the close of the month a more formidable expedition was fitted out from the Army of the Potomac for the same purpose. Kilpatrick, with 4000 cavalry, crossed the Rapidan, and passed Spottsylvania Court-house, and pushed rapidly on toward Richmond. On the first of March he had reached within less than four miles of the city, penetrating the two outer lines of defenses; but, being stopped at the third, he fell back, and the next day, concluding that the enterprise was not feasible, retreated to Yorktown. Meanwhile, at Spottsylvania Court-house, Colonel Ulric Dahlgren, with a picked body of 400 cavalry, had been detached to the right, with the view of skirting to the south, and assailing Richmond in that direction. His guide had led him out of the way. Dahlgren, believing that this was done treacherously, hung him on the spot, and rode on his way till he reached the inner line of defenses. Here he was repulsed, as Kilpatrick had been on the other side. Endeavoring to make his way eastward, he encountered a body of militia, and was shot dead, his command dispersing, a third of them being made prisoners. The Confederates assert that on his body were found an address to his men, and orders and instructions, declaring his object to be to "destroy and burn the hateful city, and not to allow the rebel leader Davis and his traitorous crew to escape. . . . . Once in the city, it must be destroyed, and Davis and his cabinet killed." The genuineness of these papers has been strenuously denied; and, apart from the intrinsic improbability, the account given of the transaction is so suspicious as to leave little doubt that these papers were either absolute forgeries or grossly interpolated. Dahlgren's body, after having been interred, was dug up and buried again secretly, and with every indignity, as that of an outlaw.

With this unfortunate enterprise closed Meade's campaign in Virginia. On the day when Kilpatrick came within sight of Richmond, Ulysses S. Grant was commissioned Lieutenant General of the Armies of the United States. The campaign soon to be opened, lasting a year lacking a month, was conducted by Grant.

[1] Meade, in *Com. Rep.*, ii., 345.

---

[1] Meade mentions incidentally that in the course of these operations Warren had about 25,000 or 26,000 men, and that this was "nearly half" of his whole army.—See *Com. Rep.*, ii., 345, 6.

[2] So Meade testifies (*Com. Rep.*, ii., 345, 6), and that Warren the next day wrote that he had suspended the attack which he had been directed to make, because the order had been based upon his judgment, and he found the enemy had been largely re-enforced. But Warren affirms (*Ibid.*, 386, 7): "I wish it to be distinctly understood that it was no scheme of mine at all to attack at this place. . . . . My idea was that, as we had plenty of provisions, we should keep on until we had passed their left and their intrenchments there, and attack the enemy where he had not any thing. . . . . That the plan of the fight did not depend upon any thing that I said that night is apparent from the fact that the troops on the right were already in position for the attack before I got to General Meade. I put the best face that I could on it then."

[3] "My movement had been apparent to the enemy, for I had made all the fires I could, my object being to make a demonstration as of a heavy force. The enemy saw also other troops moving, and during the night concentrated a large force there also. . . . . In one space, where there was not a gun before, we could then count seventeen guns in a commanding position." (Warren, in *Com. Rep.*, ii., 386, 7.)—Birney says (*Ibid.*, 373): "I think Warren's plan failed because it was attended with too much reconnoitring, fire-building, and delay, all of which fully advertised the movement to the watchful enemy, and prevented a surprise. When Warren was ready to attack he found the enemy ready to receive him. I think that in extending their right they had weakened their centre."

ULRIC DAHLGREN.

WINTER QUARTERS.—ON PICKET.

CHAPTER XXXI.
THE CHATTANOOGA CAMPAIGN.
I. THE ARMY OF THE CUMBERLAND.

The Beginnings of the Army.—Rousseau's Command at Camp Joe Holt, 1861.—Creation of the Department of the Cumberland; it includes Kentucky and Tennessee; General Robert Anderson its first Commander.—General W. T. Sherman succeeds Anderson, October, 1861.—Is succeeded by Buell in November.—The Department of the Cumberland becomes the Department of the Ohio, including Ohio, Indiana, and Michigan.—Kentucky and Tennessee soon absorbed by Halleck's Department of the Missouri.—Buell's Command styled "the District of the Ohio."—Rosecrans succeeds Buell, October 30, 1862, and the Department of the Cumberland is revived.—The Fourteenth Army Corps.—General Buell's Record.—Estimate of Rosecrans's Military Career; his Disadvantages; his subordinate Commanders, Generals Thomas, McCook, Crittenden, and Stanley.—The Organization of the Army.—Deficiency in Cavalry.—The Battle of Stone River undecisive.—Fortification of Murfreesborough.—Confederate Attack on Fort Donelson.—Actions at Spring Hill and Franklin.—Capture of McMinnville.—Colonel Streight's Raid; his Capture and Escape.—Rosecrans urged to Advance.—Decision of his War Council.—Waiting for Grant.

THE campaign for the possession of Chattanooga began with Rosecrans's advance from Murfreesborough on the 24th of June, 1863, and terminated with General Bragg's defeat on the 25th of November, just five months and one day afterward. The secure tenure of Chattanooga cost two great battles, involving a loss on both sides—if we include the killed and wounded in these battles and during the siege of Knoxville—of over 50,000 men. This campaign had two well-defined periods. With the first of these, which closed when General Rosecrans was relieved of his command (October 19th, 1863), the Army of the Cumberland is alone directly connected.

The organization of this army had its beginning in a little band of Kentuckians, summoned to Camp Joe Holt, near Louisville, early in 1861. This body of volunteers was commanded by Colonel, afterward Major General Lovell H. Rousseau, who, understanding that war must for a time silence statesmanship, had left his seat in the Kentucky Senate, and rallied about him the loyalists of his State. His eloquence, courage, and patriotism found a clear and positive utterance in this unsettled period, when Kentuckians were wavering between secession and loyalty, bound on one side by the ties of kindred and association, on the other by a strong sentiment in favor of the Union. Under the influence of the words and examples of such men as Rousseau and Anderson, this sentiment became dominant over sectional interests, and was ardently espoused by the greater portion of the state. In answer to Rousseau's call, a force of nearly 2000 men was soon assembled in his encampment. At Camp Dick Robinson there was a similar force under General Nelson, and on the 15th of August, 1861, Kentucky and Tennessee were constituted a separate military district, known as the Department of the Cumberland. General Robert Anderson, the hero of Fort Sumter, was the first commander of this department, General W. T. Sherman being second in command. Sherman succeeded Anderson in October, 1861, and established his camp on Muldraugh's Hill, about 40 miles south of Louisville. Here he awaited the arrival of troops from the states north of the Ohio. These came promptly forward, so that before the close of the year there was assembled an army of 70,000 men, over 20,000 of whom were Kentuckians.

In November Sherman was succeeded by Buell. With this change of command the Department of the Cumberland became the Department of the Ohio—Indiana, Michigan, and Ohio being added to its content, while that portion of Kentucky lying west of the Cumberland River was transferred to the Department of the Missouri, then commanded by General Halleck. Subsequently (in March, 1862), Halleck's department was extended eastward to a north and south line passing through Knoxville, and was designated the Department of the Mississippi; three months later it included all of Kentucky and Tennessee, Buell's command being then known as the "District of the Ohio." When Rosecrans succeeded Buell (October 30, 1862), the title of his command was again changed, the Department of the Cumberland being revived, including all of Tennessee and Kentucky east of the Tennessee River, and such parts of Northern Alabama and Georgia as should be conquered by the United States troops. At the same time, the Department of the Tennessee, General Grant's command, comprised Cairo, Forts Henry and Donelson, and all of Kentucky and Tennessee west of the Tennessee River. Grant's troops were designated the Thirteenth, and those of Rosecrans the Fourteenth Army Corps.

The army which thus came under Rosecrans's command had an unstained record. Under Anderson and Sherman it had been but the nucleus of an army. Buell made it formidable in numbers, and perfect in organization and discipline; he created the Army of the Cumberland. Portions of it fought at Piketon, Prestonburg, Middle Creek, Pound Gap, and Mill Spring, but the whole army was engaged in battle for the first time at Shiloh, where, on the second day, it went into the fight in as perfect order as if it had fought a score of battles.

The supersedure of Buell by Rosecrans was owing to a general lack of confidence in the former commander. During the space of nearly a year he had organized and disciplined a great army, but he had done little with it; he had gained no grand, positive success. The defeat of Bragg in Kentucky would have made Buell the great military hero of 1862. But Bragg escaped, after having compelled the Federal army to abandon its advanced position—escaped without a battle, except that of Perryville, which was precipitated by General McCook's disobedience of orders. The people were disappointed. Halleck had become dissatisfied with General Buell. Nothing but Thomas's urgent remonstrance had prevented him from making a change in the command when the Federal army reached Louisville, in the fall of 1862. Thomas declined the command which was then offered him, and urged the retention of Buell. After Bragg's retreat, Buell was court-

martialed for the affair at Perryville, but was acquitted and restored to the command. But scarcely had this been done when he was again removed, and ordered to relieve General Banks in the Department of the Gulf. Learning that the change had been made by the President immediately on the receipt of a protest from Andrew Johnson, then Military Governor of Tennessee, he very properly declined to accept the new appointment. The command of the Army of the Cumberland should have naturally devolved upon General Thomas after Buell's removal, but it so happened that just at this time it had become impossible for General Rosecrans to remain any longer in the same military department with General Grant, and Halleck gave him the Army of the Cumberland. General Buell in some respects bore a remarkable resemblance to General Thomas. In temperament they were alike. Both were cool in the presence of danger. Both were perfect soldiers in bearing, courage, and honor. It is impossible fairly to criticise Buell's military career, because it was so soon concluded. If he had any great military fault, it was an excessive regard for regularity. This was of great value in the discipline of a large army, but might easily prove an impediment in the conduct of a campaign. He was a good tactician; he was a general of extraordinary energy; yet he lacked dash and brilliancy of movement. He excited no enthusiasm, and enthusiasm is the element upon which a volunteer army mainly lives and moves. If he lacked some of the excellencies which characterized our more brilliant leaders, he was also free from many of their prominent weaknesses. He was never petulant or impatient, and never lost his dignity. He was incapable of dishonor, and the charges which were made against him in 1862, impeaching his patriotism, were unjust, and, on the part of those who ought to have known him better, were malicious.

No general could have been more widely different to Buell than his successor, General Rosecrans. Personally, and as regards physical temperament, they were as far apart as the antipodes. Nature had done little to fit Rosecrans for the highest requirements of generalship. He was too courageous to avoid danger or responsibility, yet the most critical moment of a battle would sometimes find him beside himself with nervous excitement. To such a temperament, in any large field of human effort, the highest order of achievements is denied. Other things being equal, the best general is he who has the most self-control at the decisive moment, whose powers are in most instant command, and to whom the hour of embarrassment or of peril comes, not fraught with confusion, but pregnant with suggestion. It is in such hours that battles are lost or won—lost, in nearly every instance, by the over-excitable general; and, in nearly every instance, won by the cool, self-possessed commander, who, seeing only the chances of success, is blind to the tokens of possible defeat. Rosecrans fought unequally. His early campaigns in West Virginia were in every particular admirably conducted. He very soon had the mortification of seeing other officers, who had effected less, absorb his command, and other and less promising plans adopted in preference to his own. After assuming command of the Army of the Mississippi (June 27, 1862), he fought well at Iuka and Corinth. He had never lost a battle before he took the Army of the Cumberland. His military career had been so successful as to command popular confidence, and great expectations were entertained of him, which were not fully realized.

Rosecrans was a general of more than ordinary ability. His plans were often brilliant, and led often to successful results. Then, again, they would be elaborate to an almost absurd degree, and so faulty as to embarrass himself rather than the enemy. His strategy at one time excites our admiration, and at another appals us with its manifest weakness. Now we feel that he is conducting a magnificent campaign, and the next moment he seems to be playing with his army. After weeks of steady and almost sleepless activity in preparing for movement, we behold him advancing, and at length—after a series of manœuvres, some of them admirable, and some of them, as likely as not, desperately short-sighted—in the presence of the enemy, we find him in a state of undue excitement, without any definite plan, knowing nothing about the hostile army, and incompetent to take his proper place as a commander on the field. Military critics will differ widely in their estimate of General Rosecrans; but he must be unjust who can not find much in him to admire, and he must be a very partial judge indeed who, after a mature consideration of Rosecrans's campaigns from November, 1862, to October, 1863, can pronounce him fully equal to his duties as a commander. At the same time it must be remembered that Rosecrans labored under great disadvantages, both from the difficult nature of the country through which he moved, and from the inadequate support which he received from the War Department. And so much is due to accident, or to favoring circumstances, in the final estimate which is made of public men, that probably Rosecrans, if he had had competent subordinates, and had outnumbered the enemy in his later campaigns, instead of being himself outnumbered, would to-day rank among the first generals of the war, and his faults have all been forgotten. Faults, so easily forgiven in those who succeed (upon whatsoever their success may have depended), fall with crushing weight upon those who fail.

The army which Rosecrans received from Buell was not what it had been. The ardor with which its soldiers had enlisted had been quenched by a year of fruitless labor. Over one third of the army (33,000 men) were in hospitals, on furlough, or numbered among the deserters. Every stage of Rosecrans's advance called for a strong detail of men for garrison duty. The cavalry arm of the service was far inferior to that of the enemy, and long lines of communication had to be guarded with extreme caution. The enemy, on the other hand, operating in a friendly country, could make his entire force effective against Rosecrans.

Very little alteration was made in the organization of the Army of the Cumberland on the change of its commanders. Its composition remained the same. It consisted, in about equal proportions, of veterans and raw recruits—the latter, of course, destitute of discipline, and the former poorly clothed and equipped. Thomas was given an active command, and Brigadier General Gilbert was relieved, and detailed for the protection of the railroad north of Bowling Green.

Major General George H. Thomas, commanding the centre of the army, consisting of Fry's, Rousseau's, Negley's, Dumont's, and Palmer's divisions, was Rosecrans's best general. He was now forty-six years of age. He had received a thorough military education, and acquired considerable military experience in the Florida and Mexican campaigns. At the beginning of the civil war he fought in Virginia, under Patterson and Banks, and received his appointment as brigadier general of volunteers August 17, 1861, when he was removed from Virginia to General Anderson's command. Here, early in 1862, he fought the battle of Mill Spring. From March of that year until the advance upon Corinth, his division, located at Nashville, constituted the reserve of Buell's army. He was, on the 25th of April, 1862, appointed major general of volunteers. A week later his division was transferred to the Army of the Tennessee, and he was assigned by General Halleck to the command of the right wing of that army. In June his command rejoined Buell. Upon the retreat of the latter to Louisville, Thomas was appointed his second in command. After the battle of Stone River, the Army of the Cumberland, under Rosecrans, was divided into three corps—the Fourteenth, Twentieth, and Twenty-first—General Thomas commanding the Fourteenth, which consisted of five divisions, under Rousseau, Negley, J. J. Reynolds, Fry, and R. B. Mitchell.

Major General Alexander McDowell McCook, who commanded the Twentieth Corps of Rosecrans's army, was a native of Ohio, and about thirty years of age. He was a graduate of West Point, and in 1858 had been assigned to that institution as instructor in tactics and in the art of war. He was relieved from this position at the opening of the war, and appointed colonel of the First Ohio Regiment. With this regiment he fought at Bull Run. On the 3d of September, 1861, he was made a brigadier general of volunteers, and given a command in Kentucky. In his camp on Green River he organized the Second Division, with which he fought at Shiloh on the second day of that battle. In the movement on Corinth he commanded the advance of Buell's army. He fought the battle of Perryville against orders, but with determined bravery. He commanded the right wing of Rosecrans's army at Stone River, where he was driven back by the overwhelming forces of the enemy. Although a brave soldier, he was better fitted for a division than a corps commander.

The same judgment may be passed upon Major General Crittenden, commanding the Twenty-first Corps. Before the war his military education and experience had been confined to his service in the Mexican War as aide-de-camp to General Taylor. He was a Kentuckian, being the second son of Hon. John J. Crittenden. His elder brother George was in the Confederate army. He was of about the same age as General Thomas. If Generals McCook and Crittenden, who may be termed two of Rosecrans's "disadvantages," had been displaced by more competent officers, the history of the Army of the Cumberland would have been materially changed.

Major General David S. Stanley, who had been, at Rosecrans's request, transferred from the Army of the Mississippi to take the command of the cavalry of the Army of the Cumberland, was an officer whose great worth Rosecrans had already learned to appreciate. He graduated at West Point in the class of 1852, which numbered among its members McCook, Hartsuff, Slocum, and Sheridan. At the beginning of the war he was stationed at Fort Smith, in Arkansas. He fought under Lyon at Dug Springs and Wilson's Creek, and afterward joined Fremont in the movement on Springfield. He was appointed brigadier general of volunteers September 28th, 1861. Early in 1862 he joined General Pope's command, and his division was the first to occupy the trenches before New Madrid. In the advance on Corinth he commanded the Second Division of the Army of the Mississippi. In the battle of Corinth this division especially distinguished itself, holding the left centre, supporting Battery Robinette. Stanley joined Rosecrans at Nashville in November, 1862, and devoted himself to the reorganization of the cavalry of the Army of the Cumberland.

The departments of no army were ever more completely organized or more efficient in their operation than those of Rosecrans's. Take the matter of supplies for an example. No general ever was beset by greater difficulties in this respect. He was in a barren and hostile country, and the entire subsistence of his army must be transported over a distance of from one to more than two hundred miles, either by a railroad exposed at many points to interruption from the enemy's cavalry, or by the Cumberland River, which, during a considerable portion of the year, was too low for navigation. Yet the soldiers never wanted food. In other respects they were equally well provided for. To facilitate the advance of the army, a Pioneer brigade was organized, consisting of about 3000 men, commanded by James St. Clair Morton. Every measure was taken to learn the plans and forces of the enemy; the secret service of the Army of the Cumberland was one of its characteristic excellencies, and well repaid the $10,000 per month which it cost the government. It was a service to which Rosecrans was very partial. He was the most Jesuitical of generals, and would himself have made a capital spy. It was in appreciation, probably, of his abundant mental resources in this direction that the title of "the wily Dutchman" was given him, both by ourselves and the enemy.

Before and for a long time after the battle of Stone River the enemy's superior cavalry force was a source of great anxiety and embarrassment to Rosecrans. He fought stubbornly with the War Department for the means of increasing the numbers and efficiency of this arm of the service. He wanted good horses, saddles, and revolving carbines, and his importunity in asking for them seems to have only had the effect of vexing General Halleck. His requests were always urgent, but respectful. "I must have," he writes, January 14, 1863, "cavalry or mounted infantry. I could mount infantry had I horses and saddles. . . . With mounted infantry I can drive the rebel cavalry to the wall, and keep the roads open in my rear. Not so now. . . . Will you authorize the purchase of saddles and horses for mounting, when requisite, 5000 more infantry?" "Why," he asks, two weeks later, "should the rebels command the country which, with its resources, would belong to our army, because they can muster the small percentage of six or eight thousand more cavalry than we?" Toward the close of March he again reminds the general-in-chief of his need. "Let it be clearly understood," he writes, "that the enemy have five to our one, and can, therefore, command the resources of the country and the services of the inhabitants."[1] By this time he had gained permission to mount 5000 infantry, and had succeeded in mounting 2000. But he was unable to mass his cavalry for expeditions, because they were occupied on picket duty. General Rousseau offered to raise 8000 or 10,000 infantry to increase the cavalry force if the government would mount and arm them, but he seems to have received no assurance that this would be done until the middle of summer. Of the cavalry force in hand, only forty per cent. was available for want of horses. This deficiency was repeatedly urged, but the horses were not furnished.[2]

Let us do Rosecrans ample justice in this matter. We can not over-estimate his embarrassment arising from a deficient cavalry force. What was done for Grant by the gun-boats could be done for Rosecrans only by a large and well-equipped force of cavalry or mounted infantry. It is probable that his urgent representations at length opened the eyes of the War De-

[1] *Report of Congressional Committee on Rosecrans's Campaigns*, p. 39.
[2] The two following letters to General Meigs and Secretary Stanton indicate Rosecrans's situation in respect of cavalry:

"Murfreesborough, May 10, 1863.

"GENERAL,—Your letter of the 1st instant, on the subject of cavalry horses, was yesterday received and carefully considered. I thank you for taking pains to write so fully. I will explain to you, with equal care, the true state of the case in this army, for I find you have fallen into quite a number of errors on the subject.

"1st. It is a fact that up to the 1st instant our total supply of cavalry horses was as follows:

Cavalry horses on hand	6537
Mounted infantry	1938
Total	8475
Less, at least one quarter, are not serviceable	2119
Making cavalry mounted not over	6356

"But when these troops are called out, we have at no time been able to turn out more than 5000 for active duty. The other cavalry horses, reported by Colonel Taylor, were:

Escorts and orderlies	2028
Unserviceable in Nashville	975
	3003

"You will thus see that we have not the cavalry you suppose. We are using the most strenuous and unremitting efforts to increase in care of horses and the efficiency of this arm.

"2d. But I must call your attention to the fact that this small cavalry force, effectively not half that is required for a permanent garrison of infantry equal to that of this army, have to furnish pickets, scouts, and couriers for Fort Donelson, Clarksville, Nashville, Gallatin, Carthage, and the front of this army from Franklin to this place, twenty-eight miles. You may thus form some idea of the labor imposed on our cavalry, and how our horses are worn out so rapidly.

"3d. As to the actual work of this arm, besides the routine labor, you will find it has some expedition or fight in mass nearly every week, and as yet without a single failure.

"4th. As to expeditions, we have not a sufficiently strong cavalry force to drive that of the enemy to the wall, or to risk detachments for the enterprises of which you speak to the rear of the rebels. The one which I did send out under Colonel Streight, in spite of our precautions, was captured by the superior cavalry force of the enemy, detached from Granger's front at Franklin, where Van Dorn has still left about four to our one.

"5th. As to forage, our want is for long forage, and is owing to the impossibility of getting transportation either by water or rail. You must remember we are 220 miles from our base of supplies at Louisville. You may rely on it, I am fully alive to all you have suggested, and ask for nothing which I am not fully satisfied will be an ample economy to the service. Had we a cavalry force equal to that of the enemy, we would have commanded all the forage of the country—commanded information of its inhabitants, upon whose fears we, instead of they, would thus be able to operate.

"As to the comparative value of cavalry in our and other armies, I am sure you are mistaken as to Russia at least, which has 80,000 regular cavalry, while all the outpost, picket, and courier duty is done by irregular cavalry. But, even were it otherwise, I know what cavalry would do for us here. I am not mistaken in saying that this great army would gain more from 10,000 effective cavalry than from 20,000 infantry. W. S. ROSECRANS, Major General Commanding.

"Brigadier General M. C. MEIGS, Quarter-master General, U. S. Army, Washington, D. C."

"Winchester, July 26, 1863.

"Hon. E. M. STANTON, Secretary of War:

"As you approve of General Rousseau's suggestions and views as to the advantage of raising an additional amount of force of 10,000 men to operate against the rebels from this direction, I have sent him to Washington with letters to yourself and General Halleck, and directed him to lay before you the plan which he has of obtaining from the disciplined troops recently mustered out of service in the East such a mounted force as would enable us to command the country south of us, and control its resources, cut off the enemy's means of drawing supplies from the country, destroy his lines of communication, and restore law and order to the entire country from which we have expelled the insurgents—a thing now impossible, because no one desires to avow his sentiments for fear the rebel cavalry or guerrillas will wreak vengeance on him. At the expense of repeating what I have so often laid before the War Department when urging the necessity of cavalry arms for the force we actually had in pay, but badly armed and mounted, I beg leave to state:

"1st. An adequate cavalry force would have given us control of all Middle Tennessee, with all its forage, horses, cattle, and mules, and driven the enemy from it without the battle of Stone River, and re-established civil order.

"2d. It would save us 5000 infantry now guarding our lines of communication, and the attendant expense.

"3d. We could have destroyed the enemy's lines of communication, and compelled him to relinquish East Tennessee and Chattanooga, and return to Atlanta.

"4th. We could have developed, by giving protection to the Union sentiment, which does not manifest itself much beyond the limits of our infantry lines, for fear of calling down the vengeance of the rebel cavalry and guerrillas, whose superior numbers and knowledge of the country have hitherto given almost exclusive control of it. As we advance we shall have the same condition of things renewed on our front, and must take with us a superior cavalry force to insure success. We should, moreover, require additional mounted force to control the country, protect the roads in our rear, exterminate guerrillas, and give confidence to the population, who will then readily furnish us with supplies, and give us information that will aid us to put down brigandage, and thus relieve us from the necessities of detachments of infantry at many points where otherwise they will be indispensable. The importance of General Rousseau's mission may be inferred from the value I attach to cavalry force to operate in connection with this army. To all these uses of cavalry I will add another no less important. Should we succeed in disorganizing the enemy's force, a powerful cavalry force will enable us to harass and destroy his communications, and thus make him an easy prey. Very respectfully, your obedient servant,

"W. S. ROSECRANS, Major General."

partment for the first time to the incalculable value of well-mounted cavalry. We find, at any rate, that after this period the Federal cavalry force was gradually increased and improved; but the change came too late to very materially assist Rosecrans, who, of all our commanders, was in most need of it.

Just before the battle of Stone River the Army of the Cumberland numbered 47,000 men, of whom little more than 3000 were cavalry. We have already, in a previous chapter, brought down the military operations of this army to the conclusion of the battle of Stone River. Before this battle Rosecrans had for some time been pressed to advance, but he found it hazardous to do so until Bragg had sent away his cavalry on distant expeditions. Yet so little were his real difficulties appreciated at Washington, that Halleck, in a long letter of instructions, had directed him to march to East Tennessee, a distance of over 240 miles, through a barren and mountainous region, and at the beginning of the most inclement season of the year. Even if the advance had been possible, Rosecrans's cavalry would have been ludicrously incompetent to protect his long line of communications, thus leaving the way open for Bragg to Nashville and the Ohio River.

The battle of Stone River was not decisive. Rosecrans inflicted upon Bragg greater damage than he received, and drove him from the field. It is a fact which can not be disputed, that the enemy had the advantage of superior numbers. The Federal army went into the battle 43,000 strong, and when it occupied Murfreesborough, January 5, numbered little more than 30,000. Neither army was in a condition, after the battle, to resume the offensive. The Army of the Cumberland had lost some of its bravest officers. Among these were its youngest brigadier general, J. W. Sill, who had been one of the first to join Sherman at Muldraugh's Hill in 1861; Colonel J. P. Garesché, chief of staff to General Rosecrans, whose head was

blown away by a cannon ball while he was riding over the field in execution of a special mission for his commander; and Colonels Roberts, Milliken, Shaeffer, McKee, Reed, Forman, Jones, Hawkins, and Kell. Brigadier General James A. Garfield, the hero of Middle Creek, succeeded Garesché as Rosecrans's chief of staff. This officer's skill and bravery on the battle-field was only equaled by the talent and uncompromising patriotism which he afterward displayed in the political arena.

After its occupation by the Army of the Cumberland, Murfreesborough was fortified and made a dépôt of supplies. Here the army remained encamped for six months, while General Grant was conducting the Vicksburg campaign. The rainy season soon began, but, while interfering with offensive operations, it swelled the waters of the Cumberland, and facilitated the accumulation of supplies. The monotony of camp life was relieved only by foraging excursions and encounters with the Confederate cavalry. These were conducted at some risk. Not unfrequently the men and wagons were picked up by the enemy, who succeeded sometimes, also, in capturing and burning a transport on the river.

An attempt was made by the Confederates, early in February, to obstruct the navigation of the Cumberland by the recapture of Fort Donelson. On the third of that month, Forrest, Wheeler, and Wharton advanced upon the fort from above and below, with eleven regiments of cavalry and nine guns. The garrison defending Fort Donelson at this time consisted of nine companies of the Eighty-third Illinois, with a battalion of the Fifth Iowa cavalry, and numbered less than 800 men, under the command of Colonel A. C. Harding. The only artillery defense was a battery of four rifled pieces and a single 32-pounder siege gun. A little after noon Harding was summoned to surrender, and promptly refused. The attack was then commenced. The defense was gallantly conducted, and after repeated charges, which cost them

PACK-MULES IN THE MOUNTAINS.

upward of 1000 men, the Confederates retired. Harding's loss was 16 killed, 60 wounded, and 50 prisoners.

On the 5th of March a Federal brigade, numbering 1306 men, under Colonel John Coburn, was surrounded and captured by Forrest's and Van Dorn's cavalry near Spring Hill. The cavalry and artillery of the command escaped. The Confederate force consisted of six brigades, under Generals Van Dorn, French, Armstrong, Crosby, Martin, and Jackson.

A fortnight later, Colonel A. S. Hall, with about 1400 men, encountered the Confederate General John Morgan at Milton, twelve miles northeast of Murfreesborough. Morgan attacked with a force numbering nearly 2000 men, and, after a fight of three and a half hours, withdrew from the field, defeated. The Confederate loss was about 400. Hall lost 60, killed, wounded, and missing.

About the middle of April, Van Dorn, with 9000 men, attacked General Gordon Granger's force at Franklin, consisting of Baird's and Gilbert's divisions, 1600 men and 16 guns, and Generals Smith's and Stanley's cavalry brigades of 2700 men, with four guns. The defense was materially assisted by an uncompleted fort, mounting two siege and two rifled guns, and commanding the northern approaches to Franklin. The attack was repulsed, the enemy losing about 300 men, and General Granger 37.

McMinnville, a few miles southeast of Murfreesborough, was captured on the 21st of April by General Reynolds's division, Colonel Wilder's mounted brigade, and a cavalry force under Colonel Minty, 1700 strong. About 700 Confederates were dispersed, and a few wagons taken.

In the mean time Colonel A. D. Streight had been given the command of an independent provisional brigade, consisting of his own regiment (the Fifty-first Indiana), the Eightieth Illinois, and portions of two Ohio regiments, numbering all together about 1800 men. Colonel Streight early in

April received instructions to proceed to Northern Georgia, to cut the railroads in Bragg's rear, and destroy all dépôts of supplies, manufactories of arms, clothing, etc.[1]

[1] The following is a copy of the instructions given to Colonel Streight:

"Headquarters, Department of the Cumberland, Murfreesborough, April 8, 1863.

"Colonel A. D. STREIGHT, Fifty-first Indiana Volunteers:

"By Special Field Orders No. 94, Paragraph VIII., you have been assigned to the command of an independent provisional brigade for temporary purposes. After fitting out your command with equipments and supplies, as you have already been directed in the verbal instructions of the general commanding this department, you will proceed, by a route of which you will be advised by telegraph, to some good steamboat-landing on the Tennessee River, not far above Fort Henry, where you will embark your command and proceed up the river. At Hamburg you will communicate with Brigadier General Dodge, who will probably have a messenger there awaiting your arrival. If it should then appear unsafe to move farther up the river, you will debark at Hamburg, and without delay join the force of General Dodge, which will then be en route for Iuka, Mississippi. If, however, it should be deemed safe, you will land at Eastport and form a junction with General Dodge. From that point you will then march in conjunction with him to menace Tuscumbia; but you will not wait to join in the attack unless it should be necessary for the safety of General Dodge's command or your own, or unless some considerable advantage can be gained over the enemy without interfering with the general object of your expedition. After having marched long enough with General Dodge to create a general impression that you are a part of his expedition, you will push to the southward, and reach Russelville or Moulton. From there your route will be governed by circumstances; but you will, with all reasonable dispatch, push on to Western Georgia and cut the railroads which supply the rebel army by way of Chattanooga. To accomplish this is the chief object of your expedition, and you must not allow collateral or incidental schemes, even though promising great results, to delay you so as to endanger your return. Your quarter-master has been furnished with funds sufficient for the necessary expenses of your command. You will draw your supplies and keep your command well mounted from the country through which you pass. For all property taken for the legitimate use of your command, you will make cash payments in full to men of undoubted loyalty; give the usual conditional receipts to men whose loyalty is doubtful; *but to rebels nothing.* You are particularly commanded to restrain your command from pillage and marauding. You will destroy all dépôts of supplies for the rebel army, all manufactories of guns, ammunition, equipments, and clothing for their use, which you can, without delaying you so as to endanger your return. That you may not be trammeled with minute instructions, nothing farther will be ordered than this general outline of policy and operation. In intrusting this highly important and somewhat perilous expedition to your charge, the general commanding places great reliance upon your prudence, energy, and valor, and the well-attested bravery and endurance of the officers and men in your command. Whenever it is possible and reasonably safe, send us word of your progress. You may return by way of Northern

THE COURIER LINE.

Streight's command was of about the same strength as the column under Grierson, which was at the same time setting out from La Grange for the raid through Mississippi, described in a previous chapter. It was taken on steam-boats up the Tennessee to Eastport, Alabama, where it was joined by an infantry force under General Dodge. After the capture of Tuscumbia by Streight, the two columns separated. General Dodge made a sweeping raid through Northern Alabama, and returned to Corinth. Streight struck for Northern Georgia, intending to capture Rome and Atlanta, destroying there large manufactories and magazines. He was closely followed by Forrest and Roddy, with a superior force of Confederate cavalry. He kept up a running fight for over a hundred miles, when his command, exhausted and out of ammunition, was surrendered about fifteen miles from Rome. The privates were exchanged, but Streight and his officers were kept in close confinement in Richmond, being charged with felony for having incited slaves to rebellion. Streight finally, on February 9, 1864, with 107 other Federal officers, escaped from Libby Prison. He succeeded, with about sixty of the fugitives, in making his way into the Federal lines. He surrendered 1365, and lost in the actions with Forrest 100 men. The Confederate loss in killed and wounded he claims to have been five times as large as his own.

For six months, as already stated, Rosecrans remained in camp at Murfreesborough. The Confederate army, under Bragg, lay about thirty miles south, on a branch of the Nashville Railroad running from Wartrace to Shelbyville. In May Grant was across the Mississippi fighting Pemberton and Johnston, and before the close of the month had shut up the former in Vicksburg, while the latter was straining every nerve to gather an army sufficiently large to raise the siege. At about this time the authorities at Washington supposed that Johnston was being heavily re-enforced for this purpose from General Bragg's army. Early in June, therefore, Halleck urged Rosecrans to take advantage of Bragg's weakness and drive him into Georgia, when East Tennessee would become an easy prey to the Federal forces. But the matter was looked upon in quite a different light at Rosecrans's headquarters. There it seemed better that Bragg should stay where he was. It was not believed that he had been materially weakened: it seemed evident that the Confederate War Department was resolved upon keeping its foothold in Tennessee as well as in Mississippi.[1] Again, if Rosecrans advanced and compelled Bragg's retreat, his army, for want of an adequate cavalry force, was in no condition to pursue, and the consequence would be unfavorable to Grant, who would then have to meet the bulk of Bragg's army. At a council of war called by Rosecrans, composed of seventeen officers (corps and division commanders and generals of cavalry), it was the opinion of eleven that Bragg had not been materially weakened, the other six thinking that 10,000 men had been sent to Johnston. Only four of the seventeen thought the Army of the Cumberland could then advance with a reasonable prospect of fighting a great and successful battle, and even these were doubtful. The council unanimously agreed that an advance was unadvisable.[2]

A few days later, the Vicksburg campaign seeming so near its successful termination, and it being understood that General Burnside would co-operate by an advance into East Tennessee, the Army of the Cumberland was set in motion. This advance—made under great disadvantages, which the reader has already been taught to appreciate—and the brilliant movements by which General Bragg was driven from Shelbyville to Chattanooga, form the subject of the next chapter.

CHAPTER XXXII.

THE CHATTANOOGA CAMPAIGN.

II. THE ADVANCE FROM MURFREESBOROUGH.

The Confederate Situation in Tennessee.—Estimate of Forces.—The Order to Advance.—Actions at Liberty and Hoover's Gaps.—Occupation of Shelbyville.—The Race for Elk River.—Bragg abandons Middle Tennessee.—Rosecrans brought to a Halt.

BRAGG'S army held the line of Duck River, guarding the railroad from Nashville to Chattanooga. Polk, with 18,000 men, was strongly intrenched at Shelbyville, where, by the forced labor of 3000 slaves sent from Georgia and Alabama, a line of earth-works had been constructed five miles in extent. On his right, at Wartrace, and holding the railroad, was Hardee's corps, 12,000 strong, with outposts at Liberty and Hoover's Gaps, guarding the mountain approaches from the north. In the rear, eighteen miles south of Duck River, another intrenched camp lay behind a difficult mountain range at Tullahoma. Besides Polk's and Hardee's corps north of Duck River, Bragg had another, under Buckner, in East Tennessee, numbering 10,000 effective men.

The entire Confederate army of Tennessee on the 20th of June, 1863, numbered 46,000 effective men.[1] Rosecrans's army at that time was not less than 60,000 strong, but this superiority of numbers was balanced by the inferiority of his cavalry, and by the necessity of a detachment of force at every stage of his advance into the enemy's country. It was, therefore, the obvious policy of the Federal commander to compel Bragg to fight a battle in Tennessee. It was with this idea that Rosecrans planned his summer campaign, waiting only the assurance that the retreat of Bragg's army, which must be reckoned among the things possible, would not seriously affect the Vicksburg campaign.

The Confederate General John Morgan having been sent, with a large detachment of cavalry, northward for an excursion into Kentucky, it seemed an opportune season for an advance against the enemy, orders for which were issued on the 23d of June. The movement began the next day. The direct road to Shelbyville was the easiest approach, while those farther eastward led through difficult mountain passes, strongly guarded by the enemy. An advance by the former would have terminated in a battle with the ene-

Alabama or Northern Georgia. Should you be surrounded by rebel forces and your retreat cut off, defend yourself as long as possible, and make the surrender of your command cost the enemy as many times your number as possible. A copy of the general order from the War Department in regard to paroling prisoners, together with the necessary blanks, are herewith furnished you. You are authorized to enlist all able-bodied men who desire to join the 'army of the Union.' You must return as soon as the main objects of your expedition are accomplished.

"Very respectfully, your obedient servant,

"J. A. GARFIELD, Brigadier General and Chief of Staff."

"*Additional by Telegraph.*

"April 9, 1863.

"The written instructions you have received are designed to cover the cases you allude to. It is not necessary that a manufactory be directly in the employ of the rebels to come under the rule there laid down. If it produces any considerable quantity of supplies which are likely to reach the rebel army, it is to be destroyed. Of course small mills, that can only supply the necessaries of life to the inhabitants, should not be injured. Any considerable amount of supplies likely to reach the rebel army are to be destroyed. If you dress your soldiers in the costume of the enemy, they will be liable to be treated as spies; you should not do this without the consent of the men, after they have been fully advised of the possible consequences.

"(Signed), J. A. GARFIELD, Brigadier General and Chief of Staff."

[1] This was against General Joe Johnston's advice, who said that the Confederate government must choose between Mississippi and Tennessee. He urged the retention of Tennessee, which he declared to be "the shield of the South."

[2] The following is the correspondence which passed between Rosecrans and Halleck in reference to an immediate advance:

"Murfreesborough, Tenn., June 11th, 1863.

"Your dispatch of to-day is received. You remember that I gave you, as a necessary condition of success, an adequate cavalry force. Since that time I have not lost a moment in mounting our dismounted cavalry as fast as we could get horses. Not more than three hundred remain to be mounted. The Fifth Iowa, ordered up from Donelson, arrived to-day. The First Wisconsin will be here by Saturday. My preliminary infantry movements have nearly all been completed, and I am preparing to strike a blow that will tell. But to show you how differently things are viewed here, I called on my corps and division commanders and generals of cavalry for answers in writing to the questions:

"First. From your best information, do you think the enemy materially weakened in our front? Second. Do you think this army can advance at this time with reasonable prospect of fighting a great and successful battle? Third. Do you think an advance advisable at this time? To the first, eleven answered no; six, yes, to the extent of ten thousand. To the second, four, yes, with doubts; thirteen, no. To the third, not one yes; seventeen, no.

"Not one thinks an advance advisable until Vicksburg's fate is determined. Admitting these officers to have a reasonable share of military sagacity, courage, and patriotism, you perceive that there are graver and stronger reasons than probably appear at Washington for the attitude of this army. I therefore counsel caution and patience at headquarters. Better wait a little to get all we can ready to insure the best result. If by so doing we, perforce of Providence, observe a great military maxim—not to risk two great and decisive battles at the same time—we might have cause to be thankful for it. At all events, you see that, to expect success, I must have such thorough grounds that when I say 'Forward,' my word will inspire conviction and confidence where both are now wanting. I should like to have your suggestion.

"W. S. ROSECRANS, Major General.

"To Major General H. W. HALLECK, General-in-Chief."

"Washington, June 12, 1863.

"GENERAL,—Your telegram of yesterday is just received. I do not understand your application of the military maxim not to fight two great battles at the same time. It will apply to a single army, but not to two armies acting independently of each other. Johnston and Bragg are acting on interior lines between you and Grant, and it is for their interest, not ours, that they should fight at different times, so as to use the same force against both of you. It is for our interest to fight them, if possible, while divided. If you are not strong enough to fight Bragg with a part of his force absent, you will not be able to fight him after the affair at Vicksburg is over, and his troops return to your front.

"There is another military maxim, 'that councils of war never fight.' If you say that you are not prepared to fight Bragg, I shall not order you to do so, for the responsibility of fighting or refusing to fight at a particular time or place must rest upon the general in immediate command; it can not be shared by a council of war, nor will the authorities here make you fight against your will. You ask me to counsel them to caution and patience. I have done so very often, but after five or six months of inactivity, with your force all the time diminishing, and no hope of any immediate increase, you must not be surprised that their patience is pretty well exhausted. If you do not deem it prudent to risk a general battle with Bragg, why can you not harass him, or make such demonstrations as to prevent his sending more re-enforcements to Johnston? I do not write this in a spirit of fault-finding, but to assure you that the prolonged inactivity of so large an army in the field is causing much complaint and dissatisfaction, not only in Washington, but throughout the country.

"Very respectfully, your obedient servant, H. W. HALLECK, General-in-Chief.

"Major General ROSECRANS, Murfreesborough, Tennessee."

"Headquarters, Department of the Cumberland, Murfreesborough, June 21, 1863.

"GENERAL,—In your favor of the 12th instant you say you do not see how the maxim of not fighting two great battles at the same time applies to the case of this army and to Grant's. Looking at the matter practically, we and our opposing forces are so widely separated that for Bragg to materially aid Johnston he must abandon our front substantially, and then we can move to our ultimate work with more rapidity, and less waste of material on natural obstacles. If Grant is defeated, both forces will come here, and then we ought to be near our base. The same maxim that forbids, as you take it, a single army fighting two great battles at the same time—by the way, a very awkward thing to do—would forbid this nation's engaging all its forces in the great West at the same time, so as to leave it without a single reserve to stem the current of possible disaster. This is, I think, sustained by high military and political considerations. We ought to fight here, if we have a strong prospect of winning a decisive battle over the opposing force, and upon this ground I shall act. I shall be careful not to risk our last reserve without strong grounds to expect success. W. S. ROSECRANS, Major General.

"Major General H. W. HALLECK, General-in-Chief."

In Rosecrans's letter (last quoted) to Halleck there is unnecessary impertinence. A single army might easily fight two great battles at the same time. Rosecrans speaks of it as "a very awkward thing to do," as if it were impossible.

In his testimony before the Congressional Committee on the Conduct of the War (see *Rosecrans's Campaigns*, p. 27), Rosecrans says: "I felt it my duty to sacrifice all personal gratification, and even to fall in the estimation, temporarily, of the country and friends who had high hopes and expectations of the Army of the Cumberland, to secure General Grant, in his operations before Vicksburg, from the consequences of compelling Bragg to retire, when it would not be possible for us so to pursue as to prevent him from re-enforcing Johnston, whose relative numbers to our troops under General Grant was deemed more formidable than I subsequently learned it to have been."

[1] Estimated from official returns. The following are the returns of this army from November 20, 1862, to June 20, 1863, inclusive:

	Aggregate Present and Absent.	Aggregate Present.	Present for Duty.
November 20, 1862	61,229	36.686	30,649
December 10, 1862	88,484	59,075	51,030
January, 1863	83,780	49,331	36,981
February 20, 1863	87,783	55,138	42,088
March 31, 1863	96,301	65,594	49,915
April 30, 1863	98,217	67,849	52,069
May 20, 1863	93,217	64,722	50,233
June 20, 1863	83,597	59,542	45,974

These returns show:

1. That Bragg outnumbered Rosecrans at the battle of Stone River by nearly 8000 men, the effective Federal force at the time of that battle being only 43,400 men.

2. That Bragg lost at Stone River about 14,000 men, as will appear by comparing the returns of those present for duty in December, 1862, and in January, 1863. Rosecrans's loss was 8778 killed and wounded, and nearly 3000 prisoners, altogether between 10,000 and 11,000.

3. That Bragg had not been weakened materially by any re-enforcements sent to Johnston, since the returns for April, May, and June of those *present for duty* do not vary by more than 6000 men.

4. That at the date of Rosecrans's advance, June 24, 1863, Bragg's army numbered an aggregate present of 60,000, of whom 46,000 could be brought into battle.

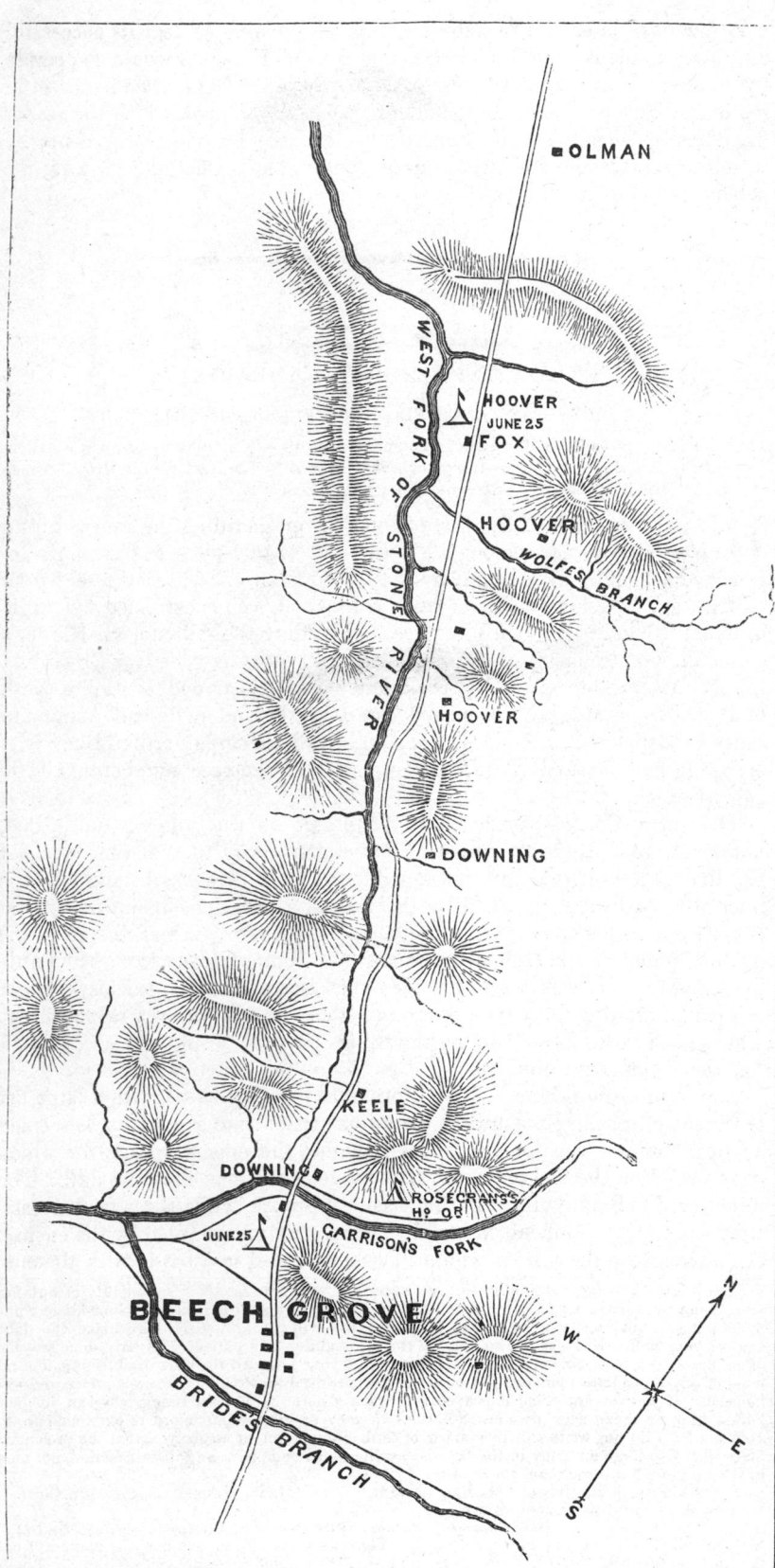

THE ADVANCE THROUGH HOOVER'S GAP.

were carried by McCook and Thomas on the 24th. The works at the entrance of Hoover's Gap, the eastern pass, were unoccupied by the enemy when Wilder's mounted infantry approached them, so sudden and unexpected was the advance, and a train of nine wagons was captured on its way to camp, with a drove of beef cattle and some prisoners. At the southern extremity of the Gap, in the vicinity of the enemy's camp at Beech Grove, there was some resistance. A miniature battle was fought between a few regiments of Wilder's brigade and a superior Confederate force, in which the Federal detachment was almost overpowered before Reynolds's division could come to its aid. The loss in Wilder's command, after two hours of fighting, was 63 killed and wounded; deserters and prisoners estimated the enemy's loss at over 500. The Confederate force defending the Gap was a part of General Pat Cleburne's division.

Another portion of Cleburne's command guarded Liberty Gap, which had in the mean time been carried by Willich's brigade of Johnson's division. Willich charged with his men, and, turning the enemy's flanks, drove him from the position, capturing his tents, baggage, and supplies. The other end of the Gap was carried with equal gallantry by Baldwin's brigade. The next day Johnson held the Gap, to keep up the delusion as to a direct advance upon Bragg's intrenchments. In the afternoon an attempt was made by the enemy to regain his lost position, and the attack was sufficiently serious to compel Johnson to send in Carlin's brigade of Davis's division. Davis was ill, but, hearing the noise of the battle, left his couch, and reached the front in time to witness the charge of Carlin's brigade and the defeat of the enemy.

Rosecrans now pushed his army on to Manchester, flanking Bragg, who immediately abandoned his useless intrenchments. These were occupied by Granger and Stanley on the 27th. Stanley, with his cavalry, had joined Granger at Christianà. Advancing on Guy's Gap, covering Shelbyville, that position was carried after a little brief skirmish. The enemy was already in retreat, and Shelbyville was captured that evening, with three guns, 500 prisoners, 3000 sacks of corn, and other supplies. The main body of Wheeler's cavalry, which had covered the retreat, escaped by swimming Duck River.

By this time all of McCook's and Thomas's corps were at Manchester. Wilder's command was ordered to Decherd to destroy the bridge over Elk River, but this was found too strongly guarded. In the race for Elk River, Bragg had come out ahead, securing his military road, which he had constructed five miles east of the railroad. Covered again by Wheeler's cavalry, he had left Tullahoma on the 30th of June, to escape the blow which Rosecrans was prepared to strike on his right flank, and succeeded in crossing the Elk at Estelle Springs without a battle. Negley's and Sheridan's divisions, with Turchin's cavalry, came up with the enemy's rear-guard, under Wheeler, July 25. Skirmishing followed, but the resistance was so stubborn that Bragg did not lose a gun. When the river, then swollen by the rains of the last nine days, was crossed by Rosecrans on the 3d, the enemy had vanished. Crittenden's corps, brought down from McMinnville, had taken possession of the road leading from Decherd by way of Tracy City to Chattanooga, thus compelling Bragg to retreat through the mountains westward. McCook had also advanced so as to keep him to the west of Winchester. But Bragg had a fair start, and these movements proved of little consequence. The Confederate army retreated across the Cumberland Mountains to Chattanooga, destroying the railroad in its rear, and crossing the Tennessee at Bridgeport.

Rosecrans was disappointed. He had hoped to fight a battle in Tennessee. He had scarcely counted upon the rapid backward movement made by Bragg. Something had been gained. He had recovered Middle Tennes-

my in his well-intrenched and chosen position—a battle which, if successful, would be gained at great sacrifice, and leave Bragg an open door for retreat. The mountain roads led to Bragg's right and rear. A strong demonstration on the Shelbyville road would compel that general to uncover the difficult approaches on his right, and once beyond these, Rosecrans, by a very rapid movement to Manchester or Winchester, would cut off retreat, and force the enemy to a battle, the conditions of which would be equal as to the field of conflict, and as to numbers much in his favor. With Morgan's command out of the way, his cavalry was able to cope with Bragg's, while he was superior in infantry by at least 20,000 men.

McCook's corps began its march early on the morning of the 24th. Phil Sheridan's division took the direct road to Shelbyville, preceded by five companies of mounted infantry. The other two divisions, under Generals Jeff C. Davis and R. W. Johnson, followed for six miles, and then turned to the left into the road to Liberty Gap. Thomas's corps, starting at the same time, moved directly on Manchester by way of Hoover's Gap. Crittenden's corps, the last to move, made a long detour to McMinnville, about forty miles southeast from Murfreesborough. Granger, commanding a reserve corps, supported McCook and Thomas. The cavalry was divided—Turchin, with one brigade, going with Crittenden, while the rest, under Stanley, were thrown out on the right flank.

For several days the weather had been clear and promising, but on the very morning of the advance from Murfreesborough it began to rain. For seventeen successive days the rain continued, swelling streams, and so badly cutting up the roads that rapid progress, the most essential element entering into the campaign, was impossible. One division occupied three days in marching twenty-one miles. Such a season at this period of the year had not been known in Tennessee for a score of years.

Both Liberty and Hoover's Gaps, about ten miles from Murfreesborough,

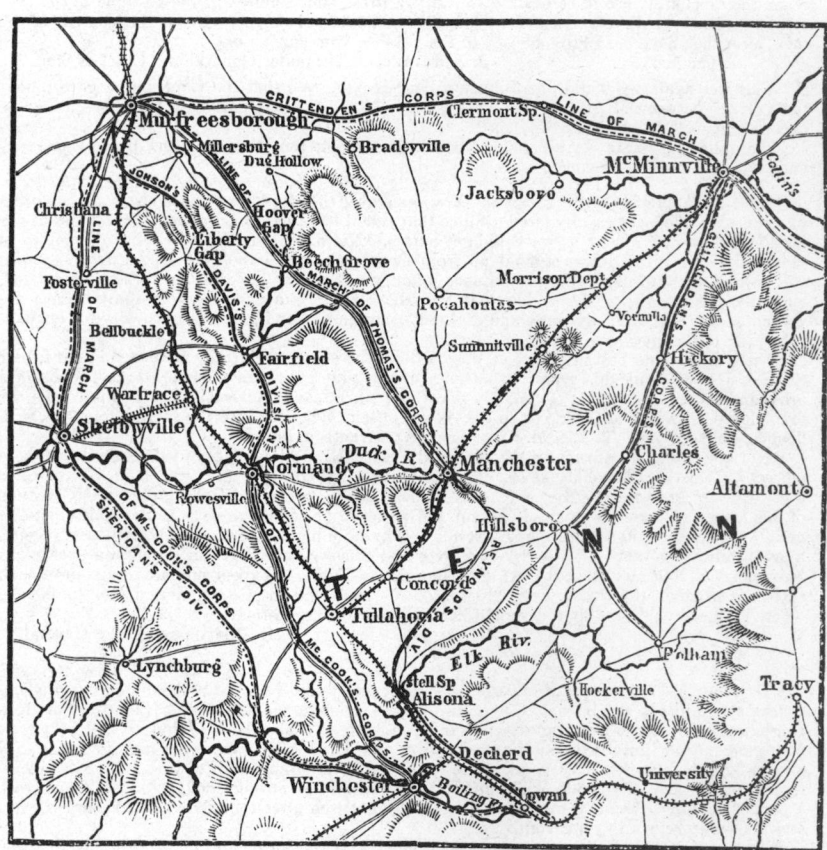

MAP ILLUSTRATING THE MIDDLE TENNESSEE CAMPAIGN.

see at a cost of less than 600 men, and had, besides causing the enemy an equal loss in killed and wounded, captured over 1600 prisoners. But Bragg had escaped. The thing which had been accomplished was not the thing which had been planned.

The worst feature of the situation in which Rosecrans found himself, after Bragg's retreat, was the impossibility of pursuit. His army occupied a line extending from McMinnville to Winchester; but his cavalry posts had followed the enemy to the Tennessee, and outposts were established from Stevenson on the right to Pelham on the left. In this position Rosecrans was brought to a halt, in order to establish his line of communications with Murfreesborough. The Middle Tennessee campaign had been concluded. The movements made by Rosecrans in this campaign were brilliant; but he had made a great mistake in too readily assuming that the enemy would fight instead of retreating. If, in place of waiting at Manchester for Crittenden, he had moved directly on Estelle Springs, Bragg must either have fought or have fallen back with an utterly demoralized army, and with great loss of artillery. If Crittenden was necessary, then he ought not, in the first instance, to have been sent so far out of the way. That which, more than any thing else, disarranged Rosecrans's plans, was the never-ceasing rain; a circumstance for which he, of course, was not accountable, and one upon which he could not have counted. Fair weather would have been the ruin of the Confederate Army of Tennessee. As it was, Rosecrans was farther than ever from his military base, and, looking forward to the next stage of his campaign, could not expect to fight a battle with the enemy under conditions as favorable as those which had just been offered him.

But Bragg's army lost by retreating. His effective force after reaching Chattanooga was only about 40,000 men, or 6000 short of his strength at Shelbyville. Two thirds of this loss is to be accounted for by straggling and desertion. His retreat, occurring at the same time with the surrender of Vicksburg and the defeat at Gettysburg, contributed much to the general despondency in the South which followed those disasters to the Confederate cause.

CHAPTER XXXIII.
THE CHATTANOOGA CAMPAIGN.

III. THE ARMY OF THE OHIO.—RECOVERY OF EAST TENNESSEE.

Burnside's Department; its Limits; Political and Military Situation.—The Ninth Corps transferred from Newport News to the West.—Pegram's Raid; his Defeat at Somerset.—New England troops at Louisville.—The three Military Districts of Kentucky and their Commanders.—Organization of the Twenty-third Corps.—The Ninth Corps is sent to Vicksburg.—This upsets Burnside's Plan for the immediate recovery of East Tennessee.—Colonel Sanders's Expedition; he breaks the East Tennessee and Virginia Railroad, and threatens Knoxville.—John Morgan's Raid.—He starts from Sparta, June 27th.—Estimate of his Force.—Fight at Tebbs's Bend, July 4th.—Colonel Moore refuses to surrender on the Glorious Fourth; his successful Defense.—Morgan crosses Green River.—Colonel Hanson surrenders Lebanon, July 5th, after seven hours' fighting; Morgan's Brother killed.—Generals Hobson, Judah, and Shackleford in pursuit of Morgan.—Morgan crosses the Ohio into Southern Indiana.—He sweeps around Cincinnati.—His perilous Situation.—He is surrounded and captured with his Command.—His subsequent Escape.—Burnside's March across the Mountains into East Tennessee.—Difficulties of the March.—Knoxville is captured without a Battle.—Burnside's Reception by the Loyalists.—Capture of Cumberland Gap.

GENERAL BURNSIDE was assigned to the Department of the Ohio on the 15th of March, 1863. He had been relieved of the command of the Army of the Potomac on the 25th of January. The interval had been spent by the general at his home in Providence, Rhode Island. One week after his new appointment he reached Cincinnati, and there established his headquarters. General Horatio G. Wright had been the commander of the Department of the Ohio, which now comprised the states of Ohio, Indiana, Illinois, Michigan, Eastern Kentucky, and East Tennessee, as soon as the latter should be occupied. The situation, political and military, of the department required the utmost tact and sagacity on the part of its commander. The Confederate cavalry was ravaging a large portion of Kentucky, and in the more northern states there existed considerable disaffection toward the national government. Martial law had been proclaimed in Kentucky, but in Indiana, Ohio, and Illinois there was no hinderance to the most licentious freedom on the part of public speakers and of the press.

In such a state of affairs, the military force then existing was not sufficient either to meet the hostile incursions of the enemy or to silence disloyalists. Burnside, therefore, had two divisions of the Ninth Army Corps, then in camp at Newport News, under Generals Willcox and Sturgis, transferred to his department. Upon this change, Sturgis was succeeded in the command of his division by General Robert B. Potter. At this time the Confederate General Pegram, with a force of 3000 men, was marching through Central Kentucky, capturing towns and plundering citizens, and had with feeble opposition penetrated as far as Danville. Louisville was almost in danger of being captured, and Indiana open to invasion. To meet these hostile intentions of Pegram, the Ninth Corps was hurried westward, and the small detachments of Federal troops scattered over Central Kentucky were concentrated at Lebanon and Hickman's Bridge, under Generals Q. A. Gillmore and Boyle. With these latter Burnside ordered an advance against Pegram on the 28th of March. The enemy was driven rapidly southward, and at Somerset, on the 30th, Gillmore, with his cavalry, routed and drove him across the Cumberland River, inflicting upon him a loss of 500 killed, wounded, and prisoners.

The two divisions of the Ninth Corps, now commanded by General John G. Parke, who had relieved "Baldy" Smith, arrived at Louisville early in April. The corps was composed for the most part of New England troops,

ROBERT B. POTTER.

against whom, as Yankees *par excellence*, the Kentuckians were prejudiced. This sentiment, however, was soon overcome by the courtesy of the officers and the general good conduct of the soldiers. Kentucky was at this time divided into three military districts: the Eastern, with headquarters at Louisa, under General Julius White; the Central, under General Q. A. Gillmore, with headquarters at Lexington; and the Western, under General J. T. Boyle, with headquarters at Louisville. Gillmore, after Pegram's defeat, was relieved by General Willcox. The line held by the troops in these three districts extended from the Big Sandy to the Cumberland River. The Ninth Corps, upon its arrival, was sent to the front. It was a part of Burnside's duty to protect so much of Rosecrans's lines of communication as lay within his department. For this purpose fortified posts were established on the railroads leading to Western Kentucky and Tennessee, and the utmost precaution was used to prevent raids on the part of guerrillas and the enemy's cavalry.

On the 27th of April, in compliance with an order from Washington, all the troops in Kentucky not belonging to the Ninth began to be organized into another corps, to be designated as the Twenty-third, and to be under the command of Major General G. L. Hartsuff. This organization was completed by the 22d of May, and a plan of operations was consulted between Burnside and Rosecrans for an immediate advance, the former marching with his two corps directly into East Tennessee, while the latter moved upon Chattanooga. Preparations were made for the campaign by both armies, and on the 2d of June Burnside moved his headquarters from Cincinnati to Lexington; but, at the very last moment, the Ninth Corps was withdrawn from Burnside to re-enforce General Grant before Vicksburg, and the East Tennessee campaign was postponed.

About the middle of June Colonel H. S. Saunders led an expedition into East Tennessee, and, striking the Virginia and Tennessee Railroad at Lenoir, moved up the road, breaking up portions of it on his route. He threatened Knoxville, burned the bridge—1600 feet long—across Holston River at Strawberry Plains, captured 10 guns and 400 prisoners, and, after destroying stores of great value, returned to Lexington on the 26th.

It was at about this time that the Confederate General John Morgan was planning his grand raid into Kentucky and the states north of the Ohio. His scheme was daring, contemplating a bold march through Kentucky, breaking through Burnside's lines, now weakened by the absence of Parke's corps, then across the Ohio River and through the southern counties of Ohio and Indiana, finally sweeping down into West Virginia, or, if fortune favored, through Pennsylvania, to join General Lee's invading army.

Morgan, starting from Sparta June 27, crossed the Cumberland River near Burkesville on the 2d of July, accompanied by General Basil Duke as second in command. His force has been variously estimated, the Confederate statements putting it at 2028 men, with four guns, and the Federal officers in Kentucky at from 4000 to 5000. The truth probably lies about midway between these estimates. Pollard states the force to have been 3000 strong, in two brigades. Burnside was scarcely prepared for this sudden invasion. His best troops were away. Saunders, with his most efficient cavalry, had only just returned from an exhausting raid. Custer's troops were at a distance from the Cumberland. Morgan's command was well organized, and would have little trouble in supplying itself in the fertile valleys of the Cumberland and Ohio. Confined to no strictly-defined line of march, it easily evaded the troops first sent to intercept it, and obtained a start of two days, moving on Columbia.

MORGAN'S RAIDERS.

IMPROMPTU BARRICADE.

Passing through Columbia, Morgan attempted to cross Green River Bridge, at Tebbs's Bend, on the 4th. Guarding the river at this point were five companies of the Twenty-fifth Michigan, under Colonel Orlando H. Moore. The position was well selected for defense, and when Morgan approached, before daylight, demanding its surrender, Moore replied, "The Fourth of July is not a proper day for me to entertain such a proposition." Morgan attacked, and was driven off with a loss of nearly 50 men, among whom were some of his best officers.[1] It had been an obstinate, and at times a hand-to-hand struggle, and the 200 brave defenders of the stockade

[1] Moore gives the Confederate loss as 50 killed and 250 wounded.

well earned the thanks which were afterward tendered them by the Kentucky Legislature. Morgan had attacked with two regiments, the rest of his force crossing the river, in the mean time, by another ford.

From the Green River Morgan swept northward, striking Lebanon the next day. The garrison at this place consisted of 400 men of the Twentieth Kentucky, under Colonel Hanson, who stood out for seven hours against Morgan's attack, placing his men in the dépôt and the neighboring houses. Surrender at length became inevitable, the enemy having charged into the town and set fire to the houses from which the garrison were firing. Here Morgan's young brother was killed while leading a charge. With the Federal cavalry now close upon him—riding swiftly on his track while he was fighting at Tebbs's Bend and Lebanon—Morgan had not time to parole his prisoners, whom he compelled to keep pace with him to Springfield, making ten miles in an hour and a half. Those who faltered were ruthlessly shot and left upon the road.

A formidable force of infantry, cavalry, and artillery, under Generals Hobson, Judah, and Shackleford, joined by Colonel Wolford, were rapidly pursuing Morgan, who was boldly advancing to the Ohio River by way of Bardstown. The experienced raider had still the best of the race, scouring the country for supplies and horses on his route, leaving behind him empty larders and stables, thus compelling his pursuers to make the most of their jaded animals. On the 7th, when the Federals reached Shepardsville, Morgan had twenty hours the start; but the exciting race was continued. Morgan, having crossed Rolling Fork, burning the bridges behind him, reached the Ohio at Brandenburg, 40 miles below Louisville, on the 8th. On board of captured steamers he ferried his command across, and his pursuers reached the southern bank just in time to witness the burning of his transports. On its swift march the Confederate command had gathered fresh accessions of force, and was now ready to fall upon the southern counties of Indiana with an army of 4000 men and 10 guns.

Taking Corydon, Greenville, and Palmyra in his way, Morgan hastened on the 9th to Salem, capturing there 350 Home Guards, breaking up the railroad, and burning the town. It was the portion of Indiana most disaffected toward the national government which Morgan was visiting with his wrath; but he had no time to distinguish friend from foe, and went on burning and ravaging. He dared not halt even to fight, and every place was secure against him which offered any serious resistance. From Salem his course veered eastward toward Lexington, which he reached on the morning of the 10th. From that point, passing northward and eastward, he menaced at once Madison and Vernon, 20 miles apart; but, finding a considerable force at the latter point, he did not venture battle, but skirmished evasively, while his men were destroying the railroads north, south, east, and west of the town. Thence he moved eastward, passing through Versailles on the 12th, seizing fresh horses as he marched, and reaching Harrison, on the Ohio border, the next day, where he gathered in his detached columns, and made a clean sweep around Cincinnati, at distances of from 7 to 18 miles. Daylight of the 14th found him 18 miles east of Cincinnati, anxiously looking for some avenue of escape.

For his position was now one of great peril. He had embarked upon a great adventure, which might have had some military consequence if he had been let alone; but, as must have been apparent to him now, it had proved little more than a bold march across one state and a portion of two others. Indeed, from a military point of view, he was more a necessity to Bragg in Tennessee than he was an injury to the Federal cause in his present position north of the Ohio. So closely had he been pursued that he had stepped lightly over the country which he had meant to crush under the heels of his horsemen. He had captured hundreds (thousands it may be, so Pollard reports) of militia, but he could do nothing with them, and their paroles placed them just where they were before. He had destroyed a large amount of property, and had broken railroad communications, but the ravages had been so slight that a single week would repair the ruin. He had only made a bold march, scarcely worthy the record which we have given it, in the event of his escape. It is the *denouement* of the little episode which gives it any historic interest. How and where did the bold march end? is the question which the reader waits to have answered. And this was the question which Morgan was trying to answer prospectively when, on the 14th, after crossing the Miami, he moved southward to the Ohio to find a crossing for his closely-meshed command.

Generals Judah, Hobson, and Shackleford had crossed the Ohio on the 8th, following Morgan in the route which we have traced. When the raiders crossed the Miami they had only four hours the start of their pursuers. Such a disposition of the Federal forces had been made as would secure Hamilton and Cincinnati against attack. Gunboats were brought up to patrol the Ohio, and to prevent Morgan's escape southward across that river. A column under Judah moved along the river roads, while Hobson and Shackleford took those in the interior. The militia sent down by Governor Morgan, of Indiana, halted at the eastern border of their own state, but the people of Ohio, along the roads in Morgan's front, blocked up his route with fallen trees, while the Federal troops hemmed him in upon the north and in his rear. For 160 miles Morgan continued his desperate flight through Williamsburg, Winchester, Piketon, and Jackson, as if running a race with the gun-boats. But the latter, under the direction of Lieutenant Commander Fitch, had been warped over the shoals, and thus had succeeded in forcing their way up the Rapids, so that when Morgan attempted to cross the river at Buffington Island, near Pomeroy, he found the "web-footed" monsters still in his front, and was driven back in confusion, and brought face to face with his pursuers, near Chester, on the 19th. Here Shackleford met him, and soon Judah, also, was upon his flank, and Hobson upon his rear. There was a good hour's fight, when Shackleford ordered a charge, and the enemy, with infantry, cavalry, and artillery attacking him upon all sides, sent in a flag of truce, and surrendered 700 men, including Dick Morgan and Basil Duke. But this was only a portion of Morgan's command. The leader himself, with the main body, had pushed up the river some 14 miles to Belleville, where he was already (about 3 P.M.) crossing his horses. Before he had got 400 men, under Colonel A. R. Johnson, across, Hobson and Shackleford were again upon him, and General Scammon's gun-boats made their appearance in his front. Here 1000 more of the raiders were surrendered.

But Morgan was not among the captured, having again disappeared with a small body of his adherents. His guns and weapons were gone, and the great raid had dwindled down into a run for dear life on Morgan's part. He fled inland to McArthur on the 21st, and thence toward Marietta, where he again made a vain attempt to cross into Virginia. Then he veered northward again to Eastport. But Shackleford, with 500 men who had volunteered to stay in the saddle without eating or drinking until Morgan should be captured, overtook the flying partisan near New Lisbon, where the latter's flight had been interrupted by an irregular force of militia and home guards. Driven to a high bluff, Morgan finally surrendered at discretion on the 27th. It was now exactly a month since he had marched from Sparta, in Tennessee. Of the command with which he first set forth, less than 400 had escaped, over 500 had been killed or wounded; the rest, with their leader, were prisoners of war.

Morgan and his officers were carried to Cincinnati, and delivered over to General Burnside. By direction of the President they were confined in Ohio penitentiaries, their heads being shaved like those of felons. Morgan, with six of his officers, managed to escape on the night of November 26 by digging their way out of their cells. Those who escaped had been confined at Columbus. Morgan, with a certain Captain Hines, took the midnight train for Cincinnati, and, just before reaching the city, put on the brakes, jumped off, and was ferried across the Ohio into Kentucky. Through Kentucky, Tennessee, and Northern Georgia, Morgan—having lost his companion by the way—proceeded to Richmond, where he was fêted and made much of. His escape from his cell, his disguise, and his flight to Virginia had been accomplished through the assistance of Confederate sympathizers outside his prison walls.

About three weeks after Morgan's capture, Burnside had at Camp Nelson, near Richmond, Kentucky, a thoroughly organized force of 20,000 men. Without waiting for the return of the Ninth Corps, he, on the 16th of August, commenced his advance to East Tennessee. Rosecrans had already driven Bragg to Chattanooga. The occupation of East Tennessee was at this time of very great importance, in order, by the destruction or possession

of the railroad from Virginia, to cut off communications between Lee's and Bragg's armies. Besides, from Knoxville, Burnside could easily and effectively co-operate with Rosecrans's next movement upon Bragg.

East Tennessee lies in the Valley of the Tennessee and Holston Rivers, and between the Cumberland and Blue Ridge ranges of mountains. It is a mountainous district, and its inhabitants were for the most part loyal to the national government. For the latter reason, it was not advisable to occupy this region before it could be permanently held. Hitherto the people had been harassed by the enemy, who had exercised his power to the utmost in order to crush out and overawe the Unionists, many of whom were already refugees.

Burnside's advance was simultaneous with Rosecrans's march from Winchester upon Chattanooga, of which we treat in the next chapter. Concentrating his forces at Crab Orchard, he moved directly upon Knoxville, through Mount Vernon, London, Williamsburg, and thence southward into Tennessee, with Hartsuff's columns upon his right, proceeding through Somerset, and Colonel Foster's cavalry upon his left. The routes taken by the several columns were those least likely to be defended by the enemy. After crossing the Cumberland River a force was sent, under command of Colonel De Courcy, to threaten Cumberland Gap, then held by Frazier's brigade of Buckner's command, while Burnside, with his main body, crossed the mountains by the gaps farther westward. It was a most difficult route; but the troops were in light marching order, and many of them mounted, with pack-mules for transportation, the few wagon trains following on the best roads, while the soldiers, on foot or on horseback, climbed over the mountains by comparatively unfrequented paths. During the fortnight after Burnside's departure from Crab Orchard, on the 21st of August, the whole army, mules and men, were tasked to the utmost limits of endurance. Up the rugged heights the artillery was with difficulty drawn, and when the mules failed from exhaustion their places were filled by the soldiers. At length the summit was reached, and the army descended into East Tennessee, its conquerors; for, surprised by the sudden and apparently formidable movement, General Buckner evacuated Knoxville and fell back to the Tennessee, leaving Frazier's command at Cumberland Gap without orders, without intelligence of his retreat, and without support.

Burnside's army had moved in five columns. The first and second joined at Jamestown, Tennessee, and, moving to Montgomery, were joined on the 30th by the third and fourth. The other column, composed of cavalry, moved directly on Jacksborough, and thence through Wheeler's Gap to Knoxville. Burnside's headquarters were established at Kingston on the 1st and at Knoxville on the 3d of September. In fourteen days he had marched his army 250 miles.

On the 5th he dispatched Shackleford to the rear of Cumberland Gap,

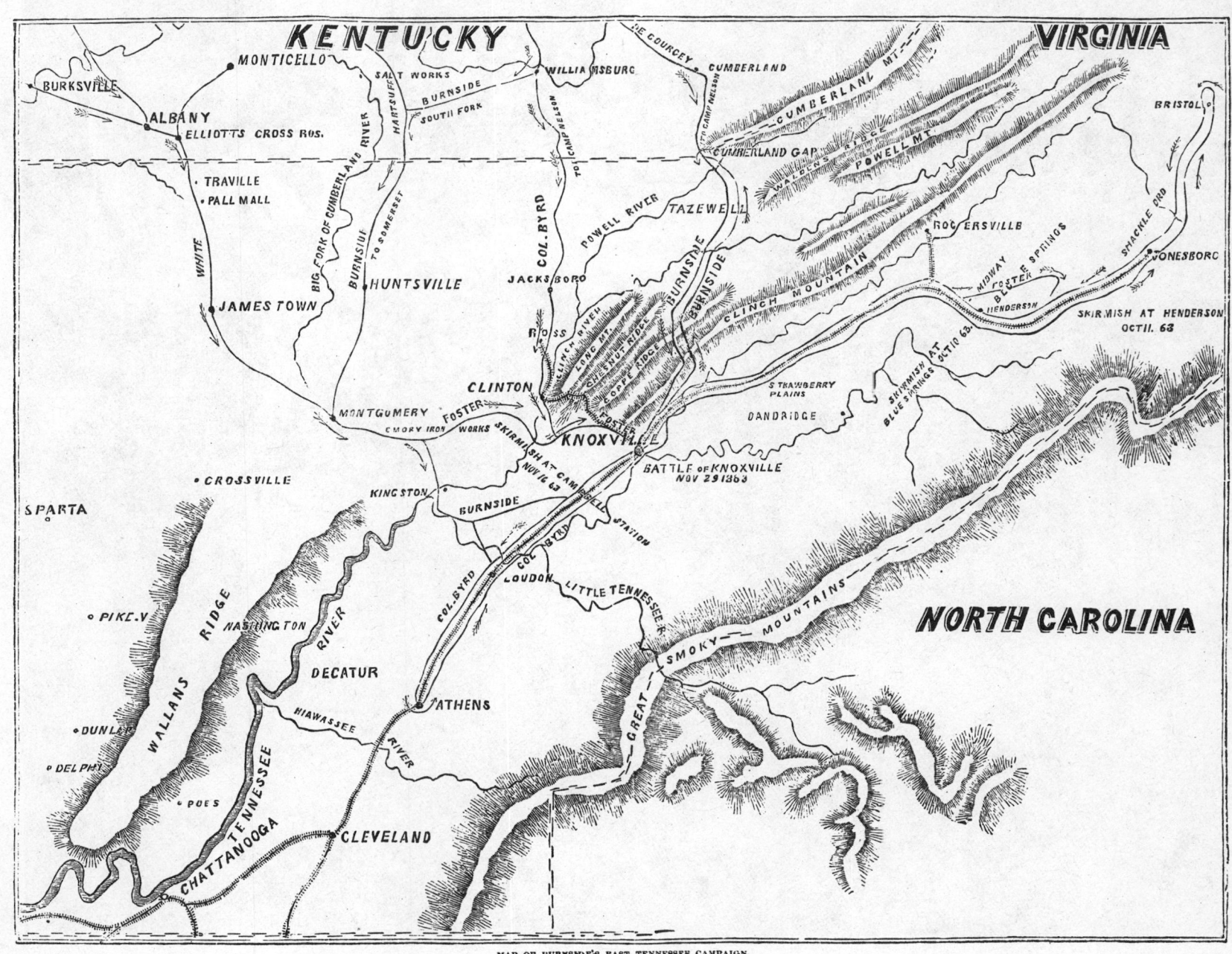

MAP OF BURNSIDE'S EAST TENNESSEE CAMPAIGN.

DRAGGING ARTILLERY OVER THE MOUNTAINS.

OCCUPATION OF CUMBERLAND GAP.

which De Courcy threatened from the north. Frazier, who occupied the Gap with four Confederate regiments, was well supplied, and confident of his ability to hold the position. But some of Shackleford's men succeeded on the 7th in creeping through the lines and burning the mill upon which the garrison depended for flour. Burnside arrived in person on the 9th, when Frazier surrendered 2000 men and 14 guns. The pursuit of a small Confederate force under Sam Jones into Virginia completed the long-sought conquest of East Tennessee. The campaign had been accomplished without a single battle.

By the Loyalists along his line of march and at Knoxville Burnside was hailed as a deliverer. His entrance into Knoxville was an ovation which might have flattered the greatest of conquerors. His wayworn troops shared the generous welcome. National flags, long concealed, came forth from the houses, and made the 3d of September seem like a 4th of July.[1] General Burnside captured at Knoxville a large quantity of ammunition, 2000 stand of small-arms, 11 guns, and 2500 prisoners.

CHAPTER XXXIV.

THE CHATTANOOGA CAMPAIGN.

IV. THE BATTLE OF CHICKAMAUGA.

Rosecrans crosses the Tennessee.—Movements of his three Corps.—Bragg retreats from Chattanooga.—Over-confidence of Rosecrans.—Why Burnside did not co-operate.—Bragg's Opportunity.—General Negley's Fight at Dug Gap discovers the Enemy.—Rosecrans alarmed.—Hurried Concentration and narrow Escape of his Army.—The Situation on the Evening of September 18.—*Battle of the 19th.*—General Thomas strikes the first Blow.—Baird's Repulse; Loss of the "Loomis" Battery.—Enemy driven, and Guns recaptured.—Confederate Attack in the Afternoon; Van Cleve driven; Hazen repulses the Enemy with Artillery.—Pat Cleburne's Night Attack.—Results of the Day's Fighting.—Council of War at the Widow Glenn's.—The

[1] Dr. W. H. Church, of Burnside's staff, thus describes the reception of the troops on the way to and in Knoxville:

"The East Tennessee troops, of whom General Burnside had a considerable number, were kept constantly in the advance, and were received with expressions of the profoundest gratitude by the people, who are described as the most heartily and generally loyal people in the United States. There were many thrilling scenes of the meeting of our East Tennessee soldiers with their families, from whom they had been so long separated.

"The East Tennesseeans were so glad to see our soldiers that they cooked every thing they had and gave it to them freely, not asking pay, and apparently not thinking of it. Women stood by the road side with pails of water, and displayed Union flags. The wonder was where all the stars and stripes came from. Knoxville was radiant with flags. At a point on the road from Kingston to Knoxville sixty women and girls stood by the road side waving Union flags, and shouting 'Hurrah for the Union!' Old ladies rushed out of their houses and wanted to see General Burnside, and shake hands with him, and cried 'Welcome, welcome, General Burnside! welcome to East Tennessee!' A meeting of the Union citizens of Knoxville was held, and addressed by General Burnside and General Carter. It was attended by about five hundred men, and a large number of women and children. The demonstrations were not boisterous, but there was intense, quiet rejoicing. Men who had been hidden for months came in, full of gratitude for their deliverance."

Confederate General Longstreet's Arrival.—*Battle of the 20th.*—Rosecrans's Dispositions.—Bragg's Plan of Attack.—Polk's Delay.—Thomas is hard pressed, but holds his Position.—Longstreet's Attack.—Hindman breaks through the Right of the Federal Line.—How the Gap was made.—Rosecrans, McCook, and Crittenden swept from the Field.—Extent of the Disorder.—Garfield goes to Thomas.—Formation of a new Line on the Slope of Mission Ridge.—General Negley's Position.—Weakness of the new Line.—Longstreet's Assault delayed.—Granger arrives in time to meet it and to save the Day.—Withdrawal of the Army by Night to Rossville and thence to Chattanooga.—Estimate of Losses.—Review of the Campaign.

WE left Rosecrans's army at Winchester, south of Elk River, with its left and rear toward McMinnville well guarded, and its outposts advanced to Pelham and Stevenson. If its progress thus far had been difficult, it was yet mere play when compared with a farther advance across the Cumberland Mountains and the broad Tennessee to Chattanooga, whither Bragg had retreated. A direct attack upon the enemy, strongly intrenched in Chattanooga, was out of the question, even if Rosecrans's army had been a hundred thousand strong. The campaign against Bragg, therefore, necessarily involved an attack upon the railroad running southward from Chattanooga through Dalton to Atlanta. The railroad connecting Chattanooga with the East would very soon be rendered useless to the Confederates by Burnside's advance to Knoxville. The valley through which the Atlanta Road runs could be reached in two ways: westwardly, by turning the head of Sequatchie Valley, or by crossing the valley at Dunlap or Thurman's, and then moving across Walden's Ridge, crossing the Tennessee above Chattanooga; or southwardly, by moving across the Cumberland range, crossing the Tennessee below Chattanooga, and then the four ranges south of the river—Raccoon, Lookout, Mission, and Taylor's.[1] Rosecrans chose the latter, or southward route, leaving the natural valley from East Tennessee to Northern Georgia open to the co-operative movement which he expected would be undertaken by Burnside.

Upon whatsoever route Rosecrans might advance, there could be little dependence upon the country for forage, none at all for the subsistence of his soldiers. Supplies of food and ammunition sufficient for the campaign must be accumulated before moving, and must be carried with the army, thus increasing the difficulties of the march. The necessity of a long halt after Bragg's retreat was therefore inevitable; yet, strange as it may seem, General Halleck, at Washington, not appreciating Napoleon's maxim that "an army crawls upon its belly," wondered and chafed at this delay, and finally issued a peremptory order directing Rosecrans to advance, and report his progress daily to the War Department.[2] Very fortunately, Rosecrans was

[1] Or, striking farther southward, after crossing the Tennessee, there would be Sand, Lookout, and Pigeon Mountains, and Taylor's Ridge.

[2] The order was issued early in August. On the 4th Rosecrans writes:

"Your dispatch, ordering me to move forward without farther delay, reporting the movement of each corps until I cross the Tennessee, is received. As I have been determined to cross the river as soon as practicable, and have been making all preparations, and getting such information

STEVENSON, ALABAMA.

nearly ready to move. He had completed the railroad from Murfreesborough to Stevenson, and thence to Bridgeport, by the 25th of July, and only waited for the opening of the road from Cowan to Tracy City. By straining to the utmost the capacities of the Stevenson Road, he had accumulated by the 8th of August a sufficient quantity of supplies to warrant his immediate advance. The enemy was in no condition to disturb his communications or to resist his advance to the Tennessee. So far, therefore, he was relieved of anxiety. While his own army covered the approaches to his rear and right, Burnside's was more than adequate to the protection of his left.

Sheridan's division had already occupied Stevenson and Bridgeport before Halleck's order was issued. The movement of the main army began on the morning of August 16th. Two of Crittenden's columns crossed the Cumberland Mountains—Palmer by Dunlap, and Wood by Thurman's—into the Sequatchie Valley, while a third, under Van Cleve, struck Pikeville at the head of the Valley. Crittenden's left, in this movement, was covered by Colonel Minty's cavalry. Thomas's and McCook's corps advanced southward to the Tennessee, occupying positions above and below Stevenson, preparatory to crossing the river. Three brigades of cavalry moved on the right, making a long detour by way of Fayetteville and Athens, to guard the river below as far as Whitesburg, about eighty miles from Stevenson.

Crittenden, upon reaching Sequatchie Valley, sent reconnoitring columns of infantry and cavalry across Walden's Ridge, Wagner's brigade and Wilder's cavalry advancing to a point opposite Chattanooga, and shelling the town on the 21st, silencing the Confederate artillery, and creating great consternation among the citizens. Another brigade (Hazen's) had also crossed the ridge farther north, at Poe's, and, with Wilder's cavalry, reconnoitred the country to Harrison's Landing, twelve miles above Chattanooga. The rest of Crittenden's command moved down the Sequatchie to the Tennessee, below Chattanooga.

On the 21st, the whole army, having crossed the Cumberland Mountains, lay upon the right bank of the Tennessee, extending over a line of 150 miles. Along this line the river flows in a southwest direction, forcing its passage through the Cumberland range, and entering Alabama at Bridgeport. The two brigades east of Walden's Ridge were prepared to enter Chattanooga in the event of its evacuation by Bragg; to force this evacuation, or to cut off the enemy from his southern communications, was the work of the main army. The preparations for crossing the river consumed ten days. During this time reconnoissances were made to discover the most available points for this purpose; the pontoons and trains were brought forward, and trestle-work and materials for improvised bridges were prepared with the utmost secrecy. The pontoons were sufficient for only two bridges, and twice that number were needed to secure rapidity of movement. The facility with which the enemy could, from the high spurs abutting on the river, overlook the whole length of the valley, prevented absolute secrecy; this, however, was of little consequence, as the intervening mountains made it impossible for Bragg to oppose any serious resistance to the movements on his left. The troops began to cross on the 29th of August, and by September 4th all were on the south side except a brigade of regulars of Baird's division, left to guard the railroad until it should be relieved by Gordon Granger's reserve corps. The crossing was conducted at four points—Shellmound, the mouth of Battle Creek, Bridgeport, and Caperton's Ferry, at the mouth of Big Crow Creek. The bridge at Bridgeport was the one mainly used for the crossing of trains. Thomas crossed one division at each of the points named; McCook crossed Woods's and Van Cleve's at Caperton's (the lowest crossing), and Sheridan's at Bridgeport; Crittenden (except Wagner's and Hazen's brigades) crossed at Shellmound, at the mouth of Battle Creek, and at Bridgeport. An accident to the bridge at Bridgeport delayed the crossing at that point for four days. The cavalry, under General Stanley, still keeping the left, crossed with McCook at Caperton's.

The plan of Rosecrans's campaign, after crossing the Tennessee, was very simple in its idea, though attended with many difficulties in its execution. Crittenden was to threaten Chattanooga by a direct advance; Thomas was to cross Raccoon Mountain, and seize Stevens's and Cooper's Gaps, leading through Lookout Mountain into McLemore's Cove, twenty miles south of Chattanooga; McCook and Stanley, in the mean time, were to move twenty miles farther southward across the mountains to Valley Head, turning the southern extremity of Pigeon Mountain, and threatening an advance on Rome. Except in its topographical features, this plan was very similar to that adopted by Hooker in his Chancellorsville campaign. In either case the enemy was flanked by the crossing of a river and an advance upon his left and rear. Hooker thought Lee would retreat, falling back upon Richmond or Gordonsville. Rosecrans was equally confident that Bragg, abandoning Chattanooga, would fall back to Rome. Both were alike mistaken; each, finding that the enemy had indeed abandoned his position, but was ready to meet the advance squarely in front, refusing to acknowledge defeat until after the test of battle. But there were three important points of difference between the Chickamauga and Chancellorsville campaigns. Hooker was able to encounter the enemy with nearly double the force of the latter, while Rosecrans, at a greater distance from his base of supplies, accepted battle with the advantage of numerical superiority against him and in Bragg's

favor. Again, Rosecrans had a more difficult country in which to operate, though this was in some degree compensated by the circumstance that the very obstacles in his own way afforded security to his rear. Finally, the sequel of the two campaigns was far different; for, although both Hooker and Rosecrans each succeeded in inflicting greater injury upon the enemy than he suffered himself, yet the former sustained a complete defeat as regarded the object of his campaign, while Rosecrans, retiring from the battle-field of Chickamauga, secured Chattanooga, the professed object of his advance from Murfreesborough.

But in carrying out this comparison we are anticipating our narrative. By the time the last divisions of the army had crossed the Tennessee, Thomas's and McCook's corps were already far advanced. Negley's division had crossed Sand Mountain into Lookout Valley, and was encamped at Brown's Spring; at the foot of the mountain, on, the west side, and ready to begin the ascent, was Reynolds's division; Brannan's had reached the summit; Jeff Davis's division, of McCook's corps, had crossed Lookout Mountain into Wills's Valley, seizing Winston's Gap; Johnson's was across Sand Mountain, while Sheridan had just reached the left bank of the Tennessee. On the 8th all the preliminary movements of the campaign had been successfully carried out. Their effect upon the enemy was immediate. Chattanooga was evidently no longer tenable. Bragg's effective force at this time was about 45,000 men.[1] He could not well afford to divide this force by sending a detachment of his army to fight the enemy, nor could he stay in Chattanooga. The capture of Vicksburg, with its garrison, was an instance, too recent to be forgotten, of the consequence of holding a position simply because of its strength, and in defiance of starvation. The nature of the country, and the presence on his right front of Burnside's army (at Knoxville on the 3d), made a counter attack upon the Federal rear, if not impossible, extremely hazardous. Reluctantly he abandoned Chattanooga, but not the campaign for its possession. The prize must be fought for, but with Rosecrans must be left the choice of the battle-field. If the Federal army emerged from the passes of Lookout Mountain into McLemore's Cove or Wills's Valley, he would meet it there; if it drew in its left in order to occupy Chattanooga in full force, and successfully evaded battle, he would still maintain the offensive, sitting down in front of the strong-hold he had so unwillingly abandoned, with his own supplies close at hand, while those of the enemy must be brought over the mountains from Murfreesborough, a hundred miles distant. His confidence in the final result was heightened by the expectation that his army, now very little inferior to that of the enemy, would soon be nearly doubled by re-enforcements from Mississippi and Virginia. Chattanooga was evacuated on the 7th and 8th. On the morning of the 9th Crittenden was apprised of this event by General Rosecrans, and ordered to push forward his entire command, with four days' rations, and make a vigorous pursuit. Bragg had waited at Chattanooga until Rosecrans had fully developed his movements southward. He then took position from Lee and Gordon's Mill to Lafayette, on the road leading southward from Chattanooga, facing the eastern slope of Pigeon Mountain. In this position he was nearer to either of Rosecrans's three corps than they were to each other.[2]

And just here Rosecrans began to base the future of his campaign upon a false calculation. His impression that Bragg's army was retreating upon Rome, demoralized and conscious of defeat, amounted to a conviction, almost to an infatuation. There was some ground for the presumption. Bragg had been flanked out of Middle Tennessee. Why not out of East Tennessee and Northern Georgia? But here Rosecrans should have remembered that in the summer campaign, his strength, as compared with that of the enemy, had been much greater than it was now. Besides its additional strength from the accession of Buckner's command, Bragg's army was now within easier reach not only of abundant supplies, but also of extensive re-enforcements. Under the circumstances, the greatest peril lurked in that presumptuous confidence with which Rosecrans was now prepared to push forward his columns.[3] There was really nothing in the way of Burnside's co-operation with over 20,000 effective men. There was every argument in its favor, and no good one against it. The moment Knoxville had been secured, Burnside ought to have been ordered to Chattanooga. He could have made

---

as may enable me to do so without being driven back like Hooker, I wish to know if your order is intended to take away my discretion as to the time and manner of moving my troops?"

And the following is General Halleck's reply (August 5):

"The orders for the advance of your army, and that its progress be reported daily, are peremptory."

Rosecrans appears to have received all this in good feeling. He writes (August 7):

"Your dispatch received. I can only repeat the assurance given before the issue of the order. This army shall move with all the dispatch compatible with the successful execution you wish. We are preparing every thing to bring up forage for our animals; the present rolling stock of the road will hardly suffice to keep us day by day here, but I have bought fifty more freight cars, which are arriving. Will advise you daily."

[1] The official returns from the Army of Tennessee for August 31, 1863, give: *Present for duty*, 45,041; *aggregate present*, 59,027; *aggregate present and absent*, 83,273. Bragg, in his official report of the battle of Chickamauga, says that at this time (September 8) his effective force, exclusive of cavalry, was a little over 35,000 men. He includes "two small divisions" just arrived from Johnston's army. The estimate given in the text is no doubt correct, as the official returns of an army are always more likely to be accurate than the numbers given in the report of a battle. It includes the cavalry force and Buckner's command.

[2] Thomas was twenty-six miles from Crittenden, on his left, and the distance to McCook's corps, on the right, was nearly as great. Rosecrans makes the distance "from flank to flank, by the nearest practicable roads," fifty miles.

[3] The idea that Bragg's army would make no stand on Rosecrans's present front seems also to have prevailed with General Halleck. On the 6th he had telegraphed to the latter: "There is no reason now to suppose that any of his troops have been detached, except, perhaps, a small force at Charleston." On the 11th he gives the following instructions: "After holding the mountain passes on the west and Dalton, or some other point on the railroad, to prevent the return of Bragg's army, it will be decided whether your army shall move farther south into Georgia and Alabama." So far is Halleck at this time from being aware of Rosecrans's danger, that he urges the latter to find out whether Bragg's army is re-enforcing Lee! If he had himself taken some pains to ascertain whether Lee was re-enforcing Bragg, a mistake on Rosecrans's part which proved next to fatal might have been avoided. As early as September 7th Rosecrans seems to have been aware of Bragg's having received re-enforcements from Johnston's army. On that day, in reply to a dispatch from Halleck (dated September 6th), inquiring about the position of Bragg and Buckner, and suggesting that, in the event of their union, it would be necessary for him to unite with Burnside, he writes:

"Your dispatch of yesterday received with surprise. You have been often and fully advised that the nature of the country makes it impossible for this army to prevent Johnston from combining with Bragg. When orders for an advance of the army were made, it must have been known that those two rebel forces could combine against it, and to some extent choose their place of fighting us. This has doubtless been done, and Buckner, Bragg, and Johnston are all near Chattanooga. The movement on East Tennessee was independent of mine. Your apprehensions are just, and the legitimate consequences of your orders. The best that can now be done is for Burnside to close his cavalry down on our left, supporting it with his infantry, and, refusing his left, threaten the enemy without getting into his grasp, while we get him in our grip, and strangle him, or perish in the attempt."

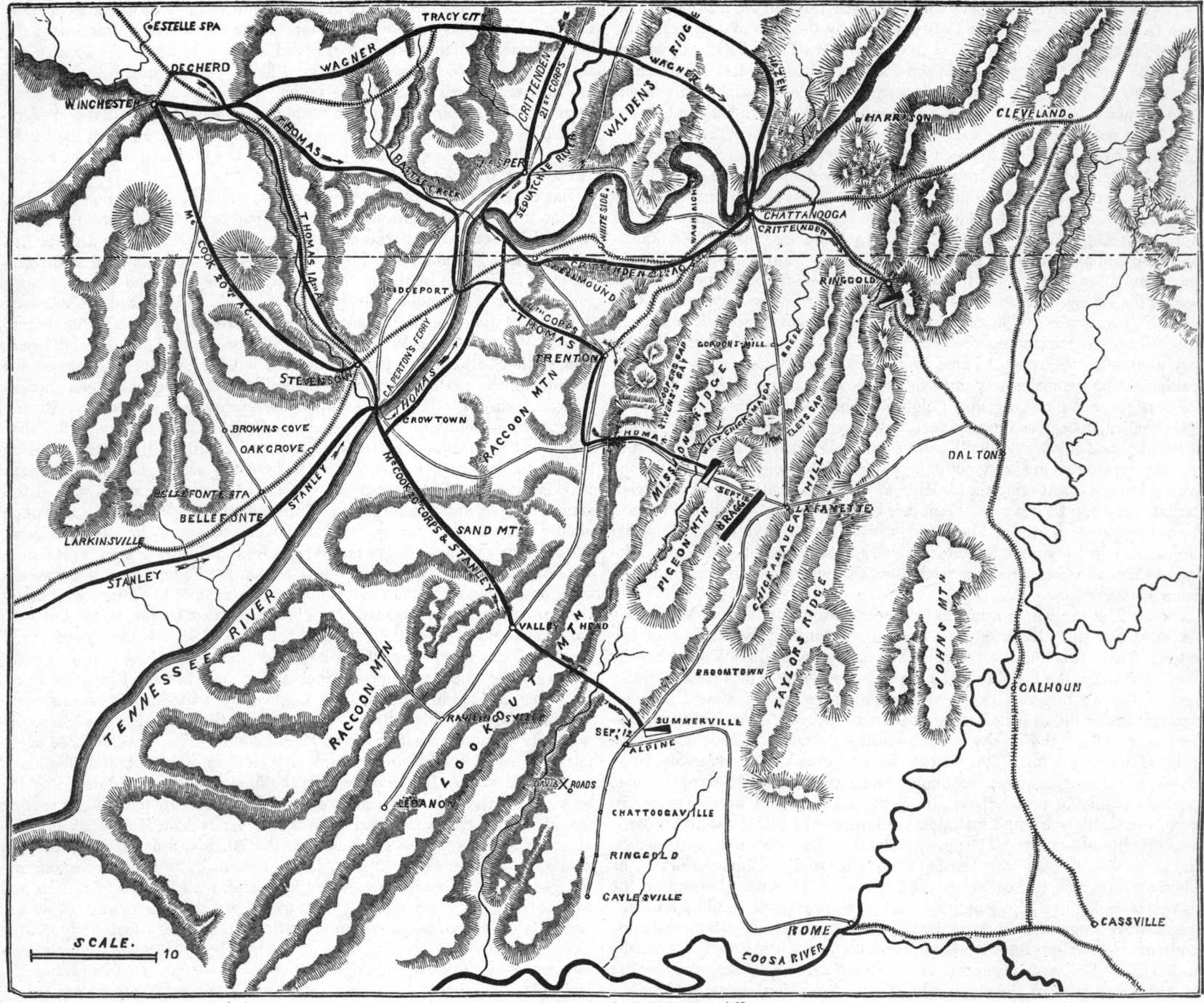

MAP ILLUSTRATING ROSECRANS'S MOVEMENTS, SEPT. 4-12.

the march in eight days,[1] connecting with Rosecrans's left within three days after Bragg's evacuation. The very fact of Buckner's precipitate withdrawal from a country abounding in strong positions for defense was sufficient evidence that the movement was something else than a mere retreat. But neither Halleck nor Rosecrans understood its real import. The former was too far from the field of operations; the latter was over-confident of the demoralization of the enemy. Before the 14th Rosecrans never asked or seemed to expect any thing from Burnside beyond a demonstration with cavalry. His chief anxiety was lest Burnside might be withdrawn to North Carolina. Even as late as the 12th he felt sufficient for the enemy in his front, but, in the case of Bragg's retreat to the Coosa River, he apprehended an advance from the line of that river into Tennessee, and thought a force from the Army of Tennessee ought to shut up that avenue.[2]

After the capture of Cumberland Gap[3] Burnside was ordered by General Halleck to concentrate on the Tennessee, connecting with Rosecrans. If this order had been issued when Burnside first reached Knoxville, and had been promptly executed, the two armies would have been by this time in co-operation.[4]

[1] Judging from the time occupied by Sherman in his march with 25,000 men to the relief of Knoxville: November 28th—December 6th.

[2] The following letter was written by Rosecrans, September 12th, to General Halleck, from Chattanooga:

"I think it would be very unwise, in the present attitude of affairs, for General Burnside to make any move in the direction of North Carolina; it would leave my left flank entirely unprotected, and open the way into Kentucky. I trust I am sufficient for the enemy now in my front; but, should he fall back to the line of the Coosa, the roads from there are short and comparatively good to the Tennessee, where it is necessary for me to cross two ranges of mountains, over very barren, rough, and difficult roads, to reach the Tennessee, and then move from thirty to fifty miles to reach the flank of a column moving from Gunter's Landing or Whitesburg on Nashville. It is desirable to have that avenue shut up. Can not you send a force from the Army of Tennessee to do it?"　　[3] September 9.

[4] "The main body of General Burnside's army was now ordered to concentrate on the Tennessee River, from Loudon west, so as to connect with General Rosecrans's army, which reached Chattanooga on the 9th. . . . As the country between Dalton and the Little Tennessee was still open to the enemy, General Burnside was cautioned to move down by the north bank of the river, so as to secure its fords, and cover his own and General Rosecrans's communications from rebel raids. With our forces concentrated near Chattanooga, the enemy would be compelled to either attack us in position or to retreat farther south into Georgia. If he should attempt a flank movement on Cleveland, his own communications would be cut off and his own army destroyed. But, although repeatedly urged to effect this junction with the Army of the Cumberland, General Burnside retained most of his command in the upper valley, which was still threatened, near the Virginia line, by a small force under Sam Jones."—Halleck's Report, 1863. This is the statement made by General Halleck, which reflects upon Burnside. But the ipsissima verba of the dispatch sent to Burnside on the 11th do not indicate that the order to co-operate with Rosecrans was very explicit, or was based upon any definite idea of the enemy's movements. The dispatch reads:

"I congratulate you on your success. Hold the gaps of the North Carolina mountains, the line of the Holston River, or some point, if there be one, to prevent access from Virginia, and connect with General Rosecrans, at least with your cavalry. General Rosecrans will occupy Dalton, or

Rosecrans does not fairly admit the fact, but it is nevertheless beyond question that, during the three days following the occupation of Chattanooga by Crittenden's corps, he had not the shadow of a doubt either as to the enemy's retreat to Rome, or as to his own secure and full possession of the object of his campaign. His only fear was that the enemy might turn his right and advance north of the Tennessee. For Rosecrans to deny that he was conducting his army under this mistaken impression is to convict himself of a folly of which the most stupid colonel in his army could not be capable. Of course he preferred the peaceable possession of Chattanooga, if that were possible. Therefore, if he had not felt secure of the place, he would have secured himself. There was nothing, absolutely nothing, in the way of his doing so. Three days, or at the most four, would have sufficed for the concentration of his entire army at Chattanooga, the fortifications of which would in the mean while have been strengthened by Crittenden. This movement demanded not one half the strategy which he had shown on numerous occasions, nor did it expose his army to any special peril. Between him and the enemy rose Lookout Mountain, "a perpendicular wall of limestone over which no wheel could pass." No change of position, open to Bragg's observation, was necessary. With the cavalry still demonstrating on the extreme right, beyond Winston's, and a portion of Thomas's corps still holding Stevens's Gap, the main army could stealthily, rapidly, and without danger, in twenty-four hours' time, have passed beyond the reach of any possible interruption from the enemy. The only thing necessary was expedition.[1]

some point on the railroad, to close all access from Atlanta, and also the mountain passes in the west. This being done, it will be determined whether the available force shall advance into Georgia and Alabama, or into the Valley of Virginia and North Carolina."

Two days after this dispatch was sent, it became apparent to General Halleck that troops were moving westward from Lee's army. He then instructed Burnside to move down his infantry "as rapidly as possible toward Chattanooga." But the reason given for the movement (namely, to secure against an advance of Bragg's army into Tennessee and Kentucky) gave Burnside no hint of Rosecrans's immediate danger. And, in any case, the order came too late to secure the arrival of Burnside before Longstreet could join Bragg.

The communications received all this time by Burnside directly from Rosecrans indicated that the latter, so far from being in embarrassment, was getting on swimmingly in Georgia, sweeping every thing before him. On the 10th Crittenden writes from Chattanooga:

"I am directed by the general commanding the Department of the Cumberland to inform you that I am in full possession of this place, having entered it yesterday, at 12 M., without resistance. The enemy has retreated in the direction of Rome, Georgia, the last of his force, cavalry, having left a few hours before my arrival. At daylight I made a rapid pursuit with my corps, and hope that he will be intercepted by the centre and right, the latter of which was at Rome. The general commanding department requests that you move down your cavalry and occupy the country recently covered by Colonel Minty, who will report particulars to you, and who has been ordered to cross the river."

[1] Rosecrans, of course, swears that this movement was impossible. He says, in his evidence before the Congressional Committee on the Conduct of the War (Rep. Com., Rosecrans's Campaigns, p. 31): "It has been a popular impression, possibly encouraged, if not believed, in high

JAMES S. NEGLEY.

Rosecrans's movements, more clearly than any thing else, indicate his misapprehension as to the situation of the Confederate army. On the evening of the 9th McCook was informed that Bragg was retreating southward, and ordered "to move rapidly upon Alpine and Summerville, Georgia, in pursuit, to intercept his line of retreat, and attack him in flank."[1] Thomas was at the same time ordered to move on Lafayette.[2] Crittenden was sent to Ringgold in pursuit. By this disposition of his army Rosecrans exposed each of his three corps to a separate and overwhelming attack of Bragg's army, which, instead of retreating to Rome, fronted the western slope of Pigeon Mountain, and was ready, holding a central position, to strike Thomas when he should emerge from Dug Gap on the way to Lafayette, Crittenden on his right, or McCook on his left. Rosecrans and his corps commanders had been alike misled by the reports of citizens and deserters, sent by Bragg within the Federal lines for the direct purpose of conveying an impression of his rapid retreat to Rome.[3] This ruse had been successful. Bragg fully appreciated his opportunity. Even on the 9th—the very day of the occupation of Chattanooga by the national troops, and while Rosecrans was urging a "vigorous pursuit" of the enemy by Crittenden, an advance by McCook and Stanley upon his flank and rear, and of Thomas's columns through the gaps of Pigeon Mountain upon Lafayette—Bragg was preparing to strike Thomas in McLemore's Cove, and by moving around his left, between him and Crittenden, to secure an easy victory over both, reserving for McCook's corps the final blow. Five hours after Rosecrans had telegraphed to Washington that Chattanooga was his "without a struggle," Bragg issued written orders to Hindman and Hill to move against Thomas.[1] The Confederate force thus ordered to move on Stevens's Gap outnumbered General Negley's division, holding that position, more than two to one.[2] Celerity was absolutely necessary to the accomplishment of Bragg's scheme. Either he should not disclose his position, waiting for the enemy to put himself more completely in his power before springing his trap, or, if he unmasked his force, he should strike a sudden and decisive blow. In this he was foiled by the dilatory execution or the refractoriness of his subordinate generals. Hill reported the order to move on Negley to be impracticable, "as General Cleburne was sick, and both the gaps, Dug and Catlett's, had been blocked by felling timber, which would require twenty-four hours for its removal."[3] Early on the morning of the 10th Bragg ordered General Buckner to execute with his corps the order issued to General Hill. Hindman had advanced promptly, and was at Morgan's (three or four miles from Davis's Cross-roads, but east of Pigeon Mountain), ready to move forward into the cove upon the arrival of a supporting column. Buckner joined him in the afternoon. To secure promptness of action, Bragg transferred his headquarters from Lee and Gordon's Mill to Lafayette. Polk was ordered to send Cheatham's division to cover Hindman's rear, and Cleburne, at Dug Gap, was instructed to attack in front. During the night of the 10th the obstructions were removed from the gap, and Walker's reserve corps was directed to join Cleburne in the front attack. Thus more than 25,000 men, besides cavalry, were, on the morning of the 11th, ready to spring upon Negley's division.

Negley in the mean time had advanced from Stevens's Gap to Bailey's Cross-roads, and thence, on the 10th, to Davis's, one mile west of Dug Gap. Until he had reached this latter position he was in utter ignorance of the fact that only the obstructions in the passes of Pigeon Mountain separated him from an overwhelming force of the enemy on his front and left; but then, just in time to save his division, his eyes began to be opened through information received from the citizens and his scouts.[4] He immediately urged Baird to support him, and made dispositions to meet the enemy. Baird was up by 8 A.M. on the morning of the 11th, with two brigades, and was posted in reserve at Davis's Cross-roads. Bragg's attack was fortunately delayed. At daylight on the 11th he went to Cleburne's position, and found him awaiting the opening of Hindman's guns, which were not heard until the middle of the afternoon, and Cleburne, on advancing, found that Negley had fallen back to Bailey's Cross-roads.[5] General Negley had found

military quarters, that because a portion of our command, including myself, entered Chattanooga, we had possession of it, in the sense of being so established there that we could have retained it without a battle. This is an error into which no good military mind cognizant of the facts could for a moment fall. Bragg was compelled or induced to fall back from Chattanooga by the menacing attitude of Thomas's corps at Frick's and Cooper's Gaps, twenty-six miles south, and of McCook's, with the cavalry corps, at Valley Head, forty-two miles from Chattanooga. Crittenden's corps, a part of which was employed in making the demonstration above Chattanooga, and the remainder in watching and covering the pass over the extremity of Lookout, passed into Chattanooga when Bragg fell back, and repaired at once to that point to ascertain the movement of the enemy; and all that was done was done promptly, and to that end only. And the instant these movements were discovered, and the enemy was found to have retired slowly toward Lafayette, not a moment was lost in making the necessary disposition, first, to secure our troops against being cut up in detail, and, secondly, to effect a most expeditious concentration at an eligible point between the enemy and Chattanooga, the goal of our efforts."

Now this is cool. Apart from the fact that Rosecrans does not here adduce the slightest argument to show *why* he could not on the 9th have commenced the concentration of his army at Chattanooga, or why such a movement must be discarded by any "good military mind cognizant of the facts" as impracticable, his entire statement gives a false impression of the theory upon which he conducted the campaign immediately after Bragg's abandonment of Chattanooga. He had only just ordered Crittenden to enter Chattanooga and vigorously pursue the retreating enemy, when he telegraphed to General Halleck (from Trenton, September 9th, 8 30 P.M): "Chattanooga is ours without a struggle, and East Tennessee is free. Our move on the enemy's *flank and rear* progresses, while the *tail of his retreating column will not escape unmolested.* Our troops from this side entered Chattanooga about noon. Those north of the river there are crossing." This dispatch, the instructions given to Burnside, through Crittenden, that he was in *full* possession of Chattanooga, and the tenor of all his dispatches to Halleck at this time, indicate, as clearly as words any way can, that Rosecrans believed that the campaign for Chattanooga was virtually ended, and that he did not concentrate at Chattanooga for the simple reason that he deemed it unnecessary, and hoped, through his advanced position, to prevent "the tail of Bragg's retreating column" from escaping unmolested. As to being "cognizant of the facts," it is certain that Rosecrans not only did not understand Bragg's movements, but misapprehended them, and acted upon his misapprehension. As we have said in the text, it is only under cover of his mistake that he can evade the imputation of folly. But no arguments, not even from Rosecrans himself, can make us believe that he was foolish enough to expose three corps of his army—each separated from the other by mountain barriers, and by a distance greater than that intervening between either of them and the enemy—to the danger of being cut up in detail. If we were not so compelled by all the circumstances of the case, we should still prefer to believe that it was a mistake, rather than deliberate recklessness, that led him to keep his army for even a single day in such a position. It is true that, after he found out his mistake, he succeeded in extricating his army from destruction, but, as we shall see, this was due to the dilatory movements of the enemy. And his manner of extricating it compelled him to accept the wager of a doubtful battle; whereas, if he had been less confident of the enemy's discomfiture, he might previously have evaded a battle, and, with his army strongly posted in Chattanooga, awaited re-enforcements.

[1] *McCook's Report.*

[2] Rosecrans does not publish this order, nor even allude to it in his report. But there is conclusive proof this order was given in the fact that, at 8 P.M. on the 9th, General Negley (commanding the advance of Thomas's corps) received instructions to move the next day to Lafayette. Negley writes to Thomas at this date, "Your order, directing me to march to Lafayette to-morrow, has been received. I will start at 8 A.M."

[3] "Thrown off his guard by our rapid movement, apparently in retreat, when in reality we had concentrated opposite his centre, and deceived by the information from deserters and others sent into his lines, the enemy pressed on his columns to intercept us, and thus exposed himself in detail."—*Bragg's Report.*

[1] The following are the orders, dated at Lee and Gordon's Mill, 11 45 P.M., September 9th:

"Major General HINDMAN, Commanding Division:

"GENERAL,—You will move with your division immediately to Davis's Cross-roads, on the road from Lafayette to Stevens's Gap. At this point you will put yourself in communication with the column of General Hill, ordered to move to the same point, and take command of the forces, or report to the officer commanding Hill's column, according to rank. If in command, you will move upon the enemy, reported to be 4000 or 5000 strong, encamped at the foot of Lookout Mountain, at Stevens's Gap. Another column of the enemy is reported to be at Cooper's Gap, number not known."

"Lieutenant General HILL, Commanding Corps:

"GENERAL,—I inclose orders given to General Hindman. General Bragg directs that you send or take, as your judgment dictates, Cleburne's division, to unite with General Hindman at Davis's Cross-roads to-morrow morning. Hindman starts at 12 o'clock to-night, and he has thirteen miles to make. The commander of the column thus united will move upon the enemy, encamped at the foot of Stevens's Gap, said to be 4000 or 5000. If unforeseen circumstances should prevent your movement, notify Hindman. A cavalry force should accompany your column. Hindman has none. Open communication with Hindman with your cavalry in advance of the junction. He marches on the road from Dr. Anderson's to Davis's Cross-roads."

[2] Negley's division numbered 5000 men. Baird's division, however, of nearly 6000 men, was moving up to his support. Brannan and Reynolds were still at Trenton, on the other side of Lookout. The two divisions ordered to move on Negley were Hindman's and Pat Cleburne's, numbering together over 11,000, with a large cavalry force, and with Bragg's whole army within easy supporting distance.

[3] *Bragg's Report.*

[4] At 8 P.M. on the 9th he writes to Thomas, "All the information I have received this evening from my scouts and others induces the belief that there is no considerable rebel force this side of Dalton." Twenty-six hours later, having discovered his danger, he writes the following dispatch to General Baird:

"Widow Davis's, September 10th, 1863—10 P.M.

"Brigadier General BAIRD:

"SIR,—There are indications of a superior force of the enemy in position near Dug Gap. Another column, estimated as a division, with twelve pieces of artillery, near Morgan's Mills, three miles to my left, in the direction of Catlett's Gap. Also a cavalry force, under Forrest, at Culp's Mills, near the road from Pond Spring to Cooper's Gap—there with the intention (as citizens and deserters report) of attacking our rear in the morning.

"My scouts all report the appearance of an offensive movement in this direction, and they confirm the reports I received this morning of a considerable force of the enemy being in the vicinity of Lafayette and Dug Gap.

"My position is somewhat advanced, and exposed to a flank approach by two roads leading from Catlett's Gap; but it is a favorable one to fight the enemy providing your division is within supporting distance, which I understood from General Thomas would be the case, and that your division would move up to Chickamauga Creek to-night. Please inform me if this will be the case.

"Have the kindness to send this information to General Thomas to-night.

"I have the honor to remain, yours very truly, JAS. S. NEGLEY, Major General."

[5] "A careful examination of the ground we occupied, which was a long, low ridge, covered with a heavy growth of small timber, descending abruptly on the north end to the Chickamauga, while the east, south, and west sides were skirted by corn-fields and commanded by high ridges, demonstrating the fact that it would be impossible to hold this or any other position south of Bailey's Cross-roads, and fight a battle, without involving the certain destruction of our trains, which, from the contour of these ridges and uneven nature of the ground, we would be obliged to park in close proximity to our position.

"The preservation of the trains, perhaps the safety of the entire command, demanded that I should retire to Bailey's Cross-roads, two miles northwest of our position, while we could get our trains under cover and fight the enemy to better advantage. I therefore directed that the trains should commence moving back slowly and in good order, and also directed General Baird to hold Widow Davis's Cross-roads until I could withdraw a portion of the second division, and take position on the north side of Chickamauga Creek, to cover the withdrawal of his two brigades and prevent the enemy from flanking us on our left.

"At 1 P.M. a heavy column of cavalry was seen moving steadily on our left flank, with the evident intention of gaining my rear. I immediately had four pieces of artillery placed in position on the ridge at John Davis's house, which commanded the valley on my left; also sent General Beatty, with one regiment and a section of artillery, to seize and hold Bailey's Cross-roads, which was reported to be in possession of the enemy's advance.

"At 2 P.M. the trains were all in motion, falling back to Bailey's Cross-roads. General Beatty and Colonel Scribner, of General Baird's division, were directed to proceed to that point without

CHATTANOOGA FROM THE NORTH BANK OF THE TENNESSEE.

his position untenable, and, after some severe fighting, retired without losing any of his artillery or transportation. His caution in observing, by means of scouts, the operations of the enemy, and his skillful disposition of his forces on the 11th, had saved his division from otherwise certain destruction. He reached Stevens's Gap with his trains at 10 o'clock P.M., and forthwith dispatched to Thomas an account of the day's operations, suggesting that the troops (Reynolds's and Brannan's divisions) moving *via* Cooper's Gap take the most direct route to Stevens's Gap, reaching that point at the earliest possible moment. He anticipated an immediate attack from the enemy; but Bragg had withdrawn his forces from the cove.

The army was still in danger. Rosecrans was as yet ignorant of the enemy's position. The weight of evidence (received through Bragg's ingenious ruse of sending deserters and citizens within the Federal lines with false information) had indicated that Bragg was moving on Rome. Information received on the 10th made it certain that the enemy had retreated by the Lafayette Road, but gave no hint of his present position. The next morning Crittenden was ordered to Ringgold, from which point he was to send a reconnoissance to Lee and Gordon's Mill. If the enemy was found in the vicinity of Lafayette, Crittenden was to support Thomas, otherwise he was to advance toward Rome.[1] In making the movement to Lee and Gordon's Mill, Crittenden drove "squads of the enemy" before him, indicating that the main body of the Confederate army was not far distant. At 3 P.M. on the 11th, Rosecrans warned Crittenden that a heavy force of the enemy was in Chattanooga Valley, and urged him to move his whole force promptly to the Rossville and Lafayette Road. This Crittenden began to do on the following morning (the 12th), moving his whole command that day to Lee and Gordon's Mill. The same day Brannan's division, of Thomas's corps, reached Negley's left, *via* Cooper's Gap, Reynolds's following close behind. In the mean while, McCook, having reached Alpine on the 10th, found "that the enemy had not retreated very far from Chattanooga."[2] He had been ordered (the day before) to move rapidly on Alpine and Summerville to intercept Bragg's line of retreat, and to attack him in flank. Finding that, after all, he was not on the enemy's flank, he communicated with Thomas, and was surprised to learn that the latter "had not reached Lafayette, as ordered." The movement to Summerville, therefore, was not made. Thomas informed McCook on the 10th that he could not reach Lafayette before the 13th. McCook, beginning to be alarmed on account of the isolated situation of his corps, on the 12th wisely returned his trains to the summit of Lookout Mountain, remaining with his command near Alpine to await the result of a cavalry reconnoissance sent out by General Stanley to ascertain the whereabouts of the enemy.

Bragg, having failed in his designs against Thomas, retired from McLemore's Cove, and sent Polk and Walker's corps in the direction of Lee and Gordon's Mill. It might not be too late for a movement northward against Crittenden. Learning from General Pegram, the Confederate cavalry commander in that direction, that this corps of the Federal army was divided, one division being at Ringgold, Bragg ordered Polk to attack this division on the morning of the 13th. His plan now was to crush Crittenden's divisions in detail, and then to turn again upon Thomas's corps in the Cove.[3] Here again he was disappointed. Polk, with double the numbers of the enemy which lay between him and Chattanooga, dispatched to Bragg (11 P.M. on the 12th) that he had taken a strong position for defense, and requesting heavy re-enforcements. He was again ordered not to delay his attack, his force already being numerically superior to the enemy, and was promised Buckner's corps the next morning. On proceeding to the front, early on the 13th, Bragg found that his orders had not been obeyed, and that Crittenden's forces were united, and on the west side of the Chickamauga.[4]

Rosecrans was at length assured from every possible source that his army was in peril, and that the theory of his movements since the occupation of Chattanooga had been founded upon a gigantic mistake.[1] He had already (on the 11th and 12th) ordered Crittenden to Lee and Gordon's Mill, bringing in his detached forces from the east side of Chickamauga Creek,[2] and directed Thomas to bring McCook and Stanley within supporting distance of his own corps. On the 13th, fully aware of his exposed situation, and that, to use his own words, "it was a matter of life and death to effect a concentration of his army," he began to hurry up his columns with the idea of shutting off the enemy from an advance on Chattanooga by the Lafayette Road. Instead of getting on the rear and flank of the enemy, his task was now to get in his front.

General Thomas, when he received, during the night of September 12th–13th, the order brought by General Mitchell from Rosecrans to bring McCook and Stanley up to his support, understood more perfectly than his commander the nature of the emergency which confronted the Union army. He immediately directed McCook to move two divisions of the Twentieth Corps over the mountain to the left of the Fourteenth, leaving the other divisions to guard the trains. Crittenden, under instructions from Rosecrans, on the 14th, leaving Wood's division at Lee and Gordon's Mill, moved the remainder of his command to Mission Ridge, and sent Wilder's cavalry up Chickamauga Creek to connect with Thomas, whose extreme left under Reynolds then touched Pond Spring.

McCook in the mean time was moving in execution of the orders which he had received; but, unfortunately, instead of taking the mountain road direct to Stevens's Gap, he crossed Lookout Mountain, and, moving down the valley, was obliged to recross at Cooper's Gap, thus losing at least a whole day at the most critical stage of the campaign.[3] This delay came near being fatal to the army.[4] By the night of the 17th McCook's command was in McLemore's Cove, and the three corps of the command were within supporting distance for the first time since the crossing of the Tennessee. The day previous Rosecrans was satisfied that Bragg was receiving re-enforcements from Lee's army. He had been advised by General Halleck to that effect on the 15th.[5] He now calls stoutly for Burnside's assistance. But it is already far too late for that to reach him.

From the morning of the 13th to the night of the 17th Bragg has now had five days since he abandoned his attempt against the detached corps of Rosecrans's army. During this time he has been contemplating an advance around the Federal left to secure the only available approaches to Chattanooga from McLemore's Cove. He has dispatched Wheeler's cavalry to the left to press the Federal forces in the Cove, in order to divert attention from

---

delay, and protect the train from the attack of a large force of cavalry approaching with tha view.

"At 3 o'clock the skirmishers of General Baird's division were ordered back across the creek, where they were placed in position to hold the enemy in check until I could get my artillery in position on the ridge this side. Two companies of the Nineteenth Illinois Infantry, concealed behind a stone fence, poured into the ranks of the enemy a destructive volley, killing, as I have since learned, thirty on the spot. This partially checked the enemy, who was advancing in three heavy lines. Meantime I had ten pieces of artillery planted on the ridge to the rear of Davis's house, which commanded that position, until another new line could be formed on a ridge to the rear.

"The enemy now occupied the south side of the creek with a heavy force, and opened two batteries of artillery at a distance of 400 yards. Two of his brigades were parallel to our position on the right. Buckner's corps was deployed, and moving up steadily on our left, within short range. Colonel Stanley's and a portion of General Starkweather's brigades sustained here a well-directed and terrific fire, which our troops returned with spirit and marked effect. The firing increased, and indicated an immediate general engagement along our entire front, and would have terminated in an assault from the enemy in a few moments, which would have been disastrous to us, considering the overwhelming force of the enemy and our very unfavorable position.

"By direction, General Baird deployed General Starkweather's brigade to our right, which checked the enemy's advance in that direction, and enabled Colonel Stanley to withdraw his brigade, which being done, we retired slowly and in good order to Bailey's Cross-roads, where a strong position of defense was assumed, and the troops were bivouacked for the night, with trains parked at Stevens's Gap. During the night the enemy withdrew to Dug Gap."—*General Negley's Report.*

[1] *Crittenden's Report.*

[2] *McCook's Report.*

[3] His orders to Polk were explicit, and were thrice repeated, as follows:

"Lafayette, Georgia, 6 P.M., September 12th.

"Lieutenant General POLK:

"GENERAL,—I inclose you a dispatch from General Pegram. This presents you a fine opportunity of striking Crittenden in detail, and I hope you will avail yourself of it at daylight to-morrow. This division crushed, and the others are yours. We can then turn on the force in the Cove. Wheeler's cavalry will move on Wilder so as to cover your right. I shall be delighted to hear of your success. Very truly yours, BRAXTON BRAGG.

"To attack at daylight on the 13th."

"Lafayette, Georgia, 6 P.M., September 12th, 1863.

"Lieutenant General POLK, Commanding Corps:

"GENERAL,—I inclose you a dispatch marked 'A,' and I now give you the orders of the commanding general, viz., to attack at daylight to-morrow the infantry column reported in said dispatch at three quarters of a mile beyond Peavine Church, on the road to Greysville from Lafayette. I am, general, etc., GEORGE W. BRENT, A. A. G."

"Lafayette, Georgia, September 12th, 1863.

"Lieutenant General POLK, Commanding Corps:

"GENERAL,—The enemy is approaching from the south, and it is highly important that your attack in the morning should be quick and decided. Let no time be lost.

"I am, general, etc., GEORGE W. BRENT, A. A. G."

[4] *Bragg's Report.* It appears, however, from Crittenden's own report, that his corps had already been concentrated at Lee and Gordon's Mill on the 12th, before the order to attack had been issued to General Polk.

[1] When was it that Rosecrans first became acquainted with the actual situation of Bragg's army? This question is not answered in his report with any degree of precision. On the evening of the 10th he was certain that the main body of Bragg's army "retired by the Lafayette Road, but uncertain whether he had gone far." At 3 30 P.M. on the 11th, he informed Crittenden that "the enemy was in heavy force in the Valley of the Chattanooga." At 3 P.M. on the 12th, he sent General R. B. Mitchell, of the cavalry corps, to General Thomas with verbal orders instructing the latter to direct McCook and Stanley to move up within supporting distance of his corps. The reason given for this movement does not imply that Rosecrans then knew that the Confederate army was near Lafayette; it was ordered "with a view of moving upon the enemy at the earliest practical moment." Mitchell (probably by taking the road east of Lookout Mountain) struck Negley's headquarters. The following is a copy of the letter written by Negley to Thomas upon Mitchell's arrival (1 A.M. on the 13th):

"Major General THOMAS:

"GENERAL,—General Mitchell, of the cavalry corps, has just arrived from General Rosecrans's headquarters, having left there at 3 o'clock P.M. He brings verbal orders from General Rosecrans to the following effect, which he desires me to communicate to you:

"That you order General McCook and Stanley, with his cavalry, to move at once within supporting distance of your corps, with a view of moving upon the enemy at the earliest practicable moment.

"General Rosecrans complains of a want of information in regard to your movements and position, and of the numbers and position of the enemy.

"*Feeling confident, from the remarks that General Rosecrans made to General Mitchell, that he is totally misinformed as to the character of the country in this vicinity, and of the position, force, and intentions of the enemy*, I write you on that point, so that you can communicate with him at once.

"Also, to inform you that one of my scouts (young Bailey), who is intelligent and reliable, has just returned from the vicinity of Bird's Mills, stating that he was informed by Mr. Paine, and other citizens, that in the affair of yesterday our force was confronted by Buckner's entire command, two other divisions of infantry from the vicinity of Dug Gap, and a force of five or six thousand cavalry. That the enemy expected to hold us at Dug Gap, while Buckner and the cavalry could pass to our rear, and take possession of Stevens's and Cooper's Gaps. That Breckinridge's command was on Pigeon Ridge, or at Lafayette. That Bragg was concentrating his entire force at or near Lafayette. That the rebel cavalry west of Pigeon Ridge had passed through Worthing Gap, and the infantry had fallen back to the top of the ridge and beyond. The smoke from their line of encampment was visible this evening.

"A similar statement was made by two other citizens on hearsay. . . . . General Brannan returned from his reconnoissance this evening. He advanced as far as Widow Davis's Cross-roads. He met with only a small cavalry picket, which fled at his approach. Indications were that the enemy were on and beyond Pigeon Ridge. . . . .

"I have the honor to remain yours very truly, JAS. S. NEGLEY, Major General."

The whole tenor of this letter indicates that the order brought by Mitchell was based upon no accurate knowledge by Rosecrans of the enemy's position. Yet it is clear, both from this order and from the instructions already issued to Crittenden to move to Lee and Gordon's Mill, that Rosecrans was, on the 12th, beginning to lose confidence in his scheme for striking the tail end of Bragg's army, and to be alarmed for his own safety. His petulant complaint of Thomas's negligence in forwarding information was an indication of his own fears. On the 13th the ground upon which he had stood slipped clean away from under his feet. On that day he received from Thomas, from McCook, and from Crittenden information which only too clearly demonstrated that Bragg's entire army was concentrated at Lafayette and along the eastern slope of Pigeon Mountain.

[2] What is throughout this chapter called "Chickamauga Creek" is really the West Fork of Chickamauga Creek.

[3] McCook probably moved upon the best instructions he had in regard to the roads. There is some discrepancy, however, between his own and Rosecrans's statements. McCook says, "It was my desire to join General Thomas by the mountain road, *via* Stevens's Gap; but not having any guide, and all the citizens concurring that no such road existed, and General Thomas also stating that the route by Valley Head was the only practicable one, I determined to join him by it." Rosecrans, in his report, states that McCook was ordered to take the mountain road. This might be explained on the supposition that McCook received an order from Rosecrans subsequent to the one received from Thomas.

[4] "The tardy arrival of McCook's corps came near being fatal to us."—*Rosecrans's Testimony before the Congressional Committee.*

[5] Rosecrans thus writes to Halleck from near Gordon's Mill, 1 30 P. M., September 16: "From information derived from various sources from my front, I have reason to believe what you assert in your dispatch of yesterday, 4 30 P.M., is true, and that they [*i.e.*, Longstreet's forces] have arrived at Atlanta at last. Push Burnside down."

his real movement, and Forrest's to the right to cover his advance. But he has not advanced. His forces, on the night of the 17th, lie along Peavine Creek, east of Pigeon Mountain. Nothing has been in his front between him and Chattanooga, except cavalry, with a small detachment of infantry, for the past four days. Chattanooga itself has only been held by Wagner's brigade, and all the while Bragg appears to have taken it for granted that the Federal army was concentrated in his front. He has been waiting also for Longstreet's corps, three brigades of which, under General Hood, have just arrived, and now, when Rosecrans's army *is* really concentrated in his front, he issues his orders for the crossing of Chickamauga Creek.[1] It is impossible to calculate the advantage of this delay to Rosecrans's army.

West Chickamauga Creek, which now separated the opposing armies, takes its rise from the junction of Mission Ridge with Pigeon Mountain at the southern extremity of the Cove, and runs northeastwardly down the Cove by Pond and Crawfish Springs, touching the Lafayette and Chattanooga Road at Lee and Gordon's Mill, and, after its junction with the main creek, empties into the Tennessee four miles above Chattanooga. About four and a half miles below Lee and Gordon's Mill, in a straight line, is Reed's Bridge, on one of the roads from Ringgold to Rossville. Here was the extreme right of Bragg's line on the night of the 17th. Between this point and Lee and Gordon's Mill there are several available crossings—at Alexander's Bridge, and at Byron's, Tedford's, Dalton's, and several other fords. The roads leading to these from the east were bad, both from their narrowness and from the mountainous character of the country. The stubborn resistance of Minty's and Wilder's cavalry delayed the crossing of Bragg's forces on the 18th. The right column, proceeding from Ringgold, was commanded by General Bushrod R. Johnson, and consisted of his division—made up of three improvised brigades from Mississippi—and Hood's,[2] which also consisted of three brigades. The two divisions numbered over 7000 men. Forrest's cavalry co-operated with this column, covering its front and right upon the march. At Peavine Creek, between Chickamauga Hill and Pigeon Mountain, an attempt was made by a small detachment of Minty's cavalry to resist the progress of Johnson's column, but without success. The attempt was repeated when the Confederates reached Reed's Bridge, again with insufficient force, and with no better result than before. Johnson succeeded in saving the bridge from destruction, and began to cross his command at 3 o'clock P.M., partly by the bridge, and partly by the ford above. He then swept southward in front of the points where Walker's and Buckner's corps had been ordered to cross.

Walker's corps, nearly 6000 strong, encountered stout resistance at Alexander's Bridge (about three miles south of Reed's), and, the Federal cavalry having, after a sharp skirmish, succeeded in destroying the bridge, was compelled to cross by night at Byron's Ford. One brigade was left east of the creek to guard the ordnance train, which could not cross with the troops.

Buckner's corps, 10,000 strong, started from a point near Rock Spring Church, and crossed Pigeon Mountain, following the route taken by Walker's, but, turning southward upon approaching the Chickamauga, secured the crossing at Tedford's Ford, but, waiting Walker's movements on the right, did not cross till the next morning.

Thus, before daylight on the 19th, Bragg had, including cavalry, over 15,000 men across the creek. Buckner's corps consisted of Stewart's and Preston's divisions. It was ready to cross, as was also Cheatham's division of Polk's corps. These, crossing early on the morning of the 19th, increased the force on the east of the creek by 16,000 men. Hindman's division of Polk's corps, and Breckinridge's and Cleburne's of Hill's corps, held the left, south and west of Lee and Gordon's Mill, on the opposite side of the creek, and did not cross until the afternoon and night of the 19th.

These movements indicate clearly the enemy's plan of operations. Anticipating no serious opposition on his extreme right, Bragg expected to secure the approach to Chattanooga by the Lafayette Road, and then to close down upon the Federal army and fight the battle upon a field from which, even in the improbable event of his defeat, he could fall back upon the strong-hold which a fortnight before he had been compelled to abandon on account of his weakness, but which now, with his army heavily re-enforced—nearly doubled, in fact[3]—he could easily hold against the combined armies of Burnside and Rosecrans. For Bragg to gain the front which he sought, and extend his army across the Lafayette and Dry Valley Roads and the intervening ridges, would have been to win the battle's prize before the battle itself had been fought. But here Bragg was again disappointed. His advance had been too long delayed, and his movements on the 18th had been unexpectedly retarded. And thus it happened that the battle of Chickamauga came to be fought for the very position which Bragg had hoped to gain before fighting it.

[1] The following is a copy of these orders.

"I. Johnson's column, on crossing at or near Reed's Bridge, will turn to the left by the most practicable route, and sweep up the Chickamauga toward Lee and Gordon's Mill.

"II. Walker, crossing at Alexander's Bridge, will unite in this move, and push vigorously on the enemy's flank and rear in the same direction.

"III. Buckner, crossing at Tedford's Ford, will join in the movement to the left, and press the enemy up the stream from Polk's front at Lee and Gordon's Mill.

"IV. Polk will press his forces to the front of Lee and Gordon's Mill, and, if met by too strong resistance to cross, will bear to the right, and cross at Dalton's Ford, or at Tedford's, as may be necessary, and join the attack wherever the enemy may be.

"V. Hill will cover our left flank from an advance of the enemy from the Cove, and, by pressing the cavalry in his front, ascertain if the enemy is re-enforcing at Lee and Gordon's Mill, in which event he will attack them in flank.

"VI. Wheeler's cavalry will hold the Gap in Pigeon Mountain, and cover our rear and left, and bring up the stragglers.

"VII. All teams, etc., not with the troops, should go toward Ringgold and Dalton, Georgia, beyond Taylor's Ridge. All cooking should be done at the trains; rations, when cooked, will be forwarded to the troops.

"VIII. The above movements will be executed with the utmost promptitude and perseverance."

[2] Hood did not take command of his division until it had crossed the creek.

[3] "Nearly half our army consisted of re-enforcements just before the battle."—*Bragg's Report.*

For Rosecrans's army had been, the last five days, marching for dear life, and when Bragg crossed the Chickamauga he found this army, which he had expected to strike near Lee and Gordon's Mill, upon his front and right, prepared to contest inch by inch the possession of the Lafayette and Chattanooga Road.[1] Its own celerity of movement, and Bragg's delay (in this case due to excessive caution), had again saved the Federal army.

While awaiting the arrival of McCook's corps, Thomas's and Crittenden's extended from the Dry Valley Road in front of Stevenson's Gap to Crawfish Spring, being connected at Pond Spring by Wilder's cavalry. Wood's division of Crittenden's corps still held a strong defensive position at Lee and Gordon's Mill,[2] and the river below that point was guarded by Minty's cavalry, which crossed and reconnoitred the country on the left front, occasionally meeting and skirmishing with the enemy. The gaps of Pigeon Mountain to the south were also carefully guarded by Thomas's command. As soon as McCook came up he closed in on Thomas's right, and Crittenden drew in his right upon Crawfish Spring, to give place for Thomas. Wilder's cavalry was then detached and sent to the left.

The 18th was a day of terrible anxiety to General Rosecrans. Reports at different periods of the day came in from Wood and Wilder of the enemy's advance upon the left. The Lafayette Road must be secured, if possible, at any hazard. Before night Palmer's and Van Cleve's divisions of Crittenden's corps were upon the creek to Wood's left and right, and all night long Thomas was marching by the road to Widow Glenn's, and past the slopes of Mission Ridge, toward Kelly's Farm on Chickamauga Creek, away off to the left of Crittenden; so that on the morning of the 19th the right of the army rested at Crawfish Spring, which the day before had been its left. Negley's division had been left by Thomas to guard the fords of the Upper Chickamauga in the vicinity of Crawfish Spring. Granger, with the reserve corps, was at Rossville.

The battle of the 19th was opened by General Thomas. The head of his column reached Kelly's at daylight, and went in on the left of Wilder (who had the night before been driven back to the heights east of the Widow Glenn's), Baird taking position first, then Brannan upon his left. At this point, Dan McCook, commanding a brigade of Granger's reserve corps, reported the presence of an isolated brigade of the enemy between Kelly's house and Reed's Bridge, and Brannan, with two brigades, was advanced on the road to the bridge to secure the capture of this detached force. Baird also advanced to keep in line with Brannan. These dispositions were made at 9 A.M. Soon after, Palmer's division, of Crittenden's corps, came up on Baird's right. The fight began at about ten o'clock.[3] It consisted at first of sharp skirmishing with Forrest on the Reed's Bridge Road. The movements of Johnston and Hood the night before toward Lee and Gordon's Mill had left Walker's corps in a somewhat isolated position on the Confederate right. Wilson's brigade, of this corps, after conducting the ordnance train across the creek, was called upon to support Forrest. Coming in contact with this force, Croxton's brigade, of Brannan's division, had become engaged, and drove the enemy for half a mile, when the latter was re-enforced by Ector's brigade, and it was necessary to send in Baird's division. The small force of the enemy engaged at this point was steadily pressed back until it was supported by the remainder of Walker's corps.[4] After an hour's severe fighting, Croxton's brigade had been withdrawn, and Baird and Brannan, uniting their forces, drove the enemy from their front.

In the mean time, Cheatham's division came up to Walker's support at noon, and, forming in rear of the latter, advanced upon Baird, striking him in the flank, and throwing two of his brigades into confusion. Baird was driven back before overwhelming numbers for some distance, when the fortunate arrival of Reynolds's and Johnson's divisions on his right again turned the tide of battle. These fresh divisions, advancing with Palmer's (which had been opportunely sent by Crittenden), struck Cheatham's flank, and thrust him back in disorder upon Walker's corps, Brannan's troops attacking him at the same time in front, and recapturing the artillery which Baird had lost in his retreat. While Cheatham was thus hotly engaged, and being driven in confusion, Stewart's division, of Buckner's corps, coming from the Confederate left to his support, attempted in vain to drive Thomas back from his advanced position. His three brigades—Clayton's, Brown's, and Bate's—advanced each in its turn. In one hour's fighting Clayton lost nearly 400 officers and men,[5] and, being withdrawn, Brown took his place, and gallantly charged through a dense underwood extending along his front, when he encountered a terrific fire from all arms. He was unable to use his artillery, while the batteries in his front and on his right flank poured into his ranks murderous volleys of grape and canister. Checked for a brief moment, he again pushed forward and up the slope, where the strength of the Federal position and an attack on his right compelled him to retreat, after the loss of many of his best officers and a large number of his men. Bate relieved him then, meeting the same fire which had driven back his brother commanders, but, with Clayton's support, succeeded in driving the Federal force in his front beyond the Chattanooga Road.

[1] "The enemy, whose left was at Lee and Gordon's Mill when our movement commenced, had rapidly transferred forces from his extreme right, changing his entire line, and seemed disposed to dispute, with all his ability, our effort to gain the main road to Chattanooga in his rear."—*Bragg's Report.*

[2] "A stronger position naturally than that which General Wood occupied can scarcely be imagined. The creek at Gordon's Mill bends round in the form of a semicircle, the convexity being toward the south, whence the enemy would have advanced toward General Wood. An eminence, forming what would be a diameter of the circle if completed, runs from east to west, uniting the extremities of the bend. Upon this General Wood had placed his artillery. The creek itself, of considerable depth, and with a bank several feet high upon our side of it, constituted a splendid ditch, and all along its bank lay Wood's men, behind a rude but efficient breastwork of logs and rails."—*National Account, Rebellion Record,* vii., p. 409.

[3] *Thomas's Report.*

[4] Forrest reports the capture of two batteries at an early stage of the engagement, but that he was unable to bring them off for want of horses.

[5] *General A. P. Stewart's Report.*

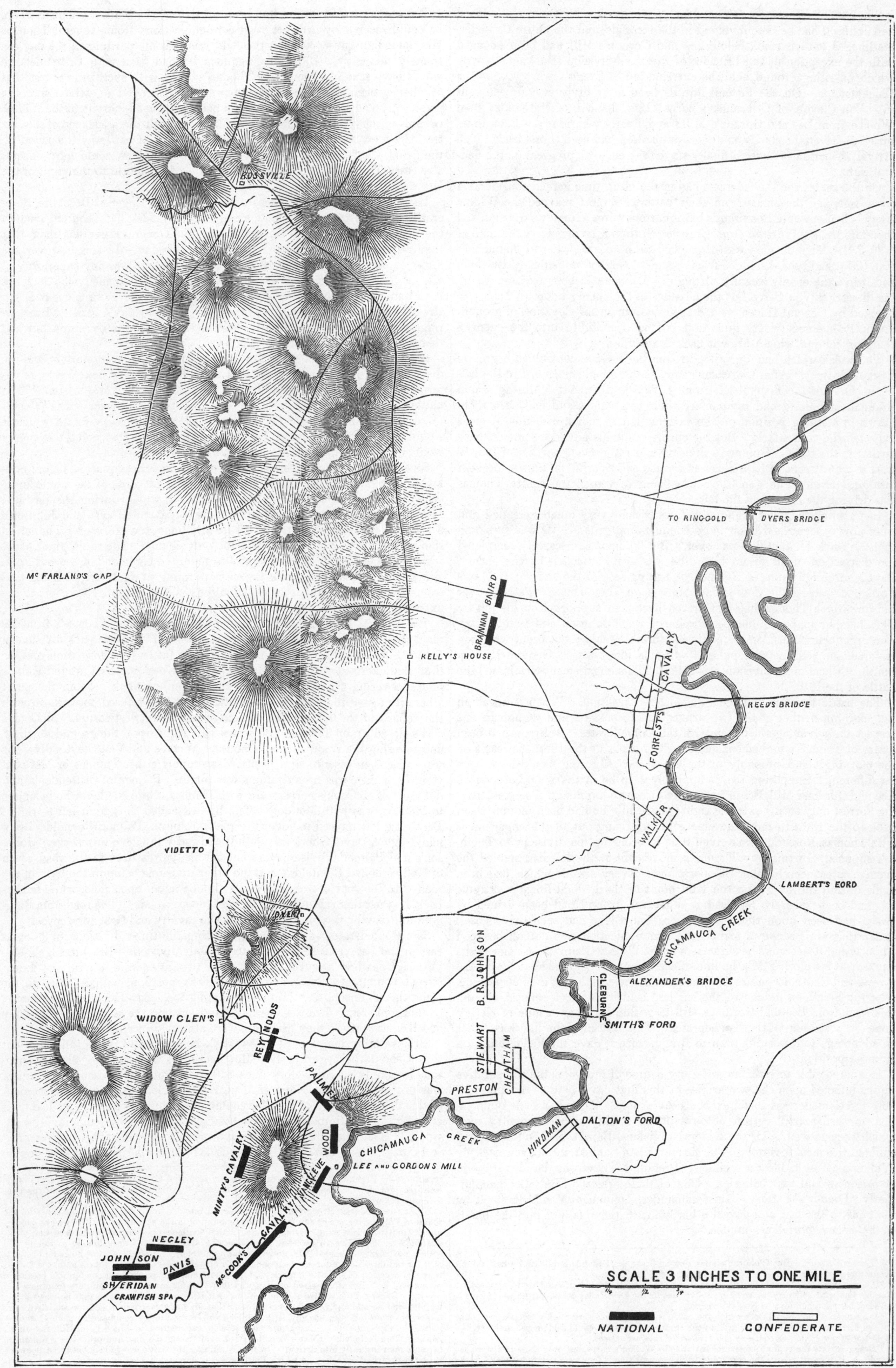

SCALE 3 INCHES TO ONE MILE

NATIONAL　　　　CONFEDERATE

POSITION OF FORCES JUST BEFORE THE OPENING OF THE BATTLE OF THE 19th.

The battle had already extended far up the creek. By two o'clock Hood and Johnson had become involved in the struggle, and the entire Confederate line, as it then stood, below Lee and Gordon's Mill, had been engaged with the exception of two brigades of Preston's division (Buckner's corps), which, on rising ground, held the extreme left of Bragg's army west of the Chickamauga. On the Federal line, division after division had been sent in—Van Cleve's, of Crittenden's corps; then Davis's, of McCook's; then Wood's, from Lee and Gordon's Mill; and, finally, Sheridan's. Each in its turn had driven the enemy, and then, outflanked, had been thrust back. The arrival of Sheridan's division finally stayed the enemy's progress on the Federal right.

On the centre the Confederates had in the mean time gained considerable advantage, and the shells from their batteries almost reached the Widow Glenn's house, where Rosecrans's headquarters were. Negley's division had therefore been withdrawn from Crawfish Spring, arriving upon the field at 4 30 P.M. This division was dispatched to the centre, where it found that Van Cleve had been dislodged from the line. Negley immediately attacked, and drove the enemy steadily till night. Palmer had been endangered by the disaster to Van Cleve, but the advance of the enemy upon his flank was checked by General Hazen, who, driven back upon an elevation of ground, promptly manned twenty guns and poured a cross-fire into the enemy's charging column, which threw it back in disorder.

The attack which had for a time broken the Federal centre had begun on Reynolds's right. After Cheatham's repulse there had been a lull in the battle in front of the Federal left from 4 o'clock till about 5, during which Brannan and Baird had reorganized their commands, and had been withdrawn to a strong position on the extreme left, in which direction Thomas expected the next attack. But the enemy made his advance some distance farther to the right. Brannan's division and the greater portion of Baird's were promptly sent to Reynolds's assistance, arriving just in time to prevent disaster. Even while Van Cleve was being driven in the centre, Thomas was driving the enemy on the left.

In pursuing the enemy Thomas's lines became very much extended, and were now concentrated upon more commanding ground. It was supposed that the battle for that day was over. But Thomas had scarcely completed the disposition of his forces before he was again attacked by the enemy. Pat Cleburne's division, of Hill's corps, having crossed the river at Tedford's Ford, had reached the Confederate right soon after sunset. Passing over the line which Thomas had just driven back, and supported on his left by Cheatham, he made an unexpected charge upon Johnson and Baird's divisions, producing considerable confusion in their ranks; but order was soon restored, and the enemy repulsed.[1] In this night attack General Preston Smith, of Cheatham's division, was killed. This engagement terminated the battle of the 19th.

The battle thus far had been waged for a position. When it began in the morning neither of the two armies had formed its line, though in this respect the advantage had been with the Confederates. If Bragg had been aware of Thomas's movement made on the night of the 18th, the result of the morning's, and, probably, of the whole day's fighting would have been far different. Supposing the Federal forces to be in the neighborhood of Lee and Gordon's Mill, Bragg had moved his own too far up the creek, leaving Forrest only on his extreme right; and while he had been moving them back to the right to meet the emergencies arising out of the engagement with Thomas, Rosecrans was given time to bring up his divisions to Thomas's support. In this way Thomas's movement to the left had spoiled the enemy's preconceived plan of operations. Every assault which had been made during the day upon the vital point of the Federal line, its extreme left, had been severely repulsed. Whatever ground had been gained by Bragg had been upon the centre, where Van Cleve had been driven back so far that, until Negley's arrival, the communication was cut off between Thomas and Rosecrans's headquarters at the Widow Glenn's.[2] Earlier in the day (say at 2 o'clock P.M.) the line of each army had extended along the Lafayette and Chattanooga Road. But upon the restoration of the Federal line, after the break on its centre, the left and centre had been refused, leaving this road, from Lee and Gordon's Mill to within less than a mile of Kelly's house, in possession of the Confederates. This refusal of the line was rather an advantage to Rosecrans than to Bragg, since it gave the Federal army a stronger position.

It is impossible to estimate, with any degree of precision, the comparative injury inflicted upon the two armies in this first day's battle. Unquestionably the Confederates sustained the heavier loss. They had little opportunity for using artillery, on account of the thickly wooded country over which they moved.[3] Of the Federal divisions, Baird's and Johnson's had suffered the most severely. The former, when flanked and driven back by Walker's corps, had lost a regiment of regulars, 411 strong, besides 100 other prisoners and two batteries. One of these was the First Michigan, formerly "Loomis's" battery. Its commander, Lieutenant Van Pelt, stood by his guns to the last, and gave up his life with them, falling into the hands of the enemy mortally wounded.[4]

Rosecrans's headquarters had been all day at the Widow Glenn's, where he could receive by a direct road communications from General Thomas. His immediate presence upon the field was at some portions of the day extremely necessary. If, just before noon, he had been with Crittenden, he would have sent in supports to Thomas's right with such promptness that Walker's corps must have been completely destroyed or driven into the river. Instead of being there, he was pacing his headquarters at the Widow Glenn's in nervous excitement, while his aids, with the assistance of the distressed widow, were attempting to locate the line of battle by the sound of the firing. The general ought to have known that he could most effectually assist Thomas by his personal direction of the battle to the right of the latter.

Leaving out the reserve corps under General Granger at Rossville, Rosecrans's whole army on the field, except two brigades, had been engaged on the 19th. Curiously, both General Bragg and General Rosecrans claim that they were opposed to superior numbers on this day. In fact, however, the forces engaged had not been far from equal; if there was any superiority, it was in Rosecrans's favor. But Bragg had full 15,000 men who had not been under fire, if we include Kershaw's and Humphreys's brigades of Longstreet's corps, which came up in time for the next day's battle. Breckinridge's and Hindman's divisions were across the river by night, but had taken no part in the battle.

A council of war was held after dark at Rosecrans's headquarters, and the disposition of forces and the conduct of the battle of the next day were determined upon. That it would be a desperate conflict was certain. The battle already fought had been for the road to Chattanooga. The attempt to secure this road would be renewed the next day with forces which it would be hard to withstand. Failing of success at this point, the enemy would do his best to crush the army which stood in his way.

General Longstreet, in person, arrived at Bragg's headquarters before midnight. To him was given the command of the left wing of the Confederate army, consisting of that portion of the troops which during the day had been under Hood's command—Buckner's corps, and Hood's and Johnson's divisions—with the fresh troops under Hindman and McLaws. The accession of Breckinridge's division was the only change made in the right wing, which had been and would still remain under the command of General Polk. Bragg ordered Polk to attack the next morning at daybreak, meaning that from his extreme right the battle should extend, division by division, to the extreme left.

The Federal line during the night was reorganized. Thomas's front remained as he had already established it, with part of Brannan's division in reserve. It extended in a semicircular form (at least its formation may be thus characterized with sufficient accuracy for our purpose) around Kelly's house, covering the road in front and on either flank. From the point where it crossed the road on the south side it was refused, to conform with the refusal of the left and centre extending southwestwardly. McCook's corps closed up on Thomas, and refused its right upon the ground north of and covering the Widow Glenn's house. Wood's and Van Cleve's divisions were placed in reserve, in a position to support either Thomas or McCook. Neither of the corps organizations was intact. Palmer, of Crittenden's, and Johnson, of McCook's corps, were with Thomas, while Negley, who belonged to Thomas, was with McCook. The line extended thus from left to right: Baird (his left refused to cover the road), Johnson, Palmer, Reynolds, Brannan, Negley, Davis, Sheridan; with Wood and Van Cleve in reserve. Johnson's and Palmer's divisions extended from Baird's lines to the road south of Kelly's house, Reynolds's and the other divisions being to the west of the road. In the rear of Johnson and Palmer was an open field, while farther back, on the other side of the road, were dense woods. The road from Ringgold to Rossville was well guarded by the cavalry and Granger's corps.

The Confederate right wing, confronting the three divisions of Thomas east of the Lafayette Road, consisted of four divisions—Breckinridge's, Cleburne's, Cheatham's, and Walker's. The two latter were in reserve. Longstreet's command extended from Cleburne's position, with Stewart on the right, then Johnson, then Hindman holding the left. Hood was in reserve, to Johnson's rear. Preston was held in reserve on the left rear. Humphrey and Kershaw, when they came up, were also held in reserve.

Bragg's army had a hard day's work before it, and it was all-important that it should be begun early. But his orders to Polk were for some reasons (certainly unsatisfactory ones to Bragg) not carried out. The attack was not begun on the right until nearly 10 o'clock A.M. Every moment of this delay had been of great advantage to Thomas, whose troops had been all night felling timber and strengthening their line by temporary breastworks.[1] And when the fight began it progressed slowly. The work assigned to Polk—namely, to thrust Thomas back from his position, and thus double

---

[1] *Thomas's Report.* But Cleburne claims that he drove the Federals a mile and a half, taking two or three hundred prisoners and two or three guns.

[2] Thomas, hearing of this break, feared that the entire right would be routed, and began to dispose his line with reference to covering its retreat to the Dry Valley Road, but he was soon relieved of his apprehensions by Negley's arrival.

[3] "As most of the ground over which the battle was fought was very thickly wooded, we could not see more than three hundred yards to the front, consequently could seldom use artillery."— *Report of Major Potter, commanding the Artillery of Buckner's Corps.*

[4] Bragg reports the capture of several batteries by Walker's corps, but only these two were secured. A. P. Stewart reports the capture of twelve guns, but only four were sent to his rear. Jackson, of Cheatham's division, reports the capture of six guns, but these were probably among the

recaptured by Brannan. Hood captured a battery from Jeff C. Davis's division, but it was afterward recaptured. On the Federal side it was claimed that there was a balance against the Confederates of three guns.

[1] "At dawn General Bragg was in the saddle, surrounded by his staff, eagerly listening for the sound of Polk's guns. The sun rose and was mounting in the sky, and still there was no note of attack from the right wing. Bragg chafed with impatience, and at last dispatched one of his staff officers, Major Lee, to ascertain the cause of Polk's delay, and urge him to a prompt and speedy movement. General Polk, notwithstanding his clerical antecedents, was noted for his fondness for military ostentation, and carried a train of staff officers whose numbers and superb dress were the occasion of singular remark. Major Lee found him seated at a comfortable breakfast, surrounded by brilliantly dressed officers, and delivered his message with military bluntness and brevity. General Polk replied that he had ordered Hill to open the action, that he was waiting for him, and he added, 'Do tell General Bragg that my heart is overflowing with anxiety for the attack—overflowing with anxiety, sir.' Major Lee returned to the commanding general, and reported the reply literally. Bragg uttered a terrible explanation, in which Polk, Hill, and all his generals were included. 'Major Lee,' he cried, 'ride along the line, and order *every* captain to take his men instantly into action.' In fifteen minutes the battle was joined, but three hours of valuable time had been lost, in which Rosecrans was desperately busy in strengthening his position."—*Pollard's Lost Cause,* p. 450.

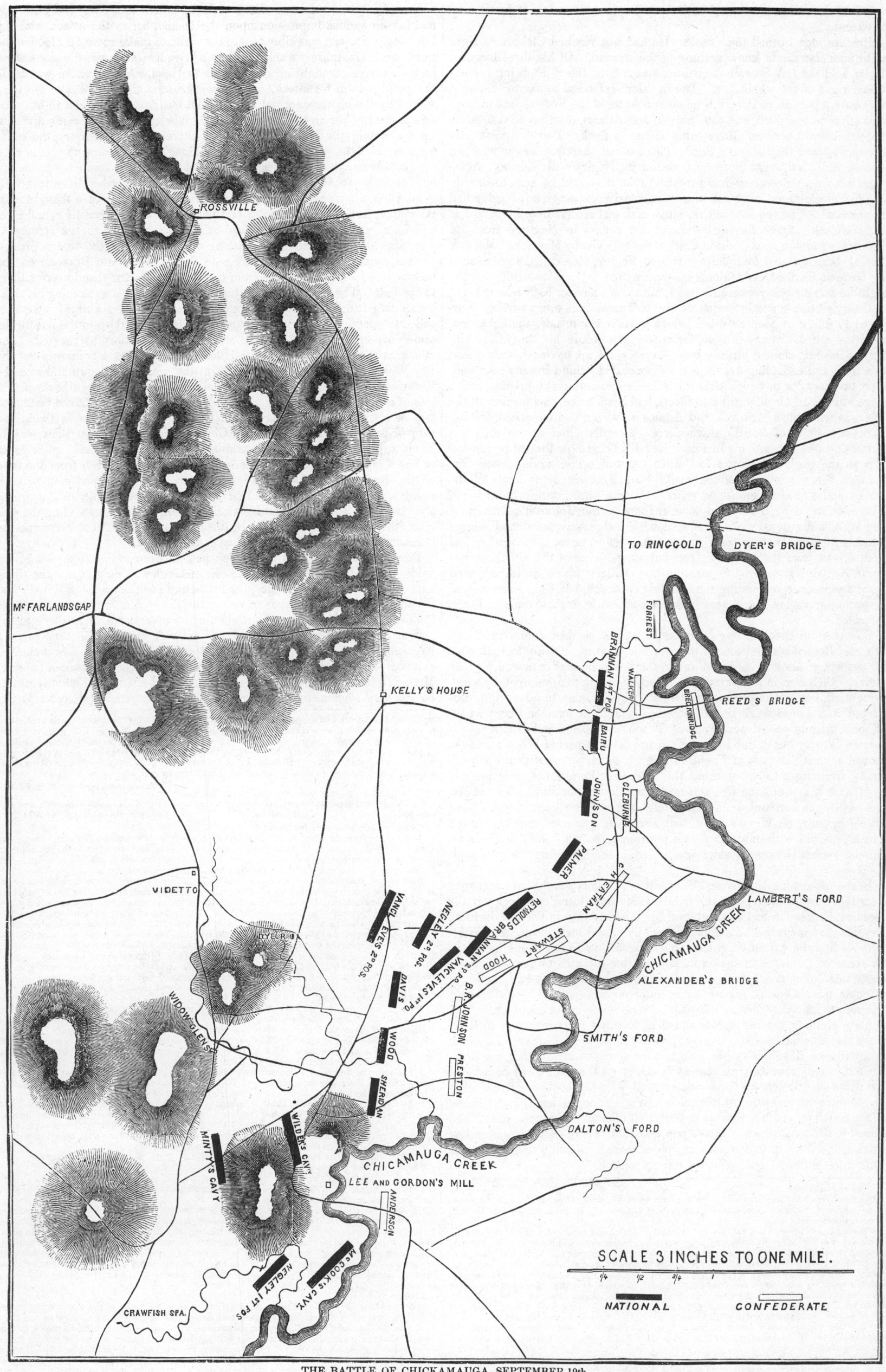

THE BATTLE OF CHICKAMAUGA, SEPTEMBER 19th.

up the Federal line, pressing it back upon Longstreet—was not found easy to execute.

Breckinridge opened the attack. He had not reached Cleburne's right until after dawn, and knew nothing of the ground. Of his three brigades Helm held the left, Stovall the centre, and Adams the right, being the extreme right of the whole line. The division extended so far to the right that only a portion of Helm's brigade encountered the Federal line in a direct advance westward, and thus Stovall and Adams, meeting no resistance, pushed forward, seriously threatening Thomas's flank. Baird's division did not quite reach the Lafayette Road; Thomas had, therefore, as early as two o'clock A.M., written to Rosecrans, asking for Negley's division to supplement his line. Rosecrans had promised that it should be sent forthwith. Seven o'clock came, an attack was momentarily expected, but Negley had not arrived. The request was repeated, and was received by Rosecrans at eight o'clock. Some demonstration of the enemy in Negley's front led Rosecrans to retain this division until it was relieved by McCook. McCook having been ordered to promptly relieve Negley, Rosecrans, accompanied by General Garfield, rode along his entire line. Upon returning to the right he found Negley where he had left him, not having been relieved.

Beatty's brigade was immediately sent to Thomas, the other two being ordered to follow as soon as other troops were ready to take their position. Beatty reached Thomas in time, fortunately, to secure his line. Breckinridge's left brigade had already been severely cut up, having been exposed to a front and enfilading fire from a foe concealed behind breastworks, and, after two assaults, in which General Helm, commanding the brigade, and a large number of his subordinate officers, had been killed, this portion of the line was withdrawn. Stovall and Adams, however, had advanced, driving back two lines of Baird's skirmishers. Stovall halted at the road, but Adams pressed forward, his line and Stovall's being now formed perpendicular to the road, to conform to Baird's position. The advance now was through the woods west of the road. Stovall attacked the angle of the works, and was soon forced to retire. Adams, encountering Baird's left, now re-enforced by Beatty and some regiments from Johnson's, Brannan's, and Wood's divisions, was severely beaten. Adams, wounded, and a large number of prisoners, were captured. Thus, before noon, Breckinridge had been driven from the field. To prevent a repetition of the attack at this point, Negley was ordered to mass all the artillery which could be spared upon a position commanding the enemy's approach, but, from some misunderstanding, Negley took a very different position from that which had been indicated.

Cleburne, on Breckinridge's left, had advanced against Johnson's, Palmer's, and Reynolds's divisions with no better success. Owing to Polk's utter neglect of his line in the morning, there was no well-arranged plan of attack. Cleburne, in the hurry occasioned by orders to dress upon Breckinridge's left, had got into some confusion. His left, also, in advancing, converged with Longstreet's line of advance in such a manner that part of Wood's brigade passed over some of Stewart's division, and Deshler's was thrown entirely out of line in Stuart's rear. Thus a part of Wood's brigade moved against that part of Thomas's line which turned westward upon the road. Crossing a field bordering the road, near Poe's house, this brigade received a heavy oblique fire, and in a few minutes sustained a loss of 500 men, killed and wounded. Deshler might then have been sent in; but Polk's brigade, on Wood's right, had also been repulsed, and Cleburne's whole line was withdrawn to a safe position some 400 yards in the rear. On the retreat General Deshler was killed, a shell piercing "fair through his chest."[1]

In the mean time, the Federal divisions on Thomas's right have met with a terrible misfortune. Upon the failure of McCook to relieve Negley in the morning, Crittenden had been ordered to do so, sending in Wood's division. But this movement had been delayed until half past nine o'clock. McCook's line, holding the extreme right, was not satisfactory to Rosecrans, being too far removed from the troops on its left. After repeated orders from Rosecrans, this difficulty was only partially remedied. Messages still continued to come from Thomas, asking for re-enforcements. Van Cleve's division was sent to his aid. Shortly after this a most unfortunate event took place. Captain Kellogg, coming across the field to bring further tidings to Rosecrans that Thomas was still heavily pressed, thought he discovered a break in the line on Reynolds's right. In fact there was no such break, but Brannan's division, from its arrangement in *echelon* at this point, had occasioned the delusion. Rosecrans forthwith ordered Wood, who had relieved Negley, to close up and support Reynolds. Wood, misapprehending the intent of the order, moved his division entirely out of line, "at double quick," and passed to Brannan's rear. Thus a gap *was made* where previously none had existed, and through this gap the enemy advanced, throwing the entire right wing into confusion, from which it did not recover.[2]

Longstreet had waited until 11 o'clock, and then, seeing that Polk was making no serious impression upon the enemy, began the attack with the left wing. Stewart was closed up to the right, to make room for Hood in the front line. Humphreys's and Kershaw's brigades (McLaws's division), were, on their arrival, brought up as supports to Hood, whose division was made the main column of attack. Longstreet's order of battle was entirely reversed by the character which the conflict had assumed on the right. His left, instead of his right, became the movable column. Stewart's division, upon reaching the Lafayette Road, was there stationed, forming the pivot upon which Longstreet's wing turned. Hood's column was up just in time to take advantage of the break occasioned by Wood's sudden withdrawal, above alluded to, and the troops on his right and left pushed the attack with great vigor. General Hood received a severe, and it was then thought mortal wound, just after his column had penetrated the Federal lines, and General Law, commanding one of his brigades, succeeded to the command. But, notwithstanding the loss of their old commander, the troops pressed their advantage, flanking Jeff Davis on the one side, and Brannan on the other, cutting off five brigades from the right of the army, and driving them to the rear. The blow had fallen just as Rosecrans was weakening his right by sending two of Sheridan's brigades to Thomas. These brigades were recalled to oppose the enemy's advance, and Davis closed up to the left for the same purpose. But the enemy's charge could not thus be resisted. The attack now extended from beyond Brannan's right to a point west of the Dry Valley Road. The Confederates at the weak point outnumbered the Federals three to one. McCook's five brigades were driven back, with a loss of nearly half their men. The right of Brannan was driven back, and two of his batteries, moving to a new position, were taken in flank, and thrown back through two of Van Cleve's brigades, then on their way to Thomas, producing inextricable confusion. In this way these two brigades of Van Cleve, with the five already mentioned, were driven from the field on the road to Rossville. Davis and Sheridan strove in vain to make a stand. Hindman's division had advanced far to their right, making resistance useless. Johnson had advanced on Hindman's right, swelling the volume of the assaulting column. In this charge of Longstreet's command the Confederates claimed a capture of seventeen guns.

Rosecrans, McCook, and Crittenden had all been swept from the battle-field. Thomas alone was left, with one of Negley's brigades, and the divisions of Baird, Johnson, Palmer, Reynolds, and such portions of Wood's and Brannan's as had not been involved in the disaster, to withstand the entire Confederate army. Negley had taken some fifty pieces of artillery to the rear, in obedience, as he supposed, of Thomas's orders. He thus saved a large number of guns from capture, and offered a somewhat formidable resistance to the enemy's advance. But the Confederate success against McCook's line compelled him to withdraw, and he went to Rossville, where he was very efficient in the reorganization of Rosecrans's scattered troops.[1]

---

[1] *Cleburne's Report.*

[2] General Wood having claimed that he did right in moving out of line, and had no discretion to do otherwise, General Rosecrans, on the 12th of January, 1864, wrote to Adjutant General Thomas the following letter:

"GENERAL,—The report of the general in chief shows that a letter from one of my division commanders at the battle of Chickamauga, commenting on the report of his commanding general, has been received at the War Department, and subsequently published by its authority. The general in chief refers to that letter as a rival authority to my own, and as raising a doubt on the accuracy of a point in my report. The letter, dated October 23, ult., four days after I left the command, is based on a quotation from my official report, to which, evidently, the writer was not at that time entitled, and which, therefore, *prima facie*, was surreptitiously obtained. It has been received and publicly used as a document disparaging my report, without having been referred to me, or passing through my hands, as required by military courtesy and army regulations.

"The War Department is therefore respectfully requested, as an act of justice, to cause the above and following observations to be filed and published as an appendix to my official report of the battle of Chickamauga:

"Brigadier General T. J. Wood writes and sends to the War Department a clandestine letter to show, contrary to the inference drawn in my report, that he did right, under an order to 'close up on General Reynolds and support him,' in taking his division out of the line of battle and in rear of Brannan's division, to a reserve position in rear of Reynolds. My report, dealing with facts, and avoiding personal censure, shows that General Reynolds sent me word, by Captain Kellogg, A.D.C. to General Thomas, that there were no troops on his immediate right, and that he wanted support there; that, supposing Brannan's division had been called away, I told an aid to write to General Wood an order to close up on Reynolds and support him, who wrote as follows:

"'Headquarters, September 20, 10 45 A.M.

"'Brigadier General T. J. WOOD, Commanding Division, etc.:

"'The general commanding directs that you close up on Reynolds as fast as possible, and support him. Respectfully, FRANK S. BOND, Major and A.D.C.'

"Now, with this order in his hand:

"1st. When General Wood found there was no interval to close, because Brannan's troops had not left, his plain duty as a division commander was to have reported that fact to the general commanding, who was not more than six hundred yards from him, and asked farther orders. His failure to do so was a grave mistake, showing want of military discretion.

"2d. When about to move, notwithstanding this, his duty, on being informed, as he was by one of his brigade commanders, that his skirmishers were engaged, and the enemy in line of battle opposite his position, General Wood was renewedly bound to have reported the facts and taken orders before leaving his position at such a critical time. But, instead of doing so, he privately withdrew his troops from the line, and let the enemy in, in the face of an order the wording of which shows that no such operation as the *opening*, but, on the contrary, the *closing* of a gap, was intended by it.

"3d. This conduct of General Wood, treated in the report with all the reserve consistent with the truth of history, contrasts most unfavorably with that of General Brannan, commanding the division next on his left, who, a little earlier in the day, when he received an order to leave his position and support the left, finding his skirmishers engaged, reported the fact to General Thomas, desiring to know if, under such circumstances, he should execute the order. He was told, 'No; stay where you are.'

"4th. It also contrasts with General Wood's own conduct and correspondence only a few days previously, when he protested against a reprimand of his corps commander for not occupying a position at Wauhatchie, lecturing his senior on the impropriety of what he termed 'blind obedience to orders,' and in upward of fifty pages of manuscript trying to prove his conduct consistent with that sound discretion which a division commander ought to exercise in removing his troops from the danger threatened by the literal execution of orders.

"The material difference of circumstances in the two cases, as appears from his own writings, being that the discretion he exercises at Wauhatchie, and the 'blind obedience' he pleads at Chickamauga, both have the effect of getting his troops out of danger.

"As the best of generals are liable to mistakes, I should have been content to leave those of General Wood to the simple historical statement of them, presuming he regretted them far more deeply than even myself. And, so feeling, I called attention to his military virtues—vigilance, discipline, providence of his commissariat, and care of his transportation. But his mean and unsoldierly defense of error shows him wrong both in head and heart.

"Respectfully, your humble servant, (Signed), W. S. ROSECRANS, Major General.

"Brigadier General L. THOMAS, Adjutant General U. S. A.

"Official: R. S. THORN, Captain, A.D.C."

[1] Both Generals Wood and Brannan, in their reports, endeavor to disparage General Negley's conduct in this connection. Brannan says:

"General Negley, so far from holding my right as he had promised, retired with extraordinary deliberation to Rossville at an early period of the day, taking with him a portion of my division, as will be seen by the report of Colonel Conwell, commanding First Brigade, leaving me open to attack from the right, as well as from the left and front (from which point the rebels attacked simultaneously on four several occasions), and my rear so far exposed that my staff officers, sent back for ammunition, were successfully cut off, and the ammunition, of such vital importance at that time, prevented from reaching me, thus necessitating the use of the bayonet as my only means of defense."

General Wood says:

"Before closing my report, I deem it my duty to bring to the notice of the commanding general certain facts which fell under my observation during the progress of the conflict on the 25th. As I was moving along the valley with my command, to the support of General Reynolds, in conformity with the order of the commanding general, I observed on my left, to the west of me, a force posted high up on the ridge. I inquired what force it was, and was informed that it was a part (a brigade, perhaps) of General Negley's division. I was informed that General Negley was with the force in person. I remember distinctly seeing a battery on the hill-side with it. At the

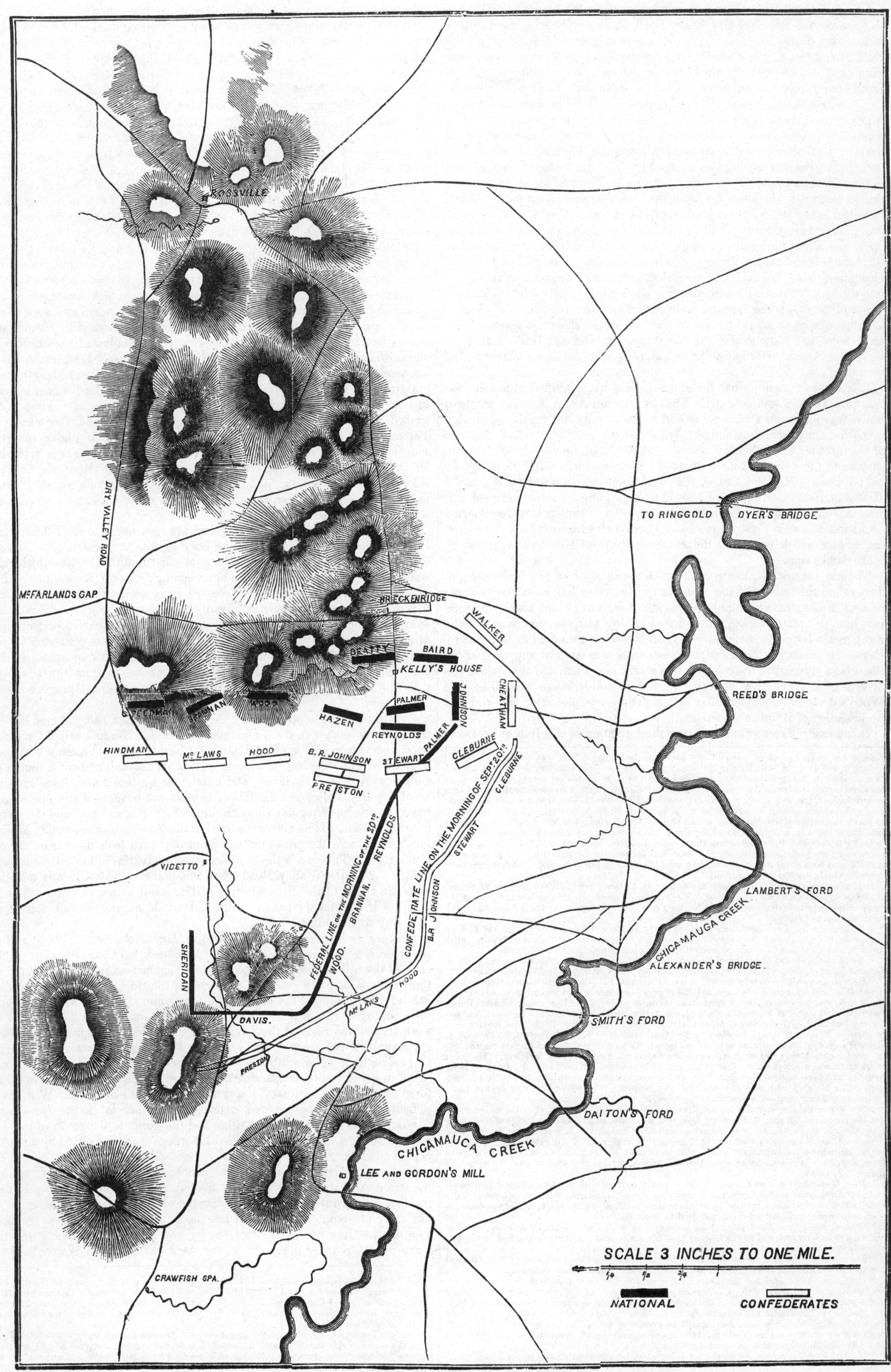

THE BATTLE OF CHICKAMAUGA, SEPTEMBER 20th.

On the Federal right there was indescribable confusion. The trains had all been pushed along the Dry Valley Road, and, mingled with the disorganized troops, blocked up the road to Rossville. Rosecrans and Garfield, his chief of staff, left the field together, taking the Rossville Road. To a retreat from this part of the field there was no alternative. As far as the eye could reach, there was no orderly array of battle, and no direct communication with the left. Was Thomas beaten also? This was the question which now agitated the minds of the general and his staff officer. If he was routed, then clearly Rosecrans's place was at Chattanooga, where he could best provide for the safety of his army and of his trains. Finally, the two officers, before reaching Rossville, came to a point where two roads led, one to Chattanooga, and the other around to Thomas's position. Firing could be heard in the latter direction with considerable distinctness. Apart from this firing, there was no hint to guide General Rosecrans. The two officers listened most intently, and reached exactly opposite conclusions. Rosecrans had already arrived at a conviction that the entire army was defeated. He judged that the firing which he heard was scattered, and indicated disorganization. Garfield, who doubtless had a more correct ear, thought it was the firing of men who were standing their ground. He felt that Thomas was not beaten, and, as General Rosecrans was determined himself to go to Chattanooga, he asked permission to go to Thomas. This was given. Rosecrans went to Chattanooga, and telegraphed to General Halleck that his army was beaten. Garfield went to Thomas; what he found *there* we shall soon discover.

It is scarcely strange that Rosecrans should have jumped at the conclusion that Thomas was defeated. That he was not seems almost a miracle; but it was just such a miracle as had twice already during this campaign saved the army from destruction. If Longstreet had known the full extent of the disorder which his first assault had produced, he would have thrown caution to the wind, and have pursued with *abandon*. But, fortunately, he did not know. His divisions on the right had met with obstinate resistance. Hindman, instead of pursuing the advantage gained on the extreme left, was moved eastward to support Johnson. Thus time was given for the formation of a new Federal line from Thomas's right, across the commanding heights which constitute the southern spurs of Mission Ridge, east of McFarland's Gap.

Thomas, meanwhile, knew nothing of the disaster to the Federal right. Just before the repulse of the enemy on his extreme left, a little after noon, he sent to Rosecrans to hurry up Sheridan's division, which had been promised him. Captain Kellogg, his aid sent for this purpose, proceeding to the right, met a large force of the enemy in the open corn-field to the rear of Reynolds, advancing cautiously. This force was at first supposed to be Sheridan's troops, but the mistake was soon discovered, and the enemy was driven back. The gap between Reynolds and Brannan was filled, and Wood's division—so much of it as remained—was placed on the right, in prolongation of Brannan's line.

It can easily be seen that if, during the formation of this line, or previous, the enemy had assaulted the Federal right with any considerable force, he must have made himself complete master of the position. Not less fortunate, nor less decisive than Longstreet's delay, was General Gordon Granger's arrival upon this part of the field just as Wood had got into position on the new line. Granger had started from Rossville at 11 o'clock with General Whittaker's and Colonel Mitchell's brigades, under the immediate command of General Steedman, leaving Colonel Dan McCook's brigade to guard the Ringgold Road. He had heard heavy firing, and judging, from the sound, that Thomas was being hard pressed, he felt that his presence upon the field was necessary. It was about three and a half miles from Rossville to the point where Thomas was then engaging Breckinridge. Granger had gone over two thirds of this distance when the enemy made his appearance in the woods to the left. This hostile force was found to be only a party of observation, and Granger pressed on with his column, leaving the enemy at this point to be taken care of by Dan McCook.

While Granger is advancing the battle has been steadily swaying to the left along Thomas's line, until it has reached Reynolds's and Brannan's divisions. Against these McLaws and Stewart, with a part of Cleburne's division, have been directing assaults as violent as those which Breckinridge and Cleburne have been making against the stronger line north and west of the Lafayette Road—stronger, because situated on more favorable ground, and more thoroughly fortified by breastworks. The result had been different: while Breckinridge and Cleburne are being driven back, Longstreet's division, though sustaining terrible loss and repeated repulse, are at length gaining ground. It is at this point that Wood withdraws from Brannan's right, and the disaster follows on the Federal right which we have already described. Brannan now withdraws from his works, and the whole of Thomas's line east of the Lafayette Road is refused, moving back upon the spurs of Mission Ridge. All this has taken place as Granger is marching for the field. Longstreet is preparing for a fresh assault upon the new position with overwhelming numbers, and, when that assault comes, Thomas feels that, so far as he can see, there is no hope for his army—no possible alternative to defeat.

At this critical moment clouds of dust are seen rising to the left and rear. In those phantom-like columns lurk hope or disaster. Some new element is about to enter into the chemistry of this doubtful battle, which now waits for the development of this approaching force for its solution. The direction from which this force is coming gives no clew as to its character: it is as like to prove hostile as friendly. At length long lines of men are seen emerging from the woods, crossing the Lafayette Road in perfect discipline, their banners fluttering above, and their bayonets glittering in the sunlight. An aid has reconnoitred, and reports that it is an infantry force. But *whose?* Soon this vital question was answered from the advanced colors—the red and blue, with the white crescent, marking Granger's battle-flag.

Granger had come up in time. Already Longstreet had gathered his columns for an assault in front and on either flank. He had called for assistance from General Polk, but the latter had been too badly beaten to respond.[1] Thomas's right rested upon a chain of heights beginning about a fourth of a mile west of Kelly's house, and extending westward about one mile toward the Dry Valley Road. These heights are covered with open woods, have a gentle but irregular slope on the south, north, and east, and their summits are a hundred feet above the level of the surrounding country.[2] McFarland's Gap—now the great strategic point of the battle-field—was on the extreme right. This gap is the entrance from the battle-field into Chattanooga Valley. The Dry Valley Road from this point to Rossville was crowded with the trains of the Federal army. The stand which was now taken by Thomas, if obstinately held till nightfall, would secure the safe retreat of the army to Rossville.

Granger, as he came up, was sent in on Brannan's right. Wood had already been formed on Brannan's left. Steedman led Granger's men up the crest of the hill, contending as he advanced against an assaulting column of the enemy which had gained the summit of the ridge. Moving forward his artillery, he dislodged the enemy and drove him down the southern slope, inflicting upon him a fearful loss in killed and wounded. The arrival of fresh troops had revived the courage of the Federals at this point, and every assault of the enemy from this time until nightfall was repulsed with great slaughter. The conflict here was desperate. Granger's command consisted in great part of troops which had never before tasted battle; but they fought with heroic obstinacy, losing nearly half their numbers. With great difficulty Longstreet succeeded in bringing his men to charge again, after they had been driven from the ridge and the gorge to the south of it. He had put in now his last division, and his troops were exhausted by their repeated assaults.

In the mean time, General Garfield, about four o'clock P.M., after running the gauntlet of the enemy's fire on the left, reached Thomas, bringing him the first official intelligence of the disaster which had befallen the right of the army at noon. Garfield had left the field with Rosecrans, as we have seen, at the time of the disaster; as he now returned to it, he found the ridge just in rear of the point where the right had been beaten, held by

time it was certainly out of reach of any fire from the enemy. This was between 11 and 12 o'clock in the day. A little later in the day, perhaps half or three quarters of an hour, when I became severely engaged, as already described, with the large hostile force that had pierced our lines and turned Brannan's right, compelling him to fall back, I looked for the force that I had seen posted on the ridge, and which, as already remarked, I had been informed was a part of General Negley's division, hoping, if I became severely pressed, it might re-enforce me, for I was resolved to check the enemy if possible. But it had entirely disappeared; whither it had gone I did not then know, but was informed later in the day it had retired to Rossville, and this information I believe was correct. By whose orders this force retired from the battle-field I do not know; but of one fact I am perfectly convinced: that there was no necessity for its retiring. It is impossible it could have been at all seriously pressed by the enemy at the time—in fact, I think it extremely doubtful whether it was engaged at all."

It is not necessary here to attempt any defense of so brave and skillful an officer as General Negley against such charges as these. We will simply quote the opinion of the Court of Inquiry called upon to investigate General Negley's conduct in the spring of 1864. The finding of this court was as follows:

"No question has any where been raised as to the conduct of General Negley on the 19th of September, the first day of the battle of Chickamauga. He commanded on that day his entire division, and it appears from the evidence that his conduct throughout was creditable.

"Early on the second day General Negley was assigned a position in the line on the right of General Brannan, from which he was relieved between 8 and 10 o'clock by Wood's division.

"He was then ordered to take a position on the extreme left; but his division having been relieved at a later hour than was expected, his reserve brigade was sent meantime in advance of the others, and became separated from him, taking a place in the line under General Baird. Subsequently another of his brigades was placed in line on the left of General Brannan, and under the command of that officer. A little later in the day, as General Negley was moving to a position on Missionary Ridge, to which he had been ordered by General Thomas, he gave up to General Brannan, on his urgent appeal for support, the largest regiment of his last brigade, retaining for himself only two weak regiments and four companies of another regiment. The point to which he was directed was in rear of the centre of the line. Here he found a battery; other batteries and parts of batteries joined him, and it appears on evidence that he had at last fifty guns under his care, with only the small infantry support above referred to, namely, two small regiments and four companies of another regiment, in all 600 or 700 men.

"The gap in the line made by the withdrawal of Wood's division, the rout of the entire right, and the unresisted advance of the enemy from that direction, as well as the advance of the enemy from the left of the line, the enemy having outflanked and driven in a portion of the left also, subjected General Negley to such hazard of losing this large park of artillery as made it expedient, in his judgment, to withdraw it to a point on the Dry Valley Road, about two or three miles from Rossville. It appears in evidence that this movement was executed in good order, and all the artillery saved.

"Here General Negley met Generals Davis and Sheridan, with portions of their command, and considerable bodies of disorganized troops from various commands. He co-operated with the division commanders above referred to in taking such measures as the exigencies of the occasion seemed to require, and toward evening retired to Rossville.

"General Negley exhibited throughout the day (the second of the battle) and the following night great activity and zeal in the discharge of his duties, and the court do not find in the evidence before them any ground of censure.

"The impression which seems to have been entertained by General Brannan that General Negley had ordered one of his brigades to the rear is not sustained by the testimony.

"It appears in the evidence that Brigadier General Wood, on one or more occasions, at the headquarters of the Army of the Cumberland, and in presence of the commander of that army and a portion of his staff, indulged in severe reflections upon the conduct of Major General Negley, applying to him coarse and offensive epithets. When placed upon the stand before the court he failed entirely to substantiate any charge or ground of accusation against him. The court deem it their duty to express their marked condemnation of such conduct, leading to vexation and unprofitable investigation prejudicial to the service.

"II. The record and opinions in the foregoing cases have been submitted to the President of the United States. He is of opinion that no farther action is required, and the Court of Inquiry is dissolved. By order of the Secretary of War, E. D. TOWNSEND, A. A. G."

[1] "About 3 o'clock in the afternoon I asked the commanding general for some of the troops of the right wing, but was informed by him that they had been beaten so badly that they could be of no service to me. I had but one division [Preston's] that had not been engaged, and hesitated to put it in, as our distress upon our right seemed to be almost as great as that of the enemy upon his right."—*Longstreet's Report.*

[2] Such is the description given in Buckner's report. In regard to the topography of the battle-field, the writer of this chapter has been compelled to depend upon Confederate reports, not finding any fair description elsewhere. Rosecrans is usually very minute in the description of the topography of his campaigns; but he probably never sufficiently explored the battle-field of Chickamauga to describe it with any degree of accuracy.

Thomas's line, which at the same time still retained the Lafayette Road. It was to him a glorious moment. He alone, of all the army which then held the field, had witnessed the advance of Hood's irresistible columns and the wreck of a whole line of battle; and he alone, of all those who had left the field, was permitted to witness the magnificent spectacle of Longstreet's repulse from the ridge. It was the fulfillment of the promise which his own heart had whispered to itself when he parted company with Rosecrans near Rossville.[1]

Shortly after Garfield's arrival, Thomas received a dispatch from General Rosecrans suggesting the withdrawal of the army to Rossville. Rosecrans had already learned from Garfield that Thomas was making a bold stand in the old tracks of the morning, and that the enemy was being repulsed. At half past five General Thomas ordered Reynolds to withdraw from his position. The line which had been assumed and obstinately held thus far, though strong in position, was weak in numbers. Only about twenty thousand men held the entire front from the Lafayette to the Dry Valley Road. Thomas, since noon, had been with his right. He saw that against the overwhelming numerical superiority of the enemy he could not hold out much longer. He, therefore, prepared to retire from the field. In passing from Wood's rear to Reynolds's position, to point out to the latter officer the position where he wished him to form line to cover the retirement of the divisions farther to the left, he found the enemy advancing in this direction to his rear. Upon this hostile force Reynolds was ordered to charge, and the enemy was driven beyond the left of the line. Wood, Brannan, and Granger were then withdrawn. Johnson's and Baird's divisions were attacked just as they were retiring, but they succeeded in moving from the field in order, and without serious loss.[2]

General Negley's presence at Rossville, where, with Sheridan's and Davis's assistance, he had rallied a considerable body of troops, and provided them with rations, was of very material assistance to General Thomas. But for these generals the retreat of the disorganized troops would have been continued to Chattanooga. Upon Thomas's arrival at Rossville, he posted Negley's division on the Ringgold Road; Reynolds's on Negley's right, stretching to the Dry Valley Road; Brannan's in reserve to Reynolds's right and rear; while McCook's corps extended from the Dry Valley Road nearly to Chattanooga Creek.

Bragg's army was too tired and too sadly worsted to attempt pursuit on the night of the 20th. On the 21st a few straggling blows were directed against the Federal army at Rossville. Thomas, feeling that he could not hold his position there against the Confederate army, suggested to Rosecrans that he be ordered to Chattanooga. The order was issued at 6 P.M. on the 21st, and by 7 o'clock the next morning Rosecrans's army was withdrawn to that place without opposition from the enemy.

Thus ended the battle. Though driven from the battle-field, the Federal army had succeeded in shutting the enemy out of Chattanooga. It had fought bravely, and had retired in good order, after having for two days held its position. Even the disaster upon its right on the 20th, taking from the field over 10,000 men, had not crushed its power of resistance. While it held the battle-field it repulsed every assault of the enemy, and withdrew only when its ammunition and supplies had given out, and it had become certain that its position could not be held for another day. The solitary advantage which the enemy had to show as a proof of his victory was his final possession of the battle-field. As to the numbers engaged on the Confederate side there are widely varying estimates.[3] After an investigation of the official returns of numbers from Bragg's army before the battle, and of the Confederate reports of the battle (which are very minute), we judge that the effective force of the enemy, including re-enforcements, amounted to 70,000 men, of whom 55,000 infantry and cavalry were directly engaged on the battle-field. Rosecrans was clearly outnumbered.[1] His entire army, including cavalry, was not far from 60,000 strong. His force actually engaged in the battle amounted to from 43,000 to 47,000 men.

The Federal army lost in the battle 1644 killed, and 9262 wounded. Bragg reports a capture of 8000 prisoners. Halleck's report (for 1863) estimates Rosecrans's missing as 4945. The loss in cavalry was 500, making a total Federal loss of 16,351. The Federal loss in artillery Bragg makes 51 guns, and Rosecrans 36 (meaning probably the net loss, subtracting from his entire loss the guns which had been captured from the enemy). The Confederate loss in killed and wounded largely exceeded that sustained by Rosecrans. Bragg reports a loss of two fifths of his command, but does not give the exact figures. Halleck, in his report, says that the Confederate journals admitted a total loss of 18,000. This is probably not far from the truth.[2] Bragg lost 2003 prisoners, leaving his loss in killed and wounded about 16,000.

[1] There is a general misapprehension in regard to this ride of Garfield's to the front from Rossville, caused probably by the publication of explanatory letters from sources which *ought* to be authentic, but which are not so. Of this nature is a letter recently (during March, 1867) published in the New York *Citizen*. This letter, entitled "Rosecrans at Chickamauga—The Question Solved," is based entirely upon information given by a member of Rosecrans's staff. Now this member of Rosecrans's staff knew absolutely nothing of what he relates as to this matter. He makes Rosecrans "fall in" with Garfield at or near Rossville, whereas it was at this very point that Garfield parted with Rosecrans, after having been with him all the time from the beginning of the battle on the 19th. By a still wider error he makes Rosecrans receive reports at this point that Thomas continued to hold his position. Rosecrans received no such reports. Neither Garfield nor Rosecrans had any thing to guide them in their conduct at this time save their own inferences. As to Rosecrans "knowing that the fate of our army depended upon our holding Chattanooga," it is clear that any such dependence upon Chattanooga could only follow upon the defeat of the entire army. Until this utter rout was established the case was exactly reversed: the ability to hold Chattanooga depended upon the fate of the army. Again, Rosecrans is made to send Thomas orders by Garfield "to hold his position at all hazards until nightfall, and then to retire to Rossville." Rosecrans sent *no* order to Thomas by Garfield. A dispatch was sent later in the day to Thomas, ordering the latter to retire to Rossville. Moreover, it is stated that the only way for Rosecrans to reach Thomas "was *via* Rossville, and thence out on the east side of the ridge, *it being impossible to cross the ridge at any intermediate point*." Certainly the advance of the enemy had not been continued so far as to prevent the crossing of the ridge at any point north of McFarland's Gap; and there was no other difficulty. From McFarland's Gap Rosecrans could have certainly gone on horseback to Thomas with as much ease as troops were a short time afterward brought over *precisely the same route* which he would have taken, the only difference being that the *direction* was opposite. The enemy at no time during the battle penetrated to the road which Rosecrans would have taken. But did Rosecrans *know* that this route was clear for him? We answer, no. And it is *here*, and not in the fact that there was no such route, that Rosecrans can find his only apology. From what he could see, he suspected that Thomas was also defeated. He says in his official report:

"Giving the troops direction to rally behind the ridge west of the Dry Valley Road, I passed down it, accompanied by General Garfield, Major McMichael, and Major Bond, of my staff, and a few of the escort, under a shower of grape and canister and musketry, for two or three hundred yards, and attempted to rejoin General Thomas and the troops sent to his support by passing to the rear of the broken portion of our lines, but found the routed troops far toward the left; and, hearing the enemy's advancing musketry and cheers, I became doubtful whether the left had held its ground, and started for Rossville. On consultation and farther reflection, however, I determined to send General Garfield there, while I went to Chattanooga to give orders for the security of the pontoon bridges at Battle Creek and Bridgeport, and to make preliminary dispositions either to forward ammunition and supplies, should we hold our ground, or to withdraw the troops into good position."

The simple fact is that Rosecrans made a great mistake. He arrived too soon at the conviction that his whole army was defeated, and upon that conviction he went to Chattanooga, because he deemed it his duty to do so. The charge of cowardice, or of an apathetic abandonment of the field, which have been made against him, are too ridiculous to be even mentioned. Rosecrans was a general against whose bravery or patriotism there can rest no reproach.

[2] The Confederate reports indicate that the entire line was carried by assault, and that Thomas was driven. This was not the case. There was no serious assault. The enemy simply occupied a position deliberately abandoned by Thomas.

[3] Rosecrans's estimate of the numbers opposed to him seems to us to be extravagant. He says (in a letter published after the battle): "The enemy reports a loss of 18,700 killed and wounded, and admits his loss to have been 20 per cent. of his entire command—a very large loss—which gave him 93,500 at Chickamauga." But this calculation is based upon a mistake which would actually *double* the enemy's numbers. Bragg distinctly states in his report that his loss amounted to *two fifths* (40 per cent.) of his entire command, which would give him—supposing his loss 18,700 (Bragg, however, does not state the exact number), 46,750 instead of 93,500. Rosecrans thinks one fifth of the numbers engaged "a very large loss." But in his official report of the battle he says, "I am fully satisfied that the enemy's loss largely exceeds ours." Now Rosecrans lost in killed and wounded 11,406, or more than one fifth of his own army.

Rosecrans (in the letter alluded to) arrives at this estimate of the enemy's numbers in another way. "Bragg," he says, "had 32,000 troops when driven from his intrenched camps at Shelbyville and Tullahoma, across the mountains and the Tennessee. Buckner joined with about 10,000 troops from East Tennessee, Johnston with about 25,000, and Longstreet with about 25,000 more, giving again 92,000 as his whole force." This also is a gross miscalculation. Bragg's force and Buckner's united, on June 20th (four days before Rosecrans advanced from Murfreesborough), amounted to 46,000 effectives—a larger estimate than Rosecrans gives. But we can find no evidence that Bragg had received 50,000 re-enforcements. At any rate, no such number was engaged in the battle. From the Army of Virginia about 12,000 men were sent under Longstreet, but Bragg reports that only 5000 of these arrived in time to participate in the battle. The re-enforcements from other sources actually engaged were B. R. Johnson's and Walker's commands, or about 15,000 men. Of Bragg's own army (the Army of Tennessee, including Buckner), the Confederate reports indicate that there were engaged about 27,000, exclusive of cavalry. This estimate would give the enemy about 47,000 infantry actually engaged at Chickamauga.

The estimate, as made up from the Confederate official reports, is the following:

LONGSTREET'S COMMAND.	
Buckner's Corps	9,207
Hindman's Division	6,122
B. R. Johnson's Division	3,683
Longstreet's Corps (proper), consisting of Hood's and McLaws's Divisions	5,000
	24,012

POLK'S COMMAND.	
Breckinridge's Division	3,769
Cleburne's Division	5,115
Walker's Corps	6,975
Cheatham's Division (approximate)	7,500
	23,359
	24,012
Total, exclusive of Cavalry	47,371

There is good reason to believe that Bragg underestimates the number of Longstreet's own troops when he puts it at 5000. Longstreet had five brigades, three under Hood (Law's, Benning's, and Robertson's), and two under McLaws (Kershaw's and Humphreys's). Kershaw had all the regiments which he had at Chancellorsville, and the Eighth North Carolina in addition. He must have had at least 2000 men. Giving Humphreys 1500 men, and Hood's three brigades 3500 (a moderate estimate in either case), Longstreet's proper command (engaged) numbered 7000. This would make the entire infantry force of the enemy, in round numbers, 50,000. The cavalry force engaged probably numbered 5000, making a total of 55,000.

This army was composed of regiments from each of the eleven Confederate States, and from Kentucky. All together there were about 115 regiments and 11 battalions; and the battalions would have made about four regiments of the average size. The average for each regiment was little over 400 men. Forty-four regiments—a little over one third of the army—were from Tennessee. Over 20 were from Alabama; 19 from Mississippi; 5 from Kentucky; 13 from Arkansas, and about the same number from South Carolina; 5 from Texas; 15 or 16 from Georgia; 6 from Louisiana; 8 from Florida; 7 from North Carolina; and from Virginia only 2. The Virginians were all in Buckner's command. B. R. Johnson's command, which Greeley (Am. Conflict, vol. ii., p. 415) makes consist of Virginians, had not a Virginia regiment. Cheatham's division consisted almost wholly of Tennesseeans. Humphreys's brigade was made up of Mississippians entirely, and Kershaw's entirely of Carolinians.

The estimate of Bragg's army which we have been considering is for the forces actually engaged. The estimate for his whole army would be largely above this. Just before his retreat from Chattanooga he had 45,000 effectives. His re-enforcements, and the additions made to his cavalry by recruiting, before the battle, increased this force to over 70,000.

[1] The last offiical returns from Rosecrans's army before the battle are those of August 31st. C. Goddard, A. A. G. of Rosecrans's staff, quoting from these returns, gives the following as the effective force of the several divisions:

Corps	Division	
Fourteenth Corps	Baird's	5,702
	Negley's	5,130
	Brannan's	6,615
	Reynolds's	6,625
		24,072
Twentieth Corps	Davis's	4,386
	Johnson's	5,607
	Sheridan's	4,352
		14,345

Corps	Division	
Twenty-first Corps	Wood's	2,964
	Palmer's	5,703
	Van Cleve's	5,308
		13,975
Granger's Reserve Corps		4,500
		13,975
		14,345
		24,072
Total		56,892

This estimate includes the entire infantry force, with the exception of Wagner's brigade left at Chattanooga. Goddard says: "I am morally certain that these returns, made previous to crossing the Tennessee, show a considerably larger force than took active part in the battle. What percentage should be deducted I can not well say. . . . . There was a regiment left at Crawfish, I think to guard the hospital. That, with the details for train guards, hospital and ambulance attendance, etc., would, I think, reduce the fighting strength at least 3000 men. I made a rough estimate at Crawfish, and put down our effectives at about 42,000, which was, I think, not far from right."

It is probable that much more than 3000 men were detailed—it would not be unfair to say 5000. Deducting this and Granger's force—which only came up at the close of the battle, and after a force more than double his own had been swept from the field—and we have left 47,392. As the cavalry on the 19th and 20th was almost entirely detached to guard the exposed flanks of the army, it ought not to be estimated as a part of the force actually engaged on the field. Rosecrans's army, all told, cavalry and infantry, numbered nearly 60,000 just before the battle.

[2] The Confederate reports give the losses in all the brigades excepting those of Gist's, Ector's, and those of Hood, McLaws's, and Cheatham's divisions. Leaving out these 10 brigades, the loss in these several commands is as follows:

	Killed.	Wounded.	Missing.	Total.	Per Cent.
Wilson's Brigade	99	426	80	605	.50
Buckner's Corps	303	2576	90	2,969	.43
Breckinridge's Division	166	909	165	1,240	.33
Cleburne's Division	204	1539	6	1,249	.34
Hindman's Division	272	1480	98	1,850	.30
Liddell's Division	162	963	277	1,462	.44
B. R. Johnson's Division	188	1081	166	1,435	.42
Total	1394	8974	882	11,250	.36

Ector's loss was about the same as Wilson's. Ector and Wilson's brigades numbered together 2400 before going into action. They lost more than half. Gist's loss is not reported, but was at least 400. The greater part of Cheatham's division was held in reserve on the 20th; but his loss on the 19th was severe. In all he must have lost 1600 men. Thus, leaving out the casualties in Longstreet's own corps, we have,

From precise data	11,250
Ector's Brigade (estimated)	600
Gist's Brigade (estimated)	400
Cheatham's Division (estimated)	1600
	13,850, or about 34 per cent.

Eighteen days after the Army of the Cumberland crossed the Tennessee it was concentrated in Chattanooga. The campaign, so far as it concerned this army alone, was over. It had been a tedious campaign of wearisome marches, terminating in a doubtful and unnecessary battle. Many mistakes had been made by both the Federal and Confederate commanders. Risks had been run on the one side which imperiled a whole army, and the disastrous results of which were only averted by delays and neglect of opportunities on the other. The battle itself was badly managed by General Rosecrans. His personal supervision of its details on the 19th would have enabled Thomas to strike blows so decisive that it is doubtful if there would have been a second day's battle. On the 20th there was, from the beginning of the fight, nothing but disorder and confusion on the right; nearly every order was either disobeyed or misunderstood. If on this day Rosecrans had devoted himself to seeing that Thomas was supported, and to such a disposition of his right as the transfer of troops to the left made necessary, there would have been no disaster, no serious loss of artillery or prisoners, and no necessity of abandoning the field to the foe. Rosecrans relied upon McCook and Crittenden to do what he ought to have known—if he knew any thing of men—would not be done by those commanders. Herein consisted his greatest blunder at Chickamauga.[1] All else—that, indeed, for which he was chiefly blamed—the historian will regard as the result of a natural mistake.

The missing, as precisely reported, we have found amounted to 882. It would be fair to suppose that the missing of Ector's and Gst's brigades and of Cheatham's division would increase this number to at least 1000. Subtracting this from the entire loss thus far estimated, we have left 12,850 as the killed and wounded, leaving out those of Longstreet's corps. Now, taking the very lowest estimate of Bragg's infantry force (as made up from official reports), it amounts to 48,000. Forty per cent. of this would give 19,200 as the number of killed and wounded in infantry alone. This would make the loss in Longstreet's corps the difference between 19,200 and 12,850, or 6350. But Bragg reports that only 5000 of Longstreet's corps took part in the battle. This estimate excludes prisoners captured from Bragg, which Rosecrans reports as 2003. We have already estimated the missing from all the other commands except Longstreet's corps as 1000; the other thousand, therefore, must have been from this corps. This would make the entire Confederate loss in infantry—killed, wounded, and missing—21,200, and Longstreet's entire loss 7350, or 2350 more men lost than, according to Bragg's report, he brought into battle.

The precise reports we are compelled to assume as correct. The error, therefore, is either in an extravagant overestimate on Bragg's part of his loss, or an equally extravagant underestimate of the number of Longstreet's corps engaged in the battle. One thing, however, is certain—namely, that the loss in Longstreet's corps was considerably above the general average. Hood's three brigades fought both days, and suffered severely on both. Kershaw's and Humphreys's brigades were engaged only on the 20th, but they sustained a fearful loss in their assaults on the afternoon of that day. It would not be extravagant, therefore, to estimate Longstreet's loss as 45 per cent. of his command. Then, supposing the entire loss of the army to have been about what Halleck says the Confederate journals stated it, 18,000, and deducting 1000 for casualties in the cavalry force, Longstreet's loss would be the difference between 17,000 and 13,850, or 3150, which would be 45 per cent. of 7000, the latter being the number which in a preceding note we gave as the probable estimate of Longstreet's force actually engaged. This calculation would decrease the percentage of loss in killed and wounded from 40 to about 30 per cent., and give Longstreet 2000 more men than Bragg gave him in his report.

The loss in some brigades of Bragg's army was almost incredible. Helm's brigade, of Breckinridge's division, went into battle with 1763 men, and came out with 432, losing over two thirds, besides its commander. Bate's brigade, of Buckner's corps, lost 608 out of 1085. Liddell's division lost 1402 out of 3175, nearly 50 per cent. In the space of a single hour, on the afternoon of the 20th, Gracie's brigade, of the same corps, lost 698 out of 2003. Another brigade (Kelly's) of this corps reports a loss of 300 out of 876. Still another reports a loss of 50 per cent. B. R. Johnson's division out of 3683 lost 1435, nearly one half. Maney's brigade, of Cheatham's division, lost half its numbers. Jackson's brigade, of the same division, lost 490 out of 1405; the loss in one of its regiments (the Fifth Georgia) was 55 per cent. Wilson's brigade lost 50 per cent., and Ector's in the same proportion.

[1] Rosecrans made no charges against McCook or Crittenden. On the contrary, in his report, he accorded them only praise. The court of inquiry which investigated Negley's conduct also considered the cases of McCook and Crittenden. We quote below the findings of the court in each case. But these opinions do not in the least affect General Rosecrans's responsibility.

Decision in McCook's Case.

"It appears from the investigation that Major General McCook commanded the Twentieth Army Corps, composed of Sheridan's, Johnson's, and Davis's divisions.

"His command on the 19th of September, 1863 (the first day of the battle of Chickamauga), consisted of Davis's and Sheridan's divisions, and of Negley's temporarily, and occupied the right of the line, Johnson's having been detached to Thomas's command. The evidence shows that General McCook did his whole duty faithfully on that day with activity and intelligence.

"Early on the 20th of September General McCook had under his command the divisions of Sheridan and Davis (the latter only 1300 to 1400 strong), and Wilder's brigade, and the senior officers of the cavalry were told they must take orders from him, though attend to their own business.

"The posting of these troops was not satisfactory to the commanding general, who in person directed several changes between 8 and 10½ o'clock P.M.

"During these changes, involving a flank movement of the whole right to the left, the enemy made a fierce attack, taking advantage of a break in the line caused by the precipitate and inopportune withdrawal of his division by Brigadier General T. J. Wood, passing through the interval, and routing the whole right and centre up to Brannan's position.

"The court deem it unnecessary to express an opinion as to the relative merits of the position taken by General McCook and that subsequently ordered to be taken by the commanding general, but it is apparent from the testimony that General McCook was not responsible for the delay in forming the new line on that occasion.

"It further appears that General McCook not only had impressed on him the vital importance of keeping well closed to the left and of maintaining a compact centre, but he was also ordered to hold the Dry Valley Road. This caused the line to be 'attenuated,' as stated in the testimony of the commanding general, who says that its length was greater than he thought it was when assumed.

"It is shown, too, that the cavalry did not obey General McCook's orders.

"The above facts, and the additional one that the small force at General McCook's disposal was inadequate to defend against greatly superior numbers the long line hastily taken under instructions, relieve General McCook entirely from the responsibility for the reverse which ensued.

"It is fully established that General McCook did every thing he could to rally and hold his troops after the line was broken, giving the necessary orders, etc., to his subordinates.

"The court are of opinion, however, that in leaving the field to go to Chattanooga, General McCook committed a mistake, but his gallant conduct in the engagements forbids the idea that he was influenced by considerations of personal safety.

"Bearing in mind that, the commanding general having previously gone to Chattanooga, it was natural for General McCook to infer that all the discomfited troops were expected to rally there, as well as to presume that a conference with the commanding general on that important subject was both desirable and necessary, the court can not regard this act of General McCook as other than an error of judgment."

Decision in Crittenden's Case.

"General Crittenden commanded the Twenty-first Army Corps, composed of Palmer's, Wood's, and Van Cleve's divisions.

"On the 19th of September, 1863 (the first day of the battle of Chickamauga), his command consisted of those divisions, except Wagner's brigade, which garrisoned Chattanooga.

"The evidence adduced respecting General Crittenden's operations on that day not only shows no cause for censure, but, on the contrary, that his whole conduct was most creditable; for by his watchfulness, and prompt and judicious support of troops engaged, serious consequences to our army were prevented, and the enemy's plans for the day disconcerted.

"Early on the morning of the 20th General Crittenden's command consisted of Wood's and Van Cleve's divisions; but as, about 8 o'clock A.M., Wood's division was detached, to take post in Thomas's line, General Crittenden is not responsible for its subsequent conduct.

"Van Cleve's division was shortly after ordered to the left, and General Crittenden was to accompany it.

The battle left Rosecrans with an army in and about Chattanooga 45,000 strong. Bragg was left with an army numbering over 50,000 men, to which re-enforcements were daily being added. It was evident, therefore, that nothing farther could be accomplished by the Army of the Cumberland until it should be largely re-enforced. Rosecrans proceeded to fortify Chattanooga. Hooker's corps was sent to him from the East on the 23d of September. Other re-enforcements were on the way from Grant's army. As soon as the latter arrived Rosecrans was relieved of his command, on the 19th of October,[1] and General Grant, with the armies of the Cumberland, the Ohio, and the Tennessee, entered upon that brilliant campaign which terminated in General Bragg's utter defeat before the close of the year.[2]

CHAPTER XXXV.
THE CHATTANOOGA CAMPAIGN.
V. THE SIEGE OF KNOXVILLE.

The Campaign for Chattanooga involved the East Tennessee Problem.—Halleck's Mistake; his Contradictory Orders.—The tardy and feeble Effort toward co-operation with Rosecrans.—Plans for subsequent Movements suggested by Burnside.—Halleck still insists upon the Occupation of the Upper Valley of the Holston and Co-operation with Rosecrans at the same Time.—Why Bragg did not move on Rosecrans's Rear directly after the Battle of Chickamauga.—The Confederates occupy Lookout Mountain, abandoned by Rosecrans.—The Mistake of Rosecrans deprives him of his shortest Line of Communication.—Wheeler's Raid north of the Tennessee.—Destruction of a Federal Train.—Capture of McMinnville.—Conflict with Crooks's Federal Cavalry near Farmington.—The Difficulty of supplying Chattanooga prevents the accession of Burnside's Army to the Defense of that Place.—The Campaign against Sam Jones in East Tennessee.—Longstreet crosses the Tennessee, November 14, 1863.—Burnside, in accordance with Grant's Instructions, falls back toward Knoxville.—The Battle at Campbell's Station.—Burnside's Situation after reaching Knoxville.—Longstreet, needed by Bragg, can not afford to wait, and Assaults on the 18th.—Death of General Sanders.—Defeat of Longstreet's second Assault, November 29th.—Grant sends Sherman to the Relief of Knoxville.—The Siege is raised, and Longstreet retreats eastward.

IN the campaign of General Rosecrans against Bragg, General Burnside's army had been utilized only to a very small extent. The advance upon Knoxville had been unresisted. The occupation of that point was of considerable importance. By his possession of the railroad connecting East Tennessee with Virginia, Burnside compelled the Confederate re-enforcements to Bragg's army from the east to make an extensive detour by way of Atlanta. His presence on Rosecrans's left and rear made his army a large reserve force relatively to Rosecrans; but the Army of the Ohio was too distant to answer the chief use of a reserve corps—that of active co-operation in case of necessity. The idea that Burnside's army, by remaining in the Valley of the Holston, secured the possession of East Tennessee, is simply absurd. It was security enough, doubtless, against Sam Jones's little army, or any other inconsiderable detachments which might straggle across the mountains from West Virginia. But these were only demonstrating columns sent for the purpose of keeping Burnside's army where it was. The Confederate force which was really fighting for East Tennessee was Bragg's army. The only force which actually contested Bragg's possession of this prize was the Army of the Cumberland; and it maintained the contest single-handed, while Burnside's army accomplished little beyond the illustration of General Halleck's pet theories. The enemy thoroughly understood that the defeat of General Rosecrans was the recovery not only of Chattanooga, but of all else which Bragg and Buckner had abandoned. If Rosecrans could be cut off from Chattanooga—and at one stage of the campaign this seemed likely to be accomplished—there was no alternative to Burnside's retreat but overwhelming disaster. The continued separation of the two armies was too auspicious to the Confederate government to be counted upon, and, therefore, Longstreet had been sent to Bragg.

"As it was moving the attack took place, and the troops were broken by our retreating artillery and infantry, as well as by the furious attack of the enemy.

"For the disaster which ensued he is in no way responsible.

"Changes were ordered to be made in the line. The break which occurred while the troops were moving by flank from the right to the left to conform to these changes was taken advantage of by the enemy, and disaster and rout ensued. It is amply proven that General Crittenden did every thing he could, by example and personal exertion, to rally and hold his troops, and to prevent the evils resulting from such a condition of affairs, but without avail.

"Believing that by his presence on the field nothing more could be effected, he left for Rossville, where he learned little else than that the commanding general had gone to Chattanooga.

"He repaired thither, where one of his brigades was stationed.

"In the opinion of the court, General Crittenden is not censurable for this act."

[1] The following is a copy of General Rosecrans's order upon leaving his army:

"*General Orders, No. 242.*

"Headquarters Department of the Cumberland, Chattanooga, Tenn., October 19th, 1863.

"The general commanding announces to the officers and soldiers of the Army of the Cumberland that he leaves them, under orders from the President.

"Major General George H. Thomas, in compliance with orders, will assume the command of this army and department.

"The chiefs of all the staff departments will report to him.

"In taking leave of you, his brothers in arms—officers and soldiers—he congratulates you that your new commander comes not to you as he did, a stranger. General Thomas has been identified with this army from its first organization. He has led you often in battle. To his known prudence, dauntless courage, and true patriotism you may look with confidence that under God he will lead you to victory.

"The general commanding doubts not you will be as true to yourselves and your country in the future as you have been in the past.

"To the division and brigade commanders he tenders his cordial thanks for their valuable and hearty co-operation in all that he has undertaken.

"To the chiefs of the staff departments and their subordinates whom he leaves behind he owes a debt of gratitude for their fidelity and untiring devotion to duty.

"Companions in arms—officers and soldiers—farewell; and may God bless you!

"W. S. ROSECRANS, Major General."

[2] We have dealt thus elaborately with the history of Rosecrans's Chickamauga campaign on account of the general misapprehension which exists in regard to many of its most important features. We have endeavored to do justice to all the actors concerned. The writer has made no statement in regard to any point in dispute without substantiating it. His materials have been abundant, consisting in no small proportion of unpublished official documents. If he has erred in any important particular, it has not been from prejudice, but because the evidence before him was, after all, incomplete. Whatever mistakes may have been made on this account, time alone can correct. A fair history of any event is not often written while the historian rests under its shadow. If the present writer has failed to do justice, still justice will be done; if he has not told the exact truth, still, sooner or later, the exact truth will be told.

Burnside had received orders instructing him to co-operate with Rosecrans, but it had all the while been insisted upon that he must hold the Valley of the Holston from Rosecrans's left to the Virginia boundary, a line of nearly 200 miles. Not till it was too late did he receive an explicit order to move to Chattanooga. The first order to this effect he got on the 16th, only three days before the battle of Chickamauga. The Ninth Corps, which had been resting for the last fortnight after its struggle in Mississippi, was now ordered to move. But the necessity for haste does not seem to have been appreciated. The next night a more urgent dispatch was received from General Halleck, who wrote, "There are several reasons why you should re-enforce Rosecrans with all possible dispatch. It is believed the enemy will concentrate to give him battle. You must be there to help him." On the 21st a peremptory order came from the President, commanding Burnside to join Rosecrans without delay. By this time all the forces had been, with great deliberation, put in motion, except a small detachment of infantry and cavalry confronting the enemy on the Watauga River. With this latter force Burnside remained. Not venturing to withdraw while the enemy was in his front, he determined to wait until the next morning, and fight a battle before obeying the President's order. The next morning disclosed the fact that the enemy had retreated, burning the bridge behind him. The Federal column at this point was then started for Knoxville, where, by the 25th, the troops were all concentrated. It was then known that the battle of Chickamauga had been fought, and the emergency was past. Some correspondence followed between Halleck and Burnside, the result of which was that the command of the latter remained in East Tennessee. Burnside proposed to the general-in-chief three separate plans for the future operations of his army.

The first of these contemplated the abandonment of the railroad and East Tennessee, leaving only a small garrison at Cumberland Gap. This would leave free an army of full 20,000 men to move down the Tennessee and re-enforce Rosecrans.

The second plan suggested the movement of his main body—say 18,000 men—along the line of the railroad against Bragg's right at Cleveland, leaving garrisons at Knoxville and Loudon, also at Cumberland Gap, and at Bull's Gap and Rogersville, to cover Cumberland Gap.

The third plan proposed the movement of a force, consisting of 7000 infantry and 5000 cavalry, south of the Tennessee River, through Athens, Columbus, and Benton, past the right flank of the enemy, "down the line of the East Tennessee and Georgia Railroad to Dalton, destroying the enemy's communications, sending a cavalry force to Rome to destroy the machine works and powder-mills at that place, the main body moving on the direct road to Atlanta, the railroad centre of Georgia, and there entirely destroying the enemy's communications, breaking up the dépôts, etc., thence moving to some point on the coast where cover could be obtained." No trains were to be taken. The troops were to live upon the country. This would divert the attention of the enemy, and materially relieve Rosecrans. The chances of escape from pursuing columns of the enemy Burnside thought were in his favor.

Burnside was partial to the plan last described, which, by the way, on a miniature scale resembled Sherman's brilliant march from Atlanta to the sea, undertaken more than a year afterward. Halleck replied somewhat testily, decidedly objecting to Burnside's proposed raid. He was in favor of immediately co-operating with Rosecrans by a movement on the north side of the Tennessee. But he still insisted upon Burnside's holding the upper valley of the Holston, 200 miles away from Chattanooga.[1]

Rosecrans favored the first of the plans proposed by Burnside, but events soon occurred which made this impracticable. While the Federal commanders had been forming plans, General Bragg had not been idle. The very next day after the battle of Chickamauga, Longstreet had suggested a movement to Rosecrans's rear, above Chattanooga, to cut off his communications, and compel him to fall back to Nashville. At first Bragg seemed inclined to adopt this plan—at least Longstreet so understood. But if Bragg for a moment entertained such a scheme, he soon gave it up as impracticable.[2] But, while keeping his main army south of the Tennessee, Bragg assumed the offensive with considerable energy.

Rosecrans's most convenient line of communication with Murfreesborough was through Bridgeport, and the shortest road from Chattanooga to this point lay along the south bank of the Tennessee. This route could be rendered secure only by holding the point of Lookout Mountain, and Stevens's and Cooper's Gaps. Rosecrans, after retreating to Chattanooga, gave up these important positions to the enemy. He claims that he could not have held them and Chattanooga at the same time.[1] The enemy immediately occupied Lookout Mountain, and thus compelled Rosecrans to transport his supplies by the more difficult route across the mountains. But even this latter route was not left undisturbed. Bragg sent Wheeler, with a large cavalry force—Wharton's, Martin's, Davidson's, and Armstrong's commands—against this line of communication. Wheeler's command crossed the Tennessee above Chattanooga, and on the 2d of November reached the Sequatchie Valley. Proceeding around Chattanooga on the north side to Jasper and Anderson's Cross-roads, two wagon trains were captured, one of them ten miles in length, consisting of from 800 to 1500 wagons, and heavily loaded with ordnance and provisions. This train was destroyed, and during the night Wheeler crossed the Cumberland Mountains, and the next morning headed his columns toward McMinnville. Although the Federal cavalry was in close pursuit, he succeeded in capturing the place, with its fortifications, and its garrison of 587 men and 200 horses. Then he moved westward to Murfreesborough. Only time was allowed for a feint on this point, but the stockade guarding the railroad bridge over Stone River was captured, and the bridge, together with the track for a distance of three miles, was destroyed. On the 5th the railroad bridges and trestles between Murfreesborough and Wartrace were destroyed, also a large quantity of stores at Shelbyville. Wheeler was now ready to withdraw; but Davidson, on the Duck River, did not retire with sufficient promptness, and was overtaken by the Federal cavalry. Rosecrans, after the battle of Chickamauga, had sent most of his cavalry north of the Tennessee to guard the fords of the river. Those nearest Chattanooga were guarded by Colonel Miller, commanding Wilder's brigade. Farther up the river were Minty's and Long's brigades, under the command of General Crook. Wheeler, as we have seen, was not thus prevented from crossing into Sequatchie Valley; but, as soon as he had crossed, the cavalry brigades along the river combined under General Crook's command, and pressed on in the pursuit. This force was soon joined by Mitchell's cavalry division. The pursuit was close, though it did not prevent the enemy from doing very great injury. There were some inconsiderable fights with the rear of Wheeler's column, but no battle until Davidson's command was engaged near Farmington. Wheeler, with Martin's division, came up just in time to relieve Davidson from his perilous situation. Both Crook and Wheeler claim each to have driven the other. Certainly Wheeler stood only long enough to secure the safety of his trains, when he withdrew.

There was, apart from any interruption from the enemy, great difficulty in supplying Rosecrans's army. Wheeler's movement had added to the embarrassment rising from this cause. Under such circumstances, the addition of Burnside's army to that which was already encamped at Chattanooga was inexpedient, unless absolutely necessary.

In the mean time the enemy, under General Sam Jones, was again threatening Burnside's left. He had advanced, by the 8th of October, as far as Blue Springs. Burnside had a small body of infantry at Morristown, and a cavalry brigade at Bull's Gap. The Ninth Corps, re-enforced by Willcox's division and Shackleford's cavalry, were on the 10th led against the enemy in front, while Colonel Foster's brigade of cavalry was sent *via* Rogersville to the enemy's rear, to intercept his retreat. The Confederates were driven by the attack in front, but escaped Foster's blow by withdrawing during the night. Shackleford pursued, driving the enemy into Virginia. Burnside lost about 100 killed and wounded, and took 150 prisoners.

A week or more after the fight at Blue Springs General Grant assumed command of the "Military Division of the Mississippi," which was now made to comprise the three departments of the Ohio, the Cumberland, and the Tennessee. Thomas succeeded Rosecrans as commander of the Army of the Cumberland, and McCook and Crittenden were ordered to Cincinnati. Sherman commanded the Army of the Tennessee, and Burnside retained his present command. Hooker's corps had come from the East, and there were now four different Federal armies operating upon the soil of Tennessee. Halleck, after so long a time, saw the necessity of unity in the action of these various commands in order to their effective co-operation, and the control of these four armies was therefore given to General Grant.

---

[1] Halleck says: "The purport of all your instructions has been that you should hold some point near the upper end of the valley, and with all your available force move to the assistance of Rosecrans. Since the battle of Chickamauga, and the wear of our force to paper, you have been repeatedly told that it would be dangerous to form a connection on the south side of the Tennessee River, and consequently that you ought to march on the north side. Rosecrans has now telegraphed to you that it is not necessary to join him at Chattanooga, but only to move down to such a position that you can go to his assistance should he require it. You are in direct communication with Rosecrans, and can learn his condition and wants sooner than I can. Distant expeditions into Georgia are not now contemplated. The object is to hold East Tennessee by forcing the enemy south of the passes, and closing the passes against his return."

[2] "The suggestion of a movement by our right, immediately after the battle to the north of the Tennessee, and thence upon Nashville, requires notice only because it will find a place among the files of the department. Such a movement was utterly impossible for want of transportation. Nearly half our army consisted of re-enforcements just before the battle, without a wagon or an artillery horse, and nearly, if not quite a third of the artillery horses on the field had been lost. The railroad bridges, too, had been destroyed to a point south of Ringgold, and in all the road from Cleveland to Knoxville. To these insurmountable difficulties were added the entire absence of means to cross the river, except by fording at a few precarious points too deep for artillery, and the well-known danger of sudden rises, by which all communication would be cut—a contingency which did actually happen a few days after the visionary scheme was proposed. But the most serious objection to the proposition was its entire want of military propriety. It abandoned to the enemy our entire line of communication, and laid open to him our dépôts of supplies, while it placed us, with a greatly inferior force, beyond a difficult, and, at times, impassable river, in a country affording no subsistence to men or animals. It also left open to the enemy, at a distance of only ten miles, our battle-field, with thousands of our wounded and his own, and all the trophies and supplies we had won. All this was to be risked and given up for what? To gain the enemy's rear, and cut him off from his dépôt of supplies by the route over the mountains, when the very movement abandoned to his unmolested use the better and more practicable route of half the length on the south side of the river. It is hardly necessary to say the proposition was not even entertained, whatever may be the inferences drawn from subsequent movements."—*Bragg's Report.*

---

[1] In his evidence before the Congressional Committee, Rosecrans says: "General Halleck, in his annual report, says I abandoned the passes of Lookout Mountain, leaving the public to imagine that these passages were within the possible control of my army, and their abandonment not justified as a military measure. I call the attention of the committee to the fact that one of these passes was forty-two miles south of Chattanooga, and the next nearest twenty-six miles south of Chattanooga, and the nearest at the extremity of Lookout Mountain in front of our lines. This latter may have been the one which gave rise to his report, and if so it ought to have been so stated. I was satisfied that I could not even hold *this* pass and Chattanooga at the same time if the enemy did his duty, and therefore withdrew my troops from it, but established batteries on the other side of the river, which rendered it practically of little, if any use to them. Subsequent events amply justified the wisdom of this decision, for the enemy, with a division and a half, were unable to hold it against General Hooker, and it was their attempt to cover this point which was one of the causes of their being beaten so easily at Missionary Ridge."

This apology is exceedingly weak. In the first place, Rosecrans, after abandoning the point of Lookout Mountain overlooking Chattanooga and its approach *via* the south bank of the Tennessee, and finding that the enemy had immediately occupied it, saw that he had made a mistake in giving it up, and ordered McCook to storm and recapture the position. McCook stoutly objected that the thing couldn't be done, and was supported in this opinion by the judgment of some of the best officers in the army. As to the other point, namely, the enemy's inability to hold the same position subsequently against Hooker, the argument is no more pertinent. Hooker did not, and *could* not have succeeded in a direct attack upon the position, such as McCook was ordered to make. He surprised the enemy by taking their works in flank. Now such a movement was impossible to the enemy in the case of Rosecrans's holding the position. This is as clear as daylight. For, of course, the *Federal* works would have fronted the enemy, and the entire disposition, both of the forces holding the position as well as of the fortifications themselves, would have been altered, so that Bragg must have assaulted in front, or not at all.

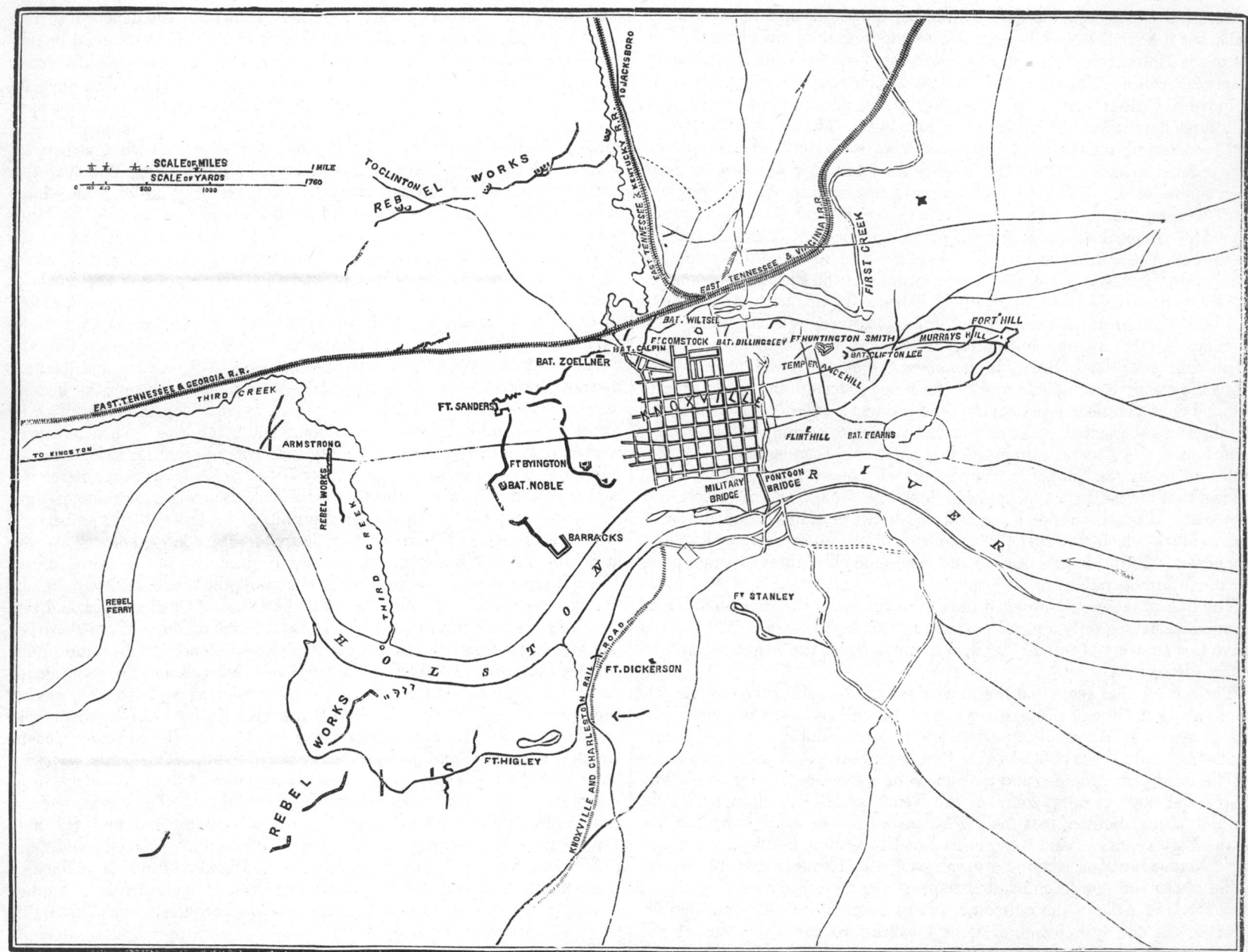

OFFICIAL MAP ILLUSTRATING THE SIEGE OF KNOXVILLE.

About the middle of October, just after Wheeler's return from Middle Tennessee, there had been indications of a movement by the enemy toward Knoxville. Bragg's right flank had begun to extend beyond Cleveland. On the 20th, Colonel Woolford, holding the Sweetwater Valley, south of the Tennessee, was attacked by a superior force of the enemy near Philadelphia, and, after several hours' fighting, finding that he was being surrounded, retired to Loudon, leaving in the enemy's hands thirty-eight wagons, six small howitzers, and between 300 and 400 prisoners. It soon became evident that Bragg was threatening Burnside with a formidable force, and the latter withdrew all his troops to the north side of the river, occupying the heights about Loudon. To this point Burnside moved his headquarters on the 28th, where he remained until the 31st, when the emergency appeared to have passed, and he returned to Knoxville. The enemy, in his operations south of the river, had captured 650 prisoners. On the 10th of November the Federal garrison at Rogersville was attacked by forces from Virginia and driven back to Morristown, with a loss of 500 prisoners, four guns, and thirty-six wagons.

Early in November, Longstreet's corps, now consisting of 12,000 men, was detached from Bragg's army, and, accompanied by 5000 cavalry under Wheeler, began to move against Burnside. Upon learning this fact, General Grant urged Burnside to concentrate his army at Kingston, where he would be in more intimate connection with the forces at Chattanooga. Burnside preferred Knoxville to Kingston. It had already been partially fortified under the superintendence of Captain O. M. Poe, who had erected two earth-works near the town. His reluctance to abandon East Tennessee was also an argument in favor of this point. About this time Charles A. Dana, Assistant Secretary of War, and Colonel Wilson, of Grant's staff, visited Knoxville. These gentlemen agreed with General Burnside, and Grant yielded the point. It seemed also to be a great advantage to Grant that Longstreet should be diverted as far as possible from Chattanooga. The movement of his corps into East Tennessee, though he had urged it at an earlier period, was at this time, it appears, opposed by Longstreet; but both Davis and Bragg insisted upon the undertaking. Longstreet was promised the support of Stevenson's and Cheatham's divisions, which would have increased his strength to over 27,000 men; but upon reaching Sweetwater (near Loudon) he discovered that they were ordered in the opposite direction. There were no indications, either, of the supplies, of which he was in pressing need, and which had been promised him. He was obliged to halt for some days at Sweetwater, losing most precious time, while he sent out his foraging expeditions in every direction to gather up corn stacked in the fields, which was then threshed and baked. His men were thinly clad; their shoes were unserviceable; they had few blankets, and no tents; but they had marched before in the same plight, and uttered no complaint.

On the morning of November 14th Longstreet's advance crossed the Tennessee at Hough's Ferry, six miles below Loudon, demonstrating against Knoxville with his cavalry at the same time. At Lenoir's General Potter was stationed, with the Ninth Corps and one division of the Twenty-third, under Brigadier General Julius White. Longstreet did not cross the river without resistance. General White fell upon his advance in the afternoon, and drove it back for two miles to the river. Burnside would have attacked again on the morning of the 15th, but he received late at night an order from General Grant to withdraw his troops. The design was to draw Longstreet on to Knoxville. The order was promptly obeyed. "If General Grant," said Burnside, "can destroy Bragg, it is of no great consequence what becomes of ourselves. Order the troops to be ready to march in the morning." Burnside fell back to Lenoir's on the 15th, and on the night of that day prepared to continue his retreat to Campbell's Station.

The enemy endeavored by a flank movement to anticipate General Burnside in the possession of Campbell's Station, but the Federal troops reached this important position first. Here a stand was made on the 16th by Hartranft's division, while the main portion of the Federal army and the trains passed along the Loudon Road toward Knoxville. Hartranft had reached the Station a quarter of an hour before Longstreet's advance came up. He succeeded in holding his ground and covering the retreat until the army and the trains had passed the threatened point. Then Burnside, forming his army upon a low range of hills, half a mile from Campbell's, covering the approaches to Knoxville, awaited the enemy's attack. Several assaults were made upon this position, which were repulsed with great loss to the enemy. Longstreet advancing upon his rear in the afternoon, Burnside withdrew to a second position, equally strong, 1000 yards in rear of the first. The enemy repeated his attack with determination, but was finally forced to withdraw, and that night Burnside's army retired within its intrenchments at Knoxville.

In the mean time General Sanders had met the enemy's cavalry south of the Holston, on the opposite bank from Knoxville. General Parke, now Burnside's chief of staff, had been left in command of the town. A pontoon bridge was thrown across the Holston, by means of which Sanders kept up communication with the garrison defending the town. Holding this position, General Sanders successfully maintained it until Burnside's army entered Knoxville.

General Burnside held a position of great strength. His force was fully equal to that of the enemy, and the hills around Knoxville, previously fortified by General Buckner, and now connected by means of rifle-pits, formed a vast fortified camp. General Sanders's force was now drawn across the river, and covered the Loudon Road. Longstreet had already lost much time. Grant was ready to move upon Bragg, and if Longstreet would be

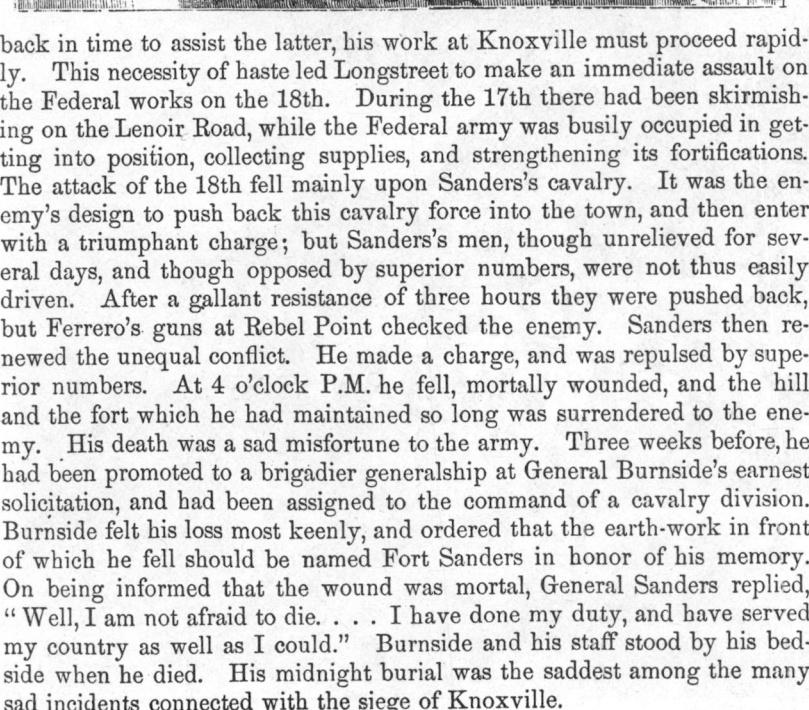

back in time to assist the latter, his work at Knoxville must proceed rapidly. This necessity of haste led Longstreet to make an immediate assault on the Federal works on the 18th. During the 17th there had been skirmishing on the Lenoir Road, while the Federal army was busily occupied in getting into position, collecting supplies, and strengthening its fortifications. The attack of the 18th fell mainly upon Sanders's cavalry. It was the enemy's design to push back this cavalry force into the town, and then enter with a triumphant charge; but Sanders's men, though unrelieved for several days, and though opposed by superior numbers, were not thus easily driven. After a gallant resistance of three hours they were pushed back, but Ferrero's guns at Rebel Point checked the enemy. Sanders then renewed the unequal conflict. He made a charge, and was repulsed by superior numbers. At 4 o'clock P.M. he fell, mortally wounded, and the hill and the fort which he had maintained so long was surrendered to the enemy. His death was a sad misfortune to the army. Three weeks before, he had been promoted to a brigadier generalship at General Burnside's earnest solicitation, and had been assigned to the command of a cavalry division. Burnside felt his loss most keenly, and ordered that the earth-work in front of which he fell should be named Fort Sanders in honor of his memory. On being informed that the wound was mortal, General Sanders replied, "Well, I am not afraid to die. . . . I have done my duty, and have served my country as well as I could." Burnside and his staff stood by his bedside when he died. His midnight burial was the saddest among the many sad incidents connected with the siege of Knoxville.

The partial success gained by Longstreet on the 18th proved of little value. To push this slight advantage against works so gallantly defended could only result in increased loss to his command, without any reasonable chance of victory. He therefore determined to reduce the garrison to surrender by famine. Burnside's army held the roads approaching Knoxville from the west; on each side of the city ran the Holston. The assault on the 18th had been on the Federal left.

Burnside was fairly besieged on the night of the 18th. The enemy had cut off communication with Cumberland Gap, and held the approaches to Knoxville on the northwest and southwest. The Federal army was supplied for three weeks; the fortifications were hourly strengthened; a *chevaux de frise* of pikes was set up in front of the rifle-pits, and the heights on the opposite side of the Holston were securely held and fortified. Burnside was urged by Grant to hold on to Knoxville. Fortunately, he was better supplied with provisions than the enemy conjectured, and had lost no time in his work upon the fortifications, which had become almost impregnable. His only hope now was Grant's speedy victory over Bragg, and the approach of a relieving force.

Grant's work, as we shall see in the next chapter, was speedily and effectually accomplished. One week after Longstreet's assault on the 18th, Bragg was defeated before Chattanooga, and Longstreet's position was rendered extremely perilous. But the latter determined to make a final effort, risking every thing upon the chances of a bold assault on Burnside's lines before a Federal force could reach his own rear. He had in the mean while

JOHN G. PARKE.

been re-enforced by two brigades of B. R. Johnson's division. The morning of the 29th of November was fixed for the assault.

The point selected for the attack was Fort Sanders, which commanded the Kingston Road, and overlooked Knoxville. The capture of this fort would be decisive, and every nerve was strained for its accomplishment. This position was held by a portion of the Ninth Corps. It was well protected by a wide ditch in front, by thickly laid abatis, and by a network of wires stretched from stump to stump.

In the gray of the morning three picked brigades of McLaws's division

appeared in front of the fort, while a Georgia regiment of sharp-shooters silenced the Federal guns. Leaving the shelter of the woods, the storming column advanced up the slope. Only at the edge of the ditch did the enemy halt. Here it was found that an important feature in the assault had been forgotten. There were no means at hand for crossing this ditch. It was now the moment of glorious opportunity to the defenders of the fort, who poured a deadly fire upon the hesitating column, checking the first impetus of its assault. But, though retarded in their movement, the courage of the assailants was indomitable. They broke through the entanglement of wires, they cut their way through the abatis; the carnage made among them by musketry and artillery could not daunt their brave spirits; they filled the ditch; some of them assailed the scarp of the fort, pushing each other up to reach the parapet; a few forced their way through the embrasures. Here, with these few, a hand-to-hand conflict was waged. One officer advanced with a flag and boldly demanded the surrender of the fort, and was dragged inside a prisoner. Those who had reached the parapet were shot and hurled back into the ditch, which now writhed with its dead and wounded, while, to increase the maddening torment, hand grenades were thrown into their midst. Meanwhile, into the rear the artillery hurled its fatal missiles, until at length, entirely baffled, this column was withdrawn and another took its place, and the carnage was renewed. But no impression was made upon the garrison. After a display of courage probably unequaled by that exhibited in any assault during this war, and never surpassed in any other war, the attack was abandoned. There followed a truce, to permit the enemy to gather up his dead and wounded—over 500 all told—and here from the lips of the enemy was heard the first tidings of Grant's victory. The loss in the fort was 8 killed, 5 wounded, and about 30 captured. An assault made at the same time upon General Shackleford on the south side of the Holston had also been repulsed.

This repulse of the enemy, though it did not immediately terminate the siege, was its last important event. The day before the assault Sherman had been ordered with 25,000 men to march to the relief of Knoxville. Elliot's cavalry division were sent in the same direction. Sherman advanced along the south side of the Tennessee, cutting off Longstreet's retreat, and by the 4th of December his army was within two or three marches of Knoxville. On the 5th the enemy retired and the siege was raised. Longstreet retired up the Holston River, but there was no pursuit. He did not entirely abandon East Tennessee until the following spring, when his command rejoined the Army of Northern Virginia.[1]

[1] With the siege of Knoxville closed the active services of General Burnside in East Tennessee. The command was transferred to General Foster. The transfer was actually made on the 11th of December. Three days afterward Burnside left Knoxville, and reached his home in Providence, R. I., on the 23d. On January 28th, 1864, President Lincoln approved a resolution "that the thanks of Congress be, and they hereby are, presented to Major General Ambrose E. Burnside, and through him to the officers and men who have fought under his command, for their gallantry, good conduct, and soldier-like endurance."

LONGSTREET'S ASSAULT ON FORT SANDERS.

LONGSTREET'S SHARPSHOOTERS ATTACKING A FEDERAL TRAIN ABOVE CHATTANOOGA.

CHAPTER XXXVI.
THE CHATTANOOGA CAMPAIGN.
VI. DEFEAT OF BRAGG.

General Grant after the Vicksburg Campaign.—He assumes Command of the Military District of the Mississippi, and of the Armies under Sherman, Thomas, Burnside, and Hooker.—His available Force for the final Struggle of the Chattanooga Campaign.—The Condition of his four Armies.—Hooker's Arrival in the West.—Chattanooga besieged by Bragg's Army.—Rosecrans's Plan for the Recovery of Lookout Valley executed by Grant.—Longstreet's Signals from Lookout Mountain interpreted by General Geary.—The Battle of Wauhatchie.—Importance of this Success.—Chattanooga relieved.—The Understanding between Grant and Burnside.—Longstreet sent against Knoxville.—Position of Bragg's Army.—Confidence of the Confederate Commander.—Grant's Plan of Attack.—Waiting for Sherman.—March of the Army of the Tennessee.—Sherman confers with Grant at Chattanooga.—Rumor of Bragg's intended Retreat.—Thomas's Reconnoissance, November 23d.—Orchard Knob carried.—Bragg strengthens his Right.—Operations on the 24th.—Sherman's attack on Tunnel Hill.—Hooker carries Lookout Mountain; the "Battle above the Clouds."—Operations on the 25th.—Bragg's altered Position.—General Corse's assault on Cleburne's Position.—Waiting for Hooker.—Thomas storms Missionary Ridge.—The Confederate Centre broken.—Hooker drives the Left.—Retreat and Pursuit.—A decisive Victory.

WE will now turn from the siege of Knoxville—an important episode in the Chattanooga campaign—to the movements of Grant's army at Chattanooga, which terminated on November 25th in the expulsion of Bragg's forces from Missionary Ridge.

Immediately after the reduction of Vicksburg, Grant dispatched expeditions in various directions in the State of Mississippi. In one of these, sent to Natchez, under General Ransom, 5000 head of cattle, which were being crossed over the Mississippi at that point for the enemy's supply, were captured. His army now became dispersed. Ord and Herron were sent to the Department of the Gulf. Steele was dispatched to Helena, to re-enforce Schofield in the Department of the Missouri. Toward the last of August General Grant proceeded upon a tour of inspection through his department. He reached New Orleans on the 2d of September. As he was returning to his hotel in that city from a review of Ord's corps, on the 4th, his horse be-

came frightened, and, violently striking a carriage, General Grant was thrown into the street, and so severely injured in the hip that he was unable either to walk, or mount his horse without assistance, until his arrival at Chattanooga, toward the close of October. Secretary Stanton met him at Indianapolis, and both together proceeded to Louisville. Here, on the 18th, the Secretary handed him the order of the President, giving him the command of the "Military District of the Mississippi," comprising the departments of the Tennessee, the Ohio, and the Cumberland. By the same order Rosecrans was relieved of his command, being superseded by General Thomas.

This order gave Grant the military control of all the territory in possession of the government from the Mississippi River to the Alleghany Mountains, and of four large armies under Sherman (who succeeded Grant in the command of the Department and Army of the Tennessee), Thomas, Burnside, and Hooker. These armies, together, numbered probably 150,000 effective men. Two thirds of this force, or about 100,000 men, was available for the Chattanooga campaign. Deducting 20,000 for Burnside's effective command, and we have left a force 80,000 strong, which could be used directly against General Bragg. General Hooker's army was 23,000 strong, and consisted of the Eleventh and Twelfth Corps. The Army of the Cumberland, now reduced to a little over 40,000 men, had been reorganized. McCook and Crittenden had been sent to Cincinnati, and their two commands, consolidated with the reserves, now constituted the Fourth Corps, under Gordon Granger. General Palmer commanded the Fourteenth, Thomas's old corps. The remaining portion of the forces brought against Bragg were to come from the Army of the Tennessee. Of this latter army, McPherson's corps remained at Vicksburg, and, by demonstrations along the Big Black, prevented Johnston from sending farther re-enforcements to Bragg. Hurlbut's corps was retained at Memphis. Upon Sherman's taking command of the Army of the Tennessee, General Blair had been assigned to that of the Fifteenth Corps.

The transfer of General Hooker's army westward to the Tennessee was

accomplished with marvelous expedition. Although accompanied by its artillery, trains, baggage, and animals, this army moved from the Rapidan, in Virginia, to Stevenson, in Alabama, a distance of 1192 miles, in seven days, crossing the Ohio twice.[1] General Hooker reached Cincinnati in person on the 29th of September, and during the first week in October his army was on Rosecrans's right flank at Stevenson. At the time of, and for a long period subsequent to Hooker's arrival, Rosecrans's army was in a state of partial siege. Bragg commanded the river road to Bridgeport, and his cavalry interrupted the communications with Bridgeport by way of Walden's Ridge, and even assailed the Nashville Railroad.[2] Rosecrans feared that the enemy would cross above Chattanooga, on his left, separating him from Burnside; but this was not his greatest danger. What Rosecrans had most reason to be apprehensive about was the subsistence of his army. To recover Lookout Valley, and the command of the river road to Bridgeport, was the important necessity of the moment. Rosecrans had already planned the movement which was to secure this road when he was relieved.

Grant met Rosecrans and Hooker at Nashville October 21st. He immediately put into execution the plan which had been adopted, and there could be no delay. The route from Stevenson over Walden's Ridge was from 60 to 70 miles in length, and the supply trains were shelled from Lookout Mountain from the very day that Rosecrans had abandoned that important position to the enemy. The roads were so bad that Wheeler's cavalry did not venture upon a raid. The animals were walking skeletons, and were dying by thousands for want of forage, and the wagons were worn out by the difficult roads. The troops were reduced to half rations. On the 19th, immediately after assuming his new command, Grant had telegraphed to Thomas to hold on to Chattanooga. Thomas replied, "I will hold the town till we starve."[3] And, as matters stood, his chance of starving was very

good. Two weeks longer, and without relief from its embarrassment, the Federal army must have abandoned its position.

Grant reached Chattanooga on the 23d of October. The next day, with General Thomas and W. F. ("Baldy") Smith, chief engineer, he made a reconnoissance of Brown's Ferry (below the mouth of Lookout Creek) and of the country lying southward. It was then decided that, in accordance with the plans already formed by Rosecrans, Hooker should cross at Bridgeport, and advance to Wauhatchie in Lookout Valley, threatening the enemy's flank. This movement was open to the observation of the enemy. So also was the movement of one of Palmer's divisions down the river to a point opposite Whiteside (11 miles west of Wauhatchie), where he was to cross and move up to Hooker's support. While attention was fixed on these movements, General Smith, with 4000 men, was to move secretly, under cover of the night, across Brown's Ferry, and seize the range of steep hills at the head of Lookout Valley, three miles below Lookout Mountain. A pontoon bridge was then to be thrown across the river at Brown's Ferry, and a line of communication being thus opened between Thomas and Hooker, the latter would be enabled to advance without danger of an attack on his left flank.

This plan was successfully carried out. The position to be gained was held by a portion of Longstreet's command, which had not yet been detached from Bragg's army. The enemy's line stretched from Lookout Mountain to Missionary Ridge. But a single brigade was posted in Lookout Valley, though the Confederate pickets lined the river down to Bridgeport. The position, from the occupation of which there was especial apprehension on the part of the Federal army, was the most feebly defended of any on the Confederate line. Hooker sent Geary's division, of Slocum's corps, across on the 26th, and by the 28th this force had reached Wauhatchie. Howard, with the Eleventh Corps, held Geary's left toward Brown's Ferry. Palmer, with the Fourteenth Corps, was moving up in the rear. Smith also had accomplished the duty assigned to his command. Of the 4000 men detailed to this command, 1800, under Hazen, embarked on sixty pontoon-boats, had floated down the river from Chattanooga on the night of the 27th, past the Confederate pickets lining the left bank, and, landing at Brown's Ferry, had taken their appointed post with a loss of only four or five men wounded. The rest of Smith's force was ferried across and joined Hazen before morning. By 10 A.M. on the 28th a pontoon bridge had been thrown across the river at Brown's Ferry, and before night Howard had connected with Smith.

This movement was, however, not accomplished without a struggle. Longstreet had a signal-station on the top of Lookout Mountain, overlooking the whole field over which Howard and Geary moved. When, on the evening of the 28th, he saw, too late, the vital importance to the Federal army of the position seized by Hooker's command, he at once communicated with Bragg, explaining the altered situation, and was directed to attack and drive back Geary and Howard at all hazards. Longstreet had already seen enough from "Signal Rock" to convince him that it was useless to attack the superior numbers on his flank directly or by daylight; but, noting the situation

ation passed the Legislature November 2, 1865. The medal is of gold, is three inches in diameter, and was wrought by Tiffany and Co., of New York City.

[1] *Secretary Stanton's Report*, November 2d, 1865.
[2] Rosecrans's letters to Halleck, at this time, indicate great anxiety for the safety of the Federal army. October 12th, he writes:
"Line from here to Kingston long; our side is barren mountain; rebel side has railroad. Our danger is subsistence; we can not bring up Hooker to cover our left, against a crossing above us, for want of means to transport provisions and horse-feed. Enemy's side of valley full of corn. Every exertion will be made to hold what we have, and gain more, after which we must put our trust in God, who never fails those who truly trust."
Again, on the 16th:
"Evidence increases that the enemy intend a desperate effort to destroy this army. They are bringing up troops to our front. They have prepared pontoons, and will probably operate on our left flank, either to cross the river and force us to quit this place and fight them, or lose our communication. They will thus separate us from Burnside. We can not feed Hooker's troops on our left, nor can we spare them from our right dépôts and communications; nor has he transportation. The rains have raised the river, and interrupted our pontoon bridge; the roads are very heavy. Our future is not bright. Had we the railroad from here to Bridgeport, the whole of Sherman's and Hooker's troops brought up, we should not, probably, outnumber the enemy. This army, with its back to the barren mountains, roads narrow and difficult, while the enemy has the railroad and the corn in his rear, is at much disadvantage. To secure this position, at least, McMinnville should be made a strong, fortified dépôt, Kingston the same, and, for ulterior operations, 20,000 or 30,000 more troops put into Tennessee, at easy points to cover the railroad, and subsist until called to the front for advance on the enemy. Additional cavalry force is indispensable to a good future for this army. Burnside must be within supporting distance of us; if we lose this point, his hold on East Tennessee is gone; if we hold it, the Rebs can not make much use of the country above, and we shall dispossess them."
[3] The accompanying illustration is a fac-simile of a medal presented to General Thomas by the State of Tennessee, after the defeat of Hood at Nashville. The resolution in favor of the present-

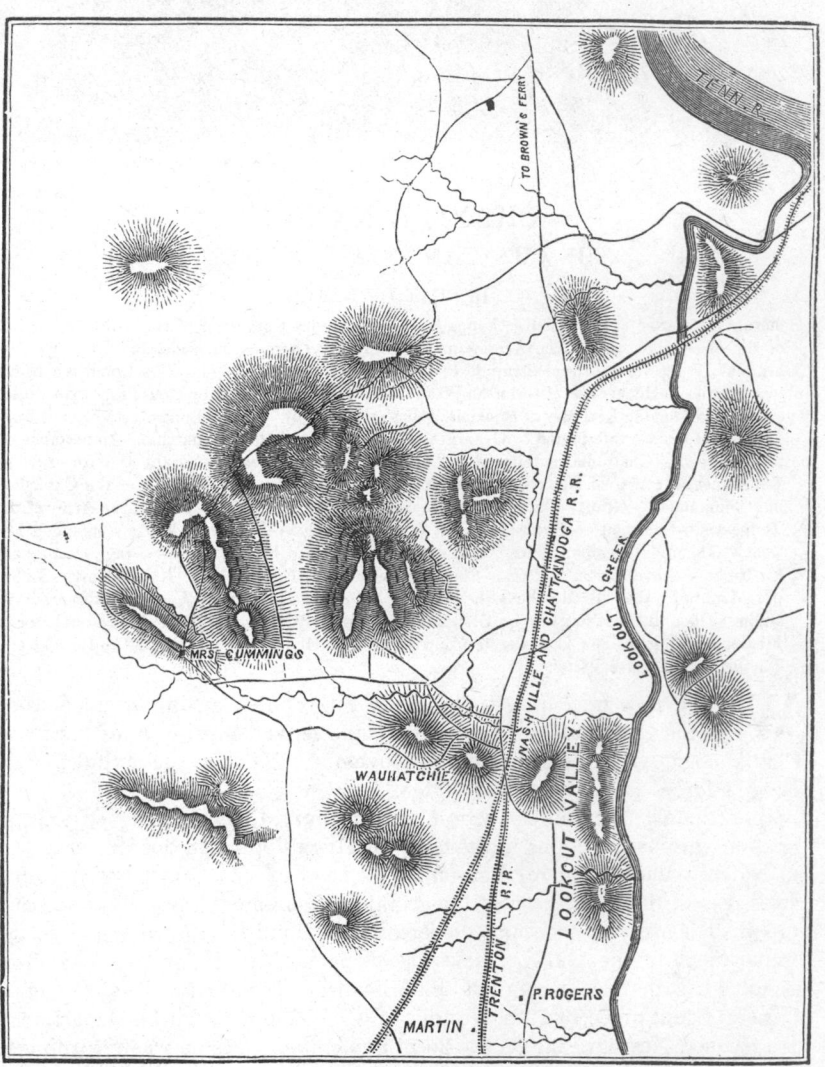

MAP ILLUSTRATING THE BATTLE OF WAUHATCHIE.

GENERAL HAZEN'S BRIGADE DESCENDING THE TENNESSEE.

of Geary's weak division at Wauhatchie, holding the road leading from Kelly's Ferry up Lookout Valley, he conceived the plan of striking this force by surprise during the night. If he succeeded in routing this force—Hooker's right flank—an easy matter as it seemed to him then—he would pursue the advantage thus gained by extending his attack against Hooker's centre and left. It was an admirable conception. But there was an important element involved in its execution which Longstreet was not, and could not be aware of, namely, Geary's precise knowledge of every movement which he might order from "Signal Rock." For some months the Federal officers had been in possession of the signal code of the enemy, and every flourish of Longstreet's signal torches on the top of Lookout, directing the assault, was at the same moment as significant to Geary as it was to Longstreet's commanders.

Thus, when, a little after midnight on the morning of the 29th, Law's division attacked Geary, the latter was fully prepared. Between the force at Wauhatchie and Howard's right was an interval of three miles. For three hours Geary defended his position without assistance, and repulsed every charge of the enemy, finally driving him from the field.[1] The success of the enemy at this point might have easily defeated the entire movement of Hooker. Of the two roads leading to Kelly's Ferry from Lookout Valley, Howard held one and Geary the other; the abandonment of one of these roads would have seriously imperiled the force holding the other.

A portion of Howard's command had in the mean time been engaged on Geary's left with equal success, and Longstreet was compelled to withdraw his command east of Lookout Creek. He still continued, however, to hold Lookout Mountain. Hooker's success, gained at the expense of only 437 men, recovered Lookout Valley, and gave Grant two good roads to Bridgeport from Brown's Ferry—one thirty-five miles long, running through Wauhatchie, Whiteside, and Shellmound; the other, from Brown's to Kelly's Ferry, a distance of eight miles by wagon, and thence by boat to Bridgeport. The enemy's position on Lookout commanded these roads, but the batteries which had been posted on Moccasin Point, north of the river, prevented the Confederate artillery from inflicting any serious damage to the supply trains. The siege of Chattanooga had been raised, and Bragg from this time was put upon the defensive. The only aggressive movement possible to him was that which he now attempted against Burnside with Longstreet's column; and this movement, unsuccessful in its special object, only accelerated his ruin. Longstreet's campaign against Knoxville was probably the result of President Davis's visit to Bragg's army, October 12.

When Grant first heard of the proposed movement against Knoxville, he seems to have regarded it as unfavorable to the development of his own plans, and intended to immediately attack Missionary Ridge in order to detain Longstreet. But after a reconnoissance he found that such an assault did not promise success, and determined to await the arrival of Sherman's troops, now well on their way from Memphis. In the mean time he established between himself and Burnside a good understanding as to the plan

JOHN W. GEARY.

[1] "For almost three hours, without assistance, he repelled the repeated attacks of vastly superior numbers, and in the end drove them ingloriously from the field. At one time they had enveloped him on three sides, under circumstances that would have dismayed any officer endowed with an iron will and the most exalted courage. Such is the character of General Geary."—*Hooker's Report.*

VIEW OF CHATTANOOGA.

AND THE FEDERAL ENCAMPMENT.

of operations which he was now about to adopt.[1] He confided to him the whole scheme of his movements against Bragg, and promised to send a force to the relief of Knoxville as soon as he had carried it out. Two things strike us forcibly in his correspondence with Burnside: first, the clearness of his plans, which read more like a history of his brief campaign, rather than a scheme of movements contemplated; and, secondly, his confidence as to their success. He almost seems to look regretfully after Longstreet's force, as if, by marching northward, it was escaping its share in the destruction which he was preparing for Bragg's entire army.

The Confederate army was intrenched upon the western slopes of Missionary Ridge, and stretched across Chattanooga Valley to the western slopes of Lookout Mountain, which, since Longstreet's departure, had been held by the divisions of Walker, Stevenson, and Cheatham.[2] His line of works, twelve miles in length, was occupied by less than 50,000 effective troops. His army was outnumbered by Grant's in about the same proportion that it had exceeded Rosecrans's at the battle of Chickamauga Creek. Nor was this inferiority in numbers balanced by superiority of position. His line, though apparently strong, was too much extended for the number of its defenders, and was really very weak. If he held the two ridges, his centre must be left vulnerable; the exposure of either of his flanks, by the abandonment of Lookout Mountain or Missionary Ridge, must be soon followed by an entire withdrawal of his army from before Chattanooga. Yet, so confident was he of the strength of his position, that when Grant moved upon his works he was just on the point of sending Cleburne's and Buckner's divisions to re-enforce Longstreet.

Grant's plan of attack was brilliant, but exceedingly simple in its general features. It involved an assault upon the strongest points in the enemy's line—its two extremes—by Hooker and Sherman, to be followed by a crushing blow from Thomas upon its centre.

But Sherman's army was not yet upon the field. It was now nearly two months since, just after the battle of Chickamauga, Sherman had been ordered to re-enforce Rosecrans. His corps, the Fifteenth, about 16,000 strong, consisted of four divisions, under P. J. Osterhaus, Morgan L. Smith, I. M. Tuttle, and Hugh Ewing.[3] Osterhaus's division had embarked for Memphis on the 23d. The other divisions followed a day later. The last of the fleet reached Memphis on the 4th of October. As soon as he reached Memphis, General Sherman was ordered to proceed with his own corps, and as many troops as could be spared from the line of the Memphis and Charleston Railroad, to Athens, Alabama. He was to look out for his own supplies. Osterhaus by this had got as far as Corinth, and J. E. Smith was on the way from Memphis. On the 11th of October the rear of the column was put in motion, and Sherman started in person for Corinth, escorted by the Thirteenth Regulars. At Collierville, about twenty-five miles east of Memphis, a Confederate cavalry force was encountered, and the general, with his staff, narrowly escaped capture. D. C. Anthony was defending the post with the Sixty-ninth Illinois against the enemy, who numbered about 3000 horse, with eight guns, under General Chalmers. Sherman's escort joined Anthony, and the Confederates were repulsed. Sherman reached Corinth on the 12th, and sent Blair forward with the divisions of Osterhaus and Morgan L. Smith. The railroad was repaired as the troops advanced. A Confederate cavalry force, about 5000 strong, kept in Sherman's front. Under these circumstances, his progress was necessarily slow. Anticipating that resistance would be made to his crossing of the Tennessee, he had requested Admiral Porter to send him two gun-boats, which he found ready upon his arrival at Eastport. Blair, after considerable skirmishing, drove the enemy from his front, and occupied Tuscumbia on the 27th.

In the mean time Sherman had been notified of his appointment to the command of Grant's former department, and had made such a disposition of the troops in his rear as would secure Mississippi and West Tennessee, leaving the former under McPherson's, and the latter under Hurlbut's control. Blair was assigned to the command of the Fifteenth Corps, and General George W. Dodge was ordered to organize from the Sixteenth a select force of 8000 men, with which he was to follow Sherman eastward. Ewing, on the 27th, was ordered to cross his division at Eastport, and advance to Florence. On the same day, a messenger, having floated down the river from Chattanooga, reached Sherman with orders to stop the work on the railroad, and advance toward Bridgeport. On the 1st of November Sherman crossed the river in person, passed to the head of the column at Florence, and, leaving the rear to be brought up by Blair, marched toward the Elk River. Not having time for ferriage or bridge-building, it was necessary to advance up that stream as far as Fayetteville, where the command crossed. Here Sherman received orders to bring the Fifteenth Corps to Bridgeport, leaving Dodge's command on the railroad at Pulaski. Blair was instructed to conduct the first and second divisions, by way of Larkinsville, to Bellefonte, while Sherman took a more northern route, *via* Winchester and Decherd, reaching Bridgeport by night on the 13th of November. Telegraphing to General Grant information of his arrival and of the disposition of his divisions, he was summoned to Chattanooga. Proceeding by boat to Kelly's Ferry, he reached Grant's headquarters on the 15th. Here his part in the coming drama was explained to him, and he was shown the enemy's fortified position on Missionary Ridge; the point which he was to attack, and the details of his march across the river at Brown's Ferry, around the mountains north of the river to the mouth of Chickamauga Creek, were here determined upon. The entire movement of his corps, after crossing Brown's Ferry till it emerged upon Bragg's right flank, was so arranged as to be concealed from the enemy by covering mountains. He saw all the arrangements which had been made for him in anticipation. "Pontoons," says Sherman, in his report, "with a full supply of bulks and chesses, had been prepared for the bridge over the Tennessee, and all things prearranged with a foresight that elicited my admiration. From the hills we looked down upon the amphitheatre of Chattanooga as on a map, and nothing remained but for me to put my troops in the desired position." To convince the enemy that his left was the especial point of attack, a division of Sherman's corps was to make a feint against Lookout Mountain from a point in the vicinity of Trenton. Sherman, from this visit to Chattanooga, was also enabled to understand the necessity of the utmost expedition on his part. The whole army he found "impatient for action, rendered almost acute by the natural apprehension felt for the safety of General Burnside in East Tennessee."[1]

It was expected that Sherman would be in position on the 19th, but the difficult roads delayed his movements. J. E. Smith's division was the first to cross. Morgan L. Smith's division crossed to the north bank at Brown's Ferry on the 21st. Ewing's was ready to cross, when the bridge broke, and occasioned a delay of two days. Ewing crossed on the 23d, when the bridge again broke, with Osterhaus on the south bank. It was therefore determined to leave Osterhaus to support Hooker, while Jeff C. Davis was sent to Sherman in his place. It was evident that Sherman could not participate in the battle before the 24th.

But, in the mean while, deserters reported that Bragg was about to fall back. A letter received by flag of truce from the Confederate commander, warning General Grant to withdraw from Chattanooga whatever non-combatants still remained, seemed to corroborate these reports. Grant had no idea of suffering Bragg to retreat without a battle, and determined to attack before Sherman's arrival.

Howard's corps had been brought to Chattanooga, and this corps, with Granger's and Palmer's, was ordered to assail the enemy's centre with such vigor as to develop his lines and detain him in front. In obedience to this order, Granger and Palmer, with Howard in support, drove in the enemy's pickets on the 23d, and carried his first line of works between Chattanooga and Citico Creeks. Although Thomas's operations had been made in full view of the Confederate pickets, no attack was expected by the enemy. The Federal troops, clad in their best uniforms, and accompanied by their bands of music, thus rapidly mustering in open view, seemed to be parading for a grand review rather than for an assault upon the outposts of Missionary Ridge. The sentries occupying the advanced rifle-pits watched the display without alarm, but about noon they discovered, to their amazement, that the spectacle was one in which they were more intimately concerned as actors than as spectators. At 1 o'clock P.M. Wood's and Sheridan's divisions, of Granger's corps, advanced in front and under the guns of Fort Wood, Palmer occupying at the same time a threatening position on their right, while Howard was held in reserve on their left. Sheridan and Wood advanced at double-quick, and drove first the enemy's pickets, then their reserves, and, capturing about 200 men, including nine commissioned officers, carried Orchard Knob before the Confederates had fairly recovered from their surprise. Upon this important position Granger intrenched himself, and the advance of the troops on his left and right obliterated the front line of the Confederate works in Thomas's front. This success was won with a loss of 111 men. But the next day promised work of a more serious character.

[1] On the 14th of November he telegraphed to Burnside:

"Your dispatch and Dana's" [in regard to the preference for Knoxville as the point to be held] "just received. Being there, you can tell better how to resist Longstreet's attack than I can direct. With your showing, you had better give up Kingston at the last moment, and save the most productive part of your possession. Every arrangement is now made to throw Sherman's force across the river just at and below the mouth of Chickamauga Creek as soon as it arrives. Thomas will attack on his" [the enemy's] "left at the same time, and together it is expected to carry Missionary Ridge, and from there rush a force on to the railroad between Cleveland and Dalton. Hooker will at the same time attack, and, if he can, carry Lookout Mountain. The enemy now seems to be looking for an attack on his left flank. This favors us. To further confirm this, Sherman's advance division will march direct from Whiteside to Trenton. The remainder of the force will pass over a new road just made from Whiteside to Kelly's Ferry, thus being concealed from the enemy, and leave him to suppose the whole force is going up Lookout Valley. Sherman's advance has only just reached Bridgeport. The rear will only reach there on the 16th. This will bring it to the 19th as the earliest day for making the combined movement as desired. Inform me if you think you can sustain yourself till that time. I can hardly conceive of the enemy breaking through at Kingston, and pushing for Kentucky. If they should, however, a new problem would be left for solution. Thomas has ordered a division of cavalry to the vicinity of Sparta. I will ascertain if they have started, and inform you. It will be entirely out of the question to send for 10,000 men, not because they can not be spared, but how could they be fed after they got one day east of here?"

On the 15th he telegraphed again as follows:

"I do not know how to impress on you the necessity of holding on to East Tennessee in strong enough terms. According to the dispatches of Mr. Dana and Colonel Wilson, it would seem that you should, if pressed to do it, hold on to Knoxville, and that portion of the valley you will necessarily possess holding to that point. Should Longstreet move his whole force across the Little Tennessee, an effort should be made to cut his pontoons on that stream, even if it sacrificed half the cavalry of the Ohio Army. By holding on, and placing Longstreet between the Little Tennessee and Knoxville, he should not be allowed to escape with an army capable of doing any thing this winter. I can hardly conceive the necessity of retreating from East Tennessee. If I did it at all, it would be after losing most of the army, and then necessity would suggest the route. I will not attempt to lay out a line of retreat. Kingston, looking at the map, I thought of more importance than any one point in East Tennessee. But my attention being called more closely to it, I can see that it might be passed by, and Knoxville, and the rich valley about it, possessed, ignoring that place entirely. I should not think it advisable to concentrate a force near Little Tennessee to resist the crossing, if it would be in danger of capture; but I would harass and embarrass progress in every way possible, reflecting on the fact that the Army of the Ohio is not the only army to resist the onward progress of the enemy."

[2] See map on page 565.

[3] FIRST DIVISION, P. T. Osterhaus: { *First Brigade*, C. K. Woods. *Second Brigade*, J. A. Williamson.

SECOND DIVISION, Morgan L. Smith: { *First Brigade*, Giles A. Smith. *Second Brigade*, J. A. D. Lightburn.

THIRD DIVISION, J. W. Tuttle: { *First Brigade*, J. A. Mower. *Second Brigade*, R. B. Buckland. *Third Brigade*, J. J. Wood.

FOURTH DIVISION, Hugh Ewing: { *First Brigade*, J. M. Corse. *Second Brigade*, Colonel Loomis. *Third Brigade*, J. R. Cockrell.

Tuttle's (Third) division was left with McPherson at Vicksburg, and its place taken by J. E. Smith's (of the Seventeenth Corps), which was also styled the Third Division. This division consisted of three brigades, commanded by General Matthias, J. B. Raum, and J. J. Alexander.

[1] *Sherman's Report.*

LOOKOUT MOUNTAIN, FROM THE FEDERAL WORKS ON CHATTANOOGA CREEK.

It now became evident to Bragg that an attempt would be made against his right flank, with a view of severing his communication with Longstreet. To strengthen this portion of his line, Walker's division was withdrawn from the western slope of Lookout Mountain, leaving Stevenson and Cheatham to hold the left.

During the night of the 23d, Giles A. Smith's brigade, of Morgan L. Smith's division, consisting of about 3000 men, manned the boats of which the pontoon bridge was to be constructed, and, dropping down the river at midnight, captured the Confederate pickets above the North Chickamauga, and landed below the mouth of the creek. By means of these boats and the steamer Dunbar, the rest of the division, together with John E. Smith's, were ferried across before daylight, so that on the morning of the 24th Sherman had a force of 8000 men ready to advance against the enemy's right. The whole valley between Citico and Chickamauga Creeks was an immense corn-field. Through this valley Howard moved on the forenoon of the 24th to connect with Sherman. The pontoon bridge had in the mean time been constructed, under "Baldy" Smith's immediate supervision. "I have never," says Sherman, "beheld any work done so quickly, so well; and I doubt if the history of the war can show a bridge of that extent (namely, 1350 feet) laid down so noiselessly and well in so short a time. I attribute it to the genius and intelligence of General W. F. Smith." By 1 o'clock P.M. the whole corps had crossed, and Davis's division was prepared to co-operate, as a reserve force, in the attack on Missionary Ridge.

Sherman's three divisions were now ordered to advance, M. L. Smith on the left, J. E. Smith in the centre, and Ewing on the right. A drizzling rain began to fall, and the clouds, resting upon the river, and low down upon the mountain sides, cloaked Sherman's movement. By 3 o'clock the northern spurs of the ridge were gained without loss. The enemy had not occupied these hills (north of the railroad tunnel) with any considerable force. Sherman fortified the heights gained by his troops, and brought up his artillery. He had supposed, from the map, that the ridge was continuous, but he now found that he was separated from the enemy by a deep gorge. The enemy attempted, later in the day, to regain the hill, attacking Sherman's left. The attack was repulsed, but in the fight Giles A. Smith was severely wounded, and carried to the rear.

While Sherman was thus confronting the enemy across the railroad on Missionary Ridge, Hooker had made better progress in his movement against the Confederate left on Lookout Mountain. The idea of an advance from Lookout Valley had been abandoned when Howard's corps was withdrawn from Hooker on the 22d. Indeed, Hooker, wishing to be with that portion of his command which would be in the fight, was on the point of following Howard, when he was ordered to remain and make a demonstration against Lookout Mountain, to divert the attention of the enemy from Sherman's movements. His command consisted of Geary's division of the Twelfth Corps, Osterhaus's of the Fifteenth, and Cruft's of the Fourth, with a small detachment of cavalry, making an aggregate of about 10,000 men. It was a conglomerate organization, no one of these three divisions having ever before seen either of the others. The presence of Osterhaus's division at this point led General Grant to resume his original plan, and he ordered Hooker to make a determined attack, and to carry the mountain if possible.

The enemy's pickets lined the east bank of Lookout Creek. His main force, under Cheatham, was encamped in a hollow midway up the slope of the mountain. The summit east of the palisaded crest was held by three brigades of Stevenson's division. The Confederate position was well protected by batteries and rifle-pits against an attack from the Tennessee or from the valleys on either side, and in the valleys also were strong lines of earth-works.

Geary, who had ascended Lookout Creek, supported by Whittaker's brigade of Cruft's division, crossed near Wauhatchie at 8 A.M. on the 24th, surprising and capturing the Confederate picket of 42 men on the river bank, and moved down the valley, his right keeping close up under the palisades, and thus avoiding the batteries on the crest. Osterhaus, with Cruft's other brigade (Grose's), at the same time gained a bridge on the road just below the point where the railroad to Chattanooga crosses the creek, and began to repair it. The enemy, not aware of the force marching in its rear, filed down from his encampment and moved into his rifle-pits in Osterhaus's front, a small force taking a position behind the embankment, which enabled it to enfilade the road which the Federal troops must take if they crossed the creek at this point. Holding the enemy here, another crossing was prepared 800 yards above. Batteries were posted enfilading the route by which the Confederates had left their encampment, and also preventing their sending re-enforcements to oppose Geary.

Before noon Geary had advanced close up to the Confederate rear. Grose's brigade, with another (Wood's) of Osterhaus's division, sprang across the creek and connected with Geary's left. All the batteries opened, and those of the enemy who escaped their fury were captured by the Federals in their rear. Meanwhile Geary, winding around the palisades, passed, says Hooker, "directly under the muzzles of the enemy's guns on the summit, climbing over ledges and boulders, up hill and down, driving the enemy from his camp, and from position after position."

By noon Geary's advance rounded the peak of the mountain. Directions had been given to halt here, as it was not known to what extent the Confederates farther to the east might have been re-enforced. But there was no such thing as "halt" for troops who, fired with success, were pressing on toward the consummation of their victory! Passing around to the eastern slope of the mountain, Osterhaus on the left, Cruft in the centre, and Geary on the right, Hooker's columns met with no formidable resistance until they emerged from the woods against the enemy's intrenchments,

which ran diagonally across an open field covering the road which leads up the mountain from Chattanooga to Summertown. Here progress was for a time interrupted. Much had been already gained. Upward of 2000 prisoners had been captured, and communication was now open across Chattanooga Creek with General Thomas. But Hooker's success thus far had been mainly the result of strategy. The enemy had been surprised. But for this, Lookout Mountain could easily have been held against Hooker's 10,000 men. The main object of the battle at this point had been secured. All that remained was to make the victory decisive by breaking Cheatham's line on the eastern slope of the mountain, thus cutting off the brigades still holding the summit.

During the operations thus far the batteries on Moccasin Point, north of the Tennessee, had been engaging the enemy's artillery on the extreme point and highest peak of Lookout. The heavy clouds, which in the morning had enveloped the mountain's summit, and thus, to some extent, favored Hooker's movement, had gradually settled into the valley, veiling it completely from view. Thus the battle of the afternoon was literally "a Battle above the Clouds."

The Confederate line had been contracted in order to give it greater strength, so that there was a considerable interval between the plateau which it held and the palisades. Geary, taking advantage of this interval, got in upon the enemy's left flank, and an advance being made by Cruft and Osterhaus in front, the entire line was carried. But it was not held by the Federals undisturbed. No sooner had it been occupied by them than the enemy turned upon it and made an assault. In the continual skirmishing which had been going on, Hooker's troops had now nearly exhausted their ammunition, and unless a fresh supply could be had from some source it seemed probable that the position which had been gained would have to be abandoned. Hooker had sent for ammunition, but it had been delayed. Just in time, fortunately, Carlin's brigade of Johnson's division arrived from Thomas, having crossed Chattanooga Creek, and brought with it 120,000 rounds strapped on the backs of the men. This fresh brigade relieved Geary's exhausted troops. The enemy was repulsed, driven back from the last position where he could make a stand, and hurled over the rocky heights down into the valley.

By this time the darkness upon the mountain rendered farther progress extremely dangerous, and Hooker's troops encamped for the night on the slope which they had so gallantly won. Lookout Mountain had been captured. The only drawback to the utmost completion of the victory was the fact that a route was left open for the retreat of Stevenson's brigades from the crest above. Before daylight the colors of the Eighth Kentucky waved from the peak of Lookout. But the enemy had abandoned his encampment, leaving behind him, in the hurry of his flight, all his camp and garrison equipage.

The morning of November 25th found Bragg's entire army stretched along Missionary Ridge from Tunnel Hill to Rossville, the valley of the Chattanooga being entirely abandoned. Lieutenant General Hardee commanded the right wing, consisting of Cleburne's, Walker's, Cheatham's, and Stevenson's divisions. The left wing—consisting of Breckinridge's old division,[1] and those of Stewart and Anderson—was under General Breckinridge. The breastworks at the foot of the rugged slope were occupied by pickets, while the infantry and artillery stretched along the ridge. Where the ascent was easy, special fortifications had been constructed to resist an assailing force. The troops on Breckinridge's right had been beaten at Lookout Mountain, had taken their position hurriedly, and had not yet recovered from the demoralization of defeat. Breckinridge's left was refused at McFarland's Gap, occupying the breastworks in which the Federals had stood in their retreat from McLemore's Cove two months before. This point connected the old battle-field of Chickamauga with that upon which the opposing forces were now contending.

About midnight on the 24th orders came from Grant, whose headquarters were on Orchard Knob, for Sherman to attack at daylight the next morning. Sherman was early in the saddle. The clouds of the previous day had cleared away, and his own position, as well as that of the enemy, was fully revealed to him as he rode along from Lightburn's brigade on the left to the position held by Ewing's division on the right. The hill held by the enemy on his front was of steep ascent, its crest narrow and wooded. Cleburne's position was well protected by log breastworks, and a higher hill beyond was held by the enemy, commanding the disputed ground. Three brigades—Lightburn's, Alexander's, and Cockrell's—one from each division, were to hold the hill, and Corse's brigade, of Ewing's division, on the right centre, was to form the assaulting column, assisted by a regiment from Lightburn, and three brigades—Loomis's, of Ewing's, and Matthias's and Raum's, of John E. Smith's divisions. Morgan L. Smith, with his remaining brigade, was to connect with Corse's left, and move around the eastern base of the ridge.

Corse moved to the attack at sunrise, and, advancing to within eighty yards of the enemy's intrenchments, established himself upon a secondary ridge. To this point the reserves were brought up. His preparations having been completed, Corse assaulted the works on Tunnel Hill. A severe conflict of more than an hour's duration followed, the issue of which was that, after gaining and losing ground, Corse made no progress beyond the

[1] Generals Polk and Hill had been relieved for disobedience of orders in the Chickamauga campaign. We also miss Hindman and Buckner. Walker, too, is absent, his division being commanded by General Gist. Hardee comes from Enterprise, Mississippi, where he had at the end of August taken command of "the paroled prisoners of Mississippi, Arkansas, Missouri, Texas, and Louisiana, recently forming the garrisons of Vicksburg and Port Hudson." These prisoners had not been exchanged up to the time of which we are writing. All of Stevenson's division, including its commander, must have violated their parole.

TOP OF LOOKOUT MOUNTAIN, SUNRISE, NOVEMBER 25 1863

REBEL BATTERY ON THE TOP OF LOOKOUT MOUNTAIN.

GENERAL HOOKER'S COLUMN STORMING LOOKOUT MOUNTAIN.

THE CREST OF LOOKOUT MOUNTAIN.

TO THE TOP OF THE MOUNTAIN.

CAPTURE OF CONFEDERATE WORKS AT THE WHITE HOUSE, ON LOOKOUT MOUNTAIN.

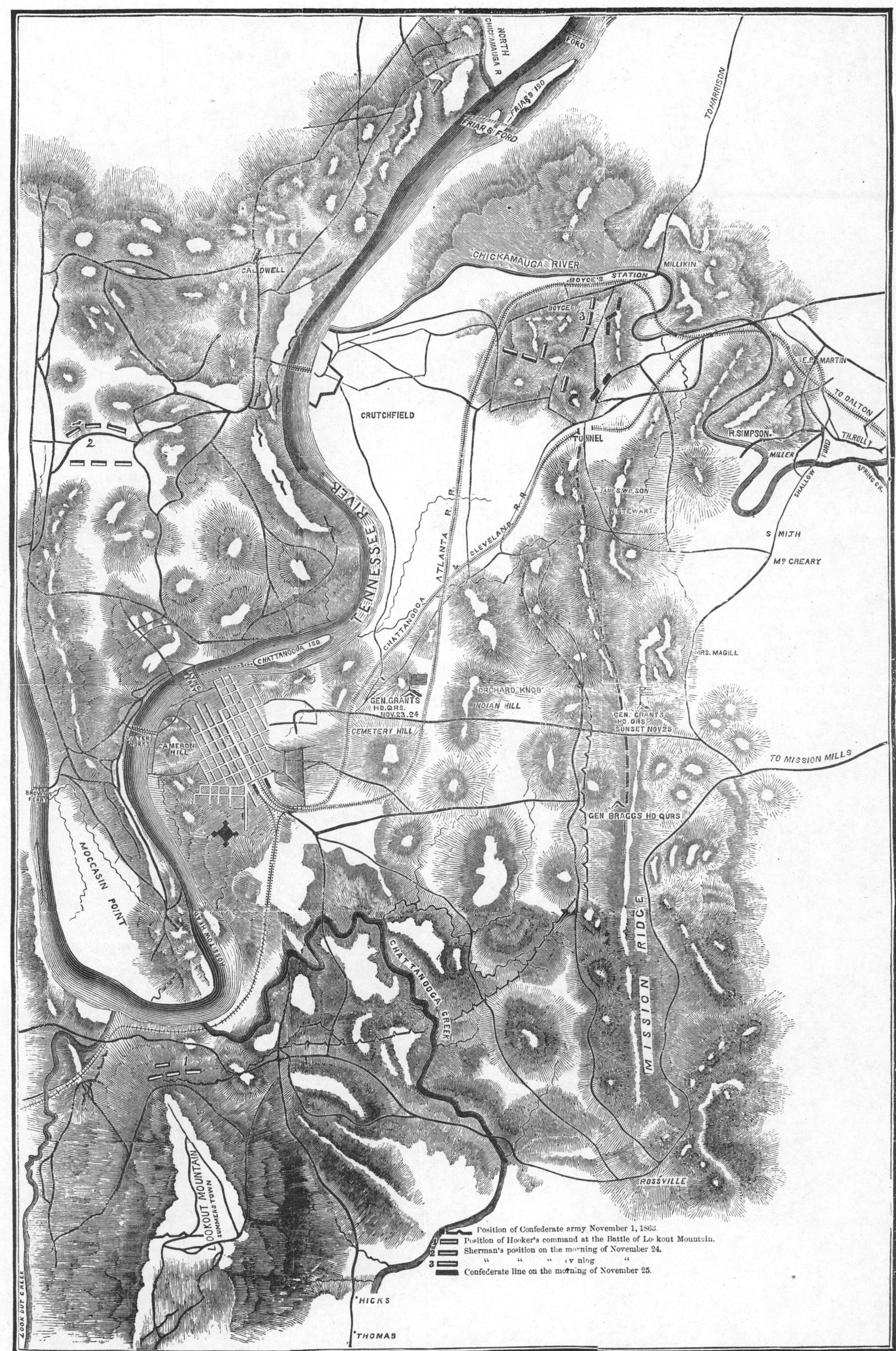

MAP ILLUSTRATING THE BATTLES ABOUT CHATTANOOGA.

THE STORMING OF MISSIONARY RIDGE.

position originally taken. Morgan L. Smith, in the mean time, had made considerable progress on the eastern slope. Loomis's brigade had got abreast of the tunnel, and, by diverting the enemy's attention, afforded some relief to General Corse. The two reserve brigades (those of John E. Smith) supporting Corse's movement had been repulsed, but the real attack was sustained. The enemy had brought to this part of the field extensive re-enforcements, and the most that Sherman could do was to maintain his position until the success of Thomas and Hooker, on the centre and right, should give him an opportunity to attack with advantage.

But the centre and right of the Federal army had been delayed. Thomas's attack was to depend upon the movements of Hooker. The latter was unexpectedly retarded in his movement from Lookout Mountain. Osterhaus's division began its march to Rossville at 10 o'clock, and the rest of Hooker's command followed, with the exception of two regiments left upon the summit of Lookout. On arriving at Chattanooga Creek it was found that the enemy had destroyed the bridge, and here Hooker was delayed for full three hours. Osterhaus was soon got across, and, pushing on to the gap in Missionary Ridge, flanked the enemy at this point, capturing artillery, ammunition, and wagons. Hooker's entire command was ready for the attack upon the enemy's left by 3 30 P.M. Cruft advanced upon the ridge, Osterhaus to the east of it, and Geary, with the artillery, along the valley, against the western slope.

Thomas in the mean time had sent Baird's division to the support of Sherman, on Granger's left. This division got into position at 2 30 P.M. Thomas then assaulted the enemy's line with his whole force, driving the enemy from his rifle-pits at the foot of the hill on the centre of his line. The troops to the right of Wood advanced up to the crest, and gained the summit of the ridge, capturing large numbers of the enemy in their trenches.[1] Against Sherman, and Baird's and Wood's divisions, the enemy still held his ground; but Hooker was well up against his left, which now, attacked in front and flank, was entirely routed, leaving behind forty pieces of artillery. Here a large number of prisoners, driven by Hooker against Palmer and Johnson, were captured. Osterhaus alone took 2000 prisoners. It was not until nightfall, however, that the enemy's right was dislodged, and the entire ridge abandoned.

At daylight on the 26th Sherman and Hooker pursued the enemy's routed columns, the former by way of Chickamauga Station, the latter by Greysville and Ringgold. The rear-guard, under Gist, was overtaken and broken up, and three more guns captured. Hooker's force came upon Cleburne in a gap in Taylor's Ridge, near Ringgold, and, attacking him, was severely repulsed, losing 65 killed and 367 wounded. Finally Cleburne was flanked and driven from his strong position, leaving 130 killed and wounded on the field. There was no farther pursuit. Grose's brigade visited the battle-field of Chickamauga, and buried the remains of many of the Federal dead, which had been left by Bragg to lie mouldering where they had fallen. Bragg attributes his defeat to a disgraceful panic on the part of his men.[2]

The real causes were the weakness of his line—a weakness not of position, but of numbers—and the demoralization which had resulted from the defeat on Lookout Mountain.

The Federal losses in the battles of the 23d, 24th, 25th, and 26th were 757 killed, 4529 wounded, and 330 missing: total, 5616. The Confederate loss in killed and wounded was probably much less; but Bragg's loss in prisoners alone amounted to 6142, of whom 239 were commissioned officers; 7000 stand of small arms had also been captured by Grant's army. By these battles Bragg's army must have been diminished by at least 10,000 men. Grant probably had engaged about 65,000 men, and Bragg between 40,000 and 45,000.

General Bragg's defeat terminated the contest for Chattanooga and East Tennessee. The tidings of Grant's victory electrified the loyal portion of the country, and President Lincoln, on the 7th of December, issued a proclamation recommending the people "to assemble at their places of worship, and render special homage and gratitude to Almighty God for this great advancement of the national cause." From this time the prospects of the Southern Confederacy were indeed desperate. The resources of the Southern States were rapidly being exhausted, while the national armies were being recruited by immense numbers, at whose backs stood thousands more ready to take the field the moment their services should become necessary. Thus closed the year 1863. It had begun with the disaster at Fredericksburg, followed soon by the defeat at Chancellorsville; but the victories of Gettysburg, Vicksburg, and Missionary Ridge crowned it with imperishable glory.[1]

---

[1] General Thomas gives the following description of this movement:

"Our troops advancing steadily in a continuous line, the enemy, seized with panic, abandoned the works at the foot of the hill and retreated precipitately to the crest, whither they were closely followed by our troops, who, apparently inspired by the impulse of victory, carried the hill simultaneously at six different points, and so closely upon the heels of the enemy that many of them were taken prisoners in the trenches. We captured all their cannon and ammunition before they could be removed or destroyed. After halting a few moments to reorganize the troops, who had become somewhat scattered in the assault of the hill, General Sherman pushed forward in pursuit, and drove those in his front who escaped capture across Chickamauga Creek. Generals Wood and Baird, being obstinately resisted by re-enforcements from the enemy's extreme right, continued fighting until darkness set in, but steadily driving the enemy before them. In moving upon Rossville, General Hooker encountered Stewart's division and other troops. Finding his left flank threatened, Stewart attempted to escape by retreating toward Greysville; but some of his force, finding their retreat threatened in that quarter, retired in disorder toward their right, along the crest of the ridge, where they were met by another portion of General Hooker's command, and were driven by these troops in the face of Johnson's division of Palmer's corps, by whom they were nearly all made prisoners."

[2] The following is General Bragg's report of the battle:

"Headquarters Army of Tennessee, Dalton, Georgia, 30th November, 1863.

"General S. Cooper, Adjutant and Inspector General, Richmond:

"Sir,—On Monday, the 23d, the enemy advanced in heavy force, and drove in our picket line in front of Missionary Ridge, but made no farther effort.

"On Tuesday morning early they threw over the river a heavy force opposite the north end of the ridge, and just below the mouth of the Chickamauga, at the same time displaying a heavy force in our immediate front. After visiting the right, and making dispositions there for the new development in that direction, I returned toward the left, to find a heavy cannonading going on from the enemy's batteries on our forces occupying the slope of Lookout Mountain, between the crest and the river. A very heavy force soon advanced to the assault, and was met by one brigade only, Walthall's, which made a desperate resistance, but was finally compelled to yield ground. Why this command was not sustained is yet unexplained. The commander on that part of the field, Major General Stevenson, had six brigades at his disposal. Upon his urgent appeal, another brigade was dispatched in the afternoon to his support—though it appeared his own forces had not been brought into action—and I proceeded to the scene.

"Arriving just before sunset, I found that we had lost all the advantages of the position. Orders were immediately given for the ground to be disputed until we could withdraw our forces across Chattanooga Creek, and the movement was commenced. This having been successfully accomplished, our whole forces were concentrated on the ridge, and extended to the right to meet the movement in that direction.

"On Wednesday, the 25th, I again visited the extreme right, now under Lieutenant General Hardee, and threatened by a heavy force, while strong columns could be seen marching in that direction. A very heavy force in line of battle confronted our left and centre.

"On my return to this point, about 11 A.M., the enemy's forces were being moved in heavy masses from Lookout and beyond to our front, while those in front extended to our right. They formed their lines with great deliberation, just beyond the range of our guns, and in plain view of our position.

"Though greatly outnumbered, such was the strength of our position that no doubt was entertained of our ability to hold it, and every disposition was made for that purpose. During this time they had made several attempts on our extreme right, and had been handsomely repulsed, with very heavy loss, by Major General Cleburne's command, under the immediate direction of Lieutenant General Hardee. By the road across the ridge at Rossville, far to our left, a route was open to our rear. Major General Breckinridge, commanding on the left, had occupied this with two regiments and a battery. It being reported to me that a force of the enemy had moved in that direction, the general was ordered to have it reconnoitred, and to make every disposition necessary to secure his flank, which he proceeded to do.

"About half past 3 P.M., the immense force in the front of our left and centre advanced in three lines, preceded by heavy skirmishers. Our batteries opened with fine effect, and much confusion was produced before they reached musket range. In a short time the roar of musketry became very heavy, and it was soon apparent that the enemy had been repulsed in my immediate front.

"While riding along the crest congratulating the troops, intelligence reached me that our line

was broken on my right, and the enemy had crowned the ridge. Assistance was promptly dispatched to that point, under Brigadier General Bate, who had so successfully maintained the ground in my front, and I proceeded to the rear of the broken line to rally our retiring troops and return them to the crest to drive the enemy back. General Bate found the disaster so great that his small force could not repair it. About this time I learned that our extreme left had also given way, and that my position was almost surrounded. Bate was immediately directed to form a second line in the rear, where, by the efforts of my staff, a nucleus of stragglers had been formed upon which to rally.

"Lieutenant General Hardee, leaving Major General Cleburne in command of the extreme right, moved toward the left when he heard the heavy firing in that direction. He reached the right of Anderson's division just in time to find it had nearly all fallen back, commencing on its right, where the enemy had first crowned the ridge. By a prompt and judicious movement, he threw a portion of Cheatham's division directly across the ridge, facing the enemy, who was now moving a strong force immediately on his left flank. By a decided stand here, the enemy was entirely checked, and that portion of our force to the right remained intact. All to the left, however, except a portion of Bate's division, was entirely routed, and in rapid flight, nearly all the artillery having been shamefully abandoned by its infantry support. Every effort which could be made by myself and staff, and by many other mounted officers, availed but little. A panic, which I had never before witnessed, seemed to have seized upon officers and men, and each seemed to be struggling for his personal safety, regardless of his duty or his character. In this distressing and alarming state of affairs, General Bate was ordered to hold his position, covering the road for the retreat of Breckinridge's command, and orders were immediately sent to Generals Hardee and Breckinridge to retire their forces upon the dépôt at Chickamauga. Fortunately, it was now near nightfall, and the country and roads in our rear were fully known to us, but equally unknown to the enemy. The routed left made its way back in great disorder, effectually covered, however, by Bate's small command, which had a sharp conflict with the enemy's advance, driving it back. After night, all being quiet, Bate retired in good order, the enemy attempting no pursuit. Lieutenant General Hardee's command, under his judicious management, retired in good order and unmolested.

"As soon as all the troops had crossed, the bridges over the Chickamauga were destroyed, to impede the enemy, though the stream was fordable in several places.

"No satisfactory excuse can possibly be given for the shameful conduct of our troops on the left in allowing their line to be penetrated. The position was one which ought to have been held by a line of skirmishers against any assaulting column; and, wherever resistance was made, the enemy fled in disorder, after suffering heavy loss. Those who reached the ridge did so in a condition of exhaustion, from the great physical exertion in climbing, which rendered them powerless, and the slightest effort would have destroyed them.

"Having secured much of our artillery, they soon availed themselves of our panic, and, turning our guns upon us, enfiladed our lines both right and left, rendering them entirely untenable. Had all parts of the line been maintained with equal gallantry and persistence, no enemy could ever have dislodged us; and but one possible reason presents itself to my mind in explanation of this bad conduct in veteran troops, who had never before failed in any duty assigned them, however difficult and hazardous. They had for two days confronted the enemy, marshaling his immense forces in plain view, and exhibiting to their sight such a superiority in numbers as may have intimidated weak minds and untried soldiers. But our veterans had so often encountered similar hosts when the strength of position was against us, and with perfect success, that not a doubt crossed my mind. As yet, I am not fully informed as to the commands which first fled, and brought this great disaster and disgrace upon our arms. Investigation will bring out the truth, however, and full justice shall be done to the good and the bad.

"After arriving at Chickamauga, and informing myself of the full condition of affairs, it was decided to put the army in motion for a point farther removed from a powerful and victorious army, that we might have some little time to replenish and recuperate for another struggle. The enemy made pursuit as far as Ringgold, but was so handsomely checked by Major General Cleburne and Brigadier General Gist, in command of their respective divisions, that he gave us but little annoyance.

"Our losses are not yet ascertained, but in killed and wounded it is known to have been very small. In prisoners and stragglers I fear it is much larger.

"The chief of artillery reports the loss of forty (40) pieces.

"I am, sir, very respectfully, your obedient servant,

"Braxton Bragg, General Commanding."

President Davis also seems to have concurred with General Bragg in attributing the blame to the troops. In his message to Congress (December 7th, 1863) he says:

"After a long and severe battle, in which great carnage was inflicted on him, some of our troops inexplicably abandoned positions of great strength, and by a disorderly retreat compelled the commander to withdraw the forces elsewhere successful, and, finally, to retire with his whole army to a position some twenty or thirty miles to the rear. It is believed that if the troops who yielded to the assault had fought with the valor which they had displayed on previous occasions, and which was manifested in this battle on other parts of the lines, the enemy would have been repulsed with very great slaughter, and our country would have escaped the misfortune, and the army the mortification, of the first defeat that has resulted from misconduct by the troops."

[1] Near the close of 1863 General Grant issued the following congratulatory order to his soldiers:

"Chattanooga, December 10th, 1863.

"The general commanding takes this opportunity of returning his sincere thanks and congratulations to the brave armies of the Cumberland, the Ohio, the Tennessee, and their comrades from the Potomac, for the recent splendid and decisive successes achieved over the enemy. In a short time you have recovered from him the control of the Tennessee River from Bridgeport to Knoxville. You dislodged him from his great stronghold upon Lookout Mountain, drove him from Chattanooga Valley, wrested from his determined grasp the possession of Missionary Ridge, repelled with heavy loss to him his repeated assaults upon Knoxville, forcing him to raise the siege there, driving him at all points, utterly routed and discomfited, beyond the limits of the state. By your noble heroism and determined courage you have most effectually defeated the plans of the enemy for regaining the possession of the states of Kentucky and Tennessee. You have secured positions from which no rebellious power can drive or dislodge you. For all this the general commanding thanks you collectively and individually. The loyal people of the United States thank and bless you. Their hopes and prayers for your success against this unholy rebellion are with you daily. Their faith in you will not be in vain. Their hopes will not be blasted. Their prayers to Almighty God will be answered. You will yet go to other fields of strife; and with the invincible bravery and unflinching loyalty to justice and right which have characterized you in the past, you will prove that no enemy can withstand you, and that no defenses, however formidable, can check your onward march."

CAPTURED CONFEDERATE CANNON IN FRONT OF GENERAL THOMAS'S HEADQUARTERS.

CHAPTER XXXVII.

SHERMAN'S MERIDIAN CAMPAIGN.

Object of the Meridian Expedition.—Condition of the Confederate Commissary.—Sherman's Plan.—Co-operative Column under W. S. Smith.—Sherman starts from Vicksburg February 3d, 1864.—His third Visit to Jackson.—The Confederate Forces, under Polk, in the Department of Mississippi.—Polk retires into Alabama.—Sherman's March unopposed.—He enters Meridian on the 14th.—Defeat of Smith's Column by General Forrest.—Sherman's Return to Vicksburg.—Forrest's Raid into Tennessee.—The Fort Pillow Massacre.—Expeditions sent against General Forrest from Memphis, under Sturgis and A. J. Smith.

SINCE the capture of Vicksburg there had been no important military movements in Mississippi during 1863. About the middle of August a small force of 1600 men, sent from General Hurlbut's command, had penetrated through the northern portion of the state to Grenada, where it captured and destroyed over 50 locomotives and about 500 cars. General McPherson two months later, with about 8000 men, comprising Logan's and Tuttle's divisions, and Colonel Winslow's cavalry, pushed out from Vicksburg nearly to Canton, driving back Wirt Adams's cavalry and three brigades of Confederate infantry. Finding himself confronted by a superior force of the enemy, he retreated to Vicksburg.

After Bragg's defeat a more formidable expedition was organized by General Sherman, having for its object the completion of the work which had been begun by the reduction of Vicksburg and Port Hudson. By the capture of those strong-holds the river itself had been conquered, and Arkansas, Louisiana, and Tennessee had been cut off from any possible connection with the main theatre of the war, which was now confined to Virginia, the two Carolinas, Georgia, Northern Florida, Alabama, and Mississippi. Winter had proclaimed a truce, so far as conflicts between the main armies were concerned. But the possession by the national troops of the east bank of the Mississippi furnished a convenient basis for a winter campaign in Mississippi and Alabama. Such a campaign would be an important preparation for the advance upon Atlanta in the following spring. If the reader will examine the map he will observe that, by the successful issue of the Chattanooga campaign, the entire network of railroads north of and including the road running from Memphis eastward to Virginia, had been secured by the national government. By General Grant's victory not only had Bragg's army been defeated and driven, but had been deprived of one of the chief sources upon which it had relied for subsistence.[1] It was forced to mainly depend upon Florida for its meat, while its supply of corn was principally derived from the rich valleys of the Alabama and Tombigbee Rivers. The Confederate Army of the West was already cut off from the immense cattle-growing region west of the Mississippi, and from the corn and bacon of Tennessee. It was proposed to still farther restrict its dependencies by operations, during the winter of 1863–4, directed against the railroads leading to Atlanta from Mississippi, Alabama, and Florida. Thus the campaigns undertaken in the beginning of 1864 by Seymour in Florida, and Sherman in Mississippi, were calculated to have an important bearing upon the progress of the main Federal army southward in the spring and summer.

Probably the principal object of Sherman's expedition against the railroads west of Atlanta was to prevent the possibility of the future concentration of a Confederate army on the east bank of the Mississippi. The destruction of these railroads would render it impossible for the enemy to approach the river with artillery and trains, and the occupation of prominent points in the interior would subject any Confederate infantry column, seeking to gain a position on the river, to an attack in its rear. In this way Sherman's army would be liberated from the necessity, hitherto imposed upon it, of remaining in strong force at Vicksburg, or some other point on the Mississippi.

The plan adopted by General Sherman was the following: He was himself to move from Vicksburg with four divisions of infantry—two of McPherson's and two of Hurlbut's corps—and Colonel Winslow's cavalry brigade, and, advancing westward, was to destroy the Southern Mississippi Railroad. At Meridian, General William Sooy Smith, General Grant's chief of cavalry, was to meet him with all the cavalry of the department, having advanced along the line of the Mobile and Ohio Railroad from Memphis, destroying the road as he moved. General Smith had a long ride of 250 miles, which he was expected to accomplish in ten days, starting from Memphis on or before the 1st of February, moving by way of Pontotoc, Okalona, and Columbus, and reaching Meridian on the 10th. He was instructed to disregard all small detachments of the enemy, and to advance rapidly to his appointed destination. Simultaneously with these movements, the Eleventh Illinois and a colored regiment, with five tin-clad gun-boats, were sent up the Yazoo to create a diversion and to protect the plantations along the banks of that river; and another force, under Brigadier General Hawkins, was to patrol the country toward the Big Black, in the rear of Vicksburg, and to collect 50 skiffs, by means of which detachments of 200 or 300 men might be moved at pleasure through the labyrinth of bayous between the Yazoo and the Mississippi, for the purpose of suppressing the bands of guerrillas then infesting that region.

Sherman began his march on the 3d of February. Hurlbut moved across the Big Black by way of Messenger's Ferry, and McPherson by the railroad bridge six miles below. The two columns, with the cavalry, numbered about 25,000 men. On the 5th both columns met the enemy, Hurlbut's at Joe Davis's plantation, and McPherson's at Champion Hills, and there was skirmishing all day, with small loss on either side, but without materially impeding the progress of the troops, who the next day entered Jackson. This was the third time that Sherman's troops had entered and occupied the capital of Mississippi, and it is fair to presume that this third occupation pretty nearly completed the work of destruction so shamelessly indulged in on two previous occasions.[1]

---

[1] Says the Knoxville *Register* (published at Atlanta, Georgia, after the Federal occupation of East Tennessee), "If any one doubts the necessity which would compel President Davis to sacrifice Richmond, Charleston, and Mobile, all to reacquire East Tennessee, he need only ask the commissary general by what agencies and from what sources the armies of the South have been sustained during the first years of the war. East Tennessee furnished the Confederate States with 25,000,000 pounds of bacon. Last year the State of Tennessee fed the army." The Richmond *Examiner* of October 31st corroborates this testimony in the following terms: "Except what was furtively obtained from Kentucky, the whole army supply of pork came from East Tennessee, and the contiguous counties of the adjoining states. The product of corn in that region was very heavy, and no portion of the Confederacy, equal in extent, afforded as large a supply of forage and winter pasturage."

The following circular, issued in November, 1863, from the office of the chief commissary in Florida, indicates the beginning of a sad era for the armies of the Confederacy:

"Office of Chief Commissary, Quincy, Fla., November 2, 1863.

"It has been a subject of anxious consideration how I could, without injury to our cause, expose to the people throughout the state the present perilous condition of our army. To do this through the public press would point out our source of danger to our enemies. To see each one in person, or even a sufficient number to effect the object contemplated, is impossible; yet the necessity of general and immediate action is imperative to save our army, and with it our cause, from disaster. The issues of this contest are now transferred to the people at home. If they fail to do their duty and sustain the army in its present position, it must fall back. If the enemy break through our present line, the wave of desolation may roll even to the shores of the Gulf and Atlantic. In discipline, valor, and the skill of its leaders, our army has proven more than a match for the enemy. But the best-appointed army can not maintain its position without support at home. The people should never suffer it to be said that they valued their cattle and hogs, their corn and money, more than their liberties and honor, and that they had to be compelled to support an army they had sent to battle in their defense. We hope it will not become necessary to resort to impressments among a people fighting for their existence, and in defense of their homes, and country, and institutions. We prefer rather to appeal to them by every motive of duty and honor—by the love they bear their wives and daughters—by the memory of the heroic dead, and the future glory and independence of their country, to come to its rescue in this darkest hour of its peril.

"A country which can afford to send forth in its defense the flower of its youth, and the best of its manhood, can afford, and are in honor bound to sustain them at any cost and sacrifice of money and property. They have sacrificed home and ease, and suffered untold hardships, and with their lives are now defending every thing we hold most sacred. Florida has done nobly in this contest. Her sons have achieved the highest character for their state, and won imperishable honors for themselves. These brave men are now suffering for want of food. Not only the men from Florida, but the whole army of the South, are in this condition. Our honor as a people demands that we do our duty to them. They must be fed. The following extracts from official letters in my possession do but partially represent the present condition of the armies of Generals Bragg and Beauregard, and their gloomy prospect for future supplies:

"Major J. F. Cumming, who supplies General Bragg's army, writes, 'It is absolutely and vitally important that all the cattle that can possibly be brought here shall be brought as promptly as possible.' And again, on the 5th of October, he says, 'I can not too strongly urge upon you the necessity, yes, the urgent necessity, of sending forward cattle promptly. It appears that all other sources are exhausted, and that we are now dependent upon your state for beef for the very large army of General Bragg. I know you will leave no stone unturned, and I must say all is now dependent on your exertions, so far as beef is concerned. In regard to bacon, the stock is about exhausted—hence beef is our only hope. I know the prospect is very discouraging, and it only remains with those of us having charge of this important work to do all we can to exhaust our resources; and when we have done this, our country can not complain of us. If we fail to do all that can be done, and our cause shall fail, upon us will rest the responsibility; therefore let us employ every means at our command.' Again, on the 6th, he says, 'Major A. can explain to you the great and absolute necessity for prompt action in the matter; for, major, I assure you that nearly all now depends on you.' And on the 19th of October he says, 'Captain Townsend, A. C. S., having a leave of absence for thirty days from the Army of Tennessee, I have prevailed on him to see you and explain to you my straitened condition, and the imminent danger of our army suffering for the want of beef.' And on the 20th of October he wrote, 'The army to-day is on half-rations of beef, and I fear within a few days will have nothing but bread to eat. This is truly a dark hour with us, and I can not see what is to be done. All that is left for us to do is to do all we can, and then we will have a clear conscience, no matter what the world may say.'

"Major Locke, Chief Commissary of Georgia, wrote, 'I pray you, major, to put every agency in motion that you can to send cattle without a moment's delay toward the Georgia borders. The troops in Charleston are in great extremity. We look alone to you for cattle; those in Georgia are exhausted.'

"Major Guerin, Chief Commissary of South Carolina, wrote, 'We are almost entirely dependent on Florida, and it is of the last importance, at this time, that the troops here should be subsisted.' Again he says, 'As it is, our situation is full of danger from want of meat, and extraordinary efforts are required to prevent disaster.' And on the 9th of October he says, 'We have now 40,000 troops and laborers to subsist. The supply of bacon on hand in the city is 20,000 pounds, and the cattle furnished by this state is not one tenth of what is required. My anxieties and apprehensions, as you may suppose, are greatly excited.'

"Major Millen, of Savannah, on the 10th of October says, 'I assure you, major, that the stock of bacon and beef for the armies of the Confederate States is now exhausted, and we must depend entirely upon what we may gather weekly. Starvation stares the army in the face—the hand-writing is on the wall.' On the 26th of October he says, 'From the best information I have, the resources of food (meat) of both the Tennessee and Virginia armies are exhausted. The remark now applies with equal force to South Carolina and Georgia, and the army must henceforth depend upon the energy of the purchasing commissaries, through their daily or weekly collections. I have exhausted the beef cattle, and am now obliged to kill stock cattle.'

"From these you perceive that there is too much cause for the deep solicitude manifested by the writers. They should excite the fears and apprehensions of every lover of his country. Truly the responsibility upon us is great, when we are expected to feed these vast armies, whether the producers will sell to us or not. The slightest reflection would teach any one that it is impossible to provide for such armies by impressments alone. The people must cheerfully yield their supplies, or make up their minds to surrender their cause. It is their cause. It is not the cause of the government. The government is theirs. The army, the government, you and I, and every one, and every thing we have, are staked upon this contest. To fail is total and irretrievable ruin, universal confiscation of every thing, and abject and ignominious submission and slavery to the most despicable and infamous race on earth. Whoever has any other thought but to fight on, at any cost of life and property, until we achieve our independence, or all perish in the struggle, deserves to be the slave of such an enemy. But, under the guidance of Providence, our cause is safe in the hands of our army, provided we do our duty at home. But Providence will not help a people who will not help themselves. Our enemies have no hope of conquering us by arms. Their only hope is that we will be untrue to ourselves, and in the blind pursuit of gain, lose sight of our country, and thus suffer our army, and with it our cause, to perish. How stands the case? You know the resources of Tennessee are lost to us; the hog cholera and other causes have cut short the prospect in Georgia and other states. It is ascertained that the last year's crop of bacon is about exhausted, and it is certain that the crop of this will be much shorter than that of last year. Now two large armies look almost solely to Florida to supply one entire article of subsistence. The entire surplus of this year's crop of bacon throughout the Confederacy, even when husbanded with the utmost economy, will be inadequate to the demands of the government. This makes it the duty of every man to economize as much as possible—to sell not a pound to any one else while there is any danger of our army suffering, and to pledge at schedule rates his entire surplus—bacon, beef, sugar, and sirup—to the government. I solemnly believe our cause is hopeless unless our people can be brought to this point.

"I have thought it my duty to address this confidential circular to the principal men in various sections of the state, and invoke their aid and co-operation with the purchasing commissaries and government agents in their districts, in inaugurating and putting into operation some system by which our armies can be more promptly supplied, and all of our resources which are necessary secured to the government. The appeals to me are more and more urgent every day; the pressure upon our state is very great. Should she now respond to the call made upon her resources as she has upon the bloodiest battle-field of the war, the measure of her glory will be full. But if we withhold our supplies, we cripple our army, and render it impossible for them to advance after achieving the most signal victories. The people at home must put themselves upon a war footing. This they have never yet done. They must sow, and plant, and gather for the government. Then, and not till then, will the bright rays of peace break through the clouds of war which overhang us.

P. W. WHITE, Major and Chief Commissary."

[1] The Northern accounts of Sherman's march indicate its character in this respect. The following extract is taken from "A National Account," published in volume viii. of the *Rebellion Record:*

"It was the expectation, when the expedition started out, that they would draw most of their supplies, and all their forage for horses and mules, from the country. There was very little difficulty in finding enough for our purpose, even in the most barren parts of the country we passed

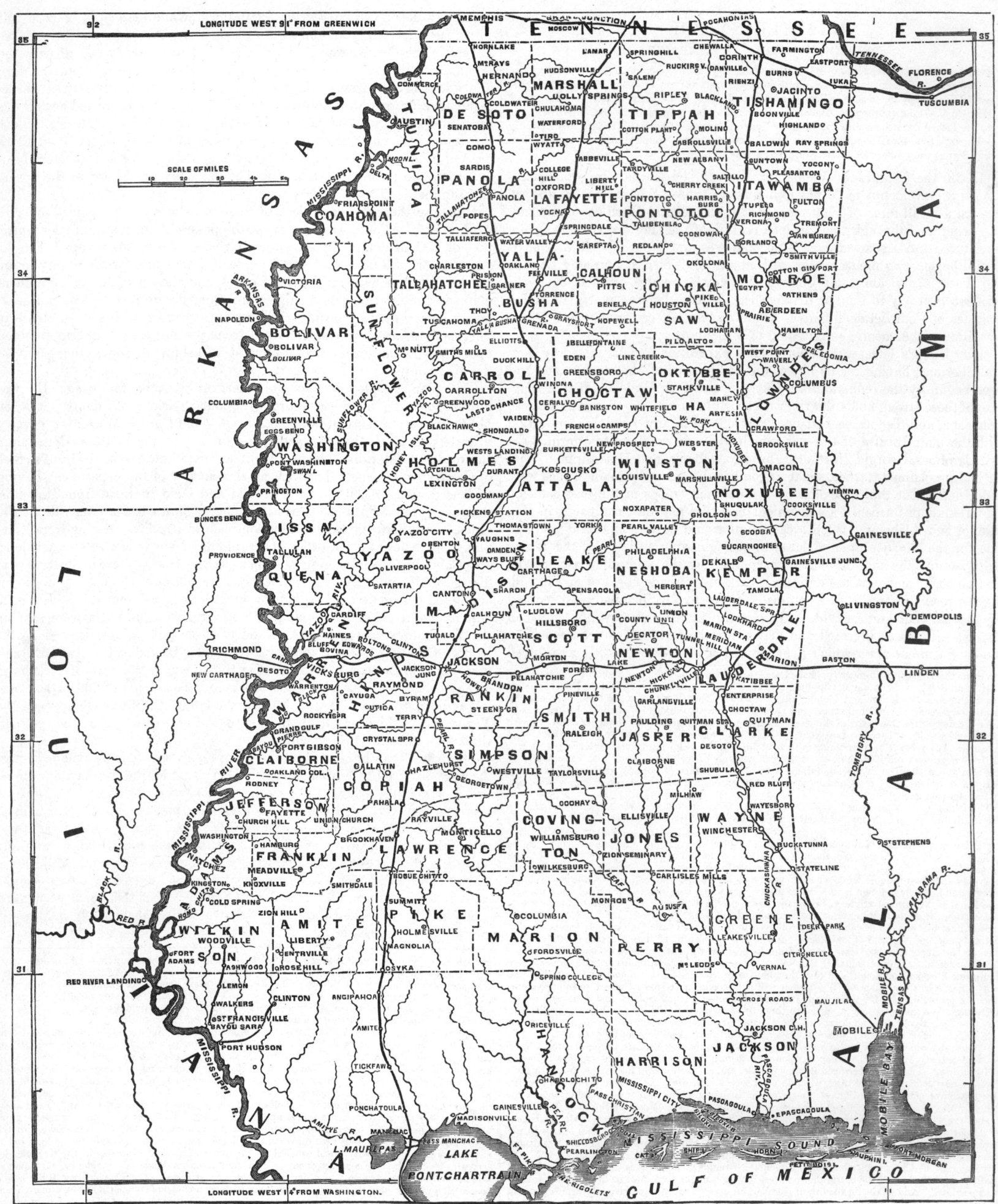

MAP OF MISSISSIPPI.

Sherman's troops marched with little other baggage than their ammunition and twenty days' provisions, and the rapidity of his movements met with very few obstacles from the enemy, who was too weak to oppose to them any formidable resistance. The entire Confederate force in the Department of Mississippi (now under General Polk's command), amounted to less than 16,000 effective men. The most which General Polk could do was to transport the supplies accumulated at the several railway stations into Alabama, behind the Tombigbee River.

Thus unopposed by the enemy, Sherman's march to Meridian was simply a promenade. He crossed the Pearl River on the pontoons which the ene-

through. There was nothing left, however, after our passage, and in many instances the people must suffer for want of food."

This was no doubt legitimate warfare, but we question whether the same excuse may be urged for the destruction of property at Jackson, described as follows by a soldier of Sherman's army (F. McC., of the Sixteenth Iowa):

"It was truly a vivid picture of war to see the streets filled with armed men, squares of large brick buildings on fire, furniture of every description, from rocking-cradles to pianos, clothing, books—in fact, almost every article of domestic utility and ornament, piled upon the sidewalks. Women and children running hither and thither, pictures of the most abject despair. There was no protection given the town, and but little mercy shown, as this was the third time our army had been compelled to come here, and we judge General Sherman rightly concluded that he would obviate all necessity of having to come again."

my had left behind in his hurried retreat from Jackson. On his route he was joined by thousands of negroes—men, women, and children—who swelled the vast column of the march. The railroad was completely demolished along the route. On the 14th, having marched 150 miles in 11 days, Sherman entered Meridian.

But where was General Smith, due four days ago? While the enemy was giving Sherman "a wide berth," he had not been blind to the importance of cutting off the supporting column of cavalry on its way to Meridian from Memphis. In fact, it was only Smith's junction with Sherman that Polk really feared. *That* must be prevented at all hazards. The accession of this cavalry force to Sherman's army would be the preliminary to a successful advance to Selma and Montgomery, and where not? Polk, covering his infantry behind the Tombigbee, ordered his cavalry to join Forrest, to whom was assigned the difficult task of heading off Smith's column.

Associated with General Smith was General B. F. Grierson, who had become thoroughly acquainted with the country on his previous raid. The column had not left Memphis till the 11th, and thus the enemy had been given time to organize his forces for effective resistance. The Federal force numbered 7000 men, and to oppose this Forrest had at length collected to-

W. S. SMITH.

gether about the same number at Okalona, nearly 100 miles north of Meridian. Up to this point Smith and Grierson continued their march without serious resistance. Thus far they were permitted by the enemy to revel in a carnival of devastation, destroying corn estimated by the millions of bushels (one account makes it 1,000,000 bushels, another 3,000,000), and two or three thousand bales of cotton. Either by lack of discipline, owing to the character of such a march, or on account of the sudden and formidable opposition encountered, the Federal command did not behave well when on the 22d it reached Okalona, as was its wont in the presence of the enemy. Almost the first onset of Forrest's cavalry was decisive. Six guns were lost by the Federals in the first attack. Probably even after the first reverse the Confederates would have been checked had it not been for the impediment to Smith's fighting force of the crowd of camp-followers, who gave way to panic, and fled to the rear, sweeping with them a portion of the troops coming into position. It was with great difficulty that Smith covered his retreat and saved his trains. The Fourth Missouri Cavalry, acting as rear-guard, stood well its ground, checking the enemy until nightfall. Under cover of night the Federals fell back to Okalona (the battle had been fought south of that place, on the border of the prairie country), where order was restored. Smith and Grierson, after losing over 300 men and a large number of horses, continued their retreat over the country which for ten days they had been laying waste.

This disaster, of course, forbid any farther advance on the part of Sherman, who had in the mean time been destroying the railroads centring in Meridian.[1] He then, with one of his columns, marched northward to Canton, continuing his work of destruction in that direction. Finding that the column from Memphis had been driven back, he returned to Vicksburg. His loss had been probably about 200 men. He brought away with him 1000 white and 5000 colored refugees. He had done the enemy very great injury, which, unfortunately, in a large measure, fell upon the population rather than the army; had, by the destruction of the railroads between Vicksburg and Meridian, secured the east bank of the Mississippi against any future attack on the part of the enemy—one of the chief objects of the raid—and had learned a lesson in regard to the facility of marching through the southern portion of the Confederacy, which was of the greatest value to him at a later period of the war.

It is possible that, but for the failure of Sherman's supporting cavalry column, an attempt would have been made in conjunction with Farragut's naval force against Mobile. Farragut did indeed make a strong demonstration against Mobile, assaulting Fort Powell, and losing a gun-boat in the operation. But this attack was only a feint, to divert attention from a pet project which the government was at this time nursing, and which regarded affairs on the other side of the Mississippi.

Forrest did not stop with his defeat of Smith and Grierson at Okalona. If he could meet all the cavalry of Grant's department in the open field, what was to hinder him—now that the garrisons of Tennessee were continually being weakened by the concentration of forces for the spring campaign—from moving into Western Tennessee and Kentucky? He passed

---

[1] "The dépôts, store-houses, arsenals, offices, hospitals, hotels, and cantonments in the town were burned, and, during the next five days, with axes, sledges, crow-bars, clam-bars, and fire, Hurlbut's corps destroyed on the north and east 60 miles of ties and iron, one locomotive, and eight bridges; and McPherson's corps, on the south and west, 55 miles of railway, 53 bridges, 61,075 feet of trestle-work, 19 locomotives, 28 steam-cars, and 3 steam saw-mills. Thus was completed the destruction of railways for 100 miles from Jackson to Meridian, and for 20 miles around the latter place, in such a manner that they could not be used against us in the approaching campaigns."—Bowman's *Sherman and his Campaigns*, p. 163.

over the frontier of Tennessee late in March, and his expedition throughout was characterized by brutality and cowardice such as is not surpassed in the record of even savage warfare. It is possible that his command was infuriated by the devastation which had marked the progress of Sherman's Mississippi expedition. But this is no fair excuse for such conduct as that which it is now our duty to expose. Wherever Sherman's troops departed from the recognized customs of war, the reader will bear us witness that we have offered no excuse in their behalf. But if against them rebuke naturally rises to our lips, our cheeks burn with shame for the brutal capabilities of our human nature as we follow the career of General Forrest from his entrance into Tennessee to the massacre at Fort Pillow.

Forrest advanced from Okalona northward by the Mobile and Ohio Railroad. His command numbered between 5000 and 6000 men.[1] The force which stood in his way, even if he looked to Cairo as his destination, did not amount to more than half his own. Jackson, in Tennessee, was captured on the 23d of March. Forrest's line of march was west of the Tennessee River, toward the Mississippi. He captured Union City, near the northern border of Tennessee, on the 24th of March. This post had been occupied by Colonel Hawkins with about 500 men. Hawkins was attacked by over three times that number, but easily repulsed four several charges of the enemy. Then a flag of truce was sent demanding a surrender, and throwing upon Colonel Hawkins the consequence of a refusal. Against the wishes of the garrison the demand was complied with, although a relieving force of 2000 men was within six miles of him. His conduct was probably influenced by the fear that the enemy in his front would soon be strongly re-enforced.[2]

The Mississippi from Paducah to Island No. 10, about 160 miles, together with the adjacent portions of Tennessee and Kentucky, was under the command of Brigadier General Mason Brayman. His whole force—distributed at Paducah, Cairo, Columbus, Hickman, Island No. 10, and Union City—amounted to 2329 men, three fourths of whom were negroes. General Hurlbut, in command of the department, had, in compliance with orders from the War Department, sent all his veteran regiments home on furlough. All his cavalry was gone save about 2000. He did not dare to leave Memphis exposed, and was therefore able to afford very little assistance to the garrisons on the Mississippi River against which Forrest was moving. As soon as Forrest approached Jackson, Grierson, with his cavalry, was sent out to develop his force, and soon reported that the enemy "was a little too strong for him."

From Union City Forrest moved upon Hickman, about fourteen miles distant on the Mississippi. The garrison at this point was withdrawn. The enemy then advanced to Wayfield, Kentucky, which is about equally distant from Paducah, Cairo, and Columbus. He was at the centre of a circle, about the edge of which General Brayman's forces were situated. The lat-

---

[1] Hurlbut thinks it could not have been less than 8000.—*Report on the Conduct of the War.*

[2] General Hurlbut says, "Contrary to the entreaties, prayers, and advice of all his officers and all his men, he did surrender his post with a relieving force within six miles of him, and surrendered it, as I have no doubt, from pure cowardice."—*Report on the Conduct of the War*: It was a tame surrender, doubtless, but other testimony before the committee fully relieves Colonel Hawkins of the charge of cowardice.

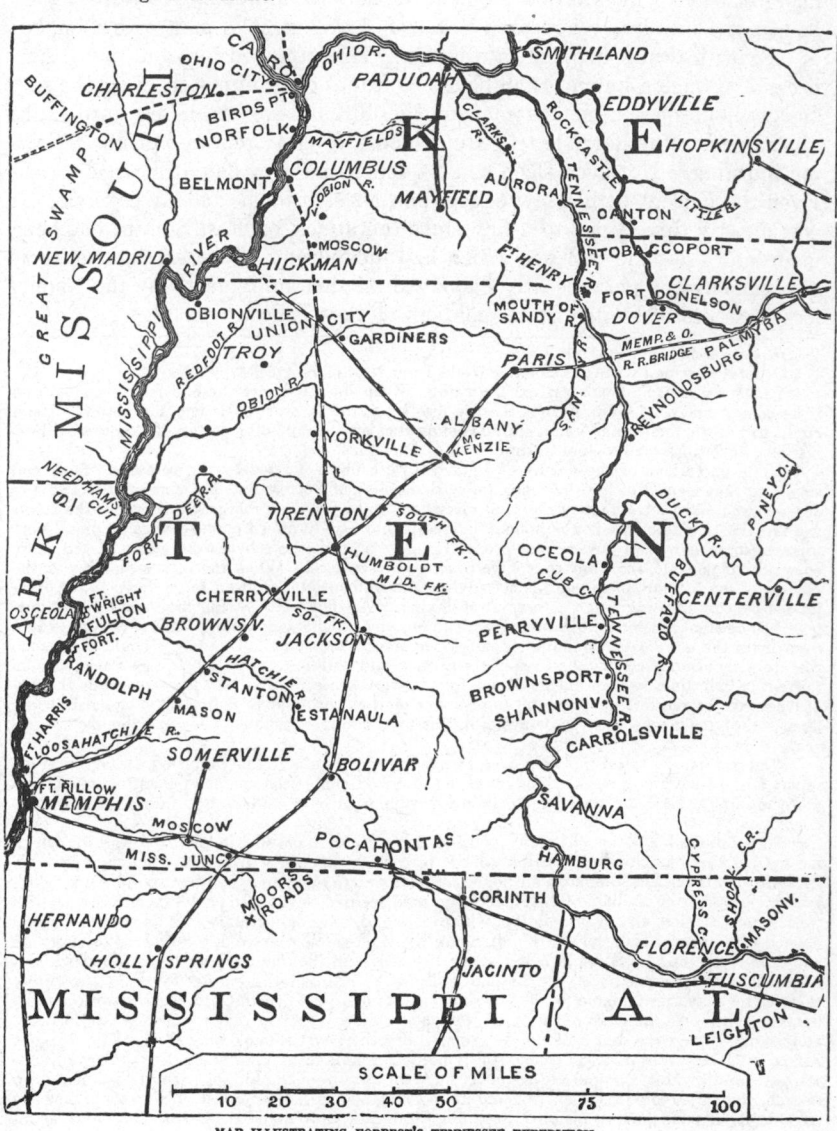

MAP ILLUSTRATING FORREST'S TENNESSEE EXPEDITION.

ter could only await attack, and send re-enforcements to such weak points in turn as the emergency might demand. "One evening," he says, "I sent 400 men to Columbus, expecting trouble there, and the next morning had them at Paducah, seventy-five miles distant."[1] No such thing as an offensive movement against Forrest could of course be contemplated, and the latter remained for three weeks subsisting upon captured stores in the very heart of a region which, almost from the beginning of the war, had been securely held by the national government. On the 25th of March an attack was made on Paducah, held by Colonel S. G. Hicks with a garrison of 650 men. The garrison retired into Fort Anderson, and there made a stand, assisted by two gun-boats, effectually repelling the enemy's assaults. Forrest then, failing to make an impression upon the defenders of the fort, demanded an unconditional surrender, closing his communication to Colonel Hicks in these words: "If you surrender you shall be treated as prisoners of war, but if I have to storm your works *you may expect no quarter.*" Hicks refused, stating, like a faithful soldier, that he had been placed there by his government to defend that post, and he should do so. Three assaults from the enemy followed, each of which was repulsed with heavy loss to the assailants. In the last, one of the Confederate general officers, General Thompson, was killed.[5] The next day Forrest retired, having suffered a loss of nearly 1500 men. The national loss was 14 killed and 46 wounded.[2] Columbus, on the Mississippi, stood out as defiantly as had Paducah, and the enemy retired without making an attack.

General Forrest appeared before Fort Pillow, 65 miles above Memphis, on the 12th of April. The garrison at this point consisted of 19 officers and 538 men, of whom 262 were negroes, commanded by Major L. F. Booth. The attack was sudden, no intimation of it being given before the pickets were driven in. Major Booth was killed early in the engagement, and Major W. F. Bradford succeeded to the command, and withdrew the forces from their outer intrenchments into the fort. The fort was situated on a high bluff, which descended precipitately to the river's edge. On either side was a ravine—the one below the fort containing several private stores and a few dwellings, constituting what is called the town. In front of the fort was an open space of level ground. The artillery defense consisted of 6 guns. The troops fought gallantly, aided by a gun-boat, and up to 2 P.M. the enemy had not gained any decisive advantage. A flag of truce was then sent in, conveying a demand for the unconditional surrender of the fort. Major Bradford asked an hour for consideration. Shortly a second flag appeared, and Bradford was allowed 20 minutes; if not out of the fort by that time an assault would be made. Bradford replied that he would not surrender. During all this time the enemy, regardless of his own flag of truce, was gaining an advantageous position for the assault. His forces were now within 100 yards of the fort, closely surrounding it. As soon as Major Bradford's reply was received, the bugle was sounded, and the Confederates, with a yell, rushed over the fortifications, raising the cry of "No quarter!" The troops composing the garrison, black and white, threw down their arms and sought to escape by running down the steep bluff on the river side, hiding behind trees, logs, bushes—any thing which could afford them cover against the maddest fiends which at that moment the sun shone upon. No wonder they fled, as it soon clearly appeared it was not a contest of men with men, but of men with brutal, fiendish murderers. The captured fort and its vicinity became at once a human shambles. Without discrimination of age or sex, and without mercy, men, women, and children were butchered until night put an end to the horrible tragedy, which was again renewed on the following morning. Not even sleep could quench the fiery hate of Forrest's men. Even the officers, with a few exceptions, assisted in the bloody carnival. It was exactly three years to a day since the attack on Fort Sumter had been made, and the same violence which had incited men to treason against their government was perhaps fitly displayed on this anniversary by the shameless massacre of United States soldiers at Fort Pillow.[3]

Forrest, in the face of his own statement that, while he lost only 20 killed and 60 wounded, he buried 228 Federals on the evening of the assault, coolly claims that all these were killed in fair fight! After this affair the enemy retreated into Mississippi. A fortnight later General S. D. Sturgis, with 12,000 men, was sent after Forrest, but the movements of the enemy were so rapid that he easily escaped this pursuing column. Early in June Sturgis was again sent against Forrest, with instructions to find and defeat his command, in order to prevent its junction with General Johnston, then resisting General Sherman's advance in Northern Georgia. The Federal column dispatched for this purpose consisted of 9000 infantry (including most of A. J. Smith's division), and 3000 cavalry under General Grierson. The campaign was terribly mismanaged by Sturgis. After advancing through West Tennessee and Northern Mississippi to Guntown on the Mobile Railroad, Grierson's cavalry encountered Forrest, pushing his cavalry back on his infantry, which was strongly posted on a semicircular ridge, protected by a creek in front. Sturgis, with the infantry, was five or six miles behind. Getting information of Grierson's position, he pushed his command forward at double-quick, and as it was a very hot day, the troops, upon confronting the enemy, were thoroughly exhausted. To make matters still worse, the train of over 200 wagons was allowed by Sturgis to rush forward with his men, filling the road and impeding their movements. No rest was given the troops, who were immediately sent to the support of the cavalry already engaged. No attempt was made to turn the enemy's strong position, and from the attack which was made no other consequence could be expected than that which followed. Both cavalry and infantry were soon routed, and driven in disorder back upon and over the abandoned train. The pursuit was momentarily checked at Ripley, but was continued with some vigor almost to Memphis. In this expedition Sturgis lost between 3000 and 4000 men, most of whom were captured.

A month later (July 7th) another command was sent against Forrest, consisting of the same number of men, but this time under command of A. J.

---

[1] *Report on the Conduct of the War.*

[2] General Sherman writes to Colonel Hicks from Nashville, April 5th, 1864:

"Your defense at Paducah was exactly right. Keep cool, and give the enemy a second edition if he comes again. I want Forrest to stay just where he is, and the longer the better. Don't credit any of the foolish and exaggerated rumors that are put afloat by design. I know what Forrest has, and will attend to him in time."

[6] "The operations of the enemy at Paducah were characterized by the same bad faith and treachery that seemed to have become the settled policy of Forrest and his command. The flag of truce was taken advantage of there, as elsewhere, to secure desirable positions which the rebels were unable to obtain by fair and honorable means, and also to afford opportunities for plundering private stores as well as government property. At Paducah the rebels were guilty of acts more cowardly, if possible, than any they have practiced elsewhere. When the attack was made, the officers of the fort and of the gun-boats advised the women and children to go down to the river for the purpose of being taken across out of danger. As they were leaving the town for that purpose, the rebel sharp-shooters mingled with them, and, shielded by their presence, advanced and fired upon the gun-boats, wounding some of our officers and men. Our forces could not return the fire without endangering the lives of the women and children. The rebels also placed women in front of their lines as they moved on the fort, or were proceeding to take positions while the flag of truce was at the fort, in order to compel our men to withhold their fire out of regard for the lives of the women who were made use of in this most cowardly manner."—*Report on the Conduct of the War.*

[3] We have not described this disgraceful tragedy in its details. The following extract from the report of the Committee on the Conduct of the War will enable the reader to examine its features more minutely. All the statements made are supported by abundant and unimpeachable evidence:

"Then followed a scene of cruelty and murder without a parallel in civilized warfare, which needed but the tomahawk and scalping-knife to exceed the worst atrocities ever committed by savages. The rebels commenced an indiscriminate slaughter, sparing neither age nor sex, white nor black, soldier or civilian. The officers and men seemed to vie with each other in the devilish work; men, women, and even children, wherever found, were deliberately shot down, beaten, and hacked with sabres; some of the children, not more than ten years old, were forced to stand up and face their murderers while being shot; the sick and the wounded were butchered without mercy, the rebels even entering the hospital building and dragging them out to be shot, or killing them as they lay there unable to offer the least resistance. All over the hill-side the work of murder was going on; numbers of our men were collected together in lines or groups and deliberately shot; some were shot while in the river, while others on the bank were shot and their bodies kicked into the water, many of them still living, but unable to make any exertions to save themselves from drowning. Some of the rebels stood on the top of the hill, or a short distance down its side, and called to our soldiers to come up to them, and as they approached, shot them down in cold blood; if their guns or pistols missed fire, forcing them to stand there until they were again prepared to fire. All around were heard cries of 'No quarter!' 'No quarter!' 'Kill the damned niggers; shoot them down!' All who asked for mercy were answered by the most cruel taunts and sneers. Some were spared for a time, only to be murdered under circumstances of greater cruelty. No cruelty which the most fiendish malignity could devise was omitted by these murderers. One white soldier, who was wounded in one leg so as to be unable to walk, was made to stand up while his tormentors shot him; others who were wounded and unable to stand were held up and again shot. One negro, who had been ordered by a rebel officer to hold his horse, was killed by him when he remounted; another, a mere child, whom an officer had taken up behind him on his horse, was seen by Chalmers, who at once ordered the officer to put him down and shoot him, which was done. The huts and tents in which many of the wounded had sought shelter were set on fire, both that night and the next morning, while the wounded were still in them—those only escaping who were able to get themselves out, or who could prevail on others less injured than themselves to help them out; and even some of those thus seeking to escape the flames were met by those ruffians and brutally shot down, or had their brains beaten out. One man was deliberately fastened down to the floor of a tent, face upward, by means of nails driven through his clothing and into the boards under him, so that he could not possibly escape, and then the tent set on fire; another was nailed to the side of a building outside of the fort, and then the building set on fire and burned. The charred remains of five or six bodies were afterward found, all but one so much disfigured and consumed by the flames that they could not be identified, and the identification of that one is not absolutely certain, although there can hardly be a doubt that it was the body of Lieutenant Akerstrom, quartermaster of the Thirteenth Tennessee Cavalry, and a native Tennesseean; several witnesses who saw the remains, and who were personally acquainted with him while living, have testified that it is their firm belief that it was his body that was thus treated.

"These deeds of murder and cruelty ceased when night came on, only to be renewed the next morning, when the demons carefully sought among the dead lying about in all directions for any of the wounded yet alive, and those they found were deliberately shot. Scores of the dead and wounded were found there the day after the massacre by the men from some of our gun-boats who were permitted to go on shore and collect the wounded and bury the dead. The rebels themselves had made a pretense of burying a great many of their victims, but they had merely thrown them, without the least regard to care or decency, into the trenches and ditches about the fort, or the little hollows and ravines on the hill-side, covering them but partially with earth. Portions of heads and faces, hands and feet, were found protruding through the earth in every direction. The testimony also establishes the fact that the rebels buried some of the living with the dead, a few of whom succeeded afterward in digging themselves out, or were dug out by others, one of whom your committee found in Mound City Hospital, and there examined. And even when your committee visited the spot, two weeks afterward, although parties of men had been sent on shore from time to time to bury the bodies unburied and rebury the others, and were even then engaged in the same work, we found the evidences of this murder and cruelty still most painfully apparent; we saw bodies still unburied (at some distance from the fort) of some sick men who had been met fleeing from the hospital, and beaten down and brutally murdered, and their bodies left where they had fallen. We could still see the faces, hands, and feet of men, white and black, protruding out of the ground, whose graves had not been reached by those engaged in reinterring the victims of the massacre; and although a great deal of rain had fallen within the preceding two weeks, the ground, more especially on the side and at the foot of the bluff, where the most of the murders had been committed, was still discolored by the blood of our brave but unfortunate men, and the logs and trees showed but too plainly the evidences of the atrocities perpetrated there.

"Many other instances of equally atrocious cruelty might be enumerated, but your committee feel compelled to refrain from giving here more of the heart-sickening details, and refer to the statements contained in the voluminous testimony herewith submitted. Those statements were obtained by them from eyewitnesses and sufferers; many of them, as they were examined by your committee, were lying upon beds of pain and suffering, some so feeble that their lips could with difficulty frame the words by which they endeavored to convey some idea of the cruelties which had been inflicted on them, and which they had seen inflicted on others.

"How many of our troops thus fell victims to the malignity and barbarity of Forrest and his followers can not yet be definitely ascertained. Two officers belonging to the garrison were absent at the time of the capture and massacre. Of the remaining officers but two are known to be living, and they are wounded and now in the hospital at Mound City. One of them, Captain Potter, may even now be dead, as the surgeons, when your committee were there, expressed no hope of his recovery. Of the men, from three hundred to four hundred are known to have been killed at Fort Pillow, of whom at least three hundred were murdered in cold blood after the post was in possession of the rebels, and our men had thrown down their arms and ceased to offer resistance. Of the survivors, except the wounded in the hospital at Mound City, and the few who succeeded in making their escape unhurt, nothing definite is known; and it is to be feared that many have been murdered after being taken away from the fort.

"In reference to the fate of Major Bradford, who was in command of the fort when it was captured, and who had up to that time received no injury, there seems to be no doubt. The general understanding every where seemed to be that he had been brutally murdered the day after he was taken prisoner.

"There is some discrepancy in the testimony, but your committee do not see how the one who professed to have been an eyewitness of his death could have been mistaken. There may be some uncertainty in regard to his fate.

"When your committee arrived at Memphis, Tennessee, they found and examined a man (Mr. McLagan) who had been conscripted by some of Forrest's forces, but who, with other conscripts, had succeeded in making his escape. He testifies that while two companies of rebel troops, with Major Bradford and many other prisoners, were on their march from Brownsville to Jackson, Tennessee, Major Bradford was taken by five rebels—one an officer—led about fifty yards from the line of march, and deliberately murdered in view of all there assembled. He fell—killed instantly by three musket-balls, even while asking that his life might be spared, as he had fought them manfully, and was deserving of a better fate. The motive for the murder of Major Bradford seems to have been the simple fact that, although a native of the South, he remained loyal to his government."

THE FORT PILLOW MASSACRE.

FORREST'S RAIDERS ATTACKING IRVING PRISON.

Smith, who advanced to Tupelo, where the enemy, about 14,000 strong, was then concentrated. A battle was here fought (July 14th), in which the enemy, thrice attacking the Federal lines, was each time repulsed. It was a drawn battle, and Smith, without advancing farther, retreated to Memphis, whence he again set out with 10,000 men on the 4th of August, moving by way of Holly Springs to the Tallahatchie River. But this time Forrest was not to be found, and Smith, after remaining in this vicinity for several days, again returned to Memphis, and was sent to the Department of the Missouri.

While General Smith was looking for Forrest in Mississippi, the latter had moved upon Memphis with 3000 men. He charged into the town on the morning of August 18th. He had heard that Generals Hurlbut, Washburne, and Buckland made their quarters at the Gayoso Hotel, but, paying them a visit at that place, he found them "not at home." He captured several staff and other officers, however, and about 300 soldiers. A number of Confederate prisoners were confined in Irving Prison. Failing in an attempt to gain possession of this prison, General Forrest left the town, and beat a hasty retreat back into Mississippi.

CHAPTER XXXVIII.

THE FLORIDA EXPEDITION.

Gillmore lands 10,000 Men at Jacksonville.—Object of the Expedition in large measure Political.—Lincoln's Amnesty Proclamation.—The President's Motives.—The Enemy surprised.—Number of Confederate Troops in Florida.—The Federal Troops occupy Baldwin.—Gillmore returns to Hilton Head.—His Instructions to General Seymour disregarded by the latter.—The Battle of Olustee.—Seymour's Blunder.—Disastrous Termination of the Expedition.

WHILE Sherman was advancing upon Meridian, a force of 10,000 men was landed at Jacksonville, on the eastern coast of Florida. These were a portion of the Tenth Army Corps, under General Q. A. Gillmore, who, on the 16th of July, 1863, had succeeded General Hunter in command of the troops operating in South Carolina. The object of this Florida expedition was in large measure a political one. President Lincoln had included in his first message to the Thirty-eighth Congress (December 7th, 1863) a proclamation of amnesty, offering a free pardon to all such rebels as would take an oath to support the Federal Constitution and Union, "and abide by and faithfully support all acts of Congress passed during the existing rebellion having reference to slaves, so long and so far as not repealed, modified, or held void by Congress, or by decision of the Supreme Court." Exceptions were made in the cases of those who were or had been officers or agents of the Confederate government; of those who had left judicial stations under the United States, or seats in Congress, or had resigned commissions in the Federal army or navy to take part in the rebellion; of Confederate military and naval officers above the rank of colonel in the army or lieutenant in the navy; and of all who had in any way treated white or black soldiers otherwise than as prisoners of war. It was also proclaimed that, as soon as in any of the Confederate States "a number of persons, not less than one tenth in number of the votes cast in such state at the presidential election of 1860, each having taken the oath aforesaid, and not having since violated it, and being a qualified voter by the election law of the state existing immediately before the so-called act of secession, and excluding all others, shall re-establish a state government which shall be republican, and in nowise contravening said oath, such shall be recognized as the true government of the state: and the state shall receive thereunder the benefits of the constitutional provision which declares that 'the United States shall guarantee to every state in this Union a republican form of government, and shall protect each of them against invasion, and, on application of the Legislature or the executive (when the Legislature can not be convened), against domestic violence.'" The President entertained somewhat extravagant expectations as to the results of this proclamation. It is not necessary to say that he had no partisan motive in issuing it; he only wished to begin the reorganization of governments in the Southern States. The movement was premature; perhaps it was ill considered. If successful, some foreign complications might be avoided; but, so far as any real reconstruction was concerned, *that* could only come as the consequence of final victory in the war. Unfortunately, the President's too sanguine hopes conduced to the embarrassment of military operations. Expeditions were undertaken which distracted forces from vital centres, and which, contemplating nothing beyond the possession of a small slice of territory in Florida and Texas, and being undertaken with numbers only adequate to such a result, had not the remotest connection with the progress of the war from a military stand-point. The disastrous results of these expeditions are not fairly attributable to the President's plan; but, apart from their unfortunate results, no such half-military and half-political projects were in place.

The objects sought to be attained by the Florida expedition are thus stated by General Gillmore:

1. To procure an outlet for cotton, lumber, timber, etc.
2. To cut off one of the enemy's sources of commissary supplies.

S. D. STURGIS.

3. To obtain recruits for any colored regiments.

4. To inaugurate measures for the speedy restoration of Florida to her allegiance, in accordance with instructions which I had received from the President by the hands of Major John Hay, Assistant Adjutant General.[1]

The troops, consisting of twelve regiments—one half of them colored troops—under the immediate command of Brigadier General Truman Seymour, left Hilton Head on the 6th of February, and landed the next day at Jacksonville, at the mouth of St. John's River. The landing of this force was a complete surprise to the enemy. In the Confederate Departments of South Carolina, Georgia, and Florida, there were at this time about 33,000 effective troops. Of these there were about 5000 in Florida, under the command of General Finnegan. The progress of the Federal troops from Jacksonville to Baldwin, in the interior, met with no opposition. Finnegan made an attempt to stand at Camp Vinegar, seven miles west of Jacksonville, but on the approach of the Federal columns he abandoned his position, having sunk the steamer St. Mary's, and burned 270 bales of cotton. On the morning of the 9th General Gillmore reports: "We have taken, without the loss of a man, about 100 prisoners, eight pieces of artillery in serviceable order and one well supplied with ammunition, and other valuable property to a large amount." Baldwin, which the Federal troops now occupied, was eighteen miles west of Jacksonville, and was the point of junction of two railroads, one running from Fernandina, a short distance north of Jacksonville, southwestwardly to Cedar Keys, on the western coast: the other from Jacksonville, across the northern part of the state to Tallahassee, the state capital. A portion of Seymour's command, under Colonel Henry, pursued the enemy almost to Lake City.

General Gillmore had accompanied the expedition in person, and remained until the 15th, when he returned to Hilton Head. On the 11th he had instructed General Seymour not to risk a repulse by an advance on Lake City, but, if possible, to hold Sanderson (forty miles west of Jacksonville), and, at any rate, the south fork of the St. Mary's. The next day he ordered the entire force to concentrate at Baldwin. Before his departure for Hilton Head he made arrangements for the construction of fortifications at Jacksonville, Baldwin, and on the south fork of the St. Mary's. At that time it was understood that no advance should be made without farther instructions from Gillmore, nor until the defensive works were well advanced.[2]

General Gillmore was therefore astonished by receiving a communication from Seymour on the 18th (dated the 17th), stating that he intended to advance to the Suwanee River, 100 miles distant from Jacksonville, and that he was already moving his troops westward. Not being able to accumulate supplies sufficient to permit him to make the movement, Seymour declared his purpose to move without supplies, even if compelled to retrace his steps to procure them. He urged Gillmore to prevent any force re-enforcing the enemy from Georgia by a naval demonstration against Savannah. He asked, also, for a general to be sent him to command his advanced troops. General Gillmore, having no intention to occupy the western part of Florida, at once dispatched General Turner, his chief of staff, to Jacksonville to prevent the movement. Upon arriving in Florida with a letter to Seymour from Gillmore protesting against the advance of the former, Turner found that the troops were already at Olustee, and engaged with the enemy.[3]

General Seymour had begun his movement on the 18th, and expected no encounter with the enemy before reaching Lake City. On the night of the 19th he halted at Barber's, a small station on the railroad 30 miles west of Jacksonville. The Confederate General Finnegan had, in the mean time, been apprized of the hostile movement, and, instead of awaiting attack at Lake City, he preferred to choose his own battle-ground, and advanced to Olustee, about 15 miles eastward, where his army took a strong position on a swamp which runs southward some distance from Ocean Pond, a small lake north of the railroad. His centre was protected by the swamp; his right rested on an earthwork protected by rifle-pits, while his left was posted on a slight elevation, sheltered by pines, and still farther guarded by cavalry. It was a position absolutely impregnable against double the numbers which held it, and the force under General Seymour was only about equal to that of the enemy; his only advantage was in artillery, of which he had sixteen pieces to the enemy's four.[1]

Seymour, without knowing any thing of the enemy's position, advanced from Barber's on the 20th, and, after a wearisome march of 15 miles over the sandy road, came suddenly upon the enemy's pickets near Olustee. The road at this point crossed the railroad to the right, to avoid the swamp on the south side. There was also a swamp on the right of the road, and between these two swamps lay the sole approach to the enemy's position. The action commenced about 2 o'clock P.M. The Federal troops, tired by their long march, went into battle under a great disadvantage. The artillery was pushed up so far to the front that both the gunners and horses were shot down with such rapidity that some of the guns were abandoned and others rendered useless. The infantry, poorly armed, were put in regiment by regiment as it arrived on the ground. There was no tactics, and the situation gave no opportunity for any. The road was so narrow that many of the men had to wade knee-deep in mud and water in order to get into action. One regiment after another went in beyond the swamps, and each fired away its ammunition, and, exposed to a murderous fire from the enemy, retired, giving place to another. The Seventh Connecticut, under the brave Colonel T. R. Hawley (late governor of Connecticut), held the advance after the preliminary skirmish. The field soon becomes too hot for this regiment,

---

[1] The following letter was addressed to General Gillmore by President Lincoln, January 13th, 1864:

"Major General GILLMORE:

"I understand an effort is being made by some worthy gentlemen to reconstruct a legal state government in Florida. Florida is in your department, and it is not unlikely that you may be there in person. I have given Mr. Hay a commission of major, and sent him to you with some blank books and other blanks, to aid in the reconstruction. He will explain as to the manner of using the blanks, and also my general views on the subject. It is desirable for all to co-operate, but if irreconcilable differences of opinion shall arise, you are master. I wish the thing done in the most speedy way possible, so that when done it may be within the range of the late proclamation on the subject. The detail labor will of course have to be done by others, but I shall be greatly obliged if you will give it such general supervision as you can find consistent with your more strictly military duties. A. LINCOLN."

On the 31st of January General Gillmore issued the following order:

"Headquarters Department of the South, Hilton Head, South Carolina, January 31st, 1864.

"In accordance with the provisions of the presidential proclamation of pardon and amnesty, given at Washington on the 8th day of December, in the year of our Lord 1863, and in pursuance of instructions received from the President of the United States, Major John Hay, Assistant Adjutant General, will proceed to Fernandina, Florida, and other convenient points in that state, for the purpose of extending to the citizens of the State of Florida an opportunity to avail themselves of the benefit of that proclamation, by offering for their signature the oath of allegiance therein prescribed, and by issuing to all those subscribing to said oath certificates entitling them to the benefits of the proclamation. Fugitive citizens of the State of Florida within the limits of this department will have an opportunity to subscribe to the same oath, and secure certificates in the office of the post commander at Hilton Head, South Carolina.

"By command of Major General Q. A. GILLMORE.

"E. W. SMITH, Assistant Adjutant General."

[2] General Gillmore's Report.

[3] The following are copies of the letters—General Seymour's announcing his movement, and General Gillmore's reply:

"Headquarters Department of the South, February 17th, 1864.

"GENERAL,—The excessive and unexpected delays experienced with regard to the locomotive, which will not be ready for two days yet, if at all, has compelled me to remain where my command could be fed. Not enough supplies could be accumulated to permit me to execute my intention of moving to the Suwanee River.

"But I now propose to go without supplies, even if compelled to retrace my steps to procure them, and with the object of so destroying the railroad near the Suwanee that there will be no danger of carrying away any portion of the track.

"All troops are therefore being moved up to Barber's, and probably by the time you receive this I shall be in motion in advance of that point.

"That a force may not be brought from Georgia (Savannah) to interfere with my movements, it is desirable that a display be made in the Savannah River; and I therefore urge that upon the reception of this, such naval force, transports, sailing vessels, etc., as can be so devoted, may rendezvous near Pulaski, and that the iron-clads in Warsaw push up with as much activity as they can exert.

"I look upon this as of great importance, and shall rely upon it as a demonstration in my favor.

"There is reason to believe that General Hardee is in Lake City, now possibly in command, and with some force at his disposal.

"But nothing is visible this side of Sanderson. Saddles, etc., for mounting the Seventh New Hampshire as rapidly as possible, are greatly needed, and I shall send a portion of that regiment to this point as soon as it can be spared subsequent to my advance.

"I have sent for the Twenty-fourth Massachusetts entire to come to this point. The Tenth Connecticut (eight companies) is to remain at St. Augustine, two companies to go to Picolata.

"I shall not occupy Picolata or Magnolia at this moment; when I do, portions of the Twenty-fourth Massachusetts will be sent from Jacksonville. The Fifty-fifth Massachusetts will remain here for the present, or until the Twenty-fourth relieves it.

"The Second South Carolina and Third South Carolina are at Camp Shaw (late Finnegan), for instruction and organization.

"The First North Carolina will be left at Baldwin, detaching three companies to Barber's.

"Colonel Barton will have the Forty-seventh, Forty-eighth, and One Hundred and Fifteenth; Colonel Hanlay will have the Seventh Connecticut, Seventh New Hampshire, and Eighth United States Colored; Colonel Montgomery the Third United States and Fifty-fourth Massachusetts Colored; Colonel Henry the cavalry and Elder's battery, and Captain Hamilton the artillery. As soon as possible, Metcalf's section will be sent back. At present I should like to use it.

"Colonel Goss is ordered to keep six companies in motion from Fernandina constantly, and at least five days out of seven (every seven) toward and beyond Camp Cooper.

"Nothing appears to have been done upon the locomotive while at Fernandina. So it is reported to me.

"The prompt use of a locomotive and a printing-press with this movement were of the most vital importance, and will continue so to be. I trust both will be economized.

"And I am, very respectfully, your obedient servant,

"T. SEYMOUR, Brigadier General Commanding.

"Brigadier General S. W. TURNER, Chief of Staff:

"Send me a general for the command of the advanced troops, or I shall be in a state of constant uncertainty. T. S."

"Hilton Head, South Carolina, February 18th, 1864.

"Brigadier General T. SEYMOUR, Commanding District of Florida:

"I am just in receipt of your two letters of the sixteenth and one of the seventeenth, and am very much surprised at the tone of the latter, and the character of your plans as therein stated. You say that by the time your letter of the seventeenth should reach these headquarters, your forces would be in motion beyond Barber's, moving toward the Suwanee River, and that you shall rely upon my making a display in the Suwanee River 'with naval force, transports, and sailing vessels,' and with iron-clads up from Warsaw, etc., as a demonstration in your favor, which you look upon as of 'great importance.' All this is upon the presumption that the demonstration can and will be made, although contingent not only upon my power and disposition to do so, but upon the consent of Admiral Dahlgren, with whom I can not communicate in less than ten days. You must have forgotten my last instructions, which were for the present to hold Baldwin and the St. Mary's south prong as your outposts to the westward of Jacksonville, and to occupy Picolata and Magnolia on the St. John's.

"Your prospect distinctly and avowedly ignores these operations, and substitutes a plan which not only involves your command in a distant movement without provisions, far beyond a point from which you once withdrew on account of precisely the same necessity, but presupposes a simultaneous demonstration of 'great importance' to you elsewhere, over which you have no control, and which requires the co-operation of the navy. It is impossible for me to determine what your views are with respect to Florida matters, and this is the reason why I have endeavored to make mine known to you so fully. From your letter of the eleventh instant from Baldwin (a very singular letter, by the way, and which you did not modify or refer to at all when you afterward saw me), I extract as follows:

"'I am convinced that a movement upon Lake City is not, in the present condition of transportation, advisable, and, indeed, that what has been said of the desire of Florida to come back now is a delusion. This movement is in opposition to sound strategy,' etc.

"And again: 'The Union cause would have been far more benefited by Jeff Davis having removed this railroad to Virginia, than by any trivial or non-strategic success you may meet. By all means, therefore, fall back to Jacksonville.'

"So much from your letters of the eleventh; and yet, five days later, you propose to push forward without instructions and without provisions, with a view to destroying the railroad which you say it would have been better for Jeff Davis to have got; and furthermore, you say in your letter of the sixteenth: 'There is but little doubt in my mind (but) that the people of this state, kindly treated by us, will soon be ready to return to the Union. They are heartily tired of the war.'

"As may be supposed, I am very much confused by these conflicting views, and am thrown into doubt as to whether my intentions with regard to Florida are fully understood by you. I will, therefore, reannounce them briefly.

"1st. I desire to bring Florida into the Union under the President's proclamation of December 8th, 1863, as accessory to the above.

"2d. To revive the trade on the St. John's River.

"3d. To recruit my colored regiments, and organize a regiment of Florida white troops; and,

"4th. To cut off in part the enemy's supplies drawn from Florida.

"After you had withdrawn your advance, it was arranged between us, at a present interview, that the places to be permanently held for the present would be the south prong of the St. Mary's, Baldwin, Jacksonville, Magnolia, and Picolata, and that Henry's mounted forces should be kept moving as circumstances might justify or require. This is my plan of present operations. A raid to tear up the railroad west of Lake City will be of service, but I have no intention to occupy now that part of the state.

"Very respectfully, etc., Q. A. GILLMORE, Major General Commanding.

"ROBERT N. SCOTT, Captain of U. S. Infantry, A. D. C.

"Headquarters of the Army, Washington, March 16th, 1864."

[1] Only about half of Seymour's force was engaged, the rest being left to hold the posts on the coast and St. John's River.

and the Seventh New Hampshire is brought up to its support, and this becoming confused, the Eighth United States colored regiment comes into action, some of the men with empty guns, standing its ground with heavy loss for nearly two hours. Barton's brigade of New York troops has at length formed on the right of the line, and Colonel Montgomery, with the Fifty-fourth Massachusetts and First North Carolina (colored), has got into position on the left. All the troops, black and white, fight nobly; but their loss had already been heavy, particularly in officers. Along the railroad an uninterrupted stream of wounded men flows to the rear, and hundreds more of wounded are left behind upon the field, as the line now is driven back, having lost nearly thirteen hundred men in this brief battle. The enemy has lost little over half that number, and nothing but the exhaustion of his ammunition holds him back from pursuit.

Such was the battle of Olustee, fought against orders, and upon the enemy's chosen field. General Seymour was present in the hottest of the fight, but neither his bravery nor that of his troops could avert the disaster which followed inevitably from the very conditions of the conflict. With this defeat active operations in Florida terminated, though the Federal troops continued to hold their position upon the coast.

CHAPTER XXXIX.

THE RED RIVER CAMPAIGN.

Another semi-Political Expedition.—Diplomatic Considerations.—Apprehensions of French Intervention.—Every military Motive in favor of a Campaign against Mobile.—The Government decides in favor of a Campaign in Texas.—The Sabine Pass Expedition; its Failure.—Coast Operations.—Occupation of Brazos Santiago, November 2, 1863; of Brownsville, November 6th; of Point Isabel, November 8th; of Aransas Pass, November 17th; and of Cavallo Pass, November 19th.—Mistake made in continuing a trans-Mississippi offensive Campaign.—Halleck advises a Movement on Shreveport.—Banks's Opinion of the Conditions necessary to a successful Red River Campaign.—These Requirements not met.—Halleck leaves the whole Affair to be settled between Banks, Sherman, and Steele.—Banks ought to have decided against the Movement.—Extent of his Responsibility.—Sherman meets Banks at New Orleans.—He sends A. J. Smith's Command to General Banks.—Steele not prepared.—Kirby Smith's Command.—Banks being detained at New Orleans, General Franklin is intrusted with the immediate command of the Expedition.—Franklin reaches Alexandria March 25th, 1864.—Admiral Porter's Co-operation.—Capture of Fort De Russy.—Difficulty in getting the Gun-boats over the Rapids at Alexandria.—Dépôt established at Alexandria, and Grover's Division detached to guard it.—Ellet's Marine Brigade recalled to Vicksburg.—T. K. Smith's division used for the Protection of Transports.—The Military Branch reduced by 8500 men on account of these Detachments.—Cotton Seizures.—The Army reaches Natchitoches April 2d and 3d, while the Navy proceeds to Grand Ecore.—The Difficulty of Navigation increases.—The Advance toward Mansfield.—Skirmishing with Confederate Cavalry.—The Enemy encountered beyond Pleasant Hill.—Banks arrives at the Front and ventures an Engagement.—He makes a great Mistake.—Federal Defeat at Sabine Cross-roads.—Causes of the Disaster.—A Stand made at Pleasant Grove.—Emory repulses the Enemy and covers the Retreat.—The Retreat continued to Pleasant Hill.—Battle of Pleasant Hill, April 9th.—Importance of this Conflict.—It is decided against the Confederates.—Retreat continued to Grand Ecore.—Admiral Porter's Troubles.—The Confederate Infantry charge upon the Gun-boats, and are worsted.—The Army and Fleet return to Alexandria.—On the way General Banks defeats the Enemy at Cane River.—The Fleet can not pass the Rapids, and is relieved by Lieutenant Colonel Bailey's Dams.—The Army retreats to Simmsport.—Operations of General Steele's Co-operative Column.—Review of the military Operations in Arkansas in 1863.—Quantrell's Raid.—Capture of Little Rock by General Steele.—Steele advances upon Shreveport from the North.—A Slow March.—Fight at Prairie d'Anne.—Steele hears of Banks's Reverse, and retreats to Little Rock.—The Political Situation in Arkansas as affected by the Campaign.

FROM the Florida expedition we turn naturally to the Red River campaign. This latter was also urged by the government without much regard to its military importance. The motives which led to its inception were more complex than those which led to the Florida expedition. In addition to political reasons, there were diplomatic considerations of still greater importance. In defiance of the Monroe Doctrine—a doctrine first promulgated in President Monroe's message of December 2, 1823, and indorsed by the whole American people, and which pronounced any interference with the affairs or destiny of any portion of the New World by the powers of the Old a hostile measure to this country, "dangerous to our peace and safety"—three European nations, France, England, and Spain, had in 1861 embarked upon an expedition against Mexico. The originally declared purposes of this joint expedition had appeared to be perfectly legitimate. The civil commotions in Mexico had endangered the liberties of foreign residents in that country, and undermined the security for its large liabilities by debt to foreign powers. The expedition proposed simply to remedy these abuses. The United States government, although its grievances were greater than those of either of the allied powers, except Great Britain, had refused to participate in the expedition, but acceded the legitimacy of its objects as openly declared. Afterward, however, the character of the movement against Mexico was essentially changed. England and Spain withdrew from the alliance, and the Emperor Napoleon entered upon the execution of a scheme which was intended to revolutionize the Mexican government, and to erect an empire upon the ruins of the republic. This was a policy hostile to this country, and, taken in connection with Louis Napoleon's expressed desire to unite with the British government in the recognition of the Confederacy, excited serious apprehension. It was deemed necessary, therefore, that the Federal government should occupy and strongly hold some point in Texas, in order to meet any emergency which might arise out of this foreign complication.

Both General Banks and General Grant, after the capture of Port Hudson and Vicksburg, were in favor of an immediate expedition against Mobile. There were good military reasons for such a movement. The full reward for the sacrifice of the army which had purchased the Mississippi could only be realized by leaving the entire trans-Mississippi region—at least all below the Arkansas River—out of the field of active military operations. The navy, with the co-operation of a few small garrisons, not amounting in the aggregate to more than 20,000 men, would have held the Mississippi against any operations of the enemy. The coast of Texas should have been occupied, and held by about 10,000 men. There should also have been an army of 20,000 men to keep down guerrillas in Missouri and Arkansas, and to prevent the enemy from advancing north of the Arkansas. Thus a Federal army, amounting in all to 50,000 men, would have maintained the defensive on and west of the Mississippi, and 50,000 men[1] would thus have been liberated for the more important, because more decisive operations in Tennessee, Georgia, and Alabama. The campaign against Mobile, if it had been undertaken immediately after the opening of the Mississippi, would have accomplished four important results:

1. It would have relieved Rosecrans—then operating against Chattanooga—more effectively than any other movement could have done.
2. It would have forestalled Sherman's Meridian raid.
3. It would have resulted in the possession of Mobile and of the fertile valleys of the Alabama and Tombigbee Rivers, upon which the Confederate Army of the West mainly relied for corn, and would have secured the Mississippi River against hostile operations from the east.
4. It would have acquired the best possible base for co-operative movements in the event either of an advance of the Federal armies southward upon Atlanta, or westward from South Carolina and Florda. Its success would have justified more formidable expeditions in the two latter states in the winter of 1863–1864, and these would in turn have materially weakened Lee's army in Virginia.

These advantages were fully appreciated by General Grant. But the government decided in favor of a trans-Mississippi campaign, the motives for which were purely of a diplomatic and political character.[2] The earliest

[1] The entire Federal force west of the Mississippi numbered at least 100,000 men.

[2] For farther illustration, we copy the correspondence on this subject between Generals Banks, Halleck, and Grant.

On the 18th of July, 1863, Banks writes to Grant:

"It is my belief that Johnston, when defeated by you . . . . will fall back upon Mobile. Such is also the expectation of the rebels. The capture of Mobile is of importance, second only in the history of the war to the opening of the Mississippi. I hope you will be able to follow him. I can aid you somewhat by land and by sea, if that should be your destination. Mobile is the last strong-hold in the West and Southwest. No pains should be spared to effect its reduction."

On the 26th of July he writes to Halleck:

"There is still strength in Mobile and in Texas which will constantly threaten Louisiana, and which ought to be destroyed without delay. The possession of Mobile and the occupation of Texas would quiet the whole of the Southwest, and every effort should be made to accomplish this. Its importance can hardly be overestimated."

And again, July 30:

"Information from Mobile leads us to believe that the force at that point is now about 5000, which is engaged industriously on the land side in strengthening the position. My belief is that Johnston's forces are moving to the East, and that the garrison of Mobile will not be strengthened, unless it be by paroled men from Vicksburg and Port Hudson; while the rebel army of the East is occupied at Charleston and at Richmond by our forces, it would be impossible for them to strengthen Mobile to any great extent. It seems to be a favorable opportunity for a movement in that direction. An attack should be made by land. Troops can be transported by the river to Mobile, with the intervention of a march of 25 miles from Portersville, on the west side of the bay and the rear of the city. We have outlines of their works, and can estimate very well their strength. I am confident that a sudden movement, such as can be made with 15,000 or 20,000 men on this line, will reduce that position with certainty and without delay. The troops of the West need rest, and are incapable of long or rapid marches. It is therefore impracticable to attack Mobile except by the river and Mississippi Sound. A portion of General Grant's forces could be transported there with but little labor to themselves, and the place could be invested before the enemy could anticipate our movement."

On August 1 he writes:

"The possession of Mobile gives the government the control of the Alabama River and the line of railways east and west from Charleston and Savannah to Vicksburg, *via* Montgomery, and places the whole of the State of Mississippi and Southern Alabama in position to return to the Union. If the rebel government loses this position, it has no outlet to the Gulf except Galveston. The operation need not last more than 30 days, and can scarcely interfere with any other movements East or West. I understand it to meet with General Grant's approval, if it be consistent with the general plans of the government, upon which condition only I urge it."

August 10, Banks writes to Grant:

"I have the honor to inclose you some memoranda concerning Mobile. I still think it of the utmost moment that that post should be in our hands. Except for Johnston's army, we should have no difficulty. He seems to occupy a position intended to cover Mobile, and if he is in force 30,000 or 40,000 strong, as I suppose, he could embarrass the operations against that point very seriously. I am unable, however, to see how he can hold his position in the Southwest with Rosecrans's army pressing down upon the rebel centre. A line extending from Mobile to Richmond, in the present shattered condition of the rebel armies—the right, centre, and left having been disastrously defeated—it seems to me impossible that they can maintain their positions if Rosecrans, with a heavy force, pushes down upon their centre, or if Charleston shall fall into our hands through the operations of the fleet and army combined. A successful movement in either direction, from Charleston or by Rosecrans, will cut their centre, and place Bragg and Johnston with their forces between the troops under Rosecrans, your troops, and mine at New Orleans. I do not believe that that condition of things can be maintained."

Halleck, on the 12th of August, replies to Banks's dispatches in regard to Mobile:

"I fully appreciate the importance of the operation proposed by you in these dispatches, but *there are reasons other than military* why those heretofore directed should be undertaken first. On this matter we have no choice, but must carry out the views of the government."

The operations "heretofore directed" were against Texas.

On the 8th of January, 1864, Halleck writes to Grant:

"In regard to General Banks's campaign against Texas, it is proper to remark that it was undertaken *less for military reasons than as a matter of state policy. As a military measure simply, it perhaps presented less advantage than a movement on Mobile and the Alabama River, so as to threaten the enemy's interior lines, and effect a diversion in favor of our armies at Chattanooga and in East Tennessee.* But, however this may have been, it was deemed necessary, as a matter of political or state policy connected with our foreign relations, and especially with France and Mexico, that our troops should occupy and hold at least a portion of Texas. The President so considered, for reasons satisfactory to himself and to his cabinet, and it was therefore unnecessary for us to inquire whether or not the troops could have been employed elsewhere with greater military advantage."

When General Banks assumed the command of the Gulf Department, his instructions from General Halleck (dated November 9, 1862) allude to operations to be undertaken after the opening of the Mississippi in the following terms:

"The river being opened, the question arises how the troops and naval forces there can be employed to the best advantage. Two objects are suggested as worthy of your attention:

"First, on the capture of Vicksburg, to send a military force directly East to destroy the railroads at Jackson and Marion, and thus cut off all connection by rail between Northern Mississippi and Mobile and Atlanta. The latter place is now the chief military dépôt of the rebel armies in the West.

"Second, To ascend, with a naval and military force, the Red River as far as it is navigable, and thus open an outlet for the sugar and cotton of Northern Louisiana. Possibly both of these objects may be accomplished, if the circumstances should be favorable. It is also suggested that, having Red River in our possession, it would form the best base for operations in Texas."

On July 24, 1863, Halleck writes to Banks:

"I suppose the first thing done by your army, after the fall of Port Hudson, was to clean out the Teche and Atchafalaya counties. That being accomplished, your next operations must depend very much upon the then condition of affairs. Texas and Mobile will present themselves to your attention. The navy are very anxious for an attack upon the latter place, but I think Tex-

NATHANIEL P. BANKS.

instructions which General Banks received, pointing to Texas as the immediate field of operations, were issued during the last week in July, 1863, shortly after the reduction of Port Hudson. They were not definite as to

the plan to be pursued, insisting only upon the occupation of some portion of Texas. Distinctly permission was given Banks to choose his own objective. The movement was again urged in a dispatch from Halleck, dated

as much the most important. It is possible that Johnston may fall back toward Mobile, but I think he will unite with Bragg. While your army is engaged in cleaning out Southwestern Louisiana, every preparation should be made for an expedition into Texas. Should Johnston be driven from Mississippi, General Grant can send you considerable re-enforcements."

July 31, 1863, he writes:

"It is important that we immediately occupy some point or points in Texas. Whether the movement should be made by land or water is not yet decided. . . . . . . If by water, Admiral Farragut will co-operate. The Navy Department recommends Indianola as the point of landing. It seems to me that this point is too distant, as it will leave the expedition isolated from New Orleans. If the landing can be made at Galveston, the country between that place and New Orleans can soon be cleared out, and the enemy be prevented from operating successively upon those places. In other words, you can venture to send a larger force to Galveston than to Indianola. I merely throw out these suggestions, without deciding upon any definite plan till I receive your answer to the former dispatch" [that of July 24].

On the 6th of August Halleck sends the following dispatch to Banks, via Vicksburg:

"There are important reasons why our flag should be restored in some point of Texas with the least possible delay. Do this by land, at Galveston, at Indianola, or at any other point you may deem preferable. If by sea, Admiral Farragut will co-operate. There are reasons why the movement should be as prompt as possible."

On the 10th, four days later, Halleck explains this order thus:

"That order, as I understood it at the time, was of a diplomatic rather than of a military char-

acter, and resulted from some European complications, or, more properly speaking, was intended to prevent such complications."

Perhaps the following from General Banks to Halleck, August 17, 1863, will throw some light upon the nature of these "foreign" complications:

"I think it my duty to represent that among the French residents of this city [New Orleans] there is evidently an expectation of some assistance from the government of France. This comes informally from the conversation of the French residents here, but too frequently to leave room for doubt that they have some grounds upon which to ground the remarks that are commonly made. This is undoubtedly the conversation of the officers of the French frigate Catinet, which has recently arrived at this port. I do not think it is more than mere surmise on their part, but have thought it worth while to direct the provost-marshal general of the department to investigate the subject and to report the facts as they are, of which I shall give you due notice."

August 20, Halleck writes:

"Mexican and French complications render it exceedingly important that the movement ordered against Texas should be undertaken without delay."

On the 28th he writes:

"Your note in regard to reports in New Orleans respecting French intervention only confirms what we have already received from other sources. While observing every caution to give no cause of offense to that government, it will be necessary to carefully observe the movements of its fleets, and to be continually on your guard. You will readily perceive the object of our immediately occupying some part of Texas."

August 6th, and Admiral Farragut's co-operation was promised, if the attack should be upon the coast. General Banks immediately made preparations for a movement against Houston by way of Sabine Pass. Grant, in obedience to orders from Washington, now sent the Thirteenth Corps to the Department of the Gulf. Including these re-enforcements, Banks had by the first of September an army of 30,000 men.[1]

If the reader will examine the map of Texas, he will find that state intersected by rivers—the Neches, Trinidad, San Jacinto, Brazos, Colorado, Guadalupe, San Antonio, and Nueces—which run from the elevated region of Northern Texas into the Gulf. The Red River, forming the northern boundary of the state, runs through Louisiana into the Mississippi; while the Rio Grande, separating Texas from Mexico, flows into the Gulf. On the eastern or Louisiana border runs the Sabine River, emptying, as does also the Neches, into Lake Sabine, which, by a narrow pass of the same name, communicates with the Gulf. From Sabine Pass, at the eastern extremity of the Texan coast, to Brazos Santiago, near the mouth of the Rio Grande, is about 375 miles. About 70 miles west of Sabine Pass is the entrance to Galveston Bay, which receives the waters of the Trinidad. Galveston Island stretches from the entrance of the harbor some 30 miles southwesterly. Houston lies west of Galveston Bay, about 40 miles inland, and by its central position as the junction of all the roads between the bay and the Rio Brazos, commands Galveston and the large and fertile district south of Montgomery. From the entrance to Galveston Bay to Velasco, the mouth of the Rio Brazos, is about 40 miles; following down the coast from this point, we reach Cavallo Pass, the entrance to Matagorda Bay, with which Aransas Bay communicates, the inlet to the latter being distant about 50

miles from Cavallo Pass. Into Aransas Bay flows the Guadalupe and San Antonio Rivers. Corpus Christi Bay, shut out from the gulf by Mustang Island, joins Aransas. From its inlet to Brazos Santiago is about 90 miles. Forty miles up the Rio Grande lies Brownsville, opposite Matamoras. The population and the commerce of the state is concentrated in a belt of counties along the Red and Sabine Rivers and the coast. This belt is narrow on the north and east as far as Shelbyville, where it widens, and from the coast stretches inland from 150 to 200 miles. It will readily be seen that the occupation of this coast by the Federal forces would command the most valuable portion of Texas, while it would also fully meet the peculiar diplomatic emergency which then confronted the government.[1]

The expedition sailed from New Orleans on the 5th of September, under the command of Major General W. B. Franklin. The military force consisted of 5000 men of the Nineteenth Corps, the number being limited to suit the means of transportation at hand. The naval force consisted of four light-draught gun-boats—the Clifton, Arizona, Sachem, and Granite City—under the command of Lieutenant Crocker. The aim of the expedition was to secure Sabine City at the mouth of Sabine River. The Pass was strongly protected by works, and the only chance of piercing or capturing these was by surprising the enemy. It was supposed that the defenses of these works consisted of two 34-pounders, a battery of field-pieces, and two boats converted into rams. The arrangement made between the naval and military commanders contemplated an attack at early dawn on the morning of

---

[1] Report on the Conduct of the War, Red River Campaign, p. 3.

[1] "The occupation of Houston would place in our hands the control of all the railway communications with Texas; give us command of the most populous and productive part of the state; enable us to move at any moment into the interior in any direction, or to fall back upon the island of Galveston, which could be maintained with a very small force, holding the enemy upon the coast of Texas, and leaving the Army of the Gulf free to move upon Mobile, in accordance with my original plan, or wherever it should be required."—Banks's Report.

MAP OF LOUISIANA

September 7th by the gun-boats, assisted by about 180 sharp-shooters from the army. After driving the enemy from the works, and repulsing the rams, the troops were to land under cover of the gun-boats, and capture the town. The gun-boats, originally lightly-built merchant vessels, were mere shells as against a well-defended fortress, and it was not expected that they would have any such encounter. If resistance was offered, General Franklin was instructed to land his troops ten or twelve miles below the Pass, and advance by land against the fortifications.[1]

The plan proposed was not carried out, and the expedition proved an utter failure. There was over a day's delay in getting into position, and for 28 hours the fleet was open to the observation of the enemy, who was thus given abundant time for preparation. Captain Crocker, with foolhardy daring, ventured upon a direct attack at 3 P.M. on the 8th. Of course the gun-boats were unable to make any impression upon the works. At 6 A.M. the Clifton stood in the bay, and opened upon the fort, which deigned no reply. The other boats soon followed, and in the afternoon the Sachem, followed by the Arizona, advanced up the eastern channel of the Pass to draw the fire of the fort, while the Clifton and Granite City moved up the western channel to cover the landing of a division under General Weitzel. The fort was silent until the gun-boats were clean abreast of it, when a fire was opened upon them from eight guns. The Clifton on one side, and the Sachem on the other, ran aground in the shallow water under the enemy's guns, and, being disabled, were compelled to surrender. The garrison of the fort consisted only of 47 men—not more than sufficient to man the guns—but it did its work as efficiently as if it had numbered a thousand. It was with great difficulty that the Arizona and Granite City escaped. With these vessels Franklin probably might still have landed the expedition below the pass, but no such attempt was made, and the troops returned on the 11th to New Orleans.[2]

The concentration of the enemy forbade any attempt to repeat the movement. Banks now directed his attention to the chances for a movement overland into Texas, either across Southern Louisiana to the Sabine, or up the Red River to Shreveport. For this purpose his troops were rapidly transferred to the Bayou Teche region. But neither of the movements in view were found practicable. That from the Teche to the Sabine proceeded over a barren country, with little water, for a distance of 300 miles from New Orleans. The route to Shreveport was 200 miles longer, through a country equally destitute of supplies, having been repeatedly overrun by both armies, and occupied by a hostile population. In either movement the army must depend entirely upon wagon transportation.

In the mean time General Herron had been sent to Morganzia, on the Mississippi, above Port Hudson, but on the opposite side. He had established a post several miles inland, garrisoned with about 700 men, under command of Major Montgomery. On the night of September 30th this force was surprised by a detachment of the enemy, who crossed the bayou, surrounded the Federal camp, and captured the artillery and 400 infantry.

The government urged the prompt occupation "of some point in Texas." If it could not be by land, it must be by sea. Accordingly, General Banks again turned to the coast, and organized a small expedition, to be under the command of Major General N. J. T. Dana, for the occupation of the lower Rio Grande. The concentration of the enemy in the southeastern part of Texas seemed to favor this movement.

Dana's expedition, consisting of 4000 men and three gun-boats—the Monongahela, Virginia, and Owasco—and accompanied by General Banks, left New Orleans October 26th. The all-important affair of raising the flag on some portion of the soil of Texas was at length accomplished on the 2d of November. On that day Brazos Santiago was occupied, and on the next the enemy was driven from his position, and the troops ordered up the Rio Grande to Brownsville, which was occupied without resistance on the 6th. The establishment of communications with the mouth of the river was assisted by the friendly offices of the Mexican government, who furnished boats for this purpose. General Dana was left in command of Brownsville, and Banks began to operate against the coast adjacent to Brazos. Point Isabel was occupied on the 8th, and by means of boats troops were transported to Mustang Island, off Corpus Christi Bay. Aransas Pass, east of this island, was occupied on the 17th by a detachment under General T. E. G. Ransom, the works defending the point having been taken by assault, with 100 prisoners and three guns. On the 19th General C. C. Washburne, of the Thirteenth Corps, moved upon Pass Cavallo, commanding the entrance to Matagorda Bay, and defended by strong works and a force of about 2000 men. Fort Esperanza was invested, and, after a brief but gallant resistance, the enemy blew up his magazines, partially dismantled the works, and evacuated the position, retreating to the main land by way of the peninsula near the mouth of Rio Brazos.

Thus, in about three weeks from the occupation of the mouth of the Rio Grande, General Banks was in possession of the whole coast of Texas, with the exception of the works at the mouth of Rio Brazos and the island of Galveston, which were still firmly held by the enemy, who would not abandon them without a desperate struggle. In order to gain possession of these remaining points on the coast—more important than all the others combined—it would be necessary to move inland, and attack them from the rear. In this case the enemy must be encountered in full force. At this point the misfortune of Franklin's failure to obtain Sabine City was painfully evident

[1] *Banks's Report.* These instructions must have been verbal. The written orders allude to no other than a direct attack.

[2] "Had a landing been effected, even after the loss of the boats, in accordance with the original plan, the success of the movement would have been complete, both as it regarded the occupation of Sabine Pass, and operations against Houston and Galveston. The enemy had at this time all his forces in that quarter, and less than a hundred men on the Sabine."—*Banks's Report.*

in its full extent, and the regret which it occasioned General Banks was intense and lasting. Still he felt confident that, by withdrawing the forces which he had left in the Teche region to the coast, he might succeed in his cherished plans against Houston and Galveston. He asked Halleck for re-enforcements to secure this object, which he deemed of the utmost importance.[1]

All the diplomatic or political measures involved in General Banks's Texas campaign had been successfully carried out. Henceforth the problem was purely military. Unquestionably the best solution of this problem would have been upon the theory of a defensive trans-Mississippi campaign. Upon this theory General Banks would have been allowed to complete his operations against Galveston, and after that would have simply held the coast of Texas with a few small garrisons, and so much of the Teche country as would suffice for the protection of New Orleans on the western side. The remainder of his army, with as many troops from the armies north of the Arkansas as could be spared after guarding against Kirby Smith's advance north of that river, would have been withdrawn to the east of the Mississippi, where they would have been occupied in offensive operations: first, during the winter, in conjunction with Sherman's troops, against Mobile, and the railroads connecting Atlanta with Montgomery in Alabama, and with Tallahassee in Florida; and, secondly, in the spring of 1864 against Atlanta, co-operating with the army advancing upon that point from Chattanooga. No greater military mistake could have been made than that which was involved in an *offensive* trans-Mississippi campaign. By such a campaign all that had been gained strategically by the possession of the Mississippi River would be thrown away. For what *was* the real strategic importance of this possession except in so far as it made the trans-Mississippi region, then in the hands of the enemy, and also the trans-Mississippi armies of the Confederacy, of as little worth to the Confederacy as if they had not existed? But to send large Federal armies into this region for offensive operations was to neutralize the vast advantage gained by this isolation—was to give the trans-Mississippi territory all the value to the Confederacy which it could possibly have had if the great river had still remained within Confederate control.

It was precisely this mistake which the government now insisted upon making. While General Banks was perfecting his plans for the capture of Galveston, he was diverted from that movement by the urgency with which preparations for an advance up the Red River were recommended by Halleck and other officers.[2] As we have seen, the political designs of the cam-

[1] "I intended to withdraw my troops to the island of Galveston, which could have been held with perfect security by less than 1000 men, which would have left me free to resume operations, suggested in August and September, against Mobile. The Rio Grande and the island of Galveston could have been held with 2000 or 3000 men. This would have cut off the contraband trade of the enemy at Matamoras and on the Texas coast. The forces occupying the island of Galveston could have been strengthened by sea at any moment from Berwick's Bay, connecting with New Orleans by railway or by the river, compelling the enemy to maintain an army near Houston, and preventing his concentrating his forces for the invasion of Louisiana, Arkansas, or Missouri. The occupation of the Rio Grande, Galveston, and Mobile would have led to the capture or destruction of all the enemy's river and sea transportation on the Gulf coast, and left the Western Gulf blockading squadron, numbering 150 vessels, and mounting 450 guns, free to pursue the pirates that infested our coast and preyed upon our commerce. The army would have been at liberty to operate on the Mississippi, or to co-operate with the Army of the Tennessee by the Alabama River and Montgomery in the campaign against Atlanta. . . . . It would have enabled the government to concentrate the entire forces of the Department of the Gulf, as occasion might require, at any point on the river or coast, against an enemy without water transportation or other means of operation than by heavy land marches, or to move by land into the rebel states east or west of the Mississippi. The winter months offered a favorable opportunity for such enterprise."—*Banks's Report.*

[2] In order to illustrate the details of the inception of the Red River campaign more fully than is possible in the text, we give the substance of the correspondence submitted as evidence before the Committee on the Conduct of the War. General Halleck, from the beginning, was partial to operations on the line of the Red River as preferable to movements on the Texan coast.

August 10, 1863, he writes:

"In my opinion, neither Indianola nor Galveston is the proper point of attack. If it is necessary, as urged by Mr. Seward, that the flag be restored to *some one point* in Texas, that can be best and most safely effected by a combined military and naval movement up the Red River to Alexandria, Natchitoches, or Shreveport, and the military occupation of Northern Texas. This would be merely carrying out the plan proposed by you at the beginning of the campaign [the beginning of the Louisiana campaign, in the spring of 1863], and, in my opinion, far superior in its military character to the occupation of Galveston or Indianola. Nevertheless, your choice is left unrestricted. In the first place, by adopting the line of the Red River you retain your connection with your own base, and separate still more the two points of the rebel confederacy. Moreover, you cut Northern Louisiana and Southern Arkansas entirely off from supplies and re-enforcements from Texas. They are already cut off from the rebel states east of the Mississippi. If you occupy Galveston or Indianola you divide your own troops, and enable the enemy to concentrate all his forces upon either of these points, or on New Orleans."

To this Banks replies, August 26:

"To enter Texas from Alexandria or Shreveport would bring us at the nearest point to Hernville, in Sabine county, or Marshall, in Harrison, due west of Alexandria and Shreveport respectively. These points are accessible only by heavy marches, for which the troops are hardly prepared at this season of the year; and the points occupied would attract but little attention; and if our purpose was to penetrate farther into the interior, they would become exposed to sudden attacks of the enemy, and defensible only by a strong and permanent force of troops.

"The serious objection to moving on this line in the present condition of the forces of this department is the distance it carries us from New Orleans—our base of operations necessarily—and the great difficulty and the length of time required to return, if the exigencies of the service should demand, which is quite possible. In the event of long absence, Johnston threatens us from the East. The enemy will concentrate between Alexandria and Franklin, on the Teche, until our purpose is developed. As soon as we move any distance, they will operate against the river and New Orleans. It is true we could follow up such a movement by falling on their rear, but that would compel us to abandon the position in Texas, or leave it exposed with but slender defenses and garrison. This view is based, as you will see, upon the impossibility of moving even to Alexandria, at the present low stage of the rivers, by water, and the inability of the troops to accomplish extended marches."

September 30, after the failure of the Sabine Pass Expedition, General Halleck writes:

"The failure of the attempt to land at Sabine is only another of the numerous examples of the uncertain and unreliable character of maritime descents. The chances are against their success."

General Banks writes, October 16:

"The movement upon Shreveport and Marshall is impracticable at present. It would require a march from Brashear City of between four hundred and five hundred miles. The enemy destroying all supplies in the country as he retreats, and the low stage of the water making it impossible for us to avail ourselves of any water communications, except upon the Teche as far as Vermillionville, it requires communication for this distance by wagon trains. Later in the season this can be done, making Alexandria the base of operations; but it could not be done now. The rivers and bayous have not been so low in this state for fifty years, and Admiral Porter informs me that the mouth of the Red River, and also the mouth of the Atchafalaya, are both hermetically sealed to his vessels by almost dry sand-bars, so that he can not get any vessels into any of the streams. It is supposed that the first rise of the season will occur early in the next month."

The following, from General Halleck to Banks, December 7, 1863, could only be construed by the latter as a censure of his coast operations:

THE ATTACK ON SABINE PASS.

LANDING OF BANKS'S EXPEDITION ON BRAZOS SANTIAGO.

CONFEDERATE EVACUATION OF BROWNSVILLE.

paign had been effected. Both General Grant and General Banks would then have preferred, after securing Galveston, that all the troops which could be spared from the Department of the Gulf should be withdrawn to the east side of the Mississippi for operations against Mobile. General

"In regard to your 'Sabine' and 'Rio Grande' expeditions, no notices of your intention to make them were received here till they were actually undertaken. The danger, however, of dividing your army, with the enemy between the two posts, ready to fall upon either with his entire force, was pointed out from the first, and I have continually urged that you must not expect any considerable re-enforcements from other departments."

To this Banks replies, December 23:

"My orders from the department were to establish the flag of the government in Texas at the earliest possible moment. I understood that the point and the means were left at my discretion. It was implied, if not stated, that time was an element of great importance in this matter, and that the object should be accomplished as speedily as possible. In addition to the instructions received from your department upon this subject, the President addressed me a letter, borne by Brigadier General Hamilton, military governor of Texas, dated September 19, 1863, in which he expressed the hope that I had already accomplished the object so much desired. In the execution of this order, my first desire was to obtain possession of Houston; and the expedition which failed to effect a landing at the Sabine was designed to secure that object. The failure of that expedition made it impossible to secure a landing at that point. I immediately concentrated all my disposable force upon the Teche, with a view to enter Texas by the way of Niblett's Bluff, on the Sabine, or by Alexandria, at some more northern point. The low stage of water in all the rivers, and the exhaustion of supplies in that country, made it apparent that this route was impracticable at this season of the year—I might say impossible within any reasonable time—and it would be accomplished by imminent peril, owing to the condition of the country, the length of marches, and the strength of the enemy, making this certain by thorough reconnoissance of the country; but, without withdrawing my troops, I concluded to make another effort to effect a landing at some point upon the coast of Texas, in the execution of what I understood to be imperative orders. For this purpose I withdrew a small force stationed at Morganzia, on the Mississippi, which had been under command of General Herron, and was then under Major General Dana, and put them in a state of preparation for this movement.

"Assisted by the commander of the naval forces, Commodore Bell, I directed a reconnoissance of the coast of Texas as far as Brazos Santiago, making my movements entirely dependent upon that report. A return from this reconnoissance was made October 16, and my troops being in readiness for movement somewhere, without the delay of a single day, except that which the state of the weather made necessary, I moved for the Brazos. You will see from these facts that it was impossible for me to give you sufficient notice of this intention to receive instructions from you upon this subject; but as soon as I had received the information necessary, or arrived at the determination to land at the Brazos, I gave you full information of all the facts in the case. It is my purpose always to keep you informed of all movements that are contemplated in this department, but it did not seem to me to be possible to do more in this instance; and, upon a review of the circumstances, I can not now see where or when I could have given you more complete and satisfactory information than my dispatches conveyed.

"I repeat my suggestion that the best line of defense for Louisiana, as well as for operations against Texas, is by Berwick's Bay and the Atchafalaya, and I also recall the suggestions made by you upon the same subject. But that line was impracticable at the time when I received your orders upon the subject of Texas. I ought to add that the line of the Atchafalaya is available for offensive or defensive purposes only when the state of the water admits the operations of a strong naval force. At the time when I made this suggestion to you it was impossible to get a boat into the Atchafalaya, either from Red River or from the Gulf, owing to the low stage of the water, and there were very few, if any, boats on the Mississippi or in this department that could have navigated these waters at that time. It was therefore impossible to avail myself of this natural line—first, for the reason that we had not sufficient naval force for this purpose, and that the navigation was impossible. As soon as the Mississippi and Red Rivers shall rise, the government can make available the advantages presented by this line of water communication."

A week later Banks again writes, urging the importance of the capture of Galveston before entering upon the Red River campaign:

"It is my desire, if possible, to get possession of Galveston. This, if effected, will give us control of the entire coast of Texas, and require but two small garrisons, one on the Rio Grande, and the other on Galveston Island, unless it be the wish of the Department of War that extensive operations should be made in the State of Texas. A sufficient number of men can probably be recruited in that state for the permanent occupation of these two posts. It will relieve a very large number of naval vessels, whose service is now indispensable to us, on the Mississippi and in the Gulf. This can occupy but a short time, and, if executed, will leave my whole force in hand to move to any other point on the Red River, or wherever the government may direct. Once possessed of Galveston, and my command ready for operation in any other direction, I shall await the orders of the government; but I trust that this may be accomplished before undertaking any other enterprise. It is impossible, at this time, to move as far north as Alexandria by water. The Red River is not open to the navigation of our gun-boats, and it is commanded by Fort De Russy, which has been remounted since our occupation of Alexandria. This position must be turned by means of a large force on land before the gun-boats can pass. To co-operate with General Steele in Arkansas, or north of the Red River, will bring nearly the whole rebel force of Texas and Louisiana between New Orleans and my command, without the possibility of dispersing or defeating them, as their movement would be directed south, and mine to the north. It is necessary that this force should first be dispersed or destroyed before I can safely operate in conjunction with General Steele. Once possessed of the coast of Texas, and the naval and land forces relieved, I can then operate against the forces in Louisiana or Texas, and I can disperse or destroy the land forces in Louisiana, and safely co-operate with General Steele, or with any other portion of the army of the United States. It was in this manner that we captured Port Hudson. It would have been impracticable to proceed against Port Hudson from the Mississippi without having first dispersed the army of Texas and Louisiana on the west of that river.

"I bear in mind the danger consequent upon the division of forces, but must suggest to you that my department is extended, and many posts must be occupied; and while I would be very glad to keep my forces concentrated, it is impossible to do so. The orders of the government seemed to be peremptory that I was to occupy a position in Texas, and those which I have in view, Brownsville and Galveston, required as little force as any other positions in that state. To this fact it may be added that there were supplies and recruits which can not be found in any other portion of this department. In all my operations you may rely upon the bulk of my forces being kept together, and prepared for any movements of the enemy. It is possible, but not probable, that they may make a successful assault upon some of the isolated positions. We shall endeavor to prevent this by all possible means. I repeat, that in any movements in which I engage I shall concentrate the available forces of my command, and peril nothing by an unnecessary division. * * * * * *

"The true line of occupation, in my judgment, offensive and defensive, for this department is the Atchafalaya and the Mississippi. The Teche country, and that between the Atchafalaya and the Mississippi, can be defended only by the assistance of the navy. It is impossible for land forces to operate on that line successfully without the assistance of gun-boats. The best position that we could occupy will be to defend this line by the aid of a strong naval force of light and heavy draught gun-boats for the different waters in which they may operate, and the disposable land forces so held as to be able to move from one point to another in a body. We should then have one complete line of water navigation from the Rio Grande to Alexandria or Shreveport during the winter and spring, and from the mouth of the Mississippi to Key West, in the Gulf, and could throw our entire force against any point of the territory occupied by the enemy, without the possibility of their anticipating our movements or purposes. I am endeavoring constantly to secure means for offensive and defensive war upon this plan, and am confident that it can be very speedily accomplished."

Halleck, in his reply to Banks, January 11, 1864, makes no allusion to Galveston. He says:

"I am assured by the Navy Department that Admiral Porter will be prepared to co-operate with you as soon as the stage of the water in the Southwest will admit of the use of his flotilla there. General Steele's command is now under the general orders of General Grant, and it is hoped that he and General Sherman may also be able to co-operate with you at an early day. General Sherman is now on the Mississippi River, and General Grant expects to soon be able to re-enforce him. . . . . It has never been expected that your troops would operate north of the Red River, unless the rebel forces in Texas should be withdrawn into Arkansas; but it was proposed that General Steele should advance to Red River if he could rely upon your co-operation, and he could be certain of receiving supplies upon that line. Being uncertain on these points, he determined not to attempt an advance, but to occupy the Arkansas River as his line of defense.

"The best military opinions of the generals in the West seem to favor operations on the Red River, provided the stage of water will enable gun-boats to co-operate. I presume General Sherman will communicate with you on this subject. If the rebels could be driven south of that river, it would serve as a shorter and better line of defense for Arkansas and Missouri than that now occupied by General Steele; moreover, it would open to us the cotton and slaves of Northeastern Louisiana and Southern Arkansas. I am inclined to think that this opens a better field of operations than any other for such troops as General Grant can spare during the winter. I have written to him and also to General Steele upon the subject."

General Banks, it will be remembered, has all along conceded that the line of the Red River was the best base of operations against Texas, but it was only practicable at high water. There were also some important difficulties connected with an advance by this route which he considered it his duty to lay before General Halleck. Hence the following correspondence. Jan. 23 he writes:

"*With the forces you propose*, I concur in your opinion, and with Generals Sherman and Steele, 'that the Red River is the shortest and best line of defense for Louisiana and Arkansas, and as a base of operations against Texas,' but it would be too much for General Steele or myself to undertake separately. With our united forces, and the assistance of General Sherman, the success of movements on that line will be certain and important. I shall most cordially co-operate with them in executing your orders. With my own command I can operate with safety only on the coast of Texas, but from the coast I could not penetrate far into the interior, nor secure control of more than the country west of San Antonio. On the other line, *with commensurate forces*, the whole state, as well as Arkansas and Louisiana, will be ours, and their people will gladly renew allegiance to the government. The occupation of Shreveport will be to the country west of the Mississippi what that of Chattanooga is to the east, and as soon as this can be accomplished the country west of Shreveport will be in condition for a movement into Texas. I have written to General Sherman and General Steele in accordance with these views, and shall be ready to act with them as soon as the Atchafalaya and Red River will admit the navigation of our gun-boats. Our supplies can be transported by the Red River until April, at least. In the mean time, the railway from Vicksburg to Shreveport ought to be completed, which would furnish communication very comfortably for the whole of Eastern Texas. I do not mean that operations should be deferred for this purpose, but, as an ultimate advantage in the occupation of these states and the establishment of governments, it would be of great importance.

"I inclose to you with this communication a very complete map of the Red River country and Texas, which embraces all the information we have been able to obtain up to this time. It has been prepared by Major D. C. Houston, of the Engineer Corps, and will show that we have not overlooked the importance of this line. Accompanying this map is a memorial which exhibits the difficulties that are to be overcome. To this I respectfully invite your attention. I have sent to General Sherman and General Steele copies of this map.

"I shall be ready to move on Alexandria as soon as the rivers are up, most probably marching by Opelousas. This will be necessary to turn the forts on the Red River and open the way for the gun-boats. From that point I can operate with General Steele, north or south of Red River, in the direction of Shreveport, or from thence await your instruction. I do not think operations will be delayed on my account. I have received a dispatch from General Sherman, in which he expresses a wish to enter upon the campaign, but had not at that time received orders upon the subject. . . . . I can concentrate on Red River all my force available for active service, except the garrisons at Matagorda and Brownsville, which will be small."

He adds, January 29:

"I shall be ready to operate with General Sherman and General Steele as soon as I receive definite information of the time when they will be ready to move. I can take possession of Alexandria at any time, but could not maintain the position without the support of the forces on the upper river. . . . . Pending information and orders in regard to the movement on Red River, but little change has occurred in the position of troops. . . . . Anxiously waiting information and instructions in regard to operations on Red River, I have done nothing in Texas except provide for the security of the positions held."

The following is a copy of Major Houston's memorial, dated January 22, 1864:

"I have the honor to submit the following information concerning the routes from the Mississippi to the interior of Texas:

"*Table of Distances.*

	Miles.		Miles.
Brashear City to Alexandria	174	Little Rock to Shreveport	225
Brashear City to Shreveport	344	Fort Smith to Shreveport	300
Natchez to Alexandria (*via* Harrisonburg)	80	Alexandria to Shreveport	170
Natchez to Natchitoches	120	Alexandria to Houston	270
Vicksburg to Shreveport	148	Shreveport to Houston	295

"The water *via* Red River commences falling about the 1st of May, and the navigation of the river for most of our gun-boats and transports is not reliable after that time. The months of March and April are unfavorable for operations in Northern and Eastern Texas, owing to the high stage of water in the Sabine, Nueces [meant for Neches], and Trinity [Trinidad] Rivers and their tributaries, and the overflow to which their banks are subject. The concentration of all the forces available for operations west of the Mississippi, in the vicinity of Shreveport, requires that the line of supply with the Mississippi be kept up. It would not be practicable to abandon the base with so large a force, with a line of operations of three hundred miles through a country occupied by the enemy to be overcome before communication could possibly be effected with points held by us on the coast. The water communication to Alexandria can not be depended on after the 1st of May, and it would be necessary to depend on the road from Natchez, a distance of eighty miles, and possibly from Harrisonburg, a distance of fifty miles.

"Boats of a very light draught, say three or three and a half feet of water, may go to Alexandria during low water at ordinary seasons, but the larger majority of our boats and gun-boats are of greater draught than this.

"The most reliable route would be by railroad from Vicksburg to Shreveport. The track is now laid from Vicksburg to Monroe. The road is graded from Monroe to Shreveport, and mostly bridged; the distance is ninety-six miles. There is a good wagon-road from Monroe to Shreveport, crossing the Washita River and other streams. It would require at least three months to rebuild this railroad, which is indispensable to the supply of our army in Northeastern Texas.

"To insure success and permanent results to the operations of a force to operate against Texas, or rather against the rebel forces west of the Mississippi, it is essential that the forces available for this purpose, viz., those now west of the Mississippi, and any additional forces that may be assigned, *should be placed under the command of a single general.* The rebel forces west of the Mississippi have a single head, and so should the force operating against them.

"*Preparations should be made to establish a line of supply independent of the water-courses*, otherwise, by the time the forces are concentrated and ready to move forward, they will be compelled to halt until a new line of supply is established, thus giving the enemy a breathing spell, and an opportunity to harass our communications with their mounted troops. It is of vital importance in operations of this kind, where the distances traveled are so great, that there should be no delays, for our main security against raids on our communications consists in keeping the enemy so well occupied in taking care of himself that he will have no time or opportunity to trouble us. Hence the importance of thorough preparation and perfect concert of action among the different corps.

"Suppose it is determined to concentrate the forces near Shreveport preliminary to a movement into Texas. This point is the principal dépôt of the enemy west of the Mississippi. There are some machine-shops and dock-yards there, and the place is fortified by a line of works with a radius of two or three miles. The position is a strong one, being on a bluff, and commanding the eastern bank. This point suggests itself at once as the proper one for such a concentration. *The most direct and only reliable line of supply to this point would be the road from Vicksburg to Monroe*—railroad as far as Monroe, fifty-two miles, and a graded road the rest of the way, ninety-six miles. It would be necessary to put the road in running order, and procure materials for completing the road. The security of this road requires that the enemy be driven out of Northern Louisiana and Southern Arkansas. This line could be held more easily than the Red River, which is very narrow and crooked, and has in many places high bluff banks, where field artillery could be placed to enfilade the channels, and have no fear of gun-boats. Such a point is Grand Ecore, where the bluff is one hundred and twenty feet high. This point, I have been informed by spies, is fortified. Concerning the mode of uniting the forces near Shreveport, I will mention no details, as it will depend much upon the enemy's movements and the character of the routes in Southern Arkansas, which I have not had time to examine fully. Our forces there have doubtless the information necessary to arrange this matter. These movements, however, should be so arranged as to drive the enemy out of Arkansas and Northern Louisiana.

"I anticipate no danger from any large force moving on New Orleans, Louisiana, from Texas. In case of this movement, our forces would immediately come in on the rear of this force and cut it off.

"The enemy will, I think, be unable to interfere seriously with our concentration of troops, and will then mass his whole force, except that at Galveston, near Shreveport, where he will fight, or retire on the line he may select.

"Suppose our force to be united at Shreveport, which would probably be effected during the season of high water, and that arrangements have been perfected to supply the army by the road from Vicksburg *via* Monroe, Arkansas and Louisiana clear of rebels, and the enemy in retreat. I assume that he will do this, as our forces should be much larger than his, and that he will continue to retreat, knowing that we will be weakened thereby, while he can select a defensive position far from our base. Whatever way he takes we must follow, and expect to have our path disputed at every point, as he will be driven to desperate efforts. The numerous streams with high banks will afford him a favorable opportunity to retard our progress and effect a secure retreat to any point he may select.

"Our subsequent movements can not well be foreseen. It does not seem probable that the enemy will retire to Houston unless his force is large, and he should propose to draw us into a trap. It is more probable that he will retire farther west, and use his cavalry to harass our flanks and rear, a species of war peculiarly adapted to Central and Western Texas. We should *then* be prepared for a most active campaign, and our force of cavalry should be especially large and efficient.

"Again recurring to the line of supply, it will be seen that the Vicksburg and Shreveport Road extends to Marshall, where there is an interval of 40 miles to Henderson, whence the road is completed to Galveston. The road from Marshall to Henderson, however, is graded, and could

Banks was by no means averse to an offensive campaign west of the Mississippi. In his evidence before the Committee on the Conduct of the War, he says: "If you cripple or scatter the enemy's army of the James, he will take refuge first in the Appalachian range of mountains, and ultimately in the country west of the Mississippi, and there reorganize. Therefore it was wise and expedient for us first to have cleared that country and held it, so that they could not cross the Mississippi. The enemy should be held on this side of the Mississippi, between the mountains and the Atlantic and the Gulf coasts." Nor was he opposed to the line of the Red River as a base of operations against Texas. He repeatedly admitted that this was the shortest and best line for that purpose. But he did insist upon certain conditions as necessary to operations from this base.

1. In the first place, the Red River campaign could not be undertaken until the waters of the river were high enough to admit Porter's gun-boats and heavy-draught transports.

---

be completed in a short time. In case the enemy should abandon the coast, this road will fall into our possession, and supplies could be obtained from two directions. Our colored troops, who are especially qualified for fighting guerrillas, would be usefully employed in guarding the entire line of the road from Vicksburg to Galveston. Texas is said to be full of blacks, who will be a valuable auxiliary in our operations in that state.

"The campaign above sketched would, I believe, be a long one. Much preparation and labor will be required to insure the army against vexatious delays, which permit the enemy constantly to elude us.

"I should estimate roughly that it would require until some time in May to effect the union of forces and be prepared with transportation for a movement into the interior. This would be about the commencement of the season most favorable for active operations in Texas. I suppose that by that time wagon trains will be provided to haul supplies from Monroe to Shreveport, that the railroad will be in running order to Monroe, and the work of completing the road well under way. The time required for subsequent operations can not be well estimated. It is highly probable that the rebel army will suffer greatly from desertion—an easy matter in active campaigning. The Arkansians will probably leave in the greatest numbers. Should their army, however, hold together, they will be able to prolong the contest some time.

"The results of this campaign will be very great. As long as we are able to keep the enemy actively engaged in Texas, Arkansas and Louisiana will be safe, and the process of reconstruction can be carried on without interruption; and should those states establish loyal state governments, there can be no doubt that desertions would be very numerous.

"This plan of operations has these advantages over that of operations from the coast of Texas. It also has the advantage of enabling us to bring a much larger force of cavalry into the field.

"It is, however, a much more difficult plan to execute, requires much more time, and is much more uncertain as to the time it will require to accomplish any of the objects undertaken.

"The movement by the coast of Texas possesses the great advantage of enabling us to deceive the enemy as to our intentions, which is not the case with the other plan. Our troops and supplies can be quickly moved by steamers to any point on the coast, landing can be threatened at different points, and the enemy kept in ignorance of our intentions. We now hold the harbor of Matagorda, the best on the coast next to Galveston. We have a secure point for the debarkation of troops and supplies. The distance by land to Houston is 150 miles, over good roads, three in number; one *via* Texana and Wharton; one *via* Matagorda and Columbia; the third along the beach to the mouth of Brazos River. Very little baggage need be required on the march, as the point of supply can be transferred to Brazos River and Sabine Pass in succession. A much less force would be required for this operation than the other. The rebel forces now in Arkansas will remain there as long as our forces are opposed to them, and we would only have to meet the force in Lower Texas. To direct and draw off this force as much as possible, the following plan could be adopted: Every preparation should be made for debarking the troops at Matagorda and transferring them to the main land. The troops intended to be sent should be designated and collected at New Orleans, so as to go aboard at a moment's notice. The steamers should be got ready and the troops assigned. All the heavy material, artillery, horses, etc., should be placed on board the light-draught vessels, having only men and light stores to be lightened. A demonstration of gun-boats, and troops in transports, could then be made at Alexandria in moderate forces, the effect of which would be to withdraw the enemy from Lower Texas. This having been effected, the force at New Orleans should be sent with all dispatch to Texas, the forces marched to Houston without delay, and Galveston be invested, and the garrison captured unless they hurriedly evacuated. This would give us entire control of the coast of Texas in a comparatively short time.

"For subsequent operations we would not be as well prepared as we would be at Shreveport with our forces concentrated. The object we started out with would have been accomplished, viz., the possession of the coast. The object proposed by the movement *via* Shreveport is much greater than the other, and hence requires more time and means. That direct object is no less than the complete destruction or scattering of the rebel forces west of the Mississippi, and it will be impracticable to stop short of this result.

"To attempt simply to hold Shreveport as a post would subject us to continued annoyance as long as an organized force remains in Texas. They would make continued raids on our flank and rear, and our resources would be gradually frittered away. The rebel army must be pursued till it is broken up, and then we can occupy the country and restore order.

"I have written the above in some haste necessarily, and have endeavored to make my ideas clear, though they may be somewhat boldly expressed. A strict comparison between the two plans of operations can hardly be made, as their objects are different. The only question is, which can be most successfully carried out. The results provided by the first plan are much more satisfactory, and they include those of the second. I do not believe, with some, in the impossibility of long land marches *with a large force*, but I am fully aware of the difficulties to be overcome, and the uncertainty of foreseeing results."

On the receipt of this memorial, General Halleck writes February 1:

"Your dispatches of January 23, transmitting report and map of Major Houston, are received. This report and map contain very important and valuable information.

"The geographical theatre of the war west of the Mississippi indicates Shreveport as the most important objective point of the operations of a campaign for troops moving from the Teche, the Mississippi, and Arkansas Rivers.

"Of course, the strategic advantages of this point may be more than counterbalanced by disadvantages of communications and supplies. General Steele reports that he can not advance to Shreveport this month unless certain of finding supplies on the Red River, and of having there the co-operation of your forces or those of General Sherman.

"If the Red River is not navigable, and it will require months to open any other communication to Shreveport, there seems very little prospect of the requisite co-operation or transportation of supplies. It has, therefore, been left entirely to your discretion, after fully investigating the question, to adopt this line or substitute any other. It was proper, however, that you should have an understanding with Generals Steele and Sherman, as it would probably be hazardous for either of those officers to attempt the movement without the co-operation of other troops.

"If the country between the Arkansas and Red Rivers is impassable during the winter, as has been represented, it was thought that a portion of General Steele's command might be temporarily spared to operate with Sherman from the Mississippi. The Department of Arkansas was therefore made subject to the orders of General Grant.

"It is quite probable that the condition of affairs in East Tennessee, so different from what General Grant anticipated when he detached General Sherman, may have caused him to modify his plans, or, at least, to postpone their execution. This may also prevent your receiving the expected aid from Sherman. Communications by the Mississippi River are so often interrupted, and dispatches delayed, that I am not advised where General Sherman now is, or what are his present plans.

"So many delays have already occurred, and the winter is now so far advanced, that I greatly fear no important operations west of the Mississippi will be concluded in time for General Grant's proposed campaign in the spring. This is greatly to be regretted, but perhaps is unavoidable, as all our armies are greatly reduced by furloughs, and the raising of new troops progresses very slowly. Re-enforcements, however, are being sent to you as rapidly as we can possibly get them ready for the field.

"Have you not over-estimated the strength of the enemy west of the Mississippi River? All the information we can get makes the whole rebel force under Magruder, Smith, and Price much less than ours under you and General Steele. Of course you have better sources of information than we have here."

On the 11th of February General Halleck writes:

"Your dispatches of January 29 and February 2 are received. In the former you speak of awaiting "orders" and "instructions" in regard to operations on Red River. If by this is meant that you are waiting for orders from Washington, there must be some misapprehension. The substance of my dispatches to you on this subject was communicated to the President and Secretary of War, and it was understood that, while stating my own views in regard to operations, I should leave you free to adopt such lines and plans of campaign as you might, after a full consideration of the subject, deem best. Such, I am confident, is the purport of my dispatches, and it certainly was not intended that any of your movements should be delayed to await instructions from here. It was to avoid any delay of this kind that you were requested to communicate directly with Generals Sherman and Steele, and concert with them such plans of co-operation as you might deem best, under all the circumstances of the case.

"My last communication from General Sherman is dated January 29, 1864, and received here to-day. He says the stage of water in Red River is such that he can not operate in that direction earlier than March or April, and that in the mean time he would operate on the east side of the Mississippi River. I think he had not then communicated with you."

Turning now for a moment from the correspondence between Halleck and Banks, we find that the former, in his dispatches to General Grant on the subject of the trans-Mississippi campaign, clearly intimates that Banks's operations west of the river must continue during the winter, and that, while he partially recommends the Red River campaign, he leaves it to General Grant's discretion as to how far or in what manner he will allow Generals Steele and Sherman to co-operate. On January 8th he writes to Grant:

"Keeping in mind that General Banks's operations in Texas, either on the Gulf coast or by the Louisiana frontier, must be continued during the winter, it is to be considered whether it will not be better to direct our efforts, for the present, to the entire breaking up of the rebel forces west of the Mississippi River, rather than divide them by operating against Mobile and the Alabama. If the forces of Smith, Pierce, and Magruder could be so scattered or broken as to enable Steele and Banks to occupy Red River as a line of defense, a part of their armies would probably become available for operations elsewhere. General Banks reports his present force as inadequate for the defense of his position and for operations in the interior; and General Steele is of the opinion that he can not advance beyond the Arkansas or Sabine unless he can be certain of co-operation and supplies on Red River. Under these circumstances, it is worth considering whether such forces as Sherman can move down the Mississippi River should not co-operate with the armies of Steele and Banks on the west side. Of course, operations of any of your troops in that direction must be subordinate, and subsequent to those which you have proposed for East and West Tennessee. I therefore present these views at this time merely that they may receive your attention and consideration in determining upon your ulterior movements."

Again, on the 17th of January:

"General Banks represents the condition of affairs in his department to be such as to require all the re-enforcements that we can possibly send him. As soon as I found that he had divided his forces by operating upon the Gulf coast, I urged that troops should be sent him from South Carolina, and that the attack on Charleston should be abandoned. It was decided otherwise. My opinion has been, and still is, that all troops not required to hold our position in Virginia and on the Atlantic coast should be sent to you and to General Banks for operations this winter, and as preparatory to a spring campaign. I hoped that by this means Tennessee, Arkansas, Mississippi, and Louisiana would be secured, and the rebel force in Texas be so reduced and hemmed in as to give us but little trouble hereafter. Our armies in the west and south could then have been so concentrated, or at least could have so co-operated as to inflict some terrible blows upon the rebels. But I fear that the unexpected condition of affairs in East Tennessee will prevent the accomplishment of these objects, or at least a part of them, this winter, and that we must soon prepare for a spring campaign. The furloughing of so many troops has greatly reduced our forces in the North, but I hope to send some more to General Banks. There is, however, much difficulty and delay in obtaining transportation by sea. This makes it still more important that the navigation of the Mississippi should be well protected, and that Sherman and Steele should so operate as to assist General Banks as much as possible. I leave it entirely to your judgment to determine how and to what extent such assistance can be rendered."

Grant appears to have been willing that Sherman, after his Meridian campaign, should co-operate with General Banks in the movement on Shreveport, provided the time occupied in this operation would not interfere with the spring campaign against Atlanta. Sherman was himself very partial to the project. On the 31st of January he writes to General Banks:

"The Mississippi, though low for the season, is free from ice and in good boating order, but I understand Red River is still low. I had a man in from Alexandria yesterday, who reported the falls or rapids at that place impassable save to the smallest boats.

"My inland expedition is now working, and will be off for Jackson, etc., to-morrow. The only fear I have is in the weather. . . . My orders from General Grant will not, as yet, justify me in embarking for Red River, though I am very anxious to operate in that direction. The moment I learned that you were preparing for it, I sent communication to Admiral Porter, and dispatched to General Grant at Chattanooga, asking if he wanted me and Steele to co-operate with you against Shreveport, and I will have his answer in time, for you can not do any thing till Red River has twelve feet of water on the rapids of Alexandria. That will be from March to June. I have lived on Red River, and know somewhat of the phases of that stream. The expedition on Shreveport should be made rapidly, by simultaneous movements from Little Rock on Shreveport, from Opelousas on Alexandria, and a combined force of gun-boats and transports directly up Red River. Admiral Porter will be able to have a splendid fleet by March 1. I think Steele could move with 10,000 infantry and 5000 cavalry. I could take about 10,000, and you could, I suppose, the same. Your movement from Opelousas simultaneous with mine up the river would compel Dick Taylor to leave Fort De Russy, near Marksville, and the whole could appear at Shreveport about a day appointed. I doubt if the enemy would risk a siege, although they are, I am informed, fortifying, and placing many heavy guns. It would be better for us that they should stand at Shreveport, as we might make large and important captures.

"But I do not believe the enemy would fight a force of 30,000 men with gun-boats. I will be most happy to take part in the proposed expedition, and hope, before you have made up your dispositions, I will have the necessary permission. . . . I think by March 1 I could put afloat for Shreveport 10,000 men, provided I succeed in my present plan of clearing the Mississippi, and breaking up the railroad about Meridian."

By the 1st of March it is clear that the Red River campaign had been fully decided upon, so far as Generals Grant, Sherman, and Banks, and Admiral Porter were concerned. Banks writes to Halleck March 6th:

"Major General Sherman, of General Grant's department, arrived in this city [New Orleans] on the evening of the 1st instant, having completed his expedition to Meridian to his entire satisfaction. He returned to Vicksburg on the evening of the 3d, to arrange for his co-operation in the Red River movement. Unless delayed by want of steam transportation, of which we have put every thing we have at his command, he will be ready to join me on the Red River by the 17th, where I hope to be at that date. He expects to furnish 10,000 men for that purpose.

"Captain Dunham, of my staff, returned from the headquarters of General Steele yesterday, bearing communications from him, copies of which will be forwarded to you. General Steele appears to have changed the plan entertained when he last communicated with me. Copies of his dispatches at that time have been forwarded to you. He then proposed to move by the way of Monroe for the Red River. He is now apprehensive, in consequence of the reduction of his force, that he can only enter upon a movement for the diversion of the enemy in the direction of Arkadelphia, without any expectation of joining us at Shreveport, or any other position on the river. General Sherman and myself have earnestly urged him to abandon this idea, that, in any event, the three forces in the course of thirty days would meet at Shreveport. General Steele represents that he will have about 6000 men at his command. I respectfully request that orders may be given to him to co-operate with us upon the point named, in accordance with the plans originally proposed by you. I see nothing to defeat its success. Admiral Porter is ready to move up the river in co-operation with us as soon as his vessels can be admitted. General McClernand has been assigned to the command of the troops in Texas, and will leave for an examination of the posts at Matagorda Bay and Brownsville to-morrow. Brigadier General Ransom will have command of the Thirteenth Army Corps, which participates in the movement on the Red River."

General Steele said the movement was earlier than he had anticipated. A large number of his troops were on furlough, and the presence of the remainder was necessary in order to secure the success of an election to be held March 14th. He writes to General Halleck March 12:

"General Banks with 17,000, and 10,000 of Sherman's, will be at Alexandria on the 17th instant. This is more than equal for any thing Kirby Smith can bring against them. Smith will run. By holding the line of the Arkansas secure, I can soon free this state from armed rebels. Sherman insists upon my moving upon Shreveport to co-operate with the above-mentioned forces with all my effective force. I have prepared to do so against my own judgment and that of the best-informed people here. The roads are most, if not quite impracticable; the country is destitute of provisions on the route we should be obliged to take. I made a proposition to General Banks to threaten the enemy's flank and rear with all my cavalry, and to make a feint with infantry on the Washington Road. I yielded to Sherman, so far as this plan is concerned. Blunt wished me to move by Monroe to Red River; Sherman wants me to go by Camden and Overton to Shreveport. The latter is impracticable, and the former would expose the line of the Arkansas and Missouri to cavalry raids. Holmes has a large mounted force. I agreed to move by Arkadelphia or Hot Springs and Washington to Shreveport. I can move with 7000, including the frontier. Our scouting-parties frequently have skirmishes with detached parties all over the state, and if they should form in my rear in considerable force I should be obliged to fall back to save my dépôts, etc."

On the 13th of March Halleck advised Steele to co-operate with the movement of Banks and Sherman on Shreveport. The appointment of Grant as lieutenant general rendered Sherman's presence necessary at Chattanooga, so that he did not in person direct the movements of his troops in the Red River campaign.

2. It should be undertaken with a commensurate force.

3. Time must be given sufficient for the accomplishment of its great object—the defeat of Kirby Smith's armies.

4. And as this prolongation of the campaign would compel the army, after the 1st of May at least, to depend upon some line of supply independent of the water-courses, it was necessary that the railroad from Vicksburg to Shreveport should be put in running order.

5. Finally, as forces from other departments must participate in the campaign, Banks urged the necessity that the operations of all should be under the control of a single general.

All these conditions were distinctly insisted upon by General Banks, and the importance of each was fully explained. If they had all been met; if the campaign had been in season, undertaken with adequate forces, free from any arbitrary limitations in regard to time, supported by land communication with Vicksburg, and controlled by a single head, even then the difficulties encountered would have been as great as in any other campaign of the war. The requirements of the campaign could not be answered—at least not in the spring of 1864.

1. The time at which the movement might commence could not be calculated with certainty. It would have been safe ordinarily to have predicted a sufficient rise of the Red River in March. But in 1864 it was not safe. The Mississippi and Red Rivers, during the winter, had been lower than they had been for years. It was reasonable, therefore, not only to anticipate unusual delay in the spring flood, but also to doubt whether, when it came, it would answer the purpose. And, if the river had been left out of view; if the possibility of efficient naval support had been left to depend upon circumstances, and reliance had been placed only upon the railroad from Shreveport, in that case not only must three months be occupied in putting the railroad in running order, but expeditions, which would occupy considerable time, must be undertaken to clear Southern Arkansas of all such hostile forces as might, if left there, interrupt this land line of supply. It was impossible, therefore, to count upon an *early* commencement of the campaign. And if not commenced early, it could not be undertaken at all, without interfering with the progress of the war east of the Mississippi.[1]

2. And this leads us to the second requirement—a sufficient force. No period of the war could have been more inopportune in this respect. The term of three years, for which the greater portion of the army had enlisted, was now expiring. It could not be safely asserted as certain that the majority of the veteran soldiers would re-enlist, though that was a probable event. The solution of the important problem thus arising ought to have been anticipated by proper measures on the part of the government. Such measures had been tried, but the result was exceedingly unsatisfactory. The conscription of 1863 had furnished only a meagre re-enforcement to the national armies. Thus, although General Halleck was partial to operations in the West, and especially partial in his estimate of the importance of the trans-Mississippi campaign, he found it extremely difficult to increase General Banks's command. He advised that operations in South Carolina be postponed for this purpose; but the government took a different view. In North Carolina the defensive could hardly be maintained, and no troops could be withdrawn from that state. To farther deplete the Army of the Potomac was also impossible. General Longstreet, after abandoning the siege of Knoxville, had occupied a position which seriously threatened East Tennessee, and from General Grant's department only about 10,000 men of Sherman's army could be detached for operations elsewhere. This small corps, and a few regiments, chiefly of cavalry, which, with great difficulty, had been secured from the East by General Halleck, were all that could be sent to the Department of the Gulf, and Sherman's troops could not co-operate with Banks until the conclusion of the Meridian expedition. The only other possible source of aid in the proposed Red River campaign must come from General Steele's department. At the most, Steele could not bring to bear upon the campaign more than 10,000 men, and his column must be independent of the direct movement on Shreveport. Advancing from Little Rock, his route to Shreveport was, at this season of the year, so difficult, and almost impracticable, that it might reasonably be apprehended that he would not be able to strike an effective blow. General Banks's own force, which could be made available for the campaign, amounted to 15,000 or 17,000 men.[2] Thus less than 40,000 troops could engage in the campaign, and only about 28,000 could be certainly counted upon in the event of an encounter with the enemy, should the latter determine to fight a battle below Shreveport.

3. The time allowed for the campaign was limited to thirty days. It was for this period, and no longer, that Sherman's troops were "loaned" to General Banks. This force was indispensable to the continuance of the campaign after reaching Shreveport. The difficulties incident to Steele's advance from Little Rock were so great that no absolute reliance could be placed upon *that* movement. The main dependence was upon A. J. Smith's

command—that portion of Sherman's troops which was loaned to Banks for a month. If the campaign was not concluded within that time, it must evidently be abandoned, except in the very improbable event of Steele's prompt arrival at Shreveport. The uncertainty of Steele's success in advancing, and the limited time allowed for the co-operation of Sherman's troops, made General Banks's command the only one to be relied upon as a permanent force.

4. This limitation as regards time of course made it out of the question to occupy several months in the establishment of communications between Vicksburg and Shreveport. For this reason, if for no other, the campaign must be concluded before the fall of the Red River, or be then abandoned.

5. No attention whatever seems to have been given to General Banks's suggestion that all the operations of the campaign should be under a single general. Four distinct commands were thus allowed to participate in the campaign—Porter's, Steele's, A. J. Smith's, and Banks's—each independent of the others. That this was the case was, in great part, General Banks's fault. In accordance with military usage, he ought to have assumed the command of Smith's troops. But he did not do so, and there was, therefore, no unity of command.[1]

The whole affair seems rather to have happened than to have been ordered. General Halleck had been recommending the campaign for months, but he would not assume the responsibility of ordering it. He left the decision entirely with Banks, Sherman, and Steele. The two former, in spite of circumstances which made failure almost certain, while success was a bare possibility, seem to have been confident of a fortunate issue. Partly from this confidence, and probably still more from the urgency with which Halleck had formerly pressed the matter, they entered upon the campaign. It is difficult to conceive what objects they expected to attain within the space of a single month. It is conceded on all hands that, even if Shreveport were reached, nothing beyond that could be accomplished, and a speedy retreat to the Mississippi was inevitable.[2] To march to Shreveport—the Richmond of the trans-Mississippi territory—to capture that place, possibly, and destroy its manufactories, and then to march back again—*this* certainly was no object commensurate with the risk or expense of the campaign, or with the forces employed. Halleck certainly dissuaded Banks from undertaking the movement unless, within the period allowed for its accomplishment, it promised an important success.

That the campaign ought not, under the circumstances, to have been undertaken, is evident. But upon whom rests the responsibility? This must lie between Halleck and Banks. Neither of them would have assumed the responsibility of ordering the movement. Banks very clearly stated the conditions upon which he could enter upon the campaign, and, upon consideration of this statement, Halleck ought to have abandoned the affair as impracticable. But he did not. He communicated with General Sherman, and the latter seemed to favor the undertaking. He reported this opinion to Banks, and advised him to communicate with Generals Steele and Sherman upon the subject. General Banks knew that his own decision was absolute in regard to the matter. He ought to have decided promptly against the movement. But, with the re-enforcements from Sherman, and General Steele's co-operation, he seems to have thought success possible. Besides, General Halleck's scarcely disguised censure of his coast operations, and the urgency with which the latter had pressed the Red River route upon his attention from the beginning, seemed to render farther opposition on his part indecorous. The matter being left to his discretion, any such consideration ought not to have influenced him. He ought to have followed his better judgment. To do otherwise was an inexcusable exhibition of weakness. We are compelled, therefore, to assume that he either weakly yielded his consent, or that his judgment had been altered in view of the co-operation which he would receive, and by "the best military opinions of the generals in the West," which Halleck urged as favorable to operations on the Red River.[3] Whichever way we may determine, he certainly consented to the campaign, and is, in so far, responsible for its results.

---

[1] General Grant's idea of the Red River expedition is shown in the following extract from a letter, written by him to Sherman, dated Nashville, February 18, 1864:

"While I look upon such an expedition as is proposed as of the greatest importance, I regret that any force has to be taken from east of the Mississippi for it. Your troops will want rest for the purpose of preparing for a spring campaign, and all the veterans should be got off on furlough at the very earliest moment. . . . .

"Unless you go in command of the proposed expedition, I fear any troops you may send with it will be entirely lost from farther service in this command. This, however, is not the reason for my suggestion that you be sent. Your acquaintance with the country, and otherwise fitness, were the reasons. I can give no positive orders that you send no troops up Red River, but what I do want is their speedy return, if they do go, and that the minimum number necessary be sent. . . . ."

[2] A large portion of his force, including all of his colored troops, was occupied in garrisoning posts, distributed as follows:

Rio Grande	3000	Key West	791	Plaquemine (colored)	620
Pass Cavallo	3277	New Orleans	1125	Port Hudson (colored)	9409
Pensacola	900	Baton Rouge	6565	Total	20,687

[1] General Sherman's orders, issued to General Smith March 4, 1864, certainly contemplated that the latter would be under General Banks's command. Sherman writes to Smith to join Banks at Alexandria. He says: "You will meet him there, *report to him, and act under his orders.*"—*Sherman's Report to the Committee on the Conduct of the War*, p. 7.

[2] The evidence before the Committee on the Conduct of the War is conclusive on this point. General Banks says (p. 20): "I believe, if any of our forces had taken Shreveport, they could not have held it for one month. . . . . We might have gone there, destroyed the place, and then come back again; but I think if the enemy had allowed us to go up there, we should never have got back with the army to the fleet." The question was asked, "How could that have been supposed to conform to the idea of going into Texas with an army?" To which Banks replied: "That is not for me to say. It was the purpose of the expedition to occupy Shreveport, and hold it. General Steele's forces were to hold it if we occupied it. But without some communication on that line, independent of river navigation, ... General Steele could not have got his supplies. It would have taken at least 10,000 men to hold Shreveport against the concentrated forces of the enemy. There was nothing in the country upon which he could subsist. They would have cut off his communications, and he would have been compelled to surrender. But there is another view of operations west of the Mississippi which, if I had had command of the forces, I should have been disposed to adopt. There were about 100,000 men west of the Mississippi, in Louisiana, Arkansas, and Missouri. If a campaign without limit of time had been set on foot, with the purpose of concentrating all disposable forces in these states, with means of supply independent of the river, and orders to follow up the enemy wherever he could be found, and then destroy him, we would have cleared the country west of the Mississippi of any organized force of the enemy; then, by constructing a railroad from the Mississippi River to Shreveport, fortifying that place, and getting supplies there sufficient for a year, and leaving troops enough there to hold it, we could cover Louisiana, Arkansas, and Missouri. The occupation of Shreveport at the conclusion of such a campaign would have been an important achievement."

[3] General Banks says in his report:

"Having made known my plan of operations on the coast, and fully stated, at different times, the difficulties to be encountered in movements by land in the direction of Alexandria and Shreveport, I did not feel at liberty to decline participation in the campaign, which had been pressed upon my attention from the time I was assigned to the command of this department, and which was now supported by the concurrent opinions of the general officers in the West, on account of difficulties which might be obviated by personal conference with commanders, or by orders from the general-in-chief. It was not, however, without well-founded apprehensions of the result of the campaign, and a clear view of the measures (which I suggested) indispensable to success, that I entered upon this new campaign. . . . In the instructions I received from government, it was left to my discretion whether or not I would join in this expedition, but I was directed to communicate with General

ADMIRAL PORTER'S FLEET ON RED RIVER.

Sherman, on the conclusion of his Mississippi expedition, went to New Orleans, and there and then the principal features of the campaign seem to have been determined upon. Returning to Vicksburg, he, on the 6th of March, instructed General A. J. Smith to report to General Banks with 7500 men of Hurlbut's (Sixteenth), and 2500 of McPherson's (Seventeenth) Corps. It was intended that Banks, Smith, and Porter should be at Alexandria by the 17th of March. General Steele was notified of this intention, and replied that he had not anticipated so early a movement; that the presence of his troops was necessary to secure the success of an election to be held at Little Rock March 14, and that he would probably only be able to make a demonstration against Shreveport.[1] After some delay, by the 13th, orders were dispatched to him to move upon Shreveport "with all his available force."

The enemy had a force nearly equal to that which was sent against him. From the official returns of the trans-Mississippi department, Kirby Smith's entire force amounted to 41,000 men, of whom 35,000 were serviceable. The greater portion of this force, probably about 20,000 men, under General Magruder, covered Galveston and Houston. General Taylor, with about 5000, held the line of the Atchafalaya and Red Rivers, while General Price, with 6000 infantry and 3000 cavalry, confronted Steele in Southern Arkansas. Probably 10,000 men could be sent from Magruder's army to re-enforce Price and Taylor. The enemy was strongly fortified at Fort De Russy, on the Red River, and at Camden, on the Washita River, in Arkansas.

Political affairs which had been set on foot by the President required General Banks's personal presence in New Orleans, and the organization of the expedition, so far as it involved his department, was intrusted to General Franklin. It was only on the 10th of March that General Franklin knew that the expedition was expected to reach Alexandria on the 17th. As Alexandria is 117 miles from Franklin, where the troops were to be concentrated for the advance, it was, of course, impossible to fulfill this expectation. Only 3000 men were then at Franklin; the remainder of the infantry, just arrived from Texas, was at Berwick's Bay, and the cavalry was still at New Orleans. On the 13th the movement commenced. General A. L. Lee, with 3300 cavalry, held the advance. Then followed two divisions of the Thirteenth Corps—Landrum's and Cameron's—under General T. E. G. Ransom, and the Nineteenth Corps under General Emory. The whole command, numbering about 18,000 men, reached Alexandria on the 25th of March.

In the mean time, Admiral Porter[2] had already arrived at Alexandria.

On the 7th he had at the mouth of Red River a fleet of fifteen iron-clad and four lighter vessels.[1] On the 11th he was joined by General Smith's command, embarked on thirty transports. There was found just sufficient water to allow the larger boats to enter the river. The Eastport was ordered to take the lead, and remove the obstructions which the enemy had placed below Fort De Russy. A portion of the fleet then accompanied the transports down the Atchafalaya, and covered the landing of troops at Simmsport. Dick Taylor's force retreated to Fort De Russy, followed by General A. J. Smith's command, and the gun-boats returned to Red River. In the

A. J. Smith (March 4), he says: "Now Red River is too low for the season, and I doubt if the boats can pass the falls or rapids of Alexandria. What General Banks proposes to do in that event, I do not know; but my own judgment is that Shreveport ought not to be attacked until the gun-boats can reach it. Not that a force marching by land can not do it alone, but it would be bad economy in war to invest the place with an army so far from heavy guns, mortars, ammunition, and provisions, which can alone reach Shreveport by water." Again (March 7) he writes to Admiral Porter: "I . . . . authorize you to use my name with General Banks that a farther move ought not to be attempted above Alexandria unless the Red River admits the navigation by your first-class gun-boats and large transports, viz., seven feet of water on the 'rapids' of Alexandria."

[1] Porter's fleet consisted of the Essex, Benton, Lafayette, Choctaw, Chillicothe, Ozark, Louisville, Carondelet, Eastport, Pittsburg, Mound City, Osage, Neosho, Ouachita, Fort Hindman, and the lighter boats Lexington, Cricket, Gazelle, and Black Hawk.

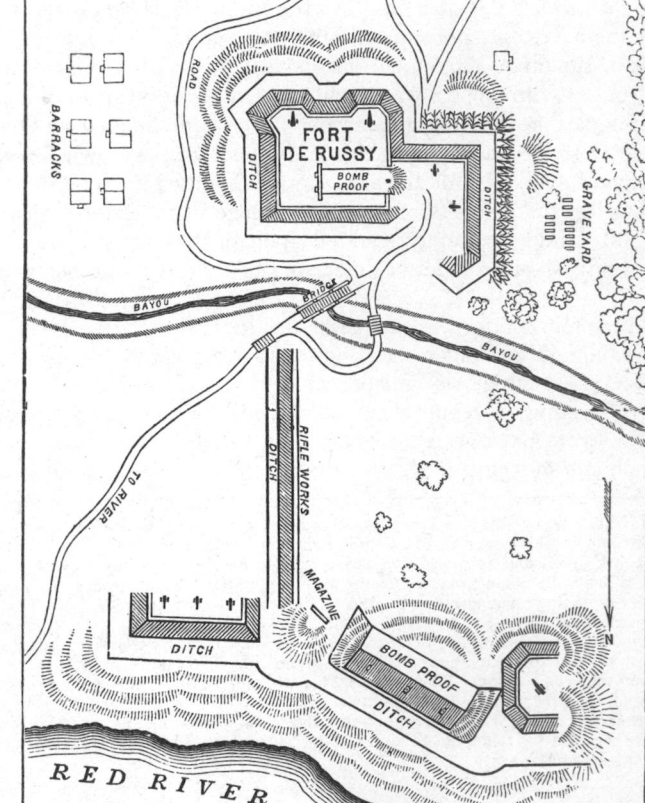

PLAN OF FORT DE RUSSY.

Sherman, and General Steele, and Admiral Porter upon the subject. I expressed the satisfaction I should find in co-operating with them in a movement deemed of so much importance by the government, to which my own command was unequal, and my belief that, *with the forces designated*, it would be entirely successful. Having received from them similar assurances, both my discretion and my authority, so far as the organization of the expedition was concerned, were at an end."

[1] Sherman writes to Steele, March 6: "I confess I feel uneasy at your assertion that you can only move with 7000 infantry, and that you prefer to wait until after the election of the 14th. *If we have to modify military plans for civil elections, we had better go home.*"

[2] The following statement is made by Porter before the Committee on the Conduct of the War: "The Red River expedition was originally proposed by General Sherman and myself; we were to have gone up there together. But while we were making the preparations for it, General Banks notified General Sherman that he was about to ascend the Red River with 30,000 men. General Banks also requested co-operation from me, showing me certain orders from General Halleck, in which he was directed to go as far as Shreveport," etc.

In explanation of this statement, it should be said that Sherman's confidence in the success of the expedition was based upon a full supply of water in Red River. In his instructions to General

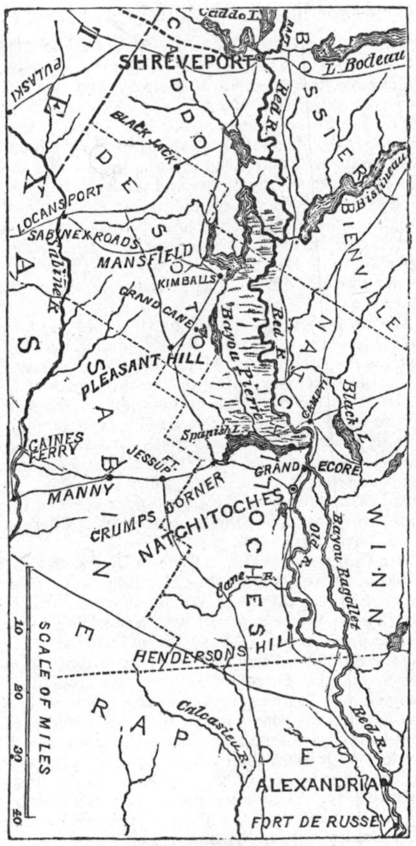

MAP OF THE RED RIVER CAMPAIGN.

mean time, the obstructions, consisting of heavy piles driven into the mud, clamped with iron plates and chains, had been removed. Just as the fleet, on the afternoon of the 14th, approached the fort, the latter was, at the same time, surrounded by the troops, who then assaulted and captured the work, with eight guns and 250 prisoners. General Smith had done a good day's work with his command. He had marched twenty-eight miles, being detained two hours to build a bridge, and had, after an action of two hours, captured the only fort which the enemy had on Red River below Shreveport. Two days afterward the fleet reached Alexandria.[1]

The work of getting the gun-boats over the rocky rapids at Alexandria was slow and difficult. Indeed, it was hazardous to advance farther up the river with the fleet, which, if it should ever reach Shreveport, would probably never return. General Banks arrived at Alexandria on the 24th. The delay caused by the slow progress of the fleet above the rapids rendered it necessary to establish a dépôt of supplies at Alexandria, and a line of wagon transportation from the steamers below to those above the falls. To guard this point, therefore, Grover's division of the Nineteenth Corps (3000 strong) had to be left behind. Ellet's marine brigade of 3000 men, of A. J. Smith's command, was recalled to Vicksburg. It was necessary that T. K. Smith's division of the same command (2500 men) should go with the fleet for the protection of the transports. Thus, when the army left for Alexandria, April 1, its number of men available for active operations on land had been reduced by 8500.

Just after the occupation of Alexandria the troops were in good spirits; indeed, the impression prevailed in the army that the Confederates in this region were demoralized, and that Shreveport would be reached without a battle. General Steele had the same feeling. This is shown in his dispatch to Halleck on March 12, where he says that Sherman's and Banks's troops were "more than equal for every thing Kirby Smith can bring against them." Smith, he said, would run. With this conviction, his co-operation must have been inefficient. At Alexandria there seems to have been some bad feeling between the military and naval forces on account of the seizure by the latter of cotton as a naval prize. Porter, during the period in which he was waiting for the army, and for the passage of his fleet above the falls, took possession of a considerable quantity of cotton. It would have been wiser to have refrained from the seizure at this time for two reasons. In the first place, it naturally created jealousy among the military forces. Then, again, it caused the cotton within the reach of the Federal forces to be burned by the inhabitants, who would otherwise have gladly disposed of it to the United States on terms advantageous to themselves and to the government. If, however, the cotton was to become a naval prize, there was no motive for its preservation. It would have been better if the existence of cotton had been ignored by the navy as well as the army until the territory in which the staple was found should be thoroughly subjugated. This was General Grant's policy. General Banks's theory was that the products of the country ought to be bought at a reasonable price. This policy was open to the objection that it added largely to the resources of the enemy, and in so far prolonged the war.

While the army was at Alexandria, a movement was made to Henderson's Hill, twenty-five miles up the river, resulting in a surprise of the enemy at that point, and the capture of 250 prisoners, 200 horses, and four guns. Three brigades of Smith's command, and one of Emory's, participated in this expedition.

On the 2d and 3d of April the army reached Natchitoches, eighty miles from Alexandria, and 100 below Shreveport. This place was about four miles inland from Grand Ecore. It is situated on the old channel of the Red River, while Grand Ecore is on the new. Lee's cavalry had skirmished with the enemy all the way to Natchitoches. The navy proceeded up to Grand Ecore. The difficulties of navigation had increased rather than diminished. The river was falling, and it was found impossible for the larger gun-boats to pass Grand Ecore. A. J. Smith's command was forced to abandon the transports and march by land. Here there was a delay of four days. On the 6th of April the army advanced from Natchitoches. The only practicable road to Shreveport lay through Pleasant Hill and Mansfield, through a barren, sandy country, with little water and scarcely any forage, and, for the most part, an unbroken pine forest. Notwithstanding the failure of Franklin at Sabine Pass, Banks still intrusted to him the active command and the regulation of the march, while he remained at Grand Ecore until the fleet advanced, on the 7th.

[1] Admiral Porter, at this time, does not seem to have had a very exalted idea of the enemy's pluck. Writing from Alexandria on the 16th, he says: "Colonel De Russy, from appearances, is a most excellent engineer to build forts, but don't seem to know what to do with them after they are constructed. The same remark may apply to his obstructions, which look well on paper, but don't stop our advance. The efforts of these people to keep up the war remind one very much of the antics of Chinamen, who build canvas forts, paint hideous dragons on their shields, turn somersets, and yell in the face of their enemies to frighten them, and then run away at the first sign of an engagement. It puts the sailors and soldiers out of all patience with them, after the trouble they have had in getting here. Now and then the army have a little brush with their pickets, but that don't often happen. It is not the intention of these rebels to fight." Admiral Porter probably had occasion to reverse his judgment before the campaign was over.

Lee's cavalry found the enemy in his front all the way to Pleasant Hill, thirty-six miles distant. Kirby Smith's design was to draw the Federal force as far as possible from its base before a general engagement. The delay of the fleet had given him time for concentration, and Green's cavalry had been withdrawn from Southern Texas.

General Banks intended that the fleet, with its six lightest boats, should reach Loggy Bayou, opposite Springfield, where communications would be established with the land forces at Sabine Cross-roads, near Mansfield, fifty-four miles from Natchitoches. The navy, with twenty transports, succeeded, though with great difficulty, in reaching Springfield. But on the way to Mansfield the army, encountering the enemy in strong force, sustained a disastrous reverse, which caused it to retreat, and finally to abandon the expedition.

On the 7th of April the advance of the Federal army reached Pleasant Hill, and there encamped for the night. General Lee had driven a small force of the enemy to Pleasant Hill and about three miles beyond, to Wilson's farm, where a fight occurred in which Lee lost sixty-two in killed, wounded, and missing. The enemy, after losing severely, was driven to St. Patrick's Bayou, nine miles from Pleasant Hill. During the action, Lee had called upon Franklin for a brigade of infantry. This was dispatched; but the firing having ceased, it was withdrawn.

As to the force of the enemy in his front, General Franklin seems to have been totally ignorant. He certainly did not expect soon to fight a battle, otherwise his order of march would not have been what it was. General Lee, with about 5000 cavalry, held the advance, skirmishing with and developing the enemy, who, whatever his force, seemed determined to retreat. Then came the train of the cavalry, consisting of over 200 wagons.[1] The size of this train is partly accounted for by the fact that it carried 20,000 rations; but even with this allowance it was very much larger than was necessary. After it came Ransom's command, consisting of two divisions of the Thirteenth Corps; then the Nineteenth Corps, Franklin's proper command, followed by A. J. Smith's troops. From the front to the rear, the line extended from twenty to thirty miles, over a single road. The cavalry train delayed the columns in the rear, and the difficulties thus experienced were increased by a rain-storm, which, lasting all day on the 7th, rendered the road next to impassable by the Nineteenth Corps and Smith's command. General Banks rode along the line that day, after having seen the fleet off from Grand Ecore, and urged on the impeded columns. He reached Franklin's headquarters, at Pleasant Hill, on the evening of the 7th, at about 9 P.M. At about the same time, Colonel Clarke, of Banks's staff, returned from the front, and reported that Lee was anxious to have infantry support, having met with strong opposition. Franklin declined to send support. If General Lee could not hold his position, he must fall back. Franklin had previously ordered Lee to crowd the enemy vigorously, and keep his train well up.[2] Lee had found his train a source of great annoyance, being obliged to detach from one third to one half of his force to guard it. He had parked about a third of his wagons, and forced the others to the rear. Franklin's order led him to keep his train close up to his column. There was evidently no proper understanding between Franklin and Lee. It ought to have been Lee's proper business to develop the enemy's force and report to his superior officer. This General Lee failed to do. All he knew of the enemy's force in his front was that it was "considerable." General Franklin's impression that the enemy would not fight interfered with the proper operations of the cavalry. Lee expected a fight near Pleasant Hill, and strongly insisted upon the probability of a battle at that point. His advice was disregarded, and the orders which he received indicated that Franklin thought him advancing too cautiously, and that the cavalry was in the way.

General Banks's arrival at Pleasant Hill on the evening of the 7th does not seem to have helped matters at all. Without being aware of the situation in the front, he ordered that a brigade of infantry should be dispatched in accordance with Lee's request. His only reason for doing this was his notion that "the advance-guard should be composed of cavalry for celerity, artillery for force, and infantry for solidity."[3] He had no idea of bringing on a general engagement. He knew what was the position of his rear columns, for he had just rode past them. Franklin's objection to moving forward the infantry was that he thought it would bring on a battle. This is clear from the conversation between him and General Banks at 11 A.M. on the 8th. At that time Franklin had moved forward with the advance of the infantry to a point about ten miles from Pleasant Hill, and was building a bridge for his train, when he was joined by Banks. He remarked to the latter that there would be no fight. Banks replied, "I will go forward and see." Lee was then five miles beyond this point. One of Ransom's brigades had been sent to him, reaching him that morning. He now reported that this brigade was much exhausted, and asked for another, which Franklin ordered forward, instructing Ransom to go with it in person. General Banks arrived

[1] The number of wagons is variously estimated. Banks speaks of it as 156. J. G. Wilson, Banks's aid-de-camp, makes it 180. General Lee, who certainly ought to have known, makes the number from 320 to 350. The enemy claims that he captured 220 at Sabine Cross-roads.

[2] These were verbal orders as delivered through Colonel Clarke in the afternoon. The written dispatch reads thus:

"The commanding general has received your dispatch of 2 P.M. A brigade of infantry went to the front; but the fire having ceased, it was withdrawn. The infantry is all here. The general commanding directs that you proceed to-night as far as possible with your whole train, in order to give the infantry room to advance to-morrow."

[3] *Report on the Conduct of the War*, p. 11.

at the extreme front at 1 P.M. He found there an unexpected force of the enemy. He felt, he says, instinctively that "we were in presence of the whole force of the enemy." He then saw with his own eyes the disadvantageous position of the cavalry train, which was stretched along for a distance of two or three miles in the rear. Skirmishing with the enemy had already commenced; a battle was imminent, and could not be avoided. There had been mismanagement, the injurious results of which it was now too late to avert entirely. The extent of the injury must depend upon the decision made at this critical moment by General Banks. If he fell back, declining a general battle, it was at some risk to the train; but if he determined upon a battle at that point, bringing up his infantry to Lee's support, the risk was much greater. Indeed, it was, under the circumstances, almost certain that he would be defeated if he ventured battle. General Banks determined to take the greater risk. He hurried up the infantry in the rear, and brought up fourteen pieces of artillery in addition to the twelve already with General Lee. Notwithstanding his own admission that he felt himself to be confronted by the full force of the enemy, Banks does not seem to have appreciated the risk which he was running. In his dispatch to Franklin half an hour after he reached Lee, he advises him that the enemy seems prepared to make a strong stand, and that he had better make arrangements to bring up his infantry, and concludes: "You had better send back and push up the trains, as manifestly we shall be able to rest here."

General Franklin, on receipt of this order, was at the point where Banks had passed him in the morning, where he had the remainder of the Thirteenth Corps under General Cameron, and Emory's division of the Nineteenth. The order to move forward quickly followed the dispatch above mentioned, and before 5 o'clock P.M. Franklin was on the field with Cameron's command. The battle had been going on then for half an hour. Ransom had reached the field at 1 30 P.M., and found that the enemy had been driven across an open field. Landrum, with the brigade sent in the morning, was advancing to a ridge which the Confederates had abandoned, and which he now occupied (at 2 P.M.), the other brigade brought up by Ransom going in to his support. Landrum's third brigade arrived soon afterward, making the infantry force under Ransom 2413 strong. This, with Lee's cavalry, made the entire force between 6000 and 7000 men. The position taken was about four miles from Mansfield, at a place called Sabine Cross-roads. It was about fifty miles south of Shreveport, and twenty miles west of Red River. Nims's battery, posted on a hill near the road, was near the left of the line, supported on either side by the Twenty-third Wisconsin and Sixty-seventh Indiana regiments. Then came the Seventy-seventh Illinois, reaching to a belt of timber 200 yards to the right of the hill. The right of the line consisted of the One Hundred and Thirtieth Illinois, the Forty-eighth Ohio, the Nineteenth Kentucky, the Ninety-sixth and Eighty-third Ohio, with a section of artillery. The Chicago Mercantile and the First Indiana batteries, brought up at a later period, were posted on a ridge in the rear, near Banks's headquarters. The cavalry was posted on the two flanks. The ground in front was open, and descended in the rear to a creek, from which it again ascended to a covered ridge.

The Confederate force was under the command of General Dick Taylor, and consisted of Walker's and Mouton's divisions, and Green's cavalry, in all probably amounting to 12,000 men. Taylor had been ordered to retreat steadily before the advance of the Federal army, leading it on to Shreveport. Two circumstances led him to disobey this order. In the first place, he saw that it would be giving Banks a great advantage to leave him in possession of the roads in the open country near Mansfield, since these would enable him to communicate with the advancing fleet. In the second place, the opportunity offered for defeating General Banks was too tempting to be rejected. Taylor had already retreated beyond Mansfield, when, acting upon these considerations, he directed Walker and Mouton to retrace their steps through the town, and take up a position three miles beyond. Thus Green, who had been skirmishing and retreating steadily, found himself, on the 8th, supported by two infantry divisions. Taylor was still undecided whether to fight the battle, when Mouton, occupying the left, advanced without orders, and gained such a decisive advantage that Walker also was ordered forward.

The attack commenced about 4 P.M. The Federal right maintained its position, but the left was soon turned, and Nims's battery was captured. The hill was now occupied by the enemy, and the position first taken by the Federals was no longer tenable. The routed cavalry, galloping to the rear, rushed through the infantry line, throwing it into confusion, and some of the regiments were cut off from retreat and surrounded. The arrival of Franklin with Cameron's command was too late to retrieve the misfortune. Out of 26 pieces of artillery engaged, all but eight had been captured. To make a stand with Cameron's fresh division, and so many of the routed troops as might be rallied, would have resulted in fresh disaster. The Thirteenth Corps and the cavalry abandoned the field in as good order as was possible under the circumstances, leaving the train in possession of the enemy. But for the position of this train fewer prisoners would have been taken by the enemy, and probably a much larger portion of the artillery would have been saved. General Banks's loss in this unfortunate battle was over 3000 men, killed, wounded, and prisoners.[1] The enemy lost about 1000. The disaster at Sabine Cross-roads must be attributed to several causes: 1st. The failure of the cavalry to obtain prompt and full infor-

[1] The responsibility for this disaster lies between Generals Banks and Franklin. The majority of the Committee on the Conduct of the War throw the weight of responsibility upon Banks. They claim that it was his duty to be cognizant of the details of the march; that if he did not know these details on the 7th, he certainly did on the 8th, before the affair at Sabine Cross-roads; and that with this knowledge he assumed the responsibility of the position by remaining where he was and sending for the troops in the rear to re-enforce him.

D. W. Gooch submits a separate report, in which he takes a different view of General Banks's connection with the disaster. He claims that both Lee and Ransom "regarded the position held by our forces as a good one; that, in addition to the cavalry and artillery which had composed Lee's advance, there were on the field, also, at that time, two brigades of infantry, and that the balance of the Thirteenth and Nineteenth Corps were respectively about five and seven miles in the rear, and probably at that time advancing." "Under these circumstances," says Gooch, "General Banks, when he arrived upon the field, was obliged to decide to abandon this favorable position, over which he would be compelled to pass in order to establish his proposed communication with the transports at Loggy Bayou, and to reach Shreveport; withdraw his artillery and the large baggage train of the cavalry, in the presence of a superior force of the enemy, on the narrow and difficult road which has been described, or remain upon the field and order up to his assistance the troops of the Thirteenth and Nineteenth Army Corps from the points heretofore mentioned. He decided to remain upon the field and take the chances of a battle. Had the enemy deferred the attack one hour longer, or had it been possible for our troops to reach the field one hour earlier, the result of that battle would undoubtedly have been reversed."

But the attack was not deferred, and Banks had no reason to suppose that it would be; nor could Cameron and the Nineteenth Corps have been up in time. Banks admits that he thought the enemy in full force in his front. But his dispatch to Franklin (received by the latter at 3 P.M. on the 8th) only ordered him to make arrangements to bring up the infantry, and to await instructions before advancing. He also ordered Franklin to push up his trains (over seven hundred wagons), "as manifestly," says Banks, "we shall be able to rest here." Ten minutes later the order came to move, and Franklin promptly advanced with Cameron's division, coming upon the field too late to prevent disaster. The Nineteenth Corps, which was also ordered forward, being still farther in the rear, could not have been brought up in time to effect any thing. It is plain, therefore, that in venturing a battle instead of withdrawing the train under cover of the troops already in front, General Banks made himself responsible for the consequences. There is no testimony to the effect that the cavalry could not have fallen back.

The responsibility for the order of march rests with General Franklin. General Banks testifies: "The order of march was perfectly proper, but it was not compact enough. The different parts of the column were not within supporting distance of each other; they were extended for from twenty to thirty miles. . . . It was certainly a great fault that the advance-guard, with a possible chance of meeting the enemy, should have had its train close upon its rear. That was inexcusable. . . . The order in which the divisions should move was the established order which had continued from our movement from Alexandria. The only addition was that General Smith's forces brought up the rear. Every thing in that respect was perfectly right. It was approved by me, and it may be said to have been changed by me somewhat, because, when the enemy in our front was found to be increasing in strength, I gave directions to General Franklin to send a brigade to the assistance of the cavalry. But the fact that this force was stretched out more than twenty miles was necessarily without my knowledge, and I am not responsible for it in any way. The responsibility rests with General Franklin. General Lee, who is responsible for the advance, received written instructions from General Franklin, which are stated in General Lee's report. My own staff officers took written instructions to General Lee from General Franklin to keep his trains close up, the theory probably being that they would not meet the enemy. When I passed General Franklin on the morning of the 8th of April, he said, 'There will be no battle.' Besides, in his instructions to General Lee he evidently supposes that the enemy was not there; for he says, 'General Banks and General Ransom have gone to the front; but it is not expected that they will remain there.'"

In answer to the question, "At what point in your advance were you expecting to meet the enemy?" Banks replies:

"My expectation was that we should meet the enemy between Mansfield and Shreveport; but it was never certain whether we should or not. . . . . I had information, upon which I relied implicitly, from a man who had been through that country, that we would have to fight at some point between Mansfield and Shreveport, at some point near Mansfield. My belief is that the plans of the enemy were changed as we approached Mansfield. [This belief is confirmed by the Confederate reports.] And it has been stated that the rebel General Taylor was suspended from his command for having attacked us at Sabine Cross-roads, General Kirby Smith being confident that if his orders had been complied with, and we had been allowed to reach Shreveport, we would have been unable to return. And of that I am assured myself. If General Taylor had not attacked us, I do not know what we would have done. But he was tempted by our position, knowing that we were in a condition where we could not get our forces together, and he knew he could gain an advantage over us. He was thereby induced to attack us against orders."

General Franklin testifies that he differed with Banks and Lee as to the policy of making the advance-guard include infantry. "If any fighting occurs, it is most likely that the infantry will do it, while the cavalry looks on; and if there be merely a march, the cavalry exhausts the infantry, or it must regulate its march by the infantry rate." He claims that the trains "had nothing to do with the defeating of the infantry and cavalry. But when the rout began, then the trains were in the way, and nothing could be got away, because the train was jammed up to where the infantry was driven back; and when the time came to turn the artillery back, there was no place for it to get through. . . . . I suppose that to a certain extent I am responsible thus far. The cavalry general had always been asking me to put his train behind the infantry troops, and let it march in front of the infantry train. I had always refused to do that; I told him it was his business to take care of his own train. The reasons which actuated me in this were these: I had about seven hundred wagons with me, which the infantry had to take care of. If it had taken the two hundred and fifty which the cavalry had, and put them in front of my infantry train, my infantry wagons would never have got into camp the day of my march. The consequence would have been that the cavalry would have had their wagons up, but at the expense of the infantry. I therefore told General Lee that he must take care of his own wagons. To that extent I am responsible for his wagons being where they were. But he writes me, at 7 30 A.M. on the 8th, 'I am keeping my train back in order that I may see the thing settled before I bring it up to the front.' That relieved my mind entirely about the train, and I had no idea that I would find it where I did find it. I was so anxious about the trains that I ordered them to close up during the day, finding that the wagons straggled badly as they passed my camp. I understand that General Lee has interpreted that to mean that I ordered his train forward, which I did not. I gave no orders to General Lee's train that day except to close up. There were several open places, between the point where the infantry was to encamp and the battle-ground, where a train much larger than the cavalry train could have been parked. The general in command at the front should, I think, have ordered the train in park at one of these places when he saw that a general battle was imminent. I could not, because I was with my immediate command."

But could not Franklin, when he received Lee's report that the train was a great annoyance to him, have issued this order to park the artillery? He could have done so but for his impression that there would be no battle at this stage of the march. It seems, therefore, that while General Franklin must be held exclusively responsible for the detached order of march, a large share of the blame attached to the position of the cavalry train should be attributed to Generals Lee and Banks, either of whom ought to have seen the necessity of parking the trains before engaging an enemy which Banks believed to be from 15,000 to 18,000 strong. If *they* failed to attend to this, it was the business of Brigadier General C. P. Stone, General Banks's chief of staff, to do so. He was on the field, and this was one of his especial duties.

Brigadier General Dwight, who, a week after the battle, succeeded General Stone as chief of staff, corroborates General Franklin's testimony as to the feasibility of parking the train. He testifies: "There was no objection to the train being on the road, provided the cavalry was not so heavily engaged with the enemy as to endanger it. There were a great many places on the road where the train could have been parked." He denies that the wagons in any way impeded the march of the Nineteenth Corps. General Lee, he says, "should by no means have permitted his train to be between the infantry of the army and the cavalry of the army when he was going to fight a battle. But he ought to have known whether there was danger of a battle; he ought to have known the enemy's force in front of him; for he had a very large force. But it is to be remarked here that he did not seem to know well; that he did not manage as if he knew the whole force of the enemy was in his front. The moment that he found the enemy was in his front in force, he should have parked the train where it would be safe; and if he found that he had got it too far in the front, he should have turned it to the rear. That is a matter of his own responsibility, of which he ought to be a competent judge." Dwight evidently thinks that Lee mismanaged the entire conduct of the advance-guard. He says the cavalry ought to have been still farther in advance of the infantry than it was; that Lee had too large a train; but that, large as it was, it could have been parked in three hours; that it was Lee's business to know that he was likely to be attacked, and thus have gained time for preparation; "it was the easiest country in the world in which to tell when you are going to be attacked, or when there was a liability to attack, because it was comparatively a narrow country. A strong advance-guard of cavalry, much less than the main body, of good cavalry scouts, could have always told where the main body of the enemy was, so that no battle should have occurred until the army was prepared for it." He thus describes Lee's command:

"This cavalry force, as it was called, of General Lee consisted of cavalry proper, of mounted infantry, and a very large proportion of artillery for such a force. It was really more infantry than it was cavalry. For the work of cavalry proper it was utterly unfit. The men were not good riders, and did not understand how to take care of their horses properly. They were infantry soldiers who had been put on horseback; they were not properly cavalry. General Lee's force, therefore, consisted of some of the very best infantry regiments that were ever in the Department of the Gulf, with cavalry proper, and a large amount of artillery. Considering the character of that force, it was an eminently proper disposition to place the whole of it, or so much of it as was in advance, in advance. The whole of it was not in advance; one brigade of it, at least, was in the

T. E. G. RANSOM.

mation concerning the enemy. 2d. General Lee's neglect to park his trains before fighting. 3d. The detached order of march, the column of infantry with its head fronting the enemy on a field over twenty miles distant from its rear. And, 4th. The decision of General Banks to venture a battle under these unfavorable circumstances. This last was the great mistake, and gave each of the disadvantages mentioned its operative force; but for this decision there need have been no defeat, at least not at this point. It would probably have been better if Banks had staid behind at Grand Ecore, or any where else, as in that case the battle, if fought at all, would have been fought with a concentrated command. For, notwithstanding General Franklin's conviction that there would be no fighting, it is clear that on the morning of the 8th his plan was to concentrate his whole command before marching beyond St. Patrick's Bayou. Had this been done, the advance would have continued to Shreveport without fighting a battle, and there it would have confronted a force of the enemy superior in numbers—Price's command united with Dick Taylor's. Still, even in that event, a far greater disaster would have befallen General Banks's army, with its immense baggage trains, and 400 miles from its base. Most certainly, in that event, the fleet—so much of it as could wriggle its way up to Shreveport—together with the transports, would have been exposed to utter destruction.

While the Thirteenth Corps and Lee's cavalry were falling back in a disorganized mass from Sabine Cross-roads, General Emory's division of the Nineteenth Corps was advancing to the field of battle. At Pleasant Grove, three miles back of where the fighting had been, this division met the fugitives, who passed through their ranks to the rear. Following these came the pursuing enemy, who just at nightfall fell upon Emory's unbroken wall of bayonets, and were repulsed after an engagement of an hour and a half. General Mouton was killed in the first onset. "The first division of the Nineteenth Corps," says General Banks, "by its great bravery in this action,

rear. . . . . I consider our force of cavalry, mounted infantry, etc., was badly commanded; that the officer commanding it did not well understand the manner of leading an advance, of obtaining proper information concerning the enemy, or of penetrating any little curtain of troops which the enemy might throw in front of him to prevent his obtaining information which he ought to have had. Our force, or that portion of the force which, on the 8th of April, advanced to the position in which it was attacked by the enemy, stood dormant in the presence of the enemy until the enemy completely enveloped it. There can be but one solution of such a conduct of affairs, and that is, that whoever directed that on our part was incapable."

"*Question.* Then, if I understand you, it is your opinion that that disaster occurred in consequence of the failure of the cavalry and its officers to do that which they should have done?"

"*Answer.* I consider that was the cause of our not having proper information. I consider that the cause of the disaster of that day was that the infantry of the army was in three detachments, one near the scene of action, and the other two respectively nine and twenty-four miles from it, and that a battle never ought to have occurred under those circumstances. The infantry of the army was not concentrated; it was in exactly the proper position to be beaten in detail, which, in fact, was what occurred."

General Dwight's opinion of General Lee's inefficiency seems to have been concurred in by a majority of the general officers of the army. General Banks says in his testimony: "General Lee was relieved from the command of the cavalry subsequent to this affair at Sabine Cross-roads, but it was not on account of this action. It was because the general officers expressed to me so positively their want of confidence in the organization and condition of the cavalry, and advised so earnestly a change. This was an act which I afterward regretted. It was done because of the demoralized condition in which the cavalry found itself after this affair, and the very important part it must have in subsequent movements. I have no complaint to make of General Lee's general conduct. He was active, willing, and brave, and suffered more or less unjustly, as all of us did, for being connected with that affair." General Arnold, formerly Chief of Artillery, succeeded General Lee.

saved the army and navy." The enemy now retreated to Mansfield, so that during the night the Federal forces occupied both battle-fields.

It was then decided to fall back to Pleasant Hill. A renewal of the attack was expected on the morning of the 9th, and it was not likely that General Smith's command would be able to reach Pleasant Grove in time to participate in the action; without his presence it would be impossible for Banks, with the Nineteenth Corps and the demoralized troops who had been driven from Sabine Cross-roads, to maintain his position. The movement to Pleasant Hill began before daylight, Emory's division covering the rear, burying the dead, and bringing off the wounded. At 8 30 A.M. the retreat had been completed, and a junction effected with Smith's command.

In the mean time the enemy had been re-enforced by Churchill's division of infantry from Arkansas—there being no immediate apprehension as to Steele's advance—so that he was able to bring into the field upward of 20,000 men. Kirby Smith had ordered Taylor to follow up Banks's force. To meet this force Banks had only 15,000 men. But a battle for the safety of the fleet would have to be fought somewhere, and General Banks concluded that it might as well take place at Pleasant Hill as farther back. A strong position was taken, and this time the trains were sent to the rear under a strong cavalry guard. The forenoon passed quietly by. The Confederates, wearied by their previous battles, and—in the case of Churchill's command—by a long march, advanced slowly, and it was not until 4 o'clock P.M. that Green's cavalry encountered the Nineteenth Corps, guarding the approaches to the open ground surrounding Pleasant Hill. The army under Banks now consisted of the Nineteenth Corps and the Western troops under A. J. Smith. The remainder had been sent to the rear with the baggage and wounded. The greater part of A. J. Smith's command was held in reserve. The troops most advanced were soon driven in, and so easily that Taylor was led to believe that he was about to fight only the rear-guard of a retreating army. Walker was ordered to attack in front. Polignac—a French gentleman of aristocratic birth who had espoused the Confederate cause—having succeeded to General Mouton's command, was held in reserve. Churchill was ordered to make a detour and strike the Federal left flank. The conflict that followed was desperate, and for a long time doubtful. The Federals held rising ground, and presented a stubborn front to every attack. Churchill found the resistance so strong in his front that he had to be supported by a brigade from Walker's division. Even with this reenforcement he was roughly handled, and driven back across the open to the cover of the woods. Walker, supported by Polignac (who was sheltered by woods), in the mean time had advanced across the valley under a galling fire, from which he suffered severe loss, against the Federal right flank. Re-enforced by Polignac, he kept advancing, and, toward night, seemed to be gaining a decisive advantage, having driven back the force in his front. But Smith's reserves were then brought up, and the Confederates were driven from the field, fairly beaten. Some guns which had been taken by the enemy in the early stage of the action were afterward recaptured. The battle had been fought by Banks for the existence of his army and of Porter's fleet, and had resulted in victory.

But what then? Should the army advance or continue its retreat? Smith, with his Western soldiers, cried out for an advance. Banks's judgment was in favor of advance; but Franklin, more wisely, advised retreat. Indeed, no folly could have been greater than to renew the attempt against Shreveport. For the army to remain where it was involved peril. A single day could add to the enemy's force sufficient re-enforcements to give him a decided advantage against Banks. With this increased force, and with proper management on Kirby Smith's part, the defeat of the Union

A. J. SMITH.

CONFEDERATE LAND ATTACK ON PORTER'S FLEET.

army was inevitable, and, following this, the capture of the gun-boats, and possibly the repossession of the Mississippi by the Confederates. Besides this, there were also other reasons for a retreat. It would consume much valuable time to turn the train back again toward Shreveport and to reorganize the army. And the enemy would certainly have attacked before Banks was fully prepared to meet him. There was no water at Pleasant Hill for man or beast. All the horses with the army had been without food for 36 hours. Without rations and without water, without tidings of the fleet with which was the supply of ammunition, General Banks, reluctantly following Franklin's advice, determined to fall back to Grand Ecore, where he could reorganize his army and be sure of communication with Porter. The losses in the campaign thus far amounted to nearly 4000 men, besides artillery, mules, and wagons. Grant was now lieutenant general, and in

March had ordered General Banks to send back Smith's command if the expedition could not be terminated successfully by the 1st of May, saying that if it should be continued beyond that date he would much rather it had never been begun. This was an additional reason for retreat. How General Banks or General A. J. Smith could have for a moment contemplated an advance under these circumstances it is difficult to imagine. But orders for such an advance had been given, and the train had been ordered to return, and it was only after consultation with his general officers that Banks countermanded these orders, and at midnight on the 9th directed preparations to be made for the return of the army to Grand Ecore. It was an unfortunate circumstance that, although this withdrawal was accomplished at leisure, a large number of the wounded were left behind for want of transportation.[1]

---

[1] The following is the testimony of Surgeon Eugene F. Sanger on this point:
Question. "What is your position in the army?"
Answer. "Surgeon of United States Volunteers."
Question. "Did you accompany the Red River expedition under General Banks?"
Answer. "I did."
Question. "Were you present at the battles of Sabine Cross-roads and Pleasant Hill?"

Answer. "I was."
Question. "What was the condition of our wounded there?"
Answer. "We brought off about half our wounded in the first battle, and in the second battle we brought off all that could walk off."
Question. "It has been said that at Pleasant Hill we won a victory; how happened it that we left our wounded in the hands of the enemy?"

The fleet had reached Loggy Bayou on the 10th, when, learning of the disaster which had happened to the army, it began to return down the narrow, snaggy channel which it had with great difficulty just ascended. Removed from the military force (except that of T. K. Smith's command, which accompanied the transports), the fleet was peculiarly exposed to attack from the bluffs on either side. Failing to destroy the army, the Confederates turned their attention to the gun-boats and transports. The river was falling, and the progress of the fleet was slow—about thirty miles per day—so that the enemy easily followed him down, continually increasing in numbers. The first attack was made at Coushutta, and a second, with 1900 of Green's cavalry and four guns, at Harrison. Both these attacks were easily met and repulsed. On the 12th of April a more determined onset was made by 2000 infantry, infuriated by Louisiana rum, from the right bank. It was a novel conflict, this, in which these reckless Texans charged upon Porter's gun-boats with the assistance of two guns! The crazy attempt was persisted in for two hours. Detachment after detachment, they were brought to the river's edge and mown down by the guns of the fleet, until at length their leader, General Tom Green, lost his head, blown off by a shell, when the enemy withdrew, leaving the river bank strewn with his killed and wounded, whose bodies, says Admiral Porter, "actually smelled" of the rum which had bedeviled them. This affair seems to have satisfied the enemy as to the chances of success in an attack by infantry upon gun-boats. On the 15th the fleet reached Grand Ecore. Here Porter found most of his larger gun-boats aground, drawing a foot more water than there was on the bar. While he was extricating them, the Eastport, eight miles below, was sunk, and was with great difficulty got afloat again.

The retreat of the army was continued on the 22d to Alexandria. The fleet followed soon, but was delayed by Porter's anxious and persistent efforts to get away the Eastport, which, finally, he was obliged to destroy. When the fleet reached Cane River, ninety miles below Grand Ecore, it was attacked by eighteen Confederate guns. Every shot from these struck the Cricket, the admiral's flag-ship, whose decks were rapidly cleared. The after gun was disabled, and every man in attendance killed or wounded. Another shell exploded her forward gun, sweeping away the crew from it, and, passing into the fire-room, left but one man there unwounded. Admiral Porter made up a crew from contrabands for the after gun, put an assistant in the place of the chief engineer, who had been killed, and ordered the

Answer. "That is a great mystery to me. I was at that time medical director of the Nineteenth Army Corps. I saw General Franklin immediately after our victory, as we assume it to be. I told him that in the hurry of sending off the supply trains in the morning, they had sent off my medical supply train. He said at that time that it should be ordered to return at once. To make sure of this matter, I went to see Major Drake, General Banks's adjutant general. He told me to give myself no uneasiness about the matter, as he would send off a courier at once and order up the medical supply train. I saw General Franklin, and told him that I should be busy all night, and in case the army moved off in any direction he must apprise me. I was told that I should be informed. That was the last I knew of the matter until between 6 and 7 o'clock the next morning, when, observing a little squad of cavalry drawn up in front of my hospital, I went out and inquired, and found that the army had retired during the night, and that this cavalry was the rearguard about leaving the place. They said they had seen the enemy approaching in the distance, whereupon I left one or two assistant surgeons with instructions, mounted my horse, and rode off.".

Question. "Did you see any real necessity for leaving our wounded in the hands of the enemy there?"

Answer. "Yes, sir; we had no transportation at that time of any kind. There was not a wagon of any kind there."

vessel to run by the battery, "which was done," says the admiral, "under the heaviest fire I have ever witnessed." Driving around the point on which were posted the enemy's guns, he shelled the latter in the rear, and by this diversion the light-draught Juliet and pump-boat Champion, lashed together, escaped from under the bank where they had drifted. The Hindman from above co-operated with the Cricket by pouring an enfilading fire into the Confederate batteries, but dared not pass them. Porter therefore went down to obtain the assistance of some of the iron-clads below, but in the trip he got aground, and was delayed for three hours. After proceeding three miles he found the Osage and Lexington engaging another Confederate battery, the latter having been hulled fifteen times, with only one man killed. It was now night, and impossible to return to the Hindman, yet the latter vessel succeeded in running the battery, but, having her wheel-ropes cut away by the enemy's fire, got badly cut up in drifting down. Three of her men were killed and four wounded. The Juliet also passed, sustaining severe injuries. The Champion was disabled and set on fire. During these operations the Cricket was hulled thirty-eight times, and fifteen of her crew were killed or wounded. After such difficulties as we have described, the fleet at length arrived at Alexandria. Admiral Porter estimates that on his way down he killed and wounded at least 500 Confederates, his own loss being less than 100.

General Banks had also met with formidable resistance on his way to Alexandria, at the crossing of Cane River, where he met a Confederate force of 8000 men, with 16 guns, under General Bee. This force, flanked by the river on one side and an impenetrable swamp on the other, was confident of checking Banks until the rest of the Confederate army could come up in his rear. Banks's only safety was in rapidity of movement. Aware of the enemy's designs, he commenced his march from Grand Ecore on the morning of the 22d, and that day and night marched 40 miles, moving upon the enemy at Monet's Bluff, on Cane River, before daybreak of the 23d. General Emory, with his own division of the Nineteenth Corps, one of the Thirteenth, and Arnold's cavalry, was ordered to attack the enemy in front. The position was found too strong to be carried by a direct attack. Therefore General H. W. Birge, with a command consisting of his own brigade (the Third of Emory's division) and Cameron's division, was dispatched across the river, three miles above, to strike the enemy's flank. Birge, after a difficult march through swamps and dense woods, reached his destination late in the afternoon. Fessenden, commanding Birge's brigade, assaulted and carried two strong positions, whose occupation forced the enemy to retreat southwestwardly into Texas. Kilby Smith, covering Banks's rear, was on the next morning unsuccessfully attacked by the Confederate force which was co-operating with Bee. The Federal loss in these engagements was 250 men. General Banks, by his promptness, had prevented the enemy from concentrating his forces and fortifying his position, otherwise the Federal army would have been compelled to cross Red River above the bluff in the presence of the enemy on both sides of both Cane and Red Rivers. The army reached Alexandria on the 25th and 26th of April, precisely a month after its occupation of the town in March.

Here, also, it was impossible to remain without the support of A. J. Smith,

GENERAL BANKS CROSSING CANE RIVER.

PORTER'S FLEET PASSING THE DAM AT ALEXANDRIA.

whose time for co-operation with Banks had already expired. But, before retreating farther, it was necessary to rescue the fleet from its perilous situation by getting it below the falls. The difficulty had been foreseen by Lieutenant Colonel Joseph Bailey, engineer of the Nineteenth Corps, who, as early as the battle of Pleasant Hill, had suggested to General Franklin a plan for its removal by means of dams. Franklin approved the project. Admiral Porter does not seem to have had much faith in it. He remarked, when the plan was first proposed to him, that "if damming would get the fleet off, he would have been afloat long before."

The plan was carried out by the army under Bailey's supervision. Between two and three thousand men were engaged in the work of damming the river, which was commenced on the 2d and completed on the 8th of May. The rapids, or falls at Alexandria, are over a mile long. At the foot of these the main dam was constructed, the river at this point being 758 feet wide, and the depth of water from four to six feet, with a swift current of about ten miles per hour. Two wing-dams were also constructed at the head of the rapids. By means of these dams the depth of water was increased by 6½ feet, and eight valuable gun-boats were thus saved from destruction. Four of the gun-boats passed immediately upon the completion of the work. The rest might have passed at the same time if Porter had been prepared to avail himself of the advantage. The pressure of the water upon the dam was very great, as might have been expected, and before the admiral was ready to get down his other boats, the works gave way. Additional wing-dams were then constructed, and on the 13th the entire fleet was safe below the falls.

Before the relief of the fleet Banks had received a dispatch from Lieutenant General Grant directing that no troops should be withdrawn from the operations against Shreveport, which were to be continued until farther orders.

But the continuance of the campaign was, of course, impracticable. As soon as the fleet had been relieved Banks evacuated Alexandria, moving from that point to Simmsport, on the Atchafalaya. On the morning of his departure a fire broke out in a building on the levee, and, under a high wind, extended to a large portion of the town.

Previous to the evacuation of Alexandria, the light gun-boats Signal and Covington, passing down the river with the transport Warner, were fired on by a large Confederate force. The Covington was burned, and the Signal, with the transport, were surrendered, with 150 soldiers. Soon afterward the transport City Belle was captured, with 225 men, who were being conveyed up to Alexandria.

The march to Simmsport was interrupted for a few hours at Mansura, near Marksville, by a Confederate cavalry force, which, after a spirited skirmish, was driven away. Simmsport was reached on the evening of May 16th. Here the army crossed the Atchafalaya by a bridge built of steam-boats on the 20th. While the wagon train was crossing the bridge, a Confederate force under Polignac attacked the rear of the army, but was repulsed by A. J. Smith's command. Having crossed the river, Banks met General E. R. S. Canby, who had been sent to relieve him of the command of the Department of the Gulf, and to whom General Banks turned over the army, proceeding himself to New Orleans. General A. J. Smith now returned to his own department. Admiral Porter descended the Red River and resumed his patrol of the Mississippi.

Before tracing the progress of Steele's co-operative column from Little Rock, let us rapidly review the military events which had taken place in Missouri and Arkansas up to the inception of the Red River campaign.

Shortly after Hindman's defeat at Prairie Grove in the latter part of 1863, a Confederate force of about 4000 men, under General Marmaduke, moved around General Blunt's command in Northern Arkansas, and marched on Springfield, in Missouri. This important station, the dépôt of munitions and supplies for the Federal troops operating in Arkansas, was partially fortified, and was held by a garrison of 1200 men under Brigadier General

E. B. Brown, consisting of state militia, a small portion of the Eighteenth Iowa, and about 300 convalescent soldiers known as the "Quinine Brigade." The main body of the Federal army under General Blunt was in the vicinity of Fayetteville, on the Arkansas border, too distant to furnish assistance, and yet dependent for its own safety upon the secure possession of Springfield. Marmaduke attacked Brown on the 8th of January, 1863, and after fighting from 10 A.M. till dark, losing some 200 men, withdrew without gaining any other advantage than the capture of a single gun. The loss of the garrison was 164 men, of whom 14 were killed. Among the wounded was General Brown, who had managed the defense of his post with great skill and bravery.

At Hartsville, 40 miles east of Springfield, Marmaduke encountered on the 10th a small detachment of Federal troops under Colonel Merrill, consisting of the Twenty-first Iowa and Ninety-ninth Illinois, with portions of the Third Missouri and Third Iowa cavalry, and a battery of artillery. Here, after a sharp skirmish, he was repulsed with a loss of 800 men; Merrill's loss amounting to 78, including 7 killed. While the Federal forces were being concentrated to intercept his retreat, Marmaduke retreated into Arkansas. At Batesville, on the 4th of February, a part of his force was attacked by Colonel Waring, who, with the Fourth Missouri cavalry, drove him across the White River.

General Curtis on the 9th of March, 1863, was relieved of the command of the Missouri Department, which about a month later was assigned to General Schofield.

In the latter part of April, Marmaduke, with a considerable force, again entered Missouri, and made an attempt on Cape Girardeau, the capture of which would have very much disturbed Grant's Vicksburg campaign, but the timely appearance of the Federal gun-boats frightened him off, sending him back to Arkansas. A month later an engagement occurred at Fort Blunt, in Indian Territory, which was occupied by the Federal Colonel Phillips with 800 cavalry and an Indian regiment. A Confederate force about 3000 strong was led by Colonel Coffey against this fort. The defense was successfully maintained, and the enemy driven south of the Arkansas.

During the summer of 1863, the more important military operations in Mississippi and Tennessee reduced both the Federal and Confederate forces in the trans-Mississippi territory to such an extent that there were no hostilities in that region of any moment. Blunt had an encounter in July with a force of the enemy under General Cooper, which was menacing Fort Blunt. The fight took place on Elk River. Cooper had about 6000 men, and Blunt 3000 infantry, 250 cavalry, and 4 guns. General Blunt crossed the river, and, after a fight of two hours, drove the enemy, who left on the field 150 killed and 77 prisoners, besides 400 wounded, which were removed. The Federal loss was 17 killed and 60 wounded. Immediately after Cooper's defeat, 3000 Texans arrived under Cabell to re-enforce the enemy, but retired during the night without a battle.

In August, 1863, the Confederate partisan "Quantrell" made his notorious raid through Western Missouri into Kansas. With a force of 300 bandits, gathered together in Western Missouri, he crossed the Kansas border, and on the morning of August 22 entered Lawrence and commenced a sack of that town. The citizens were murdered without discrimination. For a citizen to appear in the street with a defensive weapon of any sort, or to be a German or a negro, were deemed sufficient reasons why he should be shot. The finest dwellings and the public buildings were committed to the flames. The banks and stores were pillaged. Many private citizens, after surrendering to these merciless fiends all their money, were killed. Eighteen recruits found without arms in their hands were cowardly butchered. J. H. Lane, a United States senator, was at Lawrence, but, with Colonel Deitzler and others, managed to escape. General Collamore, taking refuge in a well, was suffocated, and two men in an attempt to rescue him suffered a similar fate. By 10 o'clock A.M. 140 men had been killed and nearly 200 buildings burned, when the savage monsters left the scene of their cruelties. As

RUINS OF LAWRENCE, KANSAS.

LITTLE ROCK, ARKANSAS.

they were leaving three of them were killed by the fire of some soldiers who had just reached the opposite bank of the Kansas River. The band was pursued by a small force of cavalry, but, with the loss of a few men, effected its escape.

The day after this event, Colonel Woodson, with 600 men from Pilot Knob, captured at Pocahontas, Arkansas, General Jeff. Thompson and about 50 of his men.

At the close of July, 1863, General Steele was sent to Helena to organize an expedition for the capture of Little Rock, Arkansas. The force assigned to him for this purpose consisted of 6000 men, including 500 cavalry and 22 guns. He was afterward re-enforced by General Davidson with nearly 6000 more men, most of them mounted, and 18 guns. He advanced from Helena on the 10th of August, crossing the White River at Clarendon, 60 miles east of Little Rock, on the 17th, with Davidson's cavalry in the advance. His sick at this time numbered about 1000. These were sent to Duvall's Bluff, which was made the dépôt of supplies. On the 25th Davidson reached Brownsville, 25 miles distant from Little Rock, driving Marmaduke before him to his intrenchments at Bayou Metea, from which he was dislodged and driven across the bayou. Meanwhile Steele had concentrated his forces—re-enforced by General True's brigade from Memphis—at Brownsville. Shut off from an advance north of Bayou Metea by the nature of the country, which, on account of swamps, was impracticable, he determined to advance to the Arkansas, and threaten with his cavalry the enemy's communications southward. Davidson crossed the Arkansas to carry out this plan. Marmaduke, sent out by General Holmes to resist him, was completely routed. General Price, the Confederate commander in Arkansas, then evacuated Little Rock, which was occupied by Steele on the 10th of September. Price, in some disorder and in great haste, fell back to Arkadelphia, eluding pursuit. Steele had started out on his campaign with 12,000 men, and entered Little Rock with only 7000. Of this loss less than one fiftieth was caused in battle, the remainder arising from sickness.

On the 4th of October we again hear from Quantrell, who, with 600 guerrillas disguised in Federal uniform, attacks General Blunt on his way to Fort Smith (captured by a Union force a month previous) with an escort of about 100 cavalry. General Blunt, with about 15 men, fortunately escaped. The remainder were captured, and then murdered in cold blood.

Pine Bluff, fifty miles below Little Rock, on the south bank of the Arkansas, was occupied early in October by Colonel Clayton with 350 men of the Fifth Kansas Cavalry and four guns. Marmaduke advanced against this point on the 25th of October with 12 guns and a cavalry force of between 2000 and 3000 men. In the mean time Clayton had been re-enforced by the First Indiana Cavalry and five guns. Marmaduke's attack failed. His loss was 150 killed and wounded, and 33 captured. Clayton lost 17 killed and 40 wounded.

The Confederate General Shelby, of Cabell's command, having failed in a series of unimportant attempts in Indian Territory, about this time undertook a raid into Missouri. Crossing the Arkansas between Fort Smith and Little Rock, he was joined in Southwestern Missouri by a force under General Coffey, their combined command numbering possibly 2500 men. This expedition advanced as far north as Booneville, on the Missouri River, when it commenced to retreat, pursued by General E. B. Brown with a detachment of state militia. The enemy was brought to a stand near Arrow Rock on the 13th of October. Here there was an engagement which lasted five hours, resulting finally in the defeat of the Confederates, who, besides all their artillery and baggage, lost 300 men, killed, wounded, and prisoners. On the 18th of December General McNeil superseded General Blunt as commander of the Army of the Frontier.

General Steele commenced his movement southward from Little Rock to co-operate with Banks's advance to Shreveport on the 23d of March, 1864, or about the time of Franklin's arrival at Alexandria. His army was 7000 strong. General Thayer at the same time marched from Fort Smith with 5000 men, intending to unite with Steele at Arkadelphia, while Colonel Clayton, with a small force, advanced from Pine Bluff on Steele's left. Steele reached Arkadelphia on the 29th of March; but Thayer, owing to heavy rains and almost impracticable roads, was delayed, and after waiting for him two days, the main column continued its advance. The Confederate cavalry under Shelby and Marmaduke had skirmished with its front all the way from the Sabine River, and farther down the Washita was a considerable force of infantry under General Price. Two days after Banks's defeat at Sabine Cross-roads this latter force was encountered at Prairie d'Anne, and a sharp fight, chiefly with artillery, followed. A charge of the enemy upon Steele's artillery was repulsed, and Price fell back to Washington, near the Upper Red River. From prisoners and spies, intelligence was now received of Banks's defeat. This report turned Steele from his pursuit of Price eastward to Camden. The Confederates then became bolder, attacking on the 23d of April a train of 240 wagons, which had arrived from Pine Bluff three days before, and was then returning, guarded by one of General Salomon's brigades. The attack was made 12 miles from Camden by Shelby's cavalry, and was easily repulsed. The train proceeded six miles farther, and was then parked for the night. The road was bad, and much of the distance had to be corduroyed; thus, on the 24th, only 22 miles had been made. The next morning, while crawling through a long swamp, the guard was again attacked at Marks's Mills by General Fagan's command, reported 6000 strong. The advance being cut off from the rear after a gallant resistance, which cost the Federals 250 killed and wounded —one fourth of the entire brigade—both columns surrendered, and the wagons were either captured or destroyed. According to custom, all negroes found in the command were shot after the surrender.

On the 28th of April Steele abandoned Camden, crossed the Washita, and, continually skirmishing with the enemy's cavalry, proceeded to the Sabine. By this retreat he had just escaped disaster. Kirby Smith, having thrust back General Banks, was now prepared to strike Steele. As it was, Smith assailed the rear of the retreating column as the latter was crossing the Sabine at Jenkins's Ferry. A portion of the army was already across the river, and thus the brunt of the attack fell upon the two rear brigades until re-enforcements were brought up by General Rice. The enemy succeeded finally in turning the left, but the line was restored, and by noon the attack was repulsed, and the army crossed the bridge. No artillery could be used on account of the nature of the ground. The Federal loss was 700 killed and wounded. That of the enemy was estimated as over three times that number.

With Fagan in his front menacing Little Rock, Steele's position was one of great peril. His animals were starving, compelling the destruction of nearly all his wagons. The roads were next to impassable, and over these the exhausted and hungry troops dragged their guns. Notwithstanding these difficulties, Steele succeeded in reaching Little Rock on the 2d of May.

By Steele's reverses about two thirds of the state were recovered by the Confederates, whose cavalry and partisan rangers, avoiding the few Federal strong-holds, ravaged the country without molestation or resistance. This situation was full of discomforts to those who had previously, encouraged by the prospects of restoration, which had been so flattering at the time of the capture of Little Rock in the previous autumn, committed themselves to the Union cause. During the winter of 1863-4 measures had been taken to restore the state to the Union. A Constitutional Convention was assembled at Little Rock on the 8th of January, in which 42 out of 54 counties were represented. A new State Constitution was framed, in which slavery was forever prohibited. Dr. Isaac Murphy was inaugurated provisional governor on the 22d of January. In March the new Constitution was submitted to the people, and ratified by over 12,000 votes; and state officers, three members of Congress, and a Legislature were elected. In April the Legislature convened, and elected United States senators. But all these acts were in great measure annulled by the helplessness of Steele's military force. In the autumn of 1864 a Confederate Legislature met at Washington, in Southwestern Arkansas. A message was sent to it by the Confederate Governor Hannigan, and A. P. Garland was elected to represent the state in the Confederate Senate at Richmond.

The command of the entire trans-Mississippi military division was in 1864 given to General Canby. The garrison at Matagorda had been withdrawn. After the Red River campaign, with the exception of Price's raid into Missouri in the autumn, there was no military campaign of any importance undertaken before the close of the war in 1865. Although this raid overlaps the Atlantic campaign, this is the proper connection in which it should be placed before the reader.

CHAPTER XL.

PRICE'S MISSOURI RAID.

Rosecrans assumes Command of the Department of the Missouri January 28, 1864.—Extent and Distribution of his Command.—The "Paw-paw" Militia.—Feud between Radicals and Conservatives.—Secret Organizations in Northern Missouri.—Price advances northward in September.—Rosecrans is re-enforced by A. J. Smith's Division.—Defense of St. Louis.—Price attacks Pilot Knob; Ewing retreats upon Rolla.—Rosecrans assumes the Offensive.—Pleasonton takes command of the Cavalry.—Progress of Price westward, and Movements of the Federal Forces.—General Curtis is attacked at Marshall and driven.—A good Opportunity thrown away by the Federals.—Pleasonton's Pursuit of Price.—Fight on the Big Blue.—Price is defeated, but escapes Southward.—Fight with his Rear-guard on the Osage.—Criticism of the Campaign.

ROSECRANS, after having been superseded by Thomas as commander of the Department of the Cumberland, was, on the 28th of January, 1864, assigned to the command of the Department of the Missouri. His force consisted of about 12,000 men, mainly composed of state militia, out of ten regiments of which all but one were mounted men. To this there were added four regiments of three-years' volunteers, and a similar force of cavalry. There was also in process of organization a regiment (the Second Missouri) of heavy artillery. This command was distributed through the state at the most important posts—at Springfield, Rolla, Pilot Knob, Cape Girardeau, Jefferson City, Sedalia, Macon City, and, north of the Missouri River, at St. Joseph.

There was also a force of Missouri militia, 2800 in number, in the northwestern part of the state, "provisionally enrolled," and armed by the state government. It was composed in great proportion of disloyal citizens, a large number of whom had returned home from Price's army. Pledged to obey the laws of the state and of the general government, their especial business, as they understood it, was to take care of the peaceful sympathizers with rebellion, protecting them against the indignation of the Unionists. They were called the "Paw-paw militia," to identify them with "bushwhackers"—the paw-paw being the sort of fruit upon which this class of rebel sympathizers was supposed to subsist when it took to the bush.

This Paw-paw militia was a great element of disturbance in Missouri. There was a feud at this time between the two classes of citizens in the state known respectively as Radicals, or Abolitionists, and Conservatives—the latter class being generally understood to entertain a secret preference in favor of the Confederacy. It was confidently believed that the Paw-paws were, together with the Conservatives, in league with General Price, and that they only waited his approach to throw aside their assumed disguise. The disguise, after all, seemed only partial, especially in the great slaveholding

counties on the river, where the so-called Conservatives, evidently expecting a visit shortly from Price's army, warned the Union citizens "that the Loyalists had pretty nearly had their time, and that it would soon come to an end, and then the Disloyalists would have *their* time." Carefully observing these indications, and finding that arms were plentifully coming into the northern part of the state, Rosecrans felt that the apprehensions of the Unionists were well grounded, and, determined to be on his guard, he in the mean time quietly investigated the situation. Of course Rosecrans succeeded in detecting the whole plot. If the Confederates had been leagued with the powers of darkness, Rosecrans's spies would in some way have ferreted out their machinations; and even if the delicate business had required a trip to Hades, they would surely have accomplished it and reported to headquarters!

Rosecrans soon found that the basis of the hopes of the Confederate sympathizers in Missouri was a secret society. The organization of this society took the shape of lodges, in Northern Missouri mainly. The leaders proved to be Confederates. There seemed to be no limit to the organization, which existed even in Union settlements, and extended to the backwoods. It was apparent that its designs were military in character as well as political. An intelligent physician was employed by Rosecrans, and sent into Northern Missouri with a roving commission. This man made his way into one of the lodges, and advanced in degree until finally he obtained a ritual from the grand commander of the state. A closer scrutiny detected an extension of the organization into Indiana, Kentucky, and Illinois, and finally traced it to New York. In Missouri it was designated "The Order of American Knights," or "Sons of Liberty." The exiled Vallandigham was the supreme commander in the North, and General Sterling Price in the South. It was found that about 23,000 men were sworn to join Price on his appearance in Missouri. Under the auspices of this secret society, Vallandigham was to return to Ohio to attend the Democratic Convention at Chicago on the 4th of July. Simultaneously a rising was to occur in all the states in which the order existed, the existing officials were to be put out of the way, and the arsenals, forts, and public property were to be seized. A general Northern invasion was to be made at the same time by the Confederates.

In view of these developments, Rosecrans asked for an augmentation of his force in Missouri. General Hunt was sent by General Grant to that state on a tour of observation, and reported his belief that the inhabitants would behave themselves, that Rosecrans was too apprehensive, and that the force already in the department was larger than was needed.

Rosecrans went on with his investigation, and having accumulated 1000 pages of testimony, wrote a note to General Garfield at Washington, asking the latter to state to President Lincoln that he had this testimony, and obtain permission for him to send on a staff officer to lay the whole matter before the President.[1] President Lincoln requested Rosecrans to send his depositions by mail or express. Rosecrans replied that that would not be safe. The President then sent one of his private secretaries, Major Hay, to Missouri. He read the testimony, and reported to the President. No especial notice at this time seems to have been taken of the affair at Washington.

In the mean time, it was boldly proposed in one of the lodges of the Order of American Knights to commence the assassination of Union officers in St. Louis, "beginning with the provost-marshal, and then wind up with a grab at department headquarters." This startling proposition was laid over to the next meeting. Rosecrans immediately arrested the state commander of the society—the Belgian consul at St. Louis—the deputy commander, grand secretary, lecturer, and thirty or forty leading members, and committed them to prison. A dispatch was soon received from the War Department ordering the release of the Belgian consul. Rosecrans refused to comply with the order, knowing that it would not have been given if the government had been acquainted with all the facts of the case. A full representation of the matter having been laid before the President upon the return of Major Hay, the order of release was countermanded. Rosecrans was so impressed with the necessity of his action that he would have sooner resigned his command than have released the consul.

The Democratic Convention at Chicago was postponed, but the Confederate schemes in Missouri were so fully matured that they could not be thus postponed. The hostile flag was hoisted in Platte County on the 7th of July, and these peculiar exemplars of American knighthood commenced their operations. "From that time," says Rosecrans, "until after the expiration of the invasion and the expulsion of Price, there was nothing but murder and rapine wherever they could operate."

After the Fort Pillow massacre, the four regiments of three-years' volun-

---

[1] "Having about a thousand pages of testimony, obtained in the way I have just mentioned, I wrote a note to General Garfield, in Washington, requesting him to state to the President that I had this, and to say that, as the time for the dénouement was approaching rapidly, and that as the thing was not in a sufficiently perfect state to take action on without submitting it to him, more particularly as it concerned not only my own department, but the whole West of the nation, I wished permission from him to send a staff officer, who understood the subject, with the fragments of the testimony we had collected, to lay the whole matter before him, and answer such questions as the President desired to put; that I made this request, not because I doubted my right to send a staff officer to Washington, but because, when I had before sent a staff officer on a similar occasion, on a business of importance, he had been arrested by the Secretary of War, and I did not wish to subject another officer unnecessarily to the same indignity."—*Testimony before the Committee on the Conduct of the War, Rosecrans's Campaign*, p. 52.

In regard to the arrest by the Secretary of War of one of his staff officers, General Rosecrans testified: "He [the secretary] arrested my senior aid, who brought letters to General Halleck and General Grant respecting the condition of Missouri, and the measures which I thought immediately necessary there to be of advantage to the government and to the state. He was arrested on the pretense that he had no permission to come here, under an old order that no officer should visit Washington without permission from the Secretary of War. Major Bond returned home under arrest; and, considering that the shortest way to get rid of his arrest would be to have him tried, I ordered his trial by a court composed of the highest officers in Missouri, Major General Pleasonton being president. That court unanimously and honorably acquitted him."—P. 54, *ibidem.*

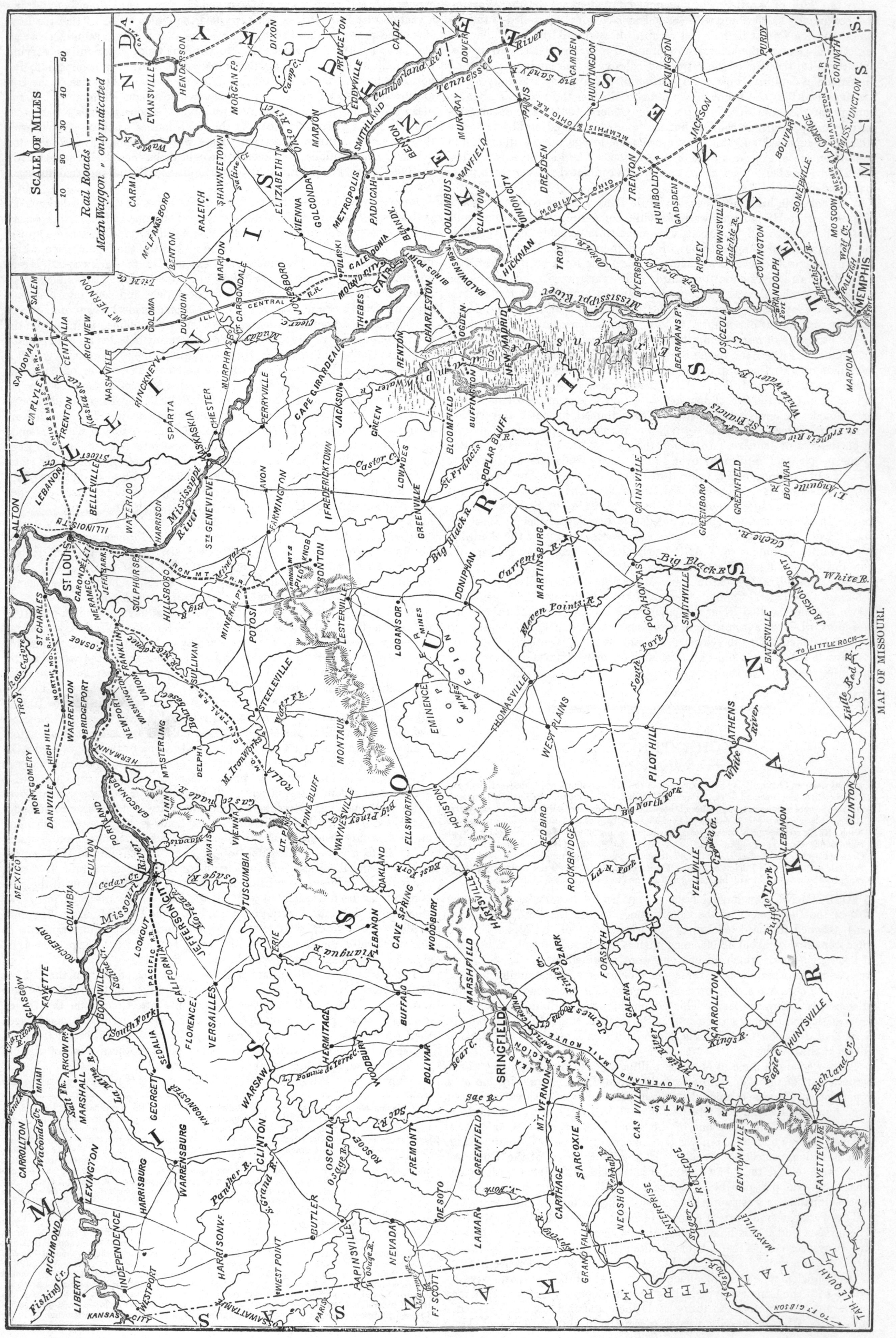

MAP OF MISSOURI.

REFUGEES FROM NORTHERN MISSOURI ENTERING ST. LOUIS.

teers which Rosecrans had at St. Louis were withdrawn from his department, as was also most of his three-years' cavalry. To supply their place, eleven regiments of twelve-months' volunteers were raised during the summer. Price's movement did not commence as early as Rosecrans had been led to anticipate. Perhaps he was deceived as to the extent and intimacy of the correspondence between the Confederate military leaders and the "Sons of Liberty;" but as to the existence of some connection between them, or as to its intent, there could be no doubt. The first sign of the invasion appeared in Arkansas early in September, 1864. On the 3d Washburn warned Rosecrans that a junction was about to be formed of Shelby's cavalry at Batesville with Price's army for the invasion of Missouri. At this time A. J. Smith's command was passing Cairo on its way to Sherman's army in Northern Georgia. At Rosecrans's request, this division was halted by order of General Halleck, and sent to St. Louis. It was decided to await Price's movements instead of advancing against him before he should cross the border.

Price by the 23d of September had crossed the Arkansas River, and was reported to be near Batesville with two divisions of mounted men, three bat-

teries, and a large wagon train; his force probably numbered 15,000 men. He entered the southeastern portion of Missouri, and advanced northward toward Rolla, with a detachment thrown out toward Pilot Knob. General Ewing was now ordered to concentrate the troops of his district at Pilot Knob and Cape Girardeau, and two of Smith's brigades were pushed out toward the front so far as seemed consistent with the safety of St. Louis. St. Louis must be protected at all hazards, being the great dépôt of supplies for the trans-Mississippi armies. This city has three approaches by railroad south of the Missouri River: one from the east, via Independence and Jefferson City; another, that against which Price was marching, from the southwest, via Rolla; and a third from Memphis, via Pilot Knob. It was important to maintain Springfield, Rolla, Jefferson City, and Pilot Knob if possible, but the capture of either of these positions by the enemy must be suffered rather than that, by a general engagement at any of these points, the safety of St. Louis should be endangered. The Federal General Mower's division was daily expected from Arkansas, but, until the arrival of this re-enforcement, it was evident that Price had a free course open to him through the state.

A portion of Price's army on the 27th of September attacked Pilot Knob, which was held by one brigade under General Ewing. The fortifications at this post were rude, but sufficiently strong to enable the garrison of 1200 men to maintain an obstinate and successful stand against several times that number. But the enemy gained commanding positions, which would have finally compelled the surrender of the post. Therefore, during the night, Ewing, having blown up his magazines and spiked his heavy guns, retreated toward Rolla. In the repulse at Pilot Knob the enemy lost over 1000 men (Ewing says 1500), while the Federal loss was less than 100. Price had already a column at Potosi, little more than twenty miles north of Pilot Knob, thus compelling Ewing to retreat in the direction of Rolla, and apparently threatening St. Louis.

Perhaps it was on account of the lesson which he had learned at Pilot Knob that Price did not make an attempt to capture St. Louis. Certainly he did not continue his advance in that direction, but turned westward, and moved on Jefferson City. Ewing retreated rapidly to Webster, and there veered northward, and struck the railroad to Springfield at Harrison, having marched about sixty-six miles in thirty-nine hours, pursued by Shelby's cavalry. The latter made an attack at this point, but Ewing held his ground for thirty hours, until re-enforced by a detachment of Sanborn's cavalry, sent from Rolla to his assistance. The apparent helplessness of Rosecrans encouraged the "conservative" guerrillas in Northern Missouri, who now grew bolder in their work of murder and plunder.[1]

It was at first hard to tell whether Price would strike for St. Louis, or for Jefferson City, or for Rolla. His delay to strike a decisive blow enabled Rosecrans to accumulate a force large enough for offensive operations. Five regiments of 100-days' men were brought from Illinois before the 1st of October, and were placed in the fortifications of St. Louis, relieving General Smith's command. A cavalry force had been raised of about 1500 men. Out of the East Missouri militia about 5000 men were organized into an effective division under General Pike. Besides these, under the direction of the mayor of St. Louis, about 5000 citizen soldiers volunteered for the defense of the city. A. J. Smith's command numbered 4500 men. General Mower's veteran division, 5000 strong, arrived at Cape Girardeau on the 5th of October. Adding to these the detachments at Rolla and Jefferson City, with Ewing's force, Rosecrans must, during the first week of October, have had a veteran army full 20,000 strong, besides over 12,000 citizen soldiers.

In the mean time the enemy, moving by Potosi, had advanced across the Meramee to Richwood, only 40 miles distant from St. Louis. Between this force and the city was A. J. Smith's command and 1500 cavalry. Demonstrating against Smith with a portion of his army, Price, on the 1st of October, after burning the railroad bridge across the Meramee at Moselle, turned toward Jefferson City, having crossed the Gasconade and the Osage by the 6th, burning Herman and the railroad bridge on his way. On the 7th he appeared before Jefferson City, garrisoned by troops from Rolla under Sanborn and McNeil, and fortified by hastily-constructed intrenchments. The garrison consisted of about 7000 men, nearly three fifths of whom was cavalry. Price drew up his forces, forming a line of battle three or four miles long about the city, but did not venture to assault; for, in addition to the intrenched force in his front, Smith, and Mower, and Winslow's cavalry were rapidly following, and would soon be upon his rear. Waiting only for his train to get a fair start, he resumed his march westward. On the 8th the Federal General Pleasonton, who had distinguished himself as a cavalry leader in Virginia, arrived at Jefferson City and assumed command. He dispatched Sanborn's cavalry with instructions to harass and delay the enemy until Mower and Smith could join the forces then in the capital. Sanborn advanced, and, in accordance with these orders, attacked Price's rear-guard at Versailles, and found that the enemy was moving to Booneville, on the Missouri. Pushing his attack with vigor, he compelled the enemy to form in line of battle; but soon finding that if he remained he would probably be surrounded, Sanborn fell back a few miles to California, where he was joined by Colonel Catherwood with A. J. Smith's cavalry on the 14th. Smith's infantry in the mean time reached Jefferson City, followed on the 16th by Winslow's cavalry, and on the 17th by nearly all of Mower's division.

[1] "Rebel agents, amnesty oath-takers, recruits, 'sympathizers,' O. A. K.'s, and traitors of every hue and stripe, had warmed into life at the approach of the great invasion. Women's fingers were busy making clothes for rebel soldiers out of goods plundered by the guerrillas; women's tongues were busy telling Union neighbors '*their time was now coming.*' General Fisk, with all his force, had been scouring the bush for weeks in the river counties in pursuit of hostile bands, composed 'argely of recruits from among that class of the inhabitants who claim protection, yet decline to perform the full duties of citizens, on the ground that they 'never tuck no sides.' A few facts will convey some idea of this warfare, carried on by Confederate agents here, while the agents abroad of their bloody and hypocritical despotism—Mason, Slidell, and Mann in Europe—have the effrontery to tell the nations of Christendom our government 'carries on the war with increasing ferocity, regardless of the laws of civilized warfare.' These gangs of rebels, whose families had been living in peace among their loyal neighbors, committed the most cold-blooded and diabolical murders, such as riding up to a farm-house, asking for water, and, while receiving it, shooting down the giver, an aged, inoffensive farmer, because he was a radical 'Union man.' In the single sub-district of Mexico the commanding officer furnished a list of near 100 Union men who, in the course of six weeks, had been killed, maimed, or 'run off' because they were 'radical Union men' or d—d Abolitionists. About the 1st of September Anderson's gang attacked a railroad train on the North Missouri, took from it twenty-two unarmed soldiers—many of them were on sick-leave—and, after robbing, placed them in a row and shot them in cold blood; some of the bodies they scalped, and put others across the track and ran the engine over them. On the 27th, this gang, with numbers swollen to 300 or 400 men, attacked Major Johnson, with about 120 men of the Thirty-ninth Missouri Volunteer Infantry, raw recruits, and, after stampeding their horses, shot every man, most of them in cold blood. Anderson, a few days later, was recognized by General Price at Booneville as a Confederate captain, and, with a verbal admonition to behave himself, ordered by Colonel Maclane, chief of Price's staff, to proceed to North Missouri and destroy the railroads, which orders were found on the miscreant when killed by Lieutenant Colonel Cox, about the 27th of October."—*Rosecrans's Report.*

By this time Price had reached Marshall, 25 miles west of Booneville. A detachment of cavalry under Shelby had crossed the Missouri at Arrow Rock, about midway between the two places last mentioned, and, moving up the river to Glasgow, which he took after a fight of seven hours, captured a part of Colonel Harding's regiment—the Forty-third Missouri—with small detachments of the Ninth Missouri militia and Seventeenth Illinois Cavalry. The Federal forces were fast closing in upon the enemy's rear, and more vigorous movement on their part ought to have resulted in an important and decisive victory. Smith and Mower had reached the Lamine River, and on the 18th and 19th the former advanced westward to Dunksburg, while still farther to the left General Pleasonton, now in command of the entire cavalry force, extended to Warrensburg.

Price leisurely proceeded to Lexington, 40 miles west of Marshall, where on the 19th he attacked General Curtis, who, after a slight skirmish, retreated to Independence. The enemy pursued to the Little Blue, where he struck General Blunt's Kansas division with such force that the retreat was continued to the Big Blue. When Rosecrans learned that the enemy was at Lexington, he ordered Pleasonton, who was demonstrating toward Waverly, to push on to Lexington, and Smith to follow. Of course the enemy had left before their arrival. Supposing that Price would be unable to cross the Big Blue in the face of Curtis's force, and would therefore move southward, Rosecrans ordered Pleasonton to harass the enemy's rear with McNeil's brigade, moving the remainder of his command to Lone Jack, to which point Smith was hurrying, having returned from his mistaken chase after the enemy. This order was unfortunately conditional; and Pleasonton, instead of complying with it, supposing that the enemy would continue his flight westward, kept on in pursuit, crossing Little Blue on the 22d, and, driving Price's rear-guard to Independence, made a charge at nightfall, capturing the place and taking two guns. Dispatching McNeil's brigade to Santa Fé to intercept the enemy, he telegraphed to Rosecrans requesting him to send Smith to Lexington. Rosecrans reluctantly complied with his request. On the morning of the 23d Pleasonton moved against the enemy at the crossing of the Big Blue, where a general engagement was fought, beginning at 7 A.M., and lasting until 1 P.M., when Shelby, finding that Marmaduke and Fagan were giving way, turned on Pleasonton, and for a moment shook Sanborn's brigade; but the skillful use of artillery and a gallant charge of the cavalry decided the fortunes of the day against the enemy, who now retired, pursued by Pleasonton and Curtis. Smith, reaching Independence at 5 P.M., was ordered to move by a forced march that night to Hickman's Mill, to strike the enemy in flank while passing that point. "Had he been ordered," reports Rosecrans, "and marched for that point instead of Independence the day before, General Smith would have arrived in time to strike the enemy's compact column and train with 9000 infantry and five batteries; but it was too late. He did not reach the mill until long after not only the enemy's, but our own columns had passed there."

Pleasonton continued the pursuit, the infantry following as rapidly as possible for support. On the banks of the Osage Price's rear-guard, composed of Marmaduke's cavalry, was overtaken, after a chase of 60 miles, on the 25th. Pleasonton here, by a furious charge, routed this Confederate force, capturing eight guns, several wagons, and nearly 1000 prisoners, including Generals Marmaduke and Cabell.

This campaign had lasted 48 days. Rosecrans reports his loss as 174 killed, 336 wounded, and 171 prisoners. Price had lost 1958 prisoners and 10 guns, and had succeeded in none of the objects for which his expedition had been undertaken. Missouri remained henceforth undisturbed by the enemy, and Price's invasion was the last important event of the war west of the Mississippi River.

Strategically the campaign on Rosecrans's part was not managed with that vigor and comprehension which we should have expected. But it was so ably conducted that, while the enemy was not made to suffer the full extent of punishment to which his audacity exposed him, he did not, on the other hand, inflict any material damage upon the Federal cause.[1]

[1] General Grant says of this campaign:

"The impunity with which Price was enabled to roam over the State of Missouri for a long time, and the incalculable mischief done by him, shows to how little purpose a superior force may be used. There is no reason why General Rosecrans should not have concentrated his forces, and beaten and driven Price before the latter reached Pilot Knob."

In view of all the circumstances of the case, and especially considering the domestic difficulties which Rosecrans encountered in Missouri, this criticism, notwithstanding its high military authority, does not seem to us to be quite fairly sustained by facts.

WILLIAM TECUMSEH SHERMAN.

CHAPTER XLI.

THE ATLANTA CAMPAIGN.

The general Military Situation at the opening of the Spring Campaign of 1864.—Richmond and Atlanta, held by the Armies of Lee and Johnston, were the Helmet and Shield of the Confederacy.—The Progress of the National Arms thus far had been in the West.—Importance of the Victories of Vicksburg and Chattanooga.—The Exhaustion of the Confederate Strength forbids offensive Operations on a large Scale by the Confederate Armies.—Comparison of the Operations during the Last Stage of the War to those of a Siege.—President Davis's Conduct of his Western Army.—Lack of Unity in Military Operations had been a great Fault on both Sides.—U. S. Grant is made Lieutenant General of the Armies of the United States.—He is ordered to Washington to receive his Commission.—His Letter to General Sherman, and Sherman's Reply.—General Sherman succeeds to Grant's former Command, and General J. B. McPherson to Sherman's.—Sherman goes to Nashville, and accompanies Grant thence to Cincinnati.—Lieutenant General Grant's Theory of prospective Operations.—Sherman's Tour of Observation.—Composition of his Army.—His Preparations for the Atlanta Campaign.—He orders the People of Tennessee to supply their own Rations.—He is ready for movement May 6th.—Review of General Thomas's Operations during the Winter.—Difficult Task assigned to General Johnston, commanding the Confederate Army.—His Correspondence with Bragg.—Can have no Re-enforcements for a Defensive Campaign.—While Johnston and Bragg discuss, Sherman moves against Dalton.—McPherson's Movement through Snake Creek Gap, threatening Resaca.—His Attack is delayed, and Hood is sent to Resaca.—Sherman moves his entire Army against Resaca.—Johnston evacuates Dalton.—The Battles of May 14th and 15th.—Johnston, again flanked, abandons Resaca, and, crossing the Oostenaula, retreats to Cassville.—Jeff. C. Davis's Division occupies Rome, Sherman's forces, in the mean time, advancing against Cassville.—Johnston consults with his Corps Commanders; Hardee advises Battle, Hood and Polk a Retreat.—Johnston, May 20th, crosses the Etowah.—Sherman follows May 23d, and, avoiding Allatoona, moves to the right against Dallas.—He finds the Enemy in his front, May 25th, at New Hope Church.—The Battle of New Hope Church.—Sherman develops toward the Left.—Battles of May 27th and 28th.—Sherman, continuing the Movement to the Left, secures the Railroad at Ackworth, June 6th, fortifies Allatoona as a secondary Base, and is re-enforced by Blair's Corps and Long's Cavalry.—Johnston also shifts his Position, and occupies Kenesaw in Sherman's Front.—Sherman hears of Morgan's Defeat in Kentucky, and of Forrest's Victory over Sturgis in Mississippi.—Lieutenant General Polk is killed June 14, and Pine and Lost Mountains are abandoned by the

Enemy.—The new Confederate Line around Kenesaw.—"Villainously bad" Weather delays Sherman.—Hooker is attacked by Hood and repulsed, June 22, near the Kulp House.—Sherman assaults the Confederate Position at Kenesaw, June 27, without success.—He extends his Right toward Marietta, and on July 2 threatens Turner's Ferry on the Chattahoochee.—The next Day Johnston abandons Kenesaw.—Sherman is foiled in the Attempt to strike the Enemy while crossing the Chattahoochee.—He secures three Crossings above Johnston's Tête de Pont, and destroys the Rosswell Factories.—Johnston crosses on the night of July 9th, and takes Position on Peach-tree Creek.—The Situation at this Stage of the Campaign.—Rousseau's Raid on the West Point Railroad.—Sherman crosses the Chattahoochee July 17th.—The same day Johnston is removed from command and succeeded by Hood.—The Battle of Peach-tree Creek, July 20. —The Battle of the 22d.—General McPherson's Death.—Stoneman's and McCook's Raids.— Sherman gives Howard command of the Army and Department of the Tennessee, and transfers that Army to the west of Atlanta.—Hooker's Resignation.—The Battle of July 28th.—Sherman extends his Lines toward East Point.—His Objective the Macon Railroad.—Hood sends Wheeler North.—Kilpatrick's Raid.—The Siege abandoned, August 25th; the Twentieth Corps guards the Chattahoochee Bridge, and the rest of Sherman's Army moves against Jonesborough and the Macon Road.—The Battles of Jonesborough, August 31st and September 1st.—Hood evacuates Atlanta on the morning of September 2d.—General Sherman occupies the City, and orders the Inhabitants to Leave.—The Exodus.—Correspondence between Generals Sherman and Hood.

IN the four last chapters we have passed round the skirts of that central field in which, during the summer and autumn of 1864, the fate of the attempted Southern Confederacy was decided. From the eastern coast of Florida to the Missouri River our survey has ranged—embracing within its scope the brief Florida campaign of General Seymour, begun February 6th, 1864, and terminating on the 20th in the disastrous battle of Olustee; General Sherman's successful expedition to Meridian, February 3–26, 1864; General Banks's operations against the coast of Texas, September 5th, 1863– January 12th, 1864; the ill-advised and mismanaged Red River expedition in the spring of 1864; the military operations in Arkansas, January 8, 1863 –May 2, 1864; and Rosecrans's campaign against Price in September and

October, 1864. From a chronological stand-point this survey ought perhaps to have included the siege of Charleston in the summer of 1863, and the operations of Admiral Farragut against the forts in Mobile Bay, August, 1864. We have determined otherwise, and shall treat of these operations in other connections—those against Mobile as a preliminary part of the campaign which finally resulted in the capture of that city, and the siege of Charleston in connection with Sherman's march from Atlanta to Goldsborough.

We turn, therefore, immediately to the consideration of Sherman's campaign against Johnston, terminating, after four months of strategical manœuvring, in the capture of Atlanta.

The spring of 1864 opened a new era for the armies of the Union. The war against the rebellion had now been going on for three years. Secretary Seward's prophetic period had already been multiplied by twelve, and still two great armies protected the Confederacy—covering Richmond, its head, and Atlanta, its heart. The helmet of the rebellion was Lee's Army of Northern Virginia; the shield before its heart was Johnston's Army of the Tennessee. To crush the one or pierce the other would be a death-blow. Thus far the Army of Northern Virginia had protected Richmond against the successive approaches of McDowell, McClellan, Burnside, and Hooker, and, after the repulse of the last, had boldly reversed the order of movement and invaded Pennsylvania, almost touching the Susquehanna in its northward march. This audacity had met its rebuke at Gettysburg, but Lee's army had resumed the defensive and still defied attack. Whatever progress had been made by the national arms had been in the West. The possession of the Mississippi had severed the western from the eastern half of the Confederacy. West of that river Kirby Smith's armies were secure from attack, not so much by their own strength as by the wastes of Texas—a sort of American Russia—from which, while they could safely whisper "Moscow" to any invader, they could not advance north of the Arkansas without disaster. Between the Mississippi River and the Appalachian range of mountains the waves of conflict had fluctuated, swaying northward and southward under the varying conditions of the war. President Davis was partial to an aggressive system of warfare. At an earlier period the invasion of the Northwestern States with a large army was practicable, and disorganized the plans of the Federal generals for pushing the war southward. Bragg's invasion of Kentucky was the last of these attempts which assumed formidable proportions. Its only success had been in the delay which it occasioned in the progress of the Union army. The secure possession of Chattanooga at the close of 1863 stayed this tendency of the war to fluctuate northward. After that the Confederate invasions were undertaken only with cavalry; flying tempests they were, sometimes violent in their ravages, but the work which they accomplished was of little military importance. These petty storms were soon past, and their wreck obliterated. It is true that, even after the capture of Nashville, Hood's army advanced northward to Nashville, but it was a desperate resort, and, as we shall soon see, illustrated at the same time its danger and its folly. But, beaten back to the mountains of Northern Georgia, the Army of the Tennessee still presented a bold front, covering the central and vital portion of the Confederacy. From Richmond to Atlanta, and on the coast from Wilmington to Mobile, the outside barriers of the Confederacy stood.[1] But let this outward shell be broken, even at a single strong point, and the whole structure must crumble into ruin. For the three past years had nearly exhausted the internal resources of the rebellion. Nearly all the strength and wealth sustaining it had been drawn to the surface. Very few able-bodied men were left at home; there was no reserved force upon which to draw, in any event. Money no longer remained a standard for the valuation of property. Gardens were now the Southern treasury; those who shared the possession of these, who were producers of any thing which sustained life, were rich to the extent of their producing power, and all others lived upon them—the soldiers by a legitimate claim, and non-combatants by the claim of necessity. The theory of the war from this time was strictly that of a siege; it had been that from the beginning, but not by so strict a construction of the term. To the garrison one problem was presented, What would be the best disposition of its forces for *defense?* Offensive operations on the part of the Confederate armies were henceforth unwise: in the first place, they could result in no material advantage, and, in the second, they involved a too rapid and extensive waste of force. Early's Shenandoah campaign, and Hood's advance to Nashville, will furnish illustrations of the folly of offensive operations in these later stages of the war. They were like sallies from a besieged fort, made by a force necessary to the defense of the fort, and at the same time insufficient to raise the siege. Certainly—whatever may have been the final result—the contest would have been prolonged if, on the part of the Confederates, a wise policy, one purely defensive, had been adopted from the commencement of the Atlanta campaign. The Confederate executive does not seem to have appreciated the full importance of the situation which was now presented. No measures were taken to secure unity of operation. To no single mind was given the control of military movements. President Davis conducted the Western campaigns, as he had done for the year past, after a very whimsical manner. By the pressure of popular opinion he had been compelled to give General Johnston command of the Army of the Tennessee, but he gave him little support, and at the first opportunity relieved him of the command. Not until it was too late was the general control of all the armies given to General Lee.

But, while the Confederate government conducted the war upon its former method, adhesion to the theories of the past was no longer suffered on the part of the general government. It is not necessary, nor would it be altogether just, to criticise with a great degree of harshness the Federal conduct of the war during these three years now concluded. The United States was not at all eminent as a military nation at the commencement of the war. The graduates of the Military Academy at West Point had not been trained in the face of war, as are European students. Besides, the study of the campaigns on the Continent of Europe during the last century, while it might have prevented very many blunders which were actually committed on both sides, would, in many important respects, have been inapplicable, on account of the peculiar topographical features of the campaigns of our civil war, and the extended area over which they were conducted. For two years, at the least, the war thus became a series of costly experiments. Then came the winnowing of our generals, and much of the chaff was blown away, though not all. A few military leaders had exhibited characteristics which entitled them to the more prominent positions in the army. Pre-eminent above all others was General Grant, who had not only been most successful, but had shown rare knowledge of men, remarkable common sense, and a persistence of purpose which was unconquerable. Gradually his sphere of control had been extended, until in 1864 he commanded all the armies in the West except that of the Gulf.[1] But still the general disposition of all the armies was subject to General Halleck at Washington. Now, without criticising Halleck's generalship, it is clear that there were several reasons why it was impossible for *any* officer in his position—whatever his military capacity—to wisely control all the military movements in so extensive a conflict. In the first place, his management *must* be simply theoretical. For Halleck had no large practical experience in war. In the Mexican War, for some successful skirmishing with the enemy he had been breveted captain. He had graduated at West Point the third in his class, and for a year was an assistant professor of engineering at the Academy. He had published some important military works. In this Civil War he had not fought a single battle, and the only march he had made was that of his Western Army to the evacuated fortifications at Corinth. Without practical experience, he must resort to theory; and frequently his theories were based upon insufficient premises. In the second place, his distance from the actual fields of conflict, and his subseqent ignorance of the circumstances which must regulate the military operations of his subordinates, led him either to make great mistakes in cases where he gave positive and peremptory orders, or to fall into the exactly opposite error of letting campaigns manage themselves in such a manner that no one could be strictly and fully responsible for their being undertaken or for their results. He assumed too much when he exercised positive and responsible control; and in cases where he was negative, and left every thing to the discretion of his subordinates, as in the case of the Red River expedition, there was no unity of action, and no absolute control by any one. The only exception to this military anarchy was in General Grant's command, simply because to him was surrendered the most complete control of the armies in his vast department. Here was a partial solution of the difficulty. Why not make an entire solution by giving to General Grant control of all the armies of the United States under the President? The voice of the people was loud and universal in favor of this; and the Thirty-eighth Congress, before the close of its first session, revived, for this purpose, the grade of lieutenant general. On the 2d of March, Grant, having been assigned to this grade

[1] The following extract from Lieutenant General Grant's Official Report shows very clearly the relative situation of the Confederate and Federal forces in May, 1864:

"At the date when this report begins the situation of the contending forces was about as follows: The Mississippi River was strongly garrisoned by Federal troops from St. Louis, Missouri, to its mouth. The line of the Arkansas was also held, thus giving us armed possession of all west of the Mississippi north of that stream. A few points in Southern Louisiana, not remote from the river, were held by us, together with a small garrison at and near the mouth of the Rio Grande. All the balance of the vast territory of Arkansas, Louisiana, and Texas was in the almost undisputed possession of the enemy, with an army of probably not less than 80,000 effective men, that could have been brought into the field had there been sufficient opposition to have brought them out. The let-alone policy had demoralized this force so that probably but little more than one half of it was ever present in garrison at any one time. But the one half, or 40,000 men, with the bands of guerrillas scattered through Missouri, Arkansas, and along the Mississippi River, and the disloyal character of much of the population, compelled the use of a large number of troops to keep navigation open on the river and to protect the loyal people to the west of it. To the east of the Mississippi we held substantially with the line of the Tennessee and Holston Rivers, running eastward to include nearly all of the State of Tennessee. South of Chattanooga a small foothold had been obtained in Georgia, sufficient to protect East Tennessee from incursions from the enemy's force at Dalton, Georgia. West Virginia was substantially within our lines. Virginia, with the exception of the northern border, the Potomac River, a small area about the mouth of James River, covered by the troops at Norfolk and Fortress Monroe, and the territory covered by the Army of the Potomac lying along the Rapidan, was in the possession of the enemy. Along the sea-coast footholds had been obtained at Plymouth, Washington, and Newbern, in North Carolina; Beaufort, Folly and Morris Islands, Hilton Head, Fort Pulaski, and Port Royal, in South Carolina; Fernandina and St. Augustine, in Florida. Key West and Pensacola were also in our possession, while all the important ports were blockaded by the navy. The accompanying map, a copy of which was sent to General Sherman and other commanders in March, 1864, shows, by red lines, the territory occupied by us at the beginning of the rebellion and at the opening of the campaign of 1864, while those in blue are the lines which it was proposed to occupy.

"Behind the Union lines there were many bands of guerrillas and a large population disloyal to the government, making it necessary to guard every foot of road or river used in supplying our armies. In the South a reign of military despotism prevailed, which made every man and boy capable of bearing arms a soldier, and those who could not bear arms in the field acted as provosts for collecting deserters and returning them. This enabled the enemy to bring almost his entire strength into the field.

"The enemy had concentrated the bulk of his forces east of the Mississippi into two armies, commanded by Generals R. E. Lee and J. E. Johnston, his ablest and best generals. The army commanded by Lee occupied the south bank of the Rapidan, extending from Mine Run westward, strongly intrenched, covering and defending Richmond, the rebel capital, against the Army of the Potomac. The army under Johnston occupied a strongly intrenched position at Dalton, Georgia, covering and defending Atlanta, Georgia, a place of great importance as a railroad centre, against the armies under Major General W. T. Sherman. In addition to these armies, he had a large cavalry force, under Forrest, in Northeast Mississippi; a considerable force of all arms in the Shenandoah Valley, and in the western part of Virginia and extreme eastern part of Tennessee, and also confronting our sea-coast garrisons, and holding blockaded ports where we had no foothold upon land.

"These two armies, and the cities covered and defended by them, were the main objective points of the campaign."

[1] Sherman suggested to Grant (January 4, 1864), in connection with the Red River expedition, that he ought to have the entire command of the Mississippi Valley. In a letter of that date, he says: "There is no doubt the whole matter would be simplified if you had command of the Mississippi Valley below Cairo. I think, if you were to name the subject to General Halleck, that he would order it, for its propriety is better known to him than to any other. Admiral Porter's command extends to and below New Orleans, and ours should also."

GRANT RECEIVING HIS COMMISSION AS LIEUTENANT GENERAL.

by the President, was confirmed by the Senate in executive session. Two days after, General Grant, then in Nashville, was ordered to report in person at Washington. This order was to him an assurance of his confirmation; and his first feeling upon receiving it seems to have been one of generous gratitude to his faithful subordinates who had so ably seconded the enterprise for which he was now to receive the highest reward which it was in the power of the people and the government to bestow.[1]

General Washington alone had previously been honored with the full title conferred upon General Grant. In 1798 our relations with France threatened war, and at this crisis Washington was made lieutenant general. In another year, if he had lived, he would have been made full general. After General Scott's unsuccessful campaign for the Presidency, the grade of lieutenant general *by brevet* was conferred upon him. The latter, by the provisions of the bill promoting General Grant to the full grade, was still to retain his "rank, pay, and allowances."

At one o'clock on the afternoon of the 9th of March, General Grant was received by the President in the cabinet chamber at Washington, and received his commission. There was no pomp, no gathering of the populace, no splendid celebration of the honor conferred. The President was there with his cabinet; General Halleck, the retiring general-in-chief; General Rawlins, Grant's chief of staff; Colonel Comstock, his chief engineer; the President's private secretary, Mr. Nicolay, and the Honorable Owen Lovejoy, of Illinois. The only other person forming a part of the group was General Grant's eldest son, a boy of fourteen years. President Lincoln having presented General Grant to the cabinet, addressed him thus:

"GENERAL GRANT,—The nation's appreciation of what you have done, and its reliance upon you for what remains to be done in the existing great struggle, are now presented with this commission constituting you lieutenant general in the army of the United States. With this high honor devolves upon you also a corresponding responsibility. As the country herein trusts you, so, under God, it will sustain you. I scarcely need to add, that with what I here speak for the nation goes my own hearty personal concurrence."

General Grant's response was equally brief. He replied:

"MR. PRESIDENT,—I accept the commission with gratitude for the high honor conferred. With the aid of the noble armies that have fought on so many fields for our common country, it will be my earnest endeavor not to disappoint your expectations. I feel the full weight of the responsibilities now devolving on me, and I know that if they are met it will be due to those armies, and, above all, to the favor of that Providence which leads both nations and men."[2]

On the 12th of March General Halleck was relieved, and made Lieutenant General Grant's chief of staff. By the same order Sherman succeeded to General Grant's former command of the Military Division of the Mississippi, and General McPherson was assigned to the command of the Department and Army of the Tennessee.[1]

Upon the receipt of the order placing him in command of all the armies, with headquarters in the field, General Grant was at Nashville, whither Sherman was forthwith summoned. Arriving at Nashville on March 17th, Sherman accompanied the lieutenant general as far on his way to Washington as Cincinnati. On this journey the two generals consulted freely together as to the plan of their future campaigns. The consultation was continued in the parlor of the Burnet House, at Cincinnati, where, over their maps, was planned the simultaneous assault upon the armies covering Richmond and Atlanta. To attack these two armies at once counteracted to a great degree the advantage of interior lines which was possessed by the enemy. To attack with vigor, and without pause, regardless of seasons, would prevent any portion of the Confederate forces from returning home on furlough during the winter to plant crops for their own sustenance. Grant's whole theory may be summed up in two sentences. Unity of operations. The attrition to powder of the Confederate armies by a continuous series of battles.[2] The main objects of attack were Lee's and Johnston's armies rather than the important strategical points which they covered. But the details of the campaigns about to be opened would necessarily depend upon the theory of defense adopted by these two Confederate generals.[3]

General Sherman's new command consisted of four departments, with their armies, those of the Ohio, the Cumberland, the Tennessee, and Arkansas.

The Army of the Ohio, now under the command of Major General John M. Schofield, consisted of the Ninth and Twenty-third Corps. Longstreet having joined Lee, the Ninth Corps was sent to re-enforce the Army of the Potomac. Two divisions of the Twenty-third Corps, those of M. S. Hascall and J. D. Cox, took the field, the other three being retained to garrison Kentucky and East Tennessee.

The Army of the Cumberland, at Chattanooga, commanded by General Thomas, consisted of the Fourth, Fourteenth, and Twentieth Corps, commanded respectively by Generals O. O. Howard, John M. Palmer, and Joseph Hooker. The Fourth Corps comprised three divisions, under Stanley, John Newton, and Wood; the Fourteenth three, under Jeff. C. Davis, R. W. Johnson, and Baird; and the Twentieth three, under A. S. Williams, Geary, and Butterfield.[4]

---

[1] Before starting for Washington he writes thus to General Sherman:

"DEAR SHERMAN,—The bill reviving the grade of lieutenant general in the army has become a law, and my name has been sent to the Senate for the place. I now receive orders to report to Washington immediately *in person*, which indicates a confirmation, or a likelihood of confirmation. I start this morning to comply with the order.

"While I have been eminently successful in this war in at least gaining the confidence of the public, no one feels more than I how much of this success is due to the energy, skill, and the harmonious putting forth of that energy and skill, of those whom it has been my good fortune to have occupying subordinate positions under me.

"There are many officers to whom these remarks are applicable to a greater or less degree, proportionate to their ability as soldiers; but what I want is to express my thanks to you and McPherson as the men to whom, above all others, I feel indebted for whatever I have had of success. How far your advice and assistance have been of help to me, you know. How far your execution of whatever has been given to you to do entitles you to the reward I am receiving, you can not know as well as I.

"I feel all the gratitude this letter would express, giving it the most flattering construction.

"The word *you* I use in the plural, intending it for McPherson also. I should write to him, and will some day, but, starting in the morning, I do not know that I will find time just now.

"Your friend, U. S. GRANT, *Major General.*"

Sherman's reply, written near Memphis March 10th, is equally characteristic. He says:

"DEAR GENERAL,—I have your more than kind and characteristic letter of the 4th instant. I will send a copy to General McPherson at once.

"You do yourself injustice and us too much honor in assigning to us too large a share of the merits which have led to your advancement. I know you approve the friendship I have ever professed to you, and will permit me to continue, as heretofore, to manifest it on all proper occasions.

"You are now Washington's legitimate successor, and occupy a position of almost dangerous elevation; but if you can continue, as heretofore, to be yourself, simple, honest, and unpretending, you will enjoy through life the respect and love of friends, and the homage of millions of human beings, that will award you a large share in securing to them and their descendants a government of law and stability.

"I repeat, you do General McPherson and myself too much honor. At Belmont you manifested your traits, neither of us being near. At Donelson, also, you illustrated your whole character. I was not near, and General McPherson was in too subordinate a capacity to influence you.

"Until you had won Donelson, I confess I was almost cowed by the terrible ray of anarchical elements that presented themselves at every point; but that admitted a ray of light I have followed ever since.

"I believe you are as brave, patriotic, and just as the great prototype Washington—as unselfish, kind-hearted, and honest as a man should be—but the chief characteristic is the simple faith in success you have always manifested, which I can liken to nothing else than the faith a Christian has in the Savior.

"This faith gave you victory at Shiloh and Vicksburg. Also, when you have completed your best preparations, you go into battle without hesitation, as at Chattanooga—no doubts—no reserves; and I tell you, it was this that made us act with confidence. I knew, wherever I was, that you thought of me, and if I got in a tight place you would help me out, if alive.

"My only point of doubts was in your knowledge of grand strategy, and of books of science and history; but, I confess, your common sense seems to have supplied all these.

"Now as to the future. Don't stay in Washington. Come West: take to yourself the whole Mississippi Valley. Let us make it dead sure; and I tell you the Atlantic slopes and the Pacific shores will follow its destiny, as sure as the limbs of a tree live or die with the main trunk. We have done much, but still much remains. Time, and time's influences, are with us. We could almost afford to sit still and let these influences work.

"Here lies the seat of the coming empire; and from the West, when our task is done, we will make short work of Charleston and Richmond, and the impoverished coast of the Atlantic.

"Your sincere friend, W. T. SHERMAN."

[2] The bill for reviving the grade of lieutenant general was presented to Congress by the Hon. E. B. Washburne, of Illinois. It was slightly amended, and was passed under the following form:

"*Be it enacted by the Senate and House of Representatives of the United States of America, in Congress assembled,* That the grade of lieutenant general be, and the same is hereby revived in the Army of the United States of America; and the President is hereby authorized, whenever he shall deem it expedient, to appoint, by and with the advice and consent of the Senate, a commander of the army, to be selected during war from among those officers in the military service of the United States, not below the grade of major general, most distinguished for courage, skill, and ability; and who, being commissioned as lieutenant general, *shall be authorized, under the direction of the President, to command the armies of the United States.*

"SEC. 2. *And be it further enacted,* That the lieutenant general appointed as is hereinbefore provided shall be entitled to the pay, allowances, and staff specified in the fifth section of the act approved May 28, 1798; and also the allowances described in the sixth section of the act approved August 23, 1842, granting additional rations to certain officers; *Provided,* That nothing in this bill contained shall be construed in any way to affect the rank, pay, or allowances of Winfield Scott, lieutenant general by brevet, now on the retired list of the army."

[1] "*General Orders, No.* 98.

"War Department, Adjutant General's Office, Washington, March 12, 1864.

"The President of the United States orders as follows:

"1st. Major General Halleck is, at his own request, relieved from duty as general-in-chief of the army, and Lieutenant General U. S. Grant is assigned to the command of the armies of the United States. The headquarters of the army will be in Washington, and also with Lieutenant General Grant in the field.

"2d. Major General Halleck is assigned to duty in Washington as chief of staff of the army, under the direction of the Secretary of War and the Lieutenant General commanding. His orders will be obeyed and respected accordingly.

"3d. Major General W. T. Sherman is assigned to the command of the Military Division of the Mississippi, composed of the Departments of the Ohio, the Cumberland, the Tennessee, and the Arkansas.

"4th. Major General John B. McPherson is assigned to the command of the Department and Army of the Tennessee.

"5th. In relieving Major General Halleck from duty as general-in-chief, the President desires to express his approbation and thanks for the zealous manner in which the arduous and responsible duties of that position have been performed.

"By order of the Secretary of War. D. E. TOWNSEND, *Assistant Adj. General.*"

[2] "From an early period in the rebellion I had been impressed with the idea that active and continuous operations of all the troops that could be brought into the field, regardless of season and weather, were necessary to a speedy termination of the war. The resources of the enemy, and his numerical strength, were far inferior to ours; but, as an offset to this, we had a vast territory, with a population hostile to the government, to garrison, and long lines of river and railroad communications to protect, to enable us to supply the operating armies.

"The armies in the East and West acted independently and without concert, like a balky team, no two ever pulling together, enabling the enemy to use to great advantage his interior lines of communication for transporting troops from east to west, re-enforcing the army most vigorously pressed, and to furlough large numbers, during seasons of inactivity on our part, to go to their homes, and do the work of producing for the support of their armies. It was a question whether our numerical strength and resources were not more than balanced by these disadvantages and the enemy's superior position.

"From the first I was firm in the conviction that no peace could be had that would be stable, and conducive to the happiness of the people both North and South, until the military power of the rebellion was entirely broken. I therefore determined, first, to use the greatest number of troops practicable against the armed force of the enemy; preventing him from using the same force at different seasons against first one and then another of our armies, and the possibility of repose for refitting and producing necessary supplies for carrying on resistance. Second, to hammer continuously against the armed force of the enemy and his resources, until by mere attrition, if in no other way, there should be nothing left to him but an equal submission with the loyal section of our common country to the Constitution and laws of the land."—*Lieut. General Grant's Official Report.*

[3] From a letter written by Lieutenant General Grant to Sherman, dated Washington, April 4, 1864, it appears that, in conjunction with the operations of his own and Sherman's armies, he intended that an attack should be made on Mobile. We give those portions of this letter which bear upon Western operations:

"It is my design, if the enemy keep quiet and allow me to take the initiative in the spring campaign, to work all parts of the army together, and somewhat toward a common centre. . . . I have sent orders to Banks by private messengers to finish up his present expedition against Shreveport with all dispatch; to turn over the defense of the Red River to General Steele and the navy, and return your troops to you, and his own to New Orleans; to abandon all of Texas except the Rio Grande, and to hold that with not to exceed 4000 men; to reduce the number of troops on the Mississippi to the lowest number necessary to hold it, and to collect from his command not less than 25,000 men. To this I will add 5000 men from Missouri. With this force he is to commence operations against Mobile as soon as he can. It will be impossible for him to commence too early. . . .

"You I propose to move against Johnston's army, to break it up, and to get into the interior of the enemy's country as far as you can, inflicting all the damage you can against their war resources. I do not propose to lay down for you a plan of campaign, but simply to lay down the work it is desirable to have done, and leave you free to execute in your own way. Submit to me, however, as early as you can, your plan of operations. . . . . I know you will have difficulties to encounter getting through the mountains to where supplies are abundant, but I believe you will accomplish it."

[4] Several changes had taken place in the Army of the Cumberland since the battle of Chattanooga. The Eleventh and Twelfth Corps were consolidated, forming the Twentieth, and General Slocum had, as a consequence, been displaced, and transferred to Vicksburg. Howard, who had commanded the Eleventh, relieved General Granger in command of the Fourth Corps. Phil Sheridan had been relieved of his command (second division, Fourth Corps), and had been succeeded by John Newton.

The Army of the Tennessee, at Huntsville, Alabama, commanded by McPherson, comprised the Fifteenth, and portions of the Sixteenth and Seventeenth Corps, under Logan, G. M. Dodge, and Frank P. Blair, Jr. The remainder of the Sixteenth and Seventeenth Corps was at Memphis and Vicksburg, under Hurlbut and Slocum, or absent on the Red River expedition. The Fifteenth Corps comprised four divisions, under Osterhaus, Herron, Morgan L. Smith, and John E. Smith; the Sixteenth three, under Ransom, Corse, and T. W. Sweeny; and the Seventeenth two, under C. R. Woods and M. D. Leggett.

The cavalry in the Army of the Ohio consisted of McCook's division, in the Army of the Cumberland of Kilpatrick's and Garrard's, and in the Army of the Tennessee of Edward McCook's brigade.

The Department and Army of Arkansas, under General Steele, was in May assigned to General Canby's trans-Mississippi division. Steele's army, therefore, must be counted out of the forces engaged in the Atlanta campaign.

General Sherman immediately prepared for active operations. On the 25th of March he set out on a general tour of inspection through his department, consulting with McPherson, Thomas, and Schofield. The value of the possession of Chattanooga was now manifest. This position was the central buttress of the Federal position. On its left East Tennessee was firmly grasped by Schofield's army; on its right the Tennessee River was guarded by a line of garrisons, which permitted the access northward of cavalry only. In the rear were two good and reliable lines of railway communication from Nashville and Memphis. During the season of navigation the Tennessee River affords a third line. Having arranged with his subordinates the disposition of their several armies—how many should take the field, and how many be retained for garrison duty—Sherman returned to Nashville. At this time the citizens of Tennessee in his rear were in large measure sustained by stores which they shared with the army. Finding that this double want could not be supplied with safety to the army, he issued orders cutting off the supply of the citizens, and leaving them to other sources of relief.[1] The 1st of May was the time fixed for the completion of preparations, and by that time the store-houses of Chattanooga contained provisions for thirty days, and the ammunition trains were fully supplied. The veteran regiments, whose time had expired, and who had been released on furlough, now returned with their ranks filled by new recruits.

Sherman had intended to move against the enemy with 100,000 men of all arms, and 250 guns. His actual force on the 1st of May was 98,797 men and 254 guns. The Army of the Cumberland, numbering 60,773 men, with 130 guns, constituted three fifths of his entire command. The Army of the Tennessee numbered 24,465, with 96 guns, and that of the Ohio 13,559, with 28 guns. Sherman's whole force was distributed as follows among the three arms of the service: the infantry of the three armies numbered 88,188 men; the artillery 4450, with 254 guns; the cavalry 6149.[2]

To General Johnston, of the Confederate army, who had succeeded Bragg at the close of 1863, was assigned a difficult task. With an army half as large as that opposing him,[3] he was to resist the approach of the latter to Atlanta. His forces were concentrated at Dalton, which he had strongly fortified. President Davis having given Johnston the command of the army much against his will,[4] did not support him by any considerable re-enforcements. Yet he

called loudly for an advance into Tennessee. Of course this would have proved immediately ruinous. Johnston, therefore, wisely declined to attempt any offensive movement, and spent the winter in preparation for the assault which he knew he must meet in the spring. During the winter desertions from his army were frequent. General Thomas reports that they averaged thirty per day, nearly all of whom desired to take the amnesty oath, and to comply with General Grant's orders in regard to deserters.[1]

Partly as a demonstration in favor of Sherman's Meridian expedition, and partly to prevent Johnston from re-enforcing Longstreet in East Tennessee, Thomas had moved against Dalton in the latter part of February, 1864. Palmer, with Johnson's and Baird's divisions, occupied Ringgold on the 22d. That night he reported to Thomas that he had reliable information that Johnston had dispatched Cheatham's and Cleburne's divisions to the relief of Polk in Alabama. This information was not correct; but, to test the enemy's strength, the next day, Davis's division having joined the two others at Ringgold, and Cruft's, of the Fourteenth Corps, with Matthias's brigade, of the Fifteenth Corps, and Long's cavalry brigade, having been sent to co-operate with Palmer, Johnston's advanced outposts beyond Tunnel Hill were attacked and driven in. Dalton is covered on its western side by Rocky Face Ridge, which runs north and south, and through which, at the pass called Buzzard Roost, passes the road from Ringgold. East of the Ringgold Road and in front of Rocky Face Ridge lies Tunnel Hill, which was occupied by Thomas on the 24th. On the 25th an attempt was made against Buzzard Roost Pass; but the enemy, contrary to anticipation, was found in full strength, and, after becoming satisfied of this, Thomas withdrew his forces to the vicinity of Ringgold. His loss in this reconnoissance was 17 killed and 255 wounded.

As soon as Johnston assumed command of the Confederate Army of the Tennessee, both the President and Secretary Seddon urged an offensive campaign. "The relative forces," reports Johnston, "including the moral effect of the affair of Missionary Ridge, condition of the artillery horses and most of those of the cavalry, and want of field transportation, made it impracticable to effect the wishes of the executive." Immediately after Thomas's reconnoissance, General Johnston, on the 27th of February, suggested to President Davis, through General Bragg, that "preparations for a forward movement should be made without farther delay." In reply, Bragg (March 4th) desired him to prepare for such a movement. He then reminded Bragg that these preparations, by the regulations of the War Department, were not left to commanders of troops, but to officers receiving orders directly from Richmond. On the 18th of March Johnston received a letter from Bragg, sketching a plan of offensive operations, and enumerating the troops to be used by the former. He replied to this letter, suggesting modifications, and urging that the re-enforcements named should be sent immediately to Dalton. General Bragg on the 21st telegraphed to Johnston: "Troops can only be drawn from other points for advance. Upon your decision of that point farther action must depend." Johnston believed that the enemy would be prepared for a movement sooner than he himself could. He wished to be prepared for the defensive as well as the offensive. From Bragg's dispatch it was evident that there were troops which might be sent to the Army of the Tennessee, but that these would not be sent for a defensive campaign. Johnston, on the 22d, explained his view of the situation to General Bragg, showing the probability of Sherman's advancing first, and urging the necessity of preparing for defensive as well as for offensive movements. No notice whatever was taken of this appeal. On the 25th Johnston renewed his request for re-enforcements, "because the enemy was collecting a larger force than that of the last campaign, while ours was less than it had been then." The only response which he received was the arrival of 1400 men, under Brigadier General Mercer, on the 2d of May, after Sherman's preparations had already been completed. Considering that Johnston might have been supported, it seems strange that, in the face of an advance, the success or re-

---

[1] "At first," he says, in his report, "my orders operated very hardly, but the prolific soil soon afforded early vegetables, and ox-wagons hauled meat and bread from Kentucky, so that no actual suffering resulted, and I trust that those who clamored at the cruelty and hardships of the day have already seen in the result a perfect justification of my course."

On May 5th Sherman writes to President Lincoln:

"We have worked hard with the best talent of the country, and it is demonstrated that the railroad can not supply the army and the people too. One or the other must quit, and the army don't intend to unless Joe Johnston makes us. The issues to citizens have been enormous, and the same weight of corn or oats would have saved thousands of the mules, whose carcasses now corduroy the roads, and which we need so much.

"We have paid back to Tennessee ten for one of provisions taken in war. I will not change my orders, and I beg of you to be satisfied that the clamor is partly humbug and for effect; and to test it, I advise you to tell the bearers of it to hurry to Kentucky, and make up a caravan of cattle and wagons, and come over the mountains by Cumberland Gap and Somerset, to relieve their suffering friends, on foot, as they used to do before a railroad was built. Tell them that they have no time to lose. We can relieve all actual suffering by each company or regiment giving of their savings. Every man who is willing to fight or work gets a full ration; and all who won't fight or work should go away, and we offer them free passage in the cars."

[2] Sherman evidently did not intend to be encumbered with baggage. April 11 he writes to Thomas: "When we move we will take no tents or baggage, but one change of clothing on our horses, or to be carried by the men, and on pack-animals by company officers. Five days' bacon, twenty days' bread, and thirty days' salt, sugar, and coffee. Nothing else but arms and ammunition in quantity proportioned to our ability. Even this will be a heavy encumbrance, but is rather the limit of our aim than what we can really accomplish. . . . . Look well to our supply of beef cattle on the hoof, and salt in large excess of the rations. Encourage drills by brigades and divisions, and let the recruits practice at the target all the time."

[3] Johnston's effective force at the commencement of the Atlanta campaign numbered about 48,000 men, one tenth cavalry. The following are the official returns from his army from December 31, 1863, to June 30, 1864:

	Present for Duty.	Aggregate Present.	Aggregate Present and Absent.
December 31, 1863	42,439	57,428	98,215
January 31, 1864	41,553	55,059	88,457
February— "	37,789	48,010	79,071
March 31, "	42,125	55,113	85,953
April 30, "	43,887	63,807	96,863
May "	Wanting.		
June 30, "	54,085	77,441	137,192

We have estimated his army at 48,000, because, in addition to the forces included in the returns for April 30, there were some 4000 cavalry scattered northward, which were afterward recalled.

[4] According to the following account of Henry S. Foote (War of the Rebellion, p. 356), it appears that Davis's hostility to Johnston began at an early period of the war, or, at any rate, before Benjamin, the Confederate Secretary of War, was displaced by Seddon. This author, Confederate representative from Tennessee, says:

"Just about the time I was laboring most assiduously to relieve the Department of War of Mr. Benjamin by calling forth, as far as it might be in my power to do so, co-operative responses from the people, an occurrence took place in social life in Richmond which had much effect, not only upon the fate of Mr. Benjamin, but which, in the sequel, had much influence also upon the course of public events. I chanced to be invited to a dinner-party, where some twenty of the most prominent members of the two houses of the Confederate Congress were congregated, including the speaker of the House of Representatives, Mr. Orr, of South Carolina, and others of equal rank. General

Joseph E. Johnston was also an invited guest. While the banquet was proceeding, Mr. Benjamin's gross acts of official misconduct becoming the subject of conversation, one of the company turned to General Johnston, and inquired whether he thought it even possible that the Confederate cause could succeed with Mr. Benjamin as war minister. To this inquiry General Johnston, after a little pause, emphatically responded in the negative. This high authority was immediately cited in both houses of Congress against Mr. Benjamin, and was in the end fatal to his hope of remaining in the Department of War. Mr. Davis, after the sending in of his nominations for cabinet appointments, under the permanent Constitution, for nearly four weeks, in order to have it in his power to persuade the Senate to confirm Mr. Benjamin as Secretary of War, in the event of his being renominated, ultimately relinquished this object in despair, that body, however accommodating it was in general to executive fancies, having been found unwilling to participate in the terrible responsibility of such an act. Mr. Benjamin was finally nominated for the Department of State, and was confirmed, by a very small majority, for that place, where he had it in his power, both abroad and at home, to perpetrate more barefaced acts of corruption and profligacy than any single individual has ever been known to commit in the same space of time in any part of Christendom. I will here remark, in passing, that this frank and manly declaration of General Johnston rendered both Mr. Davis and Mr. Benjamin alike hostile to him, and he was fated to experience the effect of their malevolence on more than one subsequent occasion previous to his ultimate deprivation of command."

[1] This order, No. 10, was issued by General Grant at Chattanooga, December 12, 1863, and was freely distributed among the Confederate soldiers. Its terms were as follow:

"I. All deserters from the enemy coming within our lines will be conducted to the commander of division or detached brigade who shall be nearest the place of surrender.

"II. If such commander is satisfied that the deserters desire to quit the Confederate service, he may permit them to go to their homes, if within our lines, on taking the following oath:

"I do solemnly swear, in the presence of Almighty God, that I will henceforth faithfully support, protect, and defend the Constitution of the United States, and the union of states thereunder, and that I will in like manner abide by and faithfully support all acts of Congress passed during the existing rebellion with reference to slaves, so far as not yet repealed, modified, or held void by Congress or by decision of the Supreme Court, and that I will in like manner abide by and faithfully support all proclamations of the President made during the existing rebellion having reference to slaves, so long and so far as not modified or declared void by decision of the Supreme Court, so help me God.

"III. Deserters from the enemy will at once be disarmed, and their arms turned over to the nearest ordnance officer, who will account for them.

"IV. Passes and rations may be given to deserters to carry them to their homes, and free passes over military railroads and on steam-boats in government employ.

"V. Employment at fair wages will, when practicable, be given to deserters by officers of the quartermaster and engineer departments.

"VI. To avoid the danger of recapture of such deserters by the enemy, they will be exempt from military service in the armies of the United States."

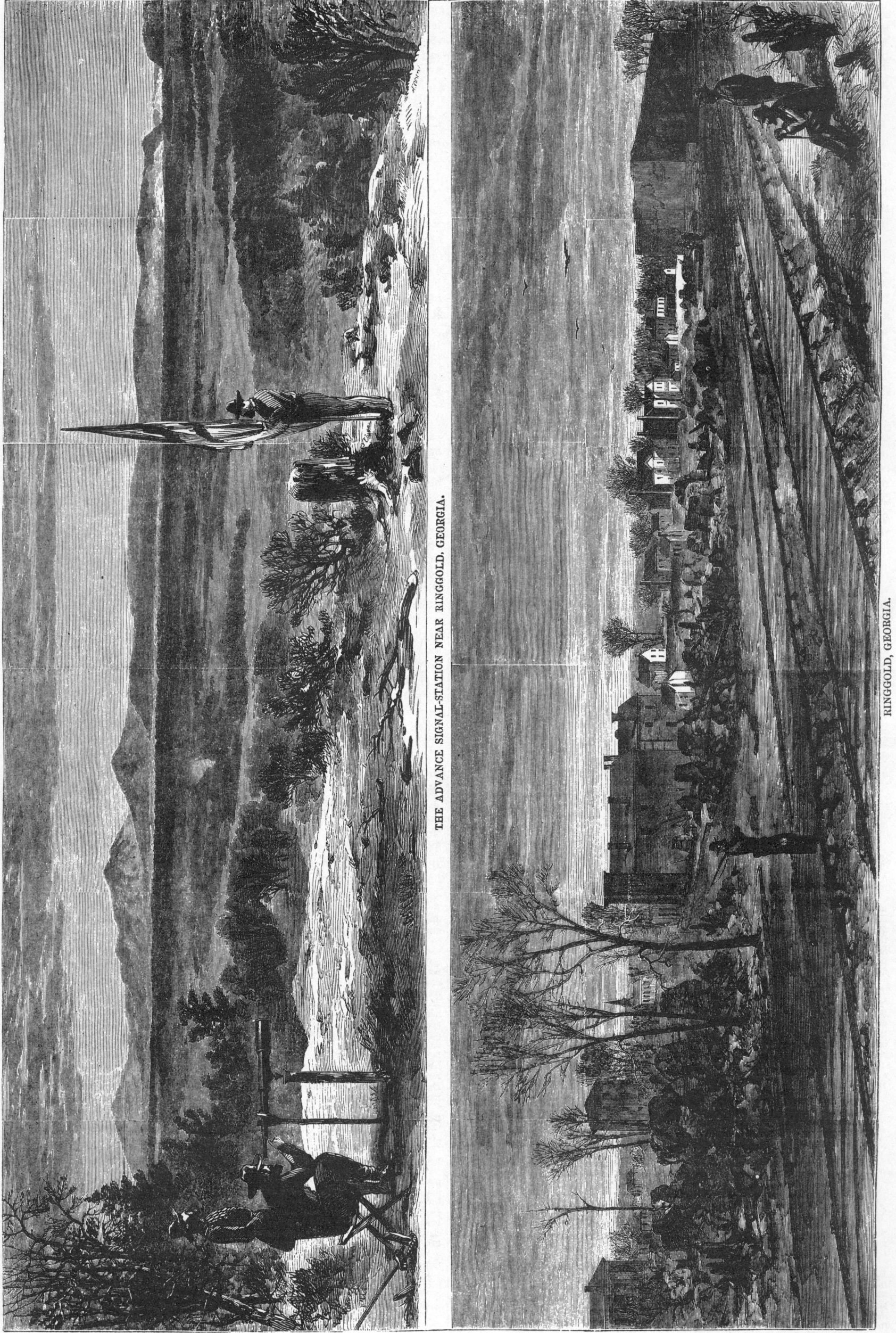

THE ADVANCE SIGNAL-STATION NEAR RINGGOLD, GEORGIA.

RINGGOLD, GEORGIA.

BUZZARD'S ROOST PASS.

pulse of which was so important to the Confederacy, he should have been left for three months with an army half as large as that which he confronted. On the 4th of May he asked for a portion of Polk's command, and was informed that this request would be granted.[1]

While the Confederate officials were disputing, Sherman had been preparing to advance. By the 1st of May, as we have before shown, he was ready to move and to strike. From Ringgold, the advanced front of the Federal army, to Atlanta was nearly one hundred miles, across a difficult country, but not so difficult as that over which Rosecrans had advanced from Murfreesborough to Chattanooga. Atlanta, the heart of Georgia, and of the Confederacy itself, was not only the principal Confederate granary, but was also the centre of a manufacturing district which supplied the Southern armies with cannon, ammunition, clothing, and equipments. To reach this point—the local objective of the campaign—three rivers had to be crossed, the Oostenaula, Etowah, and Chattahoochee. Ringgold lies amid the mountains of

Taylor's Ridge, on the road from Chattanooga to Dalton. Ten miles distant, by the road from Ringgold, is Buzzard's Roost, in Rocky Face Ridge, about four miles northwest of Dalton. The enemy held Dalton, strongly fortified, the ridge covering it, and strong outposts on the road to Ringgold. His position was almost impregnable. Sherman's command on May 7th was situated thus: On the right, at Lee and Gordon's Mill, lay the Army of the Tennessee, under McPherson; the Army of the Cumberland, under Thomas, held the centre, at and near Ringgold, more directly confronting the enemy; and under Schofield, on the Georgia border, and on the road from Cleveland southward to Dalton, which runs east of Rocky Face Ridge, was the Army of the Ohio. We have said that Atlanta was the local objective of Sherman's campaign; the *vital* objective, however, was Johnston's army at Dalton. The obvious policy of the Federal commander was to force a battle upon his opponent at the earliest stage of the campaign. Johnston's equally obvious policy—a difficult one to be pursued under the circumstances—was to evade a general engagement, opposing as obstinate resistance as was possible in his front consistent with the protection of his communications with Atlanta.

[1] General Bragg, after he was relieved from the command at Chattanooga, was called to Richmond, where President Davis, whose especial favorite he was, placed him in a position very similar to that which had been occupied by the Federal General Halleck at Washington. Certainly the management of the one was only paralleled, in the annals of war, by that of the other.

GEARY'S ASSAULT ON DUG GAP.

On the 4th of May the Army of the Potomac crossed the Rapidan, and on the same day Grant telegraphed to Sherman, reminding him that the time for his advance against Johnston had come. Sherman neither intended, nor did Johnston expect, an assault on the position covering Dalton—Buzzard's Roost Pass, which was obstructed by abatis, and flooded by means of dams across Mill Creek. Probably in no campaign of the war did the two opposing commanders so completely fathom each other's purposes, or so carefully estimate the possibilities, the one for attack and the other for defense. Sherman, on the 6th of May, with his largest army, that of the Cumberland, menaced Rocky Face Ridge with such vigor that it would seem as if an attempt like that made five months before against Missionary Ridge was to be repeated against the formidable position held by Johnston at Buzzard's Roost. Schofield threatened at the same time the enemy's right flank. McPherson's army, from Lee and Gordon's Mill, was thrown to the left and rear, moving by way of Ship's Gap, Villanow, and Snake Creek Gap to Resaca, eighteen miles south of Dalton, on the Atlanta Railroad. With this flanking column McPherson was ordered to break the railroad to the extent of his opportunity, and then to retire to Snake Creek Gap and there fortify himself.[1]

On the first day of the campaign Thomas occupied Tunnel Hill. Two days afterward Schofield closed upon Johnston's right, and Thomas renewed his demonstration upon Rocky Face with such vigor that Newton's division, of Howard's (Fourth) corps, carried a portion of the ridge; but, upon a farther advance, the crest was found too well protected by rock epaulements to hope for success in gaining the gorge. Geary's division, of Hooker's corps, in the mean time made a reconnoissance up a precipitous ridge south of Buzzard's Roost; but, though the men fought their way well up to the enemy's intrenchments on the crest, they could not gain possession of the Gap. But these movements were only demonstrations. Upon McPherson's flank movement through Snake Creek Gap Sherman had made the success of his plan to depend. But Johnston, who had expected this method of attack, had sent Canty's brigade to Resaca two days before the attack in his front had been developed. For weeks, also, he had been preparing roads in his rear, upon

which his own troops could move more rapidly than Sherman's flanking columns. McPherson had reached Snake Creek Gap on the 8th, with Logan's and Dodge's corps, preceded by Kilpatrick's division of cavalry. Debouching from the gap, McPherson found Resaca occupied by Canty's brigade. If he had made an immediate attack his success would have been certain;[1] but he over-estimated the enemy's strength both in position and numbers. While he was waiting before Resaca, and unable to get upon the railroad above or below the town, the position in his front was strengthened. On the afternoon of the 9th, Johnston, warned by Canty of this movement on Resaca, promptly dispatched to the latter point three infantry divisions under General Hood. The orders which McPherson had received had not been so explicit, perhaps, as to cover the precise case now presented for his consideration. His discretion must supply the place of definite orders. His force, over 20,000 strong, was largely superior to that of the garrison defending Resaca. The manifest intent of his orders would have favored an attack, and the probability of success, even now, was unquestionably in his favor; but there was much to be said on the other side. He was detached from the main body of the army, and the easy approaches from Dalton toward his left and rear suggested the possibility that he might be cut off and defeated. He took the safer of the alternatives offered him, and fell back to Snake Creek Gap. In doing so he probably made a mistake. Rocky Face Ridge had perfectly covered his rear during the movement. He could now easily withstand any assault which might be made on his left if he had refused that flank toward the ridge. Even if he had taken such a position without making an attack, he could have held it until he received support. But the decisive advantage gained over the enemy by his flank movement had been thrown away by his failure to attack on the 9th. The attack would have been made if General Logan had been in command, or if he had been in the advance instead of Dodge. McPherson's wagon train, which ought never to have entered the Gap at all, offered serious obstructions to the march of columns which might be sent to his support. Sherman confesses himself "somewhat disappointed at the result"[2] of his plans, but imputes no blame to McPherson. On the 11th he withdrew his army from Johnston's front, and followed McPherson, leaving only Howard's corps and a small infantry force to keep up the demonstration against Dalton. On the night of the 12th Johnston abandoned Dalton, and moved his whole army to a position

---

[1] This Snake Creek Gap movement seems to have been originally suggested by General Thomas. The latter, in his report to the Committee on the Conduct of the War, says: "Shortly after his assignment to the command of the Military Division of the Mississippi, General Sherman came to see me at Chattanooga to consult about the position of affairs, and adopt a plan for a spring campaign. At that interview I proposed to General Sherman that if he would use McPherson's and Schofield's armies to demonstrate on the enemy's position at Dalton by the direct roads through Buzzard's Roost Gap, and from the direction of Cleveland, I would throw my whole force through Snake Creek Gap, which I knew to be unguarded, fall upon the enemy's communications between Dalton and Resaca, thereby turning his position completely, and force him either to retreat toward the east through a difficult country, poorly supplied with provisions and forage, with a strong probability of total disorganization of his force, or attack me, in which latter event I felt confident that my army was sufficiently strong to beat him, especially as I hoped to gain a position on his communications before he could be made aware of my movement. General Sherman objected to this plan for the reason that he desired my army to form the reserve of the united armies, and to serve as a rallying-point for the two wings . . . . to operate from."

[1] The following is a part of the instructions given to McPherson: "I am in hopes that Garrard's cavalry will be at Villanow as soon as you. . . . . But, in any event, his movement will cover your right rear, and enable you to leave all encumbrances at Ship's Gap or at Villanow, as you deem best. I hope the enemy will fight at Dalton, in which case he can have no force there that can interfere with you; but should his policy be to fall back along the railroad, you will hit him in flank. Do not fail, in that event, to make the most of the opportunity, by the most vigorous attack possible, as it may save us what we have most reason to apprehend, a slow pursuit, in which he gains strength as we lose it. In either event you may be sure the forces north of you will prevent his turning on you alone."   [2] Sherman's Report.

SHELLING THE RAILROAD NEAR RESACA.

covering Resaca on the west. In the mean time Polk-had reached Johnston with Loring's division. Polk, Hardee, and Hood were now the corps commanders of the Confederate Army of Tennessee.

Dalton, evacuated by the enemy, was immediately occupied by Howard, who pressed on in pursuit. Sherman's columns, following upon each other's heels through Snake Creek Gap, had the advantage of Johnston in point of time. But this was counterbalanced by the more practicable and shorter route taken by the Confederates. On the 12th Sherman moved upon Resaca, McPherson on the direct road, preceded, as in his former advance, by Kilpatrick's cavalry; Thomas closed in upon McPherson's left, and Schofield upon the left of Thomas. But it was not until the 14th that Sherman was prepared to attack, and by that time he was confronted by the whole force of the enemy, who occupied the forts of Resaca behind Camp Creek, Polk's left resting on the Oostenaula, Hardee holding the centre, and Hood the right, extending northeastwardly around Resaca to the Connesauga. Loring's division, added to those already at Resaca under Hood, had on the 13th delayed Sherman's advance, thus giving time for the disposition of Hardee's and Polk's troops, then just arriving. Johnston's foresight and promptness had saved his army.[1]

Sherman now repeated against Resaca the strategic movement which had forced the enemy from Dalton; but there was this difference, that he now proceeded to threaten the enemy's communications with a lighter column, keeping almost his entire army in the enemy's front. General Sweeny's division of the Sixteenth Corps (Dodge's) crossed the Oostenaula by pontoons at Lay's Ferry and threatened Calhoun, and Garrard's cavalry division moved from its position at Villanow across the same river lower down, to destroy the railroad between Calhoun and Kingston. While these movements were in progress, Sherman attacked Johnston at Resaca, pressing him at all points during the afternoon of May 14th. Thomas, in the centre, pressed through Camp Creek Valley, sending Hooker across the creek. On the right and centre, however, the enemy successfully resisted Schofield and Thomas, and at nightfall Hood advanced from his intrenchments, and recovered a portion of the ground which the Federals had gained in the morning. McPherson's attack on Polk was more successful, the latter being driven from his position, which, commanding the Confederate bridges across the river, was immediately occupied with Federal artillery. Johnston had already given orders to Hood to attack the next morning, when he was informed of the movement by Sweeny menacing Calhoun, and of Polk's misfortune. He countermanded the orders, and sent Walker's division to Calhoun. The next day there was skirmishing along the entire front, developing on Hood's line into a severe battle in the afternoon. It appears that Walker had reported no movement on Calhoun, and Hood had been again ordered to attack, but that when the latter was prepared to do so, intelligence was received by Johnston indicating that the Federal right was crossing the river in his rear, and the order to attack was again countermanded. One of Hood's divisions—A. P. Stewart's—not being aware of this, attacked. Schofield by this time had closed down upon Hood's right, and Hooker, advancing, drove the enemy from several hills, capturing four guns and many prisoners. That night Johnston abandoned Resaca, and, crossing the Oostenaula southward, burned the railroad bridge behind him. Sherman's troops entered on the morning of the 16th just in time to save the turnpike bridge, and the whole army started in pursuit, Schofield moving by blind roads to the left, Thomas in Johnston's immediate rear, and McPherson by Lay's Ferry. In the operations around Resaca the Federal loss was between 4000 and 5000 killed and wounded. At Resaca Sherman reported to Grant that he had 1000 prisoners and eight guns.

General Sherman was now entering upon the third stage of the campaign. Johnston retreated to Cassville, four miles north of Kingston.[2] At Calhoun on the 16th, Hardee, bringing up the Confederate rear, skirmished with Howard's column. At Adairsville, farther south, there was a fight between Polk's cavalry, under Jackson, and the advance of Thomas's army, under General Newton. Polk and Hood, on the 18th, took the road from Adairsville to Cassville, while Hardee took that to Kingston. Sherman's left and centre had been delayed, Thomas having to build additional bridges across the Oostenaula, and Schofield making a detour across the two tributaries of that river—the Connesauga and Coosawattie. On the 17th the three Federal armies moved southward by different roads, and the division of Jeff. C. Davis meanwhile marched westwardly to Rome, where, meeting no resistance, it captured eight or ten heavy guns, together with some valuable mills and founderies.

On the 19th it appeared as if the enemy would make a stand at Cassville. French's division, of Polk's command, had arrived from the south, and Johnston, intrenched upon a ridge in the rear of the town, confidently ordered an advance against Thomas, who was moving southward from Adairsville. Hood, on the right, moved two miles in execution of this order, but, being deceived by the report that a Federal column was marching from

---

[1] "Nothing saved Johnston's army at Resaca but the impracticable nature of the country, which made the passage of troops across the valley almost impossible. This fact enabled his army to reach Resaca from Dalton along the comparatively good roads constructed beforehand, partly from the topographical nature of the country, and partly from the foresight of the rebel chief. At all events, on the 14th of May we found the rebel army in a strong position behind Camp Creek, occupying the forts at Resaca, and his right on some chestnut hills to the north of the town."—Sherman's Report.

[2] Johnston thus explains his continued retreat:

"The fact that a part of Polk's troops were still in the rear, and the great numerical superiority of the Federal army, made it expedient to risk battle only when position or some blunder of the enemy might give us counterbalancing advantages. I therefore determined to fall back slowly until circumstances should put the chances of battle in our favor, keeping so near the United States army as to prevent its sending re-enforcements to Grant; and hoping, by taking advantage of positions and opportunities, to reduce the odds against us by partial engagements. I also expected it to be materially reduced before the end of June by the expiration of the terms of service of many of the regiments which had not re-enlisted."

SHERMAN'S ARMY ENTERING RESAGA.

Canton to the rear and right of Cassville, he withdrew his troops to resist the approach of this fictitious column. The Federal army in the mean while concentrated about Cassville, and attacked Johnston's intrenched position with artillery. On the evening of the 19th the Confederate commanders differed as to the policy which ought now to be adopted. Hood and Polk thought that the Federal artillery would render the position untenable on the morrow, and urged immediate retreat across the Etowah River. Hardee, whose position Johnston thought much weaker than Polk's or Hood's, was still confident of his ability to hold it. Johnston inclined to Hardee's opinion, but the other commanders "were so earnest and unwilling to depend upon the ability of their corps to hold the ground," that retreat was determined upon, and on the 20th the Confederate army crossed the Etowah—"a step," reports Johnston, "which I have regretted ever since." This movement, without a battle, abandoned the whole of Etowah Valley to the Federal army. Here Sherman gave his troops rest, while supplies could be brought forward for the next stage of the campaign.

But the period of rest was brief. On the 23d of May, taking supplies in its trains for twenty days, and leaving a garrison at Rome and Kingston, Sherman's army crossed the Etowah. Satisfied that Johnston would attempt to hold Allatoona Pass, just south of the river, the Federal commander did not attempt even a demonstration against that position, but leaving the railroad, moved to the right for Dallas, southwest of Allatoona. Johnston, who had not stopped at Allatoona, but continued his retreat to the range of hills north of and covering Dallas and Marietta, detected Sherman's whole plan from the start, and concentrated his army near New Hope Church, where three roads met—from Ackworth on the north, Dallas on the southwest, and Marietta on the east. Hood's corps was posted with its centre at the church, while Polk and Hardee extended the line eastward across the Atlanta Road. Sherman's army, after crossing the Etowah, moved in three columns in the accustomed order—Schofield on the left, Thomas in the centre, and McPherson on the right. McPherson, crossing the Etowah near Kingston, joined by Davis's division from Rome, was ordered to move *via* Van Wert to a point south of Dallas. Thomas advanced *via* Euharley and Burnt Hickory, and Schofield by the road from Cassville.

Thomas's advance, under Hooker, approached New Hope Church on the 25th, and encountered the enemy's cavalry. Geary's division skirmished up to the Confederate line held by Hood, and Hooker's other divisions being well in hand by 4 P.M., Sherman ordered a bold push to be made for the cross-roads. A severe battle was fought in this position, Stewart's division by night being finally driven back to the church, but still retaining the main position. Sherman now occupied several days in deploying up to the enemy's well-intrenched lines, which extended from New Hope Church to a point north of Marietta. McPherson was pushed close up to Dallas, Thomas still confronted Hood, and Schofield was ordered to move around to the left, in order to reach and turn Johnston's right flank. Garrard's cavalry operated with McPherson, and Stoneman's with Schofield, McCook's guarding the Federal rear. The movement of the whole army was now gradually to the left, proceeding slowly over difficult, densely-wooded ground. In the course of this development there were several sharp encounters with the en-

emy, the results of which sometimes favored one side and sometimes the other. On the 27th Howard's corps assailed Cleburne's division, and was repulsed, Johnston reports, "with great slaughter."[1] In this action, and the battle of New Hope Church, Johnston estimates his own loss as 900, and that of Sherman as 6000. On the 28th the enemy attacked McPherson while the latter was on the point of closing up on Thomas. "Fortunately," says Sherman, "our men had erected good breastworks, and gave the enemy a terrible and bloody repulse." The enemy's loss in this attack was nearly 3000, and McPherson's not more than one tenth of that number. There were ten days of this undecisive work (May 25th–June 4th), when Sherman determined to leave Johnston in his intrenchments, and move eastward to Ackworth, on the railroad.[2] The roads leading back to Ackworth and Allatoona Pass were now in his possession, and he had rebuilt the railroad bridge across the Etowah and occupied the pass with his cavalry. When, on the 6th of June, he had established himself at Ackworth, he fortified and garrisoned Allatoona Pass, making it a secondary base of supplies.

Johnston, adapting his movements to those of Sherman, transferred his whole army to a point on the railroad north of Marietta, where Kenesaw on his right, Pine Mountain in the advanced centre, and Lost Mountain on his left, interposed a natural barrier to a direct approach from the north.[3] While the Confederate army was intrenching itself in this formidable position, Sherman repaired the railroad in his rear, and brought forward to his camp an abundant supply of provisions. He also received re-enforcements. General Blair, with two divisions of the Seventeenth Corps (10,500 men)

[1] Howard reports his loss as "very heavy, being upward of 1400 killed, wounded, and missing in General Wood's division alone." He adds, "Though the assault was repulsed, yet a position was secured near Pickett's Mills of the greatest importance to the subsequent movement of the army, and it has been subsequently ascertained that the enemy suffered immensely in the action, and regarded it as the severest attack made during the eventful campaign."

[2] Sherman writes to General Halleck, Grant's chief of staff, from "Near Dallas," May 28:

"The enemy discovered my move to turn Allatoona, and moved to meet us here. Our columns met about one mile east of Pumpkin-vine Creek, and we pushed them back about three miles, to the point [New Hope Church] where the road forks to Allatoona and Marietta. Here Johnston has chosen a strong line, and made hasty but strong parapets of timber and earth, and has thus far stopped us. My right is Dallas, centre about three miles north, and I am gradually working round by the left to approach the railroad any where in front of Ackworth. Country very densely wooded and broken; no roads of any consequence. We have had many sharp, severe encounters, but nothing decisive. Both sides duly cautious in the obscurity of the ambushed ground."

In a letter to Halleck, May 29, he thus alludes to the enemy's attack on McPherson the day before:

"With the intention of working to my left toward the railroad east of Allatoona, I ordered General McPherson . . . . . to withdraw his army and take General Thomas's present position, while all of General Thomas's and General Schofield's armies will be moved farther to the east, working round the enemy to the left. The enemy, who had observed, etc., ... massed against General McPherson and attacked him at 4½ P.M. yesterday, but was repulsed with great slaughter and at little cost to us. The enemy fled back to his breastworks on the ridge, leaving in our hands his dead and wounded. His loss, 2500, and about 300 prisoners. General McPherson's men being covered by log breastworks, like our old Corinth lines, were comparatively unhurt, his loss not being over 300 in all."

[3] "Kenesaw, the bold and striking twin mountain, lay before us, with a high range of chestnut hills trending off to the northeast, terminating to our view in another peak called Brusby Mountain. To our right was the smaller hill called Pine Mountain, and beyond it, in the distance, Lost Mountain. All these, though links in a continuous chain, present a sharp, conical appearance, prominent in the vast landscape that presents itself from any of the hills that abound in that region. Kenesaw, Pine Mountain, and Lost Mountain form a triangle—Pine Mountain the apex, and Kenesaw and Lost Mountain the base—covering perfectly the town of Marietta and the railroad back to the Chattahoochee. On each of these peaks the enemy had his signal stations. The summits were covered with batteries, and the spurs were alive with men, busy in felling trees, digging pits, and preparing for the grand struggle impending."—*Sherman's Report.*

LOST MOUNTAIN AT SUNRISE.

that had been on furlough, and Colonel Long's brigade of cavalry, arrived at Ackworth June 8th. This accession supplied the gaps which had been made in the original army by losses in battle and the detachments from garrison at Resaca, Rome, Kingston, and Allatoona Pass.[1] On the 9th the army moved to Big Shanty, a station on the railroad midway between Ackworth and Kenesaw. A triangular mountain fortress, of nature's construction, here confronted Sherman. Even war could not quench in Sherman his love of nature, nor interrupt "communion with her visible forms." "The scene," he says, "was enchanting—too beautiful to be disturbed by the harsh clamors of war; but the Chattahoochee lay beyond, and I had to reach it." Just beyond the Chattahoochee lay Atlanta—the object of the campaign.

While waiting before Kenesaw, Sherman received intelligence from General S. G. Burbridge, who had been left in command of the forces in Kentucky, that the Confederate General Morgan had entered that state through Pound Gap, June 4; that on the 9th he had been brought to battle and defeated with a loss of 600 prisoners; that on the 12th he had been again defeated, losing 500 killed and 400 prisoners, besides the wounded; and that his forces were scattered, demoralized, and being "pursued and picked up in every direction." Here also Sherman heard of Sturgis's defeat by Forrest, narrated in a previous chapter, and ordered a second expedition against Forrest to proceed immediately from Memphis.

Sherman paused for a brief moment and carefully scrutinized the Confederate position. He found that the enemy's line extended two miles in length, "more than he could hold with his force."[2] He had moved his armies close up by the 11th, McPherson on the left of the railroad toward Marietta, Schofield away to the right against Lost Mountain, and the larger army, under Thomas, confronting Pine and Kenesaw Mountains. It was

Sherman's object to break the line between Pine and Kenesaw. Flank movements, at this distance from his base, were too serious affairs to be attempted until they were plainly seen to be necessary. For more than 20 days Sherman tried the enemy's lines in front by cannonade, skirmish, and assault. On the 14th of June, General Polk, commanding the Confederate centre on Pine Mountain, four miles southwest of Kenesaw, was killed by a cannon-ball,[1] and was succeeded by General Loring, who immediately withdrew from his advanced position, and on the 19th Johnston's line was contracted, abandoning Pine and Lost Mountains. Hood's right rested on the Marietta Road, Loring held the centre, now transferred to Kenesaw Mountain, and Hardee extended across the Lost Mountain and Marietta Road on the left. A division of militia had in the mean time been sent to Johnston by Governor Brown. This division, commanded by General Gustavus W. Smith, was employed to guard the crossings of the Chattahoochee, to prevent the surprise of Atlanta by Federal cavalry. "The whole country," Sherman (June 23) writes to Halleck, "is one vast fort, and Johnston must have fully 50 miles of connected trenches, with abatis and finished batteries."

Sherman pressed on through the forests and difficult ravines, and finally came upon the enemy's new position, of which Kenesaw was the salient, Hood thrown back to cover Marietta, and Hardee to cover the railroad to the Chattahoochee. During these operations the weather, according to Sherman's report, "was villainously bad." Rain fell almost without pause for three weeks, making mud gullies of the narrow roads, and preventing a gen-

---

[1] The losses in Sherman's command during the month of May are not stated in his report. Thomas reports his own loss during this time as 8774.   [2] Sherman's Report.

[1] "It was on the afternoon of June 14th that Johnston, Hardee, and Polk rode out from their quarters to make some telescopic observations of the Federal position. At the time there was a brisk artillery fire going on between the two armies, but no engagement of the infantry. The generals, dismounting, walked to the front, where some of the enemy's artillerists, observing the party, fired. Their aim was too successful. One of the projectiles struck General Polk on the left arm, about the elbow, passed through his body, considerably mangling it, and carried off the right arm. He died on the spot, and his remains were immediately taken to Marietta, and thence to Atlanta, where funeral services were performed on the 15th."—Southern Generals, p. 419.

CREST OF PINE MOUNTAIN, WHERE GENERAL POLK FELL.

VIEW OF KENESAW FROM LITTLE KENESAW.

MAP OF THE ATLANTA CAMPAIGN.

eral movement; but the Federal lines with every opportunity were advanced closer to the enemy. It will be seen that Sherman had not accomplished his purpose of penetrating the Confederate line, but had only thrown it in upon itself, contracting and strengthening it. Johnston had seen the mistake of his original position, and had corrected it in time to prevent disaster. On the 21st Hood was shifted to Hardee's left, while at the same time Sherman was developing his right flank southward of Kenesaw. The next day, Hooker, having advanced his line, with Schofield on his right, was suddenly attacked by Hood near the Kulp House, southwest of Marietta. Hood appears to have gained some advantage at first, falling thus unexpectedly upon Williams's division of Hooker's corps and Hascall's of Schofield's, and driving them back; but he was checked upon reaching the main line, and himself driven back in confusion, leaving behind his dead, wounded, and many prisoners.[1]

Sherman now determined to assault Kenesaw. It was a bold and Sherman-like thing to do, and certainly failure could not have been reckoned in-

evitable.[1] The order was given on the 24th, and executed on the 27th. Two points were selected on the enemy's left centre—one at Little Kenesaw, in McPherson's front, the other a mile farther south, in front of Thomas. On the appointed day, after a vigorous cannonade, the armies of the Tennessee and the Cumberland leaped forward to their terrible work, their assault falling mainly on Loring's and Hardee's corps. With a loss of less than 500 men the Confederate position was maintained, and McPherson and Thomas were completely repulsed, losing altogether 3000 men, including General Harker, Colonel Dan. McCook, Colonel Rice, and other valuable officers. Success in this assault would have been decisive of the campaign; it would have cut the enemy in two, prevented his retreat, and exposed him to defeat in detail. But the assault was not a success.[2] Sherman gives the following explanation of his reasons for making this assault:

"Upon studying the ground, I had no alternative but to assault or turn the enemy's position. Either course had its difficulties and dangers. And

---

[1] General Thomas gives the following account of this affair:

"Williams's division of Hooker's corps skirmished itself into a position on the right of Geary's division, the right of Williams resting at Kulp's House, on the Powder Spring and Marietta Road. About 4 P. M. the enemy, in heavy force, attacked Knipe's brigade in its advanced position, before his men had time to throw up any works, and persisted in the assault until sundown, when they withdrew, their ranks hopelessly broken, each assault having been repelled with heavy loss."

---

[1] Perhaps the explanation of Sherman's hope of success is to be found in his dispatch to Halleck, June 25th, which says: "I shall aim to make him [Johnston] stretch his line until he weakens it, and then break through."

[2] General Harker commanded a brigade of Newton's division of Howard's (Fourth) corps. He led one column of the assault in Howard's front, and Wagner another. Palmer's (Fourteenth) corps at the same time assaulted on Howard's right. In regard to the result, Howard reports: "My experience is that a line of works thoroughly constructed, with the front well covered with abatis and other entanglements, well manned with infantry, whether with our own or that of the enemy, can not be carried by direct assault; the exceptions are when some one of the above conditions are wanting, or where the defenders are taken by surprise. The strength of such a line is of course increased by well-arranged batteries. Notwithstanding the probabilities against success, it is sometimes necessary to assault strong works, as has occurred in several instances during this campaign."

Colonels Dan. McCook and T. J. Mitchell (commanding brigades of Jeff. C. Davis's division) led the assaulting columns of Palmer's corps. McCook fell, dangerously wounded, and subsequently died at his home in Ohio.

CHARLES G. HARKER.

DANIEL McCOOK.

HOWARD'S CORPS CROSSING THE CHATTAHOOCHEE.

I perceived that the enemy and our own officers had settled down into a conviction that I would *not* assault fortified lines. All looked to me to out-flank. An army, to be efficient, must not settle down to one single mode of offense, but must be prepared to execute any plan that promises success. I wished, therefore, for the moral effect, to make a successful assault on the enemy behind his breastworks. . . . . Failure as it was, and for which I assume the entire responsibility, I yet claim that it produced good fruits, as it demonstrated to General Johnston that I would assault, and that boldly; and we also gained and held ground so close to the enemy's parapets that he could not show a head above them."[1]

After this repulse there was but one resource left—another flank movement. On the night of July 2d, McPherson, in front of Kenesaw, was relieved by Garrard's cavalry, and thrown around the right of the army, with instructions to advance to Nickajack Creek, and threaten Turner's Ferry, where the railroad in Johnston's rear crossed the Chattahoochee. The Confederate commander at once saw the meaning of this movement, and on the morning of the 3d Thomas found no enemy in his front. A view of the Federal skirmishers on the top of Kenesaw was the first sight which greeted Sherman's eyes at daybreak. Thomas moved forward in pursuit by the railroad, and at 8 30 A.M. Sherman in person entered Marietta just as the enemy's cavalry left the place. He hoped to strike the enemy in the confusion of crossing the Chattahoochee. Drawing Logan from McPherson's column to Marietta, the remainder of the Army of the Tennessee, with that of the Ohio, were ordered to cross the Nickajack, and attack the enemy in flank and rear.[2] Johnston, however, had covered his movement with great care, having constructed a strong *tête de pont* at the Chattahoochee, opposing also an advanced intrenched line at the Smyrna camp-meeting ground, five miles south of Marietta, his flanks resting behind Nickajack and Rottenwood Creeks. On the 5th of July this advanced position was abandoned on account of Sherman's threatening movements toward Turner's Ferry. Logan had been returned to McPherson, and Thomas was moving on Smyrna, when the enemy fell back to his *tête de pont*. The Confederate cavalry crossed the Chattahoochee, Wheeler observing the river for twenty miles above, and Jackson for the same distance below. There was skirmishing between the two armies until the 9th, Thomas's and McPherson's commands touching the river above and below the enemy, with Schofield's in reserve. While these operations were going on, Schofield had been withdrawn to Smyrna, and sent across the Chattahoochee at the mouth of Soap Creek (July 7th). This movement was successfully accomplished, Schofield surprising the Confederate guard, capturing a gun, laying a pontoon bridge across the river, and establishing himself on commanding ground on the east bank. At the same time Garrard's cavalry moved to Rosswell, farther up the river, where he destroyed the factories which had for years supplied cloth to the Confederate armies. A facetious owner of one of these mills, intent upon having his joke, even if he lost his factory, displayed a French flag above the building.[3] Having destroyed these works, Garrard secured a shallow ford, and held it until the arrival of an infantry division from Thomas's army. McPherson's whole army was soon transferred to this quarter from the Nickajack. Howard's corps, of Thomas's army, had also built a bridge at Powers's Ferry, two miles below the mouth of Soap Creek, crossed over and occupied a position on Schofield's right. These movements, securing three points of crossing the Chattahoochee above the enemy, and also a position on the east bank, from which good roads ran to Atlanta, threatened to leave Johnston at his *tête de pont* at Turner's Ferry, and turning his flank, to bring Sherman's army into Atlanta forthwith. Johnston, seeing this, followed his cavalry across the Chattahoochee on the night of the 9th, and took up a position on Peach-tree Creek and the river below,

---

[1] Sherman gives a similar explanation to Halleck shortly after the assault. He says: "The assault I made was no mistake; I had to do it. The enemy, and our own army and officers, had settled down into the conviction that the assault of lines formed no part of my game, and the moment the enemy was found behind any thing like a parapet, why, every body would deploy, throw up counter works, and take it easy, leaving it to the 'old man' [meaning Sherman] to turn the position. Had the assault been made with one fourth more vigor (mathematically), I would have put the head of George Thomas's whole army right through Johnston's deployed line, on the best ground for 'go ahead,' while my entire forces were well in hand on roads converging to my then object, Marietta. Had Harker and McCook not been struck so early, the assault would have succeeded, and then the battle would have all been in our favor, on account of our superiority in numbers and initiative."

As to the possibility of success if Harker and McCook had not fallen, General Thomas is the original authority. He reports to Sherman just after the assault: "Both General Harker and Colonel McCook were wounded on the enemy's breastworks, and all say had they not been wounded we would have driven the enemy from his works."

[2] "If you ever worked in your life," writes Sherman to McPherson on the evening of July 3, "work at daybreak to-morrow on the flank, crossing Nickajack somehow, and the moment you discover confusion pour in your fire. You know what a retreating mass across pontoon bridges means. Feel strong to-night, and make feints of pursuit with artillery. I know Johnston's withdrawal is not strategic, but for good reasons after he crosses the Chattahoochee; but his situation with that river behind him is not comfortable at all. . . . . . I don't confine you to any crossing, but press the enemy all the time in flank till he is across the Chattahoochee."

To Thomas, at the same time, he writes:

"The more I reflect, the more I know Johnston's halt is to save time to cross his material and men. No general such as he would invite battle with the Chattahoochee behind him. I have ordered McPherson and Schofield, at any cost, and work night and day, to get the enemy started in confusion toward his bridges. I know you appreciate the situation. We will never have such a chance again, and I want you to impress on Hooker, Howard, and Palmer the importance of the most intense energy of attack to-night and in the morning, and to press with vehemence, at any cost of life and material. Every inch of his line should be felt, and the moment there is a give, pursuit should be made by day with lines, and by night with a single head of column and section of artillery to each corps following a road. Hooker should communicate with McPherson by a circuit if necessary, and act in concert. You know what loss would ensue to Johnston if he crosses his bridges at night in confusion, with artillery thundering at random on his rear."

[3] This joke might easily have cost the perpetrator his life. Sherman writes to Garrard, July 7: "I will see as to any man in America hoisting the French flag, and then devoting his labor and capital to supplying armies in open hostility to our government, and claiming the benefit of his neutral flag. Should you, under the impulse of anger, natural at contemplating such perfidy, hang the wretch, I approve the act beforehand." He adds: "I repeat my orders that you arrest all people, male and female, connected with those factories, no matter what the clamor, and let them foot it, under guard, to Marietta, whence I will send them by cars to the North. . . . . The poor women will make a howl. Let them take along their children and clothing, providing they have the means of hauling, or you can spare them. We will retain them until they can reach a country where they can live in peace and security."

VIEW OF ATLANTA FROM THE SIGNAL STATION NORTH OF THE CHATTAHOOCHEE.

covering Atlanta. Thus was abandoned to Sherman all of Georgia between the Tennessee and the Chattahoochee Rivers. In the pursuit of Johnston to the Chattahoochee, 2000 prisoners were taken.

And here let us halt to review what has already been accomplished in the two months since Sherman opened the attack upon Johnston at Buzzard's Roost. Johnston had been *driven* south of the Chattahoochee; he had not retreated from strategic motives, though his retreat had been conducted with so great skill and so little waste of force that it places him in the foremost rank of Confederate generals. No great battle had been fought in the campaign, which had been a series of sieges. Assaults there had been on both sides, and in these the loss had been severe, falling mainly upon the assailants. Johnston's losses altogether had been, according to his own report, about 10,000 in killed and wounded, and 4700 from other causes. This does not include deserters, which probably numbered 2500 at the lowest, thus bringing the total loss to about 20,000. This loss had been just about covered by re-enforcements. Sherman's losses it is difficult to estimate exactly. In the Army of the Cumberland the casualties for May and June amounted to 14,521, as reported by General Thomas. Supposing the loss in McPherson's and Schofield's commands to have been in proportion, we have a total of 25,000 for the casualties of battle. These losses, and others from sickness and detachment of troops for garrison, had been made up for by re-enforcements, so that the two armies, in respect of numbers, were now nearly the same as at the opening of the campaign. In the first stage of his advance, Sherman had it in his power to compel Johnston to fight a battle upon conditions which involved the destruction of the Confederate army. It is wonderful that Johnston should have left Snake Creek Gap unguarded, but it is still more wonderful that, once having gained access through this pass to the enemy's rear, McPherson did not appreciate his advantage, and push it to the utmost. If he had done so, and had been promptly supported, Johnston's army must have been ground to powder. No such opportunity again offered. But, notwithstanding this disappointment, the fact that Johnston could hold no position north of the Chattahoochee was really a conclusive argument that he could not hold Atlanta. Sherman's sole weakness was his long line of communications; but this was so well protected that, although Johnston, after crossing the Etowah, had sent five successive detachments of cavalry to destroy it, none of these had succeeded.

Sherman's army was now within sight of Atlanta, only eight miles intervening. Atlanta is the centre of the entire network of railroads in Georgia. From it start three railway lines of communication. The road running north to Chattanooga was occupied in its entire length by Sherman. Eastward, through Decatur, another road runs to Augusta, and thence to Charleston. The road running south divides into two branches at East Point, six miles from Atlanta; one running southeastwardly through Macon to Savannah, the other southwestwardly through West Point and Opelika to Montgom-

ery, and thence with slight interruption to Pensacola. To destroy this latter or West Point Road, an expedition had been prepared, and General Rousseau had been assigned to its command. As early as the 10th of April, General Sherman, believing that Johnston would finally fall back beyond the Chattahoochee, had had this raid in view. The time for its operation had now come. On the 10th of July, when it was ascertained that Johnston had crossed the river, Rousseau started from Decatur, Alabama, with 2500 cavalry and two pieces of artillery.[1] No time more favorable could have been selected for the expedition. A. J. Smith was occupying Forrest's cavalry in Mississippi; expeditions were out inland from Vicksburg and Baton Rouge, and Canby was understood to be threatening Mobile. Rousseau's force consisted of the following cavalry regiments—the Fifth Indiana, Fifth Iowa, Second Kentucky, Fourth Tennessee, and Ninth Ohio. The party possessed 1000 Spencer repeating-rifles. At the crossing of Coosa River, on the 13th, a ferry-boat was captured, and a part of the command having crossed and effected a lodgment on the south bank, it was attacked by General Clanton with two regiments of Alabama cavalry. This Confederate detachment was routed after a few hours' skirmishing by an attack in flank, and Rousseau proceeded to Talladega on the railroad to Selma. Here a camp of about 700 conscripts was dispersed. The West Point Railroad was first struck at Chehaw Station, where the enemy was again encountered under Clanton, but was obliged to retire after a loss of 40 killed and a large number of

[1] The following instructions to Rousseau were dispatched by Sherman June 30th:

"The movement that I want you to study and be prepared for is contingent on the fact that General A. J. Smith defeats Forrest, or holds him well in check, and after I succeed in making Joe Johnston pass the Chattahoochee with his army, when I want you to go in person, or to send some good officer, with 2500 good cavalry well armed, and a sufficient number of pack-mules loaded with ammunition, salt, sugar, and coffee, and some bread or flour, depending on the country for forage, meat, and corn-meal. The party might take two light Rodman guns, with orders, in case of very rapid movements, to cut the wheels and burn the carriages, taking sledges along to break off trunnions and wedge them into the muzzles. The expedition should start from Decatur [Alabama], move slowly to Blountsville and Ashville, and, if the way is clear, cross the Coosa at the Ten Islands, or the railroad bridge, destroying it after their passage, then move rapidly for Talladega or Oxford, and then to the nearest ford or bridge over the Tallapoosa. That passed, the expedition should move with rapidity on the railroad between Tuskegee and Opelika, breaking up the road and twisting the bars of iron. They should work on that road night and day, doing all the damage possible, toward and including Opelika. If no serious opposition offer, they should threaten Columbus, Georgia, and then turn up the Chattahoochee to join us between Marietta and Atlanta, doing all the mischief possible. No infantry in position should be attacked, and the party should avoid all fighting possible, bearing in mind, for their own safety, that Pensacola, Rome, the Etowah, and my army are all places of refuge. If compelled *to* make Pensacola, they should leave their horses, embark for New Orleans, and come round to Nashville. Study this well, and be prepared to act on orders when the time comes. Selma, though important, is more easily defended than the route I have named."

On July 2d the following dispatch was sent to Rousseau:

"Now is the time for the raid to Opelika. . . . . . Forrest is in Mississippi, and Roddy has also gone there. All other rebel cavalry is here."

On July 6th the order was repeated as follows:

"That cavalry expedition must now be off, and must proceed with the utmost energy and confidence. Every thing here is favorable, and I have official information that General A. J. Smith is out from Memphis with force enough to give Forrest full occupation. Expeditions inland are also out from Vicksburg and Baton Rouge, as well as against Mobile. If managed with rapidity, the expedition can not fail of success, and will accomplish much good."

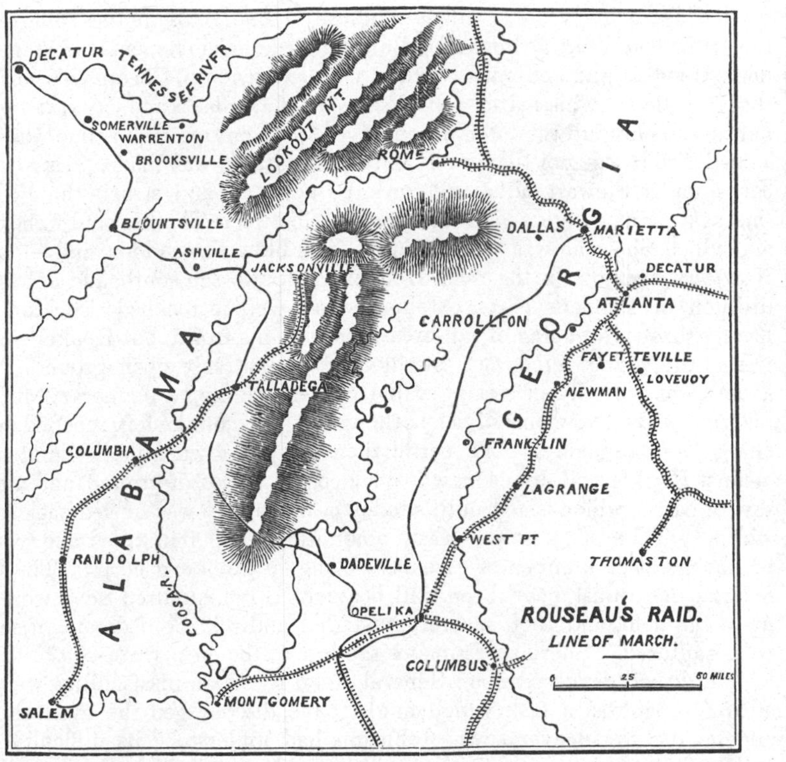

wounded. At Opelika a large quantity of stores was captured, and the railroad was obliterated. From this point, on the 19th, Rousseau began to return to Marietta, where he arrived by way of Carrolton and Villa Rica on the 22d. He had destroyed 30 miles of the railroad toward Montgomery, three miles toward Columbus, and two toward West Point. His entire loss had been 12 killed and 30 wounded. He brought in 400 mules and 300 horses.

After having collected an abundant supply of stores at Allatoona, Marietta, and Vining's Station, and strengthened the railroad guards and garrisons in the rear, General Sherman, on the 17th, crossed the Chattahoochee, a matter of no small difficulty, effected, as it was, in the face of an army 50,000 strong. Schofield was already across in an impregnable position, and was ordered to New Cross Keys. Thomas crossed at Powers's and Paice's Ferries, and was to move by way of Buckhead; and McPherson was instructed to move straight from Roswell to a point east of Decatur on the Augusta Railroad. Garrard's cavalry acted with McPherson, while Stoneman and McCook watched the rivers and roads below the railway.

At this most critical stage of the campaign, General Johnston, commanding the Confederate army, was relieved of his command. He received at 10 o'clock P.M. on the 17th a telegram from Secretary Seddon, the purport of which was that, as he had failed to arrest the Federal approach to the vicinity of Atlanta, and had expressed no confidence in his ability to defeat or repulse General Sherman, he would immediately turn the army over to General Hood.[1] Johnston, at Hood's request, continued to give orders until the afternoon of the 18th, placing his troops on the position which he had selected near Peach-tree Creek. He also fully explained to Hood the plans

[1] "Besides the causes of my removal alleged in the telegram announcing it," reports General Johnston, "various other accusations have been made against me—some published in newspapers in such a manner as to appear to have official authority, and others circulated orally in Georgia and Alabama, and imputed to General Bragg. The principal are, that I persistently disregarded the instructions of the President; that I would not fight the enemy; that I refused to defend Atlanta; that I refused to communicate with General Bragg in relation to the operations of the army; that I disregarded his entreaties to change my course and attack the enemy; and gross exaggerations of the losses of the army.

"I had not the advantage of receiving the President's instructions in relation to the manner of conducting the campaign. But as the conduct of my predecessor, in retreating before odds less than those confronting me, has apparently been approved; and as General Lee, in keeping on the defensive and retreating toward Grant's objective point, under circumstances like mine, was adding to his great fame, both in the estimation of the administration and people, I supposed that my course would not be censured. I believed then, as I do now, that it was the only one at my command which promised success.

"I think that the foregoing narrative shows that the Army of Tennessee did fight, and with at least as much effect as it has ever done before.

"The proofs that I intended to hold Atlanta are the fact that under my orders the work of strengthening its defenses was going on vigorously, the communication on the subject made by me to General Hood, and the fact that my family was in the town. That the public workshops were removed and no large supplies deposited in the town, as alleged by General Bragg, were measures of common prudence, and no more indicated the intention to abandon the place than the sending the wagons of an army to the rear on a day of battle proves a foregone determination to abandon the field.

"While General Bragg was at Atlanta, about the middle of July, we had no other conversation concerning the army there than such as I introduced. He asked me no questions regarding its operations, past or future; made no comments upon them nor suggestions, and had not the slightest reason to suppose that Atlanta would not be defended. He told me that the object of his journey was to confer with Lieutenant General Lee, and communicate with General E. K. Smith in relation to re-enforcements for me. He talked much more of affairs in Virginia than in Georgia, asserting, what I believed, that Sherman's army outnumbered Grant's, and impressed me with the belief that his visits to me were unofficial."

And here it is proper to consider General Hood's estimate of the Atlanta campaign. In the first place, he estimates General Johnston's effective force on the 6th of May, 1864, as 70,000 men. For this statement there is no authority whatsoever. "The South," he says, "had been denuded of troops to fill the strength of the Army of the Tennessee. Mississippi and Alabama were without military support, and looked for protection in decisive battle in the mountains of Georgia." Here again Hood is belied by all testimony. Forrest, whose assistance Johnston asked for, was kept in Mississippi by orders from Richmond, and not permitted to attack Sherman's communications. Besides putting Johnston's force nearly 20,000 higher than it really was, Hood says that "re-enforcements were within supporting distance." These re-enforcements were absolutely refused in a defensive campaign on Johnston's part, and no other campaign was possible.

Hood then goes on to reprimand Johnston's retreat. "In such condition," he says, "was that splendid army when the active campaign fairly opened. The enemy, but little superior in numbers, none in organization and discipline, inferior in spirit and confidence, commenced his advance. The Confederate forces, whose faces and hopes were to the north, almost simultaneously commenced to retreat. They soon reached positions favorable for resistance. Great ranges of mountains running across the line of march, and deep rivers, are stands from which a well-directed army is not easily driven or turned. At each advance of the enemy, the Confederate army, without serious resistance, fell back to the next range or river in the rear. The habit to retreat soon became a routine of the army, and was substituted for the hope and confidence with which the campaign opened. The enemy soon perceived this. With perfect security he divided his forces, using one column to menace in front and one to threaten in rear. The usual order to retreat, not strike in detail, was issued and obeyed. Those retreats were always at night. The day was consumed in hard labor. Daily temporary works were thrown up, behind which it was never intended to fight. The men became travelers by night and laborers by day. They were ceasing to be soldiers by the disuse of military duty. Thus for seventy-four days and nights, that noble army, which, if ordered to resist, no force that the enemy could assemble could dislodge from a battle-field, continued to abandon their country, to see their strength departing, and their flag waving only in retreat or in partial engagements. At the end of that time, after descending from the mountains, where the last advantage of position was abandoned, and camping without fortifications on the open plains of Georgia, the army had lost 22,750 of its best soldiers. Nearly one third was gone, no general battle fought, much of our state abandoned, two others uncovered, and the organization and efficiency of every command, by loss of officers, men, and tone, seriously diminished. These things were the inevitable result of the strategy adopted. It is impossible for a large army to retreat in the face of a pursuing enemy without such a fate. In a retreat the losses are constant and permanent. Stragglers are overtaken, the fatigued fall by the wayside, and are gathered by the advancing enemy. Every position by the rear-guard, if taken, yields its wounded to the victors. The soldiers, always awakened from rest at night to continue the retreat, leave many of their comrades asleep in trenches. This is the time for desertion. The losses of a single day are not large. Those of seventy-four (74) days will embrace the strength of an army. If a battle be fought and the field held at the close, however great the slaughter, the loss will be less than to retreat in the face of an enemy. There will be no stragglers. Desertions are in retreat, rarely, if ever, on the field of battle. The wounded are gathered to the rear, and soon recover, and in a few weeks the entire loss consists only of the killed and permanently disabled, which is not one fifth of the apparent loss on the night of the battle. The enemy is checked, his plans deranged, territory saved, the campaign suspended or won. If a retreat still be necessary, it can then be done with no enemy pressing and no loss following. The advancing party loses nothing but its killed and permanently disabled. Neither stragglers nor deserters thin its ranks. It reaches the end of its march stronger for battle than when it started. The army commanded by General Sherman and that commanded by General Johnston, not greatly unequal at the commencement of the campaign, illustrate what I have written. General Sherman, in his official report, states that his forces when they entered Atlanta were nearly the same in number as when they left Dalton. The Army of Tennessee lost twenty-two thousand seven hundred and fifty (22,750) men, nearly one third of its strength. I have nothing to say of the statement of losses made by General Johnston in his official report, except to state that, by his own figures, he understates his losses some thousands; that he excludes the idea of any prisoners, although his previous official returns show more than seven thousand (7000) under the head of 'absent without leave;' and that the returns of the army while he was in command, corrected and increased by the *records* of the army which has not been fully reported to the government, and the return signed by me, but made up under him, as soon as I assumed command, show the losses of the Army of Tennessee to be what I have stated, and a careful examination of the returns with the army will show the losses to be more than stated."

Hood's own statements belie him. He says Johnston lost 22,750 men. He gives him at the outset 70,000. This would leave 47,250. The re-enforcements during this period amounted to nearly 20,000; so that Hood should have had about as fair a start as Johnston had had. But how does Hood estimate the force which he received from Johnston? He says: "Its effective strength was, infantry, 33,750; artillery, 3500; cavalry, 10,000, with 1500 Georgia militia . . . making a total of 47,750 men." This is sufficient reason for doubting the reliability of General Hood's estimates. For, by his calculation, Johnston had received only about 500 additional men since the commencement of the campaign. The official documents tell a different story.

And here let us submit the report made by Mr. Wigfall in the Confederate Senate, March 16, 1865:

"MR. PRESIDENT,—I return the Report of General Hood, with a recommendation from the Committee on Military Affairs that it be printed. I am instructed by the committee to say that this recommendation would not have been made had the House not already ordered it to be published. No action of the Senate can now keep the report from the public, however desirable it might be. Indeed, having been sent to both houses in open session by the President without any warning as to 'its tendency to induce controversy' or cause 'prejudice to the public service,' as in the case of General Johnston's Report, the damage was already done—if damage should result from its contents being made known. The official report of the Secretary of War at the beginning of this Congress contained an attack upon General Johnston. It was sent to us by the President in open session, and published by order of Congress. General Johnston's Report, which contained his defense against this attack, was asked for promptly, but was withheld for months. It was finally sent to us *in secret session*, with a protest against its publication. A report of the operations of the Army of Tennessee *while under the command of General Hood* is asked for, and we receive this paper *in open session* as soon as it can be copied. No word of warning as to its character is given.

"Much of it is but a repetition of the charges made by the late Secretary of War, and, if they can be sustained, it is manifest that our present disasters are not to be attributed to General Johnston's removal, but to his ever having been appointed. It follows, too, that he should not be continued in his present command. It becomes necessary, therefore, to examine into the correctness of these charges. The Senate did not ask for a review of General Johnston's campaign, but for a report of the operations of the army while under the command of General Hood. Though uncalled for, it is before us and the people, and I propose to give it a fair and calm consideration.

"In reviewing the review, I shall refer to the *official* 'Field Returns' on file in the Adjutant and Inspector General's Office, made and signed by Colonel Mason, A. A. G., and approved by General Johnston, and not to those with the army, revised and 'corrected,' which I have never seen. The field returns on file here are, or should be, duplicates of those with the army, which are made up from the returns of the corps commanders. Not having the honor of a personal acquaintance with Colonel Falconer, I do not know what reliance is to be placed on his corrections of official documents. I do know Colonel Mason and General Johnston, and I do not believe either capable of making a false or fraudulent return.

"General Hood, in his review, gives the effective total of General Johnston's army 'at and near Dalton' to be 70,000 on the 6th of May, 1864. These returns appear to have been made tri-monthly, on the 1st, 10th, and 20th of each month. The last official 'field return,' previously to the 6th of May, on file in the Adjutant and Inspector General's Office, is of the 1st of May. It shows his effective total to be 40,913 infantry and artillery and 2974 cavalry, amounting in all to 43,887. This return shows, however, that two brigades of cavalry, under the command of General Johnston, were in the rear recruiting their horses, the effective total of which is not given. General Johnston, in his report, estimates his cavalry at this time at 'about 4000,' which would make the effective total of these brigades 1026, which, added to the 2974 'at' Dalton, makes the 4000. Estimating his cavalry there at 4000, it is obvious that from the official returns he had but 44,913 effective total 'at and near' Dalton on the 1st of May, the date of the last return before the 6th of that month. The official records show, then, that General Hood over-estimated General Johnston's forces 'at and near Dalton' by 25,087 men.

"If General Hood, by the term 'at or near Dalton,' refers to the forces after this date received by General Johnston from General Polk, he is again in error as to numbers. It was not till the 4th of May that General Polk was ordered to 'move with Loring's division and other available forces at your command, to Rome, Georgia, and thence unite with General Johnston.' On the 6th, the day on which General Hood says this army 'lay at and near Dalton, waiting the advance of the enemy,' General Polk telegraphs to General Cooper from *Demopolis*: 'My troops are concentrating and moving as directed.' On the 10th, at Rome, he telegraphs the President: 'The first of Loring's brigade arrived and sent forward to Resaca; the second just in; the third will arrive early to-morrow morning. * * * French's brigade was to leave Blue Mountain this morning. The others will follow in succession; Ferguson will be in supporting distance day after to-morrow; Jackson's division thirty-six hours after.' Yet General Hood asserts that four days before this the army was 'assembled' at and near Dalton, and 'within the easy direction of a single commander.' The last of these re-enforcements joined General Johnston at New Hope Church the 26th of May, nearly three weeks after they were alleged to be 'at and near Dalton,' and amounted to less than 19,000 men. If none was lost by sickness, desertion, or the casualties of battle, which is not probable, General Johnston had at New Hope about sixty-four thousand men on the 26th of May, instead of seventy thousand, at Dalton, on the 6th. A difference of six thousand; not very great, it is admitted, yet it shows General Hood to be not quite accurate in his estimates.

"General Hood asserts that General Johnston lost twenty-two thousand seven hundred men in his retreat, and offers to prove that by the record. At New Hope he had about sixty-four thousand men. The field returns of the 10th of July, the last made while the army was under his command, shows, at Atlanta, 40,656 infantry and artillery, and 10,276 cavalry—50,932—say 51,000. Deduct this from 64,000, and it leaves 13,000 loss in artillery, infantry, and cavalry, instead of 22,700, as alleged by General Hood. General Johnston does not give the losses of his cavalry for want of reports. He had 4000 at Dalton, and received 4000 (Polk's) at Adairsville on the 17th of May—8000. At Atlanta he had 10,276, showing that he had recruited his cavalry 2276 over and above his losses. Leaving out his cavalry, he had at Atlanta, 10th of July, 40,656 infantry and artillery. At New Hope he had, of all arms, 64,000. Of these, 8000 were cavalry, supposing it not to have increased by recruiting up to that time. That gives him 56,000 infantry and artillery. At Atlanta he had, of these arms, 40,656, which deduct from the 56,000, and it shows his losses to be, in infantry and artillery, 15,344.

upon which he had proposed to conduct the defense of Atlanta. In the first place, he had proposed to attack Sherman while crossing the creek, where success would be of the greatest advantage, since, in that event, both the creek and the river would intercept the Federal retreat. If he failed in this attack, his design had been to keep back the enemy by means of intrenchments constructed between the Marietta and Decatur Roads until the arrival of the state troops which had been promised by Governor Brown at the end of the month. These intrenchments he would line with the state militia which he already had, while with his main army he would attack Sherman in flank whenever the latter should approach Atlanta.

The Confederate army was now posted on high ground on the west bank of Peach-tree Creek, extending from Turner's Ferry to the Augusta Road. McPherson, on the 18th, reached a point seven miles east of Decatur, and, with Garrard's cavalry, broke up four miles of the road. Schofield the same day reached Decatur. On the 19th McPherson turned into Decatur, Schofield following a road to the right leading toward Atlanta, while Thomas, by numerous bridges, crossed Peach-tree Creek in the face of the enemy. Hood had disposed his troops so that Cheatham's (formerly Hood's) corps on the right would cut off Thomas from Schofield and McPherson. Hardee held the centre, and Stewart (commanding Polk's old corps) the left. These two

were ordered by Hood to attack Thomas at one P.M. on the 20th, before the latter could fortify himself. But the Federal movement threatened to flank Hood's right, and must be met by an extension of Cheatham's corps in that direction. This led to a displacement of Hardee's and Stewart's original line to close up the interval. In these manœuvres much time was consumed, and it was not till four P.M. that the attack was made. Hood's left corps, under Stewart, advanced toward Buckhead, and struck the Federal line at a point where a gap had been left between Thomas and Schofield, and which Sherman was trying to fill. The blow was sudden, and fell upon Newton's division on the road, Hooker's corps to the south, and Johnson's division of Palmer's corps. Johnson was well intrenched; Newton had hastily thrown up a line of rail breastworks in his front; but Hooker's corps was entirely uncovered, and fought on comparatively open ground. The assault was partially successful at first, Stewart gaining a temporary work in his front. But Newton's division, though exposed on the left, repelled every charge of the enemy. The battle then swayed toward the Federal right against Hooker and Johnson, who yielded not a foot of ground, and after a severe battle, which lasted until sundown, the enemy was hurled back to his works.[1] Thomas's loss was heavy, amounting to 1600 in killed and wounded, the greatest number of casualties being in Hooker's corps. The Confederate loss must have been still heavier. Five hundred dead were left upon the field, and 1000 severely wounded, and 360 Confederate prisoners were captured. Sherman estimates the loss of the enemy at 5000.[2]

A task had devolved upon General Hood to which his faculties were inadequate; it was a task which might have discouraged the most skillful general the world ever saw. Johnston had understood its difficulty, and had met the emergency in the only possible way which either military science or military experience suggested. His removal from command was a denunciation of his method of conducting the campaign. Hood, who, while a brave soldier, was no general, adopted an exactly opposite method. It was his well-known habit to fight battles and disregard strategy, and for this reason he had been assigned to the command. If Sherman could have made the appointment himself, he could not have more certainly or more completely served his own purpose. Hood was the commander, and Hood's theory of war was the policy which secured for him the opportunity for which he had been waiting, and out of which Johnston had all along been cheating him.

General Hood, having failed in his first plan, proceeded to execute the second, which involved an attack on McPherson. The movement of the latter to Hood's right, if not checked, would compel the evacuation of Atlanta. Thus, on the morning of the 22d, Sherman, to his surprise, found the Confederate works on Peach-tree Creek abandoned, and pushed his whole line up close to Atlanta. Hood in the mean time was constructing new fortifications, and, leaving Cheatham and Stewart to defend the city, had ordered Hardee to move south with his corps during the night of the 21st on the McDonough Road. This movement had for its object the turning of McPherson's flank. Wheeler's cavalry moved on Hardee's right, and both were to attack at daylight, or as soon thereafter as possible. Hardee's success would be followed by an attack of Cheatham on Thomas, and then, as the engagement became general, by a movement from the centre.

These combinations led to the battle of July 22. McPherson had the night before crossed the Augusta Railroad two miles west of Decatur, after severe skirmishing, and Blair, on the left of the road, had pushed forward and seized a commanding eminence not two miles distant from Atlanta. The general advance of Sherman's line on the morning of the 22d had been contracted and strengthened. Dodge's (Sixteenth) corps, on Logan's right, had been in this way displaced, and was sent around to Blair's left, to strengthen the commanding position which had been gained the previous night. Sherman in the morning had supposed that Atlanta was abandoned; but before noon Thomas and Schofield found the enemy well intrenched in their front, covering the city, and away to the left about eleven o'clock was heard the fire of musketry and artillery. In a moment Hood's design was fathomed; but it was already too late to completely avert the danger which threatened McPherson.

Sherman was at the Howard House at this time, on Thomas's left. Here McPherson met him and Schofield, and described the condition of affairs on his flank. Sherman had proposed to extend to the right, and was, therefore, not desirous to gain on the left. But the nature of the position gained by Blair led him to send Dodge to strengthen that point. This point having been settled, McPherson started from the Howard House to return to his army, reports having already reached him of an attempt on his left. The sound of musketry, increasing in volume and accompanied by artillery, led Sherman to order an advance from the right and centre, and to hold as large a portion of Schofield's corps as possible in reserve to await developments. About half an hour after McPherson's departure, his adjutant general, Lieutenant Colonel Clark, rode up with the sad and startling intelligence that his commander was either dead or a prisoner; that, riding from Sherman's headquarters to Dodge's column, and having dismissed his orderlies and staff officers on various errands, he had passed into a narrow path leading off from the extreme left of his line, and a few minutes later a sharp volley was heard in that direction, and McPherson's horse had come out riderless, with two wounds. "The suddenness of this calamity," says General Sherman, "would have overwhelmed me with grief, but the living demanded my whole thought."[3] General Logan, commanding the Fifteenth Corps, was ordered

---

"Under repeated orders from the War Department, General Johnston had before this time sent off three regiments. Supposing them to average two hundred effective total, they would amount to six hundred each; deduct that amount from the 15,344, and it leaves but 14,744 total loss in killed, wounded, deserters, stragglers, and prisoners of his infantry and artillery. From this amount deduct 10,000 killed and wounded, and we have 4744 lost from all other causes in these arms. But it appears that the cavalry had increased 2276. Deduct this from the 4744, and his losses in all arms, except in killed and wounded, amount to but 2468.

"We have, then, a loss by desertion, and straggling, and prisoners of only some 2500 from the 'digging and retreating' policy. The demoralization of the army could not have been as great as General Hood supposes, or its losses from these causes would have been greater. The 'working by night and traveling by day' would seem, too, not to be a very bad policy where the army has confidence in its leader.

"General Hood asserts that a retreating army must lose more by straggling and desertion, if it does not fight, than it would in killed and wounded if it does. He attempts to show this by what he regards well-established principles, and not by figures. Napier differs from General Hood on this point. In discussing the losses of Massena from the Torres Vedras, he says: 'It is unquestionable that a retreating army should fight as little as possible.'

"General Hood also insists that the army at Atlanta was greatly demoralized by the loss of men and officers, and by constant falling back. I do not recollect any general officer, except General Polk, who was killed while Johnston was in command; there may have been others, but certainly not many. What were his losses in general officers from Atlanta to Nashville? His march from Jonesborough to the Tennessee line was a retreat, and from Nashville to Tupelo; yet he lost by desertion but 300, and left the army in fine spirits. The demoralization of Johnston's army can not be accounted for on this theory. But was it demoralized? It fought well when he first took command. His disasters around Atlanta are not attributed by him to a want of spirit in the men, but to incompetency in the officers. He could not have his orders executed. I incline to the opinion that he is mistaken as much as to his facts as he is in his theory.

"General Hood insinuates that General Johnston attempts to dodge an acknowledgment of his full losses by 'excluding the idea of prisoners,' and charges that his official returns show more than 7000 under the head of 'absent without leave.' This is a very grave charge against an officer and a gentleman. General Hood should know that the usual, if not only mode of stating the loss of prisoners is in a marginal note opposite the column of 'absent without leave.' It can never be other than an approximate estimate; for no general can know how many of his 'absent without leave,' after a battle, have gone voluntarily to the enemy, and how many have been captured. General Hood should know also that the absent and prisoners of an army are continued on its rolls from time to time, as the 'Field Returns' are made out, without reference to a change of commanders, and that it is very possible, therefore, that a part, or even the whole, of the 7000 prisoners may have been lost when the army was under the command of General Bragg. The rout at Missionary Ridge had occurred before General Johnston took command. This is a matter, however, which especially concerns General Hood. The field return of the 10th of July shows a loss of not quite 7000 prisoners (6994). Opposite General Hood's corps is this note: '238 officers and 4597 men, prisoners of war, are reported among the "absent without leave."' This shows that, out of not quite 7000 prisoners of war, nearly 5000 (4835) were captured from his corps. He knows whether they were lost by him under Johnston, or by some one else under Bragg. For the accuracy of the statement, he, and not General Johnston, is responsible. The returns of the army is only a consolidation of the returns of the corps commanders.

"But if there were 7000 prisoners taken during the retreat from Dalton, how does he account for the fact shown by the official returns that General Johnston had, at Atlanta, on the 10th of July, leaving out his killed and wounded, within 2500 men of the number put under his command previously? How can this excess of loss in prisoners over his total loss (except in killed and wounded) be explained? Upon no other hypothesis than that his army increased by recruiting more rapidly than it decreased by straggling and loss of prisoners. The morale of the army, then, could not have been very bad—at least not as bad as it is supposed by General Hood to have been. Nor could the people of the territory which General Johnston was 'abandoning' have lost all confidence in him. It must have been from them that his recruits were gathered.

"It is alleged that at Dalton 'the enemy was but little superior in numbers, none in organization and discipline, and inferior in spirit and confidence.' The army which is described as 'inferior in spirit and confidence' to Johnston's was the one which had lately routed it at Missionary Ridge, under Bragg. An army flushed with victory is not usually wanting 'in spirit and confidence.' Did the presence of Johnston cause them to doubt their future success? What infused 'spirit and confidence' in the Army of Tennessee? Was it the consciousness that it, at last, had a commander who, careless of his own blood, was careful of that of his men, who knew when to take them under fire and how to bring them out, and whose thorough soldiership would save them from ever being uselessly slaughtered by being led to battle except when some good purpose was to be accomplished or some brilliant victory achieved? If the 'discipline and organization' of the army were as perfect as described, who produced it? For four months it had been under the control of Johnston. What evidence has General Hood to sustain his assertion that at Dalton the enemy was but little superior to us in numbers? He relies upon Sherman's statement that he was as strong at Atlanta as when the campaign opened. His army at Missionary Ridge was estimated at 80,000. He was afterward re-enforced by the army from Knoxville and the troops from North Alabama, besides others. Our scouts reported that he had been re-enforced with at least 30,000 men. General Sherman told General Govan, or said in his presence, that he had commenced the campaign with 110,000. I have never heard it estimated at less than 90,000 infantry and artillery. In July General Wheeler estimated it at between 65 and 70,000. The Northern papers, about that time, admitted his losses to be 45,000. His cavalry was estimated by General Wheeler at not less than 15,000. Johnston, in the mean time, under orders of the War Department, sent off two brigades and received one.

"General Hood charges that General Johnston did not intend to hold Atlanta. As evidence of this, he says that no officer or soldier believed it, and that General Johnston had thrown up no intrenchments in front of his lines opposite Peach-tree Creek. If General Johnston intended, as he says he did, to strike the head of Sherman's columns as soon as they appeared across Peach-tree Creek, and before they were intrenched, or had time even to deploy into line of battle, what use had he for field-works? They would have been in his way if erected, and his men would have been uselessly fatigued in constructing them. Not having been present, I can not speak of the opinion of the army. But, admitting the fact, I submit that the opinion of the army is not always evidence of the intentions of the general. Is it not possible, too, that General Hood may have mistaken his own opinion for that of the army? The evidence that General Johnston did intend to hold the place is given in his report. In addition, it may be added that he held New Hope for a fortnight, and only left it because the enemy left their intrenchments confronting it, moving to the railroad and to the rear. He then held a position in front of Kenesaw for a month, and left that, at last, because, by extending his intrenchments, Sherman had got nearer to Atlanta by several miles than we were. In all the fighting we had been successful, and that in positions frequently prepared for defense in a few hours. Is it probable, then, that General Johnston would not have attempted to hold a place fortified already to his hand under the direction of the Engineer Bureau, and previously inspected by Major General Gilmer, the chief engineer of our army? Why had he been strengthening it from the 5th of July, with all the labor he could command, if he did not intend to defend it, in the event of his failing to crush the enemy at Peach-tree Creek? Why was he strengthening it at the very moment of his removal? If the position was as weak as described by General Hood, why did Sherman not attempt to carry it by assault?"

---

[1] Thomas's Report.

[2] General Hood attributes the failure of the attack to delay, and to Hardee's failure "to push the attack as ordered."

[3] Two days after this event, it was reported as follows by General Sherman to Adjutant General Thomas:

JAMES B. McPHERSON.

to take command of the Army of the Tennessee. Sherman instructed Logan that he did not wish to gain ground on the left, but that the Augusta Railroad must be held at all hazards.

Hardee had swung around and struck the left flank of Sherman's army, his movement being covered by dense woods. Enveloping Blair's division, the attack was extended to the rear until it reached Dodge's corps in motion. There was between Blair and Dodge an interval of half a mile. The last order ever given by McPherson was that Colonel Wangelin's brigade, of Logan's corps, should cross the railroad and occupy this gap. The order had been obeyed, and its execution checked the enemy's advance. Wheeler's cavalry at the same time, having taken a wider circuit, broke in upon Decatur, capturing a portion of the trains there stationed, and driving the rest toward the Chattahoochee. Hardee had been checked, but Stewart's corps, on his left, attacked in front, sweeping across a portion of the hill which Blair was fortifying, capturing the intrenching party with its tools, and bearing down upon G. A. Smith's division, which was driven back upon that of Leggett, who still obstinately clung to the crest. Smith's line was now formed with its right touching Leggett, and the left refused, facing southeast. This position was firmly held for four hours, unmoved by the assaults of the enemy. On the extreme left Hardee had captured six guns, and Smith, in refusing his left, had abandoned two more. Hood still persisted in the attempt to turn Sherman's left flank. There was a lull at four P.M., during which the enemy felt his way to the railroad, and, suddenly breaking forth upon a regiment, which, with a section of artillery, had been advanced as a sort of picket, captured two more guns.

"It is my painful duty to report that Brigadier General James B. McPherson, United States Army, Major General of Volunteers, and commander of the Army of the Tennessee in the field, was killed by a shot from ambuscade about noon yesterday. At the time of this fatal shot he was on horseback, placing his troops in position near the city of Atlanta, and was passing by a cross-road from a moving column toward the flank of troops that had already been established on the line. He had quitted me but a few minutes before, and was on his way to see in person to the execution of my orders. About the time of this sad event the enemy had sallied from his intrenchments of Atlanta, and by a circuit had got to the left and rear of this very line, and had began an attack which resulted in serious battle; so that General McPherson fell in battle, booted and spurred, as the gallant knight and gentleman should wish. Not his the loss, but the country's; and this army will mourn his death and cherish his memory as that of one who, though comparatively young, had risen by his merit and ability to the command of one of the best armies which the nation had called into existence to vindicate its honor and integrity.

"History tells of but few who so blended the grace and gentleness of the friend with the dignity, courage, faith, and manliness of the soldier. His public enemies, even the men who directed the fatal shot, ne'er spoke or wrote of him without expressions of marked respect; those whom he commanded loved him even to idolatry; and I, his associate and commander, fail in words adequate to express my opinion of his great worth. I feel assured that every patriot in America, on hearing this sad news, will feel a sense of personal loss, and the country generally will realize that we have lost not only an able military leader, but a man who, had he survived, was qualified to heal the national strife which has been raised by designing and ambitious men. His body has been sent North in charge of Major Willard, Captains Steele and Giles, his personal staff."

7 Q

Advancing and driving back Lightburn's brigade, which held that portion of the line, he captured two full batteries, one of them 20-pounder Parrotts. By this advance of the enemy, Wood's and Harrow's divisions of Logan's corps were separated. It was important that the position should be recovered. Batteries were moved from Schofield's line to a commanding position enfilading the enemy, and while these poured in their continuous fire, Logan and a portion of Schofield's force drove the enemy from the field, recapturing the two batteries. Thus terminated the battle of the 22d. Sherman reports his loss in killed, wounded, and prisoners as 3722, and estimates that of the enemy as 8000. In this battle the Confederate general W. H. T. Walker was killed.

This day ended Sherman's operations east of Atlanta. Garrard's cavalry, whose absence had materially assisted Hood on the 22d, had been employed in the destruction of the Augusta Railroad 42 miles east of Atlanta. This movement, together with Rousseau's operations on the West Point Road, left the enemy but a single line of uninterrupted communication, that by the Macon Railroad. In order to reach this remaining road Sherman determined to transfer his army to the west of Atlanta. Rousseau, upon his return to Marietta with 2000 cavalry, was ordered to relieve Stoneman on the Chattahoochee, and to the latter was given the command of his own and Garrard's division, amounting to 5000 men. General E. M. McCook, with his own and Rousseau's cavalry, had a force 4000 strong. With these commands Stoneman and McCook were ordered to make a concerted movement against the Macon Road, while Sherman was extending his army on the right toward East Point. In respect of numbers, the cavalry designated for this expedition was sufficient for the accomplishment of its object against any opposition which it was possible for the enemy to make. Stoneman was to move by the left around Atlanta to McDonough, and McCook by the right to Fayetteville, and on the night of the 28th the two bodies were to effect a junction on the Macon Road near Lovejoy's, far south of Atlanta, and break it effectually. At the very moment of starting Stoneman begged permission, after executing the orders already given him, to proceed with his own proper command to Macon and Andersonville, and release the Union prisoners there confined. "There was something most captivating in the idea," reports Sherman, "and the execution was within the bounds of probability of success." He therefore consented.

The expedition proved a failure. There seems to have been no attempt on Stoneman's part to effect a junction at Lovejoy's with Garrard and McCook. Garrard soon returned. McCook went down the west bank of the Chattahoochee to a point near Rivertown, where he crossed, and, moving on Palmetto Station, tore up a section of the West Point Road. Thence he advanced to Fayetteville, where he destroyed about 500 wagons belonging to the enemy. Pushing on to the railroad at Lovejoy's, he burned the dépôt and destroyed a portion of the road. In the mean time the enemy was ac-

SCENE OF McPHERSON'S DEATH.

O. O. HOWARD.

cumulating forces around him, and, receiving no tidings from Stoneman, he moved south and west to Newman, on the West Point Road, where he encountered a body of infantry on the way from Mississippi to Hood's army. This body, delayed by the break at Palmetto, together with the cavalry which had been pursuing McCook, completely surrounded the latter and compelled him to fight. McCook cut his way out with great difficulty, losing 500 men. Stoneman, disregarding all the instructions which he had received, seems never to have come near Lovejoy's. Keeping east of the Ocmulgee to Clinton, he sent detachments eastward, which succeeded in inflicting great damage upon the railroad, burning the bridges over Walnut Creek and the Oconee. With his main force he appeared before Macon. He made no attempt upon the town, however, nor did he proceed toward Andersonville, but began to retrace his steps, closely followed by various detachments of Confederate cavalry under General Iverson. He was soon hemmed in by the enemy; and giving his consent to two thirds of his command to escape, with the remainder and a section of light guns he occupied the enemy. A brigade under Colonel Adams returned to Sherman almost intact. Another, commanded by Colonel Capron, was surprised on its way back, and, being scattered, a large number were killed and captured. Stoneman surrendered himself, and the small portion of his command which remained with him. Very much was sacrificed in this expedition, and very little was gained, as the breaks made in the Macon Road were of such a character as to be easily repaired.

On the 27th of July, one week after the battle of Peach-tree Creek, the Army of the Tennessee was moved from its position on the left, around Schofield and Thom-

as, to the west side of Proctor's Creek, where it prolonged the Federal line southward on the hills northwest of Atlanta—a position exactly opposite to that occupied by this army in the battle of the 22d. By orders of the Pres-

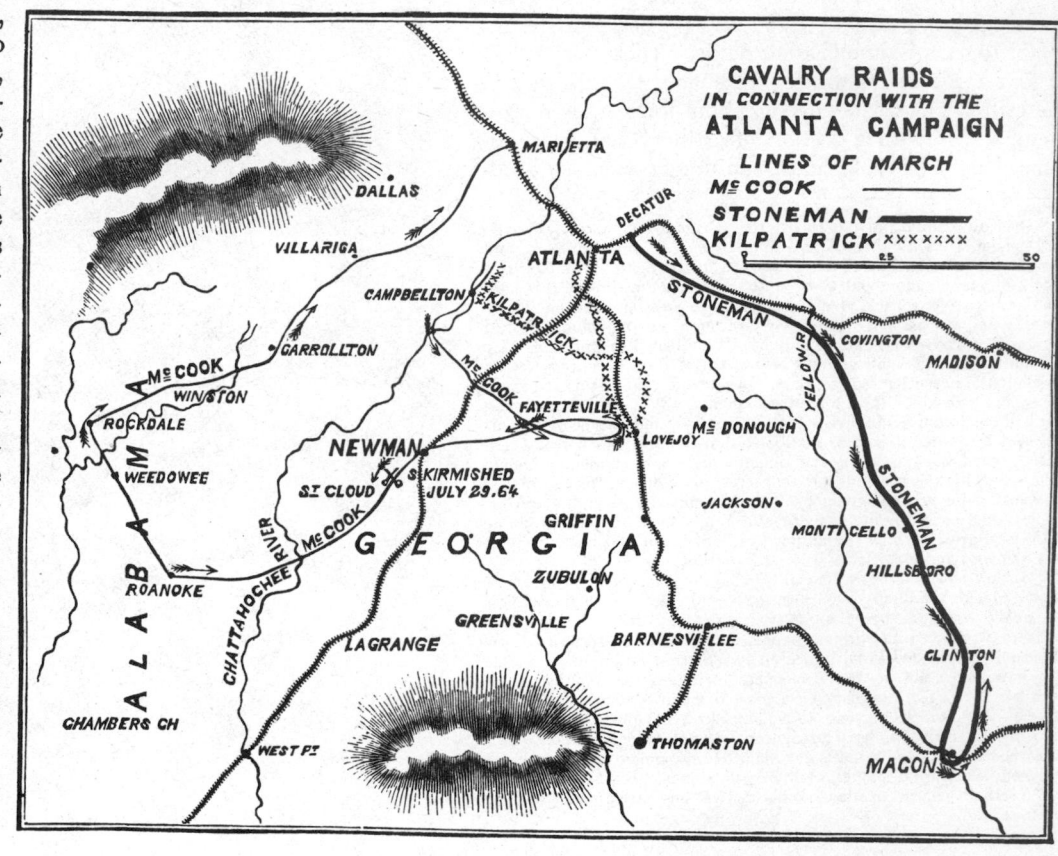

CAVALRY RAIDS IN CONNECTION WITH THE ATLANTA CAMPAIGN
LINES OF MARCH
MᶜCOOK ———
STONEMAN ━━━
KILPATRICK ×××××

SHERMAN IN COUNCIL DECIDES TO RAISE THE SIEGE OF ATLANTA

ident, given at Sherman's suggestion, General O. O. Howard had been, on the 27th, assigned to the command of the Army of the Tennessee, General Stanley succeeding to the command of the Fourth Corps. This appointment led to General Hooker's departure from Sherman's army. Howard was a junior officer as compared with Hooker, and the latter resented his promotion on the ground that, in the natural course, he should himself have been preferred. Hooker therefore threw up his command of the Twentieth Corps, and was succeeded by General H. W. Slocum. General Sherman had very properly considered that a good department commander must be selected, and for this purpose he preferred Howard to either Logan or Hooker, whom also he wished to retain in their present positions on account of their eminent efficiency as corps commanders.[1]

[1] The following letter, addressed by Sherman to Halleck, August 16, 1864, fully explains this affair:

"It occurs to me that, preliminary to a future report of the history of this campaign, I should record certain facts of great personal interest to officers of this command.

"General McPherson was killed by the musketry fire at the beginning of the battle of July 22. He had in person selected the ground for his troops, constituting the left wing of the army, I being in person with the centre, General Schofield. The moment the information reached me, I sent one of my staff to announce the fact to General John A. Logan, the senior officer present with the Army of the Tennessee, with general instructions to maintain the ground chosen by Gen-

Dodge, with the Sixteenth Corps, took a position just west of Proctor's Creek on the evening of the 27th. The next morning, Blair, with the Sev-

eral McPherson if possible, but, if pressed too hard, to refuse his left flank, but, at all events, to hold the railroad and main Decatur Road; that I did not propose to move or gain ground by that flank, but rather by the right, and that I wanted the Army of the Tennessee to fight it out unaided. General Logan admirably conceived my orders and executed them; and, if he gave ground on the left of the Seventeenth Corps, it was properly done by my orders; but he held a certain hill by the right division of the Seventeenth Corps, the only ground on that line the possession of which by an enemy would have damaged us by giving a reverse fire on the remainder of the troops. General Logan fought that battle out as required, unaided save by a small brigade sent by my orders from General Schofield to the Decatur Road, well to the rear, where it was reported the enemy's cavalry had got into the town of Decatur, and was operating directly on the rear of Logan; but that brigade was not disturbed, and was replaced that night by a part of the Fifteenth Corps next to General Schofield, and General Schofield's brigade brought back so as to be kept together on its own line.

"General Logan managed the Army of the Tennessee well during his command, and it may be that an unfair inference might be drawn to his prejudice because he did not succeed to the permanent command. I am forced to choose a commander, not only for the army in the field, but of the Department of the Tennessee, covering a vast extent of country, with troops much dispersed. It was a delicate and difficult task, and I gave preference to Major General O. O. Howard, then in command of the Fourth Army Corps in the Department of the Cumberland. Instead of giving my reasons, I prefer that the wisdom of the choice be left to the test of time. The President kindly ratified my choice, and I am willing to assume the responsibility. I meant no disrespect to any officer; and hereby declare that General Logan submitted with the grace and dignity of a soldier, gentleman, and patriot, resumed the command of his corps proper (Fifteenth), and enjoys

EZRA'S CHURCH.

enteenth Corps, extended the line south and west to Ezra Church, on the Bell's Ferry or Lickskillet Road; and Logan came in on Blair's right, his own right being refused along a well-wooded ridge south of the road. By 10 A.M. on the 28th Howard's army was in position, and was rapidly fortifying itself with breastworks of rails and logs. From that time until noon there was heavy artillery firing from the Confederate position. Evidently Hood was about to repeat the tactics of the 22d. Lieutenant General S. D. Lee, who on the 25th had relieved General Cheatham of the command of Hood's former corps, was ordered to advance and attack Howard's right, and cover the Lickskillet Road. The attack about noon fell upon the corps of General Logan, who fought alone the battle which ensued. Several assaults were made by Cheatham until 4 P.M., but were each repulsed with great loss to the enemy. Logan's loss was less than 700. But when Cheatham abandoned the field he left 642 killed, which were counted and buried, besides many others buried but not counted. Sherman estimates the Confederate loss in this battle of the 28th as "not less than 5000." He had anticipated this attack, and had made dispositions which, but for his ignorance of the topography on his right rear, must have converted Cheatham's repulse into a disastrous rout. Up to this point Hood had been acting upon the plans which General Johnston had formed, but it is very doubtful whether the latter general would have executed them in the same manner. Certainly Johnston would not have attacked Howard's army on the 28th, knowing

the love and respect of his army and of his commanders. It so happened that on the 28th of July I had again thrown the same army to the extreme right, the exposed flank, where the enemy repeated the same manœuvre, striking in mass; the extreme corps deployed in line, and refused as a flank the Fifteenth, Major General Logan, and he commanded in person, General Howard and myself being near; and that corps, as heretofore reported, repulsed the rebel army completely, and next day advanced and occupied the ground fought over and the road the enemy sought to cover. General Howard, who had that very day assumed his new command, unequivocally gave General Logan all the credit possible; and I also beg to add my unqualified admiration of the bravery and skill, and, more yet, good sense that influenced him to bear a natural disappointment, and do his whole duty like a man. If I could bestow upon him substantial reward, it would afford me unalloyed satisfaction; but I do believe, in the consciousness of acts done from noble impulses, and gracefully admitted by his superiors in authority, he will be contented. He already holds the highest commission known in the army, and it is hard to say how we can better manifest our applause.

"At the time of General Howard's selection, Major General Hooker commanded the Twentieth Army Corps in the Army of the Cumberland, made up for his special accommodation out of the old Eleventh and Twelfth Corps, whereby Major General Slocum was deprived of his corps command. Both the law and practice are and have been to fill the higher army commands by selection. Ranks or dates of commission have not controlled, nor am I aware that any reflection can be inferred, unless the junior be placed immediately over the senior; but in this case General Hooker's command was in no manner disturbed. General Howard was not put over him, but in charge of a distinct and separate army. No indignity was offered or intended; and I must say that General Hooker was not justified in retiring. At all events, had he spoken or written to me, I would have made every explanation and concession he could have expected, but could not have changed my course, because then, as now, I believed it right, and for the good of our country and cause.

"As a matter of justice, General Slocum, having been displaced by the consolidation, was deemed by General Thomas as entitled to the vacancy created by General Hooker's voluntary withdrawal, and has received it."

DEADBROOK AFTER THE BATTLE OF EZRA'S CHURCH.

SHERMAN'S ARMY DESTROYING THE MACON RAILROAD BETWEEN ROUGH AND READY AND JONESBOROUGH.

ATLANTA, GEORGIA.

that the latter was intrenched. Half a dozen of such battles would have left Hood without an army. At any rate, no farther attempt was made by General Hood to oppose Sherman's extension by flank southward. As the Federal army developed toward East Point, the enemy, without attacking, extended his intrenched line in the same direction.

By the 1st of August the Fifteenth and Seventeenth Corps had advanced beyond the Lickskillet Road. On that day Schofield's army was transferred to Howard's right, Palmer's corps, of the Army of the Cumberland, following. Palmer took a position below Utoy Creek, and Schofield extended the line to near East Point. Here a question of rank arose between Schofield and Palmer, the former being instructed by General Sherman to give orders to the latter. This difficulty finally (on the 6th of August) led to Palmer's resignation, General Jeff. C. Davis succeeding him in command of the Fourteenth Corps.

By this extension of his army southward, Sherman compelled Hood to lengthen the line of defense; and while Schofield attempted to turn the Confederate left, and reach the Macon Road, Thomas and Howard pressed vigorously on Hood's right and centre. But, though the enemy's line was fifteen miles long, extending from Decatur around to below East Point, it could easily be held by militia, and was so well masked by the shape of the ground that it was impossible for Sherman to discover its weak points. It was beginning to be evident that, in order to reach the Macon Road, the whole of Sherman's army would have to be transferred to the east and south of Atlanta. An attempt was first made to destroy the city by means of four 4½-inch rifled guns, which on the 10th arrived from Chattanooga. These did good execution, but Hood was not willing to abandon the city so long as he could keep the forts, and the battering down of every building in Atlanta would not have altered his determination.

In the mean time Hood had dispatched Wheeler, with a cavalry force 4500 strong, against the railroad in Sherman's rear. This, without frightening the Federal commander, who had no immediate cause for concern as to supplies, greatly enhanced his opportunity for offensive operations. It then seemed possible that, without moving the entire army, a raid might be made by Kilpatrick which should break up the Macon Road. Kilpatrick started out and broke the road to West Point, and then advanced to Jonesborough, on the Macon Road, where he encountered and defeated a portion of the Confederate cavalry under Ross, and held the railroad for five hours, doing it sufficient damage to give the enemy about ten days' work in repairing it. A brigade of Confederate infantry, with Jackson's cavalry, put a stop to his work here. Moving east, he again encountered the enemy at Lovejoy's, and, after defeating him and capturing four guns and a large number of prisoners, returned to Sherman's army by way of Decatur.

Not satisfied with what had been accomplished in this raid, Sherman, on the night of August 25th, raised the siege of Atlanta. General A. S. Williams,[1] with the Twentieth Corps, was ordered back to hold the intrenched position at the Chattahoochee bridge, and the remainder of the army, with 15 days' rations, was set in motion toward a position on the Macon Road, at or near Jonesborough. On the first night of the movement, Stanley, with the Fourth Corps, drew out from the extreme left to a position west of Proctor's Creek, and Williams moved back, as ordered, to the Chattahoochee, both movements being effected without loss. The next night the Army of the Tennessee moved south, well toward Sandtown, and the Army of the Cumberland to a position south of Utoy Creek, Schofield remaining in position. Only one casualty occurred in this second stage of the army's progress. A third movement, on the 27th, brought Howard's command to the West Point Road, above Fairburn, Thomas's army to Red Oak, Schofield at the same time closing in on the left. The 28th was spent in the destruction of the West Point Road, a break being made of over 12 miles.

The railroad from Atlanta to Macon follows the ridge dividing the Flint from the Ocmulgee River, and between East Point and Jonesborough makes a wide bend to the east. It was against this ridge that the Federal army moved on the 29th—Howard toward Jonesborough on the right; Thomas, in the centre, toward Couch's, on the Fayetteville Road, and Schofield on the left. As soon as Hood learned of this movement of Sherman, which, if successful, would compel the evacuation of Atlanta, he sent (on the 30th) Lee's and Hardee's corps to Jonesborough. To Hardee was given the command, Hood remaining with Stewart's corps in Atlanta, intending, in case of Hardee's success, to attack in flank. Hood does not seem to have been aware of the extent of the operation which Sherman was conducting, and supposed that Hardee, at Jonesborough, would encounter a force inferior to his own.

The battle of Jonesborough was fought on the 31st of August. Sherman was making dispositions to advance Schofield's and Davis's corps to Rough and Ready, between Atlanta and Jonesborough, when Hardee, coming out of the latter place, attacked Howard in his intrenched position. Hardee was well aware of the importance of this battle, and fought his troops with desperate obstinacy for two hours, when he withdrew from the field thoroughly beaten, having lost 1400 killed and wounded.[2]

While the battle had been in progress, Stanley's and Schofield's, and a portion of Davis's corps, had struck the railroad at several points, and were engaged in its destruction. A splendid opportunity was now offered for the destruction of Hardee's command. Sherman saw this, and ordered his three corps to turn against Jonesborough. Howard was to occupy Hardee while Thomas and Schofield moved down upon him from the north, destroying the railroad on their march. What was done must be done on the 1st of September. By noon of that day Davis's corps reached Howard's left, and faced southward across the railroad. Blair was then with the Seventeenth

---

[1] Williams commanded the Twentieth Corps until Slocum should arrive from Vicksburg.
[2] Sherman estimates Hardee's loss as 2500. We have followed General Hood's report.

CONFEDERATE PRISONERS BEING CONDUCTED FROM JONESBOROUGH TO ATLANTA.

EXODUS OF CONFEDERATES FROM ATLANTA.

Corps, and Kilpatrick's cavalry thrown across the road south of Jonesborough. About 4 P.M. Davis assaulted the enemy's lines across the open, sweeping all before him, and capturing the greater part of Govan's brigade, including its commander. Repeated orders were sent hurrying up Schofield and Stanley, but, owing to the difficult nature of the country, these two corps did not arrive until night rendered farther operations impossible; and during the night the enemy retreated southward.

During the same night, at 2 A.M. on the morning of September 2, the sound of heavy explosions was heard from the direction of Atlanta, 20 miles distant, indicating the evacuation of that place by General Hood. Without regarding these tokens, Sherman pressed on the next morning in pursuit of Hardee, but found it impossible to intercept his retreat. On the 2d Slocum entered Atlanta, followed by the whole army on the 7th. In this last movement of his army General Sherman had captured 3000 prisoners and 16 guns. His loss had been 1500 men.

In the mean time Wheeler's raid on Sherman's communications had been productive of little damage. He had broken the railroad near Calhoun, but had been checked by Colonel Laibold at Dalton until Steedman could arrive from Chattanooga, when he was headed off into East Tennessee. Finally, Rousseau, Steedman, and R. S. Granger, with their combined forces, drove him out of Tennessee.

"Atlanta is ours," telegraphed Sherman to Washington on the 3d of September, "and fairly won." The loss of this position by the Confederates was an irreparable misfortune. The wall which had hitherto protected the Cotton States was now obliterated. The victory electrified the nation; it was felt to be the consummation of the triumphs won at Vicksburg and Chattanooga, and its political effect in the loyal states can not be too highly estimated. President Lincoln wrote a letter of thanks to Sherman and his army. "The marches, battles, sieges, and other military operations that have signalized the campaign must render it famous in the annals of war, and have entitled those who have participated therein to the applause and thanks of the nation." Lieutenant General Grant, before Petersburg, on the 4th, ordered a salute to be fired in honor of the victory "with shotted guns from every battery bearing upon the enemy." On the 12th, General Sherman received from the President a commission making him a major general in the regular army.[1]

Sherman's outlook from Atlanta was magnificent. Though he had lost over 30,000 men in the numerous battles of the campaign, his army was as large as when he set out four months before. The Confederate loss must have been nearly equal to Sherman's.[2] G. A. Smith's militia had been sent to Griffin, and Hood now confronted Sherman with an army of 40,000 men of all arms. The next objective, if Hood attempted to cover Georgia, was Macon—103 miles east of Atlanta. But Sherman determined to give his army a brief period of rest before another advance. The Army of the Cumberland went into camp about Atlanta, the Army of the Tennessee about East Point, and the Army of the Ohio at Decatur.[3] At the latter point was also stationed Garrard's cavalry division, while Kilpatrick's, at Sandtown, guarded the western flank. To strengthen the railroad in the rear, two divisions—Newton's, of the Fourth, and Morgan's, of the Fourteenth Corps—were dispatched to Chattanooga, and Corse's division, of the Fifteenth Corps, to Rome. A new and more compact system of fortifications was also constructed about Atlanta, which town Sherman now proposed to make exclusively a military post.

To carry out this design, every thing in Atlanta, except churches and dwelling-houses, was burned. On the 4th of September Sherman issued an order commanding the inhabitants of the town to leave at once. "I am not willing," said Sherman, "to have Atlanta encumbered by the families of our enemies; I want it a pure Gibraltar, and will have it so by the first of October."[4] This order was a surprise to the citizens, and doubtless occasioned them much hardship. But Sherman had broken through the protecting walls of the Confederacy, and now resolved that the people of the Cotton States should feel the heavy hand of war. He would not acknowledge the impunity of treason. The city authorities and General Hood protested against the order as unnecessary and cruel. But Sherman's reply crushed all the meaning out of their words, brought them face to face with the war demon whom they themselves had invoked, and laughed to scorn their weak and impudent claims.[5] A cessation of hostilities was agreed upon between Sherman and Hood, to continue for ten days following the 12th of September. During this time 446 families were removed south from Atlanta, comprising 1644 persons, of whom 860 were children and 79 servants. During the same period arrangements were made between Hood and Sherman for the mutual exchange of 2000 prisoners.

[1] Lieutenant General Grant says in his official report:

"General Sherman's movement from Chattanooga to Atlanta was prompt, skillful, and brilliant. The history of his flank movements and battles during that memorable campaign will ever be read with an interest unsurpassed by any thing in history."

[2] Hood reports his loss in battle, since he assumed the command on the 17th of July, as 5247. It was probably, however, much higher than that. Indeed, in the four severe battles of July 20th, 22d, and 28th, and September 1st, the casualties could not have been less than 10,000. We can place no confidence in Hood's official estimates.

[3] Several changes now took place in the army, in consequence of the expiration of the terms of service of many of the regiments. "The Army of the Tennessee was consolidated into two corps, the Fifteenth and Seventeenth, respectively commanded by Major General P. J. Osterhaus and Brigadier General Thomas E. G. Ransom; the former comprising the four divisions of Brigadier Generals Charles R. Woods, William B. Hazen, John E. Smith, and John M. Corse; the latter those of Major General Joseph A. Mower, and Brigadier Generals Miles D. Leggett and Giles A. Smith, with the First Alabama Cavalry and the First Missouri Engineer regiment, having in charge a large pontoon-bridge train. This organization was effected by transferring all the troops of the Seventeenth Corps remaining on the Mississippi to the Sixteenth Corps, breaking up the detachment of the latter corps in the field, and transferring Ransom's division, now commanded by Brigadier General Giles A. Smith, and Corse's division to the Seventeenth Corps. Major Generals Logan and Blair were temporarily absent, engaged in the important political canvass then in progress. Major General Schofield returned to the headquarters of the Department of the Ohio, at Knoxville, to give his personal attention to affairs in that quarter, leaving Brigadier General Jacob D. Cox in command of the Twenty-third Corps. The cavalry was reorganized so as to consist of two divisions, under Brigadier Generals Garrard and Judson Kilpatrick."—*Bowman's Sherman and his Campaigns.*

[4] *Dispatch to General Halleck, September* 9, 1864.

[5] We quote the correspondence which followed, as given in Bowman's "*Sherman and his Campaigns:*"

"On the 11th of September, the town authorities addressed the following petition to General Sherman, praying the revocation of his orders:

"'SIR,—The undersigned, mayor and two members of Council for the city of Atlanta, for the time being the only legal organ of the people of the said city to express their wants and wishes, ask leave most earnestly, but respectfully, to petition you to reconsider the order requiring them to leave Atlanta.

"'At first view, it struck us that the measure would involve extraordinary hardship and loss; but since we have seen the practical execution of it, so far as it has progressed, and the individual condition of many of the people, and heard their statements as to the inconveniences, loss, and suffering attending it, we are satisfied that it will involve, in the aggregate, consequences appalling and heart-rending.

"'Many poor women are in an advanced state of pregnancy; others now having young children, and whose husbands are either in the army, prisoners, or dead. Some say, "I have such a one sick at home; who will wait on them when I am gone?" Others say, "What are we to do? we have no houses to go to, and no means to buy, build, or to rent any—no parents, friends, or relatives to go to." Another says, "I will try and take this or that article of property, but such and such things I must leave behind, though I need them much." We reply to them, "General Sherman will carry your property to Rough and Ready, and General Hood will take it from there on." And they will reply to that, "But I want to leave the railway at such a point, and can not get conveyance from there on."

"'We only refer to a few facts to try to illustrate in part how this measure will operate in practice. As you advanced, the people north of us fell back, and before your arrival here a large portion of the people had retired South, so that the country south of this is already crowded, and without houses to accommodate the people, and we are informed that many are now starving in churches and other out-buildings. This being so, how is it possible for the people still here (mostly women and children) to find any shelter? And how can they live through the winter in the woods—no shelter nor subsistence—in the midst of strangers who know them not, and without the power to assist them, if they were willing to do so?

"'This is but a feeble picture of the consequences of this measure. You know the woe, the horror, and the suffering can not be described by words. Imagination can only conceive of it, and we ask you to take these things into consideration.

"'We know your mind and time are constantly occupied with the duties of your command, which almost deters us from asking your attention to this matter, but thought it might be that you had not considered the subject in all its awful consequences, and that, on more reflection, you, we hoped, would not make this people an exception to all mankind, for we know of no such instance ever having occurred—surely none such in the United States; and what has this helpless people done that they should be driven from their homes, to wander as strangers, outcasts, and exiles, and to subsist on charity?

"'We do not know, as yet, the number of people still here. Of those who are here, we are satisfied a respectable number, if allowed to remain at home, could subsist for several months without assistance, and a respectable number for a much longer time, and who might not need assistance at any time.

"'In conclusion, we must earnestly and solemnly petition you to reconsider this order, or modify it, and suffer this unfortunate people to remain at home and enjoy what little means they have. Respectfully submitted,

JAMES M. CALHOUN, *Mayor.*
E. E. RAWSON, *Councilman.*
L. C. WELLS, *Councilman.*'

"To this General Sherman replied, in full and clear terms, on the following day:

"'GENTLEMEN,—I have your letter of the 11th, in the nature of a petition to revoke my orders removing all the inhabitants from Atlanta. I have read it carefully, and give full credit to your statements of the distress that will be occasioned by it, and yet shall not revoke my order, simply because my orders are not designed to meet the humanities of the case, but to prepare for the future struggles in which millions, yea, hundreds of millions of good people outside of Atlanta have a deep interest. We must have peace, not only at Atlanta, but in all America. To secure this, we must stop the war that now desolates our once happy and favored country. To stop the war, we must defeat the rebel armies that are arrayed against the laws and Constitution, which all must respect and obey. To defeat these armies, we must prepare the way to reach them in their recesses, provided with the arms and instruments which enable us to accomplish our purpose.

"'Now I know the vindictive nature of our enemy, and that we may have many years of military operations from this quarter, and therefore deem it wise and prudent to prepare in time. The use of Atlanta for warlike purposes is inconsistent with its character as a home for families. There will be no manufactures, commerce, or agriculture here for the maintenance of families, and sooner or later want will compel the inhabitants to go. Why not go *now*, when all the arrangements are completed for the transfer, instead of waiting until the plunging shot of contending armies will renew the scenes of the past month? Of course I do not apprehend any such thing at this moment, but you do not suppose this army will be here till the war is over. I can not discuss this subject with you fairly, because I can not impart to you what I propose to do, but I assert that my military plans make it necessary for the inhabitants to go away, and I can only renew my offer of services to make their exodus in any direction as easy and comfortable as possible. You can not qualify war in harsher terms than I will.

"'War is cruelty, and you can not refine it; and those who brought war on our country deserve all the curses and maledictions a people can pour out. I know I had no hand in making this war, and I know I will make more sacrifices to-day than any of you to secure peace. But you can not have peace and a division of our country. If the United States submit to a division now, it will not stop, but will go on till we reap the fate of Mexico, which is eternal war. The United States does and must assert its authority wherever it has power; if it relaxes one bit to pressure, it is gone, and I know that such is not the national feeling. This feeling assumes various shapes, but always comes back to that of *Union*. Once admit the Union, once more acknowledge the authority of the national government, and, instead of devoting your houses, and streets, and roads to the dread uses of war, I and this army become at once your protectors and supporters, shielding you from danger, let it come from what quarter it may. I know that a few individuals can not resist a torrent of error and passion such as has swept the South into rebellion; but you can point out, so that we may know those who desire a government and those who insist on war and its desolation.

"'You might as well appeal against the thunder-storm as against these terrible hardships of war. They are inevitable; and the only way the people of Atlanta can hope once more to live in peace and quiet at home is to stop this war, which can alone be done by admitting that it began in error and is perpetuated in pride. We don't want your negroes, or your horses, or your land, or any thing you have; but we do want, and will have, a just obedience to the laws of the United States. That we will have; and if it involves the destruction of your improvements, we can not help it.

"'You have heretofore read public sentiment in your newspapers, that live by falsehood and excitement, and the quicker you seek for truth in other quarters the better for you. I repeat, then, that by the original compact of government, the United States had certain rights in Georgia which have never been relinquished, and never will be, that the South began the war by seizing forts, arsenals, mints, custom-houses, etc., etc., long before Mr. Lincoln was installed, and before the South had one jot or tittle of provocation. I myself have seen, in Missouri, Kentucky, Tennessee, and Mississippi, hundreds and thousands of women and children fleeing from your armies and desperadoes, hungry, and with bleeding feet. In Memphis, Vicksburg, and Mississippi, we fed thousands upon thousands of the families of rebel soldiers left on our hands, and whom we could not see starve. Now that war comes home to you, you feel very differently—you deprecate its horrors, but did not feel them when you sent car-loads of soldiers and ammunition, and moulded shells and shot to carry war into Kentucky and Tennessee, and desolate the homes of hundreds and thousands of good people, who only asked to live in peace at their old homes, and under the government of their inheritance. But these comparisons are idle. I want peace, and I believe it can only be reached through Union and war, and I will ever conduct war purely with a view to perfect and early success.

"'But, my dear sirs, when that peace does come you may call upon me for any thing. Then will I share with you the last cracker, and watch with you to shield your home and families against danger from every quarter. Now you must go, and take with you the old and feeble; feed and nurse them, and build for them in more quiet places proper habitations to shield them against the weather, until the mad passions of men cool down, and allow the Union and peace once more to settle on your old homes at Atlanta.'

"As soon as his arrangements were completed, General Sherman wrote to General Hood, by a flag of truce, notifying him of his orders, and proposing a cessation of hostilities for ten days from the 12th of September, in the country included within a radius of two miles around Rough and Ready Station, to enable him to complete the removal of those families electing to go to the south. Hood immediately replied on the 9th, acceding to the proposed truce, but protesting against Sherman's order. He concluded:

"'Permit me to say, the unprecedented measure you propose transcends in studied and iniquitous cruelty all acts ever before brought to my attention in this dark history of the war. In the name of God and humanity, I protest, believing you are expelling from homes and firesides wives and children of a brave people.'"

WORKSHOPS—ARMY OF THE POTOMAC.

CHAPTER XLII.

THE CAMPAIGN IN VIRGINIA.—FROM THE RAPIDAN TO THE JAMES.

Result of Meade's Campaign.—Action of the Committee on the Conduct of the War.—Grant appointed Lieutenant General.—Retirement of Halleck.—Arrangements for the Campaign of 1864. —The Union Forces.—Changes in Organization and Command.—Hancock, Warren, Sedgwick, Burnside.—Sykes, French, Newton.—Kilpatrick, Pleasonton, Sheridan, Sherman.—Meade retained in command of the Army of the Potomac.—Grant's Plans of Campaign.—Position and Strength of Lee's Army.—Lee's Right Flank to be turned.—Opening of the Campaign.—How conducted by Lee and Grant.—*The Battles in the Wilderness:* Passage of the Rapidan.—Positions in the Wilderness.—Military Features of the Region.—Lee moves to the Wilderness.— Grant's proposed Line of March.—Ewell encounters Warren.—Forces him down the Turnpike. —Hill checks him on the Plank Road.—Hancock ordered up.—Getty holds the Brock Road. —Sedgwick attacks on the Right.—Hancock arrives, and attacks Hill.—The Wadsworth Movement.—Hancock repulsed.—Close of the Action of May 5.—Its Results.—Preparations for the Battle of the 6th.—Simultaneous Attack by both Armies.—Slight Engagement between Ewell and Hancock.—Hancock attacks Hill, and forces him back.—Lee on the Field.—Hancock checked.—Longstreet arrives.—Hancock forced back.—Wadsworth Killed.—Longstreet moves toward Hancock's Rear.—Is Wounded.—Burnside's Movements.—Lee assails Hancock's Intrenchments.—Close of the Action on the Left.—Night Assault upon Sedgwick.—Seymour's Division captured.—Results of the Battle.—Losses.—Grant and Lee move toward Spottsylvania. —Lee arrives First.—The whole of both Armies come up.—Fighting on the 7th.—The Action of the 9th.—Death of Sedgwick.—Fighting on the 10th.—Grant's Dispatch.—Washington Bulletins.—Losses in these Actions.—The Battle of the 12th.—Hancock carries Works, and captures Johnson's Division.—The Confederates rally.—Hancock repelled.—Other Operations.—Close of the Battle.—Results and Losses.—Grant moves for the North Anna.—Lee assails and is repulsed.—Lee's Plan of defending Rivers.—Grant crosses the North Anna.—Recrosses.—Both Armies re-enforced.—Sigel defeated at New Market.—He is superseded by Hunter.—Crooks's fruitless Expedition.—Hunter advances.—Defeats Jones at Piedmont, and moves upon Lynchburg.—Retreats northwestward.—Loses his Trains.—Butler moves up the James.—Intrenches at Bermuda Hundred.—Kautz cuts the Weldon Railroad.—Beauregard in Virginia.—Grant's Plan for Butler.—Butler attacks Fort Darling.—He is assailed by Beauregard, and retreats to his Intrenchments.—Beauregard's Plans.—The "Bottling-up" at Bermuda Hundred.—Grant moves toward the Chickahominy.—Lee's corresponding Movement.—Positions assumed.—Sheridan occupies Cold Harbor.—Is assailed.—Smith brought from Bermuda Hundred.—Action of June 1.—Value of Intrenched Positions.—Grant's Purposes.—Battle of Cold Harbor, June 3.— Hancock, Wright, and Smith attack and are repulsed.—Burnside's Movement.—Defeat of the Federal Army.—Losses.—Results of the Battle.—Both armies intrench.—Skirmishing.—Grant moves to the James River.—Lee falls back to Richmond.

THE result of the ineffective campaigns at the East brought with it the conviction that the command of the armies in Virginia must be committed to other and stronger hands. The Congressional Committee on the Conduct of the War had hardly begun their investigations into the operations conducted by General Meade when the two members by whom it had been mainly conducted[1] repaired to the President and Secretary of War, and "demanded the removal of General Meade, and the appointment of some one more competent to command." They suggested the reinstatement of Hooker, but would acquiesce in that of any other general whom the Presi-

dent might think better fitted for the place, but declared emphatically that unless some change was made "it would become their duty to make the testimony public which they had taken, with such comments as the circumstances of the case seemed to require." But events had been so shaping themselves as to obviate the necessity of farther action. Congress, after much deliberation, had passed a bill reviving the grade of lieutenant general, which had never been held except by Washington, for Scott was such only by brevet. Congress also recommended that this appointment should be conferred upon General Grant, and that he should be placed in actual command of all the armies of the United States. The bill was passed, and approved on the 2d of March, and on the 9th Grant was formally presented with his commission. "The nation's appreciation of what you have done," said the President, "and its reliance upon you for what remains to be done in the existing great struggle, are now presented with this commission constituting you lieutenant general in the armies of the United States. With this high honor devolves upon you a corresponding responsibility. As the country herein trusts you, so, under God, it will sustain you. I need scarcely add that with what I here speak for the nation goes my own hearty personal concurrence."

No man was ever more heartily rejoiced at being relieved from an onerous task than was the President when thus enabled virtually to resign his position as commander-in-chief of the army. He had at length found a man into whose hands that trust might be confided. Halleck's occupation as general-in-chief was gone. He was relieved from active duty, and made chief of staff of the army, under the direction of the President, the Secretary of War, and the Lieutenant General. He was to remain at Washington, while Grant's headquarters were to be with the Army of the Potomac in the field, whence the operations of all the Union armies were to be directed. Henceforth the war was to be carried on by a soldier uncontrolled by civilian direction. Even the strong-willed Secretary of War ceased from interfering with operations in the field.[1]

The arrangements for the spring campaign of 1864 were made for a force of a million of men. On the first of May all the armies nominally counted within 30,000 of that number; but of these 109,000 were on detached service, 117,000 were in hospitals or unfit for duty, 66,000 were absent on furlough or prisoners of war, 15,000 were absent without leave. The entire force "available and present for duty" was 662,345. Nothing was left undone to put this immense force into a condition of the utmost efficiency. Congress made appropriations with unsparing hand. Vast amounts of arms,

---

[1] Senators Wade and Chandler; see *Com. Rep.*, ii., xvii.-xix.

[1] "So far as the Secretary of War and myself are concerned, he has never interfered with my duties, never thrown any obstacles in the way of any supplies I have called for. He has never dictated a course of campaign to me, and never inquired what I was going to do. He has always seemed satisfied with what I did, and has heartily co-operated with me."—Grant's Testimony, May 18, 1865, in *Com. Rep.*, ii., 524.

ULYSSES S. GRANT.

PHILIP H. SHERIDAN.

ammunition, stores, clothing, and medical supplies were provided and distributed in dépôts. The means of transportation, by land and water, were multiplied. Of this great army 310,000 men were in Virginia and upon its borders, and in the Carolinas. The Army of the Potomac numbered 140,000, including the Ninth Corps, which acted with it from the first, and was soon formally incorporated with it. In and around Washington were 42,000. In Western Virginia were 31,000. In the Department of Virginia and North Carolina were 59,000; of these, fully 25,000, known as the Army of the James, were available for active service in the field. In South Carolina and Georgia, the Department of the South, were 18,000. In the various minor departments were 20,000. To oppose these, the Confederates had in the field not more than 125,000, in Virginia and the Carolinas. The immediate struggle was to be between the Union Army of the Potomac, 140,000 strong, and the Confederate Army of Northern Virginia, of less than half that number, probably not much exceeding 60,000.[1]

Considerable changes were made in the organization of the Army of the

Potomac. The five corps of which it had consisted were concentrated into three,[1] to be known as the Second, Fifth, and Sixth. The former First and Third Corps were broken up, the troops being distributed among the Second and Fifth. There was little room for hesitation as to the choice of corps commanders. Hancock, having recovered from his wound at Gettysburg, resumed the command of the Second. Warren, who had manifested great military capacity, was placed at the head of the Fifth. There was no question as to continuing Sedgwick in command of the Sixth. Hooker had indeed sharply censured his operations near Chancellorsville,[2] but when men came to learn the history of the disastrous operations at that place, they

---

[1] This change was suggested by Warren on the day following Grant's formal investiture. He said: "I would consolidate the army into three corps. Then I would get the best man to command the army; then I would allow him to have the choice of his corps commanders; then I would allow these corps commanders to choose their own subordinate commanders, and hold them to a strict accountability for what they did—let them understand that their position depended upon their doing well; not merely excusing themselves, but doing something."—*Com. Rep.*, ii., 384.

[2] "By his movements [after carrying the heights at Fredericksburg] I think that no one would infer that he was confident in himself, and the enemy took advantage of it. He was a perfectly brave man, and a good one; but when it came to manœuvring troops, or judging of positions, then, in my judgment, he was not able or expert."—Hooker, in *Com. Rep.*, ii., 146.

---

[1] My estimates of the Confederate forces differ considerably from those generally given. I shall hereafter give the data upon which mine are based.

GOUVERNEUR K. WARREN.

could not fail to perceive that, wherever lay the blame for that inexplicable disaster, it did not rest upon Sedgwick. Had Hooker shown half the promptitude and energy displayed by Sedgwick, the result would have been far other than what it was. The command of the Army of the Potomac had been more than once urged upon Sedgwick, and as often declined by him. Besides these three corps, there was the Ninth, under Burnside, which had just returned from Tennessee, having lately been recruited, notably by a division of colored troops. The original intention was to send it to North Carolina, and it was not until within a week of the opening of the campaign that it was decided to retain it in Virginia. Then it was proposed to hold it in reserve, but the exigencies of the campaign rendered it necessary to bring it forward. It really formed, from the first, a part of the Army of the Potomac, although for three weeks it was not under the command of Meade, but received its orders directly from Grant. Burnside was superior in rank to Meade, and could not, in military etiquette, be called upon to serve under him, but, with characteristic unselfishness, he waived his priority in rank, and served under his former subordinate.

The change in organization involved many changes in officers of high rank. Generals Sykes, French, and Newton, who had commanded corps, were relieved from services in this army, and sent to other departments. Kilpatrick was sent to Sherman to act as his chief of cavalry. Pleasonton, who had led the cavalry with great vigor, was sent to Missouri; for Grant had already fixed upon a leader for his cavalry. This was Philip Sheridan, a young man of barely thirty, who, in command of an army division in the West, had manifested a dashing bravery and a genius for command which, to the keen eye of the lieutenant general, pointed him out as the man to lead his cavalry. The people had before—not altogether unreasonably—complained that the Federal cavalry had not performed service commensurate with that of the Confederates. The fault rested not upon the men, nor of late upon the leaders, but rather upon the commanding generals, who failed to appreciate the true work of this arm of the service. They had been mainly employed as scouts and in guarding trains. Sheridan "took up the idea that our cavalry ought to fight the enemy's cavalry, and our infantry his infantry;" and he resolved to correct "the want of appreciation on the part of infantry commanders as to the power of a large and well-managed body of horse," which led to "the established custom of wasting cavalry for the protection of trains, and for the establishment of cordons around a sleeping infantry force."[1]

The general command of all the forces of the Union had been conferred upon and assumed by Grant. East of the Mississippi the bulk of these forces was concentrated into two great armies, confronting the two main armies of the Confederacy—that in Virginia under Lee, and that in Georgia under Johnston. It was evidently necessary that each of the main Union armies, so widely separated, should be under the immediate command of one general. There was no question that all the forces operating against Johnston should be confided to Sherman. No two men of great military capacity could well differ more widely in the type of their genius than did Grant and Sherman. But they had planned together for months during and after the wearisome Vicksburg campaign, and each had interpenetrated the other with his own ideas, so that it would be hard for either to say how much belonged to each other in the scheme of operations in the Southwest. They were in perfect accord; and Sherman was left in command of the

[1] Sheridan's Report.

great military division of the Mississippi. "I had," says Grant, "talked over with him the plans of the campaign, and was satisfied that he understood them, and would execute them to the fullest extent possible."

Grant having decided to take his position with the Army of the Potomac in the field, the choice of an immediate commander of that army involved very different considerations. By the necessity of the case, Grant must take upon himself the supreme direction of operations. What he here needed was an executive officer able and willing to carry out his designs. The choice fell upon Meade. The very defects which he had exhibited during his command—defects which showed him to be ill fitted for the actual leadership of a great army, proved him to be admirably fitted for any position short of the first. His patriotism and earnestness were beyond doubt; his bravery upon the field was unquestioned; his tactical abilities had been proved. His failures had all arisen from want of self-confidence. Instead of directing, he was ever in search of some one to direct him. In default of better authority, he was perpetually calling consultations and councils of war, and yielding to their decision instead of acting upon his own responsibility. A council of war, not the general in command, decided that the army should not abandon the heights of Gettysburg on the night before the last decisive day. A council of war decided by a bare majority that Lee should not be followed up when he retreated from that lost field. A council of war decided, against Meade's own judgment, that the Confederate army should not be assailed when brought to bay on the banks of the swollen Potomac. The lack of moral courage on the part of Meade caused the unaccountable retreat from Culpepper to Centreville. Fear of responsibility led him to abandon the Mine Run expedition. If Senators Wade and Chandler, of the Congressional Committee, had waited but two days more, until General Meade's own testimony had been given, they could have made out a much stronger case for demanding his removal. But if Meade lacked the faculty of command—the first requisite of a great general, he possessed the second requisite—the faculty of comprehending and executing the orders of another. As commander of the Army of the Potomac, under the immediate direction of a higher intelligence and a stronger will, he proved himself, in the long campaign which followed, to be "the right man in the right place."[1]

Grant had, in the mean while, matured his plans for the campaign. His purpose was to attack simultaneously the two great armies of the Confederacy—"to hammer continuously against the armed force of the enemy and his resources, until by mere attrition, if in no other way," they should be destroyed. Sherman, in the West, was simply instructed to "move against Johnston's army, break it up, and go into the interior of the enemy's country as far as he could, inflicting all the damage he could upon their war resources." With what vigor and skill this order was executed will be shown hereafter. The Army of the Potomac, under Grant's own eye, was to be directed upon a principle altogether new to it. The instructions to Meade read like a covert censure upon all previous operations of the Army of the Potomac. "Lee's army is to be your objective point; wherever that goes you must go." There was to be no more of that indecisive manœuvring whereby had been lost the fruit so ripe and ready for plucking at Antietam and Gettysburg. The Army of the Potomac was to move, not from, nor merely toward the enemy, but upon him. Butler, with the Army of the James, was to co-operate, at first indirectly, in this movement upon Lee. With at least 20,000 men he was to go up the James River, lay siege to Richmond, if possible, or, at all events, take up a position so threatening to the Confederate capital as to insure that none of the force which it was foreseen would be brought up from the Carolinas would be pushed forward to Lee. Sigel's 30,000 men were actually confronted by not a third of their number; but he had a large frontier to defend against raids and partisan adventurers. Yet this defense could be better performed by pushing forward a large part of his force than by lying idly in garrison. He was therefore to organize two columns, one to march up the Valley of the Shenandoah, the other to move down the western flank of the Alleghanies, and then, crossing that ridge, to fall upon the Virginia and Tennessee Railroad, one of the great avenues of supply for the Confederate army and capital, destroying also the salt-works whence was derived the main portion of the supply of this great necessary of life. All these movements were to commence simultaneously, as nearly as possible on the first of May.

The Confederate Army of Northern Virginia had lain in winter quarters along the bluffs which skirt the south bank of the Rapidan, the lines extending for a distance of twenty miles. The position, strong by nature, had been industriously fortified. Rifle-pits commanded every ford, and intrenchments crowned every hill-top. So little had an advance during the winter been apprehended, that after the demonstration at Mine Run a third of the soldiers had been allowed leave of absence upon furlough. In January and February the muster-rolls showed but 35,000 men present for duty. As spring opened the absentees were gradually recalled. On the 10th of March there were about 40,000; on the 10th of April, 53,000. The returns for May are wanting, but it may be assumed that on the first of the month, when the campaign opened, the numbers had increased to fully 60,000, probably somewhat more. Before these, at and around Culpepper, from ten to thirty miles distant, was the Union Army of the Potomac, 140,000 strong, Burnside's corps included.

An assault in front upon the Confederate lines was neither meditated by Grant nor apprehended by Lee. The attack would be made by turning,

[1] "Commanding, as I did, all the armies, I tried, as far as possible, to leave General Meade in independent command of the Army of the Potomac. My instructions for that army were all through him, and were general in their nature, leaving all the details and the execution to him. The campaigns that followed proved him to be the right man in the right place."—Grant's Report, July 22, 1865.

either upon the right or left. There were many advantages and many disadvantages in either case. If the lines were turned by the left, the Union army would still cover Washington; but if the enemy fell back, as it was assumed he would do, every step would carry the assailing force farther and farther from its base of supply. Practically it must do all that it did while the rations with which it started held out. If the turning was by the right, the distance to be marched, in case the enemy fell back to Richmond, would be much greater, and, moreover, Washington would be uncovered, and the way open for another invasion of Maryland and Pennsylvania, should Lee dare to venture it. But, on the other hand, should the enemy fall back toward Richmond, the Union base of supply could be shifted as the army moved—from Brandy Station to Acquia Creek, thence down the Rappahannock to the York, or even, as it proved, to the James. Moreover, Grant seems not to have shared in the nervous apprehension for the safety of the capital which had for two years paralyzed every fresh movement; and he had good reason to be assured that Lee, taught by Antietam and Gettysburg, would not venture to renew the experiment of crossing the border. With 60,000 men he would not attempt to perform that in which he had twice failed to succeed with 100,000. So it was decided that the turning should be made on the Confederate right, that is, to the east, not by the left, to the west. But it so happened that Lee, bearing in mind the result which had followed the movement of Burnside, and reasoning from what he presumed to be the views of the authorities at Washington—not knowing that the military power had passed from their hands—assumed that the movement would be made upon his left. He therefore massed the bulk of his force in that direction. Of the three corps of which his army was composed, those of Ewell and Hill lay behind the defenses of the Rapidan, the mass being at Orange Court-house, near the centre, while Longstreet's corps, just returned from its disastrous expedition to Tennessee, was at Gordonsville, thirteen miles farther to the southwest.

The combined operations of all the Union armies was to take place in the early days of May. On the 1st Sigel began his movement up the Valley of the Shenandoah. On the 6th, Sherman, with the combined armies of the Cumberland, the Tennessee, and the Ohio, advanced from Chattanooga. On the 4th, Butler, with the Army of the James, moved up the James River. On the night of the 3d the Army of the Potomac broke up its camps around Culpepper, and marched for the Rapidan. With this movement began the closing campaign of the war. The campaign lasted for eleven months. On the part of Lee it soon resolved itself into a purely defensive scheme, and, as such, will stand among the great defensive campaigns of history. Two of the campaigns of Frederick of Prussia may be fairly set down as its equal. That of Napoleon in 1814, when, with not more than 110,000 men, he well-nigh foiled 600,000 which the Great Alliance poured into France, is its only superior. That the one, after a hundred days, closed with the exile to Elba, and the other, after more than three hundred, with the surrender at Appomattox Court-house, detracts nothing from their merits. All that skill on the part of the Confederate commander, all that bravery on the part of his troops could do, was done to win victory in the teeth of impossibilities.

I have had occasion more than once to take exceptions to the generalship of Lee where he was successful, and where he avoided what should have been certain destruction. In this final campaign, which resulted in his total overthrow, I find little done which should have been left undone, nothing left undone which should have been done, to insure success. It has been the fashion to say that with the death of Jackson expired the dash and vigor of the Confederate Army of Virginia. Impartial history will record that its greatest achievements, whether of daring or endurance, were performed thereafter. Lee was indeed overcome, but he was overcome by forces greatly superior, wielded by generalship certainly not inferior to his own. It has sometimes been asked what would have been the result had the two commanders changed places. The careful military student will answer that the result would have been just what it was. Lee, in command of Grant's army, would have won; Grant, in command of Lee's army, would have failed. What would have been the result had each general had an equality of force and situation, no wise man will venture to say.

It has been alleged against Grant that the campaign at last assumed a shape wholly different from what he had proposed. This is only partly true. He indeed expected to fight and win a decisive battle north of Richmond; but, failing in this, he from the outset proposed to take his army to the south of the James.[1] It has also been said that after two months of marching and fighting, wherein he suffered losses far greater than he inflicted, he gained a position which he might have reached in a fortnight, without the loss of a man. But those who urge this overlook the cardinal point, that the army of Lee, not merely the geographical spot known as the capital of the Confederacy, was the thing aimed at. If that army were destroyed, the capital and all else was won. If that army remained, it mattered little where the capital of the Confederacy was placed. The army of Lee was, relatively to its opponent, far weaker when it fell back to Richmond and Petersburg than it would have been had not the great battles been fought in the Wilderness, at Spottsylvania, on the North Anna, and at Cold Harbor. War is a game in which there are two players, and it is the one who is upon the whole the stronger that wins. Looking forward, as Grant could only do, there could be little doubt as to the wisdom of his plans. Looking back, as we now can, we must still conclude that it was the wisest which could have been adopted, and brought the war to a more speedy and decisive close than any other which lay before him.

THE WILDERNESS.

Before daybreak on the morning of the 4th of May the Army of the Potomac broke up camps and commenced its march for the fords of the Rapidan. It moved in two columns—Warren's corps, followed by that of Sedgwick, on the right for Germania Ford; Hancock's, with the bulk of the trains, for Ely's Ford, six miles to the east. Burnside's corps was to remain in its position on the Alexandria Railroad, stretching as far back as Bull Run, until the passage of the Rapidan had been effected, when it was to ad-

---

[1] "My idea, from the start, had been to beat Lee's army north of Richmond, if possible. Then, after destroying his lines of communication north of the James River, to transfer the army to the south side, and besiege Lee in Richmond, or follow him south if he should retreat."—*Grant's Report.*

HANCOCK'S CORPS CROSSING THE RAPIDAN.

vance. The march of so great an army could not be effected without being perceived by a watchful enemy, and as the columns approached the fords the Confederate signal-fires were seen blazing from hill-top to hill-top, summoning the corps to concentrate. But the crossing was to be made ten miles below the extreme of the Confederate lines, at Raccoon Ford, held by Ewell, and as much farther from Orange Court-house, where Hill's corps was lying, while Longstreet was thirteen miles farther away. It was therefore impossible for Lee, had he been so inclined, to oppose the passage of the Rapidan. The vedettes at the fords were swept back by Sheridan's cavalry, and both columns, with their great train of 4000 wagons, crossed in the afternoon. Grant believed, as Hooker had done a twelvemonth before, that with the passage of the Rapidan the great danger was overpast. That evening Warren's corps, the advance of the right column, pressed on half a dozen miles, and encamped in the very heart of the Wilderness. Sedgwick halted near the bank of the river. Hancock moved to Chancellorsville, which he reached a little after noon.

On the evening of Wednesday, the 4th, the entire Army of the Potomac was thus encamped in the very heart of the Wilderness, the two columns being about five miles apart. Grant assumed that Lee, finding his position turned by a greatly superior force, would fall back toward Richmond, and his order for the next day was based upon that assumption. But Lee had resolved upon a wholly different movement—a movement apparently perilous and even desperate. With his 60,000 men, he resolved to fling himself upon the enemy, whom he knew to have twice that number. This determination was justified by the soundest military reasons. To set these forth, it is necessary to take a survey of the region.

We have before[1] described the general features of the "Wilderness," touching mainly upon that portion of it wherein were fought the battles of Chancellorsville. The Wilderness Tavern, where Grant and Meade established their headquarters on the evening of the 4th, is at the very centre of this wild region. Six miles northward is the Rapidan; as far southward begin the cleared fields of Spottsylvania; eight miles westward is Mine Run; just as far eastward is Chancellorsville. The Wilderness, stretching from a dozen to a score of miles in either direction, is traversed north and south, west and east, by two systems of roads, which, in conjunction with the jungles and chaparrals pierced by them, constitute its military features. From north to south, or more accurately from northwest to southeast, starting from Germania Ford, runs a tolerable plank road, continued after a few miles by the "Brock Road," over which Jackson in May, 1863, marched to the attack upon Hooker's weak right. Nearly parallel to this, some six miles away, starting from Ely's Ford, and passing by Chancellorsville, goes another road. These two, after many windings and turnings, come together near Spottsylvania Court-house, eight miles southeast of Chancellorsville. These are the main roads running southwardly by which Grant's two columns were to pass through the Wilderness. Running from west to east are two good roads, the northern known as the Old Turnpike, the southern as the Orange Plank Road. These, starting from Orange Court-house, run nearly parallel at a distance of about three miles, coming together again near Chancellorsville. They strike at a right angle those by which Grant would move, and the Confederates, pressing down these roads, would strike squarely upon the flank of the long Union columns slowly defiling through the tangled mazes of the Wilderness, with every probability of cutting them in two. In these labyrinths of forests, thickets, and swamps, which no eye could penetrate for more than a few yards, and where artillery could not be brought into action, Grant's preponderance of numbers would be neutralized; and indeed Lee, having two good parallel roads, might reasonably expect to be able to throw a superior force upon the decisive point. He had, moreover, the great advantage of a thorough knowledge of the country, which was wholly unknown to his opponent.

When, therefore, on the morning of the 4th, Lee learned that the Union army was heading for the Rapidan, he put his columns in motion to intercept it on its march through the Wilderness. Ewell moved by the turnpike, and the head of his column lay that night within three miles of the camp of Warren at the Wilderness Tavern. Hill moved by the plank road, but, having a longer march, was somewhat farther away. Longstreet, a day behind, was ordered up with all speed. Grant's plan for the ensuing day contemplated a leisurely march mainly for the purpose of concentrating his somewhat scattered corps. Warren was to march by a wood path southwestward till he struck the plank road, up which he was to proceed three miles to Parker's store; Sedgwick was to follow, joining upon Warren's right; Hancock was to move from Chancellorsville southward to Shady Grove Church, and stretch his right to unite with Warren's left. Meade's whole army, none of it having marched more than ten miles, would then have cleared the Wilderness, its movements being masked in front by Sheridan's cavalry. Burnside's corps would have reached Germania Ford, ready to cross and follow in the track of Meade. Grant would then be prepared for a rapid advance toward Gordonsville, whither it was taken for granted that Lee would retire.

Warren began to move at five o'clock on the morning of Thursday, the 5th. Wilson's division of cavalry had on the preceding afternoon scouted for some distance up the turnpike without encountering any enemy, for Ewell, who was coming down the road, was yet miles away. Warren, however, by way of precaution, threw Griffin's division westward up the turnpike. Ewell at the same time moved eastward down the road, and the head of the columns came unexpectedly in collision. Even now the Union commanders were wholly unaware that the enemy were approaching in force. "They have left a division here to fool us," said Meade, "while they con-

centrate and prepare a position toward the North Anna, and what I want is to prevent these fellows from getting back to Mine Run." Only a single division—that of Johnson, forming the van of Ewell's corps—had as yet come up. Griffin fell furiously upon this, and drove it back for a space. Strongly re-enforced, the Confederates turned at bay, held their ground, and soon advanced in turn, and forced Griffin back over all the space which he had won. Wadsworth, endeavoring to join Griffin, missed his way through the woods, and exposed his naked flank to a fierce fire, from which his division recoiled in confusion. In the mean time, Crawford, who had struck the plank road, and was moving up it toward Parker's store, encountered the cavalry scouts dashing back with tidings that a heavy force was pouring down that road. Crawford's movement was suspended, and his division withdrawn; one brigade, however, became isolated, and lost in prisoners nearly the whole of two regiments.

It was an hour past noon. Two hours before, Grant, perceiving that the enemy were in force and bent upon delivering battle in the Wilderness, had sent orders to Hancock to suspend his southward march, and, taking the Brock Road, to hurry to the scene of conflict. He had also sent Getty, with his division of Sedgwick's corps, to the junction of this road with the Orange Plank, with orders to hold the position, at all hazards, until Hancock, who was ten miles away, should come up. Thus far the brunt of the fight had been borne by Warren's corps, opposed to that of Ewell. Warren had been pressed back to the line whence he had started in the early morning, where he stood stoutly at bay. Ewell's on-coming brigades, spreading northward, threatened to turn Warren's right. Sedgwick's corps, or, rather, two of its three divisions, for the strongest, under Getty, had been sent elsewhere, was ordered to advance through the thick woods upon Warren's right. As they pressed on through the dense undergrowth, broken here and there by a slight clearing, they would encounter a body of Confederate skirmishers, hidden in the skirts of the chaparral. These would deliver a sharp fire, and disappear in the thickets. At length they came square in front of a strong line of battle. The Confederates charged fiercely and unavailingly upon the leading brigades, and then, with equal ill success, endeavored to turn their flank. At four o'clock they suspended their offensive movements, fell back, and began to fortify their position. The confronting lines now lay upon the opposite slopes of a swampy, wooded hollow. They were but a hundred or two yards apart, and though the ring of axes felling trees to form breastworks and abatis filled the air, not a man on either side could be discerned from the other.

At four o'clock the fight had lulled upon Warren's and Sedgwick's front. But in the mean while, and thereafter, it was raging on the plank road, barely three miles to the southward. Here Getty held grimly to the vital point at the junction of the Brock and Plank Roads, which he had been ordered to maintain, toward which Hancock was advancing. Hill's corps of the Confederates was pressing strongly down the Plank Road. Getty seemed on the point of being overwhelmed, when at three o'clock the welcome sound of Hancock's approach up the Brock Road was heard. Hancock drew up his force fronting that of Hill, and began to level the woods and throw up breastworks, designing simply to receive an assault. But Meade had ordered Getty to take the offensive, and drive Hill up the plank road. Getty had but three hundred paces to go to encounter the Confederate line. He found them in superior force, lying hidden in the woods bordering the road. Hancock backed up the attack by divisions from his own corps. The assaults were hot and furious—"repeated and desperate assaults," as Lee styles them; "a fierce fight, the lines being exceedingly close, the musketry continuous and deadly along the entire line," says Hancock. It was

ALEXANDER HAYS.

FIGHTING IN THE WILDERNESS.

all in vain. Hill could not be pushed back, and the hot volleys of musketry caused more than one of the assailing divisions to waver and break. In the effort to repair one such break, General Alexander Hays, who had won high renown at Gettysburg, was shot dead, while leading his command into the heart of the fight. So for four hours, until night closed in, the contest raged with no decisive advantage on either side.

Late in the afternoon, the fight in front of Warren and Sedgwick having been suspended, Wadsworth's division was ordered to press southward through the forest, and thus fall upon the flank and rear of Hill, who was holding his position against the hot assaults of Hancock. But, though the distance was hardly three miles, the appointed position was only reached at nightfall, when the conflict was over. Wadsworth rested on the field, in line of battle, in a position where he could strike when the fight should be opened the next morning. Hancock's and Hill's forces, who had been marching and fighting all day, lay upon their arms upon the opposite side of the Brock Road, awaiting what the next day should bring forth. But as darkness closed in, an irregular contest was opened in the woods on the extreme Union right, and the gloom of the forest was lighted up by volleys of musketry which rolled along the opposing lines. At two hours past midnight, and three hours before dawn, the noise sank away into silence.

The engagement of this day can hardly be styled a battle. It was rather a series of fierce encounters between portions of two armies, each ignorant of the position, strength, and force of the other. Neither commander had succeeded in effecting his purpose. Lee had hoped to fall upon the flank of Grant's columns while stretched out in a long, feeble line of march, cut them in two, and annihilate one portion while it was isolated from the other. If the collision had taken place two hours later, when the whole of Hill's and Ewell's divisions would have come up, while the Federals were fairly on the march, it could hardly have failed to succeed. But Grant had now been able to place his force in line of battle, opposing his front instead of his flank to the enemy. He had failed, however, to push the Confederates back upon the roads by which they had advanced. But the state of affairs was such as to warrant both in renewing the issue the next day. Grant, indeed, had no choice but to fight. He was still enmeshed in the Wilderness. He could not go southward without exposing himself to a disastrous flank assault. It would have been equally perilous to have attempted to recross the Rapidan, even had he been of a temper to give up his forward purpose. He might, indeed, have fallen back eastward toward Fredericksburg by way of the Brock Road, plank, and turnpike, and thus have got clear of the Wilderness, but there was nothing in the position of affairs to warrant such a resort. Moreover, neither general had used his whole force. Burnside's corps, 20,000 strong, had pushed on by forced marches, were crossing at Germania Ford, and could be brought into action the next day. Lee could not be aware of this accession to the numbers to be opposed to him. He also had fresh forces at hand. Longstreet's veteran corps was moving on from its cantonments forty miles away. During the afternoon he had reached a position ten miles from where the battle was raging, but in these close woods the noise of the musketry was unheard, and he was ignorant that a battle was being fought until midnight, when he received orders from Lee to advance. Two hours later he was on the march, and would come up. Anderson's division, moreover, one third of Hill's strong corps, had been left behind to watch the upper fords of the Rapidan. These were now close at hand. Longstreet and Anderson would add 20,000 fresh men to Lee's force on the field. With two thirds of his army he had gained some apparent advantage; with this addition it was not unreasonable to hope that he could win a decisive victory.

So both commanders resolved to fight; and, a rare occurrence in warfare, each proposed at daybreak to assault the lines of the other. Grant united his heretofore disjointed line by bringing forward Burnside and posting him between Warren and Hancock, so that the line from right to left ran thus: Sedgwick, as before, on the right; then Warren, who had been severely handled on the preceding day; then Burnside; then, on the left, Hancock, strengthened by detachments from Sedgwick and Warren. There was no room for the display of elaborate manœuvres or skillful combinations. Grant's plan of battle was simply a simultaneous assault along the whole line of five miles, each division attacking whatever appeared in its front. Lee, however, had two good avenues of approach. His plan was more elaborate. The main attack was to be made by Longstreet and Hill upon the Union left, while Ewell was to make an assault, or, rather, demonstration upon the right. If Longstreet succeeded, Hancock would be forced back upon the centre, and the whole Union army flung together in inextricable confusion in the almost impenetrable forests, where it could not act as an army.

Five o'clock, the hour when the gray dawn was breaking into day, was the time fixed by Grant for attack. But Ewell anticipated him by fifteen minutes, moving out of his lines upon Sedgwick's extreme right. The attack was not seriously made, and probably not seriously intended. It was easily repelled. Sedgwick and Warren then advanced, pushing the enemy back for a space until he regained the strong position from which he had sallied. Upon this no impression could be made, and the contest ceased to be a battle at this point.

Hancock, in the mean while, deploying his skirmishers, pushed half of his force through the thickets on each side of the plank road, straight westward upon Hill's front. Wadsworth, who had slept the night before hard by, advanced southward upon the Confederate flank. The attack was wholly unexpected. Longstreet, who was just coming up, was to take the position in front, relieving Hill, whose front divisions, those of Heth and Wilcox, were just preparing to retire. These divisions broke and fled back in disor-

JAMES S. WADSWORTH.

der for a mile and a half, overrunning Lee's headquarters, which were in the way, and not halting until they touched the head of Longstreet's advancing column. But here they met three regiments of Kershaw's division, who briefly stayed the flight. Other troops were hurrying up; the whole line seemed wavering and on the point of again breaking. Lee, who had narrowly escaped being shot down, flung himself at the head of Gregg's Texans, and ordered them to follow him in a charge. First one soldier, and then the whole brigade, shouted out a remonstrance, and refused to advance until their commander had retired from the front. But in the fierce rush through the pathless woods the Federal troops had likewise lost all semblance of battle array—every thing which distinguishes an army from isolated groups of Indian fighters. Coming upon a line somewhat firm, it was necessary to halt and readjust their own broken formation. This, in a tangled wilderness, was a work of time. Two hours passed—from seven to nine—before the Union line was reformed. Those hours had wrought an entire change in the aspect of the field. Longstreet's whole corps had come up, Hill's entire corps was concentrated, and the Confederate line had gained such force that it was able not only to repel assault, but to give attack. The Union force was swept back over all the space which it had won, and reformed only upon the Brock Road, whence it had started. In a vain attempt to stay the retreat of his command, which had fallen into disorder, Wadsworth was mortally wounded, and his body remained in the enemy's hands. Few as noble men have ever fallen upon the field of battle. He was the largest landholder, and one of the wealthiest men of Western New York. Past the prime of life, verging closely upon threescore, his years had been devoted to peaceful pursuits. When the war broke out he offered his purse and his person to the government. At the battle of Bull Run he acted as aid-de-camp to McDowell. Appointed brigadier general, he for a time acted as Military Governor of the District of Columbia. In the dark year of 1862 he was the Republican candidate for Governor of New York, but was defeated by Horatio Seymour. Then assigned to the command of a division in the Army of the Potomac, he did good service at Fredericksburg and Chancellorsville. At Gettysburg the heaviest brunt of the first day's fighting, whereby the Confederates were prevented from occupying the heights, fell upon his division.

Hancock had sallied out from his intrenchments with only half the force under his command. The reason of this was that Longstreet was said to be coming up by a way which, passing south of the plank road, would bring him upon the left of his position on the Brock Road, and so, if that point was abandoned, by an advance the enemy would be upon his rear. Longstreet was, indeed, at six o'clock, making this very movement; but so urgent was the stress caused by the unlooked-for attack upon Hill, that Lee was obliged to change the direction of Longstreet, and bring him to the front. When now Hancock's advance had been stayed, Lee reverted to his original plan, the execution of which was committed to Longstreet, who was to send a portion of his corps to make a detour beyond the extreme Union left, gain the Brock Road, and thus fall upon its rear. Not until this force was well in position was the front assault to be made. This took until noon, by which time Hancock's advanced right had been forced back to its intrenchments. Longstreet then rode down the plank road to direct the turning column. He met General Jenkins, an old comrade whom he had not seen for months. Mahone's brigade, a portion of his own flanking force, lay hidden in the bushes. They mistook Longstreet and others for Federal officers, and fired upon them. Jenkins fell dead, and Longstreet received a ball in his throat, which passed out through the shoulder. He was borne away fatally wounded, as was thought. But he survived, and months afterward was able to take part in the closing scenes of the war, the only survivor of the three lieutenants of Lee who fought in the battles of the Army of Northern

THE WILDERNESS—SCENE OF WADSWORTH'S DEATH.

Virginia, for Hill fell almost a year later, and Jackson had a year before received his death-wound hardly six miles from the spot where Longstreet fell wounded.

The fall of Longstreet checked for a space the execution of the operation which had been committed to him. Lee assumed immediate command of this part of the field, and at length, as the afternoon was wearing away, urged the whole strength of the two corps of Longstreet and Hill against Hancock's lines, then resting behind their intrenchments, but also preparing for a renewed assault. Much had been hoped from an advance of Burnside's corps through the woods between Hancock and Warren. Two of his three white divisions—for the colored one had been left behind to guard the trains—touched the fight somewhat sharply, losing a thousand men; but they failed to attain a place wherein their action seriously affected the fortunes of the day. Now the woods wherein the battle of the morning had been fought were on fire, and a strong westerly wind blew the flames right down upon the Federal intrenchments, forcing the foremost lines to abandon the works. The Confederates, following the fire, swept down, the foremost troops crowning the parapet and planting their colors upon the blazing breastworks. But they were met by a rush from Carroll's brigade, which came up first by flank and then straight forward, and driven back in wild disorder. With this sharp assault ended the fighting upon the left. Each side had advanced upon the other, and each, after winning some success, had been repelled. Both, as night again fell, occupied substantially the same positions which they had held when morning broke.

The battle of the day was over on the left of the field, where Hancock was struggling against Longstreet and Hill. But on the right, where the contest had lulled for hours, there was at dusk one more stirring episode. The Confederate left overlapped the Union right, held by some brigades of raw troops of Sedgwick's corps. They had wearily kept their post for thirty hours in front of breastworks which had been thrown up, behind which they might retire in case of attack. None having been made, they at dusk began to retire to this sheltered line. The vigilant enemy, perceiving this movement, made a sudden rush upon their flank, and threw every thing into confusion. One of these brigades had on that very day been given to Seymour, just released from captivity, into which he had fallen at the battle of Olustee, in Florida; another was commanded by Shaler. These brigades, four thousand strong, were enveloped, and, with their commander, captured, almost to a man. For a space it seemed that the fatal rout of the Eleventh Corps at Chancellorsville was to be renewed. But the sudden assault was soon repelled, and the Confederates fell back to the lines from which they had so suddenly emerged. This brilliant feat, wherein they made three thousand prisoners, cost the Confederates, it is said, only twenty-seven men.[1]

The morning of Saturday found both armies in a mood different from that of the day before. Each, while quite willing to be assailed in its intrenchments, was indisposed to attack the other. The losses had been heavy.

Those of the Federals numbered fully 20,000 men, of whom about 5000 were prisoners. The Confederate loss was hardly 10,000, of whom few were captured. The two days' action had otherwise been a fairly drawn battle. Both commanders had failed in their purpose. Grant had turned the impregnable position of the Rapidan only to find himself confronted in the Wilderness by the enemy in a new position equally unassailable. In this first blow the hammer had suffered more than the anvil. According to all precedent in the Army of the Potomac, Grant should have abandoned the enterprise, and cast about for something new. But of this he had no thought. To strike and keep striking, as he had done at Vicksburg, was his fixed purpose.

The first thing to be done was to flank the enemy from the Wilderness. The movement was to be upon Spottsylvania Court-house, fifteen miles southwest of the battle-field. The direct route was by the Brock Road; a more indirect one was by a detour eastward to Chancellorsville, then southward to the point of destination. Warren's and Hancock's corps were to follow the first route; Sedgwick's and Burnside's, with all the trains, were to take the latter. The wounded were to be sent through Chancellorsville to Fredericksburg. Warren was to commence his march at half past eight in the evening. If he met no obstruction he would soon after daylight reach the Court-house, of which possession in the mean time was to be taken by Wilson's cavalry. The other corps would not be long behind. Then the whole army would be again upon Lee's flank, ready to fling itself between him and Richmond.

SPOTTSYLVANIA.

But Warren, upon reaching Todd's Tavern, about half way, found the narrow road obstructed by Meade's cavalry escort, and it was an hour and a half before the way could be cleared. Two miles beyond that point the road was blocked by Stuart's Confederate cavalry, who had been posted there the day before, and which Merritt's troopers, who were in advance, had not succeeded in dislodging. It was now daylight. Warren, advancing, cleared the way and pressed on slowly, for barricades had been formed by felling trees, which could be removed only by the axe. Here and there, also, there was a slight show of opposition by dismounted troopers. At last, at half past eight, four hours behind time, the head of the column emerged from the woods into an open clearing, beyond which rose the wooded ridge whereon is the Court-house, still two miles away. Thus far there had been no intimation of any enemy except the few dismounted troopers. But when half way across the clearing the advancing column encountered a fierce musketry fire from infantry lying hidden in the opposite wood, and fell back across the plain. By one of those accidents which sometimes change the course of a whole campaign, the Confederates were first at Spottsylvania.

When Lee, on the afternoon and evening, saw the Federal trains moving due east toward Chancellorsville, he at once inferred that the enemy was heading for Fredericksburg; the Brock Road also at first trends in that direction; and when columns were perceived defiling down that road, the conclusion was confirmed. Lee was not undeceived until the next day; for on

[1] So Pollard, doubtful authority, says: *Lost Cause*, p. 516. If one chooses to see a Federal account, describing a hot fight, with charges and countercharges, he is referred to Stevens's *Three Years in the Sixth Corps*, p. 311–313.

7 U

JOHN SEDGWICK.

HORATIO G. WRIGHT.

the 8th he sent a dispatch to Richmond stating that "the enemy have abandoned their position, and are marching toward Fredericksburg. I am moving on their right flank"—that is, toward Spottsylvania. The march was at first leisurely, for it was not his purpose to overtake the Federal army, but simply to interpose between it and what was assumed to be its march down the Fredericksburg Railroad toward Richmond. It was, indeed, by accident that this march was commenced during the night of the 7th. At ten in the evening, Anderson, who now commanded Longstreet's corps, was ordered to withdraw his troops from the breastworks from before which the enemy had disappeared, and encamp in readiness to march next morning. Anderson, finding no good place to bivouac in the burning woods, kept on. Thus, during that night, Warren and Anderson were moving by roads nearly parallel upon Spottsylvania. Although Warren had the start by an hour or two, Anderson, meeting with no obstructions, as day broke was ahead. Then for the first time learning the approach of the enemy, he double-quicked his march and reached the Court-house some hours in advance. The Federal cavalry who held the place abandoned it, and Anderson drew up his men across the road by which Warren, ignorant of his presence, was advancing. He had time to throw up slight breastworks, behind which, and hidden in the woods, he awaited the approach of his enemy. Some sharp fighting here took place, continuing all the morning; and at last Warren began to intrench close in front of the Confederate line. Hancock's corps, which was following that of Warren, was delayed all day at Todd's Tavern in readiness to repel an attack upon the rear, which was apparently threatened by Lee, who, now perceiving the real aim of the Federal movement, was hurrying his whole force on toward Spottsylvania. Some time in the afternoon Sedgwick came up from Chancellorsville and took command of the field. Toward evening a slight attack was made upon the Confederate line, but nothing of

importance was effected. Lee, with his whole force, was firmly posted upon Spottsylvania ridge, and every hour was strengthening his position, from which it was clear that he could be driven only by hard fighting. Grant, whose entire army was now well in hand, and notwithstanding its severe losses in the Wilderness, was in sound heart, resolved to try what could be effected by heavy blows.

Monday, the 9th, was mainly employed by Grant in making his dispositions, and by Lee in fortifying his lines, which mainly followed the course of a wooded ridge, from the Court-house on the east, sweeping in an irregular semicircle to the north and east. Artillery and musketry firing was kept up at points from the Confederate lines, especially upon points where batteries were being established. At one of these points Sedgwick was superintending the placing of a battery. The men seemed to wince at the fire poured in upon them. "Pooh!" said Sedgwick, drawing himself up to his full height, "they can't hit an elephant at that distance." At that moment a rifle-shot struck him fairly in the face, and he fell dead. The command of the Sixth Corps now devolved upon Wright.

The 10th was spent in tentatives upon the left of the Confederate lines. These, though fiercely made, were unsuccessful, though Grant at the close sent an encouraging dispatch to Washington, which was duly published, and, for the time, was held to announce a victory; at all events, it indicated a determination which, in view of his known superiority in numbers, was held to be a sure presage of speedy and decided success.[1] He "proposed to fight it out on that line, if it took all summer." If he had known it, he was to fight all summer, and autumn, and winter, and far into the next spring. The "indecisive actions of these three days had cost wellnigh 10,000 men, the very flower of the Army of the Potomac. The enemy, fighting almost wholly behind intrenchments, could have suffered hardly a third as much."[2]

Lee's left had been found, by bitter experience, to be impregnable. But it seemed that his centre presented a weak point through which an entrance might be forced. Here his lines were thrust forward in a sharp salient which might be carried by a sudden dash. All the day of the 11th was spent in arrangements. Toward night a heavy rain set in, and under the cover of this and the darkness, Hancock's corps was brought around from the left, and posted twelve hundred yards from this salient angle. This point seemed to be so difficult of approach that it was weakly held and carelessly guarded. In the gray dawn, and through a dense fog, Hancock's men moved softly and noiselessly, sweeping over the Confederate pickets without firing a shot; then, with a shout and a rush, they dashed through the abatis, and over the breastworks on every side. Johnson's division of

FIRE-PROOF WHERE SEDGWICK FELL.

[1] Grant's Dispatch, May 11th, 8 P.M. "We have now ended the sixth day of very hard fighting. The result to this time is very much in our favor. Our losses have been heavy, as well as those of the enemy. I think the loss of the enemy must be heavier. We have taken over 5000 prisoners, while he has taken from us but few except stragglers. I propose to fight it out on this line if it takes all summer." In his report a year later, he says, "The 9th, 10th, and 11th were spent in manœuvring and fighting, without decisive results." It is worth while to recall some of the official dispatches of this period put forth by the War Department. Sunday, May 9th: "Lee's army commenced falling back on Friday. Our army commenced the pursuit on Saturday. The rebels were in full retreat for Richmond by the direct road. Hancock passed through Spottsylvania Court-house at daylight yesterday." Same day: "Dispatches have just reached here direct from General Grant. They are not fully deciphered yet; but he is on to Richmond." The President appointed a day of thanksgiving for the victories of the last five days.

[2] No returns have been rendered of the separate losses during the seven days, from May 5 to 11. The entire number is given together as follows: killed, 3288; wounded, 19,278; missing, 6844; total, 29,410. Allowing, as we have done, 20,000 for the Wilderness, there remain fully 10,000 for these three days at Spottsylvania. The Confederate loss is wholly a matter of estimate. In placing it at 15,000 during this period, we can not very greatly err.

SPOTTSYLVANIA COURT-HOUSE.

Ewell's corps, 4000 strong, were nearly all captured. Hancock sent back a hasty note to Grant, "I have finished up Johnson, and am now going into Early." But this salient was after all an outwork, adopted because the heights swelled out in that direction. Behind it, at the distance of half a mile, a second line had been laid out and partly completed. Here the Confederates rallied, Ewell in the centre, Hill rushing in from the right, and Longstreet from the left. The position was vital. If these works were carried the Confederate line would be cut in two, and their whole position forced. Hancock, struggling alone—for so rapid had been his rush that he had far outstripped Wright who was to support him—was speedily thrown back to the captured salient. The Sixth Corps now came up, and the Confederates could not gain another inch. Half of Warren's corps were sent to support Hancock and Wright, and the battle raged with hardly an interval during the whole day and far into the night. Five several assaults were made by the Confederates, and five times they were bloodily repelled. At midnight Lee withdrew to his interior line, which was still intact. During the day Burnside and Warren had demonstrated strongly upon their fronts. Burnside carried the rifle-pits, but could make no impression upon the intrenchments behind them. "The resistance," says Grant, "was so obstinate that the advantage gained did not prove decisive." The Union loss this day was probably 10,000, that of the Confederates quite as many.[1]

Grant had struck a heavy blow, but the enemy were by no means crushed. For six days longer he manœuvred in the hope of turning the lines; but, in whatever direction he moved, he found himself confronted by intrenchments which forbade assault. He was, moreover, awaiting re-enforcements which were hurried on from Washington. On the 18th, orders were given to break up the position at Spottsylvania, and move southward to the North Anna. Lee, who now seemed to divine the purposes of his opponent, saw in the preparatory movements a chance for a blow. He launched Ewell through the woods upon Grant's right flank; but the attack was easily repelled, and Ewell, after heavy loss, fell back to his intrenchments. This demonstration delayed Grant's movement until the night of the 21st. Next morning Lee saw before him no trace of the great army by which he had been confronted. Breaking up his camps, he hastened once more to fling himself athwart the line of the enemy's advance.

THE NORTH ANNA.

When, after a two days' march through a fertile region as yet untrodden by armies, Grant reached the North Anna River, he found his vigilant adversary confronting him upon the opposite bank. Lee's settled policy was never strongly to oppose the passage of a river in his front. He had not seriously contested the passage of the Chickahominy, the Rappahannock, the Antietam, or the Rapidan. He chose rather to intrench himself a little distance back, allow his adversary to cross, hoping to fight him with a stream in his rear. Here, however, he made some show of opposition to the passage, though his main line of defense was some distance beyond the stream. The opposition was speedily brushed away. Hancock and Warren crossed at two points four miles apart. But now Lee thrust his army like a sharp wedge right between the two Union columns, repelled all attempts to unite them, and was in a position to strike either. The manœuvre was a brilliant one. Grant, perceiving his peril, and the impossibility of assailing his opponent, after two days recrossed the river, and on the 26th resumed his old turning movement, which was to bring him within view of the Chickahominy.

While at Spottsylvania Grant had received re-enforcements fully equal to all his losses. Here, upon the North Anna, Lee was joined by Pickett's division and Hoke's brigade from North Carolina, and Breckinridge's command from the Valley of the Shenandoah. All told, they numbered some 15,000 men, considerably less than his losses, so that Grant was relatively stronger than at the opening of the campaign. To understand how it was possible for these re-enforcements to be given to the Army of Northern Virginia requires a rapid survey of operations in other quarters.

OPERATIONS OF SIGEL, HUNTER, AND BUTLER.

It had been a part of Grant's plan that Sigel, with 7000 men, should move up the Valley of the Shenandoah, and Crook, with 10,000, up the Kanawha. These two columns were designed to hold in check the scattered Confederate forces in that region, and destroy the salt-works in the Valley of the Kanawha, and threaten the communications between Richmond and the West by way of the Tennessee Railway. Sigel moved from Winchester on the 1st of May. On the 15th he reached Newmarket, a distance of fifty miles, having encountered no serious opposition. Here he encountered Breckinridge with a force somewhat superior.[1] Sigel suffered a severe and mortifying defeat, and fell back, leaving behind him his trains and 700 prisoners. At the instance of Grant he was superseded by Hunter. The column under Crook met with somewhat better fortune, inasmuch as it suffered no actual defeat, although Averill, who had been detached with 2000 men to destroy the lead-works at Wytheville, was foiled by Morgan; and Crook, having reached the railroad, destroyed the track for a short distance, and, on a slight encounter, defeated McCausland. But, finding the enemy gathering in his front, he retreated by the way he came. Breckinridge, thus relieved from immediate pressure, was free to join Lee with the whole of his movable force.[2] Hunter, a fortnight later, collected 20,000 men, and and moved up the valley. He encountered W. E. Jones at Piedmont on the 5th of June, defeated him, took 1500 prisoners, and, crossing the mountains, advanced upon Lynchburg. So important was the possession of this place, as the key to one of his main avenues of supply, that Lee, although Grant's whole army was in his immediate front near Cold Harbor, detached Early with a quarter of the whole Army of Northern Virginia to oppose the advance of Hunter. They reached the vicinity of Lynchburg at about the same time with Hunter. Some skirmishing ensued; but Hunter was now quite destitute of ammunition, and, not daring to seek a battle, retreated. From some unaccountable reason, instead of falling back northward down the valley, he struck northwestward down the Kanawha. His supplies were nearly exhausted, but large quantities had been collected at a point a few marches on the way. These were guarded only by a few cavalry, two regiments of hundred-days' men. Gilmor, an active partisan, dashed upon the train, destroyed the whole, and disappeared. Hunter kept up his retreat by a long detour by way of the Kanawha and Ohio, through the mountains of Western Virginia, and it was several weeks before he was able to regain the Potomac. This absence of Hunter's force gave opportunity for the annoying invasion of Maryland by Early, whereby the safety of the Federal capital was seriously endangered.

Another simultaneous co-operative movement was to be made from Yorktown by Butler. His available force consisted of the Tenth Corps under W. F. Smith, and the Eighteenth under Gillmore, which had not long before been brought from before Charleston, numbering together about 25,000 men, besides 3000 cavalry under Kautz, who were posted at Suffolk. To this force was given the name of the Army of the James. The army lay at Yorktown, apparently threatening a movement upon Richmond across the peninsula, by the route followed by McClellan two years before. Butler, on the 4th of May, embarked his infantry on board transports, passed down the

[1] The losses in the Army of the Potomac are grouped together for the period from the 12th to the 21st of May. They sum up 10,381; but after the 12th there were probably not more than 2000, leaving 8381 for the 12th. Of the Confederate losses we have no reliable statement. Pollard says (Lost Cause, 520), "The enemy had taken twenty-five pieces of artillery and about 2000 men in Johnson's division; he had inflicted a loss of 6000 or 7000." Whether he means to include the 2000 prisoners in the "loss" is uncertain; but the prisoners certainly numbered 3000; and, considering the character of the fighting, it can not be doubted that, in the main action at the salient, the Confederates lost most heavily. On the other parts of the field it is probable that the Union loss was in excess. It may be safely assumed that in a persistent assault, which is repulsed, the assailants suffer most.

[1] Breckinridge's returns for April show 6438 men; but, besides these, he collected many scattered bands, among them a company of 250 boys, cadets in the Military Academy at Lexington. These cadets were pushed to the front, and fought like veterans, losing a third of their number.
[2] According to Early, Breckinridge brought only 2500 men. Little reliance, however, can be placed upon any statement of this officer. Thus he states that the force with which he was some months later defeated by Sheridan was only 8500 men, whereas Sheridan showed that he had taken more than that number of prisoners, and Early's losses in killed and wounded were very severe.

JERICHO MILLS, NORTH ANNA.   RIFLE-PITS, NORTH ANNA.   QUARLES'S MILLS, NORTH ANNA.

York River and up the James, and next day occupied City Point, at the junction of that river and the Appomattox, and Bermuda Hundred, a narrow-necked peninsula between those rivers. Here he intrenched himself in a position which he affirmed he "could hold against the whole of Lee's army." Kautz, at the same time, made a dash upon the Weldon Railroad, by which it was known that troops from South and North Carolina were approaching Richmond.

Beauregard, who had been conducting the defense of Charleston, had not long before been placed in command of the Department of South Virginia and North Carolina. The departure of Gillmore rendered it safe to withdraw nearly all the force from South Carolina. Hoke, also, had, about the middle of April, captured Plymouth, North Carolina, almost the only point yet held by the Federals in that state, and he had been able to bring to Richmond Pickett's division, then under his command. On the 21st of April Beauregard passed through Wilmington with a considerable force, and proceeded toward Richmond. Butler supposed that most of them were still on the way, and when he found that Kautz had cut the railroad he assumed that they could not advance.[1]

Having intrenched himself at Bermuda Hundred, Butler, on the 7th, made a demonstration against the railroad from Petersburg to Richmond, and succeeded in destroying a small portion of it. Had he pushed straight to Petersburg that city would have been easily taken, for the defenses which had been begun two years before were of little account, and there were there few or no troops. But the capture of Petersburg formed no part of the plan which had been agreed upon between him and Grant. The essential part of it was that, as soon as Grant should approach Richmond from the northeast, Butler should move up southeastwardly, and the two armies would then invest Richmond on the south, west, and north, thus avoiding the almost impregnable lines of works which protected the city on the east. On the 9th he resumed his attack upon the railroad in considerable force, and with favorable results, and proposed to follow up the success next day. But that night he received the glowing dispatches from Washington announcing that Lee was in full retreat for Richmond, with Grant close upon his heels. Pausing for two days to strengthen his lines at Bermuda Hundred, on the 13th he began an attempt to carry out his part of the programme. On the 13th a portion of the outer lines near Fort Darling, which formed the extreme southern point of the defenses of Richmond, were carried. But the

[1] On the 9th he telegraphed to the Secretary of War: "Beauregard, with a large portion of his force, was left South by the cutting of the railroad by Kautz. That portion which reached Petersburg under Hill I have whipped to-day, killing and wounding many, and taking many prisoners, after a severe and well-contested fight. General Grant will not be troubled with any farther reinforcements to Lee from Beauregard's army."

interior lines were strong, and their extent was unknown. Butler, after spending two days in examination and concentrating his force, determined to attack on the morning of the 16th.

But, in the mean while, Beauregard, with all the force which he could gather, had reached the scene. What with the former garrison of Richmond of some 7000 men, and these additions, there were there some 20,000 men. Beauregard, who had studied the position from the lines at Fort Darling, conceived a bold plan for the destruction of Butler. He proposed that 15,000 men from Lee's army should be brought by rail and temporarily added to his command; with these he would overwhelm Butler's army, which lay weakly stretched over a considerable space, and then, with the whole of his victorious force, march northward. Lee was to fall back toward Richmond, Grant, of course, following. Beauregard would then fall upon Grant's left flank when on the march, while Lee, turning, should assail him in front. But Davis, who kept in his own hands the direction of all military matters, saving that he rarely interfered with Lee's operations, refused his consent, and ordered Beauregard to attack with what force he had.

The evening of the 15th was somewhat overcast, but not dark, for the moon was up. There were no indications of any movement among the Confederates. About midnight a fog arose from the river so dense that nothing could be seen at a distance of ten yards. Under this dense pall Beauregard quietly assembled his whole force, and before dawn burst upon the sleeping Federal camps. Butler, not dreaming that he would be assailed, had made the worst possible disposition of his force to resist an attack. His front was widely extended, and his right was a mile and a half from the river. Through this gap, only watched by a few cavalry, Beauregard proposed to strike this flank, cutting it off from Bermuda Hundred: this was the main assault, to be conducted by Ransom. The left was to be more lightly assaulted by Hoke, while Colquitt, held in reserve, was to act as occasion should require. But the dense fog interfered with these plans. Ransom, after gaining some ground against Smith, suffered heavy loss, and his division fell into disorder, and even with the aid of Colquitt could hardly hold its own; Gillmore, on the left, pressed severely upon Hoke; Whiting, who, with 4000 men, was to have come up from Petersburg and fall upon Butler's rear, did not make his appearance. When the fog fairly cleared away it seemed as though Beauregard had utterly failed. His elaborate plan of assault had wholly miscarried, and there was nothing to replace it. But Smith, though he had foiled every effort against him, was apprehensive that he would be cut off by a turning movement from Bermuda Hundred, and fell back a little; Gillmore, instead of swinging around and taking Beauregard in reverse, fell back to the same line with Smith; and then Butler ordered a general retreat.

Beauregard began to follow, but a heavy rain came up, and he could do no more than open a distant artillery fire upon the retreating columns. And so, as night fell, Butler found himself unassailed behind his intrenchments. A more insignificant action, save for the loss which it involved, was never fought. Beauregard took 1400 prisoners. Apart from these, the Union loss was about 2500; that of the Confederates, in killed and wounded, somewhat greater; but they lost no prisoners. Butler now began to set about strengthening his intrenchments across the narrow neck of the peninsula to keep the Confederates out. Beauregard threw up parallel works, to keep

BATTERY ON THE NORTH ANNA.

CROSSING THE NY.

the Federals in. Either line could be held against double the force that could be brought against it. Butler found himself, as he phrased it, securely "bottled up"[1] at Bermuda Hundred. And thus it happened that Beauregard was enabled to send a large part of his force to the aid of Lee; but Grant was also able, as soon as he saw fit, to draw still larger re-enforcements from the Army of the James.

> [1] This phrase of Butler's, repeated by Grant, who also speaks of Butler's being "hermetically sealed up," has really very little pertinence. Butler could not, indeed, get out toward Richmond; but he could at any time move his army down the James, as he had come, or cross the Appomattox toward Petersburg, or cross the James, having pontoons for these purposes. All three of these movements were actually made at different times without opposition, or, indeed, the possibility of any by the enemy. Grant, in fact, was as much "bottled up" at Spottsylvania and on the North Anna as was Butler at Bermuda Hundred. Neither could march straight upon Richmond, but either could move in any other direction.

COLD HARBOR.

Grant's turning movement from the North Anna brought him, by a wide detour, to the Pamunkey River, formed by the junction of the North and South Anna, and this, uniting with the Mattapony, forms the York. At the head of this was the White House, where Grant's base of supplies was to be established. Hitherto his great army had to be supplied from an ever-shifting base by wagons, over narrow roads through a densely wooded country. Now they could be brought by water close to his lines, wherever they should be posted. The Pamunkey was crossed, after several sharp skirmishes, on the 28th of May, and after three days Lee was found in his new position. The Union losses at the North Anna, and in the actions from the 21st

CROSSING THE NORTH ANNA.

HANOVER FERRY—CROSSING THE PAMUNKEY.

to the 31st, were 1607, of whom 327 were prisoners. The loss of the Confederates was much greater.

From the North Anna Lee had fallen back in a straight line, and assumed a position still covering Richmond. The two armies were now verging toward the scene where they had contended two years before. Since then, in anticipation of what was soon to happen, the ground had been thoroughly surveyed by the Confederates, lines of intrenchments and barricades laid out and partly constructed. The lines covered the upper fords and bridges of the Chickahominy. As finally developed, they formed a curve, the convex side turned toward the quarter from which Grant was advancing. The southern extremity, which was as yet only slightly held, was as far southward as Cold Harbor, a mere point where converge several roads from the fords of the Chickahominy to the Pamunkey and York. Here, in a quite isolated position, was a body of Confederate horse and foot, posted behind some slight breastworks. Torbert's and Custer's cavalry had scouted in this direction, and these generals had formed a plan to seize this point by a sudden dash. Sheridan, coming down, agreed to this. The attack was made on the 21st, and the place carried. Sheridan notified Meade of this, but said that he could not retain it, for the enemy was hard by in considerable force. He was directed to hold it at all hazards until relieved by infantry. Grant had some days before embarked two thirds of the Army of the James from Bermuda Hundred, and ordered them to join the Army of the Potomac; they were now on the march, but still some miles distant. On the morning of June 1st the enemy made efforts to drive out Sheridan; they were twice repulsed with severe loss. Meanwhile Wright's Sixth corps was sent by Grant, and Longstreet's corps by Lee, marching by roads almost parallel, to the point. Wright came up at 10 o'clock, arriving first, Longstreet halting behind intrenchments in a thick wood hard by. Smith came up soon after, and the two corps made an attack upon the Confederate position. An advanced line of rifle trenches was carried, and six hundred prisoners taken. But the second line was too strong to be forced. But the possession of Cold Harbor had been secured, though at a cost of two thousand men. Hancock's corps was now brought down and posted on the right of Wright's.

Grant had proposed to cross the Chickahominy here, having thus swung two thirds of his army around the Confederate left. Lee, anticipating this, moved Hill and Ewell in the same direction, so that now, on the 2d of June, he occupied almost the position which Fitz John Porter had occupied two years before, while Grant held that from which Lee and Jackson had advanced. The fords were then covered by Lee, as they had before been by Porter, and to cross without a battle was clearly impossible. These movements had not been effected without collision. Lee sallied out upon Burnside's corps, which was moving to take post behind Warren, who was to hold the extreme right. His skirmish line was driven through a swamp, and some hundreds of prisoners taken. But the movement had no real significance.

The Confederate position, as finally assumed, was exceedingly strong; breastworks had been thrown up, which could only be reached by passing through thickets and swamps. These thickets and swamps had, indeed, opposed Lee's advance two years before; but the breastworks and intrenchments had been wanting, for officers of that day were opposed to field-works. "It made men timid," they said. Had there been in Porter's army axes with which to have felled a few trees in his front, it is believed, by those who took part in his battle, that Lee would have suffered a disastrous repulse, and the whole issue of the seven days have been changed. Porter had that morning called for re-enforcements and axes, but the messenger, being somewhat deaf, heard only half of his order, and so the axes never came. Both armies had now grown wiser; they had learned that even a slight intrenchment will stop three fourths of the bullets which would otherwise have borne wounds or death, while an abatis that will detain an attacking force under direct fire for fifteen minutes, with the present improvements in fire-arms, more than doubles the defensive power of its defend-

COLD HARBOR.

ers. There is, indeed, hardly an instance in our war in which a line of works stoutly defended by half the assailing force has been carried.

Still, things had now come to such a pass that it seemed necessary to Grant to drive the enemy from his position. There was no longer room for any turning movement which should do more than cause Lee to retire within the defenses of Richmond, and then the campaign would resolve itself into a long siege of that city. It was his last chance to hammer against Lee in the field, and a blow sufficiently weighty might shatter to fragments the Confederate army. So he resolved to assault the enemy in his lines. If he could be forced from these he would be thrown back upon the Chickahominy, or at least be driven pell-mell up its bank, pressed in the rear by the victorious columns, while Sheridan's 10,000 horsemen, flushed by a long series of success, would assail his flank, and throw themselves in his front. The catastrophe which began at Five Forks, and ended at Appomattox Court-house, would have been antedated by ten weary months. If numbers could avail against position, Grant had good reason to hope for success. Now that he had been joined by Smith's corps, he had fully 150,000 men, while Lee had barely a third as many.

The 2d of June was spent in getting the troops into position for the battle. Hancock's corps was placed on the left, next Wright's, then Smith's, closely massed opposite the Confederate right. Then came Warren's, stretched in a long thin line, continued by Burnside's, with his right flung back. The plan of attack was simple. Hancock, Wright, and Smith, at daybreak, were to make a simultaneous assault upon the lines in their front.

In the gray dawn, under a drizzling rain, these corps, already formed into line, sprang forward from their rude parapets—for now neither army rested for a moment in front of the enemy without intrenching themselves as best they might, using, in default of better implements, the tin cups slung by their haversacks. Barlow's division, formed into two lines, was the left of Hancock's corps. The first line in a few minutes came upon a sunken road in front of the Confederate intrenchments, strongly held. This was cleared with a rush, the defenders flying to their works, the assailants hard on their heels, capturing, indeed, some hundreds of prisoners; but a solid mass of lead and flame was poured into the advancing line; for a few minutes—not fifteen, it is said, they held their ground—the second line fortunately, perhaps, lingering a little behind. It was the tragedy of Fredericksburg and Gettysburg re-enacted. The division, leaving a third of its numbers behind, recoiled, but not in rout, and only some twoscore yards, where a slight swell of ground sheltered them from the fierce fire. Gibbon's division, which had won the honors on the last day of Gettysburg, supported by Birney's, dashed on simultaneously. The story of their charge reads like that of Pickett against Cemetery Hill. They had to pass a swamp; skirting this on either side, they swept clear up to the very works, breasting the torrent of musketry. Some even mounted the parapets, crowning them with their colors. But it was all in vain; they could not pass the intrenchments, but clung to them for a space. Wright and Smith assaulted with equal and equally unavailing valor, though the contest was of longer endurance. But in an hour the contest was over. It had been virtually decided by the repulse of Barlow. Warren's division was not expected to do more than hold in check the force in its front; but Burnside, his left pivoting upon Warren's right, was to swing round and strike the Confederate left flank. The movement was made, but not till the main action had been decided. The Confederate outposts were driven in, and a little before noon Burnside was in position to make an assault upon the Confederate left. He was directed to attack at one o'clock. But just before that hour the order was countermanded, Meade judging that the failure on the right had rendered it useless. The skirmish line was drawn in, and the corps began to intrench itself in its position. The enemy made a rather feeble sortie upon this point, but was repulsed. With this closed the battle of Cold Harbor.[1] Grant's blow had utterly failed. His loss had been severe—not less than 7000, mostly in less than half an hour. That of the Confederates was far less—probably not half as many.[2]

The result of the battle of Cold Harbor decided conclusively that the campaign was to take the shape of a siege of Richmond. However Grant might manœuvre, the result would be that Lee would fall back to the lines so elaborately fortified. Two courses lay open to the Union commander. He might move around Lee's left, and invest the city upon the north; or around his right, crossing the James River, and invest it from the south. Both plans had been considered by Grant in case he should fail, as he had done, to crush the enemy in the field. Then the former seemed most feasible; but, now that the Army of the James could not co-operate in it, he determined upon the latter, meanwhile sending Sheridan's cavalry to endeavor to cut the railway connections between Richmond and the Shenandoah Valley and Lynchburg, one of the main avenues of supply for the capital and the great army soon to hold it. Meanwhile, for a few days, the army was left essentially in its position, now intrenched, facing the Confederate intrenchments upon the Chickahominy. The lines lay so close together that the sharp-shooters on either side were able to pick off many men when

[1] Swinton (Army of the Potomac, 487) says, "Some hours after the failure of the first assault, General Meade sent instructions to each corps commander to renew the attack without reference to the troops on his right or left. The order was issued through these officers to their subordinate commanders, and from them descended through the wonted channels; but no man stirred, and the immobile lines pronounced a verdict silent, yet emphatic, against farther slaughter." This statement is accepted by subsequent writers; but it is so utterly at variance with the whole conduct of the army, before and after, that I do not admit it into the text, even upon the authority of Mr. Swinton, whose statements of facts I rarely find occasion to question.

[2] "The loss on the Union side," says Mr. Swinton, p. 487, "in this sanguinary action was over 13,000, while on the part of the Confederates it is doubtful whether it reached as many hundreds." This is a singular lapsus of the author, for the very tables which he cites as authority give the entire loss, killed, wounded, and missing, during the ten days from June 1 to 10, at 13,153. Nearly every day during this period was marked by severe fighting.

MAP SHOWING OPERATIONS IN VIRGINIA, MAY, 1864—APRIL, 1865.

they showed themselves in the trenches. For ten days the army remained nearly in the same position, only gradually extending its lines to the south, and approaching the Chickahominy, covering itself with intrenchments as it moved. Lee, presuming that the purpose of Grant was to effect a crossing at Bottom's Bridge, made correspondent movements, extending his right farther and farther down the stream, likewise intrenching at every step, so that the whole arid plain was dug over until it resembled an immense prairie-dog town. General officers had their tents pitched in deep excavations fronted by high embankments. Pickets and outposts excavated burrows, in which they lay unsheltered under the fierce sun. High breastworks were thrown up, and deep trenches dug at every conceivable angle, under shelter of which the men passed to and fro, from front to rear, without being observed. The intricate system of mounds and trenches, which still scar the plain upon the north bank of the Chickahominy, were the work of these days. The Confederates made several sallies upon portions of the line, but were invariably repulsed, and after the third day ceased from formal offensive operations; yet the lines were within rifle range, and a continual fire of sharp-shooters was kept up. Not an hour passed without its quota of dead and wounded. This was interrupted only for two hours on the 7th, when a truce was entered into for removing the wounded and burying the dead.

Grant, while making preparations to transfer his army to the south bank of the James, still hoped that the enemy would make some movement which would give a favorable opportunity for a renewed attack. But Lee remained immovable in his intrenchments, which the experience of Cold Harbor had shown to be inexpugnable. On the evening of the 12th the movement for the passage of the James began. Warren, preceded by Wilson's cavalry, marched six miles down to the Long Bridge over the Chickahominy, where he crossed, masking the movements of the other corps. Hancock followed, and then, taking the advance, marched down to the James, which it struck a little below the point where McClellan had lain after the battle of Malvern Hill. Wright and Burnside moved by an exterior and longer route, crossing the Chickahominy at Jones's Bridge, six miles below the Long Bridge. The trains, making a wide detour to the south, crossed at a ferry twelve miles below. The columns moved rapidly over the sandy road, hardly stopping for a moment until the night of the 13th, when the wearied troops bivouacked upon the high lands from which they could behold the James lying broad before them, bordered by fields now ripening for the harvest. Smith's corps had in the mean while marched to the White House, whence, embarking on transports, it sailed down the York and up the James, rejoining Butler at Bermuda Hundred on the 14th, while the Army of the Potomac was crossing the James fifteen miles below.

Lee, of course, could not be for many hours ignorant of the general movement, but he was in no position to offer any resistance. He had already extended his line so far that it was as weak as he dared make it. He evidently supposed that it was Grant's purpose to march toward Richmond by the north bank of the James instead of crossing and transferring operations to the south bank. Warren, indeed, was so posted for two days near White Oak Swamp as to give color to this supposition. Lee, therefore, hastily abandoned his position, and, crossing the Chickahominy, fell back to Richmond.

The cavalry under Sheridan, 10,000 strong, had in the mean while been active. No sooner had Grant taken his position near Spottsylvania, than, on the 9th of May, Sheridan was sent toward Richmond to operate upon the enemy's lines of communication. The design was masked by a movement eastward toward Fredericksburg, which drew Stuart's Confederate cavalry in that direction. Sheridan, then turning sharply southward, struck straight for the railroad between Lee's army and Richmond. Stuart followed for a space, and ineffectually assailed Sheridan's rear. Then, imagining that Richmond was the aim of the enemy, he urged his horsemen to their utmost speed, and gained Sheridan's front, placing himself between him and Richmond. Sheridan meanwhile moved leisurely, destroying the railroad as he advanced. At Ashland Station he fell upon Lee's provision trains, which had been brought down from Orange Court-house, and destroyed a million and a half of rations, and most of the medical stores. On the 11th a sharp encounter took place between the opposing cavalry forces at Yellow Stone Tavern, a few miles north of Richmond; the Confederates were repulsed, and in the mêlée, Stuart, their ablest cavalry leader, was mortally wounded. The loss was irreparable. The Union cavalry had by this time been raised to a higher state of efficiency than that of the enemy, and, now that their ablest commander was gone, the disparity became marked. From this time forth the Union cavalry always went into action with the prestige of success. Pursuing his advantage, Sheridan crossed the Chickahominy, passed the exterior line of the defenses of Richmond, but, reaching the inner line, he found it unassailable by a cavalry force. Turning back, he crossed the Chickahominy at Meadow Bridge, skirted down its northern bank, and recrossed at a lower passage. He had been misinformed by negroes, who told him that Butler had taken up a position on the north side of the James. Then, after communicating with Butler on the James, he again recrossed the Chickahominy, made a wide detour across the Peninsula, and at length, on the 25th of May, rejoined the Army of the Potomac, and aided in its forcing the passage of the Pamunkey, and in the earlier operations at Cold Harbor.

Hunter was now supposed to be moving down the Valley of the Shenandoah toward Lynchburg, and on the 7th of June, Sheridan, with two of his three divisions, was sent in that direction to join him, and, after breaking up the Virginia Central Railroad, to unite with Hunter, when both were to join the Army of the Potomac. Sheridan did some damage to the road, and had several sharp encounters with the Confederate cavalry, the severest being on the 12th of June, at Trevillian Station, where each side lost wellnigh a thousand men, of whom a third were prisoners. Sheridan here found that Hunter, instead of coming by way of Charlottesville, as was supposed, had turned off westward toward Lexington, and, moreover, Lee had dispatched a large force toward Lynchburg, which lay right in his way. The ammunition which he had brought with him was nearly expended; his horses were fast becoming exhausted, for the region was destitute of forage. He turned eastward, passed over the battle-field of Spottsylvania, thence down the Pamunkey to the White House. The Confederate cavalry were just then about to attack the dépôt, which had not been wholly withdrawn. Sheridan drove them off after a sharp conflict, and then, crossing the James, on the 25th of June rejoined the Army of the Potomac. In these two raids he had lost 5000 men, but had inflicted a loss quite as great.

During the thirty-seven days from the Battle of the Wilderness, May 5, to the close of the fighting on the Chickahominy, Grant had lost 54,551, of whom 7289 were killed, 37,406 wounded, 9856 missing. Of the killed, 539 were officers, and 6750 privates; of the wounded, 1764 were officers, 35,642 privates; of the missing, 262 were officers, 9594 privates. This does not include the losses of the Army of the James at Bermuda Hundred. The Confederate losses, exclusive of those of Beauregard at Bermuda Hundred, were about 32,000, of whom about 8500 were prisoners, 4000 having been captured at Spottsylvania, and 2000 by Sheridan's cavalry.

CHAPTER XLIII.

THE INVESTMENT OF PETERSBURG.

Richmond to be besieged.—Prospects for its Defense.—Napoleon on the Defense of fortified Cities.—Forces of Lee and Grant.—Character of the Fortifications.—Butler's unsuccessful Attempt upon Petersburg.—Importance of Petersburg in relation to Richmond.—Smith ordered to assail Petersburg, June 15.—Delays and Misapprehensions.—The Attack suspended.—Renewed on the 16th.—The Confederates re-enforced by Beauregard.—The Confederates driven from their Lines.—Beauregard checks the Flight.—Withdraws to an inner Line, where he intrenches.—Butler advances from Bermuda Hundred, and is driven back.—Actions of June 17 and 18.—The Confederates hold their new Line.—Forces and Losses from May 5 to June 20.

EVENTS had now so shaped themselves that it was apparent that, instead of a conflict in the open field, the campaign was to resolve itself into a siege of Richmond, held by the entire Army of Northern Virginia, with such re-enforcements as could be gathered from the Carolinas and Georgia. The Confederate authorities had good right to believe, upon the soundest military reasons, that, provided they could supply their army, Richmond could hold out against any besieging force. "Empires," said Napoleon, "frequently stand in need of soldiers, but men are never wanting for internal defense if a place be provided where their energies can be brought into action. Fifty thousand National Guards, with three thousand gunners, will defend a fortified capital against an army of three hundred thousand men. The same fifty thousand men in the open field, if they are not experienced soldiers, commanded by skilled officers, will be thrown into confusion by the charge of a few thousand horse." When Lee fell back within the lines of Richmond, he had about 70,000[1] men, nearly half more than the great master of war pronounced sufficient to hold a fortified capital against 300,000; Grant had, including the Army of the James, about 150,000, half the number which Napoleon judged could be foiled by 50,000. The fortifications, indeed, bore little resemblance to the formidable works constituting the defenses of the fortified cities of Europe, which Napoleon had probably in mind. They consisted of redoubts of low profile, with ditches, parapets, and abatis, and forts at all salient points from which the lines could be swept by artillery. But Todtleben had demonstrated at Sebastopol, and Lee was to demonstrate at Petersburg, that the defensive power of such works, resolutely held by an adequate force, is fully equal to the elaborate masonry of Vauban and Cohorn. Indeed, with modern artillery, of which Napoleon never dreamed, it is doubtful whether any system of fortifications of extent sufficient to protect a great capital can be constructed on any other plan. At all events, Lee's works were never pierced until, constrained by the menaces upon his lines of supply, he virtually abandoned them.

Strangely enough, the vital importance of Petersburg seems not to have been at all appreciated on either side. While McClellan lay at Harrison's Landing, some works had been commenced on the northern and eastern sides, but upon his retreat nothing farther was done. Again, a year later, about the time of the battle of Chancellorsville, when an advance from Suffolk was threatened by Peck, a trench, not unlike the first parallel of a siege, had been dug upon the south; but there were then no works over which even cavalry could not pass. There was now here scarcely the semblance of a garrison. Butler could easily have taken it from the east at any time up to three days before he settled himself at Bermuda Hundred. On the 10th of May he made such an attempt. He had—Smith being yet with Grant—barely 7000 men in the "bottle," which was tightly enough corked at the mouth, but had no bottom. Gillmore, with 3500 men, was sent across

[1] The Confederate muster-roll of the Army of Northern Virginia, on the 30th of June, showed 51,833 "present for duty." In the Department of Richmond, that is, the proper garrison of the city, now commanded by Ewell, who had for some time been disabled from acting in the field, were 6176. In the Department of South Virginia and North Carolina, under Beauregard, were 12,592 at Richmond and Petersburg. It will be borne in mind that Lee was at this time merely commander of the Army of Northern Virginia, Davis, with Bragg for his "military adviser," keeping in his own hands the direction of all the other forces. Some months later, Lee having been appointed general-in-chief of all the armies, all of the troops at Richmond excepting the garrison proper, which was still a separate organization, was consolidated into the Army of Northern Virginia. In November this numbered 69,290 "present for duty," about 20,000 more being returned as "present," the aggregate "present and absent" being 181,826.

PETERSBURG.

the Appomattox to attack from the north, while Kautz, with 1500 cavalry, was to dash in from the south. Gillmore advanced to within two miles of the city, driving the enemy's skirmishers before him until he came to their works. These, though feeble and feebly manned, he thought yet too strong to be assailed by his small force; so he retreated. Kautz, meanwhile, had rode straight over the ditch on the south, and penetrated the town; but the retreat of Gillmore permitted the enemy to return, and Kautz was easily forced back. The whole assailing force was too weak to effect any thing unless by sheer surprise; and even if it had succeeded, they could not have held Petersburg, and Butler could spare no more to re-enforce them.

Grant now went in person to Bermuda Hundred, and saw at a glance the vital importance of Petersburg, and the ease with which it could be taken by an adequate force, provided only the attempt were made in time. Hence it was that he directed Smith's corps to be sent by water so as to reach the scene at the earliest moment, before, it was hoped, it could be re-enforced from Richmond.

Petersburg was a quiet town of 18,000 inhabitants, on the southern bank of the Appomattox. In itself it was of little consequence to either army. Its military importance arose solely from its relations to the system of railroads which connected Richmond with the region from which its supplies were almost wholly to be drawn. Had the Confederate capital been provisioned for a siege, Petersburg might safely have been abandoned. But at no time were full rations for a fortnight in advance ever accumulated—oftener there was not three days' supply in dépôt. Northward from Richmond runs the Virginia Central Railroad, which, crossing the Orange Road at Gordonsville, penetrates the fertile region known by way of eminence as "The Valley," the granary of Virginia. The Orange Road, running southwestward through Lynchburg, merges into the Virginia and Tennessee Railroad, which, with its connections, penetrates into the extreme southwest. It is the great artery of communication between the Atlantic and the Mississippi. From Lynchburg, following the windings of the James, is the James River Canal. This place, therefore, became one of the natural dépôts of the Confederacy. Next, starting from Richmond, and running southwestward, is the Danville Road, passing through North Carolina, and uniting with all the railways branching through the Carolinas and Georgia. Next, running south, is the railway to Petersburg. From Petersburg, running southward to Lynchburg, where it connects with the Tennessee Road, is the Southside Railroad. Then, running south to Wilmington, where it joins with the southern system, is the Weldon Railroad. Now the occupation of Petersburg by the Federals would not only give them the control of the Weldon and Southside Roads, but would place them in a position to strike the Danville Road at any point south of Richmond. The possession of Petersburg would insure the capture of Richmond by giving to the assailants the absolute control of the Weldon and Southside, and rendering almost certain that of the Danville railways; two certainly, and almost inevitably a third, of the five avenues of supply for the Confederate army. Moreover, Grant hoped, by means of his cavalry, and Hunter's expedition, to destroy the Central Road and the James River Canal. But, even should these latter

fail, the Danville and Central roads and the canal would be inadequate to transport supplies to the army of the capital.

Smith's corps reached Bermuda Hundred on the 14th of June, crossed the Appomattox that night, and next day were pushed forward toward Petersburg, seven miles distant. By noon, having been somewhat delayed by carrying an advanced line of rifle trenches covered with a light battery, he came upon the works, two and a half miles from the town.[1] These works were not strong, and were only feebly held. In and around Petersburg, apart from a few militia, there were but two infantry and two cavalry regiments.[2] There was, however, a considerable quantity of artillery, which was briskly served, and it was assumed that there must be a strong infantry support. Smith wore away the whole afternoon in reconnoitring and making his dispositions, and then, at sundown, instead of attacking in force, threw forward a heavy line of skirmishers. Even these were successful, and the feebly-manned lines were fairly carried at every point where they were assailed, fifteen guns and three hundred prisoners being taken. Hancock, with two divisions of his corps, now came up. He had been marching since ten o'clock, but, owing to an incorrect map, in a direction quite different from that which was intended. By some strange misadventure, also, he had not even been notified that he was to assist Smith in an attack upon Petersburg; this notice only reached him between five and six o'clock. He reached Smith's position just as the attack had been suspended. Waiving his superior rank to Smith, whom he naturally supposed must be the best judge of what should be done, he placed his troops at the disposal of that officer. Smith, instead of taking these troops and pushing straight into Petersburg, merely requested Hancock to occupy a part of the captured works.[3]

Grant came on the ground next morning. Burnside's corps was advancing, and, to give them time to aid, the attack was postponed until six in the afternoon. Another unaccountable delay;[4] for, although some slight re-en-

[1] Grant says in his Report that Smith "confronted the enemy's pickets near Petersburg before daylight." He seems to have fallen into an error as to time, for the march from the Appomattox did not begin until after daylight. He had ordered Butler to send Smith forward the night before, and probably assumed that he had marched straight on; Grant himself returned to the Army of the Potomac to hurry it on, division by division, as rapidly as possible, assuring Butler that "we could re-enforce our armies more rapidly than the enemy could bring troops against us." But this discrepancy as to time is of no real importance. There was, even after noon, as will be seen, abundant time to have assailed Petersburg with a force fourfold the number by which it was that day defended.

[2] For the details of the actions of this and the ensuing days on the Confederate side, I am indebted to Fletcher's *History of the American War.* The author, a colonel in the British service, derived his information mainly from General Beauregard, and officers of his staff.

[3] Grant's Report, and Hancock's, the latter as yet unpublished, but quoted in Swinton, *Army of the Potomac*, 502, 503.

[4] To whom this delay is to be attributed is not clear. Swinton says (p. 508, 509) that "Hancock, to whom, in the absence of Grant and Meade, the command of the field fell, was fully alive to the importance of securing all the commanding ground before heavy Confederate re-enforcements should arrive," and had the night before instructed Birney and Gibbon to attack and take all these positions before daylight, and that these instructions were not complied with. For authority he refers to, but does not quote, Hancock's Report. He also states that "Hancock was admonished by General Meade to refrain from attack until the remaining corps of the army, the Fifth and the Ninth, should arrive. Of these, the Ninth reached the front at noon, and an assault was ordered to be made about 4 P.M. by Hancock and Burnside—Smith to demonstrate merely." Grant places the time of the attack at six o'clock. From a comparison with Fletcher (p. 261), I judge the attack must have been made not later than four. Grant seems to imply that

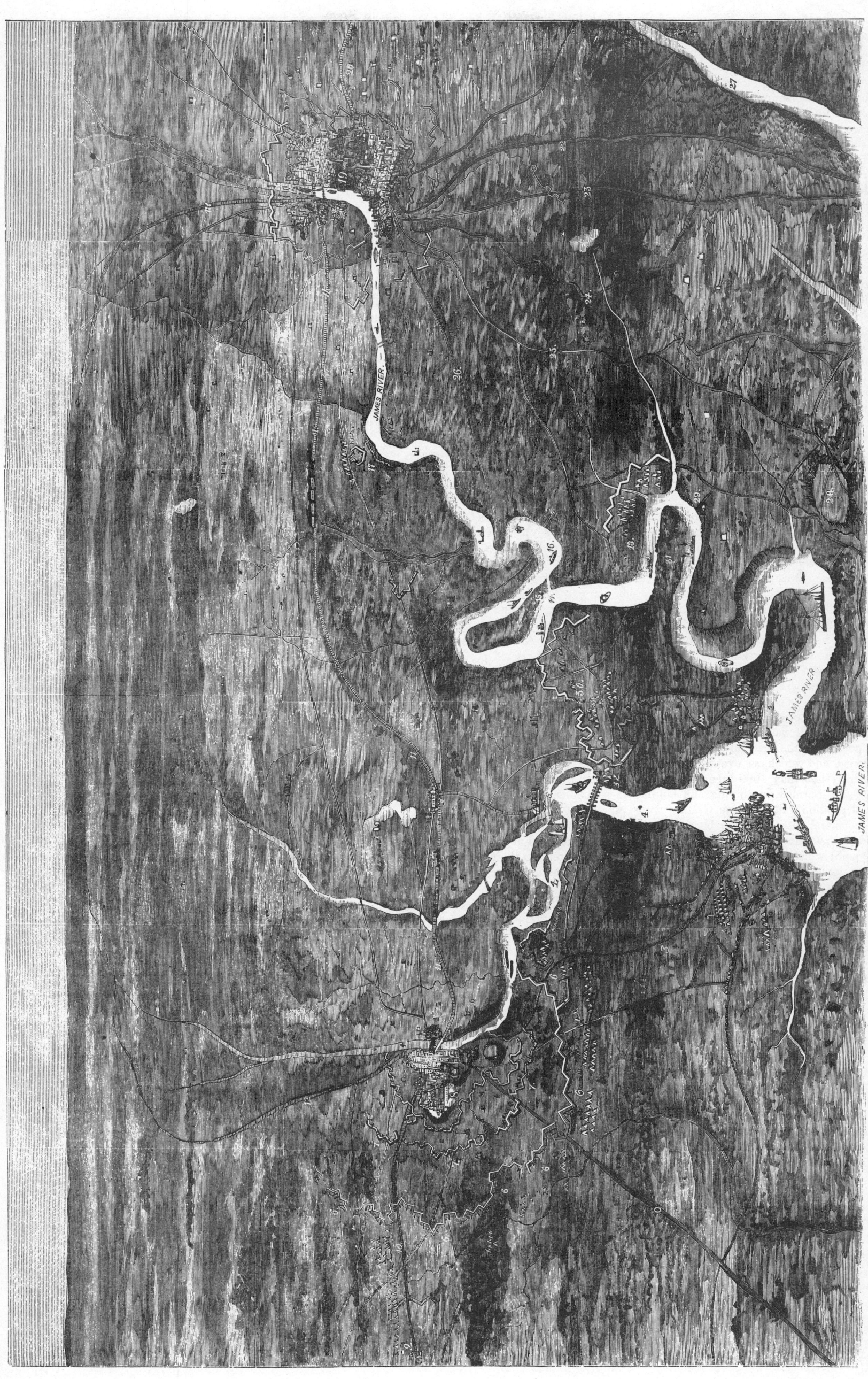

ISOMETRIC VIEW OF THE VIRGINIA CAMPAIGN [LOOKING WESTWARD].

1. City Point.—2. Bermuda Hundred.—3. City Point Railroad.—4, 4. Appomattox River.—5. Port Walthal.—6, 6, 6, 6, 6. Union lines.—7, 7, 7. Confederate lines.—8. Petersburg.—9. Reams Station.—10. Weldon Railroad.—11, 11, 11, 11. Richmond and Petersburg Railroad.—12. Southside Railroad.—13. Deep Bottom.—14. Canal at Dutch Gap.—15. Farrar's Island.—16. Confederate Gun-boats above this point.—17. Fort Darling.—18. Danville Railroad.—19. Richmond.—20. Richmond and Fredericksburg Railroad.—22, 23, 24, 25, 26. Roads leading out of Richmond.—27. The Chickahominy.—28. Malvern Hill.—30. Butler's lines.—31. Jones's Neck.—O. Norfolk Railroad.

forcements had arrived, the Federals were in overwhelming force, and had full possession of all the defensive works. Beauregard had hastened down from Richmond. By withdrawing every thing from the intrenchments at Bermuda Hundred, he had gathered 8000 men at Petersburg. In vain he telegraphed to Richmond for re-enforcements, or at least for orders. Should he abandon Petersburg or Bermuda Hundred? he could not hold both. He received neither help or orders; so, acting on his own responsibility, he evacuated the intrenchments at Bermuda Hundred, leaving only a few sentries—took the cork out of the broken bottle—and during the day concentrated his command before Petersburg. The attack on the afternoon of the 16th was made with great vigor. The Confederates held their ground stoutly, but at length began to give way. Late in the day Beauregard had left the front to snatch a hasty meal. All at once a horseman, galloping at full speed, dashed through the streets, announcing that all was lost; the enemy had broken through the defenses, and were now entering the city. Beauregard, ordering the man to be arrested and shot if his report should prove false, mounted and galloped to the front. He soon met crowds of fugitives, unarmed, hatless, panic-stricken, swarming along all the roads. In vain he essayed to check the wild rout. The fugitives poured onward, and the day seemed hopelessly lost. Just then Gracie's single brigade from Bermuda Hundred came on. Beauregard formed these and his escort across the road, with orders to shoot down every man who refused to come into line. At length order was restored; the Confederates regained their abandoned line, from which, indeed, they had not been pursued. The fighting was by no means over, but continued long after dark. It died away by midnight, and under cover of the thrice-welcome darkness Beauregard withdrew his weary troops to an inner and shorter line, which he had chosen with the quick eye of an engineer. This line was as yet wholly unfortified, and must be intrenched in the brief hours before morning should most likely renew the conflict. With bayonets, split canteens, and hands—for they had no intrenching tools—the men dug in the darkness and through the hours of the early morning. By noon of the 17th the intrenchments had assumed a defensive character, and, moreover, their defenders had been largely re-enforced. These intrenchments, so hastily flung up, were the beginning of those great works which for so long a time held in check the Union army before Petersburg.[1]

Butler meanwhile, perceiving that the lines in his front were abandoned, moved out a force upon the railroad from Petersburg to Richmond. But he had hardly touched it when he was forced back by a heavy column coming down from Richmond; for Lee, fully alive to the necessity of holding Petersburg, had sent Longstreet's corps, now commanded by Anderson, to the aid of the sorely-pressed Beauregard. Butler returned to his old position. Anderson, leaving as he passed a force to hold the lines from which Gracie had been withdrawn, hurried on his remaining troops to the defense of Petersburg.

The morning of the 17th had begun to wear away before the fighting was renewed. It was fierce but undecisive. The contest was mainly for some portion of the original Confederate line, which had not as yet been abandoned, and which, as events proved, was of great value. At heavy cost, hardly less than 4000 men, Hancock and Burnside, upon whom the brunt fell, succeeded in winning and holding these points. "The advantages of position gained," says Grant, "were very great." Next day, the 18th, a general assault was to be made early in the morning; but when the skirmishers moved forward it was found that the enemy had abandoned every point which was to be assailed, and had firmly taken up their new and interior position, from which, says Grant, "they could not be dislodged."

These attempts upon Petersburg, lasting four days, had cost fully 9000 men.[2] The result was, as expressed by Grant, that while "the advantages of position gained by us were very great, yet the enemy were merely forced into an interior position from which he could not be dislodged," and, consequently, "the army proceeded to envelop Petersburg, as far as possible without attacking fortifications."

Petersburg, which on the 10th of June had been an easy prey, which, in effect, was already taken by Smith, who needed only to have pushed on to have marched straight into the town, defended by only a mere handful of men, was now garrisoned by almost the whole of the Confederate army. Two days of heavy fighting, in which Grant employed fully three fourths of his army, had demonstrated, at a cost of wellnigh 10,000 men, that Beauregard's intrenchments, hastily flung up, but growing stronger hour by hour, could not be taken by assault, and that nothing now remained but to lay regular siege to them. The siege of Petersburg, upon which was soon concentrated the interest of the war in the East, fairly began on the 19th of June.

NOTE ON FORCES AND LOSSES FROM MAY 5 TO JUNE 20.

The numbers of the Confederate Army of Northern Virginia during the whole of this campaign, down to its final close in April, 1865, have been studiously and persistently understated. The Confederate authorities after 1862 never made public their force or losses. Pollard, the only formal historian upon the Confederate side, had no accurate means of information. Writing after the close of the war, he had every motive to understate. He says:

"The Confederate Army on the Rapidan, at the beginning of the campaign, consisted of two divisions of Longstreet's corps, Ewell's corps, A. P. Hill's corps, three divisions of cavalry, and the artillery. Ewell's corps did not exceed 14,000 muskets at the beginning of the campaign. On the 8th of May the effective strength of Hill's corps was less than 13,000 muskets, and it could not have exceeded 18,000 in the beginning of the month. Longstreet's corps was the weakest of the three when all the divisions were present, and the two with him had just returned from an arduous and exhausting winter campaign in East Tennessee. His effective strength could not have exceeded 8000 muskets. General Lee's whole effective infantry, therefore, did not exceed 40,000 muskets, if it reached that number. The cavalry divisions were weak, neither of them exceeding the strength of a good brigade. General Lee's whole effective strength at the opening of the campaign was not over 50,000 men of all arms. There were no means of recruiting the ranks of the army, and no re-enforcements were received until the 23d of May."

The captured Confederate returns (cited *ante*, p. 383, as far as relate to this army) enable us to fix the number far more accurately. On the 10th of April the returns of the Army of Northern Virginia show a nominal force of 97,576, of whom 61,218 were "present," and 52,626 "present for duty." The conscription was in operation, and was still rigorously enforced. During the preceding month Lee's army was augmented by 12,000, sent in from the various camps of instruction, and, according to their judicious system, incorporated at once into regiments already in the field. It is not at all probable that these accessions during the three weeks preceding the opening of the campaign could have been less than 10,000 or 15,000, which would raise Lee's strength at the beginning of May to between 60,000 and 70,000. This continual access went on all through the summer, quite compensating for the losses in action and from sickness. Thus, on the 30th of June, his army had present for duty 51,863—within eight hundred as many as on the 10th of April—while its nominal strength was 92,685, which includes those absent from all causes—sick, disabled, and deserters. This was after a series of sharp actions, including those of June 15 to 18, and those which, from June 23 to 28, hereafter to be described, resulting from the first attempts made upon the Weldon, Southside, and Danville Railroads. On the 10th of July the nominal force, present and absent, was 135,803, so that within ten days 43,000 were added to the muster-rolls of the army; but of these only 68,844 were present, and 57,097 present for duty, showing an actual increase of effective men only about 6000, to which should be added some small losses suffered in the interval. At the close of August the nominal strength was 146,838, of whom there were present for duty but 44,247. But at this time Early, with some 15,000 of this army, was on detached service in the Valley of the Shenandoah, and this body is not counted among those "present for duty" with the Army of Northern Virginia. Owing to a clerical error in copying the returns, this number, 44,247, is given in our table (p. 383) as the force for May instead of August. This is of some importance, as it vitiates an estimate by Mr. Swinton of Confederate losses, which will presently be referred to. The considerable apparent access to the Army of Northern Virginia after October is owing to the return of the remnants of Early's force, and the incorporation of the troops heretofore formally under Beauregard at Petersburg.

Of the losses of the Confederates during this period (May 5 to June 10) there is no report even approximating to an official character. The "impression" of General Lee's adjutant general (Swinton, 492) was that it was about 18,000. Mr. Swinton finds corroboration of this estimate in a comparison of figures. He says, in substance, that Lee opened the campaign with 52,626; that he received re-enforcements (7000 under Pickett and 2000 under Breckinridge) of 9000, making in all 61,626; that on the 31st of May he had 44,248; the difference showing a loss, up to the battle of Cold Harbor, of 17,478. To this he adds less than 1000 for Cold Harbor, making 18,000. He, however, is dubious as to the correctness of these figures, and estimates the entire loss at 20,000. This estimate is worthless, from the fact that each one of the elementary data upon which it is based is erroneous. The original force (52,626), as shown by the returns which he cites, was that of April 10 instead of May 5, during which interval it must have been considerably augmented. The re-enforcements are considerably understated. Pollard says that Breckinridge brought "2000 muskets with a battalion of artillery." Certainly not less than 3000, and probably more, for in April he had present for duty 6500, and after the defeat of Sigel at Newmarket there was no immediate necessity for retaining a man of these in the Valley. The re-enforcements brought from North Carolina were certainly more than 7000. They consisted, according to Pollard (*Lost Cause*, 505), of "Pickett's division of Longstreet's corps, and one small brigade of Early's division of Ewell's corps, which had been in North Carolina with Hoke"—Pickett being ill, and not then in actual command. Now we find that in February Pickett and Whiting had in North Carolina about 18,500; at the close of April Whiting had there about 5000; Hoke must then have brought to Richmond early in May some 12,000 or 15,000. They lost considerably in the action of May 16, which resulted in the shutting up of Butler at Bermuda Hundred; but the bulk of the command, which could hardly have been less than 10,000, were thereby at liberty to join Lee, which they did during the last week in May, simultaneously with the arrival of Breckinridge from the Valley. These conjoined re-enforcements must have been fully 15,000 instead of 9000, as stated. Finally, the number (44,247) given by Mr. Swinton as Lee's effective strength on the 31st of May should be put down as the number of the army of Northern Virginia on the 31st of August, when a quarter or more of its force was with Early in the Valley of the Shenandoah. I, as well as Mr. Swinton, was misled by a clerical error in copying these returns, whereby "May" appeared in place of "August," which error will be found in the table heretofore given.

All statements of the Confederate losses, whether based upon the impressions of officers, or upon assumed calculation of forces, being wholly unreliable, we are driven to a consideration of the character of the fighting for an approximate estimate of the loss. There can be no doubt that in the two days' battles in the Wilderness, and in the five days which followed (May 5 to 11), the Confederate loss was far less than the Federal. During these days the Federal loss, including wellnigh 7000 missing, was 29,410, of which 20,000—12,000 killed and wounded—were lost on the 5th and 6th; the Confederate loss was probably about 10,000, of whom not more than 1000 were prisoners. At Spottsylvania, previous to the great battle of the 12th, the Federal loss was about 10,000; that of the Confederates not more than 5000. In the battle of the 12th the Federals lost about 8000, and in the operations which followed up to the 20th about 2000, of whom not 300 were prisoners. The Confederate loss must have been quite equal, including the 3000 prisoners. At the North Anna, and in the turning operation which followed (May 21 to 31), the losses were about equal, not far from 2000 upon each side. At Cold Harbor, including the sharp engagement of June 1, the main action of June 3, and the subsequent skirmishing up to the 10th, the Federal loss was 13,000, of whom 2400 were captured. The Confederate loss during this time could hardly have exceeded 5000, including 2000 prisoners brought in by Sheridan from his cavalry raid. In the main assault on the 3d, where the Federals lost 8000 in less than an hour, the Confederates lost hardly 1000. On the 2d, when the Federals lost 2000, the Confederates suffered far less, probably not more than 1000, of whom 500 were prisoners. In the subsequent skirmishing and sharp-shooting from the 4th to the 10th, the losses were about equal. The entire Confederate loss from May 5 to June 10, thus approximately estimated, is 33,000. There is no statement of the Confederate losses in the actions before Petersburg from June 15 to 18, in which the Union loss in killed, wounded, and prisoners was 9665, there being 1600 prisoners. The Confederates, fighting mainly behind slight intrenchments, certainly suffered far less—probably not more than 5000, of whom about 1000 were prisoners.

The Union force at the opening of the campaign is officially given. The Army of the Potomac, including Burnside's corps, numbered, according to the Report of the Secretary of War, 141,164, of whom 10,000 were cavalry. While resting at Spottsylvania, re-enforcements were received from Washington fully equaling the losses which had been sustained. At Cold Harbor, the accession of Smith's command raised the Union force to fully 150,000; after the battles there, other re-enforcements arrived, so that when the crossing of the James was effected, Grant had still, including Butler's command, at least 140,000.

The losses in the Army of the Potomac during this period are accurately given. The following statement was furnished Mr. Coppée (*Grant and his Campaigns*, 399) by a member of Grant's staff, the report being subsequently officially indorsed. We place with it our approximate estimate of Confederate losses, merely attempting to discriminate between the killed and wounded and the prisoners. Meade, in his congratulatory address, issued May 13, claims 8000 prisoners—considerably in excess of the true numbers captured up to that time. The number actually reported from May 4 to 12 is 7000, of whom many were taken by Sheridan, of whom, at that time, Meade could know nothing. In the 2500 put down as taken at Cold Harbor are included the captures by the cavalry during the whole series of operations. With these explanations, we think that the summation in the following table gives very closely the respective losses during the period therein embraced.

LOSSES FROM MAY 5 TO JUNE 18.

Battles.	Union.				Confederate.		
	Killed.	Wounded.	Missing.	Total.	Killed and Wounded.	Missing.	Total.
Wilderness, May 5–11	3288	19,278	6,844	29,410	13,000	2,000	15,000
Spottsylvania, May 12–20...	2146	7,956	279	10,381	7,000	4,000	11,000
North Anna, May 21–31 ...	150	1,130	327	1,607	1,000	1,000	2,000
Cold Harbor, June 1–10 ...	1705	9,042	2,406	13,153	2,500	2,500	5,000
Petersburg, June 15–18	1198	6,853	2,217	9,665	4,000	1,000	5,000
	8487	44,259	12,073	64,216	27,500	10,500	38,000

he was on the ground, and that the delay for Burnside's arrival was by his order. His words are: "By the time I arrived next morning [the 16th] the enemy was in force. An attack was ordered to be made at six o'clock that evening by the troops under Smith and the Second and Ninth Corps. It required until that time for the Ninth Corps to get up and into position."

[1] Fletcher, p. 260–263.

[2] Losses from June 10 to 20: killed, 1198; wounded, 6853; missing, 1614—in all, 9665. Of these, all except a few hundred were during the days from the 15th to the 18th.

CHAPTER XLIV.

POLITICAL DEVELOPMENTS OF 1863.

The Reaction against the Administration in the Autumn of 1862.—The Elections show a Loss in the Republican Vote.—The President ahead of the People in his Emancipation Proclamation.—The need of decisive Military Victories.—The Elections in the Spring of 1863 show no better Result.—Meeting of the Second Regular Session of the Thirty-seventh Congress, December 1, 1862.—The President's Message.—His proposed Plan for compensated Emancipation.—The Arguments in its Favor.—It is not adopted by Congress.—The Change produced in the popular Sentiment by two Years of Civil War.—Repudiation of Compromise.—The political Problem made subservient to the Military.—The Tactics of the Opposition.—The Action of Congress in regard to Military Arrests.—The Case of Vallandigham.—He is arrested under Order No. 38 by General Burnside, May 4, 1863.—His Trial by a Military Commission.—His Application for a Writ of *Habeas Corpus* refused by Judge Leavitt.—The Sentence of Imprisonment commuted by the President, who orders Vallandigham to be transported beyond the Federal Lines, not to return during the War.—Vallandigham is nominated the Democratic Candidate for Governor of Ohio.—Indignation of the Democratic Party at his Arrest and Punishment.—Correspondence with President Lincoln.—The Conscription Act adopted by Congress.—Necessity and Justice of the Measure.—Its Constitutionality.—Debate upon its Passage.—The Features of the Bill.—Debate in the House on the Relation of the Insurgent States to the General Government.—Thaddeus Stevens states his Position.—Lovejoy repudiates Stevens's Theory of Subjugation.—Passage of the Bill to provide a National Currency.—Admission of West Virginia.—The Members from Louisiana admitted to the House.—Resolutions against Foreign Mediation.—Correspondence between Secretary Seward and M. Mercier.—Dissolution of the Thirty-seventh Congress, March 4, 1863.—The Political Situation in the following Summer.—The Efforts of the Opposition.—Fourth of July Speeches by Seymour and Pierce.—The New York Draft Riots; their Cause and Meaning.—The Influence of the Victories of Gettysburg and Vicksburg upon the National Politics.—The Autumn Elections.—Overwhelming Triumph of the Administration.

THE policy of the Federal and Confederate governments has already been followed in this history down to the close of the year 1862.[1] We purpose in this and the following chapter to continue the political history of the war down to the close of President Lincoln's administration. The United States government, while contending against the armies arrayed for its destruction, was from an early period of the contest embarrassed by a peculiar form of treason in the loyal states at the same time that it was also menaced by hostile intentions on the part of European powers.

The conflict with armed rebels was in itself sufficiently difficult, from its gigantic proportions, to overwhelm any other government, and at times its final issue appeared doubtful. In the darkest hours of the struggle was tested the patient endurance of the patriotic, and the treacherous infidelity of the disloyal was exposed. The universal enthusiasm which had glorified the few months immediately following the capture of Fort Sumter by the insurgents could not be sustained through a long war. This was not to be expected. Thousands upon thousands of those who had, in the April of 1861, been carried along by the tide of popular emotion when the first check was given to the progress of the national arms, wavered, hesitated, and fell back to their old landmarks. The reaction was natural. Men do not from momentary impulse, however strong, abandon sentiments which have become habitual. A majority of the Democratic party in the North were undoubtedly faithful adherents to the cause of loyalty; but a considerable number of that party believed that the Southern revolution was justifiable, both on the basis of state sovereignty, and because the long-continued and ever-increasing agitation on the subject of slavery had so menaced the slaveholding states that instant revolution was the only means of redress. Naturally, therefore, this portion of the Democratic party sympathized with the revolutionists. It was overawed for a season; but when it became evident that the rebellion was not to be put down in a few months, and that the war would be long and burdensome, then this faction found room and opportunity for political manœuvre, and began to throw aside its disguise. Every disaster to the Union army, every doubt as to ultimate victory for the nation, furnished these rebel sympathizers with arguments against the war. The boldest among them maintained their position by an open and direct appeal in favor of peace, even at the price of disunion. The more cautious resorted to strategy. Instead of making a direct assault, they moved by the flank, and sought to reach and destroy the base of supplies. Their political batteries were masked by various pretexts. Under that of conservatism they opposed the emancipation of slaves; in the name of liberty they cried out against conscription, and against interference with their own licentious use of speech and of the press; and the pretext of economy served them in their opposition to the appropriation of such vast sums of money as were needed for the prosecution of the war. The defeat of this cunning political strategy was a glorious national triumph, deserving to rank with the decisive victories achieved on the field of battle.

In any war politics becomes subservient. Whenever men appeal to the arbitration of arms, logic is silent, and waits upon victory or defeat. The victories of Vicksburg and Gettysburg, as we shall see, materially altered the political situation. There had been Union victories early in 1862—principal among them the capture of New Orleans—but they were not of a decisive character; they were not so positive as to counterbalance political prejudice against the action of the President on the question of slavery. Thus we find that, in the autumn elections of 1862, the administration was by no means supported by the popular vote. Even where the opposition candidates were not elected there was a noticeable falling off of the administrational support, as compared with the presidential election of 1860. By these elections Horatio Seymour was made governor of New York in place of Morton; Joel Parker, of New Jersey, in place of Olden; and in Pennsylvania, Ohio, Indiana, and Illinois there were opposition majorities.[2]

Thus it is clear that the President, in his proclamation for emancipation, instead of following, was far ahead of the majority of the voters in the loyal states. Of course, the other elements involved had much to do with the result of these state elections, but the sentiment in regard to slavery was the paramount and determining motive.

The elections in the spring of 1863, in New Hampshire, Rhode Island, and Connecticut, though resulting in a triumph for the administration, were closely contested, and showed a falling off in the Republican party vote as compared with that of 1860. The election in New Hampshire took place on the 10th of March; a governor and members of Congress were to be chosen. For the first time in several years a Democratic representative was returned to Congress from that state. For the office of governor there were three candidates. Eastman, the Democratic, polled 32,823 votes; Gilmore, the Republican, 29,035; Harriman, War Democrat, 4372. Eastman lacking 574 of a majority, the election devolved upon the state Legislature, and only by this circumstance was a Republican victory secured.

On the first of April, in Rhode Island, the Republicans carried both the state and congressional ticket, electing Governor Smith over Cozzens by a majority of a little over 3000—a decided reduction from that of previous years.

In Connecticut the election was held on the 6th of April. Here the two candidates for governor were exactly opposed to each other on the war question. The Republicans nominated the then incumbent, William A. Buckingham, a strenuous advocate of "coercion." Colonel Thomas H. Seymour, the Democratic nominee, was as distinctly recognized as an opponent of the war. Buckingham was elected by a majority of less than three thousand votes.

The second regular session of the Thirty-seventh Congress opened on the 1st of December, 1862.[1] The political complexion of Congress remained essentially the same as in the previous session. The President's message, in so far as it related to foreign affairs, contained very little of special importance. He announced that the treaty with Great Britain for the suppression of the slave-trade had been put into operation, with a good prospect of complete success. He alluded to the subject of African colonization. The Spanish-American republics had protested against the sending of negro colonies to their territories; only in Liberia and Hayti would the negro be received and adopted as a citizen. The negroes, however, did not seem so willing to migrate to these countries as to some others—not so willing, the President thought, as their interest demanded.

Turning from foreign to domestic affairs, the President alluded to the prosperity of our Territories, which had, with unimportant exceptions, been exempt from the ravages of war. He recommended to Congress measures for the rapid development of the mineral resources of these Territories as a means of increasing the national revenues. While he justified as necessary and expedient the legalization of the paper currency during the last session, he advised Congress to keep ever in view the speediest return to specie payments which would be compatible with the public interest. To meet the demand for a circulating medium, and at the same time to secure the advan-

[1] See Chapters VII., VIII., and IX.

[2] The following table shows the results of these elections, as compared with the presidential election of 1860:

	1860—PRESIDENT.		1862—FOR GOVERNOR OR CONGRESS.	
	Lincoln.	All Others.	Administration.	Opposition.
New York	362,646	312,510	295,897	306,649
New Jersey	58,324	62,801	46,710	61,307
Pennsylvania	268,030	208,412	215,616	219,140
Ohio	231,610	210,831	178,755	184,332
Indiana	139,033	133,110	118,517	128,160
Illinois	172,161	160,215	120,116	136,662
Michigan	88,480	66,267	28,716	62,102
Wisconsin	86,110	66,070	66,801	67,985
Iowa	70,409	57,922	66,014	50,898
Minnesota	22,069	12,668	15,754	11,442
	1,498,872	1,290,806	1,192,896	1,228,677
1860—Lincoln's majority, 208,066. 1862—Opposition majority, 35,781.				

The following table gives the comparison in regard to Representatives in Congress elected in 1860 and 1862:

	1860.		1862.	
	Republican.	Democratic.	Administration.	Opposition.
New York	23	10	14	17
New Jersey	2	3	1	4
Pennsylvania	18	7	12	12
Ohio	13	8	5	14
Indiana	7	4	4	7
Illinois	4	5	5	9
Michigan	4	0	5	1
Wisconsin	3	0	3	3
Iowa	2	0	6	0
Minnesota	2	0	2	0
	78	37	57	67
1860—Republican majority, 41. 1862—Opposition majority, 10.				

[1] The following changes in the constitution of this session should be noticed.

In the Senate, Samuel G. Arnold, of Rhode Island, succeeded James F. Simmons, resigned. Richard S. Field had been appointed for New Jersey, in place of John R. Thompson, deceased. On the 21st of January, 1863, Field was succeeded by James W. Wall, who had been elected to fill the vacancy. January 14th, 1863, Thomas H. Hicks, of Maryland, succeeded, first by appointment and then by election, James A. Pierce, deceased. Garret Davis, of Kentucky, succeeded John C. Breckinridge, expelled December 4th, 1862. Joseph A. Wright, of Indiana, succeeded Jesse D. Bright, expelled. Wright was, on the 22d of January, 1863, superseded by David Turpie. January 30th, 1863, William A. Richardson, of Illinois, superseded by election O. H. Browning. Waldo Johnson, of Missouri, expelled, had been succeeded by R. Wilson, and Trusten Polk, of the same state, expelled, by John B. Henderson. Jacob M. Howard, of Michigan, had succeeded K. S. Bingham, deceased. Edward D. Baker, of Oregon, killed at Ball's Bluff, had been succeeded by Benjamin F. Harding.

In the House, Thomas A. D. Fessenden, of Maine, had succeeded Charles A. Walton, resigned. Amasa Walker, of Massachusetts, succeeded Goldsmith F. Bailey, deceased. Samuel Hooper, of the same state, had (December 2d, 1861) succeeded William Appleton, resigned. John D. Stiles, of Pennsylvania, June 3d, 1862, had succeeded J. B. Cooper, deceased. George H. Yeaman, of Kentucky, succeeded James S. Jackson, deceased; Samuel L. Casey had, on March 10th, 1862, succeeded Henry C. Burnett, expelled. February 25th, 1863, George W. Bridges, of Tennessee, was qualified. A. L. Knapp, of Illinois, had (December 12th, 1861) been qualified in place of J. A. McClernand, resigned; June 2d, 1862, William J. Allen had been qualified in place of John A. Logan, resigned; and on January 30th, 1863, William A. Richardson withdrew to take a seat in the Senate. Thomas L. Price, of Missouri, had succeeded John W. Reid, expelled; William A. Hall had succeeded John B. Clark, expelled. James F. Wilson, of Iowa, had succeeded Samuel R. Curtis, resigned. On the 26th of January, 1863, Walter D. McIndoe, of Wisconsin, succeeded Luther Hanchett, deceased. In February, 1863, Michael Hahn and Benjamin F. Flanders, of Louisiana, were confirmed.

tages of a safe and uniform currency, he recommended the organization of bank associations by the act and subject to the regulation of Congress. For the year ending June 30th, 1862, the receipts from all sources, including loans and the balance from the preceding year, had been $583,885,247. The balance from the preceding year was $2,257,065. The loans of all forms had amounted to $529,692,460. From customs, direct tax, public lands, and miscellaneous sources, the receipts amounted to nearly $52,000,000. The balance left in the treasury, July 1st, 1862, was $13,053,546. Of the expenditures, $437,042,977 had been for the army and navy.

Notwithstanding the burdens laid upon the nation by the war, the President had favored the project for connecting the United States with Europe by an Atlantic telegraph, and a similar project to extend the telegraph from San Francisco, to connect by a Pacific telegraph with the line then being laid across Russian Asia. A Department of Agriculture had been established, and the President pressed upon Congress the claims of the Pacific Railroad project.

A very prominent feature of the President's message was his recommendation of a constitutional amendment providing for the compensated emancipation of slaves. This provision was to the effect that every slave state which should abolish slavery before January 1, 1900, should receive compensation from the United States; that this compensation should be extended to all loyal owners of slaves freed by the chances of the war; and that Congress might appropriate money, and otherwise provide for colonizing free negroes, with their own consent, at any place outside of the United States.[1] The President's proposition, coming in this form, indicates that he was not at this time fully convinced as to the justice of abolishing slavery in the loyal states, even by a constitutional amendment, without compensation to the slave owners. In regard to those states which were in open war against the government, he had no hesitation either as to the powers of the government to abolish slavery, or as to the justice of the measure. He still adhered to his proclamation of September 22d, and on the 1st of January, 1863, consummated the act therein contemplated. He believed that "without slavery the rebellion could never have existed; without slavery it could not continue." In the loyal slave states he was disposed to compromise, and would respect the opinions of all classes.

"Among the friends of the Union," he says, "there is great diversity of sentiment and of policy in regard to slavery and the African race among us. Some would perpetuate slavery; some would abolish it suddenly and without compensation; some would abolish it gradually and with compensation; some would remove the freed people from us, and some would retain them with us; and there are yet other minor diversities. Because of these diversities we waste much strength in struggles among ourselves. By mutual concessions we should harmonize and act together. This would be compromise; but it would be compromise among the friends, and not with the enemies of the Union."

The length of time contemplated in the proposed amendment, and the compensation of the owners of slaves, would, thought the President, weaken the opposition of those who did not favor emancipation. They would yield something by conceding emancipation as a fact to be accomplished, while those already in favor of emancipation would sustain the disappointment occasioned by the delay, and bear their portion of the financial burden imposed upon the country by compensation. Besides, he argued, immediate emancipation would lead to vagrant destitution; therefore the system of gradual abolition would be best for the generation of slaves now passing away, while it promised freedom to their posterity. While, by offering compensation, the government presented to every state a strong motive for adopting emancipation before the close of the century, it left to each state within that limit freedom to choose its own time and mode of effecting the object in view. In answer to the objection that by this plan some must pay who would receive nothing in return, he replied that the measure was both just and economical.

In the first place, it was just. "In a certain sense, the liberation of slaves is the destruction of property; property acquired by descent or by purchase, the same as any other property. It is no less true for having been often said that people of the South are not more responsible for the original introduction of this property than are the people of the North; and when it is remembered how unhesitatingly we all use cotton and sugar, and share the profits of dealing in them, it may not be quite safe to say that the South has been more responsible than the North for its continuance. If, then, for a common object, this property is to be sacrificed, is it not just that it be done at a common charge?"

It was also economical. The adoption of this plan, by securing an earlier termination of the war, would save more than it would cost. Besides, the expense caused by the war was an immediate burden, and must be borne all at once, whether we would or no; while the cost of compensation would be gradually incurred, and the full burden would fall upon the people thirty-seven years hence, when it would be sustained by one hundred millions instead of thirty-one millions.[1]

While the President was strongly in favor of the colonization, with their own consent, of the freed negroes, he thought the objection to their remaining in the country on the ground that they displaced white laborers was "largely imaginary, if not sometimes malicious."[2]

Even if this plan should not be adopted by the slave states, the President proclaimed his willingness that the national authority should be restored without it; also, that notwithstanding its recommendation, neither the war, nor proceedings under the proclamation of September 22d, would be stayed. It is evident, however, that in the event of the universal and immediate adoption of this plan, the President contemplated its substitution in place of sudden emancipation, except in the cases of those slaves who had been or might be freed by the chances of war, and even in these cases loyal owners would receive compensation.

"The plan is proposed," said the President, "as permanent constitutional law. It can not become such without the concurrence of, first, two thirds of Congress, and, afterward, three fourths of the states. The requisite three fourths of the states will necessarily include seven of the slave states. Their concurrence, if obtained, will give assurance of their severally adopting emancipation, at no very distant day, upon the new constitutional terms. This assurance would end the struggle now, and save the Union forever.

"I do not forget the gravity which should characterize a paper addressed to the Congress of the nation by the chief magistrate of the nation, nor do I forget that some of you are my seniors, nor that many of you have more experience than I in the conduct of public affairs; yet I trust that, in view of the great responsibility resting upon me, you will perceive no want of respect to yourselves in any undue earnestness I may seem to display.

"Is it doubted, then, that the plan I propose, if adopted, would shorten the war, and thus lessen its expenditure of money and of blood? Is it doubted that it would restore the national authority and national prosperity, and perpetuate both indefinitely? Is it doubted that we here—Congress and executive—can secure its adoption? Will not the good people respond to a united and earnest appeal from us? Can we, can they, by any other means, so certainly or so speedily assure these vital objects? We can succeed only by concert. It is not, 'Can *any* of us *imagine* better?' but, 'Can we *all* do better?' Object whatsoever is possible, still the question recurs, 'Can we do better?' The dogmas of the quiet past are inadequate to the stormy present. The occasion is piled high with difficulty, and we must rise with the occasion. As our case is new, so we must think anew, and act anew. We must disenthrall ourselves, and then we shall save our country.

"Fellow-citizens, *we* can not escape history. We, of this Congress and

---

[1] The following is a copy of the resolution recommended by the President:

"*Resolved by the Senate and House of Representatives of the United States of America, in Congress assembled* (two thirds of both houses concurring), That the following articles be proposed to the Legislatures (or Conventions) of the several states as amendments to the Constitution of the United States, all or any of which articles, when ratified by three fourths of the said Legislatures (or Conventions), to be valid as part or parts of the said Constitution, viz.:

"ARTICLE 1. Every state wherein slavery now exists, which shall abolish the same therein at any time or times before the first day of January, in the year of our Lord one thousand and nine hundred, shall receive compensation from the United States as follows, to wit:

"The President of the United States shall deliver to every such state bonds of the United States, bearing interest at the rate of — per cent. per annum, to an amount equal to the aggregate sum of $——— for each slave shown to have been therein by the eighth census of the United States, said bonds to be delivered to such state by installments or in one parcel, at the completion of the abolishment, accordingly as the same shall have been gradual or at one time within such state; and interest shall begin to run upon any such bond only from the proper time of its delivery as aforesaid. Any state having received bonds as aforesaid, and afterward reintroducing or tolerating slavery therein, shall refund to the United States the bonds so received, or the value thereof, and all interest paid thereon.

"ARTICLE 2. All slaves who shall have enjoyed actual freedom by the chances of the war at any time before the end of the rebellion shall be forever free; but all owners of such who shall not have been disloyal shall be compensated for them at the same rates as is provided for states adopting abolishment of slavery, but in such way that no slave shall be twice accounted for.

"ARTICLE 3. Congress may appropriate money, and otherwise provide for colonizing free colored persons, with their own consent, at any place or places without the United States."

[1] "Taking the nation in the aggregate, and we find its population and ratio of increase, for the several decennial periods, to be as follows:

1790	3,929,827				
1800	5,305,937	35.02	per cent.	ratio	of increase.
1810	7,239,814	36.45	"	"	"
1820	9,638,131	83.13	"	"	"
1830	12,866,020	33.49	"	"	"
1840	17,069,453	32.67	"	"	"
1850	23,191,876	35.87	"	"	"
1860	31,443,790	35.58	"	"	"

"This shows an annual decennial increase of 34.69 per cent. in population through the 70 years from our first to our last census yet taken. It is seen that the ratio of increase at no one of these seven periods is either 2 per cent. below or 2 per cent. above the average, thus showing how inflexible, and, consequently, how reliable the law of increase in our case is. Assuming that it will continue gives the following results:

1870	42,323,341	1910	138,918,526
1880	56,967,216	1920	186,984,335
1890	76,677,872	1930	251,680,914
1900	103,208,415		

"These figures show that our country *may* be as populous as Europe now is at some point between 1920 and 1930—say about 1925—our territory, at 73⅓ persons to the square mile, being of capacity to contain 217,186,000.

"And we *will* reach this, too, if we do not ourselves relinquish the chance by the folly and evils of disunion, or by the long and exhausting war springing from the only great element of national discord among us. While it can not be foreseen exactly how much one huge example of secession, breeding lesser ones indefinitely, would retard population, no one can doubt that the extent of it would be very great and injurious. The proposed emancipation would shorten the war, perpetuate peace, insure this increase of population, and proportionately the wealth of the country. With these, we should pay all that emancipation would cost, together with our other debt, easier than we should pay our other debt without it. If we had allowed our old national debt to run at 6 per cent. *per annum*, simple interest, from the end of our revolutionary struggle until to-day, without paying any thing on either principal or interest, each man of us would owe less upon that debt now than each man owed upon it then; and this because our increase of men through the whole period has been greater than 6 per cent.—has run faster than the interest upon the debt. Thus time alone relieves a debtor nation so long as its population increases faster than unpaid interest accumulates on its debt. . . . . . A dollar will be much harder to pay for the war than will be a dollar for emancipation on the proposed plan. And, then, the latter will cost no blood, no precious life."—*President's Message.*

[2] "It is insisted that their presence would injure and displace white labor and white laborers. . . . . Is it true, then, that colored people can displace any more white labor by being free than by remaining slaves? If they stay in their old places, they jostle no white laborers; if they leave their old places, they leave them open to white laborers. Logically, there is neither more nor less of it. Emancipation, even without deportation, would probably enhance the wages of white labor, and very surely would not reduce them. . . . . But it is dreaded that the freed people will swarm forth and cover the whole land. Are they not already in the land? Will liberation make them any more numerous? Equally distributed among the whites of the whole country, and there would be but one colored to seven whites. Could the one, in any way, greatly disturb the seven? There are many communities now having more than one free colored person to seven whites, and this without any apparent consciousness of evil from it. The District of Columbia, and the States of Maryland and Delaware, are all in this condition. . . . . But why should emancipation South send the freed people North? People of any color seldom run unless there be something to run from. *Heretofore* colored people, to some extent, have fled North from bondage, and now, perhaps, from both bondage and destitution. But if gradual emancipation and deportation be adopted, they will have neither to flee from. . . . . Again, as practice proves more than theory, has there been any irruption of colored people northward because of the abolishment of slavery in this district last spring?"—*President's Message.*

this administration, will be remembered in spite of ourselves. No personal significance or insignificance can spare one or another of us. The fiery trial through which we pass will light us down, in honor or dishonor, to the latest generation. We *say* we are for the Union. The world will not forget that we say this. We know how to save the Union. The world knows we do know how to save it. We—even *we here*—hold the power, and bear the responsibility. In *giving* freedom to the *slave*, we *assure* freedom to the *free*—honorable alike in what we give and what we preserve. We shall nobly save, or meanly lose, the last best hope of earth. Other means may succeed; this could not fail. The way is plain, peaceful, generous, just—a way which, if followed, the world will forever applaud, and God must forever bless."

It is clear from this proposed plan of the President, urged with such earnestness, that, notwithstanding his proclamation of September 22d, he preferred gradual and compensated to sudden and arbitrary emancipation. His reasons for this preference have already been given at some length. They may be briefly enumerated thus:

1. Gradual emancipation was better for the slave. While freedom was secured to all future generations, the present would be relieved of the destitution which it might be presumed would follow their sudden emancipation.

2. The measure proposed would reconcile differences of opinion, and therefore meet with less opposition. Undoubtedly the autumn elections of 1862 gave cogency to this argument.

3. The measure was dictated by justice, the North being no less responsible for slavery than the South.

4. By its tendency to restore peace, it would substitute for a war debt another, less in amount, and more easily borne.

The President, in a previous message to Congress (March 6, 1862), had recommended the passage of a joint resolution, declaring that the United States ought to co-operate with any state which should adopt the gradual abolition of slavery, by giving pecuniary aid to such state;[1] and this resolution had been passed by the House March 11th, 1862, and by the Senate on the 2d of April following. The President had urged the border states to embrace this opportunity, but no state had responded. It is not strange, therefore, that when the President, in the Message of December 1st, 1862, again brought the subject before Congress, it met with little consideration. On the 6th of January a bill passed the House, 83 to 50, offering compensation to Missouri in the event of that state adopting immediate emancipation. In the Senate the bill came up for consideration, and on the 14th of January Mr. Trumbull reported a substitute granting compensation to Missouri if, within twelve months, that state should adopt measures either for immediate or gradual emancipation. This substitute passed the Senate, 23 to 18, on the 12th of February; but, returning to the House, it was six days later recommitted, and never again considered. A similar bill in regard to Maryland was submitted in the House on the 19th of January, was on the 25th recommitted, and never heard of again; it did not even reach the Senate. No proposition was ever offered in Congress to incorporate into the Constitution the articles recommended by the President.

The President's proclamation of September 22d more completely met the views of Congress on the subject of slavery. This proclamation cut the Gordian knot with a single blow of the sword. By this, all the slaves within the limits of the Confederacy were henceforth and forever free. This act might be extreme; it might be arbitrary, and involve, in some measure, injustice to certain owners of slaves; it might even involve distress to the slaves thus suddenly released from bondage; but its advantage to the country was deemed so great as to outweigh such petty considerations. It was emphatically a war measure, and none but war measures, in the opinion of Congress, could hasten the termination of the war. It was bold, positive, and conclusive. It said plainly to Southern Revolutionists, "The decree of the nation has gone forth declaring absolute freedom in your fortified strongholds of slavery; only by the destruction of the nation can you nullify this decree." Clearly nothing was to be gained, as against the Confederacy, by any measure less decisive; and among Loyalists what was to be gained by a weak compromise? The offer of compensation in return for gradual emancipation had already been held out to the border states, and had been refused. Congress must choose between renewing this offer, which would certainly be again rejected, or declaring that henceforth the preservation of the nation was identified with the destruction of slavery. The moral strength thus gathered up, to be hurled against the rebellion, was as a mountain to a mole-hill when compared to the injury which could come to the nation by the repulsion of those who would identify the safety of their country with the perpetration of a monstrous wrong.

On the 15th of December, 1862, a resolution, offered by Mr. S. C. Fessenden, was adopted in the House, 78 to 52, declaring that the President's proclamation of September 22d indicated a policy of emancipation well adapted to hasten the restoration of peace, was well chosen as a war measure, and was an exercise of power with proper regard for the rights of the states and the perpetuity of free government. Two Democrats voted in favor of the resolution, and six Republicans against it.

And here it is proper to remark the change which had been effected in Congressional sentiment by two years of civil war. The burden of the conflict now began to be palpable. Every day the public debt increased by hundreds of thousands of dollars. The credit of the nation was disturbed not so much by this daily augmentation of the debt as by a prevailing disquietude as to the final success of the war. Once it had been confidently predicted that three months would conclude the struggle. But the tremendous energies which had been enlisted in the rebellion were not then appreciated. It had been hoped that compromise might neutralize and disarm treason; and in the special session of 1861, Congress had distinctly proclaimed its willingness to restore every rebellious state to its former position in the Union, with all its ancient rights and institutions undisturbed, upon the simple condition of returned allegiance. This attitude of Congress only provoked the scorn of the Revolutionists, and was interpreted by them as a sign of weakness in the national government. "We have," said these rebels, "given our challenge. We have appealed to arms. Subdue us if you can. If you can not, grant us our independence. But by no *political* overtures which you can make will we be induced either to resume our allegiance, or to abate the violence of our attempted revolution." After two years of fighting, with the exception of the capture of New Orleans, no great national victory had been won. The national reverses had been many, and were balanced only by temporary advantages and indecisive battles. One military leader and then another had been tried and set aside, but as yet no masterly generalship had been developed. The first outburst of martial enthusiasm had given place to partial discouragement. Still, the nation was not dismayed, nor did its armies shrink from the conflict because the latter had become doubtful and difficult. If the sentiment of patriotism had been in great measure exhausted, its place had been taken by patriotic good sense. As the strength and persistency of the rebellion became manifest, all attempts at political compromise were summarily set aside. The defiance of armed rebels could only be met by the confidence of the nation in its power to maintain itself by the strength of arms. In such a struggle the wisest political theories were useless, because such a struggle was, in the first instance, an appeal from the decision of statesmen to the decision of battles, in which physical and material conditions were the controlling elements—in which even moral forces could only be considered in their relations to a purely military problem. Legislation had not been able to prevent civil war, and the direct and primary authority of law was now equally powerless to procure peace. *Inter arma leges silent.* The very existence of the government was threatened, and so long as the menace endured, so long must the government stand behind its army, which was at once its representative, its shield against treason, and its uplifted arm for the punishment of traitors. The executive, the legislative, and the judicial functions of the government, in their bearing upon the war, had no significance or value except in so far as they subordinated all things else to the support of the army, and to measures which would secure its ultimate success. If this lesson had not been learned at once, two years of bitter experience had impressed it upon the popular mind. Thus the political problem which was presented for immediate solution became very simple by its subordination to military necessity. In this way there was also furnished a palpable line of separation between parties—between those who were willing to surrender every thing for national preservation, and those who preferred national dissolution to any surrender or any sacrifice whatsoever. Those who heartily supported the war did so because only by war could the nation be saved, and these were willing to legalize any method, not in itself dishonorable, which would help to secure military success, even if it involved a violation of the Constitution. In justification, no resort need be had to extraordinary statesmanship; the dictates of common sense were sufficient. The Constitution, and, *à fortiori*, all laws growing out of the Constitution, can never override the law of national existence itself. This principle needs no argument to support it, nor any amplification.

But, in fact, no great strain need be put on the Constitution, which, though not contemplating a violent civil war, yet in most respects adequately provided for the national safety in any event.

Those who opposed the war based their opposition on various grounds. Some held it to be unjust—an opinion very nearly allied to treason, and acts of opposition based upon it *were* treason. Others expected defeat, and this timidity was an insult to patriotism. Others counted the success of the war a poor recompense for its burdens; such were unworthy of their title to citizenship in the great republic. Still others, while disguising their direct opposition to the war, opposed all means proposed for its effective prosecution on the ground that they were unconstitutional. Their arguments in support of the unconstitutionality of measures thus adopted were generally baseless, and in any case were not worthy of respect.

The conflict between the two parties began early in this session of the Thirty-seventh Congress. On the first day of the session a resolution was offered by Cox, of Ohio, declaring that all arrests previously made by the United States authorities of citizens in states where there was no insurrection, were unwarranted by the Constitution, and a usurpation of power. This was laid upon the table, 80 to 40. A similar resolution offered the next day in the Senate met the same fate. A week later (December 8th), in the Senate, a resolution was offered by Saulsbury, of Delaware, calling upon the Secretary of War for information in regard to the arrest of two citizens of his state—Dr. John Laws and Whitely Meredith. In the debate which followed, Mr. Wilson, of Massachusetts, opposed the resolution on the ground that the government had been too lenient in this matter. "Instead," said he, "of the few hundred arrests we have had, we ought to have had several thousand." John Sherman, of Ohio, a leading Republican, took a different view. He thought that arrests should not be made except upon a reason which could be definitely stated to Congress. Congress ought to demand this. "The power to suspend the writ of *habeas corpus* should only be exercised with all the guards that can be thrown by wise legislation around it. Such a power, uncurbed, unregulated, and unchecked, would make this government a despotism worse than England ever saw, worse than France was in the time when *lettres de cachet* were used for the arrest of citizens, and they were confined for 40 years." Powell, of Kentucky, claimed that the right to suspend the writ of *habeas corpus* did not involve the right to make

[1] See Chapter VIII. of this History, p. 204.

CLEMENT L. VALLANDIGHAM.

arrests. The object of the writ was to relieve a man once arrested from illegal imprisonment. Neither the President nor his ministers had a right to arrest any man who was not in the military service of the United States. The claim made by Powell was not disputed by any senator. The right of the executive to make arrests in time of war, and when the public safety demanded, was too well established to admit of debate. Davis, Powell's colleague, claimed that the suspension of the writ was not within the scope of executive power. After a prolonged debate, Saulsbury's resolution was laid upon the table, 29 to 13. At the same time, a bill was passed in the House by a vote of 90 to 45, indemnifying the President and his subordinate officers for his action in making arrests, and in the suspension of *habeas corpus*.[1]

This bill went to the Senate, where it was amended. In its final shape it authorized the President to suspend the privilege of the writ of *habeas corpus* in any case throughout the United States; it directed that the Secretary of War and the Secretary of State should furnish to the judges of the Circuit and District Courts of the United States the names of all state prisoners then confined, or who should thereafter be confined, with the date of each arrest, and that those prisoners against whom the grand jury should find no indictment during the session sitting when the list was furnished should be released upon taking the oath of allegiance, either with or without recognizance or bond, as the judges of the respective courts might determine; it provided that any order of the President should be a sufficient defense in any case of prosecution for arrests made under such order, and that in any such prosecution the defendant might, by filing a petition, have it removed from the State Court to the Circuit Court of the United States. By a writ of error any case might even be transferred to the United States Supreme Court.

Not long after the close of this session Mr. Vallandigham was arrested in Ohio. The busy and persistent efforts made by domestic enemies to thwart the plans of the national government, and to prevent the enlistment of

[1] A fortnight after the passage of this bill, a resolution in the nature of a protest was submitted to the House, signed by 37 representatives. These protested for the following reasons:

"1. Because it purports to deprive the citizen of all existing, peaceful, legal modes of redress for admitted wrongs, and thus constrains him tamely to submit to the injury inflicted, or to seek illegal and forcible remedies.

"2. Because it purports to indemnify the President and all acting under his authority for acts admitted to be wrongful, at the expense of the citizen upon whom the wrongful acts have been perpetrated, in violation of the plainest principles of justice, and the most familiar precepts of constitutional law.

"3. Because it purports to confirm and make valid, by act of Congress, arrests and imprisonments which were not only not warranted by the Constitution of the United States, but were in palpable violation of its express prohibitions.

"4. Because it purports to authorize the President, during this rebellion, at any time, as to any person, and every where throughout the limits of the United States, to suspend the privilege of the writ of *habeas corpus*, whereas, by the Constitution, the power to suspend the privilege of that writ is confided to the discretion of Congress alone, and is limited to the places threatened by the dangers of invasion or insurrection.

"5. Because, for these and other reasons, it is unjust and unwise, an invasion of private rights, an encouragement to lawless violence, and a precedent full of hope to all who would usurp despotic power and perpetuate it by the arbitrary arrest and imprisonment of those who oppose them.

"6. And, finally, because in both its sections it is 'a deliberate, palpable, and dangerous' violation of the Constitution, 'according to the plain sense and intention of that instrument,' and is therefore utterly null and void."

It was signed by the following members: Geo. H. Pendleton, W. A. Richardson, J. C. Robinson, P. B. Fouke, Jas. R. Morris, A. L. Knapp, C. L. Vallandigham, C. A. White, Warren P. Noble, W. Allen, William J. Allen, S. S. Cox, E. H. Norton, Geo. K. Shiel, S. J. Ancona, J. Lazear, Nehemiah Perry, C. Vibbard, John Law, C. A. Wickliffe, Chas. J. Biddle, J. A. Cravens, Elijah Ward, Philip Johnson, John D. Stiles, D. W. Voorhees, G. W. Dunlap, Hendrick B. Wright, H. Grider, W. H. Wadsworth, A. Harding, Chas. B. Calvert, Jas. E. Kerrigan, Henry May, R. H. Nugent, Geo. H. Yeaman, B. F. Granger.

troops, led to the famous Order No. 38, issued by General Burnside from his headquarters at Cincinnati on the 13th of April. By this order, all persons found within his lines affording aid or comfort to the enemy were to be tried as spies or traitors, and upon conviction to suffer death.

Within the scope and meaning of this order were included "carriers of secret mails; writers of letters sent by secret mails; secret recruiting officers within the lines; persons who have entered into an agreement to pass our lines for the purpose of joining the enemy; persons found concealed within our lines belonging to the service of the enemy, and, in fact, all persons found improperly within our lines who could give private information to the enemy; all persons within our lines who harbor, protect, conceal, feed, clothe, or in any way aid the enemies of our country." All those who declared their sympathy with the enemy were to be arrested, either to be tried as spies or to be sent beyond the lines. This order had a very beneficial influence in Kentucky. In the states north of the Ohio it was construed by the disaffected as an extraordinary instance of military despotism.

Foremost among those who bade defiance to this order was Clement L. Vallandigham, of Ohio, lately a member of the Thirty-seventh Congress, and the leader in his state of what was known as the "Copperhead" wing of the Democratic party. He had been defeated as a candidate for the Thirty-eighth Congress by General Robert C. Schenck, but was the prospective Democratic candidate for Governor of Ohio. He was opposed to the war, and bitterly reviled the administration of President Lincoln. He was not, strictly speaking, an advocate for the rebellion; but, for the sake of peace, he was in favor of surrendering to the rebels all for which they were fighting. He preferred the re-establishment of the Union to its dissolution, if such a result could be reached by a compromise reinstating the slave oligarchy with its former prestige and power; failing in that, he would have acquiesced in secession, yielding the Confederacy its independence without farther struggle. That there should have been a war for the Union at all he denied; that this war should continue he held to be a national misfortune and manifest injustice. His voice, from first to last, was against the war; and in his opposition he was the most unscrupulous of demagogues. His convictions were strong—and to these he had a right. But at this critical period his open and violent opposition could not be without injury to the national cause, if maintained with impunity. No distinction could practically be made between a traitor in arms against the government and Vallandigham hurling against it his violent philippics, whatever distinction in favor of the latter might have existed in theory. For the government to have winked at his opposition while it was on the battle-field crushing those with whom he sympathized, and for whom his energetic co-operation was worth more than an additional army corps, would have been to convict itself of the most palpable folly and inconsistency.

It was in this light that Burnside looked upon Vallandigham's conduct, and accordingly, after an address made by the latter at Mount Vernon, about the 18th of May, he dispatched Captain Charles G. Hutton, his aid-de-camp, to Dayton, where Vallandigham resided, with orders for the arrest of the offender and his conveyance to Cincinnati for trial. The arrest took place on the night of May 4th, Hutton bringing his prisoner to Cincinnati without disturbance. The next day a charge was preferred against him for "publicly expressing, in violation of General Orders No. 38, from Headquarters Department of the Ohio, sympathy for those in arms against the government of the United States, and declaring disloyal sentiments and opinions with the object and purpose of weakening the power of the government in its efforts to suppress an unlawful rebellion." The specific charge was that he had declared the war to be "wicked, cruel, and unnecessary," "for the purpose of crushing out liberty and erecting a despotism," "for the freedom of the blacks and the enslavement of the whites;" had stated that "if the administration had so wished, the war could have been honorably terminated months ago;" had characterized the order No. 38 as a "base usurpation of arbitrary authority;" had invited resistance to this order by saying "the sooner the people inform the minions of usurped power that they will not submit to such restrictions upon their liberties, the better;" and had declared himself resolved at all times and upon all occasions "to do what he could to defeat the attempts now being made to build up a monarchy upon the ruins of our free government."

Vallandigham was tried by a military commission, of which General R. B. Potter was President, and which consisted of Colonel J. F. De Courcy, Lieutenant Colonel E. R. Goodrich, Major J. M. Brown, Major J. L. Van Buren, Major C. H. Fitch, Captain P. M. Lydig, with Captain J. M. Cutts, of the Eleventh United States Infantry, as judge advocate. The trial continued for two days. Vallandigham protested against the jurisdiction of the commission, declaring that no such charge could apply to him, as he belonged to neither the naval or military service of the United States, and that he was subject to arrest only by due process of law.[1] He demanded to be tried by

[1] The President had issued the proclamation of martial law on the 24th of September, 1862. The following are the important clauses of the proclamation:

1. "During the existing insurrection, and as a necessary means for suppressing the same, all rebels and insurgents, their aiders and abettors, within the United States, and all persons discouraging volunteer enlistments, resisting militia drafts, or guilty of any disloyal practice, affording aid and comfort to the rebels, against the authority of the United States, shall be subject to martial law, and liable to trial by courts-martial or military commission.

2. "That the writ of *habeas corpus* is suspended in respect to all persons arrested, or who are now, or hereafter during the rebellion shall be, imprisoned in any fort, camp, arsenal, military prison, or other place of confinement, by any military authority, or by the sentence of any court-martial or military commission."

This proclamation received the sanction both of Congress and of the judiciary. It violated neither the letter nor the spirit of the Constitution; and if the Constitution did not explicitly provide for martial law in case of war, it must be remembered that war proceeds not according to rules laid down by constitutions, but according to established usages. And under no government is any use more established than that of the proclamation and enforcement of martial law in time of rebellion. When the illustrious Lord Brougham addressed the House of Peers in support of a bill which empowered the Lord Lieutenant of Ireland to apprehend all persons *suspected* of con-a civil court, and in accordance with the ordinary usages adopted in his state. Witnesses were examined on both sides. But the case was submitted without argument. The validity of the prisoner's protest was not admitted, and Mr. Vallandigham was found guilty and sentenced to close confinement in some fortress of the United States, to be designated by General Burnside, there to be kept until the close of the war. Burnside, approving the finding of the court, ordered the prisoner to be confined in Fort Warren, in Boston Harbor.

In the mean time, Vallandigham, through the Hon. George H. Pugh, had applied to the Circuit Court of the United States for the Southern District of Ohio for a writ of *habeas corpus*. The case was argued before Judge H. H. Leavitt, who refused the writ. "It is clearly not a time," said the judge, "when any one connected with the judicial department of the government should allow himself, except from the most stringent obligations of duty, to embarrass or thwart the executive in his efforts to deliver the country from the dangers which press so heavily upon it." He argued that the legality of the arrest depended upon the necessity of making it, and that must be determined by the military commander. "Men should know," he said, "and lay the truth to heart, that there is a course of conduct not involving overt treason, and not, therefore, subject to punishment as such, which nevertheless implies moral guilt and a gross offense against the country. Those who live under the protection and enjoy the blessings of our benignant government must learn that they can not stab its vitals with impunity. If they cherish hatred and hostility to it, and desire its subversion, let them withdraw from its jurisdiction, and seek the fellowship and protection of those with whom they are in sympathy. If they remain with us while they are not of us, they must be subject to such a course of dealing as the great law of self-preservation prescribes and will enforce. And let them not complain if the stringent doctrine of military necessity should find them to be the legitimate subjects of its action. I have no fear that the recognition of this doctrine will lead to an arbitrary invasion of the personal security or personal liberty of the citizen. It is rare indeed that a charge of disloyalty will be made on insufficient grounds. But if there should be an occasional mistake, such an occurrence is not to be put into competition with the preservation of the nation; and I confess I am but little moved by the eloquent appeals of those who, while they indignantly denounce violation of personal liberty, look with no horror upon a despotism as unmitigated as the world has ever witnessed."

Burnside only awaited the President's confirmation of the sentence before carrying it out. But Mr. Lincoln decided to commute the punishment awarded by the military commission, and ordered the prisoner to be sent, "under a secure guard, to the headquarters of General Rosecrans, to be put by him beyond our military lines, and that, in case of his return within our lines, he be arrested and kept in close custody for the term specified in his sentence." This order was executed. General Bragg transferred the involuntary exile to Richmond, where he was very coldly received. He left the Confederacy as speedily as possible, and found an asylum in Canada, where he remained during the following autumn and winter. In the mean time he was made the Democratic candidate for Governor of Ohio, and sustained at the polls the most overwhelming defeat recorded in the political annals of this country. He returned home toward the close of the war, but it was not then considered worth while to molest him.[1]

Burnside did not content himself with banishing Vallandigham, but laid his hand upon such organs of the press as maintained the exile's cause.

---

spiracy against the British government, he said: "A friend of liberty I have lived, and such will I die; nor care I how soon the latter event may happen if I can not be a friend of liberty without being a friend of traitors at the same time—a protector of criminals of the deepest dye—an accomplice of foul rebellion and of its concomitant, civil war, with all its atrocities and all its fearful consequences."[a]

The Constitution provides that "no person shall be held to answer for a capital or otherwise infamous crime unless on a presentment or indictment of a grand jury, except in cases arising in the land or naval forces, or in the militia, when in actual service in time of war or public danger." But this provision only applies in time of peace. It has no bearing upon martial law. Says Chancellor Kent: "*Military* law is a system of regulations for the government of the armies in the service of the United States, authorized by the act of Congress of April 10, 1806, known as the Articles of War; and *naval* law is a similar system for the government of the navy, under the act of Congress of April 23, 1800. But *martial* law is quite a distinct thing, and is founded upon paramount necessity, and proclaimed by a *military chief*."

[1] The arrest of Vallandigham created considerable excitement in the Democratic party, and a vain attempt was made at his canonization as a martyr to liberty. A mass meeting was held at Albany, May 16, and strong resolutions were adopted denouncing Burnside's action. The following is a record of the meeting, as transmitted by Honorable Erastus Corning, its chairman, to President Lincoln, to which we append the President's reply:

"Albany, May 19, 1863.

"To his Excellency the President of the United States:

"The undersigned, officers of a public meeting held at the city of Albany on the 16th day of May, instant, herewith transmit to your excellency a copy of the resolutions adopted at the said meeting, and respectfully request your earnest consideration of them. They deem it proper, on their personal responsibility, to state that the meeting was one of the most respectable as to numbers and character, and one of the most earnest in the support of the Union, ever held in this city.

"Yours, with great regard,

"Erastus Corning, President.	Wm. S. Padock, Vice-President.
"Eli Perry, Vice-President.	J. B. Sanders, Vice-President.
"Peter Gansevoort, Vice-President.	Edward Mulcahy, Vice-President.
"Peter Monteith, Vice-President.	D. V. N. Radcliffe, Vice-President.
"Samuel W. Gibbs, Vice-President.	William A. Rice, Secretary.
"John Niblack, Vice-President.	Edward Newcomb, Secretary.
"H. W. McClellan, Vice-President.	R. W. Peckham, Jr., Secretary.
"Lemuel W. Rodgers, Vice-President.	M. A. Nolan, Secretary.
"William Seymour, Vice-President.	John R. Nessel, Secretary.
"Jeremiah Osborn, Vice-President.	C. W. Weeks, Secretary.

"*Resolutions adopted at the Meeting held in Albany, N. Y., on the 16th day of May*, 1863.

"*Resolved*, That the Democrats of New York point to their uniform course of action during the two years of civil war through which we have passed, to the alacrity which they have evinced in filling the ranks of the army, to their contributions and sacrifices, as the evidence of their patriotism and devotion to the cause of our imperiled country. Never, in the history of civil wars, has a government been sustained with such ample resources of means and men as the people have voluntarily placed in the hands of this administration.

"*Resolved*, That as Democrats we are determined to maintain this patriotic attitude, and, despite adverse and disheartening circumstances, to devote all our energies to sustain the cause of the Union; to secure peace through victory, and to bring back the restoration of all the states under the safeguard of the Constitution.

"*Resolved*, That while we will not consent to be misapprehended upon these points, we are determined not to be misunderstood in regard to others not less essential. We demand that the administration shall be true to the Constitution; shall recognize and maintain the rights of the states and the liberties of the citizen; shall every where, outside of the lines of necessary military occupation and the scenes of insurrection, exert all its powers to maintain the supremacy of the civil over military law.

"*Resolved*, That, in view of these principles, we denounce the recent assumption of a military commander to seize and try a citizen of Ohio, Clement L. Vallandigham, for no other reason than words addressed to a public meeting, in criticism of the course of the administration and in condemnation of the military orders of that general.

"*Resolved*, That this assumption of power by a military tribunal, if successfully asserted, not only abrogates the right of the people to assemble and discuss the affairs of government, the liberty of speech and of the press, the right of trial by jury, the law of evidence, and the privilege of *habeas corpus*, but it strikes a fatal blow at the supremacy of law and the authority of the state and federal Constitutions.

"*Resolved*, That the Constitution of the United States—the supreme law of the land—has defined the crime of treason against the United States to consist 'only in levying war against them, or adhering to their enemies, giving them aid and comfort,' and has provided that 'no person shall be convicted of treason unless on the testimony of two witnesses to the same overt act, or on confession in open court.' And it farther provides that 'no person shall be held to answer for a capital or otherwise infamous crime unless on a presentment or indictment of a grand jury, except in cases arising in the land or naval forces, or in the militia, when in actual service in time of war or public danger;' and farther, that 'in all criminal prosecutions the accused shall enjoy the right of a speedy and public trial by an impartial jury of the state and district wherein the crime was committed.'

"*Resolved*, That these safeguards of the rights of the citizen against the pretensions of arbitrary power were intended more especially for his protection in times of civil commotion. They were secured substantially to the English people after years of protracted civil war, and were adopted into our Constitution at the close of the Revolution. They have stood the test of seventy-six years of trial under our republican system, under circumstances which show that, while they constitute the foundation of all free government, they are the elements of the enduring stability of the republic.

"*Resolved*, That, in adopting the language of Daniel Webster, we declare 'it is the ancient and undoubted prerogative of this people to canvass public measures and the merits of public men.' It is a 'homebred right,' a fireside privilege. It had been enjoyed in every house, cottage, and cabin in the nation. It is as undoubted as the right of breathing the air or walking on the earth. Belonging to private life as a right, it belongs to public life as a duty, and it is the last duty which those whose representatives we are shall find us to abandon. Aiming at all times to be courteous and temperate in its use, except when the right itself is questioned, we shall place ourselves on the extreme boundary of our own right, and bid defiance to any arm that would move us from our ground. 'This high constitutional privilege we shall defend and exercise in all places—in time of peace, in time of war, and at all times. Living, we shall assert it; and should we leave no other inheritance to our children, by the blessing of God we will leave them the inheritance of free principles, and the example of a manly, independent, and constitutional defense of them.'

"*Resolved*, That in the election of Governor Seymour, the people of this state, by an emphatic majority, declared their condemnation of the system of arbitrary arrests and their determination to stand by the Constitution. That the revival of this lawless system can have but one result—to divide and distract the North, and destroy its confidence in the purposes of the administration. That we deprecate it as an element of confusion at home, of weakness to our armies in the field, and as calculated to lower the estimate of American character, and magnify the apparent peril of our cause abroad. And that, regarding the blow struck at a citizen of Ohio as aimed at the rights of every citizen of the North, we denounce it as against the spirit of our laws and Constitution, and most earnestly call upon the President of the United States to reverse the action of the military tribunal which has passed 'a cruel and unusual punishment' upon the party arrested, prohibited in terms by the Constitution, and to restore him to the liberty of which he has been deprived.

"*Resolved*, That the president, vice-presidents, and secretary of this meeting be requested to transmit a copy of these resolutions to his excellency the President of the United States, with the assurance of this meeting of their hearty and earnest desire to support the government in every constitutional and lawful measure to suppress the existing rebellion."

President Lincoln's Reply.

"Executive Mansion, Washington, June 12, 1863.

"Hon. Erastus Corning, and others:

"Gentlemen,—Your letter of May 19, inclosing the resolutions of a public meeting held at Albany, New York, on the 16th of the same month, was received several days ago.

"The resolutions, as I understand them, are resolvable into two propositions—first, the expression of a purpose to sustain the cause of the Union, to secure peace through victory, and to support the administration in every constitutional and lawful measure to suppress the rebellion; and, secondly, a declaration of censure upon the administration for supposed unconstitutional action, such as the making of military arrests. And, from the two propositions, a third is deduced, which is, that the gentlemen composing the meeting are resolved on doing their part to maintain our common government and country, despite the folly or wickedness, as they may conceive, of any administration. This position is eminently patriotic, and, as such, I thank the meeting and congratulate the nation for it. My own purpose is the same; so that the meeting and myself have a common object, and can have no difference, except in the choice of means or measures for effecting that object.

"And here I ought to close this paper, and would close it if there were no apprehension that more injurious consequences than any merely personal to myself might follow the censures systematically cast upon me for doing what, in my view of duty, I could not forbear. The resolutions promise to support me in every constitutional and lawful measure to suppress the rebellion, and I have not knowingly employed, nor shall knowingly employ, any other. But the meeting, by their resolutions, assert and argue that certain military arrests, and proceedings following them, for which I am ultimately responsible, are unconstitutional. I think they are not. The resolutions quote from the Constitution the definition of treason, and also the limiting safeguards and guarantees therein provided for the citizen on trials of treason, and on his being held to answer for capital or otherwise infamous crimes, and, in criminal prosecutions, his right to a speedy and public trial by an impartial jury. They proceed to resolve 'that these safeguards of the rights of the citizen against the pretensions of arbitrary power were intended more *especially* for his protection in times of civil commotion.' And, apparently to demonstrate the proposition, the resolutions proceed: 'They were secured substantially to the English people *after* years of protracted civil war, and were adopted into our Constitution at the *close* of the Revolution.' Would not the demonstration have been better if it could have been truly said that these safeguards had been adopted and applied *during* the civil wars and *during* our Revolution, instead of *after* the one and at the *close* of the other? I, too, am devotedly for them *after* civil war, and *before* civil war, and at all times 'except when, in cases of rebellion or invasion, the public safety may require' their suspension. The resolutions proceed to tell us that these safeguards 'have stood the test of seventy-six years of trial under our republican system, under circumstances which show that, while they constitute the foundation of all free government, they are elements of the enduring stability of the republic.' No one denies that they have so stood the test up to the beginning of the present rebellion, if we except a certain occurrence at New Orleans, nor does any one question that they will stand the same test much longer after the rebellion closes. But these provisions of the Constitution have no application to the case we have in hand, because the arrests complained of were not made for treason—that is, not for *the* treason defined in the Constitution, and upon conviction of which the punishment is death; nor yet were they made to hold persons to answer for any capital or otherwise infamous crimes; nor were the proceedings following, in any constitutional or legal sense, 'criminal prosecutions.' The arrests were made on totally different grounds, and the proceedings following accorded with the grounds of the arrests. Let us consider the real case with which we are dealing, and apply to it the parts of the Constitution plainly made for such cases.

"Prior to my installation here it had been inculcated that any state had a lawful right to secede from the national Union, and that it would be expedient to exercise the right whenever the devotees of the doctrine should fail to elect a President to their own liking. I was elected contrary to their liking; and, accordingly, so far as it was legally possible, they had taken seven states out of the Union, had seized many of the United States forts, and had fired upon the United States flag, all before I was inaugurated, and, of course, before I had done any official act whatever. The rebellion thus began soon ran into the present civil war; and, in certain respects, it began on very unequal terms between the parties. The insurgents had been preparing for it more than thirty years, while the government had taken no steps to resist them. The former had carefully considered all the means which could be turned to their account. It undoubtedly was a well-pondered reliance with them that, in their own unrestricted efforts to destroy Union, Constitution, and law all together, the government would, in great degree, be restrained by the same Constitution and law from arresting their progress. Their sympathizers pervaded all departments of the government, and nearly all communities of the people. From this material, under cover of 'liberty of speech,' 'liberty of the press,' and '*habeas corpus*,' they hoped to keep on foot among us a most efficient corps of spies, informers, suppliers, and aiders and abettors of their cause in a thousand ways. They knew that in times such as we were now inaugurating, by the Constitution itself the '*habeas corpus*' might be suspended; but they also knew they had friends who would make a question as to who was to suspend it; meanwhile their spies and others might remain at large to help on their cause. Or if, as has happened, the executive should suspend the writ, without ruinous

[a] *Hansard's Debates*, 3d Series, vol. 100, p. 635.

The Chicago *Times* was suppressed, and a military guard placed over the office; and the circulation of the New York *World* was prohibited within the lines of the department. These latter acts were soon afterward annulled by the President.

The most important measure adopted in the last session of the Thirty-seventh Congress was the act of conscription. It was one of the latest acts passed by this Congress. Almost a year had passed since the Confederate government had resorted to conscription as a means of recruiting its armies. Hitherto no such measure had been adopted by the national government. But the time had now come when both necessity and justice demanded its adoption.

The necessity of such a measure was obvious. Over a million of men had volunteered for periods varying from three months to three years.[1] Of these there remained in the service between 600,000 and 700,000. About 160,000 of those who had disappeared from the field had been enlisted for three or nine months. Over one fourth, therefore, of those who had volunteered had been killed or wounded in battle, had become the victims of disease, had been discharged for physical disability, or had deserted. The large number of men drawn from industrial pursuits had increased the demand for labor, and the price thereof. The depreciation of the national currency had still farther increased the price of labor. These circumstances, taken in connection with the diminution of martial enthusiasm, made it impossible any longer to depend upon volunteers.

But, apart from this consideration, it was not fitting that the entire burden of the battle should be borne by those alone whose patriotism was sufficient for the sacrifice. Especially in a struggle which involved national honor, and even national existence, was it the duty of the government to insist upon its claim to the military service of every able-bodied citizen. By enrolling the entire militia of the states, which would thus become the grand reserve of the army, and by drafting from the whole number as many men, and at such periods, as the exigencies of the service might demand, seemed both the most efficient and the most impartial method of obtaining recruits. There could be no question either as to the constitutional power of Congress to enroll the militia, or as to the power of the executive, with the consent of Congress, to make requisition by draft. The Constitution authorizes Congress—

"To provide for calling forth the militia to execute the laws of the Union, suppress insurrections, and repel invasions;

waste of time, instances of arresting innocent persons might occur, as are always likely to occur in such cases, and then a clamor could be raised in regard to this which might be, at least, of some service to the insurgent cause. It needed no very keen perception to discover this part of the enemy's programme so soon as by open hostilities their machinery was fairly put in motion. Yet, thoroughly imbued with a reverence for the guaranteed rights of individuals, I was slow to adopt the strong measures which, by degrees, I have been forced to regard as being within the exceptions of the Constitution, and as indispensable to the public safety. Nothing is better known to history than that courts of justice are utterly incompetent to such cases. Civil courts are organized chiefly for trials of individuals, or, at most, a few individuals acting in concert, and this in quiet times, and on charges of crimes well defined in the law. Even in times of peace bands of horse-thieves and robbers frequently grow too numerous and powerful for ordinary courts of justice. But what comparison, in numbers, have such bands ever borne to the insurgent sympathizers even in many of the loyal states? Again, a jury too frequently has at least one member more ready to hang the panel than to hang the traitor. And yet, again, he who dissuades one man from volunteering, or induces one soldier to desert, weakens the Union cause as much as he who kills a Union soldier in battle. Yet this dissuasion or inducement may be so conducted as to be no defined crime of which any civil court would take cognizance.

"Ours is a case of rebellion—so called by the resolutions before me—in fact, a clear, flagrant, and gigantic case of rebellion; and the provision of the Constitution that 'the privilege of the writ of *habeas corpus* shall not be suspended, unless when, in cases of rebellion or invasion, the public safety may require it, is *the* provision which specially applies to our present case. This provision plainly attests the understanding of those who made the Constitution that ordinary courts of justice are inadequate to 'cases of rebellion'—attests their purpose that, in such cases, men may be held in custody whom the courts, acting on ordinary rules, would discharge. *Habeas corpus* does not discharge men who are proved to be guilty of defined crime; and its suspension is allowed by the Constitution on purpose that men may be arrested and held who can not be proved to be guilty of defined crime, 'when, in cases of rebellion or invasion, the public safety may require it.'

"This is precisely our present case—a case of rebellion, wherein the public safety does require the suspension. Indeed, arrests by process of courts, and arrests in cases of rebellion, do not proceed altogether upon the same basis. The former is directed at the small percentage of ordinary and continuous perpetration of crime, while the latter is directed at sudden and extensive uprisings against the government, which, at most, will succeed or fail in no great length of time. In the latter case, arrests are made not so much for what has been done as for what probably would be done. The latter is more for the preventive and less for the vindictive than the former. In such cases the purposes of men are much more easily understood than in cases of ordinary crime. The man who stands by and says nothing when the peril of his government is discussed can not be misunderstood. If not hindered, he is sure to help the enemy; much more if he talks ambiguously—talks for his country with 'buts,' and 'ifs,' and 'ands.' Of how little value the constitutional provisions I have quoted will be rendered if arrests shall never be made until defined crimes shall have been committed may be illustrated by a few notable examples. General John C. Breckinridge, General Robert E. Lee, General Joseph E. Johnston, General John B. Magruder, General William B. Preston, General Simon B. Buckner, and Commodore Franklin Buchanan, now occupying the very highest places in the rebel war service, were all within the power of the government since the war began, and were nearly as well known to be traitors then as now. Unquestionably, if we had seized and held them, the insurgent cause would be much weaker. But no one of them had then committed any crime defined in the law. Every one of them, if arrested, would have been discharged on *habeas corpus*, were the writ allowed to operate. In view of these and similar cases, I think the time not unlikely to come when I shall be blamed for having made too few arrests rather than too many.

"By the third resolution the meeting indicate their opinion that military arrests may be constitutional in localities where rebellion actually exists, but that such arrests are unconstitutional in localities where rebellion or insurrection does not actually exist. They insist that such arrests shall not be made 'outside of the lines of necessary military occupation and the scenes of insurrection.' Inasmuch, however, as the Constitution itself makes no such distinction, I am unable to believe that there is any such constitutional distinction. I concede that the class of arrests complained of can be constitutional only when, in cases of rebellion or invasion, the public safety may require them, and I insist that in such cases they are constitutional *wherever* the public safety does require them, as well in places to which they may prevent the rebellion extending as in those where it may be already prevailing; as well where they may restrain mischievous interference with the raising and supplying of armies to suppress the rebellion, as where the rebellion may actually be; as well where they may restrain the enticing men out of the army, as where they would prevent mutiny in the army; equally constitutional at all places where they will conduce to the public safety, as against the dangers of rebellion or invasion. Take the peculiar case mentioned by the meeting. It is asserted, in substance, that Mr. Vallandigham was, by a military commander, seized and tried 'for no other reason than words addressed to a public meeting, in criticism of the course of the administration, and in condemnation of the military orders of the general.' Now, if there be no mistake about this; if this assertion is the truth and the whole truth; if there was no other reason for the arrest, then I concede that the arrest was wrong. But the arrest, as I understand, was made for a very different reason. Mr. Vallandigham avows his hostility to the war on the part of the Union; and his arrest was made because he was laboring, with some effect, to prevent the raising of troops, to encourage desertions from the army, and to leave the rebellion without an adequate military force to suppress it. He was not arrested because he was damaging the political prospects of the administration or the personal interests of the commanding general, but because he was damaging the army, upon the existence and vigor of which the life of the nation depends. He was warring upon the military, and this gave the military constitutional jurisdiction to lay hands upon him. If Mr. Vallandigham was not damaging the military power of the country, then his arrest was made on mistake of fact, which I would be glad to correct on reasonably satisfactory evidence.

"I understand the meeting, whose resolutions I am considering, to be in favor of suppressing the rebellion by military force—by armies. Long experience has shown that armies can not be maintained unless desertion shall be punished by the severe penalty of death. The case requires, and the law and the Constitution sanction, this punishment. Must I shoot a simple-minded soldier-boy who deserts, while I must not touch a hair of a wily agitator who induces him to desert? This is none the less injurious when effected by getting a father, or brother, or friend into a public meeting, and there working upon his feelings till he is persuaded to write the soldier-boy that he is fighting in a bad cause, for a wicked administration of a contemptible government, too weak to arrest and punish him if he shall desert. I think that, in such a case, to silence the agitator and save the boy is not only constitutional, but, withal, a great mercy.

"If I be wrong on this question of constitutional power, my error lies in believing that certain proceedings are constitutional when, in cases of rebellion or invasion, the public safety requires them, which would not be constitutional when, in absence of rebellion or invasion, the public safety does not require them; in other words, that the Constitution is not, in its application, in all respects the same in cases of rebellion or invasion involving the public safety, as it is in times of profound peace and public security. The Constitution itself makes the distinction; and I can no more be persuaded that the government can constitutionally take no strong measures in time of rebellion, because it can be shown that the same could not be lawfully taken in time of peace, than I can be persuaded that a particular drug is not good medicine for a sick man because it can be shown not to be good food for a well one. Nor am I able to appreciate the danger apprehended by the meeting, that the American people will, by means of military arrests during the rebellion, lose the right of public discussion, the liberty of speech and the press, the law of evidence, trial by jury, and *habeas corpus*, throughout the indefinite peaceful future which I trust lies before them, any more than I am able to believe that a man could contract so strong an appetite for emetics during temporary illness as to persist in feeding upon them during the remainder of his healthful life.

"In giving the resolutions that earnest consideration which you request of me, I can not overlook the fact that the meeting speak as 'Democrats.' Nor can I, with full respect for their known intelligence, and the fairly presumed deliberation with which they prepared their resolutions, be permitted to suppose that this occurred by accident, or in any way other than that they preferred to designate themselves 'Democrats' rather than 'American citizens.' In this time of national peril I would have preferred to meet you on a level one step higher than any party platform, because I am sure that, from such more elevated position, we could do better battle for the country we all love than we possibly can from those lower ones where, from the force of habit, the prejudices of the past, and selfish hopes of the future, we are sure to expend much of our ingenuity and strength in finding fault with, and aiming blows at, each other. But, since you have denied me this, I will yet be thankful, for the country's sake, that not all Democrats have done so. He on whose discretionary judgment Mr. Vallandigham was arrested and tried is a Democrat, having no old party affinity with me; and the judge who rejected the constitutional view expressed in these resolutions, by refusing to discharge Mr. Vallandigham on *habeas corpus*, is a Democrat of better days than these, having received his judicial mantle at the hands of President Jackson. And still more, of all those Democrats who are nobly exposing their lives and shedding their blood on the battle-field, I have learned that many approve the course taken with Mr. Vallandigham, while I have not heard of a single one condemning it. I can not assert that there are none such. And the name of President Jackson recalls an instance of pertinent history. After the battle of New Orleans, and while the fact that the treaty of peace had been concluded was well known in the city, but before official knowledge of it had arrived, General Jackson still maintained martial or military law. Now, that it could be said the war was over, the clamor against martial law, which had existed from the first, grew more furious. Among other things, a Mr. Louaillier published a denunciatory newspaper article. General Jackson arrested him. A lawyer by the name of Morel procured the U. S. Judge Hall to order a writ of *habeas corpus* to relieve Mr. Louaillier. General Jackson arrested both the lawyer and the judge. A Mr. Hollander ventured to say of some part of the matter that 'it was a dirty trick.' General Jackson arrested him. When the officer undertook to serve the writ of *habeas corpus*, General Jackson took it from him, and sent him away with a copy. Holding the judge in custody a few days, the general sent him beyond the limits of his encampment, and set him at liberty, with an order to remain till the ratification of peace should be regularly announced, or until the British should have left the southern coast. A day or two more elapsed, the ratification of the treaty of peace was regularly announced, and the judge and others were fully liberated. A few days more, and the judge called General Jackson into court and fined him $1000 for having arrested him and the others named. The General paid the fine, and there the matter rested for nearly thirty years, when Congress refunded principal and interest. The late Senator Douglas, then in the House of Representatives, took a leading part in the debates, in which the constitutional question was much discussed. I am not prepared to say whom the journals would show to have voted for the measure.

"It may be remarked, First, that we had the same Constitution then as now; secondly, that we then had a case of invasion, and now we have a case of rebellion; and, thirdly, that the permanent right of the people to public discussion, the liberty of speech and the press, the trial by jury, the law of evidence, and the *habeas corpus*, suffered no detriment whatever by that conduct of General Jackson, or its subsequent approval by the American Congress.

"And yet let me say that, in my own discretion, I do not know whether I should have ordered the arrest of Mr. Vallandigham. While I can not shift the responsibility from myself, I hold that, as a general rule, the commander in the field is the better judge of the necessity in any particular case. Of course, I must practice a general directory and revisory power in the matter.

"One of the resolutions expresses the opinion of the meeting that arbitrary arrests will have the effect to divide and distract those who should be united in suppressing the rebellion, and I am specifically called on to discharge Mr. Vallandigham. I regard this as, at least, a fair appeal to me on the expediency of exercising a constitutional power which I think exists. In response to such appeal, I have to say, it gave me pain when I learned that Mr. Vallandigham had been arrested—that is, I was pained that there should have seemed to be a necessity for arresting him—and that it will afford me great pleasure to discharge him so soon as I can, by any means, believe the public safety will not suffer by it.

"I farther say, that as the war progresses, it appears to me opinion and action, which were in great confusion at first, take shape and fall into more regular channels, so that the necessity for strong dealing with them gradually decreases. I have every reason to desire that it should cease altogether, and far from the least is my regard for the opinion and wishes of those who, like the meeting at Albany, declare their purpose to sustain the government in every constitutional and lawful measure to suppress the rebellion. Still, I must continue to do so much as may seem to be required for the public safety.
A. LINCOLN."

[1] It is impossible to calculate exactly the number of volunteers in 1861 and 1862, but the following table gives an approximate estimate:

STATES.	3 Months.	9 Months.	3 Years.	Total.
Maine	779	7,493	24,771	33,043
New Hampshire	800	2,023	14,915	17,738
Vermont	782	4,777	13,457	19,006
Massachusetts	3,736	16,896	50,406	71,038
Rhode Island	3,147	2,069	9,410	14,626
Connecticut	2,340	5,697	20,182	28,219
New York	15,922		176,783	192,705
New Jersey	3,105	10,714	16,395	30,214
Pennsylvania	20,979	15,100	164,257	194,558
Ohio	26,893		143,228	170,121
Indiana	4,698		93,840	104,316
Illinois	4,901		130,539	135,440
Michigan	780		44,890	45,670
Wisconsin	810	491	39,345	40,646
Minnesota	930	1,200	10,136	12,266
Iowa	959		47,855	48,814
Missouri			27,407	27,407
Kentucky		878	41,163	42,041
Delaware	No Returns.			
Maryland				
Virginia				
Tennessee				
California				
	91,561	67,335	1,068,769	1,227,758

This estimate does not include 30,131 men enlisted in New York for two years, 2589 twelve-months' men enlisted in Pennsylvania, nor 15,853 men raised for the defense of Maine, Pennsylvania, Missouri, and Kentucky. Including these, the grand total reaches 1,276,331.

"To provide for organizing, arming, and disciplining the militia, and for governing such part of them as may be employed in the service of the United States, reserving to the states respectively the appointment of the officers, and the authority of training the militia according to the discipline prescribed by Congress."

With the exception of official appointments and the authority of training the militia, the state governments, under the Constitution, have nothing whatsoever to do with the raising of armies for the United States service.

On the 5th of February a bill for enrolling and drafting the militia was reported to the Senate by Mr. Wilson, of Massachusetts, chairman of the Committee on Military Affairs. The batteries of the opposition were immediately opened against it. As there was no valid constitutional objection to the bill, it is fair to consider the attempt on the part of certain members in the two houses to defeat it as an indication of their opposition to the war itself. Apart from this, they were also influenced by a political motive of the most contemptible sort. They knew that so long as the nation depended upon volunteers its armies would be filled from the ranks of those who heartily supported the administration, while those who were politically opposed to the war would remain at home, and support by their votes the opposition party. If, however, the government called upon all its citizens alike, in the method proposed by this bill, then the soldiers would be drawn in just proportion from among the supporters and opponents of the administration. The bill would also, if successful, defeat the purposes of the opposition leaders, who hoped to see the army dwindle away under the volunteer system, which, they knew, must prove inadequate. It is easy to understand, therefore, how these men in Congress pronounced the bill one "of doubtful propriety and doubtful constitutionality," "despotic," "conferring upon the President of the United States more power than belongs to any despot in Europe or any where else."[1] This bill passed the Senate, the yeas and nays not being called. The vote on Mr. Bayard's motion, that the measure be indefinitely postponed, shows the exact strength of the opposition. Eleven Democrats voted in favor of postponement; 35 voted against it, including every Republican present, with Messrs. McDougall, of California, and Harding and Nesmith, of Oregon.

The bill came up for consideration in the House on the 23d of February. The same objections were urged which had been offered in the Senate. Mr. Thomas, of Maryland, who was strongly opposed to emancipation, to the use of negro soldiers, and to confiscation, but who yet had no sympathy with rebellion, supported the measure as necessary.[2] Mr. Crittenden, of Kentucky, while agreeing with Mr. Thomas as to the causes of the difficulty experienced by the government in sustaining its military strength by the volunteer system, still opposed the measure.[1] The bill was finally passed, on the 3d of March, by a vote of 115 to 49.

---

[1] In the Senate Mr. Wilson strongly urged the passage of the bill. "We are now," he said, "engaged in a gigantic struggle for the preservation of the life of the nation, menaced by the foulest and most wicked rebellion recorded in the annals of mankind. The young men of the republic for more than twenty months have been thronging to the field to uphold the cause of their periled country. They left their homes in the pride and bloom, and filled with the high hopes of young manhood. Those noble regiments of volunteers that left their homes full of lusty life, and in all the pride and strength of assured manhood, are now thinned and wasted by the diseases of the camp and the storms of battle.

"The old regiments hardly average now more than four hundred men in the field fit for the stern duties of war. Many who rallied at the call of their country, and who followed its flag with unswerving devotion, now sleep in bloody graves, or linger in hospitals, or, bending beneath disease and wounds, can no longer fill the ranks of our legions in camp or on the battle-field. If we mean to maintain the supremacy of the Constitution and the laws, if we mean to preserve the unity of the republic, if we mean that America shall live and have a position and name among the nations, we must fill the broken and thinned ranks of our wasted battalions.

"The issue is now clearly presented to the country for the acceptance or rejection of the American people—an inglorious peace, with a dismembered Union and a broken nation on the one hand, *or war*, fought out until the rebellion is crushed beneath its iron heel. Patriotism, as well as freedom, humanity, and religion, accepts the bloody issues of war, rather than peace purchased with the dismemberment of the republic and the death of the nation.

"If we accept peace, disunion, death, then we may speedily summon home again our armies; if we accept war until the flag of the republic waves over every foot of our united country, then we must see to it that the ranks of our armies, broken by toil, disease, and death, are filled again with the health and vigor of life. To fill the thinned ranks of our battalions we must again call upon the people. The immense numbers already summoned to the field, the scarcity and high rewards of labor, press upon all of us the conviction that the ranks of our wasted regiments can not be filled again by the old system of volunteering. If volunteers will not respond to the call of the country, then we must resort to the involuntary system."

[2] "The policy," said he, "inaugurated on the 1st of December, 1861, has been fruitless of good. It has changed the ostensible, if not the real issue of the war. That policy, and the want of persistent vigor in our military counsels, render any farther reliance upon voluntary enlistments futile. The nostrums have all failed. Confiscation, emancipation by Congress, emancipation by the proclamation of the President, compensated emancipation, arbitrary arrests, paper made legal tender, negro armies, will not do the mighty work. Nothing will save us now but victories in the field and on the sea, and then the proffer of the olive-branch, with the most liberal terms of reconciliation and reunion. We can get armies in no other way but by measures substantially those in the bill before us, unless the administration will retrace its steps, and return to the way of the Constitution—for us the strait and narrow way which leads unto life. At any rate, the war on paper is at an end. The people have, for a time, been dèluded by it. That delusion exists no longer. If you are to suppress this rebellion, all instrumentalities will fail you but the power of your own right arm. Mr. Speaker, the measures and policy heretofore pursued have not been merely fruitless of good, they have been fruitful of evil. They have made, or largely contributed to make, a united South; they have made for you a divided North; they have alienated from the administration the confidence and affection of large portions of the people; they have paralyzed your arm, and divided your counsels. Gentlemen flatter themselves this alienation and disaffection are the work of Democrats; that the people have been misled and deceived by their wiles. Sir, the people of this country read, and keep their eyes open, and comprehend, and the plain fact is, you can not unite them upon the policy you now pursue. They do not believe in destroying the Union and the Constitution in the hope of building up better by force of arms. You may unite them on the issue of maintaining the Union and the government at every price and cost, but upon no other.

"Having distracted the public mind, having alienated to a great degree the affection and confidence of the country, what is left to you? To resort to those constitutional powers vested in you for the preservation of the government which you have in trust, and which you must use or be false to that trust. Gentlemen say the people will not bear this measure. I will not believe it. I believe the people of this country are ready to do and to endure every thing for the preservation of their unity, their national life, and, through that unity and that national life, all that makes life precious to men. They will submit to it. In view of the infinite interests at stake in this great controversy; in the solemn conviction that there is to-day no hope of peace except in disintegration; that as a nation we must conquer in arms or perish, they will meet and respond to this imperative call of duty. Such is my hope and trust.

"But, Mr. Speaker, suppose they hesitate; suppose they do not submit; you can but try; you have no other hope; the negro will not save you, paper money will not save you, your infractions of personal liberty will not save you. If persisted in in the peaceful and loyal states, they will ruin you. Go firmly to the people, and present to them the issue. They will understand the terrible exigency in which the country is placed, and they will be true to that country if you show clearly to their comprehension the length, and breadth, and height, and depth of that exigency. Mr. Speaker, the issue must be met at all hazards. If the people will not support you, if they will not do this highest act of duty, the days of this republic are numbered, and the end is nigh. Satisfy them that you mean to be true to the Constitution and the Union, and they will be true to you.

"The issue, I repeat, must be met. You die without this measure; you can do no more with it, except you die, as cowards die, many times. I go, therefore, for appealing from these panaceas, and makeshifts, and paper bullets, to this highest, most solemn, and imperative duty of the citizen to proteet the life of the state, and I believe that appeal will be answered."

[1] "The measure, it seems to me," said he, "is but the natural result of the course of policy which this Congress has pursued from the commencement, or very near the commencement of this war.

"When this war first broke out, it was a national war, with a single national object; and upon that one purpose and object all hearts were united. That object was the re-establishment of this great republic—our republic. Upon that great object, I repeat, we were all united. There was no division; and in order to satisfy the country more effectually of the fact of our unity, but little more than eighteen months ago a resolution offered by me was passed, almost unanimously, declaring that this was our sole object. We then declared that this was our only object. We pledged ourselves that no interference should be made in any of the institutions of the states having a special reference to the institution of slavery.

"Mr. Speaker, had the pledges then solemnly made by this Congress been adhered to, how different would be the condition of the country to-day! There was then but one sentiment pervading the whole people of the country. The people then flocked to your standard by hundreds of thousands, filling the ranks of such an army as the world never saw. There was then but one sentiment in the people of the country. No coercion was then talked of. What has produced the change that now presents itself? What, as my friend from Massachusetts says, has united the South in one solid iron phalanx? What has crushed out, and destroyed to a great extent, if not wholly, the confidence and enthusiasm that swelled up in the heart of the people of the nation? What has done all this? It is our departing from our faith. It is our departing from that object which we declared to be the only just and patriotic one. What else has done it? Have you not departed from the policy of that faith? Have you not, in a manner considered perfidious, violated pledges which you gave the country more than eighteen months ago? Was there any discontent expressed at that time? I heard of none. The hearts of the loyal people North and South were fired with a common purpose to preserve the integrity and honor of the republic. Every man felt himself under every honorable obligation to step forward, and abandon his private affairs, and look after the welfare of the Union. That was the undivided, pervading, patriotic sentiment of the whole body of the people. Nowhere in the North or Northwest was heard a murmur of discontent; and the same confidence and patriotic feeling was as strong among the Union men of the border states as it was any where in the North and West. It was every where the same. We were willing to suffer to the last extremity to preserve the government. That was the feeling of the people then; we all know it.

"What has brought this mighty change? What has done it, Mr. Speaker? Do not we all know? Can there be any doubt on the subject? It has been our infidelity to the pledges made to the people. It has been because of the reckless course of the dominant power. It is because of the impolicy of which Congress has been guilty. Is it not time to learn that the course we have pursued and are pursuing has produced a state of division and dissension even in the remaining states? Yes, sir, the policy that has been recently pursued has been the fruitful source of these disastrous dissensions. It has been our departure from our policy of not attacking the institution of slavery, and fighting only for the government, for the Union, and the Constitution.

"What have we seen at this session? We have passed bills changing the rules and articles of war in order that slavery might be encroached upon. We deprive the loyal people of the South of all protection by the army for their property. You have passed a law taking the slaves from any of the citizens of the country. You have passed a law for organizing an army of three hundred thousand negroes. This, you know, is against the deep-rooted prejudices of at least one half our people. Such a bill would have been rejected with one common voice eighteen months ago. Even the mention of the subject created profound indignation. You have done this and more. You have passed laws, in the opinion of the people, which violate the Constitution. You have scorned the friends of the government. You have turned away from us the hearts of the people by these measures. We have sown deep the seeds of future disasters to the government. I implore the House to pause before it sanctions any more measures of that kind.

"Mr. Speaker, can we carry on the war more successfully by transcending the Constitution than we can by obeying it? I have always said that the Constitution was our bulwark; that it was the best defense; that our strongest defense was to keep within the clearly-defined powers of that instrument. But what have we done? We have assumed powers not delegated by the Constitution. We have acted, not according to the provisions of the Constitution, but according to the sentiment which actuated us at the moment. We seem to have been controlled by the petty spirit of party rather than by the spirit of patriotism and a determination to obey the Constitution and the laws. You have lost the heart of the people, and you have lost it by the dogmas you have inaugurated and established rather than follow the Constitution.

"The gentleman from Pennsylvania (Mr. Stevens) said the other day that we have every man in the field that we can get voluntarily. Why is that? Because the object is clearly proclaimed of abolishing slavery throughout the United States. You have done this while you have had an accidental majority here. Hence it is that the people have changed. This is the only time when that party ever had a majority in the House—I mean a majority of Abolitionists. With this accidental power, what has it done? It has declared emancipation by law. It has declared by law for the raising of negro armies. It has declared emancipation and confiscation by law. By these means, I say, you have lost the hearts of the people. Why do not the people have the same enthusiasm in the war that they had at first? Then they put a million of men into the field. The country is still in peril, in more peril than at first, and why is not an army of two million men now put into the field? It is only because of the bad policy by which you have established the dogmas of the Abolitionists, of emancipation of slavery throughout the country. It is that which has induced them to lose confidence in you. It is not for the country, it is not for the white man, it is for the negro this war is to be waged; and for that war I am not. The logical conclusion from the impolitic course we have pursued is, that we have lost the hearts of the people.

"You say that this bill is framed on the idea that the people will no longer volunteer—that the people will no longer stand a draft. Why not? Because the people will not do one thing or another; they will neither volunteer nor stand a draft, and you are obliged by law to coerce them. That is the condition in which we are placed, and this bill is nothing more than the logical conclusion of what we have previously done. We have created a necessity for it. The people are no longer with us, and therefore we must force the people, by coercive and penal laws, by new jurisdictions, provost-marshals scattered through the land, and by a new sort of military judicature to which the people have not been accustomed. And knowing that you have an unwilling people to deal with, you make that law as coercive as possible, and accompany it with every sort of inquisitorial and compulsory power, judicial and executive, in order to insure obedience, willing or unwilling, to that law. Is not that our condition fairly considered?

"There is but one sort of consistency which deserves the respect of honest men, and that is to let your acts be consistent with your convictions at the time you are called upon to vote. It is not what we did yesterday that we are to consider alone. We have lived through a time of trial and of trouble. Have we learned nothing? Up to this time I fear we have learned very little. Our lessons have been very severe, and the fear of more dangerous lessons hereafter ought to instruct us. The life of the country is attacked, and that life is upon your hands, and its preservation depends in a great measure upon your wisdom, upon your solemn deliberations, and your solemn consideration of all the mighty questions upon us.

"If we want to get back the Union, how must we do it? We must change our policy. This will not answer your purpose. You must get back what you have lost. You have lost the heart of the people, and the confidence of the people. The people's affections are turned away from us, and will they bear more exactions and burdens laid upon them? No, sir; you are mistaken in the remedy. Your only remedy is to regain the confidence and heart of the people, to substitute for the distrust which now exists confidence that your object is a national one, and not a mere public one; not the abolition of slavery, but the salvation of the country. Get that back, and you do not want this bill; fail to get it back, and this bill will be just as inoperative as if there was not a word written upon it.

"You say a draft will not do; that a draft will not be submitted to. I know nothing about that. Will, then, this more exacting provision be submitted to? In a country like ours, laws which do not carry along with them the assent of the people are but blank paper. Have you not cause to fear that unless you win back the hearts of the people, and their confidence, this bill will do no good? You are mistaking the disease altogether. The disease of the public heart is loss of confidence in us, members of Congress. It is the Abolition element here which has destroyed every thing; that has clouded the great ideas of nationality—the pride of the American heart.

"That is the disease of the public heart, and you should endeavor to administer measures which will reclaim it, and that will heal discontent. And yet in the last moments of our existence you are endeavoring to consummate a policy which the people have condemned, and to put the people beyond the means of redress. The remedy, and the sole remedy, is by reversion, by retracing our steps, and making this again a national war. Then you will not want this bill, nor will you want a draft. You will have volunteers enough. I do not speak rashly, because you had volunteers enough, and more than you knew what to do with, when you stood upon that ground. But you chose to change that ground. Political abolitionists thought the time had come for them to introduce the sword and the spear into the public arena, and to make use of this war to carry out the ends which they have long cherished—the abolition of slavery."

OWEN LOVEJOY.

This act, as passed by Congress, included, as a part of the national forces, all able-bodied male citizens of the United States between the ages of twenty-one and forty-five years, except such as should be rejected as physically or mentally unfit for the service. The militia thus enrolled were to be divided into two classes—the first to contain those under thirty-five and all unmarried persons under forty-five; the second, all others liable to military duty. The country was to be divided into districts, in each of which an enrollment board was to be established. Those enrolled were subject to be called into service for two years from July 1st, 1863, and to continue in service for three years. Any person drafted might furnish an acceptable substitute, or pay $300, and be discharged from farther liability under that draft. Those who, after being drafted, failed to report, were to be treated as deserters. No choice was given to those drafted as to the corps or regiment, or as to the branch of the service in which they should serve.[1]

In the House a bill had already been passed, 83 to 54, authorizing the President "to enroll, arm, and equip, and receive into the land or naval service of the United States, such numbers of volunteers of African descent as he may deem useful to suppress the present rebellion, for such term as he may prescribe, not exceeding five years." This bill was not passed by the Senate, on the ground that the authority thereby granted had already been given in the act of July 17, 1862.

Early in the session a discussion was opened in the House which brought out an expression of views as to the position of the insurgent states in their relation to the general government. On the 8th of January, the appropriation bill being under consideration, an amendment was offered to add to the clause for the compensation of thirty-three revenue commissioners and twelve clerks (with salaries amounting to $112,000) a proviso that their compensation should be collected in the insurgent states. Thaddeus Stevens, of Pennsylvania, insisted that the Constitution did not embrace a state in arms against the government. "The establishment of a blockade," he said, "admitted the Southern States, the Confederates, to be a belligerent power. Foreign nations have all admitted them as a belligerent power. Whenever that came to be admitted by us and by foreign nations, it placed the rebellious states precisely in the position of an alien enemy with regard to duties and obligations." He held, therefore, that all obligations or contracts previously existing between these states and the general government were abrogated, and that the former were to be treated simply in accordance with the laws of war. "With regard to all the Southern states in rebellion the Constitution has no binding influence and no application." In his opinion these states were not members of the Union, nor under the laws of the government. He proposed to levy the tax and collect it as a war measure.

In this expression of opinion Mr. Stevens was not sustained by his party. Abram Olin, of New York, held this doctrine in utter abhorrence—equally unsound and mischievous as that of the so-called right of secession. Mr. Thomas, of Massachusetts, favored the amendment, but would collect the tax under the provisions of the Constitution, "because to-day, as always heretofore, the authority of the national government covers every inch of the territory of the national domain; because that law which we call the Constitution is to-day the supreme law of the land.[1] Mr. Lovejoy, of Illinois, emphatically repudiated Mr. Stevens's theory.[2]

On the 18th of February the bill to provide a national currency came up for consideration in the Senate. The President, in his message, had urged the passage of this bill. It passed the Senate by a majority of two votes—23 to 21—and the House by a vote of 78 to 64.[3]

[1] The following persons were exempted: The Vice-President, the judges of United States courts, the heads of executive departments, and the governors of the several states; the only son, laible to military service, of a widow dependent upon his labor for support; the only son of aged or infirm parent or parents dependent upon his labor for support; also, where there are two or more sons of aged or infirm parents subject to draft, the father, or, if he be dead, the mother, may elect which son should be exempt; also the father of motherless children under twelve years of age, dependent upon his labor for support; also, where there were a father and sons in the same family and household, and two of them were in the military service as non-commissioned officers, musicians, or privates, the residue of such family should be exempt; and all were exempt who had been convicted of any felony.

[1] Mr. Stevens did not claim to speak for his party. "I desire," he said, "to say that I know perfectly well . . . . I do not speak the sentiments of this side of the house as a party. I know more than that: that, for the last fifteen years, I have always been a step ahead of the party I have acted with in these matters; but I have never been so far ahead, with the exception of the principles I now enunciate, but that the members of the party have overtaken me and gone ahead; and they, together with the gentleman from New York (Mr. Olin), will again overtake me, and go with me, before this infamous and bloody rebellion is ended. They will find that they can not execute the Constitution in the seceding states; that it is a total nullity there, and that this war must be carried on upon principles wholly independent of it. They will come to the conclusion that the adoption of the measures I advocated at the outset of the war—the arming of the negroes, the slaves of the rebels—is the only way left on earth by which these rebels can be exterminated. They will find that they must treat those states now outside of the Union as conquered provinces, and settle them with new men, and drive the present rebels as exiles from this country; for I tell you they have the pluck and endurance for which I gave them credit a year and a half ago, in a speech which I made, but which was not relished on this side of the house, nor by the people in the free states. They have such determination, energy, and endurance, that nothing but actual extermination, or exile, or starvation will ever induce them to surrender to this government. I do not now ask gentlemen to indorse my views, nor do I speak for any body but myself; but, in order that I may have some credit for sagacity, I ask that gentlemen will write this down in their memories. It will not be two years before they will call it up, or before they will adopt my views, or adopt the other alternative of a disgraceful submission by this side of the country."

[2] "I repudiate," said he, "the theory which, if I understand the gentleman from Pennsylvania, is his theory, that, if I own a vessel, the mere fact that pirates come and take possession of it destroys the validity of my title to it. I may not be in possession; I may go and demand the possession to which I am legally and constitutionally entitled, and force may prevent my taking possession; but that does not invalidate my rightful claim.

"I hold that if one third of the citizens of Kentucky are loyal, the state belongs to that third; that if one fourth of the citizens of Tennessee are loyal, the state belongs to that fourth; and that just as soon as the government can enforce their rights, it is bound to enforce them; and the whole machinery of state government can be set going by those who remain, who are loyal, whether one half, one fourth, one tenth, or one hundredth. The right of the federal government never was invalidated, and never ceased for a moment."

[3] The provisions of the bill, the objections to it, and the arguments in its favor, will be best shown by the following speeches of Senators Collamer, of Vermont, and Sherman, of Ohio:

Mr. Collamer opposed the bill. "What," asked he, "are its great purposes and objects as stated by those who framed, recommended, and support it? It is said to be to institute a great national paper currency through the medium of banks, to be organized under this act, who are to take United States stocks and deposit them in the Treasury, and take ninety per cent. of them in notes to circulate as money, with which to do banking business, and that they shall have twenty-five per cent. more than this circulating part as a permanent capital to work upon. They are to pay two per cent. on their circulation to the United States government annually, or one per cent. every six months, and the United States are to pay them six per cent. per annum on the bonds in gold. The United States further agree that they will take all this money in circulation, receive it for and pay it out on all public dues, and declare it to be in the act a national currency. Besides that, the United States agree that they will guarantee to the bill-holders the payment of these bills at the Treasury. If the banks do not redeem them in currency when asked for their redemption, they may be protested and presented at the Treasury, and the Treasury is to pay them, and to pay them in full, whether the stocks left upon deposit are able to meet them or not. Besides this investment, the property put into these associations is itself to be clear of taxation.

"Now, Mr. President, it is to be further understood, and is an integral part of the very system, without which it is good for nothing, that the circulation of the existing banks of the country is to be withdrawn. Measures are to be taken with those banks that shall induce or compel them to take home their circulation and put it out no more, so that this shall be a national currency. Unless this latter part of the scheme is secured, its great professed object of making a uniform national currency throughout the United States is not and can not be effected. It therefore implies all this, and we must understand that if we enter upon this proposition and entertain this plan, we are to take measures in order to perfect it to do the other thing; that is, to destroy, put out of existence, the circulation of the present state banks.

"The Supreme Court, in the case of McCullough *vs.* Maryland, decided that the United States had the right to make a United States Bank, with branches in different states, and they said the states could not tax that United States Bank. Why? Because the exercise of that power in the extreme would destroy it, and therefore you would make it out that the Congress had a power to establish a bank; but, after all, it was subject to the power of the states to put it down. In the case of Kentucky, the Supreme Court decided that the long-continued usage in this country in states to make banks was constitutional, and that a state had a right to make a bank of issue. There were other questions in that case which it is not necessary now to bring in here. It was decided that a state had a right, not to make a bank to issue the state paper, but a bank to issue paper currency.

"Now, sir, if a state has that right, it has that right certainly independent of the consent of Congress. Does it hold it at the will of Congress? Certainly not. The United States, in making a United States Bank, held it independent of state action, and it was so decided. If the state has this right, and has it independent of the consent of Congress, it can not have that right if the United States can tax it out of existence. Hence I say the United States has no more power to tax a state institution out of existence than a state has to tax a United States institution out of existence. I should like to see that answered. I have sometimes proposed that question, but I have never received any answer to it. In most of the states, the State of New York, for instance, almost all their banks are founded upon their own state stocks. It is a part of their financial system to make their stocks valuable, and to enable them to make internal improvements. All these state banks are more or less connected with and ramified in with the business of their several states. Can they be taxed out of existence by the United States? Why, sir, you might just as well tell me that the United States, under the power of taxation, could go on and extinguish all the schools in New England by taxing its schools, its colleges, and its academies, and their books, and their buildings, and the salaries of the professors, and in that way destroy them under the very general principle of the power of universal taxation. I shall not dwell any longer upon that point. I have stated my view upon it.

"But, Mr. President, there is another principle involved in this measure, and I am looking at it now in its great national aspects, as a national principle, without regard to the time. I say it is to establish corporations in all the states and Territories, entirely independent of any power of visitation by those states or Territories. This, to say the least of it, is an extremely questionable power. What may be the number of these institutions? As the capital is to be $300,000,000, that will make three thousand banks of $100,000 each; and the bill provides that they may be made $50,000 banks, which will make six thousand $50,000 banks. I believe we have now, in what are called the loyal states, between thirteen and fourteen hundred banks altogether; and this bill proposes to make at least three thousand, or perhaps six thousand of these bank corporations, established all over the states.

"That is not all. It is proposed that there shall be no other banks but these; the whole banking capital is to be put into these banks, and the whole of that property is removed from all state taxation. I ask gentlemen to reflect on what will be the effect in their different states of closing up the present banks, and taking the capital belonging to the stockholders, putting it into the banks under this bill, and removing the whole of it from all the forms of state taxation—state, county, city, and town. Many of our states derive their school-fund from what they obtain from these state banks. I believe it is so in New Hampshire. They have their school-fund in that way.

"The next point to which I desire to call attention is the propriety of our undertaking as a nation to say that we will be responsible for the ultimate redemption of these bills by the securities that are deposited. I am aware that the honorable senator who is the parent of the bill here thinks he has got in it something very valuable, in the provision about the liability of individual stockholders, and requiring twenty-five per cent. of the amount of their circulation to be kept on hand. All these things, to my mind, are hardly worth the paper on which they are written; they are good for nothing at all. How can you follow the responsibility of stockholders? The very stocks are assignable; they are personal property. They are bought and sold in the market every day for more or less, according to their worth. Although one of these banks may start with some very responsible men when it first sets up, the moment it becomes at all doubtful or troublesome it quickly passes off into the hands of men who have no responsibility. You can never pursue it in that way. As to the provision that they shall retain twenty-five per cent. on their circulation on hand, that is their own money; it is not United States money. The fact is just this: whenever your bonds that you hold for your security to redeem these bills depreciate essentially, the bank will wind up, and they will do it without any sort of disparagement or any dishonesty. The stockholders will say at once to themselves, 'We have noticed the fall of these stocks; we know

The bill for the admission of West Virginia passed both houses during this session. It first came up before the House of Representatives on the 9th of December, 1862. The senators elected by West Virginia had already been admitted into the Senate. The question as to the admission of West Virginia as a separate state was involved in great difficulty. While it was consistent to recognize the Legislature of this portion of Virginia as the Legislature of the state, to the exclusion of that assembled at Richmond, it was still a violation of the Constitution to admit West Virginia as a separate state. To do this was to take the ground which Mr. Stevens held—that the Constitution had no longer any application to the states engaged in rebellion. Probably not more than one third of the proposed new state were in favor of its separation from Virginia. But the bill passed the House 96 to 55, and the Senate without debate.

On the 9th of February, 1863, resolutions were adopted by the House admitting to seats in that body Benjamin F. Flanders and Michael Hahn, elected from the first and second Congressional districts of Louisiana. The adoption of these resolutions was a protest on the part of the House against the political theories of Thaddeus Stevens.

Resolutions were adopted in both houses toward the close of the session repudiating foreign mediation in our civil war. These were passed in the Senate 31 to 5, and in the House 103 to 28.[1] The occasion for this action

that they are very much down; we will not redeem any more of these bills; we will leave them to be redeemed by the government; we gave them $100,000 and deposited it with them in bonds; they only allowed us $90,000; that is all we have had of them; we leave these notes in their hands to redeem; we will let them redeem them; we gave them a great deal more than they ever gave us, and let them redeem them.' When would that occur? Why, sir, in great national calamities such as those under which we already suffer by the unfortunate proceedings of this war, we know that public stocks rise and fall with the prosperity or decline of the nation.

"Again, I will take the very reverse of this state of things. Suppose we should close this unfortunate controversy and return to peace. The moment you are at peace every man wants all the money he has got to go into business. He has lent it to the United States, taken this, that, or the other sort of stock, in order to have it earn something while this public controversy and difficulty was going on. The moment that is ended he wants his money to go into business again in our cities and towns—importing and the like. He immediately cashes these bonds, and a very large portion of these bonds will at once be thrown on the market at a discount the moment you are at peace. In either of these cases, whether from public calamity or from peace, there comes a deterioration upon the value of these bonds; these banks are wound up, the bills are protested and presented to the Treasury here in bundles for payment. What will you do? It is said in the bill that they are to be paid here. You may take the stocks the bank left as security and go and sell them in the market, and thus get money to pay them. If they have deteriorated so much that the banks do not want to pay their bills, it will be a pretty hard bargain for us to pay them with those bonds. We should have to sell at as much discount as they. Besides, we do not get rid of any thing in that way. We have to anticipate our bonds. They run twenty years. We have got to pay these notes when they are presented; and if we sell our bonds at a discount in the market to get some money to redeem them with, we have got to meet that bond in the end, have we not? We do not get rid of it at all; but we are compelled to get the money about twenty years before it is due. I do not see the policy, the expediency, or the profit of such a bargain.

"The next aspect to which I will call attention is this: we once had, or twice had, a United States Bank. The history of the last one is within the recollection of most of those who hear me. That bank had a capital of $35,000,000. The proposition now is to make United States banks with a capital of $300,000,000. The United States took $7,000,000 of that stock. They paid nothing in, but put in their stock for it on time. They had directors of their own appointed to keep watch of that bank. They had the right to borrow money at that bank. The bank was bound to loan it to them at a certain rate and limitation. They went on with that bank during the whole period of its existence. They took their dividends from year to year by extinguishing the payment of interest on their bonds; and at the close of the whole they received back their stock and ten per cent. upon it of accumulated profits that had not been divided. Every body concerned in it was paid, the stock was paid back; and the United States made that money.

"Now, sir, why did that institution go down; or, rather, why was it not renewed, and enlarged, and adapted to the condition of the country? It was because it was said to be a dangerous political engine in the hands of whatever political party existed at the time; that it would be used as a great machine in the different states by the favor which the government would give it, or the control which they would exercise over it; and it was dangerous, as it was said then, and I think it was demonstrable.

"Mr. President, look at the proposition now before us in this aspect. It provides that the Secretary of the Treasury shall nominate the Comptroller of the Currency. He can be appointed by the President only on the nomination of the Secretary of the Treasury; and he is given any number (not limited at all) of clerks and agents. There are established, if you please, three thousand of these banks under this bill, of $100,000 each, scattered through all the country. They can be visited by agents appointed here under this bill, and inspected from time to time, and reported upon. The Secretary is authorized to make such of them as he thinks proper depositories of the public revenue, and he is to distribute this stock, one half of the $300,000,000 to the different states according to their representative population, and the other half according to the banking resources of the country; there is no limitation upon him whatever. If the old United States Bank furnished well-grounded apprehensions of its dangerous political tendency as a political agency, permit me to ask gentlemen to reflect for a moment on what you have got here, with $300,000,000 of capital, with three thousand banks subject to inspection, and to be troubled just as much as the head of the Treasury Department pleases, if they do not support his views; or to receive favors by way of being made depositories for the public dues; and the Secretary having the power to appoint agents and clerks *ad libitum*. I do not wish to enlarge upon this point at all, but I say this: if a Secretary of the Treasury can be furnished with these powers and chooses to use them, he must be a very bungling politician if he can not make himself President any day.

"Then, putting it in plain English, you propose to hire these people to go into these associations, take these bonds, and deposit them. They are to pay two per cent. on their circulation, and you pay them six on their bonds. I will call it four per cent.; though it is more, as the gentleman knows, because the two per cent. they pay in currency, and the six per cent. we pay in gold. The amount of it is this: we say to them, 'If you will do this to the amount of $300,000,000, and put out notes to the extent of ninety per cent. of the bonds, we will pay you $12,000,000 in gold every year for doing it.' You may talk about its being in the form of bonds, but that does not alter it at all. We are to enter into that arrangement with them. If they take their money, buy these bonds, put them on deposit, issue paper to the extent of ninety per cent. of those bonds and circulate it, and pay two per cent. on that circulation, we pay them six on the bonds; that is, we pay them four per cent. on the bonds, if they will do us this great service! There is all there is about it. You may discuss it as you please, and use a great many financial expressions and schemes; but that is the English of it; that is the simple common sense of it. Instead of circulating that amount of our own currency upon our own responsibility and paying nothing, we are to hire them to circulate that amount of our currency, and pay them $12,000,000 a year in gold for doing it; and we are to be responsible after all. That is all there is of it. Yankee as I am, I am unable to perceive how it is possible that that can be a good trade for us, or how any shrewd man would ever think of entering into an agreement of that kind.

"It is said, however, that it is a fair tax in proportion to our other war taxes. Let us look at this for a moment. My neighbor here has $100,000 saved, we will say, and having retired from business, he lives by loaning out that money, and he realizes six per cent. a year on it. How much do we tax him? One hundred and eighty dollars, three per cent. on what he gets. I am going now upon the ground that he has got $6000 income in some other way. We tax him three per cent. on his *gain;* and that is $180, although he has used $100,000. Here are three other neighbors of mine—I will not include myself, because that would make the supposition too improbable—who have $100,000, and they bank with it according to the law of their state. What do they make? Perhaps they make eight per cent. If they do make $8000 on the $100,000, they have to pay a tax of three per cent. on that now, and it goes into the Treasury. But what is the proposition here? The government says to them, 'You have got $100,000 invested in banking; you will therefore probably have about $150,000 of circulation; we will tax you on the $150,000 one per cent. every six months, or two per cent. a year.' How much will that be? Three thousand dollars. 'For the use of your $100,000 in banking you shall pay $3000 a year.' The other man, for the use of his $100,000, pays but $180 a year. Do you call that fair and equal taxation? The one pays $180, while the other, on the same amount of capital, pays $3000. It is perfectly monstrous.

"But, in the next place, I think it a mere matter of figures, and capable of mathematical certainty about this problem of whether banks will be set up in my part of the country under this bill, even if the existing banks are all destroyed. To illustrate it, I will take the plain case of a $100,000 bank, because that is the ordinary size of a country bank in my part of the country, and it is, in round numbers, easy of calculation. You are to take $100,000, go and buy bonds with it, leave them there, and take out $90,000 of circulating notes. As to exchange, that is to be the same all over the country, and that is to be no item in the profit of a bank hereafter.

"Now let us see how it will work. In the first place, I believe I am borne out by examination of experienced men in saying that you can not operate a country bank, or any bank of the amount of $100,000, with less than $2500 per year. Pay your cashier, open your office, warm it, light it, take care of it, pay your expresses, and do all your business, and it can not be done for less than $2500, and that is putting it very low. Now a $100,000 bank, under this bill, will, in the first place, get from the government of the United States $4000 a year interest, after paying the tax. We understand that. They lend the $90,000 which they receive, and they get six per cent. interest on that. That interest would amount to $5400. There is all they can make without stealing. It is all that can be made. What does it cost? It costs $2500 to operate the bank, the ordinary expenses, and they lose the use of $22,500 for that year, because they are to keep on hand twenty-five per cent. on their circulation. They have kept that on hand, and of course the use of it is lost. That is over $1300. That expense and loss makes $3800. The interest from the government and the interest on the $90,000 amounts to $9400. Deducting the one from the other, it leaves $5600. Now what did it make that on? On the $100,000 put in, and the $22,500 which was kept on hand. The investment was $122,500, and the profit is $5600; that is, about four per cent. That is all that can be made under it. They are to run the risk in their loans of all the loanings of $90,000, and getting it out and in, and can not make five per cent., if all works smoothly and there are no losses at all. I say that is not a matter of speculation; that is a matter of certainty. Those figures which I have given in this instance can not lie."

Mr. Sherman, of Ohio, followed in defense of the bill. "That bankers can make a reasonable profit under this bill I have no doubt. They have the benefit of four per cent. on the bonds deposited by them. They have the benefit of interest on the notes given them for circulation. They have the benefit of exchange; not the rates of exchange formerly paid, but that incidental exchange which every bank charges in drawing a draft, probably a quarter or a half of one per cent. They have the profits they can make from deposits. They have other profits from the ordinary incidents of banking. I have no doubt, from all these various profits, they will make what banks in ordinary times under specie payments could make, that is, seven or eight per cent. a year.

"But, sir, the principal point made by the honorable senator, and one most likely to influence the judgment of senators, is this: he asks what benefit the United States derives from this arrangement, and he endeavors by argument to show that the United States derives no benefit. I would put to him this simple proposition: there are now $167,000,000 of local bank circulation in the country. Suppose we can induce through their interests—I do not propose to do it by any arbitrary mode—the retirement of $100,000,000 of this circulation, taking the smallest sum that will probably be used in the course of a year; suppose we can induce the banks to withdraw $100,000,000 of their circulation, is it no benefit to the United States? Now the United States gets no benefit whatever from their circulation. The United States can not receive it in their ordinary business transactions. It fills the channels of circulation to the exclusion of the greenbacks. Suppose we can induce the banks to withdraw $100,000,000 of their circulation, and invest that much money in our bonds, and receive United States circulation, does not the honorable senator see that we should derive a great advantage from it? That is the object of this bill. The object is, by appealing to the patriotism and the interest of the people and the banks, to induce the banks to withdraw their local circulation and convert it into a national circulation. If it fails, as a matter of course it does no harm. But suppose it succeeds, does not the United States derive a benefit from it? Certainly; because at once a demand is created for the purchase of $100,000,000 of United States bonds. We are anxious to sell these bonds. They are now below the par of gold. The creation of a demand for $100,000,000 will, as I showed yesterday, by the well-known and recognized laws of trade, probably create a demand for $500,000,000. There is the benefit, there is the advantage we seek to derive. We shall make a market at once for the sale of $100,000,000 worth of our bonds, and the additional market which is always created by making a demand for a particular commodity, which is equivalent at least to five times the amount of the real demand. The government of the United States is willing to borrow money from the honorable senator at six per cent. and pay the interest in gold coin. Any person who desires to loan money to the United States may receive six per cent. interest on it, and we are very glad to sell our bonds at that rate in this time of war; but to those who avail themselves of the privileges of this law we only pay four per cent., so that we save one third of the interest on the amount of our bonds used for banking; and more than that, we get a circulation which by the laws of the United States may be used in the collection of our dues; and in the ordinary operations of our government these banking agencies may be made useful and beneficial as depositories. There is the answer. The benefit derived to the government is by making a market for its bonds, by having fiscal agencies throughout the United States, so that it may the more readily collect its debts, and by saving one third of the interest on the payment of its bonds, and by securing to the people of the country a uniform national currency which can be passed from hand to hand in all parts of the country without loss by exchange, or deterioration, or alteration.

"But the honorable senator says that the power granted by this bill would render the Secretary of the Treasury a very dangerous person, or a very powerful person; probably that is the meaning. He says that this bill would create a dangerous political power. According to all experience, if you invest in any particular person the power to appoint men to office, or the power to manage banks or control a scheme of this kind, it rather weakens him. Sir, it will be a dangerous power in one sense; not to the American people, but it will be dangerous to the individual who exercises the power. Any man in this country who is clothed with the power of appointing men to office, or selecting certain persons to have certain privileges, loses more than he makes, by the well-known law that he disappoints more than he benefits. And if you confer upon the Secretary of War or the Secretary of the Treasury the power to appoint twenty clerks, as we did the other day, there are five hundred applicants at once; and you disappoint four hundred and eighty, and make them enemies, for the sake of gaining twenty friends. No, sir, the administration of patronage, the power to select depositories, all the power conferred by this bill, the power of visitation, all these are powers which tend rather to decrease the influence of the Secretary of the Treasury, because they are more likely to make him enemies than friends."

[1] The following is the text of the resolutions as offered in the Senate, March 3d, by Mr. Sumner:

"*Whereas*, it appears from the diplomatic correspondence submitted to Congress that a proposition, friendly in form, looking to pacification through foreign mediation, has been made to the United States by the Emperor of the French, and promptly declined by the President; and whereas the idea of mediation or intervention in some shape may be regarded by foreign governments as practicable, and such governments, through this misunderstanding, may be led to proceedings tending to embarrass the friendly relations which now exist between them and the United States; and whereas, in order to remove for the future all chance of misunderstanding on this subject, and to secure for the United States the full enjoyment of that freedom from foreign interference which is one of the highest rights of independent states, it seems fit that Congress should declare its convictions thereon: Therefore,

"*Resolved* (the House of Representatives concurring), That while, in times past, the United States have sought and accepted the friendly mediation or arbitration of foreign powers for the pacific adjustment of international questions, where the United States were the party of the one part and some other sovereign power the party of the other part; and while they are not disposed to misconstrue the natural and humane desire of foreign powers to aid in arresting domestic troubles, which, widening in their influence, have afflicted other countries; especially in view of the circumstance, deeply regretted by the American people, that the blow aimed by the rebellion at the national life has fallen heavily upon the laboring population of Europe; yet, notwithstanding these things, Congress can not hesitate to regard every proposition of foreign interference in the present contest as so far unreasonable and inadmissible, that its only explanation will be found in a misunderstanding of the true state of the question, and of the real character of the war in which the republic is engaged.

"*Resolved*, That the United States are now grappling with an unprovoked and wicked rebellion, which is seeking the destruction of the republic that it may build a new power, whose corner-stone, according to the confession of its chiefs, shall be slavery; that for the suppression of this rebellion, and thus to save the republic and prevent the establishment of such a power, the national government is now employing armies and fleets, in full faith that through these efforts all the purposes of conspirators and rebels will be crushed; that while engaged in this struggle, on which so much depends, any proposition from a foreign power, whatever form it may take, having for its object the arrest of these efforts, is, just in proportion to its influence, an encouragement to the rebellion and to its declared pretensions, and, on this account, is calculated to prolong and embitter the conflict, to cause increased expenditure of blood and treasure, and to postpone the much-desired day of peace; that, with these convictions, and not doubting that every such proposition, although made with good intent, is injurious to the national interests, Congress will be obliged to look upon any further attempt in the same direction as an unfriendly act, which it earnestly deprecates, to the end that nothing may occur abroad to strengthen the rebellion or to weaken those relations of good-will with foreign powers which the United States are happy to cultivate.

"*Resolved*, That the rebellion from its beginning, and far back even in the conspiracy which preceded its outbreak, was encouraged by the hope of support from foreign powers; that its chiefs frequently boasted that the people of Europe were so far dependent upon regular supplies of the great Southern staple, that sooner or later their governments would be constrained to take side with the rebellion in some effective form, even to the extent of forcible intervention, if the milder form did not prevail; that the rebellion is now sustained by this hope, which every proposition of foreign

on the part of Congress was the offer of mediation made by the French government early in the year. During the year 1862 the Emperor Napoleon had proposed to the Russian and British governments to join him in trying to bring about an armistice of six months between "the federal government and the Confederates of the South." The proposition was in both cases declined. On the 9th of January, 1863, M. Drouyn de l'Huys, the French Minister of Foreign Affairs, addressed M. Mercier, the French minister at Washington, on this subject. The government, he said, in proffering its good offices, had been guided by its friendship toward the United States. "We can not," he added, "regard without profound regret this war, worse than civil, comparable to the most terrible distractions of the ancient republics, and whose disasters multiply in proportion to the resources and valor which each of the belligerent parties develop." It was urged, also, that recourse to the good offices of one or several neutral powers contained nothing incompatible with the pride of a great nation, and that mediation might be as useful in civil as in international wars. Plainly the French emperor ill understood the real temper of the government to which he made this offer. Undoubtedly he would have been joined by the British government in his offer had not the latter been recently (November, 1862) advised by Lord Lyons that such an offer at the present crisis would be injurious to the peace party in the North. Perhaps, also, Napoleon was deceived as to the real import of the autumn elections of 1862, mistaking them for an indication of a popular desire for peace even at the price of disunion.

Secretary Seward's reply was at once courteous and firm. It was acknowledged that the people of France were "faultless sharers with the American nation" in the misfortunes of the war. The traditional friendship between France and the United States had not been forgotten. The land and naval forces of the United States had steadily advanced, until now the Confederates retained "only the states of Georgia, Alabama, and Texas, with half of Virginia, half of North Carolina, two thirds of South Carolina, half of Mississippi, and one third respectively of Arkansas and Louisiana." The determination to preserve the integrity of the country had not relaxed. "This government," said the secretary, "if required, does not hesitate to submit its achievements to the test of comparison; and it maintains that, in no part of the world, and in no times, ancient or modern, has a nation, when rendered all unready for combat by the enjoyment of eighty years of almost unbroken peace, so quickly awakened at the alarm of sedition, put forth energies so vigorous, and achieved successes so signal and effective as those which have marked the progress of this contest on the part of the Union. M. Drouyn de l'Huys, I fear, has taken other light than the correspondence of this government for his guidance in ascertaining its temper and firmness. He has probably read of divisions of sentiment among those who hold themselves forth as organs of public opinion here, and has given to them an undue importance. . . . . . While there has been much difference of popular opinion and favor concerning the agents who shall carry on the war, the principles on which it shall be waged, and the means with which it shall be prosecuted, M. Drouyn de l'Huys has only to refer to the statute-book of Congress, and the executive ordinances, to learn that the national activity has hitherto been, and yet is, as efficient as that of any other nation—whatever its form of government—ever was under circumstances of equally grave import to its peace, safety, and welfare. Not one voice has been raised any where, out of the immediate field of the insurrection, in favor of foreign intervention, mediation, or arbitration, or of compromise, with the relinquishment of one acre of the national domain, or the surrender of even one constitutional franchise. At the same time, it is manifest to the world that our resources are yet abundant, and our credit adequate to the existing emergency." To surrender the subject to neutral arbitration amounted to nothing less than for the government, while engaged in the suppression of insurrection, to enter into diplomatic discussion with the insurgents. Either the government or the insurgents must yield the whole question in dispute, which neither was prepared to do; therefore the end of arbitration would only be a recommittal of the question to the decision of battle. "It is a great mistake," continued the secretary, "that European statesmen make if they suppose this people are demoralized. Whatever, in the case of an insurrection, the people of France, or of Great Britain, or of Switzerland, or the Netherlands would do to save their national existence, no matter how the strife might be regarded by or affect foreign nations, just so much, and certainly no less, the people of the United States will do, if necessary, to save for the common benefit the region which is bounded by the Pacific and Atlantic coasts, and by the shores of the Gulfs of St. Lawrence and Mexico, together with the free and common navigation of the Rio Grande, Missouri, Arkansas, Mississippi, Ohio, St. Lawrence, Hudson, Delaware, Potomac, and other national highways by which this land—which to them is at once the land of inheritance and a land of promise—is opened and watered. Even if the agents of the American people now exercising their power should, through fear or faction, fall below this height of the national virtue, they would be speedily, yet constitutionally replaced by others of sterner character and patriotism." The time for peace would finally come, and then there would be conference, but it would be between states and in the congressional forum, and not between the United States and foreign powers.

The Thirty-seventh Congress was dissolved on the 4th of March, 1863, at a time of great national despondency. This Congress had first been convened at the special call of the President, on the 4th of July, 1861, to meet the emergencies of a rebellion already inaugurated. It had witnessed the conclusion of the first period of the war—that in which the enthusiasm of the nation at first aroused had proved sufficient for its safety. It had also anticipated the second period—in which the government must put forth its utmost power, setting aside compromise, striking at the very heart of treason, compelling the services of every citizen, and at the same time sealing the mouths and binding the hands of such opponents as, in the midst of the loyal, sought to perfect the work begun by traitors.

The spring and early summer of 1863 was the most doubtful period of the war. The Confederate armies were at their maximum of strength. At Vicksburg they held Grant at bay; in middle Tennessee they defied Rosecrans, and in Virginia they were preparing for an invasion of the Northern states. These were the days of sunshine in which the opposition leaders made hay which they never could garner. Vallandigham, indeed, rushed into the clutches of martial law, was arrested, sentenced, and banished, as has been already related; but the others thundered at their will against the administration. As the national anniversary approached, it seemed as if it were to be a repetition of its gloomy predecessor of 1862. The "Copperheads"—as the peace-at-any-price party in the North was styled—looked forward to the Fourth of July as the grand harvest-day of the rebellion, and, when it came, their leaders were prepared for its celebration. On that day Franklin Pierce, a former President of the United States, in an oration delivered to the citizens of his own state, at Concord, New Hampshire, while he had not one word to say against the sectionalism which had raised its arm against the nation, denounced the war for the Union as sectional and parricidal. "Nor is that all," said he; "for in those states which are exempt from the actual ravages of war, in which the roar of the cannon, and the rattle of the musketry, and the groans of the dying are heard but as a faint echo from other lands, even here in the loyal states the mailed hand of military usurpation strikes down the liberties of the people, and its foot tramples on a desecrated Constitution." Not a word had he to say about the desecration of the Constitution by traitors. The chief grievance of which he complained was that it was "made criminal for that noble martyr of free speech, Mr. Vallandigham, to discuss public affairs in Ohio." And for this speech Franklin Pierce, of New Hampshire, will go down to history hand in hand with Vallandigham, who could enlist a larger share of his sympathy than his own nation in peril.

On the same day Governor Seymour addressed a large audience assembled at the Academy of Music in New York City. The prelusion of his elaborate oration was an amplification of the calamities of the nation. These calamities, he said, had been predicted years ago by Democrats as the consequence of the refusal of the people to be ruled by a Southern policy. But the fears of Democrats had been laughed at. When the war commenced they had implored for compromise. Their prayers had been unheeded. On this account the country had been brought "to the very verge of destruction." He therefore had come before them to repeat the warning and the prayer which had hitherto been scorned. There was not only a bloody civil war, but the hostile attitude of the two parties at the North threatened a second revolution. "Remember," he warned Republicans, "that the bloody, and treasonable, and revolutionary doctrine of public necessity can be proclaimed by a mob as well as by a government."

But Governor Seymour and ex-President Pierce were moderate in expression when compared to others throughout the North, who threatened to revolutionize the government if a Democratic success could be gained in no other way. Among the motives used to excite to violence, the principal was that furnished by the impending conscription. These harangues produced their natural effect upon the ignorant and the evil-disposed. Undoubtedly there would have been an immediate explosion of this inflamed sedition but for the fact that even while these demagogues were throwing their torches into the magazine, their malicious work was spoiled by the two greatest and most decisive national victories of the war. It is scarcely too much to declare that Gettysburg and Vicksburg prevented a Democratic revolution in the North. It is true they did not prevent an attempt at revolution, but they deprived the opposition of popular support. Our Seymours, Vallandighams, and Pierces suffered pangs as keen, on account of these great national victories, as did their confederates in the South. With lowering faces they witnessed the revival of martial enthusiasm, which, during months of disaster and discouragement, they had seen diminish and fail. They had been ready to ring its knell when it rose from the dead and overcame them with its fury. Henceforth they could number among their friends and supporters only the most ignorant and debased—the offscouring of our great cities. But they did not therefore desist from their base efforts. Willingly they accepted the only alliance left them, and bravely defied the sure verdict of history.

Thus it was that, during the month of July, New York city became the scene of the most disgraceful drama ever enacted in America. Three journals which had surrendered themselves to the enemies of the government sounded the prelude and announced the argument. The draft which had

interference quickens anew, and that without this life-giving support it must soon yield to the just and paternal authority of the national government; that, considering these things, which are aggravated by the motive of the resistance thus encouraged, the United States regret that foreign powers have not frankly told the chiefs of the rebellion that the work in which they are engaged is hateful, and that a new government, such as they seek to found, with slavery as its acknowledged corner-stone, and with no other declared object of separate existence, is so far shocking to civilization and the moral sense of mankind, that it must not expect welcome or recognition in the commonwealth of nations.

"*Resolved*, That the United States, confident in the justice of their cause, which is the cause also of good government and of human rights every where among men; anxious for the speedy restoration of peace, which shall secure tranquillity at home, and remove all occasion of complaint abroad; and awaiting with well-assured trust the final suppression of the rebellion, through which all these things, rescued from present danger, will be secured forever, and the republic, one and indivisible, triumphant over its enemies, will continue to stand an example to mankind, hereby announce, as their unalterable purpose, that the war will be vigorously prosecuted, according to the humane principles of Christian states, until the rebellion shall be overcome; and they reverently invoke upon their cause the blessing of Almighty God.

"*Resolved*, That the President be requested to transmit a copy of these resolutions, through the Secretary of State, to the ministers of the United States in foreign countries, that the declaration and protest herein set forth may be communicated by them to the governments to which they are accredited."

HORATIO SEYMOUR.

been ordered to begin in the city on Saturday, July 11th, these journals pronounced the work of evil-minded men, intended to accomplish their own selfish ends. Those who had determined to strike at slavery, the chief support of the rebellion, were styled "neither more nor less than murderers." The administrators of the government were styled "weak and reckless men." The draft was declared to be "a measure which could not have been ventured upon in England, even in those dark days when the press-gang filled the English ships-of-war with slaves, and dimmed the glory of England's noblest naval heroes—a measure wholly repugnant to the habits and prejudices of our people." It was asserted that the aim of the government, in conscription, was "to lessen the number of Democratic votes at the next election." "The miscreants at the head of the government," said the *Daily News*, "are bending all their powers, as was revealed in the late speech of Wendell Phillips at Framingham, to securing a perpetuation of their ascendency for another four years; and their triple method of accomplishing this purpose is to kill off Democrats, stuff the ballot-boxes with bogus soldiers' votes, and deluge recusant districts with negro suffrage." The operation of the draft was declared to have been unfair. One out of about two

and a half of our citizens was to be brought off into Lincoln's charnel-house. Governor Seymour was quoted as having openly expressed "his belief that neither the President nor Congress, without the consent of the state authorities, has any right to enforce such an act as is now being carried out under the auspices of the War Department." Every possible argument was adduced to excite violence on the part of the people against the government.

On Saturday, the 11th, after several postponements, Colonel Nugent, the provost-marshal of New York city, was directed to proceed with the draft, and the several deputies were instructed accordingly. In compliance with these instructions, Provost-marshal Jenkins, of the Ninth Congressional district, commenced operations at a building on the corner of Forty-sixth Street and Third Avenue. There was a large crowd assembled at the place of drawing, and it seemed to be in good humor, saluting well-known names with cheers. No disturbance was apprehended, and the draft was to be continued on the following Monday. But in the vicinity there were residing a large number of foreigners of Irish birth, and some of these had been drafted on Saturday. Here the turbulent element, encouraged by the utterances of a disloyal press, began to exhibit itself. Secret meetings were held, and

FIGHT WITH THE MILITARY.

NEW YORK RIOTERS HANGING A NEGRO.

it was determined to resort to force. On Monday morning organized parties proceeded from place to place, compelling workmen to desist from their accustomed labors, and join the processions already wending their way to the corner of Third Avenue and Forty-sixth Street.

Scarcely had the drawing recommenced when it was interrupted by the turbulent crowd assembled outside. Paving-stones were hurled through the windows. The crowd was in an instant transformed into a mob. The doors were broken down, and the crowd rushed in, demolishing every thing connected with the office, and taking complete possession. Only the drafting-wheel escaped destruction. Provost-marshal Jenkins escaped, and the reporters; but one of the deputies, Lieutenant Vanderpoel, was badly beaten, and taken home for dead. Having possession of the office, the rioters, regardless of the women and children residing in the stories above, poured camphene over the floor and set the place ablaze. In two hours the entire block was a smoking ruin. Officers of the Fire Department, under Chief Engineer Decker, arrived, but the hydrants were in possession of the mob, and it was only after the most persistent persuasion on the part of Decker that the firemen were allowed to prevent the farther progress of the conflagration. In the mean time, Police Superintendent Kennedy had·been attacked by the mob and nearly killed.

There were no troops in the city, the militia being absent on duty in Pennsylvania. A small force of the Invalid Corps appeared on the ground soon after the disturbance commenced, armed with muskets loaded with blank cartridges. Of course these were promptly overpowered by the mob, which had now swollen to thousands. A detachment of the police was in like manner beaten and forced to retreat. The mob was composed almost entirely of Irishmen. Now it is a curious circumstance that, while no class of our foreign population is more jealous of its own liberties than the Irish, there is also none which more strongly resents every liberty accorded to the negro race. The rioters took possession of hotels and restaurants whose servants were negroes, destroyed the furniture, maltreated the guests, and

sought the lives of the poor servants. These things were done deliberately, and not in the heat of passion. The writer of this chapter passed through the mob on the afternoon of the 14th, as they were burning down the Colored Orphan Asylum at the corner of Fifth Avenue and Forty-sixth Street. He saw no tumult, no exhibition of rage, but only a cruel, fiendish, and deliberate purpose to persecute to the death an innocent race, against whom they were only moved by a political prejudice. The asylum was burned to ashes, while the female friends of the rioters lugged off to their shanties the plundered furniture. At about the same hour the armory on Twenty-ninth Street and Second Avenue was burned. Another portion of the mob had made its way to the City Hall Park, and made an attack upon the *Tribune* office, but were severely handled and dispersed by the police.

It is supposed that about a dozen negroes were, on Monday, brutally murdered by the rioters. A colored man residing in Carmine Street was seized by the mob, and, after his life had been nearly beaten out, his body was suspended from a tree, a fire was kindled under him, and, in the midst of excruciating torments, he expired.

On Tuesday the spirit of the rioters was even more malignant. Governor Seymour, who had been absent in New Jersey, arrived in the city, and issued proclamations commanding the rioters to disperse, and declaring the city and county of New York to be in a state of insurrection. In the afternoon he addressed the mob from the steps of the City Hall. After their courteous acknowledgment of his leadership, he could not well address them otherwise than as his "friends." He assured them of his friendship, and informed them that he had sent his adjutant general to Washington "to con-

CHARGE OF THE POLICE AT THE TRIBUNE OFFICE.

THE RIOTERS BURNING THE COLORED ORPHAN ASYLUM, CORNER OF FIFTH AVENUE AND FORTY-SIXTH STREET, NEW YORK CITY.

8 c

ANDREW G. CURTIN.

JOHN BROUGH.

fer with the authorities there, and to have this draft suspended and stopped."
He gave over to these friends of his the charge over the property and persons of all other citizens, and the good order of the city, and then advised them to retire peaceably. This step on the part of the governor had little effect. The riot continued for four days, and this day was the worst of them all. All stores were closed, and no business was transacted. A small military force had been marshaled, and, wherever it encountered the mob, the latter was dispersed. But the police were far more efficient than the military, and in every conflict subdued the rioters. But neither the police nor the small military force could be omnipresent, and the most cruel atrocities were inflicted upon negroes wherever they were found. It was on Tuesday that Colonel O'Brien was killed. Commissioned to disperse a mob in Third Avenue, he had successfully accomplished his duty with the troops in his command. He had sprained his ankle in the excitement, and, stepping into a drug-store, had become separated from his troops. Here he was surrounded by the mob, and suffered a cruel death.

On the 16th several militia regiments returned from Pennsylvania, and after that there was no farther trouble. It is estimated that during the excitement over 1000 of the rioters had been killed, while of those opposed to them less than 50 lives were lost. The property destroyed by the mob was estimated at $2,000,000. The municipal authorities had, in the mean time, passed a relief bill, to pay $300 commutation, or substitute money, to every drafted man unable to pay that sum for himself.

Riots of a less serious nature occurred at the same time in Boston and other cities, but in all these were principally the disturbing element.

Governor Seymour strongly urged upon the President to postpone the draft until its constitutionality was determined upon by the courts. The President replied that he did not object to abide the decision of the courts, but he could not consent to lose the time while it was being obtained.

The subjects which had for the past few months agitated the loyal states—the emancipation proclamation, the enlistment of negro soldiers, arbitrary arrests, and the conscription—were submitted in the autumnal elections of 1863 for the decision of the people. The result was a decisive success for the administration. In Vermont, on the 1st of September, J. G. Smith, the Republican candidate for governor, was elected by a majority of nearly 18,000. In California, two days later, a Republican governor, F. F. Low, was elected by 20,000 majority. On the 14th of September Maine gave 18,000 majority to Governor Cony, Republican. In October Pennsylvania re-elected Governor Curtin by a majority of 15,000. His opponent was George W. Woodward, a peace man, whose election was regarded by General McClellan as "called for by the interests of the nation." In the same election Chief Justice Lowrie, who had declared the enrollment act unconstitutional, was defeated by over 12,000 votes. In the State of Ohio the success of the administration was most strongly marked. In 1862 the Democratic Secretary of State had received a majority of 5000 votes. But now a governor was to be elected, and the opposing candidates were the exiled "martyr" Vallandigham and Brough. Vallandigham was defeated by over 100,000 votes, of which 40,000 were polled by soldiers. The Legislature of this state, elected at the same time, stood 27 to 5 in the Senate, and 73 to 24 in

the House. Iowa elected a Legislature almost entirely Republican, and a Republican governor and judge. Similar results followed in Wisconsin, Minnesota, and Michigan. In New York the Republican majority amounted to 30,000, against a Democratic majority in 1862 of over 10,000. In Massachusetts the Republican majority was over 40,000. Even Maryland supported the administration by a majority of 20,000. When we compare these results with those of the preceding year, it is clear that the people of the loyal states had not yet deserted the administration, and that their determination to sustain the war had increased rather than diminished.

CHAPTER XLV.

POLITICAL DEVELOPMENTS OF 1864.

The Spring Elections of 1864.—Meeting of the Thirty-eighth Congress, December 7, 1863.—Position of Parties.—Colfax elected Speaker.—The President's Message.—The Amnesty Proclamation.—Arbitrary Arrests.—The Test-Oath reaffirmed.—Repeal of the Fugitive Slave Law.—The Montana Bill and Negro Suffrage.—The Anti-Slavery Amendment; its Defeat in the House.—Reverdy Johnson's Argument in favor of the Amendment.—Negro Soldiers declared free.—Congress presents a Gold Medal to General Grant.—Views of the Thirty-eighth Congress in regard to Reconstruction.—The Theory of Lincoln's Amnesty Proclamation.—Stevens's Ideas as expressed in Debate on the Confiscation Act.—The Civil Code and the Laws of War.—Henry Winter Davis's Bill for the Appointment of Provisional Governors over rebel States; passed by the House May 4, 1864, by the Senate July 2d.—Lincoln refuses to Sign the Bill; his Proclamation.—The Wade and Davis Manifesto.—Debate on the Expulsion of Alexander Long.—Financial Measures.—Resolutions on the Mexican Imbroglio.—The Presidential Campaign of 1864.—Radical Convention at Cleveland; Fremont and Cochrane nominated for President and Vice-President.—The Republican Convention at Baltimore; President Lincoln renominated, and Andrew Johnson nominated for Vice-President.—The military Situation.—Peace Missions.—Meeting of the Democratic Convention at Chicago.—Character and Purposes of the Convention; its Platform and Resolutions; Nomination of McClellan and Pendleton.—McClellan's Letter of Acceptance.—Victory at Atlanta.—Other Victories in the Shenandoah Valley.—Brighter Prospects.—Democratic Defeat at the Polls.—The Vote for President.—Lincoln and Johnson elected.—Ratification of the new Constitution in Maryland.—The Peace Commission at Hampton Roads.

IN the spring elections of 1864 we can estimate the weight of General Grant's success in the battles around Chattanooga, won in November, 1863. In New Hampshire, Gilmore, the Republican candidate for governor, was elected by a majority of nearly 6000 votes over Harrington. In Connecticut, Buckingham (Republican) was elected over O. S. Seymour by a majority of 5658 votes. In Rhode Island, also, the Republican candidate for governor, J. Y. Smith, was elected over G. H. Browne by a majority of 1538.

The first session of the Thirty-ninth Congress assembled on the 7th of December, 1863.[1] The position of parties was not far different to that of the

---

[1] The following is a list of the members of the Thirty-eighth Congress, with their political designation. Those marked A. were adherents of the administration; its opponents are marked O. An asterisk precedes those who were members of the Thirty-seventh Congress.

SENATE.

California	John Conness, A.	*Delaware*	*James A. Bayard, O.
	*James A. McDougall, O.		*Willard Saulsbury, O.
Connecticut	*James Dixon, A.	*Illinois*	William A. Richardson, O
	*Lafayette S. Foster, A		*Lyman Trumbull, A.

previous Congress. In the Senate there was a gain of two members for the administration. Of 40 senators, only 13 were in the ranks of the opposition. In the House of Representatives, of 183 members, 101 were adherents of the administration. There were 115 new members in the House and 12 in the Senate. Thus there were in the Thirty-eighth Congress 106, or nearly one half of the members which had composed the Thirty-seventh.

Indiana	Thomas A. Hendricks, O.
	*Henry S. Lane, A.
Iowa	*James W. Grimes, A.
	*James Harlan, A.
Kansas	*Samuel C. Pomeroy, A.
	*James H. Lane, A.
Kentucky	*Garrett Davis, O.
	*Lazarus W. Powell, O.
Maine	*William P. Fessenden, A.
	*Lot M. Morrill, A.
Massachusetts	*Charles Sumner, A.
	*Henry Wilson, A.
Maryland	*Thomas H. Hicks, A.
	Reverdy Johnson, O.
Michigan	*Zachariah Chandler, A.
	*Jacob M. Howard, A.
Minnesota	*Morton S. Wilkinson, A.
	Alexander Ramsay, A.
Missouri	*John B. Henderson, A.
	B. Gratz Brown, A.
New Hampshire	*Daniel Clark, A.
	*John P. Hale, A.
New Jersey	*John C. Ten Eyck, A.
	William Wright, O.
New York	*Ira Harris, A.
	Edwin D. Morgan, A.
Ohio	*Benjamin F. Wade, A.
	*John Sherman, A.
Oregon	*Benjamin F. Harding, O.
	*James W. Nesmith, O.
Pennsylvania	*Edgar Cowan, A.
	Charles R. Buckalew, O.
Rhode Island	*Henry B. Anthony, A.
	William Sprague, A.
Vermont	*Solomon Foot, A.
	*Jacob Collamer, A.
Virginia	*John S. Carlile, O.
	Lemuel J. Bowden, A.
West Virginia	P. G. Van Winkle, A.
	*Waitman T. Willey, A.
Wisconsin	*James R. Doolittle, A.
	*Timothy O. Howe, A.

Lemuel J. Bowden, of Virginia, died January 2, 1864. His vacancy was not filled. J. A. Bayard, of Delaware, resigned January 29, 1864, and his place was filled by G. R. Riddle (A.).

HOUSE OF REPRESENTATIVES.

California	Thomas B. Shannon, A.
	William Higby, A.
	Cornelius Cole, A.
Connecticut	Henry C. Deming, A.
	*James E. English, O.
	Augustus Brandegee, A.
	John H. Hubbard, A.
Delaware	Nathaniel B. Smithers, A.
Illinois	*Isaac N. Arnold, A.
	John F. Farnsworth, A.
	*Elihu B. Washburne, A.
	Charles M. Harris, O.
	*Owen Lovejoy, A.
	Jesse O. Norton, A.
	John R. Eden, O.
	John T. Stewart, O.
	Lewis W. Ross, O.
	*Anthony L. Knapp, O.
	*James C. Robinson, O.
	William R. Morrison, O.
	*William J. Allen, O.
	James C. Allen, O.
Indiana	*John Law, O.
	*James A. Cravens, O.
	Henry W. Harrington, O.
	*William S. Holman, O.
	*George W. Julian, A.
	Ebenezer Dumont, A.
	*Daniel W. Vorhees, O.
	Godlove S. Orth, A.
	*Schuyler Colfax, A.
	Joseph K. Edgerton, O.
	James F. McDowell, O.
Iowa	*James F. Wilson, A.
	Hiram Price, A.
	William B. Allison, A.
	J. B. Grinnell, A.
	John A. Kasson, A.
	A. W. Hubbard, A.
Kansas	A. Carter Wilder, A.
Kentucky	Lucien Anderson, A.
	*George H. Yeaman, O.
	*Henry Grider, O.
	*Aaron Harding, O.
	*Robert Mallory, O.
	Green Clay Smith, A.
	Brutus J. Clay, O.
	William H. Randall, A.
	*William H. Wadsworth, O.
Maine	Lorenzo D. M. Sweat, O.
	Sidney Perham, A.
	James G. Blaine, A.
	*John H. Rice, A.
	*Frederick A. Pike, A.
Maryland	John A. J. Creswell, A.
	*Edwin H. Webster, A.
	Henry Winter Davis, A.
	*Francis Thomas, A.
	Benjamin G. Harris, O.
Massachusetts	*Thomas D. Eliot, A.
	Oakes Ames, A.
	*Alexander H. Rice, A.
	*Samuel Hooper, A.
	*John B. Alley, A.
	*Daniel W. Gooch, A.
	George S. Boutwell, A.
	John D. Baldwin, A.
	William B. Washburn, A.
	*Henry L. Dawes, A.
Michigan	*Fernando C. Beaman, A.
	Charles Upson, A.
	John W. Longyear, A.
	*Francis W. Kellogg, A.
	Augustus C. Baldwin, O.
	John F. Driggs, A.
Minnesota	*William Windom, A.
	Ignatius Donnelly, A.
Missouri	*Francis P. Blair, Jr., A.
	Henry T. Blow, A.
	John G. Scott, O.
	Joseph W. McClurg, A.
	Samuel H. Boyd, A.
	Austin A. King, O.
	Benjamin F. Loan, A.
	*William A. Hall, O.
	*James S. Rollins, O.
New Hampshire	Daniel Marcy, O.
	*Edward H. Rollins, A.
	James W. Patterson, A.
New Jersey	John F. Starr, A.
	George Middleton, O.
	*William G. Steele, O.
	Andrew J. Rogers, O.
	*Nehemiah Perry, O.
New York	Henry G. Stebbins, O.
	Martin Kalbfleisch, O.
	*Moses F. Odell, O.
	*Benjamin Wood, O.
	Fernando Wood, O.
	*Elijah Ward, O.
	John W. Chanler, O.
	James Brooks, O.
	Anson Herrick, O.
	William Radford, O.
	Charles H. Winfield, O.
	Homer A. Nelson, O.
	*John B. Steele, O.
	John V. L. Pruyn, O.
	John Q. Griswold, O.
	Orlando Kellogg, A.
	Calvin T. Hulburd, A.
	James W. Marvin, A.
	Samuel F. Miller, A.
	*Ambrose W. Clark, A.
	Francis Kernan, O.
	De Witt C. Littlejohn, A.
	Thomas T. Davis, A.
	*Theodore M. Pomeroy, A.
	Daniel Morris, A.
	Giles W. Hotchkiss, A,
	*Robt. B. Van Valkenburg, A.
	Freeman Clark, A.
	*Augustus Frank, A.
	John B. Gunson, O.
	*Reuben E. Fenton, A.
Ohio	*George H. Pendleton, O.
	Alexander Long, O.
	Robert C. Schenck, A.
	J. F. McKinney, O.
	Frank C. Le Blond, O.
	*Chilton A. White, O.
	*Samuel S. Cox, O.
	William Johnson, O.
	*Warren P. Noble, O.
	*James M. Ashley, A.
	Wells A. Hutchins, O.
	William E. Finck, O.
	John O'Neill, O.
	George Bliss, O.
	*James R. Morris, O.
	Joseph W. White, O.
	Ephraim E. Eckley, A.
	Rufus P. Spaulding, A.
	James A. Garfield, A.
Oregon	John R. McBride, A.
Pennsylvania	Samuel J. Randall, O.
	Charles O'Neill, A.
	Leonard Myers, A.
	*William D. Kelley, A.
	M. Russell Thayer, A.
	*John D. Stiles, O.
	John M. Broomall, A.
	*Sydenham E. Ancona, O.
	*Thaddeus Stevens, A.
	Myer Strause, O.
	*Philip Johnson, O,
	Charles Dennison, O.
	Henry M. Tracy, A.
	William H. Miller, O.
	*Joseph Baily, O.
	Alexander H. Coffroth, O.
	Archibald McAllister, O.
	*James T. Hale, A.
	Glenni W. Scofield, A.
	Amos Myers, A.
	John L. Dawson, O.
	*James K. Moorhead, A.
	Thomas Williams, A.
	*Jesse Lazear, O.
Rhode Island	Thomas A. Jenckes, A.
	Nathan F. Dixon, A.
Vermont	Fredk. E. Woodbridge, A.
	*Justin S. Morrill, A.
	*Portus Baxter, A.
West Virginia	*Jacob B. Blair, A.
	*William G. Brown, A.
	*Killian V. Whaley, A.
Wisconsin	James S. Brown, O.
	*Ithamar C. Sloan, A.
	Amasa Cobb, O.
	Charles A. Eldridge, O.
	Ezra Wheeler, O.
	*Walter D. McIndoe, A.

On the 11th of June, 1864, Francis P. Blair, Jr., of Missouri, was unseated, and four days afterward Samuel Knox was qualified in his place. On March 25th, 1864, Owen Lovejoy died, and Eben C. Ingersoll was qualified as his successor.

Colfax, of Indiana, and Cox, of Ohio, were the prominent candidates for speaker—the former representing the administration, and the latter the opposition. Colfax was elected on the first ballot, receiving 101 votes, every Republican member supporting him except Francis P. Blair, who was absent, and one Democrat, Brutus J. Clay, of Kentucky. Cox received 42 votes.

The President's Message was communicated to Congress on the second day of the session. After commenting upon the foreign relations of the government, which were undisturbed at this time, the President announced the successful conduct of the Treasury under the national banking law of the previous Congress. Every demand had been promptly met, and the people had cheerfully borne the burden of taxation. The receipts for the fiscal year had been $901,125,674 86; the expenditures $895,796,630 65. The naval force of the United States had been increased to 588 vessels, completed or in process of construction, of which 75 were iron-clad steamers. Since the blockade had been instituted over 1000 vessels had been captured, and the prizes already sent in for adjudication amounted to more than $13,000,000. The number of seamen in the public service had since the spring of 1861 increased from 7500 men to about 34,000, notwithstanding the injurious effect of the high bounties paid to army recruits.

The President contrasted the present condition of the country with that which had confronted the previous session. "When Congress assembled a year ago," said he, "the war had already lasted twenty months, and there had been many conflicts on both land and sea, with varying results. The rebellion had been pressed back into reduced limits; yet the tone of public feeling and opinion, at home and abroad, was not satisfactory. With other signs, the popular election, just then past, indicated uneasiness among ourselves, while, amid much that was cold and menacing, the kindest words coming from Europe were uttered in accents of pity that we were too blind to surrender a hopeless cause. Our commerce was suffering greatly by a few armed vessels built upon and furnished from foreign shores, and we were threatened with such additions from the same quarter as would sweep our trade from the sea and raise our blockade. We had failed to elicit from European governments any thing hopeful upon this subject. The preliminary emancipation proclamation, issued in September, was running its assigned period to the beginning of the new year. A month later the final proclamation came, including the announcement that colored men of suitable condition would be received into the war service. The policy of emancipation and of employing black soldiers gave to the future a new aspect, about which hope, and fear, and doubt contended in uncertain conflict. According to our political system, as a matter of civil administration, the general government had no right to effect emancipation in any state, and for a long time it had been hoped that the rebellion could be suppressed without resorting to it as a military measure. It was all the while deemed possible that the necessity for it might come, and that, if it should, the crisis of the contest would then be presented. It came, and, as we anticipated, it was followed by dark and doubtful days.

"Eleven months having now passed, we are permitted to take another view. The rebel hordes are pressed still farther back, and, by the complete opening of the Mississippi, the country dominated by the rebellion is divided into distinct parts, with no practical communication between them. Tennessee and Arkansas have been substantially cleared of insurgent control, and influential citizens in each, owners of slaves and advocates of slavery at the beginning of the rebellion, now declare openly for emancipation in their respective states. Of those states not included in the emancipation proclamation, Maryland and Missouri, neither of which three years ago would tolerate any restraint upon the extension of slavery into new territories, only dispute now as to the best mode of removing it within their own limits. Of those who were slaves at the beginning of the rebellion, full one hundred thousand are in the United States military service, about one half of which number actually bear arms in the ranks, thus giving the double advantage of taking so much labor from the insurgent cause, and supplying the places which otherwise must be filled with so many white men. So far as tested, it is difficult to say they are not as good soldiers as any. No servile insurrection, or tendency to violence or cruelty, has marked the measures of emancipation or arming the blacks. These measures have been much discussed in foreign countries, and contemporary with such discussion the tone of public sentiment there is much improved. At home the same measures have been fully discussed, supported, criticised, and denounced, and the annual elections following are highly encouraging to those whose official duty it is to bear the country through this great trial. Thus we have the new reckoning. The crisis which threatened to divide the friends of the Union is past."

In this changed condition of public affairs the President had seen fit to put forth an amnesty proclamation. The Constitution authorized the President to grant or withhold pardon for offenses committed against the United States at his own absolute discretion, and this involved the power to grant pardon on terms. The constitutional obligation to guarantee to every state in the Union a republican form of government was explicit and full. But why tender the benefits of this provision to governments only in such states as could show a loyal tenth of their population ready to take the oath of allegiance to the government and of support to the enactments of Congress which had been occasioned by the war? "This section of the Constitution," said the President, "contemplates a case wherein the element within a state favorable to republican government in the Union may be too feeble for an opposite and hostile element external to or even within a state, and such are precisely the cases with which we are now dealing. . . . . There must be a test by which to separate the opposing elements, so as to build only from the sound; and that test is a sufficiently liberal one which accepts as sound whoever will make a sworn recantation of his former un soundness." "I shall not attempt," he added, "to retract or modify the emancipation proclamation, nor shall I return to slavery any person who is free by that proclamation, or by any of the acts of Congress. For these and other reasons, it is thought best that the support of these measures shall be included in the oath; and it is believed the executive may lawfully claim it in return for pardon and restoration of forfeited rights, which he has clear constitutional power to withhold altogether, or to grant upon the terms which he shall deem wisest for the public interest."

The message thus concluded:

"In the midst of other cares, however important, we must not lose sight of the fact that the war power is still our main reliance. To that power alone can we look, yet for a time, to give confidence to the people in the contested regions, that the insurgent power will not again overrun them. Until that confidence shall be established, little can be done any where for what is called reconstruction. Hence our chiefest care must still be directed to the army and navy, who have thus far borne their harder part so nobly and well. And it may be esteemed fortunate that, in giving the greatest efficiency to these indispensable arms, we do also honorably recognize the gallant men, from commander to sentinel, who compose them, and to whom, more than to others, the world must stand indebted for the home of freedom disenthralled, regenerated, enlarged, and perpetuated."

It was a new Congress, and many of the contests already decided in favor of the administration had to be fought over again. The House had been in session scarcely a week when the subject of arbitrary arrests was introduced. By a vote of 90 to 67 the decision of the previous Congress was reaffirmed. This was purely a party vote, if we except the name of Brutus J. Clay, who, though nominally a Democrat, in all important matters supported the administration. On the 29th of February, Pendleton, of Ohio, offered a resolution denouncing the arrest of Vallandigham as an arbitrary act, and a violation of the Constitution, which the House rejected by 77 votes against 47. Here also Clay was the only Democrat in favor of rejection. Other resolutions of a similar character in regard to the general subject of arrests were introduced during the session, but were invariably tabled.

In the Senate, on the 17th of December, Sumner offered as a new rule for the Senate that the oath prescribed for senators by the act of July 2, 1862, should be taken and subscribed by every senator in open Senate before entering upon his duties. Thus the whole subject was again laid open to discussion, and the next day a substitute was moved by Saulsbury, of Delaware, instructing the Judiciary Committee to inquire whether members of Congress were included within the provisions of the act of July 2, 1862, and whether this act was constitutional. The substitute was rejected, and Sumner's resolution was adopted. Bayard, of Delaware, who had been reelected for the term ending March 3, 1869, was the only senator who had not taken the oath. On the 26th of January he subscribed to the oath, and then resigned his seat.[1] His place was supplied by George R. Riddle, a supporter of the administration.

It is curious and suggestive to trace the steady progress of negro emancipation in the congressional history of the war. Undoubtedly this progress was in a large degree due to a sense of moral justice on the part of the Northern people, which had been for many years repressed by the supposed necessity of sanctioning and actually upholding a system of gross injustice, in order to preserve the Constitution and the Union. But when it became evident that this system, thus nursed, was a serpent in the bosom of the people—a serpent whose fangs were now thrust into both the Union and the Constitution—this monstrous incubus was thrown off, and justice breathed unshackled. And it should also be remembered that in this case the dictates of freedom and justice were uttered in the very teeth of a prejudice against the negro race which was far stronger in the North than it was in the South. No greater tribute could be paid to the virtue of republican institutions than this victory of the moral sense over prejudice. But in this case the suppression of the prejudice against the negro was made easy by the aid of a stronger prejudice against treason. Then, again, the *military* necessity of striking at slavery in order to weaken treason, and the *political* necessity of emancipation in order to prevent a future reign of discord, were overmastering motives, helping on the great revolution in behalf of an oppressed race—a moral revolution, in comparison with which the war itself, and its immense sacrifices of blood and treasure, would become almost insignificant, were they not inseparably linked therewith in the sequences of Providence.

During this session a bill "to repeal the Fugitive Slave Law of 1850, and all acts and parts of acts for the rendition of fugitive slaves," was passed. It was reported in the Senate by Sumner on the 19th of April. An amendment offered by Sherman, of Ohio, excepting the act of 1793, was adopted 24 to 17. Among those voting in the affirmative were Senators Collamer, Cowan, Dixon, and Doolittle. Fessenden voted in the negative. This bill was not again acted upon. But on the 13th of June the House passed a bill reported from the Judiciary Committee by Morris, of New York, repealing the acts of 1793 and 1850 by a vote of 90 to 62, Griswold, of New York, being the only opposition member voting in the affirmative. On the 22d of June the bill passed the Senate 27 to 12, and was approved by President Lincoln on the 28th.

On the 26th of February a bill was reported in the Senate proposing to repeal the law prohibiting negroes from being employed as carriers of the mail, with an amendment providing that in the courts of the United States there should be no exclusion of any witnesses on account of color. The amendment was not passed in this connection, but subsequently was attached as a provision to the Civil Appropriation Bill—a favorite device of Senator Sumner.[1] It was afterward approved in the House and became a law.

On the 31st of March the House bill, in the usual form, providing a temporary government for Montana, was considered in the Senate, and an amendment was passed ignoring any distinction based on color in the organization of the territorial government. The House refused to concur. A conference committee was appointed, and the bill was finally passed without the amendment. As there was not a negro in the territory, the subject was of no practical importance, but in any case probably the amendment would not have been adopted; for, in a joint resolution amending the charter of the District of Columbia, which passed both houses a few weeks later, Sumner's amendment providing that there should be no exclusion from the register on account of color was rejected. Congress at this time certainly was not in favor of negro suffrage even in the district over which it had legislative control. In the bill, however, incorporating the Metropolitan Railroad Company of the District of Columbia, which passed both houses, provision was incorporated that there should be no regulation excluding any person from any car on account of color. On the 24th of June Sumner succeeded in attaching to the Civil Appropriation Bill a section prohibiting the coastwise slave-trade, which passed both houses.

About the end of March a joint resolution was offered in the Senate, proposing to the Legislatures of the several states the following article as an amendment to the Constitution:

"ARTICLE XIII., *Section* 1. Neither slavery nor involuntary servitude, except as a punishment for crime, whereof the party shall have been duly convicted, shall exist within the United States, or in any place subject to their jurisdiction.

"*Section* 2. Congress shall have power to enforce this article by appropriate legislation."

"When this amendment shall be consummated," said Senator Wilson, "the shackles will fall from the limbs of the hapless bondsman, and the lash drop from the weary hand of the task-master. . . . . Then the slave-mart, pen, and auction block, with their clanking fetters for human limbs, will disappear from the land they have brutalized, and the school-house will rise to enlighten the darkened intellect of a race imbruted by long years of enforced ignorance. Then the sacred rights of human nature, the hallowed family relations of husband and wife, parent and child, will be protected by the guardian spirit of the law which makes sacred alike the proud homes and lowly cabins of freedom. Then the sacred earth, blighted by the sweat and tears of bondage, will bloom again under the quickening culture of rewarded toil. Then the wronged victim of the slave system, the poor white man, and sand-hiller, the clay-eater of the wasted fields of California, impoverished, debased, dishonored by the system that makes toil a badge of disgrace, and the instruction of the brain and soul of man a crime, will lift his abashed forehead to the skies, and begin to run the race of improvement, progress, and elevation. Then the nation, 'regenerated, and disenthralled by the genius of universal emancipation,' will run the career of development, power, and glory, animated and guided by the spirit of the Christian Democracy, that 'pulls not the highest down, but lifts the lowest up.'" The resolution was adopted by a vote of 38 to 6. In the House it failed of the necessary two thirds majority. Reverdy Johnson, of Maryland, on most subjects a member of the opposition, and himself a slaveholder, strongly advocated the passage of the amendment in the Senate. "There was a period," said he, "in our own time when there was but one opinion upon the question of right, or almost but one opinion upon that question. The men who fought through the Revolution, those who survived its peril and shared in its glory, and who were called to the Convention by which the Constitution of the United States was drafted and recommended to the adoption of the American people, almost without exception, thought that slavery was not only an evil to any people among whom it might exist, but that it was an evil of the highest character, which it was the duty of all Christian people, if possible, to remove, because it was a sin as well as an evil.

"I think the history of those times will bear me out in the statement, that if the men by whom that Constitution was framed, and the people by whom it was adopted, had anticipated the times in which we live, they would have provided by constitutional enactment that that evil and that sin should at some comparatively remote day be removed. Without recurring to authority, the writings, public or private, of the men of that day, it is sufficient for my purpose to state what the facts will justify me in saying, that every man of them who largely shared in the dangers of the revolutionary struggle, and who largely participated in the deliberations of the Convention by which the Constitution was adopted, earnestly desired, not only upon grounds of political economy, not only upon reasons material in their character, but

[1] "With a firm conviction," said he, "that your decision inflicts a vital wound upon free representative government, I can not, by continuing to hold the seat I now occupy under it, give my personal assent and sanction to its propriety. To do so, I must forfeit my own self-respect, and sacrifice my clear conviction of duty, for the sake merely of retaining a high trust and station with its emoluments. That will I never do; but, retiring into private life, shall await, I trust, with calmness and firmness, though certainly with despondency, the farther progress of a war which it is apparent to my vision will, in its continuance, subvert republican institutions, and sever this Federal Union into many arbitrary governments.

"Among these, wars for dominion will arise and continue until, from exhaustion, the different divisions subside into separate nationalities, leaving not the vestige of a republic remaining. If the lessons of history be not deceptive and valueless, such will be the inevitable result of protracted war; for a single centralized government over so vast a territory, inhabited by so intelligent and energetic a people, could it be organized through military genius and power, and be successful for the hour, would not outlive the generation in which it was established."

[1] The entire amendment reads thus:

Provided, That in the courts of the United States there shall be no exclusion of any witness on account of color, nor in civil actions because he is a party to or interested in the issue tried.

CHARLES SUMNER.

upon grounds of morality and religion, that sooner or later the institution should terminate.

"The present incumbent of the presidential chair was elected—elected by a sectional vote—and the moment the news reached Charleston, where some of the leading conspirators were, and here in this chamber, where others were to be found, it was hailed, not with regret, but with delight. Why? Because, as they thought, it would enable them to drive the South to madness by appealing to the danger in which such an event involved this institution, which the people were made to believe was so essential to their power and to their happiness, and that will be repeated over and over again just as long as the institution is suffered to remain. Terminate it, and the wit of man will, as I think, be unable to devise any other topic upon which we can be involved in a fratricidal strife. God and nature, judging

by the history of the past, intend us to be one. Our unity is written in the mountains and rivers in which we all have an interest. The very difference of climate render each important to the other and alike important. That mighty horde which from time to time have gone from the Atlantic, imbued with all the principles of human freedom which animated their fathers in running the perils of the mighty deep and seeking liberty here, are now there, and as they have said, and will continue to say until time shall be no more: 'We mean that the government in the future shall be as in the past, one, an example of human freedom for the light and example of the world, and illustrating in the blessings and the happiness it confers the truth of the principles incorporated into the Declaration of Independence, that life and liberty are man's inalienable right.'"

This able senator, on a former occasion during this session, when the section providing for the freedom of negro soldiers, their wives and their children, was under discussion, had very plainly demonstrated the wickedness of slavery. "I doubt very much," he said, "if any member of the Senate is more anxious to have the country composed of free men and free women than I am. I understand the bill to provide that upon the enlistment as a soldier of any man of African descent, his wife and children are at once to be free. No provision is made to compensate the owner of the wife and children if they happen to be slaves, and it of course only applies to such wives and children as are slaves—those who are to be set free, and not those who are now free.

"The bill provides that a slave enlisted any where, no matter where he may be, whether he be within Maryland or out of Maryland, whether he be within any of the loyal states or out of the loyal states altogether, is at once to work the emancipation of his wife and his children. He may be in South Carolina; and many a slave in South Carolina, I am sorry to say it, *can well claim to have a wife, and perhaps wives and children, within the limits of Maryland.* It is one of the vices, and the *horrible vices* of the institution—one that has shocked me from infancy to the present hour—the whole marital relation is disregarded. They are made to be, practically and by education, forgetful or ignorant of that relation. When I say they are educated, I mean to say they are kept in absolute ignorance, and out of that *immorality of every description* arises, and among the other immoralities is that the connubial relation does not exist.

"The men who were here preaching their treason from these desks, telegraphing from these desks—I saw it, though I was not a member, and my heart burned within me—for their minions, or the deluded masses at home, to seize upon the public property of the United States, its forts, its means, its treasure, its material of war, and who were seeking to seduce from their allegiance officers of the army and navy of the United States—they have done it; and they were told that such would be the result. They did not believe it. They believed that your representatives would not have the firmness to try the wager of battle. They believed—I have heard them say so—that a Southern regiment could march without resistance successfully from Washington to Boston, and challenge for themselves independence in Faneuil Hall. Sad delusion! Gross ignorance of the character of your people! You were free, and you knew its value. You are free, and you are brave because you are free; and as I have told them over and over again, let the day come when in their madness they should throw down the gage of battle to the free states of the Union, and the day of their domestic institution will have ended. They have done it. I have said it was, as against them, retributive justice. Hoping and believing that their effort will be fruitless, that their treason will fail in its object, that the authority of the government will be sustained, and the Union be preserved, I thank God that as a compensation for the blood, the treasure, and the agony which have been brought into our households, and into yours, it has stricken now and forever this institution from its place among our states."

Though the section providing for the freedom of the families of negroes engaged in the military service was not passed, yet the soldiers themselves were by another act declared free, and provision was made for their receiving the same payment as white soldiers.[1]

In legislating upon slavery, Congress did not forget the army. One of the first acts of the session was a joint resolution directing that the thanks of Congress be presented to General Grant, and to the officers and soldiers under him, and requesting the President to cause a gold medal to be struck, with suitable emblems, devices, and inscriptions, to be presented to General Grant. A copy of the joint resolutions engrossed on parchment was directed to be transmitted with the medal, to be presented to the general in the name of the people of the United States.

No act of Congress relating to the war was of so much importance as that approved by the President on the 29th of February, reviving the grade of lieutenant general. The circumstances connected with General Grant's nomination to and confirmation in this office have already been narrated in a previous chapter.

Resolutions were offered in December by Johnson, of Pennsylvania, and by Eldridge, of Wisconsin, in opposition to the Conscription Act of the previous Congress, but these were promptly laid on the table. Toward the close of the session the commutation clause was repealed, and no exemption was allowed except for alienage, previous service of two years, or physical disability.

The President's Amnesty Proclamation naturally introduced the subject of reconstruction early in the session. On the 15th of December, Henry

Winter Davis, of Maryland, moved the reference of that portion of the President's message which related to reconstruction to a select committee of nine, to be named by the speaker. He objected to the use of the term reconstruction as vague and inaccurate, as there had been "no destruction of the Union, no breaking up of the government." "The fact," said he, "as well as the constitutional view of affairs in the states enveloped by rebellion, is that a force has overthrown, or the people, in a moment of madness, have abrogated the governments which existed in those states under the Constitution, and were recognized by the United States prior to the breaking out of the rebellion. The government of the United States is engaged in two operations. One is the suppression of armed resistance to the supreme authority of the United States, and which is endeavoring to suppress that opposition by arms. Another—a very delicate and perhaps as high a duty—is to see, when armed resistance shall be removed, that governments shall be restored in those states republican in their form."

Lovejoy, of Illinois, expressed very similar views of the subject. "I do not believe," said he, "strictly speaking, that there are any rebel states. I know there are states which rebels have taken possession of and overthrown the legitimate governments for the time being; and I hold, with the gentleman from Maryland, as I understood him, that those governments still remain, and that as soon as we can get possession of them we will breathe into them the spirit of republican life—a free soul once again. I am for the Constitution as it is and the Union as it was. Yes, I am for the Constitution as it is, and not as it has been falsely interpreted, and for the Union as it was before it was taken possession of by slaveholding tyrants."

The House adopted Davis's proposition[1] by a vote of 91 to 80. Thus it will be seen that even at this time there was a great difference of opinion in regard to the restoration of the insurrectionary states to their normal relations in the Union. The dividing line was already being drawn between those who were willing to base restoration upon the returning allegiance to the Constitution of the people of the South, and upon their support of the action of the government in regard to slavery, and those who, insisting upon the right and expediency of treating the Southern people as a conquered nation of aliens, would impose additional conditions of a harsher and more humiliating character. The majority of the members of Congress belonged at this time to the former class, and adopted the views of Henry Winter Davis and Lovejoy. The President's Amnesty Proclamation was a practical expression of the same views. The proclamation consists of two parts—one declaring the executive pardon upon certain conditions and with certain exceptions; the other declaring the willingness of the government to recognize state governments, republican in form, whenever re-established by loyal voters, not less than one tenth in number of the votes cast in the respective states at the presidential election of 1860.

1. The subject of pardon was purely within executive control. The Constitution expressly declares that the President "shall have power to grant reprieves and pardons for offenses against the United States, except in cases of impeachment." Of course, the power to grant pardon includes the power to grant it upon conditions and with exceptions. The condition required by the President was the taking of the following oath:

"I, —— ——, do solemnly swear, in presence of Almighty God, that I will henceforth faithfully support, protect, and defend the Constitution of the United States and the Union of the states thereunder; and that I will, in like manner, abide by and faithfully support all acts of Congress passed during the existing rebellion with reference to slaves, so long and so far as not repealed, modified, or held void by Congress, or by decision of the Supreme Court; and that I will, in like manner, abide by, and faithfully support all proclamations of the President made during the existing rebellion, having reference to slaves, so long and so far as not modified or declared void by decision of the Supreme Court. So help me God."

The following persons were excepted: "All who are or shall have been civil or diplomatic officers of the so-called Confederate government; all who have left judicial stations under the United States to aid the rebellion; all who are, or shall have been, military or naval officers of said so-called Confederate government above the rank of colonel in the army, or of lieutenant in the navy; all who left seats in the United States Congress to aid the rebellion; all who resigned commissions in the army or navy of the United States, and afterward aided the rebellion; and all who have engaged in any way in treating colored persons, or white persons in charge of such, otherwise than lawfully as prisoners of war, and which persons may have been found in the United States service as soldiers, seamen, or in any other capacity."

2. The second part of the proclamation also rested upon a constitutional basis. The Constitution provides that "the United States shall guarantee to every state in this Union a republican form of government, and shall protect each of them against invasion, and, on application of the Legislature or the executive (when the Legislature can not be convened), against domestic violence." It was only in cases like this—where loyal governments had been subverted—that such a guaranty could become necessary. It was a guaranty to loyal men as against rebels—a guaranty backed by the whole military power of the government. It was granted in good faith, and sustained by every pledge which it was in the power of the executive to give. So far as it went, it was authoritative, without the sanction of any legislative or judicial body. It was a proclamation by the executive declaring a mode by which loyal men in the disturbed states might restore the latter to their

---

[1] The *American Annual Cyclopædia* for 1864 thus enumerates the several acts relating to slavery which were passed by the Thirty-seventh and during the first session of the Thirty-eighth Congress: "Slaves used for military purposes by the enemy were declared to be free; an additional article of war dismissed from service all officers who should surrender escaped fugitives coming within the lines of the armies; three thousand slaves in the District of Columbia were emancipated, and slaveholding forbidden; it was enacted that colored persons in the District should be tried for the same offenses, in the same manner, and be subject to the same punishment as white persons, and that such persons should not be excluded as witnesses on account of color; and that colored schools should be provided, and the same rate of appropriation made to them as to schools for white children; and that there should be no exclusion from any railway car in the District on account of color; slavery was forever prohibited in all territory of the United States; a joint resolution was passed pledging the faith of the nation to aid non-seceding states to emancipate their slaves; all slaves of persons aiding the enemy who should take refuge within the lines of the army were declared free; it was enacted that no slave should be surrendered to any claimant until such person had made oath that he had not given aid and comfort to the rebellion; the President was authorized to receive into the military service persons of African descent, and such person, his mother, wife, and children, owing service to any person giving aid to the rebellion, were declared free; the mutual right of search was arranged within certain limits with Great Britain in order to suppress the slave-trade; the independence of Hayti and Liberia were recognized, and diplomatic relations with them authorized; colored persons, free or slave, to be enrolled and drafted the same as whites, the former to have the same pay as the latter, and the slave to be free; all fugitive slave acts were repealed; the coastwise slave-trade was declared illegal; colored persons enabled to testify in all the courts of the United States; colored persons were authorized to carry the mails of the United States. Other measures were introduced, but failed to pass."

[1] "'That so much of the President's message as relates to the duty of the United States to guarantee a republican form of government to the states in which the governments recognized by the United States have been abrogated or overthrown, be referred to a select committee of nine, to be named by the speaker, which shall report the bills necessary and proper for carrying into execution the foregoing guarantee.'"

normal relations with the executive. The direct participation of these states in the Federal government by means of representation was left entirely to Congress. "Whether members sent to Congress from any state shall be admitted to seats constitutionally, rests exclusively *with the respective houses*, and not, to any extent, with the executive." We have said that the provisions of this proclamation were made for loyal men; yet the proclamation was by its very terms addressed to rebels, to induce them to return to their allegiance to the government, and time was given for its operation upon the minds of the people. The amnesty had no reference to the *past*, but only to *prospective* allegiance. Only those were excluded from participation in the work of restoration who refused to take this oath, and who were not qualified voters by the election laws of their respective states. This work might proceed in any of the eleven so-called Confederate States "*whenever*" (not *if now*, or *if immediately*) one tenth of the voters in the state should have taken the amnesty oath in good faith.

Thus the real burden of restoration, according to President Lincoln's method, was thrown upon the people of the disturbed states. The only conditions imposed were the modification of the new governments to suit the altered situation of the negro, and that the governments should be republican in form. That otherwise than in regard to slavery Lincoln's method did not contemplate any radical revolution in the revived state governments is evident from the fact that he saw no impropriety in maintaining "the name of the state, the boundary, the subdivisions, the Constitution, and the general code of laws, as before the rebellion." Negro suffrage was not even alluded to either as necessary or desirable. It was simply declared that any provision which might be adopted in relation to the freed people, recognizing and declaring their permanent freedom, providing for their education, or meeting their present condition as a laboring, landless, and homeless class, would "not be objected to by the executive."

It must be remembered that this plan, so liberal in its provisions, was offered while the war was yet in progress, though no longer doubtful as to its result. Perhaps there is no stronger evidence of the blindness and persistency of the rebellion, or of the want of foresight among its leaders, than the fact that this generous plan was not immediately and universally adopted. The nation would have been thus delivered not only from sixteen months of useless strife, but also from the dissensions which, after the close of the war, arose in regard to the methods of restoration. Whether, on the whole, so sudden a deliverance would have been better for the interests of freedom on this continent, there is room for doubt. If treason had thus suddenly and of its own motion been transformed into loyalty, in order to save itself from impending woes, it would not then have been utterly slain; if it had thus willingly put off its own armor, and resigned the conflict while yet in its full might of resistance, might it not then again have proudly stepped into the political arena, changed only in respect of *prudence?* The nation would have lost that complete sense of the victory of right over wrong which followed the forced surrender of the Confederate armies; and who can estimate the moral power lodged in that sublime exaltation which thrilled the whole loyal people in the spring of 1865? But in that way also lay fearful temptation and possible madness, arising out of the very completeness of a victory by which the people of an entire section were laid prostrate at the feet of that of another. But even this test, if it could be borne, it were a pity to have lost—losing, as we should have done, at the same time, so much of moral force; escaping at once inestimable good and the possibility of inestimable harm. If the war had thus concluded, slavery would have been abolished indeed; but whatever of positive liberty the negro might gain he must owe to the magnanimity or the fears of his former masters, or else to his own utility as a political dummy.

By the amnesty proclamation, property forfeited under the Confiscation Act of Congress, and not already sold, was restored to all persons taking the oath of allegiance.

In Congress the general subject of reconstruction came up in the course of a discussion relating to the Confiscation Act of 1862, and its application to the perpetual forfeiture of property. During the debate in the House on the 22d of January, Thaddeus Stevens reiterated the views upon which he had so strongly insisted in the previous session. It had been argued by some members that the Constitution permitted no forfeiture of real estate beyond the natural life of the offender, and by others that no such meaning was intended by the framers, whose design was merely to prevent the act of forfeiture from original application after the offender's decease. Stevens claimed that the Confiscation Act was not affected, either directly or indirectly, by the provisions of the Constitution; that its operation was not under the Constitution, but in accordance with the laws of war. The seizure of property operated not as against traitors, but as against alien enemies. "It is, however," said he, "essential to ascertain what relation the seceded states bear to the United States, that we may know how to deal with them in reestablishing the national government. There seems to be great confusion of ideas and diversity of opinion on that subject. Some think that those states are still in the Union, and entitled to the protection of the Constitution and laws of the United States, and that, notwithstanding all they have done, they may at any time, without any legislation, come back, send senators and representatives to Congress, and enjoy all the privileges and immunities of loyal members of the United States; that whenever those 'wayward sisters' choose to abandon their frivolities and present themselves at the door of the Union and demand admission, we must receive them with open arms, and throw over them the protecting shield of the Union, of which it is said they had never ceased to be members. Others hold that, having committed treason, renounced their allegiance to the Union, discarded its Constitution and laws, organized a distinct and hostile government, and by force of arms

having risen from the condition of insurgents to the position of an independent power *de facto*, and having been acknowledged as a belligerent both by foreign nations and our own government, the Constitution and laws of the Union are abrogated so far as they are concerned, and that, as between the two belligerents, they are under the laws of war and the laws of nations alone, and that whichever power conquers may treat the vanquished as conquered provinces, and may impose upon them such conditions and laws as it may deem best.

"It is obvious that this question is of vast importance. If the first position should be established, then the rebel states, after having been conquered and reduced to helplessness through the expenditure of many billions of money and the shedding of oceans of loyal blood, may lay down their arms, which they can no longer wield, claim to be legitimate members of the Union, send senators and representatives to Congress, retain all their lands and possessions, and leave the loyal states burdened with an immense debt, with no indemnity for their sufferings and damages, and with no security for the future.

"If the latter proposition prevails, then Congress will readjust the government on the firm basis of individual and public justice; will protect the innocent and pardon the least guilty; will punish the leading traitors, seize their lands and estates, sell them in fee-simple, pay the proceeds into the national treasury to discharge the expenses and damages of the war, and provide a permanent fund for pensions to the widows and orphans, and the maimed and mangled survivors of this infamous war; and, above all, will forever exclude the infernal cause of this rebellion—human bondage—from the continent of North America."

Stevens then proceeded to argue—from the corporate capacity in which the war was waged by the Confederate States, and from the concession to them of belligerent rights, both by ourselves and foreign powers—that the operation of the war was exactly the same as if it were being waged between two hostile nations, and that all treaties or compacts previously existing between the same were therefore annulled.[1] The concession of belligerent rights to the seceding states, he claimed, was an admission that they were out of the Union. These states, as minor corporations, and also as confederated together in a major corporation, styled the "Confederate States," were waging war against the United States. It was idle to claim "that townships, and counties, and parishes within such states are at peace, while the states, by acknowledged majorities, have declared war;" and still more idle was the claim that the loyal individuals, who were a small minority, in each of the belligerent states, constituted the state, and that hence the states were not at war. "This," said he, "is ignoring the fundamental principle of democratic republics, which is, that majorities must rule; that the voice of the majority, however wicked and abandoned, is the law of the state. If the minority choose to stay within the misgoverned territory, they are its citizens, and subject to its conditions. The innocence of individuals forms no protection (except in a personal point of view) to those residing in a hostile territory. Even the innocence of women and children does not screen them from the fate of their nation." There could be no neutrals in a hostile state. "From all this," said he, "the legitimate conclusion is, that all the people and all the territory within the limits of the organized states which, by a legitimate majority of their citizens, renounced the Constitution, took their states out of the Union, and made war upon the government, are, so far as they are concerned, subject to the laws of the state, and, so far as the United States government is concerned, subject to the laws of war and of nations, *both while the war continues and when it shall be ended.* If the United States succeed, how may she treat the vanquished belligerent? Must she treat her precisely as if she had always been at peace? If so, then this war on the part of the United States has been not only a foolish, but a very wicked one. But there is no such absurd principle to restrain the hands of the injured victor. By the laws of war, the conqueror may seize and convert to his own use every thing that belongs to the enemy. This may be done when the war is raging, to weaken the enemy, and when it is ended the things seized may be retained to pay the expenses of the war and the damages caused by it. Towns, cities, and provinces may be held as a punishment for an unjust war, and as security against future aggressions. The property thus taken is not confiscated under the Constitution after conviction for treason, but is held by virtue of the laws of war. No individual crime need be proved against the owners. The fact of being a belligerent enemy carries the forfeiture with it. To my mind there can be no doubt as to *what we have a right to do* if, as I will not permit myself to doubt, we should finally conquer the Confederate States. *What it will be policy to do* may be more difficult to determine. My mind is fixed. The rebels have waged the most unjust, cruel, and causeless war that was ever prosecuted by ruthless murderers and pirates. They have compelled the government in self-defense to expend billions of money. Every inch of the soil of the guilty portion of this usurping power should be held responsible to reimburse all the costs of the war, to pay all the damages to private property of loyal men, and to create an ample fund to pay pensions to wounded soldiers and to the bereaved friends of the slain. Who will object to this? Who

---

[1] He quoted from Vattel, p. 424, 425:

"When, in a republic, the nation is divided into two opposite factions, and both sides take up arms, this is called a civil war. The sovereign, indeed, never fails to bestow the appellation of *rebels* on all such of his subjects as openly resist him; but when the latter have acquired sufficient strength to give him effectual opposition, and oblige him to carry on the war against them according to the established rules, he must necessarily submit to the use of the term 'civil war.'

"On earth they have no common superior. They stand precisely in the same predicament as two nations who engage in a contest, and, being unable to come to an agreement, have recourse to arms."

Also from the same, book iii., chap. x., sec. 125:

"The conventions, the treaties made with a nation, are broken or annulled by a war arising between the contending parties."

will consent that his constituents and their posterity shall be burdened with an immense load caused by these bloody traitors? Their lands, if sold in fee, would produce enough for all these purposes, and leave a large surplus."

Broomall, of Pennsylvania, thought that the government should be confined absolutely neither to the position of those who would for all purposes treat those engaged in the rebellion as public enemies, nor to that of those who would for all purposes treat them as "our fellow-citizens, and entitled to the benefits of the Constitution and laws of the United States." The rebels were wrong by their own voluntary act, and, while not entitled to any of the advantages of their position, were subject to all its disadvantages. They could not claim to be treated either as subjects or as public enemies, but the government might at its own election treat them in either capacity. Sometimes, as in the case of prisoners, the more humane laws of war ought to step in in the place of civil law. But the power to enforce civil law still remained. In regard to the property of rebels either code might be applied. This property might be confiscated absolutely under the laws of war, and in this case the confiscation would not be penal in its nature, would have nothing to do with attainder for treason, and would therefore fall outside of the scope of constitutional provisions; or, under the civil code this property could be fined or forfeited as a penalty of treason, and in the latter case the effects of the attainder could not extend beyond the life of the offender.

But both Stevens and Broomall were wrong in assuming that because the general laws of war are applicable to civil wars, therefore under and by virtue of those laws private property on land belonging to the enemy might be confiscated. By modern usage, the private property of a public enemy on land is exempt from capture except when taken as a penalty for military offenses, as a forced contribution for the support of invading armies, or to pay the expenses of maintaining order and affording protection to the conquered. It was necessary, therefore, to resort to the civil code in order to reach the private property of rebels. The inhabitants of the states engaged in rebellion must, in this respect at least, be regarded as subjects, or escape the penalty of confiscation.

The House was disposed, therefore, to consider the provision of the Constitution in regard to attainder for treason as applicable to the Confiscation Act. By a vote of 83 to 74, a joint resolution was passed amending the joint resolution explanatory of the Confiscation Act, and adopted at the President's suggestion, so that no punishment or proceeding under the act might be construed to work the forfeiture of the offender's estate contrary to the Constitution. In the Senate, the clause of the joint resolution of 1862, limiting forfeiture to the life of the offender, was repealed, 23 to 15. Returning to the House, the subject was postponed to the next session, and the act of 1862 remained as it was.

The President's amnesty proclamation had only spoken for the executive. It was also deemed necessary that Congress should speak for itself in terms equally explicit, either adopting the President's plan or proposing some other. Accordingly, in the House, on the 15th of February, Henry Winter Davis, from the Select Committee, reported a bill to guarantee to certain states a republican form of government.[1] The plan thus offered differed from that proposed by the President in several important particulars. It provided for the supervision, by a provisional governor, of the work of restoration. It postponed this work in any state until the rebellion in that state should have been suppressed, and until a majority had taken the oath of allegiance. No person was allowed to vote for, or act as a delegate in the Convention who had held any civil, military, state, or Confederate office under the rebel occupation, or who had voluntarily borne arms against the United States. Three distinct articles were dictated to the Convention for insertion in the state Constitution: the first disfranchising, in elections for governor and Legislature, all citizens who had held any military or civil office (except offices merely ministerial and military offices below that of colonel) under the usurpng power; the second abolished slavery, and guaranteed the freedom of all persons; and the third prohibited the recognition or payment of the Confederate debt. The assent of Congress was made a necessary condition precedent to the President's proclamation recognizing the government thus established. From the date of such recognition, and not before, could senators, representatives, and presidential electors be elected in any of the states included within the provisions of the bill. The bill also emancipated all slaves in these states, and affixed a distinct penalty to any attempt to re-enslave those who had been thus declared free. It disfranchised all those whom it required the several state Conventions to disfranchise. It agreed with the President's proclamation in ignoring negro suffrage.

[1] The bill authorized the President to appoint in each of the states declared in rebellion a provisional governor, with the pay and emoluments of a brigadier, to be charged with the civil administration until a state government therein shall be recognized. As soon as the military resistance to the United States shall have been suppressed, and the people sufficiently returned to their obedience to the Constitution and the laws, the governor shall direct the Marshal of the United States to enroll all the white male citizens of the United States resident in the state, in their respective counties; and wherever a majority of them take the oath of allegiance, the loyal people of the state shall be entitled to elect delegates to a Convention to act upon the re-establishment of a state government—the proclamation to contain details prescribed. Qualified voters in the army may vote in their camps. No person who has held or exercised any civil, military, state, or Confederate office under the rebel occupation, and who has voluntarily borne arms against the United States, shall vote or be eligible as a delegate. The Convention is required to insert in the Constitution provisions—

"1. No person who has held or exercised any civil or military office (except offices merely ministerial and military offices below a colonel), state or Confederate, under the usurping power, shall vote for, or be a member of the Legislature or governor.

"2. Involuntary servitude is forever prohibited, and the freedom of all persons guaranteed in said state.

"3. No debt, state or Confederate, created by or under the sanction of the usurping power, shall be recognized or paid by the state."

Upon the adoption of the Constitution by the Convention, and its ratification by the electors of the state, the provisional government shall so certify to the President, who, after obtaining the assent of Congress, shall, by proclamation, recognize the government as established, and none other, as the constitutional government of the state; and from the date of such recognition, and not before, senators and representatives, and electors for President and Vice-President may be elected in such state. Until reorganization, the provisional governor shall enforce the laws of the Union and of the state before rebellion.

The remaining sections are as follows:

"*Sec.* 12. That all persons held to involuntary servitude or labor in the states aforesaid are hereby emancipated and discharged therefrom, and they and their posterity shall be forever free. And if any such person or their posterity shall be restrained of their liberty, under pretense of any claim to such service or labor, the courts of the United States shall on habeas corpus discharge them.

"*Sec.* 13. That if any person declared free by this act, or any law of the United States, or any proclamation of the President, be restrained of liberty, with intent to be held in or restored to involuntary labor, the person convicted before a court of competent jurisdiction of such act shall be punished by fine of not less than $1500, and be imprisoned not less than five nor more than twenty years.

"*Sec.* 14. That every person who shall hereafter hold or exercise any office, civil or military, except offices merely ministerial and military offices below the grade of colonel, in the rebel service, state or Confederate, is hereby declared not to be a citizen of the United States."

This bill was passed by the House on the 4th of May, 74 to 66. Every affirmative vote was Republican, and only six Republicans voted in opposition. On the 27th, B. F. Wade, of Ohio, reported the bill in the Senate. In the course of the discussion which followed, Wade, in the most emphatic terms, repudiated as "most hazardous" the theory that the states could lose their organization, their rights as states, or their corporate capacity by rebellion.[1] The Senate passed the bill July 2d, yeas 18, and nays 14. Among those voting nay were Senators Doolittle, Lane (of Indiana), and Trumbull. The President refused to sign the bill, but on the 9th of July he issued a proclamation concerning it. It had, he said, been presented to him less than one hour previous to the close of the session, and he had not signed it. He declared that he was "unprepared, by the formal approval of this bill, to be inflexibly committed to any single plan of restoration;" to set aside the free state constitutions and governments already adopted and installed i Arkansas and Louisiana, thus discouraging loyal citizens from farther effort; or to declare the constitutional competency of Congress to abolish slavery in the states. Yet he was "fully satisfied with the system for restoration contained in the bill as one very proper for the loyal people of any state choosing to adopt it," and was prepared to give executive aid and assistance in carrying out such a method, and he would appoint military governors for this purpose so soon as military resistance to the government should have been suppressed in any state, and the people thereof sufficiently returned to their obedience to the Constitution and laws of the United States. This proclamation called forth a political manifesto from Davis and Wade, which was published in the New York *Tribune* for August 5, 1864, censuring the President, and charging him with usurpation and unworthy motives.[2]

[1] The following is an extract from Mr. Wade's speech:

"It has been contended in the House of Representatives, it has been contended upon this floor, that the states may lose their organization, may lose their rights as states, may lose their corporate capacity by rebellion. I utterly deny that doctrine. I hold that once a state of this Union, always a state; that you can not by wrong and violence displace the rights of any body or disorganize the state. It would be a most hazardous principle to assert that. No, sir; the framers of your Constitution intended no such thing. They did not leave this great question untouched; and when we study that great instrument, I can hardly help but stop and contemplate the all-embracing wisdom that seemed to actuate them; for you can find hardly an exigency that may arise in the complicated affairs of government that they did not anticipate and provide for. They did foresee that in the progress of the government some of the states might go into rebellion; that they might undertake themselves to absolve their connection with the general government and set up some hostile government of their own; and they expressly provided for just such a case; and how gentlemen with this principle of the Constitution staring them in the face can fancy that states can lose their rights because more or less of the people have gone off into rebellion, is marvelous to me. The principle of law every where is that no honest man shall lose a right by wrong or usurpation. The act of rebellion is void. It may have physical force for the moment to displace rights; but the law never yields to any such power as that. The law never any where acknowledges that right can be overthrown by wrongful action. They, then, who contend that the state governments are lost, obliterated, blotted out, are contending against the face and eyes of the Constitution. Has that said any such thing? No, sir. It has said that the Federal government shall guarantee to every state a republican form of government; and if a portion of the people undertake to overthrow their government and set up another, it is the manifest duty of the general government immediately to interfere, and, if necessary, to interpose the strong arm of its power to prevent such a state of things. Precisely that state of things is upon us, and this bill proceeds upon that idea, and discards absolutely the notion that states may lose their rights, and that they may be abrogated and may be reduced to the condition of Territories. It denies any such thing as that. No sound principle can be adopted that warrants any such thing."

[2] *Protest of Senator Wade and H. Winter Davis, M. C., to the supporters of the Government.*

"We have read without surprise, but not without indignation, the proclamation of the President of the 8th of July, 1864.

"The supporters of the administration are responsible to the country for its conduct; and it is their right and duty to check the encroachments of the executive on the authority of Congress, and to require it to confine itself to its proper sphere.

"It is impossible to pass in silence this proclamation without neglecting that duty; and, having taken as much responsibility as any others in supporting the administration, we are not disposed to fail in the other duty of asserting the rights of Congress.

"The President did not sign the bill 'to guarantee to certain states whose government have been usurped, a republican form of government'—passed by the supporters of his administration in both houses of Congress after mature deliberation.

"The bill did not, therefore, become a law, and it is, therefore, nothing.

"The proclamation is neither an approval nor a veto of the bill; it is, therefore, a document unknown to the laws and Constitution of the United States.

"So far as it contains an apology for not signing the bill, it is a political manifesto against the friends of the government.

"So far as it proposes to execute the bill which is not a law, it is a grave executive usurpation.

"It is fitting that the facts necessary to enable the friends of the administration to appreciate the apology and the usurpation be spread before them.

"The proclamation says:

"'And whereas the said bill was presented to the President of the United States for his approval less than one hour before the *sine die* adjournment of said session, and was not signed by him—'

"If that be accurate, still this bill was presented with other bills which were signed.

"Within that hour the time for the *sine die* adjournment was three times postponed by the votes of both houses; and the least intimation of a desire for more time by the President to consider this bill would have secured a farther postponement.

"Yet the committee sent to ascertain if the President had any further communication for the House of Representatives reported that he had none; and the friends of the bill, who had anxiously waited on him to ascertain its fate, had already been informed that the President had resolved not to sign it.

"The time of presentation, therefore, had nothing to do with his failure to approve it.

"The bill has been discussed and considered for more than a month in the House of Representatives, which it passed on the 4th of May. It was reported to the Senate on the 27th of May, without material amendment, and passed the Senate absolutely as it came from the House on the 2d of July.

"Ignorance of its contents is out of the question.

"Indeed, at his request, a draft of a bill substantially the same in material points, and identical in the points objected to by the proclamation, had been laid before him for his consideration in the winter of 1862–3.

"There is, therefore, no reason to suppose the provisions of the bill took the President by surprise.

"On the contrary, we have reason to believe them to have been so well known that this method of preventing the bill from becoming a law without the constitutional responsibility of a veto had been resolved on long before the bill passed the Senate.

The Senate, a short time before its adjournment, declared by a vote 27 to 6 that W. M. Fishback and Elisha Baxter, claiming seats from Arkansas,

"We are informed by a gentleman entitled to entire confidence, that before the 22d of June, in New Orleans, it was stated by a member of General Banks's staff, in the presence of other gentlemen in official position, that Senator Doolittle had written a letter to the department that the House Reconstruction Bill would be staved off in the Senate to a period too late in the session to require the President to veto it in order to defeat it, and that Mr. Lincoln would retain the bill, if necessary, and thereby defeat it.

"The experience of Senator Wade, in his various efforts to get the bill considered in the Senate, was quite in accordance with that plan; and the fate of the bill was accurately predicted by letters received from New Orleans before it had passed the Senate.

"Had the proclamation stopped there, it would have been only one other defeat of the will of the people by the executive perversion of the Constitution.

"But it goes farther. The President says:

"'And whereas the said bill contains, among other things, a plan for restoring the states in rebellion to their proper practical relation in the Union, which plan expresses the sense of Congress upon that subject, and which plan it is now thought fit to lay before the people for their consideration—'

"By what authority of the Constitution? In what forms? The result to be declared by whom? With what effect when ascertained?

"Is it to be a law by the approval of the people, without the approval of Congress, at the will of the President?

"Will the President, on his opinion of the popular approval, execute it as a law?

"Or is this merely a device to avoid the serious responsibility of defeating a law on which so many loyal hearts reposed for security?

"But the reasons now assigned for not approving the bill are full of ominous significance.

"The President proceeds:

"'Now, therefore, I, Abraham Lincoln, President of the United States, do proclaim, declare, and make known that, while I am (as I was in December last, when by proclamation I propounded a plan for restoration) unprepared by a formal approval of this bill to be inflexibly committed to any single plan of restoration—'

"That is to say, the President is resolved that people shall not *by law* take *any* securities from the rebel states against a renewal of the rebellion, before restoring their power to govern us.

"His wisdom and prudence are to be our sufficient guarantees! He farther says:

"'And while I am also unprepared to declare that the free state Constitutions and governments already adopted and installed in Arkansas and Louisiana shall be set aside and held for naught, thereby repelling and discouraging the loyal citizens who have set up the same as to farther effort—'

"That is to say, the President persists in recognizing those shadows of governments in Arkansas and Louisiana which Congress formally declared should not be recognized—whose representatives and senators were repelled by formal votes of both houses of Congress—which it was declared formally should have no electoral vote for President and Vice-President.

"They are mere creatures of his will. They are mere oligarchies, imposed on the people by military orders under the form of election, at which generals, provost-marshals, soldiers, and camp-followers were the chief actors, assisted by a handful of resident citizens, and urged on to premature action by private letters from the President.

"In neither Louisiana nor Arkansas, before Banks's defeat, did the United States control half the territory or half the population. In Louisiana, General Banks's proclamation candidly declared, 'The fundamental law of the state is martial law.'

"On that foundation of freedom he erected what the President calls 'the free Constitution and government of Louisiana.'

"But of this state, whose fundamental law was martial law, only sixteen parishes out of forty-eight parishes were held by the United States; and in five of the sixteen we held only our camps.

"The eleven parishes we substantially held had 233,185 inhabitants; the residue of the state not held by us, 575,617.

"At the farce called an election, the officers of General Banks returned that 11,346 ballots were cast; but whether any or by whom the people of the United States have no legal assurance; but it is probable that 4000 were cast by soldiers or employés of the United States, military or municipal, but none according to any law, state or national, and 7000 ballots represent the State of Louisiana.

"Such is the free Constitution and government of Louisiana; and like it is that of Arkansas. Nothing but the failure of a military expedition deprived us of a like one in the swamps of Florida; and before the presidential election like ones may be organized in every rebel state where the United States have a camp.

"The President, by preventing this bill from becoming a law, holds the electoral votes of the rebel states at the dictation of his personal ambition.

"If those votes turn the balance in his favor, is it to be supposed that his competitor, defeated by such means, will acquiesce?

"If the rebel majority assert their supremacy in those states, and send votes which elect an enemy of the government, will we not repel his claims?

"And is not that civil war for the Presidency inaugurated by the votes of rebel states?

"Seriously impressed with these dangers, Congress, 'the proper constitutional authority,' formally declared that there are no state governments in the rebel states, and provided for their erection at a proper time; and both the Senate and the House of Representatives rejected the senators and representatives chosen under the authority of what the President calls the free Constitution and government of Arkansas.

"The President's proclamation 'holds for naught' this judgment, and discards the authority of the Supreme Court, and strides headlong toward the anarchy his proclamation of the 8th of December inaugurated.

"If electors for President be allowed to be chosen in either of those states, a sinister light will be cast on the motives which induced the President to 'hold for naught' the will of Congress rather than his government in Louisiana and Arkansas.

"That judgment of Congress which the President defies was the exercise of an authority exclusively vested in Congress by the Constitution, to determine what is the established government in a state, and in its own nature and by the highest judicial authority binding on all other departments of the government.

"The Supreme Court has formally declared that, under the 4th section of the IVth article of the Constitution, requiring the United States to guarantee to every state a republican form of government, 'it rests with Congress to decide what government is the established one in a state;' and 'when senators and representatives of a state are admitted into the councils of the Union, the authority of the government under which they are appointed, as well as its republican character, is recognized by the proper constitutional authority, and its decision is binding on every other department of the government, and could not be questioned in a judicial tribunal. It is true that the contest in this case did not last long enough to bring the matter to this issue; and as no senators or representatives were elected under the authority of the government of which Mr. Dorr was the head, Congress was not called upon to decide the controversy. Yet the right to decide is placed there.'

"Even the President's proclamation of the 8th of December formally declares that 'whether members sent to Congress from any state shall be admitted to seats constitutionally rests exclusively with the respective houses, and not to any extent with the executive.'

"And that is not the less true because wholly inconsistent with the President's assumption in that proclamation of a right to institute and recognize state governments in the rebel states, nor because the President is unable to perceive that his recognition is a nullity if it be not conclusive on Congress.

"Under the Constitution, the right to senators and representatives is inseparable from a state government.

"If there be a state government the right is absolute.

"If there be no state government there can be no senators or representatives chosen.

"The two houses of Congress are expressly declared to be the sole judges of their own members.

"When, therefore, senators and representatives are admitted, the state government under whose authority they were chosen is conclusively established; when they are rejected, its existence is as conclusively rejected and denied; and to this judgment the President is bound to submit.

"The President proceeds to express his unwillingness 'to declare a constitutional competency in Congress to abolish slavery in states' as another reason for not signing the bill.

"But the bill nowhere proposes to abolish slavery in states.

"The bill did provide that all *slaves* in the rebel states should be *manumitted.*

"But as the President had already signed three bills manumitting several classes of slaves in states, it is not conceived possible that he entertained any scruples touching *that* provision of the bill respecting which he is silent.

"He had already himself assumed a right by proclamation to free much the larger number of slaves in the rebel states, under the authority given him by Congress to use military power to suppress the rebellion; and it is quite inconceivable that the President should think Congress could vest in him a discretion it could not exercise itself.

"It is the more unintelligible from the fact that, except in respect to a small part of Virginia and Louisiana, the bill covered only what the proclamation covered—added a Congressional title and judicial remedies by law to the disputed title under the proclamation, and perfected the work the President professed to be so anxious to accomplish.

"Slavery, as an institution, can be abolished only by a change of the Constitution of the United States, or of the law of the states; and this is the principle of the bill.

"It required the new Constitution of the state to provide for that prohibition; and the President, in the face of his own proclamation, does not venture to object to insisting on that condition. Nor will the country tolerate its abandonment—yet he defeated the only provision imposing it.

"But when he describes himself, in spite of this great blow at emancipation, as 'sincerely hoping and expecting that a constitutional amendment abolishing slavery throughout the nation may be adopted,' we curiously inquire on what his expectation rests, after the vote of the House of Representatives at the recent session, and in the face of the political complexion of more than enough of the states to prevent the possibility of its adoption within any reasonable time; and why he did not indulge his sincere hopes with so large an instalment of the blessing as his approval of the bill would have secured?

"After this assignment of his reasons for preventing the bill from becoming a law, the President proceeds to declare his purpose to execute it as a law by his plenary dictatorial power.

"He says: 'Nevertheless, I am fully satisfied with the system for restoration contained in the bill as one very proper plan for the loyal people of any state choosing to adopt it; and that I am, and at all times shall be, prepared to give the executive aid and assistance to any such people as soon as the military resistance to the United States shall have been suppressed in any such state, and the people thereof shall have sufficiently returned to their obedience to the Constitution and the laws of the United States—in which cases military governors will be appointed, with directions to proceed according to the bill.'

"A more studied outrage on the legislative authority of the people has never been perpetrated.

"Congress passed a bill; the President refused to approve it, and then, by proclamation, puts as much of it in force as he sees fit, and proposes to execute those parts by officers unknown to the laws of the United States, and not subject to the confirmation of the Senate.

"The bill directed the appointment of provisional governors by and with the advice and consent of the Senate.

"The President, after defeating the law, proposes to appoint, without law and without the advice and consent of the Senate, military governors for the rebel states!

"He has already exercised this dictatorial usurpation in Louisiana, and defeated the bill to prevent its limitation.

"Henceforth we must regard the following precedent as the presidential law of the rebel states:

"'Executive Mansion, Washington, March 15, 1864.

"'His Excellency Michael Hahn, Governor of Louisiana:

"'Until farther orders, you are hereby invested with the powers exercised hitherto by the military governors of Louisiana. Yours, ABRAHAM LINCOLN.'

"This Michael Hahn is no officer of the United States; the President, without law, without the advice and consent of the Senate, by a private note not even countersigned by the Secretary of State, makes him dictator of Louisiana!

"The bill provided for the civil administration of the laws of the state—but it should be in a fit temper to govern itself—repealing all laws recognizing slavery, and making all men equal before the law.

"These beneficent provisions the President has annulled. People will die, and marry, and transfer property, and buy and sell; and to these acts of civil life courts and officers of the law are necessary. Congress legislated for these necessary things, and the President deprives them of the protection of the law!

"The President's purpose to instruct his military governors 'to proceed according to the bill'—a makeshift to calm the disappointment its defeat has occasioned—is not merely a grave usurpation, but a transparent delusion.

"He can not 'proceed according to the bill' after preventing it from becoming a law.

"Whatever is done will be at his will and pleasure, by persons responsible to no law, and more interested to secure the interests and execute the will of the President than of the people; and the will of Congress is to be 'held for naught,' 'unless the loyal people of the rebel states choose to adopt it.'

"If they should graciously prefer the stringent bill to the easy proclamation, still the registration will be made under no legal sanction; it will give no assurance that a majority of the people of the states have taken the oath; if administered, it will be without legal authority and void; no indictment will lie for false swearing at the election, or for admitting bad or rejecting good votes; it will be the farce of Louisiana and Arkansas acted over again, under the forms of this bill, but not by authority of law.

"But when we come to the guaranties of future peace which Congress meant to enact, the forms, as well as the substance of the bill, must yield to the President's will that none should be imposed.

"It was the solemn resolve of Congress to protect the loyal men of the nation against three great dangers: (1) the return to power of the guilty leaders of the rebellion; (2) the continuance of slavery, and (3) the burden of the rebel debt.

"Congress required assent to those provisions by the Convention of the state; and if refused, it was to be dissolved.

"The President 'holds for naught' that resolve of Congress, because he is unwilling 'to be inflexibly committed to any one plan of restoration,' and the people of the United States are not to be allowed to protect themselves unless their enemies agree to it.

"The order to proceed according to the bill is therefore merely at the will of the rebel states; and they have the option to reject it, accept the proclamation of the 8th of December, and demand the President's recognition!

"Mark the contrast! The bill requires a majority, the proclamation is satisfied with one tenth; the bill requires one oath, the proclamation another; the bill ascertains voters by registering, the proclamation by guess; the bill exacts adherence to existing territorial limits, the proclamation admits of others; the bill governs the rebel states *by law*, equalizing all before it—the proclamation commits them to the lawless discretion of military governors and provost-marshals; the bill forbids electors for President, the proclamation and defeat of the bill threaten us with civil war for the admission or exclusion of such votes; the bill exacted exclusion of dangerous enemies from power and the relief of the nation from the rebel debt, and the prohibition of slavery forever, so that the suppression of the rebellion will double our resources to bear or pay the national debt, free the masses from the old domination of the rebel leaders, and eradicate the cause of the war—the proclamation secures neither of these guaranties.

"It is silent respecting the rebel debt and the political exclusion of rebel leaders, leaving slavery exactly where it was by law at the outbreak of the rebellion, and adds no guaranty even of the freedom of the slaves he undertook to manumit.

"It is summed up in an illegal oath, without sanction, and therefore void.

"The oath is to support all proclamations of the President, during the rebellion, having reference to slaves.

"Any government is to be accepted at the hands of one tenth of the people not contravening that oath.

"Now that oath neither secures the abolition of slavery, nor adds any security to the freedom of the slaves the President declared free.

"It does not secure the abolition of slavery; for the proclamation of freedom merely professed to free certain slaves while it recognized the institution.

"Every Constitution of the rebel states at the outbreak of the rebellion may be adopted without the change of a letter; for none of them contravene that proclamation; none of them establish slavery.

"It adds no security to the freedom of the slaves, for their title is the proclamation of freedom.

"If it be unconstitutional, an oath to support it is void. Whether constitutional or not, the oath is without authority of law, and therefore void.

"If it be valid and observed, it exacts no enactment by the state, either in law or Constitution, to add a state guaranty to the proclamation title; and the right of a slave to freedom is an open question before the state courts on the relative authority of the state law and the proclamation.

"If the oath binds the one tenth who take it, it is not exacted of the other nine tenths who succeed to the control of the state government, so that it is annulled instantly by the act of recognition.

"What the state courts would say of the proclamation, who can doubt?

"But the master would not go into court—he would seize his slaves.

"What the Supreme Court would say, who can tell?

"When and how is the question to get there?

"No *habeas corpus* lies for him in a United States court; and the President defeated with this bill the extension of that writ to his case.

"Such are the fruits of this rash and fatal act of the President—a blow at the friends of his administration, at the rights of humanity, and at the principles of republican government.

"The President has greatly presumed on the forbearance which the supporters of his administration have so long practiced, in view of the arduous conflict in which we are engaged, and the reckless ferocity of our political opponents.

"But he must understand that our support is of a cause and not of a man; that the authority of Congress is paramount and must be respected; that the whole body of the Union men of Congress will not submit to be impeached by him of rash and unconstitutional legislation; and if he wishes our support, he must confine himself to his executive duties—to obey and execute, not make the laws—to suppress by arms armed rebellion, and leave political reorganization to Congress.

"If the supporters of the government fail to insist on this, they become responsible for the usurpations which they fail to rebuke, and are justly liable to the indignation of the people whose rights and security, committed to their keeping, they sacrifice.

"Let them consider the remedy of these usurpations, and, having found it, fearlessly execute it.

"B. F. WADE, Chairman Senate Committee.

"H. WINTER DAVIS, Chairman Com. House of Rep. on the Rebellious States."

were not entitled to them. This was as emphatic a rejection of the President's plan of restoration as was possible. In the House, A. C. Rogers, J. M. Johnson, and T. M. Jacks, claiming seats from Arkansas, were not admitted. In the same body the claims of A. P. Fields and Thomas Cotton, from Louisiana, were rejected by a vote of 100 to 71.

During this session several resolutions were offered concerning the object and conduct of the war. A number of these reiterated the resolutions adopted by the Thirty-seventh Congress to the effect that the war was not waged for the purpose of conquest or subjugation, or of overthrowing or interfering with the rights or established institutions of the insurgent states, "but to defend and maintain the supremacy of the Constitution, and to preserve the Union with all the dignity, equality, and rights of the several states unimpaired." Such resolutions were invariably tabled, laid over, or referred to the Select Committee, never to be heard of again.

On the 8th of April, the House sitting in Committee of the Whole on the State of the Union, Alexander Long, of Ohio, rose, and in a long speech prophesied the ultimate failure of the war, and declared himself in favor of the recognition of the Confederacy. General Garfield, his patriotic colleague, as soon as Long took his seat, rose and asked that a white flag might be placed between his colleague and himself. "I recollect," said he, "that on one occasion, when two great armies stood face to face, that under a white flag just planted I approached a company of men dressed in the uniform of the rebel Confederacy, and reached out my hand to one of the number, and told him I respected him as a brave man. Though he wore the emblems of disloyalty and treason, still underneath his vestments I beheld a brave and honest soul. I would reproduce that scene here this afternoon. I say were there such a flag of truce—but God forgive me if I should do it under other circumstances!—I would reach out this right hand and ask that gentleman to take it, because I honor his bravery and honesty. . . . . He has done a brave thing. It is braver than to face cannon and musketry." Then, in a speech—the most thrilling of that session—General Garfield analyzed and developed the significance of Long's proposition. "Now," said he, "when hundreds of thousands of brave souls have gone up to God under the shadow of the flag, and when thousands more, maimed and shattered in the contest, are sadly awaiting the deliverance of death ; now, when three years of terrific warfare have raged over us, when our armies have pushed the rebellion back over mountains and rivers, and crowded it into narrow limits, until a wall of fire girds it; now, when the uplifted hand of a majestic people is about to let fall the lightning of its conquering power upon the rebellion ; now, in the quiet of this hall, hatched in the lowest depths of a similar dark treason, there rises a Benedict Arnold and proposes to surrender us all up, body and spirit, the nation and the flag, its genius and its honor, now and forever, to the accursed traitors to our country ! And that proposition comes —God forgive and pity my beloved state!—it comes from a citizen of the honored and loyal commonwealth of Ohio. . . . . . .

"For the first time in the history of this contest, it is proposed in this hall to give up the struggle, to abandon the war, and let treason run riot through the land ! * * * *

"Suppose the policy of the gentleman were adopted to-day. Let the order go forth ; sound the 'recall' on your bugles, and let it ring from Texas to the far Atlantic, and tell the armies to come back. Call the victorious legions back over the battle-fields of blood, forever now disgraced. Call them back over the territory they have conquered and redeemed. Call them back, and let the minions of secession chase them with derision and jeers as they come. And then tell them that that man across the aisle, from the free state of Ohio, gave birth to the monstrous proposition."

The next day Speaker Colfax took the floor, and offered a resolution for the expulsion of Long. He did this, he said, in the performance of a high public duty—a duty to his constituents and to the soldiers in the field. He believed in the freedom of speech, and had during this Congress heard nothing, save this single speech, which could have prompted him to offer such a resolution. The flag of the Confederacy had been boldly unfurled by a gentleman who had taken an oath at the opening of the session that up to that time he had not given aid, countenance, or encouragement to the enemies of the United States. If such an oath was necessary to membership, then he who could thus publicly give the encouragement which he had sworn not to have given in the past was an unworthy member, and ought not to remain. The soldiers who deserted did not more surely turn their backs upon the obligation they had assumed than had the member from Ohio. If the House allowed such sentiments to go unquestioned, they should stop shooting deserters. Could the United States go to war with a foreign nation recognizing the Confederacy, while from the halls of Congress an opinion was permitted to go forth in favor of such recognition, and unaccompanied by the highest expression of Congressional censure ?

Cox, of Ohio, while opposing the resolution, and pleading for the utmost freedom of discussion, emphatically disavowed for himself and his Democratic colleagues the sentiments expressed by Long. On the other hand, Harris, of Maryland, as emphatically indorsed those sentiments, and in terms far more distinct than Long had adopted. "I am," said he, "a peace man, a radical peace man, and I am for peace by the recognition of the Confederacy. I am for acquiescence in the doctrine of secession. I thought I was alone ; but now, thank God ! there is another soul saved. . . . . The South asked you to let them go in peace. But no, you said you would bring them into subjection. That is not done yet, and God Almighty grant that it may never be. I hope that you may never subjugate the South." Washburne, of Illinois, called him to order, and then moved his expulsion. The vote upon this motion was 81 ayes to 58 nays, and thus lacked the necessary two thirds majority. But a motion of censure was voted 93 to 18.

HENRY WINTER DAVIS.

Probably there was no man who more completely commanded the attention of the House, whenever he spoke, than Henry Winter Davis. His eloquence and impressiveness were only matched by his profound culture and his elegance of expression. On this occasion he addressed a silent and crowded house in support of the resolution for Long's expulsion. In the course of his speech, he said:

"Mr. Speaker, if it be said that a time may come when the question of recognizing the Southern Confederacy will have to be answered, I admit it; and it is answering the strongest and the extreme case that gentlemen on the other side can present. I admit it. When a Democrat shall darken the White House and the land ; when a Democratic majority here shall proclaim that freedom of speech secures impunity to treason, and declare recognition better than extermination of traitors ; when McClellan and Fitz John Porter shall have again brought the rebel armies within sight of Washington City, and the successor of James Buchanan shall withdraw our armies from the unconstitutional invasion of Virginia to the north of the Potomac ; when exultant rebels shall sweep over the fortifications and their bomb-shells shall crash against the dome of the Capitol ; when thousands throughout Pennsylvania shall seek refuge on the shores of Lake Erie from the rebel invasion, cheered and welcomed by the opponents of extermination ; when Vallandigham shall be Governor of Ohio, and Bright Governor of Indiana, and Woodward Governor of Pennsylvania, and Seymour Governor of Connecticut, and Wall be Governor of New Jersey, and the gentleman from New York city sit in Seymour's seat, and thus, possessed of power over the great centre of the country, they shall do what they attempted in vain before in the midst of rebel triumphs—to array the authorities of the states against those of the United States ; to oppose the militia to the army of the United States ; to invoke the *habeas corpus* to discharge confined traitors ; to deny to the government the benefit of the laws of war, lest it exterminate its enemies ; when the Democrats, as in the fall of 1862, shall again, with more permanent success, persuade the people of the country that the war should not be waged till the integrity of the territory of the Union is restored, cost what it might, but that such a war violates the spirit of free institutions, which those who advocate it wish to overthrow, and should stop, for the benefit of the Democratic party, somewhere this side of absolute triumph, lest there be no room for a compromise ; when gentlemen of that party in New York shall again, as in November, 1862, hold illegal and criminal negotiations with Lord Lyons, and avow their purposes to him, the representative of a foreign and unfriendly power, and urge him to arrange the time of proffering mediation with a view to their possession of power and their preparation of the minds of the public to receive suggestions from abroad ; and when mediation shall appear by the event to be the first step toward foreign intervention, swiftly and surely followed by foreign armed enemies upon our shores to join the domestic enemies ; when the war in the cars shall begin, which was menaced at the outbreak of the rebellion, and the friends of Seymour shall make the streets of New York run with blood on the eve of another Gettysburg less damaging to their hopes ; when the people, exhausted by taxation, weary of sacrifices, drained of blood, betrayed by their rulers, deluded by demagogues into believing that peace is the way to union, and submission the path to victory, shall throw down their arms before the advancing foe; when vast chasms across every state shall make apparent to every eye, when too late to remedy it, that division from the South is inauguration of anarchy at the North, and that peace without union is the end of the republic—THEN the independence of the South will be an accomplished fact, and gentlemen may, without treason to the dead republic, rise in this migratory house, wherever it may then be in America, and declare themselves for *recognizing* their masters at the South rather than exterminating them! Until that day, in the name of the American nation—in the name of every house in the land where there is one dead for the holy cause—in the name of those who stand before us in the ranks of battle—in the name of the liberty our ancestors have confided to us, I devote to eternal execration the name of him who shall propose to destroy this blessed land rather than its enemies."[1]

On the side of the opposition, Pendleton, of Ohio, one of the most popular leaders of his party, closed the debate with an able argument in favor of free discussion. It was in reply to Davis's speech of the night before. "The gentleman from Maryland," said he, "told us last night, in terms of eloquence which I can not emulate, that when Lord Chatham, aged, feeble, wrapped in flannel and suffering from disease, came, resting upon the arm of his still greater son, to address for the last time the British House of Lords, and to die upon the floor, he came to speak against the dismemberment of the British empire. It is true; and what did he say? 'I told you this war would be disastrous; I predicted its consequences; I told you you could not conquer America; I begged you to conciliate America; you would not heed my advice. You have exhausted the country; you have sacrificed its men; you have wasted its treasures; you have driven these colonies to declare their independence; you have driven them into the arms of our ancient and hated enemy, and now, without striking a blow, without firing a shot, cowardly under difficulties as you were truculent in success, you propose to yield through fear to France what you have refused as justice to America.' Did it not occur to the gentleman from Maryland that possibly at a future day, when the history of that civil strife shall have been reproduced in this land, another Chatham may come to this House, and hurl against those who are now in power these bitter denunciations because they have shown themselves unable to make an honorable peace even as they have been unable to make a victorious war? . . . .

"Sir, if there be depths of public opinion where eternal stillness reigns, there gather, even as festering death lies in those ocean depths, the decaying forms of truth, and right, and freedom. Eternal motion is the condition of their purity. Did he think this resolution would for one instant retard its progress? Did he not know that the surging waves would wash away every trace of its existence? Did he suppose this puny effort would avail him? The rocks of the eternal hills alone can stay the waves of the ever-rolling sea. Nothing but the principles of truth and right can stay the onward progress of public opinion in this our country as it swells, and sways, and surges in this mad tempest of passion, and seeks to find a secure resting-place."

The resolution was finally changed to one of censure in place of expulsion, and in that shape passed 80 to 70. If any evidence were needed of the jealous regard for freedom of debate in the American Congress, it is furnished by the fact that Harris and Long were only censured and not expelled.

During the session enabling acts were passed for the formation of state governments in Colorado, Nevada, and Nebraska. The people of Colorado voted against a Convention, preferring to remain for the present under the territorial organization. The pay of soldiers was increased to $16 per month,[2] and a Bureau of Military Justice was established. The government was authorized to borrow $400,000,000 on coupon bonds running from 5 to 30 years, at not less than 6 per cent. interest, payable in coin. These and the 5.20 bonds might be disposed of in Europe at the discretion of the Secretary of the Treasury. All United States bonds were declared exempt from taxation.[3] Provision was also made for the issue of $50,000,000 in fractional or postage currency. A separate bureau was established, to be charged with the execution of all laws respecting a national currency, secured by United States bonds.[4] At the head of this bureau the President placed

Hugh McCullough, afterward Secretary of the Treasury. A special income tax was levied at the rate of five per cent. on all sums exceeding $600 clear income, to be collected under the rules of the Internal Revenue Department.

At this time the relations between this government and that of France were exceedingly critical, and it required all the skill and prudence of Secretary Seward to avert war.

Maximilian, the oldest brother of the reigning Emperor of Austria, had been proclaimed Emperor of Mexico, July 10th, 1863, by an assembly of "Notables" summoned by a government established under the auspices of the French army. The choice of Maximilian was of course made by Louis Napoleon. But the French emperor had commanded that the question as between an empire and a republic should be submitted to the Mexican people. Accordingly, at the same time that the Mexican deputation was proceeding to Europe with the vote of the Notables engrossed on parchment and inclosed in a golden sceptre, instructions were on their way from Paris to the French commander in Mexico to carry out the emperor's instructions to the letter. Thus Maximilian's acceptance was delayed. An election was held under the impressive authority of French bayonets, and on the 10th of April, 1864, the Mexican deputation was again at Miramar, and Maximilian was informed that the vote of the "Notables" had been ratified by an immense majority. Maximilian accepted the sceptre, which, at first the badge of empire, became in the end, to him, the wand of martyrdom. He visited the Pope, and, having received the blessing of the latter, embarked with his consort, the Empress Carlotta, for Mexico, where he arrived on the 28th of May, and entered upon his imperial career.

The French occupation of Mexico, resulting in the subversion of its republican government, was construed as an act of hostility both by the people and the government of the United States. The full expression of this feeling on the part of the executive was held in check by the civil war. No pledge was given to France that this question—now held in abeyance—would not arise for settlement, and in the mean while every honorable effort was made by the government to prevent a foreign war. That this was the wisest policy is too evident to require argument. It was the policy adopted both by the President and the Senate. In the latter body, McDougall, of California, on January 11th, introduced a series of resolutions, declaring that the French attempt to subvert the Mexican republic was an act hostile to the United States, and that it was the duty of our government to require France to withdraw her armed forces from Mexico. These resolutions were referred to the Committee on Foreign Relations, and not heard of again. On the 14th of June McDougall sought in vain to introduce a resolution, which was in form a general expression of the Monroe doctrine.

The House took an entirely different view as to the question of an immediate protest. On the 4th of April, Henry Winter Davis reported from the Committee on Foreign Affairs the following joint resolution, which passed without a single dissentient voice: "That the Congress of the United States are unwilling, by silence, to leave the nations of the world under the impression that they are indifferent spectators of the deplorable events now transpiring in the republic of Mexico, and they therefore think fit to declare that it does not accord with the policy of the United States to acknowledge a monarchical government erected on the ruins of any republican government in America, under the auspices of any European power." The resolution

---

[1] Mr. Davis thus illustrated the freedom of opinion and its limitations:
"Surely, sir, opinion is the life of our nation. It is the measure of every right, the guarantee of every privilege, the protection of every blessing. It is opinion which creates our rulers. It is opinion that nerves or palsies their arms. It is opinion which casts down the proud and elevates the humble. Its fluctuations are the rise and fall of parties; its currents bear the nation on to prosperity or ruin. Its free play is the condition of its purity. It is like the ocean, whose tides rise and fall day by day at the fickle bidding of the moon; yet it is the great scientific level from which every height is measured—the horizon to which astronomers refer the motion of the stars. But, like the ocean, it has depths whose eternal stillness is the condition of its stability. Those depths of opinion are not free, and it is they that are touched by the words which have so moved the House. Men must not commit treason and say its guilt is a matter of opinion, and its punishment a violation of its freedom. Men can not swear to maintain the integrity of the nation, and avow their intention to destroy it, and cover that double crime by the freedom of speech. *That* is to break up the fountains of the great deep on which all government is borne, and to pour its flood in revolutionary ruin over the land. To punish that is not a violation of the freedom of opinion or its expression. It is to protect its normal ebb and flow, its free and healthy fluctuations, that we desire to relieve it from the opprobrium of being confounded with the declarations of treasonable purposes here, in the high and solemn assemblage of the Union."   [2] Chapter cxlv.

[3] Chapter clxxii. This act also provided that in lieu of so much of this loan, the secretary might issue $200,000,000 of treasury notes redeemable within three years, bearing interest of seven and three tenths per cent., convertible into bonds. The secretary might also cancel all treasury notes heretofore issued, and issue these in their stead. These notes were not to be a legal tender. Bonds might be exchanged for seven and three tenths notes. The secretary might receive temporary loans, and issue certificates of deposit therefor, at six per cent., the certificates to be payable on ten days' notice—such deposits not to exceed $150,000,000.

[4] Chapter cvi.—*National Currency*—establishes a separate bureau, to be charged with the execution of this and all laws respecting a national currency, secured by United States bonds, and names the officers of said bureau, together with the securities conditioned by their assumption of office. Every certificate, assignment, and conveyance shall be as valid as when the comptroller's seal is stamped on the paper. Associations for carrying on the business of banking may be formed by any number of persons not less than five, who shall enter into articles of association, signed by the members of the association, a copy of which shall be forwarded to the Comptroller of the Currency. The requisite capital for the organization of associations of this kind shall be not less than two hundred thousand dollars in a city exceeding fifty thousand inhabitants, and not less than one hund-

red thousand dollars in a city whose population is less than fifty thousand; provided, however, that banks may be organized, with a capital of not less than fifty thousand dollars, in any place not exceeding six thousand inhabitants, with the approval of the Secretary of the Treasury. Such association shall transact no business, except such as may be incidental to its own organization, until authorized by the Comptroller of the Currency. The number of directors must be not less than five, one of whom shall be president. The capital stock of any association shall be in shares of one hundred dollars each, deemed personal property, and transferable on the books of the association. The shareholders shall be held individually responsible, equally and ratably, and not one for another, for all contracts, debts, and engagements of their association, according to the par value of their amount of stock therein, in addition to the amount invested in such shares; except in the case of shareholders in present existing state banking institutions, of not less than five millions of dollars of capital, and a surplus of twenty per centum on hand, who shall be liable only to the amount invested in their shares. It shall be lawful for an association, formed under this act, to provide for an increase of its capital from time to time, subject to the limitations of this act; provided that the maximum of such increase shall be determined by the comptroller; and that no increase of capital shall be valid until the whole amount of such increase shall be paid in. And every association shall have power, by a vote of shareholders owning two thirds of its stock, to reduce the capital of such association to any amount not below the amount required by this act for its outstanding circulation. Every association, preliminary to commencing business, shall deliver to the Treasurer of the United States United States registered bonds to an amount equal to one third of the capital stock; the deposit to be increased as the capital is paid up or increased; while an association, desiring to diminish its capital or to close up its business, may take up its bonds, upon returning to the comptroller its circulating notes. The comptroller shall examine and determine if any association can commence business. All transfers of United States bonds shall be made to the Treasurer of the United States, in trust for the association, the comptroller to keep the transfer-book. Associations, after the transfer and delivery of bonds to the treasurer, may receive from the comptroller circulating notes, in blank, equal in amount to ninety per centum of the current market value of the United States bonds so transferred; but at no time shall the total amount of such notes exceed the amount of its capital stock actually paid in. The entire amount of circulating notes to be issued under this act shall not exceed three hundred millions of dollars. Such notes shall be received at par in payment of all indebtedness to the United States except for duties on imports; and also for all indebtedness of the United States except interest on the public debt, and in redemption of the national currency. Associations shall, annually or oftener, examine its bonds deposited, and execute to the treasurer a certificate, setting forth the different kinds, and the amounts thereof; such examination to be made by a duly appointed officer or agent of the association, whose certificate shall be of full force and validity. The deposited bonds shall be held exclusively for the security of the association's circulating notes, the association having the benefit of the interest on the bonds which it may have deposited so long as it may redeem its circulating notes. The total liabilities to any association, of any person, company, corporation, or firm, shall at no time exceed one tenth part of the capital stock of such association actually paid in; provided that the discount of commercial paper actually owned by the person, company, etc., negotiating the same, shall not be considered as money borrowed. The established interest of the state or territory wherein the banking association is located shall govern its charge of interest on loans, notes, bills, etc., and, when there is no established interest in such state or territory, the association may take interest not exceeding seven per centum. The penalty for taking greater interest than herein prescribed shall be a forfeiture of the entire interest which has been agreed to be paid; and the person or persons who may have paid a greater interest may recover back from the association receiving the same twice the amount of the interest thus paid, provided that such action for recovery is commenced within two years after the occurrence of the usurious transaction. The circulating notes of the different associations shall be redeemed in New York at par by associations selected for that purpose.

WILLIAM L. DAYTON.

was introduced into the Senate and referred, but not again reported during the session.

This torch, which the House had thrown into a magazine already almost on the point of explosion from other causes, was snatched away by the Secretary of State before it had done its destructive work. A letter of instructions was immediately forwarded to Mr. Dayton, our minister at the French court. A copy of the resolution was inclosed. It was admitted by the secretary that this resolution truly interpreted the unanimous sentiment of the people of the United States. But it had not passed the Senate, and, even if it had, the form of expression which the government might choose to adopt toward that of France on this subject depended, not upon Congress, but upon the executive. "While the President," he added, "receives the declaration of the House of Representatives with the profound respect to which it is entitled as an exposition of its sentiments on a grave and important subject, he directs that you inform the government of France that he does not at present contemplate any departure from the policy which this government has hitherto pursued in regard to the war which exists between France and Mexico."

The passage of the resolution produced a great degree of excitement in France. When Mr. Dayton visited M. Drouyn de l'Huys on the 21st of April, the first words addressed to him by the latter were, "Do you bring us peace or bring us war?" Mr. Dayton had not then received his instructions from the secretary. When these were made known to the French government the excitement subsided, and the *Moniteur*, the official organ of the emperor, announced that satisfactory explanations had been received from the United States government.

On the 27th Mr. Davis made a long report, closing with a recommendation that a resolution be passed declaring the constitutional right of Congress to an authoritative voice in determining the foreign policy of the United States, and that a proposition in regard to such policy while pending and undetermined is not a fit topic of diplomatic explanation with any foreign power. This report was ordered to be printed, but did not again come up for action during the session.

The people of Kentucky—so strongly opposed to secession and to sympathizers with rebellion that they had (August 3, 1863) elected Bramlette, the Union candidate, over Wickliffe, the Democratic, by a majority of over 50,000—were still so bitterly opposed to emancipation and to the enrollment of negroes for military service, that their governor was compelled, when these measures were adopted, to issue a proclamation, counseling them against unlawful resistance. But the President remained firm. He had 130,000 soldiers to show as the result of a policy which had been tried for one year, and this, to him, was a sufficient argument why that policy should be maintained. The fact that the Union delegates from Kentucky would be sent to the Democratic Convention to be assembled at Chicago for the nomination of a presidential ticket was not deemed a compensatory argument to the contrary.

In the autumn of 1864 a presidential election was to be decided in the midst of war, as the one four years previous had been decided under its projected shadow. Many of the more radical members of the Republican party were dissatisfied with Abraham Lincoln for various reasons, but chiefly because he was considered too slow to adopt their own revolutionary theories on the subject of emancipation and reconstruction. This faction of the party held its National Convention at Cleveland, Ohio, on the 31st of May, pursuant to a call addressed "to the Radical Men of the Nation." Of the 350 persons who answered this call, few, if any, were properly delegates representing constituencies. These men, representing their own principles rather than the people, nominated General John C. Fremont for President, and for Vice-President General John Cochrane. The distinctive articles of the platform adopted by this Convention were those declaring that the President ought to be elected for a single term and by a direct vote of the people, that the question of reconstruction belonged to Congress and not to the executive; and that justice required the confiscation of rebel property and its distribution among "the soldiers and actual settlers." This policy of general confiscation was repudiated by General Fremont in his letter accepting the nomination.

Just a week later—June 7th—the Republican Convention proper assembled at Baltimore, in response to a call issued by the Executive Committee, which had been created by the Chicago Convention of 1860. Senator Morgan, of New York, chairman of that committee, called the Convention to order, and proposed Dr. Robert J. Breckinridge, of Kentucky, as temporary president. Breckinridge and the ten other delegates from Kentucky did not claim to fairly represent that party in their state which would cast the majority of votes. Hon. William Dennison, of Ohio, was elected president in the permanent organization of the Convention.[1] The work of the Convention was soon accomplished. The platform of resolutions, as reported by H. J. Raymond, of New York, and unanimously adopted, maintained the integrity of the Union; the paramount authority of the Constitution and laws of the United States; the suppression of the rebellion and the punishment of rebels; the repudiation of compromise, and of any terms of peace except those based on the unconditional surrender of hostility on the part of the enemies arrayed against the government; the abolition of slavery by constitutional amendment; the policy and measures of the administration, especially the Emancipation Proclamation and the employment of negro soldiers; the recognition of the valor and patriotism of the soldiers and sailors, and provision — ample and permanent — for those disabled by wounds; prompt and full redress for the violation of the laws of war in the treatment by the enemy of our soldiers, without distinction of color; the encouragement of immigration; the inviolability of the public debt; and the Monroe doctrine.[2]

---

[1] There were 520 delegates admitted, from the following States and Territories:

From Maine, 14.	From Maryland, 14.	From Wisconsin, 16.
New Hampshire, 10.	Louisiana, 14.	Iowa, 16.
Vermont, 10.	Arkansas, 10.	Minnesota, 8.
Massachusetts, 24.	Missouri, 22.	California,-10.
Rhode Island, 8.	Tennessee, 15.	Oregon, 6.
Connecticut, 12.	Kentucky, 21.	West Virginia, 10.
New York, 66.	Ohio, 42.	Kansas, 6.
New Jersey, 14.	Indiana, 26.	Nebraska, 6.
Pennsylvania, 49.	Illinois, 32.	Colorado, 6.
Delaware, 6.	Michigan, 16.	Nevada, 6.

[2] The following is a copy of these resolutions:

Resolved, That it is the highest duty of every American citizen to maintain against all their enemies the integrity of the Union, and the paramount authority of the Constitution and laws of the United States; and that, laying aside all differences of political opinion, we pledge ourselves as Union men, animated by a common sentiment, and aiming at a common object, to do every thing in our power to aid the government in quelling by force of arms the rebellion now raging against its authority, and in bringing to the punishment due to their crimes the rebels and traitors arrayed against it.

Resolved, That we approve the determination of the government of the United States not to compromise with rebels, nor to offer any terms of peace except such as may be based upon an "unconditional surrender" of their hostility and a return to their just allegiance to the Constitution and laws of the United States, and that we call upon the government to maintain this position and to prosecute the war with the utmost possible vigor to the complete suppression of the rebellion, in full reliance upon the self-sacrifice, the patriotism, the heroic valor, and the undying devotion of the American people to their country and its free institutions.

Resolved, That, as slavery was the cause, and now constitutes the strength of this rebellion, and as it must be always and every where hostile to the principles of republican government, justice and the national safety demand its utter and complete extirpation from the soil of the republic; and that we uphold and maintain the acts and proclamations by which the government, in its own defense, has aimed a death-blow at this gigantic evil. We are in favor, furthermore, of such an amendment to the Constitutton, to be made by the people in conformity with its provisions, as shall terminate and forever prohibit the existence of slavery within the limits of the jurisdiction of the United States.

Resolved, That the thanks of the American people are due to the soldiers and sailors of the army and navy, who have periled their lives in defense of their country and in vindication of the honor of the flag; that the nation owes to them some permanent recognition of their patriotism and valor, and ample and permanent provision for those of their survivors who have received disabling and honorable wounds in the service of the country; and that the memories of those who have fallen in its defense shall be held in grateful and everlasting remembrance.

Resolved, That we approve and applaud the practical wisdom, the unselfish patriotism, and unswerving fidelity to the Constitution and the principles of American liberty with which Abraham Lincoln has discharged, under circumstances of unparalleled difficulty, the great duties and responsibilities of the presidential office; that we approve and indorse, as demanded by the emergency and essential to the preservation of the nation, and as within the Constitution, the measures and acts which he has adopted to defend the nation against its open and secret foes; that we approve especially the Proclamation of Emancipation, and the employment as Union soldiers of men heretofore held in slavery; and that we have full confidence in his determination to carry these and all other constitutional measures essential to the salvation of the country into full and complete effect.

Resolved, That we deem it essential to the general welfare that harmony should prevail in the national councils, and we regard as worthy of public confidence and official trust those only who cordially indorse the principles proclaimed in these resolutions, and which should characterize the administration of the government.

Resolved, That the government owes to all men employed in its armies, without regard to distinction of color, the full protection of the laws of war; and that any violation of these laws or of the usages of civilized nations in the time of war by the rebels now in arms, should be made the subject of full and prompt redress.

Resolved, That the foreign immigration, which in the past has added so much to the wealth and development of resources and increase of power to this nation, the asylum of the oppressed of all nations, should be fostered and encouraged by a liberal and just policy.

Resolved, That we are in favor of the speedy construction of a railroad to the Pacific.

Resolved, That the national faith, pledged for the redemption of the public debt, must be kept inviolate; and that for this purpose we recommend economy and rigid responsibility in the public expenditures, and a vigorous and just system of taxation; that it is the duty of every loyal state to sustain the credit and promote the use of the national currency.

Resolved, That we approve the position taken by the government that the people of the United States never regarded with indifference the attempt of any European power to overthrow by force, or to supplant by fraud, the institutions of any republican government on the Western continent, and that they view with extreme jealousy, as menacing to the peace and independence of this our country, the efforts of any such power to obtain new footholds for monarchical governments, sustained by a foreign military force, in near proximity to the United States.

The nomination of Mr. Lincoln for President was already a foregone conclusion when the Convention met. On the first ballot he received the vote of every delegation except that from Missouri, which had been instructed to vote for General Grant. This delegation changing its vote, the nomination was made unanimous.

For Vice-President there were three candidates—Andrew Johnson, Military Governor of Tennessee, Hannibal Hamlin, the then incumbent, and Daniel S. Dickinson. On the first ballot the vote stood, Johnson, 200; Dickinson, 108; Hamlin, 150; scattering, 59. Several delegations changed their vote in favor of Johnson, who, on the second ballot, received 494 votes, and was then declared unanimously nominated.

In his letter accepting the nomination, President Lincoln announced, to avoid misunderstanding, that the position of the government in relation to the action of France in Mexico, as assumed through the State Department, and indorsed by the Convention, would be maintained so long as it was pertinent and applicable.

When the Republican Convention met it was confidently expected that the war would soon close by the downfall of Atlanta and Richmond. But in the interval that elapsed before the meeting of the Democratic Convention, which was postponed from July 4th to August 29th, the situation was materially changed. Grant, in his march from the Rapidan to the James, inflicted great losses upon the Confederate army, but he suffered far greater losses himself, and had not captured Richmond. The progress of the Atlanta campaign seemed slow to the people who, a few weeks before, were confident of speedy victory. Since the defeat of Bragg at Chattanooga, no important and decisive triumph had been won by the Union armies. Numerous failures there had been, and, though none of them were of great magnitude or decisive in character, yet they added a sting to the disappointment of looking over a nine months' calendar barren of any palpable success. There was no doubt as to final results—it was simply a period of gloomy disappointment. There was no flinching either on the part of the army or the people. The army pushed grimly on, and met partial discomfiture with soldierly fortitude; the people afforded it a grim but determined support, though their efforts had been unrewarded by immediate success.

If there was much in the military situation which gave encouragement to the opposition party, the financial aspect of the country afforded them a still more palpable fulcrum upon which to swing their lever for the overthrow of the administration. The amount of the public debt was rapidly climbing

CHIEF JUSTICES OF THE UNITED STATES.

JOHN JAY.   OLIVER ELLSWORTH.   JUSTICE.   LIBERTY.   JOHN MARSHALL.   ROGER B. TANEY.

up to two billions.[1] In July, 1864, gold was quoted at 290, having reached that point from 195 since Grant and Sherman began their campaigns in May.

Just at this crisis, Salmon P. Chase, the Secretary of the Treasury, resigned, and there were not a few who attributed his resignation to the financial difficulties of the nation. It is probable, however, that he was influenced chiefly by political reasons, arising out of the relations which, during the presidential canvass, had grown up between himself and Mr. Lincoln. That there was no hostility toward the secretary on the part of the President is evident from the fact that, upon the death of Roger B. Taney, October 12, 1864, he appointed Mr. Chase chief justice of the United States Supreme Court.[2]

During the summer of 1864, two attempts were made by irresponsible parties, apparently having for their object the conclusion of the war through mutual accommodation, but in reality influenced solely by political motives. It is a curious fact that, at the same time, President Lincoln was sounded on the subject of peace by Confederate agents in Canada, for the express purpose of drawing out of him a distinct refusal to afford accommodation—a refusal which might be used both to incite the South to renewed efforts to gain Confederate independence, and to strengthen the cause of the opposition in the North; and President Davis was sounded upon the same subject for the purpose of drawing out from him a like refusal, to be used for a similar purpose in behalf of the supporters of the administration.

On the 5th of July, George N. Sanders, from the Clifton House, Niagara Falls, addressed a letter to Horace Greeley, stating that he himself, and Clement C. Clay, of Alabama, and James P. Holcombe, of Virginia, were willing to go to Washington if full protection were accorded them. Nothing was said in the letter as to the object of the proposed visit to Washington. But from other sources Greeley understood that Clay and Holcombe had full powers from Richmond to treat on the subject of peace. He therefore forwarded the application to President Lincoln, urging a response, and suggesting terms of accommodation. The "plan of adjustment" suggested by him proposed the restoration of the Union; the abolition of slavery, the Union paying $400,000,000 in 5 per cent. bonds as compensation to the owners of slaves, whether loyal or rebel; the representation in Congress of the slave states on the basis of their total population; and a National Convention, to be convened as soon as possible, for the ratification of these terms. He added: "I do not say that a just peace is now attainable, though I believe it to be so. But I do say that a frank offer by you to the insurgents of terms which the impartial must say ought to be accepted, will, at the worst, prove an immense and sorely needed advantage to the national cause. It may save us from a Northern insurrection."

The President forthwith deputed Greeley to Niagara to communicate with the Confederate agents. Greeley went to Niagara, and on the 17th informed Messrs. Clay and Holcombe that, if they were duly accredited agents from Richmond, the President would grant them a safe-conduct to Washington. These gentlemen replied that they were not accredited agents, but thoroughly understood the views of the Confederate government on the subject of peace. Upon learning this the President sent a message, addressed "to whom it may concern," in the following terms:

"Any proposition which embraces the restoration of peace, the integrity of the whole Union, and the abandonment of slavery, and which comes by and with an authority that can control the armies now at war with the United States, will be received and considered by the executive government of the United States, and will be met by liberal terms on other substantial and collateral points, and the bearer or bearers thereof shall have safe-conduct both ways."

This, of course, was final, being all the Confederate gentlemen had waited for. They had now their text, and they issued their manifesto against the tyranny which could thus rudely spurn the offer of peace. But President Lincoln had simply been honest with them, and certainly had not been discourteous. Nor had he rejected their overtures. His design in addressing his mission "to all whom it may concern" is evident. These gentlemen had admitted that they were not accredited agents of the Confederate government, but had expressed their confidence that they could obtain the requisite power. But they might be, and probably were, indulging false hopes as to the accommodation which the government would be willing to grant. It was only fair, therefore, that both they and the Confederate government—all whom it might concern—should be made to understand the ultimatum of the government which must be met before the door could be open to ne-

---

[1] The public debt was thus estimated at the close of each fiscal year since 1860:

1860—June 30th......... $ 64,769,703	1863—June 30th....... $1,097,274,360
1861— " 90,867,828	1864— " 1,740,036,689
1862— " 514,211,371	

[2] JOHN JAY, the first chief justice of the United States, was born in New York, December 12, 1745. He graduated at King's (now Columbia) College in 1764, and was admitted to the bar four years later. When the Revolutionary troubles came on he took a prominent part in the contest. He was the youngest member of the first Congress which convened in 1774. In 1777 he prepared the draft of the Constitution of the State of New York, and was appointed the first chief justice of the state. In 1779 he was sent on a mission to Spain. That government demanded as a condition of recognizing the independence of the United States that the possession of Florida and the exclusive right to navigate the Mississippi should be guaranteed to Spain. Jay refused to consent that the mouth of our great river should be shut up by a foreign power. In conjunction with Adams, Franklin, and Laurens, Mr. Jay negotiated the treaty by which Great Britain recognized the independence of the United States. In 1784 he returned to his country, and was appointed Secretary for Foreign Affairs. When the Union took the place of the old Confederation, Washington requested him to select any office which he might prefer. He chose that of Chief Justice of the United States, to which he was appointed in 1789. In 1794 he was sent to Great Britain as envoy extraordinary to negotiate an important treaty. This treaty, which settled the questions in dispute between the two nations, was violently opposed by the Democratic party, especially at the South. He was absent a year, during which time he was elected Governor of New York. He then resigned the chief justiceship, was twice re-elected governor, and then, in 1801, at the age of fifty-six, resolved to retire from public life. President Adams, wishing to retain his services for the public, nominated him for his former place as chief justice, then vacant by the resignation of Oliver Ellsworth. Jay declined, on the ground that he had deliberately made up his mind to retire from public life, and duty to his country did not then require him to accept office. He retired to his farm in Bedford, New York, where he died May 17, 1829, in the eighty-fourth year of his age. Mr. Jay was one of the noblest and purest characters in our history. No man, except a few violent partisans in South Carolina, however much he might oppose his public policy, dared to asperse the perfect integrity of John Jay.

Upon the resignation of Mr. Jay, JOHN RUTLEDGE was nominated by the President as chief justice of the United States, but was not confirmed.

The President then nominated as chief justice Judge WILLIAM CUSHING, of Massachusetts; the nomination was confirmed; but Mr. Cushing, after holding the commission a few days, resigned on account of ill health. As he never acted in that capacity, his name does not properly belong to the list of chief justices.

OLIVER ELLSWORTH was then nominated and confirmed as chief justice. He was born at Windsor, Connecticut, April 29, 1745. His studies commenced at Yale, were completed at Princeton, where he graduated at the age of twenty-three. For a time he was a teacher, then commenced the study of theology, but subsequently decided on the profession of law. He had then married, and his father gave him a farm of wild land and an axe. While slowly working his way at the bar he cleared his wild farm with his own hands. His early career gave no promise of future eminence; but the first upward steps once taken, his progress was sure. He was appointed state's attorney, and yearly elected to the General Assembly. In 1777 he was chosen delegate to Congress, 1784 Judge of the Superior Court of Connecticut, and in 1789 senator in Congress. In 1796 he was appointed chief justice of the United States. His unquestioned probity and the soundness of his judicial decisions gained him the highest respect. In 1799 he was sent, against his wishes, as minister to France, though still retaining for two years his seat on the bench. His health failing, he resigned his office in 1801. He died November 26, 1807, at the age of sixty-two.

JOHN MARSHALL, the most eminent of our chief justices, was born in Fauquier County, Virginia, September 24, 1755. His father was a farmer in narrow circumstances, but of decided ability. By his own unaided exertions he subsequently became a fair classical scholar, and was intimately acquainted with English literature. He had just begun the study of law when the war of the Revolution broke out. In 1775 he was appointed lieutenant in a company of minute-men. He afterward became captain in a Virginia regiment of the Continental army, and was present at the battles of Brandywine, Germantown, and Monmouth. He pursued his legal studies at intervals during the war, and at its close commenced practice. He soon rose to eminence at the bar and in politics. He was one of the small but distinguished body of men through whose influence Virginia was induced to accept the Federal Constitution. In 1794 Washington offered him the post of attorney general, and subsequently the mission to France. Both offers were declined. The French government having refused to receive Mr. Pinckney as minister, Mr. Adams, who was then President, appointed Mr. Marshall as one of three envoys to that country. Shortly after his return he yielded to the personal solicitations of Washington, and consented to become a candidate for Congress. President Adams at the same time offered him a seat on the bench of the Supreme Court, which was declined. He was elected to Congress after a sharp contest, taking his seat in December, 1799. During the excited session which followed he was one of the ablest supporters of the administration of Mr. Adams. In May, 1800, he was nominated and confirmed as Secretary of War, but he declined to accept the appointment. Shortly after he accepted the post of Secretary of State. On the 31st of January, 1801, he was appointed chief justice of the United States, a position which he held for thirty-five years, until his death in July, 1835, at the age of eighty years. His unquestioned character, sound judgment, and felicitous diction, added to the long period during which he held his seat, and the magnitude of the questions which came before him for decision, entitle Mr. Marshall beyond all question to the first place in the noble list of our chief justices. Besides his judicial labors, he was the author of a History of the American Colonies and of a Life of Washington.

ROGER BROOKE TANEY was born in Calvert County, Maryland, March 17, 1777. In 1831 President Jackson appointed him attorney general of the United States. Two years later, Mr. Duane, then Secretary of the Treasury, refused to remove the government deposits from the United States Bank; he was removed, and Mr. Taney was appointed in his place. The Senate refused to confirm the nomination; but in the mean while Mr. Taney had obeyed the orders of the President and removed the deposits. Jackson then nominated him as associate justice of the Supreme Court, to fill a vacancy occasioned by the resignation of Judge Duval. The Senate refused to confirm the nomination. Chief Justice Marshall died in 1835, and Jackson at once nominated Mr. Taney for the place. The Democrats, having now a majority in the Senate, confirmed the nomination, and Mr. Taney became chief justice—a position he retained until his death, October 12, 1864, a period of twenty-seven years. Chief Justice Taney is best known by his famous "decision," or rather "opinion," in the Dred Scott case, in which, going beyond the question before the court, he endeavored to settle the general question of the *status* of persons of African descent in the United States. Undeserved obloquy has been attached to him on account of a sentence in this opinion which apparently affirmed that blacks had no rights which whites were bound to respect. The context shows that this was the very reverse of the meaning intended to be conveyed by Judge Taney. He says that it is now difficult to realize the state of opinion on this subject held at the formation of our government. Blacks were then regarded as beings of an inferior order, "*and so far inferior that they had no rights which the white man was bound to respect.*" This outrageous sentiment is mentioned only to be impliedly condemned. The "opinion" of the chief justice, harsh enough as he gave it, being to the effect that no person whose ancestors were imported to this country and sold as slaves had any right to sue in a court of the United States, or could become citizens of the United States. It is due to the honor of our highest judicial tribunal to state that the opinion of the chief justice did not affirm, but did by plain implication condemn, the doctrine that such persons "had no rights which whites were bound to respect." Mr. Taney's last notable public act was in May, 1861, when the case of John Merryman came before him. This man was arrested near Baltimore, on charge of being an officer in a company raised to aid the rebellion. He was imprisoned by the military authorities in Fort M'Henry. He prayed for a writ of *habeas corpus*, which was granted by Judge Taney. General Cadwalader, the commander, refused to obey, on the ground that the execution of the writ of *habeas corpus* had been suspended by the President in the State of Maryland. The judge issued an order for the arrest of General Cadwalader. The marshal was not allowed to serve the writ. Judge Taney thereupon prepared an opinion, denying the right of the President to suspend the writ, and affirming that it was the duty of all military officers to obey it. He added that if the officer had been brought before him he should have punished him by fine and imprisonment; but as he had no force capable of carrying his order into effect, he should report the whole case to the President, and call upon him to en-

force the process of the court. No farther action was had on the case. Mr. Taney died October 12, 1864, at the age of eighty-seven, having filled the chief judicial chair of the nation for twenty-seven years. He owed his appointment to the purely partisan services which he rendered to President Jackson. As a jurist he can not be ranked with the great men who had occupied his seat before him. His judicial integrity has never been impeached, even in the case of his unfortunate opinion in the Dred Scott case, or the later and equally unfortunate course in the Merryman case, by which he will be chiefly remembered in after years.

SALMON PORTLAND CHASE, now chief justice of the United States, was born in Cornish, New Hampshire, January 13, 1808. His father having died, he was sent at the age of twelve to Ohio, and placed under the care of his uncle, Bishop Chase. After studying for a year at Cincinnati College, he entered Dartmouth College in New Hampshire, from which he graduated in 1829. He went to Washington, where he opened a school, at the same time studying law under the direction of William Wirt. Having been admitted to the bar, he went to Cincinnati, and entered upon the practice of his profession. To this for some years he applied himself exclusively, taking no prominent part in politics, although he belonged to the Democratic party. In 1841 he first took a decided part in politics. He was then a member of the Convention of those opposed to the farther extension of slavery, and was the author of the address unanimously adopted by that body. He took a prominent part in all the subsequent movements having this end in view, and was president of the Free Soil Democratic Convention at Buffalo in 1848. The Democratic party in Ohio had at this time assumed the position of hostility to slavery in the Territories. Mr. Chase was chosen United States Senator in February, 1849, receiving the votes of all the Democratic members of the Legislature, together with those of others who were in favor of free soil. Though elected as a Democrat, he declared that if the party withdrew from its position in regard to slavery he should withdraw from it. This he did formally, in consequence of the action of the Democratic Convention held at Baltimore in 1852. When the Republican party was organized, Mr. Chase took the position of one of its acknowledged leaders. Soon after the close of his senatorial term in 1855 he was elected Governor of Ohio. He was re-elected, his second term closing in 1860. In the Republican Convention at Chicago in that year, he was, next after Mr. Lincoln and Mr. Seward, the leading candidate for the presidency. He had in the mean time been again elected to the Senate of the United States, and had he taken his place would undoubtedly have been the leader in that body. But he resigned his seat in order to accept the position of Secretary of the Treasury—a position for which he was especially pointed out by the success of his financial policy while Governor of Ohio. As the presidential canvass of 1864 approached, a strong effort was made to bring forward Mr. Chase as the Union candidate; but the current of popular feeling was so unmistakably in favor of the re-election of Mr. Lincoln that Mr. Chase refused to become a candidate, and gave his cordial support to Mr. Lincoln. Meanwhile, finding that Congress hesitated to carry out the financial system which he proposed, Mr. Chase had, on the 30th of June, 1864, resigned the post of Secretary of the Treasury. Almost the first important public act of Mr. Lincoln after his re-election has been to appoint Mr. Chase to the most important position within the executive nomination. Mr. Chase enters upon the duties of his high office at the age of fifty-six, with a sound legal reputation, and with a physical vigor which gives reason to hope that he may be able to perform its duties for a period as long as that of his predecessor.

gotiation. This ultimatum was simply the integrity of the Union and the abandonment of slavery.

Undoubtedly the people of the South longed for peace. The whole people longed for peace, except a few to whom war was money. But peace was impossible until either the government or the rebels were defeated, except by the abandonment on one side or the other of the very object for which it was fighting. No proposition indicating the willingness of the Confederate government to surrender its independence upon any conditions had ever been made. That no such disposition existed in the summer of 1864 is shown by the result of a visit made to Richmond by Colonel Jacques and J. R. Gilmore while Greeley was in communication with Clay and Holcombe at Niagara. These gentlemen went to Richmond with no credentials. They were not sent by the government. They did not expect to accomplish any thing in the way of peace. Yet in a certain sense they were commissioners, not of the government, but of a party, sent to receive a distinct expression of the unwillingness of Mr. Davis to negotiate for peace except on the basis of Confederate independence. This they obtained in the most explicit terms. Davis told them that the "war must go on till the last of this generation falls in his tracks, and his children seize his musket and fight our battle, unless you acknowledge our right to self-government. We are not fighting for slavery; we are fighting for independence, and that or extermination we will have." Certainly this declaration did not improve the prospects of the opposition party in the North in the approaching elections.

On the 29th of August the National Democratic Convention assembled at Chicago. The next day it was permanently organized, with Governor Seymour, of New York, as president. Upward of 250 delegates were present. Among these, and master spirits of the Convention, were Vallandigham—recently returned from exile—Price, and Long. A large portion of the audience consisted of the most disaffected men of the Northwestern states, among whom were mingled Confederate spies from Canada, who, with their friends, were at this very moment meditating a scheme for the liberation of the 8000 Confederate prisoners at Camp Douglas, near the city, the execution of which scheme was to be followed by a general uprising of the disloyal in all the Northwestern states. This movement was only prevented by the preparations which had been made to thwart it through the vigilance of Colonel B. J. Sweet, the commander at Camp Douglas.

Governor Seymour, upon assuming the chair, addressed the delegates and the audience. Seymour, while he was thoroughly identified with the peace party, was the most astute and prudent member of that party. Not turbulent himself, he rejoiced in the turbulence of others. His style of eloquence was modeled upon that which Mark Antony (as rendered by Shakspeare) adopted over the corpse of Cæsar. His thunderbolts, like those of Wendell Phillips, always fell out of a clear sky. There was no measure of the opposition, however extreme, which he did not heartily indorse; and yet the problem to be solved in this Convention, as it seemed to him, was to at the same time apparently ignore all such measures, and adopt such as would secure their execution. The task was not an easy one. There was a great diversity of opinion among the members of the Convention. Only the utmost tact could prevent such a division as had occurred at the Charleston Convention four years ago. Seymour counseled them to select such men for their candidates as enjoyed the popular confidence. He reminded them of the Republican Convention held in that city in 1860, and that while the party which it represented had there declared that it would not interfere with the rights of states, the sentiment by which it was animated—its sectional prejudices and fanaticism—had overruled this declaration. Even now, under the shadow of impending ruin, this party would not let the shedding of blood cease even for a little, "to see if Christian charity or the wisdom of statesmanship" might not save the Union. But, even if it would, the administration could not save the country. It had, by its proclamations and vindictive legislation, placed obstacles in its own way which it could not overcome; its freedom of action was hampered by its own unconstitutional acts. Seymour then proceeded to pay a tribute to our soldiers, which falls upon our ears like mockery when we remember that he did all he could to weaken the armies in the field by his opposition to conscription. But his compliment to the soldiers was of a very doubtful sort when he intimated that they were more lenient toward traitors than was the administration.

"But if the administration can not save the Union," said he, "we can. . . . There are no hinderances to our pathways to union and to peace." He forgot under what administrations disunion had blossomed and matured to ripeness. And when he added, "we have no hates, no prejudices, no passions," did he remember the fiendish, negro-hunting mob, whom a little more than a year ago he had addressed in New York city as "my friends?" Yes, this astute statesman could look down into the face of Long, who had a few weeks before, in the halls of Congress, advocated the recognition of the Confederacy, and into the faces of others who had applauded his words to the echo, and say, "the administration can not save the Union, but we can do it." He had complained of the lack of wise statesmanship in the Republican party to secure the fruit of victories won in the field. Was wise statesmanship in this trying hour of the nation's life confined to such men as Price, Vallandigham, and the Seymours? With remarkable coolness he alluded to the military edict which three days before had gone forth, forbidding the transportation of arms or ammunition into Ohio, Indiana, Illinois, and Michigan. Did he know of the existence of secret organizations in those states, the members of which were the sworn enemies of the national government, waiting only their opportunity to aid the Confederate armies by domestic insurrection in the North? Did he know that he was addressing men who directly controlled and sustained these organizations? So well did he understand the character of his audience, that he especially guarded those who

were not delegates against an unbecoming expression of their opinion by applause or condemnation. He had noticed with chagrin that the loudest cheers followed the expression of disloyal sentiments, and feared the result of the impression which would thus be made upon the people at large. Indeed, he had scarcely given this prudent bit of advice when he was interrupted by loud calls for Vallandigham.

Seymour to a great degree succeeded in impressing his own temper upon the Convention, but he could not control the members in their conduct outside of the wigwam. From the balconies of hotels and on street-corners sentiments were uttered which more fully represented the temper of the crowd which had naturally gathered about this Democratic Convention. Here C. Chauncey Burr, Vallandigham, and Henry C. Dean could speak out clearly their sympathy with rebels without disguise or circumlocution. Here they could charge Lincoln with spoon-stealing and negro-stealing; could declare that the South, fighting for her honor, could not honorably lay down her arms, and that Lincoln's army, already the slaughter-pen of two millions of men, could not again be filled either by enlistment or conscription; and could utter their prayers for the failure of the national arms. Here they could call Lincoln a usurper, traitor, tyrant, blood-thirsty old monster, or any other odious name which the Democratic vocabulary of that day readily furnished. And yet these men belonged to a party which, Seymour said, had "no hates, no prejudices, no passions." War-Democrats received their share of this wholesale vituperation and execration. Between a War-Democrat and an Abolitionist, said Judge Miller, of Ohio, there is no real difference; "they are links of one sausage, made out of the same dog," and the crowd yelled its applause. Judge Miller was a fair representative of that "insulted judiciary" which Seymour in his speech had declared "would again administer the laws of the land" when the Democratic administration should have displaced that of Mr. Lincoln.

The platform of resolutions was constructed by a committee, of which Vallandigham was a member. In the contest for the chairmanship of this committee, Vallandigham received 8 votes and Guthrie 12. This man was the master-spirit of the Convention, so far as its objects were concerned, while Seymour furnished the model for its style of utterance. In the Committee on Resolutions, James Guthrie, of Kentucky, its chairman, acted the same part which Seymour played in the conduct of the entire Convention. Vallandigham was the irrepressible soul of the resolutions, and it was the business of Guthrie to hide this wretched soul within a becoming body, to disguise sympathy with treason by sandwiching it in between a declaration of fidelity to the Union and one of pity toward unnecessarily slaughtered soldiers.[1] The resolutions as adopted pretended to speak for a party, a large and the most respectable and patriotic portion of which repudiated them; they declared as a sentiment of the Convention "unswerving fidelity to the Union under the Constitution." But how many members of this Convention had publicly declared that under the Constitution the right of secession was justifiable? They declared in behalf of the Convention and as the sense of the American people that the experiment of war, tried for four years, had proved a failure, and that "justice, humanity, liberty, and the public welfare demand that immediate efforts be made for a cessation of hostilities, with a view to an ultimate Convention of the states, or other peaceable means, to the end that at the earliest practicable moment peace may be restored on the basis of the Federal Union of the states."[2] It is in vain that one inquires after the reasons for this demand by either "justice," "humanity," "liberty," or the "public welfare." It was known—it had been the undeviating declaration of the Confederate government, one from which it had not swerved even in order to assist this peace party of the North—that no peace was practicable (except a conquered peace) on any other basis than that of Confederate independence. And this Convention knew that the peace for which they declared must result in the recognition of the Confederacy. How justice, or humanity, or liberty, or the public welfare were to be advanced by that inglorious consummation it is not easy to discover. Let us suppose for an instant that this peace party should succeed, and that the leaders who controlled its action should come into possession of the executive and legislative

---

[1] The following is the platform adopted by the Convention:

Resolved, That in the future, as in the past, we will adhere with unswerving fidelity to the Union under the Constitution, as the only solid foundation of our strength, security, and happiness as a people, and as a framework of government equally conducive to the welfare and prosperity of all the states, both Northern and Southern.

Resolved, That this Convention does explicitly declare, as the sense of the American people, that, after four years of failure to restore the Union by the experiment of war, during which, under the pretense of a military necessity of a war power higher than the Constitution, the Constitution itself has been disregarded in every part, and public liberty and private right alike trodden down, and the material prosperity of the country essentially impaired, justice, humanity, liberty, and the public welfare demand that immediate efforts be made for a cessation of hostilities, with a view to an ultimate Convention of all the states, or other peaceable means, to the end that at the earliest practicable moment peace may be restored on the basis of the Federal Union of the states.

Resolved, That the direct interference of the military authority of the United States in the recent elections held in Kentucky, Maryland, Missouri, and Delaware, was a shameful violation of the Constitution, and the repetition of such acts in the approaching election will be held as revolutionary, and resisted with all the means and power under our control.

Resolved, That the aim and object of the Democratic party is to preserve the Federal Union and the rights of states unimpaired; and they hereby declare that they consider the administrative usurpation of extraordinary and dangerous powers not granted by the Constitution, the subversion of the civil by military law in states not in insurrection, the arbitrary military arrest, imprisonment, trial, and sentence of American citizens in states where civil law exists in full force, the suppression of freedom of speech and of the press, the denial of the right of asylum, the open and avowed disregard of state rights, the employment of unusual test-oaths, and the interference with and denial of the right of the people to bear arms, as calculated to prevent a restoration of the Union and the perpetuation of a government deriving its just powers from the consent of the governed.

Resolved, That the shameful disregard of the administration to its duty in respect to our fellow-citizens who now and long have been prisoners of war in a suffering condition, deserves the severest reprobation, on the score alike of public interest and common humanity.

Resolved, That the sympathy of the Democratic party is heartily and earnestly extended to the soldiery of our army, who are and have been in the field under the flag of our country; and, in the event of our attaining power, they will receive all the care and protection, regard and kindness, that the brave soldiers of the republic have so nobly earned.

[2] This resolution, the second and most important one of the platform, was written by Vallandigham. So Vallandigham himself states in a letter written to the New York *Daily News* from Chicago, October 22d.

SOLDIERS VOTING FOR PRESIDENT.

powers of the nation. Suppose an armistice declared under such auspices. The armies, with ultimate victory already in sight, rest upon their arms, while these men try their boasted "statesmanship" in the interests of peace. Soldiers levied by conscription, and on their way to the field, are halted, released from obligation, and returned to their homes. Recruiting and conscription cease. Military ardor is already dead, or this peace party could not else have come into power. What would be the action of Davis and his associates, and of the Southern people? They seceded under the auspices of Buchanan's administration; but now an administration is in power which is pledged to desist from war in any event. The storming of cannon, the musketry attack, the strong hands of soldiers already about to clutch this demon of treason and strangle it to death, silently vanish from the scene, and are replaced by this nest of cooing doves, who from the national capital seek to woo traitors back to their spurned allegiance. Can there be any doubt as to the result of this innocent, amicable sport? Would the Confederacy dance to the piping of these men of peace? No, it would claim the right of secession, which these men would instantly yield; it would become a nation which these doters would forthwith recognize. The armies in the field would then slink back to their homes, cursing the people who had betrayed them. Grant, and Sherman, and Thomas, and Farragut, would hide their faces for shame, and quietly receive their reward—the brand of murder placed upon their foreheads by Peace Democrats and an unworthy people. The uncoffined, living corpse of Lincoln—more than murdered by these political assassins—would proceed from Washington to Springfield amid the jeers of faithless multitudes. And this was to be the Democratic apotheosis of justice, humanity, and liberty!

We do not wonder, after this declaration, that the Convention tendered its sympathy to the Union soldiers, who would need so much sympathy in the event of its political success.

The members of the Convention, after the adoption of this platform, named various candidates for President, and spent the remainder of the day in discussing their comparative merits. General McClellan was the only nominee who stood any fair chance of success, but there was certainly room for discussion as to the propriety of asking a major general of the United States army to stand upon the platform adopted by the Convention. On the 31st the voting commenced. On the first ballot it stood: McClellan, 174; Thomas H. Seymour, 38; Horatio Seymour, 12. This was revised so that McClellan stood 202½, and Thomas H. Seymour 28½. On the motion of Vallandigham, the nomination of McClellan was made unanimous. No less than eight candidates were offered on the first ballot for Vice-President. James Guthrie received the largest number of votes—65; George H. Pendleton stood next, receiving 55; and the third on the list was Lazarus W. Powell, who received 36. But the New York delegation, commanding 33 votes, went over to Pendleton, who was finally declared the nominee of the Convention.

McClellan's letter accepting the nomination expressed sentiments at vari-

ance with those of the Convention. "If a frank, earnest, and persistent effort," said he, "to obtain these objects [peace and union] should fail, the responsibility for ulterior consequences will fall upon those who remain in arms against the Union. But the Union must be preserved at all hazards." This idea—that of resuming the war in the event of the failure to obtain peace on the basis of the Union—came up before the Committee on Resolutions in the Convention, and was *unanimously* rejected.[1] "I could not," adds McClellan, in allusion to one of the resolutions adopted at Chicago, "look in the face of my gallant comrades of the army and navy, who have survived so many bloody battles, and tell them that their labors and the sacrifice of so many of our slain and wounded brethren had been in vain; that we had abandoned that Union for which we have so often periled our lives. A vast majority of our people, whether in the army and navy or at home, would, as I would, hail with unbounded joy the permanent restoration of peace on the basis of the Union under the Constitution, without the effusion of another drop of blood. But no peace can be permanent without the Union." He differed with the Convention also in postponing the effort to procure peace by the exhaustion of "all the resources of statesmanship" until it should become clear or probable "that our present adversaries are ready for peace upon the basis of the Union." A similar proposition coming before the Convention Committee on Resolutions in exactly the same terms used in this letter, received only three votes out of twenty-four.[2]

Pendleton very cautiously refused to commit himself except in so far as to state that he deprecated and would persistently oppose the establishment of another government over any portion of the territory within the limits of the Union. With one hand he clung to Vallandigham, and with the other to McClellan, while the latter shouldered Pendleton, Vallandigham, and the Chicago platform—protesting against the burden, but still bearing it—and with this incubus ran the race with Lincoln for the presidential chair. Even without these entanglements his prospects of success were doubtful, as his success involved the abandonment of the emancipation policy, which had already grown as dear to the American people as to President Lincoln.

Scarcely had the members of the Convention returned home, and begun to mingle with the people again, when they discovered too late that they had made a great mistake. As Gettysburg and Vicksburg had followed the harangues of Seymour, Pierce, and others on the 4th of July, 1863, so now the people got up from reading the Chicago platform to celebrate the capture of Atlanta, which was the sternest rebuke and most striking refutation of that document. Men who were disposed to split hairs with the Chicago statesmen were knocked down by Sherman's more palpable arguments. As Seward truly said at the time, "Sherman and Farragut had knocked the bottom out of the Chicago nominations."

---

[1] Vallandigham, in a public speech at Sidney, Ohio, September 24th, makes this statement in the most positive terms, and it has never been denied.
[2] See Vallandigham's speech alluded to in the previous note.

GEORGE H. PENDLETON.

Fremont now withdrew from the contest, and while still pronouncing Lincoln's administration "politically, militarily, and financially a failure," he abandoned the field, "not to aid the triumph of Lincoln," but to do his part to prevent the election of McClellan. The latter would establish the Union *with* slavery, while the former was pledged to re-establish it *without* slavery, and thus the great issues of the day were fairly joined, and there ought to enter into the contest no disturbing element to diminish the full strength of the victory of emancipation. Sheridan's victories over Early in the Valley of the Shenandoah, though not necessary to a Republican triumph, doubtless increased the popular majority for Lincoln.

The state elections in October and November, preceding that for presidential electors, betokened a certain victory for the administration. In Vermont the Republican candidate for governor was elected by a majority larger than that of 1863. In Maine there was a slight loss as compared with the election of 1863. In Indiana, O. P. Morton, the Republican candidate for governor, was elected by a majority of over 20,000. In Pennsylvania there was no general election for state officers, but the delegation from that state to Congress was changed from 12 against 12 to 15 against 9—a gain of three Republican Congressmen. In New York, Reuben E. Fenton was elected by 8000 majority over Seymour.

The presidential election, November 8th, resulted in an overwhelming victory for the administration. McClellan received the electoral votes of three states—Delaware, New Jersey, and Kentucky—21 in all; the remainder—212—were cast for Lincoln and Johnson. Lincoln's popular majority was 411,428.[1] In the twelve states whose vote by soldiers was counted so as to be distinguished, the success of the administration was even more signal, its majority being over 3 to 1. Such was the decision of the soldiers on the questions of peace and emancipation.[2]

An important issue in this election had been to secure a House of Representatives which would adopt the constitutional amendment abolishing slavery. The returns indicated that in the Thirty-ninth Congress the Republican majority would be so great that the members of that party, as compared with the Democrats, would number over 4 to 1. But it was not necessary to wait for another Congress.

The Thirty-eighth Congress reassembled for its second session December 5th, 1864.[1] The important act of this short session was the passage by the House of the joint resolution to amend the Constitution so as to abolish slavery. The President had in his message strongly urged this action. On the 31st of January the question was brought to a final issue. The form of the amendment remained the same as when it came from the Senate. The resolution passed by the requisite majority, receiving 119 ayes to 56 nays.[2] In this connection it is proper to mention the death of Owen Lovejoy, of Illinois, which occurred on the 25th of March, 1864. This old advocate of emancipation did not live to see the anti-slavery amendment passed, but he died in the faith that both Congress and the President would maintain justice.

In Maryland, on the 24th of June, in Constitutional Convention, the abolition of slavery in that state was declared as the twenty-third article of the Bill of Rights. In the following October this article was ratified by the people of the state. The vote stood 30,174 for, to 29,699 against the ratification. The majority was very small, and the measure would have failed but for the preponderance of the soldiers' vote in its favor. The soldiers' vote stood 2633 to 163.

Early in February, 1865, an attempt was made to open negotiations for peace. Alexander H. Stephens, the Confederate Vice-President, R. M. T. Hunter, and John A. Campbell, were permitted to pass through Grant's lines to Hampton Roads, where they were met by President Lincoln and Secretary Seward. The conference was soon concluded, President Lincoln refusing to treat on the basis of Confederate independence. Upon the return of the Confederate commissioners a great meeting was held to revive the drooping spirits of the Confederacy, and it was unanimously resolved that the conditions of peace offered by President Lincoln were a gross and premeditated insult to the Southern people. Three days later a war meeting was held, R. M. T. Hunter presiding, and it was there resolved that the Confederates would never lay down their arms until they should have achieved their independence.

The events—political and military—which from this point followed fast upon each other—the reinauguration of President Lincoln; the surrender of the Confederate armies; the attempt of a conspiracy to overthrow the government by the assassination of its principal officers; the succession of President Johnson; and the detailed history of reconstruction, belong properly to other chapters.

[1] The vote in the twenty-five loyal states stood as follows:

	LINCOLN.	McCLELLAN.		LINCOLN.	McCLELLAN.
Maine	72,278	47,736	Indiana	150,422	130,233
New Hampshire	36,595	33,034	Illinois	189,487	158,349
Vermont	42,422	13,325	Missouri	72,991	31,026
Massachusetts	126,742	48,745	Michigan	85,352	67,370
Rhode Island	14,343	8,718	Iowa	87,331	49,260
Connecticut	44,693	42,288	Wisconsin	79,564	63,875
New York	368,726	361,986	Minnesota	25,060	17,375
New Jersey	60,723	68,014	California	62,134	43,841
Pennsylvania	296,389	276,308	Oregon	9,888	8,457
Delaware	8,115	8,767	Kansas	14,228	3,871
Maryland	40,153	32,739	West Virginia	23,223	10,457
Kentucky	27,786	64,301	Nevada	9,826	6,594
Ohio	265,154	205,568	Total	2,213,665	1,802,237

[2] The army vote is shown in the following table. The soldiers of New York sent their ballots home to be deposited there, and so can not be distinguished. The vote of Minnesota soldiers, and a large portion of the Vermont soldiers' votes reached the canvassers too late to be counted:

	LINCOLN.	McCLELLAN.		LINCOLN.	McCLELLAN.
Maine	4,174	741	Michigan	9,402	2,957
New Hampshire	2,066	690	Iowa	15,178	1,364
Vermont	243	49	Wisconsin	11,372	2,458
Pennsylvania	26,712	12,349	Kansas	2,867	543
Maryland	2,800	321	California	2,600	237
Kentucky	1,194	2,823	Total	119,754	34,291
Ohio	41,146	9,757			

[1] The following changes occurred from the last session: In the Senate, Wm. Pitt Fessenden, of Maine, resigned to become Secretary of the Treasury, was succeeded by Nathan A. Farwell. On the 1st of February, 1865, William W. Stewart and James W. Nye took their seats as senators from Nevada—the former for the term expiring March 3, 1867, the latter for the term expiring March 3, 1869. On the 13th of February, Thomas H. Hicks, of Maryland. His successor, John A. Cresswell, was not qualified until March 10th, during the special executive session of the Senate.

In the House, Dwight Townsend, of New York, succeeded Henry G. Stebbins, resigned. December 21, Henry G. Worthington, of Nevada, was qualified.

[2] The vote in detail was as follows:

YEAS.

Alley	Mass.	Dixon	R. I.	King	Mo.	Rollins, E. H.	N. H.
Allison	Iowa.	Donnelly	Minn.	Knox	Mo.	Rollins, J. S.	Mo.
Ames	Mass.	Driggs	Mich.	Littlejohn	N. Y.	Schenck	Ohio.
Anderson	Ky.	Dumont	Ind.	Loan	Mo.	Schofield	Pa.
Arnold	Ill.	Eckley	Ohio.	Longyear	Mich.	Shannon	Cal.
Ashley	Ohio.	Elliot	Mass.	Marvin	N. Y.	Sloan	Wis.
Bailey	Pa.	English	Conn.	McAllister	Pa.	Smith	Ky.
Baldwin, A. C.	Mich.	Farnsworth	Ill.	McBride	Oregon.	Smithers	Del.
Baldwin, J. D.	Mass.	Frank	N. Y.	McClurg	Mo.	Spaulding	Ohio.
Baxter	Vt.	Ganson	N. Y.	McIndoe	Wis.	Starr	N. J.
Beaman	Mich.	Garfield	Ohio.	Miller	N. Y.	Steele	N. Y.
Blaine	Me.	Gooch	Mass.	Moorhead	Pa.	Stevens	Pa.
Blair	W. Va.	Grinnell	Iowa.	Morrill	Vt.	Thayer	Pa.
Blow	Mo.	Griswold	N. Y.	Morris	N. Y.	Thomas	Md.
Boutwell	Mass.	Hale	Pa.	Myers, A.	Pa.	Tracy	Pa.
Boyd	Mo.	Herrick	N. Y.	Myers, L.	Pa.	Upson	Mich.
Brandagee	Conn.	Higby	Cal.	Nelson	N. Y.	Van Valkenburg	N. Y.
Broomall	Pa.	Hooper	Mass.	Norton	Ill.	Washburne	Ill.
Brown	W. Va.	Hotchkiss	N. Y.	Odell	N. Y.	Washburne	Mass.
Clarke, A. W.	N. Y.	Hubbard, A. W.	Iowa.	O'Neill, C.	Pa.	Webster	Md.
Clarke, Freeman	N. Y.	Hubbard, J. H.	Conn.	Orth	Ind.	Whaley	W. Va.
Cobb	Wis.	Hurlburd	N. Y.	Patterson	N. H.	Wheeler	Wis.
Coffroth	Pa.	Hutchins	Ohio.	Perham	Me.	Wilder	Kansas.
Cole	Cal.	Ingersoll	Ill.	Pike	Me.	Williams	Pa.
Colfax	Ind.	Jenckes	R. I.	Pomeroy	N. Y.	Wilson	Iowa.
Creswell	Md.	Julian	Ind.	Price	Iowa.	Windom	Minn.
Davis, H. W.	Md.	Kasson	Iowa.	Radford	N. Y.	Woodbridge	Vt.
Davis, T. T.	N. Y.	Kelley	Pa.	Randall	Ky.	Worthington	Nev.
Dawes	Mass.	Kellogg, F. W.	Mich.	Rice, A. H.	Mass.	Yeaman	Ky.
Deming	Conn.	Kellogg, O.	N. Y.	Rice, J. H.	Me.		

NAYS.

Allen, J. C.	Ill.	Eldridge	Wis.	Law	Ind.	Scott	Mo.
Allen, W. H.	Ill.	Finck	Ohio.	Long	Ohio.	Steele, W. G.	N. J.
Ancona	Pa.	Grider	Ky.	Mallory	Ky.	Stiles	Pa.
Bliss	Ohio.	Hall	Mo.	Miller, W. H.	Pa.	Strouse	Pa.
Brooks	N. Y.	Harding	Ky.	Morris, J. R.	Ohio.	Stuart	Ill.
Brown, J. S.	Wis.	Harrington	Ind.	Morrison	Ill.	Sweat	Me.
Chanler	N. Y.	Harris, B. G.	Md.	Noble	Ohio.	Townsend	N. Y.
Clay	Ky.	Harris, C. M.	Ill.	O'Neill, J.	Ohio.	Wadsworth	Ky.
Cox	Ohio.	Holman	Ind.	Pendleton	Ohio.	Ward	N. Y.
Cravens	Ind.	Johnson, P.	Pa.	Perry	N. J.	White, C. A.	Ohio.
Dawson	Pa.	Johnson, W.	Ohio.	Pruyn	N. Y.	White, J. W.	Ohio.
Dennison	Pa.	Kalbfleisch	N. Y.	Randall, S. J.	Pa.	Winfield	N. Y.
Eden	Ill.	Kernan	N. Y.	Robinson	Ill.	Wood, B.	N. Y.
Edgerton	Ind.	Knapp	Ill.	Ross	Ill.	Wood, F.	N. Y.

NOT VOTING.

Lazear	Pa.	Marcy	N. H.	McKinney	Ohio.	Rogers	N. J.
Le Blond	Ohio.	McDowell	Ind.	Middleton	N. J.	Voorhees	Ind.

CHAPTER XLVI.
AFTER ATLANTA.

Sherman's Position after the Capture of Atlanta.—What to do next?—Hood's Army in his Front, and the Railroad to Chattanooga untenable.—Hood gets out of Sherman's Way.—President Davis makes another Western Tour.—His Speech at Macon.—He discloses his Plans to the Enemy.—An Advance northward determined on.—Forrest's prelusive Invasion of Tennessee.—Thomas is sent to Nashville.—Hood shifts to the West Point Road, and at length crosses the Chattahoochee.—Sherman follows to Kenesaw.—Slocum left at Atlanta.—The Battle of Allatoona is fought, and the Confederates are repulsed.—Hood across the Coosa, followed by Sherman through Allatoona Pass.—Resaca held, but Hood takes Dalton, and, avoiding a Battle, retreats to Gadsden.—Is joined there by Beauregard.—The Confederate Plan of a Campaign against Nashville.—Sherman, tired of chasing Hood, prepares for his March to the Sea.—He sends the Fourth and Twenty-third Corps to Thomas.—His Theory of the grand March.—He puts his Plan into Operation.

THE period immediately following the campaign which had closed with the capture of Atlanta was full of contingencies and uncertainties. What shall I do next? was the question which occupied the minds both of Hood and Sherman. It was a brief period; for Hood could not wait long, and Sherman would not. The Federal commander, while he was compelling the exodus of citizens from Atlanta, reorganizing his army, protecting his rear, and making arrangements with General Hood for an exchange of prisoners, and for the relief of some of the inconveniences suffered by Union prisoners in the South,[1] was revolving great schemes in his mind. He must secure the position which he had already gained in the heart of the enemy's country. But when secured, Atlanta was of no consequence to him except as a point from which to strike. Of one thing he was well satisfied. Hood would not divide his army; it would remain, therefore, a compact organization, whether in his front or moved against his rear. Sherman's desire was to march through Georgia to the Atlantic coast. While guarding the railroad to Chattanooga, his eyes were fixed upon Savannah. But, so long as Hood's army remained in his front, no such scheme could be ventured, at least not until the Savannah River was in the possession of the Federal navy.[2] The Confederate cavalry swarmed about his army, and he could not advance far from Atlanta eastward or southward and protect the railroad in his rear without detaching forces which were necessary to his advance. If Canby should be heavily re-enforced and advance to Columbus, Georgia, and establish a new base for Sherman by way of the Alabama

River, the difficulty would be obviated. Under all the circumstances, Sherman had little expectation that this would be accomplished.

But General Hood speedily relieved Sherman of all his difficulties by removing the Confederate army out of his way. Hood was the most accommodating general that we have ever heard or read of. No sooner was the truce which had been agreed upon concluded, than he proceeded to shift his entire army to Sherman's rear.[1] If he had not already determined upon this movement he would yet have been forced to make it by the Confederate President, who proceeded from Richmond about three weeks after the fall of Atlanta to urge its execution. On his way to Hood's army, Davis, on the 23d of September, reached Macon, and addressed the citizens of that town. Among the many impolitic acts of President Davis during his administration, this speech stands prominent. In the first place, it informed General Sherman of plans which, if adopted at all, should never have been discovered till the latest possible moment. And the abusive denunciation of Governor Brown, of Georgia, and of General Johnston, were so undignified, that the reported address was at once pronounced a forgery in the Richmond papers. Even the enemies of Davis refused to credit its authenticity. Governor Brown was denominated "a scoundrel" by Davis, and contempt was thrown upon Johnston's retreat from Dalton to the Chattahoochee. His speech was not, on the whole, very encouraging. He reported two thirds of the Confederate army as absent, most of them without leave. He said it was impossible to lend Georgia any aid from Virginia, where the disparity of forces was just as great as it was in Georgia. He disclosed to his hearers, to Georgia, to the world, the extremities to which the Confederacy had been reduced. He told of mothers who had given their last son for the war, and informed Georgians that Macon, and of course the whole route eastward to the Atlantic, if threatened, must not call upon Hood's army for protection, but that their old men must stand in the breach, reminding them that they had not many men left between the ages of 18 and 45. But that which must have seemed most ominous to his audience was the declaration that he was going to the army to confer with General Hood and his subordinates. In view of evident facts, and of the situation of the Confederacy which he had so fully disclosed, his predictions were ludicrous. The burden of his prophecy was that Sherman must retreat, like Napoleon from the deserts of Russia, escaping only with a body-guard![2]

---

[1] The relief which was proposed by General Sherman is indicated in the following letter from him to Hood, September, 1864:

"My latest information from Andersonville is to the 12th, and from what I learn, our prisoners of war confined there, and being removed to Savannah, Charleston, and Millen, need many articles which we possess in superfluity, and can easily supply with your consent and assistance, such as shirts and drawers, socks, shoes, soap, candles, combs, scissors, etc.

"If you will permit me to send a train of wagons, with a single officer to go along under a flag of truce, I will send to Lovejoy's or Palmetto a train of wagons loaded exclusively with 10,000 or 15,000 of each of these articles, and a due proportion of soap, candles, etc., under such restrictions as you may think prudent to name. I would like to have my officer go along to issue these things, but will have no hesitation in sending them if you will simply promise to have them conveyed to the places where our prisoners are, and have them fairly distributed."

Sherman expected a refusal. He writes to James G. Yeatman, President of the Western Sanitary Commission (date same as above): "I doubt if he [Hood] will consent. These Confederates are as proud as the devil, and hate to confess poverty, but I know they are unable to supply socks, drawers, undershirts, scissors, combs, etc., which our men need more than any thing else to preserve cleanliness and health."

In the same letter he says: "The condition of the prisoners at Andersonville has always been present to my mind, and, could I have released them, I would have felt more real satisfaction than to have won another battle." General Hood acceded to Sherman's request, and the articles were sent.

[2] We see clearly what Sherman's designs were from his dispatches during the month of September to Generals Halleck, Canby, and Grant. He writes to Halleck on the 4th (before he had in person entered Atlanta), evidently on the supposition that Hood would cover Macon:

"For the future I propose that of the drafted men I receive my due share, say 50,000 men; that an equal or greater number go to General Canby, who should now proceed with all energy to get Montgomery and the reach of the Alabama River above Selma; that when I know he can move on Columbus, Georgia, I move on La Grange and West Point, keeping to the coast of the Chattahoochee; that we form a junction, repair roads to Montgomery, and open up the Appalachicola and Chattahoochee Rivers to Columbus, and move from it as a base straight on Macon."

On the 10th he writes to Canby:

"We must have the Alabama River now, and also the Appalachicola at the old arsenal, and up to Columbus. My line is so long now that it is impossible to protect it against cavalry raids; but if we can get Montgomery and Columbus, Georgia, as bases in connection with Atlanta, we have Georgia and Alabama at our feet."

The same day he writes to Grant:

"I do not think we can afford to operate farther, dependent on the railroad, it takes so many men to guard it, and even then it is nightly broken by the enemy's cavalry that swarms about us. Macon is distant 103 miles, and Augusta 175 miles. If I could be sure of finding provisions and ammunition at Augusta or Columbus, Georgia, I can march to Milledgeville, and compel Hood to give up Augusta or Macon, and could then turn on the other. The country will afford forage and many supplies, but not enough in any one place to admit of delay.... If you can manage to take the Savannah River as high as Augusta, or the Chattahoochee as far up as Columbus, I can sweep the whole state of Georgia; otherwise I would risk the whole army by going too far from Atlanta."

The above was in reply to Grant's suggestion that Canby should operate against Savannah and Sherman against Augusta.

On the 12th he writes to Grant:

"I don't understand whether you propose to act against Savannah direct from Fort Pulaski, or by way of Florida, or from the direction of Mobile. If you take Savannah by a sudden coup de main, it would be valuable."

On the 20th again: "It [Savannah] once in our possession, I would not hesitate to cross the State of Georgia with 60,000 men, hauling some stores, and depending on the country for the balance. Where a million of people find subsistence my army won't starve; but, as you know, in a country like Georgia, with few roads and innumerable streams, an inferior force could so delay an army and harass it that it would not be a formidable object; but if the enemy knew that we had our boats on the Savannah, I could rapidly move to Milledgeville, where there is abundance of corn and meat, and I could so threaten Macon and Augusta that he would give up Macon for Augusta; then I would move to interpose between Augusta and Savannah, and force him to give me Augusta, with the only powder-mills and factories remaining in the South, or let us have the Savannah River. Either horn of the dilemma would be worth a battle. I would prefer his holding Augusta, as the probabilities are, for then, with the Savannah River in our possession, the taking of Augusta would be a mere matter of time. This campaign would be made in the winter. But the more I study the game, the more am I convinced that it would be wrong for me to penetrate much farther into Georgia without an objective beyond. It would not be productive of much good. I can start east, and make a circuit south, and back, doing vast damage to the state, but resulting in no permanent good; but by merely threatening to do so I hold a rod over the Georgians, who are not over loyal to the South. I will therefore give my opinion that your army and Canby's should be re-enforced to the maximum; that after you get Wilmington you strike for Savannah and the river; that General Canby be instructed to hold the Mississippi River, and send a force to get Columbus, Georgia, either by way of the Alabama or Appalachicola; and that I keep Hood employed, and put my army in fine order for a march on Augusta, Columbus, and Charleston. ... The possession of the Savannah River is more than fatal to the possibility of a Southern independence. They may stand the fall of Richmond, but not of all Georgia.... If you can whip Lee, and I can march to the Atlantic, I think Uncle Abe will give us twenty days' leave of absence to see the young folks."

---

[1] Hood's explanation of this movement is a weak apology for his folly. He says:

"A serious question was now presented to me. The enemy would not certainly long remain idle. He had it in his power to continue his march to the South, and force me to fall back upon Alabama for subsistence. I could not hope to hold my position. The country, being a plain, had no natural strength, nor was there any advantageous position upon which I could retire. Besides, the morale of the army, greatly improved during the operations around Atlanta, had again become impaired in consequence of the recurrence of retreat, and the army itself was decreasing in strength day by day. Something was absolutely demanded, and I rightly judged that any advance, at all promising success, would go far to restore its fighting spirit. Thus I determined, in consultation with the corps commanders, to turn the enemy's right flank, and attempt to destroy his communications and force him to retire from Atlanta. The operations of the cavalry under Wheeler in Georgia, and under Forrest in Tennessee, proved to me conclusively, and beyond a doubt, that all the cavalry in the service could not permanently interrupt the railroad communications in the enemy's rear sufficiently to cause him to abandon his position. To accomplish any thing, therefore, it became necessary for me to move with my entire force."

Instead of having any hope of forcing Hood to fall back upon Alabama for subsistence, Sherman was in doubt as to the possibility of his advance, so long as Hood was in his front, until he could dispense with dependence upon his present line of communications. As to the morale of Hood's army, he was not likely to improve it by leaving Georgia open to Sherman's destructive march.

[2] The following is a copy of Davis's Macon speech as reported in the Macon Telegraph:

LADIES AND GENTLEMEN, FRIENDS AND FELLOW-CITIZENS,—It would have gladdened my heart to have met you in prosperity instead of adversity. But friends are drawn together in adversity. The son of a Georgian, who fought through the first revolution, I would be untrue to myself if I should forget the state in her day of peril. What though misfortune has befallen our arms from Decatur to Jonesboro', our cause is not lost. Sherman can not keep up his long line of communication, and retreat sooner or later he must; and when that day comes, the fate that befell the army of the French empire in its retreat from Moscow will be reacted. Our cavalry and our people will harass and destroy his army as did the Cossacks that of Napoleon; and the Yankee general, like him, will escape with only a body-guard. How can this be the most speedily effected? By the absentees of Hood's army returning to their posts; and will they not? Can they see the banished exiles; can they hear the wail of their suffering countrywomen and children and not come? By what influences they are made to stay away it is not necessary to speak. If there is one who will stay away at this hour, he is unworthy of the name of Georgian. To the women no appeal is necessary. They are like the Spartan mothers of old. I know of one who has lost all her sons except one of eight years. She wrote that she wanted me to reserve a place for him in the ranks. The venerable General Polk, to whom I read the letter, knew that woman well, and said it was characteristic of her; but I will not weary you by turning aside to relate the various incidents of giving up the last son to the cause of our country known to me. Wherever we go we find the hearts and hands of our noble women enlisted. They are seen wherever the eye may fall or the step turn. They have one duty to perform—to buoy up the hearts of our people. I know the deep disgrace felt by Georgia at our army falling back from Dalton to the interior of the state. But I was not of those who considered Atlanta lost when our army crossed the Chattahoochee. I resolved that it should not be, and I then put a man in command who I knew would strike a manly blow for the city, and many a Yankee's blood was made to nourish the soil before the prize was won. It does not become us to revert to disaster. Let the dead bury the dead. Let us, with one arm and one effort, endeavor to crush Sherman. I am going to the army to confer with our generals. The end must be the defeat of our enemy. It has been said that I abandoned Georgia to her fate. Shame upon such falsehood. Where could the author have been when Walker, when Polk, and when General Stephen D. Lee were sent to her assistance. Miserable man. The man who uttered this was a scoundrel. He was not a man to save our country. If I knew that a general did not possess the right qualities to command, would I not be wrong if he was not removed? Why, when our army was falling back from Northern Georgia, I even heard that I had sent Bragg with pontoons to cross it to Cuba. But we must be charitable. The man who can speculate ought to be made to take up his musket. When the war is over, and our independence won—and we will establish our independence—who will be our aristocracy? I hope the limping soldier. To the young ladies I would say that, when choosing between an empty sleeve and the man who had remained at home and grown rich, always take the empty sleeve. Let the old men remain at home and make bread. But should they know of any young man keeping away from the service, who can not be made to go any other way, let them write to the executive. I read all letters sent me from the people, but have not the time to reply to them. You have not many men between eighteen and forty-five left. The boys—God bless the boys!—are, as rapidly as they become old enough, going to the field. The city of Macon is filled with stores, sick and wounded. It must not be abandoned when threatened; but when the enemy comes, instead of calling upon Hood's army for defense, the old men must fight, and when the enemy is driven beyond Chattanooga, they too can join in the general rejoicing. Your prisoners are kept as a sort of Yankee capital. I have heard that one of their generals said that their exchange would defeat Sherman. I have tried every means, conceded every thing to effect an exchange, but to no purpose. Butler, the Beast, with whom no commissioner of exchange would hold intercourse, had published in the newspapers that if we would consent to the exchange of negroes all difficulties might be removed. This is reported as an effort of his to get himself whitewashed, by holding intercourse with gentlemen. If an exchange could be effected, I don't know but I might be induced to recognize Butler. But in the future every effort will be given, as far as possible, to effect the end. We want our soldiers in the field, and we want the sick and wounded to return home. It is not proper for me to speak of the number of men in the field, but this I will say, that two thirds of our men are absent—some sick, some wounded, but most of them absent without leave. The man who repents and goes back to his commander vol-

JAMES D. MORGAN.

A new problem was now presented to General Sherman. He was astonished at Hood's withdrawal from the Macon Road. It was true the Confederate army was at West Point, in a position to move on his flank; but Davis's Macon speech, which he had read in full in the Southern papers, left him no room for doubt that an attempt would be made by the enemy, moving in full force to his rear, to compel him to release his hold upon Georgia. He could not decide at once as to his future movements. It was still a question with him whether, while protecting Tennessee against Hood's invasion, he would have men enough left for the execution of his favorite project—the march eastward to Georgia. This question was soon settled by General Grant's generous co-operation[1] and encouragement, and by the patriotism of the loyal states. Every day increased Sherman's confidence. In the mean time he carefully watched the enemy's movements. Tennessee must be protected at all hazards. The devastation of Georgia and the capture of Savannah would not compensate for the surrender of Nashville and Chattanooga to the Confederates.

Hood had already sent Forrest with a cavalry force 7000 strong into Middle Tennessee as a prelude to the march of his whole army. Forrest, on the 20th of September, crossed the Tennessee near Waterloo, Alabama, and destroyed a portion of the railroad between Decatur and Athens. On the 23d he appeared before the latter place, and drove the garrison of 600 men into their fort. The commander of this post was Colonel Campbell, who, in a personal interview with Forrest on the 24th, was persuaded that it was useless to resist the odds against him, and induced to surrender. In half an hour two regiments of Michigan and Ohio troops came to his assistance, and were driven back. Before Forrest reached Pulaski, General Rousseau had collected a force sufficient to defend that place, and the Confederate cavalry on the 29th swung around upon the Nashville and Chattanooga Road, and began to break it up between Tullahoma and Decherd. Rousseau had also moved promptly eastward, and at Tullahoma again barred the progress of Forrest northward. Steadman also, with 5000 men from Chattanooga, had crossed the Tennessee, and put his force in front of the enemy, compelling the latter to fall back through Fayetteville. The injuries done to the road were repaired in the course of a single day. Forrest now divided his force into two columns, commanded by Buford and himself, his own consisting of 3000 men. Buford demanded the surrender of Huntsville on the 30th, and being refused, proceeded against Athens, which General R. S. Granger had ordered to be reoccupied by the Seventy-third Indiana, and, attacking the

untarily appeals strongly to executive clemency. But suppose he stays away until the war is over, and his comrades return home, and when every man's history will be told, where will he shield himself? It is upon these reflections that I rely to make men return to their duty; but, after conferring with our generals at headquarters, if there be any other remedy it shall be applied. I love my friends and I forgive my enemies. I have been asked to send re-enforcements from Virginia to Georgia. In Virginia the disparity in numbers is just as great as it is in Georgia. Then I have been asked why the army sent to the Shenandoah Valley was not sent here. It was because an army of the enemy had penetrated that valley to the very gates of Lynchburg, and General Early was sent to drive them back. This he not only successfully did, but, crossing the Potomac, came well-nigh capturing Washington itself, and forced Grant to send two corps of his army to protect it. This the enemy denominated a raid. If so, Sherman's march into Georgia is a raid. What would prevent them now, if Early were withdrawn from taking Lynchburg, and putting a complete cordon of men around Richmond? I counseled with that great and grave soldier, General Lee, upon all these points. My mind roamed over the whole field. With this we can succeed. If one half the men now absent without leave will return to duty, we can defeat the enemy. With that hope I am going to the front. I may not realize this hope; but I know there are men there who have looked death in the face too often to despond now. Let no one despond. Let no one distrust; and remember that if genius is the beau ideal, hope is the reality.

[1] Grant writes him September 27:
"It is evident from the tone of the Richmond press, and all other sources, that the enemy intend making a desperate effort to drive you from where you are. I have directed all new troops from the West, and from the East too, if necessary, if none are ready in the West, to be sent to you."

garrison, was repulsed, without having effected any thing of any consequence. Forrest's command recrossed the Tennessee southward about the 3d of October.

Forrest retreated just in time; for before the end of September, Newton's (now Wagner's) division of Stanley's corps had relieved Steadman's command at Chattanooga; Morgan's division of Jeff. C. Davis's corps was on the way to Stevenson; and Rousseau was in pursuit of Forrest with 4000 cavalry and mounted infantry, and was soon to be joined by General C. C. Washburne with 3000 cavalry and 1500 infantry from Memphis. On the 29th, General Thomas had been sent to Nashville to take command of the forces covering Tennessee. Thomas reached Nashville on the 3d of October, and had made such a disposition of his command that, but for the rise of the Elk River, Forrest would have had great difficulty in effecting his escape. Corse's division had been dispatched to Rome, and all the new recruits and such detachments of troops as could be spared from the more northern posts of the West had been ordered to Nashville as reserves.

In the mean time Hood was moving to accomplish his daring scheme of Northern invasion. Removing the rails from the Augusta and Macon Roads for forty miles out from Atlanta, he repaired the West Point Road, toward which he began to shift his army on the 18th of September. Here he remained in the vicinity of Palmetto, with his left touching the Chattahoochee, and, having accumulated provisions for his march, began to cross the river on the 29th. By the 3d of October his army reached the neighborhood of Lost Mountain, with his cavalry on his front and right. The next day he dispatched Stewart's corps with orders to strike the railroad at Ackworth and Big Shanty. The garrisons at both these stations, numbering about 400 men, were captured. Hood's three corps d'armee were at this time commanded by Stewart, Cheatham, and Lee.

The entire Confederate army having crossed the Chattahoochee, Sherman, leaving Slocum's corps to occupy Atlanta and guard the crossing of the Chattahoochee, moved the rest of his army—the Fourth, Fourteenth, Fifteenth, Seventeenth, and Twenty-third Corps—northward, reaching Kenesaw on the 5th of October. The position of the Confederate army threatened Allatoona, where a million of rations were stored. This post was held by three regiments (890 men) under Colonel Tourtellotte, and was well protected by redoubts. General Sherman had anticipated an attack upon Allatoona, and had, by means of signals, ordered General Corse to re-enforce that post from Rome. The enemy had already got upon the railroad, as we have seen, by the 4th, destroying the railroad and cutting the telegraph; and on the night of that day, General Corse, with Rowett's brigade and 165,000 rounds of ammunition, reached Allatoona just in time to meet the attack made on the morning of the 5th by French's division of Stewart's corps. Sherman reached the top of Kenesaw Mountain at 10 A.M., and from that point—a distance of 18 miles—he could see the smoke of the battle and hear faintly the sound of the artillery. He could not reach the scene of conflict in time, nor was it probable that he could afford any assistance from his main army; but he sent General J. D. Cox, with the Twenty-third Corps, to attack the assailants in the rear, on the Dallas and Allatoona Road. Signals were exchanged between Sherman and General Corse, and as soon as the Federal commander learned that the latter was at the point of danger, all his anxiety vanished. Corse's arrival increased the number of the garrison to 1944 men. By 8 30 A.M. French had turned Allatoona, reaching the railroad north, and cutting off communication with Cartersville and Rome. At this time he sent a flag of truce summoning the garrison to surrender, "to avoid needless effusion of blood." Corse promptly replied that he was prepared for "the needless effusion of blood," whenever it would be agreeable to General French. The enemy then attacked with great fury, the first assault falling upon Colonel Rowett, who held the western spur of the ridge. This onset was successfully resisted, but the assault was repeated over and over again, and as often repulsed. On the north side, a brigade of the enemy under General Sears made an attack in flank with better success. "The enemy's line of battle," reports General Corse, "swept us like so much chaff." But Tourtellotte from the eastern spur poured on Sears's advancing troops a fire which caught them in flank and broke their ranks. The battle thus far had been going on outside of the fort, into which, by the volume and impetuosity of the enemy's assaults, the garrison was driven before noon. But, notwith-

LOVELL H. ROUSSEAU.

HOOD'S ATTACK ON ALLATOONA.

standing the odds against them, they had inflicted sufficient injury upon French's division to make it pause, and consider whether it was worth the while to attack the fort, held by men who, outside of its walls, had fought with such obstinacy. The delay gave Corse time to dispose his force in the trenches and behind the parapet. From noon till almost night the enemy closed around the fort, enfilading its trenches, and making death almost certain to those who ventured to expose themselves. The unyielding temper of the garrison baffled the enemy, who, learning that a hostile force was almost upon his rear, gave up the contest. In this action General Corse was wounded in the face.[1] The loss of the garrison was about 700 men—over one third of the entire command. Corse reports that he buried 231 of the enemy's dead and captured 411 prisoners, one of whom, Brigadier General Young, estimated the Confederate loss at 2000. In no instance during the war was the value of the Signal Corps more fully illustrated than in the affair at Allatoona. The service which it rendered here, General Sherman afterward said, more than paid its entire expense from the time of its origination.

The army with which Hood had crossed the Chattahoochee, if we include Wheeler's command which subsequently joined him, numbered about 36,000, of which one fourth was cavalry. After his failure at Allatoona, Hood moved northwestwardly across the Coosa. Sherman followed by the railroad, marching through Allatoona Pass on the 8th, and reaching Kingston on the 10th. Here he found that, making a feint on Rome, the enemy had crossed the river about 11 miles below that place. The next day, therefore, he advanced to Rome, pushing forward Garrard's cavalry and the Twenty-third Corps, with instructions to cross the Oostenaula and threaten Hood's right flank, if the latter continued his movement northward. But the Confederates, by reason of their superior cavalry force, moved more rapidly, and on the 12th Hood summoned the garrison of Resaca to surrender, threatening to take no prisoners if the surrender was refused. Colonel Weaver, the commander at Resaca, saw no cause for alarm, and bluntly refused. He had been re-enforced by Sherman, and the enemy, deeming it prudent to avoid a battle, pushed on toward Dalton, destroying the railroad in his progress. Capturing the garrison at Dalton, he moved through Tunnel Hill to Villanow.

Sherman reached Resaca on the 15th, and endeavored to force Hood to a battle by moving upon his flank and rear. Howard's army was ordered to Snake Creek Gap, where the enemy was found occupying the former Federal defenses. Here Howard tried to hold Hood until Stanley, with the Fourth Corps, could come up in his rear at Villanow. But the Confederate commander did not intend to fight Sherman's army; he was well content with being chased. Covering his rear with Wheeler's cavalry, he fell back to Gadsden, Alabama. Sherman followed as far as Gaylesville. Here there was a pause on the part of both armies. At Gadsden, General Beauregard, commanding the military division of the West, joined Hood. The latter had anticipated that Sherman would divide his forces, and give him a chance, but he had been disappointed. To venture a general engagement in the open field with an enemy whom he had been unable to oppose behind the

fortifications of Atlanta was a step too reckless for even General Hood to take. To retreat utterly at this stage of affairs would be the ruin of his own not-too-well-established reputation, and would demoralize his army. It was therefore finally determined between him and General Beauregard that Sherman should be drawn north of the Tennessee.

But Sherman had long been growing weary of chasing an army that would not, and could not be made to fight. He had now a splendid position for defense, covering Bridgeport, Rome, Chattanooga, and the railroad thence to Atlanta. It was necessary that he should hold this position for a time, until his plans were matured. The strategy to which Hood was about to tempt him was not the strategy suited to his nature. If Hood would only cross the Tennessee, he would soon gratify him by a division of the Federal army. The railroads were speedily repaired, and Atlanta was being supplied with an abundance of provisions. Sherman was urging upon Grant his project of the march through Georgia to Savannah, and anxiously watching the accumulation of an army under Thomas sufficient to oppose Hood, leaving himself free to use his main army for offensive operations.[1]

[1] Sherman says in his report: "Hood's movements and strategy had demonstrated that he had an army capable of endangering at all times my communications, but unable to meet me in open fight. To follow him would simply amount to being decoyed away from Georgia, with little prospect of overtaking and overwhelming him. To remain on the defensive would have been bad policy for an army of so great value as I then commanded, and I was forced to adopt a course more fruitful in results than the naked one of following him to the southwest. I had previously submitted to the commander-in-chief a general plan, which amounted substantially to the destruction of Atlanta and the railroad back to Chattanooga, and sallying forth from Atlanta, through the heart of Georgia, to capture one or more of the great Atlantic sea-ports. This I renewed from Gaylesville, modified somewhat by the change of events."

Sherman's dispatches during this period contain a very complete history of the progress of his favorite scheme of the March to the Sea. They are so characteristic that we here give all of them which have a direct bearing upon the subject:

September 29, 1864. To General HALLECK: "I prefer for the future to make the movement on Milledgeville, Millen, and Savannah River."

September 30. To General COX: "I may have to make some quick counter-moves east and southeast. Keep your folks ready to send baggage into Atlanta, and to start on short notice. . . . . . There are fine corn and potato fields about Covington and the Ocmulgee bottoms. . . . If we make a counter-move I will go out myself with a large force, and take such a route as will supply us, and at the same time make Hood recall the whole or part of his army."

September 30. To General THOMAS: "If he [Hood] moves his whole force to Blue Mountain, you watch him from the direction of Stevenson, and I will do the same from Rome; and as soon as all things are ready, I will take advantage of his opening to me all of Georgia."

October 30. To General GRANT: "Hood is evidently on the west side of Chattanooga, below Sweetwater. If he tries to get on my road this side of the Etowah, I shall attack him; but if he goes on to the Selma and Talladega Road, why would it not do for me to leave Tennessee to the forces which Thomas has, and the reserves soon to come to Nashville, and for me to destroy Atlanta, and then march across Georgia to Savannah or Charleston, breaking roads, and doing irreparable damage? We can not remain on the defensive."

There is no immediate reply to this from Grant.

October 1. To Generals HOWARD and COX: "It is well for you to bear in mind that if Hood swings over to the Alabama Road, and thence tries to get into Tennessee, I may throw back to Chattanooga all of General Thomas's men as far down as Kingston, and draw forward all else, send back all cars and locomotives, destroy Atlanta, and make for Savannah or Charleston via Milledgeville and Millen. If Hood aims at our road this side of Kingston, and in no manner threatens Tennessee, I will have to turn on him. Keep these things to yourselves. The march I propose is less by 200 miles than I made last fall, and less than I accomplished in February, and we could make Georgia a break in the Confederacy by ruining both east and west roads, and not running against a single fort until we get to the sea-shore, and in communication with our ships."

October 1. To General THOMAS: "Use your own discretion as to the matters north of the Tennessee River. If I can induce Hood to swing across to Blue Mountain, I shall feel tempted to start for Milledgeville, Millen, and Savannah or Charleston, absolutely destroying all Georgia, and taking either Savannah or Charleston. In that event, I will order back to Chattanooga every thing the other side of Kingston, and bring forward all else, destroy Atlanta and the bridge, and absolutely scour the Southern Confederacy. In that event, Hood would be puzzled, and would follow me; or, if he entered Tennessee, he could make no permanent stay. But if he attempts the road this side of Kingston or Rome, I will turn against him."

[1] The day after the battle, Corse writes to Sherman: "I am short a cheek-bone and one ear, but am able to whip all hell yet."

Sherman had already submitted to Grant the general outlines of his scheme of a march to the Atlantic. But at that time Hood was in his front, on the Macon Road. He was not, under these circumstances, willing to make the venture unless he could be sure of some objective point, like Savannah, al-

October 7. To General CORSE: "Keep me well advised, for I now think Hood will rather swing against Atlanta and the Chattahoochee Bridge than against Kingston and the Etowah Bridge; but he is eccentric, and I can not guess his movements as I could those of Johnston, who was a sensible man, and only did sensible things. If Hood does not mind, I will catch him in a worse snap than he has been in yet."

October 9. To General THOMAS: "I came up here to relieve our road. Twentieth Corps at Atlanta. Hood reached our road and broke it between Big Shanty and Ackworth, and attacked Allatoona, but was repulsed. . . . . I want to destroy all the road below Chattanooga, including Atlanta, and make for the sea-coast. We can not defend this long line of road."

October 9. To General GRANT: "It will be a physical impossibility to protect the road, now that Hood, Forrest, and Wheeler, and the whole batch of devils, are turned loose, without home or habitation. . . . . I propose that we break up the railroad from Chattanooga, and strike out with wagons for Milledgeville, Millen, and Savannah. Until we can repopulate Georgia it is useless to occupy it, but the utter destruction of its roads, houses, and people will cripple their military resources. By attempting to hold the roads we will lose a thousand men monthly, and will gain no result. I can make the march, and make Georgia howl. We have over 8000 cattle, and 3,000,000 rations of bread, but no corn; but we can forage in the interior of the state."

October 10. To General GRANT: "Hood is now crossing the Coosa, twelve miles below Rome, bound West. If he passes over to the Mobile and Ohio Road, had I not better execute the plan of my letter sent by Colonel Porter, and leave General Thomas, with the troops now in Tennessee, to defend the state. He will have an ample force when the re-enforcements ordered reach Nashville."

The same day Thomas writes to Sherman: "I will not say positively that I can hold Hood with the present force I have and the re-enforcements expected, because I do not know how many re-enforcements are coming. I will do my best, however, and, as you direct, will concentrate the infantry force about Stevenson and Huntsville, leaving a portion of the cavalry to watch the river between Decatur and Eastport."

October 11. To General GRANT: "Hood moved his army from Palmetto Station across by Dallas and Cedartown, and is now on the Coosa River, south of Rome. He threw one corps on my road at Ackworth, and I was forced to follow. I hold Atlanta with the Twentieth Corps, and have strong detachments along my line. These reduce my active force to a comparatively small army. We can not remain now on the defensive. With 25,000 men, and the bold cavalry he has, he [Hood] can constantly break my road. I would infinitely prefer to make a wreck of the road, and of the country from Chattanooga to Atlanta, including the latter city, send back all my wounded and worthless, and with my effective army move through Georgia, smashing things to the sea. Hood may turn into Tennessee and Kentucky, but I believe he will be forced to follow me. Instead of being on the defensive, I would be on the offensive. Instead of guessing at what he means to do, he would have to guess at my plans. The difference in war is full 25 per cent. I can make Savannah, Charleston, or the mouth of the Chattahoochee (Appalachicola). Answer quick, as I know we will not have the telegraph long."

October 16. To General SCHOFIELD: "I want the first positive fact that Hood contemplates an invasion of Tennessee. Invite him to do so. Send him a free pass in."

October 17. Slocum telegraphs to Sherman the statement made in a Montgomery paper that Beauregard is with Hood, and that the army is going to cross the Tennessee.

October 17. Sherman is advised by Thomas to "adopt Grant's idea of turning Wilson loose rather than undertake the plan of a march with the whole force through Georgia to the sea." Again, the next day, Thomas writes: "I don't want to be in command of the defense of Tennessee, unless you and the authorities in Washington deem it absolutely necessary."

October 19. To General HALLECK: "The enemy will not venture into Tennessee except around by Decatur. I propose to send the Fourth Corps to General Thomas, and leave him with that corps, the garrisons, and new troops, to defend the line of the Tennessee, and with the rest to push into the heart of Georgia and come out at Savannah, destroying all the railroads of the state."

October 19. To General THOMAS: "Make a report to me as soon as possible of what troops you now have in Tennessee, what are expected, and how disposed. I propose, with the armies of the Tennessee and the Ohio, and two corps of yours, to sally forth, and make a hole in Georgia and Alabama that will be hard to mend. Hood has little or no baggage, and will escape me. He can not invade Tennessee except to the west of Huntsville. . . . . I will send back into Tennessee the Fourth Corps, all dismounted cavalry, all sick and wounded, and all encumbrances whatever, except what I can haul in our wagons, and will probably, about November, break up the railroad and bridges, destroy Atlanta, and make a break for Mobile, Savannah, or Charleston. I want you to remain in Tennessee, and take command of all my division not actually present with me. Hood's army may be set down at 40,000 of all arms fit for duty; he may follow me or turn against you. If you can defend the line of the Tennessee in my absence of three months is all I ask."

October 19. To Colonel BECKWITH (Act'g Q. M. at Atlanta): "Hood will escape me. I want to prepare for my big raid. On the 1st of November I want nothing in Atlanta but what is necessary to war. Send all trash to the rear, and have on hand thirty days' food and but little forage. I propose to abandon Atlanta and the railroad back to Chattanooga, and sally forth to ruin Georgia and bring up on the sea-shore."

October 19. To General HALLECK: "We must not be on the defensive, and I now consider myself authorized to execute my plan, to destroy the railroad from Chattanooga to Atlanta, including the latter city . . . . strike out into the heart of Georgia, and make for Charleston, Savannah, or the mouth of the Appalachicola. General Grant prefers the middle one, Savannah, and I understand you to prefer Selma and the Alabama. I must have alternatives, else, being confined to one route, the enemy might so oppose that delay and want would trouble me; but, having alternatives, I can take so eccentric a course that no general can guess at my objective. Therefore, when you hear I am off, have look-outs at Morris Island, South Carolina, Ossabaw Sound, Georgia, Pensacola, and Mobile Bays. I will turn up somewhere, and believe I can take Macon, Milledgeville, Augusta, and Savannah, Georgia, and wind up with closing the neck back of Charleston, so that they will starve out. This movement is not purely military or strategic, but it will illustrate the vulnerability of the South. They don't know what war means; but when the rich planters of the Oconee and Savannah see their fences, and corn, and hogs, and sheep vanish before their eyes, they will have something more than a mean opinion of the 'Yanks.' Even now our poor mules laugh at the fine corn-fields, and our soldiers riot on chestnuts, sweet potatoes, pigs, chickens, etc. The poor people come to me and beg us for their lives; but my customary answer is, 'Your friends have broken our railroads which supplied us bountifully, and you can not suppose our soldiers will suffer when there is abundance within reach.'

"It will take ten days to finish up our roads, during which I will eat out this flank, and along down the Coosa [Sherman, when writing this, was at Summerville, Georgia], and then will rapidly put into execution 'the plan.' In the mean time I ask that you will give General Thomas all the troops you can spare of the new levies, that he may hold the line of the Tennessee during my absence of, say, ninety days."

October 19. To General WILSON: "General Garrard has about 2500 cavalry, General Kilpatrick 1500, General McCook 600; there may be about 1000 other cavalry with my army. These embrace all the cavalry ready for battle. I wish you would . . . . bring to me about 2500 new cavalry, and then go to work to make up three divisions, each of 2500, for the hardest fighting of the war. I am going into the very bowels of the Confederacy, and propose to leave a trail that will be recognized fifty years hence."

October 20. To General THOMAS: "I think I have thought over the whole field of the future, and, being now authorized to act, I want all things bent to the following general plan of action for the next three months.

"Out of the forces now here and at Atlanta I propose to organize an efficient army of 60,000 to 65,000 men, with which I propose to destroy Macon, Augusta, and, it may be, Savannah and Charleston; but I will also keep open the alternatives of the mouth of the Appalachicola and Mobile. By this I propose to demonstrate the vulnerability of the South, and make its inhabitants feel that war and individual ruin are synonymous terms. To pursue Hood is folly, for he can twist and turn like a fox, and wear out any army in pursuit; to continue to occupy long lines of railroads simply exposes our small detachments to be picked up in detail, and forces me to make countermarches to protect lines of communication. I know I am right in this, and shall proceed to its maturity. As to details, I propose to take General Howard and his army, General Schofield and his, and two corps of yours, viz., Generals Davis's and Slocum's. I propose to remain along the Coosa watching Hood until all my preparations are made, viz., until I have prepared the railroad, sent back all surplus men and material, and stripped for the work. Then I will send General Stanley, with the Fourth Corps, across by Will's Valley and Caperton's to Stevenson, to report to you. If you send me 5000 or 6000 new conscripts, I may also send back one of General Slocum's or Davis's divisions, but I prefer to maintain organizations. I want you to retain command in Tennessee, and before starting I will give you delegated authority over Kentucky and Mississippi, Alabama, etc., whereby there will be unity of action behind me. I will want you to hold Chattanooga and Decatur in force; and on the occasion of my departure, of which you will have ample notice, to watch Hood close. I think he will follow me, at least with his cavalry, in which event I want you to push south from Decatur and the head of the Tennessee for Columbus, Mississippi, and Selma—not absolutely to reach those points, but to divert or pursue, according to the state of facts. If, however, Hood turns on you, you must act defensively on the line of the Tennessee. I will ask, and you may also urge, that at the same time General Canby act vigorously up the Alabama River.

"I do not fear that the Southern army will again make a lodgment on the Mississippi, for past events demonstrate how rapidly armies can be raised in the Northwest on that question, and how easily handled and supplied. The only hope of a Southern success is in the remote regions difficult of access. We have now a good entering wedge, and should drive it home. It will take some time to complete these details, and I hope to hear from you in the mean time. We must preserve a large amount of secrecy, and I may actually change the ultimate point of arrival, but not the main object."

October 20. To General SLOCUM: "Use all your energies to send to the rear every thing not needed for the grand march. I will take your corps along. We will need 1,500,000 rations of bread, coffee, sugar, and salt, 500,000 rations of salt meat, and all else should be shipped away. . . . . I want to be near Atlanta and ready by November 1st."

October 22. To General GRANT: "I feel perfectly master of the situation here. I still hold Atlanta, and the road with all bridges and vital points well guarded, and I have in hand an army before which Hood has retreated precipitately down the Coosa. It is hard to divine his future plans; but by abandoning Georgia, and taking position with his rear to Selma, he threatens the road from Chattanooga to Atlanta, and may move up to Tennessee by Decatur. He can not cross the Tennessee except at Muscle Shoals, for all other points are patroled by our gun-boats.

"I am now perfecting arrangements to put into Tennessee a force able to hold the line of the Tennessee while I break up the railroad in front of Dalton, including the city of Atlanta, and push into Georgia and break up all its railroads and dépôts, capture its horses and negroes, make desolation every where, destroy the factories at Macon, Milledgeville, and Augusta, and bring up with 60,000 men on the sea-shore about Savannah or Charleston. I think this far better than defending a long line of railroad. I will leave General George H. Thomas to command all my military division behind me, and take with me only the best fighting material. Of course I will subsist on the bountiful corn-fields and potato-patches, as I am now doing, luxuriously."

October 23. To General SLOCUM: "Go on; pile up the forage, corn, and potatoes, and keep your artillery horses fat; send back all unserviceable artillery, and, at the last moment, we can count up our horses, and see what we can haul, and send back all else. One gun per thousand men will be plenty to take along. Hood is doubtless now at Blue Mountain, and Forrest over about Corinth and Tuscumbia, hoping by threatening Tennessee to make me quit Georgia. We are piling up men in Tennessee enough to attend to them, and to leave me free to go ahead. The railroad will be done in a day or two. We find abundance of corn and potatoes out here, and we enjoy them much; they cost nothing a bushel. If Georgia can afford to break our railroads, she can afford to feed us."

October 23. To General THOMAS: "Hood is now at Blue Mountain, and Forrest evidently over about Tuscumbia. No doubt they will endeavor conjointly to make me come out of Georgia, but I don't want them to succeed. All Georgia is now open to me, and I do believe you are the man best qualified to manage the affairs of Tennessee and North Mississippi.

"I want approximate returns of all troops subject to your orders, and, as I wrote you, I can spare you the Fourth Corps and about 5000 men not fit for my purposes, but which will be well enough for garrison at Chattanooga, Murfreesborough, and Nashville. What you need is a few points fortified and stocked with provisions, and a movable column of 25,000 men that can strike in any direction."

October 24. To General HALLECK: "Beauregard announces his theorem to be to drive Sherman out of Atlanta, which he still holds defiantly, and dares him to the encounter, but is not willing to chase him all over creation."

October 26. To General THOMAS: "A reconnoissance pushed down to Gadsden to-day reveals the fact that the rebel army is not there, and the chances are it has moved West. If it turns up at Guntersville I will be after it, but if it goes, as I believe, to Decatur and beyond, I must leave it to you at present, and push for the heart of Georgia."

October 28. To General THOMAS: "I have already sent the Fourth Corps, which should reach Wauhatchee to-morrow; use it freely, and if I see that Hood crosses the Tennessee I will send Schofield. On these two corps you can ingraft all the new troops; with the balance I will go south."

October 29. To General THOMAS: "Ingraft on Stanley and Schofield all the new troops. Give Schofield a division of new troops. Give General Tower all the men you can to finish the forts at Nashville, and urge on the navy to pile up gun-boats in the Tennessee."

October 29. To General ROSECRANS: "I have pushed Beauregard to the west of Decatur, but I know he is pledged to invade Tennessee and Kentucky, having his base on the old Mobile and Ohio Road. I have put Thomas in Tennessee, and given him as many troops as he thinks necessary, but I don't want to leave it to chance, and therefore would like to have Smith's and Mower's divisions up the Tennessee River as soon as possible. . . . . I propose myself to push straight down into the heart of Georgia, smashing things generally."

November 1. To General GRANT: "As you foresaw, and as Jeff. Davis threatened, the enemy is now in the full tide of execution of his grand plan to destroy my communications and defeat this army. His infantry, about 30,000, with Wheeler and Roddy's cavalry, from 7000 to 10,000, are now in the neighborhood of Tuscumbia and Florence, and the water being low, are able to cross at will. Forrest seems to be scattered from Eastport to Jackson, Paris, and the Lower Tennessee, and General Thomas reports the capture by him of a gun-boat and five transports. General Thomas has near Athens and Pulaski Stanley's corps, about 15,000 strong, and Schofield's corps, 10,000, *en route* by rail, and has at least 20,000 to 25,000 men, with new regiments and conscripts arriving all the time also. General Rosecrans promises the two divisions of Smith and Mower, belonging to me, but I doubt if they can reach Tennessee in less than ten days. If I were to let go Atlanta and North Georgia and make for Hood, he would, as he did here, retreat to the southwest, leaving his militia, now assembling at Macon and Griffin, to occupy our conquests, and the work of last summer would be lost. I have retained about 50,000 good troops, and have sent back 25,000, and have instructed General Thomas to hold defensively Nashville, Chattanooga, and Decatur, all strongly fortified and provisioned for a long siege. I will destroy the railroads of Georgia, and do as much substantial damage as is possible, reaching the sea-coast near one of the points hitherto indicated, trusting that Thomas with his present troops, and the influx of new troops promised, will be able in a very few days to assume the offensive. Hood's cavalry may do a good deal of damage, and I have sent Wilson back with all dismounted cavalry, retaining only about 4500. This is the best I can do, and shall, therefore, when I get to Atlanta the necessary stores, move south as soon as possible."

The same day Grant writes to Sherman: "Do you not think it advisable, now that Hood has gone so far north, to entirely ruin him before starting on your proposed campaign? With Hood's army destroyed, you can go where you please with impunity. I believed, and still believe, if you had started south while Hood was in the neighborhood of you, he would have been forced to go after you. Now that he is so far away, he might look upon the chase as useless, and he will go in one direction while you are pushing the other. If you can see the chance for destroying Hood's army, attend to that first, and make the other move secondary."

November 2. To General THOMAS: "According to Wilson's account, you will have, in ten days, full 12,000 cavalry, and I estimate your infantry force, independent of railroad guards, full 40,000, which is a force superior to the enemy."

November 2. To General GRANT: "If I could hope to overhaul Hood, I would turn against him with my whole force; then he would retreat to the southwest, drawing me as a decoy from Georgia, which is his chief object. If he ventures north of the Tennessee, I may turn in that direction and get between him and his line of retreat, but thus far he has not gone above the Tennessee. Thomas will have a force strong enough to prevent his reaching any country in which we have an interest, and he has orders, if Hood turns to follow me, to push for Selma. No single army can catch him, and I am convinced the best results will follow from our defeating Jeff. Davis's cherished plan of making me leave Georgia by manœuvring. Thus far I have confined my efforts to thwart his plans, and have reduced my baggage so that I can pick up and start in any direction; but I would regard a pursuit of Hood as useless. Still, if he attempts to invade Middle Tennessee, I will hold Decatur, and be prepared to move in that direction; but, unless I let go Atlanta, my force will not be equal to his."

To this Grant replies the same day: "Your dispatch of 9 A.M. yesterday is just received. I dispatched you the same date, advising that Hood's army, now that it had worked so far north, ought to be looked upon more as the object. With the force, however, you have left with General Thomas, he must be able to take care of Hood and destroy him. I really do not see that you can withdraw from where you are to follow Hood, without giving up all we have gained in territory."

November 2. To General GRANT: "General Thomas reports to-day that his cavalry reconnoitred within three miles of Florence yesterday, and found Beauregard intrenching. I have ordered him to hold Nashville, Chattanooga, and Decatur, all well supplied for a siege; all the rest of his army to assemble about Pulaski, and to fight Beauregard cautiously and carefully; at the same time, for A. J. Smith and all re-enforcements to get up to enable him to assume a bold offensive, and to enable Wilson to get a good amount of cavalry. I think Jeff. Davis will change his tune when he finds me advancing into the heart of Georgia instead of retreating, and I think it will have an immediate effect on your operations at Richmond."

November 3. To General HALLECK: "The situation of affairs now is as follows: Beauregard, with Hood's army, is at Florence, with a pontoon bridge protected from our gun-boats from below by the Colbert Shoals, from above by the Muscle Shoals. He has with him Wheeler's and Roddy's cavalry. Forrest's cavalry is down about Fort Heiman. The country round about Florence has been again and again devastated during the past three years, and Beauregard must be dependent on the Mobile and Ohio Railroad, which also has been broken and patched up in its whole extent. He purposes and promises his men to invade Middle Tennessee for the purpose of making me let go Georgia. The moment I detected that he had passed Gadsden, I dispatched the Fourth Corps, General Stanley, 15,000 strong, who is now at Pulaski, and subsequently the Twenty-third Corps, General Schofield, 10,000, who is now on cars moving to Nashville. This gives General Thomas

ready in possession of the national armies. But, as soon as Hood moved from his front, the way seemed open for an advance through Georgia to the sea-coast. He had then to consider whether he could make the march, and at the same time protect Chattanooga and Nashville. This was a question which could only be answered when it was certainly ascertained what re-enforcements would be received. By the middle of October Hood had been driven off from the Chattanooga and Atlanta Railroad. About the 1st of November he threatened to cross the Tennessee in the neighborhood of Decatur. This, indeed, was the only point at which he could effect a crossing, the rest of the river—from Muscle Shoals above and Colbert Shoals below—being guarded by gun-boats. Sherman had, by this time, dispatched Stanley's Fourth and Schofield's Twenty-third Corps—about 25,000 infantry—to General Thomas. Brevet Major General James Wilson had arrived from the Army of the Potomac, to take command of Sherman's cavalry, and it seemed probable that in the course of a few days he would be able to mount 12,000 men. New regiments of recruits were continually coming into Nashville, and Sherman ordered these to be ingrafted into the veteran corps of Stanley and Schofield. Hood would be delayed for some days in the accumulation of supplies, and in the mean time A. J. Smith's and Mower's divisions could be brought over from Missouri. With these divisions added to his other forces, Sherman thought Thomas would have a force sufficient to attend to Hood. He thought, however, that Hood, learning of his march eastward, would follow him, at least with his cavalry. In any event, he had no uneasiness in regard to Tennessee.

But Thomas was not so confident. He thought it would be better to send Wilson's cavalry through Georgia, and fight Hood with the whole of Sherman's army. Grant also urged this at first; but Sherman's arguments finally convinced him that Thomas could take care of Tennessee, and that it was better that Sherman should carry out his project. Thomas also, in the end, reached the same conclusion.

Sherman's perfect confidence in his own scheme excites our admiration. He had no doubts. He had carefully balanced the forces on both sides, and knew that Thomas would be a match for Hood. To protect his long line of railroad, garrison Atlanta, and pursue Hood "all over creation" involved, in his judgment, the waste of 60,000 men. To make a wreck of Atlanta and Rome, and of the railroad from Atlanta to Dalton, left nothing for the enemy to occupy, nothing for himself to guard. The four army corps which he still retained—60,000 strong—contained the best fighting material of his command. North of Atlanta they were not needed. If they should operate with Thomas against Hood, the latter, "turning and twisting like a fox," would slip out of their hands, and thus time, energy, and opportunity would be wasted, without any adequate results. In the strict economy of war, therefore, Sherman was justified in using this superfluous army elsewhere, striking instead of waiting, marching, and countermarching. It is true there were no armies in his front to strike, southward or eastward. Still, there were several important ends to be attained by his march.

In the first place, the march of an organized army, as strong in numbers as that with which Sherman proposed to move through the interior of the enemy's country, from its easternmost to its westernmost limit, would at the same time illustrate the inherent weakness of the Confederacy and the strength of the national armies. Such a march, with such an army, would demonstrate to the world that the ultimate triumph of the nation over the rebellion was an assured fact. In connection with President Lincoln's re-election, it would ruin the hopes of the peace party in the loyal states. It would also destroy all confidence on the part of the Southern people that their usurped government could afford them protection. Well might Sherman say that, "even without a battle, the results, operating upon the minds of sensible men, would produce fruits more than compensating for the expense, trouble, and risk."

But it would not be simply a political demonstration. The military con-

two full corps and about 8000 cavalry, besides 10,000 dismounted cavalry and all the new troops recently sent to Tennessee, with the railroad guards, with which to encounter Beauregard, should he advance farther. Besides which, General Thomas will have the active co-operation of the gun-boats both above and below the Shoals, and the two divisions of Smith and Mower, *en route* from Missouri. I therefore feel no uneasiness as to Tennessee, and have ordered General Thomas to assume the offensive in the direction of Selma, Alabama. With myself I have the Twentieth Corps at Atlanta, the Fifteenth and Seventeenth near Kenesaw, and the Fourteenth here [near Kingston]. I am sending to the rear, as fast as cars will move, the vast accumulation of stuff that, in spite of my endeavors, has been got over the road, and am sending forward just enough bread and meat to enable me to load my wagons, destroy every thing of value to the enemy, and start on my contemplated trip. I can be ready in five days, but am waiting to be more certain that Thomas will be prepared for any contingency that may arise. It is now raining, which is favorable to us and unfavorable to the enemy. Davis has utterly failed in his threat to force me to leave in thirty days, for my railroad is in good order from Nashville to Atlanta, and his army is farther from my communications now than it was twenty days ago. . . . . . I propose to adhere, as near as possible, to my original plan, and, on reaching the sea-coast, will be available for re-enforcing the army in Virginia, leaving behind a track of desolation, as well as a sufficient force to hold fast all that is of permanent value to our cause."

November 6. To General GRANT:

"DEAR GENERAL,—I have heretofore telegraphed and written you pretty fully, but I still have some thoughts in my busy brain that should be confided to you as a key to future developments.

"The taking of Atlanta broke on Jeff. Davis so suddenly as to disturb the equilibrium of his usually well-balanced temper, so that at Augusta, Macon, and Columbia, South Carolina, he let out some of his thoughts, which otherwise he would have kept to himself. As he is not only the President of the Southern Confederacy, but also its commander-in-chief, we are bound to attach more importance to his words than we would to those of a mere civil chief magistrate.

"The whole burden of his song consists in the statement that Sherman's communications *must* be broken and his army destroyed. Now it is a well-settled principle that, if we prevent his succeeding in his threat, we defeat him, and derive all the moral advantages of a victory. Thus far Hood and Beauregard conjointly have utterly failed to interrupt my supplies or communications. My railroad and telegraph are now in good order from Atlanta back to the Ohio River. His losses in men at Allatoona, Resaca, Ship's Gap, and Decatur exceed in number ours at the block-houses at Big Shanty, Allatoona Creek, and Dalton; and the rapidity of his flight from Dalton to Gadsden takes from him all the merit or advantage claimed for his skillful and rapid lodgment on my railroad. The only question in my mind is whether I ought not to have dogged him far over into Mississippi, trusting to some happy accident to bring him to bay and to battle; but I then thought that by so doing I would play into his hands, by being drawn or decoyed too far away from our original line of advance. Besides, I had left at Atlanta a corps, and guards along the railroad back to Chattanooga, which might have fallen an easy prey to his superior cavalry. I felt compelled, therefore, to do what is usually a mistake in war—divide my forces—send a part back into Tennessee, retaining the balance here.

"As I have before informed you, I sent Stanley back directly from Gaylesville, and Schofield from Rome, both of which have reached their destination; and thus far Hood, who has brought up at Florence, is farther from my communications than when he started; and I have in Tennessee a force numerically greater than his, well commanded and well organized, so that I feel no uneasiness on the score of Hood reaching my main communications.

"My last accounts from General Thomas are to 9 30 last night, when Hood's army was about Florence in great distress about provisions, as it well must be, and that devil Forrest was down about Johnsonville, making havoc among the gun-boats and transports; but Schofield's troops were arriving at Johnsonville, and a fleet of gun-boats was reported coming up from below, able to repair that trouble. You know that line of supplies was only opened for summer's use, when the Cumberland is not to be depended upon. We now have abundant supplies at Atlanta, Chattanooga, and Nashville, with the Louisville and Nashville Railroad and the Cumberland River unmolested, so that I regard Davis's threat to get his army on my rear, or on my communications, as a miserable failure.

"Now as to the second branch of my proposition. I admit that the first object should be the destruction of that army; and if Beauregard moves his infantry and artillery up into the pocket about Jackson and Paris, I will feel strongly tempted to move Thomas directly against him, and myself move rapidly by Decatur and Purdy to cut off his retreat. But this would involve the abandonment of Atlanta, and a retrograde movement, which would be very doubtful of expediency or success; for, as a matter of course, Beauregard, who watches me with his cavalry and his friendly citizens, would have timely notice, and slip out and escape, to regain what we have earned at so much cost. I am more than satisfied that Beauregard has not the nerve to attack fortifications, or it would be a great achievement for him to make me abandon Atlanta by mere threats and manœuvres.

"These are the reasons which have determined my former movements.

"I have employed the last ten days in running to the rear the sick, wounded, and worthless, and all the vast amount of stores accumulated by our army in the advance, aiming to organize this branch of my army into four well-commanded corps, encumbered by only one gun to a thousand men, and provisions and ammunition which can be loaded up in our mule-wagons, so that we can pick up and start on the shortest notice. I reckon that by the 10th instant this end will be reached, and by that date I also will have the troops all paid; the presidential election over and out of the way; and I hope the early storms of November, now prevailing, will also give us the chance of a long period of fine healthy weather for campaigning. Then the question presents itself, 'What shall be done?' On the supposition always that Thomas can hold the line of the Tennessee, and very shortly be able to assume the offensive as against Beauregard, I propose to act in such a manner against the material resources of the South as utterly to negative Davis's boasted threat and promises of protection. If we can march a well-appointed army right through his territory, it is a demonstration to the world—foreign and domestic—that we have a power which Davis can not resist. This may not be war, but rather statesmanship; nevertheless, it is overwhelming to my mind that there are thousands of people abroad and in the South who will reason thus: If the North can march an army right through the South, it is proof positive that the North can prevail in this contest, leaving only open the question of its willingness to use that power. Now Mr. Lincoln's election (which is assured), coupled with the conclusion thus reached, makes a complete logical whole. Even without a battle, the results, operating upon the minds of sensible men, would produce fruits more than compensating for the expense, trouble, and risk.

"Admitting this reasoning to be good, that such a movement *per se* be right, still there may be reasons why one route should be better than another. There are three from Atlanta—southeast, south, and southwest—all open, with no serious enemy to oppose at present.

"*The first* would carry me across the only east and west railroad remaining to the Confederacy, which would be destroyed, and thereby the communication between the armies of Lee and Beauregard severed. Incidentally I might destroy the enemy's dépôts at Macon and Augusta, and reach the sea-shore at Charleston and Savannah, from either of which points I could re-enforce our armies in Virginia.

"*The second* and easiest route would be due south, following substantially the valley of Flint River, which is very fertile and well supplied, and fetching up on the navigable waters of the Appalachicola, destroying *en route* the same railroad, taking up the prisoners of war still at Andersonville, and destroying about 400,000 bales of cotton near Albany and Fort Gaines. This, however, would leave the army in a bad position for future movements.

"*The third*, down the Chattahoochee to Opelika and Montgomery, thence to Pensacola or Tensas Bayou, in communication with Fort Morgan. This latter route would enable me at once to co-operate with General Canby in the reduction of Mobile, and occupation of the line of the Alabama.

"In my judgment, the first would have a material effect upon your campaign in Virginia; the second would be the safest of execution; but the third would more properly fall within the sphere of my own command, and have a direct bearing upon my own enemy, 'Beauregard.' If, therefore, I should start before I hear farther from you, or before farther developments turn my course, you may take it for granted that I have moved *via* Griffin to Barnsville; that I break up the road between Columbus and Macon *good*, and then, if I feign on Columbus, will move *via* Macon and Millen to Savannah, or, if I feign on Macon, you may take it for granted I have shot off toward Opelika, Montgomery, and Mobile Bay or Pensacola.

"I will not attempt to send couriers back, but trust to the Richmond papers to keep you well advised. I will give you notice by telegraph of the exact time of my departure."

To this Grant replies, November 7: "I see no present reason for changing your plan; should any arise, you will see to it, or if I do, I will inform you. I think every thing here favorable now. Great good fortune attend you. I believe you will be eminently successful, and at worst can only make a march less fruitful of results than hoped for."

November 8. To G. W. TYLER, *Louisville, Ky.*: "Dispatch me to-morrow night and the next night a summary of all news, especially of elections, that I may report them to Governor Brown at Milledgeville, where I expect a friendly interview in a few days. Keep this very secret, for the world will lose sight of me shortly, and you will hear worse stories than when I went to Meridian. Jeff. Davis's thirty days are up for wiping us out, and we are not wiped out yet by a good deal."

November 10. To C. A. DANA, *Assistant Secretary of War*: "If indiscreet newspaper men publish information too near the truth, counteract its effect by publishing other paragraphs calculated to mislead the enemy—such as Sherman's army has been much re-enforced, especially in the cavalry, and he will soon move in several columns in a circuit, so as to catch Hood's army. Sherman's destination is not Charleston, but Selma, where he will meet an army from the Gulf," etc.

November 11. To General HALLECK: "My arrangements are now all complete. Last night we burned all founderies, mills, and shops of every kind in Rome, and to-morrow I leave Kingston, with the rear-guard, for Atlanta, which I propose to dispose of in a similar manner, and to start on the 16th on the projected grand raid. All appearances still indicate that Beauregard has gone back to his old hole at Corinth, and I hope he will enjoy it; my army prefers to enjoy the fresh sweet-potato fields of the Ocmulgee. I have balanced all the figures well, and am satisfied that General Thomas has in Tennessee a force sufficient for all probabilities, and I have urged him, the moment Beauregard turns south, to cross the Tennessee at Decatur and push straight for Selma. To-morrow our wires will be broken, and this is probably my last dispatch. I would like to have Foster break the Savannah and Charleston Road about Pocotaligo about the 1st of December. All other preparations are to my entire satisfaction."

The same day Colonel Beckwith reports to Sherman as follows: "The Army of the Tennessee have obtained and have got in their wagons all they can haul and all they want; same of the Twentieth Army Corps. There is great plenty of salt, coffee, meat, pepper, and soap here. The Fourteenth Army Corps may want a little more bread, and perhaps a little more sugar. I have about 100,000 rations of bread for the Fourteenth Army Corps; 22,000 rations sugar. I do not know how much General Davis may have on hand, but presume he has 200,000 rations of bread. Every thing is loaded in Atlanta save what is held for the Fourteenth Army Corps. There are at least 11,200,000 rations of the principal rations in hands of troops and available."

November 11. To General THOMAS: "All right. I can hardly believe Beauregard would attempt to work against Nashville from Corinth as a base at this stage of the war, but all information points that way; if he does, you will whip him out of his boots. But I rather think you will find commotion in his camp in a day or two. Last night we burned Rome, and in two days more will burn Atlanta, and he must discover that I am not retreating, but, on the contrary, fighting for the very heart of Georgia. . . . . By using detachments of recruits and dismounted cavalry in your fortifications, you will have Schofield, and Stanley, and A. J. Smith strengthened by eight or ten new regiments, and all of Wilson's cavalry; you could safely invite Beauregard across the Tennessee, and prevent his ever returning. I still believe, however, that public clamor will force him to turn and follow me, in which event you should cross at Decatur, and move directly toward Selma as far as you can transport supplies. The probabilities are the wires will be broken to-morrow, and that all communication will cease between us. . . . . You may act, however, on the certainty that I sally from Atlanta on the 16th, with about 60,000 men, well provisioned, but expecting to live liberally on the country."

Thomas replies the next day: "I have no fears that Beauregard can do us any harm now, and if he attempts to follow you I will follow him as far as possible; if he does not follow you, I will then thoroughly organize my troops, and, I believe, shall have men enough to ruin him unless he gets out of the way very rapidly. The country of Middle Alabama, I learn, is teeming with supplies this year, which will be greatly to our advantage. . . . . I am now convinced that the greater part of Beauregard's army is near Florence and Tuscumbia, and that you will at least have a clear road before you for several days, and that your success will fully equal your expectations."

This was the last dispatch received by Sherman from Thomas before starting out on the great march. Sherman replied "All right," and the wires were cut.

sequences of such a march must be important and decisive. The cities of the Atlantic sea-board were doomed the moment Sherman's army should reach their rear. At Savannah or Charleston this army could be transported by sea, or could march by land through the Carolinas, and, re-enforcing Grant, terminate the long-protracted conflict with Lee's army.

But what if Thomas should be conquered by Hood? Then, indeed, Sherman's march would have demonstrated only his own folly. He would have ascended like a rocket and come down a stick. But to have anticipated such an event would have been an insult to General Thomas, and to the armies of Schofield, Stanley, and Smith. Sherman had no apprehensions on that score. Not until Thomas had himself expressed his faith in his own power to ruin Hood, if the latter advanced, or to assume the offensive against him if he retreated, did Sherman move from Atlanta.

By the 14th of November, the Fourteenth, Fifteenth, Seventeenth, and Twentieth Corps were grouped about Atlanta, constituting an army 60,000 strong, with an additional force of cavalry under Brigadier General Judson Kilpatrick, numbering 5500 men. The artillery consisted of about 60 guns, or one piece to every thousand men. Every thing had been sent to the rear which could not be used in the campaign. The railroad north had been destroyed as far as Dalton. Rome and Atlanta had been burned, only the dwelling-houses and churches escaping destruction. On the 16th of November Sherman commenced his grand March to the Sea. While he is advancing eastward through the fruitful fields of Georgia, let us follow the counter-movement of Hood against Nashville.

CHAPTER XLVII.
BATTLE OF NASHVILLE.

Hood attacks Decatur and is repulsed.—Forrest's Demonstration against Johnsonville.—Hood north of the Tennessee.—Estimate of the opposing Forces.—Schofield abandons Pulaski.—Retreat from Columbia to Franklin.—Narrow Escape at Spring Hill.—Battle of Franklin.—Its Results.—Hood in front of Nashville.—Demonstration against Murfreesborough.—Preparations for Battle on both sides.—Inclement Weather.—General Thomas assumes the Defensive.—Battles of December 15th and 16th.—Defeat of Hood's Army.—The Pursuit.—Results of the Nashville Campaign.—Gillem defeated by Breckinridge.—Stoneman drives Breckinridge into North Carolina.—Destruction of the Works at Saltville.

FORREST had intended to cross the Tennessee in the vicinity of Gunter's Landing and threaten Bridgeport, thus compelling Sherman to abandon Georgia in order to protect Tennessee. Beauregard had ordered Forrest to move with his cavalry into Tennessee, Hood not having a sufficient cavalry force to protect his trains north of the river.[1] These orders did not reach Forrest in time, and Hood was therefore compelled to move down the Tennessee and await Forrest's arrival. On the 26th of October a portion of Hood's infantry appeared before Decatur, on the south side of the river, at the southern terminus of the Nashville and Decatur Railroad, and on the afternoon of that day made a feeble attack on the garrison, which was commanded by R. S. Granger. Granger was re-enforced by two regiments from Chattanooga, and instructed to hold his post at all hazards. The next day the enemy established a line of rifle-pits within 500 yards of the town. On the 28th a sortie was made by a part of the garrison, which, advancing under cover of the guns of the fort, down the river bank and around to the rear of the enemy's rifle-pits, dislodged the Confederates, capturing 120 prisoners. Forrest in the mean while had reached Corinth, and advanced from that point upon Fort Heiman, on the west bank of the Tennessee, about 75 miles from Paducah. Here he captured the gun-boat No. 55 and two transports on the 31st, having previously burned the steamer Empress. He had about 17 regiments of cavalry, probably numbering altogether 5000 men, and 9 pieces of artillery. On the 2d of November he planted batteries above and below Johnsonville, one of General Thomas's bases of supplies on the river, isolating, at that place, three gun-boats and eight transports. The gun-boats made an unsuccessful attack upon the lower batteries, but, though repulsed, they recaptured from the enemy one of the transports which he had taken, and forced him to destroy the gun-boat No. 55. On the 4th Forrest made an attack on the gun-boats and the garrison, consisting of 1000 men. The gun-boats, being disabled, were burned to prevent their falling into the enemy's hands, and the fire, spreading to the buildings of the commissary and quartermaster's departments, and to the stores on the levee, caused the government a loss estimated at $1,500,000. The next morning Forrest repeated his attack upon the garrison, and, after a furious cannonade of over an hour's duration, withdrew from Johnsonville.

Hood's army arrived at Florence on the 31st of October, one month after it had been transferred from Sherman's front. This long delay, caused partly by the difficulties attending the transportation of supplies, had thwarted the sole object of Hood's campaign. It had given Sherman and Thomas time for completing their preparations, the former for his march eastward, and the latter for the accumulation of an army large enough to protect Tennessee.

Hood's force, including all arms, on the 1st of November did not number over 40,000 effective men. Thomas had in his command a considerably larger force. After deducting the garrisons of Nashville, Decatur, and Chattanooga, however, his army available for battle numbered about 30,000 men.[2]

---

[1] Hood's Report.

[2] Thomas says in his report: "At this time (November 5th) I found myself confronted by the army which, under General J. E. Johnston, had so skillfully resisted the advance of the whole active army of the military division of the Mississippi from Dalton to the Chattahoochee, re-enforced by a well-equipped and enthusiastic cavalry command of over 12,000, led by one of the boldest and most successful commanders in the rebel army. My information from all sources confirmed the reported strength of Hood's army to be from 40,000 to 45,000 infantry, and from 12,000 to 15,000

DESTRUCTION OF THE DEPÔTS, PUBLIC BUILDINGS, AND MANUFACTORIES AT ATLANTA.

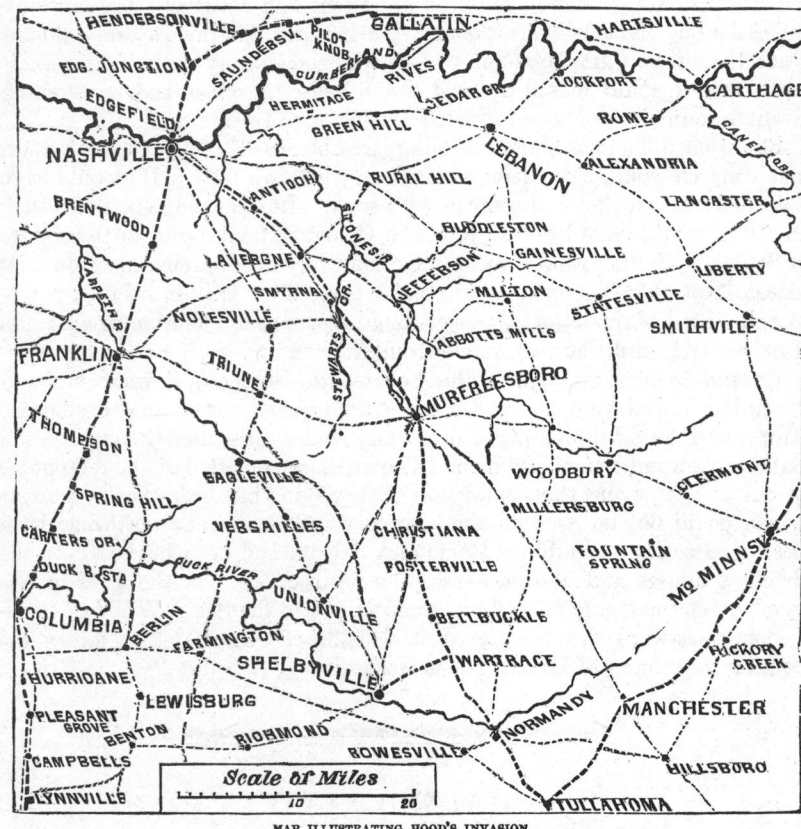

MAP ILLUSTRATING HOOD'S INVASION.

Hood persisted in his scheme of invading Tennessee. General Beauregard does not seem to have exercised a very potent influence in this matter. The problem now presented puzzled him, and he could not solve it. He therefore left it to Hood's option to do as he pleased—either to divide his forces, sending a part against Sherman and advance with the other, or to move against Thomas with his whole force. Hood had delayed on the banks of the Tennessee till past the middle of November, and until Sherman was on his march. He had laid a pontoon bridge across the river, mooring it to the piers of the old railroad bridge at Florence, and had crossed Lee's corps and two divisions of cavalry. Stewart and Cheatham still remained on the south side until November 17th. On the 21st Forrest's cavalry joined the main army, and the movement northward was commenced.

If the Confederate army of Tennessee had been under the disposition of General Grant to move where it would best suit him, he would not, he declares in his official report, have made any other disposition of it than that made by General Hood. Hood's reasoning upon the proper course for him to take is exceedingly shallow. He says: "The enemy having for the first time divided his forces, I had to determine which of the two parts to direct my operations against. To follow the forces about to move through Georgia under Sherman would be to again abandon the regained territory to the forces under Thomas, with little hope of being able to reach the enemy in time to defeat his movement, and also to cause desertion and greatly impair the *morale*, or fighting spirit of the army, by what would be considered a compulsory retreat." It was, indeed, of no use to follow Sherman except with cavalry. But the reason which Hood gives for advancing against Thomas is simply ludicrous. For what had he gained thus far in his campaign that he should hesitate to abandon? He had advanced from Jonesborough to Dalton, capturing some unimportant stations which he had hastily released, destroying a few miles of railroad which it had taken less than a fortnight to repair, then had fallen back to Gadsden, and had moved thence to Corinth and Florence. He held no post of any military value to himself or to his foe. Indeed, he had nothing to abandon except his design of invasion. But the chief motive of the invasion—namely, to compel Sherman to leave Georgia for the protection of Tennessee—no longer existed,

for Sherman had defied his projected invasion in the boldest and bluntest terms. The railroad from which Hood had been driven Sherman had destroyed with his own hands. Atlanta, which Hood had hoped to recover, Sherman had made a useless possession to the enemy as well as to himself. And Georgia, which Hood was pledged to redeem, was already being trampled down under the heels of 60,000 men, whom, with his own army, he could not reach if he would, and whom, if he could have reached, he dared not encounter. As to the *morale* of his army, Hood's invasion thus far had certainly not improved *that*; for since he had started from Jonesborough he had lost 10,000 men, or one fourth of his army, though in that time he had only fought a single serious battle—that of Allatoona. Hood could have lost nothing by a judicious retreat which could be compared with what he risked by an advance against Thomas. To allow the Federal forces to assume the defensive was to give them such advantages as must be decisive. The advance was the result of the infatuation of both Hood and Davis. The threat had been uttered, the pledge given, and it was too late now to hesitate or falter.

The wager which Hood had offered Thomas was ready to accept. The latter would have preferred an encounter with the enemy south of Duck River: this would have been possible if the Confederate army had delayed its movements for a week or ten days. The Federal cavalry guarding the Tennessee about Florence had already been driven back, so that Croxton was on the east side of Shoal Creek, and Hatch occupied Lawrenceburg. Schofield, with the Twenty-third Corps, had arrived at Nashville November 5th, and was directed to join the Fourth Corps at Pulaski, take the command of the troops at that point, and, as far as possible, retard Hood's advance into Tennessee. It was obviously Thomas's policy to impede Hood's movements, gradually withdrawing Schofield and Stanley, until he could receive the re-enforcements under A. J. Smith, and organize Wilson's cavalry and the new regiments. Hood's army moved by parallel roads to Waynesborough and eastward of that place, with Forrest on the right flank. On the 22d of November Hatch's cavalry was driven from Lawrenceburg. Hood desired to push his army up between Nashville and Schofield's command; but on the 23d the Federal forces evacuated Pulaski, and fell back to Columbia, on the Duck River. The retreat was ably conducted, all the public property being removed beforehand from Pulaski, and the trains carefully guarded. Thomas had meanwhile received some 7000 men which had been sent back from Atlanta by General Sherman; his command had also been re-enforced by 20 new one-year regiments, very many of which were absorbed in the veteran corps, replacing old regiments whose term of service had expired. R. S. Granger had withdrawn the garrisons at Athens, Decatur, and Huntsville, Alabama, taking a part of the force thus collected to Stevenson, and sending back five regiments to Murfreesborough. The garrison at Johnsonville was withdrawn to Clarkesville.

Hood's movement on Columbia was slow; not until the evening of November 27th had his advance reached Schofield's front. During that night Schofield crossed Duck River, taking a position on the north bank, where he was not disturbed during the 28th. General Wilson's cavalry, 4300 strong, guarded the crossings of the river above and below. On the afternoon of the 29th Wilson was pressed back and cut off from Schofield, while Hood's infantry crossed the river, and threatened to turn Schofield's flank by an advance on Spring Hill, about 15 miles north of Columbia. Schofield, therefore, sending Stanley with Wagner's division to Spring Hill to head off the enemy at that point and cover the retreat, prepared to fall back toward Franklin. Stanley reached Spring Hill just in time to check Forrest's advance and save the trains. The Confederate infantry coming up to Forrest's assistance, a doubtful battle was maintained till dark, in which the enemy nearly succeeded in dislodging Stanley from his position. Schofield, having sent back his trains, was at the same time occupied in resisting the enemy's attempts to cross Duck River in his front, and, after having several times repulsed the Confederate force opposed to him, retreated at night, his command making 25 miles under cover of the darkness, and, passing Spring Hill in safety, got into position at Franklin, 18 miles south of Nashville, on the morning of the 30th.

With Cheatham's corps supported by Stewart's, it seems that the enemy ought to have defeated Stanley at Spring Hill and cut off Schofield's retreat. But Stanley maintained his position and saved the army.[1] He was re-enforced toward night by Ruger's division of the Twenty-third Corps. But, even after this re-enforcement, the enemy had the advantage. With two

cavalry. My effective force at this time consisted of the Fourth Corps, about 12,000, under Major General D. S. Stanley; the Twenty-third Corps, about 10,000, under Major General John M. Schofield; Hatch's division of cavalry, about 4000; Croxton's brigade, 2500, and Capron's brigade of about 1200. The balance of my force was distributed along the railroad, and posted at Murfreesborough, Stevenson, Bridgeport, Huntsville, Decatur, and Chattanooga, to keep open our communications and hold the posts above named, if attacked, until they could be re-enforced, as up to this time it was impossible to determine which course Hood would take—advance on Nashville or turn toward Huntsville."

According to this report, Hood had from 52,000 to 57,000 men, and Thomas about 30,000, exclusive of his detachments on the railroad and at the posts mentioned.

As to the numbers of Hood's army, the best authority is the official return of the Confederate Army of Tennessee for November 6th, 1864, which gives a force of 30,600 men. This is exclusive of Forrest's cavalry, which probably did not reach 10,000.

As to Thomas's command, Sherman represents the Fourth Corps as 15,000 strong; but, taking Thomas's estimate, we have his available force (November 5th):

Stanley's Corps	12,000	Croxton's Cavalry	2,500
Schofield's Corps	10,000	Capron's Cavalry	1,200
Hatch's Cavalry	4,000		29,700

But to this must be added Washburne's command, 4500, which makes 34,200. It must also be remembered that, in case of an important battle, at least 6000 veteran troops, in addition to those above enumerated, could be brought into action. And in this estimate no notice whatever is taken of four elements which would soon give Thomas a very great preponderance of force as compared with Hood's, namely: 1st, new regiments of recruits constantly arriving at Nashville; 2d, A. J. Smith's two divisions on the way from Missouri; 3d, Wilson's cavalry, which in a few days would amount to about 12,000 men; and, 4th, about 7000 men suitable for garrison duty which would soon be sent back to Thomas from Sherman's army, on account of their unfitness for the great march.

In connection with the official return of Hood's army for November 6th, one thing is worthy of notice. On the 20th of September, before Hood moved from the Macon Road, his army numbered 40,406. It is plain, therefore, that in the course of the advance to Dalton, the retreat to Gadsden, and the movement to Florence, Hood had lost about 10,000 men; and a large proportion of this loss must be attributed to desertion. Hood, it is clear, had not by his invasion very much improved the *morale* of his army.

[1] General Hood, in his report, gives the following account of the affair at Spring Hill:

"When I had gotten well on his flank, the enemy discovered my intention, and began to retreat on the pike toward Spring Hill. The cavalry became engaged near that place about midday, but his trains were so strongly guarded that they were unable to break through them. About 4 P.M. our infantry forces, Major General Cheatham in the advance, commenced to come in contact with the enemy, about two miles from Spring Hill, through which place the Columbia and Franklin Pike passes. The enemy was at this time moving rapidly along the pike, with some of his troops formed on the flank of his column to protect it. Major General Cheatham was ordered to attack the enemy at once, vigorously, and get possession of this pike, and, although these orders were frequently and earnestly repeated, he made but a feeble and partial attack, failing to reach the point indicated. Had my instructions been carried out there is no doubt that we could have possessed ourselves of this road. Stewart's corps and Johnson's division were arriving upon the field to support the attack. Though the golden opportunity had passed with daylight, I did not at dark abandon the hope of dealing the enemy a heavy blow. Accordingly, Lieutenant General Stewart was furnished a guide, and ordered to move his corps beyond Cheatham's, and place it across the road beyond Spring Hill. Shortly after this General Cheatham came to my headquarters, and when I informed him of Stewart's movement, he said that Stewart ought to form on his right. I asked if that would throw Stewart across the pike. He replied that it would, and a mile beyond. Accordingly, one of Cheatham's staff officers was sent to show Stewart where his (Cheatham's) right rested. In the dark and confusion, Stewart did not succeed in getting the position desired, but about 11 P.M. went into bivouac. About 12 P.M., ascertaining that the enemy was moving in great confusion—artillery, wagons, and troops intermixed—I sent instructions to General Cheatham to advance a heavy line of skirmishers against him, and still farther impede and confuse his march. This was not accomplished. The enemy continued to move along the road in hurry and confusion, within hearing, nearly all the night. Thus was lost a great opportunity of striking the enemy, for which we had labored so long, the greatest this campaign had offered, and one of the greatest during the war."

G. D. WAGNER.

full corps of Forrest's cavalry in the vicinity of Spring Hill, Schofield ought to have been cut off at least from the direct road to Franklin. His main army did not leave Duck River, where it had been fighting Lee, until after dark, and passed Spring Hill about midnight. It certainly had a narrow escape. General Wagner's division of Stanley's corps held on to its position at Spring Hill until near daylight. Notwithstanding the superior numbers of the enemy, the only disturbances suffered in the retreat was from a slight attack made north of Thompson's by Forrest's cavalry, causing the loss of a few wagons. General Cooper, who had been left to guard the crossing at Duck River, was cut off from the direct road to Franklin, and proceeded to Nashville.

When Schofield reached Franklin he found no wagon bridge across the Harpeth River, and the fords in a bad condition. The railroad bridge was rapidly repaired and a foot-bridge was constructed, which was also available for the use of wagons. He sent his train across, and intended to cross with his army. But the enemy was in too close proximity. As the Federal troops arrived they were placed in position on the south side of the river, the Twenty-third Corps, under General Cox, on the left and centre, covering the approaches from Columbia and Lewisburg, and Kimball's division of Stanley's corps on the right; both flanks of the army resting on the river. Wood's division of Stanley's corps was sent to the north side of the river to cover the flanks, in the event of Hood's crossing above or below. Two brigades of Wagner's division—the last to reach Franklin—were left in front, to retard the advance of the enemy.

At daylight Hood had commenced the pursuit, which was pushed with great vigor. Stewart was in the advance, Cheatham following, while Lee, with the trains, brought up the rear from Columbia. Hood determined to make a direct attack with Stewart's and Cheatham's corps without waiting for Lee. No flank movement which he could now make would prevent Schofield from reaching Nashville.[1] Stewart advanced on the right, Cheatham on the left, with the cavalry on either flank, the main body of the latter, under Forrest, moving to the right. Johnson's division of Lee's corps arrived during the engagement, and went in on the left.

Fortunately for Schofield, Hood's attack was delayed until 4 o'clock on the afternoon of the 30th. In the mean time the Federal troops were constructing breastworks and protecting them by a slight abatis on the left. To them, with the river in their rear, and with the roads, by which alone retreat was possible, crowded with the wagon trains, defeat would have been a terrible disaster, affecting the safety of Nashville. On both sides the decisive nature of the contest was fully appreciated. It was a brief battle, for at this season of the year 4 P.M. was the verge of twilight.[2] Wagner's men, holding the outposts, "imprudently brave," reports Schofield, maintained the conflict outside of the intrenchments longer than was necessary, suffering heavy loss. When they fell back it was at a full run, and this movement swept back a portion of the first line in the works, allowing the enemy to

enter in large numbers. In this attempt to fight a battle with outposts Wagner lost over a thousand men. The enemy had gained an advantage, which, if pressed, might have resulted in success. Victory seemed almost within his grasp. The Federal line had been broken in the centre; two batteries of four guns each had been captured. But at this moment Opdyke, commanding the remaining brigade of Wagner's division, which had been held in reserve inside the works, leading his men on, shouting "Forward to the lines!" rushed forward, recovered the lost batteries, and captured 400 prisoners. The gap had been closed; but the enemy, though disappointed, was not disheartened. He charged the works, making four distinct attacks, and was each time hurled back with heavy loss. "So vigorous and fierce were these assaults that the enemy reached the exterior slope of the rude intrenchments, and hand-to-hand encounters occurred between the enraged combatants across the works."[1] Between the assaults, the enemy, covered by the undulations of the ground, pressed his sharp-shooters close to the works, and kept up a galling fire.

The Confederates persistently assailed Schofield's line until after dark, continuing the attack at intervals until near midnight, but were repulsed in every attempt to carry the works. The Confederate loss was between 4500 and 6000 men. Schofield lost 2326, of which number of casualties 1241 occurred in Wagner's division.[2] On the Federal side, General Stanley was severely wounded in the neck. The Confederate loss in general officers was very great, including among them Major General Pat. Cleburne, and Brigadier Generals Gist, John Adams, Strahl, and Granbury; Brigadier Generals Carter, Manigault, Quarles, Cockrell, and Scott were wounded, and Brigadier General Gordon was captured.[3] At midnight Schofield withdrew from the trenches which he had held against the repeated assaults of far superior numbers, and fell back to Nashville.

Hood's orders to his corps commanders to drive Schofield into the river, and for Forrest to advance and capture the trains, had failed of execution. General Thomas's position was now secure. On the 1st of December he had behind the fortifications of Nashville and covering its southern approaches an investing force superior to General Hood's, and a cavalry force in process of organization at Edgefield, north of the river, which in a few days would in numbers be at least equal to Forrest's command. A. J. Smith's command of three divisions had also reached Nashville. Smith was placed on the right of the line, Wood, now commanding the Fourth Corps, in the centre, and Schofield on the left.

The next day, December 2d, the enemy advanced to within two miles of Nashville, and invested the town on the south side, General Lee holding the centre of the line, Cheatham the right, and Stewart the left; the cavalry on either flank extended to the river. The whole line was intrenched, and strong detached works were constructed to guard the flanks against attack. On Hood's right, Murfreesborough was held by a Federal force 8000 strong under General Rousseau, which cut off all communication with Georgia and Virginia. Bates's division of Cheatham's corps attacked the block-house at Overall's Creek, four miles north of Murfreesborough, on the 4th of December. The garrison maintained its position, and being soon re-enforced from Murfreesborough with three infantry regiments, four companies of cavalry, and a section of artillery, the enemy was driven off. During the 5th, 6th, and 7th, Bates, re-enforced by the greater portion of Forrest's cavalry, demonstrated against Fortress Rosecrans at Murfreesborough. As the enemy hesitated to make a direct assault, Rousseau determined to assume the offensive himself. Accordingly, on the 8th, General Milroy, with seven infantry regiments (3325 men), proceeded to the Wilkinson Pike, there encountered Bates and Forrest, and drove them from their temporary breastworks, capturing 207 prisoners.[4] The Federal loss in killed and wounded was 205. Buford's division of Forrest's cavalry entered the town of Murfreesborough the same day, but was speedily driven out by a single infantry regiment and a section of artillery. Forrest's cavalry, retiring from before Murfreesborough, proceeded northward to Lebanon, and threatened to cross the Cumberland above Nashville and cut off Thomas's communications by the Louisville Road. This movement was thwarted by a division of gun-boats and a detachment of Wilson's cavalry.

From the 3d to the 15th of December was spent by both armies in preparation for the conflict which was to decide the fate of Nashville. Hood was furnishing his army with supplies and with shoes. From the 7th to the 14th both armies were ice-bound. Thomas thus had time to remount Wilson's cavalry, increase the strength of his works, bring up re-enforcements of new recruits and temporary volunteers, and to mature his plan of operations. Nashville was well fortified when Thomas entered it with his army. The southern approaches were covered by Forts Negley, Morton, Confiscation, Houston, and Gillem. Some of these had been constructed in the latter part of 1862, when the city was threatened by a portion of Bragg's army. These forts were situated on commanding hills near the city, and some distance beyond ran the line now held by Thomas's army. From Fort Morton westward an interior line of defense was also constructed, along the range of hills nearer Nashville.[5]

---

[1] "I learned from dispatches captured at Spring Hill, from Thomas to Schofield, that the latter was instructed to hold that place till the position at Franklin could be made secure, indicating the intention of Thomas to hold Franklin and his strong works at Murfreesborough. Thus I knew that it was all-important to attack Schofield before he could make himself strong, and, if he should escape at Franklin, he would gain his works about Nashville. The nature of the position was such as to render it inexpedient to attempt any farther flank movement, and I therefore determined to attack him in front, and without delay.—Hood's Report.

[2] On the 30th of November, 1864, the sun set at 4 39. Schofield's report makes the battle to have commenced at 3 30 P.M.

---

[1] General T. J. Wood's Report.
[2] Hood reports his own loss as 4500. Schofield, from information obtained afterward, makes the enemy's loss "1750 buried upon the field, 3800 disabled, and 702 prisoners." Hood claims that he captured 1000 prisoners. This tallies well with Schofield's report, in which he admits 1104 missing, 670 of whom were from Wagner's division.   [2] Hood's Report.
[4] Hood reports that Bates's division behaved badly.
[5] Thomas's army at Nashville consisted of the following forces:

Schofield's Twenty-third Corps	9,000 men.
Woods's Fourth Corps	11,000 "
A. J. Smith's Corps, say	11,000 "
Steadman's Command, which arrived at Nashville from December 1	5,200 "
Wilson's Cavalry	12,000 "
Quartermaster's Troops under Brigadier General Donaldson, and other forces under General Miller used in the immediate defense of Nashville, say	8,000 "
Total	56,200 "

MAP OF THE BATTLE OF NASHVILLE.

The severity of the weather began to relax on the 14th, and on the afternoon of that day Thomas issued orders to his corps commanders for an advance against the enemy. His army was now 50,000 strong, and fully prepared for battle. A large portion of Forrest's cavalry was still absent from the Confederate army. Hood seems in his infatuation to have been absolutely confident of victory in the event of Thomas's assuming the offensive.[1] He even dreamed of besieging Nashville. But the swollen river, patroled by gun-boats, hindered an advance against the Louisville Road, and, even if this road had been reached and broken by Confederate cavalry, Thomas was well supplied at Nashville with all that was necessary for either a defensive or offensive campaign. The term siege would be scarcely applicable to General Hood's operations.

Upon his first approach to the city on the 2d of December, Hood had seized Montgomery Hill, within 600 yards of the Federal centre, and thrown up strong lines of earth-works on the hills south and parallel with those occupied by Thomas. His infantry stretched from the Nolensville Pike, on the right, along the high ground south and east of Brown's Creek, and across the Franklin and Granny White Pikes to the hills bordering the Hillsborough Pike. A wide interval, therefore, separated his left from the river. This—as also the corresponding interval between the Nolensville Pike and the river—was held by the cavalry, who had established batteries about eight miles below Nashville, blockading the river. The weak point of the Confederate position was its left flank, which, though strongly intrenched, was easily turned.

Thomas's long silence appeared to have increased Hood's confidence. It also led to considerable apprehension on the part of Lieutenant General Grant, who, at so great a distance from the field, was not aware of the rigorous cold which hindered Thomas's advance, and was also a serious inconvenience to the poorly-clad soldiers of Hood's army. He thought that Thomas ought to have moved upon Hood as soon as the latter had made his appearance in front of Nashville, and before he was fortified, and that by waiting to remount Wilson's cavalry he had made a great mistake. Perhaps, also, the narrow escape of Schofield's army in the retreat from Columbia to Franklin—an escape which could only be attributed to either the stupidity of the Confederate generals or to their want of confidence in their commander—led him to suspect that the campaign was not being properly conducted. At any rate, so great was his impatience that he started West with the idea of superintending matters there in person. He had only reached Washington when he received a dispatch from Thomas announcing the successful commencement of the battle of Nashville.[2]

General Thomas's plan of the battle was very simple, involving the turning of the enemy's left flank by a sudden and irresistible blow to be struck with the bulk of his army, and to be followed up until Hood's army was destroyed or dispersed in utter rout. Success was as certain as the event of a battle ever could be. The execution of this plan was so perfect in all its details that it justly conferred upon General Thomas the first rank among the Union generals as a tactician.[3] He had delayed for the purpose of organizing an efficient cavalry corps, in order that, in the event of victory, he might reap its full fruits by a relentless pursuit of the defeated army. He was prepared to attack a week before he did, but the weather, as we have said, was unfavorable. On the 12th Wilson's cavalry had crossed the Cumberland from Edgefield to the left of the Hillsborough Pike.

The morning of the 15th of December was every way favorable to the immediate execution of Genetal Thomas's plans. The sheet of ice which had covered the earth for nearly a week was broken up; and, in addition to the undulations of the ground, a heavy mist, lasting until noon, completely masked the preparations for battle. Under these auspicious circumstances, Smith advanced immediately in front of his works, with Wilson's cavalry on his right. Wood and Schofield, leaving strong skirmish lines in their trenches, marched to the right, Wood forming in line on Smith's left, and Schofield supporting Wood, guarding the left flank against attack. Steedman, who had charge of the defenses of Nashville, leaving Donaldson's and Miller's troops to hold the interior line of defense, advanced with his main force against the enemy's right. Steedman's operations were demonstrative, and preceded the main attack. His force consisted of three brigades—Thompson's, Morgan's, and Grosvenor's, the two former being composed of disciplined negro soldiers. Though unsuccessful in his attack on the Confederate right, he succeeded in diverting the enemy's attention from the centre and left, leaving the way open for Wilson, Smith, Wood, and Schofield, 40,000 strong, to sweep around against the enemy's works on the Hillsborough Pike.

JAMES B. STEEDMAN.

The advance of Smith and Wilson commenced as soon as Steedman's movement was completely developed on either side of the Hardin Pike. Over difficult and broken ground, their movement proceeded from the Cumberland and the hills adjoining it across and along the Hardin Pike, and then swept eastward, enveloping the Confederate left on the Hillsborough Pike, threatening to strike Brentwood, in Hood's rear, on the road to Franklin. Hood was completely surprised, and his cavalry, a great portion of which was in the vicinity of Murfreesborough and along the Cumberland, was too weak to meet the sudden blow. Hatch's cavalry division moved on Smith's right, with Croxton's brigade on his own right, and Knipe's division in support. McArthur's infantry division held the right, and therefore the advance of Smith's corps, and, with Hatch's cavalry, encountered the enemy a little after noon. On the right of the Hillsborough Pike the enemy had some advanced works protecting his left. The Confederates were driven from this position by Hatch and McArthur, who, swinging to the left, came upon a redoubt containing four guns, which was carried by a portion of Hatch's division, and the captured artillery turned upon the enemy. A second redoubt was then carried, with four guns and about 300 prisoners. McArthur justly shared the glory of these captures.

While the enemy's left was being driven back on the Granny White Pike, the Fourth Corps, under Wood, was assaulting the centre at Montgomery Hill. This position was carried by Post's brigade of Wagner's division, and several prisoners were captured. Wood now connected with Smith's left, and Schofield's corps was moved from the reserve to Smith's right, the cavalry, at the same time, being thrown still farther around against the enemy's rear. But, while Wilson, Schofield, and Smith pressed forward during the afternoon, sweeping every thing before them, Wood had still another line of works to assault on his front. This was at length carried, and 700 prisoners, 8 guns, and 5 caissons were captured. By night, Hood's army had been driven out of its original line of works, and back from the Hillsborough Road, but still held possession of two lines of retreat to Franklin by the main road through Brentwood and the Granny White Pike. Thomas had won substantial trophies of victory, his captures consisting of 1200 prisoners, 16 guns, 40 wagons, and a large number of small-arms. Owing to the unexpectedness of the attack, and the brilliant tactics of the Federal commander, these results had been gained with slight Union loss, while the Confederate loss was heavy. During the afternoon, Johnson's division of Wilson's cavalry had, with the co-operation of the gun-boats, captured the Confederate batteries blockading the river below Nashville at Bell's Landing. At 9 P.M. Thomas telegraphed to Washington: "I shall attack the enemy again to-morrow if he stands to fight, and if he retreats during the night I will pursue him, throwing a heavy cavalry force in his rear to destroy his trains, if possible."

But Hood did not yet give up the contest. During the night he withdrew

---

[1] "Should he attack me in position, I felt that I would defeat him, and thus gain possession of Nashville, with abundant supplies for the army. This would give me possession of Tennessee."—*Hood's Report.*

[2] In his official report, Grant says:

"Before the battle of Nashville I grew very impatient over, as it appeared to me, the unnecessary delay. This impatience was increased upon learning that the enemy had sent a force of cavalry across the Cumberland into Kentucky. I feared Hood would cross his whole army and give us great trouble there. After urging upon General Thomas the necessity of immediately assuming the offensive, I started West to superintend matters there in person. Reaching Washington City, I received General Thomas's dispatch announcing his attack upon the enemy, and the result as far as the battle had progressed. I was delighted. All fears and apprehensions were dispelled. I am not yet satisfied but that General Thomas, immediately upon the appearance of Hood before Nashville, and before he had time to fortify, should have moved out with his whole force and given him battle, instead of waiting to remount his cavalry, which delayed him until the inclemency of the weather made it impracticable to attack earlier than he did. But his final defeat of Hood was so complete that it will be accepted as a vindication of that distinguished officer's judgment."

[3] The following is a copy of Thomas's order issued to his corps commanders on the 14th:

"As soon as the state of the weather will admit of offensive operations, the troops will move against the enemy's position in the following order: Major General A. J. Smith, commanding detachment of the Army of the Tennessee, after forming his troops on and near the Hardin Pike, in front of his present position, will make a vigorous assault on the enemy's left. Major General Wilson, commanding the cavalry corps, Military Division of the Mississippi, with three divisions, will move on and support General Smith's right, assisting, as far as possible, in carrying the left of the enemy's position, and be in readiness to throw his force upon the enemy the moment a favorable opportunity occurs. Major General Wilson will also send one division on the Charlotte Pike to clear that road of the enemy, and observe in the direction of Bell's Landing, to protect our right rear until the enemy's position is fairly turned, when it will rejoin the main force. Brigadier General T. J. Wood, commanding Fourth Army Corps, after leaving a strong skirmish line in his works from Laurens's Hill to his extreme right, will form the remainder of the Fourth Corps on the Hillsborough Pike to support General Smith's left, and operate on the left and rear of the enemy's advanced position on Montgomery Hill. Major General Schofield, commanding the Twenty-third Army Corps, will replace Brigadier General Kimball's division of the Fourth Corps with his troops, and occupy the trenches from Fort Negley to Laurens's Hill with a strong skirmish line. He will move with the remainder of his force in front of the works, and co-operate with General Wood, protecting the latter's left flank against an attack of the enemy. Major General Steedman, commanding the District of Etowah, will occupy the interior line in front of his present position, stretching from the reservoir on the Cumberland River to Fort Negley with a strong skirmish line, and mass the remainder of his force in its present position, to act according to the exigencies which may arise during these operations. Brigadier General Miller, with the troops forming the garrison of Nashville, will occupy the interior line from the battery on hill 210 to the extreme right, including the inclosed work on the Hyde's Ferry Road. The quartermaster's troops, under command of Brigadier General Donaldson, will, if necessary, be posted on the interior line from Fort Morton to the battery on hill 210. The troops occupying the interior line will be under the direction of Major General Steadman, who is charged with the immediate defense of Nashville during the operations around the city. Should the weather permit, the troops will be formed to commence operations at 6 A.M. on the 15th, or as soon thereafter as practicable."

NASHVILLE, FROM EDGEFIELD.

NASHVILLE FROM THE OPPOSITE BANK OF THE CUMBERLAND.

EASTPORT, TENNESSEE.

his right and centre to conform to the left. Cheatham's corps was transferred from right to left, leaving Stewart in the centre and Lee on the right. Thus, when Wood advanced at 6 A.M. on the morning of the 16th, he found only skirmishers in his front. He advanced, therefore, directly south from Nashville on the Franklin Pike until he developed the enemy's main line. Then Steedman came up by the Nolensville Pike on Wood's left, and Smith on his right. These troops faced southward, while Schofield, facing to the east, held the position which he had gained the evening before. Wilson extended away off to the enemy's rear, still threatening Brentwood, at the same time that he guarded the Federal right, and was ready, in case of Hood's retreat, to fall upon his flank. Hood's right rested upon Overton's Hill, four miles north of Brentwood, and his left upon the hills bordering the Granny White Pike. His centre was weaker than either flank. The whole line, about three miles long, had been hastily but strongly intrenched, with abatis thrown up in front.

Not until mid-afternoon were Thomas's preparations for attack completed. About 600 yards separated the opposing armies. On the right, Wilson had extended well to Hood's rear and across the Granny White Pike. The tactics of the day before were repeated in the attack of the 16th. Wood and Steedman proceeded to assault Overton Hill. The movement, commencing at 3 P.M., was open to the enemy's observation, and troops were hurried from the Confederate left and centre to meet the attack at this point. Post's brigade, which the day before had stormed Montgomery Hill, again formed the main column of assault, Steedman's colored troops co-operating on the left. The result is thus briefly reported by General Thomas: "The assault was made, and received by the enemy with tremendous fire of grape and canister, and musketry. Our men moved steadily onward up the hill until near the crest, when the reserve of the enemy rose and poured into the assaulting column a most destructive fire, causing the men first to waver and then to fall back, leaving their dead and wounded, black and white indiscriminately mingled, lying amid the abatis, the gallant Colonel Post among the wounded."

Wood again reformed his command in its first position, and prepared to renew the attack. Hood, in the momentary enthusiasm following his partial success, began to hope that the day was already won. But his anticipations were doomed to disappointment; for Smith and Schofield had heard of Hood's weakening his lines in their front to support Lee's corps, and rushed forward upon the enemy's right and centre, "carrying all before them, irreparably breaking his lines in a dozen places, and capturing all his artillery and thousands of prisoners."[1] Among the latter were four general officers, including Major General Edward S. Johnson, and Brigadier Generals Jackson and Smith. Wilson made a simultaneous advance in the rear, falling upon the flank of the routed enemy and cutting him off from the Granny White Pike. This was a fitting prelude to Wood's second assault on Overton Hill. Once again the slopes of that eminence were ascended in the face of the enemy's fire. The summit was gained, the enemy was swept like chaff from his works, so many, at least, as were not taken prisoners, and all the artillery was captured. Hood's army, routed as no army had been in the history of the war, with but a remnant of artillery, abandoning its wagons and flinging aside its muskets, blankets, and every thing which might impede its own flight, or, clogging the road behind, might delay the pursuit of its victorious enemy, scattered in irrecoverable confusion down the Franklin Pike through Brentwood Pass.

If the battle could have been fought in the forenoon instead of in the afternoon, nothing could now have saved Hood's army from annihilation. The Fourth Corps pursued rapidly for several miles, capturing more prisoners, until darkness kindly enveloped the enemy's retreat. As soon as Hatch's dismounted men received their horses they also pursued on the Granny White Pike, Croxton and Knipe closely following. After proceeding about a mile, Hatch encountered Chalmers's Confederate cavalry, posted across the road behind barricades. The Twelfth Tennessee, Colonel Spaulding, charged and broke the enemy's lines, scattering the Confederates, and capturing, among other prisoners, Brigadier General G. W. Rucker.

Thus ended the two days' battle of Nashville. Hood's dead and wounded were left upon the field; besides these, he had lost 4462 prisoners, including 287 officers of all grades, from major general down, 53 guns, and thousands of small-arms.

The next morning the pursuit was continued. The Fourth Corps was followed by Steedman, and Wilson's cavalry by Schofield and Smith. Johnson's cavalry division was dispatched directly across the Harpeth to menace Franklin. Upon reaching the point where the Granny White runs into the Franklin Pike, Wilson took the advance, and encountered the Confederate rear-guard, under Stevenson, four miles north of Franklin, and charging in front and flank, dispersed the enemy and captured 413 prisoners. The presence of Johnson's cavalry division near Franklin compelled Hood to abandon that town, leaving in the hospitals over 2000 Confederate wounded. Wilson's cavalry still pursued. Now, more than ever, did Hood feel his need of Forrest, whom, in an evil moment, he had sent off on a bootless errand, just as formerly he had sent off Wheeler's cavalry at the very crisis of the Atlanta campaign. Forrest had been ordered back, but, owing to the swollen streams which barred his progress, he did not join Hood until the latter had reached Duck River. About five miles south of Franklin, the rear-guard, toward nightfall, made a temporary stand in the road, posting a battery of artillery on some rising ground. But Wilson, sending Hatch to the left and Knipe to the right of the road, with their batteries, charged Stevenson with his own body-guard, the Fourth Regular Cavalry, 180 strong. Freely using their sabres, the Union horsemen broke the Confederate centre,

[1] Thomas's Report.

Knipe and Hatch at the same time falling upon the flanks. Stevenson was thus swept from his chosen position for the second time, leaving his artillery in the road.

The 18th, like the day before, was rainy and dismal. The pursuit was continued to Duck River, where Hood had intrenched to make a stand, but wisely repented of his rash design and continued his flight to the Tennessee, leaving some of his guns at the bottom of Duck River. On reaching Ruth-erford's Creek, three miles north of Columbia, that stream was found impass-able by the national troops. Sherman had taken the best pontoon train along with his army, and another, which had been hurriedly constructed at Nashville, was incomplete, and did not arrive in time. The delay thus oc-casioned relieved Hood from instant danger. But his army was reduced—so far as organization was concerned—to a simple rear-guard. Hood was retreating from Tennessee in precisely the same condition in which Davis had three months before predicted that Sherman would retreat from Georgia. Still, Thomas, as soon as possible, continued the pursuit to the Tennessee River. The route of the flying enemy—if toilsome dragging along the miry roads could be called flight—was easily traced by ruins of baggage wagons, by small-arms and blankets, and other *débris* of a demoralized army. At Pulaski, four guns were abandoned and thrown into Richland Creek; and a mile beyond, twenty wagons loaded with ammunition, and belonging to Cheatham's corps, were destroyed. All along the road Hood's stragglers lined the wayside, where they had fallen out, tired and discouraged.[1] The Confederate army, or rather its disorganized remnant, crossed the Tennessee on the 27th of December, and fell back to Tupelo, Mississippi. Here Hood, overwhelmed by the denunciations which beat upon him heavily from all sides, resigned his command of the wreck of an army which he had brought back, and was succeeded by General Dick Taylor, who had managed to get across from the west of the Mississippi.[2] But the Confederate Army of Ten-nessee, as an organized force, had fought its last campaign.

Thomas, on December 30th, announced to his army the successful com-pletion of the campaign. It was an army which had been hastily gathered together from all quarters to meet Hood's invasion. Its numbers and effi-ciency were indications at the same time of the prompt and unyielding pa-triotism of the West, and of the generalship of Thomas. He it was who had moulded its segregate parts into a mobile army. And in all military histo-ry probably no army was ever more skillfully wielded. Thomas had quiet-ly manifested his military capacity in the early battles of 1862; he had greatly distinguished himself, in a situation more adapted to a larger display of tactical skill, on the battle-field of Chickamauga, in 1863; but the battles of Nashville were the seal and impress of his military genius. In these lat-ter battles he saw the end from the beginning; the victorious event was as clear to him on the morning of the 15th as on the night of the next day, when Hood had been routed; with him no mistake was possible, and thus upon victory followed its full fruits. For the first time in the history of the war, a Confederate army 40,000 strong had been destroyed on the field of battle and in its flight. The numbers *directly* brought to bear upon Hood's army had not been far superior; the result is therefore to be attributed to the admirable tactics of General Thomas. The battles of Nashville deserve to rank with those of Lookout Mountain and Missionary Ridge. A very memorable feature of these battles is the slight loss of the Federals in killed and wounded.[3] The grand result had been accomplished rather by skillful manœuvre than by an enormous sacrifice of life. The Confederate loss had been heavier in killed and wounded, and, in addition, over 8000 prisoners had been captured. During the Tennessee campaign Hood lost 13,189 pris-oners, and by desertion over 2000, besides 72 guns.

At the close of 1864 Thomas disposed of his army as follows: Smith's corps was stationed at Eastport, Mississippi; Wood's was concentrated at

---

[1] "With the exception of his rear-guard, his army had become a disheartened and disorganized rabble of half-armed and barefooted men, who sought every opportunity to fall out by the wayside and desert their cause, to put an end to their sufferings. The rear-guard, however, was undaunted and firm, and did its work bravely to the last."—*Thomas's Report.*

[2] "Here, finding so much dissatisfaction throughout the country as in my judgment to greatly impair, if not destroy, my usefulness and counteract my exertions, and with no desire but to serve my country, I asked to be relieved, with the hope that another might be assigned to the command who might do more than I could hope to accomplish. Accordingly, I was so relieved on the 23d of January by authority of the President."—*Hood's Report.*

[3] General Thomas reports his loss in killed, wounded, and missing during the entire campaign as 10,000.

Huntsville and Athens, Alabama; Schofield's at Dalton, Georgia; and Wil-son's cavalry at Eastport and Huntsville.

In the mean time the cavalry force, 800 strong, which, under General Lyon, had been sent by Hood across the Cumberland to operate against Thomas's communications in Kentucky, had been defeated and driven back into Alabama, after some 600 of its number had been scattered or captured. The small remnant was about the middle of January surprised in camp be-tween Warrenton and Tuscaloosa, where General Lyon, with about 100 of his men, was captured. Lyon was taken in bed, and, having been permitted to dress himself, he watched his opportunity and treacherously shot his sen-tinel, escaping in the darkness.

To finish this chapter, it remains only for us to glance at the operations which, toward the close of the year, had been going on east of Knoxville, on the yet contested border of East Tennessee and West Virginia.

General Morgan had been captured and killed on the 4th of September, 1864, at Greenville, in East Tennessee, and his command had passed into the hands of his confederate and recent biographer, General Basil Duke. In November General Breckinridge proceeded to East Tennessee, and took command of the operations in that quarter. On the 13th of November, with about 3000 men, he attacked Brigadier General A. C. Gillem, near Morris-town, routing him and capturing his artillery (6 guns), with about 500 pris-oners. The remainder of Gillem's command escaped to Strawberry Plains, and thence to Knoxville. Gillem's command, 1500 strong, had formerly be-longed to the Army of the Cumberland, but at the instance of Governor An-drew Johnson had been made an independent command. It was this sep-aration, and the consequent lack of co-operation between Gillem and the offi-cers of Thomas's army, which doubtless led to this disaster.

Breckinridge followed up his success, moving through Strawberry Plains to the immediate vicinity of Knoxville, but on the 18th of November be-gan hastily to retrace his line of advance. For General Thomas, in all his preparations against Hood, had not weakened his rear, and the force under Breckinridge was not competent to meet that suddenly brought to his front. On the 18th—the day of Breckinridge's retreat—General Ammen's troops, re-enforced by 1500 men from Chattanooga, reoccupied Strawberry Plains.

General Schofield had left Stoneman at Louisville to take charge of the Department of the Ohio during his absence with Thomas's army. Stone-man started for Knoxville, having previously ordered Brevet Major General Burbridge to march with all his available force in Kentucky, by way of Cumberland Gap, to Gillem's relief. On his way to Knoxville, Stoneman re-ceived instructions from Thomas to concentrate as large a force as possible in East Tennessee against Breckinridge, and either destroy his force or drive it into Virginia, and destroy the salt-works at Saltville, in West Virginia, and the railroad from the Tennessee line as far into Virginia as practicable.

Having rapidly concentrated the commands of Burbridge and Gillem at Bean's Station, on the 12th of December General Stoneman advanced against the enemy. Gillem struck Duke at Kingsport, on the north fork of the Hol-ston River, killing, capturing, or dispersing the whole command. Burbridge, at Bristol, came upon the enemy under Vaugn, and skirmished with him un-til Gillem's troops came up. Vaugn then retreated. Burbridge pushed on to Abingdon, to cut the railroad between Wytheville and Saltville, to pre-vent re-enforcements from Lynchburg. Gillem also reached Abingdon on the 15th, and the next day struck the enemy at Marion, routed him, and cap-tured all his artillery and trains, and 198 prisoners. Wytheville, with its stores and supplies, was destroyed, as also the extensive lead-works near the town, and the railroad bridge over Reedy Creek. Stoneman, having made a demonstration on Saltville, proceeded to join Burbridge at Marion, where Breckinridge had collected the scattered remnants of his command. But the Confederates avoided battle, retreating into North Carolina. Stoneman then moved on Saltville with his entire command, capturing at that place eight guns, a large amount of ammunition, and two locomotives. The salt-works were destroyed by breaking the kettles, filling the wells with rubbish, and burning the buildings. Stoneman then returned to Knoxville, accom-panied by Gillem's command, while General Burbridge, by way of Cumber-land Gap, fell back into Kentucky. The country marched over by Stone-man's troops during these operations was laid waste, and all mills, factories, and bridges were destroyed.

SALTVILLE, VIRGINIA.

SALT VALLEY.

THE FOURTEENTH AND TWENTIETH CORPS MOVING OUT OF ATLANTA.

CHAPTER XLVIII.

SHERMAN'S CAMPAIGN.—THE MARCH TO THE SEA.

After the Battle of Nashville the East becomes the Theatre of the War.—Estimate of General Sherman's Generalship.—He marches from Atlanta.—Constitution of his Army.—The Order of March.—The Movement not simply "a big Raid."—The Country traversed.—Occupation of Milledgeville.—Action at Griswoldville.—Crossing of the Oconee.—Sandersville occupied.—Kilpatrick's Movement on Millen.—Destruction of Railroads.—Apprehension in the North.—Crossing of the Ogeechee.—The Approaches to Savannah.—Capture of Fort McAllister, and communication with Dahlgren's Fleet.—Investment of Savannah.—Sherman demands a Surrender.—Hardee declines.—Movement against the Charleston and Savannah Railroad.—Hardee's Retreat.—Sherman enters Savannah.—Results of the March.—The Amount of Property captured or destroyed.—Character of the Defenses of Savannah.—Conduct of Sherman's Army on the March.

BY Thomas's victory at Nashville the Confederate army of Tennessee had been eliminated from the problem of the war. After this event the continuance of the struggle on the part of the Confederate government involved a useless waste of human life. The interest of the war from this point is transferred to the East. With the exception of the conflict terminating in the capture of Mobile, there were, after the battle of Nashville, no great military operations in the West. We are therefore prepared to follow Sherman's March to the Sea, and thence to Goldsborough in North Carolina.

Since General Sherman had been given an independent command in the West, he had fully illustrated his characteristic qualities as a great captain. As a subordinate he had shown these qualities only in a limited degree, because in that capacity he could only display his power to execute operations which were conceived and planned by others. No officer had so completely won the confidence of General Grant. At Shiloh his military talents were so conspicuous that Grant afterward acknowledged that the final triumph of the national arms on that occasion was chiefly due to Sherman. Of course, in this acknowledgment, we must make large allowances on the score of General Grant's natural modesty; but, if he was modest, he was also just. Sherman's prompt and unquestioning obedience to the orders of his superior officer ought not, perhaps, to be remarkable, but it was, nevertheless. He was never behind time. His comprehension of the task assigned him made misconception or mistake impossible, and he never lacked in vigor of execution. It is true that he sometimes failed in the object sought. His assault on the Confederate works at Chickasaw Bayou has been frequently adduced as proof of his indiscretion. But it must be remembered, in the first place, that he was acting in obedience of positive orders, and, secondly, that he was ignorant of the failure that had attended General Grant's movement in the rear, and it was this latter circumstance alone which made the assault indiscreet, or its success impossible. The assault on Kenesaw has also been adduced for a similar purpose. But here, too, the critics have a losing case, unless they can withstand the testimony of General Thomas and the best officers of Sherman's army, who assert that success must have followed the attempt but for the fall of Harker and McCook at a critical moment. The popular conception of General Sherman is greatly at fault. It has been the fashion to accord him brilliancy of conception—great strategic powers—and to ignore those characteristic qualities of his mind without which his strategy would have been ludicrous and useless.

In the first place, a factitious distinction has been made between *strategy* and *tactics*, and Sherman has been pronounced a great strategist, but an inferior tactician. Strategy properly includes tactics. The commander who can so determine and control the movements of his army as to, in the surest way, and with the least friction and waste, accomplish the object in view, is a great strategist.[1] If we confine these movements to the disposition of an army upon the field of battle, then we have what is properly termed tactics. Of course the original conception of the object and plan of a campaign is back of both strategy and tactics, and depends upon the speculative side of military genius—the power of ideal combination. This power of combination *may* exist without the practical knowledge or experience necessary to successful strategy or to successful tactics. But this is rarely the case, for the very practicability of the theoretical scheme must be determined by a knowledge of the material elements involved. So also it might happen that a great strategist should not be a great tactician—that a commander might be successful in large movements, and fail in his combinations on the battlefield and in the presence of the foe. But such cases must of necessity be very exceptional; for the skillful disposition of an army on a large scale would naturally involve its skillful manipulation on a limited field of operations. The exception could only occur by reason of certain elements involved in actual battle which demand peculiar qualities in the commander. Thus a general might exhibit brilliant strategic powers in bringing his army upon a well-chosen field of battle, or in forcing a battle upon his antagonist, and yet utterly fail in the battle itself through a lack either of promptness or of self-control in the presence of the enemy. Certainly Sherman lacked none of the qualities demanded upon the battle-field. In what, then, did his poor tactics consist? Was it for his strategy or his tactics that Grant commended him at Shiloh? Or upon what battle-field did he illustrate his weakness in tactics? If the battle of Chickasaw Bayou was a failure, that certainly was not Sherman's fault. No general on earth could have succeeded there, and Sherman only obeyed orders in fighting there. Under the circumstances he had no discretion, any more than he had at Tunnel Hill, in the battle of Chattanooga. But if we consider the tactics displayed by Sherman in the Atlanta campaign, where he had an independent command, do we find him deficient? It is true that, at Resaca, Sherman failed to destroy Johnston's army, where that result was possible. But why? Simply because his orders were not executed. But the order given is to decide his tactical ability, and not its execution by a subordinate. Surely all the op-

---

[1] This is clear from the very etymology of the term *strategy*, which is from two Greek words—*stratos*, an army, and *ago*, to move.

Howard. Kilpatrick. Logan. Hazen. Sherman. Jeff. C. Davis. Slocum. Blair. Mower.

SHERMAN AND HIS GENERALS.

erations of the Atlanta campaign were tactical as well as strategic, and the success of these operations was as much due to skillful tactics as it was to skillful strategy.

It must be admitted that Johnston, by leaving open the approach to Resaca through Snake Creek Gap at the beginning of the campaign, afforded Sherman a splendid opportunity to destroy the Confederate army. And Sherman designed to accomplish this. He only failed through the excessive caution of McPherson. A similar opportunity was offered by Hood at the close of the Atlanta campaign by the division of his army. And here again, while Sherman's tactics were faultless, his subordinate officers failed him. But in both cases—at Resaca and Jonesborough—if Sherman's orders had been executed, the result would have involved the annihilation of the Confederate army.

It has also been said that Sherman could not organize and discipline an army. To this we only need reply that, so far as the purposes of war are concerned, Sherman's army was as well disciplined and efficient as any other. Beyond that it would be too curious to inquire.

General Sherman's conceptions were always bold, and his daring was only equaled by his confidence in ultimate success. No movement ever made by General Thomas or General Grant surpassed that by which Sherman transferred the bulk of his army to Jonesborough. Sherman was never vacillating or irresolute. His plans, once formed, were immutable. He was also as remarkable for discretion as for boldness. Thus his audacity never verged upon rashness. He was the Centaur general, being at once the fiery horse and the curbing rider. No pet military project could infatuate him. No better illustration of Sherman's caution can be given than his manner of undertaking the boldest movement of the war—his March to the Sea. With Hood in his front, he would not attempt the movement without an objective point on the coast already secured and awaiting his arrival. And even when Hood moved to the rear, leaving him an open path eastward, Sherman followed him, and, driving him far westward, waited and watched until he was over 200 miles west of Atlanta, and Thomas was prepared to meet his invasion.

Sherman's foresight was almost prophetic. At the beginning of the war he discerned the gigantic proportions which it would assume. He was laughed at, and thought insane, when he asserted that 200,000 men were necessary to prosecute the first great Western campaign; but time proved that he was right, and that the insanity with which he had been charged was lodged in other brains than his. He predicted Butler's failure at Fort Fisher. No military man ever had a clearer discernment between the practicable and the impracticable, or as to what might be accomplished with given means. He was as sure of the success of his grand march before he set out as when he reached its termination; he predicted the time of his arrival upon the coast, and anticipated the full effect of the movement in its bearings upon the war.

This foresight is not so strange when we consider Sherman's wonderful knowledge of the minute details of the conflict. He had been not only a careful student of military science, but also a careful observer of the country in which the war was conducted. He knew its mountains, its rivers, its railroads, its resources, and its people. His experience in regard to all these matters had been large before the war began, but since that time he had made them an especial study. What he once learned he never forgot. The movements of Cape Fear River were as well known to him as those of the Red River, upon whose banks he had lived. The whole Southern country was a grand chart before his mind; no geographical feature escaped him; he knew the natural products of each district, its population, its proportion of slaves, its cattle, its horses, its factories. This kind of knowledge his mind seemed to absorb and retain almost without effort. Yet, with all this attention to the *minutiæ* of campaigning, Sherman always based his plans upon general principles. Therefore, while he knew perfectly how to feed, march, and fight an army of a hundred thousand men, the conceptions which controled him in the use of this army, and which formed the basis of his campaign, were calculated to accomplish the grandest results possible with the means employed. Sherman's military economy, as illustrated in the Atlanta campaign, and the operations which were its natural sequel, will hereafter be to the military student the most instructive portion of the American Civil War. The greatest results were accomplished with the smallest possible waste of force.

Perhaps the most characteristic point of Sherman's generalship was his perfect appreciation of the American soldier and of the discipline best adapted to his peculiarities. He was *par eminence* the American general, and his army was the military microcosm of the republic, for the maintenance of which it fought and marched. Both on the part of the general and his army there was perfect military subordination; but there was, at the same time, absolute freedom from conventional or arbitrary restraint in minor details. The martial enthusiasm of the soldier was not held in check by petty restrictions. Sherman scouted the idea that the American army must be made a mere machine. In the place of a purely mechanical discipline he substituted one which recognized the intelligence, not only of his subordinate officers, but of every private in the army. To inspire his soldiers with his own ideas appeared to him a more efficient means of control than the establishment over them of a military autocracy. The result fully vindicated his peculiar mode of discipline. His army moved as if by inspiration; but its movements, like that of the tides, were mathematically accurate and certain. There was no lagging from the march, there was no shrinking from battle.

It was a grand moment for Sherman when he had been, by Hood's folly, released from his dependence upon the railroad in his rear. In the event of an advance upon an army in his front, this long line of communication was a serious and unavoidable perplexity. From Atlanta to Allatoona, Sherman's sub-base was 40 miles. Thence to Chattanooga was 98 miles. But Chattanooga itself was only a dépôt, and was exposed to siege and capture, unless a large portion of the army was detached for its protection. Thus Sherman's real base of supplies is pushed back to Nashville, 290 miles from Atlanta, and, in the case of a successful Confederate attack on Nashville, back to Louisville, nearly 500 miles. This perplexity, as we have seen, was removed by Hood's invasion of Tennessee; and by giving Thomas an army sufficient to meet Hood, Sherman was permitted to ignore his connection with the North, and move eastward with from 60,000 to 70,000 men.

On the 16th of November, Sherman's army, with the smoking ruins of Atlanta in his rear, began its great march.[1] The right wing of the army, under General Howard, with Kilpatrick's cavalry, was put in motion in the direction of Jonesborough, and McDonough, with orders to make a strong feint on Macon, to cross the Ocmulgee near Planter's Mills, and rendezvous in the neighborhood of Gordon in seven days. At the same time, Slocum, with the Twelfth Corps of the left wing, moved by Decatur, with orders to tear up the railroad from Social Circle to Madison, to burn the railroad bridge across the Oconee, east of Madison, and, turning south, to reach Milledgeville on the same day that Howard should reach Gordon. General Sherman in person accompanied Jeff. C. Davis's corps—the Fourteenth—on the road through Covington, directly to Milledgeville. All the troops were provided with good wagon trains, loaded with ammunition and supplies, approximating 20 days' bread, 40 days' sugar and coffee, with a double allowance of salt, and beef-cattle sufficient for 40 days' supplies. The wagons were supplied with three days' rations in grain. Each brigade commander was instructed to organize a foraging party, to gather near the route corn, forage, meat, and vegetables, aiming at all times to keep in the wagon trains at least 10 days' provisions and three days' forage. The cavalry was to receive orders direct from General Sherman. Soldiers were forbidden to enter the dwellings of the inhabitants or to commit any trespass, but were permitted, during a halt or when in camp, to gather vegetables, and to drive in stock in their front. On the march the gathering of provisions was to be left entirely to regular foraging parties. Army commanders were permitted to destroy mills, houses, cotton-gins, etc., but such destruction must only take place in regions where the army should be molested. Horses, mules, and wagons were to be appropriated as they were needed, but discrimination must be made in these captures, the rich rather than the poor being made the victims. No family was to be deprived of any thing necessary to its maintenance. Able-bodied negroes might be taken along, in so far as this would not cause embarrassment in the matter of supplies. The troops were to start each morning at 7 o'clock, and make about 15 miles per day.[2]

---

[1] Major Nichols thus describes the spectacle of Atlanta in flames: . "A grand and awful spectacle is presented to the beholder in this beautiful city, now in flames. By order, the chief engineer has destroyed by powder and fire all the store-houses, dépôt buildings, and machine-shops. The heaven is one expanse of lurid fire; the air is filled with flying, burning cinders; buildings covering two hundred acres are in ruins or in flames: every instant there is the sharp detonation or the smothered booming sound of exploding shells and powder concealed in the buildings, and then the sparks and flame shoot away up into the black and red roof, scattering cinders far and wide.

"These are the machine-shops where have been forged and cast the rebel cannon, shot and shell that have carried death to many a brave defender of our nation's honor. These warehouses have been the receptacle of munitions of war, stored to be used for our destruction. The city, which, next to Richmond, has furnished more material for prosecuting the war than any other in the South, exists no more as a means for injury to be used by the enemies of the Union.

"A brigade of Massachusetts soldiers are the only troops now left in the town: they will be the last to leave it. To-night I heard the really fine band of the Thirty-third Massachusetts playing 'John Brown's soul goes marching on,' by the light of the burning buildings. I have never heard that noble anthem when it was so grand, so solemn, so inspiring."

[2] The following is a copy of the general orders for the march, issued by General Sherman at Kingston, November 9th:

"I. For the purpose of military operations, this army is divided into two wings, viz., the right wing, Major General O. O. Howard commanding, the Fifteenth and Seventeenth Corps; the left wing, Major General H. W. Slocum commanding, the Fourteenth and Twentieth Corps.

"II. The habitual order of march will be, whenever practicable, by four roads, as nearly parallel

ATLANTA IN RUINS.

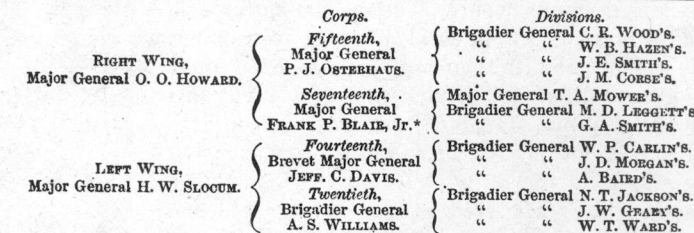

JUDSON C. KILPATRICK.

The line of march of the several corps of Sherman's army we shall not attempt to follow in detail, but will merely trace the general features of the movement. In the first place, it must be distinctly asserted that Sherman's

as possible, and converging at points hereafter to be indicated in orders. The cavalry, Brigadier General Kilpatrick commanding, will receive special orders from the commander-in-chief.

"III. There will be no general trains of supplies, but each corps will have its ammunition and provision train, distributed habitually as follows: Behind each regiment should follow one wagon and one ambulance; behind each brigade should follow a due proportion of ammunition wagons, provision wagons and ambulances. In case of danger, each army corps should change this order of march by having his advance and rear brigade unencumbered by wheels. The separate columns will start habitually at seven A.M., and make about fifteen miles per day, unless otherwise fixed in orders.

"IV. The army will forage liberally on the country during the march. To this end, each brigade commander will organize a good and sufficient foraging party, under the command of one or more discreet officers, who will gather near the route traveled corn or forage of any kind, meat of any kind, vegetables, corn meal, or whatever is needed by the command; aiming at all times to keep in the wagon trains at least ten days' provisions for the command and three days' forage. Soldiers must not enter the dwellings of the inhabitants or commit any trespass; during the halt or a camp they may be permitted to gather turnips, potatoes, and other vegetables, and drive in stock in front of their camps. To regular foraging parties must be intrusted the gathering of provisions and forage at any distance from the road traveled.

"V. To army corps commanders is intrusted the power to destroy mills, houses, cotton-gins, etc., and for them this general principle is laid down: In districts and neighborhoods where the army is unmolested, no destruction of such property should be permitted; but should guerrillas or bushwhackers molest our march, or should the inhabitants burn bridges, obstruct roads, or otherwise manifest local hostility, then army corps commanders should order and enforce a devastation more or less relentless, according to the measure of such hostility.

"VI. As for horses, mules, wagons, etc., belonging to the inhabitants, the cavalry and artillery may appropriate freely and without limit; discriminating, however, between the rich, who are usually hostile, and the poor or industrious, who are usually neutral or friendly. Foraging parties may also take mules or horses to replace the jaded animals of their trains, or to serve as pack mules for the regiments or brigades. In all foraging, of whatever kind, the parties engaged will refrain from abusive or threatening language, and may, when the officer in command thinks proper, give written certificates of the facts, but no receipts; and they will endeavor to leave with each family a reasonable portion for their maintenance.

"VII. Negroes who are able-bodied, and can be of service to the several columns, may be taken along; but each army commander will bear in mind that the question of supplies is a very important one, and that his first duty is to see to those who bear arms.

"VIII. The organization at once of a good pioneer battalion for each corps, composed, if possible, of negroes, should be attended to. This battalion should follow the advance-guard, should repair roads and double them if possible, so that the columns will not be delayed after reaching bad places. Also, army commanders should study the habit of giving the artillery and wagons the road, and marching their troops on one side; and also instruct their troops to assist wagons at steep hills or bad crossings of streams.

"IX. Captain O. M. Poe, Chief Engineer, will assign to each wing of the army a pontoon train, fully equipped and organized, and the commanders thereof will see to its being properly protected at all times."

Sherman's army on the march, besides Kilpatrick's cavalry, 5500 strong, included the following forces:

march was not simply "a big raid." It accomplished all the purposes of a raid—the destruction of railroads and supplies. The large force with which Sherman marched of course more effectually accomplished these purposes than could have been done by a cavalry expedition. To destroy the railroads by which Georgia was connected with the Carolinas and with Virginia, and to consume the supplies upon which the Confederate armies depended, was a very important object. But, after all, this was only incidental. The Grand March was at once a magnificent raid and a decisive campaign. Sherman was conducting offensive operations against Lee's army, threatening his rear and flank.

Again, it was not Sherman's object to capture important strategic points upon his route to Savannah. Macon and Augusta were the main points likely to be defended by the enemy. Sherman could not afford to delay his columns in consideration of the results to be gained by the capture of either place; accordingly, he determined to demonstrate against each and avoid both. Kilpatrick, therefore, until the army was past Macon, kept on the right flank, and from that point covered the left wing, demonstrating against Augusta. Sherman's line of march followed the Georgia Central Railroad, covering a wide belt on either side, and, east of Louisville, extended over the entire tract—the most fertile in Georgia—between the Ogeechee and Savannah Rivers.

On the 23d of November Slocum occupied Milledgeville, the capital of Georgia, and Howard had reached Gordon. Slocum gained possession of

	Corps.	Divisions.
Right Wing, Major General O. O. Howard.	Fifteenth, Major General P. J. Osterhaus.	Brigadier General C. R. Wood's. " " W. B. Hazen's. " " J. E. Smith's. " " J. M. Corse's.
	Seventeenth, Major General Frank P. Blair, Jr.*	Major General T. A. Mower's. Brigadier General M. D. Leggett's. " " G. A. Smith's.
Left Wing, Major General H. W. Slocum.	Fourteenth, Brevet Major General Jeff. C. Davis.	Brigadier General W. P. Carlin's. " " J. D. Morgan's. " " A. Baird's.
	Twentieth, Brigadier General A. S. Williams.	Brigadier General N. T. Jackson's. " " J. W. Geary's. " " W. T. Ward's.

Brigadier General Judson C. Kilpatrick's cavalry division consisted of two brigades, commanded by Colonels Eli H. Murray and Smith D. Atkins.

* Brigadier General T. E. G. Ransom had commanded this corps during the pursuit of Hood, though suffering from a severe attack of dysentery, and too weak to mount his horse. He died at Rome, October 29, 1864, aged thirty years.

EXTERIOR VIEW OF THE PRISON PEN AT MILLEN.

INTERIOR VIEW OF THE PRISON PEN AT MILLEN.

DESTRUCTION OF MILLEN JUNCTION.

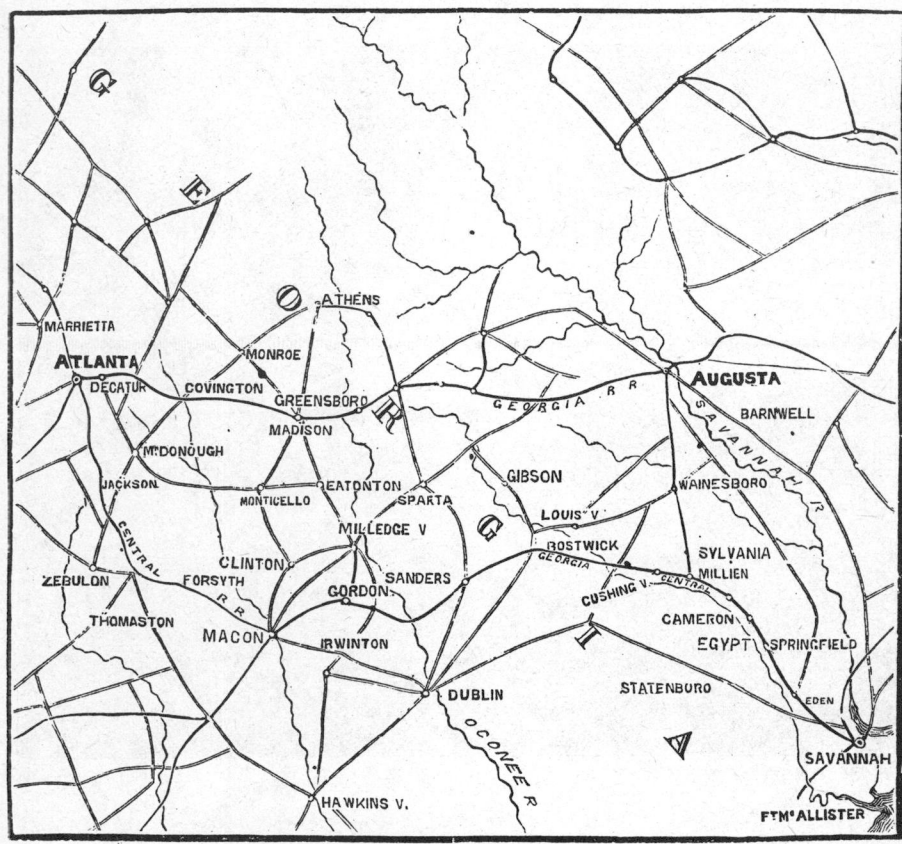

MAP ILLUSTRATING THE MARCH TO THE SEA.

cold ground, while near by lay the graves of 700 dead, marked only by head-boards designating them by the fifties.

By the last of November Sherman's army had crossed the Ogeechee River. still covered by Kilpatrick's cavalry—an impenetrable cloud to the enemy. The railroad was destroyed all along the line of march.[1] In the mean while the Confederates have been predicting the ruin of Sherman's army: They do not seem to have had any accurate knowledge of its numbers. Hood and Beauregard estimated it as about 36,000 strong. In the North there was great anxiety for Sherman's fate. Both the confidence of the enemy and the apprehensions of the loyal are indications of the impression which then prevailed as to the audacity of Sherman's movement.

After Sherman crossed the Ogeechee there was no opportunity for the enemy to oppose his march to the city of Savannah. "No opposition from the enemy worth speaking of," says Sherman, "was encountered until the heads of the columns were within fifteen miles of Savannah, where all the roads leading to the city were obstructed more or less by felled timber, with earth-works and artillery. But these were easily turned and the enemy driven away, so that by the 10th of December the enemy was driven within his lines at Savannah." There were five approaches to the city—the two railroads and three dirt pikes—but they were narrow causeways through otherwise impassable swamps, and were strongly guarded by artillery. The entrance of the Ogeechee River to Ossibaw Sound was guarded by Fort McAllister. To invest the city and to reduce this fort, so as to command an outlet to the sea, were the next things to be accomplished. Admiral Dahlgren's fleet was awaiting Sherman off Tybee, Warsaw, and Ossibaw Sounds; and, although the latter had an abundant supply of beef-cattle and breadstuffs, still he held it of the utmost importance that he should connect with the fleet outside. Captain Duncan, one of Howard's best scouts, had passed down the Ogeechee in a canoe to Dahlgren's fleet, giving full information of Sherman's present situation. But, in order to establish a line of communication with the sea by way of the Ogeechee River, it was necessary to reduce Fort McAllister.

the bridge across the Oconee. The day before, a force of the enemy, consisting mainly of Cobb's militia, had advanced from Macon to Griswoldville, and attacked Walcott's infantry brigade and a portion of Kilpatrick's cavalry, but was severely punished, losing over 2000 men. In this affair General Walcott was wounded. A few days before Slocum's occupation of Milledgeville, the State Legislature, then assembled at the capital, had hurriedly absconded on hearing of Sherman's approach. The panic seems to have spread to the citizens, and the trains out of Milledgeville were crowded to overflowing, and at the most extravagant prices private vehicles were also pressed into service by the fugitives. Only a few of the Union troops entered Milledgeville. The magazines, arsenals, dépôts, factories, and storehouses, containing property belonging to the Confederate government, were burned; also some 1700 bales of cotton. Private dwellings were respected, and no instances occurred of pillage or of insult to the citizens. Sherman occupied the executive mansion of Governor Brown, who had not waited to receive the compliments of his distinguished visitor, but had removed his furniture, taking good care, it is said, to ship even his cabbages.

Slocum continued his progress eastward, crossing the Oconee, when it was discovered that Wheeler, with a large body of Confederate cavalry, had also crossed, and was covering the approaches to Sandersville, to which point he was driven by the advancing Federal column. On the 26th the Fourteenth and Twentieth Corps entered the town. Howard, in the mean time, accomplished the passage of the Oconee lower down, in the face of a Confederate cavalry force under Wayne, and proceeded to Tennille Station, opposite Sandersville.

Before reaching Milledgeville, Kilpatrick had been ordered to move rapidly eastward to break the railroad from Augusta to Millen, and, turning upon the latter place, to rescue the Union prisoners there confined. He skirmished with Wheeler all the way to Waynesborough, destroying there the railroad bridge across Brier Creek, between Augusta and Millen. But at Millen he found only the empty prison pens in which the Union soldiers had been confined. For some time past the Confederates had been removing these prisoners to points far remote from Sherman's line of march. But they had left behind the traces of their cruel neglect. The corpses of several of those who had died in the prison were found yet unburied on the

CAPITOL AT MILLEDGEVILLE.

To Hazen's division of the Fifteenth Corps was allotted this work. On the 13th of December this division crossed to the southwest bank of the Ogeechee. The fort was commanded by Major Anderson, who had a garrison of about 200 men; it was mounted by 23 guns *en barbette*, and one mortar. As Hazen was crossing the Ogeechee, Generals Sherman and Howard went to Dr. Cheves's rice-mill on the river bank, whence they had a full view of the fort. About noon they heard the guns of the fort open inland, and Hazen's skirmishers were seen firing in response. By means of signals, Hazen was ordered to take the work that day, if possible. He soon accomplished his mission. The guns, being *en barbette*, were not available for defense. With a loss of only about 90 men, the Union troops carried the work by assault and captured the garrison. That very night Sherman and Howard, in a small boat, passed down the river to the fort, and thence down to a steamer which during the conflict had passed up from the fleet within view of the army.

[1] "The destruction of railroads in this campaign has been most thorough. The work of demolition on such long lines of road necessarily requires time, but the process is performed as expeditiously as possible, in order to prevent any serious delay of the movement of the army. The method of destruction is simple, but very effective. Two ingenious instruments have been made for this purpose. One of them is a clasp, which locks under the rail. It has a ring in the top, into which is inserted a long lever, and the rail is thus ripped from the sleepers. The sleepers are then piled in a heap and set on fire, the rails roasting in the flames until they bend by their own weight. When sufficiently heated, each rail is taken off by wrenches fitting closely over the ends, and, by turning in opposite directions, it is so twisted that even a rolling-machine could not bring it back into shape. In this manner we have destroyed thirty miles of rail which lay in the city of Atlanta, and all on the Augusta and Atlanta Road from the last-named place to Madison, besides the entire track of the Central Georgia line, from a point a few miles east of Macon to the station where I am now writing."—*Nichols's Story of the Great March.*

FORT McALLISTER.

ASSAULT ON FORT McALLISTER.

WILLIAM B. HAZEN.

By the route thus opened abundant supplies were soon brought from Hilton Head, and heavy ordnance for the reduction of Savannah. Sherman's army had already invested the city, shutting up every avenue of supply, and the only possible way of retreat left to General Hardee, who now, with about 10,000 men, mostly militia, conducted the defense of Savannah, was in the northeast toward Charleston. On the 17th General Sherman demanded the surrender of the city. He wrote to Hardee that he held all the avenues by which Savannah was supplied, and that if the city was surrendered he would grant liberal terms to the garrison, while, if he was compelled to assault, or depend upon the slower process of starvation, he should feel justified in resorting to the harshest measures, and should make little effort to restrain his army, "burning to avenge the great national wrong

they attach to Savannah and other large cities, which have been so prominent in dragging our country into civil war." To this communication Sherman added: "I inclose you a copy of General Hood's demand for the surrender of the town of Resaca, to be used by you for what it is worth."

General Hardee declined to surrender on the ground that he still maintained his line of defense, and was in communication with his superior officer. In order to complete the investment of Savannah on the north, and across the plank road on the South Carolina shore, known as the "Union causeway," it would be necessary for Sherman to throw his left across the Savannah River. This would be scarcely safe, since the enemy still held the river opposite the city with gun-boats, and could easily destroy the pontoon bridge and isolate any force which might cross to that side. General Foster, with Admiral Dahlgren's co-operation, had established a division of troops on the narrow neck between the Coosawatchee and Tullifiny Creeks, at the head of Broad River, threatening the Savannah and Charleston Railroad, which was within easy range of his artillery. On the 20th Sherman started for Port Royal by water to confer with Foster and Dahlgren. He intended to increase the forces operating up Broad River, which would thus be able to break the railroad, and then turn upon the single line of retreat held by Hardee. He left instructions for his army commanders to prepare for an attack on the enemy's lines before Savannah.

But, before Sherman's arrangements were concluded, Hardee evacuated the city, retreating to Charleston, and on the morning of the 21st the Federal army took possession of the enemy's lines. The next morning Sherman, having returned up the Ogeechee, rode into the city of Savannah. Then, in a brief note to President Lincoln, Sherman thus announced the termination of his campaign:

"I beg to present you, as a Christmas gift, the city of Savannah, with 150 heavy guns and plenty of ammunition, and also about 25,000 bales of cotton."

Between the 16th of November and the 10th of December, Sherman's entire army had marched 255 miles.[1] For the greater portion of the army, the march really commenced at Rome and Kingston, and extended over 300 miles. The railroads had been rendered completely useless along the line of march, and a belt of country from Atlanta to Savannah, thirty miles wide, had been exhausted of supplies. If we include the devastation involved in the Atlanta campaign, Sherman's immense army had spread itself over more than one third of the State of Georgia. Georgia, as a feeder of the Confederacy, had been wholly annihilated. Sherman estimates the damage done to the state as fully $100,000,000, one fifth of which had been of use to his

[1] It is 190 miles in a straight line from Atlanta to Savannah. The following is a table of distances on the road followed by the Twentieth Corps:

	Miles.		Miles.
Atlanta to Decatur	7	Milledgeville to Hebron	18
Decatur to Rockbridge	14	Hebron to Sandersville	10
Rockbridge to Sheffield	13	Sandersville to Davisboro'	10
Sheffield to Social Circle	14	Davisboro' to Louisville	12
Social Circle to Rutledge	7	Louisville to Millen	30
Rutledge to Madison	9	Millen to Springfield	30
Madison to Eatonton	20	Springfield to Savannah	30
Eatonton to Milledgeville	21	Atlanta to Savannah	255

SHERMAN'S ARMY ENTERING SAVANNAH.

FORT JACKSON, SAVANNAH.

REBELS EVACUATING SAVANNAH, DEC. 20, 1864.

CONFEDERATES EVACUATING SAVANNAH.

own army, and the rest sheer waste and destruction. "This," he adds, "may seem a hard species of warfare, but it brings the sad realities of war home to those who have been directly or indirectly instrumental in involving us in its attendant calamities." About 7000 negroes followed the march through to the coast, and General Slocum estimates that as many more joined the Federal columns, but through weakness or old age were unable to hold out to the end. Over 10,000 horses and mules were captured on the march. A large quantity of cotton, estimated at about 20,000 bales, was destroyed before reaching Savannah. As regards the provisions captured, the estimate given is almost incredible, including 10,000,000 pounds of corn, and an equal amount of fodder. Slocum reports the capture of 1,217,527 rations of meat, 919,000 of bread, 483,000 of coffee, 581,534 of sugar, 1,146,500 of soap, and

137,000 of salt. Howard estimates the breadstuffs, beef, sugar, and coffee captured by the Fifteenth and Seventeenth corps as amounting in value, at the government cost of rations at Louisville, to $283,202.[1]

The grand prize of the campaign, however, was the city of Savannah. This was indeed a precious "Christmas gift" to the nation. It had been gained—if we count out the assault on Fort McAllister—without a battle. The whole number of casualties on the march had not amounted to 1000 in killed and wounded. With Savannah were captured 25,000 bales of cotton, and, as was found on a careful reckoning, about 200 guns. The city was almost impregnable against a purely naval attack. Both the north and the south branch of the Savannah River, at the head of Elba Island, were obstructed by a double line of cribs, to remove which, so as to allow a channel in each branch a little over 100 feet wide, occupied the navy for

[1] Howard's report includes the following statistics of property captured and destroyed, negroes freed, and prisoners taken by the right wing:

Negroes set free (estimated number)..............................		3,000
Prisoners captured.—By Fifteenth Army Corps:		
Commissioned officers..	32	
Enlisted men..	515	547
By Seventeenth Army Corps:		
Commissioned officers..	2	
Enlisted men..	117	119
Total prisoners captured.................................		666
Escaped Federal prisoners:		
Commissioned officers..	6	
Enlisted men..	43	49
Bales of cotton burned...		3,523
Ocmulgee Mills, 1500. Spindles and large amount of cotton cloth burned, value not known.		
Subsistence captured; namely, breadstuffs, beef, sugar, and coffee, at government cost of ration in Louisville................................		$283,202
Command started from Atlanta with head cattle.....................	1,000	
Took up as captured...	10,500	11,500
Consumed on the trip..	9,000	
Balance on hand December 18, 1864.............................		2,500
Horses captured.—By the Fifteenth Army Corps.....................	369	
By the Seventeenth Army Corps.................................	562	931
Mules captured.—By the Fifteenth Army Corps......................	786	
By the Seventeenth Army Corps.................................	1,064	1,850
Corn.—By the Fifteenth Army Corps........................lbs.	2,500,000	
By the Seventeenth Army Corps............................"	2,000,000	4,500,000
Fodder.—By the Fifteenth Army Corps......................"	2,500,000	
By the Seventeenth Army Corps............................"	2,000,000	4,500,000
Miles of railroad destroyed....................................		191

Slocum's report gives the following estimate for the left wing:

"It was thirty-four days from the date my command left Atlanta to the day supplies were received from the fleet. The total number of rations required during this period was 1,360,000. Of this amount there were issued by the Subsistence Department 440,900 rations of bread, 142,473 rations of meat, 876,800 of coffee and tea, 778,466 of sugar, 213,500 of soap, and 1,123,000 of salt. As the troops were well supplied at all times, if we deduct the above issues from the amount actually due the soldiers, we have the approximate quantities taken from the country, namely, rations of bread, 919,000; meat, 1,217,527; coffee, 483,000; sugar, 581,534; soap, 1,146,500; salt, 137,000. The above is the actual saving to the government in issue of rations during the campaign, and it is probable that even more than the equivalent of the above supplies was obtained by the soldiers from the country. Four thousand and ninety (4090) valuable horses and mules were captured during the march, and turned over to the Quartermaster's Department. Our transportation was in far better condition on our arrival at Savannah than it was at the commencement of the campaign.

"The average number of horses and mules with my command, including those of the pontoon train and a part of the Michigan engineers, was fourteen thousand five hundred. We started from Atlanta with four days' grain in wagons. Estimating the amount fed the animals at the regulation allowance, and deducting the amount on hand on leaving Atlanta, I estimate the amount of grain taken from the country at five million pounds; fodder, six million pounds; besides the forage consumed by the immense herds of cattle that were driven with the different columns. It is very difficult to estimate the amount of damage done the enemy by the operations of the troops under my command. During the campaign one hundred and nineteen miles (119) of railroad were thoroughly and effectually destroyed, scarcely a tie or rail, a bridge or culvert, on the entire line being left in a condition to be of use again. At Rutledge, Madison, Eatonton, Milledgeville, Tensnille, and Davisboro', machine-shops, turn-tables, dépôts, water-tanks, and much other valuable property was destroyed. The quantity of cotton destroyed is estimated by my subordinate commanders at seventeen thousand bales. A very large number of cotton-gins and presses were also destroyed.

"Negro men, women, and children joined the column at every mile of our march, many of them bringing horses and mules, which they cheerfully turned over to the officers of the Quartermaster's Department. I think at least fourteen thousand of these people joined the two columns at different points on the march; but many of them were too old and infirm, and others too young, to endure the fatigues of the march, and were therefore left in the rear. More than one half of the above number, however, reached the coast with us. Many of the able-bodied men were transferred to the officers of the Quartermaster and Subsistence Departments, and others were employed in the two corps as teamsters, cooks, and servants."

nearly three weeks. These obstructions were commanded by four works—Forts Lee and Jackson, Battery Lawton, and a water battery—mounted with 26 heavy guns, of which 13 were Columbiads. The river is so completely lined with marshes that the attack in front could have no co-operation from troops on either side. To guard against the approach by St. Augustine Creek there were also formidable batteries—Turner's Rocks, Thunderbolt, and Barton, with its outpost Causton's Bluff—mounting 34 heavy cannon; and obstructions were sunk in the narrow channel of the creek. But this entire net-work of defenses could be turned by troops landing on the Vernon and Ogeechee Rivers. To prevent this, the former was closed with obstructions commanded by Fort Beaulieu, 9 guns, while Big Ogeechee, in addition to the obstructions, was guarded by Fort McAllister with 23 guns. On the Little Ogeechee stood Fort Rosedew, with 6 guns. In the land works around the city there were 116 cannon of less calibre. Altogether the defensive works of Savannah mounted 229 cannon. It is clear, therefore, that, without a great sacrifice of life, Savannah could not have been captured in any other way than that adopted by General Sherman.

In justice to General Sherman and to the United States government, it is necessary that we should, in our comments upon the Great March, allude to the conduct of the army. It must be candidly admitted that many outrages were committed, or, to use the words of General Sherman, his soldiers "did some things they ought not to have done." We can safely affirm, however, that, with the same opportunities for wantonness, no European and no other American army would have accomplished the march with less violence. The only way in which outrage could have been absolutely prevented by the commander would have been the disbandment before the march of every soldier who would, under strong temptation, disobey the Decalogue. It is simply nonsense to attribute the violence of scattered foraging parties to the lack of discipline in Sherman's army. The strictest orders were given forbidding soldiers to enter the dwellings of the inhabitants, or to commit any trespass. If General Sherman could have been every where present these orders would have been obeyed. It must be remembered that whatever supplies could in any way assist the Confederates in prolonging the war were a legitimate prize. In many cases there was wanton plunder. Many of the wealthy planters had fled suddenly on the approach of Sherman's army, and had hastily concealed their treasures of gold, silver, and precious stones in the earth. Aided by the disclosures of the negroes, these places were diligently sought and rifled wherever opportunity offered. This gave color to extravagant reports, which had no other basis of credibility than the imagination of those who circulated them. But the violence actually perpetrated was far less than, under the circumstances, might have been expected. While we do not exculpate the wrong, we entirely exonerate General Sherman in the matter. No restrictions imposed by discipline would have prevented the evil done; and that there was no serious want of discipline in Sherman's army is clearly shown by the promptness with which the march was accomplished, and the perfect efficiency of the army as an organization when it reached Savannah. This would have been impossible if the army had not been held under restraint. There is universal and undisputed testimony that, in connection with the occupation of Savannah, there was no breach of good order.[1]

[1] In regard to this, General Sherman reports: "The behavior of our troops in Savannah has been so manly, so quiet, so perfect, that I take it as the best evidence of discipline and true courage. Never was a hostile city, filled with women and children, occupied by a large army with less disorder, or more system, order, and good government. The same general and generous spirit of confidence and good feeling pervades the army which it has ever afforded me especial pleasure to report on former occasions."

SHERMAN'S HEADQUARTERS AT SAVANNAH.

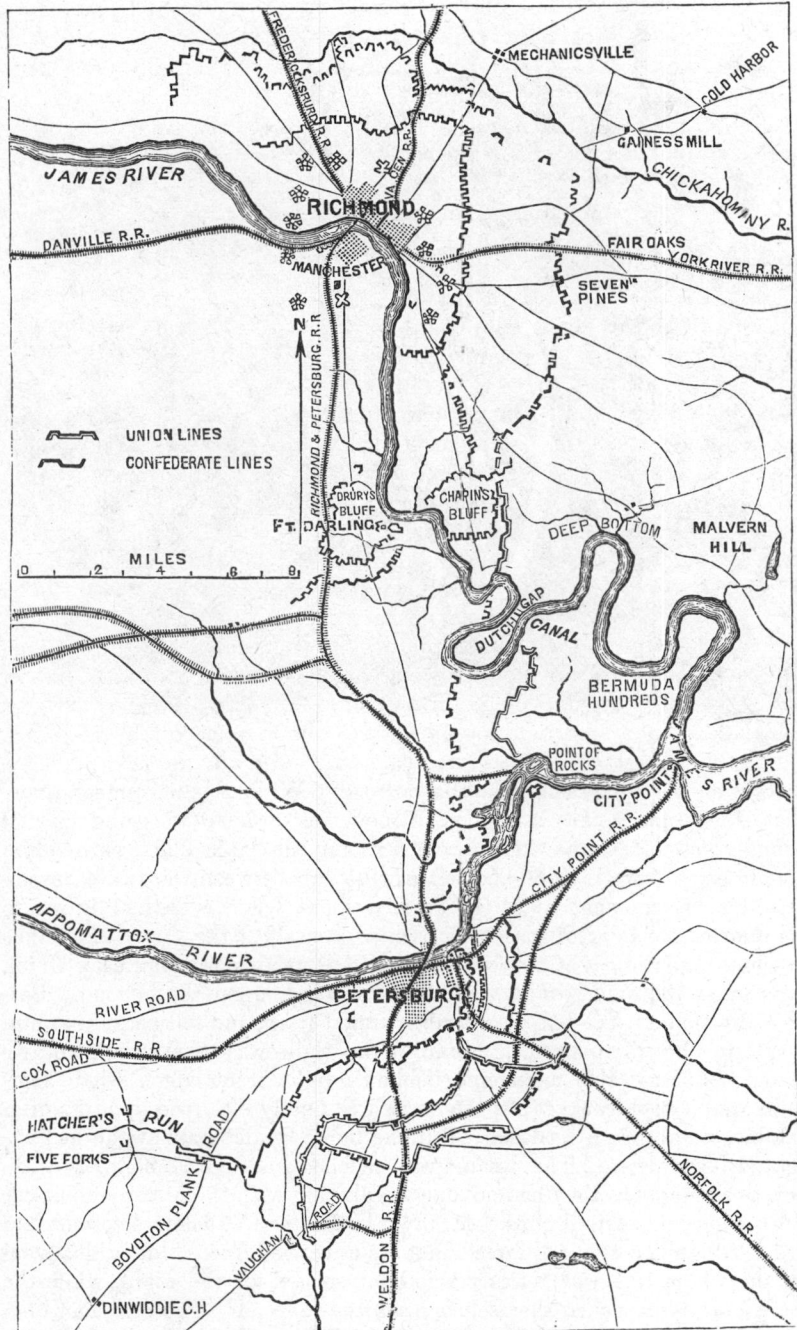

THE LINES AT PETERSBURG AND RICHMOND.

CHAPTER XLIX.

THE SIEGE OF PETERSBURG.

Opening of the Siege.—Strategic Relations of Petersburg and Richmond.—The Defenses of Richmond.—The Confederate Commissariat.—The Weldon, Southside, and Danville Railroads.—Birney and Wright's Attempt on the Weldon Road.—Character of the Region.—Hill drives back Birney, and is repulsed.—Anderson assails Wright.—Results of the Movement.—Wilson and Kautz's Cavalry Raid.—They cut the Railroads.—Are assailed, and return with Loss.—Results of the Expedition.—The Financial Effects of the Destruction of the Railroads.—Condition of the Federal Army.—Early sent to the Shenandoah.—Grant demonstrates before Richmond.—Burnside's Mine before Petersburg.—Grant resolves to assail the Confederate Works.—Condition of Burnside's Corps.—He wishes to put the Colored Division in Front.—This is refused by Meade and Grant.—The leading Division chosen by Lot.—Delay in the Explosion of the Mine.—The Explosion.—Burnside's Plan of Assault.—The Assault after the Explosion.—The Confederates paralyzed.—They rally.—Potter attempts to advance.—Meade orders a general Assault.—Advance and Repulse of the Colored Division.—Meade orders a Withdrawal.—Losses at the Mine.—The Opinions of the Court of Inquiry.—Grant's Opinion as to the Causes of the Failure.—The Situation after the Mine Failure.—Lee re-enforces Early.—Grant again demonstrates North of the James.—The Operation fails.—Warren's Movement against the Weldon Railroad.—Warren holds the Road.—Hancock's Movement upon Reams's Station.—The Action.—Both Parties withdraw.—Prisoners and Deserters.—Period of Repose.—Assaults upon Forts Harrison and Gilmer.—Fight at Peebles's Farm.—First Movement upon Hatcher's Run.—Butler's Co-operative Movement.—The Army in Winter Quarters.—The Dutch Gap Canal.—Warren destroys the Weldon Railroad.—Raid of the Confederate Iron-clads.—Another Movement upon Hatcher's Run.

THE fatal misapprehension and delay of the 15th of June forfeited the golden opportunity when Petersburg, defended only by a mere handful, would have fallen at a touch. During the next three days it had been demonstrated, at a cost of 10,000 men, that its improvised defenses had become so strong, and were so strongly held, as to preclude all hope of carrying them by assault. This siege could be conducted only by gaining the avenues through which the defending army received its supplies. Richmond itself was even more impregnable to direct assault than Petersburg, for the elaborate system of works by which it was encircled had been the leisurely work of two years. The James River, coming in from the west, makes a sharp bend, almost a right angle, to the south. Here, on the north bank, at the head of navigation, stands Richmond. The river runs straight northward for ten miles, then turns eastward, and, after a tortuous course, alternating to every point of the compass, receives the Appomattox at City Point. The Appomattox, coming also from the west, bends northward. At this bend, upon the southern bank, stands Petersburg. The Appomattox approaches within three miles of the James, at the point where it makes its eastward turn; then bends to the east, running parallel with the James, which at length turns southwestward to meet it. The peninsula inclosed by these rivers is styled Bermuda Hundred; it is of irregular shape, from six

8 N

to ten miles in either direction. Here, upon the northern bank of the Appomattox and the southern bank of the James, lay the Army of the James, shut in upon the landward side by the Confederate lines thrown up across the narrow neck of the peninsula. The Army of the Potomac lay upon the south bank of the Appomattox, over which had been thrown pontoon bridges, which, with the gun-boats, afforded ready means of connection between the two armies. Richmond and Petersburg were thus separated by the two rivers; but bridges at the two cities, and pontoons across the James ten miles below Richmond, enabled an army to pass without interruption from one to the other. The cities are connected by a railroad and highway running parallel with the James and Appomattox at the distance of a mile or two. The rivers, except for the space of three miles across the neck of the peninsula at Bermuda Hundred, effectually covered the Confederate line from any assault from either of the Federal armies. Had the Confederate works across the isthmus been taken, a way would have been opened for a direct assault upon the line of the railway. This, if successful, would have severed the connections of Richmond with the south as effectually as would have been done by the capture of Petersburg. This might easily have been done on the 16th, for during that day Beauregard had abandoned these works, and for hours they were occupied only by a few sentries. An attempt was indeed made to occupy these lines on that day; they were held for hours by a mere picket-guard, and the failure to retain them forms a conspicuous part of the first ill-judged operations around Petersburg.[1] This opportunity lost was never again presented. Thereafter no attempt was made to disturb the communications between Petersburg and Richmond.

The defenses of Richmond had long been complete. The exterior line, not in itself very strong except at one or two points, covered the city on the east at a distance varying from four to ten miles, terminating on the south at Chapin's Bluff, on the north bank of the James, opposite to which, on the south bank, is Fort Darling, which effectually bars the passage of the river. From this fort a line of works was extended westward across the railroad. This exterior line, saving at its southern extremity, was never occupied in force. Kilpatrick and Sheridan, in their raids, rode through it, back and forth, but were brought up before the inner line. This line enveloped the city, at a distance of about two miles, from the northeast to the southwest, both extremities resting upon the James, which completed the circuit. The works, extending fully ten miles, were never assailed. They were never even seen by any part of the Union army, save the cavalry, until they were finally abandoned. During the long siege, really of Richmond, though apparently of Petersburg, it is doubtful whether any Federal soldier, save as a prisoner, ever caught sight of the spires of the Confederate capital, or whether the noise of the great battles which were waged for its defense were ever heard in its streets.

Richmond, as fortified, was clearly invulnerable to assault, and could be held so long as the great army which defended it could be fed. But, as has been seen, the capture of Petersburg would involve the loss of the avenues of supply for that army, which must then, of necessity, abandon Richmond. But, as matters stood during the summer and autumn of 1864, the abandonment of Richmond involved the probability of the speedy disbandment of the Army of Northern Virginia. Not only would the abandonment of Richmond be looked upon as the virtual surrender of the cause, but there was then no point in Virginia or the Carolinas at which sufficient supplies could be concentrated. Richmond was the focus upon which converged all the lines of railway from the producing regions, which were soon practically reduced to portions of the states of Georgia, Alabama, and Mississippi. What with the ravages of both armies, the conscription of every able-bodied man, thus reducing the area planted, and finally the general failure of crops, Virginia was practically exhausted.[2] Supplies from these distant and widely spread regions, and from abroad through the port of Wilmington, could reach the army only over the Weldon, Southside, and Danville railways. These, then, were the vital and assailable points of attack; and to gain these, not the intrenchments which guarded the two cities, or rather fortified camps, was the aim of Grant. To hold these, not to waste his strength in

1 "On the 16th the enemy, to re-enforce Petersburg, withdrew from a part of his intrenchments in front of Bermuda Hundred [that they withdrew entirely from these intrenchments is shown by Fletcher, vol. iii., 260; referred to ante, p. 640], expecting, no doubt, to get troops from the north of the James to take the place of those withdrawn before we could discover it. General Butler, taking advantage of this, at once moved a force on the railroad between Petersburg and Richmond. As soon as I was apprised of the advantage thus gained, to retain it I at once ordered two divisions of the Sixth Corps, General Wright commanding, to report to General Butler at Bermuda Hundred, of which General Butler was notified, and the importance of holding a position in advance of his present line urged upon him. About two o'clock in the afternoon General Butler was forced back to the line the enemy was forced from in the morning. General Wright, with his two divisions, joined General Butler on the morning of the 17th, the latter still holding with a strong picket line the enemy's works. But, instead of putting these divisions into the enemy's works to hold them, he permitted them to halt and rest some distance in the rear of his own line. Between four and five o'clock in the afternoon the enemy attacked and drove in his pickets, and reoccupied his old line."—Grant's Report.

2 See Pollard, Lost Cause, 648.—In October, before Sherman's march had cut off the supplies from Georgia, the chief of the Bureau of Subsistence reported to President Davis: "The commissariat is in an alarming condition. Georgia, Alabama, and Mississippi are the only states where we have an accumulation, and from these all the armies of the Confederacy are now subsisting, to say nothing of the prisoners. The chief commissary of Georgia telegraphs that he can not send forward another pound. Alabama, under the most urgent call, has recently shipped 125,000 pounds, but can not ship more. Mississippi is rendering all the aid possible to the command of General Beauregard in supplying beef: she is without bacon. South Carolina is scarcely able to subsist the troops at Charleston and the prisoners in the interior of the state. During my late visit to North Carolina I visited every section of the state for the purpose of ascertaining the true condition of affairs, and under your orders to send forward every pound of meat possible to the Army of Northern Virginia, and to supply the forts at Wilmington; I was unable to ship one pound to either Virginia or Wilmington. We have on hand in the Confederate States 4,105,048 rations of fresh meat, and 3,426,519 rations of beef and pork, which will subsist 300,000 men twenty-five days. We are now compelled to subsist, independent of the armies of the Confederacy, the prisoners of war, the Navy Department, and the different bureaus of the War Department."—This statement was furnished in the autumn, after the harvests had been gathered. Before that time the state of things could not have been better in this respect. Thus Pollard says that "at the opening of the campaign Lee had urged that rations for thirty days should be kept in reserve at Richmond and Lynchburg, yet on the 2d of May there were at Richmond rations for only two days, and on the 23d of June rations for only thirteen days."

BATTERY BEFORE PETERSBURG

the almost hopeless task of dislodging the beleaguering force from its position, was the policy of Lee. Only twice during the siege, and in both cases under extraordinary circumstances, was any real attempt made by either army upon the intrenchments of the other, and both attempts resulted in disaster.

The siege of Petersburg really began immediately after the repulse of the assault of the 18th of June. Within two days the Union army had thrown up strong lines parallel to those of the Confederates. On the 21st Grant made his first attempt to seize or destroy the railroads. Hancock's and Wright's corps, the Second and the Sixth, were moved out of their intrenchments. Hancock's wound, received at Gettysburg, had broken out afresh, and Birney was now in command of the Second Corps. The object of the movement was to capture the lines to the Weldon Road, and, while holding that, to push the investment of Petersburg farther to the west. The region to be traversed was covered by forests and swamps filled with a dense undergrowth, and cut up by small creeks and runs which fall mainly southward into the streams emptying into Albemarle Sound. These had all to be crossed by the advancing force, while between them ran several tolerable roads by which the Confederates could strike the advancing columns in the flank. The position was, on a smaller scale, not unlike that of the Wilderness. Birney, having the advance, soon came upon the enemy, posted behind earth-works three miles south of Petersburg, but beyond the line of the regular intrenchments. A slight attempt was made upon these by Barlow's division of the Second Corps; but this was soon recalled, and a position taken up for the night. Next morning Wright, who had marched in the rear of Birney, was pushed forward, with the design of taking up a

position on his left, reaching to the railroad. While this movement, somewhat slowly made, was going on, Birney was ordered to swing his left around, so as to take the Confederate works in the flank. This carried him directly away from Wright, and left a wide gap between the two corps, increased every moment by Wright's movement. Hill, who had drawn to this quarter the bulk of his corps, availed himself of the opportunity thus presented, and flung a strong column into the opening, striking each Union corps upon the flank. The weightiest blow fell upon the Second. Barlow's division, on the left, was doubled upon itself, and fell back in confusion, losing heavily; Mott, the next on the right, was then struck, and retreated with loss; this uncovered Gibbon's right, from which whole regiments were swept away. But the corps was finally reformed upon its original line, where it was assailed. But the fierce Confederate swoop had exhausted its impetus. The assault was repelled; and Hill's columns withdrew as suddenly as they had advanced, carrying with them many hundreds of prisoners and several guns. Meanwhile another Confederate column had struck Wright's corps, and forced back its advanced line. But in the evening the whole line was reformed and intrenched for the night, while the Confederates intrenched themselves upon the railroad. The next morning, the 23d, Wright sent a small reconnoitring force to the railroad, which was reached at a point below the Confederate position. But hardly had they cut the telegraph wires when Anderson, at the head of Longstreet's division, fell upon their flank, drove them away, capturing many prisoners, and assailed the main line, which was withdrawn to the cover of the breastworks.

This attempt, which cost from 3300 to 4000 men in killed, wounded, and prisoners, resulted in no advantage. The line of investment was indeed somewhat extended to the left; but, as the railroad was not reached, the extension was of no use; and after it had been held without molestation for a

GERSHOM MOTT.

DAVID B. BIRNEY.

BUILDING WORKS.

few days, most of it was abandoned, and the advanced force was withdrawn to its former intrenchments in front of the Confederate lines.[1]

Simultaneously with this infantry movement, a cavalry expedition, consisting of Wilson's and Kautz's divisions, 8000 strong, was sent against the railroads. On the 22d they struck the Weldon Road at Reams's Station, ten miles below Petersburg, seven miles from the point where Birney and Smith were engaged. Having burned the dépôt and water-tank, and destroyed a considerable stretch of the road, they pushed on for the Southside Road, which they struck at a point fifteen miles from Petersburg. Kautz rode forward to Burkesville, the junction of the Southside and Danville roads, 50 miles from Petersburg, where he began to destroy the track. Wilson pushed ten miles down the Southside Road, which he destroyed in his way. Here he was met by Fitzhugh Lee's cavalry, which he defeated after a brisk fight, and thence moved on to rejoin Kautz. Both divisions then pushed down the Danville Road, damaging it for eighteen miles to Roanoke Bridge. This was found defended by a considerable body of militia, hastily gathered

from the adjacent parts of Virginia and North Carolina. The whole region was now aswarm, and on the 24th the expedition, having accomplished its purpose, set out on its return. At Stony Creek, on the Weldon Road, they had a sharp but indecisive action with a force of Confederate cavalry. Finding these too strong to be dislodged, by a wide detour to the left they struck for Reams's Station, which was supposed to be in possession of the Union forces. But, instead of this, it was held by a strong force of Confederate cavalry and infantry, sent down from Petersburg after the abandonment of Birney's and Wright's attempt. Wilson was forced to fall back in every direction, losing all his artillery and trains. The two divisions became separated, and only succeeded in making their way back within the Federal lines in straggling parties and most wretched plight, having lost at least 1000 men.[1]

Although this expedition terminated so disastrously, it had accomplished much for which it was undertaken. The destruction of the railroads was so thorough, that, urgent as was the need of their repair, it required twenty-three days to accomplish this. Lee had then but thirteen days' rations for his army. To feed them the commissary general had to offer the market price for wheat still standing uncut or shocked in the field. This market price was then twenty dollars a bushel in Confederate money; for specie it could be bought for a dollar. The price rose almost at a bound to forty dollars. That is, Confederate paper, which had for months been received and paid at the rate of twenty dollars for one in specie, fell suddenly to forty, and thence steadily declined to sixty for one. For months, indeed, it would have wholly lost all recognized value had not the government steadi-

[1] It is singular that this costly attempt upon the Weldon Road is not even alluded to in Grant's otherwise comprehensive Report. For the losses we are compelled to resort mainly to conjecture. Swinton, p. 512, states that the Second Corps lost 2500 prisoners, and the Sixth several hundreds. I do not find the authority upon which the statement is made, and think it an over-estimate. The semi-official statement furnished to Coppeé (*Grant and his Campaigns*, 399) gives the entire loss in the Army of the Potomac from June 20 to July 30 at 5316, of whom 605 were killed, 2494 wounded, and 2217 missing. It does not certainly appear whether this includes the losses in the cavalry expedition of Wilson and Kautz, in which Lee claims to have taken 1000 prisoners; and whether among these are to be included several hundred negroes who had followed this expedition on its return, does not appear. Although in these forty days there was no active battle, there was continued picket-firing between the lines. Burnside, whose corps was most exposed, gives (*Testimony, Battle of Petersburg*, 144) the loss in his corps during this time at 1138 men killed and wounded. The other corps undoubtedly lost many; probably the entire loss in the trenches was about 1500 (for the eighteen days following August 1 it was 868). Assuming that in the foregoing 5315 are included the losses of the cavalry expedition, and that these amounted, exclusive of captured negroes, to 1000, and that the losses in the trenches were 1500, there remain 2836 for this attempt upon the railroad, of whom probably more than 1800 were prisoners, leaving about 400 for the captures from the cavalry. From the best accessible data, I judge the foregoing estimates to be a close approximation to the truth.

[1] Lee, in his dispatch, says: "In the various conflicts with the enemy's cavalry in their late expedition against the railroads, besides their killed and wounded left on the field, 1000 prisoners, 13 pieces of artillery, and 30 wagons and ambulances were taken." As before noted, we think that among the prisoners are included some hundreds of negroes who had attached themselves to the expedition.

A MORTAR BATTERY.

RETURN OF KAUTZ'S CAVALRY.

SIGNAL STATION.

ly sold gold at nearly or quite that rate. Bankruptcy of the government had quite as much to do with the sudden collapse of the Confederacy as the defeats which it suffered in the field. For a time, indeed, under a rigid despotism, soldiers can be kept in the ranks without pay. The Confederate government succeeded in doing this for months. Indeed, it is said that "there were thousands of soldiers who had not received a cent of pay in the last two years of the war." When a "loaf of bread was worth three dollars in Richmond, and a soldier's monthly pay would hardly buy a pair of socks,"[1] it mattered little whether this nominal pay was ever received. But to feed, clothe, and equip an army requires money. Any government which has exhausted all its resources, actual and possible, must go down. The bankruptcy of the French monarchy under Louis XVI. was the immediate cause of its overthrow; for without this, the States-General, which inaugurated the Revolution, would never have been convened. This raid of Wilson hurried on the bankruptcy of the Confederacy. But for this it might have had a longer lease of life, with all the innumerable possibilities of the chapter of accidents. Grant, therefore, looking back after a year, was justified in affirming that "the damage suffered by the enemy in this expedition more than compensated for all the losses we sustained."

But for the time the attitude of the Army of Northern Virginia was more defiant, and seemingly more threatening than at any former period during the campaign. It was, after all its losses, nearly as strong as when it moved upon the Wilderness; stronger than when it foiled Grant at Spottsylvania, held him in check upon the North Anna, and defeated him upon the Chickahominy. The efficiency of the Federal army, in the mean while, had been greatly impaired. Its numbers, perhaps, had been kept up, but it had lost well-nigh half of its best officers and men; the remainder had suffered fearfully by their arduous labors under a fierce midsummer sun, through a drought of unexampled intensity, with a sky of brass overhead, and a soil of ashes underfoot. Not a few of the recruits, brought in by the enormous bounties then paid, were poor material for soldiers; and even the good material needed time to transform them into efficient soldiers. Even the tried veterans lacked much of their old determination. More than one leader of a storming-party in the fresh assaults upon the outworks of Petersburg was compelled to admit that his men did not charge as they had done a month before. But when, in the Weldon movement, the Second Corps, which had come to be recognized as the best in the army, fell back, division after division, almost routed by an inferior foe, losing twice as many in prisoners as in killed and wounded, it became clear that there must be a pause for reorganization and recuperation. Five weeks passed before another active operation was undertaken, and that also resulted in disaster.

[1] Pollard, Lost Cause, 647. For the effect of Wilson's raid upon Confederate finances, see Ibid., 647, 652.

Lee, indeed, was now so confident of the invulnerability of his position, that he ventured to detach a quarter of his army from Petersburg and Richmond to threaten once more the Federal capital. Hunter's eccentric retreat from Lynchburg had left the Valley of the Shenandoah bare of troops. The defenses of Washington had been stripped of almost every man to re-enforce the Army of the Potomac. Lee, reasoning justly from all former experience, was warranted in believing that a demonstration upon Washington would induce the recall of a large part of the force in his front, and not improbably even to the entire abandonment of the siege. Early had been already sent with a part of his corps to check the advance of Hunter upon Lynchburg. Now re-enforced by a part of Longstreet's corps, he was directed to march down the Valley of the Shenandoah to the Potomac, thus separating him by a perilous distance from the main army. This movement failed in its main purpose of causing Grant to detail any considerable part of his force from the lines before Petersburg. The Sixth Corps was sent thence, and to these was added the Nineteenth, under Emory, which had just arrived at Hampton Roads from the unlucky Red River expedition of Banks, and, without even disembarking, sailed up the Potomac to Washington. Grant's army was thus reduced by about the same number of men which Early had taken from that of Lee. Of the career of Early in this expedition, ending months after, in the annihilation of his forces, we shall speak hereafter.

As the month of July drew toward a close, signs of movement began to appear in the Federal army upon the James. Butler had, simultaneously with the attempt on the railroads, crossed a division over to the north bank of that river, which had intrenched itself securely at Deep Bottom, ten miles below Richmond. This position formed a point from which a force might, upon occasion, be directed against Richmond. Grant now planned an operation with a twofold object. The immediate purpose was by means of a cavalry expedition to cut the railroads north of Richmond, and thus make Lee wary of the situation of Early, who, having failed in his demonstration upon Washington, was lying in the Valley of the Shenandoah. The secondary purpose was, by apparently threatening a movement against Richmond, to force Lee to withdraw a considerable force from Petersburg, which was then to be assaulted. On the night of the 26th of July, Hancock's corps, with three divisions of cavalry, crossed the James. On the two following days offensive movements were made in such force as to convince Lee that Richmond was to be assailed. He brought over five of his eight divisions, leaving but three at Petersburg. This force was sufficient to prevent the Union cavalry from moving to the railroad, but its withdrawal across the James seemed to promise success to a sudden attack upon the lines at Petersburg, to be opened by the explosion of a mine which had been excavated under a fort which formed a part of the Confederate works.

This mine had been prepared with the consent rather than the approval of Meade. Burnside's corps had held the line upon the right. At one point his intrenchments approached within a hundred and forty yards of the Confederate works. Just in the rear of the advanced position was a deep hollow, where work could be carried on unseen by the enemy. One of Burnside's regiments was made up of miners from Pennsylvania. Some of the soldiers suggested that a mine should be dug right under this Confederate fort, perched upon the brow overhanging the hollow. The talk passed from grade to grade, until it reached Colonel Pleasants, the commander of the regiment, by whom it was communicated to his division commander, and by him to Burnside, who at once gave permission for the commencement of the work. So little confidence had Meade in its success that only the slightest facilities were afforded for its execution. Nothing better than empty cracker-boxes were furnished to carry out the earth. In spite of all obstacles, Pleasants pushed on the work. It was begun on the 25th of June, and was finished on the 23d of July. It consisted of a main shaft four or five feet in diameter, five hundred and twenty feet long, terminating in lateral branches forty feet in either direction. Four days after, Grant having finally resolved upon assaulting Petersburg, orders were given to charge the mine with 8000 pounds of powder. Burnside asked for 12,000 pounds, but the engineers at headquarters decided that this was too much.

Daybreak of the 30th was the time fixed upon for the attack. The mine was to be exploded at half past three. Burnside was to dash through the

CARRYING POWDER TO THE MINE.

EXPLOSION OF THE MINE.

breach, and seize a crest a few hundred yards in the rear, which was appa rently unfortified. This crest, known as Cemetery Hill, commanded Petersburg. Warren, upon Burnside's right, was to mass his whole corps, except just enough to hold his intrenchments, and join in the assault. Ord, who had replaced Gillmore in the command of the Eighteenth Corps of the Army of the James, was to support Burnside on the left. Thus fully 50,000 men were appointed for the attack. Hancock, moreover, who had been secretly withdrawn from the north side of the James, was to hold himself in readiness to support the assaulting column; while Sheridan, with his whole cavalry corps, was to move against the enemy's left. It seemed that the operation could hardly fail of success, for the entire Confederate force holding the intrenchments at Petersburg was barely 15,000 men.

But in the execution of this well-conceived plan every thing went awry. Burnside had proposed to put Ferrero's division of colored troops in the front. They had not as yet been engaged, and were comparatively fresh, while the other divisions had performed arduous duty during the whole campaign, and ever since they had occupied the position before Petersburg had been so close to the enemy that no man could safely raise his head above the parapet. In forty days, without being engaged in any formal action, they had lost more than 1100 men out of 9000. They had acquired the habit of seeking shelter, and it could be hardly expected that they would at once forego the habit, and be efficient in the fierce and sudden charge upon which depended success. The colored division, on the contrary, had been for several weeks trained for just such an enterprise. Meade disapproved of the plan of putting the colored troops in the front. He averred that, should the operation prove unsuccessful, it would be said that these men had been pushed ahead because we did not care for them. Burnside was, however, so urgent that the question was referred to Grant, who agreed with Meade. Then Burnside left it to be decided by lot which of his three white divisions should lead. The chance fell upon Ledlie's, the poorest probably, certainly the worst commanded, of all. The fuse was lighted at the appointed moment. An hour passed, and no explosion followed. Two

brave men, Lieutenant Douty and Sergeant Rees, volunteered to creep into the mine and ascertain the cause. They found that the fuse had parted within fifty feet of the magazine. They relighted it, and had just emerged from the mine when the explosion took place. A solid mass of earth, mingled with timbers, rose two hundred feet into the air, and fell sullenly back, leaving where the fort had stood a crater two hundred feet long, sixty feet wide, and thirty deep. At the instant the guns from all the batteries opened fire. The enemy were taken completely by surprise, and replied but feebly, and this feeble fire was soon almost silenced. Ledlie's men dashed over the lip of the crater, and plunged wildly into its depths. Between them and the commanding crest there was nothing but the rough, steep sides of the crater. A determined rush would have crowned the crest with the loss of hardly a man.

Burnside's original plan of assault, submitted to Meade four days before, was judiciously conceived. The fort occupied a re-entering angle where the Confederate intrenchments receded from the general direction of the lines. This fort being demolished, not only were the defenses pierced, but the works to the right and left were taken in reverse. Believing that his colored division might be relied upon for a vigorous charge, he proposed that it should be massed into two close columns; as soon as the heads of these had passed through the breach caused by the explosion, the two leading regiments of each were to sweep to the right and left, seizing the enemy's lines, while the remainder of the columns should dash straight forward upon Cemetery Hill, to be followed by the other divisions as rapidly as they could be thrown in. The crest gained, the colored division was to push right into the town. He seems to have supposed that his corps was sufficient for the assault, merely suggesting that the other corps should co-operate indirectly, and be in readiness to hold the crest, while he pushed forward toward Petersburg.[1] But the refusal of Meade to permit the colored divi-

[1] The sending the whole of the Ninth Corps to Cemetery Hill would, says Burnside, "involve the necessity of relieving these divisions by other troops before the movement, and of holding columns of other troops in readiness to take our place on the crest in case we gain it and sweep down

sion to take the advance materially changed Burnside's plans; and Meade's general order, issued on the evening before the assault, was so worded as apparently to ignore the movement to the right and left, or at least to leave the seizure of the lines to be performed by Warren and Ord.[1] There was one important part of the order of Meade with which Burnside failed to comply. He directed that Burnside should "prepare his parapets and abatis for the passage of the columns." Nothing of the kind was done. Burnside declares that "this part of the order was necessarily inoperative, because of the lack of time and the close proximity of the enemy, the latter of which rendered it impossible to remove the abatis from the front of our line without attracting not only a heavy fire of the enemy, but letting him know exactly what we were doing." Thus it was that the only approach to the breach was by two crooked covered ways, only wide enough to admit the passage of two to four men abreast.[2]

The explosion of the mine took the enemy completely by surprise. Hardly had the concussion ceased when the head of Ledlie's division began to move for the breach. Climbing the rim, they saw before them the deep crater, its sides of loose sand, from which protruded masses of clay, mingled with beams and timbers, the ruins of the fort. It presented an obstacle over which it was impossible to pass in military order. Into this the men pressed and huddled in inextricable confusion. The enemy abandoned their lines for a space on each side of the chasm. Into these the troops spread themselves, and, although as yet no fire was opened upon them, they sought shelter, and refused to move. Brigade after brigade poured in, until the crater was crowded with a disorganized mass. A single regiment climbed the slope, and advanced a few hundred yards toward the crest, to seize which was the first object of the assault, but, seeing no others following them, fell back into the shelter of the crater and the abandoned Confederate lines. So an hour passed, the confusion growing momentarily greater. Ledlie all this time was safely ensconced in a bomb-broof in the rear of the Union lines, which he hardly left for a moment. In the mean while the enemy, recovering from his first astonishment, began to plant batteries so as to sweep the approaches to the crater, toward and upon each side of which Burnside's divisions were now pressing. Potter, on the right, endeavored to extricate his division from the crowded gulf and gain the crest in its rear. But he found the way blocked up by Ledlie's men lying in the shelter of the works which they had seized, and from which they made no attempt to advance. Potter at length got two or three regiments across, and had formed them into something like order. It was now six o'clock, an hour and a quarter after the explosion. Meade, who had taken his position a mile from the scene of action, imperfectly informed of what was going on, sent orders to Burnside to push his men, white and black, forward at all hazards; to lose no time in making formations, but to rush for the crest. Ferrero's colored division dashed forward gallantly toward the crater, although the approach was swept by a heavy cross-fire right and left. A part of these troops rushed straight for the chasm and plunged into it, filling it so that there was barely standing-room. Some of them pressed through the troops near the crater, partially formed, and charged toward the crest, capturing two or three hundred prisoners—the only semblance of success on this fatal day. But they were met by a counter-charge, and broke and fled in utter confusion, sweeping back in their flight many of the white troops. It was clear that all chance of success was past. Orders had been given to Warren and Ord to support Burnside; these were countermanded, and at a quarter to ten Burnside was directed to abandon the crater and withdraw to his intrenchments. Burnside was chagrined at this order. He still hoped against hope that he could carry the crest. Ord, who had advanced a brigade of his division, declared that this was impossible, and the order to cease all further efforts was reiterated.

But to withdraw now was a work of difficulty and danger. The space over which the troops must retire was now swept by a furious fire of musketry and artillery. The men within the crater were sheltered by the declivity from a direct fire; but the Confederates had planted mortars, from which shells were rained down among the densely packed masses. To remain was as perilous as to retreat, more perilous than it would have been to advance. The troops swarmed out in squads, losing fearfully on the way. The enemy charged fiercely down to the edge of the crater, and were repulsed; a second charge was made; the whole mass broke and fled. It was now past noon. For eight hours the men had been crowded, without water, under a fierce July sun, within that narrow slaughter-pen. This disastrous attempt cost 4000 men, of whom 1900 were prisoners, who surrendered rather than run the fierce gauntlet of fire. In Burnside's corps of hardly 15,000 men, the loss was 3828. With the exception of a single brigade of Ord's corps, none of the 50,000 men who had been prepared for this assault, save Burnside's corps, were put into action. Burnside had no authority to call upon Warren or Ord, and Meade delayed until too late to order them into action.

This affair of the mine was made the subject of searching investigation by a Court of Inquiry and by the Congressional Committee. Their conclusions as to the causes of the failure were somewhat different. The court found that this was owing to the injudicious formation of the troops, the movement being made by flank instead of extended front; to the halting of the troops in the crater instead of going forward to the crest when there was no fire of consequence from the enemy; that some parts of the assaulting column were not properly led; and to the want of a competent common head at the scene of assault to direct affairs as occurrences should demand. They mildly censured Burnside for all except the last of these, and sharply censured Ledlie and Ferrero for absolute inefficiency, if not cowardice in, keeping themselves habitually in a bomb-proof instead of being present at the assault. The Congressional Committee attribute the failure primarily to the refusal of Meade, sanctioned by Grant, to permit the colored division to lead the assault, and generally to the fact that "the plans and suggestions of the general who had devoted his attention for so long a time to the subject, who had carried out to a successful completion the project of mining the enemy's works, and who had carefully selected and drilled his troops for the purpose of securing whatever advantages might be attainable from the explosion of the mine, should have been so entirely disregarded by a general who had evinced no faith in the successful prosecution of that work, had aided it by no countenance or open approval, and had assumed the entire direction and control only when it was completed, and the time had come for reaping any advantages that might be derived from it." Grant, in his testimony, attributes the disaster to the utter inefficiency of the division commanders, and especially of the one who was to lead the advance of the attacking columns. Meade's order, he says, was all that was required; "if the troops had been properly commanded, and been led in accordance with this order, we should have captured Petersburg, with all the artillery, and a good portion of its support, without the loss of five hundred men. There was a full half hour when there was no fire against our men, and they could have marched past the enemy's intrenchments just as they could in the open country; but that opportunity was lost in consequence of the division commanders not going with their men, but allowing them to go into the enemy's intrenchments and spread themselves there without going on farther, thus giving the enemy time to collect and organize against them. If they had marched through to the crest of that ridge they would have taken every thing in the rear. I do not think there would have been any opposition at all to our troops had that been done." Although Grant afterward believed that, if Burnside had been allowed to put his colored division in the advance, "it would have been a success," he still thought his own refusal and that of Meade to permit this was at the time right and proper. "We had," he says, "but one division of colored troops in the whole army about Petersburg at that time, and I do not think it would have been proper to put them in front, for nothing but success would have justified it. The cause of the disaster was simply the leaving the passage of orders from one to another down to an inefficient man. I blame his seniors, also, for not seeing that he did his duty, all the way up to myself." He thought this commander the poorest of all; he knew that he had been chosen simply by lot; yet he adds, "I did nothing in regard to it." This great effort, for which such abundant preparations had been made, was conducted without any common head. Although the lieutenant general and the second in command were all the while close at hand, neither gave any practical orders until the crisis was past. Neither even took adequate measures to know what had been done or left undone. They seem to have thought success so certain that they neglected all precaution to secure it. It is inexplicable that, out of the 50,000 men who stood drawn up in battle order for this very purpose, not a third were ordered to advance for the hours during which the operation continued. In Warren's front the fire of the enemy was silenced, and yet he was never permitted to move a man from his lines. "Thus terminated in disaster what promised to be the most successful assault of the campaign."[1] It cost more than 4000 men to the assailants, while the entire loss to the Confederates, including the regiment blown up in the fort, and the prisoners captured by the colored division, were hardly a quarter as many.

The mine enterprise had been undertaken under a conjuncture of favorable circumstances, a recurrence of which could not be looked for. It had failed utterly and disastrously. The failure had demonstrated that the works about Petersburg could not be carried by direct assault upon their strong centre. But the whole line necessary for the defense of the two cities was so extended that it seemed certain that there must be weak points somewhere, and that these points were to be found at the extremities. Grant had thrown up works opposite those of the enemy, in front of Petersburg, so strong that they could be held by a fraction of his army, leaving the bulk of it free to operate upon either flank of the Confederate lines. These lines nominally extended from the north side of Richmond around to the James, thence to and around Petersburg. As finally developed north-

it. It would, in my opinion, be advisable, if we succeed in gaining the crest, to throw the colored division right into the town. There is a necessity for the co-operation, at least in the way of artillery, by the troops on our right and left. Of the extent of this General Meade will necessarily be the judge. I think the chances of success in a plan of this kind are more than even."—Burnside, however, had good reason to avoid more than a mere suggestion as to the employment of other corps. Nearly a month before, when asked for his opinion as to the practicability of making an assault in front of his lines, he had said: "If the assault be delayed until the completion of the mine, I think we should have a more than even chance of success. If the assault be made now, I think we have a fair chance of success, provided my corps can make the attack, and it is left to me to say when and how the other two corps shall come to my support." Meade replied, somewhat curtly: "The recent operations in your front," that is, the mine, "as you are aware, though sanctioned by me, did not originate in any orders from these headquarters. Should it, however, be determined to employ the army under my command in offensive operations, I shall exercise the prerogative of my position to control and direct the same, receiving gladly, at all times, any suggestions which you may think proper to make. I consider these remarks necessary in consequence of certain suggestions which you have thought proper to attach to your opinion, acceding to which in advance would not, in my judgment, be consistent with my position as commanding general of this army."

[1] "Major General Burnside will spring his mine, and his assaulting columns will immediately move rapidly upon the breach, seize the crest in the rear, and effect a lodgment there. He will be followed by Major General Ord, who will support him on the right, directing his movement to the crest indicated, and by Major General Warren, who will support him on the left." Meade, however, says: "General Burnside submitted for my consideration a plan of attack of which I never disapproved. The only question of difference was in regard to the troops to be employed. I never objected to the handling of his troops; I only objected to the colored troops being placed in the advance. General Burnside afterward seemed to be under the impression that I objected to all of his plans. But as to his tactical formation, and what he was to do with his troops, I made no objection."

[2] Many officers attribute mainly to this neglect to remove the abatis and parapets the disastrous result of the operation. This forms one of the four grounds upon which the Court of Inquiry censured General Burnside.

[1] Grant's Report.

IN THE TRENCHES BEFORE PETERSBURG.

CONFEDERATE WORKS AT HATCHER'S RUN.

ward to Hatcher's Run, their whole extent from the north of Richmond to the south of Petersburg was forty miles. But Grant, in placing his army on the south side of the James, had abandoned all purpose of assailing, or even menacing Richmond from the north or east. The works immediately around the Confederate capital were therefore held only by Ewell, who had been disabled from active service in the field. The garrison of Richmond was really nothing more than a body of militia, nominally numbering about 10,000; but of these there were never during the summer 5000 reported as present for duty. During the whole siege, indeed, the gay people of the Confederate capital—and Richmond was never so gay as during this period—never saw a regiment of the veteran troops who were defending it.

The real line which Lee had to hold began upon the James River, ten miles below Richmond. Here, at Chapin's Bluff, on the north bank, and Fort Darling, opposite on the south bank, strong works had been erected. Thence to Petersburg the distance is fifteen miles. But this space, as has been shown, was protected by the two rivers, and by the works across the narrow neck of Bermuda Hundred. So perfect were the natural defenses of this space of fifteen miles that it was never occupied in force. It could be assailed only by the narrow isthmus. During the whole siege this space was never even menaced. At the time of the mine affair a demonstration here was suggested, but the idea was pronounced impracticable. Lee's Army of Northern Virginia was then posted in two great divisions: the left, under Longstreet, who was slowly recovering from the wound received in the Wilderness, at Chapin's Bluff; the right, with which was Lee, at Petersburg. An attack any where upon the centre, from Petersburg to Fort Darling, being out of the question, Grant was shut up to the alternative of assailing one flank or both of the Confederate lines; that is, to move upon the left from Deep Bottom, where a part of Butler's force had a secure lodgment, up the north bank of the James, and thus threaten Richmond directly, or to operate upon the right flank, assailing, not Petersburg directly, but the railroads whereby the Confederate armies were mainly fed.[1] Grant's theory of operations was to make a strong demonstration upon one flank, and then to follow it up with a movement upon the other, each being made in such force as to be converted into a real attack should circumstances warrant. It was assumed throughout that the enemy could not strengthen one flank without greatly weakening the other. The capture of Richmond, though important, was still a secondary consideration, for the Confederate army occupying Petersburg would still remain to be destroyed before any decisive advantage was gained; whereas, if the railroads were destroyed or seized, the enemy, deprived of sustenance, must become a certain prize. Hence

Grant's main efforts were always directed against the enemy's right, while Lee, equally aware of the nature of the case, massed the bulk of his force in the works around Petersburg, leaving at Chapin's Bluff hardly more than a corps of observation, yet always ready to strengthen it whenever a menace was made in that quarter.

The terrain south of Petersburg presented great natural obstacles for attack, and furnished admirable facilities for an offensive defense. The roads radiate like the sticks of an expanded fan. First running south is the Jerusalem Plank Road. This was now in the possession of the Union force. Next, parallel to it, is the Weldon Railroad; then come several minor roads, and then the Boydton Plank Road running southwest; and, lastly, the Southside Railroad, running almost west. Hatcher's Run, a small stream threading through swamps and thickets, flows eastwardly from near the Southside Railroad, crossing the Boydton Plank Road, when it bends southward, forming a sort of wet ditch to the south side of Petersburg, at a distance of six miles. The Confederate works closely encircled Petersburg until they reached the Boydton Plank Road, which they then followed to Hatcher's Run, crossing it and continuing for a space along its southern bank. They thus effectually covered the Southside Railroad for a space of many miles. To reach this vital artery the assailants must pass westward clear around the Confederate lines, and then turn northwest, involving a march of at least thirty miles by any practicable roads. A column making this march was exposed to a blow upon its flank from any one of the roads leading from Petersburg. The Confederates could sally from their intrenchments, strike any exposed part of the column, and return, in case of check, to their fortified position. The Union lines followed the general course of those of the enemy. But the complete development of both was a work of months. Early in August the Confederate intrenchments had only reached the Weldon Railroad, while the extreme left of the Federal line was on the Jerusalem Plank Road.

After the repulse of the mine assault, Lee felt his position so strong as to warrant him in detaching re-enforcements to Early, who, having given up the invasion of Maryland, was still hovering in the Valley of the Shenandoah. Only Kershaw's division was actually dispatched, although orders were ostentatiously given that Anderson, who yet commanded Longstreet's corps, should take the command. This would leave the north bank of the James only weakly defended, and Grant perceived in this a favorable occasion to menace Richmond. On the 13th of August, Hancock, with the Second Corps, and Birney, who had replaced Smith, and now commanded the Tenth, followed by Gregg's cavalry division, were sent across the James. To mask the movement, Hancock's force was embarked on transports, which were ostentatiously towed down the river as though their destination was Fortress Monroe, and thence up the Potomac to Washington. But, as soon as darkness set in, their course was reversed, and next morning, after some vexatious delays, they were landed at Deep Bottom, whence they advanced in the direction of Richmond. In the afternoon they came upon the enemy's intrenched line, upon the right of which an attack was made by Barlow with two of Hancock's divisions. This was vigorously repelled, and nothing was effected. Birney, on their left, gained some slight advantage. During the four succeeding days a series of brisk but undecisive en-

[1] It has indeed been suggested that the works in front of Petersburg might have been operated against by a system of regular approaches. "Two saps," it is said, "might have been run, and, in the course of a month, there is every likelihood that the Confederate line might have been carried." But during that month the enemy would have had ample time to fortify an inner line to which he could fall back, and so the work would have to be repeated. Lee was too accomplished an engineer to neglect such an obvious precaution. When, in the end, the line of works, having been almost stripped of troops, was carried, there was found an inner line before which the overwhelming Union force was held in check. This inner line was never actually carried. It was abandoned by the Confederates when defeats in another quarter had rendered the abandonment of Petersburg a necessity. Those who suggest this course quite overlook the essential difference between the siege of a fortress, the capture of whose works involve the loss of every thing, and operations against a line defended by a series of parallel or concentric works, which may be continued to any number, the seizure of any one of which involves only the gain of a few rods of space.

UNION WORKS ON THE WELDON ROAD.

gagements was kept up, Hancock trying in vain to discover some weak point. Lee, in the mean while, by detaining two of the three divisions ordered to the Shenandoah, and withdrawing largely from those at Petersburg, had accumulated a force too strong to be formally assaulted. He even ventured, on the 18th, to assume the offensive by an attack upon Birney; but the assault was repelled with heavy loss. In this operation the Union loss was about 1500, of which two thirds fell upon the corps of Hancock. The Confederate loss was about the same.

The operation had failed in its ostensible and perhaps its immediate purpose to secure a position more directly menacing Richmond. It had, however, accomplished two ulterior objects. It had prevented large re-enforcements being sent to Early, and had, by weakening the force at Petersburg,

given a promising occasion for a movement against the Weldon Railroad. This was committed to Warren. On the 18th he moved quietly from his position on the extreme left, and struck the railroad without serious opposition at a point four miles below Petersburg. Leaving Griffin's division to hold this, he pushed Ayres's and Crawford's divisions for a mile up the road, until they found themselves confronted by the enemy drawn up in line of battle. Warren's position was a critical one. His corps was isolated, for its march had left a wide gap between itself and the troops on his right. The left of his advanced division also was approached by an obscure road of which he had no knowledge. Down this came the enemy, striking heavily upon Ayres, forcing him back for a space with heavy loss. The troops rallied, and the Confederates were repulsed in turn, Warren still holding

BRINGING IN PRISONERS BY NIGHT.

fast to and intrenching himself upon the railroad. This was of too great importance to be surrendered without a struggle. The next day Lee, having concentrated a powerful force, burst suddenly upon Warren. The wide space between Warren and Burnside had by some mischance been left uncovered. Into this broad gap Lee thrust Mahone's division, striking Warren's right, and, gaining its rear, pressed fiercely along it toward the left, throwing the whole line into confusion, and sweeping away more than 2000 prisoners, while at the same time Heth's division assailed the left. The core of Warren's troops still stood firm, and opportunely at the moment 2000 men from the Ninth Corps came upon the scene. With his whole force Warren now struck back upon his assailants right and left, and drove them back in confusion within their lines. On the 20th all was quiet along the lines, and Warren wisely passed it in strengthening the position against an attempt which he could not doubt would be made to regain it. On the morning of the 21st, Lee, having massed thirty guns, opened a fierce fire, under cover of which a heavy infantry force moved upon Warren's front, while another body endeavored to turn the left flank. The front attack was speedily repelled; the turning force met with still worse success; pushing heedlessly on, they encountered a fire so severe that they broke and fled in confusion, leaving behind 500 prisoners. So the Weldon Railroad was won, but at heavy cost. In the three days' struggle the Union loss was 4543, of whom more than two thirds were "missing."[1]

It was now resolved to destroy the railroad for a dozen of miles south of the point where it was held by Warren. For this purpose a part of Hancock's corps, which had been withdrawn from across the James, with a brigade of cavalry, 8000 men in all, was dispatched on the 21st. In the course of the next two days the work was effectually performed for four miles, as far as Reams's Station, where hasty and ill-planned breastworks were erected. On the morning of the 24th it was pursued three miles farther, and orders were given that on the next day five miles more should be destroyed. Up to this time no enemy had been encountered, and none was looked for. But Lee had in the mean while sent a strong force under Hill down the Boydton Road, which showed itself on the morning of the 25th. Hancock then withdrew his infantry behind the breastworks at Reams's Station, the cavalry having been pushed some distance to the left. Two sharp attacks were made and repulsed. Hill then, assuming a position where his artillery could take Hancock's line in reverse, opened a hot fire, throwing the Federals into some confusion. This was followed by an impetuous charge, by which the disordered lines were broken through and three batteries captured. The breastworks were carried after a feeble resistance, and all seemed lost. Miles, whose lines had been broken through, succeeded in rallying upon a new line, where the advance of the enemy was checked, and one of the lost batteries regained. Night put an end to the contest, and Hancock in the darkness withdrew. Hill, not suspecting how small was the force opposed to him, also withdrew at the same time, and when morning broke the place was vacant save of the dead. Out of his 8000 men, Hancock had lost 2400, of whom almost three fourths were missing.[2]

Five weeks of almost unbroken quiet now ensued. To all seeming the armies of Lee and Grant had come to a dead-lock. Each lay behind intrenchments which it was hopeless for the other to assail. Men's eyes were turned to other quarters—to Georgia, where Sherman at Atlanta was watching the heady manœuvres of Hood, ready to take advantage of the first false move, and meditating the great March to the Sea; to the Valley of the Shenandoah, where Sheridan was operating against Early, who had for a month menaced the Federal capital; to Mobile, where Farragut was sealing up that important port, precious to the Confederacy as the last save Wilmington hitherto open to blockade-runners. Grant, meanwhile, was steadily tightening his grasp upon what he had won, and seeking to make this a base for farther acquisitions. The extension of his lines across the Weldon Road had compelled Lee in like manner to stretch his, so that it seemed that he could have left few troops north of the James, and that there was most likely an opportunity of gaining something in the direction of Richmond. On the 28th of September, Ord and Birney, with the two divisions of the Army of the James, crossed the river, and fell fiercely upon the strong works near Chapin's Bluff. One of these, Fort Harrison, was captured, but an assault upon Fort Gilmer was repulsed with heavy loss. Fort Harrison occupied a commanding position, and was the main defense of that part of the Confederate lines. Desperate attempts were made to retake it, but they were unavailing, and Butler held a secure position from which to threaten Richmond. This compelled Lee to maintain a larger force than before upon the north bank of the James.

DESTRUCTION OF THE WELDON RAILROAD.

[1] Killed and wounded, 1367; missing, 3176. The Confederate loss in killed and wounded was probably quite as great; in prisoners, hardly a sixth as many.
[2] Killed and wounded, 663; missing, 1769. The Confederate loss is stated by Pollard (*Lost Cause*, 607) to have been "720 killed, wounded, and missing;" of prisoners there were very few, so that the respective losses in killed and wounded were about equal. When we consider the character of the fighting during the seven days from August 18 to 25, and note the inordinate ratio of Union prisoners to the killed and wounded (2000 killed and wounded, 5000 missing), we are forced to the conclusion that the greater part of the prisoners were really deserters—the scum of the army who had been brought in by the enormous bounties which had been for some months paid for recruits and substitutes, the loss of whom was really a gain to the effective strength of the army. Of the 24,000 losses in the army of the Potomac during what may be strictly considered the siege of Petersburg, from June 20 to November 1, considerably more than 12,000 were "missing;" yet during this period there was no action excepting that at the mine, in which the Union forces were really defeated. The Confederates during that period, while losing fully 10,000 in killed and wounded, lost barely 2000 prisoners. There were, indeed, some thousands of deserters who sought refuge in the Union lines, and a still larger number who managed to escape from the army and regain their homes. Pollard (*Lost Cause*, 647), speaking of the manner in which, during the last year, the Confederate ranks were recruited, says: "It was not unusual to see at the railroad stations long lines of squalid men, with scraps of blankets in their hands, or small pine boxes of provisions, or whatever else they might snatch in their hurried departure from their homes, whence they had been taken almost without an hour's notice, and ticketed for the various camps of instruction in the Confederacy. In armies thus recruited, it is no wonder that desertions were numerous; but for every Confederate soldier who went over to the Federal lines, there were hundreds who dropped out from the rear and deserted to their homes."

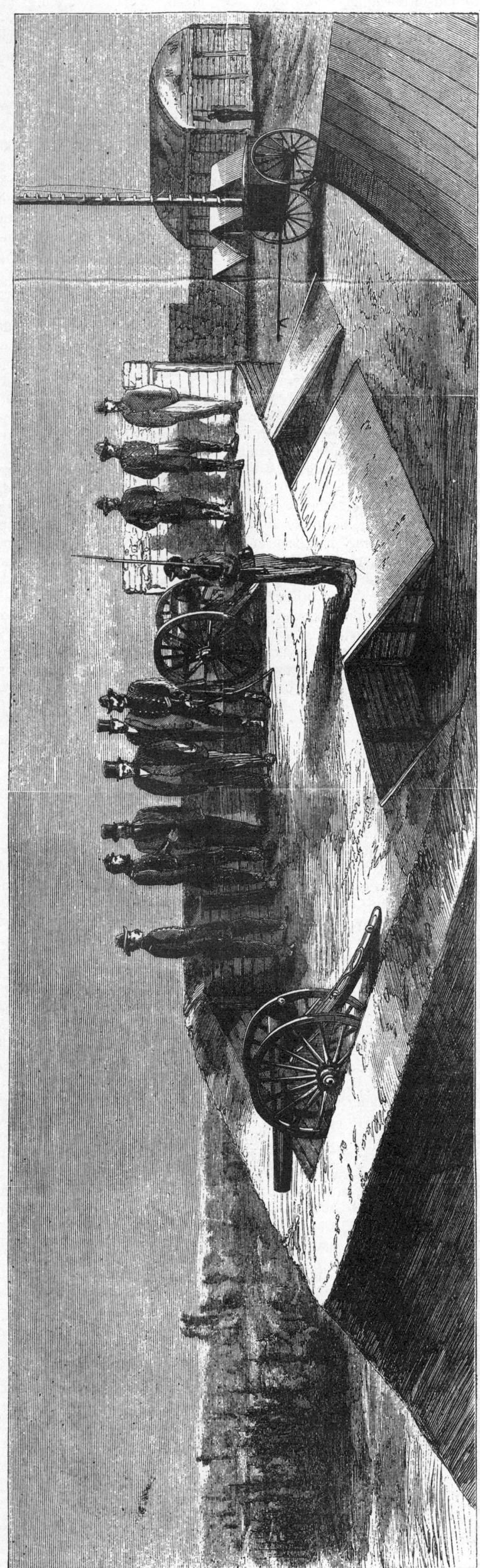

UNION WORKS BEFORE PETERSBURG.

The Confederates being thus strong upon their left, it was assumed that they must be weak on their right. To ascertain this, Warren was directed on the 30th to make a strong reconnoissance with two divisions of his own corps and two of the Ninth, now commanded by Parke. The reconnoissance was to be converted into an attack should the enemy prove to be in small force. Some works at Peebles Farm were taken and held; but Parke, pushing on, came upon the enemy in force, who charged upon him, threw Potter's division into rout, and swept off a thousand prisoners. Wilcox's and Griffin's divisions coming up, checked the pursuit, and the corps returned to the works which they had captured. Next day a fierce storm suspended operations. On the 2d of October a reconnoissance was pushed out, but the enemy had fallen back to his intrenchments. The loss in this operation was 2685, of whom 1756 were missing, mainly the unreliable recruits which had been added to Parke's corps. But the line had been extended three miles westward, and now reached within five miles of the Southern Railroad.

If this railroad could be seized, it would be equivalent to the capture of Petersburg. Grant, after long and careful preparation, attempted this with a force greater than he had put forth upon any one operation during the siege. The plan was to find the extremity of the Confederate intrenched line, turn it, gain the rear, and then move westward and strike the railroad. On the morning of the 27th of October the whole Army of the Potomac, leaving only sufficient men to hold the fortified line, was put in motion, both Grant and Meade accompanying the expeditionary force. Parke, who was posted at the extreme left, in the position which had been won ten days before, was to move out toward the Boydton Road, and, if possible, force the Confederate lines as far down as the crossing of Hatcher's Run. Warren was to support Parke, and, in case he was successful, was to closely press the retreating enemy; otherwise Warren was to cross the stream, march up its south side beyond the plank road, then recross, thus gaining the rear of the enemy's line, in front of which Parke would be posted. Meanwhile the main movement to the railroad was to be executed by Hancock. Marching down southwardly in the rear of Parke and Warren, he crossed the Run with slight opposition, then turning sharply to the northwest, he reached by noon the Boydton Road, whence a march of six miles would bring him to the railroad. Here he received an order from Meade to halt; for Parke, upon coming in front of the line which he was to carry, found it impenetrable. He therefore halted and intrenched himself. Hancock's corps was now wholly isolated, and the halt was ordered to give Warren time to execute his alternative movement, which would connect him with Hancock. Grant had by this time become convinced that it would be impossible to reach the railroad, and ordered the troops to be withdrawn to the fortified lines from which they had set out. Up to this time the enemy had not moved from his intrenchments, or shown any disposition to attack. Grant, having received an erroneous report that Warren had connected with Hancock, rode off to his headquarters at City Point, whence in the evening he sent a dispatch to Washington stating that there had been no serious fighting, intimating that he intended no offensive operation, but should hold his advanced position for a few hours to invite an attack from the enemy.[1]

But there was no need to invite an attack upon a force so isolated as was that of Hancock. Warren had, indeed, promptly endeavored to connect with Hancock. Crawford's division crossed Hatcher's Run, and moved up the south bank through dense woods, wherein whole regiments lost their way. But by the middle of the afternoon he reached a point opposite the enemy's intrenchments on the opposite side of the stream, and within a mile of Hancock's right, which had been extended to meet him. Yet such was the difficult character of the intervening space, that each command was unaware of the precise position of the other. Hill meanwhile, apparently unaware of the approach of Crawford, had arranged an assault upon Hancock. Heth crossed the run between Hancock and Crawford, fairly turned the right of the former, and fell upon Mott's division, which, looking for an attack from another direction, was struck in the rear. Pierce's brigade gave way for a space, losing a number of guns. But Egan promptly changed front with his division, so as to face Heth, who had now become aware that Crawford was close upon his left. The Confederates, bewildered, changed front so as to expose their flank to Egan, who, with his own regiment and one of Mott's brigade, swept on, while De Trobriand's brigade and Kerwin's dismounted cavalry struck in front. The Confederates, overborne by the fierce rush, gave way, and were driven from the field, leaving behind them nearly a thousand prisoners. Had Crawford in the mean while advanced, the whole Confederate force, isolated by the stream, must have been captured. But, though so close at hand, the noise of the musketry was not heard through the forest. Two hundred of the Confederates, bewildered in

[1] "The Army of the Potomac, leaving only sufficient men to hold its fortified lines, moved by the enemy's right flank. The Second Corps, followed by two divisions of the Fifth, with the cavalry in advance, forced a passage of Hatcher's Run, and moved up the south side of it toward the Southside Railroad, which I had hoped by this movement to reach and hold; but, finding that we had not reached the end of the enemy's fortifications, and no place presenting itself for a successful assault by which he might be doubled up and shortened, I determined to withdraw within our fortified line. Orders were given accordingly. Immediately upon receiving a report that General Warren had connected with General Hancock, I returned to my headquarters."—Grant's Report. "Our line now extends from its former left to Armstrong's Mill; thence by the south bank of Hatcher's Run Creek to its crossing at the Boydton Plank Road. At every point the enemy was found intrenched and his works manned. No attack was made during the day farther than to drive pickets and cavalry inside of the main work. Our casualties have been light, probably less than 200 killed, wounded, and missing; the same is probably true of the enemy. I shall keep the troops out where they are until toward noon to-morrow, in hopes of inviting an attack."—Grant's Dispatch. From the wording of the report, it might be inferred that the withdrawal was ordered to be made during the afternoon of the 27th, and that therefore the fighting which ensued was in consequence of a violation of orders. But the dispatch shows that the withdrawal was not to be made till next day. Grant's direction for holding on until then was subsequently modified by Meade, who left it optional with Hancock to withdraw during the night of the 27th. For this whole operation, see especially Swinton (Army of the Potomac, 540–546), where will be found citations from the as yet unpublished reports of Hancock and Warren.

DUTCH GAP CANAL.

the woods, strayed within Crawford's lines, and gave themselves up as prisoners. Meanwhile Hampton, with five brigades, assailed Gregg's cavalry upon the Union left and rear. But Hancock, sending thither all of his force not actually engaged with Heth, held his ground. The Confederates had met a decided repulse; but Hancock's position was still critical. He was yet isolated and in front of the enemy in unknown strength, who would undoubtedly attack next morning with increased force. His ammunition was well-nigh exhausted, and it was not likely that it could be replenished in time. So, the option having been given by Meade, he withdrew that night, and retraced his way to the lines from which he had set out. It was well that he did so, for during the night Hill had massed 18,000 infantry and cavalry, with which he proposed to renew the attack at daybreak. The entire Union loss was 1900, of whom a third were missing. Most of this fell upon Hancock's corps, Parke's losing only 150, and Warren's probably about as many. The Confederate loss was probably greater in killed and wounded, certainly twice as great in prisoners, of whom 1200 were taken.[1]

Butler's co-operative movement was feebly made and ineffectual. He pushed out two columns toward the Williamsburg Road and the York Railroad. The first column was checked at the outset, losing 400 prisoners; the second column carried a small fortified work, which it forthwith abandoned, and both returned to their former position. Thus the operation for which such ample preparation had been made, and from which so much had been expected, resulted in nothing beyond gaining some slight knowledge of the region, a knowledge which proved that the Southside Railroad could not be reached by that line. Yet the same costly experiment was made three months later, and with the like result.

The army now took up winter quarters behind its intrenchments, and during the remainder of the year no important operation was undertaken around Petersburg, although the quiet of the camps was broken by the continual picket-firing and artillery duels inevitable when two great armies lie intrenched face to face. Butler, indeed, was prosecuting a scheme from

---

[1] Lee's dispatch gives a very inadequate view of this affair. He says: "General A. P. Hill reports that the attack of General Heth upon the enemy upon the Boydton Plank Road was made by three brigades under General Mahone in front, and General Hampton in the rear. Mahone cap-

tured 400 prisoners, three stands of colors, and six pieces of artillery. The latter could not be brought off, the enemy having possession of the bridge. In the attack subsequently made by the enemy, General Mahone broke three lines of battle, and during the night the enemy retired from the Boydton Plank Road, leaving his wounded and more than 250 dead on the field."

RAID OF THE CONFEDERATE IRON-CLADS.

which he, and he alone, expected large results.　Above Bermuda Hundred the James makes a double bend, first to the west, then south, thence east, and after a course of six miles returns to within less than half a mile of its starting-point.　This tortuous bend was commanded by batteries which barred the farther ascent of the river.　Butler proposed to dig a canal through the narrow isthmus, by which gun-boats could ascend the river and assail the Confederate works at Chapin's Bluff, and perhaps even force a passage to Richmond.　The work, begun late in the summer, was prosecuted all through the autumn, mainly by details from the colored troops, not without considerable annoyance from the hostile batteries.　At the close of the year the excavation was completed, save a narrow bulkhead at the upper end.　On New-year's day this was blown up, but the earth fell back into the channel, leaving only space for a little rivulet.　The Confederates forthwith established a battery opposite the mouth of the canal, which completely swept its whole length, and the scheme came to naught.

The Weldon Railroad meanwhile, though crossed by the Union intrenchments, and destroyed for some distance below, had not been rendered wholly useless to the Confederates.　Cars still ran to within a few miles of the Union lines, and then freight, mainly supplies brought to Wilmington by blockade-runners, was hauled by wagons to Richmond.　On the 7th of December Warren started out to destroy the road still farther down.　The work was thoroughly and systematically done.　The troops were formed in line of battle along the road.　Each division destroyed that in its front; then each one moved down to the left, and so on in succession.　In two days twenty miles of road were destroyed.　At length the enemy were encountered in some force, strongly posted across the road.　The expedition then returned, having marched a hundred miles in six days.

The communication with Wilmington was rendered somewhat more difficult, but was not wholly interrupted, for at this very period the supplies from hence saved the Confederate army in one of its sorest straits.　On the 9th of December the commissary general reported that there were but nine days' food for Lee's army, producing also a letter from the commander stating that his men were deserting on account of short rations.　On the 14th Lee telegraphed to Davis that his men were without meat.　This disaster was only averted by the opportune arrival at Wilmington of several vessels loaded with supplies, which were then on their way to the army.[1]

The capture of Fort Fisher on the 15th of January effectually closed the port of Wilmington, and thus compelled Lee to rely solely upon the Southside and Danville roads.　Taking advantage of the absence of the iron-clads at Wilmington, the Confederates made a bold attempt to destroy the Union shipping in the James.　On the night of the 23d of January, their three iron-clads, the Virginia, Richmond, and Fredericksburg, accompanied by five steamers and three torpedo-boats, dropped silently down the river, passed

Fort Brady, which covered the upper extremity of Butler's position, and broke the chain which had been stretched across the river opposite the lower end of the Dutch Gap Canal.　The Fredericksburg got through the obstructions; the other iron-clads and the steamer Drewry grounded.　The iron-clads returned, the Virginia being severely injured by a bolt from a monitor.　The Drewry, being immovable, was abandoned and blown up.

As spring approached, and Sherman was beginning to move northward through the Carolinas, Grant wished to prevent Lee from dispatching any part of his army to the south.　The immediate problem to be solved was entirely changed.　Before it had been how to drive Lee out of Petersburg; now it was to keep him there for a space, until Sherman had swept away the forces opposed to him.　An offensive operation must be undertaken, and there seemed to be no one except an essential repetition of that which had been attempted in October.[1]

On the 5th of February, Warren's corps, accompanied by Gregg's cavalry, was sent to turn the Confederate lines at Hatcher's Run, while Humphreys, who now commanded the Second Corps—Hancock having been ordered north to organize a new corps—was to assail in front.　Warren's route was nearly the same as that formerly taken by Hancock.　Humphreys advanced to the Run, and was furiously assailed; but the attack was repelled, and at night the position was firmly held.　Next morning Warren, who, having crossed the Run, had moved in the rear, came up, and the two corps were connected.　Warren then pushed his left under Crawford up the west bank of the stream, through tangled woods and miry sloughs.　Pushing before him a Confederate force under Pegram, Crawford went as far as he had gone in October.　Here Pegram, re-enforced by Evans, made a stand, and in turn forced Crawford back.　Meanwhile a Confederate force had made a detour around his left and rear.　They struck Ayres's division, which was advancing to the support of Crawford, drove it in confusion upon Crawford, whose division also gave way and fell into rapid retreat.　They fell back wildly to the position on Hatcher's Run, where Humphreys had hastily intrenched himself.　The Confederates pursued fiercely; but, as they emerged into an open space, they encountered a sharp fire, and hastily withdrew into the shelter of the woods, whence they fell back within their lines.　The Union loss in these two days was 2000; that of the Confederates less—probably not more than 1000.　The only gain to the Federals was a farther extension of their line to the westward—an extension which might have been made without a battle.　With this unsuccessful endeavor fell the curtain of the great drama, soon to be raised for the final short and stirring act.

[1] Thus only can we explain the movement now undertaken.　Grant, in his report, refers to it only incidentally.　He says: "The operations in front of Petersburg and Richmond until the spring campaign of 1865 were confined to the defense and extension of our lines, and to offensive movements for crippling the enemy's lines of communication, and to prevent his detaching any considerable force to send south.　By the 7th of February our lines were extended to Hatcher's Run, and the Weldon Railroad had been destroyed to Hicksford."

CUTTING THE CHESAPEAKE AND OHIO CANAL.

CHAPTER L.

THE CAMPAIGN IN VIRGINIA.—EARLY AND SHERIDAN.

Hunter's Advance upon Lynchburg.—His Retreat through Western Virginia.—Early sent to the Valley of the Shenandoah.—Sigel driven from Martinsburg.—Early crosses the Potomac into Maryland.—Defeats Wallace on the Monocacy.—Threatens Washington.—Troops arrive for its Defense.—Early repulsed at Fort Stevens.—Recrosses the Potomac.—Is followed by Crook, who is defeated at Kernstown.—Early's Raid into Pennsylvania.—The Burning of Chambersburg.—Sheridan appointed to the command of the Middle Department.—His Instructions.—Opening Movements.—Position in September.—Sheridan to go in.—The Battle of the Opequan, or Winchester.—Early defeated.—Battle of Fisher's Hill.—Early routed.—The Pursuit.—Sheridan Returns.—Devastation of the Valley of the Shenandoah.—Early advances.—Battle of Middletown, or Cedar Creek.—The Federals surprised and driven back.—Sheridan comes upon the Field.—He attacks and routs Early.—Early's Address to his Troops.—Results of the Campaign.

EARLY in June, while, as has been narrated, Grant, after the battle of Cold Harbor, lay upon the Chickahominy, Hunter was successfully pressing down the great Valley of Virginia. Crossing the Blue Ridge, he emerged into the tide-water region, and on the 16th appeared before Lynchburg, whither Lee had already sent the small command of Breckinridge. This, joined to the few troops scattered in that region, was altogether insufficient to oppose the threatening movement of Hunter, and Early was hurried thither by railroad, reaching Lynchburg just in advance of the Union force. Hunter had expended most of his ordnance stores in the long march through a hostile country. On the 17th and 18th, while the first battles were waged before Petersburg, Hunter made some demonstrations, but, finding the enemy strong in his front, and with constantly increasing force, he hastily recrossed the Blue Mountains; then, apprehending that his return would be intercepted, and thinking himself in no condition to risk a battle, he continued his retreat westward, crossing the Alleghanies into the mountain region of West Virginia, whence he could regain his position on the Potomac only by a wide detour. This retreat left Washington and the whole northern frontier almost bare of troops, for every effective regiment had been sent to re-enforce Grant. The operations before Petersburg had convinced Lee that he could still hold his lines with a portion of the force which he had; and he reasoned, also, that the threat of a renewed invasion of the North would compel his opponent to detach largely from the force at Petersburg, and most likely compel him to raise the siege.

In the latter days of June, Early was therefore ordered to move down the Valley of the Shenandoah. The force with which this movement was made compared ill with the great armies which had twice before marched along this beaten track. Instead of the 100,000 men with which Lee had moved on the campaigns which closed at Antietam and Gettysburg, Early had not more than 20,000 men of all arms. But the force for the defense was still weaker in proportion, and it was within the limits of possibility that even the Federal capital might be seized by a sudden dash. Early moved with

the rapidity which had always characterized the Confederate marches. In spite of the fierce summer heat, the troops made twenty miles a day, and on the 2d of July he was close upon Martinsburg. Sigel, who was there with a small force guarding a large quantity of stores, fell back toward Harper's Ferry, abandoning every thing which he could not carry off. Taught by the experience of the past, he was not entrapped into halting at Harper's Ferry, but, crossing the Potomac, took post upon Maryland Heights. Here he was safe from attack, but useless for obstructing the passage of the river, had his force been five times as great. Hunter was far away, making his toilsome circuit through the mountain wilds of Western Virginia. There was nothing to hinder Early from making a raid into Maryland and Pennsylvania. Crossing the Potomac, he sent scouting-parties in every direction. One destroyed the Baltimore and Ohio Railroad for miles, and cut the embankments of the Chesapeake and Ohio Canal in various places; another pushed on to Hagerstown, where they levied a heavy contribution and went off. The main body pushed on toward Frederick City by the same route over which Lee had marched two years before, threatening both Baltimore and Washington. Wallace was at Baltimore in the command of a few disjointed fragments of troops, but he knew that the veteran Sixth Corps was coming to his aid from the James. He therefore advanced and took position on the Monocacy River, where he covered the roads to both Baltimore and Washington, and hoped to hold the enemy in check until the arrival of Wright with the Sixth Corps, and Emory with the Nineteenth. This latter had been brought from Louisiana, had opportunely arrived at Fortress Monroe, and, without disembarking there, was sent up the Potomac to Washington. Ricketts's division of the Sixth Corps had joined him at Baltimore, and the other divisions were on the point of embarking at City Point; two days would bring them up.

On the morning of the 9th of July, Early, after some skirmishing, came upon Wallace at the Monocacy. The Confederates were more than two to one. Their first and second assaults were repelled; but the third, made in greater force, was successful. The Federals retreated, some in good order, toward Baltimore, but the greater part fled in utter confusion in every direction. The Union loss was 1959; of them, 1282 were "missing," of whom fully half were stragglers. The Confederate loss was vaguely reported at 600. It was apparently somewhat greater, since two days after 400 of those too severely wounded to be removed were found in the hospitals at Frederick.

The approach to Washington was now fairly opened, and Early moved the next day in that direction. He had with him about ten thousand men, for detachments had been sent in every direction to gather supplies and plunder. Had he pushed straight on with even this small force, he might, in all likelihood, have entered the capital, and, after doing what damage he pleased,

PILLAGING AT HAGERSTOWN.

SACKING A FLOUR MILL.

have retired by the way he came. A delay of a single day forfeited an opportunity for striking a blow which might have changed the current of history. On the evening of the 10th Early's whole force was within half a dozen miles of Washington. Between him and the Federal capital there were only a few isolated forts manned by militia, invalids, and convalescents from the hospitals. For one day it was not Richmond, but Washington that was in peril. Few men in the Federal capital believed that it could be saved from capture. On the afternoon of the 12th Early made demonstrations looking toward an assault. He advanced his line close up to Fort Stevens, an isolated work half a dozen miles north of the city, covering one of the roads. But during the previous night the whole aspect of things had been changed. The Nineteenth Corps, and the two remaining divisions of the Sixth, had steamed up the Potomac, and were disembarked. A great weight was lifted from the heart of the man upon whose calm courage rested more than even upon any general in the field the destiny of the nation. As the tried veterans stepped ashore, they saw upon the wharf the gaunt figure of Abraham Lincoln. He greeted them with kindly words and the winning smile which was wont to light up his homely features, munching at intervals a bit of army bread. No wonder that he had that day missed his dinner. As the foremost men filed swiftly through the streets, they were greeted with acclamation. "It is the old Sixth Corps, the men who took Marye's Heights; the danger is over." That night it was felt that the peril was over-past. Toward evening of the 12th a brigade of the Sixth Corps moved out to dislodge the Confederates, who had all day kept up annoying demonstrations in front of Fort Stevens. A hot conflict ensued, for the combatants were veterans who had encountered each other on more than one stricken field. Each side lost heavily in proportion to the numbers engaged. The Union brigade, a thousand strong, lost a quarter of its numbers. The Confederates lost more, and were driven from the field.

Early saw that his opportunity was past. The Federal capital was held by a force too strong in number and quality to be encountered by his little army. Under the cover of night he withdrew, recrossing the Potomac, and thus closing the last invasion of the North. This attempt, however, had not been an entire failure. He had won one considerable battle, and swept back with him no inconsiderable booty, not the least valuable part of which was 5000 horses and 2500 cattle.

Having placed the Potomac between himself and the enemy, Early moved leisurely up the Valley of the Shenandoah. Wright, who was now placed at the head of the Sixth and Nineteenth Corps, followed by the same route and with the same undecided steps wherewith McClellan and Meade had before gone after Lee. Passing through Snicker's Gap, he came up on the 19th of July with the retreating Confederate column at the crossing of the Shenandoah. When half way over, Early turned, repelled him, and then fell back leisurely to Winchester; while Wright, under orders from Grant, returned to Washington.

It was supposed that Early's command was returning to join Lee at Pe-

tersburg, and the Federal commander proposed to recall the Sixth Corps to the Army of the Potomac. But Lee, who was aware of the importance of maintaining a force in the Valley of the Shenandoah, and thus keeping up a constant menace of raids across the Potomac, had no thought of withdrawing Early. The Federals soon had reason to find to their cost that Early was yet close at hand. On the 23d of July, Crook, who was in command at Harper's Ferry, pushed up the Valley, which he supposed had been abandoned by the enemy. At Kernstown, four miles beyond Winchester, hard by where Jackson had suffered his only defeat in the Valley, his small force encountered Early, was defeated, and driven back in rout to Martinsburg, losing 1200 men. It then recrossed the Potomac, leaving the way open for a raid across the river. Early took prompt advantage of the opportunity. His cavalry, 3000 strong, under McCausland, passed the Potomac, and, making a wide sweep so as to conceal their real destination, reached Chambersburg on the 30th. The purpose of this raid was destruction. McCausland demanded $200,000 in gold as a ransom for the town. Compliance was out of the question, and orders were at once given to burn the town. The execution of this was committed to Gilmor, a Marylander, who had joined the Confederates, and in an hour two thirds of that flourishing town of 4000 inhabitants was in flames. This is the only instance during the war in which a town was wantonly, and by express order, destroyed, without any pretense of military advantage; for the destruction of Atlanta by Sherman was ordered as a military necessity, and the burning of Columbia was not by any order from the Union commander. The raiding party now made their way back across the Potomac, after several skirmishes, in which the losses were about equal upon either side.

These annoying occurrences upon the frontier were owing quite as much to defective military arrangements on the Federal side as to skill on the part of the Confederates. It seemed as though this region was looked upon as a hospital for incapable commanders. The departments were so divided and subdivided that no commander had any real authority or responsibility. Thus Washington, Baltimore, and the adjacent region formed one department; parts of Pennsylvania and Maryland another; West Virginia another; the region of the Shenandoah another. Grant saw clearly that the first thing to be done was to form all these into one military department. This was done, and Hunter, who had now got back from his long wandering, was placed in command. But Grant had fixed his eye upon another man for the position. Hunter intimated his willingness to be relieved. The intimation was promptly acted upon, and Sheridan, who had just been sent to Washington in anticipation of such a contingency, was placed in the command of these departments, which were constituted the Middle Military Division, the forces there being designated as the Army of the Shenandoah.

Sheridan assumed command on the 7th of August. The Army of the Shenandoah consisted of the Sixth Corps, one division of the Nineteenth, two small divisions under Crook, known as the Eighth Corps, with Averill's and Torbert's divisions of cavalry, the latter having just come up from the

EARLY RECROSSING THE POTOMAC.

RUINS OF CHAMBERSBURG.—THE MAIN STREET.

James. In all it numbered 18,000 infantry and 3500 cavalry disposable for active operations. As many more were required for garrisons and to guard the railroad. The Confederates, with the addition of Anderson's command, were in about equal force. To Sheridan were turned over the instructions just given to Hunter. He was to concentrate all his available force near Harper's Ferry, whence he was to operate against Early: pursue and fight him if he crossed the Potomac; follow him if he retreated south; first or last he would have to pursue the enemy up the Valley of the Shenandoah, where he must leave nothing which could invite the return of the Confederates. Dwellings were to be spared, but such provisions, forage, and stock as could not be used were to be destroyed. The people must be made to understand that, so long as a Confederate army could subsist among them, raids would be of continual occurrence, and these it was determined to stop at all hazards. This stern order was soon to be sternly executed.

Sheridan at once moved up the Valley toward Winchester, where he expected to find the enemy; but they had fallen back. Then, being notified from Grant that re-enforcements had been sent to Early, raising his force to 40,000 men, he drew back and took up a strong defensive position near Harper's Ferry, to await the development of the intentions of his opponent. For a month the outposts and cavalry parties of the armies were in almost daily collision, with no important results. Early having been re-enforced by Anderson, in command of Kershaw's division of infantry and Fitzhugh Lee's cavalry, and Sheridan by Grover's division of the Nineteenth Corps and Wilson's cavalry, the respective forces were not greatly disproportionate—the Confederates numbering about 22,000, and the Federals about 27,000. There was some question as to the command between Early and Anderson. Both had been made lieutenant generals on the same day; but Anderson's commission as major general was prior to that of Early, which gave him the military seniority; but he had been sent to Early's department. There was thus a question of rank, and the two commanders never cordially co-operated.

At the middle of September the Confederates were concentrated around Winchester, and the Federals near Berryville, ten miles to the east, the Opequan running between. The armies were so posted that either could bring on an action; but neither commander was disposed to attack the other in a position of his choosing. Grant indeed for a while held Sheridan in check, for defeat would lay Maryland and Pennsylvania open to a renewed invasion. At length he left the James, and came to the Potomac to confer with Sheridan. At the very time of his arrival, Sheridan had learned that Kershaw's division had been recalled. Lee was meditating an offensive operation at Petersburg, and wished Kershaw to be at hand in case it should be undertaken. He was therefore directed to fall back as far as Culpepper, whence he could reach Richmond by rail in a few hours. This left Early with from 15,000 to 18,000.[1] Sheridan had resolved to attack Early, and, on submitting his plans to Grant, received the emphatic order to "go in."

Sheridan proposed to march upon Newtown, above Winchester, and thus throw himself upon the Confederate rear; but on the 18th of September, just as the movement was to have commenced, he learned that Early had sent two of his four divisions to Martinsburg, twenty-two miles from Winchester, with the purpose of destroying the Baltimore and Ohio Railroad at that point. He therefore changed his plan, and resolved to catch the two divisions left near Winchester, and, having routed them, to fall upon those sent to Martinsburg. Thus ensued the action called by him the Battle of

[1] Early indeed asserts that his effective force was only 8500 muskets—say 9000 infantry, and less than 3000 cavalry, with three battalions of artillery: not more than 13,000 men in all. But, as will be seen hereafter, this is evidently an under-statement; for, taking into account his statement of all the re-enforcements which he at any time received, Sheridan captured during this campaign nearly as many prisoners as the whole of Early's alleged force. His losses in killed and wounded were also very heavy, and a considerable remnant of his army rejoined Lee at Petersburg. Pollard (*Lost Cause*, p. 593) adopts Early's statement; but Pollard's own accounts elsewhere show that this must be erroneous.

RUINS OF CHAMBERSBURG.—THE TOWN HALL.

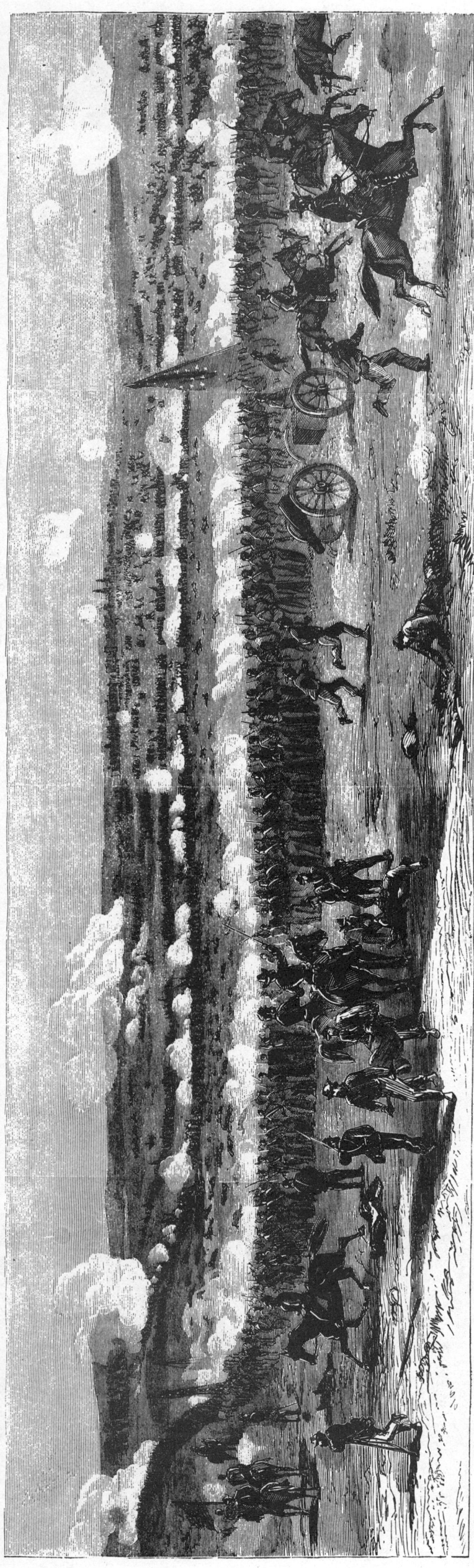

THE CONFEDERATE ROUT AT WINCHESTER.

the Opequan, by the Confederates that of Winchester. As it happened, however, Early marched only half way to Martinsburg, and was able to bring his whole force upon the field. Before dawn of the 19th Sheridan was in motion. Torbert's cavalry, in front, was to cross the Opequan, and clear the passage of the stream in one direction. Wilson, supported by the Sixth and Nineteenth Corps, was to move rapidly down the defile through which ran the direct road from Berryville, and thus fall upon the portion of the enemy lying directly in front of Winchester, Crooks's corps being held in reserve. Wilson charged into the deep gorge, drove back the enemy's pickets, and captured the earthworks at its mouth. Wright and Emory defiled through the narrow gorge, and emerged, under a heavy artillery fire, into an irregular undulating valley, dotted over with ledges of rock and patches of wood, sloping gradually up to the semicircular heights of Winchester. Time was lost in making these movements, and it was nine o'clock before the order to advance was given. The attack and defense were alike obstinate, and, neither being sheltered except by the natural cover afforded by the formation of the ground, the loss on both sides was heavy. Ramseur, upon whom the attack first fell, held his ground stoutly for two hours. But the whole of Wright's and Emory's corps having at length passed through the gorge, he began to give way. At this moment Rodes came back from the direction of Martinsburg and joined in the fight. Rodes was shot dead, the centre of Early's first line was broken, and the Federals rushed on. They now encountered Gordon, who had followed hard after Wharton. The advance was checked, and then Gordon made a counter-charge, which, striking Sheridan's centre, where the Sixth and Nineteenth Corps joined, forced it back in confusion, which threatened to become a total rout. Gordon pushed on in pursuit so fiercely that his flank was exposed to Russell's brigade, of the Sixth, which was on the left. He was in turn driven back, and Sheridan's line was soon re-established, most of the two or three thousand men who had gone to the rear being brought back.

Still the battle hung in even scales. Breckinridge, with the last of the cavalry, the last of Early's absent men, now came up from the rear, and took position on the Confederate left. Now ensued the fiercest fighting of the day. Early sought to extend his left so as to outflank Sheridan's right; then, sweeping round, to seize the mouth of the narrow gorge and cut off the retreat. Sheridan's quick eye perceived that his opportunity had now come. Crook's corps had not yet been brought into action. He had kept them in reserve upon his right, intending also to turn the enemy's left and cut off his retreat. Crook was now directed to the left, turn the Confederate right, strike it in flank and rear, and, as soon as it was broken, the Federal left should swing round and strike on the other flank. Both movements were made with the utmost precision. On what was now the decisive point the Federals were in great preponderance. They fairly overlapped the Confederates, who were powerless to prevent the turning of their flank. Crook's line swept steadily on over the open fields in the face of a fierce musketry fire, under which 900 men went down in a few minutes. Emory's corps now sprung from the ground where they had been lying to shelter themselves from the artillery, by which they had for three hours been sorely pelted, poured in a fire so rapid that in five minutes their ammunition was exhausted, and then dashed straight upon a patch of woodland where was the extreme left of the Confederate line, into the other side of which Crook was already pouring. The enemy rushed out in utter rout, many of them in their flight throwing away their guns and accoutrements.

The battle was irretrievably lost. To hold this wood Early had brought in his last two divisions, those of Breckinridge. These divisions had all the morning, and until far in the afternoon, held in check Merritt's and Torbert's cavalry. These magnificent horsemen had then pressed up, sweeping before them the Confederate cavalry, and circling round to the Confederate flank and rear. They charged fiercely upon the disorganized mass, which broke and fled in confusion back to Winchester. The fragments of the routed army entered the town as night was falling. But here was no rest. In the darkness they kept on their flight, only halting until they reached Fisher's Hill, a strong position eight miles south of Winchester, and twelve from the battle-field. It had been a well-fought action, and decisive, won indeed by superior force, but with equal bravery. Sheridan's losses summed up 4990, of whom 653 were killed, 3719 wounded, and 618 missing. The heaviest loss, 1956, fell upon Emory's corps, among whom were 450 missing, captured when they were repulsed early in the day. In Wright's corps there were 1637 killed and wounded, and 48 missing. In Crook's corps, which struck the final decisive blow, out of a total loss of 953, there were but 8 missing. The cavalry lost 441, of whom 109 were missing. The Confederate loss is not stated, but in all it could not have been less than 6000. Upon the field and in the pursuit 2500 prisoners were taken; 2000 wounded were found in the hospitals at Winchester.

On the next morning Sheridan set out in pursuit, and soon came in front of the position which Early had taken up at Fisher's Hill. Here the valley is split by an intervening ridge, the main branch contracting to the breadth of three and a half miles, overhung on each side by precipitous bluffs. Early had availed himself of the brief respite to throw up breast-works across the valley. Here he thought himself secure, for it was a position which could be held against a direct assault from a fivefold force. So safe did Early think himself that his ammunition-boxes were taken from the caissons and placed behind the breastworks. Sheridan determined to drive him out of his position by turning his left. To do this, the turning force must gain the summit of the North Mountain, and, marching for a space along the crest, plunge down into the valley. The movement must be made by night, for from a signal station the enemy could observe every movement made by daylight.

GEORGE CROOK.

Crook's corps was at night placed in a mass of wood, where they lay hidden all through the 21st, while Wright's and Emory's corps were drawn up in front of the Confederate centre, ready to join in the assault. Crook made his movement without being perceived. Noon had passed before he was in position. Sheridan then, posting Ricketts in front of the Confederate left, sent Averill, with his cavalry, to drive in the enemy's skirmish line. The movement succeeded beyond expectation. It was reported from the Confederate signal station that a turning column was moving against their left front. Early massed his force to check this. At that moment Crook burst in upon his rear. The Confederates broke and fled after some show of resistance in front, and Wright's corps, swinging round, joined with Crook's.

The victory was complete, and won at little cost—not 300 in all, of whom 237 were in Wright's corps, and 60 in Emory's. Crook, whose mere presence in position won the fight, appears not to have lost a man. The Confederate loss in killed and wounded was not much greater; but they left behind them 1100 prisoners. Complete as was the success, Sheridan had expected to render it still more decisive. He had hoped to capture Early's whole army. For this purpose he had sent Torbert down the parallel Luray Valley, whence it was to cross over into that of the Shenandoah, and intercept the enemy's retreat. But Torbert was held in check at a narrow gorge by the Confederate cavalry and a small body of infantry until the fugitives had passed the point.

It was almost dark when the fight at Fisher's Hill was begun. The remnants of Early's broken divisions fled rapidly down the Valley, hardly a company preserving its organization. Sheridan pushed on the pursuit for a day and night as rapidly as possible, but the fugitives were too fleet for the infantry, and there was present of cavalry only Devins's small division, for Torbert was in Luray Valley, on the opposite side of the dividing range, and Averill had unaccountably gone into camp immediately after the fight. On the morning of the 23d Devins came up with the enemy's rear at Mount Jackson, twenty-five miles from Fisher's Hill. Here, not in sufficient force to attack, he waited for Averill, who arrived late in the afternoon, and then fell back again. Averill was here superseded by Powell. Early's divisions kept on their flight by different routes until they reached New Market, where several roads converge. Here the shattered force got itself partly reorganized, but kept on its retreat, now presenting a line of battle too strong for the cavalry to assail. The Federal infantry pushed on in columns, but were unable to bring on an action. Torbert, in the mean time, had beaten the enemy in Luray Valley; and on the 25th Wright's and Emory's corps had reached Harrisburg, Crook's having been left a little behind until the movements of Early were ascertained. Kershaw, with his fresh division, now rejoined Early, and the Confederates, nearly as strong as they had been at the Opequan, made a show of advancing.

Sheridan was now in doubt what course to pursue—whether to again assault or to fall back. He finally decided on the latter course. He was little, if any, superior to the enemy; his transportation would not keep him in supplies for a much farther advance; and, moreover, it was by no means sure that Grant would be able to hold the entire Confederate force in the lines at Petersburg. Lee might secretly detach a sufficient number, which, moving rapidly by rail, could overwhelm him, and then return before their absence should be perceived. He had, moreover, in a week, accomplished more than he had dared to count upon. He had destroyed or captured half

of Early's army, and driven the remainder so far to the south that it no longer threatened Maryland and Pennsylvania. He therefore determined to terminate the active campaign and return northward. But on the way back he was to carry out his original instructions to devastate the valley which had so long served as a granary for the Confederate army and an avenue for an invading force. This done, he could give back to Grant at Petersburg the bulk of the infantry which had been sent to check the diversion made by Lee. The plan was carried out, but not for three weeks, and after Early had once more staked all in a desperate venture and lost.

On the 6th of October Sheridan commenced his return march. The cavalry swept across the whole breadth of the Valley of the Shenandoah from the Blue Ridge to the eastern slope of the Alleghanies. The order to transform the Valley into a barren waste, with nothing which should tempt the enemy to return, was carried out with unsparing severity. Before the army was a fertile region filled with the stores of an abundant harvest just gathered in; behind was a desert and devastated region. Sheridan himself shall describe his work of destruction: "In moving back to Woodstock, the whole country from the Blue Ridge to the North Mountain has been rendered untenable for a rebel army. I have destroyed over two thousand barns filled with wheat, and hay, and farming implements; over seventy mills filled with flour and wheat; have driven in front of the army over four thousand head of stock, and have killed and issued to the troops not less than three thousand sheep. This destruction embraces the Luray Valley and the Little Fort Valley, as well as the main Valley; a large number of horses has also been obtained." This was the work of but two days. Dwelling-houses were indeed spared save in a single retributive case. One of the Union engineer officers was murdered, and for this act all the houses within an area of five miles were burned.

It is hard, in the midst of peace, to decide where the military right of destruction and retribution begins and ends. Early, in retreating from Maryland, had seized more cattle and horses than Sheridan took in the Valley. The numerous guerrilla parties who had made the Valley their lair plundered at will. "Since I came in the Valley," continues Sheridan, "every train, every small party has been bushwhacked by the people, many of whom have protection papers from commanders who have hitherto been in the Valley." Sheridan spared dwellings, although the ruins of Chambersburg, fired without pretense of military necessity, had hardly ceased to smoke. But this devastation only partly accomplished its purpose. The Valley was not rendered untenable to a Confederate force until a fortnight later, when the army there ceased to exist.

The Confederate cavalry followed Sheridan's return at a distance, and at length came into conflict with Torbert's division, by whom they were defeated; and when, four days after the commencement of the return march, Sheridan, passing Fisher's Mountain, took up his post four miles beyond, Early, strengthened by Kershaw, was close behind. Here he suffered the final crushing defeat which put an end to the war in the Valley of the Shenandoah.

On the 15th of October, Sheridan, having posted his army at Cedar Creek, set out for Washington to consult with the Secretary of War as to the route by which Wright's corps should be sent back to Petersburg. He had just started on the journey when he received a message from Wright, who was left in command, inclosing a dispatch deciphered from the enemy's signal-flag. It purported to be from Longstreet to Early, and read, "Be ready to move as soon as my forces join you, and we will crush Sheridan." Suspecting it to be, as it undoubtedly was, a ruse, Sheridan sent back word to Wright, "If Longstreet's dispatch be true, he is under the impression that we have largely detached. If the enemy should make an advance, I know that you will defeat him. Look well to your ground, and be well prepared."

On the night of the 18th of October the Federal army lay encamped in a position apparently unassailable. It was disposed upon three parallel ridges of no great height, facing southward. To the west, four miles away, lay Early in unknown force at the wooded base of Fisher's Hill. The left of the Union army—the corps farthest from the Confederate position—was occupied by Crook. At the foot of this crest ran a deep valley. Next, and half a mile in the rear, across the turnpike, and to the right, was Emory. Then, somewhat farther to the right, and considerably in the rear of all, was Wright. From the extreme right to the extreme left was a space of three miles, and still farther to the right was Torbert's cavalry. The fronts and flanks of Crook and Wright were protected by breastworks and batteries. The position, unless turned by surprise and taken in the rear, was impregnable to any force which the enemy could by any possibility have. Early resolved to turn both flanks by surprise. The march toward Emory upon the right flank presented no great natural difficulty; but to reach the left flank the assailants had to descend a rugged gorge so steep that a man must here and there support himself by holding fast upon the bushes, then wade the Shenandoah, recross it again, enter the Valley, skirting Crook's front, and go up it for three miles, moving scarcely four hundred yards from the picket line. If we may credit Early's express averment, he had an effective force of less than 10,000 men of all arms. This was hardly half the number that was to be opposed to him; of this, however, he was not aware; for he supposed that a considerable portion of Sheridan's army was miles away, at Front Royal, where he knew them to have been a few days before, or still farther away on the way to Washington.

Early commenced his march at midnight. His left column, with the artillery and cavalry, moved over easy ground, and at dawn began to demonstrate against Emory. Meanwhile the other column, consisting of the divisions of Gordon, Ramseur, Pegram, Kershaw, and Wharton, the remnants of those who had just a month before fled in rout from the Opequan and Fish-

ALFRED TORBERT.

er's Hill, moved silently down the mountain slope, forded the Rappahannock, and crept stealthily along Crook's front. So imperative was the necessity for silence that they had left their canteens behind, lest their rattling should betray them. Before dawn they had pursued their dark-long march of seven miles. These three divisions passed beyond Crook's left flank, and turned it without having been perceived, and were fairly within striking distance of its rear, while the other two crouched in his front. Once, indeed, the pickets reported that they had heard a suspicious rustling, and a part of the front line was sent into the trenches; but, so little was danger apprehended, that many 'went in with unloaded muskets. The gaps left in the line were not filled, and no reconnoissance was made. There was just then a slight stir in Emory's camp, for he was to send out a reconnoissance at daybreak toward Fisher's Hill. His aid was in the saddle, ready to report the exact time when the troops moved. The gray dawn was just breaking through a dense mist which shrouded mountain and valley when this impatient aid heard far to the left a sudden sharp rattle of musketry, and the fierce yell which denoted a Confederate charge.[1] The five divisions had broken on front, flank, and rear, through the lines of the sleeping Eighth Corps. In fifteen minutes it was perfectly routed and streaming back in confusion upon the Nineteenth, its guns being captured and turned upon the fugitives. Simultaneously a brisk artillery fire, with demonstrations of cavalry, was opened upon Emory's right; while his front and left flank were assailed as Crook's had been, and the enemy were already sweeping around his rear. The Nineteenth Corps was now fighting the whole Confederate force. Desperate, but brief and unavailing efforts were made to hold their lines until the Sixth Corps could come up; but from point to point they were driven back before the furious rush of Kershaw in front, while Gordon and Ramseur poured in a fire upon their left flank. The camps of the Eighth and Nineteenth Corps were now in possession of the Confederates, and what remained of these corps were pushed back upon the Sixth, which alone maintained the fight. This also fell back, but slowly and in order, from one position to another, until at length, after three miles of retreat, it had fairly outstripped Gordon, and stood with its left flank free from his pertinacious assault. Here at last they held fast, and awaited the attack. The assailants had now exhausted their impulse. Most of them, weary and hungry, scattered through the captured camps, eager for food and plunder; only a distant artillery fire was kept up. Wright fell back undisturbed a little farther to a position where he could cover the high road to Winchester, and began, at nine o'clock, to form his broken lines. He had been beaten, but was not routed, and now stood prepared to repel any farther attack.

Sheridan, in the mean while, was on his way back from Washington. He had slept that night at Winchester. At seven in the morning a picket there reported that he had heard artillery firing; but Sheridan, supposing that it proceeded from the reconnoissance which he had ordered that morning, gave little heed. He rode leisurely on until nine o'clock, when, a mile and a half beyond the town, the head of the foremost fugitives appeared in sight—men and trains rushing to the rear with a rapidity which betokened

[1] A graphic account of this battle, by Captain De Forest, the aid in question, is given in *Harper's Magazine* for February, 1865.

a great disaster. There happened to be a brigade at Winchester. Stopping briefly to halt the trains and draw out this brigade to stem the flight, Sheridan pushed rapidly on, and soon approached the front. His very presence stayed the flight of the fugitives, who were running from they knew not what. "Face about!" he shouted; "we're going back to our camps! We're going to lick them out of their boots!" Hundreds turned and followed his black steed. He found Getty—the same who had held the road in the Wilderness—far in front of the remainder of the line of the Sixth Corps, confronting the enemy, and momentarily expecting an attack. The other divisions of Wright and Emory were brought forward, and soon were ready for the enemy.

Two hours and more passed. Then Early pushed a column toward Emory. No sooner was it within range than a single volley sent it whirling back, and Sheridan was about to order an advance, when word came to him from the cavalry far off to the left that a fresh infantry column of Confederates were pressing toward Winchester to gain his rear. The report was erroneous, but it delayed the order to advance. At four o'clock the order came. Early had now thrown up breastworks and taken strong positions under cover of stone fences. For a space he fought bravely, and gave way slowly and sullenly, but surely. Once, indeed, by a flank movement, he wheeled Gordon's division around Emory's right, and threw it into some confusion; but the movement was a fatal one. McMillan's brigade dashed into the angle thus formed in the Confederate line, pressed through, and cut off the turning column, upon which Custer's cavalry charged. At the same moment the whole Union line rushed forward, and swept the enemy before them. Gordon first broke, then Kershaw, then Ramseur, and all rushed in wild tumult down the turnpike which led to their position at Fisher's Hill, charged by cavalry on both flanks, and pressed by infantry in the centre. The fugitives outran their foot-pursuers, who, weary and thirsty, toiled after them. But the swift cavalry were on their heels. At the crossing of Cedar Creek Custer and Devin charged the train without provoking a shot. A little farther on was another bridge; this broke down, and the whole train, guns and wagons, was abandoned. At length, once more behind the lines at Fisher's Hill, which cavalry could not pass, Early had a brief respite; but in the darkness the whole crowd rushed on, never halting for thirty miles. There was no need for pursuit the next day. So utterly destroyed was Early's army that there was nothing worth chasing.

With this battle ended the fighting in the Valley of the Shenandoah. The remnant of Early's force rejoined Lee, by swift marches, at Petersburg, only enough of his own three divisions being left in the Valley to form one small division. Early put forth a bitter address to his troops. After recounting the brilliant success of the morning, he added: "I have the mortification of announcing to you that, by your subsequent misconduct, all the benefits of that victory were lost, and a serious disaster incurred. Many of you, including some commissioned officers, yielding to a disgraceful propensity to plunder, deserted your colors to appropriate the abandoned property of the enemy; and subsequently those who had previously remained at their posts, seeing their ranks thinned by the absence of the plunderers, when the enemy, late in the afternoon, with his shattered columns, made but a feeble effort to retrieve the failures of the day, yielded to a needless panic, and fled the field in confusion."

The defeat was indeed as total as "Lee's bad old man" represented it; but the reproach was undeserved. The troops had fought themselves out in the morning. The victory was won by surprise against superior numbers. The surprise was over in the afternoon, and the numbers were still largely against them,[1] while the advantage of position was not great. Early appears once more for a moment in the history of the war, when, four months after, a little band of 1500 men whom he had gathered was rode over and captured almost to a man by a single division of Sheridan's cavalry.

The Federal victory was complete and absolute, but it was purchased at a heavy cost. The losses numbered 5990, of whom 1890 were missing, mostly prisoners, more than a third of them from Crook's corps, captured in the surprise. This corps lost but 65 killed, while it had 654 missing. Early's loss was barely half as great. There were 1500 prisoners, and probably about as many killed and wounded, nearly all in the final fight in the afternoon. He lost also 30 guns, all that he brought into action, besides 16 which he had captured in the morning.

Sheridan's decisive campaign in the Valley was comprised within just a month, counting from the time when he commenced direct offensive operations. In that month he completely annihilated his opponent, capturing fully 13,000 prisoners, and killing and wounding quite 10,000. His own losses in killed and wounded indeed were greater. Including the three great battles and about thirty skirmishes, which mainly took place in the six weeks while he was watching the enemy, preparatory to striking, they amounted to 13,831; the missing 3121—a total loss of 16,952; of whom 11,327 were in the great battles, and 5625 in minor engagements.[2]

[1] I accept Early's statement of his force as an approximation to the truth. I do not think it possible that his force exceeded 12,000 infantry, although many endeavor to make it twice as great. To do this, they speak of a re-enforcement of 12,000 or 16,000 of Longstreet's corps, received the day before the battle. Of these I can find no credible information. I find with Early only that half of his army which had escaped from the Opequan and Fisher's Hill — say not more than 8000 men, and Kershaw's one division of probably 4000. Pollard says definitely 2750 muskets—say 3000 men.

[2] The following is a summary of the losses of Sheridan during his whole campaign in the Shenandoah Valley, from August 7 to October 19:

Battle of the Opequan	5,035	Battle of Cedar Creek	5,995
Battle of Fisher's Hill	297	Minor Engagements	5,625
			16,952

The Confederate loss in prisoners is officially given. Of the killed and wounded we can only conjecture.

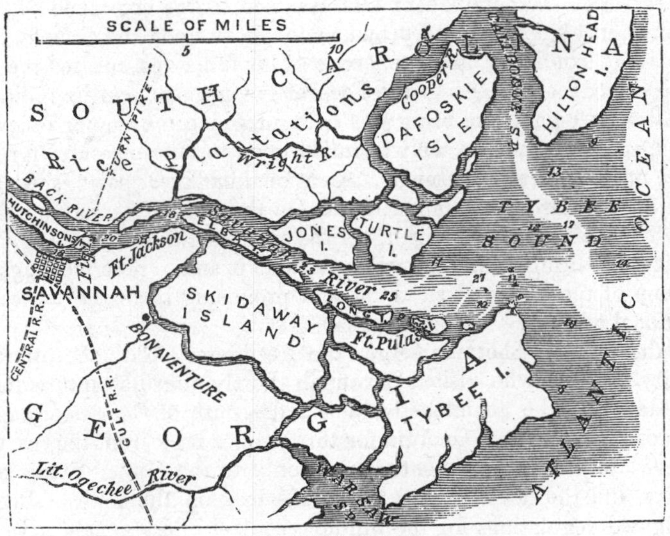

APPROACHES TO SAVANNAH.

CHAPTER LI.

SHERMAN'S CAMPAIGN.—THE CAROLINA MARCH.

Correspondence between Grant and Sherman.—The Idea of transporting Sherman's Army to Virginia by Sea abandoned.—Sherman's Preparations for a March through the Carolinas.—Civil Administration at Savannah.—Trade Regulations.—Sherman's Orders respecting Freedmen.—Regulations for the Government of Savannah.—Cotton taken as a Prize of War.—Howard's Movement on Pocotaligo.—A Flood in the Savannah River impedes Slocum's Operations.—Comparison of the Carolina March with that from Atlanta to Savannah.—Sherman's Acquaintance with the Country.—Feint Movement on Charleston.—Crossing of the Salkehatchie.—Destruction of the Railroad connecting Augusta with Charleston.—Crossing of the South Edisto.—Sherman declines Wheeler's Cotton Compromise.—Union of the two Wings south of the Congaree.—Capture of Columbia.—Explanation of the Burning of Columbia.—Occupation of Winnsborough.—Crossing of the Catawba.—Sherman retaliates for the Murder of his Foragers.—Correspondence with Wheeler on this Subject.—Occupation of Cheraw.—Charleston Evacuated.—Affair between Kilpatrick and Wade Hampton.—Sherman's Army at Fayetteville, on the Cape Fear River.—Concentration of the Enemy's Forces under Johnston.—Sherman communicates with Terry and Schofield.—Crossing of the Cape Fear.—Battle of Averysborough.—Battle of Bentonville.—Sherman, re-enforced by Terry and Schofield, concentrates his Army at Goldsborough, and establishes Communications with Newbern and Morehead City.

WHEN General Sherman, after the capture of Fort McAllister, passed down the Ogeechee into Ossibaw Sound, and to the flag-ship of Admiral Dahlgren, he found two communications waiting him from Lieutenant General Grant. When these were written Sherman was still marching through Georgia, and had not "struck bottom." But they express no fear as to the ultimate success of the extraordinary campaign which Sherman had undertaken. The second of these communications, of date December 6th, indicated Grant's intention to transport Sherman's army, after it had established a base on the coast, to the James River, to co-operate in the campaign against Lee.[1]

Sherman, although his original plan had contemplated a continuation of his march through the Carolinas to Virginia,[2] immediately set out to obey General Grant's instructions. In the delay incident to the transportation of his army he determined to capture Savannah. As we have seen, he accomplished that object on the 21st. The next day he announced his success to the lieutenant general.

In the mean time General Sherman had heard of Hood's defeat at Nashville, which was at once a vindication of his march and the indispensable seal of its success. The tidings of the capture of Savannah following close upon Hood's defeat illustrated to the outside world what had all along been present to the prophetic eye of Sherman—the tremendous significance of the March to the Sea. In a twinkling, the doubts of the loyal, and the rash confidence of the rebellious and of their sympathizers, were dispersed. It was to the Northern people the breaking of a glorious dawn after terribly dark hours of anxiety and apprehension. A period of suspense had passed, during which few opened their mouths to judge General Sherman or to predict the issue of a movement which was almost universally believed too bold to rank among the legitimate ventures of war; and now, suddenly, out of this ominous silence arose a universal shout at once of triumph and of praise to the victor, who had been no less signally crowned by his own success at Savannah than by that of his subordinate at Nashville, 657 miles away.[1] General Grant, even before the capture of Savannah, congratulated General Sherman and his army upon the successful termination of his "brilliant campaign." It is true, he had heard of Hood's defeat; but he says, "I never had a doubt of the result. When apprehensions for your safety were expressed by the President, I assured him, with the army you had, and you in command of it, there was no danger but you would strike bottom on salt water some place; that I would not feel the same security, in fact would not have intrusted the expedition to any other living commander." On the 26th, in answer to Sherman's note presenting him with Savannah as a Christmas gift, President Lincoln replied:

"MY DEAR GENERAL SHERMAN,—Many, many thanks for your Christmas gift. When you were about leaving Atlanta for the Atlantic coast, I was anxious, if not fearful; but, feeling that you were the better judge, and remembering that 'nothing risked, nothing gained,' I did not interfere. Now, the undertaking being a success, the honor is all yours; for I believe none of us went farther than to acquiesce. And, taking the work of General Thomas into the count, as it should be taken, it is indeed a great success. Not only does it afford the obvious and immediate military advantages, but, in showing the world that your army could be divided, putting the stronger part to an immediate new service, and yet leaving enough to vanquish the old opposing force of the whole—Hood's army—it brings those who sat in darkness to see a great light. But what next? I suppose it will be safer to leave General Grant and yourself to decide."[2]

General Grant, after Thomas's victory at Nashville, was shaken in his determination to transport Sherman's army by sea to the James River. It would be impossible to effect this in less than two months, and in that time Sherman could make the march by land, and in doing so strike the enemy a far heavier blow. He writes on the 18th of December: "If you capture the garrison of Savannah, it will certainly compel Lee to detach from Richmond, or give us nearly the whole South. My own opinion is, Lee is averse to going out of Virginia; and, if the cause of the South is lost, he wants Richmond to be the last place surrendered. If he has such views, it may be well to indulge him until we get every thing else in our hands." General Sherman was delighted at the modification of Grant's plan, as he would thus be permitted to carry out his original scheme of a march through the Carolinas.[3]

---

[1] The following are copies of both these letters. The first, from City Point, Virginia, December 3, reads thus:

"The little information gleaned from the Southern press indicating no great obstacle to your progress, I have directed your mails, which previously had been collected in Baltimore by Colonel Markland, special agent of the Post-office Department, to be sent as far as the blockading squadron off Savannah, to be forwarded to you as soon as heard from on the coast. Not liking to rejoice before the victory is assured, I abstain from congratulating you and those under your command until bottom has been struck. I have never had a fear, however, as to the result.

"Since you left Atlanta no great progress has been made here. The enemy has been closely watched, though, and prevented from detaching against you. I think not one man has gone from here except some 1200 or 1500 dismounted cavalry. Bragg has gone from Wilmington. I am trying to take advantage of his absence to get possession of that place. Owing to some preparations Admiral Porter and General Butler are making to blow up Fort Fisher, and which, while I hope for the best, do not believe a particle in, there is a delay in getting this expedition off. I hope they will be ready to start by the 7th, and that Bragg will not have started back by that time.

"In this letter I do not intend to give you any thing like directions for future action, but will state a general idea I have, and will get your views after you have established yourself on the sea-coast. With your veteran army I hope to get control of the only two through routes, from east to west, possessed by the enemy, before the fall of Atlanta. This condition will be filled by holding Savannah and Augusta, or by holding any other post to the east of Savannah and Branchville. If Wilmington falls, a force from there can co-operate with you.

"Thomas has got back into the defenses of Nashville, with Hood close upon him. Decatur has been abandoned, and so have all the roads, except the main one leading to Chattanooga. I hope Hood will be badly crippled or destroyed. After all becomes quiet, and the roads up here are so bad that there is likely to be a week or two that nothing can be done, I will run down the coast and see you."

On the 6th he writes again:

"On reflection, since sending my letter by Lieutenant Dunn, I have concluded that the most important operation toward closing out the rebellion will be to close out Lee and his army. You have now destroyed the roads of the South so that it will probably take them months, without interruption, to establish a through line from east to west. In that time, I think, the job here will be effectually completed. My idea now is, that you establish a base on the coast, fortify, and leave in it all your artillery and cavalry, and enough infantry to protect them, and, at the same time, so threaten the interior that the militia of the South will have to be kept at home. With the balance of your command, come here with all dispatch. Select yourself the officer to leave in command, but you I want in person. Unless you see objections to this plan which I can not see, use every vessel going to you for the purpose of transportation."

[2] In reply to Grant's communications of the 3d and 6th, Sherman incidentally remarks that with his army he "had expected, after reducing Savannah, instantly to march to Columbia, South Carolina, thence to Raleigh," etc.

On the 18th he again writes to Grant, as a sort of postcript to a letter dealing with other matters: "I do sincerely believe that the whole United States, North and South, would rejoice to have this army turned loose on South Carolina, to devastate that state in the manner we have done in Georgia, and it would have a direct and immediate bearing on your campaign in Virginia."

Again, on the 22d, at the close of his letter announcing the capture of Savannah, he says: "I have now completed my first step, and should like to go on to you *via* Columbia and Raleigh, but will prepare to embark as soon as vessels come. Colonel Babcock will have told you all, and you know better than any body else how much better troops arrive by a land march than when carried by transports. . . . . The capture of Savannah, with the incidental use of the rivers, gives us a magnificent position in this quarter, and if you can hold Lee, and if Thomas can continue as he did on the 18th, I could go on and smash South Carolina all to pieces, and also break up roads as far as the Roanoke. But, as I before remarked, I will now look to coming to you as soon as transports are ready."

[1] That General Sherman looked upon the defeat of Hood by Thomas as necessary to justify his march is evident from the following letter, written by him to General J. D. Webster (at Nashville), December 23:

"Major Dixon arrived last night, bringing your letter of the 10th of December, for which I am very much obliged, as it gives me a clear and distinct view of the situation of affairs at Nashville up to that date. I have also from the War Department a copy of General Thomas's dispatch, giving an account of the attack on Hood on the 15th, which was successful, but not complete. I await farther accounts with anxiety, as Thomas's complete success is necessary to vindicate my plans for this campaign, and I have no doubt that my calculations that Thomas had in hand (including A. J. Smith's troops) a force large enough to whip Hood in fair fight were correct. I approve of Thomas's allowing Hood to come north far enough to enable him to concentrate his own men, though I would have preferred that Hood should have been checked about Columbia. Still, if Thomas followed up his success on the 15th, and gave Hood a good whaling, and is at this moment following him closely, the whole campaign in my division will be even more perfect than the Atlanta campaign, for at this end of the line I have realized all I had reason to hope for except in the release of our prisoners, which was simply an impossibility."

[2] General Sherman's reply to this is equally characteristic. Writing January 6th, he says: "I am gratified at the receipt of your letter of December 26th at the hands of General Logan, especially to observe that you appreciate the division I made of my army, and that each part was duly proportioned to its work.

"The motto, 'Nothing venture, nothing win,' which you refer to, is appropriate; and, should I venture too much and happen to lose, I shall bespeak your charitable inference.

"I am ready for the 'great next' as soon as I can complete certain preliminaries, and learn of General Grant his and your preferences of intermediate 'objectives.'"

[3] He replies to General Grant, December 24: "I am gratified that you have modified your former orders, as I feared that the transportation by sea would very much disturb the unity and *morale* of my army, now so perfect.

"The occupation of Savannah . . . . completes the first part of our game, and fulfills a great part of your instructions; and I am now engaged in dismantling the rebel forts which bear upon the sea and channels, and transporting the heavy ordnance and ammunition to Fort Pulaski and Hilton Head, where they can be more easily guarded than if left in the city.

"The rebel inner lines are well adapted to our purpose, and, with slight modifications, can be held by a comparatively small force, and in about ten days expect to be ready to sally forth again. I feel no doubt whatever as to our future plans. I have thought them over so long and well that they appear as clear as daylight. I left Augusta untouched on purpose, because the enemy will be in doubt as to my objective point after crossing the Savannah River, whether it be Augusta and Charleston, and will naturally divide his forces. I will then move either on Branchville or Columbia by any curved line that gives me the best supplies, breaking up in my course as much railroad as possible, then ignoring Charleston and Augusta both. I would occupy Columbia and Camden, pausing there long enough to observe the effect. I would then strike for the Charleston and Wilmington Railroad, somewhere between the Santee and Cape Fear Rivers, and, if possible, communicate with the fleet under Admiral Dahlgren (whom I find a most agreeable gentleman, in every way accommodating himself to our wishes and plans). Then I would favor Wilmington, in the belief that Porter and Butler will fail in their present undertaking. Charleston is now a mere desolated wreck, and is hardly worth the time it would take to starve it out. Still I am aware that historically and politically, much importance is attached to the place, and it may be that, apart from its military importance, both you and the administration would prefer I should give it more attention; and it would be well for you to give me some general idea on that subject, as otherwise I would treat it, as I have expressed, as a point of little importance, after all its railroads leading into the interior are destroyed or occupied by us. But on the hypothesis of ignoring

General Grant fully sanctioned Sherman's scheme before the close of 1864. There was nearly a month's delay at Savannah. This time was occupied in gathering supplies, in disposing of captured property, and in local administration. The march through Georgia had already led to some important political results in that state. In Liberty and Tatnall counties, south of Savannah, Union meetings were held by the citizens, and patriotic resolutions were adopted. Sherman recognized the movement, and promised his aid, encouragement, and defense to all citizens who would "stay quietly at home, and call back their sons and neighbors to resume their peaceful pursuits." He invited all such to bring their produce to Savannah, to be sold to the highest bidder or to his commissary. Merchants and attorneys in Savannah were required to acknowledge the national supremacy in order to the continuance of their avocations. But, in Sherman's judgment, all matters relating to reconstruction in Georgia were of secondary importance until the final victory of the nation should be secured.

Sherman caused a thorough examination to be made of the defenses of Savannah, which city was now to become an important dépôt of supplies. New lines of fortification were constructed, "embracing the city proper, Forts Jackson, Thunderbolt, and Pulaski, with slight modifications in their

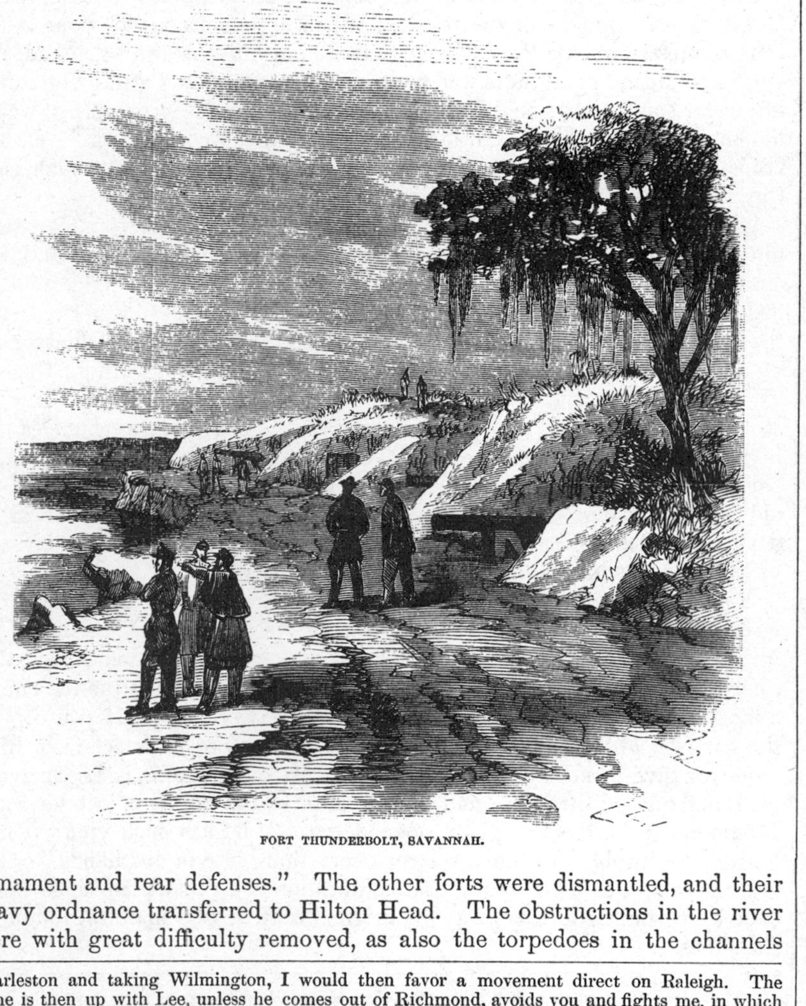

FORT THUNDERBOLT, SAVANNAH.

armament and rear defenses." The other forts were dismantled, and their heavy ordnance transferred to Hilton Head. The obstructions in the river were with great difficulty removed, as also the torpedoes in the channels below the city. General Geary was assigned to the command of the city. His policy, just but conciliatory, had a good effect upon the citizens. Mayor R. D. Arnold, continued in the exercise of his functions, advised the citizens to yield a ready obedience to the Federal government and its military representative. A public meeting was held, in which the mayor's views were adopted, and Governor Brown was called upon to take measures for the restoration of Georgia to the Union. A national bank was established, and the city enjoyed undisturbed tranquillity. On the 14th of January, 1865, General Sherman issued orders regulating the internal trade of the state, inviting the citizens to bring their produce to Savannah, and to hold meetings for the discussion of their present situation, and promising them the protection of the national army.[1]

Nor did General Sherman forget the freedmen. With the approval of Secretary Stanton, who visited Savannah shortly after its capture, he issued orders devoting the abandoned sea islands south of Charleston, and rice-fields along the rivers of Georgia for thirty miles back from the sea, to their exclusive use and management, subject only to the United States military authority and the acts of Congress.[2] He had, on the 26th of December, promulgated regulations for the military control of Savannah.[3] In his or-

---

Charleston and taking Wilmington, I would then favor a movement direct on Raleigh. The game is then up with Lee, unless he comes out of Richmond, avoids you and fights me, in which case I should reckon on your being on his heels.

"Now that Hood is used up by Thomas, I feel disposed to bring the matter to an issue as quick as possible. I feel confident that I can break up the whole railroad system of South Carolina and North Carolina, and be on the Roanoke, either at Raleigh or Weldon, by the time spring fairly opens; and if you feel confident that you can whip Lee outside of his intrenchments, I feel equally confident that I can handle him in the open country.

"One reason why I should ignore Charleston is this: That I believe they will reduce the garrison to a small force, with plenty of provisions, and I know that the neck back of Charleston can be made impregnable to assault, and we will hardly have time for siege operations.

"I will have to leave in Savannah a garrison, and, if Thomas can spare them, I would like to have all detachments, convalescents, etc., belonging to these four corps, sent forward at once. I don't want to cripple Thomas, because I regard his operations as all-important, and I have ordered him to pursue Hood down into Alabama, trusting to the country for supplies.

"I reviewed one of my corps to-day, and shall continue to review the whole army. I don't like to boast, but I believe this army has a confidence in itself that makes it almost invincible."

Grant replied on the 27th of December, giving Sherman permission to follow out his plan, and making some suggestions. He says:

"Your confidence in being able to march up and join this army pleases me, and I believe it can be done. The effect of such a campaign will be to disorganize the South, and prevent the organization of new armies from their broken fragments. Hood is now retreating, with his army broken and demoralized. His loss in men has probably not been far from 20,000, besides deserters. If time is given, the fragments may be collected together, and many of the deserters reassembled. If we can we should act to prevent this. Your spare army, as it were, moving as proposed, will do this.

"In addition to holding Savannah, it looks to me that an intrenched camp ought to be held on the railroad between Savannah and Charleston. Your movements toward Branchville will probably enable Foster to reach this with his own force. This will give us a position in the South from which we can threaten the interior without marching over long, narrow causeways, easily defended, as we have heretofore been compelled to do. Could not such a camp be established about Pocataligo or Coosawatchie?

"I have thought that, Hood being so completely wiped out for all present harm, I might bring A. J. Smith with from 10,000 to 15,000. With this increase I could hold my lines, and move out with greater force than Lee has. It would compel him to retain all his present force in the defenses of Richmond, or abandon them entirely. The latter contingency is probably the only danger to the easy success of your expedition. In the event you should meet Lee's army, you would be compelled to beat it or find the sea-coast. Of course I shall not let Lee's army escape if I can help it, and will not let it go without following it to the best of my ability.

"Without waiting farther directions, then, you may make preparations to start on your Northern expedition without delay. Break up the railroads in South and North Carolina, and join the armies operating against Richmond as soon as you can.

"I will leave out all suggestions about the route you should take, knowing that your information, gained daily in the progress of events, will be better than any that can be obtained now. It may not be possible for you to march to the rear of Petersburg; but, failing in this, you could strike either of the sea-coast ports in North Carolina held by us. From there you could easily take shipping. It would be decidedly preferable, however, if you could march the whole distance. From the best information I have, you will find no difficulty in supplying your army until you cross the Roanoke. From there here is but a few days' march, and supplies could be collected south of the river to bring you through. I shall establish communication with you there by steam-boat and gun-boat. By this means your wants can be partially supplied."

[1] The following is a copy of these orders:

"It being represented that the Confederate army and armed bands of robbers, acting professedly under the authority of the Confederate government, are harassing the people of Georgia and endeavoring to intimidate them in the efforts they are making to secure themselves provisions, clothing, security to life and property, and the restoration of law and good government in the state, it is hereby ordered and made public:

"I. That the farmers of Georgia may bring into Savannah, Fernandina or Jacksonville, Florida, marketing, such as beef, pork, mutton, vegetables of any kind, fish, etc., as well as cotton in small quantities, and sell the same in open market, except the cotton, which must be sold by or through the treasury agents, and may invest the proceeds in family stores, such as bacon and flour, in any reasonable quantities, groceries, shoes, and clothing, and articles not contraband of war, and carry the same back to their families. No trade-stores will be attempted in the interior, or stocks of goods sold for them, but families may club together for mutual assistance and protection in coming and going.

"II. The people are encouraged to meet together in peaceful assemblages to discuss measures looking to their safety and good government, and the restoration of state and national authority, and will be protected by the national army when so doing; and all peaceable inhabitants who satisfy the commanding officers that they are earnestly laboring to that end must not only be left undisturbed in property and person, but must be protected as far as possible consistent with the military operations. If any farmer or peaceful inhabitant is molested by the enemy, viz., the Confederate army of guerrillas, because of his friendship to the national government, the perpetrator, if caught, will be summarily punished, or his family made to suffer for the outrage; but if the crime can not be traced to the actual party, then retaliation will be made on the adherents to the cause of the rebellion. Should a Union man be murdered, then a rebel selected by lot will be shot; or if a Union family be persecuted on account of the cause, a rebel family will be banished to a foreign land. In aggravated cases, retaliation will extend as high as five for one. All commanding officers will act promptly in such cases, and report their action after the retaliation is done."

[2] The following are the orders:

"I. The islands from Charleston south, the abandoned rice-fields along the rivers for thirty miles back from the sea, and the country bordering the St. John's River, Florida, are reserved and set apart for the settlement of the negroes now made free by the acts of war and the proclamation of the President of the United States.

"II. At Beaufort, Hilton Head, Savannah, Fernandina, St. Augustine, and Jacksonville, the blacks may remain in their chosen or accustomed vocations; but on the islands, and in the settlements hereafter to be established, no white person whatever, unless military officers and soldiers detailed for duty, will be permitted to reside, and the sole and exclusive management of affairs will be left to the freed people themselves, subject only to the United States military authority and the acts of Congress. By the laws of war and orders of the President of the United States, the negro is free, and must be dealt with as such. He can not be subjected to conscription, or forced into military service, save by the written orders of the highest military authority of the department, under such regulations as the President or Congress may prescribe; domestic servants, blacksmiths, carpenters, and other mechanics will be free to select their own work and residence; but the young and able-bodied negroes must be encouraged to enlist as soldiers in the service of the United States, to contribute their share toward maintaining their own freedom, and securing their rights as citizens of the United States.

"Negroes so enlisted will be organized into companies, battalions, and regiments, under the orders of the United States military authorities, and will be paid, fed, and clothed according to law. The bounties paid on enlistment may, with the consent of the recruit, go to assist his family and settlement in procuring agricultural implements, seed, tools, boats, clothing, and other articles necessary for their livelihood.

"III. Whenever three respectable negroes, heads of families, shall desire to settle on lands, and shall have selected for that purpose an island or a locality clearly defined within the limits above designated, the inspector of settlements and plantations will himself, or by such subordinate officer as he may appoint, give them a license to settle such island or district, and afford them such assistance as he can to enable them to establish a peaceable agricultural settlement. The three parties named will subdivide the land, under the supervision of the inspector, among themselves and such others as may choose to settle near them, so that each family shall have a plot of not more than forty acres of tillable ground, and, when it borders on some water-channel, with not more than etght hundred feet water-front, in the possession of which land the military authorities will afford them protection until such time as they can protect themselves, or until Congress shall regulate their title.

"The quartermaster may, on the requisition of the inspector of settlements and plantations, place at the disposal of the inspector one or more of the captured steamers to ply between the settlements and one or more of the commercial points heretofore named in orders, to afford the settlers the opportunity to supply their necessary wants, and to sell the products of their land and labor.

"IV. Whenever a negro has enlisted in the military service of the United States, he may locate his family in any one of the settlements at pleasure, and acquire a homestead and all other rights and privileges of a settler as though present in person.

"In like manner, negroes may settle their families and engage on board the gun-boats, or in fishing, or in the navigation of the inland waters, without losing any claim to land or other advantages derived from this system. But no one, unless an actual settler as above defined, or unless absent on government service, will be entitled to claim any right to land or property in any settlement by virtue of these orders.

"V. In order to carry out this system of settlement, a general officer will be detailed as inspector of settlements and plantations, whose duty it shall be to visit the settlements to regulate their police and general management, and who will furnish personally to each head of a family, subject to the approval of the President of the United States, a possessory title in writing, giving, as near as possible, the description of boundaries, and who shall adjust all claims or conflicts that may arise under the same, subject to the like approval, treating such titles altogether as possessory. The same general officer will also be charged with the enlistment and organization of the negro recruits, and protecting their interests while absent from their settlements, and will be governed by the rules and regulations prescribed by the War Department for such purposes."

[3] Of which the following is a copy:

"The city of Savannah and surrounding country will be held as a military post and adapted to future military uses, but, as it contains a population of some twenty thousand people who must be provided for, and as other citizens may come, it is proper to lay down certain general principles, that all within its military jurisdiction may understand their relative duties and obligations.

"I. During war, the military is superior to civil authority, and where interests clash the civil must give way; yet, where there is no conflict, every encouragement should be given to well-disposed and peaceful inhabitants to resume their usual pursuits. Families should be disturbed as little as possible in their residences, and tradesmen allowed the full use of their shops, tools, etc. Churches, schools, all places of amusement and recreation, should be encouraged, and streets and roads made perfectly safe to persons in their usual pursuits. Passes should not be exacted within the line of outer pickets; but if any person shall abuse these privileges by communicating with the enemy, or doing any act of hostility to the government of the United States, he or she will be punished with the utmost rigor of the law.

"Commerce with the outer world will be resumed to an extent commensurate with the wants of the citizens, governed by the restrictions and rules of the Treasury Department.

"II. The chief quartermaster and commissary of the army may give suitable employment to the people, white and black, or transport them to such points as they choose, where employment may

ders regulating trade he had excluded cotton from ordinary commerce, holding this staple to be a legitimate prize of war, and the property of the United States.[1] These trade regulations included within their scope the whole Department of the South, which, though still under the immediate command of General Foster, was now subordinate to General Sherman.

By the 19th of January Sherman was ready to move. Grover's division of the Nineteenth Corps had been withdrawn from Sheridan's Army of the Shenandoah to Savannah, relieving Geary's division, and forming thereafter a part of General Foster's command. General Schofield, with the Twenty-third Corps, had been transferred from the West to re-enforce Generals Terry

SLOCUM'S ARMY CROSSING THE SAVANNAH AT SISTER'S FERRY.

be had, and may extend temporary relief in the way of provisions and vacant houses to the worthy and needy, until such time as they can help themselves. They will select, first, the buildings for the necessary uses of the army; next, a sufficient number of stores to be turned over to the treasury agent for trade-stores. All vacant store-houses or dwellings, and all buildings belonging to absent rebels, will be construed and used as belonging to the United States until such times as their titles can be settled by the courts of the United States.

"III. The mayor and city council of Savannah will continue and exercise their functions as such, and will, in concert with the commanding officer of the post and chief quartermaster, see that the fire-companies are kept in organization, the streets cleaned and lighted, and keep up a good understanding between the citizens and soldiers. They will ascertain and report to the chief commissary of subsistence, as soon as possible, the names and number of worthy families that need assistance and support.

"The mayor will forthwith give public notice that the time has come when all must choose their course, namely, to remain within our lines and conduct themselves as good citizens, or depart in peace. He will ascertain the names of all who choose to leave Savannah, and report their names and residence to the chief quartermaster, that measures may be taken to transport them beyond the lines.

"IV. Not more than two newspapers will be published in Savannah, and their editors and proprietors will be held to the strictest accountability, and will be punished severely, in person and property, for any libelous publication, mischievous matter, premature news, exaggerated statements, or any comments whatever upon the acts of the constituted authorities: they will be held accountable even for such articles though copied from other papers."

[1] This led to some dissatisfaction on the part of the citizens of Savannah and of foreign consuls. On the 2d of January Sherman writes to Secretary Stanton in regard to this matter as follows:

"I have just received from Lieutenant General Grant a copy of that part of your telegram to him of 26th December relating to cotton, a copy of which has been immediately furnished to General Eaton, my chief quartermaster, who will be strictly governed by it.

"I had already been approached by all the consuls and half the people of Savannah on this cotton question, and my invariable answer has been that all the cotton in Savannah was prize of war, and belonged to the United States, and nobody should recover a bale of it with my consent; and that as cotton had been one of the chief causes of this war, it should help pay its expenses; that all cotton became tainted with treason from the hour the first act of hostility was committed against the United States, some time in December, 1860, and that no bill of sale subsequent to that date could convey title.

"My orders were that an officer of the quartermaster's department, United States army, might furnish the holder, agent, or attorney a mere certificate of the fact of seizure, with description of the bales, marks, etc.; the cotton then to be turned over to the agent of the Treasury Department, to be shipped to New York for sale. But since the receipt of your dispatch I have ordered General Eaton to make the shipment himself to the quartermaster at New York, where you can dispose of it at pleasure. I do not think the Treasury Department ought to bother itself with the prizes or captures of war.

"Mr. Barclay, former consul at New York—representing Mr. Molyneux, former consul, but absent since a long time—called on me in person with reference to cotton claims by English subjects. He seemed amazed when I told him I should pay no respect to consular certificates, and that in no event would I treat an English subject with more favor than one of our own deluded citizens; and that, for my part, I was unwilling to fight for cotton for the benefit of Englishmen openly engaged in smuggling arms and munitions of war to kill us; that, on the contrary, it would afford me great satisfaction to conduct my army to Nassau and wipe out that nest of pirates. I explained to him, however, that I was not a diplomatic agent of the general government of the United States; but that my opinion, so frankly expressed, was that of a soldier, which it would be well for him to heed. It appeared also that he owned a plantation on the line of investment to Savannah, which, of course, is destroyed, and for which he expected me to give him some certificate entitling him to indemnification, which I declined emphatically.

"I have adopted in Savannah rules concerning property, severe but just, founded upon the laws of nations and the practice of civilized governments; and am clearly of opinion that we should claim all the belligerent rights over conquered countries, that the people may realize the truth that war is no child's play."

and Palmer, who were operating on the coast of North Carolina, and preparing the way for General Sherman's arrival. On the 24th of December an unsuccessful attack had been made on Fort Fisher, at the mouth of Cape Fear River, by Admiral Porter. The failure of the expedition was due to a want of proper management on the part of General Butler, the military commander. On the 15th of January the attack was renewed, General Butler being replaced by General Terry, and was successful. The remaining works of the enemy at the mouth of the Cape Fear soon followed the fate of Fort Fisher. This victory was auspicious for Sherman, who was then setting out upon his northward march.

General Howard was ordered to effect a lodgment on the Savannah and Charleston Railroad, at Pocotaligo. He embarked with the Seventeenth Corps at Thunderbolt, and proceeded to Beaufort, and there landing his troops, succeeded in reaching Pocotaligo Station. Leggett's division dislodged the enemy, and a secure dépôt for supplies was established at the mouth of Pocotaligo Creek, within easy communication by Broad River with Hilton Head. Three divisions of Logan's corps (the Fifteenth) followed Blair; but Corse's division was cut off by the freshets, and compelled to move with the left wing.

Slocum, with the left wing and Kilpatrick's cavalry, was ordered to move directly across the Savannah River up to Coosawatchie, on the Charleston Road, and to Robertsville, on the road to Columbia. He had established a good pontoon bridge across the river opposite the city, and the Union causeway, over which Hardee had retreated a month before, had been repaired and corduroyed; but before the time appointed for his march the heavy rains of January had swollen the river, swept away the bridge, and overflowed the whole bottom, so that the causeway was four feet under

POCOTALIGO DEPÔT.

MARCHING THROUGH THE SWAMPS.

water. Driven thus from the route originally determined upon, Slocum, on the 26th of January, ascended the river to Sister's Ferry. But even there the river was three miles wide, and his command was prevented from crossing until the 7th of February. Two divisions of the Twentieth Corps—Jackson's and Geary's—had crossed the river at Pureysburg, and, proceeding to Hardeeville, on the Charleston Road, secured communication with Howard at Pocotaligo.

Sherman, in the mean time, on the 22d, embarked for Hilton Head, where he conferred with Admiral Dahlgren and General Foster in regard to their co-operative movements. General Foster was to follow Sherman's army inland, and occupy in succession Charleston and such other points on the sea-coast as would be of any military value. Thus Sherman's army was free to move directly upon Goldsborough.

In all its general features, the march through the Carolinas was a repetition of that through Georgia, already accomplished. No important stronghold of the enemy was attacked. As Sherman in the Georgia promenade had feigned on Macon and Augusta, and passed between without striking either, so now he purposed to demonstrate against Augusta and Charleston, avoiding both, and make the quickest possible march to Goldsborough. In boldness, his present scheme exceeded the one already executed. The country to be traversed was more difficult, and the enemy had been given time to concentrate his fragmentary forces in Sherman's front. But Sherman had

no doubts. "I think," he says,[1] "the time has come now when we should attempt the boldest moves, and my experience is that they are easier of execution than more timid ones, because the enemy is disconcerted by them."[2] He was as familiar with the country over which he was about to march as with Georgia. "I have hunted it over many a time," he says, "from Santee

[1] Letter to General Halleck, December 24th, 1864.
[2] He adds in the same letter: "I also doubt the wisdom of concentration beyond a certain point, as the roads of this country limit the amount of men that can be brought to bear in any one battle; and I don't believe that any one general can handle more than 60,000 men in battle. I think any campaign of the last month, as well as every step I take from this point northward, is as much a direct attack upon Lee's army as though I were operating within the sound of his artillery. . . . . . I attach more importance to these deep incisions into the enemy's country, because this war differs from European wars in this particular—we are not only fighting hostile armies, but a hostile people, and must make old and young, rich and poor, feel the hard hand of war, as well as their organized armies. I know that this recent movement of mine through Georgia has had a wonderful effect in this respect. Thousands who had been deceived by their lying papers into the belief that we were being whipped all the time, realized the truth, and have no appetite for a repetition of the same experience. To be sure Jeff. Davis has his people under a pretty good shape of discipline, but I think faith in him is much shaken in Georgia, and I think before we are done South Carolina will not be so tempestuous. . . . . I felt somewhat disappointed at Hardee's escape from me. . . . Still, I know that the men that were in Savannah will be lost, in a measure, to Jeff. Davis, for the Georgia troops, under G. W. Smith, declared they would not fight in South Carolina, and they have gone north *en route* for Augusta; and I have reason to believe the North Carolina troops have gone to Wilmington."

ENTERING BLACKVILLE, SOUTH CAROLINA.

CROSSING THE SOUTH EDISTO.

SHERMAN'S ARMY ENTERING COLUMBIA, SOUTH CAROLINA.

to Mount Pleasant." His army did not lack enthusiasm, and the prospect of a march through South Carolina was one which it relished exceedingly. The general feeling of the North toward Charleston may be inferred from General Halleck's suggestion to Sherman: "Should you capture Charleston, I hope that by *some* accident the place may be destroyed; and if a little salt should be sown upon its site, it may prevent the growth of future crops of nullification and secession."[1] Poor South Carolina! she was sandwiched between two states who looked upon her as the original source of their past madness and their present woes.

Perhaps if Sherman had had Johnston as an antagonist in his immediate front he would not have been so confident. He calculated on the same Confederate scheme for the defense of the Carolinas which he had baffled in Georgia. He knew that they would hold on to Augusta and Charleston as they had, six weeks before, to Augusta and Macon, leaving him the route between, molested only by Wheeler's cavalry and a mob of disorganized militia, which would be swept like chaff before his march.

General Sherman accompanied the right wing of his army. On the 25th of January, with a small force, he demonstrated against the Combahee Ferry and the railroad bridge across the Salkehatchie, which river the enemy had adopted as his line of defense covering Charleston. After amusing the enemy at this point for nearly a week, the real march of Howard's army began on the 1st of February. Still keeping up the feint on Charleston, the main body of the army moved westward up the Salkehatchie. All the roads northward had been held for weeks by Wheeler's cavalry; the bridges

had been burned and trees had been felled to obstruct Sherman's movements. But the pioneer battalions soon cleared the way and rebuilt the bridges. On the 2d the Fifteenth Corps was well advanced at Loper's Cross-roads, while the Seventeenth had reached River's Bridge, and was ready to cross the Salkehatchie.

Slocum's army in the mean time, as we have seen, was still struggling with the Savannah floods. Kilpatrick, however, and two of Williams's divisions, had crossed on pontoons. The latter were ordered to Beaufort's Bridge, and Kilpatrick to Blackville. Howard crossed the Salkehatchie in the face of the enemy at River's and Beaufort's bridges. The position of the enemy at River's Bridge was on the 3d carried by Mower's and G. A. Smith's divisions of the Seventeenth Corps, who crossed the swamp, nearly three miles wide, through water reaching from knee to shoulder, and in bitter cold weather, and making a lodgment below the bridge, turned on the Confederate brigade posted there, driving it in confusion toward Branchville. The Confederate killed and wounded, numbering eighty-eight, were sent back to Pocotaligo. The Fifteenth Corps, with less resistance, but with equal success, effected the crossing at Beaufort's Bridge, a short distance above.

The line of the Salkehatchie being broken, the enemy fell back behind the Edisto River to Branchville, and Sherman occupied the South Carolina Railroad connecting Augusta with Charleston. While waiting for the remainder of Slocum's army, this road was thoroughly destroyed from the Edisto to Blackville, Kilpatrick in the mean time being dispatched eastward to Aiken to threaten Augusta. Slocum reached Blackville on the 10th. The destruction of the railroad was continued to Windon. The whole army was on the 11th well concentrated about midway between Augusta and Charleston, thus dividing the forces of the enemy covering those two points.

Crossing the South Edisto, the right wing appeared in front of Orangeburg on the 12th, swept away a detachment of the enemy intrenched at that

---

[1] Sherman, in the letter already quoted, replies to this: "I will bear in mind your suggestion as to Charleston, and don't think "salt" will be necessary. . . . . . The whole army is burning with an insatiable desire to wreak vengeance on South Carolina. I almost tremble at her fate, but feel that she deserves all that seems in store for her. Many and many a person in Georgia asked me why we did not go to South Carolina, and when I answered that I was *en route* for that state, the invariable reply was, 'Well, if you will make those people feel the severities of war, we will pardon you for your desolation of Georgia.'"

MAP OF SHERMAN'S CAROLINA MARCH.

struction of the railroad to Columbia. Slocum's army moved by roads farther to the west, covered by Kilpatrick on its left. On the morning of February 16th the advance of Sherman's army beheld Columbia from the south bank of the Congaree.

In the mean time Sherman had received a communication from Wheeler, in which the latter promised not to burn cotton if Sherman would not burn houses. Sherman replied, "I hope you will burn all the cotton and save us the trouble. We don't want it, and it has proved a curse to our country. All you don't burn I will. As to private houses occupied by peaceful families, my orders are not to molest or disturb them, and I think my orders are obeyed. Vacant houses, being of no use to any body, I care little about, as the owners have thought them of no use to themselves."

On the south bank of the Congaree the two wings of the army were again united, but forthwith began to diverge again. Slocum was ordered to cross the Saluda at Zion Church, above Columbia, and proceed direct to Winnsborough, destroying the bridges and railroads about Alston. Howard crossed at the same time a little below the point selected for Slocum, and, turning the enemy's position at Columbia, moved upon the town from the north. The next morning, February 17th, under cover of Stone's brigade of Wood's division (Logan's corps), a pontoon bridge was thrown across Broad River, and, while the remainder of the corps was crossing, the Mayor of Columbia rode out and formally surrendered the city to General Stone, who marched his brigade directly into the town. Sherman, crossing the pontoon bridge accompanied by General Howard, rode into the capital of South Carolina. They found perfect quiet in the city, the citizens and soldiers mingling together in the streets. General Wade Hampton, commanding the rear guard of the Confederate cavalry, had, before leaving, ordered all the cotton in the town to be burned. The bales had been piled in the streets, the ropes and bagging cut, and tufts of cotton were thrown about by the wind, which was blowing a perfect gale, lodging in the trees and upon the houses. As this threatened the destruction of the entire town, the soldiers assisted the citizens in putting out the flames. Sherman had ordered the destruction of the arsenals, of all public property not needed for the use of the army, and of the railroads, dépôts, and such machinery as could assist the enemy in carrying on war. But, before this order began to be executed, the smouldering fires of the morning had been rekindled by the wind and communicated to the surrounding buildings. By night they had spread into a conflagration that baffled the efforts of both citizens and soldiers to allay its fury. It was not until about 4 A.M. on the 18th that the fire was got under control. It was due to the assistance of Sherman's soldiers that any portion of the city was left standing. After this matter had been attended to, during the 18th and 19th, Sherman's orders for the destruction of the arsenals, railroads, etc., were properly carried out.[1]

point, and followed, pushing him across the north branch of the Edisto, where he took refuge behind a rampart, supported by a battery, and, having partially burned the bridge, threatened to dispute the crossing. From this position he was soon flanked, and Blair's corps, having crossed, began the de-

[1] The origin of the destructive conflagration in Columbia has been the subject of much discussion, which we can not give here in full. The statements of General Sherman, Major G. W. Nichols, a member of Sherman's staff, General Wade Hampton, and James McCarter (a Confederate citizen who was in Columbia when the event took place), form the body of evidence so far as published. The statements made in Confederate journals at the time are of no value, except in their details as to the exact time the conflagration commenced, the direction of the wind, etc. In regard to the four principal authorities above mentioned, it is assumed that each is reliable so far as he states facts within the scope of his own personal observation.

Sherman, in his official report, says: "Without hesitation, I charge General Wade Hampton with having burned his own city of Columbia, not with a malicious intent, or as the manifestation of a silly 'Roman stoicism,' but from folly and want of sense in filling it with lint, cotton, and tinder. Our officers and men on duty worked well to extinguish the flames; but others not on duty, including the officers who had long been imprisoned there, rescued by us, may

WADE HAMPTON.

STATE CAPITOL and PALMETTO MEMORIAL TO THE S. CAROLINA REGT.S IN THE MEXICAN WAR.

PLAN OF COLUMBIA, SOUTH CAROLINA.

COLUMBIA ON FIRE.

Slocum reached Winnsborough on the 21st of February, and the Twentieth Corps crossed the Catawba River on the 23d, Kilpatrick following the

same night, and then demonstrating against Charlotte, in North Carolina, to which place Beauregard and the Confederate cavalry had retreated. There also might soon be expected Cheatham's corps, of Hood's old army, which had been cut off by Sherman's rapid movement on Columbia and Winnsborough. On the 26th the Twentieth Corps reached Hanging Rock, where it waited for the Fourteenth to cross the Catawba, now swollen by recent heavy rains. As soon as Davis came up with the Fourteenth Corps, Slocum moved direct to Cheraw, North Carolina, nearly 70 miles south of west from Charlotte.

On the 22d Kilpatrick reported to Sherman that 18 of his men had been murdered by Wade Hampton's cavalry, and left in the road with labels upon them threatening a similar fate to all foragers. Sherman replied that this conduct left Kilpatrick no alternative; he must retaliate man for man. "Let it be done at once," ordered Sherman. "We have a perfect war right to the products of the country we overrun, and may collect them by foragers or otherwise. Let the whole people know the war is now against them because their armies flee before us, and do not defend their country or frontier as they should. It is pretty nonsense for Wheeler and Beauregard, and such vain heroes, to talk of our warring against women and children. If they claim to be men they should defend their women and children, and prevent us reaching their homes. Instead of maintaining their armies, let them turn their attention to their families, or we will follow them to the death; they should know that we will use the produce of the country as we please. I want the foragers to be regulated and systematized, so as not to degenerate into common robbers; but foragers, as such, to collect corn, bacon, beef, and such other products as we need, are as much entitled to our protection as skirmishers and flankers. . . . . If our foragers commit excesses, punish them yourself, but never let an enemy judge between our men and the law."[1]

have assisted in spreading the fire after it once had begun, and have indulged in unconcealed joy to see the ruin of the capital of South Carolina." In regard to the origin and progress of the flames he says, "Before one single public building had been fired by [my] order, the smouldering fires set by Hampton's order were rekindled by the wind, and communicated to the buildings around. About dark they began to spread, and got beyond the control of the brigade on duty within the city. The whole of Wood's division was brought in, but it was found impossible to check the flames, which by midnight had become unmanageable, and raged until about 4 A.M., when, the wind subsiding, they were got under control. I was up nearly all night, and saw Generals Howard, Logan, and Wood, and others laboring to save the houses, and to protect families thus suddenly deprived of shelter, and of bedding and wearing apparel. I disclaim on the part of my army any agency in this fire, but, on the contrary, claim that we saved what of Columbia remains unconsumed." It must be remembered in this connection that the only soldiers of Sherman's army in Columbia were those of Wood's division.

General Wade Hampton, in a letter to Hon. Reverdy Johnson, of Georgia, says: "I pledge myself to prove . . . that he [General Sherman] promised protection to the city, and that, in spite of his solemn promise, he burned the city to the ground, deliberately, systematically, and atrociously." He also asserts in the same letter, "I gave a positive order, by direction of General Beauregard, that no cotton should be fired." Of course Hampton's testimony in regard to Sherman's conduct is unreliable, as he had no means of knowing that which he affirmed. We accept his statement that he gave the order against the destruction of cotton; but the only mode of reconciling this statement with the fact that his soldiers really *did* set the cotton on fire, is to suppose either that the order against the burning came too late, and subsequent to a former order directing the cotton to be burned, or that the burning was against orders.

Major Nichols came with Sherman into Columbia about noon on the 17th. He notices the prevalence of a strong wind, and that it came from the south. It was in the southern portion of the city that the cotton was burning. "It seemed to me," he says, "I had never experienced a more powerful gale of wind." Both he and Sherman testify that the air was filled with smoking tufts of cotton, catching in trees and falling on the shingled roofs of houses. Nichols admits that, apart from the fires occasioned by the burning cotton, "there were fires which must have started independent of the above-mentioned cause. The source of these is ascribed to the desire for revenge from some 200 of our prisoners who had escaped from the cars as they were being conveyed from this city to Charlotte. Again it is said that the soldiers who first entered the town, intoxicated with bad liquor, which was freely distributed among them by designing citizens, in an insanity of exhilaration, set fire to unoccupied houses." Nichols testifies to the efforts made by officers and soldiers to put out the fire which broke out in the afternoon. He says: "I saw Sherman, Howard, Logan, Woods, and other general officers, with their staffs, working with heart and hand to stay the progress of the flames. . . . . During the progress of the fire, and afterward, while the army was in the city, every effort was made for the relief of the sufferers. They were furnished with bedding and food, and were quartered in the houses which had been deserted by their owners who had fled the city the day before. General Sherman gave up his own quarters to a family of ladies, with their children, who were fed from his table; I know from personal observation that he and the officers and men of his army could not have made greater exertions to alleviate the sufferings of these homeless ones if they had been their own kith and kin."

Mr. James McCarter entirely exonerates General Sherman from any responsibility for the conflagration, and states his belief that "Sherman intended to protect the persons and private property of the citizens." Still, he charges the burning and plundering of Columbia upon the soldiers of Sherman's army. He adduces as an argument leading to this conclusion that the wind was from the north. Here Mr. McCarter not only contradicts Major Nichols's testimony, but that of the *Columbia Daily Phœnix*, which asserts that the wind throughout the day "had steadily prevailed from southwest by west, and bore the flames eastward." This is the main argument adduced by McCarter to prove his sweeping assertion; and this, as we have seen, is based upon false premises. The only other argument presented by him is the fact that Wade Hampton's men left Columbia ten hours before the conflagration which so desolated the city. This is true; but it is also true that Sherman's soldiers, on entering the city, found the cotton burning, and assisted the soldiers in putting out the flames. But, as Sherman states in his report, the fire which had been subdued still smouldered in the cotton, and was rekindled by the wind in the afternoon, baffling every effort made by his army to resist its progress.

The above is the testimony bearing upon the case, from which it is clear,

First, that the burning of Columbia was due to two causes, the carelessness of Hampton's men in their manner of destroying the cotton, and the incendiarism of a number of prisoners burning with a desire to wreak vengeance upon the people whom they held responsible for the cruelties which they had experienced in confinement.

Secondly, that Sherman and his army proper not only had no agency in producing the conflagration, but worked heartily and persistently to subdue it, and made every exertion to alleviate the sufferings which followed it.

We have given this matter of the burning of Columbia so much space simply for the purpose of presenting the facts of the case before the reader. We are making no apology—that is not the business of the historian. It is worthy of note, however, that, though Sherman and his army *felt* that South Carolina deserved destruction, after they entered that state they marched through it like an army, and not like a mob of marauders and incendiaries. Although Sherman, in his letter of December 24th, 1864, had said to General Halleck, "I look upon Columbia as quite as bad as Charleston, and I doubt if we shall spare the public buildings there as we did at Milledgeville," still, upon entering Columbia, he found his pity larger than his wrath, and did his best to protect the citizens against a destruction of their property for which he was in no way responsible; just as at Savannah, notwithstanding his menace of punishment in case the city was not surrendered, when he entered the city he saved it from devastation by a mob of its own citizens.

[1] Sherman writes thus to Wade Hampton in regard to this matter, February 24:

"It is officially reported to me that our foraging parties are murdered after being captured, and labeled 'death to all foragers;' one instance of a lieutenant and seven men near Chesterfield, and another of twenty 'near a ravine eighty rods from the main road,' about three miles from Feasterville. I have ordered a similar number of prisoners in our hands to be disposed of in like manner.

"I hold about 1000 prisoners captured in various ways, and can stand it about as long as you, but I hardly think these murders are committed with your knowledge, and would suggest that you give notice to the people at large that every life taken by them results in the death of one of your confederates.

"Of course you can not question my right to 'forage on the country.' It is a war right as old as history. The manner of exercising it varies with circumstances, and if the civil authorities will supply my requisitions, I will forbid all foraging. But I find no civil authorities who can respond to calls for forage and provisions, therefore must collect directly from the people. I have no doubt this is the occasion of much misbehavior on the part of our men, but I can not permit an enemy to judge, and punish with wholesale murder.

"Personally I regret the bitter feelings engendered by this war, but they are to be expected, and I simply allege that those who struck the first blow and made war inevitable, ought not in

WINNSBOROUGH, SOUTH CAROLINA.

HANGING ROCK, SOUTH CAROLINA.

FORAGERS STARTING OUT.

FORAGERS RETURNING TO CAMP.

The right wing, after destroying the railroad to Winnsborough, crossed the Catawba at Peay's Ferry. Detachments were sent from the Fifteenth Corps to Camden to burn the bridge over the Wateree, a tributary of the Santee River, and to break up the railroad between Florence and Charleston. The latter object was not accomplished, as Captain Duncan, commanding the expedition, met Butler's division of Confederate cavalry, and was forced to return.

On the 3d of March Sherman's army had reached Cheraw. Charleston

had in the mean time been evacuated by the Confederates, and at Cheraw were found many of the guns which had been brought from that city. From this point the weather was unfavorable and the roads bad; but, crossing the Great Pedee, the Fourteenth and Seventeenth corps entered Fayetteville on the 11th. During the night of the 9th, Kilpatrick's three brigades guarding the roads east of the Pedee were divided. General Wade Hampton, detecting this, dashed in at daylight, got possession of the camp of Colonel Spencer's brigade, and the house in which Kilpatrick and Spencer had their quarters. Nothwithstanding the completeness of the surprise and the temporary confusion which followed, Kilpatrick succeeded in rallying his

fairness to reproach us for the natural consequences. I merely assert our 'war right' to forage, and my resolve to protect my foragers to the extent of life for life."

UNITED STATES ARSENAL AT FAYETTEVILLE.

THE TUG-BOAT DONALDSON MOVING UP THE CAPE FEAR.

men, and by a prompt attack regained the artillery which he had lost and the camp from which he had been so suddenly ousted.

The 12th, 13th, and 14th of March were passed by Sherman's army at Fayetteville. The Arsenal and the machinery which had formerly belonged to the Harper's Ferry Arsenal were completely destroyed. "Every building. was knocked down and burned," General Sherman reports, "and every piece of machinery utterly broken up and ruined."

Sherman's army was now on the Cape Fear River. Up to this point he had, by admirable strategy, succeeded in dividing the enemy's forces. But now Cheatham's corps had joined Beauregard, and Hardee had got across Cape Fear River in advance of Sherman; and these forces were all on their way to join the Confederate troops in North Carolina, and were under the command of General Joseph E. Johnston, Sherman's old antagonist. In cavalry Johnston's command had somewhat the advantage of Sherman's, and, taking into consideration the military genius of its leader, its artillery and infantry were sufficiently formidable to justify extreme caution on the part of the Federal commander. Before reaching Fayetteville, Sherman had dispatched from Laurel Hill to Wilmington—then in possession of the national troops—two of his best scouts. These men succeeded in their somewhat difficult adventure, and on the morning of the 12th of March Sherman beheld the army tug Donaldson approaching Fayetteville, "bringing me," he says, "full intelligence of the outer world." This tug-boat returned the same day, conveying to General Terry at Wilmington, and to General Schofield at Newbern, intelligence that on the 15th Sherman would move upon Goldsborough. Both Terry and Schofield were ordered to the same point.

In the mean time pontoon bridges had been thrown across the Cape Fear River. Kilpatrick was ordered to move to Averysborough and beyond, in advance of the left wing. Four of Slocum's divisions were to follow, while his two remaining divisions moved as an escort to the trains. Howard moved by a more eastward route to Goldsborough. The idea of this march was to feign on Raleigh and make Goldsborough. But four of Howard's divisions were to preserve communication with Slocum, ready to support the latter in the event of a battle. These movements commenced on the 15th of March. General Sherman went with Slocum's army.

Before reaching Averysborough, Slocum encountered General Hardee's force[1] on the 16th, at a point where the road branches off toward Goldsborough through Bentonville. The enemy must be dislodged both in order to gain the Goldsborough Road and to continue the feint on Raleigh. Hardee's position was difficult to carry, not by reason of its intrinsic strength, but on account of the difficult nature of the ground, which was so soft as to swamp the horses, and even the infantry could scarcely make its way over the pine barren. The Twentieth Corps had the lead, Ward's division in the advance. The latter was deployed, and a skirmish developed the position of a brigade of Charleston heavy artillery, armed as infantry, and commanded by Rhett, posted across the road behind a light parapet, enfilading the approach across a cleared field. Williams dispatched Casey's brigade to the left, turning this position, and Rhett's line was broken, and three guns were captured, with 217 prisoners. Besides these, 108 Confederate dead were afterward buried by Sherman's men.

Ward's division, advancing, developed a second and stronger line, and Jackson's came up on his right, and the Fourteenth Corps on his left, well toward Cape Fear River. Kilpatrick at the same time was ordered to mass his cavalry on the right, and to feel forward for the road to Goldsborough. A brigade of the cavalry gained this road, but was driven back by McLaws's Confederate division. Late in the afternoon the whole Federal line advanced, drove the enemy within his intrenchments, from which, during the stormy night of the 16th, he retreated over the wretched road in his rear. Ward's division followed the next day, beyond Averysborough, and found that Hardee had fallen back on Smithfield. General Slocum's loss in the action at Averysborough was 12 officers and 65 men killed, and 477 wounded.

The Goldsborough Road was now open to the left wing, which, on the night of the 18th, encamped five miles from Bentonville and 27 from Golds-

borough. Howard was two miles farther south, and as no farther resistance was expected from the enemy, was directed to move to Goldsborough via Tulling Creek Church. Sherman joined this wing of the army. But he had not got six miles away from Slocum when he heard artillery to the left. His apprehensions were aroused, but were soon quieted by information conveyed through Slocum's staff officers that the leading division (Carlin's) had encountered Dibbrell's cavalry, which he was driving easily. Shortly after this pleasant intelligence, other staff officers from Slocum reported that the latter had developed the whole of Johnston's army near Bentonville.[1]

Turning, therefore, to the left wing, we find that it has been attacked by the enemy, who has gained a temporary advantage, capturing three of Carlin's guns and driving back his two advanced brigades. General Williams, however, is aware of the danger which threatens him in its full extent, and promptly brings up his whole force, with which, behind hastily-constructed barricades, he assumes the defensive, knowing that Sherman will bring the whole right wing, if necessary, to his assistance.

While Hardee had been fighting Sherman near Averysborough, Johnston was concentrating his medley army at Smithfield, and immediately after that action moved forward with great rapidity, intending to strike and overwhelm Slocum's army before it could be relieved by re-enforcements from Howard. "But," says Sherman, "he 'reckoned without his host.' I had expected just such a movement all the way from Fayetteville, and was prepared for it." During the night of the 19th Slocum got up his wagon train, with the two divisions guarding it, and Hazen's division of the Fifteenth Corps, and made his position impregnable. Johnston could only effect his purpose by placing his whole army between Sherman's two wings, which would, under the circumstances, have proved his ruin. His cavalry, of course, was unable to cut off communication with Howard. Logan's corps, therefore, approached Bentonville without serious resistance, compelling Johnston to refuse his left flank and intrench. Thus the Confederate army was put upon the defensive on the 20th, having three corps of Sherman's army in his front, and unassailable. Johnston's flanks were well protected by swamps, and as it was not Sherman's purpose to fight a battle here, unless forced to do so, the Federal army simply continued to hold its position in the enemy's front. The next day, March 21st, Schofield entered Goldsborough with little opposition, and Terry connected with Blair's corps at Cox's Bridge, on the Neuse, so that, stretching from Goldsborough around to Bentonville, Sherman had now under his command an army of 100,000 men in an impregnable position. Johnston very sensibly, therefore, retreated to Smithfield before his retreat could be cut off by a portion of this immense army. The Federal loss at Bentonville amounted in the aggregate to 1646. Johnston's loss must have been at least 3000 men, including the prisoners which he left to be captured when he abandoned his intrenchments.

The objects of the Carolina campaign had been accomplished in the full possession of Goldsborough, with its two railroads leading to Beaufort and Wilmington. By the 25th of March Sherman's army was concentrated at Goldsborough, and his line of communication with Newbern and Morehead City was firmly established. The co-operative movements which had been conducted while Sherman was marching, by Generals Terry, Foster, and Schofield, next invite our attention.

[1] Johnston's army had not yet been joined by Hoke's command, some 9000 strong. The Confederate force at Bentonville consisted of Stewart's and Cheatham's corps from Hood's old army, together amounting to about 10,000 men; of Hardee's force from Charleston, 9000 strong, and of Wade Hampton's cavalry, numbering about 5000. This made up an army of about 24,000 men.

A. S. WILLIAMS.

[1] Sherman reports this force as 20,000, but this is an exaggeration.

8 U

WILMINGTON AND ITS APPROACHES.

W. B. CUSHING.

CHAPTER LII.
RECOVERY OF THE ATLANTIC COAST.
I. WILMINGTON.

Capture of Plymouth.—Lieutenant Cushing's Expedition for the Destruction of the Albemarle.—Naval Actions in North Carolina Sounds.—Organization of the First Expedition for the Capture of Wilmington.—Delays.—Butler's Powder-boat Strategy.—His Connection with the Expedition.—Explosion of the Powder-boat.—Bombardment of Fort Fisher.—Re-enforcements received by the Enemy.—Landing of Butler's Forces.—Weitzel advises against an Assault.—Reembarkation and Withdrawal of the Troops.—Causes of Failure.—Butler relieved of Command.—The Second Expedition.—Terry in Command.—Plan of Attack.—Assault and Capture of Fort Fisher.—Explosion of the Magazine.—Schofield comes East with the Twenty-third Corps.—Assumes command of the North Carolina Department.—Operations against Wilmington.—Capture of the City.

AT the beginning of 1865 only three important positions on the Atlantic and Gulf coasts east of the Mississippi were retained by the Confederates—Wilmington, Charleston, and Mobile. Of these, Wilmington alone afforded an outlet for even a partial and restricted commerce with Europe.

On the last day of October, 1864, Plymouth, near the mouth of the Roanoke River—a town which had been captured from the Federals early in the year—had been surrendered. Though the possession of this place was of no vital importance, yet the gallant exploit of Lieutenant W. B. Cushing,

which led to its surrender, is so memorable as an instance both of a heroism which has never been surpassed, and of a success which, gained as it was by a single hand, stands unparalleled in the annals of war, that it can not here be forgotten.

In the spring of 1864, the Federal forces had met with several reverses on the North Carolina coast. On the 1st of February, the Confederate General G. E. Pickett captured the Federal outpost at Bachelor's Creek, eight miles from Newbern, with a considerable number of prisoners. During the following night, a party of the enemy in barges captured the United States steamer Underwriter, lying in the Neuse River, and covering the Newbern fortifications. Surprising the garrison at Plymouth on the 17th of April, the Confederates, after a severe struggle, captured that town on the 20th. This was accompanied by the co-operation of the Confederate iron-clad ram Albemarle, which, descending the river, sunk the Federal gun-boat Southfield. The Miami, the only other national gun-boat off Plymouth, with-

THE CONFEDERATE RAM ALBEMARLE ATTACKING THE FEDERAL GUN-BOATS OFF PLYMOUTH.

THE SASSACUS RAMMING THE ALBEMARLE.

drew. General Wessels, thus cut off from communication with the fleet in Albemarle Sound, surrendered the town, with 1600 men and 25 guns, to General Hoke. Washington, at the head of Pamlico River, was evacuated by the Federals in the latter part of the same month, the town having been previously burned by some soldiers of the Seventeenth Massachusetts and Fifteenth Connecticut Regiments.

Albemarle Sound was still held by the national gun-boats. But besides the Albemarle, other Confederate rams were being prepared to recover the naval supremacy of the North Carolina sounds. Captain Melancthon Smith was accordingly sent to assume command in these sounds, with several double-enders. On the afternoon of May 5th the Albemarle came out of the Roanoke, followed by the Bombshell, a small armed tender, and engaged the national fleet collected together off the mouth of the river. A brisk little fight followed. The gun-boats succeeded in dodging the ram, but their guns made no impression. About five o'clock the Sassacus, watching her opportunity, struck the enemy behind her starboard beam, causing her to careen until her deck was washed by the waves. In this position the two vessels remained for some time, and prompt assistance on the part of one of the larger gun-boats might have accomplished the destruction of the Albemarle. Before this was effected the ram swung clear of the Sassacus, and, maintaining the fight until dark, retreated up the river, leaving her tender, the Bombshell, behind in the hands of the Federals. She appeared again on the 24th, but did not venture to renew the contest. The next day a bold attempt was made by a party of five volunteers from the gun-boat Wyalusing to destroy the Albemarle by means of a torpedo, but proved unsuccessful. Thus the affair rested, so far as the Albemarle was concerned, through the summer of 1864.

Notwithstanding the failure of the expedition to blow up the Albemarle in May, Lieutenant Cushing thought the thing practicable, and formed a scheme for accomplishing this object, which, having been submitted to Admiral Lee, he was permitted to carry out. He had formed his plan in June, at which time he was commanding the Monticello. Proceeding to New York, he, in conjunction with Admiral Gregory, Captain Boggs, and Chief Engineer W. W. Wood, applied to one of the new steam pickets a torpedo arrangement, which had been invented by Wood, and then returned to the Sound. The Albemarle was lying off Plymouth at its moorings, and formed the defense of that town. On the night of October 27th, with a select crew of 13 men, six of whom were officers, he proceeded up the river with his engine of destruction. The distance to Plymouth was eight miles. Passing the Confederate picket stationed on the wreck of the Southfield, a mile below the town, without causing alarm, he found the ram protected with a boom of pine logs 30 feet from her side. As the party approached, it encountered a fire from the enemy's infantry on shore, to which the howitzer from Cushing's boat replied. Almost at the same moment the boat ran its bows against the logs guarding the ram. With his own hands Lieutenant Cushing fixed the torpedo in its proper position. "The torpedo boom," says Cushing, "was then lowered, and I succeeded in diving the torpedo under the overhang, and exploding it at the same time that the Albemarle's gun was fired. A shot seemed to go crashing through my boat, and a dense mass of water rushed in from the torpedo, filling the launch and completely disabling her. The enemy then continued his fire at 15 feet range, and demanded our surrender, which I twice refused, ordering the men to save themselves, and removing my overcoat and shoes. Springing into the river, I swam, with others, into the middle of the stream, the rebels failing to hit us." The ram had been destroyed by the torpedo, but the necessity of immediate flight had prevented Cushing from observing the extent and efficiency of his work. All but one of the party accompanying him met death or capture. Cushing escaped, with a bullet in his wrist, by floating down the river, hid himself among the woods on the bank, and finally found a skiff, in which, after eight hours paddling, he reached the Valley City on the

DESTRUCTION OF THE ALBEMARLE.

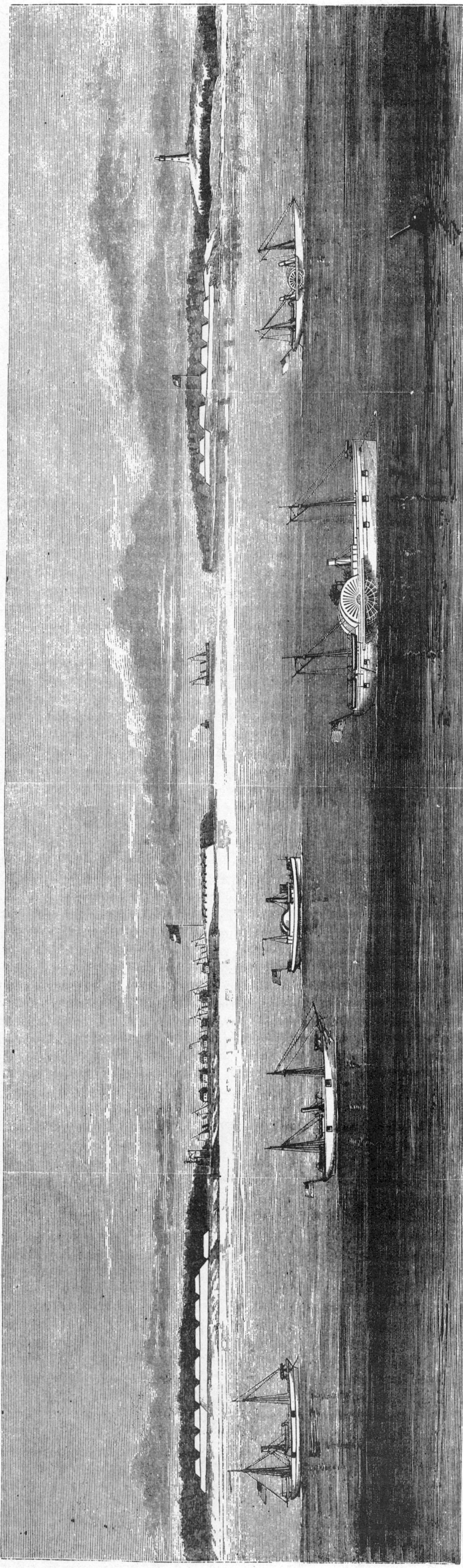

BLOCKADING FLEET OFF WILMINGTON—OLD INLET.

BLOCKADING FLEET OFF WILMINGTON—NEW INLET.

night of the 30th. The next day Plymouth was surrendered to the naval squadron.

The capture of Wilmington would have been undertaken in the earlier stages of the war if it could have been accomplished by a naval force alone. But military co-operation was indispensable, and the instant, ever-pressing need of the military forces on more important fields caused the expedition to be postponed until the autumn of 1864. In September—after the capture of Atlanta, and while the Federal army under Meade was besieging Petersburg, waiting its own opportunity and the accomplishment of Sherman's plans in the West—it was thought forces could be spared from Butler's Army of the James to co-operate with the Navy Department in the reduction of Fort Fisher and the capture of Wilmington.

The naval preparations were promptly made, and it was intended that Vice-Admiral Farragut, then operating on the Gulf Coast, should have command of this branch of the expedition. This was impossible on account of the impaired health of that distinguished officer, and the command was assigned to Rear Admiral Porter, who had been identified with the most important naval victories of the West. After considering the subject, Porter offered to take Fort Fisher in three days if he could have all the heaviest frigates, with 300 guns, and a co-operative military force of 13,000 men.[1] Upon consultation with Grant, the latter said he could not then detach so large a force, but could raise it within 24 hours after Porter had assembled his fleet. No definite time was fixed for the expedition, but it was expected to move by the middle of October. In the mean time Grant collected what information he could about Cape Fear River, with maps and charts, and placed this in the hands of General Weitzel, commanding the Eighteenth Corps, to whom, with General Butler's knowledge, the command of the military force was assigned. As the enemy had in some way been informed of the expedition, it was postponed, but the preparations for it were continued. The small force which Grant could detach rendered it necessary that the attack should be a surprise. The War Department had proposed General Gillmore as the military commander, but to this Grant objected on the ground that he had shown timidity on a former occasion, and appointed Weitzel.

General Butler took a great interest in this affair. It was to be carried out by his own troops, and within the limits of his own department. General Grant preferred that he should not participate in the expedition, but did not choose to interfere, though strict military propriety would have dictated Butler's remaining with the larger portion of his army instead of following a detachment which had been already assigned to an able commander. General Butler's chief interest in the affair was connected with a novel experiment which he had suggested for blowing up Fort Fisher by the explosion near it of 200 or 300 tons of powder. He had heard of the destruction caused by the explosion of a large quantity of gunpowder at Erith, England. The remarkable effect of this explosion for many miles around led him to speculate as to the possibility of destroying military fortifications by similar means. He had first proposed this matter to General Grant in connection with Charleston, which he wanted to blow up with a vessel loaded with 1000 tons of powder. But Grant was skeptical as to the effect of such an experiment. About the time the Fort Fisher expedition was ready to start, Butler again broached his gunpowder plot. Some high authorities had come to his support. Grant referred the matter to Colonel Comstock, of his staff, who reported that the explosion of 300 or 400 tons of powder out at sea would do no damage. General Delafield, Chief Engineer, said the explosion would have about the same effect on the fort that firing feathers from muskets would have on the enemy. The Navy Department and Admiral Porter looked upon the scheme with more favor. General Butler himself was perfectly confident of success. Grant therefore consented to the experiment, but would have no waiting for the powder-boat.

Sherman was at this time in the heart of Georgia, and the enemy, having nearly recovered from his apprehensions of an attack on Wilmington, had left a very small force at Fort Fisher in order to assist in impeding Sherman's march. This was the time to strike. Butler having determined to join the expedition to see that the powder-boat was properly exploded, General Grant ordered him to get off with 6500 men, General Weitzel to have the immediate command. Still Grant had no idea that Butler would go with the expedition until the latter passed his headquarters on the way to Fortress Monroe.[2] Of course, as a matter of military courtesy, all orders for Weitzel had passed through General Butler. On the 4th of December Grant had telegraphed to the latter to get the expedition off without delay, with or without the powder-boat. Instead of moving directly, Butler opened a telegraphic correspondence with Porter about their "little experiment." He issued his orders for the movement to General Weitzel on the 6th. The next day thirteen of the transports were ready. Four—and those the largest—were yet to arrive. On the 10th Butler had reached Fortress Monroe, and telegraphed to General Grant that he was waiting for the navy. Porter was waiting at Norfolk for the powder-boat. He left Hampton Roads on the 13th. The powder-boat had on board 200 tons of powder, and was to receive 90 tons more at Beaufort. "She has delayed us a little," writes Porter to Butler before starting, "and our movements had to depend on her." Butler's transports arrived off Masonborough Inlet, eighteen miles from Fort Fisher, on the 15th. The next day Porter reached Beaufort, and off that point wrote to Butler that he would start for the rendezvous (twenty-five miles east of Cape Fear River) the next day, and, in case of fair weather, would be able to blow up the powder-boat on the night of the 18th. Butler was not ready to land, and the weather did not promise favorably; it was therefore agreed to postpone the explosion. In the mean time, Butler returned to Beaufort for a fresh supply of coal and provisions. Porter remained with the fleet at the appointed rendezvous, and rode out the gale, which was one of unusual violence. His vessels, however, seem to have got in sight of Fort Fisher, for on the 20th their presence was reported to General Hoke. But for the delay occasioned by the powder-boat, the three days of fine weather (the 16th, 17th, and 18th) would have been improved, the troops would have been landed without difficulty, the enemy surprised, and Fort Fisher captured.

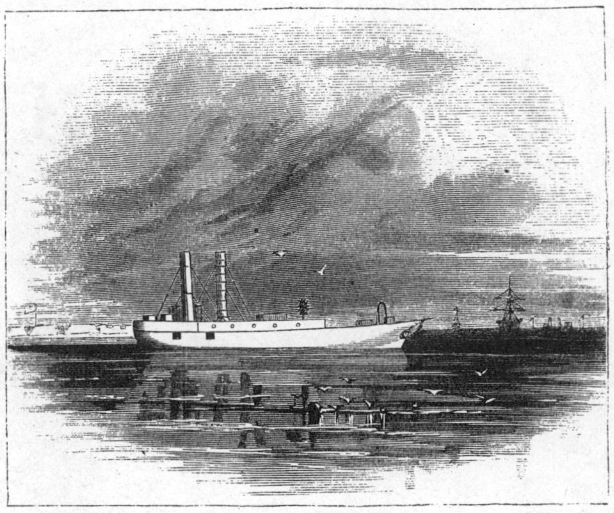

THE POWDER-BOAT LOUISIANA.

Finally, the mountain gave birth to the mouse. On the night of the 23d the powder-boat was exploded at a distance from Fort Fisher of 830 yards. Not a Federal gun-boat or transport dared venture an approach nearer than to a point twelve miles from the scene, and even at a much greater distance the steam in the boilers was lowered to prevent disaster. But, after all, the effect was insignificant. It is true, the explosion was heard at the fort, but it was there supposed that some unfortunate gun-boat had got aground, and been blown up to prevent its falling into the hands of the enemy. The Louisiana had been chosen for this experiment, and had on board, at the time of the explosion, 235 tons of powder. Commander A. C. Rhind had charge of the affair, and associated with him in this perilous service were Lieutenant Assistant Engineer A. T. Mullan, of the Agawam, Paul Boyden, acting master's mate, and seven men. Undoubtedly the effect of the explosion would have been very great if the powder had been properly confined, and if the fuses could have been so arranged that the ignition of the whole mass of powder would be instantaneous. As it was, there were four distinct explosions, and a large amount of the powder was blown away before it ignited.[1] But, in any case, the experiment ought to have been incidental; and Butler and Porter, in making it so prominent a matter, disregarded General Grant's instructions.

It was designed that the troops should be ready to land as soon as possible after the powder-boat explosion. But General Butler was delayed in collecting water, coals, and other supplies, and did not come up until the evening of the 24th, and then with only a few of his transports. Admiral Porter had that morning (11 30 A.M.) commenced the bombardment of Fort Fisher from a fleet of naval vessels, surpassing in numbers and equipments any which had assembled during the war.[2] The attack was made

[1] "I think it was about the 20th of September last that I was on my way to Cairo to resume my command of the Mississippi squadron. Secretary Welles sent me word to meet him that evening at Mr. Blair's. I had arranged to leave for the West the next morning. I went to Mr. Blair's, and found Secretary Welles and Assistant Secretary Fox, who had a number of charts of Cape Fear River, which were spread out for examination. Secretary Welles said that he thought it most important that some attempt should be made to get possession of Cape Fear River; that he had always been in favor of making the attempt, and had, time and time again, invited the co-operation of the army for that purpose, but had received no encouragement. He said he thought there was then a prospect of getting troops for that purpose, and asked me what was my opinion about the matter. I told him I had never seen Cape Fear River, and knew nothing about the defenses the rebels had erected there. He said he would put me in possession of all the papers he had from Admiral Farragut, Admiral Lee, and others who had investigated the subject, and then let me give my opinion about it. I read over carefully all the papers, and examined the charts. Admiral Lee decided most positively that the place could not be taken with 50,000 men, it was so strong; and Admiral Farragut decided that we had not ships in the navy to do any thing with it. Under these circumstances, I told the secretary that I should require time to consider this matter. I went back to the secretary the next morning, and told him that if he would give me the force I named, I would promise to take the fort in three days. That was encouraging to him, for his whole heart was bent upon the matter. . . . . I told him I wanted 300 guns on board ship, and all the heaviest frigates . . . . . that it would require 13,000 men to land with intrenching tools."—*Porter's Testimony before the Committee on the Conduct of the War: Fort Fisher*, p. 88.

[2] At City Point Butler met Grant, and explained his presence with the expedition. He said: "This expedition is a matter of very grave responsibility. (I had known Admiral Porter somewhat in the Mississippi River. General Weitzel and himself, I had understood, had some little difference upon the report as to the damage done by Admiral Porter's bombardment to Fort Jackson and St. Philip.) General Weitzel is a very able general, but a very young man. I am anxious to see this powder experiment go on and succeed, for it is a very grave one; and I think I had better go with the expedition, to take the responsibility off General Weitzel, being an older officer."—*Butler before Committee*, p. 11. This explanation would never have been given if Butler had not felt its necessity to account for his presence with the expedition. It is a conclusive corroboration of Grant's statement that he was surprised to see Butler on the way to Fort Fisher.

[1] See General Butler's and A. C. Rhind's testimony before the Committee.

[2] Porter's haste in exploding the powder vessel, and in commencing the bombardment on the morning of the 24th, before the land force was ready to co-operate, gave rise to considerable feeling. On the night of the 23d Butler sent his staff officer, Captain Clarke, to visit Porter, and inform the latter that the transports would arrive the next day. General Weitzel, in his testimony, says: "Captain Clarke returned just before we left the harbor, and reported that the admiral had said he would explode the powder vessel during the night of Friday, and commence the attack as soon thereafter as possible. It was a question of discussion between us, while sailing toward New Inlet, whether the admiral would commence the attack before we were there to co-operate with him. Several—I think General Butler among the number—doubted that he would do so. I did not doubt it, having been with the admiral on two or three previous expeditions. . . . . I know the opinion expressed on board our vessel by several officers when it was found that the navy had made the attack as they did. There was one officer who particularly surprised me by expressing the opinion he did. He said that he believed Admiral Porter made the attack in the way he did because he believed he could knock the fort all to pieces, and would thus get all the credit of taking it to himself. This officer is generally very quiet in the way of expressing his opinions."

FORT FISHER.

THE IRON-CLAD MONITOR MONADNOCK.

with thirty-seven vessels, five of which were iron-clads; and, besides these, there was a reserve force of nineteen vessels.[1] The main attack was made with the iron-clads and seven other vessels on the land face of the fort. The fleet had upward of 500 guns.

Fort Fisher is situated on Federal Point, on the north bank and at the mouth of Cape Fear River, 20 miles below Wilmington. The original plan of the expedition, as proposed in September, 1864, contemplated the passage of the fleet by the fort up the Cape Fear River. This had been abandoned on account of its impracticability. The channel was intricate, and was commanded by strong forts. It was also full of torpedoes. It was extremely difficult to cross the bar except at high tide, and even when this was accomplished it was unsafe for the vessels to enter without good pilots, or until the channel had been buoyed and the torpedoes removed. The only way in which the fort could be reduced was to land troops north of the work, and then either assault or lay siege to it. It was an earth-work mounting over 40 guns, and though the latter might be dismounted or silenced, the work itself could not be materially injured by a bombardment.[2] This fort, probably the strongest which had been attacked during the war, was manned on the 18th of December by a garrison of 677 men, under General W. H. C. Whiting; Colonel Lamb, who had himself erected the greater portion of the work, being second in command. Within five miles of the fort, at Sugar Loaf, was a reserve force of 800 men.[3] On the 20th the alarm had been given, and on the 22d the advance of General Hoke's division reached Wilmington, and re-enforcements were rapidly sent to Sugar Loaf. Thus, on the 23d, the garrison of the fort was increased to 1087 men.[4]

Very little damage was done to Fort Fisher by the bombardment on the 24th. Twenty-three of the garrison were wounded, all but three only slightly. Five gun-carriages were

The distance between Fort Fisher and Beaufort Harbor was about seventy miles. Porter's explanation of his prompt attack is this: "Captain Clarke said he could make fourteen miles an hour. This would bring him in five hours to Beaufort, with information to General Butler as to the precise time of the explosion of the powder-boat (1 30 A.M. on the 24th). Butler would therefore have plenty of time to reach Fort Fisher before the commencement of his attack, at 11 30 A.M." But it seems Butler, although starting from Beaufort when Clarke returned, did not reach the fleet until night. It is clear, therefore, that Admiral Porter took too much for granted. If he had waited till the night of the 24th for the explosion of the powder-boat, and given Butler prompt notice of this—as he could have done through Captain Clarke—then Butler would have been on hand with the transports, and the attack, taking place on the 25th, would have been a combined one of the navy and army. The reader, however, should understand that, as the affair turned out, this lack of combination on the 24th had nothing whatever to do with the failure of the expedition.

[1] The five iron-clads were the New Ironsides, Canonicus, Monadnock, Saugus, and Mahopac. The four last were turreted monitors.

[2] The following description of the fort is given by General Grant's engineer, Colonel Comstock:

"The land front consists of a half bastion on the left or Cape Fear River side, connected by a curtain with a bastion on the ocean side. The parapet is 25 feet thick, averages 20 feet in height, with traverses rising 10 feet above it and running back on their tops, which are from 8 to 12 feet in thickness, to a distance of from 30 to 40 feet from the interior crest. The traverses on the left half bastion are about 25 feet in length on top. The earth for this heavy parapet and the enormous traverses at their inner ends, more than 30 feet in height, was obtained partly from a shallow exterior ditch, but mainly from the interior of the work. Between each pair of traverses there was one or two guns. The traverses on the right of this front were only partially completed. A palisade, which is loop-holed and has a banquette, runs in front of this face, at a distance of 50 feet in front of the exterior slope, from the Cape Fear River to the ocean, with a position for a gun between the left of the front and the river, and another between the right of the front and the ocean. Through the middle traverse on the curtain is a bomb-proof postern, whose exterior opening is covered by a small redan for two field-pieces, to give flank-fire along the curtain. The traverses are generally bomb-proofed for men or magazines. The slopes of the work appear to have been reveted with marsh sods or covered with grass, and have an inclination of 45 degrees or a little less. . . . There were originally on this front 21 guns and three mortars. . . . The sea front consists of a series of batteries, mounting in all 24 guns, the different batteries being connected by a strong infantry parapet, so as to form a continuous line. The same system of heavy traverses for the protection of guns is used as on the land front, and these traverses are also generally bomb-proofed."

[3] The Confederate Department of North Carolina was under the command of General Bragg, as it had been since October.

[4] These facts were stated by General Whiting after his capture.

Malvern.

Juniata, 14.

Ticonderoga, 16.

FEDERAL FLEET AT HAMPTON ROADS.

Mackinaw, 10.

Minnesota, 48.

Mohican, 11. Monadnock, 4. Osceola, 10. New Ironsides, 18. Colorado, 48. Tuscarora, 11. Wabash, 42. Powhatan, 16. su-quehanna, 16. Shenandoah, 13. Brooklyn, 24. Massasoit, 10.

TRANSPORT FLEET OFF FEDERAL POINT.

THE MONITORS IN A GALE.

disabled, but this and every other injury done to the work was repaired during the night.

The next day, the 25th, was at once Sabbath and Christmas. The bombardment was renewed in the morning, and was more effective. The casualties in the fort were 46, three men being killed and nine mortally wounded. Four gun-carriages and one 10-inch gun were disabled. While the bombardment was going on, and under cover of the fleet, the landing of the troops began about noon. About this time Admiral Porter's flag-ship came alongside Butler's. After an exchanged greeting, the admiral hallooed through his speaking-trumpet, "There is not a rebel within five miles of the fort. You have nothing to do but to land and take possession of it."

The military force was 6500 strong, consisting of General Ames's division of the Twenty-fourth Corps, and General Paine's division of the Twenty-fifth. Paine's division consisted of colored troops. Between 2100 and 2300 men were landed. General Weitzel went with the first 500 (General Curtis's brigade of Ames's division) to reconnoitre. In advancing upon the fort about 300 prisoners were captured by the reconnoitring column. The skirmishers were pushed up by General Curtis to within 150 yards of the fort. Weitzel mounted an artificial knoll, and took a view of the fort. As a defensive work, it did not appear to be injured by the terrific bombardment which it had sustained, and which was still going on. He counted 16 guns, all in proper position, on the land face. Even the grass slopes of the traverses and parapet remained unbroken, and their regular shapes undisturbed. The row of palisades in front of the ditch presented no opening. "It was a stronger work," he says, "than I had ever seen or heard of being assailed during this war." Weitzel remembered Fort Wagner; he recalled his experience in regard to assaults upon works not nearly so strong as this, and which had all proved failures; he remembered, also, that he had been appointed by General Grant to command the expedition instead of Gillmore on the ground that the latter had once shown timidity; that he himself had just been appointed to a major generalship, and that his confirmation depended largely upon his present conduct. He had every possible motive for boldness. Yet he considered that it would be murder to assail the fort, which, if skillfully defended (as he must assume it would be, knowing nothing to the contrary), ought to repulse any attack which he could make; and he advised General Butler against an assault. In the mean time another brigade had landed, and Curtis's skirmishers advanced boldly up to the par-

ADELBERT AMES.

apet. One man crept through the palisade and brought off the flag of the fort, which had been shot down and fallen outside the parapet. But this exploit did not change Weitzel's opinion. He knew that a portion of an assaulting column might even enter a fort, and yet the main body be repulsed. Curtis's advance had not been resisted, but this might be due either to the severity of the bombardment or to a deliberate design on the part of the garrison to tempt an assault. Even if it was due to the bombardment, the latter must cease at the moment of assault, and the garrison would spring again to its guns. General Curtis thought that, if allowed to advance, he could capture the fort. But as there was no well understood and skillfully arranged plan of attack, and no feint to cover his operations, it is very

General Butler thereupon proceeded to re-embark his troops. He gives two reasons for taking this step. In the first place, a storm was approaching, and he feared that it would be impossible to supply his troops on the shore. In the second place, a considerable force of the enemy was on his right flank at Sugar Loaf, and he thought that, under these circumstances, the position was untenable. There was nothing in the way of his landing the remainder of his force, and nothing prevented the landing of supplies until midnight.[1] The fleet would probably outride the gale, and would see to it that his force was supplied and protected against attack. Besides, General Butler had been ordered by General Grant to remain if he effected a landing. The question of immediate assault was left to his discretion; but,

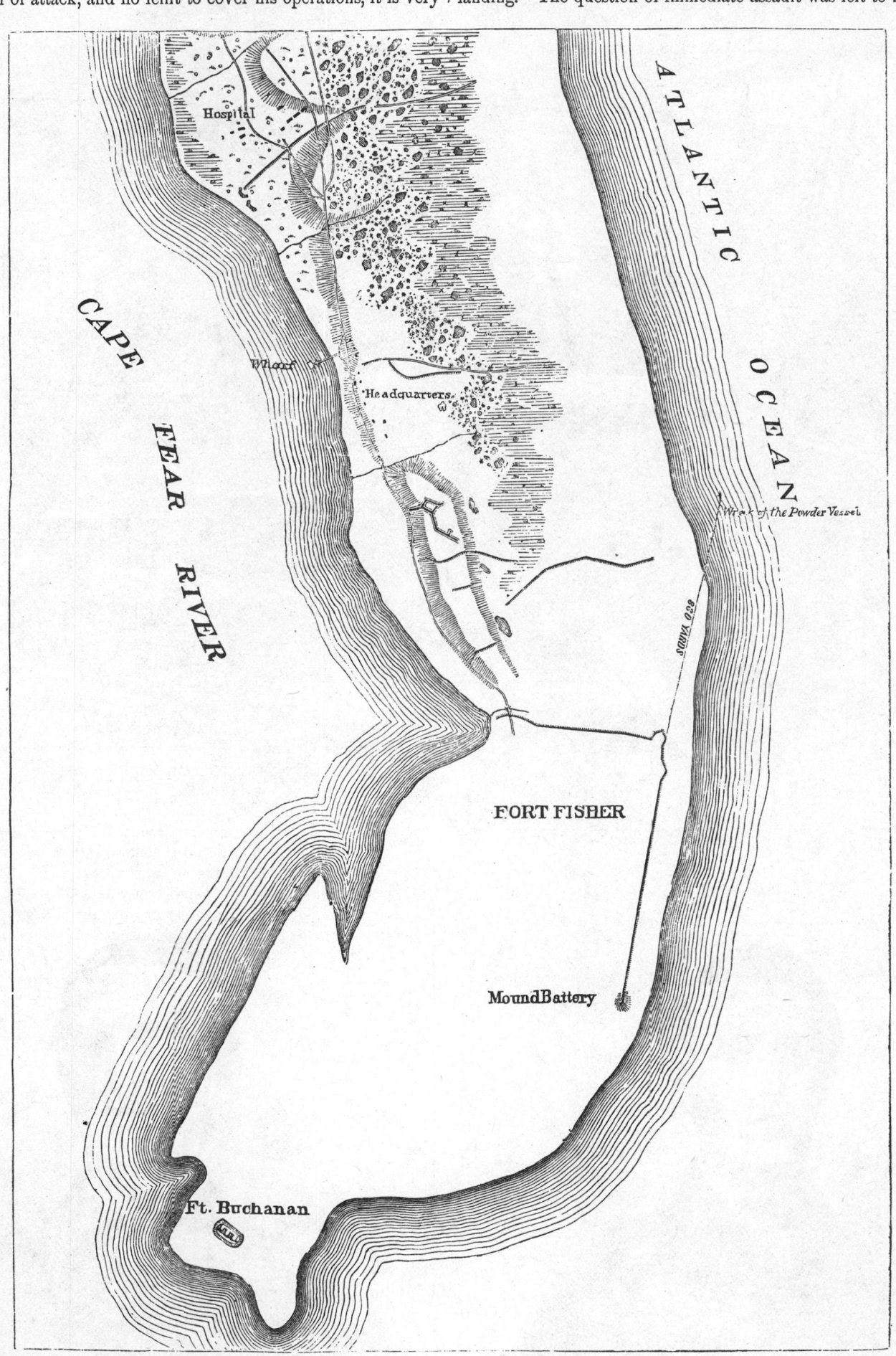

MAP OF FORT FISHER.

probable that, if General Curtis's force had even entered the fort, every man of it would have been captured.[1]

[1] The statement made by General Whiting, who was captured in the second attack on Fort Fisher, certainly confirms the wisdom of General Weitzel's opinion. He says that "the garrison was in no instance driven from its guns, and fired in return, according to orders, slowly and deliberately, 662 shot and shells;" that on the land front 19 guns were in position, and the palisade was in perfect order; and that, while it was possible that 3000 or 6000 men might have carried the work by assault, such an event was not probable. "The work," he adds, "was very strong, the garrison in good spirits, and ready; and the fire on the approaches (the assaulting column having no cover) would have been extraordinarily heavy. In addition to the heavy guns, I had a battery of Napoleons, on which I placed great reliance. The palisade alone would have been a most formidable obstacle."

In his official report he says: "During the day [the 25th] the enemy landed a large force, and at half past four advanced a line of skirmishers on the left flank of the second curtain, the fleet at the

giving due weight to the reasons alleged by Butler for the re-embarkation of his troops, it was clearly a disobedience of orders. It is a curious fact that, although Weitzel was understood to have the immediate command of the expedition, he never saw the orders issued by General Grant for its conduct, and was not aware, until some time afterward, of Grant's intention that the land force should maintain its position after landing.[2]

same time making a concentrated and tremendous enfilading fire upon the curtain. The garrison, however, at the proper moment, when the fire slackened to allow the approach of the enemy's land force, drove them off with grape and musketry; at dark the enemy withdrew."
[1] See Captain Alden's testimony.—Committee Report, p. 60.
[2] See General Weitzel's testimony. He says (Committee Report. p. 79): "The order of General Grant to General Butler, which I saw published in the papers—I never saw the original of the

DAVID D. PORTER.

BENJAMIN H. PORTER.

SAMUEL W. PRESTON.

LANDING OF TROOPS ABOVE FORT FISHER.

Thus the expedition failed, and the failure was due to mismanagement. It had been delayed, in the first place, until the enemy had gained time for re-enforcement. There was no well-arranged plan of attack. And there was no attempt made to maintain the position secured by the military force on Federal Point.[1] The loss in life, however, had been slight. Upward of forty casualties occurred in the navy from the bursting of 100-lb. Parrott guns on several of the vessels. The loss thus caused was greater than that inflicted by the enemy.

The popular disappointment which followed the failure of an expedition from which, chiefly on account of the extent of the naval force, so much had been expected, was diversified with the mutual recriminations between the army and navy commanders. But these find no proper place in history. The Committee on the Conduct of the War (Benjamin F. Wade, chairman) investigated the affair, and acquitted General Butler of blame. But General

Grant gave his own decision in another way by relieving General Butler of his command of the Army of the James.

Admiral Porter determined to remain until a more efficient military commander should be sent to co-operate with him. He even proposed to take the fort with his sailors.

While the altercation occasioned by the first attack on Fort Fisher was going on, a second expedition was organized, in which the command of the military force was assigned to Major General Alfred H. Terry, who, after the death of General D. B. Birney, stood next to Weitzel in the Army of the James. His command was the same as that with which Butler had sailed, with a single brigade added, bringing its number up to about 8000 men. General Terry, though not a graduate of West Point, had carefully studied the art of war theoretically and practically.

Porter, after experimenting on Fort Fisher for two or three days subsequent to Butler's departure, had returned to Fortress Monroe, where he was joined by Terry before the middle of January. On the 12th of that month the combined expedition reached New Inlet, and the next day the troops were landed. General Whiting and Colonel Lamb still commanded the garrison, which now numbered 2500 men, more than double the force which had confronted Butler. At 2 P.M. on the 13th the debarkation was completed, and the bombardment commenced again, and was more precise and effective than in the first attack. The garrison were driven from their guns, which were soon silenced, and many of them disabled. All night the bom-

order—stated that in certain cases he was to intrench and hold his position, and co-operate with the navy in the reduction of the fort. General Grant said to me the other night that when he ordered the expedition to sail he knew that Wilmington and the works there were nearly devoid of troops, and he thought if we moved down there and landed quickly, the mere effect of landing the troops, together with the presence of such a fleet, would be to compel them to surrender. But in consequence of the delay the enemy got troops down there. But he said that his intention was, after we had made a landing there, finding that it was not possible to assault, that General Butler should intrench there."

Question. "What was there to prevent compliance with such an order?"

Answer. "There was nothing to prevent a compliance with it. There would have been difficulties to contend with at that season of the year. The landing of supplies would have been one difficulty; the annoyance from the rebel gun-boats in the river would have been another. But they might, and probably would have been driven off by our artillery. . . . . If I had had the instructions that General Grant gave to General Butler . . . . I would have intrenched and remained there. . . . . No matter what the difficulties were, that order would have covered him from any consequences."

General Grant testifies (*ibidem*, p. 54): "There is no question that General Butler could have remained, in obedience to my instructions; but I do not think he was guided by them; I do not think he paid any particular attention to them."

[1] The following correspondence passed between General Butler and Admiral Porter just after the re-embarkation:

General Butler writes: "Upon landing the troops and making a thorough reconnoissance of Fort Fisher, both General Weitzel and myself are fully of the opinion that the place could not be carried by assault, as it was left substantially uninjured as a defensive work by the navy fire. We found seventeen guns protected by traverses, two only of which were dismounted, bearing up the beach and covering a strip of land, the only practicable route, not more than wide enough for a thousand men in line of battle.

"Having captured Flag-pond Hill Battery, the garrison of which, sixty-five men and two commissioned officers, were taken off by the navy, we also captured Half-moon Battery and seven officers and 218 men of the Third North Carolina Junior Reserves, including its commander, from whom I learned that a portion of Hoke's division, consisting of Kirkland's and Haygood's brigades, had been sent from the lines before Richmond on Tuesday last, arriving at Wilmington Friday night.

"General Weitzel advanced his skirmish line within fifty yards of the fort, while the garrison was kept in their bomb-proofs by the fire of the navy, and so closely that three or four of the men of the picket line ventured upon the parapet and through the sally-port of the work, capturing a horse, which they brought off, killing the orderly, who was the bearer of a dispatch from the chief of artillery of General Whiting to bring a light battery within the fort, and also brought away from the parapet the flag of the fort.

"This was done while the shells of the navy were falling about the heads of the daring men who entered the work, and it was evident, as soon as the fire of the navy ceased because of the darkness, that the fort was fully manned again, and opened with grape and canister upon our picket line.

"Finding that nothing but the operations of a regular siege, which did not come within my instructions, would reduce the fort, and in view of the threatening aspect of the weather, wind rising from the southeast, rendering it impossible to make farther landing through the surf, I caused the troops, with their prisoners, to re-embark, and see nothing farther that can be done by the land forces. I shall therefore sail for Hampton Roads as soon as the transport fleet can be got in order.

"My engineers and officers report Fort Fisher to me as substantially uninjured as a defensive work."

To this Porter replies:

"I beg leave to acknowledge the receipt of your letter of this date, the substance of which was communicated to me by General Weitzel last night.

"I have ordered the largest vessels to proceed off Beaufort and fill up with ammunition, to be ready for another attack, in case it is decided to proceed with this matter by making other arrangements.

"We have not commenced firing rapidly yet, and could keep any rebels inside from showing their heads until an assaulting column was within twenty yards of the works.

"I wish some more of your gallant fellows had followed the officer who took the flag from the parapet, and the brave fellow who brought the horse out from the fort. I think they would have found it an easier conquest than is supposed.

"I do not, however, pretend to place my opinion in opposition to General Weitzel, whom I know to be an accomplished soldier and engineer, and whose opinion has great weight with me.

"I will look out that the troops are all off in safety. We will have a west wind presently, and a smooth beach about three o'clock, when sufficient boats will be sent for them.

"The prisoners now on board the Santiago de Cuba will be delivered to the provost-marshal at Fortress Monroe, unless you wish to take them on board one of the transports, which would be inconvenient just now."

ALFRED H. TERRY.

bardment went on, giving the enemy no opportunity to repair injuries. On the 14th the fleet continued the battle with the silent fort, its efforts being chiefly directed to dismount the guns. In the mean time preparations were made for the assault, which was to take place on the afternoon of the 15th. Up to this time shot and shell from 500 guns had been beating upon the earth-work, doing the work itself little damage, but breaking the palisade and dismounting its guns. About 1400 sailors and marines had landed, and were to participate in the assault, the plan of which had been most skillfully arranged. The marines and sailors were to attack the sea-face of the fort, while Terry's three brigades should carry the land front. The assault by the sailors was to be covered by an intrenched party on the beach. A perfect system of signals was agreed upon between the military commander and the admiral. No precaution was neglected, no measure overlooked which would assist in securing success.

At 3 P.M. the preconcerted signal was given for the commencement of the assault, and the admiral turned his guns from the parapet and against the upper batteries (on the centre mound). The attack by the marines appears to have been mistaken by the garrison for the main assault. The intrenched party of sharp-shooters did not well cover the advance of the sailors, and the latter were repulsed, losing Lieutenants Preston and Porter, who were bravest among the brave.[1] In the mean while the soldiers had gained the northeastern rampart. The guns of the fleet were turned upon the traverses, while the brave men of Terry's command fought their way from traverse to traverse,[2] overpowering the garrison, and driving it back to the Mound Battery. Both Generals Whiting and Lamb had been wounded. Dispirited by the loss of their leaders, the Confederates were easily driven from their last refuge, and the entire command surrendered, with 75 guns. The fighting had been desperate, and had lasted from 3 o'clock till 10 P.M. The

---

[1] K. R. Breese thus alludes to the death of these gallant officers in a special report:

"North Atlantic Squadron, U. S. Flag Ship Malvern, off Fort Fisher, January 18, 1865.

"ADMIRAL,—In my report of the assault on Fort Fisher I have scarcely mentioned the names and services of Lieutenant S. W. Preston, your flag-lieutenant, and Lieutenant B. H. Porter, your flag-captain, thinking that by a little delay I might the more do justice, yet I seem to feel that impossible in me. Preston, after accomplishing most splendidly the work assigned him by you, which was both dangerous and laborious, under constant fire, came to me, as my aid, for orders, showing no flagging of spirit or body, and returning from the rear, whither he had been sent, fell among the foremost at the front, as he had lived the thorough embodiment of a United States naval officer. Porter, conspicuous by his figure and uniform, as well as by his great gallantry, claimed the right to lead the headmost column with the Malvern's men he had taken with him, carrying your flag, and fell at its very head. Two more noble spirits the world never saw, nor had the navy ever two more intrepid men. Young, talented, and handsome, the bravest of the brave, pure in their lives, surely their names deserve something more than a passing mention, and are worthy to be handed down to posterity with the greatest and best of naval heroes.

"Were you not so well acquainted with their characters I should deem it my duty to speak of their high merits; but as chief of your staff, to which they belonged, I must speak of their wonderful singleness of purpose to do their whole duty; always most cheerful and willing, desirous of undertaking any thing which might redound to the credit of the service, giving me at all times the most ready assistance in my duties, combining with their intelligence a ready perception as to the best mode of accomplishing their orders, the country has lost two such servants as could illy be spared, and your staff its brightest ornaments.

"Very respectfully, your obedient servant,
                                        K. R. BREESE,
"Fleet Captain, North Atlantic Squadron."

"Rear-Admiral DAVID D. PORTER, Commanding North Atlantic Squadron."

[2] "These traverses," says Admiral Porter, "are immense bomb-proofs, about sixty feet long, fifty feet wide, and twenty feet high—seventeen of them in all, being on the northeast face. Between each traverse, or bomb-proof, are one or two heavy guns. The fighting lasted until ten o'clock at night, the *Ironsides* and Monitors firing through the traverses in advance of our troops, and the level strip of land called Federal Point being enfiladed by the ships to prevent re-enforcements reaching the rebels."

Federal loss in Terry's command was 110 killed and 536 wounded, including among the latter all three of the brigade commanders engaged in the assault—Generals Curtis, Bell, and Pennybacker. The casualties in the fleet amounted to 309, making a total loss of nearly 1000 men.

In a great degree this success had been due to surprise, or rather to an attack made in an unexpected quarter with the main column. This column, advancing out of the woods, suddenly approached the western extremity of the land front, and one brigade (Bell's) charged along a narrow causeway in the face of four guns.[1] Nothing, however, was accomplished by the second expedition which might not, under good management, have been as well accomplished by the first.

The next morning a sad event occurred, which to some extent marred the cheer of victory. By some culpable negligence, the soldiers were allowed to approach the magazine with lighted candles. In this way an explosion was occasioned, resulting in the loss of about 200 men. Among the severely wounded was Colonel Alonzo Alden, of the One Hundred and Sixty-ninth New York regiment.

As a result of the fall of Fort Fisher, the surrounding work—Fort Caswell, a large work at the West Inlet, mounting 29 guns, all the works on Smith's Island, those between Caswell and Smithville up to the battery on Reeves's Point, on the west side of the river, were abandoned. Including the guns taken at Fort Fisher, 169 were captured in all.

The same day that Fort Fisher was assaulted and carried by Terry's troops, Major General Schofield, with the Twenty-third Corps, 21,000 strong, left Thomas's army for the East. In February Schofield was appointed commander of the Department of North Carolina, just created. He then commenced a campaign, the ultimate object of which was the occupation of Goldsborough, in order to prepare for the arrival of Sherman's army by opening railway communication from that point with the sea-coast, and accumulating supplies. Wilmington was to be captured first, because it would be a valuable auxiliary base to Morehead City if Sherman should reach Goldsborough, and absolutely necessary in the event of Sherman's concentrating his army farther south.

Schofield, with the Third division (J. D. Cox's) of his corps, reached the mouth of Cape Fear River on the 9th of February, landing near Fort Fisher. Terry and Porter had already made the port of Wilmington useless to blockade runners. The former, still retaining his command, and having the co-operation of the North Atlantic Squadron, held a line across the peninsula two miles above Fort Fisher, and occupied Smithville and Fort Caswell. The Cape Fear had been entered by a portion of the fleet, so that both of Terry's flanks were secure. The enemy, under General Hoke, still covered Fort Anderson on the west bank, and the immediate defenses of Wilmington, in position impregnable against a direct attack. The Confederate line must be turned either on its left by the fleet passing above Masonborough Inlet, or by a march of the army around the swamp covering its right. The

---

[1] Admiral Porter says in his report:

"I have since visited Fort Fisher and its adjoining works, and find their strength greatly beyond what I had conceived. An engineer might be excusable in saying they could not be captured except by regular siege. I wonder even now how it was done. The work, as I said before, is really stronger than the Malakoff Tower, which defied so long the combined powers of France and England; and yet it is captured by a handful of men, under the fire of the guns of the fleet, and in seven hours after the attack commenced in earnest."

PORTER'S FLEET CELEBRATING THE CAPTURE OF FORT FISHER.

latter movement was adopted. The result was successful. On the 19th of February Fort Anderson was abandoned, and the enemy retreated behind Town Creek, where he again intrenched. Terry meanwhile occupied the force on the peninsula. The next day, the 20th, General Cox crossed Town Creek, gained the enemy's flank, attacked and routed him, taking two guns and 375 prisoners. Cox continued his advance, and threatened to cross the Cape Fear above Wilmington. General Hoke then gave up the struggle, set fire to his steamers, cotton, and other stores, and abandoned Wilmington on the night of the 21st. The next morning Cox entered the town without opposition. In these operations the Federal loss was very slight, amounting to about 200 in killed and wounded. That of the enemy is estimated at 1000 men, besides 30 guns. Goldsborough was occupied by General Schofield on the 21st of March, where he effected a junction with Sherman's army.

FORT SUMTER.

CHAPTER LIII.
RECOVERY OF THE ATLANTIC COAST.
II. CHARLESTON.

Defenses of Charleston.—Its Approaches.—The Department of the South.—Hunter's Operations against Charleston.—Federal Repulse at Secessionville, May, 1862.—Attack on the Blockading Fleet by the Palmetto State and Chicora.—Beauregard's *Ruse de Guerre*.—Admiral Dupont's Bombardment, April, 1863.—The Obstructions in the Harbor defeat the Undertaking.—Results of the Bombardment.—Sinking of the Keokuk.—How the Monitors came out of the Fight.— Dupont succeeded by Dahlgren, and Hunter by Gillmore.—The Situation when Gillmore assumed Command.—Capture of Morris's Island.—Terry's co-operative Movement on James's Island. —The First Assault on Fort Wagner.—Second Assault.—Death of Strong and Shaw.—Siege of the Fort.—Operations of the Fleet.—The "Swamp Angel."—Correspondence between Gillmore and Beauregard.—Demolition of Fort Sumter.—Dahlgren's Error in not immediately advancing upon Charleston.—Fort Johnson strengthened by the Confederates during the delay.— Confederate Evacuation of Forts Wagner and Gregg.—Williams's Night Attack on Fort Sumter. —Result of the Conquest of Morris's Island.—General Foster's Operations in 1865.—He is relieved by Gillmore.—Charleston is turned by Sherman's Movement.—Capture of the City by Gillmore.—Raising of the old Flag over Fort Sumter.

FORT Sumter was captured by the Confederates on the 13th of April, 1861. The defenses of Charleston at that time consisted of the following works, which had been constructed by the United States government:

1. Fort Sumter, a strong casemated brick work of five faces, with three tiers of guns, two in embrasure and one *en barbette*. This fort is distant a little more than three miles from the city, and is on the south side of the channel, about midway between Morris's Island on the south, and Sullivan's Island on the north. Its full armament would comprise 135 guns. At the time of its capture by the Confederates the fort mounted 78 guns.

2. Fort Moultrie, 1700 yards from Fort Sumter, on Sullivan's Island. This also is a brick work, with one tier of guns *en barbette*. In 1860 it mounted 52 guns.

3. Castle Pinckney, a brick work on Shute's Folly Island, distant one mile east of the lower end of the city, and mounting, at the beginning of the war, 28 guns.

The city of Charleston is situated at the head of Charleston Harbor, on the point of the narrow peninsula formed by Ashley and Cooper Rivers. Across the entrance of the harbor—between Sullivan's and Morris's Islands —stretches a bar, seven miles below the city. The islands on either side are each about three and a half miles in length, low, narrow, and sandy, and separated from the main land by deep and impenetrable marshes, which are submerged by the spring tides. The distance from their nearest point to Charleston is between three and four miles. Charleston Harbor itself is bounded by James's Island on the south, and on the north by the main land. Its entrance is 2700 yards in width. James's Island, south of the city, is limited on the west by Stono River, which separates it from John's Island. Stono River is connected with the Ashley, south of Charleston, by Wappoo Creek. South of James's Island is Cole's Island, which is for the most part marsh, with Folly River on the south separating it from Folly Island. Lighthouse Inlet, at its mouth, separates Morris's and Folly Islands. The formation of all these islands is thin quartz sand.

The fortifications of Charleston at the opening of the war were only adapted to resist a naval attack. To these, other works were rapidly added. On Sullivan's Island were erected, in addition to Fort Moultrie, the following works: Marion, Beauregard, Marshall, and Battery Bee. On Morris's

Island a battery had been constructed at Cummings's Point, and a mile farther south Fort Wagner. Forts Sumter and Moultrie were strengthened, and their armament increased. Old Fort Johnson, on James's Island, was rebuilt and armed with heavy guns, and north of it was constructed Fort Ripley. The preparations against a land attack were formidable. On the James a line of works was built fronting Stone River, with Fort Pemberton near its northern extremity. An inclosed work on Cole's Island covered the Stono Inlet and harbor. Heavy guns were mounted on the wharves of Charleston, and in the rear of the city formidable works were erected. Such and so extensive were the defenses of Charleston under the command of the Confederate General Beauregard.

On the 15th of March, 1862, the Department of the South was created, embracing South Carolina, Georgia, and Florida, and was assigned to General Hunter. Port Royal had been occupied by a military force under General T. W. Sherman and Dupont's squadron late in 1861. Edisto Island, farther north, was taken possession of by Sherman in February, 1862. The expeditionary force commanded by General Sherman in March became subject to General Hunter's control. During the month which followed, General Q. A. Gillmore captured Fort Pulaski.

In December, 1861, a Federal fleet of sixteen vessels, heavily laden with granite, was sunk on the bar in Charleston Harbor to obstruct the channel and obviate the necessity of a blockade. This operation excited a great degree of indignation on the part of foreign governments. The elements of nature expressed their dissent in a more quiet way, but with much more effect. In a few weeks the Ashley and Cooper Rivers made for themselves a new channel, better than the previous one.

Shortly after General Hunter assumed command of the Department of the South, operations were commenced against Charleston by way of Stono River and James's Island. The Confederates had made a great mistake in abandoning Cole's Island, which commanded the entrance of the Stono. Admiral Dupont, with three gun-boats—the Unadilla, Pembina, and Ottawa —entered the river on the 29th of May, 1862. At the approach of the gun-boats all the works of the enemy along the Stono up to the Wappoo were abandoned. Early in June Generals Hunter and Benham arrived with a considerable detachment of troops—too weak, however, for operations on James's Island, where the enemy was not only strongly intrenched from Secessionville to Fort Johnson, but had an easy and open communication with the rear, and could bring up re-enforcements at his pleasure. On the 16th of June an attack was made on Secessionville by General I. I. Stevens's and General H. G. Wright's divisions of General Benham's command—some 6000 strong—but was repulsed by the enemy, the Federal loss amounting to over 500 men.

After this action for nearly a year the operations against Charleston were suspended. The Charleston campaign from the beginning of 1863 till the close of the war may be treated under three heads:

I. Admiral Dupont's bombardment, April 7, 1863.

II. General Gillmore's operations on Morris's Island during the summer of 1863.

III. General Foster's and Gillmore's movements co-operative with Sherman's Carolina campaign, resulting in the occupation of Charleston, February 21, 1865.

I. Admiral Dupont's expedition was an experiment, in which the offensive and defensive power of monitors was to be put to the severest test. The original Monitor—whose name came to be applied to all iron-clads of similar construction—had been lost on her way to join Dupont's squadron (the South Atlantic) in the autumn of 1862.[1] The popular expectation as to the omnipotence of the monitors was extravagant and unfounded. The Merrimac had been beaten by the original Monitor, and the Nashville had been sunk by another vessel of the same class. Fort Pulaski had fallen, not before the gun-boats of Dupont's fleet, but from the effect of batteries on shore.[2] It is true, Dupont had at that time no monitors, but the presence of these could scarcely have affected the result. The monitors, however, had undergone a pretty fair trial in the attack on Fort McAllister. The only vessel of this class engaged in the assault was the Montauk. The result seemed to prove the invulnerability of the monitor, but its offensive power as

---

See Chapter XIII., p. 258.   [2] Gillmore's Operations against Charleston, p. 240.

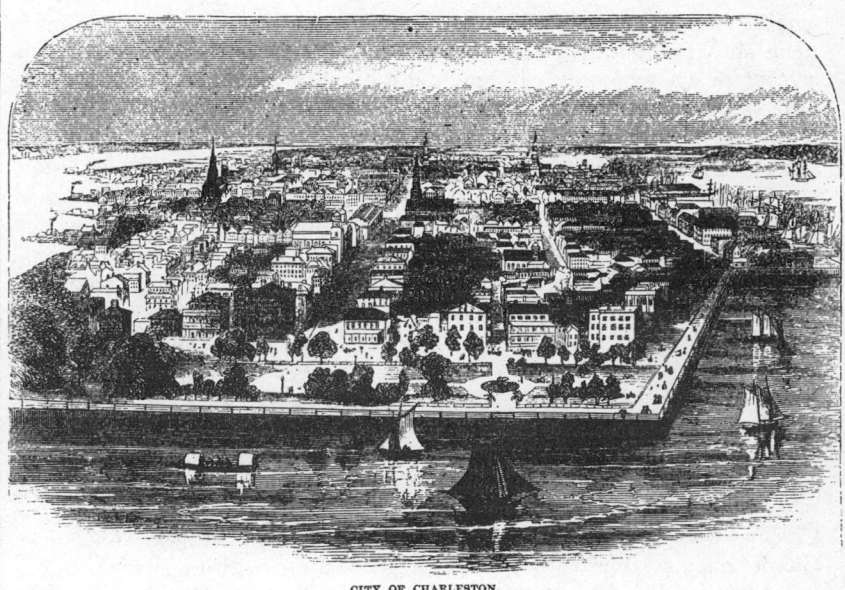

CITY OF CHARLESTON.

SAMUEL F. DUPONT.

against forts was not so well established. A visible impression was made upon McAllister, but not of such a character as to destroy either its offensive or defensive power. It was still a question whether a large number of monitors might not do what one alone had failed to accomplish. Indeed, it was confidently expected that the monitor fleet which Dupont commanded in April, 1863, would batter down Fort Fisher and ride up to Charleston, while a military force about 10,000 strong, under General Hunter, would occupy and hold that city under the guns of the fleet.

Previous to the attack on Charleston an event occurred which showed the insufficiency of blockading vessels against rams. Early on the morning of January 29th, 1863, the Princess Royal was captured while attempting to pass through the blockading squadron into Charleston Harbor. Her cargo would have been of great value to the enemy, consisting of two engines intended for iron-clads, with rifled guns, arms, ammunition, and medicines. Her loss was a severe blow to the Confederates, who, ascertaining that she was still at anchor off the harbor, organized an expedition for her recapture. Before light on the morning of the 31st two Confederate iron-clad steam rams—the Palmetto State, commanded by Lieutenant Rutledge, and the Chicora, Commander Tucker—ran out by the main ship channel from Charleston, and attacked the blockading squadron with great vigor. The latter consisted of 10 vessels—the Housatonic, Mercedita, Ottawa, Unadilla,

Keystone State, Quaker City, Memphis, Augusta, Stettin, and Flag—most of them being light vessels, and incompetent to resist such an onslaught. The iron-clads and two of the heaviest men of war, the Powhatan and Canandaigua, were off at Port Royal. The Palmetto State, with Flag-officer D. N. Ingraham on board, almost immediately disabled the Mercedita with a 7-inch shell, which entered her side, exploded in one of her boilers, and in its exit killed and wounded several men. One blow from the ram settled the case of this ship, which, as it seemed to be sinking, was surrendered. Both the Palmetto and Chicora then attacked the Keystone State. The latter bore down rapidly upon the Palmetto, intending to sink her. But a shot from the ram passed through both her steam chests; 10 rifle shells struck her near and below water mark, and almost simultaneously a fire broke out in her forehold. Commander Le Roy hauled down his flag. The enemy still continued to fire, and the flag was again hoisted and the battle renewed. The Augusta, Memphis, and Quaker City came up and relieved the suffering vessel, one fourth of whose crew had been killed or wounded. Together with the Mercedita, whose leak had been stopped and who had not been secured by the enemy, the Keystone State went to Port Royal. The other vessels of the squadron kept at a prudent distance from the rams. Soon, however, the Housatonic came up, and the rams, refusing battle, fled back into the harbor.

CONFEDERATE RAMS ENGAGING THE BLOCKADING FLEET OFF CHARLESTON.

DEPARTURE OF DUPONT'S EXPEDITION FROM BEAUFORT.

BOMBARDMENT OF FORT SUMTER.

Upon the return of his rams a bright idea occurred to Beauregard. He knew that the reports of Admiral Dupont could not reach the North for some three days at least. His own communication by telegraph with Richmond was uninterrupted, and the Richmond papers soon found their way to New York. Here, then, was a splendid opportunity for a *ruse de guerre*, which, if it involved considerable lying, might—so thought the chivalrous, honor-loving general—be excused on the maxim that "all is fair in war." Accordingly, over his own signature and that of Flag-officer Ingraham, he dispatched to Richmond an official proclamation, stating that the Confederate naval force at Charleston had attacked the blockading fleet off the harbor, and had sunk, dispersed, and drove off the same, and declaring the blockade of Charleston to be raised from and after the 31st of January, 1863. This proclamation, with Beauregard's account of the affair, asserting that, as a result of the naval engagement on the 31st, two Federal vessels were sunk, four set on fire, and the rest driven away, was published in the Richmond papers of February 2d. As if this were not enough in the way of falsification, another dispatch was added, declaring that on the afternoon of the 31st the British consul, on board the British war steamer Petrel, had gone five miles beyond the usual anchorage of the blockaders, and could see nothing of them with glasses.

Now, without characterizing these declarations by the plain English term that is applicable to them, it is sufficient to say that they are false in every particular. And they were recognized as false by every European government. The raid with the rams had not succeeded in the object for which it was undertaken—the recovery of the Princess Royal; they had retreated on the appearance of the Housatonic, and did not venture out again. Not a single Federal steamer was sunk, not one was burned, and only two were in any way disabled. The position of the blockading squadron was not shifted, and no vessel advanced from Charleston, after the affair, beyond the bar of the harbor.[1]

By the 7th of April the preparations for the bombardment of Fort Sumter were completed. At noon of that day the vessels of Dupont's fleet, having crossed the bar by the new channel formed since the sinking of the stone fleet, proceeded to the attack. The attacking fleet consisted of nine vessels, all of which were monitors except the New Ironsides and Keokuk, which were iron-clad and turreted. The five strongest vessels of the blockading squadron were held in reserve.[2] The orders issued by the admiral were that the fleet should pass up the main ship channel, open fire upon Fort Sumter when within range of that work, disregarding the batteries on Morris's Island, advance to a position northwest of Sumter in order to attack its weakest face, fire upon the work with precision rather than rapidity, and, having reduced the fort, turn against the Morris's Island batteries. The advance had been delayed till noon, waiting for the tide, and from the fleet, in the mean while, could be seen the steeples and roofs of Charleston crowded with spectators, just as they had been two years before, when Fort Sumter was attacked by its present defender. It is a novel conflict whose spectacle is now anxiously awaited—that of a fleet mounting 32 guns arrayed against forts which mount 300. The forts know little of the monitors, but stand defiant. The monitors know little of the forts, or the obstructions to their progress, but defiantly they advance.

The reserve fleet lies outside the bar, while the monitors approach Sumter. The Weehawken has the lead, and as she advances, a raft attached to her prow looks out for torpedoes. Scarcely has she started, however, before the grappling irons attached to this raft become fouled in the anchor cable, and an hour's delay is occasioned. Then the movement is resumed. The entire fleet passes Morris's Island, but no gun opens upon her. Now (3 P.M.) she rounds to enter the harbor, and comes within range of Fort Sumter and the batteries on Sullivan's Island. A broadside from the upper tier of guns (*en barbette*) greets the Weehawken, who is seeking, according to orders, to reach the left face of the fort. Suddenly she halts midway between Sumter and Moultrie. Her progress has been stopped by an unforeseen obstacle—a stout hawser stretches between the two forts, strung with torpedoes. The fleet has been proceeding along the right channel thus far, and, meeting this obstruction in the way of reaching its desired position, it changes its course,

and tries the left channel, between Fort Sumter and Cummings's Point. This also is blockaded, and more effectually than the other, by a row of piles stretching across the channel. Beyond is seen another row extending between Forts Johnson and Ripley, and more careful scrutiny discloses a third row, beyond which lie three Confederate rams.

Thus the original design of reaching Fort Sumter's weakest face is frustrated at the outset. And there is no help for it. The fort could probably be reduced but for these obstructions which cover its weakness: the obstructions might be removed but for the thundering guns of the fort.

To make matters worse, the New Ironsides—the flag-ship—caught by the tide, refuses to obey her rudder, and becomes unmanageable. The Catskill and the Nantucket fall foul of her, and thus remain a full quarter of an hour. While, in the midst of these difficulties, the vessels are taking such positions as they can gain, they are in a circle of fire, which concentrates upon them from Cummings's Point Battery, Battery Bee, and Forts Beauregard, Moultrie, and Sumter. The range is less than 800 yards, and the fire is from guns of the heaviest calibre that could be obtained from the Tredegar works of Richmond or from the armories of Europe. This fire has been going on from the time of its first opening by Sumter; but now for thirty minutes it pours upon the fleet the white heat of its fury. One hundred and sixty shots are counted in a single minute; they strike the iron plates of the monitors as rapidly as the ticking of a watch. It is estimated that from all the forts, in this brief engagement, not less than 3500 rounds have been fired. In reply, only 139 shots have been delivered by the fleet.

And what is the result to the fort? What to the fleet? A few marks are visible on Fort Sumter, and the parapet near the eastern angle shows a huge crater.[1] If the monitors could remain where they are, time would solve the problem of the reduction of the fort. But they can not. Apart from the embarrassments under which they are working as regards effective offense—their confined space; their tendency to drift against the obstructions or upon submerged batteries; and the clouds of smoke which hang over the water, obscuring their range—they have sustained injuries which compel their withdrawal, and at 5 P.M. the signal is given for their retreat. Already the Keokuk, which advanced to within 570 yards of Fort Sumter, has left the field in a sinking condition, having been completely riddled with shots. It is her last fight. The Ironsides also has lost one of her port-shutters, her gun-deck is thus exposed, and her bows have been penetrated with red-hot shot. But these are not monitors. How is it with the latter? The Nahant has received thirty wounds, her turret has been jammed so that it will not turn, and her pilot-house is in such a rickety condition that every bolt in it flies about when it is struck, killing and wounding its tenants. The turret of the Passaic is broken and unmanageable. The Nantucket's turret is jarred so that the cover of the port can not be opened, and consequently her 15-inch gun can not be used. The other four monitors are essentially uninjured.[2]

After the withdrawal of the fleet, Admiral Dupont having been informed as to the conditions of his vessels, decided not to renew the conflict, and the next day returned to Port Royal. The Keokuk sank on the morning of the 8th abreast of Morris's Island, and her armament was thus left in the hands of the enemy. In the action of the 7th only one man was mortally wounded. The entire casualties were twenty-six.

Within the short space of about two hours had been decided the question of monitors against forts. The result was decisive on two points: first, that the defensive powers of these vessels was not sufficient to withstand the concentrated fire of half a dozen forts heavily armed; and, secondly, that while the reduction of brick forts might result from a long-continued bombardment, yet the limits of endurance on the part of the monitors were such as to render this impracticable.[3]

II. The War Department was not satisfied with the result of the experiment, and determined to renew the attack, but upon a somewhat different plan. Admiral Dupont was relieved of the command, and would have been succeeded by Admiral Foote but for the death of the latter on the way to Port Royal. The command of the South Atlantic squadron was therefore, on the

---

[1] Beauregard's statements are fully refuted by that subsequently made by Admiral Dupont, and signed by nearly all the commanding officers of the fleet lying off Charleston Harbor on the 31st. We make the following extract from this statement:

"We deem it our duty to state that the so-called results are false in every particular—no vessels were sunk, none were set on fire seriously. . . . . So hasty was the retreat of the rams that, although they might have perceived that the Keystone State had received serious damage, no attempt was ever made to approach her. The Stettin and Ottawa, at the extreme end of the line, did not get under way from their position till after the firing had ceased, and the Stettin merely saw the black smoke as the rams disappeared over the bar. The rams withdrew hastily toward the harbor, and on their way were fired at by the Housatonic and Augusta until both had got beyond reach of their guns. They anchored under the protection of their forts, and remained there. No vessel, iron-clad or other, passed out over the bar after the return of the rams inshore. The Unadilla was not aware of the attack until the Housatonic commenced firing, when she moved out toward that vessel from her anchorage. The Housatonic was never beyond the usual line of the blockade. We do not hesitate to state that no vessel came out beyond the bar after the return of the rams, at between 7 and 8 A.M., to the cover of the forts. We believe the statement that any vessel came any where near the usual anchorage of any of the blockaders, or up to the bar, after the withdrawal of the rams, to be deliberately and knowingly false. If the statement from the papers, as now before us, has the sanction of the captain of the Petrel and the foreign consuls, we can only deplore that foreign officers can lend their official positions to the spreading before the world, for unworthy objects, untruths patent to every officer of this squadron."

[2] The vessels of the monitor fleet, including the New Ironsides and Keokuk, advanced in the following order:
1. Weehawken, Captain John Rodgers.
2. Passaic, Captain Percival Drayton.
3. Montauk, Commander John L. Worden.
4. Patapsco, Commander Daniel Ammen.
5. New Ironsides, Commodore Thomas Turner.
6. Catskill, Commander George W. Rodgers.
7. Nantucket, Commander Daniel McN. Fairfax.
8. Nahant, Commander John Downes.
9. Keokuk, Lieutenant Commander A. C. Rhind.
The reserve squadron consisted of the Canandaigua, Unadilla, Housatonic, Wissahickon, and Huron, under the command of Captain Joseph H. Green.

[1] Mr. William Swinton gives the following graphic description of the inside of a monitor during the engagement:
"Could you look through the smoke, and through the flame-lit ports, into one of those revolving towers, a spectacle would meet your eye such as Vulcan's stithy might present. Here are the two huge guns which form the armament of each monitor—the one eleven, and the other fifteen inches in diameter of bore. The gunners, begrimed with powder and stripped to the waist, are loading the gun. The charge of powder—thirty-five pounds to each charge—is passed up rapidly from below; the shot, weighing four hundred and twenty pounds, is hoisted up by mechanical appliances to the muzzle of the gun, and rammed home, the gun is run out to the port, and tightly "compressed;" the port is open for an instant, the captain of the gun stands behind, lanyard in hand—"Ready, fire!" and the enormous projectile rushes through its huge parabola, with the weight of 10,000 tons, home to its mark."

[2] The following estimate was made of the shots received by each vessel:

New Ironsides	65	Nantucket 51
Keokuk	90	Catskill 51
Weehawken	60	Patapsco 45
Montauk	20	Nahant 80
Passaic	53	Total 515

[3] A year after the attack on Charleston Admiral Dupont thus alludes to the affair:
"I am well aware," he says, "that the results at Charleston were not all that were wished for, and I quite agree with the department that there was, nevertheless, much in them that was gratifying, particularly that the loss of life was so small, and that the capacity of the iron-clads for enduring the hot and heavy fire brought to bear upon them, which would have destroyed any vessels of wood heretofore used in warfare, was made so evident. But I must take leave to remind the department that ability to endure is not a sufficient element wherewith to gain victories; that endurance must be accompanied with a corresponding power to inflict injury on the enemy; and I will improve the present occasion to repeat the expression of a conviction which I have already conveyed to the department in former letters, that the weakness of the monitor class of vessels, in this important particular, is fatal to their attempts against fortifications having outlying obstructions, as at the Ogeechee and at Charleston, or against other fortifications upon elevations, as at Fort Darling, or against any modern fortifications before which they must anchor or lie at rest, and receive much more than they can return. With even their dismantled surface they are not invulnerable, and their various mechanical contrivances for working their turrets and guns are so liable to immediate derangement, that, in the brief though fierce engagement at Charleston, five out of eight were disabled, and, as I mentioned in my detailed report to the department, half an hour more fighting would, in my judgment, have placed them all *hors de combat*."

SINKING OF THE KEOKUK.

6th of July, assigned to Admiral Dahlgren, and General Q. A. Gillmore succeeded Hunter in the command of the Department of the South. Toward the close of May, 1863, Gillmore had received orders to repair to Washington, to consult with General Halleck and Secretary Welles as to future operations against Charleston. No more troops could be spared for the Department of the South. Gillmore did not ask for more, although he knew that his operations must, on account of his small military force, be restricted to Morris's Island. With this force he proposed to occupy that island, capture Forts Wagner and Gregg, and demolish Fort Sumter by means of shore batteries. The way would thus be open for Dahlgren to advance with his fleet, remove the obstructions in the harbor, and command Charleston. Even if the city was not captured, the full possession of Morris's Island would effectually blockade the harbor.

General Gillmore assumed command of the department on the 12th of June. At that time the coast from Light-house Inlet to St. Augustine, Florida—a distance of 250 miles—was in possession of the national forces. The positions actually occupied by troops were Folly Island, Seabrook Island, on the North Edisto, St. Helena Island, Port Royal Island, Hilton Head Island, the Tybee Islands, Fort Pulaski, Ossibaw Island, Fort Clinch and Amelia Island, and the city of St. Augustine. Off or inside the principal inlets lay the blockading squadron.[1]

Folly Island was occupied by a brigade under General Vogdes, strongly intrenched, with heavy guns mounted on the south end of the island to control the entrance of the Stono River. Vogdes had also constructed a road, practicable for artillery, and affording a means of concealed communication between the several parts of the island. In Stono and Folly Rivers a naval force was stationed, consisting of two gun-boats and a mortar schooner, to secure Folly Island against attack, and to hold the Stono against the light-draught gun-boats of the enemy. Folly Island was necessarily the base of operations against Morris's Island.[2] The dense undergrowth with which it

[1] Gillmore's Operations against Charleston, p. 42.
[2] "The question has been asked why the route across James's Island from Stono River, the same that Brigadier General Benham attempted, was not selected to operate upon.

"The answer is simple. The enemy had more troops available for the defense of Charleston than we had for the attack. The general-in-chief, in the preliminary discussions of the project, had mentioned 10,000 men as the approximate number that could be collected in the Department of the South for this operation. The force actually got together there did not vary much from 11,500 men, including engineers and artillerists. Upon Morris's Island, on account of its narrowness, this force was ample, and it was not until the command had been reduced one third by sickness and casualties that re-enforcements were asked for. But James's Island presents a different case. There our progress would soon have been arrested by the concentration of a superior force in our front. Upon Morris's Island both parties had all the force that could be applied with advantage. Our superiority in artillery, ashore and afloat—particularly in the use of mortars in the trenches—the successful application of new devices, the energy and skill of our engineers, and a strictly maintained initiative, gave us the controlling elements of success. Moreover, according to the programme of joint operations, the demolition of Fort Sumter was what the land forces had to accomplish, and that could be done with more ease and certainty from Morris's Island than from any other position. James's Island was too wide to operate upon, with a fair promise of success, with our small force."—Gillmore's Operations, p. 22.

was covered afforded cover for batteries on the north end, within musket range of the enemy's picket on the opposite side of Light-house Inlet.

The forces in Ossibaw Sound and on the North Edisto were withdrawn. Gillmore's entire command available for offensive operations then consisted of 11,500 men and 66 guns, besides about 30 mortars.

The descent upon Morris's Island was made July 10th, 1863. It was an operation which required boldness and great skill, as it involved the storming of a fortified position, not by the regular approaches of a siege, but by an advance covered by a few batteries, and made in small boats exposed to the enemy's fire. There were two co-operative expeditions—one conducted by General A. H. Terry, with 3800 men, on James's Island, which was eminently successful, diverting a portion of the garrison from Morris's Island; and a second, sent from General Saxton's command at Beaufort to cut the Charleston and Savannah Railroad at Jacksborough, in order to delay re-enforcements from Savannah. This latter expedition proved a signal failure, involving the loss of two guns and a small steamer, which was burned to prevent its capture.

The main column engaged in the attack on Morris's Island—about 2000 men of General Strong's brigade—was embarked in Folly River, and passed by night during high tide through the shallow creeks into Light-house Inlet. This movement was first fixed for the night of the 8th of July, but had been postponed until the night of the 9th. At daybreak on the 10th the column halted, having reached Light-house Inlet, the boats keeping close to the east shore of the creek, where they were screened by the marsh grass from hostile observation. Shortly after daybreak the batteries on the north end of Folly Island—10 in number, and mounting 47 guns—opened against the opposite shore, the undergrowth having been previously cleared away in their front to give them an unobstructed view. Four monitors joined their fire to that of the batteries. For two hours this bombardment continued, and then Strong's brigade moved across the inlet to the assault.

The movement had been planned with much skill and secrecy, and was a surprise to the enemy. At Oyster Point, and on the firm land lower down, the Federal troops were landed under a hot fire of musketry and artillery. But the column never faltered, and by 9 o'clock A.M. all the hostile batteries south of Fort Wagner were overrun and captured. This success closed the operations of that day. The troops were within musket range of Fort Wagner, and were exhausted by the intense heat and three hours' hard fighting. Throughout the day the bombardment from the monitors was kept up, directed chiefly at Fort Wagner.

On the morning of the 11th an assault was made upon Fort Wagner. The advance, led by General Strong in person, reached and gained the parapet of the fort. But the supports could not be brought up in face of a fire from which they had no protection, and the attack failed. In the actions

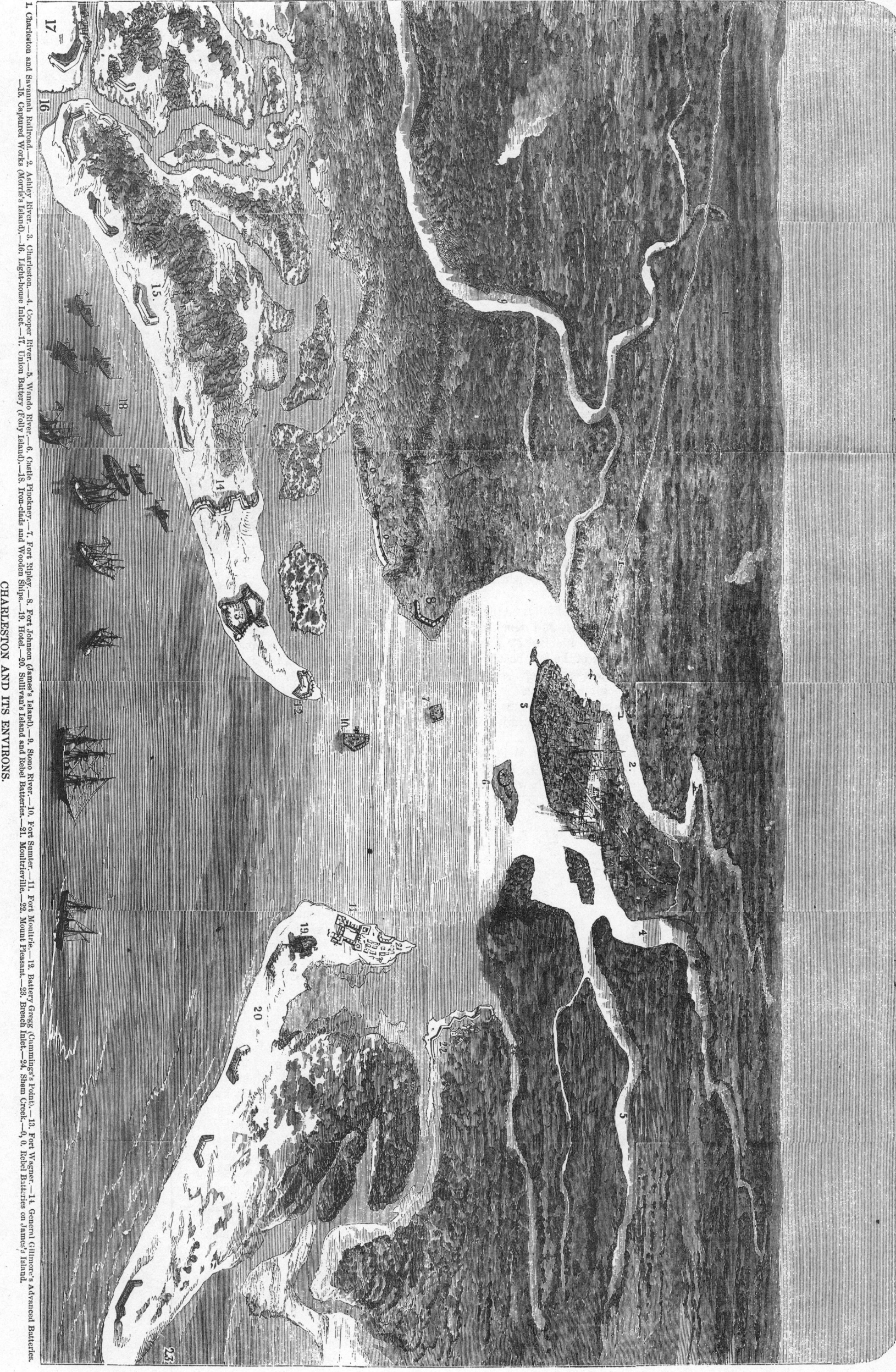

CHARLESTON AND ITS ENVIRONS.

1. Charleston and Savannah Railroad.—2. Ashley River.—3. Charleston.—4. Cooper River.—5. Wando River.—6. Castle Pinckney.—7. Fort Ripley.—8. Fort Johnson (James's Island).—9. Stono River.—10. Fort Sumter.—11. Fort Moultrie.—12. Battery Gregg (Cumming's Point).—13. Fort Wagner.—14. General Gillmore's Advanced Batteries. —15. Light-house Inlet.—16. Captured Works (Morris's Island).—17. Union Battery (Folly Island).—18. Iron-clads and Wooden Ships.—19. Hotel.—20. Sullivan's Island and Rebel Batteries.—21. Moultrieville.—22. Mount Pleasant.—23. Breach Inlet.—24. Shem Creek.—0, 0. Rebel Batteries on James's Island.

Q. A. GILLMORE.

ROBERT G. SHAW.

on the 10th and 11th the Federal loss was about 150. General Beauregard admits a loss of 300, including 16 commissioned officers.[1] He had also lost 11 heavy guns.

In the mean time, General Terry, on James's Island, had followed the route taken by Benham's two divisions on the 16th of June, and demonstrated against Secessionville. On the 16th of July he was attacked by a largely superior force of the enemy; but with the assistance of the gun-boat Pawnee in the Stono, and two smaller vessels, the attack was easily repulsed. Terry's command was the next day withdrawn from James's Island.

On the 18th, just one week after the failure of the first assault on Fort Wagner, a second was undertaken. In the interim, four batteries—Reynolds, Weed, Hays, and O'Rourke—mounting twenty-nine guns and fourteen mortars, had been erected on Morris's Island bearing upon Fort Wagner, and at a distance from that work of from 1330 to 1920 yards. In addition to the four monitors (the Catskill, Montauk, Nahant, and Weehawken), which

[1] Gillmore's Operations, p. 75.

were across the bar on the 10th, two other vessels—the Patapsco and the New Ironsides—now lay abreast of Morris's Island. The guns of this fleet and of the shore batteries bombarded the fort all day. At twilight, in the midst of a thunder-storm, the assaulting columns, commanded by Brigadier General T. Seymour, advanced. Strong's brigade—consisting of Colonel Shaw's Fifty-fourth Massachusetts (colored) Regiment; the Sixth Connecticut, Colonel Chatfield; a battalion of the Seventh Connecticut; the Forty-eighth New York, Colonel Barton; the Third New Hampshire, Colonel Jackson; the Ninth Maine, Colonel Emery; and the Seventy-sixth Pennsylvania, Colonel Strawbridge—was in the advance, and was supported by Colonel H. S. Putnam's brigade. The whole force engaged in the attack numbered about 6000 men. The approach of darkness, hastened by the storm, made it impossible for the fleet to discern friend from foe, so that the advance was exposed to the fire of Forts Wagner, Gregg (on Cummings's Point), and Sumter, assisted by the works on James's and Sullivan's Island. Never, during the war, was an assault made in the face of such opposition. As soon as the columns approached the fort, and the Federal guns in the batteries and on the monitors were silent, the garrison of Wagner, 1000 strong, sprang to its guns and muskets. Notwithstanding this tremendous fire from four different quarters, and although the leading regiment was thrown into such disorder that Putnam's supporting brigade had to be sent in, still the troops went forward, and the southeast bastion of Fort Wagner was gained and held for nearly three hours. The darkness was so great an advantage to the garrison that it more than compensated for the partial success of the assailants, and a retreat was ordered. The Federal loss was very

GEORGE C. STRONG.

RUINS OF LIGHT-HOUSE ON MORRIS'S ISLAND.

severe, especially in officers. General Strong, and Colonels Chatfield, Putnam, and Shaw, were either killed on the spot, or died subsequently of their wounds. Colonel Shaw was killed upon the parapet of the fort. If, as was reported at the time, he was buried with the fallen negroes of his gallant regiment, it can only be said that what was intended for a disgrace will in the light of history be regarded as a monumental honor. General Seymour and several regimental commanders were severely wounded. The entire loss sustained in the assault must have amounted to 1200 killed and wounded.

This repulse revived the faltering hopes of the citizens of Charleston, who regarded Fort Wagner as the key to the city. They had looked upon the conflict with anxiety and doubt. They remembered that this same General Gillmore had once demolished Fort Pulaski—which they considered in impregnability next to Sumter—as easily as if it had been a house built of cards.[1] They had trembled, therefore, for the fate

SHARPSHOOTERS BEFORE WAGNER.

of Wagner and Sumter, but now they breathed more freely.

But General Gillmore had as yet scarcely commenced operations. His principal object was the demolition of Fort Sumter, in order to allow the iron-clads an entrance to the harbor. Failing in this, there was still left a secondary object to be accomplished—namely, to secure a perfect blockade of the port. This could be effected by the reduction of Forts Wagner and Gregg.

Fort Wagner was an inclosed work, one fourth of a mile in width, extending from high-water mark on the east, to Vincent's Creek and the impassable marshes on the west. It had an excellent garrison, and was constructed of sand, upon which the heaviest bombardment could make little impression, with a ditch in front. Its bomb-proof shelter was capacious and secure, and its armament consisted of between fifteen and twenty guns, covering the solitary approach to it on the south. This approach was in many places scarcely half a company front in width, and was swept by Fort Sumter, the batteries on James's Island, and that at Cummings's Point. Its communication with the rear was secure, thus giving opportunity for the increase of its armament or garrison.[2]

[1] See the *Augusta Sentinel* of July 15, 1863.   [2] Gillmore's Operations, p. 105.

Fort Wagner was neared by regular approaches. Immediately after the repulse of the 18th, the first parallel was established about 1300 yards from Fort Wagner.[1] On the night of the 23d the second parallel was established 600 yards in advance of the first, on a line running diagonally across the island northwest and southeast. In the creek on the left two booms of floating timber were stretched across, to resist the approach of the enemy's boats. It must be remembered that these approaches to Fort Wagner were chiefly *defensive* as to that work, and were preliminary to offensive operations against Fort Sumter. The third parallel was established within less than 400 yards of Fort Wagner. The fire from the fort now became so severe that it was determined to operate against Sumter before another advance.

Breaching batteries had been constructed for this purpose in rear of the several parallels. By the 11th of August 12 of these batteries were ready

[1] "A row of inclined palisading, reaching entirely across the island, was planted about 200 yards in advance of the line, with a return of fifty yards on the right. This return was well flanked by two guns on the right of the parallel. The parallel was arranged for infantry defense; a bomb-proof magazine was constructed, and the armament of the line modified and increased, so that the parallel contained eight siege and field guns, ten siege mortars, and three Requa rifle batteries."—Gillmore's Operations, p. 114.

THE "SWAMP ANGEL."

PORTION OF CHARLESTON EXPOSED TO THE FIRE OF THE FEDERAL FLEET.

for operation, mounting 28 heavy guns and 12 mortars. Their distance from Fort Sumter ranged from 3516 to 4290 yards. The bombardment commenced on the morning of the 17th, and the guns were served steadily and deliberately for several days, until Fort Sumter was literally knocked out of all shape and deprived of its offensive power. During this time the fleet also bombarded Fort Wagner, whose fire, unless silenced, would interfere with the operations of the batteries on shore.

On the 21st of August a demand was made upon General Beauregard for the surrender of Morris's Island and Fort Sumter, accompanied by the assurance that, if the demand was not complied with during the four hours following its delivery, fire would be opened upon Charleston from batteries already established within range of the city. For three weeks Gillmore had been locating a battery, commonly known among the troops as the "Swamp Angel," mounted with an 8-inch Parrott rifle, and within range of Charleston, on the marsh between Morris's and James's Islands. He waited ten hours beyond the time specified in his notice to the Confederate general, and, receiving no reply, opened fire on the city.[1]

On the 24th of August the military force operating against Charleston had accomplished its primary object—the elimination of Fort Sumter. This fort was not obliterated, and its offensive power was only temporarily removed.[1] For at least ten or fifteen days it could oppose to the monitors no serious resistance. Fort Wagner still remained in the hands of the enemy, but could be easily avoided by the fleet. But Admiral Dahlgren did not embrace the opportunity, and in the mean time the enemy strengthened Fort Johnson, converting it into an earth-work. This work is on the north end of James's Island, and commands the channel.

Gillmore continued his parallel approaches up to within 150 yards of Fort Wagner, and on the 5th of September commenced a bombardment of that work, which was continued for forty-two consecutive hours. Seventeen siege and Coehorn mortars dropped their shells into the work, thirteen heavy Parrott rifles pounded away at the southwest angle of the bombproof, while by day the New Ironsides poured an uninterrupted stream of eleven-inch shells from her eight-gun broadside against the parapet. An assault would have been made on the morning of the 7th upon the now silent fort; but during the night of the 6th the Confederates, convinced of their inability to maintain their position on Morris's Island, slipped away from Forts Wagner and Gregg, and all but seventy men effected their escape. Eighteen guns were captured in Fort Wagner, and seven in Fort Gregg.

This success concluded General Gillmore's work. From Cummings's Point an irregular bombardment was commenced upon the city, and continued till the evacuation of the latter in 1865. The "Swamp Angel" battery had long discontinued its fire upon Charleston. At the thirty-sixth round its gun—a 100-lb. Parrott—had exploded, and the guns mounted afterward were directed against the James's Island batteries.

Admiral Dahlgren was unwilling to attempt the entrance to the harbor until Fort Sumter was in possession of the national forces. This possession could only be effected by an open assault, involving great sacrifice of life; and after the acquisition of the fort, Gillmore could not expect to hold it against the formidable works of the enemy which bore upon its weakest points. Gillmore, on the 27th of September, offered to remove the obstruc-

[1] The following is a copy of the correspondence which passed between Generals Gillmore and Beauregard:

No. 1.

"Headquarters Department of the South, Morris's Island, S. C., August 21, 1863.

"General G. T. BEAUREGARD, Commanding Confederate Forces about Charleston, S. C.:

"GENERAL,—I have the honor to demand of you the immediate evacuation of Morris's Island and Fort Sumter by the Confederate forces.

"The present condition of Fort Sumter, and the rapid and progressive destruction which it is undergoing from my batteries, seem to render its complete demolition within a few hours a matter of certainty. All my heaviest guns have not yet opened. Should you refuse compliance with that demand, or should I receive no reply thereto within four hours after it is delivered into the hands of your subordinate at Fort Wagner for transmission, I shall open fire on the city of Charleston from batteries already established within easy and effective range of the heart of the city.

"I am, general, your obedient servant,

"Q. A. GILLMORE, Brigadier General Commanding."

No. 2.

"Headquarters South Carolina, Georgia, and Florida, Charleston, S. C., August 22, 1863.

"SIR,—Last night, at 15 minutes before 11 o'clock, during my absence on a reconnoissance of my fortifications, a communication was received at these headquarters, dated 'Headquarters Department of the South, Morris's Island, S. C., August 21, 1863,' demanding the immediate evacuation of Morris's Island and Fort Sumter by the Confederate forces on the alleged ground that 'the present condition of Fort Sumter, and the rapid and progressive destruction which it is undergoing from my batteries, seem to render its complete demolition within a few hours a matter of certainty,' and if this letter was not complied with, or no reply was received within four hours after it was delivered into the hands of my subordinate commander at Fort Wagner for transmission, a fire would be opened on the city of Charleston from batteries already established within easy and effective range of the heart of the city. This communication to my address was without signature, and, of course, returned. About half past one o'clock one of your batteries did actually open fire and throw a number of heavy shells into the city, the inhabitants of which, of course, were asleep and unwarned.

"About 9 o'clock the next morning the communication alluded to was returned to these headquarters, bearing your recognized official signature, and it can now be noticed as your deliberate official act. Among nations not barbarous, the usages of war prescribe that where a city is about to be attacked, timely notice shall be given by the attacking commander, in order that non-combatants shall have an opportunity of withdrawing beyond its limits. Generally the time allowed is from one to three days; that is, time for the withdrawal in good faith of at least the women and children. You, sir, gave only four hours, knowing that your notice, under existing circumstances, could not reach me in less than two hours, and not less than that time would be required for an answer to be conveyed from this city to Battery Wagner.

"With this knowledge you threaten to open fire on this city, not to oblige its surrender, but to force me to evacuate those works which you, assisted by a great naval force, have been attacking in vain for more than 40 days. Batteries Wagner and Gregg and Fort Sumter are nearly due north from your batteries on Morris's Island, and in distance therefrom ranging from half a mile to two and a quarter miles. This city, on the other hand, is to the northwest, and quite five miles distant from the battery which opened against it this morning. It would appear, sir, that, despairing of reducing these works, you now resort to the novel measure of turning your guns against the old men, women, and the hospitals of a sleeping city—an act of inexcusable barbarity, from your own confessed point of sight, inasmuch as you allege that the complete demolition of Fort Sumter within a few hours by your guns seems a matter of certainty. Your omission to attach your signature to such a grave paper must show the recklessness of the course upon which you have adventured. While the facts that you knowingly fixed a limit for receiving an answer to your demand, which made it almost beyond the possibility of receiving any reply within that time, and that you actually did open one, and threw a number of the most destructive missiles ever used in war into the midst of a city taken unawares and filled with sleeping women and children, will give you a bad eminence in history—even in the history of this war. I am only surprised, sir, at the limits you have set to your demand. If, in order to obtain the abandonment of Morris's Island and Fort Sumter, you feel authorized to fire on this city, why did you not include the works on Sullivan's and James's Islands, nay, even the city of Charleston, in the same demand? Since you have felt warranted in inaugurating this method of reducing batteries in your immediate front which were otherwise found to be impregnable, and a mode of warfare which I confidently declare to be atrocious and unworthy of a soldier, I now solemnly warn you, that, if you fire again on the city from your Morris's Island batteries, without giving a somewhat more reasonable time to remove the non-combatants, I shall feel impelled to employ such stringent means of retaliation as may be available during the continuance of this attack. Finally, I reply that neither the works on Morris's Island nor Fort Sumter will be evacuated on the demand you have been pleased to make. Already, however, I am taking measures to remove all non-combatants, who are now fully aware and alive to what they may expect at your hands. Respectfully, your obedient servant,

"G. T. BEAUREGARD, General Commanding.

"To Brigadier General Q. A. GILLMORE, Commanding U. S. Forces, Morris's Island."

No. 3.

"Headquarters Department of the South, Morris's Island, S. C., August 22, 1864—9 P.M.

"General G. T. BEAUREGARD, Commanding Confederate Forces, Charleston, S. C.:

"SIR,—I have the honor to acknowledge the receipt of your communication of this date, complaining that one of my batteries has opened upon the city of Charleston, and thrown 'a number of heavy rifled shells into the city, the inhabitants of which, of course, were asleep and unwarned.'

"My letter to you demanding the surrender of Fort Sumter and Morris's Island, and threatening, in default thereof, to open fire upon Charleston, was delivered near Fort Wagner at 11 15 o'clock A.M. on the 28th instant, and should have arrived at your headquarters in time to have permitted your answer to reach me within the limit assigned, viz., four hours. The fact that you were absent from your headquarters at the time of its arrival may be regarded as an unfortunate circumstance for the city of Charleston, but one for which I clearly am not responsible. This letter bore date at my headquarters, and was officially delivered by an officer of my staff.

"The inadvertent omission of my signature doubtless affords ground for special pleading, but is not the argument of a commander solicitous only for the safety of sleeping women and children, and unarmed men. Your threats of retaliation for acts of mine, which you do not allege to be in violation of the usages of civilized warfare except as regards the length of time allowed as notice of my intentions, are passed by without comment. I will, however, call your attention to the well-established principle, that the commander of a place attacked, but not invested, having its avenues of escape open and practicable, has no right to expect any notice of an intended bombardment other than that which is given by the threatening attitude of his adversary. Even had this letter not been written, the city of Charleston has had, according to your own computation, forty days' notice of her danger.

"During that time my attack on her defenses has steadily progressed; the ultimate object of that attack has at no time been doubtful. If, under the circumstances, the life of a single non-combatant is exposed to peril by the bombardment of the city, the responsibility rests with those who have first failed to remove the non-combatants or secure the safety of the city, after having held control of all its approaches for a period of nearly two years and a half, in the presence of a threatening force, and who afterward refused to accept the terms upon which the bombardment might have been postponed.

"From various sources, official and otherwise, I am led to believe that most of the women and children of Charleston were long since removed from the city; but upon your assurance that the city is still "full" of them, I shall suspend the bombardment until 11 o'clock P.M. to-morrow, thus giving you two days from the time you acknowledge to have received my communication on the 21st instant. Very respectfully, your obedient servant,

"Q. A. GILLMORE, Brigadier General Commanding."

[1] "The barbette fire of the work was entirely destroyed. [It was this plunging fire from the barbette tier from which the monitors had most to fear.] A few unserviceable guns still remaining on their carriages were dismounted a week later. The casemates of the channel fronts were more or less thoroughly searched by our fire, and we had trustworthy information that but one serviceable gun remained in the work, and that pointed up the harbor toward the city. The fort was reduced to the condition of a mere infantry outpost, alike incapable of annoying our approaches to Fort Wagner, or of inflicting injury upon the iron-clads.

"The enemy soon after commenced removing the dismounted guns by night, and not many weeks elapsed before several of them were mounted in other parts of the harbor. The period during which the weakness of the enemy's interior defenses was most palpable was during the ten or fifteen days subsequent to the 23d of August, and that was the time when success could have been most easily achieved by the fleet. The concurrent testimony of prisoners, refugees, and deserters represented the obstacles in the way as by no means insurmountable."—Gillmore's Operations, p. 149, 150.

General Gillmore gives the following tabular statement of the firing from seven of his batteries on Fort Sumter, August 17–23:

NAME OF BATTERY.	No. and Calibre of Parrott Rifles.	Distance from Battery to centre of Gorge Wall in yards.	Whole No. of Projectiles thrown.	Total Weight of Metal thrown.	No. of Projectiles which struck Fort.	No. which struck Gorge Wall, and helped to form Breach.	Weight of Metal which formed Breach.
Strong	One 300-pr.	4290	76	19,142	46	22	5,500
Brown	Two 200-prs.	3516	542	82,070	299	198	32,670
Hays	One 200-pr.	4172	531	86,129	225	196	33,320
Reno	One 200-pr.	4272	333	115,171	480	316	38,940
	Two 100-prs.	4272	784				
Rosecrans	Three 100-prs.	3447	1173	105,807	587	392	37,240
Meade	Two 100-prs.	3428	1004	98,282	502	336	98,392
Stevens	Two 100-prs.	4278	566	46,082	340	208	43,924
Total			5000	552,683	2479	1668	289,98[illegible]

CONFEDERATE EVACUATION OF MORRIS'S ISLAND.

E. R. S. CANBY.

tion with his soldiers, but Dahlgren would not agree to this, considering it his own "proper work." He promised to proceed as soon as his monitors were repaired, if the musketry fire from Fort Sumter should be completely silenced. Delays followed, and finally the attempt was abandoned.

The same day that Gillmore occupied the forts on the north end of Morris's Island, an expedition more gallant than judicious was undertaken by a hundred marines under Lieutenant Commander Williams. This force approached Fort Sumter in 30 boats, but was driven back before a fire of musketry and hand-grenades, which killed or wounded about 50 men.

III. No serious attack was made on the defenses of Charleston by sea. New fortifications were built on Morris's Island, and named after the brave men who had fallen in the second assault on Fort Wagner. The capture of Morris's Island secured a more perfect blockade of the port, but proved of no great value from any other point of view. After all the labor and cost involved in the defense of Charleston by the Confederates, and in offensive operations against it by the national forces—naval and military—the city was finally captured without a battle. As soon as General Sherman had reached Branchville in his march through South Carolina, and had, by his destruction of the railroad in that neighborhood, left General Hardee only a single line of retreat, the latter determined to evacuate Charleston. Beauregard, who had been in command at Charleston, was at this time on the North Carolina border, collecting forces, and awaiting Hill's troops from Augusta, and the remnants of Hood's army from the West.

General Foster had been relieved by General Gillmore shortly after Sherman's departure from Savannah. The available forces in the Department of the South had been making demonstrations against Charleston from James's Island on the south, and Bull's Bay on the north. On the 10th of February General Schemmelfennig effected a lodgment on James's Island, and, covered by a naval force on the Stono, advanced and carried the works of the enemy with a loss of 70 or 80 men. The movement from Bull's Bay was under the immediate command of General Potter, Admiral Dahlgren co-operating. Hardee evacuated Charleston on the night of the 17th of February, and moved northward so rapidly that he managed to join Johnston's forces in North Carolina before he could be intercepted by General Sherman.

The plan of defense against Sherman's march was extremely novel. Wilmington, Augusta, and Charleston were held until the latest moment. These points ought all to have been abandoned the moment General Sherman entered South Carolina, and, with the forces from the West, been concentrated in his front.

On the morning of the 21st General Gillmore's army entered Charleston. Lieutenant Colonel A. G. Bennett, with two companies of the Fifty-second Pennsylvania regiment, and about 30 men of the Third Rhode Island Artillery, had entered the city on the 18th. Fort Sumter and the works on Sullivan's Island had been abandoned, and that morning Lieutenant Colonel Bennett had hoisted over Fort Sumter the United States flag. He then moved toward the city, having then with him only 22 men, replacing the national colors on Fort Ripley and Castle Pinckney in his progress, and at 10 A.M. landed at Mills's Wharf, Charleston, where he learned that a part of the Confederate troops yet remained in the city, and that mounted patrols "were out in every direction, applying the torch and driving the inhabitants before them." He addressed a communication to Mayor Macbeth, demanding the surrender of Charleston in the name of the United States, and then awaited re-enforcements. Mayor Macbeth, probably astonished at the audacity of this meagre force, replied, addressing "the general commanding the army of the United States at Morris's Island," that the Confederate military authorities had evacuated the city, and that he himself remained to enforce order until the national forces took possession. Bennett replied, offering to move into the city with his command and assist in extinguishing the fires. Having received re-enforcements, he landed, and took measures for putting out the fires, and for the preservation of the United States Arsenal and the railroad dépôts. With Charleston were captured 450 guns. These guns, and the importance which had been attached to Charleston on account of its historic connection with the origin of the rebellion, were the only considerations which made its possession valuable to the captors.

On the 14th of April, 1865—just four years after the evacuation of Fort Sumter by Major Anderson—the old flag which had once been hauled down at the bidding of rebels was again raised above the fort by the hands of Major Anderson. On this occasion the Reverend Henry Ward Beecher delivered an oration which will be recognized by posterity as the ablest production of that orator, and worthy to hold a place by the side of the most brilliant efforts of Burke or Demosthenes.

CHAPTER LIV.
THE MOBILE CAMPAIGN.

Situation and Defenses of Mobile.—Canby assumes command of the Mississippi Department, May 11, 1864.—The proposed Campaign against Mobile frustrated by the failure of the Red River Expedition.—Attack on Fort Gaines, in Mobile Bay.—Fort Powell evacuated.—Farragut passes Forts Morgan and Gaines.—Sinking of the Tecumseh.—Naval Engagement in Mobile Bay.—Capture of the Tennessee.—Surrender of Forts Gaines and Morgan.—Suspension of Operations against Mobile.—Opening of a new Campaign in March, 1865.—The Situation.—Military and Naval Forces.—Investment of Spanish Fort.—Bombardment of April 8th.—The Enemy evacuates.—Steele's Movement against Montgomery.—Evacuation of Forts Huger and Tracy.—The Fleet again moves up in Front of Mobile.—Capture of Fort Blakely.—Surrender of Mobile.—Losses.

MOBILE—the last surrendered of the Confederate strong-holds—is the chief city and port of Alabama. It is situated on low ground at the mouth of Mobile River, and on the western shore of Mobile Bay. At the outset, the city was not in favor of secession; but the false prediction of Yancey, which promised such an extraordinary development of its com-

GORDON GRANGER.

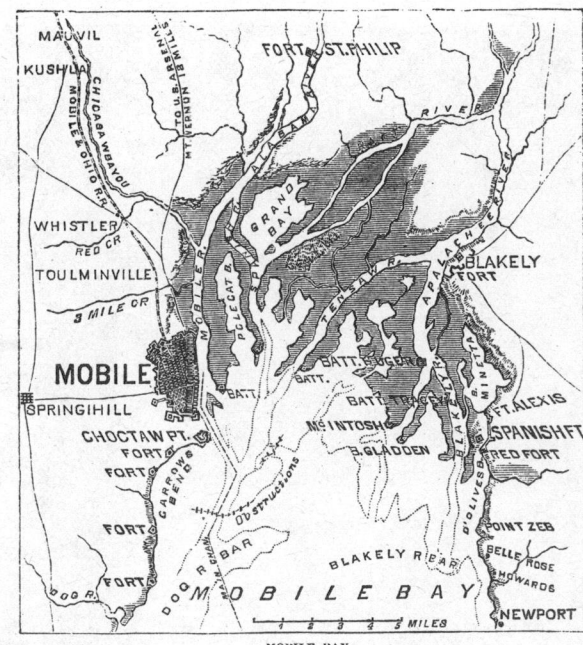

MOBILE BAY.

merce as a consequence of rebellion that the only peril to be dreaded would be the excess of luxury that must follow, had overcome its scruples.

Mobile had often been threatened with attack, but no blow was directed against the city until the summer of 1864. At this time it was considered the best fortified city in the Confederacy. It had three lines of defenses. The outer was constructed three miles distant from the city, upon commanding ground, and comprised fifteen redoubts. Through the suburbs of the city, after the fall of Vicksburg, a line of works was built with sixteen inclosed forts. Midway between these two lines still another was constructed in 1864, including nineteen bastioned forts and eight redoubts. Below the city ten batteries swept the channel, which was also obstructed by long rows of piles with narrow openings here and there for blockade-runners. Besides these obstacles on the Spanish River Channel, Forts Huger and Tracy had been erected on the eastern shore, close to the Appalachee River, and obstructions placed in the river to prevent the ascension of national gun-boats up that stream, and their progress thence into the Tensas River to the front of the city.

At the entrance of the bay stood two walled forts—Morgan and Gaines— four miles apart, built by the United States, but seized by the Confederates early in 1861. Fort Gaines, on Little Dauphin Island, mounted 30 guns, and had a garrison of 900 men. Fort Morgan, at the western extremity of Mobile Point, was a more formidable work, armed with 60 guns, with a water battery in its front. Fort Powell—a small work, mounting 98 guns —commanded Grant's Pass, west of Little Dauphin Island. A large number of torpedoes had been planted in the channel abreast of Fort Morgan, but the strength of the current at this point hindered their efficiency.

Behind these forts, in the bay, lay a small Confederate fleet, consisting of the ram Tennessee, and the gun-boats Gaines, Morgan, and Selma. Such were the defenses of Mobile against approach by land and sea.

In General Grant's plan of operations for 1864, a campaign against Mobile held a prominent place. But among the other unfortunate consequences of the disastrous Red River campaign was the impossibility of carrying out this part of the lieutenant general's programme. On the 11th of May, 1864, General Canby assumed command of the military division of West Mississippi. He had been instructed to make the movement on Mobile, if possible. But he found Kirby Smith's forces, encouraged by Banks's repulse and Steele's retreat, threatening both the Arkansas and Mississippi. Thus the forces under Canby, as well as those under Steele, were for a time put on the defensive. This attitude was rendered all the more necessary by the withdrawal of 6000 men of the Nineteenth Corps to Virginia.

Admiral Farragut, commanding the West Gulf Squadron, attacked Fort Gaines on the 5th of August. Fort Powell was that day blown up and evacuated by the Confederates. On the 3d, General Gordon Granger joined Farragut with 1500 men, who were landed on Dauphin Island. The military force marched up the island under cover of the fleet, and on the 4th intrenched within half a mile of Fort Gaines. The next morning, with fifteen vessels, Farragut—having promised his men that they should breakfast in Mobile Bay—steamed up to Fort Morgan, the admiral being bound to the main rigging of his flag-ship, the Hartford. Forts Morgan and Gaines sim-

FEDERAL FLEET IN MOBILE BAY.

CAPTURE OF THE TENNESSEE.

FORT MORGAN AFTER ITS SURRENDER.

ultaneously opened upon the fleet. Scarcely had the Tecumseh, the leading vessel, fired her first shot, when she struck a torpedo, and with her gallant Captain Craven and 120 of the crew, sank to the bottom of the channel. Under a galling fire from Fort Morgan, ten of the crew were rescued by a boat's crew of the Metacomet. The Hartford then took the lead, and, after an hour's engagement, passed the fort and entered the bay. The forts have been passed. Now the Confederate navy opposes a new obstacle to the advance of the fleet. But this affair is soon settled. In about an hour after entering the harbor the Metacomet has captured the Selma, with her crew—90 officers and men. The Morgan, more fortunate, has escaped, and the Gaines, disabled, has sought refuge under the protecting guns of Fort Morgan. But the ram Tennessee bids defiance to the entire Federal fleet. She makes for the Hartford, but, in the mean time, is attacked on every side. A desperate struggle follows, lasting two full hours. At length a 15-inch shot from the Manhattan penetrates her armor, and at the same time a shell from one of the monitors, reaching her steering apparatus, disables her, and she surrenders, with 20 officers and 170 men. Admiral Buchanan, her commander, has been seriously wounded, and she has lost eight or ten of her crew by death or wounds. The Federal loss in the engagement with the forts and the hostile fleet is 52 killed and 170 wounded. But the battle—so far as Mobile Bay is concerned—has been fought and won.

On the 8th, at 9 A.M., Fort Gaines was surrendered by its commander, Colonel Anderson, with 900 men. Fort Morgan still held out. Granger's land force was then transferred to Mobile Point, and siege operations were commenced. On the 22d there was a general bombardment. At night a fire broke out in the fort, compelling the garrison to throw 90,000 pounds of powder into the cisterns. The interior of the fort soon became a mass of smoking ruins. All night the bombardment was kept up at intervals, and on the morning of the 23d the Confederate General Page surrendered the fort, with its garrison.

Admiral Farragut removed the torpedoes planted in the bay. But, with the exception of some demonstrative movements made by Granger from Pascagoula, and by cavalry expeditions from Baton Rouge and Memphis, no farther attack was made on Mobile until the spring of 1865. Without doubt 8000 could have, immediately after Farragut's entrance to Mobile Bay, moved up Dog River and captured the city; but, until after General Hood's defeat in December, so large a force could not be spared for this purpose. The capture of Forts Gaines, Morgan, and Powell had secured a perfect blockade of the port, and it was the best policy of the national commanders to let the Confederates weaken themselves by detaching large garrisons for the protection of their coast cities, and then to disregard them, and rapidly concentrate against the two great armies of the Confederacy.

But after Hood's defeat, and when, by Sherman's strategic marches, the field of conflict had been limited to the states of Virginia and North Carolina, there were two motives which urged a campaign against Mobile. In the first place, a portion of Hood's, now Dick Taylor's army, would be prevented from joining Johnston against Sherman; and, in the second place, forces could be thus occupied on the Federal side which were not available or necessary elsewhere.

In March, 1865, a force of 45,000 men was collected for operating against Mobile. It consisted of three commands—General Granger's Thirteenth Corps, 13,200 strong; A.J. Smith's Sixteenth Corps, 16,000 strong, to which must be added 3000 for engineers, artillery, and cavalry; and Steele's column, 13,200 strong. At this time Dick Taylor had his headquarters at Meridian, Mississippi, and Major General D.H. Maury commanded the District of the Gulf, with headquarters at Mobile. The garrison of Mobile numbered about 9000 men. The defenses near the city had been strengthened, and on the eastern shore a system of defenses, known as Spanish Fort, had been erected.

The movement against Mobile was made from the east side. On the 17th of March the Thirteenth Corps marched from Fort Morgan along the peninsula, and on the 24th reached Danley's, on Fish River. The Sixteenth Corps had already reached this point, being conveyed thither by transports from Fort Gaines. A demonstration was at the same time made by Colonel J.B. Moore, with one brigade of the Sixteenth Corps, west of Mobile.

General Steele's command arrived at Barrancas on the 28th of February, and on the 19th of March reached Pensacola. It was designed with this column to cut the railroad from Mobile to Montgomery, and, if possible, capture the latter city.

The naval force, which had been increased by several light-draught ironclads from the Mississippi, and which was now under the command of Admiral Thatcher, in the absence of Farragut, had covered the landing of the troops on Fish River.

On the 27th of March Spanish Fort was invested by the national troops—A.J. Smith's corps on the right, and Granger's on the left. This fort—or rather system of defenses—was seven miles east of Mobile, and was flanked on the one side by D'Olieve's Creek and Bay, and on the other by Minette Bay. It was held by three thousand Confederates under Generals Gibson, Holtzclaw, and Ector. The line of works was two miles in length, and was weakest on its extreme left, opposite General Carr's division. The siege lasted 13 days, during which the investing force made regular approaches to the fort. On the ninth day of the siege (April 4th) a bombardment was opened from 38 siege-guns and 37 field-pieces, but little was accomplished either in the way of injuring the fort or its garrison. At this time the advance parallels of the besiegers were within a hundred yards of the enemy's works. The Confederate General Gibson, who commanded the fort, telegraphed to Maury on the 5th: "Enemy sweeps my flanks with heavy batteries, and presses on at all points. . . . My line is extended now to the water and in it. My men are worked all the time, and I don't believe I can possibly do the work necessary in the dense flats on the flanks. Can't you take a look at the situation to-morrow? . . . My men are wider apart than they ever were under Generals Johnston and Hood. The works not so well managed nor so strong, and the enemy in larger force, more active, and closer. Can't you send me the detachment belonging to Ector and Holtz-

LIGHT-HOUSE AT FORT MORGAN.

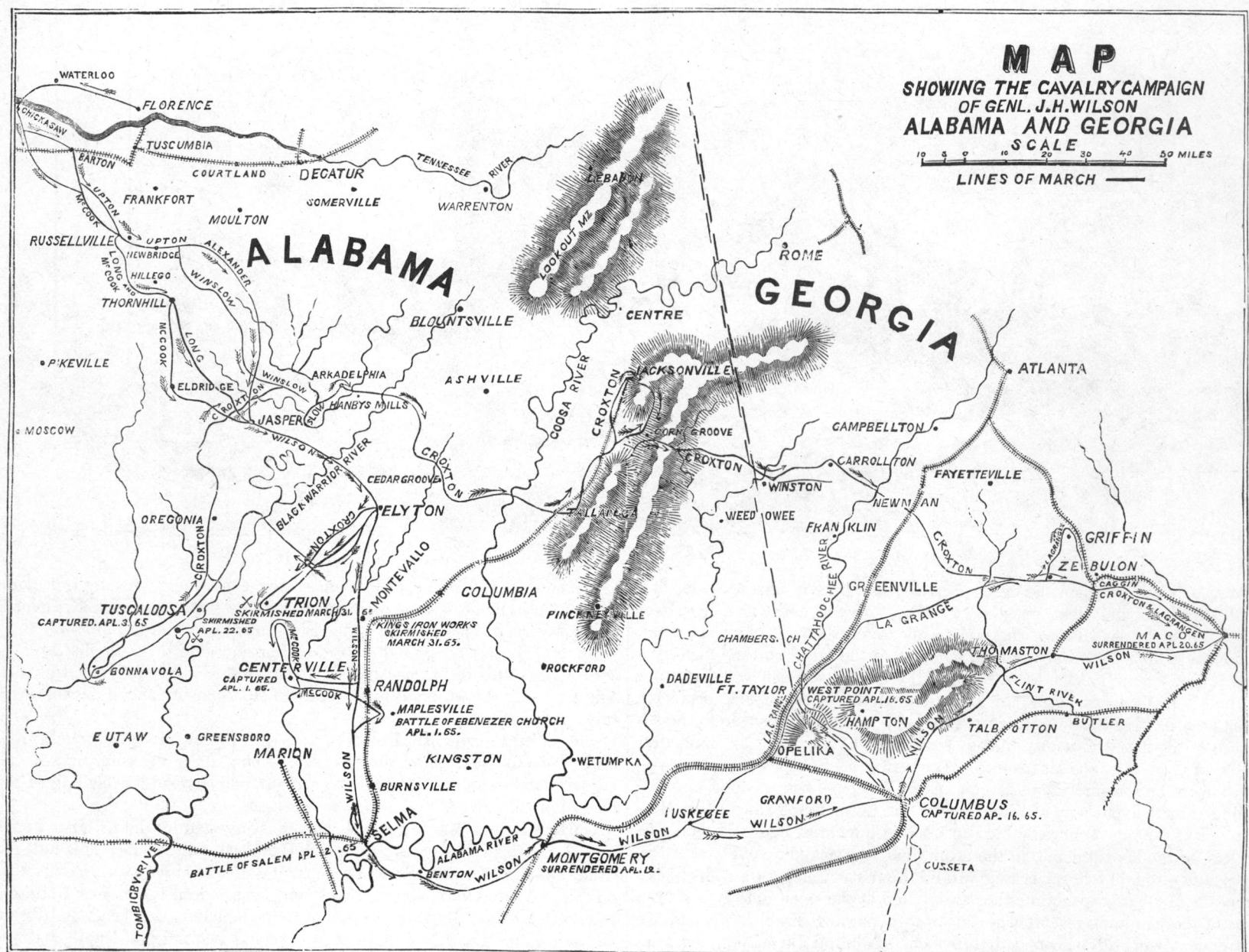

MAP
SHOWING THE CAVALRY CAMPAIGN
OF GENL. J. H. WILSON
ALABAMA AND GEORGIA
SCALE
LINES OF MARCH —

claw? Can't you send a force of negroes with axes? I can make good soldiers of the negroes."

On the 8th of April the bombardment was renewed, continuing from 5 30 to 7 30 P.M. General Canby intended to assault on the morning of the 9th, but had instructed his corps commanders in their operations on the 8th to take advantage of every opportunity for assault which promised decisive success. Such an opportunity was offered during the bombardment. General Carr, on the extreme Federal right, had advanced his works as close to the enemy's as was practicable. In his front was Ector's brigade, 659 strong. By attacking this brigade on the flank, it seemed to him possible to gain some 200 yards on the Confederate left, and secure a commanding crest well covered with pines, where a battery might be erected which would take the enemy in reverse. A little after 6 P.M., the Eighth Iowa, led by Colonel Bell, advanced boldly, and, in the face of a sharp musketry fire, gained the crest and a portion of the parapet. Then a hand-to-hand struggle ensued between the Iowans and the garrison in their immediate front. The fight was severe, but the enemy was forced to yield. The clamor of the bombardment had covered this brief combat so effectually that those of the garrison occupying the detached pits next to those who had been worsted were surprised. Advancing from pit to pit, Colonel Bell captured 300 yards of the Confederate works, and over one half of Ector's brigade. His own loss had been five killed and 20 wounded. Then supports came up, until a whole Federal brigade was inside the works and had begun to intrench.

General Gibson, hearing of the reverse on his left, determined to evacuate Spanish Fort under cover of a bold attack on Carr's division. While, therefore, some two or three hundred men maintained the unequal struggle against the Federals already in the works, the remainder of the garrison, under General Gibson, silently and barefooted, glided out by the narrow treadway leading to Fort Huger, and crossed the Appalachee in boats. Five hundred prisoners and fifty guns were captured by Canby's army, which entered the fort on the 9th—the same day that, hundreds of miles away, General Lee was surrendering to Grant the Confederate Army of Northern Virginia.

In the mean time General Steele's column had made its demonstration against Montgomery, moving with great difficulty through the swamps of Florida northward on the Pollard Road. A few miles south of Pollard the Confederate General Clanton's brigade was encountered and defeated. General Clanton was seriously wounded, and 130 prisoners captured. Steele's advance entered Pollard on the 26th of March, and destroyed a portion of the railroad. From this point he turned again southward, and joined the main army in front of Mobile at the close of the month. His command was then moved against Fort Blakely. This work is about five miles north of Spanish Fort, on the east bank of the Appalachee River, opposite its point of junction with the Tensas. The garrison occupying the defenses at this point consisted of French's division, then under General Cockrell, on the left, and General Thomas's division of Alabama reserves on the right, and numbered 3500 men. The general command of the works had been assigned to General St. John Lidell.

Fort Blakely—which, like Spanish Fort, is a name designating a system of defenses rather than the fort proper—was stronger than Spanish Fort. The works were more extended, being about three miles in length, and were held by a stronger garrison, which, after the capture of Spanish Fort, might also be re-enforced by a large portion of Gibson's escaped command. On the 2d of April these works were invested by General Steele.

On the evening of the 11th of April Forts Huger and Tracy were evacuated by the enemy. Thus the way was open for the fleet to move up the river into the Tensas. Contrary to the expectation of the enemy, the iron-clads had been able to cross Blakely Bar, but in doing so the Milwaukee and Osage had both been sunk. After the evacuation of Forts Huger and Tracy, the obstructions were removed from the channel of the river, and on the 13th Admiral Thatcher, with the Octorara and iron-clads, anchored off Mobile.

But before this time the fate of Blakely had been decided. The siege of the Confederate works at this point was not essentially different from that of Spanish Fort. After the fall of the latter the entire army moved upon Blakely. The works were carried on the evening of the 9th by an assault, in which General Hawkins's negro troops especially distinguished themselves. They captured nine guns, twenty-two officers, and 200 enlisted men. The entire garrison was captured—3423 men—and forty guns. The loss of the Federals in the assault was 654 in killed and wounded.

Mobile, now left with a garrison less than 5000 strong—a force too weak to oppose resistance to nearly ten times that number of men, assisted by a powerful fleet—was evacuated on the 11th of April. The remnant of General Maury's command retreated up the Tombigbee to Meridian. On the 12th Mayor R. H. Slough surrendered the city to General Granger and Admiral Thatcher. In this Mobile campaign 5000 Confederate prisoners were captured. General Canby's entire loss in killed and wounded was 1500 men.

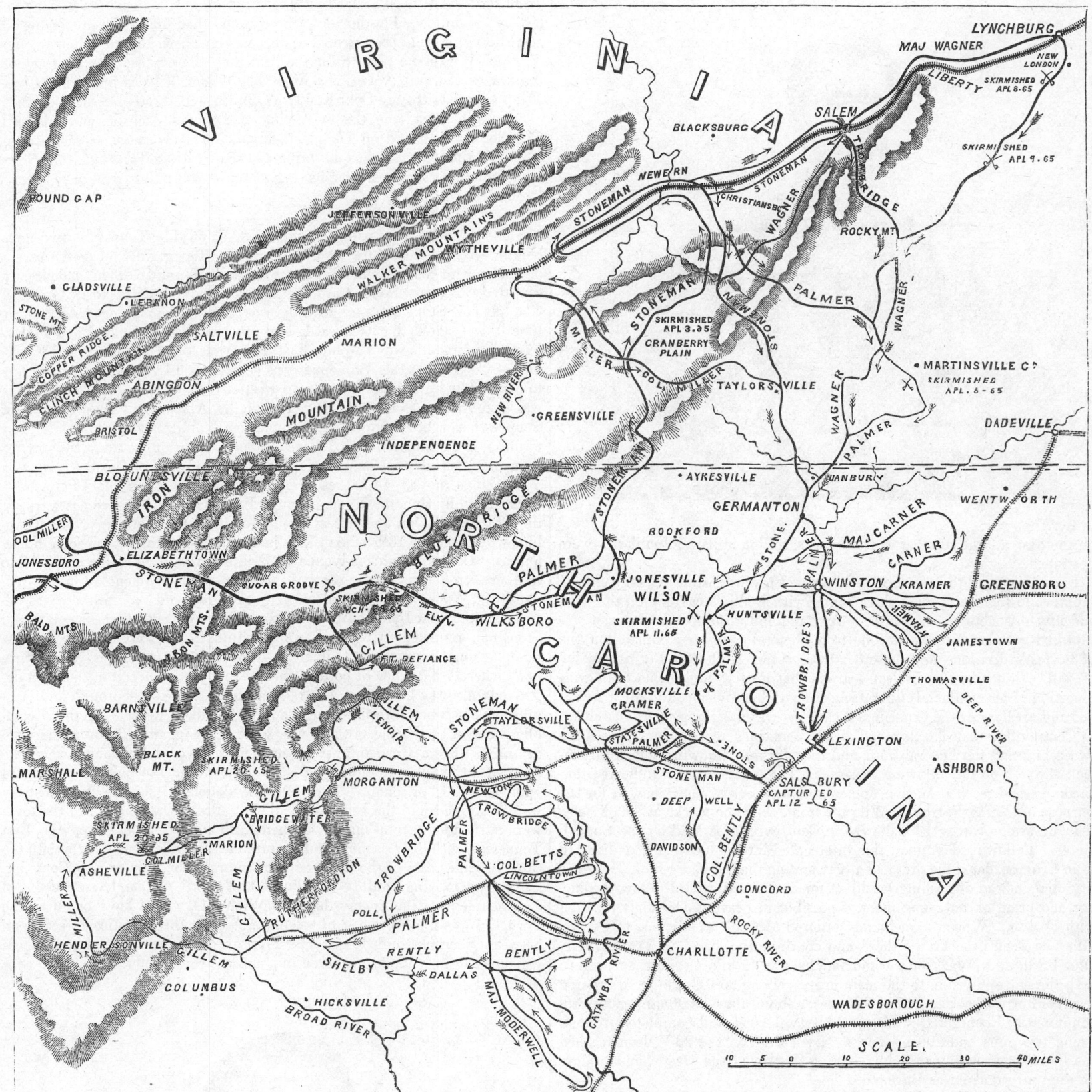

MAP OF STONEMAN'S NORTH CAROLINA RAID.

CHAPTER LV.

WILSON'S AND STONEMAN'S RAIDS.

Situation in the West at the close of January, 1865.—Organization of two Co-operative Expeditions under Wilson and Stoneman.—The Object of these Movements.—Wilson's Raid.—Intercepted Confederate Dispatches.—Capture of Selma.—Surrender of Montgomery.—Capture of Fort Taylor at West Point.—Macon surrendered under Protest.—Croxton joins Wilson at Macon.—Stoneman's Raid.—Change of Plan.—Stoneman enters Southwestern Virginia.—Capture of Towns, Destruction of Railroads, etc.—Stoneman returns to North Carolina.—Fight at Salisbury.—Gillem defeats the Confederate Detachment covering Ashville.—Is checked by the Sherman-Johnston Armistice.

AT the close of January, 1865, General Thomas's army consisted of A. J. Smith's and Stanley's corps—the Sixteenth and Fourth—and of Wilson's cavalry command, then about 22,000 strong. The only organized Confederate forces in the West this side of the Mississippi amounted to about 21,000 men, of which 12,000 were in Mississippi and the remainder at Mobile. As we have seen, A. J. Smith's corps and 5000 of Wilson's cavalry were sent in February to re-enforce General Canby. Thus Thomas retained the Fourth Corps and 17,000 of Wilson's cavalry. General Stoneman's command was also subject to his control.

Dick Taylor's army at Meridian, Mississippi, consisted of one infantry corps and 7000 cavalry under Forrest. It was not sufficiently large for an offensive campaign, and not an element of enough importance in the operations now contemplated by Thomas to justify the latter in attempting its elimination. In accordance with instructions received from the lieutenant general, Thomas determined to use the Federal forces under his control in co-operative movements. Two expeditions were organized; one to consist of Stoneman's command supported by the Fourth Corps, and the other of 12,000 cavalry under General Wilson. The former was designed to penetrate North Carolina and South Carolina toward Columbia, to co-operate

with General Sherman, destroying the railroads and supplies on its march; the latter was to co-operate with Canby by an advance, conducted upon a similar plan, against Selma, Montgomery, and Macon.

Wilson's expedition, delayed by unfavorable weather and the exhausted condition of the horses, caused by the recent pursuit of Hood, did not leave Chickasaw, Alabama, until the 22d of March. It consisted of three cavalry divisions, commanded by Generals Upton,[1] Long, and McCook. The dismounted men of the three divisions, numbering 1500, acted as an escort to the supply train, which consisted of about 250 wagons. Wilson's instructions from the lieutenant general allowed him the largest discretion as an independent commander.[2] By divergent roads the command moved upon Russellville, and reached Elyton on the 30th of March, after an extremely difficult march over bad roads and swollen streams. At Jasper, on the 27th, Wilson had been informed that a part of Forrest's force, under Chalmers, was moving toward Tuscaloosa, and he knew that as soon as the direction of his movement was discovered the balance of the enemy's cavalry would move to the same point. The country so recently overrun by Hood's army was nearly destitute of supplies, and Wilson's train was consequently very large. Obviously Forrest would make every effort to destroy this train. Wilson therefore ordered his wagons to be left between the two branches of the Black Warrior, and his troops to fill their haversacks and load the pack animals with supplies, and advance as rapidly as possible to Montevallo. At Elyton, Croxton's brigade, of McCook's division, was detached, and sent to Tuscaloosa, "to burn the public stores, military school, bridges, and founderies" at that place. In the neighborhood of Montevallo,

---

[1] Upton commanded the Fourth Division. Wilson says in his report: "Brigadier General B. H. Grierson had been originally assigned to the command of this division, but, failing to use diligence in assembling and preparing it for the field, he was replaced by Brevet Major General E. Upton, an officer of rare merit and experience."

[2] Wilson's Report.

9 D

JAMES H. WILSON.

on the 31st, a large number of iron works, rolling-mills, and collieries were destroyed.

From this point the advance was resumed toward Selma. Just south of Montevallo there was some skirmishing with Roddy's cavalry there on the 31st, and fifty prisoners were captured. At Randolph a Confederate courier was captured with two dispatches, one from General Jackson, commanding one of Forrest's divisions, and the other from Major Anderson, Forrest's chief of staff. From the first Wilson learned that Forrest was in his front with a portion of his command; that Jackson, with his division, and all the wagons and artillery of the Confederate cavalry, was marching from Tuscaloosa to Centreville; that Croxton had struck Jackson's rear, and interposed between him and the Federal train, and that Jackson, knowing this, would attack Croxton on the following morning. The other dispatch indicated that Chalmers had reached Marion, and was about to cross the Cahawba for the purpose of joining Forrest in Wilson's front, or in the works at Selma; also that the bridge across the Cahawba at Centreville was held by the Confederates. Following fast upon this intercepted intelligence came a dispatch from Croxton, dated the previous night, stating that he had struck Jackson's rear, and, instead of pushing on direct for Tuscaloosa, would follow the enemy, and bring on an engagement, if possible, to prevent Jackson's junction with Forrest. Wilson immediately ordered McCook to advance to Centreville and secure the bridge there, and continue the march to Trion, where, after breaking up Jackson's command, he was to join Croxton and return with the entire division to the main army. Long and Upton were ordered to press Forrest back to Selma. Forrest's force, about 5000 strong, was encountered at Ebenezer Church on the 1st of April, and completely routed, losing two guns and 200 prisoners. By 4 P.M. on the 2d Wilson reached the immediate vicinity of Selma, having destroyed the trestle and bridges on the railroad as far as Burnsville.

Selma is situated on the north bank of the Alabama River. A line of bastioned fortifications extended three miles distant from the city, on the north side, from the river below to the river above, flanked on the west by Valley Creek, and on the east by an almost impracticable swamp. Including the citizen militia, the garrison numbered about 7000 men. On the approach of the Federal columns, Dick Taylor left the city under the command of General Forrest. The works were carried by assault on the 2d. The loss in Long's division, which was mainly engaged in the direct assault, was 40 killed and 260 wounded. Forrest, Armstrong, Roddy, and Adams escaped with the main portion of their commands under cover of the darkness. Thirty-two guns and 2700 prisoners—including 150 officers—and a large quantity of stores were captured. Selma was the principal Confederate dépôt in the southwest. In anticipation of its capture, 25,000 bales of cotton had been burned by the enemy.

On the 5th McCook came in with the train, not having attacked Jackson or effected a junction with Croxton. After having constructed a bridge 870 feet long across the Alabama, General Wilson crossed his troops on the 10th, leaving the arsenal, founderies, and stores of Selma a complete ruin. Montgomery was on the 12th surrendered by the city authorities, the Confederate General Adams having fallen back before Wilson, after the destruction of 90,000 bales of cotton. The Federal cavalry then entered Georgia, and on the 16th General Upton, with 400 dismounted men, captured Columbus, saving the bridges over the Chattahoochee, and taking 52 field-guns and 1200 prisoners. The Confederate ram Jackson, nearly ready for sea, and carrying an armament of six 7-inch guns, was destroyed, together with the navy yard, arsenal, armory, factories, 200 cars, and an immense amount of cotton. The same day La Grange's brigade, of McCook's division, captured Fort Taylor at West Point, above Columbus, taking three guns and 300 prisoners.

On the 20th Wilson arrived at Macon, which was surrendered under protest by the municipal authorities, who claimed that, under the provisions of armistice which had been agreed upon between Sherman and Johnston, and of which Wilson now heard for the first time, the capture was contrary to the usages of war. Notwithstanding this, Wilson held as prisoners of war Major Generals Howell Cobb and G. W. Smith, and three brigadier generals.

Croxton's brigade, in the mean time, had eluded Jackson, and captured Tuscaloosa on the 3d of April, and, advancing a few miles farther southwest, had then turned back to Jasper, and thence, via Talladega and Newman, joined Wilson at Macon, having marched 650 miles in 30 days.

Stoneman's expedition had started from Knoxville, Tennessee, two days before Wilson's departure from Chickasaw. Its original purpose was cooperation with General Sherman; but before it set out Sherman had already captured Columbia, South Carolina, and was moving into North Carolina. The plan of Stoneman's expedition was therefore modified. About this time it was feared that General Lee might evacuate Richmond and Petersburg, and force his way through East Tennessee, via Lynchburg and Knoxville. To prevent this, Stoneman was sent toward Lynchburg, with orders to completely annihilate the railroad west of that point. The Fourth Corps was also ordered to advance from Huntsville, Alabama, as far up into East Tennessee as it could supply itself, repairing the railroad as it advanced, and forming, in conjunction with Tillson's infantry division, a strong support for Stoneman's cavalry in the event of the latter being driven back.

Stoneman moved with three brigades—Brown's, Miller's, and Palmer's—commanded by General Gillem, through Bull's Gap, and thence eastward up the Watauga River, and across Iron Mountain to Boone, in North Carolina, where, on the 18th of April, he had a slight skirmish with some horseguards. Continuing his advance to Wilkesborough, he then moved into southeastern Virginia. By the main column and detachments from it, Christiansburg, Wytheville, and Salem were captured, and the railroad was destroyed from near Lynchburg to Wytheville. Concentrating his command, Stoneman returned to North Carolina through Jacksonville and Taylorsville. From Germantown Palmer's brigade was sent to Salem (North Carolina), where 7000 bales of cotton were burned and the cotton factories destroyed; also the bridges on the railroad between Greensborough and Danville, and between Greensborough and the Yadkin River. In the accomplishment of these objects there was some fighting, and 400 prisoners were captured. From Germantown Stoneman moved on Salisbury, where he charged a Confederate force 3000 strong defending the place, capturing 14 guns and 1364 prisoners. The immense dépôts of supplies in Salisbury were destroyed, and the bridges on all the railroads leading out of the town were burned for several miles. Stoneman then returned to Greenville, East Tennessee, with his prisoners and captured artillery, leaving Gillem with the three brigades east of the mountains to intercept or disperse any Confederate troops moving south. On the 23d of April, Gillem, having defeated a detachment of the enemy defending Ashville, would have captured the town, but was met by a flag of truce announcing the armistice agreed upon between Sherman and Johnston. This armistice, and the circumstances which led to it, will be considered in a subsequent chapter.

ALVIN C. GILLEM.

GRANT'S HEADQUARTERS, CITY POINT.

CHAPTER LVI.

THE CAPTURE OF PETERSBURG AND RICHMOND.

Position in the Autumn of 1864.—Davis's Macon Speech.—Political Aspect.—Presidential Election at the North.—The Democratic Convention.—How McClellan's Nomination was regarded at the South.—Views of Alexander H. Stephens.—Moral Effect of Sherman's Campaign.—Forces of Johnston.—Military Situation in the Spring of 1865.—Actual Boundaries of the Confederacy.—Forces in the Field.—Strength of Lee's Army.—Project for arming the Slaves.—Opposed by the President and Secretary of War.—Favored by Lee.—Act passed for this purpose.—Protest by Mr. Hunter.—Provisions of the Act.—Confederate Finances.—Enormous Issue of Paper Money.—Practical Repudiation.—Depreciation of the Currency.—The Confederate Commissariat.—Difficulty in Feeding the Armies in Virginia.—New Tax Laws.—Lee determines to abandon Richmond.—His Plans.—Grant's Plans.—His Orders to Sheridan.—Sheridan moves up the Valley.—Routs Early at Waynesborough.—Destroys Canal and Railroads.—Joins Grant at Petersburg.—Designs of Lee and Grant.—Changes in the Organization of the Federal Army.—Commanders and Position.—The Confederate Lines.—Strategical Position of the Five Forks.—General Confederate Position.—The Confederates assault Fort Steadman.—The Fort surprised and taken.—The Confederates checked by Hartranft.—They are cut off, and surrender.—The Confederate Picket Line assaulted and carried.—Losses on both Sides.—Grant's Plans unchanged.—The Idea of the Operations.—Special Directions to Sheridan.—Strength of Sheridan's Cavalry.—Advance of Warren's Corps.—Lee's Counter-movement.—He masses Troops against Sheridan and Warren.—Operations suspended by a Storm.—Battle of White Oak Ridge, March 31.—Sheridan reaches Five Forks, and is forced back.—Action at Dinwiddie Court-house.—Warren directed to join Sheridan.—The Orders received by him.—The Confederates fall back to the Five Forks.—Sheridan's Movements.—Sheridan and Warren.—The Battle of the Five Forks.—The Fifth Corps captures the Confederate Lines.—Cavalry Operations.—The last Confederate Stand.—Their Rout.—How Lee received the Tidings.—Warren superseded.—Sheridan's Reasons.—Bombardment of Petersburg.—The general Assault.—The Ninth Corps carries the first Lines in their Front, and is checked.—The Sixth Corps pierces the Confederate Lines.—Capture of Fort Gregg.—Movements of Sheridan and Humphreys.—Death of A. P. Hill.—Lee determines to abandon his Position.—His Strength at the Time.—He concentrates his Force, and assaults the Union Lines.—Fort Mahone captured and recaptured.—Petersburg abandoned.—Davis notified of the intended Evacuation.—Scenes in Richmond.—Davis leaves Richmond.—Riots and Pillaging.—Ewell fires the Warehouses.—The Conflagration at Richmond.—In the Lines.—Musical Interlude.—Weitzel enters Richmond.—Hoisting of the Union Flag upon the Capitol.—Shepley appointed Military Governor.—His Orders.—The Conflagration checked.—Jefferson Davis reaches Danville.—His last Proclamation.

AS the spring of 1865 drew near, all men might see that the end of the Confederacy was close at hand. Late into the autumn of the preceding year its fortunes had seemed far from desperate. Never had it borne itself to the world more defiantly than in October. The two great armies east of the Mississippi, for the destruction of which the campaign of 1864 had been planned, were in October as strong as they had been in May. In Virginia Grant had been brought to a dead stand by Lee before Petersburg. Early lay in the Valley of the Shenandoah, threatening a renewed invasion of Maryland and Pennsylvania. Sherman had indeed penetrated far into Georgia, and had won Atlanta—a heavy blow, but one lighter than others from which the Confederacy had apparently recovered. Sherman's position, indeed, seemed full of peril. He was 300 miles from his only source of supplies, with which he was connected by two slender lines, and if these should be severed his army would be starved out. So it seemed to Jefferson Davis, who had[1] gone on a tour of inspection to the West. The army of Sherman, he declared in public speeches, "would meet the fate that befell the army of the French empire in its retreat from Moscow." "Our cavalry and our people," he said, "will harass and destroy his army as did the Cossacks that of Napoleon, and the Yankee general will, like him, escape with only a body-guard." "Be of good cheer," he said to a division of Tennessee troops; "for within a short time your faces will be turned homeward, and your feet pressing Tennessee soil."[2] All thoughts of peace which did not start with the recognition of the absolute independence of the Confederacy were scouted.

While the military operations of the campaign had not been decidedly unfavorable, and it needed only a sanguine spirit to consider them rather favorable than otherwise to the Confederate cause, there was much in the apparent political aspect of affairs to encourage the South. To all appearance the Confederacy was yet thoroughly united for the prosecution of the war to the utmost extremity. It is now known that a general feeling of dissatisfaction with the government was growing up, but hitherto it had hardly manifested itself openly. All the functions of authority had been merged in the executive. Congress was little more than a debating club.

Vehement opposition speeches were indeed made, but, as the sessions were mainly held in secret, they had little influence upon public opinion. It was different in the Union. There had all along been an active party opposed to the administration and to the conduct of the war, if not, as was believed at the South, to the war itself. The presidential election was approaching; all the elements of opposition had combined in the nomination of McClellan. The Chicago Convention had embraced in its platform a proffer of thanks to the soldiery of the army and the sailors of the navy, who had fought upon land and water under the flag of the country; but it had also declared that the four years of war had been a failure, and that immediate efforts should be made for a cessation of hostilities, with a view to an ultimate Convention of the states, or other means, for the restoration of peace. It was indeed added that the restoration should be "on the basis of the Federal Union of the states." But so emphatic had been the declaration of the South against any restoration or reconstruction of the Union, that it was firmly believed that, should the opposition come into power, hostilities be suspended, and a Convention called, the North would yield this point, and consent to a separation. So the South looked with much anxiety and something of hope to the result of the coming election at the North.[1]

These hopes, political and military, were soon dispelled. Lincoln was re-elected as President; Sherman accomplished his march through Georgia, and thence traversed South Carolina, and penetrated the very heart of North Carolina, with scarcely a show of opposition. Hood's army was crushed, and in effect annihilated in Tennessee. Sherman's march demonstrated to both parties and to the world the exhaustion of the Confederacy. It was not so much that the march was effected, but that there was no force left to dispute it. Johnston, once more called to the rescue, and placed in command of all the Confederate forces east of the Mississippi up to the very lines of Petersburg, swept together all the troops left in that wide region. Saving those shut up at Mobile, he drew together almost every man from Mississippi to Alabama, from Alabama to Georgia, with all in the two Carolinas. By the Confederate muster-rolls there were still enough for a great army. But to gather them was like collecting water with a sieve. On the last day of January Hardee had in South Carolina 23,000 men present for duty. Three weeks after he evacuated Charleston with 18,000; three weeks later, when he joined Johnston in North Carolina, he had but 6000. The Governor of South Carolina had withdrawn from him 1100 state troops; the remaining 11,000 missing had deserted on the march.[2] All told, the garrisons of Savannah, Charleston, Wilmington, and Augusta, with the relics of Hood's army, Johnston could not gather more than 40,000 men.[3] Pressing hard upon these was Sherman, now re-enforced by Schofield from Thomas's victorious army, raising his force to fully 100,000.

Before the last week of March, when the active operations of the campaign were opened, the field of contest had been restricted within narrow

---

[1] September and October, 1864.　　　[2] Davis's speech at Macon, September, 1864.

[1] "The action of the Chicago Convention, so far as its platform of principles goes, presents a ray of light which, under Providence, may prove the dawn of day to this long and cheerless night—the first ray of real light I have seen from the North since the war began." (Alexander H. Stephens, September 22, 1864.)—"I look upon the election of McClellan as a matter of vast importance to us in every view of the case, and hence I thought it judicious, patriotic, and wise to do every thing that could properly be done to aid in his election. Whatever may be his individual opinions, he is the candidate of the State Rights party at the North, in opposition to the Centralists and Consolidationists, whose hobby now is abolitionism. . . . Some think that if what they term a Conservative man should be elected, or any on the Chicago platform even, that such terms for a restoration of the Union would be offered as our people could accept. The spectre of reconstruction rears its ghastly head at every corner, and haunts their imagination. These apprehensions, I doubt not, are sincere, but I entertain none such myself. The old Union and the old Constitution are both dead—dead forever, except so far as the Constitution has been preserved by us. There is for the Union as it was no resurrection by any power short of that which brought Lazarus from the tomb. These fears of voluntary reconstruction are but chimeras of the brain. No one need entertain any such from McClellan's election. But, on the contrary, I think that peace—and peace on the basis of a separation of the states and our independence—would be the almost certain result. . . . . So, in any and every view I can take of the subject, I regard the election of McClellan and the success of the State Rights party at the North, whose nominee he is, as of the utmost importance to us. . . . . On the question of reconstruction, I stand now just where I did in October, 1861, when I wrote to a gentleman, in answer to a letter from him stating that I was charged with such sentiments, that I looked upon such charges as no less an imputation upon my intelligence than upon my integrity. The issue of this war, in my judgment, was subjection or independence." (Alexander H. Stephens, November 5, 1864.)　　　[2] Pollard, Lost Cause, 676.

[3] Johnston surrendered 31,243; but in this number were included many not actually present with him in front of Sherman. By his own statement, which must pass unquestioned, he had with him near Raleigh about 24,000, of whom 18,578 were infantry and artillery, and a little more than 5000 cavalry. In the interval he had lost some thousands in battle, and it is presumable many more by desertion. Our estimate of 40,000 will unquestionably cover his force when the largest.

FIELD HOSPITAL OF NINTH CORPS.

limits. There was still a considerable Southern force beyond the Mississippi, but this was so thoroughly isolated from the remainder of the Confederacy that it could effect nothing toward the general result. The West was swept clear of Confederate troops. In Alabama they held useless and precarious possession of Mobile, with feeble garrisons at a few points in the interior. The remainder of the state, together with Georgia, South Carolina, and two thirds of North Carolina, were held by the Federals. Wilson's and Stoneman's cavalry, sent out by Thomas, rode at will, with none to molest or hinder them. If they gained no great victories, it was because there was no enemy to encounter save in trifling skirmishes. All Northern and Eastern Virginia, down to the banks of the James, had been wrested from the hands of the Confederates. As a military, and, by consequence, as a political power, the Confederacy now embraced only the southern third of Virginia and the northern third of North Carolina. Its boundaries were the James on the North and the Neuse on the south, the Atlantic on the east and the Alleghanies on the west—one hundred and fifty miles from Raleigh to Richmond, and cutting off a broad strip on the sea-board, practi-

cally in Federal hands, as far from the mountains toward the ocean—a territory of 22,500 square miles, less than one half of the area once comprised in the State of Virginia. Within these boundaries the Confederate armies numbered about 100,000, with no prospect of the addition of a single regiment; the Union forces numbered fully 250,000, with 100,000 more ready to be launched thither, and still another 100,000 in arms, which could be sent in a few weeks.[1] Lee, indeed, still held his strong lines at Petersburg with a powerful army. On paper it numbered 175,000 men; but of these more than half were absent, and only about 65,000 present for

[1] The Federal force "available and present for duty" on the 1st of March numbered 602,598, of whom about 150,000 were with Grant, and 100,000 with Sherman. There were 40,000 in the departments of Washington and West Virginia; these, with quite 60,000 from various departments of the West where hostilities had ceased, could have been sent at once to Virginia and North Carolina, leaving 252,000 for operations in the extreme South and elsewhere, from which another 100,000 could, in case of need, have been spared for operations on the actual scene of war. Besides the 602,000, there were 180,000 in hospitals or on sick leave, and 50,000 absent as prisoners of war or without leave; there were 132,000 on detached service in the different military departments, many of whom could have been brought into active service. The entire nominal force of the Union armies on the 1st of March was 965,591.—See Report of the Secretary of War for 1865.

NEGRO QUARTERS ARMY OF THE JAMES.

duty.[1] With such an army, according to the dictum of Napoleon, Lee might have held Richmond against the whole Federal army, had that been the simple problem presented to him for solution. But, as we have seen, the maintenance of Richmond involved also the holding of a long line of intrenchments, designed to cover the only communications by means of which his army could be fed.

But the depletion of the army was only an external symptom of the general infirmity which had fallen upon the Confederate state. As usual, the patient tried to remove the symptom rather than heal the disease. The project began to be broached of replenishing the army by arming the slaves. A proceeding so utterly at variance with every idea upon which Southern society was based met at first with little favor. Slaves had, indeed, from the very first, been employed as laborers upon fortifications, and gradually as teamsters and pioneers in the field. In September, 1864, the Governor of Louisiana urged upon the Secretary of War that the time had come to put into the army every able-bodied negro as a soldier. "I would," he said, "free all able to bear arms, and put them into the field at once." In his message in November Mr. Davis discussed the question. It was to be viewed, he said, "solely in the light of policy and our domestic economy. When so regarded, I must dissent from those who advise a general levy and arming of the slaves for the duty of soldiers; but," he added, "should the alternative ever be presented of subjugation or the employment of the slave as a soldier, there seems no reason to doubt what should then be our decision." Mr. Seddon, then Secretary of War, took the same view. So long as there were whites who could be brought into the army, it was not safe to "risk our liberties and safety on the negro. For the present, it seems best to leave the subordinate labors of society to the negro, and to impose its highest, as now existing, on the superior class." But it became apparent that few more whites could be brought into the depleted armies. Late in February, 1865, Lee strongly urged the employment of negroes as soldiers. "I think," he said, "the measure not only important, but necessary. I do not think our white population can supply the necessities of a long war. I think those who are employed should be freed. It would not be just or wise to require them to remain as slaves." An impressment or draft he thought would not bring out the best class; he would rather call upon those who were willing to come, with the consent of their owners. "If," he wrote, "Congress would authorize their reception, and empower the President to call upon individuals or states for such as they are willing to contribute, with the condition of emancipation to all enrolled, a sufficient number would be forthcoming to enable us to try the experiment." Soon after an act was passed by Congress for this purpose. It had passed the House, and was lost in the Senate by a single vote; but the Legislature of Virginia having instructed the senators from that state to vote for it, it was reconsidered, and passed by one majority. Mr. Hunter, who had before voted against the bill, in now voting for it in obedience to the instructions of the Legislature, accompanied his vote with an emphatic protest. "When we left the old government," he said, "we thought we had got rid forever of the slavery agitation. We insisted that Congress had no right to interfere with slavery. We contended that whenever the two races were thrown together, one must be master and the other slave. We insisted that slavery was the best and happiest condition of the negro; now, if we offer slaves their freedom as a boon, we confess that we were insincere and hypocritical. Yet, if the negroes were made soldiers, they must be made freemen. There is something in the human heart that tells us that when they come out scarred from this conflict they must be free. If we can make them soldiers—the condition of the soldier being socially equal to any other—we can make them officers, perhaps to command white men. If we are right in passing this measure, we were wrong in denying to the old government the right to interfere with the institution of slavery and to emancipate slaves." The measure, he said, would also injure the Confederacy abroad. It would be regarded as a confession of despair, and an abandonment of the ground upon which secession was based. As a matter of expediency, it was, he declared, worse than as a question of principle. No considerable body of negro troops could be got together without stripping the country of the labor absolutely necessary to produce food. Moreover, the negroes abhorred the profession of a soldier. They would not volunteer, and if they were impressed they would desert to the Yankees, who could give them a better price than the Confederacy could do. The act, as passed, empowered the President to ask for and accept from owners of slaves such number of negroes as he should deem expedient, for and during the war, "to perform military service in whatever capacity he may direct." They were to be formed into companies and regiments by the general-in-chief, and commanded by such officers as the President should appoint, and to receive the same pay and rations as other troops in the same branch of the service. If a sufficient number was not thus raised, the President might call upon each state for her quota of any number not exceeding 300,000 troops, in addition to those subject to military service under existing laws, "to be raised from such classes of the population, irrespective of color, in each state as the proper authorities thereof may determine." But it was provided that "nothing in this act shall be construed to authorize a change in the relation of the said slave;" and that not more than a quarter of the male slaves between the ages of eighteen and forty-five should be called for. Whatever might have been the effect of such a law if enacted at an earlier period, it came too late. The Confederacy had now no arms to put into their hands, and no means of producing them at home or procuring them from abroad;[1] and, moreover, long before the requisition could be made and complied with, the Confederacy had ceased to exist.

The finances of the Confederacy were even in a worse condition than its armies. It had long since practically ceased to pay its soldiers. It was hardly worth the trouble even to go through the form, when a month's pay of a soldier in paper money would not buy a pair of shoes. Yet, for many purposes, the government must have something to represent money; and at last notes and bonds were put forth with a profusion limited only by the ability of the printing-press to execute them. What the total sum was no man can tell with any approach to accuracy.[2] The financial measures of the government have been made the subject of unbounded animadversion; but it is hard to see how the wisest financier could have materially changed the general results. Most of the twenty millions of specie in the Confederacy was loaned to government, or soon became absorbed in the tempting business of blockade-running; all that government could borrow or raise by the export of cotton was spent abroad for vessels, arms, munitions, and military supplies. Bank-notes, themselves in the end to become almost worthless, were carefully hoarded, and the government could only pay its home expenses in its own notes and bonds; and these, as the expenses accumulated, must be issued in larger and still larger quantities, accelerated by what was styled the universal advance in prices, but which was really the depreciation in the estimate put upon the circulating medium. The Confederate financiers had laid upon them a task more grievous than that imposed by the Egyptians upon the Hebrews. They had to make bricks not only without straw, but without clay—with nothing but sand. No wonder that their bricks crumbled at a touch. The Confederate paper depreciated until it had a real purchasing power of only a twentieth, a fortieth, and finally a sixtieth of its nominal value. It grew to be a common jest, that when one went to market he needed a basket to carry his money, and only a wallet to bring home his purchases.

A vigorous government may for a long time keep armies in the field without pay, but not without food. The Confederate commissariat was in worse plight than its treasury. The South, though essentially agricultural, and abundantly supplied with food, had yet no large accumulations. It had no great dépôts where supplies were collected in advance. The crops were consumed in the year of their harvesting, and mainly in the region of their production. The means were scanty for their transportation from place to place. Hence, when the sudden necessity arose for accumulating large amounts at Richmond, it was with the utmost difficulty that this want could be met. We have already[3] seen how sorely this difficulty pressed upon Lee in the summer and autumn of 1864. As weeks passed on, the difficulty became greater and greater. The immediate region was well-nigh exhausted. Early in the winter the state of things was thus set forth in secret session of Congress:[4] There was not meat enough in the Confederacy for the armies it had in the field. In Virginia there was not meat enough for the armies within her limits. The supply of even bread depended upon keeping open railroad connections with the South. Meat must be obtained from abroad; and bread could no longer be had by impressment, but must be paid for at market rates, and in a better currency than that in circulation.

Grave as were these difficulties, they grew rapidly graver. The capture of Fort Fisher, by closing the port of Wilmington, shut off all possibility of obtaining meat from abroad. The wharves at Nassau might be piled with meat purchased for the Confederacy, but not a barrel could reach the army. Sherman's march though Georgia and the Carolinas had severed all connection with the regions where bread was mostly to be found. Even if it was to be found, whence was to come that better currency wherewith to purchase it? Congress, near the close of its last session, made a desperate ef-

[1] The strength of Lee's force has been most persistently and strangely understated. Pollard (*Lost Cause*, 679) asserts that "in the first months of 1865 Lee held both Richmond and Petersburg with not more than 33,000 men." Swinton (*Army of the Potomac*, 573) says: "At the opening of the spring campaign General Lee had on paper 160,000 men, but, in reality, less than 50,000, from which, if there be deducted the 10,000 troops on detached duty, it will appear that he had 40,000 men wherewithal to defend forty miles of intrenchments." It is somewhat strange that Mr. Swinton should have failed to refer to the Confederate reports which he had in his possession. These reports give the following as the sum of Lee's force at the close of February:

	Present and Absent.	Present.	Present for Duty.
Army of Northern Virginia	160,411	73,349	59,094
Department of Richmond	9,675	5,431	4,692
Total	170,086	78,780	64,786

The troops in the Department of Richmond, under Ewell, were the actual garrison of Richmond; they marched out at the evacuation, and formed the rear-guard of the retreating army. Upon what "detached duty" any of Lee's force could have been engaged, it is hard to see. The one thing to be done was to defend his lines. It is probable that Lee's force was slightly increased during the three weeks between the date of this report and the commencement of operations; for, as will be seen hereafter, about 65,000 are definitely accounted for as killed and wounded, captured on the field, or surrendered; and it is certain that considerable numbers escaped, and were not included in the lists of paroled prisoners.

[1] At the time when "Congress was debating a bill to put 300,000 negroes into the Confederate armies, there were not five thousand spare arms in the Confederacy, and our returned prisoners could not actually find muskets with which to resume their places in the field."—Pollard, *Lost Cause*, 660.

[2] Pollard (*Lost Cause*, 420) says: "The total cost of the war to the Confederate government had reached at its close, according to the opinion of intelligent officers of the Treasury, about thirty-five hundred millions of dollars. Of this total about twenty-five hundred millions consisted of eight, six, and four per cent. bonds of long dates, of treasury notes, unsettled accounts," etc.; the remaining thousand millions being in the form of unpaid claims for property purchased or impressed and damages sustained at the hands of the enemy. He elsewhere (page 651) puts down the amount of treasury notes in circulation as money at three hundred and twenty-five millions; but, as appears, many millions had been practically repudiated by the government a year before. At that time the amount of notes was more than six hundred millions. By the law of February 17, 1864, holders of these notes above the denomination of five dollars were for a few months to be allowed to exchange them for four per cent. bonds; after that they should cease to be current, but might be exchanged for new notes at the rate of three of the old for two of the new. Old notes of one hundred dollars could not be exchanged for the new ones, but only for four per cent. bonds; all of them outstanding after April 1 were to be taxed ten per cent. a month until January, 1865, when they should be taxed one hundred per cent.—that is, repudiated wholly. Notes of the new issue, and the small ones of the old scaled down to two thirds of their value, might be exchanged for certificates bearing four per cent. interest, and payable two years after the notification of a treaty of peace with the United States. A large majority of the note-holders, it is added, exchanged the old notes for new ones under the conviction that the reduction of the amount of the currency would make the two dollars worth more than three now were. If we suppose that this large majority held two thirds of the whole six hundred millions, the scaling down was in effect a repudiation of one hundred and fifty millions of dollars.

[3] *Ante*, p. 693.

[4] Pollard (*Lost Cause*), 649.

UNION AND CONFEDERATE WORKS SOUTHWEST OF PETERSBURG, FROM SIGNAL STATION.

fort to grapple with this last difficulty. Early in March a tax-bill was passed, more stringent than any civilized people had ever endured. Agriculturists must pay in kind a tenth of their produce. All property, real and personal, not otherwise provided for, must pay eight per cent.; specie, bullion, and bills of exchange, twenty per cent.; paper money five per cent.; incomes five per cent.; all profits of above twenty-five per cent. upon sales, twenty-five per cent. Upon all prescribed taxes, of whatever kind, there was to be an addition of one eighth, to be applied toward the increased pay of soldiers. On the 17th of March another act was passed, "to raise coin for the purpose of furnishing necessaries for the army." A tax of twenty-five per cent. was imposed upon all coin held by banks or individuals in excess of two hundred dollars; not, however, to go into effect in case banks and individuals would, within a month, raise a loan of two millions to the government. The tax was also commuted in cases where the owners of coin would exchange it for cotton at the rate of fifteen cents a pound. On the 28th, the very day before Grant opened the final ten days' campaign, the State of Virginia advanced three hundred thousand dollars in coin, taking in exchange an order from the Secretary of the Treasury for two millions of pounds of cotton, "with the right to export the same free of all conditions except the payment of the export duty of seventy-five cents a pound." This duty, being payable in paper, was, at the then existing rate, equivalent to one and a quarter cents a pound in coin.

Thus threatened with starvation, imminent at the best, and certain in case either of the two railroads running southward were interrupted even for a week, Lee at last determined that his position was no longer tenable. He resolved to abandon it, and unite with Johnston somewhere near the borders of Virginia and North Carolina. If the retreat could be successfully executed, he would have a force of nearly or quite 100,000. Perhaps he might be able to crush Sherman, and thus regain possession of the Carolinas and Georgia, and then, gathering together the troops beyond the Mississippi, inaugurate a new war. At worst, the contest could be prolonged for a while, for it would be a work of months for the Federal army, with its material, to concentrate upon this new and difficult field of operations, and who could tell what changes a few months might not bring? Would the North hold out for another campaign? At all events, the army would escape immediate peril of starvation. If its food could not come to it, it would be going toward its food. This resolution was formed early in March, and the arrangements for its execution concerted with Johnston. But time was required to carry these arrangements into effect. Dépôts of provisions must be gathered at different points on the way, and the march could not begin until opening spring should make the roads practicable for an army and its trains of material.

Grant, on his part, was aware of the situation of Lee, and divined what must be the means which he would essay to extricate himself. Day after day was spent by him in anxiety lest each morning should bring the report that his opponent had retreated the night before. He had before meditated bringing Sherman, by water or land, upon the rear of Lee's position, but he became convinced that Sherman's crossing the Roanoke would be the signal for Lee to march toward Johnston. To forestall the junction of these two armies, and thus prevent a long and tedious campaign, seemed the thing nearest at hand to be done. Perhaps, also, he wished that the armies of the East, after their long and as yet not successful struggle, should have the glory of destroying their stout opponent, and thus match the achievements of their heretofore more fortunate comrades of the West. Something which seemed almost an accident now favored the execution of this design.

Early in February Grant had begun to make dispositions for the campaign. In the far South, Canby was moving upon Mobile, while Thomas was to send his cavalry to raid in different directions. Sheridan had wintered at Winchester, where he had recruited his cavalry until he had more than 10,000 in excellent condition. These, Merritt being Chief of Cavalry, had been organized into two divisions, under Devin and Custer. On the 20th Grant sent his orders, or rather suggestions, to Sheridan. As soon as the roads would permit, he would find no difficulty in going with cavalry alone up the Valley of the Shenandoah, and thence crossing the Blue Ridge still farther southward to Lynchburg. From there he was to destroy the canal and railroads in every direction, so that they would be of no farther use to the enemy. Grant was desirous to re-enforce Sherman with cavalry, in which arm he was greatly inferior to the enemy. Accordingly, when Sheridan had reached Lynchburg, and done his work in that region, he might, if circumstances should warrant, strike southward, heading the streams in Virginia, and push on to join Sherman, whom he would be likely to find somewhere near Raleigh.

Sheridan set out from Winchester on the 27th of February, his men carrying five days' rations in haversacks, and each horse bearing thirty pounds of forage; fifteen days' rations of coffee, sugar, and salt were borne in wagons. Besides the ammunition trains, a pontoon train of eight boats, eight ambulances, and one wagon for each division headquarters, no vehicle was permitted to accompany the march. Thus lightly equipped, the command moved rapidly, though the weather was bad. The mountains were covered with snow, rapidly disappearing under the heavy rains, rendering most of the streams past fording. Small parties of guerrillas hovered upon the flanks of the column; but they kept at a respectful distance, and no notice was taken of them. Once, however, Rosser, with one or two hundred cavalry, attempted to impede the march by burning a bridge over a fork of the Shenandoah, but was driven off with loss of men and material. In three days Staunton was reached, the farthest point which any Union force had hitherto attained by this route. Early, with a miscellaneous force of 2000 men, had been hovering in this region ever since his defeat at Cedar

River. He retreated eastward, leaving word behind that he would fight at Waynesborough, which commanded the only practicable gorge through the Blue Mountains, which Sheridan must pass to debouch into the Valley of the James, and reach Lynchburg. Custer's division was pushed in pursuit. He found Early, true to his word, well posted, with two divisions of infantry and Rosser's cavalry, behind breastworks. Without even pausing to reconnoitre, with his troopers partly dismounted and partly in the saddle, Custer dashed straight at the works, drove the enemy out, pursued them until they were brought up by the river, where they threw up their hands in token of surrender, "with cheers at the suddenness with which they had been captured."[1] The fruits of this brilliant dash were 1600 prisoners, 11 guns, and 200 wagons, with ammunition and subsistence. Early escaped with two of his staff. Rosser's cavalry also rode off, to appear for a moment a few days later. Herewith Early disappears from the war. On the 30th of March Lee wrote, dismissing him from command, couching his order in the kindest terms possible: He himself had full confidence in Early's zeal, ability, and discretion; but he had lost public confidence, and a commander must be sought for who could secure this. Lee had no occasion to make this search; for, before Early had received the order of dismissal, Lee was forced from Petersburg, and was on his disastrous retreat, which ten days after closed in his surrender.

Sheridan pushed through the gorge in the Blue Mountains thus opened to him, and reached Charlottesville in the Valley of the James, where he was obliged to wait two days for his trains to make their slow way through the thick mud. The prisoners, meanwhile, were sent under a strong escort toward Winchester. Rosser followed this body, and at Mount Jackson made an attack, hoping to rescue the prisoners. He was repulsed, and left behind some of his own men. The delay at Charlottesville enabled the Confederates to gather at Lynchburg a force too strong to be assailed by cavalry. Sheridan abandoned the purpose of reaching that point, but sent his troopers in every direction to destroy the canal, railroad, and public property. The James River Canal was for miles so thoroughly destroyed as to be impassable, and thus one important means of supply for Lee's army was cut off. Sheridan then proposed to cross the James between Lynchburg and Richmond, and, pressing southward, to reach the Southside Railroad fifty miles in the rear of Lee's lines. But the Confederates succeeded in destroying every bridge between these two points, and the pontoons would not half span the still swollen stream.

Sheridan now, exercising the discretion which had been wisely given him, resolved, instead of endeavoring to join Sherman in North Carolina, to more thoroughly destroy the railroads leading northward from Richmond, and then, pressing eastward to the York River, bend southward, and, after eight months' absence, rejoin Grant in front of Petersburg. After raiding hither and yon for a week, destroying every thing destructible down to within ten miles of Richmond, he resumed his march. Nature imposed obstacles to this march such as had been heretofore pronounced insurmountable. It was the worst season of the Virginian year. There were incessant rain, deep and almost impassable streams, swamp and mud to be endured or overcome. The animals suffered much, mostly from hoof-rot. The men, buoyed up by the thought that they had completed their work in the Valley of the Shenandoah, and were now on their way to aid in what remained to be done upon the Appomattox, bore up bravely. The whole loss on the march was not more than a hundred men, and some of these were left by the wayside, overborne by fatigue. Crossing the South and North Anna Rivers, passing hard by many famous battle-fields whereon there was now no hostile force, this cavalry force reached the site of the memorable White House upon the 19th of March. Sheridan's march from Winchester had occupied twenty days. In its course he had traversed thirteen counties in Virginia, and, by the almost utter destruction of the James River Canal and of the railroads, had effectually deprived the Confederate army at Richmond of all subsistence from the region of Virginia lying north and east of the James River. After resting and refitting for a week at the White House, Sheridan resumed his route. Crossing the Chickahominy and the James, he encamped near Petersburg on the evening of the 26th of March.

Here, at points only a few score rods apart, two men, neither of them to a casual observer notable for any thing but the rare faculty of saying little, however much they might think, yet both somehow having that power of command which more showy men never cared to question, had fixed upon measures the result of which was to determine the issue of the war. Each of these two men, Grant and Lee, had by this time learned to value the other; each knew nearly the condition of the other, and so could gauge what he should, and therefore would endeavor. Either could then play the part of his opponent almost as well as his own. Lee's main purpose toward the close of March was to withdraw his army, with its materials, from the James and the Appomattox, and, joining Johnston, to carry on the fight in North Carolina, or, events favoring, far to the southward. Grant's purpose was to prevent this orderly retreat, either by shutting up Lee within his lines, and therein forcing him to surrender by assault or famine, or to drive him out by sheer force, in which case he would be able to follow hard on in pursuit.[2]

[1] Sheridan's Report.

[2] Neither Lee himself, nor any one qualified by position or knowledge to speak for him, has as yet undertaken to set forth the purpose of the Confederate commander at this period; but his operations, soon to be described—such as bringing to Petersburg only the food needed from day to day, accumulating supplies at different points on the railroads, and the assault upon Fort Steadman—can be explained and justified only upon this theory. Grant, in a few significant sentences, clearly sets forth his design. He says: "The greatest source of uneasiness to me was the fear that the enemy would leave his strong lines about Petersburg and Richmond, for the purpose of uniting with Johnston, before he was driven from them by battle or I was prepared to make an effectual pursuit. . . . With Johnston and him combined, a long, tedious, and expensive campaign, consuming most of the summer, might become necessary. By moving out I would put the army in better condition for pursuit, and would at least, by the destruction of the Danville Road, retard

BRIDGE ON MILITARY RAILROAD.

Important changes had within a few months taken place in the organization of the Federal armies in Virginia. Not long after the failure of the mine enterprise, and in consequence of the censure of the Court of Inquiry, Burnside, at his own request, received leave of absence. He wished to resign his commission, but the President refused to accept it, thinking that there would arise occasion to place him again in active service. The command of the Ninth Corps was in the mean time given to Parke, who happened to be the ranking general in command of a corps, and who consequently found himself at an imminent moment in command of the whole army. Hancock, never fully recovered from his wound at Gettysburg, had given up the command of the Second Corps, and gone East to recruit a new corps, to be known as the First. Humphreys, who had acted as chief of staff to Meade, was placed at the head of the Second Corps, Webb taking his place as Meade's chief of staff. Wright retained the command of the Sixth Corps, to which he had acceded upon the death of Sedgwick at Spottsylvania. This corps, having done brave service in the annihilation of Early in the Valley of the Shenandoah, had returned to the Appomattox, and to it was reserved the honor of giving two out of the three great blows which decided the issue of the war.[1] Warren still retained the command of the Fifth Corps. Butler had been, at the special request of Grant, removed from the command of the Department of Virginia and North Carolina, including what was known as the Army of the James. This army had been reorganized. The former Tenth and Eighteenth Corps had been discontinued, and the troops, to which was added the colored division formerly attached to Burnside's corps, were formed into two corps, designated as the Twenty-fourth and Twenty-fifth. Ord, having performed brilliant service in the West and Southwest, had been ordered to the North, and had replaced Smith at the head of the old Eighteenth Corps, and was at length placed in command of the department vacated by the removal of Butler, the newly-arranged Twenty-fourth and Twenty-fifth Corps, constituting the Army of the James, being confided to Gibbon and Birney. Thus it happened that, of the six generals who commanded corps in the combined armies of the East at the opening of operations in May, 1864, Warren only retained his place in March, 1865. Sheridan also, though now with his troopers upon the James, was still nominally commander of the Army of the Shenandoah. But the distinction between the armies of the Potomac, the James, and the Shenandoah had been practically set aside. The entire force around Richmond and Petersburg was directly under Grant, Meade being second in command, Sheridan coming next in grade, the corps commanders following in order of seniority in the date of their commissions. The combined force of all arms numbered about 150,000 men present for duty, of whom about two thirds were available for direct offensive operations in the field, the remainder being required for guards, camp duty, and other multifarious work.[2] As posted, Ord lay on the right, north of the James, and at Ber-

muda Hundred; next, and before Petersburg, Parke; then Wright; then Humphreys; and upon the extreme left, Warren.

Lee had, during the winter, continued his intrenchments two miles farther westward, bending the extremity in a sharp crotchet to the north. Farther he could not go from sheer want of men to hold the lines; otherwise there was no reason why they might not have stretched across the continent. Four miles beyond where the works ceased was a point as important as any other. Here three roads came together, the point of junction being known as the Five Forks. . One, the White-oak Road, ran westward from the Boydton Plank Road, nearly parallel with the vital Southside Railroad, from which at the Five Forks it was but three miles distant, by way of the Ford Road, running north and south. An enemy, having gained the Five Forks, could in an hour strike the railroad, and in a few hours so damage it that days would be required for its repair. It was of prime importance that the Five Forks should be guarded. Intrenchments were therefore laid out here, stretching for two miles north and south behind the White-oak Road. This, between the Forks and the extremity of the regular lines, ran along a slight ridge, southward of which the region was woody and swampy. The White-oak Road thus formed practically a covered way by which troops could, in case of a menaced movement by the enemy, be hurried to the defense of the Forks. Thus, at the opening of spring, the absolute right of the Confederate line was a mile to the west of the Five Forks: this was watched by the bulk of the cavalry under Fitzhugh Lee. Thence it stretched eastward and northward, girdling Petersburg and Richmond. Ewell commanded the few thousand men which formed the proper garrison of Richmond. Longstreet commanded below the city, north of the James, and across the river to within a few miles of Petersburg. Then came Gordon at Petersburg, the bulk of his force consisting of the remnants of the three divisions reduced to the numbers of one in the disastrous campaign in the Valley of the Shenandoah. Lastly came Hill with three strong divisions, holding the long line south and west of Petersburg. Lee's headquarters were with Hill's division.

On the 24th of March Grant issued his order for a grand movement to be commenced on the 29th against the Confederate right. Lee, knowing the imminency of such a movement, and perceiving that the time had now come for the evacuation of his position, resolved to anticipate the movement of his antagonist by an offensive thrust which should facilitate his own withdrawal. The thing to be done was to prevent Grant from adding to the strength upon his left, and, if possible, to cripple for a space the forces already there, so as to leave open his own meditated line of retreat. He therefore planned a sudden assault upon the Federal right, the point farthest removed from that upon which the effect of the blow was to be felt.

The point chosen was Fort Steadman, close by the crater where Burnside's mine had so signally failed. This fort occupied a salient projected forward toward the Confederate works, the distance between being only one hundred and fifty yards. The fort itself was of no great strength. It was a small earthwork, without bastions, slightly constructed originally, and now much dilapidated by the frosts and rains of winter. So completely was it covered by the enemy's artillery that it was impossible to make any repairs except imperfectly and by stealth. This, however, was of less consequence, as the hill[1] upon which it stood was commanded in the immediate rear by a crest of nearly equal height, and covered upon each side by flanking batteries. Still it seemed to Lee that if the fort and a few of the flanking batteries could be taken by surprise, an opening could be made through which a strong column could be thrust, which should carry the

the concentration of the two armies of Lee and Johnston, and cause the enemy to abandon much material that he might otherwise save." As late as March 27, just two days before active operations commenced, Grant concerted with Sherman, who had come to City Point from North Carolina, a plan of campaign based on the supposition that Lee would continue to hold his lines at Petersburg and Richmond. Sherman, on the 20th of April, was to move northward, his army fully equipped and rationed for twenty days. He would, as circumstances should indicate, strike the Danville and Southside Railroads at their junction at Burkesville, 52 miles in the rear of Lee's lines, or join the armies operating in front of Richmond. Sherman, unless otherwise directed, was to begin this movement on the 10th of April; but, as events finally shaped themselves, on the very day before, Lee, having been forced from Richmond and Petersburg, surrendered his army at Appomattox Court-house. It may be safely assumed that, at the opening of the spring campaign of 1865, both of the opposing commanders so well understood the whole situation, that the immediate aim of each was to prevent the other from accomplishing the thing which at the moment he most desired. As, therefore, Grant's main purpose was to prevent Lee from getting safely away from his lines, it may be safely assumed that thus to get away was the main purpose of Lee. Each general, of course, was eager to avail himself of any advantage which circumstances should throw into his hands. In this view of the plans of the opponents—that is, Lee wishing to carry off his army and material, and Grant wishing to prevent him from so doing—the operations of the last fortnight of this long campaign are clearly explicable.

[1] The three great blows were: (1st) The battle of the Five Forks, won April 1 by Warren's Fifth Corps and Sheridan's Cavalry; (2d) The piercing of the Confederate lines, April 2, by the Sixth Corps; (3d) The capture of Ewell's Corps at Sailor's Creek, April 6, mainly by the Sixth Corps. These three blows cost the Confederates a loss of 20,000 prisoners, and probably 5000 in killed and wounded—nearly a half of the nominal, and more than a half of the real fighting force which Lee had left to him on the 31st of March.

[2] Force present for duty, March 1: Army of the Potomac, Meade, 103,273; Department of

Virginia, Ord, 45,986, some thousands being at Fortress Monroe and elsewhere, and so not available for direct operations; cavalry of Middle Division, 12,980, of whom there were, at the close of March, about 9000 under Sheridan, at hand on the James. The actual movable force may be estimated from the fact that when Warren moved on the 29th of March, his corps counted 15,300 men. The corps appear to have been of about equal strength, so that the six would have contained 91,800 movable men. Add to these 9000 cavalry, and there will be 100,800 at Grant's command for immediate offensive operations.

[1] Known as Hare's Hill. Confederate writers usually denominate the action which here ensued as the battle of Hare's Hill.

heights in the rear, and thus effectually pierce the Federal lines. Thence a sudden rush of less than two miles would reach the military railroad which Grant had constructed from City Point southwestward, by which the left of the Union army received its supplies. Such an attack, it was not unreasonably anticipated, would induce Grant to bring all his force from both extremities of his lines. If nothing more than this was accomplished, Longstreet and Hill, relieved from immediate pressure in front and on flank, could start southward without obstruction, while the assaulting column would be suddenly withdrawn and follow in their rear, and, before the Federal commander could reorganize his army for pursuit, would, with its material, be fairly on its way, with two full days' start, to unite with Johnston, and could so obstruct the roads behind them that they could not be overtaken until the junction already prepared for was effected. It was not wholly impossible that still greater results might be accomplished. The railroad destroyed, City Point itself might perhaps be reached, and in a brief space the great accumulation of stores there be given to the flames. The plan was a bold one; but Lee was now in such case that he must venture much. In its very audacity lay its best augury of success.

Lee left nothing undone which it was in his power to do to insure success. The initial blow was to be struck by Gordon with two of his divisions, while 20,000 more were massed to follow up the blow in case an opening was made at Fort Steadman and the crest in its rear was gained. The first blow must be given by surprise. Accident favored this. The Federal picket-line was advanced fifty yards in front of the fortifications, and within a hundred yards of the Confederate works. Across this narrow space deserters, often in squads and with arms in their hands, had been wont to make their way within the Union lines. At four o'clock on the morning of March 25 the officer on duty made his rounds along the picket-line; the men were alert, and there was no indication of any movement on the part of the enemy. Soon after, squad after squad, announcing themselves as deserters, began to drop in. The occurrence had come to be so common that no alarm was taken. Suddenly these squads dashed upon the pickets, and overpowered them with scarcely a show of resistance. At the same moment the near Confederate abatis was opened and three strong columns emerged. The central column struck straight for Fort Steadman; the others diverged to the right and left, taking in reverse small advanced batteries which flanked the fort on either hand. All these were carried with a rush, the garrison, five hundred strong, being made prisoners. A gap of a quarter of a mile wide had been made into, but not through the Union lines—an opening large enough to give passage to the 20,000 who had been massed to follow up the assault. If they had followed promptly in the gray dawn no man can say what would have been the result. They might possibly have won the commanding crest in the rear, and thence dashed upon the railroad; they might thus have won a great success, or they might have been cut off to a man, shut in by the enemy closing in behind them. By whose merit or whose fault it was that the 5000 whom Gordon pushed forward were left unsupported has been left untold.[1]

The lines, for a long distance to the right and left of Fort Steadman, were held by Parke's Ninth Corps. At half past five, when the attempt of the enemy was apparent, he sent tidings of it to headquarters. Three times within half an hour the message was repeated without an answer. Then came the reply through the telegraph operator: "General Meade is not here, and the command devolves upon you." Hurrying couriers to City Point to inform Grant and Meade of what was going on, Parke summoned Wright and Warren to move troops toward the point assailed. But before they could come up the Ninth Corps had done the work. Tidball, chief of artillery, was ordered to post his batteries upon the hill in the rear. These effectually stopped the advance of the central column. The two other assailing columns soon came to grief. The right column met Hartranft's division, which had sprung to arms; they were checked, and soon forced back. The left gained some success, capturing momently two batteries, but were in like manner checked and forced back. The three columns were now drawn together within the captured works of Fort Steadman; but these were commanded by Fort Haskell on the left, as well as by the batteries in the rear. After making a feeble attempt to take this fort, the troops of Gordon crouched in disorder behind the breastworks which they had captured, for the way of retreat was by this time closed upon them. Forts Haskell on the left, and McGilvery on the right, swept the narrow space to the Confederate lines with a fire under which no troops could live. Hartranft, upon whom the immediate direction of operations had devolved, had posted his own division and portions of others so as to cover their front and both flanks.[2] Hartranft now dashed upon the works, and carried them with hardly a show of resistance. Some of the Confederates ran the terrible cross-lines of fire and got back to their own lines, but nearly 2000 of them surrendered. Their loss in killed and wounded is unknown, but it must have exceeded that of the Federals, which amounted to 500. Of the 5000 men whom Gordon led to the attack, about 3000 were killed, wounded, or captured.

The Confederate disasters of the day were not yet over. The conflict at Fort Steadman was finished before nine o'clock, only a part of the Ninth Corps having taken part in it. Wright and Humphreys, whose corps were now well in hand, were anxious to follow up the advantage by an assault in their fronts; but Parke considered that his accidental and temporary command of the entire army would not warrant him in forcing a general engagement. Meade, who soon after came upon the field, forbade a general attack, but later in the day pushed forward the Second and Sixth Corps to feel the enemy in their respective fronts. After a fierce struggle the strong Confederate picket-lines were carried, and held in spite of desperate attempts to retake them. This cost the Federals 1100 men, of whom 200 were missing. The Confederates lost 800 prisoners, and probably as many in killed and wounded. The entire Confederate loss on this day was not far from 4500, that of the Federals 2000.[1]

There was nothing in the result of the affair on the 25th of March to induce Grant to change his order issued the day before, to be carried into effect four days later. The essential thing contemplated in this plan was that Sheridan, with all the cavalry of all the armies upon and near the James and the Appomattox, should, by a wide detour, pass clear beyond the utmost westward extension of Lee's lines, and cut the railroads by which the Confederate army was fed, nearly half way to the point where Johnston was presumably awaiting the approach of the Army of Northern Virginia. This movement was rendered feasible only by what we have already styled the "accident" whereby Sheridan was in Virginia, instead of far away in North Carolina, ready to operate with Grant instead of with Sherman. Subsidiary to this cavalry movement, the infantry was to make a determined effort to turn the enemy out of his position around Petersburg. To effect this, every available man of the two armies of the Potomac and the James was to be brought against the Confederate right before Petersburg, and to its south and southwest.

Ord, leaving Weitzel in command north of the Potomac, was to bring half of his two corps over, and, sweeping around in the rear of the lines before Petersburg, pass toward the left of the position. Parke was to hold the position which his corps had so long maintained; Wright, next to him, was to be ready to hold his lines or to move; Humphreys, and the movable part of Ord's corps, and that of Warren, were to form the great turning column whose movements, it was hoped, would force the abandonment of Petersburg; the general purpose of all being "not to attack the enemy in his intrenched position, but to turn him out of it if possible." But, at the same time, all corps and division commanders were to hold themselves ready for offense should the enemy weaken himself in their front. Above all things, no commander of a corps or division, in case of attack, was to wait for special orders from headquarters. The strength of the enemy was pretty well ascertained. Should he appear in great force at any one point, it could only be by weakening himself elsewhere. Advantage should be promptly taken of every weakening, and every advantage any where gained should be promptly followed up. For the rest, the men of the moving column were to take four days' rations in their haversacks, twice as much following in wagons. The artillery was to be kept within the smallest compass, six or eight guns to a division being the utmost to be taken; for in the woody and swampy region where operations were to be carried on, artillery would be an incumbrance rather than aid. Such was the substance of the general order of the 24th.

The order to Sheridan, given on the 28th, just as he was setting out, was to the same purport, but with some special additions: First and foremost, he was to aim at the railroads; "but if the enemy should come out of his own lines and attack, or put himself in a position where he can be attacked, move in your own way; the army will engage or follow, as circumstances will dictate. Having accomplished the destruction of the two railroads," so concluded the order, "which are now the only avenues of supply to Lee's army, you may return to this army, selecting your road farther south, or may go on into North Carolina, and join General Sherman." No wider discretion was ever given to a general than this of Grant to Sheridan. Next day, indeed, March 29, when matters had apparently taken shape, this order was modified: "I feel like ending this matter, if it is possible to do so, before going back," wrote Grant. "I do not want you, therefore, to cut loose and go after the enemy's roads at present. In the morning, push around the enemy's rear, if you can, and get on to his right rear. We will act all together as one army here until it is seen what can be done with the enemy." How nearly this last plan failed of the success which it finally attained is now to be shown.

[1] Pollard (*Lost Cause*, 686) says: "Had this opportunity" (that is, the capture of the fort and batteries) "been taken advantage of, there is no telling the result; but the troops could not be induced to leave the breastworks they had taken from the enemy, and to advance beyond them and seize the crest in rear of the line they had occupied." But nothing can be clearer than that the force which had effected the capture was inadequate for any thing more. Swinton (*Army of the Potomac*, 597) says: "It is well known that there was great dereliction on the part of the supporting columns, for Gordon's attack was left almost wholly unsupported, notwithstanding that Lee had massed in the vicinity all his available force." He, however, fails to give his authority for this representation, and does not state upon whom rests the blame of this dereliction. The one thing certain is, that this supporting force was not pushed forward. We can hardly suppose that a movement upon which so much was staked should have been made except under the direct supervision of Lee. In the light of the account given in the text, which shows how rapidly the Union troops recovered from their momentary surprise, we think that the failure to follow up the attack was wise. Twenty thousand men could not then have carried the lines. It was better to submit to the inevitable loss of a fifth than to risk the almost certain destruction of the whole of the force assigned to the adventure.

[2] "At half past seven o'clock the position of affairs was thus: Batteries 11 and 12 had been recaptured; a cordon of troops, consisting of Hartranft's division, with regiments belonging to McLaughlin's and Ely's brigades, was formed around Fort Steadman and battery 10, into which the enemy was forced. There he was exposed to a concentrated fire from all the artillery in position bearing on these points, and the reserve batteries in the rear."—*Parke's Report.*

[1] The entire Federal loss is officially given. It was, at Fort Steadman, 68 killed, 337 wounded, 506 missing—in all, 911; at the picket-lines, 52 killed, 864 wounded, 207 missing—in all, 1123: a total of 2034. The number of Confederate prisoners taken is also given: these were, at Fort Steadman, 1900; at the picket-lines, 834—in all, 2734. Their loss in killed and wounded is purely conjectural. From the facts that at Fort Steadman they were for two or three hours under heavy fire, and that at the picket-lines they were repulsed after desperate charges, it is safe to assume that it was in both cases considerably greater than that of their opponents. Grant, in his final Report, says: "Their loss in killed and wounded was far greater than ours." In his first dispatch, he says: "Humphreys estimates the loss of the enemy in his front at three times his own, and Wright, in his front, as double that of ours." This would indicate the entire Confederate loss to have been greater than we have estimated it. But those who have had occasion to compare these guesses, on either side, with actual facts as subsequently verified, will place little reliance upon them. In the absence of authenticated reports, they will rather rely upon estimates based upon the nature of the operations. Thus, in the case under consideration, the Union loss in killed and wounded having been shown to have been 1300, and that of the Confederates considerably greater, though far from two or three times as large, by placing it at about 1700 we reach approximately at the result given in the text.

EWELL'S HEADQUARTERS, NEAR RICHMOND.

Sheridan had a month before set out from Winchester with 10,000 horsemen. Of these, 1500 had been sent back to guard the prisoners taken from Early at Waynesborough. In his great ride up the Valley, and thence through thirteen counties, he had lost by casualty hardly a hundred men. But his animals had suffered severely, and when he joined Grant, his two divisions, under Devin and Custer, numbered 5700 men in saddle;[1] but Crook, with 3300, was ready to join him, and he thus set out with 9000. In a day or two, McKenzie, with 1000 horsemen from the Army of the James, was added to his mounted command, making 10,000 in all. The Confederate cavalry under Fitzhugh Lee could hardly have reached a third of this number. With this magnificent force Sheridan swept southward and then westward, until, after encountering a few mounted pickets, who were easily brushed away, he reached Dinwiddie Court-house. Here several roads centred, along some of which his proposed raid would be conducted. Here, on the evening of the 29th, he received the order from Grant countermanding the plan of a raid, and directing him to co-operate with the infantry in the effort to turn the right flank of Lee's army.

Warren's corps—the Fifth—consisting of the three divisions of Crawford, Griffin, and Ayres, 15,300 strong in all, with twenty guns, marched out at three o'clock on the morning of the 29th.[2] They moved southwestward until they struck the Quaker Road running straight north to the Confederate lines. Turning up this, Griffin, whose division was in the advance, encountered a force of the enemy pushed in front of their lines, and after a sharp conflict, in which some four hundred were killed and wounded on each side, forced them back within the shelter of their intrenchments. Humphreys, also moving to the right of Warren, got close up to the Confederate fortified line without meeting opposition. It seemed now that the enemy was shut up in his lines to their utmost westward reach; and now, if this could be turned by Sheridan, it was as sure as any thing can be in warfare that the matter might be ended. To secure this, Grant was prepared, if need were, to give up every thing south of the position still held by Parke, flinging upon Lee's right his cavalry, with the entire corps of Warren, Humphreys, and Wright, with the three divisions detached from Ord. It was then that the order was sent to Sheridan to abstain from his projected raid upon the railroads.

Lee had in the mean time learned something of the mighty effort to be put forth against him. He still misconceived its ultimate purport. He thought it only a more determined repetition of the old efforts to reach the railroads, for the great sweep of Sheridan's cavalry was still unknown to him. Yet this must be thwarted at all hazards, and those roads protected for a few days, or all was lost; for, these roads seized, he had no means of feeding his army for a week, and no means of escaping from his position. So, stripping his intrenchments in front of Petersburg until to guard ten miles of works there were hardly as many thousand men, he gathered a mobile force, which, added to the cavalry on his right, numbered in all some

15,000 or 20,000, to meet the endeavor of Grant.[1] This column was only sent out after nightfall, and there was a fearful probability that it would not reach the scene of operations, fifteen miles away, until it was too late. But a fortune which neither general could anticipate intervened in favor of Lee. During the night a furious rain set in, which lasted all through the next day, the 30th. The region through which Warren was working his way was a low land covered mainly with tangled woods, threaded every where with swampy brooks, which a sharp shower would render difficult of passage. The soil of mingled sand and clay, upheaved by the winter frosts, was still soft, and the rain quickly converted the ill-made roads into mortar-beds. Any thing on wheels could hardly move a rod unless the road was laboriously corduroyed. Footmen and cavalry could indeed advance slowly; so, during the 30th, Warren and Sheridan worked their way a little onward, the former toward the White-oak Road, the latter toward the Five Forks. Lee's column had much farther to go, but they had the advantage of a less intolerable road, and thus, on the morning of the 31st, had passed beyond the extremity of the intrenched line, and occupied the White-oak Road toward the Five Forks.

On the morning of Friday, March 31, Warren's corps had worked itself up in sight of the White-oak Road, clear beyond the line of the enemy's intrenchments. On account of the woods and swamps, they could not form a regular line of battle, but each division was so massed that it could fight in any direction. Humphreys's corps had connected with Warren on the right. Just before nine o'clock Warren received an order from Meade, informing him that there was firing along Humphreys's front, and directing him to be ready to support Humphreys, if necessary, adding that there would be no movement of troops that day. Warren replied that he thought it best, if possible, to drive the enemy from the road, and in two hours received permission to make the attempt. Winthrop's brigade of Ayres's division was sent to make the attempt. The Confederates, at the same time, had planned a counter-move to drive Warren off. They rushed forward from both north and west. Ayres's division was forced back in confusion upon Crawford's, which lay next behind. This also gave way, and both fell back upon Griffin, who was posted in an opening in the woods large enough to give room for all. The two divisions which had fallen back, bewildered by the fierce assault in front and flank, amidst the unknown forests and swamps, rallied with that of Griffin, and held their ground. Humphreys, in the mean while, had sent Miles's division against the enemy's left flank. Warren, at two o'clock, finding that the enemy had ceased from his onset, advanced upon him with all his force. To his surprise, he met with little resistance; only one of his brigades was seriously engaged, and this swept up nearly a whole Confederate regiment, with its flags. At half

---

[1] These two divisions formed Merritt's command; Sheridan directing all the cavalry, together with such infantry as were at times added to it for special operations.

[2] For the movements of March 29, 30, 31, and April 1, culminating in the battle of the Five Forks, one needs to compare Sheridan's Report with Warren's Account of Operations. For the operations of the Fifth Corps we rely upon Warren; for those of the cavalry, upon Sheridan. Grant's report of this critical period is very meagre. Confederate reports are wholly wanting.

[1] The numbers of this body are given conjecturally from the indicia afforded by its known losses. Swinton (Army of the Potomac, 585; Decisive Battles, 485) gives the number at 15,000, apparently exclusive of the cavalry, which could not then have been more than 3000. In this statement he apparently follows Pollard (Lost Cause, 689), whose words are: "In the night of the 29th, General Lee, having perceived Grant's manœuvre, dispatched Pickett's and Bushrod Johnson's divisions, Wise's and Ransom's brigades, Huger's battalion of infantry, and Fitzhugh Lee's division—in all about 17,000 men—to encounter the turning column of the enemy." But Fitzhugh Lee's cavalry division were already upon the right, falling back before Sheridan. Taking into account the ascertained losses in this force, we think that Pollard's statement is a very close approximation to the actual number.

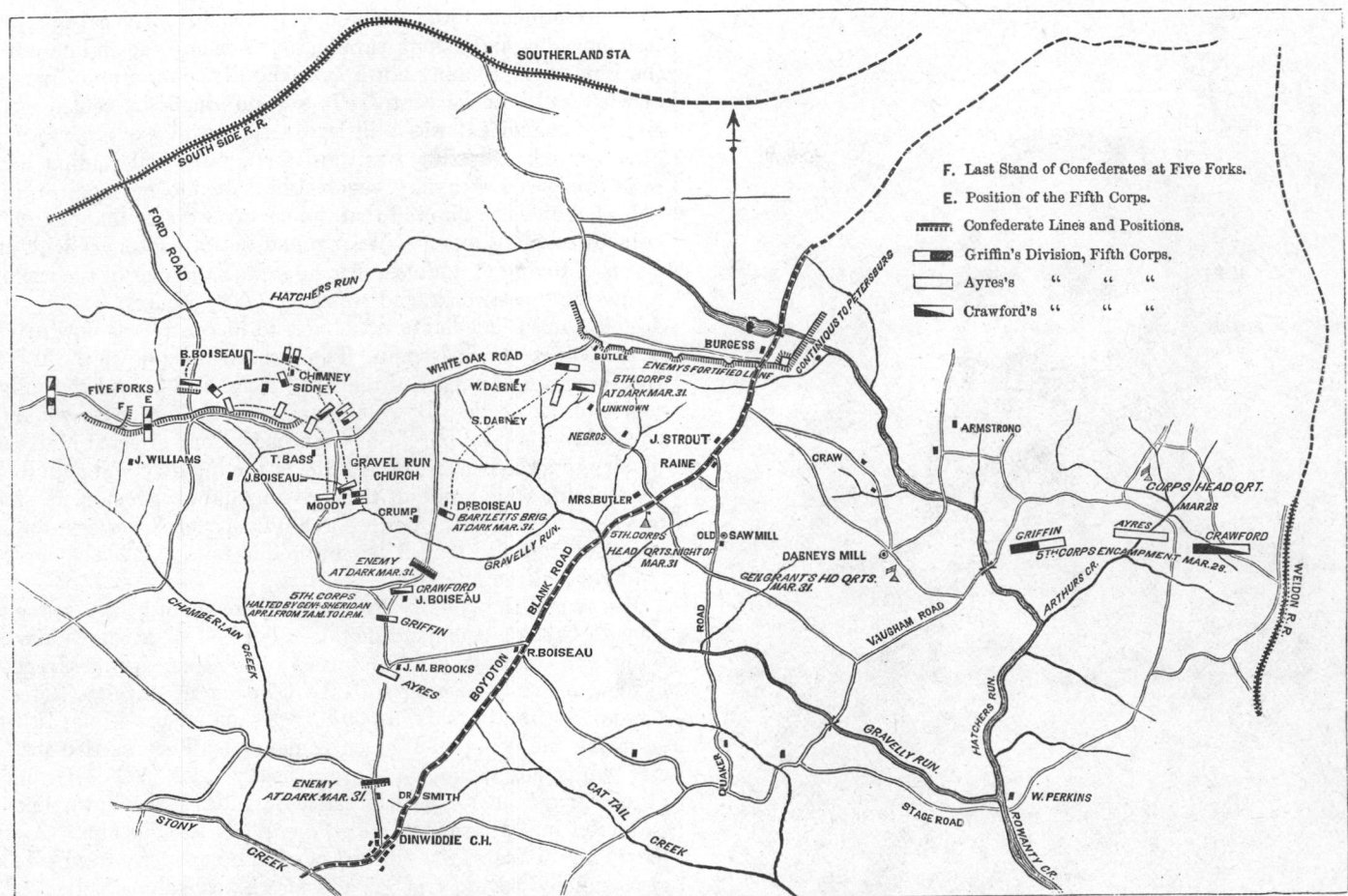

FIVE FORKS—MOVEMENTS OF THE FIFTH CORPS, MARCH 28–APRIL 1.

past three he wrote from the White-oak Road to Meade's chief of staff: "We have driven the enemy, I think, into his breastworks. The prisoners report General Lee here to-day, and also that their breastworks are filled with troops. We have prisoners from a portion of Pickett's and Johnson's divisions." He had, to appearance, won a decided victory on the White-oak Ridge, though at heavy cost, for his losses in killed and wounded numbered 1400.

Lee had, indeed, recoiled from the attack. Possibly he would in any case have given it up after having forced Warren back a space from his threatening position, for he was in no condition to run great risks, unless urged by imperative necessity. But the immediate occasion was that he was called upon to meet a still more imminent peril. To understand this, we must look to Sheridan's movements.

On the 30th, Sheridan, in spite of the rain, had pushed a part of his command toward the Five Forks, forcing the Confederate cavalry westward, and right away from the army of Lee. In the forenoon of the 31st a division of the cavalry reached the Forks. This point must be regained by Lee at all hazards, so the force which had been engaged with Warren was withdrawn and sent down the White-oak Road, and, falling upon the Union cavalry, drove them from the Forks. Then, uniting with the cavalry of Fitzhugh Lee, the whole force pressed upon Sheridan's cavalry, who were much scattered, and, in spite of strong resistance, forced them back upon Dinwiddie Court-house. The two divisions of Devin and Davies were cut off from a direct retreat, and compelled to make a wide detour to gain the main body at Dinwiddie, reaching it only after the fight which there ensued was over. But Sheridan's horsemen, dismounting, took post behind a slight breastwork of rails, where they recovered and repulsed the assault of the enemy, who at dark withdrew a little, and lay upon their arms within a hundred yards. During the evening, Sheridan was informed by a dispatch from Grant that Warren's corps were ordered to report to him, and would reach him by midnight. This dispatch was written hours before—Grant's headquarters being ten miles away—and in ignorance of what had transpired. Warren also, some time before, had begun to receive orders from Meade. At five o'clock he was told that Sheridan was pushing up the White-oak Road, and he might send down a small force to communicate with him, but must be careful not to fire into his advance. An hour and a half later, the tidings to Warren were that a portion of Pickett's force had penetrated between him and Sheridan. Warren had learned this before. An hour and a half more, and tidings came that Sheridan had been forced back to Dinwiddie by a strong force of cavalry, supported by infantry. Close upon the heels of this came an intimation from Meade that "the probability is that we shall have to contract our lines to-night." To contract the lines was equivalent to a retreat. All the indications at the moment were that this movement would be a repetition of those which had gone before. Warren urged that, instead of retreating, he might be allowed to move down to Dinwiddie, and attack the enemy on one side, while Sheridan assailed him on the other. Orders for movements were given, few of which, owing to the darkness, were capable of exact literal execution, but the general purport of all was that Warren should advance to the aid of Sheridan.[1] He obeyed the intent of his orders, and moved as rapidly as possible.

But, in the mean time, the Confederates had their own difficulties to encounter. They had found it impossible to shake Sheridan away from Dinwiddie; and, knowing that re-enforcements were coming to him, they began a little after midnight to retire cautiously toward the Five Forks. Sheridan suspected that this movement was going on, and so notified Meade by verbal message; but he could not be sure, for at three o'clock he sent an order to Warren stating that he was holding on at Dinwiddie with Custer's division, where he might be attacked at daybreak. In that case, Warren, who was thought to be nearer than he was, should also attack in flank and rear. "Do not fear," added Sheridan, "my leaving here. If the enemy remain I shall fight at daylight." But just after daylight, when Ayres's division, the advance of Warren's corps, came in sight, the enemy "hastily decamped,"[1] and hurried back toward their intrenchments at the Five Forks. Merritt followed hard after with the cavalry, until he saw the enemy fairly within their works, and had even driven them from two lines of temporary works.

The whole of Warren's corps were united at seven o'clock on the morning of April 1 at a point three miles from the Forks, and somewhat to the right of the extremity of the Confederate works, which had in the mean while been much strengthened. Here they were halted for four hours by Sheridan until he could complete his arrangements for attack, for he proposed nothing less than to dispose absolutely of this body, crushing it if possible, and driving westward any who might escape, isolating them from the main army at Petersburg. There was a likelihood that Lee, comprehending the peril, might venture to send re-enforcements down the White-oak Road to the Forks. Fortunately, Sheridan had just been joined by McKenzie's fresh cavalry, a thousand strong. These were sent straight to the White-oak Road, with orders to attack any force of the enemy which they might find. The prevision was justified. McKenzie met a force coming down, and drove it back.

The day was wearing away when Sheridan had completed his preliminary dispositions. His plan was beautiful in its simplicity. Merritt was to hold the enemy in front with a part of the cavalry, while with the remainder he should demonstrate as if proposing to turn their right flank. Warren was to move the infantry up to the White-oak Road, and then, by a sharp wheel to the right, strike the enemy's left, and, doubling it up, gain their rear. This plan presupposed a great superiority of force, but that was at hand. Sheridan had of cavalry and infantry quite 20,000; the Confederates could hardly number more than 10,000 infantry, with only a few guns; and they do not appear to have brought their cavalry behind their intrenchments, where they could be of little service.

Having, as was his wont, made his plans with careful deliberation, Sheridan was eager for their prompt execution. He chafed at every thing which looked like delay. Warren, quite as earnest, strove to repress all outward manifestations of impatience, which he thought would tend to impair the confidence of his troops. "When every thing possible is being done," he argued, "it is important to have the men think it is all that success demands." So Sheridan rode off firmly impressed with the idea that Warren was not exerting himself to get his corps up as rapidly as he should have done, and that "he wished the sun to go down before the dispositions for the attack could be completed."[2]

---

[1] The last order from Meade to Warren, written a quarter of an hour before midnight, and received an hour after, contained these sentences: "Sheridan can not maintain himself at Dinwiddie without re-enforcements, and yours are the only ones that can be sent. Time is of the utmost importance. Use every exertion to get troops to him as soon as possible. If Sheridan is not re-enforced, and is compelled to fall back, he will retire by the Vaughan Road."

[1] Ayres's Report.

[2] *Sheridan's Report.*—Sheridan had also been previously dissatisfied with Warren. He had, very naturally, asked that Wright's corps, which had been with him in the Valley of the Shenandoah, should be sent to him instead of that of Warren. This, owing to its position, could not be

ROMEYN B. AYRES.

But the sun was still more than two hours high when Warren advanced from the point where his corps had been formed, a thousand yards from the White-oak Road. In the operations of the three days about 2000 of his corps had been disabled, and 1000 more had fallen out from weariness, or been sent on detached duty, so that the corps went into action 12,000 strong. Ayres's division, the weakest, was on the left; next came Crawford's, with Griffin's as a support, in its rear, and a little to the right. It was supposed that upon reaching the road they would strike just upon the enemy's left; then, pivoting upon Ayres's division, the others were to wheel round, so that Crawford's would just fall upon the flank. But, on reaching the road, it was found that they were some distance from the hostile line, which was also hidden in a thick wood beyond an open space. This mistake, slight in itself, changed the whole order of the battle. The division of Ayres, forming that part of the radius nearest to the centre of the semi-circle to be described in the turning movement, and thus having the shortest distance to be traversed, effected its change of front earliest, and moved across the open space toward the enemy's position. The order given to each division was to keep closed upon that to its left; and as the region where they were to move was wholly unknown, the direction to march was to be maintained by keeping the sun over their left shoulders. But now, Crawford having the larger distance to sweep, his left became disjoined from Ayres's right, which was thus thrown out into the air, in the open space over which both were advancing. At this moment, also, a sharp fire was poured from the woods upon these exposed flanks—Ayres's right and Crawford's left. The effect was that the right of Ayres became disordered, many of the men rushing back to the rear, while Crawford's left obliqued to the right, where the woods and a slight ridge gave shelter. Thus the interval between the two became still wider. The firing, however, was more noisy than destructive, owing to the dense wood through which the shot had to pass. Ayres soon rectified his line; the portions which had become unsteady "moved up and bore their part of the action in a handsome manner."[1] Pressing forward, he soon came upon the enemy's position. The Confederate line ran from west to east, but its extremity was turned at a right angle northward for a hundred yards. This crochet, fronting to the east, was that part of the line facing Ayres. It was a strong breastwork secured behind a dense undergrowth of pines. Through this undergrowth and over the breastwork Ayres's corps charged with the bayonet, and captured a thousand prisoners—more than a third of its own number.[2] Here it was halted by Sheridan, who was now on this part of the field, awaiting the result of what was transpiring elsewhere. It was soon "apparent that the enemy were giving way generally," and Ayres pushed forward rapidly, holding his men in hand, and marching steadily in line of battle.[3]

Crawford, having completed his wider circuit, moved steadily westward, urged on by both Sheridan and Warren. His way lay through bogs, tangled woods, and thickets of pines, interspersed here and there with open spaces. The Confederate skirmishers spread northward from the extremity

of their intrenched line. These were steadily driven back; and so Crawford moved straight along parallel to the enemy's main line until he reached the Ford Road, running north from the Five Forks, and directly in the rear of what had been its centre. It was no longer its centre. Griffin, whose circle of movement was a little exterior to that of Crawford, moved on a little behind. Pressing westward for a mile, and finding nothing on his front except a few cavalry vedettes, he halted to reconnoitre. Heavy firing to his left and rear showed that the enemy were in that direction, and thither he directed his march. Warren had sent a messenger with orders to that effect. Moving at double-quick, he struck the rear of the enemy's left, capturing the breastworks, and securing 1500 prisoners.

The whole Confederate left almost to its centre was now driven in. Half or more of it were prisoners. The rest streamed down the White-oak Road. But Crawford had reached the Ford Road, and barred the only avenue of escape to the north. Down this pressed Crawford, with whom Warren had now taken his position. Sheridan had before directed McKenzie with his cavalry to sweep clear to the right of the infantry and gain the Ford Road. He took too wide a circuit through an unknown region, and found himself moving away from the battle; and, turning back, reached the road, not till after Crawford had won it, but in time to take part in the closing scenes of the fight and the pursuit.

Meanwhile the cavalry had borne their share in the action. Two divisions of Crook's command had been left behind at Dinwiddie to guard the trains and crossings of the streams; the other, that of Gregg, was on the left and rear, skirmishing with the Confederate cavalry. Merritt, with the divisions of Devin and Custer, charged the enemy's lines in front, the signal being the firing of Warren's infantry. They carried the lines at several points, not without enduring heavy loss. While Griffin and Ayres pressed upon the routed left flank, Crawford came down upon their rear. One brief but determined effort was made to stop him. A stiff line, supported by artillery, was formed across the road, from which Coulter's brigade suffered severely. But the effort was vain. Entrapped, assailed in front, flank, and rear, almost the whole of the force surrendered to Crawford.

Warren now rode on to the coveted Five Forks, thence westward along the White-oak Road. A mile beyond the Forks the remnant of the Confederates made one more attempt to stand. Their line was formed at a right angle, one branch facing southward toward Merritt's cavalry, the other eastward to confront Warren, whose three divisions had come up in pursuit. These were somewhat disordered by their long march and fighting through the woods. They halted, but kept up a rapid fire. Warren, with a few of his staff, dashed to the front, shouting to those at hand to follow. He was met with a single sharp fusilade; his horse was shot under him, an aid at his side was killed, and Colonel Richardson, who had sprung right between him and the enemy, fell sorely wounded. But Warren's appeal had not been in vain. All along the line officers and color-bearers sprang to the front; and the troops, advancing at a run, and without firing, captured every man in their front. Those who had been trying to make a stand against Merritt broke and fled in wild confusion by the only way open to them—that leading westward. Merritt and McKenzie dashed forward in pursuit, which was kept up for six miles, and until long after darkness had set in. The two divisions upon which Lee had counted for the salvation of his army were gone. Johnson's was utterly annihilated; of Pickett's we find, five days later, note of a remnant of a few hundred men. Whether they had been in the fight and escaped, or whether they had been kept back, is not recorded. The Union loss in the battle of the Five Forks was about 1000, of which 634 were of Warren's corps. Of the Confederate killed and wounded there is no statement. They lost in prisoners between 5000 and 6000, of whom 3244 were captured by Warren.

The blow to Lee was a crushing one. It is said that upon the receipt of the tidings of his loss, he for the only time gave utterance to any reproach in the field. The next time his troops were taken into the field he would put himself at their head; and, turning to one of his generals, he ordered him sharply to gather up and put under guard all the stragglers in the field —officers as well as men. It may be granted that the Confederates fought at Five Forks with less than their wonted vigor; but they must have felt that, after Sheridan had fairly shut them up within their lines, victory was impossible; and, moreover, could they have made their escape, now that their lines were fairly turned, it would be but to prolong for a few days a hopeless struggle.

When Warren had captured the last of the enemy opposed to him, he sent to Sheridan a report of the result, and asked for farther instructions. The reply was that his instructions had been sent. They reached him at seven o'clock. Surely no general who had just gained a victory so brilliant and decisive ever before received upon the field which he had won such a message. The order ran thus: "Major General Warren, commanding Fifth Corps, is relieved from duty, and will report at once for orders to Lieutenant General Grant, commanding armies U.S." The command of the corps was conferred upon Griffin.[1]

---

[1] That the general credit of the victory of the Five Forks must be given to Sheridan is undoubted. The plans were his, and they were, as he affirms, "successfully executed." But the essential feature of these plans, without which all else would have been comparatively fruitless, was the operations of the Fifth Corps. These operations were conducted by Warren. After the movement was begun, there is record of but a single order given by Sheridan to any portion of this corps. The main allegation brought by Sheridan against Warren is that "General Warren did not exert himself to get up his corps as rapidly as he might have done, and his manner gave me the impression that he wished the sun to go down before dispositions for the attack could be completed." But the dispositions were made and the attack commenced while the sun was yet more than two hours high, and in time to win the victory before it had set. Moreover, each of Warren's division commanders—and no one more explicitly than Griffin, who succeeded him—aver that their divisions were formed without any unnecessary delay. Sheridan, indeed, makes two other specifications against Warren: (1.) "Had General Warren moved according to the expectations of the Lieutenant General, there would appear to have been but little chance for the escape of the enemy's

---

[2] Ayres's division marched out on the 29th not quite 4000 strong. In the interval it had lost about 1000.—Warren's Narrative.   [3] Ayres's Report.

CHARLES GRIFFIN.

While the result of the movements of Sheridan and Warren were uncertain, active operations directly before Petersburg were suspended to await the issue upon the extreme Union left. When, at nightfall, Sheridan had utterly routed the force directly opposed to him, his position was not free from peril. His command, now numbering about 18,000 cavalry and infantry, was widely separated from the main army, and there was reason to apprehend that Lee would, during the night, abandon his lines, and, falling upon Sheridan, drive him off, and thus open the way for retreat. To guard against this, Miles's division of Humphreys's corps was sent to the support of Sheridan, while a furious bombardment was opened along the whole line, sweeping from the north of Petersburg clear around to Hatcher's Run. The Union batteries had gradually crept closer to the city, and for the first time during the siege the balls fairly crashed through the streets of Petersburg. This fierce fire was kept up until almost daybreak, when the general assault was ordered. Parke and Wright had before expressed their belief that they could carry the lines in their front.

The assault commenced just before daybreak on the morning of Sunday, April 2. Parke's Ninth Corps was in front of the strongest portion of the Confederate defenses. The general plan for this corps was that Wilcox's division should make a feint in front of Fort Steadman, while the divisions of Potter and Hartranft were to make the assault to the left, at the very points which it had been hoped would have been opened by the explosion of the mine eight months before. Each column was accompanied by pioneers with axes, and details of artillerists to work any guns that might be captured. Wilcox's feint was successful. His division carried the whole outer line in its front, causing the Confederates to concentrate a heavy force to stay their farther advance. Then, at half past four, the signal was given for the opening of the main assault. The troops, eager to avenge their former repulse, sprang forward with a rush, and in the teeth of a deadly storm of grape, canister, and musketry, plunged through the ditch, tore away the

abatis, mounted the parapet, and carried the line of works. Here Hartranft's division captured 12 guns and 800 prisoners. Potter's division, next on the left, attacked with equal vigor, and, in spite of the most gallant opposition, pressed the enemy clear back to his interior cordon of works. This inner line had within the last few months been most elaborately fortified. From it the position gained by Parke was swept on the right and the left by an enfilading fire of artillery. Potter made a determined but unsuccessful effort to force this inner cordon. He fell severely wounded, and the command of his division fell upon Griffin.[1] But the assault in other quarters had met with such success that there was no need for the Ninth Corps to essay to carry the lines opposed to them. Parke was directed not to advance unless he saw the way clear to success, but to strengthen his position so as to hold it against any assailing force.

The Sixth Corps, under Wright, was next on the left to that of the Ninth. As it lay, it occupied a salient where the Union lines, after trending away from the Confederate works, again closely approached them. Here, during the darkness, this corps had been formed into a mighty wedge, which was, in the result, to be driven straight through the Confederate lines which had for so long bidden defiance to all assault. At half past four a single gun gave signal for the advance of the Sixth. It happened that the very point where the edge of the wedge was to strike had been left weakly held by the withdrawal of the force which had held it to defend a point which seemed of more pressing importance. The Confederate pickets and skirmishers were swept away in a moment, the three lines of abatis overpassed, the works crowned, the long lines which had guarded Petersburg and its railway communications pierced. The Confederate army, a quarter of which had twelve hours before been annihilated by Sheridan and Warren, was again cut in two, a quarter of what remained being to all appearance wholly severed from the main body. Wright swept leftward for a space down the line of the Confederate intrenchments, repeating Warren's movement at Five Forks, and capturing some thousands of prisoners; and then, being joined by portions of Ord's command and Humphreys's corps, who had carried every thing in their own fronts, turned to the right, and moved straight toward Petersburg, leaving that portion of the Confederate force which had been severed from the main army to be disposed of by Sheridan, whose command had in the mean while been augmented by Miles's division of Humphreys's corps.

Miles was ordered by Sheridan to move up the White-oak Road and attack the extreme right of the enemy. This, in the mean time, had been cut off from Petersburg by Wright and by Humphreys, who, with the divisions of Hays and Mott, carried a redoubt in their front, and then swept round and took up their position upon the left of Wright. The Confederates here made no opposition, and their isolated right fled northward, crossing Hatcher's Run, and took up a position at Southerland's Station, on the Southside Railroad. Miles was anxious to attack, and Sheridan gave him permission to do so; but at this moment Meade directed that Miles should be returned to the command of Humphreys, and the attack, to Sheridan's regret, was not made. Sheridan, who had been moving in the same direction with the Fifth Corps, now retraced his steps, and moved back to the Five Forks. Thence they struck the railroad, and, after destroying it for

[1] General S. G. Griffin, who commanded the division during the few remaining days of the campaign with such ability that he received therefor the brevet rank of major general. He is to be distinguished from General Charles Griffin, who was now in command of the Fifth Corps.

NATHANIEL A. MILES.

infantry in front of Dinwiddie Court-house" on the morning of the 1st of April. Whether or not Warren could, either with or without the expectation of Grant, have made movements which would have had this result, it is certain that Sheridan, on the evening of that day, could have had no adequate means of knowing. (2.) "During this attack I again became dissatisfied with General Warren. In this engagement, portions of his line gave way when not exposed to a heavy fire, and simply from want of confidence on the part of the troops, which General Warren did not exert himself to inspire. I therefore relieved him from the command of the Fifth Corps, authority for this action having been sent to me before the battle unsolicited."—Leaving out of view Sheridan's emphatic testimony to the gallantry of the troops in this engagement, there is no mention of any part of Warren's line giving way under any fire, light or heavy, saving the very brief one of a part of Ayres's division, and this was soon rectified; and these very men, in a few minutes, "bore a part in a handsome manner in the first brilliant charge which took place." In any case, Warren could not personally inspire them with confidence, for he was in a different part of the field; and he, as commander of the corps, had a right to judge on what portion of the field his presence was most required, subject, of course, to the ultimate decision of his superiors, upon due consideration, as to the military soundness of his judgment. In any case, Sheridan, being on a still different part of the field, could have had no personal knowledge on this point; and, in the interval of less than two hours between any possible giving way and the order of supersedure, could not have had opportunity to ascertain the facts in the case with sufficient certainty to warrant such a summary procedure. The misconduct, if any had existed, could no longer produce any evil effect, for the victory had been fully won when the supersedure took place. The order was certainly overhasty, and we think no one who examines the question will hesitate to say unjust. There is, indeed, no reason to suppose that Sheridan was moved by any unworthy personal feeling, for the two generals had never happened to serve together. Sheridan was likely somewhat annoyed that Warren's corps, instead of Wright's, was sent to him; for on the day before, in writing his plans to Grant, he said: "I believe I could, with the Sixth Corps, turn the enemy's left or break through his lines, but I would not like the Fifth Corps to make such an attempt." But the Fifth Corps, under his own dispositions, did make the attempt, and with a success which did not fall short of his most sanguine anticipations of what the Sixth would have accomplished. Warren, on reporting to Grant, was at once assigned to the command of the defenses at City Point and Bermuda Hundred. Just a month after his supersedure from the command of the Fifth Corps he was assigned to the command of the Department of the Mississippi, the only one in which there was then any prospect of farther hostilities.

a space, moved up it toward Southerland's Station, upon the flank of the Confederates who still held position there. His cavalry meanwhile had been sent westward to break up the Confederate cavalry, who had gathered in some force, but not sufficient to offer any resistance. These operations consumed the whole day. Toward evening Miles attacked the enemy at Southerland's, and, after a brief conflict, routed them, capturing 600 prisoners, and driving them in confusion to the Appomattox. It was supposed that the river was impassable, and that this body, shut in by Sheridan on the one side and Humphreys on the left, must surrender. But there happened to be a ford, over which they escaped, leaving their guns behind, and next day joined Lee in his retreat.

Two or three hundred yards behind the lines which Wright had carried a series of strong forts had been erected to guard against just such results as had ensued. In the movement which had followed, Gibbon's division of Ord's command came right upon the two strongest of these, Forts Alexander and Gregg, which were all that stood in the way of the Federal forces marching straight upon Petersburg by the rear. Gibbon dashed upon these. Fort Alexander was carried with a rush. Within Fort Gregg had been gathered a mixed garrison from the very extremities of the Confederacy. There were Virginians and Louisianians, North Carolinians and Mississippians. Its commander was Captain Chew, of Maryland. Gibbon marched straight for this fort, but was met by a fire so fierce and deadly that the troops recoiled for a moment. Then the charge was renewed; the assailants, unchecked by the fusilade which met them, swarmed up the parapet. Once, twice, and thrice they were pressed back; but at length the crest was gained, and a brief hand-to-hand conflict ensued. The fort was carried. Of its two hundred and fifty defenders, only thirty survived; of the assailants, five hundred lay dead or wounded.

It was now barely seven o'clock, hardly three hours from the time when the grand assault had been commenced; but within that time the whole outer line of defenses had been carried, and what remained of the Confederate army was shut up within the interior lines. Lee, with Hill and Mahone, was within the city, listening to the noise of battle which sounded from every side, and endeavoring from it to judge how the fight was going, and to decide upon what remained to be done. The reports grew momently nearer and nearer. "How is this, general?" exclaimed Lee to Hill; "your men are giving way!" Hill, buttoning around him a rough citizen's coat, upon the shoulders of which were only the stars of a colonel, and accompanied by a single orderly, rode out to reconnoitre. In a wooded ravine he came upon half a dozen soldiers in the blue Federal uniform. They had penetrated in advance of their comrades. He ordered them to surrender. For an instant they were confounded by the very audacity of the demand. The next instant their answer was given from their rifles, and Hill fell dead from his horse. Of all the great generals in the Confederate army, no other one had borne part in so many of the great battles in Virginia, Maryland, and Pennsylvania, from Bull Run onward. No one division of the Army of Northern Virginia had been engaged in so many fights as his. After the seven days on the Peninsula, it had formed part of Jackson's command while that daring general lived. It bore the brunt of the fight at Groveton, saved the lost day at Antietam, won the action at Chancellorsville, was foremost in the Wilderness, and to it, during this last campaign, was confided the most important task, that of holding the Confederate lines on the right, the vital point in Lee's system of defense.

Sheridan's victory at the Five Forks and Wright's piercing of the Confederate lines had in a few hours solved the long-questioned problem of the siege of Petersburg. The place was no longer tenable, for its avenues of supply were lost beyond all hope of recovery. Lee resolved upon a speedy abandonment of the lines which he had held so long. The bells were ringing for church on that Sunday morning when a dispatch was sent to President Davis, at Richmond, giving notice of what had happened, and informing him that the two besieged cities would be abandoned by the army, and advising that the authorities should make preparations to leave the capital that night.

Lee, indeed, was shut up to the alternative to surrender or to make his escape, and try the almost desperate chance of a race for life or death with a victorious army of thrice his force close upon his rear and flank. He chose the latter course, and in the execution of it manifested energy and skill not exceeded in any other portion of his career. After all the losses of the two days, he had still an army of more than 40,000 men; but they were widely scattered. Some 5000, cut off from the rest, were at Southerland's, fifteen miles west of Petersburg; as many more were in Richmond, a score of miles to the north; Longstreet, with half the remainder, was on the James; leaving 15,000 at and around Petersburg, confronting the corps of Parke, Wright, and Humphreys, with half that of Ord—in all not less than 50,000 men ready for action; while upon the flank of his line of retreat was Sheridan with well-nigh 20,000 cavalry and infantry.[1] The obstinate defense of Fort Gregg gave Lee a breathing space, and enabled him to assume a strong defensive position which could be held for a brief space. It must be held for twelve hours at all hazards; for the retreat could not be begun until darkness had come on, veiling the movement from the eyes that were keenly watching every sign of the abandonment, which all saw was speedily inevitable.

---

[1] The data upon which I estimate the present force of Lee will be stated hereafter. In giving that of Grant, I only include the numbers actually available for immediate pursuit from before Petersburg. Besides these 70,000, there was a considerable force at City Point, and half of the Army of the James, left under Weitzel on the north side of the James. The actual number in each corps available for instant action in the field at the commencement of operations on the 29th was about 15,000, or 90,000 in all. To these are to be added 10,000 cavalry. The losses in the interval had been not far from 10,000 in killed, wounded, and prisoners.

WORKS CAPTURED BY THE SIXTH CORPS.

THE EVACUATION OF PETERSBURG.

Lee was still ignorant that the force north of the James had been reduced to three divisions. But immediately after the tidings of the disaster at Five Forks he had ordered Longstreet to send re-enforcements from the James to the Appomattox. That veteran commander, with a few brigades, arrived just in time to stay the Federal advance, and enable Lee to form his new line. This, in a narrow semicircle, girdled Petersburg, each flank resting upon the Appomattox. A show of offense was the best defensive, and at intervals, from ten o'clock until dark, blows were struck at various parts of the Federal line closely encircling his own. These attempts were mainly directed upon that part of the line held by the Ninth Corps. In one of these assaults Fort Mahone fell again into the hands of the Confederates.[1] So threatening were these assaults, that two brigades were ordered up from City Point and one from the Sixth Corps to re-enforce the Ninth. Fort Mahone was soon recaptured, and Parke wished to renew the assault which had been closed in the morning; but, finding that his men were greatly exhausted, he decided merely to make his position perfectly secure, and await the operations of the next day, but in the mean while to be in a position to take advantage of any movement which the enemy might make showing an intention of evacuating his position.

The night had almost passed before any such indications were perceived. At two o'clock in the morning the Confederate pickets were still out; but the evacuation had been commenced in the darkness hours before. By three o'clock the troops were all across the river, and the only bridge in flames, while the air was luminous with the glare of the burning warehouses. At this moment the heavily-charged magazine of the battery of siege-guns before Bermuda Hundred was blown up; then followed the explosion of that of Fort Clifton on the James. The explosion was taken up all along the line to Richmond, giving some tokens that the evacuation was accomplished, and the Confederate army in full retreat. The skirmishers of the Ninth were at once pushed forward, but found no trace of an enemy. The entire corps went forward, Ely's brigade leading. They were met by the mayor and a deputation from the Common Council, who announced that the city, having been evacuated, was formally surrendered, and asked for the protection of the persons and property of the inhabitants. At half past four the flag of the First Michigan Regiment was raised upon the Court-house of Petersburg.

The dispatch of Lee, announcing his purpose to evacuate the cities, was received by Davis while in church. Three years before, lacking a month, he had been baptized and confirmed on the same day, and had since been a devout worshiper. As nearly as such hurried moments can be noted, the message reached the church just when the Litany, with its solemn responses, "Good Lord, deliver us!" was being uttered. The Confederate President rose from his knees and left the house with his wonted stately step. But men remembered, or thought they remembered, that he seemed to have grown older by years since he had entered the sacred edifice an hour before. Evil tidings find speedy messengers. Though no announcement was made, within an hour every inhabitant knew that the Confederate capital was to be abandoned. In the leading Presbyterian Church, the minister, at the close of his sermon, announced to the congregation that there was sad news; the army had met with great reverses, and it was not likely that the congregation would ever again assemble in that house of God.

Never since when the Babylonians learned that Cyrus had penetrated their walls, or when the dwellers in New Carthage assembled in the theatre were told that the Vandals of Genseric were upon them, was there a greater surprise than at Richmond when on that bright April Sabbath it was made known that within a few hours the city was to fall into the hands of the beleaguering force. They could see no signs of siege. They knew, indeed, that for months a great hostile force was encamped not far away, but between them and it was their own invincible army under its indomitable commander, who had three years before driven off a like threatening force, and had held this at bay so that not a sound of battle had reached their ears, and who had vowed that he would die before he would abandon their defense. Richmond had been notably gay all through the winter and spring, so much so that the clergy had been constrained to institute special religious services to counteract the prevailing current of dissipation. The newspapers were allowed to give only brief scraps of tidings furnished by the War Department, and these amounted simply to nothing. But in the absence of all true accounts there was a superabundance of rumors and reports. One day it was said that a messenger was making his way overland with a treaty duly signed, whereby the French emperor, and, by consequence, the British queen, had formed an alliance with the Confederacy against the Union. Again it was reported that Johnston had crushed Sherman, and was in full march to unite with Lee, and that by the combined force the army of Grant would be swept away, as that of McClellan had been swept away not three years before. Of the great battles which had been fought not a score of miles away, not a word was told; but on the very day before they commenced, the morning train from Petersburg brought reports that Lee had made a night attack, in which he had crushed the enemy along his whole line. That day John Daniel, the editor of the leading Richmond paper, and the wielder of the most trenchant pen in the Confederacy, had died. Next morning his obituary appeared in the papers, closing with a regret that "the great Virginian" had passed away just as the decisive victory had been won which was likely to prove the turning-point to the success of the Southern Confederacy. So, of all the days in the year, this bright April Sabbath seemed the last which was to be the day of doom to the Confederacy.

---

[1] Fort Mahone was at a point where the two lines had approached most closely. Opposite to it was Fort Sedgwick. So fierce and continuous had been the fire from these forts that the latter was known in the army as "Fort Hell," and the former as "Fort Damnation."

THE OCCUPATION OF PETERSBURG.

St. Paul's. 2d Baptist Church Presbyterian Church. City Hall. 1st Baptist Church. Capitol. Governor's House. Custom-house.

RICHMOND, FROM GAMBLE'S HILL.

When, therefore, the authentic tidings came that before another sun should rise the Confederate capital was to be abandoned, they were like a thunder-clap from a cloudless sky. All was confusion and dismay. Those who rushed to the government offices could learn nothing; but the hasty packing of archives, and the long lines of wagons conveying them to the railroad dépôts, told the story. A special train during the afternoon bore the President and a part of his cabinet toward Danville. This was now the only avenue for those who hoped to escape from the apprehended horrors of a sacked city. They could not forget how the Confederates had wantonly burned Cumberland; they knew what had befallen Columbia. So the great throng of those who had means of paying their fare pressed to the dépôt of the Danville Road. They found the doors guarded by lines of soldiers, with orders to allow no one to enter without a special pass from the Secretary of War. To find that functionary was hopeless. Now and then one who knew the premises, or had special means of influence, succeeded in getting within, only to find the waiting trains loaded to twice their regulated capacity with the employés and effects of the government.

In the streets the disorder grew fiercer and fiercer till it rose to tumult and riot. As night closed in all the rascality of the city seemed let loose, and surged around every spot where there was a chance of pillage. There were numerous stores and warehouses filled with goods which, having run the blockade, were rated at prices which, reckoned in Confederate currency, were worth a prince's ransom. These were broken open, and their contents borne away with scarcely a pretense of opposition. The poorest scoundrel in the city was for the moment a richer man than he had ever hoped to become. For a few hours there had been a lingering hope that Lee would be able to escape the necessity of withdrawing his army. But when at last the mayor announced that this hope was vain, and that the evacuation was a foregone conclusion, the city council proposed to get together some regiments of militia to preserve order, and to establish a regular patrol for the night. Above all, every drop of liquor in the shops and warehouses was to be destroyed. This was partially executed, and the gutters ran with a liquor freshet whose reeking fumes filled the air. But the destruction could be only partial. Not a few who were to carry out the order chose to drink rather than destroy the liquor. The militia slipped through the hands of their officers; the patrols disappeared; soldiers, half famished during the long months in the intrenchments, straggled from their commands, maddened by the thirst for liquor, which they now found it easy to satiate. The city was given up to pillage; stores were entered and stripped; the sidewalks were strewn with a mingled rubbish of costly goods, provisions, and broken glass. The early night was made hideous by the shouts of the mob, the yells of drunken men, and wild cries of distress from women and children.

But the horrors of that night had only begun. The great body of troops from the fortifications had been passing through the city, and had crossed the river. Their presence had some effect in checking the outrages. To Ewell's corps, the rear-guard, had been committed the task of destroying the bridges across the James, and blowing up the iron-clad vessels which lay in the stream, and, in general, of making way with every thing which could be of use to the enemy. In the very heart of the town were four warehouses filled from top to bottom with tobacco; close by were the great Gallego Flour-mills, the largest in the world, with all the combustible materials which gather around such establishments. To these Ewell ordered the torch to be applied. A fire breaking out here at any time would be disastrous; now, when all means of checking it were paralyzed, a general conflagration was inevitable. The mayor and a committee of citizens remonstrated against the execution of this order. The warehouses were fired, the flames spread from building to building, and from street to street, over whole acres of ground whereon was the whole business part of Richmond. Within its area were all the banks, insurance offices, auction stores, newspaper offices, and nearly all the mercantile houses. Here, too, were arsenals stored with shells and munitions of war: the successive explosion of these sounded like a continuous peal of thunder. While this great conflagration was raging, without even an effort to check it, the tumult, and riot, and ravaging, and pillaging grew madder and madder all through that long night.

When the sun rose in the morning it looked upon a strange and sorrowful scene. The streets were crowded with a motley throng—drays loaded with goods, men toilsomely rolling barrels, women and children of all colors staggering under heavy loads, their own goods or that which they had plundered. The Capitol Square, seeming to be safest from the conflagration, was covered over with piles of furniture dragged from the burning houses, among which were huddled together women and children, whose only homes were now beneath the open sky; even here the air was dim with smoke, and blinding with a snow of fiery cinders. The sun was an hour high when from the rear of the motley crowd pressing up Main Street arose the ominous cry of "The Yankees! The Yankees!"

During the three days while fighting had been going on around Petersburg there had been perfect quiet on the James. Confederates and Federals seemed aware that nothing which could be done there would influence the issue. When that Sabbath night closed in, each was aware that the result was decided. All the bands in Weitzel's lines struck up the national airs. They were answered with corresponding music from the Confederate lines. Until midnight the air was vocal with the strains of "Hail Columbia" and "Dixie," the "Star-spangled Banner" and the "Bonnie Blue Flag." Then came a brief interval of absolute repose, during which the Confederate troops were silently withdrawn, and, as morning was breaking, the glare of the flames, and the dense masses of smoke which rose over Richmond, proclaimed to Weitzel that the Confederate capital, the prize of such long endeavor,

RUINS OF RICHMOND—MAIN STREET.

was probably at his mercy. Slowly and cautiously at first he put his troops in motion. They threaded the intricate lines of works before which they had so long lain, and for the first time learned how formidable they were. Every thing showed how hasty had been the abandonment. Around Fort Field, the first approached, were three lines of abatis and one of torpedoes. The flags which marked the place of the torpedoes had not been taken down. The torpedoes were carefully removed by the advance-guard. A second and third line, each commanding that exterior to it, was passed. The camps were entered, the tents still standing, and all the furniture within. Then, when, for the first time, Richmond was fairly in view by a Federal army, Weitzel sent forward a squad of cavalry, twoscore strong, to enter the city. It was this little body whose coming aroused the cry of "The Yankees!" They proceeded at a leisurely walk up the main street. The crowd fled cursing and trampling up the main street and down the by-streets. The troopers then broke into a trot for the public square, and in a few minutes their guidons were fluttering from the Capitol. Soon afterward a regular flag was raised. This was the same which had been hoisted over the head-quarters of Butler at New Orleans. It had been brought there by Shepley, who hoped to raise it over the Capitol at Richmond. It had been given in charge of Johnston de Peyster, a young aid of Shepley, who had asked permission to hoist it himself when the Confederate capital should be captured. By some misapprehension, the flag was raised over the "State" end of the Capitol instead of over the "Confederate States" end. Those who believed in omens saw in this an augury that Federal authority had now triumphed over the cherished theory of "States Rights."

Soon they were followed by all the troops, marching in order, but with cheers and martial music. It was noted with bitter indignation that a regiment of colored cavalry, as if moved by an irrepressible impulse as they swept by the principal hotel, drew their sabres and broke into wild shouts. Mayo, the mayor, had gone out to surrender the city, but missed his way. Three years before he had declared that "when the citizens of Richmond demand of me to surrender the capital of Virginia and the Confederacy, they must find some other man to fill my place." But the scenes of the past night, and the flames which were still surging and spreading, were enough to convince him that there was something worse even than surrender to the Yankees. The city had been fired against his earnest remonstrance, and now the conquering army alone could put a stop to the conflagration, and prevent a general pillage which was going on.

General Shepley, the same who had been appointed military governor of New Orleans, was placed in command of Richmond. He issued orders at once. The first duty of the army was to save the city, which the Confederate army, unable to hold, had sought to destroy. The fire department of the city would report to the provost-marshal, who would aid them with a detachment of troops; all attempts at plunder, whether by soldiers or citizens, would be summarily punished; no officer or soldier should enter any private dwelling without express orders; no soldier should use offensive words or gestures toward citizens; no treasonable expressions, or insults to the national flag or cause, would be allowed; the rights and duties of the citizens were laid down in the proclamations of the President; and, finally, "with the restoration of the flag of the Union, the citizens might expect the restoration of that peace, prosperity, and happiness which they enjoyed under the Union of which that flag was the glorious symbol."

All attempts to check the conflagration seemed unavailing; but toward evening the wind changed, blowing the flames back in the direction from which they had spread, and the fire died out for lack of fuel. A third part of Richmond had been burnt. The pencil of the surveyor could not have more distinctly marked out the business portion of the city. For a night and a day the Confederate capital had undergone all the horrors of a sacked town; but they had been inflicted by its own populace, not by the victors. The bitterest enemies of the conquerors find hardly an instance of the slightest outrage committed by the Federal troops.[1] Men have wrongly, we think, in the main, charged the burning of Columbia upon the Federal troops; but no one has ventured to charge upon them the far more destructive conflagration of Richmond. The responsibility for this wanton act, palliated by no possible pretext of military necessity, rests solely upon Ewell, who had for well-nigh a year commanded the garrison of the city. Deliberately, and against all remonstrance, he applied the torch where there was no human possibility that the result could have been other than what it was.

Jefferson Davis had in the mean while reached Danville, where, on the next day, he issued a characteristic proclamation. The general-in-chief, he said, had found it necessary to make such movements of his troops as to uncover the capital. The loss of the capital was certainly a great misfortune; for months the finest army of the Confederacy had been obliged, in order to defend Richmond, to forego many promising enterprises. But now a new phase of the struggle had begun. The army, free from the necessity of guarding particular points, was free to move, and could strike the enemy in detail far from his base. Virginia, and no part of it, should be permanently abandoned. If compelled temporarily to withdraw, the army would return until the baffled and exhausted enemy should give over the contest; and no peace should ever be made with the infamous invaders. The people of Richmond only knew of this proclamation when they read it in the Northern newspapers. Before that time arrived the Confederate army had surrendered. Davis, indeed, returned to Virginia, but it was as a prisoner of state, captured in the vain attempt to escape to a foreign soil.

[1] The best account of the incidents at the capture of Richmond is that given by the Rev. Dr. Leyburn, in *Harper's Magazine* for June, 1866. From this we cite a few sentences: "The curtain had now fallen on one act of the stupendous drama. It was soon to rise on what, in its opening at least, would prove even more striking and impressive. The government and army which for years had protected us was gone; that other army, which had come so near that they could hear the sound of our church-bells, and we could see the flash and smoke of their guns—that army, probably by this time exasperated and infuriated to the last degree, was to be upon us with the dawn of the coming day, and we helplessly at their mercy. . . . . Imagine our condition, left by our own army and anticipating the enemy's; the entire business part of the city on fire—stores, warehouses, mills, depôts, and bridges, all covering acres, one sea of flame; and as an accompaniment, the thunder of exploding shells, and in the midst of it that long-threatening, hostile army entering to seize its prey. . . . . Up to this time I do not remember to have seen a fire-engine at work. I went to one of the Federals and told him that, unless they went to work to arrest the conflagration, the entire city would be swept away. Soon after, the military authorities organized the crowds of blacks as a fire corps, and this, with their own efforts and the steam-engines at length brought to play, was instrumental in checking, and at length stopping the tempest of fire. But all the forenoon, and till well on in the afternoon, flame and smoke, and burning brands, and showers of blazing sparks filled the air. Seldom has a city in proportion to its population and wealth suffered so terribly. Very agreeable was the disappointment at the behavior of the victorious army. The fact was that, with few exceptions, the troops behaved astonishingly well, and were remarkably courteous and respectful. Some cases of outrage were committed in the suburbs, but every attempt of the sort in the city of which I heard was followed by condign punishment."

McLEAN'S HOUSE.

CHAPTER LVII.

THE RETREAT AND SURRENDER OF LEE.

The Line of Retreat.—Number of Lee's Army.—The Pursuit.—Lee reaches Amelia Court-house.
—Finds no Supplies.—Sheridan reaches Jettersville.—Position of Lee.—He resumes his Retreat.—Sheridan's Plan of Assault.—Engagement at Sailor's Creek.—Capture of Ewell's Corps.
—Straggling from the Confederate Army.—Ord's Column reaches Farmville.—Reade attacks
and is repulsed.—The Confederates recross the Appomattox, make a stand, and repulse Humphreys.—They continue their Retreat.—Sheridan's Movements.—A Scout reports Supplies at
Appomattox Station.—Custer sent forward.—He captures the Trains and heads off Lee's Retreat.—Ord and Griffin urged forward.—The Confederate Retreat on the 8th of April.—Reach
Appomattox Station.—Are assailed by Custer and driven back.—Situation on the 9th.—Gordon
attempts to break through.—He fails.—Asks a Suspension of Hostilities.—Lee and Grant.—
Their Correspondence.—Conference of Confederate Generals.—Lee seeks Grant.—Their Meet-
ing.—Terms of Surrender.—The Correspondence between Grant and Lee.—The Paroles.—Lee's
Farewell Address to his Army.—His Return to Richmond.—The formal Surrender.

WHEN Lee abandoned Richmond and Petersburg, his purpose was to
retreat to Danville, where he hoped to unite with Johnston. The
first necessity was to concentrate his widely-spread forces. The point of
junction fixed upon was Chesterfield Court-house, midway between Petersburg and Richmond, but to the west of both cities. The forces at Petersburg thus at first headed northwestward, those at Richmond southwestward.
Leaving the burning warehouses of Petersburg and the fast-spreading conflagration of Richmond behind them, the troops plunged into the thick darkness of a moonless night. When all were brought together there were
about 40,000 men.[1] The men, unencumbered by rations, moved rapidly,
and at dawn had put nearly a score of miles between them and Petersburg.
All the next day they pressed on with no signs of an enemy on their track.
To Lee it seemed that the great peril was overpast. His troubled brow
lightened. He had accomplished the almost hopeless task of getting his
army safely on its way, and had gained a start of many miles. One more
day unmolested, and he would have passed the junction of the Southside and
Danville Railroads, and then, by destroying roads and bridges behind him,
he could easily keep ahead of any possible pursuit. But he had now to
deal with a different opponent from the one who had suffered him after Antietam to slip quietly across the Potomac, or that other who failed to follow
up the retreat from Gettysburg.

Early on Monday morning Grant put his pursuing columns in motion, not
following the line of Lee's retreat, but moving so as to intercept him before
he should reach the junction of the Southside and Danville roads. This is
at Burkesville, fifty-two miles almost due west from Petersburg. If the
Confederates passed that point, they were safely on their way to Danville,
and could laugh at present pursuit. If the Federals reached that place, or
any other on the railroad nearer Richmond ahead of the Confederates, Lee's
purpose of joining Johnston would be frustrated.

The Appomattox River, rising in the county of the same name, runs east-

ward for fifty miles toward Richmond. At a distance of thirty miles from
the capital it bends sharply southward for twenty miles, and then, resuming
its eastward course, reaches Petersburg. The Danville Railroad, along which
lay Lee's proposed line of retreat, runs southwestward, crossing the Appomattox just at its southward bend. For a rapid day's march Lee's line of
retreat lay on the north side of the river, which he had then to cross in order
to head toward Danville. Grant's pursuing, or rather intercepting columns,
moved upon the south side of the river, which ran between, and thus it
happened that for the first two days the two armies, though heading for the
same point, never came in sight of each other. The Union army moved in
two parallel lines. Ord, with his two half corps of the Army of the James,
marched along the Southside Railroad straight for the junction at Burkesville. The other and larger column, to the north, kept close to the Appomattox. This column consisted of the cavalry and the Fifth Corps under
Sheridan, followed closely by the corps of Wright and Humphreys. In the
rear of this was the Ninth Corps, which was left behind to occupy Petersburg, form the rear-guard of the whole army, and cover the communications
with City Point.

As the morning of Monday, April 3, broke, it was doubtful whether pursuers or pursued would first reach the Danville Road. The chances were
rather in favor of Lee, for he had about the same distance, with the advantage of better roads, and was at the outset unencumbered with provision
trains. So all day he marched cheerily on. Making a brief halt during the
night, he crossed the Appomattox at Goode's Bridge, and early on the morning of the 4th reached Amelia Court-house, on the Danville Road. Here,
according to his carefully-planned arrangements, he was to have found supplies for his troops, who had started out with only food for a single day.
He had ordered that trains from the South, loaded with a quarter of a million of rations, should await him here. The trains arrived duly on the
evening of Sunday. They were met by orders from Richmond to press on
to the capital in order to carry off the persons and archives belonging to
the government. In the hurry and confusion of the moment, no order was
given for the unloading of the trains, and so, with all their stores of food,
they moved on to Richmond, and when Lee reached the Court-house he
found not a morsel of food for his famishing troops. Thus, at a moment
when every hour was precious, Lee had no alternative but to halt, break up
his force into foraging squads, and sweep the region round for such scanty
supplies of food as might be picked up. This enforced delay proved fatal.

Sheridan, on the other side of the Appomattox, had kept up a neck-and-
neck race with Lee. His cavalry, striking that of the enemy at Deep
Creek, routed them, capturing many prisoners, and leaving Griffin, who was
close behind, to pick up whatever spoils were left behind. Lee's enforced
delay at Amelia Court-house enabled Sheridan's cavalry to push ahead of
him, and strike the Danville Road. Up this they moved, and late in the
afternoon the Fifth Corps also gained the railroad at Jettersville, seven miles
south of the Court-house. Here they intrenched themselves, resolved to contest the passage until the main body could come up. Had Lee been able
to move his army that afternoon, he might possibly have broken through,[1]
and kept up his retreat. Such, indeed, was apparently Lee's design; for he
sent on a dispatch, here intercepted, to the commissaries at Danville and
Lynchburg, directing 200,000 rations to meet him at Burkesville. But the
Confederate troops were in no condition to fight, much less to make a rapid
march that day. They had been pushed to the utmost limits of human en-

---

[1] I am aware that this number is far in excess of that usually assigned. Thus Pollard (*Lost
Cause*, 703) says: "With the additions made to the Petersburg section of troops from the Richmond lines and from Lee's extreme right which had crossed the Appomattox above Petersburg"
[that is, those who, having been cut off by Wright, retreated before Miles], that resourceful commander had now well in hand more than 20,000 troops." There is some ambiguity in this statement, as it is not clearly said whether in this number are to be included those from the north of
the James and from Richmond, 15,000 at least. Elsewhere (*Southern History of the War*, ii., 507)
he says, "Lee had on the lines he had abandoned between 27,000 and 28,000." This would seem
not to include that portion cut off by Wright. Swinton (*Army of the Potomac*, 605) puts the entire number at 25,000; and (*Twelve Decisive Battles*, 499) says "the army was reduced to almost
20,000 effective men." But the official returns show that Lee finally surrendered 27,805 men (*Report of the Secretary of War*, 1865, p. 45); and Pollard (*Lost Cause*, 711) says, "About 7500
men laid down their arms; but the capitulation included in addition some 18,000 stragglers, who
were unarmed, and who came up to claim the benefit of surrender and accept paroles."—Besides
these there were, as will be seen, not far from 10,000 prisoners captured during the retreat; and
there were, moreover, considerable losses in killed and wounded. Perfect accuracy where official
reports are wanting is impossible; but I think, in placing Lee's entire force when the retreat was
begun at 40,000, I am rather below than above the true number.

[1] "It seems to me that this was the only chance the army of Northern Virginia had of saving
itself, which might have been done had General Lee promptly attacked and driven back the comparatively small force opposed to him, and pursued his march to Burkesville Junction."—*Sheridan's Report.*

durance. Half of them were broken up into foraging parties, and all were in a state of starvation. Moreover, their long trains of ammunition, stretching for thirty miles, must at all hazards be protected, for these, if lost, could not be replaced. So Lee, sending forward a portion of his trains under a cavalry escort, was compelled to lie at Amelia Court-house all that day and until the afternoon of the next. Humphreys's corps now came up, Meade accompanying it, but, being unwell, he placed it under the charge of Sheridan. Sheridan pushed out Davies with a brigade of cavalry to strike the moving trains. Davies routed the escort, destroyed 180 wagons, and captured five guns, with many prisoners. Meade now requested that the Fifth Corps should be returned to his immediate command. Sheridan complied with reluctance. He had learned the worth of that corps, with which not a week before he had been loth to undertake an offensive operation.

Wright's corps now came up, and three fourths of the army of the Potomac were concentrated at Jettersville. On the morning of the 6th it was put in motion toward Amelia Court-house; but Lee, anticipating such a movement, had the evening before moved off. Bending a little to the north, he turned the head of the advancing force, and Sheridan, upon nearing Amelia, found that Lee had given him the slip, and had gained a full half day's march to the westward.

The faces of the pursuing force were now turned from the north to the west. To secure greater rapidity, it was divided into three columns, Humphreys in the rear of the retreating enemy, Griffin on the south, and Wright on the north of it. Lee's retreat was now painfully slow. Worn out, half famished, and encumbered by the wagons, which the half-starved animals could hardly drag over the rough roads, they could barely move half a mile an hour. The advantage of the start was soon lost. Sheridan, whose command was now reduced to the cavalry, soon came upon the left flank of the long column. The trains were the tempting objects of attack, and against these Sheridan directed his fiery energy. Crook, who was in the advance, was to attack; if he found the enemy too strong, he was to hold them in check, while another division passing was to strike farther on, and so on alternating until a weak point was at last found. Crook found the enemy too strong to be driven; he held his own, while Custer passed him and found a weak point at Sailor's Creek, a small tributary of the Appomattox. Crook and Devin coming up, the whole force charged the train, dispersed the guards, capturing hundreds of prisoners and sixteen guns, destroying four hundred wagons, and cutting off a large body of the enemy from their line of retreat.

The troops thus cut off were Ewell's corps and the remnants of Pickett's division who had escaped from the disaster of Five Forks—in all, some six or eight thousand strong. This force thus isolated was a prize so tempting that Sheridan, not for the first time, deviated from the principle that he had laid down that cavalry should not be employed to attack infantry in position, and gave Merritt permission to make a mounted charge against their lines. The charge was gallantly made by Stagg's brigade, which dashed up to, but were unable to break the hostile lines. But the charge accomplished its main purpose. It detained the enemy for a space. Sheridan, who had waited behind, sent back a message urging Wright's corps to come up with the utmost speed. He was still unaware of Custer's complete success in cutting the Confederate line two miles beyond. But information came to him in an unexpected way. A single horseman dashed up. He was one of Custer's men, who had rode right into the enemy's works, had been a prisoner for a brief space, and then, getting clear of his captors, had fairly passed through the hostile troops and brought tidings of what had been accomplished, and that Custer and Crook were pressing hard upon the opposite side. Sheridan, in the hurry of the moment, forgot the name of the trooper, but he must have kept the exploit in mind, for in a note added long after to his report he mentions that he had ascertained that it was private William Richardson, of the Ohio Veteran Cavalry. The head of Wright's division now came up, and Ewell and Pickett faced about and met them with such a hot fire that Seymour's division was checked until Wheaton's came up to its support. Pickett's remnant was overpowered and broke into rout. Ewell made a brief stand, and from a commanding position poured in a fire which broke a portion of the assailants who were advancing over a patch of open ground. But now a general charge was made. Stagg struck one flank, Custer the rear, while Wright assailed in front. Humphreys, a little to the right, also struck a body of the enemy, destroyed two hundred wagons, and made many prisoners. Ewell was outnumbered and completely surrounded. His whole corps threw down their arms. Ewell, Custis Lee, and Kershaw, with six or eight thousand men, surrendered themselves as prisoners.[1]

The straggling from Lee's army had become enormous. Quite a quarter of its remaining effective force was now lopped off at a blow. The remainder had, however, won a brief respite, and moved on. Their sufferings from hunger during the last days had been fearful. Save the single ration which they had brought with them, and the scanty scraps gathered by some foraging parties, they had been without food since they had left Petersburg. Company after company was sent out into the woods to browse upon the tender shoots of the trees just bursting into bud.[2] More pitiable even than the condition of the troops was that of the animals. At every step the jaded horses and mules sank down. At every difficult place the way was blocked up with wagons which could not be moved, and which were set on fire to save them from falling into the hands of the enemy. The exploding ammunition sounded like the continuous noise of a great battle. The spirits of the men gave way at every step. They threw away their arms by regi-

ments, too weak to carry them. Thousands of these unarmed men wandered away, the officers finally ceasing to make any effort to restrain the straggling. Other thousands dragged themselves along mechanically by the side or at the rear of the few who yet kept their ranks, and held on to their arms; for there was yet, after the disaster at Sailor's Creek, a solid core of some ten thousand in whom was now concentrated all the vitality of the great Army of Northern Virginia. So the army struggled on, heading for Farmville, where they hoped to recross the Appomattox, and, by burning the bridges behind them, place the river once more between them and their eager pursuers.

While the Army of the Potomac thus pressed hard upon the Confederates, Ord, with his command from the Army of the James, had, on the evening of the 5th, reached Burkesville. Next morning he moved northward toward Farmville, hoping to head off the enemy there. Approaching this place, he sent Reade forward with a couple of regiments and a squadron of cavalry. He encountered the head of Lee's column and charged it vigorously. His small force was repulsed with heavy loss, he himself being among the slain. But this attack delayed the crossing until the remainder of Ord's force came up, whereupon the Confederates intrenched themselves too strongly to be assailed. During the night they began to cross the river at various points, proposing to destroy the bridges behind them. This was delayed an hour too long. The last of the stragglers had just got over, and the fuel which was to consume the bridges was just lighted, when Barlow's division of the Sixth Corps came up, drove off the Confederate rear-guard, saved the highway bridge close by the high railroad bridge, and secured the means of crossing the river. The Confederates fell back step by step to positions which had been previously selected until toward night, when their whole remaining force was seen drawn up in line of battle in a position covering the roads, their batteries sweeping a gentle slope of half a mile in their front. Humphreys, keeping Barlow in their front, sent Miles around to attack them upon their left. The assault was repelled with heavy loss; and then, under cover of night, the Confederates resumed their retreat eastward toward Appomattox Station, where supplies were awaiting them. They hoped that the start thus gained would enable them to reach Lynchburg, a score of miles beyond, where they would pass the mountains, and emerge into the great Valley of Virginia. Here they might hope for at least a temporary respite from pursuit.

Sheridan, having learned that Ord had failed to cut off the enemy at Farmville, apprehended that it might be Lee's purpose to sweep southwestwardly by rapid marches, heading the pursuing columns, and, regaining the Danville Road, follow up his original plan of joining Johnston in North Carolina. He therefore sent his cavalry in that direction. Reaching Prince Edward Court-house and discovering no traces of the enemy, he sent his divisions to reconnoitre in various directions to find the whereabouts of Lee's army. Crook, crossing the Appomattox, struck the main body near Farmville, assailed their trains, was repulsed, and recrossed the river. On the morning of the 8th the cavalry was concentrated at Prospect Station. Here Sheridan was informed by one of his scouts that at Appomattox Station, twenty-eight miles distant, were four trains of cars laden with provisions for Lee's army. The report of this scout, as the event proved, gave shape to the events of the two closing days of the campaign. It showed just whither Lee was now heading. Instead of aiming at Danville, he was moving straight for Lynchburg. The cavalry were forthwith pushed forward to seize these trains. Custer, who was in the advance, reached Appomattox Station at midnight. The Confederate van had reached the point just before, and had gone into camp. Dashing upon the rear of the trains, Custer cut them off from returning to Lynchburg, captured them, sent them to the rear, and then, without even waiting to reform, burst upon the Confederate force, and drove it pell-mell northward toward Appomattox Court-house, capturing, besides the trains, twenty-five guns and a park of wagons. Sheridan was little behind. He sent back word to Ord and Griffin, who, with their infantry corps, were behind, that if they only pressed on there was no escape for the enemy. Meanwhile he disposed of his cavalry in such a manner as to cover the roads toward Lynchburg, resolving to contest them step by step until the infantry could come up.

The Confederates having, on the evening of the 7th as it seemed, fairly shaken off the attack of Humphreys on their rear, pressed forward all that night and the next day with renewed hopes. If one from a balloon could have overlooked the region lying directly under his eye, he would have seen at a glance that the whole issue turned upon the relative speed of the pursuers and pursued for a few hours. Lee's line of retreat lay along a narrow neck of land between the Appomattox and the James, which here ran parallel at a distance of seven or eight miles. The only avenue of escape was to the west, for on the north was the James, the bridges over which had all been destroyed two months before to prevent the march of Sheridan; on the south was the Appomattox, difficult of passage, and covered on its opposite side by Ord, Griffin, and Sheridan; eastward, and pressing after in the rear, were Humphreys and Wright. For the first few hours of the day the retreating army moved slowly along by-paths running through thickets of oak and pine. At noon they struck the main road, and then moved rapidly. Every hour they appeared to be gaining upon the pursuers, for the noise of a single gun could not be heard in their rear. When, as night was falling, the head of the column came to Appomattox Station, the rear being but four miles behind, they went into camp with a feeling of security to which they had long been strangers. The wearied soldiers lay down to rest, while the bands played merrily. Just then, like a thunderbolt, Custer's cavalry burst upon them. Orders were hastily given that all the extra artillery should be cut down and the commands disbanded.

---

[1] No actual count of the prisoners at Sailor's Creek seems to have been made. Sheridan roughly estimates them at 10,000. Grant, probably more accurately, states the number at 6000 or 7000. Pollard gives the number of Ewell's and Pickett's men at about 5000.

[2] Fletcher, iii., 516, upon authority of one of Longstreet's staff.

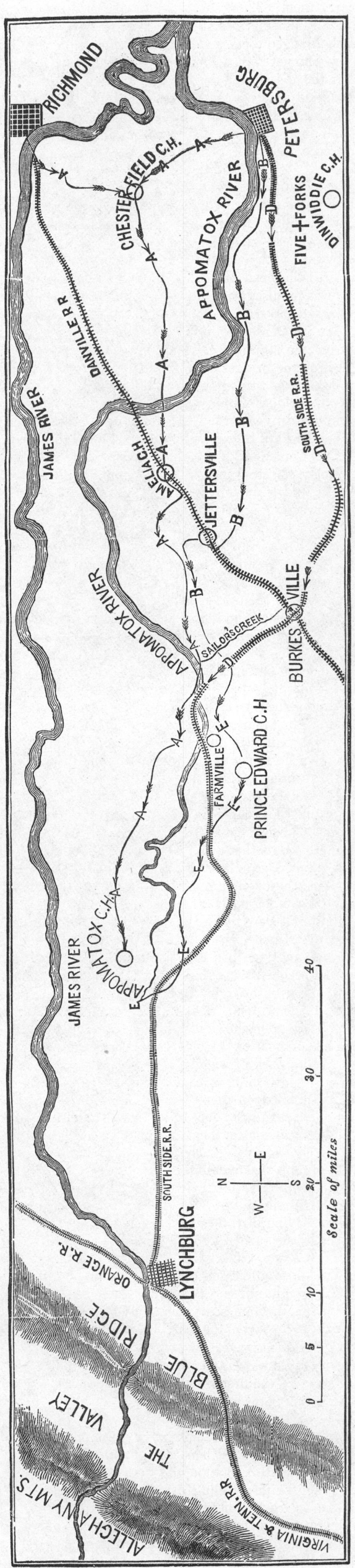

THE RETREAT AND PURSUIT OF LEE.

This plan represents, in a general way, the routes pursued in the retreat and pursuit. A A indicates the line of Lee's retreat, the two columns from Richmond and Petersburg joining at Chesterfield Court-house.—B B indicates the march of Grant's right column, Sheridan's cavalry, with Griffin's, Humphreys's, and Wright's divisions, to Jettersville.—D D shows the route of the left column, Ord's command, along the Southside or Lynchburg Railroad to Burkesville, and thence to Farmville.—E E shows the march of Sheridan's cavalry, followed by Griffin and Ord, from Jettersville and Farmville to Appomatox Court-house.—From near Farmville the corps of Humphreys and Wright followed directly after Lee, in the line from that point indicated by A A.—Lee's original design was to move from Amelia Court-house, through Burkesville, and thence on to Danville, seventy miles southwestward, where he expected to be joined by Johnston. Headed off at Jettersville, he next proposed to go to Lynchburg, and thence through the passes of the Blue Mountains into the Valley of Virginia.

But in the gathering darkness the extent of the peril could only be conjectured. There was certainly a Federal force right in their front; but it was apparently only cavalry, through which a way might most likely be forced. So, gathering together his army as best he might, Lee made preparations to attempt the passage at dawn. Gordon, who had brought up the rear, was sent to the front, passing the remnants of the wagon train, around which lingered thousands of men who, too weak to carry their arms, had flung them away along every mile of the road from Amelia Court-house. Early in the morning Gordon made reconnoissances in his front. He could see nothing but a line of dismounted cavalry to oppose his march. At ten o'clock his line was ordered to advance. Sheridan had directed his troops to fall back slowly, keeping a steady front, until Ord and Griffin, who had been marching all night, should come up and form in their rear. Gordon pressed on, flushed with what seemed an easy victory, when all at once Sheridan's dismounted cavalry moved to one side, like the withdrawing of a curtain, and disclosed a long line of infantry bearing straight down, while at the same moment the troopers sprang to saddle, ready to charge upon the flank of the unarmed men in the centre of the Confederate column. Had that charge been made, the whole Confederate force would have been ridden over like stubble. Gordon sent word to Lee in the rear that he was being driven back. What was to be done in such a case had already been decided. Lee mounted his horse and rode back toward the Union lines, while Gordon sent a flag of truce to the front, asking for a suspension of hostilities, for negotiations for surrender were then in progress.

Sheridan was in no mood for trifling. He had just been assailed; the smoke of the guns fired at him had hardly lifted. He had no wish to shed more blood; but, before he would order a suspension of an attack, the issue of which was patent to all, he must have positive assurance that a surrender was decided upon. Gordon came to the front and gave the required assurance. In a few moments officers of high rank upon both sides were mingling in friendly concourse, as though for four long years they had not confronted each other on a hundred battle-fields. There were men on each side who had been cadets together at West Point, and who had since fought side by side during the Mexican War, and later in the wearisome operations on the wide frontier. Now, bridging over the fatal four years, they could at last meet as friends. War has its amenities as well as its hostilities.

Lee, accompanied by two aids, was riding toward the Federal lines to meet Grant, prepared at this supreme moment to give an unconditional surrender of what remained of the remnant of the great army which had so long been under his command; for to this issue it had at last come. He hoped, indeed, to gain favorable terms, and in this hope he was encouraged by what had within a day or two occurred between himself and the commander of the Federal forces. The surrender of the Confederate Army of Northern Virginia had for some days been a foregone conclusion on both sides. On the 6th, directly after the disaster at Sailor's Creek, such of the Confederate generals as could come together met at Anderson's tent, and concluded that the end was at hand, and the surrender must soon take place. They would take upon themselves the sole responsibility of advising the surrender. Pendleton was deputed to see that this opinion was presented to Lee; if possible, Longstreet was to be induced to act as intermediary. Events following closely after rendered superfluous any direct action upon this suggestion.

On the 7th Grant took the initiative. To Lee he wrote: "The result of the last week must convince you of the hopelessness of farther resistance on the part of the Army of Northern Virginia," and so, to shift from himself the responsibility of more bloodshed, he asked that Lee should surrender the army under his immediate command. Lee replied diplomatically, and in phrases which perhaps were meant to bear a double sense. He was not entirely of the opinion that farther resistance was hopeless; but yet, hoping to avoid useless bloodshed, he asked the terms which would be offered to him on condition of surrender. Grant, understanding this to be an offer of surrender, replied that peace being his only desire, the sole terms he would insist upon were that the men surrendered should not again take up arms against the government of the United States until properly exchanged; and he was ready to arrange with Lee, either personally or by representatives, for the definite terms of surrender. Lee's answer could not well be other than a surprise to Grant. He had not intended to propose to surrender, but only to ask the terms which Grant would propose. Indeed, "to be frank," he said, "I do not think the emergency has arisen to call for surrender." He could not, therefore, meet Grant with a view to surrender his army, but would be pleased to meet him to talk over the subject of the restoration of peace, "which should be the sole object of all." To understand Lee's motive in this reply, it is only necessary to look at the operations of the day. He had flung back the assault upon his rear, and was, to all appearance, safely on his way toward Lynchburg, and at least temporary safety. This was by no means the first time in which an attempt had been made to induce Grant to transcend his authority and undertake to make peace. He, indeed, knew clearly the limits of his functions. Moreover, if more had been needed, he had the express order of the President prohibiting him from dealing with the general question of the restoration of peace. So to Lee's letter Grant responded sharply, but still with a kindly addition which left the way open for each military commander to do what he properly might. I have no authority, he said, to treat on the subject of peace, and so the meeting which you propose would do no good; but the terms upon which peace can be had are well understood: the South has only to lay down its arms.

So matters rested through the 8th of April and the night following. As day dawned on the 9th, raw and gusty, three Confederate generals sat around

POSITION OF THE CONFEDERATE ARMY WHEN THE SURRENDER WAS ANNOUNCED.

a camp-fire. They were Lee, dressed in a new uniform just donned, and contrasting with the rough garb by which he had long been best known in the army; Longstreet, his arm still in a sling, his old Wilderness wound yet unhealed; and Mahone, perhaps the best of Longstreet's surviving subordinates, who had come up from the rear to hold part in the informal council there assembled. These three were to decide upon what could be and must be done. Mahone, being junior officer, according to army rules was to speak first. His own division, he said, and one or two others, were able to fight; the rest of the army was so worn out as to be fit only for surrender. Longstreet corroborated this statement; yet both declared that the Army of Northern Virginia should surrender only upon honorable terms. Lee then, for the first time, imparted to his subordinates the substance of what had passed between himself and Grant. The terms proposed were honorable; but now, after two days' rejection, it was not certain that they would be conceded. Then—for some hours had passed in deliberation—came the message from Gordon that he was overmatched and falling back. The crisis had come and gone. Surrender on the best terms that could be obtained was all that was left. "General Longstreet," said Lee, "I leave you in charge here; I am going to hold a conference with General Grant." How that conference must result was no longer a matter of doubt. It must be surrender at all events, no matter upon what terms, for the remnant of the Confederate army, outnumbered, worn out, and surrounded, could neither fight nor fly. Its only alternative was to die or surrender. And so Gordon in front was warranted in assuring Sheridan that the surrender was now a foregone conclusion. The last shot fired by the Army of Northern Virginia was by the Richmond Howitzers, who had fired the first gun at Bethel just four years before, lacking a month and a day.

Lee rode to that part of the Union line where he expected to find Grant. Here he was met by Grant's note declining an interview to treat of the general question of peace. Grant had gone to meet Sheridan. Lee wrote a hasty note: "I received your note on the picket-line, whither I had come to meet you and ascertain definitely what terms were embraced in your proposition of yesterday with reference to the surrender of this army. I now request an interview in accordance with the offer contained in your letter of yesterday for that purpose." Two hours passed, and noon came before this request reached Grant. He returned a courteous reply, explaining the delay, and expressing his readiness to meet Lee at any point which he should select.

Appomattox Court-house, a hamlet of a half score houses, which had now become neutral ground, was the place chosen. The best house, that of Mr. McLean, was fixed upon for the interview. The owner was naturally astounded at the honor thus suddenly thrust upon him. The two great commanders, after due introduction, seated themselves at a little table in his quiet parlor to settle what each knew was in effect to end the war. The two men had certainly seen each other before, for both had served under Scott almost a score of years before at the capture of Mexico. Most likely Grant remembered Lee, but Lee could hardly be expected to remember Grant. The brilliant Virginian, the favorite of the commander, and already looked upon as the rising man of the army, could hardly be expected to have taken special note of a certain second lieutenant Grant, acting as regimental quartermaster, even though he was breveted first lieutenant for "meritorious services" at Molino del Rey; and a few days afterward, at Chapultepec, as was duly reported by General Worth and Colonel Garland, "acquitted himself most nobly" under the observation of his regimental, brigade, and division commanders.

The afternoon was wearing away when the interview began. There was really little to be said, and both men had the faculty of not spending words upon trifles. Grant's original proposition embraced all the terms that Lee could ask. The question was, were these still open to acceptance. Grant still offered them; Lee said they were lenient, and he would leave to Grant to express them in form. Lee asked a few explanations respecting certain phrases used in the formal agreement. Both commanders understood them alike. The purport of the whole was that this Confederate army surrendered, giving up all public property, the officers retaining their side-arms, baggage, and their own horses. Officers were to give their personal paroles not to take up arms against the government of the United States until properly exchanged, and also to give a like parole for the men under their command. This being done, every officer and man might return to his home, "not to be disturbed by the United States authority so long as they observe their paroles and the laws in force where they may reside." Terms so magnanimous were never before offered and accepted. So clearly were they defined, that never, amid all the complications that have ensued, has there been any question as to their import, or any serious dispute as to the exact fulfillment of the terms of surrender.[1]

The momentous interview which virtually closed the war lasted hardly an hour, for it wanted but ten minutes of noon when Grant, miles away, received the letter of Lee asking for a meeting, and at half past three the Confederate commander rode quietly back to his quarters. There was no need of inquiring what had been done. All saw at a glance that the surrender had been made. Officers and men rushed up to bid farewell to their leader. He received their greeting quietly. "We have fought through the war together," he said, "and I have done the best I could for you." The next day he issued a formal address to his army, and then rode off toward Richmond. On the afternoon of the 12th, attended by half a dozen of his staff, he rode into the smoking city which he had so long and stoutly defended. Entering his home, he disappeared from the history of the war, of which his surrender had, indeed, been the actual conclusion, though nominally it lasted a few weeks longer.

The surrender of the Army of Northern Virginia was virtually performed by the two men who sat quietly together in McLean's parlor at Appomattox Court-house. All that remained to be done was performed as quietly. There were to be none of the formal ceremonies heretofore practiced

[1] The following—mere formal terms of courtesy being omitted—is the text of the correspondence between Grant and Lee:

I. Grant to Lee, *April* 7. "The result of the last week must convince you of the hopelessness of farther resistance on the part of the Army of Northern Virginia in this struggle. I feel that it is so, and regard it as my duty to shift from myself the responsibility of any farther effusion of blood by asking of you the surrender of that portion of the Confederate States army known as the Army of Northern Virginia."

II. Lee to Grant, *April* 7. "I have received your note of this date. Though not entertaining the opinion you express on the hopelessness of farther resistance on the part of the Army of Northern Virginia, I reciprocate your desire to avoid useless effusion of blood, and therefore, before considering your proposition, ask the terms you will offer on condition of its surrender."

III. Grant to Lee, *April* 8. "Your note of last evening, in reply to mine of same date, asking the conditions on which I will accept the surrender of the Army of Northern Virginia, is just received. In reply I would say, that *peace* being my great desire, there is but one condition I would insist upon, namely, That the men and officers surrendered shall be disqualified for taking up arms again against the government of the United States until properly exchanged. I will meet you, or will designate officers to meet any officers you may name for the same purpose at any point agreeable to you, for the purpose of arranging definitely the terms upon which the surrender of the Army of Northern Virginia will be received."

IV. Lee to Grant, *April* 8. "I received at a late hour your note of to-day. In mine of yesterday I did not intend to propose the surrender of the Army of Northern Virginia, but to ask the terms of your proposition. To be frank, I do not think the emergency has arisen to call for the surrender of the army; but as the restoration of peace should be the sole object of all, I desire to know whether your proposals would lead to that end. I can not, therefore, meet you with a view to surrender the Army of Northern Virginia; but, as far as your proposal may affect the Confederate States forces under my command, and tend to the restoration of peace, I should be pleased to meet you at 10 A.M. to-morrow, on the old stage road to Richmond, between the picket-lines of the two armies."

V. Grant to Lee, *April* 9. "Your note of yesterday is received. I have no authority to treat on the subject of peace; the meeting proposed for 10 A.M. to-day could lead to no good. I will state, however, general, that I am equally anxious for peace with yourself, and the whole North entertains the same feeling. The terms upon which peace can be had are well understood. By the South laying down their arms they will hasten that most desirable event, and save thousands of human lives, and hundreds of millions of property not yet destroyed. Seriously hoping that all our difficulties may be settled without the loss of another life, I subscribe myself, etc."

VI. Lee to Grant, *April* 9. "I received your note this morning on the picket-line, whither I had come to meet you, and ascertain definitely what terms were embraced in your proposal of yesterday with reference to the surrender of this army. I now ask an interview in accordance with the offer contained in your letter of yesterday for that purpose."

VII. Grant to Lee, *April* 9. "Your note of this date is but this moment, 11 50 A.M., received. In consequence of my having passed from the Richmond and Lynchburg Road to the Farmville and Lynchburg Road, I am at this writing about four miles west of Walter's Church, and will push forward to the front for the purpose of meeting you. Notice sent to me on this road where you wish the interview to take place will meet me."

VIII. Grant to Lee, *April* 9. "In accordance with the substance of my letter to you of the 8th instant, I propose to receive the surrender of the Army of Northern Virginia upon the following terms, to wit: Rolls of all the officers and men to be made in duplicate, one copy to be given to me, the other to be retained by such officers as you may designate. The officers to give their individual paroles not to take up arms against the government of the United States until properly exchanged, and each company or regimental officer to sign a like parole for the men of their commands. The arms, artillery, and public property to be parked and stacked, and turned over to the officers appointed by me to receive them. This will not embrace the side-arms of the officers, nor their private horses or baggage. This done, each officer and man will be allowed to return to their homes, not to be disturbed by the United States authority so long as they observe their paroles and the laws where they may reside."

IX. Lee to Grant, *April* 9. "I received your letter of this date, containing the terms of the surrender of the Army of Northern Virginia as proposed by you. As they are substantially the same as those expressed in your letter of the 8th instant, they are accepted. I will proceed to designate the proper officers to carry the stipulations into effect."

The last two documents, though put in the form of letters, the former dated at "Appomattox Court-house," the latter at the "Headquarters Army of Northern Virginia," were drawn up and signed by Grant and Lee at their meeting at McLean's residence, near the Court-house.

The paroles were in the following form:

"We, the undersigned, prisoners of war belonging to the Army of Northern Virginia, having been this day surrendered by General R. A. Lee, commanding the said army, to Lieutenant General Grant, commanding the armies of the United States [in the officers' parole for the men the reading was, I, the undersigned, commanding ——, do, for the within-named prisoners of war this day surrendered, etc., give my solemn parole of honor that the within-named shall not], will not hereafter serve in the armies of the Confederate States, or in any military capacity whatever [in parole for privates, In military or any capacity whatever] against the United States of America, or render aid to the enemies of the latter, until properly exchanged in such manner as shall be mutually approved by the respective authorities."

This parole was countersigned by the provost-marshal: "The above officer or officers [in the parole for privates, the within-named] will not be disturbed by the United States authorities so long as they observe their parole and the laws in force where they may reside."

Lee's formal parting address to his army, issued on the 10th, the day following the surrender, was as follows:

"After four years of arduous service, marked by unsurpassed courage and fortitude, the Army of Northern Virginia has been compelled to yield to overwhelming numbers and resources. I need not tell the survivors of so many hard-fought battles, who have remained steadfast to the last, that I have consented to this result from no distrust of them; but feeling that valor and devotion could accomplish nothing that would compensate for the loss that would have attended the continuation of the contest, I have determined to avoid the useless sacrifice of those whose past services have endeared them to their countrymen. By the terms of the agreement, officers and men can return to their homes, and remain there until exchanged. You will take with you the satisfaction that proceeds from the consciousness of duty faithfully performed; and I earnestly pray that a merciful God will extend to you His blessing and protection. With an unceasing admiration of your constancy and devotion to your country, and a grateful remembrance of your kind and generous consideration of myself, I bid you an affectionate farewell."

THE LAST SHOT.

EDMUND RUFFIN.

when an army laid down its arms—the vanquished general courteously delivering his sword to the victor, to be as courteously returned to him. Neither Lee nor Grant even appeared on the scene. Gibbon's infantry and McKenzie's cavalry, of Ord's command, with the Fifth Corps—the victors of Five Forks, now under Griffin—remained at Appomattox Court-house to take charge of the surrendered property. The remainder of the army marched back to Burkesville, for it seemed that one more blow might have to be struck, whereby Johnston's army should share the fate of that of Lee. Sheridan with his cavalry, and an infantry corps, Wright's being chosen, was to march to aid Sherman. They had fairly started on the way when tidings came that Johnston had surrendered to Sherman.

Meanwhile the commissioners appointed by Grant and Lee had been busily at work making out the list of prisoners to be paroled. Their work was completed on the 11th, and on the next day the Confederate Army of Northern Virginia had its last formal parade. It marched to the place appointed, stacked its arms, and piled up its accoutrements. The list of paroled prisoners contained 27,805 names, but of these scarcely 8000 had arms in their hands. Thirty cannon and three hundred and fifty wagons were turned over. These comprised all the material and munitions left to this Confederate army. A week before it had set out on its retreat with fully two hundred cannon and more than a thousand wagons, bearing ammunition and material, all save food, sufficient for an army of 100,000 men.

The military history of the Confederacy covers exactly four years. On the 9th of April, 1861, the Confederate commissioners, in view of the pro-

posed provisioning of Fort Sumter, formally announced to the government of the United States that this could not be accomplished without the effusion of blood; and that they, "in behalf of their government and their people, accept the gage of battle thus thrown down to them."[1] On the 9th of April, 1865, Lee signed the surrender to Grant. On the 12th of April, 1861, fire was opened upon Fort Sumter by Edmund Ruffin, a Virginian of threescore and ten, who asked permission thus to open the war. On the 12th of April, 1865—just four years to a day—the army of Northern Virginia laid down its arms and dispersed, thereby in effect formally closing the war. A few weeks later Ruffin committed suicide, leaving behind him a memorandum that he preferred to die rather than to live under the government of the United States.

There was to be one more formal review of Confederates in Virginia. For two years there had been a band of partisans under Mosby, operating in Northeastern Virginia. It consisted at the outset of only a few score men, but gradually accumulated to a considerable force. They received no pay, but were allowed to keep all the plunder which they could secure, and this formed an inducement for many reckless individuals to join the band. They were kept in subjection by their leader by the understanding that for any failure in obedience they would be sent to the regular army, which was "regarded in the light of a Botany Bay."[2] Even after the complete annihilation of Early's command, they managed to maintain themselves in the valley east of the Blue Ridge. Their depredations became so annoying that one of the last acts of Sheridan in the Department of Washington was to order[3] the complete devastation of the region in which they operated. All forage and subsistence was to be destroyed, all barns and mills burnt, and all stock driven off; no buildings, however, were to be burnt, and no personal violence offered to citizens. "The ultimate result of the system of guerrilla warfare," said Sheridan, "is the total destruction of all private rights in the country occupied by such parties. This destruction may as well commence at once, and the responsibility of it must rest upon the authorities at Richmond, who have acknowledged the legitimacy of guerrilla bands."[4] This band, at the time of Lee's surrender, numbered about 600 men, all well mounted. On the 15th of April, having been informed of the surrender of Lee, Mosby wrote to Hancock, then commanding this department, that, while he thought there had not arisen any emergency which would justify the surrender of his men, he was yet indisposed "to cause the useless effusion of blood, or to inflict on a war-worn population any unnecessary distress." He therefore proposed an armistice until he could communicate with his own authorities, and obtain sufficient information to determine his farther action. Hancock replied that he might have reasonable time, but that he could not communicate with Lee, who was no longer in command. Grant, having been communicated with, directed Hancock: "You may receive all rebel officers and soldiers who surrender to you on exactly the same terms that were given to General Lee, except have it distinctly understood that all who claim homes in states that never passed ordinances of secession have forfeited them, and can only return on compliance with the amnesty proclamation. Maryland, Kentucky, Delaware, and Missouri are such states. They may return to West Virginia on their parole." On the 21st of April Mosby assembled his band for their last review. "I have," he said, "summoned you together for the last time. The vision that we cherished of a free and independent country has vanished, and that country is now the spoil of the conqueror. I disband your organization in preference to surrendering to our enemies. I am no longer your commander."[5]

[1] Ante, p. 52.   [2] Scott's Partisan Life with Mosby, 395.   [3] November 27, 1864.   [4] Sheridan's Report, 47.   [5] Partisan Life with Mosby, 476.

THE LAST REVIEW.

CHAPTER LVIII.

JOHNSTON'S SURRENDER.

Sherman's Preparations for an advance on Raleigh.—Contemporaneous Events.—Change of Plan after the Capture of Richmond.—Johnston retreats Westward.—Sherman enters Raleigh.—Johnston puzzled.—He inquires of Sherman as to Terms of Surrender.—The Reply.—Sherman's Letters to Grant.—Conference with Johnston, April 17th.—The Latter explains his Situation.—He offers, on favorable Terms, to surrender all the remaining Confederate Armies.—Conference renewed on the 18th.—Semi-political Nature of the Conversation.—Breckinridge admitted to the Conference.—Reagan's Memorandum ruled out.—Sherman pens one of his own.—"Glittering Generalities."—Substance of the Memorandum.—Sherman's Position in the Matter.—Letters to Washington.—The Cabinet Meeting.—Rejection of the Memorandum.—Grant goes to Morehead City.—His Consideration for Sherman.—Johnston's Surrender.—Secretary Stanton's Telegrams.—Injustice to Sherman.—Halleck's Interference.—Sherman's Indignation.—Surrender of Taylor and Kirby Smith.—The End of the War.

AT the close of March, 1865, Sherman's army was being reorganized at Goldsborough, and awaiting the repair of railroads and the accumulation of supplies and clothing preliminary to an advance against General Johnston, who then covered Raleigh with an army of over 40,000 men. The Twenty-third and Tenth corps were united under the designation of the Army of the Ohio. Slocum's command was now styled the Army of Georgia, while Howard's retained its former title. Wilson's and Stoneman's expeditions were in full and successful operation, and General Canby was investing the defenses of Mobile.

Sherman's preparations could not be completed before the 10th of April. In the mean time Mobile had fallen; Selma had been occupied by Wilson, who was fast approaching Montgomery; Stoneman had broken up the railroad west of Lynchburg, and had pushed down to the Catawba River, in North Carolina, destroying the railroad through Greensborough and Salisbury; Richmond and Petersburg had been abandoned, and the Confederate Army of Northern Virginia had been routed and captured.

Tidings of the battles about Petersburg reached Sherman on the 6th. Up to this time Sherman's plan was to make a feint on Raleigh, cross the Roanoke, and, securing by the Chowan River communication with Norfolk as a base of supplies, to strike for Burkesville, interposing between Johnston and Lee. But the Army of the Potomac, under General Grant's leadership, had eliminated Lee's army from the problem to be solved. This led General Sherman to change his plan. On the 5th Grant warned him that Lee would attempt to reach Danville, and urged an immediate movement against Johnston. "Rebel armies now," he writes, "are the only strategic points to strike at." Instead of making a feint on Raleigh, Sherman, on the 11th, made a real movement on that place. Hearing of Lee's surrender in the mean time, Johnston had retreated westward, and on the morning of the 13th Sherman's army entered the capital of North Carolina.

Johnston had but a single line of retreat left—that by Greensborough and Charlotte. Of course it was folly for him to venture a battle with Sherman. He could not retreat as an organized army. He had therefore to choose between the surrender and the disbandment of his forces. The consequence of the latter step would be to let loose upon the citizens of North Carolina 40,000 men with arms in their hands, who would inaugurate a reign of terror. Johnston looked upon farther opposition as criminal. But how to dispose of his army was a perplexing problem. Lee's army had been defeated on the field of battle—in effect, it had been actually surrounded and captured, and in this case no such considerations had been involved as now presented themselves to Johnston. To the army of the latter escape was possible by disorganization; it had not been defeated or surrounded. The same considerations applied with equal force to Dick Taylor's and Kirby Smith's armies. As soon as it was fully realized that farther resistance was hopeless, immediate disorganization would follow, and the Confederate armies would resolve themselves into armed bands of lawless, irresponsible marauders, scattered over the entire South, unless some motive was offered sufficient to hold these armies until they could be paroled and disarmed.

Sherman had taken measures to cut off Johnston's retreat southward when, on the 14th, he received by flag of truce a letter from the Confederate commander, asking an armistice, and information as to the best terms on which he would be permitted to surrender his army. Sherman replied that he was willing to confer with him as to the terms of surrender, and added: "That a basis of action may be had, I undertake to abide by the same terms and conditions entered into by Generals Grant and Lee at Appomattox Court-house, Virginia, on the 9th instant." Arrangements were made for a conference on the 17th.

Up to this time Sherman had entertained no other terms of surrender than those proposed by Grant in the case of Lee's army. After Lee's surrender, he wrote to the lieutenant general: "The terms you have given Lee are magnanimous and liberal. Should Johnston follow Lee's example, I shall, of course, grant the same." The very day after he had agreed to meet and confer with Johnston, he again wrote: "I will grant the same terms as General Grant gave General Lee, and be careful not to complicate any points of civil policy."

During the interval between the first correspondence between Sherman and Johnston and their meeting on the 17th, no movement was made by either army.[1] At noon of the day appointed, the two generals met at a house five miles from Durham Station under a flag of truce. They had never met before in person, though for two years they confronted each other on

many battle-fields. The interview, says Sherman, was frank and soldier-like. Johnston freely acknowledged that the war was at an end, and that every sacrifice of life after Lee's surrender was simply murder. He admitted that the terms conceded to Lee were magnanimous. He had no right to ask any better conditions for himself. But the situation of his army was peculiar. The sudden revelation of the hopelessness of farther resistance was likely to operate on the fears and anxieties of his soldiers. The consequence would be to relax military restraint. He therefore asked that some general concessions might be made which would enable him to maintain his control over his troops until they could be got back to the neighborhood of their homes. He suggested, also, that the proposition agreed upon should extend to all the Confederate armies then existing. Sherman asked Johnston what authority he had as to the armies beyond his own command. Johnston admitted he had no such power, but thought he could obtain it. He did not know where Davis was, but he could find Breckinridge—the Confederate Secretary of War—whose orders would be every where respected. It was then agreed to postpone the farther consideration of the subject till noon on the next day.

Sherman returned to Raleigh and conferred with his general officers, every one of whom pronounced in favor of a conclusion of the war upon terms which seemed so favorable, and which involved no sacrifice of the national honor.

The conference with Johnston was renewed on the 18th. The territory within the immediate command of Johnston comprised the states of North and South Carolina, Georgia, and Florida. He was now able to satisfy Sherman of his power to disband also the armies in Alabama, Mississippi, Louisiana, and Texas. He then asked Sherman what he was willing to do. Sherman replied that he could only deal with belligerents—that no military man could go beyond that. He was willing to make terms for the Confederate soldiers in accordance with President Lincoln's amnesty proclamation; that is, all of the rank of colonel and under should have pardon upon condition of taking the oath of allegiance to the United States. He was also willing to go farther than this—he would grant what had been conceded to Lee's army, that *every* officer and soldier who would return home, observe his parole and obey the laws, should be free from disturbance by United States authority. But Johnston did not seem to be quite satisfied. He expressed great solicitude lest the Southern States should be dismembered, and denied representation in Congress or any separate political existence; also, lest the absolute disarming of his men might leave the South powerless, and exposed to the depredations of assassins and robbers. Sherman listened with great courtesy to all this, which both commanders equally well knew lay outside the scope of a military surrender. In reply, he simply expressed his own personal assurance that if the Southern people submitted to the lawful authority of the nation, as defined by the Constitution, the courts, and the authorities of the United States, supported by the courts, there would be no occasion for solicitude; they would "regain their position as citizens of the United States, free and equal in all respects."

While the conversation was thus drifting off from the main question, Johnston suggested that Breckinridge be allowed to come in. Sherman was never fond of politicians, and had very good reasons for not being partial to this one in particular. He reminded Johnston that it had been agreed that the negotiation must be confined to belligerents. Johnston replied that he understood that perfectly. "But," said he, "Breckinridge, whom you do not know, save by public rumor, as the secretary of state, is, in fact, a major general. Have you any objection to his being present as a major general?" Sherman then consented, and Breckinridge came in; and though it was understood that he was only present as a part of Johnston's personal staff, he joined in the conversation. Soon a courier entered and handed Johnston a package of papers, over which he and Breckinridge held a conversation, and then put the papers in their pockets. One of these was a memorandum, written, as Johnston told Sherman, by the Confederate Post-master General Reagan. It was preceded by a preamble, and concluded with some general terms. Sherman read it, and, being the court in this case, ruled it out.

The conversation then became general, touching upon slavery, which was acknowledged "to be as dead as any thing can be," and upon reconstruction. Then it occurred to General Sherman—possibly it may have been suggested by Reagan's document—to write out a memorandum consisting of some general propositions, meaning little or much, according to the construction of parties, and send them to Washington for the assent or rejection of the government. No delay would result from this, as he would be obliged to communicate with his government in any case, in order to obtain authority by which he could receive the surrender of armies beyond the limits of his proper department.

These propositions Sherman himself calls "glittering generalities." The following is the substance of the memorandum:

The contending armies were to remain as they then were, but the armistice would cease forty-eight hours after a notice to that effect should be given by either commander to the other. All the Confederate armies were to be disbanded and conducted to their several state capitals, where their arms were to be deposited in the state arsenal, subject to the control of the general government. There, also, each officer and man was to be paroled. The several state governments of the South were to be recognized by the President on their officers and Legislatures taking the oath prescribed by the Constitution of the United States. The people of these states were to be guaranteed their political rights and franchise, and their rights of person and property, as defined by federal and state Constitutions. They were not to be disturbed so long as they lived peaceably and obeyed the laws. The war was to cease, and a general amnesty to be granted, on condition of the

---

[1] "I was both willing and anxious thus to consume a few days, as it would enable Colonel Wright to finish our railroad to Raleigh. Two bridges had to be built, and 12 miles of new road made. We had no iron except by taking up that on the branch from Goldsborough to Weldon. Instead of losing time, I gained in every way, for every hour of delay possible was required to reconstruct the railroad to our rear, and improve the condition of our wagon roads to the front, so desirable in case the negotiations failed, and we be forced to make the race of near 200 miles to head off or catch Johnston, then retreating toward Charlotte."—Sherman's Report.

disbandment and disarmament of the Confederate armies, and the resumption by the soldiers of their peaceful pursuits.

This memorandum was signed by Generals Johnston and Sherman, who, recognizing their want of authority to carry its terms into effect, pledged themselves to promptly obtain such authority, and to endeavor to carry out the programme indicated.[1]

So far as Sherman allowed himself to take a political view of the crisis then upon the nation, this memorandum doubtless expressed, though somewhat crudely, his real sentiments. He said, some time afterward, "I stand by the memorandum." He put his signature to the document meaning thereby to give to its propositions all the sanction he could. He had hastily penned the memorandum. The act was wholly due to the suggestion of a moment; it had not been the subject of an hour's deliberation. From the beginning of the conference he had steadily resisted the encroachment of politics upon the negotiation for surrender. He would have persisted in this resistance if Johnston's army alone had been concerned. But Johnston had made a proposition for the surrender of all the Confederate armies from the Roanoke to the Rio Grande. This proposition Sherman would have rejected at once if it had not been backed by authority which seemed to him sufficient, or if it could possibly have been intended as a ruse on the part of the enemy to gain time. He had neither motive for its rejection. He was confident that the authority supporting the proposition would be respected by every Confederate soldier, and he was equally confident of its sincerity. It was, moreover, a proposition which, from its very terms, was not made to him, but through him to the United States government. Its rejection by him without reference to the government, and without a sufficient military motive, would have been as clearly a usurpation of authority as its acceptance would have been without such reference.

But why not submit the proposition to the government in the simplest terms and unaccompanied by the memorandum? Simply because the proposition was not thus submitted to him. Johnston had admitted that the terms granted to Lee's army were sufficiently magnanimous, but had begged that some official assurance might be given by the general government in regard to its future treatment of Southern citizens. Some general concessions were asked which might prevent the Confederate soldiers from resorting to a species of guerrilla warfare, from which the people of the South must suffer heavily. It must be remembered, also, that from Kentucky almost to Virginia, General Sherman was the military commander of the South, and that from the first the regulation of civil affairs had, in a large measure, been committed to military commanders within their several departments. The consideration of civil affairs—the regulation of trade, of the affairs of freedmen, of municipal government—was a part of the manifold duties of department commanders. On two previous occasions—in a letter to the mayor of Atlanta, and subsequently in a communication addressed to a citizen of Savannah—General Sherman had expressed his sentiments as to the policy which would be adopted by the government upon the return of the South to its allegiance. "Both these letters," says Sherman, "asserted my belief that, according to Mr. Lincoln's proclamations and messages, when the people of the South had laid down their arms and submitted to the lawful power of the United States, *ipso facto*, the war was over as to them; and furthermore, that if any state in rebellion would conform to the Constitution of the United States, 'cease war,' elect senators and representatives to Congress, if admitted (of which each house of Congress alone is the judge), that state becomes *instanter* as much in the Union as New York or Ohio. Nor was I rebuked for these expressions, though it was universally known and commented on at the time. And again, Mr. Stanton in person, at Savannah, speaking of the terrific expense of the war, and difficulty of realizing the money necessary for the daily wants of the government, impressed me most forcibly with the necessity of bringing the war to a close as soon as possible for *financial reasons*."

Some memorandum must accompany the submission of Johnston's proposition, in order that the government might understand what concessions were expected: once before the government, this basis might be modified, entirely changed, or rejected altogether. There was nothing final, nothing in the nature of an *ultimatum* about the memorandum.

In the midst of the negotiations with Johnston, Sherman had heard of the murder of the President, but saw in that event no reason to modify these negotiations. In that respect it probably had no more influence over him than did the information received from General Halleck that a man by the name of Clark had been detailed for his own assassination.[1]

Major Hitchcock, an officer on Sherman's staff, proceeded to Washington to lay the memorandum before President Johnson. No moment could have been more unfavorable for the consideration of concessions to be granted to rebels than that which witnessed Major Hitchcock's arrival at Washington. The country was buried in a sea of sorrow—a sea which, while it moaned in hopeless regret for one lost, whose need was now felt more than ever before, boiled also with indignation against the spirit of treason which had impelled the assassin's blow. It was, perhaps, too much to be expected of our poor human nature that President Johnson and his cabinet, meeting under these circumstances, would consider fairly and calmly the propositions submitted by Sherman. The document was read, and every word was listened to very much as if it had been a proclamation of pardon to Booth and his fellow-conspirators. Sherman, the scourge, with the fire and the sword, was the man for that moment, not Sherman, the liberal-minded soldier, who disdained to strike a fallen foe. No one seemed able to preserve calmness save Lieutenant General Grant, who was present at the meeting, and who, while he disapproved of the propositions submitted, was not willing to denounce his brother commander.

General Grant offered to go in person to Raleigh, and notify Sherman of the disapproval of the memorandum by the government. He arrived at Morehead City on the evening of the 23d, and from that point communicated with General Sherman. The latter gave Johnston notice of the close of the armistice, informed him of the fate of their agreement, and demanded the surrender of his army on the same terms which had been granted to General Lee. On the 26th Johnston complied with this demand.[2] So great confidence had General Grant in Sherman's ability to manage his own command, that, during these final negotiations, Johnston was not aware of his presence at Raleigh.

---

[1] The following is a copy of the memorandum in full:

"*Memorandum, or Basis of Agreement, made this, the* 18*th day of April, A.D.* 1865, *near Durham's Station, in the State of North Carolina, by and between General Joseph E. Johnston, commanding the Confederate Army, and Major General W. T. Sherman, commanding the Army of the United States, both present.*

"I. The contending armies now in the field to maintain the *status quo* until notice is given by the commanding general of any one to his opponent, and reasonable time, say forty-eight hours, allowed.

"II. The Confederate armies now in existence to be disbanded and conducted to their several state capitals, there to deposit their arms and public property in the state arsenal; and each officer and man to execute and file an agreement to cease from acts of war, and to abide the action of both state and federal authorities. The number of arms and munitions of war to be reported to the chief of ordnance at Washington City, subject to the future action of the Congress of the United States, and in the mean time to be used solely to maintain peace and order within the borders of the states respectively.

"III. The recognition by the executive of the United States of the several state governments, on their officers and Legislatures taking the oath prescribed by the Constitution of the United States; and where conflicting state governments have resulted from the war, the legitimacy of all shall be submitted to the Supreme Court of the United States.

"IV. The re-establishment of all federal courts in the several states, with powers as defined by the Constitution and laws of Congress.

"V. The people and inhabitants of all states to be guaranteed, so far as the executive can, their political rights and franchise, as well as their rights of person and property, as defined by the Constitution of the United States and of the states respectively.

"VI. The executive authority or government of the United States not to disturb any of the people by reason of the late war, so long as they live in peace and quiet, and abstain from acts of armed hostility, and obey the laws in existence at the place of their residence.

"VII. In general terms, it is announced that the war is to cease; a general amnesty, so far as the executive of the United States can command, on condition of the disbandment of the Confederate armies, the distribution of arms, and the resumption of peaceful pursuits by officers and men hitherto composing said armies.

"Not being fully empowered by our respective principals to fulfill these terms, we individually and officially pledge ourselves to promptly obtain authority, and will endeavor to carry out the above programme."

[1] The following letters were written by General Sherman on the 18th to Washington—the first to accompany the memorandum, and the second having reference to President Lincoln's assassination:

No. 1.

"Headquarters Middle Department of the Mississippi, in the Field, Raleigh, N. C., April 18, 1865.

"To Lieutenant General U. S. GRANT, or Major General HALLECK, Washington, D. C.:

"GENERAL,—I inclose herewith a copy of an agreement made this day between General Joseph E. Johnston and myself, which, if approved by the President of the United States, will produce peace from the Potomac to the Rio Grande. Mr. Breckinridge was present at the conference in the capacity of a major general, and satisfied me of the ability of General Johnston to carry out to the full extent the terms of this agreement; and if you will get the President to simply indorse the copy, and commission me to carry out the terms, I will follow them to the conclusion. You will observe that it is an absolute submission of the enemy to the lawful authorities of the United States, and disperses his armies absolutely; and the point to which I attach most importance is, that the disposition and dispersement of the armies is done in such a manner as to prevent them breaking up into a guerrilla crew. On the other hand, we can retain just as much of an army as we please. I agree to the mode and manner of the surrender of armies set forth, as it gives the states the means of suppressing guerrillas, which we could not expect them to do if we strip them of all arms.

"Both Generals Johnston and Breckinridge admitted that slavery was dead, and I could not insist on embracing it in such a paper, because it can be made with the states in detail. I know that all the men of substance South sincerely want peace, and I do not believe they will resort to war again during this century. I have no doubt but that they will in the future be perfectly subordinate to the laws of the United States. The moment my action in this matter is approved, I can spare five corps, and will ask for and leave General Schofield here with the Tenth Corps, and go myself with the Fourteenth, Fifteenth, Seventeenth, Twentieth, and Twenty-third Corps, *via* Burkesville and Gordonsville, to Frederick or Hagerstown, there to be paid and mustered out.

"The question of finance is now the chief one, and every soldier and officer not needed ought to go home at once. I would like to be able to begin the march north by May 1st.

"I urge on the part of the President speedy action, as it is important to get the Confederate armies to their homes, as well as our own. I am, with great respect, your obedient servant,

"W. T. SHERMAN, Major General Commanding."

No. 2.

"Headquarters Military Department of the Mississippi, in the Field, Raleigh, N. C., April 18, 1865.

"General H. W. HALLECK, Chief of Staff, Washington, D. C.:

"GENERAL,—I received your dispatch describing the man Clark detailed to assassinate me. He had better be in a hurry or he will be too late. The news of Mr. Lincoln's death produced a most intense effect on our troops. At first I feared it would lead to excesses, but now it has softened down, and can easily be quieted. None evince more feeling than General Johnston, who admitted that the act was calculated to stain his cause with a dark hue; and he contended that the loss was most severe on the South, who had begun to realize that Mr. Lincoln was the best friend the South had.

"I can not believe that even Mr. Davis was privy to the diabolical plot, but think it the emanation of a lot of young men of the South, who are very devils. I want to throw upon the South the care of this class of men, who will soon be as obnoxious to their industrious class as to us.

"Had I pushed Johnston's army to an extremity, it would have dispersed and done infinite mischief. Johnston informed me that General Stoneman had been at Salisbury, and was now about Statesville. I have sent him orders to come to me.

"General Johnston also informed me that General Wilson was at Columbus, Ga., and he wanted me to arrest his progress. I leave that to you. Indeed, if the President sanctions my agreement with Johnston, our interest is to cease all destruction. Please give all orders necessary, according to the views the executive may take, and inform him, if possible, not to vary the terms at all, for I have considered every thing, and believe that the Confederate armies are dispersed. We can adjust all else fairly and well. I am yours, etc.,

"W. T. SHERMAN, Major General Commanding."

[2] "*Terms of a Military Convention entered into this twenty-sixth* (26*th*) *day of April*, 1865, *at Bennett's House, near Durham's Station, North Carolina, between General Joseph E. Johnston, commanding the Confederate Army, and Major General W. T. Sherman, commanding the United States Army in North Carolina.*

"All acts of war on the part of the troops under General Johnston's command to cease from this date. All arms and public property to be deposited at Greensborough, and delivered to an ordnance officer of the United States army. Rolls of all officers and men to be made in duplicate, one copy to be retained by the commander of the troops, and the other to be given to an officer to be designated by General Sherman. Each officer and man to give his individual obligation in writing not to take up arms against the government of the United States until properly released from this obligation. The side-arms of officers, and their private horses and baggage, to be retained by them.

"This being done, all the officers and men will be permitted to return to their homes, not to be disturbed by the United States authorities so long as they observe their obligations and the laws in force where they may reside.

"W. T. SHERMAN, Major General Commanding the Army of the United "States in North Carolina.

"J. E. JOHNSTON, General Commanding Confederate States Army in "North Carolina.

"Approved: U. S. GRANT, Lieutenant General.

"Raleigh, N. C., April 26, 1865."

JAMES BENNET'S HOUSE, WHERE JOHNSTON SURRENDERED.

The fact that only about 30,000 men and some 10,000 small-arms were included in the surrender shows that Johnston's apprehensions as to the scattering of his command were well founded.

The conduct of the lieutenant general in this affair between the government and Sherman was noble and characteristic. Unfortunately, some of the officers in the cabinet, in their treatment of General Sherman in this connection, were neither just nor generous. It was perfectly proper for the government to reject the basis of agreement between Sherman and Johnston. But the very reasons given for this repudiation, and which must have been published by official authority, the terms of the memorandum not having yet been made public, cast reflections upon General Sherman's patriotism. These reasons were thus reported in the newspapers of April 22d:

"1st. It was an exercise of authority not vested in General Sherman, and on its face shows that both he and Johnston knew that General Sherman had no authority to enter into any such arrangement.

"2d. It was an acknowledgment of the rebel government.

"3d. It is understood to re-establish rebel state governments that had been overthrown at the sacrifice of many thousands of loyal lives and immense treasure, and placed arms and munitions of war in the hands of rebels, at their respective capitals, which might be used as soon as the armies of the United States were disbanded, and used to conquer and subdue loyal states.

"4th. By the restoration of the rebel authority in their respective states, they would be enabled to re-establish slavery.

"5th. It might furnish a ground of responsibility, by the federal government, to pay the rebel debt, and certainly subjects loyal citizens of the rebel states to debts contracted by rebels in the name of the states.

"6th. It put in dispute the existence of loyal state governments, and the new State of Western Virginia, which had been recognized by every department of the United States government.

"7th. It practically abolished the confiscation laws, and relieved rebels of every degree who had slaughtered our people from all pains and penalties for their crimes.

"8th. It gave terms that had been deliberately, repeatedly, and solemnly rejected by President Lincoln, and better terms than the rebels had ever asked in their most prosperous condition.

"9th. It formed no basis of true and lasting peace, but relieved the rebels from the pressure of our victories, and left them in condition to renew their effort to overthrow the United States government, and subdue the loyal states, whenever their strength was recruited, and any opportunity should offer."

In the first place, the people were led to suppose that Sherman had actually usurped authority, which was not the case. The assertion that the memorandum in any way recognized the Confederate government was entirely without foundation. Nor did the memorandum re-establish Confederate state governments except in the same way that President Lincoln had re-established the state government of Virginia.[1] Indeed, Sherman had in-

troduced this feature into his memorandum on the basis of President Lincoln's action in the case of Virginia. It was not until after the rejection of his own scheme that he heard that the invitation accorded to the Virginia Legislature had been retracted.

Again, the arms to be deposited in the state capitals were subject to the control of the United States, and it could only be through the fault of the government that they could be used in another rebellion.

There was not a word or phrase in the memorandum that indicated by the remotest suggestion the liability of the United States for the Confederate debt, or any thing which might be a basis for such liability. Nor did it acknowledge the legitimacy of the obligations of that debt as binding upon the citizens of the states which had incurred it. The recognition of the state governments in no way legalized their contracts made during the rebellion any more than it sanctioned their repudiation of debts due to Northern citizens.

Instead of putting in dispute the existence of West Virginia, the memorandum left that matter to be settled by proper authority. Nor was the Confiscation Bill passed by Congress in any way touched by the guarantee of the rights of person and property to Southern citizens, so far as such guarantee could be given by the executive, for the President is bound to execute the laws of Congress. It relieved no one of the penalty of their crimes any farther than Grant's terms with Lee had done.

The assertion that the memorandum was contrary to the policy of President Lincoln was so far from being true, that it was exactly false in every particular. And President Johnston's subsequent policy of reconstruction is a curious comment on his rejection of Sherman's memorandum.

The final reason given is simply absurd. If the memorandum left the Confederate armies in a favorable situation for a renewal of the war, pray where did it find those armies? It certainly did not increase their efficiency

they attempt it, give them permission and protection, until, if at all, they attempt some action hostile to the United States, in which case you will notify them, give them reasonable time to leave, and at the end of which time arrest any who remain. Allow Judge Campbell to see this, but do not make it public."

Thus authorized, General Weitzel approved a call for the meeting of the Virginia Legislature. This was after Lee's surrender. The call approved by General Weitzel read thus:

"The undersigned, members of the Legislature of the State of Virginia, in connection with a number of citizens of the state, whose names are attached to this paper, in view of the evacuation of the city of Richmond by the Confederate government and its occupation by the military authorities of the United States, the surrender of the Army of Northern Virginia, and the suspension of the jurisdiction of the civil power of the state, are of the opinion that an immediate meeting of the General Assembly of the state is called for by the exigencies of the situation. The consent of the military authorities of the United States to a session of the Legislature of Richmond, in connection with the governor and lieutenant governor, to their free deliberation upon the public affairs, and to the ingress and departure of all its members under safe-conduct, has been obtained.

"The United States authorities will afford transportation from any point under their control to any of the persons before mentioned.

"The matters to be submitted to the Legislature are the restoration of peace to the State of Virginia, and the adjustment of the questions involving life, liberty, and property, that have arisen in the state as a consequence of war.

"We therefore earnestly request the governor, lieutenant governor, and members of the Legislature to repair to this city by the 25th of April, instant.

"We understand that full protection to persons and property will be afforded in the state, and we recommend to peaceful citizens to remain at their homes and pursue their usual avocations with confidence that they will not be interrupted.

"We earnestly solicit the attendance in Richmond, on or before the 25th of April, instant, of the following persons, citizens of Virginia, to confer with us as to the best means of restoring peace to the State of Virginia. We have secured safe-conduct from the military authorities of the United States for them to enter the city and depart without molestation."

---

[1] On the 6th of April (three days before Lee's surrender), President Lincoln wrote to General Weitzel: "It has been intimated to me that the gentlemen who have acted as the Legislature of Virginia in support of the rebellion, may now desire to assemble at Richmond and take measures to withdraw the Virginia troops and other support from resistance to the general government. If

JOHNSTON'S SURRENDER.

by disbanding them, sending them home, and rendering their arms subject to the disposition of the United States.

The memorandum ought to have been rejected, on the ground that the subject of reconstruction could not be settled except by the deliberate action of the executive and Congress, and should not, therefore, be introduced in connection with the surrender of the Confederate armies. But the reasons for its rejection which were published then by official sanction not only had no validity, but almost seem to have been chosen for publication because of their reflections upon General Sherman.

On the same day that these reasons were published, Secretary Stanton telegraphed to General Dix:

"Yesterday evening a bearer of dispatches arrived here from General Sherman. An agreement for a suspension of hostilities, and a memorandum of what is called 'a basis of peace,' had been entered into on the 18th instant by General Sherman with the rebel General Johnston, the rebel General Breckinridge being present at the conference.

"A cabinet meeting was held at 8 o'clock in the evening, at which the action of General Sherman was disapproved by the President, by the Secretary of War, by General Grant, and by every member of the cabinet. General Sherman was ordered to resume hostilities immediately, and he was directed that the instructions given by the late president, in the following telegram, which was penned by Mr. Lincoln himself, at the Capitol, on the night of the 3d of March, were approved by President Andrew Johnson, and were reiterated to govern the action of military commanders.

"On the night of the 3d of March, while President Lincoln and his cabinet were at the Capitol, a telegram from General Grant was brought to the Secretary of War, informing him that General Lee had asked for a conference to make arrangements for terms of peace. The letter of General Lee was published in a message of Davis to the rebel Congress. General Grant's telegram was submitted to Mr. Lincoln, who, after pondering a few minutes, took up his pen, and wrote with his own hand the following reply, which he submitted to the Secretary of State and the Secretary of War. It was then dated, addressed, and signed by the Secretary of War, and telegraphed to General Grant:

"'Washington, March 3, 1865, 12 30 P.M.

"'Lieutenant General GRANT:

"'The President directs me to say to you that he wishes you to have no conference with General Lee, unless it be for the capitulation of General Lee's army, or some minor and purely military matters. He instructs me to say you are not to decide or confer upon any political questions. Such questions the President holds in his own hands, and will submit them to no military conference or conditions. Meantime you are to press to the utmost your military advantages. EDWIN M. STANTON, Secretary of War.'

"The orders of General Sherman to General Stoneman to withdraw from Salisbury and join him, will probably open the way for Davis to escape to Mexico or Europe with his plunder, which is reported to be very large, including not only the plunder of the Richmond banks, but previous accumulations. A dispatch received by this department from Richmond says:

"'It is stated here by respectable parties that the amount of specie taken south by Jefferson Davis and his partisans is very large, including not only the plunder of the Richmond banks, but previous accumulations. They hope, it is said, to make terms with Sherman, or some other Southern commander, by which they will be permitted, with their effects, including the gold plunder, to go to Mexico or Europe. Johnston's negotiations look to this end.'

"After the cabinet meeting last night, General Grant started for North Carolina, to direct future operations against Johnston's army."

This telegram was sent to General Dix for the purpose of publication. It would have been courteous in the secretary to have withheld this report until the circumstances under which Sherman had acted were more fully known. In the first place, it was implied, though not stated, that the same instructions had been received by Sherman which, on the 3d of March, had been addressed to the lieutenant general. This would naturally be inferred from the date of those instructions. Thus Sherman was somewhat cruelly exposed, for a time at least, to a suspicion of disobedience of orders. But Sherman had not received these instructions. The statement that Grant had gone to North Carolina to direct future operations against Johnston's army was also likely to be misunderstood. Grant had gone to Raleigh to communicate to General Sherman the action of the government in regard to the memorandum. Of course, if more than that was necessary, Grant would do more. As lieutenant general, he directed the operations of all the national armies. Any instructions from Secretary Stanton could give him no power which he had not before. But he never for a moment contemplated the necessity of interference with, or personal direction of, Sherman's movements—and, in fact, did not interfere or direct. Unfortunately, Stanton's dispatch implied, and was popularly understood to imply, that Grant's presence at Raleigh was necessary.

But the matter did not end here. On the 26th of April, General Halleck, then at Richmond in command of the Military Division of the James, dispatched to Secretary Stanton that he had ordered Generals Meade, Sheridan, and Wright to move into Sherman's proper department, and pay no regard to either the orders or truce of the latter. He also advised that Sherman's own subordinates should receive similar orders. The pretext given for moving into Sherman's department was "to cut off Johnston's retreat." Now Johnston was not retreating, and could not retreat if he would, on account of the disposition which Sherman had already made of his forces.

This dispatch also was sent by Stanton to Dix for publication. A few hours later the public was informed through the same channel that the Secretary of War had instructed General Thomas, and, through him, his subcommanders, to disregard Sherman's orders. These bulletins, succeeding each other with such rapidity, excited at once serious apprehension and a tumult of indignation. Every body read and wondered. What had Sherman been doing? Had he allied himself with traitors? Could he no longer be trusted? For a time some terrible danger was supposed to hang like the sword of Damocles over the republic. It did not seem possible that the government could itself thus excite popular apprehension without good reason. Where orders were given to violate a truce—an act punishable with death by the laws of war—certainly there must be some peril impending which could only thus be averted. For a brief period a storm of denunciation was directed against General Sherman. And while all this was going on in the North, it must be remembered that Sherman was accepting Johnston's surrender, and that not one word had been said or written to him indicating the displeasure of the government.[1] He received the announcement of the rejection of the memorandum with entire good feeling. He wrote to Stanton on the 25th admitting his "folly in embracing in a military convention any civil matters." He adds: "I had flattered myself that, by four years of patient, unremitting, and successful labor, I deserved no reminder such as is contained in the last paragraph of your letter to General Grant."[2] It was not until several days afterward that Sherman saw Stanton's bulletins, and then his indignation was aroused, especially against Halleck, with whom he refused to have any friendly intercourse.[3]

---

[1] The following were the instructions which Grant received from Stanton when he started for Raleigh, and which were there shown to General Sherman:

"GENERAL,—The memorandum or basis agreed upon between General Sherman and General Johnston having been submitted to the President, they are disapproved. You will give notice of the disapproval to General Sherman, and direct him to resume hostilities at the earliest moment.

"The instructions given to you by the late President, Abraham Lincoln, on the 3d of March, by my telegram of that date addressed to you, express substantially the views of President Andrew Johnson, and will be observed by General Sherman. A copy is herewith appended.

"The President desires that you proceed immediately to the headquarters of General Sherman, and direct operations against the enemy."

[2] See previous note.

[3] The following extract from General Sherman's report shows the manner in which he regarded the treatment which he had received:

"On the evening of the 2d of May I returned to Hilton Head, and there, for the first time, received the New York papers of April 28th, containing Secretary Stanton's dispatch of 9 A.M. of the 27th of April to General Dix, including General Halleck's, from Richmond, of 9 P.M. of the night before, which seems to have been rushed with extreme haste before an excited public, namely, morning of the 28th. You will observe from the dates that these dispatches were running back and forth from Richmond and Washington to New York, and there published, while General Grant and I were together in Raleigh, North Carolina, adjusting, to the best of our ability, the terms of surrender of the only remaining formidable rebel army in existence at the time east of the Mississippi River. Not one word of intimation had been sent to me of the displeasure of the government with my official conduct, but only the naked disapproval of a skeleton memorandum sent properly for the action of the President of the United States.

"The most objectionable features of my memorandum had already (April 24th) been published to the world in violation of official usage, and the contents of my accompanying letters to General Halleck, General Grant, and Mr. Stanton, of even date, though at hand, were suppressed.

"In all these letters I had stated clearly and distinctly that Johnston's army would *not* fight, but, if pushed, would 'disband' and 'scatter' into small and dangerous guerrilla parties, as injurious to the interests of the United States as to the rebels themselves; that all parties admitted that the rebel cause of the South was abandoned, that the negro was free, and that the temper of all was most favorable to a lasting peace. I say all these opinions of mine were withheld from the public with a seeming purpose; and I do contend that my official experience and former services, as well as my past life and familiarity with the people and geography of the South, entitled my opinions to at least a decent respect.

"Although this dispatch (Mr. Stanton's of April 27th) was printed 'official,' it had come to me only in the questionable newspaper paragraph headed 'Sherman's Truce Disregarded.'

"I had already done what General Wilson wanted me to do, namely, had sent him supplies of clothing and food, with clear and distinct orders and instructions how to carry out in Western Georgia the terms for the surrender of arms and paroling of prisoners made by General Johnston's capitulation of April 26th, and had properly and most opportunely ordered General Gillmore to occupy Orangeburg and Augusta, strategic points of great value at all times, in peace or war; but, as the secretary had taken upon himself to order my subordinate generals to disobey my 'orders,' I explained to General Gillmore that I would no longer confuse him or General Wilson with 'orders' that might conflict with those of the secretary, which, as reported, were sent, not through me, but in open disregard of me and of my lawful authority.

"It now becomes my duty to paint in justly severe character the still more offensive and dangerous matter of General Halleck's dispatch of April 26th to the Secretary of War, embodied in his to General Dix of April 27th.

"General Halleck had been chief of staff of the army at Washington, in which capacity he must have received my official letter of April 18th, wherein I wrote clearly that if Johnston's army about Greensborough were 'pushed,' it would 'disperse,' an event I wished to prevent. About that time he seems to have been sent from Washington to Richmond to command the new Military Division of the James, in assuming charge of which, on the 22d, he defines the limits of his authority to be the 'Department of Virginia, the Army of the Potomac, and such part of North Carolina as may not be occupied by the command of Major General Sherman.' (See his General Orders, No. 1.) Four days later, April 26th, he reports to the secretary that he has ordered Generals Meade, Sheridan, and Wright to invade that part of North Carolina which was occupied by my command, and pay 'no regard to any truce or orders of' mine. They were ordered to 'push forward, regardless of

SMALL-ARMS SURRENDERED BY JOHNSTON.

ACCOUTREMENTS SURRENDERED BY JOHNSTON.

The surrender of Johnston included all the Confederate forces east of the Chattahoochee River, numbering altogether about 50,000 men. On the 4th of May Dick Taylor surrendered to General Canby all the remaining Confederate forces east of the Mississippi. On the 26th of May Kirby Smith surrendered his army. The war was concluded.

CHAPTER LIX.

FLIGHT AND CAPTURE OF DAVIS.

A memorable Sabbath.—Davis receives a startling Message.—Richmond must be abandoned.—Panic in the City.—Davis, with his Cabinet, fly by night.—Incidents of the Journey.—Danville enjoys a brief Celebrity as the Capital of the Confederacy.—Semmes's Marine Guard.—Trenholm's Treasury Department.—Davis's Proclamation to his People.—Tidings of Lee's Surrender.—Evacuation of Danville.—The Flight resumed.—Interview with Johnston at Greensborough.—The Confederacy in a Railroad Car.—Dispersion of the Cabinet.—Flight through Georgia.—General Wilson's Arrangements for the Capture of Davis.—Harnden gets upon the Track of the Fugitives.—Close Pursuit.—Pritchard anticipates Harnden, and captures the Confederate Party near Irwinsville, Georgia.—Incidents connected with the Capture.—General Wilson's Report.

WE now turn back to that memorable Sabbath—April 2, 1865—which suddenly disclosed to the Confederate capital its inevitable fate. The battle of Five Forks had been fought on Saturday, and its loss by the Confederates involved the woful necessity of evacuating Richmond. The disaster was unknown in Richmond except to Davis and his cabinet, and even these had no full knowledge of the situation, having no other intimation of what had happened than what was contained in a brief but ominous telegram received early in the morning from General Lee. The President and his cabinet, with the exception of J. P. Benjamin, who was an Israelite, were all at their respective places of worship at the usual hour of morning service. Davis was at St. Paul's, looking care-worn, but still confident. Mallory attended mass at St. Peter's. Reagan was at the Baptist church. Benjamin was probably enjoying his pipe on the veranda of his mansion in Main Street.

During the service at St. Paul's the sexton walked up to Davis's pew, and whispered a few words in the ear of the President. Another dispatch had come, and his presence was wanted immediately. The members of the cabinet received a similar call. Thus, from church to church, the note of warning was communicated, and those who were only spectators were agitated with apprehensions which were certainly not less fearful because they were

based upon no definite information. The dispatch which met Mr. Davis at the door of St. Paul's conveyed to him intelligence of a startling character. That morning the outer defenses of Petersburg had been carried. A single interior line still resisted Grant's approach, but that could be held but a few hours longer. In the mean time, both Petersburg and Richmond must be evacuated. By two o'clock every body in Richmond knew that the city was to be abandoned, and a scene of dismay and confusion followed. Already the orders had been issued for the removal of the archives of the government, and for the destruction of stores for which there was no transportation. This must be completed by 7 o'clock P.M., and by 8 the military and civil authorities of the capital were to meet Davis at the Danville dépôt. By the railroad to Danville a way of escape was still open, but how long it would continue open was uncertain.

The panic in the city was almost universal. The negroes alone were jolly, and they worked with a hearty good will to help off as much of the Confederacy as they could. But, while these were placid and satisfied, nearly all others were either helpless with consternation, or were preparing to leave the city without exactly knowing where they were going. All the coaches in Richmond were waiting at the doors of private houses, and, as the afternoon wore away, the streets were filled with voluntary exiles. Of course there was transportation for a very small fraction of those who crowded toward the dépôt. The rest were compelled to return to the pandemonium from which they could not escape. The presidential party with difficulty made its way through the excited crowd which thronged and blocked the streets. At the dépôt the scramblers were concentrated in an almost impenetrable mass, which was kept back from the platform only by military force. Davis and his cabinet took their seats in a close car. Among this party were Adjutant General Samuel Cooper and a few other military officers. In an adjoining car were the heads of bureaus. A privileged few were admitted to fill up the train. In a car between the engine and that occupied by Davis was a guard of 200 picked men. The principal Confederate officers were spurred, and horses were ready for them in another car in case of an emergency. At 10 o'clock the train left the dépôt, leaving immediately behind it indescribable tumult, and further behind in the city an uncontrollable mob, which had already begun to sack the city. When Weitzel entered Richmond the next morning he found the city in flames.

Very soon the fugitive Confederacy—for it was all crowded into this train—*ubi Davis ibi Confederatio*—was beyond observation of the havoc it had left behind in the doomed city. To Davis and his fellow-conspirators the events of the last few hours must have seemed like a dream. Twenty-four hours ago Richmond was deemed an impregnable fortress. For four years it had been the Confederate capital, and had withstood five separate attempts made by large armies for its capture, and had, during a siege of nine months, repulsed every assault made upon Petersburg, its outpost. Several times its doom had been anticipated, but the fatal day had been so long postponed, it was thought that day might never come. Davis and his confederates, under as calm a sky as ever overarched Virginia, on this night of disaster vigorously rubbed their eyes, but could not escape the reality of the fate of Richmond or of their own flight. In a few hours the national flag would float over the rebel capital, and as to themselves the immediate future was misty and dark. But the dream of empire is not easily dissipated. Davis was troubled, but he did not yet despair. The hope and consolation which he had administered to his followers after the loss of Vicksburg and Atlanta he now whispered to his own agitated soul after the fall of Richmond. His capital was gone, but he said to himself, "All is not lost," and even as he fled he dreamed of newly-mustered armies that should rise at his bidding. Davis was not a matter-of-fact man. Probably no man was ever called to hold so important a position as he had held who had less appreciation of facts or knowledge of men. He did not reflect upon the actual circumstances of his present situation. He never asked himself whence these armies of his imagination were to come. He forgot that, if marshaled at all, their ranks must be filled with the old and the decrepit, beardless boys, and Southern amazons. His determination outran his judgment and transgressed common sense. He could only understand fate when he was crushed by her final blow.

any orders save those of Lieutenant General Grant, and cut off Johnston's retreat.' He knew at the time he penned that dispatch and made out those orders that Johnston was not retreating, but was halted under a forty-eight hours' truce with me, and was laboring to surrender his command and prevent its dispersion into guerrilla bands, and that I had on the spot a magnificent army at my command, amply sufficient for all purposes required by the occasion.

"The plan for cutting off a retreat from the direction of Burkesville and Danville is hardly worthy one of his military education and genius. When he contemplated an act so questionable as the violation of a 'truce' made by competent authority within his sphere of command, he should have gone himself and not sent subordinates, for he knew I was bound in honor to defend and maintain my own truce and pledge of faith, even at the cost of many lives.

"When an officer pledges the faith of his government, he is bound to defend it, and he is no soldier who would violate it knowingly.

"As to Davis and his stolen treasure, did General Halleck, as chief of staff or commanding officer of the neighboring military division, notify me of the facts contained in his dispatch to the secretary? No, he did not. If the Secretary of War wanted Davis caught, why not order it, instead of, by publishing it in the newspapers, putting him on his guard to hide away and escape? No orders or instructions to catch Davis or his stolen treasure ever came to me; but, on the contrary, I was led to believe that the Secretary of War rather preferred he should effect an escape from the country, if made 'unknown' to him. But even on this point I inclose a copy of my letter to Admiral Dahlgren, at Charleston, sent him by a fleet steamer from Wilmington, on the 25th of April, two days before the bankers of Richmond had imparted to General Halleck the important secret as to Davis's movement, designed doubtless to stimulate his troops to march their legs off to catch their treasure for their own use.

"I know now that Admiral Dahlgren did receive my letter on the 26th, and had acted on it before General Halleck had even thought of the matter; but I do not believe a word of the treasure story—it is absurd on its face—and General Halleck or any body has my full permission to chase Jeff. Davis and cabinet with their stolen treasure through any part of the country occupied by my command.

"The last and most obnoxious feature of General Halleck's dispatch is wherein he goes out of his way and advises that my subordinates, Generals Thomas, Stoneman, and Wilson, should be instructed not to obey 'Sherman's' commands.

"This is too much; and I turn from the subject with feelings too strong for words, and merely record my belief that so much mischief was never before embraced in so small a space as in the newspaper paragraph headed 'Sherman's Truce Disregarded,' authenticated as 'official' by Mr. Secretary Stanton, and published in the New York papers of April 28th."

After a ride of 23 miles the train stopped abreast of Petersburg. Here Breckinridge left the party to go to Lee's headquarters. Then the flight was resumed. Benjamin was soon asleep, and Mallory followed his example. Whether Davis slept or not there is no chronicler to tell us, but, whether asleep or awake, he still dreamed of the impossible. Burkesville was reached shortly after daybreak. As the train approached Danville, the question of destination for the first time began to be discussed. Hitherto the only concern of the party had been to get beyond the reach of Sheridan's cavalry. Where was the new capital to be established? Davis expressed his determination to cling to Virginia to the last, and, after some discussion, Danville was honored with all the glory which had departed from Richmond. It was a small town, incapable of receiving the full weight of honor which had been thrust upon it, and it was accordingly settled that the subordinate officials should proceed to Charlotte, North Carolina.

The fugitives were received with great hospitality at Danville, and on the 4th of April they began to establish the new seat of government. Trenholm opened the Treasury at one of the banks, and delighted the citizens of Danville by dispensing silver in return for Confederate notes, one dollar for seventy. In two days $40,000 in coin was disposed of in this way. Eligible structures were impressed for the other departments. Admiral Semmes organized a brigade of marines for the defense of the new capital, and mounted guns on all the hills about the town. Thousands of fugitives had followed the President from Richmond in subsequent trains, and all the able-bodied men among these were armed with muskets and pressed into the service.

On the 5th Davis issued a proclamation to his people. He announced that General Lee had been compelled to make movements which uncovered Richmond, the loss of which had, he admitted, inflicted moral and material injury upon the Confederate cause. But the energies of the people must not falter, nor their efforts be relaxed. Lee's army—"the largest and the finest in the Confederacy"—had been for months trammeled by the necessity of protecting Richmond. "It is for us, my countrymen," he urged, "to show, by our bearing under reverses, how wretched has been the self-deception of those who have believed us less able to endure misfortune with fortitude than to encounter dangers with courage. We have now entered upon a new phase of the struggle. Relieved from the necessity of guarding particular points, our army will be free to move from point to point, to strike the enemy in detail far from his base. Let us but will it, and we are free. Animated by that confidence in spirit and fortitude which never yet failed me, I announce to you, fellow-countrymen, that it is my purpose to maintain your cause with my whole heart and soul; that I will never consent to abandon to the enemy one foot of the soil of any one of the states of the Confederacy. That Virginia—noble state—whose ancient renown has been eclipsed by her still more glorious recent history; whose bosom has been bared to receive the main shock of this war; whose sons and daughters have exhibited heroism so sublime as to render her illustrious in all time to come—that Virginia, with the help of the people and by the blessing of Providence, shall be held and defended, and no peace ever be made with the infamous invaders of her territory. If by the stress of numbers we should ever be compelled to a temporary withdrawal from her limits, or those of any other border state, again and again will we return, until the baffled and exhausted enemy shall abandon in despair his endless and impossible task of making slaves of a people resolved to be free. Let us, then, not despond, my countrymen; but, relying on God, meet the foe with fresh defiance, and with unconquered and unconquerable hearts."

Brave words, but vain, uttered in the face of defeat, and falling upon the ears like the sound of the droppings of dust upon numberless graves, to be filled by a useless strife which could have no other name but murder! The words of this proclamation could not reach the ears of Davis's "countrymen" before events, already near their consummation, would expose their ludicrous insignificance. For three whole days Davis had not heard one word of tidings from General Lee or his army. This suspense continued until the 10th, and then came the startling intelligence that Lee had been defeated, and had surrendered his army. Then at Danville, on a diminished scale, was repeated the scene which had been witnessed eight days before at Richmond. The new capital was abandoned amid just such tumult as had attended the evacuation of Richmond. Narrowly escaping a raiding party, the presidential train reached Greensborough, North Carolina, on the 11th, bearing with it the disastrous tidings. Here Johnston and Beauregard met Davis. Breckinridge soon arrived with the details of Lee's surrender. The four officers then held a consultation on the slope of a hill where Nat. Green, of Revolutionary memory, had held his council of war the night before the battle of Guilford Court-house. Davis thought the struggle ought to be continued, and even ordered Johnston to fight. That general, however, did not agree with him, and refused obedience. Davis was powerless. He distrusted Johnston, and left Breckinridge with him to foil any movement which he might make to the prejudice of the Confederate cause. How Johnston acted afterward has already been told in these pages.

The people of Greensborough, unlike those of Danville, did not recognize the presence of the Confederate chief, or tender to him any offer of hospitality. The Confederacy was, therefore, now cooped up in a railroad car! On the 14th it left inhospitable Greensborough, uncertain of its destination, but too painfully conscious of the gad-fly Necessity, which urged it to "move on." A good part of the way to Charlotte was passed in wagons. At the latter place the news of Johnston's surrender and Lincoln's murder reached the fugitives. Here Breckinridge rejoined the party. From this point Davis threw off the semblance of authority which he had partially sustained thus far. The movement of the entire party was henceforth simply a flight. Davis now conceived the idea of reaching Texas. With his cabinet and staff, he left Charlotte under a cavalry escort of 2000 men. On the way to the Catawba River, Trenholm, the Secretary of the Treasury, and George Davis, attorney general, resigned their positions, and left the President to his fate. The flight was continued through Abbeville, South Carolina, Washington, Georgia, and then past Milledgeville and Macon southward, as if making for the coast of Florida. No one showed respect to the ruined President. Benjamin left the party before it reached Washington, and Mallory soon afterward. Breckinridge also broke away, and only Reagan was left of the whole cabinet.

Davis had started from Charlotte shortly after the expiration of the truce made between Johnston and Sherman. Preparations on an extensive scale were then made for his capture by General Wilson. Stoneman's three brigades—Brown's, Miller's, and Palmer's—then in Western North Carolina, were ordered to start in pursuit. These forces were commanded by General Palmer in Gillem's absence. They succeeded in crossing the Savannah River in Davis's front, and thus cut off his retreat toward the Mississippi. Wilson's cavalry was stretched over the whole country, from Kingston in Georgia to Tallahassee in Florida. In the mean time, also, a reward of $100,000 had been offered by President Johnson for the apprehension of Davis, as an accomplice of Booth in the assassination of Lincoln. Stoneman's and Wilson's cavalry now formed a network through whose meshes Davis could hardly hope to escape.

On the evening of May 7th, four days after Davis left Washington, Lieutenant Colonel Henry Harnden, of the First Wisconsin Cavalry—belonging to Wilson's command—ascertained at Dublin, on the Oconee, that during the day the fugitives had crossed the river, and were moving on the Jacksonville Road. Harnden followed close the next day, and at night reached the camp which had four hours before been occupied by Davis between the forks of Alligator Creek. He pursued the trail to Gum Swamp Creek, and there encamped for the night. On the 9th he pushed on to the Ocmulgee, crossed at Brown's Ferry, and at Abbeville learned that Davis had left that place at one o'clock that morning, and was now on the way to Irwinsville. Colonel Pritchard, of the Fourth Michigan Cavalry—also belonging to Wilson's command—had by this time reached Abbeville, and, taking a more direct route than was followed by Harnden's detachment, reached Irwinsville at two A.M. on the 10th, where he learned that Davis was encamped about a mile from the town, on another road leading to Abbeville. Sending a part of his force to the north to intercept Davis's return to Abbeville, he cautiously approached the camp from both sides, completely cutting off all escape. At daylight he surprised the encampment, and captured Davis, with his family, Postmaster General Reagan, two aid-de-camps, Davis's private secretary, four other officers, and eleven soldiers. Various details have been published in connection with the capture of the Confederate President. It was reported, soon after the event, that Davis was captured in female attire, and a recent official report by General Wilson confirms the report.[1]

---

[1] General Wilson's report here referred to is dated January 17, 1867, and gives the following details of the capture of Davis:

"The first direct information which I received of Davis's movements was on the 23d or 24th of April, from a citizen who had seen him at Charlotte, N. C., only three or four days before, and had learned that he was on his way, with a train and an escort of cavalry, to the South, intending to go to the trans-Mississippi Department. This information was regarded as entirely reliable, and hence the officers in charge of the different detachments afterward sent out were directed to dispose of their commands so as to have all roads and crossings vigilantly watched. It was thought at first that Davis would call about him a select force, and endeavor to escape by marching to the westward through the hilly country of Northern Georgia. To prevent this, Colonel Eggleston was directed to watch the country in all directions from Atlanta. Brevet Brigadier General A. J. Alexander, with the second brigade of Upton's division, having reached Atlanta in advance of the division, was directed by General Winslow to scout the country to the northward as far as Dalton, or until he should meet the troops under General Steedman in that region. On beginning his march from Macon, General Alexander was authorized to detach an officer and twenty picked men, disguised as rebel soldiers, for the purpose of trying to obtain definite information of Davis's movements. This party was placed under the command of Lieutenant Joseph O. Yoeman, First Ohio Cavalry, and at the time acting inspector general of the brigade. Verbal instructions were also given to other brigade and division commanders to make similar detachments. General Croxton was directed to send a small party toward Talladega, by the route upon which he had marched from that place, while Colonel Eggleston was directed to send a party by rail to West Point. By these means it was believed that all considerable detachments of rebels would be apprehended, and that such information might be obtained as would enable us to secure the principal rebel leaders if they should undertake to pass through the country in any other way than as individual fugitives.

"In declaring the armistice of Sherman null and void, the Secretary of War had directed that my command should resume active operations and endeavor to arrest the fugitive rebel chiefs. I accordingly notified him and General Thomas by telegraph of the dispositions I had made, and that I had no doubt of accomplishing the desired object; but having forwarded the records of my command to the Adjutant General's Department, as required by army regulations, and having been denied copies of the documents relating to these matters, I can not now fix the exact dates of these dispatches.

"After a rapid march toward the upper crossings of the Savannah River, in Northwestern Georgia, Lieutentant Yoeman's detachment met and joined Davis's party, escorted by Debrill and Ferguson's divisions of cavalry, probably under Wheeler in person, and continued with them several days, watching for an opportunity to seize and carry off the rebel chief. He was frustrated by the vigilance of the rebel escort. At Washington, Ga., the rebel authorities must have heard that Atlanta was occupied by our troops, and that they could not pass that point without a fight. They halted, and for a short time acted with irresolution in regard to their future course. The cavalry force which had remained true to Davis, estimated at five brigades, and probably numbering two thousand men, now became mutinous, and declined to go any farther. They were disbanded and partially paid off in coin which had been brought to that point in wagons. Lieutenant Yoeman lost sight of Davis at this time, but, dividing his party into three or four detachments, sought again to obtain definite information of his movements, but for twenty-four hours was unsuccessful. Persevering in his efforts, he became convinced that Davis had relinquished his idea of going into Alabama, and would probably try to reach the Gulf or South Atlantic coast and escape by sea. Couriers were sent with this information to General Alexander, and by him duly transmitted to me at Macon. The same conclusion had already been forced upon me by information derived from various other sources, and from the nature of the case it seemed quite probable. With railroad communication through most of Northern Georgia, and with a division of four thousand national cavalry operating about Atlanta, it would have been next to impossible for a party of fugitives, however small, to traverse that region by the ordinary roads. This must have been clear to the rebels. From these circumstances I became convinced that Davis would either flee in disguise and unattended, or endeavor to work his way sonthward into Florida. With the view of intercepting him in this attempt, I directed the crossings of the Ocmulgee River to be watched with renewed vigilance all the way from the neighborhood of Atlanta to Hawkinsville, and on the evening of May 6th I directed Brigadier General Croxton to select the best regiment in his division and send it, under its best officer, with orders to march eastward, via Jeffersonville, to Dublin, on the Oconee River, with the greatest possible speed, scouting the country well to the northward, and leaving detachments at the most important cross-roads with instructions to keep a sharp look-out for all detachments of rebels. By these means it was hoped that Davis's line of march would be intersected and his

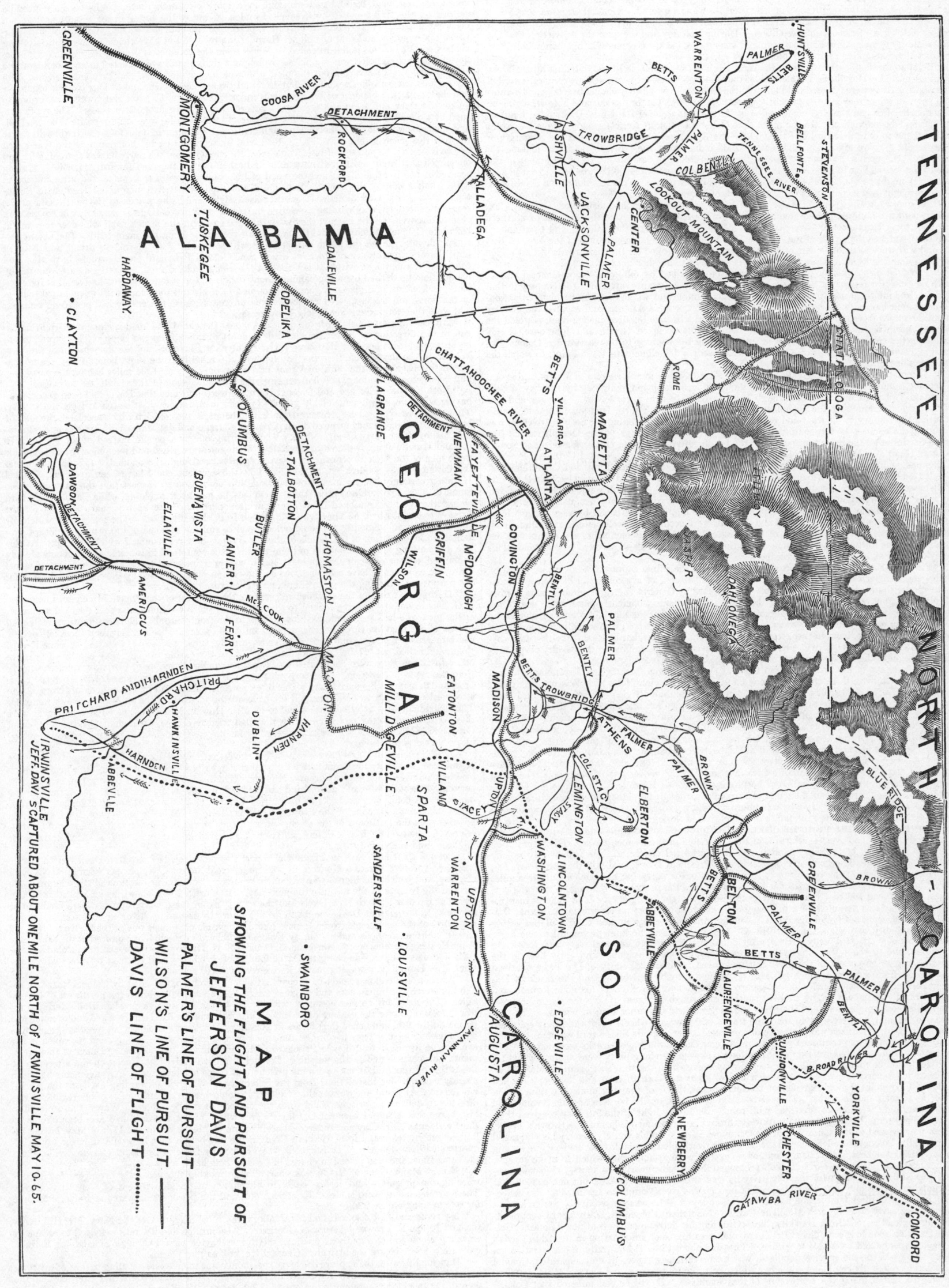

MAP
SHOWING THE FLIGHT AND PURSUIT OF
JEFFERSON DAVIS
PALMER'S LINE OF PURSUIT ——
WILSON'S LINE OF PURSUIT ——
DAVIS LINE OF FLIGHT ....

IRWINSVILLE.
JEFF. DAVIS CAPTURED ABOUT ONE MILE NORTH OF IRWINSVILLE MAY 10-65.

About the same time Alexander H. Stephens and Secretary Mallory were captured by other portions of General Wilson's command. Before the close of the month Davis was confined in Fortress Monroe, where he remained for two years, subject to trial. He was indicted for treason, but the trial was postponed time after time, and at length he was released upon bail of $100,000, exactly the same amount which was awarded to his captors. The Confederate Vice-President A. H. Stephens was also confined for a brief period in Fort Warren, Boston Harbor.

Thus closed at once the official and military career of the Confederacy.

---

movements discovered, in which event the commanding officer was instructed to follow it, wherever it might lead, until the fugitives should be overtaken and captured. General Croxton selected for this purpose the First Wisconsin Cavalry, commanded by Lieutenant Colonel Henry Harnden, an officer of spirit, experience, and resolution. During that day and the next the conviction that Davis would try to escape into Florida became so strong that I sent for General Minty, commanding the Second Division, and in person directed him to select his best regiment, and order it to march without delay to the southeastward along the right bank of the Ocmulgee River, watching all the crossings between Hawkinsville and the mouth of the Ohoopee River. In case of discovering the trail of the fugitives, they were directed to follow it to the Gulf coast, or till they should overtake and capture the party of whom they were in pursuit. General Minty selected for this purpose his own regiment, the Fourth Michigan Cavalry, commanded by Lieutenant Colonel Benjamin D. Pritchard, an excellent and dashing officer. In the mean time General Upton, at Augusta, had sent me a dispatch advising me to offer a reward of $100,000 for the capture of Davis, urging that the Secretary of War would approve my action, and that it would induce even the rebels to assist in making the capture. Not caring, however, to assume the responsibility of committing the government in this way, I authorized him to issue a proclamation offering a reward of $100,000, to be paid out of such money as might be found in the possession of Davis or his party. This was done, and copies scattered throughout the country as early as the 6th of May.

"As soon as it was known at Atlanta that Davis's cavalry escort had disbanded, General Alexander, with five hundred picked men and horses of his command, crossed to the right or northern bank of the Chattahoochee River, occupied all the fords west of the Atlanta and Chattanooga Railroad, watched the passes of the Altoona Mountains and the main crossings of the Etowah River, and with various detachments of his small command patrolled all the main roads in that region day and night, until he received news of Davis's capture in another quarter.

"The final disposition of my command may be described as follows: Major General Upton, with parts of two regiments, occupied Augusta, and kept a vigilant watch over the country in that vicinity, and informed me by telegraph of every thing important which came under his observation. General Winslow, with the larger part of that division, occupied Atlanta, and scouted the country in all directions from that place. General Alexander, with five hundred picked men, patroled the country north of the Chattahoochee, while detachments occupied Griffin and Jonesboro, closely watching the crossings of the Ocmulgee, and scouting the country to the eastward. Colonel Eggleston, commanding the post of Atlanta, had also sent a detachment to West Point, to watch the Alabama line in that quarter.

"General Croxton, with the main body of the First Division in the vicinity of Macon, had sent a detachment under my direction to the mountain region of Alabama, marching by the way of Carrolton to Talladega, and another through Northeastern Georgia toward North Carolina, and was also engaged in watching the Ocmulgee from the right of the Fourth Division to Macon, and in scouting the country to his front and rear. General Minty, commanding the Second Division, was scouting the country to the southeast, watching the lower crossings of the Ocmulgee, and had small parties at all the important points on the Southwestern Railroad, and in Western and Southwestern Georgia. Detachments of the Seventh Pennsylvania Cavalry occupied Cuthbert, Eufaula, Columbus, and Bainbridge, and kept a vigilant watch over the Lower Flint and Chattahoochee. While General McCook, with a detachment of his division at Albany, and 700 men between there and Tallahassee, Florida, was scouting the country to the north and eastward, we also had rail and telegraphic communication from my headquarters at Macon with Atlanta, Augusta, West Point, Milledgeville, Albany, and Eufaula. By inspecting the map herewith it will be seen that my force of nearly 15,000 cavalry, well mounted and vigilant, were occupying a well-defined and almost continuous line from Kingston, Georgia, to Tallahassee, Florida, with detachments and scouts well out in all directions to the front and rear. From this it will be difficult to perceive how Davis and his party could possibly have hoped to escape.

"From the time they were reported at Charlotte till their final capture I was kept informed of their general movements, and was enabled thereby to dispose of my command in such a manner as to render the capture morally certain. As reported by General Winslow, rumors came in from all directions, but by carefully weighing them, the truth became sufficiently manifest to enable me to act with confidence. It is to be regretted now, however, that the hurry of events precluded the use of written orders. In nearly every instance my instructions were given verbally to the division commanders, and by them, in turn, transmitted verbally to their subordinates. Such written dispatches and orders as were given are preserved in the records pertaining to the cavalry corps, Military Division of the Mississippi, now on file in the Adjutant General's office.

"In pursuance of my instructions to General Croxton, heretofore recited, Lieutenant Colonel Henry Harnden, with three officers and one hundred and fifty men of the First Wisconsin Cavalry, left Macon, Ga., on the evening of May 6, 1865, and marched rapidly via Jeffersonville toward Dublin, on the Oconee River. At Jeffersonville Colonel Harnden left one officer and thirty men, with orders to scout the country in all directions for reliable information as to Davis's flight. With the balance of his command he continued the march all night, and the next day, about seven P.M., reached Dublin. During the night and day he had sent out scouts and small parties on all the side roads, in the hope of finding the trail of the party for whom he was looking. Nothing of importance occurred until after he had bivouacked for the night. The white inhabitants of that place expressed entire ignorance and indifference in regard to the movement of important rebels, but were unusually profuse in their offers of hospitality to Colonel Harnden. This, together with the conduct of the colored servants, excited his suspicions, though he gained no valuable intelligence till about midnight, at which time he was informed by a negro man, who went to his camp for that purpose, that Davis, with his wife and family, had passed through Dublin that day, going south on the river road. The negro reported that the party in question had eight wagons with them, and that another party had gone southward on the other side of the Oconee River. His information seems to have been of the most explicit and circumstantial character. He had heard the lady called 'Mrs. Davis,' and a gentleman spoken of as 'President Davis,' and said that Mr. Davis had not crossed the river at the regular ferry with the rest of the party, but had gone about three miles lower down, and crossed on a small flat-boat, and rejoined the party with the wagons near the outskirts of the town, and that they had all gone toward the south together. The colored man reported Mr. Davis as mounted on a fine bay horse, and told his story so circumstantially that Colonel Harnden could not help believing it. The ferryman was called up and examined, but, either through stupidity or design, succeeded in withholding whatever he knew in regard to the case. But in view of the facts already elicited, after detailing Lieutenant Lane and sixty men to remain at Dublin, and to scout the country in all directions, Colonel Harnden, at an early hour in the morning, began the pursuit of the party just mentioned. Five miles south of Dublin he obtained information from a woman which left him no room to doubt that he was on the track of Davis in person. He dispatched a messenger to inform General Croxton of his good fortune, and pushed rapidly in pursuit. The trail led southward through a region of pine forests and cypress swamps, almost uninhabited, and therefore affording no food for either men or horses. The rain began to fall, and, as there was no road, the tracks of the wagon-wheels upon the sandy soil were soon obliterated. A citizen was pressed, and compelled to act as guide till the trail was again discovered. The pursuit was continued with renewed vigor, but as the wagon-tracks were again lost in the waters of the swamp bordering on Alligator Creek, the pursuing party were again delayed till a citizen could be found to guide them to the road upon which the trail was again visible. Colonel Harnden reports this day to have been one of great toil both to men and horses; they had marched forty miles through an almost trackless forest, much of the way under the rain, and in water up to their saddle-girths. They bivouacked after dark on the borders of Gum Swamp, and during the night were again drenched with rain. Before daylight of the 9th they renewed their march, their route leading almost southwest through swamp and wilderness to Brown's Ferry, where they crossed to the south side of the Ocmulgee River. In his anxiety to ferry his command over rapidly, Colonel Harnden allowed the boat to be overloaded; a plank near the bow was sprung loose, causing the boat to leak badly, and, as no means were at hand with which to make repairs, lighter boat-loads had to be carried. This prolonged the crossing nearly two hours. Colonel Harnden learned from the ferryman that the party he was pursuing had crossed about one o'clock that morning, and were only a few hours ahead of him on the road leading to Irwinsville. At Abbeville, a village of three families, he halted to feed, and, just as he was renewing his march, he met the advance party of the Fourth Michigan Cavalry, Lieutenant Colonel B. D. Pritchard commanding, moving on the road from Hawkinsville. Ordering his detachment to continue its march, Colonel Harnden rode to meet Colonel Pritchard, and gave him such information in regard to Davis's movements as he had been able to gather. This was about three P.M. After a conversation between these officers, the precise details of which are variously reported, they separated, Colonel Harnden to rejoin his command, already an hour or more in advance, and Colonel Pritchard continuing his march along the south side of the Ocmulgee. It will be remembered that Colonel Pritchard had begun his march from the vicinity of Macon on the evening of May 7, under verbal orders given him by General Minty, in pursuance of my instructions. His attention was particularly directed to the crossings of the Ocmulgee River, between Hawkinsville and Jacksonville, near the mouth of the Ohoopee, with the object of intercepting Davis and such other rebel chiefs as might be making their way out of the country by the roads in that region. He had not gone more than three miles before he obtained such additional information in regard to the party as convinced him that it was his duty to join in the pursuit. In this he was clearly right, and had he done otherwise would have been censurable for negligence and want of enterprise. Colonel Harnden having informed him that he had force enough to cope with Davis, Colonel Pritchard determined to march another road, leading to Irwinsville by a more circuitous route. Why he did not send a courier on the trail pursued by Colonel Harnden to notify the latter of his intentions has not been explained. This would probably have prevented the collision which afterward occurred between his regiment and that of Colonel Harnden, and would not have rendered the capture of Davis less certain. This is not intended to reflect upon the conduct of Colonel Pritchard, for it is believed that this omission was simply an oversight which might have occurred to any confident and zealous officer. In carrying out the plan which he had adopted, Colonel Pritchard selected from his regiment seven officers and one hundred and twenty-eight men, and at four o'clock began the march, leaving the balance of his regiment under command of Captain Hathaway, with orders to picket the river and scout the country in accordance with previous instructions. The route pursued by Colonel Pritchard led down the river nearly twelve miles to a point opposite Wilcox's Mill, and thence southwest for a distance of eighteen miles, through the pine forest to Irwinsville. He reached this place at one A.M. of the 10th, and by representing his command as the rear-guard of Davis's party, he succeeded in learning from the citizens that the party he was searching for had encamped that night at dusk about a mile and a half out on the road toward Abbeville. Having secured a negro guide, he turned the head of his column toward that place, and after moving to within half a mile of the camp, halted and dismounted twenty-five men under Lieutenant Purinton. This party were directed to move noiselessly through the woods to the north side of the camp, for the purpose of gaining a position in its rear and preventing the possibility of escape. In case of discovery by the enemy, they were directed to begin the attack from wherever they might be, while Colonel Pritchard would charge upon the camp along the main road. Lieutenant Purinton having reached the point assigned him without exciting an alarm, the attack was delayed until the first appearance of dawn, at which time Colonel Pritchard put his troops in motion, and continued his march to within a few rods of the camp undiscovered. Having assured himself of his position, he dashed upon the camp without delay, and in a few moments had secured its occupants and effects, and placed a guard of mounted men around the camp, with dismounted sentries at the tents and wagons. No resistance was offered, because the enemy had posted no sentries, and were therefore taken completely by surprise.

"Almost simultaneously with the dash of Colonel Pritchard and his detachment sharp firing began in the direction of Abbeville, and only a short distance from the camp. This turned out to be an engagement between the party under Lieutenant Purinton and the detachment of the First Wisconsin Cavalry, which, it seems, had followed the rebel trail the night before till it was no longer distinguishable in the dark, had gone into camp only two or three miles behind the party they had been pursuing so long, and had renewed the pursuit as soon as they could see to march.

"Both Colonel Pritchard and Colonel Harnden were informed that Davis had been reported as having with him a well-armed body-guard of picked men, variously estimated at from ten to fifty. They therefore expected desperate resistance, and hence, in the collision which occurred, the men of both detachments seemed inspired by the greatest courage and determination. It was several minutes before either party discovered they were fighting our own people instead of the enemy. In this unfortunate affair two men of the Fourth Michigan were killed and one officer wounded, while three men of the First Wisconsin were severely and several slightly wounded. It is difficult, under the circumstances as detailed, to perceive how the accident could have been avoided. Colonel Harnden certainly had no means of knowing, and no reason to suspect that the party whom he found in his front were any other than the rebels he had been pursuing, while Colonel Pritchard claims that he had cautioned Lieutenant Purinton particularly to keep a sharp look-out for the First Wisconsin, which he knew would approach from that direction. The hurry with which my command was subsequently mustered out of service, and the absence of the principal officers, prevented an investigation of the details of this affair, and the circumstances which led to it. At this late day nothing more can be said of them than what is contained in the official documents already submitted, except that not the slightest blame was ever intended to be cast by me upon Colonel Harnden, as seems to have been assumed by the commission convened by the Secretary of War for the purpose of awarding the prize offered for the capture of Davis.

"During the firing of the skirmish referred to, the adjutant of the Fourth Michigan, Lieutenant J. G. Dickinson, after having looked to the security of the rebel camp, and sent forward a number of the men who had straggled, was about to go to the front himself, when his attention was called by one of the men 'to three persons dressed in female attire,' who had apparently just left one of the large tents near by, and were moving toward the thick woods. He started at once toward them, and called out 'Halt!' but, not hearing him, or not caring to obey, they continued to move off. Just then they were confronted by three men under direction of Corporal Munger, coming from the opposite direction. The corporal recognized one of the persons as Davis, advanced carabine, and demanded his surrender. The three persons halted, and by the actions of the two, who afterward turned out to be women, all doubt as to the identity of the third person was removed. The individuals thus arrested were found to be Miss Howell, Mrs. Davis, and Jefferson Davis. As they walked back to the tent from which they had tried to escape, Lieutenant Dickinson observed that Davis's high top-boots were not covered by his disguise, which fact probably led to his recognition by Corporal Munger.

"As the friends of Davis have strenuously denied that he was disguised as a woman, it may not be improper to specify the exact articles of woman's apparel which he had upon him when first seen by Lieutenant Dickinson and Corporal Munger. The former states that he was one of the three persons 'dressed in woman's attire,' and had a 'black mantle wrapped about his head, through the top of which could be seen locks of his hair.' Captain G. W. Lawton, Fourth Michigan Cavalry, who publishes an account of the capture in the Atlantic Monthly for September, 1865, states explicitly, upon the testimony of the officers present, that Davis, in addition to his full suit of Confederate gray, had on 'a lady's waterproof (cloak), gathered at the waist, with a shawl drawn over the head, and carrying a tin pail.'

"Colonel Pritchard says in his official report that he received from Mrs. Davis, on board the steamer Clyde, off Fortress Monroe, 'a waterproof cloak or robe,' which was worn by Davis as a disguise, and which was identified by the men who saw it on him at the time of the capture. He secured the balance of the disguise the next day. It consisted of a shawl, which was identified in a similar manner by both Mrs. Davis and the men. From these circumstances there seems to be no doubt whatever that Davis sought to avoid capture by assuming the dress of a woman, or that the ladies of the party endeavored to pass him off upon his captors as one of themselves.

"In addition to Davis and his family, Colonel Pritchard's detachment captured at the same time John H. Reagan, rebel postmaster-general, Colonel B. N. Harrison, private secretary, Colonels Lubbock and Johnson, aids-de-camp to Davis, four inferior officers, and thirteen private soldiers, besides Miss Howell, two waiting-maids, and several colored servants.

"As soon as breakfast could be prepared, Colonel Pritchard, preceded by Colonel Harnden, began his march, with prisoners and wagons, for Macon, about 120 miles to the northwest of Irwinsville. The next day he met a courier with copies of the President's proclamation offering a reward of $100,000 for the capture of Davis. This proclamation had been received and promulgated by me on the 9th, and hence the officers in pursuit of Davis were in no way inspired by the promise which it contained. They performed their part from a higher sense of duty, and too much praise can not be awarded to Colonels Pritchard and Harnden, and the officers and men of their regiments who participated in the pursuit. Colonel Pritchard arrived at Macon on the afternoon of the 13th, and reported at once with his prisoners at corps headquarters. Arrangements had been already made, under instructions from the Secretary of War, for forwarding Davis to the North, via Atlanta, Augusta, and Savannah. Colonel Pritchard, with a detachment of his regiment, was directed to deliver his prisoner safely into the custody of the Secretary of War. I also placed in his charge the person of Clement C. Clay, Jr., for whose arrest a reward had also been offered by the President. Mr. Clay surrendered himself to me at Macon about the 11th of May, having informed me by telegraph from Western Georgia the day before that he would start for my headquarters without delay. A. H. Stephens was arrested by General Upton, at Crawfordsville, about the same time, and also placed in charge of Colonel Pritchard.

"Brevet Major General Upton was charged with making the necessary arrangements for forwarding the prisoners and escort safely to Savannah, in the department of General Gillmore. These arrangements were successfully carried out, and the prisoners delivered at Fortress Monroe for safe keeping on the 22d of May.

"My command had also arrested Mr. Mallory, the rebel Secretary of the Navy, Mr. Hill, senator, and Joseph E. Brown, governor of Georgia. Breckinridge and Toombs managed to escape by traveling alone and as rapidly as possible, the former having passed through Tallahassee, Florida, only a few hours before the arrival of General McCook at that place.

"Immediately after the capture of Davis, the small detachments and scouting parties of my command were assembled by their respective brigade and division commanders, and after paroling the bulk of the rebel forces, amounting to about 59,000 men that had been serving in Florida, Georgia, North and South Carolina, the various regiments were ordered to be mustered out.

"From the foregoing narrative, it will be seen that the first perfectly reliable information in regard to the movements of Davis was sent in by Lieutenant Joseph O. Yeoman, of General Alexander's staff; that the route actually pursued by Davis and his party after leaving Washington was first discovered by Lieutenant Colonel Harnden at Dublin, and that the capture was actually made one and a half miles north of Irwinsville, Georgia, at dawn of May 10, by Lieutenant Colonel Benjamin D. Pritchard, with a detachment of 7 officers and 128 men of the Fourth Michigan Cavalry."

LINCOLN AT HOME.

CHAPTER LX.

THE DEATH OF LINCOLN.

The Mission of Abraham Lincoln.—His Conservatism.—Characteristic Peculiarities.—Charitable Disposition toward the Southern People.—Closing Days of Lincoln's Life.—His second Inaugural.—Visit to City Point.—Entrance into Richmond.—The last Day.—The Evening at Ford's Theatre.—Lincoln's Assassination.—His Death-bed.—Attempt to Assassinate Secretary Seward.—The Effect upon the Country.—The Fate of the Conspirators.—Death of John Wilkes Booth.—The Trial before the Military Commission.—Flight and final Capture of John H. Surratt.—Connection of the Conspiracy with the Confederate Government.—Burial of President Lincoln.

NEVER before, in the history of the world, was a single fortnight so thronged with events of thrilling interest, concerning not alone one continent, but commanding the attention of the world, as that which commenced on the 1st, and ended with the 14th of April, 1865. As, in the denouement of a great tragedy, events which have hitherto crept along, in light or darkness, leap forward, thronging and culminating toward their conclusion, so was it in the closing period of that antagonism in which, for four years, the republic had met, grappled, and finally put under its feet the rebellion of states against its sovereignty. This national drama had had its

prelude in years of plotting and conspiracy on the part of Southern statesmen, who sought to array their states against the general government. Still its first outward act was a violent shock. The American people was raised clean off the ground; but it soon regained its footing, and saw that the crisis upon it ought not to have been a surprise. It was a long time before the intense violence of the rebellion was understood; but at length the nation put on its complete armor, and gathered up its full strength. From that moment doubt was thrust aside, and victory crowned its banners. But Gettysburg, Vicksburg, Atlanta, Nashville, and Savannah, although great national victories, had not been crushing defeats to the Confederate armies. Then within the confines of Virginia and North Carolina was marshaled the combined strength of both antagonists. The curtain uplifted to disclose the last act of the drama. It disclosed Grant's army in motion. One blow from the national arm swept away the defenses of Lee's army and uncovered the Confederate capital. A second blow crushed the finest army of the Confederacy, and its fragments were left at the mercy of the conqueror. The Confederate President was a fugitive, bearing with him to Greensborough the tidings of terrible disaster, the very weight of which crushed and crumbled Johnston's army. The rebel government, with its armies, vanished like the

LINCOLN'S HOME, SPRINGFIELD, ILLINOIS.

clouds of an April day. The winter of national discontent was passed, followed by glorious summer. The national colors floated on innumerable eminences, wafting fragrance more grateful than that of flowers. Exultation filled the whole atmosphere, and pervaded the hearts of all men. It was like a heaven from which Satan and his angels had been thrust out into the abyss. Strong men wept for joy. Inspired with awe, the people expressed their triumph, not in shouts, but in anthems.

In this sublime awe, in this inspiration of joyous triumph, Lincoln had participated not as others. He was wrapped in a cloud of glory which no man could penetrate. It was a glory which was hid from his own eyes, in which he was somehow buried, but which had not yet blossomed into the full flower. He had been chosen of God for great ends. When the Republican National Convention assembled at Chicago on the 16th of May, 1860, it was almost universally assumed that William H. Seward would be nominated for President. On the first ballot he stood far ahead of Lincoln; on the second he was three votes ahead; but on the third Lincoln stood fifty-one votes ahead of Seward, and his nomination was then made unanimous. The people were scarcely as yet familiar with the name of Lincoln. They soon learned that he was an awkward, ungainly man, one who had risen from obscurity by perseverance, a man shrewd in debate and plain in speech, and who was known simply as "Honest old Abe." But this awkward, plain man, without culture, and without that despotism of genius which commands admiration, God had taken by the hand, and had chosen as the champion of the republic at the most critical moment of its history. His very election was made the pretext for rebellion. But he accomplished nobly and wisely his great mission. Against the violence of rebellion he opposed the firmness of national authority, supported by the strong arms of patriots. The subtle machinations of those who opposed his administration were foiled by his good sense. Thus he won the confidence of the people. He had no love of arbitrary power, and indulged no radical or revolutionary theories which could tempt him to such use of power. He was a conservative in the best sense of that term: not a conservator of party, but of national integrity. Thus he was the better fitted to accomplish his divine mission. For it must be remembered that God, the great Disposer of all events, works not with the haste of man. Tares and wheat He lets grow together until the harvest, lest by rooting up the tares upon impulse He uproot the wheat also. While Lincoln never vacillated, he was never in haste. He hesitated long before he issued his proclamation of emancipation. He laid it away, and weeks passed before he signed it—and then he acted in accordance with a solemn vow which he had made to God. Even after he issued this document he doubted whether the system of gradual and compensated emancipation might not be more just and better for the slaves. He looked on every side of every question, and was therefore slow in reaching conclusions. In Lincoln thought and prayer were mingled, and thus the final word which came in answer to thought and prayer sounded solemnly in his ears like the commandment of God. Following that voice, he had no doubt as to results: it was, "This do, and thou shalt be saved."

In no life, perhaps, more than in Lincoln's, did the outward appearance contradict the inward fact and experience. A casual acquaintance with him would lead to the inference that he looked upon every subject only as the occasion of a joke or the point for an anecdote. But those who came near-

er to him, or who carefully study the man, can not thus judge. Upon no man ever fell the weight of sadder care than upon him. Day by day he labored under a burden which he could not lay aside. Thus to his intimate friends he always seemed weary and sorrowful. In an equal degree his external awkwardness curiously contrasted with an inward grace and sweetness not common among men. He was as gentle as a woman. His compassion was infinite. As the hour of victory approached, when the enemies of the nation would lie prostrate at its feet, the desire nearest to his heart was to heal the wounds which the strife left open and bleeding, to pardon and restore. Thus, when the summer of triumph came, its glory wrapped him all about. He saw a nation restored, a race emancipated. He saw the seal of God set upon all which he had done. He looked upon a people inspired with solemn joy, and as their souls went up in anthems, his rose supreme above them all, crowned with an aureola such as never graced the head of Cæsar or king.

But how easily is the summer sky overcast with gloom! The serpent's head has been bruised, but his venomous fangs have not been plucked. Treason, which wears the semblance of honor on the battle-field, and whose proud crest flashing at the head of armies is an image of something glorious, is, after all, a creeping thing with a devilish instinct. And thus it is that at one moment we look upon the great leader of the people crowned with the highest honors which the hands or hearts of his countrymen can bestow, and the next are called to witness his martyrdom.

On the 4th of March Lincoln had been reinaugurated President. On that occasion he thus alluded to the war, and to the two parties engaged in it:

"Each looked for an easier triumph, and a result less fundamental and astounding. Both read the same Bible and pray to the same God, and each invokes his aid against the other. It may seem strange that any men should dare to ask a just God's assistance in wringing their bread from the sweat of other men's faces. But let us judge not that we be not judged. The prayers of both could not be answered; that of neither has been answered fully. The Almighty has his own purposes. 'Woe unto the world because of offenses, for it must needs be that offenses come, but woe to that man by whom the offense cometh.' If we shall suppose that American slavery is one of those offenses which, in the providence of God, must needs come, but which, having continued through his appointed time, he now wills to remove, and that he gives to both North and South this terrible war as the woe due to those by whom the offense came, shall we discern therein any departure from these divine attributes which the believers in a loving God always ascribe to him? Fondly do we hope, fervently do we pray that this mighty scourge of war may speedily pass away. Yet if God wills that it continue until all the wealth piled by the bondman's two hundred and fifty years of unrequited toil shall be sunk, and until every drop of blood drawn with the lash shall be paid by another drawn with the sword, as was said three thousand years ago, so still it must be said, 'The judgments of the Lord are true and righteous altogether.'

"With malice toward none, with charity for all, with firmness in the right, let us strive on to finish the work we are in, to bind up the nation's wounds, to care for him who shall have borne the battle, and for his widow and his orphan, to do all which may achieve and cherish a just and a lasting peace among ourselves and with all nations."

FORD'S THEATRE, WASHINGTON.

A few days afterward he went to City Point, and was there when Grant defeated Lee. The day after Richmond was taken he entered that city, coming, not as the conqueror, but the deliverer, and was welcomed with acclamation, especially by the poor negroes, who kissed the hands which had broken their bonds. After Lee's surrender he returned to Washington. Here, on the evening of the 11th, in the midst of the universal rejoicings, he addressed his fellow-citizens, calling upon them to remember Him to whom they owed the preservation of the nation, and the soldiers and sailors who, under God, had won the victory. He also, on this occasion, announced his purpose to issue another proclamation to the people of the South, in order to hasten the work of restoration.

On the morning of the 14th—the last day of Lincoln's life—his son Robert breakfasted with him, and told him all the details of Lee's surrender, from the scene of which he had just returned. The President then spent an hour with Schuyler Colfax, speaker of the House. The conversation naturally turned upon the immediate future of the nation, and every word uttered by Lincoln breathed a pardon toward repentant rebels. After a brief interview with some of his old Illinois friends, the President met his cabinet between 11 and 12 o'clock. He seemed more joyous than was his wont. The lieutenant general was also present. Then, in the afternoon, he drove out with Mrs. Lincoln, and conversed of the happier days which seemed in store for them. He seemed to be looking forward to four years of peaceful administration, and after that to retirement and a quiet conclusion of an eventful life in the midst of old and familiar scenes. But even then the weapon of death in the hands of the assassin was laden with the fatal bullet. A peace such as the world can not give was nearer to the weary heart of Lincoln than he then dreamed.

In the evening he met Colfax again, with George Ashmun, who had presided at the Chicago Convention which nominated him for the presidency. It was well understood in Washington that the President and General Grant would that evening attend Ford's Theatre, and a private box had been especially prepared and decorated for the presidential party. General Grant, owing to another engagement, could not attend. Mr. Colfax was invited to accompany the party, but declined, to his subsequent regret.[1] The President himself was reluctant, as his mind was on other things, but he was not willing to disappoint the people in this hour of public rejoicing. At nine o'clock, with his wife, Mr. Lincoln reached the theatre, and, as usual, was received with an outburst of applause. The other members of the party were Miss Harris, daughter of Senator Harris, of New York, and Major Rathbun, of the regular army. The play for the evening was "Our American Cousin." The American flag drooped over Lincoln's head, and his thoughts were occupied with a grander drama than that which was presented to the audience. Four years ago this day the flag had been hauled down from Fort Sumter, and this very day the same old flag had been restored by the hands of Major Anderson. It was natural, therefore, that the President's mind should range over the weary years which had intervened, and of which he was so great a part. His face wore a happy smile, such as had not been there since the beginning of the war.

But still another play was in progress of which neither Lincoln nor the audience knew. Shortly after the President entered the theatre three men were noticed by one Sergeant M. Dye, who was sitting in front of the theatre. They seemed to be in earnest consultation, and to be waiting for some one to come out. They went to a neighboring saloon, and in a few minutes returned. One was a well-dressed gentleman, another was a rough-looking fellow, and the third was a younger man than either of the other two. This latter stepped up and called out the time, and then started up the street. Soon he reappeared and called out "ten minutes after ten," this time louder than before. The well-dressed gentleman then entered the theatre by the door in the rear leading to the stage. He passed up the stairs and through

the gallery leading to the box occupied by the President, and overlooking the stage on its right. He stood for a moment surveying the audience, and then, taking out a card, gave it to the President's messenger, and immediately followed the latter into the box. As he entered he fired, taking unerring aim at the President's head. Major Rathbun attempted to seize the assassin, but was thrust aside, receiving at the same time a wound in the breast. The assassin advanced to the front brandishing his knife, and leaped upon the stage, shouting "Sic semper tyrannis," the motto of Virginia. In a moment he was gone.

Lincoln was carried, unconscious, from the theatre to Mr. Peterson's house opposite, where he was laid upon a bed. In ten minutes all Washington was apprised of the deed which had been committed, but the extent of the injury was yet unknown. Surgeon General Barnes was hastily summoned, and the members of the cabinet were assembled in the death-chamber of the President. There also were Senator Sumner and Speaker Colfax. The wound which had been received in the back of the head was probed by the surgeon general and pronounced mortal. As the fatal word was uttered, the hearts of all present sank within them. "Oh no! general, no!" cried out Stanton, and, sinking into a chair, he wept like a child. Sumner, who held the hand of the martyred President, sobbed as if his great heart would break with sorrow. It was the night of Good Friday, and it seemed as if another had been crucified, the just for the unjust!

All night the watchers stood about the death-bed. Lincoln remained unconscious to the last. His wife and son Robert several times entered the chamber, but in their grief could not bear the scene, and they remained most of the time in an adjoining room. Lincoln lived until twenty-two minutes past seven o'clock on the morning of the 15th.

The same hour that the President was shot, a man appeared at the door of Secretary Seward and pretended that he was a messenger from the physician who was then attending upon the secretary. Being refused admittance, he forced his way to the secretary's chamber. Frederick Seward and an attendant rushed to the rescue, but were both severely wounded. The assassin—probably the rough-looking fellow observed by Sergeant Dye in front of Ford's Theatre—entered the chamber and inflicted several wounds upon the secretary, and then escaped. It had been intended by the assassins to kill Secretary Stanton, Lieutenant General Grant, and Vice-President Johnson, and thus paralyze the government. But even if all this had been accomplished the conspirators would have been disappointed. Secretary Seward survived the blows inflicted upon him, but to his dying day will wear the honorable scars which associate him in the thoughts of the people with the martyrdom of their President.

The tidings of the assassination spread rapidly over the country. In all history there was never national sorrow to be compared with this. Literally the whole people wept. Thousands there were who would willingly have received the fatal bullet in their own hearts if thereby they could have saved the precious life of their leader. Even those who had for four years reviled Lincoln, who had called him a boor and a despot, now vied with his friends in their adulation. A few rejoiced in the murder, but their lips were closed partly from fear and partly from the universal expression of sorrow which struck them dumb.

But who and where were the murderers? The assassin of the President, as he escaped across the stage, was recognized by one of the actors as John Wilkes Booth. Other evidence was soon found which fixed upon this person the guilt of the murder. But, though he left traces of his guilt behind, he was not to be found. The rendezvous of the conspirators was discovered. It was the house of Mrs. M. E. Surratt, located in the very heart of Washington. On the night of April 17th the officers of the government proceeded thither and arrested the occupants—Mrs. Surratt, her daughter Anna, Miss Fitzpatrick, and Miss Holahan. Before leaving the house a light knock was heard at the door. It was opened, and a young man appeared, evidently in disguise. He was dressed like a common laborer, and carried a pick upon his shoulder. But his hands were white and soft, apparently unused to labor, and his answers to questions put to him were unsatisfactory. During the investigation he produced the certificate of an oath of allegiance, purporting to have been taken by Lewis Payne, of Fauquier County, Virginia. He was arrested, and it was afterward proved that he was the man who had attempted to murder Secretary Seward, and that his real name was Powell. Three days later George A. Atzerott was captured

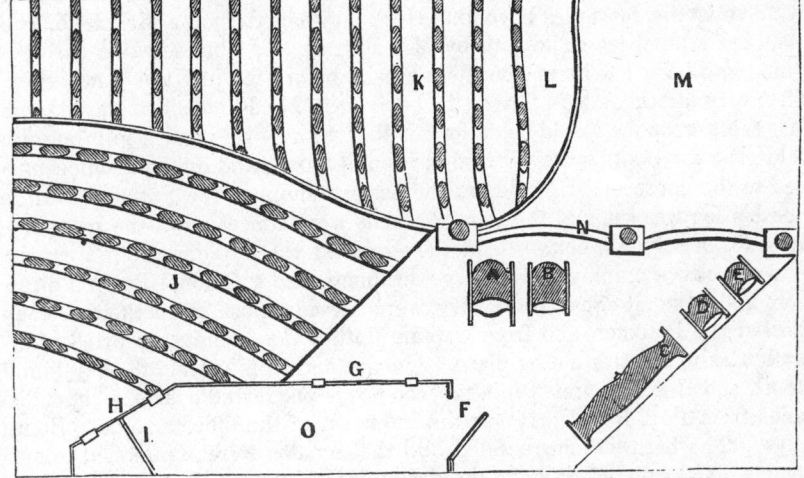

PLAN OF THE BOX OCCUPIED BY PRESIDENT LINCOLN AT FORD'S THEATRE, APRIL 14, 1865.

O. Dark Corridor leading from the Dress Circle to Box.—H. Entrance to Corridor.—I. The Bar used by Booth to prevent entrance from without.—J. Dress Circle.—K. The Parquette.—L. The Foot-lights.—M. The Stage.—F. Open door to the President's Box.—G. Closed door.—N. Place where Booth vaulted over to the Stage below.

near Middleburg, in Maryland. He had on the 14th of April occupied a room in the Kirkwood House, Washington, where Vice-President Johnson was staying. In this room a revolver was found the next day, hid under the pillow of the bed, and some bowie-knives between the mattresses. There was also found evidence of his complicity with Booth.

The principal assassin, John Wilkes Booth, was not found until eleven days after the murder. When he leaped upon the stage at Ford's Theatre, his foot became entangled in the folds of the flag decorating the box occupied by Lincoln, and his leg was broken. He had engaged one of the swiftest steeds in Washington, which was held by one of the attendants of the theatre during the accomplishment of the crime. Limping across the stage with great difficulty, he mounted his horse and was joined by one Harold, who had been on the look-out. They crossed the navy-yard bridge and rode to Surrattsville, ten miles beyond. Here they called upon a Mr. Lloyd, who occupied a hotel leased to him by Mrs. Surratt, and obtained two carbines which had been left there about six weeks before for just this emergency. That very afternoon Mrs. Surratt had driven to Mr. Lloyd's and warned him that these weapons would be called for that night. She had also brought a field-glass for Booth's use. From this point Booth and his companion hurried to the house of Dr. Mudd, on the eastern shore of the Potomac. Here Booth's leg was set, and the two criminals were concealed in the neighborhood for nearly a week. Then they crossed the Potomac into Virginia. The detectives employed by the government, under Colonel Baker's direction, and a small squad of cavalry, were already close upon them. They crossed the Potomac, and from Captain Jett, a Confederate, extorted information as to Booth's hiding-place. On the night of April 25th they found Booth and Harold secreted in a tobacco-house on Garrett's farm, a short distance from Port Royal. It was the intention of the officers to take Booth alive. The barn was surrounded, and the inmates were summoned to surrender. Colonel Baker made the demand, and suggested as an alternative "a bonfire and a shooting-match." Harold came out, but Booth wanted "fair play," and proposed that the officers stand off and give him a chance

for his life. As he persisted in his refusal to surrender, the barn was fired. Booth made a desperate plunge toward the door, and at that moment was shot in the back of the head by Sergeant Boston Corbett. This act of Corbett was clearly a disobedience of orders.

Booth was taken out of the barn, and was laid upon the grass in a dying condition. The wound which he had received was in its location very similar to that which he had inflicted upon the President, but it did not deprive him of consciousness. Water was given him, and he revived. Baker put his ear close to the murmuring lips of the dying man, and heard him say, "Tell mother I die for my country." He was carried to the veranda of Garrett's house. Here he again revived, and said, "I thought I did for the best." He asked that his hands might be raised so that he could see them. As he looked upon them he muttered, "Useless! useless!" These were his last words. Ay, indeed, wretched man, how useless!

Upon Booth's body a diary was found, with some of its leaves torn out, and containing some photographs of female acquaintances. The pages removed were at the beginning of the book, and as the diary purported to be one for 1864, they probably related to events preliminary to his bloody act, and of which he did not care to leave behind him a record. What was left pertained solely to the assassination, and implicated no one else in the murder. The words written were those of a man who felt that a curse rested upon him—a mark like that which was set upon Cain. In almost the same breath he commends himself as having done well, and yet doubts if there can be pardon for him in heaven.[1]

---

[1] The following is a copy of the writing, which was in pencil, found in this diary:
"Te amo.   April 13–14.   Friday, the ides.
"Until to-day nothing was ever thought of sacrificing to our country's wrongs. For six months we had worked to capture; but our cause being almost lost, something decisive and great must be done. But its failure was owing to others, who did not strike for their country with a heart. I struck boldly, and not as the papers say. I walked with a firm step through a thousand of his friends, and was stopped, but pushed on. A colonel was at his side. I shouted "Sic semper!" before I fired. In jumping, broke my leg. I passed all his pickets, rode sixty miles that night with the bone of my leg tearing the flesh at every jump. I can never repent it, though we hated to kill. Our country owed all her troubles to him, and God simply made me the instrument of his punishment. The country is not (April, 1865) what it was. This forced Union is not what I have

BOSTON CORBETT.

There was a *post-mortem* examination of the body, which was taken to Washington. This examination took place on board the Montauk, on the Potomac. On the night of the 27th of April a small row-boat received the remains of the murderer. The place and manner of his sepulture were for

loved. I care not what becomes of me. I have no desire to outlive my country. This night, before the deed, I wrote a long article and left it for one of the editors of the *National Intelligencer*, in which I fully set forth our reasons for our proceeding. He or the government—

"*Friday, 21st.* After being hunted like a dog through swamps, woods, and last night being chased by gun-boats till I was forced to return, wet, cold, and starving, with every man's hand against me, I am here in despair. And why? For doing what Brutus was honored for, what made Tell a hero. And yet I, for striking down a greater tyrant than they ever knew, am looked upon as a common cut-throat. My action was purer than either of theirs. One hoped to be great; the other had not only his country's, but his own wrongs to avenge. I hoped for no gain. I knew no private wrong. I struck for my country, and that at once; a country that groaned beneath this tyranny and prayed for this end. And yet now behold the cold hand they extend to me. God can not pardon me if I have done wrong. Yet I can not see my wrong, except in serving a degenerate people. The little, the very little I left behind to clear my name, the government will not allow to be printed. So ends all. For my country I have given up all that makes life sweet and holy; brought misery upon my family, and am sure there is no pardon in the Heaven for me, since man condemns me so. I have only heard of what has been done, except what I did myself, and it fills me with horror. God, try and forgive me, and bless my mother. To-night I will once more try the river, with the intent to cross, though I have a greater desire and almost a mind to return to Washington and in a measure clear my name, which I feel I can do. I do not repent the blow I struck. I may before my God, but not to man. I think I have done well, though I am abandoned, with the curse of *Cain upon— When, if the world* knew my heart, that one blow would have made me great, though I did desire no greatness. To-night I try to escape these blood-hounds once more. Who—who can read his fate? God's will be done. I have too great a soul to die like a criminal. May He spare me that and let me die bravely. I bless the entire world; have never hated or wronged any one. This last was not a wrong unless God deems it so, and it's with Him to damn or bless me. Hard for this brave boy with me, who often prays—yes, before and since, with a true and sincere heart. Was it crime in him? If so, why can he pray the same? I do not wish to shed a drop of blood, but I must fight the course. 'Tis all that's left me."

Upon a piece of paper found in the diary, and supposed to have been torn from it, is written the following:

"My dea [piece torn out.] Forgive me, but I have some little pride. I can not blame you for want of hospitality; you know your own affairs. I was sick, tired, with a broken limb, and in need of medical advice. I would not have turned a dog from my door in such a plight. However, you were kind enough to give us something to eat, for which I not only thank you, but, on account of the rebuke and manner in which to [piece torn out.] It is not the substance, but the way in which kindness is extended that makes one happy in the acceptance thereof. The sauce to meat is ceremony. *Meeting were bare* without it. Be kind enough to accept the inclosed five dollars, although hard to spare, for what we have received.

"Most respectfully, from your obedient servant."

A letter had been (November, 1864) left by Booth in the hands of his brother-in-law, J. S. Clarke. It was opened by the latter on the Monday after the assassination, and was published in the *Philadelphia Press* of April 19th. The following is a copy:

"——, ——, 1864.

"My dear Sir,—You may use this as you think best. But as some may wish to know when, who, and why, and as I know not how to direct, I give it (in the words of your master)—

"'To whom it may concern:'

"Right or wrong, God judge me, not man. For, be my motive good or bad, of one thing I am sure, the lasting condemnation of the North.

"I love peace more than life. Have loved the Union beyond expression. For four years have I waited, hoped, and prayed for the dark clouds to break, and for a restoration of our former sunshine. To wait longer would be a crime. All hope for peace is dead. My prayers have proved as idle as my hopes. God's will be done. I go to see and share the bitter end.

"I have ever held the South were right. The very nomination of Abraham Lincoln four years ago spoke plainly war—war upon Southern rights and institutions. His election proved it. 'Await an overt act.' Yes; till you are bound and plundered. What folly! The South were wise. Who thinks of argument or patience when the finger of his enemy presses on the trigger? In a foreign war, I too could say, 'Country, right or wrong.' But in a struggle such as ours (where the brother tries to pierce the brother's heart), for God's sake choose the right. When a country like this spurns justice from her side, she forfeits the allegiance of every honest freeman, and should leave him, untrammeled by any fealty soever, to act as his conscience may approve.

"People of the North, to hate tyranny, to love liberty and justice, to strike at wrong and oppression, was the teaching of our fathers. The study of our early history will not let me forget it, and may it never.

"This country was formed for the white, not for the black man. And, looking upon African slavery from the same stand-point held by the noble framers of our Constitution, I, for one, have ever considered it one of the greatest blessings (both for themselves and us) that God ever bestowed upon a favored nation. Witness heretofore our wealth and power; witness their elevation and enlightenment above their race elsewhere. I have lived among it most of my life, and have seen less harsh treatment from master to man than I have beheld in the North from father to son. Yet, Heaven knows, no one would be willing to do more for the negro race than I, could I but see a way to still better their condition.

"But Lincoln's policy is only preparing the way for their total annihilation. The South are not, nor have they been, fighting for the continuance of slavery. The first battle of Bull Run did away with that idea. Their causes since for war have been as noble and greater far than those that urged our fathers on. Even should we allow they were wrong at the beginning of this contest, cruelty and injustice have made the wrong become the right, and they stand now (before the wonder and admiration of the world) as a noble band of patriotic heroes. Hereafter, reading of their deeds, Thermopylæ will be forgotten.

"When I aided in the capture and execution of John Brown (who was a murderer on our western border, and who was fairly tried and convicted before an impartial judge and jury, of treason, and who, by the way, has since been made a god), I was proud of my little share in the transaction, for I deemed it my duty, and that I was helping our common country to perform an act of justice. But what was a crime in poor John Brown is now considered (by themselves) as the greatest and only virtue of the whole Republican party. Strange transmigration! Vice to become a virtue simply because more indulge in it!

"I thought then, as now, that the Abolitionists were the only traitors in the land, and that the entire party deserved the same fate as poor old Brown; not because they wish to abolish slavery, but on account of the means they have ever endeavored to use to effect that abolition. If Brown were living, I doubt whether he himself would set slavery against the Union. Most, or many in the North do, and openly, curse the Union, if the South are to return and retain a single right guaranteed to them by every tie which we once revered as sacred. The South can make no choice. It is either extermination or slavery for themselves (worse than death) to draw from. I know my choice.

"I have also studied hard to discover upon what grounds the right of a state to secede has been denied, when our very name, United States, and the Declaration of Independence, both provide for secession. But there is no time for words. I write in haste. I know how foolish I shall be deemed for undertaking such a step as this, where, on the one side, I have many friends and every thing to make me happy, where my profession alone has gained me an income of more than twenty thousand dollars a year, and where my great personal ambition in my profession has such a great field of labor. On the other hand, the South have never bestowed upon me one kind word; a place now where I have no friends except beneath the sod; a place where I must either become a private soldier or a beggar. To give up all of the former for the latter, besides my mother and sisters whom I love so dearly (although they so widely differ with me in opinion), seems insane; but God is my judge. I love justice more than I do a country that disowns it; more than fame and wealth; more (Heaven pardon me if wrong)—more than a happy home. I have never been upon a battle-field; but oh! my countrymen, could you all but see the reality or effects of this horrid war as I have seen them (in every state save Virginia), I know you would think like me, and would pray the Almighty to create in the Northern mind a sense of right and justice, even should it possess no seasoning of mercy), and that he would dry up this sea of blood between us, which is daily growing wider. Alas! poor country, is she to meet her threatened doom? Four years ago I would have given a thousand lives to see her remain (as I had always known her) powerful and unbroken. And even now I would hold my life as naught to see her what she was. Oh! my friends, if the fearful scenes of the past four years had never been enacted, or if what has been had been but a frightful dream, from which we could now awake, with what overflowing hearts could we bless our God and pray for his continued favor! How I have loved the old flag can never now be known. A few years since, and the entire world could boast of none so pure and spotless. But I have of late been seeing and hearing of the bloody deeds of which she has been made the emblem, and would shudder to think how changed she had grown. Oh! how I have longed to see her break from the mist of blood and death that circles round her folds, spoiling her beauty and tarnishing her honor. But no, day by day has she been dragged deeper and deeper into cruelty and oppression, till now (in my eyes) her once bright red stripes look like bloody gashes on the face of heaven. I look now upon my early admiration of her glories as a dream. My love (as things stand to-day) is for the South alone. Nor do I deem it a dishonor in attempting to make for her a prisoner of this man, to whom she owes so much of misery. If success attend me I go penniless to her side. They say she has found that 'last ditch' which the North have so long derided and been endeavoring to force her in, forgetting they are our brothers, and that it is impolitic to goad an enemy to madness. Should I reach her in safety, and find it true, I will proudly beg permission to triumph or die in that same 'ditch' by her side.

"A Confederate doing duty upon his own responsibility. J. Wilkes Booth."

RUINS OF GARRETT'S BARN AND OUT-HOUSES NEAR PORT ROYAL, WHERE BOOTH WAS SHOT.

LEWIS PAYNE (POWELL).

a long time unknown to the world. It were better that thus it should remain forever. This man had attempted to build his fame upon the ruins of the government. There was an ancient villain—Erostratus by name—who deliberately purposed to perpetuate the memory of his name among men by shocking sacrilege, and he burned the temple of the Ephesian Diana. John Wilkes Booth once remarked to a company of his friends that this man's name had survived, while that of the builder of the temple was forgotten. It was thus that Booth sought to leave his name to posterity, preferring to be detested rather than not be remembered at all. By bringing a whole nation to tears, he would secure immortality for himself. It is not probable that either he or his fellow-conspirators in the inception of their scheme contemplated murder. But it soon came to that. It is evident that Booth attempted to poison the President in the summer of 1864, but failed. In a room of the McHenry House, Meadville, Pennsylvania, there was found on the pane of window-glass the following inscription in Booth's handwriting: "Abe Lincoln departed this life, Aug. 13th, 1864, by the effects of poison." A conspiracy long existed which contemplated the capture of Lincoln, but was at length given up. At last, when the defeat of the Confederate armies was an accomplished fact, the conspirators reverted to assassination as the surest means of destroying the government, and inaugurating a period of anarchy in which, as they confidently believed, the Confederates would, under the leadership of some master mind, gain by murder what they had lost in battle. There is no doubt that when this scheme was adopted it was a matter of deliberation; nor can there be any question but the chief accomplices—Harold, Powell, Atzerott, Mrs. Surratt and her son John H. Surratt—were, at least for some hours previous to the murder, aware of Booth's intention, and were thus, in their several ways, participators in his guilt.

John Wilkes Booth was the third son born in America of the eminent English tragedian, Junius Brutus Booth. There were three brothers, Junius Brutus Jr., Edwin, and John Wilkes, all of whom inherited a predilection for the stage. Of these three, Edwin alone has attained an eminent distinction as an actor, and he is probably unsurpassed by any living man. No suspicion rests upon his loyalty, and after the assassination, the sympathy

elicited in his behalf was only equaled by the popular abhorrence of his unworthy brother. John Wilkes, the assassin, was born in 1839, and was only twenty-six years of age at the date of his crime. He had never achieved any marked success upon the stage, and but for his connection with the death of Lincoln, would never be known by even the next genera-

tion. In his soul inhered no nobility which could relieve his crime. He was an advocate of human slavery, and his dissolute life culminated in an act alike cowardly and despicable. Only the blank, vulgar act of murder remains as the basis of his unenviable fame. Instances there have been where brutality, allied with intellect and power, has formed the pedestal for a monument. But here the case was different: here brutality stood forth

JOHN H. SURRATT.

in its nakedness; men shrank away from the monster, and cared not to know the place of his sepulture.

The other conspirators were tried in Washington by a military commission, and on the 6th of July they received their sentence. The next day four of them—Harold, Atzerott, Powell, and Mrs. Surratt—were hung. Dr. Mudd, O'Loughlin, and Arnold were committed to a life-long imprisonment, and Spangler[1] was imprisoned for a term of six years. John H. Surratt had escaped, but he also was finally overtaken by justice, and while we write he awaits his second trial. He fled to Canada after the assassination, and there remained until September, 1865, when he started for Liverpool. In the spring of 1866 Mr. Seward was informed by Mr. King, at Rome, that Surratt had enlisted in the papal guards under the name of John Watson. He was arrested at Teroli, in Italy, but managed to escape by plunging down a ravine, making a leap of twenty-three feet. Wounded by his fall, he crawled off to a hospital, and after a few days resumed his flight. He went to Egypt, and was there again captured by our minister, Mr. Hale, and sent to

[1] The charge against O'Loughlin was that he designed the murder of Lieutenant General Grant. Arnold was charged with having rendered assistance to Booth, Powell, Atzerott, and O'Loughlin; and Spangler with having assisted in Booth's escape.

this country. He every where boldly acknowledged his connection with the assassination, and seemed to think that the world had not only forgiven the crime, but admired its atrocity.

On the morning of Mr. Lincoln's death Andrew Johnson was inaugurated President. A few days afterward—on the 2d of May—he issued a proclamation offering large rewards for the capture of Jefferson Davis, Jacob Thompson, Clement C. Clay, Beverly Tucker, George N. Saunders, and William C. Cleary, on the ground that they were implicated in the assassination by evidence then in the possession of the Bureau of Military Justice.[1] It

[1]   "*By the President of the United States of America:*

"A PROCLAMATION.

"Whereas, it appears from evidence in the Bureau of Military Justice that the atrocious murder of the late President, Abraham Lincoln, and the attempted assassination of the Honorable William H. Seward, Secretary of State, were incited, concerted, and procured by and between Jefferson Davis, late of Richmond, Virginia, and Jacob Thompson, Clement C. Clay, Beverly Tucker, George N. Saunders, William C. Cleary, and other rebels and traitors against the government of the United States, harbored in Canada:

"Now, therefore, to the end that justice may be done, I, Andrew Johnson, President of the United States, do offer and promise for the arrest of said persons, or either of them, within the limits of the United States, so that they can be brought to trial, the following rewards:

"One hundred thousand dollars for the arrest of Jefferson Davis.

"Twenty-five thousand dollars for the arrest of Clement C. Clay.

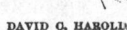
DAVID C. HAROLD.

MRS. SURRATT'S HOUSE, WASHINGTON.

was afterward proved that a cipher found in Booth's trunk corresponded to that used by the Confederate Secretary of State, J. P. Benjamin, and that Jefferson Davis had referred to his Secretary of War for consideration a letter from one L. W. Alston, who proposed to rid the Confederacy "of some of her deadliest enemies, by striking at the very heart's blood of those who seek to enchain her in slavery."[1]

In the mean while the people were burying their president. As soon as his death was known, business for a time ceased. Every house, from the palatial mansion to the lowest hovel, was draped with mourning. The nation was one vast funeral. From every pulpit, on the following Sabbath, there was uttered a funeral sermon. On Monday, April 17th, all the members of Congress then at Washington met at the Capitol to make arrangements for the funeral. It was finally determined that the remains of the President should be taken to his old home at Springfield, Illinois, and a Congressional Committee was appointed to accompany them, consisting of the entire Illinois delegation, and one member from each other state and each territory. The consignment of Lincoln's remains to Illinois was due to the urgent request of Governor Oglesby, Senator Yates, and others of that state. Sumner and many others desired that the body should be placed under the dome of the Capitol, at Washington, where a vault had been prepared for the Father of his Country, but had not been used for that purpose.

On Wednesday, the 19th, the funeral services were held in the east room of the White House. The coffin rested upon a canopied catafalque, and was decorated with wreaths of moss and evergreen, with white flowers and lilies. Around the catafalque at noon were gathered the late President's family, the officiating clergymen, the cabinet, the governors of several states, the Supreme Court, and the diplomatic corps. The Episcopal service for the dead was read by the Rev. Dr. Hall. Bishop Simpson, of the Methodist Episcopal Church, followed with a prayer. This portion of the service was most impressive, and, as the bishop concluded with the Lord's Prayer, the whole audience, dissolved in tears, joined as with one voice. Rev. Dr. Gurley, pastor of the church which Mr. Lincoln and his family were in the habit of attending, preached the funeral discourse. Then the concluding prayer was offered by Rev. Dr. Gray, chaplain of the Senate.

From the White House, at the close of the service, the procession passed up Pennsylvania Avenue to the Capitol, and up the steps, underneath the very spot from which, six months before, Lincoln had delivered his second inaugural, his funeral car was carried and deposited in the rotunda. Here the body remained until the 21st, when it was removed, under escort, to the dépôt of the Baltimore and Ohio Railroad. Then commenced the funeral procession of the President from Washington to Springfield—from the scene of his divinely-directed labors to his final resting-place. At each of the principal cities on the route—at Baltimore, Harrisburg, Philadelphia, New York, Albany, and Chicago—the body of the President lay for some hours in state, and hundreds of thousands of citizens were thus permitted to look upon the face which they had greeted four years before—then turned toward the national capital, now returning thence to meet the silence of the tomb. *Then* the malice of his foes had compelled Lincoln to proceed in disguise through Baltimore to Washington; now also he is in disguise, wearing the mask of death, through which all, bending over the silent features in loving reverence, discover his worthiness. His work has been all done, and this funeral procession is, after all, one of triumph. Well did Beecher say: "And now the martyr is moving in triumphal march, mightier than when alive. The nation rises up at every stage of his coming. Cities and states are his pall-bearers, and the cannon speaks the hours with solemn progression. Dead, dead, dead, he yet speaketh. Is Washington dead? Is Hampden dead? Is David dead? Is any man that was ever fit to live dead? Disenthralled of flesh, risen to the unobstructed sphere where passion never comes, he begins his illimitable work. His life is now grafted upon the infinite, and will be fruitful as no earthly life can be. Pass on, thou that hast overcome! Your sorrows, oh people, are his pæans; your bells, and bands, and muffled drums sound triumph in his ears. Wail and weep here; God makes it echo joy and triumph there. Pass on! Four years ago, oh Illinois, we took from thy midst an untried man, and from among the people; we return him to you a mighty conqueror. Not thine any more, but the nation's; not ours, but the world's. Give him place, oh ye prairies. In the midst of this great continent his dust shall rest, a sacred treasure to myriads who shall pilgrim to that great shrine to kindle anew their zeal and patriotism. Ye winds that move over the mighty places of the West, chant his requiem! Ye people, behold the martyr whose blood, as so many articulate words, pleads for fidelity, for law, for liberty!"

As the procession moved through New York on the 25th, it was witnessed by nearly a million of people. Among the most interesting of the incidents connected with the lying in state at this city was the visit to the remains of the aged soldier, General Scott, who was soon to follow the President. The funeral train reached Springfield on the 3d of May. Since his departure from that city in 1861, when he had asked his friends and neighbors to accompany him with their prayers, he had never returned till this time and in this manner. As it was beautifully expressed in one of the mottoes displayed by the citizens:

"He left us borne up by our prayers,
He returns embalmed in our tears."

Lincoln was buried at Oak Ridge Cemetery, about two miles from Springfield. The funeral oration was pronounced by Bishop Simpson.

"Here," said the bishop, "are gathered around his tomb the representatives of the army and navy, senators, judges, governors, and officers of all the branches of the government. Here, too, are members of civic processions, with men and women from the humblest as well as the highest occupations. Here and there, too, are tears as sincere and warm as any that drop, which come from the eyes of those whose kindred and whose race have been freed from their chains by him whom they mourn as their deliverer. More persons have gazed on the face of the departed than ever looked upon the face of any other departed man. More races have looked on the procession for sixteen hundred miles or more—by night and by day—by sunlight, dawn, twilight, and by torchlight, than ever before watched the progress of a procession."

He concluded with the following *Vale:*

"Chieftain, farewell! The nation mourns thee. Mothers shall teach thy name to their lisping children. The youth of our land shall emulate thy virtues. Statesmen shall study thy record and learn lessons of wisdom. Mute though thy lips be, yet they still speak. Hushed is thy voice, but its echoes of liberty are ringing through the world, and the sons of bondage listen with joy. Prisoned thou art in death, and yet thou art marching abroad, and chains and manacles are bursting at thy touch. Thou didst fall not for thyself. The assassin had no hate for thee. Our hearts were aimed at, our national life was sought. We crown thee as our martyr, and humanity enthrones thee as her triumphant son. Hero, martyr, friend, farewell!"

"Twenty-five thousand dollars for the arrest of Jacob Thompson, late of Mississippi.

"Twenty-five thousand dollars for the arrest of George N. Saunders.

"Twenty-five thousand dollars for the arrest of Beverly Tucker.

"Ten thousand dollars for the arrest of William C. Cleary, late clerk of Clement C. Clay.

"The Provost-marshal General of the United States is directed to cause a description of said persons, with notice of the above rewards, to be published.

"In testimony whereof, I have hereunto set my hand and caused the seal of the United States to be affixed.

"Done at the City of Washington, this second day of May, in the year of our Lord one thousand [L.S.] eight hundred and sixty-five, and of the independence of the United States of America the eighty-fifth.
ANDREW JOHNSON.

"By the President: W. HUNTER, Acting Secretary of State."

[1] The following is an abstract of a portion of the evidence relating to this subject, offered before the Military Commission at the trial of the conspirators:

Charles A. Dana, Assistant Secretary of War, testified that he went to Richmond April 6, and there found in Benjamin's office the key to an official cipher. It is a machine about a foot long and eight inches high, and consists of a cylinder of wood which has a paper envelope inscribed with letters; the cylinder revolves on pivot-holes at each end, and a bar across the top contains wooden indices pointing down to the letters.

Major Eckert then being sworn, testified that a cipher found in Booth's trunk corresponded with that of which Dana had spoken. Rebel dispatches of October 13th and 19th (1860) had fallen into his hand which were deciphered on the same principle. The following are the dispatches translated:

"October 13, 1864.

"We again urge the necessity of our getting immediate advantages. Strain every nerve for victory. We now look upon the re-election of Lincoln in November as almost certain, and we need to whip his hirelings to prevent it. Besides, with Lincoln re-elected, and his armies victorious, we need not hope even for recognition, much less the help mentioned in our last. Holcomb will explain this. Those figures of the Yankee armies are correct to a unit. Your friend shall be immediately set to work as you direct."

"October 19, 1864.

"Your letter of the 13th is at hand. There is yet time enough to colonize many voters before November. A blow will shortly be stricken here. It is not quite time. General Longstreet is to attack Sheridan without delay, and then move north as far as practicable toward unprotected points. This will be made instead of the movement before mentioned. He will endeavor to assist the Republicans in collecting their ballots. Be watchful and assist him."

That of the 13th passed from Canada to Richmond; that of the 19th from Richmond to Canada.

Robert A. Campbell, first teller of the Ontario Bank of Montreal, testified Jacob Thompson had kept an account with the bank from May 30, 1864. The account closed April 11, 1865. The aggregate amount of credit was $649,872 23; there was a balance due Thompson. Since March 1st he had drawn $300,000. Since the assassination Thompson had left Montreal. He said he was going overland to Halifax *en route* to Europe. This was about two weeks before navigation opened. To Mr. Campbell it seemed strange that Thompson should have gone overland, when, by waiting two weeks, he could have taken a steamer. Booth also had a small account with the Ontario Bank.

C. F. Hall testified that he had found the following paper, taken from a box marked "Adjutant General's Office. Letters received July to December, 1864."

"Montgomery, White Sulphur Springs, Va.

"To his Excellency President C. S. A.

"DEAR SIR,—I have been thinking for some time I would make this communication to you, but have been deterred from doing so on account of ill health.

"I now offer you my services, and if you will favor me in my designs, I will proceed, as soon as my health will permit, to rid my country of some of her deadliest enemies, by striking at the very heart's blood of those who seek to enchain her in slavery. I consider nothing dishonorable having such a tendency. All I want of you is to favor me by granting the necessary papers, etc., to travel on while in the jurisdiction of this government. I am perfectly familiar with the North, and feel confident that I can execute any thing I undertake. I have just returned now from within their lines. I am a lieutenant in General Duke's command. I was on a raid last June in Kentucky, under General John A. Morgan. I and all my command, except two or three commissioned officers, were taken prisoners; but, finding a good opportunity while being taken to prison, I made my escape from them. In the garb of a citizen I attempted to pass out through the mountains, but, finding that impossible, narrowly escaping two or three times being retaken, directed my course north and west through the Canadas; by the assistance of Colonel J. P. Holcombe I succeeded in making my way round through the blockade; but, having taken the yellow fever, etc., at Bermuda, I have been rendered unfit for service since my arrival. I was reared up in the State of Alabama, and educated in its University. Both the Secretary of War and his assistant, Judge Campbell, are personally acquainted with my father, William J. Alston, of the Fifth Congressional District of Alabama, having served in the time of the old Congress in 1849, 1850, and 1851. If I do any thing for you I shall expect your full confidence in return. If you can give this, I can render you and my country very important service. Let me hear from you soon. I am anxious to be doing something, and having no command at present, all or nearly all being in garrison, I desire that you favor me in this a short time. I would like to have a personal interview with you in order to perfect arrangements before starting. I am, very respectfully, your obedient servant, L. W. ALSTON.

"Address me at the Springs, in hospital."

On the above letter were the following indorsements:

"1. Brief of letter without signature.

"2. Respectfully referred by direction of the President to Honorable Secretary of War. Burton N. Harrison, Private Secretary. Received November 29, 1864. Record book A. G. O., December 8, 1864.

"3. A. G. for attention. By order, J. A. Campbell, A. S. W."

CHAPTER LXI.

CONDUCT OF THE WAR.

Grand Review at Washington.—Mustering out of the Troops.—The two Periods of the War.—Our Generals.—Connection of Negroes with the War.—The Foreign Element in our Armies.—Confederate Conscription.—The War Department and Secretary Stanton.—The Question of Supplies with the Confederates.—Sanitary Commissions.—Treatment of Prisoners.—Irregular Warfare.—Confederate Agents in Canada.—The War upon the Sea.—Anglo-Confederate Cruisers.—The Alabama Claims.—Withdrawal of the French from Mexico.—The Political Situation at the Close of the War.

UPON the surrender of the Confederate armies the war for the Union was concluded. The battles had been all fought, and the nation was victorious. It was, by reason of its victory, secure against traitors in arms. Treason might still remain, but it was a disarmed prisoner. The reward of four years of bitter strife had been grasped by a patriotic people. Peace had come, not through conciliation or compromise, but as a conquest. For a brief period the popular enthusiasm knew no bounds, until too soon it was tempered by the death of Lincoln. No one talked of political theories; all felt that such theories had no share in the glory of this triumph. The battle had been won by blood and sacrifice. With one accord the nation turned toward its armies, and showered its blessings upon them. The successful generals, the brave soldiers—these were the heroes of that time. Four years before, regiment after regiment had marched through our cities, with new banners, bright arms, and fresh, youthful faces. They were followed by hopes and prayers. Two soldiers—Ladd and Whitney—in the van of this southward march, had been slain in the streets of Baltimore, and their death so impressed the people that they received a monument, and passed into history sacredly, and by the association of time, linked with the revolutionary heroes of Lexington. These were the first victims of the war. They led that glorious march of the dead which, ere the end, numbered among its ranks over a quarter of a million of just such heroes as they, victims, by disease or mortal wounds, of this protracted struggle for a nation's life. Closing up the rear of this procession, thousands were still gathering from many hospitals.[1] But, though so large a number had disappeared by discharge, death, or wounds, their places had been filled by others. All together a million and a half of men had entered the United States service, and at the close of the war a million still remained,[2] of whom 650,000 were available for active duty. There were as many effective soldiers in the army when the Confederate forces surrendered as when, in May, 1864, Grant and Sherman entered upon their final campaigns.

Now the record of blood was all written, and the scene of four years ago was reversed. The soldiers were returning to their homes, and as they passed through our streets were welcomed back with grateful shouts. Their banners now were tattered, and their arms and uniform battle-soiled; many an absent one was mourned; and the fresh faces which went forth from us returned worn with the hardships of war. But they had served their country, and their step was proud and triumphant.

The armies of Grant and Sherman, who had shared in the latest struggle, as they passed through Washington, were marshaled in review. Over two hundred thousand soldiers made up the grand spectacle. They were assembled in one body for the first time. They were gathered together from every battle-field of the war—from the Ohio to New Orleans, from New Orleans to Olustee, and from Olustee to the Potomac. Those who looked upon that spectacle were reminded of that first stage of the war when the national capital was threatened, and when the first recruits rushed to its rescue. They looked upon a living, moving demonstration of the fact that treason in a republic *could* be subdued, though every rebel leader, from Davis and Stephens down to the most petty demagogue of the South, had prophesied to the contrary. There were some things to mar the triumph. A general who had marched and fought his army from Chattanooga through the fortifications of Atlanta to the sea, and thence to Goldsborough and Washington, still felt the wrong which had been studiously thrust upon him by some officers of the government. Sherman could not take Halleck by the hand. The soldiers also grievously missed the presence of Lincoln, who had called them to the conflict, and to whom they had always looked as father and friend. But may we not suppose that Lincoln, though withdrawn from the earth, looked down upon the sublime spectacle? Did he not, as one of our poets has imagined, marshal another host, composed of those who, like him, had been victims of this civil war, and who now participated in this grand review?[1]

---

[1] It is estimated that during the war 56,000 national soldiers were killed in battle, while about 35,000 died in hospital of wounds, and 184,000 by disease. The mortal casualties of the war, if we include those dying subsequent to their discharge, probably did not fall short of 300,000. The Confederates lost less in battle, owing to the defensive character of the struggle on their part; but they lost more from wounds and disease, on account of their inferior sanitary arrangements. The total loss of life caused by the rebellion must have been over half a million, while nearly as many more were disabled.

[2] The calls made during the war amount to nearly three millions of men. The following table shows the date of the several demands, the length of the period of service required, and the number obtained:

Date of Call.	Number called for.	Periods of Service.	Number obtained.	Date of Call.	Number called for.	Periods of Service.	Number obtained.
April 15, 1861........	75,000	3 mos.	93,326	October 17, 1863	300,000	3 yrs. }	374,807
May and July, 1861 ..	582,748	3 yrs.	714,231	February 1, 1864....	200,000	3 yrs. }	
May and June, 1862..		3 mos.	15,007	March 14, 1864......	200,000	3 yrs.	284,021
July 2, 1862	300,000	3 yrs.	431,958	April 23, 1864........	85,000	100 days.	83,652
August 4, 1862.......	300,000	9 mos.	87,588	July 18, 1864.........	500,000	1, 2, & 3 yrs.	384,882
June 15, 1863	100,000	6 mos.	16,361	December 19, 1864...	300,000	1, 2, & 3 yrs.	204,568
				Total........	2,942,748		2,690,401

The following table shows the number of men furnished by the several states, in the aggregate, and reduced to three years' standard:

States.	Aggregate.	Aggregate reduced to Three Years' Standard.	States.	Aggregate.	Aggregate reduced to Three Years' Standard.
Maine	71,745	56,595	District of Columbia....	16,872	11,506
New Hampshire	34,605	30,827	Ohio....................	317,133	239,976
Vermont................	35,256	29,052	Indiana.................	195,147	152,283
Massachusetts	151,785	123,844	Illinois	258,217	212,694
Rhode Island...........	23,711	17,878	Michigan	90,119	80,865
Connecticut	57,270	50,514	Wisconsin	96,118	78,985
New York..............	455,568	380,980	Minnesota..............	25,034	19,675
New Jersey	79,511	55,785	Iowa	75,860	68,182
Pennsylvania	366,326	267,558	Missouri	108,773	86,192
Delaware	13,651	10,303	Kentucky..............	78,540	70,348
West Virginia..........	30,003	27,653	Kansas	20,097	18,654
Maryland	49,730	40,692	Total	2,653,062	2,129,041

It is impossible to give an exact estimate of the number of *different* men who entered the service. It is generally conceded, however, to have been about a million and a half. Scarcely less than three quarters of a million different men entered the Confederate armies, not including state militia. So that the number of men withdrawn from industrial pursuits by the war was over two millions.

---

[1] Henry Howard Brownell, in a poem originally published in the *Atlantic Monthly*—a poem which is certainly the greatest of the many called forth by the war—thus expresses this imagination:

"So, from the fields they win,
Our men are marching home—
A million are marching home!
To the cannon's thundering din,
And banners on mast and dome;
And the ships come sailing in
With all their ensigns dight,
As erst for a great sea-fight.

"Let every color fly,
Every pennon flaunt in pride;
Wave, Starry Flag, on high!
Float in the sunny sky,
Stream o'er the stormy tide!
For every stripe of stainless hue,
And every star in the field of blue,
Ten thousand of the brave and true
Have laid them down and died.

"And in all our pride to-day
We think, with a tender pain,
Of those so far away
They will not come home again.

"And our boys had fondly thought,
To-day, in marching by,
From the ground so dearly bought,
And the fields so bravely fought,
To have met their Father's eye.

"But they may not see him in place,
Nor their ranks be seen of him;
We look for the well-known face,
And the splendor is strangely dim.

"Perished?—who was it said
Our Leader had passed away?
Dead? Our President dead?
He has not died for a day!

"We mourn for a little breath
Such as, late or soon, dust yields;
But the dark flower of death
Blooms in the fadeless fields.

"We looked on a cold, still brow,
But Lincoln could yet survive;
He never was more alive,
Never nearer than now.

"For the pleasant season found him,
Guarded by faithful hands,
In the fairest of Summer Lands;
With his own brave staff around him,
There our President stands.

"There they are all at his side,
The noble hearts and true,
That did all men might do—
Then slept, with their swords, and died.

"Of little the storm has reft us
But the brave and kindly clay—
('Tis but dust where Lander left us,
And but turf where Lyon lay).

"There's Winthrop, true to the end,
And Ellsworth of long ago
(First fair young head laid low!),
There's Baker, the brave old friend,
And Douglas, the friendly foe.

"(Baker, that still stood up
When 'twas death on either hand:
''Tis a soldier's part to stoop,
But the senator must stand.')

"The heroes gather and form—
There's Cameron, with his scars,
Sedgwick, of siege and storm,
And Mitchell, that joined his stars.

"Winthrop, of sword and pen,
Wadsworth, with silver hair,
Mansfield, ruler of men,
And brave McPherson are there.

"Birney, who led so long,
Abbott, born to command,
Elliott the bold, and Strong,
Who fell on the hard-fought strand.

"Lytle, soldier and bard,
And the Ellets, sire and son;
Ransom, all grandly scarred,
And Redfield, no more on guard
(But Allatoona is won!).

"Reno, of pure desert,
Kearney, with heart of flame,
And Russell, that hid his hurt
Till the final death-bolt came;

"Terrill, dead where he fought,
Wallace, that would not yield,
And Sumner, who vainly sought
A grave on the foughten field

"(But died ere the end he saw,
With years and battles outworn).
There's Harker of Kenesaw,
And Ulric Dahlgren, and Shaw,
That slept with his hope forlorn.

"Bayard, that knew not fear
(True as the knight of yore),
And Putnam, and Paul Revere,
Worthy the names they bore.

"Allen, who died for others,
Bryan, of gentle fame,
And the brave New England brothers
That have left us Lowell's name.

"Home, at last, from the wars—
Steadman, the stanch and mild,
And Janeway, our hero-child,
Home, with his fifteen scars!

"There's Porter, ever in front,
True son of a sea-king sire,
And Christian Foote, and Dupont
(Dupont, who led his ships
Rounding the first ellipse
Of thunder and of fire).

"There's Ward, with his brave death-wounds,
And Cummings, of spotless name,
And Smith, who hurtled his rounds
When deck and hatch were aflame;

"Wainwright, steadfast and true,
Rodgers, of brave sea-blood,
And Craven, with ship and crew
Sunk in the salt sea flood.

"And, a little later to part,
Our captain, noble and dear—
(Did they deem thee, then, austere?
Drayton! O pure and kindly heart!
Thine is the seaman's tear).

"All such, and many another
(Ah, list how long to name!),
That stood like brother by brother,
And died on the field of fame.

"And around—(for there can cease
This earthly trouble)—they throng,
The friends that had passed in peace,
The foes that have seen their wrong.

"(But, a little from the rest,
With sad eyes looking down,
And brows of softened frown,
With stern arms on the chest,
Are two, standing abreast—
Stonewall and Old John Brown.)

"But the stainless and the true,
These by their President stand,
To look on his last review,
Or march with the old command.

"And lo, from a thousand fields,
From all the old battle-haunts,
A greater army than Sherman wields,
A grander review than Grant's!

"Gathered home from the grave,
Risen from sun and rain—
Rescued from wind and wave
Out of the stormy main—
The legions of our brave
Are all in their lines again!

"Many a stout corps that went,
Full-ranked, from camp and tent,
And brought back a brigade;
Many a brave regiment,
That mustered only a squad.

"The lost battalions,
That, when the fight went wrong,
Stood and died at their guns—
The stormers steady and strong,

"With their best blood that bought
Scarp, and ravelin, and wall—
The companies that fought
Till a corporal's guard was all.

"Many a valiant crew,
That passed in battle and wreck—
Ah, so faithful and true!
They died on the bloody deck,
They sank in the soundless blue.

"All the loyal and bold
That lay on a soldier's bier—
The stretchers borne to the rear,
The hammocks lowered to the hold.

"The shattered wreck we hurried,
In death-fight, from deck and port—
The Blacks that Wagner buried—
That died in the Bloody Fort!

"Comrades of camp and mess,
Left, as they lay, to die,
In the battle's sorest stress,
When the storm of fight swept by;
They lay in the Wilderness—
Ah! where did they not lie?

"In the tangled swamp they lay,
They lay so still on the sward!—
They rolled in the sick-bay,
Moaning their lives away—
They flushed in the fevered ward.

"They rotted in Libby yonder,
They starved in the foul stockade—
Hearing afar the thunder
Of the Union cannonade!

"But the old wounds all are healed,
And the dungeoned limbs are free—
The Blue Frocks rise from the field,
The Blue Jackets out of the sea.

"They've 'scaped from the torture-den,
They've broken the bloody sod,
They're all come to life agen!—
The third of a million men
That died for thee and for God!

"A tenderer green than May
The Eternal Season wears—
The blue of our summer's day
Is dim and pallid to theirs—
The horror faded away,
And 'twas heaven all unawares!

"Tents on the Infinite Shore!
Flags in the azuline sky,
Sails on the seas once more!
To-day, in the heaven on high,
All under arms once more!

"The troops are all in their lines,
The guidons flutter and play;
But every bayonet shines,
For all must march to-day.

"What lofty pennons flaunt?
What mighty echoes haunt,
As of great guns, o'er the main?
Hark to the sound again—
The Congress is all ataunt!
The Cumberland's manned again!

"All the ships and their men
Are in line of battle to-day—
All at quarters, as when
Their last roll thundered away—
All at their guns, as then,
For the fleet salutes to-day.

"The armies have broken camp
On the vast and sunny plain,
The drums are rolling again;
With steady, measured tramp,
They're marching all again.

"With alignment firm and solemn,
Once again they form
In mighty square and column—
But never for charge and storm.

"The old flag they died under
Floats above them on the shore,
And on the great ships yonder
The ensigns dip once more—
And once again the thunder
Of the thirty guns and four!

"In solid platoons of steel,
Under heaven's triumphal arch,
The long lines break and wheel,
And the word is 'Forward, march!'

"The colors ripple o'erhead,
The drums roll up to the sky,
And with martial time and tread
The regiments all pass by—
The ranks of our faithful Dead,
Meeting their President's eye.

"With a soldier's quiet pride
They smile o'er the perished pain,
For their anguish was not vain—
'For thee, O Father, we died!
And we did not die in vain.'

"March on, your last brave mile!
Salute him, Star and Lace!
Form round him, rank and file,
And look on the kind, rough face;
But the quaint and homely smile
Has a glory and a grace
It never had known erewhile—
Never, in time and space.

"Close round him, hearts of pride!
Press near him, side by side—
Our Father is not alone!
For the Holy Right ye died,
And Christ, the Crucified,
Waits to welcome his own."

GRAND REVIEW AT WASHINGTON.—SHERMAN'S VETERANS MARCHING THROUGH PENNSYLVANIA AVENUE.

Immediately after Lee's surrender the government began to return to a peace establishment. Four days after this surrender Secretary Stanton issued orders stopping all drafting and recruiting, curtailing purchases of arms and supplies, and reducing the number of general and staff officers. Before the close of April, 1865, preparations were made for mustering out the volunteers. On November 15th, 900,000 soldiers had been discharged.[1] The stability of the republic was not more surely demonstrated by the success of the war for the Union than by the speedy and quiet return of its defenders to civil pursuits after the suspension of hostilities.

The course of the war has been traced in the pages of this history. Of the minor actions, many have been omitted because they had no bearing upon the result; but the principal campaigns have been developed as accurately and elaborately as has been possible. We who have written, while aware of the fact that many events might have been more fully developed and illustrated by private and unofficial intelligence, still feel confident that the general outlines of the war, as we have delineated them, will thus remain forever. It is unnecessary for us here to enter into a minute review of the contest. Two eras of the war are distinctly marked. The first ended in the summer of 1863, in the victories at Gettysburg and Vicksburg. In this first period no distinction can be made between the martial enthusiasm or military skill displayed on the two sides of the struggle. In the peninsular campaign of 1862, it is difficult to say which general committed the most serious blunders—Lee or McClellan. At Shiloh we are no more astonished by Grant's negligence as to any preparation for the conflict which he knew was sure to come, than by the panic which two gun-boats created among the Confederates, depriving them of the victory of which they were already assured by their preponderance of numbers. If we wonder why Hooker, at Chancellorsville, outnumbering the enemy almost two to one, was compelled to recross the Rappahannock, we are not less surprised that Johnston and Pemberton did not prevent Grant from reaching the rear of Vicksburg after the latter general had placed his army at the mercy of his antagonists. But after the defeat of the Confederates at Gettysburg, involving severe losses on their side, and after the surrender of Vicksburg and Port Hudson, involving a loss of nearly 50,000 more, we find the conflict not only contracted to smaller proportions, but proceeding upon far more favorable conditions for the national armies. After this time the Confederate forces dwindle away by discouragement and desertion, and never again reach their former numbers. The decisive victories won by Grant at Missionary Ridge and Lookout Mountain, in November, 1863, began to illustrate the new conditions of this second era of the war. At the same time, Meade was hesitating in the East; but in May, 1864, Grant was at the head of the Army of the Potomac. Then simultaneously began the campaigns against Richmond and Atlanta, and in both the Union armies were twice as large as those which confronted them. The exhaustion of the enemy now went on rapidly, and the memorable blunder of Hood's invasion hastened the final crisis. Sherman proceeded upon his two bold marches, and in the spring of 1865 the war was terminated in Virginia and North Carolina. The crushing political defeat of the peace party in the North, while it did not create military victories, insured the ultimate success of our armies, and took away from the insurgents their last hope.

Upon a careful study of the campaigns of this war, and comparing them with those of the Old World in other times, although we find much that excites admiration, we do not find upon either side a general who could rank with the first-class generals of the world. The comparison of Lee, or Johnston, or Grant, or even of Sherman, with Napoleon or Frederick, is unwarranted, while either of the American generals named might be fitly matched with the Duke of Wellington. Republics do not, in the ordinary course of events, naturally beget Cæsars, Napoleons, nor Fredericks. Few of our generals entered the war to satisfy a personal ambition, and those who did failed utterly. Whatever success was attained was the result of a desire to faithfully serve the country. It is fortunate, on the whole, that such was the case, and that the people might claim for themselves the victory.

The fact that over one eighth of the population of the country consisted of slaves, and the relation of this servile race to the war, demands our attention. The negroes of the South expected that the war would result in their emancipation, and they were not surprised when the government broke their fetters. They waited for their freedom, but not one blow of their own motion did they strike for it. When they came within our lines, their poverty and dependence made them willing conscripts. Their sympathy with the national cause is evident from the many instances in which they furnished valuable information to our officers, and assisted our fugitive prisoners in escaping northward. Their assistance, however valuable, was not absolutely necessary, and had no important bearing upon the final result of the war. About 175,000 negroes entered the United States service, and a large portion of these were employed in garrison duty. It is a very suggestive fact, and speaks well for the peaceful disposition of the Southern negro, that while thousands of opportunities were afforded, no case of servile insurrection occurred during the war. In the early part of 1865, when every other resource had apparently been exhausted, the question of enrolling the negro as a soldier, and giving him his freedom, was quite generally discussed in the South, but it did not meet with the favor of the Confederate President. If this measure had been adopted by the Confederate government at an early stage of the war, there is no reason to doubt that the slaves would have fought for the enemies of the national government as willingly as they built their fortifications or performed other offices. The disposition by the nation of the emancipated slave after the war closed did not rest so much upon the basis of gratitude as upon general considerations affecting the common welfare.

It has been frequently asserted that the foreign element of our population was indispensable to victory, but this assertion is contradicted by the fact that over nine tenths of our soldiers were native-born citizens. The triumph of the nation would have been certain if neither foreigners nor slaves had engaged in the contest. But this fact ought not to diminish the nation's gratitude toward the negroes and foreigners who fought in its behalf, and who acquitted themselves well on the field of battle.

The two ideas upon which the Confederacy rested were those of state sovereignty and the untrammeled development of negro slavery. Scarcely, however, had the Southern States been, for these purposes, launched upon their novel voyage—scarcely had they entered upon the conflict for independence, when the necessities of war threatened the ruin of both state sovereignty and slavery. The concentration of power in the Confederate executive—more formidable and despotic than had ever before been exercised over the states of the republic—left scarcely a vestige of liberty either to states or individuals. And, on the other hand, the progress of the national arms—slow, but steady and sure—threatened the destruction of slavery. The people of the South, therefore, could not, without apprehension, look forward to either success or defeat. They had espoused a cause which, if won, placed them at the mercy of the despotism to which they had committed themselves, and the loss of which would lay them prostrate at the feet of a power whose just claim to their allegiance they had defied and resisted. To one of these evils they had committed themselves so absolutely that no release from that lay within their power; to the other evil they *would* not yield but by compulsion. They were embarked upon a ship whose pilots would surely deliver it into the jaws of Scylla, unless Fate should deliver it over to the opposite Charybdis. Fate was rapidly deciding in favor of Charybdis; but, in the mean time, they, without heart, and in their desperation, shouted their pilots on Scylla-ward. It was a pitiable situation, but they had brought it upon themselves by weakly yielding their property and their lives at the bidding of ambitious traitors. In a moment of enthusiasm, believing that no power could withstand "Southern chivalry," and that Northern enterprise, industry, and intelligence were but synonyms for cowardice, and would easily be driven from every battle-field by an effete slave aristocracy, they had dared every thing, had invoked war by an outrage upon the national flag, had pledged their estates, their honor, and their lives to treason. A few months of war exposed their mistake, both as to the character of their leaders and of the struggle in which they were engaged; but then there was no escape for a people already demoralized by rebellion.

It was only by the most arbitrary exercise of power that the Confederate armies were recruited after the first year of the war. Those who volunteered at the beginning were forcibly retained after the expiration of their terms of service. On the 16th of April, 1862, a Conscription Bill passed the Confederate Congress which placed in the service for three years all white men between the ages of 18 and 35 not legally exempted. On the 15th of July, 1863, Davis issued a proclamation which included in the service all between 18 and 45. But even this act was not sufficient. The Confederate armies did not reach their former standard. This was due largely to desertion. In February, 1864, a Conscription Bill was passed by the Confederate Congress declaring all white men between the ages of 17 and 50 "in the military service for the war." By this law, the exemption of those who had furnished substitutes was revoked. The only persons exempted were ministers of the Gospel who were in the actual performance of their duties; superintendents of deaf, dumb, and blind or insane asylums; one editor for each newspaper, and such employés as he might upon oath declare indispensable; public printers and their necessary assistants; one apothecary to each drug-store; physicians over 30 years of age of seven years' practice; presidents and teachers of colleges, academies, and schools, who had 30 or more pupils; the superintendents of public hospitals, with such physicians and nurses as were indispensable for the management of the same; and one agriculturist on each farm where there was no white male adult not liable to military duty, and which employed 15 able-bodied slaves. This act left no resource untouched. Only those were excluded from service who were absolutely necessary to the production of supplies and for the execution of the functions of government. According to an estimate published at Richmond at the close of 1864, there were in the Confederacy in 1860, between the ages of 17 and 50, 1,299,700 white men. Since that time it was estimated that 331,650 had arrived at the age of 17. And this addition would probably be balanced by the ordinary mortality added to the number of those who had advanced beyond the age of 50. But, deducting the population within the Federal lines, the losses in battle and by unusual disease, exemptions for disability, prisoners held by the Federals, and those who had left the country, there were less than half a million of soldiers left to the Confederacy, and of these full 250,000 were already in the Confederate armies. From this estimate it appears that by the close of 1864 the Confederacy was nearly exhausted of its fighting men.

The Conscription Act passed by the United States Congress did not directly increase the army to any considerable extent. But the number of substitutes obtained, and the high bounties offered under the influence of the act, increased the Federal armies to the full measure required.

It would be unjust to leave unnoticed Secretary Stanton's admirable and efficient administration of the War Department. By this department a million of men were fed, clothed, armed, and supplied with ammunition, and with all the war material necessary to organized armies; an immense

[1] Troops mustered out to August 7... 640,806
" " " August 22.. 719,338
" " " Sept. 14.... 741,107
Troops mustered out to October 15... 785,205
" " " November 15 800,963

fleet of transports moved at its bidding, laden with supplies; and under its orders thousands of miles of railroad were constructed and put in operation. Upon its prompt and efficient efforts our armies depended not only for subsistence, but also, to a great degree, for the successful issue of their marches and battles. At the head of this vast organization stood the secretary, untiring, conscientious, kind-hearted, but often brusque, as men are apt to be upon whom rest weighty responsibilities. His character was irreproachable, and his management was characterized by scrupulous economy. He had his failings, doubtless, and made many enemies; but no man probably could have been more wisely selected to move, adjust, and keep in harmonious operation the intricate machinery of a great war.

The task of supplying the national armies involved only a financial problem; with the Confederates it was a question of possibilities, and in 1863 it became a difficult and embarrassing question. The Confederate currency had depreciated until a dollar in paper was only worth six cents in coin. There were not in the South, as in the North, large capitalists to buy up the government bonds, and the banks were rapidly exhausted. The agriculturists were willing to sell their produce only at the highest market price in currency, and many refused to sell at all. The most fertile portion of the soil was devoted to the production of cotton, tobacco, and rice, and the substitution of other crops was a measure very reluctantly adopted. To add to the embarrassment of the situation, the year 1863 was remarkable for scarcity in every crop. The possession of the Mississippi cut off all supplies from the fertile states west of that river, and the occupation of East Tennessee deprived the Confederate armies of bacon. The stringency of the blockade made any extensive importation of supplies or exportation of cotton impossible; and an important consequence was the absorption of a large proportion of labor in the production of war material. The conscription of all the able-bodied men in the Confederacy between 18 and 45 left a small laboring population, if we except women, children, and slaves. It is easily seen, therefore, that the slaves of the South were already become an indispensable support of a war for the perpetuation of their own bondage. If at this crisis the Confederate government had proclaimed the emancipation of slaves, it would have stood on a high vantage-ground both as regarded foreign powers and the conduct of its struggle for independence. But such an act was, under the circumstances, a moral impossibility.

The Confederate government met the difficulty of obtaining supplies just as it had met that of obtaining soldiers. As it had forced the latter by conscription, so now it began to impress the former. If its despotic will could demand the lives of men, it could certainly demand their property. Thus the government obtained supplies at its own price. But this action created great popular discontent and much distress. The natural desire on the part of agriculturists to evade impressment led them to refuse their products to the public markets. Besides this, the extent to which impressment was carried on in the vicinity of the principal dépôts left a scanty supply of provisions for the people, and especially for women and children whose natural protectors were in the army. Famine cursed the large cities, and the instances were not a few in which women marched through the streets with arms in their hands, and compelled the satisfaction of their hunger which they had no money to appease.

What food there was in the Confederacy was not made fully available for the supply of the army or of the principal towns. The railroads were giving way, and there were no means at hand for their repair. The wooden ties rotted, the machinery was almost exhausted, the rails were worn out, and thus the speed and capacity of the trains were greatly reduced. This embarrassment in regard to supplies weakened and discouraged the Confederate armies, and produced disaffection among the people.

In another respect a great contrast is presented upon a comparison of the National and Confederate armies. We allude to sanitary arrangements. No nation ever took such care of its armies in the field as did the United States in this war. Scarcely had the President issued his first call for 75,000 men before, in our cities and rural districts, hundreds of soldiers and societies sprang up to furnish lint, bandages, hospital clothing, nurses, and delicacies for the sick and the wounded. It was at this time that the Women's American Association of Relief was organized in New York City. Associated with this organization were a number of eminent medical men, prominent among whom was Rev. Henry W. Bellows, D.D. This society united with the advisory committee of the Board of Physicians and Surgeons of New York, and the New York Medical Association for furnishing supplies in aid of the army, in sending a delegation to Washington to offer their co-operation with the medical bureau of the government. Accordingly, H. W. Bellows, and Drs. W. H. Van Buren, Elisha Harris, and Jacob Harsen, on the 18th of May, 1861, addressed a communication to the Secretary of War recommending the organization of a commission of civilians, medical men, and military officers, having for its object the regulation and development of the active benevolence of the people toward the army. With some reluctance the organization was permitted to exist under the name of a "Commission of Inquiry and Advice in respect of the Sanitary Interests of the United States Forces." Subsequently it was styled simply the United States Sanitary Commission.[1] From duties which at first were simply advisory, the commission soon advanced to such as were executive. Its representatives were found upon every transport, at every camp and

every fort, in every hospital and on every battle-field. It carefully investigated the character of the original *material* of the army from a sanitary point of view. The diet and clothing of the recruits, the cleanliness of their persons, their camping-grounds, were all subjects of its care. Disease was thus, to a great degree, prevented in the incipient stages of the soldier's career. Every provision was made for the relief of the sick and the wounded. The ambulances of the commission followed the army into battle, took the soldier almost as he fell, and prompt and sufficient relief was applied where relief was possible, and the most tender care taken of the dead. When the soldiers of the hostile army fell into our hands, they also shared in these beneficent provisions.

The officers and agents of the commission received no compensation for their labors. The people generously supplied them with the necessary means for carrying out their designs, both by the contribution of money and supplies. There were other organizations formed for similar objects, prominent among which were the Christian and the Western Sanitary Commissions. It is estimated that through these channels, and other means used for the benefit of the soldier, not less than $500,000,000 were expended. At a single fair in New York City over a million of dollars was realized by the United States Sanitary Commission.

It must not be supposed that the Confederates at home did not make sacrifices for their soldiers in the field, but from the lack of extensive and well-regulated organizations like those which we have described, their armies suffered far heavier losses both from diseases in the camp, which might have been largely prevented, and from casualties in the field, which proved fatal for want of prompt relief.

In this general review of the war there is one page upon which the historian is loth to enter. Whatever instances of barbarity may have occurred in the heat of battle or in the excitement of the march on either side, and although in some sections of the West there was a prevailing disregard of the usages of civilized war, still, to the soldiers of both armies, history must yield the honor always due to bravery. But the treatment of national prisoners by the Confederate government, especially in the later stages of the war, is a disgrace which the conscientious historian can neither palliate nor gloss over, though his cheek burn with shame for his own countrymen.

The question of the exchange of prisoners was at the outset one beset with a legal difficulty. At first the prevailing opinion was in favor of hanging as traitors every prisoner captured by the government. The rebellion was regarded as an insurrection which could soon be put down by energy and severity, and it seemed derogatory to the national dignity to recognize the belligerent rights of rebels by negotiations with them of any sort. But it was soon found necessary to adopt a different view of the whole question.

The first prisoners captured by the government were the captain and crew of the privateer Savannah, who fell into the hands of the United States brig Perry on the 3d of June, 1861. These men were tried as pirates; but, while their trial was pending, the Confederate government threatened to visit upon the prisoners captured at Bull Run the precise punishment which should be inflicted upon the privateersmen. By this threat of retaliation, the national government was induced to abandon its position. There still remained an unwillingness on its part to directly sanction exchanges, and the whole matter was for a time submitted to the various commanders, to be arranged under flags of truce. But in this way only a few exchanges took place. Without instructions from the general government, our generals declined to receive communications on the subject from the other side. Thus, after the battle of Belmont, in November, 1861, General

HENRY W. BELLOWS.

[1] The commission was composed of the following gentlemen: Rev. H. W. Bellows, D.D., New York; Professor A. D. Bache, Vice-President, Washington; Elisha Harris, M.D., Corresponding Secretary, New York; George W. Cullum, U. S. A., Washington; Alexander E. Shiras, U. S. A., Washington; Robert C. Wood, M.D., U. S. A., Washington; W. H. Van Buren, M.D., New York; Wolcott Gibbs, M.D., New York; Cornelius R. Agnew, M.D., New York; George T. Strong, New York; Frederick Law Olmstead, New York; Samuel G. Howe, M.D., Boston; J. S. Newberry, M. D., Cleveland, Ohio. Others were afterward included, and there were nearly 600 associate members in all parts of the country.

THE CHRISTIAN COMMISSION ON THE BATTLE-FIELD.

CAMP OF CONFEDERATE PRISONERS AT ELMIRA, NEW YORK.

Grant refused to treat with General Polk for a general exchange of prisoners captured in that action. The shyness of the national government in this matter was as ridiculous as it was unnecessary. The existence of the blockade was a recognition of belligerent rights as full as that involved in a cartel for the exchange of prisoners. In neither case did the recognition of belligerent rights involve a recognition of sovereignty. If the necessities of war justified the blockade, the necessities of humanity justified and demanded an arrangement in regard to prisoners.

In the latter part of December, 1861, a joint resolution was adopted by Congress, requesting the President to take immediate measures to effect a general exchange. During the following January Secretary Stanton appointed two commissioners, the Rev. Bishop Ames and the Hon. Hamilton Fish, "to visit the prisoners belonging to the army of the United States now in captivity at Richmond, in Virginia, and elsewhere, and under such regulations as may be prescribed by the authorities having custody of such prisoners, relieve their necessities and provide for their comfort at the expense of the United States." The authorities at Richmond refused to admit the commissioners, but declared their readiness to negotiate for a general exchange of prisoners. Negotiations for this purpose were accordingly opened at Norfolk, Virginia. These resulted in an agreement for an equal exchange. The Confederates at this time held 300 prisoners in excess of those captured by the national troops. These they proposed to release on parole, provided the United States would release the same number of those who might afterward be captured by them. The exchanges were commenced in the latter part of February, 1862, but were interrupted on the 18th of March by a message from President Davis to the Confederate Congress, recommending that all the Confederate prisoners who had been paroled by the United States government be released from the obligations of their parole. In the mean time, the captures made at Roanoke Island and Fort Donelson left an excess of many thousands of prisoners in the hands of the national government.

On the 22d of July a cartel was agreed upon for a general exchange, based upon that established between the United States and Great Britain in 1812. According to the provisions of this cartel, an equal exchange was to be made. All prisoners taken on either side were to be released in ten days after their capture; and those for whom no exchange could be rendered were to be bound by parole not to perform military duty until exchanged.[1]

---

[1] The following is the text of this cartel:

                 "Haxall's Landing, on James River, Va., July 22, 1862.

"The undersigned, having been commissioned by the authorities they respectively represent to make arrangements for a general exchange of prisoners of war, have agreed to the following articles:

"ARTICLE 1. It is hereby agreed and stipulated that all prisoners of war held by either party, including those taken on private armed vessels, known as privateers, shall be discharged upon the conditions and terms following:

"Prisoners to be exchanged man for man and officer for officer; privates to be placed on the footing of officers and men of the navy.

"Men and officers of lower grades may be exchanged for officers of a higher grade, and men and officers of different services may be exchanged according to the following scale of equivalents:

"A general commander-in-chief or an admiral shall be exchanged for officers of equal rank, or forty-six privates or common seamen.

The provisions of this cartel were carried out generally in good faith on both sides; but in some instances its perfect execution was interrupted.

"A flag officer or major general shall be exchanged for officers of equal rank, or for forty privates or common seamen.

"A commodore carrying a broad pennant, or a brigadier general, shall be exchanged for officers of equal rank, or twenty privates or common seamen.

"A captain in the navy, or a colonel, shall be exchanged for officers of equal rank, or for fifteen privates or common seamen.

"A lieutenant colonel, or a commander in the navy, shall be exchanged for officers of equal rank, or for ten privates or common seamen.

"A lieutenant commander or a major shall be exchanged for officers of equal rank, or eight privates or common seamen.

"A lieutenant or a master in the navy, or a captain in the army or marines, shall be exchanged for officers of equal rank, or six privates or common seamen.

"Masters' mates in the navy, or lieutenants and ensigns in the army, shall be exchanged for officers of equal rank, or four privates or common seamen.

"Midshipmen, warrant officers in the navy, masters of merchant vessels, and commanders of privateers, shall be exchanged for officers of equal rank, or three privates or common seamen; second captains, lieutenants, or mates of merchant vessels or privateers, and all petty officers in the navy, and all non-commissioned officers in the army or marines, shall be severally exchanged for persons of equal rank, or for two privates or common seamen; and private soldiers and common seamen shall be exchanged for each other, man for man.

"ART. 2. Local, state, civil, and militia rank held by persons not in actual military service will not be recognized, the basis of exchange being of a grade actually held in the naval and military service of the respective parties.

"ART. 3. If citizens held by either party on charge of disloyalty or any alleged civil offense are exchanged, it shall only be for citizens, captured sutlers, teamsters, and all civilians in the actual service of either party, to be exchanged for persons in similar position.

"ART. 4. All prisoners of war to be discharged on parole in ten days after their capture, and the prisoners now held and those hereafter taken to be transported to the points mutually agreed upon at the expense of the capturing party. The surplus prisoners not exchanged shall not be permitted to take up arms again, nor to serve as military police or constabulary force in any fort, garrison, or field-work held by either of the respective parties, nor as guards of prisoners, dépôts, or stores, nor to discharge any duty usually performed by soldiers, until exchanged under the provisions of this cartel. The exchange is not to be considered complete until the officer or soldier exchanged for has been actually restored to the lines to which he belongs.

"ART. 5. Each party, upon the discharge of prisoners of the other party, is authorized to discharge an equal number of their own officers or men from parole, furnishing at the same time to the other party a list of their prisoners discharged and of their own officers and men relieved from parole, enabling each party to relieve from parole such of their own officers and men as the party may choose. The lists thus mutually furnished will keep both parties advised of the true condition of the exchanges of prisoners.

"ART. 6. The stipulations and provisions above mentioned to be of binding obligation during the continuance of the war, it matters not which party may have the surplus of prisoners, the great principle involved being,

"1. An equitable exchange of prisoners, man for man, officer for officer, or officers of higher grade exchanged for officers of lower grade or for privates, according to the scale of equivalents.

"2. That privates and officers and men of different services may be exchanged according to the same rule of equivalents.

"3. That all prisoners, of whatsoever arm of service, are to be exchanged or paroled in ten days from the time of their capture, if it be practicable to transfer them to their own lines in that time; if not, as soon thereafter as practicable.

"4. That no officer, soldier, or employé in the service of either party is to be considered as exchanged and absolved from his parole until his equivalent has actually reached the line of his friends.

"5. That the parole forbids the performance of field, garrison, police, or guard or constabulary duty.   JOHN A. DIX, Major General.

"D. H. HILL, Major General C. S. Army."

Supplementary Articles.

"ART. 7. All prisoners of war now held on either side, and all prisoners hereafter taken, shall be sent with all reasonable dispatch to A. H. Aikens, below Dutch Gap, on the James River, in Virginia, or to Vicksburg, on the Mississippi River, in the State of Mississippi, and there exchanged, or paroled until such exchange can be effected, notice being previously given by each party of the number of prisoners it will send, and the time when they will be delivered at those points respectively; and in case the vicissitudes of war shall change the military relations of the places designated in this article to the contending parties, so as to render the same inconvenient for the delivery and exchange of prisoners, other places, bearing as nearly as may be the present local relations of said places to the lines of said parties, shall be, by mutual agreement, substituted. But nothing

The execution of William B. Mumford by order of General Butler at New Orleans; the measures taken by Federal generals to prevent private citizens not in the regular service of the Confederates from engaging in acts of war; the orders of General Pope for the impressment of property required for the use of his army in Virginia; and the action of Generals Hunter and Phelps in regard to slaves, led to a series of retaliatory orders from Richmond, issued partly for popular effect, but which were only partially executed. They contributed, however, to exaggerate the animosity of the war. Still the exchanges went on regularly at City Point during the year, and the excess of prisoners on either side was not sufficient to occasion apprehension as to the good faith of the other.

But, in the mean time, President Lincoln had issued his Emancipation Proclamation, and measures had been taken by the United States government for the employment of negroes in its military service. These measures produced consternation and fear in the minds of the Southern people. President Davis, in his message (January 14, 1863), declared his determination to deliver over to the state authorities all commissioned officers of the United States thereafter captured in any of the states embraced in the Emancipation Proclamation, to be punished as criminals engaged in exciting servile insurrection. This determination was supported by the Confederate Congress.[1]

The cartel remained in operation until July, 1863. On the third of that month, an order was issued by the Adjutant General at Washington requiring all prisoners to be delivered at City Point and Vicksburg, there to be exchanged, or paroled until exchange could be effected. The only exception allowed was in the case of the two opposing commanders, who were authorized to exchange prisoners or to release them on parole at other points agreed upon. This order was issued to prevent unauthorized paroles, and in order that the balance of exchanges might be accurately kept. The very next day General Lee was defeated at Gettysburg, and released a number of prisoners which he was unable to take with him into Virginia. He therefore paroled them, and the parole was not recognized by the United States, as it had not been made in strict accordance with the cartel, nor by the mutual agreement of the opposing commanders. At the same time, a large number of Confederate prisoners fell into the hands of the Federals by the captures of Vicksburg and Port Hudson. These were paroled by mutual agreement between the Federal and Confederate commanders. The Confederate government, without any plausible reason, declared these prisoners released from their parole, and thousands of them fought under Bragg in the battles about Chattanooga in November. But this violation of good faith did not permanently interrupt the exchange of prisoners.

The real difficulty, however, soon presented itself in the refusal of the Confederate government to recognize negro soldiers captured as prisoners of war. That government refused to exchange negro prisoners or the commissioned officers of negro regiments. The United States could not honorably make any distinction between its soldiers on the ground of color. When, therefore, the Confederate government adopted the policy of reducing to slavery all negro prisoners, and of delivering over to the state governments for punishment the commissioned officers of negro regiments, President Lincoln issued a proclamation ordering that for every national soldier killed a Confederate soldier should be executed, and for every negro in the national service sold into slavery, a Confederate prisoner should be placed at hard labor on the public works.[1] This proclamation prevented the Confederate government from carrying out its inhuman policy; but it persisted in refusing to exchange negro prisoners. This refusal interrupted the execution of the cartel of exchange. At the close of 1863 there had been captured from the Confederates one hundred and fifty thousand prisoners, of whom about 30,000 remained in the hands of the government.

In 1864 the situation in regard to prisoners remained unchanged. The positions occupied by the two governments were so antagonistic that agreement was impossible. The national government refused to exchange white for white, because the enemy would thus be relieved of the burden of maintaining his white prisoners, and, getting back his soldiers, he would dispose of the negro as he chose, since there would be left no means of retaliation. Finally, the excess of prisoners in the hands of the government became so large that the discussion ceased. It was certainly the policy of the Confederate government to yield the point in dispute. The prisoners which it held, if returned, would not, in most cases, resume their places in the field, their terms of service having expired. The Confederate prisoners, on the other hand, were soldiers for the war, and could be made immediately available. Their presence in the field was, moreover, a necessity which became every day more pressing.

What it could not accomplish by negotiation the Confederate government sought to extort by cruelty. The prison camps at Belle Isle, Andersonville, Millen, and Salisbury were each transformed into human shambles. Thousands of men were huddled together within narrow limits. In the midst of a country abounding in timber, they were deprived of all means of shelter. Exposure to rains, dews, and frost generated disease, and there was neither medical relief at hand nor suitable food. No opportunities were afforded for cleanliness, and the prisoners were covered with vermin, which, in many cases, they were too weak to remove. They were shot by those guarding them for offenses the most trivial; they were plundered of every thing which was deemed valuable by their captors; supplies sent for their relief were in many cases appropriated by Confederate officers in charge; and the charities of Southern citizens excited in their behalf were repelled. Thousands died in those prison Golgothas, and many, from weakness induced by starvation, became idiots.[2] These barbarities were not only known to the Confederate authorities, but seem to have been encouraged by them. The officers placed over the prison appear to have been selected for their brutal capacity to carry out this system of cruelty. Among these was the notorious Captain Henry Wirz, the Anderson jailer, who was after the war tried by a military commission, and executed on the 10th of November, 1865.[3]

---

in this article contained shall prevent the commanders of two opposing armies from exchanging prisoners or releasing them on parole at other points mutually agreed on by said commanders.

"ART. 8. For the purpose of carrying into effect the foregoing articles of agreement, each party will appoint two agents, to be called Agents for the Exchange of Prisoners of War, whose duty it shall be to communicate with each other by correspondence and otherwise, to prepare the list of prisoners, to attend to the delivery of the prisoners at the places agreed on, and to carry out promptly, effectually, and in good faith, all the details and provisions of the said articles of agreement.

"ART. 9. And in case any misunderstanding shall arise in regard to any clause or stipulation in the foregoing articles, it is mutually agreed that such misunderstanding shall not interrupt the release of prisoners on parole, as herein provided, but shall be made the subject of friendly explanations, in order that the object of this agreement may neither be defeated nor postponed.

"JOHN A. DIX, Major General.

"D. H. HILL, Major General C. S. A."

[1] The following joint resolutions were adopted by the Confederate Congress:

"*Resolved*, by the Congress of the Confederate States of America, in response to the message of the President, transmitted to Congress at the commencement of the present session, That, in the opinion of Congress, the commissioned officers of the enemy ought not to be delivered to the authorities of the respective states, as suggested in the said message; but all captives taken by the Confederate forces ought to be dealt with and disposed of by the Confederate government.

"*Sec.* 2. That, in the judgment of Congress, the proclamations of the President of the United States, dated respectively September 22d, 1862, and January 1st, 1863, and the other measures of the government of the United States and of its authorities, commanders, and forces, designed or tending to emancipate slaves in the Confederate States, or to abduct such slaves, or to incite them to insurrection, or to employ negroes in war against the Confederate States, or to overthrow the institution of African slavery and bring on a servile war in these states, would, if successful, produce atrocious consequences, and they are inconsistent with the spirit of those usages which in modern warfare prevail among civilized nations; they may, therefore, be properly and lawfully repressed by retaliation.

"*Sec.* 3. That in every case wherein, during the present war, any violation of the laws and usages of war among civilized nations shall be, or has been, done and perpetrated by those acting under the authority of the government of the United States, on the persons or property of the citizens of the Confederate States, or of those under the protection of the land or naval service of the Confederate States, or of any state of the Confederacy, the President of the Confederate States is hereby authorized to cause full and complete retaliation to be made for every such violation, in such manner and to such extent as he may think proper.

"*Sec.* 4. That every white person, being a commissioned officer, or acting as such, who, during the present war, shall command negroes or mulattoes in arms against the Confederate States, or who shall arm, train, organize, or prepare negroes or mulattoes for military service against the Confederate States, or who shall voluntarily aid negroes or mulattoes in any military enterprise, attack, or conflict in such service, shall be deemed as inciting servile insurrection, and shall, if captured, be put to death, or be otherwise punished at the discretion of the court.

"*Sec.* 5. Every person, being a commissioned officer, or acting as such in the service of the enemy, who shall, during the present war, excite, attempt to excite, or cause to be excited servile insurrection, or who shall incite or cause to be incited a slave to rebel, shall, if captured, be put to death, or be otherwise punished, at the discretion of the court.

"*Sec.* 6. Every person charged with an offense punishable under the preceding resolutions shall, during the present war, be tried before the military court attached to the army or corps by the troops of which he shall have been captured, or by such other military court as the President may direct, and in such manner and under such regulations as the President shall prescribe, and, after conviction, the President may commute the punishment in such manner and on such terms as he may deem proper.

"*Sec.* 7. All negroes or mulattoes who shall be engaged in war or be taken in arms against the Confederate States, or shall give aid or comfort to the enemies of the Confederate States, shall, when captured in the Confederate States, be delivered to the authorities of the state or states in which they shall be captured, to be dealt with according to the present or future laws of such state or states."

"Executive Mansion, Washington, July 30th.

[1] "It is the duty of every government to give protection to its citizens, of whatever class, color, or condition, and especially to those who are duly organized as soldiers in the public service. The law of nations, and the usages and customs of war, as carried on by civilized powers, permit no distinction as to color in the treatment of prisoners of war as public enemies. To sell or enslave any captured person on account of his color, and for no offense against the laws of war, is a relapse into barbarism and a crime against the civilization of the age. The government of the United States will give the same protection to all its soldiers; and if the enemy shall sell or enslave any one because of his color, the offense shall be punished by retaliation upon the enemy's prisoners in our hands.

"It is therefore ordered that for every soldier of the United States killed in violation of the laws of war, a rebel soldier shall be executed, and for every one enslaved by the enemy or sold into slavery, a rebel soldier shall be placed at hard labor on the public works, and continue at such labor until the other shall be released and receive the treatment due a prisoner of war.

"ABRAHAM LINCOLN."

[2] A letter of the Confederate Inspector General Chandler, dated July 5, 1864, and addressed to Colonel Chilton, of Richmond, thus describes Andersonville:

"No shelter whatever, nor materials for constructing any, had been provided by the prison authorities, and the ground being entirely bare of trees, none is within reach of the prisoners, nor has it been possible, from the overcrowded state of the inclosure, to arrange the camp with any system. Each man has been permitted to protect himself as best he can by stretching his blanket, or whatever he may have about him, on such sticks as he can procure. Of other shelter there has been none. There is no medical attendance within the stockade. Many (twenty yesterday) are carted out daily who have died from unknown causes, and whom the medical officers have never seen. The dead are hauled out daily by the wagon-load, being first mutilated with an axe in the removal of any finger-rings they may have. Raw rations have to be issued to a very large portion, who are entirely unprovided with proper utensils, and furnished with so limited a supply of fuel that they are compelled to dig with their hands in the filthy marsh before mentioned for roots, etc. No soap or clothing has ever been issued. After inquiry, the writer is confident that, with slight exertions, green corn and other antiscorbutics could readily be obtained. The present hospital arrangements were only intended for the accommodation of ten thousand men, and are totally insufficient, both in character and extent, for the present needs, the number of prisoners being now more than three times as great. The number of cases requiring medical treatment is in an increased ratio. It is impossible to state the numbers of sick, many dying within the stockade whom the medical officers have never seen or heard of till their remains are brought out for interment. The transportation of the post is also represented to be entirely insufficient, and authority is needed by the quartermaster to impress wagons and teams, and saw-mills when not employed by the government, and kept diligently occupied, and instructions given to the quartermaster in charge of transportation to afford every facility practicable for transporting lumber and supplies necessary for prisoners."

[3] The following testimony, given before the Committee on the Conduct of the War, January 30, 1865, by Albert D. Richardson, a *Tribune* correspondent, describes the situation of our prisoners at Salisbury, North Carolina:

"I am a *Tribune* correspondent, and was captured by the rebels May 3, 1863, at midnight, on a hay-bale in the Mississippi River, opposite Vicksburg. After confinement in six different prisons I was sent to Salisbury, N. C., February 3, 1864, and kept there until December 18, when I escaped. For several months Salisbury was the most endurable rebel prison I had seen. The six hundred inmates exercised in the open air were comparatively well fed and kindly treated. But early in October 10,000 regular prisoners of war arrived there, and it immediately changed into a scene of cruelty and horrors. It was densely crowded; rations were cut down and issued very irregularly; friends outside could not even send in a plate of food. The prisoners suffered constantly and often intensely for want of water, bread, and shelter. The rebel authorities placed all the prison hospitals under charge of my two journalistic comrades (Messrs. Brown and Davis) and myself. Our positions enabled us to obtain exact and minute information. Those who had to live or die on the prison rations always suffered from hunger. Very frequently one or more divisions of a thousand men would receive no rations for twenty-four hours; sometimes they were without a morsel of food for forty-eight hours. The few who had money would pay from five to twenty dollars, rebel currency, for a little loaf of bread. Most of the prisoners traded the buttons from their blowses for food. Many, though the weather was very inclement and snows frequent, sold coats from their backs and shoes from their feet. Yet I was assured, on authority entirely trustworthy, that the great commissary warehouse near the prison was filled with provisions; that the commissary found it difficult to obtain storage for his flour and meal; that when a subordinate asked the post commandant, Major John H. Gee, 'Shall I give the prisoners full rations?' he replied, 'No, God damn them, give them quarter rations.' I know, from personal observation, that

THE ANDERSONVILLE BURIAL-GROUNDS WHERE WERE INTERRED 14,000 UNION PRISONERS.

In the latter part of 1864, Lieutenant General Grant made an arrangement for an exchange of prisoners man for man, according to the old cartel, until on one side or the other the number of prisoners held was exhausted. The war seemed so near its close that the exchange could afford no substantial aid to the Confederacy, and every motive on the score of humanity demanded that the government, under these circumstances, should waive the old dispute respecting negro prisoners.[1]

During the last few months of the war, when the prospects of Confederate success through regularly conducted warfare seemed desperate, a series of attempts were made to paralyze and subvert the national government by means which desperation naturally suggested to bold and unscrupulous men. The capture of the Confederate archives at the close of the war disclosed letters which showed that propositions for the destruction of officers connected with the government had not only, at various stages of the war, been received by the Confederate executive, but had been subjects of consideration. As early as June 19th, 1861, one C. L. V. De Kalb, representing himself to be the grandson of Baron De Kalb, of Revolutionary fame, addressed a letter to L. P. Walker, the Confederate Secretary of War, reminding the latter that the Federal Congress would assemble on the 4th of July, and that the Capitol and public buildings at Washington were undermined. In regard to this matter, he begged "the honor of a few moments' private audience." The letter is indorsed "About blowing up the Capitol at Washington." Another letter, dated the next day, was also found, from which it appears that De Kalb had been granted an audience on the 19th, but that Walker had hesitated to consent to the diabolical scheme proposed, not on account of its nature, but because De Kalb was a stranger to him. In this letter of the 20th De Kalb discloses his antecedents, his relation to Baron De Kalb, his service in the Crimean War as second lieutenant of Engineers, his arrival at Quebec in November, 1860, and at Washington three weeks ago. "Does the Southern Confederacy," he adds, "consider the explosion of the Federal Capitol, at a time when Abe, his myrmidons, and the Northern Congress members are all assembled together, of sufficient importance as to grant me, in case of success, a commission as colonel of Topographical Engineers, and the sum of one million of dollars?" Walker, instead of spurning the proposition, indorsed the letter with the following phrase: "See this man with Benjamin." He proposed to make the matter a subject of consideration at an interview between himself, this murderous villain, and the Confederate Secretary of State. In the Confederate archives was also found a letter addressed to Jefferson Davis, September 12th, 1861, by J. S. Parramore, in which the writer offers "to dispose of the leading characters of the North," and upon the letter was Davis's indorsement indicating the object of the communication, and referring it to the Secretary of War. After due consideration, both De Kalb's and Parramore's schemes appear to have been rejected as unadvisable.

On the 17th of August, 1863, we find another letter written to Davis by H. C. Dunham, of Georgia, a volunteer in the Confederate service, in which the writer states that the evidences of Davis's Christian humility encourage him to propose the organization of from 300 to 500 men, "to go into the United States, and assassinate the most prominent leaders of our enemies—for instance, Seward, Lincoln, Greeley, Prentice, etc." This communication was also referred to the Secretary of War.

Still later, Lieutenant W. Alston, in November, 1864, offered to rid the Confederacy "of some of her deadliest enemies," and his communication is referred to the Confederate Secretary of War. These various propositions for the assassination of the prominent officers of the Federal government appear to have been considered and rejected for prudential reasons. The time for such desperate measures had not yet arrived. But still they were matters of deliberate consideration.

Other schemes also were proposed. In February, 1865, W. S. Oldham, of Texas, in company with Senator Johnson, of Missouri, conferred with Davis "in relation to the prospect of annoying and harassing the enemy by burning their shipping, towns, etc." The Confederate President interposed objections as to the practicability of the scheme proposed. These objections were subsequently rebutted by Oldham. "I have seen enough," says the latter, "of the effects that can be produced to satisfy me that in most cases, without any danger to the parties engaged, and in others but very slight, we can, first, burn every vessel that leaves a foreign port for the United States; second, we can burn every transport that leaves the harbor of New York, or other Northern port, with supplies for the armies of the enemy in the South; third, burn every transport or gun-boat on the Mississippi River, as well as devastate the country of the enemy, and fill his people with terror and consternation. I am not alone of this opinion, but many other gentlemen are as fully and thoroughly impressed with the conviction as I am. I believe we have the means at our command, if promptly appropriated and energetically applied, to demoralize the Northern people in a very short time. For the purpose of satisfying your mind upon the subject, I respectfully but earnestly request that you will have an interview with General Harris, formerly a member of Congress from Missouri, who, I think, is able, from conclusive proof, to convince you that what I have suggested is perfectly feasible and practicable." Davis requested the Secretary of War to confer with Harris, "and learn what plan he has for overcoming the difficulty heretofore experienced."

What was the "difficulty heretofore experienced?" A number of Confederates—George N. Sanders, Beverly Tucker, Jacob Thompson, William C. Cleary, and Clement C. Clay—had been sent to Canada as agents of the Confederate government. Jacob Thompson appears to have been the treasurer of this special organization, the objects of which were the terror and consternation of the North through the destruction of shipping, the burning of hotels, the introduction of pestilence, and the assassination of the prominent officers of the national government. In the latter part of 1864 the attempt at arson had been tried without success, and the principals engaged were executed. John Y. Beall, detected in the act of destroying Federal vessels in the Northwest, was tried and condemned as a spy, and suffered death. One Kennedy, on the night of November 25th, 1864, with his confederates, attempted to set fire to four hotels in New York City. The attempt did not succeed, but Kennedy was apprehended and hung on the 19th of October. Three days later, Lieutenant Bennet H. Young, with from 30 to 40 Confederate associates, made a raid upon St. Albans, Vermont, 15 miles from the Canadian border. Over $200,000 was captured from the banks, horses were seized, and several citizens were wantonly murdered. An unsuccessful attempt was also made to fire the town. The raiders were pursued, but escaped into Canada. Here they were arrested and brought before the Court of Quarter Sessions at Montreal. The judge, Mr. Coursol, released them from custody on the ground that the court had no jurisdiction over the case. Judge Coursol was afterward suspended for this action, and the raiders were rearrested, but the prisoners finally were again released without punishment.

These expeditions all originated in Canada, and proceeded under Confed-

---

corn and pork are very abundant in the region about Salisbury. For several weeks the prisoners had no shelter whatever. They were all thinly clad; thousands were barefooted; not one in twenty had either overcoat or blanket; many hundreds were without shirts, and hundreds were without blowses. At last one Sibley tent and one 'A' tent were furnished to each squad of one hundred. With the closest crowding these sheltered about one half the prisoners. The rest burrowed in the ground, crept under buildings, or shivered through the nights in the open air upon the frozen, muddy, or snowy soil. If the rebels, at the time of their capture, had not stolen their shelter-tents, blankets, clothing, and money, they would have suffered little from cold. If the prison authorities had permitted a few hundred of them, either upon parole or under guard, to cut logs within two miles of the garrison, the prisoners would gladly have built comfortable and ample barracks in one week. But the commandant would never, in a densely wooded region, with the cars which brought it passing by the wall of the prison, even furnish half the fuel which was needed.

"The hospitals were in a horrible condition. By crowding the patients thick as they could lie upon the floor they would contain six hundred inmates. They were always full to overflowing, with thousands seeking admission in vain. In the two largest wards, containing jointly about two hundred and fifty patients, there was no fire whatever. The others had small fireplaces, but were always cold. One ward, which held forty patients, was comparatively well furnished. In the other eight the sick and dying men lay upon the cold and usually naked floor, for the scanty straw furnished us soon became too filthy and full of vermin for use. The authorities never supplied a single blanket, or quilt, or pillow, or bed, for those eight wards. We could not procure even brooms to keep them clean, or cold water to wash the faces of the inmates. Pneumonia, catarrh, and diarrhœa were the prevailing diseases, but they were directly the result of hunger and exposure. More than half who entered the hospitals died in a very few days. The deceased, always without coffins, were loaded in a dead-cart, piled upon each other like logs of wood, and so driven out to be thrown into a trench and covered with earth.

"The rebel surgeons were generally humane and attentive. They endeavored to improve the shocking condition of the hospitals, but the Salisbury and Richmond authorities both disregarded their complaints and protests.

"On November 25 many of the prisoners had been without food for forty-eight hours. Desperate from hunger, without any matured plan, a few of them said, 'We may as well die in one way as another; let us break out of this horrible place.' Some of them wrested the guns from a relief of fifteen rebel soldiers just entering the yard, killing two who resisted and wounding five or six. Others attempted to open the fence, but they had neither adequate tools nor concert of action. Before they could effect a breach every gun in the garrison was turned upon them, two field-pieces operated with grape and canister, and they dispersed to their quarters. Five minutes from the beginning the attempt was quelled, and hardly a prisoner was to be seen in the yard. My own quarters were a hundred and fifty yards from the scene of the insurrection. In our vicinity there had been no participation at all in it, and yet for twenty minutes after it was ended the guards upon the fence on each side of us, with deliberate aim, fired into the tents upon helpless and innocent men. They killed, in all, fifteen, and wounded about sixty, not one tenth of whom had taken part in the attempt, many of whom were ignorant of it until they heard the guns.

"Deliberate cold-blooded murders of peaceable men, where there was no pretense that they were breaking any prison regulation, were very frequent. On October 16, Lieutenant Davis, of the 155th New York Infantry, was thus shot dead by a guard, who the day before had been openly swearing that he would 'kill some damned Yankee yet.' November 6, Luther Conrod, of the 45th Pennsylvania Infantry, a delirious patient from one of the hospitals, was similarly murdered. November 30, a chimney in one of the hospitals fell down, crushing several men under it. Orders were immediately given to the guard to let no one approach the building, on the pretext that there might be another insurrection. Two patients from that hospital had not heard the order, and were returning to their quarters, when I saw a sentinel on the fence, within twenty feet of them, without challenging them, raise his piece and fire, killing one and wounding the other. Major Gee, at the time, was standing immediately beside the sentinel, who must have acted under his direct orders. December 16, Moses Smith, of 7th Maryland (colored) Infantry, while standing beside my quarters, searching for scraps of food from the sweepings of the cook-house, was shot through the head. There were very many similar murders. I never knew any pretense, even, made of investigation or punishing them. Our lives were never safe for one moment; any sentinel, at any hour of the day or night, could deliberately shoot down any prisoner, or into any group of prisoners, black or white, and he would not even be taken off his post for it.

"Nearly every week an officer came into the prison to recruit for the rebel army. Sometimes he offered bounties; always he promised good clothing and abundant food. Between 1200 and 1800 of our men enlisted in two months. I was repeatedly asked by prisoners, sometimes with tears in their eyes, 'What shall I do? I don't want to starve to death. I am growing weaker daily; if I stay here I shall follow my comrades to the hospital and dead-house; if I enlist I may live until I can escape.'

"I had charge of the clothing left by the dead, and reissued it to the living. I distributed articles of clothing to more than 2000 prisoners; but when I escaped there were fully 500 without a shoe or a stocking, and more yet with no garment above the waist except one blouse or one shirt. Men came to me frequently upon whom the rebels, when they captured them, had left nothing whatever except a light cotton shirt and a pair of light ragged cotton pantaloons.

"The books of all the hospitals were kept, and the daily consolidated reports made up, under my supervision. During the two months between October 18 and December 18, the average number of prisoners was about 7500. The deaths for that period were fully 1500, or twenty per cent. of the whole. I brought away the names of more than 1200 of the dead; some of the remainder were never reported; the others I could not procure on the day of my escape without exciting suspicion. As the men grew more and more debilitated, the percentage of deaths increased. I left 6500 remaining in the garrison, December 18, and they were dying then at the average rate of 28 a day, or thirteen per cent. a month.

"The simple truth is, that the rebel authorities are murdering our soldiers at Salisbury by cold and hunger, while they might easily supply them with ample food and fuel. They are doing this systematically, and, I believe, intentionally, for the purpose of either forcing our government to an exchange, or forcing our prisoners into the rebel army."

[1] General Grant's testimony (February 11, 1865) before the Committee on the Conduct of the War fully answers the charge which has been made against the government that it refused to consent to an exchange of prisoners because we found ours starved, diseased, and unserviceable when we received them. "There never," testifies General Grant, "has been any such reason as that for making exchanges. I will confess that if our men who are prisoners in the South were really well taken care of, suffering nothing except a little privation of liberty, then, in a military point of view, it would not be good policy for us to exchange, because every man they get back is forced right into the army at once, while that is not the case with our prisoners when we receive them. In fact, the half of our returned prisoners will never go into the army again, and none of them will until after they have had a furlough of thirty or sixty days. Still, the fact of their suffering as they do is a reason for making this exchange as rapidly as possible. . . . . Exchanges having been suspended by reason of disagreement on the part of agents of exchange on both sides before I came in command of the armies of the United States, and it then being near the opening of the spring campaign, I did not deem it advisable or just to the men who had to fight our battles to reenforce the enemy with thirty or forty thousand disciplined troops at that time. An immediate resumption of exchanges would have had that effect, without giving us corresponding benefits. The suffering said to exist among our prisoners South was a powerful argument against the course pursued, and I so felt it."

erate authority. None of them had succeeded in accomplishing what they had attempted. Some difficulties had been experienced, and the Confederate government was now considering how these difficulties might be overcome. Soon, however, other and more desperate plans were found necessary. The old scheme of assassination, formerly laid aside, was reconsidered. Ready agents were found for its accomplishment. President Lincoln was murdered, but the conspirators did not succeed in subverting the government.

The war carried on by sea against the United States by the Confederates presents many novel features. Over 200 of the officers registered in 1864 as belonging to the Confederate navy were formerly United States naval officers. Although President Davis at the outset had issued letters of marque, a Confederate navy was impossible. There were many iron-clads and rams on the Southern rivers; the defenses of the Southern harbors by means of forts, ships, torpedoes, and obstructions were very formidable; but upon the sea the Confederacy had no chance, in so far as it depended upon its own resources. But what the Confederates lacked the people of Great Britain furnished, and thus it happened that while the United States was threatened with dissolution by intestine civil war, it was compelled also, at the same time, to contend on the ocean against a British fleet—British in every sense except that it did not receive its commissions from the English government—built at Liverpool and Glasgow, sailing from those ports by the connivance of the British government, armed with British guns, and manned, for the most part, with British crews.

In the early part of the war a number of strictly Confederate privateers were fitted out. Most of these, however, did not venture far from the coast. The Sumter and Nashville, who were bolder, had a short career, which has already been traced in these pages. The only vessels which materially injured the commerce of the United States were those built in British ports, and some of which were never in a port belonging to the Confederacy.

The history of the Alabama and the Florida has already been given. In 1864, three new British vessels—the Tallahassee, Olustee, and Chickamauga—were furnished to the Confederates by the British ship-builders, and contributed each its full share in the work of destruction and plunder. By their depredations American merchantmen were almost entirely driven from the seas.

The Georgia commenced her career in 1863. She was built at Glasgow, and left Greenock as the Japan. Off the French coast she received her armament and set out upon her cruise. After a short raid upon our commerce she was sold to a Liverpool merchant. Setting out again for Lisbon, she was captured twenty miles out from that port by Captain Craven, of the Niagara, who landed her crew at Dover, in England.

Early in 1865 two new vessels—the Stonewall and Shenandoah—were added to this British tribe of corsairs. The iron-clad ram Stonewall, Captain Page, was originally built for the Danish government, and afterward purchased by the Confederates. She arrived at Ferrol, in Spain, February 4th, closely followed by the United States steamers Niagara and Sacramento. The Stonewall shifted quarters to Lisbon in March, and the Federal vessels again followed her. The Portuguese government ordered the privateer to leave, and by maritime law the national vessels were required to remain for 24 hours before entering upon the pursuit. While changing their anchorage in the Tagus, these vessels were fired upon from Belem Tower under the supposition that they were about to leave the port. No injury was done, and ample apology was rendered by the Portuguese government. On the 11th of May the Stonewall arrived at Havana. Here she was closely blockaded by Admiral Godon, with several iron-clads, and soon surrendered herself to the Spanish authorities, by whom she was given over to the United States.

The Shenandoah was built at Glasgow in 1863, and was called the Sea King. In September, 1864, she was sold to Richard Wright, of Liverpool, and thus passed into the hands of the Confederacy. She cleared at London for Bombay ostensibly as a merchant vessel. On the same day that she left London, another vessel, the Laurel, left Liverpool with armament, stores, Confederate officers, and several men enlisted in the Confederate service. At Madeira the two vessels met; the Laurel fitted out the Sea King, which then became the Shenandoah, and set forth on her piratical cruise. She destroyed a few vessels in the neighborhood of St. Helena, and on February 8th, 1865, sailed for the North Pacific from Melbourne, Australia. Between April 1st and July 1st she destroyed or bonded 29 vessels, thus breaking up the whaling season in that locality. Waddell, her captain, although aware of the surrender of the Confederate armies, continued his cruise until four months after the fall of Richmond. He then returned to England, never having been in a Confederate port, and surrendered his vessel to the English government, and by the latter was given up to the American consul at Liverpool.

It is estimated that during the war 30 vessels of all descriptions were employed by the enemy as privateers. Only seven of these were very formidable, and of these seven five were British vessels. 275 vessels were captured, comprising four steamers, 78 ships, 43 brigs, 82 barks, and 68 schooners. On the other hand, 1143 vessels were captured by blockading squadrons, valued at $24,500,000, and 355 destroyed, worth about $7,000,000.[1]

In regard to one at least of the privateers issuing from British ports, the circumstances appeared to justify the United States in claiming redress by way of compensation for the injurious consequences to American commerce. This was the case of the Alabama. The facts of the case were briefly these: The Oreto had already been permitted to sail from a British port, notwithstanding the protest of Mr. Francis Adams, the United States minister in England. Afterward Mr. Adams and the American consul at Liverpool were satisfied, upon competent evidence, that a vessel known as the 290 had been built for the Confederate service in the dock-yard of persons, one of whom was then sitting as a member of the House of Commons. This evidence was laid before the Lords Commissioners of Her Majesty's Treasury, but the latter decided that nothing had yet transpired which appeared to demand a special report. Farther evidence was procured and submitted, which, in the opinion of the queen's solicitor, was sufficient to justify the Liverpool collector in seizing the vessel. But, while the Lords Commissioners were deliberating upon the matter, the 290 sailed from Liverpool without register or clearance. Earl Russell explained to Mr. Adams that the delay in determining upon the case had been caused by the sudden illness of Sir John D. Harding, the Queen's Advocate.

It was apparent, therefore, that the fault, with its responsibility, rested upon the British government. Mr. Adams was therefore directed "to solicit redress for the national and private injuries already thus sustained, as well as a more effective prevention of any repetition of such lawless and injurious proceedings in her majesty's ports hereafter." Earl Russell replied to this demand that her majesty's government could not admit that they were under any obligation to render compensation to United States citizens for the depredations of the Alabama. There has since been a voluminous correspondence upon the subject, but the matter still stands just where it stood in 1863. Certainly it is a case in which the interests of the British government are more jeopardized by its refusal to grant compensation than its treasury could suffer by payment; and it is equally true that the United States government can well afford to waive its claim, and let the whole matter rest just as it lies.

The foreign complications with the French government arising out of the ill-advised Mexican expedition, and which at one period of the war threatened serious danger to the United States, were, soon after the suspension of hostilities, removed by the withdrawal of the French troops from Mexico. From that moment the Mexican empire which had been established rapidly waned until early in 1867, when it fell, and the Emperor Maximilian became a martyr to the cause of imperialism, which he had fought out to the bitter end.

At the close of the civil war our political sky was bright with promise. The defeated Confederates seemed disposed to accept the situation in good faith, and, on the other hand, the victorious party exhibited signs of noble magnanimity. It is true that there were in the South those who still retained the spirit which had brought on the war. Such a one was that old man Edmund Ruffin, of South Carolina, who fired the first gun against his country's flag, and who, when the national triumph was fully consummated, committed suicide. So also, on the other side, there were those who nursed a vindictive spirit against a conquered people. But, notwithstanding these exceptions, a glorious future seemed about to dawn upon the republic. How this situation was changed, and a political strife engendered which agitated the country for a series of years, and postponed the restoration and harmony which ought to have followed immediately upon the close of the war, will form the subject of the concluding chapter of this history.

---

[1] The number of vessels captured and sent to the United States Admiralty Courts for adjudication from May 1, 1861, to the close of the war, was 1143, of which there were—steamers, 210; schooners, 569; sloops, 139; ships, 13; brigs and brigantines, 29; barks, 25; yachts, 2; small boats, 139; rams and iron-clads, 6; gun-boats, torpedo-boats, and armed schooners and sloops, 10; class unknown, 7—making a total of 1149. The number of vessels burned, wrecked, sunk, and otherwise destroyed during the same time were—steamers, 85; schooners, 114; sloops, 32; ships, 2; brigs, 2; barks, 4; small boats, 96; rams, 5; iron-clads, 4; gun-boats, torpedo-boats, and armed schooners and sloops, 11; total, 355—making the whole number of vessels captured and destroyed 1504. During the war of 1812, the naval vessels, of which there were 301 in service at the close, made 291 captures. There were 517 commissioned privateers, and their captures numbered 1428. Nearly all the captures of value in the recent war were vessels built in so-called neutral ports, and fitted out and freighted for the purpose of running the blockade. The gross proceeds of property captured since the blockade was instituted, and condemned as prize prior to the 1st of November, 1865, amount to $21,829,543 96; costs and expenses, $1,616,223 96; net proceeds for distribution, $20,501,927 69. At the close of the year there were a number of important cases still before the courts, which will largely increase these amounts. The Secretary of the Navy estimates that the value of the 1143 captured vessels will not be less than $24,500,000, and of the 355 vessels destroyed at least $7,000,000, making a total valuation of not less than $31,500,000, much of which was British property.—American Cyclopædia, 1865.

ANDREW JOHNSON.

CHAPTER LXII.

RECONSTRUCTION.—1865-1867.

Difficulties incident to Restoration from the sudden Termination of the War.—The prevailing Sentiment of the North after Lee's Surrender one of Magnanimity.—Effect of Lincoln's Assassination.—Andrew Johnson's Accession to the Presidency.—Biographical Sketch.—Johnson's Inaugural Speech.—"Treason is a Crime, and must be punished as a Crime."—His View of the Situation.—His Cabinet.—Reconstruction under Lincoln's Administration.—Johnson follows the Policy of his Predecessor.—The Constitutional Provision guaranteeing to the States "a Republican Form of Government."—Meaning of this Provision.—What was involved in a Return to Allegiance on the Part of the South.—The popular Demand.—Johnson's Amnesty Proclamation.—Establishment of Provisional Governments.—The Blockade rescinded.—Release of Stephens and Trenholm.—Martial Law suspended in Kentucky.—Partial Restoration of the Writ of *Habeas Corpus*.—Southern State Conventions.—Nullification of Secession Ordinances.—Prohibition of Slavery.—Repudiation of the Rebel Debt.—Legislation in regard to Freedmen.—Its oppressive Features.—The Temper of the Southern People.—Johnson's Disappointment.—Official Announcement of the Ratification of the Anti-Slavery Amendment.—Meeting of the Thirty-ninth Congress.—Composition of the two Houses.—The new Vice-President, L. S. Foster.—The Clerk of the House, Edward McPherson, and his Disposition of the Call-roll.—Colfax re-elected Speaker of the House.—His Speech.—President Johnson's Message.—Johnson's Mistake.—He establishes a Basis for Conflict between himself and Congress.—Ought to have convened Congress in special Session at the Outset.—The Select Congressional Committee of Fifteen on Reconstruction.—Debate in the Senate.—Reports by President Johnson, Carl Schurz, and General Grant on the Southern Situation.—Unnecessary Delay of the Reconstruction Committee.—Report of the Committee by Bill, January 22, 1866.—Joint Resolution for the Amendment of the Constitution.—Its Provisions.—The President's Views on the Readjustment of the Basis of Representation.—Debate in the House.—Roscoe Conkling's Statement.—Position of Henry J. Raymond.—The Resolution referred back to the Committee, amended, and again reported.—Stevens's Speech.—Resolution passed in the House.—Debate on the Resolution in Congress.—It fails of a two-thirds Vote.—Senator Sumner's Opposition.—Second Report of the Committee, April 30, 1866.—Features of the new Amendment proposed.—Its Passage in the House and Senate.—The President's Protest.—The Prospects of the Amendment.—Full Reports of the Reconstruction Committee, June 18, 1866.—Resolution passed to exclude Southern Representatives until both Houses should consent to their Admission.—Fessenden's Support of the Resolution.—Sherman's Opposition.—His Defense of President Johnson.—Tennessee ratifies the Amendment, and her Representatives are admitted in both Houses.—The Freedmen's Bureau Bill.—The President's Veto.—The Bill fails of a two-thirds Vote.—A new Bill passed over the President's Veto.—Bill for the admission of Colorado, vetoed by the President, fails of a two-thirds Vote.—Passage of the Bill for Negro Suffrage in the District of Columbia over the Veto.—Close of the Congressional Session.—History of the Conflict between Congress and the President.—Johnson's Speech denouncing Congress, February 22, 1866.—Division in the Republican Party.—The National Union Executive Committee of Washington.—Serenade of the President and Cabinet, May 23, 1866.—Views of the Cabinet.—Resignation of Harlan and Speed.—The Political Situation in the Summer of 1866.—The Appeal to the People, and the Issues presented.—The conflicting Arguments.—The National Union Convention at Philadelphia.—Its Character and Proceedings.—The Southern Loyalists' Convention at Philadelphia.—Cleveland Convention of Soldiers and Sailors in support of the President.—Similar Convention at Pittsburg in support of Congress.—The New Orleans Riots.—Johnson's Tour to the Tomb of Douglas.—Address of the Republican National Executive Committee in support of Congress.—The Autumn Elections of 1866.—Decisive Victory of Congress.—Passage of the Military Bill.—Provisions of the Bill.—Supplementary Act of the Fortieth Congress.—Universal Suffrage in the South.—Operation of this Act.—Southern Conventions.—Reaction in the North.—Autumn Elections of 1867.—Their Significance.—A Glance at the Future.—Conclusion.

IT is always difficult to write a fair and impartial history of contemporaneous events—almost impossible for one to write such a history who has been a prominent actor in the events which he records. The position of the actor is not that of the spectator. The field which the former occupies is executive, that held by the latter is judicial. The historian is a judicial spectator, whose business it is to reproduce before his readers not simply the facts, the bare plot of a drama, but also the ideas involved in the connections between facts, the moral and physical powers by which the drama is evolved. The strength of action depends upon concentration, which precludes extensive generalization. Strong impressions upon the world are made with clenched fists, while many-sided thought tends to relax the muscles, and leads to weak and random blows, "beating the air." Especially is this true in politics, where progress is usually marked by the fluctuations of a conflict between parties. Each of the conflicting parties lives through its own distinctive ideas, and undergoes dissolution or modification only by the destruction or change of these ideas. Neither party monopolizes either all the right or all the wrong of the contest. The political actor is generally strong in the proportion that he avails himself, and becomes the representative of the one or the other class of ideas involved in the struggle. His action does not assimilate all the good of both parties, and exclude all the evil. He is, therefore, of necessity, partial, one-sided. He who will fight under neither banner, who is unwilling to identify himself with either of the great party organizations of his time, by this isolation weakens his power to strike. But with the historian it is different. The necessity of partisanship does not exist for him. Partisan history is not history, but special pleading. The historian must generalize, must be many-sided, must be impartial. His standard of truth and justice is not a party standard.

In the present case, where the writer is about to enter upon the history of the political struggle which immediately followed the Civil War, it is peculiarly appropriate that this distinction between the necessities which obligate party leaders and those which obligate the historian should be clearly drawn. If the reader, however partisan, will remember that the historian, in his judgment of men and events, is bound by a more absolute criterion of truth than is possible in party conflict, the writer will also bear in remembrance that many political acts which involved or threatened serious evils, were rendered necessary by the inevitable political conditions which controlled the development of the time of which he writes.

The manner in which the war closed, and some of the accidents of its conclusion, largely influenced subsequent political movements. If the collapse of the Confederacy had not been sudden, but gradual, the problem of reconstruction would, indeed, have been the same in its essential elements, but much of the difficulty attending its development would have been obviated. If state after state had been brought back to its allegiance, while the war still went on in others, restoration would have been immediate and thorough in each particular case, and would not have been beset with legal doubts and difficulties. The vastness of the problem was increased by the sudden cessation of hostilities, and many of its complications arose from the universal peace which all at once settled upon the country, and seemed to demand the immediate revival of constitutional civil law. Under these circumstances, there was great danger lest restoration might come in the form of reaction, by which the country would be swept along without mature de-

WILLIAM PITT FESSENDEN.

liberation, or a prudent regard for future security. The disturbance by war of the relations between the states and the central government had been violent, and their readjustment demanded the deepest thought and the most prudent caution. The domestic revolution produced in the South by the war, giving freedom to nearly four millions of slaves, added fresh and obvious reasons for such deliberation.

The prevailing feeling in the North after the surrender of Lee's army was one of magnanimity. That was generous and proper. But there might easily grow out of this such hasty action as must afterward occasion vain regret. The murder of Lincoln—the natural result of the personal abuse which had been heaped upon him by the Southern press and by Northern Copperheads—served to temper and restrain this sentiment of generosity. It recalled to mind the malevolence of those who had sought to overthrow the government; it generated distrust. The apprehensions entertained by prudent men at that time may have been extravagant, but in the light of the past they could not be deemed baseless. Certainly they were safer than the sentiment which they displaced.

Another result of Lincoln's death was a memorable change in the national administration. Andrew Johnson succeeded Abraham Lincoln.

Johnson, by the circumstance of his birth, occupied a position similar to that of Lincoln. He was born a poor Southern white. The difference between the two men arose from their different natures rather than from the outward conditions of their lives. Both were self-educated men. Neither of them knew of any school but that of experience, and thus from the first they were kept near to the people, and in close contact with the practical facts and conditions of the popular life in America. From such a relation they might have been removed by a more scholastic education and more classic culture. They knew nothing but America. Two circumstances gave Lincoln an immense superiority. The first was his moral and mental constitution, which made him a statesman of deep and unwavering convictions, and of great reasoning powers; the second was his connection with the young, free, and enterprising West. Johnson, on the other hand, by mental

constitution and by the circumstances of his political career, became a demagogue rather than a statesman.

The biography of Andrew Johnson up to the time of his accession to the presidency may be condensed into a single paragraph. He was born at Raleigh, North Carolina, December 29, 1808. While a mere child he lost his father, and at the age of ten years was apprenticed as a tailor. He worked at his trade in South Carolina for seven years, and during this time acquired the rudiments of a plain English education. Removing to Greenville, Tennessee, in 1825, he was five years later elected mayor of that town. He was elected to the State Legislature in 1835, and to the State Senate in 1841. From 1843 to 1853 he was a representative in Congress from Tennessee, and during the latter year was elected governor of that state. In 1857 he was chosen United States senator for the long term, expiring in 1863. But in 1862 he was appointed by President Lincoln military governor of Tennessee. In politics he had always been identified with the Democratic party, accepting Andrew Jackson, of whose name his own was a parody, as his model. He was prominently connected with the passage of the Homestead Law. In the Thirty-sixth Congress, he alone, of all the senators from the South, remained faithful to the Union. His bold denunciation of treason created the wildest sort of popular enthusiasm in the North, and as military governor of Tennessee his action was wise and firm, strengthening the hands of the loyal men of that state, and favoring the emancipation of slavery. In 1864 the Union Convention met at Baltimore to nominate candidates for President and Vice-President. President Lincoln was renominated by acclamation, but it was not considered advisable to renominate Mr. Hamlin. The Convention was styled a "Union" Convention, and many of its delegates were not strictly Republicans. To renominate the Chicago ticket of 1860 would appear too partisan. In Andrew Johnson, however, Providence kindly, as it then seemed, furnished a candidate who had been always a Democrat, but who had been conspicuous for loyalty during the war. His nomination was effected by the friends of Mr. Seward as a conservative movement, and Andrew Johnson was elected Vice-President.

HUGH McCULLOCH.

In the Presidential campaign of 1864 Johnson was repudiated by the opposition party in the North. His inauguration as Vice-President in the following March was an occasion of humiliation to himself, and afforded an opportunity for the most vehement and scurrilous abuse on the part of his political enemies. Evidently Johnson was at this time under the influence of liquor. He was unwell, and had, at the request of some of his friends, taken stimulants previous to entering the Senate Chamber. The closeness of the room exaggerated the effect of the artificial stimulant, and under these circumstances Johnson very unwisely allowed himself to make a speech, the incoherency of which was only too evident. It was an unfortunate affair, and his enemies made the most of it, and even some Republican journals described it as a national disgrace. Others, who knew the circumstances, were charitably silent.

Six weeks later, by the death of Lincoln, Johnson became President of the United States. The oath of office was quietly administered to him at his rooms in the Kirkwood Hotel, by Chief Justice Chase, in presence of the cabinet and several members of Congress. He felt incompetent, he said, to perform the important and responsible duties which had so suddenly devolved upon him. His policy must be left for development, as the administration progressed. The only assurance he could give as to the future was by a reference to the past. He believed that the government, in passing through its present trials, would settle down upon principles consonant with popular rights, more permanent and enduring than heretofore. "Toil," said he, "and an honest advocacy of the great principles of free government, have been my lot. The duties have been mine—the consequences are God's." In conclusion, he asked the gentlemen present for their encouragement and countenance. In the addresses made at this time by President Johnson, he carefully avoided self-committal as to his future policy. He expressed, however, a strong determination to punish conscious traitors. "The American people," said he, "must be taught to know that treason is a crime. Arson and murder are crimes, the punishment of which is the loss of liberty and life. . . . . Treason is a crime, and must be punished as a crime. It must not be regarded as a mere difference of political

opinion. It must not be excused as an unsuccessful rebellion, to be overlooked and forgiven. It is a crime before which all other crimes sink into insignificance; and in saying this, it must not be considered that I am influenced by angry or revengeful feelings. Of course a careful discrimination must be observed, for thousands have been involved in this rebellion who are only technically guilty of the crime of treason. They have been deluded and deceived, and have been made the victims of the more intelligent, artful, and designing men, the instigators of this monstrous rebellion. The number of this latter class is comparatively small. The former may stand acquitted of the crime of treason—the latter never; the full penalty of their crimes should be visited upon them. To the others I would accord amnesty, leniency, and mercy."[1] There is no question but that Johnson, following his own inclination, would have doomed to the scaffold every traitor of the class which he deemed guilty of crime, had not the whole people united in unanimous protest against such an extreme and unnecessary measure.

In regard to the situation in which the Southern States were left by the rebellion, he was explicit. "Some," he said, "are satisfied with the idea that states are to be lost in territorial and other divisions—are to lose their character as states. But their life-breath has only been suspended, and it is a high constitutional obligation we have to secure each of these states in the enjoyment of a republican form of government. A state may be in the government with a peculiar institution, and by the operation of rebellion lose that feature. But it was a state when it went into rebellion, and when it comes out without the institution, it is still a state. . . . . Then, in adjusting and putting the government upon its legs again, I think the progress of this work must pass into the hands of its friends. If a state is to be nursed until it again gets strength, it must be nursed by its friends, and not *smothered* by its enemies."[2]

President Johnson retained the entire cabinet of his predecessor. William Pitt Fessenden had resigned his position as Secretary of the Treasury March 4th, 1865, to take the position of senator from Maine, and Hugh

[1] Address to the New Hampshire delegation.
[2] Address to the Indiana delegation, April 21, 1865.

9 R

McCulloch had been appointed in his stead. Hon. William Dennison, of Ohio, had succeeded Montgomery Blair, October 1, 1864, as Postmaster General, the latter having resigned at Lincoln's request. In December, 1864, Edward Bates, of Missouri, Attorney General, had been succeeded by James Speed, of Kentucky. John P. Usher, Secretary of the Interior, had succeeded Caleb B. Smith, January 8th, 1863.

The subject of reconstruction did not come into President Johnson's hands as a new affair which had never before been handled or discussed. His predecessor had not been entirely silent upon this important question, and the matter had been somewhat discussed in Congress. Lincoln's Amnesty Proclamation is the best indication as to his convictions in this matter, and as to the general principles which would have characterized his administration if he had lived. In the previous pages of this history we have considered the provisions of this proclamation. Certain prominent officers of the Confederate government were excepted from the privileges which it granted. The ultimatum, as presented by Lincoln to the insurgent states, was allegiance to the government and the emancipation of slaves. Lincoln believed that the abolition of slavery would "remove all cause of disturbance in the future." Congress had incorporated in the Constitution an amendment prohibiting slavery; he only asked that this amendment should be ratified by the requisite number of states. On the 6th of April he ordered General Weitzel to permit the Virginia Legislature to assemble, and this body was to be broken up only in the event of its attempting some action hostile to the United States. Three days before his assassination President Lincoln gave his views as to the government established in Louisiana in accordance with his Amnesty Proclamation. Every member of his cabinet, he said, had approved of the plan. As to sustaining the Louisiana government he had given his promise, and had not yet been convinced that the keeping of this promise was adverse to the public interest. The question as to whether the seceded states were in the Union or out of it he regarded as not practically material, and that its discussion "could have no effect other than the mischievous one of dividing our friends." "As yet," he added, "that question is bad as the basis of a controversy, and good for nothing at all—a merely pernicious abstraction. We all agree that the seceded states, so called, are out of their proper practical relation with the Union, and that the sole object of the government, civil and military, in regard to those states, is to again get them into that proper practical relation. I believe it is not only possible, but, in fact, easier to do this without deciding or even considering whether these states have ever been out of the Union, than with it. Finding themselves safely at home, it would be utterly immaterial whether they had ever been abroad. Let us all join in doing the acts necessary to restoring the proper practical relations between these states and the Union, and each forever after innocently indulge his own opinion whether, in doing the acts, he brought the states from without into the Union, or only gave them proper assistance, they never having been out of it."

The simple question with Lincoln was how best to bring the insurgent states back to their proper relation with the Union. To him this question appeared to have a solution in his amnesty proclamation.

Congress had not accepted Lincoln's plan of restoration, nor had it, except in the "Wade and Davis Bill," which had been virtually vetoed, announced any other. The only members of Congress who seemed to have any definite ideas of reconstruction were Senator Sumner and Thaddeus Stevens, who proposed to treat the Southern States as subjugated provinces. These two men stood alone, and without substantial support in either house. But, for all that, they held a high vantage-ground from the very fact that they alone presented any positive and definite method of reconstruction. Probably there had never before been a time in the history of the republic when Congress was so utterly barren of a high order of statesmanship as during and immediately after the war. The Thirty-ninth Congress was certainly not superior in this respect to its immediate predecessors. It first regular session would commence in December, and thus for eight months President Johnson was left alone in the work of reconstruction. As we have said, no fixed principles had been furnished by previous Congresses for his guidance, and he would have been confused beyond redemption if he had attempted to frame a policy in accordance with the crude and random expressions of opinion which had from time to time been made by our statesmen. He could not and ought not have accepted the sweeping theories of Sumner and Stevens.

Johnson appears at first to have followed closely the general features of the plan adopted by Lincoln. He was compelled to act. The dissolution of the Confederacy left the Southern States without any government which could be recognized by national authority. Certain movements had already been inaugurated by President Lincoln in Arkansas and Louisiana. Johnson saw no objection to the continuance of the work after the manner in which it had been begun by his predecessor. Nor was the Constitution entirely silent and inapplicable to the pressing questions of the moment. Although its framers never contemplated the existence of such a crisis, yet it contained at least one provision which in its general meaning was fully adequate to the emergency. It provides (Art. IV., Sec. 4) that "the United States shall guarantee to every state in this Union a republican form of government, and shall protect each of them against invasion; and, on application of the Legislature, or of the executive (when the Legislature can not be convened), against domestic violence."

The latter clause of this constitutional provision evidently applies to cases where the government of a state is not wholly subverted or paralyzed by domestic violence. It is only the first clause which was applicable to the situation in which the states were left by the rebellion. But what was meant by "a republican form of government?" This phrase has been va-

riously understood. Some have declared it to mean nothing definitely, and therefore every thing in an indefinite way; that it was a constitutional sanction for the establishment in a disturbed state of any government which the President and Congress might prescribe. Others have supposed that the term "republican" was simply opposed to the term "monarchical." It is clearly evident, however, that any state in the Union has a republican form of government so long and in so far as its government has not been so disturbed by any agency as to be out of harmony with the republic, i. e., with the general government of the United States. The Constitution being the organic law of the United States government, it follows that the guaranty of a republican form of government to any state presupposes a case in which by some disturbing agency the government of such state has assumed a form inconsistent or out of harmony with the Constitution. It is immaterial what the nature of such disturbing agency may have been, whether it was usurpation from within or from without.

The question, therefore, naturally arises, How far had the rebellion been such a disturbing agency? The Confederate Constitution, under which the Southern state governments had been organized during the rebellion, was not materially different from the Constitution of the United States. Comparing the situation of the Southern States in 1865 with their situation in 1860, the chief difference which we find was the fact of a transferred allegiance. The simple return of these states to their allegiance to the United States would be also a resumption of a form of government which in 1860 was deemed "republican." But such a government of the Southern States as was in harmony with the Constitution in 1860 was not in harmony with the Constitution after the war. By the war all slaves had been emancipated. The Congress of the United States had passed a resolution proposing the anti-slavery constitutional amendment. It was eminently proper that the ratification of this amendment should be insisted upon as a condition of reconstruction. It was a measure rendered necessary by the war, and the acceptance of the situation by the Southern States in good faith involved the ratification. This general condition gave rise to others as incidental. The freedom of the negro race in the South involved also the equality of that race with white men before the law. It did not involve the enfranchisement of the negro, because the Constitution, even after the war, contained no provision to that effect. But in every other respect the negro must be placed upon an equality with the white man.

There was another important feature to be insisted upon by the government, and which was also a result of the national victory. This was a repudiation by the Southern States of the debt which they had incurred for treasonable purposes. The possibility of a repudiation of the national debt must also be obviated.

The emancipation of slaves introduced still another element. Before the war representation was apportioned among the several states "according to their respective numbers, which shall be determined by adding to the whole number of free persons, including those bound to service for a term of years, and excluding Indians not taxed, three fifths of all other persons." But after the war all persons were declared free. The "other persons" no longer existed. Thus the entire negro population of the South would be counted in the basis of representation, and the Southern States would, by emancipation, gain a political advantage which they did not have before the war. It was therefore proper that a new adjustment of the basis of representation should be insisted upon as an incidental condition of the situation arising out of emancipation. It ought also have been distinctly and permanently settled that there should be no compensation for emancipation.

Thus the allegiance demanded of the insurgent states was not simply that from which they had departed. They had made war upon the nation, and this conflict had not been without consequences, the principal of which were a Confederate debt, a National debt, and Emancipation. If the Confederacy had been victorious, it would have gained its independence—its recognition as a separate nation. Its defeat was not simply a forfeiture of this independence, but it involved submission to several important conditions, imposed, not as terms to a vanquished foe, not as penalties for treason, but for the security of the nation. Under these circumstances, a republican form of government in the disturbed states involved the acceptance by the latter of the following conditions:

1. Nullification of the theory of secession.
2. Repudiation of the Confederate debt.
3. Security of the national debt.
4. Ratification of emancipation, waiving all claim to pecuniary compensation.
5. Readjustment of the basis of representation.
6. Concession of civil rights to the colored race.
7. Disfranchisement of leading traitors for such time as Congress might deem expedient.

When it is considered that the nation could in justice demand indemnity for the national debt caused by the war, and the punishment of leading traitors, these conditions could not be considered harsh or unreasonable. Every one of them ought to have been embodied by Congress in the form of a constitutional amendment. Many of them demanded congressional sanction, and could not be imposed by the President alone. It was therefore Johnson's duty to have called the Thirty-ninth Congress together in special session to meet this new emergency. His failure to do this was a blunder from which his administration never recovered.

The President proceeded to his work alone. On the 29th of May, 1865, he issued his amnesty proclamation, granting pardon to all who had participated in the rebellion, with restoration of property except as to slaves, and except in cases where legal proceedings had been instituted under the laws of the United States providing for the confiscation of property. From the benefits of this proclamation the following classes were excepted:

1. All who are or shall have been pretended civil or diplomatic officers, or otherwise domestic or foreign agents of the pretended Confederate government.

2. All who left judicial stations under the United States to aid the rebellion.

3. All who shall have been military or naval officers of said pretended Confederate government above the rank of colonel in the army or lieutenant in the navy.

4. All who left seats in the Congress of the United States to aid the rebellion.

5. All who resigned or tendered resignations of their commissions in the army or navy of the United States to evade duty in resisting the rebellion.

6. All who have engaged in any way in treating otherwise than lawfully as prisoners of war persons found in the United States service as officers, soldiers, seamen, or in other capacities.

7. All persons who have been or are absentees from the United States for the purpose of aiding the rebellion.

8. All military and naval officers in the rebel service who were educated by the government in the Military Academy at West Point or the United States Naval Academy.

9. All persons who held the pretended offices of governors of states in insurrection against the United States.

10. All persons who left their homes within the jurisdiction and protection of the United States, and passed beyond the Federal military lines into the so-called Confederate States, for the purpose of aiding the rebellion.

11. All persons who have been engaged in the destruction of the commerce of the United States upon the high seas, and all persons who have made raids into the United States from Canada, or been engaged in destroying the commerce of the United States upon the lakes and rivers that separate the British Provinces from the United States.

12. All persons who, at the time when they seek to obtain the benefits hereof by taking the oath herein prescribed, are in military, naval, or civil confinement or custody, or under bonds of the civil, military, or naval authorities or agents of the United States as prisoners of war, or persons detained for offenses of any kind either before or after conviction.

13. All persons who have voluntarily participated in said rebellion, and the estimated value of whose taxable property is over twenty thousand dollars.

14. All persons who have taken the oath of amnesty as prescribed in the President's proclamation of December 8, A.D. 1863, or an oath of allegiance to the government of the United States since the date of said proclamation, and who have not thenceforward kept and maintained the same inviolate—provided that special application may be made to the Presideut for pardon by any person belonging to the excepted classes, and such clemency will be liberally extended as may be consistent with the facts of the case and the peace and dignity of the United States.

Johnson had, on the 9th of May, re-established by an executive order the authority of the United States in the State of Virginia. The Secretary of the Treasury was instructed to nominate for appointment assessors of taxes, and collectors of customs and internal revenue, and all other officers necessary to put in execution the revenue laws; the Postmaster General was directed to establish post-offices and post-routes, and put in execution the postal laws; the Federal Courts were re-established; the Secretary of War was ordered to assign the necessary provost-marshal generals and provost-marshals, and the Secretary of the Navy to take possession of all public property belonging to the Navy Department. The acts of the political, military, and civil organizations of the state during the war were declared null and void, and Francis H. Pierpont was recognized as the lawful governor.[1]

On the same day that he issued his Amnesty Proclamation, Johnson appointed William W. Holden Provisional Governor of North Carolina. He declared it to be the duty of the provisional governor to prescribe at the earliest practicable period the rules and regulations for the assembling of a Convention, to be chosen by the loyal people of North Carolina, for the purpose of amending the state Constitution. No person could be an elector or member of such Convention unless he should have previously taken the amnesty oath, and should be a qualified voter by the laws of the state. The heads of departments were directed to resume their respective relations with the state, and the Federal Courts were re-established as in Virginia.[1]

The instructions to the heads of departments, and for the re-establishment of Federal Courts, were the same as in the case of Virginia.

During the months of June and July, similar provisional governments were established in all the other insurgent states except Louisiana, Arkansas, and Tennessee. On the 13th of June William L. Sharkey was appointed Provisional Governor of Mississippi; on the 19th, James Johnson, of Georgia, and Andrew J. Hamilton, of Texas; on the 21st, Lewis E. Parsons, of Alabama; on the 30th, Benjamin F. Perry, of South Carolina; and on July 13th, William Marvin, of Florida.

In all these cases only loyal men were allowed to become electors or members of the several Conventions, and the heads of departments were instructed to give the preference to qualified loyal men in the distribution of offices, and where such were not to be obtained in the several states they were to be appointed from other states. Neither in the Amnesty Proclamation, nor in those establishing provisional governments, was any intimation given as to what actions would be required of the several states in order to insure the recognition of their governments by the United States as republican in form.

In Louisiana, J. Madison Wells, who had succeeded Michael Hahn, March 4th, 1865, was recognized and sustained by President Johnson as the lawful governor of the state. In like manner, William G. Brownlow, elected March 4th, 1865, was recognized as Governor of Tennessee; and Isaac Murphy, elected March 14, 1864, as Governor of Arkansas. In these three states, movements toward reconstruction were already at an advanced stage under President Lincoln's administration. In each of them loyal state governments existed, with a Constitution abolishing slavery; but these governments did not rest upon a popular majority. They were instituted and put in operation during the war, at a time when large portions of the territory over which they had jurisdiction were within the control of the Confederacy, and they had not as yet received the sanction of the United States Congress.

On the 23d of June the President rescinded the blockade, and on the 29th of August removed all restrictions upon internal, domestic, and coastwise commerce, so that articles declared by previous proclamations to be contraband of war might be imported into or sold in the insurgent states, "subject only to such regulations as the Secretary of the Treasury may prescribe." On the 11th of October he released John A. Campbell, of Alabama; John H. Reagan, of Texas; Alexander H. Stephens, of Georgia; George A. Trenholm, of South Carolina, and Charles Clark, of Mississippi, from confinement, upon their parole to answer any charge which might be preferred against them, and to abide in their respective states until farther orders. On the 12th of October martial law was suspended in Kentucky, and on the 1st of December the suspension of *habeas corpus* was annulled except in the states of Virginia, Kentucky, Tennessee, North Carolina, Georgia, Florida, Alabama, Mississippi, Lousiana, Arkansas, and Texas, the District of Columbia, and the Territories of New Mexico and Arizona.

Before the assembling of the Thirty-ninth Congress, each of the states in

---

[1] "Executive Chamber, Washington City, May 9, 1865.

"Ordered—*First*. That all acts and proceedings of the political, military, and civil organizations which have been in a state of insurrection and rebellion within the State of Virginia against the authority and laws of the United States, and of which Jefferson Davis, John Letcher, and William Smith were late the respective chiefs, are declared null and void. All persons who shall exercise, claim, pretend, or attempt to exercise any political, military, or civil power, authority, jurisdiction, or right by, through, or under Jefferson Davis, late of the city of Richmond, and his confederates, or under John Letcher or William Smith and their confederates, or under any pretended political, military, or civil commission or authority issued by them, or either of them, since the 17th day of April, 1861, shall be deemed and taken as in rebellion against the United States, and shall be dealt with accordingly.

"*Second*. That the Secretary of State proceed to put in force all laws of the United States, the administration whereof belongs to the Department of State, applicable to the geographical limits aforesaid.

"*Third*. That the Secretary of the Treasury proceed without delay to nominate for appointment assessors of taxes, and collectors of customs and internal revenue, and such other officers of the Treasury Department as are authorized by law, and shall put into execution the revenue laws of the United States within the geographical limits aforesaid. In making appointments, the preference shall be given to qualified loyal persons residing within the districts where their respective duties are to be performed. But if suitable persons shall not be found residents of the districts, then persons residing in other states or districts shall be appointed.

"*Fourth*. That the Postmaster General shall proceed to establish post-offices and post-routes, and put into execution the postal laws of the United States within the said state, giving to loyal residents the preference of appointment. But if suitable persons are not found, then to appoint agents, etc., from other states.

"*Fifth*. That the district judge of said district proceed to hold courts within said state, in accordance with the provisions of the acts of Congress. The Attorney General will instruct the proper officers to libel and bring to judgment, confiscation, and sale property subject to confiscation, and enforce the administration of justice within said state in all matters civil and criminal within the cognizance and jurisdiction of the Federal Courts.

"*Sixth*. That the Secretary of War assign such assistant provost-marshal general, and such provost-marshals in each district of said state as he may deem necessary.

"*Seventh*. The Secretary of the Navy will take possession of all public property belonging to the Navy Department within said geographical limits, and put in operation all acts of Congress in relation to naval affairs having application to the said state.

"*Eighth*. The Secretary of the Interior will also put in force the laws relating to the Department of the Interior.

"*Ninth*. That to carry into effect the guarantee of the Federal Constitution of a republican form of state government, and afford the advantage and security of domestic laws, as well as to complete the re-establishment of the authority of the laws of the United States, and the full and complete restoration of peace within the limits aforesaid, Francis H. Pierpont, Governor of the State of Virginia, will be aided by the Federal government, so far as may be necessary, in the lawful measures which he may take for the extension and administration of the state government throughout the geographical limits of said state.

[L. S.] "In testimony whereof, I have hereunto set my hand and caused the seal of the United States to be affixed. Andrew Johnson.

"By the President: W. Hunter, Acting Secretary of State."

[1] "*Whereas*, The fourth section of the fourth article of the Constitution of the United States declares that the United States shall guarantee to every state in the Union a republican form of government, and shall protect each of them against invasion and domestic violence; *and whereas* the President of the United States is, by the Constitution, made commander-in-chief of the army and navy, as well as chief civil executive officer of the United States, and is bound by solemn oath faithfully to execute the office of President of the United States, and to take care that the laws be faithfully executed; *and whereas* the rebellion which has been waged by a portion of the people of the United States against the properly constituted authorities of the government thereof in the most violent and revolting form, but whose organized and armed forces have now been almost entirely overcome, has, in its revolutionary progress, deprived the people of the State of North Carolina of all civil government; *and whereas* it becomes necessary and proper to carry out and enforce the obligations of the United States to the people of North Carolina in securing them in the enjoyment of a republican form of government:

"Now, therefore, in obedience to the high and solemn duties imposed upon me by the Constitution of the United States, and for the purpose of enabling the loyal people of said state to organize a state government, whereby justice may be established, domestic tranquillity restored, and loyal citizens protected in all their rights of life, liberty, and property, I, Andrew Johnson, President of the United States and Commander-in-chief of the Army and Navy of the United States, do hereby appoint William W. Holden Provisional Governor of the State of North Carolina, whose duty it shall be, at the earliest practicable period, to prescribe such rules and regulations as may be necessary and proper for convening a Convention composed of delegates to be chosen by that portion of the people of said state who are loyal to the United States, and no others, for the purpose of altering and amending the Constitution thereof; and with authority to exercise within the limits of said state all the powers necessary and proper to enable such loyal people of the State of North Carolina to restore said state to its constitutional relations to the Federal government, and to present such a republican form of state government as will entitle the state to the guarantee of the United States therefor, and its people to protection by the United States against invasion, insurrection, and domestic violence. Provided that in any election that may be held hereafter for choosing delegates to any state Convention as aforesaid, no person shall be qualified as an elector or shall be eligible as a member of such Convention unless he shall have previously taken and subscribed the oath of amnesty as set forth in the President's proclamation of May 29, A.D. 1865, and is a voter qualified as prescribed by the Constitution and laws of the State of North Carolina in force immediately before the 20th day of May, 1861, the date of the so-called Ordinance of Secession. And the said Convention, when convened, or the Legislature that may be thereafter assembled, will prescribe the qualification of electors and the eligibility of persons to hold office under the Constitution and laws of the state—a power the people of the several states composing the Federal Union have rightfully exercised from the origin of the government to the present time."

which provisional governments had been established had elected and held its Convention and had also inaugurated a permanent government, displacing the provisional, under the auspices of President Johnson. In all cases the Ordinance of Secession was either annulled or repealed by the state Conventions, and slavery was forever prohibited. In the Georgia Convention, there was incorporated in the ordinance abolishing slavery a provision that this acquiescence in the action of the government of the United States was not intended to operate as a relinquishment of any claim made by the citizens of that state for compensation. The constitutional amendment was also ratified by the new Legislatures except in the case of Mississippi. In Alabama, South Carolina, and Florida, the ratification was made with the understanding that the clause giving Congress the power to carry out the provisions of the amendment by appropriate legislation did not give that body the right to legislate as to the political status of the freedmen.[1] The Confederate debt was also repudiated in every state save South Carolina, whose Legislature adjourned before taking final action on this subject.

The legislation in regard to freedmen seemed to have for its object the perpetuation of the spirit of slavery after its body had been decently buried. Some of the enactments passed by the various Legislatures were judicious and benevolent, but most of them were expressly designed to establish a distinction of caste between the white and the colored race. While, on the one hand, the right to sue and be sued, and to give testimony in all cases where their own interests were involved, was granted to the negroes, and marriage was legalized among them, on the other the penal code in nearly all the states abounded with oppressive distinctions against the colored race. By emancipation a very large proportion of the freedmen were left in a dependent condition, which demanded instant relief through a generous and well-considered system for the reorganization of the Southern system of labor on the principles of freedom. But, instead of the establishment of such a system, a deliberate scheme was planned to take advantage of the unfavorable condition of the negro by an enactment that all freedmen having no visible means of support should be regarded as vagrants and bound to apprenticeship. Every effort was also made to prevent any organization of the freedmen for their own relief, and making it a misdemeanor for whites to assemble or associate with them.[2] Some of this legislation was so oppressive to the freedmen that it was annulled by the order of military commanders.

It was evident that the late Confederate States misunderstood their situation. President Johnson had thrown upon them the burden of reconstruction, and properly it belonged to them. They, in turn, ought to have shown their good faith by the prompt and voluntary fulfillment of all the con-

---

[1] The following persons were elected permanent governors of the several states: Jonathan Worth, of North Carolina; Benjamin G. Humphreys, of Mississippi; Charles J. Jenkins, of Georgia; R. M. Patton, of Alabama; James L. Orr, of South Carolina; Andrew J. Hamilton, of Texas; and D. S. Walker, of Florida.

[2] The legislation in regard to freedmen may be briefly epitomized in a few paragraphs.

North Carolina.—March 10, 1866, an act was passed declaring that one eighth part of African blood constituted a person a negro. It provided that, so soon as jurisdiction in matters relating to freedmen should be committed to the courts of the state, negroes should have all the privileges of white men in the prosecution of suits, and be eligible as witnesses in cases involving their own interests. It extended the criminal laws to all persons, making no distinction in punishment except for rape, which, if committed upon a white female, was made a capital crime for a black. It legalized marriages contracted during slavery. All contracts, to which one of the parties was a colored person, for the sale or purchase of any horse, mule, jennet, ass, neat cattle, hog, sheep, or goat, whatever the value, and in the case of other articles contracts involving the value of ten dollars, were declared void, except when made in writing, and witnessed by a white person who could read and write. Marriages between whites and blacks were forbidden.

Mississippi.—November 22, 1865, an act was passed to regulate the relation of master and apprentice relative to freedmen. It provided for the apprenticeship to suitable persons, former masters being preferred, of all freedmen under the age of 18 who are orphans, or who are not supported by their parents, to be bound in the case of males till the age of 21, and to the age of 18 in case of females. Power was given to the masters to inflict moderate corporal punishment. Where the age of the freedman was uncertain, it could be fixed by the judge of the county clerk.

November 24, 1865, the vagrant act was passed.

Section 2 provides that all freedmen, free negroes, and mulattoes in this state, over the age of 18 years, found on the second Monday in January, 1866, or thereafter, with no lawful employment or business, or found unlawfully assembling themselves together, either in the day or night time, and all white persons so assembling with freedmen, free negroes, or mulattoes, or usually associating with freedmen, free negroes, or mulattoes on terms of equality, or living in adultery or fornication with a freedwoman, free negro, or mulatto, shall be deemed vagrants, and on conviction thereof shall be fined in the sum of not exceeding, in the case of a freedman, free negro, or mulatto, fifty dollars, and a white man two hundred dollars, and imprisoned at the discretion of the court, the free negro not exceeding ten days, and the white man not exceeding six months.

Section 5 provided that all negroes failing to pay any fine or forfeiture imposed should be hired out, or, if that were impossible, should be treated as paupers.

Section 6 provided that a tax not exceeding one dollar should be levied upon every negro between the ages of 18 and 60 to make up a "freedmen's pauper fund."

November 25, 1865, an act was passed to confer civil rights upon freedmen.

Section 1 provided that negroes might sue and be sued, and acquire personal property, but should not be allowed to rent or lease any lands or tenements except in incorporated towns and cities, in which places the corporate authorities should be the controlling powers.

Section 2 provided for the intermarriage of negroes, the clerk of probate to keep separate records of the same.

Section 3 declared intermarriage between whites and negroes a felony, to be punished by imprisment for life.

Section 4 gave negroes the right to give testimony in cases where negroes were plaintiffs or defendants.

Seotion 5 provided that on the second Monday of January, 1866, every negro must have a lawful home or employment, and must have either a license to do irregular and job work, or a written contract for regular labor.

Section 6 provided that negroes quitting the service of employers without good cause before the expiration of their written contract should forfeit their wages.

November 29, 1865, an act was passed prohibiting negroes not in the military service of the United States to "keep or carry arms of any kind, or any ammunition, dirk, or bowie knife." Upon conviction for this event, the penalty was a fine of ten dollars and forfeiture of the weapons. Section 4 of this act provided that all the penal and criminal laws in force in that state "defining offenses and prescribing the mode of punishment for crimes and misdemeanors committed by slaves, free negroes, or mulattoes," were thereby re-enacted, and declared in full force as against freedmen.

Georgia.—December 15, 1865, negroes were made competent witnesses in cases to which freedmen were parties, and marriages between persons of color were legalized.

March 12, 1866, all vagrants or persons leading an immoral or profligate life were made subject to fine, imprisonment, or forced labor for one year, or to be bound out for one year in apprenticeship.

March 17, 1865, it was enacted that persons of color should have the right to make and enforce contracts, to sue and be sued, to give evidence, to inherit, purchase, lease, sell, hold, and convey real and personal property, and that they should not be subjected to any other or different punishment for the commission of any offense than such as were prescribed for white persons committing the same.

Alabama.—December, 1865, a bill was passed "making it unlawful for any freedman, mulatto, or free person of color to own fire-arms, or carry about his person a pistol or other deadly weapon," under a penalty of one hundred dollars fine or three months' imprisonment.

December 9, 1865, it was enacted that negroes and mulattoes should have the right to sue and be sued, and to testify in cases in which negroes were parties.

Early in 1866 Governor Patton vetoed three bills. One of these provided for the regulation of contracts with freedmen, for which the governor thought no special law was necessary. "Information," said he, "from various parts of the state shows that negroes are every where making contracts for the present year upon terms that are entirely satisfactory to the employers. They are also entering faithfully upon the discharge of the obligations contracted. There is every prospect that the engagement formed will be observed with perfect good faith. I therefore think that special laws for regulating contracts between whites and freedmen would accomplish no good, and might result in much harm." He also vetoed a bill extending the criminal laws of the state (which were applicable to free persons of color) to freedmen. The bill applied to the freedmen a system of laws enacted for free negroes in a community where slavery existed. "I have," said the governor, "carefully examined the laws which, under this bill, would be applied to the freedmen, and I think that a mere recital of some of their provisions will show the impolicy and injustice of enforcing them upon the negroes in their new condition." Governor Patton also vetoed "a bill entitled an act to regulate the relations of master and apprentice as relate to freedmen, free negroes, and mulattoes," because he deemed the present laws amply sufficient for all purposes of apprenticeship, without operating upon a particular class of persons.

South Carolina.—October 19, 1865, an act was passed providing that the statutes and regulations concerning slaves were now inapplicable to persons of color. Negroes, though not entitled to social or political equality with white persons, were allowed the right to acquire, own, and dispose of property, to make contracts, to enjoy the fruits of their labor, and to sue and be sued.

December 19, 1865, an act was passed amending the criminal law.

Section 1 provided "that either of the crimes specified in this first section shall be felony, without benefit of clergy, to wit: For a person of color to commit any willful homicide, unless in self-defense; for a person of color to commit an assault upon a white woman with manifest intent to ravish her; for a person of color to have sexual intercourse with a white woman by personating her husband; for any person to raise an insurrection or rebellion in this state; for any person to furnish arms or ammunition to other persons who are in a state of actual insurrection or rebellion, or permit them to resort to his house for advancement of their evil purpose; for any person to administer, or cause to be taken by any other person, any poison, chloroform, soporific, or other destructive thing, or to shoot at, stab, cut, or wound any other person, or by any means whatsoever to cause bodily injury to any other person, whereby, in any of these cases, a bodily injury dangerous to the life of any other person is caused, with intent, in any of these cases, to commit the crime of murder, or the crime of rape, or the crime of robbery, burglary, or larceny; for any person who had been transported under sentence to return to the state within the period of prohibition contained in the sentence; or for a person to steal a horse or mule, or cotton packed in a bale ready for market."

Section 10 provided "that a person of color who is in the employment of a master engaged in husbandry shall not have the right to sell any corn, rice, peas, wheat, or other grain, any flour, cotton, fodder, hay, bacon, fresh meat of any kind, poultry of any kind, animal of any kind, or any other product of a farm, without having written evidence from such master, or some person authorized by him, or from the district judge or a magistrate, that he has the right to sell such product; and if any person shall, directly or indirectly, purchase any such product from such person of color without such written evidence, the purchaser and seller shall each be guilty of a misdemeanor."

Section 13 declared that negroes should constitute no part of the state militia, and that they should not be permitted to keep fire-arms, except in the case of farm owners, who were allowed to keep a shot-gun or rifle.

Section 22 provided that no person of color should migrate into and reside in South Carolina unless within 20 days after his arrival he should enter into a bond in a penalty of $1000 dollars, with two good freeholders as security, for his good behavior and support.

December 21. "*An act to establish and regulate the domestic relations of persons of color, and to amend the law in relation to paupers and vagrancy,*" establishes the relation of husband and wife, declares those now living as such to be husband and wife, and provides that persons of color desirous hereafter to marry shall have the contract duly solemnized. A parent may bind his child over two years of age as an apprentice to serve till 21 if a male, 18 if a female. All persons of color who make contracts for service or labor shall be known as servants, and those with whom they contract as masters.

"Colored children between 18 and 21, who have neither father nor mother *living in the district in which they are found*, or whose parents are paupers, or unable to afford them a comfortable maintenance, *or whose parents are not teaching them habits of industry and honesty*, or are persons of notoriously bad character, or are vagrants, or have been convicted of infamous offenses, and colored children, *in all cases where they are in danger of moral contamination*, may be bound as apprentices by the district judge or one of the magistrates for the aforesaid term."

It "provides that no person of color shall pursue or practice the art, trade, or business of an artisan, mechanic, or shopkeeper, or any other trade, employment, or business (besides that of husbandry, or that of a servant under a contract for service or labor), on his own account and for his own benefit, or in partnership with a white person, or as agent or servant of any person, until he shall have obtained a license therefor from the judge of the District Court, which license shall be good for one year only. This license the judge may grant upon petition of the applicant, and upon being satisfied of his skill and fitness, and of his good moral character, and upon payment by the applicant to the clerk of the District Court of one hundred dollars if a shopkeeper or peddler, to be paid annually, and ten dollars if a mechanic, artisan, or to engage in any other trade, also to be paid annually.

Florida.—January 11, 1866, an act was passed providing that the judicial tribunals of the state should be accessible to all persons without distinction of color, and repealing all laws heretofore passed with reference to slaves, free negroes, and mulattoes, except the acts to prevent their migration into the state and the sale to them of fire-arms.

January 11, 1866, an act was passed legalizing the marriage relation among persons of color.

January 12, 1866, an act was passed in relation to contracts, similar in its provisions to those enacted by the other states.

January 15, 1866, it was enacted "that if any negro, mulatto, or other person of color shall intrude himself into any religious or other public assembly of white persons, or into any railroad car or other public vehicle set apart for the exclusive accommodation of white people, he shall be deemed to be guilty of a misdemeanor, and upon conviction shall be sentenced to stand in the pillory for one hour, or be whipped not exceeding thirty-nine stripes, or both, at the discretion of the jury; nor shall it be lawful for any white person to intrude himself into any religious or other public assembly of colored persons, or into any railroad car or other public vehicle set apart for the exclusive accommodation of persons of color, under the same penalties."

Virginia.—Early in 1866 a vagrant act was passed providing that vagrants should be hired out for a period of three months.

Tennessee.—1866, January 25, this bill became a law:

"That persons of African and Indian descent are hereby declared to be competent witnesses in all the courts of this state, in as full a manner as such persons are by an act of Congress competent witnesses in all the courts of the United States, and all laws and parts of laws of the state excluding such persons from competency are hereby repealed: *Provided, however*, That this act shall not be so construed as to give colored persons the right to vote, hold office, or sit on juries in this state; and that this provision is inserted by virtue of the provision of the 9th section of the amended Constitution, ratified February 22, 1865."

May 26, this bill became a law:

"An act to define the term 'persons of color,' and to declare the rights of such persons.

"SEC. 1. That all negroes, mulattoes, mestizoes, and their descendants, having any African blood in their veins, shall be known in this state as 'persons of color.'

"SEC. 2. That persons of color shall have the right to make and enforce contracts, to sue and be sued, to be parties and give evidence, to inherit, and to have full and equal benefits of all laws and proceedings for the security of person and estate, and shall not be subject to any other or different punishment, pains, or penalty for the commission of any act or offense than such as are prescribed for white persons committing like acts or offenses.

"SEC. 3. That all persons of color, being blind, deaf and dumb, lunatics, paupers, or apprentices, shall have the full and perfect benefit and application of all laws regulating and providing for white persons, being blind, or deaf and dumb, or lunatics or paupers, or either (in asylums for their benefit), and apprentices.

"SEC. 4. That all acts, or parts of acts or laws inconsistent herewith, are hereby repealed: *Provided*, That nothing in this act shall be so construed as to admit persons of color to serve on a jury; *And provided further*, That the provisions of this act shall not be so construed as to require the education of colored and white children in the same school.

"SEC. 5. That all free persons of color who were living together as husband and wife in this state while in a state of slavery are hereby declared to be man and wife, and their children legitimately entitled to an inheritance in any property heretofore acquired, or that may be hereafter acquired by said parents, to as full an extent as the children of white citizens are now entitled by the existing laws of this state."

May 26, all the freedmen's courts in Tennessee were abolished by the assistant commander, the law of the state making colored persons competent witnesses in all civil courts.

Louisiana.—An act was passed in relation to vagrants, providing that the latter, failing to obtain security for good behavior and industry, should be hired out for a period of twelve months.

ditions necessary to restoration. It was not expected that their military defeat would result in their conversion from secession to loyalty, but it seemed certain that the war must at least have convinced them of their folly. It did so to some extent, but it did not bring them wisdom. They appeared determined to do as little as possible to show their appreciation of the significance of the conflict which had gone against them. It was only at the earnest solicitation of the President that certain states repudiated their rebel debt. The manner in which they abolished slavery, with "insamuches," "ifs," and "buts," showed their reluctance and their desire to find some possible chance of evasion.

Johnson was disappointed. He had calculated upon very different action. He knew that the people would not be satisfied with this half-hearted, evasive sort of allegiance. In his correspondence with the provisional governors he had scarcely been able to conceal his impatience on account of the manner in which the Southern States were moving. Some features of the criminal code adopted by these states seemed to him exceedingly unsatisfactory. He almost begged them to be sensible, and not to neglect the opportunity which had been so generously offered them; but he pleaded in vain. He knew that every mistake made by these states in the movement which he had inaugurated would give force and plausibility to the theories which such men as Stevens, Sumner, and Wendell Phillips were urging upon the country. It is probable that the Southern States still retained a vivid remembrance of the persistent efforts made in their behalf, even while they were in armed rebellion, by the Northern faction led by Seymour, Vallandigham, Pendleton, Long, Bayard, and a host of others, and that, exaggerating the power of this faction, they hoped by union and co-operation with it to obtain in the political arena what they had lost on the field of battle. It is difficult upon any other hypothesis to understand the attitude which they now so defiantly assumed.

The constitutional amendment abolishing slavery had been ratified by the requisite number of states, and on the 18th of December, 1865, Secretary Seward publicly announced this fact, certifying the validity of the amendment "to all intents and purposes as a part of the Constitution of the United States."[1]

The Thirty-ninth Congress was convened at Washington December 4, 1865.[2] The Senate was organized with Lafayette S. Foster as President *pro tempore*. He had been chosen for this position in the extra session of the Senate, and thus became acting Vice-President of the United States. He had been a senator from Connecticut since 1855, and was eminently fitted both by natural qualities and by experience for the duties of a presiding officer. In the House, the members were called to order by the clerk, Edward McPherson, of Pennsylvania. The office of clerk of the House at this time was beset with difficulties of the most delicate nature. By law, his decision as to the members who might be properly placed upon the call-roll and take part in the organization of the House was absolute. By one party it was claimed that for him to exclude the names of Southern members was an assumption on his part of the right to reject members before they had been rejected by the House. By another party it was claimed that, by including those names, McPherson would equally anticipate the action of Congress by presuming to accept members before the House had acted in the matter. McPherson very wisely concluded to let the matter rest exactly where he found it. The members from the Southern States had not been admitted, and there were peculiar circumstances incident to their election which did not usually exist in ordinary cases. He determined, therefore, to leave the whole subject to Congress. It is evident, also,

---

[1] "*To all to whom these presents may come, greeting:*

"Know ye, that whereas the Congress of the United States, on the 1st of February last, passed a resolution which is in the words following, namely: 'A resolution submitting to the Legislatures of the several states a proposition to amend the Constitution of the United States.

"'*Resolved by the Senate and House of Representatives of the United States of America, in Congress assembled* (*two thirds of both houses concurring*), That the following article be proposed to the Legislatures of the several states as an amendment to the Constitution of the United States, which, when ratified by three fourths of said Legislatures, shall be valid, to all intents and purposes, as a part of the said Constitution, namely:

"'ARTICLE XIII.

"'SEC. 1. Neither slavery nor involuntary servitude, except as a punishment for crime, whereof the party shall have been duly convicted, shall exist within the United States, or any place subject to their jurisdiction.

"'SEC. 2. Congress shall have power to enforce this article by appropriate legislation.'

"*And whereas* it appears from official documents on file in this department that the amendment to the Constitution of the United States, proposed as aforesaid, has been ratified by the Legislatures of the states of Illinois, Rhode Island, Michigan, Maryland, New York, West Virginia, Maine, Kansas, Massachusetts, Pennsylvania, Virginia, Ohio, Missouri, Nevada, Indiana, Louisiana, Minnesota, Wisconsin, Vermont, Tennessee, Arkansas, Connecticut, New Hampshire, South Carolina, Alabama, North Carolina, and Georgia—in all, twenty-seven states;

"*And whereas* the whole number of states in the United States is thirty-six; *and whereas* the before specially-named states, whose Legislatures have ratified the said proposed amendment, constitute three fourths of the whole number of states in the United States:

"Now, therefore, be it known that I, William H. Seward, Secretary of State of the United States, by virtue and in pursuance of the second section of the act of Congress approved the twentieth of April, eighteen hundred and eighteen, entitled 'An Act to provide for the publication of the Laws of the United States and for other purposes,' do hereby certify that the amendment aforesaid has become valid, to all intents and purposes, as part of the Constitution of the United States.

"In testimony whereof I have hereunto set my hand and caused the seal of the Department of State to be affixed.

"Done at the City of Washington, this eighteenth day of December, in the year of our Lord one thousand eight hundred and sixty-five, and of the Independence of the United States of America the ninetieth.

[L. S.] WILLIAM H. SEWARD, Secretary of State."

[New Jersey, Oregon, California, and Iowa ratified subsequently to the date of this certificate, as did Florida in the same form as South Carolina and Alabama.]

[2] The following is a list of the members of this Congress. Those marked with an asterisk were new members:

SENATE.

California—James A. McDougall, John Conness.
Connecticut—Lafayette S. Foster, James Dixon.
Delaware—George Read Riddle, Willard Saulsbury.
Illinois—Lyman Trumbull, Richard Yates.*
Indiana—Henry S. Lane, Thomas A. Hendricks.
Iowa—James W. Grimes, Samuel J. Kirkwood.*
Kansas—Samuel C. Pomeroy, James H. Lane.
Kentucky—Garret Davis, James Guthrie.*
Maine—Lot M. Morrill, William Pitt Fessenden.*
Massachusetts—Charles Sumner, Henry Wilson.
Maryland—John A. J. Creswell,* Reverdy Johnson.
Michigan—Zachariah Chandler, Jacob M. Howard.
Minnesota—Alexander Ramsay, Daniel S. Norton.*
Missouri—B. Gratz Brown, John B. Henderson.
Nevada—William M. Stewart,* James W. Nye.*
New Hampshire—Daniel Clerk, Aaron H. Cragin.*
New Jersey—William Wright, John P. Stockton.*
New York—Ira Harris, Edwin D. Morgan.
Ohio—John Sherman, Benjamin F. Wade.
Oregon—James W. Nesmith, George H. Williams.*
Pennsylvania—Edgar Cowan, Charles R. Buckalew.
Rhode Island—William Sprague, Henry B. Anthony.
Tennessee—David D. Patterson,* J. S. Fowler.*
Vermont—Luke P. Poland,* Solomon Foot.
West Virginia—Peter G. Van Winkle, Waitman T. Willey.
Wisconsin—Timothy O. Howe, James R. Doolittle.

HOUSE.

California—Donald C. McRuer,* William Higby, John Bidwell.*
Connecticut—Henry C. Deming, Samuel L. Warner,* Augustus Brandegee, John H. Hubbard.
Delaware—John A. Nicholson.*
Illinois—John Wentworth,* John F. Farnsworth, Elihu B. Washburne, Abner C. Harding, Ebon C. Ingersoll, Burton C. Cook,* H. P. H. Bromwell,* Shelby M. Cullom,* Lewis W. Ross, Anthony Thornton,* Samuel S. Marshall,* Jehu Baker,* Andrew J. Kuykendall,* at large, S. W. Moulton.*
Indiana—William E. Niblack,* Michael C. Kerr,* Ralph Hill,* John H. Farquhar,* George W. Julian, Ebenezer Dumont, Daniel W. Voorhees,* Godlove S. Orth, Schuyler Colfax, Joseph H. Defrees,* Thomas N. Stillwell.*
Iowa—James F. Wilson, Hiram Price, William B. Allison, Josiah B. Grinnell, John A. Kasson, Asahel W. Hubbard.
Kansas—Sidney Clarke.*
Kentucky—L. S. Trimble,* Burwell C. Ritter,* Henry Grider, Aaron Harding, Lovell H. Rousseau,* Green Clay Smith, George S. Shanklin,* William H. Randall, Samuel McKee.*
Maine—John Lynch,* Sidney Perham, James G. Blaine, John H. Rice, Frederick A. Pike.
Maryland—Hiram McCullough, John L. Thomas, Jr.,* Charles E. Phelps,* Francis Thomas, Benjamin G. Harris.
Massachusetts—Thomas D. Eliot, Oakes Ames, Alexander H. Rice, Samuel Hooper, John B. Alley, Nathaniel P. Banks,* George S. Boutwell,* John D. Baldwin, William B. Washburn, Henry L. Dawes.
Michigan—Fernando C. Beaman, Charles Upson, John W. Longyear, Thomas W. Ferry,* Rowland E. Trowbridge,* John F. Driggs.
Minnesota—William Windom, Ignatius Donnelly.
Missouri—John Hogan,* Henry T. Blow, Thomas E. Noell,* John R. Kelso,* Joseph W. McClurg, Robert T. Van Horn,* Benjamin F. Loan, John F. Benjamin,* George W. Anderson.*
Nevada—Delos R. Ashley.*
New Hampshire—Gilman Marston,* Edward H. Rollins, James W. Patterson.
New Jersey—John F. Starr, William A. Newell,* Charles Sitgreaves,* Andrew J. Rogers, Edwin R. V. Wright.*
New York—Stephen Tabor,* Tunis G. Bergen,* James Humphrey,* Morgan Jones,* Nelson Taylor,* Henry J. Raymond,* John W. Chanler, James Brooks, William A. Darling,* William Radford, Charles H. Winfield, John H. Ketcham,* Edwin N. Hubbell,* Charles Goodyear,* John A. Griswold,* Robert S. Hale,* Calvin T. Hulburd, James M. Marvin, Demas Hubbard, Jr.,* Addison H. Laflin,* Roscoe Conkling,* Sidney T. Holmes,* Thomas T. Davis, Theodore M. Pomeroy, Daniel Morris, Giles W. Hotchkiss, Hamilton Ward,* Roswell Hart,* Burt Van Horn,* James M. Humphrey, Henry Van Aernam.*
Ohio—Benjamin Eggleston, Rutherford B. Hayes,* Robert C. Schenck, William Lawrence,* F. C. Le Blond, Reader W. Clark,* Samuel Shellabarger,* James H. Hubbell,* Ralph P. Buckland,* James M. Ashley, Hezekiah S. Bundy,* William E. Finck, Columbus Delano,* Martin Welker,* Tobias E. Plants,* John A. Bingham,* Ephraim R. Eckley, Rufus P. Spalding, James A. Garfield.
Oregon—John H. D. Henderson.*
Pennsylvania—Samuel J. Randall, Charles O'Neill, Leonard Myers, William D. Kelley, M. Russell Thayer, B. Markley Boyer,* John M. Broomall, Sydenham E. Ancona, Thaddeus Stevens, Myer Strouse, Philip Johnson, Charles Denison, Ulysses Mercur,* George F. Miller,* Adam J. Glossbrenner,* William H. Koontz,* Abraham A. Barker,* Stephen F. Wilson,* Glenni W. Schofield, Charles Vernon Culver,* John L. Dawson, James K. Moorhead, Thomas Williams, George V. Lawrence.*
Rhode Island—Thomas A. Jenckes, Nathan F. Dixon.
Tennessee—Nathaniel G. Taylor,* Horace Maynard,* William B. Stokes,* Edmund Cooper,* William B. Campbell,* S. M. Arnell,* Isaac R. Hawkins, John W. Leftwich.*
Vermont—Frederick E. Woodbridge, Justin S. Morrill, Portus Baxter.
West Virginia—Chester D. Hubbard,* George R. Latham,* Killian V. Whaley.
Wisconsin—Halbert E. Paine,* Ithamar C. Sloan, Amasa Cobb, Charles A. Eldridge, Philetus Sawyer,* Walter D. McIndoe.

The members from Tennessee were not admitted to either house until near the close of the session. Henry P. Stockton's seat in the Senate was declared vacant. Solomon Foote, of Vermont, died March 28, and was succeeded by George F. Edmunds. In the House the seat of D. W. Voorhees was given to Henry D. Washburne. That of James Brooks was given to William E. Dodge.

The following members were elected to Congress from the Southern States, but were not admitted:

SENATE.

Alabama—George S. Houston, Lewis E. Parsons.
Arkansas—E. Baxter, William D. Snow.
Louisiana—R. King Cutler, Michael Hahn.
Mississippi—William L. Sharkey, J. L. Alcorn.
North Carolina—John Pool, William A. Graham.
South Carolina—John L. Manning, Benjamin F. Perry.
Virginia—John C. Underwood, Joseph Segar.
Florida—William Marvin, Wilkerson Call.
Georgia—Alexander H. Stephens, Herschel V. Johnson.

HOUSE.

Alabama—C. C. Langdon, George C. Freeman, Cullen A. Battle, Joseph W. Taylor, B. T. Pope, T. J. Foster.
Arkansas—William Byers, George H. Kyle, J. M. Johnson.
Florida—F. McLeod.
Georgia—Solomon Cohen, Philip Cook, Hugh Buchanan, E. G. Cabaniss, J. D. Matthews, J. H. Christy, W. T. Wofford.
Louisiana—Louis St. Martin, Jacob Barker, Robert C. Wickliffe, John E. King, John S. Young.
Mississippi—A. E. Reynolds, R. A. Pinson, James T. Harrison, A. M. West, E. G. Peyton.
North Carolina—Jesse R. Stubbs, Charles C. Clark, Thomas C. Fuller, Josiah Turner, Jr., Bedford Brown, S. H. Walkup, A. H. Jones.
South Carolina—John D. Kennedy, William Aiken, Samuel McGowan, James Farrow.
Virginia—W. H. B. Custis, Lucius H. Chandler, B. Johnson Barbour, Robert Ridgway, Beverly A. Davis, Alexander H. H. Stuart, Robert Y. Conrad, Daniel H. Hoge.

Of those elected to the Senate, Mr. A. H. Stephens was a delegate from Georgia to the Convention which framed the "Confederate" Constitution, and was Vice-President of the "Confederacy" until its downfall. Mr. H. V. Johnson was a senator in the rebel Congress in the first and second Congresses, as was Mr. Graham from North Carolina. Mr. Pool was a senator in the Legislature of North Carolina. Mr. Perry was a "Confederate States" judge. Mr. Manning was a volunteer aid to General Beauregard at Fort Sumter and Manassas. Mr. Alcorn was in the Mississippi militia.

Among those elected to the House, of the *Alabama* delegation, Mr. Battle was a general in the rebel army, and Mr. Foster a representative in the first and second rebel Congresses.

Of the *Georgia* delegation, Messrs. Cook and Wofford were generals in the rebel service.

Of the *Mississippi* delegation, Messrs. Reynolds and Pinson were colonels in the rebel service; Mr. Harrison was a member of the rebel Provisional Congress.

Of the *North Carolina* delegation, Mr. Fuller was a representative in the first rebel Congress, and Mr. Turner was a colonel in the rebel army, and a representative in the second rebel Congress; Mr. Brown was a member of the State Convention which passed the Secession Ordinance in 1861, and voted for it.

Of the *South Carolina* delegation, Mr. Kennedy was colonel and Mr. McGowan brigadier general in the rebel army; Mr. Farrow was a representative in the first and second rebel Congresses.

Of the *Virginia* delegation, Messrs. Stuart and Conrad were members of the Secession Convention of Virginia in 1861, and continued to participate after the passage of the ordinance and the beginning of hostilities.

LAFAYETTE S. FOSTER.

that President Johnson did not expect McPherson to come to any different conclusion in the matter, from his letter to Provisional Governor Perry, November 27, a week before the assembling of Congress. In this letter he said it was not necessary for the members elect from South Carolina to be present at the organization of Congress. On the contrary, he thought it would be better policy to present their certificates of election after the organization of the two houses, and then it would be "a simple question under the Constitution of the members taking their seats." "Each house," he added, "must judge for itself the election, returns, and qualifications of its own members."

An attempt was made by Brooks, of New York, to bring up the question as to the credentials of members previous to organization, but it proved unsuccessful. In the vote for speaker the House divided by a strictly party separation between Brooks and Colfax; 175 votes being cast, of which the former received 36, and the latter 139. Thus Schuyler Colfax was re-elected speaker. Being conducted to the chair, he addressed the House. He alluded to the circumstances under which this new Congress was assembled. The Thirty-eighth Congress had closed its existence while the war was still in progress, but now there was peace from shore to shore. The duties of this Congress, he said, "are as obvious as the sun's pathway in the heavens. Representing, in its two branches, the states and the people, its first and highest obligation is to guarantee to every state a republican form of government. The rebellion having overthrown constitutional state governments in many states, it is yours to mature and enact legislation which, with the concurrence of the executive, shall establish them anew on such a basis of enduring justice as will guarantee all necessary safeguards to the people, and afford what our Magna Charta, the Declaration of Independence, proclaims is the chief object of government—protection to all men in their inalienable rights. The world should witness in this great work the most inflexible fidelity, the most earnest devotion to the principles of liberty and humanity, the truest patriotism, and the wisest statesmanship. Heroic men, by hundreds of thousands, have died that the republic might live. The emblems of mourning have darkened White House and cabin alike; but the fires of civil war have melted every fetter in the land, and proved the funeral-pyre of slavery. It is for you, representatives, to do your work as faithfully and as well as did the fearless saviors of the Union on their more dangerous arena of duty. Then we may hope to see the vacant and once abandoned seats around us gradually filling up, until this hall shall contain representatives from every state and district, their hearts devoted to the Union for which they are to legislate, jealous of its honor, proud of its glory, watchful of its rights, and hostile to its enemies; and the stars on our banner, that paled when the states they represented arrayed themselves in arms against the nation, will shine with a more brilliant light of loyalty than ever before."

The speaker then took the test oath, which still remained in operation.

In the Senate, excluding Tennessee, there were 10 new members out of 50; in the House, excluding Tennessee, 93 out of 184, or fully one half, were new members. The political complexion of the Senate remained unchanged; but in the House the change was very great. In the Thirty-eighth Congress about four ninths of the members were Democrats, now they numbered less than one fourth. This change simply indicated the popular opposition to the schemes of the peace party in 1864. The Thirty-

ninth Congress had been elected, not on the special issues of reconstruction, but on issues directly connected with the prosecution of the war.

President Johnson's message was anxiously awaited by the people. The President of the United States holds a peculiar position. He is, *par excellence*, the representative of the republic. He is directly elected by the whole people, while the legislative officers are elected either by states, as in the case of the Senate, or by local districts, as in the case of the House; therefore the people naturally look to him as to one whom they have expressly chosen as the exponent of their own views. He is elected by the majority of the whole people, and is therefore supposed to represent the nation rather than any section. To him is intrusted more power than resides in the head of a constitutional monarchy, because he is the choice of the people, and not a hereditary imposition. If Johnson's present position was different from that of a President elected as such, and not as Vice-President, that was the fault of the party which had elected him.

Johnson was a Democrat elected by the Republican party as Vice-President, and who, by accident, had become President. He had been a supporter of Breckinridge in the presidential contest of 1860. Although he was an ardent advocate of the Union, his political principles had not changed. He could scarcely find a name harsh enough by which to designate the rebellion. Following his own inclinations, he would have hanged the leading men engaged in it. In his view traitors should be "punished and impoverished." He knew that slavery was dead, but he was no mourner over its corpse. As military governor of Tennessee, he had been deemed one of the most radical members of the Republican party; and such indeed he had been, so far as war measures were concerned. Yet, now that the war was over, he was satisfied with what had been accomplished, and desired the immediate restoration of the Southern States to the Union upon the basis of the Constitution as it then stood, without farther modification. He would have preferred that the Southern Conventions should have extended the elective franchise to all negroes who could "read the Constitution of the United States in English and write their names," or who owned real estate to the value of $250. He even went so far as to urge such a measure upon the Mississippi Convention. He foresaw, or thought he did, that the Republican party would demand universal negro suffrage as a condition of restoration, and thought that the adoption of partial suffrage for the colored race would satisfy the people, and, as he expressed it, "disarm the adversary." But what was the "adversary" which Johnson wished to disarm? The party which had elected him. From the extremists of this party he feared more danger to the country than from the just subdued rebellious states. The very fact that these states had not appreciated the opportunity which he had given them, and had not heartily co-operated with him in his efforts in their behalf, only increased his apprehension; for he knew that their reluctant, half-hearted submission, and their ill-considered attempts to evade the consequences of the war, would give power to the faction of whose future action he had the most serious apprehension. With all their mistakes, he preferred to trust the Southern States rather than extreme Republicans. If

SCHUYLER COLFAX.

he was dissatisfied with the former, he was more apprehensive of the latter. He would sooner forgive rebels who had laid down their arms, however sullen their submission, than support those who desired to make the victory of the nation an occasion for the aggrandizement of their party. The former were powerless for injury; the danger threatened by the latter he deemed imminent and formidable.

During the few months preceding the assembling of Congress the speculations as to Johnson's position were numerous. He was every day pardoning rebels belonging to the classes excepted from his Amnesty Proclamation of May 29th. Of course the applications for pardon were many, but the exceptions had been made to exclude a few, and there was no impropriety in the President's pardoning all others. In some cases, however, where there was a special reason for refusal, pardon was not refused.

During this period, also, the Democratic press had undergone a somewhat remarkable change. Those journals which had hitherto been foremost in abusing Johnson now altered their tone. The Democratic party had been shamefully defeated in the election of 1864, but now there seemed to be a chance for its recovery. Somewhat curiously, this party supposed that Johnson was coming over to it, while Johnson, on the other hand, supposed that this party was coming over to him. And here we are reminded of the interview between George L. Stearns and the President, October 3d, 1865. "The Democratic party," said Johnson at this interview, "finds its old position is untenable, and is coming over to ours; if it has come up to our position, I am glad of it." At the same time the President expressed his views in detail. He said the states were in the Union, "which was whole and indivisible." "We must not," he remarked, "be too much in a hurry; it is better to let them reconstruct themselves than to force them to it; for if they go wrong, the power is in our hands, and we can check them in any stage to the end, and oblige them to correct their error; we must be patient with them." He expressed his opposition both to giving too much power to the states, and also to a great consolidation of power in the central government. "Our only safety," he said, "lies in allowing each state to control the right of voting by its own laws, and we have the power to control the rebel states if they go wrong. . . . . If the general government controls the right to vote in the states, it may establish such rules as will restrict the vote to a small number of persons, and thus create a central despotism." Universal negro suffrage now he thought would breed a war of races; but he was in favor of a gradual introduction of the black race to participation in political power. He said the negro would rather vote with his master whom he did not hate, than with the non-slaveholding population of the South, against whom he had an hereditary prejudice. This prejudice was shown by the fact that outrages committed originated either from non-slaveholding whites against negroes, or from negroes against non-slaveholding whites.

To understand Johnson's position at this time we must call to mind the considerations which influenced him. In the first place, there was his theory of the situation, according to which he believed that the burden of reconstruction rested upon the South, and not upon the executive or legislative departments of the government. The rebellion had ceased, and, whatever might be the decision of government as to the punishment of individual traitors, the states in which the rebellion had existed were still states, with all their powers unimpaired, and with all their social institutions intact save that of slavery. Allegiance, as it seemed to him, consisted in the performance of constitutional obligations. It is true that by the Constitution every man who had borne arms against the government might be hung for treason, or be punished in any other way, at the option of the government; but, even after that had been done, it would still remain true that the only claim which the government had upon the Southern people was a claim to their allegiance—not their allegiance to the Republican party, but to the Constitution. The ratification of the anti-slavery amendment he deemed necessary as a recognition of what had been accomplished by the war. The nullification of secession ordinances and the repudiation of the rebel debt were, in his view, directly involved in the abandonment of the struggle by the South. His views had not changed from what they had been in 1862, when in the Senate he introduced the resolution declaring that the object of the war was simply the suppression of the rebellion, and that, so soon as this should be accomplished, the war ought to cease, leaving the Southern States with all their original powers under the Constitution. Since then slavery had been abolished, and thus far the views expressed in this resolution had been changed, but no farther. Johnson did not regard the resumption of their former functions by the late Confederate States as a privilege granted them, but as a duty—a constitutional obligation which even the existence of civil war had no power to relax. Whatever farther changes in the organic law of the nation might seem necessary in the new situation consequent upon restoration ought, in his opinion, to be made in the ordinary way, and by all the states acting in common, and upon terms of equality.

But, apart from his theory as to the basis of restoration, there were certain practical considerations which influenced the President. So long as the Southern States were prevented from resuming their normal relations to the government, the balance of political power would remain disturbed. By the very election which had given him his present position a Congress also had been chosen which was more than three fourths Republican. He foresaw, or at least feared, that this Congress, in which there was so heavy a preponderance of power on the Republican side, would be partisan in its legislation, and would use its advantages for the concentration and perpetuation of party power. The immediate representation of the South in Congress, while it would counteract this tendency, could not, it seemed to him, be productive of evil, inasmuch as each house, by its power to decide upon the qualification of its members, had a safeguard against the admission of the disloyal, and inasmuch, moreover, as, even after the admission of every Southern member, the Republicans would still maintain a majority in both houses.

These principles constituted the basis of President Johnson's policy of reconstruction as laid before Congress in his first annual message. The first question, he said, which had presented itself for decision was whether the territory of the South should be held as conquered territory under military authority emanating from the President as commander-in-chief of the army. He had decided the question in the negative. Military governments, while they would not alleviate, would, on the other hand, exaggerate existing discontent; they would envenom hatred rather than restore affection; once established, no precise limit to their continuance was conceivable; the expense occasioned by them would be incalculable and exhausting; they would operate unfavorably against emigration from the Northern to the Southern States—one of the best means for the restoration of harmony; the powers of patronage and rule thus exercised under the President over a vast, populous, and naturally wealthy region, were greater than he would, unless under extreme necessity, intrust to any one man—greater than he would consent to exercise himself except on occasions of great emergency; and the willful use of such powers for a series of years would endanger not only the purity of the general administration, but also the liberties of the states which remained loyal.

But, argued the President, there was another and more vital objection to the establishment of military governments over the Southern States. Such a policy would imply that the states whose inhabitants had participated in the rebellion had, by the act of those inhabitants, ceased to exist. The true theory, on the other hand, was "that all pretended acts of secession were from the beginning null and void." States could not commit treason, nor screen individual traitors, any more than they could make treaties with foreign powers. The vitality of the seceding states had been by the rebellion impaired, but not extinguished, and their functions suspended, but not destroyed.

"But," proceeds the argument, "if any state neglects or refuses to perform its offices, there is the more need that the general government should maintain all its authority, and, as soon as practicable, resume the exercise of all its functions. On this principle I have acted, and have gradually and quietly, and by almost imperceptible steps, sought to restore the rightful energy of the general government and of the states. To that end provisional governors have been appointed for the states, Conventions called, governors elected, Legislatures assembled, and senators and representatives chosen to the Congress of the United States. At the same time, the courts of the United States, as far as could be done, have been reopened, so that the laws of the United States may be enforced through their agency. The blockade has been removed, and the custom-houses re-established in ports of entry, so that the revenue of the United States may be collected. The Post-office Department renews its ceaseless activity, and the general government is thereby enabled to communicate promptly with its officers and agents. The courts bring security to persons and property; the opening of the ports invites the restoration of industry and commerce; the post-office renews the facilities of social intercourse and of business. And is it not happy for us all that the restoration of each one of these functions of the general government brings with it a blessing to the states over which they are extended? Is it not a sure promise of harmony and renewed attachment to the Union that, after all that has happened, the return of the general government is known only as a beneficence?"

This policy was attended with some risk; its success involved the acquiescence of the states concerned. But the risk must be taken, and in the choice of difficulties it was the smallest risk. To diminish the danger involved in his policy he had asserted his power to pardon.

"The next step which I have taken," said the President, "to restore the constitutional relations of the states has been an invitation to them to participate in the high office of amending the Constitution. Every patriot must wish for a general amnesty at the earliest epoch consistent with public safety. For this great end there is need of a concurrence of all opinions, and the spirit of mutual conciliation. All parties in the late terrible conflict must work together in harmony. It is not too much to ask, in the name of the whole people, that, on the one side, the plan of restoration shall proceed in conformity with a willingness to cast the disorders of the past into oblivion; and that, on the other, the evidence of sincerity in the future maintenance of the Union shall be put beyond any doubt by the ratification of the proposed amendment to the Constitution, which provides for the abolition of slavery forever within the limits of our country. So long as the adoption of this amendment is delayed, so long will doubt, and jealousy, and uncertainty prevail. This is the measure which will efface the sad memory of the past; this is the measure which will most certainly call population, and capital, and security to those parts of the Union that need them most. Indeed, it is not too much to ask of the states which are now resuming their places in the family of the Union to give this pledge of perpetual loyalty and peace. Until it is done, the past, however much we may desire it, will not be forgotten. The adoption of the amendment reunites us beyond all power of disruption. It heals the wound that is still imperfectly closed; it removes slavery, the element which has so long perplexed and divided the country; it makes of us once more a united people, renewed and strengthened, bound more than ever to mutual affection and support."

Thus President Johnson explained the policy which he had thus far pursued. The completion of the work of restoration would be accomplished by the resumption on the part of the states of their places in the two branches of the national Legislature. "Here," he added, "it is for you, fellow-citizens of the Senate, and for you, fellow-citizens of the House of Representatives, to judge, each of you for yourselves, of the elections, returns, and qualifications of your own members."

After advocating the speedy restoration by Congress of the Circuit Courts in the late rebel states, in order that those charged with the commission of treason might have fair and impartial trials, the President proceeded thus to consider the situation of the freedmen in those states:

"The relations of the general government toward the four millions of inhabitants whom the war has called into freedom have engaged my most serious consideration. On the propriety of attempting to make the freedmen electors by the proclamation of the executive, I took for my counsel the Constitution itself, the interpretations of that instrument by its authors and their contemporaries, and recent legislation by Congress. When, at the first movement toward independence, the Congress of the United States instructed the several states to institute governments of their own, they left each state to decide for itself the conditions for the enjoyment of the elective franchise. During the period of the Confederacy, there continued to exist a very great diversity in the qualifications of electors in the several states; and even within a state a distinction of qualifications prevailed with regard to the officers who were to be chosen. The Constitution of the United States recognizes these diversities when it enjoins that in the choice of members of the House of Representatives of the United States 'the electors in each state shall have the qualifications requisite for electors of the most numerous branch of the state Legislature.'

"After the formation of the Constitution, it remained, as before, the uniform usage for each state to enlarge the body of its electors according to its own judgment; and, under this system, one state after another has proceeded to increase the number of its electors, until now universal suffrage, or something very near it, is the general rule. So fixed was this reservation of power in the habits of the people, and so unquestioned has been the interpretation of the Constitution, that during the civil war the late President never harbored the purpose—certainly never avowed the purpose—of disregarding it; and in the acts of Congress, during that period, nothing can be found which during the continuance of hostilities, much less after their close, would have sanctioned any departure by the executive from a policy which has so uniformly obtained. Moreover, a concession of the elective franchise to the freedmen, by act of the President of the United States, must have been extended to all colored men, wherever found, and so must have established a change of suffrage in the Northern, Middle, and Western States, not less than in the Southern and Southwestern. Such an act would have created a new class of voters, and would have been an assumption of power by the President which nothing in the Constitution or laws of the United States would have warranted.

"On the other hand, every danger of conflict is avoided when the settlement of the question is referred to the several states. They can, each for itself, decide on the measure, and whether it is to be adopted at once and absolutely, or introduced gradually and with conditions. In my judgment, the freedmen, if they show patience and manly virtues, will sooner obtain a participation in the elective franchise through the states than through the general government, even if it had power to intervene. When the tumult of emotions that have been raised by the suddenness of the social change shall have subsided, it may prove that they will receive the kindliest usage from some of those on whom they have heretofore most closely depended."

But, while the President thought it was not competent for the general government to extend the elective franchise in the several states, it seemed equally clear to him that good faith required the security of the freedmen in their liberty and property, their right to labor, and to just compensation therefor. "It is," said he, "one of the greatest acts on record to have brought four millions of people into freedom. The career of free industry must be fairly opened to them; and then their future prosperity and condition must, after all, rest mainly on themselves. If they fail, and so perish away, let us be careful that the failure shall not be attributable to any denial of justice. In all that relates to the destiny of the freedmen we need not be too anxious to read the future; many incidents which, from a speculative point of view, might raise alarm, will quietly settle themselves."

This message was as able a political document as had ever been laid before the American Congress. But, for all that, the President, as we have said already, had committed a terrible blunder. He had assumed that the executive might *independently* determine the conditions necessary to restoration, and that to Congress was only left the consideration on the part of the two houses respectively of the qualifications of their members, and such action as might be deemed necessary to secure the freedmen against oppression. His mistake was not that he had not established military governments over the Southern States; it was not that he had usurped any power in re-establishing the relations between those states and the executive, which it was clearly his duty to do; but he had created an impression among the people of the South that simply by nullifying secession, repudiating the rebel debt, and ratifying the anti-slavery amendment, they had done all which was necessary to satisfy the people that the security of the country was fully established. Here was his mistake. The people were not satisfied by what had been done. They did not feel secure as to the future. On the contrary, they were greatly agitated with apprehension lest Southern politicians, combining with Northern Democrats, and assisted by the increased numerical representation resulting from the abolition of slavery, might imperil the security of the national debt, demand compensation for their freed slaves, inaugurate a system of legislation injurious to freedmen, and neutralize the results of the war. Congress also was dissatisfied, not only for the reasons which had occasioned popular discontent, but because

it had not been admitted to participation in the first stages of reconstruction. In this work there were some things demanded by the people which belonged alone to the national Legislature, and could not be touched by the President. Thus, for instance, he had no right to demand the readjustment of the basis of representation.

All this difficulty might have been avoided if the President had called an extra session of Congress in July, 1865. There were two urgent reasons for such a session:

1. The perfection of the preliminary steps toward restoration in such features as required the supplementary action of Congress could only thus be secured.

2. It was an emergency which demanded harmonious action on the part of the government. This harmony implied no usurpation by the executive of the functions of Congress, or by Congress of executive powers. The President would still be perfectly independent in his own sphere, and a like independence would belong to the national Legislature. The very fact of the President's consulting with Congress would have conduced to harmony. And if, after all, there should arise a difference, and the President should deem it his duty to do his share of the work upon one plan, while Congress, after mature deliberation, should decide upon a different policy in regard to its own action, each would have shown a proper respect for the other, and thus the antagonism which might have been inevitable, however unfortunate, would have been free from bitterness. Each department of the government, moreover, would at the outset have given a full expression of its policy, and the Southern States would have been prevented from entertaining false hopes as to the result of their own action. The questions involved in the two different policies—if there must be two—would have thus been brought immediately before the people for calm discussion, and not in such a way as to lead on to an angry and acrimonious dispute.

But Johnson, as we have said, preferred another course, and proceeded to his work alone. Thus he laid the basis for a conflict between himself and Congress, for popular dissatisfaction, and for unreasonable expectations on the part of the Southern people. Whether these results followed with or without the President's design, they were equally unfortunate. It was certainly in his power to prevent them, but he did not use the power. Whatever might afterward be done by Congress to deepen and exacerbate the conflict between the executive and legislative departments of the government, it would still remain true that the President had taken the first steps toward such a conflict. Did he distrust Congress, and therefore attempt to forestall its action? Then it must be answered, first, that his distrust had no good foundation, as there was no indication that Congress was disposed to act unreasonably toward the South; and, secondly, that if Congress had been thus disposed, its action *could* not be forestalled by the President. It was the Congress of the United States; its action was as independent within its own sphere as was that of the President; so long as it remained in power, its decision as to the representation of the Southern States was irrevocable by any power on earth. And, moreover, the President could, by his distrust of Congress, or by an attempt to anticipate its action in the preliminary stages of restoration, only put that body upon its guard, and generate in it a corresponding distrust of himself, thus rendering future harmony between the executive and legislative departments almost impossible.

Previous to the organization of Congress, it had been determined in a caucus of Republicans to reject all delegations from the Southern States until both houses had agreed upon some plan of action respecting them. On the first day of the session, Thaddeus Stevens offered a resolution, which was adopted by the House, 133 to 36, "that a joint committee of fifteen members shall be appointed, nine of whom shall be members of the House and six members of the Senate, who shall inquire into the condition of the states which formed the so-called Confederate States of America, and report whether they, or any of them, are entitled to be represented in either house of Congress, with leave to report at any time by bill or otherwise; and until such report shall have been made and finally acted upon by Congress, no member shall be received into either house from any of the so-called Confederate States; and all papers relating to the representation of said states shall be referred to the said committee without debate." The previous question was demanded by Stevens, and all debate was forestalled. This resolution came before the Senate for action on the 12th of December, and was amended on motion of Senator Anthony, of Rhode Island, so as to become a concurrent instead of a joint resolution, thus making the signature of the President unnecessary. Anthony then moved another amendment, to strike out the provision preventing either house from admitting any of the members concerned until the committee should have reported and Congress should have taken final action upon the subject. This led to debate. Senator Howard, of Michigan, opposed the amendment. He held that the late Confederate States were conquered communities, without the right of self-government; we held them, not by their free will, but by the exercise of military power. Under these circumstances, he considered either house incompetent to admit members from those states without the consent of both. Senator Anthony replied that it was intended that both houses should act in concert, and it was also desirable that the executive and Congress should act in concert; "that all branches of the government shall approach this great question in a spirit of comprehensive patriotism, with confidence in each other, and that each branch of the government, and all persons in each branch of the government, will be ready, if necessary, to concede something of their own views in order to meet the views of those who are equally charged with the responsibility of public affairs." The Constitution confided to each house separately its own independent right of judgment of the elections, returns, and qualifications of its members.

Under the resolution as it came from the House, it would be necessary to refer the credentials of those claiming seats in the Senate to a committee, the majority of which was from the House. Besides, the resolution provided that papers should be referred to the committee without debate. This was contrary to the practice of the Senate.

Senator Doolittle, of Wisconsin, objected to the preponderance given to the House in the proposed committee, and said the injurious result of this could only be obviated by the amendment under consideration. He alluded to the restriction upon debate, and said the Senate was "to be led like a lamb to the slaughter, bound hand and foot, shorn of its constitutional power, and gagged." Again, the resolution, as it stood, would exclude 11 states from representation in the Union, thus accomplishing what rebellion had failed to accomplish—it was the "dissolution of the Union by act of Congress." The doctrine of Senator Howard, involving the theory of state destruction, was, he claimed, opposed to the ground taken by the Union party from the first, which was that states could not withdraw from the Union. They could not do it peacefully; they had undertaken to do it by arms; "we crushed the attempt; we trampled their armies under our feet; we captured the rebellion; the states are ours; and we entered them to save, and not to destroy." He alluded to the fact that the resolution originated in a secret caucus dominated by Thaddeus Stevens, the zealous advocate of confiscation, and to the hot haste with which this shrewd leader had pressed it through the House in the short space of 10 minutes, without debate, and before the President's message had been communicated. In conclusion, Doolittle urged upon the Senate the duty of that body to act in harmony with the President. We claim, he said, to be here acting as the friends of the late lamented President, and the friends of him upon whom had lately fallen the responsibilities of executive power. We aided in the election of both. When they were nominated, the experiment of reconstruction had already begun. For nearly a year Lincoln had been pursuing substantially the same policy which had been since followed by his successor. Their election, he claimed, was a popular support of this policy, and he predicted that Johnson would be sustained by the people. This was as certain, he said, as the revolutions of the earth.

Senator Fessenden then arose. He had at first favored the resolution as it came from the House because he sympathized with its object. The Senate ought not to adopt the convictions of the President without examination. This was a subject of infinite importance, involving the integrity and welfare of the republic in all future time, and it was the duty of senators to examine the subject with care and fidelity, and act upon their own convictions and not upon those of others. The resolution looked toward calm and deliberate consideration before action, and so far he approved it. But, upon a more careful reading, he had come to the conclusion, for the reasons already given by Senator Anthony, that the resolution perhaps went a little too far. It was important that the committee should be appointed, to secure harmony of action between the two houses. The subject would thus be carefully considered, and the delay necessary to secure deliberation was not so great an evil as party action. He concurred, however, in the objections made by Senator Anthony. From the passage of the amendment moved by that senator, the inference was not deducible, as Senator Howard thought it was, that the Senate was in favor of the immediate or hasty admission of any of the Southern members. He was himself certainly not in favor of such action, and yet he should vote for the amendment. Neither did he agree with Senator Doolittle that the appointment of this committee was any intimation with regard to the opinion entertained by the Senate of the President's policy. The Senate simply chose to consider the whole subject for itself before acting upon it.

Anthony's amendment was agreed to, and on the next day the House concurred in the amendments of the Senate, and the resolution was adopted. The House subsequently adopted for its own guidance the provisions which had been stricken out by the Senate. On the 14th the speaker announced as members of the joint committee on the part of the House, Thaddeus Stevens, of Pennsylvania; Elihu B. Washburne, of Illinois; Justin S. Morrill, of Vermont; Henry Grider, of Kentucky; John A. Bingham, of Ohio; Roscoe Conkling, of New York; George S. Boutwell, of Massachusetts; Henry T. Blow, of Missouri; and Andrew J. Rogers, of New Jersey. In the Senate, on December 21st, the following members were announced by the President *pro tem.*: Fessenden, Grimes, Harris, Howard, Johnson, Williams.

On the 12th the Senate adopted a resolution requesting the President to furnish information as to the condition of that portion of the Union lately in rebellion. The President replied on the 18th that the rebellion had been suppressed; that, so far as possible, United States courts had been restored, the post-offices re-established; and steps taken to put in operation the revenue laws. The late Confederate States, he said, had reorganized their governments, and were yielding obedience to the laws and government of the United States with more willingness and greater promptitude than under the circumstances could reasonably have been anticipated." The anti-slavery amendment had been ratified except in the case of Mississippi, and in nearly all the states measures had either been adopted or were now pending to confer upon freedmen the rights and privileges essential to their comfort, protection, and security. The aspect of affairs, in the President's opinion, was more promising than could have been anticipated. "The people," he said, "throughout the entire South evince a laudable desire to renew their allegiance to the government, and to repair the devastations of war by a prompt and cheerful return to peaceful pursuits. An abiding faith is entertained that their actions will conform to their professions, and that, in acknowledging the supremacy of the Constitution and laws of the United

States, their loyalty will be unreservedly given to the government, whose leniency they can not fail to appreciate, and whose fostering care will soon restore them to a condition of prosperity. It is true that in some of the states the demoralizing effects of the war are to be seen in occasional disorders; but these are local in character, not frequent in occurrence, and are rapidly disappearing as the authority of civil law is extended and sustained. Perplexing questions were naturally to be expected from the great and sudden change in the relations between the two races; the systems are gradually developing themselves under which the freedman will receive the protection to which he is justly entitled, and by means of his labor make himself a useful and independent member of the community in which he has his home. From all the information in my possession, and from that which I have recently derived from the most reliable authority, I am induced to cherish the belief that sectional animosity is surely and rapidly merging itself into a spirit of nationality, and that representation, connected with a properly adjusted system of taxation, will result in a harmonious restoration of the relations of the states to the national Union."

With this brief message, which was somewhat rose-colored in its construction of Southern loyalty, and evidently designed to hasten the admission of Southern representatives to Congress, two reports were transmitted — from Major General Carl Schurz and Lieutenant General Grant, who had each recently made a tour of inspection through the Southern States. Schurz's report was more consonant with what was termed the "radical" sentiment, but was so prolix that, notwithstanding Senator Sumner's urgent request that it should be read by the secretary, the majority of the Senate preferred to see it in print. The lieutenant general was concise in his statements, which, though eminently conservative, were to the point. He had left Washington on the 27th of November, and his tour had only occupied little more than one week. His mission had been principally military in its nature, regarding the necessary distribution of the United States forces in the several states. He expressed himself satisfied that the "mass of thinking men of the South accepted the present situation of affairs in good faith, and that they regarded the questions of slavery and state rights as having been finally settled by the war, regarding this decision not only as final, but as a fortunate one for the whole country, 'they receiving like benefits from it with those who opposed them in the field and in council.'" But, adds the lieutenant general, "four years of war, during which law was executed only at the point of the bayonet throughout the states in rebellion, have left the people possibly in a condition not to yield that ready obedience to civil authority the American people have generally been in the habit of yielding." Therefore he thought small garrisons throughout those states necessary "until such time as labor returns to its proper channels, and civil authority is fully established." Neither the officers under the government nor the Southern citizens thought the present withdrawal of the military practicable. "The white and the black mutually require the protection of the general government." The military force needed was small. "There is," said the lieutenant general, "such universal acquiescence in the authority of the general government throughout the portions of country visited by me, that the mere presence of a military force, without regard to numbers, is sufficient to maintain order." He thought the good of the country and economy required that the force kept in the interior where there were many freedmen should consist of white troops. The presence of black troops demoralized labor not only by its direct influence, but as furnishing a resort for the freedmen for long distances around. No violence would be offered to black troops by thinking men, but it might by the ignorant; and, adds the lieutenant general, "the late slave seems to be imbued by the idea that the property of his late master should by right belong to him, or at least should have no protection from the colored soldier." He thought it was to be regretted that at this time there could not be a commingling of the two sections, especially in Congress.

In regard to the operations of the Freedmen's Bureau, there appeared to the general to have been in some of the states a lack of good judgment and economy. The agents of the Bureau had caused an idea to prevail among the freedmen that the lands of their former masters would be divided among them, and this belief had seriously interfered with the willingness of the freedmen to make contracts for the coming year. In some form the continuance of the Bureau was a necessity, and many of the disorders and much of the expense might, he thought, be removed by making every officer on duty in the Southern States an agent of the Bureau.

The Select Committee on Reconstruction, instead of being an organ of progress, proved one of obstruction. Its object had been sufficiently definite, namely, to inquire into the condition of the Southern States in respect of their fitness for representation. The elements involved in this investigation were very simple. If the entire committee had resolved itself into a board of inspectors, and had traveled over every one of the Southern States, it would have discovered no new aspect of the case presented. The primary question which they were expected to answer was, Does the security of the nation require other measures than those already included in the President's policy before Southern representatives ought to be admitted? The answer was just as plain when the committee was appointed as it was six months later. Other measures were necessary, not only in the view of Congress, but in that of the people. Then came the secondary question, What were these measures? And it was for conference concerning this question that the committee had been appointed. But here again the answer was clear, demanding the removal of no obscurity, for there was none to remove; requiring no great delay, but only careful deliberation as to details. The necessary measures to be insisted upon had been subjects of popular discussion for months, and among those whose past had proved their steadfast loyalty and patriotism there was no expression of doubt as to what these measures were. By a constitutional amendment, said the popular voice, must it be declared that the rebel debt is repudiated, the adoption of the national debt secured, the basis of representation so readjusted as to give the South no advantage on account of rebellion, the civil rights of the freedmen firmly established, and the leaders of the late rebellion disfranchised until they can be safely admitted to a share in the government which they did their best to destroy. If these conditions had been written upon the sky in letters of fire they could not have been plainer. They were not conditions dependent upon any decision which might be rendered as to the present state of the South, or as to dangers clearly in prospect; they were necessary in any case for absolute security. Delay is not deliberation, and there were no good reasons why the committee should not have been ready to report in full within a fortnight from the time of its appointment. There was no necessity for long delay; and, on the other hand, the necessity was urgent that Congress should soon and fully declare its policy. Nothing could be done before the committee reported, and several of its members boldly expressed their idea that the South was not to be represented, nor to participate in the election of President for a series of years; and some of them went so far as to confess that this exclusion was designed to perpetuate the Republican party. Thus there was occasioned popular distrust of Congress, and within that body opposition began to be shown by members, who, while they did not object to a single one of the conditions demanded by the people, grew dissatisfied with the manner and spirit in which the development of the congressional policy was proceeding.

The committee did not report in full until six months after its appointment. It did not even report by bill until January 22d, 1866. On that day Thaddeus Stevens reported a joint resolution to amend the Constitution in regard to the basis of representation. This amendment declared that representatives and direct taxes should be apportioned among all the states according to their respective numbers, excluding Indians not taxed, *provided* that whenever the elective franchise should be denied or abridged in any state on account of race or color, all persons of such race and color should be excluded from the basis of representation. In this connection Stevens said that there were twenty-two states whose Legislatures were then in session, some of which would adjourn within two or three weeks. It was therefore desirable, he said, that this amendment, if adopted, should be adopted promptly. "It does not," he added, "deny to the states the right to regulate the elective franchise as they please; but it does say to a state, 'if you exclude from the right of suffrage Frenchmen, Irishmen, or any particular class of people, none of that class of people shall be counted in fixing your representation in this House.'"

This amendment was necessary, just, and impartial. It did not meet with any strong objection from the President, who, while he doubted the propriety of making farther amendments to the Constitution, was not opposed to the readjustment of the basis of representation. In an interview with Senator Dixon, of Connecticut, January 28th, 1866, he expressed his preference for a proposition making the number of qualified voters the basis of representation. The President's proposition offered the Southern States a motive for the partial extension of suffrage to negroes, while that reported by the Reconstruction Committee made it impossible for those states to gain in representation in any other way than by establishing impartial negro suffrage. The congressional proposition did not necessarily invite to universal suffrage; it excluded the entire colored race from representation only in the event of the elective franchise being denied to any of that race *because of color*. The exclusion would not result from any restriction upon the franchise which was applicable to white and black alike. The amendment thus favored impartial suffrage in the Southern States.

The whole case was fully stated by Roscoe Conkling, of New York, a member of the Reconstruction Committee. He began his argument by alluding to the constitutional provision which had hitherto regulated the apportionment of taxes and representation. These had been apportioned among the several states according to numbers, to be determined by adding to free persons three fifths of the slaves. This provision was one of the compromises of the Constitution; but, like the present amendment, it owed its existence to the principle that political representation belongs only to those who have political existence. The slaves of the South formed no part of the political society which framed the Constitution. They were without either natural or political rights. From this it naturally followed that they should not be represented. But direct taxes and representation ought to be distributed uniformly among the members of a free government. All alike should bear the burdens—all alike should share the benefits. The exception of aliens or unnaturalized foreigners from representation was not permanent or fixed. Slaves alone were forever excluded from the political community. He was a man and not a man; in flesh and blood alive, but politically dead—the representative of nothing but value. It could not be maintained by the slaveholding states that slaves were persons to be represented; it could neither be claimed that they were persons to be taxed. For these purposes slaves were excluded altogether by the principle on which the government was built. Without some special provision, therefore, they would have been altogether ignored. Taxes, however, were desirable on the one side, and representation on the other, and, for mere convenience, a compromise was invented for the sake of both. Thus a purely arbitrary agreement was inserted in the Constitution, supported by nothing but the consent of the parties, based upon the facts as they then stood. It was agreed in substance that the free people of all the states should be counted alike, and that the people of the slaveholding states should have as much power besides as would be measured by counting every slave as three fifths

of one person; direct taxes to follow the same rule. The power thus agreed upon was not exercised by the slaves, but by their masters. This covenant was operative so long as there was any thing to operate upon. That time was now past. The provision had become impotent. The fall of slavery had superseded it. To continue the compromise now that the thing upon which it rested had passed from under it would lead to results which, when the Constitution was made, were condemned by the judgment of all. An anomaly had been introduced. Four millions were suddenly among us not bound to any one, and yet not clothed with any political rights—not slaves, and not, in a political sense, "persons." No figment of slavery remained with which to spell out a right in somebody else to wield for them a power which they might not wield themselves. Their masters had a fraction of power, on their account, while they were slaves, but now there were no masters and no slaves. Did this fraction of power still survive? If so, to whom did it belong? The blacks were pronounced unfit to wield even a fraction of power, and must not have it. That answered the question. If the answer was true, it was an end of controversy. If the blacks were unfit to have the power, then the power had no belonging whatsoever, and was at once resumed by the nation. This fractional power, then, was extinct. A moral earthquake had turned fractions to units, and units to ciphers. If a black man counted at all now, he was a whole man, not three fifths of one. Revolutions had no such fractions in their arithmetic; war and humanity joined hands to wipe them out. Four millions were to be reckoned, and these four millions, we were told, were unfit for political existence. The framers of the Constitution never dreamed of reckoning in the basis of representation those who were denied all political rights. Our fathers trusted to gradual and voluntary emancipation, which would go hand in hand with education and enfranchisement. They never peered into the bloody epoch when four million fetters would be at once melted off in the fires of war—four millions, each a Caspar Hauser, long shut up in darkness, and suddenly led out into the full flash of noon, and each, it was said, too blind to walk politically. No one foresaw such an event, and no provision was made for it. The three-fifths rule gave the slaveholding states over and above their just representation as a political community eighteen representatives. The new situation would enable these states to claim 28 representatives besides their just proportion. These 28 votes were to be controlled by those who once betrayed the government, and for those so destitute, it was claimed, of intelligence as not to be fit to vote for themselves. The result of this would be that while 127,000 white people in New York cast but one vote in the House, the same number of white men in Mississippi would cast three votes. Thus the death of slavery would add two fifths to the power which slavery exercised while it lived. Should one white man have as much share in the government as three other white men merely because he lived where blacks outnumbered whites two to one? Should this inequality exist, and exist only in favor of those who, without cause, drenched the land with blood, and covered it with mourning? Should such be the reward of those who did the foulest and guiltiest act which crimsons the annals of recorded time? To prevent this, three modes had been proposed:

1. To make the basis of representation in Congress and the Electoral College consist of sufficiently qualified voters alone.

ROSCOE CONKLING.

2. To deprive the states of the power to disqualify or discriminate politically on account of race or color.

3. To leave every state free to decide who should belong to its political community, and who should vote. Those decided unworthy to vote to be excluded from the basis of representation.

The last of these methods had been adopted by the committee. If voters alone were made the foundation of representation, the actual ratio would differ infinitely among different states. In the strife of unbridled suffrage, a state might give the franchise to women, minors, and aliens. In the second method, a great objection was encountered on the very threshold, because this plan denied to states the right to regulate their own affairs. The plan adopted by the committee had several advantages over the others.

1. It provided for representation going hand in hand with taxation.

2. It brought into the basis both sexes and all ages, and thus counteracted casual and geographical inequalities of population.

3. It put every state on an equal footing in the requirement prescribed.

4. It left every state free to enumerate all its people for representation or not, as it might choose.

If the amendment was adopted, and suffrage remained confined, as it was now, upon the census of 1860, the gains and losses would be these: Wisconsin, Indiana, Illinois, Ohio, Pennsylvania, Massachusetts, New Jersey, and Maine would gain one representative each, and New York would gain three; Alabama, Kentucky, North Carolina, South Carolina, and Tennessee would each lose one; Georgia, Louisiana, and Virginia would each lose two, and Mississippi three.[1]

Such was the argument of Roscoe Conkling—a statement so full and so conclusive in its reasoning that it is unnecessary to introduce the other arguments presented in favor of the proposition. When Stevens introduced the proposition, he demanded its adoption or rejection before the going down of the sun. The committee, of which he was so prominent a member, might be allowed weeks for deliberation, but the moment any of its measures were brought before the House, he deemed a few hours sufficient for their disposition. The House, however, did not seem inclined to amend the Constitution of the United States with such haste, and Stevens yielded.

The debate in the House was continued for several days. The proposition of the committee was opposed by those who desired to prevent the Southern States from disfranchising races, and also by those who, for political purposes, objected both to the enfranchisement of the negro race and to the equalization of representation, one or the other of which results would necessarily follow the adoption of the amendment. There was also a large number of Republicans who preferred that representation should be based upon the number of voters. This, it will be remembered, was the preference of the President. The objections to this basis (that of voters) which had been offered by Roscoe Conkling could easily be obviated, it was argued, by restrictions excluding women, minors, and aliens. But still it would remain true that such restrictions would limit the power of the states to regulate the franchise of their citizens—a power which they would not willingly abdicate, and thus the amendment might be defeated. The basis furnished by the committee's amendment was open to the somewhat serious objection that it left room for evasion on the part of the Southern States. Negroes or other races were excluded from representation only in case they were denied "franchise on account of race and color." But might not the Southern States prescribe as a qualification that no one should vote who had ever been a slave, and thus secure at once the exclusion of negroes from the franchise, and their inclusion in the basis of representation? Or might they not secure the same results by establishing a property qualification and then making negroes incompetent to own real estate? But, it was answered, these were evasions so evident that the courts would prevent their success. The object of the amendment was not to invite to negro suffrage, but simply to equalize representation upon a just and impartial basis, and the arguments brought forward in the course of the debate as to the probable effect of the amendment upon negro suffrage were of secondary importance, and foreign to the object which was meant to be accomplished. The amendment, if passed, would leave the subject of suffrage just where it was before.

There were a few gentlemen on the Republican side of the House who opposed the amendment of the committee because they agreed with the President that there was no good reason why Southern representatives should not be immediately admitted, if loyal, and who opposed any farther amendments to the Constitution as conditions to complete restoration. The most prominent of these was Henry J. Raymond, of New York, whose argument may stand as an exemplification of the views of those members of the House who adopted the President's policy. This argument was presented on the 28th of January, toward the close of the debate. Raymond was a man 46 years of age. He had graduated at the University of Vermont in 1840. The next year after his graduation he became managing editor of the New York *Tribune*. Subsequently he became leading editor of the New York *Courier and Enquirer*, performing at the same time the duties of reader for the firm of Harper & Brothers. In 1849 he was elected to the New York State Assembly; was re-elected and made Speaker. In 1851 he established the New York *Times*. Five years afterward he became a leader in the Republican party, and was subsequently chosen Lieutenant Governor of New York. He had been a delegate to the Chicago Convention of 1860, and, after having again served in the New York Legislature, was in 1864 elected representative from New York to the Thirty-ninth Congress. He was one of the most influential members of that Congress, and his opinions were always worthy of consideration. His speech on the 29th of January, 1866, was his first elaborate effort in Congress. He began his argument by stating that he looked upon all propositions for the amendment of the Constitution with hesitation and distrust. The Constitution had proved itself adequate to all the emergencies of peace and war. It had not been made for days or for years, but for all time. Yet he recognized the wisdom and necessity of amendments to meet changed circumstances and an altered condition of facts. In the fact that slavery was destroyed, he recognized the propriety of so amending the Constitution as to make the re-establishment of that institution impossible. The specific evil which the amendment of the Reconstruction Committee was intended to remedy properly demanded attention. By emancipation, 1,600,000 had been added to the representative population of the South. Thus arose an inequality which demanded attention and remedy. The committee had reported this amendment as a remedy. He did not suppose it would be possible to propose any remedy which would not be open to some objections. He thought, however, that this amendment was open to objections of a very serious nature. It changed the basis of representation from population to something else, and the same objection applied to the other remedies which had been proposed. It was a fundamental principle of free government that the population, the inhabitants, all who were subjects of law, should be represented in the enactment of law, "and in the election of men by whom the law is to be executed, either directly by their own votes, or through the votes of others, so connected with them as to afford a fair presumption that their wishes, their rights, and their interests will be consulted." This proposition departed from that principle, and thus disturbed the corner-stone of our Democratic institutions. Another objection was that it deprived of representation the whole of any race in a state if the state should extend to a portion only of that race the elective franchise. Thus the anomaly was introduced of having voters for representatives who were not themselves entitled to representation. It held out to the states no encouragement to enfranchise any portion of the colored race without enfranchising all. The effect of this would be most disastrous upon the relations of the Union to the Southern States, and upon the welfare of the states themselves and of the colored people within their borders. But he could not regard this as a distinct proposition standing upon its own merits alone, but as one of a series of amendments which, as the House had been given to understand, were yet to be proposed as preliminary to the admission of Southern representatives. He thought the House was entitled to know the whole programme before it acted upon specific features of it. It should know the relation of this proposition to those which were to follow. It should know "whether the powers of the general government of the United States are to be so enlarged as to destroy the rights which those states now hold under the Constitution." He was not willing to act on this proposition till he knew the rest of the schedule. He could not help believing that this was part of a scheme for reconstructing the government and the Constitution upon a distinct principle which had been announced over and over again in the House—that by the rebellion certain states had ceased to exist as states, the people of which were to be treated as vanquished enemies, subject to no law but our own discretion. He denied *in toto* the fact of such subjugation. Of defeated rebels we had a right to demand the surrender of their arms and of the principles on which their rebellion had been based. This surrender had been made and accepted. But the states still remained with all their constitutional powers. Raymond went on to illustrate the present situation of the Southern States by comparing it with that of a state whose government had been disturbed by a foreign power. The only conquest which had been made of the Southern States was their subjugation to the Constitution and the laws. He showed conclusively that every department of the government had recognized the late Confederate States as in the Union. It was possible that

[1] The following is the estimate for the several states:

Free States.	Apportionment under Census of 1860.	Based on Three fifths Slave Population.	Based on Population including Blacks.	Based on White Suffrage.	Based on Equal Suffrage.	According to proposed Amendment.
California	3	—	3	6	*6	3
Connecticut	4	—	4	5	4	4
Illinois	14	—	13	15	13	15
Indiana	11	—	10	11	10	12
Iowa	6	—	5	5	5	6
Kansas	1	—	1	1	1	1
Maine	5	—	5	6	5	6
Massachusetts	10	—	9	12	10	11
Michigan	6	—	6	7	6	7
Minnesota	2	—	2	2	2	2
New Hampshire	3	—	3	3	3	3
New Jersey	5	—	5	6	5	6
New York	31	—	29	35	31	34
Ohio	19	—	18	19	17	20
Oregon	1	—	1	1	1	1
Pennsylvania	24	—	22	24	22	25
Rhode Island	2	—	2	2	2	2
Vermont	3	—	3	3	3	3
Wisconsin	6	—	6	7	6	7
Total	156	—	147	170	152	168

Slave States.	Apportionment under Census of 1860.	Based on Three fifths Slave Population.	Based on Population including Blacks.	Based on White Suffrage.	Based on Equal Suffrage.	According to proposed Amendment.
Alabama	6	1	7	4	7	5
Arkansas	3	1	3	3	3	3
Delaware	1	—	1	1	1	1
Florida	1	—	1	1	1	1
Georgia	7	2	8	5	7	5
Kentucky	9	1	9	8	8	8
Louisiana	5	2	6	4	6	3
Maryland	5	—	5	5	5	5
Mississippi	5	2	6	3	6	3
Missouri	9	1	9	9	9	10
North Carolina	7	2	8	5	7	6
South Carolina	4	2	5	3	5	3
Tennessee	8	1	9	7	8	7
Texas	4	1	5	4	5	4
Virginia	11	2	12	9	11	9
Total	85	18	94	71	89	73

* Not including Chinamen.

"NOTE.—In these several plans of apportionment the results are arrived at in the mode practiced under the present law, namely, the total representative population of all the states is first ascertained; this number is divided by 233, the number of representatives provided by law at the time of the taking of the last census. This gives the requisite ratio to a member. The representative population of each state is then divided by the ratio, and the result, rejecting fractions, shows the number of representatives to each state. The number unapportioned, in consequence of the fractions, is then added to the eight additional members provided by the law of 1862, and these are apportioned to the states having the largest fractions.

The ratio under the present apportionment is	127,000
The ratio on the basis of population, including the negroes, is	133,700
The ratio on the basis of white suffrage is	29,300
The ratio on the basis of equal suffrage, white and black, is	33,500
The ratio on the basis of the proposed amendment is	114,800

"Entirely accurate data of the number of voters in the several states can not be obtained from any recorded statistics. It is not shown by the presidential vote of 1860, for the reason that in some of the states where there was little real contest the vote was far from full. The number of males above the age of twenty years, aliens included, as given by the census of 1860, is taken as the nearest approximate to the number of voters. The proportion of aliens will not hold alike in all the states, there being a larger ratio in the northern than in the southern section of the Union; but it is believed the results indicated in the table will be sufficiently accurate for present purposes."—*Congressional Globe*, 39th Session, p. 357–8.

THADDEUS STEVENS.

Congress might attempt to expel them, but he did not think it would. He traced the various stages of the President's action since the close of the war, and added that it only remained for Congress to complete the work of restoration by the admission of the Southern representatives. If these representatives were loyal men, and each house was judge of that, then their action could not be disloyal, and there was no occasion for apprehension. We needed just the information which such loyal representatives could bring us. But Congress had given the whole subject over to a committee "which sits with closed doors, which deliberates in secret, which shuts itself out from the knowledge and observation of Congress, and which does not even deign to give us the information it was appointed to collect, and on which we are to base our action—but which sends its rescripts into this house, and demands their ratification, and without reasons and without facts, before the going down of the sun!" He thought the House ought to emancipate itself from the domination of this committee, and take the subjects assigned to it into its own keeping. There was too great reliance, he thought, placed in constitutional amendments as guarantees of the national safety. The Constitution had not prevented rebellion; was it probable that amendments could be more efficient? We must depend upon the patriotism of the American people—upon the national will and conscience. When these ceased to be efficient, what dependence was to be placed upon "paper Constitutions?" In conclusion, Raymond thus expressed his views as to what the government ought to do:

"In the first place, I think we ought to accept the present *status* of the Southern States, and regard them as having resumed, under the President's guidance and action, their functions of self-government in the Union. In the second place, I think this house should decide on the admission of representatives by districts, admitting none but loyal men who can take the oath we may prescribe, and holding all others as disqualified; the Senate acting, at its discretion, in the same way in regard to representatives of states. I think, in the third place, we should provide by law for giving to the freedmen of the South all the rights of citizens in courts of law and elsewhere. In the fourth place, I would exclude from federal office the leading actors in the conspiracy which led to the rebellion in every state. In the fifth place, I would make such amendments to the Constitution as may seem wise to Congress and the states, acting freely and without coercion. And, sixth, I would take such measures and precautions, by the disposition of military forces, as will preserve order and prevent the overthrow, by usurpation or otherwise, in any state, of its republican form of government. . . . . Above all, I beg this house to bear in mind, as the sentiment that should control and guide its action, that we of the North and they of the South are at war no longer. The gigantic contest is at an end. The courage and devotion on either side which made it so terrible and so long, no longer owe a divided duty, but have become the common property of the American name, the priceless possession of the American republic through all time to come.

The dead of the contending hosts sleep beneath the soil of a common country and under one common flag. Their hostilities are hushed, and they are the dead of the nation forever more. The victor may well exult in the victory he has achieved. Let it be our task, as it will be our highest glory, to make the vanquished, and their posterity to the latest generation, rejoice in their defeat."

Raymond's argument may be fairly called a statement of the views entertained by the President, and it was open to precisely the same objections. It overlooked the necessity not only of the proposed amendment, but of others equally important. It underrated the value of constitutional provisions for national security. It is true that in extraordinary emergencies, like that presented at the opening of the rebellion, a section of the country might, in the madness of treason, throw the Constitution to the winds; but that was an appeal to arms. Congress was now considering the motives which regulate and restrain men in times of peace, and when obedience is universally yielded to law. In such a time, certainly, an amendment to the Constitution would be more efficient than a resolution or a sentiment.

The proposition was referred back to the committee for amendment, and was again reported in the House, January 31, so altered as to leave out the matter of taxation, but in no other respect. Thaddeus Stevens called the previous question, but yielded ten minutes of his time to other gentlemen. His address to the House on this occasion was characteristic. He had been informed, he said, by high authority "at the other end of the avenue," introduced through an unusual conduit (the "unusual conduit" being intended to designate Raymond), that no amendment to the Constitution was necessary. He then proceeded to consider the present amendment. He denied that it contained an implied permission to the general government to regulate the franchise of states. It left the rights of states just where they were. But it punished the abuse of this right. In making this statement Stevens committed a blunder. The object of the amendment was to remove an inequality which had hitherto existed in the basis of representation. If New York or South Carolina has the admitted right to exclude negroes from the franchise, then their exercise of that right could not be called an abuse, subject to legal penalty. Under the operation of the amendment, each state had to choose between impartial suffrage and a diminution of its representation, and its choice was not controlled. If the Southern States, continued Stevens, adopt the colored population as a part of their political community, they will have 83 votes in the House; if not, they will only have from 45 to 48, and with this diminution of their power all the Copperhead assistance they might receive could not enable them to do injury. He preferred that to an immediate declaration that all should be represented; "for, if you make them all voters, and let them into this hall, not one beneficial act for the benefit of the freedmen or for the benefit of the country would ever be passed. Their 83 votes, with the representatives from the Five Points and other dark corners, would be sufficient to overrule the friends of progress here, and this nation would be in the hands of secessionists at the very next congressional election, and at the very next presidential election. I do not, therefore, want to grant them this privilege, at least for some years. I want, in the mean time, our Christian men to go among them—the philanthropists of the North, the honest Methodists, my friends the Hardshell Baptists, and all others; and then, four or five years hence, when these freedmen shall have been made free indeed—when they shall have become intelligent enough, and there are sufficient loyal men there to control the representation from those states, I shall be glad to see them admitted here; but I do not want them to have representation—I say it plainly—I do not want them to have the right of suffrage before this Congress has done the great work of regenerating the Constitution and laws of this country according to the principles of the Declaration of Independence."

Stevens did not disguise his opinion that this amendment would result in the exclusion of Southern representatives for a period of years. It was for this reason that he preferred it to that which had been proposed fixing the representation upon voters. The latter would be more readily acceded to. An encouragement would thus be offered to extend the suffrage to the colored race. That, said Stevens, is the very objection. The Southern States would admit those whose political action they could control, and then, on this basis, enter Congress and make our laws for us; but they would not accede now to the present amendment—he did not expect to see that during his lifetime. In the mean time the freedmen would be educated, and finally receive universal suffrage (how many years hence Stevens did not conjecture), and then the Southern representatives might be admitted.

Stevens went on to say that he had a proposition which was the genuine one for the present situation—one which he loved, and which he hoped Congress would educate itself to the idea of adopting: "That all national and state laws shall be equally applicable to every citizen, and that no discrimination shall be made on account of race or color." But he was content to take what was practicable—what would be carried by the states. He then alluded to Raymond's argument, which he pronounced not pertinent to the question, but proceeded to controvert by an argument equally impertinent. He endeavored to prove, by Vattel, that the late Confederate States were out of the Union.

Stevens had already, on the 18th of December, announced his theory of the situation. He had then insisted upon two things as of vital importance:

1. That the principle should be established that none of the late Confederate states should be counted in any of the amendments to the Constitution before they were "duly admitted into the family of states by the law-making power of their conqueror." "I take no account," said he, "of the aggregation of whitewashed rebels who, without any legal authority, have assembled in the capitals of the late rebel states and simulated legislative bodies; nor do I regard with any respect the cunning by-play into which they deluded the Secretary of State by frequent telegraphic announcements that 'South Carolina has adopted the amendment,' 'Alabama has adopted the amendment, being the twenty-seventh state,' etc. This was intended to delude the people, and accustom Congress to hear repeated the names of these extinct states as if they were alive; when, in truth, they have now no more existence than the revolted cities of Latium, two thirds of whose people were colonized, and their property confiscated, and their right of citizenship withdrawn by conquering and avenging Rome."

2. It was also important that it should then be solemnly decided what power could revive, recreate, and reinstate these provinces into the family of states, and invest them with the rights of American citizens. It was time that Congress should assert its sovereignty, and assume something of the dignity of the Roman Senate.

The doctrine, added Stevens on that occasion, "of a white man's government is as atrocious as the infamous sentiment that damned the late chief justice to everlasting fame, and, I fear, to everlasting fire."

Stevens's argument upon the present proposition regarding the basis of representation did not improve its prospect of adoption. He adroitly managed to connect it with his own peculiar theories. In his entire argument he assumed that its ratification by three fourths of the states then represented in Congress was sufficient. He distinctly advocated a postponement of restoration until it could be accomplished upon the principles asserted by the extremists of the Republican party. This connection of the proposed amendment with Stevens's peculiar theories was not necessary, and tended to misrepresent its object to Congress and the people. It furnished more arguments for the enemies than for the friends of the amendment. Notwithstanding this speech, however, the joint resolution passed the House 120 to 46. Eleven Republicans voted in the negative.[1]

In the Senate the resolution failed to receive a two-thirds vote. Indeed, it only passed by a bare majority.[2] One of its principal opponents was Senator Sumner. Charles Sumner differed from Thaddeus Stevens. Both were theorists on a grand scale, but the latter could let slip his splendid theory for a moment in order to grasp tangible objects in his way, while the former would accept nothing which did not to him seem true when tested by the plummet of absolute truth and eternal justice.[3] Of the 22 votes cast against the resolution in the Senate, one half were Republican. This opposition arose from motives so various that we find in the list of Nays the names of Democrats, and of the most extreme as well as of the most moderate Republicans.

The Reconstruction Committee after this defeat—which was due to the dissensions that divided the Republican party—again proceeded to deliberate, and on the 30th of April Thaddeus Stevens offered another resolution for the amendment of the Constitution. This new proposition covered a great deal of ground. It contemplated four results:

1. The equal protection of all citizens under the laws;

2. The equalization of representation;

3. The exclusion of all who had engaged in rebellion from the right to vote for representatives in Congress and presidential electors until July 4, 1870; and,

4. The repudiation of the rebel debt, and of any claim for compensation on account of the loss of slaves.[1]

In explaining the provisions of this amendment,[2] Stevens said they were not all that he desired, but all that he expected he could obtain, by the ratification of nineteen of even the loyal states. The idea that the ratification of amendments by the other states were to be counted he considered absurd. He would take all he could get in the cause of humanity, and leave it to be perfected by better men in better times. It might be that he would not be here to enjoy that glorious triumph, but it was as certain to come as that there is a just God. He animadverted with some bitterness to the manner in which the amendment formerly offered by the committee had been slaughtered in the Senate—in the house of its friends—by "puerile and pedantic criticism." The present amendment was, he thought, less efficient, but some way had to be devised "to overcome the united forces of self-righteous Republicans and unrighteous Copperheads." Evidently Thaddeus Stevens was disgusted with his brethren; but, said he, "it will not do for those who for thirty years have fought the beasts at Ephesus to be frightened by the fangs of modern catamounts." He wanted to secure more than was secured by this amendment. We should not approach the measure of justice until we gave every adult freedman a homestead on the land where he had toiled and suffered. Forty acres of land and a hut would be more valuable to the negro than the right to vote. Unless we gave this we should receive the censure of mankind and the curse of Heaven. The section excluding rebels from voting for a period of years he considered the mildest of all punishments ever inflicted on traitors. He might not consent to the extreme severity denounced upon them by a provisional governor of Tennessee—"the late lamented Andrew Johnson of blessed memory"—but he would have increased the severity of this section. On the 10th of March, the resolution, as presented by the committee, was passed 128 to 37.[3] Baldwin, Hale, Eliot, Jenckes, W. H. Randall, and Raymond—Republicans who had voted against the former amendment, gave their support to this one.

The resolution passed the Senate, after numerous amendments, on the 8th of June, by a two-thirds vote (33 to 11),[4] and went back to the House, where the Senate amendments were adopted, June 13th. The following is the text of the proposed amendment as finally passed:

"ARTICLE XIV. *Sec.* 1. All persons born or naturalized in the United States, and subject to the jurisdiction thereof, are citizens of the United States and of the state wherein they reside. No state shall make or enforce any law which shall abridge the privileges or immunities of citizens of the United States, nor shall any state deprive any person of life, liberty, or property without due process of law, nor deny to any person within its jurisdiction the equal protection of the laws.

"*Sec.* 2. Representatives shall be apportioned among the several states according to their respective numbers, counting the whole number of persons

---

[1] Baldwin, Eliot, Hale, Jenckes, Latham, Phelps, W. H. Randall, Raymond, Rousseau, Smith, and Whaley.

The following is the vote in detail:

YEAS.—Messrs. Alley, Allison, Ames, Anderson, James M. Ashley, Baker, Banks, Barker, Baxter, Beaman, Benjamin, Bidwell, Bingham, Blaine, Blow, Boutwell, Brandegee, Bromwell, Broomall, Buckland, Bundy, Reader W. Clarke, Sidney Clarke, Cobb, Conkling, Cook, Cullom, Darling, Davis, Dawes, Defrees, Delano, Deming, Dixon, Donnelly, Eckley, Eggleston, Farnsworth, Farquhar, Ferry, Garfield, Grinnell, Griswold, Abner C. Harding, Hart, Hayes, Hill, Holmes, Hooper, Hotchkiss, Asahel W. Hubbard, Chester D. Hubbard, Demas Hubbard, John H. Hubbard, James H. Hubbell, Hulburd, James Humphrey, Ingersoll, Julian, Kasson, Kelley, Kelso, Ketcham, Kuykendall, Laflin, George V. Lawrence, William Lawrence, Longyear, Lynch, Marston, Marvin, McClurg, McIndoe, McKee, Mercur, Miller, Moorhead, Morrill, Morris, Moulton, Myers, O'Neill, Orth, Paine, Patterson, Perham, Pike, Plants, Pomeroy, Price, Alexander H. Rice, John H. Rice, Rollins, Sawyer, Schenck, Schofield, Shellabarger, Sloan, Spalding, Starr, Stevens, Stillwell, Thayer, Francis Thomas, John L. Thomas, Upson, Van Aernam, Burt Van Horn, Robert T. Van Horn, Ward, Warner, Elihu B. Washburne, William B. Washburn, Welker, Wentworth, Williams, James F. Wilson, Stephen F. Wilson, Windom, and Woodbridge—120.

NAYS.—Messrs. Baldwin, Bergen, Boyer, Brooks, Chanler, Dawson, Denison, Eldridge, Eliot, Finck, Grider, Hale, Aaron Harding, Harris, Hogan, Edwin N. Hubbell, James M. Humphrey, Jenckes, Johnson, Kerr, Latham, Le Blond, Marshall, McCullough, Niblack, Nicholson, Noell, Phelps, Samuel J. Randall, William H. Randall, Raymond, Ritter, Rogers, Ross, Rousseau, Shanklin, Sitgreaves, Smith, Strouse, Taber, Taylor, Thornton, Trimble, Voorhees, Whaley, and Wright—46.

NOT VOTING.—Messrs. Ancona, Delos R. Ashley, Culver, Driggs, Dumont, Glossbrenner, Goodyear, Henderson, Higby, Jones, Loan, McRuer, Newell, Radford, Trowbridge, and Winfield—16.

[2] March 9, 1866. The following is the vote in detail:

YEAS.—Messrs. Anthony, Chandler, Clark, Conness, Cragin, Creswell, Fessenden, Foster, Grimes, Harris, Howe, Kirkwood, Lane of Indiana, McDougall, Morgan, Morrill, Nye, Poland, Ramsey, Sherman, Sprague, Trumbull, Wade, Williams, and Wilson—25.

NAYS.—Messrs. Brown, Buckalew, Cowan, Davis, Dixon, Doolittle, Guthrie, Henderson, Hendricks, Johnson, Lane of Kansas, Nesmith, Norton, Pomeroy, Riddle, Saulsbury, Stewart, Stockton, Sumner, Van Winkle, Willey, and Yates—22.

ABSENT.—Messrs. Foot, Howard, and Wright—3.

[3] The following is a recapitulation of Sumner's argument against the amendment:

"Following it from the beginning, you have seen, first, how this proposition carries into the Constitution itself the idea of inequality of rights, thus defiling that unspotted text; secondly, how it is an express sanction of the acknowledged tyranny of taxation without representation; thirdly, how it is a concession to State Rights at a moment when we are recovering from a terrible war waged against us in the name of State Rights; fourthly, how it is the constitutional recognition of an oligarchy, aristocracy, caste, and monopoly founded on color; fifthly, how it petrifies in the Constitution the wretched pretension of a white man's government; sixthly, how it assumes what is false in constitutional law, that color can be a 'qualification' for an elector; seventhly, how it positively ties the hands of Congress in fixing the meaning of a republican government, so that under the guaranty clause it will be constrained to recognize an oligarchy, aristocracy, caste, and monopoly founded on color, together with the tyranny of taxation without representation, as not inconsistent with such a government; eighthly, how it positively ties the hands of Congress in completing and consummating the abolition of slavery according to the second clause of the constitutional amendment, so that it can not for this purpose interfere with the denial of the elective franchise on account of color; ninthly, how it installs recent rebels in permanent power over loyal citizens; and, tenthly, how it shows forth in unmistakable character as a compromise of human rights, the most immoral, indecent, and utterly shameful of any in our history."

[1] The following is the text of the proposed amendment as first presented by Stevens:

"ARTICLE —. *Sec.* 1. No state shall make or enforce any law which shall abridge the privileges or immunities of citizens of the United States; nor shall any state deprive any person of life, liberty, or property without due process of law, nor deny to any person within its jurisdiction the equal protection of the laws.

"*Sec.* 2. Representatives shall be apportioned among the several states which may be included within this Union according to their respective numbers, counting the whole number of persons in each state, excluding Indians not taxed. But whenever in any state the elective franchise shall be denied to any portion of its male citizens not less than twenty-one years of age, or in any way abridged, except for participation in rebellion or other crime, the basis of representation in such state shall be reduced in the proportion which the number of male citizens shall bear to the whole number of such male citizens not less than twenty-one years of age.

"*Sec.* 3. Until the 4th day of July, in the year 1870, all persons who voluntarily adhered to the late insurrection, giving it aid and comfort, shall be excluded from the right to vote for representatives in Congress, and for electors for President and Vice-President of the United States.

"*Sec.* 4. Neither the United States nor any state shall assume or pay any debt or obligation already incurred, or which may hereafter be incurred, in aid of insurrection or war against the United States, or any claim for compensation for loss of involuntary service or labor.

"*Sec.* 5. The Congress shall have power to enforce by appropriate legislation the provisions of this article."

[3] March 8.

[2] YEAS.—Messrs. Alley, Allison, Ames, Anderson, Delos R. Ashley, James M. Ashley, Baker, Baldwin, Banks, Barker, Baxter, Beaman, Benjamin, Bidwell, Bingham, Blaine, Blow, Boutwell, Bromwell, Broomall, Buckland, Bundy, Reader W. Clark, Sidney Clarke, Cobb, Conkling, Cook, Cullom, Darling, Davis, Dawes, Defrees, Delano, Deming, Dixon, Dodge, Donnelly, Driggs, Dumont, Eckley, Eggleston, Eliot, Farnsworth, Ferry, Garfield, Grinnell, Griswold, Abner C. Harding, Hart, Hayes, Henderson, Higby, Holmes, Hooper, Hotchkiss, Asahel W. Hubbard, Chester D. Hubbard, Demas Hubbard, James R. Hubbell, Hulburd, James Humphrey, Ingersoll, Jenckes, Julian, Kasson, Kelley, Kelso, Ketcham, Kuykendall, Laflin, George V. Lawrence, William Lawrence, Loan, Longyear, Lynch, Marston, McClurg, McIndoe, McKee, McRuer, Mercur, Miller, Moorhead, Morrill, Morris, Moulton, Myers, Newell, O'Neill, Orth, Paine, Patterson, Perham, Pike, Plants, Price, William H. Randall, Raymond, Alexander H. Rice, John H. Rice, Rollins, Sawyer, Schenck, Schofield, Shellabarger, Spalding, Stevens, Stillwell, Thayer, Francis Thomas, John L. Thomas, Trowbridge, Upson, Van Aernam, Burt Van Horn, Robert T. Van Horn, Ward, Warner, Elihu B. Washburne, Henry D. Washburn, William B. Washburn, Welker, Williams, James F. Wilson, Stephen F. Wilson, Windom, Woodbridge, and the Speaker—128.

NAYS.—Messrs. Ancona, Bergen, Boyer, Chanler, Coffroth, Dawson, Eldridge, Finck, Glossbrenner, Goodyear, Grider, Aaron Harding, Harris, Kerr, Latham, Le Blond, Marshall, McCullough, Niblack, Phelps, Radford, Samuel J. Randall, Ritter, Rogers, Ross, Rousseau, Shanklin, Sitgreaves, Smith, Strouse, Tabor, Taylor, Thornton, Trimble, Whaley, Winfield, and Wright—37.

NOT VOTING.—Messrs. Brandegee, Culver, Denison, Farquhar, Hale, Hill, Hogan, John H. Hubbard, Edwin N. Hubbell, James M. Humphrey, Johnson, Jones, Marvin, Nicholson, Noell, Pomeroy, Sloan, Starr, and Wentworth—19.

[4] YEAS.—Messrs. Anthony, Chandler, Clark, Conness, Cragin, Creswell, Edmunds, Fessenden, Foster, Grimes, Harris, Henderson, Howard, Howe, Kirkwood, Lane of Indiana, Lane of Kansas, Morgan, Morrill, Nye, Poland, Pomeroy, Ramsey, Sherman, Sprague, Stewart, Sumner, Trumbull, Wade, Willey, Williams, Wilson, and Yates—33.

NAYS.—Messrs. Cowan, Davis, Doolittle, Guthrie, Hendricks, Johnson, McDougall, Norton, Riddle, Saulsbury, and Van Winkle—11.

ABSENT.—Messrs. Brown, Buckalew, Dixon, Nesmith, and Wright—5.

in each state, excluding Indians not taxed. But when the right to vote at any election for the choice of electors for President and Vice-President of the United States, representatives in Congress, the executive and judicial officers of a state, or the members of the Legislature thereof, is denied to any of the male inhabitants of such state, being twenty-one years of age and citizens of the United States, or in any way abridged except for participation in rebellion or other crime, the basis of representation therein shall be reduced in proportion which the number of such male citizens shall bear to the whole number of male citizens twenty-one years of age in such state.

"*Sec.* 3. No person shall be a senator or representative in Congress, or elector of President and Vice-President, or hold any office, civil or military, under the United States or under any state, who, having previously taken an oath, as a member of Congress, or as an officer of the United States, or as a member of any state Legislature, or as an executive or judicial officer of any state, to support the Constitution of the United States, shall have engaged in insurrection or rebellion against the same, or given aid and comfort to the enemies thereof. But Congress may, by a vote of two thirds of each house, remove such disability.

"*Sec.* 4. The validity of the public debt of the United States authorized by law, including debts incurred for payment of pensions and bounties for services in suppressing insurrection and rebellion, shall not be questioned. But neither the United States nor any state shall assume or pay any debt or obligation incurred in aid of insurrection or rebellion against the United States, or any claim for the loss or emancipation of any slave, but all such debts, obligations, or claims shall be held illegal and void.

"*Sec.* 5. The Congress shall have power to enforce, by appropriate legislation, the provisions of this article."

The joint resolution did not require the assent of the President. But a resolution having been passed by the House requesting the President to transmit the proposed amendment to the several state Legislatures, he took occasion to reply, expressing his opinion, and protesting that the ministerial act of transmitting the amendment to the state Legislatures did not commit the executive to an approval or recommendation of it.[1]

The amendment covered the whole ground of reconstruction, so far as Congress was concerned. There was no reason why its ratification might not be properly required of every Southern State as an evidence of its good faith, which would not also apply to the amendment abolishing slavery. Just after the war closed its ratification would have been readily acceded; but it was certain to be refused now by almost every Southern State on account of the encouragement afforded by President Johnson's policy, and the hope that this might prevail sooner or later with the Northern people. No other attitude could have been expected of the South under the circumstances. It was in the condition of an army which acknowledges its defeat, but insists upon the best terms of accommodation which there is the slightest ground to hope the conqueror will grant.

The Reconstruction Committee submitted its full report to Congress on the 18th of June, 1866—or rather it submitted two reports, one representing the views of the majority of its members, and the other those of the minority, consisting of Reverdy Johnson, A. J. Rogers, and Henry Grider. The latter report almost entirely ignores the fact of the war, and the nature of the situation immediately consequent. It refuses the right of the government to deny even temporarily, and for its own safety, to states which have been in rebellion, the resumption of all their rights and privileges; whereas, if there is any political principle clearly established and beyond dispute, it is, that the security of government lies back of even its written Constitution, and is the supreme law of national existence.

The report of the majority we shall consider more in detail. It contains many false constructions of the Constitution, based upon the erroneous theories of some members of the committee, and to which exception might be taken. Its denial to the President of any other powers, outside of his position as commander-in-chief of the army and navy, except those involved in the execution of the laws of Congress, is inconsistent with the whole spirit of the Constitution, according to which the executive is a *co-ordinate* branch of the government, and not vested merely with *subordinate* and *ministerial* functions. It is inconsistent also with the President's oath of office, by which he is bound not simply to execute the laws, but to protect the Constitution. The assumption made in the report that upon Congress alone devolves the duty to guarantee to every state a republican form of government, is contradicted by the very words of the constitutional provision making this guaranty the duty of the United States; and, as if with the very purpose of not confining it to either the President or to Congress exclusively, this provision occurs in neither of the articles defining respectively the powers of the executive and of Congress. This assumption that Congress is, in an exclusive sense, the government of the United States, pervades the whole report.

But, laying aside all matters which might be made the subject of criticism, we must regard this report as a conclusive argument in justification of the action of Congress in refusing representation to the Southern States until

[1] "Even in ordinary times," said the President, "any question of amending the Constitution must be justly regarded as of paramount importance. This importance is at the present time enhanced by the fact that the joint resolution was not submitted by the two houses for the approval of the President, and that, of the thirty-six states which constitute the Union, eleven are excluded from representation in either house of Congress, although, with the single exception of Texas, they have been entirely restored to all their functions as states in conformity with the organic law of the land, and have appeared at the national capital by senators and representatives, who have applied for and have been refused admission to the vacant seats. Nor have the sovereign people of the nation been afforded an opportunity of expressing their views upon the important questions which the amendment involves. Grave doubts, therefore, may naturally and justly arise as to whether the action of Congress is in harmony with the sentiments of the people, and whether state Legislatures elected without reference to such an issue should be called upon by Congress to decide respecting the ratification of the proposed amendment."

certain measures necessary to the national safety should be secured beyond the possibility of doubt through constitutional amendment. The nature and extent of the outrage which had been committed against the government, argues the committee, gave the government the right to exact indemnity for the injuries done, and security against their recurrence. The decision as to what that security should be, as to what proof should be required of returned allegiance, must depend upon grave considerations of the public safety and the general welfare. If it were true that, the moment when rebels lay down their arms and actual hostilities cease, all political rights of the rebellious communities are at once restored—if their right to participate in the government of the country must be allowed under these circumstances—then the government would be powerless for its own protection, "and flagrant rebellion, carried to the extreme of civil war, is a pastime which any state can play at, not only certain that it can lose nothing in any event, but may even be the gainer by defeat. If rebellion succeeds, it accomplishes its purpose and destroys the government. If it fails, the war has been barren of results, and the battle may still be fought out in the legislative halls of the country. Treason, defeated in the field, has only to take possession of Congress and the cabinet."

"It is desirable," continues the report, "that the Union of all the states should become perfect at the earliest moment consistent with the peace and welfare of the nation; that all these states should become fully represented in the national councils, and take their share in the legislation of the country. The possession and exercise of more than the just share of power by any section is injurious, as well to that section as to all others. Its tendency is distracting and demoralizing, and such a state of affairs is only to be tolerated on the ground of a necessary regard to the public safety. As soon as that safety is secured it should terminate."

Before the restoration of the states to their original privileges, the rights, as free men and citizens, of millions belonging to the colored race must be secured, and the basis of representation must be altered to prevent some states from exercising a disproportionate share in the government. Accordingly, the committee had submitted the constitutional amendment embracing these provisions, together with others, "after a long and careful comparison of conflicting opinions."[1]

[1] We subjoin the concluding portion of this report:

"Your committee have been unable to find, in the evidence submitted to Congress by the President, under date of March 6, 1866, in compliance with the resolutions of January 5 and February 27, 1866, any satisfactory proof that either of the insurrectionary states, except perhaps the State of Tennessee, has placed itself in a condition to resume its political relations to the United States. The first step toward that end would necessarily be the establishment of a republican form of government by the people. It has been before remarked that the provisional governors, appointed by the President in the exercise of his military authority, could do nothing by virtue of the power thus conferred toward the establishment of a state government. They were acting under the War Department, and paid out of its funds. They were simply bridging over the chasm between rebellion and restoration. And yet we find them calling Conventions and convening Legislatures. Not only this, but we find the Conventions and Legislatures thus convened acting under executive direction as to the provisions required to be adopted in their Constitutions and ordinances as conditions precedent to their recognition by the President. The inducement held out by the President for compliance with the conditions imposed was, directly in one instance, and presumably, therefore, in others, the immediate admission of senators and representatives to Congress. The character of the Conventions and Legislatures thus assembled was not such as to inspire confidence in the good faith of their members. Governor Perry, of South Carolina, dissolved the Convention assembled in that state before the suggestion had reached Columbia from Washington that the rebel war debt should be repudiated, and gave as his reason that it was a 'revolutionary body.' There is no evidence of the loyalty or disloyalty of the members of those Conventions and Legislatures except the fact of pardons being asked for on their account. Some of these states now claiming representation refused to adopt the conditions imposed. No reliable information is found in these papers as to the constitutional provisions of several of these states, while in not one of them is there the slightest evidence to show that these 'amended Constitutions,' as they are called, have ever been submitted to the people for their adoption. In North Carolina alone an ordinance was passed to that effect, but it does not appear to have been acted on. Not one of them, therefore, has been ratified. Whether, with President Johnson, we adopt the theory that the old Constitutions were abrogated and destroyed, and the people 'deprived of all civil government,' or whether we adopt the alternative doctrine that they were only suspended, and were revived by the suppression of the rebellion, the new provisions must be considered as equally destitute of validity before adoption by the people. If the Conventions were called for the sole purpose of putting the state government into operation, they had no power either to adopt a new Constitution or to amend an old one without the consent of the people. Nor could either a Convention or a Legislature change the fundamental law without power previously conferred. In the view of your committee, it follows, therefore, that the people of a state where the Constitution has been thus amended might feel themselves justified in repudiating altogether all such unauthorized assumptions of power, and might be expected to do so at pleasure.

"So far as the disposition of the people of the insurrectionary states, and the probability of their adopting measures conforming to the changed condition of affairs can be inferred from the papers submitted by the President as the basis of his action, the prospects are far from encouraging. It appears quite clear that the anti-slavery amendments, both to the State and Federal Constitutions, were adopted with reluctance by the bodies which did adopt them, while in some states they have been either passed by in silence or rejected. The language of all the provisions and ordinances of these states on the subject amounts to nothing more than an unwilling admission of an unwelcome truth. As to the Ordinance of Secession, it is in some cases declared 'null and void,' and in others simply 'repealed;' and in no instance is a refutation of this deadly heresy considered worthy of a place in the new Constitution.

"If, as the President assumes, these insurrectionary states were, at the close of the war, wholly without state governments, it would seem that, before being admitted to participation in the direction of public affairs, such governments should be regularly organized. Long usage has established, and numerous statutes have pointed out the mode in which this should be done. A Convention to frame a form of government should be assembled under competent authority. Ordinarily this authority emanates from Congress; but, under the peculiar circumstances, your committee is not disposed to criticise the President's action in assuming the power exercised by him in this regard. The Convention, when assembled, should frame a Constitution of government, which should be submitted to the people for adoption. If adopted, a Legislature should be convened to pass the laws necessary to carry it into effect. When a state thus organized claims representation in Congress, the election of representatives should be provided for by law, in accordance with the laws of Congress regulating representation, and the proof that the action taken has been in conformity to law should be submitted to Congress.

"In no case have these essential preliminary steps been taken. The Conventions assembled seem to have assumed that the Constitutions which had been repudiated and overthrown were still in existence, and operative to constitute the states members of the Union, and to have contented themselves with such amendments as they were informed were requisite in order to insure their return to an immediate participation in the government of the United States. Not waiting to ascertain whether the people they represented would adopt even the proposed amendments, they at once ordered elections of representatives to Congress, in nearly all instances before an executive had been chosen to issue writs of election under the state laws, and such elections as were held were ordered by the Conventions. In one instance, at least, the writs of election were signed by the provisional governor. Glaring irregularities and unwarranted assumptions of power are manifest in several cases, particularly in South Carolina, where the Convention, although disbanded by the provisional governor on the ground that it was a revolutionary body, assumed to redistrict the state.

"It is quite evident from all these facts, and indeed from the whole mass of testimony submitted by the President to the Senate, that in no instance was regard paid to any other consideration than obtaining immediate admission to Congress under the barren form of an election in which

The committee had been working hard for six months, and with the results of its deliberations no reasonable ground of complaint can be found. But the necessity of every measure which it had submitted to Congress was just as clear at the beginning of the session as at the close. It had accu-

no precautions were taken to secure regularity of proceedings or the assent of the people. No Constitution has been legally adopted except perhaps in the State of Tennesee, and such elections as have been held were without authority of law. Your committee are accordingly forced to the conclusion that the states referred to have not placed themselves in a condition to claim representation in Congress, unless all the rules which have, since the foundation of the government, been deemed essential in such cases should be disregarded.

"It would, undoubtedly, be competent for Congress to waive all formalities, and to admit these Confederate States to representation at once, trusting that time and experience would set all things right. Whether it would be advisable to do so, however, must depend upon other considerations of which it remains to treat. But it may well be observed that the inducements to such a step should be of the very highest character. It seems to your committee not unreasonable to require satisfactory evidence that the ordinances and constitutional provisions which the President deemed essential in the first instance will be permanently adhered to by the people of the states seeking restoration after being admitted to full participation in the government, and will not be repudiated when that object shall have been accomplished. And here the burden of proof rests upon the late insurgents who are seeking restoration to the rights and privileges which they willingly abandoned, and not upon the people of the United States who have never undertaken, directly or indirectly, to deprive them thereof. It should appear affirmatively that they are prepared and disposed in good faith to accept the results of the war, to abandon their hostility to the government, and to live in peace and amity with the people of the loyal states, extending to all classes of citizens equal rights and privileges, and conforming to the republican idea of liberty and equality. They should exhibit in their acts something more than an unwilling submission to an unavoidable necessity—a feeling, if not cheerful, certainly not offensive and defiant; and they should evince an entire repudiation of all hostility to the general government by an acceptance of such just and reasonable conditions as that government should think the public safety demands. Has this been done? Let us look at the facts shown by the evidence taken by the committee.

"Hardly is the war closed before the people of these insurrectionary states come forward and claim as a right the privilege of participating at once in that government which they had for four years been fighting to overthrow. Allowed and encouraged by the executive to organize state governments, they at once placed in power leading rebels, unrepentant and unpardoned, excluding with contempt those who had manifested an attachment to the Union, and preferring, in many instances, those who had rendered themselves the most obnoxious. In the face of the law requiring an oath which would necessarily exclude all such men from federal offices, they elect, with very few exceptions, as senators and representatives in Congress, men who had actively participated in the rebellion, insultingly denouncing the law as unconstitutional. It is only necessary to instance the election to the Senate of the late Vice-President of the Confederacy, a man who, against his own declared convictions, had lent all the weight of his acknowledged ability and of his influence as a most prominent public man to the cause of the rebellion, and who, unpardoned rebel as he is, with that oath staring him in the face, had the assurance to lay his credentials on the table of the Senate. Other rebels of scarcely less note or notoriety were selected from other quarters. Professing no repentance; glorying apparently in the crime they had committed; avowing still, as the uncontradicted testimony of Mr. Stephens and many others proves, an adherence to the pernicious doctrine of secession, and declaring that they yielded only to necessity, they insist, with unanimous voice, upon their rights as states, and proclaim that they will submit to no conditions whatever as preliminary to their resumption of power under that Constitution which they still claim the right to repudiate.

"Examining the evidence taken by your committee still farther, in connection with facts too notorious to be disputed, it appears that the Southern press, with few exceptions, and those mostly of newspapers recently established by Northern men, abound with weekly and daily abuse of the institutions and people of the loyal states; defends the men who led, and the principles which incited the rebellion; denounces and reviles Southern men who adhered to the Union; and strives, constantly and unscrupulously, by every means in its power, to keep alive the fire of hate and discord between the sections, calling upon the President to violate his oath of office, overturn the government by force of arms, and drive the representatives of the people from their seats in Congress. The national banner is openly insulted, and the national airs scoffed at, not only by an ignorant populace, but at public meetings, and once, among other notable instances, at a dinner given in honor of a notorious rebel who had violated his oath and abandoned his flag. The same individual is elected to an important office in the leading city of his state, although an unpardoned rebel, and so offensive that the President refuses to allow him to enter upon his official duties. In another state the leading general of the rebel armies is openly nominated for governor by the speaker of the House of Delegates, and the nomination is hailed by the people with shouts of satisfaction, and openly indorsed by the press.

"Looking still farther at the evidence taken by your committee, it is found to be clearly shown, by witnesses of the highest character, and having the best means of observation, that the Freedmen's Bureau, instituted for the relief and protection of freedmen and refugees, is almost universally opposed by the mass of the population, and exists in an efficient condition only under military protection, while the Union men at the South are earnest in its defense, declaring with one voice that without its protection the colored people would not be permitted to labor at fair prices, and could hardly live in safety. They also testify that without the protection of United States troops, Union men, whether of Northern or Southern origin, would be obliged to abandon their homes. The feeling in many portions of the country toward the emancipated slaves, especially among the uneducated and ignorant, is one of vindictive and malicious hatred. This deep-seated prejudice against color is assiduously cultivated by the public journals, and leads to acts of cruelty, oppression, and murder, which the local authorities are at no pains to prevent or punish. There is no general disposition to place the colored race, constituting at least two fifths of the population, upon terms even of civil equality. While many instances may be found where large planters and men of the better class accept the situation, and honestly strive to bring about a better order of things by employing the freedmen at fair wages and treating them kindly, the general feeling and disposition among all classes are yet totally averse to the toleration of any class of people friendly to the Union, be they black or white; and this aversion is not unfrequently manifested in an insulting and offensive manner.

"The witnesses examined as to the willingness of the people of the South to contribute, under existing laws, to the payment of the national debt, prove that the taxes levied by the United States will be paid only on compulsion and with great reluctance, while there prevails, to a considerable extent, an expectation that compensation will be made for slaves emancipated and property destroyed during the war. The testimony on this point comes from officers of the Union army, officers of the late rebel army, Union men of the Southern States, and avowed secessionists, almost all of whom state that, in their opinion, the people of the rebellious states would, if they should see a prospect of success, repudiate the national debt.

"While there is scarcely any hope or desire among leading men to renew the attempt at secession at any future time, there is still, according to a large number of witnesses, including A. H. Stephens, who may be regarded as good authority on that point, a generally prevailing opinion which defends the legal right of secession, and upholds the doctrine that the first allegiance of the people is due to the states, and not to the United States. This belief evidently prevails among leading and prominent men, as well as among the masses every where, except in some of the northern counties of Alabama and the eastern counties of Tennessee.

"The evidence of an intense hostility to the Federal Union, and an equally intense love of the late Confederacy, nurtured by the war, is decisive. While it appears that nearly all are willing to submit, at least for the time being, to the federal authority, it is equally clear that the ruling motive is a desire to obtain the advantages which will be derived from a representation in Congress. Officers of the Union army on duty, and Northern men who go South to engage in business, are generally detested and proscribed. Southern men who adhered to the Union are bitterly hated and relentlessly persecuted. In some localities prosecutions have been instituted in state courts against Union officers for acts done in the line of official duty, and similar prosecutions are threatened elsewhere as soon as the United States troops are removed. All such demonstrations show a state of feeling against which it is unmistakably necessary to guard.

"The testimony is conclusive that, after the collapse of the Confederacy, the feeling of the people of the rebellious states was that of abject submission. Having appealed to the tribunal of arms, they had no hope except that by the magnanimity of the conquerors their lives, and possibly their property, might be preserved. Unfortunately, the general issue of pardons to persons who had been prominent in the rebellion, and the feeling of kindness and conciliation manifested by the executive, and very generally indicated through the Northern press, had the effect to render whole communities forgetful of the crime they had committed, defiant toward the federal government, and regardless of their duties as citizens. The conciliatory measures of the government do not seem to have been met even half way. The bitterness and defiance exhibited toward the United States under such circumstances is without a parallel in the history of the world. In return for our leniency we receive only an insulting denial of our authority. In return for our kind desire for the resumption of fraternal relations we receive only an insolent assumption of rights and privileges long since forfeited. The crime we have punished is paraded as a virtue, and the principles of republican government which we have vindicated at so terrible cost are denounced as unjust and oppressive.

"If we add to this evidence the fact that, although peace has been declared by the President, he has not, to this day, deemed it safe to restore the writ of habeas corpus, to relieve the insurrectionary states of martial law, nor to withdraw the troops from many localities, and that the commanding general deems an increase of the army indispensable to the preservation of order and the protection of loyal and well-disposed people in the South, the proof of a condition of feeling hostile to the Union and dangerous to the government throughout the insurrectionary states would seem to be overwhelming.

"With such evidence before them, it is the opinion of your committee—

"I. That the states lately in rebellion were, at the close of the war, disorganized communities, without civil government, and without Constitutions or other forms by virtue of which political relations could legally exist between them and the federal government.

"II. That Congress can not be expected to recognize as valid the election of representatives from disorganized communities which, from the very nature of the case, were unable to present their claim to representation under those established rules the observance of which has been hitherto required.

"III. That Congress would not be justified in admitting such communities to a participation in the government of the country without first providing such constitutional or other guarantees as will tend to secure the civil rights of all citizens of the republic; a just equality of representation; protection against claims founded in rebellion and crime; a temporary restoration of the right of suffrage to those who have not actively participated in the efforts to destroy the Union and overthrow the government; and the exclusion from positions of public trust of at least a portion of those whose crimes have proved them to be enemies to the Union, and unworthy of public confidence.

"Your committee will, perhaps, hardly be deemed excusable for extending this report farther; but inasmuch as immediate and unconditional representation of the states lately in rebellion is demanded as a matter of right, and delay, and even hesitation, is denounced as grossly oppressive and unjust, as well as unwise and impolitic, it may not be amiss again to call attention to a few undisputed and notorious facts, and the principles of public law applicable thereto, in order that the propriety of that claim may be fully considered and well understood.

"The State of Tennessee occupies a position distinct from all the other insurrectionary states, and has been the subject of a separate report, which your committee have not thought it expedient to disturb. Whether Congress shall see fit to make that state the subject of separate action, or to include it in the same category with all others, so far as concerns the imposition of preliminary conditions, it is not within the province of this committee either to determine or advise.

"To ascertain whether any of the so-called Confederate States 'are entitled to be represented in either house of Congress,' the essential inquiry is whether there is, in any one of them, a constituency qualified to be represented in Congress. The question how far persons claiming seats in either house possess the credentials necessary to enable them to represent a duly qualified constituency is one for the consideration of each house separately, after the preliminary question shall have been finally determined.

"We now propose to restate, as briefly as possible, the general facts and principles applicable to all the states recently in rebellion.

"1st. The seats of the senators and representatives from the so-called Confederate States became vacant in the year 1861, during the second session of the Thirty-sixth Congress, by the voluntary withdrawal of their incumbents, with the sanction and by direction of the Legislatures or Conventions of their respective states. This was done as a hostile act against the Constitution and government of the United States, with a declared intent to overthrow the same by forming a Southern Confederation. This act of declared hostility was speedily followed by an organization of the same states into a confederacy, which levied and waged war by sea and land against the United States. This war continued four years, within which period the rebel armies besieged the national capital, invaded the loyal states, burned their towns and cities, robbed their citizens, destroyed more than 250,000 loyal soldiers, and imposed an increased national burden of not less than $3,500,000,000, of which seven or eight hundred millions have already been met and paid. From the time these confederated states thus withdrew their representation in Congress and levied war against the United States, the great mass of their people became and were insurgents, rebels, traitors, and all of them assumed and occupied the political, legal, and practical relation of enemies of the United States. This position is established by acts of Congress and judicial decisions, and is recognized repeatedly by the President in public proclamations, documents, and speeches.

"2d. The states thus confederated prosecuted their war against the United States to final arbitrament, and did not cease until all their armies were captured, their military power destroyed, their civil officers, state and confederate, taken prisoners or put to flight, every vestige of state and confederate government obliterated, their territory overrun and occupied by the federal armies, and their people reduced to the condition of enemies conquered in war, entitled only by public law to such rights, privileges, and conditions as might be vouchsafed by the conqueror. This position is also established by judicial decisions, and is recognized by the President in public proclamations, documents, and speeches.

"3d. Having voluntarily deprived themselves of representation in Congress for the criminal purpose of destroying the Federal Union, and having reduced themselves, by the act of levying war, to the condition of public enemies, they have no right to complain of temporary exclusion from Congress; but, on the contrary, having voluntarily renounced the right to representation, and disqualified themselves by crime from participating in the government, the burden now rests upon them, before claiming to be reinstated in their former condition, to show that they are qualified to resume federal relations. In order to do this, they must prove that they have established, with the consent of the people, republican forms of government in harmony with the Constitution and laws of the United States, that all hostile purposes have ceased, and should give adequate guarantees against future treason and rebellion—guarantees which shall prove satisfactory to the government against which they rebelled, and by whose arms they were subdued.

"4th. Having, by this treasonable withdrawal from Congress, and by flagrant rebellion and war, forfeited all civil and political rights and privileges under the Constitution, they can only be restored thereto by the permission and authority of that constitutional power against which they rebelled and by which they were subdued.

"5th. These rebellious enemies were conquered by the people of the United States, acting through all the co-ordinate branches of the government, and not by the executive department alone. The powers of conqueror are not so vested in the President that he can fix and regulate the terms of settlement, and confer congressional representation on conquered rebels and traitors. Nor can he in any way qualify enemies of the government to exercise its law-making power. The authority to restore rebels to political power in the federal government can be exercised only with the concurrence of all the departments in which political power is vested; and hence the several proclamations of the President to the people of the Confederate States can not be considered as extending beyond the purposes declared, and can only be regarded as provisional permission by the commander-in-chief of the army to do certain acts, the effect and validity whereof is to be determined by the constitutional government, and not solely by the executive power.

"6th. The question before Congress is, then, whether conquered enemies have the right, and shall be permitted, at their own pleasure and on their own terms, to participate in making laws for their conquerors; whether conquered rebels may change their theatre of operations from the battle-field, where they were defeated and overthrown, to the halls of Congress, and, through their representatives, seize upon the government which they fought to destroy; whether the national treasury, the army of the nation, its navy, its forts and arsenals, its whole civil administration, its credit, its pensioners, the widows and orphans of those who perished in the war, the public honor, peace, and safety, shall all be turned over to the keeping of its recent enemies without delay, and without imposing such conditions as, in the opinion of Congress, the security of the country and its institutions may demand.

"7th. The history of mankind exhibits no examples of such madness and folly. The instinct of self-preservation protests against it. The surrender by Grant to Lee, and by Sherman to Johnston, would have been disasters of less magnitude, for new armies could have been raised, new battles fought, and the government saved. The anti-coercive policy, which, under pretext of avoiding bloodshed, allowed the rebellion to take form and gather force, would be surpassed in infamy by the matchless wickedness that would now surrender the halls of Congress to those so recently in rebellion, until proper precautions shall have been taken to secure the national faith and the national safety.

"8th. As has been shown in this report, and in the evidence submitted, no proof has been afforded by Congress of a constituency in any one of the so-called Confederate States, unless we except the State of Tennessee, qualified to elect senators and representatives in Congress. No state Constitution, or amendment to a state Constitution, has had the sanction of the people. All the so-called legislation of state Conventions and Legislatures has been had under military dictation. If the President may, at his will, and under his own authority, whether as military commander or chief executive, qualify persons to appoint senators and elect representatives, and empower others to appoint and elect them, he thereby practically controls the organization of the legislative department. The constitutional form of government is thereby practically destroyed, and its powers absorbed in the executive. And while your committee do not for a moment impute to the President any such design, but cheerfully concede to him the most patriotic motives, they can not but look with alarm upon a precedent so fraught with danger to the republic.

"9th. The necessity of providing adequate safeguards for the future, before restoring the insurrectionary states to a participation in the direction of public affairs, is apparent from the bitter hostility to the government and people of the United States yet existing throughout the conquered territory, as proved incontestably by the testimony of many witnesses and by undisputed facts.

"10th. The conclusion of your committee therefore is, that the so-called Confederate States are not at present entitled to representation in the Congress of the United States; that, before allowing such representation, adequate security for future peace and safety should be required; that this can

mulated volumes of testimony in regard to the condition of the Southern States. That was proper enough, but it was not necessary to wait for the development of all this evidence before submitting to Congress the measures which it finally proposed. By the delay of Congress to declare its policy, its measures did not come before the country until after the conflict between the President and Congress had produced dissensions in the Republican party, increased agitation throughout the country, and exaggerated the contumacious spirit of the Southern people to such an extent as to greatly diminish the prospect that the latter would accede to the conditions offered for its acceptance. Early in the session the resistance to the Congressional plan of restoration would not have been formidable; now it was plain that it would be resisted by the executive, by the Southern States, and by a large portion of the Republican party. This delay was only less unfortunate in its consequences than the President's hasty action and his failure to convene Congress at the beginning of his administration.

Some time before the full report of the Reconstruction Committee, the latter had presented a concurrent resolution declaring "that, in order to close agitation upon a question which seems likely to disturb the action of the government, as well as to quiet the uncertainty which is agitating the minds of the people of the eleven states which have been declared to be in insurrection, no senator or representative shall be admitted into either branch of Congress from any of the said states until Congress shall have declared such state entitled to such representation." As usual, Stevens cut off debate in the House by demanding the previous question, and the resolution was adopted in that body without discussion, 109 to 40.[1]

It was a strange measure, when considered in reference to its declared purpose, "to close agitation" and "to quiet the uncertainty" of the unrepresented section! The reasons which induced the committee to introduce this resolution were more clearly stated by Fessenden in the Senate, where the measure was debated at length, than in the resolution itself. In his speech upon the resolution, Senator Fessenden confessed that the committee introduced the resolution because President Johnson had denounced it as "an irrepressible central directory" in which was lodged the concentrated power of a few, and because in his veto (February 19th) of the Freedman's Bureau Bill he had indicated "that no legislation affecting the states which have recently been in rebellion would meet with the approval of the President while those states were not represented." Under these circumstances, he thought the resolution necessary "in order that Congress may assert distinctly its own rights and its own powers; in order that there may be no mistake any where, in the mind of the executive or in the minds of the people of this country, that Congress, under the circumstances of this case, with this attempted limitation of its powers with regard to its own organization, is prepared to say to the executive and to the country, respectfully but firmly, over this subject they have, and they mean to exercise, the most plenary jurisdiction; they will be limited with regard to it by no considerations arising from the views of others than themselves, except so far as those considerations may affect the minds of individuals; we will judge for ourselves not only upon credentials, and the character of men and the position of men, but upon the position of the states which sent those men here. In other words, to use the language of the President again, when the question is to be decided whether they obey the Constitution, whether they have a fitting Constitution of their own, whether they are loyal, whether they are prepared to obey the laws as a preliminary, as the President says it is, to their admission, we will say whether those preliminary requirements have been complied with, and not he, and nobody but ourselves." The war, admitted the senator, was not commenced with the idea of subjugation; "but if subjugation must come in order to accomplish what we desire to accomplish and what we must accomplish, it is not our fault." We could not, he added, consider the country safe when the President himself does not withdraw his suspension of the writ of *habeas corpus*.

only be found in such changes of the organic law as shall determine the civil rights and privileges of all citizens in all parts of the republic, shall place representation on an equitable basis, shall fix a stigma upon treason, and protect the loyal people against future claims for the expenses incurred in support of rebellion and for manumitted slaves, together with an express grant of power in Congress to enforce those provisions. To this end they offer a joint resolution for amending the Constitution of the United States, and the two several bills designed to carry the same into effect, before referred to.

"Before closing this report, your committee beg leave to state that the specific recommendations submitted by them are the result of mutual concession, after a long and careful comparison of conflicting opinions. Upon a question of such magnitude, infinitely important as it is to the future of the republic, it was not to be expected that all should think alike. Sensible of the imperfections of the scheme, your committee submit it to Congress as the best they could agree upon, in the hope that its imperfections may be cured, and its deficiencies supplied by legislative wisdom; and that, when finally adopted, it may tend to restore peace and harmony to the whole country, and to place our republican institutions on a more stable foundation.

"W. P. FESSENDEN, ELIHU B. WASHBURNE,
"JAMES W. GRIMES, JUSTIN S. MORRILL,
"IRA HARRIS, JOHN A. BINGHAM,
"J. M. HOWARD, ROSCOE CONKLING,
"GEORGE H. WILLIAMS, GEORGE S. BOUTWELL."
"THADDEUS STEVENS,

[1] YEAS.—Messrs. Allison, Anderson, James M. Ashley, Baker, Baldwin, Banks, Baxter, Beaman, Benjamin, Bidwell, Bingham, Blaine, Boutwell, Brandegee, Bromwell, Broomall, Buckland, Sidney Clarke, Cobb, Conkling, Cook, Cullom, Dawes, Defrees, Deming, Donnelly, Driggs, Eckley, Eggleston, Eliot, Farnsworth, Farquhar, Ferry, Garfield, Grinnell, Griswold, Abner C. Harding, Hart, Hays, Henderson, Higby, Holmes, Hooper, Hotchkiss, Asahel W. Hubbard, Chester D. Hubbard, Demas Hubbard, John H. Hubbard, James R. Hubbell, Hulburd, Ingersoll, Jenckes, Julian, Kelley, Kelso, Ketcham, Laflin, George V. Lawrence, William Lawrence, Loan, Longyear, Lynch, Marston, McClurg, McIndoe, McKee, McRuer, Mercur, Moorhead, Morrill, Morris, Moulton, Myers, O'Neill, Orth, Paine, Patterson, Perham, Pike, Plants, Pomeroy, Price, William H. Randall, John H. Rice, Sawyer, Schenck, Scofield, Shellabarger, Sloan, Spalding, Starr, Stevens, Thayer, John L. Thomas, Trowbridge, Upson, Van Aernam, Burt Van Horn, Ward, Warner, Elihu B. Washburne, William B. Washburn, Welker, Wentworth, Williams, James F. Wilson, Stephen F. Wilson, Windom, and Woodbridge—109.

NAYS.—Messrs. Bergen, Boyer, Brooks, Chanler, Coffroth, Dawson, Eldridge, Finck, Glossbrenner, Goodyear, Grider, Hale, Aaron Harding, Hogan, James M. Humphrey, Kerr, Latham, Marshall, McCullough, Newell, Niblack, Nicholson, Phelps, Radford, Samuel J. Randall, Raymond, Ritter, Rogers, Ross, Rousseau, Shanklin, Sitgreaves, Smith, Taber, Taylor, Thornton, Trimble, Voorhees, Whaley, and Wright—40.

NOT VOTING.—Messrs. Alley, Ames, Ancona, Delos R. Ashley, Barker, Blow, Bundy, Reader W. Clarke, Culver, Darling, Davis, Delano, Denison, Dixon, Dumont, Harris, Hill, Edwin N. Hubbell, James Humphrey, Johnson, Jones, Kasson, Kuykendall, Le Blond, Marvin, Miller, Noell, Alexander H. Rice, Rollins, Stillwell, Strouse, Francis Thomas, Robert T. Van Horn, and Winfield—34.

Senator Sherman, of Ohio, followed in opposition to the resolution. He did not differ from Fessenden as to the power of Congress or as to the propriety of the two houses acting in concert upon this subject of admitting Southern representatives. He considered the adoption of the resolution, therefore, as unnecessary, and as calculated to increase rather than to close agitation. The true way to assert the proper powers of Congress was to exercise them. He held that the real difficulty in this whole matter had been the unfortunate failure of the executive and legislative branches of the government to agree upon the plan of reconstruction. The blame on this account did not rest wholly with the President. If Congress had, at its last session, provided a law by which these states might be guided in their efforts toward restoration, the controversy would have been at an end. He alluded to the Wade and Davis bill, which had been passed at the first session of the Thirty-eighth Congress,[1] but which failed to receive the signature of President Lincoln. Here Senator Sumner remarked that President Lincoln, in an interview with him, had expressed his regret that he had not accepted that bill. Sherman thought every patriotic citizen would express his regret not so much that the President did not approve that bill, but that Congress did not, in connection with the President, agree upon some plan for reconstruction. Why, he asked, now arraign Andrew Johnson for following out the plan which he deemed best, especially when it was the same plan which had been adopted by Lincoln, and which had the apparent ratification of the people in Lincoln's re-election? "One whole session intervened after this vote, as I may call it, of President Lincoln, and no effort was made by Congress to reconcile this conflict of views; and when President Johnson came suddenly, by the hand of an assassin, into the presidential chair, what did he have before him to guide his steps? The forces of the rebellion had been subdued; all physical resistance was soon after subdued. . . . . Who doubts, then, that if there had been a law upon the statute-book by which the people of the Southern States could have been guided in their efforts to come back into the Union, they would have cheerfully followed it, although the conditions had been hard?" Lincoln and Johnson had both been obliged to follow out a plan of their own. We might find fault with the conditions imposed by them, but Lincoln's plan had been substantially sanctioned by the people in his re-election. At the very time Johnson was nominated for Vice-President he was, as military governor of Tennessee, executing the very plan which he subsequently adopted as President. There was now no difference between the President and Congress as to the condition of the Southern States. By both they were treated as states in insurrection, but still as states. It only remained for Congress to provide a method by which the condition of states might be tested, and they might come back, one by one, each upon its own merits, upon complying with such conditions as the public safety demands. Senator Sherman then proceeded to explain the policy which Johnson had adopted. He had retained Lincoln's cabinet, and had thus far received its full support. He had executed every law passed by Congress. He had in his proclamations adopted almost the precise words used by Lincoln in like cases, only that he had extended and made more severe the policy of the latter. In carrying out his plans he had adopted all the main features of the Wade and Davis bill—the only law bearing upon the subject ever passed by Congress. In his amnesty proclamation of May 29th he had excepted from pardon some fourteen classes of persons, "more than quadrupling the exceptions of the previous proclamation of Mr. Lincoln; so that, if there was any departure in this connection from the policy adopted by Mr. Lincoln, it was a departure against the rebels, and especially against those wealthy rebels who gave life, and soul, and power to the rebellion." He had required of the Southern States the adoption of the constitutional amendment abolishing slavery, had enforced the test oath in the case of every officer receiving his commission under the law, and had insisted upon the full protection of the freedmen. Now what were the objections to this policy? It was said that the pardoning power had been abused; but this power had been sanctioned by Congressional enactment. It was also objected that Johnson had not extended the suffrage to negroes; but there were only six of the Northern States in which negroes had the right to vote, and until the present session the proposition to give negroes this right in the District of Columbia had never been seriously considered, although Congress had complete jurisdiction over the district. Even in the Territories, also under the unrestricted jurisdiction of Congress, the franchise had never been extended to the colored race. In the Wade and Davis bill Congress expressly refused to make negro suffrage a part of their plan.

We have given Senator Sherman's arguments so much space not only on account of his recognized position as one of the most eminent statesmen of the country, but because they furnish the fullest possible defense of President Johnson's policy. This defense was just, so far as it went, but still it must be remembered that the senator's argument entirely ignored the peculiar features of the political situation at the time he spoke. The President's policy could not be separated from the President's conduct of that policy. Johnson had not confined himself to issuing proclamations and to vetoes of Congressional enactments. He had in an unbecoming manner entered into a bitter antagonism with Congress in occasional harangues before the people. Perhaps Sherman paid less regard to the objectionable features of the President's conduct because these features had not as yet assumed their peculiarly offensive character. Sherman defended the President in

[1] See page 660 of this History.

February, 1866—what his judgment would have been five months later is another question.

Notwithstanding his speech, Sherman voted in favor of the resolution, which was passed 29 to 18.[1]

The House on the 19th, and the Senate on the 21st of July, passed a resolution declaring the State of Tennessee entitled to representation in Congress, that state having ratified the constitutional amendment proposed by the Thirty-ninth Congress. The President signed the resolution on the 24th, and at the same time sent a message to the House, scolding Congress for its previous contumacy, and denying its right to pass laws preliminary to the admission of duly qualified members from any of the states. The members elected from Tennessee were then duly qualified.

Two important bills were passed during this session, having for their principal object the protection of freedmen, both of which were vetoed by the President, but afterward became laws by a two-thirds vote.

The first of these was a bill to enlarge the powers of the Freedmen's Bureau. This bureau had been established by the previous Congress, while the war was still in progress, and was styled "a Bureau of Refugees, Freedmen, and Abandoned Lands."[2] It passed Congress March 3d, 1867, and received within the week following the approval of President Lincoln, who appointed Major General O. O. Howard as commissioner. This choice was very judicious, as General Howard was not only an able military officer, but had also a thorough knowledge of the South, and of the special duties of the office to which he was assigned. He was, moreover, a conscientious Christian gentleman. He was retained at the head of the bureau by President Johnson. The abandoned lands consisted of some 770,000 acres of lands scattered over the Southern States, the most valuable portion of which were the sea islands off the South Carolina coast, which had been given to the freedmen by General Sherman, acting in consultation with the Secretary of War.

By President Johnson's amnesty proclamation the most valuable lands were restored to their original owners, and this circumstance seriously embarrassed the operations of the bureau. Notwithstanding this obstacle, however, the bureau proved a beneficent institution to the freed slave and refugee. It secured them many educational privileges hitherto denied, stood between them and the avarice of their employers, and provided medical relief to their sick, and assistance to the old and decrepit. Great opposition was manifested to the education of freedmen. The educational statistics of October 31, 1865, show that there were at that time 560 schools in operation, with 1135 teachers, and 68,241 pupils. Toward the close of the year, General Howard estimated the number of persons receiving rations from the bureau at 45,035, which he thought would be increased during the ensuing winter to 100,000. The expenses of the bureau for 1865 amounted to nearly $12,000,000.

The bill enlarging the powers of the Freedmen's Bureau passed the Senate January 24, 1866, by a party vote. A substitute for this bill passed the House, which was subsequently accepted by the Senate. This bill continued in force the bureau until otherwise ordered by law, and provided for its extension to freedmen and refugees in all parts of the United States, the entire section containing such persons to be divided into twelve districts, over each of which an assistant commissioner should preside. These districts, in turn, were to be subdivided, so that there should be one for each county or parish, each of which was to be controlled by an agent. It provided for the issue by the Secretary of War of provisions, clothing, fuel, and other supplies, including medical stores and transportation; and that the secretary might afford such aid as was necessary for the temporary shelter and supply of destitute freedmen and refugees, with their wives and children. The President was authorized to reserve from sale and set apart unoccupied public lands in the South for the use of freedmen and loyal refugees, the amount thus appropriated not to exceed three millions of acres of good land, to be allotted in parcels of not more than forty acres each, the tenants to be protected in the use thereof for such time and at such rental as should be agreed upon between the commissioners and freedmen. This land might ultimately be purchased by the occupants. Those occupying land under General Sherman's special order of January 16, 1865, were confirmed in possession for three years. This act also provided for the erection of asylums and

[1] YEAS.—Messrs. Anthony, Brown, Chandler, Clark, Conness, Cragin, Creswell, Fessenden, Foster, Grimes, Harris, Henderson, Howe, Kirkwood, Lane of Indiana, Morrill, Nye, Poland, Pomeroy, Ramsey, Sherman, Sprague, Sumner, Trumbull, Wade, Willey, Williams, Wilson, and Yates—29.

NAYS.—Messrs. Buckalew, Cowan, Davis, Dixon, Doolittle, Guthrie, Hendricks, Johnson, Lane of Kansas, McDougall, Morgan, Nesmith, Norton, Riddle, Saulsbury, Stewart, Stockton, and Van Winkle—18.

ABSENT.—Messrs. Foot, Howard, and Wright—3.

[2] The bill established in the War Department for the war and one year thereafter a Bureau of Refugees, Freedmen, and Abandoned Lands, for the supervision and management of all abandoned lands, and the control of all subjects relating to refugees and freedmen from rebel states, or from any district of the country within the territory embraced in the operations of the army, under rules to be approved by the President. The bureau to have a commissioner at $3000 year, and $50,000 bonds, with an assistant commissioner for each rebel state, not exceeding ten, at $2500 a year, and $20,000 bonds. The assistants to make quarterly reports to the commissioner, and he a report at each session of Congress.

Section 2 authorizes the Secretary of War to direct such issues of provisions, clothing, and fuel as he may deem needful for the immediate and temporary shelter and supply of destitute and suffering refugees and freedmen, and their wives and children, under such rules and regulations as he may direct.

The bill also gives the commissioner, under the direction of the President, authority to set apart for the use of loyal refugees and freedmen such tracts of land within the insurrectionary states as shall have been abandoned, or to which the United States shall have acquired title by confiscation, or sale, or otherwise. And to every male citizen, whether refugee or freedman, as aforesaid, there shall be assigned not more than forty acres of such land, and the persons to whom it is so assigned shall be protected in the use and enjoyment of the land for the term of three years, at an annual rent not exceeding six per cent. upon the value of said land as it was appraised by the state authorities in 1860 for the purpose of taxation, and in case no such appraisal can be found, then the rental shall be based upon the estimated value of the land in said year, to be ascertained in such manner as the commissioner may, by regulation, prescribe. At the end of said term, or at any time during said term, the occupants of any parcels so assigned may purchase the land and receive such title thereto as the United States can convey upon paying therefor the value of the land, as ascertained and fixed for the purpose of determining the annual rent as aforesaid.

schools. It also contained provisions for the protection of the civil rights of freedmen.[1]

This bill was vetoed by the President February 19th, 1866. His objections may be briefly stated thus:

1. The act was unnecessary, the original act not having yet expired. That act was considered sufficiently stringent in time of war. Before its expiration, farther experience may lead to a wise policy for a time of peace.

2. The act contained provisions not warranted by the Constitution. It substituted military for civil tribunals, and military law for civil law in time of peace.

3. The exercise of such arbitrary power by so vast a number of agents must be attended by acts of caprice, injustice, and passion. From these officers of the bureau there was no appeal.

4. The continuance of this military establishment was not limited to any definite period of time.

5. While it was intended to protect the negro, it deprived other citizens of constitutional rights. "I can not," said the President, "reconcile a system of military jurisdiction of this kind with the words of the Constitution, which declare that 'no person shall be held to answer for a capital or otherwise infamous crime unless upon a presentment or indictment of a grand jury, except in cases arising in the land and naval forces, or in the militia when in actual service in time of war or public danger;' and that 'in all criminal prosecutions the accused shall enjoy the right to a speedy and public trial by an impartial jury of the state or district wherein the crime shall have been committed.'"

6. It placed too much power in the hands of the President. It would enable him to control four millions of people for his own political ends.

7. A system for the support of indigent persons in the United States was never contemplated by the framers of the Constitution, nor could any good reason be given why it should be founded for one class of our people more than another. The idea on which the slaves were assisted to freedom was that, on becoming free, they would be a self-sustaining population.

8. It was an expensive system.

9. It deprived the rightful owners of certain lands of their property without due process of law.

10. It was injurious to the freedman, encouraging him to entertain idle and vague expectations.

11. Eleven states were still unrepresented, and these were the very states most nearly concerned in the operations of the bill.

The House passed the bill over the President's veto, but it failed to receive a two-thirds vote in the Senate, and thus failed to become a law. Before the end of May a new bill was presented in the House by Thomas D. Eliot, of Massachusetts, apparently obviating many of the objections which had been urged by the President against the former enactment. This new bill simply sought to supplement the act already in operation by provisions applicable to the altered situation since that act had been passed. It continued that act in force for two years; appropriated one million instead of three millions of acres for the use of the freedmen, and embodied the provisions of the Civil Rights Bill. This bill, after various amendments, passed both houses, and was presented to the President for his approval. On the 16th of July Johnson returned the bill with objections similar to those urged against the previous act. It was again passed in both houses by a two-thirds vote, and became a law.

In the mean time Congress had passed the Civil Rights Bill. This act was supported in both houses by the entire Republican party.[2] It was

[1] "*Sec.* 7. That whenever in any state or district in which the ordinary course of judicial proceedings has been interrupted by the rebellion, and wherein, in consequence of any state or local law, ordinance, police or other regulation, custom, or prejudice, any of the civil rights or immunities belonging to white persons, including the right to make and enforce contracts, to sue, be parties, and give evidence, to inherit, purchase, lease, sell, hold, and convey real and personal property, and to have full and equal benefit of all laws and proceedings for the security of person and estate, including the constitutional right of bearing arms, are refused or denied to negroes, mulattoes, freedmen, refugees, or any other persons, on account of race, color, or any previous condition of slavery or involuntary servitude, or wherein they or any of them are subjected to any other or different punishment, pains, or penalties for the commission of any act or offense than are prescribed for white persons committing like acts or offenses, it shall be the duty of the President of the United States, through the commissioner, to extend military protection and jurisdiction over all cases affecting such persons so discriminated against.

"*Sec.* 8. That any person who, under color of any state or local law, ordinance, police, or other regulation or custom, shall, in any state or district in which the ordinary course of judicial proceedings has been interrupted by the rebellion, subject, or cause to be subjected, any negro, mulatto, freedman, refugee, or other person, on account of race or color, or any previous condition of slavery or involuntary servitude, or for any other cause, to the deprivation of any civil right secured to white persons, or to any other or different punishment than white persons are subject to for the commission of like acts or offenses, shall be deemed guilty of a misdemeanor, and be punished by fine not exceeding one thousand dollars, or imprisonment not exceeding one year, or both; and it shall be the duty of the officers and agents of this bureau to take jurisdiction of, and hear and determine all offenses committed against the provisions of this section, and also of all cases affecting negroes, mulattoes, freedmen, refugees, or other persons who are discriminated against in any of the particulars mentioned in the preceding section of this act, under such rules and regulations as the President of the United States, through the War Department, shall prescribe. The jurisdiction conferred by this and the preceding section on the officers and agents of this bureau shall cease and determine whenever the discrimination on account of which it is conferred ceases, and in no event to be exercised in any state in which the ordinary course of judicial proceedings has not been interrupted by the rebellion, nor in any such state after said state shall have been fully restored in all its constitutional relations to the United States, and the courts of the state and of the United States within the same are not disturbed or stopped in the peaceable course of justice."

[2] The following is the text of the bill:

"*Be it enacted, etc.*, That all persons born in the United States and not subject to any foreign power, excluding Indians not taxed, are hereby declared to be citizens of the United States; and such citizens of every race and color, without regard to any previous condition of slavery or involuntary servitude, except as a punishment for crime whereof the party shall have been duly convicted, shall have the same right in every state and territory in the United States to make and enforce contracts; to sue, be parties, and give evidence; to inherit, purchase, lease, sell, hold, and convey real estate and personal property; and to full and equal benefit of all laws and proceedings for the security of person and property as is enjoyed by white citizens, and shall be subject to like punishment, pains, and penalties, and to none other, any law, statute, ordinance, regulation, or custom to the contrary notwithstanding.

"*Sec.* 2. That any person who, under color of any law, statute, ordinance, regulation, or custom, shall subject, or cause to be subjected, any inhabitant of any state or territory to the deprivation of any right secured or protected by this act, or to different punishment, pains, or penalties on account of such person having at any time been held in a condition of slavery or involuntary servitude, except as a punishment for crime whereof the party shall have been duly convicted, or by

vetoed by the President March 27, 1866. This veto was not based upon sound reasoning, and the message of the President totally disregarded the obvious necessity of the Congressional enactment. The bill was again passed by both houses over the executive veto.

A bill was passed early in May admitting Colorado as a state, but it was vetoed by the President on the ground that it was doubtful whether the majority of the people of that Territory desired a state government, that the population was insufficient, and that, until the Southern section of the country was represented in Congress, it was undesirable to admit new states. The bill was not repassed.

A bill was introduced early in the session to extend the right of suffrage to negroes in the District of Columbia. It passed the House, after an unsuccessful attempt on the part of a Republican member to obtain its postponement, by a vote of 116 to 54. It was not brought to a vote in the Senate until the next session, when it passed, was vetoed by the President, and on the 7th and 8th of January, 1867, was repassed by a two-thirds vote in the Senate and House.[1]

The first session of the Thirty-ninth Congress closed on the 28th of July, after a continuance of nearly eight months. During this period the political situation had been radically changed. When the Thirty-ninth Congress assembled, there was no strongly-marked popular dissatisfaction on account of the measures adopted by President Johnson in the early stages of reconstruction. Now the people murmured against the administration; the President had lost his hold upon the popular confidence. Radical Republicans now as vehemently denounced him as Copperheads had at the time of his inauguration. The latter, from calling him a boor, had come to grant him a place among the gods; the former, who had once shouted his praises to the echo, now not only took the scoffers' place, but boldly proclaimed him a traitor.

There had been in the ranks of the dominant party some apprehension of Johnson's policy at the outset, but it scarcely found a voice before the meeting of Congress. There was a feeling of insecurity, caused by the prospect of a too hasty admission of the Southern representatives to Congress, and enhanced by the half-hearted expression of loyalty on the part of the Southern Conventions and Legislatures; but this was to a great degree counteracted by the hope that Congress and the President would unite upon some plan by which harmony would soon be restored, the wounds occasioned by civil strife healed, and the national safety secured. No conflict between the executive and Congress—at least none which would prove irreconcilable—was apprehended. The war record of President Johnson, his vehement denunciation of treason, his oft-repeated expressions of deference to the popular will, and the fact that thus far he had been carrying out the policy of restoration which Lincoln had inaugurated, and had only modified that policy by severer features as against rebels—all these were taken as assurances that he, at least, would not be a ready party to such a conflict. And, on the other hand, the popular confidence in the wisdom of Congress was a source of encouragement. It was well known that there were in that body certain members who would push their extreme and impracticable theories to the utmost; but, if Sumner, and Stevens, and Boutwell, and Ashley were there, there also were Fessenden, Sherman, Trumbull, Colfax, Conkling, Doolittle, and Raymond. The factious disposition and the partisan fury of the few, it was thought, would be controlled and overruled by the unsectional patriotism of wiser and better-tempered statesmen.

But scarcely had Congress assembled before this feeling of assurance, this anticipation of harmony, began to be disturbed. We regret that we must attribute to President Johnson's policy so much of the responsibility for the discord—the more shameful because it was unnecessary—which now began to develop into the most violent antagonism. He had already established a basis for this conflict by not convening and consulting Congress at the outset. Undoubtedly he thought that the policy which he had adopted was supported by the people, and that nothing more than that was necessary. He had good reasons for judging thus. But, in carrying out this policy, some circumstances presented themselves to which he did not pay

---

reason of his color or race, than is prescribed for the punishment of white persons, shall be deemed guilty of a misdemeanor, and on conviction shall be punished by fine not exceeding one thousand dollars, or imprisonment not exceeding one year, or both, in the discretion of the court.

"Sec. 3. That the District Courts of the United States, within their respective districts, shall have, exclusively of the courts of the several states, cognizance of all crimes and offenses committed against the provisions of this act, and also, concurrently with the Circuit Courts of the United States, of all causes, civil and criminal, affecting persons who are denied or can not enforce in the courts or judicial tribunals of the state or locality where there may be any of the rights secured to them by the first section of this act; and if any suit or prosecution, civil or criminal, has been or shall be commenced in any state court against any such person, for any cause whatsoever, or against any officer, civil or military, or other person, for any arrest or imprisonment, trespasses, or wrongs done or committed by virtue or under color of authority derived from this act, or the act establishing a bureau for the relief of freedmen and refugees, and all acts amendatory thereof, or for refusing to do any act upon the ground that it would be inconsistent with this act, such defendant shall have the right to remove such cause for trial to the proper District or Circuit Court in the manner prescribed by the 'Act relating to *Habeas Corpus* and regulating Judicial Proceedings in certain cases,' approved March 3, 1863, and all acts amendatory thereof. The jurisdiction in civil and criminal matters hereby conferred on the District and Circuit Courts of the United States shall be exercised and enforced in conformity with the laws of the United States so far as such laws are suitable to carry the same into effect; but in all cases where such laws are not adapted to the object, or are deficient in the provisions necessary to furnish suitable remedies and punish offenses against law, the common law, as modified and changed by the Constitution and statutes of the state wherein the court having jurisdiction of the cause, civil or criminal, is held, so far as the same is not inconsistent with the Constitution and laws of the United States, shall be extended to and govern said courts in the trial and disposition of such cause, and, if of a criminal nature, in the infliction of punishment on the party found guilty.

"Sec. 4. That the district attorneys, marshals, and deputy marshals of the United States, the commissioners appointed by the Circuit Court and territorial courts of the United States, with powers of arresting, imprisoning, or bailing offenders against the laws of the United States, the officers and agents of the Freedmen's Bureau, and every other officer who may be specially empowered by the President of the United States, shall be, and they are hereby specially authorized and required, at the expense of the United States, to institute proceedings against all and every person who shall violate the provisions of this act, and cause him or them to be arrested and imprisoned, or bailed, as the case may be, for trial before such court of the United States or territorial court as by this act has cognizance of the offense. And with a view to affording reasonable protection to all persons in their constitutional rights of equality before the law, without distinction of race or color, or previous condition of slavery or involuntary servitude, except as a punishment for crime, whereof the party shall have been duly convicted, and to the prompt discharge of the duties of this act, it shall be the duty of the Circuit Courts of the United States and the Superior Courts of the Territories of the United States, from time to time to increase the number of commissioners, so as to afford a speedy and convenient means for the arrest and examination of persons charged with a violation of this act. And such commissioners are hereby authorized and required to exercise and discharge all the powers and duties conferred on them by this act, and the same duties with regard to offenses created by this act, as they are authorized by law to exercise with regard to other offenses against the laws of the United States.

"Sec. 5. That it shall be the duty of all marshals and deputy marshals to obey and execute all warrants and precepts issued under the provisions of this act when to them directed; and should any marshal or deputy marshal refuse to receive such warrant or other process when tendered, or to use all proper means diligently to execute the same, he shall, on conviction thereof, be fined in the sum of one thousand dollars, to the use of the person upon whom the accused is alleged to have committed the offense. And the better to enable the said commissioners to execute their duties faithfully and efficiently, in conformity with the Constitution of the United States and the requirements of this act, they are hereby authorized and empowered, within their counties respectively, to appoint, in writing, under their hands, any one or more suitable persons, from time to time, to execute all such warrants and other process that may be issued by them in the lawful performance of their respective duties; and the persons so appointed to execute any warrant or process as aforesaid shall have authority to summon and call to their aid the by-standers or the *posse comitatus* of the proper county, or such portion of the land and naval forces of the United States, or of the militia, as may be necessary to the performance of the duty with which they are charged, and to insure a faithful observance of the clause of the Constitution which prohibits slavery, in conformity with the provisions of this act; and said warrants shall run and be executed by said officers any where in the state or territory within which they are issued.

"Sec. 6. That any person who shall knowingly and willfully obstruct, hinder, or prevent any officer, or other person charged with the execution of any warrant or process issued under the provisions of this act, or any person or persons lawfully assisting him or them, from arresting any person for whose apprehension such warrant or process may have been issued, or shall rescue or attempt to rescue such person from the custody of the officer, other person or persons, or those lawfully assisting as aforesaid, when so arrested pursuant to the authority herein given and declared, or shall aid, abet, or assist any person so arrested as aforesaid, directly or indirectly, to escape from the custody of the officer or other person legally authorized as aforesaid, or shall harbor or conceal any person for whose arrest a warrant or process shall have been issued as aforesaid, so as to prevent his discovery and arrest after notice or knowledge of the fact that a warrant has been issued for the apprehension of such person, shall, for either of said offenses, be subject to a fine not exceeding one thousand dollars, and imprisonment not exceeding six months, by indictment and conviction before the District Court of the United States for the district in which said offense may have been committed, or before the proper court of criminal jurisdiction, if committed within any one of the organized territories of the United States.

"Sec. 7. That the district attorneys, the marshals, their deputies, and the clerks of the said District and Territorial Courts shall be paid for their services the like fees as may be allowed to them for similar services in other cases; and in all cases where the proceedings are before a commissioner, he shall be entitled to a fee of ten dollars in full for his services in each case, inclusive of all services incident to such arrest and examination. The person or persons authorized to execute the process to be issued by such commissioners for the arrest of offenders against the provisions of this act shall be entitled to a fee of five dollars for each person he or they may arrest and take before any such commissioner as aforesaid, with such other fees as may be deemed reasonable by such commissioner for such other additional services as may be necessarily performed by him or them, such as attending at the examination, keeping the prisoner in custody, and providing him with food and lodging during his detention, and until the final determination of such commissioner, and in general for performing such other duties as may be required in the premises; such fees to be made up in conformity with the fees usually charged by the officers of the courts of justice within the proper district or county, as near as may be practicable, and paid out of the treasury of the United States on the certificate of the judge of the district within which the arrest is made, and to be recoverable from the defendant as part of the judgment in case of conviction.

"Sec. 8. That whenever the President of the United States shall have reason to believe that offenses have been, or are likely to be committed against the provisions of this act within any judicial district, it shall be lawful for him, in his discretion, to direct the judge, marshal, and district attorney of such district to attend at such place within the district, and for such time as he may designate, for the purpose of the more speedy arrest and trial of persons charged with a violation of this act; and it shall be the duty of every judge or other officer, when any such requisition shall be received by him, to attend at the place and for the time therein designated.

"Sec. 9. That it shall be lawful for the President of the United States, or such person as he may empower for that purpose, to employ such part of the land or naval forces of the United States, or of the militia, as shall be necessary to prevent the violation and enforce the due execution of this act.

Sec. 10. That upon all questions of law arising in any cause under the provisions of this act, a final appeal may be taken to the Supreme Court of the United States."

---

[1] The following is the text of this enactment:

"*Be it enacted by the Senate and House of Representatives of the United States of America, in Congress assembled,* That from and after the passage of this act, each and every male person, excepting paupers and persons under guardianship, of the age of twenty-one years and upward, who has not been convicted of any infamous crime or offense, and excepting persons who may have voluntarily given aid and comfort to the rebels in the late rebellion, and who shall have been born or naturalized in the United States, and who shall have resided in the said District for the period of one year, and three months in the ward or election precinct in which he shall offer to vote next preceding any election therein, shall be entitled to the elective franchise, and shall be deemed an elector, and entitled to vote at any election in said District, without any distinction on account of color or race.

"Sec. 2. *And be it further enacted,* That any person whose duty it shall be to receive votes at any election within the District of Columbia, who shall willfully refuse to receive, or who shall willfully reject, the vote of any person entitled to such right under this act, shall be liable to an action of tort by the person injured, and shall be liable, on indictment and conviction, if such act was done knowingly, to a fine not exceeding five thousand dollars, or to imprisonment for a term not exceeding one year in the jail of said District, or to both.

"Sec. 3. *And be it further enacted,* That if any person or persons shall willfully interrupt or disturb any such elector in the exercise of such franchise, he or they shall be deemed guilty of a misdemeanor, and, on conviction thereof, shall be fined in any sum not to exceed one thousand dollars, or be imprisoned in the jail in said District for a period not to exceed thirty days, or both, at the discretion of the court.

"Sec. 4. *And be it further enacted,* That it shall be the duty of the several courts having criminal jurisdiction in said District to give this act in special charge to the grand jury at the commencement of each term of the court next preceding the holding of any general or city election in said District.

"Sec. 5. *And be it further enacted,* That the mayors and aldermen of the cities of Washington and Georgetown respectively, on or before the first day of March in each year, shall prepare a list of the persons they judge to be qualified to vote in the several wards of said cities in any election: and said mayors and aldermen shall be in open session to receive evidence of the qualification of persons claiming the right to vote in any election therein, and for correcting said list, on two days in each year, not exceeding five days prior to the annual election for the choice of city officers, giving previous notice of the time and place of each session in some newspaper printed in said District.

"Sec. 6. *And be it further enacted,* That on or before the first day of March, the mayors and aldermen of said cities shall post up a list of voters thus prepared in one or more public places in said cities respectively, at least ten days prior to said annual election.

"Sec. 7. *And be it further enacted,* That the officers presiding at any election shall keep and use the check-list herein required at the polls during the election of all officers, and no vote shall be received unless delivered by the voter in person, and not until the presiding officer has had opportunity to be satisfied of his identity, and shall find his name on the list, and mark it, and ascertain that his vote is single.

"Sec. 8. *And be it further enacted,* That it is hereby declared unlawful for any person, directly or indirectly, to promise, offer, or give, or procure, or cause to be promised, offered, or given, any money, goods, right in action, bribe, present, or reward, or any promise, understanding, obligation, or security for the payment or delivery of any money, goods, right in action, bribe, present, or reward, or any other valuable thing whatever, to any person with intent to influence his vote to be given at any election hereafter to be held within the District of Columbia; and every person so offending shall, on conviction thereof, be fined in any sum not exceeding two thousand dollars, or imprisoned not exceeding two years, or both, at the discretion of the court.

"Sec. 9. *And be it further enacted,* That any person who shall accept, directly or indirectly, any money, goods, right in action, bribe, present, or reward, or any promise, understanding, obligation, or security, for the payment or delivery of any money, goods, right in action, bribe, present, or reward, or any other valuable thing whatever, to influence his vote at any election hereafter to be held in the District of Columbia, shall, on conviction, be imprisoned not less than one year, and be forever disfranchised.

"Sec. 10. *And be it further enacted,* That all acts and parts of acts inconsistent with this act be, and the same is hereby repealed."

sufficient regard. He had thrown the burden of reconstruction upon the Southern people, which was right. But they had not taken up this burden in the proper spirit; he was himself dissatisfied, and he must have known that the loyal people would not be less so; yet, although he had expressed his disappointment, he had shown a lack of firmness and of judgment in allowing this spirit to have full sway; in finally sanctioning it by his assent, however reluctant, and without consultation with Congress; in encouraging the idea that the Southern States might hope for representation in that body on the basis of their imperfectly expressed allegiance. Congress, with good reason, felt aggrieved by this action of the President.

Congress, upon its meeting, did exactly what it would have done if Lincoln had been President. It appointed a joint committee to investigate the whole subject. Upon mature consideration, it felt that it could not, with a proper regard to the national safety, respond to the expectations which the President had encouraged the Southern people to entertain. Thus the divergence between the executive and Congress began. On the part of the majority there was no misconstruction of the motives of the President and no ill temper; but there were some members who could not refrain from denouncing "the man at the other end of the avenue." Stevens went so far as to say that the President's usurpation of authority was no less heinous a crime than that which had cost Charles the First his head.

And just here it was that President Johnson began to show his most extraordinary lack of judgment. Harmony of action was still possible between the two branches of government. The only necessity on the President's part was that he should keep his temper. Whether he ought to have kept or abandoned his policy may be a debatable question, about which much might be said on both sides; but certainly he ought not to have lost his temper and self-control, since that loss would prove fatal alike to his own good fame and to his policy. Unfortunately, Johnson belonged to that class of politicians who can never refuse a challenge to antagonism, and foolishly took up the gauntlet which Stevens had so adroitly flung. The challenge did not come from Congress. It did come from a man who, without self-conceit, could boast that he had the power arbitrarily to control the debates of the House, but that was no excuse for such an acceptance of the challenge by the President of the United States as that into which Johnson was betrayed in his speech at Washington on the 22d of February, 1866. He then and there publicly declared that, after one rebellion had been subdued, another had just begun. An attempt, he said, was being made "to concentrate all power in the hands of a few at the federal head, and thereby bring about a consolidation of the republic, which is equally objectionable with its dissolution. We find a power assumed and attempted to be exercised of a most extraordinary character. We see now that governments can be revolutionized without going into the battle-field, and sometimes the revolutions most distressing to a people are effected without the shedding of blood; that is, the substance of your government may be taken away, while there is held out to you the form and the shadow. And now, what are the attempts, and what is being proposed? We find that by an irresponsible central directory nearly all the powers of Congress are assumed, without even consulting the legislative and executive departments of the government. By a resolution reported by a committee, upon whom and in whom the legislative power of the government has been lodged, that great principle in the Constitution which authorizes and empowers the legislative department, the Senate and House of Representatives, to be the judges of elections, returns, and qualifications of its own members, has been virtually taken away from the two respective branches of the national Legislature, and conferred upon a committee, who must report before the body can act on the question of the admission of members to their seats. By this rule they assume a state is out of the Union, and to have its practical relations restored by that rule before the House can judge of the qualifications of its own members. What position is that? You have been struggling for four years to put down a rebellion. You contended at the beginning of that struggle that a state had not a right to go out. You said it had neither the right nor the power, and it has been settled that the states had neither the right nor the power to go out of the Union. And when you determine by the executive, by the military, and by the public judgment that these states can not have any right to go out, this committee turns around and assumes that they are out, and that they shall not come in." In this strain the President continued. Not satisfied with denouncing a proceeding of Congress which was evidently proper, and the purport of which he wholly misconstrued, he, in answer to a call from the crowd, went so far as to mention the names of Thaddeus Stevens, Charles Sumner, and Wendell Phillips as men "opposed to the fundamental principles of the government, and now laboring to destroy them." He called the Secretary of the Senate a "dead duck." He said he did not intend to be governed by real or pretended friends, nor to be bullied by his enemies. When he was beheaded, like Charles the First, he wanted the American people to be the witness. He foolishly attached serious importance to Stevens's equally foolish insinuation about his deserving execution. "I do not want," he said, "by innuendoes of an indirect character in high places, to have one say to a man who has assassination broiling in his heart, 'there is a fit subject,' and also exclaim that the 'presidential obstacle' must be got out of the way, when possibly the intention was to institute assassination. Are those who want to destroy our institutions and change the character of the government not satisfied with the blood that has been shed? Are they not satisfied with one martyr? Does not the blood of Lincoln appease the vengeance and wrath of the opponents of this government? Is their thirst still unslaked? Do they want more blood? Have they not honor and courage enough to effect the removal of the presidential obstacle otherwise than through the

hands of the assassin? I am not afraid of assassins; but if it must be, I would wish to be encountered where one brave man can oppose another. I hold him in dread only who strikes cowardly. But if they have courage enough to strike like men (I know they are willing to wound, but they are afraid to strike)—if my blood is to be shed because I vindicate the Union and the preservation of this government in its original purity and character, let it be so; but when it is done, let an altar of the Union be erected, and then, if necessary, lay me upon it, and the blood that now warms and animates my frame shall be poured out in a last libation as a tribute to the Union; and let the opponents of this government remember that when it is poured out the blood of the martyr will be the seed of the Church. The Union will grow. It will continue to increase in strength and power, though it may be cemented and cleansed with blood."

Nothing could have been more unwise than this speech of Johnson's. He showed himself too ready to answer vituperation with vituperation. It was the speech of a demagogue and not of a statesman. It manifested his incapacity to become a popular leader, whatever might be the merits of his policy.

Thus the conflict progressed and continually increased in bitterness. Johnson committed himself to it with gladiatorial eagerness. He was in no fit temper to listen to the wisest and most potent arguments which Congress might suggest. All hope of reconciliation soon disappeared. In his veto messages he plumply denied the right of Congress to adopt legislative measures preliminary to the admission of duly qualified members from the Southern States, and Congress, in its turn, denied his right to adopt the measures which he had adopted preliminary to his recognition of those states. The appeal, therefore, was to the people.

The Republican party was divided. The people were divided, and it appeared for a long time difficult to decide whether its verdict would be for the executive or for Congress. In the mean time, a decision had been rendered by the Supreme Court of the United States against the constitutionality of test oaths. Certain Republicans in Washington, coinciding with the views of the President, formed an organization known as the "National Union Club." This organization was subsequently united with another of similar character in Washington, and a National Union executive committee was appointed. On the 23d of May the members of this league serenaded the President and the officers of his cabinet to elicit an expression of views on the existing crisis. In most cases, and especially in that of Secretary McCulloch, the ministerial advisers of the President sustained his policy of restoration. Secretary Stanton did not commit himself. He said that "no one better than Johnson understood the solemn duty imposed upon the national executive to maintain the national authority, vindicated at so great a sacrifice, and the obligation not to suffer the just fruits of so many battles and victories to slip away or turn to ashes." After a calm and full discussion, he said that he had yielded to the President's opinion against negro suffrage. He distinctly declared that the plan reported by the Congressional Committee on Reconstruction did not receive his assent. Postmaster General Dennison regretted the difference between the President and Congress. He did not believe it rested upon any good reasons, and thought that time and discussion would bring reconciliation. Secretary Seward was absent at Auburn, New York, but he there indulged in a frank expression of his views. He was hopeful—"hopeful of the President, hopeful of Congress, hopeful of the National Union party, hopeful of the unrepresented states—above all, hopeful of the favor of Almighty God." He ought ever afterward to be styled "Secretary Hopeful."

On the 25th of June a call was issued for a National Union Convention, to be composed of at least two delegates from each Congressional District in every state, two from each Territory, two from the District of Columbia, and four delegates at large from each of the states, to meet at Philadelphia August 14. This call was signed by A. W. Randall, J. R. Doolittle, O. H. Browning, Edgar Cowan, Charles Knapp, and Samuel Fowler, members of the executive committee of the National Union Club. The delegates, however, were to agree upon the following principles: That the Union could not be dissolved even by Congressional action; that each state has the undoubted right to prescribe the qualifications of its own electors, and no external power rightfully can or ought to dictate, control, or influence the free and voluntary action of the states in the exercise of that right; that the maintenance inviolate of the rights of the states, and especially of the right of each state to order and control its own domestic concerns, according to its own judgment exclusively, subject only to the Constitution of the United States, is essential to the balance of power on which the perfection and endurance of our political fabric depend, and the overthrow of that system by the usurpation and centralization of power in Congress would be a revolution dangerous to republican government and destructive of liberty; and that each house of Congress is made, by the Constitution, the sole judge of the elections, returns, and qualifications of its members; but the exclusion of loyal senators and representatives, properly chosen and qualified under the Constitution and laws, is unjust and revolutionary.

This call was followed on the 4th of July by an address to the people, signed by 41 Democratic members of Congress, who approved the call and the principles therein set forth. The executive committee addressed letters to each member of the cabinet, to obtain, in reply, an expression of their views as to the propriety of such a Convention, and as to the principles upon which the call had been based. Seward replied that he considered restoration the most vital interest of the country. Nothing could complete this but the admission of loyal members from the Southern States. Every day's delay increased our domestic and foreign embarrassment. It seemed not only proper, but expedient, therefore, that all parties should unite in remonstrance against the Congressional policy. Secretary Welles was not less strong and explicit in the position taken by him in favor of the Convention. Attorney General Speed expressed far different views. Many of the principles set forth in the call for the Convention he deemed unobjectionable. But the formation of this new party would dissolve the old Union party, which had, in face of the prophecies of half the New and all the Old world, saved the government from demoralization and utter ruin. The scheme of this new party was, in his view, a distraction from the real and all-absorbing question of the moment—the acceptance or rejection by the people of the Congressional amendment. Being himself decidedly in favor of the amendment, he could not identify himself with an organization which ignored its importance and smothered its discussion. Postmaster General Dennison replied on July 11th by tendering his resignation, which was accepted by the President, who appointed A. W. Randall, of Wisconsin, to act as his successor. The causes given by Dennison for his resignation were his difference of opinion with the President in regard to the proposed amendment and the movement for the Philadelphia Convention. The attorney general soon after resigned, and was succeeded by Henry Stansberry, of Ohio. The Secretary of the Interior, Mr. Harlan, of Iowa, having been elected senator, resigned, and Orville H. Browning, of Ohio, was appointed in his stead.

And here let us pause for a moment to look at the various phases of the political situation which presented itself in the summer of 1866, just before the meeting of the Philadelphia Convention. In this connection the mistakes of the President or of Congress are not to be considered; for, even if we admit that Congress had erred as well as the President, these errors belonged to the past, and could not be reversed. It was evident that the conflict between the two departments of the government now admitted of no reconciliation. We are not now to consider how previously reconciliation could have been effected; it was not now possible. We must also concede both to the President and to Congress the constitutional right to act precisely as they had acted. Whatever want of tact there may have been on the part of either is not here a subject for consideration. Neither party to the conflict had been in the slightest degree guilty of any usurpation. We are to forget all extraneous and incidental considerations, and confine ourselves to the precise issue presented to the people. For the moment we are to banish both the President and Congress from a place in our thoughts, and weigh the two policies between which the people must decide. We must not forget, however, that the people had not been all this while a silent party to the contract. The President believed that his policy was supported by the people, and Congress had been restrained from the adoption of more radical measures by the fear that these would not obtain the popular assent. Both the President and Congress appealed to the people. And the issue presented was a very plain one: it was simply a question whether it should ignore the President and accept the Congressional amendment as a preliminary to the admission of Southern representatives, or ignore Congress and decide in favor of immediate representation on the President's plan.

It was a plain question. Either the policy of the President or that of Congress must receive the popular sanction. But, although the line drawn between the two policies was so clearly defined, the motives influencing the popular judgment were various and complex. The question resolved itself into one of expediency. Which plan, under the circumstances, ought to be adopted? Thus all mere theories were swept out of the arena of discussion. The issue was intensely practical, and pressed instantly for decision—neither time nor room was left for speculation. There were dangers to be avoided, there were benefits to be maintained and secured. Which plan most surely averted danger? Which secured the most lasting good?

The plea put in for each policy was strong, and urgently demanded careful and calm consideration. The advocates of the executive plan for restoration claimed that the war had a distinct purpose which had already been accomplished—the extinction of armed rebellion. Slavery also had been extinguished with rebellion. Thus the root and seed of all our strife had been removed. But, although the slave had departed, the negro remained. In many of the states the negro population at the close of the war exceeded the white. The two races would naturally abide together, for each needed the other. The white race needed the black for labor, not because it would not itself labor, but because of the extraordinary resources of the southern section of the country, which demanded for their full development not only all the white and black inhabitants already occupying it, but thousands upon thousands more who would come from the Northern States as immigrants, and from all the nations of Europe. The black race stood in no less need of the white, because the latter had intelligence in a greater degree, was used to the exercise of political power, and must therefore, of necessity, be the regulative and controlling race. Not regulative in the despotic sense, in which it had been hitherto as the task-masters over the black, but, because of its greater civilization, it was more competent to carry out the ends of civilization. To change this relation, to give the black race all the political mastery to which it might be entitled merely on the basis of numbers, would be to fight Nature, who gives sovereignty not to numbers, but to developed capacity. Such a revolution against Nature would necessarily put back the civilization of one half of the nation by a foolish surrender of power to ignorance or incompetency. We must trust to Nature, whose movements, if they are large in their cycles and slow of accomplishment, are nevertheless efficient. Before the war, Nature had already decreed the death of slavery, and the war itself had grown out of an attempt on the part of slaveholders to defy Nature; for they saw that slavery, restricted as it must be by the nation under the pressure of moral opinion, would

surely die. They said, therefore, we will resist the pressure; we will make a new nation, with slavery for the corner-stone; there shall be no restriction, and this peculiar institution shall live forever! They defied Nature, and were defeated; and the very institution which by revolution they hoped to save, was by revolution destroyed. By this revolution the society of the South was reduced back to first principles—to a new beginning. A new era was opened to labor, now emancipated. A period of transition was now commenced. Might we not trust to Nature, and to the new influences in operation, and to time for results? Labor, free, must have a destiny of its own. Intelligence must follow, and the development of political capacity in the masses. The revolution had been radical. All things were new, and must grow out of a new beginning. Might we not trust to this new growth? Would we not best help it on by an era of mutual trust and good feeling? Might not the North say to the South, "Work out your destiny for yourself under these new and better influences, and we will await with patience the result, and will not interfere?" Would not legislative interference, defying Nature, defeat its own purpose? Was it necessary to add to the changes produced by the war any change in the organic law beyond the declaration of the death of slavery? That dead, would not the new life of the South, under the new circumstances, develop satisfactory results?

Thus questioned and reasoned those, who, without partisan motives and from simple patriotism, supported the President's policy. Among the best representatives of this class was Rev. Henry Ward Beecher.

But to all this reasoning Congress, and the supporters of Congress, had a reply. It is true, said they, that we are to begin anew, and that we must largely trust to the working of Nature and the influences of time. But the South does not begin anew as a separate section, but as a part of a great nation. The responsibilities of the moment do not rest upon a part alone, but upon the whole. The whole nation is beginning anew, and not one section alone. The South does not stand by itself in this new era. The national Legislature, acting under the organic law—the Constitution—is the regulative power. The revolution which has taken place must be recognized here, in this Legislature, in this organic law. It is true that Nature is large in movement, slow, and in the end efficient. But Nature is sometimes diseased, abnormal in its action, and may be helped by remedies. The diseases of the past, the result of slavery, still cling to the ruling, regulative race in the South, and will injuriously affect not only Southern development, but the national growth. Labor in the South is emancipated, but, in those who control labor there, the oppressive spirit developed by slavery still remains. With this oppressive class, whose political power in the national councils is rather increased than diminished by the death of slavery, there is a party in the North at this moment ready to strike hands and unite in a treaty, offensive and defensive, for the control of the country. It is within our power, and is therefore a duty for which we are responsible, to avert this possible evil. So far as possible, we must start aright and upon correct principles on this new era upon which the nation is entering. We can not act arbitrarily, we can not exercise the power of despotism, but we can submit to the people such changes in the organic law of the nation as, if the people will ratify them, will establish the new nation upon a secure basis. We therefore submit to the people an amendment to the Constitution which will give to all citizens equal rights and equal representation, secure the repudiation of the rebel debt and the adoption of the national debt in good faith, and disable leading traitors for such time as we may deem expedient.

Such were the pleas in behalf of the Presidential and Congressional policies. And the appeal was to the people.

On the 14th of August the National Union Convention assembled at Philadelphia. Every state and Territory was represented excepting Arizona, Montana, and Utah. General John A. Dix was chosen temporary Chairman, and Senator Doolittle President. At the opening of the Convention quite a sensation was created by the entrance of the delegates from Massachusetts and South Carolina arm in arm. The Convention did its work rapidly. On the third day an address was read by Henry J. Raymond, and approved by the Convention, and resolutions were adopted, declaring that the rights, dignity, and authority of the states were perfect and unimpaired; that Congress had no right to deny representation to any state; that the right to regulate the elective franchise was reserved to the states; that amendments to the Constitution might be made in the usual way, and that in rectifying the same all the states of the Union had an equal and indefeasible right to a voice and a vote thereon; that slavery was abolished, and the enfranchised slaves should receive equal protection with other citizens in every right of person or property; that any debt incurred in the execution of rebellion was invalid, and that the national debt was sacred and inviolable; and that President Johnson was a chief magistrate worthy of the nation, and equal to the great crisis upon which his lot was cast.[1]

[1] "The National Union Convention now assembled in the city of Philadelphia, composed of delegates from every state and territory in the Union, admonished by the solemn lessons which, for the last five years, it has pleased the Supreme Ruler of the Universe to give to the American people; profoundly grateful for the return of peace; desirous, as are a large majority of their countrymen, in all sincerity, to forget and forgive the past; revering the Constitution as it comes to us from our ancestors; regarding the Union in its restoration as more sacred than ever; looking with deep anxiety into the future, as of instant and continuing trials, hereby issues and proclaims the following declaration of principles and purposes, on which they have, with perfect unanimity, agreed:

"1. We hail with gratitude to Almighty God the end of the war and the return of peace to our afflicted and beloved land.

"2. The war just closed has maintained the authority of the Constitution, with all the powers which it confers, and all the restrictions which it imposes upon the general government, unabridged and unaltered, and it has preserved the Union, with the equal rights, dignity, and authority of the states perfect and unimpaired.

"3. Representation in the Congress of the United States and in the electoral college is a right recognized by the Constitution as abiding in every state, and as a duty imposed upon the people, fundamental in its nature, and essential to the existence of our republican institutions, and neither

A committee was appointed to present to the President a copy of the proceedings of the Convention. Senator Reverdy Johnson acted as the representative of this committee. The President, in his reply, spoke of Congress as a body which was preventing the restoration of peace and harmony—a body which, pretending to be a Congress of the United States, but which was, in fact, a Congress of only part of the states—a body "hanging upon the verge of the government."

Other Conventions also were held. The Southern Loyalists' Convention met at Philadelphia on the 1st of September, and adopted resolutions in favor of the Congressional policy. On the 17th of September, the Convention of soldiers and sailors assembled at Cleveland, Ohio, and adopted resolutions of a similar character with those adopted by the Philadelphia Convention of August 14th. Of this Convention Major General Gordon Granger was President. On the 25th of September, a Convention of soldiers and sailors sustaining the action of Congress assembled at Pittsburg, Pennsylvania, and Major General J. D. Cox was elected President. A series of resolutions was reported by Major General B. F. Butler, of which the two following were the most characteristic:

"*Resolved,* That the President, as an executive officer, has no right to a policy as against the legislative department of the government. That his attempt to fasten his scheme of reconstruction upon the country is as dangerous as it is unwise; his acts in sustaining it have retarded the restoration of peace and unity; they have converted conquered rebels into impudent claimants to rights which they have desecrated. If consummated, it would render the sacrifices of the nation useless, the loss of the lives of our buried comrades vain, and the war in which we have so gloriously triumphed what his present friends at Chicago, in 1864, declared it to be, a failure.

"*Resolved,* That the right of the conqueror to legislate for the conquered has been recognized by the public law of all civilized nations. By the operation of that law for the conservation of the good of the whole country, Congress had the undoubted right to establish measures for the conduct of the revolted states, and to pass all acts of legislation that are necessary for the complete restoration of the Union."

In the mean time, an event had occurred which had created the most intense excitement throughout the country. In 1864, the Louisiana State Convention had made a new Constitution, and submitted it to the people of that state. This Constitution had been ratified. Among its provisions was one for its amendment, requiring that the proposition for amendment should proceed from the state Legislature. Two years had passed, and the Convention was dissatisfied with its own work, and had grown rabid for negro suffrage. It was no longer a legitimate organization after the ratification of its Constitution. It attempted, however, to revive itself; it obtained the support of Governor Wells, who appointed an election to secure delegates from the parishes not represented in the original Convention, and the 30th of July was appointed for the revival of the Convention. The plan proposed by this Convention involved the overturning of its own Constitution, which had already been sanctioned by the people. It was a revolutionary body. It is not wonderful that its scheme occasioned excitement. As if for the purpose of revolution and tumult, this Convention held a preliminary meeting in New Orleans, at which speeches were made appealing to the negroes to come forth in force for the protection of the Convention. The mayor of New Orleans at this time was John T. Monroe. His antecedents were not of a favorable character. In company with Lieutenant Governor Voorhees, he had waited upon General Absalom Baird, who, in the absence of Major General Sheridan, commanded the United States military force at New Orleans, to ascertain whether, if the members of the Convention were arrested, the military would interfere. General Baird's answer was, that the sheriff, attempting such an arrest, would himself be arrested; that the Convention, meeting peaceably, could not be interfered with by the officers of the law. But the Convention could not be said to have met peaceably, having directly provoked tumult. A telegram was sent to the President inquiring whether the process of the court to arrest the members could be thwarted by the military. The President replied that the military would sustain, and not interfere with the proceedings of the courts. The Convention met on the 30th, but there was not a quorum. Plainly either the majority of the members were timid, or were satisfied of the irregularity of the Convention. The negroes whom Dr. Dostie, a member of that body, had called forth in prospect of a conflict, were ready at the time appointed. The citizens of New Orleans were, on the other hand, also ready. The collision was inevitable. Just how the riot began is uncertain. But there is no question of the fact that both the negroes and the citizens were gathered together for no other purposes than those of strife. The result was disgraceful to the negroes, to the citizens, to the Convention, and to the New Orleans police, whose brutality can scarcely be distinguished from murder.[1]

This occurrence was made use of by both parties as political capital. The supporters of Congress pointed to it as an indication of the disloyalty of the Southern people, and the Democrats, on the other hand, held up the revolutionary Convention as an example of radical violence. The prevailing popular impression acquitted the negroes of any desire to disturb the peace, and threw the blame partly upon the Convention, which, by the incendiary speech of at least one of its members, had incited tumult; but chiefly upon the white citizens of New Orleans, who had been organized for a riot, and who had met at a preconcerted signal for the purpose of violently dispersing the Convention. The mayor, John T. Monroe, was supposed to be on the side of the rioters, and was held by General Sheridan to be largely responsible for their action. President Johnson suffered much loss in the people's estimation from his support of Mayor Monroe hitherto, but he can not be held consciously responsible for the violence of July 30th.

On the 28th of August President Johnson left Washington for Chicago, to be present at the laying of the corner-stone of a monument to be erected to the memory of Stephen A. Douglas. He was accompanied by Secretaries Seward and Welles, by General Grant and Admiral Farragut. In all the cities through which the President passed, he was accorded that courteous welcome which the people are always ready to extend to their chief magistrate. His speeches on the route were full of the most bitter denunciation of Congress, which he described as a body hanging upon the verge of the government. In some cases he descended to bandy words with a crowd, and to answer ill-tempered jeers at himself by an echo of their bad temper. His utter lack of tact disgusted even his friends. He too clearly proved that, whatever might be the merits of his policy, he could not be safely trusted as leader with any policy. As Henry Ward Beecher soon afterward aptly said, "The greatest obstacle to the success of Andrew Johnson's policy is Andrew Johnson."

The autumn elections of 1866 were now at hand. The President, sure of Democratic support, desired also to retain a good portion of the Republican vote. His especial favorites—those who received the largest share of his patronage, were Republicans of the Philadelphia Convention school. But the defection from the Republican ranks caused by the Philadelphia Convention movement was not large. The old Union party still maintained its ranks unbroken, and refused to be distracted from the main issue—the Congressional amendment to the Constitution. The national executive committee, which had been appointed in 1864, held its regular meeting at Philadelphia. Governor Marcus L. Wood, of New Jersey, was elected chairman. The places on that committee of Henry J. Raymond, and others who had participated in the Philadelphia Convention, were filled, and an address was issued to the people calling upon them to support the Congressional plan of restoration.

The late riots in New Orleans, the President's tour to the tomb of Douglas, the attempt of the President to influence the prospective elections by the distribution of patronage to his special adherents, and his evident determination to use Democrats, pardoned rebels, and every possible available element to carry out his policy, tended to consolidate the Republican party in opposition. Another circumstance which conduced to this result was the fact that the nominees of the so-called Conservatives were in most cases men in whom the Union party of the country had no confidence.

The popular vote was decidedly in favor of the Congressional policy. In Maine, Chamberlain, the Republican candidate, was elected over Pillsbury

---

Congress nor the general government has any authority or power to deny this right to any state, or to withhold its enjoyment under the Constitution from the people thereof.

"4. We call upon the people of the United States to elect to Congress as members thereof none but men who admit this fundamental right of representation, and who will receive to seats therein loyal representatives from every state in allegiance to the United States, subject to the constitutional right of each house to judge of the elections, returns, and qualification of its own members.

"5. The Constitution of the United States, and the laws made in pursuance thereof, are the supreme law of the land, any thing in the Constitution or laws of any state to the contrary notwithstanding. All the powers not conferred by the Constitution upon the general government, nor prohibited by it to the states, are reserved to the states, or to the people thereof; and among the rights thus reserved to the states is the right to prescribe qualifications for the elective franchise therein, with which right Congress can not interfere. No state or combination of states has the right to withdraw from the Union, or to exclude, through their action in Congress or otherwise, any other state or states from the Union. The Union of these states is perpetual.

"6. Such amendments to the Constitution of the United States may be made by the people thereof as they may deem expedient, but only in the mode pointed out by its provisions; and in proposing such amendments, whether by Congress or by a Convention, and in ratifying the same, all the states of the Union have an equal and indefeasible right to a voice and a vote thereon.

"7. Slavery is abolished and forever prohibited, and there is neither desire nor purpose on the part of the Southern States that it should ever be re-established upon the soil, or within the jurisdiction of the United States; and the enfranchised slaves in all the states of the Union should receive, in common with all their inhabitants, equal protection in every right of person and property.

"8. While we regard as utterly invalid, and never to be assumed or made of binding force, any obligations incurred or undertaken in making war against the United States, we hold the debt of the nation to be sacred and inviolable; and we proclaim our purpose in discharging this, as in performing all other national obligations, to maintain unimpaired and unimpeached the honor and faith of the republic.

"9. It is the duty of the national government to recognize the services of the Federal soldiers and sailors in the contest just closed, by meeting promptly and fully all their just and rightful claims for the services they have rendered the nation, and by extending to those of them who have survived, and to the widows and orphans of those who have fallen, the most generous and considerate care.

"10. In Andrew Johnson, President of the United States, who, in his great office, has proved steadfast in his devotion to the Constitution, the laws, and interests of his country, unmoved by persecution and undeserved reproach, having faith unassailable in the people and in the principles of free government, we recognize a chief magistrate worthy of the nation, and equal to the great crisis upon which his lot is cast; and we tender to him, in the discharge of his high and responsible duties, our profound respect, and assurance of our cordial and sincere support."

[1] The views of General Sheridan, in military command of the Department, are expressed in the following dispatches:

"New Orleans, August 1, 1866.

"U. S. GRANT, General:

"You are doubtless aware of the serious riot which occurred in this city on the 30th. A political body, styling itself the Convention of 1864, met on the 30th, for, as it is alleged, the purpose of remodeling the present Constitution of the state. The leaders were political agitators and revolutionary men, and the action of the Convention was liable to produce breaches of the public peace. I had made up my mind to arrest the head men if the proceedings of the Convention were calculated to disturb the tranquillity of the Department, but I had no cause for action until they committed the overt act. In the mean time official duty called me to Texas, and the mayor of the city, during my absence, suppressed the Convention by the use of the police force, and, in doing so, attacked the members of the Convention and a party of two hundred negroes with fire-arms, clubs, and knives, in a manner so unnecessary and atrocious as to compel me to say that it was murder. About forty whites and blacks were thus killed, and about one hundred and sixty wounded. Every thing is now quiet, but I deem it best to maintain a military supremacy in the city for a few days, until the affair is fully investigated. I believe the sentiment of the general community is great regret at this unnecessary cruelty, and that the police could have made any arrrest they saw fit without sacrificing lives.   P. H. SHERIDAN, Major General Commanding.

"New Orleans, Louisiana, August 2, 1866.

"U. S. GRANT, General, Washington, D. C.:

"The more information I obtain of the affair of the 30th in this city, the more revolting it becomes. It was no riot; it was an absolute massacre by the police, which was not excelled in murderous cruelty by that of Fort Pillow. It was a murder which the mayor and police of the city perpetrated without the shadow of a necessity. Furthermore, I believe it was premeditated, and every indication points to this. I recommend the removing of this bad man. I believe it would be hailed with the sincerest gratification by two thirds of the population of the city. There has been a feeling of insecurity on the part of the people here on account of this man, which is now so much increased that the safety of life and property does not rest with the civil authorities, but with the military.   P. H. SHERIDAN, Major General Commanding."

by twenty-seven thousand votes, and every Republican delegate to Congress was chosen by a considerable majority. In New Hampshire, the Republican majority for Governor Smyth over Sinclair was nearly 5000. In Connecticut, the Republican candidate, General Joseph R. Hawley, was elected over English by a few hundred votes. General Burnside was chosen Governor of Rhode Island by a majority of over 5000. Alexander H. Bullock, in Massachusetts, received a majority over Sweetser of over 65,000. Among the members elected to the state Legislature were two colored men. In Vermont, Paul Dillingham received a majority of nearly 23,000 over Davenport, the Democratic candidate for governor. In New Jersey, out of five members elected to the Fortieth Congress, three were Republican. In New York, Governor Fenton was elected over Hoffman, the Democratic candidate, by a majority of nearly 14,000. In Delaware, Saulsbury, the Democratic candidate for governor, was elected by some 1200 votes. In Kentucky, the election was not for the principal officers, but the Democratic majority was about 38,000. In California, a judge of the Supreme Court was elected by the Republican party by a majority of 7000. In Oregon, the Republican majority for Woods as governor was 327. In Ohio, the Republican majority for secretary of state was nearly 43,000. In Indiana also a Republican secretary was elected by 14,000 majority. Kansas gave a Republican majority for Crawford, as governor, of over 11,000. In Iowa, the Republican majority for secretary of state was over 35,000. In Pennsylvania, Major General Geary, the Republican candidate, was elected governor over Heister Clymer by 17,000 majority. In Michigan, Crapo, Republican candidate for governor, was elected over Williams by a majority of 29,000. Minnesota elected Republican representatives to Congress by about 10,000 majority. In Illinois, General John A. Logan was elected Congressman at large over Dickey by nearly 56,000. Wisconsin gave a Republican majority of 24,000 for Congressmen.

From this estimate, it is clear that the people repudiated the President's policy, and by overwhelming majorities in nearly all the states supported Congress. This was not more decisively shown in the election of state officers than in the vote for members of the Fortieth Congress.

From this point a new stage in the reconstruction movement commenced. The antagonism of the President was still continued against Congress, notwithstanding the popular decision in favor of the Congressional amendment. The Southern States still refused to accept the conditions submitted by Congress and supported by the loyal people. Thus there was a dead-lock in the process of restoration. There were then two methods of procedure. Either Congress and the whole country could wait until the Southern States should accept the amendment, or they could take the whole affair into their own hands, and decide arbitrarily that the movement should go on, and upon what conditions. Congress adopted the latter method. Just before the close of its second session, the Thirty-ninth Congress passed an act known as the Military Bill. This act declared that no legal state governments existed in the late rebel states (excluding Tennessee), and that in these states there was no adequate protection for life or property. These states were therefore distributed into military districts, subject to the military authority of the United States, as follows:

I. Virginia.
II. North Carolina and South Carolina.
III. Georgia, Alabama, and Florida.
IV. Mississippi and Arkansas.
V. Louisiana and Texas.

The President was to appoint as a commander of each district an officer of the army not below the rank of brigadier general, and to detail a sufficient military force to enable such officer to perform his duties and enforce his authority.

The duties of these commanders were—to protect all persons in their rights of person and property, to suppress insurrection, disorder, and violence, and to punish, or cause to be punished, all disturbers of the public peace and criminals. To this end they might allow local civil tribunals to take jurisdiction of and try offenders, or, at their discretion, might organize military commissions for the trial of offenders, and this exercise of military authority should exclude interference on the part of the state government. No sentence of death should be carried into effect without the approval of the President.

The fifth section of this act provided that when the people of any of these states should have formed a Constitution in conformity with the Constitution of the United States in all respects, and which should be framed by delegates elected by the male citizens of said state 21 years old and upward, "of whatever race, color, or previous condition, resident in the state for one year, excepting those disfranchised for participation in rebellion," and when such Constitution should provide for universal suffrage, with the exception of those disfranchised for participation in rebellion, and be ratified by the people and approved by Congress, and the Congressional amendment should have been adopted, the said state should be admitted to representation in Congress.

The sixth section of the bill provided that until this admission of representatives to Congress the civil government of each state should be considered as provisional only.

The President vetoed this bill, and it was passed over his veto by both houses March 2, 1867. He then, in obedience to the act thus passed against his remonstrance, appointed Brevet Major General John M. Schofield, commander of the First District; Major General Daniel E. Sickles, commander of the Second; Major General Pope, commander of the Third; Major General E. O. C. Ord, commander of the Fourth; and Major General Philip H. Sheridan, commander of the Fifth.

The Fortieth Congress assembled on the 4th of March, 1867, immediately succeeding and receiving the mantle of the Thirty-ninth. Soon after its assembling it passed an act supplementary to the Military Bill adopted at the previous session. This supplementary act provided in detail for the registration of voters.[1] It was vetoed by the President, and then passed over the veto by each house.

The supplementary act was vetoed as the original act had been, but was on the 23d of March passed, notwithstanding the President's objections.[2]

---

[1] *An Act supplementary to an Act entitled "An Act to Provide for the more efficient Government of the Rebel States," passed March 2d, 1867, and to facilitate Restoration.*

"Be it enacted by the Senate and House of Representatives of the United States of America, in Congress assembled, That before the first day of September, 1867, the commanding general in each district defined by an act entitled 'An Act to Provide for the more efficient Government of the Rebel States,' passed March 2d, 1867, shall cause a registration to be made of the male citizens of the United States, twenty-one years of age and upward, resident in each county or parish in the state or states included in his district, which registration shall include only those persons who are qualified to vote for delegates by the act aforesaid, and who shall have taken and subscribed the following oath or affirmation: 'I, ——, do solemnly swear (or affirm), in the presence of Almighty God, that I am a citizen of the State of ——; that I have resided in said state for — months next preceding this day, and now reside in the county of ——, or the parish of ——, in said state (as the case may be); that I am twenty-one years old; that I have not been disfranchised for participation in any rebellion or civil war against the United States, nor for felony committed against the laws of any state or of the United States; that I have never been a member of any state Legislature, nor held any executive or judicial office in any state, and afterward engaged in insurrection or rebellion against the United States, or given aid or comfort to the enemies thereof; that I have never taken an oath as a member of Congress of the United States, or as an officer of the United States, or as a member of any state Legislature, or as an executive or judicial officer of any state, to support the Constitution of the United States, and afterward engaged in insurrection or rebellion against the United States, or given aid or comfort to the enemies thereof; that I will faithfully support the Constitution and obey the laws of the United States, and will, to the best of my ability, encourage others so to do: so help me God;' which oath or affirmation may be administered by any registering officer.

"Sec. 2. And be it further enacted, That after the completion of the registration hereby provided for in any state, at such time and places therein as the commanding general shall appoint and direct, of which at least thirty days' public notice shall be given, an election shall be held of delegates to a Convention for the purpose of establishing a Constitution and civil government for such state loyal to the Union, said Convention in each state, except Virginia, to consist of the same number of members as the most numerous branch of the state Legislature of such state in the year 1860, to be apportioned among the several districts, counties, or parishes of such state by the commanding general, giving each representation in the ratio of voters registered as aforesaid as nearly as may be. The Convention in Virginia shall consist of the same number of members as represented the territory now constituting Virginia in the most numerous branch of the Legislature of said state in the year 1860, to be apportioned as aforesaid.

"Sec. 3. And be it further enacted, That at said election the registered voters of each state shall vote for or against a Convention to form a Constitution therefor under this act. Those voting in favor of such a Convention shall have written or printed on the ballots by which they vote for delegates as aforesaid the words 'For a Convention,' and those voting against such a Convention shall have written or printed on such ballot the words 'Against a Convention.' The persons appointed to superintend said election, and to make return of the votes given thereat, as herein provided, shall count and make return of the votes given for and against a Convention; and the commanding general to whom the same shall have been returned shall ascertain and declare the total vote in each state for and against a Convention. If a majority of the votes given on that question shall be for a Convention, then such Convention shall be held as hereinafter provided; but if a majority of said votes shall be against a Convention, then no such Convention shall be held under this act: Provided, That such Convention shall not be held unless a majority of all such registered voters shall have voted on the question of holding such Convention.

"Sec. 4. And be it further enacted, That the commanding general of each district shall appoint as many boards of registration as may be necessary, consisting of three loyal officers or persons, to make and complete the registration, superintend the election, and make return to him of the votes, list of voters, and of the persons elected as delegates by a plurality of the votes cast at said election; and upon receiving said returns he shall open the same, ascertain the persons elected as delegates, according to the returns of the officers who conducted said election, and make proclamation thereof; and if a majority of the votes given on that question shall be for a Convention, the commanding general, within sixty days from the date of election, shall notify the delegates to assemble in Convention, at a time and place to be mentioned in the notification, and said Convention, when organized, shall proceed to frame a Constitution and civil government according to the provisions of this act, and the act to which it is supplementary; and when the same shall have been so framed, said Constitution shall be submitted by the Convention for ratification to the persons registered under the provisions of this act at an election to be conducted by the officers or persons appointed or to be appointed by the commanding general, as hereinbefore provided, and to be held after the expiration of thirty days from the date of notice thereof, to be given by said Convention; and the returns thereof shall be made to the commanding general of the district.

"Sec. 5. And be it further enacted, That if, according to said returns, the Constitution shall be ratified by a majority of the votes of the registered electors qualified as herein specified, cast at said election, at least one half of all the registered voters voting upon the question of such ratification, the president of the Convention shall transmit a copy of the same, duly certified, to the President of the United States, who shall forthwith transmit the same to Congress, if then in session, and if not in session, then immediately upon its next assembling; and if it shall moreover appear to Congress that the election was one at which all the registered and qualified electors in the state had an opportunity to vote freely, and without restraint, fear, or the influence of fraud, and if the Congress shall be satisfied that such Constitution meets the approval of a majority of all the qualified electors in the state, and if the said Constitution shall be declared by Congress to be in conformity with the provisions of the act to which this is supplementary, and the other provisions of said act shall have been complied with, and the said Constitution shall be approved by Congress, the state shall be declared entitled to representation, and senators and representatives shall be admitted therefrom as therein provided.

"Sec. 6. And be it further enacted, That all elections in the states mentioned in the said 'Act to Provide for the more efficient Government of the Rebel States' shall, during the operation of said act, be by ballot; and all officers making the said registration of voters and conducting said elections shall, before entering upon the discharge of their duties, take and subscribe the oath prescribed by the act approved July 2d, 1862, entitled 'An Act to prescribe an Oath of Office:' Provided, That if any person shall knowingly and falsely take and subscribe any oath in this act prescribed, such person so offending and being thereof duly convicted shall be subject to the pains, penalties, and disabilities which by law are provided for the punishment of the crime of willful and corrupt perjury.

"Sec. 7. And be it further enacted, That all expenses incurred by the several commanding generals, or by virtue of any orders issued, or appointments made by them, under or by virtue of this act, shall be paid out of any moneys in the treasury not otherwise appropriated.

"Sec. 8. And be it further enacted, That the Convention for each state shall prescribe the fees, salary, and compensation to be paid to all delegates and other officers and agents herein authorized or necessary to carry into effect the purposes of this act not herein otherwise provided for, and shall provide for the levy and collection of such taxes on the property in such state as may be necessary to pay the same.

"Sec. 9. And be it further enacted, That the word 'article,' in the sixth section of the act to which this is supplementary, shall be construed to mean 'section.'"

[2] To the original bill President Johnson objected on the following grounds:

1. That "the mass of the Southern people, while they entertain diverse opinions on questions of federal policy, are completely united in the effort to reorganize their society on the basis of peace, and to restore their mutual prosperity as rapidly and completely as the circumstances of the case will permit."

2. The military rule established by the bill is "to be used, not for any purpose of order or for the prevention of crime, but solely as a means of coercing the people into the adoption of principles and measures to which it is known that they are opposed, and upon which they have an undeniable right to exercise their own judgment." Thus it was in "palpable conflict with the plainest provisions of the Constitution."

3. The power given by the bill "is that of an absolute monarch, his mere will taking the place of all law; it places at his free disposal all the lands and goods in his district; and he may distribute them to whom he pleases; he may make a criminal code of his own, and he may make it as bloody as any recorded in history, or he may reserve the privilege of acting upon the impulse of his private humors in each case that occurs. . . . . It is plain that the authority here given to the military officer amounts to absolute despotism. But, to make it still more unendurable, the bill provides that it may be delegated to as many subordinates as he chooses to appoint; for it declares that he shall 'punish or cause to be punished.' Such a power has not been wielded in England for more than 500 years. . . . . It reduces the whole population of the ten states—all per-

The President's objections to both the original and the supplementary acts were theoretically just; but, for all that, they did not touch the question as it offered itself to Congress. He could see in the establishment of military power and the suffrage given to the blacks only three things: a design on the part of the Republican party to perpetuate its own power; an absolute despotism; and a violation of the Constitution. There may have been, and probably were, a few members in both houses of Congress who were partisans in the sense that they preferred the success of their party to the interests of their country; there may have been those who lightly regarded constitutional liberty and constitutional law; but this was not the light in which Congress, as a body, looked upon the situation which confronted it. An appeal had been made to the people of the Northern States, and the result had been a Congressional victory. An opportunity had already been afforded to the Southern States to regain their representation in Congress by doing exactly what Tennessee had done—*i. e.*, by accepting a Constitutional amendment, which involved no imposition upon them of negro suffrage, nor indeed any conditions not really demanded by the situation at the close of the war. But they had rejected the advances of Congress, and stood defiantly upon "their rights" as interpreted for them by Andrew Johnson. The work of restoration could not, then, proceed upon the plan originally proposed by Congress. But the work must go on upon some plan. Either the people must surrender to the President against their own good sense, by reverting to his plan, now that their own had failed, or they must adopt still another. And what other was possible? Only one; and that was to appeal from the whites of the South to the whole people, white and black. In order to do this, it was necessary to give the negroes of the South the privilege of voting for Conventions in the several states. This plan evidently could not be carried into execution except under the supervision of military commanders. We are not, however, in vindicating the necessity of the Military Bill, defending every feature of that bill. Undoubtedly it would have been better if Congress had omitted that provision by which so large a portion of Southern whites were disfranchised. This provision was not essential in order to secure the objects sought.

It must indeed be admitted that the Military Bill was unconstitutional. But so in a greater or less degree had been every measure in the entire process of reconstruction, whether adopted by the President or by Congress. Lincoln's Emancipation Proclamation was unconstitutional, and was only defensible on the plea of military necessity. But the necessities of war are no more binding than those of peace. The object of the war was to conquer peace; and after the war there still remained the no less difficult work of securing the peace which had been conquered. Was the security of the conquest any less important than the conquest itself? Lincoln issued his proclamation after long hesitation and with evident reluctance. But he stood face to face with a great necessity, and was compelled to act. The deliberations of the Thirty-ninth Congress in 1866 show that that body was equally reluctant to interfere directly with the right of states to regulate their own system of franchise. But the necessity came, and came as the result of the attitude assumed by the Southern people. Congress yielded, as Mr. Lincoln had done.

At first the bill did not strike the South unfavorably. This is probably to be accounted for by the fact that the political leaders of the South anticipated that the votes of the freedmen could easily be regulated by their former masters. Every attempt was made to influence the freedmen in this direction. Thus General Wade Hampton said to them,[1] "Give your friends at the South a fair trial; when they fail you will be time enough to go abroad for sympathy; it is for your interest to build up the South, for as the country prospers you will prosper." Similar arguments were used in every Southern state. Disfranchised white men addressed assemblages mainly composed of enfranchised blacks. But they did not hold the field alone, else their success might have been assured. Several Northern men traversed the South, and urged the freedmen to act with the Republican party. Prominent among these were Senator Wilson, of Massachusetts, and Mr. Kelley, representative from Pennsylvania. Their speeches were moderate in tone, but very effective. White men attended these meetings, apparently willing that both parties should have a fair chance in this contest for the negro vote. There was a slight disturbance in Mobile, in which Mr. Kelley was placed in some peril; but in New Orleans, at a meeting addressed by Senator Wilson, the Confederate General Longstreet was one of the Vice-Presidents. Whatever may have been the hopes entertained by the Southern whites as to the possibility of securing the support by the freedmen of what was termed the Conservative policy, they were not realized. So soon as it became evident that the negroes would support Congress, there began to be developed a bitter opposition to the Military Bill, both in the South and among those in the North who supported Mr. Johnson. Very many, also, who were opposed to Johnson's policy, thought that the disfranchisement of so many whites in the South, and the evident purpose shown by those who controlled registration to give political supremacy to the blacks, were not only unnecessary, but also injurious to the Republican party.

Although President Johnson had protested so strongly against the establishment of military governments, yet after the passage of the Congressional acts he proceeded promptly to their execution. Even in the appointment of the military commanders he seems to have sought just those officers in the army which would be most likely to meet the approbation of Congress. In the case of General Sheridan particularly, the President feared that the conduct of that officer might be needlessly arbitrary. Still he yielded to the popular sentiment in favor of the general, and gave him the most difficult of the five military districts. The President sought, however, in every possible way, to regulate the operations of the military government in such a manner as to relieve those features which were most obnoxious. But the legislation of Congress left him a very limited sphere of action. He could not prevent the subordination of the civil governments of the South to the military commanders; the provisions of the original Military Bill were explicit on that point, and could not be avoided. On the same day that this bill was finally passed, the Tenure of Office Bill was also passed over the President's veto. The provisions of this bill, by limiting his authority in making official appointments, almost entirely deprived him of the power to check any proceedings, however arbitrary, on the part of the military commanders; it took from him the power of removing even the members of his cabinet except by and with the consent of the Senate. Indeed, more executive power was delegated to each of the military commanders than was left to the executive head of the government.

Thus cramped and fettered by Congress, the President had recourse to Mr. Stansberry, his attorney general. Was there no way in which the executive might lay his hand upon the registration of voters in the South, and prevent the sweeping disfranchisement contemplated by Congress? Stansberry thought there was. Surely the legal opinion of the highest legal officer in the nation ought to avail somewhat. So the attorney general gave an opinion—and a very ingenious and elaborate opinion it was, we must admit.[1] The most important point in this opinion is the statement that the

sons, of every color, sex, and condition, and every stranger within their limits—to the most abject and degrading slavery. No master ever had a control over his slaves so absolute as this bill gives to the military officers over both white and colored persons."

4. The bill is unconstitutional in conferring the right of suffrage upon the freedmen. "The negroes have not asked for the privilege of voting; the vast majority of them have no idea what it means. This bill not only thrusts it into their hands, but compels them, as well as the whites, to use it in a particular way. If they do not form a Constitution with prescribed articles in it, and afterward elect a Legislature which will act upon certain measures in a prescribed way, neither blacks nor whites can be relieved from the slavery which the bill imposes upon them. Without pausing here to consider the policy or impolicy of Africanizing the southern part of our territory, I would simply ask the attention of Congress to that manifest, well-known, and universally-acknowledged rule of constitutional law which declares that the federal government has no jurisdiction, authority, or power to regulate such subjects for any state. To force the right of suffrage out of the hands of the white people and into the hands of the negroes is an arbitrary violation of this principle."

5. "We should remember that all men are entitled to at least a hearing in the councils which decide upon the destiny of themselves and their children. At present ten states are denied representation; and when the Fortieth Congress assembles on the 4th day of the present month, sixteen states will be without a voice in the House of Representatives. This grave fact, with the important question before us, should induce us to pause in a course of legislation which, looking solely to the attainment of political ends, fails to consider the rights which it transgresses, the law which it violates, or the institutions which it imperils."

The veto to the supplementary act reiterates the objections to the original bill, and adds some others. "By the oath required at registration," says the President, "every elector must decide for himself, under peril of military punishment if he makes a mistake, whether he has been disfranchised for participation in rebellion. . . . . Almost every man—the negro as well as the white—above 21 years of age, who was resident in the ten states during the rebellion, voluntarily or involuntarily, at some time and in some way, did participate in resistance to the lawful authority of the general government." Besides, urges the President, as the people themselves have no voice in conducting the registration and the subsequent election, the Conventions elected can not be considered as representing the citizens of those states.

[1] At Columbia, South Carolina, March 18.

[1] The principal points are as follows: 1. All who are registered, and none others, have the right to vote. 2. No one who is not a citizen of the United States, and of the special state, can properly take the oath; but if an alien not naturalized chooses, he can take it, and mnst be registered; but "he takes it at his peril, and is liable to prosecution for perjury." 3. The person who applies for registry must be of the age of twenty-one years when he applies; but the requirement for a residence of one year applies to the time of voting, not of registration.

He next proceeds to consider the various grounds of disfranchisement provided for in the bills. In his opinion, (4), the sections which "deny the right to vote to such as may be disfranchised for participation in the rebellion or felony at common law," must be interpreted to mean that "the mere fact of such participation, or the commission of the felonious act, does not of itself work as a disfranchisement. It must be ascertained by the judgment of a court, or by a legislative act, passed by competent authority." But the applicant for registration must swear that "I have never been a member of any state Legislature, nor held any executive or judicial office, and afterward engaged in insurrection or rebellion against the United States; that I have never taken an oath as a member of the Congress of the United States, or as an officer of the United States, or as a member of any state Legislature, or as an executive or judicial officer of any state, to support the Constitution of the United States, and afterward engaged in insurrection or rebellion against the United States." This provision, in the opinion of the attorney general, certainly excludes (5) members of Congress, of state Legislatures, and of Conventions which passed ordinances of secession. Then as to who are to be considered as intended by executive and judicial officers of the state, he gives his opinion that (6) officers of the militia of a state are not as such intended; that (7) governors, state treasurers, and others, commonly designated as "state officers," who "exercise executive functions at the seat of government," and also judicial officers whose jurisdiction extends through the state, are included; but that (8) those functionaries commonly known as "county, township, and precinct officers," sheriffs, county judges, commissioners of public works and improvements, and the like, are not included.

Under the provision working disfranchisement on account of the person having taken an oath to support the Constitution, and afterward engaged in insurrection, he holds that (9) the two things must concur, and "in the order of time mentioned: First, the office and the oath; and afterward engaging in the rebellion or giving aid and comfort." Hence (10) "a person who has held an office within the meaning of this law, and taken the official oath, and who has not afterward participated in the rebellion; and so too the person who has fully participated in the rebellion, but has not prior thereto held an office and taken the official oath, may with safety take the oath" required for registration.

The attorney general then proceeds to consider "what acts, within the meaning of the law, make a party guilty of engaging in insurrection or rebellion against the United States, or of giving aid or comfort to the enemies thereof?" As to official acts, he thinks that the phrase "enemies," to whom "aid and comfort" has been given, should in strict law be limited to mean only "foreign enemies;" but he adds, (11), "I am not quite prepared to say that Congress may not have used it as applicable to the late rebellion," and therefore he goes on to inquire "what is meant by engaging in insurrection or rebellion against the United States?" It implies, he thinks, (12), "active rather than passive conduct, voluntary rather than compulsory action." Hence it does not include (13) such cases as that of a person who has been forced into the ranks by conscription, or a slave who, by command of his master, or by military order, has been engaged upon military works or served in the ranks of the army. But (14) it does include many who, without having actually been in arms, were engaged in the furtherance of the common unlawful purpose, such as "members of Congress and rebel Conventions, diplomatic agents of the rebel Confederacy, or such other officials whose duties more especially appertained to the support of the rebel cause." Yet, on the other hand, it does not (15) include "officers in the rebel states who, during the rebellion, discharged duties not incident to the war. The interests of humanity," the attorney general argues, "require such officers for the performance of such official duties in time of war or insurrection as well as in time of peace, and the performance of such duties can never be considered as criminal."

From official participation the attorney general goes on to discuss what constitutes, in the view of this law, individual participation in the rebellion, premising that in the case of a great insurrection, which for a time excluded the people from the protection of the lawful government, the "obligations of allegiance are necessarily modified," and that many things should be considered as "rightfully done which in the case of a mere local insurrection would have no color of legality." He concludes, therefore, (16), that "some direct overt act, done with the intent to further the rebellion, is necessary to bring the party within the purview and meaning of the law." The expression of disloyal sentiments, the performance of acts of ordinary charity and humanity, the payment of taxes or forced contributions and the like, are not sufficient. But (17) "voluntary contributions in furtherance of the rebellion, or subscriptions to the rebel loan, and even organized contributions of food and clothing or necessary supplies, except of a strictly sanitary character, are to be classed with acts which disqualify."

mere fact of participation in the rebellion does not of itself work disfranchisement, except as it had been declared to have that effect by the judgment of a court or by a legislative act passed by competent authority. The attorney general also construed the Military Bill as not intending the disfranchisement of those who had held minor executive offices of a local nature under the Confederate government, nor those who had not *voluntarily* engaged in rebellion. He declared also that, under the law, registering officers could not refuse to permit every applicant to take the oath required; and that the oath once taken, and the applicant's name once registered, the privilege of voting could not be withdrawn.

Invested with this legal authority, President Johnson issued an order to each of the military commanders, directing them to conform to the opinion of the attorney general. The value of a legal opinion had such an impression upon the President that he shortly afterward obtained another from the same source, the purport of which was that the military commanders had no right to remove civil officers, and that therefore Mr. Wells, whom Sheridan had removed, was still the rightful governor of Louisiana, and John T. Monroe (also removed by the same officer) was mayor of New Orleans.

Congress met again July 4, and continued in session for sixteen days. In this brief period a new bill was matured and passed, defining the military acts of the two previous sessions.[1] This explanatory act completely annulled the attorney general's opinions, and left no room for doubt as to the intentions of Congress in its plan of Southern reconstruction. The President returned the bill with his objections July 19. In this veto message he denounced with equal bitterness the despotic powers conferred upon military commanders, and the limitations imposed, against the manifest intent of the Constitution, upon the executive.[2] The bill was passed over Johnson's veto.

But the President did not relinquish his claim to the authority which he conceived rightfully belonged to him as the executive head of the nation. Scarcely had Congress adjourned when he addressed a note[1] to Secretary Stanton, stating that "grave public considerations" constrained him to request the secretary's resignation. Mr. Stanton replied, "Grave public considerations constrain me to continue in the office of Secretary of War until the next meeting of Congress." The secretary had originally co-operated with the President's plan of Southern restoration, but after the elections of 1866 he went over to Congress. His position in the cabinet thus became very embarrassing. He could not resign his position without disappointing Congress, and, as he believed, the people; nor could he retain the secretaryship without violating the hitherto well understood principles of official courtesy. But Johnson relieved him of his embarrassment on the 12th of August by removing him, ordering General Grant to assume the duties of acting Secretary of War. Stanton then submitted, "under protest," as he said, "to the superior force of the President." The general satisfaction of the people with the administration of the war office by General Grant soon reconciled them to the change, and the President's palpable defiance of the Tenure of Office Bill was for a time substantially ignored.

Five days after the removal of Secretary Stanton, the President drew up an order removing General Sheridan from the command of the Fifth Military District, and appointing General Thomas in his stead. This did not meet with General Grant's approbation. The general boldly defended Sheridan on the ground that the military district was the most difficult one in the South to manage; that this difficulty had grown out of the prevailing impression among the people of that district that the President was about to remove Sheridan; and that, under these circumstances, General Sheridan had been compelled to resort to the arbitrary measures which the President disapproved. General Grant also objected to the change as being an impolitic one at the time. But the President insisted; Grant submitted, and the order was issued on the 26th. General Thomas declined the appointment, and General Hancock finally assumed the important office from which Sheridan had been removed.

Almost simultaneously, General Sickles was removed from the command of the Second District, embracing North and South Carolina, and General Canby was appointed in his stead. The removals of Stanton, Sheridan, and Sickles, following each other in quick succession, excited considerable apprehension in the North, which was exaggerated by flying rumors that the President was now prepared to resist Congress by force, that Maryland militia were being trained for his support, and that the country was on the verge of a *coup d'etat*. Indeed, it was impossible to say what thunderbolts the President was *not* prepared to fulminate against the legislative department of the government. The autumn elections were at hand, in which a second appeal was to be made to the people, and these popular fears were used by Republican orators as an argument for the support of Congress and its military reconstruction enactments.

The results of the autumn elections of 1867 were a surprise to the Republican party. In California, on the 4th of September, the Democratic candidate for governor was elected by a majority of 7466 over both the opposing Republican candidates; a Democratic Legislature was also elected, involving the loss of a Republican United States senator. Five days later, the Maine election resulted in a falling off from Republican majority of 14,000 votes. On the 8th of October elections took place in Pennsylvania, Ohio, Indiana, Iowa, and West Virginia. In Pennsylvania there was a Republican loss of 18,000 as compared with the previous year. Ohio elected a Republican governor, but lost so largely in the Legislature as to secure a Democratic United States senator at the expiration of Benjamin F. Wade's term. There was a Republican loss in that state of 40,000 votes. In Indiana only local officers were elected. In Iowa there was a Republican loss of over 10,000. On the 5th of November, elections were held in New York, New Jersey, Massachusetts, Maryland, Illinois, Wisconsin, Minnesota, and Kansas, and with similar results. In New York, a Democratic secretary of state was elected by a majority of 48,922. There was in that state a Republican loss of over 62,000 votes. In Massachusetts, Governor Bullock, Republican, was re-elected by 25,000 majority, showing a falling off of 32,000 from the majority of 1866. In New Jersey there was a Democratic majority of about 15,000, the Republican loss being about 18,000. Maryland went Democratic by a majority of 40,000, against 13,000 in 1866. In Illinois the elections were local. Wisconsin elected a Republican governor by 4000, a loss from the previous year of 20,000. In Minnesota there was a falling off of over 6000 from the Republican majority of 1866. Estimating by majorities, the Republican loss indicated in all the elections was over 250,000.

In Kansas, Minnesota, Ohio, and Pennsylvania, the people voted upon a constitutional amendment, allowing negroes to vote in these states. The amendment was defeated by heavy majorities in all except Minnesota.

In respect to the functions of the Boards of Registration and Election, the attorney general holds (18) that they can impose no oath other than that prescribed by this law; that (19) they must administer the oath to all who will take it, "the oath being the only and sole test of the qualification of the applicant;" that (20) if a person takes the oath his name must go upon the register; and that (21) his name being on the register, he must be allowed to vote. "There is no provision," adds the attorney general, "to surcharge or falsify, or add a single name to the registration, or erase a single name that appears upon it."

[1] The following are in brief the provisions of this explanatory act:

Sec. 1. "That it is hereby declared to have been the true intent and meaning of the act of the 2d day of March, 1867, entitled an Act to Provide for the more efficient Government of the Rebel States, thereto passed the 23d of March, 1867, that the governments then existing in the rebel states of Virginia, North Carolina, South Carolina, Georgia, Mississippi, Alabama, Louisiana, Florida, Texas, and Arkansas were not legal state governments, and that thereafter said governments, if continued, shall be subject in all respects to the military commanders of the respective districts, and to the paramount authority of Congress."

Sec. 2. "That the commander of any district named in said act shall have power, subject to the disapproval of the general of the army of the United States, and to have effect till disapproved, whenever, in the opinion of such commander, the proper administration of said act shall require it, to suspend or remove from office, or from the performance of official duties and the exercise of official powers, any officer or person holding or exercising, or professing to hold or exercise, any civil or military office or duty in such district, under any power, election, appointment, or authority, derived from, or granted by, or claimed under any so-called state or the government thereof, or municipal or other division thereof; and upon such suspension or removal such commander, subject to the disapproval of the general as aforesaid, shall have power to provide from time to time for the performance of the said duties of such officer or person so suspended or removed by the detail of some competent officer or soldier of the army, or by the appointment of some other person to perform the same, and to fill the vacancies occasioned by death, resignation, or otherwise."

Sec. 3. "That the general of the army of the United States be invested with all the powers of suspension, removal, appointment, and detail granted in the preceding section to district commanders."

Sec. 4. "That the acts of the officers of the army already done in removing, in said districts, persons exercising the functions of civil officers, and appointing others in their stead, are hereby confirmed, provided that any person heretofore or hereafter appointed by any district commander to exercise the functions of any civil office may be removed, either by the military officer in command of the district or by the general of the army, and it shall be the duty of such commander to remove from office as aforesaid all persons who are disloyal to the government of the United States, or who use their official influence in any manner to hinder, delay, prevent, or obstruct the due and proper administration of this act and the acts to which it is supplementary."

Sec. 5 makes it the duty of the Boards of Registration, before allowing any person to be registered, to ascertain whether he is entitled to registration; and the oath of the person is not to be conclusive evidence; and no person shall be registered unless the board decides that he is entitled thereto; and "no person shall be disqualified as member of any Board of Registration by reason of race or color."

Sec. 6 declares that the true intent and meaning of the oath prescribed in the supplementary act is, among other things, "that no person who has been a member of the Legislature of any state, or who has held any executive or judicial office in any state, whether he has taken an oath to support the Constitution or not, and whether he was holding such office at the commencement of the rebellion, or had held it before and who has afterward engaged in rebellion against the United States, or given aid and comfort to the enemies thereof, is entitled to be registered or vote; and the words 'executive or judicial office in any state,' in said oath mentioned, shall be construed to include all civil officers created by law for the administration of any general law of a state, or for the administration of justice."

Sec. 7 authorizes the commander of any district to extend the period for registration until the 1st of October, 1867. Makes it their duty, commencing fourteen days previous to any election under the act, and for a period of five days, to revise the registration list, strike off the names of all persons not entitled thereto, and add any names of persons so entitled which have not been registered; "and no person shall at any time be entitled to be registered or to vote by reason of any executive pardon or amnesty for any act or thing which, without such pardon or amnesty, would disqualify him from registration or voting."

Sec. 8. "That all members of said Boards of Registration, and all persons hereafter elected or appointed to office in said military districts, under any so-called state or municipal authority, or by detail, or appointment of the district commanders, shall be required to take and subscribe to the oath of office prescribed by law for the officers of the United States."

Sec. 9. "That no district commander or member of the Board of Registration, or any officers or appointees acting under them, shall be bound in his action by any opinion of any civil officer of the United States."

Sec. 10. "That section 4 of said last-named act shall be construed to authorize the commanding general named therein, whenever he shall deem it needful, to remove any member of a Board of Registration, and to appoint another in his stead, and to fill any vacancy in such board."

Sec. 11. "That all the provisions of this act, and of the acts to which this is supplementary, shall be construed liberally, to the end that all the intents thereof may be fully and perfectly carried out."

[2] The President thus concludes his message:

"Within a period less than a year the legislation of Congress has attempted to strip the executive department of the government of some of its essential powers. The Constitution, and the oath provided in it, devolve upon the President the power and duty to see that the laws are faithfully executed. The Constitution, in order to carry out this power, gives him the choice of the agents, and makes them subject to his control and supervision; but, in the execution of these laws, the constitutional obligation upon the President remains, but the power to exercise that constitutional duty is effectually taken away. The military commander is, as to the power of appointment, made to take the place of the President, and the general of the army the place of the Senate, and any attempt on the part of the President to assert his own constitutional power may, under pretense of law, be met by official insubordination. It is to be feared that these military officers, looking to the authority given by these laws rather than to the letter of the Constitution, will recognize no authority but the commander of the district and the general of the army. If there were no other objections than this to this proposed legislation, it would be sufficient. While I hold the chief executive authority of the United States, while the obligation rests upon me to see that all the laws are faithfully executed, I can never willingly surrender that trust or the powers given for its execution. I can never give my assent to be made responsible for the faithful execution of laws, and at the same time surrender that trust and the powers which accompany it to any other executive officer, high or low, or to any number of executive officers. If this executive trust, vested by the Constitution in the President, is to be taken from him and vested in a subordinate officer, the responsibility will be with Congress in clothing the subordinates with unconstitutional power, and with the officer who assumes its exercise. This interference with the constitutional authority of the executive department is an evil that will inevitably sap the foundations of our federal system; but it is not the worst evil of this legislation. It is a great public wrong to take from the President powers conferred on him alone by the Constitution; but the wrong is more flagrant and more dangerous when the powers so taken from the President are conferred upon subordinate executive officers, and especially upon military officers. Over nearly one third of the states of the Union military power, regulated by no fixed law, rules supreme. Each of the five district commanders, though not chosen by the people, or responsible to them, exercises at this hour more executive power, military and civil, than the people have ever been willing to confer upon the head of the executive department, though chosen by and responsible to themselves."

[1] August 5, 1867.

It is evident from these estimates that there had been a popular reaction. In 1866, the people had decided against President Johnson—now they appeared to mutter against Congress. It must be remembered, however, that in most of the states the elections were of such a character as not to draw out the full strength of the Republican party. Still, even making this allowance, the people evidently disapproved of the temper and spirit which characterized the proceedings of Congress in this matter of reconstruction. It would hardly be fair to infer from the elections that the people were opposed to *what* Congress had done; but the manner in which Congress proceeded, apparently assuming that any measures, however extreme, would receive popular support, indicated that some check must be put upon that body. There was another consideration of the utmost importance, and which largely affected the popular vote. Before another general election could take place, the party Conventions would meet for the nomination of presidential candidates. The prominent leaders of the Republican party were evidently determined to select some one representing the extreme views of that party. It was important that this should not be done, and yet quite certain that it would be attempted, if in the elections the Republican party should receive the same support as in 1866. This consideration materially affected the result of the elections. Thousands of Republicans staid away from the polls, wishing neither to support Democratic candidates, nor to give their sanction to the extreme views of their own party leaders. As to the vote in four of the states upon negro suffrage, the result had no special significance, for the issue presented had none. The refusal of Ohio to allow colored citizens to vote did not by any means imply opposition to negro suffrage as a feature of the military reconstruction bill. In Ohio, as in all the Northern States, the only question involved in this matter was one between an abstract principle and the prejudice of race; but not so in the Southern States, one third of whose entire population was colored. Here there were questions of expediency as well as of abstract justice to be considered. The exclusion of the vast colored population of the South from negro suffrage involved dangers not only to the future tranquillity of the states themselves, but to the peace of the nation. The perils which many feared from this universal or impartial suffrage were mainly imaginary. President Johnson predicted that it would bring on a war of races; but it would seem far more reasonable to expect such a war to follow the exclusion of a very large class from all political power. The moment the negro becomes invested with political rights, the very basis for the antagonism of races is removed.

When Congress again assembled on the 21st of November, its proceedings were characterized by greater moderation, but it steadfastly adhered to its policy of restoration. The President's message was for the most part a reiteration of the arguments upon which he had insisted from the beginning of his administration. He urged the repeal of those "acts of Congress which place ten of the states under the domination of military masters." He denounced the policy of negro suffrage and white disfranchisement as the "subjugation of these states to negro domination, and worse than military despotism." He alluded to certain cases in which it would become the President's duty to resist Congressional enactments by force, "regardless of consequences." "If, for instance," said he, "the legislative department should pass an act, even through all the forms of law, to abolish a co-ordinate branch of the government, in such a case the President must take the high responsibility of his office, and save the nation at all hazards."

In January, the Thirty-ninth Congress had passed a resolution looking toward the impeachment of President Johnson, and directing the judiciary committee to investigate his official conduct. This committee, at the close of the session on March 4th, had delivered over its duties and the results of its inquiry to its natural successor. In June, the judiciary committee of the Fortieth Congress, after a careful sifting of the testimony offered, stood four for and five against impeachment. But one of the members, who in June had been opposed to impeachment—Mr. John C. Churchill—changed his mind before the beginning of the November session, and thus the measure came before the House on the 25th supported by a majority report.[1] Two minority reports were also submitted. It is clear that the President had been guilty of no offense indictable by law; and both the American and British law on this subject determine that impeachment can not rest except upon offenses of this character. Besides, the impeachment of President Johnson, simply because his policy was opposed to that of the legislative department of the government, would establish a dangerous precedent, which could be used against any president by any dominant political party opposed to him. The House wisely, therefore, refused to adopt the report of the majority.

President Johnson, after having once entered into the conflict against Congress, fought obstinately for the success of his own policy of reconstruction. His legal arguments, however wise in theory, were almost always practically false. His angry denunciation of his opponents weakened the popular confidence in his wisdom and capacity for the successful leadership of any party. His subsidizing of all the subordinate offices of the government for his own purposes promised to reinaugurate the system of official corruption under which the national politics had degenerated through a long series of administrations previous to the election of Mr. Lincoln. This excited greater fear and distrust, because an enormous national debt, involving a most intricate system of internal revenue, had infinitely increased the opportunities for corruption. Johnson's administration completely disappointed the American people. It was notoriously corrupt. It misled the Southern people, sharpening continually the edge of their defiance. It drove Congress and the loyal people to the alternative of a surrender to what they believed a mistaken policy, or of adopting extreme measures, which otherwise they would have reluctantly sanctioned. It was a failure as regarded its own purposes, and an obstruction to the national development.

As we write (December, 1867) the Congressional plan of reconstruction is still in its preliminary stages. Registrations have been completed in all the ten states under military rule, and in most of them show a majority of colored voters. Elections have been held in several of these states, and in some the Conventions are now in session. The delegates of these Conventions are almost all supporters of the Congressional policy; and it is probable that the Constitutions framed by them will be ratified by the several states, and that they will include provisions for impartial or universal suffrage. Whether in other respects—for example, in the disfranchisement of a large number of whites—they will meet the approbation of Congress after the recent elections in the North, we can not predict. It seems certain, however, that, whatever else may fail, the principle of "equal rights for all men, without distinction of color," will be maintained in the next presidential election and in the election of a new Congress. But prophecy belongs not to the historian. We will not seek to lift the veil of our future. With the recital of the events of the last seven years our proper work concludes. What remains to be written we leave to other hands; what we have written we now submit to the charitable but impartial judgment of our readers.

---

[1] The charges brought in this report against the President were the following:

"1st. That the President of the United States, assuming it to be his duty to execute the constitutional guarantee, has undertaken to provide new governments for the rebellious states without the consent or co-operation of the legislative power, and upon such terms as were agreeable to his own pleasure, and then to force them into the Union against the will of Congress and the people of the loyal states, by the authority and patronage of his high office.

"2d. That to effect this object he has created offices unknown to the law, and appointed to them, without the advice or consent of the Senate, men who were notoriously disqualified to take the test oath, at salaries fixed by his own mere will, and paid those salaries, along with the expenses of his work, out of the funds of the War Department, in clear violation of law.

"3d. That, to pay the expenses of the said organizations, he has also authorized his pretended officers to appropriate the property of the government, and to levy taxes from the conquered people.

"4th. That he has surrendered, without equivalent, to the rebel stockholders of Southern railroads captured by our arms, not only the roads themselves, but the rolling-stock and machinery captured along with them, and even roads constructed or renovated at an enormous outlay by the government of the United States itself.

"5th. That he has undertaken, without anthority of law, to sell and transfer to the same parties, at a private valuation and on a long credit, without any security whatever, an enormous amount of rolling-stock and machinery, purchased by and belonging to the United States, and after repeated defaults on the part of the purchasers, has postponed the debt due to the government in order to enable them to pay the claims of other creditors, along with arrears of interest on a large amount of bonds of the companies, guaranteed by the State of Tennessee, of which he was himself a large holder at the time.

"6th. That he has not only restored to rebel owners large amounts of cotton and other abandonded property that had been seized by the agents of the treasury, but has presumed to pay back the proceeds of actual sales made thereof, at his own will and pleasure, in utter contempt of the law directing the same to be paid into the treasury, and the parties aggrieved to seek their remedy in the courts, and in manifest violation of the true spirit and meaning of that clause of the Constitution of the United States which declares that no 'money shall be drawn from the treasury but in consequence of appropriations made by law.'

"7th. That he has abused the pardoning power conferred on him by the Constitution, to the great detriment of the public, in releasing, pending the condition of war, the most active and formidable of the leaders of the rebellion, with a view to the restoration of their property and means of influence, and to secure their services in the furtherance of his policy; and, further, in substantially delegating that power for the same objects to his provisional governors.

"8th. That he has further abused this power in the wholesale pardon, in a single instance, of 193 deserters, with restoration of their justly forfeited claims upon the government for arrears of pay, without proper inquiry or sufficient evidence.

"9th. That he has not only refused to enforce the laws passed by Congress for the suppression of the rebellion, and the punishment of those who gave it comfort and support, by directing proceedings against the delinquents and their property, but has absolutely obstructed the course of public justice, by either prohibiting the initiation of legal proceedings for that purpose, or, where already commenced, by staying the same indefinitely, or ordering absolutely the discontinuance thereof.

"10th. That he has further obstructed the course of justice by not only releasing from imprisonment an important state prisoner, in the person of Clement C. Clay, charged, among other things, as asserted by himself in answer to a resolution of the Senate (Ex. Doc., 39th Congress, No. 7), 'with treason, with complicity in the murder of Mr. Lincoln, and with organizing bands of pirates, robbers, and murderers in Canada, to burn the cities and ravage the commercial coasts of the United States on the British frontier,' but has even forbidden his arrest on proceedings instituted against him for treason and conspiracy in the State of Alabama, and ordered his property, when seized for confiscation by the district attorney of the United States, to be restored.

"11th. That he has abused the appointing power lodged with him by the Constitution:

"1. In the removal, on system, and to the great prejudice of the public service, of large numbers of meritorious public officers, for no other reason than because they refused to indorse his claim of the right to reorganize and restore the rebel states on conditions of his own, and because they favored the jurisdiction and authority of Congress in the premises.

"2. In reappointing, in repeated instances, after the adjournment of the Senate, persons who had been nominated by him and rejected by that body as unfit for the place for which they had been so recommended.

"12th. That he has exercised a dispensing power over the laws by commissioning revenue officers and others unknown to the law, who were notoriously disqualified by their participation in the rebellion from taking the oath of office required by the act of Congress of July 2, 1862, allowing them to enter upon and exercise the duties appertaining to their respective offices, and paying to them salaries for their services therein.

"13th. That he has exercised the veto power conferred on him by the Constitution in its systematic application to all the important measures of Congress looking to the reorganization and restoration of the rebel states, in accordance with a public declaration that 'he would veto all its measures whenever they came to him,' and without other reasons than a determination to prevent the exercise of the undoubted power and jurisdiction of Congress over a question that was cognizable exclusively by them.

"14th. That he has brought the patronage of his office into conflict with the freedom of elections by allowing and encouraging his official retainers to travel over the country, attending political conventions and addressing the people, instead of attending to the duties they were paid to perform, while they were receiving high salaries in consideration thereof.

"15th. That he has exerted all the influence of his position to prevent the people of the rebellious states from accepting the terms offered to them by Congress, and neutralized, to a large extent, the effects of the national victory by impressing them with the opinion that the Congress of the United States was bloodthirsty and implacable, and that their only hope was in adhering to him.

"16th. That, in addition to the oppression and bloodshed that have every where resulted from his undue tenderness and transparent partiality for traitors, he has encouraged the murder of loyal citizens in New Orleans by a Confederate mob pretending to act as a police, by holding correspondence with its leaders, denouncing the exercise of the constitutional right of a political Convention to assemble peacefully in that city as an act of treason proper to be suppressed by violence, and commanding the military to assist instead of preventing the execution of the avowed purpose of dispersing them.

"17th. That he has been guilty of acts calculated, if not intended, to subvert the government of the United States by denying that the Thirty-ninth Congress was a constitutional body, and fostering a spirit of disaffection and disobedience to the law and rebellion against its authority, by endeavoring, in public speeches, to bring it into odium and contempt."

INDEX.

THE END.